EUROPEAN ADMINISTRATIVE LAW

For Werner von Simson

EUROPEAN ADMINISTRATIVE LAW

JÜRGEN SCHWARZE

*Professor of Law, University of Freiburg and
European University Institute, Florence*

OFFICE FOR OFFICIAL PUBLICATIONS OF
THE EUROPEAN COMMUNITIES

SWEET AND MAXWELL

1992

Published in 1992 by
Sweet and Maxwell Limited of
South Quay Plaza, 183 Marsh Wall, London E14
and
Office for Official Publications of the European Communities
2 rue Mercier, L-2985 Luxembourg

First published in German as Europäisches Verwaltungsrecht
by Nomos Verlagsgesellschaft, Baden-Baden, 1988
© Nomos Verlagsgesellschaft, Baden-Baden

Computerset by
MFK Typesetting Limited, Hitchin, Herts.
Printed and bound in Great Britain by
Hartnolls Limited, Bodmin

British Library Cataloguing in Publication Data

A catalogue record for this book is
available from the British Library

Sweet and Maxwell, South Quay Plaza, London E14
ISBN 0-421-45490-3

Office for Official Publications of the European Communities,
2 rue Mercier, L-2985 Luxembourg
ISBN 92-826-3460-4
Catalogue Number CM-72-91-786-EN-C

PREFACE

This work reflects the results of a research project which has been generously funded by the Volkswagen Foundation. The original German version (1988) has now been translated into English with the invaluable support of the Commission of the European Communities, for which I am most grateful.

The work is devoted to the evolution of a new legal system: the origins and development of a corpus of European administrative law on the basis of comparative law in the context of the European Community.

As explained in greater detail in the Introduction, this work pursues a number of aims. It sets out to show, as a kind of handbook, the state of development currently reached in European administrative law. Moreover, as a contribution to the elaboration of a theoretical system, it reveals the possibilities for and limits to the further development of European administrative law. Finally, in the form of a programme of comparative law, it not only highlights the influences of national principles of administrative law on European Community law but it also reveals the repercussions of the newly elaborated European law on the national systems of administrative law.

The question subjected to investigation of the origins and development of a corpus of European administrative law must therefore be appreciated not just in the narrower sense of a corpus of administrative law for the European Community, that should be as unified as possible when Community law is being enforced, but at the same time in a wider sense as an enquiry into the possible further development and convergence of national administrative laws in Europe.

This comprehensive investigation could not have been carried out without the dedicated support of tried and trusted colleagues in my Hamburg seminar, among whom special mention must be made of Dr. Armin Hatje, Hans-Holger Herrnfeld, Dr. Jan-Peter Hix, Klaus Rainer Kirchhoff, Ulrike von der Ohe and Dr. Adrian Glaesner.

v

In addition, I am especially grateful to numerous colleagues and institutes at home and abroad. To represent them all, may I mention my colleagues, staff and students at the European University Institute in Florence, who have fulfilled the aims of the Institute by providing a wide range of ideas and assistance for research on a European basis.

Freiburg and Florence   Jürgen Schwarze
January 1992

SUMMARY OF CONTENTS FOR THE COMPLETE WORK

PART I

Page

Chapter 1   Introduction   3

Chapter 2   Essential characteristics of the administrative law systems of the E.C. Member States   97

Chapter 3   Legal constraints on and freedom of decision for the administration   207

Chapter 4   The principle of equality and the prohibition of discrimination as obligatory maxims of government action   545

PART II

Chapter 5   The principle of proportionality   677

Chapter 6   Legal certainty and the protection of legitimate expectations   867

Chapter 7   Principles of administrative procedure under the rule of law   1173

Chapter 8   Conclusion   1433

Bibliography   1467
Index   1515

CONTENTS

	Page
Preface	*v*
Cases before the European Court of Justice: Numerical List	*xxxvii*
Cases before the European Court of Justice: Alphabetical List	*lix*
Council and Commission Regulations	*lxxv*
Cases before National Courts	*lxxxi*
EEC Treaty: Articles referred to	*xci*
National Legislation	*xcv*
Abbreviations	*ci*

PART I

CHAPTER 1 **INTRODUCTION**	3

Section 1	The European Community as a Community of administrative law	3

Section 2	The European concept of administration	11
A.	The concept of administration in the Member States	11
B.	The concept of administration in the European Community	20

Section 3	The areas of administrative implementation of Community law	25
A.	Direct implementation	25
I.	Internal Community administration	25
II.	Administration external to the Community	27
B.	Indirect implementation	34
I.	The Common Agricultural Policy	34
II.	The external protection of the Common Market through the Common Customs Tariff	36

Section 4 Sources of general administrative law of the
European Community

A.	Written law	38
I.	Primary law	39
II.	Secondary law	42
	1. The present position	42
	(a) Direct implementation	43
	(b) Indirect implementation	45
	2. The legal basis of an act—the power to legislate	47
	(a) Direct implementation	48
	(b) Indirect implementation	50
	3. Summary	53
	(a) The inadequacy of the written law	53
	(b) The admissibility of reasoning by analogy	54
	(c) Conclusion	55
B.	Customary law	55
C.	Judge-made law and general legal principles	59
I.	Judge-made law	59
II.	General principles of law	64
	1. Authenticity	66
	2. Status	68
	3. Methods for determining the content of general principles	71
	4. Summary	75

Section 5 The emergence of a European administrative law
through comparative method | 76

A.	The fundamentals of comparative law	76
I.	Concept	77
II.	Aims and functions	78
	1. The creation of new law by the legislature	78
	2. The unification of law	79
	3. Judicial law making and the interpretation of statutes	81
III.	Method	82
B.	Comparative public law	85
I.	Characteristics of public law	85
II.	The methodology of comparative law	87
III.	The chances of a unification of laws	88
C.	Comparative administrative law in particular	89
D.	Towards a European *ius commune* in the area of administrative law	93

CHAPTER 2 ESSENTIAL CHARACTERISTICS OF THE
ADMINISTRATIVE LAW SYSTEMS OF
THE E.C. MEMBER STATES   97

Section 1   France   100

Section 2   Federal Republic of Germany   114

Section 3   Italy   128

Section 4   United Kingdom   140

Section 5   Belgium   154

Section 6   Denmark   161

Section 7   Greece   167

Section 8   Ireland   173

Section 9   Luxembourg   181

Section 10 The Netherlands   187

Section 11 Portugal   193

Section 12 Spain   199

CHAPTER 3 LEGAL CONSTRAINTS AND THE
FREEDOM OF DECISION OF THE
ADMINISTRATION   207

Part 1   Introduction   207

Part 2   The principle of the legality of the administration   212

Section 1   The legality of the administration in the Member
States   212

A.   A comparative legal analysis   212
I.   The principle of legality in France   212
II.   The principle of legality in the Federal Republic of
      Germany   214
      1.   The primacy of statute law   214
      2.   The requirement that there be a statute   215
      (a)   Field of application   215
      (b)   Content of the statutes in the reserved area   217
      3.   The constraints placed on the administration by
            fundamental rights and general principles of law   218
      4.   Unlawful administrative conduct   218
      (a)   The unlawful administrative act   218
      (b)   Unlawfulness in delegated rule-making   219
III. The principle of legality in Italy   220
IV.   The principle of legality in the United Kingdom   220
V.   The principle of legality in Belgium   222
VI.   The principle of legality in Denmark   223
      1.   Content and form of the principle of legality   223
      2.   Unlawful administrative conduct   225
VII. The principle of legality in Greece   225
      1.   The applicability of the principle of legality   225
      2.   Unlawful administrative conduct   226
VIII. The principle of legality in Ireland   226
IX.   The principle of legality in Luxembourg   227
X.   The principle of legality in the Netherlands   227
      1.   The primacy of statute   227
      2.   The requirement that there be a statute   228
XI.   The principle of legality in Portugal   229
XII. The principle of legality in Spain   230
B.   Conclusions from the survey State practice   230
I.   Foundations of the principle of legality in the national
      constitutions   230
II.   Variations in the figuration of the principle of legality   231
III. Unlawful administrative conduct   232

Section 2   The principle of legality in European Community
             law   233

A.   Introduction—terminology   233
B.   The principle of legality in the legal system of the
      European Communities—the underlying structures   233

I.   The primacy accorded to superior law   234
        1.   The principle   234
        2.   Survey of European Community law   235
        (a)   The distinction between binding instruments and
                non-binding statements   235
        (aa)   Positive law distinctions   235
        (bb)   Distinguishing criteria used by the European Court 236
        (b)   Effectiveness, nullity and invalidity of legal
                instruments   239
        (aa)   Effectiveness of legal acts   239
        (bb)   Nullity according to Article 33 ECSC Treaty,
                Article 173 EEC Treaty, Article 146 Euratom
                Treaty   239
                (1)   Grounds of action   239
                (a)   EEC and Euratom Treaties   239
                (b)   ECSC Treaty   240
                (2)   Legal consequences of annulment of
                        legal acts   240
                (a)   General   240
                (b)   Validity pending annulment   241
                (c)   Effects of annulment under Article 173 EEC
                        Treaty   242
                (d)   Continuing applicability of a void regulation 242
                (3)   Effects of a declaration of invalidity under
                        subparagraph (b) of Article 177 EEC Treaty 243
                (a)   Preliminary remark on tests of validity under
                        subparagraph (b) of Article 177 EEC Treaty 243
                (b)   Invalidity according to subparagraph (b) of
                        Article 177 EEC Treaty   244
        (c)   Authority to act and legal acts—sources of legality 247
        3.   The hierarchy of rules in Community law   248
        (a)   Hierarchy within Community law   248
        (b)   Hierarchy of rules in the relationship between the
                Community and the Member States   252
II.   "Requirement of a statute" in Community law   253
        1.   Terminology   253
        2.   The principle   253
        (a)   Reserved treaty powers   253
        (b)   Treaty reservation in secondary legislation   256
III.   Principles of interpretation   257

C.	Unlawful administrative conduct	258
I.	Sources of error	258
II.	The principle of the revocability of unlawful administrative acts	259
Part 3	Elements which moderate legal constraints— undefined legal terms and discretion	261
Section 1	Administrative freedom of decision in the legal systems of the Member States	261
A.	A comparative legal analysis	261
I.	Statutory constraints and discretion in France	261
	1. The fundamentals of the doctrine of discretion in France	261
	2. The extent of judicial review of discretionary decisions	263
II.	Statutory constraints and discretion in the Federal Republic of Germany	270
	1. Fundamentals of the German doctrine of discretion	270
	2. Judicial Review of discretionary decisions	277
III.	Statutory constraints and discretion in Italy	279
IV.	Statutory constraints and discretion in the United Kingdom	281
	1. Fundamentals of administrative discretion in the United Kingdom	281
	2. The *ultra vires* doctrine	282
	3. The principle of natural justice	286
V.	Statutory constraints and discretion in Belgium	287
VI.	Statutory constraints and discretion in Denmark	289
VII.	Statutory constraints and discretion in Greece	290
VIII.	Statutory constraints and discretion in Ireland	290
IX.	Statutory constraints and discretion in Luxembourg	291
X.	Statutory constraints and discretion in the Netherlands	291
XI.	Statutory constraints and discretion in Portugal	293
XII.	Statutory constraints and discretion in Spain	294
B.	Conclusion	294
Section 2	Executive freedom of decision in the European Community	296
A.	Introduction	296
I.	The terminology of Community law	296

II. Administrative and legislative discretion 298
III. Judicial protection against discretionary decisions 299
IV. The link between discretion and the obligation to
substantiate 301
V. Explanation of the mode of procedure 301
B. The case law—a survey and appraisal 302
I. The law of the Community civil service 302
   1. Civil service law in general 303
   2. The operation of legal constraints in European civil
service law, as demonstrated in typical cases in
selected fields 304
   (a) Review of the formal conditions of a decision 304
   (aa) Functional authority and procedure 304
   (bb) Formal rules for decisions 306
   (b) Review of the subject-matter of decisions 307
   (aa) Completeness and accuracy of the underlying facts 307
   (bb) Limits to discretionary power in the source of
authority 308
      (1) Case 59/81, *Commission* v. *Council of the
European Communities* 308
      (a) Subject-matter and grounds of the decision 308
      (b) The evaluation process 311
      (2) The adjustment of salary weightings in Case
59/81 312
   (cc) Self-regulation by the administration 313
      (1) Example: how discretion in appointments is
constrained by the conditions of recruitment 313
      (2) Example: the force of discretionary
guidelines on remuneration 316
   (dd) Misuse of discretion as a limit to discretionary
powers 319
      (1) The *Bernhard Schloh* case 320
      (2) An assessment 322
   (ee) General principles of law as a limit on the freedom
of decision 324
   3. Conclusion 325
II. The Common Market in coal and steel 325
   1. Executive freedom of decision and the framework
for its judicial review 326
   2. The standards of judicial review of discretionary
decisions 327

(a) The aims of the Treaty as a standard of conduct for the ECSC executive   327

(b) Misuse of powers   330

(aa) The concept of misuse of powers in the case law of the European Court   330

(bb) Procedural irregularity   334

(cc) The effectiveness of the plea of misuse of powers in reviewing administrative decisions   336

(c) Manifest failure to observe a rule of law   337

(d) The standards of review for the other causes of action   339

(aa) The binding nature of powers conferred by the Treaty   340

(1) Preliminary remarks   340

(2) Case law   340

(bb) How institutional rules constrain discretionary powers   351

(cc) How the ECSC executive is bound by general principles of law   355

3. Conclusion   359

III. The competition law of the EEC   360

1. Introduction   360

2. The subject-matter of Articles 85 and 86 of the EEC Treaty   361

(a) The ban on cartels (Article 85)   361

(aa) The subject-matter of Article 85(1) of the EEC Treaty   362

(bb) Exemptions under Article 85(3) of the EEC Treaty   366

(cc) Conclusion   369

(b) Abuse of a dominant position (Article 86)   370

(aa) How the term "abuse of a dominant position" is applied in individual cases   370

(bb) Summary   378

(c) Enforcement   378

3. The prohibition of aid by Articles 92 et seq. of the EEC Treaty   381

(a) Introduction   381

(b) The prohibition of State aids in Article 92(1) of the EEC Treaty   384

(aa) The concept of State aids   384

(a)	The concept of subsidy under the ECSC Treaty	384
(bb)	The approval of aids which are incompatible with Article 92(3) of the EEC Treaty	387
(c)	Conclusion	389
IV.	Community law on external trade, and especially the rules against dumping	389
V.	The Common Agricultural Policy	395
1.	Introduction	395
2.	The Council's prerogative of market regulation	396
(a)	The task of policy-making	397
(b)	The legal limits of constitutive authority	398
(aa)	Formal constraints—proper authority and procedure	398
(bb)	The limits of the subject-matter	404
(1)	General requirements clarity of rules	404
(2)	The compulsory objectives of Article 39(1) of the EEC Treaty	406
(3)	Reviewing the underlying facts	411
(4)	Misuse of powers	415
(5)	How general principles of law constrain policy-making	415
(a)	Article 40(3), second paragraph, of the EEC Treaty, and the general principle of equality as a limit to freedom of decision	416
(b)	How the proportionality principle limits policy-making in the law of market organisation	423
(c)	How the demands of legal certainty limit the discretion of policy-makers	431
(d)	How fundamental rights limit policy-making in the law of market organisation	435
(c)	Assessment of the Council's freedom in policy-making in agricultural law	439
3.	The authority to implement by the Commission	440
(a)	The limitation of powers by the source of authority and by the Treaty	441
(aa)	Establishing and weighing the facts	443
(bb)	Constraints arising from the source of authority and the Treaty	448
(b)	How executive discretion is constrained by general principles of law	451

(c) Concluding comments on executive freedom in policy-making 452
4. How the Member States implement agricultural law 453
(a) Preliminary observation 453
(b) How States exercise scope for decision-making 454
(c) The legal constraints on rule-making in the Member States 455
(aa) The enactment of "substantive" agricultural law by the Member States 455
(bb) The enactment of "formal" implementing law 457
(1) Competence 457
(2) The freedom of States to decide in procedural law matters 459
(d) Selected examples from the case law on problems associated with the application of agricultural law at national level 462
(aa) Definition of terms 463
(bb) The remission of levies on grounds of equity 469
(cc) Reclaiming Community subsidies paid unlawfully 474
(e) Concluding assessment of the legal constraints found in the indirect (national) implementation of the agricultural law of the European Community 479
VI. The customs union 480
1. The significance of the customs union 480
2. Legal constraints in customs policy: the essential points 481
3. Applying the customs tariff nomenclature (CCT) 482
(a) Explanations of the CCT by the Community and the Member States 483
(b) The Court's review of the application of the CCT 486
4. Conclusion 494
VIII. The legal constraints on the administration in the social security law of the European Community 494
1. Introduction 494
2. The Community's competence in social policy, and how it is exercised 495
3. Executive freedom of decision in European social law, illustrated in Regulation 1408/71 on social security for migrant workers 497

Part 4 The non-contractual liability of the Community 504

Section 1 The development of non-contractual liability in
Community law 505

Section 2 Circumstances giving rise to liability 508

A. Administrative wrongs 508
I. General principle 508
II. Particular conditions 508
  1. Official capacity 508
  2. The conduct of Community institutions or officials 510
  3. The "illegality" of the conduct 511
  4. The "culpability" of the conduct which incurs
     liability 513
III. Damage which can be made good 515
  1. The nature of the compensation 516
  2. The extent of compensation 517
B. The prerequisites of liability for legislative wrongs 524

Section 3 Other forms of liability 531

A. Liability for illegal acts not involving fault 531
B. Liability for lawful acts 532
C. Absolute liability 533

Section 4 Delimitation of liability systems in the
Communities and the Member States 535

Part 5 Summary and conclusion 539

A. The present situation 539
B. Prospects for development 542

CHAPTER 4 **THE PRINCIPLE OF EQUALITY AND THE
PROHIBITION OF DISCRIMINATION AS
OBLIGATORY MAXIMS OF
GOVERNMENT ACTION** 545

A. Introduction 545
I. General problems and the development of the principle;
structure and method of the survey 545

xix

II.	The concept of equality	548
III.	Possible orientations of the principle	550
	1. The requirement of formal equality in the application of the law	550
	2. The requirement of substantive equality before the law	551
IV.	The concept of arbitrary action	553
V.	The binding nature of the equality principle as a legal rule	555
	1. General validity	555
	2. Special national features	556
	(a) French law	556
	(b) British law	558
	(c) Danish law	560
VI.	The equality principle and prohibitions of discrimination	561
	1. The concept of discrimination and discrimination prohibitions in general	561
	2. The structure of discrimination prohibitions in Community law	562
B.	The concept of discrimination	563
I.	Elements of a discriminatory act	564
	1. Unlike treatment of like matters	564
	2. Like treatment of unlike matters	571
II.	Discrimination and arbitrary action	574
	1. Arbitrary action as regards the facts	575
	2. Arbitrary action and justification	584
III.	Other characteristics and forms of discrimination	601
	1. Occurrence of damage	601
	2. Distortion of competition	602
	3. "Natural" differences	606
	4. "Contributory fault"	610
	5. Failure to take a measure	614
	6. Hidden discrimination	616
IV.	Summary	625
C.	Recognition of the equality principle as a general legal principle	625
I.	As a fundamental principle of Community law	625
II.	As an administrative-law principle	641
III.	Summary	644
D.	Limits to the application of the equality principle	645
I.	The Community's external relations	645

II.	Member States' jurisdiction	649
III.	Summary	657
E.	The equality of Member States under Community law	658
I.	Incomplete application of a legal act	658
	1. Refusal to implement or execute	658
	2. Delay in implementation or performance	661
II.	Unilateral supplementary or amending measures	663
	1. Formal measures	663
	2. Substantive measures	667
III.	Summary	669
F.	Conclusion	670

PART II

Page

CHAPTER 5   THE PRINCIPLE OF PROPORTIONALITY   677

A.   Introduction   677
B.   The concept of proportionality   678
I.   Historical origins   678
II.   The role of the proportionality principle   679
C.   The proportionality principle in the legal systems of the
      Member States and in international law   680
I.   The legal systems of the Member States   680
      1.   France   680
      2.   Federal Republic of Germany   680
      3.   Italy   692
      4.   United Kingdom   695
      5.   Belgium   697
      6.   Denmark   698
      7.   Greece   699
      8.   Ireland   699
      9.   Luxembourg   700
      10.   The Netherlands   700
      11.   Portugal   701
      12.   Spain   702
II.   The proportionality principle in international law   703
      1.   General international law   703
      2.   The principle of proportionality under the
            European Convention on Human Rights   704
      (a)   The case law of the European Commission of
            Human Rights   705
      (b)   The proportionality principle in the case law of the
            European Court of Human Rights   706

D.	The proportionality principle in Community law	708
I.	Introduction	708
II.	The sources of the proportionality principle	710
	1. Express provisions in the Treaty	710
	2. Deriving the proportionality principle from that of the rule of law	712
	3. The proportionality principle as derived from national rules	714
	4. The proportionality principle as deduced from the Treaty provisions	715
	5. Summary and evaluation	716
III.	The proportionality principle as an objective rule	717
	1. Its status	717
	2. Its function as a substitute for fundamental rights	719
IV.	The practical application of the proportionality principle in the case law of the European Court of Justice	726
	1. The organisation of agricultural markets	727
	(a) Introduction	727
	(b) Cases featuring deposits	727
	(aa) Introduction	727
	(bb) The legal nature of deposits	729
	(cc) The amount of the deposit	732
	(dd) Forfeiture of deposits	732
	(c) Skimmed-milk powder cases	747
	(d) Other cases concerning intervention	752
	(aa) Guarantee	753
	(bb) Co-responsibility levy	753
	(cc) Fixing of threshold prices	754
	(dd) Fixing the amount of the levy	756
	(ee) Quota system	759
	(ff) Minimum prices system	760
	(gg) Monetary compensation system	762
	(hh) Subsidies and denaturing premiums	766
	2. The free movement of goods	773
	(a) Introduction	773
	(b) The field of application of Article 30 EEC	775
	(aa) Measures relating to the quality of food	776
	(bb) Measures concerning the marketing of products	779
	(cc) Penalties	781
	(c) Measures restricting exports (Article 34 EEC)	783
	(d) The case law relating to "mandatory requirements"	785
	(e) Article 36 EEC	789

(aa)	Protection of health	790
(bb)	Protection of public security and public policy	798
(cc)	Protection of industrial and commercial property	800
(dd)	Recent legal developments	803
3.	The foreign trade law of the Community	806
4.	Freedom of movement	814
5.	Freedom to provide services and freedom of establishment	827
6.	Competition law	833
(a)	Introduction	833
(b)	Administrative procedure in European competition law	834
(c)	Fines	837
(d)	Substantive competition law	841
7.	ECSC	842
(a)	Introduction	842
(b)	Scrap metal equalisation cases	844
(c)	The production quota system	845
(d)	Procedural questions	850
8.	Staff law cases	853
V.	Summary	853
1.	Content of the proportionality principle in Community law	854
(a)	Suitability	855
(b)	Necessity	857
(c)	Proportionality in the strict sense	859
2.	Differentiation according to the field of application and the form taken by the official action	861
E.	Conclusion	864

CHAPTER 6   LEGAL CERTAINTY AND THE PROTECTION OF LEGITIMATE EXPECTATIONS — 867

Section 1   The origins — 867

A.	Introduction	867
B.	Emergence as principles of law	868
I.	Recognition in national law	868
II.	Recognition in Community law	870

Section 2   The principles of legal certainty and the protection of legitimate expectations in the law of the Member States — 874

A.   France — 874
I.   General recognition of the principles — 874
II.   Application to individual cases — 875
   1.   Action by the administration — 876
   (a)   Annulment of administrative decisions — 876
   (aa)   Retrait — 877
      (1)   Individual decisions (*actes individuels*) — 877
      (2)   Regulations (*actes réglementaires/règlements*) — 881
   (bb)   Abrogation — 882
      (1)   Individual decisions — 883
      (2)   Regulations — 883
   (b)   Reclaiming benefits paid without legal justification — 884
   2.   Legislation—retroactivity of statutes and regulations — 885
B.   Germany — 886
I.   General recognition of the principles — 886
II.   Application to individual cases — 887
   1.   Action by the administration — 887
   (a)   Revocation and withdrawal of administrative decisions — 887
   (aa)   Revocation — 888
      (1)   Revocation of administrative decisions imposing burdens — 888
      (2)   Revocation of administrative decisions conferring benefits — 889
   (bb)   Withdrawal — 891
      (1)   Withdrawal of administrative decisions imposing burdens — 891
      (2)   Withdrawal of administrative decisions conferring benefits — 892
   (b)   Pledges — 894
   (c)   Recovery of payments having no legal basis — 895
   (aa)   Recovery of payments made by the State — 895
   (bb)   Recovery of duties wrongly levied by the State — 897
   2.   Legislation—retroactivity of statutes and regulations — 898
   3.   The retrospective effect of court decisions — 900

C.	United Kingdom	901
I.	General recognition of the principles	901
	1. Legitimate expectations	902
	2. Estoppel	903
II.	Application to individual cases	904
	1. Action by the administration	904
	(a) Revocation of administrative decisions	904
	(b) Recovery of payments having no legal basis	907
	2. Legislation—retroactivity of statutes and regulations	910
D.	Italy	911
I.	General recognition of the principles	911
II.	Application to individual cases	912
	1. Action by the administration	912
	(a) Annulment of administrative decisions	912
	(aa) Withdrawal of unlawful administrative decisions (*annullamento*)	912
	(bb) Revocation of inappropriate administrative decisions (*revoca*)	914
	(b) Recovery of payments having no legal basis	915
	2. Legislation—retroactivity of statutes	916
E.	Belgium	918
I.	General recognition of the principles	918
II.	Application to individual cases	918
	1. Annulment of administrative decisions	918
	2. Retroactivity of administrative decisions and rules	920
	3. Recovery of wrongly levied duties	921
F.	Denmark	921
G.	Greece	923
H.	Ireland	924
I.	Luxembourg	925
J.	The Netherlands	926
I.	General recognition of the principles	926
II.	Application to individual cases	928
	1. Action by the administration	928
	(a) Annulment of administrative decisions	928
	(aa) Annulment of lawful administrative decisions conferring benefits	928
	(bb) Annulment of unlawful administrative decisions conferring benefits	929
	(b) Recovery of State benefits wrongly paid	930

	(c) Recovery of wrongly levied duties	930
	2. Legislation—retroactivity of statutes and regulations	931
K.	Portugal	932
L.	Spain	933
I.	General recognition of the principles	933
II.	Application to individual cases	934
	1. Action by the administration—annulation of administrative decisions	934
	(a) Revocación	935
	(b) Anulación	935
	2. Legislation—retroactivity of statutes and regulations	937

Section 3	The principles of legal certainty and of the protection of legitimate expectations in Community law	938

A.	Introduction	938
I.	The development of these principles in the case law of the Court of Justice	938
II.	Legal certainty and the protection of legitimate expectations as principles of constitutional and administrative law	940
III.	The areas in which these principles apply	942
	1. Legal certainty and the protection of legitimate expectations as applied to direct executive action by the administration	942
	2. Legal certainty and the protection of legitimate expectations in the field of indirect executive action by the administration	944
	3. Legal certainty and the protection of legitimate expectations as applied to Community legislative action	945
IV.	The principles of legal certainty and the protection of legitimate expectations as concepts	946
	1. The principle of legal certainty	946
	2. The principle of the protection of legitimate expectations	949
	3. Vested rights	953

B.	Direct executive action	956
I.	Administrative acts	957
	1. Conditions which must be met by Community administrative acts	957
	2. Differentiating administrative acts from regulations	964
	3. Classification of administrative acts	970
	(a) Declaratory administrative acts and acts establishing rights	970
	(b) Administrative acts conferring benefits and imposing burdens	972
	(c) Unlawful administrative acts which are completely null and void	975
II.	Revocation of administrative acts	979
	1. Introduction	979
	2. The revocation of administrative acts in written law	980
	(a) Revocation under Article 65(2), fourth paragraph, ECSC	981
	(b) Revocation under Article 8(3) of Regulation 17 (EEC)	983
	(c) Revocation in the Staff Regulations	984
	3. General legal principles regarding the revocation of administrative acts	986
	(a) The revocation of lawful administrative acts	986
	(b) The revocation of unlawful administrative acts	991
	(c) Special characteristics of the revocation of measures imposing burdens	1010
	(d) Special grounds for revocation	1011
	(aa) Revocation as laid down by statute	1011
	(bb) Measures explicitly subject to revocation	1012
	(cc) Revocation on the grounds of false or incomplete information	1013
	(dd) Changes in the legal situation	1015
	(ee) Changes of circumstances	1022
	(e) Summary	1024
	4. General conditions for the lawful nature of revocation decisions	1025
	(a) Where no forfeiture has occurred	1025
	(b) Principles governing form and procedure	1027
	(c) The exercise of discretion and the duty to observe the law	1029

5. Legal implications of an infringement of legitimate expectations in the event of revocation of administrative measures ... 1031

III. Time limits for remedies and administrative procedures ... 1032
1. Time limits for remedies and the formal validity of measures ... 1032
(a) Conditions for and consequences of the existence of formal validity ... 1035
(b) Exceptions to the principle of formal validity ... 1044
(aa) The absolute nullity of administrative measures ... 1044
(bb) New circumstances ... 1045
(cc) The plea of illegality ... 1051
2. Time limits in administrative proceedings ... 1054

IV. Recovery and subsequent assessment ... 1061
1. Recovery of payments wrongly made ... 1061
(a) Article 85 of the Staff Regulations ... 1062
(aa) Absence of legal basis ... 1062
(bb) Other conditions for the recovery of payments ... 1066
(cc) The procedural context of the right of recovery ... 1067
(b) The principle of unjustified enrichment ... 1068
2. Subsequent collection of duties which were incorrectly not levied ... 1069

V. Retroactivity of administrative measures ... 1072
1. General observations ... 1072
2. Examples of the retroactivity of administrative measures ... 1072
(a) The law on the supervision of subsidies ... 1072
(b) Authorisations for protective measures ... 1075
(c) Regulations challengeable under the second paragraph of Article 173 EEC as being decisions ... 1078

VI. Self-binding action by the authorities and the protection of legitimate expectations ... 1079
1. Principles ... 1079
2. Administrative practice and linked administrative measures ... 1080
3. Information and explanation ... 1085
4. Undertakings and pledges ... 1089

C. Indirect executive action ... 1093
I. Principles ... 1093
1. Introduction ... 1093
2. Case law of the Court of Justice ... 1095

II. Relevance of the principles of the protection of legitimate expectations and of legal certainty in indirect executive action — 1096
  1. Introduction — 1096
  2. Recovery of amounts paid contrary to Community law — 1097
  3. Subsequent recovery of amounts not levied contrary to Community law — 1101
  (a) Regulation 1697/79 — 1102
  (b) The application of national law as a complementary tool — 1102
  4. Repayment of amounts levied contrary to Community law — 1104
  (a) Regulation 1430/79 — 1104
  (b) The application of national law as a complementary tool — 1109
III. Summary — 1112
D. Normative instruments — 1113
I. The duty of the legislator to observe, in principle, the rules of legal certainty and the protection of legitimate expectations — 1114
II. The protection of legitimate expectations in relation to changes in legal positions—the retroactivity of rules — 1119
  1. Principles relating to the validity of legal rules in time and in substance — 1119
  (a) Actual retroactivity — 1120
  (b) Apparent retroactivity — 1121
  2. The conditions for the admissibility of actual retroactivity—a detailed survey — 1122
  3. The conditions for the operation of apparent retroactivity of normative acts — 1130
  (a) The protection of legitimate expectations as a restriction on the legislator's freedom to legislate — 1130
  (b) Legal consequences — 1145
  (c) The special case of the retroactivity of directives — 1148
III. Other means by which the legislature can be bound by the principles of legal certainty and the protection of legitimate expectations — 1151
  1. Expectation of changes in the legal position — 1151
  2. The clear and predictable nature of the legal position — 1152

Section 4 Summary   1154

A. Legal certainty and the protection of legitimate
expectations as general legal principles   1154
B. Revocation of administrative measures   1156
C. Recovery of payments made without a legal basis   1160
I. The obligation to repay in the case of unlawfully paid
public levies   1161
II. The recovery of payments wrongly made by the State   1166
D. The retroactivity of rules   1168
E. Concluding observations   1170

CHAPTER 7   **PRINCIPLES OF ADMINISTRATIVE
PROCEDURE UNDER THE RULE OF LAW**   1173

A. Introduction   1173
I. The subject-matter of the investigation   1173
II. The changing meaning of the law of administrative
procedure   1175
    1. The notion of procedure in the Member States   1175
    2. The significance of the notion of procedure within
the Community   1186
III. Summary   1197
B. Competence   1198
I. Community competence   1198
II. Institutional competence   1202
III. The competence of the decision-making institution   1209
C. The language question   1212
D. Administrative powers to collect information, and the
legal limits governing them   1215
I. The Commission's powers to collect information   1216
    1. Powers to collect information provided for in the
Treaties   1216
    2. Powers to collect information provided for in
secondary legislation   1218
    (a) Regulation 17   1218
    (aa) The request for information under Article 11 of
Regulation 17   1219
    (bb) The authority to conduct investigations under
Article 14 of Regulation 17   1220
    (b) Powers to collect information under anti-dumping
law   1222

II.   The duty to make a complete investigation—as
elaborated by the Court of Justice   1223
    1.   The earlier case law   1223
    (a)   Individual examples from a variety of fields of law   1223
    (b)   The special problems arising in the law of customs
    duties and levies   1231
    2.   The more recent case law   1236
    3.   Conclusion   1238
III.   Limits placed upon investigatory powers   1239
    1.   The principle of proportionality and "legal
    privilege"   1239
    2.   Prohibitions on the use of evidence   1241
    3.   Various limitations on the powers of investigation
    in the context of competition proceedings and anti-
    dumping proceedings   1242
E.   Rights of the defence   1243
I.   Survey   1243
II.   A comparison of Member States' laws   1245
    1.   The "droits de la défense" in France   1245
    (a)   The development of a general legal principle   1245
    (b)   The formulation of statutory protective rights   1251
    2.   The right to a hearing in German administrative
    procedure   1255
    (a)   General observations   1255
    (b)   Those entitled to be heard   1258
    (c)   Exceptions to the duty to grant a hearing   1259
    (d)   The type and scope of the hearing   1261
    (e)   Rights of objection   1262
    (f)   Complementary rights   1263
    (g)   The consequences of non-observance or
    inadequate observance of the procedural rights   1268
    3.   The rights of the defence in Italy   1269
    (1)   The preparatory phase   1271
    (2)   The constitutive phase   1273
    (3)   The phase in which the act becomes fully
    effective   1273
    4.   The rules of natural justice in the United Kingdom   1273
    (a)   The current significance of the general principle of
    law   1278
    (b)   Statutory rules   1284
    (aa)   Tribunals   1285

(bb)	Inquiries	1288
(c)	Legal consequences	1290
5.	The rights of defence in Belgium	1292
6.	The right to a hearing in Denmark	1296
7.	The rights of defence in Greece	1300
8.	The right to a hearing in Ireland	1305
9.	The "droits de la défense" in Luxembourg	1309
10.	The right to a hearing in the Netherlands	1311
11.	The rights of defence in Portugal	1314
12.	The right to a hearing in Spain	1315
III.	Rights of the defence in Community law	1320
1.	Normative rules	1320
2.	The existence of a general principle of law	1324
3.	Rights of defence for third parties	1325
4.	General limitations upon the rights of the defence	1328
(a)	The risk that the purpose of the decision may be defeated	1328
(b)	The gathering of evidence	1330
(c)	Insignificant interferences	1332
(d)	Danger in delay	1332
(e)	The impossibility of granting protection	1333
(f)	The petition of the person concerned	1334
5.	The content of the rights of the defence at the different phases of the procedure	1335
(a)	The opening of the procedure	1335
(b)	Explanation about the content of the objections (communication of the statement of objections)	1338
(c)	Access to files	1341
(aa)	The duty to communicate individual documents	1341
(bb)	Limits and exceptions	1347
(1)	General limits	1347
(2)	Confidential documents	1348
(d)	The nature and extent of the provision of a hearing	1358
(aa)	The object and degree of the hearing	1358
(bb)	Procedure for the hearing	1363
IV.	Summary	1370
F.	The decision-making process	1371
I.	The formulation of the decision	1371
1.	General comments	1371
2.	The possibilities of informal settlement	1373
3.	The possibilities of adopting interim measures	1378

	4.	The process for adopting the decision	1380
	5.	The presentation of the decision	1381
	6.	Information about remedies	1382
II.		The duty to give reasons	1384
	1.	Introduction	1384
	2.	The duty to give reasons in the legal orders of the Member States	1385
	(a)	The duty to give reasons in France	1385
	(b)	The duty to give reasons in the Federal Republic of Germany	1386
	(c)	The duty to give reasons in Italy	1388
	(d)	The duty to give reasons in the United Kingdom	1389
	(e)	The duty to give reasons in Belgium	1390
	(f)	The duty to give reasons in Denmark	1391
	(g)	The duty to give reasons in Greece	1392
	(h)	The duty to give reasons in Ireland	1393
	(i)	The duty to give reasons in Luxembourg	1395
	(j)	The duty to give reasons in the Netherlands	1396
	(k)	The duty to give reasons in Portugal	1398
	(l)	The duty to give reasons in Spain	1399
	3.	The duty to give reasons in European Community law	1400
	(a)	The significance of the duty to give reasons	1400
	(b)	Measures which are subject to the duty to give reasons	1403
	(c)	The form of the statement of reasons	1405
	(d)	The scope of the duty to give reasons	1406
	(aa)	Individual acts	1407
	(bb)	Normative acts	1412
III.		Notification	1416
G.		Legal consequences of procedural defects	1420
H.		Summary	1430

CHAPTER 8   CONCLUSION   1433

I.	The evolution of European administrative law	1433
II.	The interdependence of national (European) administrative legal orders and the development of a common European law	1434

CONTENTS

III.   European administrative law between case law and
statute   1446
IV.   The integration function of European constitutional and
administrative law   1455
V.   Final remarks   1465

Bibliography   1467
Index   1515

CASES BEFORE THE EUROPEAN COURT OF JUSTICE
(Numerical List)

1/54   France v. High Authority [1954–56] E.C.R. 1 .... 331, 332, 549
2/54   Italy v. High Authority [1954–56] E.C.R. 37 1420
6/54   Netherlands v. High Authority [1954–56] E.C.R. 103 .... 327, 337, 338, 339,
                                                                                                412, 1380, 1422
7A/54   Groupement des Industries Sidérurgiques Luxembourgeoises v. High
           Authority [1954–56] E.C.R. 222 .... 564, 565, 657, 964, 1197
1/55   Kergall v. Common Assembly [1954–56] E.C.R. 151 .... 988, 1406, 1424, 1425
8/55   Fédération Charbonnière de Belgique v. High Authority [1954–56] E.C.R.
           292 .... 48, 65, 225, 325, 330, 333, 337, 567, 572, 577, 677, 710, 843, 965
9/55   Soc. des Charbonnages de Beeringen v. High Authority [1954–56] E.C.R.
           311 .... 567, 572, 577
7/56 & 3–7/57   Algera v. Common Assembly [1957–58] E.C.R. 39 .... 5, 67, 83,
                          236, 303, 324, 523, 872, 938, 941, 951, 955, 957, 971, 976, 985,
                   992, 997, 1004, 1006, 1009, 1013, 1024, 1027, 1030, 1131, 1435, 1446, 1456
8/56   Alma v. High Authority [1957–58] E.C.R. 95 .... 1417, 1456
10/56   Meroni & Co., Industrie Metallurgische SpA v. High Authority [1957–58]
           E.C.R. 157 .... 329, 524, 870, 1051, 1069, 1205, 1206, 1207, 1376
1/57   Soc. des Usines & Tubes de la Sarre v. High Authority [1957–58] E.C.R.
           105 .... 976, 1420
8/57   Groupement des Hauts Fourneaux et Aciéries Belges v. High Authority
           [1957–58] E.C.R. 245 .... 328, 329, 331, 335, 554, 575, 674, 844, 1196
9/57   Chambre Syndicale de la Sidérurgie Française v. High Authority [1957–58]
           E.C.R. 319 .... 554, 566, 575, 674
11/57   Soc. d'Electro-Chimie, d'Electro-Metallurgie et des Aciéries d'Ugine v.
           High Authority [1957–58] E.C.R. 575 .... 554, 566
12/57   Syndicat de la Sidérurgie du Centre-Midi v. High Authority [1957–58]
           E.C.R. 375 .... 556, 575, 674
13/57   Wirtschaftsvereinigung Eisen-und Stahlindustrie v. High Authority
           [1957–58] E.C.R. 265 .... 65, 329, 333, 337, 554, 566
15/57   Compagnie des Hauts Fourneaux de Chasse v. High Authority [1957–58]
           E.C.R. 211 844
18/57   I. Nold KG v. High Authority [1959] E.C.R. 41 .... 333, 342, 358, 436,
                                                                                                956, 976, 1420, 1459, 1414
3–18, 25 & 26/58   Barbara Erzbergbau AG v. High Authority 549, 601, 1224,
                                                                                                1230, 1370, 1419
20/58   Phoenix-Rheinrohr AG v. High Authority [1959] E.C.R. 75 .... 328, 962, 1061,
                                                                                                1422, 1425
27/58   Compagnie des Hauts Fourneaux et Fonderies de Givors v. High Authority
           [1960] E.C.R. 241 328
32–33/58   Soc. Nouvelle des Usines de Pontlieve Aciéries du Temple v. High
           Authority [1959] E.C.R. 127 .... 572, 579, 603
3/59   Germany v. High Authority [1960] E.C.R. 53 .... 975, 977, 1051, 1052
14/59   Soc. des Fonderies de Pont à Mousson v. High Authority [1959] E.C.R.
           215 .... 565, 672
15 & 29/59   Soc. Métallurgique de Knutange v. High Authority [1960]
           E.C.R. 1 .... 327, 845, 979

16–19/59 'Geitling' Ruhrkohlen-Verkaufsgesellschaft mbH, 'Mausegatt' Ruhrkohlen-Verkaufsgesellschaft mbH, 'Präsident' Ruhrkohlen-Verkaufsgesellschaft v. High Authority [1960] E.C.R. 17 .... 349, 1087, 1224, 1384, 1403
20/59 Italy v. High Authority [1960] E.C.R. 325 .... 48, 256, 1361
27 & 39/59 Campolongo v. High Authority E.C.R. 391 1447
30/59 De Gezamenljkce Steenkolnmijnen in Limburg v. High Authority [1961] E.C.R. 50 .... 389, 956, 963, 1054
31/59 Acciaieria v. High Authority [1960] E.C.R. 71 837
33/59 Compagnie des Hauts Fourneaux de Chasse v. High Authority [1962] E.C.R. 408 514
36–38 & 40/59 'Präsident' Ruhrkohlen-Verkaufsgesellschaft mbH, 'Geitling' Ruhrkohlen-Verkaufsgesellschaft mbH, I. Nold KG v. High Authority [1960] E.C.R. 423 .... 981, 1385, 1410
42 & 49/59 Soc. Nouvelles des Usines de Pontlieue-Aciéries du Temple (SNU-PAT) v. High Authority [1961] E.C.R. 53 .... 6, 65, 68, 237, 259, 260, 867, 872, 939, 940, 947, 948, 957, 959, 971, 973, 974, 975, 988, 994, 995, 997, 998, 999, 1010, 1014, 1019, 1020, 1025, 1029, 1034, 1042, 1045, 1070, 1225, 1325
43, 45 & 48/59 Eva von Lachmüller v. Commission [1960] E.C.R. 463 .... 65, 1405
44/59 Fiddelaar v. Commission [1960] E.C.R. 535 1405
6/60 Humblet v. Belgian State [1960] E.C.R. 559 .... 1118, 1190
9 & 12/60 Vloeberghs v. High Authority [1961] E.C.R. 197 .... 511, 513, 521
14/60 Meroni v. High Authority [1961] E.C.R. 161 673
15/60 Simon v. European Court of Justice [1961] E.C.R. 115 .... 957, 971, 973, 989, 990, 991, 1023
19/60 Soc. Fives Lille Cail, Soc. Union Sidérurgique du Nord de la France 'Usina', Soc. des Forges et Ateliers de Creusot and Soc. Marrel Frères v. High Authority [1961] E.C.R. 281 .... 238, 514, 978, 1081, 1045
25/60 De Bruyn v. Parliamentary Assembly [1962] E.C.R. 21, [1962] C.M.L.R. 167 .... 1029, 1405, 1429
7/61 Commission v. Italy [1961] E.C.R. 317, 802 [1962] C.M.L.R. 39 .... 300, 800
13/61 Kledingverkoopbedrijf De Geus en Uitdenbogerd v. Robert Bosch GmbH [1962] E.C.R. 45, [1962] C.M.L.R. 1 .... 6, 871
14/61 Koninklijke Nederlandsche Hoogovens en Staalfabrieken NV v. High Authority [1962] E.C.R. 253, [1963] C.M.L.R. 73 .... 48, 65, 876, 877, 878, 881, 913, 938, 939, 948, 952, 957, 958, 959, 963, 971, 973, 974, 979, 990, 992, 993, 994, 994, 997, 998, 1003, 1005, 1009, 1010, 1014, 1020, 1024, 1025, 1027, 1029, 1034, 1070, 1224, 1225
16/61 Acciaierie Ferriere & Fonderie di Modena v. High Authority [1962] E.C.R. 289, [1962] C.M.L.R. 221 .... 289, 578
17/61 Klöckner-Werke AG and Hoesch AG v. High Authority [1962] E.C.R. 325 .... 359, 564, 579, 603, 1081, 1089, 1090, 1091, 1365, 1415
19/61 Mannesmann AG v. High Authority [1962] E.C.R. 357 .... 436, 564, 579, 603, 714, 914, 957, 971, 978, 1061, 1064, 1069, 1081
5–11, 13–15/62 Soc. Industriale Acciaierie San Michele v. High Authority [1962] E.C.R. 449; [1963] C.M.L.R. 13 .... 719, 851, 1447
19–22/62 Féderation Nationale de la Boucherie en Gros et du Commerce en Gros des Viandes v. Council [1962] E.C.R. 491, [1963] C.M.L.R. 160 960
25/62 Plaumann & Co v. Commission [1963] E.C.R. 95, [1964] C.M.L.R. 29 1191
26/62 NV Algemene Transport-en Expeditie Onderneming Van Gend en Loos v. Nederlandse Belastingadministratie [1963] E.C.R. 1, [1963] C.M.L.R. 105 .... 252, 481, 1236, 1457
31 & 33/62 Milchwerke Heinz Wöhrmann & Sohn KG and Alfons Lütticke GmbH v. Commission [1962] E.C.R. 501, [1963] C.M.L.R. 152 1021

32/62   Alvis v. Council [1963] E.C.R. 49, [1963] C.M.L.R. 396 1325
34/62   Germany v. Commission [1963] E.C.R. 131, [1963] C.M.L.R. 369 .... 338, 339,
398, 1403, 1404
36/62   Soc. des Aciéries du Temple v. High Authority [1963] E.C.R. 289, [1963]
C.M.L.R. 49 517
1/63   Macchiorlati Dalmas & Figli v. High Authority [1963] E.C.R. 303, [1964]
C.M.L.R. 223 1091
13/63   Italy v. Commission [1963] E.C.R. 165, [1963] C.M.L.R. 289 .... 417, 562, 563,
564, 571, 581
18/63   Wollast née Schmitz v. E.E.C. [1964] E.C.R. 85 .... 853, 861
23–24 & 52/63   Usines Emile Henricot SA v. High Authority [1963] E.C.R. 217
[1963] C.M.L.R. 119 .... 958, 959, 961
26/63   Pistoj v. Commission [1964] E.C.R. 341 .... 1358, 1369
27/63   Raponi v. Commission [1964] E.C.R. 129 .... 307, 308, 1231, 1408
55–59 & 61–63/63   Soc. Acciaierie Fonderie Ferriere di Modena v. High Authority
[1964] E.C.R. 211, [1964] C.M.L.R. 401 250
66/63   Netherlands v. High Authority [1964] E.C.R. 533, [1964] C.M.L.R. 522 1403
80/63   Degreef v. Commission [1964] E.C.R. 391 1325
90 & 91/63   Commission v. Luxembourg and Belgium [1964] E.C.R. 625, [1965]
C.M.L.R. 58 251
94 & 96/63   Bernusset v. Commission [1964] E.C.R. 297 .... 296, 307, 1408, 1409
97/63   De Pascale v. Commission [1964] E.C.R. 515 322
100/63 Kalsbeek née Van der Veen v. Bestuur der Sociale Verzekeringsbank
[1964] E.C.R. 565, [1964] C.M.L.R. 548 1123
102/63 Boursin v. High Authority [1964] E.C.R. 691 304
106/63 Alfred Toepfer KG and Getreide-Import Gesellschaft mbH v. Commission
[1965] E.C.R. 405, [1966] C.M.L.R. 111 407
108/63 Officine Elettromeccaniche Ing. A. Merlini v. High Authority [1965]
E.C.R. 1, [1965] C.M.L.R. 109 .... 971, 1038, 1404
109/63 & 13/64   Muller v. Commission [1964] E.C.R. 663 1046
110/63 Willame v. Euratom Commission [1965] E.C.R. 649, [1966] C.M.L.R.
231 296
111/63 Lemmerzwerke GmbH v. High Authority [1965] E.C.R. 677, [1968]
C.M.L.R. 280 ....: 6, 260, 340, 673, 938, 958, 971, 973, 999,
1000, 1001, 1002, 1009, 1014, 1025, 1029, 1070
3/64   Chambre Syndicale de la Sidérurgie Française v. High Authority [1965]
E.C.R. 441 330
6/64   Costa v. E.N.E.L. [1964] E.C.R. 585 [1964] C.M.L.R. 425 1457
21/64   Macchiorlati Dalmas & Figli v. High Authority [1965] E.C.R. 175, [1966]
C.M.L.R. 46 .... 1052, 1091
27 & 30/64   Fonzi v. Euratom Commission [1965] E.C.R. 481 322
36/64   S.O.R.E.M.A. v. High Authority [1965] E.C.R. 329, [1966] C.M.L.R.
28 .... 975, 977, 981, 982, 1012, 1013, 1037, 1052, 1084
40/64   Sgarlata v. Commission [1965] E.C.R. 215, [1966] C.M.L.R. 314 61
46/64   Schoffer v. Commission [1965] E.C.R. 811 .... 1045, 1051
50–51, 53–54 & 57/64   Loebisch v. Council [1965] E.C.R. 825 1051
56 & 58/64   Consten and Grundig-Verkaufs-GmbH v. Commission [1966] E.C.R.
299, [1966] C.M.L.R. 418 .... 366, 841, 1229, 1326, 1344, 1359,
1410, 1411, 1420
2/65   Ferriera Ernesto Preo & Figli v. High Authority [1966] E.C.R. 219 .... 343, 971,
1225
8/65   Accaierie & Ferriere Pugliesi SpA v. High Authority [1966] E.C.R. 1 343
16/65   Firma C, Schwarze v. Einfuhr-und Vorratsstelle für Getreide und Futtermittel [1965] E.C.R. 877, [1966] C.M.L.R. 172 .... 244, 1195, 1409, 1423
18A/65 Gutmann v. Euratom Commission [1967] E.C.R. 61 .... 1406, 1407, 1425

20/65   Collotti v. European Court of Justice [1965] 847 .... 1033, 1037
34A/65   Mosthaf v. Euratom Commission [1966] E.C.R. 541 1034
52 & 55/65   Germany v. Commission [1966] E.C.R. 159, [1967] C.M.L.R. 22 661
54/65   Compagnie des Forges de Châtillon, Commentry et Neuves-Maisons v. High
        Authority [1966] E.C.R. 185, [1966] C.M.L.R. 525 ..... 238, 988, 1001, 1002, 1087
56/65   La Technique Minière v. Maschinenbau GmbH [1966] E.C.R. 235, [1966]
        C.M.L.R. 357 .... 365, 1228, 1229
59/65   Schreckenberg v. Euratom Commission [1966] E.C.R. 543 1164
3/66   Alfieri v. European Parliament [1966] E.C.R. 437, [1967] C.M.L.R. 110 1364
5, 7 & 13–24/66   Firma E Kampffmeyer v. Commission [1967] E.C.R.
        245 .... 9, 71, 408, 467, 505, 506, 512, 518, 531, 535
8–11/66   Re Noordwijks Cement Acoord : Cimenteries C.B.R. Cementzbedrijven
        NV v. Commission [1967] E.C.R. 75, [1967] C.M.L.R. 77 .... 236, 958, 959,
                                                              962, 976, 989, 1420, 1421
28/66   Netherlands v. Commission [1968] E.C.R 1 .... 495, 1230
3/67   Fonderie Acciaierie Giovanni Mandelli v. Commission [1968] E.C.R.
        25 .... 344, 1330, 1380
4/67   Muller née Collignon v. Commission [1967] E.C.R. 365 .... 1033, 1034, 1035
5/67   Beus (W.) GmbH & Co v. Hauptzollamt München-Landsbergerstrasse
        [1968] E.C.R. 83, [1968] C.M.L.R. 131 .... 406, 409, 411, 1406, 1412
17/67   Firma Max Neumann v. Hauptzollamt Hof/Saale [1967] E.C.R. 441 939,
                                                                          1115, 1120
29/67   Soc. De Wendel SA v. Commission [1968] E.C.R. 263, [1969] C.M.L.R.
        354 .... 1370, 1411, 1422
2/68   Ufficio Imposte v. Commission [1968] E.C.R. 434 1425
4/68   Schwarzwaldmilch GmbH v. Einfuhr-und Vorratsstelle für Fette [1968]
        E.C.R. 377, [1969] C.M.L.R. 406 .... 249, 463, 733
7/68   Commission v. Italy [1968] E.C.R. 423, [1969] C.M.L.R. 1 798
12/68   Commission v. E.C. Audit Commission [1969] E.C.R. 109 ...... 1364, 1366, 1425
13/68   Salgoil SpA v. Ministero per il Commercio con l'Estero [1968] E.C.R. 453,
        [1969] C.M.L.R. 181 798
14/68   Wilhelm v. Bundeskartellamt [1969] E.C.R. 1 [1969] C.M.L.R. 100 .... 368, 379,
                                                                          591, 651
25/68   Schertzer v. Parliament [1977] E.C.R. 1729 .... 1212, 1405
4/69   Alfons Lütticke GmbH v. Commission [1971] E.C.R. 325 .... 508, 514, 517, 518
6 & 11/69   Commission v. France [1969] E.C.R. 523, [1970] C.M.L.R. 43 ..... 976, 977,
                                                                          1045, 1052
9/69   Sayäg v. Leduc [1969] E.C.R. 329 .... 505, 506, 509, 511, 513, 521
10/69   Portelange SA v. Smith Corona Marchant International SA [1969] E.C.R.
        309, [1974] 1 C.M.L.R. 397 1229
13/69   Van Eick v. Commission [1970] E.C.R. 3 .... 324, 1366, 1369
19–20, 25 & 30/69   Richez-Parise v. Commission [1970] E.C.R. 325 .... 1085, 1372
23/69   Fiehn v. Commission [1970] E.C.R. 547 1086
24/69   Nebe v. Commission [1970] E.C.R. 145 .... 1033, 1034, 1038, 1041, 1402, 1405
29/69   Stauder v. City of Ulm [1969] E.C.R. 419, [1970] C.M.L.R. 112 .... 625, 720,
                                                                          1459
31/69   Commission v. Italy [1970] E.C.R. 25, [1970] C.M.L.R. 175 661
40/69   Hauptzollamt Hamburg-Oberelbe v. Firma Paul G. Bollmann [1970] E.C.R.
        69, [1970] C.M.L.R. 141 455
41/69   ACF Chemiefarma NV v. Commission [1970] E.C.R. 661 .... 55, 1057, 1059,
                                                    1215, 1345, 1382, 1383, 1384, 1402, 1427, 1430
44/69   Buchler & Co v. Commission [1970] E.C.R. 733 .... 1057, 1368, 1450
45/69   Boehringer Mannheim GmbH v. Commission [1970] E.C.R. 769 ..... 1057, 1338,
                                                              1339, 1357, 1368, 1450
46/69   Reinarz v. Commission [1970] E.C.R. 275 322

48/69   ICI Ltd v. Commission [1972] E.C.R. 619, [1972] C.M.L.R. 557 .... 363, 1111,
                                        1201, 1202, 1211, 1418, 1419, 1450
49/69   Badische Anilin-und Sodafabrik AG v. Commission [1972] E.C.R. 713,
        [1972] C.M.L.R. 557 .... 363, 1058, 1368
51/69   Bayer AG v. Commission [1972] E.C.R. 745, [1972] C.M.L.R. 557 1058,
                                                    1342, 1344, 1365, 1368
52/69   J.R. Geigy AG v. Commission [1972] E.C.R. 787, [1972] C.M.L.R.
        557 .... 363, 1058, 1201, 1418, 1419
53/69   Sandoz AG v. Commission [1972] E.C.R. 845, [1972] C.M.L.R. 557 363,
                                                            1058, 1201
54/69   Francolor v. Commission [1972] E.C.R. 851, [1972] C.M.L.R. 557 ..... 363, 1058
55/69   Cassella Farbwerke Mainkur AG v. Commission [1972] E.C.R. 887, [1972]
        C.M.L.R. 557 1058
56/69   Farbwerke Hoechst AG v. Commission [1972] E.C.R. 927, [1972] C.M.L.R.
        557 .... 363, 1058
57/69   Azienda Colori Nazionali Affini SpA (A.C.N.A.) v. Commission [1972]
        E.C.R. 933, [1972] C.M.L.R. 557 .... 363, 1058, 1336
67/69   Società Industriale Metallurgica di Napoli (S.I.M.E.T.) v. Commission
        [1971] E.C.R. 197 .... 236, 1456
68/69   Bundesknappschaft Bochum v. Brock [1970] E.C.R. 171, [1971] C.M.L.R.
        55 1132
73/69   Firma Oehlmann & Co v. Hamptzollamt Münster [1970] E.C.R. 467, [1970]
        C.M.L.R. 409 757
74/69   Hauptzollamt Bremen-Freihafen v. Waren-Import Gesellschaft Krohn & Co
        [1970] E.C.R. 451, [1970] C.M.L.R. 466 484
2/70   Acciaierie e Ferriere Riva SpA v. Commission [1971] E.C.R. 97 .... 868, 959,
                                        971, 974, 1010, 1011, 1037, 1070, 1450
9/70   Franz Grad v. Finanzamt Traunstein [1970] E.C.R. 825, [1971]
        C.M.L.R. 1 1148
11/70   Internationale Handelsgesellschaft mbH v. Einfuhr-und Vorratsstelle für
        Getreide und Futtermittel [1970] E.C.R. 1125, [1972] C.M.L.R. 255 .... 6, 85,
                            435, 467, 625, 710, 721, 731, 732, 733, 780, 843, 1459
12/70   Craeynest v. Belgian State [1970] E.C.R. 905 666
14/70   Deutsche Bakels GmbH v. Oberfinanzdirektion München [1970] E.C.R.
        1001, [1971] C.M.L.R. 188 485
19/70   Almini v. Commission [1971] E.C.R. 623 .... 1338, 1362
21/70   Rittweger v. Commission [1971] E.C.R. 7 .... 322, 1345, 1420
22/70   Commission   v.   Council   [1971]   E.C.R.   263,   [1971]   C.M.L.R.
        335 .... 236, 242, 958, 1018, 1047, 1236
25/70   Einfuhr-und Vorratsstelle für Getreide und Futtermittel v. Fa. Köster
        Berodt & Co. [1970] E.C.R. 1161, [1972] C.M.L.R. 255 .... 399, 400,
                                        428, 430, 732, 856, 1201, 1207, 1376
31/70   Deutsch Getreide-und Futtermittel Handelsgessellschaft mbH v. Haupt-
        zollamt Hamburg Altona [1970] E.C.R. 1055; [1971] C.M.L.R. 205 ..... 418, 607,
                                                                    711
33/70   SACE v. Ministero delle Finanze [1970] E.C.R. 1213, [1971] C.M.L.R.
        123 .... 252, 481
36/70   Getreide-Import GmbH v. Einfuhr-und Vorratsstelle für Getreide und
        Futtermittel [1970] E.C.R. 1107 .... 463, 464
37/70   Rewe Zentrale des Lebensmittel-Großhandels GmbH v. Hauptzollamt
        Emmerich [1971] E.C.R. 23, [1971] C.M.L.R. 238 .... 446, 1016
38/70   Deutsch Tradax GmbH v. Einfuhr-und Vorratsstelle für Getreide und
        Futtermittel [1971] E.C.R. 145, [1972] C.M.L.R. 213 249
39/70   Norddeutsches Vieh-und Fleischkontor GmbH v. Hauptzollamt
        Hamburg-St. Annen [1971] E.C.R. 49, [1971] C.M.L.R. 281 .... 669, 727

xli

40/70   Sirena Srl v. Eda Srl [1971] E.C.R. 69, [1971] C.M.L.R. 260   378
41–44/70   International Fruit Company BV v. Commission [1971] E.C.R. 411,
    [1975] 2 C.M.L.R. 515   814
45 & 49/70   Bode v. Commission [1971] E.C.R. 465 ....   1019, 1030
48/70   Bernardi v. Parliament [1971] E.C.R. 175   1212
59/70   Netherlands v. Commission [1971] E.C.R. 639 .... 871, 1032, 1055, 1057, 1449
62/70   Bock KA v. Commission [1972] C.M.L.R. 160 .... 807, 1076, 1077, 1144
76/70   Ludwig Wünsche & Co v. Hauptzollamt Ludwigshafen am Rhein [1971]
    E.C.R. 393 ....   418, 525
79/70   Müllers v. Economic and Social Committee [1971] E.C.R. 689 .... 961, 1032,
    1035, 1040, 1041, 1384
80/70   Defrenne v. Belgian State [1971] E.C.R. 445, [1974] 1 C.M.L.R. 494   673
2/71   Germany v. Commission [1971] E.C.R. 669, [1972] C.M.L.R. 431 ...... 1035, 1043
3/71   Gebrüder Bagusat AG v. Hauptzollamt Berlin Packhof [1971] E.C.R. 577,
    [1972] C.M.L.R. 761   1232
5/71   Aktien-Zuckerfabrik Schöppenstedt v. Council [1971] E.C.R. 975 .... 506, 507,
    514, 524, 525, 563, 752
6/71   Fa Rheinmühlen Düsseldorf v. Einfuhr-und Vorratsstelle für Getreide
    und Futtermittel (No. 1) [1971] E.C.R. 823, [1972] C.M.L.R. 401 .... 460, 568
9 & 11/71   Compagnie d'Approvisionnement de Transport et de Credit SA and
    Grands Moulins de Paris SA v. Commission [1972] E.C.R. 391, [1973]
    C.M.L.R. 529 .... 507, 532, 535, 563, 653, 673
20/71   Sabbatini née Bertoni v. Parliament [1972] E.C.R. 345, [1972] C.M.L.R.
    945 .... 52, 652, 1035, 1049, 1409
22/71   Béguelin Import Co v. G.L. Import Export SA [1971] E.C.R. 949, [1972]
    C.M.L.R. 81   1201
32/71   Chollet née Bauduin v. Commission [1972] E.C.R. 363, [1972] C.M.L.R.
    945   1035
36/71   Firma Günter Henck v. Hauptzollamt Emden [1972] E.C.R. 187, [1972]
    C.M.L.R. 785   486
43/71   Politi S.A.S. v. Ministero dello Finanze [1971] E.C.R. 1039, [1973]
    C.M.L.R. 60   252
46/71   Brandau v. Council [1972] E.C.R. 373, [1973] C.M.L.R. 99 .... 319, 641, 642
48/71   Commission v. Italy [1972] E.C.R. 527, [1972] C.M.L.R. 699   52
49/71   Hagen OHG v. Einfuhr-und Vorratsstelle für Getreide und Futtermittel
    [1972] E.C.R. 23, [1973] C.M.L.R. 35 ....   455, 465
77/71   Gervais-Danone AG v. Hauptzollamt München-Schwanthalerstrasse
    [1971] E.C.R. 1127, [1973] C.M.L.R. 415   1123
82/71   Pubblico Ministero v. SpA Soc. Agricola Industria Latte (S.A.I.L.) [1972]
    E.C.R. 119, [1972] C.M.L.R. 723   1123
93/71   Leonesio v. Ministero dell' Agricoltura e delle Foreste [1972] E.C.R. 287,
    [1973] C.M.L.R. 343   669
94/71   Firma Schlüter & Maack v. Hauptzollamt Hamburg-Jonas [1972] E.C.R.
    307, [1973] C.M.L.R. 113 ....   475, 663
96/71   R. & V. Haegeman Sprl v. Commission [1972] E.C.R. 1005, [1973]
    C.M.L.R. 365   536
1/72   Frilli v. The State [1972] E.C.R. 457, [1973] C.M.L.R. 386   498
6/72   Europemballage Corp. and Continental Can Co. Inc. v. Commission [1973]
    E.C.R. 215, [1973] C.M.L.R. 199 .... 377, 1201, 1214, 1418
21–24/72   International Fruit Company NV v. Produktschap voor Groenten en
    Fruit (No. 3) [1972] E.C.R. 1219, [1975] 2 C.M.L.R. 1 .... 251, 449, 457, 458,
    459, 963, 965, 967, 1195, 1402, 1412
27/72   Aimer v. Einfuhr-und Vorratsstelle für Getreide und Futtermittel [1972]
    E.C.R. 1091, [1973] C.M.L.R. 612   766
28/72   Tontodonati v. Commission [1973] E.C.R. 779   1047

33/72   Gunnella v. Commission [1973] E.C.R. 475 1043
35/72   Kley v. Commission [1973] E.C.R. 679 1407
36/72   Meganck v. Commission [1973] E.C.R. 527 .... 1063, 1065, 1066
39/72   Commission v. Italy [1973] E.C.R. 101, [1973] C.M.L.R. 439 .... 658, 663, 673
40/72   Schroeder KG v. Bundesamt für Ernährung und Forstwirtschaft [1973]
        E.C.R. 125, [1973] C.M.L.R. 824 .... 447, 761
42/72   Firma Alfons Lütticke GmbH v. Hauptzollamt Passau (No. 2) [1973]
        E.C.R. 57, [1973] C.M.L.R. 309 .... 408, 418, 445, 537, 595, 657
43/72   Merkur-Au Benhandels GmbH v. Commission [1973] E.C.R. 1055 ...... 593, 655
46/72   De Greef v. Commission [1973] E.C.R. 543 ..... 324, 1192, 1212, 1366, 1367, 1420
48/72   Brassiere de Haecht v. Wilkin (No. 2) [1973] E.C.R. 77, [1973] C.M.L.R.
        287 871
57/72   Westzucker GmbH v. Einfuhr-und Vorratsstelle für Getreide und Futtermit-
        tel [1973] E.C.R. 321 673
59/72   Firma Wünsche Handelsgesellschaft v. Commission [1973] E.C.R. 791,
        [1974] 1 C.M.L.R. 61 .... 507, 762
63–69/72 Wilhelm Werhahn Hansamühle v. Council [1973] E.C.R. 1229 408,
                                                      506, 531, 533, 607, 614, 616, 655
70/72   Commission v. Germany [1973] E.C.R. 813, [1973] C.M.L.R. 741 .... 258, 388,
                                                                                                              1073
71/72   Kuhl v. Council [1973] E.C.R. 705 .... 1062, 1066
72/72   Einfuhr-und Vorratsstelle für Getreide und Futtermittel v. Baer-Getreide
        GmbH [1973] E.C.R. 377 858
81/72   Commission v. Council [1973] E.C.R. 575, [1973] C.M.L.R. 639 .... 6, 23, 117,
        119, 243, 316, 643, 872, 939, 940, 1141, 1115, 1138
1/73   Westzucker GmbH v. Einfuhr-und Vorratsstelle für Zucker [1973] E.C.R.
        723 .... 6, 432, 939, 940, 947, 1116, 1119, 1120, 1122, 1169
4/73   J. Nold K.G. v. Commission [1974] E.C.R. 491, [1974] 2 C.M.L.R. 338 436,
                                                                                      625, 722, 723, 1420
5/73   Balkan-Import-Export-GmbH v. Hauptzollamt Berlin-Packhof [1973]
        E.C.R. 1091 .... 6, 244, 405, 407, 409, 410, 412, 443, 445, 446, 593, 746, 762,
                                                                                                  763, 848, 1130
15–33, 52, 53, 57–109, 117, 123, 132 & 135–137/73 Schots née Kortner v. Council,
        Commission and Parliament [1974] E.C.R. 177 .... 6, 975, 978, 1019, 1021, 1028,
                                                      1033, 1035, 1036, 1039, 1048, 1049
34/73   Fratelli Variola SpA v. Amministrazione Italiana delle Finanze [1973]
        E.C.R. 981 1132
40/73   'Suiker Unie' UA v. Commission [1975] E.C.R. 1663, [1976] 1 C.M.L.R.
        295 .... 1214, 1345, 1364, 1365, 1370
120/73 Gebrüder Lorenz GmbH v. Germany [1973] E.C.R. 1471 ...... 383, 1059, 1075
121/73 Markmann KG v. Germany [1973] E.C.R. 1495 .... 383, 1060
122/73 Nordsee, Deutsche Hochseefischerei GmbH v. Germany [1973] E.C.R.
        1511 .... 383, 1060
131/73 Italy v. Grosoli [1973] E.C.R. 1555, [1974] 2 C.M.L.R. 40 669
141/73 Fritz Lohrey v. Germany [1973] E.C.R. 1527 1060
143/73 S.O.P.A.D. v. F.O.R.M.A. [1973] E.C.R. 14331 [1977] 1 C.M.L.R.
        227 .... 432, 1122
148/73 Louwage v. Commission [1974] E.C.R. 81 .... 67, 68, 643, 962, 1079
149/73 Otto Witt KG v. Hauptzollamt Hamburg-Ericus [1973] E.C.R. 1587 1236
152/73 Sotgiu v. Deutsche Bundespost [1974] E.C.R. 153 .... 21, 617, 621, 622, 822
153/73 Holtz & Willemsen GmbH v. Council and Commission [1974] E.C.R.
        675 .... 409, 417, 595
169/73 Compagnie Continentale France v. Council [1975] 1 C.M.L.R. 578, [1975]
        E.C.R. 117 .... 517, 533
175/73 Union Syndicale v. Council [1974] E.C.R. 917, [1975] 1 C.M.L.R. 131 1189

186/73 Norddeutsches Vieh-und Fleischkontor GmbH v. Einfuhr-und Vorrats-
stelle für Schlachtvieh [1974] E.C.R. 533 734
188/73 Grassi v. Council [1974] E.C.R. 1099 .... 307, 322, 1231, 1407
2/74 Reyners v. Belgian State [1974] E.C.R. 631, [1974] 2 C.M.L.R. 305 832
3/74 Einfuhr-und Vorratsstelle für Getreide und Futtermittel v. Pfützenreuter
[1974] E.C.R. 589 .... 404, 463, 467
8/74 Procureur du Roi v. Dassonville [1974] E.C.R. 837, [1974] 2 C.M.L.R.
436 .... 773, 779, 780, 786
10/74 Becker v. Commission [1974] E.C.R. 867 1149
11/74 Union des Minotiers de la Champagne v. French Government [1974] E.C.R.
877, [1975] 1 C.M.L.R. 75 .... 408, 417, 418, 563, 585
15/74 Centrafarm v. Sterling Drug [1974] E.C.R. 1147, [1974] 2 C.M.L.R. 480 800
17/74 Sadolin & Holmblad A/S v. Commission [1974] E.C.R. 1063, [1974] 2
C.M.L.R. 459 .... 6, 368, 1192, 1229, 1324, 1329, 1434
18/74 Syndicat Général du Personnel des Organismes Européens v. Commission
[1974] E.C.R. 933, [1975] 1 C.M.L.R. 144 1189
25/74 Firma Günter Henck v. Einfuhr-und Vorratsstelle für Getreide und
Futtermittel [1974] E.C.R. 1017, [1975] 1 C.M.L.R. 49 .... 418, 489
26/74 Soc. Roquette Frères v. Commission [1976] E.C.R. 677 .... 51, 636, 640
28/74 Gillet v. Commission [1975] E.C.R. 463 1015
33/74 Van Binsbergen v. Bestuur van de Bedrijfsvereniging voor de Metaalnij-
verheid [1974] E.C.R. 1299, [1975] 1 C.M.L.R. 298 .... 725, 824
41/74 Van Duyn v. Home Office [1974] E.C.R. 1337, [1975] 1 C.M.L.R. 1 .. 252, 258,
816, 1148
43/74 Guillot v. Commission [1977] E.C.R. 1309 1364
56–60/74 Kurt Kampffmeyer v. Commission and Council [1976] E.C.R.
711 .... 594, 615
64/74 Firma Adolf Reich v. Hauptzollamt Landau [1975] E.C.R. 261, [1975] 1
C.M.L.R. 396 758
71/74 Nederlandse Vereniging voor de Fruit en Groentenimporthandel 'Frubo' v.
Commission [1975] E.C.R. 563, [1975] 2 C.M.L.R. 123 .... 368, 1090
74/74 C.N.T.A. SA v. Commission [1975] E.C.R. 533, [1977] 1 C.M.L.R.
171 .... 6, 941, 955, 1113, 1117, 1119, 1122, 1132, 1133, 1135, 1141, 1145
95–98/74, 15–75 & 100/75 Union Nationale des Coopératives Agricoles de Céréales
v. Commission [1975] E.C.R. 1615 .... 1139, 1140, 1142
100/74 C.A.M. SA v. Commission [1975] E.C.R. 1393 368
2/75 Einfuhr-und Vorratsstelle für Getreide und Futtermittel v. Firma C. Mackprang [1975] E.C.R. 607, [1977] 1 C.M.L.R. 198 .... 432, 753, 1076, 1077, 1142
5/75 Deuka, Deutsche Kraftfutter GmbH B.J. Stolp v. Einfuhr-und Vorratsstelle
für Getreide und Futtermittel [1975] E.C.R. 759 .... 872, 955, 1113, 1141,
1146, 1407
29/75 Kaufhof AG v. Commission [1976] E.C.R. 431 .... 808, 1076, 1077
36/75 Rutili v. Ministre de l'Intérieur [1975] E.C.R. 1219, [1976] 1 C.M.L.R.
140 .... 717, 818
39/75 Coenen v. Sociaal-Economische Raad [1975] E.C.R. 1547, [1976] 1
C.M.L.R. 30 .... 725, 827
43/75 Defrenne v. S.A.B.E.N.A. (No. 2) [1976] E.C.R. 455, [1976] 2 C.M.L.R.
98 .... 495, 496, 652, 673, 925, 1103, 1165, 1347
47/75 Germany v. Commission [1976] E.C.R. 569, [1977] 1 C.M.L.R.
149 1082,
1118
48/75 Belgium v. Royer [1976] E.C.R. 497 882
54/75 De Dapper v. Parliament [1976] E.C.R. 1381 307
55/75 Balkan-Import-Export GmbH v. Hauptzollamt Berlin-Packhof [1976]
E.C.R. 19 .... 633, 647

56/75   Elz v. Commission [1976] E.C.R. 1097 .... 972, 1004, 1065
67–85/75   Lesieur Cotelle et Associés SA v. Commission [1976] E.C.R. 391, [1976]
    2 C.M.L.R. 185 445
91/75   Hauptzollamt Göttingen und Bundesfinanzminister v. Wolfgang Miritz
    GmbH & Co [1976] E.C.R. 217 .... 243, 1018
95/75   Effem GmbH v. Hauptzollamt Lüneburg [1976] E.C.R. 361, [1976] 2
    C.M.L.R. 86 .... 445, 756
104/75   Officier van Justitie v. De Peijper [1976] E.C.R. 613, [1976] 2 C.M.L.R.
    271 779
105/75   Giuffrida v. Council [1976] E.C.R. 1395 .... 305, 324
110/75   Mills v. European Investment Bank [1976] E.C.R. 955 .... 83, 1405
113/75   Frescassetti v. Amministrazione delle Finanze dello Stato [1976] E.C.R.
    983 638
118/75   The State v. Watson and Belmann [1976] E.C.R. 1185, [1976] 2 C.M.L.R.
    552 .... 58, 592, 724, 818, 862
123/75   Küster v. Parliament [1976] E.C.R. 1701 .... 322, 1427, 1428
124/75   Perinciolo v. Council [1976] E.C.R. 1953 1368
130/75   Prais v. Council [1976] E.C.R. 1589, [1976] 2 C.M.L.R. 708 324
1P/76   Laying Up Fund for Inland Waterway Vessels [1977] E.C.R. 741, [1977]
    2 C.M.L.R. 278 1206
7/76   Industria Romana Carni e Affini SpA v. Amministrazione delle Finanze dello
    Stato [1976] E.C.R. 1213 .... 432, 655, 939, 1076, 1118, 1124, 1169
15/76   France v. Commission [1979] E.C.R. 321 .... 667, 1424
26/76   Metro-SB-Großmärkte GmbH & Co KG v. Commission [1977] E.C.R.
    1875, [1978] 2 C.M.L.R. 1 1194
27/76   United Brands Company v. Commission [1978] E.C.R. 207, [1978] 1
    C.M.L.R. 429 .... 370, 379, 1201, 1365, 1369, 1370, 1483
33/76   Rewe-Zentralfinanz eG and Rewe-Zentral AG v. Landwirtschaftskammer
    für das Saarland [1976] E.C.R. 1989, [1977] 1 C.M.L.R. 533 .... 51, 945
36/75   Rutili v. Minister of the Interior [1975] E.C.R. 1219 .... 717, 818
37/76   Simmenthal SpA v. Ministero delle Finanze (No. 1) [1976] E.C.R. 1871,
    [1977] 2 C.M.L.R. 1 794
41/76   Criel née Donckerwolcke v. Procureur de la République [1976] E.C.R. 1921,
    [1977] 2 C.M.L.R. 535 .... 773, 781, 782, 858
45/76   Comet BV v. Produktschap voor Siergewassen [1976] E.C.R. 2043, [1977] 1
    C.M.L.R. 533 .... 51, 945
46/76   Bauhuis v. Netherlands State [1977] E.C.R. 5 .... 792, 798
50/76   Amsterdam Bulb BV v. Produktschap voor Siergewassen [1977] E.C.R.
    137, [1977] 2 C.M.L.R. 218 664
52/76   Beneditti v. Munari Fratelli SAS [1977] E.C.R. 163 244
54–60/76   Compagnie Industrielle et Agricole du Comté de Loheac v. Council and
    Commission [1977] E.C.R. 645 .... 525, 1151
61/76   Geist v. Commission [1977] E.C.R. 1349 1422
64/76   Dumortier Frères SA v. Council [1979] E.C.R. 3091 529
68/76   Commission v. France [1977] E.C.R. 515, [1977] 2 C.M.L.R. 161 457
69/76   Firma Rolf H. Dittmeyer v. Hauptzollamt Hamburg-Waltershof [1977]
    E.C.R. 231 484
71/76   Thieffry v. Conseil de l'Ordre des Avocats à la Cour de Paris [1977] E.C.R.
    765, [1977] 2 C.M.L.R. 373 832
78/76   Firma Steinike & Weinlig v. Bundesamt für Ernährung und Forstwirtschaft
    [1977] E.C.R. 595, [1977] 2 C.M.L.R. 688 .... 388, 673
79/76   Fossi v. Bundesknappschaft [1977] E.C.R. 667 498
83 & 94/76, 4, 15 & 40/77   Bayerische HNL Vermehrungsbetriebe GmbH & Co. KG
    v. Council and Commission [1978] E.C.R. 1209, [1978] 3 C.M.L.R.
    566 .... 525, 526, 533, 719, 751, 752

85/76   Hoffmann-La Roche & Co AG v. Commission [1979] E.C.R. 461, [1979] 3
C.M.L.R. 211 .... 6, 65, 377, 1192, 1194, 1201, 1324,
1325, 1350, 1356, 1423, 1425

88/76   Soc. pour l'Exportation des Sucres SA v. Commission [1977] E.C.R.
709 .... 1118, 1147

99 & 100/76   Roomboterfabriek De Beste Boter NV v. Bundesanstalt für Landwirtschaftliche Marktordnung [1977] E.C.R. 861 426

101/76   Koninklijke Scholten-Honig NV v. Council & Commission [1977] E.C.R.
797, [1980] 2 C.M.L.R. 669 .... 968, 1140, 1147, 1360

111/76   Officier van Justitie v. Van den Hazel [1977] E.C.R. 901, [1980] 3 C.M.L.R.
12 .... 425, 456

112/76   Manzoni v. Fonds National de Retraite des Ouvriers Mineurs [1977]
E.C.R. 1647, [1978] 2 C.M.L.R. 416 245

114/76   Bela-Mühle Josef Bergmann KG v. Grows Farm GmbH & Co KG [1977]
E.C.R. 1211, [1979] 2 C.M.L.R. 83 .... 6, 420, 424, 718, 747, 748

116/76   Granaria v. Hoofdproduktschap voor Akkerbouwprodukten (No. 1) [1977]
E.C.R. 1247, [1979] 2 C.M.L.R. 83 .... 718, 747

117/76 & 16/77   Firma Albert Ruckdeschel & Co and Dramalt AG v. Hauptzollamt
Hamburg-St Annen and Hauptzollamt Itzehoe [1977] E.C.R. 1753, [1979]
2 C.M.L.R. 445 .... 6, 65, 245, 416, 417, 561, 562, 597, 626, 632, 670, 715

118/76   Balkan-Import-Export GmbH v. Hauptzollamt Berlin-Packhof [1977]
E.C.R. 1177 .... 637, 746

119–120/76   Ölmühle Hamburg AG and Firma Kurt A. Becher v. Hauptzollamt
Hamburg-Waltershof and Haupzollamt Bremen-Nord [1977] E.C.R. 1269,
[1979] 2 C.M.L.R. 83 .... 420, 747

121/76   Moli v. Commission [1977] E.C.R. 1971 .... 1325, 1348

124/76 & 20/77   Moulin et Huileries de Pout-à-Mousson SA v. Office National
Interprofessionnel des Céréales [1977] E.C.R. 1795, [1979] 2 C.M.L.R.
445 .... 245, 562, 626, 627, 632, 670

2/77   Hoffmann's Stärkefabriken AG v. Hauptzollamt Bielefeld [1977] E.C.R.
1375 .... 416, 596

6/77   Schouten BV v. Hoofdproduktschap voor Akkerbouwprodukten [1978]
E.C.R. 769 755

7/77   Ritter von Wüllerstorff und Urbair v. Commission [1978] E.C.R.
769 .... 322, 1402

8/77   Sagulo [1977] E.C.R. 1495, [1977] 2 C.M.L.R. 585 .... 725, 819, 828

19/77   Miller International Schallplatten GmbH v. Commission [1978] E.C.R. 131,
[1978] 2 C.M.L.R. 334 1236

22/77   Fonds National de Retraite des Ouvriers Mineurs v. Mura [1977] E.C.R.
1699, [1978] 2 C.M.L.R. 416 .... 572, 651

29/77   Roquette Frères SA v. Administration des Douanes [1977] E.C.R.
1835 .... 407, 409, 410, 414, 418, 445, 763

30/77   Regina v. Bouchereau [1977] E.C.R. 1999 [1977] 2 C.M.L.R. 800 817

34/77   Oslizlok v. Commission [1978] E.C.R. 1099 1338

52/77   Cayrol v. Giovanni Rivoira e Figli snc [1977] E.C.R. 2261, [1978] 2
C.M.L.R. 253 .... 782, 830

54/77   Herpels v. Commission [1978] E.C.R. 585 .... 972, 1006, 1007, 1022,
1023, 1025

56/77   Agence Européenne d'Interims SA v. Commission [1978] E.C.R. 2215,
[1979] 2 C.M.L.R. 57 1405

59/77   Establissements A. de Bloos Sprl v. Bouyer SCA [1977] E.C.R. 2359 [1978]
1 C.M.L.R. 511 1054

61/77   Commission v. Ireland [1978] E.C.R. 417, [1978] 2 C.M.L.R. 466 619

62/77   Carlsen Verlag GmbH v. Oberfinanzdirektion Köln [1977] E.C.R. 2343
[1978] 3 C.M.L.R. 14 489
68/77   Intercontinentale Fleischandelsgesellschaft mbH & Co KG (IFG) v. Commission [1978] E.C.R. 353 [1978] 2 C.M.L.R. 733 .... 516, 607, 1136, 1140
72/77   Universiteitskliniek Utrecht v. Inspecteur der Invoerrechten en Accijnzen
[1978] E.C.R. 189 [1979] 2 C.M.L.R. 514 489
74/77   Allgayer née Parzinger v. Parliament [1978] E.C.R. 977 315
75/77   Mollet v. Commission [1978] E.C.R. 897 1348
78/77   Firma Johann Lührs v. Hauptzollamt Hamburg-Jonas [1978] E.C.R. 169
[1978] 1 C.M.L.R. 657 .... 434, 1141, 1147
79/77   Kühlhaus Zentrum AG v. Hauptzollamt Hamburg-Harburg [1978] E.C.R.
611 .... 418, 569
87/77   Greco v. Fonds National de Retraite des Ouvriers Mineurs [1977] E.C.R.
1711 1087
88/77   Minister for Fisheries v. Schonenberg [1978] E.C.R. 473, [1978] 2 C.M.L.R.
519 622
90/77   Hellmut Stimming KG v. Commission [1978] E.C.R. 995 ...... 517, 941, 955, 1136
92/77   An Bord Bainne Co-operative Ltd v. Minister for Agriculture [1978] E.C.R.
497, [1978] 2 C.M.L.R. 567 244
94/77   Fratelli Zerbone Snc v. Amministrazione delle Finanze dello Stato [1978]
E.C.R. 99 455
96/77   Ancienne Maison Marcel Bauche SA v. Administration des Douanes [1978]
E.C.R. 383, [1978] 3 C.M.L.R. 133 .... 432, 1122, 1141
102/77   Hoffman-La Roche v. Centrafarm [1978] E.C.R. 1139, [1978] 3 C.M.L.R.
217 801
103 & 145/77   Royal Scholten-Honig (Holdings) Ltd and Tunnel Refineries Ltd v.
Intervention Board for Agriculture Produce (1978) E.C.R. 2037, [1979] 1
C.M.L.R. 675 .... 416, 421, 562, 611, 628, 671
111/77   Bleiindustrie KG v. Hauptzollamt Hamburg-Waltershof [1978] E.C.R.
659 489
112/77   August Töpfer & Co. GmbH v. Commission [1978] E.C.R. 1019 ...... 872, 941,
955, 1075, 1114, 1118, 1143, 1148
113/77   NTN Toyo Bearing Co Ltd v. Council [1979] E.C.R. 1185, [1979] 2
C.M.L.R. 257 .... 389, 393, 964, 1191, 1324, 1340, 1359,
1360, 1361, 1383, 413, 1421, 1440, 1463
118/77   Import Standard Office v. Council [1979] E.C.R. 1277, [1979] 2 C.M.L.R.
257 .... 389, 1413
119/77   Nippon Seiko KK v. Council and Commission [1979] E.C.R. 1303, [1979] 2
C.M.L.R. 257 .... 389, 965, 1413
120/77   Koyo Seiko Co Ltd v. Council and Commission [1979] E.C.R. 1337, [1979]
2 C.M.L.R. 257 .... 389, 965, 1413
121/77   Nachi Fujikoshi Corp v. Council and Commission [1979] E.C.R. 1363
[1979] 2 C.M.L.R. 257 965
125/77   Koninklijke   Scholten-Honig   NV   v.   Hoofdproduktschap   voor
Akkerbouwprodukten   [1978]   E.C.R.   1991,   [1979]   1   C.M.L.R.
675 .... 432, 562, 628, 670, 1122, 1139
131/77   Firma Milac v. Hauptzollamt Saarbrücken [1978] E.C.R. 1041 764
139/77   Denkavit Futtermittel GmbH v. Finanzamt Warendorf [1978] E.C.R. 1317,
[1979] 1 C.M.L.R. 108 .... 586, 591
146/77   British Beef Co Ltd v. Intervention Board for Agricultural Produce [1978]
E.C.L. 1347, [1978] 3 C.M.L.R. 47 .... 1141, 1147
149/77   Defrenne v. SABENA (No. 3) [1978] E.C.R. 1365, [1978] 3 C.M.L.R.
312 .... 626, 651, 673
151/77   Peiser & Co KG v. Hauptzollamt Hamburg-Ericus [1979] E.C.R.
1469 .... 764, 1118, 1147

xlvii

156/77   Commission v. Belgium [1978] E.C.R. 1881 .... 1032, 1034, 1053
1/78   Kenny v. Insurance Officer [1978] E.C.R. 1489, [1978] 3 C.M.L.R.
651 .... 622, 651
2/78   Commission v. Belgium [1979] E.C.R. 1761, [1980] 1 C.M.L.R. 216 780
6/78   Union Française de Céréales v. Hauptzollamt Hamburg-Jonas [1978] E.C.R.
1675 54
8/78   Milac GmbH v. Hauptzollamt Freiburg [1978] E.C.R. 1721 .... 417, 445,
573, 574, 596
11/78   Italy v. Commission [1979] E.C.R. 1527 764
12/78   Italy v. Commission [1979] E.C.R. 1731, [1980] 2 C.M.L.R. 573 .... 445, 764
14/78   Denkavit Srl and Denkavit BV v. Commission [1978] E.C.R. 2497, [1979] 2
C.M.L.R. 135 510
16/78   Choquet [1978] E.C.R. 2293, [1979] 1 C.M.L.R. 535 823
21/78   Delkvist v. Anklagemyndigheden [1978] E.C.R. 2327, [1979] 1 C.M.L.R.
372 252
30/78   The Distillers Company Ltd v. Commission [1980] E.C.R. 2229 [1980] 3
C.M.L.R. 121 .... 1348, 1425
31/78   Bussone v. Ministero dell'Agricoltura e delle Foreste [1978] E.C.R. 2429
[1979] 3 C.M.L.R. 18 .... 458, 649
34/78   Yoshida Nederland BV v. Kamer Van Koophandel en Fabrieken voor
Friesland [1979] E.C.R. 115, [1979] 2 C.M.L.R. 747 249
35/78   N.G.J. Schouten BV v. Hoofdproduktschap voor Akkerbouwprodukten
[1978] E.C.R. 2643 947
83/78   Pigs Marketing Board (Northern Ireland) v. Redmond [1978] E.C.R.
2347 456
84/78   Tomadini SNC v. Amministrazione delle Finanze dello Stato [1979] E.C.R.
1801, [1980] 2 C.M.L.R. 573 .... 432, 1135, 1143
86/78   SA des Grandes Distilleries Peureux v. Directeur des Services Fiscaux de la
Haute-Saône [1979] E.C.R. 897, [1980] 3 C.M.L.R. 337 .... 657, 673
87/78   Welding & Co v. Hauptzollamt Hamburg-Waltershof [1978] E.C.R.
2457 .... 418, 757, 1406, 1412
88/78   Hauptzollamt Hamburg-Jonas v. Hermann Kendermann OHG [1978]
E.C.R. 2477 599
92/78   Simmenthal SpA v. Commission [1979] E.C.R. 777, [1980] 1 C.M.L.R.
25 .... 445, 762, 792, 1022
95/78   Dulciora SpA v. Amminstrazione delle Finanze dello Stato [1979] E.C.R.
1549 .... 764, 1141
98/78   Firma A. Racke v. Hauptzollamt Mainz [1979] E.C.R. 69 947
99/78   Weingut Gustav Decker KG v. Hauptzollamt Landau [1979] E.C.R.
101 .... 433, 1121, 1125
101/78   Granaria BV v. Hoofdproduktschap voor Akkerbouwprodukten (No. 2)
[1979] E.C.R. 623, [1979] 3 C.M.L.R. 124 .... 241, 420, 466, 713, 714, 716, 718
120/78   Rewe-Zentral AG v. Bundesmonopolverwaltung für Branntwein [1979]
E.C.R. 649, [1979] 3 C.M.L.R. 494 .... 773, 787, 859
122/78   Buitoni SA v. Fonds d'Orientation et de Regularisation des Marchés
Agricoles [1979] E.C.R. 677, [1979] 2 C.M.L.R. 665 .... 6, 735
128/78   Commission v. United Kingdom [1979] E.C.R. 419, [1979] 2 C.M.L.R.
45 661
138/78   Stolting v. Hauptzollamt Hamburg-Jonas [1979] E.C.R. 713, [1979] 3
C.M.L.R. 588 .... 6, 410, 425, 754
139/78   Coccioli v. Bundesanstalt für Arbeit [1979] E.C.R. 991, [1979] 3 C.M.L.R.
144 824
148/78   Pubblico Ministero v. Ratti [1979] E.C.R. 1629, [1980] 1 C.M.L.R.
96 .... 252, 1148
153/78   Commission v. Germany [1979] E.C.R. 2555, [1980] 1 C.M.L.R. 198 790

154, 205–206, 226–228, 263-264/78 & 31, 39, 83 & 85/79   Ferriera Valsabbia *v.*
Commission [1980] E.C.R. 907, [1981] 1 C.M.L.R. 613 848
157/78   Travigo GmbH & Co KG *v.* Hamptzollamt Aachen-Nord [1979] E.C.R.
1657 764
158/78   Biegi *v.* Hauptzollamt Bochum [1979] E.C.R. 1103 .... 484, 1123
166/78   Italy *v.* Council [1979] E.C.R. 2575, [1981] 3 C.M.L.R. 770 .... 297, 412
171/78   Commission *v.* Denmark [1980] E.C.R. 447, [1981] 2 C.M.L.R. 688 623
179/78   Procureur de la République *v.* Rivoira and Giovanni Rivoira & Figli SNC
[1979] E.C.R. 1147, [1979] 3 C.M.L.R. 456 783
180/78   Brouwer-Kaune *v.* Bestuur van de Bedrijfsvereniging voor het Kledingbedrijf [1979] E.C.R. 2111, [1980] 2 C.M.L.R. 145 54
181/78   Ketelhandel P. van Paassen BV *v.* Inspecteur der Invoerrechter en
Accijnzen [1979] E.C.R. 2063, [1980] 2 C.M.L.R. 47 1422
185–204/78   Firma J. Van Dam en Zonen [1979] E.C.R. 2345, [1980] 1 C.M.L.R.
350 650
209/78   Heintz van Landewyck Sàrl, Fédération Belgo-Luxembourgeoise des
Industries du Tabac Asbl (FEDETAB) *v.* Commission [1980] E.C.R. 3125,
[1981] 3 C.M.L.R. 134 .... 1345, 1357, 1363, 1366, 1369, 1370
216/78   Beljatzky *v.* Hauptzollamt Aachen-Süd [1979] E.C.R. 2273 1101
217/78   Nicolas Corman & Fils SA *v.* Hauptzollamt Aachen-Süd [1979] E.C.R.
2287 1101
222/78   I.C.A.P. Distribution Srl *v.* Beneventi [1979] E.C.R. 1163 [1979] 3
C.M.L.R. 475 657
230/78   Eridania-Zuccherifici Nazionali SpA *v.* Minister of Agriculture and Fore-
stry [1979] E.C.R. 2749 .... 400, 401, 573, 574, 582, 759, 1130
231/78   Commission *v.* United Kingdom [1979] E.C.R. 1447, [1979] 2 C.M.L.R.
427 668
237/78   Caisse Regionale d'Assurance Maladie de Lille *v.* Palermo née Toia [1979]
E.C.R. 2645, [1980] 2 C.M.L.R. 31 622
238/78   Ireks-Akady GmbH *v.* Council and Commission [1979] E.C.R. 2955 507
240/78   Atlanta Amsterdam BV *v.* Produktschap voor en Vlees [1979] E.C.R.
2137 736
241, 242 & 245-250/78   Deutsche Getreideverwertung und Rheinische Kraftfutter-
werke GmbH (DGV) *v.* Council and Commission [1979] E.C.R.
3017 .... 6, 507, 519
251/78   Denkavit *v.* Minister für Ernährung [1979] E.C.R. 3369, [1980] 3 C.M.L.R.
513 791
253/78   Procureur de la Republique *v.* Giry [1980] E.C.R. 2327, [1981] 2 C.M.L.R.
99 1374
258/78   L.C. Nungesser KG and Kwit Eisele *v.* Commission [1982] E.C.R. 2015
[1983] 1 C.M.L.R. 278 842
265/78   H. Ferwerda BV *v.* Produktschap voor Vee en Vlees [1980] E.C.R. 617,
[1980] 3 C.M.L.R. 737 .... 51, 455, 475, 634, 671, 674, 1097, 1098
4/79   Soc. Cooperative (Providence Agricole de la Champagne) *v.* Office National
Interprofessionnel des Céréales (ONIC) [1980] E.C.R. 2823 .... 245, 445,
605, 670, 674, 1107
12/79   Hans-Otto Wagner GmbH Agrarhandel KG *v.* Commission [1979] E.C.R.
3657 538
15/79   P.B. Groenveld BV *v.* Produktschap voor Vee en Vlees [1979] E.C.R. 3409,
[1981] 1 C.M.L.R. 207 776
22/79   Greenwich Film Production *v.* Soc. des Auteurs, Compositeurs et Editeurs
de Musique (SACEM) and Société des Editions Labrador [1979] E.C.R.
3275, [1980] 1 C.M.L.R. 629 378
30/79   Land Berlin *v.* Wigei Wild-Geflügel-Eier-Import GmbH & Co KG [1980]
E.C.R. 151, [1981] 3 C.M.L.R. 746 792

33/79   Kuhner v. Commission [1980] E.C.R. 1677 .... 306, 1332, 1362, 1384,
                                                            1407, 1426, 1427
36/79   Denkavit Futtermittel GmbH v. Finanzamt Warendorf [1979] E.C.R.
      3439 588
37/79   Marty v. Lander [1980] E.C.R. 2481, [1981] 2 C.M.L.R. 143 1374
40/79   Mrs P v. Commission [1981] E.C.R. 361 1122
41, 121 & 796/79   Testa v. Bundesanstalt für Arbeit, Nürnberg [1980] E.C.R. 1979,
      [1981] 2 C.M.L.R. 552 .... 502, 825
44/79   Hauer v. Land Rheinland Pfalz [1979] E.C.R. 3727, [1980] 3 C.M.L.R.
      42 .... 426, 434, 435, 723, 859, 863, 1459
49/79   Pool v. Council [1980] E.C.R. 569, [1980] 3 C.M.L.R. 279 525
52/79   Procureur du Roi v. Debauve [1980] E.C.R. 833, [1981] 2 C.M.L.R.
      362 .... 606, 614, 830
61/79   Amministrazione delle Finanze dello Stato v. Denkavit Italiana Srl [1980]
      E.C.R. 1205, [1981] 3 C.M.L.R. 694 945
66, 127 & 128/79   Amministrazione delle Finanze dello Stato v. Meridionale
      Industria Salumi Srl [1980] E.C.R. 1237, [1981] 1 C.M.L.R. 1 .... 638, 671, 674,
                                          871, 1102, 1150, 1152, 1169
68/79   Hans Just I/S v. Ministeriet for Skatter og Afgifter [1980] E.C.R. 501, [1981]
      2 C.M.L.R. 714 .... 51, 624, 916, 922, 945, 1163
89/79 Bonu v. Council [1980] E.C.R. 553 .... 1409, 1427, 1384
98/79   Pecastaing v. The Belgian State [1980] E.C.R. 691, [1980] 3 C.M.L.R.
      685 .... 6, 433, 445, 1120, 1121, 1125, 1127, 1151, 1343
99/79   SA Lancôme and Cosparfrance Nederland BV v. Etos BV and Albert Heijn
      Supermart BV [1980] E.C.R. 2511, [1981] 2 C.M.L.R. 164 .... 6, 433, 445,
                                452, 1120, 1121, 1125, 1127, 1151, 1343, 1374
101/79   Vecchioli v. Commission [1980] E.C.R. 3069 1212
106/79   Vereniging ter Bevordering van de Belangen des Boekhandels v. Eldi
      Records BV [1980] E.C.R. 1137, [1980] 3 C.M.L.R. 719 .... 1061, 1065, 1067
109/79   Maïseries de Beauce Sàrl v. Office National Interprofessionnel des Céréales
      [1980] E.C.R. 2883 .... 246, 450, 764
119 & 126/79   Lippische Hauptgenossenschaft eG v. Bundesanstalt für Landwirt-
      schaftliche Marktordnung [1980] E.C.R. 1863 .... 55, 475, 1099
122-123/79   Schiavo v. Council [1981] E.C.R. 473 .... 1032, 1038
129/79   Macarthys Ltd v. Smith [1980] E.C.R. 1275, [1980] 2 C.M.L.R.
      205 .... 236, 601
130/79   Express Dairy Foods Ltd v. Intervention Board for Agricultural Produce
      [1980] E.C.R. 1887, [1981] 1 C.M.L.R. 451 .... 51, 247, 968, 1095,
                              1099, 1106, 1110, 1111, 1449
131/79   R. v. Secretary of State for Home Affairs, ex p. Santillo [1980] E.C.R. 1585,
      [1980] 2 C.M.L.R. 308 .... 1345, 1434
133/79   Sucrimex SA and Westzucker GmbH v. Commission [1980] E.C.R. 1299,
      [1981] 2 C.M.L.R. 479   510
136/79   National Panasonic (UK) Ltd v. Commission [1980] E.C.R. 2033, [1980] 3
      C.M.L.R. 169 .... 6, 835, 1195, 1218, 1229, 1239, 1324, 1328,
                             1329, 1330, 1331, 1332, 1337, 1383, 1421
138/79   Roquette Frères SA v. Council [1980] E.C.R. 3333 .... 402, 413, 759,
                                  1127, 1386, 1422
139/79   Maizena GmbH v. Council [1980] E.C.R. 3393 .... 501, 584, 610, 759, 1044,
                                  1127, 1456
149/79   Commission v. Belgium [1980] E.C.R. 3881, [1981] 2 C.M.L.R. 413 .... 20, 21,
                            246, 249, 450, 822, 823, 1107
155/79   Australian Mining & Smelting Europe Ltd v. Commission [1982] E.C.R.
      1575, [1982] 2 C.M.L.R. 264 .... 714, 1193, 1221, 1240, 1346, 1352, 1434

532, 534, 567, 600, 618 & 660/79   Amesz v. Commission and Council [1981] E.C.R.
    2569 1016
543/79   Birke v. Commission and Council [1981] E.C.R. 2669 .... 1016, 1164
730/79   Philip Morris Holland BV v. Commission [1980] E.C.R. 2671, [1981] 2
    C.M.L.R. 321 388
788/79   Italy v. Gilli [1980] E.C.R. 2071, [1981] 1 C.M.L.R. 146 .... 777, 787
792/79R   Camera Care Ltd v. Commission [1980] E.C.R. 119, [1980] 1 C.M.L.R.
    334 .... 1346, 1379
808/79   Fratelli Pardini SpA v. Commission [1980] E.C.R. 2103, [1981] 2 C.M.L.R.
    603 .... 783, 856
811/79   Amministrazione delle Finanze dello Stato v. Ariete SpA [1980] E.C.R.
    2545, [1981] 1 C.M.L.R. 316 945
816/79   Klaus Mecke & Co v. Hauptzollamt Bremen-Ost [1980] E.C.R. 3029 489
817/79   Buyl v. Commission [1982] E.C.R. 245 .... 1016, 1131, 1139
819/79   Germany v. Commission [1981] E.C.R. 21 .... 460, 665
827/79   Amministrazione delle Finanze dello Stato v. Acampora [1980] E.C.R.
    3731, [1981] 2 C.M.L.R. 349 1101
1252/79   Acciaierie e Ferriere Lucchini SpA v. Commission [1980] E.C.R. 3753
    [1981] 3 C.M.L.R. 487 .... 1081, 1083
2/80   Dautzenberg v. Court of Justice [1980] E.C.R. 3107 .... 322, 1089, 1091
8/80   Danks Supermarked v. Imerco [1981] E.C.R. 181, [1981] 3 C.M.L.R.
    590 .... 801, 802
22/80   Boussac Saint-Frères SA v. Gerstenmeier [1980] E.C.R. 3427 [1982] 1
    C.M.L.R. 202 .... 614, 622
25/80   De Briey v. Commission [1981] E.C.R. 637 .... 1405, 1408, 1422
27/80   Fietje [1980] E.C.R. 3839, [1981] 3 C.M.L.R. 722 787
31/80   L'Oréal v. De Nieuwe A.M.C.K. Pvba [1980] E.C.R. 3775, [1981] 2
    C.M.L.R. 235 .... 983, 1374
35/80   Denkavit Nederland BV v. Produktschap voor Zuivel [1981] E.C.R.
    45 .... 415, 445
53/80   Officier van Justitie v. Koninklijke Kaasfabriek Eyssen BV [1981] E.C.R.
    409, [1982] 2 C.M.L.R. 20 791
64/80   Giuffrida and Campogrande v. Council [1981] E.C.R. 693 .... 955, 969
66/80   SpA International Chemical Corporation v. Amministrazione delle
    Finanze dello Stato [1981] E.C.R. 1191, [1983] 2 C.M.L.R. 593 245
95/80   Soc. Havraise Dervieu-Delahais SA v. Directeur Général des Douanes
    et Droits Indirects [1981] E.C.R. 317 445
96/80   Jenkins v. Kingsgate (Clothing Productions) Ltd. [1981] E.C.R. 911, [1981] 2
    C.M.L.R. 24 .... 599, 622
98/80   Romano v. Institut Nationale d'Assurance Maladie-Invalidité (INAMI)
    [1981] E.C.R. 1241, [1983] 2 C.M.L.R. 698 1207
100–103/80   Musique Diffusion Française SA v. Commission [1983] E.C.R. 1825,
    [1983] 3 C.M.L.R. 221 .... 838, 1237, 1242, 1325, 1339, 1342, 1345, 1428
112/80   Firma Anton Dürbeck v. Hauptzollamt-Frankfurt am Main-Flughafen
    [1981] E.C.R. 1095, [1982] 3 C.M.L.R. 314 .... 414, 809, 859, 867,
    1115, 1136, 1144
113/80   Commission v. Ireland [1981] E.C.R. 1625, [1982] 1 C.M.L.R. 706 786
115/80   Demont v. Commission [1981] E.C.R. 3147 .... 1342, 1346, 1362, 1366, 1368,
    1400, 1409, 1423
125/80   Arning v. Commission [1981] E.C.R. 2539 .... 324, 1362
127/80   Grogan v. Commission [1982] E.C.R. 869 .... 939, 1015, 1016, 1017, 1114,
    1118, 1131, 1138, 1142
130/80   Fabriek voor Hoogwaardige Voedingsprodukten Kelderman BV [1981]
    E.C.R. 527 787

132/80   United Foods v. Belgian State [1981] E.C.R. 995, [1982] 1 C.M.L.R.
          273 .... 787, 792
143/80   Amministrazione delle Finanze dello Stato v. Carlo Salengo [1981] E.C.R.
          1413 236
151/80   De Hoe v. Commission [1981] E.C.R. 3161 .... 322, 1402
152/80   Debayser SA v. Directeur du Fonds d'Intervention et de Régularisation du
          Marché du Sucre [1981] E.C.R. 1291 .... 765, 1141
155/80   Oebel [1981] E.C.R. 1993, [1983] 1 C.M.L.R. 390 .... 499, 776, 803
158/80   Rewe Handelsgesellschaft Nord mbH and Rewe Markt Steffen v. Haupt-
          zollamt Kiel [1981] E.C.R. 1805, [1982] 1 C.M.L.R. 449 ...... 404, 605, 1402, 1412
164/80   De Pascale v. Commission [1982] E.C.R. 909 .... 1138, 1405
167/80   Curtis v. Commission and Parliament [1981] E.C.R. 1499 ...... 1015, 1016, 1122,
                                                                                              1131, 1138
169/80   Administration des Douanes v. Gondrand Frères SA [1981] E.C.R.
          1931 .... 404, 1153
173/80   Blasig v. Commission [1981] E.C.R. 1649 1047
182/80   Gauff, Ingenieure GmbH & Co KG v. Commission [1982] E.C.R. 799,
          [1982] 3 C.M.L.R. 402 .... 958, 961
188-190/80 France v. Commission [1982] E.C.R. 2545, [1982] 3 C.M.L.R.
          144 .... 69, 248
193/80   Commission v. Italy [1981] E.C.R. 3019 .... 777, 787, 789
195/80   Michel v. Parliament [1981] E.C.R. 2861 1424
196/80   Anglo-Irish Meat Co. v. Minister for Agriculture [1981] E.C.R. 2263 1123
197–200, 243, 245 & 247/80   Ludwigshafener Walzmühle Erling KG v. Council
          and Commission [1981] E.C.R. 3211 .... 410, 414, 517, 649, 755, 1130, 1242
258/80   Metallurgica Rumi SpA v. Commission [1982] E.C.R. 487 .... 1118, 1128
272/80   Frans-Nederlandse Maatschappij voor Biologische Producten BV [1981]
          E.C.R. 3277, [1982] 2 C.M.L.R. 497 791
275/80   Krupp Stahl AG v. Commission [1981] E.C.R. 2489 .... 1211, 1382, 1411
276/80   Ferriera Padana SpA v. Commission [1982] E.C.R. 517 .... 845, 1118, 1128
279/80   Webb [1981] E.C.R. 3305 [1982] 1 C.M.L.R. 719 .... 618, 831
280/80   D'Aloya née Bakke v. Council [1981] E.C.R. 2887 .... 314, 315
1/81   Pfizer Inc v. Eurim-Pharm GmbH [1981] E.C.R. 2913, [1982] 1 C.M.L.R.
          406 .... 801, 802, 803
7/81   Sinatra v. Fonds National de Retrâite des Ouvriers Mineurs [1982] E.C.R.
          137, [1982] 3 C.M.L.R. 77 1370
14/81   Alpha Steel Ltd v. Commission [1982] E.C.R. 749 .... 951, 957, 972, 993, 1008,
                                                                                  1024, 1030, 1131, 1139
19/81   Burton v. British Railways Board [1982] E.C.R. 555, [1982] 2 C.M.L.R.
          136 .... 653, 673
36/81   Seton v. Commission [1983] E.C.R. 1789 .... 1360, 1361, 1409
37/81   Seton v. Commission [1981] E.C.R. 813 .... 1360, 1361, 1409
39/81   Halyvourgiki Inc v. Commission [1982] E.C.R. 593 .... 297, 345
44/81   Germany v. Commission [1982] E.C.R. 1855, [1983] 2 C.M.L.R. 656 1060
52/81   Faust v. Commission [1982] E.C.R. 3745 .... 415, 645, 812, 1131, 1139
54/81   Firma Wilhelm Fromme v. Bundesanstalt für Landwirtschaftliche Marktord-
          nung [1982] E.C.R. 1449 .... 416, 475, 771, 1099
60/81   IBM v. Commission [1981] E.C.R. 2639, [1981] 3 C.M.L.R. 635 .... 73, 133,
                                                                961, 963, 964, 1331, 1409, 1420, 1421, 1423
62 & 63/81   Seco SA v. Establissement d'Assurance contre la Vieillesse et
          l'Invalidité [1982] E.C.R. 223 .... 618, 829
67/81   Ruske v. Commission [1982] E.C.R. 661 314
75/81   State v. Blesgen [1982] E.C.R. 1211, [1983] 1 C.M.L.R. 431 803
77/81   Zuckerfabrik Franken GmbH v. Germany [1982] E.C.R. 681 .... 769, 1104

84/81 Staple Dairy Products Ltd v. Intervention Board for Agricultural Produce
[1982] E.C.R. 1763 .... 432, 434, 1126
95/81 Commission v. Italy [1982] E.C.R. 2187 802
106/81 Julius Kind KG v. EEC [1982] E.C.R. 2885 .... 408, 416, 417, 589
108/81 Amylum v. Council [1982] E.C.R. 3107 .... 433, 527, 940, 952, 1078, 1127
110/81 Roquette Frères SA v. Council [1982] E.C.R. 3159 .... 433, 1019, 1078
113/81 Otto Reichelt GmbH v. Hauptzollamt Berlin-Süd [1982] E.C.R. 1957 1106
114/81 Tunnel Refineries Ltd v. Council [1982] E.C.R. 3189 1127
115–116/81 Adoui and Cornuaille v. Belgian State [1982] E.C.R. 1665, [1982] 3
C.M.L.R. 631 .... 47, 821
119/81 Klöckner-Werke AG v. Commission [1982] E.C.R. 2627 672
124/81 Commission v. United Kingdom [1983] 2 C.M.L.R. 1 793
126/81 Wünsche Handelsgesellschaft v. Germany [1982] E.C.R. 1479 ..... 446, 447, 449
141–143/81 Holdijk [1982] E.C.R. 1299, [1983] 2 C.M.L.R. 635 655
146, 192 & 193/81 BayWa AG v. Bundesanstalt für Landwirtschaftliche Markt-
ordnung [1982] E.C.R. 1503 .... 772, 1436
147/81 Merkur Fleisch-Import GmbH v. Hauptzollamt Hamburg-Ericus [1982]
E.C.R. 1389 .... 442, 730, 736
206/81 Alvarez v. Parliament [1982] E.C.R. 3369 1342
210/81 Demo-Studio Schmidt v. Commission [1983] E.C.R. 3045, [1984] 1
C.M.L.R. 63 .... 338, 398, 1194
217/81 Compagnie Interagra SA v. Commission [1982] E.C.R. 2233 .... 510, 537
220/81 Robertson [1982] E.C.R. 2349, [1983] 1 C.M.L.R. 556 788
230/81 Luxembourg v. Parliament [1983] 2 C.M.L.R. 726 62
232/81/ Agricola Commerciale Ohio Srl v. Commission [1981] E.C.R.
2193 .... 75, 967, 969, 988, 1022, 1079
233/81 Denkavit Futtermittel GmbH v. Germany [1982] E.C.R. 2933 649
236A/81 Celanese Chemical Co Inc v. Council and Commission [1982] E.C.R.
1183 1352
245/81 Edeka Zentrale AG v. Germany [1982] E.C.R. 2745 .... 562, 631, 648, 671,
810, 1131, 1139, 1141
247/81 Commission v. Germany [1984] E.C.R. 1111, [1985] 1 C.M.L.R. 640 797
249/81 Commission v. Ireland [1982] E.C.R. 4005, [1983] 2 C.M.L.R. 104 787
255/81 Grendel GmbH v. Finanzamt für Körperschaften, Hamburg [1982] E.C.R.
2301, [1983] 1 C.M.L.R. 379 1149
256/81 Paul's Agriculture v. Council and Commission [1983] E.C.R. 1707, [1983] 3
C.M.L.R. 176 .... 507, 523
261/81 Walter Rau Lebensmittelwerke v. De Smedt Pvba [1982] E.C.R. 3961,
[1983] 2 C.M.L.R. 496 788
265/81 Giannini v. Commission [1982] E.C.R. 3865 322
272/81 RU-MI Sàrl v. F.O.R.M.A. [1982] E.C.R. 4167 .... 452, 737, 738, 743
273/81 Société Laitière de Gacé v. F.O.R.M.A. [1982] E.C.R. 4193, [1984] 1
C.M.L.R. 542 767
280/81 Hoffmann v. Commission [1983] E.C.R. 889 315
286/81 Openbaar Ministerie v. Oosthoek's Uitgeversmaatschappij BV [1982]
E.C.R. 4575, [1983] 3 C.M.L.R. 428 657
289/81 Mavridis v. Parliament [1983] E.C.R. 1731 .... 949, 953, 1088, 1093
292/81 Lion et Cie v. F.I.R.S. [1982] E.C.R. 3887 .... 612, 613, 1402, 1412
294/81 Control Data Belgium NV v. Commission [1983] 2 C.M.L.R.
357 .... 491, 1194, 1401
301/81 Commission v. Belgium [1983] E.C.R. 467, [1984] 2 C.M.L.R. 430 1404
307/81 Alusuisse Italia SpA v. Council and Commission [1982] E.C.R.
3463 .... 966, 967, 1191
322/81 Michelin v. Commission [1983] E.C.R. 3461, [1985] 1 C.M.L.R. 282 1339,
1344, 1349, 1356

2–4/82   Delhaize Fréres 'Le Lion' SA v. Belgium [1983] E.C.R. 2973, [1985] 1
          C.M.L.R. 561 .... 792, 1084
5/82   Hauptzollamt Krefeld v. Maizena GmbH [1982] E.C.R. 4601 599
8/82   KG in der Firma Hans-Otto Wagner GmbH Agrarhandel v. Bundesanstalt
          für Landwirtschaftliche Marktordnung [1983] E.C.R. 371 .... 564, 573, 583
9/82   Ohrgaard v. Commission [1983] E.C.R. 2379 322
10/82   Mogensen v. Commission [1983] E.C.R. 2397 322
40/82   Commission v. United Kingdom [1982] E.C.R. 2793, [1982] 3 C.M.L.R.
          497 .... 625, 792
42/82   Commission v. France [1983] E.C.R. 1013, [1984] 1 C.M.L.R. 160 792
43 & 63/82   VBVB and VBBB v. Commission [1982] E.C.R. 1241, [1985] 1
          C.M.L.R. 27 1344
64/82   Tradax Graanhandel BV v. Commission [1984] E.C.R. 1359 74
66/82   Fromançais SA v. F.O.R.M.A. [1983] E.C.R. 395, [1983] 3 C.M.L.R.
          453 739
85/82   Schloh v. Council [1983] E.C.R. 2105 .... 308, 320 et seq.
86/82   Hasselblad v. Commission [1984] E.C.R. 883, [1984] 1 C.M.L.R. 559 840
92/82   Gutmann v. Commission [1983] E.C.R. 3127 1063
107/82   AEG v. Commission [1983] E.C.R. 3151, [1984] 3 C.M.L.R. 325 .... 839, 1339,
                                                                          1341, 1356, 1423, 1428
126/82   Smit Transport BV v. Commissie Grensoverschrijdend Beroepsgoederen-
          vervoer [1983] E.C.R. 73, [1983] 3 C.M.L.R. 106 651
129/82   Lux v. Court of Auditors [1984] E.C.R. 4127 643
144/82   Detti v. Court of Justice [1983] E.C.R. 2421 306
155/82   Commission v. Belgium [1983] E.C.R. 531, [1983] 2 C.M.L.R. 566 794
159/82   Verli-Wallace v. Commission [1983] E.C.R. 2711 .... 971, 972, 973, 998
167/82   Nordgetreide v. Hauptzollamt Hamburg-Jonas [1983] E.C.R. 1149 441
174/82   Officier van Justitie v. Sandoz BV [1983] E.C.R. 2445, [1984] 3 C.M.L.R.
          43 794
179/82   Lucchini Sidérurgica SpA v. Commission [1983] E.C.R. 3083 352
188/82   Thyssen v. Commission [1983] E.C.R. 3721 .... 645, 846, 1879, 1081,
                                                                          1089, 1092, 1196, 1368
191/82   Fediol v. Commission [1983] E.C.R. 2913, [1984] 3 C.M.L.R. 244 ...... 29, 299,
                                                                          390, 1194, 1345, 1443
199/82   Amministrazione delle Finanze dello Stato v. San Giorgio [1983] E.C.R.
          3595, [1985] 2 C.M.L.R. 658 .... 916, 945, 1163
205–215/82   Deutsche Milchkontor v. Germany [1983] E.C.R. 2633, [1984] 3
          C.M.L.R. 586 .... 46, 51, 60, 460, 474, 674, 772, 872, 1095, 1099, 1100
216/82   University of Hamburg v. Hauptzollamt Hamburg-Kehrureder [1983]
          E.C.R. 2771 1053
224/82   Meiko-Konservenfabrik v. Germany [1983] E.C.R. 2539 .... 432, 1114,
                                                                          1121, 1129, 1130, 1147
226/82   Thyssen Aktiengesellschaft v. Commission [1984] E.C.R. 951 .... 335, 848
228/82   Ford v. Commission [1984] E.C.R. 1129, [1984] 1 C.M.L.R. 649 1379
235/82   Ferriere San Carlo SpA v. Commission [1983] E.C.R. 3949 1118
237/82   Jongeneel Kaas v. Netherlands [1984] E.C.R. 483, [1985] 2 C.M.L.R. 53 777
238/82   Duphar v. Netherlands [1984] E.C.R. 523, [1985] 1 C.M.L.R. 256 804
239/82   Allied Corporation v. Commission [1984] E.C.R. 1005, [1985] 3 C.M.L.R.
          572 966
263/82   Klöckner-Werke AG v. Commission [1983] E.C.R. 4143 847
264/82   Timex v. Council and Commission [1985] E.C.R. 849, [1985] 3 C.M.L.R.
          550 .... 29, 299, 389, 1195, 1345, 1354, 1357, 1429
265/82   USINOR v. Commission [1983] E.C.R. 3105 .... 1033, 1037, 1051, 1089, 1092
267/82   Développement SA v. Commission [1986] E.C.R. 1907, [1989] 1 C.M.L.R
          309 .... 508, 532

270/82   Estel NV v. Commission [1984] E.C.R. 1195 1051
276/82   BV Roomboterfabrik "De Beste Boter" v. Produktschap voor Zuivel
         [1983] E.C.R. 3331 1141
281/82   Unifrex Sàrl v. Commission and Council [1984] E.C.R. 1969 1152
283/82   Schoellershammer v. Commission [1983] E.C.R. 4219 492
296 & 318/82   Holland v. Commission [1985] E.C.R. 809, [1985] 3 C.M.L.R. 380 387
323/82   Intermills v. Commission [1984] E.C.R. 3809, [1986] 1 C.M.L.R. 614 387
345/82   Wünsche Handelsgesellschaft GmbH v. Germany [1984] E.C.R. 1995 813
348/82   I.R.O. v. Commission [1984] E.C.R. 1409 1051
352/82   Commission v. Germany [1984] E.C.R. 777 .... 1402, 1404
9/83   Eisen-und Metall AG v. Commission [1984] E.C.R. 2071 .... 1238, 1358, 1363,
                                                                    1370, 1422, 1463
15/83   Denkavit Nederland v. Hoofproduktschap voor Akkerbouwprodukten
        [1984] E.C.R. 2171 .... 768, 784
23/83   Liefting v. Academisch Ziekenhuis bij de Universiteit van Amsterdam
        [1984] E.C.R. 3225, [1984] 3 C.M.L.R. 702 673
25/83   Buick v. Commission [1984] E.C.R. 1773 .... 67, 316
41/83   Italy v. Commission [1985] E.C.R. 873, [1985] 2 C.M.L.R. 368 1194
46/83   Gerlach v. Inspecteur der Invoerrechten en Accijzen [1984] E.C.R. 841 486
52/83   Commission v. France [1983] E.C.R. 3707, [1985] 3 C.M.L.R. 278 .... 871, 1032,
                                                                    1033, 1052
53/83   Allied Corporation v. Council [1985] E.C.R. 1622, [1986] 3 C.M.L.R.
        605 .... 1191, 1223, 1414
59/83   SA Biovilac v. E.E.C. [1984] E.C.R. 4057, [1987] 2 C.M.L.R. 881 .... 75, 562,
                                                                    632, 671, 1130
63/83   R. v. Kent Kirk [1984] E.C.R. 2689, [1984] 3 C.M.L.R. 522 1123
69/83   Lux v. Court of Auditors [1984] E.C.R. 2447 .... 319, 1194, 1196
70/83   Kloppenburg v. Finanzamt Leer [1984] E.C.R. 1075, [1985] 1 C.M.L.R.
        205 .... 1147, 1153, 1447
72/83   Campus Oil v. Minister for Industry and Energy [1984] E.C.R. 2727, [1986] 3
        C.M.L.R. 544 .... 700, 798, 817
76/83   Usines Gustave Böel v. Commission [1984] E.C.R. 859 1033
81/83   Acciaierie e Ferriere Busseni SpA v. Commission [1984] E.C.R.
        2951 .... 1033, 1052, 1196, 1216, 1331, 1352, 1385, 1411, 1429
94/83   Officier Van Justitie v. Heijn [1984] E.C.R. 3263 796
97/83   Melkunie BV [1984] E.C.R. 2367, [1986] 2 C.M.L.R. 318 795
106/83   Sermide SpA v. Cassa Conguaglio Zucchero [1984] E.C.R. 4209 632
107/83   Ordre des Avocats au Barreau de Paris v. Klopp [1984] E.C.R. 2971, [1985]
         1 C.M.L.R. 99 833
112/83   Société des Produits de Mäis SA v. Administration des Douanes et Droits
         Indirects [1985] E.C.R. 719, [1988] 1 C.M.L.R. 459 1107
145/83   Stanley Adams v. Commission [1985] E.C.R. 3539, [1986] 1 C.M.L.R.
         506 .... 521, 523, 1193, 1194, 1352, 1353
182/83   Fearon v. Irish Land Commission [1984] E.C.R. 3677, [1985] 2 C.M.L.R.
         228 831
185/83   Rijksuniversiteit te Groningen v. Inspector of Customs and Excise [1984]
         E.C.R. 3623 1194
188/83   Witte v. Parliament [1984] E.C.R. 3465 672
194 & 206/83   Asteris v. Commission [1985] E.C.R. 2815 530
214/83   Germany v. Commission [1985] E.C.R. 3053, [1987] 1 C.M.L.R. 566 388
222/83   Municipality of Differdange v. Commission [1984] E.C.R. 2889, [1985] 3
         C.M.L.R. 638 .... 61, 967
227/83   Moussis v. Commission [1984] E.C.R. 3133 .... 1032, 1038, 1039
235/83   Mulligan v. Commission [1984] E.C.R. 3379 1063
244/83   Meggle Milchindustrie v. Council and Commission [1986] E.C.R. 1101 510

246/83   De Angelis v. Commission [1985] E.C.R. 1254 672
290/83   Commission v. France [1985] E.C.R. 440, [1986] 2 C.M.L.R. 546 1187
294–296/83   'Les Verts': Parti Ecologiste v. Parliament [1986] E.C.R. 1339, [1987]
         2 C.M.L.R. 343 .... 4, 62, 1191
298/83   CICCE v. Commission [1985] E.C.R. 1105, [1986] 1 C.M.L.R. 486 1327
326/83   Aschermann v. Commission [1984] E.C.R. 2253 1045
1/84   Ilford v. Commission [1984] E.C.R. 423 .... 1076, 1077
20/84   De Jong Verenigde NV v. Voedselvoorzienings In-en Verkoopbureau
         [1985] E.C.R. 2061 70
33/84   Fragd SpA v. Amministrazione delle Finanze dello Stato [1985] E.C.R.
         1606 .... 1106, 1109
39/84   Maizena GmbH v. Hauptzollamt Hamburg-Jonas [1985] E.C.R. 2115 74
44/84   Hurd v. Jones [1986] E.C.R. 29, [1986] 2 C.M.L.R. 1 58
59/84   Tezi Textiel BV v. Commission [1986] E.C.R. 887, [1987] 3 C.M.L.R. 64 531
64/84   Queensborough Rolling Mill Co. v. Commission [1985] E.C.R. 1830, [1986]
         2 C.M.L.R. 211 .... 848, 1051
110/84   Municipality of Hillegom v. Hillenius [1985] E.C.R. 3947, [1986] 3
         C.M.L.R. 422 1349
127/84   Esly v. Commission [1985] E.C.R. 1437 1045
134/84   Williams v. Court of Auditors [1985] E.C.R. 2225 672
141/84   De Compte v. Parliament [1985] E.C.R. 1952 .... 1193, 1333, 1369
142/84   BAT v. Commission [1987] E.C.R. 4566, [1988] 4 C.M.L.R. 24 ...... 1328, 1354
107/84   Commission v. Germany [1985] E.C.R. 2655, [1986] 2 C.M.L.R. 177 .... 21, 92
169/84   Compagnie Française de l'Azote v. Commission [1986] E.C.R. 391, [1986] 3
         C.M.L.R. 385 .... 1073, 1194
174/84   Bulk Oil v. Sun International [1986] E.C.R. 559, [1986] 2 C.M.L.R. 732 1195
178/84   Commision v. Germany [1987] E.C.R. 1227, [1988] 1 C.M.L.R. 780 796
181/84   Man Sugar v. IBAP [1985] E.C.R. 2889, [1985] 3 C.M.L.R. 759 ..... 6, 742, 743
183/84   Söhlein Rheingold v. Hauptzollamt Weisbanden [1985] E.C.R. 3351 470
205/84   Commission v. Germany [1986] E.C.R. 3755, [1987] 2 C.M.L.R. 69 831
222/84   Johnston v. R.U.C. [1986] E.C.R. 1651, [1986] 3 C.M.L.R. 240 62
226/84   British Leyland v. Commission [1986] E.C.R. 3263, [1987] 1 C.M.L.R.
         184 372
228/84   Pauvert v. Court of Auditors [1985] E.C.R. 1969 .... 952, 1089, 1092
234/84   Belgium v. Commission [1986] E.C.R. 2263, [1988] 2 C.M.L.R.
         331 369,
                                                                            1349
236/84   MALT GmbH v. Hauptzollamt Düsseldorf [1986] E.C.R. 1923 ... 412, 445, 645
248/84   Germany v. Commission [1987] E.C.R. 4013, [1985] 3 C.M.L.R. 710 1402
255/84   Nachi Fujikoshi Corporation v. Council [1987] E.C.R. 1861, [1989] 2
         C.M.L.R. 76 .... 296, 368, 369, 1413
279, 280, 285 & 286/84   Lebensmittelwerke v. Commission [1987] E.C.R. 1069,
         [1988] 2 C.M.L.R. 704 .... 296, 407, 409, 417, 426, 443, 445, 856
299/84   Neumann v. BALM [1985] E.C.R. 3663, [1987] 3 C.M.L.R. 4 .... 6, 744
303/84   Commission v. Germany [1986] E.C.R. 1171, [1987] 2 C.M.L.R. 867 .... · 27
307/84   Commission v. France [1986] E.C.R. 1725, [1987] 3 C.M.L.R. 555 21
9/85   Nordbutter v. Germany [1986] E.C.R. 2831, [1988] 2 C.M.L.R. 245 ...... 739, 772
15/85   Consorzio Cooperative d'Abruzzo v. Commission [1987] E.C.R. 1005,
         [1988] 1 C.M.L.R. 841 .... 994, 1027, 1158
21/85   Maas & Co. SA v. B.A.L.M. [1986] E.C.R. 3537, [1987] 3 C.M.L.R.
         794 .... 141, 744
26/85   Vaysse v. Commission [1986] E.C.R. 3131 .... 307, 315
40/85   Belgium v. Commission [1986] E.C.R. 2321, [1988] 2 C.M.L.R. 301 .. 387, 1358
42/85   Cockerill-Sambre v. Commission [1985] E.C.R. 3749, [1987] 1 C.M.L.R.
         325 1417

45/85   Verband der Sachversicherer *v.* Commission [1987] E.C.R. 405, [1988] 4
C.M.L.R. 264 368
53/85   AKZO Chemie *v.* Commission [1986] E.C.R. 1965, [1987] 1 C.M.L.R.
231 .... 1194, 1243, 1326, 1328, 1337, 1346, 1350, 1354, 1355, 1357, 1369, 1371
66/85   Lawrie Blum *v.* Land Baden-Württemberg [1986] E.C.R. 2121, [1987] 3
C.M.L.R. 389 .... 21, 823
75/85   Ragnelli *v.* Commission [1986] E.C.R. 2775 1408
80/85   Nederlandse Bakkerij Stichting *v.* Edah BV [1986] E.C.R. 3359, [1988] 2
C.M.L.R. 113 .... 657, 673
89, 104, 114, 116–117 & 125–129/85   Ahlström o/y *v.* Commission [1988] E.C.R.
5193, [1988] 4 C.M.L.R. 901 1200
91/85   Clemen *v.* Commission [1986] E.C.R. 2853 599
92/85   Hamai *v.* Court [1986] E.C.R. 3157 .... 324, 641
130/85   Wulro BV [1986] E.C.R. 2035, [1988] 1 C.M.L.R. 496 456
133–136/85   Lebensmittel *v.* B.A.L.M. [1987] E.C.R. 2289 856
137/85   Maizena *v.* B.A.L.M. [1987] E.C.R. 4587, [1989] 2 C.M.L.R. 336 744
148/85   Direction Générale des Impôts *v.* Forest [1986] E.C.R. 3449, [1988] 2
C.M.L.R. 577 456
185/85   Usinor SA *v.* Commission [1986] E.C.R. 2079 .... 342, 1411
201 & 202/85   Klensch *v.* Secrétaire d'Etat à l'Agriculture [1986] E.C.R. 3477,
[1988] 1 C.M.L.R. 151 .... 562, 599
215/85   Bundesanstalt für Landwirtschaftliche Marktordnung *v.* Raiffeisen Hauptgenossenschaft [1987] E.C.R. 1279 .... 416, 626, 671
223/85   Rijn-Schelde-Verolme *v.* Commission [1987] E.C.R. 4617, [1989] 2
C.M.L.R. 259 1083
237/85   Rummler *v.* Dato-Druck GmbH [1986] E.C.R. 2101, [1987] 3 C.M.L.R.
127 673
249/85   ALBAKO Margerinefabrik *v.* B.A.L.M. [1987] E.C.R. 2345 296
281, 283–285 & 287/85   Germany *v.* Commission [1987] E.C.R. 3203, [1988] 1
C.M.L.R. 11 .... 495, 1199
288/85   Hauptzollamt Hamburg-Jonas *v.* Plange Kraftfutterwerke GmbH & Co.
[1987] E.C.R. 611 1160
309/85   Barra *v.* Belgian State [1988] E.C.R. 355, [1988] 2 C.M.L.R. 409 945
310/85   DEUFIL GmbH & Co. KG *v.* Commission [1987] E.C.R. 901, [1988] 1
C.M.L.R. 553 1074
355/85   Commissionaire de Police Driancourt *v.* Michel Coguet [1986] E.C.R.
3231, [1987] 3 C.M.L.R. 942 657
34/86   Council *v.* Parliament [1986] E.C.R. 2155, [1986] 3 C.M.L.R.
94 .... 26, 62, 1191
38/86   Neumann *v.* B.A.L.M. [1987] E.C.R. 1675, [1988] 1 C.M.L.R.
523 .... 428, 746
170/86   Deetzen *v.* Hauptzollamt Hamburg-Jonas [1988] E.C.R. 2355, [1989] 2
C.M.L.R. 327 .... 941, 1114, 1136
222/86   Heylens [1987] E.C.R. 4097, [1989] 1 C.M.L.R. 901 .... 1401, 1431, 1462
316/86   Hauptzollamt Hamburg-Jonas *v.* Krücken [1988] E.C.R. 2213 1084
302/87   Parliament *v.* Council [1988] E.C.R. 5615 1205

CASES BEFORE THE EUROPEAN COURT OF JUSTICE
(Alphabetical List)

Acciaierie di Modena v. High Authority (55–59 & 61–63/63) 250
Acciaierie Ferriere & Fonderie di Modena v. High Authority (16/61) 289, 578
Acciaierie & Ferriere Pugliesi v. High Authority (8/65) 343
Acciaierie & Ferriere Busseni SpA (81/83) 1033, 1052, 1196, 1216, 1331,
1352, 1385, 1411, 1429
ACF Chemiefarma N.V. v. Commission (41/69) 55, 1057, 1058, 1059, 1215, 1345,
1382, 1383, 1384, 1402, 1427, 1430
ACNA Spa v. Commission (57/69) 363, 1058, 1336
Adams (Stanley George) v. Commission (145/83) 521, 523, 1193, 1194, 1352, 1353
Administration des Douanes v. Gondrand Frères (169/80) 404, 1153
Adoui & Cornuaille v. Belgium (115–116/81) 47, 821
AEG v. Commission (107/82) 839, 1339, 1341, 1356, 1423, 1428
AETR (22/70) 236, 242, 958, 1018, 1047, 1236
Agence Européenne d'Interims v. Commission (56/77) 1405
Agricola Commerciale Olio Srl & SPA Savma v. Commission (232 &
264/81) 75, 967, 969, 988, 1022, 1079
Ahlström o/y v. Commission (89, 104, 114, 116–117 & 125–129/85) 1200
Aimer v. Einfuhr-und Vorratsstelle für Getreide (27/72) 766
Aktien-Zuckerfabrik Schöppenstedt v. Council (5/71) see Schöppenstedt v.
Council 506, 507, 514, 524, 525, 563, 752
AKZO Chemie v. Commission (53/85) 1194, 1243, 1326, 1328, 1337, 1346,
1350, 1354, 1355, 1357, 1369, 1371
ALBAKO Margarinefabrik v. BALM (249/85) 296
Alfieri v. European Parliament (3/66) 1364
Algera v. Common Assembly (7/56 & 3–7/57) 5, 67, 68, 83, 236, 303,
324, 523, 872, 938, 941, 951, 955, 957, 971, 976, 985, 986, 987,
988, 992, 993, 997, 998, 1004, 1006, 1009, 1013, 1024, 1025,
1027, 1028, 1030, 1031, 1131, 1435, 1446, 1456, 1457
Allied Corporation v. Commission (239 & 275/82) 966
—— v. Council (53/83) 1191, 1223, 1414
Allgayer (Magdalena) v. Parliament (74/77) 315
ALMA v. High Authority (8/56) 1417, 1456
Almini v. Commission (19/70) 1338, 1362
AlphaSteel v. Commission (14/81) 951, 957, 972, 993, 1008, 1024, 1030, 1131, 1139
Alusuisse v. Council and Commission (307/81) 966, 967, 1191
Alvarez v. Parliament (206/81) 1342
Alvis v. Council (32/62) 1325
AM&S Europe Ltd. v. Commission (155/79) 714, 1193, 1221, 1240, 1346,
1352, 1434
Amesz v. Commission and Council (532, 534, 567, 600, 618 & 660/79) 1016
Amministrazione delle Finanze v. Acampora (827/79) 1101
Amministrazione delle Finanze dello Stato v. Ariete (811/79) 945
—— v. Denkavit Italiana (61/79) 945
—— v. Carlo Salengo (143/80) 236

lix

Amministrazione delle Finanze dello Stato v. Meridionale Industria Salumi (66, 127
    & 128/79) 638, 671, 674, 871, 1102, 1150, 1152, 1169
—— v. San Giorgio (199/82) 916, 945, 1163
Amsterdam Bulb B.V. v. Produktschap voor Siergewassen (50/76) 664
Amylum v. Council (108/81) 433, 527, 940, 952, 1078, 1127
An Bord Bainne Cooperative Ltd. v. Minister for Agriculture (92/77) 244
Ancienne Maison Marcel v. France (96/77) 432, 1122, 1141
Anglo-Irish Meat Company v. Minister for Agriculture (196/80) 1123
Arning v. Commission (125/80) 324, 1362
Aschermann v. Commission (326/82) 1045
ASSIDER v. High Authority (3/54) 268, 279, 332, 336
Asteris AE v. Commission (194 & 206/83) 530
Atalanta BV v. Produktschap voor Vee en Vlees (240/78) 736
Azienda Colori Nazionali v. Commission (57/69) 363, 1058, 1336

BASF v. Commission (49/69) 363, 1058, 1368
BAT v. Commission (142/84) 1328, 1354
BV Roomboterfabriek "De Beste Boter" v. Produktschap voor Zuivel (276/82) 1141
Bakels v. Oberfinanzdirektion München (14/70) 485
Bakke-d'Aloya v. Council (280/80) 314, 315
Balkan-Import-Export v. Hauptzollamt Berlin-Packhof (5/73) 6, 244, 405, 407, 409,
                    410, 412, 443, 445, 446, 593, 746, 762, 763, 848, 1130
Balkan-Import-Export GmbH v. Hauptzollamt Berlin-Packhof (118/76) 637, 746
BALM v. Raiffeisen Hauptgenossenschaft (215/85) 416, 626, 671
Barra v. City of Liège (309/85) 945
Bayer v. Commission (51/69) 1058, 1342, 1344, 1365, 1368
Bayerische HNL Vermehrungsbetriebe v. Council and Commission (83 & 94/76, 4,
    15 & 40/77) 525, 526, 533, 719, 751, 752
Bauhuis v. Netherlands (46/76) 792, 798
Baywa v. BALM (146, 192–193/81) 772, 1436
Becker v. Commission (10/74) 1149
Béguelin Import Co. v. G.L.Import Export SA (22/71) 1201
Bela Mühle v. Grows Farm (114/76) 6, 420, 424, 718, 748
Belgium v. Commission (234/84) 369, 1349
—— v. Commission (40/85) 387, 1358
Beljatzky v. HZA Aachen-Süd (216/78) 1101
Benedetti v. Munari (52/76) 244
Berlin v. Wigei (30/79) 792
Berlin Butter (133–136/85) 856
Bernardi v. Parliament (48/70) 1212
Bernusset v. Commission (94 & 96/63) 296, 307, 1408, 1409
Bertoni v. Parliament (20/71) 52, 1035, 1049
Beste Boter und Hoche v. Bundesanstalt für Landwirtschaftliche Marktordnung
    (99 & 100/76) 426,
Beus (W) v. Hauptzollamt München-Landsbergerstrasse (5/67) 406, 409, 411, 1406,
                                                   1412
Biegi v. Hauptzollamt Bochum (158/78) 484, 1123
Birke v. Commission and Council (543/79) 1016, 1164
Blasig v. Commission (173/80) 1047
Bleiindustrie v. Hauptzollamt Hamburg-Walltershof (111/77) 489
Blesgen (75/81) 803
Bock v. Commission (62/70) 807, 1076, 1077, 1144
Bode v. Commission (45 & 49/70) 1019, 1030
Boehringer v. Commission (45/69) 1057, 1338, 1339, 1357, 1368, 1450

Bouchereau (30/77) 817
Boursin (Jacques) v. High Authority (102/63) 304
Boussac Saint-Frères S.A. v. Brigitte Gerstenmeier (22/80) 614, 622
Bonu v. Council (89/79) 1409, 1427, 1384
Brandau (George) v. Council (46/71) 319, 641, 642
Brasserie de Haecht v. Wilkin-Janssen (48/72) 871
British Beef Co. Ltd. v. Intervention Board (146/77) 1141, 1147
British Leyland v. Commission (226/84) 372
Brouwer-Kaune v. Bestuur van de Bedrijfsvereniging voor het Kledingbedrijf
    (180/78) 54
Buchler v. Commission (44/69) 1057, 1368, 1450
Buick v. Commission (25/83) 67, 316
Buitoni v. FORMA (122/78) 6, 735
Bulk Oil v. Sun International (174/84) 1195
Bundesknappschaft v. Brock (68/69) 1132
Bundesrepublik Deutschland v. Commission see Germany v. Commission
    (34/62) 338, 339, 398, 407, 1403, 1404
Burton (Arthur) v. British Railways Board (19/81) 653, 673
Bussone v. Italian Ministry of Agriculture (31/78) 458, 649
Buyl v. Commission (817/79) 1016, 1131, 1139

Caisse Régionale d'Assurance Maladie v. Diamante Toia, épouse Palermo
    (237/78) 622
CAM v. Commission (100/74) 368
CICCE v. Commission (298/83) 1327
CNTA v. Commission (74/74) 6, 941, 955, 1113, 1117, 1119, 1122, 1132,
                                                                    1133, 1135, 1141, 1145
COFAZ v. Commission (169/84) 1073, 1194
Camera Caree v. Commission (792/79R) 1346, 1379
Campus Oil Ltd v. Minister for Industry and Energy (72/83) 700, 798, 817
Campolongo v. High Authority (27 & 39/59) 1447
Caribou see Witt v. HZA Hamburg-Ericus (149/73) 1236
Carlsen Verlag v. Oberfinanzdirektion Köln (62/77) 489
Cassella Farbwerke Mainkur AG v. Commission (55/69) 1058
Cassis de Dijon see Rewe v. Bundesmonopolverwaltung (120/78) 773, 787, 859
Cayrol v. Rivoira (52/77) 782
Celanese Chemical & Co. v. Commission and Council (236/81) 1352
Centrafarm (15/74) 800
Chambre Syndicale (9/57) 554, 566, 575, 674
Chambre Syndicale de la Sidérurgie Française v. High Authority (3/64) 330
Châtillon v. High Authority (54/65) 238, 988, 1001, 1002, 1087
Chollet-Bauduin v. Commission (32/71) 1035
Choquet (16/78) 823
Christmas Butter (279, 280, 285 & 286/84) 296, 407, 409, 417, 426, 443, 445, 856
Cimenteries Cementzbedrijven N.V. v. Commission (8–11/66) 236, 958, 959, 962,
                                                                    976, 989, 1420, 1421
Clemen (Anne-Marie) v. Commission (91/85) 599
Coccioli v. Bundesanstalt für Arbeit (139/78) 501, 824, 1044
Cockerill-Sambre v. Commission (42/85) 1417
Coenen (39/75) 725, 827
Colloti v. Court of Justice (20/65) 1033, 1037
Comet v. Produktschap voor Siergewassen (45/76) 51, 945
Commissionaire de Police Driancourt v. Michel Coguet (355/85) 657
Commission v. Belgium and Luxembourg (90 & 91/63) 251
—— v. Belgium (156/77) 1032, 1034, 1053

Commission v. Belgium (149/79) 21, 246, 249, 450, 822, 823, 1107
—— v. —— (149/79R) 20
—— v. —— (301/81) 1404
—— v. —— (155/82) 794
—— v. Council (22/70) 236, 242, 958, 1018, 1047, 1236
—— v. —— (81/72) 6, 23, 117, 119, 243, 316, 643, 872, 939, 940, 1114, 1115, 1138
—— v. Denmark (171/78) 623
—— v. France (6 & 11/69) 976, 977, 1045, 1052
—— v. —— (68/76) 457
—— v. —— (42/82) 792
—— v. —— (52/83) 871, 1032, 1033, 1052
—— v. —— (290/83) 1187
—— v. —— (307/84) 21
—— v. Germany (70/72) 258, 383, 1073
—— v. —— (153/78) 790
—— v. —— (247/81) 797
—— v. —— (325/82) 1402, 1404
—— v. —— (107/84) 21, 92
—— v. —— (178/84) 796
—— v. —— (205/84) 831
—— v. —— (303/84) 27
—— v. Ireland (61/77) 619
—— v. Ireland (113/80) 786
—— v. —— (249/81) 787
—— v. Italy (7/61) 300, 800
—— v. —— (7/68) 798
—— v. —— (48/71) 52
—— v. —— (39/72) 658, 663, 673
—— v. United Kingdom (128/78) 661
—— v. —— (231/78) 668
—— v. —— (124/81) 793
—— v. —— (40/82) 625, 792
Compagnie Continentale v. Council (169/73) 517, 533
Compagnie d'Approvisionment de Transport et de Crédit SA and Grands Moulins
    de Paris SA v. Commission (9 & 11/71) 507, 532, 535, 563, 653, 673
Compagnie des Hauts (33/59) 514
Compagnie des Hauts Fourneaux v. High Authority (27/58) 328
Compagnie Industrielle du Comté de Loheac v. Council and Commission
    (54–60/76) 525, 1151
Compagnie des Forges de Châtillon, Commentry et Neuves-Maisons v. High
    Authority (54/65) 238, 988, 1001, 1002, 1087
Consorzio Cooperative d'Abruzzo v. Commission (15/85) 994, 1027, 1158
Consten and Grundig v. Commission (56 & 58/64) 366, 841, 1229, 1326, 1344,
    1359, 1410, 1411, 1420
Control Data Belgium v. Commission (294/81) 491, 1194, 1401
Coopératives Agricoles de Céréales v. Commission (95–98/74, 15/75 &
    100/75) 1139, 1140, 1142
Corman und Fils v. HZA Aachen-Süd (217/78) 1101
Costa v. ENEL (6/64) 1457
Council v. Parliament (34/86) 26, 62, 1191
Craeynest (Paul) v. Belgian State (12/70) 666
Curtis v. Commission and European Parliament (167/80) 1015, 1016, 1122,
    1131, 1138

DGV v. Council and Commission (241, 242 & 245–250/78) 6, 507, 519
DEUFIL GmbH & Co. KG v. Commission (310/85) 1074
Dautzenberg v. Court of Justice (2/80) 322, 1089, 1091
Dansk Supermarked v. Imerco (8/80) 801, 802
Dassonville see Procureur du Roi v. Dassonville (8/74) 773, 779, 780, 786
De Angelis (246/83) 672
de Bloos v. Bouyer (59/77) 1054
de Briey (Alain) v. Commission (25/80) 1405, 1408, 1422
De Bruyn v. Parliament (25/60) 1029, 1405, 1429
De Compte v. Parliament (141/84) 1193, 1333, 1369
De Dapper v. Parliament (54/75) 307
De Gezamenlijke Steenkolenmijnen in Limburg v. High Authority (30/59) 389, 956,
                                                                                      963, 1054
De Greef v. Commission (46/72) 324, 1192, 1212, 1366, 1367, 1420
De Hoe v. Commission (151/80) 322, 1402
De Pascale v. Commission (97/63) 322
De Peijper (104/75) 779
De Smedt (261/81) 788
De Wendel v. Commission (29/67) 1370, 1411, 1422
Debauve (52/79) 606, 614, 830
Debayser v. FIRS (152/80) 765, 1141
Decker v. Hauptzollamt Landau (99/78) 433, 1121, 1125
Deetzen (Georg von) v. HZA Hamburg-Jonas (170/86) 941, 1114, 1136
Defrenne (II) v. SABENA (43/75) 495, 496, 652, 693, 925, 1103, 1165, 1347
Defrenne (III) v. SABENA (149/77) 626, 651, 673
Degreef v. Commission (80/63) 1325
Delhaize v. Belgium (2–4/82) 792
Delkvist v. Anklagemyndigheden (21/78) 252
Demont v. Commission (115/80) 1342, 1346, 1362, 1366, 1368, 1400, 1409, 1423
Demo-Studio Schmidt v. Commission (210/81) 338, 398, 1194
Denkavit 36/79 588
—— (233/81) 649
—— v. Commission (14/78) 510
—— v. Produktschap voor Zuivel (35/80) 415, 445
Denkavit Futtermittel GmbH v. Finanzamt Warendorf (139/77) 586, 591
Denkavit Nederland v. Hoofdproduktschap voor Akkerbouwprodukten
     (15/83) 768, 784
Dervicu-Delahais v. Directeur Général des Douanes et Droits Indirects (95/80) 445
Detti (Armelle) v. Court of Justice (144/82) 306
Deuka v. Einfuhr-und Vorratsstelle für Getreide (5/75) 872, 955, 1113, 1137,
                                                                                      1141, 1146, 1407
Deutsche Getreide-und Futtermittel Handelsgesellschaft mbH v. Hauptzollamt
     Hamburg-Altona (31/70) 418, 607, 711
Deutsche Milchkontor GmbH v. Bundesrepublik Deutschland (205–215/82) 46, 51,
                                         60, 460, 474, 674, 772, 872, 1095, 1099, 1100
Developpement S.A. v. Commission (267/82) 508, 532
Direction Générale des Impôts v. Forest (148/85) 456
Distillers Co. v. Commission (30/78) 1348, 1425
Dittmeyer v. Hauptzollamt Hamburg-Waltershof (69/76) 484
Donckerwolcke (41/76) 773, 781, 782, 858
Dulciora Spa v. Amministrazione delle Finanze dello Stato (95/78) 764, 1141
Dumortier Frères SA v. Council (64/76) 529
Duphar v. Netherlands (238/82) 804
Dürbeck v. Hauptzollamt Frankfurt (112/80) 414, 809, 859, 867, 872,
                                                                                      1115, 1136, 1144

Edeka-Zentrale AG. *v.* Germany (245/81) 562, 631, 648, 671, 810, 1131, 1139, 1141
Effem GmbH *v.* Hauptzollamt Lüneburg (95/75) 445, 756
Einfuhr-und Vorratsstelle für Getreide *v. Baer-Getreide (72/72)* *507, 858*
Einfuhr-und Vorratsstelle für Getreide und Futtermittel *v.* Köster, Berodt
    (25/70) 399, 400, 428, 430, 732, 856, 1201, 1207, 1376
—— *v.* Mackprang (2/75) 432, 753, 1076, 1077, 1142
—— *v.* Pfützenreuter (3/74) 404, 463, 467
Eisen-und Metall AG *v.* Commission (9/83) 1238, 1358, 1363, 1370, 1422, 1463
Eisen-und Stahlindustrie *v.* High Authority (13/57) 65, 329, 333, 337, 554, 566
Elz (Raymond) *v.* Commission (56/75) 972, 1004, 1065
Eridania *v.* Minister of Agriculture and Forestry (230/78) 400, 401, 573, 574, 582,
                                                                                                                759, 1130
Erzbergbau (Barbara) *v.* High Authority (3–18, 25 & 26/58) 549, 601, 1224, 1230
                                                                                                            1370, 1419
Esly *v.* Commission (127/84) 1045
Estel NV *v.* Commission (270/82) 1051
Europemballage and Continental Can Company *v.* Commission (6/72) 377, 1201,
                                                                                                                1214, 1418
Eximo *v.* Commission (62/83) 1152
Exportation des Sucres *v.* Commission (88/76) 1118, 1147
Express Dairy Foods *v.* Intervention Board for Agricultural Produce
    (130/79) 51, 247, 968, 1095, 1099, 1106, 1110, 1111, 1449

Faust *v.* Commission (52/81) 415, 645, 812, 1131, 1139
Fearon *v.* Irish Land Commission (182/83) 831
Fédération Charbonnière de Belgique *v.* High Authority (8/55) 48, 65, 225, 325, 330,
                                                                                        333, 337, 567, 572, 577, 677, 710, 843, 965
Fédération Nationale de la Boucherie *v.* Council (19–22/62) 960
Fediol *v.* Commission (191/82) 29, 299, 390, 1194, 1345, 1443
Ferriera Ernesto Preo *v.* High Authority (2/65) 343, 971, 1225
Ferriere San Carlo SpA *v.* Commission (235/82) 1118
Ferwerda *v.* Produktschap voor Vee en Vlees (265/78) 51, 455, 475, 634, 671, 674,
                                                                                                                1097, 1098
Fiddelaar *v.* Commission (44/59) 1405
Fiehn *v.* Commission (23/69) 1086
Firma Bock *v.* Commission (62/70) 807, 1076, 1077, 1144
Firma IRCA *v.* National Tax Authority (7/76) 432, 655, 939, 1076, 1118,
                                                                                                                1124, 1169
Firma Kühlhaus Zentrum AG *v.* Hauptzollamt Hamburg (79/77) 418, 569
Firma Nold KG *v.* High Authority (18/57) 333, 342, 358, 956, 976, 1420, 1459, 1464
Firma Racke *v.* Hauptzollamt Mainz (98/78) 947
Firma Schlüter & Maack *v.* Hauptzollamt Hamburg-Jonas (94/71) 475, 663
Firma Schwarze *v.* Einfuhr-und Vorratsstelle für Getreide und Futtermittel
    (16/65) 244, 1195, 1409, 1423
Firma Schwarzwaldmilch GmbH *v.* Einfuhr-und Vorratsstelle für Fette (4/68) 249,
                                                                                                                463, 733
Firma Stimming K.G. *v.* Commission (90/77) 517, 941, 955, 1136
Firma J. van Dam en Zonen (185–204/78) 650
Firma Werner Faust OHG *v.* Commission 52/81 645
Firma Wilhelm Fromme *v.* Bundesanstalt für Lanwirtschaftliche Marktordnung
    (54/81) 416, 475, 771, 1099
Firma Wünsche Handelsgesellschaft *v.* Commission (59/72) 507, 762
Fish Research (132/80) 787, 792
Fleischkontor *v.* Einfuhr-und Vorratsstelle (186/73) 734
Fonderie Acciaierie Giovanni Mandelli *v.* Commission (3/67) 344, 1330, 1380
Fonzi *v.* Commission of Euratom (27 & 30/64) 322

Ford v. Commission (228/82) 1379
Fossi v. Bundesknappschaft (79/76) 498
France v. Commission (15/76) 667, 1424
—— v. —— (188–190/80) 69, 248
—— v. High Authority (1/54) 331, 332, 549
Francolor v. Commission (54/69) 363, 1058
Fratelli Zerbone v. Amministrazione delle Finanze dello Stato (94/77) 455
Frecassetti (113/75) 638
Frilli v. Belgium (1/72) 498
Fromançais SA v. FORMA (66/82) 739
Fromme v. BALM (54/81) 416, 475, 771, 1099
Frubo v. Commission (71/74) 368, 1090

Gauff v. Commission (182/80) 958, 961
Gebrüder Bagusat v. HZA Berlin-Packhof (3/71) 1232
Geigy v. Commission (52/69) 363, 1058, 1201, 1418, 1419
Geist v. Commission (61/76) 1422
Geitling v. High Authority (16-19/59) 349, 1087, 1224, 1384, 1403
Gelders-Deboeck v. Commission (106/79) 1061, 1065, 1067
Gemeinde Hillegom v. Hillenius (110/84) 1349
Gerlach v. Inspecteur der Invoerrechten en Accijzen (46/83) 486
Germany v. Commission (3/59) 975, 977, 1051, 1052
—— v. —— (34/62) 338, 339, 398, 1403, 1404
—— v. —— (52 & 55/65) 661
—— v. —— (2/71) 1035, 1043
—— v. —— (47/75) 1082, 1118
—— v. —— (819/79) 460, 665
—— v. —— (44/81) 1060
—— v. —— (248/84) 1402
—— v. —— (281, 283–285 & 287/85) 495, 1199
Germany and Wirtschaftsvereinigung Eisen-und Stahlindustrie v. Commission
    (214/83) 388
Gervais-Danone v. Hauptzollamt München (77/71) 1123
Gesellschaft zur Verwertung von Leistungsschutzrechten v. Commission (7/82) 1370
Getreide Import GmbH v. Einfuhr-und Vorratsstelle für Getreide und Füttermit-
    tel (36/70) 463, 464
Giannini v. Commission (265/81) 322
Giuffrida v. Council (105/75) 305, 324
Guiffrida and Campogrande v. Council (64/80) 955, 969
Gillet v. Commission (28/74) 1015
Grad v. Finanzamt Traunstein (9/70) 1148
Granaria BV v. Hoofdproduktschap voor Akkerbouwprodukten (101/78) 241, 420,
                                                            466, 713, 714, 718
—— v. —— (No.1) (116/76) 718, 747
Grandes Distilleries Peureux v. Directeur des Services Fiscaux de la Haute-Saône et
    du Territoire de Belfort (86/78) 657, 673
Grassi v. Council (188/73) 307, 322, 1231, 1407
Greenwich Film Production v. SACEM (22/79) 378
Grendel v. Finanzamt für Körperschaften (255/81) 1149
Groenveld v. Produktschap voor Vee en Vlees (15/79) 776
Grogan v. Commission (127/80) 939, 1015, 1016, 1017, 1114, 1118, 1131, 1138, 1142
Grosoli (131/73) ....,.. 669
Groupement des Hauts Fourneaux et Aciéries Belges v. High Authority
    (8/57) 328, 329, 331, 335, 554, 566, 575, 674, 844, 1196

Groupement des Industries Sidérurgiques Luxembourgeoises v. High Authority
(7 & 9/54) 564, 565, 657, 964, 1189
Guillot v. Commission (43/74) 1364
Gunnella v. Commission (33/72) 1043
Günter Henck v. Einfuhr-und Vorratsstelle für Getreide und Futtermittel
(25/74) 418, 489
Gutmann v. Commission (92/82) 1063
——— v. ——— (18/65) 1406, 1407, 1425

Haegeman v. Commission (96/71) 536
Hagen v. Einfuhr-und Vorratsstelle für Getreide und Futtermittel (49/71) 455, 465
Halyvourgiki v. Commission (39/81) 297, 345
Hamai v. Court (92/85) 324, 643
Handelsgesellschaft Ferriera Ernesto Preo & Figli v. High Authority (2/65) 343, 971,
                                                                                                           1225
Hasselblad v. Commission (86/82) 840
Hauer v. Land Rheinland Pfalz (44/79) 426, 434, 435, 723, 859, 863, 1459
HZA Göttingen v. Miritz (91/75) 243, 1018
HZA Jonas v. Krüken (316/86) 1084
HZA Kreteld v. Maizena (2/82) 1084
Hauptzollamt Bremen-Freihafen v. Waren-Import-Gesellschaft Krohn & Co.
(74/69) 484
Hauptzollamt Hamburg v. Bollmann (40/69) 455
Hauptzollamt Hamburg-Jonas v. Hermann Kendermann OHG (88/78) 599
——— v. Plange Kraftfutter GmbH (288/85) 1166
Heijn (94/83) 796
Henck v. Hauptzollamt Emden (36/71) 486
Herpels (Anton) v. Commission (54/77) 972, 1006, 1007, 1022, 1025
Heylens (222/86) 1401, 1431, 1462
Hirschberg v. Commission (129/75) 236
Hoechst v. Commission (56/69) 363, 1058
Hoffmann (Christiane) v. Commission (280/81) 315
Hoffmann-La Roche v. Centrafarm (102/77) 801
——— v. Commission (85/76) 6, 65, 377, 1192, 1194, 1201, 1324,
                                                                          1325, 1350, 1356, 1423, 1425
Hoffmann's Stärkefabriken AG v. Hauptzollamt Bielefeld (2/77) 416, 596
Holdijk (141-143/81) 655
Holtz & Willemsen GmbH v. Council and Commission (153/73) 409, 417, 595
Hoogovens v. High Authority (14/61) ... 48, 65, 876, 877, 878, 881, 913, 938, 939, 948, 952,
                                                                957, 958, 959, 963, 971, 973, 974, 979, 990, 992,
                                                                993, 994, 997, 998, 1003, 1005, 1009, 1010, 1014,
                                                                1020, 1024, 1025, 1027, 1029, 1034, 1070, 1224, 1225
Humblet v. Belgium (6/60) 1188, 1190
Hurd v. Jones (44/84) 58

IBM v. Commission (60/81) 73, 133, 961, 962, 964, 1331, 1409, 1420, 1421, 1423
ICAP v. Beneventi (222/78) 657
ICI v. Commission (48/69) 363, 1111, 1201, 1202, 1211, 1418, 1419, 1450
IRCA v. Amiministrazione delle Finanze dello Stato (7/76) 432, 657, 939, 1076,
                                                                                                      1118, 1124, 1169
IRO v. Commission (348/82) 1051
Ilford v. Commission (1/84) 1076, 1077
Import Standard Office v. Council (118/77) 389, 1413
Interagra v. Commission (217/81) 510, 537

Intercontinentale Fleischhandelsgesellschaft v. Commission (68/77) 516, 607, 1136, 1140
Intermills SA (323/82) 387
Internationale Handelsgesellschaft v. Einfuhr-und Vorratsstelle Getreide (11/70) 6, 85, 435, 467, 625, 710, 721, 731, 732, 733, 780, 843, 1459
International Fruit Company (21-24/72) 251, 449, 457, 458, 459, 963, 965, 967, 1195, 1402, 1412
Ireks-Arkady GmbH v. Council and Commission (238/78) 507
Isoglucose see Amylum v. Council (108/81) 433, 527, 940, 952, 1078, 1127
Italian Public Ministry v. SAIL (82/71) 1123
Italy v. Commission 13/63 .... 417, 562, 563, 564, 571, 581
—— v. Commission (173/72) 387
—— v. —— (11/78) 764
—— v. —— (12/78) 445, 764
—— v. —— (41/83) 1194
—— v. Council (166/78) 297, 412
—— v. High Authority (2/54) 1420
—— v. —— (20/59) 48, 256, 1361
IRCA v. Amministrazione delle Finanze (7/76) 432, 655, 939, 1076, 1118, 1124, 1169

Jenkins v. Kingsgate (Clothing Productions) Ltd (96/80) 599
Johnston v. RUC (222/84) 62
Jongeneel Kaas v. Netherlands (237/82) 777
Just v. Danish Ministry for Fiscal Affairs (68/79) 51, 624, 916, 922, 945, 1163

Kalsbeek-van der Veen v. Sociale Verzekeringsbank (100/63) 1123
Kampffmeyer v. Commission (5, 7 & 13–24/66) 9, 71, 408, 467, 505, 506, 512, 518, 531, 535
Kaufhof v. Commission (29/75) 808, 1076, 1077
Keldermann (130/80) 787
Kenny v. Insurance Officer (1/78) 622, 651
Kergall v. Common Assembly (1/55) 988, 1406, 1424, 1425
Kind v. EEC (106/81) 408, 416, 417, 419
Klaus Mecke & Co. v. Hauptzollamt Bremen-Ost (816/79) 489
Kledingverkoopbedrijf De Geus en Uitenbogerd v. Bosch (13/61) 6, 871
Klensch (Martha) v. Secrétaire d'Etat à l'Agriculture (201 & 202/85) 562, 599
Kley v. Commission (35/72) 1407
Klöckner Werke AG, Hoesch AG v. High Authority (17/61) 359, 564, 579, 603, 1081, 1089, 1090, 1091, 1365, 1415
Kloppenburg v. Finanzamt Leer (70/83) 1147, 1153, 1447
Koninklijke Scholten-Honig v. Hoofdproduktschap voor Akkerbouwprodukten (125/77) 45, 408, 413, 416, 432, 562, 628, 670, 1122, 1139
Kortner Schots v. Council, Parliament and Commission (15–33, 52, 53, 57-109, 117, 123, 132 & 135–137/73) 975, 978, 1019, 1021, 1028, 1033, 1035, 1036, 1037, 1048, 1049
Koyoseiko Co. Ltd. v. Council and Commission (120/77) 389, 965, 1413
Krupp v. Commission (275/80) 1211, 1382, 1411
Kuhl v. Council (71/72) 1062, 1066
Kuhner (Richard) v. Commission (33/79) 306, 1332, 1362, 1384, 1407, 1426, 1427
Kurt Kampffmeyer v. Commission and Council (56–60/74) 594, 615
Küster v. Parliament (123/75) 322, 1427, 1428

Lachmüller v. Commission (43, 45 & 48/59) 65, 1405
Lancôme v. Etos (99/79) 6, 443, 445, 452, 1120, 1121, 1125, 1127, 1151, 1343, 1374

Lawrie Blum *v*. Land Baden-Württemberg (66/85) 21, 823
Laying-up Fund for Inland Waterway Vessels (1/76) 1206
Lemmerz-Werke *v*. High Authority (111/63) 6, 260, 340, 673, 938, 958, 971, 973, 999,
1000, 1001, 1002, 1009, 1014, 1025, 1029, 1070
Leonesio (Orsolina) *v*. Italian Ministry of Agriculture (93/71) 669
Lesieur Cotelle *v*. Commission (67–85/75) 445
"Les Verts" *see* Parti Ecologiste *v*. Parliament 294/83 .... 4, 62, 1191
Leuwardener Papierfabrieken *v*. Commission (296 & 318/82) 387
Liefting *v*. Academisch Ziekenhuis bij de Universiteit van Amsterdam (23/83) 673
Lion *v*. FIRS (292/81) 612, 613, 1402, 1412
Lippische Hauptgenossenschaft *v*. Bundesanstalt für Landwirtschaftliche Marktord-
nung (119 & 126/79) 55, 475, 1099
Loebisch *v*. Council (50–51, 53–54 & 57/64) 1051
Lohrey *v*. Germany (141/73) 1060
L'Oréal *v*. De Nieuwe AMCK (31/80) 983, 1374
Lorenz *v*. Germany and Rheinland Pfalz (120/73) 383, 1059, 1075
Louwage *v*. Commission (née Marianne) (148/73) 67, 68, 643, 962, 1079
Lucchini *v*. Commission (1252/79) 1081, 1083
Lucchini Siderurgica SpA *v*. Commission (179/82) 352
Ludwig Wünsche & Co. *v*. Hauptzollamt Ludwigshafen/Rhein (76/70) 418, 525
Ludwigshafener Walzmühle *v*. Council and Commission (197-200, 243, 245 &
247/ 80) 410, 414, 517, 649, 755, 1130, 1242
Lührs *v*. HZA Hamburg-Jonas (78/77) 434, 1141, 1147
Luigi de Pascale *v*. Commission (164/80) 1016, 1138, 1405
L'Union des Minotiers de la Champagne *v*. France (11/74) 408, 417, 418, 563, 585
Lütticke *v*. Commission (4/69) 508, 514, 517, 518
Luxembourg *v*. Court of Auditors (129 & 274/82) 643
—— *v*. —— (69/83) 319, 1194, 1196
—— *v*. European Parliament (230/81) 62

Macarthys Ltd. *v*. Wendy Smith (129/79) 236, 601
Macchiorlati Dalmas *v*. High Authority (21/64) 1052, 1091
Macchiorlati Dalmas & Figli *v*. High Authority (1/63) 1091
Maiseries de Beauce *v*. ONIC (109/79) 246, 450, 764
Maizena (5/82) 599
Maizena GmbH *v*. Council (139/79) 501, 584, 610, 759, 1044, 1127, 1456
—— *v*. HZA Hamburg-Jonas (39/84) 74
MALT GmbH *v*. Hauptzollamt Düsseldorf (236/84) 412, 445, 645
Man Sugar *v*. IBAP (181/84) 6, 742, 743
Mandelli *v*. Commission (3/67) 344, 1330, 1380
Mannesmann AG *v*. High Authority (19/61) 436, 564, 579, 603, 714, 914, 957,
971, 978, 1061, 1064, 1069, 1081
Manzoni *v*. FNROM (112/76) 245
Markmann *v*. Germany and Schleswig-Holstein (121/73) 383, 1060
Marty *v*. Lauder (37/79) 1374
Mavridis *v*. Parliament (289/81) 949, 953, 1088, 1093
Meganck *v*. Commission (36/72) 1063, 1065, 1066
Meggle Milchindustrie *v*. Council and Commission (244/83) 510
Meiko Konservenfabrik *v*. Bundesrepublik Deutschland (224/82) 432, 1114, 1121,
1129, 1130, 1147
Melkunie BV (97/83) 795
Merkur-Aussenhandels-GmbH *v*. Commission (43/72) 408, 418, 445, 537, 593, 655
Merkur-Fleisch-Import *v*. Hauptzollamt Hamburg-Ericus (147/81) 442, 730, 736
Merlini *v*. High Authority (108/63) 971, 1038, 1404
Meroni *v*. High Authority (10/56) 329, 524, 870, 1051, 1069, 1205, 1206, 1207, 1376
Metro-SB-GroBmärkte GmbH & Co. KG *v*. Commission (26/76) 1194

Michel v. Parliament (195/80) 1424
Michelin v. Commission (322/81) 1339, 1344, 1349, 1356
Milac v. Hauptzollamt Freiburg (8/78) 417, 445, 573, 574, 596
Miller International Schallplatten GmbH (19/77) 1236
Mills v. Investment Bank (110/75) 83, 1405
Ministre des Pêcheries v. C.A. Schonenberg (88/77) 622
Minotiers (11/74) 408, 417, 418, 563, 585
Mogensen v. Commission (10/82) 322
Moli v. Commission (121/76) 1325, 1348
Mollet v. Commission (75/77) 1348
Mosthaf v. Commission (34/65) 1034
Moulins et Huileries de Pont-à-Mousson and Providence (124/76 & 20/77) 245, 562,
                                                                626, 627, 632, 670
Moussis (Sophie) v. Commission (227/83) 1032, 1038, 1039
Mrs. P. v. Commission (40/79) 1122
Müller v. Commission (4/67) 1033, 1034, 1038
—— v. —— (109/63 & 13/64) 1046
—— v. Economic and Social Committee (79/70) 961, 1032, 1035, 1040, 1041, 1384
Mulligan v. Commission (235/83) 1063
Municipality of Differdange v. Commission (222/83) 61, 967
Musique Diffusion Française v. Commission (100–103/80) 838, 1237, 1242, 1325,
                                                                1339, 1342, 1345, 1428

NTN Toyo Bearing Co. v. Council (113/77) 389, 393, 964, 1191, 1324, 1340, 1359,
                                          1360, 1361, 1383, 1413, 1421, 1440, 1463
NV De Jong Verenigde and Coöperatieve "Dorno-Bedum" GA v. Voedsel-
     voorzienings In-en Verkoopbureau (V.I.B.) 20/84 70
NV L'Oreal v. PVBA De Nieuwe AMCK (31/80) 983, 1374
NVA Maas & Co. SA v. BALM (21/85) 141, 744
Nachi Fujikoshi (121/77) 965
Nachi Fujikoshi Corporation v. Council (255/84) 296, 368, 389, 1413
National Panasonic v. Commission (136/79) 6, 835, 1195, 1218, 1229, 1239, 1324,
                                          1328, 1329, 1330, 1331, 1332, 1337, 1383, 1421
Nebe v. Commission (24/69) 1033, 1034, 1038, 1041, 1402, 1405
Netherlands v. Commission (66/63) 1403
—— v. —— (28/66) 495, 1230
—— v. —— (59/70) 871, 1032, 1055, 1057, 1449
—— v. High Authority (6/54) 327, 337, 338, 339, 412, 1380, 1422
Neumann (17/67) 939, 1115, 1120
Neumann v. BALM (299/84) 6, 744
—— v. —— (38/86) 428, 746
Nippon Seiko v. Council and Commission (119/77) 389, 965, 1413
Nold v. Commission see Firma Nold KG v. Commission (4/73) 356, 436, 625, 722,
                                                                        723, 1420
Noordwijks Cement Accord v. Commission (8-11/66) 236, 958, 959, 962, 976,
                                                                        989, 1420, 1421
Nordbutter v. Germany (9/85) 739, 772
Norddeutsches Vieh-und Fleischkontor GmbH v. Hauptzollamt Hamburg St.
     Annen (39/70) 669, 727
Nordgetreide v. Hauptzollamt Hamburg-Jonas (167/82) 441
Nordsee, Deutsche Hochseefischerei v. Germany and Rheinland-Pfalz
     (122/73) 383, 1060
Nungesser v. Commission (258/78) 842

Oebel (155/80) 499, 776, 803

Oehlmann (73/69) 757
Oelmühle u. Becher v. HZA Hamburg u. HZA Bremen-Nord (119–120/76) 420, 747
Officier van Justitie v. Van den Hazel (111/76) 425, 456
Ohrgaard v. Commission (9/82) 322
Ordre des Avocats au Barreau de Paris v. Klopp (107/83) 833
Oslizlok v. Commission (34/77) 1338

Padana v. Commission (276/80) 845, 1118, 1128
Papierfabrik Schoellershammer v. Commission (83/82) 492, 1105
Pardini (808/79) 783, 856
Parliament v. Council (302/87) 1205
Parti Ecologiste v. Parliament (294–296/83) 4, 62, 1191
Paul's Agriculture v. Council and Commission (256/81) 507, 523
Pauvert v. Court of Auditors (228/84) 952, 1089, 1092
Pecastaing v. Belgium (98/79) 6, 433, 445, 1120, 1121, 1125,
                                                                                        1127, 1151, 1343
Peiser v. Hauptzollamt Hamburg-Ericus (151/77) 764, 1118, 1147
Perinciolo v. Council (124/75) 1368
Pesticides (272/80) see Frans-Nederlandse Maatschappij voor Biologische Produk-
      ten BV 791
Pfizer v. Eurim-Pharm (1/81) 801, 802, 803
Philip Morris BV v. Commission (730/79) 388
Phoenix-Rheinrohr v. High Authority (20/58) 328, 962, 1061, 1422, 1425
Pigs Marketing Board v. Redmond (83/78) 456
Pistoj v. Commission (26/63) 1358, 1369
Plaumann v. Commission (25/62) 1191
Pool v. Council (49/79) 525
Portelange v. Corona Marchant International (10/69) 1229
Politi v. Italy (43/71) 252
Prais v. Council (130/75) 324
Präsident Ruhrkohlenverkaufsgesellschaft mbH v. High Authority (36-38 &
      40/59) 981, 1385, 1410
Procureur de la République v. Giry & Guerlain (253/78) 1374
——— v. Rivoira (179/78) 783
Procureur du Roi v. Dassonville (8/74) 773, 779, 780, 786
——— v. Marc JVC Debauve (52/79) 606, 614, 630
Providence Agricole de la Champagne v. ONIC (4/79) 245, 445, 764, 1107

Queensborough Rolling Mill Company v. Commission (64/84) 848, 1051

R. v. Kent Kirk (63/83) 1123
——— v. Secretary of State for Home Affairs (131/79) ex p. Santillo 1345, 1434
Racke v. Hauptzollamt Mainz (98/78) 6, 433, 445, 947, 1120, 1121, 1125, 1127, 1151
Ragnelli (Valerio) v. Commission (75/85) 1408
Raponi v. Commission (27/63) 307, 308, 1231, 1408
Ratti (148/78) 252, 1148
Rau (Walter) v. Commission (279, 280, 285 & 286/84) 296, 407, 409, 417,
                                                                                        426, 443, 445, 856
Reich (Adolf) v. HZA Landau (64/74) 758
Reichelt v. Hauptzollamt Berlin-Süd (113/81) 1106
Reinarz v. Commission (46/69) 322
Rewe v. Landwirtschaftskammer Saarland (33/76) 51, 945
Rewe-Handelsgesellschaft Nord mbH v. Hauptzollamt Kiel (158/80) 404, 605,
                                                                                        1402, 1412

Rewe-Zentral AG v. Bundesmonopolverwaltung für Branntwein (120/78) 773, 787, 859
Rewe-Zentrale v. Hauptzollamt Emmerich (37/70) 446, 1076
Reyners v. Belgium (2/74) 832
Rheinmühlen v. Einfuhr-und Vorratsstelle für Getreide und Füttermittel (6/71) 460, 568
Richez-Parise v. Commission (19–20, 25 & 30/69) 1085, 1372
Rijksuni Versiteit (185/83) 1194
Rijn-Schelde-Verolme v. Commission (223/85) 1083
Ritter von Wüllerstorff und Urbair v. Commission (7/77) 322, 1402
Rittweger v. Commission (21/70) 322, 1345, 1420
Riva v. Commission (2/70) 868, 959, 971, 974, 1010, 1011, 1037, 1070, 1450
Robertson (220/81) 788
Romano v. INAMI (98/80) 1207
Roquette v. Commission (26/74) 51, 636, 640
Roquette Frères v. Council (138/79) 402, 413, 759, 1127, 1380, 1422
—— v. Council (110/81) 433, 1019, 1078
—— v. France (29/77) 407, 409, 410, 414, 418, 445, 763
—— v. French Customs Administation (145/79) 246, 249, 450, 1107
Royal Scholten-Honig (Holdings) Ltd. v. International Board for Agricultural Produce (103 & 145/77) 416, 421, 562, 611, 628, 671
Ruckdeschel v. Hauptzollamt Hamburg-St. Annen (117/76 & 16/77) 6, 65, 245, 416, 417, 561, 562, 597, 626, 632, 670, 715
Rumi v. Commission (258/80) 1118, 1128
Rummler (Gisela) v. Dato-Druck GmbH (237/85) 673
Ruske v. Commission (67/81) 314
Rutili v. Minister for the Interior (36/75) 717, 818

SA Biovilac NV v. EEC (59/83) 75, 562, 632, 671, 1130
SA des Grande Distilleries Peureux v. Directeur des Services Fiscaux de la Haute-Saône et du Territoire de Belfort (86/78) 657, 673
SACE v. Ministry for Italian Finance (33/70) 252, 481
SOREMA v. High Authority (36/64) 975, 977, 981, 982, 1012, 1013, 1037, 1052, 1084
Sabbatini-Bertoni (20/71) 652, 1035, 1049
Sagulo (8/77) 725, 819, 828
Salerno (87/77) 1087
Salgoil (13/68) 798
San Michele v. High Authority (5–11, 13–15/62) 719, 851, 1447
Sandoz v. Commission (53/69) 363, 1058, 1201
Sàri Unifrex v. Commission and Council (281/82) 1152
Sayag v. Leduc (9/69) 505, 506, 509
Sgarlata v. Commission (40/64) 61
Schertzer v. Parliament (25/68) 1212, 1405
Schiavo v. Council (122–123/79) 1032, 1038
Schlüter & Maack v. Hauptzollamt Hamburg-Jonas (94/71) 475
Schmitz v. Commission (18/63) 853, 861
Schoellershammer v. Commission (283/82) 492
Schoffer v. Commission (46/64) 1045, 1051
Schloh v. Council (85/82) .... 308, 320 et seq
Scholten-Honig (125/77) 432, 564, 630, 672, 1122, 1139
—— (101/76) 968, 1140, 1147, 1360
Schoppenstedt v. Council (5/71) 506, 507, 514, 524, 525, 565, 754
Schouten B.V. (35/78) 947
Schreckenberg v. Commission (59/65) 1164

Schröder v. Germany (40/72) 447, 761
Schwarze v. Einfuhr-und Vorratsstelle für Getreide (16/65) 224, 1195, 1409, 1423
Schwarzwaldmilch GmbH v. Einfuhr-und Vorratsstelle für Fette (4/68) 249, 463, 733
Seco v. Etablissement d'Assurance contre la Vieillesse et l'Invalidité (62 &
    63/81) 618, 629
Sermide SpA v. Cassa Conguaglio Zucchero (106/83) 632
Seton v. Commission (37/81) 1360, 1361, 1409
SIMET v. Commission (67/69) 236, 1456
Simmenthal v. Commission (92/78) 445, 762, 792, 1022
Simon v. Court of Justice (15/60) 957, 971, 973, 989, 990, 991, 1023
Sirena v. EDA (40/70) 378
Smit (D.J.) Transport BV v. Commissie Grensoverschrijdend Beroepsgoederen-
    vervoer (126/82) 651
SNUPAT v. High Authority (42 & 49/59) 6, 65, 68, 237, 259, 260, 867, 872, 939, 940,
        947, 948, 957, 959, 971, 973, 974, 975, 988, 994, 995, 997, 998, 999, 1010,
            1014, 1019, 1020, 1025, 1029, 1034, 1042, 1045, 1070, 1225, 1325
Société Coopérative, Providence Agricole de la Champagne v. ONIC (4/79) .. 245, 445,
                                                                605, 670, 764, 1107
Société des Acieries du Temple v. High Authority (36/62) 517
Société des Charbonnages de Beeringen v. High Authority (9/55) 567, 572, 577
Société d' Electro-Chimie v. High Authority (11/57) 556, 568, 577, 676
Sociétés des Fonderies de Pont-à-Mousson v. High Authority (14/59) 565, 672
Société des Produits de Mais SA v. Administration des Douanes et des Droits
    Indirects (112/83) 1107
Société des Usines à Tubes v. High Authority (1/57) 976, 1420
Société Fives Lille Cail v. High Authority (19/60) 238, 514, 978, 1081, 1045
Société Métallurgique de Knutange v. High Authority (15 & 29/59) 327, 845, 979
Societé RU-MI v. FORMA (272/81) 452, 737, 738
Société Technique Minière v. Maschinenbau Ulm (56/65) 365, 1228, 1229
Söhnlein Rheingold v. Hauptzollamt Wiesbaden (183/84) 470
SOPAD v. FORMA and Firs (143/73) 432, 1122
Sotgiu v. Deutsche Bundespost (152/73) 21, 617, 621, 622, 822
SpA Fragd v. Amministrazione delle Finanze dello Stato (33/84) 1106, 1109
SpA International Chemical Corporation v. Amministrazione delle Finanze delle
    Stato (66/80) 245
Staple Dairy Products v. Intervention Board (84/81) 432, 434, 1126
Stauder v. Staut Ulm-Sozialamt (29/69) 625, 720, 1459
Steinike & Weinlig v. Germany (78/76) 388, 673
Stimming v. Commission (90/77) 517, 941, 955, 1136
Stölting v. Hauptzollamt Hamburg-Jonas (138/78) 6, 410, 425, 754
Suiker Uni v. Commission (40/73) 1214, 1348, 1364, 1365, 1370
Sucrimex (133/79) 510
Syndicat de la Sidérurgie du Centre-Midi v. High Authority (12/57) . 556, 566, 575, 674,
                                                                    675, 674
Syndicat Général du Personnel des Organismes Européens v. Commission (18/74) ... 1189
—— v. Council (175/73) 1189

Testa v. Bundesanstalt für Arbeit (41, 121 & 796/79) 502, 825
Tezi Textiel BV v. Commission (59/84) 531
Thieffry v. Conseil de l'Ordre des Avocats à la Cour de Paris (71/76) 832
Thyssen A.G. v. Commission (188/82) 846, 1079, 1081, 1089, 1092, 1196, 1368
Timex v. Council and Commission (264/82) 29, 299, 389, 1195, 1345, 1354, 1357, 1429

Tomadini SNC v. Amministrazione delle Finanze dello Stato (84/78) 432, 1135,
1143
Tontodonati v. Commission (28/72) 1047
Töpfer (Alfred) v. Commission (106/63) 407
Töpfer & Co. GmbH v. Commission (112/77) 872, 941, 955, 1075, 1114, 1118, 1143,
1148
Tradax Graenhandel BV v. Commission (38/70) 249
Tradax Graanhandel B.V. v. Commission (64/82) 74
Transocean Marine Paint v. Commission (17/74) 6, 368, 1192, 1229, 1324, 1329, 1434
Travigo v. Hauptzollamt Aachen-Nord (157/78) 764
Tubes de la Sarre v. High Authority (1/57) 976, 1420
Tunnel Refineries v. Council (114/81) 1127

Ufficio imposte v. Commission (2/68) 1425
Union Française de Céréales v. HZA Hamburg-Jonas (6/78) 54
Union Malt v. Commission (44-51/77) 434, 951, 1141
United Brands Company v. Commission (27/76) ... 370, 379, 1201, 1365, 1369, 1370, 1423
United Foods and van den Abeele v. Belgium (132/80) 787, 792
Universiteitskliniek Utrecht v. Inspecteur der Invoerrechten en Accijnzen (72/77) ... 489
University of Hamburg v. HZA Hamburg-Kehrureder (216/82) 1053
Usines Emile Henricot v. High Authority (23–24 & 52/63) 958, 959, 961
Usines Gustave Böel and Fabrique de fer de Maubeuge v. Commission (76/83) 1033
USINOR v. Commission (265/82) 1033, 1037, 1051, 1089, 1092
—— v. —— (185/85) 342, 1411

VBVB v. Commission (43 & 63/82) 1344
Valsabbia v. Commission (154, 205–206, 226–228, 263–264/78 & 31, 39, 83 &
85/79) 327, 337, 339, 848, 1384
Van Binsbergen (33/74) 725, 827
Van Duyn v. Home Office (41/74) 252, 258, 816, 1148
Van Eick v. Commission (13/69) 324, 1366, 1369
Van Gend en Loos v. Nederlandse Belastingadministratie (26/62) .. 252, 481, 1236, 1457
Van Landewyck v. Commission (209/78) 1345, 1357, 1363, 1366, 1369, 1370
Van Paassen v. Staatssecretaris (181/78) 1422
Variola SpA v. Amministrazione Italiana delle Finanze (34/73) 1132
Vaysse v. Commission (26/85) 307, 315
Vecchioli v. Commission (101/79) 1212
Verband der Sachversicherer v. Commission (45/85) 368
Verli-Wallace v. Commission (159/82) 971, 972, 973, 998
Vloeberghs v. High Authority (9 & 12/60) 511, 513, 521

Wagner (8/82) 564, 573, 583
Wagner (12/79) 538
Walzstahl-Vereinigung and Thyssen v. Commission (140, 146, 221 & 226/82) 335
Watson and Belmann (118/75) 58, 592, 724, 818, 862
Webb (279/80) 618, 829
Werhahn v. Council (63-69/72) 408, 506, 531, 533, 607, 614, 616, 755
Weingut Gustav Decker KG v. Hauptzollamt Landau (99/78) 433, 452, 1121, 1125
Welding and Co. v. Hauptzollamt Hamburg-Waltershof (87/78) 418, 757, 1406, 1412
Westzucker v. Einfuhr-und Vorratsstelle für Getreide und Futtermittel (57/72) 673
Westzucker GmbH v. Einfuhr-und Vorratsstelle für Zucker (1/73) 6, 432, 939, 940,
947, 1116, 1119, 1120, 1122, 1169
Wilhelm (Walt) v. Bundeskartellamt (14/68) 368, 379, 591, 651

Willame (Alfred) v. Commission of the European Atomic Energy Community
(110/63) 296
Williams (134/84) 672
Wirtschaftsvereinigung Eisen-und Stahlindustrie v. High Authority (13/57) 65, 329,
333, 337, 554, 566
Witt v. NZA Hamburg-Ericus (149/73) 1236
Witte (Hermann) v. Parliament (188/83) 672
Wöhrmann and Lütticke v. Commission (31 & 33/62) 1021
Wüllerstorff v. Commission (7/77) 322, 1402
Wulro BV (130/85) 456
Wünsche v. Germany (126/81) 446, 447, 449

X v. Audit Board (12/68) 1364, 1366, 1425

Yoshida v. Kamer van Koophandel en Fabriken voor Friesland (34/78) 249

Zuckerfabrik Franken GmbH v. Germany (77/81) 769, 1100, 1104

COUNCIL AND COMMISSION REGULATIONS

Council Regulation 1/58, J.O. 1958,
L385; O.J. Sp.Ed. 1952–1958,
59 .... 42, 1213, 1215
Council Regulation 17/62; J.O.
1962, 204; O.J. Sp.Ed. 1959–
1967, 87 .... 28, 44, 362, 366, 1187, 1218,
1237, 1242, 1376
Art. 2 983
Art. 3 1218
    (2)(b) 1346
Art. 4 367
    (2) 1303, 1327
Art. 6 (1) 983
Art. 8 1030
    (3) 983, 1011, 1014
    (b)–(d) 984
    (4)(c) 1022
    (12) 1014
Art. 9 (3) 1338
Art. 10 (3) 1356
Art. 11 .... 839, 1218, 1219, 1243
    (5) 1337, 1383, 1404
Art. 14 .... 837, 838, 1212, 1218, 1221,
1240, 1329
    (2)–(3) 1220
    (3) 1243
    (3)–(4) 1337
Art. 15 .... 379, 839
    (2) 840
    (5) 960, 1190
    (6) 958, 959, 963, 966
Art. 17 839
    (2) 838
Art. 19 .... 1321, 1322
    (1) 1338, 1356
    (2) 1326
Arts. 19–20 1355
Art. 20 .... 1349, 1350, 1424
    (2) 1328
Art. 24 1322
Council Regulation 27/62, J.O.
1962, 1118; O.J. Sp.Ed. 1959–
1962, 132 44
Council Regulation 31/62, J.O.
1962, 45/1385; O.J. Sp.Ed. 1959–
1962, 135 (Staff Regulations) 1187,
1321

Council Regulation 31/62—*cont.*
Art. 2 642
    (1) 1212
Art. 4 (3) 1035
Art. 9 (b) 1022
Art. 13 985
Art. 14 1064
    (1) 1063
Art. 17 (1)–(2) 1005
Art. 20 320
Art. 25   306, 985, 1036, 1361, 1405,
1422
    (1) 1407
    (2) 1404
Art. 26 1321
    (6) 1342
Art. 27 .... 320, 322, 323
    (3) 323
Art. 28 985
Art. 29 308
    (1)(b) 304
    (2) 319, 1088, 1362
Arts. 39–40 985
Art. 41 (4)–(5) 984
Art. 45 1231
    (1) 307
    (2) 305
Art. 47 989
    (3) 989, 990
Arts. 49–50 985
Art. 50 1362
Art. 67 (2) 1065, 1066
Art. 65 .... 311, 316, 317, 318, 319, 323,
1115, 1116
    (1) 309, 310
    (2) 313
Art. 85 .... 324, 988, 1007, 1061, 1065,
1066, 1162, 1165
Art. 86 (2) (f) 985
Art. 87 1321
Art. 88I 1379
Art. 90 .... 1036, 1038
    (2) 1039
    (3) 1372
Art. 91 .... 1036, 1372, 1373
    (1) 303

Council Regulation 31/62—*cont.*
  Art. 91—*cont.*
    (2) 1036, 1039, 1040
  Art. 102 (1) 1358
Council Regulation 87/62 760
Council Regulation 99/63, J.O.
  1963, 2268, O.J. Sp.Ed. 1963–
  1964, 47 .... 44, 362, 1187, 1211, 1237,
          1322, 1334, 1339, 1375, 1417
  Art. 2 964
  Art. 9 1363
    (2) 1368
Commission Regulation 102/64 427
Council Regulation 136/64—
  Art. 6 465
Council Regulation 141/64; O.J.
  1964, 2666 571
Council Regulation 142/64, J.O.
  1964, 2673 628
Commission Regulation 164/64,
  O.J. 1964, 2739 .... 570, 571
Commission Regulation 19/65, J.O.
  1965, 533; O.J. Sp.Ed. 1965–
  1966, 35 1376
Council Regulation 136/66, J.O.
  1966, L172/3025; O.J. Sp.Ed.
  1965–1966, 221 597
Council Regulation 120/67, J.O.
  1967, L117/2269; O.J. Sp.Ed.
  1967, 33 .... 461, 469, 587, 599,
         610, 617, 618, 628, 733
  Art. 10 611
  Art. 11 (11) 629
Council Regulation 131/67, J.O.
  1967, L120/2362; O.J. Sp.Ed.
  1967, 70 587
Council Regulation 132/67 469
Council Regulation 371/67, J.O.
  1967, L174/40; O.J. Sp.Ed. 1967,
  219 .... 599, 600
Council Regulation 876/67, J.O.
  1967, L281/7 597
Council Regulation 1009/67, J.O.
  1967, 308/1 666
Commission Regulation 1041/67,
  O.J. 1967, L314/9 .... 636, 664, 666
Council Regulation 259/68, J.O.
  1968, L56/1; O.J. Sp.Ed. 1968
  (I), 30 .... 25, 45
Council Regulation 459/68—
  Arts. 14, 17 .... 393, 394
  Art. 15 393
Council Regulation 802/68, J.O.
  1968, L148/1; O.J. Sp.Ed. 1968,
  165 482

Council Regulation 805/68 .... 732, 739
Council Regulation 865/68, O.J.
  Sp.Ed. 1967–8, 225 .. 1232, 1233, 1234,
                            1235
Council Regulation 950/68, J.O.
  1968 L172/1; O.J. Sp.Ed. 1968
  (I) 275 .... 36, 482, 485, 1233
Council Regulation 986/68, J.O.
  1968, L169/4 667
Council Regulation 1017/68, J.O.
  1968, L175/1; O.J. Sp.Ed. 1968,
  302—
  Art. 12 1374
Council Regulation 1028/68—
  Art. 5 469
Council Regulation 1612/68, J.O.
  1968, L257/2; O.J. Sp.Ed. 1968
  (II), 475 .... 619, 621, 816
  Art. 7 620
    (1) 619
Council Regulation 95/69—
  Art. 5 458
Council Regulation 97/69, J.O. 1969
  L14/1; O.J. Sp.Ed. 1969, 12 ... 37, 483
  Art. 3 484
Council Regulation 1191/69, J.O.
  1969, L156/1; O.J. Sp.Ed. 1969,
  276 44
Council Regulation 441/69, J.O.
  1969, L59/1; O.J. Sp.Ed. 1969
  (I), 91 .... 636, 637
Council Regulation 1192/69, J.O.
  1969, L156/8; O.J. Sp.Ed. 1969,
  283 44
Commission Regulation 1403/69,
  J.O. 1969, L180/3; O.J. Sp.Ed.
  1969 (II), 345 768
Council Regulation 1544/69 1412
Council Regulation 1586/69, O.J.
  1969, L202/1 .... 656, 657
Commission Regulation 1670/69,
  O.J. 1969, L214/7 656
Commission Regulation 1957/69,
  J.O. 1969, L250/1; O.J. Sp.Ed.
  1969 (II), 417 .... 636, 637
Council Regulation 1975/69, O.J.
  1969, L252/1 .... 661, 662, 663
Commission Regulation 2195/69,
  O.J. 1969, L278/6 .... 661, 663
Council Regulation 2464/69, J.O.
  1969, L312/4; O.J. Sp.Ed. 1969
  (II) 527 .... 589, 591
Council Regulation 459/70, J.O.
  1970, L57/19; O.J. Sp.Ed. 1970,
  L57/145 967

Council Regulation 729/70, O.J.
Sp.Ed. 1970 (I), 218 .... 46, 475, 476, 638, 639
Arts. 2–3 462
Art. 8 ...... 461, 476, 477, 773, 1097, 1098
(1) 474, 475, 774
Commission Regulation 756/70 770
Council Regulation 816/70, J.O.
1970, L99/1; O.J. Sp.Ed. 1970, 234 669
Council Regulation 849/70 1146
Council Regulation 983/70, J.O.
1970, L116/35 967
Council Regulation 1107/70, J.O.
1970, L130/1; O.J. Sp.Ed. 1970, 360 44
Council Regulation 1210/70, J.O.
1970, L142/20 588
Council Regulation 1432/70, O.J.
1970, L159/20 .... 656, 657
Commission Regulation 1505/70,
O.J. 1970, L166/33 656
Council Regulation 974/71, J.O.
1971, L106/1; O.J. Sp.Ed.
1971 .... 246, 410, 443, 444, 446, 450, 595, 596, 649, 650, 764, 766
Art. 1 (3) 445
Art. 2 442
Art. 4 (2) (b) 766
Art. 6 595
Commission Regulation 1014/71,
J.O. 1971, L110/10 595
Council Regulation 1054/71, J.O.
1971, L115/8 610
Council Regulation 1120/71, J.O.
1971, L118/3 610
Council Regulation 1182/71, J.O.
1971, L124/1; O.J. Sp.Ed. 1971, 354 .... 43, 49, 53
Council Regulation 1408/71, J.O.
1971, L149/2, O.J. Sp.Ed. 1971, 416 .... 46, 54, 496, 501
Art. 4 (1) 497
(4) 497
Art. 12 574
Art. 13 497
Art. 45 574
Art. 68 826
Art. 69 (2) 501, 502, 827
Council Regulation 1427/71, J.O.
1971, L151/5 762
Council Regulation 1428/71, J.O.
1971, L151/6 .... 448, 763

Council Regulation 1530/71, J.O.
1971, L162/13 .... 610, 611
Commission Regulation 1643/71,
O.J. 1971, L171/2 763
Commission Regulation 1687/71,
J.O. 1971, L173/1 596
Commission Regulation 189/72 1134
Council Regulation 766/72, O.J.
1972, 191/1 669
Council Regulation 858/72, J.O.
1972, L101/3; O.J. Sp.Ed. 172, 253 45
Commission Regulation 990/72,
J.O. 1972, L115/1 .... 667, 668
Council Regulation 1035/72, J.O.
1972, L118/1; O.J. Sp.Ed. 1972, (II), 437 .... 810, 811
Council Regulation 1259/72 426
Commission Regulation 1259/72 743
Council Regulation 1473/72, J.O.
1972, L160/1 .... 1039, 1061
Council Regulation 2707/72—
Art. 3 811
Council Regulation 2746/72, O.J.
Sp.Ed. 1972, 64 638
Council Regulation 907/73, O.J.
1973, L89/2 .... 49, 1208
Commission Regulation 330/74,
O.J. 1974, L359/1 .... 401, 402
Council Regulation 1125/74, O.J.
1974, L128/12 .... 599, 629, 630
Council Regulation 1132/74, O.J.
1974, L128/24 .... 600, 601
Commission Regulation 1608/74,
O.J. 1974, L170/38 .... 470, 471, 472, 473, 767
Commission Regulation 2107/74,
O.J. 1974, L218/54 648
Council Regulation 2988/74, O.J.
1974, L319/1 .... 43, 1451
Council Regulation 3113/74, O.J.
1974, L332/1 .... 600, 601
Council Regulation 3330/74 .... 422, 585
Council Regulation 3331/74, O.J.
1974, L359/18 584
Commission Regulation 192/75,
O.J. 1975, L25/1 .... 636, 637
Commission Regulation 193/75,
O.J. 1975, L25/10 785
Commission Regulation 231/75,
O.J. 1975, L24/4 600
Commission Regulation 232/75 743
Council Regulation 337/75, O.J.
1975, L139/1 1208

Council Regulation 665/75, O.J.
1975, L72/14 .... 529, 629
Council Regulation 724/75, O.J.
1965, L73/1 31
Council Regulation 1035/75—
Art. 29 (1) (1) 809
Council Regulation 1365/75, O.J.
1975, L139/1 1208
Commission Regulation 1380/75,
O.J. 1975, L139/37 .... 572, 573
Council Regulation 2727/75, O.J.
1975, L28/1 631
Council Regulation 2742/75, O.J.
1975, L281/57 .... 631, 632
Council Regulation 2772/75—
Arts. 17 (1) and 26 454
Council Regulation 101/76, O.J.
1976, L20/19 .... 621, 623
Council Regulation 563/76, O.J.
1976, L67/18 .... 241, 420, 421, 720,
749, 750, 754
Council Regulation 1162/76, O.J.
1976, L135/32 .... 426, 437, 725
Commission Regulation 1687/76,
O.J. 1976, L190/1 730
Council Regulation 1862/76, O.J.
1976, L206/3 .... 631, 632, 633
Council Regulation 1358/77 586
Commission Regulation 2158/76,
O.J. 1976, L241/21 .... 630, 632
Council Regulation 222/77, O.J.
1977, L38/1 482
Council Regulation 280/77, O.J.
1977, L40/1 .... 37, 483
Council Regulation 516/77, O.J.
1977, L73/1 633
Council Regulation 521/77, O.J.
1977, L73/28 634
Art. 2 (2) 634
Commission Regulation 938/77 451
Council Regulation 1079/77 O.J.
1977, L131/6 755
Council Regulation 1111/77 .... 403, 421,
422, 423, 527, 528, 613
Council Regulation 1775/77 488
Council Regulation 1778/77 .... 393, 965
Art. 3 393
Council Regulation 3023/77 1412
Council Regulation 240/78 738
Council Regulation 572/78 732
Commission Regulation 1102/78,
O.J. 1978, L139/26 .... 633, 634, 635,
648, 812
Council Regulation 1298/78 422

Commission Regulation 1998/78,
O.J. 1978, L231/5 .... 575, 585
Commission Regulation 3016/78,
O.J. 1978, L359/11 615
Commission Regulations 3085–
86/87 .... 1016, 1146
Council Regulation 214/79, O.J.
1979, L35/1 31
Council Regulation 262/79, O.J.
1979, L41/1 735
Commission Regulation 262/79,
O.J. 1979 L41/1—
Art. 22 730
Art. 23 .... 730, 735
Commission Regulation 687/79,
O.J. 1979, L86/18 811
Commission Regulation 779/79,
O.J. 1979, L101/7 811
Commission Regulation 1152/79,
O.J. 1979, L144/73 811
Council Regulation 1293/79 .... 403, 613,
759, 1078
Council Regulation 1430/79, O.J.
1979, L175/1 .... 45, 51, 52, 1061,
1104, 1105, 1106, 1109,
1113, 1164, 1165, 1171
Council Regulation 1697/79, O.J.
1979, L197/1 .... 45, 1069, 1102
Commission Regulation 1725/79,
O.J. 1979, L199/1 770
Commission Regulation 2173/79,
O.J. 1979, L251/12 747
Council Regulation 3017/79, O.J.
1978, L339/1 .... 52, 391, 966, 1340
Art. 2 397
Art. 5 (5) 390
Art. 13 (2) 966
Commission Regulation 1091/80,
O.J. 1980, L114/18 730
Commission Regulation 1092/80,
O.J. 1980, L114/22 730
Council Regulation 1224/80, O.J.
1980, L134/1 482
Council Regulation 1575/80, O.J.
1980, L161/13 1105
Council Regulation 1592/80 1078
Council Regulation 1837/80, O.J.
1980, L183/1 .... 591, 592, 593
Commission Regulation 2946/80,
O.J. 1980 1129
Commission Regulation 3183/80,
O.J. 1980, L338/1 730
Art. 33 745

Council Regulation 3429/80, O.J. 1980, L358/66—

Art. 1 815

Council Regulation 71/81 969

Commission Regulation 731/81, O.J. 1981, L74/27 746

Council Regulation 1785/81, O.J. 1981, L117/4 422

Art. 8 441

Art. 41 442

Council Regulation 1468/81, O.J. 1981, L144/1 46

Council Regulation 3245/81, O.J. 1981, L328/1 1208

Council Regulation 288/82, O.J. 1982, L35/1 30

Council Regulation 1967/82, O.J. 1982, L214/7 .... 966, 1105

Commission Regulation 1880/83, O.J. 1983, L187/5—

Art. 6 (3) 744, 745

Council Regulation 2176/84, O.J. 1984, L202/1 .... 29, 44, 334, 389, 390, 1187, 1218, 1320, 1333, 1340, 1346

Art. 7 .... 123, 1222, 1417, 1418

(1) (a) 1326

(3) 1222

(4) (a) 1347

(4)–(7) 1324

(5)–(6) 1363

(7) (b) 1222

Art. 10 1377

Art. 11(5) 1378

Art. 12 (2) 1378

Commission Regulation 2349/84, O.J. 1984, L219/5 1374

Council Regulation 2626/84, O.J. 1984, L247/1 49

Council Regulation 2641/84, O.J. 1984, L252/1 29

Commission Regulation 417/85, O.J. 1985, L53/1 1374

Commission Regulation 418/85, O.J. 1985, L53/1 1374

Council Regulation 1676/85, O.J. 1985, L164/1 1451

Council Regulation 1677/85, O.J. 1985, L164/6 1451

Commission Regulation 2220/85, O.J. 1985, L205/5 1451

Council Regulation 1761/87, O.J. 1987, L167/9 .... 29, 389, 1187

DIRECTIVES

Council Directive 64/221, J.O. 1964, 156/850; O.J. Sp.Ed. 1963–1964, 117 .... 47, 817, 818, 1343

Council Directive 68/360, J.O. 1968, L275/13 .... 817, 820

Council Directive 69/73, J.O. 1969, L58/1; O.J. Sp.Ed. 1969, 75 482

Council Directive 70/156, J.O. 1970, L42/1; O.J. Sp.Ed. 1970, 96 47

Council Directive 75/117, O.J. 1975, L45/19 .... 39, 496

Council Directive 75/329, O.J. 1975, L48/29 496

Council Directive 76/207, O.J. 1976, L39/40 .... 39, 496

Council Directive 77/187, O.J. 1977, L61/26 496

Council Directive 78/453, O.J. 1978, L146/19 46

Council Directive 79/7, O.J. 1979, L6/24 .... 39, 496

Council Directive 80/987, O.J. 1980, L283/23 496

CASES BEFORE NATIONAL COURTS

Belgium

A.S.B.L. Enseignement moyen de l'évêché de Liège, 3 January 1968, A.D.C.E., 5 920
Allard 21.595, 25 November 1981 ...... 1293, 1295
Baudrin, 20.347, 22 May 1980 1296
Benelux, No. 20561, 17 September 1980 919
Blondiau, 3.956, 24 December 1954 1296
Blomme (Conseil d'Etat) No. 17, 127, 9 July 1975 157
Boschloos, 22.149, 26 March 1982 ...... 1295, 1296
Bury, 2.937, 20 November 1953 1295
Buyle, 16.686, 22 October 1974 1295
Creteur, 2558, 11 June 1953 1293
De Graeve, 16.938, 19 March 1975 .. 1295
De Kerpel, 11.430, 6 October 1965 1295
De Laer, 15.038, 2 December 1971 1293
De Meyer, 4.168, 22 March 1955 1295
De Nul, 17.022, 20 May 1975 1295
De Roo, 12.878, 19 March 1968 1296
De Troyer, Nos. 1339 and 1340, 3 March 1952 919
Decafmeyer, 23.626, 26 October 1983 1295
Dekeyser, 9.206, 27 February 1962 .. 1296
Demarest, 13.783, 12 November 1969 1295
Demolin, 906, 4 June 1951 1296
Detournay 16.328, 26 March 1974 1294
Detry, 3, 748, 26 October 1954 288
Doyen 15.467, 26 July 1972 1295
Exelmans, 985, 30 June 1951 288
Freney, 4.539, 29 July 1955 1295
Gemeinde Schoten 8477, 7 March 1961 1391
Gielen, 12.086, 2 December 1966 1296
Goethals, 16.284, March 6 1974 1295
Grynpas 18.208, 1 April 1977 1295

Belgium—cont.

Hubert, No. 6091, 21 February 1958 919
Huybrechts, 15.581, 27 November 1972 1294
Janssens, 8, 712, 3 July 1961 288
Jong-Bloet et C.A.P. Ostende, 15.150, 9 1972 1295
Lamalle, 13.939, 5 February 1970 1295
Lannaj, 6 June 1969, 1970 R.J.D.A. 149 920
Labijn, 16.217, 30 January 1984 ...... 1293, 1294
Magery, 13.363, 9 January, 1969 1295
Mahy, 7.212, 15 September 1959 1295
Marceli, 22.672, 19 November 1982 1296
Matthys, 2, 574, 16 June 1953 288
Meulepas, 14.067, 21 April 1970 1295
Michel, 5.480, 1 February 1957 1295
Mombach 4.163, 18 March 1955 1295
Municipality of Boechout (Conseil d'Etat) No. 20, 040, 15 January 1980 157
Paternotte, 905, 4 June 1951 1296
Piette, 13.407, 14 February 1969 1296
Piron, 24 April 1964, A.A.C.E. 375 920
Regniers (Conseil d'Etat) No. 23, 455, 26 July 1983 157
Rochet (Conseil d'Etat) No. 18,207, 1 April 1977 ...... 157, 1293, 1295
Roulen 22.577, 12 October 1982 1294
Rummens, 15.419, 4 July 1972 1295
Schiepers and de Plecker, 16.358, 9 April 1974 1391
Schollaert 16.022, 26 September 1973 1295
Schraepen 1, 632, 11 June 1952 288
Speleers 21.037, 17 March 1981 1293
Sonet 11.288, 3 June 1965 1295
Stocker and L'on, 4, 590, 7 October 1955 289
Tedesco (Conseil d'Etat) No. 17,024, 20 May 1975 157

Belgium—*cont.*

Van Bergen 19.281, 5 December 1978 .... 1293, 1294

Van Brussel, 21.437, 6 October 1981 1295

Van Daele 18.398, 18 July 1977 1294

Van den Bulcke, 21.236, 11 June 1981 1294

Van den Eynde, 20.710, 14 November 1980 1295

Van Guembergen, 16.993, 22 April 1975 1294

Van Loo, 5.580, 28 March 1957 1295

Vandenbussche, 4.510, 14 July 1955 1295

Vandermotten, 9.086, 22 December 1961 1296

Vanhaeverbeke, 13 March 1950, R.J.D.A. 129 920

Vercanteren, 20.097, 5 February 1980 1296

Willockx, 14.864, 5 July 1971 1295

Wouters (Conseil d'Etat) No. 20,887, 20 January 1981 157

Zoete (Conseil d'Etat) No. 21,167, 12 May 1981 157

Decision No. 3405, 20 May 1954 1293

Decision No. 14.865, 5 July 1971 1293

Denmark

Decision 1932 U.F.R. 505 560

Decision 1940 U.F.R. 1030 560

Decision 1958 U.F.R. 455 560

Decision 1958 U.F.R. 868 560

France

Abbé Barthélémy (Conseil d'Etat) 9 July 1926, Recueil 713 345

Aramu (Conseil d'Etat) 26 October 1945, Recueil Lebon 213 .... 106, 126

Armand Pelleriri et Cie et Fédération nationale du négoce du tissu RDP 1981, 1036 1182

Association des anciens élèves de l'Institut Commercial de Nancy (Conseil d'Etat) 23 November 1962, A.J.D.A. 1962, 677 879

France—*cont.*

Azoulay (Conseil d'Etat) 17 December 1948, Recueil 474 267

Bailler (Conseil d'Etat) 10 March 1976, R.P.D. 1976, 1373 880

Baudrin, No. 20, 347, 22 May 1980 ... 698

Bontemps. (Conseil d'Etat) 15 October 1954, Rec. 438 1248

Brian (Conseil d'Etat) 15 July 1936, Recueil Lebon 777 1246

Buissière (Conseil d'Etat) 15 October 1967, Rec. 419 .... 877, 878

Cabot (Conseil d'Etat) 22 May 1985, RDP, 1987, 233 1251

Canal, Robin and Godat (Conseil d'Etat) 19 October 1962, G.A.J.A. 511 682

Car (Conseil d'Etat) 11 May 1960, Recueil 319 266

Casanova (Conseil d'Etat) G.A. No. 8, 35 110

Chegtba (Conseil d'Etat) 24 June 1981, Recueil 853 266

Clary (Conseil d'Etat) 4 November 1946, Recueil Lebon 252 1246

Cohn-Bendit (Conseil d'Etat) C.E. 1978, 524, EUR 1979, 292, DUBI. 1980, 126 252

Concerts du Conservatoire (Conseil d'Etat) G.A. No. 181, 355 106

Constantin (Conseil d'Etat) 30 June 1950, Rec. 840 1250

Constantin (Conseil d'Etat) 17 July 1953, Rec. 381 880

Crédit foncier de France (Conseil d'Etat) 11 December 1970, Recueil 750 268

Damas, Dol and Laurent, 28 February 1919, G.A.J.A. 150 681

Dame Cachet (Conseil d'Etat) 3 November 1922, R.D.P. 1922, 522 .... 878, 919

Dame Cozic-Savoure (Conseil d'Etat) 20 February 1953, Rec. 86 1333

Dame Denayer (Conseil d'Etat) 18 February 1949, Recueil 80 346

Dame Ingrand (Conseil d'Etat) 21 March 1947, Rec. 430 878

Dame Ruard (Conseil d'Etat) 4 May 1962, Rec. 296 1268

De Fontbonne (Conseil d'Etat) 3 February 1956, R.D.P. 1956, 859 880

France—*cont.*

Decock (Conseil d'Etat) (1979/80)
Rechtskundig Weekblad, 2757 ... 698
Diaw (Conseil d'Etat) 7 March 1980
Recueil 127 266
Dlle. Achille Fould (Conseil d'Etat)
19 January 1938, Rec. 55 879
Dlle. Mollet (Conseil d'Etat) 6 February 1948, Rec. 20 880
d'Oriano (Conseil d'Etat) 23 October 1964, Recueil Lebon 486 1247
Druard (Conseil d'Etat) 28 April
1950, Rec. 243 879
Du Chalard (Conseil d'Etat) 18 May
1939, Recueil Lebon 1246
Epoux Speter (Conseil d'Etat) 7
March 1958, Rec. 152 1248
Foerst (Conseil d'Etat) 20 February
1953, Rec. 83 1250
Fuster (Conseil d'Etat) 9 July 1937,
Recueil Lebon, 690 1246
G.I.S.T.I. (Conseil d'Etat) G.A.
No. 112, 587 106
Garysao (Conseil d'Etat) 12 December 1955 RDD 1956, 333 1249
Gauthier (Conseil d'Etat) 17 June
1936, Recueil Lebon, 659 1246
Gornel (Conseil d'Etat) 4 April
1914, Recueil 488 266
Grassin (Conseil d'Etat) 26 October
1973, Rec. 598 682
Hollender (Conseil d'Etat) 20 January 1939, Rec. 20 880
Imbach (Conseil d'Etat) 14 May
1948, Recueil 215 266
Kremer (Conseil d'Etat) 12 June
1936, Rec. 638 879
La Fleurette (Conseil d'Etat) 14
January 1938, Recueil Lebon
25 533
Lagrange (Conseil d' Etat) 15
February 1961, Rec. 121 682
Laiterie Saint-Cyprien (Conseil
d'Etat) 8 January 1960, Rec.
10 883
Leboucher et Tarendon (Conseil
d'Etat) 12 May 1976, A.J.D.A.
1977, 261 883
Manufacture de produits chimiques
de Tournan (Conseil d'Etat) 4
March 1966, Recueil 174 266
Manufacture française de Pneumatiques Michelin (Conseil d'Etat)
29 March 1968, A.J.D.A. 1968,
342 878

France—*cont.*

Marcin-Kowsky (Conseil d'Etat) 28
November 1951, Recueil 548 345
Matherey (Conseil d'Etat) 9 December 1974, Rec. 830 1248
Ministère de l'Aménagement du territoire, de l'Equipement, du
Logement et du Tourisme *v.*
Thooris (Conseil d'Etat) 23 July
1974, Rec. 442 880
Ministre de l'Education Nationale *v.*
Dufresne (Conseil d'Etat) 28
March 1958, Rec. 204 1250
Ministère de l'Education et Nguyen
Van Nang (Conseil d'Etat) 7
February 1973, A.J.D.A. 1975,
248 883
Ministre de l'Economie et des
Finances *v.* Société Saumat et
Cie (Conseil d'Etat) 10 March
1967, Rec. 113 877
Ministère du Travail *v.* Sociètè Afrique Europe Transaction (Conseil
d'Etat) 30 January 1981, Rec.
32 883
Ministre de L'Intérieur *v.* Gay (Conseil d'Etat) 23 July 1974, Rec.
441 878
Ministre de l'Interieur *v.* Sideyn et
Desonneville, RDP 1970, 1042 ... 1249
Mytteis-Hager (Conseil d'Etat) 22
July 1977, Recueil 366 266
Nègre (Conseil d'Etat) 24 June 1949
Rec. 304 .... 1249, 1250
Palm (Conseil d'Etat) 20 January
1956, RDP 1956, 569 1250
Reynaud (Conseil d'Etat) 25 May
1928, Rec. 1928 879
Silberstein (Conseil d'Etat) 17 June
1955, R.P.D.A. 310 880
Sirey (Conseil d'Etat) 1949, Recueil
40 346
Société Civile Sainte-Marie de l'Assomption (Conseil d'Etat) 20
October 1972, Recueil 657 .... 268, 682
Société Duchet et Cie (Conseil
d'Etat) 27 June 1947, Rec. 283 877
Société Laboratoires Geigy (Conseil
d'Etat) 25 April 1958, Rec. 236 ... 1333
Société Leroi et autres (Conseil
d'Etat) 26 January 1973,
A.J.D.A. 1973, 252 883
Société Libraire François Maspero,
2 November 1973, Rec. 611 .. 682, 683

France—cont.

Société Toni (Conseil d'Etat) 27 April 1951, Recueil 312 267

Sté Establissement Cruse (Conseil d'Etat) A.J.D.A. 1980, 483 .... 1247, 1248

Sté Varoise de Transport (Conseil d'Etat) 6 February 1981, Rec. 52 1248

Syndicat chrétien du Ministère de l'Industrie et du Commerce (Conseil d'Etat) 12 June 1959, A.J.D.A. 1960, *IT*, 62 879

Syndicat de la raffinerie du soufre française et Société française des Etablissements Koch et Reis (Conseil d'Etat) 26 November 1954, Rec. 620 881

Syndicat des Patrons coiffeurs de Limoges (Conseil d'Etat) G.A. No. 18, 69 110

Syndicat des sylviculteurs du Sud-Ouest (Conseil d'Etat) 6 October 1967, Rec. 356 881

Syndicat national de la meunerie à siegle (Conseil d'Etat) 25 June 1954, Rec. 379 883

Syndicat national des statistiques (Conseil d'Etat) 13 February 1948, Rec. 74 881

Thomet (Conseil d'Etat) 15 January 1943, Rec. 9 .... 877, 878

Thibault (Conseil d'Etat) 5 December 1956, Recueil 463 265

Trompier-Gravier (Conseil d'Etat) G.A. No. 66, 281 106

Ville de Bagreux (Conseil d'Etat) 6 May 1966, A.J.D.A. 498 886

Ville Nouvelle Est (Conseil d'Etat) 28 May 1971, Recueil 409 ..... 265, 268

Vogler (Conseil d'Etat) 14 May 1947, Recueil Lebon 777 1246

Decision No. 17, 101 (Conseil d'Etat) 26 June 1975 697

Decision (Conseil d'Etat) 19 May 1933 680

Decision (Conseil d'Etat) 15 February 1949 Rec. 98 875

Germany

BAG, NJW 1984, 2374 901

BFHE 137, 202, 205 901

Germany—cont.

BGHZ 15, 305 1264

BVerfGE 2, 266 (282) 691

BVerfGE 7, 377 760

BVerfGE 8, 155, 172 887

BVerfGE 11, 139, 146 900

BVerfGE 13, 97 (113) 754

BVerfGE 13, 261, 270 899

BVeftGE 13, 261, 271 .... 898, 946, 948

BVerfGE 13, 261, 272 899

BVerfGE 13, 339 [1987] 3 C.M.L.R. 225 1449

BVerfGE 14, 19 (27) 688

BVerfGE 15, 226 (234) 688

BVerfGE 16, 147 (118) 754

BVerfGE 18, 224, 240 901

BVerfGE 18, 254, 261 898

BVerfGE 18, 353 (362) 688

BVerfGE 18, 429, 439 899

BVerfGE 19, 1 (5) 691

BVerfGE 19, 119 (126 *et seq.*) 754

BVerfGE 19, 348 688

BVerfGE 20, 230 896

BVerfGE 20, 351 (361) 687

BVerfGE 21, 173 (183) 686

BVerfGE 27, 1; DVB (1971) 892 836

BVerfGE 27, 297 892

BVerfGE 28, 122, 126 901

BVerfGE 28, 122, 127 892

BVerfGE 29, 402 (410 *et seq.*) 754

BVerfGE 30, 272, 285 899

BVerfGE 30, 292 (316) 754

BVerfGE 30, 367, 386 .... 887, 899

BVerfGE 30, 367, 389 899

BVerfGE 30, 392, 401 887

BVerfGE 32, 1, 22 899

BVerfGE 33, 171 (187) 754

BVerfGE 34, 384 (386) 689

BVerfGE 35, 202 (221) 690

BVerfGE 36, 73, 82 900

BVerfGE 37, 271, [1974] 2 C.M.L.R. 540 .... 1449, 1460

BVerfGE 38, 139, 148 898

BVerfGE 38, 386, 397 901

BVerfGE 39, 210 (230) 754

BVerfGE 40, 196 (222) 754

BVerfGE 43, 242, 288 900

BVerfGE 44, 336 892

BVerfGE 45, 142, 173 899

BVerfGE 45, 142, 167 887

BVerfGE 45, 142, 168 898

BVerfGE 48, 1, 25 .... 898, 899

BVerfGE 52, 187; [1980] 2 C.M.L.R. 531 1460

BVerfGE 55, 185, 203 900

Germany—*cont.*

BVerfGE 57, 361, 391	899
BVerfGE 59, 128, 164	900
BVerfGE 59, 128, 165	901
BVerfGE 63, 144	687
BVerfGE 63, 312, 329	900
BVerfGE 63, 343, 357	900
BVerfGE 65, 1	1267
BVerfGE 67, 1, 15	900
BVerfGE 71, 255, 273	900
BVerfGE 73, 339; [1987] 3 C.M.L.R. 225	61, 1460
BVerfG (E63, 343, 353)	899
BVerfG, RIW 1986, 651	899, 1121
1956 BVerwGE 4, 89	273
1961 BVerwGE 11, 168	273
BVertGE, 11 October 1966	890
r1971 BVerwGE 39, 197	273
BVertGE, 8 April 1987, 74, 223	1147
DVertGE [1988] 3 C.M.L.R. 19	1448
BVerwGE 8, 261	895
BVerwGE 9, 251	892
BVerwGE 16, 156	1264
BVerwGE 17, 178	1264
BVerwGE 19, 188	892
BVerwGE 37, 293, 300	898
BVerwGE 38, 191	1388
BVerwGE 45, 41 (59)	689
BVerwGE 48, 199 (302)	686
BVerwGE 67, 129, 131	898
BVerwGE 67, 305	895
BVerwG, N J W 1961, 1130	46
BVerwG, DÖV9, 142	1040
BVerwG, DVB1. 1982, 1004	890
BVerwG, NVwZ 1983, 608	1040
BVerwG, 12 July 1985, DÖV 1986, 74	1443
BVerwG 1986, DVB1.1202	896
BVerwG, 14 August 1986, DVB 1 1986, 1205	1100
BVerwG, 5 December 1986, NVwZ 1987, 578	1443
DVB1 1957, 503	892
OVG Münster, NJW 1981, 936	1388
OVG Münster, NVwZ 1982, 326	1387
VGH München, NJW 1981, 1001	1387
Federal Administrative Court Decision—	
13 (28, 31)	219
Federal Constitutional Court Decisions—	
33 (1, 9)	216
(125, 157)	216
(303, 346)	216
44 (251)	216

Germany—*cont.*

Berlin (Conseil d'Etat) 19 May 1953, Rec. 208	1255
Kloppenburg (Gerda) *v.* Finanzamt Leer (German Federal Finance Court) 25 April 1985	252
Decision 39, 210	754
Decision 40, 196	754
Decision 9, NJW 1960, 692	869
Decision 13, NJW 1962, 291	869
Decision (Federal Administrative Court) NJW 1986, 796	276
Decision 10/1983/66/101, Dr. Sigurd Barthold *v.* Germany (1985) EUGRZ 170	706

Greece

Decision 2309/1964	1304
Decision 2281/1968	1304
Decision 2196/1969	1302
Decision 3485/1971	1304
Decision 2184/1973	1393
Decision 657/1976	1304
Decision 2078/1976	1304
Decision 2383/1976	1304
Decision 3291/1976	1304
Decision 539/1977	1304
Decision 1003/1977	1304
Decision 1652/1977	1304
Decision 1900/1977	1304
Decision 1965/1977	1304
Decision 1134/1978	1304

Ireland

Abenglen Properties Ltd. *v.* Dublin Corporation (1982) 17 Irish Jurist 32	177
Byrne *v.* Ireland and Attorney General (1976) 11 Irish Jurist 11	174, 1394
Dunleary's Estate, *Re* [1952] I.R. 86	1394
East Donegal Co-op Ltd. *v.* Attorney-General [1970] I.R. 317	1306
Geraghty *v.* Minister for Local Government [1976] I.R. 153	1308
Haughey, *Re* [1971] I.R. 217	174, 1309

Ireland—*cont.*

Ingle v. O'Brien [1975] 109 *Irish Law Times Reports* 7 1307

Irish Family Planning Association v. Ryan [1979] I.R. 295 .... 1306, 1307, 1309

Kiely v. Minister for Social Welfare [1977] I.R. 267 1308

Local Government Board v. Aldridge [1915] A.C. 120 1394

Macauley v. Minister for Posts and Telegraphs [1966] I.R. 345 .... 174, 1307, 1394

McDonald v. Bord na glon [1965] I.R. 217 1305

Moran v. Attorney-General [1976] I.R. 400 1307

Murphy v. Attorney-General [1982] I.R. 241 .... 925, 1165

—— v. Lord Mayor of Dublin [1972] I.R. 215 .... 1308, 1394, 1437

O'Brien v. Bord na Móna [1983] I.L.R.M. 314 1309

Pigs Marketing Board v. Donnelly (Dublin) Ltd. [1939] I.R. 413 174

Russel v. Minister for Local Government [1976] I.R. 195 1394

State (Duggan) v. Tapley [1952] I.R. 67 176

The State (Gleeson) v. Minister for Defence and the Attorney-General [1976] I.R. 286 ...... 177, 1181

The State (Lynch) v. Cooney [1982] I.R. 337 1308

The State (McGeough) v. Louth County Council I.L.T.R. 107, 13 1394

State (Quinn) v. Ryan [1965] I.R. 70 176

Italy

Decision (Turin Court of Appeal) 18 May 1869, (1869) Giur.it.II, 340 129

Decision (Florence Court of First Instance) 31 May 1875, (1875) Legge I, 673 129

Decision (Corte di Cassazione, Rome) 15 April 1880, (1880) Giur.it.II, 789 129

Decision (Corte di Cassazione, Rome) 3 December 1881, (1882) Legge I, 806 129

Italy—*cont.*

Decision (Bologna Court of Appeal) 23 December 1882, (1883) Legge II, 596 129

Decision No. 3357 (Corte di Cassazione) 7 October 1954 915

Decision No. 297, 30 April 1955 917

Decision No. 2994 (Corte di Cassazione) 11 October 1955 135

Decision No. 261 (Consiglio di Stato) 28 June 1956 135

Decision No. 508, 11 July 1956 917

Decision No. 118, 8 July 1957 917

Decision No. 857 (Corte di Cassazione) 14 November 1958 915

Law No. 654, 6 May 1948 135

Decision No. 1142 (Corte di Cassazione) 8 May 1963 912

Decision No. 475, 27 September 1963 913

Decision No. 12, 28 November 1970 914

Decision No. 674 (Corte di Cassazione) 10 March 1971 135

Decision No. 7, 5 October 1971 914

Decision No. 1036, 23 November 1971 914

Decision No. 279, 29 February 1972 913

Decision 183/73; [1974] 2 C.M.L.R. 372 1460

Decision No. 713 (Corte di Cassazione) 14 March 1974 137

Decision No. 25 (Consiglio di Stato) 26 October 1975 136

Decision (Cds, Sez. II) No. 375/75 ... 1389

Decision No. 6 (Corte di Cassazione) 9 January 1976 136

Decision No. 264, 29 December 1976, (1977) Foro H.I., 565 693

Decision No. 100, 2 June 1977, (1977) Foro it. 1, 1609 693

Decision (CdS, Sez. VI) No. 798/77 1389

Decision No. 5831 (Corte di Cassazione) 1 December 1978 912

Decision No. 72 (Corte di Cassazione) 9 February 1979 915

Decision No. 73, 16 July 1979, (1979) Foro it. I, 2181 693

Decision No. 5172, (Corte di Cassazione) 6 October 1979 135

Decision No. 47, 14 April 1980, (1980) Foro it. I, 2673 693

Decision No. 72, 20 May 1980, (1980) Foro it.I, 1828 693

Italy—*cont.*

Decision No. 539 (T.A.R. Piedmonte) 15 July 1980 136

Decision No. 5838 (Corte di Cassazione) 7 October 1983 135

Decision No. 654, September 30 1984 913

Netherlands

Decision (Centrale Raad van Beroep) 31 October 1935, Dutch O.J. 1936, 168 931

Decision (Centrale Raad van Beroep) 23 March 1937, Dutch O.J. 1937, 497 930

Decision (Hoge Raad) 25 February 1949 (1949) N.J. 558 701

Decision (Centrale Raad van Beroep) 2 October 1951, A.A. II, 116 .... 869, 926

Decision (Centrale Raad van Beroep) 30 December 1952, A.A. III, 44 926

Decision, 6 August 1956, Bull. de doc. communale, No. 4, 26 925

Decision (Centrale Raad van Beroep) 3 April 1963, Dutch O.J. 1964, 75 931

Decision (Centrale Raad van Beroep) 24 November 1971, Dutch O.J. 1972, 269 930

Decision (Centrale Raad van Beroep) 18 February 1975, Dutch O.J. 1976, 68 929

Decision, 17 December 1975, Bull. de doc. communale, No. 16, 163 925

Decision (Koninklijk Besluit) 4 June 1976, Dutch O.J. 1976, 182 930

Decision (Centrale Raad van Beroep) 19 December 1977, Dutch O.J. 1978, 258 929

Decision (College van Beroep voor het Bedrijsleven) 27 December 1977, Dutch O.J. 1978, 334 929

Decision (Koninklijk Besluit) 23 June 1978, Dutch O.J. 1979, 9 929

Decision (Hoge Raad) 7 March 1979, N.J. 1979, 319 931

Decision (Koninklijk Besluit) 29 November 1979, Dutch O.J. 1980 177 930

Netherlands—*cont.*

Decision, 13 June 1978, Dec. C.E. 1978 926

Decision 17 May 1982, De Gemeenrestem 679 927

Decision (Hoge Raad) 23 June 1982, A.B. 1982, 121 926

Decision (Centrale Raad van Beroep) 20 October 1983, Dutch O.J. 1984, 100 931

Decision, O.J. 1983, 417 189

CBB February 11, 1972, AB 1972, 100 1397

CBB, 6 November 1959 1397

Rapport ABAR. 141 1397

Rapport ABAR. 166 1397

Rapport ABAR. 172 1397

SEW 1960, 37 1397

Portugal

Naulilaa Wb V.R. II 577 703

Spain

Decision (Tribunal Supremo) 26 January 1961 936

Decision 62/1982, R.A.-70 702

Decision (Supreme Court) 28 February 1962 1310

Decision (Supreme Court) 8 January 1963 1319

Decision (Tribunal Supremo) 6 April 1963 936

Decision (Supreme Court) 25 January 1966 1319

Decision (Tribunal Supremo) 15 March 1971 936

Decision (Supreme Court) 17 May 1972 1319

Decision (Supreme Court) 23 September 1974 1319

Decision 185/1980 702

Decision 402/1981 702

Decision (Supreme Court) 22 January 1982 1319

Decision (Supreme Court) 8 February 1982 1319

Decision 3/1983, CJ–8, 222/1982 (BJC) 1983 702

United Kingdom

Anisminic Ltd. v. Foreign Compensation Commission [1969] 2 A.C. 147; [1969] 1 All E.R. 208, H.L. 149, 1290

Att.-Gen. v. Great Eastern Ry. [1880] A.C. 473 146

Att.-Gen. of Hong Kong v. Ng Yuen Shiv [1983] A.C. 629; [1983] 2 W.L.R. 735; (1983) 127 S.J. 188 901

Bugg's Case 1615, 77 Eng.Rep. 1271 (K.B. 1615) 1274

Balen v. Inland Revenue Commissioners [1978] 2 All E.R. 1033; [1978] T.R. 181; [1978] S.T.C. 420 1281

Bates v. Lord Hailsham [1972] 1 W.L.R. 1373; [1972] 3 All E.R. 1019 1275

Bilbie v. Lumley (1802) 2 East 469 ... 908

Board of Education v. Rice [1911] A.C. 179 1277

Breen v. A.E.U. [1971] 2 Q.B. 175; [1971] 2 W.L.R. 742; 115 S.J. 203 .... 143, 1390

Bushell v. Secretary of State for the Environment [1981] A.C. 75; [1980] 3 W.L.R. 22; [1980] 2 All E.R. 608 1288

C.C.S.U. v. Minister for the Civil Service [1984] 3 All E.R. 935 ...... 697, 902, 903, 1437

Camberwell (Wingfield News) No. 2 Clearance Order 1936, Re [1939] 1 E.R. 590 284

Canterbury Building Society v. Baker [1979] 2 All E.R. 247 1282

Cinnamond v. British Airports Authority [1980] 1 W.L.R. 582; (1980) 124 S.J. 221; [1980] 2 All E.R. 368 1291

Cooper v. Wandsworth Board of Works [1863] 14 C.B. (N.S.) 180 .... 147, 1276

Denby (William) & Sons Ltd. v. Minister of Health [1936] 1 K.B. 337 1283

Denton Road, 56, Twickenham, Re [1953] Ch. 51 .... 905, 906, 907

Dimes v. Grand Junction Canal (1852) 3 H.L.C. 759 147

Durajappah v. Fernando [1967] 2 A.C. 337; [1967] 3 W.L.R. 294; [1967] 2 All E.R. 152 1284

United Kingdom—cont.

Giraundan & Co. v. Minister of Housing [1966] All E.R. 1390

Glynn v. Keele University [1971] 1 W.L.R. 487; [1971] 2 All E.R. 89 1291

Employment and Immigration Commission v. Macdonald Tobacco Inc. (1981) 905

Hanily v. Minister of Local Government and Planning [1952] 2 Q.B. 444 1285

Hoffmann-La Roche & Co. A.G. v. Secretary of State for Trade Industry [1975] A.C. 295; [1975] 3 W.L.R. 104 1290

Hounslow London Borough Council v. Twickenham Garden Developments Ltd. [1971] Ch. 233; [1971] 3 W.L.R. 538 1290

Inland Revenue Commissioners v. National Federation of Self-Employed and Small Businesses Ltd. [1982] A.C. 617 .... 143, 149

(H) (an infant) Re [1967] 1 All E.R. 226 1279

Kanda v. Government of Malaya [1962] A.C. 322; [1962] 2 W.L.R. 1153 1283

Kruse v. Johnson [1898] 2 Q.B. 91 .... 286, 559

L. (A.C.) Re [1971] 3 All E.R. 743 ... 904

Lavender v. Minister of Housing and Local Government [1970] 1 W.L.R. 1231; 114 S.J 636 282

Lazarus Estates Ltd. v. Beasley [1956] 1 Q.B. 702; [1956] 2 W.L.R. 502; [1956] 1 All E.R. 341 906

Lee v. Dept. of Education and Science [1967] 66 L.G.R. 195 1285

Lever Finance Ltd. v. Westminster Corporation [1971] 1 Q.B. 222; [1970] 3 W.L.R. 732 904

Local Government Board v. Amidge [1915] 1283

London County Council v. Attorney General [1902] A.C. 165 283

Lovelock v. Minister of Transport (1980) 40 P. & C.R. 366 1290

Minister of National Revenue v. Wrights Canadian Ropes Ltd. [1947] A.C. 109 1390

McInnes v. Onslow-Fane [1978] 1 W.L.R. 520; (1978) 122 S.J. 944 .... 903, 1390

United Kingdom—*cont.*

Malloch *v.* Aberdeen Corporation [1971] 1 W.L.R. 1578; [1971] 2 All E.R. 1278 1291

Maritime Electric Co. Ltd. *v.* General Dairies Ltd. [1937] 907

Master Ladies Taylors Organisation *v.* Minister of Labour and National Service [1950] W.N. 386 910

Nakkudo Ali *v.* Jayaratne [1951] A.C. 66 1275

Norwest Holst Ltd. *v.* Secretary of State for Trade [1978] Ch. 201; [1978] 3 W.L.R. 73 1282

O'Reilly *v.* Mackmann [1983] 2 A.C. 237; [1982] 3 W.L.R. 1096 901

Padfield *v.* Minister of Agriculture, Fisheries and Food [1968] A.C. 997 284

Pearlberg *v.* Varty [1972] 1 W.L.R. 534; [1972] 2 All E.R. 6 .... 1281, 1285

Phillips *v.* Eyre [1870] 6 Q.B. 1, 23 ... 910

Prescott *v.* Birmingham Corporation [1955] Ch. 210; [1954] 3 W.L.R. 990; [1954] 3 All E.R. 698 286

R. *v.* Chancellor of Cambridge University (1723) 1 Star. 557 ... 1244, 1274

—— *v.* Commission for Racial Equality, *ex p.* Cottrell and Rothon [1980] 1 W.L.R. 1580; [1980] 3 All E.R. 265 1284

—— *v.* Darlington School Governors (1844) 6 Q.B. 682 1280

—— *v.* Gaming Board for Great Britain, *ex p.* Benairn and Khaida [1970] Q.B. 417; [1970] 2 W.L.R. 1009 1282

—— *v.* Goldstein [1983] 1 W.L.R. 157 696

—— *v.* Secretary of State for Home Department, *ex p.* Hosenball [1977] 1280, 1281

—— *v.* Home Secretary, *ex p.* Khan [1984] 1 W.L.R. 1337; [1985] 1 All E.R. 40 901

—— *v.* Home Secretary, *ex p.* Khawaja [1984] A.C. 74; [1983] 2 W.L.R. 321 906

—— *v.* Liverpool Corporation, *ex p.* Liverpool Taxi Fleet Operators' Association [1972] 2 Q.B. 229; [1972] 2 W.L.R. 1262 902

—— *v.* Home Secretary, *ex p.* Santillo [1981] Q.B. 778 1279

—— *v.* Home Secretary, *ex p.* Venicott [1920] 3 K.B. 72 283

United Kingdom—*cont.*

R. *v.* Home Secretary, *ex p.* Zamir [1980] A.C. 930; [1980] 3 W.L.R. 249; (1980) 124 S.J. 527 906

—— *v.* Lambeth London B.C., *ex p.* Sharp, *The Times*, December 28, 1984 1285

—— *v.* Metropolitan Police Commissioner, *ex p.* Panar [1953] 1 W.L.R. 1150; [1953] 2 All E.R. 717 1275

—— *v.* Paddington and St. Marylebone Rent Tribunal [1948] 2 K.B. 413 283

Ridge *v.* Baldwin [1964] A.C. 40 .... 147, 1180, 1276, 1277, 1278, 1280, 1284

Robertson *v.* Minister of Pension [1949] 1 K.B. 227; [1949] L.J.R. 323 904

Rootkin *v.* Kent County Council [1981] 1 W.L.R. 1186; (1980) 125 S.J. 496; [1981] 2 All E.R. 227 .... 906, 907

Russell *v.* Duke of Norfolk [1949] 1 All E.R. 109 1284

Secretary of State for Education *v.* Tameside Metropolitan Borough Council [1976] 3 All E.R. 665 697

Secretary of State for the Environment, *ex p.* Ostler [1977] Q.B. 122; (1976) 75 L.G.R. 45; (1976) 238 E.G. 971 1290

Schmidt *v.* Secretary of State for Home Affairs [1969] 2 Ch. 149; [1969] 2 W.L.R. 337 ..... 902, 903, 1280

Selvarajan *v.* Race Relations Board [1975] 1 W.L.R. 1686; [1976] 1 All E.R. 12 1390

Simms Motor Units Ltd. *v.* Minister of Labour [1946] 2 All E.R. 201 .. 286

Southend-on-Sea Corporation *v.* Hodgson (Wickford) Ltd. [1962] 1 Q.B. 416 907

Ward *v.* Bradford Corp. 115 S.J. 606 1291

Wells *v.* Minister of Housing and Local Government [1967] 1 W.L.R. 1000; 131 J.P. 431, 111 S.J 519; [1967] 2 All E.R. 1041 904

Western Fish Products Ltd. *v.* Penrith District Council (1978) 122 S.J. 471; [1981] 2 All E.R. 204; (1978) 38 P. & C.R. 7 904

United Kingdom—*cont.*
Wiseman *v.* Borneman [1971] A.C.
297; [1969] 3 W.L.R. 706 .. 1281, 1285
White and Collins *v.* Minister of
Health [1939] 2 K.B. 838 283

United States

Board of Regents of State Colleges
v. Roth 408 U.S. 564 (1972) 1181

United States—*cont.*
Federal Trade Commission *v.*
Ruberoid Co. 343 U.S. 470, 487/
488 (1952) 20
Goldberg *v.* Kelly 397 U.S. 254
(1976) 1181
McNabb *v.* U.S. 318 U.S. 332
(1943) 147

EEC TREATY: ARTICLES REFERRED TO

Art. 2 46
Arts. 2–3 411
Art. 3 234
    (1) 817
Art. 4 .... 40, 59
    (1) 61
Art. 5 .... 457, 1098, 1217
Art. 6 785
Art. 7 .... 39, 46, 547, 561, 571, 581, 591,
        592, 614, 619, 650, 785
    (1) 596
Art. 8a 53
Art. 9 .... 36, 457
    (1) 480
Art. 12 722
Art. 13 (2) 945
Art. 14 (6) 1217
Art. 15 (1) 1217
Art. 17 36
Art. 18 36
Art. 25 34
Art. 28 485
Art. 30 .... 431, 457, 625, 657 et seq., 668,
       774, 775, 780, 781, 783, 786, 789,
       790, 795, 798, 800, 803, 805, 806
Art. 31 798
    (2) 1217
Art. 33 239
Art. 34 .... 777, 783, 784
Art. 36 .... 625, 657, 715, 722, 726, 773,
      775, 786, 789, 790, 792, 793, 794,
      795, 796, 797, 798, 799, 801, 802,
         803, 858, 1118, 1463
Arts. 36–37 547
Art. 38 .... 34, et seq., 396, 439
    (2) 411
Art. 39 .... 34, 407, 408, 410, 417, 420,
      447, 457, 528, 588, 616, 632, 710,
      711, 712, 721, 748, 750, 755, 762,
         763, 808, 811, 813
    (1) ... 397, 411, 415, 416, 423, 439,
                  856
    (2) 588
Arts. 39–40 .... 302, 409
Art. 40 .... 34, 397, 411, 416, 417, 426,
      574, 582, 596, 710, 754, 813

Articles referred to—*cont.*
Art. 40—*cont.*
    (1) 856
    (2) 415, 425
    (3) ... 413, 416, 423, 425, 430, 528,
      562, 570, 573, 574, 583, 584, 585,
      586, 588, 589, 590, 591, 593, 594,
      596, 607, 610, 612, 613, 615, 616,
      627, 633, 645, 650, 653, 656, 657,
       670, 715, 748, 767, 771
    (3) (2) 439
Art. 42 (2) 34
Art. 43 ..... 35, 46, 52, 401, 403, 410, 411,
       426, 430, 754, 760, 1216
    (2) 403, 660
    (2) (3) 398
    (3) 451
    (3b) 451
Art. 44 (2) 412
Art. 46 457
Art. 47 41
Art. 48 .... 21, 496, 814, 1431, 1462
    (2) 547, 561
    (3) 715, 815
    (3) (2) 547
    (4) 20, 21, 815, 821, 822,
                 823, 832
Art. 49 1380
    (c) 547, 561
Art. 51 .... 46, 500
Art. 52 .... 547, 561
Art. 55 832
Art. 56 (1) 815
    (2) 47
Art. 57 .... 833, 1380
Art. 58 1197
Art. 59 .... 657, 725, 827, 828
Arts. 59–60 .... 606, 618
Art. 60 .... 547, 561, 607, 668
    (2) 669
Art. 63 1380
Art. 65 .... 28 et seq.
Art. 66 815
Art. 67 .... 547, 561
Art. 75 .... 43, 1216
Art. 77 32
Art. 79 .... 43, 547, 561, 1216

Articles Referred to—*cont.*

Art. 84 362
Art. 85 ..... 28 *et seq.*, 44, 302, 361 *et seq.*,
391, 541, 833, 834, 837, 841,
1200, 1230
   (1) .... 361 *et seq.*, 592, 839, 842,
958, 959, 1228, 1237,
1375, 1376
      (a) 547
   (2) .... 361 *et seq.*
   (3) .... 302, 350, 361 *et seq.*, 771,
842, 958, 959, 983, 984, 1090,
1229, 1322, 1329
Arts. 85–86 .... 1218, 1239, 1355
Art. 86 .... 362 *et seq.*, 370 *et seq.*, 391,
541, 833, 834, 837
      (a) 547
Art. 87 ..... 43, 48, 362, 834, 1216, 1380
Art. 89 834
   (2) 1418
Art. 90 .... 60, 69, 218
Art. 91 60
Art. 92 ... 28 *et seq.*, 382, 387, 1072, 1074
   (1) ... 382, 384, 386, 387, 388, 389,
1074, 1402
   (3) 387, 389, 771
Art. 93 1059
   (2) 383, 388, 1052, 1053, 1072,
1073, 1320
   (3) 382, 383, 1059, 1074
Art. 94 .... 48, 383
Art. 95 (1) 623
Art. 100 .... 36, 46, 47, 52, 479, 1172
Art. 100a 53, 1172, 1380
Art. 103 .... 654, 655, 1216
Art. 106 722
Art. 107 655
Art. 110 811
Art. 111 485
Art. 113 .... 44, 394, 457, 806
Art. 115 .... 807, 808, 1075, 1077
   (2)–(3) 715
Art. 117 .... 486, 653
Arts. 117–128 495
Art. 118 .... 495, 653, 1199
Art. 119 .... 39, 495, 496, 600, 622, 623,
650, 651, 653
Art. 123 30
Art. 124 .... 21, 26, 30
Art. 127 .... 45, 48
Art. 129 .... 32, 248
Art. 130 32
Art. 132 (5) 547, 1561
Art. 137 1380
Art. 141 26
Art. 145 .... 398, 440
   (3) 1202, 1205

Articles Referred to—*cont.*

Art. 155 .... 248, 398, 399, 400, 401, 1204
   (4) 35, 256, 446, 1202,
1203, 1380
Art. 163 593
Art. 164 .... 59, 61, 62, 67, 299, 1192
Art. 169 .... 27, 33, 383, 459, 621, 661,
662, 663, 1187, 1320, 1404
Art. 172 .... 60, 244, 300, 379
Art. 173 .... 4, 40, 61, 62, 234, 240, 492,
516, 536, 941, 956, 958, 961, 962,
965, 966, 975, 977, 978, 1020, 1035,
1053, 1054, 1060, 1075, 1078, 1105,
1108, 1114, 1147, 1164, 1191, 1205,
1209, 1237, 1360, 1401, 1413, 1416,
1419, 1420, 1421, 1424, 1425, 1430,
1434
   (1) 239, 240, 1402
   (2) 60, 61, 239, 370, 393, 433,
1383, 1401, 1413
   (3) 1383, 1419
Arts. 173–174 .... 241, 1018, 1021, 1030
Art. 174 ..... 142, 241, 243, 244, 246, 949,
1047, 1048, 1107, 1108, 1112, 1165
Art. 175 .... 240, 516, 1054, 1055, 1060,
1372
   (3) 60
Art. 176 .... 240, 241, 242, 403, 1018,
1019, 1032, 1047, 1067, 1108
Art. 177 ... 37, 60, 63, 241, 243, 244, 247,
257, 378, 439, 464, 486, 537, 538,
542, 727, 742, 745, 798, 804, 818,
823, 939, 1053, 1103, 1108, 1109,
1117, 1205, 1436
   (1) 252
Art. 178 1242
Art. 179 .... 25, 60, 303
Art. 184 ..... 241, 1020, 1021, 1022, 1030,
1048, 1054
Art. 188 .... 248, 532
Art. 189 ..... 235, 249, 461, 660, 956, 962,
965, 964, 1078
   (2) 366
Art. 190 .... 4, 40, 301, 404, 1186, 1380,
1384, 1385, 1400, 1402, 1403, 1405,
1416
Arts. 190–209 635
Art. 191 .... 41, 239, 1079, 1115, 1119,
1148, 1416, 1418
   (1) 1417
Art. 193 .... 41 *et seq.*
Art. 196 26
Art. 198 1380
Art. 199 26
Art. 205 .... 26, 27

Articles referred to—*cont.*

Art. 209 .... 45, 247
Art. 213 .... 41, 1216
Art. 214 .... 42, 1328, 1349, 1352, 1353
Art. 215 ..... 307, 504, 505, 506, 507, 508,
510, 511, 512, 515, 516, 518, 523,
527, 531, 532, 812, 872, 1117, 1163,
1164, 1242
(2) 60, 752
Art. 217 .... 42, 1187, 1198, 1213
Art. 222 722
Art. 223 .... 1217, 1220
Art. 226 .... 571, 581, 1075
Art. 228 (1) 251
(2) 251
Art. 235 ..... 31, 43, 46, 47, 49, 50, 52, 53,
254, 255, 496, 1172, 1198, 1216, 1380
Art. 248 258

EURATOM TREATY

Art. 4 31
Art. 15 1416
Art. 30 32
Art. 40 .... 32, 515, 516
Art. 46 (2) 1187
Art. 52 .... 32, 33
Art. 53 23
Arts. 53–56 33
Art. 124 256
(4) 1203
Art. 136 59
Art. 141 .... 33, 1187
Art. 144 300
Art. 146 .... 62, 234, 239, 956, 962, 963,
975, 978, 1020, 1047
(2) 1401
Arts. 146–147 1030
Art. 147 .... 241, 1018, 1047
Art. 148 .... 1054, 1055
Art. 149 .... 240, 242, 1047, 1067
Art. 150 257
Art. 152 303
Art. 161 .... 235, 956, 964
Art. 162 .... 301, 1403, 1405
Arts. 162, 163 41
Art. 163 239
Art. 165 41
Art. 171 26
Art. 180 26
Art. 183 247
Art. 187 1216
Art. 188 .... 504, 505, 509, 534
Art. 190 42
Art. 203 .... 47, 48, 254
Art. 207 248

EUROPEAN COAL AND STEEL COMMUNITY TREATY

Art. 2 385
(2) 603, 604
Arts. 2–4 332
Arts. 2–5 .... 44, 328, 331
Art. 3 329
(b) 576, 331, 603, 604
(1) 234
(b) 577
Arts. 3–4 331
Art. 4 .... 39, 330, 384
(b) 547, 554, 561, 562, 564,
565, 569, 576, 577, 601,
605, 657
(c) 385, 386
Art. 5 .... 40, 327, 386, 850, 976
(2) 1320
Art. 8 329
Art. 14 ... 235, 238, 327, 956, 1197, 1238,
1386
Art. 15 .... 301, 976, 1186, 1404, 1405
(1) 41
(2) 41, 239
Art. 16 .... 1188, 1197
Art. 18 1197
Arts. 18–19 41
Art. 19 (1) 1380
Art. 20 1380
Art. 26 .... 565, 1380
(2) 844
Art. 28 236
Art. 31 59
Art. 33 .... 4, 40, 61, 234, 240, 325, 330,
331, 962, 963, 975, 978, 1018, 1020,
1030, 1035, 1047, 1055, 1430, 1449
(1) ... 237, 299, 326, 327, 338, 342,
345, 357
(1)–(2) 334
(2) 240, 328, 332, 956, 1118,
1401
Art. 34 .... 242, 1032, 1047, 1067
Art. 35 ...... 1054, 1055, 1056, 1057, 1449
Art. 36 .... 325, 355, 1052, 1238
(1) 41, 1187, 1320
(2) 300
Art. 40 .... 505, 506, 513, 514
Art. 46 (2) 1320
Art. 47 .... 837, 850, 851, 1216
(1) 41
(2)–(4) 42
Art. 48 330
Art. 49 1071
Art. 50 1071

European Coal and Steel Community Treaty—*cont.*

Art. 53 .... 236, 328, 331, 1206
  (a) 575
  (1) (a) 327
  (b) 328, 334, 341
Art. 54 .... 386, 976
  (1) 31
  (4) 1157, 1320
Art. 58 ...... 335, 346, 348, 349, 845, 1196
  (1) 297, 340, 346, 347, 1380
  (2) 340, 348, 349, 1320
  (4) 31, 353
Arts. 58–59 31
Art. 59 334
  (1) 340
Art. 60 .... 331, 603, 604
  (1) 547, 554, 561, 562, 576, 578
Arts. 60–61 332
Art. 61 .... 31, 337, 849
Art. 62 327
Art. 65 .... 332, 349, 350
  (1) 1410
  (2) ... 342, 350, 356, 981, 982, 984,
          1013, 1030, 1084
  (1)–(2) (c) 349
Arts. 65–66 1216
Art. 66 356
  (1) 356
  (2) 357, 1187
  (5) 1320
Art. 67 .... 603, 604
Art. 70 (1) 601
  (4) 34, 1224
Art. 71 511
Art. 74 ` 347, 348
Art. 78 26
  (e) 26
  (h) 247
Art. 83 722
Art. 84 249
Art. 88 33

European Coal and Steel Community Treaty—*cont.*

• Art. 88—*cont.*
  (1) 1187, 1320
Art. 92 578
Art. 95 .... 47, 48, 254
  (1) 44
Art. 139 139
Art. 141 1320

EUROPEAN CONVENTIONS AND TREATIES

European Convention on Human Rights—
  Art. 6 .... 62, 1431
  Art. 7 1123
  Art. 8 836
    (2) 836
  Arts. 8–11 .... 716, 818
  Art. 10 .... 706, 707
  Art. 11 705
  Art. 13 .... 62, 1431
  Art. 14 705
Single European Act 1986 53
  Art. 10 1202
  Art. 145 257
Merger Treaty—
  Art. 1 234
  Art. 9 234
  Art. 16 26
  Art. 28 248
Vienna Convention—
  Arts. 8–11 704
  Art. 60 704
International Labour Organisation—
  Convention No. 111, 25 June
    1958 652

NATIONAL LEGISLATION

AUSTRIA

Austrian National Basic Law—
Art. 2 555

BELGIUM

Civil Code—
Art. 1235 921
Arts. 1376, 1377 921
Constitution—
Arts. 1–3 156
Arts. 6–24 156
Art. 6 (2) 555
Art. 29 159
Art. 31 .... 159, 160
Art. 66 159
Arts. 66-67 156
Arts. 92–93 .... 154, 156
Art. 93 158
Art. 107 .... 159, 223
Arts. 107–108 156
Art. 108 .... 159, 160
Décret sur la presse, 20 July 1831 1292
Law of the Council of State—
Art. 14 .... 288, 289
Law Relating to Communes—
Art. 86 919
Law Relating to the Establishment
of the Conseil d'Etat, 23
December 1946 .... 156, 159

DENMARK

Constitution—
s. 43 225
s. 55 165
ss. 62-63 162
s. 63 (2) 164
Danish Law No. 274, 22 December
1908 922
Law No. 258, 9 June 1971 165

Denmark—cont.
Law No. 280, 10 June 1970 163
Law No. 342, 1 December 1961 165
Law No. 488, 2 October 1978 164
Law No. 571, 19 December
1985 .... 163, 1183, 1297
ss. 7–14 1300
Law No. 572, 19 December
1985 .... 163, 1297
Law No. 572, 19 December 1985 163
ss. 2–16 1298
s. 9 1297
ss. 17–26 1299

FRANCE

Civil Code—
Art. 2 .... 875, 885
Art. 4 5
Arts. 1235, 1376 854
Art. 2011 729
Constitution—
Arts. 2–3 556
Art. 16 1247
Art. 34 213
Arts. 34 et seq 103, 104
Art. 37 213
Art. 55 .... 213, 250
Art. 72 112
Decret No. 83–1025, 28 November
1983, J.O. 1983, 3492 1182
Law Concerning Competition, 7 July
1977 1251
Law Relating to Judicial Organisa-
tion of August 16–24, 1790 100
Law Relating to the Election of the
President of the Republic by
Universal Suffrage 62–1292,
November 6, 1962 103
Law of April 22, 1905 1245
Law of October 19, 1946—
Art. 67 1246
Law No.52–432, J.O. April 1952,
4349 246

France—*cont.*

Law No. 53–934 Concerning Reform
of Administration, 30 Septem-
ber, 1953 108
Law No. 66–481, 6 July 1966 105
Law No. 75/587, 11 July 1979 264
Law No. 77-806, 19 July 1977 1251
Law of 17 July, J.O. 1978,
277 .... 104, 1182, 1252, 1255
Arts. 1 (i) — 1 (b) 1253
Law No. 78–753, 17 July 1978 104
Law No. 78–787, J.O. 12 July 1979,
1711 1182
Law No. 79–18, 3 January
979 104
Law No. 79/587, 7 November
1979 .... 104, 1254
Art. 1 882
Law No. 82–213, 4 February 1982 111
Law No. 83–8, 7 January 1983 111
Law No. 83–663, 22 July, 1983 111
Law No. 83–1186, 29 December
1983 111
Law No. 86–14, 6 January 1986 108
Ordonnance No. 86–1243 1251
Arts. 23–24 1252
Art. 44 1251

GERMANY

Abgabenordnung (AO) BGB1.I
1976, 613
s. 88 1265
s. 89 1263
s. 91 .... 1257, 1259
s. 127 1269
Administrative Procedures Act—
s. 35 218
Basic Law—
Art. 1 (3) 214, 218
Art. 2 722
(2) 1171
Art. 3 (1) 555
Art. 4 722
Art. 5 707
Art. 12 722
(1) 1177
Arts. 12–14 436
Art. 13 835
Art. 14 .... 722, 898
(3) (4) 124
Art. 19 (4) 272, 473
(1) 122, 125

Germany—*cont.*

Basic Law—*cont.*
Art. 20 (3) 120, 214, 272
Art. 25 250
Art. 28 886
Art. 34 513
(3) 124
Art. 46 888
Art. 51 (1) 888
(2) 216, 405, 443
Art. 80 (1) 219, 539
Basic Law—
Art. 87 126
Art. 103 (2) 898
(3) 1256
Art. 108 126
Art. 44 (4) 896
Bonn Basic Law 127
Employment Promotion Act—
ss. 106, 110 (3) 826
BVerfGG—
Art. 79 (2) 898, 1165
BVwVFG—
Art. 48–49 980
Federal Civil Service Remuneration
Act—
Art. 12 897
GVG—
s. 137 *et seq* 119
Land Act 1965—
Art. 35 832
Law of 18 December 1978 117
Law on Administrative Procedure—
s. 40 277
s. 48 (1) 461, 477
(2) 461, 478, 1031
Law on Protection against Damag-
ing Enviromental Pollution 1262
Law Relating to Aliens—
s. 15 819
s. 47 820
Law Relating to Federal Adminis-
trative Procedure (Verwal-
tungsrerfahrensgesetz des
Bundes-Vw VfG), 25 May
1976 117
s. 13 1266
(2) 1258
s. 25 .... 1263, 1264, 1265
s. 28 1256
(2)–(4) 1259
(3) 1260
s. 29 1266
s. 38 (2) 891
(2)–(3) 894

Germany—*cont.*
Law Relating to Federal Administrative Procedure—*cont.*
s. 43 (2) 888
s. 44 897
s. 45 (1) 1269
s. 46 1269
s. 48 120
ss. 48 (4), 49 (2) 1158, 1026
ss. 48–49 .... 888 *et seq*
s. 79 (2) (4) 898
Law Relating to Restrictions on
Competition—
Art. 46 (1) 850
Law Relating to Social Courts—
s. 51 123
Law Relating to Summonses issued
to the Administration, 3 July
1952 118
Law Relating to the Acceleration of
Administrative and Financial
Judicial Proceedings, 4 July
1985 123
Law Relating to the Enforcement of
Administrative Action (Vw
VG) 27 April 1953 118
Order Relating to Administrative
Courts (VwGO)—
s. 11 (4) 119
s. 40 122
(2) 124
ss. 40–42 897
s. 68 *et seq* 122
ss. 70, 74 897
ss. 80, 123 123
(1) 126
s. 114 124
Penal Code—
s. 264 (6) 386
Revaluation Compensation Act
1969 587
Rules of Procedure for Administra-
tive Courts—
s. 114 .... 277, 278
Rules Relating to Disciplinary
Tribunals—
s. 15 123
Rules Relating to the Financial
Courts—
s. 33 123
Sozialgestzbuch (Social Code,
SGB)—
ss. 14–16 1263
s. 20 1265
s. 24 1255

Germany—*cont.*
Sozialgestzbuch—*cont.*
s. 25 1266
s. 42 1269
Turnover Tax Act—
Art. 24 (2) 587
Weimer Constitution 1918—
Art. 109 546

GREECE

Constitution—
Art. 2 923
Art. 4 555
Art. 7 (1) 923
Art. 10 .... 168, 171
Art. 20 .... 1185, 1301
(2) 168, 169, 1302
Art. 26 (2) 223
Art. 50 .... 168, 225
Arts. 77 (2), 78 (2) 923
Art. 83 168
Arts. 87 *et seq* 167
Art. 95 .... 170, 290
Art. 100 171
Arts. 101–102 171
Art. 103 (4) (2) 170
Law No. 1406/83, 11 June 1985 171
Presidential Order No. 933/1975 172
Statutory Order No. 2189/1952 172

IRELAND

Act of Union 1800 173
Constitution—
Art. 3 693
Art. 3.1 555
Art. 15.2 174
Art. 15.5 924
Art. 28.3.3 175
Art. 40 699
Art. 40.1 555
Art. 40.3.1 177
Art. 40.4 178
Art. 43 699
Arts. 44–40 175
Sea Fisheries (Conservation and
Rational Exploitation) Order
1977 620
Seanad Resolution 1978 925

ITALY

Civil Code—
Art. 1 133
Arts. 1153, 1175, 1337, 1414,
1433, 1445 911
Arts. 2041–2042 915
Constitution—
Art. 3 131
    (1) 555
    (2) 131
Art. 5 137
Art. 24 (1) 134
Art. 25 (2) 917
Art. 73 916
Art. 97 (1) 1270
Art. 113 (1) (2) 131
Arts. 116–118 (3) 138
Decree Law No. 59, 20 February
1968 662
Draft Law on Administrative
Procedure—
s. 26 1272
s. 28 1272
s. 36 1272
s. 41 (4) 1272
Law No. 752 Relating to Religious
Works, 3 August 1862 129
Law No. 800, Relating to the
Establishment of the Court of
Auditors, 14 August 1862 129
Law No. 2248, Relating to a
Uniform System of Administra-
tion, 20 March 1865 129
Art. 5 913
Law No. 2359, Relating to
Expropration, 25 June
1865 129
Law No. 5992 129
Law No. 303, 13 May 1966 139
Law No. 312, 11 July 1980 1271
Arts. 21–22 1271

LUXEMBOURG

Constitution—
Arts. 11–31 182
Art. 33 227
Art. 36 227
Art. 45 181
Arts. 63–69 181
Arts. 84–85 181
Arts. 86–87 181

Luxembourg—cont.
Constitution—cont.
Arts. 91 et seq 182
Art. 95 185
Law of 16 January 1886 183
Law of 10 April 1946 185
Law of 1 March 1952—
Art. 7 185
Law of 8 January 1961—
Art. 31 183
Law of March 1974 1310
Règlement, 8 June 1979 .... 1309, 1310

NETHERLANDS

Administrative Court Law 1975—
Art. 7 41
Basic Law 1972—
Art. 57 228
Art. 66 228
Basic Law 1983—
Art. 89 225
Art. 94 228
Constitution—
Art. 1 (1) 555
Art. 16 931
Art. 89 189
Art. 107 (2) 189
Art. 108 192
Art. 110 189
General Regulations resulting to
State Officials—
Art. 98 929
Koninklijk Besluit, 8 September
1961 656
Law Governing Enviromental
Protection—
Arts. 21–22 1311
Law Governing the Council of
State—
Arts. 34, 38 1311
Law Governing the Provinces—
Art. 109 1311
Law of Immigration—
Art. 31 (2) 1311
Law of 1 May 1975 O.J. 283 188
Law of 11 November 1978, O.J.
581 189
Law on Housing Accommodation—
Art. 7 292
Law on Openness of Admin-
istration—
Art. 1 (1)–(2) 1313
Art. 5 1313

Netherlands—*cont.*

Law on Public Service 1929	293
Law Relating to Aliens—	
Art. 12 (a)	929
Law Relating to Imports and Exports—	
Art. 9	929
Law Relating to Legislation—	
Art. 4	931
Pension Act—	
Art. 132	930
State Employees Law—	
Art. 58 (2)	700
Wet ARBO	190
Art. 8 (1)	189, 228
(b)	293
(c)	701
Art. 14	1311
Wet BAB—	
Art. 4	190
(b)	293

PORTUGAL

Administrative Code—	
Art. 83	933
Constitution—	
Art. 6 (1)	198
Art. 9 (3)	934
Art. 18 (3)	933
Art. 20	197
Art. 23	198
Art. 29	933
Art. 35 I	195, 1315
Art. 114 (1)	195
Art. 200	195
Art. 201	229
Arts. 201–204	195
Art. 212 (2)	197
Arts. 237 *et seq*	198
Art. 266	195
Arts. 266–267	1314
Art. 267 (1)	195
(4)	196
Arts. 267–268	1184, 1315
Art. 269	197
(1)	195
(3)	195, 1315
Art. 271	195
Art. 272	195, 702
Law Relating to the Supreme Administrative Court—	
Art. 18	933

Portugal—*cont.*

Law No. 81/77, 22 November 1977	198
Law No. 129/84, 27 April 1984	197
Law No. 267/85, 16 July 1985	197

SPAIN

CodeCivil—	
Art. 2 (3)	937
Constitution—	
Art. 1	200
Art. 2	204
Art. (1)	200, 230
(2)	702
(3)	200, 937
Art. 13	555
Art. 14	202, 203, 555
Art. 24 (1)	203
Art. 53 (1)	200
(2)	230
Art. 54	204
Art. 81	201
Art. 97	200, 230
Art. 103 (1)	200
Art. 105	201, 1185
(c)	1317
Art. 106 (1)	201
Art. 137	204
Art. 143	204
Art. 159	203
Law No. 10/1973, 17 March 1973	203
Law No. 311, 29 December 1978	230
Law No. 2/1979, 3 October 1979	203
Law No. 3/1979, 22 December 1979	204
Law No. 4/1979, 22 December 1979	204
Law Relating to the Legal Status of the Administration, 16 July 1957	201
Ley de Bases de Procedimiento Administrativo, 19 October 1889	1316
Ley de Procedimiento Administrativo, 17 July 1958	1316
Art. 23	1317, 1318
Art. 48 (2)	1319
Art. 91 (1)	1318
(3)	1318
Arts. 109–110	936
Outline Law 1889	201

SWITZERLAND

Swiss Constitution—
  Art. 4 555

UNITED KINGDOM

Old Age Pension Act 1908 142
National Insurance Act 1911 142
Administrative Procedure Act
  1946 144
Statutory Instruments Act 1946 142
Crown Proceedings Act 1947 149
Agricultural Marketing Act 1958 284
Tribunals and Inquiries Acts 1958 &
  1971 .... 1180, 1285, 1286, 1288, 1412
Agricultural Act 1970—
  s. 29 (4) 909
European Communities Act 1972—
  s. 3 (1) 908
Local Goverment Act 1972 151

United Kingdom—*cont.*
Interpretation Act 1978—
  s. 12 905
Limitation Act 1980—
  s. 9 (1) 908
Supreme Court Act 1981 149
Industrial Development Act 1982 90

STATUTORY INSTRUMENTS

S.I. 1977 No, 1955 148
S.I. 1977 No. 212 909

UNITED STATES OF AMERICA

American Constitution—
  14th amendment 555

Abbreviations

ACP States	African, Caribbean and Pacific States (Member States of the Lomé Agreement)
AFDI	Annuaire Français de Droit International
A-G	Advocate-General
AJDA	Actualités Juridiques de Droit Administratif
AJIL	American Journal of International Law
AktG	Aktiengesetz (German Companies Act)
AO	Abgabenordnung (German Tax Code)
AöR	Archiv des öffentlichen Rechts
ArchVR	Archiv des Völkerrechts
AROB	(Wet) Administratieve Rechtspraak Overheidsbeschikkingen
Art.	article
AufenthG	Aufenthaltsgesetz (EEC law on residence)
AWD	Aussenwirtschaftsdienst (Foreign trade service)
AWG	Aussenwirtschaftsgesetz (German Foreign Trade and Payments Act)
BA	Beitrittsakte (Act of Accession)
BAG	Bundesarbeitsgericht (German Federal Labour Court)
BAGE	Decisions of the Federal Labour Court
BAnz	Bundesanzeiger
BArbBl.	Bundesarbeitsblatt
BArbG	Bundesarbeitsgericht (Federal Labour Court)
BArbGE	Decisions of the Federal Labour Court
BayVBl	Bayerische Verwaltungsblätter
BaZ	temporary employee
BB	Der Betriebs-Berater
Benelux States	Belgium, Netherlands, Luxembourg
BfA	Bundesversicherungsanstalt für Angestellte (German Federal Insurance Office for Salaried Employees)
BFH	Bundesfinanzhof (German Federal Finance Court)
BGB	Bürgerliches Gesetzbuch (German Code of Civil Law)
BGBl.	Bundesgesetzblatt
BGH	Bundesgerichtshof (German Federal Court of Justice)
BGHZ	Decisions of the Federal Court of Justice in civil cases
BIS	Bank for International Settlements
BSB	Conditions of employment for general employees of the European Communities
BSG	Bundessozialgericht (German Federal Social Court)
BT-Drucks.	Drucksache des Deutschen Bundestages
BullEC	Bulletin of the European Communities

BVerfG	Bundesverfassungsgericht (German Federal Constitutional Court)
BVerfGE	Decisions of the Federal Constitutional Court
BVerwG	Bundesverwaltungsgericht (German Federal Administrative Court)
BVerwGE	Decisions of the Federal Administrative Court
BYIL	British Yearbook of International Law
CCT	Common Customs Tariff
CDE	Cahiers de droit européenne
CEE	Communauté Economique Européenne
cf.	compare
CMEA	Council for Mutual Economic Assistance (COMECON)
CMLR	Common Market Law Review
Dept.	department
DG	Directorate-General
DÖV	Die Öffentliche Verwaltung
DS	Droit Social
DVBl.	Deutsches Verwaltungsblatt
DVO	Durchführungsverordnung (implementing regulation)
EA/D	Europa-Archiv (documents)
EA	Europa-Archiv
EAGGF	European Agricultural Guidance and Guarantee Fund
EC	European Communities
ECHR	European Convention on Human Rights
ECJ	Court of Justice of the European Communities
ECLR	European Competition Law Review
ECR	Reports of Cases before the Court of Justice of the European Communities
ECSC	European Coal and Steel Community
ECU	European Currency Unit
ed.	edited by
EDF	European Development Fund
edn.	edition
EEC	European Economic Community
EFTA	European Free Trade Area
EGBGB	Einführungsgesetz zum Bürgerlichen Gesetzbuch (Introductory Law of the Civil Code)
EIB	European Investment Bank
ELR	European Law Review
EMA	European Monetary Agreement
EMCF	European Monetary Cooperation Fund
EMS	European Monetary System
EP	European Parliament
EPU	European Payments Union
EPZ	Europäische Politische Zusammenarbeit
ESC	Economic and Social Committee
esp.	especially
et seq.	and following pages
EUA	European Unit of Account
EuGRZ	Europäische Grundrechte-Zeitschrift
EuR	Europarecht
Eur.Arch.	Europa-Archiv
Euratom	European Atomic Energy Community
EurBSt.	Europäisches Beamtenstatut (Staff Regulations of the European Communities)

FAO	Food and Agricultural Organization of the United Nations
FAZ	Frankfurter Allgemeine Zeitung
FG	Finance Court
FIDE	Fédération Internationale de Droit Européen
Fin.Arch	Finanzarchiv
FS	Festschrift
FusV	Fusionsvertrag (Merger Treaty)
GATT	General Agreement on Tariffs and Trade
GG	Grundgesetz (Basic Law [Constitution] of the Federal Republic of Germany)
GO	Geschäftsordnung (rules of procedure)
GRUR	Gewerblicher Rechtsschutz und Urheberrecht
GRUR Int.	Gewerblicher Rechtsschutz und Urheberrecht (foreign and international section)
GU	Gazetta Uffiziale
GVBl.	Gesetz- und Verordnungsblatt
Gw.	Grondwet
GWB	Gezetz gegen Wettbewerbsbeschränkungen (Act against Restraints of Competition)
HER	Handbuch für Europäisches Recht (formerly Handbuch für Europäische Wirtschaft)
HEW	Handbuch für Europäische Wirtschaft (now Handbuch für Europäisches Recht)
HGB	Handelsgesetzbuch (German Code of Commercial Law)
HO	Haushaltsordnung (Financial regulation)
HZA	Hauptzollamt (Principal customs office)
ibid.	the same
ICJ Reports	International Court of Justice: Reports of Judgments, Advisory Opinions and Orders
ICJ	International Court of Justice
ICLQ	International and Comparative Law Quarterly
ILA	International Law Association
ILO	International Labour Organization
IMF	International Monetary Fund
IPR	Internationales Privatrecht
JBL	Journal of Business Law
JDI	Journal du Droit international
JIR	Jahrbuch des Internationalen Rechts
JöR	Jahrbuch des öffentlichen Rechts der Gegenwart
JR	Juristische Rundschau
JT	Journal des Tribunaux
JuS	Juristische Schulung
JWTL	Journal of World Trade Law
JZ	Juristen-Zeitung
KSE	Kölner Schriften zum Europarecht
LIEI	Legal Issues of European Integration
loc. cit.	in the previously quoted work

MDR	Monatsschrift für Deutsches Recht
MFA	Arrangement regarding International Trade in Textiles — Multifibre Arrangement
Montanunion	European Coal and Steel Community
n.F.	neue Folge (new series)
NCI	New Community Instrument for bonds and loans
NIMEXE	Nomenclature of Goods for the External Trade Statistics of the Community and Statistics of Trade between Member States
NJW	Neue Juristische Wochenschrift
OAS	Organization of American States
OECD	Organization for Economic Cooperation and Development
OEEC	Organization for European Economic Cooperation
OJ	Official Journal of the European Communities
OJ ECSC	Official Journal of the European Coal and Steel Community
p.	page
para.	paragraph
RabelsZ	Rabels Zeitschrift für ausländisches und internationales Privatrecht
RdA	Recht der Arbeit
Rec.	Recueil des Cours de l'Académie de Droit International de la Haye
RGBl.	Reichsgesetzblatt
RIDC	Revue Internationale de Droit Comparé
Riv.dir.eur.	Rivista di diritto europeo
Riv.dir.int.	Rivista di diritto internazionale
RiW	Recht der internationalen Wirtschaft
RLT	Raccolta delle lezioni Trieste, published by the Istituto per lo studio dei Trasporte nell'integrazione economica europea
RMC	Revue du Marché commun
RMT	Rechtsgeleerd Magazijn Themis
RTDE	Revue trimestrielle de droit européen
RVO	Reichsversicherungsordnung (Reich Insurance Code)
SE	Societas Europaea
SEA	Single European Act
SEW	Sociaal Economische Wetgeving
SonstBed.	Sonstige Bedienstete (general employees)
StGB	Strafgesetzbuch (German Code of Criminal Law)
StPO	Strafprozessordnung (Code of Criminal Procedure
UA	Unit of account
UNO	United Nations Organization
UWG	Gesetz gegen den unlauteren Wettbewerb (German Law against Unfair Competition
VerfO	Rules of procedure
VG	Verwaltungsgericht (Administrative Court)
VGH	Verwaltungsgerichtshof (Higher Administrative Court)
VO	Verordnung (Regulation)
Vol.	volume
VVDStRL	Veröffentlichungen der Vereinigung Deutscher Staatsrechtslehrer
VWD	Vereinigter Wirtschaftsdienst

WB	Wettbewerbsbericht
WEU	Western European Union
WHO	World Health Organization
WiR	Wirtschaftsrecht
WRP	Wettbewerb in Recht und Praxis
WRV	Weimarer Reichsverfassung (Weimar Constitution)
WuW	Wirtschaft und Wettbewerb
ZaöRV	Zeitschrift für ausländisches öffentliches Recht und Völkerrecht
ZBeamtenrecht	Zeitschrift für Beamtenrecht und Beamtenpolitik
ZGR	Zeitschrift für Unternehmens- und Gesellschaftsrecht
ZgS	Zeitschrift für die gesamte Staatswissenschaft
ZHW	Zeitschrift für das gesamte Handels- und Wirtschaftsrecht
ZPO	Zivilprozessordnung (German Code of Civil Procedure)
ZRP	Zeitschrift für Rechtspolitik
ZStaatsw.	Zeitschrift für die gesamte Staatswissenschaft
ZVerglRW	Zeitschrift für vergleichende Rechtswissenschaft
ZVP	Zeitschrift für Verbraucherpolitik
ZZP	Zeitschrift für Zivilprozess

PART I

CHAPTER 1: INTRODUCTION

SECTION 1

THE EUROPEAN COMMUNITY AS A COMMUNITY OF ADMINISTRATIVE LAW

Administrative law as a field of law and a scientific discipline has in the past been almost entirely limited to the intellectual confines of the exclusively domestic administrative legal order, taken as a closed system and source of knowledge. The truth of this basic contention is in no way impugned by the fact that Otto Mayer, generally regarded as the father of modern German administrative law, had already produced a book on French Administrative Law[1] even before he wrote his *Deutsches Verwaltungsrecht*,[2] or that he made use of French models for the development of the German doctrine of administrative law.[3] Indeed, the principles of French administrative law, in the development and determination of which the Conseil d'Etat[4] has played a crucial role, have exercised a significant influence on systems of administrative law throughout Europe.[5]

Nevertheless, administrative law has emerged only reluctantly and under pressure from comparative law from the cocoon of its national

---

[1] O. Mayer, *Theorie des französischen Verwaltungsrechts*, Strasbourg 1886, p. 2.

[2] O. Mayer, *Deutsches Verwaltungsrecht*, 2 Vols. (1st ed., Leipzig 1895/96).

[3] See on this also J. Schwarze, "Der Schutz des Gemeinschaftsbürgers durch allgemeine Verwaltungsrechtsgrundsätze im EG-Recht," NJW 1986, pp. 1067 *et seq.*

[4] On the crucial role of the Conseil d'Etat in the development of French administrative law see recently M. Fromont in H.-U. Erichsen (ed.), *Festschrift für F.C. Meyer*, Cologne/Berlin/Bonn/Munich 1985, pp. 886 *et seq.*

[5] On the influence exercised by French administrative law, which in turn has been decisively determined by the Conseil d'Etat, see principally the volume *Le Conseil d'Etat, Livre Jubilaire*, Paris 1949, pp. 481 *et seq.* ("Le rayonnement du Conseil d'Etat et le droit administratif à l'étranger").

isolation. A perspective which truly stretches beyond and across frontiers was achieved only after the foundation of the European Community.[6]

On the one hand, European Community law itself is primarily made up of rules of administrative law, drawn in particular from the area of law governing the management of the economy.[7] To that extent, the European Community, already described by the European Court of Justice as a community based on law,[8] could more precisely be termed a community based on administrative law.

On the other hand, the need for a cross-cultural perspective and the search for similarities and differences in the resolution of administrative law problems within the European legal system is not the result simply of a thirst for knowledge on a theoretical level on the part of modern comparative law, but also and above all the product of practical necessity. As a continuously evolving legal order, European Community law is particularly dependent upon appropriate supplementation and growth.[9] Of course, there are a number of essential principles such as the duty to state reasons (Article 190 EEC) or the grounds for review drawn from French law and incorporated in the judicial review provisions (Article 33 ECSC; Article 173 EEC),[10] which are set out in the Treaties themselves. A number of rules of administrative law of notable scope have also been written into secondary sources of law in some fields of Community policy.[11]

However, by far the greatest number of legal principles governing administrative activity recognised today in Community law originate in

---

[6] See principally J. Rivero, "Vers un droit européen: nouvelles perspectives en droit administratif," in M. Cappelletti (ed.), *New Perspectives for a Common Law of Europe*, Publications of the European University Institute, Vol. 1, Florence 1978, pp. 389 *et seq.* Informative on the doctrinal history of European administrative law is the contribution under that title by H. Bülck, in *Festschrift für H. Kraus*, Würzburg 1964, pp. 29 *et seq.*

[7] *cf.* H. P. Ipsen, *Europäisches Gemeinschaftsrecht*, Tübingen 1972, 1/11–12.

[8] In the case law see on this most recently the judgment of the European Court of Justice in Case 294/83 "*Les Verts*" [1986] E.C.R. 1339, para. 23: "une communauté de droit." In the literature, see principally W. Hallstein, *Die Europäische Gemeinschaft.* (5th ed., Düsseldorf/Vienna 1979), pp. 51 *et seq.* See also C.-D. Ehlermann in *Festschrift für K. Carstens*, Vol. 1, Cologne/Berlin/Bonn/Munich 1984, pp. 81 *et seq.*

[9] See on this in more detail J. Schwarze in *Festschrift für K. Carstens*, Vol. 1, *op. cit.* footnote 8, pp. 259 *et seq.*

[10] *cf.* also on this P. Becker, *Der Einfluss des französischen Verwaltungsrechts auf den Rechtsschutz in den Europäischen Gemeinschaften*, Hamburg 1963, pp. 55 *et seq.*; H.-W. Daig, *Nichtigkeits- und Untätigkeitsklagen im Recht der Europäischen Gemeinschaften*, Baden-Baden 1982, pp. 125 *et seq.*

[11] Core provisions of an administrative law nature are reprinted in the appendix to the volume *Europäisches Verwaltungsrecht im Werden* (ed. J. Schwarze), Baden-Baden 1982, pp. 125 *et seq.*

the creative law-making and decision-making process of the European Court of Justice.[12] As is characteristic of the development of national administrative law systems,[13] administrative law in the European Community has expanded primarily through judicial decisions.[14]

The well known case of *Algera*[15] constitutes the starting point and benchmark for the judicial practice of the European Court in the area of general administrative law. In this case, the Court established its own unique method for decision-making in the evolution of administrative law principles. The Court was faced with the necessity of expressing a view on the revocation of administrative acts. It was expressly recognised in the Court's reasoning that the Treaty itself contained no special provisions, although the case law and literature of all the Member States of the Community were already well acquainted with the question. The Court felt constrained to hold that:

"Unless the Court is to deny justice, it is therefore obliged to solve the problem by reference to the rules acknowledged by the legislation, the learned writing and the case-law of the member countries."[16]

Since that time, the Court of Justice has given recognition to an impressive array of such general administrative law principles: the general

---

[12] See in more detail J. Schwarze, *Die Befugnis zur Abstraktion im europäischen Gemeinschaftsrecht*, Baden-Baden 1976, pp. 224 *et seq.*

[13] *cf.* on the significance of judge-made law in German administrative law generally H. Sendler in J. H. Kaiser (ed.), *Verwaltung und Verwaltungswissenschaften in der Bundesrepublik Deutschland*, Schriften der Deutschen Sektion des Internationalen Instituts für Verwaltungswissenschaften VIII, 1983, pp. 29 *et seq.*; F. Ossenbühl in H. U. Erichscn/W. Martens (ed.), *Allgemeines Verwaltungsrecht* (7th ed., Berlin/New York 1986), pp. 107 *et seq.*; H. Maurer, *Allgemeines Verwaltungsrecht* (5th ed., Munich 1986), pp. 55 *et seq.*; R. Mussgnug, "Das allgemeine Verwaltungsrecht zwischen Richterrecht und Gesetzesrecht," in *Festschrift der Juristischen Fakultät zur 600-Jahr-Feier der Ruprecht-Karls-Universität Heidelberg*, Heidelberg 1986, pp. 203 *et seq.*

[14] On the function and significance of judge-made law in the European Community in general see in particular U. Everling in J. Schwarze (ed.), *Der EuGH als Verfassungsgericht und Rechtsschutzinstanz*, Baden-Baden 1983, pp. 137 *et seq.*

[15] Joined Cases 7/56 & 3–7/57 *Algera* v. *Common Assembly* [1957] E.C.R. 39.

[16] [1957] E.C.R. 39 at 55; the reference to the Court's obligation to avoid a denial of justice demonstrates clearly the influence of French legal thinking. The well-known prohibition on the denial of justice in Article 4 of the Code Civil runs as follows: "Le juge qui refusera de juger, sous prétexte du silence, de l'obscurité ou de l'insuffisance de la loi, pourra être poursuivi comme coupable de déni de justice."

principle of administration through law,[17] the principle of non-discrimination,[18] the principle of proportionality,[19] the principles of legal certainty[20] and of the protection of legitimate expectations[21] and the right to a hearing before an adverse decision is taken by a public authority.[22]

This list sets out in the form of key words the central substance of the following investigation. We are concerned here in particular to establish, using the example of selected principles of administrative law, the extent to which a European administrative law can now be said to exist and what possibilities and limits condition its further evolution.[23] The investigation is limited to the 12 Member States of the European Community, which offer, through their alliance, a special set of interactions of an administrative nature.[24]

Just as there are certain matters needing regulation within national administrative law, on the European level the principles of administration through law, equal and non-discriminatory administrative conduct, proportionality, legal certainty and the protection of legitimate expecta-

---

[17] cf. Cases 42 & 49/59 SNUPAT v. High Authority [1961] E.C.R. 53 at 87; Case 113/77 NTN Toyo Bearing Company v. Council [1979] E.C.R. 1185 at 1209.

[18] cf. Case 117/76 & 16/77 Ruckdeschel v. Hauptzollamt Hamburg-St. Annen [1977] E.C.R. 1753 at 1770; Case 138/78 Stölting v. Hauptzollamt Hamburg-Jonas [1979] E.C.R. 713 at 722; Joined Cases 241–242 & 245–250/78 DVG v. Council and Commission [1979] E.C.R. 3017 at 3038; Case 52/79 Debauve v. Procureur du roi [1980] E.C.R. 833.

[19] Case 11/70 Internationale Handelsgesellschaft v. Einfuhr- und Vorratsstelle Getreide [1970] E.C.R. 1125 at 1137; Case 5/73 Balkan Import-Export v. Hauptzollamt Berlin-Packhof [1973] E.C.R. 1091 at 1110; Case 114/76 Bela Mühle v. Grows Farm [1977] E.C.R. 1211 at 1221; Case 122/78 Buitoni v. FORMA [1979] E.C.R. 677 at 684; Case 136/79 National Panasonic v. Commission [1980] E.C.R. 1033 at 2059; Case 299/84 K.H. Neumann v. BALM [1985] E.C.R. 3663 at 3687; Case 181/84 Man Sugar v. IBAP [1985] E.C.R. 2889 at 2902.

[20] Case 13/61 Kledingverkoopbedrijf de Geus en Uidenbogerd v. Bosch [1962] E.C.R. 45 at 52; Joined Cases 15–33, 52–53, 57–109, 116–117, 123, 132 & 135–137/73 Kortner Schots et al. v. Council, Parliament and Commission [1974] E.C.R. 177 at 190; Case 98/78 Racke v. Hauptzollamt Mainz [1979] E.C.R. 69 at 86.

[21] cf. Case 111/63 Lemmerz-Werke v. High Authority [1965] E.C.R. 677 at 690; Case 81/72 Commission v. Council [1973] E.C.R. 575 at 584; Case 1/73 Westzucker v. Einfuhr- und Vorratsstelle Zucker [1973] E.C.R. 723 at 729; Case 74/74 CNTA v. Commission [1975] E.C.R. 533 at 548.

[22] Case 17/74 Transocean Marine Paint Association v. Commission [1974] E.C.R. 1063 at 1081; Case 85/76 Hoffmann-La Roche v. Commission [1979] E.C.R. 461 at 511; Case 136/79 National Panasonic v. Commission [1980] E.C.R. 2033 at 2058.

[23] On this see previously J. Schwarze (ed.), Europäisches Verwaltungsrecht im Werden, Baden-Baden 1982.

[24] This does not mean of course that this work has no regard to the work of the Council of Europe on the unification of laws, or that the administrative law systems of other Western European states are ignored. On occasion reference may also be made in relevant areas to parallels in U.S. administrative law.

6

tions, and the maintenance of a balanced and fair administrative process, have emerged as essential issues. They represent the core and the point of crystallisation for European administrative law, and therefore form the framework for the following detailed analysis.

In adopting this framework, this work is pursuing a number of goals. In the first place, it seeks to illustrate how far administrative law on the European level, which has often gone unnoticed,[25] now extends. To this end, it is necessary not only to describe the law to be found in codes, the basic characteristics of which are set out below, but also to conduct a highly detailed analysis of the relevant judge-made legal rules in the area of administrative law. Since there now exists a bulk of judicial decisions which is becoming more and more difficult to survey, it is the aim of this analysis, along the lines of a handbook, to facilitate the practical application of law in this increasingly important area and to help to make it easier and quicker to pinpoint the applicable rules of law.

The investigation is therefore located within the framework of theoretical doctrinal development in the area of administrative law.[26] It proceeds from the recognition that without doctrinal development in this area it will not be possible to guarantee either the necessary efficacy of administrative measures or the level of transparency and comparability of administrative action required for the protection of citizens.

A systematic recording of the essential elements of European administrative law contains "an assertion of its present day stability and generates expectations for the future."[27]

---

[25] *cf.* on this already U. Everling, "Elemente eines europäischen Verwaltungsrechts," DVBl. 1983, pp. 649 *et seq.*; H.-W. Rengeling, "Rechtsgrundsätze beim Verwaltungsvollzug des Europäischen Gemeinschaftsrechts," KSE Vol. 27, Cologne/Berlin/Bonn/Munich 1977; *ibid.* "Fragen zum allgemeinen Verwaltungsrecht in der Europäischen Gemeinschaft," in *Festschrift für H. U. Scupin*, Berlin 1983, pp. 475 *et seq.*; *ibid.* "Die Entwicklung verwaltungsrechtlicher Grundsätze durch den Gerichtshof der Europäischen Gemeinschaften," EuR 1984, pp. 331 *et seq.*; J. Schwarze (ed.) *Europäisches Verwaltungsrecht im Werden*, Baden-Baden 1982; *ibid.* "Der Schutz des Gemeinschaftsbürgers durch allgemeine Verwaltungsrechtsgrundsätze im EG-Recht," NJW 1986, pp. 1067 *et seq.*; V. Götz, "Probleme des Verwaltungsrechts auf dem Gebiete des gemeinsamen Agrarmarkts," EuR 1986, pp. 29 *et seq.*; A. Weber, "Verwaltungskollisionsrecht der Europäischen Gemeinschaften im Lichte neuerer Rechtsentwicklungen," EuR 1986, pp. 1 *et seq.*; M. Akehurst, "The Application of General Principles of Law by the Court of Justice of the European Communities," BYIL 1981, pp. 29 *et seq.*; H. G. Schermers, "Algemene rechtsbeginselen als bron van gemeenschapsrecht," SEW 1983, pp. 514 *et seq.*

[26] See on this in particular E. Schmidt-Assmann, *Das allgemeine Verwaltungsrecht als Ordnungsidee und System*, Heidelberg 1982. *cf.* also J. Schwarze, "Zum Nutzen einer Systembildung für die Kontrolle der Staatsgewalt," DVBl. 1983, pp. 893 *et seq.*

[27] U. Everling, "Elemente eines europäischen Verwaltungsrechts," DVBl. 1983, pp. 649 *et seq.* at p. 658.

A more precise consideration of future possibilities for development can be undertaken only on the basis of a reliable analysis of the existing legal situation. Thus perspectives for the further evolution of administrative law in the European Community represent a specific requirement intrinsic to that system. If the European Community as a new legal order wishes to guarantee the supremacy and direct effect of Community law and equal treatment for all citizens of the Community,[28] then it must in principle have access to its own implementation mechanisms.[29] The need for these is all the more urgent, since Community law is in fact directly administered only to a very small extent by the Commission as a Community institution, but rather is implemented above all by national administrative authorities.[30]

Finally, this investigation pursues comparative law goals in the sense that it aims to clarify not just the influence of national administrative law principles on European Community law, but also the legal effects of the newly developed European law on the national administrative legal systems.[31] Thus the question of the creation and evolution of a European administrative law, which underpins the investigation, should not be understood simply in the narrow sense of isolating a single unified administrative law for the European Community in the implementation of Community law, but also in the wider sense of pursuing the further development and convergence of national administrative law systems in Europe. In future national legal systems will continue to be able to resist unifying tendencies[32] even though similar demands and difficulties operate on public administration in both the Member States and the Community, with the demands at a national level being at least as pressing as those on the Community. However, against this background, the following fundamental question must be asked. How far have the same principles of administrative conduct evolved or emerged[33] in the Member

---

[28] On these pillars of Community law see in particular H. P. Ipsen, *Europäisches Gemeinschaftsrecht*, Tübingen 1972, 2/29–57.

[29] See H.-W. Rengeling, *op. cit.* footnote 25.

[30] See in more detail M. Hilf, *Die Organisationsstruktur der Europäischen Gemeinschaften*, Berlin/Heidelberg/New York 1982; M. Schweitzer, "Die Verwaltung der Europäischen Gemeinschaften," Die Verwaltung 1984, pp. 137 *et seq*.

[31] On the interactions in the relationship between national and European administrative law see a forceful analysis in O. Bachof, "Die Dogmatik des Verwaltungsrechts vor den Gegenwartsaufgaben der Verwaltung," VVDStRL Vol. 30, p. 193 at p. 236.

[32] See a full account in U. Scheuner, "Der Einfluss des französischen Verwaltungsrechts auf die deutsche Rechtsentwicklung," DÖV 1963, pp. 714 *et seq*.

[33] J. Rivero, "Vers un droit commun européen: nouvelles perspectives en droit administratif," in M. Cappelletti (ed.), *New Perspectives for a Common Law of Europe*, Publications of the European University Institute, Vol. 1, Florence 1978, pp. 389 *et seq*.

States and the Community, and has the system that created an adequate balance between an effective and efficient administration and the subjective rights and expectations of the individual.

The investigation must not, in any case, be blind to the reservations and opposition which in the foreseeable future will continue to dog all attempts to effect a systematic bringing together of the facets of European administrative law as so defined. The traditional resistance of administrative law to all attempts to bring about unification has already been mentioned. A further specific doubt is found in the area of legal technique, which can be observed in the field of judicial decision-making in European Community law and which constitutes the core of this legal analysis.

In attempting to develop a set of principles for European administrative law it must be borne in mind that there is no recognisable strict doctrine based on deductive reasoning at the heart of the case law of the European Court of Justice. This is a consequence of the special legal position and function of the Court. In its case law, where conflicts arise, the various approaches of the French, German and more recently English legal systems as well as those of the other Member States must be balanced. In addition, the judgments of the Court of Justice, at least as regards their effect on individual cases, can sometimes have considerable political repercussions. To that extent, parallels with the well-known practice of the French Conseil d'Etat are appropriate, for that body proceeds in its task of guaranteeing the protection of the rule of law on the basis of the needs of the particular case before it, rather than on the basis of some easily comprehensible doctrine.

To analyse the case law of the Court of Justice in terms of methodology, an individual approach focusing on individual cases is required. Only thus can one guarantee that a basis for establishing a doctrinal content of the case law will emerge.[34]

We are therefore aware that a set of principles or doctrines for European administrative law can only gradually be developed by bringing together, examining and differentiating individual cases. As Advocate-General Gand so rightly put it in conclusions presented to the Court: "But, as in any legal work, theory can be built only by successive strokes and emerges from the reconciliation of judgments; it is a culmination."[35]

---

[34] See in more detail J. Schwarze, *Die Befugnis zur Abstraktion im Europäischen Gemeinschaftsrecht*, Baden-Baden 1976, p. 22.

[35] Advocate-General Gand, Joined Cases 5, 7 & 13–24/66 *Kampffmeyer* v. *Commission* [1967] E.C.R. 361 at 367.

Subsequent sections of this text will broaden and deepen the analysis of administrative law principles by expanding upon the principal difficulties which have resulted from the development of a corpus of European administrative law. Clearly determining which body bears responsibility for European administration is a starting point. The notion of administration on a European level will first be contrasted and defined by reference to national concepts of administration. That accomplished, there follows a description of the different ways in which Community law is implemented in the European Community today.

This investigation will thus reveal the most important individual areas of Community policy. We shall then move on to an overview of the sources of law within the Community which are of most significance for administrative law. Finally, problems will emerge which are relevant to the use of comparative law as a means for creating a generally unified law with an emphasis on European administrative law. Because of the close links between the national administrative laws of the Member States and the administrative law of the European Community, a special chapter will be devoted to setting out the basic features of the administrative law systems of the Member States.

SECTION 2

THE EUROPEAN CONCEPT OF ADMINISTRATION

A. THE CONCEPT OF ADMINISTRATION IN THE MEMBER STATES

The concept of public administration has its origins in the realm of the State. Aristotle distinguished three forms of the expression of sovereign activity. These can be translated, using modern terminology, as the legislative power, the executive power and the judicial power.[1] The absolutist State, however, combined all three functions in one hand, so that the distinctions between them were of purely theoretical interest.[2] The Aristotelian differentiation of forms of State activity acquired practical relevance only with the coming of the Enlightenment, which along with the fundamental notion of equality and freedom of the individual gave rise to the demand for personal freedom to be guaranteed against the absolute all-powerful State through an organisational separation of the three powers.[3] Whereas in the absolutist State the State activities as a whole were termed "administration" or "government,"[4] the organisational separation of powers led to a narrowing of the concept of administration.[5] Administration accordingly became a component of the executive power, which was separated from the legislative and judicial powers.

In this organisational scheme there remained no place for the

---

[1] cf. W. Jellinek, *Verwaltungsrecht* (3rd ed., Offenburg 1931), pp. 6 *et seq.*

[2] cf. F. Fleiner, *Institutionen des Verwaltungsrechts*, (reprint of the 8th ed., Tübingen 1928 (1960)), pp. 9 *et seq.*

[3] cf. on the distinction between different forms of power and the organisational separation of powers, E. Forsthoff, *Verwaltungsrecht I* (10th ed., Munich 1973), pp. 2 *et seq.*; on their role in guaranteeing freedom, K. Hesse, *Grundzüge des Verfassungsrechts* (15th ed., Karlsruhe 1985), pp. 184 *et seq.*

[4] O. Mayer, *Deutsches Verwaltungsrecht* (3rd ed., Munich/Leipzig 1924), Vol. 1, pp. 2 *et seq.* See also F. Fleiner, *op. cit.*, footnote 2, pp. 3 *et seq.*

[5] cf. W. Merk, *Deutsches Verwaltungsrecht*, Berlin 1962, Vol. 1, pp. 24 *et seq.* at p. 25; R. Mayntz, *Soziologie der öffentlichen Verwaltung*, Heidelberg/Karlsruhe 1978, pp. 3 *et seq.*

"government" as an independent source of power, but only the managing role within the State, a task in the nature of administration.[6]

The principle of the separation of powers gained access in the eighteenth and nineteenth centuries into the constitutions of Europe.[7] However, this statement should be qualified by adding that the principle was put into practice with varying degrees of strictness. As a consequence, there was often a discrepancy between the substantive functions and the organisation of powers. This led to the evolution of different notions of administration, one material and another organisational. Public administration in a material sense constitutes administrative activity, therefore the material concept of administration focuses on the specifics of administrative State activity. Public administration in the organisational sense is, on the other hand, the totality of administrative organs as opposed to the organs of the legislature, the judiciary and the government.[8] In all European legal systems it is possible to discern the search to bring together the various forms of the expression of state power in one definition and so to give a conceptual outline to "administration" as well. The most pronounced are the endeavours to find a satisfactory definition in France and Germany.[9] In France the starting point for the material concept of administration was the three-way split of state power into *législation, administration* plus *gouvernement* and *juridiction*. The *législation* sets out the general rules for the polity:

> "Légiférer, c'est poser les règles générales qui régissent dans la communauté nationale l'ensemble des activités, privées ou publiques."[10]

---

[6] O. Mayer, *op. cit.*, footnote 4, pp. 2 *et seq.*; *cf.* also F. Fleiner, *op. cit.*, footnote 2, pp. 4 *et seq.*, who ranks the government alongside the executive within the administration in the narrow sense; L. von Stein, *Handbuch der Verwaltungslehre und des Verwaltungsrechts*, Stuttgart 1870, p. 21: "The function of government is of its very essence simply the execution of the will of the State." E. Forsthoff, *op. cit.*, footnote 3, pp. 16 *et seq.*, makes reference to this.

[7] *cf.* H. Peters, *Lehrbruch der Verwaltung*, Berlin/Göttingen/Heidelberg 1949, pp. 7 *et seq.*

[8] In addition, a further concept of administration in the formal sense is to some extent being developed; this covers all the activities exercised in a particular society by the organs whose primary task is administration in the material sense, whether those activities are in the material sense administrative, governmental, legislative or judicial. *cf.* H. J. Woff & O. Bachof, *Verwaltungsrecht I* (9th ed., Munich 1974), pp. 16 *et seq.*; H. Maurer, *Allgemeines Verwaltungsrecht* (5th ed., Munich 1986), pp. 1 *et seq.*

[9] On the causes of this from the point of view of the sociology of administration, R. Mayntz, *Soziologie der öffentlichen Verwaltung*, Heidelberg/Karlsruhe 1978, pp. 3 *et seq.*

[10] J. Rivero, *Droit administratif* (11th ed., Paris 1985), pp. 12 *et seq.*

12

On the other hand, "administration" is described as follows:

> "L'administration, elle assume une gestion: administrer, c'est accomplir la série des actes que requiert, au fil des jours, la poursuite d'un certain but. L'action administrative est donc, tout à la fois, continue et concrète, deux traits par lesquels elle se distingue de l'activité législative."[11]

Finally, judicial power is separate from administration as regards its relationship to the law:

> "Le juge a pour fonction d'appliquer le droit à la solution de litiges, ... L'administration est, elle aussi, soumise au droit, mais, contrairement au juge, elle agit de son propre mouvement, en dehors de toute contestation. D'autre part, le droit constitue pour elle une limite, non un but; elle agit dans le cadre du droit, mais non pas seulement—comme le juge—pour faire respecter le droit."[12]

In other words, for judicial power the engagement with law is an end in itself; for the administration, law represents the limits of the realisation of non-legal goals.

The concept of *administration*, thus distinguished from *législation* and *juridiction*, has a further counterpart in the form of the *gouvernement*.[13] *Gouvernement* is understood not as an independent source of power, but in the sense of an authority set above the administration in political terms, which, without being legally separate from it,[14] determines in the form of directives the actions of the administration.

In France, the precise definition of the term "public administration" evolved with particular reference to the scope of administrative law. It has thus been relevant specifically in distinguishing between the competences of administrative and ordinary law courts.

In the nineteenth century, the concept of *puissance publique* (public authority) was most prominent. There was a distinction between *actes d'autorité*, which were subordinated to the *puissance publique*, and *actes de gestion* carried out with private law means. Starting from the *Blanco* case (1873),[15] in which the Tribunal des Conflits for the first time focused

---

[11] *Ibid., op. cit., loc. cit.*
[12] *Ibid., op. cit., loc. cit.*
[13] J. Rivero, *op. cit.*, footnote 10, p. 12; C. Eisenmann, *Cours de droit administratif*, Paris 1982, Vol. 1, pp. 139 *et seq.*
[14] J. Rivero, *op. cit.*, footnote 10, p. 12.
[15] T.C. 8.2.1873, G.A. No. 1, p. 5.

on the criterion of *service public* (public service), in order to determine the jurisdiction of the administrative courts, the *Ecole du service public* (Duguit, Jèze, Bonnard, Rolland *et al.*) began to gain in influence towards the end of the nineteenth century. It was no longer the concept of *puissance publique* but rather that of *service public* which came to be seen as the determining feature of the administration, the task of which was increasingly redefined as the fulfilment of the objectives of the providing State. Meanwhile, even the criterion of *service public* later came to be questioned, which led as a result to a partial rehabilitation of the criterion of *puissance publique* (Hauriou, Berthélémy). If it is the case that today there is a broad consensus that *service public* does not cover all aspects of public administration, this concept nevertheless represents now as then the most frequent starting point for any attempts to achieve a satisfactory definition.[16]

Service public describes (in the material sense) "une activité assumée par une collectivité publique en vue de donner satisfaction à un besoin d'intérêt général."[17] The requirement of general or public interest as the goal of administrative action represents a link with those definitions of administration which are oriented around the concept of *puissance publique*. As Rivero put it[18]:

"L'administration apparaît donc comme l'activité par laquelle les autorités publiques pourvoient en utilisant le cas échéant les prérogatives de la puissance publique, à la satisfaction des besoins d'intérêt public."

Whereas this material concept of "administration" is focused on administrative activities, the organisational concept refers rather to the organs concerned with administrative tasks:

"L'administration est l'ensemble des organismes qui, sous l'autorité du Gouvernement, participent à l'exécution des multiples tâches d'intérêt général, qui incombent à l'Etat."[19]

---

[16] On the historical development and current relevance of this see in more detail, A. de Laubadère, J.-C. Venezia & Y. Gaudemet, *Traité de droit administratif* (9th ed., Paris 1984), Vol. 1, pp. 41 *et seq.*, pp. 643 *et seq.*
[17] *Ibid.*, p. 644.
[18] J. Rivero, *op. cit.*, foonote 10, p. 14.
[19] J.-M. Auby & R. Ducos-Ader, *Institutions administratives* (4th ed., Paris 1978), pp. 2 *et seq.*

From the German perspective, the approach of Carré de Malberg (1920) appears instructive, at least from a historical point of view. He asserts, on the basis of the constitution of the Third Republic and in explicit contrast to German constitutional law:

> "La Constitution française, en effet, ne définit pas la législation mais seulement l'administration, dont elle dit que le domaine coincide avec l'exécution des lois; de là se déduit alors la définition de la puissance législative: celle-ci comprend tous les actes qui ne rentrent pas dans la fonction d'exécution."[20]

De Malberg's technique defines in positive terms the concept of administration and then goes on to define in negative terms legislation as everything which does not involve the execution of legislation and judicial activities. It was adopted for many years in German administrative law in precisely the opposite sense. Thus, according to the standard doctrine developed by Otto Mayer, "administration" is the "activity of the State towards the realisation of its objectives within its legal system with the exception of the judicial power."[21] Building on this, Walter Jellinek defined the administration as "the activity of the State or some other bearer of public power apart from the legislative and judicial power."[22] In contrast to the negative definition which long held sway and is still adhered to today,[23] Wolff and Bachof offer instead a positive definition for the material concept of administration:

> "Administration in the material sense is thus the diverse actions of the agents of the polity entrusted with such tasks on behalf of the polity and of its members as such. Such actions are conditionally or only objective-determined, that is externally determined, only partially of a planning nature, and undertaken and organized on the basis of an autonomous power of decision."[24]

---

[20] R. Carré de Malberg, *Contribution à la Théorie générale de l'Etat*, Paris 1920, Vol. 1, pp. 500 *et seq.* at p. 501. See also on this C. Eisenmann, *op. cit.*, footnote 13, p. 169.

[21] O. Mayer, *op. cit.*, footnote 4, p. 13; see similarly F. Fleiner, *op. cit.*, footnote 2, pp. 7 *et seq.*

[22] W. Jellinek, *op. cit.*, footnote 1.

[23] *cf.* I. von Münch in H.-U. Erichsen & W. Martens (eds.), *Allgemeines Verwaltungsrecht*, (7th ed., Berlin/New York 1986), pp. 3 *et seq.*

[24] *Verwaltungsrecht I*, p. 12; *cf.* also L. von Stein, *Handbuch der Verwaltungslehre und des Verwaltungsrechts*, Stuttgart 1870, p. 14: "It (administration) is the great mediation between the will of the State and its real, natural and personal circumstances. It permeates the whole State and is active in every sphere."

In spite of this wide-ranging and sufficiently abstract definition, Wolff and Bachof also concede that there is no concept of administration which can be used in every circumstance.[25] Forsthoff even works from the premise that administration cannot be defined but only described.[26] But even a purely descriptive conceptual construction presupposes for the selection of the descriptive phenomena an abstract notion of the basic outline of the conceptual picture which is to be filled in. Thus in the conceptualisation of administration in the material sense in German administrative law today, a combined approach involving the construction of abstract notional outlines and a descriptive listing of detailed phenomena has become current. Thus, for instance, H. Maurer proposes the following characteristics as typical:

— administration is a "social arrangement";
— it is concerned with "the public interest";
— it is above all an "active arrangement aimed at the future";
— administration takes "concrete measures for the regulation of individual cases."[27]

Public administration in the organisational sense includes all institutions which for the most part undertake administrative activities. Building on this, all activities belong to public administration in the formal sense which are undertaken by the administration in the organisational sense.[28] To this extent the picture in German administrative law reflects the conception current in French law.

The situation is different in the United Kingdom, because there public administration came to be regarded as an object of legal significance later than in the countries of Continental Europe.

"Administrative law," the existence of which A. V. Dicey still denied in his principal work, which appeared in 1885 but remained highly influential until well into the twentieth century,[29] is still a comparatively

---

[25] *Verwaltungsrecht I*, p. 7.

[26] *Lehrbuch des Verwaltungsrechts*, Vol. 1, General Part, p. 1.

[27] H. Maurer, *Allgemeines Verwaltungsrecht* (5th ed., Munich 1986), pp. 4 *et seq. cf.* also H. Peters, *Lehrbuch der Verwaltung*, Berlin/Göttingen/Heidelberg 1949, p. 5: "Even though it is difficult to give a short conceptual definition of administration, it is nonetheless important to achieve a description which at least brings to the fore the typical features of administration."

[28] *cf.* H. Maurer, *op. cit.*, footnote 27, pp. 1 *et seq.*; H. J. Wolff & O. Bachof, *op. cit.*, footnote 8, p. 16; I. von Münch, *op. cit.*, footnote 23, p. 2; W. Thieme, *Verwaltungslehre* (4th ed., Cologne/Berlin/Bonn/Munich 1984), p. 4 on the functional concept of administration.

[29] A. V. Dicey, *Introduction to the Law of the Constitution* (9th ed.), pp. 203 & 330.

16

youthful discipline in the United Kingdom. This fact may—together with the characteristic features of English legal thinking—have contributed to the fact that British scholarly work on administrative law is marked by pragmatic rather than doctrinal definitional endeavours in the conceptualisation of its main object. Thus E. C. S. Wade and A. W. Bradley describe administrative law as "the law relating to public administration."[30] The administrative or executive function is distinguished from the legislative function: "the functions of government have often been divided into three broad classes—legislative, executive (or administrative) and judicial."[31] The concept of "government" includes here therefore the whole of state power, whereas at other times it simply describes the executive power or the government in the narrow sense, which, together with its complementary partner, the administration, exercises the executive function. The legislative role is in an institutional sense principally located in Parliament and is superior to both the executive and the judiciary: "Parliament as the legislature is sovereign and beyond legal control."[32] The supremacy of Parliament is the dominant characteristic of the separation of powers in England.

On the distinction between the executive and legislative functions, O. Hood Phillips has this to say:

"The executive or administrative function is the general and detailed carrying on of government according to law, including the framing of policy and choice of the manner in which the law may be made to render the policy possible."

In contrast, the judicial function consists of "the interpretation of the law and its applications by rule or discretion to facts of particular cases."[33]

The classification of the state powers and in particular the distinction between administrative and judicial acts fulfilled in England, at least in

---

[30] E. C. S. Wade & A. W. Bradley, *Constitutional and Administrative Law* (10th ed., London/New York 1985), p. 593: "Administrative law is a branch of public law which is concerned with the composition, powers, duties, rights and liabilities of the various organs of government which are engaged in administration. Or, more concisely, the law relating to public administration."

[31] *Op. cit.* p. 47.

[32] H. W. R. Wade, *Administrative Law* (5th ed., Oxford 1982), pp. 4 *et seq.* Fundamental to an understanding of parliamentary sovereignty is A. V. Dicey *op. cit.*, footnote 29, pp. 39 *et seq.* On the meaning today of what they term "parliamentary supremacy," see O. Hood Phillips & P. Jackson, *Constitutional and Administrative Law* (6th ed., London 1978), pp. 50 *et seq.* and E. C. S. Wade & A. W. Bradley, *op. cit.*, footnote 30, pp. 60 *et seq.*

[33] O. Hood Phillips & P. Jackson, *op. cit.*, footnote 32, p. 13.

the past, has essentially two functions.[34] First, this distinction was relevant to the scope of application of the claims of "certiorari" and "prohibition."[35] These "prerogative writs" originally served only to control the lower courts and those organs which acted in a judicial capacity. Secondly, the procedural guarantees of natural justice[36] bound only those organs which were exercising a judicial function. Both as regards the admissibility of such claims and as regards the application of the standards of natural justice the possibilities of securing legal protection against acts of the State thus increased to the extent that these acts were classified as judicial rather than administrative. It was often useful to describe actions of administrative authorities as "quasi-judicial" and thus to subject them to a more comprehensive legal control.

In the other Member States of the European Community, the search for a conceptual understanding of public administration has led to more or less comprehensive attempts at definitions.[37] As in France, Germany and the United Kingdom, the difficulties of achieving a unified concept of public administration have largely been a result of the fact that the administrative organs which grew up as a consequence of the separation

---

[34] cf. E. C. S. Wade & A. W. Bradley, op. cit., footnote 30, pp. 604 et seq.

[35] See in more detail below, Chapter 2, section 12.

[36] See in more detail below, Chapter 2, section 12.

[37] *Belgium*: as in French administrative law doctrine a distinction is drawn between a functional and an organisational concept of public service (service public, openbaare dienst). The latter is defined as "un organisme public, créé par les gouvernements, placé sous leur haute direction, soumis à un régime spécial, qui a pour but de répondre à l'obligation que les gouvernants estimant avoir de donner satisfaction à des besoins collectifs du public d'une façon régulière, continue et en respectant la loi d'égalité des usagers." (*cf.* A. Buttgenbach, *Manuel de Droit Administratif*, p. 63; J. Dombow, *Droit administratif*, p. 91 follows this position; A. Mast & J. Dujardin, *Overzicht van het Belgisch Administratief Recht*, Gent 1984, p. 62).

Denmark: in Danish administrative doctrine the "negative definition" can once more be found, according to which public administration is described as that part of State activities which is neither legislative nor judicial. *cf.* G. T. Nielsen, "Constitutional and Administrative Law," in H. Gammeltoft-Hansen, B. Gomard & A. Philip (eds.), *Danish Law—A General Survey*, Copenhagen 1982, p. 49.

Greece: In Greece also the distinction between formal and material concepts of administration is current; *cf.* for instance P. Dagtoglou, "Verfassung und Verwaltung" in *Südosteuropa—Handbuch*, Greece, (ed. K.-D. Grothusen), Vol. III, p. 45 in conjunction with the definition of the administrative act. Of the older doctrine *cf.* also N. N. Saripoulos, *Das Staatsrecht des Königreichs Griechenland*, Tübingen 1909, p. 97.

Ireland: The central administration, local authorities and state-funded bodies are usually included in the concept of administration in the organisational sense; although it must be noted that these bodies, from a functional point of view, undertake not only executive but also legislative and judicial tasks. (*cf.* A. K. Asmal, *Administrative Law in Ireland*, RISA

of powers not only undertook executive functions in the narrow sense, but were simultaneously active in the quasi-judicial field (*e.g.* in the

1968, pp. 109 *et seq.* at p. 110; R. M. Stout, *Administrative Law in Ireland*, Dublin 1985, pp. 27 *et seq.*). Otherwise the terminology follows the British model.

Italy: According to G. Landi & G. Potenza, *Manuale di Diritto Amministrativo* (7th ed., Milan 1983), pp. 7 *et seq.*, the executive function can be distinguished from the legislative and judicial functions through its limitation to the pursuit of concrete objectives. For more detail on the objectives of administrative activities, see pp. 8 *et seq.* Otherwise, from a conceptual point of view, a distinction is drawn between the activities of the administration (attività amministrativa) and public administration in the subjective sense (pubblica amministrazione); *cf.* A. M. Sandulli, *Manuale di diritto amministrativo* (14th ed., Naples 1984), pp. 20 *et seq.*

Luxembourg: As it did originally in France, the concept of "service public" forms the core of the definition of administration: "l'administration publique est l'ensemble des services publics qui, sous l'impulsion générale des organes de la puissance souveraine, assurent les multiples activités de l'Etat, en vue de la réalisation du bien public," (P. Majerus, *L'Etat Luxembourgeois*, Luxembourg 1983, p. 285).

Netherlands: The concept of public administration (openbaar bestuur) describes both the totality of administrative organs and also the function of the administration. The function of the administration is determined in negative terms by reference to the legislature and the judiciary (*cf.* Rapport ABAR, p. 2) or in positive terms as the "official undertaking of public affairs by the public service," (A. M. Donner, *Nederlands Bestuursrecht, Algemeen Deel*, Alphen a.d. Rijn 1974, pp. 4 *et seq.*). *cf.* also for the Netherlands H. van den Brink, in E. V. Heyen, *Geschichte der Verwaltungswissenschaft in Europa*, Frankfurt a.M. 1982, pp. 117, 118 on the concepts of bestuursrecht ("administrative law for the public administration") and administratiefrecht ("administrative law for the legislature and the judiciary.")

Portugal: M. Caetano, *Manual de Direito Administrativo*, Coimbra 1983, Vol. 1, pp. 2 *et seq.* distinguishes between an organisational concept of administração pública and the concept of administração pública in a material sense. The latter is defined as the totality of decisions and measures through which the State and other public bodies acting within politically determined guidelines—directly or through encouragement, advice and co-ordination of private activities—secures the regular fulfilment of the needs of the community for security and the welfare of the individual. To this end appropriate means are provided and employed on a national basis (*cf. op. cit.* p. 5).

Spain: R. Entrena, *Curso de derecho administrativo* (8th ed., Madrid 1983), Vol. I/1, pp. 26 *et seq.*, distinguishes between a subjective, an objective and a formal concept of public administration; *cf.* also F. Garrido Falla, *Tratado de derecho administrativo* (9th ed., Madrid 1985), Vol. 1, which in the first chapter ("El concepto de administración pública"), starting from the etymological meaning of the expression and making use of comparative references, attempts a detailed explanation of the concepts of public administration (pp. 33–87); see also E. Garcia de Enterria & T.-R. Fernandéz, *Curso de derecho administrativo I*, (reprint of the 4th ed., Madrid 1984), pp. 23 *et seq.*

formal administrative procedures and through "administrative tribunals") and the quasi-legislative field (*e.g.* through delegated legislation).[38] Taken individually, the functional realm of public administration is determined by the particular form of separation of powers laid down in accordance with each national constitution. Therefore, for that reason alone none of the conceptual definitions thus reached can lay claim to any general validity.

B. THE CONCEPT OF ADMINISTRATION IN THE EUROPEAN COMMUNITY

The concept of public administration can be found also in the EEC Treaty, even if only in a very specific context. According to Article 48(4), the provisions on the free movement of workers have no application to employment in the public service. This provision refers to public service in the Member States. In order not to impair the uniform and effective application of Community law, however, the provision must be interpreted and applied uniformly across the whole Community. In *Commission* v. *Belgium*, the European Court of Justice held that the reservation in Article 48(4) applies only to "posts which involve direct or indirect participation in the exercise of powers conferred by public law and duties designed to safeguard the general interests of the State or of other public authorities."[39] On the other hand, this provision does not apply to posts "which, whilst coming under the State or other organisations governed by public law, still do not involve any association with tasks belonging to the public service properly so called . . ."[40] The Court of Justice thus deve-

---

[38] This finding is of particular relevance to public administration in the U.S.A. There special administrative agencies are active and are independent of the executive, which is led by the President. *cf.* in this context Justice Jackson in *Federal Trade Commission* v. *Ruberoid Co.* 343 U.S. 470, 487/488 (1952): "They (administrative bodies) have become a veritable fourth branch of the Government, which has deranged our three-branch legal theories much as the concept of a fourth dimension unsettles our three-dimensional thinking. Courts have differed in assigning a place to these seemingly bodies in our constitutional system. Administrative agencies have been called quasi-legislative, quasi-executive or quasi-judicial, as the occasion required, in order to validate their functions within the separation-of-powers scheme of the Constitution. The mere retreat to the qualifying 'quasi' is implicit with confession that all recognized classifications have broken down, and 'quasi' is a smooth cover which we draw over our confusion as we might use a counterpane to conceal a disordered bed." See also K. C. Davies, *Administrative Law, Cases-Text-Problems* (6th ed., Minnesota 1978), pp. 28 *et seq.*

[39] Case 149/79R *Commission* v. *Belgium* [1980] E.C.R. 3881 at 3900 (interim order).

[40] *Ibid.* at 3901. *cf.* also the final judgment in the same case, [1982] E.C.R. 1845 at 1851, where the Court of Justice presupposed a link between the post and the specific activities

20

lops a concept of "public service" in the "actual" functional sense for the purposes of interpreting Article 48(4).[41]

Whereas Article 48 EEC may be concerned with a uniform Community concept of public service in the Member States,[42] the following discussion is concerned rather with the concept of administration within the European Community itself. In this sense, Article 124 EEC talks of the administration (of the European Social Fund) without defining the concept. The ECSC treaty uses the concept of the High Authority, whereby is simply meant administrative activity.

The literature has defined European administration functionally as the implementation of Community law in individual cases or concrete situations.[43] The idea of the "individual case" or the "concrete situation" is wide and flexible enough to cover normative rules which aim at a specific object as well as legal acts of an individual nature. The attempt to delimit European administration in functional terms from the legislature and the judiciary or to locate it in organisational terms in any one Community institution runs up against the objection in principle that these concepts formed on the level of the nation State cannot simply be transferred without more ado to the supranational level.[44] Of course, Community law recognises that a distribution of functions[45] on an organisational basis is

of the public service. See also Case 152/73 *Sotigu* v. *Deutsche Bundespost* [1974] E.C.R. 153 at 162 and Case 307/84 *Commission* v. *France* [1986] E.C.R. 1725 as well as Case 66/85 *Lawrie Blum* [1986] E.C.R. 2121, a reference from the Federal Administrative Court (DVBl. 1985, 742) on the admission of a British national to training for work in grammar schools in Baden Württemberg, which refers expressly to both the judgments in Case 149/79 *Commission* v. *Belgium*.

[41] On the scope of Article 48(4) EEC see P. Karpenstein, "Zur Tragweite des Art. 48 Abs. 4 EWG-Vertrag," in *Gedächtnisschrift für Constantinesco* (eds. G. Lücke, G. Ress and M. R. Will), Cologne/Berlin/Bonn/Munich 1983, p. 377.

[42] In Case 107/84 *Commission* v. *Germany* [1985] E.C.R. 2655 the European Court interpreted the concept of "public postal services" similarly in the light of the varying definitions in the different language versions of the Treaties, paras. 10 *et seq*.

[43] *cf.* U. Everling, "Elemente eines europäischen Verwaltungsrechts," DVBl. 1983, 649; see similarly H.-W. Rengeling, *Rechtsgrundsätze beim Verwaltungsvollzug des Europäischen Gemeinshaftsrechts*, Cologne/Berlin/Bonn/Munich 1977, pp. 8 *et seq*.; M. Zuleeg, *Das Recht der Europäischen Gemeinschaften im innerstaatlichen Bereich*, Cologne 1969, pp. 47 *et seq*.

[44] *cf.* as on the following H. P. Ipsen, *Europäisches Gemeinschaftsrecht*, Tübingen 1972, 11/1–3 *et seq*.; *ibid., Fusionsverfassung Europäische Gemeinschaften*, Bad Homburg/Berlin 1969, pp. 28 *et seq*.; N. Achterberg, review of H. Petzold, *Die Gewaltenteilung in den Europäischen Gemeinschaften*, EuR 1968, pp. 240 *et seq*.

[45] *cf.* in general on the "distribution of functions in the constitutional law of European organisations" the standard monograph by H. J. Hahn, *Funktionenteilung im Verfassungsrecht europäischer Organisationen*, Baden-Baden 1977, in particular pp. 86 *et seq*. on the executive tasks of international associations.

necessary in order to effect a separation of and legal control over sovereign powers. Instead of the traditional separation of powers as is usual at the national level, what is at issue in the European Community is rather a classification of functions which is appropriate to the goals of integration and which is specific to the needs of Community law, limiting the powers of the Community in particular through the instrument of the limited vesting of powers on an individual rather than a general basis.

Any attempt to ascribe specific functions to Community institutions must start from the four-cornered structure for the Community laid down in the Treaties. This "quadripartisme communautaire"[46] is characterised by P. Pescatore in the following terms:

> "le pôle interétatique représenté par le Conseil; la représentation de l'intérêt commun par la Commission, véritable exécutif communautaire; la représentation des forces populaires au sein du Parlement; la matérialisation des valeurs juridiques par la Cour de justice."

The Council, according to Pescatore, has the essential function of promulgating regulations and directives. It is the true legislature of the Community, albeit a non-parliamentary legislature, the legitimacy of which is grounded in the international sphere and not directly in the people. Pescatore continues:

> "Ceci dit, il apparaît plus clairement que la Commission est effectivement plus proche de la notion traditionnelle d'exécutif, caractérisée précisément par des fonctions telles que, d'une part, l'initiative, d'autre part, la mise en oeuvre d'une politique, l'application d'une législation, la gestion et la surveillance. Certes, on n'a jamais permis à la Commission d'acquérir le profil qui est celui des gouvernements nationaux, mais quelles que soient les inhibitions et les limites existantes, quelles que soient les interférences, positives et négatives, du Conseil dans le domaine d'action réservé à la Commission (que l'on songe, par exemple, au domaine des relations extérieures), il reste que celle-ci possède, du moins partiellement et en puissance, les prérogatives essentielles qui définissent l'exécutif dans la conception de la séparation des pouvoirs."[47]

---

[46] P. Pescatore, "L'exécutif communautaire: justification du quadripartisme institué par les traités de Paris et de Rome," Cahiers de droit européen 1978, pp. 387 *et seq.* at p. 393.
[47] *Ibid.*, p. 393.

Thus within the classification of functions according to Community law, the Commission fulfils essential executive functions. That does not however mean that the executive and in particular the administrative tasks are undertaken exclusively by the Commission. Many Council regulations can be characterised in the sense of the definition of administration used above as being the implementation of Community law in individual cases and in concrete situations. Thus the Court has held that a Council Regulation which provides for the adjustment of the remuneration of Community officials in execution of Article 65 of the Staff Regulations is expressly to be seen as a "measure of an administrative rather than a legislative nature," which means that it is important to protect the confidence of those affected by the measures in assumed obligations which the Council has previously bound itself to observe.[48] For the rest, Community administration, just like administration in the Member States, is familiar with various forms of deconcentration and decentralisation.[49] Thus for instance the European Social Fund can be cited as an example of deconcentrated administration and the Supply Agency of Euratom (Article 53 Euratom), which is a body with its own legal personality, can be cited as an example of functional decentralisation. In addition, Community law is implemented not only by the institutions of the Community, but above all by the institutions of the Member States. The first instance is an example of direct administrative implementation (through Community institutions), the second of indirect implementation (through institutions of the Member States).[50] The addressees of direct implementation include Member States and indivi-

---

[48] Case 81/72 *Commission* v. *Council* [1973] E.C.R. 575 at 584.

[49] See already J. Mertens de Wilmars, "De europese gemeenschappen en het administratief recht," S.E.W. 1962, pp. 660 *et seq.* at p. 666. On the tendencies towards a decentralised development of Community administration and on the causes of this see in more detail R. Priebe, *Entscheidungsbefugnisse vertragsfremder Einrichtungen im Europäischen Gemeinschaftsrecht*, Baden-Baden 1979, pp. 15 *et seq.* In more detail on administrative organisation within the Communities themselves see M. Hilf, *Die Organisationsstruktur der Europäischen Gemeinschaften*, Berlin/Heidelberg/New York 1982; see also M. Schweitzer, "Die Verwaltung der Europäischen Gemeinschaften," *Die Verwaltung 1984*, pp. 137 *et seq.* at p. 150.

[50] *cf.* H.-W. Rengeling, *op. cit.*, footnote 43 at pp. 9 *et seq.*; *ibid.*, "Die Entwicklung verwaltungsrechtlicher Grundsätze durch den Gerichtshof der Europäischen Gemeinschaften," EuR 1984, pp. 331 *et seq.* at p. 333; U. Everling, DVBl. 1983, pp. 649 *et seq.* at p. 650. The further distinction which is sometimes drawn between direct and indirect implementation by the Member States focuses on the legal basis for the administrative action; however, this distinction adds nothing to the understanding of the organisation of the administration. The decisive distinction for the approach taken here is the identity of the responsible body: Community or Member States.

dual persons. The legal forms used in this context may be decisions, regulations or directives. The addressees of indirect implementation are the individual citizens of the Community. The national implementing bodies act according to the legal mechanisms which are otherwise at their disposal.

Taking into account also the many mixed forms of administration[51] and the types of action which have developed within administrative practice, in particular in intra-administrative relations,[52] a comprehensive and complete explication of the concept of European administration hardly seems attainable. It would be forced to slip into generalisations, from which it would hardly be possible to focus on the substantive core of Community administration. Instead, we shall give in the following section an overview of the organisational features of administrative implementation in individual sectors. From this it will also become clear which administrative tasks must be undertaken within the Community and which administrative bodies are responsible for these.

---

[51] *cf.* on this M. Zuleeg, *Das Recht der Europäischen Gemeinschaften im innerstaatlichen Bereich*, Cologne 1969, p. 209.

[52] *e.g.* the practice of issuing "communications" and "information notes" in the course of the audit procedure, which has fundamentally altered the institutional relationship between the Commission and national administrations; see in more detail J. Scherer, "Das Rechnungsabschlussverfahren—Ein Instrument zur Durchsetzung europäischen Verwaltungsrechts?" EuR 1986, pp. 52 *et seq.* at p. 72. The relations between the Community administration and European interest groupings are ultimately only partly comprehensible in terms of legal categories; see in more detail R. Hrbek, "Relations of Community Bureaucracy with the Social-Political Environment," in J. Jamar & W. Wessels (eds.), *Community Bureaucracy at the Crossroads*, Bruges 1985, pp. 105 *et seq.*

SECTION 3

THE AREAS OF ADMINISTRATIVE IMPLEMENTATION OF COMMUNITY LAW

A. DIRECT IMPLEMENTATION

Community law is implemented primarily by the Member States. The Community institutions are limited in most areas to the task of setting normative standards. There are however areas in which the institutions of the Community themselves implement Community law, in the sense of applying normative standards to individual cases. These areas of direct administrative implementation concern matters internal and external to the Community.

I. INTERNAL COMMUNITY ADMINISTRATION

The three Communities employ more than 20,000 people.[1] The questions of recruitment, career structure, social provision, old-age pensions, dismissal, etc. as regards these people are dealt with in the Staff Regulations of Officials of the European Communities[2] and in the Conditions of Employment of other Servants.[3] From an organisational point of view there are special administrative units responsible for personnel matters within the individual institutions. In cases of dispute before the European Court the institution represented by the official involved is the plaintiff or defendant.[4]

Alongside personnel management, management of material resources and a series of service agencies—language service, legal service, secretariat, etc.—ensure that the European institutions, agencies and other bodies continue to function. The legal bases for these administrative units

---

[1] *cf.* the final adoption of the budget of the European Communities for the budgetary year 1987, O.J. 1987, L86/1.

[2] Regulation 259/68/EEC/Euratom/ECSC, J.O. 1968, L56/1; O.J. Sp. Ed. 1968 (I), 30.

[3] *Loc. cit.*

[4] *cf.* H.-W. Daig & D. Rogalla, in v.d. Groeben v. Boeckh, Thiesing & Ehlermann, *Kommentar zum EWG-Vertrag* (3rd ed., Baden-Baden 1983), Article 179 EEC, notes 7 *et seq.*

can be found in the treaties, either as a mere reference to "internal powers of organisation" in the form of authority to lay down rules of procedure,[5] or as specific organisational rules in the treaty provisions themselves.[6] In so far as agencies are not provided for in the treaties themselves, their internal structure can be found either in constitutive or secondary legal acts.[7]

The budget is a special legal act provided for in Articles 199 *et seq.* EEC, Articles 171 *et seq.* Euratom and Articles 78 *et seq.* ECSC.[7a] The budgetary power includes the power to authorise, implement and control the implementation of the budget.[8] According to Articles 205 EEC, 180 Euratom and 78e ECSC, the Commission implements the budget on its own responsibility. This gives the Commission a significant administrative jurisdiction,[9] which includes the area of income and expenditure of resources.[10]

The implementation of the income side is regulated in detail in the Financial Regulation (FR) of 1977. In this context there is co-operation between national financial authorities and the Commission. The national authorities provide assistance in implementation as regards the collection of the Community's own resources independent of national budgets and are ultimately responsible in this to the Commission.[11]

As regards the expenditure side of the budget, Article 18(2) FR provides for implementation in a manner which departs from Article 205 EEC: in so far as administrative expenditure is concerned, each institution is responsible for its own appropriations. At the same time the Commission bears the overall legal responsibility, so that the requirements of Article 205 EEC are observed. In any case, the Commission's own budget constitutes the operational and thus the most important part

---

[5] *cf.* for example Article 16 of the Merger Treaty as regards the Commission; Article 141 EEC: European Parliament; Article 196 EEC: Economic and Social Committee.

[6] *cf.* Article 124 EEC as regards the Committee which assists the Commission in administering the Social Fund.

[7] See in more detail on the so-called tertiary organisational structure M. Hilf, *Die Organisationsstruktur der Europäischen Gemeinschaften*, Berlin/Heidelberg/New York 1982, pp. 109 *et seq.*

[7a] On the legal nature of the budget and in particular on the question whether it is subject to judicial review, see Case 34/86 *Council* v. *European Parliament* [1986] E.C.R. 2155. See on this H.-J. Glaesner, EuR 1987, pp. 157 *et seq.*

[8] *cf.* also on the following D. Strasser, *The Finances of Europe* (2nd ed., Luxembourg 1982).

[9] See on this the Financial Regulation of December 21, 1977, O.J. 1977, L356/1.

[10] *cf.* Articles 17 *et seq.* of the Financial Regulation. On this see Heck, in v.d. Groeben *et al.*, *op. cit.*, footnote 4, Article 205 EEC, paras. 5 *et seq.*, p. 741.

[11] *cf.* on the nature of own resources, Bull.Suppl. 8/78–1978 II, 17, point 19.

of the budget. As regards this part, Article 18(2) again adheres to the rule laid down in Article 205 EEC.

In so far as the Commission is directly implementing Community policies, it has sole right of decision over the allocation of resources. However, only a relatively small part of the expenditure under the budget is implemented directly by the Community. By far the greater part is subject to national implementation.

This portrayal of the different forms of implementation also defines the various areas of control of execution.[12] As regards the raising of revenues the Commission must ensure that the correct transfers of the resources due to the Communities are made by the Member States.[13] As regards the execution of expenditure the lawful and economical use of finances is to be secured through controls. This occurs internally above all through financial controllers, who supervise the budgetary conduct of each institution and the notional authorities. Financial commitments entered into through Member States' executive institutions are of particular interest to the construction of a European administrative law.

For the Commission, which also carries the ultimate executive responsibility for the indirect implementation of the budget, it is particularly important to ensure the supervision of the legality and economy of expenditure by national authorities in a manner which is both effective and uniform across the Community. Above all the questions of demands for the return of subsidies wrongly paid and of the charging of unlawfully paid subsidies which have not been reclaimed to national budgets represent fertile objects for inquiry which can only be referred to here.[14]

II. ADMINISTRATION EXTERNAL TO THE COMMUNITY

One of the most important areas of direct administration, that is administration actually carried out by Community institutions, which is

---

[12] See on this in detail C.-D. Ehlermann, *Der Rechnungshof der Europäischen Gemeinschaften*, Baden-Baden 1976.

[13] If a Member State fails to comply with this obligation, the Commission can bring an action for enforcement under Article 169 EEC. The European Court so held in Case 303/84 *Commission* v. *Germany* [1986] E.C.R. 1171, finding that the Federal Republic of Germany had breached its obligations under the Treaty by failing to determine within the prescribed period certain sugar production levies, by failing to credit the corresponding amounts to the Commission within the prescribed period and by refusing to pay interest on those arrears.

[14] See in more detail below the Chapter on legal certainty and the protection of legitimate expectations.

external to the Community is competition law. Articles 85 *et seq.* EEC and 65 *et seq.* ECSC lay down rules for the regulation of cartels, abuses, mergers and subsidies. The Commission has exclusive competence to apply the ECSC competition rules (prohibition of cartels and control over mergers in accordance with Articles 65 and 66 ECSC). The distribution of administrative powers between the Commission and national authorities in EEC competition law is dealt with in detail in Regulation 17,[15] which governs competition procedures.

The Commission is primarily responsible for the application of the directly effective prohibition of cartels (Article 85(1) EEC) and the prohibition of the abuse of a dominant position (Article 86 EEC). In so far as the Commission has not yet instituted proceedings, the competition authorities of the Member States remain competent. The Commission has exclusive responsibility for granting exemptions under Article 85(3) EEC.[16]

The most common form of action which the Commission takes in the context of competition law is that of the individual decision. The competition procedure thus represents a typical example of management of the economy on the supranational level. The Commission's ultimate sanction against undertakings acting in breach of the rules of the Treaty is the imposition of fines.

Articles 92 *et seq.* EEC regulate a further important area of the economy: the granting of national subsidies. These are in principle incompatible with the common market, in so far as they distort or threaten to distort competition and affect trade between Member States (Article 92(1) EEC).

In times of economic crisis and high unemployment in all Member States of the European Community, this paragraph of the Treaty has acquired increasing significance. In accordance with Article 92(2) EEC certain subsidies are regarded as compatible with the common market, and Article 92(3) EEC provides that certain types of subsidies may be regarded as compatible with the common market. The control of state subsidies is a matter for the Commission in accordance with Article 93 EEC. The efficiency and practical effectiveness of the Commission's

[15] Council Regulation 17 of February 2, 1962, J.O. 1962, 204, O.J. Sp. Ed. 1959–1962, 87.
[16] For more details on national and Community competences in competition law, see the discussion by the E.C. Commissioner (then) responsible for competition law, P. Sutherland, VWD of January 13, 1986, p. 10.

review of subsidies has long met with massive criticism from some quarters.[17]

Council Regulation 2176/84 of July 23, 1984[18] currently regulates the Community's protective mechanisms against dumped or subsidised imports from third countries. Thus there is dumping in principle if the "export price [of a product] to the Community is less than the normal value of the like product" (Article 2). In this case a countervailing duty may be applied if the import of the dumped products either threatens to cause or already has caused significant injury in a branch of the Community economy.[19] Subject to the same conditions, a countervailing duty "may be imposed for the purpose of offsetting any subsidy bestowed, directly or indirectly, in the country of origin or export, upon the manufacture, production, export or transport of any product" (Article 3).

Under Regulation 2176/84 the undertakings that may be affected by dumping or subsidies have the right to seek the introduction of an anti-dumping or anti-subsidy duty.[19a] The Commission is responsible for the investigation of the relevant facts. Any anti-dumping or anti-subsidy duty ultimately imposed is laid down in a Council Regulation.[20] In 1984 the so-called New Trade Policy Instrument was introduced by Council Regulation 2641/84 of September 17.[21] It is aimed at illicit trade practices and is intended to strengthen the common commercial policy of the Community.

The Regulation permits measures to be taken against "illicit commercial practices with a view to removing the injury resulting therefrom" and "to ensure the unrestricted exercise of the rights of the Community as regards the commercial practices of non-Member States" (Article 1). Article 2 defines illicit commercial practices as being those "which are incompatible with international law or with the generally accepted rules."

---

[17] See on this B. Börner, "Subventionen—Unrichtiges Europarecht?" in *Festschrift für K. Carstens*, Vol. 1, Cologne/Berlin/Bonn/Munich 1984, pp. 63 *et seq.*

[18] O.J. 1984, L201/1, amended by Regulation 1761/87 of June 22, 1987, O.J. 1987, L167/9.

[19] See in more detail C.-D. Ehlermann, "Neuere Entwicklungen im Aussenhandelsrecht der Europäischen Gemeinschaften," in J. Schwarze (ed.) *Integrationsrecht*, Vol. 1, Baden-Baden 1985, p. 105 at 112.

[19a] On the legal status of the complainant in anti-dumping procedures see Case 264/82 *Timex* v. *Council and Commission* [1985] E.C.R. 849 at 867 (para. 16); Case 191/82 *FEDIOL* v. *Commission* [1983] E.C.R. 2913 at 2935 (para. 28).

[20] On the problem of the legal protection of undertakings affected against the anti-dumping measures taken by the Community see recently J. Schwarze, "Rechtsschutz gegen Anti-Dumpingmassnahmen der EG—Zu Verfahren und richterlicher Kontrolle auf dem Gebiet der Aussenwirtschaftsverwaltung der Gemeinschaft," EuR 1986, pp. 217 *et seq.*

[21] O.J. 1984, L252/1.

Community rights subject to protection are "those international trade rights of which it may avail itself either under international law or under generally accepted rules." The right to investigate in this area lies with the Commission, the right to decide on measures to counter such practices lies on the other hand with the Council, which decides on a qualified majority on a proposal from the Commission.

The external protection of the common market includes in "the normal case" customs duties, agricultural levies and to a very small extent quantitative restrictions.[22] For emergencies there exists a series of so-called protective clauses in Community rules.

The oldest and long standardised protective clause can be found in all basic regulations governing common organisations of the market in agricultural products.[23] In the area of industrial goods Council Regulation 288/82 of February 5, 1982 today contains the relevant protective clause as regards common rules on imports.[24] The decision whether to apply it lies with the Commission. The Council may, however, at the request of a Member State, and acting by a qualified majority, decide otherwise.[25]

The substantive scope of the common social policies is determined by Article 123 EEC and is institutionally secured by the setting up of the European Social Fund. The objective of this body is described in Article 123 EEC as that of improving employment opportunities and raising living standards, which is to be achieved by rendering the employment of workers easier and by increasing their geographical and occupational mobility within the Community. The administration of the Social Fund set up to achieve this aim lies, according to Article 124 EEC, with the Commission. It is assisted in this by a Committee, which is composed of representives of governments and employers' and employees' organisations (Article 124 EEC). A request for assistance to promote particular measures of social policy can however be made only by the Member States.[26]

The absence of a comprehensive regional policy in the EEC Treaty was to some extent mitigated by Council Regulation 724/75 of March 18, 1975

---

[22] C.-D. Ehlermann, "Neuere Entwicklungen im Aussenhandelsrecht der EG," in J. Schwarze *Integrationsrecht*, Baden-Baden 1985, pp. 108 *et seq.*
[23] C.-D. Ehlermann, *op. cit.*, footnote 22, p. 109.
[24] O.J. 1982, L35/1.
[25] C.-D. Ehlermann, *op. cit.*, footnote 22, pp. 111 *et seq.*
[26] On the details of the provision of financial assistance see W. Stabenow in v.d. Groeben *et al.*, op. cit., footnote 4, Article 124, paras. 5 *et seq.*

based on Article 235 EEC.[27] Under this regulation only Member States, but not subdivisions of them, are authorised to apply for financial assistance. The criteria for financial assistance are laid down in the Regulation setting up the Fund and various implementing regulations.[28] The decisional competence lies with the Commission, which decides on the basis of proposals from the so-called Fund Committee. If there are differences of opinion between the two, the Council decides. Thus in this sector there are significant traces of an administrative hierarchy.

The oldest area of European administration, and one which has proved to be particularly significant in the economic crisis, is the European Coal and Steel Community. The precise wording of the ECSC Treaty reveals it to be a supranational amalgamation which undertakes the tasks of managing an area of the economy which has been taken out of the sovereign control of the Member States.[29] The Coal and Steel Community has the right to increase rates, to take out and offer loans,[30] to fix minimum and maximum prices[31] and to fix binding production quotas for undertakings,[32] as well as the right to impose fines for infringements against any of its decisions.[33] Because the ECSC Treaty itself represents a well-developed regulatory framework, the area of secondary law passed on the basis of the Treaty is less well developed than under the European Economic Community. Thus the Treaty itself here represents the central source of administrative law.

The European Atomic Energy Community is similar in nature to the ECSC: this is an administrative community which is once more sectorally limited and basically technocratic and apolitical. The detailed regulations contained in the Treaty represent the chief source of law. There is little distinctive development to the secondary law. The tasks of the EAEC include, for example, the promotion of research (Articles 4 *et seq.* Euratom), the laying down of standards for the protection of health and

---

[27] O.J. 1975, L73/1; as amended by Council Regulation 214/79 of February 6, 1979, O.J. 1979, L35/1. There is now a legal basis in the SEA for the Regional Fund, in Article 130c EEC.

[28] *cf.* P. Wäldchen, in: v.d. Groeben *et al.*, *op. cit.*, footnote 4, Vol. II Appendix 6, p. 1587, para. 8, with a review of the primary legal acts on the Regional Fund.

[29] G. Nicolaysen, *Europäisches Gemeinschaftsrecht*, Stuttgart/Berlin/Cologne/Mainz 1979, p. 6.

[30] Article 54(1) ECSC.

[31] Article 61 ECSC.

[32] *cf.* Articles 58 & 59 ECSC.

[33] *cf.* Article 58(4) ECSC.

safety (Article 30 Euratom) and the promotion of investment programmes in the nuclear field (Article 40 Euratom) as well as the setting up
of Joint Undertakings and the supply of fissile materials to the Community (Articles 52 *et seq.* Euratom). According to Articles 77 *et seq.* the
Commission has comprehensive rights to supervise activities within the
territories of the Member States, so that it can satisfy itself that source
materials and in particular fissile materials are not diverted from their
intended uses as declared by the users and that the provisions relating to
supply and any particular safeguarding obligations assumed by the Community under an agreement concluded with a third State or an international organisation are complied with.

A number of the administrative tasks entrusted to the Community are
undertaken by special bodies. These include *inter alia* the European
Investment Bank (EIB) and the Supply Agency of the EAEC (Euratom).
It is the task of the EIB, within the framework of the economic and
integration policies of the Community, to make a financial contribution
to those policies using the credit mechanisms at its disposal (Article 130
EEC). In order to guarantee the greatest possible independence and
business flexibility, under Article 129 EEC, the Bank has legal personality.[34] The extensive institutional autonomy of the EIB should be contrasted with a functional link to the Community through the obligation to
have regard to the interests of the Community and the obligation to
operate on a non-profit-making basis. Although the EIB may operate
like any other bank on the capital markets, these obligations take it out of
the ranks of normal credit institutions and allow it to be included within
the administration of the European economy. The significance of the EIB
for the financial economy of the Community has grown steadily since its
foundation, not least through its role in administering E.C. borrowing
and lending activities.[35] Article 129 EEC, as already mentioned, regulates the status of the Bank. Its tasks and the means at its disposal are
described in Article 130 EEC. The rules governing its organisation are
laid down in the EIB Statute, which forms a protocol to the Treaty.

The goal of the EAEC to ensure a secure supply of ores and nuclear
fuels to consumers in the Member States has already been referred to.
For the performance of this task the Treaty provides for an agency with

---

[34] *cf.* on its legal status, M. Hilf, *Die Organisationsstruktur der Europäischen Gemeinschaften*, Berlin/Heidelberg/New York 1982, pp. 31 *et seq.*
[35] *cf.* M. Hilf, *op. cit.*, footnote 34 at p. 31; Beutler, Bieber, Pipkorn & Streil, *Die
Europäische Gemeinschaft—Rechtsordnung und Politik* (3rd ed., Baden-Baden 1987),
p. 161; D. Strasser, *The Finances of Europe* (2nd ed., Luxembourg 1982), pp. 158/159.

legal personality and financial autonomy, which has a right of option on all ores and nuclear fuels produced in the territories of the Member States and an exclusive right to conclude supply contracts with countries inside and outside the Community.[36] Article 53 Euratom contains a strict right of supervision for the Commission over the Agency. The Commission can issue directives to it, exercise a right of veto over its decisions and even appoint its Director-General and Deputy Director-General. In addition the Statute of the Agency, passed by the Council, imposes on it a duty to have regard to the welfare of the Community and prohibits it from pursuing its activities on a profit-making basis.[37] Thus there are some parallels to the EIB, although the strict supervision by the Commission over the Supply Agency represents a distinctive feature which distinguishes it sharply from the EIB.[38]

The direct implementation of Community law in the wider sense may also include certain tasks of the Commission in the enforcement or qualified suspension of the Treaty obligations of the Member States, although these could not be described as being exclusively administrative functions.[39] Articles 169 EEC, 88 ECSC and 141 Euratom lay down the procedure for ensuring that Member States comply with Community law. If, in the opinion of the Commission, there is a breach of obligations arising under the EEC or Euratom Treaties, then it first gives the Member State the opportunity to submit its observations. If it still believes that the State is acting in breach of the Treaty, the procedure is concluded by the delivery of a reasoned opinion by the Commission. If the State does not comply with the opinion, then the Commission has the discretion to bring an action for enforcement before the Court of Justice. In the field of Coal and Steel the procedure ends with a binding decision by the Commission, against which the Member State concerned may bring proceedings (Article 88 ECSC).

The Treaties also contain provisions which give the Commission the right to suspend individual treaty obligations for particular Member States. They cannot all be mentioned here. Examples which can be sited are the granting of tariff quotas at a reduced rate of duty or duty free

---

[36] cf. Articles 52, 53–56 Euratom.
[37] Statute of November 6, 1958, J.O. 1958, 534 et seq.; recently amended by the Decision of the Council of March 8, 1973, O.J. 1973, L83/20, on the occasion of the accession of the new Member States.
[38] cf. the detailed analysis of the status of the Agency in M. Hilf, op. cit., footnote 34, pp. 51 et seq., in particular the conclusion on p. 64/5.
[39] cf. M. Schweitzer, "Die Verwaltung der Europäischen Gemeinschaften," Die Verwaltung 1984, pp. 137 et seq. at p. 141.

(Article 25 EEC); the authorisation of the grant of national subsidies for the protection of agricultural enterprises handicapped by structural or natural conditions or for development programmes in the agricultural sector (Article 42(2) EEC); the application of special internal rates for transport (Article 70(4) ECSC) as well as the authorisation of Member States by the Commission, with the assent of the Council, to take measures against a Member State in breach of the Treaty in order to correct the effects of that breach (Article 88(3) ECSC).

B.   INDIRECT IMPLEMENTATION

The greater part of Community law is implemented by national authorities (indirect implementation). These bodies act either directly on the basis of provisions of Community law or on the basis of national rules which render Community law, in particular Community Directives, concrete and apt for implementation. Both forms of execution may occur together in respect of one and the same measure.[40]

The main areas of indirect implementation are the common agricultural policy and the external protection of the Community through the common customs tariff. There is of course frequently co-operation in these areas between Community and national authorities. This co-operation, which occurs as a matter of administrative reality, is only sufficiently expressed through the original strict declaratory model of administrative organisation, namely the distinction between direct and indirect implementation.

I.   THE COMMON AGRICULTURAL POLICY

The provisions of Articles 38 *et seq.* EEC leave a wide discretion to the responsible institutions of the Community in the formation of a common agricultural policy. Article 38 EEC lays down the scope of the provisions, Article 39 EEC establishes the objectives of the common agricultural policy, and Article 40 EEC describes the means available for achieving these objectives.

---

[40] U. Everling, "Elemente eines europäischen Verwaltungsrechts," DVBl. 1983, p. 649; H.-W. Rengeling, "Die Entwicklung verwaltungsrechtlicher Grundsätze durch den Gerichtshof der Europäischen Gemeinschaften," EuR 1984, pp. 331 *et seq.* at p. 333.

The determination of the basic structure of the European agricultural market took the form of Community legislation, which it was for the Council to pass (Article 43 EEC). The Council made use of the broad discretion left to it in the Treaty and through the creation of common organisations of the market laid the cornerstone of what in the 1960s was still intended to be an exemplary integrated economic sector.

The common agricultural policy is now a field of the highest regulatory density, and its implementation is an instructive subject for an investigation of the problems facing European administrative law. The basic source of law in agriculture is a network of market regulations which cover almost every agricultural product at the most varied points during the production process and which establish the instruments for market dirigism from above. Very often this occurs in the form of Community price guarantees or subsidies for specific products. Some market regulations lay down quality requirements for products. One or two market regulations provide for production levies or thresholds, or sometimes both, which are intended to regulate the production of surpluses.

In addition to market regulations, the Common Agricultural Market includes "supporting intervention systems," such as agricultural levies and refunds at the border in respect of imports from or exports to third countries of agricultural products, and monetary compensation amounts payable in intracommunity trade and in trade with third countries.

All market regulations contain delegations of power to the Commission in accordance with Article 155(4) EEC allowing it to pass the necessary executory measures. Such delegations of power are frequently to be exercised in accordance with a so-called management committee procedure. The decisions of the Commission must be put before a Committee, chaired by a representative of the Commission, which is made up of representatives of the Member States. In contrast to the position in other sectors of the economy where such committees are used, in the agricultural sector the Commission may still pass the measure in question notwithstanding a negative opinion from the Committee, but the Council may within one month replace that decision with one of its own.[41]

The implementing provisions concern for example procedural matters, the adjustment of certain parameters within a market regulation (fixing of levels and refunds, etc.) and the control of financial implementation. However, an application of the rules of the common agricultural policy to every single person affected would exceed the administrative capacity of the Commission. For this reason alone, it is necessary to revert to

[41] *cf.* Beutler *et al.*, *op. cit.*, footnote 35, p. 136.

national enforcement mechanisms, which in consequence now bear the greater part of the administrative burden.

Nonetheless, many even normative measures of the Commission should be qualified as administrative acts, for they either refer to individual cases or are at least applicable to concrete situations. Thus the agricultural policy involves co-operation between Community and national executive organs, thus demonstrating a characteristic trait of European administration.[42]

II. THE EXTERNAL PROTECTION OF THE COMMON MARKET THROUGH THE COMMON CUSTOMS TARIFF

According to Article 9 EEC the customs union is one of the pillars of the Community. It includes in particular a uniform external tariff. Articles 18 *et seq*. EEC contain the instruments provided for the achievment of this goal.

The right to levy tariffs within the EEC Treaty envisages a separation between the common customs tariff (CCT) and the application of tariffs to individual cases.[43] The competence to establish the CCT lies with the E.C. and was confirmed with the passing of Council Regulation 950/68.[44] The CCT contains around 3,000 tariff positions, which provide for duties expressed as a percentage of the value of the goods. The application of the CCT is a matter for national customs authorities. The Member States also have the competence to issue customs rules which, for example, regulate the methods for calculating the value of goods.

The danger which thus arises that the CCT may not be uniformly applied because, for example, a variety of methods of calculation are used in the Member States, means that approximation of laws is necessary within the area of customs law. Thus Article 17 EEC provides for the approximation of national legal and administrative provisions by the Member States on the recommendation of the Commission. However, the "recommendation" has no binding legal force, so that the issuing of Directives under Article 100 EEC, which the Member States would then be under a duty to incorporate and which would ensure a greater level of

---

[42] *cf*. M. Zuleeg, *Das Recht der Europäischen Gemeinschaften im innerstaatlichen Bereich*, Cologne/Berlin/Bonn/Munich 1969, p. 209.
[43] *cf*. Beutler *et al.*, *op. cit.*, footnote 35 at p. 277.
[44] J.O. 1968, L172/1; O.J. Sp. Ed., 1968 (I), 275.

uniformity among the national rules thus put into effect, would be more effective in the interests of integration.

However, it is not only national customs law which can be the cause of a varied application of the CCT. Even the CCT itself often leads to divergences in customs practice. Most particularly, there are the problems of interpretation of individual tariff positions in relation to particular goods crossing frontiers. In an attempt to ensure a uniform interpretation of the tariff the Council passed Regulation 97/69 of January 16, 1969 on measures to be taken for uniform application of the nomenclature of the Common Customs Tariff.[45]

This represents the legal basis for interpretative regulations passed by the Commission using the so-called committee procedure.[46] These regulations explain the provisions of the CCT without amending them.[47] Even so the numerous cases on the CCT which have come before the Court of Justice, primarily through the Article 177 EEC preliminary ruling procedure, show that there are difficulties of interpretation which still remain.

---

[45] *cf.* Article 1(1) of Regulation 97/69 of January 16, 1969, J.O. 1969, L14/1; O.J. Sp. Ed., 1969, 12 as amended by Council Regulation 280/77 of February 8, 1977, O.J. 1977, L40/1. See on this also M. Beschel in v.d. Groeben *et al.*, *op. cit.*, footnote 4, introductory note to Articles 18–29, para. 11.

[46] *cf.* para. 3 of the preamble of Regulation 97/69, *op. cit.*, footnote 45 at p. 1.

[47] *cf.* Beutler *et al.*, *op. cit.*, footnote 35 at p. 278.

SECTION 4

SOURCES OF GENERAL ADMINISTRATIVE LAW OF THE EUROPEAN COMMUNITY

In describing the various fields of direct and indirect implementation of Community law a large number of relevant legal provisions in the Treaties and secondary legislation have already been mentioned. These rules form the basis for the management of the different sectors of the European economy. In so far as they constitute economic administrative law, using German terminology they fall within the special part of administrative law (das besondere Verwaltungsrecht).[1]

At the centre of this investigation, however, should be the principles which represent, in the various fields of administrative activity, the basic standard of legality, that is, to use once more German terminology, what could be described as the general part of administrative law (das allgemeine Verwaltungsrecht).[2]

The sources of law[3] to which regard must be had in the general part of European Community administrative law are written law, customary law, general principles of law and judge-made law.[4]

A. WRITTEN LAW

There are a large number of administrative law rules to be found in

---

[1] See H.-W. Rengeling, "Die Entwicklung verwaltungsrechtlicher Grundsätze durch den Gerichtshof der Europäischen Gemeinschaften," EuR 1984, pp. 331 *et seq.* at p. 332.

[2] *Ibid.*

[3] On the concept of a source of law see the basic work by A. Ross, *Theorie der Rechtsquellen*, 1929 (see p. 291 on the definition of a source of law as a "reason for recognising something as law"). On sources of law and their hierarchy, see an instructive comparative study in L.-J. Constantinesco, *Rechtsvergleichung*, Die rechtsvergleichende Wissenschaft, Vol. III, Cologne/Berlin/Bonn/Munich 1983, pp. 411 *et seq.*

[4] On sources of law in European Community law in general *cf.* H.-G. Schermers, *Judicial Protection in the European Communities* (3rd ed., Deventer 1983), pp. 8 *et seq.*; A. Bleckmann, *Europarecht* (4th ed., Cologne/Berlin/Bonn/Munich 1985), pp. 93 *et seq.* Of the older literature see in particular P. Pescatore, *L'ordre juridique des Communautés européennes—Etudes des sources du droit communautaire*, Liège 1975; C. F. Ophüls, "Quellen und Aufbau des Europäischen Gemeinschaftsrechts," NJW 1963, pp. 1697 *et seq.*

written law. However, they remain far from offering comprehensive and uninterrupted coverage of the whole area of administrative activity. On the contrary, these are isolated provisions which tend to give the impression of being of a random nature.

With regard to the provisions which aim to regulate the administrative implementation of Community law on a number of levels, it is first necessary to investigate how far these rules have penetrated primary and secondary Community law. In addition, it is important to mention on what legal basis they have been adopted and to what extent they count as legal principles. In sum, the following account of the relevant sources of law is intended to be a basic review of the state of the law, but not a complete account of the content of existing individual rules.

I. PRIMARY LAW

If one examines the provisions of the Treaties which may be of use in the control of administrative action under Community law, it emerges that in the ECSC context there are more and more detailed rules available than in the EEC or Euratom contexts.

That is not surprising when one takes into account that the ECSC Treaty was formulated in much more specific terms in order to regulate a concrete sector of the economy (Traité Loi) than the EEC Treaty, the conclusion of which was intended to leave more detailed matters of regulation to the Community legislator (Traité Cadre). The Euratom Treaty occupies a intermediate position.[5]

As an unqualified standard against which administrative activity is to be judged, the prohibition of discrimination to be found in Article 4 ECSC and Article 7 EEC is of considerable relevance. This prohibition, which is supplemented by specific prohibitions of discrimination to be found in the Treaties[6] and in secondary sources of law,[7] contains an instruction to act in a particular way aimed specifically at the executive

---

[5] cf. G. Nicolaysen, *Europäisches Gemeinschaftsrecht*, Stuttgart/Berlin/Cologne 1979, p. 6; Beutler, Bieber, Pipkorn & Streil, *Die Europäische Gemeinschaft—Rechtsordnung und Politik* (3rd ed., Baden-Baden 1987), p. 39 with further references.

[6] e.g. in Article 119 EEC.

[7] e.g. in Directive 75/117 of February 10, 1975, O.J. 1975, L45/19; Directive 76/207 of February 9, 1976, O.J. 1976, L39/40; Directive 79/7 of December 19, 1978, O.J. 1979, L6/24.

bodies which are responsible for putting Community law into effect, both on the national level and on the level of the Community itself.[8]

There are also crucial substantive rules in the provisions on judicial protection. In particular, the four grounds for review, which are derived from French models[9]—lack of competence, infringement of an essential procedural requirement, infringement of the Treaty or of any other rule relating to its application, and misuse of powers (Article 173 EEC, Article 33 ECSC). These heads of review offer, in addition to their function as preconditions for the admissibility of individual claims, standards generally adhered to for determining the legality of administrative action.

It is thus clearly expressed in the Treaties, through the influence of French legal thinking, that the Community powers are subject to the rule of law, and this is to be achieved primarily through the objective principles of administrative law. As Ernst-Werner Fuss,[10] Gottfried Zieger[11] and Hans Peter Ipsen[12] in particular have rightly pointed out, the rule of law and the protection of the law should be realised primarily not by safeguarding the legal situation of individuals, but by means of generally binding principles of administrative law.

The so-called "compétence d'attribution" principle governing the Treaties creates a further decisive limitation of Community powers. Unlike States, the Communities do not possess unlimited sovereign powers, but only the powers which the Treaties have expressly attributed to them (Article 4 EEC; Article 5 ECSC).

In so far as the Treaties themselves provide that infringement of an essential procedural requirement is a ground for reviewing the legality of a Community act, it is important to read the judical review provisions in conjunction with the special provisions on procedural matters which are included in the Treaties or in the secondary legislation. Thus, for instance, Article 190 EEC provides that all legal acts must state the

---

[8] *cf.* for a comprehensive analysis of the significance of the prohibition of discrimination H. P. Ipsen, *Europäisches Gemeinschaftsrecht*, Tübingen 1972, §30/1, pp. 531 *et seq.* with further references.

[9] On the influence of French administrative law on the European system of judicial protection see in more detail, J. Schwarze, "Der Schutz des Gemeinschaftsbürgers durch allgemeine Verwaltungsrechtsgrundsätze im EG-Recht," NJW 1986, pp. 1067 *et seq.*, at p. 1072 with further references.

[10] E.-W. Fuss, *Die Europäischen Gemeinschaften und der Rechtsstaatsgedanke*, Heule 1967, pp. 38 *et seq.*

[11] G. Zieger, *Das Grundrechtsproblem in den Europäischen Gemeinschaften*, Tübingen 1970, p. 39.

[12] H. P. Ipsen, *op. cit.*, footnote 8, §41/21 and 23, pp. 730, 733.

reasons on which they are based, and there are similarly worded provisions in Articles 15(1) ECSC and 162 Euratom. Further, in this context, Articles 15(2) and (3) ECSC, 191 EEC and 163 Euratom contain specific rules on the publication and notification of legislative acts and individual decisions of Community institutions.

Finally in this context it is important to mention that the Treaties frequently require an institution which proposes to pass a particular measure (in particular legislative measures) to consult a special committee before doing so.

In the Coal and Steel and Euratom contexts in particular, these committees also include representatives of those parties directly affected by the measures.[13] The participation of these committees thus facilitates a formalised hearing for affected parties.[14] Failure to involve or consult these committees will render the measures thus taken voidable for infringement of an essential procedural requirement.

The Treaties only exceptionally and in well-disguised instances give those directly affected by a measure the right to be heard. For instance, Article 36(1) ECSC provides that before imposing a pecuniary sanction or ordering a periodic penalty payment the High Authority must give the party concerned the opportunity to submit its comments. Similarly clearly formulated rights to a hearing can otherwise be found only in secondary legislation.

Finally, all the Treaties contain provisions which give the Commission the right to request information from individual undertakings and citizens (Article 213 EEC, Article 187 Euratom, Article 47(1) ECSC).

A codified right to refuse to make a statement does not as yet exist.[14a] However, some attempt is made to offer protection to the interests of the parties concerned by requiring that the substance of information thus provided must be treated confidentially by the body receiving it, in

---

[13] Such committees are provided for in particular in Articles 18, 19 ECSC, 47, 193 *et seq.* (especially 198) EEC as well as Articles 165 *et seq.* Euratom.

[14] On the consultation of interest groups in national administrative law see for example in Germany §14 para. 3 of the Güterkraftverkehrsgesetz, §29 para. 1 of the Bundesnaturschutzgesetz and §51 of the Bundesimmissionsschutzgesetz. On the legal situation in the Netherlands, see D. H. Kok, *Due Process in Netherlands administrative procedure*, FIDE 1978, p. 99, which refers to the right to be heard of legal persons affected (Article 7 of the Administrative Court Law 1975), which exists also where an interest in the substance of a measure can be discerned from the objectives of an organisation as defined in its constitution.

[14a] See in more detail on this question J. Schwarze, "Grenzen für die Ermittlungstätigkeit der Kommission als Wettbewerbsbehörde der EG," in *Der Gemeinsame Markt—Bestand und Zukunft in wirtschaftsrechtlicher Perspektive*, (ed. J. Schwarze), Baden-Baden 1987, pp. 159 *et seq.* at p. 163.

particular where business secrets or statistical information constitute the object of the request for information (*cf.* Articles 214 EEC and 47(2), (4) ECSC). In sum, it can be seen that the primary law contains provisions covering a relatively wide spectrum of questions which form in domestic law elements of general administrative law.

However, it is also apparent that the intensity and meaningfulness of the treaty provisions are relatively insignificant; rather, to use geographical terminology, we are dealing here with basic measuring points, which facilitate and alleviate the task of determining the position and specification of further rules.

II. SECONDARY LAW

Since the provisions of primary law do not provide sufficient measures to ensure the control of the administration, it is also necessary to examine to what extent the Community legislator has filled or been able to fill any existing gaps by passing secondary legislation. Provisions of secondary law with application to general administrative law may, depending on the level of administrative implementation at which they are functioning, be directed either towards the institutions of the Community themselves or towards the authorities of the Member States which are responsible for applying Community law.

The Treaties do not grant any express power to undertake a comprehensive codification of the general administrative law of the European Community. That applies equally to administration by the Community itself and to administrative implementation by national authorities.

1. The Present Position

Only a small number of secondary administrative law provisions with general rather than particular scope within a limited substantive area have so far been passed. These include Regulation 1 on the language question, according to which *inter alia* individual acts directed at national authorities or private person in a Member State are to be written in the language of the Member State to which jurisdiction that authority or person is subject.[15] This regulation is based on the express power contained in Article 217 EEC (Article 190 Euratom).

[15] Regulation 1 of April 15, 1958, J.O. 1958, 385; O.J. Sp. Ed. 1952–1958, 59.

Regulation 1182/71 determining the rules applicable to periods, dates and time limits is also of general application to the implementation of Community law.[16] It is intended to ensure the uniform operation of Community law and establishes for this purpose rules on the exact point in time when the legal acts of the Community are to come into force. This Regulation is based on Article 235 EEC.

There are many more provisions of secondary law which are not of general application to the implementation of Community law, but rather apply only to one or more substantive areas or even simply to the implementation of a particular regulation, but which nonetheless from the point of view of their substance correspond to the rules of the general part of administrative law.[17] These include substantive law provisions as well as rules on organisational and procedural aspects of administration. These provisions of secondary law are based for the most part on provisions of the Treaty which specifically include a power to regulate the relevant substantive area. It is sufficient here merely to cite the following examples:

(a) Direct implementation

The Council passed Regulation 2988/74 based on Articles 75, 79 and 87 EEC concerning limitation periods in proceedings and the enforcement of sanctions under the rules of the European Economic Community relating to transport and competition.[18] It governs limitation periods in proceedings concerning cases of fines or penalties imposed in consequence of an infringement of the transport and competition provisions as well as concerning the enforcement of any fines, penalties or periodic penalty payments imposed by the Commission in such circumstances. In particular also, the issues of the interruption or suspension of the limitation periods are dealt with in the Regulation.

[16] Regulation 1182/71/EEC/Euratom of June 3, 1971, J.O. 1971, L124/1, O.J. Sp. Ed. 1971, 354.
[17] *cf.* M. Schweitzer, "Die Verwaltung der Europäischen Gemeinschaften," Die Verwaltung 1984, pp. 137 *et seq.* at p. 145; H.-W. Rengeling, "Fragen zum allgemeinen Verwaltungsrecht in der Europäischen Gemeinschaft," in *Festschrift für Ulrich Scupin*, Berlin 1983, p. 477.
[18] Regulation 2988/74 of November 26, 1974, O.J. 1974, L319/1.

Individual procedural provisions for the fields of transport and state aids are to be found in Regulations 1191/69, 1192/69 and 1107/70[19] concerning the elimination of distortions of competitive conditions in the transport market based on Articles 75, 77 and 94 EEC.

In addition, one should also mention in particular Competition Regulation 17[20] as well as implementing Regulations 27[21] and 99/63.[22] Regulation 17 establishes the procedure for the application of the community competition rules contained in Articles 85 *et seq*. EEC. General procedural questions are dealt with in this Regulation for competition law as a whole, such as the conditions governing the revocation of favourable administrative acts (Article 8(3)). Regulation 27 lays down specific requirements of form for competition procedures.

In application of the general principle of the right to a hearing, Regulation 99/63 gives effect to Article 19 of Regulation 17 by providing for the hearing of persons affected by a competition investigation and interested third parties.

Regulations on limitation periods in proceedings and enforcement of sanctions in the context of the ECSC Treaty can be found in Decision 715/78/ECSC.[23] These measures, which are based on Articles 2–5 and 95(1) ECSC, govern limitation periods in cases involving infringements of the provisions in Articles 47, 54, 58, 59, 64, 65, 66 and 68 or of provisions based on Article 95(1) and (2) ECSC for which financial penalties are threatened.

Further procedural rules can be found in Regulation 2176/84 concerning protection against dumped or subsidised imports from non-EEC third countries.[24] This Regulation, which is based on Article 113 EEC, contains provisions in Article 5 which govern the right to lodge a complaint and procedures in anti-dumping questions.[24a] Article 16 provides for the

---

[19] Regulation 1191/69 of June 26, 1969, J.O. 1969, L156/1; O.J. Sp. Ed. 1969, 276; Regulation 1192/69 of June 26, 1969, J.O. 1969, L156/8; O.J. Sp. Ed. 1969, 283; Regulation 1107/70 of June 4, 1970, O.J. 1970, L130/1; O.J. Sp. Ed. 1970, 360.

[20] Regulation 17 of February 6, 1962, J.O. 1962, 204; O.J. Sp. Ed. 1959–1962, 87.

[21] Regulation 27 of February 6, 1962, J.O. 1962, 1118; O.J. Sp. Ed. 1959–1962, 132.

[22] Regulation 99/63 of July 25, 1963, J.O. 1963, 2268; O.J. Sp. Ed. 1963–1964, 47.

[23] Decision 715/78/ECSC of April 6, 1978, O.J. 1978, L94/22.

[24] Regulation 2176/84 of July 23, 1984, O.J. 1984, L201/1; *cf.* on this A. Weber, "Das Verwaltungsverfahren im Antidumpingrecht der EG," EuR 1985, pp. 1 *et seq.*; J. Schwarze, "Rechtsschutz gegen Anti-Dumpingmassnahmen der EG—Zu Verfahren und richterlicher Kontrolle auf dem Gebiet der Aussenwirtschaftsverwaltung der Gemeinschaft," EuR 1986, pp. 217 *et seq.*

[24a] See in more detail on this J. Schwarze, *op. cit.*, footnote 24, pp. 217 *et seq.*

reimbursement of excess anti-dumping duties on the application of the importer concerned.

In addition, Regulation 858/72 on certain administrative and financial procedures for the operation of the European Social Fund should also be cited.[25] This legal measure, based on Articles 127 and 209 EEC, contains numerous procedural provisions governing the distribution of financial assistance from the European Social Fund.

Finally, a plethora of organisational and procedural questions, which from the point of view of their content should be treated as belonging to the general part of the administrative law of the European Community, are dealt with in the rules of procedure of the various institutions[26] and in the Staff Regulations.[27] These govern many issues concerning Community administrative implementation.

(b) Indirect implementation

In the area of import and export levies, that is, for customs duties, charges having equivalent effect and levies and other measures within the framework of the CAP, Regulation 1430/79[28] on the repayment or remission of import and export duties and Regulation 1697/79[29] on the post-clearance recovery of import and export duties establish the conditions in which a Community duty which has been wrongly paid or not claimed may be reclaimed or be subject to post-clearance recovery.[30] These regulations, with their rules on the revocation and retrospective adoption

---

[25] Regulation 858/72 of April 4, 1972, J.O. 1972, L101/3; O.J. Sp. Ed. 1972, 353.

[26] Provisional Rules of Procedure of the Commission, Decisions 67/426/EEC and 67/24/Euratom of July 6, 1967, J.O. 1967, L147/1; in conjunction with the Rules of Procedure of the Commission of the European Economic Community of January 9, 1963, J.O. 1963, 181; O.J. Sp. Ed. 1963, 181 amended most recently by Commission Decision 81/2/Euratom/ECSC/EEC of January 6, 1981, O.J. 1981, L8/16; Commission Decision 73/2/ECSC/EEC/Euratom of January 6, 1973 on the delegation of signature, O.J. 1973, L7/2; cf. on this Commission Decision 75/461/Euratom/ECSC/EEC of July 23, 1975, O.J. 1975, L199/43; Rules of Procedure of the Council 79/868/ECSC/EEC/Euratom of July 24, 1979, O.J. 1979, L268/1. A leading work on the problems of rules of procedure is R. Bieber, "Verfahrensregeln—Skizze einer verborgenen Quelle des Gemeinschaftsrechts" in F. Capotorti et al. (eds.) Festschrift für P. Pescatore, Baden-Baden 1987.

[27] cf. Council Regulation 259/68/EEC/Euratom/ECSC of February 29, 1968, J.O. 1968, L56/1; O.J. Sp. Ed. 1968, 30 reprinted in v.d. Groeben, Thiesing, Ehlermann, Handbuch des Europäischen Rechts, IA 67.11, pp. 1 et seq.

[28] Regulation 1430/79 of July 2, 1979, O.J. 1979, L175/1.

[29] Regulation 1697/79 of July 24, 1979, O.J. 1979, L197/1.

[30] cf. in more detail on this, P. Karpenstein, "Die Entwicklung des Gemeinschaftsrechts," EuR 1980, pp. 258 et seq., p. 260.

of administrative acts, are concerned with a core question of general (European) administrative law. They were adopted on the basis of Articles 43 and 235 EEC.

Also in the area of agricultural and customs law is Regulation 1468/81, which governs the procedure for mutual assistance among the administrative authorities of the Member States and co-operation between the latter and the Commission to ensure the correct application of the law on customs and agricultural matters.[31] This Regulation is also based on Articles 43 and 235 EEC.

Regulation 729/70 on the financing of the common agricultural policy[32] also contains organisational and procedural provisions, which refer as regards the important question of the recovery of sums paid as a result of irregularities to the legal and administrative provisions of the individual Member States. According to the case law of the Court, this reference applies not only as regards rules of procedure and forms to be followed in recovering such sums, but also to the substantive conditions for their recovery.[33] The legal bases of this Regulation are Articles 43 and 209 EEC.

Substantive and procedural provisions which constitute part of the general part of administrative law from the point of view of their content are also to be found in Directives harmonising the legal and administrative provisions of the Member States. Reference should be made here to Directive 78/453 based on Article 100 EEC, which provides for the harmonisation of provisions concerning deferred payment of import and export duties.[34]

Furthermore, the individual market regulations of the common agricultural policy contain procedural and organisational provisions.[35]

As regards other areas, special procedural rules are contained for instance in Regulation 1408/71[36] on the application of social security systems to employed persons, to self-employed persons and to members of their families moving within the Community (Articles 84 *et seq.*). In addition, the Regulation on the co-ordination of the application of this Regulation based on Articles 2, 7 and 51 EEC provides in Articles 80 *et*

---

[31] Regulation 1468/81 of May 19, 1981, O.J. 1981, L144/1.

[32] Regulation 729/70 of April 21, 1970, J.O. 1970, L94/13; O.J. Sp. Ed. 1970, 218.

[33] Joined Cases 205–215/82 *Deutsche Milchkontor GmbH et al.* v. *Bundesrepublik Deutschland* [1983] E.C.R. 2633 at 2670.

[34] Directive 78/453/EEC of May 22, 1978, O.J. 1978, L146/19.

[35] *cf.* on this the overview in the collection Sartorius II No. 177.

[36] Regulation 1408/71 of June 14, 1971, J.O. 1971, L149/2; O.J. Sp. Ed. 1971, 416 as amended by Regulation 1660/85 of June 13, 1985, O.J. 1985, L160/1.

seq. for the setting up of an administrative commission and an advisory committee on social security for migrant workers.

Finally, two further harmonising Directives should be mentioned. Organisational and procedural provisions are contained in Directive 64/221[37] on the co-ordination of special measures concerning the entry and residence of foreign nationals which are justified on grounds of public policy, public security or public health, which is based on Article 56(2) EEC. Article 9 of this Directive ensures that persons affected by an expulsion order are given minimum procedural guarantees. In particular, they have certain rights to be heard and rights of defence, where there is no right of appeal to court of law against the decision in the relevant Member State or where such an appeal may be made only in respect of the legal validity of the decision (not its expediency) or cannot have suspensory effect.[38]

Procedural provisions are also contained, for instance, in Directive 70/156 EEC[39] on the approximation of the laws of the Member States relating to type-approval of motor vehicles and their trailers. As regards all decisions taken in pursuance of this Directive and refusing or withdrawing type approval or refusing registration or prohibiting sales or use, Article 14 obliges Member States to state in detail the reasons on which the decisions are based and to notify the parties affected of the remedies available to them.

2. The Legal Basis of an Act—The Power to Legislate

When one considers the general question of the potential powers of the Community to lay down administrative law rules, it must be pointed out at the outset, with regard to practice thus far in this field, that any attempts to codify general administrative law, which are currently contained in numerous specific measures for the various substantive areas, are in each case based either on express powers in the Treaty to lay down necessary executive measures[40] or additionally or exclusively on the "general powers" provided for in Articles 100, 235 EEC, 95 ECSC and 203 Euratom.

---

[37] Directive 64/221 of February 25, 1964, J.O. 1964, 850; O.J. Sp. Ed. 1963–1964, 117.
[38] *cf.* on this Joined Cases 115–116/81 *Adoui & Cornaille* v. *Belgium* [1982] E.C.R. 1665 at 1710.
[39] Directive 70/156 of February 6, 1970, J.O. 1970, L42/1; O.J. Sp. Ed. 1970, 96.
[40] *cf.* for instance Articles 43, 51, 56(2), 57, 75, 79, 87, 94, 113, 127 and 217 EEC.

Defining the Community's area of jurisdiction makes it necessary to draw the following distinction between direct and indirect implementation.

(a) Direct implementation

In the context of the implementation of Community law by the Community's own institutions or authorities, their power to lay down substantive law is linked to their authority to regulate administrative implementation, having regard to any attendant organisational and procedural rules which may be necessary. In so far as their administrative authority in an individual case does not result expressly from the provisions of the Treaty—such as for instance in the case of Articles 87, 94 and 127 EEC—it can be based in part on the doctrine of "implied powers."[41]

As the Court of Justice held in some of its earlier cases,[42] it is permissible to apply a rule of construction generally recognised both in international law and in domestic law, according to which the provisions of an international treaty or of a statute are assumed to contain those provisions without which they would lack meaning or could not reasonably be applied.

A wider competence to adopt general administrative law provisions in the context of direct implementation is further to be seen in Articles 235 EEC, 95 ECSC and 203 Euratom.[43] Under this provision, the Council has in principle the power to adopt appropriate measures if action by the Community is necessary in order to attain the objectives of the Community and the Treaty has not specifically provided the necessary powers. As

---

[41] H.-W. Rengeling, *Rechtsgrundsätze beim Verwaltungsvollzug des Europäischen Gemeinschaftsrechts*, Cologne/Berlin/Bonn/Munich 1977, p. 14. On the foundations of administrative implementation and on the theory and concretion of legal principles having regard to comparative law, see KSE Vol. 27, Cologne, etc., p. 34 at 37. *cf.* on this also G. Nicolaysen, "Zur Theorie von den Implied Powers in den Europäischen Gemeinschaften," EuR 1966, pp. 129 *et seq.*; H. P. Ipsen, *Europäisches Gemeinschaftsrecht*, 20/43 *et seq.*; I. Schwartz, in v.d. Groeben, v. Boeckh, Thiesing, Ehlermann, *Kommentar zum EWG-Vertrag* (3rd ed., Baden-Baden 1983), Art. 235, paras. 26 *et seq.*; H. P. Ipsen, *Fusionsverfassung*, Bad Homburg/Berlin 1969, p. 71.

[42] Case 8/55 *Fédération Charbonnière de Belgique* v. *High Authority* [1954–1956] E.C.R. 245; Case 20/59 *Italy* v. *High Authority* [1960] E.C.R. 325 at 336; Case 25/59 *Netherlands* v. *High Authority* [1960] E.C.R. 355 at 372.

[43] *cf.* the discussion reports in *Europäisches Verwaltungsrecht im Werden* (ed. J. Schwarze), p. 93 at 123.

we have seen, the Council has also made use of this broad competence to regulate general questions of administrative law.[44]

In so far as the Treaty itself authorises the Community to implement its own policies, it is possible to establish, on the basis of Article 235 EEC and the corresponding provisions in the other Treaties, a power to regulate the general part of Community administrative law. Thus there could be a need, for instance, to regulate the question of when it is permissible to revoke or adopt retrospectively an administrative act on a uniform basis for all fields of direct implementation, as well for the area of the ECSC Treaty as for competition law enforcement under the EEC Treaty and for the law governing the rights and duties of Community officials.

It is quite another matter, of course, to consider whether, by means of the adoption of organisational and administrative measures based on Article 235 EEC, the arena of direct implementation of substantive Community law can be extended.

This concern does not limit the authority of Community institutions to lay down administrative measures to implement the new so called supporting policies, which may be validly based on Article 235 EEC. An example of this is the creation of the European Monetary Co-operation Fund[45] as well as the creation of the European Monetary System.[46] Within the framework of its tasks, the Fund (or its administrative council) was given an autonomous administrative power which in particular included the authority to adopt independently the administrative rules to be applied within a specific framework.[47]

On the other hand, it is doubtful whether it is permissible to extend direct Community implementation at the expense of the Member State's power over indirect implementation.

---

[44] Regulation 1182/71/EEC/Euratom of June 3, 1971 determining the rules applicable to periods, dates and time limits, J.O. 1971, L124/1; O.J. Sp. Ed. 1971, 354; ECSC Decision 715/78 of April 6, 1978, O.J. 1978, L94/22, on limitation periods in proceedings and the enforcement of sanctions.

[45] Regulation 907/73 of April 3, 1973, O.J. 1973, L89/2 in the version of Regulation 2626/84 of September 15, 1984, O.J. 1984, L247/1.

[46] The EMS can be traced back to the Resolution of the European Council of December 5, 1978 on the establishment of the European Monetary System (Europa Archiv 1979, p. D124) and the agreement between central banks made thereafter. It is now recognised in the Treaty in Article 102a(1) EEC, inserted by the Single European Act, cf. on this Beutler et al., op. cit., footnote 5, pp. 431 et seq.

[47] Article 4 of Regulation 907/73; on the Community's power to regulate in the area of monetary co-operation see C.-D. Ehlermann, "Die Errichtung der Fonds für währungspolitische Zusammenarbeit," EuR 1973, p. 193 at 196 et seq.

In the context of the implementation of Community law by Community institutions or authorities, their power to make substantive law is linked to their authority to lay down accompanying administrative measures, having regard to any organisational and procedural rules.[48] In the absence of other Community competences, this principle provides that Community law will be implemented by the Member States on the basis of the authority which they have retained.[49] Of course, the principle of "compétence d'attribution," in application of Article 235 EEC, may bring about a partial break from this approach. A precondition for this is, however, always that it is "necessary" in order to attain a goal of the Community. The need for the uniform application of Community law in all Member States may not alone be sufficient to constitute the "necessity" for a comprehensive centralist administration. The existing administrative structures and national characteristics of the Member States, the fact that they are closer both to the things and to the people they are administering as well as finally the structural features ("traité cadre") which clearly distinguish the EEC Treaty from, for instance, the ECSC Treaty, all speak against an unlimited extension of direct implementation of Community law at the cost of indirect implementation, at least in so far as it is proposed to use Article 235 EEC to this end.[50]

(b) Indirect implementation

In so far as the law as it stands requires implementation in central areas of Community policy to remain with the authorities of the Member States, the question must then arise whether the Community, even though it may not itself take over the implementation, may at least regulate it.

In so far as the authorities of the Member States implement Community law in the fields of customs and agriculture, for instance, they act primarily to apply substantive Community administrative law belonging to the special part. Organisation and procedure in these activities are, however, governed according to national administrative law, in so far as these questions are not in individual cases also regulated by Community law. The appropriate national substantive administrative law is also to be

---

[48] M. Schweitzer, "Die Verwaltung der Europäischen Gemeinschaften," Die Verwaltung 1984, pp. 137 et seq. at p. 139. Beutler et al., op. cit., footnote 5, p. 75.

[49] See on this H.-W. Rengeling, op. cit., footnote 41, p. 30; U. Everling, "Elemente eines europäischen Verwaltungsrechts," DVBl. 1983, pp. 649 et seq., at p. 651.

[50] H.-W. Rengeling, op. cit., footnote 41, p. 27; U. Everling, op. cit., footnote 49, p. 651.

applied where such fundamental administrative law questions as the revocability and retroactive adoption of administrative acts are concerned.[51]

Breaking down legal and administrative responsibilities in this way for the indirect implementation of Community law is obviously not without its problems. On the one hand, the law of the Member States must be recognised, and decisions must be taken using their administrative organisation, administrative procedures and general administrative law; on the other hand there is a risk that competitive conditions will be distorted and interested parties will not have equal chances if national authorities are proceeding on the basis of different standards in their application of Community law.[52]

If Community law is applied unevenly by national administrative authorities, this will mean that it does not have a uniform effect throughout the Community. As is shown in detail elsewhere,[53] the case law of the Court of Justice demonstrates in numerous cases[54] the need, now partially satisfied in the form of Regulations 1430/79 and 1697/79,[55] for uniform rules on the repayment or remission/post-clearance recovery of import and export duties which have been either wrongfully levied or incorrectly not levied.

In any case, even in the absence of Community law rules on administrative implementation, the Member States are not completely free to enlist the support of "domestic legal and administrative provisions"[56] for the

---

[51] Joined Cases 205–215/82 *Deutsche Milchkontor GmbH* v. *Bundesrepublik Deutschland* [1983] E.C.R. 2633 at 2634.

[52] *cf.* on this for instance the reasons given in the preamble to the Commission's draft Directive on the harmonisation of provisions laid down by law, regulation or administrative action concerning the exercise of the right to appeal in respect of customs matters; presented on January 29, 1981, O.J. 1981, C33/2.

[53] *cf.* also M. Hilf, "Möglichkeiten und Grenzen des Rückgriffs auf nationale verwaltungsrechtliche Regeln bei der Durchführung von Gemeinschaftsrecht," in J. Schwarze, *op. cit.*, footnote 28, pp. 67 *et seq.*

[54] *cf.* for example, Case 33/76 *Rewe* v. *Landwirtschaftskammer Saarland* [1976] E.C.R. 1989 *et seq.*; Case 45/76 *Comet* v. *Produktschap voor Siergewassen* [1976] E.C.R. 2043; Case 68/79 *Just* v. *Ministerium für das Steuerwesen* [1980] E.C.R. 501; Case 26/74 *Roquette* v. *Commission* [1976] E.C.R. 677; Case 265/78 *Ferwerda* v. *Produktschap voor Vee en Vlees* [1980] E.C.R. 617; Case 130/79 *Express Dairy Foods* v. *Intervention Board for Agricultural Produce* [1980] E.C.R. 1887; Joined Cases 205–215/82 *Deutsche Milchkontor GmbH* v. *Bundesrepublik Deutschland* [1983] E.C.R 2633.

[55] O.J. 1979, L175/1 and L197/1.

[56] These are sometimes expressly referred to, as for instance in Article 8 of Regulation 729/70 of April 21, 1970, J.O. L94/13; O.J. Sp. Ed. 1970, 218; otherwise an implicit reference is recognised, see Case 265/78 *Ferwerda* v. *Produktschap voor Vee en Vlees* [1980] E.C.R. 617 at 629 para. 12).

purpose of implementing Community law. On the contrary, the principle of loyalty to the Community laid down in Article 5 EEC requires them to guarantee the proper application of Community law in their territory.[57] As the Court held in Case 48/71 *Commission* v. *Italy* in 1972, it must be ensured that Community law is "fully applicable at the same time and with identical effects over the whole territory of the Community" without the Member States being able to invoke any "provisions whatsoever of national law" to override it.[58]

The scope and significance of this obligation on the Member States in combination with principles of Community law can be determined more precisely from individual examples.

In so far as the uniform application of Community law cannot be guaranteed simply by reference to the administrative law provisions of the Member States, a power to regulate selectively both procedural and organisational matters as well as the general substantive administrative law can be found in the relevant provisions of the Treaty[59]—for agriculture, for instance, in Article 43 EEC—and more widely in the general clauses contained in Articles 100 and 235 EEC.

The same conditions apply here to the adoption of Regulations under Article 235 EEC as those applicable in the field of direct implementation: that is, such a measure is permissible only where it is necessary, in the context of the common market, in order to attain one of the objectives of the Community and an express power has not been provided. Having regard to the absence of any other power, the Council thus adopted Regulations 1430/79 and 1697/79 on customs duties referred to above on the basis of Article 235 EEC, as well as on the basis of Article 43 EEC as regards agricultural levies.

A harmonisation of legal and administrative provisions of the Member States is possible under Article 100 EEC through the adoption of directives, if the national provisions directly affect the establishment or functioning of the common market. This does not of course give the Community the power to eliminate all differences among national provisions which may emerge in the implementation of Community law. The power to approximate laws begins only where these differences have a

---

[57] U. Everling, *op. cit.*, footnote 59, p. 653; H.-W. Rengeling, *op. cit.*, footnote 41, p. 35; v.d. Groeben *et al.*, *op. cit.*, footnote 41, Article 5, paras. 3 *et seq.*; Case 265/78 *Ferwerda* v. *Produktschap voor Vee en Vlees* [1980] E.C.R. 617 at 629 (para. 10).

[58] Case 48/71 *Commission* v. *Italy* [1972] E.C.R. 529 at 534 (paras. 5 to 10).

[59] For a competence based on so-called "implied powers" see H.-W. Rengeling, *op. cit.*, footnote 41, pp. 14 *et seq.*; *ibid.*, in *Festschrift für Ulrich Scupin, op. cit.*, footnote 17, p. 485.

deleterious effect, in the sense of interfering with the establishment or functioning of the common market.[60]

A harmonising directive has the advantage over a regulation adopted on the basis of Article 235 EEC in that it allows Member States the choice of form and methods (Article 189(3) EEC) thus allowing them to have regard to special national characteristics.[61] However, given the narrow conditions of Article 100 EEC, such directives can be used only selectively.

Neither Article 100 nor Article 235 EEC by their terms grant a power to the Community to lay down comprehensive rules governing the general part of administrative law which is to be applied when national authorities are implementing Community law.[62]

3. Summary

(a) The inadequacy of the written law

This overview has shown that in the area of secondary law as well, the written rules so far adopted with regard to questions of general administrative law are as yet insufficient. The relevant measures deal primarily with individual problems, or are limited in their application to individual substantive spheres of Community competence.

Thus, for instance, there are no rules on the revocation or retrospective adoption of administrative acts or on limitation periods and the payment of interest on claims for recovery or reimbursement. The only regulations which are not limited in their application to specific substantive areas or individual problems are the Regulation on the language question[63] and the Regulation determining the rules applicable to periods, dates and time limits.[64]

---

[60] H. C. Taschner, in v.d. Groben *et al.*, *op. cit.*, footnote 41, Article 100, paras. 11, 28. The adoption of directives under Article 100 EEC requires unanimity on the part of the Council. Under the Single European Act of February 17 and 28, 1986, Articles 100a and 8a provide that a qualified majority will be sufficient for the adoption of measures for the approximation of legal and administrative provisions which have as their object the establishment and functioning of the internal market. See in more detail the contributions of H. J. Glaesner and P. Pescatore, in EuR 1986, pp. 119 *et seq.* and 153 *et seq.*

[61] On this discussion see the Discussion Report, in *Europäisches Verwaltungsrecht im Werden* (ed. J. Schwarze), Baden-Baden 1982, pp. 117, 123.

[62] M. Hilf, *op. cit.*, footnote 61, pp. 67 *et seq.* at p. 89.

[63] Regulation 1 J.O. 1958, 17/385; O.J. Sp. Ed. 1952–1958, 59.

[64] Regulation 1182/71 J.O. 1971, L124/1; O.J. Sp. Ed. 1971, 354.

Certainly, the codification of a general administrative law for the European Community cannot be an end in itself. Thus, if there were for the individual substantive fields rules which, while comprehensive, were in some respects different, then a general codification of administrative law would clearly be a less urgent task. The numerous judgments of the European Court concerning the application of general unwritten legal principles in Community law demonstrate, however, that even the measures of secondary law already adopted for individual cases do not in themselves always offer a sufficient basis for decision where the legality of Community measures or of measures taken by national authorities entrusted with the implementation of Community law is to be determined.

(b) The admissibility of reasoning by analogy

The potential for alleviating this situation by adopting analogies with other legal provisions is limited given the general thinness of existing European administrative law. However, it is generally recognised that it is in principle permissible within Community law to reason by analogy.[65] The European Court has occasionally made use of this approach. Thus in a 1978 judgment, the Court applied the existing provisions on the maintenance of a claim for an export refund where the goods have perished as a result of force majeure by analogy to the similarly situated but unregulated (in Community law) case of a claim for currency compensatory amounts.[66]

Also in the context of Regulation 1408/71 on the application of social security rules to migrant workers, the European Court has used an application of the law by analogy in order to close a gap in the law by applying a provision aimed at a similarly situated case.[67]

However, in so far as special substantive or procedural administrative law rules are laid down for specific fields of Community law, these are rarely suitable, given "the necessarily technical and detailed nature of

---

[65] cf. H. P. Ipsen, *Europäisches Gemeinschaftsrecht*, Tübingen 1972, §5/82, p. 134; H. Kutscher, "Methods of Interpretation as seen by a judge of the Court of Justice," in Judicial and Academic Conference, Luxembourg 1976, I–10; R. Voss, "Nationale Vorschriften zur Durchführung des EWG-Rechts im Bereich des Zoll- und Agrarverwaltungsrechts," RIW 1979, pp. 657 *et seq.* at p. 658.

[66] Case 6/78 *Union Française de Céréales* v. *HZA Hamburg-Jonas* [1978] E.C.R. 1675 at 1684.

[67] Case 180/78 *Brouwer-Kaune* v. *Bestuur van de Bedrijfsvereniging voor het Kledingbedrijf* [1979] E.C.R. 2111 at 2120.

such provisions,"[68] to be applied by analogy to other fields or even to other sets of circumstances.

Thus for instance the Court in Case 119, 126/79 *Lippische Hauptgenossenschaft* refused to apply limitation periods contained in other measures to the unregulated case of the recovery of premiums for denaturing mistakenly granted under Community law and asserted instead that the matter was to be dealt with under national law.[69] As Advocate-General Capotorti rightly declared with reference to an earlier decision of the Court,[70] limitation periods must be set in advance for each field of Community law by the Community legislature so that they can "fulfil their function of ensuring legal certainty."[71]

(c) Conclusion

It thus remains to state that the existing written Community law barely contains sufficient legal rules to ensure administrative implementation. The possibilities of making good the existing lack of rules through an application of law by analogy are clearly limited. The decisive question is thus to what extent further standards for the control and review of administrative action according to the principles of the rule of law have been developed in unwritten law.[72]

B. CUSTOMARY LAW

The classic form of unwritten law is customary law. One speaks of customary law where a practice has been for a long time in regular and continuous usage and the "colleagues-at-law" accept this practice as

---

[68] See Case 265/78 *Ferwerda* v. *Produktschap voor Vee en Vlees* [1980] E.C.R 617 at 628, with regard to Regulation 1430/79 and Regulation 1679/79; *cf.* also M. Hilf, *op. cit.*, footnote 62, p. 76.

[69] Joined Cases 119 & 126/79 *Lippische Hauptgenossenschaft et al.* v. *Bundesanstalt für landwirtschaftliche Marktordnung* [1980] E.C.R. 1863 at 1879, para. 9.

[70] Case 41/69 *ACF Chemiefarma N.V.* v. *Commission* [1970] E.C.R. 661 at 686, para. 17.

[71] Advocate-General Capotorti, [1980] E.C.R. 1863 at 1885.

[72] See in general on the significance of unwritten law in Community law F. Capotorti, "Il diritto communitario non scritto," Dir. Comun. e degli Scambi Internaz. 1983, pp. 409 *et seq.*

legally imperative, so that both a *consuetudo* and an *opinio juris necessitatis* are present.[73]

In principle, customary law is recognised in all the Member States. However, customary law plays a significant role above all in the Anglo-Saxon legal sphere,[74] not only at the level of simple law but also, in the form of the so-called "constitutional conventions," in the realm of constitutional law.[75] These "ancient customs" are not new creations, for according to Blackstone's still applicable test[76] they require the proof that they have been practised since time immemorial ("time whereof the memory of man runneth not to the contrary").[77] The usage must be both continuous and unbroken since that time, with the belief that it is a lawful and reasonable way of behaving.[78]

Within the French legal sphere too the recognition of customary law (droit coutumier) presupposes both material and conscious elements.[79] However, in contrast to the common law, it is assumed with regard to the objective element (continuous usage) that a period of time is sufficient when a form of behaviour has come to be seen as a fully established way of acting.

In German law too,[80] as in the legal systems of the other Member States of the European Community, the classic approach to customary law applies, whereby customary law exists only where objective and subjective conditions are both present.

The preconditions for the recognition of customary law are thus quite

---

[73] *cf.* K. Larenz, *Methodenlehre der Rechtswissenschaft* (5th ed., Berlin 1983), p. 341; "Customary law in the original sense is a rule of conduct between people in practice overwhelmingly followed during the course of a long period of time, which is adhered to in the belief that a precept of the law is thereby being observed".

[74] R. David, *Les grands systèmes de droit contemporains* (8th ed., Paris 1982), pp. 392 *et seq.*; N. Michelsen, *Das rechtliche Gehör im Verwaltungsverfahren der Europäischen Gemeinschaften*, Diss. Hamburg 1974, p. 146 with further references.

[75] *cf.* on constitutional conventions O. Hood Phillips, *Constitutional and Administrative Law* (6th ed. by O. Hood Phillips and P. Jackson, London 1978), p. 29 as well as K.-U. Meyn, *Die Verfassungskonventionalregeln im Verfassungssystem Grossbritanniens*, Göttingen 1975.

[76] W. Blackstone, *Commentaries on the Laws of England* (12th ed., London 1973), Vol. 1, pp. 76 *et seq.*

[77] C. Allen, *Law in the Making* (6th ed., Oxford 1958), p. 130 with further references.

[78] C. Allen, *op. cit.*, footnote 77, pp. 132 *et seq.* On the significance of custom in English law see also R. David, *op. cit.*, footnote 74, pp. 392 *et seq.*

[79] R. David, *op. cit.*, footnote 74, pp. 129 *et seq.*

[80] On the role of customary law in Germany see Ch. Tomuschat, *Verfassungsgewohnheitsrecht?—Eine Untersuchung zum Staatsrecht der Bundesrepublik Deutschland*, Heidelberg 1972 and F. Ossenbühl in *Allgemeines Verwaltungsrecht* (eds. H.-U. Erichsen & W. Martens) (7th ed., Berlin/New York 1986), pp. 103 *et seq.* with further references.

similar in the different legal systems of the Member States of the Community, although there are to some extent significant differences, in particular with regard to the length of usage necessary before a practice is recognised as custom. The function which customary law[81] plays in the different legal orders also appears to vary.

According to continental legal thought, rules of customary law serve primarily to reflect in the legal order itself changes in the meaning of law which occur at first incrementally and unnoticed.[82] The formation of customary law is a lengthy process. The newly developed belief that some matter constitutes law is finally secured through relevant court decisions and is thus documented for the outside world.[82a]

Customary law does not have such a role to play in the English legal system. In spite of the notion of binding judicial precedent in the common law and the rule of *stare decisis*, adaptation to changing conceptions of law is possible using the process of "distinguishing" or by limiting the *ratio*, thus diminishing the precedent effect of the earlier decision with regard to the present case. In the common law system the court can, within limits, thus take account of the changed conception of law and, by recognising the new conception as a "rule," make it part of binding law.[83] Customary law itself has in the English legal system, as Blackstone's definition has already indicated, a more strongly conservative character than on the continent.[84]

These differences in approach make it clear that the formation of customary law, although essentially similar as regards certain substantive conditions, also depends on the function accorded to customary law within each legal order. Having regard in particular to this latter point of view, it is possible to understand the demand that, given the special characteristics of the European Community, there should be no exaggerated requirements placed on the formation of customary law in this context and that here in particular a short period of time should suffice before a practice can be recognised as custom.[85] In this context a comparison with public international law might be useful, where, under the

---

[81] *cf.* on this aspect A. Bleckmann, "Zur Funktion des Gewohnheitsrechts im Europäischen Gemeinschaftsrecht," EuR 1981, pp. 101 *et seq.*
[82] H. Lecheler, *Der Europäische Gerichtshof und die allgemeinen Rechtsgrundsätze*, Berlin 1971, p. 175 with further references.
[82a] E. Forsthoff, *Lehrbuch des Verwaltungsrechts* (10th ed., Munich 1973), Vol. I, pp. 146 *et seq.*
[83] R. David, *op. cit.*, footnote 74, pp. 373 *et seq.*
[84] R. David, *ibid.*
[85] H. P. Ipsen, *op. cit.*, footnote 75, §5/25, p. 115.

keyword "instant customary law," a practice will begin to take root in response to the need for a greater capacity for change.[86]

Apart from these details it is recognised in principle that given the general conditions already cited, customary law may also arise in the European Community legal system.[87] It is however debatable whether a body of rules of customary law has already been formed. It appears that the Court of Justice has not yet referred to customary law. In the case of *Watson and Belman*, Advocate-General Trabucchi affirmed the possibility that "the Community system can evolve of its own accord" in a case where the Community institutions and the Member States have recognised particular principles since the time when the Treaty was first applied.[88] However, the Court of Justice did not find it necessary in its decision to consider expressly Trabucchi's question whether it is "possible to conclude that, in this way, there has been established in the Community legal order a rule of custom and practice on the basis of which tourists can assert a right to claim the same treatment as the States are bound to give to persons providing services."[89]

In academic literature, the existence of legal rules which have the character of customary law is affirmed by some in the area of administra-

---

[86] *cf.* International Court of Justice, ICJ Rep. 1969, 3 (43) (*North Sea Continental Shelf Case*): "Although the passage of only a short period of time is not necessarily, or of itself, a bar to the formation of a new rule of customary international law on the basis of what was originally a purely conventional rule, an indispensable requirement would be that within the period in question, short though it might be, State practice, including that of States whose interests are specially affected, should have been both extensive and virtually uniform in the sense of the provision invoked;—and should moreover have occurred in such a way as to show a general recognition that a rule of law of legal obligation is involved." *cf.* also E. Menzel & K. Ipsen, *Völkerrecht* (2nd ed., Munich 1979), pp. 79 *et seq.*; D. W. Greig, *International Law* (2nd ed., London 1976), pp. 19 *et seq.* with further references; I. Brownlie, *Principles of Public International Law* (3rd ed., Oxford 1979), pp. 6, 9.

[87] *cf.* H. P. Ipsen, *op. cit.*, footnote 65, p. 115, who cites examples from the inter-institutional context; P. Pescatore, *L'ordre juridique des Communautés européennes*, Liège 1975, p. 74. The most detailed treatment of this theme is to be found in A. Bleckmann, "Zur Funktion des Gewohnheitsrechts im Europäischen Gemeinschaftsrecht," EuR 1981, pp. 101 *et seq.*

[88] Case 118/75 *Watson & Belmann* [1976] E.C.R. 1185 at 1204. *cf.* also Advocate-General Slynn, who expressed doubts in his conclusions in Case 44/84 *Hurd* v. *Jones* [1986] E.C.R. 29 at 39 whether "the concept of a non-binding instrument acquiring binding force with the passage of time through the customs and practices of the Member States forms part of the Community law." The case gave no further clarification of the controversy concerning the question of the incorporation of customary international law into Community law. On this question see J. Schwarze, "Das allgemeine Völkerrecht in den innergemeinschaftlichen Rechtsbeziehungen," EuR 1983, pp. 1 *et seq.* at pp. 3 *et seq.*, which rejects incorporation.

[89] Case 118/75 *Watson & Belmann* [1976] E.C.R. 1185 at 1205.

tive law. Thus E.-W. Fuss cites the general principles of equality and proportionality as examples of this.[90] However, a blanket qualification of legal principles in general as customary law stands in contradiction above all to the creative role which the Court of Justice plays in the evolution and detailed development of these principles and which tends to indicate that the general doctrine of legal sources applying to national legal orders cannot simply be adopted without modification in Community law.[91]

C. JUDGE-MADE LAW AND GENERAL LEGAL PRINCIPLES

I. JUDGE-MADE LAW

Given the sketchy nature of written law and the absence of customary law, case law in the Community as in national legal orders,[92] has a particular significance precisely in the area of administrative law.

The constitutive treaties accorded a powerful position to the Court of Justice of the European Communities. Article 4 EEC lists the Court as an institution with equal status beside the Council, Commission and Parliament. According to Article 164 EEC (Articles 136 Euratom, 31 ECSC) it is the task of the Court to ensure that in the interpretation and application of the Treaties, the law is observed. The various legal actions are laid down in the Treaties themselves.[93]

---

[90] E.-W. Fuss, "Rechtsstaatliche Bilanz der Europäischen Gemeinschaften," in *Festschrift für Günther Küchenhoff*, Berlin 1972, pp. 781, 794; adopting the same view see H.-W. Daig, in v.d. Groeben *et al.*, *op. cit.*, footnote 41, Art. 164, para. 33; K. Zweigert speaks of a customary law in the process of development in "Das Grosse Werk Ipsens über Europäisches Gemeinschaftsrecht," EuR 1972, pp. 308 *et seq.* at p. 317.

[91] See thus also G. Zieger, "Die Rechtsprechung des Europäischen Gerichtshofs, eine Untersuchung der Allgemeinen Rechtsgrundsätze," JöR Vol. 22, NF 1973, pp. 299 *et seq.* at p. 348.

[92] *cf.* for instance P. Pescatore, *Introduction à la science du droit*, Luxembourg 1960, p. 115, on the significance of the French Conseil d'Etat for the development of administrative law. See also the references in Chapter 2 (national reports).

[93] In the following only a limited number of important legal actions under the EEC Treaty are dealt with. On the other actions see in detail in particular G. Bebr, *Development of Judicial Control of the European Communities*, The Hague 1981; L. Neville Brown & F. G. Jacobs, *The Court of Justice of the European Communities*, London 1977; H.-W. Daig, in v.d. Groeben, *et al.*, *op. cit.*, footnote 41 on Articles 164 *et seq.*; *ibid. Nichtigkeits- und Untätigkeitsklagen im Recht der Europäischen Gemeinschaften*, Baden-Baden 1985; U. Everling, *Das Vorabentscheidungsverfahren vor dem Gerichtshof der EG*, Baden-Baden 1986; R. Joliet, *Le droit institutionnel des Communautés européennes: le contentieux*, Liège 1981; B. Chr. Ortlepp, *Das Vertragsverletzungsverfahren als Instrument zur Sicherung der Legalität im Europäischen Gemeinschaftsrecht*, Baden-Baden 1987; H. G. Schermers, *Judicial Protection in the European Communities* (3rd ed.,

The administrative jurisdiction of the Court covers actions by private individuals (or servants of the Community) against an institution of the Community.[94]

The action for annulment allows private individuals to challenge decisions of the Council and the Commission which are addressed to them, or decisions which although in the form of a regulation or a decision addressed to another person are of direct and individual concern to them (Article 173(2) EEC). Related to the action for annulment is the action against measures imposing penalties (Article 172 EEC). According to Article 17 of Regulation 17 of the Council, the Court has unlimited jurisdiction to review fines or periodic penalty payments imposed by the Commission in competition proceedings.

Whereas actions for annulment are brought quite frequently, actions under Article 175(3) EEC for failure to act are rather seldom brought by private parties against the Community institutions.

Under Article 178 in conjunction with Article 215(2) EEC the Court has jurisdiction to decide on the non-contractual liability of the Community as an official body. In the realm of non-contractual liability the Community must make good any loss caused by its institutions or servants in the exercise of their official functions according to general principles common to the laws of the Member States.

Finally, mention should be made of the actions by servants of the Community against their appointing institution covered by Article 179 EEC and Articles 90 and 91 of the Staff Regulations.

The decisions of the Court of Justice which concern administrative law are not limited to those dealing with the actions of private individuals against the Community institutions which belong within the administrative jurisdiction in the narrower sense. Equally important are the statements concerning administrative law which the Court makes in the course of preliminary rulings under Article 177 EEC and in actions between Community institutions and Member States, or amongst the Community institutions themselves, which properly belong to the constitutional jurisdiction of the Court. A sharp distinction between these two main functions of the Court as a constitutional court and as a court for the protection of individual interests[95] seems, in the light of the close connec-

---

Deventer 1983); G. Vandersanden & A. Barav, *Contentieux communautaire*, Brussels 1977.

[94] *cf.* H. Kutscher, "Der Gerichtshof der Europäischen Gemeinschaften," EuGRZ 1978, pp. 503 *et seq.* at p. 504.

[95] See in more detail the contributions in *Der Europäische Gerichtshof als Verfassungsgericht und Rechtsschutzinstanz*, (ed. J. Schwarze), Baden-Baden 1983. On the role of the

tion between the substance of constitutional and administrative law, also to make little sense.

Just like the other Community institutions (Article 4(1) EEC), the Court may act only within the limits of the powers conferred upon it by the Treaties. Article 164 EEC, according to which the Court is to ensure that the law is observed in the interpretation and application of the Treaty, does not contain a general clause which would make it possible for the Court to bypass the jurisdictional conditions attached to each type of action.[96] Thus in the case of Scarlata the plaintiffs' contention that a narrow construction of Article 173 EEC would deprive them of the full protection of the law, in contradiction to the fundamental legal principles prevailing in all Member States, was rejected by reference to the narrow wording of Article 173 EEC.[96a] In a further case,[96b] what was at issue was the admissibility of actions by a number of Luxembourg municipalities which sought the annulment of a decision of the Commission on subsidies granted by the Luxembourg government to the steel industry and based on both the EEC and ECSC Treaties. The municipalities feared that the closure of the factories situated in their areas would lead to a reduction of the municipal tax revenue.

With regard to the admissibility of their claims, the municipalities referred to an administrative law principle which applied in a number of the Member States whereby the interests of the inhabitants resident in the municipalities and of the undertakings established in those areas were to be regarded as the interests of the municipalities themselves. This principle, it was claimed, also applied in Community law.[96c] Without going into this principle in more detail, the Court of Justice rejected the claims as inadmissible, since the municipalities did not belong to the group of legal subjects referred to in Article 33 ECSC as being entitled to bring an action for a declaration that a measure is void, and because the decision addressed to the Grand-Duchy of Luxembourg was not of direct and individual concern to the municipalities as laid down in Article 173(2) EEC. The appeal to general principles of law cannot therefore of itself make it possible to bypass the limitations on the jurisdiction of the Court and on the possible actions which are provided for in the relevant provisions of the Treaties.

Court in European integration see recently H. Rasmussen, *On law and policy in the European Court of Justice*, Dordrecht 1986.
[96] *cf.* H. Kutscher, *op. cit.*, footnote 94, p. 504.
[96a] Case 40/64 *Scarlata et al.* v. *Commission* [1965] E.C.R. 295 at 312.
[96b] Case 222/83 *The Municipality of Differdange et al.* v. *Commission* [1984] E.C.R. 2889.
[96c] *Ibid.* at pp. 2893 and 2895.

On the other hand the Court of Justice recently referred back on a number of occasions to Article 164 EEC and interpreted the conditions of admissibility for the action for annulment in the light of this provision. In the Case of *Luxembourg* v. *European Parliament* (1st judgment) it raised, obiter, the question whether "the principles appertaining to observance of the law and review in that respect by the Court as embodied in Article 164 EEC Treaty and Article 136 Euratom Treaty required that Article 173 EEC Treaty and Article 146 Euratom Treaty be interpreted as meaning that the Parliament may be a party to proceedings before the Court."[97]

In the dispute between the Parti écologiste "Les Verts" and the European Parliament, in which the question of the Parliament being a party to proceedings for annulment under Article 173 EEC before the Court was at issue, the court recently stated that it would contradict the spirit of the Treaty as it finds expression in Article 164 EEC as well as its system, if sovereign measures taken by a Community institution were not subject to judicial control.[98] For: "it must be emphasized that the European Economic Community is a community based on law inasmuch as both the Member States and the institutions are subject to judicial review of the conformity of measures adopted by them with the basic constitutional charter represented by the Treaty."[99]

In a further case,[100] the Court established with regard to the protection of the individual against acts of State power in breach of Community law, that the requirement of an effective judicial control is the expression of a general legal principle which lies at the heart of the constitutional traditions of the Member States and is also set out in Articles 6 and 13 of the European Convention on Human Rights.[101]

The Court of Justice has so far realised its function of ensuring the protection of the law in an exemplary fashion. European administrative law is remarkable for the decisive contribution of case law to its development. The scope and limits of the task of the European Court in creating the law are determined by the particular character of the Community legal order. The fragmented nature of Community law and the insuffi-

---

[97] Case 230/81 *Luxembourg* v. *European Parliament* [1983] E.C.R. 255 at 283.
[98] Case 294/83 *Parti écologiste "Les Verts"* v. *European Parliament* [1986] E.C.R. 1339 at 1365. *cf.* also Case 34/86 *Council* v. *Parliament* [1986] E.C.R. 2155, paras. 5, 12 and 13 (action by the Council against the adoption of the budget by the President of the European Parliament).
[99] Case 294/83 *Parti écologiste "Les Verts"* v. *European Parliament supra* at 1365 (para. 23).
[100] Case 222/84 *Johnston* v. *RUC* [1986] E.C.R. 1651.
[101] *Ibid.* at 1682, paras. 17 and 18.

ciency of written norms caused by the decisional weaknesses of the Council stand in contrast to the claim to autonomy of Community law, which makes it impossible to fall back directly on national or international law. It follows from the relationship of tension between these two competing demands that the Court of Justice should acquire the authority to abstract from the particular in the sense of developing a quasi-normative function.[102] Only thus could the functional capacity of the Community and the developmental capacity of its new autonomous legal order be maintained. The particular structural conditions of the Community legal order have thus meant that the degree of judicial law-making, in comparison both with the traditions of international law and with those of national constitutional law, is striking.[103]

Although the quasi-normative decisions of the Court of Justice are here described as judge-made law, that is not intended to mean that they have the effect as such of binding "precedents" in the Common law sense.[104] In particular, the effect of preliminary rulings of the Court under Article 177 EEC is both problematic and as yet unsettled.[105] The view previously held by most commentators was that they could not have an effect erga omnes, but this has now been abandoned in favour of a more nuanced approach.[105a] Thus decisions on the validity of Community law in preliminary rulings have in practice an effect erga omnes. Of course national courts are quite free to make a further reference, which would seem to indicate that a decision is binding only on the particular case at issue. But in instances where the Court has declared a provision of Community law to be invalid, it is hardly likely—in particular for reasons of legal certainty—to come to the conclusion in a further reference that

---

[102] For details see J. Schwarze, *Die Befugnis zur Abstraktion im europäischen Gemeinschaftsrecht*, Baden-Baden 1976, pp. 182 *et seq.*

[103] So also A. Bleckmann, "Die Rolle der richterlichen Rechtsschöpfung im Europäischen Gemeinschaftsrecht," in *Gedächtnisschrift L.-J. Constantinesco* (eds. G. Lüke *et al.*), *Rechtsvergleichung, Europarecht und Staatenintegration*, Cologne 1983, pp. 61, 73.

[104] Lord Mackenzie Stuart & J.-P. Warner go further in "Judicial Decision as a source of Community Law," in *Festschrift Hans Kutscher* (eds. W. G. Grewe, H. H. Rupp & H. Schneider), *Europäische Gerichtsbarkeit und nationale Verfassungsgerichtsbarkeit*, Baden-Baden 1981, pp. 273, 281; *cf.* also T. Koopmans, "Stare decisis in European Law," in *Essays in European Law and Integration. To mark the silver jubilee of the Europa Institute, Leiden 1957–1982*, (eds. D. O'Keeffe & H. G. Schermers), Deventer 1982, pp. 11 *et seq.*

[105] For more detail see J. Schwarze, *op. cit.*, footnote 102, p. 125 with references to the different viewpoints.

[105a] To that extent I no longer adhere to the view put forward in *Die Befugnis zur Abstraktion*, at pp. 124 *et seq.*

the measure is in fact valid.[105b] The position is rather different where the Court has established that a measure is valid. Here the European Court frequently uses the formula that the "consideration of the question submitted has disclosed no factor of such a kind as to affect the validity of the . . . Regulations." It would seem as if other or new arguments could perhaps do so. In practice this possibility should be regarded as rather insignificant, because the Court will have examined the validity of the norm from all possible points of view before making its decision. So even in this instance it is not to be expected that the Court of Justice will depart in future from its previous ruling.[105c]

Decisions on the interpretation of Community law given in the context of a preliminary ruling are, in comparison with those concerning validity, much more closely linked to the individual case. They take into account in particular the background to the preliminary reference. These decisions have no generally binding legal effect, but fulfill a sort of guiding function. A further reference from national courts will not lead to a different decision so long as the underlying facts are essentially identical and no alterations in the economic and social circumstances have occurred which would justify such a departure. So long as this is not the case, decisions which depart from the original ruling of the Court should not be allowed to stand[105d] when higher courts are considering the fulfilment of their duty to refer.[105e]

The concept of the "presumptive binding force of preliminary rulings"[106] put forward by M. Kriele with regard to German law accurately describes also the binding effect of the decisions of the European Court of Justice.

II. GENERAL PRINCIPLES OF LAW

In the case law of the European Court general principles of administra-

---

[105b] U. Everling, *Das Vorabentscheidungsverfahren vor dem Gerichtshof der Europäischen Gemeinschaften*, Baden-Baden 1986, pp. 63 *et seq.*; G. Bebr, "Preliminary Rulings to the Court of Justice: Their Authority and Temporal Effect," (1981) C.M.L.Rev. 475 at pp. 476 *et seq.*

[105c] U. Everling, *op. cit.*, p. 65; *cf.* also G. Bebr, *op. cit.* pp. 483 *et seq.*

[105d] U. Everling, *ibid.*

[105e] H. Rassmussen, *On Law and Policy in the European Court of Justice*, Dordrecht 1986, p. 244.

[106] M. Kriele, *Theorie der Rechtsgewinnung—entwickelt am Problem der Verfassungsinterpretation*, Schriften zum öffentlichen Recht, Vol. 41 (2nd ed., Berlin 1976), pp. 243 *et seq.*

tive law occupy a particularly important position. The concept of general principles of law is unsettled. A great variety of terminology is used both in the literature and in the case law of the Court. In part the differences relate simply to the choice of words,[106a] as when the Court of Justice and the Advocates-General refer to a generally accepted rule,[107] to a generally accepted principle,[108] to a basic principle of law,[109] to a fundamental principle,[110] to a general principle,[111] to a principle[112] or to the general principle of equality, which is one of the fundamental principles of Community law.[113]

In literature, however, contradictory views on the basis and status of the general principles of law do appear in the various analyses.[114] These conceptual differences could clearly be relevant to the application of the general principles of law.[115]

There is at least agreement that the general principles are of great importance in the case law of the Court of Justice for filling gaps and as aids to interpretation. This is a result, not least, of the fact that the European Community is a legal order in the process of development which, given its sensitivity to the progress of integration, necessarily contains gaps and requires extensive interpretation. In recognition of this, the Court of Justice has avoided undertaking a precise classification of the general principles of law in order to retain the flexibility which it needs so as to be able to decide the substantive questions which come before it irrespective of terminological differences.

[106a] The origin of the terminological differences could lie in the problems of translating decisions given in another language.

[107] Case 8/55 *Fédération Charbonnière de Belgique* v. *High Authority* [1955] E.C.R. 292 at 299.

[108] Case 13/57 *Wirtschaftsvereinigung Eisen- und Stahlindustrie* v. *High Authority* [1958] E.C.R. 265 *et seq.* at 280.

[109] Joined Cases 42 & 49/59 *SNUPAT* v. *High Authority* [1961] E.C.R. 53 at 84.

[110] Case 85/76 *Hoffmann-La Roche* v. *Commission* [1979] E.C.R. 461 at 511.

[111] Joined Cases 43, 45 & 48/59 *Lachmüller et al.* v. *Commission* [1960] E.C.R. 463 at 472.

[112] Case 14/61 *Hoogovens* v. *High Authority* [1962] E.C.R. 253 at 275.

[113] Joined Cases 117/76 & 16/77 *Ruckdeschel* v. *HZA Hamburg-St. Annen* [1977] E.C.R. 1753 at 1769.

[114] *cf.* for example B. J. Boulois, *Droit institutionnel des Communautés européennes*, pp. 153 *et seq.*, who distinguishes between "principes inhérents à tout système de droit organisé," "principes généraux communs aux droits des Etats membres" and "principes déduits de la nature des Communautés"; H. G. Schermers, "Algemene rechtsbeginselen als bron van gemeenschapsrecht," SEW 1983, p. 514 at 515, *et seq.* ("Beginselen van regelend recht" and "Beginselen van dwingend recht"); H.-W. Rengeling *op. cit.*, footnote 41, at p. 172 ("Allgemeine Rechtsgrundsätze," "Besondere Rechtsgrundsätze" und "Allgemeine Verwaltungsrechtsgrundsätze").

[115] *cf.* H.-W. Daig, in v.d. Groeben *et al.*, *op. cit.*, footnote 41, Article 164, para. 16.

Where Community law is subject to indirect enforcement, the statement of the Court that national authorities when implementing Community regulations act in accordance with their own national law "in so far as Community law, including its general principles, does not include common rules to this effect"[116] deserves particular attention.

Does it follow implicitly from this statement that the Community possesses the competence to pass regulations governing the implementation of Community law by national authorities? In the same judgment it held that "if disparities in the legislation of the Member States proved to be such as to compromise the equal treatment of producers and traders in different Member States or to distort or impair the functioning of the common market, it would be for the competent Community institutions to adopt the provisions needed to remedy such disparities."[117] Is this statement to be understood as meaning that the Court of Justice sees the outer limit of the control of the legality of national administrative action using the general principles of law developed by the Court itself as having been reached? These questions and distinctions will be considered not in this introduction but in the course of the analysis of the case law on the individual administrative law principles.

The issues here primarily concern the authenticity, status and methods for determining the substance of the general principles of law considered as a matter of principle.

1. Authenticity

The question of the authenticity of the general principles of law has been most widely discussed in the German literature on European law. Matters of controversy have included in particular whether the principles of law possess a direct authenticity as independent sources of Community law, or whether they can lay claim to only a subordinate authenticity in so far as they are recognised by written law, customary law or judge-made law.[118] As a result of these discussions there is now widespread agreement that the principles of law, irrespective of their authenticity as original or

---

[116] Joined Cases 205–215/82 *Deutsche Milchkontor GmbH et al.* v. *Bundesrepublik Deutschland* [1983] E.C.R. 2633 at 2665.

[117] *Ibid.* at 2667.

[118] *cf.* in more detail H.-W. Rengeling, *op. cit.*, footnote 41, pp. 205 *et seq.*; K. M. Meessen, "Zur Theorie allgemeiner Rechtsgrundsätze des internationalen Rechts: Der Nachweis allgemeiner Rechtsgrundsätze des Europäischen Gemeinschaftsrechts," in JIR, Vol. 27 (1974), pp. 283 *et seq.* at pp. 287 *et seq.*; G. Hoffmann-Becking, *Normaufbau und Methode—Eine Untersuchung zur Rechtsprechung des Gerichtshofs der Europäischen*

derivative sources of law, are to be applied by the Community institutions and that the Court of Justice may condemn a breach of these principles just like a breach of any written norm.

To that extent it is not surprising that the Court of Justice has made no clear pronouncements on the rather theoretical question of authenticity. On the one hand it frequently refers when dealing with the principles of law to its task laid down in Article 164 EEC to ensure that the law is observed.[119] That could be understood as meaning that the principles of law are to be regarded as part of the already existing law and are thus to be observed. On the other hand, it is also possible to find in its judgments statements which refer to its law-creating role. Thus in the case of *Algera*, having held that a gap in the law existed, the Court regarded itself as being under a duty "to solve the problem" in order to avoid the reproach of a denial of justice.[120]

As will be shown below in more detail, the Court of Justice has offered no specific Community or national law basis for such paramount principles as good faith, legal certainty or proportionality. On the contrary, it has simply assumed their authenticity or has established their special characteristic as principles of Community law with the most brief of formulas.

On the other hand, the law-making task of the Court of Justice, which should not be underestimated, involves shaping these principles by applying them to actual cases. Yet this is not simply a matter for the Court alone.[121] In addition, through continuing practices, the administrative authorities can lend actual substance to the principles of law by making them legally effective above and beyond the individual case, since the principle that the administration may bind itself applies in European law also.[122] The binding force of such practices is of course less than that of decisions of the Court of Justice, since any articulation of a principle undertaken by the administration is subject to subsequent review by the

---

Gemeinschaften, Tübingen 1973, pp. 349 *et seq.*; H. J. Lecheler, *Der Europäische Gerichtshof und die allgemeinen Rechtsgrundsätze*, Berlin 1971, pp. 181 *et seq.*; G. Zieger, "Die Rechtsprechung des Europäischen Gerichtshofs—Eine Untersuchung der allgemeinen Rechtsgrundsätze," JöR, N.F., Vol. 22 (1973), pp. 299 *et seq.* at p. 352; J. Schwarze, *op. cit.*, footnote 102, pp. 223 *et seq.*

[119] *cf.* for example Case 29/69 *Stauder* v. *Stadt Ulm* [1969] E.C.R. 419 at 425.

[120] Joined Cases 7/56 & 3–7/57 *Algera* v. *Common Assembly* [1957] E.C.R. 39 at 76.

[121] H.-W. Rengeling, *op. cit.*, footnote 41, p. 204; G. Zieger, *op. cit.*, footnote 118, JöR, N.F. (1973), pp. 299 *et seq.* at p. 352.

[122] Case 148/73 *Louwage* v. *Commission* [1974] E.C.R. 81 at 89; see on this J. Schwarze, *op. cit.*, footnote 102 at p. 70; *cf.* also Case 25/83 *Buick* v. *Commission* [1984] E.C.R. 1773 and 1783.

Court and the administration may depart from an existing practice if special circumstances apply.[122a] Above all, however, it is for the Community legislators to facilitate the positive application of general principles of law. If, for instance, the legislature were to decide to develop general rules for the revocation and retrospective adoption of administrative acts in the course of the implementation of Community policies, then just like the court it would be bound to undertake an evaluation of the respective weight of the principle of administration according to law on the one hand, and of the protection of legitimate expectations on the other.[123] In so far as the legislature has not acted, however, it is a matter for the Court of Justice, in order to avoid a denial of justice,[124] to ensure that substance is given to these principles. The Court's solutions are of course provisional. The legislature could later adopt a different solution in order to close the gap in the law, thus departing from the concept developed by the Court of Justice. So long as the legislature has taken no decision, the rule put forward by the Court will continue to operate, until such time as the Court itself replaces or amends it.[125]

2. Status

In the Community there exists a very complex and hierarchical edifice of norms and types of activity; the question arises with regard to each of these how the general principles of law are to operate as standards of lawfulness against which they are to be judged.

The edifice is topped by primary law, which is today widely regarded as being of a constitutional nature.[126]

[122a] Case 148/73 *Louwage* v. *Commission* [1974] E.C.R. 81 at 89 and Case 25/83 *Buick* v. *Commission* [1984] E.C.R. 1773 at 1783.

[123] On this requirement see Joined Cases 42 & 49/59 *SNUPAT* v. *High Authority* [1961] E.C.R. 53 at 87.

[124] Joined Cases 7/56 & 3–7/57 *Algera et al.* v. *Common Assembly* [1957] E.C.R. 39 at 55.

[125] J. Schwarze, *op. cit.*, footnote 102, p. 110.

[126] *cf.* on this in detail J. Schwarze, in *Eine Verfassung für Europa* (eds. J. Schwarze & R. Bieber), Baden-Baden 1984, p. 15 at pp. 23 *et seq.*; H. P. Ipsen, *op. cit.*, footnote 65, 2/33 *et seq.*, pp. 64 *et seq.*; *ibid.* "Zur Tragfähigkeit der Verfassungsprinzipien der Europäischen Gemeinschaft," in *Integrationskonzepte auf dem Prüfstand*, Baden-Baden 1983, pp. 9 *et seq.*, p. 12; see further R. Bernhardt, in *Thirty Years of Community Law* (ed. Commission of the E.C.), Luxembourg 1983, pp. 77 *et seq.*; J. V. Louis, *The Community Legal Order*, Brussels 1980, pp. 45 *et seq.*; Lord Mackenzie Stuart, *The European Communities and the Rule of Law, The Hamlyn Lectures, 29th Series*, London 1977, pp. 30, 63; H. Matthies, "Die Verfassung des Gemeinsamen Marktes," in *Gedächtnisschrift für Christoph Sasse*, Vol. 1, Baden-Baden 1981, pp. 115 *et seq.*; *Europäische*

Below this are Council regulations, which the Council has adopted directly on the basis of primary law. Furthermore, the Commission has also acquired powers in certain circumstances to adopt normative rules with general application.[127] In this context there are on the one hand provisions which authorise the Commission to act on its own initiative; other authorisations to act incorporate limitations, in particular those which are subject to so-called administrative or regulatory committee proceedings.[128] Finally, the Commission may also adopt administrative acts in the form of individual decisions.

On the other hand, the general principles of law reveal a variety of structures. There are, first, those of which it can be said that they are rules which are patently reasonable and which flow from the very principle of justice. Other principles of law are very specific. These might include deductions from general norms which may in certain circumstances be in conflict, which are applicable only within a narrow and circumscribed sphere. Between these two extremes there are numerous mixed forms. At this point it is sufficient to make a small number of general observations on the relationship of these two groups of norms to each other.

Some general principles of law are, as a matter of principle, of only subordinate application,[129] which means that they are intended in particular to fill gaps in the law which, as has been shown, represent a typical and desired facet of the Community legal order. It is clear that a more or less arbitrary appeal to general principles of law cannot override or repeal a legal provision put in place for precisely the matter in question, which is

---

Gemeinschaft. Verfassung nach drei Jahrzehnten (eds. G. Nicolaysen & H.-J. Rabe), Baden-Baden 1982; E. Stein, "Lawyers, Judges and the Making of a transnational Constitution," (1981) Vol. 75 AJIL pp. 1 *et seq.*, at pp. 3, 26. *cf.* also the opinions of E. Stein, G. Casper, J. W. Bridge and P. VerLoren van Themaat on the theme: "The Emerging European Constitution" in American Society of International Law, Proceedings of the 72nd Annual Meeting, Washington 1978, pp. 166 *et seq.* Walter Hallstein in his famous speech before the European Parliament on October 17, 1962 (see Bull. 11–1962, 5, *et seq.*) had already spoken of the "constitutional problems of the EEC."

[127] It is clear from the case law (*cf.* Joined Cases 188–190/80 *French Republic et al.* v. *Commission* (transparency directive) [1982] E.C.R. 2545) that it is not the Council alone which has an autonomous power to legislate, with the Commission simply possessing supervisory and implementing authority. Specific provisions of the Treaty, such as Article 90 EEC, may also grant the Commission the power to legislate.

[128] See on this H. Schmitt von Sydow, in v.d. Groeben *et al.*, *op. cit.*, footnote 41, Article 155, paras. 48 *et seq.*

[129] H.-W. Rengeling *op. cit.*, footnote 41, p. 214; P. Aubin, *Die Haftung der Europäischen Wirtschaftsgemeinschaft und ihrer Mitgliedstaaten bei gemeinschaftsrechtswidrigen nationalen Verwaltungsakten*, Baden-Baden 1982, p. 58; J. Schwarze, *op. cit.*, footnote 102, p. 224.

not itself the subject of challenge on legal grounds. This can be illustrated by the following decision of the European Court.

This case concerned a request for a preliminary ruling involving the question whether an undertaking, which had for a considerable period of time been buying up, processing and reselling quantities of butter within the framework of the intervention system for butter, could claim the return of certain processing securities, even though it had not fulfilled the relevant conditions.[130] The undertaking based its case on the fact that it had acted in reliance on the correctness of certain official checks undertaken in the case of earlier transactions, which had only later turned out to be insufficient. The Court held that according to the text of the Regulation aimed at the disposal of surplus butter each transaction was to be considered separately. The fact that some transactions had proceeded normally could not therefore be a legitimate ground for expecting subsequent transactions to proceed normally. The obligation to provide a processing security for each quantity of butter awarded would in practice become completely meaningless if a plea invoking general principles of law and based on the fact that the competent authorities had, rightly or wrongly, issued the required documents in some transactions were to be sufficient to obtain the release of other securities even where the requisite proof had not been furnished.[131]

On the other hand this does not mean that written norms are not to be judged against the standards set by general principles of law. On the contrary, in many cases the Court of Justice has examined whether specific normative acts of the Commission or the Council are compatible with principles of law to which it attributes "constitutional status."[132]

It is therefore very difficult to develop any rules of general application which go beyond these basic observations. The decisive factors here are the structure and meaning of each individual principle of law, which will be examined in detail below. They determine the relationship of each principle to written rules of Community law within the framework of the hierarchy of norms under the Community legal order. Nonetheless it is conceivable that, as it is in German public law, a specific general principle

---

[130] cf. Case 20/84 N.V. De Jong Verenigde and Coöperatieve "Domo-Bedum" GA v. Voedselvoorzienings In—en Verkoopbureau (V.I.B.) [1985] E.C.R. 2106.

[131] Ibid. at p. 2112, para. 19.

[132] cf. on the development of the case law in which the general principles of law have been used first to scrutinise individual acts of the Commission and later increasingly as "constitutional law principles" in order to scrutinise normative acts of the administration, H. Kutscher, "Der Schutz von Grundrechten im Recht der Europäischen Gemeinschaften," in Der Grundrechtsschutz im Europäischen Gemeinschaftsrecht (eds. H. Kutscher, K. Rogge and F. Matscher), p. 35 at p. 40.

of law, with a different substantive scope and a different level of precision, may have both constitutional status and status as a principle of administrative law.[132a]

A further controversial question in this context, which will be answered below in the individual analyses, asks whether and to what extent Community law principles may also constitute the standard against which administrative action in the Member States is to be measured.

3. Methods for Determining the Content of General Principles

The view was earlier put forward by some that general principles of law apply in Community law only if they have valid status as law or a legal institution in each of the participating legal orders in the same way.[133] This conception comes down to a minimalist solution, for in this way the measure of Community law in this area is reduced to the smallest common denominator. A further disadvantage of this theory is that an alteration of the law of one Member State must have an automatic consequence for Community law. It is difficult to square this conclusion with the position which has since acquired general support that the Community legal order is an autonomous legal order,[134] which is in principle independent of the legal orders of the Member States.

In addition to the minimalist solution, there is also a so-called maximalist theory.[135] According to this, Community law should incorporate the provisions of the Member State which offers the most extensive protection of the individual. Such a theory makes an impartial search for the "best" solution for the Community impossible, irrespective of the question, itself difficult to answer, as to which national law, taking into

---

[132a] On the varying status and degree of concretisation of principles relating to the application of the rule of law in German public law see only K. Hesse, *Grundzüge des Verfassungsrechts der Bundesrepublik Deutschland* (15th ed., Heidelberg 1985), para. 185.

[133] A. Heldrich, "Art. 215 Abs. 2 des Vertrages über die Europäische Wirtschaftsgemeinschaft—Ein Irrweg zu europäischer Rechtseinheit," JZ 1960, p. 681. Heldrich abandoned this position in his note on the judgment in Joined Cases 5, 7 & 13–24/66 *Kampffmeyer et al.* v. *Commission*, EuR 1967, pp. 337 *et seq.* at p. 349; [1967] E.C.R. 245. *cf.* on this also G. Zieger, *op. cit.*, footnote 118, pp. 299 *et seq.*, at p. 345, footnote 332.

[134] *cf.* H. P. Ipsen, "Über Supranationalität," in *Festschrift für Ulrich Scheuner*, Berlin 1973, p. 211, at p. 220; L.-J. Constantinesco, *Das Recht der Europäischen Gemeinschaften I*, Baden-Baden 1977, paras. 468 *et seq.*; B. Beutler, in Beutler *et al.*, *op. cit.*, footnote 5 at p. 88.

[135] *cf.* H. Schwaiger, "Mitgliedstaatliche Verfassungsmässigkeit und sekundäres Gemeinschaftsrecht," AWD/RIW 1972, pp. 265 *et seq.* at p. 271.

account the special characteristics and functional requirements of the Community, in fact does have the most "progressive" solution to the problems of protecting individual rights. Because of these disadvantages, both extreme positions are rarely put forward in practice. Today, essentially two different points of view are supported.

On the one hand, it is suggested that general principles of law are to be recognised where in a particular legal question there is a consensus in the solutions adopted in the various national legal orders, regardless of the legal construction applied in order to achieve this consensus.[136] More problematic and in dispute even among those who represent this view is the question as to the extent of common ground among the national legal orders which is required. It is suggested by some that the relevant principle of Community law must be present in all the national legal orders at least in its most general form.[137] Others believe that "a certain similarity" or "a certain degree of concurrence" will suffice.[138] On the other hand, it is very widely accepted that the correct approach to determining general principles of law involves an "evaluative comparison of laws."[139] That means that comparable legal rules or legal principles do not need to exist in all Member States. This approach also appears to be followed by the European Court in its decisions. For it has applied general principles of law in a variety of cases, even where the Advocate General was not able to find comparable rules in all Member States.[140]

Those who put forward this view suggest that for the purposes of determining the substance of the general principles of law, a weighted evaluation of the results of a comparative survey should primarily be adopted. According to this view, a general principle of law is not that "which appears in concurrent form in the majority of legal orders. A general principle of law is rather that which represents the best solution

---

[136] H. Lecheler, *Der Europäische Gerichtshof und die allgemeinen Rechtsgrundsätze*, Berlin 1971, p. 189 with further references; K. Feige, *Der Gleichheitssatz im Recht der EWG*, Tübingen 1973, p. 142; P. Pescatore, "Die Menschenrechte und die europäische Integration," Integration 1969, pp. 103, 125.

[137] H. Lecheler, *op. cit.*, footnote 136, at p. 189.

[138] K. Feige, *op. cit.*, footnote 136 at p. 142; P. Pescatore, *op. cit.*, footnote 136 at p. 125.

[139] H. P. Ipsen, *op. cit.*, footnote 65, 5/20 p. 113; K. Zweigert, "Der Einfluss des Europäischen Gemeinschaftsrechts auf die Rechtsordnung der Mitgliedstaaten," RabelsZ. Vol. 28, (1964), pp. 601 *et seq.* at p. 611; A. Heldrich, Note on the Judgment of the Court of Justice of July 14, 1967 in Joined Cases 5, 7 & 13–24/66 *Kampffmeyer et al.* v. *Commission*, *op. cit.*, footnote 133, pp. 337 *et seq.*, at p. 349; K. M. Meessen, *op. cit.*, footnote 118, pp. 281 *et seq.* at pp. 300 *et seq.*

[140] See in detail on this M. Akehurst, "The Application of General Principles of Law by the Court of Justice of the European Communities," BYIL 1981, pp. 29 *et seq.* at pp. 32–40 with references to the case law.

based on a critical analysis of the various solutions offered which results from a comparative survey."[141] That raises the question, of course, of what distinguishes the best solution.

The starting point should, in the view of the authors who are involved in this debate, be the consideration that Community law represents an autonomous legal order. Thus there is a presumption in favour of the coherence of the Community legal order. In consequence, the legal principle which is the "best" following a comparative analysis is the one which is most compatible with the legal order of Community law and which most closely corresponds to the functional capacity and the goals of the Community.[142]

This view is also put forward by the Court. It is particularly apparent in its decisions on fundamental rights. Thus in a number of cases the Court has stressed that while it is guided in the recognition of Community fundamental rights by the "constitutional traditions common to the Member States," these principles must be compatible with the "structure and objectives of the Community."[143]

The criterion requiring principles to be appropriate to the requirements of integration applies equally to the determination on a comparative basis of general principles of administrative law. The principal concern in this area is to reconcile the legal rights of individuals to protection with the requirements of an effective and efficient Community administration. The Court expressed these thoughts in the *IBM* decision on the rejection of a claim for the annulment of a decision instituting a competition procedure and the communication of the statement of objections, arguing that such a claim would be "incompatible with the system of the division of powers between the Commission and the Court and of the remedies laid down by the Treaty, as well as the requirement of the sound administration of justice and the proper course of the administrative procedure to be followed in the Community."[144]

---

[141] K. Zweigert, *op. cit.*, footnote 139, p. 611. *cf.* also J. Schwarze, *op. cit.*, footnote 102 at p. 222 with further references.

[142] K. Zweigert, *op. cit.*, footnote 139, p. 611; *cf.* also G. Zieger, *op. cit.*, footnote 118 at p. 346, footnote 345 with further references.

[143] Case 11/70 *Internationale Handelsgesellschaft mbH* v. *Einfuhr- und Vorratsstelle Getreide* [1970] E.C.R. 1125 at 1134. On the more recent case law of the Court in this field see J. Schwarze, "Schutz der Grundrechte in der Europäischen Gemeinschaft—Grundlagen und heutiger Entwicklungsstand" EuGRZ 1986, pp. 293 *et seq.*

[144] Case 60/81 *IBM* v. *Commission* [1981] E.C.R. 2639 at 2654.

In other contexts too, the Court also takes into account, in addition to the citizen's interest in the protection of the law, so-called "administrative reasons."[145] The following example will serve as an illustration of this. In the *Tradax* case,[146] the European Court was called upon to determine the scope of the Commission's duties to provide information and give reasons for its actions with regard to operation of the common organisations of the market in the agricultural field. The plaintiff contended that the Commission was obliged to provide the comprehensive information requested. Such a duty, it argued, flowed from the general principles of good administration and the legality of administrative action, from the guarantee of the protection of legal rights, legal certainty and the protection of legitimate expectations. The Commission and the Advocate General rejected this approach for lack of a legal basis. In particular Advocate-General Slynn referred to the fact that such a comprehensive duty to provide information would cause "administrative chaos" and in view of the otherwise adequate protection of the individual was not supportable.[147] The Court essentially followed these approaches and rejected the claim.

The evaluative comparative method, which has regard to the structure and objectives of the Community, plays a considerably greater role in the extrapolation of administrative law principles before the Court of Justice than would appear simply from the decisions of the Court themselves.[148] The Court of Justice may simply rely upon the conclusions of the Advocates General. Examples of the articulation of general principles of Community administrative law on the basis of comparative investigations can be found for instance in the conclusions of Advocate-General Lagrange on the concept of misuse of discretion,[149] of Advocate-General Warner on the extent to which an administrative body may bind itself in advance and on the principle of the right to be heard in administrative proceedings,[150] of Advocate-General Roemer on the principle of the

---

[145] *cf.* Case 39/84 *Maizena GmbH* v. *HZA Hamburg-Jonas* [1985] E.C.R. 2115 at 2130, para. 22 with respect to the deduction of the monetary compensatory amounts paid on the basic product for the purposes of calculating the monetary compensatory amounts on the secondary product.

[146] Case 64/82 *Tradax Graanhandel B.V.* v. *Commission* [1984] E.C.R. 1359 *et seq.*

[147] *Ibid.* at pp. 1385 *et seq.*

[148] *cf.* H. Kutscher, "Methods of interpretation as seen by a judge at the Court of Justice" in Court of Justice of the European Communities (ed.), Judicial and Academic Conference, Luxembourg 1976.

[149] [1954–55] E.C.R. 74 *et seq.*

[150] [1973] E.C.R. 592 *et seq.*

protection of legitimate expectations in the case of the artificial retro-active effect of statutes,[151] and[152] of Advocate-General Mayras on the right to make complaints against the periodic reports drawn up on Community officials.[153] Moreover, the Court of Justice has access to a Documentation Service, one of the most important tasks of which is the preparation of comparative reports.[154]

4. Summary

This discussion has moved the legal instrument of comparative law for the development of the general principles of law in Community administrative law to the centre of the stage.

The function of comparative law in the evolution of a European, administrative law is not however limited to the process of the concretion of general principles of law by the Court of Justice. Both the Council and the Commission too must make use of it in order to achieve through legislation a unified form of European administrative law which pays sufficient attention to national characteristics but is also appropriate to the structure and objectives of the Community.

Finally, above and beyond the limited concerns of Community law itself, comparative law may also contribute to a mutual enrichment of the administrative legal orders of the Member States. A number of basic points about this approach are developed in the following section.

---

[151] [1973] E.C.R. 736 *et seq.*
[152] [1974] E.C.R. 1090 *et seq.*
[153] [1977] E.C.R. 894 *et seq.* The Advocates-General often refer back to comparative law submissions made by the parties to the case; *cf.* for example Advocate-General Slynn, in Case 59/83 *SA Biovilac* v. *EEC*, opinion of September 18, 1984 [1984] E.C.R. 4082 at 4091 (liability for acts with legal effects: "special victim" "rupture le l'égalité devant les charges publiques"); Advocate-General Lenz, Joined Cases 232 & 264/81 *Agricola Commerciale Olio S.r.l. & SPA Savma* v. *Commission*, opinion of September 25, 1984 [1984] E.C.R. 3900 at 3911 (interference analogous to expropriation).
[154] *cf.* H.-W. Daig, "Zur Rechtsvergleichung und Methodenlehre im Europäischen Gemeinschaftsrecht," in *Festschrift für Konrad Zweigert*, Tübingen 1981, p. 395 at p. 414.

SECTION 5

THE EMERGENCE OF A EUROPEAN ADMINISTRATIVE LAW
THROUGH COMPARATIVE METHOD

A. THE FUNDAMENTALS OF COMPARATIVE LAW

Studies in comparative law have so far been undertaken principally in the area of private law in its widest sense.[1] This fact is all the more remarkable when one recalls that the historical roots of comparative law are grounded in public law[2] and that the transfer of the legal experiences of the "older" states to assist the development of the public and in particular the constitutional law of the "younger" states, has made an unmistakable contribution towards the former having exercised and continuing to exercise today a considerable influence on the latter.[3]

The reason for this one-sided orientation of comparative law towards civil law matters may lie primarily in the fact that the practical need to call it in aid has been concentrated above all in areas of private law. Commercial and personal relations across national boundaries are traditionally closer and more highly developed between individual citizens than they

---

[1] cf. for example, R. Bernhardt, "Eigenheiten und Ziele der Rechtsvergleichung im Öffentlichen Recht," ZaÖRV, Vol. 24 (1964), pp. 431 et seq. at p. 431; J. H. Kaiser, "Vergleichung im Öffentlichen Recht, Einleitung," ZaÖRV, Vol. 24 (1964), pp. 391 et seq. at p. 402; J. Rivero, "Vers un droit commun européen: nouvelles perspectives en droit administratif," in M. Cappelletti (ed.), New perspectives for a Common Law of Europe, Publications of the European University Institute, Vol. 1, Florence 1978, pp. 389 et seq., at p. 391. General comparative investigations in the field of public law are unusual. See in particular, M. Cappelletti & W. Cohen, Comparative Constitutional Law, Indianapolis/New York/Charlottesville Virginia 1979 and T. Koopmans, Vergelijkend publiekrecht, Deventer 1979.

[2] This was impressively demonstrated by Montesquieu, the founder of modern comparative law, with his work De l'Esprit des Lois. It is also interesting that Aristotle also collected Greek constitutions and in his Politics developed both a comparative and an evaluative theory of the State. cf. on this J. H. Kaiser, op. cit., footnote 1, pp. 392, 399; F. Münch, "Einführung in die Verfassungsvergleichung," ZaÖRV, Vol. 33 (1973), pp. 126 et seq., at pp. 128 et seq.

[3] cf. R. Bernhardt, op. cit., footnote 1, p. 443; J. H. Kaiser, op. cit., footnote 1, p. 400. See the examples in M. Bothe, Die Kompetenzstruktur des modernen Bundesstaates in rechtsvergleichender Sicht, Beiträge zum ausländischen öffentlichen Recht und Völkerrecht, Vol. 69, Berlin/Heidelberg/New York 1977, pp. 12 et seq.; F. Münch, op. cit., footnote 2, pp. 132 et seq.

are between national administrations or between the citizens of one state and the administration of another.[4] In the case of administrative law in particular, it should also be added that this is a relatively youthful field of law which developed in European states only during the course of the nineteenth century as the administration came to be subject to the rule of law. Since that time the tasks and authority of the administration *vis-à-vis* citizens have continually grown; indeed to such an extent that the legal relations between the individual and the administration have today in quantitative terms matched the volume of legal relations between citizens themselves.[5] Against the background of the ever extending influence of western civilisation and of the approximation of moral, economic and even legal standards in different states through the mutual exchange of goods and ideas, it is therefore hardly imaginable that administrative law will remain for long untouched by comparative law.[6] In the words of Joseph H. Kaiser:

> "Every legal theory today must gain and evaluate its insights using comparative law, bearing in mind the ever growing similarities between living conditions, and between notions of law in large parts of the world, and indeed the more that state power intervenes in legal relations, the more important it is to proceed through a comparison of public laws."[7]

Before we examine the specifics of the comparative process in public law and in particular in administrative law, a few remarks on the concept, function and methods of comparative law in general may be useful.

I. CONCEPT

A unified, generally recognised definition of comparative law cannot

---

[4] *cf.* J. Rivero, *op. cit.*, footnote 1, p. 392; see also K. Zweigert & H. Kötz, *Einführung in die Rechtsvergleichung auf dem Gebiete des Privatrechts, Vol. 1: Grundlagen* (2nd ed., Tübingen 1984), p. 29 (specifically on the (partial) unification of laws by statute).

[5] Thus J. Rivero, *op. cit.*, footnote 1, p. 392. On the historical evolution of administrative law in the Federal Republic of Germany see in particular P. Badura, *Verwaltungsrecht im liberalen und sozialen Rechtsstaat*, Tübingen 1966; *ibid. Das Verwaltungsrecht im liberalen Rechtsstaat*, Göttingen 1967.

[6] *cf.* on this J. H. Kaiser, *op. cit.*, footnote 1, p. 393; J. Rivero, *op. cit.*, footnote 1, p. 392; R. Bernhardt, *op. cit.*, footnote 1, p. 440; see also K. Hailbronner, "Ziele und Methoden völkerrechtlich relevanter Rechtsvergleichung," ZaÖRV, Vol. 36 (1976), pp. 190 *et seq.*, at p. 224.

[7] J. H. Kaiser, *op. cit.*, footnote 1, p. 393, see also p. 400.

be found either in individual national legal orders, or at a European level.[8] Using the textual meaning of the expression as a starting point, comparative law can be described as the setting against each other of different legal orders, bearing in mind that this process may extend both to the spirit and style of entire legal systems (so-called macro-comparisons) and to the solutions of individual problems as they occur in the various legal systems in question (so-called micro-comparisons).[9]

II. AIMS AND FUNCTIONS

Comparative law is above all a method of gaining knowledge.[10] In so far as it displays this characteristic it is capable of offering a variety of solutions to problems which is far greater and in itself more diverse than that offered by a nationally introverted legal science. Comparative law enriches and extends the "supply of solutions" and gives the person who uses this method critically the opportunity of finding a "better solution" to a concrete problem.[11]

Furthermore, comparative law also pursues certain specific goals relevant to practice. Thus comparative studies are often useful when undertaken during the preparatory stage of the legislative process, and to that extent the methods of comparative law facilitate both the creation of new law (1) and also the task of the supranational unification of laws (2). Finally, comparative law can also be of assistance to judges in the interpretation of law and in their creative role as law makers (3).

1. The Creation of New Law by the Legislature

In so far as national law is concerned, legislators frequently have

---

[8] A collection of the various definitions can be found in L.-J. Constantinesco, *Rechtsvergleichung, Vol. 1, Einführung*, Cologne/Berlin/Bonn/Munich 1971, pp. 206 *et seq.*, and A. F. Schnitzler, *Vergleichende Rechtslehre* (2nd ed., Basel 1961), pp. 106 *et seq.*, at p. 118.

[9] K. Zweigert, Entry on "Rechtsvergleichung," in K. Strupp & H.-J. Schlochauer, *Wörterbuch des Völkerrechts*, Vol. 3, Berlin 1962, p. 79.

[10] K. Zweigert & H. Kötz, *op. cit.*, footnote 4, p. 16; L.-J. Constantinesco, *Rechtsvergleichung, Vol. III, Die rechtsvergleichende Wissenschaft*, Cologne/Berlin/Bonn/Munich 1983, p. 33.

[11] M. Cappelletti *et al.* (eds.), "Integration Through Law: Europe and the American Federal Experience. A General Introduction," in *ibid.* (eds.), *Integration Through Law*, Vol. 1, Book 1, Berlin/New York 1986, pp. 1 *et seq.* at pp. 5 *et seq.*, on comparative law as a "third school" between legal positivism and natural law thinking.

recourse in many areas and in many countries to the material elaborated by legal scientists using comparative law methods.[12]

In the law of international organisations, the use of comparative law is, on grounds of legal policy, a necessary precondition for any type of law creation; thus it is used on the one hand for the creation of the organisation itself (formulation of the foundation treaty), and on the other hand for the autonomous regulation of its internal sphere (creation of secondary law).[13] The reason for this is that the knowledge to be gleaned from the various national legal orders of the member states of an international organisation does not simply represent a reservoir of welcome ideas for the formation of the law of this organisation. On the contrary, a closer analysis of the national legal orders will demonstrate which values are capable of positive implementation within a community of states and which processes are most suitable for ensuring the maximum realisation of common principles.[14] In other words, comparative law may be able to make a decisive contribution to the development of a functionally effective international organisation and to the acceptance of its internal law.

2. The Unification of Law

By far the most important function of comparative law is the preparation of a transnational (partial) unification of law, to be implemented by national legislatures, the goal of which is "to reduce or eliminate in so far as is desirable and possible" disparities between national legal systems.[15] As experience has taught us, such projects can be successfully undertaken only on the basis of the intensive use of comparative law. Unification of laws is less a question of power, and more a question of persuasion and the development of a consensus.[16] To this it should be added that existing differences in national legal orders become truly apparent only through comparative law and that the unification of laws

---

[12] *cf.* K. Zweigert & H. Kötz, *op. cit.*, footnote 4, p. 17; see also F. Münch, *op. cit.*, footnote 2, p. 132 (with examples from historical experience).

[13] *cf.* G. Ress, "Die Bedeutung der Rechtsvergleichung für das Recht internationaler Organisationen," ZaÖRV, Vol. 36 (1976), pp. 227 *et seq.* at p. 233.

[14] K. Zemanek, "Was kann die Vergleichung staatlichen öffentlichen Rechts für das Recht der internationalen Organisationen leisten?," ZaÖRV, Vol. 24 (1964), pp. 452 *et seq.* at p. 462; G. Ress, *op. cit.*, footnote 13, p. 234.

[15] *cf.* K. Zweigert & H. Kötz, *op. cit.*, footnote 4, p. 23.

[16] G. Kegel, "Sinn und Grenze der Rechtsangleichung," in *Angleichung des Rechts der Wirtschaft in Europa*, Kölner Schriften zum Europarecht, Vol. 11 (1971), pp. 9 *et seq.* at pp. 39–40.

and comparative law are thus for that reason irrevocably linked one to the other.

A unification of laws on the basis of statute can occur in two ways: on the one hand it occurs through "unified laws" ("lois uniformes") negotiated between states and put into effect in each state, and on the other hand through the supranational legislative activities of international organisations.[17] The latter form of unification of laws is typical for communities aimed at regional economic integration. Economic integration is in fact barely imaginable without simultaneous unification of trade rules, that is, without legal integration.[18] Article 100 EEC illustrates graphically the link between economic and legal integration within the context of the Treaties establishing the European Community. This clause establishes the competence of the Council to adopt directives approximating those legal and regulatory provisions of the Member States which "directly affect the establishment or functioning of the common market."

The utility of every instance of transnational unification of laws lies in the achievement of a significant facilitation of legal dealings across frontiers. Unified law renders the application of what are in part very complicated and confusing rules governing the conflict of laws (private international law) just as superfluous as it does the need which sometimes arises as a result of the application of these rules for national judges to apply largely unfamiliar foreign law.[19] At a time of ever closer economic and personal contacts with foreign countries the unification of laws can make a considerable contribution to the foreseeability and certainty of law.[20] It should not, however, be forgotten that unified law, when it is established in a binding form, may, in spite of all the progress that it may represent in terms of the development of law, also demonstrate conservative effects.[21] If it is desired to avoid inhibiting any future legal developments, then the unified law should primarily be used in order to regulate those constellations of factual circumstances in which disparities in

---

[17] cf. K. Zweigert & H. Kötz, op. cit., footnote 4, p. 26; G. Ress, op. cit., footnote 13, at p. 237.
[18] cf. G. Ress, op. cit., footnote 13, at p. 237.
[19] cf. K. Zweigert & H. Kötz, op. cit., footnote 4, at p. 27.
[20] Ibid.
[21] cf. P. Behrens, "Voraussetzungen und Grenzen der Rechtsfortbildung durch Rechtsvereinheitlichung," p. 5 of the photocopied summary of a paper presented to a symposium of the Max-Planck-Institut für ausländisches und internationales Privatrecht, Hamburg (February 15/16, 1985).

national laws lead to serious disturbances of international legal transactions.[22]

For close and permanently established economic communities, unified law brought into being using the methods of comparative law represents a significant aspect of integration.[23] If, when such a community is established, there is no common language and no common legal tradition, then it is inevitable and necessary that the step-by-step bringing together of national laws will occur by legislative harmonisation as part of the development of a common law.[24]

3. Judicial Law Making and the Interpretation of Statutes

In judicial law making as well as in the interpretation of statutes there is potential at both national and international/supranational level for reliance to be placed on comparative law studies where the problem is that of clarifying conceptual confusions based on language or of closing a gap in the written law using general principles of law.[25] The judge is generally not permitted to make more extensive use of comparative law, as adherence as a general principle to the unambiguous text of a national law is the very core of every civilised legal order and clear statutory rules may not simply be bypassed using arguments based on comparative law.[26]

Since the judge also has a role to play in the making of law and even, in the context of the interpretation of statutes, acts in some ways akin to the legislature by formulating abstract rules, comparative law may also prove

---

[22] P. Behrens, *op. cit.*, footnote 21 at p. 7.
[23] The President of the (German) Bundesgerichtshof G. Pfeiffer has also described the unification of law as the "most effective instrument on the road to a unified Europe": *Ansprache zum Gedenken des 175. Geburtstages von Eduard von Simson*, Bull. des Presse- und Informationsdienstes der Bundesregierung, No. 126 of November 13, 1985, p. 1100, at p. 1104.
[24] *cf.* G. Ress, *op. cit.*, footnote 13 at p. 241.
[25] *cf.* K. Zweigert & H. Kötz, *op. cit.*, footnote 4 at p. 20; G. Ress, *op. cit.*, footnote 13, at p. 253, and pp. 258 *et seq.*; T. Koopmans, *op. cit.*, footnote 1, p. 1; K. Zweigert, *op. cit.*, footnote 9 at p. 80.
[26] See K. Zweigert & H. Kötz, *op. cit.*, footnote 4 at p. 20.

useful here as it is to the legislature when it is making new laws.[27] To this should be added the fact that supranational legislative acts all have the goal of achieving the unification of laws. If this fact is not to be lost sight of, then the later interpretation and further development of that law must proceed upon the same assumption.[28] This means that the judge must make use, albeit indirectly, of comparative law as a working tool in this context too. For without a comparative law basis it would in practice be difficult to achieve a common standard in the judicial interpretation and development of the newly created common law.

III. METHOD

The principle of functionality is generally recognised as the basic methodological principle of every comparison of laws.[29] The initial question must be focused on a concrete problem and must aim at the method of the solution offered.

In this type of approach, care must be taken to ensure that the substantive problem is formulated in terms which are wherever possible free from the specific doctrinal conceptions of the legal order in which it occurs. Only thus is it possible to recognise a rule to be found in a foreign legal order, which as a matter of doctrine may be differently formulated or situated, as a functionally equal solution (the so-called negative side of the principle of functionality).[30]

---

[27] R. Bernhardt is still sceptical about the use of comparative law to assist in the interpretation of national (public) law: *op. cit.*, footnote 1 at p. 443; *cf.* however on the current practice of the courts: K. Zweigert & H. Kötz, *op. cit.*, footnote 4 at p. 21 with regard to the German Bundesgerichtshof, the Swiss Bundesgericht and the French Cour de Cassation; J. M. Mössner, "Rechtsvergleichung und Verfassungsrechtsprechung," AöR, Vol. 99 (1974), pp. 192 *et seq.* at pp. 201 *et seq.*, with regard to the German Bundesverfassungsgericht. On the practice of the European Court of Justice *cf.* H.-W. Daig, "Zur Rechtsvergleichung und Methodenlehre im Europäischen Gemeinschaftsrecht," in H. Bernstein, U. Drobnig & H. Kötz (eds.), *Festschrift für Konrad Zweigert*, Tübingen 1981, pp. 395 *et seq.* at pp. 411 *et seq.*; G. Ress, *op. cit.*, footnote 13 at pp. 255, 270 *et seq.*; R. Bernhardt, *op. cit.*, footnote 1, p. 448; F. Münch, *op. cit.*, footnote 2 at p. 147. See in this context also K. Zemanek, *op. cit.*, footnote 14 at pp. 464 *et seq.*, 466 *et seq.*

[28] *cf.* K. Zweigert & H. Kötz, *op. cit.*, footnote 4 at p. 21.

[29] *cf.* K. Zweigert & H. Kötz, *op. cit.*, footnote 4, p. 34; J. M. Mössner, *op. cit.*, footnote 27, p. 197; F. Münch, *op. cit.*, footnote 2, p. 139. R. Bernhardt, *op. cit.*, footnote 1, p. 436 is again of a different view, believing a comparison with public law possible only with regard to institutions; see on this also J. H. Kaiser, *op. cit.*, footnote 1, p. 403; H. Bülck, "Zur Dogmengeschichte des europäischen Verwaltungsrechts," in Göttinger Arbeitskreis (ed.) *Recht im Dienste der Menschenwürde, Festschrift für Herbert Kraus*, Würzburg 1964, pp. 29 *et seq.*

[30] *cf.* on this the discussion by K. Zweigert & H. Kötz, *op. cit.*, footnote 4, pp. 35, 37.

Furthermore, it is possible properly to discover possible equivalents of the solution to a problem given in one's own legal system only where every unnecessary restriction is avoided with regard to the types of sources of law to be taken into consideration: a source of law must, in this type of comparative legal analysis, be everything which regulates the legal essence of a society or at least contributes to its ordering.[31]

In particular, the application of the principle of functionality will give rise on the one hand to a negative effect as regards the process of comparison; that is that the solutions taken from the legal systems under investigation will have to be divested as far as possible from all specific conceptual content in order to facilitate their separation from specifically national doctrine and their proper evaluation.[32] On the other hand, the use of the principle of functionality has a positive effect in this context in so far as each solution is to be examined as a single unit with respect to its function and is thus to be drawn in to the comparison. Quite irrelevant in this context is the question whether individual steps or elements within the "whole" solution, when evaluated in accordance with the approach followed in the particular national legal order studied, are in fact different and whether in this approach they are ascribed a different significance.[33]

The first hints of this form of functional comparative law are to be found also in the case law of the European Court of Justice. Thus in the Algera decision, when examining the conditions governing the revocation of administrative acts, the European Court does not limit itself to looking at the time limits laid down in many legal systems; it also takes into account the concepts of waiver (Verzicht) and forfeiture (Verwirkung), which have a similar function in German law.[34]

The functional approach to comparative law appears particularly clearly in the final pleas of Advocate-General Warner in the case of Mills.[35] Mr. Mills brought an action against the termination of his contract of employment as a translator in the European Investment Bank. In determining the validity of the dismissal, the European Court made reference to the "general principles of the law of master and servant," which were referred to in the Staff Regulations of the Bank. The case concerned, *inter alia*, the question whether the personnel of the

---

[31] *cf.* K. Zweigert & H. Kötz, *op. cit.*, footnote 4, p. 36.
[32] *cf.* K. Zweigert & H. Kötz, *op. cit.*, footnote 4, p. 48; K. Zemanek, *op. cit.*, footnote 14, p. 46; on constitutional law in particular see F. Münch, *op. cit.*, footnote 2, p. 138.
[33] *cf.* K. Zweigert & H. Kötz, *op. cit.*, footnote 4, p. 48.
[34] Joined Cases 7/56 & 3–7/57 *Algera* v. *Common Assembly* [1957] E.C.R. 39 at 56.
[35] Case 110/75 *Mills* v. *Investment Bank* [1976] E.C.R. 955 at 972 *et seq.*

Investment Bank had an employment relationship governed by public or private law.

Advocate-General Warner referred in his comparative review of the legal situation in the Member State to the absence of a distinction between public law and private law in the United Kingdom and Ireland. The nature of the employment relationship with the Investment Bank should therefore not be described using the terminology of public law or private law. On the contrary, the real question was whether the personnel of the Bank belonged to the category, existing in every Member State, of public servants, whose rights were protected in different ways through special legal provisions and who enjoyed a certain privilege derived from the sovereign power of the State.

In this context the statements of Advocate-General Warner concerning the role of the functional method of comparative law in the determination of general principles of law are instructive[36]: "In the search for the 'general principles common to the laws of the Member States' it is to my mind unhelpful to use terms derived from particular national systems and unknown, or bearing different meanings, in others. Rather should one look for the reality behind the labels: seek to identify the substance of the legal rights, powers and obligations recognized and enforced in the different systems."

The comparative study ends with a critical evaluation of the results gained through the comparison.[37] This means that in every individual case it is necessary to consider and determine which of a number of solutions is more appropriate and just and thus preferable as the "better" solution.[38]

While this evaluation is in principle a matter of considering in isolation the existing national solutions, where the law of international organisations is concerned, a legal evaluation of the aims of the organisation in question must also be considered, because only then will the comparative process acquire a framework and a standard against which it is to judge the different solutions.[39] This becomes particularly clear if one looks at the principles of legality developed by the European Court and prevailing

---

[36] *Ibid.* p. 979.
[37] *cf.* K. Zweigert & H. Kötz, *op. cit.*, footnote 4, p. 52.
[38] *cf.* K. Zweigert & H. Kötz, *op. cit.*, footnote 4, p. 53. It may, for example, emerge from the "critical evaluation" that the different solutions are essentially equally valid. It is, however, also possible that one of the solutions will be superior to the others and thus preferable. If none of the solutions considered satisfies the requirements of a "best" solution, it may be appropriate to develop a new solution through a combination of all other solutions (see K. Zweigert & H. Kötz, *op. cit.*, p. 52).
[39] *cf.* G. Ress, *op. cit.*, footnote 13, p. 232.

within the Community. An "autonomous" comparative study which simply considered the relevant national systems would of course in any case give significant hints towards the development of a common position as regards specific problems. However, in the interests of an appropriate realisation of the tasks and goals of the Communities, it is not sufficient simply to rely on these common elements alone in the formulation of the legal principles of Community law.[40] In addition there must be an evaluation of these elements against the standards of the particular goal of integration pursued in the Treaty.

This point emerges too from the Court's judgment in the *Internationale Handelsgesellschaft* case of December 17, 1970[41] when it expressly stated that:

"respect for fundamental rights forms an integral part of the general principles of law protected by the Court of Justice. The protection of such rights, whilst inspired by the constitutional traditions common to the Member States, must be ensured within the framework of the structure and objectives of the Community."[42]

B. COMPARATIVE PUBLIC LAW[43]

I. CHARACTERISTICS OF PUBLIC LAW

Public law is characterised by a multiplicity of distinctive features which are not to be found to the same extent or in the same combination in other areas of law. From the point of view of their possible effect on comparative law the most important of these characteristics can be summarised as follows[44]:

The regulatory scope of public law extends both to the structure and tasks of State power and to the relationship between State owner and individual citizens. Thus public law has from its very objective its own

---

[40] *cf.* on this G. Ress, *op. cit.*, footnote 13 at p. 231.
[41] Case 11/70 [1970] E.C.R. 1125.
[42] [1970] E.C.R. 1135.
[43] The concept "public law" is used in the following section as a generic term covering constitutional and administrative law.
[44] See on this R. Bernhardt, *op. cit.*, footnote 1, pp. 432–434, who of all the authors goes into most detail on the characteristics of public law and their significance for comparative law; see also T. Koopmans, *op. cit.*, footnote 1, p. 1 and J. H. Kaiser, *op. cit.*, footnote 1, p. 396.

distinctive outlook: it is concerned with the essential structural elements of the State.[45] This means, furthermore, that public law is determined to a greater extent than other areas of law by extra-legal factors, which are grounded in historical tradition, in political style and specific ideologies.[46] In consequence, the concepts of public law are formulated to a greater extent than for example those of private law by national beliefs and value concepts. Its true content can be determined only if political influences, social pressures, the effectiveness of the constitution and other factors are taken into account.[47]

In the nature of things, large areas of public law are determined less by an inherent substantive legality than by the political desire for change on the part of the forces currently holding power. Of course, there are rules in public law, particularly within administrative law, which are politically more or less neutral. In administrative law, however, decisions are taken which have a significant impact on the conception and legal policy of a State. One need think only of how the law governing the public order and security is formulated, or of the various positions on the citizen's right to challenge acts of the administration before independent courts.[48]

The various areas of public law consist traditionally of a mixture of layers of written and unwritten law.[49] Thus administrative law in particular has developed in virtually all countries less through statute law and more in the form of case law.[50] But even case law in some areas of constitutional and administrative law is in many respects rudimentary, so that it is necessary to bring in subsidiary sources of law such as, for example, academic literature and State practice to clarify the law.[51] In addition it should be remembered that the interpretation of written law by courts is often of greater significance than the legal rules themselves. This point applies above all to constitutional law.[52]

Public law employs traditionally and to a greater extent than other areas of law framework provisions and value-laden concepts which need to be articulated through interpretation. Good examples of this include the concepts of "public security and order," "due process of law" and

---

[45] *cf.* R. Bernhardt, *op. cit.*, footnote 1, p. 432.
[46] See on this the examples given in T. Koopmans, *op. cit.*, footnote 1, p. 2 and in R. Bernhardt, *op. cit.*, footnote 1, p. 441; see also J. H. Kaiser, *op. cit.*, footnote 1, p. 401.
[47] *cf.* J. H. Kaiser, *op. cit.*, footnote 1, p. 396; R. Bernhardt, *op. cit.*, footnote 1, p. 438.
[48] *cf.* R. Bernhardt, *op. cit.*, footnote 1, p. 432.
[49] *cf. ibid.* p. 433.
[50] *cf. ibid.* p. 433.
[51] *cf. ibid.* p. 434.
[52] *cf. ibid.* p. 433.

"Sozialstaat." In the case of these and similar concepts formal canons of construction are in no way sufficient for the purposes of articulating a concrete legal standard. Without knowledge of concrete practice it is even less possible to determine the meaning of each term than it is with regard to the general clauses of private law.[53]

In conclusion reference should be made to the fact that public law of its very nature is continually subject to particularly strong pressure through the exercise of political power. It follows from this that in particular where there is no "contrary pressure" through clear legal provisions or where there is no comprehensive legal protection through the courts, the body of law characterised as public law is capable of changing more or less unnoticed and within a very short space of time.[54]

II. THE METHODOLOGY OF COMPARATIVE LAW

The general principles of comparative law set out above also govern the methodology of comparisons within public law.[55] It would be wrong as a matter of substantive logic for there to be a specific public law comparative method.[56] However, one or two decisive features must be taken into account, which emerge when public law is made the subject of a comparative investigation.[57]

The key characteristics of public law have been set out above. Having regard to the general principles of comparative law, it emerges from these characteristics that the precise recording and assessment of the various sources of law within public law will be relatively difficult, bearing in mind their nature and in particular their responsiveness to change. Because of the uncertainties set out above, statements about the actual substance of a norm as a guarantee and the effective meaning of a source of law employed in an individual case can be made only with certain reserves in the context of comparisons of public law.[58]

---

[53] cf. ibid. p. 433; T. Koopmans, op. cit., footnote 1, p. 6.

[54] cf. R. Bernhardt, op. cit., footnote 1, p. 434; T. Koopmans, op. cit., footnote 1, pp. 250 et seq. on the dynamics of public law.

[55] K. Zweigert makes some general points on this in his entry on "Rechtsvergleichung," op. cit., footnote 9, p. 79 and J. M. Mössner, op. cit., footnote 27, p. 242 makes these points in particular for constitutional law. See also L.-J. Constantinesco, Rechtsvergleichung, Vol. II, Cologne/Berlin/Bonn/Munich 1972, pp. 33, 66–68, 331 et seq.

[56] cf. J. M. Mössner, op. cit., footnote 27, p. 224.

[57] cf. J. M. Mössner, op. cit., footnote 27, p. 224.

[58] Thus also T. Koopmans, op. cit., footnote 1, p. 1; J. H. Kaiser, op. cit., footnote 1, pp. 395, 396.

It has further become clear that the relativity of legal concepts, which has already been relied upon by Ernst Rabel in order to argue against the type of doctrinal system which is grounded in national legal systems,[59] is harder to accept in the context of public law than it is, for example, in private law, because the concepts of public law are particularly strongly linked to their nation-state context on the grounds of their primarily political shaping.[60] It is thus possible in general terms to establish that comparisons in the field of public law are more successful the lower the political content of the individual rules and constructs; in other words, the more "technical" the legal material is in total, the easier any attempted comparison will be.[61] The recognition of this fact may give some encouragement to the extension of the as yet rather feeble attempts to undertake comparative projects in this field into further wide areas of modern administrative law.[62]

III. THE CHANCES OF A UNIFICATION OF LAWS

Because of the universal grounding of public law in established political spheres and historical traditions, the chances of a gradual transnational unification of laws in this field on the basis of comparative law naturally do not seem too great. In the light of a discernible and sustained internationalisation of the standards of constitutional and administrative law, however, the limits of comparative law based on traditional practices which have hitherto prevailed are today becoming increasingly irrelevant.[63] Thus the chances of the unification of laws in the field of public law are also improving.

Of course, the partial or even complete acceptance of a foreign rule into one's own legal order is most likely to be contemplated where more or less politically neutral questions require a solution—in other words, questions which require measures which deal only with their substance.[64] The following maxim thus applies equally to the goal of the unification of laws: the more the political content of a legal provision decreases, the

---

[59] Quoted in J. H. Kaiser, *op. cit.*, footnote 1, p. 396.
[60] *cf.* J. H. Kaiser, *op. cit.*, footnote 1, p. 396; K. Zemanek, *op. cit.*, footnote 14, p. 461.
[61] *cf.* R. Bernhardt, *op. cit.*, footnote 1, p. 437.
[62] Thus R. Bernhardt, *op. cit.*, footnote 1, p. 437.
[63] Thus J. H. Kaiser, *op. cit.*, footnote 1, p. 403. M. Cappelletti, "Introduction" in *ibid.* (ed.), *New Perspectives for a Common Law of Europe, op. cit.*, footnote 1, p. 24; *cf.* however also J. D. B. Mitchell, "Law, Democracy and Political Institutions," in M. Capelletti, *op. cit.*, footnote 1, p. 361, pp. 362 *et seq.*
[64] *cf.* R. Bernhardt, *op. cit.*, footnote 1, p. 445.

more its comparability grows and with that the prospect of creating unified law.[65] As far as constitutional law and many parts of traditional administrative law, such as the law relating to public order, are concerned, it is unlikely that the comparability of individual rules will in the end be sufficient in order to bring about a worthwhile unification of laws. Because of the specific characteristics of these areas of law in particular, there is an additional requirement that the States in question should share to a significant extent the same ideological and political positions.[66] In the case of close communities of states which demonstrate essentially the same political, cultural, social and economic structure, the chances of a transnational unification of public law would appear to be highest.[67] Since these conditions seem to be largely present within the European Community and the Council of Europe, it would appear legitimate to hope that moves towards a *ius commune* across Europe can develop in the public law field as well.[68] Whether and to what extent this has already happened today, will be demonstrated in detail by this study.

C. COMPARATIVE ADMINISTRATIVE LAW IN PARTICULAR

In the context of a study of the influence of French administrative law on the development of German law Ulrich Scheuner[69] wrote in 1963 that administrative law belongs to those areas of law "in which the national characteristics of the people and the State are revealed most starkly."[70] It is not just that in administrative law traditional institutional forms prove to be resistant to change. Even the legal position of administrative personnel, the relationship between the administration and the citizen, the level of centralisation and the entire style of administration are,

---

[65] *cf.* R. Bernhardt, *op. cit.*, footnote 1, p. 450.
[66] Thus R. Bernhardt, *op. cit.*, footnote 1, p. 450.
[67] *cf.* R. Bernhardt, *op. cit.*, footnote 1, p. 450.
[68] *cf.* on this thought with regard to civil law H. Kötz, "Gemeineuropäisches Zivilrecht," in: H. Bernstein, U. Drobnig & H. Kötz (eds.), *Festschrift für Konrad Zweigert, op. cit.,* footnote 27, pp. 481 *et seq.*, in particular p. 490. *cf.* also T. Koopmans, *op. cit.,* footnote 1, p. 252, who sees in European union the first attempt to achieve a "constitutional ius gentium"; (he is, however, rather sceptical about the possibilities of unification of laws in public law); J. D. B. Mitchell, *op. cit.*, footnote 63, pp. 362 *et seq.*, p. 387 disagrees with this.
[69] U. Scheuner, "Der Einfluss des französischen Verwaltungsrechts auf die deutsche Rechtsentwicklung," DÖV 1963, pp. 714 *et seq.*
[70] U. Scheuner, *op. cit.*, footnote 69, p. 714.

according to Scheuner, "to a large extent the expression of national particularities."[71]

In so far as this view might suggest the conclusion that administrative law as a whole is unsuitable material for study in comparative law, it is necessary to point out up one or two doubts. Even at the turn of the century, when the scholarly exposition of administrative law was beginning to take hold, numerous studies of foreign administrative law systems were undertaken. It is notable that Otto Mayer, even before he published his fundamentally important work on German administrative law,[72] wrote a book in 1886 on French administrative law and made French models accessible to German administrative law doctrine.[73] Edouard Lafferrière, one of the founders of French administrative law doctrine, deals in his *Traité de la juridiction administrative et des recours contentieux*, which appeared in 1887, with the administrative law protection offered in other states.[74] Furthermore Albert V. Dicey's basic introduction to English constitutional law, which appeared in 1885,[75] also deals with French "droit administratif." Whereas Dicey denied the existence of an "administrative law" comparable to "droit administratif" in English law,[76] the American administrative law teacher Frank J. Goodnow discussed not only France and Germany, but also England and the United States in his two volume *Comparative Administrative Law* (1893). In his foreword, Goodnow wrote[77]: "The great problems of modern public law are almost exclusively administrative in character. While the age that has passed was one of constitutional, the present age is one of administrative reform. Our modern complex social conditions are making enormous demands of the administrative side of the government, demands which will not be satisfied at all or which will be inadequately met, unless a greater knowledge of administrative law and science is possessed by our

---

[71] U. Scheuner, *op. cit.*, footnote 69, p. 714. *cf.* also *Cours de droit administratif comparé (rédigé d'après les notes et avec l'autorisation de J. Rivero)* Paris 1957–1958, pp. 18 *et seq.* on the particular difficulties of comparative administrative law.

[72] O. Mayer, *Deutsches Verwaltungsrecht*, 2 Vols., (1st ed., Leipzig 1895/6).

[73] O. Mayer, *Theorie des französischen Verwaltungsrechts*, Strasbourg 1886. On the influence of French law on the work of O. Mayer, see for instance R. David, *Les grands systèmes de droit contemporains* (8th ed., Paris 1982), p. 87.

[74] *cf.* on the influence of German and French scholarly works in the field of administrative law J. Rivero, "Droit administratif français et droit administratif étranger," in A. de Laubadère, Mathiot, J. Rivero & G. Vedel (eds.), *Pages de doctrine*, pp. 475, 479.

[75] A. V. Dicey, *Introduction to the study of the law of the Constitution* (1st ed., London 1885).

[76] *Ibid.* p. 330. See in more detail below Chap. 2, Section "United Kingdom."

[77] J. F. Goodnow, *Comparative Administrative Law*, New York/London 1893, p. IV.

legislators and moulders of opinion. This knowledge can be obtained only by study, and by comparison of our own with foreign administrative methods."

In the early days of comparative administrative law, the focus was primarily on making the experiences of foreign, more highly developed administrative law systems accessible in practice for one's own doctrine. Above all, it was the case law of the French Conseil d'Etat which exercised an extensive influence, through the medium in part of comparative scholarly works, on the administrative law of many European and non-European States.[78] Danish administrative law, to name but one more example, was decisively influenced by Poul Andersen's comparative study "on invalid administrative acts" (1924), the conclusions of which were shaped to a great extent by French and German law.[79]

Increasingly comparative law considerations are being taken into account in the preparation of laws in the field of administrative law.[80]

Thus the Franks Committee, whose Report on Administrative Tribunals and Enquiries led to the most important postwar administrative reform in the United Kingdom, also listened to foreign experts.[81] On the possibilities and limits of comparative administrative law, the Franks Committee had this to say in its final report[82]:

> "In these matters each country seeks to work out for itself, within the framework of its own institutions and way of life, the proper balance between public and private interest. It follows that translation of the practice of one country into the procedures of another is not likely to be appropriate, although since the basic issue, the relationship between the individual and the administration, is common, there will continue to be advantage in comparative study."

After the Second World War comparative administrative law gained a new dimension through the co-operation of European States in the Council of Europe and the European Community. Within the context of the Council of Europe, the European Commission and the European

---

[78] cf. in particular the various contributions in *Le Conseil d'Etat, Livre jubilaire*, Paris 1952 (*seconde partie, Le rayonnement du Conseil d'Etat et le droit administratif à l'étranger*), pp. 481 *et seq.*; J. Rivero, *op. cit.*, footnote 74, pp. 475 *et seq.*

[79] In German translation: P. Andersen, *Ungültige Verwaltungsakte*, Mannheim/Berlin/Leipzig 1927. See in more detail below Chapter 2, Section "Denmark."

[80] cf. for example A. Holleaux, "Les nouvelles lois françaises sur l'information du public," RISA 1981, pp. 191, 192 *et seq.* on "foreign inspiration."

[81] These were in fact Professors M. Letourneur (France) and B. Schwartz (U.S.A.).

[82] Report of the Committee on Administrative Tribunals and Enquiries (Cmnd. 218) Pt. IV, Ch. 30, No. 408.

Court of Human Rights have to pay great attention to comparative law in the interpretation and application of the European Convention on Human Rights, in order to give the provisions of the Convention an autonomous meaning which is not tied to any particular national characteristics.[83] Wherever the alleged human rights violations have concerned measures of the administration, the comparative statements of the Court are also of relevance to administrative law.

Within the context of the European Community, the European Court has been particularly concerned with the fruits of comparative administrative law.[84] Comparative law is of particular relevance where Community law must be interpreted in the light of the various linguistic versions. One example of this is the case *Commission* v. *Federal Republic of Germany*.[85] The Court was there required to decide whether the Federal Republic had breached the 6th Turnover Tax directive when it provided an exemption from value added tax for certain services provided by transport undertakings for the Deutsche Bundespost. According to the directive a tax exemption is provided for "the supply of services by the public postal services." The Court examined the text of the provision in question in all the linguistic versions and came to the conclusion that only the services provided by the public postal services in the organisational sense were covered by the exemption from tax.[86] The Federal Republic had thus breached the directive in so far as it had extended the exemption to the services provided by other transport undertakings.

Furthermore, comparative administrative law, as already shown, plays a significant role in the development and concretion of the general principles of administrative law by the Court of Justice.

---

[83] On comparisons made by the European Court of Human Rights see in more detail R. Bernhardt, "Rechtsvergleichung bei Auslegung und Anwendung internationaler Menschenrechtskonventionen," Paper delivered at the Tagung der Gesellschaft für Rechtsvergleichung on September 18, 1985 in Göttingen, Manuscript, pp. 11 *et seq.* See also J. A. Frowein & W. Peukert, *Europäische Menschenrechtskonvention, EMRK-Kommentar*, Kehl/Strasbourg/Arlington 1985, Introduction 8, p. 4 on the "evaluative comparison" of national legal orders.

[84] *cf.* already on this *Cours de droit administratif comparé (rédigé d'après les notes et avec l'autorisation de J. Rivero)*, Paris 1957–1958, in particular pp. 52 *et seq.*

[85] Case 107/84 *Commission* v. *Federal Republic of Germany* [1985] E.C.R. 2655.

[86] *Ibid.* paras. 10 *et seq.*

D.   TOWARDS A EUROPEAN IUS COMMUNE IN THE AREA OF ADMINISTRATIVE LAW

Using general principles of administrative law it is possible to illustrate through examples the mutual influences of European and national administrative law upon each other. On the one hand, in developing general principles of Community law the European Court of Justice has regard to the principles recognised in the national legal systems. On the other hand, the synthesis of administrative law carried out at Community level reflects back on to national administrative systems. Otto Bachof has already drawn attention with some emphasis to this relationship in a paper on the "doctrinal system of administrative law in the face of the current tasks of the administration" read to the Association of German Teachers of Public Law. Taking into account the central importance of the European Court of Justice for the progressive development of Community law, he had this to say:

"Different views for instance on the nature of the administrative act, its illegality and the consequences of that illegality, on abuse of discretion under the German and détournement de pouvoir under the French system all have to be weighed up against each other in the European case law. National doctrinal systems cannot remain untouched by this. It is difficult to imagine that in the long term a German, a French, an Italian, etc., as well as a common European doctrinal system of administrative action can exist alongside each other."[87]

The possibilities and limitations of a common European administrative law were first fully considered as a comprehensive problem by Jean

---

[87] O. Bachof, "Die Dogmatik des Verwaltungsrechts vor den Gegenwartsaufgaben der Verwaltung," VVDStRL, Vol. 30 (1972), pp. 193 *et seq.* In this sense see also J. Rivero, *op. cit.*, footnote 1, p. 403; H. Kutscher, "Zum Grundsatz der Verhältnismässigkeit im Recht der Europäischen Gemeinschaften," in H. Kutscher, G. Ress, F. Teitgen, F. Ermacora & G. M. Ubertazzi (eds.), *Der Grundsatz der Verhältnismässigkeit in europäischen Rechtsordnungen, Rechtsstaat in der Bewährung*, Vol. 15, 1984, pp. 89 *et seq.* at p. 95; *ibid.* "Der Gerichtshof der Europäischen Gemeinschaften 1952–1982, Rückblick-Ausblick," Integration 4/83, pp. 149 *et seq.* at p. 153; J. A. Frowein, "Eigentumsschutz im Europarecht," in W. G. Grewe, H. H. Rupp & H. Schneider (eds.), *Europäische Gerichtsbarkeit und nationale Verfassungsgerichtsbarkeit, Festschrift für Hans Kutscher*, Baden-Baden 1981, pp. 189 *et seq.* at p. 200; J. Schwarze, "Entwicklungsstufen des Europäischen Gemeinschaftsrechts," in B. Börner, H. Jahrreiss & K. Stern (eds.), *Festschrift für Karl Carstens*, Vol. 1, Karlsruhe 1984, pp. 259 *et seq.* at p. 266.

Rivero.[88] In spite of all the links with national peculiarities, Rivero could see against the background of similar problems and similar attempts at solutions in national administrative systems a strong possibility of achieving a unification of administrative law in Europe.

Indeed the Member States of the European Community are all (more or less) highly developed industrial countries, the national administrations of which are faced with essentially the same problems. Throughout Europe the urgent tasks of modern administrative law are at the forefront, whether in the area of building law, planning and development control, environmental protection, public health or social law.[89]

Furthermore the administrative law systems of the Member States of the European Community are built on common political and legal conceptions. The control of the administration by law is the primary goal of the administrative laws of the Member States, whether they use the idea of the "rule of law," of the "Rechtsstaat" or of the "principe de légalité" in order to seek to achieve it.[90]

The conditions set out above for a convergence between different administrative laws are certainly not limited to the European context, but apply equally to other democracies of the Western type. The traditional close co-operation within (Western) Europe naturally greatly favours development in the direction of a common European administrative law. This applies not just to the European Community but also to the States belonging to the Council of Europe. The Commission and the Court of Human Rights are developing through the interpretation and application of the European Convention on Human Rights something akin to a

---

[88] J. Rivero, *op. cit.*, footnote 1; there are already some indications of this approach in *Cours de droit administratif comparé*, *op. cit.*, footnote 84, p. 159: "Perspectives euro-péennes de 'droit commun.' "

[89] *cf.* J. Schwarze, "Europäisches Verwaltungsrecht im Werden—Einführung und Problemaufriss," in J. Schwarze (ed.), *Europäisches Verwaltungsrecht im Werden*, Baden-Baden 1982, p. 20 with further references.

[90] *cf.* J. Rivero, *op. cit.*, footnote 1, p. 390. See also A. Bleckmann, "Der Rechtsstaat in vergleichender Sicht. Zugleich ein Beitrag zur Rechtsquellenlehre des Europäischen Gemeinschaftsrechts," in GYIL 20 (1977), pp. 406 *et seq.*; D. N. MacCormick, "Der Rechtsstaat und die rule of law," JZ 1984, pp. 65 *et seq.* In contrast to this, in the States of Eastern Europe which are dominated by the Soviet Union the primacy of politics in all areas of social activity including the law applies, *cf.* in more detail on this H. Krüger, "Die Funktion der Verwaltungs- und Verfassungsgerichtsbarkeit in einigen Staaten Osteuropas," DÖV 1986, p. 45 at pp. 49 *et seq.* on the "different quality of administrative law in Eastern Europe." On the other hand, K.-J. Kuss, "Die sowjetische Diskussion um den gerichtlichen Verwaltungsrechtsschutz," Verwaltungsarchiv, Vol. 77 (1986), pp. 145 *et seq.* at p. 156 considers the outcome of the struggle "between the dominance of politics over law and that of law over politics" to be "still open."

"common law for Europe based on democracy and the rule of law,"[91] which in turn has an influence on the administrative laws of the signatory states. The Committee of Ministers of the Council of Europe contributes through recommendations and resolutions to the development of a common European administrative law standard.[92] The "Resolution of the Protection of the Individual in Relation to the Acts of the Administration"[93] adopted in 1977, which offers as guidelines for administrative proceedings the principles of the right to a hearing, access to information, legal representation, the duty to give reasons and the duty to inform the citizen of his or her remedies, is based expressly on the consideration that "in view of the increasing co-operation and mutual assistance between Member States in administrative matters and the increasing international movement of persons, it is desirable to promote a common standard of protection in all Member States."

Whether and to what extent such common standards of administrative law have already developed within Europe[94] and in particular within the framework of the European Community can of course be demonstrated only through a review of the principles of administrative law, which will be dealt with individually below in detail.

First, however, it is appropriate to set out the basic features of the various national administrative systems of the Member States to ensure that the later overall evaluation is properly grounded.

---

[91] R. Bernhardt, Paper delivered at the Tagung der Gesellschaft für Rechtsvergleichung, September 18, 1985 in Göttingen, Manuscript, p. 13.

[92] Resolution (77) 31 of the Council of Europe on the Protection of the Individual in Relation to the Acts of Administrative Authorities, September 28, 1977 (Council of Europe, Information Bulletin on legal activities, June 1978, p. 45); Recommendation No. R(80)2 of the Committee of Ministers concerning the Exercise of Discretionary Powers by Administrative Authorities, March 28, 1977 (Council of Europe, Information Bulletin on legal activities, June 1980, p. 50). Both are reprinted in J. Schwarze (ed.), *op. cit.*, footnote 89, pp. 163 and 165.

[93] See above footnote 92.

[94] Building on the arguments of L. von Stein, *Handbuch der Verwaltungslehre und des Verwaltungsrechts, mit Vergleichung der Literatur und der Gesetzgebung von Frankreich, England und Deutschland,* Stuttgart 1870 (2nd ed., 1876; 3rd ed. in three volumes 1883/88) it is possible to speak within the European area, having regard to the legal systems of the States of the former Deutsche Bund (including Austria), of a "ius commune" of administrative law. *cf.* on this W. Brauneder, "Formen und Tragweite des deutschen Einflusses auf die österreichische Verwaltungswissenschaft 1850–1914," in E. V. Heyen (ed.), *Wissenschaft und Recht der Verwaltung seit dem Ancien Régime,* Frankfurt 1984, pp. 249 *et seq.* at p. 278.

CHAPTER 2

ESSENTIAL CHARACTERISTICS OF THE ADMINISTRATIVE LAW SYSTEMS OF THE E.C. MEMBER STATES

The administrative law systems of the Member States are relevant to E.C. administrative law in several respects.

On the one hand, the European Court of Justice resorts to applying the general legal principles of the Member States where gaps appear in the written Community law, thus making these principles available to Community law by the selective use of comparative law methods.[1] Occasionally, the Community law principles thus obtained influence in turn the administrative law of the Member States. However, individual legal principles, such as the conformity of administrative action with the relevant statute, equality of treatment, the proportionality rule, the protection of legitimate expectation and the right to fair administrative proceedings, cannot be considered in isolation from their legal context. Legal principles can assume different forms and take on different meanings according to their legal context.

On the other hand, Community law is applied on a large scale by the Member States' authorities.[2] The domestic administrative authorities are embedded in the administrative structure of their respective national legal systems and, in the absence of any Community rule to the contrary, act in accordance with the relevant principles of national administrative law.

For these reasons, a survey of the Member States' administrative law systems can be a useful additional tool in gaining an understanding of European administrative law.

---

[1] *cf. supra* (Chapter 1, Section 4, C.II.3) for more detailed explanation.
[2] *cf. supra* (Chapter 1, Section 3, B) for more detailed explanation.

This survey is basically confined to five aspects, which are examined in the legal systems of the twelve Member States. The first aspect features the origin and development of each administrative law system. The continuity with which French administrative law has developed since the end of the eighteenth century on the one hand, and the hesitancy with which the existence of a separate system of administrative law was recognised in the United Kingdom and in Ireland on the other hand, constitute the two opposing extremes.

The second aspect focuses on the constitutional basis of administrative law. In this connection, the United Kingdom assumes a special place in view of the unwritten and flexible nature of its constitution.[3]

In the third section, the sources of administrative law (at a lower level than the constitution) are examined. Although administrative law has found its most frequent expression as judge-made law, whether in the form of keynote decisions under the continental law systems (especially the pioneering decisions by the French Conseil d'Etat), or in the form of precedents under the common law systems,[4] it is possible to discern an increasing tendency nowadays towards codifying administrative law, in particular the law relating to administrative procedure. The codification of Spanish administrative law is a particularly early and extensive example of this trend.[5]

Fourthly, there follows a survey of the various forms of administrative law protection. Essentially, a distinction is drawn under this heading between the British system (protection by the ordinary courts), the French system (protection by a judicial organ belonging to the executive, *i.e.* the Conseil d'Etat) and the German system (protection by an independent system of administrative courts). Attention is also given to the forms of protection involving a mixture between these different systems, and to the non-judicial forms of legal protection.

---

[3] On the "unwritten" and "flexible" nature of the British constitution *cf.* O. Hood Philips, P. Jackson, *Constitutional and Administrative Law* (6th ed., London 1978), pp. 6 *et seq.*, 22 *et seq.*

[4] On the convergence of both systems of judicial decision-making, *cf.* K. Zweigert, H. Kötz, *Einführung in die Rechtsvergleichung* (2nd ed., Tübingen, 1984), Vol. 1, pp. 296 *et seq.* In particular in relation to administrative law, *cf.* also G. Vedel, "Le Précédent Judiciaire en Droit Public," in U. Blaurock (ed.), (1985) Frankfurt, *Die Bedeutung von Präjudizien im deutschen und französischen Recht*, Frankfurt 1985, pp. 75 *et seq.* (especially p. 82).

[5] The first Outline Law relating to administrative procedure dates from 1889 (Ley de Bases sobre el Procedimiento Administrativo of October 19, 1889). *cf. infra* (Section 12) for more detailed explanation concerning the current state of administrative law codification in Spain.

Under the fifth heading, a brief survey of the various administrative structures is given. This ranges from the federal structure of the Federal Republic of Germany to the unitary state, with its varying degrees of decentralisation and deconcentration.

The survey that follows examines in the first place the administrative law systems of the four large Member States (*i.e.* France, the Federal Republic of Germany, Italy and the United Kingdom), then the systems which apply in the other Member States in alphabetical order.

SECTION 1

FRANCE

(1) Present-day French administrative law has its origin in the final years of the eighteenth century. Already in the ancien régime, a centralised and hierarchical system of administration had become established. Although this administrative system, which was controlled by the King, was not subject to a system of administrative law in the current sense of the term, there nevertheless had appeared by the end of the ancien régime a system of administrative rules, influenced initially by Roman and canon law, and increasingly during the eighteenth century by the philosophy of the Enlightenment.[1]

The 1789 revolution and the Declaration of the Rights of Man and the Citizen marked the transition from a police state to a state based on the rule of law. This meant that for the first time the essential prerequisite for the creation of a modern system of administrative law was fulfilled, *i.e.* making the public administration subject to the rule of law.[2]

The subsequent development of administrative law was strongly influenced by the development of various forms of legal protection. After 1789, a strict separation between the executive and the judiciary was observed, under which any involvement by the courts in the administration was prohibited.[3] The fact that supervision of the administration by independent courts was prohibited is explained by the reactionary attitude of the courts during the ancien régime. The pre-revolutionary courts

---

[1] *cf.* J.-L. Mestre, "Les fondements historiques du droit administratif français," in [1982–83] E.D.C.E. No. 34, pp. 63 *et seq. cf.* in this context also F.-P. Bénoit, "Les fondements de la justice administrative," Mél. M. Waline, (1974) Paris, pp. 283 *et seq.* (on the development of the autonomous nature of administrative law).

[2] *cf.* J. Rivero, "Vers un droit commun européen: nouvelles perspectives en droit administratif" in M. Cappelletti (ed.) *New Perspectives for a Common Law of Europe*, (1978) Florence, pp. 389, 393 *et seq.*

[3] Law (relating to judicial organisation) of August 16–24, 1790, Article 13: "Les fonctions judiciaires sont distinctes et demeureront toujours séparées des fonctions administratives. Les juges ne pourront, à peine de forfaiture, troubler, de quelque manière que ce soit, les opérations des corps administratifs, ni citer devant eux les administrateurs pour raison de leurs fonctions."

("Parlements") had impeded attempts at reforming the administration and shown themselves hostile towards the ideas of the Revolution.[4]

Because of this strict regime of separation of powers, it was not for the courts, but for the administration itself to adjudicate in complaints against administrative actions. This task was assigned to the Conseil d'Etat, which was established by the Constitution of the Year VIII (1799) as a consultative body to the government. It was not long before its opinions enjoyed a high degree of authority and became to all intents and purposes binding on lower authorities. In 1872, the Conseil d'Etat acquired a special Litigation Section.[5] In institutional terms, the Conseil d'Etat should still be considered as forming part of the executive, its members being civil servants rather than judges.[6] In the meantime, however, the Litigation Section of the Conseil d'Etat has emancipated itself from its original role and currently operates as an independent administrative court.

However, it was not the Conseil d'Etat, but the Tribunal des Conflits which was the first to point clearly to the independence enjoyed by administrative law in relation to private law. In its keynote *Blanco* decision of 1873, it held that the liability of the public authorities was to be made subject, not to the fundamental principles of the Code Civil, which regulates the relations between individuals, but to those "règles spéciales qui varient suivant les besoins du service et la nécessité de concilier les droits de l'Etat avec les droits privés."[7] Thus the liability of the public authorities was made subject to a special set of rules of public law.

The starting-point for the decision by the Tribunal des Conflits was the question of the boundaries of competence between the administration and the (ordinary) courts in the area of state liability. In the past, questions of jurisdiction have often formed the basis of substantive administrative law theory.[8] The fundamental question of finding a deci-

---

[4] *cf.* A. de Laubadère, J.-C. Venezia, Y. Gaudemet, *Traité de droit administratif* (9th ed., Paris 1984), Vol. 1, pp. 431 *et seq.*
[5] Further details on the history of the Conseil d'Etat: *Le Conseil d'Etat, son histoire à travers les documents d'époque, 1799–1974*, (1974) Paris; *cf.* also J. M. Auby, R. Drago, *Traité de contentieux administratif* (3rd ed., Paris 1984), Vol. 1, pp. 233–243.
[6] *cf.* M. Fromont, "Der französische Staatsrat und sein Werk" (1978) DVBl., 89.
[7] Decision of the Tribunal of February 8, 1873; M. Long, P. Weil, G. Braibant, *Les grands arrêts de la jurisprudence administrative* (G.A.) (8th ed., Paris 1984), p. 5.
[8] *cf.* H. D. Jarass, "Besonderheiten des französischen Verwaltungsrechts im Vergleich," (1981) DÖV, 813, 814, who cites by way of example the distinction between "domaine public" and "domaine privé," "contrat administratif" and "contrat privé," "gestion publique" and "gestion privée," "agents publics" and "salariés privés," "travaux publics" and "travaux privés."

sive criterion for what constitutes administrative law, which finds its clearest expression in the controversy surrounding the concepts of "public authority" (puissance publique) and "public service" (service public)[9] can be traced back to the demarcation between the jurisdiction of the administrative courts and that of the ordinary courts. It is mainly in the procedural field that French administrative law has been designed to accommodate this distinction.

Thus the administrative courts were not created on the basis that the available administrative law required specific organs for its enforcement. In fact the opposite was the case: "The legal review organs of the administration created their own subject-matter, namely administrative law."[10]

Following the establishment of the Litigation Section of the Conseil d'Etat (1872) on the one hand and the leading *Blanco* decision by the Tribunal des Conflits on the other, administrative law, from the end of the nineteenth century onwards, developed as a separate branch of the law having its own theoretical basis. Among the leading authors who staked out the field for this development, special mention must be made of Edouard Laferrière,[11] whose work *Traité de la juridiction administrative et des recours contentieux*, which appeared in 1887, was for a long time regarded as the administrative law bible (R. Drago).[12] It was, however, chiefly the Conseil d'Etat which, through its case law, exercised a decisive influence over French administrative law. The main body of French administrative law can essentially be regarded as its creation.[13]

---

[9] On this point, *cf.* J.-B. Geffroy, "Service public et prérogatives de puissance publique, Réflexions sur les déboires d'un couple célèbre," (1987) RDP, pp. 49 *et seq.*; on the development of the concept of administrative law, *cf.* J. Rivero, *Droit administratif* (11th ed., Paris 1985), pp. 31 *et seq.*, Ch. Eisemann, *Cours de droit administratif*, Part 1, (1982) Paris, pp. 21 *et seq.*

[10] H. D. Jarass, (1981) DÖV, 813, 814.

[11] On the important place occupied by Laferrière in the development of French administrative law as a discipline, *cf.* G. Langrod, "France" in: E. V. Heyen (ed.), *Geschichte der Verwaltungsrechtswissenschaft in Europa*, pp. 67, 68 *et seq.* The following major works played an important part in the subsequent development of French administrative law as a discipline: L. Duguit, *Traité de droit constitutionnel*, 5 Vol., (1921, 1928); M. Hauriou, *Précis de droit administratif* (12th ed., 1933); G. Jèze, *Principes généraux du droit administratif*, 6 Vol. (1925–36); M. Waline, *Droit administratif* (9th ed., 1963).

[12] Quoted by G. Langrod, *loc. cit.*, footnote 11, p. 71.

[13] *cf.* M. Fromont, (1978) DVBl., 89, 91; J.-M. Woehrling, "Die französische Verwaltungsgerichtbarkeit im Vergleich mit der deutschen," (1985) NVwZ, 21.

(2) Otto Mayer's famous dictum that "constitutional law passes away, administrative law remains"[14] applies particularly to the development of French law, influenced as it is by the continuity of the Conseil d'Etat's case law.[15] Nevertheless, the many various forms of government and types of state organisation which France has experienced between the Revolution and the Fifth Republic[16] have not been completely without influence on the administrative law of the day.

The main distinguishing feature of the Constitution of the Fifth Republic of October 4, 1958, as compared both with the previous Constitution of the Fourth Republic and with the forms of state organisation in Germany and the United Kingdom, for example, is the particularly powerful position of the executive. The latter has a dual structure and consists of the President of the Republic, who is elected by the people,[17] and of the Government, led by the Prime Minister. The relationship between the Government and the Parliament is governed by Articles 34 *et seq.* of the Constitution. Only those very important matters which are listed in those Articles may be the subject of Laws adopted by Parliament. However, the Government may be empowered to issue regulations in these fields by a Law adopted by Parliament. In relation to all other matters the Government has the power, acting independently, to issue regulations (Article 37).[18]

The courts are not entitled to deliberate on the constitutionality of promulgated Laws adopted by Parliament. It is the Conseil Constitutionnel which exercises a preventive review of those Laws, which must be submitted to it before being promulgated. On the other hand, the courts may in principle be called upon to review the legality of administrative actions. The increased powers of administrative regulation have also enhanced the importance of the Conseil d'Etat, which, since 1958, also

---

[14] O. Mayer, *Deutsches Verwaltungsrecht* (3rd ed.), München-Leipzig, Vol. 1, foreword.
[15] Vedel (Mél. Waline [1974] Paris, Part II, p. 777) refers to the "Discontinuité du droit constitutionnel et continuité du droit administratif"; *cf.* also J. Rivero, *loc. cit.*, footnote 9, p. 24.
[16] *cf.*, *e.g.* P. Pactet, *Institutions politiques—Droit constitutionnel* (7th ed., Paris 1985), pp. 262 *et seq.*
[17] Since the constitutional amendment brought about by the Referendum of October 28, 1962 (Loi No. 62–1292 du 6 novembre, 1962 relative à l'élection du Président de la République au suffrage universel).
[18] On the government's rule-making powers, *cf.* G. Burdeau, *Droit constitutionnel et institutions politiques* (20th ed., Paris 1984) Paris, pp. 603 *et seq.*; also R. Klisch, *Gesetz und Verordnung in der Verfassung der 5. französischen Republik vom 4. Oktober, 1958,* (1971) Berlin.

has the power to review the legality of those regulations which have been issued independently by the Government.

The Constitution does not confine itself to defining the competence, and consequently also the position, of the executive in relation to the legislature and the courts. It also establishes the limits within which the administration may act against the citizen by referring in its preamble to the Declaration of the Rights of Man and the Citizen of 1789 and to the provisions of the 1946 Constitution which confirmed and completed them. By virtue of this reference the *libertés publiques* included in these provisions have been incorporated into the present Constitution. As the Conseil Constitutionnel has decided, these freedoms are constitutionally binding.[19]

(3) Although the fundamental principles of administrative law are thus already embodied in the Constitution, they remain too abstract to constitute adequate guidance for the settling of administrative disputes. In addition to the Constitution, the sources of administrative law include other written legislation, customary law and judge-made law.[20]

As to written legislation, Laws adopted by Parliament concern themselves only with particular items of general administrative law and procedure.[21] Prominent among these Laws are the 1978/79 Laws relating to certain duties to provide information and to give reasons.[22] There is an increasing tendency towards codifying specific subjects of "special" administrative law, *e.g.* the Code de l'administration communale, the Code de l'environnement and the Code de l'urbanisme. However, these Codes essentially restrict themselves to the grouping together of the relevant legal texts, and as such serve the purpose of clarifying the law rather than fulfilling a creative role of further development. Finally, rules of

---

[19] Decision of the Conseil of July 16, 1971, J.O. 1971, 7114 = G.D. No. 20, p. 222. On the question of the legal status of the preamble to the 1958 Constitution, *cf.* also J. Gicquel, A. Hauriou, *Droit constitutionnel et institutions politiques* (8th ed., Paris 1985), pp. 169 *et seq.*; on the general question of the "libertés publiques," *cf.* the work of the same name by J. Morange, (1985) Paris.

[20] Further details in J. Rivero, *loc. cit.*, footnote 9, pp. 52 *et seq.*

[21] The law-making powers of Parliament in the field of administrative law are based on Article 34 of the Constitution, in particular in relation to those issues which concern (a) "the fundamental guarantees for the benefit of the citizen which enable him/her to exercise his/her civil liberties," (b) "the judicial system" and (c) "the fundamental principles of autonomy and of social security."

[22] *cf.* Law No. 78–17 of January 6, 1978; Law No. 78–753 of July 17, 1978; Law No. 79–18 of January 3, 1979; Law No. 79–587 of November 7, 1979. These Laws are extensively dealt with in A. Holleaux, "Les nouvelles lois françaises sur l'information du public," (1981) RISA, pp. 191 *et seq.*, especially pp. 192 *et seq.* (on foreign influences).

administrative law can also be found in the regulations (règlements) issued by the executive. European Community directives are also in principle incorporated into French law by means of regulations.[23]

Although in principle customary law is acknowledged as being a source of law, it plays only a subordinate role in administrative law.[24]

In view of the fragmentary nature of the available legislation and customary law, it is case law which has donned the mantle of principal agent in the development of administrative law. Through a liberal interpretation of Laws which do not completely cover the cases before them, and by the creative process of filling gaps in the existing legislation,[25] the administrative courts have contrived to create a separate system of general administrative law. The demarcation between administrative law and private law, the theory of the various forms of administrative action (*i.e.* the acte administratif as a unilateral, specifically individual or generally abstract rule on the one hand and the contrat administratif as a bilateral form of regulation on the other), as well as the conditions as to substance and form for the legality of administrative action, can all be traced back to the case law of the Conseil d'Etat. This "jurisprudence" constitutes a system of law which is flexible and capable of adjusting to the particular circumstances of each individual case to be decided.[26] Although under the Constitution the courts are not formally empowered to issue binding and generally-applicable rules, the leading decisions (arrêt de principe) of the Conseil d'Etat are generally acknowledged as constituting valid law. The Conseil d'Etat itself only very rarely deviates from these decisions, the administration considers itself to be bound by its "jurisprudence," and an infringement of the case law is punished in the same way as an infringement of the written law, *i.e.* by a declaration of nullity or liability of the public authorities. Rivero is right when he says on the status of the "jurisprudence" as a source of law:

[23] *cf.* Law No. 66–481 of July 6, 1966. On the subject of European Community law as a (direct) source of French administrative law, *cf.* B. Genevois, "Der Conseil d'Etat und das Gemeinschaftsrecht: Antagonismus oder Komplementarität?" (1985) EuR, 355, 364 *et seq.*

[24] *cf.* A. de Laubadère, J.-C. Venezia, Y. Gaudemet, *loc. cit.*, footnote 4, Vol. 1, p. 31.

[25] *cf.* also, however, G. Vedel, P. Delvolvé, *Droit administratif* (9th ed., Paris 1984), p. 404: "Le juge 'découvre' le droit plus qu'il ne 'l'invente.' "

[26] On the characteristics of the règles jurisprudentielles, *cf.* J. Rivero, *loc. cit.*, footnote 9, p. 76.

"La règle jurisprudentielle au double point de vue objectif—existence d'une sanction—et subjectif—sentiment d'obligation pesant sur les assujettis—présente tous les caractères de la règle de droit."[27]

Of great practical importance, although subject to controversy as to their theoretical basis, are the general principles of law (principes généraux de droit). The following can be mentioned as examples of principles recognised by the Conseil d'Etat: substantive civil rights (in particular those relating to public freedom, individual rights and the equality rule), constitutional rights in relation to the administration and to administrative law procedure (in particular the right to defend oneself and the right to a hearing) and finally the principle of administration conducted in accordance with the rule of law.[28] In substance, these principles are essentially aimed at the legal protection of the citizen, yet they also seek to be compatible with the requirements of the administration. This is why the principle of the *continuité du service public* was invoked to justify a restriction of the civil servants' right to strike.[29] Although the Conseil d'Etat, which made *de facto* use of these principles as far back as the 1940s and applied them explicitly in the 1950s,[30] is sometimes said to be the "inventor" of the theory of fundamental legal principles,[31] we must not

[27] J. Rivero, *loc. cit.*, footnote 9, p. 77. On the role of precedents in French administrative law, *cf.* also G. Vedel, "Le précédent judiciaire en droit public" in U. Blaurock (ed.), *Die Bedeutung von Präjudizien im deutschen und französischen Recht*, (1985) Frankfurt, pp. 75 *et seq.* (especially. p. 82: "La structure du droit administratif français est donc paradoxale et plus anglaise que française").

[28] The various legal principles are extensively listed in G. Vedel, P. Delvolvé, *loc. cit.*, footnote 25, pp. 390 *et seq.* and in H. Krech, *Die Theorie der allgemeinen Rechtsgrundsätze im französischen öffentlichen Recht*, (1973) Göttingen, pp. 176–181.

[29] Leading decision by Conseil d'Etat of July 7, 1950 (Dehaene), G.A. No. 79, p. 339, *cf.* G. Vedel, P. Delvolvé, *loc. cit.*, footnote 25, pp. 1110 *et seq.*; *cf.* also A. Bleckmann, (*Europarecht* (4th ed., Köln/Berlin/Bonn/München (1985), pp. 114 *et seq.*) on the possibility of incorporating this principle into European Community law.

[30] Conseil d'Etat decisions of May 5, 1944 (*Trompier-Gravier*), G.A. No. 66, p. 281; of October 26, 1945 (*Aramu*), Rec. 213; and in particular March 9, 1951 (*Concerts du Conservatoire*), G.A. No. 81, p. 355: "principe d'égalité qui régit le fonctionnement des services publics" and June 26, 1959 (*Syndicat général des ingénieurs-conseils*) G.A. No. 98, p. 474. Among the more recent Conseil d'Etat decisions, particular attention should be given to the decision of December 8, 1978 (*G.I.S.T.I.*), G.A. No. 112, 587, by which the right to lead a normal family life was also recognised in relation to foreigners living in France. By creating its "own" principles, the Conseil d'Etat avoids applying the European Human Rights Convention. *cf.* also on this point J.-F. Flauss, "Le juge administratif français et la Convention européenne des droits de l'homme," (1983) AJDA, 387.

[31] *cf.* A. de Laubadère, J.-C. Venezia, Y. Gaudemet, *loc. cit.*, footnote 4, Vol. 1, p. 266.

lose sight of the fact that the Conseil Constitutionnel[32] and the leading authors[33] have also made a considerable contribution to this trend.

The definition, legal nature and hierarchical place of the principes généraux remain the subject of continued controversy, even in France. It is of course rare to find any such theoretical considerations in the statements of reasons for court decisions. Statements made by the members of the Conseil d'Etat give the impression that the courts merely restrict themselves to confirming the existence of already discovered fundamental principles.[34] The leading authors, however, have tended to adhere to the view that the Conseil d'Etat is acting in a creative capacity; the fundamental legal principles were included in the substantive law for the first time by the courts and must therefore be regarded as being part and parcel of case law.[35]

The hierarchical place of the principes généraux in law has yet to be definitively clarified.[36] There is general agreement that fundamental legal principles, where they have not been expressly designated as being of subsidiary importance, take precedence over any regulations, including the *règlements autonomes*, and consequently constitute a criterion for their legality.[37] In addition, the Conseil Constitutionnel has accorded constitutional status to a number of legal principles.[38] The implication

---

[32] *cf.* in particular the Decision by the Conseil Constitutionnel of June 26, 1969, G.D. No. 19, p. 208. On the increasingly important role played by the Conseil Constitutionnel in the development of general legal principles, *cf.* B. Jeanneau, "La théorie des principes généraux du droit à l'epreuve du temps," (1981–82) E.C.D.E. pp. 33, 36 *et seq.*

[33] *cf.* essentially B. Jeanneau, *Les principes généraux du droit dans la jurisprudence administrative*, (1954) Paris, as well as M. Letourneur, "Les principes généraux du droit dans la jurisprudence du Conseil d'Etat," (1951) E.D.C.E., p. 19. On the present stage reached in this development, *cf.* A. de Laubadère, J.-C. Venezia, Y. Gaudemet, *loc. cit.*, footnote 4, Vol. 1, pp. 266 *et seq.*; B. Jeanneau, (1981–82) E.D.C.E., 33 *et seq.*

[34] A similar opinion can be found in G. Braibant, *Le droit administratif français*, (1984) Paris, p. 221. Prior to this, *cf.*, *e.g.* R. Latournerie, "Essai sur les méthodes juridictionnelles du Conseil d'Etat," *Le Conseil d'Etat, livre jubilaire*, (1952) Paris, pp. 177, 204 *et. seq.*

[35] *cf.* esp. J. Rivero, *loc. cit.*, footnote 9, p. 78; A. de Laubadère, J.-C. Venezia, Y. Gaudemet, *loc. cit.*, Vol. 1, p. 269. For a contrary opinion, *cf.* esp. M. Waline, *Droit administratif* (9th ed., Paris 1963), p. 468.

[36] For a summary: B. Jeanneau, (1981–82) E.D.C.E., pp. 33, 38 *et seq.*

[37] *cf.* Decision of Conseil d'Etat of June 26, 1959 (*Syndicat général des ingénieurs-conseils*), G.A. No. 98, pp. 474 *et seq.*: "les principes généraux du droit qui, résultant notamment du préambule de la Constitution, s'imposent à toute autorité réglementaire même en l'absence de dispositions législatives."

[38] *cf.* Decisions by the Conseil Constitutionnel of July 16, 1971, G.D. No. 20, p. 222 (Freedom of assembly) and of December 27, 1973, G.D. No. 24, p. 274 (principle of equality). However, here we are dealing with principles which can be traced back to the written law, *cf.* G. Vedel, P. Delvolvé, *loc. cit.*, footnote 25, 399.

that these legal principles could derogate from Laws adopted by Parliament becomes a practical proposition only where the Conseil Constitutionnel reviews Laws before their entry into force.

Legal writing cannot qualify as a source of law in the true sense of the term, although it has exercised a considerable influence on the courts in many fields. Because of the brevity of the statements of reasons for judgment, annotations on decisions are of considerable assistance in understanding the various trends in administrative law.

(4) The specific ways in which judicial review can be exercised are judicial proceedings (recours contentieux), administrative complaint (recours administratif) or intervention by the mediator (recours au médiateur).

Judicial protection against the administration has, as has already been mentioned, been shaped by the central position occupied by the Conseil d'Etat. In certain forms of litigation, designated by law, the Conseil d'Etat acts as a court of first and last instance. In other cases there are essentially two levels of judicial action. In its role as appeal court, the Conseil d'Etat essentially reviews decisions of the *tribunaux administratifs*, which since 1953 have acted as general administrative courts of first instance and as such have jurisdiction in principle over all administrative litigation.[39] In its role as Supreme Court, the Conseil d'Etat reviews the decisions taken at first instance by the majority of special administrative courts. These include not only the disciplinary courts, but also certain quasi-judicial administrative commissions. Actions may be brought before the ordinary courts for disputes which relate to administrative action which comes within the sphere of private law (*e.g.* contracts governed by private law) or for certain forms of administrative litigation especially designated by law. The civil courts also have jurisdiction over the so-called *voies de fait* committed by the administration, *i.e.* administrative action which has no statutory basis, which is clearly illegal, and which constitutes a serious infringement of basic civil liberties.[40]

---

[39] *cf.* Décret No. 53–934 of September 30, 1953, Portant réforme du contentieux administratif. On the legal position of the judges with the tribunaux administratifs, *cf.* the recent Law No. 86–14 of January 6, 1986, and commenting on it, M. Tourdias, "La loi du 6 janvier 1986," (1986) AJDA, 275 *et seq.*; L. Richer, "Des droits du juge à ceux du justiciable," (1986) AJDA, 278 *et seq.*

[40] For a more detailed discussion: *cf.* G. Vedel, P. Delvolvé, *loc. cit.*, footnote 25, p. 151.

Conflicts of jurisdiction between the administrative courts and the ordinary courts are settled by the Tribunal des Conflits.[41]

The types of action are, as is normally the case, classified in accordance with the extent of the relevant court's jurisdiction.[42] Under the *contentieux de l'annulation* (action for annulment) it is only the courts which may annul unlawful administrative action. The most important type of action under this heading is the *recours pour excès de pouvoir*. Under the *contentieux de pleine juridiction* (litigation involving unlimited jurisdiction) the court also has the power to amend or replace the administrative decision. With the exception of the action for damages, which may result in the administration being ordered to make a financial payment, the courts are reluctant to issue directives to the administrative authorities. An action seeking to compel the administration to perform a certain obligation would be incompatible with the French interpretation of the separation of powers.[43]

By far the most important type of action is the recours pour excès de pouvoir,[44] which can be used to act against all forms of activity by an administration (actes administratifs unilatéraux). These include both individual acts and regulations. In order to be admissible, the action brought must not only observe the prescribed time limits and formalities, but also—and above all—seek to protect a legal interest. The courts have brought a very liberal interpretation to bear on the concept of intérêt pour agir. Thus the inhabitant of a municipality who paid municipal taxes was found to be entitled to sue for the purpose of challenging any measure

---

[41] For a more detailed discussion see R. Kutscher, *Das französische Konfliktsgericht—sein Beitrag zur Kompetenzverteilung zwischen ordentlichen Gerichten und Verwaltungsgerichten in Frankreich*, (1983), Diss. Mainz, 1983.

[42] Apart from the "contentieux de l'annulation" and the "contentieux de pleine juridiction," there are also the "contentieux de l'interprétation" and the "contentieux de la répression" (Examples in A. de Laubadère, J.-C. Venezia, Y. Gaudemet, *loc. cit.*, footnote 4, Vol. 1, p. 548. In recent times, authors have tended to draw a distinction according to the object (*e.g.* Debbasch, *Contentieux administratif* (3rd ed., Paris 1981), p. 698) or the nature of the action (contentieux objectif/subjectif and contentieux de la légalité/des droits respectively) (*cf.* J.-M. Auby and R. Drago, *loc. cit.* (footnote 5), Vol. 2, pp. 79 *et seq.*).

[43] *cf.* J.-M. Woehrling, (1985) NVwZ, 21, 22; also A. de Laubadère, J.-C. Venezia, Y. Gaudemet, *loc. cit.*, footnote 4, Vol. 1, p. 539.

[44] On the historical development of this concept, *cf.* P. Landon, *Histoire abrégée du recours pour excès de pouvoir des origines à 1954*, (1962) Paris. A critical assessment of the effectiveness of the recours pour excès de pouvoir for the purpose of protecting individual rights, *cf.* J. Rivero, "Le système français de protection des citoyens contre l'arbitraire administratif à l'épreuve des faits," in Mél. J. Dabin, (1966) Brussels, pp. 813 *et seq.*, and, most recently, P. Delvolvé, "L'exécution des décisions de justice contre 'l'administration' " (1983–84) E.D.C.E., pp. 111 *et seq.*

adopted by the communal authorities with financial implications.[45] In addition, associations may seek to represent the interests of their members in court actions.[46] Unlike the position in Germany, where admissibility is conditional upon the plaintiff's claiming the infringement of a subjective right, French court action challenging the administration is geared more to the objective interest served by the opportunity to review the lawfulness of administrative action.[47] Where the action is admissible, the administrative action is assessed for its defects. The grounds for review include lack of competence, procedural irregularity, statutory infringement and misuse of powers (détournement de pouvoir).[48]

Proceedings before the administrative courts are based on the principle of preliminary examination and that of the written nature of the procedure. The *Commissaire du Gouvernement* has an important role in the conduct of these proceedings.[49] He examines the dispute before the court independently of the *juge rapporteur* and makes his submissions. The position of Commissaire du Gouvernement served as the inspiration for that of Advocate-General with the European Court of Justice.[50]

Before the commencement of court proceedings, the citizen may apply

---

[45] Decision of Conseil d'Etat of March 29, 1901 (*Casanova*), G.A. No. 8, p. 35.
[46] Decision of Conseil d'Etat of December 28, 1906 (*Syndicat des patrons coiffeurs de Limoges*), G.A. No. 18. p. 69.
[47] *cf.* J.-M. Woehrling, (1985) NVwZ, 21, 23; M. Fromont, *Rechtsschutz gegenüber der Verwaltung in Deutschland, Frankreich und den Europäischen Gemeinschaften*, pp. 203 *et seq*. A critical note regarding exaggerated emphasis on this distinction can be found in G. Vedel, P. Delvolvé, *loc. cit.*, footnote 25, p. 744.
[48] For more detailed discussion, *cf.* M. Degen, "Klageverfahren und Klagegründe im französischen Verwaltungsprozess," (1981) *Die Verwaltung*, 157, 166 *et seq*.
[49] On the historical development and the role of the Commissaires du Gouvernement, *cf.* A. Bernard, "Aperçu sur l'oeuvre juridictionnelle des commissaires du Gouvernement durant la seconde moitié du XIXe siècle," as well as F. Gazier, "Aperçu sur l'oeuvre jurisprudentielle des commissaires du Gouvernement depuis 1900," both in: *Le Conseil d'Etat, Livre jubilaire*, (1947) Paris, pp. 299 and 303 respectively; *cf.* also Sauvel, "Les origines des commissaires du Gouvernement auprès du Conseil statuant au contentieux," (1949) RDP, pp. 299 *et seq.*, J.-M. Auby, R. Drago, *Traité de contentieux administratif*, pp. 261 *et seq*. On the role and personal profile of J. Romieu and L. Blum, two important Commissaires du Gouvernement, *cf.* the contributions by G. Cahen-Salvador and P. Juvigny, *Le Conseil d'Etat, Livre jubilaire*, pp. 323 and 337 respectively.
[50] *cf.* C. O. Lenz, "Aus der Praxis des Generalanwalts am EuGH," lecture given at the College of Europe in Hamburg on November 22, 1985, *Vorträge und Berichte aus dem Institut für Integrationsforschung der Stiftung Europa-Kolleg Hamburg* (J. Schwarze, ed.), pp. 1 *et seq.*; G. Reischl, "Die Funktion der Generalanwälte in der Europäischen Rechtsprechung," *Der EuGH als Verfassungsgericht und Rechtsschutzinstanz* (J. Schwarze, ed.), (1983) Baden-Baden, pp. 121 *et seq*.

for an internal administrative review, under which he challenges an administrative decision before the department which took the decision (recours gracieux) or before its hierarchical superior (recours hiérarchique). This type of procedure with full argument on both sides is, in principle, optional. However, the action will be admissible only if an administrative decision has actually been taken (règle de la décision préalable). Four months' silence on the part of the administration is taken as a refusal.

Finally, the administration is subject to supervision through a Mediator (médiateur), who is appointed by the Government but acts independently.[50a] The latter is invited by a Member of the National Assembly or by a senator, mostly on application by a citizen, to investigate shortcomings in the administration and, where appropriate, to propose improvements. The office of Mediator, created in 1973, was inspired by the Scandinavian Ombudsman model, although his position is clearly weaker and is closer to that of the British Parliamentary Commissioner, who similarly cannot be approached directly by the general public.

(5) The organisation of the administration is characterised by a high degree of centralisation, which dates back to the Ancien Régime and became even more pronounced during Napoleon's reign. However, since the 1970s it has been possible to discern a trend towards decentralisation (i.e. the devolution of decision-making powers from the State to legally autonomous administrative authorities) and towards deconcentration (i.e. the devolution of decision-making powers from central to subordinate and local departments of the central administration),[51] which found their clearest expression in the regional and municipal reforms of 1972 and 1982/83.[52] However, this has done little to change the fact that France is essentially administered from Paris.[53]

The direct central administration (Fonction publique d'Etat) has a hierarchical structure. It is led by the President of the Republic and by the

---

[50a] On the legal nature of the function of the Médiateur, cf. J.-P. Costa, "Le médiateur peut-il être autre chose qu'une autorité administrative?" (1987) AJDA, pp. 341 et seq.
[51] For more details on the notions of décentralisation and déconcentration, cf. G. Vedel, P. Delvolvé, loc. cit., footnote 25, pp. 849 et seq.
[52] Law No. 82.213 of February 4, 1982, amended by the Law of June 22, 1982; Law No. 83.8 of January 7, 1983; Law No. 83.663 of July 22, 1983; Law No. 83.1186 of December 29, 1983. On the progress recorded so far by these reforms, particularly Law No. 86.16 of January 6, 1986 relative à l'organisation des régions, cf. A. Delcamp, "La région, nouvelle collectivité territoriale," (1986) AJDA, pp. 195 et seq.; cf. also the contributions in (1987) 3 AJDA, special issue, "La décentralisation cinq ans après" (pp. 139 et seq.).
[53] cf. also M. Fromont, "Die französische Kommunalverfassung," (1985) DVBl., 421, 425.

Prime Minister. The specialist Ministers head each specific department. The State is represented in the Départements by a "Commissaire de la République." The latter has taken the place of the Prefect, who, until the 1982/83 reforms, exercised the dual function of State representative and of executive officer of the Département.[54] The current executive functions of the Départements are exercised by the elected President of the Conseil Général, this development realising one of the aims of these reforms, namely to create more "local democracy."[55]

The indirect administration (Fonction publique territoriale) consists of the territorial authorities (municipalities, Départements and regions). Article 72 of the Constitution guarantees the autonomy of these authorities subject to state supervision. The functions of these territorial authorities have been extended by the above-mentioned reforms. New functions have been conferred on the municipalities, especially in the field of town planning, on the Départements, in the field of social administration and public health, and on the regions in the field of regional planning and economic assistance. State supervision has been relaxed and is currently limited to legal review.

Municipalities, Départements and regions have been constituted so as to conform to a uniform model, which does not invariably take into account the actual geographical, electoral or economic dividing lines. The resulting lack of flexibility may have contributed towards the proliferation of new types of administrative units.[56] In this context, mention must be made of the public corporations (établissements publics), *i.e.* legal entities subject to public law, on whom specific public functions, to be exercised with a considerable degree of autonomy, have been conferred, and whose action is subject to state supervision. More specifically, this concept covers a great variety of administrative units, ranging from institutions whose structures are of a corporate nature to the *établissements publics de caractère industriel et commercial*, which, although constituted according to public law, are nevertheless exempt from certain public law rules.[57]

---

[54] *cf.* M. Fromont, (1985) DVBl., 421; for more details of the role of the Commissaires de la République, *cf.* A. de Laubadère, J.-C. Venezia, Y. Gaudemet, *loc. cit.* footnote 4, Vol. 1, pp. 76 *et seq.*

[55] For more details, *cf.* M. Fromont, (1985) DVBl., 421, 422 *et seq.*

[56] *cf.* M. Hilf, *Die Organisationsstruktur der Europäischen Gemeinschaften*, (1982) Berlin/Heidelberg/New York, pp. 270 *et seq.*

[57] For more details of recent date, *cf.* F. Gazier, "Etude sur les établissements publics," E.D.C.E. No. 36 (1984–85), pp. 13 *et seq.*

(6) A summary of the main characteristics of French administrative law[58] should feature in the first instance the crucial role played by the Conseil d'Etat, whose case law has shaped general administrative law, especially by developing its fundamental legal principles. The fact that administrative law has developed through court procedure geared to legal disputes explains the extent to which even substantive administrative law has been influenced by procedural law; thus the demarcation of court jurisdiction has in many cases constituted the basis for fundamental principles of administrative law. At the same time, the administrative law system has been geared towards the correction of administrative errors.

In theoretical terms, French administrative law has been shaped by the objectives of administrative action.[59] The aim of ensuring the effective and continuous functioning of the administration is a major consideration here. The strong position occupied by the executive and the principle of the strict separation of powers mean that, for the purposes of legal protection, actions seeking the performance of obligations are normally inadmissible and that the degree of supervision exercised by the judicial review of administrative action tends to be on the low side compared with German law. This applies to both the number of decisions and the extent to which the substance of the various cases is subjected to review.[60]

French administrative procedure is essentially geared to the objective supervision of administrative action, although it also seeks to enforce the citizen's subjective rights. This explains why entitlement to sue is not subject to any particularly onerous conditions, and why even rules having a general and abstract scope, which do not affect the citizen, are open to challenge. This is also directly why the instituting of an action has no suspensive effect.[61] In spite of the recent decentralising legislation, French administrative organisation remains extremely centralist.

---

[58] Summary descriptions of the main characteristics of the most recent developments in French administrative law can be found in M. Fromont, "Le système français de protection juridictionnelle du citoyen contre l'administration," *Festschrift für C.-F. Menger* (H.-U. Erichsen, W. Hoppe, A. v. Mutius [ed.]), (1985) Köln/Berlin/Bonn/München, pp. 887 *et seq.*; J.-M. Woehrling, (1985) NVwZ, 21 *et seq.*; H. D. Jarass, (1981) DÖV 813 *et seq.*

[59] *cf.* also H. D. Jarass, (1981) DÖV, 813, 818.

[60] *cf.* J.-M. Woehrling, (1985) NVwZ, 21, 22; H. D. Jarass, (1981) DÖV 813, 815.

[61] For a critical assessment of the absence of suspensive effect in French administrative law, *cf.* M. Fromont, *Festschrift für C.-F. Menger*, *loc. cit.*, footnote 58, pp. 887, 896. *cf.* also by the same author, RISA (1984) 309 *et seq.* on the provisional legal protection in the E.C. Member States from a comparative viewpoint.

SECTION 2

FEDERAL REPUBLIC OF GERMANY

(1) The prevailing administrative law in the Federal Republic of Germany is the result of an evolution whose main stages run from the police state administration of the seventeenth and eighteenth centuries, through the administration under the liberal constitutional State of the nineteenth century, to that of the twentieth century social constitutional State and its distinctive shape under the Bonn constitution.[1]

The absolutist State, which took shape initially in Germany's statelets, exercised its functions not only with a view to raising revenue for the purpose of maintaining an army and a royal household, but also in order to improve the lot of its citizens, which made it a "mercantilist welfare state."[2] The policing authority covered practically the entire internal administration. The increase in administrative functions, which extended to virtually every form of human activity, was accompanied by the growth of a bureaucracy formed by a professional civil service. The public authorities were not subject to a binding set of legal rules. The sovereign had virtually freed himself from the limitations imposed on his power by the estates under the legal system of the Middle Ages, and his role as the unfettered creator of law grew accordingly.[3] The individual had to accept the sovereign's intrusions, but he could claim damages from the State which was conceived as a separate legal entity (subject to private law), distinct from the monarch acting with his sovereign power (the so-called Fiskustheorie: "accept and liquidate").

The constitutional movement of the nineteenth century, which was led by the bourgeoisie, was aimed in the first place against the numerous and legally unimpeded intrusions by the monarch. The objectives of this movement, namely the separation of powers (enabling representatives of the people to participate in the law-making process), the equality before

---

[1] *cf.* on this trend H. J. Wolff, O. Bachof, *Verwaltungsrecht I* (9th ed., München 1974), pp. 38 *et seq.*; H. Maurer, *Allgemeines Verwaltungsrecht* (5th ed., München 1986), pp. 12 *et seq.*; E. Forsthoff, *Lehrbuch des Verwaltungsrechts* Vol. 1: General Considerations, (10th ed., München 1973), pp. 19 *et seq.*; P. Badura, *Verwaltungsrecht im liberalen und im sozialen Rechtsstaat* (1966) Tübingen, and, by the same author, *Das Verwaltungsrecht des liberalen Rechtsstaates* (1967) Göttingen.
[2] *cf.* H. J. Wolff, O. Bachof, *loc. cit.*, footnote 1, p. 39.
[3] *Ibid.*, p. 41.

the law of all citizens, and the recognition of areas of individual freedom in which the State was unable to interfere, were all to a greater or lesser extent realised by the Land constitutions of the mid-nineteenth century. Henceforth, any infringement of the citizen's freedom and property rights required the authority of a statute, obtained with the co-operation of the people's representatives. Instruments issued by the administrative authorities, including their regulations, were made subordinate in rank to statutes. The establishment of these principles, which ensured that the administration abided by the law, laid the foundations for the development of a modern system of administrative law. A classical description of administrative law under a liberal constitutional system can be found in Otto Mayer's *Deutsches Verwaltungsrecht*,[4] published in 1895–96, which exercised a lasting influence on the practice and theory of administrative law and found acclaim beyond the German borders.

The second half of the nineteenth century also saw the establishment of autonomous administrative courts, which led a separate existence from the administration and from the ordinary courts.[5] Contrary to what occurred in France, where the development of administrative jurisdiction was shaped by a central institution, the Conseil d'Etat, the German judicial system developed "from the bottom up," *i.e.* from the Länder.[6] After administrative courts had been established in Baden as early as 1863, the next decisive stage in the development of administrative jurisdiction was the establishment of the Prussian Higher Administrative Court (the OVG) between 1872 and 1875.

Under the Weimar Constitution (1919) and under the Bonn Basic Law of 1949, which followed the period of the totalitarian National Socialist State,[7] public administration evolved from a liberal constitutional

---

[4] *cf.* O. Mayer, *Deutsches Verwaltungsrecht*, Vols. 1 and 2 (1895/96) Leipzig; also E. V. Heyen, *Otto Mayer—Studien zu den geistigen Grundlagen seiner Verwaltungswissenschaft*, (1981) Berlin.

[5] For the conflicting viewpoints on the introduction of administrative courts, *cf.* the arguments by O. Bähr, *Der Rechtsstaat* (1st ed., Kassel/Göttingen 1864), and R. Gneist, *Der Rechtsstaat und die Verwaltungsgerichte in Deutschland* (2nd ed.), (1879); *cf.* also H.-U. Erichsen, *Verfassungs- und verwaltungsrechtsgeschichtliche Grundlagen der Lehre vom fehlerhaften belastenden Verwaltungsakt und seiner Aufhebung im Prozess*, (1971) Frankfurt, pp. 270 *et seq.*

[6] *cf.* M. Fromont, "Der französische Staatsrat und sein Werk," (1978) DVBl., 89.

[7] On the administrative court decisions during this period, *cf.* W. Hempfer, *Die nationalsozialistische Staatsauffassung in der Rechtssprechung des Preussischen Oberverwaltungsgerichts*, (1974) Berlin; *cf.* also M. Stolleis, "Verwaltungsgerichtsbarkeit im Nationalsozialismus," *Festschrift für C.-F. Menger* (H.-U. Erichsen, W. Hoppe, A. v. Mutius, ed.), (1985) Köln/Berlin/Bonn/München, pp. 57 *et seq.*

system to a State system which integrated social laws and customs. Whereas the nineteenth century administration essentially confined itself to guaranteeing state security and maintaining law and order, its role now increasingly became that of a provider of services.[8] The industrialisation and urbanisation of society, the social upheavals which followed both World Wars, as well as a series of economic crises, led to demands for "welfare provision" (Forsthoff's "Daseinsvorsorge")[9] by the State, which the administration attempted to satisfy by setting up municipal public utilities and public transport corporations and through the provision of social and cultural services. In addition to this shift in emphasis in the tasks of the administration, there occurred, as a result of the creation of the Federal Republic of Germany, a fundamental transformation in the administrative law system and its constitutional framework.[10]

(2) Under the Basic Law of May 23, 1949,[11] the Federal Republic of Germany is constituted as a federally structured, democratic State based on the rule of law and social justice (Article 20(1) and Article 28(1)(1)). In addition to these fundamental structural principles, it is especially the fundamental rights, including the general equality principle and the provisions relating to administrative organisation (especially respecting the division of administrative powers between the Federal State and the Länder), which constitute the basic tenets of administrative law, which is characterised as a whole by its special relationship with the Constitution. This relationship also finds expression in the oft-quoted dictum by F. Werner, former President of the Federal Administrative Court,

---

[8] cf. in particular E. Forsthoff, loc. cit., footnote 1, pp. 36, 368 et seq.

[9] Initially, cf. E. Forsthoff, Die Verwaltung als Leistungsträger (1938) Stuttgart/Berlin; on the current interpretation of the concept of welfare provision, cf. E. Forsthoff, loc. cit., footnote 1, p. 370 and the works cited there (Note 2).

[10] We shall refrain from discussing below the separate development of the public authorities in the German Democratic Republic, which H. J. Wolff and O. Bachof place under the heading of "Administrations in totalitarian states," loc. cit., footnote 1, pp. 46, 48 et seq. For more details on this subject, cf. M. Bullinger, Das Verwaltungsrecht in der DDR (1966); by the same author, "Umbildung des Verwaltungsrechts durch Planung in der DDR," Planung I (J. H. Kaiser, ed.), (1965) Baden-Baden, pp. 189 et seq.; C. H. Ule, "Gesetzlichkeit in der Verwaltung durch Verwaltungsverfahren und gerichtliche Kontrolle in der DDR," (1985) DVBl., 1029 et seq.; also, in general terms, on the function of the administrative and constitutional courts in the Eastern European states, cf. H. Krüger, (1986) DÖV, 45 (on the GDR in particular, p. 49); on the position occupied by administrative law theory in the GDR, cf. E. V. Heyen, "Deutschland," Geschichte der Verwaltungsrechtswissenschaft in Europa (E. V. Heyen, ed.), (1982) Frankfurt, pp. 29, 46–50.

[11] German Official Journal III, No. 100–1.

that administrative law is "constitutional law in concrete form."[12] The current President of the Court, H. Sendler, has pointed out that this relationship is reflected not only in the manner in which constitutional law finds its concrete expression in administrative rules, but also in the many principles of administrative law which the courts derive directly from the Constitution (*e.g.* the balanced judgment and proportionality principles).[13]

(3) The legislators, the courts and learned authors have co-operated in developing administrative law within its constitutional context. The crucial items of legislation here have been the Law relating to Federal Administrative Procedure (Verwaltungsverfahrensgesetz des Bundes— VwVfG) of May 25, 1976,[14] and the Laws relating to Administrative Procedure in the Länder, which essentially have the same contents as the former.[15] The single most decisive factor in bringing about the codi-

---

[12] *cf.* F. Werner, "Verwaltungsrecht als konkretisiertes Verfassungsrecht" (1959) DVBl., 527 *et seq.*; for an extensive contemporary view of the constitutional basis for administrative law, *cf.* N. Achterberg, *Allgemeines Verwaltungsrecht* (2nd ed., Heidelberg 1986), pp. 91 *et seq.*

[13] *cf.* H. Sendler, "Die Entwicklung des Verwaltungsrechts in der Bundesrepublik Deutschland," *Verwaltung und Verwaltungswissenschaften in der Bundesrepublik Deutschland* (J. H. Kaiser, ed.), (1983) Baden-Baden, pp. 27, 28 *et seq.*

[14] VwVfG of May 25, 1976 (German Official Journal I 1253).

[15] Even prior to the adoption of the VwVfG, Schleswig-Holstein had enacted a Law relating to Land Administration (April 18, 1967, GVOBl. p. 131) which was brought in line with the VwVfG by the Law of December 18, 1978 (GVOBl. 1979, p. 2) and currently applies in the version published on March 19, 1979 (GVOBl. p. 181). Following the adoption of the VwVfG, the following Länder adopted Laws which *mutatis mutandis* have the same wording:

Bremen (BremVwVfG) on November 15, 1976 (GBl. p. 243), amended by the Law of April 9, 1979 (GBl. p. 123).

Hessen (NVwVfG) on December 1, 1976 [GVBl. p. 454 (1977) p. 95].

Niedersachsen (provisional Law) (Nds.VwVfG) on December 3, 1976 (GVBl. p. 311), amended by the Law of June 2, 1982 (GVBl. p. 139).

Berlin on December 8, 1976 (GVBl. p. 2735 at p. 2898).

Saarland (Law No. 1056) (SVwVfG) on December 15, 1976 (ABl. p. 1151).

Nordrhein-Westfalen (VwVfG.NW.) on December 21, 1976 (GV NW p. 438).

Bavaria (BayVwVfG) on December 23, 1976 (GVBl. p. 544), amended by the Law of September 7, 1982 (GVBl. p. 722).

Rheinland-Pfalz (LVwVfG) on December 23, 1976 (GVBl. p. 308).

Baden-Württemberg (LVwVfG) on June 21, 1977 (GBl. p. 227) amended by the Law of July 18, 1983 (GBl. p. 369).

Hamburg (HmbVwVfG) on November 9, 1977 (GVBl. p. 333, at p. 402).

On the scope of the Federal VwVfG, *cf.* Sections 1, 2 of the Law: in principle the Law applies only to administrative action undertaken by the Federal authorities.

fication of the law of administrative procedure was the set of recommendations máde at the 43rd German Lawyers' Conference of 1960,[16] which pronounced itself in favour of a uniform set of rules governing administrative procedure, including those aspects of general administrative law which were closely related to it.[17] The VwVfG was to promote such uniformity by integrating disparate special provisions into a single set of rules. At the same time, the relevant procedural rules themselves were to be simplified and rationalised. Finally, an effort was also made to lay down express rules for the participation by the citizen in the administrative procedure.[18] In addition to the principles applicable to general administrative procedure and to special formal proceedings, the Law also regulates the manner in which administrative instruments are issued and their scope, as well as the conditions under which public contracts may be concluded.

In many areas, the legislator was able to bring the contents of the relevant statutes into line with the unwritten general principles of administrative law as expresssed in administrative law theory and in the relevant court decisions. Controversial questions were either settled one way or another by statute, or deliberately left open for further development by the courts and academic writers. In addition to the VwVfG, there exists a range of other statutes regulating individual areas of general administrative law[19] and a virtually limitless number of statutes in the field of special administrative law.[20] Finally, administrative law statements are also found in subordinate legislation and regulations.

At present, it is only at the enforcement stage (at the local authority level) that customary law, whose existence is dependent on prolonged and continuous usage, as well as the belief by those participating in it that this usage is legally justified, presents any relevance.[21] Thus a develop-

---

[16] Proceedings of the 23rd German Lawyers' Conference, "Empfiehlt es sich, den Allgemeinen Teil des Verwaltungsrechts zu kodifizieren?" (Vol. II, Part D 149—Conclusion).

[17] On the origins of the VwVfG, *cf.* in particular P. Badura, *Allgemeines Verwaltungsrecht* (H.-U. Erichsen, W. Martens, ed.) (7th ed., Berlin/New York 1986), pp. 337 *et seq.*

[18] *cf.* H. Maurer, *loc. cit.*, footnote 1, pp. 68 *et seq.*

[19] *e.g.* the Law relating to Summonses issued to the Administration (VwZG) of July 3, 1952 (German Official Journal III 201–3); the Law relating to the Enforcement of Administrative Action (VwVG) of April 27, 1953 (German Official Journal III 201–4) and the corresponding Länder Laws.

[20] A collection of important administrative Laws is contained in Sartorius, Vol. 1, *Verfassungs- und Verwaltungsgesetze.*

[21] *cf.* H. Maurer, *loc. cit.*, footnote 1, pp. 50 *et seq.*

ment plan laid down in the form of a bye-law can be set aside by local customary law.[22]

The courts have made important contributions towards the development of administrative law. As has already been mentioned, the Federal Administrative Court has had a decisive influence on the shaping of the principles laid down in the VwVfG. The Federal Court of Justice (Bundesgerichtshof—BGH), the highest ordinary judicial authority in the Federal Republic, has made important contributions, particularly in the field of compensation for forced renunciation and expropriation. The Federal Constitutional Court (Bundesverfassungsgericht—BVerfG) has given a fundamentally new direction to the scope of statutory reservation.[23] The "detainee decision" by the Federal Constitutional Court[24] provided the breakthrough for the application of the statutory reservation principle to the so-called "special relationships between authorities" (the penal system, the education system, the status of civil servants, etc.), which, under traditional assumptions, could be regulated by means of straightforward administrative regulations.[25] In the meantime, the established case law of the Federal Constitutional Court has detached statutory reservation from the concept of "intervention" and extended it to "all essential decisions" in "the major areas of rule-making"[26] (*i.e.* the "essential decision" theory[27]).

The statement that "the laying down of general legal principles is a task which naturally appertains to the higher courts," made by the Federal Constitutional Court in another case,[28] is not disputed, particularly in administrative law, in view of the many gaps presented by the legislation. In certain referral proceedings, the Plenary Chamber of the Federal Administrative Court is explicitly called upon to develop the law further.[29] It

---

[22] *cf.* BVerwGE 26, 282, 284 *et seq.*: 54, 5, 7 *et seq.* For further evidence of the judicial recognition of customary law, *cf.* H. Maurer, *loc. cit.*, footnote 1, p. 52.

[23] *cf.* M. Kloepfer, "Der Vorbehalt des Gesetzes im Wandel," JZ 1984, 685 *et seq.* with extensive references from case law and doctrine; K. Stern, "Das Staatsrecht der Bundesrepublik Deutschland," Vol. I) (2nd ed., München 1984), pp. 805 *et seq.*

[24] BVerfGE 33, 1.

[25] From the viewpoint of constitutional administrative law theory at the end of the nineteenth century: *cf.* O. Mayer, *loc. cit.*, footnote 4, Vol. 1, pp. 101 *et seq.* On the "special administrative relationships" in the light of the Bonn Basic Law, *cf.* H. J. Wolff, O. Bachof, *loc. cit.*, footnote 1, pp. 212 *et seq.*

[26] BVerfGE 49, 89, 126 with references to previous decisions.

[27] *cf. e.g.* H. Maurer, *loc. cit.*, footnote 1, p. 82.

[28] BVerfGE 26, 327, 337.

[29] *cf.* Section 11(4) VwGO. *cf.* also Sections 137 *et seq.* GVG on the jurisdiction of the Plenary Chambers for civil or criminal matters and of the Combined Plenary Chambers for the resolution of fundamental legal questions.

is, however, a matter for debate whether this confers on this "judge-made law" the status of a source of law: this depends essentially on the terminological definitions used.[30] However that may be, it must be stressed that, as Article 20(3) of the Basic Law explicitly states, the courts are "bound by statute and law" in taking their decisions.

A question which has yet to be settled is that of the legal nature of the general principles of administrative law (the proportionality principle, the protection of legitimate expectation, etc.).[31] In many cases, these have been codified into legislation. This applies especially to the rules relating to the principles of court procedure under the VwVfG. The others have been recognised mainly by the available case law or by customary law. In many cases the general principles of administrative law have been developed as concrete applications of fundamental constitutional principles. Thus the Federal Administrative Court originally derived the rule relating to the revocation of administrative acts bestowing illegitimate favours (which has in the meantime been codified under Article 48 VwVfG) from a combination of the principles of the protection of legitimate expectations and conformity with statute, which are both embedded in the principle of the rule of law. In view of the fact that the general principles of administrative law are currently, "in accordance with established case law, applied in the same way as written rules,"[32] the question whether these principles constitute legal sources in their own right, which is the subject of academic controversy,[33] presents hardly any practical relevance.

---

[30] On this subject, *cf.* the recent contribution by F. Ossenbühl, *Allgemeines Verwaltungsrecht* (H.-U. Erichsen, W. Martens, ed.) (7th ed., Berlin/New York 1986), pp. 107 *et seq.* with further examples (note 192).

[31] *cf.* H.-J. D. Hardt, "Die allgemeine Verwaltungsgrundsätze" (1971) DÖV, 685 *et seq.*; C.-F. Menger, "Die allgemeinen Grundsätze des Verwaltungsrechts als Rechtsquellen," *Festschrift für W. Bogs*, (1967) Wiesbaden, pp. 89 *et seq.*; F. Ossenbühl, *loc. cit.*, footnote 30, pp. 112 *et seq.*; H. Wolff, O. Bachof, *loc. cit.*, footnote 1, pp. 121 *et seq.*; H.-W. Rengeling, *Rechtsgrundsätze beim Verwaltungsvollzug des Europäischen Gemeinschaftsrechts*, (1977) Köln/Berlin/Bonn/München, pp. 90 *et seq.* Prior to the enactment of the Laws relating to administrative procedure, the debate focused mainly on the extent to which the general legal principles were capable of revision; on this subject, *cf.*, in addition to the contributions cited above, especially H.-J. D. Hardt, "Die Revisibilität der allgemeinen Verwaltungsrechtsgrundsätze" (1973) DVBl, 235 *et seq.*; and a recent contribution, P. Kirchof, "Revisibles Verwaltungsrecht," *Festschrift für C.-F. Menger, loc. cit.*, footnote 7, pp. 813 *et seq.*, 819 *et seq.*

[32] *cf.* the decision of the Federal Social Court of September 21, 1962, (1963) DÖV, 182, 183, which is also cited by F. Ossenbühl, *loc. cit.*, footnote 30, p. 114.

[33] *cf.* the authors cited in footnote 31.

The general part of German administrative law is characterised by a highly systematic approach, to which academic studies of administrative law have made a not inconsiderable contribution.[34] At the centre of this systematic approach, which is mainly aimed at the forms of action adopted by the administration, lies invariably the concept of the administrative measure which, contrary to the French use of this term, covers in principle only individually specific measures adopted by the administration.[35]

Recently, administrative practice and theory have been faced with a number of new challenges which the law has not always been capable of meeting adequately. Thus environmental law in particular has been the scene of many far-reaching departures from traditional administrative law theory.[36] The desire to provide "the public authorities with sufficient scope of action, using options ranging from legislation to judicial review,"[37] also constitutes a major challenge for present-day administrative law. The extension of the concept of statutory reservation, which is at times held responsible for the rising tide of legislation and the intensity of judicial review, has given rise to a debate concerning a possible "administration reservation" (Verwaltungsvorbehalt), which is to secure

---

[34] Following the important work by O. Mayer (cf. supra, footnote 4) particular mention should be made of F. Fleiner, *Institutionen des Deutschen Verwaltungsrechts* (8th ed., Tübingen 1928); W. Jellinek, *Verwaltungsrecht* (3rd ed., Offenburg 1931); H. Peters, *Lehrbuch der Verwaltung* (1949) Berlin/Göttingen/Heidelberg; E. Forsthoff, *loc. cit.*, footnote 1; H. J. Wolff, O. Bachof, *Verwaltungsrecht* Vol. 1, (9th ed., München 1974), Vol. 2, (5th ed., 1987), Vol. 3, (4th ed., 1978). On the subject of administrative theory, an important contribution is L. von Stein, *Die Verwaltungslehre*, 8 parts in 10 vols., (1st–2nd ed., Stuttgart 1866–1884) (reprinted Aalen 1962), and currently W. Thieme, *Verwaltungslehre* (4th ed., Köln/Berlin/Bonn/München 1984).

[35] cf. Section 35(1) VwVfG; however, on the concept of the "general enactment," cf. Section 35(2) VwVfG. By contrast with the escalating degree of involvement of law in administrative action, attention is being focused on the extent to which administrative action embodied in legal form is being complemented by informal forms of action which have no legal substance: cf. J. Becker, "Informales Verwaltungshandeln zur Steuerung wirtschaftlicher Prozesse im Zeichen der Deregulierung" (1985) DÖV 1003 *et seq*.

[36] On the subject mentioned below, cf. also H. Sendler, *loc. cit.*, footnote 13, pp. 27, 30 *et seq*.

[37] This was the topic of a symposium organised in 1985 in Göttingen, cf. V. Götz, H. H. Klein, C. Starck (ed.), *Die öffentliche Verwaltung zwischen Gesetzgebung und richterlicher Kontrolle* (1985) München. On this subject, cf. also H. Sendler, "Die öffentliche Verwaltung zwischen Scylla und Charybdis," (1986) NJW 1084 *et seq*.

for the administration a sphere of decision-making under its own responsibility.[38]

(4) Among the many institutions and procedures supervising administrative action, ranging from auditing procedures at the State and local authority level, through parliamentary supervision in the shape of ministerial responsibility, to informal social supervision through the mass media, we shall merely sketch here the possibility of self-supervision by the administration in objection proceedings and judicial review.

The objection procedure (Widerspruchsverfahren) is an extra-judicial preliminary procedure in which the legality and expediency of the enactment of an administrative act, or of the refusal to issue an administrative act, is examined by the administration itself, in most cases by the superior authority.[39] The preliminary procedure is a precondition for obtaining a judgment on the merits of an action for annulment or for the performance of an administrative action. This extensive examination, which also enables the expediency of discretionary decisions to be examined, leads in many cases to a decision which is favourable to the applicant and at the same time provides relief for the administrative courts.[40]

Article 19(4)(1) of the Basic Law guarantees judicial protection against infringements committed by the public authorities. Under the general clause of Section 40 of the Order relating to Administrative Courts (Verwaltungsgerichtsordnung—VwGO) all public law disputes[41] which are not constitutional in nature come within the jurisdiction of the administrative courts, subject to special rules on the attribution of jurisdiction laid down by Federal statute. The general judicial system relating to adminstrative law provides two stages of appeal: above the Verwaltungsgericht (administrative court of first instance), there are the Oberverwaltungsgericht (or the Verwaltungsgerichtshof) and the

---

[38] *cf.* the conference papers by H. Maurer and F. E. Schnapp given at the Meeting of the Association of German Teachers of Public Law in Göttingen, VVDStRL 43(1985), pp. 135 *et seq.* and pp. 172 *et seq.*; E. Schmidt-Assmann, "Funktionen der Verwaltungsgerichtsbarkeit," in *Festschrift für C.-F. Menger, loc. cit.*, footnote 7, pp. 107, 113; *cf.* also BVerfGE 67, 100, 139; 68, 1, 87 on the "key area of executive autonomy" of the government.

[39] *cf.* Sections 68 *et seq.* VwGO.

[40] *cf.* also C. H. Ule, *Verwaltungsprozessrecht* (8th ed., München 1983), pp. 113 *et seq.*, who refers to the "filtering effect" of the preliminary procedure.

[41] On the concept of the "public law dispute," *cf.* F. O. Kopp, *Verwaltungsgerichtsordnung* (Commentary), (7th ed., München 1986), Section 40 Nos. 6–30 with examples from the available case law.

Bundesverwaltungsgericht.[42] In addition to the above, there are also several special administrative courts.[43]

According to the nature of the legal protection sought, a distinction is made between actions seeking a new legal status, actions for performance, and declaratory actions. The "most typical administrative action"[44] is the action seeking a new legal status (Gestaltungsklage) in the form of an objection (Anfechtungsklage), which is aimed at the judicial annulment of an administrative act. The action for performance seeks to have the administration ordered by the court to perform, or to refrain from performing, a certain administrative action. Here, a distinction is made between general actions for performance and actions seeking to obtain the adoption of an administrative act (Verpflichtungsklage). The declaratory action (Feststellungsklage) can be used to have a legal relationship covered by public law declared existent or non-existent. A particular form of declaratory action is the application for the review of rules (Normenkontrolle). This action seeks to have certain non-statutory rules examined as to their validity. Finally, there are certain proceedings seeking provisional legal protection (*cf.* sections 80 and 123 of the VwGO).

For these various forms of action and application certain detailed preconditions must be met before a judgment on their merits can be given. In addition to the observance of certain requirements as to form and deadline, and the prior use of the objection procedure mentioned above, the plaintiff in the *Anfechtungsklage*, the *Verpflichtungsklage* and the general *Leistungsklage*[45] must plead the infringement of a subjective

---

[42] Under the Law of July 4, 1985 on the acceleration of administrative and financial judicial proceedings (German Official Journal 1274), which came into force on July 17, 1985, the appeals procedure against large-scale technical plans (*e.g.* power stations, airfields) was shortened in that the jurisdiction at first instance was transferred from the administrative courts to the higher administrative courts. For more details *cf.* H. J. v. Oertzen, "Zur erstinstanzlichen Zuständigkeit des OVG nach dem Beschleunigungsgesetz" (1985) DÖV, 749 *et seq.*

[43] *cf.* in particular Section 51 of the Law relating to the Social Courts, Section 33 of the Rules relating to the Financial Courts, Section 15 of the Rules relating to Disciplinary Tribunals. On the Bill for a uniform set of rules governing administrative proceedings, including the special administrative courts, *cf.* C. H. Ule, "Ein neuer Anlauf?" (1985) DVBl. 939 *et seq.*

[44] *cf.* C. H. Ule, *loc. cit.*, footnote 40, p. 146.

[45] On the general actions for performance, *cf.* F. O. Kopp, *loc. cit.*, footnote 41, Section 42, No. 38.

right. Interests of a purely moral or economical nature, on the other hand, cannot confer *locus standi*.[46]

If the action is found to be admissible once the above conditions have been complied with, the court examines the merits of the action. The legality of the administrative act which forms the basis of the action is subjected to a thorough examination. This judicial examination is, however, restricted where the legislator has allowed the administration a certain degree of discretion and freedom of evaluation and thus given it a "right of final decision" in the area concerned. Where discretionary decisions are involved, the court merely examines whether the statutory limits of the discretion have been exceeded, or whether the discretion was used in a manner which was inconsistent with the intent of the statutory decision in conferring this discretion (Section 114 VwGO).

Contrary to the practice before the civil courts, the rule in administrative proceedings is that the court examines the facts of the case *ex officio* without being bound by the submissions made by the parties. For the rest, administrative proceedings are subject to the right of disposal (*i.e.* the control exercised by the parties over the subject-matter of the dispute) and the principles of the oral nature, the immediacy and the public nature of the proceedings.[47]

The disputes involving the public authorities which have been traditionally allocated to the ordinary courts and not to the administrative courts include claims relating to public authority liability, expropriation and enforced surrender compensation as well as certain property disputes.[48]

Finally, the Federal Constitutional Court provides judicial protection against the administration in certain cases. Any citizen may bring a constitutional action before the Federal Constitutional Court on the grounds that his or her fundamental rights have been infringed by the public authorities.[49] However, the constitutional action is admissible only after all the available remedies have been exhausted, which results in most actions being brought not against administrative acts, but against decisions of the highest appeal courts. Questions of administrative law may also be brought before the Constitutional Court through the medium

---

[46] For more details on *locus standi*, *cf.* F. O. Kopp, *loc. cit.*, footnote 41, Section 42, No. 37 *et seq.*
[47] For more details on the basic principles of administrative proceedings, *cf.* C. H. Ule, *loc. cit.*, footnote 40, pp. 129 *et seq.*
[48] *cf.* Section 40(2) VwGO, Article 14(3)(4) Basic Law, Article 34(3) Basic Law.
[49] Article 93(1) No. 4a; Sections 13, No. 8a, 90–96 BVerfGG.

of other proceedings, in particular the abstract review of rules. As has already been mentioned, the Constitutional Court has exercised a decisive influence on present-day administrative law.

R. Herzog, the distinguished constitutional lawyer and President of the Federal Constitutional Court, has described the exceptionally strong "third power" as being probably the most striking characteristic of the Basic Law.[50] It must be acknowledged that the legal protection against the executive is very advanced.[51] By contrast with the traditional French approach, under which the role of the courts in securing legal protection has traditionally consisted in the objective supervision of the executive, the German approach towards administrative proceedings is first and foremost the protection of the individual's subjective rights.[52] That much is already expressed in the legal protection guaranteed by Article 19(4)(1) of the Basic Law, under which anyone whose rights have been infringed by the public authorities has access to legal remedies.[53]

The notion of the protection of subjective rights also explains the requirements which must be met in German administrative proceedings if the action is to be admissible, *i.e.* the ability to claim a subjective public right belonging to the plaintiff, the redress of which is sought through the action. Finally, the idea of protecting the individual is also expressed in the rules governing temporary legal protection: whilst in most legal systems it is possible to obtain provisional legal protection only by means of a decision by a court in summary proceedings,[54] the mere filing of an objection (or an application for annulment in Germany is sufficient to

---

[50] *cf.* R. Herzog, "Die Verfassung der Bundesrepublik Deutschland" in *Verwaltung und Verwaltungswissenschaften in der Bundesrepublik Deutschland*, *loc. cit.*, footnote 13, pp. 12, 24.

[51] On the special importance of judicial protection for the German model of the "perfect" state based on the rule of law, *cf.* from the French viewpoint M. Fromont, "République Fédérale d'Allemagne—L'état de droit," (1984) RDP, 1203 *et seq.* (1214 *et seq.*). On the problems which this question entails, *cf.* the recent contribution by W. Brohm, "Die staatliche Verwaltung als eigenständige Gewalt und die Grenzen der Verwaltungsgerichtsbarkeit" (1986) DVBl. 321 *et seq.*

[52] *cf.* especially M. Fromont, *Rechtsschutz gegenüber der Verwaltung in Deutschland, Frankreich und den Europäischen Gemeinschaften*, (1967) Köln/Berlin/Bonn/München, p. 203; *cf.* also the comparative law study in A. Bleckmann, "Das Ziel des gerichtlichen Rechtsschutzes: Schutz des Einzelnen oder objektive Kontrolle der vollziehenden Gewalt? Die Rolle der Klagebefugnis," *Gerichtsschutz gegen die Exekutive*, Vol. 3 (H. Mosler, ed.), Köln/Berlin/Bonn/München (1971) pp. 21 *et seq.*

[53] *cf.* E. Schmidt-Assmann, *loc. cit.*, footnote 38, pp. 107, 109 *et seq.*

[54] *cf.* M. Fromont, "La protection provisoire des particuliers contre les décisions administratives dans les Etats Membres des Communautés européennes," (1984) RISA 309, 312 *et seq.*

prevent the implementation of the administrative action involved.[55] It would scarcely be possible to explain the so-called "suspensive effect" of the application merely by reference to the procedural significance of the objective supervision of administrative action.[56]

(5) The administrative organisation of the Federal Republic of Germany has been shaped by the federal structure of the State. The Basic Law regulates the allocation of administrative jurisdiction between the federal authorities and the Länder.[57] The Länder have jurisdiction where no special powers have been attributed to the federal authorities. Thus it is for the Länder to enforce the Länder statutes and the majority of federal statutes as well; the federal authorities have been given the right to supervise this process.

The enforcement of Community law is effected in principle in accordance with the allocation of jurisdiction between the federal authorities and the Länder.[58] Thus, for example, the Länder administrative authorities will have jurisdiction to enforce not only those Länder statutes which implement E.C. Directives but also directly applicable Community law in areas which would come within the scope of statutes enacted by the Länder.[59] However, the centre of gravity for the enforcement of Community law remains with the federal authorities, which exercise their administrative function in customs matters through the Federal Financial Authorities and in agricultural matters through the Federal Board for Agricultural Market Regulation and the Federal Department of Food and Forestries.[60]

Both the federal authorities and the Länder may exercise their administrative functions either directly through their own organs or indirectly through autonomous legal entities.[61] Where these functions are

---

[55] *cf.* Section 80(1) VwGO.
[56] *cf.* M. Fromont, *loc. cit.*, footnote 52, p. 150.
[57] Articles 30, 83–91b, 108, 115f, 115i, 120a. On the allocation of federal powers in the administrative sphere, *cf.* for further details P. Badura, *Staatsrecht*, (1986) München, pp. 411 *et seq.*
[58] *cf.* H. P. Ipsen, *Europäisches Gemeinschaftsrecht*, (1972) Tübingen p. 220; *contra* D. H. Scheuing, "Rechtsprobleme bei der Durchsetzung des Gemeinschaftsrechts in der Bundesrepublik Deutschland," (1985) EuR, 229, 249 *et seq.*
[59] *cf.* D. H. Scheuing, (1985) EuR, p. 249.
[60] *cf.* Article 108 Basic Law; Article 87 Basic Law of August 31, 1972, in conjunction with Section 3 of the Law governing the Establishment of the Common Organisation of the Market (German Official Journal I, 1617). For more details, *cf.* D. H. Scheuing, (1985) EuR, pp. 249 *et seq.*
[61] For more details, *cf.* H. Maurer, *loc. cit.*, footnote 1, Sections 22, 23 (pp. 432 *et seq.*).

exercised directly through the legal personality of the federal authorities or the Länder, there is a general power to issue directives, from the relevant Minister to the lowest administrative units. Where these functions are exercised indirectly, the legally autonomous administrative bodies, such as corporations, boards and foundations, are subject only to legal review by the State. In respect of the municipal territorial bodies (*i.e.* the local authorities and districts), they have the express right under the Basic Law to regulate all matters relating to the local community within the scope of the relevant legislation under their own responsibility (Article 28(2)). Finally, a number of administrative tasks are also transferred to private parties (*e.g.* transport companies), especially in the field of public welfare, on the understanding that certain public-law provisions remain binding on the parties concerned.[62] Administrative reality has witnessed the formation of numerous deviations from the model structures described, producing intermediate bodies and types of mixed organisation.[63]

(6) The above can be summarised by stating that the administrative law of the Federal Republic of Germany has been particularly shaped by the Constitution. The legislator,—especially through the enactment of the VwVfG—the courts and academic writers have all contributed to giving practical expression to the essential provisions of the Basic Law. Legal protection against the executive is particularly solid. The administrative courts are mainly designed to protect the subjective rights of the citizens. The administrative functions have been divided, as far as their organisation is concerned, between the federal authorities and the Länder.

[62] *Ibid.*, p. 410.
[63] *cf.* M. Hilf, *Die Organisationsstruktur der Europäischen Gemeinschaften*, (1982) Berlin/Heidelberg/New York, pp. 262–269.

SECTION 3

ITALY

(1–2) The formative period of Italian administrative law is generally said to be the period between the end of the eighteenth century (following the French Revolution) and the end of the nineteenth century.[1] During the first half of the nineteenth century the legal regime applicable to the administration developed to a large extent in accordance with the ordinary law (*ius commune*), which applied to administrative authorities and private parties alike. Legal theory during this period was dominated by the personality of G. D. Romagnosi, who, unlike his contemporaries, recognised that administrative law could no longer be satisfactorily accommodated within the various categories of Roman law, but required its own basic principles. By virtue of his work *Principi fondamentali di diritto amministrativo*,[2] which was published in 1814, he became the founding father of Italian—some would say, of European[3]—administrative law.

Whilst under Napoleonic rule, the administrative law system of the Italian states was influenced by the French model. This influence extended well beyond the Restoration period and the proclamation of Italy as a kingdom (1861).

---

[1] For more details *cf.* M. S. Giannini, *Diritto amministrativo* (1970) Milan, Vol. 1, pp. 23 *et seq.*; by the same author, "Diritto amministrativo," EdB, Vol. XII (1964) pp. 855–870; M. D'Alberti, *Le concessioni amministrative. Aspetti della contrattualità delle pubbliche amministrazioni* (1981) Naples, pp. 49 *et seq.*; V. E. Orlando, "Introduzione generale" in *Primo trattato completo di diritto amministrativo* (V. E. Orlando, ed.), Vol. 1 (1900) Milan, pp. 48 *et seq.*; B. Sordi, *Giustizia e amministrazione nell'Italia liberale (La formazione della nozione di interesse legittimo)* (1985) Milan, Giuffrè; F. D'Alessio, "Dalla dichiarazione dei diritti dell'uomo al moderno stato di diritto," in "Scritti Romano" (1940) Padua, Vol. 1, p. 493; S. Cassese, *La formazione dello Stato amministrativo* (1974) Milan, Giuffrè; I. Santangelo Spoto, "Diritto amministrativo," *Il Italiano*, Vol. 9, II, 1898–1901, pp. 771–829.

[2] G. D. Romagnosi, *Principi fondamentali di diritto amministrativo* (1814) Milan.

[3] *cf.* V. E. Orlando, *loc. cit.*, footnote 1, p. 49. On the significance of Romagnosi's writing, *cf.* also "Atti del Convegno di studi in onore di G. D. Romagnosi," in Studi Parmensi (1961); E. A. Albertoni, *La vita degli Stati e l'incivilimento dei popoli nel pensiero giuridico di Gian Domenico Romagnosi* (1979) Milan; by the same author, *Per cognoscere Romagnosi* (R. Ghiringhelli-F. Invernici, ed.) (1982) Milan.

In the period that followed, a series of important laws relating to public administration were enacted.[4] In the first instance, mention must be made of the Law relating to the Creation of a Uniform System of Administration of March 20, 1865, which was regarded as a type of Administrative Code. It contains the Laws on the organisation of the municipalities, the provinces, the police force, public health, the Council of State (Consiglio di Stato) as well as a Law abolishing the previous system of protection under administrative law and a Law on public works.

The Law abolishing the system of protection under administrative law did away with the special *Tribunali del contenzioso amministrativo*, which had been dependent on the executive. The jurisdiction in disputes between the citizen and the administration which involved the citizen's subjective rights was transferred to the ordinary courts. The Law of March 31, 1889[5] established a judicial section of the Consiglio, which was to have jurisdiction in disputes concerning the legality of administrative action, where the latter infringed a citizen's legitimate interest.[6]

Whilst initially the case law was firmly placed within the sphere of private law,[7] by the end of the nineteenth century the theory that relations

---

[4] In particular the Laws of August 3, 1862, No. 752 (religious works), of August 14, 1862, No. 800 (the establishment of the Court of Auditors), of March 20, 1865, No. 2248 (a uniform system of administration) and of June 25, 1865, No. 2359 (expropriation). *cf.* on this subject *Atti del congresso celebrativo del centenario delle leggi amministrative di unificazione* (Firenze, 1965), 11 Vol., (1967–68) Vicenza, especially Vol. II; G. Astuti, *L'unificazione amministrativa del Regno d'Italia* (1966) Naples; C. Ghisalberti, *Contributi alla storia delle amministrazioni preunitarie* (1963) Milan; E. Ragionieri, *Politica e amministrazione nella storia dell'Italia unita* (1967) Bari.

[5] Law No. 5992.

[6] On the genesis and development of the Italian system of administrative courts, *cf.* M. Stipo, *Le origini del riparto di giurisdizione verso la pubblica amministrazione e la doppia tutela*, (1979) Rome; F. Scoca, "Linee evolutive della giustizia amministrativa," in Annali Fac. giur. Perugia, N. 3 (1975); G. Berti, "Momenti di trasformazione della giustizia amministrativa" (1972) Riv. trim. dir. pubbl., pp. 1861 *et seq.*; M. Nigro, *Giustizia amministrativa* (1983) Bologna, pp. 67 *et seq.*; *Il controllo giurisdizionale della pubblica amministrazione* (Piras, ed.) (1971) Turin; F. Schupfer, "I precedenti storici del diritto amministrativo vigente in Italia," *Primo trattato completo di diritto amministrativo italiano* (V. E. Orlando, ed.), Vol. I, pp. 1089 *et seq.*; A. Salandra, *La giustizia amministrativa nei governi liberi* (1904) Turin.

[7] *cf., e.g.* Decision by Bologna Court of Appeal of December 23, 1882, in (1883) Legge II, p. 596; Decision by the Corte di Cassazione in Rome of December 3, 1881, in (1882) Legge I, p. 806, on the status of municipal government employees; and Decision by the Turin Court of Appeal of May 18, 1869, in (1869) Giur. it., II, p. 340; Decision by the Florence Court of First Instance of May 31, 1875, in (1875) Legge I, p. 673; Decision by the Corte di Cassazione in Rome of April 15, 1880, in (1880) Giur. it. I,1 p. 789 on permits.

between the administration and private subjects belonged essentially to the field of public law had, under the influence of administrative law theory,[8] increasingly gained acceptance.

In the course of the twentieth century, Italian administrative law experienced far-reaching changes. The continuing crisis which enveloped the limited-suffrage State over extension of the right to vote, led to the creation of the "stato pluri-classe,"[9] which among other things strove to provide social security for the poorer classes. This change had already become noticeable towards the end of the previous century, especially through the adoption of social legislation and the establishment of public enterprises. The increase in public intervention proceeded side by side with technological progress and the industrial revolution, which led *inter alia* to an increase in the number of people using public welfare services.[10]

As a result of the development from a liberal state to a welfare state,[11] traditional attitudes towards the separation of powers changed. This

---

[8] As the founder of the new Italian school of public law, V. E. Orlando deserves special mention. Among his numerous works (*Principi di diritto amministrativo* (1891) Florence, "I criteri tecnici per la ricostruzione giuridica del diritto pubblico" in (1889) Arch. giur., and now in Diritto pubblico generale; Scritti vari (1941) Milan, pp. 3 *et seq.*; "Studi giuridici sul governo parlementare," *ibid.*, pp. 345 *et seq.*, etc.) a prominent place is occupied by the *Primo trattato completo di diritto amministrativo italiano*, published between 1897 and 1925 under his direction.

[9] *cf.* M. S. Giannini, *Diritto amministrativo* (1970) Milan, Vol. I, pp. 45 *et seq.*

[10] Evidence of this development can be found in, for example, the increase in the relevant budgets, (*cf.* on this subject A. Caracciolo, *Stato e società civile. Problemi dell'unificazione italiana* (1960) Turin; A. Salandra, "La progressione dei bilanci negli Stati moderni," in *Politica e legislazione* (1915) Bari, pp. 112 *et seq.*) and the growth of the civil service (*cf.* on this subject G. Abignente, *La riforma delle amministrazioni pubbliche in Italia* (1913) Bari, pp. 3 *et seq.* For more general information, *cf.* also F. Tessitore, *Crisi e trasformazioni dello Stato (Ricerche sul pensiero giuspubblicistico italiano tra Otto e Novecento)* (1971) Naples.

[11] *cf.* on this subject in general A. Barbera, *Le instituzioni del pluralismo* (1977) Bari; M. S. Giannini, *Diritto pubblico dell'economia* (1977) Bologna; by the same author, "Stato sociale: una nozione inutile" in *Scritti in onore di C. Mortati* (1978) Milan, Vol. I; *Diritto e transformazione sociale* (E. Resta, ed.) (1978) Bari; F. Galgano, *Storia del diritto commerciale* (1977) Bologna; *Lo Stato moderno* (E. Rotelli and P. Schiera, ed.) (1971–74) Bologna, 3 Vol.; G. Poggi, *La vicenda dello Stato moderno* (1978) Bologna; G. Treves, "Considerazioni sullo Stato di diritto," in *Studi Crosa*, Vol. II; G. Grasso, "Osservazioni sullo Stato sociale," in (1965) Quad. sc. soc.; by the same author, "Stato di diritto e Stato sociale nell'attuale ordinamento italiano" in *Il Politico* (1961); U. Pototschnig, *I pubblici servizi* (1964) Padua; S. Lener, *Lo Stato sociale contemporaneo* (1966) Rome; A. M. Sandulli, "Stato di diritto e Stato sociale," in *Nord e Sud* (1963), pp. 8 *et seq.*; by the same author, "Verso lo Stato sociale," in *Studi centenario Corte dei Conti*, (1963) Milan; P. Barcellona, *Stato e mercato tra monopolio e democrazia* (1976) Bari; by the same author, *La Repubblica in trasformazione* (1978) Bari, and *Oltre lo Stato sociale* (1980) Bari; F.

trend found its clearest expression in the Constitution of the Italian Republic which entered into force on January 1, 1948. The government is no longer merely an executive body, but takes part in the enactment of legislation through the adoption of *decreti legge*[12] and *leggi delegate*[13] (Articles 76 and 77). Parliament no longer restricts its activity to the enactment of general and abstract laws, but also makes increasing use of laws setting out detailed measures. In addition, the legislative and executive functions are no longer the exclusive prerogative of the State, but are increasingly delegated to other institutions subject to public law. For example, the regions have the power to enact their own laws in specific areas (Article 117).

The equality principle enshrined in Article 3 of the republican Constitution must not only be taken as a formal legal statement, for it also has a substantive sense. Under Article 3(2) the Republic has the duty to "remove such economic and social obstacles as constitute an effective restriction on the freedom and equality of the citizens and prevent them from realising their full potential and also obstruct the participation by anyone actively employed in the political, economic and social development of the nation."[14] The extension of the functions of the public authorities to include the development of a welfare state, which is clearly expressed in this provision, caused a further growth in the size of the administration. The simultaneous increase in the rule-making powers of the administration caused it to become more and more independent of

Galgano, *Le istituzioni dell'economia capitalistica* (1974) Bologna; by the same author, *Le istituzioni dell'economia di transizione* (1978) Rome; Castronovo, *L'industria italiana dall' 800 ad oggi* (1980) Milan; G. Amato, "L'interesse pubblico e le attività economiche private" in *Pol. dir.* (1980); C. Conte, *L'ordinamento elettorale italiano. L'elettorato politico* (1963) Empoli.

[12] Provisional legislative acts issued by the Government which require subsequent approval by Parliament within a short period.

[13] Delegated legislation.

[14] For further details *cf.* D. Sorace, "Il governo dell' economia," in *Manuale di diritto pubblico* (G. Amato and A. Barbera, ed.), pp. 899 *et seq.*; B. Cavallo-G. Di Plinio, *Manuale di diritto pubblico dell'economia* (1983) Milan, pp. 59 *et seq.*; G. Amato, *Economia, politica e istituzioni in Italia* (1976) Bologna; "La Costituzione economica," in *Trattato di diritto commerciale e di diritto pubblico dell'economia* (F. Galgano, ed.), Vol. I; A. Pizzorusso, *Che cos'è l'eguaglianza. Il principio etico e la norma giuridica nella vita reale* (1983) Rome; C. Esposito, "Eguaglianza e giustizia nell'art. 3 della Costituzione," in *La Costituzione italiana* (1954); Saggi, Padua, pp. 15 *et seq.*; L. Paladin, *Il principio costituzionale di eguaglianza* (1965) Milan; A. S. Agro-U. Romagnoli, "Commento all'art. 3 della Costituzione," in *Commentario della Costituzione* (G. Branca, ed.). On the jurisprudence of the Italian constitutional court referring to the equality principle A. Cerri, *L'eguaglianza nella giurisprudenza della Corte Costituzionale. Esame analitico ed ipotesi ricostruttiva* (1976) Milan.

government and legislature alike.[15] The resulting crisis which afflicted the administration prompted a number of reforming measures, which sought to reorganise the administration and the legal position of civil servants on the one hand[16] and to rationalise administrative procedures on the other.[17]

Recent trends in administrative law have been conditioned by two factors. On the one hand, administrative law, as a set of public law rules, has declined under the impact of the extension of those aspects of administrative action which are governed by private law.[18] On the other hand, the relationship between administrative law and constitutional law, which often forms the basis for the development of fundamental principles of administrative law, has been strengthened.

(3) Constitutional principles relating to administrative law have found their concrete expression in the available case law and theoretical writing rather than in the relevant legislation.

[15] *cf.* on this subject S. Cassese, *Il sistema amministrativo italiano* (1983) Bologna, p. 12; M. S. Giannini, "Parlamento e amministrazione," in *L'amministrazione civile* (1961) pp. 145 *et seq.*; A. M. Sandulli, "Governo e amministrazione," in *Riv. trim. dir. pubbl.*, 1966 pp. 752 *et seq.*; L. Elia, *Problemi costituzionali della amministrazione centrale* (1966) Milan; A. S. Agro, *Rapporti costituzionali tra governo e pubblica amministrazione*; N. Speranza, *Governo e amministrazione nel sistema costituzionale italiano* (1971) Naples; P. Calandra, *Parlamento e amministrazione* (1971) Milan.

[16] *cf.* on the reforms of the public authorities G. Pastori, "La pubblica amministrazione," in *Manuale di diritto pubblico* (G. Amato and A. Barbera, ed.), pp. 601 *et seq.*; G. Marongiu, *Il riordinamento della amministrazione pubblica* (1979) Palermo; *La riorganizzazione dei ministeri nel quadro della riforma della amministrazione* (Meeting held in Catania in 1974) (1975) Padua; CISL, *Azione sindicale e pubblica amministrazione* (1977) Milan; the main literature relating to the post-1979 reforms can be found in *Riv. trim. dir. pubbl.*, 1982, No. 3. On the changes which have occurred in the administration as a result of technological developments, *cf.* P. Melito and R. Granata, "Progresso tecnologico e pubblica amministrazione," in Centro nazionale di prevenzione e difesa sociale, *Studi sul progresso technologico e la società italiana—aspetti giuridici* (1960) Milan, pp. 41 *et seq.* The general changes are described by V. Bachelet ("Evoluzione del ruolo e delle strutture della pubblica amministrazione," in *Scritti Mortati*, II (1977) Milan, and, currently, in *L'amministrazione in cammino, una guida alla lettura degli scritti giuridici di Vittorio Bachelet* (1984) Milan. On the organisation of and reforms in the civil service, *cf.* G. Pastori, *La burocrazia* (1967) Padua; M. Rusciano, *Il pubblico impiego in Italia*, (1978) Bologna; P. Virga, *Il pubblico impiego* (1973) Milan; A. Orsi Battaglini, *Gli accordi sindacali nel pubblico impiego. Pluralismo giuridico, separazione degli ordinamenti e forme di comunicazione* (1982) Milan; Pubblico impiego e contrattazione collettiva (XXVth Meeting, Varenna) (1980) Milan.

[17] For more details, *cf. infra*, footnotes 19 and 20.

[18] The increased use, by the administration, of contracts and transactions governed by private law (the so-called "fuga dell'amministrazione nel privato") reveals a growing reluctance to use the unilateral administrative instrument. *cf.* on this subject M. Nigro,

It is a fact that in the course of the nineteenth century, Italian administrative law was already the subject of extensive statutory law, particularly the Law of March 20, 1865 mentioned above, which sought to impart greater uniformity to the administration. However, general principles of administrative law which apply equally to all administrative departments have not been codified either by Parliamentary statute or by rules made by the executive. Current endeavours concentrate on the adoption of a Law relating to administrative procedure. Since 1948, a series of Bills has been drawn up but never adopted.[19] On September 7, 1984[20] two Committees of Experts on Institutional Problems were attached to the Council of Ministers. One of these concerned itself, among other things, with the question of administrative procedure and has prepared a Bill.

Under Article 1 of the General Provisions of the Civil Code, customary law occupies third place in the hierarchy of legal sources, after statute law and regulations. As a result, customary law may not apply *contra legem*, but only *secundum legem* and *praeter legem*.[21] The same principles apply to administrative practice. However, in most cases they lack the elements of *voluntas populi* and *opinio juris et necessitatis*, which are regarded as the preconditions for the application of customary law. Nevertheless, the administration may not, in the absence of justifying reasons, deviate from or change established practice without being guilty of exceeding its powers.[22] Some of the general principles of administrative law have

"Lineamenti generali," in *Manuale di diritto pubblico* (Amato and A. Barbera, ed.), pp. 839 *et seq.*, and, generally, A. Amorth, "Osservazioni sui limiti all'attività amministrativa di diritto privato" in *Arch. dir. pubbl.*, 1938; G. Pericu, "Note in tema di attività di diritto privato della pubblica amministrazione," in *Annali Facoltà giurisprudenza Università di Genova* (1965); G. Guarino, "Pubblico e privato nell'organizzazione e nella disciplina delle imprese," in *Scritti degli allievi offerti ad A. Tesauro* (1968) Milan, Vol. 1, pp. 7 *et seq.*

[19] For more details, *cf.* G. Cataldi, *Il procedimento amministrativo nei suoi attuali orientamenti giuridici e non giuridici* (1967) Milan; ISAP, *La procedura amministrativa* (1964) Vicenza, in particular the articles by Pastori and Benvenuti.

[20] *cf.* Atti parlam., Camera dei deputati, leg. IX.

[21] On the customary law aspect, *cf.* N. Bobbio, "Consuetudine (teoria gen.)" in EdD Vol. IX (1961) p. 426; by the same author, *La consuetudine come atto normativo* (1942) Padua; G. Ferrari, *Introduzione allo studio del diritto pubblico consuetudinario* (1950) Milan; R. Franceschelli, *Consuetudine (diritto moderno)*, Nss. Dig. Vol. II (1980) App. p. 456.

[22] S. Sandulli, *Manuale di diritto amministrativo* (1982) Naples, p. 73; on administrative practice, *cf.* L. Majorano, *Appunti per una teoria della prassi amministrativa* (1975) Bari; A. Carullo, *La prassi amministrativa* (1979) Padua. The Corte di Cassazione denies administrative practice the status of a legal source (Civil chamber, decision of March 14, 1974, No. 713).

been entrenched in the constitution, whereas others have been the creation of the courts and learned authors. Thus, for example, Article 97(1), under which the public authorities are to be legally organised in such a way as to ensure the proper functioning (buon andamento) and the impartiality of the administration, is invoked as the constitutional basis for the principles of the compliance of the administration with the relevant legislation,[23] its impartiality,[24] and its proper functioning and efficient organisation.[25] The protection of *bona fides* is regarded by the authors in part as an unwritten constitutional principle, on which the protection of the citizen's legitimate expectations *vis-à-vis* the public authorities is based.[26]

(4) Judicial protection against the public administration is guaranteed by Articles 24(1) and Article 113(1) and (2) of the Constitution. In accordance with these provisions, it is possible to appeal to the ordinary and administrative courts, even against acts of the public authorities. The Constitution took over the already existing two-tier judicial system, under which normally the ordinary courts had jurisdiction to hear disputes about subjective rights and the administrative courts had jurisdiction to hear those about legitimate interests. The traditional

---

[23] *cf.* C. Marzuoli, *Principio di legalità e attività di diritto privato della pubblica amministrazione* (1982) Milan, pp. 19 *et seq.*; L. Carlassare, *Amministrazione e potere politico* (1973) Padua, pp. 132 *et seq.*; Ottaviano, "Poteri dell' amministrazione e principi costituzionali," in *Riv. trim. dir. pubbl.*, 1964, p. 926; P. Gasparri, "I Concetti di 'legislazione,' 'amministrazione' e 'potere politico' nella terminologia della Costituzione," in *Studi in onore di S. Lessona*, I (1963) Bologna, p. 360.

[24] D. Sorace, A. Orsi Battaglini and R. Ruffili, *Diritto pubblico* (1981) Florence, p. 251; C. Mortati, *Istituzioni di diritto pubblico* (1976) Vol. I, p. 373, and C. Marzuoli, *Principio di legalità, loc. cit.*, p. 24; who demonstrate that the administration continues to represent "the interests of a party" (*i.e.* the public interest). On the notion of the impartiality of the administration, *cf.* also U. Allegretti, *L'imparzialità amministrativa* (1965) Padua; P. Barile, "Il dovere di imparzialità della pubblica amministrazione," in *Scritti giuridici in memoria di P. Calamandrei*, IV (1958) Padua, p. 28: A. Cerri, *Imparzialità ed indirizzo politico nella pubblica amministrazione* (1973) Padua; S. Cassese, "Imparzialità amministrativa e sindacato giurisdizionale," in *Riv. ital. per le scienze giuridiche*, 1968. On the principle of equality laid down in Article 3, *cf. supra* in footnote 14.

[25] *cf.* M. Giannini, *Istituzioni di diritto amministrativo* (1981) Milan, p. 263; S. Sandulli, *Manuale, loc. cit.*, footnote 22, p. 516; A. Andreani, *Il principio costituzionale di buon andamento della pubblica amministrazione* (1979) Padua.

[26] *cf.* F. Merusi, *L'affidamento del cittadino* (1970) Milan, and "Buona fede e tutela dell'affidamento nella programmazione economica" in *Studi sulla buona fede* (1975) Milan, pp. 731 *et seq.*; similarly, G. Guarino, "Sul regime costituzionale delle leggi di incentivazione e di indirizzo," in *Scritti di diritto pubblico dell'economia e di diritto dell'energia* (1962) Milan, p. 125; V. Bachelet, "Leggi o superleggi di incentivazione?" in

distinction between subjective (private or public) rights (diritti sogget-
tivi) and legitimate (*i.e.* legally protected) interests (interessi legittimi) is
the subject of controversy as to detail.[27] Conflicts of jurisdiction are
decided by the Corte di Cassazione, which thus determines the effective
scope of the jurisdiction of the administrative courts.[28]

The administrative judicial system has two stages of appeal. The
regional administrative courts (Tribunali Amministrativi Regionali),[29]
established in 1971, pronounce judgment at the first stage, whereas at the
second stage the Judicial Section of the Consiglio di Stato[30] adjudicates.
In addition to the general administrative courts, there are also special
administrative courts. The administrative courts have general jurisdiction to take decisions concerning the legality of administrative acts which
infringe the legally protected interests of the plaintiff (competenza di
legittimità). The action succeeds if the administrative measure is illegal.
The following grounds for annulment are examined: lack of jurisdiction
(incompetenza), misuse of powers (eccesso di potere) and infringement
of legislation (violazione di legge). Special legislative provisions have also
attributed to the administrative courts certain extended powers of examination and adjudication (competenza di merito), under which they may

Legge e attività amministrativa nella programmazione economica (1975) Milan; in a
critical sense, A. Barbera, *Leggi di piano e sistema delle fonti* (1968) Milan, pp. 58, 61–62,
71, 83; L. Benadusi, "Attività di finanziamento pubblico, Aspetti costituzionali e amministrativi," in *Riv. trim. dir. pubbl.*, 1966, pp. 931 *et seq.*; C. Mortati, *Istituzioni di diritto
pubblico* (1975) Padua, Vol. I, p. 285.
[27] For more details, *cf.* E. Casetta, "Diritto soggettivo e interesse legittimo: problemi della
loro tutela giurisdizionale," in *Riv. trim. dir. pubbl.*, 1952, p. 611 containing further
references; A. Romano, "Diritto soggettivo, interesse legittimo e assetto costituzionale,"
in *Foro it.*, 1980, V, p. 258; M. Nigro, *Giustizia amministrativa* (1983) Bologna, pp. 115 *et
seq.* containing further references to case law as well.
[28] *cf.* P. Manca, "Conflitti di attribuzione e conflitti di giurisdizione nella giurisprudenza
della Cassazione," in *Riv. trim. dir. pubbl.*, 1932; E. Cannada Bartoli, "Giurisdizione
(conflitti di)," EdD, XIX, pp. 295 *et seq.*; M. Nigro, *Giustizia amministrativa, loc. cit.*,
footnote 27, pp. 183 *et seq.*, containing further references; Decision by the Corte di
Cassazione of October 6, 1979, N. 5172; and of October 7, 1983, N. 5838.
[29] Established by the Law of December 6, 1971, N. 1034, in accordance with Article 125(2)
of the Constitution.
[30] Sicily has its own administrative court, the Consiglio di giustizia amministrativa della
Regione siciliana (*cf.* Decree-Law of May 6, 1948, N. 654; G. Landi, "Profili e problemi
della giustizia amministrativa per la regione siciliana" *Giust. civ*, 1955; S. De Fina,
"Consiglio di giustizia amministrativa per la Regione siciliana," EdD, Vol. IX, p. 227).
According to the available case law, this court is part of the Consiglio di Stato (*cf.*
Decisions by the Corte di Cassazione of October 11, 1955, N. 2994; of March 10, 1971, N.
674; of November 11, 1973, N. 2896, and Decision by the Consiglio di Stato of June 28,
1956, N. 261).

also pronounce judgment on the expediency of administrative acts,[31] as well as certain matters for which they have "exclusive jurisdiction" (competenza esclusiva), under which they may adjudicate on specifically defined subjective rights.[32]

It is possible to have recourse to the ordinary courts for the protection of subjective rights against measures taken by the administration. The ordinary courts have no power to amend or revoke administrative acts.[33] They may, however, take decisions which find for the citizen making a claim, and order the administration to pay compensation. Finally, the Constitutional Court (Corte Costituzionale) can also deal with questions of administrative law, e.g. where it is called upon to exercise judicial review of legislative measures taken by the administration.[34]

In addition to invoking judicial protection, the citizen may lodge three types of complaint which are internal to the administration itself.[35] The "opposizione" is directed to the authority which issued the act; it is admissible in specific circumstances which are laid down by law.[36] Hierarchical complaints[37] are made to the superior authority. They may be made about any administrative act issued by a lower body which has no exclusive jurisdiction. Special complaints to the President of the Republic may be made within 120 days against any definitive administrative act.

[31] On this subject, cf. M. Nigro, Giustizia amministrativa, loc. cit., footnote 27, pp. 108, 295, containing further references.

[32] On the exclusive jurisdiction, cf. Decision by the Corte di Cassazione of January 9, 1976, N. 6; Decision by the TAR Piemonte of July 15, 1980, N. 539; Decision by the Consiglio di Stato (Ad. plen.) of October 26, 1979, N. 25; M. Nigro, Giustizia amministrativa, loc. cit., footnote 27, pp. 110, 166, 279, 315 et seq., containing further references.

[33] On this subject, cf. M. Nigro Giustizia amministrativa, loc. cit., footnote 27, pp. 223 et seq., containing further references.

[34] For more details of the jurisdiction of the Italian Constitutional Court, cf. Th. Rittersprach, "Probleme der italienischen Verfassungsgerichtsbarkeit—20 Jahre Corte Costituzionale." A.ö.R., Vol. 104 (1979), pp. 137 et seq., and, more recently, H. J. Faller, "Zur Entwicklung der nationalen Verfassungsgerichte in Europa" (1986) EuGRZ, 42 (at 46 et seq.).

[35] On the subject of internal complaints, cf. A. Sandulli, Manuale, loc. cit., footnote 22, p. 1052 containing further references. On the relationship between judicial actions and administrative complaints, cf. Decisions by the Corte Costituzionale of February 27, 1974, N. 46, and of July 26, 1979, N. 93.

[36] Article 7 d.P.R. November 24, 1971, N. 1199.

[37] Article 1–6 d.P.R. 1199.

The protection of the citizen against the administration, of which merely the bare outlines are provided here,[38] is complemented by the political supervision exercised by Parliament over the executive, which takes the form of Parliamentary questions, examinations and inquiries on the one hand, and of debates concerning the approval of the budget and of the final accounts on the other.

(5) As to the organisation of the administration, the organisation State administration reveals a pyramidal structure, at the summit of which stands the relevant Minister. Subordinate to the Ministries are the local authorities. At this level special mention should be made of the Prefect, an official whose jurisdiction covers a province and who comes under the authority of the Ministry for Internal Affairs.[39]

Article 5 of the Constitution states that the Republic shall be based on the principles of local administrative autonomy and of maximum decentralisation of services provided by the State. These principles, which have not as yet been fully realised, constitute one of the chief institutional changes brought about by the Republican constitution. From the viewpoint of political organisation, the Italian Republic can be described as a *Stato delle autonomie*. The territorial decentralisation secures for the local authorities, *i.e.* the regions, the provinces and the municipalities, extensive rights of self-government. Under the Constitution and the 1934 Law relating to the Provinces and Municipalities, the local authorities are

[38] For more details in German, *cf.* D. Karwiese, *Kontrolle der Verwaltung durch ordentliche Gerichte und allgemeine Verwaltungsgerichte nach italienischem Recht* (1986) Frankfurt; F. Marriuzzi, "Struktur und Wirkungskreis der italienischen Verwaltungsgerichsbarkeit" *Bayerische Verwaltungsblätter*, 1984, pp. 737 *et seq.*, and, from a comparative law point of view, R. Grawert, "Grenzen und Alternativen des gerichtlichen Rechtsschutzes in Verwaltungsstreitsachen, Rechtsvergleichender Bericht: Bundesrepublik Deutschland—Italien" (1983) DVBl., pp. 973 *et seq.*; M. Fromont, "Verwaltungsgerichtsbarkeit in Frankreich und Italien," in *Festschrift zum 100jährigen Bestehen des österreichischen Verwaltungsgerichtshofs* (Lehne, Loebenstein, Schimetschek, eds.).

[39] On the official organisation of the administration, *cf.* G. Treves, *L'organizzazione amministrativa* (1975) Turin; S. Cassese, *Il sistema amministrativo italiano, loc. cit.*, footnote 15; V. Mortara, *Introduzione alla pubblica amministrazione italiana* (1983) Milan. On the organisation of the ministry, *cf.* D. Serrani, *L'organizzazione per Ministeri* (1963) Milan and (1979) Rome; G. Arena, "Ministeri," in *Dizionario amministrativo* (Guarino, ed.) (1983) Milan; F.O.R.M. E.Z., *Ricera sull'organizzazione e il funzionamento delle amministrazioni centrali e periferiche dello Stato* (1983) Rome.

governed by a council (the regional, provincial or municipal council) elected by direct universal suffrage. Every council elects its own chairman and executive committee. The Mayor is the chairman of the municipal council.

The regions have legislative powers in certain defined areas, in the sense that they enact concurrent legislation in the ordinary regions and exclusive legislation for specific matters in the special regions (Articles 116 and 117). The autonomous powers of the regions extend to the areas specifically designated in Article 117 (Article 118(1)). In other areas the State may confer on the regions wider administrative powers (Article 118(2)), whereas the regions normally exercise their authority by transferring their administrative powers to the provinces or to the municipalities (Article 118(3)).

For a number of years attempts have been made to reform the regional and local administrations and to adapt them to constitutional developments.[40] A particularly acute problem is posed by the financial system, since all local authorities have only limited tax revenue at their disposal and obtain the bulk of their financial resources from the State (the so-called Derived Financing System).[41] This constitutes a restraint on autonomy and decentralisation.

In addition to the local authorities, the decentralised system of administration also covers the public utilities (organised by the State, the regions, the provinces and the municipalities), which have the status of corporate bodies constituted under public law and have varying degrees

---

[40] On the reform of the Local Authorities Regulation, cf. B. Dente, "Il governo locale in Italia," in Il governo locale in Europa (1977) Milan; L. Vandelli, Le autonomie locali verso la riforma. Progetti e documenti (1981) Rimini; La riforma dell'amministrazione locale (1977) Turin. On the principle of autonomy laid down in the Constitution, cf. Benvenuti, L'ordinamento repubblicano (1979) Venice; C. Esposito, "Autonomie locali e decentramento amministrativo nell'art. 5 Cost.," in La Costituzione italiana (1954) Padua; G. Berti, "Art. 5," in Commentario della Costituzione (von Branca, ed.), (1975) Bologna, p. 277; G. Volpe, Autonomie locali e garantismo (1974) Milan; Orsi Battaglini, Le autonomie locali nell'ordinamento regionale (1975) Milan; F. Pizzetti, Il sistema costituzionale delle autonomie locali (1970) Milan; A. Pubusa, Sovranità popolare e autonomie locali nell'ordinamento costituzionale italiano (1983) Milan.

[41] On the method of financing local authorities, cf. M. Bertolissi, L'autonomia finanziaria regionale: lineamenti costituzionali (1983) Padua; E. Buglione and I. Pierantoni, I rapporti finanziari tra Stato e Regioni (1980) Milan; P. Giarda, Finanza locale. Idee per una riforma (1982) Milan.

of self-governing power.[42] Special functions are conferred on the autonomous corporations ("aziende autonome"),[43] which have only some of the attributes of a corporate body constituted under public law. The A.I.M.A. (Azienda autonoma per gli interventi sul mercato agricolo) is such an azienda autonoma, which has its own legal personality. It was established by the Law of May 13, 1966[44] under the Ministry for Agriculture, and its main function is to carry out E.C. agricultural regulations and directives. This the A.I.M.A. does through the Federconsorzi (Federazione nazionale dei consorzi agrari), which is a private organisation consisting of *consorzi agrari*.[45]

---

[42] On the public corporations, *cf.* CIRIEC (Centro italiano di richerche e d'informazione sulle economie delle imprese pubbliche e di pubbliche interesse), *Gli enti pubblici italiani. Anagrafe legislativa e giurisprudenziale dal 1861 al 1970* (1972) Milan; D. Cosi and F. P. Pugliese, *I modelli organizzativi degli enti pubblici* (1975) Milan; D. Serranti, *Il potere per enti. Enti pubblici e sistema politico in Italia* (1978) Bologna; N. Capria, "Amministrazione per enti," in Archivio ISAP, 1983, Vol. I (1983) Milan, pp. 365 *et seq.*

[43] On the "aziende autonome", *cf.* M. La Torre, "Aziende autonome e uffici autonomi," in *Scritti giuridici in onore di S. Romano*, Vol. II, pp. 687 *et seq.*; G. Treves "Aziende (diritto pubblico)," EdD IV, pp. 741 *et seq.*

[44] N. 303, recently amended by the Laws of August 14, 1973, N. 496 and of February 16, 1980, N. 59.

[45] *cf.* on this subject A. Brancasi and M. Carrà, "Rapport du droit italien," in Centre Interuniversitaire de droit comparé A.S.B.L., *Régime juridique des relations entre les opérateurs économiques et les organismes d'exécution du droit communautaire*, Vol. II, pp. 419 *et seq.* For general comments on the problems presented by the co-ordination of Community policy in Italy, *cf.* also R. Lazzareschi, "Problems and Structure of Community Policy Co-ordination," in *National and Supranational Powers in the Shaping of Community Policies* (F. Francioni, G. Grottanelli de' Santi, eds.) (1984) Milan, pp. 1 *et seq.*, as well as G. Grottanelli de' Santi, *Formulating and Implementing Community Policies—Italian Constitutional Aspects, ibid.*, pp. 15 *et seq.*

SECTION 4

UNITED KINGDOM*

(1) The most distinctive characteristic of the British administrative law system is the absence of a formal separation between private law and public law. The public authorities are subject to the common law as modified by Parliamentary statute. The judicial review of administrative action is, in principle, exercised not by a special administrative judiciary, but by the ordinary courts.

The traditional constitutional basis for these principles is supplied by A. V. Dicey in his *Introduction to the Study of the Law of the Constitution*, which appeared in 1885. He derives these principles essentially from the "rule of law" doctrine,[1] which is the second major pillar of England's unwritten constitution (the other being the sovereignty of Parliament). According to Dicey, the "rule of law" doctrine entails in the first instance the rule that the executive is bound by the law and that all arbitrary action should be excluded,[2] secondly, the principle of equality before the law, which excludes the possibility of a separate legal order or judicial system for administrative action,[3] and thirdly, the conclusion that the Constitution is the result of private law as applied by the ordinary courts and binding upon the Crown and its servants.[4] Dicey's analysis culminates in the statement that "In England . . . the system of administrative law and the very principles on which it rests are in truth unknown."[5] Dicey stresses the superiority of English law over French administrative law and the

---

* Within the United Kingdom of Great Britain and Northern Ireland, there exist three separate legal systems, each one having its own judicial organisation, *i.e.* England and Wales, Scotland and Northern Ireland (for more details *cf.* E. C. S. Wade, A. W. Bradley, *Constitutional and Administrative Law* (10th ed., London–New York, 1985). The points on which the administrative law of Northern Ireland (*cf.* A. G. Donaldson, *Some Comparative Aspects of Irish Law*, pp. 181 *et seq.*) and that of Scotland (*cf.* J. D. B. Mitchell, *Constitutional Law* (2nd ed., Part 3) differ from English administrative law are not discussed here.

[1] *cf.* A. V. Dicey, *Introduction to the Study of the Law of the Constitution* (10th ed., 1959, reprinted London 1979), pp. 183 *et seq.*, in particular the summary featured on pp. 202 *et seq.*

[2] *Ibid.*, p. 188.

[3] *Ibid.*, p. 193.

[4] *Ibid.*, p. 195.

[5] *Ibid.*, p. 330.

protection it provides, ascribing to the latter the essential function of exempting civil servants from liability, or at least lightening its burden.[6] Although Dicey's misconception of *"droit administratif"* was criticised even in his lifetime, his theories continued to exert a great deal of influence until well into the twentieth century.[7]

In the meantime, the individual tradition of English administrative law, whose origins date back to the late seventeenth century, continues to exercise the legal mind.[8] Even before this period, an elementary form of supervision of administrative action had been developed, which culminated, during the Tudor dynasty, in the establishment of the Star Chamber court, which exercised a certain degree of supervision over the lower administrative authorities. Subsequently, however, this court degenerated into an instrument in the service of the arbitrary power exercised by the Stuarts. In the course of the constitutional struggle between the Stuart dynasty and its prerogative courts on the one hand, and Parliament together with the Common Law courts on the other, the Star Chamber and consequently its jurisdiction over administrative action, which was "tainted with the stigma of tyrannical rule,"[9] were abolished. At the end of the seventeenth century, following the "Glorious Revolution" of 1688/89, the fundamental principles of modern administrative law in England were established: disputes relating to administrative action were to be decided by the ordinary courts, more particularly through the mechanism of the writs of certiorari, prohibition and mandamus.[10] Many of the principles of substantive administrative law which continue to apply at present were moulded into shape by case law during this period.[11] Even though they continued to develop as a result of many individual reforms, these principles remained essentially intact until the end of the nineteenth century.

---

[6] *Ibid.*, Chapter XII ("Rule of Law compared with Droit Administratif"), pp. 328 *et seq.*, in particular pp. 336 and 403 *et seq.*

[7] *cf.* in particular the introduction by E. C. S. Wade in A. V. Dicey, *loc. cit.*, footnote 1, pp. XCVI *et seq.*; E. H. Riedel, *Kontrolle der Verwaltung im englischen Rechtssystem* (1976) Berlin, pp. 242 *et seq.*; O. Hood Phillips, P. Jackson, *Constitutional and Administrative Law* (6th ed., London 1978, pp. 36 *et seq.*; J. Jowell, "The Rule of Law Today" in *The Changing Constitution* (J. Jowell, D. Oliver, eds.) (1985) Oxford, pp. 3 *et seq.*

[8] *cf.* H. W. R. Wade, *Administrative Law* (5th ed., Oxford 1982) Oxford, p. 15.

[9] *cf.* E. H. Riedel, *loc. cit.*, footnote 7, p. 284.

[10] For further details, *cf. infra* at 57.

[11] *cf.* H. W. R. Wade, *loc. cit.*, footnote 8, pp. 15 *et seq.*

It was finally the effects of the industrial revolution and the creation of the welfare state, together with the consequent changes in the role of the administration, which led to the modernisation of traditional administrative law theory.[12] Technological progress meant that Parliament was no longer in a position to regulate satisfactorily complex issues such as the railways (and, later, road transport), safety standards in the course of mass production, etc. As a result, increasing use was made of the practice of delegating legislative powers to the government or to specially selected administrative bodies, whose specialist staff was in a better position to issue detailed regulations and to react flexibly to new developments. Thus the practice of delegating legislation to the administration increased considerably towards the end of the nineteenth century.[13] The welfare legislation of the early twentieth century created a new field of activity for the administration, particularly in the sphere of social security.[14] Also, in the course of the First World War the powers of the executive to issue ministerial regulations and to set up special administrative tribunals were considerably enlarged.

These developments gave rise to a mounting chorus of criticism levelled at the excessive power wielded by the executive, which was condemned by the then Lord Chief Justice, Lord Hewart, as "the new despotism."[15] As a result of this criticism, a Committee was established with the brief of examining ministerial powers. The committee submitted its Report in 1932 (the Donoughmore Report).[16] One of its recommendations, namely the reform of democratic control over delegated legislation,[17] was realised in part by the Statutory Instruments Act 1946. However, the unsupervised transfer of judicial and quasi-judicial powers to ministers and to certain tribunals,[18] which was also the subject of criticism in the Report, actually increased after the Second World War. It was not until the 1958 Tribunals and Inquiries Act, which essentially

---

[12] cf. J. F. Garner, "England," in Geschichte der Verwaltungsrechtswissenschaft in Europa (E. V. Heyen, ed.) (1982) Frankfurt, pp. 49, 55 et seq.; K. Loewenstein, Staatsrecht und Staatspraxis von Grossbritannien (1967) Berlin/Heidelberg/New York, Vol. 2, pp. 71 et seq. ("Umwandlung des Gesetzgebungs- in den Verwaltungsstaat").

[13] An important step in this development was made by the Report of the Committee on Ministers' Powers (1932), Cmd. 4060, in particular sec. II, 4; II, 11.

[14] e.g. through the 1908 Old Age Pension Act and the 1911 National Insurance Act.

[15] cf. Lord Hewart of Bury, The New Despotism (1929) London.

[16] Report of the Committee on Ministers' Powers (1932) Cmd. 4060.

[17] Ibid., sec. I, 15.

[18] Ibid., sec. II, 21 et seq.

followed the recommendations of the Franks Report,[19] that this situation was remedied to a certain extent.

Following a period of judicial restraint during the 1940s and 1950s, in the course of which an exceptionally broad interpretation was brought to bear on the powers of the administration, it is possible to discern since the 1960s a reaffirmation and extension of the principles of judicial review of administrative action.[20] As early as 1971, Lord Denning M.R. concluded that this period witnessed the creation of a sophisticated system of administrative law in England.[21] Ten years later, Lord Diplock described this development as "that progress towards a comprehensive system of administrative law that I regard as having been the greatest achievement of the English courts in my judicial lifetime."[22]

(2–3) What is the general picture of present-day British administrative law, and what are its sources? It is worth noting that, in the absence of a written constitution,[23] there is also no written record of the constitutional principles of administrative law, in particular that of the rule of law. On the subject of the general sources of law, and consequently also the sources of administrative law, since the latter is deemed to form part of "ordinary law," mention must be made in the first place of legislation and case law.[24]

Customary law, in so far as it has not found expression in case law, has little relevance for administrative law.[25] The "opinions of the learned writers" constitute a subsidiary source.[26] Although not binding, "quasi-law," *i.e.* "near legislation" (discretionary directives and codes of conduct issued by the administration) and "near precedents" (especially the

---

[19] Report of the Committee on Administrative Tribunals and Enquiries (1957) Cmnd. 218.
[20] On the subject of this development, *cf.* H. W. R. Wade, *loc. cit.*, footnote 8, pp. 18 *et seq.*, and S. A. de Smith, J. M. Evans, *Judicial Review of Administrative Action* (4th ed., London 1980), p. 8, which trace back this evolution to the influence exerted by the more active systems of administrative courts in the U.S., France and certain Commonwealth states.
[21] *cf.* Lord Denning, M.R., in *Breen* v. *A.E.U.* [1971] 2 Q.B. 175, 189.
[22] *cf.* Lord Diplock, in *Inland Revenue Cmrs.* v. *National Federation of Self-Employed and Small Businesses Ltd.* [1982] A.C. 617; the decision is reproduced in J. Beatson, M. H. Matthews, *Administrative Law: Cases and Materials* (1983) Oxford, pp. 346 *et seq.* (at p. 354).
[23] On the "unwritten" and "flexible" nature of the British Constitution, *cf.* O. Hood Phillips, P. Jackson, *loc. cit.*, footnote 7, pp. 6 *et seq.*, 22 *et seq.*
[24] P. S. James, *Introduction to English Law* (11th ed., 1985), pp. 8 *et seq.*
[25] *cf.* on the subject of customary law as a source of law, O. Hood Phillips, P. Jackson, *loc. cit.*, footnote 7, pp. 24 *et seq.*
[26] *Ibid.*, pp. 25 *et seq.*

decisions by the administrative tribunals), play an important part in practice.[27] Finally, mention must also be made of the reports submitted by the Reform Committees, whose role in the development of the law should not however be overstated.[28] In addition to the reports of the ad hoc committees[29]—such as the Donoughmore Report (which, according to Loewenstein, constitutes "one of the most significant political documents in contemporary Britain")[30] and the Franks Report mentioned earlier the reports submitted by the English and Scottish Law Commissions[31] and the independent lawyers' organisation "Justice"[32] which exert particular influence on the development of administrative law.

Acts of Parliament and delegated legislation, *i.e.* the Statutory Instruments and Regulations issued by the administration on the basis of statutory powers, regulate a considerable number of questions of special administrative law. In most cases, these enabling Acts also contain provisions relating to the administrative procedure for each individual section of the administration. Britain does not have a general statute relating to procedure, such as the American Administrative Procedure Act.[33] The Tribunals and Inquiries Act (1958/1971) did, however, introduce a certain measure of uniformity to administrative procedure. Thus, for example, Section 12 lays down a general duty to give reasons for all decisions by ministers or administrative tribunals taken under this Act.[34]

General administrative law can be found chiefly in case law, *i.e.* court precedents. Under the *stare decisis* doctrine[35] the lower courts are bound by the decisions taken by the higher courts within the same jurisdiction. It is however only the *ratio decidendi* which is binding, *i.e.* the rule based on the material facts which is essential to the decision. The principles which form the basis for the individual rationes are not as such

---

[27] *cf.* J. F. Garner, *Administrative Law* (5th ed., London 1979), pp. 28 *et seq.*

[28] *Ibid.*, pp. 27 *et seq.*

[29] *cf. supra*, footnotes 16 and 19.

[30] *cf.* K. Loewenstein, *loc. cit.*, footnote 12, Vol. 2, p. 74.

[31] *cf.*, *e.g.*, Report on Remedies in Administrative Law (1976) Cmnd. 6407.

[32] *cf.*, *e.g.*, Report by Justice, Administration under Law (1971).

[33] Administrative Procedure Act 1946.

[34] *cf.* also the relevant proposals in: Report of the Committee on Administrative Tribunals and Enquiries, Cmnd. 218, sec. 98.

[35] *cf.* (also in relation to the footnotes below) P. S. James, *loc. cit.*, footnote 24, pp. 16 *et seq.*, in particular at p. 18 on the Practice Statement of the House of Lords made in 1966; *cf.* also T. Koopmans, "Stare decisis in European Law," in *European Law and Integration* (D. O'Keeffe, H. G. Schermers, eds.) (1982) Deventer *et al.*, pp. 11 *et seq.*, and Lord Mackenzie Stuart, J.-P. Warner, "Judicial Decision as a Source of Community Law" in FS Kutscher (Grewe, Rupp, Schneider, eds.) (1981) Baden-Baden, p. 273 on the first signs of *stare decisis* in the case law of the European Court of Justice.

vested with binding force. As starting points for the legal reasoning process, and as guiding summaries of series of decisions, they are capable of further development.[36] Thus the *ultra vires* and natural justice principles, which are fundamental to administrative law, have experienced various stages of judicial restriction and extension.[37]

As a result of the rising tide of legislation, the original judge-made law has increasingly moved in the direction of statutory interpretation.[38] Even the general principles of administrative law are often considered as being the outcome of statutory interpretation and are construed as an integral part (which, although unwritten, is nevertheless vested with statutory authority) of special administrative legislation.[39] In view of the development of the general principles of administrative law through the body of precedents, which is shaped by the material facts of cases, and through the interpretation of special administrative legislation, it is understandable that no systematic theory has yet emerged concerning these principles.

These principles of administrative law, especially the various constructions of the *ultra vires* doctrine and the concept of natural justice, have a function and legal significance similar to the general principles of administrative law developed by the Continental legal systems.[40] There is, however, an essential difference arising from the British constitutional doctrine of Parliamentary sovereignty,[41] which excludes in particular the possibility of any judicial appraisal of Acts of Parliament. This principle means that Parliament may at all times derogate from the legal principles laid down by the courts or change their field of application.[42]

---

[36] *cf.* J. Esser, *Grundsatz und Norm in der richterlichen Fortbildung des Privatrechts* (2nd ed., 1964) Tübingen, pp. 185 *et seq.*

[37] *cf.* H. W. R. Wade, *loc. cit.*, footnote 8, pp. 18 *et seq.*

[38] *cf.* K. Loewenstein, *loc. cit.*, footnote 12, Vol. 1, p. 51.

[39] *cf.* H. W. R. Wade, *loc. cit.*, footnote 8, p. 38.

[40] This view is shared by H.-W. Rengeling, *Rechtsgrundsätze beim Verwaltungsvollzug des Europäischen Gemeinschaftsrechts* (1977) Köln/Berlin/Bonn/München, p. 156. *cf.* also, however, L. Collins, *European Community Law in the United Kingdom* (3rd ed., London 1984), pp. 199 *et seq.* (on the various points of distinction between the principles of administrative supervision under English law and the general legal principles of Community law).

[41] The standard work on the concept of Parliamentary Sovereignty is A. V. Dicey, *loc. cit.*, footnote 1, pp. 39 *et seq.*; on the current significance of what they term "Parliamentary Supremacy," *cf.* O. Hood Phillips, P. Jackson, *loc. cit.*, footnote 7, pp. 50 *et seq.*, and E. C. S. Wade, A. W. Bradley, *Constitutional and Administrative Law* (10th ed., London/New York 1985), pp. 60 *et seq.*

[42] *cf.* J. F. Garner, in *Geschichte der Verwaltungsrechtswissenschaft in Europa, loc. cit.*, footnote 12, p. 61.

The principle which is central to English administrative law, *i.e.* the *ultra vires* doctrine, is however itself a logical outcome of British constitutional thinking and can be viewed as resulting from a combination of Parliamentary sovereignty and the "rule of law" concept. In essence, this doctrine implies that no administrative body may exceed the bounds of the authority conferred upon it, especially where such authority has been conferred by an Act of Parliament.[43] This applies both to the individual acts issued by the administration and to the general rules adopted within the framework of delegated legislation.

An essential distinction is drawn between substantive and procedural errors.[44] An administrative action is substantively *ultra vires* if essential requirements of the enabling provision have not been met, or if an administrative authority exercises the powers conferred on it for unlawful purposes, in bad faith, unreasonably or on the basis of false evidence.[45] Administrative action is held to be procedurally *ultra vires* where it infringes mandatory procedural requirements. This involves the process of establishing in each individual case, by interpreting the enabling provision, whether the procedural requirements contained therein are mandatory or not. Examples of mandatory formal requirements are the right to be heard and the rule that legal remedies must be notified to the party concerned.

In addition to the *ultra vires* doctrine, the "rule of natural justice" constitutes the second fundamental principle of administrative law.[46] This rule includes the minimum requirements which are necessary for a fair procedure, which is a duty imposed by common law on any person or

---

[43] A leading case on the limits of the scope of this theory is particularly the important House of Lords decision in *Attorney-General* v. *Great Eastern Ry.* 5 [1880] A.C. 473 at 478, where it is stated that "whatever may fairly be regarded as incidental to, or consequential upon, those things which the legislature has authorized, ought not (unless expressly prohibited) to be held, by judicial construction, to be ultra vires." On the origins and historical development of the *ultra vires* doctrine, *cf.* also R. Glücksmann, *Die Grenzen der Betätigung englischer Verwaltungsbehörden* (1984) Frankfurt.

[44] In addition, other categories have been formed and others restricted in their scope. *Cf.* J. F. Garner, B. L. Jones, *Administrative Law* (6th ed., London 1985), pp. 109–136; H. W. R. Wade, *loc. cit.*, footnote 8, pp. 38 *et seq.* and 213 *et seq.*; D. Foulkes, *Administrative Law* (5th ed., London 1982), pp. 169 *et seq.*

[45] *cf.* H. W. R. Wade, *loc. cit.*, footnote 8, pp. 38, 391 ("good faith") 353 ("Reasonableness"), 287 ("no evidence"), each concept being illustrated with examples from the relevant case law.

[46] *cf.* H. Marshall, *Natural Justice* (1959); P. Jackson, *Natural Justice* (1973) and the relevant passages from the general works on administrative law: S. A. de Smith, J. M. Evans, *loc. cit.*, footnote 20, pp. 156 *et seq.*; J. F. Garner, B. L. Jones, *loc. cit.*, footnote 44, pp. 136 *et seq.*; H. W. R. Wade, *op. cit.*, footnote 8, pp. 414 *et seq.*; D. Foulkes, *loc. cit.*, footnote 44, pp. 221 *et seq.*

body obliged to take judicial decisions, in particular the various administrative tribunals.[47] This "code establishing a fair administrative procedure"[48] essentially[49] involves the right to a fair hearing (audi alteram partem)[50] and the rule that no-one may be a judge in his own cause (nemo iudex in causa sua).[51]

It becomes apparent from the principles of procedural *ultra vires* and of natural justice that the shape of English administrative law has been conditioned mainly by considerations of administrative procedure. The notion that substantive rights are to be secured mainly by procedural rules is particularly entrenched in Anglo-American legal thinking[52] and also finds expression in the case law of the United States Supreme Court relating to the due process clause in the American constitution.[53] The oft-quoted words of Justice Frankfurter: "The history of liberty has largely been the history of the observance of procedural safeguards"[54] are also particularly apt for describing the development of British administrative law.

(4) The predominance of the procedural aspect also characterises the relationship between the substantive administrative law and its procedural counterpart. The original English system, under which the plaintiff would succeed only if he could designate one of the writs appropriate to his claim (ubi remedium, ibi ius) is still visible in its effects in spite of the

---

[47] *cf.* S. A. de Smith, H. Street, R. Brazier, *Constitutional and Administrative Law* (4th ed., Harmondsworth (Middlesex) 1981), p. 569.

[48] *cf.* H. W. R. Wade, *loc. cit.*, footnote 8, p. 414.

[49] In addition, other categories have been formed, such as the "duty to act fairly," the duty to give reasons and the principle that proceedings must be public; *cf.* the literature cited *supra* (footnote 47).

[50] Leading cases on this subject are *Cooper* v. *The Board of Works for the Wandsworth District* (1863) 14 C.B.N.S. 180 and, recently, especially *Ridge* v. *Baldwin* [1964] A.C. 40. Extracts from both decisions can be found in J. Beatson, M. H. Matthews, *loc. cit.*, footnote 22, pp. 211 *et seq.*, 214 *et seq.*

[51] A leading case on this subject is *Dimes* v. *Grand Junction Canal* (1852) 3 H.L.C. 759 (extracts in: O. Hood Phillips, *Leading Cases in Constitutional and Administrative Law* (5th ed., London 1979), p. 146).

[52] *cf.* R. David, *Les grands systèmes de droit contemporains* (8th ed., Paris 1982), pp. 361 *et seq.* In Continental Europe, the emphasis on procedure is particularly marked in Austrian administrative law. For more details: *cf.* W. Antoniolli, F. Koja, *Allgemeines Verwaltungsrecht* (2nd ed., Vienna 1986), pp. 554 *et seq.*

[53] *cf.* H. D. Jarass, "Besonderheiten des amerikanischen Verwaltungsrechts im Vergleich— zugleich ein Beitrag zum Stellenwert des Verwaltungsverfahrens" DÖV (1985), 377, 378 *et seq.*; J. Schwarze, *Der funktionale Zusammenhang von Verwaltungsverfahrensrecht und verwaltungsgerichtlichem Rechtsschutz* (1974) Berlin, pp. 28 *et seq.*

[54] *McNabb* v. *U.S.* 318 U.S. 332, 347 (1943).

fundamental reforms to which it has been subjected.[55] Thus many of the theories surrounding substantive administrative law can be understood only in the context of the development of legal remedies and the manner in which they have been extended and adjusted.[56] This also explains why the British legal system has never drawn a clear distinction between substantive and procedural administrative law.

The available remedies against administrative action break down into the statutory appeal on the one hand, and judicial review, which traditionally comes within the jurisdiction of the courts, on the other. Since the statutory remedies concern only certain specific questions, the "prerogative writs," which were originally actions developed by the royal courts for the enforcement of the rights of the Crown, have retained their important role in administrative law protection. They may seek to challenge sovereign acts which have been adopted, to prohibit sovereign acts whose adoption is imminent, or to compel the adoption of a measure deemed necessary by the court (orders of certiorari, prohibition, mandamus) on the one hand, or to secure a verdict on a restraint of liberty (writ of habeas corpus)[57] on the other. An age-old distinction has been drawn between these "public law" actions and the "ordinary private law" actions for damages, declarations and injunctions (which involve an order to do or not to do something).[58] This distinction has, however, lost a good deal of its significance, since from 1978 onwards any designated action (with the exception of the writ of habeas corpus, which is irrelevant to administrative law) can be brought by means of a uniform application to the relevant court and is subject to a standardised procedure.[59] The appropriate court is the Divisional Court of the Queen's Bench Division of the High Court. The applicant must make the application within a certain time-limit and prove that he has a legitimate interest in the dispute (locus standi). The legitimate interest requirement has recently been inter-

---

[55] cf. E. H. Riedel, loc. cit., footnote 7, p. 23.

[56] cf. H. W. R. Wade, loc. cit., footnote 8, p. 513.

[57] The individual actions are extensively dealt with in S. A. de Smith, J. M. Evans, loc. cit., footnote 20, Part 3, pp. 379 et seq. and Appendix 2 (Habeas Corpus); in German, cf. especially E. H. Riedel, loc. cit., footnote 7, Chapters 1–5.

[58] cf. H. W. R. Wade, loc. cit., footnote 8, pp. 513, 514.

[59] These reforms have their origin in a proposal by the Law Reform Commission (Report on Remedies in Administrative Law, Cmnd. 6407 (1976)). It was initially realized by an amendment of the Rules of the Supreme Court (Amendment No. 3), S.I. 1977 No. 1955; its essential parts were entrenched in statutory form in 1981 through the Supreme Court Act.

preted very liberally by the House of Lords and in certain cases does not exclude the use of popular actions.[60]

Present-day Acts often contain a clause to the effect that the decision of the Minister or of the authority shall be final. Occasionally the judicial review of any such decision is expressly excluded. The courts, however, appear unwilling to apply such clauses automatically. The leading case in this connection is *Anisminic Ltd.* v. *Foreign Compensation Commission*, in which the House of Lords established that such clauses do not in principle exclude the possibility of judicial review where the administrative decision is based on an error of jurisdiction.[61]

The restrictive interpretation of such exclusion clauses reflects, as does the liberal application of the *locus standi* requirement, the concern of the courts that every action by the authorities should, if at all possible, be subject to judicial review.

Until the enactment of the 1947 Crown Proceedings Act, the liability of the Crown and of the public authorities was dominated by the principle that "The King can do no wrong". In view of the historical identity of the King with the system of justice, the notion that the King or his servants could be sued for damages appeared absurd. The Crown continues to enjoy certain privileges under the law of torts, which have become the subject of mounting criticism. In principle, actions in tort against the Crown or against local authorities are currently decided in accordance with general common law principles.

In addition to supervision by the ordinary courts, the judicial review of administrative action by special tribunals has gained in importance.[62] There currently exist well over 2,000 different types of tribunal, set up mainly as a result of the enactment of welfare legislation, *e.g.* in the fields of social security and labour law. These judicial bodies adjudicate in complaints brought against measures adopted by the administration. The detailed rules concerning the composition of these tribunals, which in

---

[60] *cf.* in particular *Inland Revenue Cmrs.* v. *National Federation of Self-Employed and Small Businesses Ltd.* [1982] A.C. 617 (extracts in J. Beatson, M. H. Matthews, *loc. cit.*, footnote 22, pp. 346 *et seq.*); *cf.* also on this case H. W. R. Wade, *loc. cit.*, footnote 8, pp. 587 *et seq.*

[61] [1969] 2 A.C. 147; [1969] 1 All E.R. 208 (H.L.). Reproduced in S. H. Bailey, C. A. Cross, J. F. Garner, *Cases and Materials in Administrative Law* (1977) London, pp. 199 *et seq.* More details on the statutory preclusion clause in H. W. R. Wade, *loc. cit.*, footnote 8, pp. 598 *et seq.* (in particular pp. 603 *et seq.* on the *Anisminic* case).

[62] *cf.*, also in relation to the items below, H. W. R. Wade, *loc. cit.*, footnote 8, pp. 776 *et seq.*, and E. H. Riedel, *loc. cit.*, footnote 7, p. 120 (both references applying also to the Inquiries procedure, which is not dealt with here); C. v. Loeper, *Verwaltungsrechtspflege in England* (1983) Frankfurt, pp. 158 *et seq.*

most cases consist of a lawyer as chairman and two lay persons, the procedure to be followed and the review of tribunal decisions by the ordinary courts, reveal considerable variations from one type to another. Since the balance of judicial and administrative characteristics varies considerably from one tribunal to another, there would appear to be little point in trying to decide whether this institution is a special type of administrative court or part of the administrative machinery.[63] It is precisely the fact that they present a combination of administrative and (quasi-) judicial characteristics that gives tribunals their particular appearance.

The increasing establishment of new tribunals after the First World War produced a rising tide of criticism directed at the inadequacy of their procedural guarantees and the defective nature of the legal protection against tribunal decisions. Following the public outcry over the misuse of administrative power in the *Crichel Down* case,[64] the above-mentioned Committee on Administrative Tribunals and Enquiries (Franks Committee) was established in 1955. Its recommendations,[65] published in 1957, were essentially given statutory recognition barely a year later.[66] In particular, a Council on Tribunals was set up, which supervises the various tribunals and submits an annual report to Parliament. Other measures include a strengthening of the procedural rights of the citizen concerned and an improvement in the opportunities for judicial review of tribunal decisions.

Finally, the administration is also subject to Parliamentary supervision. Apart from the responsibility before Parliament of Ministers and Question Time, which is used by MPs individually, the various administrative departments are supervised largely through the medium of the so-called Select Committees, which are organised by Parliament for the purpose of supervising certain sections and powers of the administration.[67] The creation, in 1967, of the institution of the Parliamentary

---

[63] *cf.* E. H. Riedel, *loc. cit.*, footnote 7, pp. 123 *et seq.*, pp. 133 *et seq.*, with references to dissenting viewpoints.

[64] *cf.* on the *Crichel Down* case and its implications for the reform of English administrative law; M. Bernhardt, *Zur rechtlichen Bedeutung der Erklärung einer "Policy" in der englischen Verwaltungspraxis. Dargestellt am Beispiel der Rückübereignung enteigneter Grundstücke*, Diss. Freiburg, undated, pp. 49 *et seq.*

[65] Report of the Committee on Administrative Tribunals and Enquiries (1957) Cmnd. 218.

[66] Tribunals and Inquiries Act 1958 (replaced by the Tribunals and Inquiries Act 1971).

[67] *cf.* on the select committees S. A. de Smith, H. Street, R. Brazier, *loc. cit.*, footnote 47, pp. 296 *et seq.*; O. Hood Phillips, P. Jackson, *loc. cit.*, footnote 7, pp. 230 *et seq.*, pp. 569 *et seq.* Of particular importance to European Community law are the Joint Select Committee on Statutory Instruments, which also examines the Acts implementing Com-

Commissioner for Administration[68] was inspired by the Danish model, *i.e.* the Ombudsman,[69] but is in many respects but a pale reflection of its Danish counterpart, in that the Commissioner is appointed by the Prime Minister (and not elected by Parliament), and he may act only where a case has been referred to him by a Member of Parliament rather than being approached directly by the citizen concerned.[70]

(5) The organisational structure of the United Kingdom administration will be sketched only in its broad outlines, without going into the special features of the Scottish and Northern Irish systems. A distinction is made between "central government," "local government" and "public corporations."

It is interesting to note that the legal representative of the central administration is not the State as such, but the Crown.[71] The executive powers of the Crown are derived from Acts of Parliament and from the Royal prerogative (*i.e.* from the common law) and are exercised by Ministers in the name of the Crown. Normally the Ministers are empowered directly by Act of Parliament, but even then they act in their capacity as Crown servants.[72] Since the seventies, an increasing number of quasi-governmental and quasi-non-governmental organisations ("quagos" and "quangos") have been detached from the ministerial departmental structure.[73]

The structure of the local authorities was reorganised by the 1972 Local Government Act,[74] which came into force in 1977, under which a reduction in the number of local bodies was matched by an enhancement of their powers. England and Wales are divided into counties, and the latter

---

munity directives, and the Select Committees on European Legislation (House of Commons) and on the European Communities (House of Lords).

[68] Parliamentary Commissioner Act 1967. *cf.* also R. Gregory, P. Hutchesson, *The Parliamentary Ombudsman* (1975) London.

[69] *cf.* E. H. Riedel, *loc. cit.*, footnote 7, pp. 161 *et seq.*, who draws attention to the approaches made at the time to Danish Ombudsman Hurwitz.

[70] In the meantime, the institution of the Ombudsman has been extended to the National Health Service and to local government through the appointment of Health Service Commissioners and Local Commissioners.

[71] *cf.* D. Foulkes, *loc. cit.*, footnote 44, p. 11.

[72] *Ibid.*

[73] *cf.* M. Hilf, *Die Organisationsstruktur der Europäischen Gemeinschaften* (1982) Berlin/Heidelberg/New York, pp. 283 *et seq.* On the present-day challenges faced by the British administrative authorities generally, *cf.* Lord Scarman, "The Shifting State: Public Administration in a Time of Change" (1985) Public Administration, Vol. 63, pp. 1 *et seq.*

[74] *cf.* (also in relation to the items below) *e.g.* O. Hood Phillips, P. Jackson, *loc. cit.*, footnote 7, pp. 527 *et seq.*

into districts. Each of these local authorities is run by an elected council. Their powers are derived from the authority granted by Act of Parliament and are subject to judicial review under the *ultra vires* rule. In addition, central government departments exercise administrative supervision, in particular in the field of financial management. On the whole, the self-governing bodies have been assigned extremely important administrative powers, which they exercise with a great deal of autonomy. In particular, the maintenance of public order is to a large extent the concern of the self-governing bodies and not, as is the case in the majority of Continental states, that of the local agent of central government.[75] To this extent the traditionally distinctive system of local autonomy in England, which reached its zenith in the self-governing status of the counties in the eighteenth century, continues to apply at present.

The third category of administrative authority is constituted by the "public corporations." These are legally responsible organisational units, established by Act of Parliament and entrusted with the performance of certain public duties. They act as commercial enterprises in the nationalised industries, as bodies administering social benefits conferred by the State, or as special supervisory or consultative organs.[76] The rapid and unco-ordinated expansion of this type of entity has been the target of a great deal of criticism.[77] Particularly problematic is the effectiveness of the supervision exercised by the relevant Minister over these corporations and consequently also that which is exercised by Parliament.[78]

(6) Finally, it can be stated that the characteristics of British administrative law which have been mentioned at the beginning of this chapter, namely the absence of an independent body of public law which is formally distinct from private law on the one hand and of a system of administrative courts separate from the ordinary judiciary on the other, have survived only in a considerably diluted form.[78a]

The legislators, inspired by proposals tabled by various Reform Committees, and the courts, with leading judicial figures like Lord Denning, Lord Diplock and Lord Reid in the vanguard,[79] have in the meantime developed a body of administrative rules which is entirely comparable

---

[75] *cf.* J. F. Garner, *Administrative Law* (5th ed., London 1979), p. 15.
[76] *cf.* the examples given in O. Hood Phillips, P. Jackson, *loc. cit.*, footnote 7, pp. 547 *et seq.*
[77] *cf.* M. Hilf, *loc. cit.*, footnote 73, pp. 285 *et seq.*
[78] *cf.* O. Hood Phillips, P. Jackson, *loc. cit.*, footnote 7, pp. 555 *et seq.*
[78a] *cf.* also J. Beatson, " 'Public' and 'Private' in English Administrative Law," (1987) LQR, pp. 34 *et seq.*
[79] *cf.* H. W. R. Wade, *loc. cit.*, footnote 8, Preface (v).

with the Continental system of administrative law, even though it is not as sophisticated and individualised as the latter. Judicial protection against the administration has, since the 1977 reforms,[80] essentially been the concern of the Queen's Bench Divisional Court, which thus has come to fulfil the role of administrative division of the High Court.[81] All in all, this system of administrative law and the judicial protection it provides is characterised by a particular emphasis on procedural safeguards.

It remains to be seen whether the proposals for a more fundamental reform of constitutional and administrative law are realisable[82]: the enactment of a Bill of Rights enjoying a special status, the establishment of a constitutional court, the codification of other areas of the common law, particularly administrative law, the adoption of a list of principles of good administration and the setting up of an independent system of administrative courts.

Regardless of the above, it is already possible to discern at this moment an increased convergence between British administrative law and its Continental counterpart—a change in which the European Convention on Human Rights and the European Communities have played no mean part.[83]

---

[80] On the amendment of the Rules of the Supreme Court (1977) cf. supra at footnote 60.

[81] cf. H. W. R. Wade, loc. cit., footnote 8, p. 13.

[82] On the proposals for constitutional reform, cf. in particular Lord Scarman, English Law—The New Dimension (Hamlyn Lecture) (1974) London, especially pp. 76 et seq.; cf. also A. Geisseler, Reformbestrebungen im Englischen Verfassungsrecht (1985) Frankfurt/Bern/New York; on the enactment of a list of "principles of good administration" cf. Report by Justice, Administration under Law (1971): on the establishment of an administrative court, J. D. B. Mitchell, 1965 Public Law 95 (1966); cf. also C. v. Loeper, loc. cit., footnote 63, pp. 130 et seq.

[83] cf. Lord Mackenzie Stuart, "Recent Developments in English Administrative Law—The Impact of Europe" in FS Pescatore (1987) Baden-Baden; cf. also S. A. de Smith, J. M. Evans, loc. cit., footnote 20, pp. 8 et seq.; Sir Gordon Slynn, "Statement," in Eine Verfassung für Europa (J. Schwarze, R. Bieber, eds.) (1984) Baden-Baden, pp. 121, 123: ". . . the doctrine of proportionality . . . which has dominated much of the thinking of the European Court and may be about to slip across the channel into the United Kingdom's legal system." On the effect of Community Law and of the European Convention on Human Rights on British constitutional law, cf. Lord Scarman, loc. cit., footnote 82, pp. 9 et seq., and its review by W. von Simson, "Das Common Law als Verfassungsrecht," Der Staat (Vol. 16) (1977), pp. 75 et seq.; J. A. Usher, "General Principles derived from the laws of the member states as a source of Community law—the interaction between Community law and national law, United Kingdom Report," FIDE Rapports, 12e Congrès I (1986) Paris, pp. 312 et seq.; D. N. Clarke, B. E. Sufrin, "Constitutional conundrums. The impact of the United Kingdom's membership of the Communities on constitutional theory," in The Effect on English Domestic Law of Membership of the European Communities and of Ratification of the European Convention on Human Rights (M. P. Furmston, R. Kerridge, B. E. Sufrin, eds.), (1983) The Hague/Boston/London, p. 32 with a comprehensive list of references; O. Hood Phillips, P. Jackson, loc. cit., footnote 7, pp. 74 et seq.

SECTION 5

BELGIUM

(1) Belgian administrative law is a product of the French Revolution, which was instrumental, especially through the introduction of the principle of legality of administrative action, in effecting the transition from a police state to a state based on the rule of law.[1] During the period of French rule from 1795 to 1814, the French bureaucratic type of administration replaced the corporate model of the *ancien régime*. In spite of the French influence on Belgian administrative law, there are fundamental differences between the two systems.[2] Although Belgian administrative law has, like the French system, adopted the subordination of the administration to the law, the 1831 Constitution,[3] which together with its subsequent amendments remains in force today, gives, unlike French law, jurisdiction to the ordinary courts in settling disputes between the citizens and the administration.[4] This reveals not only a refusal to establish a separate system of administrative courts, but also a disinclination to create a body of administrative law independent of ordinary law.[5] However, the Belgian system does not go as far as that in England, which for many years, under Dicey's influence, denied the existence of an independent body of administrative law.[6]

---

[1] Y. Chapel, "Belgique," in E. V. Heyen (ed.), *Geschichte der Verwaltungsrechtswissenschaft in Europa* (1982) Frankfurt am Main, p. 1.

[2] J. Velu, "La protection juridictionnelle du particulier contre le pouvoir exécutif en Belgique," in H. Mosler (ed.), *Gerichtsschutz gegen die Exekutive, Vol. 1, Länderberichte* (1969) Köln/Berlin/Bonn/München, pp. 55, 58; Y. Chapel, *loc. cit.*, footnote 1, p. 1.

[3] Reproduced in P. C. Mayer-Tasch and I. Contiades (eds.), *Die Verfassungen der nichtkommunistischen Staaten Europas* (2nd ed., München 1975), p. 40.

[4] Articles 92 and 93 of the Belgian Constitution; *cf.* J. Velu, *loc. cit.*, footnote 2, p. 58; J.-M. Auby and M. Fromont, *Les recours contre les actes administratifs dans les pays de la Communauté Economique Européenne* (1971) Paris, p. 140; A. Mast and J. Dujardin, *Overzicht van het Belgisch Administratief Recht* (9th ed., Ghent 1984), No. 502.

[5] Y. Chapel, *loc. cit.*, footnote 1, p. 3; *cf.* also on this subject C. Cambier, *Droit administratif* (1968) Brussels, p. 13; the legal history relating to this topic is extensively dealt with by A. Mast, *loc. cit.*, footnote 4, Nos. 500 *et seq.*

[6] C. Cambier, *loc. cit.*, footnote 5, p. 13, footnote 2.

The opportunities available to the ordinary courts to provide legal protection against the administration were limited.[7] Thus, these courts had no powers to set aside the instruments issued by the administrative authorities, except where such powers were specifically laid down by statute.[8]

As the administration extended the scope of its activities and governed ever-increasing fields of economic and social activity, the weaknesses and difficulties inherent in the Belgian system became more apparent.[9] In 1906 the Belgian Prime Minister Auguste Beernaert commented on the problems posed by inadequate legal protection:

> "In no other country does it (the administration) wield such extensive powers; no other system, however, provides fewer remedies against the excesses committed by the public authorities. As soon as the administration makes a pronouncement, that is the end of the matter."[10]

This situation was amended only in 1948 by the creation of the Belgian Conseil d'Etat (Raad van State). It was introduced into the Belgian legal system by a simple ordinary statute and constitutes part of the Executive. Like its French model, the Belgian Conseil d'Etat consists of two sections: the legislative section, which acts in an advisory capacity in the enactment of legislation, and the administrative section, which is a consultative body in administrative matters and also acts in a judicial capacity for certain categories of administrative law disputes.[11] Where it acts as a judicial organ, the Conseil d'Etat has extensive jurisdiction to adjudicate in actions for annulment concerning either administrative acts and regulations issued by the administrative authorities or decisions taken in

---

[7] cf. J. Velu, loc. cit., footnote 2, p. 59; Y. Chapel, loc. cit., footnote 1, p. 6; J.-M. Auby, M. Fromont, loc. cit., footnote 4, p. 140.

[8] cf. J. Velu, loc. cit., footnote 2, p. 59; Y. Chapel, loc. cit., footnote 1, p. 6.

[9] Y. Chapel, loc. cit., footnote 1, p. 6; A. Mast, "Le Conseil d'Etat belge au 1er janvier 1980" (1979) RISA (Revue internationale des sciences administratives), 307.

[10] As quoted by H. Velge, La loi du 23 décembre 1946 instituant en Belgique le Conseil d'Etat (1947) Brussels, p. 22: "Nulle part elle (l'administration) n'a de pouvoirs plus étendus, nulle part les abus eux-mêmes ne comportent moins de remèdes; quand l'administration a parlé, tout est dit." cf. also on this subject H. Buch, "Einführung Belgien," in C. H. Ule (ed.), Verwaltungsverfahrensgesetze des Auslandes, Erster Teilband (1967) Berlin, pp. 91 et seq.

[11] A Mast, loc. cit., footnote 4, No. 542; by the same author, (1979) RISA, 307; J.-M. Auby, M. Fromont, loc. cit., footnote 4, pp. 146 et seq.

disputes conducted before the administrative authorities, on grounds of infringement of essential procedural requirements or of the violation of formalities whose infringement necessarily entails annulment because the relevant authority has exceeded its powers or abused its discretion.[12]

(2–3) There is no general Law relating to administrative procedure in Belgium. Apart from the codification of certain fragmented areas, Belgian administrative law has been shaped mainly by case law and by the writings of legal authors.[13] The 1831 Constitution forms the basis of Belgian public and administrative law and occupies the highest position in the hierarchy of norms. It is from the Constitution that all the organs of the public authorities derive their powers either directly or indirectly.[14] It contains many provisions which are relevant to the administrative law system. Thus Articles 1bis, 3bis, 31, 107quater, 108, 108bis and 108ter contain the basic rules concerning the regional, provincial, municipal and supra-municipal subdivisions and institutions. Articles 6 to 24 lay down civil rights which are guaranteed. Articles 66 and 67 regulate the powers conferred on the King to appoint officials and to implement statutes, whereas Articles 92 and 93 establish the jurisdiction of the ordinary judiciary and of the administrative courts.[15]

Case law, especially that which emanates from the Conseil d'Etat, plays a decisive role in the Belgian system of administrative law. The annulment decisions of the Conseil d'Etat now apply *erga omnes* and exercise a considerable influence on the development of this branch of law.[16] This applies also to general legal principles which, although they do not possess the same importance in Belgium as they do in the Netherlands[17] or in France,[18] are one of the recognised sources of Belgian

---

[12] Article 9 of the Law of December 23, 1946, relating to the establishment of the Conseil d'Etat, which entered into force on August 23, 1948; *cf.* on this subject also J.-M. Auby, M. Fromont, *loc. cit.*, footnote 4, pp. 1245 *et seq.*; J. Velu, *loc. cit.*, footnote 2, pp. 59 and 85.

[13] J. Dembour, *Droit administratif* (3rd ed., Liège 1978), No. 11.

[14] A. Mast, *loc. cit.*, footnote 4, No. 19.

[15] *cf.* on this subject J. Dembour, *loc. cit.*, footnote 13, No. 18.

[16] A. Mast, *loc. cit.*, footnote 4, No. 36; also J. Dembour, *loc. cit.*, footnote 13, No. 27.

[17] *cf. Rapport van de commissie inzake algemene bepalingen van administratief recht (Rapport ABAR)* (5th ed., Alphen a/d Rijn 1984), p. 116.

[18] *cf., e.g.,* J. Rivero, *Droit administratif* (9th ed., Paris 1980), No. 235; C. Huberlant, "Le droit administratif belge comprend-il des principes généraux non écrits?" in *Mélanges en l'honneur de J. Dabin* (1963) Brussels, Pt. II, p. 661.

administrative law.[19] The legal principles sanctioned by the Conseil d'Etat include of "fair play,"[20] equality before the law, which is also enshrined in the Constitution,[21] careful administration,[22] legal certainty,[23] equitable justice,[24] the right to be heard[25] and the obligation to give reasons.[26] The debate surrounding the general legal principles has been strongly influenced by Dutch authors, commencing with G. J. Wiarda,[27] and by the case law of the French Conseil d'Etat after 1945.[28] It is possible to discern here a preference for one legal system or the other according to the language group of the author concerned.[29]

Customary law is a recognised legal source, but plays merely a secondary role in Belgian administrative law.[30]

(4) The citizen has two opportunities to obtain legal protection against administrative action. He may apply to have the legality of an

---

[19] A. Mast, *loc. cit.*, footnote 4, No. 37; J. Dembour, *loc. cit.*, footnote 13, No. 22; L. P. Suetens, "Algemene beginselen van behoorlijk bestuur in de rechtspraak van de Raad van State," Tijdschrift voor bestuurswetenschappen en publiek recht (TvB), 81, 88 *et seq.*

[20] *cf.*, *e.g.*, Decision by the Conseil d'Etat no. 20,040 of January 15, 1980, *Municipality of Boechout*.

[21] *cf.* Decision by the Conseil d'Etat no. 17,127 of July 9, 1975, *Blomme*.

[22] *cf.* Decision by the Conseil d'Etat no. 23,455 of July 26, 1983, *Regniers*.

[23] *cf.* Decision by the Conseil d'Etat no. 17,024 of May 20, 1975, *Tedesco*.

[24] *cf.* Decision by the Conseil d'Etat no. 21,167 of May 12, 1981, *Zoete*.

[25] *cf.* Decision by the Conseil d'Etat no. 18,207 of April 1, 1977, *Rochet*.

[26] *cf.* Decision by the Conseil d'Etat no. 20,887 of January 20, 1981, *Wouters*; this whole subject is extensively dealt with by L. P. Suetens, *loc. cit.*, footnote 19, (1981) TvB 8189, with references from case law; J. Dembour, *loc. cit.*, footnote 13, No. 22; A. Mast, *loc. cit.*, footnote 4, No. 37 with numerous references from the recent case law (footnote 56).

[27] G. J. Wiarda, "Algemene beginselen van behoorlijk bestuur," Geschriften van de Vereniging voor Administratief Recht, XXIV (1952) Haarlem, pp. 55–94; this author is cited in A. Mast, *loc. cit.*, footnote 4, No. 37; L. P. Suetens, "Algemene rechtsbeginselen en algemene beginselen van behoorlijk bestuur in het Belgisch administratiefrecht" (1970) TvB, 379 *et seq.*; by the same author, *loc. cit.*, footnote 19, (1981) TvB 81 *et seq.*; W. van Gerven, "Beginselen van behoorlijk handelen" (1982–83) Rechtskundig Weekblad, 961 *et seq.*

[28] *cf.* W. J. Ganshof van der Meersch, "Le droit de la défense, principe général du droit. Réflexions sur des arrêts récents," in *Mélanges en l'honneur de Dabin*, Part II (1963) Brussels, pp. 569, 587; C. Huberlant, *loc. cit.*, footnote 18, 661 *et seq.*; M. Somerhausen, "Les principes généraux du Droit Administratif," in *Perspectivas del Derecho Público en la segunda mitad del siglo XX*, Festschrift for Enrique Sayagues-Laso, Vol. IV (1969) Madrid, pp. 463, 478; by the same author, "De Raad van State en de algemene beginselen van het administratief recht" (1970) TvB, 481.

[29] *cf.* the examples given in footnotes 27 and 28.

[30] A. Mast, *loc. cit.*, footnote 4, No. 39; J. Dembour, *loc. cit.*, footnote 13, No. 24.

administrative act examined by the administration itself by filing a complaint,[31] or he may bring an action before the courts.[32]

Administrative complaints may be filed either with the authority which originally issued the instrument (recours gracieux—oneigenlijk beroep) or with an authority superior to it (recours hiérarchique—hierarchisch beroep).[33] In addition, it is possible to request the supervisory department to annul an unlawful measure adopted by a decentralised organ.[34] In certain cases the Conseil d'Etat makes it a precondition for the admissibility of an action that the complaints procedure shall have been used before the action is initiated.[35]

The judicial examination of the legality of administrative acts and regulations may come within the jurisdiction of either the ordinary courts or the administrative courts. The basic rules for the resolution of questions of jurisdiction are Articles 92 and 93 of the Constitution. According to these, the ordinary courts have exclusive jurisdiction in civil law disputes. These include claims for compensation from the public authorities and disputes concerning administrative contracts.[36] Under Article 93 of the Constitution, the ordinary courts also have jurisdiction to hear cases involving "political rights." This jurisdiction may, however, be transferred by statute to the administrative judiciary.[37] Thus the administrative courts have merely that jurisdiction which is assigned to them, confined to cases involving subjective rights which do not come within the purview of civil law.[38]

In addition to the Conseil d'Etat, which is the most important administrative court having general jurisdiction for administrative law disputes, there are approximately 400 judicial bodies set up pursuant to Article 93 of the Constitution, to whom the legislature has assigned powers to adjudicate in specific administrative areas.[39] These include the

---

[31] This is extensively dealt with by A. Mast, *loc. cit.*, footnote 4, No. 485 *et seq.*; *cf.* also J.-M. Auby and M. Fromont, *loc. cit.*, footnote 4, pp. 151 *et seq.*; A. Buttgenbach, *Manuel de Droit Administratif* (3rd ed., Brussels 1966), No. 492.

[32] A. Mast, *loc. cit.*, footnote 4, Nos. 490 *et seq.*; A. Buttgenbach, *loc. cit.*, footnote 31, No. 492.

[33] A. Mast, *loc. cit.*, footnote 4, No. 486; A. Buttgenbach, *loc. cit.*, footnote 31, p. 493.

[34] This is extensively dealt with by A. Mast, *loc. cit.*, footnote 4, No. 339 *et seq.*

[35] A. Mast, *loc. cit.*, footnote 4, No. 489; J. Velu, *loc. cit.*, footnote 2, p. 84.

[36] J.-M. Auby and M. Fromont, *loc. cit.*, footnote 4, pp. 177 *et seq.*; A. Mast, *loc. cit.*, footnote 4, No. 520; C. Cambier, *loc. cit.*, footnote 5, pp. 573 *et seq.*

[37] A. Mast, *loc. cit.*, footnote 4, No. 502; J.-M. Auby, M. Fromont, *loc. cit.*, footnote 4, p. 177.

[38] A. Mast, *loc. cit.*, footnote 4, No. 502; by the same author, RISA, 1979, 309.

[39] J. Velu, *loc. cit.*, footnote 2, p. 74; A. Mast, *loc. cit.*, footnote 4, Nos. 538 *et seq.*

Standing Committees of the provincial councils and the administrative judicial organs in military matters.[40]

The jurisdiction of the Conseil d'Etat in administrative law disputes is derived from the Law relating to the Conseil d'Etat of December 23, 1946. Article 14 of this Law regulates the action which in practice is the most important, the action for annulment (recours en annulation—annu-latieberoep). This provision specifies three grounds for annulment: *excès de pouvoir—machtsoverschrijding* (the relevant authority has exceeded its powers), *détournement de pouvoir—machtsafwending* (misuse of powers) and infringement of procedural requirements.[41] The judicial review exercised by the Conseil d'Etat concerns points of law rather than questions of fact.[42] It does not involve an assessment of the manner in which discretionary powers were used (exercice du pouvoir discrétion-naire) or of questions of policy (opportunité).[43]

Whereas the decisions of the Conseil d'Etat in cases involving the illegality of the challenged administrative instrument or regulation lead to their being annulled and apply *erga omnes*, the judgments issued on the basis of Article 107 of the Belgian Constitution by the ordinary courts apply only inter partes and leave intact the administrative acts or reg-ulations which are held to be illegal. They are merely declared to be non-binding or inapplicable.[44] Even where the citizen has other oppor-tunities to compel the public authorities to comply with statute law, the action for annulment on grounds of *excès de pouvoir* is the most appro-priate means for ensuring compliance with the relevant statute, as it is capable of being brought against any measure adopted by the administration.[45]

(5) The organisational structure of the Belgian administration is based on the principle of the decentralised unitary state.[46] The most important example of the centralised, hierarchically structured public authority is provided by the ministries, at whose head stands, at least according to the Constitution, the King.[47] Articles 31 and 108 of the Belgian Constitution

---

[40] Further examples can be found in A. Mast, *loc. cit.*, footnote 4, Nos. 538 *et seq.*; J.-M. Auby, M. Fromont, *loc. cit.*, footnote 4, p. 148.

[41] *cf.* J. Velu, *loc. cit.*, footnote 2, p. 85; A. Mast, *loc. cit.*, footnote 4, No. 561.

[42] J. Velu, *loc. cit.*, footnote 2, p. 85.

[43] J. Velu, *loc. cit.*, footnote 2, p. 85; A. Mast, *loc. cit.*, footnote 4, No. 568.

[44] A. Mast, *loc. cit.*, footnote 4, No. 520.

[45] A. Mast, *loc. cit.*, footnote 4, No. 559, referring to J. Rivero, *loc. cit.*, footnote 18, No. 235.

[46] A. Mast, *loc. cit.*, footnote 4, No. 68.

[47] Articles 29 and 66 of the Belgian Constitution; *cf.* A. Mast, *loc. cit.*, footnote 4, No. 69.

lay down the constitutional rules regarding the decentralised organs of the administration. Article 31 stipulates that matters which are exclusively the concern of the municipalities and provinces are to be regulated by the municipal or provincial councils respectively in accordance with the principles laid down in the Constitution.[48] In Article 108, the powers of the provincial and municipal authorities are regulated, matters of provincial or municipal concern are defined, and the powers of the supervisory authorities are specified.[49]

[48] This is extensively dealt with by A. Mast, *loc. cit.*, footnote 4, No. 293.
[49] A. Mast, *loc. cit.*, footnote 4, Nos. 68 and 290 *et seq*.

SECTION 6

DENMARK

(1) Danish administrative law shows clear signs of having been influenced by the French and German systems. The rules relating to legal protection against the administration, on the other hand, have followed the British system and give jurisdiction to the ordinary courts. In addition, the administration is subject to supervision by the Ombudsman, appointed by Parliament, this being an institution[1] which is characteristic of the entire Nordic system of public law.[2]

Although in Denmark, as in Britain, judicial review of administrative action is exercised by the ordinary courts, the development of a separate system of administrative law which is independent private law does not appear to have encountered the same theoretical objections as had been the case in Britain. Certainly Denmark also had to wait a long time before it acquired a distinct system of administrative law. The chief impulse for this development came from the writers, in particular Professor Poul Andersen of Copenhagen.[3] Until the publication of his key monograph on the subject of "Invalid Administrative Acts" (1924)[4] which was followed in 1936 by his "Danish Administrative Law,"[5] neither the courts nor the legislature had developed a coherent body of administrative law principles. Andersen's monograph is, as is stated in the Introduction, "the result of comparative law studies . . . whose object, besides Nordic law, was German and French administrative law in particular."[6]

---

[1] In the relevant theoretical circles, which are mainly inclined towards civil law, the Nordic school is held to include Denmark, Sweden, Norway, Finland and Iceland; cf. K. Zweigert, H. Kötz, *Einführung in die Rechtsvergleichung*, Vol. 1 (2nd ed., Tübingen 1984), p. 321; on the initial steps towards the development of a Nordic public law, cf. N. Herlitz, "Legal Remedies in Nordic Administrative Law" AJCL, 1966–67, 687, 688.

[2] The post of Ombudsman has existed in Sweden since 1809, in Finland since 1919, in Denmark since 1954 and in Norway since 1962, cf. N. Herlitz, *loc. cit.*, footnote 1, p. 705.

[3] cf. P. Meyer, in *Geschichte der Verwaltungsrechtswissenschaft in Europa* (E. V. Heyen, ed.) (1982) Frankfurt, pp. 19, 21 *et seq.*

[4] German translation in P. Andersen, *Ungültige Verwaltungsakte* (1927) Mannheim/Berlin/Leipzig.

[5] Referred to by P. Meyer, in *Geschichte der Verwaltungsrechtswissenschaft in Europa*, *loc. cit.*, footnote 3, pp. 19, 22, footnote 10.

[6] cf. P. Andersen, *loc. cit.*, footnote 4, p. IX (Introduction by R. Thoma).

161

Many of the principles of administrative law, developed by Andersen on the basis of comparative law, have in the meantime become firmly entrenched in the practices followed by the Danish courts.[7]

(2) Whereas Danish law has constituted a kind of "melting pot"[8] in assimilating foreign influences, the Danish monarchy, which has been in existence for more than 1,000 years, has simultaneously developed its own legal tradition.

The current Constitution of June 5, 1953[9] has many points of similarity with the 1849 Constitution, which marked the transition from an absolute to a constitutional monarchy. The separation of powers was considered a fundamental constitutional principle.[10] The legislative power is exercised by Parliament (the Folketing), its statutes requiring formal assent by the monarch.[11] Under Section 3(2) of the Constitution the executive power is vested in the monarch. In practice, however, the monarch is entirely bound by the directives issued by the Government (or the Minister).[12] The judicial function is exercised by the independent courts. Although they have the power to assess statutes in the light of the Constitution, the role of the courts in Danish constitutional practice tends to be a secondary one.[13] Sections 62 and 63 of the Constitution expressly provide that court proceedings must be kept separate from public administration and that the courts shall also adjudicate on the extent of the powers exercised by the administrative authorities. Statutory clauses which exempt certain

---

[7] cf. P. Meyer, in Geschichte der Verwaltungsrechtswissenschaft in Europa, loc. cit., footnote 3, pp. 19, 22.

[8] cf. W. Steiniger, Einführung in das dänische Rechtssystem (1982) Kiel, p. 9. Specifically on the French and British influence on Danish administrative organisation, cf. P. Andersen and B. Christensen, "Le Conseil d'Etat et le droit administratif danois," in Le Conseil d'Etat, Livre Jubilaire (1952) Paris, pp. 595 et seq.

[9] A German translation of the text of the Constitution (and of the Law relating to the Succession to the Throne of March 27, 1953) can be found in P. C. Mayer-Tasch, Die Verfassungen Europas (2nd ed., München 1975), pp. 67 et seq. On the guaranteed civil rights under the Constitution, cf. R. Gralla, Der Grundrechtsschutz in Dänemark (1987) Frankfurt/Bern/New York.

[10] cf. G. T. Nielsen, "Constitutional and Administrative Law," in Danish Law—A General Survey (H. Gammeltoft-Hansen, B. Gomard, A. Philip, eds.) (1982) Copenhagen, p. 38, who also points out the participation by the monarch in the executive and legislative processes as provided for in Sections 2 and 3.

[11] Ibid., loc. cit., p. 41.

[12] Ibid., p. 39.

[13] Ibid., pp. 37, 43.

administrative decisions from judicial review ("definitive validity" clauses) are regarded as admissible by the courts, although they are interpreted very restrictively.[14]

(3) With the adoption of the Law on Public Administration of December 19, 1985,[15] and the Law on the Public Character of the Administration[16] of the same date, the Danish system of administrative procedural law has become extensively codified.[16a] The Law on Public Administration covers the following areas: the exclusion of biased civil servants, the rights of parties involved in administrative law proceedings to obtain legal advice and representation, the right to consult the relevant files and to receive a fair hearing, and the duty of the administrative authorities to give reasons for their decisions, to advise the parties of any available remedies, and to observe confidentiality. The Law on the Public Character of the Administration guarantees the right of any citizen, and not just the parties involved in administrative law proceedings, to consult the records of the public authorities. At the same time, the administration is obliged to record in writing certain facts involved in any administrative dispute. Exceptions to the right to consult public documents include the internal working papers of the administration.

The considerable extent to which the administration is open to the public is characteristic of Danish administrative law. This is reflected in the extensive rules safeguarding the right to consult documents which are contained in the Law on Public Administration[17], and in the provisions of the Law on the Public Character of the Administration. Before the adoption of these Laws, access by the public to administrative documents was regulated by the Law of June 10, 1970, which was superseded by them.[18] As to its contents, the Danish law of administrative procedure is

---

[14] *cf.* in particular O. Krarup, "Judicial Control of Administrative Powers" *Scand. Studies in Law*, 1971, 143, 151 *et seq.*; *cf.* also B. Christensen, "Der gerichtliche Rechtsschutz des Einzelnen gegenüber der vollziehenden Gewalt in Dänemark," in *Gerichtsschutz gegen die Exekutive*, Vol. 1 (H. Mosler, ed.) (1969) Köln/Berlin/Bonn/München, pp. 113/114.

[15] Law No. 571 of December 19, 1985 (Forvaltningslov).

[16] Law No. 572 of December 19, 1985 (om offentlighed i forvaltningen).

[16a] This subject is extensively dealt with by K. Borgsmidt, "Ein Verfahrensgesetz und Neugestaltungen im dänischen Verwaltungsrecht" (1988) DÖV, p. 70.

[17] *Loc. cit.*, footnote 15, chapter 4, sections 9–18.

[18] Law No. 280 of June 10, 1970; on this subject, *cf.* N. Eilschou Holm, "The Danish system of Open Files in Public Administration" *Scand. Studies in Law* (1975), pp. 153 *et seq.*; (with an English translation of the text of the Law, pp. 173 *et seq.*). As early as 1964 a Law had been adopted giving the parties to administrative proceedings the right to consult the

modelled on the procedural legislation of other Nordic states (particularly Sweden), which already had a system of preventive administrative supervision by means of procedural rules.[19]

Customary law, whose status as a legal source is also acknowledged in Denmark, is of little relevance to administrative law.[20]

The general principles of law are granted only secondary status where they are not entrenched in the Constitution or in statute law.[21] Even before the adoption of the new Laws governing Public Administration, Danish law recognised certain general principles of administrative law, whose origins can be traced back to case law, administrative practice (especially that of the ministerial departments) and juridical literature.[22]

(4) The organisation of the courts and the law of procedure are laid down in the Law relating to Judicial Proceeding.[23] There is no separate system of administrative courts.[24] Legal protection against the executive is provided by one judicial system only, through the medium of civil proceedings.[25] Of the three judicial stages over which an action may be conducted (the lower courts, the district courts and the Supreme Court (højesteret)), only two are normally used. Both the substance and the effect of the decisions depend on the nature of the claim. Denmark has no system featuring different types of action. Where the plaintiff has claimed a legal interest, the courts examine both individual acts and rules issued by the administration; on an incidental plea the courts may also review the constitutional validity of Parliamentary statutes.[26] The scope of the

---

files, which was incorporated into the Law of 1970. Both Laws were enacted as a result of a report submitted by an independent committee established in 1956 (Betænkning om Offentlighed i Forvaltningen, No. 325/1963).

[19] cf. N. Eilschou Holm, loc. cit., footnote 18, p. 172.

[20] cf. G. T. Nielsen, loc. cit., footnote 10, p. 52.

[21] cf. H.-W. Rengeling, Rechtsgrundsätze beim Verwaltungsvollzug des Europäischen Gemeinschaftsrechts (1977) Köln/Berlin/Bonn/München, p. 147.

[22] cf. N. Eilschou Holm, "Danish report on due process in administrative procedures," in FIDE, Due process in the administrative procedure Vol. 3 (1978) Copenhagen, pp. 3.1, 3.3 et seq. On the current significance in Danish law of the general principles of administrative law and their links with the principles of European Community law, cf. J. K. Skadhauge, "Danish report on general principles derived from the law of member states as source of Community law. Interaction between Community law and national law," FIDE Reports, 12th Congress, I (1986) Paris.

[23] Law No. 488 of October 2, 1978, on judicial procedure (om rettens pleje).

[24] However, under Section 63(2) of the Constitution, the establishment of administrative courts by statute is permitted.

[25] cf. W. Steiniger, loc. cit., footnote 8, pp. 20 et seq.

[26] cf. B. Christensen, loc. cit., footnote 14, p. 122.

of the court's powers of review is restricted to a review of the legality of the act concerned. The courts appear to base such reviews on the traditional French list of administrative defects, giving particular prominence to the "détournement de pouvoir" theory.[27]

The main forms of extra-judicial review of administrative action are the complaint procedures and the institution of the Ombudsman. Apart from these, the political supervision exercised by Parliament through the medium of ministerial responsibility does not have a particularly important part to play in practical terms.

Instruments and rules issued by the administration may be challenged within the administration itself by means of a complaint lodged with the immediately superior authority, who may assess the decision as to its propriety. In addition, there exist a number of complaint commissions.[28] These are separate from the administration both in functional terms and, to a certain extent, in their personnel, and take their decisions in accordance with quasi-judicial rules of procedure. These commissions, which are established by special legislation and resemble the British administrative tribunals, exist in many different forms.[29] Normally, legal remedies are available against their decisions.

Particular mention must be made of the Ombudsman, originally a Nordic instrument of administrative review, though it has subsequently been imitated by other countries.[30] Under Section 55 of the Constitution, the Ombudsman is appointed by the Folketing, and his function is to supervise the civil and military administration. Special legislation[31] has given him the power to conduct investigations, to require the public authorities to produce documents and to deliver opinions. He may act on his own initiative or at the request of a citizen, who must, however, have exhausted the complaint procedure first. He submits an annual report to the Folketing. Although the Ombudsman has practically no powers of coercion, his statements enjoy a high degree of authority. In a number of cases the Ombudsman has delivered opinions on the application and scope of general legal principles, in particular that of fair administrative

[27] *Ibid.*, p. 119; G. T. Nielsen, *loc. cit.*, footnote 10, p. 52; on a critical note, O. Krarup, *loc. cit.*, footnote 14, pp. 143 *et seq.*

[28] *cf.* on this subject B. Christensen, *loc. cit.*, footnote 14, p. 124; N. Herlitz, (1966–67) A.J.C.L. 687, 704.

[29] Complaint commissions have been set up especially in the field of social legislation.

[30] This subject is extensively dealt with by G. T. Nielsen, *loc. cit.*, footnote 10, pp. 62 *et seq.*, containing further references; N. Herlitz (1966–67) A.J.C.L. 687, 705 *et seq.*

[31] Law No. 342 of December 1, 1961, amended by Law No. 258 of June 9, 1971.

proceedings. These opinions, which are based on a detailed analysis of the relevant legislation, case law, administrative practice and literature, are, virtually without exception, followed as constituting authoritative statements of the applicable law.[32]

(5) Finally, we examine the organisational structure of the Public Administration.[33] The Public Administration is directed by the Government. The Ministers are responsible for their respective departments, which are hierarchically structured. For the purpose of co-ordinating the various departments whose competences cover E.C. matters, co-ordinating committees have been established at various levels ever since Denmark's accession to the European Communities in 1972, the most important being the Cabinet Committee and the E.C. Committee.[34] The task of implementation has been increasingly delegated to subordinate organisational units and, by statute, to independent administrative organs authorised to perform actions with legal implications.[35]

Local government is exercised by the municipalities and districts, which currently enjoy a virtually uniform structure as a result of the municipal reforms completed in 1981. They are managed by bodies representative of the community (municipal assemblies, district councils) and by their elected chairman, *i.e.* the mayor of the municipality or of the district.[36]

---

[32] *cf.* N. Eilschou Holm, *loc. cit.*, footnote 22, Vol. 3, p. 3.4; *cf.* also G. T. Nielsen, *loc. cit.*, footnote 10, p. 64. On the significance of the Ombudsman in the development of Danish administrative law, *cf.* also K. Borgsmidt, *loc. cit.*, footnote 16a.

[33] *cf.* G. T. Nielsen, *loc. cit.*, footnote 10, pp. 52 *et seq.*

[34] *cf.* K. Hagel-Sørensen and H. Rasmussen, "The Danish Administration and its Interaction with the Community Administration" (1985) C.M.L.Rev. 273, 274 *et seq.*; H. Rasmussen, "Über die Durchsetzung des Gemeinschaftsrechts in Dänemark" *EuR*, 1985, 66 *et seq.* In general terms, on the legal problems raised by Denmark's accession to the Communities, *cf.* O. Due, C. Gulmann, "Constitutional Implications of the Danish Accession to the European Communities" (1972) C.M.L.Rev. 256.

[35] *cf.* M. Hilf, *Die Organisationsstruktur der Europäischen Gemeinschaften* (1982) Berlin/Heidelberg/New York, pp. 288 *et seq.*

[36] For further details, *cf.* W. Steiniger, *loc. cit.*, footnote 8, pp. 33 *et seq.*

SECTION 7

GREECE

(1) The administrative law and the system of legal protection against the Public Administration in Greece are largely based on French law. It is only relatively recently that Greek administrative law has developed into a systematically treated and independent subject. This is possibly connected with the tortuous path charted by Greek constitutional history,[1] as a result of which the organisation of the courts was subjected to constant changes until well into the twentieth century. This was a major obstacle to the development of a consistent body of administrative case law, such as France was able to secure through the Conseil d'Etat.[2]

(2) The current Greek Constitution came into force on June 11, 1975[3] and picked up the thread of the 1952 Constitution, which had been reinstated in 1974 after the fall of the military dictatorship.[4] This allowed Greece to return to the fold of representative parliamentary democracies. The principle of the separation of powers, which is characteristic of a state based on the rule of law, finds its clearest expression in the independent status of the courts (Articles 87 *et seq.*). Parliament shares the power of legislation with the President, and the Government shares with the latter the executive power.[4a] Dagtoglou[5] considers the characteristics of the Constitution to be: the prominence it gives to international law and to the European Community,[6] the protection afforded to

---

[1] *cf.* in more detail P. Dagtoglou, "Verfassung und Verwaltung," in *Südosteuropa-Handbuch*, Vol. 3 (K. D. Grothusen, ed.) Göttingen 1980, pp. 14 *et seq.*

[2] *cf.* (also in relation to the development of the study of administrative law in Greece) T. I. Panagopoulos, "Griechenland," in *Geschichte der Verwaltungsrechtswissenschaft in Europa* (E. V. Heyen ed.), Frankfurt 1982, pp. 81 *et seq.*

[3] German translation of the Constitution in JöR, New Series 32 (1983), 360–393.

[4] Several articles were also inspired by other European constitutions, notably the German Basic Law, *cf.* J. Iliopoulos-Strangas, "Grundrechtsschutz in Griechenland," JöR, New Series 32 (1983), 395, 401 with references; P. Dagtoglou, "Die Griechische Verfassung von 1975," JöR, new series 32 (1983), 355.

[4a] On the transfer of the preponderance of authority from the State President to the Prime Minister following the constitutional amendment of March 12, 1986, *cf.* J. Catsiapis, "Les dix ans de la Constitution grecque du 9 juin 1975," RDP 1987, pp. 399 *et seq.*

[5] P. Dagtoglou, JöR, New Series 32 (1983), 355, 356.

[6] *cf.* also Th. Antoniou, *Europäische Integration und griechische Verfassung*, Frankfurt/Bern/New York, 1985.

fundamental rights,[7] the general legal protection it guarantees, and the bolstering of the executive. The latter characteristic is particularly evident in the manner in which the rule-making powers of the executive were extended.[8]

The Constitution also contains important principles of general administrative law. Thus the principle that the Public Administration is bound by the relevant legislation was derived from Article 50 (limited powers of the President) and from Article 83 (powers vested in the Ministers).[9] Under Article 10, every citizen has the right to address petitions to the public authorities. Article 20(2) guarantees the right to a fair hearing before any administrative measure is taken which imposes a burden.

(3) There is no statute codifying administrative law in Greece. Various attempts to introduce a statute on administrative procedure foundered a long time ago.[10] Only a few limited areas of general administrative law have been statutorily entrenched. Thus the fundamental principles of Greek administrative law can be found in the case law of the Council of State, which has been since 1929 the supreme administrative court of Greece. The recognised forms of administrative action are (a) the administrative instrument, as in France, which includes individual instruments and regulations, and (b) the public contract.[11] The discretionary powers of the administration have been restricted by the prohibi-

---

[7] Detailed comments on the protection of fundamental rights in J. Iliopoulos-Strangas, JöR, New Series 32 (1983), 395 *et seq.* On the principle of equality and the legal protection of women under the 1975 Constitution, *cf.* D. Kontogeorga-Theocharopoulou, "La situation juridique de la femme dans le droit administratif hellénique (Le droit des femmes hellènes d'exercer toutes les fonctions publiques)" in *Hellenic Review of International Relations*, Vol. 2, No. 1, pp. 161, 207 *et seq.*

[8] On the rule-making powers of the administration (compared with French law) in more detail, *cf.* W. Skouris, "Les incidences de la Constitution hellénique de 1975 sur le droit administratif," RDP 1982, pp. 113, 118 *et seq.*

[9] P. Dagtoglou, *op. cit.*, footnote 1, p. 44. On the legitimacy and legality of the administration from the point of view of state liability, *cf.* most recently W. Skouris, "L'illégalité de l'action administrative comme fondement de la responsabilité de la puissance publique en Grèce," in *Journées de la Société de Législation Comparée* 1984, pp. 51 *et seq.*; A. Manitakis, "L'illicéité comme élément de la responsabilité de l'état en droit hellénique," in *Journées de la Société de Législation Comparée* 1984, pp. 17 *et seq.*

[10] *cf.* the administrative procedure Bill based on the proposals of the Commission for the Reorganisation of the Public Services (1958) and the proposals by M. Stassinopoulos (1967). For further details *cf.* T. I. Panagopoulos, DVBl. 1977, 154 *et seq.*

[11] The fundamental work on the theory of administrative instruments is M. Stassinopoulos, *Traité des actes administratifs*, Paris 1954.

tion of "détournement de pouvoir", whereas the Council of State has recognised the following principles as constituting limits to the administration's discretionary powers: equality before the law, the impartiality of the administration, the rule that the administration must act in good faith, and the proportionality rule (in its initial stages).[12] In relation to administrative procedure, the main principles to be observed[13] are the duty to give reasons for decisions[14] and the rule that each party affected must be heard.

It is especially the development of the right to a fair hearing which provides a telling illustration of the interaction between the case law and the Constitution. This principle was recognised initially by the Council of State; however, its scope and its place in the hierarchy of rules remained the subject of controversy.[15] Its incorporation in the 1975 Constitution (Article 20(2)) not only entrenched it as a principle of constitutional rank, but also served to extend its scope to all measures adopted by the administration which could affect the rights or interests of individual citizens. Subsequently this Article of the Constitution has received a more definite shape as a consequence of decisions of the Council of State. The incorporation of the *audi alteram partem* rule in the Constitution was hailed by Greek legal writers as the first step towards a rational system of administrative procedure.[16]

For the substance of its decisions, the Council of State is inspired by French law, in particular by the principes généraux developed by the French Conseil d'Etat. M. Stassinopoulos, a former President of the Republic and Honorary President of the Greek Council of State, has emphasised the important role played by French law, stating that ". . . la jurisprudence (du Conseil d'Etat hellénique) est amplement redevable à la jurisprudence française, qui a donné toute la matière nécessaire pour solidifier son oeuvre, depuis 1929."[17] Recently, Greek administrative law

---

[12] *cf.* P. Dagtoglou, *op. cit.*, footnote 1, p. 44.
[13] Further procedural principles in T. I. Panagopoulos, DVBl. 1977, 154, 157.
[14] *cf.*, *e.g.*, Council of State 188/58, 216/59, 804/71.
[15] For more details *cf.* M. Stassinopoulos, *Le droit de la défense devant les autorités administratives*, Paris 1976, pp. 117 *et seq.*
[16] See P. Pavlopoulos, A. Calogeropoulos & S. Lytras, "Procédure administrative non contentieuse et problèmes juridiques en Grèce," *Annuaire européen d'administration publique* I, 1978, pp. 427, 436; *cf.* also W. Skouris, "Les incidences de la Constitution hellénique de 1975 sur le droit administratif," RDP 1982, pp. 113, 115 *et seq.*
[17] *cf.* M. Stassinopoulos: "Long, Weil et Braibant, Les grands arrêts de la jurisprudence administrative" (review), RDP 1970, 820, 828.

studies appear to have been increasingly influenced by German theories.[18]

(4) Greece reinstated its separate system of administrative courts in 1929. Even during the initial years of the modern Greek state, administrative disputes were settled before special administrative courts.[19] The year 1835 saw the establishment, inspired by the French model, of the Council of State, which, in addition to its consultative functions, also performed judicial duties. The 1844 Constitution, which provided for the transition from an absolute to a constitutional monarchy, once again abolished the administrative judiciary, which was associated with the absolutist tradition, and introduced a judicial system with only one type of court. It was only in 1928/1929 that the Council of State was resurrected, the 1911 and 1927 Constitutions having created the conditions which enabled its re-creation to take place. Under Article 95 of the current 1975 Constitution the Council of State has jurisdiction, in the first and last instance, to adjudicate on applications for the annulment of enforceable acts issued by the administrative authorities on the grounds that the latter had exceeded their powers or infringed statute law, and further on such disputes concerning the substance of administrative action as were specifically assigned to it by the Constitution or by statute.[20] The application for annulment is, as regards the conditions for its admissibility and the grounds on which it may be granted, based on the French "recours pour excès de pouvoir."[21] The main condition for its admissibility is that the claim should involve an immediate, current and personal interest on the applicant's part.[22] In addition to its jurisdiction in the first instance, the Council of State adjudicates on applications for the review of decisions taken by the administrative courts. The establishment

---

[18] cf. T. I. Panagopoulos, op. cit., footnote 2, p. 87, who draws attention to the increasingly frequent separation between general administrative law and the law of administrative procedure.

[19] cf. also on the development of the possibilities of legal protection Tsatsos, in Gerichtsschutz gegen die Exekutive, Vol. 1 (H. Mosler ed.), Köln/Berlin/Bonn/München 1969, pp. 278 et seq., and on the history of the Council of State M. Poulitsas; "L'influence de l'institution du Conseil d'Etat français sur le Conseil d'Etat hellénique," in Le Conseil d'Etat, Livre jubilaire, Paris 1952, pp. 539 et seq.

[20] e.g. Article 103(4)(2) of the Constitution in conjunction with the Civil Service Act.

[21] cf. P. Dagtoglou, op. cit., footnote 1, p. 52.

[22] The Council of State therefore does not require a subjective right to be claimed (as under §42(2) of the VwGO) but on the other hand appears to deal more restrictively with the qualification of interest than does the French Conseil d'Etat. cf. on this point, from a comparative law point of view, W. Skouris, Verletztenklagen und Interessentenklagen im Verwaltungsprozess, Köln/Berlin/Bonn/München 1979, esp. pp. 120–122.

of a general system of administrative courts, prescribed by the 1975 Constitution, was realised by Law No. 1406/83, which came into force on June 11, 1985. This was followed by the organisation of general administrative courts and an administrative appeal court.[23] In its capacity as supreme special court, which at the same time fulfils the function of a constitutional court, the Areopagus adjudicates in conflicts of jurisdiction between the administrative courts and the civil courts.[24]

Extra-judicial review of administrative action is exercised through the accountability of the Ministers and the Government to Parliament and through a system of internal review by the administration. The latter process can be initiated by lodging an administrative complaint, in the course of which the citizen concerned uses his right of petition (under Article 10 of the Constitution) to challenge the administrative action before the issuing authority or that which is immediately superior to it, or by lodging a complaint, similar in character to an appeal, on the basis of a special legal provision to that effect. The completion of the preliminary procedure initiated by this "quasi-appeal" is a precondition for the admissibility of an application for annulment before the Council of State.[25]

(5) As regards the organisational structure of the administration, a distinction is made between the direct State administration (Article 101 of the Constitution) and local government (Article 102). The State administration is managed at the central level by the appropriate Ministers[26] and at the regional level (Nomoi) by Prefects (Nomarchos). The Prefect has the status of a general administrative organ in the regions, a status which he shares with the special organs of the various Ministries. Local

---

[23] For more detail cf. *Institutions judiciaires des états membres (Cour de justice des Communautés européennes)* (2nd ed., Luxembourg 1987), pp. EL–6 *et seq.*
[24] cf. Article 100 of the Constitution.
[25] cf. in detail on the complaint procedure P. Pavlopoulos, A. Calogeropoulos & S. Lytras, "Les recours administratifs et le recours pour excès de pouvoir en droit grec," in *Annuaire européen d'administration publique*, I, 1978, pp. 437 *et seq.*
[26] cf. in more detail P. Pavlopoulos, A. Calogeropoulos & S. Lytras, "Les structures de l'administration central grecque," in *Annuaire européen d'administration publique*, I, 1978, pp. 446 *et seq.* The Minister for Co-ordination is responsible for dealing with E.C. matters; cf. A. Calogeropoulos, "L'administration chargée des relations avec les Communautés Européennes," in *Annuaire européen d'administration publique*, II, 1979, pp. 564 *et seq.*

government is administered by the cities and municipalities.[27] These are corporate bodies constituted under public law, which do not, however, enjoy any rule-making powers. In the course of managing local affairs and such attributes of the state administration as are conferred on them by statute, they are subject to supervision by the State, which normally merely concerns itself with the question whether the measures adopted by local authorities are in accordance with the law or not (administrative supervision). In addition to local government, there is also the special autonomous administration. This consists of individual administrative units, operating mostly as corporate bodies constituted under public law (*e.g.* colleges of higher education) or private law (*e.g.* public enterprises).[28]

---

[27] Local government law is laid down in Statutory Order no. 2189/1952 as amended by Presidential Order no. 933/1975 (the "Code of Municipal Law"). *cf.* for more detail E. Spiliotopoulos, "Les compétences du pouvoir local en Grèce," in *Annuaire européen d'administration publique*, III, 1980, pp. 267 *et seq.*

[28] *cf.* in detail on the administrative structure D. Kontogeorga-Theocharopoulou, "Les bases constitutionnelles de l'organisation administrative de l'Etat en Grèce (L'influence de la Constitution hellénique de 1975 sur l'organisation administrative de l'Etat)," in *Journées de la Société de Législation Comparée* 1981, pp. 525 *et seq.* and P. Dagtoglou, *op. cit.*, footnote 1, pp. 38 *et seq.* On the organisation of the administration and the legal position of civil servants *cf.* also D. Corsos, in *Festschrift für C. H. Ule*, Köln/Berlin/ Bonn/München 1977, pp. 529 *et seq.*

SECTION 8

IRELAND

(1) Like the United Kingdom, Ireland has neither a special system of administrative courts nor a separate set of rules independent of private law on remedies applicable to the administration. One essential difference from the British system, however, resides in the availability of a written Constitution and the opportunity to assess the compliance of statutes with the Constitution.

The development of Irish administrative law reflects the way in which relations between the Irish and British legal systems have developed in general.[1] With the invasion of Ireland by the Normans in the twelfth century, a process began, lasting many centuries, whereby ireland adopted the common law and judicial system of England. Both legal systems were finally integrated comprehensively by the Act of Union of 1800. The Westminster Parliament became the overall legislator, and the House of Lords also heard final appeals against decisions of the Irish courts. This guaranteed the uniform application and development of the principles of judicial review of the administration, in particular the *ultra vires* doctrine.[2]

Once Ireland had secured its independence from Britain in 1921, the principle of the constitutional review of rules by the courts was incorporated in the Constitution of the Irish Free State.[3] In practical terms, however, this did not entail any fundamental departure from the British system.[4] The flexible mechanisms for amending the Constitution, as well as the possibility, recognised by the Supreme Court, of amending the Constitution by an Act of Parliament conferred on the latter quasi-sovereign powers. The courts were also extremely reticent in relation to the executive. The development of special principles of administrative supervision was impeded to a considerable extent by the objections raised

---

[1] *cf.* on the historical development of Irish law, and in particular on the English influences to which it has been subjected: R. Grimes, P. Horgan, *Introduction to Law in the Republic of Ireland* (1981) Portmarnock (Dublin), pp. 16 *et seq.*

[2] *cf.* J. P. Casey, "Ireland," in *Geschichte der Verwaltungsrechtswissenschaft in Europa* (E. V. Heyen, ed.) (1982) Frankfurt, p. 90.

[3] On the Constitution of the Irish Free State of 1922, *cf.* B. Chubb, *The Constitution and Constitutional Change in Ireland* (1978) Dublin, pp. 7 *et seq.*

[4] *cf.* A. K. Asmal, "Administrative Law in Ireland," RISA 34 (1968), 109.

by Dicey against the French *droit administratif*, which also exerted a great deal of influence on Irish legal thinking.[5] This inaction by the courts prevented in particular the development of effective supervision of the discretionary powers wielded by the executive.

It is only with the adoption of the 1937 Constitution that it is possible to discern a degree of disaffection with traditional British attitudes, as well as an increase in creative intervention by the courts in the field of administrative law, which resulted particularly in a reduction in the prerogatives exercised by the State. This trend became even more marked from the 1960s onwards.[6]

(2) The basis for this development and for the current state of Irish law is the 1937 Constitution. The principle of the separation of powers, entrenched in Article 6,[7] is given its true shape, as in other modern constitutions, by the many ways in which, both in legal and in practical terms, the interaction between the legislature, the executive and the judiciary is limited.[8] The legislative function is undertaken by a Parliament (Oireachtas) consisting of two chambers, the possibility of delegating legislative powers being expressly recognised.[9] The executive power is

---

[5] *Ibid.*

[6] *cf.* Finbarr Murphy, "Report on due process in administrative proceedings in Ireland," in FIDE, *Due Process in the Administrative Procedure*, Vol. 3 (1978) Copenhagen, pp. 6.1, 6.4 *et seq.*; J. P. Casey, in *Geschichte der Verwaltungsrechtswissenschaft in Europa*, pp. 100 *et seq.*; A. K. Asmal, RISA 34 (1968), 109.

Particularly on the reduction of state prerogatives and the extension of state liability, *cf.* the leading decisions in (a) *Macauley* v. *Minister for Posts and Telegraphs* (1966) I.R. 345, which held that the rule that proceedings could be taken against Ministers only after prior approval by the Attorney-General was unconstitutional, and (b) *Byrne* v. *Ireland and A.-G.* [1972] I.R. 241, which led to the removal of state immunity for unlawful acts. (For more details, *cf.* W. N. Osborough, "The State's Tortious Liability: Further Reflections on *Byrne* v. *Ireland and A.G.*, (1976) 11 Irish Jurist, pp. 11 *et seq.*, 279 *et seq.*).

On the significance of Ireland's accession to the E.C. for the development of Irish administrative law, *cf.* J. Temple Lang, "European Community Law, Irish Law and the Irish Legal Profession—Protection of the Individual and Co-operation between Member States and the Community," (1983) 5 Dublin University Law Journal pp. 1, 5 *et seq.* For a discussion on further reforms, *cf.* especially the Report of Public Services Organisation Review Group 1966–69, especially Appendix I, "Note on Administrative Law and Procedure" (Devlin Report); The Law Reform Commission, Working Paper no. 8, *Judicial Review of Administrative Action: The Problem of Remedies* (1979) Dublin; Report of the All-Party Informal Committee on Administrative Justice (1977).

[7] *cf.* also O'Dálaigh C.J., *in re Haughey* [1971] I.R. 217: "The Constitution of Ireland is founded on the doctrine of the tripartite division of the powers of government—legislative, executive, judicial."

[8] *cf.* B. Chubb, *The Constitution and Constitutional Change in Ireland*, pp. 33 *et seq.*; J. M. Kelly, *The Irish Constitution* (2nd ed., Dublin 1984), p. 31.

[9] *cf.* Article 15.2 and *Pigs Marketing Board* v. *Donnelly (Dublin) Ltd.* [1939] I.R. 413.

exercised by the Government, which is dependent on the prevailing Parliamentary majority. The judicial function is undertaken by the independent courts. However, the transfer of certain limited judicial functions to non-judicial organs is permitted and given practical substance by the establishment of administrative tribunals. The judicial function of the High Court and the Supreme Court includes the power to assess the constitutional validity of Acts—with the exception of certain Emergency Powers Acts[10]—and, where appropriate, to declare them null and void.

Articles 40 to 44 of the Constitution contain a comprehensive list of fundamental rights, including the general principle of equality before the law as well as the right to property and freedom. The Christian order of values as well as the influence of Catholic theories of society are clearly expressed not only in the Articles relating to fundamental rights,[11] but also in other provisions of the Constitution.[12] In the field of administrative law, the fundamental rights have a particularly important role to play in extending the opportunities available to the citizen for bringing complaints against the administration and in ensuring adequate procedural safeguards where the administration intervenes in society.[13]

(3) In addition to the Constitution, as the main legal source, the sources of Irish law in general, and consequently also of administrative law, comprise the Acts of Parliament and case law, as well as customary law and the opinions of leading writers by way of secondary sources.[14]

Acts of Parliament, as well as the regulations and orders issued by the Government, the Ministers and the municipalities (*i.e.* delegated legislation), govern a number of areas of administrative law ranging from

---

[10] Under Article March 28, 3, Acts adopted for the protection of public safety and the maintenance of the State in time of war or national emergency are not subject to assessment [or only to a restricted form of assessment—*cf. In re Art. 26 and the Emergency Powers Bill 1976* [1977] I.R. 159] as to their constitutional validity. A state of war (or of emergency) was declared in 1939 and subsists to this day, having been renewed in 1976. For more details, *cf.* J. M. Kelly, *The Irish Constitution*, pp. 163 *et seq.*

[11] *cf.* in particular the Preamble (and the case law which relates to it, cited in J. M. Kelly, *The Irish Constitution*, p. 6), Article 6 and Article 45.

[12] *cf.* B. Chubb, *The Constitution and Constitutional Change in Ireland*, pp. 46–50; by the same author, *The Government and Politics of Ireland* (1974) London/Oxford/New York, pp. 53 *et seq.* (on the subject of Irish Catholicism as a characteristic of Irish "political culture").

[13] *cf.* A. K. Asmal, (1968) RISA 109, 110. *cf.* also J. Temple Lang (1983) 5 Dublin University Law Journal pp. 1, 2 *et seq.* on the influence of the fundamental rights enshrined in European Community law and the European Convention on Human Rights on Irish law.

[14] *cf.* R. Grimes, P. Horgan, *Introduction to Law in the Republic of Ireland* pp. 54 *et seq.*

protection against various hazards to welfare provision. Some of these Acts also contain provisions on administrative procedure. Thus, for example, the Housing Act stipulates that local authorities may exercise their right to purchase plots of land only after having informed the owner thereof and invited him to submit his opinion.[15] Statutory provisions enacting general rules of administrative law or procedure which are not restricted to a particular area of the administration are comparatively rare.

General principles of administrative law as described above can be found especially in the decisions of the High Court and of the Supreme Court, which in principle follow the *stare decisis* theory.[16] Its basis is the *ultra vires* doctrine, under which the administration may not exceed its statutory powers. The *ultra vires* test also applies in principle to the rule-making and (quasi-) judicial powers of the administration (*i.e.* delegated legislation and the decisions of the administrative tribunals). More particularly, an administrative action is illegal if it has been carried out by an authority which has no powers to do so, if the statutory conditions contained in the authorising provision have not been met, if its legal implications are not covered by the authorising provision, if discretion has been exercised in contradiction of the principles of good faith (particularly where the discretionary decision is based on irrelevant considerations), if the principles of constitutional justice, *i.e.* the *audi alteram partem* and *nemo judex in causa sua* rules, have been infringed, or if it involves any other constitutional infringement (*e.g.* illegal breach of fundamental rights).[17]

These principles run broadly in parallel with British theories. If anything, the protection of the individual under Irish administrative law generally appears to reach further than under the British system. In the first place, important principles entrenched in the Constitution cannot, as is the case in Britain, be set aside by a mere Act of Parliament. This

---

[15] Housing Act no. 21 of 1966, Section 79(1).

[16] The Supreme Court, however, no longer considers itself to be bound by its own decisions, and bases this practice in particular on the special features of the Irish Constitution which depart from British tradition: *cf. State (Duggan)* v. *Tapley* [1952] I.R. 62 and *State (Quinn)* v. *Ryan* [1965] I.R. 70. The High Court is bound by the decisions of the Supreme Court, but not in every case by its own decisions. On the position regarding *stare decisis* in Ireland, *cf.* R. Grimes, P. Horgan, *Introduction to Law in the Republic of Ireland*, pp. 60–67.

[17] *cf.* on this category of cases D. G. Morgan, *Constitutional Law of Ireland* (1985) pp. 209 *et seq.*, with references to the case law; *cf.* also R. M. Stout, *Administrative Law in Ireland* (1985) Dublin, pp. 92–101 and (for an extensive study of the constitutional justice principle) pp. 133–217.

applies both to the fundamental rights and to the procedural guarantees of constitutional justice, which can be derived from Article 40.3.1.[18] Secondly, the Irish courts have also given broader substance to the principle of constitutional justice than the British courts have in their interpretation of the natural justice principle.[19] This has prompted D. G. Morgan to conclude that:

> "the Irish judges have set the balance between administrative efficiency and fair procedure for individuals further in favour of the individual than the British judges."[20]

(4) As regards the remedies available against administrative action, a distinction is made, as in Britain, between "appeal" and "review."[21] Any appeal brought before a higher administrative authority or a court seeks the setting aside, either wholly or in part, of the challenged decision and must be authorised by statute. Applications for review, on the other hand, are not aimed at obtaining a new decision but seek an examination of the question, in particular, whether the original measure had been adopted *ultra vires*. They are set in motion by means of the original prerogative writs of certiorari, prohibition and mandamus (the so-called State-side orders) or through a declaration or injunction.[22] The court

---

[18] *cf.* D. G. Morgan, *Constitutional Law of Ireland*, p. 213.

[19] *Ibid. cf.* also Henchy J. in *The State (Gleeson)* v. *Minister for Defence and the Attorney General* [1976] I.R. 280 at 294 *et seq.*: "while the common-law concept of natural justice is usually taken to comprehend no more than what is encompassed by the maxims *nemo judex in sua causa* and *audi alteram partem*, the requirements of what was there called "constitutional justice" and is sometimes called "constitutional due process" cover a wide field. . . . The necessary implementation of express or necessarily implied constitutional guarantees means that decisive acts and procedures may be impugned for a variety of reasons . . . for instance, because justice was not administered in public; or the decision was given by an unconstitutional tribunal; or the decision applied an unconstitutional law; or the accused was deprived of a fair, competent and impartial jury; or the person affected received unjustifiably unequal treatment; or the evidence was obtained in a manner not constitutionally permissible." (Quoted from R. M. Stout, *Administrative Law in Ireland*, pp. 134 *et seq.*).

[20] D. G. Morgan, *loc. cit.*, footnote 17, p. 213.

[21] *cf.* D. G. Morgan, *Constitutional Law of Ireland*, p. 214; in general, on the question of legal protection against the administration, *cf.* also A. K. Asmal, RISA 34 (1968), 109, 112 *et seq.*, and J. M. Kelly, "Judicial Protection of the Individual against the Executive in the Republic of Ireland," in *Gerichtsschutz gegen die Exekutive*, Vol. 1 (H. Mosler, ed.) (1969) Köln/Berlin/Bonn/München, pp. 425 *et seq.*

[22] For more details concerning the various forms of action, R. M. Stout, *Administrative Law in Ireland*, pp. 80 *et seq.* In particular on the action of certiorari, G. W. Hogan, "Remoulding Certiorari: A Critique of the State (*Abenglen Properties Ltd.* v. *Dublin Corporation*), (1982) 17 The Irish Jurist pp. 32 *et seq.*

which has jurisdiction in these matters is normally the High Court, which forms part of the ordinary judicial system.

The various conditions of admissibility, rules of procedure and criteria which determine the scope of the reviewing powers envisaged vary from one action to another.[23] The fact that it is often very difficult for the citizen to select the action most appropriate for his claim, and the resulting shortcomings in terms of legal protection, have prompted the Law Reform Commission, inspired by the reform of the Supreme Court Rules (1977) in Britain, to propose the introduction of a uniform application for judicial review which would constitute a combination of the various existing actions.[24] The original habeas corpus procedure now forms the subject-matter of a special set of rules contained in Article 40.4 of the Constitution.

The Irish legal system has also witnessed an increase in the number of judicial functions which have been developed to special ministerial bodies and administrative tribunals.[25] Examples of these "judicial substitutes,"[26] are the Employment Appeals Tribunal, which hears labour law disputes, and the tribunals set up in the field of welfare provision. The requirements which must be met by the procedure before these tribunals, as well as the extent of judicial and extra-judicial supervision of these tribunals, form the subject of considerable controversy among the leading Irish writers.[27]

In addition to the recently introduced position of Ombudsman,[28] the informal "benevolent intervention"[29] by Members of Parliament, who not infrequently, at the request of their constituents, follow up allegations of defective administration, constitutes an effective mechanism for

---

[23] For an extensive study of the admissibility and scope of judicial review (including certain comparative law aspects), *cf.* R. M. Stout, *Administrative Law in Ireland*, pp. 420 *et seq.*

[24] The Law Reform Commission, Working Paper no. 8–1979, *Judicial Review of Administrative Action: The Problem of Remedies*, pp. 77 *et seq.* On this subject, E. Graham, "Judicial Review—Where to Reform" (1984) 6 Dublin University Law Journal, pp. 25 *et seq.*, which analyses the Irish proposals for reform against the background of the reforms occurring in the United Kingdom.

[25] For more details, *cf.* A. K. Asmal, RISA 34 (1968), 109, 112 *et seq.*; J. P. Casey, in *Geschichte der Verwaltungsrechtswissenschaft in Europa* (E. V. Heyen, ed.) (1982) Frankfurt, pp. 97 *et seq.*

[26] *cf.* J. P. Casey, *loc. cit.*, footnote 25, p. 98.

[27] *cf.* the Report of the Public Services Organisation Review Group (Devlin Report), Appendix I, and J. P. Casey, *loc. cit.*, footnote 25, pp. 98 *et seq.* with further references.

[28] The first Ombudsman was appointed in 1984 on the basis of the 1980 Ombudsman Act. On the legal status and function of the Ombudsman, *cf.* R. M. Stout, *Administrative Law in Ireland*, pp. 484 *et seq.*

[29] *cf.* J. M. Kelly, in *Gerichtsschutz gegen die Exekutive, loc. cit.*, footnote 21, p. 436.

supervising the administration, which is eminently accessible because of the relatively high number of senators and Members of Parliament in relation to the population.[30]

(5) The structure of the administration breaks down into the central administration, the local authorities and the so-called "state-sponsored bodies." The central administration[31] is directed by the Ministers, who are accountable to Parliament, according to their departmental remit. Notwithstanding reforms, the structure of the central administration is marked by a continuity of development which dates back to the period of union with Britain.[32] Even today, the manner in which the body of state employees is organised closely resembles the structure of the British Civil Service.[33] The Attorney-General, appointed by the President, occupies a special position. In the course of constitutional and administrative disputes he may, according to the type of procedure involved, plead the public interest either as defendant or as plaintiff.[34]

The structure of local government was also for a long period based on the British model. In Ireland, however, as Chubb points out,[35] contrary to British traditions, the democratic element takes second place to increasing the efficiency of local government. This is apparent from, *inter alia*, the post of County Manager, who, although accountable to the elected municipal council, is appointed by a special nominating body and is vested with specific executive powers conferred on him by statute. Especially since the early 1970s the municipalities have yielded some of their administrative tasks to independent state-sponsored bodies, in particular in the field of health provision.

The state-sponsored bodies, following a period of rapid growth since the 1940s, currently exercise a considerable proportion of the tasks incumbent on the public authorities, especially in the field of welfare provision.[36] Each of these bodies has its own individual structure and legal capacity. They can be established by Act of Parliament or by ministerial order, or take the form of an enterprise governed by private

---

[30] *cf.* B. Chubb, *The Government and Politics of Ireland*, p. 307.
[31] Contrary to the position in Great Britain, the State, as a legal person, is deemed to be the legal representative of the central administration, *cf.* J. M. Kelly, *The Irish Constitution*, pp. 21 *et seq.*
[32] *cf.* J. P. Casey, in *Geschichte der Verwaltungsrechtswissenschaft in Europa*, p. 95.
[33] *cf.* B. Chubb, *The Government and Politics of Ireland*, pp. 235 *et seq.*
[34] For a detailed study, *cf.* J. P. Casey, *The Office of the Attorney General in Ireland* (1980).
[35] B. Chubb, *The Government and Politics of Ireland*, p. 271.
[36] For a list of state-sponsored bodies, *cf.* B. Chubb, *loc. cit.*, footnote 35, Appendix D, p. 345.

law. They are vested with specific powers and duties and are subject to supervision, in varying degrees of intensity, by the relevant Ministers.[37]

The unsystematic way in which the tasks of the state-sponsored bodies have been extended, as well as the fact that a large number of organisational units, which do not have legal capacity, have freed themselves from the control of various ministerial departments, has led to a rising tide of criticism directed at the organisation of the Irish administration.[38]

---

[37] For more details, cf. B. Chubb, *The Government and Politics of Ireland*, pp. 246 *et seq.*
[38] cf. in particular Report of the Public Services Organisation Review Group (Devlin Report) (1969); cf. also M. Hilf, *Die Organisationsstruktur der Europäischen Gemeinschaften*, (1982) Berlin/Heidelberg/New York, pp. 287 *et seq.*

SECTION 9

LUXEMBOURG

(1) The fact that in the course of its history Luxembourg has at various times been attached to its neighbouring states of France, Belgium and the Netherlands[1] has inevitably left its mark on the structure of Luxembourg administrative law. Even today French administrative case law exercises considerable influence on the development of the Luxembourg legal system.

Under the 1841 Constitution, the citizen was afforded legal protection against the administration by the Council of Government, which adjudicated on the types of administrative dispute assigned to it by statute. Appeal against its enforceable decisions was to the Grand-Duke.[2] The liberal 1848 Constitution, which was influenced by the Belgian Constitution of 1841, also assigned the task of supervising the Public Administration to the Government or its individual members, *e.g.* in tax matters.[3] It was already under this Constitution that the ordinary courts (tribunaux judiciaires) were given exclusive jurisdiction to hear disputes concerning civil or political rights.[4] The current Constitution reaffirms the general jurisdiction of the ordinary courts for the above-mentioned disputes.[5]

In contrast to French law, which in principle prohibited the ordinary courts from adjudicating cases involving administrative action on the grounds of "dualité de juridiction," the Luxembourg legal system, after

[1] French rule from 1795 to 1815; government under a personal union between the Netherlands and Luxembourg from 1815, during which period the Grand Duchy was subjected to the Netherlands Constitution; following the outbreak of the Belgian revolution, the Luxembourg state was placed under Belgian rule in 1830.

[2] Article 45 of the Constitution of October 12, 1841; Regulation of the Council of Government of June 2, 1842, approved by Grand-Ducal Decree of August 29, 1842, Articles 63–69.

[3] In this context, mention should be made of the Law of November 26, 1849, which established the *conseil de révision* as a complaints authority in tax matters, against whose decisions appeal lay to the Head of the Ministry of Finance. *cf.* A. Bonn, *Der Staatsrat des Grossherzogtums Luxemburg* (1984) Luxembourg, pp. 93 *et seq.*

[4] Articles 86, 87 of the 1848 Constitution.

[5] Articles 84, 85 of the 1868 Constitution. *cf.* J. M. Auby and M. Fromont, *Les recours contre les actes administratifs dans les pays de la Communauté Economique Européenne* (1971) Paris, p. 364; P. Majerus, *L'Etat luxembourgeois* (5th ed., M. Majerus, Luxembourg 1983), p. 245.

an initial period of uncertainty, adopted the position that the ordinary courts could establish the defective nature of administrative action.

However, for the sake of safeguarding the principle of the separation of powers,[6] this jurisdiction by the ordinary courts merely consists of the power to exercise supervision by way of incidental plea in decisions on claims for compensation brought against the public authorities.[7] Decisions on conflicts of jurisdiction between the ordinary and administrative courts are also currently the prerogative of the ordinary courts.[8] Administrative disputes as such, are not dealt with by members of the Government but have been settled by the Conseil d'Etat (more particularly by its judicial section (comité de contentieux)), ever since its establishment under the 1856 Constitution. The Conseil d'Etat was inspired by French public law and forms part of the executive.[9]

(2) The basis of the prevailing system of constitutional and administrative law is the 1868 Constitution, now more than a century old, in its revision of June 13, 1979. It contains, in Articles 11–31, a comprehensive list of fundamental rights,[10] the text of which closely resembles the corresponding provisions in the Belgian Constitution.[11] The constitutional revision of 1919 replaced the constitutional monarchy with the State based on democracy, which the constitutional amendment of 1948, in Article 51(1), proclaimed as a parliamentary democracy.[12] This form of separation of powers finds its clearest expression in the principles of ministerial accountability and of judicial independence (Articles 91 *et seq.*). In 1919, the possibility of holding a referendum in cases specified by statute was incorporated in Article 51.

(3) The administrative law of Luxembourg is no more the subject of a coherent administrative law code than its French or Belgian counter-

---

[6] *cf.* P. Majerus, *loc. cit.*, footnote 5, p. 140; for more details concerning the separation of powers, *cf.* F. Welter, "Discours prononcé à l'occasion du Centenaire du Conseil d'Etat," in *Le Conseil d'Etat du Grand-Duché de Luxembourg, Livre Jubilaire* (1957) Luxembourg, p. 33 (49–51).

[7] *cf.* A. Bonn, *loc. cit.*, footnote 3, pp. 88 *et seq.*

[8] *cf.* J.-M. Auby, M. Fromont, *loc. cit.*, footnote 5, p. 343.

[9] *cf.* A. Bonn, *loc. cit.*, footnote 3, pp. 17, 94; since 1939 the Conseil d'Etat has been totally independent.

[10] For a recent analysis, *cf.* L. Liesch, "Bestand und Bedeutung der Grundrechte in Luxemburg," (1981) EuGRZ, 84 *et seq.*

[11] Articles 4–24 of the Belgian Constitution, parts of which have, however, been interpreted differently; *cf.* B. Delvaux, "L'égalité des Luxembourgeois devant le service public," L'Association Henri Capitant (1965), 399 (400).

[12] *cf.* P. Majerus, *loc. cit.*, footnote 5, pp. 136 *et seq.*

parts. Of considerable importance for administrative law and legal protection against the administration are the Law of February 8, 1961 relating to the organisation of the Conseil d'Etat , and the Law of January 16, 1866.

The grounds for annulment or review, inspired by the French system as developed by the French Conseil d'Etat, were already included in a specific list set out in the Law of 1866 (Article 36) and are currently contained in Article 31 of the Law of February 8, 1961[13]:

(a) lack of competence of the administrative authority is the only ground for judicial review which is checked ex officio[14]; .

(b) under the *violation des formes destinées a protéger les intérêts privés*, an infringement of form is relevant only where the form was laid down with a view to the benefit of individuals also;

(c) under the prohibition of *violation de la loi*, the administration may not take any decisions which infringe the written law;

(d) the defect of *détournement de pouvoir* (misuse of power),[15] which was introduced by the Law of July 20, 1939, has the same meaning as in French administrative law.[16] It renders illegal the exercise of discretion for any purpose other than that laid down in the relevant statute;

(e) the ground for annulment termed *excès de pouvoir* is generally acknowledged to constitute the appropriate mechanism for annulment when the Conseil d'Etat has established that there has been an infringement of general, unwritten legal principles.[17] Whereas under French law the *recours pour excès de pouvoir* is possible against both written and unwritten law, Luxembourg law makes a distinction between *violation de la loi* (infringement of written law) and *excès de pouvoir* (infringement of unwritten legal

---

[13] For more details, *cf.* J.-M. Auby and M. Fromont, *loc. cit.*, footnote 5, 357 *et seq.*; P. Majerus, *loc. cit.*, footnote 5, p. 202.

[14] *cf.* J.-M. Auby and M. Fromont, *loc. cit.*, footnote 5, p. 358.

[15] For a general analysis of the discretion exercised by the administration, *cf.* A. Bonn, "L'examen du fait par le Conseil d'Etat," *Livre jubilaire*, *loc. cit.*, footnote 6, p. 529 (540–542).

[16] H.-W. Rengeling, *Rechtsgrundsätze beim Verwaltungsvollzug des Europäischen Gemeinschaftsrechts* (1977) Köln/Berlin/Bonn/München, p. 274.

[17] *cf. inter alia* A. Loesch, "Le Conseil d'Etat, Comité du Contentieux," *Livre Jubilaire, loc. cit.*, footnote 6, p. 507 (517 *et seq.*). For a different opinion, *cf.* P. Majerus, *loc. cit.*, footnote 5, p. 202, who considers this ground for annulment to be a case of an authority exceeding its powers by interfering with another authority.

principles). The following are among the recognised general legal principles: equality before the administration which provides services and the administration which takes intervening action; the continuity of the administration, and the basic rules concerning the revocation of administrative instruments.[18]

The law of administrative procedure is also based on case law. The duties to hear the parties and to give reasons are the subject of a few sporadic Laws relating to certain specific sections of the administration, but have been developed above all by the courts. The desire for a Law on administrative procedure has, for a long period now, never proceeded beyond the proposal stage.[19]

(4) Under the 1961 Law, the Conseil d'Etat has the following jurisdiction: (a) as an appeal court in actions aimed at reforming decisions (contentieux de réformation), in the course of which its judgment may, where appropriate, replace the administrative decision referred to it, and (b) for actions for annulment (contentieux d'annulation).[20] The action for annulment constitutes the most far-reaching mechanism for the legal protection of the individual against arbitrary action by the administration, and consequently forms the main focus for the procedure before the Conseil d'Etat.[21] The action for annulment must be directed at an individual administrative decision which may infringe a personal and legitimate interest, not necessarily a subjective right, of the applicant.[22] Accordingly, legislative action is exempted from judicial review. However, the same applies to instruments issued by the Government and, contrary to

---

[18] For a more comprehensive list, cf. A. Loesch, "Le Conseil d'Etat, Comité du Contentieux," *Livre Jubilaire, loc. cit.*, footnote 6, p. 507 (517 *et seq.*).

[19] For more details concerning administrative procedure, cf. F. Schockweiler, in FIDE, *Due process in the administrative procedure*, Vol. 3 (1978) Copenhagen, p. 8.1; F. Welter, A. Goldmann, R. Maul and F. Baden, "La procédure d'élaboration des actes administratifs en droit luxembourgeois," in *Rapports présentés aux colloques entre les Conseils d'Etat Belge, Néerlandais, Français, Italien, Luxembourgeois et le Bundesverwaltungsgericht, Colloque de Rome* (1968), pp. 165 *et seq.*.

[20] The jurisdiction of the Conseil in reform procedure arises from Articles 30 and 33 of the Law and the relevant special Laws; for actions for annulment, it arises from Article 31 of the Law of February 8, 1961.

[21] cf. A. Bonn, *loc. cit.*, footnote 3, p. 69; J.-M. Auby, M. Fromont, *loc. cit.*, footnote 5, p. 350; the action for annulment can be compared with the *recours pour excès de pouvoir* under French law.

[22] cf. J.-M. Auby and M. Fromont, *loc. cit.*, footnote 5, p. 352; P. Majerus, *loc. cit.*, footnote 5, pp. 200 *et seq.*

the case law of the French Conseil d'Etat, acts of a general and abstract nature issued by the administration.[23]

As regards the general *règlements* (*i.e.* regulations made by the executive), Article 95 of the Constitution provides a certain degree of judicial supervision of the administration in the shape of a procedural objection. The ordinary courts may apply the general or local decisions and *règlements* only where these comply with the relevant statutes. The logical outcome of the sovereignty of the legislature is that the examination of the legitimacy of these executive instruments is not matched by an assessment of the constitutionality of statutes after their enactment. However, the Conseil d'Etat does deliver an opinion on the constitutional validity of laws before their adoption.[24]

Whereas in France a number of administrative courts were set up in 1953 which are subordinate to the Conseil d'Etat as the highest judicial authority in the field of administrative law, Luxembourg has no administrative courts of first instance (tribunaux administratifs), against whose decisions appeal would lie to the Conseil d'Etat. Instead, the task of adjudicating in this field is assigned to the administrative organs, *i.e.* the so-called *juridictions administratives*, which are complaints authorities subordinate to the Conseil d'Etat and whose decisions are partly enforceable;—it is an ordinary court, the Cour de Cassation, which takes the final decision in administrative disputes under a different judicial hierarchy.[25] Accordingly, Luxembourg administrative law draws a distinction between two types of action:

(a) especially in tax cases, objections against administrative decisions are raised before a higher administrative organ. However, in the field of trade tax, objections are lodged with a different authority, against whose decisions appeal lies to the Conseil d'Etat, which consequently adjudicates as an administrative court of first and of last instance[26];

---

[23] The so-called *règlements d'administration publique, arrêtés ministériels ou locaux d'ordre général*, which cover, *e.g.* town planning; *cf.* A. Bonn, *loc. cit.*, footnote 3, p. 98.

[24] *cf.* A. Bonn, *loc. cit.*, footnote 3, pp. 90 *et seq.* On the sovereignty of the legislature, *cf.* T. Biever, "De l'irresponsabilité de l'Etat législateur, Esquisse de droit luxembourgeois," *Livre jubilaire, loc. cit.*, footnote 6, p. 457 (458–461).

[25] *cf.* A. Bonn, *loc. cit.*, footnote 3, pp. 92–94; P. Majerus, *loc. cit.*, footnote 5, who describes the various possible forms of action before the *jurisdictions administratives*, pp. 248–253.

[26] *cf.* arrêté ministériel of April 10, 1946 and the Law of March 1, 1952, Article 7 of which provides a remedy against the fixing of the trade tax before the Minister of Internal Affairs, as well as the possibility of appeal to the Conseil d'Etat.

(b) a different judicial hierarchy applies where certain *juridictions administratives* adjudicate at the bottom of the hierarchy, especially in the field of social security. Subsequently, appeal against an administrative decision can be lodged with a court of lower instance, whose decisions can be challenged at the highest instance before the Cour de Cassation.

(5) The division of the territory of the Grand-Duchy into three administrative areas (*arrondissements administratifs*), twelve cantons and 126 municipalities forms the basis for the four-level structure of the Public Administration, *i.e.* the State, the area, the canton and the municipality.[27]

The central authorities, *i.e.* the Grand-Duke and the Ministers who have responsibility for the areas coming within their jurisdiction, direct and supervise the administration of the public services in their entirety (*l'ensemble des services publics*), assisted by the Ministerial departments and the *services généraux*, which are dependent on the latter. The *services généraux* belong to the legal entity which constitutes the State and are deconcentrated rather than decentralised, since they come directly under the Ministerial departments concerned. Thus they occupy a position which is the direct opposite of (a) the municipalities, which enjoy a considerable degree of self-government (*décentralisation territoriale*), and (b) the public corporations (*établissements publics*), which are independent of the State and of the municipalities and on whom the management of certain administrative tasks, which are guaranteed under the Constitution, has been conferred (*décentralisation par services*). Examples of these corporations are the social security organs and the professional associations. However, these independent corporations are also, in spite of the freedom of action they enjoy, subject to supervision by the central authorities, in this case the relevant Minister, in the sense that the latter exercise what is known as a *tutelle administrative*.

---

[27] *cf.* (also in relation to the text *infra*) P. Majerus, *loc. cit.*, footnote 5, pp. 286 *et seq.*

SECTION 10

THE NETHERLANDS

(1) Both the system of administrative law and the legal protection against the administration in the Netherlands have been exposed to a great number of foreign influences in the course of their varied history. To this day, the Dutch system reveals traces of English law, and—increasingly of late—of the French and German systems.[1]

As early as the mid-nineteenth century, a clear distinction was established between private law and public law.[2] In its capacity as fiscal authority, the State acted through private law procedures, whereas it exercised public law powers when acting as the public authority. Legal protection against the administration could be sought before the ordinary courts, which had jurisdiction for all matters involving property rights or claims for the repayment of debts. For the rest, complaints could be addressed to superior organs of the executive, in particular to the Crown, which adjudicated after having heard the opinion of the Raad van State (the Dutch Council of State). As a result of the increase in State intervention at the end of the nineteenth century, it was not long before the available legal protection was experienced as being unsatisfactory. For the purpose of obtaining compensation on grounds of unlawful intervention by the administration, private law was, at the turn of the century, considered to constitute the normally applicable body of rules, which also applied to the public authorities. Specific administrative law provisions were complementary by nature and constituted the exception.[3]

The change from a liberal state based on the rule of law to a welfare state saw the development of new instruments for the provision of services and for planning purposes, which could not be satisfactorily accommodated by either private law theory or traditional administrative

---

[1] cf. J.-M. Auby and M. Fromont, *Les recours contre les actes administratifs dans les pays de la Communauté Economique Européenne* (1971) Paris, p. 371; M. Fromont, "Der Rechtsschutz des Einzelnen im niederländischen Verwaltungsrecht," (1972) DÖV, 405; cf. also T. Koopmans, *Vergelijkend publiekrecht* (1978) Deventer, p. 132.

[2] cf. H. van den Brink, "Niederlande," in *Geschichte der Verwaltungsrechtswissenschaft in Europa* E. V. Heyen, ed., Frankfurt, 1982, pp. 117, 119.

[3] *Ibid.*

law theory, which was geared to the individual administrative act.[4] As a result of this development, the notion of administrative law as a complementary and exceptional body of rules increasingly lost ground to that of an independent system of administrative law,[5] which also covered the field of the provision of services, which occupied an intermediate position between state intervention and the law of contracts.

The development of substantive administrative law was matched in the twentieth century by the enhancement of legal protection against the administration.[6] Initially, special administrative courts (*e.g.* for tax cases and for social security matters) were established and complaints authorities set up within the administration itself. In 1962/63, the opportunities to challenge decisions made by the central authorities were extended and approximated to a quasi-judicial procedure.[7] In 1976, a judicial section of the Raad van State, inspired by the French model, was set up, with jurisdiction to adjudicate on challenges to administrative decisions (including those made by regional authorities).[8]

(2) The basis of the constitutional and administrative law of the Netherlands is the Constitution of February 17, 1983.[9] The 1815 Constitution, which had applied up to that date, had, a spate of amendments notwithstanding, lost a great deal of its authority. In many departments, all the new Constitution did was to adjust to constitutional reality. No fundamental alterations were made to the existing type of State or form of government—the constitutional and parliamentary monarchy, individual ministerial accountability, the precedence of statute law and the independence of the judiciary were all maintained. Of particular importance to

---

[4] *cf.* in particular A. M. Donner, *Nederlands Bestuursrecht*, Vol. 1 (4th ed., Alphen a/d Rijn 1974, Preface to the 4th ed., p. VII.

[5] *cf.* P. de Haan, T. G. Drupsteen and R. Fernhout, *Bestuursrecht in de Sociale Rechtsstaat* (1978) Deventer, pp. 6 *et seq.*, 17 *et seq.*

[6] For an extensive study of the development of administrative law protection, *cf.* N. Rothenbücher, *Verwaltungsrechtsschutz in den Niederlanden*, Dissertation, (1978) Heidelberg, pp. 21 *et seq.*

[7] This was by virtue of the Law concerning challenges to administrative decisions of June 20, 1963, Dutch Official Journal 268 (Wet BAB).

[8] *cf.* the Law of May 1, 1975, Dutch Official Journal 283 and the Law of May 1, 1975, Dutch Official Journal 284 (Wet administratieve rechtspraak overheidsbeschikkingen, "AROB"). A German translation by Rothenbücher can be found in (1977) ZaöRV 37, 292 *et seq.*

[9] A German translation can be found in (1983) J.Ö.R., New Series 32, 277 *et seq.*; *cf.* C. A. J. M. Kortmann, "Das niederländische Grundgesetz vom 17.2.1983" (1984) J.Ö.R., new series 33, 175 *et seq.* For a general study of the Constitution of the Netherlands seen from a European angle, *cf.* F. C. L. M. Crijns, *Het Europese perspektief van het Nederlandse staatsrecht* (1984) Zwolle (in particular pp. 20 *et seq.* on Article 94).

administrative law was the extension of those matters which were reserved to the legislator under Article 89.[10] Article 110 raised to the status of a constitutional rule the principle of the public nature of the administration, which had already been recognised by statute.[11] Article 107(2) provides that "statutes shall contain rules relating to general administrative law." This provision is to be interpreted as an injunction to legislate here in the continued absence of a general code of administrative law, which had already been deemed necessary by J. R. Thorbecke, a legal writer who was later to become a Minister, as early as 1871.[12] Since 1983, however, a legislative committee, established by the Government, has been engaged in the task of formulating a set of general administrative law provisions.[13] This Committee submitted its first intermediate report in October 1985.[14]

(3) Another important instrument (also in relation to substantive administrative law) is the Law relating to actions against administrative decisions before the Raad van State.[15] This Law contains, *inter alia*, a definition of the concept of "administrative decision"[16] and specifies four grounds for an action for judicial review[17]:

(a) the decision infringes a provision which has general applicability;
(b) in taking the decision concerned, the administrative body clearly used its powers for a purpose other than that envisaged by the statute;
(c) had the administrative body considererd all the interests involved, it could not equitably have arrived at the decision concerned, or
(d) the administrative body had taken a decision which contravenes

---

[10] *cf.* C. A. J. M. Kortmann, (1984) J.Ö.R., new series 33, 175, 185.
[11] Wet openbaarheid van bestuur, of November 11, 1978, Dutch Official Journal 581; *cf.* also Besluit openbaarheid van bestuur, of October 12, 1979, Dutch Official Journal 590.
[12] *cf.* A. M. Donner, *Nederlands Bestuursrecht*, Vol. 1, p. 74.
[13] *cf.* Decision of August 23, 1983, Dutch Official Journal 417; *cf.* also the Bill which had already been proposed in 1974 by the Administrative Law Association, Commissie Van Maarseveen, "Rapport ABAR," V.A.R.—Geschrift LXXII, pp. 14 *et seq.*
[14] *cf.* Voortgangsrapport Commissie wetgeving inzake algemene regels van bestuursrecht (1985) 's Gravenhage.
[15] Wet AROB of May 1, 1975, Dutch Official Journal 284 (*cf. supra*, footnote 8).
[16] Article 2(1) Wet AROB; on how this compares with the concept of "administrative instrument" under Article 35 VwVfG *cf.* N. Rothenbücher, *Verwaltungsrechtsschutz in den Niederlanden*, pp. 107 *et seq.*
[17] Article 8(1) Wet AROB.

basic notions of proper administration entrenched in the general legal consciousness.

These grounds for contesting administrative action, which find their origins in previous statutes,[18] to a certain extent amount to a codification of existing case law.[19] Although these grounds have certain parallels in French and German legal theory (the second ground corresponds to *détournement de pouvoir* and the third can be interpreted as amounting to a prohibition of arbitrary action), they have, at least as far as their wording and method of application are concerned, assumed a dimension in their own right under the legal system of the Netherlands.[20]

This applies in particular to the fourth category, namely infringement of the principle of proper administration (beginsel van behoorlijk bestuur). This concept was created by reference to unwritten general legal principles. In his 1952 report to the Administrative Law Association, Wiarda held these to include the principles of fair play, careful administration, honourable intentions, consistency and legal certainty.[21] These principles have been developed especially by the case law, not only of the various administrative courts,[22] but also of the ordinary courts (*e.g.* the fair play rule).[23] The precise delimitation of the concept of "infringement of proper administration" in relation to the other grounds for contesting administrative action is not entirely clear. Thus, for example, the second ground, *i.e.* the prohibition of *détournement de pouvoir*, could also be considered to be a general legal principle (in the broad sense of the term).[24] The question whether the general legal principles, or established case law on a particular point, constitute legal sources in their own right

---

[18] *cf.* in particular Article 4 Wet BAB (*supra*, footnote 7); Article 5 Wet administratieve rechtspraak bedrijfsorganisatie (ARBO) of September 16, 1954, Dutch Official Journal 416.

[19] *cf.* M. Fromont, (1972) DÖV 405, 408.

[20] *Ibid.* pp. 408 *et seq.*

[21] *cf.* G. J. Wiarda, "Algemene beginselen van behoorlijk bestuur," V.A.R.—Geschrift XXIV (1952) Haarlem; for a recent study of the general legal principles in the legal system of the Netherlands, *cf.* S. Prechal and T. Heukels, "Algemene beginselen in het Nederlandse en het Europese recht: rechtsvergelijking en interactie" (1986) SEW, pp. 287 *et seq.*

[22] *cf.* P. de Haan, T. G. Drupsteen and R. Fernhout, *Bestuursrecht in de Sociale Rechtsstaat*, pp. 38 *et seq.*; Rapport Algemene bepalingen van administratief recht, pp. 116 *et seq.* with comprehensive references to the relevant case law.

[23] *cf.* decision by the Hoge Raad of June 28, 1951 (1951) N.J. 528, commented on by P. de Haan, T. G. Drupsteen and R. Fernhout, *loc. cit.*, footnote 22, p. 38.

[24] For a detailed study of the four grounds for contesting administrative decisions, *cf.* N. Rothenbücher, *Verwaltungsrechtsschutz in den Niederlanden*, pp. 109 *et seq.*

has received a wide variety of replies.[25] Customary law is recognised as being a legal source by most authorities, but has hardly any relevance to general administrative law.[26]

(4) The legal protection against administrative action appears a "labyrinth of instances and procedures surrounding the various actions."[27] In essence, a distinction must be made among three forms of complaint or action. The first is the action brought before a higher administrative authority, especially the provincial authorities (administratief beroep) – here, both the legality and the propriety of the decision made by the subordinate authority are assessed. The second is the action before the administrative courts. These include the special administrative courts whose jurisdiction covers specific fields of public law (in particular the Centrale Raad van Beroep)[28] and the judicial section of the Raad van State, which, under the AROB Law,[29] has subsidiary jurisdiction for actions contesting administrative decisions.[30] Both actions result in a thorough assessment of the legality of the decision in question, with reference to both the relevant statutes and the general legal principles. The third category covers actions instituted before the ordinary courts; the latter may have jurisdiction on the basis of statutory provisions relating to administrative disputes. The scope of the assessment carried out by these courts is the same as that before the administrative courts. In addition, the ordinary courts have jurisdiction for actions brought against public authorities and claiming damages in consequence of their unlawful actions. The scope of the assessment carried out in such cases is confined to a marginal appraisal of the merits of the case based on equitable considerations. The criteria which form the basis for the assessment are the relevant statute, the prohibition of *détournement de pouvoir* and the

---

[25] *cf.* E. Reiners, *Die Normenhierarchie in den Mitgliedstaaten der europäischen Gemeinschaften* (1971) Hamburg, first half-volume, pp. 184 *et seq.* with references; *cf.* also on the general legal principles H. W. Rengeling, *Rechtsgrundsätze beim Verwaltungsvollzug des Europäischen Gemeinschaftsrechts* (1977) Köln/Berlin/Bonn/München, pp. 142 *et seq.*

[26] *cf.* E. Reiners, *loc. cit.*, footnote 25.

[27] *cf.* P. de Haan, T. G. Drupsteen and R. Fernhout, *Bestuursrecht in de Sociale Rechtsstaat*, p. 347.

[28] The case law of the Centrale Raad van Beroep constitutes one of the most important sources of the general principles of proper administration, *cf.* P. de Haan, T. G. Drupsteen and R. Fernhout, *loc. cit.*, p. 355.

[29] *Supra*, footnote 8.

[30] For a detailed study, *cf.* P. de Haan, T. G. Drupsteen and R. Fernhout, *loc. cit.*, pp. 363 *et seq.*; N. Rothenbücher, *Verwaltungsrechtsschutz in den Niederlanden*, pp. 91 *et seq.*

principle of equitableness, whilst the principles of proper administration are generally excluded from this assessment.

Finally, a form of administrative supervision which has also recently been introduced in the Netherlands is the Ombudsman.[31]

(5) The structure of the administration in the Netherlands is shaped by the principle of the decentralised unitary state.[32] The public authorities are organised at three levels, *i.e.* the State administration, that of the provinces and that of the municipalities. The State administration is directed by the Government, consisting of the King and the Ministers. Within the Council of Ministers, to which all Ministers belong and which is chaired by the Prime Minister, the principle of collective responsibility applies.[33] Each Minister is accountable to Parliament for his particular portfolio. The provincial administration also includes a "Royal Commissioner," who may, by statute, be assigned the task of enforcing the directives issued by the Government.[34] Although the provincial and municipal authorities are subject to supervision by the State, they nevertheless enjoy a great deal of freedom.[35] New tasks for the administration are in most cases introduced at the local level.[36] To this extent, the municipalities fulfil the role of a "laboratory for the administration"[37] and thus make a considerable contribution to the development of administrative law.

The remaining administrative organs, in addition to the local authorities, are the functional corporations.[38] These include the trade and professional associations,[39] whose jurisdiction covers the entire nation, and the water authorities, whose jurisdiction is restricted to a well-defined area. From an organisational viewpoint, they are at the same level as the municipalities and are subject to supervision by the provincial authorities and the State.

---

[31] *cf.* Article 108 of the Constitution.
[32] *cf.* D. W. P. Ruiter, "Die niederländische Kommunalverfassung" (1983) DVBl., 658 *et seq.*; *cf.* also A. M. Donner, *Nederlands Bestuursrecht*, Vol. 1, p. 76.
[33] *cf.* C. A. J. M. Kortmann, (1984) J.Ö.R., new series 33, 175, 183.
[34] *cf.* Article 125 *et seq.* of the Constitution.
[35] *cf.* P. de Haan, T. G. Drupsteen and R. Fernhout, *Bestuursrecht in de Sociale Rechtsstaat*, p. 65.
[36] *cf.* H. van den Brink, in *Geschichte der Verwaltungsrechtswissenschaft in Europa*, p. 122.
[37] *Ibid.*
[38] *cf.* P. de Haan, T. G. Drupsteen and R. Fernhout, *loc. cit.*, footnote 35.
[39] The Social and Economic Council, established by the Law on Economic Organisation of January 27, 1950, occupies a special position in this context: it is both a consultative organ of the Government and an autonomous institution capable of acting at law. *cf.* R.-P. Geidel, "Der sozial-ökonomische Rat der Niederlande" (1983) J.Ö.R., New Series 32, pp. 219 *et seq.*

SECTION 11

PORTUGAL

(1) The development of Portuguese administrative law has been influenced considerably by French law. The most influential author on the administrative law of his country,[1] M. Caetano (a former professor at Lisbon University who was later to become Head of Government) discerns three periods in this development.[2]

The formative stage commences with the administrative reform of 1832, under which the judiciary, the administrative and the financial departments were separated in organisational terms and made subject to their own sets of rules.[3] Whereas the liberal revolution of 1820, which marked the end of the monarch's power and the beginning of a constitutional system, was influenced by the ideas on which the French revolution was based, the 1832 reforms revealed clear traces of French legislation and theories, in particular those expounded in the writings of C. J. Bonnin.[4]

The second stage, identified as the period of codification and of exegetic interpretation, commenced in 1842 with the adoption of the Código Administrativo, which set out the fundamental principles of local government.[5] In 1845, a Council of State, inspired by the French Conseil d'Etat, was established, whose judicial section was transformed in 1870 into the supreme administrative court (Supremo Tribunal Administrativo). The interpretation of the provisions laid down in the Código Administrativo formed the basis for the administrative case law of the day.

It is only at the beginning of the twentieth century that Portuguese administrative law began to develop its own independent set of admin-

---

[1] For the significance of Caetano's work for the development of Portuguese administrative law, cf. F. de Quadros, "Portugal," in Geschichte der Verwaltungsrechtswissenschaft in Europa (E. V. Heyen, ed., Frankfurt 1982), pp. 161, 166 et seq.

[2] cf. M. Caetano, Manual de Direito Administrativo, Vol. 1, (10th ed., 3rd impression— updated by D. Freitas do Amaral, Coimbra 1984), pp. 165–173.

[3] Decrees Nos. 22–24 of May 16, 1832.

[4] On Bonnin's influence, cf. also F. de Quadros, loc. cit., footnote 1, pp. 161 et seq.; M. Caetano, "L'influence française sur l'évolution du droit administratif portuguais," in Le Conseil d'Etat, Livre Jubilaire (1952) Paris, p. 535.

[5] cf. M. Caetano, loc. cit., footnote 2, pp. 167 et seq.

istrative law theories.[6] These were shaped by (a) the considerable influence exerted by the case law of the French Conseil d'Etat (as communicated by French writers) and (b) an increased awareness of the special features of Portugal's national legislation and case law on the one hand, and of its political and social situation on the other.[7] The study of administrative law as a science, and in particular the task of adapting French administrative law to specifically Portuguese situations, has been mainly the concern of the academic world as long as the administrative case law had failed to acquire a significance in its own right.[8] During this phase, the relevant legislation is characterised by an increasing trend towards uniformity, which finds its clearest expression in the new Código Administrativo of 1936–40.

(2) Following the fall of the Salazar regime and the failure of Caetano's reform programme, the adoption of the 1976 Constitution ended the transitional period which followed the 1974 uprising.[9] The struggle between the socialists and the conservatives to achieve a constitutional compromise between on the one hand the Marxist concept of a classless society and on the other the principles of the sovereignty of the people and a State based on the rule of law (inspired by the liberal-democratic notion of freedom), is clearly reflected in the text of the Constitution (cf. in particular the Preamble and Articles 1 and 2).[10] The formula which emerged as a compromise between the concept of socialist legitimacy and that of a State based on the rule of law was the notion of "democratic legality."[11] However, with the constitutional revision of 1982[12] this was for

---

[6] cf. F. de Quadros, loc. cit., footnote 1, p. 165, and M. Caetano, loc. cit., footnote 2, p. 171, who situate the beginning of this stage in 1914, the latter by referring to the monograph Concessões de serviços públicos by João Telo de Magalhães Colaço, which appeared in that year.

[7] cf. M. Caetano, loc. cit., footnote 4, pp. 536 et seq.

[8] cf. F. de Quadros, loc. cit., footnote 1, p. 168.

[9] On the legal and political background of this development, cf. A. Thomashausen, Verfassung und Verfassungswirklichkeit im neuen Portugal (1981) Berlin.

[10] cf. A. Thomashausen, loc. cit., footnote 9, pp. 176 et seq. and, by the same author, "Der Freiheitsbegriff, die Grundrechte und der Grundrechtsschutz in der neuen Portugiesischen Verfassung vom 2. April 1976" (1981) EuGRZ, 1, 3 et seq.

[11] cf. A. Thomashausen, (1981) EuGRZ 1, 11.

[12] cf. A. Thomashausen, "Die revidierte Verfassung der Republik Portugal von 1976—Eine Einführung" (1983) J.Ö.R., new series 32, 443 et seq. (For a German translation of the revised Constitution, cf. pp. 446–501).

the most part replaced by the concept of a democratic state based on the rule of law.[13]

Article 114(1) provides for the "division and interlinking of powers" among the President of the Republic, the Government, the Assembly and the courts. The executive function is exercised by the President and the Government, which is dependent on the confidence vested in it by the Assembly. In addition to its political and executive functions,[14] the Government also has legislative powers in its own right—on matters which are not reserved for the Assembly—which it exercises by adopting statutory regulations, which must be ratified by the Assembly.[15] The Constitution also contains a comprehensive list of fundamental rights,[16] which, in addition to the traditional basic rights, also contains items such as the citizen's right to information concerning the recording of his personal data.[17]

One chapter of the Constitution which relates to the public authorities contains a large number of constitutional principles.[18] Article 266 provides that (a) the public administration shall endeavour to safeguard the public interest whilst observing the rights and interests of the citizen which are guaranteed by law, and (b) the organs and representatives of the administration shall be subject to the Constitution and the relevant statutes and shall exercise their functions lawfully and with due regard for impartiality.

The principle that the administration is subject to the Constitution and to the law is confirmed by Article 269(1), under which those employed in the public services shall act in the interest of the public good as defined by the relevant Law, and by Article 272, under which the police shall observe the principles of lawfulness and necessity. Article 271 regulates the responsibility of civil servants. Article 269(3) guarantees the accused in disciplinary proceedings the right to a fair hearing and to proper defence. Article 267(1) provides that bureaucratisation of the administration is to be avoided and that the citizen is to be granted statutory rights of

---

[13] The concept of a (democratic) state based on the rule of law can be found, for example, in the Preamble, in Article 2 and Article 9, whereas the notion of "democratic legality" can be found in Article 3(2) and in Article 272(1).

[14] *cf.* Articles 200 and 202.

[15] *cf.* Article 201.

[16] For more details, *cf.* A. Thomashausen (1981) EuGRZ, 1 *et seq.*

[17] Article 35(1).

[18] D. Freitas do Amaral (Direito Administrativo, Vol. 1 (1986) Lisbon, p. 132) describes these principles, which form part of the substantive administrative law and the formal constitutional law, as "Direito Constitucional administrativo."

participation in the taking of decisions which concern him/her. Over and above this, Article 267(4) lays down that "the performance of administrative tasks shall be the subject of a special Law, which shall ensure the rational use of the resources to be deployed by the administrative departments and the participation of the citizen in the taking of decisions and decrees which affect him/her." To this end, the Constitution provides for the enactment of a Law relating to administrative procedure.[19]

(3) At the time of writing, this constitutional assignment has yet to be implemented—during the intervening period, all that has been forthcoming is a Bill relating to administrative procedure.[20] As for the other areas of general administrative law, these too have been regulated only in part by statute. The above-mentioned Código Administrativo essentially covers only local government and administration.[21]

The administrative case law does not have the significance its counterpart enjoys in France. Nevertheless, the courts put their stamp on administrative law by applying and developing further the relevant statutory provisions and by applying and lending authority to general legal principles.[22] The leading Portuguese authorities on administrative law have also concerned themselves with the theory of general legal principles. Thus a distinction is made among general legal principles, general principles of public law and general principles of administrative law.[23] The following constitute, in order of importance, the principles which are relevant to administrative action (and which have in most cases been enshrined in the Constitution): the pursuit of the public interest, and the principles of legality, equality and impartiality, justice, proportionality, proper administration and judicial hearing.[24]

---

[19] *cf.* on this subject J. J. Gomes Canotilho, Vital Moreira, *Constituição da República Portuguesa, Anotada*, Coimbra Editora (1980), Article 268 no. III (now: Article 267(IV)).

[20] Projecto de Código de Processo Administrativo Gracioso, ed. da Presidência do Conselho (1980). On the codification of administrative procedure, *cf.* also D. Freitas do Amaral, *loc cit.*, footnote 18, pp. 114 *et seq.*

[21] For a general study of the question of a more far-reaching codification of administrative law, *cf.* M. Caetano, *loc. cit.*, footnote 2, pp. 162 *et seq.* and D. Freitas do Amaral, *loc. cit.*, footnote 18, pp. 116 *et seq.*

[22] For more details, *cf.* D. Freitas do Amaral, *loc. cit.*, footnote 18, pp. 94 *et seq.*

[23] *cf.* M. Caetano, *loc. cit.*, footnote 2, pp. 136 *et seq.*

[24] For more details, *cf.* M. Estevas de Oliveira, *Direito Administrativo*, Vol. 1,2 a Reimpressão (1984) Coimbra, pp. 287–342.

(4) Legal protection against the administration is guaranteed by the Constitution. The general clause of Article 20 lays down the right of access to the courts. Article 268(3) guarantees judicial protection for the citizen affected by definitive and enforceable administrative action.[25]

Article 212(2) permits the establishment of administrative and financial courts. The judicial organisation, jurisdiction and rules of procedure which relate to the administrative courts are regulated in detail in the Decree-Law which governs the status of the administrative and tax courts[26] on the one hand and in the Law relating to administrative procedure[27] on the other. The general administrative courts are organised on two levels and consist of the circuit administrative courts[28] and the Supreme Administrative Court (Supremo Tribunal Administrativo). The main type of action to be brought is the action for annulment (recurso contencioso de anulação), which is reminiscent of the French recours pour excès de pouvoir.

Following the Constitutional revision of 1982, the Constitutional Committee, which had already shown some promising signs of developing a case law which tended to place the accent on freedom, especially as regards the protection of fundamental rights,[29] was converted into a constitutional court. This new constitutional court may be independent, but the judges are selected (and possibly reselected) by Parliament, which is intended to prevent the display of too much independence by the constitutional judiciary.[30] It remains to be seen what will be the effect of this reform on the case law surrounding the principles of administrative law which are entrenched in the Constitution.

In addition to judicial protection and supervision within the administration itself, which can be initiated especially by means of a complaint lodged by the person affected before the superior administrative department, mention must be made of the position of the Ombudsman. The latter may be approached directly by the citizens and intervene in the

---

[25] For more details on this subject, cf. J. J. Gomes Canotilho, Vital Moreira, loc. cit., footnote 19, Article 269 no. III (now amended to Article 268(III)); cf. also J. J. Gomes Canotilho, Direito Constitucional (2nd ed., Coimbra 1980), pp. 584 et seq.

[26] Estatuto dos Tribunais Administrativos e Fiscais, Decreto-Lei no. 129/84 of April 27, 1984.

[27] Lei de Processo nos Tribunais Administrativos, Decreto-Lei no. 267/85 of July 16, 1985.

[28] Tribunais administrativos de circulo; in addition, there is also the Tribunal Administrativo de Macau.

[29] cf. A. Thomashausen, (1981) EuGRZ, 1, 11 et seq.

[30] cf. A. Thomashausen, J.Ö.R., new series 32 (1983), 443, 444.

administrative decision-making process through mediation or by means of recommendations.[31]

(5) In relation to the structure of the administration, Article 6(1) of the Constitution states that:

"Portugal is a unitary State, whose structure respects the principles of the autonomy of local government and of the democratic decentralisation of the public administration."

The local authorities, *i.e.* the municipalities, communes and administrative regions, are subject to such supervision as is determined by the relevant statutes.[32]

---

[31] Article 23 of the Constitution, Law no. 81/77 of November 22, 1977.
[32] For more details, *cf.* Articles 237 *et seq.* The Azores and Madeira island groups have a separate political and administrative status, *cf.* Article 6(2), Articles 227 *et seq.*

SECTION 12

SPAIN

(1) Spanish administrative law has its origins in the first half of the nineteenth century.[1] The monopoly of power wielded by the monarchy having already revealed a degree of diversity according to subject-matter during the period which preceded constitutional rule,[2] the Cadiz Constitution of 1812 was the first instrument to lay down expressly the separation of the legislative, executive and judicial powers. The constitutional amendment—and the resulting changes in the administration—which took effect in 1833, after the death of Fernando VII, led to public administration becoming centralised and laid the foundations for the development of a coherent system of administration. The procedural rules governing complaints against certain decisions of a financial nature having already been laid down by statute in 1881, an Outline Law relating to general administrative procedure was adopted in 1889[3] and brought into effect over the next few years by Implementing Regulations issued by various ministerial departments.[4] This, the first statute relating to administrative procedure in Europe, was replaced by a new Law as part of the administrative reforms which took place in the 1950s.

The development of a system of administrative courts commenced in 1845, when a Royal Council (later to become the Council of State), inspired by the French model, was established containing a judicial section, whose decisions were, however, subject to various reservations by the Government.[5] This judicial section gave rise, in 1888, to an administrative court forming part of the Council of State, which had the task of adjudicating in administrative law disputes using quasi-judicial

---

[1] For an extensive study of this topic, cf. J. A. Santamaría Pastor, *Sobre la génesis del Derecho Administrativo español en el siglo XIX (1812–1845)* (1973).

[2] cf. F. Garrido Falla, "Der gerichtliche Rechtsschutz des Einzelnen gegenüber der vollziehenden Gewalt in Spanien," in *Gerichtsschutz gegen die Exekutive*, Vol. 2 (H. Mosler, ed.) (1970) Köln/Berlin/Bonn/München, pp. 990 *et seq.*

[3] Ley de Bases sobre el procedimiento Administrativo of October 19, 1889.

[4] For further details, cf. F. Garrido Falla, "Introduction," in *Verwaltungsverfahrensgesetze des Auslandes*, Vol. 2 (C. H. Ule, ed., Berlin 1967), pp. 743 *et seq.*

[5] cf. (also in relation to subsequent passages) F. Garrido Falla, in *Gerichtsschutz gegen die Exekutive*, Vol. 2, pp. 991–998. On the history of the Spanish Council of State, cf. also L. Jordana, "Le Conseil d'Etat espagnol et les influences françaises au cours de son évolution," in *Le Conseil d'Etat, Livre jubilaire* (1952) Paris, pp. 521 *et seq.*

procedures. In 1904, its powers were conferred on a special Senate of the Supreme Court and thus transferred to the jurisdiction of the ordinary courts. The reorganisation of the administrative courts in 1956 maintained the situation whereby administrative law disputes were, in principle, assigned to judicial organs which, although numbered among the ordinary courts, nevertheless were granted a certain degree of independence.

(2) The basis of the current system of administrative law in Spain is the Constitution of December 27, 1978,[6] which was adopted after the Franco regime had ended. Under Article 1 of the Constitution, Spain constitutes a democracy based on social justice and on the rule of law founded on the principle of the sovereignty of the people and taking the form of a parliamentary monarchy. Article 9(1) lays down that the State authorities are bound by the Constitution and by the other rules of the legal system. Article 9(3) establishes the principles of legality, the hierarchy of rules, the public nature of the legal rules, the non-retrospective nature of rules imposing penalties, legal certainty and the accountability of the public authorities as well as the prohibition of arbitrary action by the latter. The list of fundamental rights and duties specified in the subsequent Articles must, under Article 53(1), be compulsorily observed by all State authorities. Considerable parts of this list are safeguarded by a special type of legal protection, based on the principles of priority and expedition, to be provided by the ordinary courts and by the Constitutional Court.[7] The above constitutional provisions, which affect all the State authorities, already constitute, from the viewpoint of the Executive, the essential framework for the development of administrative law. A number of special provisions are contained in Section IV of the Constitution, entitled "The Government and the Administration." The Government performs the tasks of the Executive and exercises statutory power in accordance with the Constitution and the relevant Laws (Article 97). The public administration is to serve the general interest and act in accordance with the principles of effectiveness, order of rank, decentralisation, "deconcentration" and co-ordination, while remaining totally subject to the relevant statutes and the law (Article 103(1)). The courts supervise on

---

[6] Constitución Española de 1978, B.O.E. no. 311 of December 29, 1978; *cf.* on this subject A. Weber, "Die Spanische Verfassung von 1978," (1980) J.Ö.R., new series 29, 209; the Appendix (pp. 252 *et seq.*) contains a German translation of the Constitution.

[7] For further details, *cf.* K.-P. Sommermann, *Der Schutz der Grundrechte in Spanien nach der Verfassung von 1978—Ursprünge, Dogmatik, Praxis* (1984) Berlin.

the one hand the exercise of the power to issue regulations and on the other the compliance with the relevant statutes of the actions performed by the administration as well as the conformity of these actions with the objectives which justify them (Article 106(1)). It is interesting to note that this section also contains a number of special principles of administrative law, such as the right of persons affected by administrative acts or other types of decision to be heard before their adoption and the citizen's right of access to the archives and registers kept by the administration, it being the task of the legislator to define and elaborate these principles further (Article 105).

(3) At a level below that of the Constitution, the general administrative law is largely laid down in the relevant statutes and regulations.[8] In the first place, mention must be made of the Law relating to administrative procedure of 1958,[9] which finds its origin in the Outline Law of 1889 which has already been mentioned.[10] The object of the reorganisation of the law of procedure was to standardise and simplify proceedings, to improve the level of citizen participation and to reduce the number of rules.[11] The Law not only regulates procedure in the narrow sense, but also covers the substantive administrative law, in particular the various aspects of administrative acts and the conditions for their applicability. Individual areas of general administrative law are regulated in a large number of Laws other than that relating to administrative procedure, in particular the Law relating to the legal status of the administration.[12] Thus the general administrative law of Spain is, contrary to the situation in most other European legal systems, essentially written law. F. Garrido Falla considers the rules contained in the Law relating to administrative procedure and in the Law relating to the legal status of the

---

[8] Under Articles 81 *et seq.* of the Constitution, a distinction is made between the so-called "Organic Laws" (leyes orgánicas), which regulate matters seeking to elaborate further constitutional provisions and enjoy a higher formal status, Outline Laws (leyes de bases) and Ordinary Laws (leyes ordinarias). Certain law-making Regulations and Decrees issued by the Provinces and the Municipalities have an equal rank with Ordinary laws. A survey of these instruments is given in A. Weber, "Die Spanische Verfassung von 1978," (1980) J.Ö.R., new series 29, 209, 232 *et seq.*; *cf.* also E. García de Enterría, T. R. Fernández, *Curso de derecho administrativo*, Vol. 1, (4th ed., revised impression, Madrid 1984), pp. 147 *et seq.*

[9] Ley de Procedimiento Administrativo of July 17, 1958, amended by the Law of December 2, 1963.

[10] *cf. supra*, footnote 3.

[11] *cf.* the speech by L. López Rodó to the Cortes defending the proposed legislation, July 15, 1958, B. O. de las Cortes Españolas no. 601.

[12] Ley de Régimen Jurídico de la Administración del Estado of July 16, 1957.

administration to be so comprehensive as to constitute in their entirety a codification of the general part of administrative law.[13]

It is a matter of controversy in Spain whether customary law is to be acknowledged as a source of substantive law in the context of the applicable system of administrative law.[14] What is clear is that customary law has hardly any practical relevance for general administrative law. Administrative practice as such does not have any rule-making authority; however, arbitrary departures by the administration from established practice may in certain cases constitute an infringement of the principle of equality (Article 14 of the Constitution) or of the bona fides principle.[15]

Case law is not generally acknowledged as constituting a legal source in Spain.[16] There is controversy surrounding the rule-making authority of general legal principles. According to García de Enterría and Fernández,[17] general legal principles express the fundamental values of a legal system, on which society bases its principles of legal ethics. They manifest themselves in the practical application of the law by the courts and by the leading writers. Thus the Tribunal Supremo has recognised, *inter alia*, the following legal principles: (a) that of administrative proportionality and of restricting intervention to the required minimum, (b) the bona fides rule and the prohibition of *venire contra factum proprium*, and (c) the rule that no one may be condemned without a judicial hearing or without having had the opportunity to defend himself/herself.[18] Many legal principles which in France found their expression in the case law of the Conseil d'Etat have in Spain been embodied in various Laws and even in the Constitution. To this extent, they are undoubtedly binding and have overriding applicability.[19]

---

[13] *cf.* F. Garrido Falla, *Tratado de derecho administrativo*, Vol. I (9th ed., Madrid 1985), p. 414.

[14] For a detailed study, *cf.* E. García de Enterría, T.-R. Fernández, *Curso de derecho administrativo*, Vol. 1, pp. 66 *et seq.*; F. Garrido Falla, *Tratado de derecho administrativo*, Vol. I, pp. 389 *et seq.*; R. Entrena Cuesta, *Curso de derecho administrativo*, Vol. I/1 (8th ed., Madrid 1983), pp. 152 *et seq.*

[15] *cf.* E. García de Enterría, T.-R. Fernández, *loc. cit.*, pp. 67 *et seq.* with references to the case law.

[16] *cf.* F. Garrido Falla, *Tratado de derecho administrativo*, Vol. 1, pp. 408 *et seq.*, R. Entrena Cuesta, *Curso de derecho administrativo*, Vol. I/1, p. 158 (an "indirect" legal source only).

[17] *Curso de derecho administrativo*, Vol. 1, pp. 73 *et seq.*

[18] *cf.* the references given in R. Entrena Cuesta, *Curso de derecho administrativo*, Vol. I/1, p. 156.

[19] *cf.* in particular the decision by the Constitutional Court of February 2, 1981 (cited in E. García de Enterría, T.-R. Fernández, *Curso de derecho administrativo*, Vol. 1, p. 80), in

(4) Article 24(1) of the Constitution guarantees the right to effective and comprehensive legal protection in the exercise of legitimate rights and interests. The judicial review of administrative action is performed in the first instance by the administrative law senates of the ordinary courts. Under the general provisions relating to the applicable jurisdiction contained in the rules relating to the administrative courts, these senates have jurisdiction for all actions performed by the public administration.[20] For each action there is one stage of appeal. The administrative law senates of the Audiencias Territoriales adjudicate in complaints against local administrative authorities.[21] The administrative law senates of the Audiencia Nacional or of the Tribunal Supremo adjudicate in complaints against the authorities whose jurisdiction extends to the entire national territory. The Tribunal Supremo acts as a review body in relation to decisions issued by the Audiencias Territoriales and those pronounced by the Audiencia Nacional.[22] The specific precondition for the admissibility of these actions before the courts is that a procedure involving a fair hearing of both parties must have resulted in a negative decision by the administration, it being understood that silence on the administration's part is construed as a refusal.[23]

Legal protection against the administration is also guaranteed by the Constitutional Court (Tribunal Constitucional)[24] established in 1979. Its jurisdiction is similar to that of the German Federal Constitutional Court (Bundesverfassungsgericht).[25] Supervision of the administration can be exercised in particular by means of the Constitutional Action (Recurso de Amparo) where it is claimed that certain fundamental freedoms have been infringed.[26] In the course of the procedure which involves an

which the Court held that the general legal principles contained in the Constitution (in this case the principle of equality in Article 14) also take effect as part of the Constitution.

[20] cf. (also in relation to the allocation of specific jurisdiction to other courts) Article 1 (et seq.) of the Ley reguladora de la Jurisdicción contencioso-administrativa of December 27, 1956.

[21] Under Law 10/1973 of March 17, 1973, these Senates also adjudicate on certain instruments issued by the administrative authorities whose jurisdiction extends over the entire national territory.

[22] For more details concerning this extremely complex allocation of jurisdiction, cf. R. Entrena Cuesta, *Curso de derecho administrativo*, Vol. I/1, pp. 327 et seq.

[23] On the case where the administration is silent, cf. ibid. pp. 228 et seq.

[24] Articles 159 et seq. of the Constitution, in conjunction with Ley Orgánica 2/1979 of October 3, 1979, B.O.E. no. 239 (32709) of October 5, 1979.

[25] For more details, cf. A. Weber, (1980) J.Ö.R., new series 29, 209, 236 et seq., as well as K.-P. Sommermann, loc. cit. footnote 7, pp. 311 et seq. (at 329 et seq.).

[26] cf. on this subject M. Reckhorn-Hengemühle, *Der spanische "recurso de amparo" und die deutsche Verfassungsbeschwerde*, Law Dissertation (1987) Osnabrück.

abstract or concrete assessment of rules, the regulations issued by the administration are also capable of review where they have the status of Law.

In the field of extrajudicial supervision, one institution which must be mentioned is the Advocate of the People (Defensor del Pueblo). Under Article 54 of the Constitution, in conjunction with the Organic Law of 1981,[27] it is the task of the Advocate of the People, who is elected by Parliament, to supervise the compliance of administrative action with the fundamental rights and the basic principles of social and economic policy. It is precisely in the field of the constitutionally guaranteed basic principles of social and economic policy that this supervisory task is of particular importance, since in these instances the protection of the courts is not normally available to the individual.[28] The Defensor may intervene on his own initiative or at the citizen's request. He is granted comprehensive rights to receive information and carry out checks. He has the power to formulate proposals, issue admonitions and lodge certain types of complaint. He presents an annual report to Parliament. The Defensor thus has a status comparable to that of the Swedish Ombudsman and possesses more extensive powers than his counterparts under English and French law.[29]

(5) As to the structure of the administration, Article 2 of the Constitution guarantees both the unity of the Spanish nation and the right to autonomy of the various nationalities and regions. The national territory is divided into municipalities, provinces and such autonomous communities as establish themselves; they all enjoy autonomy in the pursuit of their respective interests.[30] By providing the opportunity to establish autonomous communities, the new Constitution gives official recognition to the traditionally independent stance adopted by certain regions, in particular Catalonia and the Basque country. The powers of these communities are laid down in the Constitution and are given substance by each charter of self-government.[31] Although they are not comparable with the powers of the German Bundesstaaten (States of the Federation), they are

---

[27] Ley orgánica 3/1981 of April 6, 1981, B.O.E. no. 109 of May 7, 1981.
[28] cf. K.-P. Sommermann, "Der Defensor del Pueblo: ein spanischer Ombudsman" (1985) A.ö.R. 267, 272.
[29] Ibid., p. 286; K. P. Sommermann, loc. cit., footnote 7, p. 333.
[30] cf. Article 137 of the Constitution.
[31] cf. Articles 143 et seq. of the Constitution in connection with the Statute for the Basque country (Ley Orgánica 3/1979 B.O.E. no. 306 of December 22, 1979) and that for Catalonia (Ley Orgánica 4/1979 B.O.E. no. 306 of December 22, 1979). On the alloca-

nevertheless more extensive than those of the French regions. As regards the allocation of administrative powers, a distinction must be drawn between those powers which are intrinsic to the community and those which are exercised by means of delegation.[32] The direct state administration as it applies within the territory of the autonomous communities is directed by a delegate from central government and is to be co-ordinated with the administration which is intrinsic to the community itself.[33] Both the central authorities and the above-mentioned self-governing bodies may establish further organs capable of exercising their "indirect" administration which are subject to their supervision, such as corporations (*e.g.* the professional associations) and services (such as the National Social Insurance Service or the municipal transport companies).[34]

tion of legislative and administrative powers based on the Catalonian model, *cf.* A. Weber, (1980) J.Ö.R., new series 29, 209, 246–251.

[32] *cf.* A. Weber, (1980) J.Ö.R., new series 29, 209, 245.

[33] *cf.* Article 154 of the Constitution.

[34] For a detailed study, *cf.* E. García de Enterría, T.-R. Fernández, *Curso de derecho administrativo*, Vol. 1, pp. 368 *et seq.*

CHAPTER 3

LEGAL CONSTRAINTS AND THE FREEDOM OF DECISION OF THE ADMINISTRATION

PART 1: INTRODUCTION

"The State should be a state governed by law; that is the watchword and in truth the impetus for the development of the modern age. It should set out exactly and steadfastly guarantee the directions and limitations of its effectiveness just as it docs for the freedom of its citizens in the form of law and should not seek to realise (or impose) ethical ideas as State policy any more than appropriately belongs to its legal competence: that is, the restrictions should only be those which are absolutely necessary."[1]

Thus Julius Stahl formulated the idea of the state governed by law at a time when the citizens of Europe had only just begun to gain their individual freedoms from the restrictions of the absolutist state. The contents of this basically very general concept of Order delineating the relationship between the state and its subjects were defined more precisely in a series of principles influenced by the loosening of the monopoly of power as exercised by the sovereign princes in favour of the sovereignty of the people.

An essential feature of the state governed by law is the principle of "the legality of the administration," which, together with the organisational division of the power of the state into three component elements, is

---

[1] J. Stahl, *Rechts- und Staatslehre* (3rd ed.), Pt. 2, p. 137; on the German doctrine of the Rechtsstaat (the state governed by law) in general, *cf.* also Otto Bähr, *Der Rechtsstaat* (1st ed.), Kassel and Göttingen 1864, photocopy reprint 1963; Rudolf Gneist, *Der Rechtsstaat und die Verwaltungsgerichte in Deutschland*, photocopy reprint of the second, revised edition of 1879, issued in 1966.

intended to guarantee the freedom of the citizen against the untrammelled intervention of the executive.

The development of the principles of the equality of individuals before the law and of legal certainty, and the protection of individual rights by independent courts,[2] played a major role in completing the subjection of the state to the rule of law.

Limitation of the previously all-powerful executive through Parliament-created statutes was the first step towards the effective guarantee of freedom for the individual. This development did not, however, come to a halt just with legal constraints but led to a far-reaching subjection of administration to the law, which also encompassed constraints under constitutional law.[3]

There is agreement in the Member States of the European Community—in spite of their differing historical development—about what constitutes the underlying principles of the safeguarding of the freedom of the individual and about the fundamental rules for the democratic exercise of state power. Accordingly, in all Member States, the executive is bound by Law, Loi, Wet, Statut or Lov or whatever is the appropriately designated term for parliamentary legislation.

The principles of law developed by the (national) States for the legal delimitation of sovereign power cannot however be directly transferred to the European Community itself and the legal order which it has established. Although, to start with, the temptation arose to clarify the Community structures authoritatively with the help of national legal principles, what in fact has happened is the development of specific Community interpretations.

To deal with the special nature of this newly formed Community power,[4] specific guidelines have been developed in order to deal with the problem of sovereign legal control. This does not mean, however, that essential elements of sovereign legal control of power developed for the nation state have no meaning or validity for the Community. In basic

---

[2] cf. in the German literature on this subject K. Hesse, *Grundzüge des Verfassungsrechts* (15th enlarged ed., Karlsruhe 1985), pp. 78 *et seq.*; for a survey of the concept of the state governed by law in other countries cf. A. Bleckmann, "Der Rechtsstaat in vergleichender Sicht," in *German Yearbook of International Law*, Vol. 20 (1977), pp. 406 *et seq.*

[3] This development can be seen very clearly in German constitutional and administrative law.

[4] This expression ("Gemeinschaftsgewalt") was coined by H. P. Ipsen, *Europäisches Gemeinschaftsrecht*, Tübingen 1972, p. 196, with the express comment that this term told one nothing about the legal position of the Communities but merely characterised the features distinguishing them from national and international associations for integration.

questions to do with the exercise of sovereign power the founders of the Community had no intention of eschewing essential principles of their own constitutional experience in the sphere of a supra-national Association. Certainly, the realisation of the democratic principle was rather neglected.[5] This was however necessary, not least in order to be able to take sufficient account of the continuing sovereignty of the Member States as well as of the authoritative legislative direction of the Community by the Council of Ministers. To this end the role of Law in the limitation of "sovereign" Community power was particularly emphasised.

The Communities are not the holders of all-embracing power, but are empowered to act only in specifically designated spheres, which are laid down in often precisely defined and formal provisions.[6] Moreover, they have at their disposal a fully fledged system for the protection of rights, of which the European Court of Justice forms the centre-piece. Hence there exists a structural concurrence with the Member States to the extent that the concept of the state governed by law in its most general terms has been realised, in consequence of which every exercise of executive power must be directed and limited by the law.[7]

Thus the concept of "the legality of the administration" applies in Community law, if only in a form specially adapted to the circumstances. The most important source of legality is the written law of the E.C. In addition, however, unwritten legal principles are also of significance, as described in the Introduction.[8]

In the subjection of Community power to written law, the same problems arise as for the control of state power in the Member States. In reality, what appears to be an absolute subjection of the administration to the rule of law cannot be achieved. If the adaptability and flexibility of the executive are to be ensured, then the express concession of freedom of decision-making (discretion) to the administration becomes a legislative

---

[5] On the intensive discussion about the E.C. and the democratic principle *cf.*, *e.g.* K.-H. Nassmacher, *Demokratisierung der Europäischen Gemeinschaften*, 1972, and the clear analysis given by P. C. Müller-Graff, *Die Direktwahl des Europäischen Parlaments*, 1977.

[6] *cf.* B. Beutler, R. Bieber, J. Pipkorn and J. Streil, *Die Europäische Gemeinschaft-Rechtsordnung und Politik* (3rd ed., Baden-Baden 1987), p. 75; E. W. Fuss, *Die Europäischen Gemeinschaften und der Rechtsstaatsgedanke*, Heule 1967, p. 24, regards the principle of limitation as definitely a "specific system" for keeping power in check (p. 23).

[7] *cf.* A. Bleckmann, "Der Rechtsstaat in vergleichender Sicht," in *German Yearbook of International Law*, Vol. 20 (1977), pp. 406 *et seq.*

[8] E.-W. Fuss, *Die Europäischen Gemeinschaften und der Rechtsstaatsgedanke*, Heule 1967, p. 13, points out however that legality as such does not create a State governed by law; other principles must play their part as well; *cf. ibid. op. cit.*, p. 17.

necessity.[9] But even where legal rules *per se* deny any freedom of decision to the administration, the itemisation in concrete form of largely undefined concepts leads to an at least factual relativisation of legal constraints.

The varied nature of life's contingencies can frequently be dealt with fairly by the legislature only when it uses flexible, undefined legal concepts which the administration can apply in the light of the actual necessities of the individual case. Moreover, the difficulty arises of formulating sufficiently precise legal provisions, especially in the field of economic administrative law. The complexity of the subject-matter of the rules is paralleled by a rather vague conceptual formulation and the application of provisions taking the form of blanket clauses. This is particularly apparent in the case of Community law, which is primarily designed to achieve economic aims.[10]

The principle of limited individual powers in treaties on the one hand and the complexity of the subject-matter of the rules on the other, in addition to the tendency towards flexibility inherent in any integration process, throw into relief the legal difficulties associated with undefined legal concepts and discretionary powers when considered in the light of treaty obligations. This is also to be seen at very nearly all levels of secondary rights as well as in the national law promulgated for the execution of Community law. The purpose of this examination is served less by the theoretical determination of the nature of the various forms which the relaxation of the rule of law takes[11] than by the most unambiguous definition of the limits of administrative freedom of action.

The decisive limitations on the exercise of sovereign power in this context are probably most vividly illustrated by an examination of the case law of the European Court of Justice. The principle of legality in the law of the European Community will first be examined from this aspect (see Part 2). Part 3, which follows, will examine the relaxation of administrative constraints and the legal restrictions on the freedoms created

---

[9] *cf.* on this point J. Schwarze, *Die Befugnis zur Abstraktion im europäischen Gemeinschaftsrecht*, Baden-Baden 1976, p. 152, with reference to the particular requirements of an integration process.

[10] *cf. ibid. loc. cit.*

[11] As far as we are aware, no attempt has yet been made to do this, in marked contrast to German legal theory, for example; on this point *cf.* merely the comprehensive explanations by D. Jesch, "Unbestimmter Rechtsbegriff und Ermessen in rechtstheoretischer und verfassungsrechtlicher Sicht," AöR Vol. 82 (1957), pp. 163 *et seq.*

in consequence. The recognition of legal limits on sovereign action leads then to the question raised in Part 4: what happens when the state or the Community breaks the law and individuals suffer in consequence?

How far the system of legal protection in Community law is complemented by adequate protection of property will be examined in detail in the penultimate part of this chapter. Finally the question is posed whether reciprocal effects between the Community legal order and the national legal orders can be seen in the development of relevant legal principles.

PART 2: THE PRINCIPLE OF THE LEGALITY OF THE ADMINISTRATION

SECTION 1

THE LEGALITY OF THE ADMINISTRATION IN THE MEMBER STATES

A. A COMPARATIVE LEGAL ANALYSIS

To obtain a more precise definition of the principle of the legality of the administration as applied in the Community, we shall begin by looking at the law of the Member States from the perspective of comparative law. This will give a clearer idea of the origins and characteristic forms of the principle in Community law.

I. THE PRINCIPLE OF LEGALITY IN FRANCE

The French system of administrative law, already outlined in Chapter 2,[1] is inspired by the principle of legality.[2] Legality in this context is not to be understood simply in a narrow sense of legal positivism, as the constraints imposed by statute; it has a broader definition, according to the classic notion of the rule of law, as any legal constraint to which the executive is subject.[3]

> "Le principe de légalité appliqué à l'Administration exprime donc la règle selon laquelle l'Administration doit agir conformément au droit."[4]

---

[1] *cf.* Chapter 2, Section 1.
[2] See A. de Laubadère, *Traité de droit administratif* (9th ed., Paris 1984), Vol. 1, by J.-C. Venezia and Y. Gaudemet, p. 257 no. 537.
[3] *cf.* A. de Laubadère, *op. cit.*, footnote 2, p. 260, no. 544; J. Rivero, *Droit administratif* (11th ed., Paris 1985), pp. 81 *et seq.*
[4] G. Vedel, P. Delvolvé, *Droit administratif*, Paris, 1984, pp. 373 *et seq.*

This means that the executive must act in conformity with written law (Constitution, statutes, regulations). The Constitution of the Fifth Republic, which is at the apex of the legal order, has a central significance in the basic division of powers among the organs of the State, but is of less importance as a measure of the legality of administrative conduct.[5] The French Constitution differs from the German, for example, in that the Parliament in France has only limited legislative authority, as defined in Article 34, paragraph 2 of the Constitution; this authority guarantees that any encroachments on freedom and property rest on a basis legitimated by Parliament.[6] In other fields, the executive has legislative functions of its own under Article 37, and these are exercised by promulgating ordinances or regulations.[7] The administration may also be empowered under statute to make rules in matters governed by the authority of Parliament.[8]

The discretionary powers enjoyed by the executive are nonetheless constrained by the written *principes généraux du droit*.[9] However, customary law (*coutumes*) plays no noteworthy role.[10] The administration must also comply with international treaties. Under Article 55 of the present Constitution, duly ratified treaties and agreements have precedence over national statutes. Finally, the administration has to observe the law of the European Community, which is now acknowledged by the Conseil d'Etat, after some initial hesitation, to have direct effect and primacy.[11]

In France, the guarantee of administrative legality is exercised in the first place by the Tribunaux administratifs, and ultimately by the Conseil d'Etat, which, historically speaking, has played a decisive role in limiting the powers of the executive.[12] The most important procedural means for testing the legality of administrative acts after the event is the *recours pour excès de pouvoir*, through which claims can be grounded on lack of

---

[5] See above, Chapter 2, Section 1.
[6] See H. D. Jarass, "Besonderheiten des französischen Verwaltungsrechts im Vergleich," DÖV 1981, pp. 813 *et seq.* (816).
[7] For the promulgation of ordinances by the executive in France, see A. de Laubadère, *op. cit.*, footnote 2, pp. 305 *et seq.*; G. Vedel, P. Delvolvé, *op. cit.*, footnote 4, pp. 288 *et seq.*
[8] On the legal regime of subsidiary legislation (*ordonnances*) see G. Vedel, P. Delvolvé, *op. cit.*, footnote 4, pp. 310 *et seq.*
[9] See G. Vedel, P. Delvolvé, *op. cit.*, footnote 4, pp. 387 *et seq.*
[10] See A. de Laubadère, *op. cit.*, footnote 2, p. 265 Nos. 555 *et seq.*
[11] *cf.* A. de Laubadère, *op. cit.*, footnote 2, p. 263 No. 552; G. Vedel, P. Delvolvé, *op. cit.*, footnote 4, pp. 381 *et seq.*, with references to the case law.
[12] This is fully dealt with in Chapter 2, Section 1 above.

jurisdiction, procedural and formal defects, breach of statute or abuse of discretionary power.[13]

II. THE PRINCIPLE OF LEGALITY IN THE FEDERAL REPUBLIC OF GERMANY

According to Article 20, paragraph 3 of the Basic Law, executive authority must be exercised in accordance with statute and law; and under Article 1, paragraph 3 of the Basic Law, its exercise is also subject to respect for fundamental rights. Hence the traditional principle of the legality of the administration is broadened to form a general principle of the constitutionality of the administration.[1] The legality principle itself consists of two elements: the primacy of statute (see 1) and the requirement of a statute (see 2). These principles will be considered first. We shall then look at the other legal constraints on the administration, those which go beyond the legality principle itself.

1. The primacy of statute law

The primacy of statute is a term used to describe the superiority of the formal statutory source[2] over all secondary sources of law (for instance, ordinances or regulations, articles of association or administrative guidelines). All acts which the administration performs under statute must be in accordance with statutory authority. The primacy of statute law applies unreservedly to the whole of the administration.

This relationship between administration and statute can be defined in relatively simple terms, but the definition of the concepts involved poses considerable difficulties when it comes to the scope and content of the requirement of a statute.[3]

---

[13] cf. ibid.
[1] C. H. Ule, in *Evangelisches Staatslexikon* (2nd ed.), Stuttgart 1975, p. 848; O. Bachof, *Verwaltungsrecht I*, München 1974, p. 176.
[2] F. Ossenbühl, in H.-U. Erichsen, W. Martens, *Allgemeines Verwaltungsrecht* (7th ed.), 1986, p. 61; *cf.* also F. Fleiner, *Institutionen des deutschen Verwaltungsrechts*, reprint of the updated edition, J. C. B. Mohr, Tübingen 1928, p. 68. For the concept of statute, see K. Hesse, *Grundzüge des Verfassungsrechts der Bundesrepublik Deutschland* (15th ed., 1985), pp. 194 *et seq.*; D. Jesch, *Gesetz und Verwaltung* (2nd unchanged ed., Tübingen 1968), pp. 9 *et seq.*; N. Achterberg, *Allgemeines Verwaltungsrecht* (2nd ed., Heidelberg 1986), p. 330, marginal note 2.
[3] F. Ossenbühl, *op. cit.*, footnote 2, p. 61.

2. The Requirement that there be a Statute

(a) *Field of application*

In the area where this requirement exists, the administration may act only if authorised by statute to do so.[4] The principle raises the question, which matters are reserved for Parliament alone to decide and resolve through statute.[5] For a better understanding of the problems which arise in this field, it is necessary to recall the historical circumstances in which the requirement of a statute arose. The question, which decisions should be "reserved" to Parliament in the form of a statute and should therefore be withheld from the executive, could arise only following a distribution of power, hitherto absolute, among different bodies.[6] This was the aim of the liberal constitutional movement, which at the end of the eighteenth century sought to limit the monopoly power of the sovereign through a separation of powers, thereby securing the individual rights of citizens.

This movement held that the executive could encroach upon the sphere of individual rights—consisting of personal freedom and the right to property—only if Parliament, as the representative of the citizens concerned, had previously given its consent through legislation.[7]

The citizens' sphere of influence was defined by reserving to statute the authority to encroach on their personal freedom and property. However, outside the reserved area the monarch continued to enjoy unfettered powers of decision-making.[8] This shows that the concept of reservation to statute describes a particular combination of historical circumstances, and it was only natural that the concept should be considered afresh in the light of the Basic Law.[9]

Insofar as legal restrictions of fundamental rights were to be expressly subjected to statute, there were no problems of interpretation. It was a

---

[4] *cf.* H. Maurer, *Allgemeines Verwaltungsrecht* (5th ed., München 1986), p. 79, marginal note 3; H. Faber, *Verwaltungsrecht* Tübingen 1987, p. 87; N. Achterberg, *op. cit.*, footnote 2, p. 330, marginal note 2.

[5] F. Ossenbühl, *op. cit.*, footnote 2, p. 61.

[6] F. Ossenbühl, *op. cit.*, footnote 2, p. 62; H. Maurer, *op. cit.*, footnote 4, p. 14, marginal note 5 and p. 81, marginal note 9.

[7] *cf.* H. Maurer, *op. cit.*, footnote 4, p. 81, marginal note 9; H. Faber, *op. cit.*, footnote 4, p. 87.

[8] On the dual system of government by Crown and citizenry, see D. Jesch, *op. cit.*, footnote 2, pp. 102 *et seq.*, especially pp. 108 *et seq.*

[9] H. Maurer, *op. cit.*, footnote 4, p. 81, marginal note 10:; F. Ossenbühl, *op. cit.*, footnote 2, p. 58.

moot point, however, whether statutory authority was required in order to encroach upon fundamental rights in the area of what are known as special situations of authority (such as the situation of civil servants, school children, prisoners, etc., who have a particularly close relationship with the State). This point will require special consideration below.

Once more, the answer to the question of the requirement that there be a statute in the area of rules made and imposed on the public by the administration is to be found in the Constitution itself. According to Article 80, paragraph 1(2) of the Basic Law, ordinances must in every case be based on clearly defined statutory authority. Hence the executive has no independent powers in the making of ordinances or regulations, unlike the executive in France.

A further problem which developed when the Basic Law came into force was whether, and to what extent, the administration of services requires statutory authority. It had become obvious that the individual must be protected, not merely from unbridled attempts to interfere with his rights, but also from the arbitrary decision to withhold State benefits. Taking this argument to its logical conclusion, there are some who advocate a so-called total reservation; they argue from the mandatory system of democracy[10] and the rule of law in the Constitution[11] that the whole of the administrative conduct which affects citizens should be governed by comprehensive statutory reservation.

Even though this view, for various reasons, has not prevailed, it is now widely held that it is insufficient for the requirement for a statute to be confined to encroachments on freedom and property. Because of the steady growth in public services over the past 100 years, and the resulting increase in the dependency of individuals on State welfare, an extension of the reserved area was felt to be unavoidable.[12]

Accordingly, the Federal Constitutional Court developed the "theory of substantiality," whereby legislation is always necessary if the question to be resolved is one of "substantial" importance for the citizen or the public,[13] regardless of whether the measures contemplated by the State constitute "interventions" or "services." This will be the case whenever

---

[10] See D. Jesch, *op. cit.*, footnote 2.

[11] See H. H. Rupp, *Grundfragen der heutigen Verwaltungsrechtslehre*, Tübingen 1965, p. 135.

[12] For a rejection of "total reservation" see B. H. Maurer, *op. cit.*, footnote 4, p. 82, marginal note 10; *cf.* the detailed commentary in N. Achterberg, *op. cit.*, footnote 2, pp. 333 *et seq.*, marginal notes 10 *et seq.*

[13] For the basis of the so-called "theory of substantiality" see Federal Constitutional Court Decisions, 33, 1(9); 33(125, 157); 33(303, 346); 44(251).

the question to be resolved has a bearing on fundamental rights, *i.e.* whenever fundamental rights are encroached upon, hence also in the special situation of authority,[14] but it will also apply to administrative activities which are of "substantial" importance for securing the fundamental rights of individuals.[15] No less "substantial" in their nature are the essential organisational aspects of the public services, and their regulation likewise falls in principle within the area reserved to statute.[16]

Since the first decision of the Constitutional Court[17] on the question of statutory reservation in penal matters, the academic controversy concerning the need to extend statutory reservation beyond the areas to which it traditionally applies has somewhat abated. However, certain practical instances to which the expanded statutory reservation applies are still controversial, such as the granting of State subsidies.[18]

(b) Content of the statutes in the reserved area

There are also problems in determining how precise legislation must be in the area reserved to statute. Here the question arises how far the conduct of the administration must be determined by the statutes. Here too, the cardinal principle is the "substantiality" theory developed by the Federal Constitutional Court, according to which the need for legislation and the nature of the statute are dictated by the importance to individuals or the public at large of the issue to be decided. This means that the greater the threat to, or effect on, the individual's fundamental rights, the more precise and restrictive must be the statutory authority.[19]

[14] *cf.* Federal Constitutional Court Decision 33, 1 (Penal provisions).
[15] *cf.* Federal Constitutional Court Decision 47, 46 *et seq.* (79) (Sex education).
[16] *cf.* Federal Constitutional Court Decision 40, 237 (247 *et seq.*) (Competence of public authorities and administrative procedures).
[17] See above, note 14.
[18] For detailed comment and references, see F. Ossenbühl, *op. cit.*, footnote 2, pp. 62 *et seq.*; *cf.* also H. P. Bull, *Allgemeines Verwaltungsrecht* (2nd ed., Heidelberg 1986), p. 112, marginal note 335 *et seq.*
[19] *cf.* H. Maurer, *op. cit.*, footnote 4, p. 82, marginal note 11; on statutory reservation see also F. Rottmann, *Der Vorbehalt des Gesetzes und die grundrechtlichen Gesetzesvorbehalte*, EuGRZ 1985, pp. 277 *et seq.*

3. The Constraints Placed on the Administration by Fundamental
   Rights and General Principles of Law

As already explained, under Article 1, paragraph 3 of the Basic Law
the fundamental rights in the Basic Law are also directly binding in law on
the executive. Hence the administration, in its activities, must also pay
constant heed to fundamental rights, and this affects the interpretation of
the underlying basis of authority as well as the exercise of discretion.

Even where the administration, in the nature of things, has to carry out
public functions according to private law procedures, it is constrained by
fundamental rights, so that there cannot be any "escape into private
law."[20]

According to prevailing theory, fundamental rights do not in principle
apply in the area of so-called fiscal administration, *i.e.* in meeting needs
according to private law and in administering the property of the State. In
this area, however, the ban on arbitrary action found in Article 3 of the
Basic Law continues to apply.[21]

Constitutional status is assigned to those general principles of law
which must guide administrative conduct: the proportionality principle
and the principle of respect for legitimate expectations. There are also,
however, other principles, which are described as "general principles of
administrative law" and which impose tighter legal obligations and restrictions on the conduct of the administration.[22]

4. Unlawful Administrative Conduct

German administrative law, in section 35 of the Administrative Procedures Act, draws a conceptual and theoretical distinction between administrative acts as individual decisions, and ordinances or regulations as
general or abstract rulings by the administration.

(a) *The unlawful administrative act*

To be lawful, an administrative act must be issued by the responsible

---

[20] *cf.* I. von Münch, in H.-U. Erichsen, W. Martens, *Allgemeines Verwaltungsrecht* (7th ed.,
1986), p. 50; H. P. Bull, *op. cit.*, footnote 18, p. 125, marginal note 389.
[21] As above, *op. cit.*
[22] There is a good survey in Ossenbühl, *op. cit.*, footnote 2, pp. 113 *et seq.*

authority through due process and in the correct form, and may not contain any substantive defect.[23] If any of these requirements are not fulfilled, the administrative act is unlawful or, according to the definition of the Federal Administrative Court[24]:

> "An administrative act is unlawful if it occurs through improper application of the existing legal rules."

The formal requirements for an administrative act to be lawful—pertaining to authority, procedure and form—need not be further explained here. However, some explanation is needed of the requirements as to content.

First, as already stated, the legality principle demands that the measure be in conformity with superior law, including fundamental rights. In addition, an administrative measure in the area reserved to statute must rest on a formal statute, which in turn must accord with the Constitution, and especially with fundamental rights. Fundamental rights also apply, significantly, in the interpretation of any undefined concepts in the statute and in setting limits to the exercise of administrative discretion. This highly-developed chapter in German legal theory will be considered in detail later.

(b) Unlawfulness in delegated rule-making

Owing to the unfortunate effects of the broadly-drawn decree powers of the Weimar Republic, the "fathers" of the Basic Law adopted a restrictive approach in determining the legislative powers to be delegated to the executive.[25]

Article 80, paragraph 1 of the Basic Law stipulates that rule-making authority is subject to statutory authorisation, and this authorisation must specify the content, the purpose and the extent of the delegated authority. Only in this context can the administration exercise a rule-making function.

---

[23] See H.-U. Erichsen and W. Martens, in Erichsen, Martens, *Allgemeines Verwaltungsrecht* (7th ed., 1986), pp. 214 *et seq.* (215).

[24] Federal Administrative Court Decision 13, 28 (31).

[25] The Weimar Constitution had no general rule-making authority, only the authority for rules in individual cases; on this, see B. O. Bryde, in I. von Münch (editor), *Grundgesetzkommentar* (2nd ed., Munich 1983), Vol. 3, Art. 80, p. 245; especially p. 246 on the historical background.

III. THE PRINCIPLE OF LEGALITY IN ITALY

Although it is not disputed that in Italy, administrative functions are governed by the principle of legality,[1] its legal basis is open to a variety of interpretations. The basis is said by most writers to be Article 97, paragraph 1 of the Constitution, which states that:

"The public institutions are organized according to statute, to assure the proper functioning and the impartiality of the administration."[2]

From the *principio di legalità* it follows, first, that the administration may encroach upon the freedom and property of the individual citizen only where it has statutory authority to do so.[3] Secondly, this general principle of the Italian legal system imposes on the executive the duty to comply with both law and statute, hence also with the *principi generali del diritto*.[4]

IV. THE PRINCIPLE OF LEGALITY IN THE UNITED KINGDOM

In the United Kingdom, the statutory constraints on the administration are derived from the interlinkage of two fundamental constitutional principles. The starting point is the sovereignty of Parliament, and on this basis the British Parliament in combination with the monarch, a second source of sovereignty, enjoys a legislative power which in principle is unlimited.[1] The second governing principle of the British constitutional

---

[1] Marzuoli, *Principio di legalità e attività di diritto privato della pubblica amministrazione*, Milan 1982, pp. 19 *et seq.*; Fois, "Legalità (principio di)," in EdD, Vol. XXII, 1973, pp. 659 *et seq.*; Carlassare, *Amministrazione e potere politico*, Padua 1973, pp. 132 *et seq.*

[2] Ottaviano, "Poteri dell'amministrazione e principi costituzionali," in Riv. trim. dir. publ. 1964, p. 926; Gasparri, "I Concetti di 'legislazione,' 'amministrazione' e 'potere politico' nella terminologia della Costituzione," in *Studi in onore di S. Lessona*, I, Bologna 1963, p. 360.

[3] On this, see Di Giovine, *Introduzione allo studio della riserva di legge nell'ordinamento italiano*, Turin 1969; F. Levi, "Legittimità," in EdD Vol. XXIV 1974, pp. 124 *et seq.* and Marzuoli, *op. cit.*, footnote 1, p. 22, according to whom Article 97, paragraph 1 of the Constitution enshrines the principle of the legitimacy of administrative action and the principle of statutory reservation in administrative organisation.

[4] A detailed commentary is in H.-W. Rengeling, *Rechtsgrundsätze beim Verwaltungsvollzug des Europäischen Gemeinschaftsrechts*, Köln, Berlin, Bonn, München 1977, pp. 138 *et seq.*, with a survey of Italian sources.

[1] *cf.* A. V. Dicey, *Introduction to the study of the law of the constitution* (8th ed., London 1931), pp. 36 *et seq.*, especially 37 *et seq.*; O. Hood Phillips, P. Jackson, *Constitutional and administrative law* (6th ed., London 1975), pp. 42 *et seq.*

system, the rule of law, has a force equal to the sovereignty of Parliament and postulates that the administration is subject to common law in the form in which it is modified by Parliament,[2] or, in the words of the English administrative lawyer H. W. R. Wade[3]: "Its primary meaning is that everything must be done according to law. Applied to the powers of government, this requires that every government authority which does some act which would otherwise be a wrong (such as taking a man's land), or which infringes a man's liberty (as by refusing him planning permission), must be able to justify its action as authorised by law—and in nearly every case this will mean authorised by Act of Parliament."

Administrative measures which affect the rights, duties and freedoms of individuals must rest on a firm statutory foundation[4]:

> "Every act of governmental power, *i.e.* every act which affects the legal rights, duties or liberties of any person, must be shown to have a strictly legal pedigree. The affected person may always resort to the courts of law, and if the legal pedigree is not found to be perfectly in order the court will invalidate the act, which he can then safely disregard."

Parliamentary authority is also required whenever the executive seeks to promulgate general, abstract rules (delegated legislation). The extent of administrative legislative power depends mainly on the content of the authorisation. By contrast with Germany, however, it is open to Parliament to decide this itself.[5]

A further component of the rule of law is equality before the law, which ensures formal equality in the application of the law. The definition given by the English constitutional lawyer A. V. Dicey was highly influential in the development of an independent British concept of administrative law[6]:

> "It means, again, equality before the law, or the equal subjection of all classes to the ordinary law of the land administered by the ordinary Law Courts; the 'rule of law' in this sense excludes the idea of any exemption of officials or others from the duty of obedience to

---

[2] A. V. Dicey is the authority for this *op. cit.*, footnote 1, pp. 198 *et seq.*
[3] H. W. R. Wade, *Administrative Law* (5th ed., Oxford 1982), p. 22.
[4] *Ibid.*
[5] For a detailed commentary on delegated legislation, see H. W. R. Wade, *op. cit.*, footnote 3, pp. 733 *et seq.*, especially on the fields to which it applies, pp. 736 *et seq.*
[6] *Op. cit.*, footnote 1, p. 198.

the law which governs other citizens or from the jurisdiction of the ordinary tribunals; there can be with us nothing really corresponding to the 'administrative law' (*droit administratif*) or the 'administrative tribunals' (*tribunaux administratifs*) of France."

Dicey's view that there could be no administrative law in Britain rested, as already pointed out, on a misapprehension of the function of "droit administratif" in France. For many years, however, its consequence was to prevent the emergence of a British administrative law as an independent branch of law and a scientific discipline.[7] Although this view is now considered outdated and Britain now has a developed "administrative law," this has not so far affected in any way the fundamental competence of the ordinary courts in disputes concerning administrative questions.[8] At the same time, the "administrative tribunals" specially created for the administration have acquired considerable importance in the resolution of conflicts.

The legality of administrative conduct is guaranteed partly by means of the doctrine of *ultra vires*: if the executive acts outside the area in which it has authority, its action is "*ultra vires*" and therefore unlawful.[9]

Administrative discretion is not however limited only by written law. Significant procedural constraints also arise from the principles of "natural justice," including, for example, the rule that no one may be judge in his own cause or that an individual has a right to a judicial hearing. These principles, which at first applied only to judicial proceedings, are now also applied to administrative decision-making.[10]

V. THE PRINCIPLE OF LEGALITY IN BELGIUM

In a country like Belgium, with its traditional democratic system, the rule of law is a principle universally recognised. The Belgian administration is subject to law, *i.e.* to the principle of legality .[1] This means that the

---

[7] *cf.* Chapter 2, Section 3.

[8] *Ibid.*

[9] On the *ultra vires* doctrine, see H. W. R. Wade, *op. cit.*, footnote 3, pp. 348 *et seq.*; O. Hood Phillips, P. Jackson, *op. cit.*, footnote 1, pp. 596 *et seq.*, and for further detail R. Glücksman, *Die Grenzen der Betätigung englischer Verwaltungsbehörden*, Frankfurt am Main, 1981.

[10] On natural justice, see H. W. R. Wade, *op. cit.*, footnote 1, pp. 413 *et seq.*; O. Hood Phillips, *op. cit.*, footnote 1, pp. 602 *et seq.*

[1] J. Dembour, *Droit administratif* (3rd ed., Liège 1978), no. 9; also A. Mast, J. Dujardin, *Overzicht van het Belgisch Administratief Recht* (9th ed., Ghent 1984), no. 14.

public authorities are bound by objective law; they must ensure the application of the law, and their powers are circumscribed by the law.[2]

The principle of the legality of the administration means that the actions of an administrative organ are lawful only if they are in accordance with the decisions reached by a superior organ of the public authority. This is described as the "hierarchy of legal norms."[3]

Article 107 of the Belgian Constitution, under which the courts are bound to reject general rules and regulations made by the provinces and municipalities if they are contrary to the law, and Article 14 of the law on the Council of State, according to which any person with interest to act may seek from the Council of State the revocation of unlawful administrative decisions, are both expressions of the principle of legality.[4]

Although the Constitution ranks highest in the hierarchy of legal norms, the courts have no power to decide whether legislation is compatible with the Constitution, so that there is no sanction if a statute is unconstitutional.[5]

The case law of the Council of State has developed from the legality principle, as a general rule of law, the rule that an administrative authority may not enact provisions contrary to its own general rulings (principle of *patere legem quam ipse fecisti*).[6] For instance, a royal decree on the appointment or dismissal of a civil servant may not conflict with another royal decree containing general rules on the appointment and dismissal of civil servants. The earlier decree can be altered only by a royal decree of general scope.[7]

VI.   THE PRINCIPLE OF LEGALITY IN DENMARK

1.   Content and Form of the Principle of Legality

In Denmark too, it is recognised that a statutory authority is needed in

---

[2] A. Mast, *op. cit.*, footnote 1, no. 14.

[3] *Ibid.*

[4] *Ibid.*

[5] A. Mast, no. 14; further comment on this in A. Mast, *Overzicht van het Belgisch Grondwettelijk Recht* (7th ed., Ghent 1983), nos. 387–397.

[6] A. Mast, *op. cit.*, footnote 1, no. 15; however, L. P. Suetens, in "Algemene rechtsbeginselen en algemene beginselen van behoorlijk bestuur in het Belgisch administratief recht," *Tijdschrift voor bestuurswetenschappen en publiek recht* (TvB), 1970, pp. 379, 385 *et seq.*, derives this principle from the equality principle.

[7] *cf.* on the principle "patere legem quam ipse fecisti"—the administration is bound by its own rules—J. Schwarze, *Die Befugnis zur Abstraktion in europäischen Gemeinschafts-*

order to encroach upon freedom or property.[1] Legislation also defines the boundaries of permissible administrative conduct.

In 1927 P. Andersen[2] showed that the legality principle in the Danish administration largely accords with German law. From a modern perspective, the interesting question is whether the scope of statutory reservation has been extended to cover the administration of public services, as in Germany, but the question is a difficult one to answer. It is not emphasised in Danish sources to the same degree as in German literature. Poul Meyer, for instance, writes that the actions of the public administration must "in every case" be defined and covered by an Act of Parliament.[3] This suggests a wider statutory reservation, extending beyond the traditional area of encroachments on freedom and property.

The same conclusion is suggested by G. T. Nielsen, who explains[4]:

"As mentioned previously in the section dealing with the executive power within the constitutional framework, it is a characteristic feature of Danish administration that it has only such powers as have been granted by statute."

Elsewhere he offers the following definition of executive power:

". . . the government does not have any independent authority in this respect, but is constantly obliged to take action only by fiat of the law."[5]

It is beyond doubt, however, that statutory reservation applies to administrative legislation. The administration may make regulations only on

---

recht, Baden-Baden 1976, p. 70 and ibid. footnote 53: J. Dembour, op. cit., footnote 1, no. 222°. Key decisions on this question by the Council of State are Judgment no. 115 of August 26, 1949, François; for the later case law, see the references in A. Mast, No. 15 footnote 28; for the historical background to this principle see M. Sommerhausen, "Les principes généraux du Droit Administratif," in Perspectivas del Derecho Publico en la segunda mitad del siglo XX, Festschrift für Enrique Sayagues-Laso, Vol. IV, Madrid 1969, pp. 463, 482 et seq.; also, De Raad van State en de algemene beginselen van het administratief recht, TvB 1970, p. 481, 483.

[1] cf. P. Andersen, Ungültige Verwaltungsakte—mit besonderer Berücksichtigung der Ungültigkeitsgründe, Mannheim/Berlin/Leipzig 1927, translated into German by Walther Pappenheim, p. 316.

[2] Op. cit., footnote 1, p. 317.

[3] P. Meyer, in Geschichte der Verwaltungsrechtswissenschaft in Europa, edited by E. V. Heyen, Frankfurt am Main 1982, p. 20.

[4] G. T. Nielsen, Danish Law—A General Survey, edited by H. Gammeltoft-Hansen, B. Gomard, A. Philip, Copenhagen, 1982, p. 49.

[5] Op. cit., footnote 4, p. 40.

the basis of an Act of Parliament. It does not have any authority of its own to do so.[6] The limits of delegated parliamentary authority are defined in the Constitution. For instance, taxes may be levied only on the basis of a statute (clause 43 of the Danish Constitution).

As regards the other legal constraints on the Danish executive, mention must be made of the pertinent unwritten principles of law.[7] Hence in Denmark the legality principle also embraces the legality of the administration, a phenomenon which has also been observed in other national legal systems described here.

2. Unlawful Administrative Conduct

Rules made by the administration and individual administrative acts may be challenged under similar conditions and on similar grounds. The court examines the facts and ascertains whether there are any of the classic defects defined in French law, such as breach of statute or absence of statutory authority, want of competence, defective composition of the official body concerned, procedural and formal defects or *détournement de pouvoir*.[8]

VII. THE PRINCIPLE OF LEGALITY IN GREECE

1. The Applicability of the Principle of Legality

In many of its provisions, the Greek Constitution of June 9, 1975 implicitly enshrines the notion of the constitutional state. The legality of the executive is therefore a governing principle of the Greek administration.[1] The individual and social rights defined in Article 4 of the Constitution of July 9, 1975 can be restricted, where such restrictions are not expressly provided for in the Constitution itself, only by a corresponding statute. The statutory constraints on the executive also help to explain Article 50 of the Constitution, under which the President of the Hellenic Republic, as the head of the executive (Article 26, no. 2), has only such

---

[6] G. T. Nielsen, *op. cit.*, footnote 4, p. 42.
[7] *Ibid. op. cit.*, footnote 6, p. 50.
[8] *cf.* Christensen, *Gerichtsschutz gegen die Exekutive*, Vol. 1, pp. 118 *et seq.*
[1] P. Dagtoglou, *Südosteuropa-Handbuch*, Vol. III Griechenland, p. 27, ed. Klaus-Detlev Grothusen, Göttingen 1980.

authority as is expressly conferred on him by the Constitution and by statute. But the Greek administration is not bound simply by written law. Its activities are guided and regulated by unwritten general principles of law, as in other Member States of the European Community.[2]

Hence in Greece also, the legality of the administration has been extended to mean that administration must comply not only with statute but with law generally.

2.   Unlawful Administrative Conduct

The Greek procedure for challenging administrative decisions is modelled on the French example of the *cas d'ouverture du recours pour excès de pouvoir*. The grounds for contesting a decision are therefore want of jurisdiction, defects of form or procedure, misuse of authority and breach of statute.[3] The concept of unlawfulness also includes the infringement of general principles of law, which are binding on the administration.[4]

Rule-making acts by the executive, where an individual is affected or injured by the rule, can be directly contested before the Council of State of Greece by a plea in revocation.[5] With the exception of cases of *détournement de pouvoir*, the Council of State investigates the legality of the decision[6] in the light of the above categories of defects.[7]

VIII.   THE PRINCIPLE OF LEGALITY IN IRELAND

As in the United Kingdom, in Ireland the "rule of law" means that the administration must act in accordance with law and statute.[1] As in English law, the doctrine of *ultra vires* also has an important place in Irish constitutional law. If an administrative organ acts outside the area of competence assigned to it by statute, the act is *ultra vires* and therefore

---

[2] T. Tsatsos, *Gerichtsschutz gegen die Exekutive*, Vol. I, Köln/Berlin/Bonn/München 1969, p. 310 with references.

[3] *cf.* W. Skouris, "L'illégalité de l'action administrative comme fondement de la responsabilité de la puissance publique en Grèce," in *Journées de la Société de Législation comparée*, 1984, pp. 51 *et seq*. (54).

[4] *Ibid.*

[5] T. Tsatsos, *op. cit.*, footnote 2, p. 318.

[6] T. Tsatsos, *ibid.* but a contrary view.

[7] *Ibid. op. cit.*, footnote 2; p. 319.

[1] Kelly in: *Gerichtsschutz*, Vol. I, p. 426.

unlawful.[2] This applies both to individual acts of the administration and to the field of delegated legislation. For other administrative defects and the control exercised over them by the courts, reference may be made to the description of the legal situation in the United Kingdom.

IX. THE PRINCIPLE OF LEGALITY IN LUXEMBOURG

Under the Luxembourg Constitution, executive power lies wholly in the hands of the Grand Duke (Article 33 of the Constitution). His authority *vis-à-vis* the legislature is limited, under Article 36 of the Constitution, to the implementation of statutes. For this purpose he has a right to issue ordinances and decrees, but this right may not be used to amend laws or hinder their execution.[1]

A further constraint derives from general principles of law, such as the right to a judicial hearing and to equality of treatment in public taxation and benefits.[2] These principles are similar in their origin and development to French principles, because legal developments in France have had a powerful impact on administrative law in Luxembourg. This is equally true of the treatment of error in administrative conduct, which corresponds to the French model[3] but unlike the latter is regulated in a positive law sense, through a statute.[4]

X. THE PRINCIPLE OF LEGALITY IN THE NETHERLANDS

The principle of the legality of the administration is recognised in Dutch administrative law. As in German law, a distinction is drawn between the primacy of statute and reservation to statute.

1. The Primacy of Statutes

In the Kingdom of the Netherlands primacy is accorded to statute, which gives priority to laws jointly enacted by the Crown and the States

---

[2] Kelly, *op. cit., ibid.*
[1] *cf.* also P. Majerus, *L'Etat Luxembourgeois* (5th ed., Luxembourg 1983), p. 140.
[2] *cf.* H.-W. Rengeling, *Rechtsgrundsätze beim Verwaltungsvollzug des Europäischen Gemeinschaftsrechts*, Köln/Berlin/Bonn/München 1977, p. 136 with further references.
[3] *cf.* P. Majerus, *op. cit.*, footnote 1, p. 202.
[4] *cf. ibid., op. cit.*, footnote 1, pp. 200 *et seq.*

General above all derived sources of law[1] and which also stipulates that the administration is bound by statute. An example of this statutory constraint on the administration is the ground for contesting a decision found in Article 8, paragraph 1a of the AROB law, according to which administrative decisions can be contested if it is alleged that they infringe a generally binding provision.[2]

The primacy of statute is restricted by Article 94 of the Basic Law (Gw.) of 1983,[3] according to which a national law is not applied if its application cannot be reconciled with generally binding provisions of international treaties and decisions of international organisations.[4] This rule is chiefly important in the area of European Community law.[5]

2. The Requirement that there be a Statute

The liberal constitutional state of the nineteenth century was characterised by a strict separation of powers and the grant of individual fundamental rights and freedoms in a basic law.[6] From this followed the basic principle that the administration must act in conformity with statute, and according to this principle the freedom of the individual citizen may not be encroached upon except on the basis of statute (the requirement of a statute).[7] This principle of legality is expressed in Article 89, paragraph 2, Gw. of 1983.[8] According to this provision, rules in general administrative orders which carry a penalty for non-observance may be promulgated only by virtue of a statute. When it is also borne in mind that

---

[1] cf. A. M. Donner, Nederlands Bestuursrecht, Algemeen Deel (4th ed.), Alphen a/d Rijn 1974, p. 77; C. W. van der Pot, Handboek van het Nederlandse Staatsrecht, edited by A. M. Donner (9th ed., Zwolle 1972), p. 387.

[2] Rapport van de commissie inzake algemene bepalingen van administratief recht (Rapport ABAR), (5th ed.), Alphen a/d Rijn 1984, p. 55, footnote 2: a provision is generally binding if it is enacted by the public authorities on the basis of a power to impose rules resting directly or indirectly on statute.

[3] Previously Article 66 of the 1972 Basic Law.

[4] A. M. Donner, op. cit., footnote 1, p. 77.

[5] Ibid.

[6] cf. P. de Haan, Th.G. Drupsteen, R. Fernhout, Bestuursrecht in de sociale rechtsstaat (2nd ed., Deventer 1978), p. 11.

[7] P. de Haan, Th.G. Drupsteen, R. Fernhout, op. cit., footnote 6, p. 11; A. M. Donner, op. cit., footnote 1, p. 31.

[8] Previously Article 57 of the 1972 Basic Law.

subsidiary public organs may be authorised to enact regulations only through or under statute, and that a transfer of powers, *e.g.* to a Minister, through general administrative orders will invariably require some statutory authority, this leads to the conclusion that the principle of legality in the sense of a comprehensive requirement of a statutory basis for administrative provisions which impose obligations, has been applied to the fullest possible extent.[9]

The general rule that a citizen is bound only by decisions based, directly or indirectly, on a statutory source is subject to one class of exceptions, which has acquired significance with the transition from the liberal to the social constitutional state. These are internal administrative rules (comparable to administrative provisions in German law), with a bearing on particular functional relationships and on the law on subsidies.[10] The area of subsidies, in particular, has continued to grow in importance. Since subsidies, however, being administrative provisions which confer rights, do not require a statutory basis,[11] a substantial area of administrative activity is excluded from statutory control.

XI. THE PRINCIPLE OF LEGALITY IN PORTUGAL

In Portuguese administrative law since 1974, the legality principle has developed in a conceptual fashion which is typical of the political upheaval. The term "democratic legality," coined as a compromise between the concepts of "socialist legality" and "constitutional State," was largely replaced, as a consequence of the 1982 constitutional revision, by the concept of the "democratic constitutional State."[1] However, apart from terminological peculiarities both the Government and the administration in Portugal are subject to statute. Meanwhile the Government, by contrast with the constitutional arrangements of most of the other Member States of the EEC, has an independent legislative competence in the areas not attributed to Parliament, and it exercises this competence by promulgating statutory orders.[2] In any case, intervention by the admin-

---

[9] A. M. Donner, *op. cit.*, footnote 1, pp. 78 *et seq.*; ABAR Report, *op. cit.*, footnote 1, pp. 55 and 104.

[10] A. M. Donner, *op. cit.*, footnote 1, pp. 79 *et seq.*; *cf.* also P. de Haan, Th.G. Drupsteen, R. Fernhout, *op. cit.*, footnote 6, p. 150.

[11] P. de Haan, Th.G. Drupsteen, R. Fernhout, *op. cit.*, footnote 6, p. 150; *cf.* here also the critique of this trend.

[1] See above, Chapter 2, Section 11.

[2] Article 201 of the revised Constitution.

istration in the fundamental rights guaranteed by the Constitution requires legitimation through an Act of Parliament.[3]

XII. THE PRINCIPLE OF LEGALITY IN SPAIN

The Constitution of December 12, 1978 makes Spain a democratic, social constitutional State in the form of a parliamentary monarchy.[1] Under Article 9, paragraph 1 the State authorities are subject to the Constitution and to the legal system in general. Article 9, paragraph 3 defines the classic elements of the constitutional State, such as the principles of legality, the hierarchy of legal norms, the public character of legal norms, the non-retroactivity of sanctions and legal certainty, as well as responsibility and the veto on arbitrary action by the public authorities. Chapter IV of the Constitution, on "Government and administration," assigns to the Government the executive function and the power of enacting regulations, powers which it must exercise in accordance with the Constitution and with statute (Article 97). Restrictions on the fundamental rights of the citizen are subject to the requirement of a statute and are ultimately limited by the "substantive guarantee" in Article 53, paragraph 1(2).[2]

B. CONCLUSIONS FROM THE SURVEY OF STATE PRACTICE

1. Foundations of the Principle of Legality in the National Constitutions

The principle of the legality of the administration is the cardinal element in the practice of the liberal bourgeois democratic constitutional state. The idea of the State governed by law is the underlying principle of organisation in the constitutions of all Member States. Regardless of the name it is given or the form it takes, the powers of the state are limited in

---

[3] cf. A. Thomashausen, "Der Freiheitsbegriff, die Grundrechte und der Grundrechtsschutz in der neuen Portugiesischen Verfassung vom 2. April 1976," EuGRZ 1981, pp. 1 et seq. (4).

[1] Constitución Española de 1978, B.O.E. no. 311 of December 29, 1978; cf. A. Weber, "Die spanische Verfassung von 1978," J.ö.R. new series 29 (1980), p. 209; there is an annex (p. 252 et seq.) containing a German translation.

[2] See A. Weber, op. cit., footnote 1, p. 221.

every country by law, for the purpose of protecting civil liberties. Under the influence of the democratic principle, Acts of Parliament have become the most significant legal constraint on the State's area of influence.

In all Member States, the rule of law has been further developed to become a set of broader legal constraints on the administration. In some States this also covers constitutional law, especially the securing of fundamental rights, which, as directly applicable legal principles, are decisive in shaping the pattern of administrative decisions, especially in the Federal Republic of Germany.

II. VARIATIONS IN THE FIGURATION OF THE PRINCIPLE OF LEGALITY

That the principle is expressed in a variety of different ways is due to the role of the various parliaments under the different constitutional arrangements in ensuring the legality of the administration in the narrow sense.

In all the States of the European Community, formal parliamentary statutes take priority over secondary legislation. In this respect, there is no difference in the position of the various representative assemblies. Such differences as exist become apparent only if we inquire which state decisions may be made only through, or on the basis of, a statute.

In all the Member States we have considered, statutory reservation applies wherever freedom and property are encroached upon. Here we see the common heritage of the conceptual tradition of the liberal bourgeois constitutional movement.

The French Constitution has the characteristic feature that it gives Parliament only a limited range of legislative powers and assigns to the executive a general right to make regulations in other fields. However, in France too the classic forms of intervention in civil liberties are subject to statutory reservation. The same applies to Portugal, although the Portuguese Constitution limits the autonomous legislative powers of the Government by requiring parliamentary agreement.

This is not the case in the other Member States—apart from the royal prerogative. Generally speaking, statutory reservation applies to rule-making by the administration; in the Federal Republic of Germany there is even a qualified statutory reservation, under which the content, the purpose and the extent of the delegated authority must be defined by statute. What is relatively new, and has therefore apparently excited little comment, is the extension of statutory reservation to the administration.

231

The extension of statutory reservation seems to have generated most interest in the Federal Republic of Germany. But in Denmark and the United Kingdom too, some trends are now emerging along these lines. It may be concluded that in all Member States there is a tendency to subject administrative conduct to closer scrutiny and regulation.

III. UNLAWFUL ADMINISTRATIVE CONDUCT

The emergence of legal flaws in administrative conduct is closely linked to the development of a proper judicial review procedure. For lack of space it is not possible to describe this development here even briefly. It will suffice to say that the French *contentieux administratif* with its *cas d'ouverture* has had great influence on the concept of legal protection in a number of other European States. The United Kingdom is an exception; because of its independent legal system, almost inevitably it has had to take a different path. But the German system of administrative law, too, despite some intellectual borrowings from its French neighbour, has also formed its own standards for scrutinising administrative conduct.

SECTION 2

THE PRINCIPLE OF LEGALITY IN EUROPEAN COMMUNITY LAW

A. INTRODUCTION—TERMINOLOGY

The concept of the legality principle has to be adjusted to conditions in the Communities. A national law, in whatever language it is framed, is a binding instrument freely adopted by the representative assembly of the country concerned. The idea of law is inspired by democracy.[1]

In the literature it has often been said that the European Community has no law, in a constitutional sense. In the first place, it lacks a parliament with full legislative powers; in the second place, there are structural differences between Community and national legal systems which forbid the drawing of any such parallel.[2] However, adapting the principle of legality to Community conditions, a necessary process in these circumstances, does not mean that it is wholly foreign to the structural principles found in State practice. In the preceding comparative law survey it has been shown that even in the modern State, the "legality of the administration" is a phrase which only partly defines the relationship of the executive to the law. What was originally thought of as "legality" (conformity with statute) has long since become the more general concept of compliance by the administration with law generally. If this latter concept is here used for the Community legal system, it comes unencumbered by any national associations or implications. The only question it poses is the relationship between the Community authorities and the law, a question which will be examined in more detail below.

B. THE PRINCIPLE OF LEGALITY IN THE LEGAL SYSTEM OF THE EUROPEAN COMMUNITIES—THE UNDERLYING STRUCTURES

The problem raised in this section touches upon the very foundations of

---

[1] On the democratic concept of law in general, see D. Jesch, *Gesetz und Verwaltung* (2nd ed., Tübingen 1968), pp. 26 *et seq.*
[2] *cf.* H. P. Ipsen, *Europäisches Gemeinschaftsrecht*, Tübingen 1972, p. 320.

the Community, and the related questions which arise are no less complex.

Even in the context of this study, it is impossible to do more than sketch in the various aspects of the legality principle. Almost every one of these would warrant a separate study of its own, whereas all that can be covered here is the basic elements of a principle fundamental to the Community legal system.

I. THE PRIMACY ACCORDED TO SUPERIOR LAW

1. The Principle

The priority accorded to statute in the various national legal systems, understood in a broader sense as the priority of the superior legal rule, is reflected in Community law by a corresponding principle.[3] There is a clear connection with positive law in Article 3, paragraph 1 of the ECSC Treaty, in the requirement that the institutions of the Coal and Steel Community should fulfil their functions "within the limits of their respective powers." According to Article 3, paragraph 1 of the EEC Treaty, the European Economic Community carries out its functions "as provided in this Treaty."

The Council and the Commission act in specific fields, according to the three Treaties, within the limits of the functions and responsibilities entrusted to them (Articles 1 and 9 of the Merger Treaty and Articles 145 and 155 of the EEC Treaty).

Moreover, decisions and regulations in breach of the Treaty or of one of the legal rules under which it is implemented will be declared void by the European Court (Article 33 of the ECSC Treaty, Article 173 of the EEC Treaty, Article 146 of the Euratom Treaty). The highest category of rules is therefore to be found in the Treaty provisions, and secondary legislation must be judged in the light of those provisions. The status of the other sources of law is considered in detail below.

---

[3] H.-W. Rengeling, *Rechtsgrundsätze beim Verwaltungsvollzug des Europäischen Gemeinschaftsrechts*, Cologne/Berlin/Bonn/Munich 1977, p. 260.

2. Survey of European Community Law

The law of the European Community comprises normative rules such as treaty provisions or regulations, and also individual acts, such as the decisions mentioned in the EEC and Euratom treaties. In the past it has always been sufficient merely to state that this European Community law exists. But when, it may be asked, does a rule belong to the "law of the European Community"? The Treaty provisions undoubtedly possess legal force. With the actions of the Community institutions, however, it is more difficult to distinguish legal from non-legal acts (see (a) below). It is also necessary to consider when, and for how long, a legal act is effective and under what circumstances it can be contested (see (b)). Finally, by classifying the various kinds of binding legal acts, it is possible to arrange them into a hierarchy of Community law and thereby to answer the question which takes priority in individual cases (see (c)).

(a) The distinction between binding instruments and non-binding statements

(aa) Positive law distinctions

The Treaties are the starting-point when determining the legal character of an act by a Community institution. Article 14 of the ECSC Treaty distinguishes between decisions, recommendations and opinions. According to Article 14, paragraph 2 of the ECSC Treaty, decisions shall be binding in their entirety, whereas according to paragraph 3 of the same provisions, recommendations are binding only as to the aims to be pursued, those to whom the recommendations are addressed being free to choose the methods. Opinions, on the other hand, are expressly (paragraph 4) defined as having no binding force. The same concept is found in Article 189 of the EEC Treaty, although different terms are used for the legal acts in question. Regulations, like decisions, are binding in their entirety; directives are binding only as to the result to be achieved. EEC recommendations and opinions, like the opinions of the ECSC, have no binding force. The same applies to Article 161 of the Euratom Treaty, which is identical to Article 189 of the EEC Treaty. The list of acts of Community organs found in these key provisions could be considerably lengthened by the addition of the various modes of expression of the

Community found in the Treaty and in secondary legislation.[4] Provision is made for communications, declarations, information statements, etc., but in most cases they are defined as lacking any positive law effects. The European Court was therefore obliged, at an early stage, to develop generally applicable criteria for distinguishing binding from non-binding acts of the E.C. institutions.

(bb) Distinguishing criteria used by the European Court

The distinction between binding acts of the E.C. organs and non-binding statements has been a major concern of the European Court, initially in the framework of the Coal and Steel Community, and later also in the area of the EEC,[5] especially in cartel proceedings.[6] The judgment in Joined Cases 7/56 and 3/57 to 7/57 *Algera and others* v. *Common Assembly*,[7] which has attracted much attention on other grounds, is also worthy of mention in this connection.

These cases concerned the regrading of the complainants, all salaried staff of the Common Assembly, to a different salary category, a move which they vehemently contested. The contested decision was contained in a letter addressed to the complainants by the Vice-President of the Assembly and in a communication from the Deputy Secretary-General to the staff of the Common Assembly, from which the consequences for the complainants could be inferred if they persisted in refusing the regrading. The Court found that the letter from the Vice-President constituted a decision[8]:

> "That letter makes sufficiently clear the action which the Common
> Assembly intended to take in relation to the applicants' situation if

---

[4] *cf.* B. Beutler, R. Bieber, J. Pipkorn, J. Streil, *Die Europäische Gemeinschaft*, (3rd ed., Baden-Baden 1987), p. 186.

[5] *cf.* the judgment in the *AETR* Case, 22/70 [1971] E.C.R. 263 *et seq.* on the legal character of a Council decision; pp. 276 *et seq.*, esp. p. 278, paras. 52 to 55 of the judgment. *cf.* also Case 67/69, *Semet* v. *Commission* [1971] E.C.R. 197 *et seq.*, concerning a Council recommendation in the case of an assent according to Articles 28 and 53 of the ECSC Treaty; Case 143/80 *Amministrazione delle Finanze dello Stato* v. *Essevi Spa and others* [1981] E.C.R. 1413 *et seq.*, esp. p. 1433, paras. 16 and 17; Case 129/75, *Hirschberg* v. *Commission* [1976] E.C.R. 1259 *et seq.* (1269 *et seq.*) (law of E.C. civil service).

[6] Joined Cases 8–11/66, *Noordwijks Cement Accord* v. *Commission* [1967] E.C.R. 100 *et seq.*

[7] 1957, pp. 83 *et seq.*

[8] *Op. cit.*, p. 116.

236

they persisted in refusing to accept the proposals which had previously been made to them in Mr Vanrullen's letter of 27 June 1956."

As for the communication from the Deputy Secretary-General, the question arose whether it constituted a decision in respect of the complainants. This communication was directed to all salaried staff of the Assembly. On this point the European Court found as follows[9]:

"It may be asked whether Communication No. 56/13 of 15 October 1956 constitutes a decision in relation to the applicants or only a source of information from which they could infer that they would no longer receive the salary to which they were entitled under the orders of 12 December 1955. The decision of the Bureau of the Assembly not to apply the Staff Regulations to the applicants and not to grant them the salary provided for by the orders of 12 December 1955 was not expressly communicated to them. However, this behaviour on the part of the defendant cannot deprive the applicants of their right of appeal.
For that reason, the Court also admits the Application directed against Communication No. 56/13 of 15 October 1956, since it is only by that communication that the applicants were informed that Mr Vanrullen's proposals had been confirmed by the Bureau, which Communication No. 56/12 expressed only indirectly. Thus, in claiming the annulment of the 'decision of 15 October 1956,' the applicants have in view the implied decision of the defendant not to allow them either the salary or the classification which had been conferred on them by the orders of 12 December 1955."

The decision in Joined Cases 42 and 49/59 *SNUPAT* v. *High Authority*[10] clearly defines the principles according to which the Court distinguishes between binding decisions and non-binding communications.

The relevant object of claim in these cases was a letter from the Director of the Market Division of the High Authority, dated August 7, 1959, rejecting compensation claims which had been entered by the SNUPAT company for the exemption of existing scrap reserves from an equalisation levy payable by competing firms. The question arose whether SNUPAT could proceed against the statement in the letter under Article 33, paragraph 1 of the ECSC Treaty. For it to do so, the

---

[9] *Op. cit.*, pp. 116 *et seq.*
[10] 1961, pp. 111 *et seq.*

letter would have to constitute a decision by the High Authority within the meaning of Article 14 of the ECSC Treaty.

The Court found that the letter did not constitute a decision[11]:

> "In fact the letter in question does not constitute a decision of the High Authority either in its form or in its content.
> As regards its form, this letter was signed solely by the Director of the Market Division, acting in his own name and not in the name and on behalf of the High Authority; it cannot therefore be regarded as a decision of the High Authority. As regards its content, it merely states that the judgments of the Court of Justice of 17 July 1959 will be considered by the departments of the High Authority which will take the necessary decisions, and that the Market Division sees no basis for the claim for compensation for a wrongful act or omission. Such a statement does not establish any general rule and does not conclusively affect any individual interest."

This method of differentiation is confirmed by the judgment of the European Court of June 16, 1966, in Case 54/65, *Compagnie des Forges de Châtillon, Commentry et Neuves-Maisons* v. *High Authority of the ECSC*. Here the Court stated[12]:

> "... the declarations ... in no way constitute genuine 'decisions.' A decision must in fact appear as a measure emanating from the competent authority, intended to produce legal effects and constituting the culmination of procedure within that authority, whereby the latter gives its final ruling in a form from which its nature can be identified.
> In this instance, certain of these conditions were absent."

To sum up, a binding act—in this case, a decision—will therefore exist if:

— it is a measure emanating from the competent authority[13]

---

[11] *Op. cit.*, p. 154.

[12] 1966, pp. 529 *et seq.*

[13] *cf.* Case 19/60, *Société Fives Lille Cie and others* v. *High Authority*, [1961] E.C.R. 611 *et seq.*, in which Advocate-General Roemer, on a comparative law basis (pp. 699 *et seq.*), describes an instrument issued in clear breach of authority as a non-act.

- which culminates in a procedure in which the authority gives its final ruling, and
- the ruling, in its outward form, can be identified as a decision relating to the recipient (the addressee).

(b) Effectiveness, nullity and invalidity of legal instruments

(aa) Effectiveness of legal acts

According to Article 15, paragraph 2 of the ECSC Treaty, decisions and recommendations of an individual character become binding upon being notified to the party concerned. Decisions and recommendations of a general nature take effect when they have been published (paragraph 3).

EEC and Euratom regulations are published in the Official Journal and come into force either on the date specified in them or on the twentieth day following their publication (Article 191, paragraph 1 of the EEC Treaty, Article 163, paragraph 1 of the Euratom Treaty). Directives and decisions take effect when notified to those to whom they are addressed.

(bb) Nullity according to Article 33 ECSC Treaty, Article 173 EEC Treaty, Article 146 Euratom Treaty

(1) Grounds of Action

(a) EEC and Euratom Treaties

Under Article 173, paragraph 1 of the EEC Treaty and Article 146 of the Euratom Treaty, the Member States, the Council or the Commission may contest acts of the Council or the Commission on the grounds of lack of competence, infringement of an essential procedural requirement or of the Treaties, or of any rule of law relating to their application, or misuse of powers.

Article 173, paragraph 2 of the EEC Treaty provides that a person to whom the decision is addressed may contest it under the same conditions as in paragraph 1. In addition, individuals may contest decisions which take the form of regulations or are addressed to other persons, but which are of direct and individual concern to themselves.[14]

(b) ECSC Treaty

The comparable provision in the ECSC Treaty to Article 173 of the EEC Treaty is Article 33, whereby Member States and the Council, according to paragraph 1, may contest decisions and recommendations on the same grounds as in Article 173, paragraph 1 of the EEC Treaty. Article 33, paragraph 2 of the ECSC Treaty distinguishes between decisions and recommendations of an individual character, which may be contested by undertakings and certain types of associations under the conditions laid down in paragraph 1, and general decisions and recommendations,[15] which may be contested by such undertakings and selected associations only if it is contended that there is a misuse of powers.

A special feature of the ECSC Treaty is that failure to act, in the sense of a manifest refusal by the negligent organ to do so, is treated as a ground for avoidance. In Article 175 of the EEC Treaty and Article 148 of the Euratom Treaty, this legal remedy becomes an action for a declaratory judgment, which, however, is given compulsory effect through Article 176 of the EEC Treaty and Article 149 of the Euratom Treaty.[15a] But what is crucial to the point here at issue, the binding character of EEC instruments, is the consequence of a successful claim.

(2) Legal Consequences of Annulment of Legal Acts

(a) General

If a claim is justified under Article 173 of the EEC Treaty or Article 146 of the Euratom Treaty, the Court declares the act concerned to be void

---

[14] On the restricted right of private individuals to institute proceedings, see: H. W. Daig, in Groeben, Boeckh, Thiesing, Ehlermann, *Kommentar zum EWG-Vertrag* (3rd ed., Baden-Baden 1983), Article 73, no. 5 *et seq.*, pp. 320 *et seq.*; *cf.* also Case 97/85 *Union Deutsche Lebensmittelwerke and others* v. *Commission* [1987] E.C.R. 2265, para. 10.

[15] On the distinction between individual and general decisions, see B. Börner, *Die Entscheidungen der Hohen Behörde*, 1965, pp. 117 *et seq.*, with references to the case law.

[15a] *cf.* H. W. Daig, *op. cit.*, footnote 14, Article 175, no. 6, p. 363.

(Article 174 EEC Treaty, Article 147 Euratom Treaty). The same legal consequence follows from Articles 33 and 34 of the ECSC Treaty, but it must also be asked: what are the effects?

(b) Validity pending annulment

A nullity declaration by the Court is a judgment *in rem*; it therefore has a constitutive effect. The contested act is therefore treated as effective until judgment is delivered, as the European Court pointed out in Case 101/78, *Granaria BV* v. *Hoofdproduktschap voor Akkerbouwprodukten.*[16]

This case, brought under Article 177 of the EEC Treaty, dealt with the legal consequences for certain trade sectors of the earlier invalidation of a Council regulation on the compulsory purchase of skimmed milk powder.

> "The first question asks, in essence, whether the competent national administrative authority was obliged to refuse to issue a 'protein certificate' pursuant to Regulation 563/76 to all those persons who did not fulfil the conditions laid down by that regulation as long as it had not been declared to be invalid.
>
> Every regulation which is brought into force in accordance with the Treaty must be presumed to be valid as long as a competent court has not made a finding that it is invalid.
>
> This presumption may be derived, on the one hand, from Articles 173, 174 and 184 of the Treaty, which reserve to the Court of Justice alone the power to review the legality of regulations and to determine, where necessary, to what extent they are to be declared to be invalid and, on the other hand, from Article 177, which empowers the same Court to give rulings as a court of last instance on the validity of regulations where a dispute on that issue has been brought before a national court."[17]

The Court also explains why validity can be presumed[18]:

> "Thus it follows from the legislative and judicial system established by the Treaty that, although respect for the principle of the rule of

---

[16] [1979] E.C.R. 623 *et seq.*
[17] *Op. cit.*, p. 636, para. 4.
[18] *Op. cit.*, p. 637, para. 5.

law within the Community context entails for persons amenable to Community law the right to challenge the validity of regulations by legal action, that principle also imposes upon all persons subject to Community law the obligation to acknowledge that regulations are fully effective so long as they have not been declared to be invalid by a competent court."

(c) Effects of annulment under Article 173 EEC Treaty

A declaration that a legal act is void takes effect *ex tunc* and *erga omnes*.[19] The *AETR* decision, which is the basis of the Community's capacity to conclude external agreements, explains that[20]:

> "Under Article 174, 'If the action is well-founded the Court of Justice shall declare the act concerned to be void.' If that were done, the Council's proceedings would have to be deemed non-existent in so far as they had been annulled by the Court; the parties to the dispute would then be restored to their original position, and would have to reconsider the disputed questions so as to resolve them in accordance with Community law."

There is also a duty under Article 34 of the ECSC Treaty, Article 176 of the EEC Treaty and Article 149 of the Euratom Treaty, on the institutions whose acts are declared void, to take the steps required by the judgment.

(d) Continuing applicability of a void regulation

By way of exception, under the second paragraph of Article 174 of the EEC Treaty the Court may determine that certain effects of a regulation declared void shall be considered as definitive. Here the Treaty allows for the special character of a regulation which also forms the basis of rights and duties for citizens throughout the Community.

This ensures that the annulment of a basic regulation cannot cause the collapse of the body of law derived from it, since the lawfulness of the

---

[19] J. Streil, *op. cit.*, footnote 4, p. 258; H. W. Daig, *op. cit.*, footnote 14, Article 174, no. 7, p. 360.
[20] Case 22/70 *Commission of the European Communities* v. *Council of the European Communities* [1971] E.C.R. 263 *et seq.* (279).

latter depends in turn on the validity of the underlying legal act.[21] Considerations of legal certainty and the protection of legitimate expectations are central to this treaty provision.[22]

The case law on the second paragraph of Article 174 of the EEC Treaty is somewhat sparse. One case in point was Case 81/72,[23] which concerned a regulation on salary payments for officials, certain articles of which had been declared void. The reasoning of the decision stated, on the point in question regarding the continuing application of certain effects, that[24]:

> "These Articles 1 to 4 must therefore be declared void. However, to avoid discontinuity in the system of remuneration, the second paragraph of Article 174 of the Treaty should be applied so that the Articles declared void shall continue to have effect until the Council passes a new Regulation in consequence of the present judgment."[25]

One reason for the reluctance to apply the second paragraph of Article 174 of the Treaty may be that in legal proceedings, the validity of regulations is tested chiefly according to Article 177, and if the second paragraph of Article 174 of the EEC Treaty is applied it must be done in a similar manner.

(3) Effects of a declaration of invalidity under subparagraph (b) of Article 177 EEC Treaty

(a) Preliminary remark on tests of validity under subparagraph (b) of Article 177 EEC Treaty

Because of the overriding importance of Article 177 of the EEC Treaty in monitoring the legality of regulations and of other legal acts, special interest attaches to the effects of a finding of invalidity under this provision.

Whereas Article 173 of the ECSC Treaty refers to the "legality" of a legal act, subparagraph (b) of Article 177 of the EEC Treaty uses

---

[21] H. W. Daig, *op. cit.*, footnote 14, Article 174, no. 3, p. 358.
[22] *Ibid.* see also Advocate-General Trabucchi in Case 91/75, *HZA Göttingen* v. *Miritz* [1976] E.C.R. 217 *et seq.* (238).
[23] *Commission* v. *Council* [1973] E.C.R. 575 *et seq.*
[24] *Op. cit.*, footnote 23, p. 586.
[25] *Op. cit.*, footnote 23, p. 586, para. 15 of the judgment.

the term "validity." Although the language of that subparagraph of the EEC Treaty suggests that the test should be confined to the existence or otherwise of a rule of law,[26] the Court, in its case law, has consistently used this clause as a comprehensive test of legality, although restricting it to the grounds of claim stated in Article 173 of the EEC Treaty and to the questions actually submitted.[27] In practice a reference under subparagraph (b) of Article 177 of the EEC Treaty, contrary to the original intentions of the treaty's authors, has acquired much wider significance than a claim for annulment under Article 173 of the EEC Treaty. The question of the effects of invalidity is therefore extremely important.

(b) Invalidity according to subparagraph (b) of Article 177 EEC Treaty

A finding by the European Court that a provision is invalid will at once render it inapplicable to the case before it.[28] It is questionable, however, whether a finding of invalidity also takes effect "erga omnes." Advocate-General Gand, in Case 16/65, *Firma G. Schwarze* v. *Einfuhr und Vorratsstelle für Getreide und Futtermittel* argued that the decision took effect only for the case in question[29]:

> "It seems that the problem should be formulated as follows: When this Court rules, on a point referred to it by a national court within the framework of Article 177 procedure, that a measure is invalid, what are the consequences of the *res judicata* effect of its judgment? Are they relative, or do they bind all and sundry? Although authorities are divided on this point, I have no hesitation in adopting the first solution. A detailed distinction must be drawn between the extent and the effects of an annulment of a measure on application under Article 173, and a declaration of illegality under Article 177.

---

[26] On the matter of restriction to a test of legal existence, see H. W. Daig, *op. cit.*, footnote 14, Article 172, no. 22, pp. 395 *et seq.*

[27] *cf.* the Court's standard utterance, that an examination of the questions in issue had revealed no elements capable of affecting the validity of the provision concerned. Examples from a wide body of case law include: Case 92/77 *An Bord Bainne Cooperative Limited* v. *Minister for Agriculture* [1978] E.C.R. 497 *et seq.* (p. 515, paras. 38 to 39); Case 5/73 *Balkan-Import Export GmbH* v. *HZA Berlin-Packhof* [1973] E.C.R. 1091 *et seq.* (1116, para. 42). On certain views which require official consideration see J. Streil, *op. cit.*, footnote 4, p. 242, which argues for an independent examination by the Court in the context of Article 177 of the EEC Treaty on the basis that, under Article 164 of the Treaty, the Court is the guardian of the law.

[28] *cf.* Case 52/76 *Benedetti* v. *Munari* [1977] E.C.R. 67 *et seq.* (p. 183, paras. 26 to 27).

[29] [1965] E.C.R. 1152 (1181 *et seq.*).

In the first case, the action is initiated by a person who enjoys a right to appeal; it is covered by a strict time-limit, to avoid prolonging the period of doubt. The wide effects of a successful appeal are balanced by the restrictions on its admissibility. A national court or tribunal, on the other hand, can at any time ask for your opinion on the validity of a measure against which the time for appealing has long since expired. It refers a dispute to you in order to enable it to decide a case before it, and it is sufficient if the effects of your judgment are confined to the framework of that case. Were we to do otherwise and give general effect to the declaration of illegality, we would, in effect, be reviving a right of action time-barred under Article 173 every time a case before a national court raised a question as to the validity of a measure of one of the Community institutions. I therefore consider that a decision which is declared to be unlawful is deprived of its force only in relation to the parties to the principal action; in other words, if you consider the decision of 24 January 1964 not to be valid, Schwarze may rely on your judgment, but not the other importers, who are not parties to the action but who are affected by the same levies. Thus the reply to Question 4 which I would suggest does not fall into any of the categories suggested by the Finanzgericht."

By contrast, in Case 112/76, *Manzoni* v. *FNROM* Advocate-General Warner expressed a more cautious view.[30]

In Case 4/79, *Providence Agricole de la Champagne* v. *ONIC* the Court ruled as follows on the consequences of invalidity[31]:

"Although the Treaty does not expressly lay down the consequences which follow from a declaration of invalidity within the framework of a reference to the Court for a preliminary ruling, Articles 174 and 176 contain clear rules as to the effects of the annulment of a regulation within the framework of a direct action. Thus Article 176 provides that the institution whose act has been declared void shall be required to take the necessary measures to comply with the judgment of the Court of Justice. In its judgments of 19 October 1977 in Joined Cases 117/76 and 16/77 (*Ruckdeschel und Hansa Lagerhaus Ströh (Quellmehl)* [1977] E.C.R. 1753) and in Joined Cases 124/76 and 20/77 (*Moulins et Huileries de Pont-à-Mousson and Providence*

---

[30] [1977] E.C.R. 1647 *et seq.* (1622 *et seq.*).
[31] [1980] E.C.R. 2823 (2853, para. 44).

Agricole de la Champagne (Maize groats and meal) [1977] E.C.R. 1975) the Court has already referred to that rule within the context of a reference to it for a preliminary ruling."

The Court considers that the provisions cited here, which apply to nullity judgments under Articles 174 and 176 of the EEC Treaty, are applicable by analogy to proceedings under subparagraph (b) of Article 177. In paragraph 45 of the judgment, the Court's position on the effects of invalidity also emerges indirectly:

"In this case it is necessary to apply by analogy the second paragraph of Article 174 of the Treaty, whereby the Court of Justice may state which of the effects of the regulation which it has declared void shall be considered as definitive, for the same reasons of legal certainty as those which form the basis of that provision. On the one hand the invalidity of the regulation in this case might give rise to the recovery of sums paid but not owed by the undertakings concerned in countries with depreciated currencies and by the national authorities in question in countries with hard currencies which, in view of the lack of uniformity of the relevant national legislation, would be capable of causing considerable differences in treatment, thereby causing further distortion in competition. On the other hand, it is impossible to appraise the economic disadvantages resulting from the invalidity of the fixing of the monetary compensatory amounts under the system of calculation adopted by the Commission without making assessments which that institution alone is required to make under Regulation No. 974/71, having regard to other relevant factors, for example the allocation of the maximum permissible amount amongst the various derived or dependent producers."

The Court, by applying the requirements resulting from this decision in different countries, clearly shows what general effect it attributes to a declaration of invalidity. Indeed it is inconceivable that the Court would rely on the second paragraph of Article 174 of the EEC Treaty if it assumed that the effects applied only to the case before it.[32] The Court's

---

[32] See H. W. Daig, *op. cit.*, footnote 4, Article 177, no. 52, p. 407; for an effect of nullity see C. Tomuschat, *Die gerichtliche Vorabentscheidung nach den Verträgen über die europäischen Gemeinschaften*, Cologne, Berlin 1964, p. 180. Other examples of the Court's case law include: Case 109/79 *Maiseries de Beauce* v. *ONIC* [1980] E.C.R. 2913 *et seq.* (2915, para. 2); Case 149/79, *Roquette Frères* v. *French Customs Administration* [1980] E.C.R.

judgment of May 13, 1981, *International Chemical Corporation* v. *Amministrazione delle Finanze* makes this clear[33]:

> "Although a judgment of the Court given under Article 177 of the Treaty declaring an act of an institution, in particular a Council or Commission regulation, to be void is directly addressed only to the national court which brought the matter before the Court, it is sufficient reason for any other national court to regard that act as void for the purposes of a judgment which it has to give."

Since this does not, however, mean that national courts lose the powers conferred on them by Article 177 of the EEC Treaty, it is for these courts to determine whether they are of interest if the Court has found an action by a Community institution to be invalid. Such an interest may exist, principally, if uncertainty remains as to the grounds, the scope and perhaps the consequences of the invalidity which has already been established.

(c) *Authority to act and legal acts—sources of legality*

The concept of a legal source has already been explained in the Introduction and defined, in the sense attributed to it by Alf Ross, as "the basis for recognising something as law."[34] What follows is a glance at the essential sources of Community law. In the Community system, treaties, known as primary Community law, form the apex of the hierarchy of rules. What is known as secondary Community law, enacted on the basis of the treaties, consists of regulations, directives, general decisions (ECSC Treaty) and recommendations (ECSC Treaty).

Mention should also be made in this context of decisions addressed to States, the budget of the European Community (Article 78(h) of the ECSC Treaty, Article 209 of the EEC Treaty, Article 183 of the Euratom Treaty) and of the rules of procedure of Community institutions and other organisational arrangements of the Communities.

Decisions of the Council and of the Commission may also have legal effects. Finally, the international agreements of the Community also

---

2946 (2948); Case 66/80, SpA *International Chemical Corporation* v. *Amministrazione delle Finanze dello Stato* [1981] E.C.R. 1191 *et seq.* (1215 *et seq.*); Case 130/79 *Express Dairy Foods* v. *Intervention Board for Agricultural Produce* [1980] E.C.R. 1887 *et seq.* (1899, esp. pp. 1900 *et seq.*).

[33] [1981] E.C.R. 1191 *et seq.* (1216).

[34] A. Ross, *Theorie der Rechtsquellen*, 1929, pp. 298 *et seq.*

have binding force, as do the unwritten general principles of Community law.

3. The Hierarchy of Rules in Community Law

Sources or principles of law will be described here, in general terms, according to their "validity ranking."[35]

(a) Hierarchy within Community law

(aa) The Community treaties, including legal instruments of equivalent force,[36] and the regulations of the Council and of the Commission are inter-related according to a hierarchical order of priority.[37]

This applies unreservedly to the relationship between the Treaty and Council regulations; however, some qualification is needed for the relationship between the regulations of the Council and of the Commission.

When the Commission issues a regulation directly on the basis of the Treaties, in principle it will have the same status as a Council regulation.[38] However, when the Commission has authority to act under Article 155, fourth indent, of the EEC Treaty, a Commission regulation will have a

---

[35] H. J. Wolff, O. Bachof, *Verwaltungsrecht*, (9th ed., Munich, Berlin 1974), Vol. I, pp. 139 *et seq.*

[36] On the same level as the Treaties are supplementary agreements and protocols concluded among the Member States. The chief ones are: Protocol on the Statute of the European Court (Article 188, first paragraph, EEC Treaty) and of the European Investment Bank (Article 129, third paragraph, EEC Treaty), Protocol on the Privileges and Immunities of the European Communities, (Article 28 of the Merger Treaty); Protocol on intra-German trade and associated questions; Article 84 ECSC Treaty, Article 139 ECSC Treaty, Article 207 Euratom Treaty.

[37] *cf.* J. H. Kaiser, *Zur Anwendung von Artikel 85 Abs. 3 des EWG-Vertrags auf Gruppen von Kartellverträgen*, Cologne/Berlin/Bonn/Munich 1964, p. 16; on the application of a hierarchical principle to Community law, see also E. W. Fuss, *Die Europäischen Gemeinschaften und der Rechtsstaatsgedanke*, Heule 1967, pp. 61 *et seq.*; J. Schwarze, *Die Befugnis zur Abstraktion im Europäischen Gemeinschaftsrecht*, Baden-Baden 1976, p. 47.

[38] According to the case law of the European Court (*cf.* Joined Cases 188–190/80 *France* v. *Commission* [1982] E.C.R. 2545 on "transparency of financial relations") it cannot be inferred from the division, in the Treaties, of powers and responsibilities among the Community institutions that only the Council possesses the power to enact legislation, the Commission having only the functions of supervision and implementation. The Commission also may have the power to legislate under the special provisions of the Treaty, such as Article 90 EEC. Advocate-General Reischl has also commented to this effect in his opinion on these cases, *ibid.*, 2584 *et seq.*

status subsidiary to that of a basic Council regulation. If a Commission regulation infringes the underlying Council authorisation, it will be unlawful. This illustrates the principle that the bounds of delegated legislation are defined by the rule of delegation. In proceedings before the European Court, considerable attention is devoted to the question of reconciling implementing regulations under Article 155, fourth indent, of the EEC Treaty with the pertinent Council authorisation. From a substantial body of case law, one case may be selected to show the consequences of infringing the rule of delegation.[39]

In Case 34/78, *Yoshida* v. *Kamer van Koophandel en Fabrieken voor Friesland* (determination of the origin of slide fasteners),[40] the European Court had to decide whether an implementing regulation was compatible with the underlying Council regulation. Since, in its view, the Commission had exceeded the authority conferred on it in the Council regulation, it declared Article 1 of the regulation in question, No. 2067, to be "invalid."[41] This illustrates both the inter-relationship of Council and Commission regulations and the legal consequence of infringing the authorisation.

(bb) In descending order, the next level consists of individual administrative acts, which must be in conformity with the Treaties and with the general line of conduct of the Community institution.[42] The difficulties involved in drawing a dividing line between the rule and the individual act can only be mentioned here. This question is chiefly significant for purposes of judicial protection.[43] There are some indications in Article 189 of the EEC Treaty of where the dividing line should be drawn. One determining factor is to whom the sovereign measure is addressed. If the act issued by the EEC is directed to an undefined number of persons, it is a regulation or, in the ECSC Treaty, a general decision.[44] If, however, a

---

[39] *cf.* also Case 145/79 *SA Roquette Frères* v. *French State—Customs Administration* [1980] E.C.R. 2917 *et seq.* (2940, 2945).

[40] [1979] E.C.R. 115 *et seq.*

[41] *cf.* the Court's headnote at [1979] E.C.R. 115. See also earlier, Case 38/70 [1971] E.C.R. 145 ("*Tradax*"), according to which an implementing regulation—which in this case was issued by the Council itself, not the Commission—cannot alter the provisions of the basic regulation from which it is derived.

[42] E. W. Fuss, *op. cit.*, footnote 37, p. 62.

[43] *cf.* Article 173, paragraphs 1 and 2, of the EEC Treaty; Article 146, paragraphs 1 and 2, of the Euratom Treaty.

[44] *cf.* as examples from the Court's case law: Case 4/68 *Schwarzwaldmilch GmbH* v. *Einfuhr- und Vorratsstelle für Fette* [1968] E.C.R. 377 *et seq.* (headnote nos. 3 and 4, see also p. 620); in this case the opinion delivered by Advocate-General Roemer (624 *et seq.*) is instructive, distinguishing between norms and individual acts on a comparative law

Community act contains a conclusive definition of the persons to whom it is addressed, or indeed names these persons, it is a decision in the sense of an individual instrument.[45]

(cc) There is no particular difficulty in deciding what priority should be given to an EEC or Euratom directive, or a recommendation under the ECSC Treaty, provided they are clearly subordinate within the hierarchy of Community law.

If the authority to issue a directive is conferred by a legal act of the Council, the same principles apply as in the relationship between a basic Council regulation and an implementing regulation of the Commission, *i.e.* a hierarchical relationship. Directives issued directly on a treaty basis pose considerable problems as regards their hierarchical relationship to the other forms of action under the Treaties. There is no simple hierarchical category to cover the relationship between these and a regulation, a general decision and an individual decision. E. W. Fuss, somewhat hesitantly, has classified directives issued directly on the basis of the Treaties as lying between a regulation and an individual decision.[46] The Court has not yet had to rule on this problem. However, as long as the respective functions of regulations and directives are kept separate, there is little likelihood of any overlap between them.

(dd) It is no less problematic to reconcile general and specific international law with the system of rules prevailing in the Communities. Unlike, for instance, Article 25 of the German Basic Law or Article 55 of the French Constitution, the European Treaties contain no express provision on the applicability and status of general norms of international law.

As a result, how these norms are to be applied and what status they are to have can be inferred only from the "nature" of the Communities. A distinguishing feature of the Community legal system is that it is independent both constitutionally and as a system of regulation and dispute

---

basis, with reference to the case law of the European Court. Joined Cases 55–59 & 61–63/63, *Acciaierie di Modena* v. *High Authority* [1964] E.C.R. 211 *et seq.* (at 492); *cf.* also the opinion expressed by Advocate-General Roemer, on a comparative law basis (at 321 *et seq.*).

[45] *cf.* E. W. Fuss, *op. cit.*, footnote 37, p. 63.

[46] *Ibid.*, *op. cit.*, footnote 37, p. 64.

settlement[47]; there is no gap to be filled by general international law, which in principle is not applicable in intra-Community legal relations.[48]

In its jurisprudence, the Court has confirmed this principle, for example by refusing to admit conduct by a Member State contrary to the Treaties as a justification for breaches of the Treaties by another Member State, or by the Community itself.[49] If the Court were to allow such a plea in justification, this would be tantamount to allowing retorsion as a protective measure of general international law within the system of Community law.[50]

In determining the applicability and status of international treaty law, a pointer can be found in Article 228, paragraph 2 of the EEC Treaty, whereby agreements with non-Member States and international organisations are binding upon the Community institutions and upon the Member States.

Under Article 228, paragraph 1 of the EEC Treaty, the Community may conclude agreements which are incompatible with the Treaty only following an amendment of the Treaty according to Article 236. Under that article, international agreements are inferior in status to Treaty law.[51] Finally, from the language of Article 228, paragraph 2 of the EEC Treaty, it may be assumed that Community agreements are superior to secondary law, since their binding effect is expressed without reservation.[52] Even if this line of argument is rejected, the Court's case law at least points to such a conclusion. Joined Cases 21 to 24/72 *International Fruit Company*[53] were concerned with the validity of a Community regulation, which in the plaintiff's view was in contravention of GATT. The

---

[47] *cf.* the detailed exposition in J. Schwarze, "Das allgemeine Völkerrecht in den innergemeinschaftlichen Rechtsbeziehungen," EuR 1983, pp. 5 *et seq.*, esp. p. 34, considering the state of the controversy in the literature and surveying the case law on the question.

[48] *Ibid., op. cit.*, footnote 47, p. 33.

[49] The important cases for reliance on conduct contrary to the Treaty and the refusal to admit such conduct are Joined Cases 90 & 91/63 *Commission* v. *Belgium and Luxembourg* [1964] E.C.R. 1329 *et seq.* (esp. 1344).

[50] On the concept of retorsion, see: F. Berber, Lehrbuch des Völkerrechts (2nd ed., Munich 1977), Vol. 3, p. 94.

[51] For the generally held view see, among many other sources, L. J. Constantinesco, *Das Recht der europäischen Gemeinschaften I* (1st ed., Baden-Baden 1977), p. 219; A. Bleckmann, *Europarecht* (4th ed., Cologne/Berlin/Bonn/Munich 1985), p. 126.

[52] *cf.* L. J. Constantinesco, *op. cit.*, footnote 51, p. 219; see also A. Bleckmann, *op. cit.*, footnote 51, p. 126, which concludes that recognition by the jurisprudence of the European Court has the force of customary law.

[53] [1972] E.C.R. 1219 *et seq.*

European Court admitted the plea and commented as follows on the grounds for invalidity[54]:

> "Under that formulation (Art. 177, para. 1 of the EEC Treaty), the jurisdiction of the Court cannot be limited by the grounds on which the validity of those measures may be contested.
>
> Since such jurisdiction extends to all grounds capable of invalidating those measures, the Court is obliged to examine whether their validity may be affected by reason of the fact that they are contrary to a rule of international law."

(ee) Finally, mention must be made of the hierarchical status of general principles of law.[55] This topic has already been discussed in the Introduction and will be treated in detail in the specific sections, since it must be considered in context.

(*b*) *Hierarchy of rules in the relationship between the Community and the Member States*

The relationship of Community law to the law of the Member States is governed by the principle of direct effect and by the primacy of Community law. The cardinal principles laid down by case law on this point will be mentioned here only in summary fashion.[56]

In the administrative execution of Community law, the rule of primacy offers solutions for those cases where conflict would otherwise occur,

---

[54] *Op. cit.*, footnote 53, p. 1227, paras. 5 to 6.

[55] *cf.* also the investigation by H.-W. Rengeling *Rechtsgrundsätze beim Verwaltungsvollzug des europäischen Gemeinschaftsrechts*, Cologne/Berlin/Bonn/Munich 1977, pp. 212 *et seq.*

[56] The key cases for the direct effect of Community law are: Case 26/62 *Van Gend En Loos* v. *Nederlandse Belastingadministratie* [1963] E.C.R. 1; on the direct effect of regulations: Case 43/71 *Politi* v. *Italy* [1971] E.C.R. 1039; on the direct effect of directives: Case 33/70 *SACE* v. *Ministry for Finance of the Italian Republic* [1970] E.C.R. 1213 *et seq.*; Case 41/74 *Van Duyn* v. *Home Office* [1974] E.C.R. 1337 *et seq.*; Case 21/78 *Delkvist* v. *Anklagemyndigheden* [1978] E.C.R. 2329 *et seq.*; Case 148/78 *Ratti* [1979] E.C.R. 1629 *et seq.*

By contrast, see the judgment of the German Federal Finance Court of April 25, 1985, *Gerda Kloppenburg* v. *Finanzamt Leer* (on this see EuR 1985, pp. 191 *et seq.*), which holds that directives which have not been incorporated into national law within the time limit cannot have direct effect. From the French case law, *cf.* Conseil d'Etat, *Cohn-Bendit*, C.E. 1978, 524 *et seq.*, EuR 1979, p. 292 = DVBl. 1980, p. 126. For the legal position in Germany, however, *cf.* also the decision of the Federal Constitutional Court of April 8, 1987, rescinding the above-mentioned judgment of the Federal Finance Court in response to a constitutional complaint.

according to the definition of the scope and application of the Community rule, with national legislation having the same purpose.[57] The precise boundaries of the sphere of influence of Community law, as it can be defined with the aid of the precedence rule, will be clearer from the individual examples given.

II. "REQUIREMENT OF A STATUTE" IN COMMUNITY LAW

1. Terminology

We have had to look repeatedly at the terminological difficulties which invariably occur in any pronouncement on the question of "legality" in Community law. This is especially true of the question of "requirement of a statute" in the European legal system. This principle, in the form in which it is commonly found in national law, has no equivalent in Community law. The decisive factor, briefly described, in the division of functions among the Community institutions is the attempt to secure the interests of the Member States despite the Community's powers of decision-making. Primarily, therefore, it is not a question of protecting the individual sphere from the exercise of sovereign power, but of drawing a dividing line between Community and national powers of decision-making. As a result of this particular rule of interpretation, it is better to use for Community law terms which differ from those used in national law, such as reserved treaty powers or treaty reservation.

2. The Principle

(a) Reserved treaty powers

A determining principle of all conduct by the Community institutions is the principle of *compétence d'attribution*, also referred to as the principle of restricted or specific compctcncc.[58]

---

[57] On the conflicts which may also occur between substantive E.C. law and procedural national law, such as the time limits for appeals, see K. E. Huthmacher, *Der Vorrang des Gemeinschaftsrechts bei indirekten Kollisionen*, Cologne/Berlin/Bonn/Munich 1985.

[58] B. Beutler, R. Bieber, J. Pipkorn, J. Streil, *op. cit.*, footnote 4, p. 75: "Grundsatz der enumerativen Einzelermächtigung."

According to this principle, the Communities exercise responsibility only to the extent that the Treaties expressly confer authority on their institutions for the taking of specific measures. No institution possesses any general power of legislation.[59] The Treaties (*cf.* Article 4 of the EEC Treaty) express this principle as follows:

"Each institution shall act within the limits of the powers conferred upon it by this Treaty."

In their provisions the Treaties frequently establish not merely the actual scope of the acts issued by Community institutions, but also the manner in which the institutions must act. Freedom of action is thus restricted by the requirement for express authority, the constraints placed on that authority and the modes of action specified therein.

Where the scope for action is broadly defined, the Treaty establishes the principle of limitation in a variety of ways, by tighter requirements for voting majorities or by specifying that other institutions must take part in the process of decision-making.[60] If, however, no specific modes of action are prescribed in the authorisation itself, an interpretation must be made in order to determine what legal procedures are possible.[61]

The reserved treaty powers are the same regardless of the type of administrative act concerned—whether it confers rights, imposed duties, or exercises planning or other functions. In principle, the reservation always applies,[62] and is subject to only two exceptions: the creation of new powers under Article 235 of the EEC Treaty, Article 203 of the Euratom Treaty or Article 95 of the ECSC Treaty, and the exercise of so-called implied powers.[63]

Under the provision in Article 235 of the EEC Treaty which seeks to extend the powers of the Community through the inherent potential of the system, where action by the Community appears necessary in order to achieve one of the aims of the common market and the power to act is not

---

[59] H. P. Ipsen, *Europäisches Gemeinschaftsrecht*, Tübingen 1972, p. 427, 20/26.

[60] *cf.* H. P. Ipsen, *op. cit.*, footnote 59, p. 425; B. Beutler, J. Pipkorn, J. Streil, *op. cit.*, footnote 4, p. 75, top of left-hand column.

[61] H. P. Ipsen, *op. cit.*, footnote 59, p. 427.

[62] *cf.* H.-W. Rengeling, *op. cit.*, footnote 55, p. 260; H. Lecheler, *Der Europäische Gerichtshof und die allgemeinen Rechtsgrundsätze*, Diss. jur. 1967, p. 23, both with references to the case law.

[63] Ipsen, *op. cit.*, footnote 59, p. 432, 20/37, refers to a "correction" of the principle of limited individual competence through "special authority to fill gaps in the Treaties."

provided for, the Council may, on a proposal by the Commission and after consulting the Parliament, enact appropriate provisions by a unanimous decision.

The E.C.'s power to act under Article 235 of the EEC Treaty and the corresponding provisions of the other Treaties is not, therefore, derived from any express or specific conferment, but from the over-riding general aims of the Treaty, where these cannot be achieved by any other means.[64]

A further source of authority is found in the theory of "implied powers."[65] The European Court has made use of this theory to flesh out the existing powers of the Community in the following manner.[66]

The key case, 8/55 *Fédéchar* v. *High Authority*, concerned price-fixing by the High Authority for Belgian coal. For production reasons, the price of this coal was above the level in the other Member States, and it was supposed to be adjusted to the general level by means of price reductions and equalisation payments. This adjustment was to take place under Article 26 of the Convention on the Transitional Provisions, which did not, however, specify how it was to be achieved. The High Authority decided that prices should be fixed by itself. The complainant objected on the ground that the High Authority had no express power to fix prices.[67]

The Court found that the High Authority had no other practical option, and then turned to the question of its competence to make such a decision[68]:

> "The Court considers that without having recourse to a wide interpretation it is possible to apply a rule of interpretation generally accepted in both international and national law, according to which the rules laid down by an international treaty or a law presuppose the rules without which that treaty or law would have no meaning or could not be reasonably or usefully applied.

---

[64] See the detailed commentary by I. Schwartz, in Groeben, Boeckh, Thiesing, Ehlermann, *op. cit.*, footnote 14 on Article 235, with other references from the numerous sources; with special reference to the conditions, *op. cit.*, nos. 11 *et seq.*, pp. 1165 *et seq.* On the question of the extent to which it is still possible to rely on Article 235 of the EEC Treaty, following the extension of Community competence by the Single European Act, see J. A. Usher, "The gradual widening of EEC policy, in particular on the basis of Articles 100 and 235 EEC Treaty," in *Structure and Dimensions of European Community Policy* (ed. J. Schwarze–H. G. Schermers), Baden-Baden 1988.

[65] See G. Nicolaysen, "Zur Theorie von den Implied Powers in den Europäischen Gemeinschaften," EuR 1966, pp. 129 *et seq.*

[66] Case 8/55 *Fédéchar* v. *High Authority* [1955–56] E.C.R. 245.

[67] *Ibid.*, at 311.

[68] *Ibid.*, at 259.

As, in this instance, it is necessary to achieve the aim of Article 26 of the Convention, the High Authority has the power, if not the duty, to adopt—within the limits laid down by that provision—measures to reduce the prices of Belgian coal.

The result is that the accomplishment of its task in this instance assumes a power to fix prices on the part of the High Authority. It must be acknowledged, however, that that power extends only to the aim of ensuring that all consumers of Belgian coal benefit from a reduction in the price of that product from the beginning of the transitional period and within the limits laid down in Article 26 of the Convention.

The judgment in Case 20/59, *Government of the Italian Republic* v. *High Authority* confirmed the principle[69]:

"Writers and case-law agree in recognizing that the rules established by a treaty imply the principles without which these rules cannot effectively or reasonably be applied."

In this particular case, however, the European Court decided that the High Authority had no unwritten competence of this kind.[70]

(b) Treaty reservation in secondary legislation

In the EEC, the focus of secondary legislative power is the Council. The Commission itself, apart from individual treaty-based functions for setting norms, has only the right to propose legislation.[71] Article 155, paragraph 4 of the EEC Treaty and Article 124 of the Euratom Treaty also place the Commission under a duty "to exercise the powers conferred on it by the Council for the implementation of the rules laid down by the latter."[72]

---

[69] [1960] E.C.R. 325 (at 336).

[70] *Ibid.*, at 338 *et seq.*

[71] *cf.* H. Schmitt von Sydow, in Groeben, Boeckh, Thiesing, Ehlermann, *op. cit.*, footnote 14, Article 155, no. 26, p. 181.

[72] Because the relationship between the Council and the Commission (High Authority) is fundamentally different in the ECSC Treaty, there is no delegated authority under this treaty; see H. P. Ipsen, *Europäisches Gemeinschaftsrecht*, Tübingen 1972, p. 440, 20/50.

If the delegation of authority is to be lawful, the Council must possess the power to legislate in the area in question. This authority, including the manner of delegation, is exercised in the form prescribed by the basic treaty rule. In its subsequent exercise of transferred functions, the Commission is no longer bound by the procedural requirements imposed on the Council.[73] However, its freedom of manoeuvre is limited, as already explained, by the rule of delegation,[74] the Treaty provisions and general principles of law. The key principles for the transfer of powers of implementation in the relationship between Council and Commission have been redefined and elucidated by the Single European Act in Article 145, third indent, of the EEC Treaty.

III. PRINCIPLES OF INTERPRETATION

When a legal system develops, there must be not only legal principles, but also rules for interpreting these principles.[75] There are few applications of the law in which a real-life situation can be mechanically allotted to a certain rule. What is required is an "interpretation" of the provision in question, to bring it into service in resolving the dispute.[76]

All the institutions which have to apply Community law, *i.e.* Community organs, national authorities and courts, have to interpret it. The ultimate decision on the "correct" interpretation of E.C. law rests with the European Court (Article 177 of the EEC Treaty, Article 150 of the Euratom Treaty).

Community law makes use of the same methods of interpretation as are found in national law—literal, systematic, historical and teleological.[77] However, because of the special character and historical context of Community law, different weighting has to be given to the individual methods. The guiding principle of interpretation is the integration called for by the Treaties.[78]

In Community law, literal interpretation is difficult to apply because the text to be interpreted, the EEC Treaty, is binding in several different

---

[73] H. *Schmitt von Sydow, op. cit.*, footnote 71, p. 186, no. 45.
[74] See above for the explanation of the hierarchy of norms in the area of Commission legislation under Article 155, fourth indent, of the EEC Treaty.
[75] On the task of interpretation in general, see: K. Larenz, *Methodenlehre der Rechtswissenschaft* (5th ed., Berlin/Heidelberg/New York/Tokyo 1983), pp. 298 *et seq.*
[76] *Ibid., op. cit.*, footnote 75, p. 198.
[77] On this point see A. Bleckmann, *Europarecht* (4th ed., 1985), pp. 95 *et seq.*, p. 200, with examples.
[78] H. P. Ipsen *op. cit.*, footnote 72, p. 131, 5/72.

languages (Article 248 of the EEC Treaty). Accordingly, where the different methods of interpretation would lead to conflicting results, they are supplemented by the systematic and teleological methods.[79]

The historical method of interpretation plays only a minor role, and in interpreting the Treaties scarcely any, because the materials on the negotiations are largely secret.[80] Even if these were known, to revert to earlier negotiating positions would involve the risk of reopening old wounds, which were supposed to have been healed through the compromise formulas in the Treaties.

The systematic and teleological methods of interpretation, on the other hand, are of greater significance. Systematic interpretation is carried out at different levels. It may involve only one clause or section of a legal document, or the whole of it.[81]

The teleological procedure is somewhat similar. In ascertaining the purpose of the Treaties, an individual provision or specific groups of rules may form the centre of interest. One form of the teleological method is the search for the "effet utile" of a provision, *i.e.* its "useful" or "most useful" effect. The quest is for approaches which make it possible to achieve the general effect intended by the legislator. This quest for the "effet utile" has been a central focus of many European Court decisions.[82]

However, the most important variant of the teleological method of interpretation is the approach to the subject in terms of the aims of the Treaty, an approach which can be broadly described as integrative.[83] Applied in this way, the method has the result of blending systematic and goal-oriented interpretation into a single whole which reflects the dynamics of a process of integration.[84]

C.   UNLAWFUL ADMINISTRATIVE CONDUCT

I.   SOURCES OF ERROR

In dealing with administrative errors in the implementation of Com-

---

[79] B. Beutler, R. Bieber, J. Pipkorn, J. Streil, *op. cit.*, footnote 4, p. 222.
[80] *cf.* H. P. Ipsen, *op. cit.*, p. 134, 5/80.
[81] See A. Bleckmann, *op. cit.*, footnote 77, p. 96, with references.
[82] See, for example, Case 41/74 *Van Duyn* v. *Home Office* [1974] E.C.R. 1337 at 1348; Case 70/72 *Commission* v. *Federal Republic of Germany* [1973] 813 at 829.
[83] See Ipsen, *op. cit.*, footnote 78.
[84] B. Beutler, R. Bieber, J. Pipkorn, J. Streil, *op. cit.*, footnote 4, p. 224.

munity law, it is necessary to distinguish between direct and indirect performance. Indirect performance, in turn, has both direct and indirect aspects.[85]

In direct performance (that is, implementation by the Community institutions), the act of an institution may be unlawful because of want of authority, procedural or formal defects, breaches of the Treaties or of secondary legislation, or abuse of authority. In indirect performance (that is, where a national authority directly applies Community law), any breach of the EEC rule will render the administrative act unlawful.

If a national rule of implementation is applied in an intermediate role between the law of the E.C. and the subject governed by it, any error in the administrative act will be judged initially according to the national legal system, but the latter must, in turn, conform to Community law if the act of implementation is to be lawful.

II. THE PRINCIPLE OF THE REVOCABILITY OF UNLAWFUL ADMINISTRATIVE ACTS

It has already been shown how the Court eliminates unlawful acts by Community institutions from the body of law in force. However, a judicial decision is not always necessary. The administration—which, at the Community level, will normally be the Commission—can itself revoke unlawful administrative acts. Where the administrative conduct in question is of the kind which imposes duties, this is usually a straight-forward process. However, difficulties arise where the administrative act to be revoked is one which confers rights.[86]

The principle of the "legality of the administration," according to which the lawful situation has to be re-established, may in this case conflict with the principle of legal certainty (in the form of the legitimate expectations of the holder of the rights).[87]

Two questions arise: How can the conflict between the two principles be resolved, and what kind of effects—*ex nunc* or *ex tunc*—may the revocation have?

The first question has been answered by the Court in Joined Cases 42 and 49/59, *SNUPAT* v. *High Authority*, where it stated that in each

---

[85] For these concepts and the administrative context in which they are used, see H.-W. Rengeling, "Die Entwicklung verwaltungsrechtlicher Grundsätze durch den Gerichtshof der Europäischen Gemeinschaften," EuR 1984, pp. 331 *et seq*. (333).

[86] See above for the commentary on void, contestable and invalid acts of EEC institutions.

[87] See H. Lecheler, *Allgemeine Rechtsgrundsätze in der Rechtsprechung des Europäischen Gerichtshofs* Diss. jur. 1967, pp. 31 *et seq*.

individual case the public interest, represented by the principle of legality, must be weighed against the private interest in maintaining the right acquired.[88]

On the second question the Court took the position, in the *SNUPAT* decision, that revocation *ex tunc* is a possibility:

> "Furthermore, according to the law of all the Member States, retroactive withdrawal is generally accepted in cases in which the administrative measure in question has been adopted on the basis of false or incomplete information provided by those concerned."[89]

In Case 111/63, *Lemmerz-Werke* v. *High Authority* the Court's stance was even more decisive[90]:

> "The High Authority can revoke illegal decisions, even retroactively, provided that in certain exceptional cases proper consideration is given to the principle of legal certainty. Such consideration is in the first instance a matter for the High Authority; it is, however, subject to review by the Court."

So much for the main circumstances in which unlawful administrative acts in the direct execution of Community law may be revoked. Chapter 6 contains a fuller treatment of this question, which has some very complex ramifications, with special emphasis on the difficult questions of legal certainty and the protection of legitimate expectations in the framing of legal rules. It also examines in greater depth the various national arrangements for revocation.

[88] [1961] E.C.R. 53 at 87.
[89] [1961] E.C.R. 109 at 173.
[90] [1965] E.C.R. 677 at 690.

PART 3: ELEMENTS WHICH MODERATE LEGAL CONSTRAINTS—UNDEFINED LEGAL TERMS AND DISCRETION

SECTION 1

ADMINISTRATIVE FREEDOM OF DECISION IN THE LEGAL SYSTEMS OF THE MEMBER STATES

A. A COMPARATIVE LEGAL ANALYSIS

I. STATUTORY CONSTRAINTS AND DISCRETION IN FRANCE

1. The Fundamentals of the Doctrine of Discretion in France

The predominant role of the Conseil d'Etat in the development of French administrative law is also evident in determining the nature and scope of administrative freedom of action. Of course, theory has always played a part in the emergence of a doctrine of discretion which reconciles the demands of the administration with the individual's search for legal protection.[1] But unlike what has happened in Germany, this has not led to the creation of two separate categories of legal effects derived from a rule of law, *i.e.* one in which the facts are entirely open for judicial appraisal and the legal concepts are not defined, and another which constitutes an area of discretion in the choice of legal consequences, where the courts may only test the boundaries set by law.[2]

In French administrative law, the concept of discretion (pouvoir or compétence discrétionnaire) is a general term denoting the freedom of

---

[1] *cf.* the survey of sources in A. de Laubadère, *Traité de droit administratif* (9th ed., Paris 1984), Vol. I, by J.-C. Venezia, Y. Gaudemet, p. 284, no. 593; M. Fromont, *Rechtsschutz gegenüber der Verwaltung in Deutschland, Frankreich und den Europäischen Gemeinschaften*, Cologne, Berlin, Bonn, Munich 1967, p. 170, writes that the role of theory is "very modest."

[2] *cf.* A. de Laubadère, *op. cit.*, footnote 1, pp. 291 *et seq.*, no. 603.

decision and action enjoyed by the executive within the law, or, as Michou's classic definition puts it[3]:

"Il y a pouvoir discrétionnaire, toutes les fois qu'une autorité agit librement, sans que la conduite à tenir lui soit dictée à l'avance par une règle de droit."

G. Braibant sums up the essence of administrative discretion in one succinct sentence[4]:

"Le pouvoir discrétionnaire se definit pour l'administration par sa liberté d'appréciation, d'action et de décision."

An important element of the freedom of decision enjoyed by the administration is that it alone has authority to determine the expediency (opportunité) of a particular course of action.[5] This is also the essence of discretion. As well as these attempted definitions of discretion in its own terms, there is also a description which contrasts it with tied authority (pouvoir lié). Tied authority exists wherever a principle of administrative law requires, in particular circumstances, that a particular line of conduct be adopted. A. de Laubadère offers the following definition[6]:

"Il y a ... pouvoir (ou compétence) lié lorsque, dès lors qu'il se trouve en présence de telle ou telle circonstance de fait, l'administrateur est tenu de prendre telle ou telle décision; il n'a plus le choix entre plusieurs décisions, sa conduite lui est dictée à l'avance par la règle de droit."

G. Braibant puts it more tersely[7]:

"La compétence d'une autorité administrative est liée lorsque cette autorité est tenue d'agir dans un sens determiné, sans disposer de possibilités d'appréciation ou de choix."

---

[3] Extract from the Encyclopédie Dalloz, p. 730, no. 575.
[4] G. Braibant, *Le droit administratif français*, 1984, p. 239.
[5] See A. de Laubadère, *op. cit.*, footnote 1, p. 286, no. 595. *cf.* also G. Vedel, P. Delvolvé *Droit administratif* (7th ed., Paris 1980), pp. 426 *et seq.*
[6] *Op. cit.*, footnote 1, p. 285, no. 594.
[7] *Op. cit.*, footnote 4, p. 237.

However, discretion is only one of the ways in which the force of law may be moderated for the administration in France. There is also the theory of *circonstances exceptionnelles*, which may justify departures from the applicable law in emergency situations, for the sake of the public weal.[8] Finally, the theory of the *acte de gouvernement*, according to which government measures are not subject to judicial review, moderates the legal constraints placed on the executive.[9]

In what follows, the two last-named ways of mitigating legal constraints should be disregarded. If seen in the context of the full legal regime which governs administrative conduct, they are exceptional cases, and it is therefore reasonable to confine ourselves to the problems of discretionary authority. We shall attempt to describe here the chief features of the judicial review process as exercised by the Conseil d'Etat.

2. The Extent of Judicial Review of Discretionary Decisions

In France there is no single monolithic theory of discretionary power, such as we still find in Germany, in spite of continuing criticism.[10] This imposes the greatest caution when seeking to generalise about the extent of the review powers found in French administrative case law. Although decisions are made on a case-by-case basis, there are discernible guidelines for the review process, which will be described below.

To begin with the procedure which is the most important in practice, the *recours pour excès de pouvoir* has four causes of action (cas d'ouverture). As well as the procedural significance these possess, they have become general standards for the legality of an administrative act. They have already been mentioned several times in this study.[11]

Under the general heading of causes of error, the following aspects of an administrative decision are investigated:

---

[8] On the theory of "circonstances exceptionnelles," see: J. Rivero, *Droit administratif* (9th ed., Paris 1980), pp. 87 *et seq.*; G. Braibant, *op. cit.*, footnote 4, pp. 249 *et seq.*; A. de Laubadère, *op. cit.*, footnote 1, pp. 401 *et seq.*

[9] *cf.* J. Rivero, *op. cit.*, footnote 8, pp. 161 *et seq.*, nos. 155 *et seq.* This also deals with the problem of distinguishing between "actes administratifs" and "actes de gouvernement," and lists the government measures which are now acknowledged to be free from judicial control. See also G. Braibant, *op. cit.*, footnote 4, p. 263, who treats "actes de gouvernement," from a legal point of view, as occupying a halfway position between legislative instruments and administrative acts.

[10] See above, Pt. 2, Section I, A. I.

[11] See above, Pt. I, Section I, A. I.

In every instance, due authority and the observance of the prescribed procedure and of the prescribed form are looked for.[12] In the area of due authority there is no room for discretion, but the administration occasionally has some freedom of choice as regards procedural and formal requirements.[13]

In deciding whether there has been a breach of law (violation de la loi) the French administrative courts seek to ascertain whether the ruling made by the administration conflicts with the law in force (illégalité relative à l'objet)[14] or whether the legal and factual grounds are defective (illégalité relative aux motifs).[15] There is *illégalité relative à l'objet* where the administration seeks to order a legal effect which is inadmissible, such as by imposing on a public official a disciplinary penalty which is not provided by statute,[16] or where it fails to act in the face of a strict obligation (compétence liée).[17]

Illégalité relative aux motifs relates to defective grounds, whether legal or factual. The legal grounds will be defective whenever the administration relies on a legal basis which is either ineffectual or inapplicable, or makes a wrong interpretation of the relevant source of authority.[18] The latter situation includes, in particular, cases where the administration believes itself to be bound by law, but on a correct interpretation possesses discretionary authority.[19]

The factual grounds are extremely important when discretionary decisions have to be reviewed. The facts will be found defective if the administration has based its decision on mistaken or incomplete facts or has made an erroneous appraisal of the facts.[20]

Before the enactment of Law no. 79/587 of July 11, 1979, the problem for the courts in ascertaining the facts was that the administration had no general duty to give reasons for its actions.[21] If the administration failed to comply with its duty to present the facts which prompted its decision, the

---

[12] This is called *contrôle minimum*; cf. J. Rivero, *op. cit.*, footnote 8, p. 262, no. 265.
[13] cf. R. Hoffmann, *Das Ermessen der Verwaltungsbehörden in Frankreich*, Berlin 1967, p. 126.
[14] See above, Pt. I, Section I, A.I.
[15] *Ibid.*
[16] C.E. March 22, 1957, *Clausi*, Recueil p. 198.
[17] C.E. July 24, 1936, *Syndicats de défense des grands vins de la Côte d'Or*, Recueil p. 861.
[18] M. Fromont, *op. cit.*, footnote 1, p. 264.
[19] C.E. December 1, 1950, *Escalon*, Recueil p. 589.
[20] See M. Degen, "Klageverfahren und Klagegründe im französischen Verwaltungsprozess," *Die Verwaltung* 1981, pp. 157 *et seq.* (171).
[21] cf. *Journal Officiel* of July 12, 1979, p. 1711.

court would act on the presumption that the facts adduced by the plaintiff were correct.[22]

The next step is the legal appraisal of the facts in the light of the applicable rule of law (qualification juridique des faits). Here we find that, unlike the German Federal Constitutional Court, the Conseil d'Etat does not in principle carry out a complete review of whether the case has been correctly assigned to a particular legal concept.[23] No general rule can be discerned from which it is possible to predict how far the review process will go.

Instead, the scope of the investigation is determined individually, in each subject area, by any major public and private interests which happen to be at stake and by the extent to which the court's power of appraisal permits it to examine accordingly the particular administrative measure concerned.[24]

In its decision in the *Ville Nouvelle Est* case,[25] concerning an objection to a planning decision for the siting of a stretch of motorway, the Conseil d'Etat conducted a full judicial inquiry into the notion of the "public benefit" (utilité publique) of an expropriation. The inquiry involved weighing public gain against private loss, and in the end the Conseil d'Etat decided that the results of a similar process undertaken by the administration were unobjectionable.[26]

Similarly, the Conseil d'Etat decided to carry out its own investigation of the alleged "danger to young people" posed by a press publication.[27] It should be remembered here that in a similar case, the German Federal Administrative Court decided that a judgment of this nature by the administration should not be subject to review. Again, the Conseil d'Etat made its own assessment of the "commemorative character" of a certain

---

[22] C.E. May 28, 1954, *Barel*, Recueil p. 308.
[23] H. D. Jarass, "Besonderheiten des französischen Verwaltungsrechts im Vergleich," DÖV 1981, pp. 813 *et seq.* (815).
[24] M. Bullinger, "Unbestimmte Gesetzesbegriffe in der neueren deutschen und französischen Verwaltungsrechtsprechung," *Festschrift für H. Jahrreiss*, 1974, pp. 19 *et seq.* (33).
[25] C.E. May 28, 1971, Recueil p. 409.
[26] See M. Bullinger, *op. cit.*, footnote 24; J. Schwarze, *Die Befugnis zur Abstraktion im Europäischen Gemeinschaftsrecht*, Baden-Baden 1976, p. 162, footnote 30; *cf.* also A. de Laubadère, "Le contrôle juridictionnel du pouvoir discrétionnaire dans la jurisprudence récente du Conseil d'Etat français," *Mélanges offerts à Marcel Waline*, Paris, 1974, Vol. 2, pp. 531 *et seq.*, with a critical appraisal of this judicial practice from the viewpoint of the new constraints it places on the administration (*op. cit.*, pp. 543 *et seq.*).
[27] C.E. December 5, 1956, *Thibault*, Recueil p. 463.

site and rescinded the official refusal to grant planning consent, on the ground that the intended structure would not disturb it.[28]

In economic administrative law, too, the courts have sometimes chosen to test the administration's interpretation and application of certain undefined concepts. There was, for instance, the *Manufacture de produits chimiques de Tournan* case,[29] turning on the concept of a "substantial disadvantage" for a French economic sector, this concept being a vital factor in an anti-dumping decision by the Finance and Economics Minister. The Conseil d'Etat took the view that no such risk existed, and rescinded the decision in question.[30]

Another area of stringent control is police law. This is a traditional area for intervention by the authorities, and one in which the public interest (intérêt public) and the individual citizen's rights and freedoms are mutually opposed.[31] The individual's interest in legal protection carries special weight in this field because of the risk of an unacceptable threat to basic freedoms, and this explains why police measures are subject, in principle, to maximum scrutiny by the courts.

On the other hand, the supervision of foreigners, which also belongs to the functions of the police in a broad sense, is subject to only a limited degree of judicial control.[32] Where expulsion orders are concerned, the only matter for review apart from due authority, procedure and form and the abuse of discretionary power, is the accuracy of the facts which prompted the order, if it is a question of a risk to law and order arising from the presence of the foreigner. The courts do not place any interpretation on the facts, this being a role reserved to the administration.[33]

Similarly, in principle no legal interpretation is made of the facts in areas which presuppose special technical knowledge. A well-known example of this is the refusal of the Conseil d'Etat to check on the official

---

[28] C.E. April 4, 1914, *Gomel*, Recueil p. 488. Also see M. Long, P. Weil, G. Braibant, *Les grands arrêts de la jurisprudence administrative* (8th ed., Paris 1984), no. 32, p. 123.

[29] C.E. March 4, 1966, Recueil 174.

[30] *Loc. cit.*

[31] *cf.* M. Degen, *op. cit.*, footnote 20, p. 173.

[32] *cf.* R. Hoffmann, *op. cit.*, footnote 13, pp. 122 *et seq.*; C.E. May 14, 1948, *Imbach*, Recueil p. 215; C.E. May 11, 1960, *Car*, Recueil p. 319.

[33] See the references in footnote 32; on legal protection in the law on foreigners, *cf.* C.E. July 22, 1977, *Mytteis-Hager*, Recueil p. 366: a residence permit may be refused on grounds of "ordre public" and the interests of national defence. C.E. March 7, 1980, *Diaw*, Recueil 127 *et seq.* the refusal to issue a residence permit on the ground that the applicant was without visible means of support was rescinded, because he earned his living as an itinerant trader. C.E. June 24, 1981, *Chegkba*, Recueil p. 853: to uphold an expulsion order despite blameless conduct at the time of an application for review of the decision is proof of a manifest error of judgment.

description of a hair-growth preparation as "poisonous."[34] This means that the administration retains the ultimate right to make such judgments, in the light of its own knowledge of the field. The power which the authorities possess to make their own appraisal of the relevant facts is conveyed by the description originally given of discretionary power: *liberté d'appréciation* (G. Braibant). Liberté d'appréciation (or "pouvoir d'appréciation") corresponds to freedom of appraisal in German administrative law, although unlike the latter it does not include the function of determining facts by incorporating a degree of discretion restricted to considering the legal consequences of a rule, while retaining the essential dichotomy between an undefined legal concept and discretionary power. In France, this concept denotes only a certain kind of administrative freedom of decision.[35]

The Conseil d'Etat has devised a special limit for this purpose: manifest error in the appraisal of the facts (erreur manifeste d'appréciation).[36] G. Braibant observes[37]:

> "L'administration a le droit de se tromper dans son appréciation, mais elle n'a pas le droit de commettre une erreur manifeste, c'est-à-dire une erreur qui se caractérise à la fois par sa gravité et par son évidence."

But the "right to error" within the freedom of decision enjoyed by the administration does not entitle it to make an "absurd choice" (faire des choses absurdes). Significantly, G. Braibant assigns erreur manifeste to the classic quartet of causes of error which may lead to a recours pour excès de pouvoir, as follows[38]:

> "L'erreur manifeste est, dans la domaine de la logique, ce qu'est le détournement de pouvoir dans le domaine de la morale."

As well as being bound by positive rules of law, the administration has also to pay heed to unwritten principles of law—*principes généraux du droit*.[39] Among these, special mention should be made of the principle of

---

[34] C.E. April 27, 1951, *Société Toni*, Recueil p. 312.
[35] M. Bullinger, *op. cit.*, footnote 24, pp. 19 *et seq.* (23).
[36] See A. de Laubadère, *op. cit.*, footnote 1, p. 290, no. 602; G. Vedel, P. Delvolvé, *op. cit.*, footnote 5, pp. 766 *et seq.* J.-P. Henry, "Une nouvelle fonction pour l'erreur manifeste," A.J.D.A. 1979, pp. 17 *et seq.*
[37] *Op. cit.*, footnote 4, p. 240.
[38] *Op. cit., ibid.*
[39] C.E. December 17, 1948, *Azoulay*, Recueil p. 474.

equality,[40] the bar on retroactivity,[41] the rights of due process and to a fair hearing,[42] and the principle of proportionality,[43] which is a relatively new idea. The principle of proportionality has made its appearance in French administrative law chiefly as a result of the decision of the Conseil d'Etat in the *Ville Nouvelle Est* case.[44] As for the role to be played by administrative guidelines when exercising discretion, the Conseil d'Etat initially rejected them, but has now accepted that they are binding in principle, in order to achieve uniformity in administrative practice.[45] In individual cases, however, they are no bar to the exercise of discretion.

Finally, it must be remembered that administrative conduct is always constrained by the rule that discretion may not be abused—*détournement de pouvoir*.[46] There is a misuse of discretion whenever the executive knowingly exercises the authority it has been granted for a purpose other than the one for which it was intended.[47]

As a cause of action, misuse of discretion plays only a minor role among the remedies afforded by modern French administrative law.[48] This is chiefly due to the disadvantage the complainant suffers in having to shoulder the burden of proof. Although administrative proceedings are essentially inquisitorial, whenever a détournement de pouvoir is alleged the burden of proof falls on the complainant, who must therefore adduce the facts which bear out his claim. Proceedings against the administration for acting contrary to the spirit of a rule of law often fail for want of convincing evidence.[49] On the other hand, actions based on alleged

---

[40] *cf.* A. de Laubadère, *op. cit.*, footnote 1, p. 267, no. 559, with numerous references to the case law.

[41] See A. de Laubadère, *op. cit.*, footnote 1, p. 349, no. 728.

[42] *cf.* G. Braibant, *op. cit.*, footnote 4, pp. 230 *et seq.*; G. Vedel, P. Delvolvé, *op. cit.*, footnote 5, p. 375; A. de Laubadère, *op. cit.*, footnote 1, p. 344, no. 717: "droits de la défense" (ou principe *Audi alteram partem*).

[43] G. Braibant, *op. cit.*, footnote 4, p. 241.

[44] In this case in the form of a cost-benefit analysis; see also the successful avoidance action in the *Société civile Sainte-Marie de l'Assomption* case, C.E. October 20, 1972, Recueil pp. 657 *et seq.* (esp. 660), challenging the administration's claim that an expropriation was of "public benefit." There is also a survey of the current case law, by J.-M. Auby, RDP, Fascicule I, 1986, Vol. 102, pp. 281 *et seq.*

[45] See C.E. December 11, 1970, *Crédit foncier de France*, Recueil pp. 750 *et seq.* (751). This is considered in detail by G. Braibant, *op. cit.*, footnote 4, pp. 241 *et seq.*

[46] For a fuller treatment, see A. de Laubadère, *op. cit.*, footnote 1, pp. 598 *et seq.*, no. 1182 *et seq.*, with a list of sources.

[47] G. Braibant, *op. cit.*, footnote 4, p. 240.

[48] *cf.* M. Degen, *op. cit.*, footnote 20, p. 169; also the opinion of Advocate-General Lagrange in Case 3/54 *Assider* v. *High Authority* [1954–55] E.C.R. 131 *et seq.* (161) in the context of comparative law reflections on the misuse of discretion in Community law.

[49] See M. Degen, *op. cit.*, footnote 20, p. 169.

breaches of law have become much more frequent in recent decades.[50] This is due partly to more stringent controls on administrative conduct, and a remedy which consists of an objective test of legality offers the individual an effective form of legal protection.

Brief though it is, this survey points to the flexibility shown by the French administrative courts in measuring the scope of administrative decision-making, whether in a broader or a narrower sense, by investigating the facts in depth if need be, and judging them against the degree of legitimate authority.

To summarise, judicial control of discretionary decisions can be classified into three stages of ascending importance[51]:

— Minimal control (contrôle minimum) involves testing for procedural and formal defects, testing the accuracy of the supporting facts and ascertaining that there is no abuse of authority. One example is the review of administrative decisions in the law on foreigners and in specialised technical fields.
In principle, there is no check on the legal weight given to the facts adduced, unless the plaintiff is alleging manifest error (erreur manifeste d'appréciation).
— The ordinary extent of the test (contrôle normal) may extend beyond minimum control to a legal appraisal of the facts.
— Exceptionally, maximum control (contrôle maximum) may also include a test of the necessity and proportionality of the administrative measure. Here the court invariably intrudes into areas which are otherwise governed by the principle of expediency (opportunité) and are properly the preserve of the administration. One example of a legal area with maximum judicial control of the administration is police law.

---

[50] cf. Advocate-General Lagrange, op. cit., footnote 48; also A. de Laubadère, op. cit., footnote 1, p. 602, no. 1196.
[51] See J.-M. Auby, R. Drago, Traité de contentieux administratif (3rd ed., Paris 1984), pp. 370 et seq., no. 1257, which includes a separate category for "contrôle moyen."

II. STATUTORY CONSTRAINTS AND DISCRETION IN THE FEDERAL REPUBLIC OF GERMANY

1. Fundamentals of the German Doctrine of Discretion

Few systems of administrative law have been more thoroughly debated than the German, in terms of statutory constraints on the executive and its use of undefined legal concepts and discretion.[1] A dominant feature of German administrative law has always been the frequency with which the topic of administrative freedom comes to the forefront.[2]

This intensive study of the problems of discretionary decision is justified chiefly by the fact that administrative freedom of decision touches on the essence of the relationship between the executive and the other two powers, although it remains true that interest focuses mainly on the jurisdictional aspect.[3] Yet apart from the administrative law aspect in the narrow sense, this is a constitutional problem which has dogged German history as a result of the disastrous experience of the National Socialist period, with a Parliament voluntarily shorn of power, an executive with excessive power and administrative courts almost bereft of their role. The situation under the "Third Reich" was no doubt the principal reason why,

---

[1] See the comprehensive survey of sources in H. Meyer, H. Borgs, *Kommentar zum Verwaltungsverfahrensgesetz* (2nd ed., Frankfurt a.M. 1982), para. 40, pp. 338 *et seq*. On the theory of discretion and the scope for appraisal in Switzerland, see F. D. A. Bertozza, *Der Beurteilungsspielraum*, Bern 1984; on discretion in Swiss administrative law in general, see T. Fleiner-Gerster, *Grundzüge des allgemeinen und schweizerischen Verwaltungsrechts* (2nd ed., Zürich 1980), 119 *et seq*. For Austria, see L. K. Adamovich, B. C. Funk, *Allgemeines Verwaltungsrecht* (2nd ed., Vienna/New York, 1984), pp. 114 *et seq*.

[2] O. Bachof, address on the anniversary of the Association of Teachers of German Constitutional Law in 1975, VVDSTRL Vol. 34 (1976), p. 275 (276); see also C. H. Ule, p. 305, who disputes the idea that there is any "recurring trend" of this kind in the administration of justice.

[3] *cf.* H.-U. Erichsen, "Die sog. unbestimmten Rechtsbegriffe als Steuerungs- und Kontrollmassgaben im Verhältnis von Gesetzgebung, Verwaltung und Rechtsprechung," DBVl. 1985, pp. 22 *et seq*. (22), who locates the origins of the theory of the indeterminate legal concept in the controversy surrounding the scope and extent of the review powers enjoyed by the administrative courts over administrative conduct. H. Ehmke, *"Ermessen" und "unbestimmter Rechtsbegriff" im Verwaltungsrecht*, Tübingen 1960, p. 7, says that almost everything written about discretionary power since the end of the last century treats the problem as a question of how the law is applied by the administration and then reviewed by the courts.

even now, discussion of statutory constraints on the administration is marked by a certain distrust of executive authority.[4] The efforts in the post-war period to construct a constitutional State, *i.e.* to bring the conduct of the State as far as possible under the law, led to the idea that administrative discretion was, if anything, an element foreign to the constitutional system, rather than a necessary means of achieving administrative flexibility.[5]

The German doctrine of discretion was largely imbued with the jurisprudence of the administrative courts, which derive their review powers in all public law disputes not of a constitutional law character from the general clause in paragraph 40 of the Statute of the administrative courts (VwGO), unless such disputes are to be referred to other courts.[6] This doctrine is based on a sharp division between the conditions for acting in the circumstances covered by a rule of law, and a definition of the legal consequences which follow from the existence of those circumstances.[7]

Following on from this, a distinction is drawn between undefined legal or statutory concepts which govern the application of the law in the existence of a legal principle, and discretion, as the freedom to decide which of a number of possible legal consequences will be adopted.[8] As regards the factual conditions for administrative action, in the post-war period the courts were anxious to leave as little room as possible for discretionary measures.[9] The concrete formulation of undefined concepts is therefore seen as conferring a legal blessing on what, in a specific case,

---

[4] *cf.* M. Bullinger, "Das Ermessen der öffentlichen Verwaltung," JZ 1984, pp. 1001 *et seq.* (1003). On the destruction of the constitutional state by National Socialism, see also C. H. Ule, "Rechtsstaat und Verwaltung," *Verwaltungs-Archiv*, Vol. 76, 1985, pp. 1 *et seq.* (3 *et seq.*). On the mistrust of the executive, see H. Reuss, "Das Verwaltungsverfahren—psychologisch betrachtet," DÖV 1958, pp. 656 *et seq.*

[5] *cf.* H. H. Rupp, *Grundfragen der heutigen Verwaltungsrechtslehre*, Tübingen 1965, pp. 200 *et seq.*, 207 *et seq.*: M. Bullinger, *op. cit.*, footnote 4, pp. 1001 and 1003.

[6] See G. Schmidt-Eichstaedt, "Der Konkretisierungsauftrag der Verwaltung beim Vollzug öffentlich-rechtlicher Normen," DVBl., 1985, pp. 645 *et seq.* (646). See also H. Maurer, *Allgemeines Verwaltungsrecht* (5th ed., Munich 1986), p. 93, paras. 3 *et seq.*

[7] G. Schmidt-Eichstaedt, *ibid.* (footnote 6).

[8] See H. Reuss, "Der unbestimmte Rechtsbegriff," DVBl., 1953, p. 649; R. Jarosch, "Die Prüfung unbestimmter Rechtsbegriffe durch die Verwaltungsgerichte," DVBl., 1954, p. 521; E. Forsthoff, *Lehrbuch des Verwaltungsrechts* (10th ed., Munich 1973), Vol. I, pp. 85 *et seq.*; see also H. J. Wolff, O. Bachhof, *Verwaltungsrecht* I, (9th ed., Munich 1974), pp. 188 *et seq.*, with extensive comment on how the courts test the administration's application of undefined concepts; also H.-U. Erichsen, W. Martens (editors), *Allgemeines Verwaltungsrecht* (7th ed., Berlin, New York 1986), p. 193 (for a critical view); H. Faber, *Verwaltungsrecht*, Tübingen 1987, pp. 92 *et seq.*

[9] See the numerous references in F. Ossenbühl, *Verwaltungsvorschriften und Grundgesetz*, Berlin/Zürich 1968, p. 317.

will be one correct result only, being merely an application of the law and therefore fully open to judicial review.[10]

On the other hand, discretion also represents a range of possible types of conduct, all equally lawful, which the administration may adopt in implementing statutes.[11] Hence the decision on how to act in a concrete case is made not merely from the viewpoint of legality—as already explained, all possible courses of action are equally lawful—but also in the light of expediency. These expediency considerations underpin and form the area reserved to the administration, in which it can take its decisions free of statutory constraints and judicial control.[12] The administrative courts may examine only whether the legal limits of discretion have been observed.[13]

The idea of the constitutional state, as expressed in Article 20, paragraph 3 of the Basic Law (GG), and the requirements of due process in Article 19, paragraph 4 GG, whereby anyone whose rights are infringed by public authorities has a remedy at law, also create a general presumption in favour of strict legal controls on the administration and against the free use of discretionary power within the law.[14]

Which of the two forms is to be followed is a matter for the lawmakers.[15] Discretionary powers are indicated chiefly by the use of "can," "may" and "should" in the drafting.[16] Where these "code-words" are absent, it can be assumed that the decision to be made is non-dis-

---

[10] See H.-U. Erichsen, W. Martens *op. cit.*, footnote 8, p. 191, where a distinction is drawn between "empirical" or "descriptive" and "normative" or "value-free" concepts, each of which poses different demands when the law has to be applied. On the value concepts and the need to determine their specific meaning in individual cases, see E. Forsthoff, *op. cit.*, footnote 8, pp. 87 *et seq*.

[11] *cf.* H. Maurer, *op. cit.*, footnote 6, p. 81, nos. 9 *et seq*.

[12] M. Bullinger, *op. cit.*, footnote 4, p. 1001, defines discretion in its broadest sense as the freedom of manoeuvre enjoyed by the public administration where its conduct is not completely prescribed by statute and is not completely subject to judicial review.

For the different legal effects which are equally permissible in the context of discretionary authority, see E. Forsthoff, *op. cit.*, footnote 8, p. 84, with a definition of discretion as an act of choice in the process of assigning value, *op. cit.*, p. 87; H.-U. Erichsen, W. Martens, *op. cit.*, footnote 8, pp. 195 *et seq*.

[13] See H.-U. Erichsen, W. Martens *op. cit.*, footnote 8, pp. 196 *et seq*.; N. Achterberg, *Allgemeines Verwaltungsrecht* (2nd ed., Heidelberg 1986), p. 346, nos. 54 *et seq*. A comparative law survey of discretion will be found in H. Soell, *Das Ermessen der Eingriffsverwaltung*, Heidelberg 1973.

[14] *cf.* O. Bachof, "Beurteilungsspielraum, Ermessen und unbestimmter Rechtsbegriff im Verwaltungsrecht," JZ 1955, p. 98 (100 VI); E. Forsthoff, *Lehrbuch des Verwaltungsrechts* (10th ed., Munich 1973), Vol. I, p. 90.

[15] *cf.* Forsthoff, *op. cit.*, footnote 14, pp. 94 *et seq*.

[16] H. Maurer, *op. cit.*, footnote 6, p. 96, no. 7.

cretionary, *i.e.* the administrative authority is bound, in the circumstances indicated, to prescribe certain legal effects.[17] Although the relationship of the administration to the laws and regulations by which it is governed is now divided into non-discretionary and discretionary areas, historically this was not the case. Originally, in the early constitutional State, discretion meant being outside the laws and the courts; this was the freedom of action enjoyed by the king's officers, enabling them to pursue their own ends.[18] Discretion was therefore a particular phenomenon, not tied to the existence of a rule of law and its legal effects, which expressed the continuance of the monarchical system. It was only later, with the growth of the democratic constitutional State, that discretionary authority was narrowed down and finally relegated to the category of legal effects of a rule of law.[19]

The essential distinction between the full review powers which apply to undefined legal expressions and the limited degree of control which applies to discretionary authority has now been somewhat modified by the acceptance of what is called scope for appraisal in the interpretation of certain undefined concepts within a rule of law.

The tendency to which we have referred, to use the law to restrict the powers of the executive as far as possible, has already had a marked influence on case law in the Federal Republic of Germany. This was why, for example, the concept of the "interest of public transport" was transformed from a discretionary concept to an undefined one, fully subject to review by the courts.[20] But even the administrative courts had to admit that there are concepts for which the dogma of the only correct decision in individual cases is sheer fiction. The chief precedent for this in the case law of the Federal Administrative Court dates from 1971.[21] The judgment of the Court related to a decision of the Federal inspection agency for publications dangerous to young people, to include a certain magazine in the list of dangerous publications. According to the relevant statute, for

---

[17] H. J. Wolff, O. Bachof, *op. cit.*, footnote 8, p. 186.
[18] M. Bullinger, "Das Ermessen der öffentlichen Verwaltung," JZ 1984, pp. 1001 *et seq.* (1002).
[19] *Ibid., op. cit.*, footnote 15, p. 1003.
[20] *cf.* from the year 1956, BVerwGE 4, p. 89 (esp. 92) and, by contrast, from the year 1961, BVerwGE 11, p. 168 (191 *et seq.*).
[21] BVerwGE 39, pp. 197 *et seq.*; but as early as 1955 O. Bachof, *op. cit.*, footnote 14, pp. 97 *et seq.*, argued that the administration's scope for appraisal should be recognised, although treated with caution. See also C. H. Ule, "Zur Anwendung unbestimmter Rechtsbegriffe im Verwaltungsrecht," *Gedächtnisschrift für W. Jellinek*, Munich 1955, pp. 309 *et seq.*

such a decision to be made there must be a "tendency to pervert youth." The Federal Administrative Court commented[22]:

> "Inclusion in the list creates the presumption that there is a tendency to pervert youth. This was previously treated as an undefined legal concept, which permits of only one correct decision. But including an item on this list is not simply a matter of establishing facts and drawing inferences from them. Rather, a decision that there is a tendency to pervert involves a predictive judgment, which sets a guideline and also involves a considerable element of appraisal. The idea that in applying the concept of a tendency to pervert, only one correct solution is possible, is found to be a fiction. In this case several solutions are conceivable; there is a 'range of possible decisions' (Redeker, DÖV 1971, 757, 762) which may be equally admissible from a legal viewpoint. Because the Federal agency's decision involves a prediction for the future, it is essentially unsustainable . . ."

The Court describes the consequent impact on the judicial review process in the following terms[23]:

> "This does not mean that the decisions of the Federal agency are outside the scope of judicial review. It is for the administrative courts to examine whether the Federal agency proceeded on the basis of an accurate and complete representation of the facts, and whether it kept to the bounds of its "prerogative of appraisal" (Wolff, *Verwaltungsrecht* I (8th ed.), 1981, no. 31 I c 4 p. 182), and applied the correct standards, as illustrated in Section 1, para. 1(2) GjS. The Federal agency must justify its decision in a manner which permits of judicial examination, showing the standards of appraisal on which its decision was based. Otherwise, a decision to include a certain item on the index may be rescinded by a court."

With the recognition that there is a scope for appraisal—or, as the Federal Administrative Court has it, a prerogative of evaluation (*Ein-*

---

[22] *Op. cit.*, footnote 21, p. 203.
[23] *Op. cit.*, footnote 21, p. 204.

schätzungsprärogative)[24]—the German doctrine of discretionary authority has become much more flexible. Ossenbühl called this an "almost sensational decision."[25]

Nevertheless, there are not many admitted instances of such administrative prerogatives.[26] This can be explained by what we have already noted to be a prevailing tendency to aim for the maximum degree of judicial control and to tie the administration to statutory rules. The legal notion of a "scope for appraisal" is therefore largely academic. What it means, at least in theory, is that the facts underlying a legal ruling may include an element of administrative decision-making. Here discretion becomes once more, in practice at least, an essential component of the ruling and not merely of its legal effects.[27]

It is not possible to trace here all the ramifications of the academic debate about administrative discretion.[28] One new tendency should, however, be singled out, by way of contrast with the prevailing theory of discretion as described above. Its common denominator lies in a breakdown of the hitherto rigid categorisation into undefined legal concepts on the one hand, with the facts, and discretion on the other, with the legal effects of a ruling. Here discretion is treated as a problem inherent in the administration's relationship to statute law, and not simply as a way, restricted to legal effects, of moderating the legal constraints on the administration when it is implementing statute.[29]

This view, already challenged at the beginning of the 1960s by H. Ehmke,[30] appears to be undergoing a revival as a result of the large number of court cases relating to approvals for large technical installations, cases in which ideas such as "the state of the art" have taxed the

---

[24] This particular term has become current, but is criticised by H. J. Wolff, O. Bachof, *op. cit.*, footnote 8, p. 192, who claim that to describe officialdom's prerogative of evaluation as "scope for appraisal" is based on a misunderstanding.

[25] On the revival of the administrative power of appraisal, see DÖV 1972, p. 401.

[26] M. Bullinger *op. cit.*, footnote 18, p. 1004; on the frequency of precedent in the case law of the Federal Administrative Court, see H.-U. Erichsen, "Die sog. unbestimmten Rechtsbegriffe als Steuerungs- und Kontrollmassgaben im Verhältnis von Gesetzgebung, Verwaltung und Rechtsprechung," DVBl. 1985, pp. 23 *et seq.* (24).

[27] W. Schmidt went so far as to refer to the "end of the undefined legal concept" in NJW 1975, pp. 1753 *et seq.*

[28] See the sources listed in footnote 1.

[29] *cf.* W. Schmidt, *op. cit.*, footnote 27, esp. pp. 1754 *et seq.*; E. Less, "Begriffsherrschaft und Verwaltungstätigkeit," DÖV 1957, pp. 418 *et seq.*; M. Bullinger, "Das Ermessen der öffentlichen Verwaltung," JZ 1984, pp. 1001 *et seq.*; G. Schmidt-Eichstaedt, "Der Konkretisierungsauftrag der Verwaltung beim Vollzug öffentlich-rechtlicher Normen," DBVl 1985, pp. 645 *et seq.*

[30] H. Ehmke, *"Ermessen" und "unbestimmter Rechtsbegriff" im Verwaltungsrecht*, Tübingen 1960, esp. p. 45.

limits of the courts' review powers. It must also be said that nearly 40 years of proper constitutional administration under the Basic Law have done much to allay the initial mistrust. It is becoming clearer that increasingly detailed legislation in ever more areas of life does not necessarily guarantee the citizen a greater degree of legal security and justice.[31] Quite the opposite: the over-abundance of statutory rules and regulations paralyses the ability of the administration to ensure a proper balance of interests in individual cases. There is one further point which fuels doubts about the modern German theory of discretionary power. The sheer rigour of the tests to which undefined expressions are subjected and the restrictive treatment of the legal notion of the scope for appraisal create a very rigid and inflexible review system, with an inner logic which compels the courts in certain cases—for example, those concerning the approval of major technical installations—to reach a final decision in a subject area so complex that it is bound to tax the ability of even the most knowledgeable appeal body.[32] To shift the burden of decision in this way from the administration to the courts does not always lead to an objectively "better" result. A glance through the judgments of the administrative courts will show, however, that the tendency to subject even the most undefined of concepts to exhaustive testing is still prevalent.[33]

A more loosely-conceived theory of discretion, avoiding the dual classification of the undefined legal concept and discretion and geared instead to the citizen's need for legal protection, could offer a way out of this dilemma.[34] However, in the immediate future the courts are unlikely to abandon their firmly-held principles.[35] The survey which follows of the judicial review of discretionary decisions by the administration will there-

---

[31] On this problem, see F. Wagener, "Der 'Vorbehalt des Gesetzes' im Industriestaat," in H. J. von Oertzen (editor), Antworten der öffentlichen Verwaltung auf die Anforderungen der heutigen Gesellschaftssysteme, *Schriften der Deutschen Sektion des Internationalen Instituts für Verwaltungswissenschaften* Bonn 1980, Vol. 5, pp. 13 *et seq.* (21 *et seq.*).

[32] See, with examples, H.-U. Erichsen, *op. cit.*, footnote 26, p. 24; see also H.-W. Rengeling, "Anlagenbegriff, Schadensvorsorge und Verfahrensstufung im Atomrecht—Bemerkungen zu dem Urteil des Bundesverwaltungsgerichts vom 19.12.1985 betreffend das Kernkraftwerk Wyhl im Hinblick auf den Begriff 'Stand von Wissenschaft und Technik' in § 7, Abs. 2 Nr. 3 AtomG," (regarding the evaluation of risk for compensation purposes), DVBl. 1986, pp. 265 *et seq.*

[33] See M. Bullinger, *op. cit.*, footnote 26, p. 25.

[34] See, for example, H. Ehmke, *op. cit.*, footnote 30, pp. 48 *et seq.*, suggesting other criteria for the extent of judicial review.

[35] See the judgment of the Federal Administrative Court (BVerwG) of July 27, 1985, N.J.W. 1986, pp. 796 *et seq.*, esp. p. 798, on the idea of the "hospital which is efficient, cost-effective and adapted to need" and which, in the court's view, does not allow for either appraisal or planning judgments.

fore focus on discretion in the narrow sense of a choice of legal effects. As for the undefined concepts, it has already been explained that they can be fully tested by the courts and that the review process is only occasionally limited by the presence of some scope for appraisal.

2. Judicial Review of discretionary decisions

According to section 40 of the Law on Administrative Procedure (VwVfG), public authorities must "exercise their discretionary power in conformity with the purpose for which authority has been granted, and must observe the statutory limits of discretion." The review of discretionary decisions of the administration is expressly governed by section 114 of the Rules of Procedure for Administrative Courts (VwGO) of January 21, 1960:

> "Where the administrative authority is empowered to use its discretion, the court will also satisfy itself that the acts or omissions of the administration are not unlawful because the statutory limits of discretion have been exceeded, or because discretion has been exercised in a manner not in conformity with the authority granted."

Section 114 of the VwGO refers to the material aspects, or the content, of a discretionary decision. There is no mention here of the formal limits, since these apply to all administrative conduct, not simply to the exercise of discretion.[36] They include the rule that the administrative body must possess proper authority and must observe the prescribed procedure and form.[37] The formal requirements set for administrative conduct are significant in so far as the exercise of discretion is governed by rules of procedure; this does not of course prejudge the outcome, but does offer a sounder guarantee that it will be the correct one, chiefly because there is a right to a hearing and other rights of participation.[38] The courts have

---

[36] B. Drews, G. Wacke, K. Vogel, W. Martens, *Gefahrenabwehr* (9th ed., Cologne/Berlin/ Bonn/Munich 1986), p. 376, interpret Section 114 of the VwGO in a broader sense, to include procedural errors (p. 377). Similarly, H.-U. Erichsen, W. Martens, *op. cit.*, footnote 8, p. 197, footnote 40, explain the absence in Section 114 of the VwGO of any test of procedure and content by the theory that judicial control "naturally" extends to these aspects of an administrative decision.

[37] Where procedural and formal requirements are not governed by special legislation, the laws on administrative procedure of the Bund or the Länder will apply, depending on whether the authority is a Federal or Land authority.

[38] On the relationship between procedural and substantive law in the case of limited judicial control of administrative decisions, see J. Schwarze, *Der funktionale Zusammenhang von Verwaltungsverfahrensrecht und verwaltungsgerichtlichem Rechtsschutz*, Berlin, 1974, pp. 64 *et seq*.

wide-ranging powers to test for compliance with the formal rules governing discretionary decisions, unless the administration has been specifically exempted.

As regards the material aspects of judicial control, section 114 of the VwGO mentions two causes of error: exceeding the bounds of discretion, and making wrongful use of discretionary power. The statutory bounds of discretion will be exceeded whenever the decision fails to observe the outer legal limits of administrative discretion. For example, the bounds of discretion will be exceeded if the public authority orders a result which is not contemplated by statute.[39]

Another error in the exercise of discretion is covered by the prohibition against its wrongful use.[40] This prohibition sets certain requirements for the points considered by the authorities in exercising their discretion. They must be sufficient, not unreasonable, relevant and appropriate to the purpose, and must observe the ban on unconstitutional excesses and the principle of equality.[41]

Misuse of discretion is a subordinate category of the wrongful use of discretion; it covers cases in which irrelevant views, such as personal preferences (friendship or hostility) have played a part in the discretionary decision.[42] This will render the administrative decision unlawful, even if it observes the outer limits of discretion. Where the motives of an individual administrator are subjective and therefore unacceptable, this is similar to the French *détournement de pouvoir*, which is generally used to mean a subjective exercise of official authority, contrary to the purpose of a statute.[43] Finally, a public authority may not attach a condition to a discretionary decision requiring some form of payment by the citizen

---

[39] B. Drews, G. Wacke, K. Vogel, W. Martens *op. cit.*, footnote 36, p. 378; N. Achterberg, *op. cit.*, footnote 13, p. 347, no. 57.

[40] *Ibid.*, the term previously in general use was misuse of discretion. Nowadays, misuse of discretion is treated as a subsidiary category of wrongful use of discretion.

[41] *Ibid.*

[42] *Ibid.* see also H.-U. Erichsen, W. Martens (editors), *op. cit.*, footnote 8, p. 198; H. P. Bull, *Allgemeines Verwaltungsrecht* (2nd ed., Heidelberg 1986), p. 151, no. 480.

[43] See the opinion of Lagrange A.-G. in Case 3/54 *Assider* v. *High Authority* [1954–55] E.C.R. 63, at 83, esp. 85. See also W. Rupprecht, *Die Nachprüfungsbefugnis des Europäischen Gerichtshofs gegenüber Ermessenshandlungen der Exekutive in der Montanunion und der Europäischen Wirtschaftsgemeinschaft*, Kiel 1962, p. 51, which finds the German concept of misuse of discretion more meaningful than the French *détournement de pouvoir*.

where this would be extraneous to the legal purpose of the desired administrative act.[44]

A further cause of error is the failure to exercise discretion when required to do so, also called discretionary negligence.[45] This occurs whenever the administration mistakenly supposes that it is under a precise legal obligation and neglects to use the discretionary power which it possesses. If there is a provision calling for the use of discretion, the administration is bound to exercise it in a manner appropriate to the circumstances.[46] Finally, a statement of fact which is incorrect or incomplete in any important respects will lead to error in the use of discretion, since this will preclude adequate and appropriate consideration of the different views involved.[47]

III. STATUTORY CONSTRAINTS AND DISCRETION IN ITALY

The development of Italian administrative law, and especially the role of the administrative courts, has been briefly described in Chapter 2.[1] The administrative courts share with the ordinary courts the task of protecting individuals from unlawful administrative conduct.[2] As in the other legal systems already described, judicial control of the actions of the administration ends at the point where the scope for administrative discretion

---

[44] H.-U. Erichsen, W. Martens (editors), *op. cit.*, footnote 8, p. 167; H. Faber, *op. cit.*, footnote 8, pp. 191 *et seq.*

[45] F. Mayer, F. Kopp, *Allgemeines Verwaltungsrecht* (5th ed., Stuttgart/Munich/Hanover 1985), p. 159, defines it as a constituent element of the wrongful use of discretion. Similarly, B. Drews, G. Wacke, K. Vogel, W. Martens, *op. cit.*, footnote 36, p. 378; but these writers treat the relative categories simply as different aspects of discretionary error. By contrast, H.-U. Erichsen, W. Martens (editors), *op. cit.*, footnote 8, p. 197, equate failure to use discretion with its excessive use, both being failures to observe the statutory limits. In the case law, see BVerwGE 15, p. 196 (199); 37, p. 112 (115 *et seq.*); 48, p. 81 (84).

[46] This does not affect the administration's right to apply internal guidelines in order to achieve greater consistency in its use of discretion. For a full treatment of this question, see F. Ossenbühl, *Verwaltungsvorschriften und Grundgesetz*, Berlin/Zürich 1968. See also B. Drews, G. Wacke, K. Vogel, W. Martens, *op. cit.*, footnote 36, pp. 393 *et seq.*, which points out that administrative rules must make some allowance for the exercise of discretion, to provide for the main function of discretion, which is to enable the public authority to take account of the particular features of an individual case.

[47] *cf.* B. Drews, G. Wacke, K. Vogel, W. Martens, *op. cit.*, footnote 36, p. 376.

[1] See also the "Introduction" chapter.

[2] *cf.* D. Karwiese, *Kontrolle der Verwaltung durch ordentliche Gerichte und allgemeine Verwaltungsgerichte nach italienischem Recht*, Frankfurt a.M. 1986, pp. 31 *et seq.*

begins.[3] Hence in Italy too, discretionary power (*discrezionalità*) signifies that, in certain defined areas, how the administration is to act is not laid down in any statute, nor are its actions open to judicial review.[4] In Italy there is no strict division, such as we find in German administrative law, between undefined concepts and discretion.[5]

The standards of review applied by the administrative courts are borrowed from French law,[6] but with some modification, since only three of the four traditional grounds for revocation have been taken over into the Italian system: want of competence (incompetenza), breach of statute (violazione di legge) and wrongful use of discretion (eccesso di potere),[7] the latter, in the contemporary case law of the Consiglio di Stato, is a blanket term for all discretionary errors.[8]

The grounds for revocation, like the French "cas d'ouverture," are only a rough framework for the review of administrative decisions, hence particularly of discretionary decisions. Within this framework, academic writers and the courts have combined to formulate a wide range of discretionary errors.[9] Thus the court must first satisfy itself in general terms that the administration was not only properly authorised to act as it did and followed the prescribed procedure, but also that it proceeded on the basis of a complete and relevant statement of facts, and that these have been correctly subsumed under the applicable rule of law.[10] An important additional factor is that in Italian administrative proceedings, the inquisitorial principle applies only to a very limited extent.[11] Hence the court relies mainly on examining the facts adduced by the public authority or by the plaintiff. If this reveals any error as to the facts, the administrative decision will be voidable (travisamento dei fatti).

The category *illogicità manifesta* covers cases where there is obviously no logical connection between the result decided by the administration

---

[3] On the nature of discretion, see A. M. Sandulli, *Manuale di diritto amministrativo* (14th ed., Naples 1984), no. 122, pp. 571 *et seq.*

[4] *Ibid., op. cit.*, footnote 3.

[5] Instead, in recent times a distinction has been drawn between the application of undefined statutory concepts, defined as "technical discretion," and what is called "free discretion" in the fulfilment of legal aims. See A. M. Sandulli, *op. cit.*, footnote 3, no. 122, pp. 573 *et seq.*

[6] See B. W. Meister, *Ermessensmissbrauch oder détournement de pouvoir als Fehlertatbestand der Nichtigkeitsklage des Montanvertrages*, Bielefeld 1971, p. 78.

[7] A. M. Sandulli, *op. cit.*, footnote 3, no. 144, p. 685; G. Landi, G. Potenza, *Manuale di diritto amministrativo*, (7th ed., Milan 1983), p. 258.

[8] *cf.* B. W. Meister, *op. cit.*, footnote 6, p. 80.

[9] There is a detailed comment in D. Karwiese, *op. cit.*, footnote 2, p. 46.

[10] *cf.* G. Landi, G. Potenza, *op. cit.*, footnote 7, p. 260.

[11] See Chapter I "Introduction."

and the reasons for its decision; this implies a faulty intention on the part of the authorities.[12] Again, inconsistent treatment of similar cases, not warranted by the circumstances, will render the administrative decision voidable.[13] Similarly, the principle of equal treatment will render unlawful an administrative decision which conflicts with an internal administrative guideline.[14] Discretionary error also occurs where a decision conflicts outright with a previous, or simultaneous, decision by the same administration (incoerenza manifesta).[15]

An administrative decision which is obviously inequitable or inappropriate (ingiustizia manifesta) will also be unlawful.[16] Finally, mention should be made of the classic *eccesso di potere*, misuse of discretion in the sense of the French *détournement de pouvoir*. This error occurs where the public authority, in making its decision, pursues an aim other than the aim prescribed in law. If it acts from a mixture of motives, the unlawful motive will be treated as uppermost.[17]

IV. STATUTORY CONSTRAINTS AND DISCRETION IN THE UNITED KINGDOM

1. Fundamentals of Administrative Discretion in the United Kingdom

Although Dicey, in defining the rule of law, apparently precluded any scope for discretion by the executive,[1] "discretionary power" may be seen nowadays as an accepted part of the English system of administrative law, and indeed an indispensable part in an era of expanding state functions. Many statutes endow the administration with a broad authority to decide as it thinks fit.

In line with the generally pragmatic character of English administrative law, there is no elaborate doctrine of discretion such as we find in Germany, Switzerland or Austria.[2] Instead, the amount of freedom

---

[12] G. Landi, G. Potenza, *op. cit.*, footnote 7, p. 260.
[13] *Ibid.*
[14] *Ibid.*, *op. cit.*, footnote 7, p. 261.
[15] See B. W. Meister, *op. cit.*, footnote 6, p. 82.
[16] G. Landi, G. Potenza, *op. cit.*, footnote 7, p. 261.
[17] *Ibid.*, *op. cit.*, footnote 7, p. 259, gives these defects the name *sviamento di potere*, to distinguish them from the broader concept of *eccesso di potere*.
[1] *cf.* A. V. Dicey, *Introduction to the Study of the Law of the Constitution* (9th ed., London 1948), p. 202.
[2] For Germany, see Chapter II above; for Switzerland, see T. Fleiner-Gerster, *Grundzüge des allgemeinen und schweizerischen Verwaltungsrechts* (2nd ed., Zürich 1980), pp. 119 *et seq.*; for Austria, see L. K. Adamovich, B.-C. Funk, *Allgemeines Verwaltungsrecht* (2nd ed., Vienna/New York 1984), pp. 114 *et seq.*

enjoyed by the administration in its decision-making matches the extent of the review powers which the courts consider necessary in each area of administrative authority. Decisions made under the prerogative of the Crown are exempt from judicial review, although even in this area there is a trend towards tighter control. The courts' powers of investigation are limited by certain types of plea, with their accompanying "grounds of review." Two governing standards have been formulated to control discretionary decisions: the doctrine of *ultra vires* and the principles of natural justice.[3] Because they originated in the practice of the courts, neither of these standards for the legality of administrative conduct has been given any full or precise definition.[4] A whole range of suggested definitions can be found in English learned sources, but the practical applications, by contrast, are remarkably uniform.

2. The Ultra Vires Doctrine

If a public authority acts outside the scope of its authority—which is mostly defined by statute—it is acting *ultra vires*.[5] In an attempt to put some flesh on the bones of this general statement, different types of cases have been described.

It is plain from the first of these groups of cases how broad the concept can be. Cases of "procedural *ultra vires*" relate to formal and procedural defects, some of which are also covered by the principles of natural justice.[6] Procedural *ultra vires* involves action by a wrongly constituted authority, or by one lacking in due authority, for instance if a decision in a case is referred from the responsible authority to one without responsibility (*delegatus non potest delegare*).

An interesting case to illustrate the latter group of procedural defects was the decision in *Lavender* v. *Minister of Housing and Local Govern-*

---

[3] See H. W. R. Wade, *Administrative Law* (5th ed., Oxford 1982), pp. 348 *et seq.* and pp. 413 *et seq.*; O. Hood Phillips, P. Jackson, *Constitutional and Administrative Law* (6th ed., London 1978), pp. 596 *et seq.* on the *ultra vires* doctrine, also pp. 602 *et seq.* on natural justice. For a detailed explanation of the *ultra vires* doctrine, see R. Glücksmann, *Die Grenzen der Betätigung englischer Verwaltungsbehörden*, Frankfurt a.M. 1984.

[4] E. H. Riedel, *Kontrolle der Verwaltung im englischen Rechtssystem*, Berlin 1976, p. 91 on the *ultra vires* doctrine, also referring to natural justice, pp. 106 *et seq.*

[5] O. Hood Phillips, P. Jackson, *op. cit.*, footnote 3, p. 595.

[6] See E. H. Riedel, *op. cit.*, footnote 4, p. 92; *cf.* also H. W. R. Wade, *Administrative Law*, Oxford 1961, p. 45.

ment.[7] The plaintiff had applied to the Minister of Housing for permission to extract minerals on a site used for agriculture. Consent was refused because the Minister of Agriculture raised objections on agricultural grounds. The court which dealt with the consequent appeal rescinded the refusal as *ultra vires*, because the Minister of Housing had given his colleague in the agriculture ministry a sort of right of veto, this being equivalent to a delegation of authority which he was not entitled to make. Similarly, a decision to fix the rents in a block of dwellings at a flat rate, rather than on the individual basis required by the statutory authority, was found to be unlawful.[8]

By contrast, cases of "substantive *ultra vires*"[9] relate to the substance of official decisions. Review practice is extremely varied for cases of this type, and no firm rules have been developed to fix the precise extent of the courts' review powers in any particular instance. In one particular case the local authority had the power to expropriate parcels of land which did not form part of a private park. The court therefore found that an order for expropriation which affected a part of the park was *ultra vires*.

In the court's view, this was a question of fact, and the court was within its rights to consider the interpretation of the facts unless prevented by statute from doing so.[10]

In the law on aliens, which, in the United Kingdom also, leaves a substantial measure of discretion to the public authorities, the courts also consider whether the facts have been wrongly interpreted. For instance, in *R. v. Home Secretary, ex parte Venicoff*, they had to consider whether the person concerned was, or was not, an alien.[11]

A legal question of a different kind was involved in *London County Council v. A.-G.*[12] The council of Greater London had statutory authority to acquire trams. The statute referred only to "trams," but the council had construed it to mean that the city was empowered to take over the operation of the fleet of buses belonging to a tram company. Hence in this case the facts were not in dispute, but merely the extent of a permissible interpretation of the word "trams." The court decided that "buses" and "trams" could not be treated as interchangeable concepts.

---

[7] [1970] 3 All E.R. 871 at 880.
[8] *R. v. Paddington and St. Marylebone Rent Tribunal*, [1949] 1 All E.R., 720.
[9] *cf.* E. H. Riedel, *op. cit.*, footnote 4, p. 94.
[10] *White and Collins* v. *Minister of Health*, [1939] 2 K.B. 838.
[11] [1920] 3 K.B. 72.
[12] [1902] A.C. 165.

Another decision turned on the question whether certain buildings were to be treated as "houses" within the meaning of a statute. The judge commented[13]:

"Whether or not a particular building falls under that word is a mixed question of law and of fact—fact in so far as it is necessary to ascertain all the relevant facts relating to the building, and law in so far as the application of the word 'houses' to those facts involves the construction of the Act."

Hence in his view, it was a mixed question of fact and of law, and therefore within the competence of the court.

The *ultra vires* doctrine also encompasses cases in which the administration has either failed to pay sufficient heed to the purpose of a law, or has pursued aims which fall wholly outside it. The case which became known as the *Padfield Case* is a significant example of the former group.[14] It rested on the Agricultural Marketing Act 1958, which defined the English system for the marketing of agricultural produce. This law provided that disputes and complaints arising from the individual marketing regulations would be dealt with by a committee of investigation, if the Minister responsible ordered one to be set up ("if the Minister in any case so directs"). Problems arose in the context of the milk marketing system. This system provided that milk would be delivered to the so-called Milk Marketing Board, which paid different prices for it, depending on which of the 11 regions into which England and Wales had been divided under the milk marketing system had supplied the milk. The price differences among regions reflected the differing costs of transporting the milk from the producer to the consumer. However, the cost structure had altered over the years to such an extent that the fixed differentials in transport costing no longer corresponded to the true situation. As a result of the changed situation, the producers in the south-west of the country felt themselves to be disadvantaged. Although they had a seat and a vote on the crucial decision-making bodies of the Milk Marketing Board, they were numerically too small to secure a majority for their views on pricing. They therefore applied to the responsible Minister to set up the committee of investigation provided for by statute, to ensure that the situation

---

[13] *Re Camberwell (Wingfield News) No. 2 Clearance Order 1936* [1939] 1 All E.R. 590 at 597.

[14] *Padfield* v. *Minister of Agriculture, Fisheries and Food* [1968] A.C. 997; see also D. C. U. Yardley, "The Abuse of Powers and its Control in English Administrative Law," *The American Journal of Comparative Law*, Vol. 18 (1970), pp. 565 *et seq.* (571 *et seq.*).

and their demands would be examined by a neutral body. If the committee were to find that the producers' complaints were justified, the Minister would have powers under the Agricultural Marketing Act to instruct the Marketing Board at his discretion (if he thinks fit).

However, the Minister rejected the application on the ground that the committee of investigation was not the proper forum to resolve a problem of milk pricing structures, which touched on wider political issues. Furthermore, because of its democratic structure, the Milk Marketing Board, of which the plaintiff was himself a member, was a more suitable body for taking a decision.[15] The House of Lords held that his decision was unlawful, since it conflicted with the purpose of the statutory authority. Lord Upjohn commented[16]:

> "(A) decision of the Minister stands on quite a different basis; he is a public officer charged by Parliament with the discharge of a public discretion affecting Her Majesty's subjects; if he does not give any reason for his decision it may be, if circumstances warrant it, that a court may be at liberty to come to the conclusion that he had no good reason for reaching that conclusion and order a prerogative writ to issue accordingly.
>
> The Minister in my opinion has not given a single valid reason for refusing to order an inquiry into the legitimate complaint (be it well founded or not) of the South-Eastern Region; all his disclosed reasons for refusing to do so are bad in law."

There will also be an unlawful use of discretion where the public authority uses its powers for unlawful ends (improper purposes).[17] In one famous case a railway company brought an action to restrain the City of Westminster from building a street subway crossing.[18] The statute in question provided only for the construction of toilets, not for the building of a subway at the same time. The complaint of the railway company was rejected, but the House of Lords admitted that to build a public toilet solely for the purpose of building a subway would have been *ultra vires*. An intention to do this could not, however, be reliably proved.[19] This

---

[15] See [1968] A.C. 999 *et seq.*; *cf.* also D. C. U. Yardley, *op. cit.*, footnote 14, pp. 571 *et seq.*
[16] [1968] A.C. 1062.
[17] *cf.* J. F. Garner, B. L. Jones, *Administrative Law* (6th ed., London 1985), pp. 126 *et seq.*, with references.
[18] [1905] A.C. 426.
[19] E. H. Riedel, *op. cit.*, footnote 4, p. 96.

form of *ultra vires* conduct is perceptibly akin to the French *détournement de pouvoir*.

Further instances of the *ultra vires* doctrine are found where a public authority unlawfully limits its own use of discretion through administrative directives which preclude any examination of individual cases.[20] This does not mean that guidelines may not be set for the use of discretion; it means only that such guidelines must offer sufficient flexibility for an examination of individual cases, and for the possibility of departing from the guideline when they are resolved.

Finally, inequitable or inappropriate decisions are *ultra vires* and therefore unlawful.[21] This group consists mainly of cases showing the so-called "unreasonableness" of an administrative act. One example is the judgment in *Prescott* v. *Birmingham Corporation*.[22] This turned on a decision by the city of Birmingham to grant the old-age pensioners of the city free use of public transport, leading to a substantial loss of revenue. A ratepayer instituted proceedings against the city corporation. The Court of Appeal quashed the decision as *ultra vires*, since it did not represent a reasonable transport policy.

The above brief sketch is an attempt to bring out the basic principles of judicial review of administrative conduct in Britain through the doctrine of *ultra vires*. The main applications of this doctrine, at least, should become clear through examples of cases. The flexibility of the review practice of the courts reflects the pragmatic approach of English law, although critics feel that it detracts from the legal protection available to citizens.[23] It is obvious, however, that the courts are seeking to tighten the legal constraints on the use of discretion by the administration.

3.   The Principle of Natural Justice

The second part of this survey has already referred to natural justice and its function, and this theme is further examined in the chapter dealing with procedural rights. Only a few additional remarks will be made here. Natural justice is purely procedural in character, and relates to the circumstances in which an administrative decision is made and takes

---

[20] See *Simms Motor Units, Ltd.* v. *Minister of Labour*, [1946] 2 All E.R. 201.
[21] *cf.* the leading case of *Kruse* v. *Johnson*, [1898] 2 Q.B. 91.
[22] 1955, 1 Ch. 210; see O. Hood Phillips, *Leading Cases in Constitutional and Administrative Law* (5th ed., London 1979), pp. 311 *et seq.*
[23] See, *e.g.* E. M. Riedel, *op. cit.*, footnote 4, p. 120.

effect. The chief rules by which it is inspired are the generally accepted principle *audi alteram partem*[24] and the principle *nemo iudex in causa sua debet esse*.[25] As we have already said in connection with the doctrine of *ultra vires*, this overlaps to some extent with procedural *ultra vires*. We see here that there is no sharp distinction between the two; this is reflected in K. Löwenstein's comment that an offence against natural justice will stamp an administrative decision as *ultra vires*, although in a formal sense there is no breach of authority.[26]

V. STATUTORY CONSTRAINTS AND DISCRETION IN BELGIUM

Belgian administrative law also distinguishes between administrative decisions subject to restriction and those which may be made at the discretion of a public authority.

Although the law recognises that the administration is free to use its discretion, it is for the latter to decide which step seems most appropriate for achieving the goal set. It can judge for itself whether its conduct is advisable in the circumstances, and the courts are forbidden to substitute their own judgment for this.[1] As in Dutch law, no clear distinction is made between discretion (pouvoir discrétionnaire/discretionaire bevoegdheid) and scope for appraisal (beoordelingsbevoegdheid).[2]

The concept of discretion is contrasted with the idea of being bound by statute. A statutory compulsion exists whenever the law prescribes the nature or the subject-matter of a decision which the administration is obliged to take if the preconditions specified in the statute are fulfilled.[3] The lawmaker seeks to reconcile the advantages for the citizen of statutory constraints with the requirement of expediency, which warrants a measure of discretion being granted to the administration. This explains

---

[24] O. Hood Phillips, P. Jackson, *op. cit.*, footnote 3, pp. 604 *et seq.*; for a full commentary, see S. A. de Smith, J. U. Evans, *Judicial Review of Administrative Action* (4th ed., London 1980), pp. 175 *et seq.*

[25] O. Hood Phillips, P. Jackson, *op. cit.*, footnote 3, pp. 603 *et seq.*

[26] K. Löwenstein, *Staatsrecht und Staatspraxis von Grossbritannien*, Vol. II, Berlin/Heidelberg/New York, 1967, p. 101.

[1] A. Mast, J. Dujardin, *Overzicht van Belgisch Administratief Recht* (9th ed., Gent 1984), no. 567; *cf.* also C. Cambier, *Droit administratif*, Brussels 1968.

[2] *cf.* A. Mast, *op. cit.*, footnote 1, no. 567.

[3] A. Mast, *op. cit.*, footnote 1, no. 568.

why administrative laws often contain provisions allowing for discretionary judgment in certain aspects of a decision, but none at all in other aspects.[4]

Discretion must be exercised within the limits defined in the statute. The Council of State requires the administration to weigh up the conflicting public and private interests involved before reaching a decision. Moreover, the reasons for the decision must bear out the lawfulness and reasonableness of the decision.[5] Hence discretionary freedom is limited, as in the Netherlands, by a so-called principle of reasonableness.[6]

As in Dutch administrative law, in Belgium the prohibition against *détournement de pouvoir* is governed expressly by statute.[7] *Détournement de pouvoir* exists where the administration acts with the intention of harming someone,[8] when it uses its authority for the advantage of a particular individual or individuals without heed to public welfare,[9] or when it exercises its functions for a public purpose other than the one for which the authority was conferred.[10]

However, instances of *détournement de pouvoir* are extremely rare in the case law of the Council of State. As far as can be ascertained, this principle has not been applied since 1961.[11] The reason for this is that a case of *détournement de pouvoir* can be proven only if the following conditions are fulfilled[12]:

1. The (unlawful) intention must have been the only deciding factor in the administrative decision.
2. There must be no connection between this intention and the statutory authority which has been exercised.

---

[4] A. Mast, *op. cit.*, footnote 1, no. 568; for example, the laws of August 3, 1919 and May 27, 1947 on the special rights of war combatants and similar categories confer both discretionary and non-discretionary authority.

[5] A. Mast, *op. cit.*, footnote 1, no. 568.

[6] A. Mast, *op. cit.*, footnote 1, no. 568; see also L. P. Suetens, "Algemene beginselen van behoorlijk bestuur in de rechtspraak van de Raad van State." *Tijdschrift voor bestuurswetenschappen en publiek recht* (TvB), 1981, pp. 81, 86 *et seq.*

[7] Article 14 of the Law of the Council of State.

[8] J. Dembour, *Droit administratif* (3rd ed., Liège 1978), no. 212, 1.

[9] J. Dembour, *op. cit.*, footnote 8, no. 212, 2.

[10] J. Dembour, *op. cit.*, footnote 8, no. 212, 3.

[11] L. P. Suetens, "Algemene rechtsbeginselen en algemene beginselen van behoorlijk bestuur in het Belgisch administratief recht," TvB 1970, pp. 379, 383; *ibid.* TvB 1981, p. 86; relevant cases: Council of State judgment no. 985 of June 30, 1951, *Exelmans*; 1,632 of June 11, 1952, *Schraepen*; 2,574 of June 16, 1953, *Matthys*; 3,748 of October 26, 1954, *Detry*; 8,712 of July 3, 1961, *Janssens*.

[12] See L. P. Suetens, TvB 1970, p. 383; F. Debaedts, *Machtsafwending, Algemene praktische rechtsverzameling*, Ghent 1956, nos. 197–199.

3. There must be a causal link between the facts and grounds for suspicion indicating the existence of an unlawful intention, and the decision impugned.

The Council of State is more likely to annul an administrative decision because of defective grounds than because of *détournement de pouvoir*. In any case, the broad interpretation placed on another ground for revocation under Article 14 of the Law of the Council of State—namely, *excès de pouvoir*—often renders the legal notion of *détournement de pouvoir* unnecessary.[13]

VI. *STATUTORY CONSTRAINTS AND DISCRETION IN DENMARK*

As already explained in Part 2 of this chapter, control of administrative conduct in Denmark is exercised by means of the four traditional French causes of action: want of due authority, procedural and formal defects, breach of statute and *détournement de pouvoir*.[1] Unlike French procedure, the degree of judicial control is determined not by a variety of "voies de recours," but according to the extent to which the administrative decision is determined by statute.[2] Hence the administration can be ordered to adopt a particular course of action if the prior conditions and the result to be achieved are prescribed by law.[3] Examples of this include payments made on the basis of social welfare legislation, or the payment of compensation by the administration.[4]

On the other hand, the courts cannot go beyond setting aside of the administrative decision, if it is a discretionary one; they cannot substitute any other decision for it.[5] Their review powers are confined to the legality of the administrative decision; it is for the executive to decide whether the decision is advisable in itself.[6]

---

[13] L. P. Suetens, TvB 1970, p. 384; *cf.* Council of State judgment no. 4,590 of October 7, 1955, *Stocklet* and *Lion*.

[1] See Pt. 2, Section I, VIII, 2.

[2] B. Christensen, in *Gerichtsschutz gegen die Exekutive*, Cologne/Berlin/Bonn/Munich 1969, Vol. 1, p. 119.

[3] *Ibid.*

[4] G. T. Nielsen, *Constitutional and Administrative Law*, in H. Gammeltoft-Hansen, B. Gomard, Λ. Philip (editors): *Danish Law—A General Survey*, G.E.C. Gads Publishing House, Copenhagen 1982, p. 61.

[5] B. Christensen, *op. cit.*, footnote 2, p. 119.

[6] *Ibid., op. cit.*, footnote 2, p. 118.

VII. STATUTORY CONSTRAINTS AND DISCRETION IN GREECE

Under Article 95 of the 1975 Constitution, the Council of State may entertain applications to annul enforceable decisions by the administrative authorities.[1] The standards of review are the *cas d'ouverture* taken from the French *recours pour excès de pouvoir*: want of due authority, procedural and formal defects, breach of statute and misuse of powers.[2] Discretionary decisions by the administration will be unlawful and open to revocation if they transgress statutory limits or breach general principles of law, or if the administrative authority has misused its discretion.[3] The plea of misuse of discretion has gained in importance in Greece, as it has in French administrative law, by comparison with the plea of breach of statute.[4]

As in all the administrative law systems surveyed in this study, judgments of the expediency or otherwise of an administrative decision are beyond the reach of the courts.[5] The Greek doctrine apparently does not distinguish sufficiently between undefined legal concepts and discretion so as to affect the degree of judicial control. T. Tsatsos observes, however, that the value judgments which are necessarily involved in applying undefined concepts cannot form discretionary decisions, since they do not allow for a number of equally valid alternative outcomes in individual cases.[6] He sees this form of statutory constraint as ultimately a kind of intermingling of non-discriminatory and discretionary administration, which the courts can scarcely review unless the reasons for the decision are adequately explained.[7]

VIII. STATUTORY CONSTRAINTS AND DISCRETION IN IRELAND

Because of the historical background, the development of judicial review procedures for administrative decisions in Ireland has followed a

---

[1] See also Introduction.
[2] *cf.* P. Dagtoglou, in *Südosteuropa-Handbuch*, Vol. 3, p. 52.
[3] See W. Skouris, "L'illégalité de l'action administrative, comme fondement de la responsabilité de la puissance publique en Grèce," *Journées de la Société de législation comparée*, 1984, pp. 51 *et seq.* (57).
[4] *Ibid.*
[5] T. Tsatsos, in *Gerichtsschutz gegen die Exekutive*, Cologne/Berlin/Bonn/Munich 1969, Vol. I, pp. 277 *et seq.* (310).
[6] *Ibid., op. cit.*, footnote 5, 309.
[7] *Ibid.*

pattern similar to that in the United Kingdom.[1] This is especially true of the doctrine of *ultra vires*,[2] from which have emerged a range of standards for judicial review, including investigation of the facts relevant to the decision and of purely legal questions.[3] Finally, the doctrine of "natural justice," with its procedural guarantees, is also of great importance in reviewing administrative decisions.[4]

IX. STATUTORY CONSTRAINTS AND DISCRETION IN LUXEMBOURG

In Luxembourg, as already explained, the judicial control of administrative conduct largely follows the French model.[1] Hence discretionary decisions by the executive are reviewed by the Council of State (Conseil d'État) in its capacity as an administrative court, on the basis of *recours pour excès de pouvoir*, which in Luxembourg are incorporated in legislation.[2] However, judicial review powers do not extend to the expediency (opportunité) of a decision.[3]

X. STATUTORY CONSTRAINTS AND DISCRETION IN THE NETHERLANDS

Dutch administrative law distinguishes between bound and discretionary decisions. Bound decisions tend to be the exception.[1] One reason for this is that Dutch administrative law—like French law—does not distinguish expressly between discretion and scope for appraisal.[2] Hence there is no uniform terminology; reference is sometimes made to *beleidsvrijheid* (free discretion),[3] and sometimes to *beoordelingsruimte*

---

[1] See above, Pt. 2, Section 1, A. IV; *cf.* also R. M. Stout, *Administrative Law in Ireland*, Dublin 1985, pp. 92 *et seq.*

[2] See J. M. Kelly, *Gerichtsschutz gegen die Exekutive*, Cologne/Berlin/Bonn/Munich 1969, Vol. I, pp. 425 *et seq.* (432). See also R. M. Stout, *op. cit.*, footnote 1, p. 93.

[3] R. M. Stout, *op. cit.*, footnote 1.

[4] R. M. Stout, *op. cit.*, footnote 1, pp. 456 *et seq.*

[1] *cf.* above, Chapter 2.

[2] See P. Majerus, *L'Etat Luxembourgeois* (4th ed., Luxembourg 1983), p. 201.

[3] *Ibid.*

[1] A. M. Donner, *Nederlands Bestuursrecht*, Algemeen Deel, (4th ed., Alphen a/d Rijn 1974), p. 226.

[2] A. M. Donner, *op. cit.*, footnote 1, pp. 227 *et seq.*; *cf.* also D. de Haan, Th. G. Drupsteen, R. Fernhout, *Bestuursrecht in de Sociale Rechtsstaat*, Kluwer-Deventer 1978, p. 414.

[3] D. de Haan, Th. G. Drupsteen, R. Fernhout, *op. cit.*, footnote 2, p. 20.

(scope for appraisal).[4] However, both ideas carry the same meaning.[5] To explain them, borrowings are often made from German or French terminology.[6]

Although there is no express distinction between discretion and scope for appraisal, the two are distinguished in practice. The administration has no discretion when dealing with undefined legal concepts, as long as their meaning is clear or can be elucidated.[7] The fact that the lawmakers leave it to the executive to interpret them in practice does not exempt the latter from legal constraints.[8] The situation is somewhat different with undefined legal concepts which call for a weighing-up of the respective interests involved.[9] For example, Article 7 of the Law on Housing Accommodation empowers the administration to "secure an appropriate allocation of housing-space in the local community," taking account of individual interests. Ideas such as "general needs" indicate that the executive has room to exercise its discretion.[10]

Express authority to act on a discretionary basis is found in terms such as "in the cases determined by the mayor and municipal governor" or "in the opinion of," as also in provisions which state that the administration "may" do something.[11] In the area of discretion, a distinction is drawn between discretionary decisions and discretionary choices.[12]

By granting discretionary power, the legislature gives the executive room to choose for itself which methods to adopt and how it will make its decisions. Within this context several different and indeed conflicting outcomes may be perceived as being equally lawful.[13] Discretion must be properly exercised, *i.e.* in accordance with the purpose of the rule, and in the light of the interests which it seeks to promote.[14] The limits of discretionary freedom are furthermore derived from the general principles of sound administration.[15]

---

[4] A. M. Donner, *op. cit.*, footnote 1, p. 227; here, however, using the concept in the sense of "free discretion" and "pouvoir discrétionnaire."

[5] *cf.* A. M. Donner, *op. cit.*, footnote 1, p. 232.

[6] T. Koopmans, *Vergelijkend publiekrecht*, Deventer 1978, pp. 104 *et seq.*

[7] A. M. Donner, *op. cit.*, footnote 1, pp. 227 *et seq.*

[8] A. M. Donner, *op. cit.*, footnote 1, p. 228.

[9] A. M. Donner, *op. cit.*, footnote 1, pp. 228 *et seq.*

[10] A. M. Donner, *op. cit.*, footnote 1, p. 230; D. de Haan, Th. G. Drupsteen, R. Fernhout, *op. cit.*, footnote 2, p. 414.

[11] A. M. Donner, *op. cit.*, footnote 1, p. 232.

[12] A. M. Donner, *op. cit.*, footnote 1, p. 231.

[13] A. M. Donner, *op. cit.*, footnote 1, p. 227.

[14] A. M. Donner, *op. cit.*, footnote 1, p. 232.

[15] A. M. Donner, *op. cit.*, footnote 1, pp. 232 *et seq.*

Mention should here be made of the special prohibition against *détournement de pouvoir*, which is found in Article 8, paragraph 1b of the Arob Law. This legal notion, which is borrowed from the case law of the French Conseil d'Etat,[16] is directed against the exercise of authority for a purpose other than the one prescribed by law.[17] In Dutch administrative law, as in the French system,[18] this means failure to achieve the intended aim.

The prohibition against *détournement de pouvoir*, as a statutory cause of action, was first recognised in the 1929 Law on the Public Service and was later incorporated, in a similar form of wording, in Article 5b of the ARBO Law, Article 4b of the BAB Law and Article 8 1b of the Arob Law. Nowadays, the prohibition against *détournement de pouvoir* is understood as the duty of the administration to exercise a function in accordance with the aim of the lawmaker, and to be guided in so doing by untainted motives and intentions.[19]

The prohibition against *détournement de pouvoir*, as an independent cause of action, plays only a subordinate role in the administrative case law. This can be attributed primarily to the absence of clear guidelines for applying the principle.[20] The courts tend, in cases where this principle would apply, to revoke administrative provisions[21] on the grounds that they are not in conformity with the law[22] or that they fail to satisfy the principle of sufficient motivation (*motiveringsbeginsel*).[23]

XI. STATUTORY CONSTRAINTS AND DISCRETION IN PORTUGAL

The Portuguese system of administrative law also moderates the impact of legal constraints on the executive by providing for discretionary powers[1] and enabling the administrative courts to review the exercise of these powers by ascertaining whether the public authority, in deciding on a certain course of action, has observed the legal limits of discretion. The

---

[16] *cf.* C.E. November 26, 1875, *Pariset*, Recueil 934.
[17] A. M. Donner, *op. cit.*, footnote 1, p. 97; D. de Haan, Th. G. Drupsteen, R. Fernhout, *op. cit.*, footnote 2, p. 37; Rapport ABAR, p. 146.
[18] *cf.* A. de Laubadère, *Traité de droit administratif*, Vol. I, (9th ed., Paris 1984), by J.-C. Venezia, Y. Gaudemet, no. 1182.
[19] Rapport ABAR, p. 147.
[20] *cf.* Rapport ABAR, pp. 147 *et seq.*
[21] See, for example, Article 8, para. 1a of the AROB Law.
[22] See below, Section VI. 5, and Rapport ABAR, pp. 166 *et seq.*
[23] Rapport ABAR, pp. 150 *et seq.*
[1] M. Caetano, *Manual de Direito Administrativo* Vol. I, Coimbra 1984, pp. 484 *et seq.*

governing standards of review for the legality of administrative conduct are akin to the *cas d'ouverture* in French administrative proceedings.[2]

XII. STATUTORY CONSTRAINTS AND DISCRETION IN SPAIN

Spanish administrative law distinguishes between bound and discretionary decisions. The decision is bound whenever the law to be applied in particular circumstances has precisely defined legal effects.[1] By com-

parison, discretionary power exists where a rule leaves it to the administration to choose, on its own responsibility, among several lawful courses of action.[2] The competent courts are empowered to review administrative discretionary decisions only to ascertain that they conform with the prescribed legal limits.[3]

B. CONCLUSION

This comparative survey has shown clearly that every legal system allows the executive some room for decision-making. In this respect administrative law systems all display some similarity. However, it has also been shown that discretion is not merely a question of administrative practice, but in essence touches on a matter of principle, namely the inter-relationship which prevails among state authorities.

The fact that administrative discretion is so strongly rooted in the individual constitutional systems sets clearly-defined limits to any future approximation of the various national rules governing the use and control of discretion. It is to be expected that the constitutional separation and balance of powers among the Parliament, the administration and the courts, which in some cases has taken centuries to develop and which has contributed to the various theories of discretion, will prove resistant to change and will hamper efforts to achieve convergence among the various

---

[2] Further detail in M. Caetano, *op. cit.*, footnote 1, pp. 495 *et seq.*
[1] *cf.* E. García de Enterría, T.-R. Fernandez, *Curso de derecho administrativo* I, (4th ed., Madrid 1984), p. 429.
[2] *Ibid., op. cit.*, footnote 1, p. 434.
[3] *Ibid., op. cit.*, footnote 1, pp. 439 *et seq.*; see also R. Entrena Cuesta, *Curso de derecho administrativo* (8th ed., Madrid 1983), Vol. I/I, pp. 170 *et seq.*; F. Garrido Falla, *Tratado de derecho administrativo* (7th ed., Madrid 1985), Vol. I, pp. 286 *et seq.*

administrative law rules. The relationship of the administration to the courts especially determines how much freedom the executive enjoys in its decision-making. The various systems of legal protection are also of crucial significance in determining the extent of administrative discretion.

SECTION 2

EXECUTIVE FREEDOM OF DECISION IN THE EUROPEAN COMMUNITY

A. INTRODUCTION

I. THE TERMINOLOGY OF COMMUNITY LAW

The judgments of the European Court, in their German translations, refer to the decision-making functions of the executive in a colourful mixture of terms. Discretionary powers and authority appear as *Ermessensbefugnis*,[1] *Beurteilungsspielraum*,[2] and *Beurteilungsermessen*,[3] to name only a few examples.

For German jurists, these terms have a certain dogmatic flavour, which has already been explained in the comparative survey.[4] The use of such familiar concepts as discretion and discretionary powers may well persuade the German jurist that the Court is following the German model and is drawing a clear distinction between undefined legal terms and discretion. Where the judicial review of administrative acts is concerned, this would mean that decisions based on undefined legal terms must be completely open to review.[5] Where the decisions have been made on the basis of discretionary powers, they would be open to only a limited measure of judicial review, limited by considerations of expediency.[6] The study which follows shows, however, that the European Court has not followed the theory prevalent in Germany. Nor would it be correct, generally speaking, to say that the Court adopts the French model of the

---

[1] See, for example, Joined Cases 94 & 96/63 *Pierre Bernusset* v. *Commission* [1964] E.C.R. 297; Case 255/84 *Nachi Fujikoshi Corporation* v. *Council* [1987] E.C.R. 1861.

[2] See, for example, Case 144/82 *Detti* v. *Court of Justice* [1983] E.C.R. 2421 *et seq.* (2436, para. 27); for agriculture, see Joined Cases 279–280 & 285–286/84 *Walter Rau and others* v. *Commission* [1987] E.C.R. 1069 and Case 249/85 *ALBAKO Margarinefabrik* v. *BALM* [1987] E.C.R. 2345.

[3] See, for example, Case 110/63 *Alfred Willame* v. *Commission of the European Atomic Energy Community (Euratom)* [1965] E.C.R. 649.

[4] See above, pp. 254 *et seq.*

[5] See above, p. 256.

[6] See above, p. 256.

296

pouvoir d'appréciation, and that when it refers to value judgments (*Beurteilungsspielraum*) it means the executive's freedom to weigh up the legal significance of the facts. No such consistency can be discerned in the Court's use of terms.[7]

Instead, we shall find in the course of our study that for the European Court, the use of undefined legal terms and the conferment of discretionary powers are only two particular dimensions of a more general phenomenon, which can be broadly described as the executive's freedom to decide and order matters for itself.[8]

How does this affect our approach? We cannot divide our treatment of this phenomenon into two categories: undefined legal terms on the one

---

[7] This is clear, for example, from Case 166/78 *Italy* v. *Council* [1979] E.C.R. 2575 at 2599, para. 14. Here the Court comments on the assessment of the economic factors involved when the Council introduced a premium for potato starch:

"In such circumstances the discretion which the Council has when it assesses a complex economic situation is not only exercisable in relation to the nature and scope of the provisions which are to be adopted but also, to a certain extent, to the findings as to the basic facts, especially in this sense that the Council is free to base its assessment, if necessary, on findings of a general nature."

But the Court took a somewhat different view in Joined Cases 197–200, 243, 245 & 247/80 *Ludwigshafener Walzmühle and others* v. *Council and Commission* [1981] E.C.R. 3211 *et seq.* (3251, para. 37), which dealt with a claim for compensation entered on the basis that the threshold price set for imported durum wheat was too high:

"It should be remembered that, in determining their policy in this area, the competent Community institutions enjoy wide discretionary powers regarding not only establishment of the factual basis of their action but also definition of the objective to be pursued, within the framework of the provisions of the Treaty, and the choice of the appropriate means of action."

If we compare this extract from the judgment with the corresponding passage in the French series, we find a small but significant difference:

"Il convient de rappeler que, dans la détermination de leur politique en la matière, les institutions communautaires compétentes jouissent d'un large pouvoir d'appréciation en ce qui concerne non seulement l'établissement des bases actuelles de leur action, mais encore la définition des objectifs poursuivis, dans le cadre des prévisions du traité, et le choix des instruments d'action appropriés."

Here the term discretion ("Ermessen") has been added in the German version; the French text has only a wide "pouvoir d'appréciation." This shows that to attempt to derive legal notions from the choice of words alone is to start on the wrong tack; instead of clarifying, this further obscures the overall problem of the executive's freedom to decide. See also Joined Cases 39 & 45/81 *Halyvourgiki* v. *Commission* [1982] E.C.R. 593 *et seq.*, at 616, para. 22, where the Court draws a connection between the need to assess a complex economic situation, according to Article 58(1) ECSC, and a corresponding "discretion" to do so. It does not, as might have been expected, refer specifically to a power of assessment.

[8] See M. Bullinger, "Das Ermessen der öffentlichen Verwaltung," JZ 1984, p. 1001, which explains discretion in its broadest sense as the area "within which a public administration acts whenever its conduct is not laid down by statute and is not open to complete judicial review."

hand, discretion on the other.[9] Instead, we begin our analysis with the general problem of executive freedom of decision. We use the term "discretion" in the sense of "freedom of decision," but without looking to any national school of thought. What this chiefly means is that "discretion" in this sense can be thought of not simply as enabling or "may" clauses, but as having a role in the application of undefined legal concepts.[10]

II.   ADMINISTRATIVE AND LEGISLATIVE DISCRETION

Basically, there are two relationships in which the granting of freedom of decision to the administration can become a legal problem: the relationship between the lawmaker and the administration on the one hand, and that between the administration and the courts on the other.

In Member States which have developed a system of constitutional courts to review legislation, jurists have to deal with legislative as well as executive discretion.[11] Legislative discretion is the freedom of drafting enjoyed by the lawmaker under the constitution, as opposed to the freedom of the executive under the law and *vis-à-vis* the courts.

The legislature generally has greater freedom of decision than the executive. In other words, the constitution does not define what the lawmaker may do quite as closely as the law determines the actions of the executive.[12] The study which follows will show to what extent the distinction made in national law between administrative and legislative discretion is also relevant and useful in Community law, although the latter system makes no rigid distinction between the executive and the legislature, such as we find in national legal systems.

---

[9] It should be remembered that German theory has become more flexible as a result of introducing a "scope for appraisal" in the interpretation of undefined legal concepts; see above, Part 3, Section 1, A. II.

[10] For examples from the case law, see J. Schwarze, *Die Befugnis zur Abstraktion im Europäischen Gemeinschaftsrecht*, Baden-Baden 1976, pp. 179 *et seq.*

[11] For the Federal Republic of Germany, see BVerfGE 4, p. 7 (18), which refers expressly to the lawmaker's "discretion"; for the limits to this, see P. Badura, AÖR 92 (1967), pp. 382 *et seq.* (393).

[12] This is an inherent characteristic of the step-by-step method for putting law into practice. It is also apparent from the frequent vagueness of the language found in national constitutions.

III. JUDICIAL PROTECTION AGAINST DISCRETIONARY DECISIONS

According to Article 164 of the EEC Treaty, the Court is to ensure that in the interpretation and application of the treaty, the law is observed. Here, the mandate for judicial review of the actions of Community organs also defines the point at which discretionary decisions are no longer justiciable. Judicial review begins at the boundary between application of the proper law and the deployment of other considerations relevant to the decision, such as the expediency or political advisability of a certain proposal.[13] A distinguishing feature of discretion is that admissible non-legal considerations set the bounds of judicial review.[14]

In Case 191/82, *Fediol* v. *Commission* the Court commented on the essential relationship between discretion and judicial review[15]:

> "In that respect, the Court is required to exercise its normal powers of review over a discretion granted to a public authority, even though it has no jurisdiction to intervene in the exercise of the discretion reserved to the Community authorities by the aforementioned regulation."

The wider the specific competence of the Community institutions, the narrower will be the review function exercised by the Court.[16] The Court often refuses, for instance, to exercise it on complex economic matters, where the executive is better informed than itself.

This judicial reserve is endorsed in Article 33, paragraph 1, second sentence of the ECSC Treaty, whereby "The Court may not . . . examine the evaluation of the situation, resulting from economic facts or circumstances, in the light of which the High Authority took its decisions or

---

[13] But the courts may intrude into the domain of the executive where expediency is a necessary part of legality: for instance, by reviewing the relationship between ends and means in the context of proportionality. See E. Steindorff, *Die Nichtigkeitsklage im Recht der Europäischen Gemeinschaften für Kohle und Stahl*, Frankfurt am Main 1952, p. 65, on the case law of the French Conseil d'Etat.

[14] For these limits to judicial review, see K. Stern, *Ermessen und unzulässige Ermessensausübung*, Berlin 1964, p. 21, explaining the limits on review of discretionary decisions by the duty of administrative courts to exercise their review powers without duplicating the task of the executive. See also H. Ehmke, *"Ermessen" und "unbestimmter Rechtsbegriff" im Verwaltungsrecht*, Tübingen 1960, p. 45.

[15] [1983] E.C.R. 2913 *et seq.* (2935–2936, para. 30); also Case 264/82 *Timex Corporation* v. *Council* [1985] E.C.R. 849 *et seq.*, at 866, para. 16.

[16] See also H.-W. Daig, *Nichtigkeits- und Untätigkeitsklagen im Recht der Europäischen Gemeinschaften*, Baden-Baden 1985, p. 163.

made its recommendations." Hence the treaty law here expressly confers on the administration a prerogative to assess the facts of the situation.

Further indications that judicial review may be limited will be found in Article 172 of the EEC Treaty, Article 144 of the Euratom Treaty and Article 36(2) of the ECSC Treaty. These treaty clauses stipulate that the Court, exceptionally, has unlimited review powers for discretionary decisions in certain cases.[17] This implies that in ordinary circumstances, judicial review of discretionary decisions is limited.

In the ECSC Treaty, however, the second sentence of Article 33(1) permits review of the evaluation of the overall economic situation in some cases, notably where the High Authority (now the Commission) is accused of misusing its discretion. This cause of action, which appears in the French text of the Treaty as *détournement de pouvoir*, has generated a wealth of discussion and comment.[18] It has been asked whether this term has the same meaning as the famous plea in French law of the *recours pour excès de pouvoir*.[19] It is enough to say here that the Court has not fully espoused the French approach, although the idea of "acts contrary to the purpose of the official authority conferred" also justifies, in its case law, the finding of a misuse of powers.[20] Apart from the explicit rules for review of discretionary acts which have been mentioned here, the following survey of case law will consider, one by one, the aspects which influence the Court when reviewing discretionary decisions. Only in this way is it possible to obtain a clear picture of the legal constraints on the administration on the one hand, and the legal protection of the individual on the other.

---

[17] As well as in the cases covered by the Treaties, complete review of discretionary decisions is possible under Article 90, paragraph 1, second sentence, of the Staff Regulations, and under Article 17 of Regulation 17 (on cartel procedures). Judicial review of this kind follows the French model of "contentieux de pleine juridiction." See H. W. Daig, in: Groben, Boeckh, Thiesing, Ehlermann, *Kommentar zum EWG-Vertrag*, (3rd ed., 1983), Article 172, p. 309 no. 3.

[18] See E. Steindorff, *op. cit.*, footnote 13, pp. 157 *et seq.*; see also W. Rupprecht, *Die Nachprüfungsbefugnis des Europäischen Gerichtshofes gegenüber Ermessenshandlungen der Exekutive in der Montanunion und der Europäischen Wirtschaftsgemeinschaft*, Diss. jur. Kiel 1962, pp. 47 *et seq.*; B. Meister, *Ermessensmissbrauch oder détournement de pouvoir als Fehlertatbestand der Nichtigkeitsklage des Montanvertrages*, Bielefeld 1971; F. Clever, *Ermessensmissbrauch und détournement de pouvoir nach dem Recht der Europäischen Gemeinschaften*, Berlin 1967.

[19] See E. Steindorff, *op. cit.*, footnote 13, pp. 157/158.

[20] See W. Rupprecht, *op. cit.*, footnote 18, p. 53.

IV. THE LINK BETWEEN DISCRETION AND THE OBLIGATION TO SUBSTANTIATE

There is no essential outward distinction between a discretionary decision and one which the executive has no choice but to make. In the latter type of decision, however, the outcome is in principle laid down in advance by the law[21]; where the law allows a measure of discretion, it is much less easy to foresee what the result will be. But the practical necessity and inevitability of dispensing with complete regulation of administrative conduct does not allow the making of decisions on arbitrary or irrelevant grounds. A public authority must therefore state the reasons for its decision, so that the public can see why that particular decision has been made.

The statement of reasons for a decision is a means by which the executive can regulate its own conduct; it also enables the person affected by the decision to judge whether an appeal is likely to succeed.[22] The statement of reasons also gives a court some insight into the otherwise hidden process by which the executive made up its mind, so that the court is not faced simply with the actual outcome, in the form of the appealed decision itself, which is seldom very enlightening.

The duty to give reasons is expressly laid down in Article 15 of the ECSC Treaty, Article 190 of the EEC Treaty and Article 162 of the Euratom Treaty. It applies regardless of whether the decision is favourable or unfavourable to the individual, or merely confirmatory. These points will be examined further in the chapter on procedural rights.

V. EXPLANATION OF THE MODE OF PROCEDURE

In the introduction we have already surveyed the main fields of executive action under Community law. Because there are so many of these, an enormous range of questions has to be regulated by the Community's executive organs or by those of the Member States.

The nature of the regulations and their strictness depend on the subject-matter. The freedom of decision which the administration enjoys will vary accordingly, and the legislation which bestows this freedom and sets its boundaries is equally varied.

---

[21] The extent to which this is true will depend, of course, on the vagueness or otherwise of the terms found in a rule of law.

[22] See the chapter on "Procedural rights."

For example, Article 39 of the EEC Treaty defines only the aims of the agricultural policy, which are to be put into effect by methods deployed at the discretion of the Council under Article 40 of the EEC Treaty. Article 85 of the Treaty, however, contains a relatively precise statement of its subject, and this is followed by an outright ban on cartels, from which a waiver can be granted only through a discretionary decision of the Commission under Article 85(3) of the EEC Treaty.

Both these regulations deal with complex economic matters, where Community action is of comparable significance in the creation of a common market. Yet the Treaty rules relating to them are framed in very different ways. In one area, agriculture, a broad political mandate has to be discharged through legislative action by the Community organs themselves; in another area, cartel law, a ban on cartels is expressed in relatively narrow terms, and the Commission has limited discretion to grant exemptions in certain specific circumstances.

This brief description of the disparity between the two areas indicates that executive freedom of decision in agricultural law, where the basic political decisions are made by the executive itself, is not the same thing as in cartel law, which is based on a decision already incorporated as a treaty rule, derogations from which are permitted only under strict conditions.

The objection may of course be made that there is no real point of comparison between the two areas. But it is this very difference in the formulation of the law which suggests that discretionary power should be considered in each area in turn. By doing this, we can see what kind of subject is normally governed by free decision-making, and how the decisions themselves are reached.

A whole group of subjects will fall into a single category from the perspective of judicial review, where common standards apply in the form of causes of action.

We shall consider these areas of law separately, depending on whether Community law, as explained in Chapter I, is applied directly or indirectly.

B.   THE CASE LAW—A SURVEY AND APPRAISAL

I.   THE LAW OF THE COMMUNITY CIVIL SERVICE

Proceedings instituted by Community officials comprise about a quarter of all cases brought before the Court.

Discretion plays a greater role in civil service law than in almost any other area of law. This in itself warrants a study of the subject, although naturally the numbers of persons directly affected are much smaller than in other branches of law.

It is one of the peculiarities of Community civil service law that the Community organs are independent in these disputes and have little need to resort to national considerations.

The "insular position" of Community civil service law means, however, that the solutions devised in this area have only limited application to other areas of law. Nevertheless, decisions such as *Algera* v. *Common Assembly*[1] set precedents which are sometimes crucial for the whole of Community law.

Our survey is confined to the interesting area of civil service law itself, which is highly significant as regards discretionary power. The legal relationships of other Community employees are not touched upon.

Some selection must be made from a large number of decisions, where the case law, based on detailed staff regulations, is often highly specialised. The survey here is presented according to the causes of action, which form the standards of judicial review and enable the judicial material to be organised in a systematic manner. A series of cases will illustrate how the legal constraints on the European institutions operate.

1. Civil service law in general

The civil service law of the European Community is governed by the Staff Regulations of Officials and by the Conditions of Employment of Other Employees.[2] Under Article 179 of the EEC Treaty and Article 152 of the Euratom Treaty, it is the European Court which resolves disputes arising between the Community and its employees.

Article 91(1) of the Staff Regulations expressly confers jurisdiction in staff cases on the Court. According to the second sentence of this paragraph, the Court has unlimited jurisdiction to review and to alter or annul discretionary decisions on financial questions as well as those in cases covered by the Staff Regulations.

[1] [1957] E.C.R. 39.
[2] J.O. 1968, L56/1, O.J. Sp. Ed. 1968 (I), 30.

2. The operation of legal constraints in European civil service law, as demonstrated in typical cases in selected fields

(*a*) *Review of the formal conditions of a decision*

(*aa*) *Functional authority and procedure*

One almost automatic condition is that the decision must have been taken by the proper authority. Because of the complex internal structure of the official machinery, it is sometimes difficult to decide which is the proper authority.[3]

Secondly, the prescribed procedure for reaching the decision must have been followed. We shall consider this further in the chapter on procedural principles, in particular the right to a court hearing.

Here we shall look only at cases where the executive abuses its freedom to choose how a particular decision will be made, for instance in filling a staff vacancy under Article 29(1) of the Staff Regulations, which sets a fixed order of priority for the different appointment procedures.

The appointing authority is, of course, free to decide how to proceed from one stage of the appointment process to the next. However, it must always begin by considering the opportunities for promotion and transfer within the institution.

If the appointing authority has decided against an internal promotion or transfer it must, under Article 29(1)(b) of the Staff Regulations, consider the possibility of an internal selection procedure. Article 29 of the Staff Regulations distinguishes between an internal selection procedure and a general selection procedure. The internal procedure will take priority, in order to give effect to the principle that those already in the service are to be preferred when a post has to be filled. However, European Community officials may compete alongside external candidates in a general selection procedure.

---

[3] See, for instance, Case 102/63 *Jacques Boursin* v. *High Authority* [1964] E.C.R. 691 and Advocate-General Roemer, at 715–716.

Under Article 45, paragraph 2 of the Staff Regulations, an internal appointment procedure is compulsory whenever officials are to transfer to a higher career grade.

In all other cases, the appointing authority has the sole prerogative to decide whether an internal selection procedure is required.

However, the limit set by the Court in Case 105/75 on discretionary authority in the choice of appointment procedures must be observed.[4] The appointing authority will be guilty of a misuse of powers if it institutes an internal selection procedure solely because it wishes to appoint to a particular post an official who does not satisfy the conditions for promotion.

This case is also important because on that occasion the complaint of misuse of powers was upheld.

The case dealt with an action, brought by another candidate, against the appointment of a certain official, in other words a complaint under the rules of civil service law governing competitions. The chief complaint was, as already indicated, that the internal selection process, based on evidence of qualifications, had been carried out solely in order to secure the vacant post in question for the person ultimately appointed.

The appointing authority argued that its decision had been intended to remove an "anomaly" in the service, namely that an official was performing duties assigned to a higher career grade than the one he was in.[5] The Court clearly did not consider this sufficient justification[6]:

> "It is clear from the abovementioned note and from the foregoing statements that Internal Competition No. A/108 was organized by the appointing authority for the sole purpose of remedying the anomalous administrative status of a specific official and of appointing that same official to the post declared vacant. The pursuit of such a specific objective is contrary to the aims of any recruitment procedure, including the internal competition procedure, and this constitutes a misuse of powers."

The Court found evidence of a misuse of powers in the fact that the conditions of the selection procedure were tailored exactly to the official

---

[4] *Franco Giuffrida* v. *Council* [1976] E.C.R. 1395 at 1402 *et seq.*; see also Advocate-General Warner, at 1411 *et seq.*, referring to the case law of both the European Court and the House of Lords.

[5] *Op. cit.*, footnote 4, at 1402, nos. 10–11.

[6] *Op. cit.*, footnote 4, at 1402 *et seq.*, nos. 10–11.

in question, and also in the fact that—contrary to the standing administrative practice—no tests were made to supplement the evidence of qualifications submitted.[7]

A misuse of procedural powers of this kind is known in French administrative law as a *détournement de pouvoir*—a misuse of procedure.[8]

(bb) *Formal rules for decisions*

According to Article 25, paragraph 1 of the Staff Regulations, every decision based on the Regulations must be communicated forthwith, in writing, to the official concerned. Reasons must be given for any unfavourable decision. The written format is intended chiefly to supply proof and to offer a measure of certainty.

The written statement of reasons must explain the decision to the person concerned and show clearly on what basis it was made. It will also afford judicial protection, especially where the executive's decision is a discretionary one.[9] Particularly where the nature of the authority conferred imposes few legal requirements, the statement of reasons will indicate whether the outcome is lawful.[10]

The case law of the European Court shows how the extent of a discretionary power relates to the detail required in the statement of reasons. In principle, the wider the powers used, the more fully the executive must substantiate its action.[11]

The chapter on administrative procedures will show, however, that this principle may be modified where there are resource constraints on the executive, *e.g.* for letters of rejection in a selection procedure involving several thousand applicants—so that the statement of reasons may be kept short, even where there is wide discretion.

---

[7] *Op. cit.*, footnote 4, at 1403, paras. 12 to 14 and 15 to 17.

[8] See A. de Laubadère, *Traité de droit administratif* (8th ed., Paris 1980), p. 573 no. 954, with references.

[9] *cf.* Case 144/82 *Armelle Detti* v. *Court of Justice* [1983] E.C.R. 2421 *et seq.* at 2436, para. 27. For the link between discretionary power and the duty to supply reasons, see also Case 33/79 *Richard Kuhner* v. *Commission* [1980] E.C.R. 1677 *et seq.*, at 1695, para. 14.

[10] See the section on "The obligation to state reasons."

[11] *cf.* footnote 10.

(b) Review of the subject-matter of decisions

(aa) Completeness and accuracy of the underlying facts

Because the powers conferred by the Staff Regulations are often wide-ranging, the Court places special value on completeness and accuracy in the facts underlying a decision. This is clear from an example of a case involving a promotion, Case 27/63 *Raponi*, where the Court decided[12]:

> "The appointing authority has . . . wide discretionary powers. Such powers presuppose that, while great freedom is allowed in making the decision, there must at the same time be a scrupulous consideration of personal files. . . ."

The personal files must be complete, and the data supplied must be accurate.[13]

In Case 27/63 *Raponi*, the career history on which the promotion procedure was based did not match the one in the plaintiff's personal file or the one which he had submitted with his application for promotion. The Court concluded from this that the appointing authority might be insufficiently informed. Together with a second procedural defect, this led to the annulment of the contested decision for an infringement of the first subparagraph of Article 45(1) of the Staff Regulations.[14]

Similarly, a refusal to promote, in a procedure which omitted a standard performance evaluation, was annulled. The Court decided[15]:

> "Consideration of the merits of candidates whose periodic reports had already been drawn up under Article 43 and of others in whose case this had not yet been done fails to meet the requirements of Article 45 with regard to consideration of the comparative merits of officials."

---

[12] [1964] E.C.R. 129 at 137; see also Case 188/73 *Grassi* v. *Council* [1974] E.C.R. 1099 *et seq.*, at 1109, paras. 25 to 26, and Case 26/85 *Vaysse* v. *Commission* [1986] E.C.R. 3131, para. 26.

[13] *cf.* Case 94/63 *Pierre Bernusset* v. *Commission* [1964] E.C.R. 297 *et seq.*; see also Advocate-General Roemer, *op. cit.*, with reference also to Case 27/63 *Raponi* v. *Commission* [1964] E.C.R. 314. This was a special case in which the regular performance evaluation was omitted owing to the transition to Community-wide staff regulations; *cf.* also Case 26/85 *Vaysse* v. *Commission* [1986] E.C.R. 3131, para. 20.

[14] [1964] E.C.R. 129.

[15] *De Dapper* v. *European Parliament* [1975] E.C.R. 35, at 41, paras. 13 to 15.

The guiding principle, in sum, according to the case law of E.C.J. in Case 27/63 *Raponi*[16] mentioned above, is that a decision taken on the basis of inaccurate facts is defective and must therefore be annulled.

This review does not therefore focus on the stage at which the merits of the candidates are judged, but on an earlier stage, the facts pertinent to the decision. This prompts the question whether the Court has ever identified a transgression of the bounds of discretion, or any glaring error, at the evaluation stage. Apparently, it never has, perhaps because of the difficulty of proof.

However, even the few decisions mentioned here reveal how the Court has developed its approach to reviewing cases. It looks chiefly at the elements in the decision-making process which can be objectively examined, that is, the underlying facts and the procedural guarantees.

The same approach is adopted with regard to selection procedures under Article 29 of the Staff Regulations.[17]

(bb) Limits to discretionary power in the source of authority

The foregoing examples were drawn from staff appointments, an area in which the delegated authority is framed in broad terms and confers similarly wide powers of decision. We shall now turn to another source of authority, which poses tighter constraints.

(1) Case 59/81, Commission v. Council of the European Communities

(a) Subject-matter and grounds of the decision

Case 59/81 concerned the adjustment of salaries under Article 65(1) of the Staff Regulations.[18]

For the sake of clarity, we quote here the wording of Article 65:

---

[16] *Op. cit.*, footnote 12, at 139.
[17] See also below, Case 85/82 *Schloh* v. *Council* [1983] E.C.R. 2105 *et seq.* For a detailed commentary on the selection of staff in EEC civil service law, see A. Hatje, *Der Rechtsschutz der Stellenbewerber im Europäischen Beamtenrecht*, Baden-Baden 1988.
[18] [1982] E.C.R. 3329.

"1. The Council shall each year review the remunerations of the officials and other servants of the Communities. This review shall take place in September in the light of a joint report by the Commission based on a joint index prepared by the Statistical Office of the European Communities in agreement with the national statistical offices of the Member States; the index shall reflect the situation as at 1 July in each of the countries of the Communities.

During this review the Council shall consider whether, as part of (the) economic and social policy of the Communities, remuneration should be adjusted. Particular account shall be taken of any increases in salaries in the public service and the needs of recruitment."

The factual basis for the Council's decision is therefore to be found in paragraph 1, subparagraph 1.

Under subparagraph 2, the Council must ascertain whether, on this basis, an adjustment of remuneration is warranted "as part of the economic and social policy of the Communities."

The Commission complained that in February 1981, when it made an adjustment, the Council had been guided by the poor overall economic situation rather than by the economic and social policy of the Communities.

It also complained that the Council had infringed the second sentence of the second subparagraph of Article 65(1) of the Staff Regulations, since the adjustment had reduced the purchasing power of European officials at a time when salaries in national civil services had been increased.[19]

The Court begins by defining the limits of the Council's discretionary power[20]:

"Whilst Article 65 leaves the Council free to choose the most suitable means and forms for implementing its policy with regard to remuneration, the first sentence of the second subparagraph of Article 65(1) requires the Council to pursue its policy in adjusting remuneration 'as part of the economic and social policy of the Communities,' and the second sentence of that subparagraph requires the Council to take 'particular' account of 'any increases in salaries in the public service.' "

[19] *Op. cit.*, footnote 18, at 3355, para. 17.
[20] *Op. cit.*, footnote 18, at 3356, para. 20.

309

As to the criterion for salary development in the Member States the Court concludes[21]:

> "Article 65, paragraph 1, subsection 2, second sentence indicates that when the Council exercises its discretionary power it must, when making the annual review of the level of remuneration, include any increases in the public sector as one of all the factors to be taken into consideration.
>
> It is true that the word 'particular' implies that Article 65 does not require the Council to take account exclusively of changes in the salaries of national civil servants when adjusting salaries for Community civil servants. Nevertheless, the requirement imposed by that provision means that the Council cannot, by reason of the fact that it takes other criteria into consideration, omit to take account of one of the criteria expressly referred to in the second sentence of the second subparagraph of Article 65(1)."

The Court then considers the data on salary trends in the public service in the Member States[22]:

> "It is common that during the reference period July 1979 to June 1980 salaries in the national public service showed an average increase in purchasing power of 0.2%, and even 1.6% after correction of the figures for Italy. In addition, according to the Annual Report on the Economic Situation of November 1979 for the year 1979/80 the Council, which is expressly required in the second subparagraph of Article 65(1) to make its decision as part of the economic and social policy of the Communities, merely recommended to the Member States that for the period from July 1979 to June 1980 the average increase in real income in the Community must be virtually nil, that is to say, it must be restricted to maintaining purchasing power, and no more.
>
> By contrast, the Council regulation at issue has the effect of reducing the purchasing power of Community salaries for the same reference period by an average of 1.6%. The Council has thus disregarded a criterion which by virtue of the second subparagraph of Article 65(1) of the Staff Regulations it has a duty to apply, namely any increase in salaries in the public service in the Member

---

[21] *Op. cit.*, footnote 18, at 3356, paras. 21 and 22.
[22] *Op. cit.*, footnote 18, at 3356 *et seq.*, paras. 24 *et seq.*

States, whereas its assessment of 'the economic and social policy of the Communities' for the period in question had led it to recommend that purchasing power be maintained."

The Court finally concludes[23]:

"It follows that in deciding to reduce the purchasing power of Community salaries by an average of 1.6% when for the same reference period that of salaries in the public services in the Member States rose by 0.2% (and even by 1.6% after correction of the figures for Italy) the Council failed to comply with Article 65(1) of the Staff Regulations."

(b) The evaluation process

Article 65 of the Staff Regulations is a good example of rules which confer discretionary power while simultaneously setting express legal standards for the use of discretion.

As we have seen, this also applies to the rules governing the selection of officials and the filling of vacant posts.

The Court appears to have been guided by the criterion of the "increases in salaries in the public service of the Member States," something which is statistically ascertainable. This keeps it within the bounds of certainty and avoids the risk involved in making a value judgment of complex economic factors, which would have been unavoidable if it had ventured to interpret the expression "part of the economic and social policy of the Communities." The "increases in salaries in the public service" comprise a substantial portion of the facts underlying the Council's decision and at the same time set a limit on discretionary power.

It must be borne in mind, however, that the Court does not investigate how this parameter was established, but takes it simply as "common ground." This is a phenomenon regularly found in national administrative law: where the concepts involved are of a technical and mathematical kind, the courts simply agree to accept the outcome of a non-judicial investigation of facts, a process which they cannot review adequately.

The allocation of responsibility for the decision which emerges from this process is simply noted by the courts. This is particularly striking in

---

[23] *Op. cit.*, footnote 18, at 3357, para. 26.

view of the considerations relevant in this area of civil service law which are listed in subparagraph 1 of Article 65(1) of the Staff Regulations.

(2) *The adjustment of salary weightings in case 59/81*

Case 59/81 also dealt with the adjustment of the salary weightings for the various duty stations. These weightings are supposed to adjust salaries to actual purchasing power at the duty station to which an official is posted.[24]

According to Article 65(2), if a "substantial change in the cost of living" takes place, the Council, within two months at most, must take steps to adjust the weightings and, if necessary, to make them retroactive.

The Commission attacked the refusal to make a quarterly adjustment of the weightings, on the grounds that in 11 countries—some Member States, some non-Members—the cost of living had risen by 10 per cent. in six months. According to previous practice, this meant that the conditions in Article 65(2) for altering the weightings were fulfilled.

The Commission also alleged that the Council was infringing the principle of equal treatment, whereby all officials, irrespective of their station, must be guaranteed parity of purchasing power.[25]

In the Court's view, the Council has less discretion under Article 65(2) of the Staff Regulations than in adjusting salaries under paragraph 1[26]:

> "The drafting of paragraph (2) indicates that the Council's discretion is less wide in that matter than in relation to the annual adjustment of salaries. The provision reads: 'In the event of a substantial change in the cost of living, the Council *shall decide* ... what adjustments should be made to the weightings,' which implies that when the cost of living rises substantially the Council has a duty to take steps to adjust the weightings."

The meaning of the expression "a substantial change" is therefore decisive. The Court seems to be giving the Council discretion only to determine whether a substantial change has taken place, without defining more precisely the limits of that discretion[27]:

---

[24] *Op. cit.*, footnote 18, pp. 3357 *et seq.*
[25] *Op. cit.*, footnote 18, p. 3357, para. 28.
[26] *Op. cit.*, footnote 18, p. 3358, para. 32.
[27] *Op. cit.*, footnote 18, p. 3358, para. 34.

> "It follows that the power available to the Council is not to determine whether weightings should be adjusted at intervals of six months or quarterly, but to decide whether or not there has been a substantial increase in the cost of living and, if there has, to draw the appropriate conclusions."

Since the Council itself considered the 10 per cent. rise in living costs to be substantial, the Court annulled its refusal to adjust the weightings.[28]

From the standpoint of German administrative law theory, Article 65(2) of the Staff Regulations is a legal rule expressed in terms which confer discretionary power as to the facts, while prescribing the legal result to be achieved, in the sense of the action to be taken under certain conditions. When considering the legal consequences of Article 65(2) of the Staff Regulations, a distinction must be drawn between the discretionary power to decide—notably the Council's freedom to make the adjustment—and the discretion involved in determining the actual amount of the adjustment.

The Court's statement that where substantial changes in the cost of living have taken place, the appropriate conclusions must be drawn, implies that in taking account also of the meaning and purpose of Article 65(2) of the Staff Regulations (similar purchasing power irrespective of station), there is only a narrow measure of discretion, either in making the determination or in reaching the decision.

However, the administration is not bound merely by legal rules; it may also limit its own discretionary power by means of self-regulation.

(cc) Self-regulation by the administration

Once again, there is some instructive material in the case law dealing with the appointment and remuneration of Community officials.

(1) Example: how discretion in appointments is constrained by the conditions of recruitment

In choosing the criteria by which vacant posts are to be filled, the appointing authority has a discretionary power, which it must exercise

---

[28] *Op. cit.*, footnote 18, p. 3359, paras. 36 and 37.

according to the needs of the rational organisation of posts. In the Court's words, in Case 280/80[29]:

"It is for the administration to determine its criteria for selection in the exercise of its discretion, having regard to the exigencies of the rational organization of its various departments."

There is a further reason why this case is worthy of mention. The Court approved the selection criterion set by the appointing authority: "In English shorthand the applicant did not satisfy the requirement of 150 syllables per minute which the appointing authority was entitled to lay down." But the next paragraph contains a noticeable criticism of the appointing authority whose decision was being appealed[30]:

"However, the criteria laid down in Staff Note No. 184/79 may appear to be inflexible in certain respects and, at least with regard to certain officials, they bear little relationship to the actual work to be done and the merits of the persons concerned. In particular, the note makes no provision for the possibility of reliance on other merits to compensate for the absence of proved shorthand skill at the required speed in the first working language or of taking into account knowledge of shorthand in other languages, even where that knowledge is actually used in practice and is recorded in the periodic reports."

Where the appointing authority, in advertising the post, has stated that it is looking for certain qualities in the applicants, it will be bound by these for the rest of the appointment procedure. In Case 67/81 *Ruske* v. *Commission*, which concerned an internal selection procedure, the Court decided[31]:

"It should be emphasized in the first place that although the appointing authority enjoys a wide discretion to determine the conditions governing a competition, the Selection Board is bound by the text of the notice of competition as published."

[29] *Bakke-d'Aloya* v. *Council* [1981] E.C.R. 2887 *et seq.* (2900, para. 17).
[30] *Op. cit.*, footnote 29, p. 2900, para. 16.
[31] [1982] E.C.R. 661 *et seq.*, at 672, para. 9.

Its discretionary power is therefore limited by the published text of the vacancy notice. It may be asked how far the Court exercises its review powers in this area.

In the promotion process, the appointing authority and its promotion committees enjoy a wide measure of discretion when evaluating and comparing the evidence available on the officials and their performance reports (Article 45(1), second sentence of the Staff Regulations). This has been consistently recognised in the case law of the Court. For instance, in Case 280/80 *Bakke-d'Aloya* v. *Council*, the Court stated[32]:

> "It should be emphasized in the first place that in order to evaluate the interests of the service and the merits to be taken into account in connection with the decision provided for in Article 45 of the Staff Regulations, the appointing authority has a wide discretion and that, in that respect, the Court's review must be confined to the question whether, regard being had to the bases and procedures available to the administration for its assessment, it remained within the proper bounds and did not use its authority in a manifestly incorrect manner."

The Court takes the same line in its review of decisions made in selection procedures.[33]

One example is Case 74/77:

> "It is therefore for the Selection Board to determine whether the documents produced by a candidate are such as to justify that candidate's being allowed to enter the competition being held."

Here the executive is essentially self-regulating, and whether it observes its own rules is a matter which cannot be fully tested.

A slightly different picture emerges from the following examples of the Court's case law.

---

[32] *Op. cit.*, footnote 29, p. 2898, judgment para. 10; see also Case 280/81 *Christiane Hoffmann* v. *Commission* [1983] E.C.R. 889 *et seq.*; Advocate-General Rozès p. 907; also Case 26/85 *Vaysse* v. *Commission* [1986] E.C.R. 3131, para. 26.

[33] *Magdalena Allgeyer* v. *Commission* [1978] E.C.R. 977 *et seq.*, at 984 para. 4.

(2) Example: the force of discretionary guidelines on remuneration

Case 81/72 *Commission* v. *Council* is particularly illuminating in this regard.[34]

The case concerned a decision by the Council on March 20 and 21, 1972 to adjust officials' remuneration in the light of two indicators: salary trends in the public service in the Member States during the previous year, and the total figure for per capita wages and salaries in the public service in those States. Trends in the purchasing power of salaries in the Member States were to be judged by those criteria.[35]

Although the Commission calculated that in the first half of 1972 there had been a growth of purchasing power in the Member States of 3.6 per cent. or 3.9 per cent., the Council issued a regulation to fix the increase in remuneration at 2.5 per cent.[36]

The Commission treated this as an infringement of Article 65 of the Staff Regulations and of the Council's own decision, since it had failed to observe its own parameters.

The Court had therefore to decide first on the legal force of the original decision[37]:

"The nature and effect of the Decision of 21 March 1972 must be appraised within the framework of the Council's implementation of the task assigned to it by Article 65 of the Staff Regulations.

This provision thus leaves to the Council the choice of the means and forms best suited to carry out an emoluments policy in conformity with the criteria laid down by Article 65.

The Council, which is responsible for the organization of the staff, may, as part of the means of implementation of Article 65, incorporate procedures of collective bargaining, similar to those practised in the Member States, according to their various methods.

The Council is free to divide up the decision-making process into successive phases, in accordance with a practice usual in the Com-

---

[34] [1973] E.C.R. 575 *et seq.*; but see also Case 25/83 *Buick* v. *Commission* [1984] E.C.R. 1773 *et seq.*, at 1783, para. 15; the guideline used within the service is described as a standard of reference.

[35] *Op. cit.*, footnote 34, p. 582, para. 4.

[36] *Op. cit.*, footnote 34, p. 582, para. 5.

[37] *Op. cit.*, footnote 34, pp. 583 *et seq.*, paras. 6 *et seq.*

munity, and to decide certain questions of principle first, in order to facilitate the application of subsequent implementing measures.

There is no doubt that in deciding on the act of 21 March 1972, the Council had gone beyond the stage of preparatory consideration and had entered on the phase of decision-making.

The Council acted, on the proposal of the Commission, following consultations between the latter and the organizations representing the staff.

Both the antecedents and the terms of the Decision taken make it clear that the Council intended to bind itself to observe fixed criteria, in the working out of subsequent measures relative to the periodic determination of remunerations. This intention shows itself particularly in the provisions whereby the system established by the Decision 'shall be applied' as an experiment and for a period of three years, from the affirmation that 'it is within the framework of the provisions of the present Article 65 of the Staff Regulations,' from the statement of an 'operative date' and finally from the insertion of an express reservation by which the application of the new method for an experimental period 'cannot give rise to vested rights.'

In the course of the oral procedure, moreover, the Council repeatedly emphasized that it acknowledged itself to be bound by this act, that it still intended to respect it, and that the disagreement turned exclusively on the interpretation of the Decision.

It appears, therefore, that by its Decision of 21 March 1972, the Council, acting within the framework of the powers relating to the remunerations of the staff conferred on it by Article 65 of the Staff Regulations, assumed obligations which it has bound itself to observe for the period it has defined."

The Court justified this binding effect as follows[38]:

"Taking account of the particular employer-staff relationship which forms the background to the implementation of Article 65 of the Staff Regulations, and the aspects of consultation which its application involved, the rule of protection of the confidence that the staff could have that the authorities would respect undertakings of this nature, implies that the Decision of 21 March 1972 binds the Council in its future action.

---

[38] *Op. cit.*, footnote 34, p. 584, para. 10.

Whilst this rule is primarily applicable to individual decisions, the possibility cannot by any means be excluded that it should relate, when appropriate, to the exercise of more general powers.

Furthermore, the adjustment each year of remunerations provided for in Article 65 only constitutes an implementing measure of an administrative rather than a legislative nature, and is within the framework of the Council's application of that provision."

The justification of the binding effect of the decision through the rule of protection of legitimate expectations is clearly borrowed from the maxim *legem patere quam ipse fecisti*. However, Advocate-General Warner, relying chiefly on the English legal tradition, argued that the Council could not be bound in its exercise of discretion by the decision.[39] Here the Court did not follow his opinion.

It is also noteworthy that the Court appears to agree with the Council in its express refusal to accept that the decision creates vested rights, but holds that the staff have an expectation deserving of protection.

However, the following passage from the Court's reasoning shows that it conceives the binding effect only in limited terms[40]:

"The circumstances that Article 65, by endowing the Council with a wide power of appraisal with regard to the economic and social policy of the Communities, requires it to take account of all possible relevant factors, does not prevent it from pre-determining, under certain circumstances and conditions, in a first stage and for a limited time, the framework of, and the factors to be taken into account in, its decision.

In this respect, to justify its new attitude, the Council has invoked the risks of inflation, which have been aggravated in the interval between the time when the Decision was adopted and the passing of the contested Regulation.

Furthermore, it appears that all the relevant factors had already been considered, both in the course of the preparatory studies and in the proceedings prior to the Decision of 21 March 1972.

Further, neither the minutes of the Council's proceedings of 5, 6 and 8 December 1972 nor the recitals of the contested Regulation, establish circumstances sufficient to justify the abandonment, after

[39] *Op. cit.*, footnote 34, pp. 592 *et seq.*
[40] *Op. cit.*, footnote 34, pp. 584 *et seq.*, para. 11.

nine months, of the system which the Council had bound itself to respect.

There is reason to consider that this system, by its very nature, has a slowing-down effect, since it provides for the adjustment of the remuneration of the officials and other servants of the Community only after a finding that national remunerations have already increased, and since, within the framework of Article 65 this adjustment is only made once a year, at a fixed interval. In the circumstances, the Council has failed to found the contested Regulation on grounds sufficient to justify it in departing from its prior undertakings."

According to this, the Council could have quite easily departed from the decision, if there had been special circumstances to warrant its doing so. Indeed the Court's decision in Case 46/71 indicates that in spite of an existing guideline, the exercise of discretion in individual cases may not be anticipated.[41]

When a specific decision has to be made, the circumstances of the case must be weighed separately in spite of the discretionary guideline, so that it may even be essential to adopt a measure which departs from it.

Here we see the parallels with English law, which forbids legislative and administrative organs to set prior guidelines to predetermine what use they will make of their discretionary powers.[42]

However, this does not alter the fact that such directives are in principle allowable means by which the administration can pattern its own conduct.

(dd) Misuse of discretion as a limit to discretionary powers

In the *Schloh* case against the Council, the proceedings turned on the appointment procedure under Article 29(2) of the Staff Regulations for filling a Director post.[43] It makes no difference that this was an exceptional procedure under Article 29(2) of the Staff Regulations, since this does not resolve the problem of how far discretion should go: indeed this

---

[41] Case 46/47 *George Brandau* v. *Council* [1972] E.C.R. 373 at 380, paras. 11 to 14.
[42] *cf.* also J. Schwarze, *Die Befugnis zur Abstraktion*, Baden-Baden 1976, p. 67. See also Advocate-General Warner, *op. cit.*, footnote 34, pp. 592–593.
[43] [1983] E.C.R. 2105 *et seq.*; see for instance the unsuccessful procedure in Case 69/83 *Luxembourg* v. *Court of Auditors* [1984] E.C.R. 2447 at 2465, para. 29.

problem is highlighted by the special requirements posed for the applicants.

(1) The Bernhard Schloh case

This case began with a Council advertisement for the newly created post of a "Director of the Budget and the Staff Regulations," in Category A, Grade 2.[44] The plaintiff, who belonged to Category A3, and 16 other Council officials, including a Luxembourg national and Mr. Kasel, also a Luxembourg national working temporarily for the Commission, applied for the post within the set time-limit. One application was received after the time-limit had expired.

The Secretary-General of the Council rejected all the applications made by Council officials. The rejection of the applicants not of Luxembourg nationality was justified on the ground that it was necessary to re-establish a geographical balance among the staff.

One point should here be added concerning the background to the case: following the resignation of a Council Secretary-General of Luxembourg nationality, that nationality was under-represented in the Secretariat of the Council.

However, the application of the official of Luxembourg nationality was also rejected, not on grounds of proportionality, but because he was said to be insufficiently qualified for the advertised post. Instead, the Mr. Kasel mentioned above was appointed to the post.

It should be noted that the Luxembourg official had attached to his application an "explanatory note," stating that he was fully aware that he had no chance of succeeding in his application, because the post in question, by political agreement, had already been reserved for a specific individual of a specific nationality.

When the prescribed preliminary proceedings had been completed, Bernhard Schloh finally petitioned the Court. He sought to have the rejection of his application and the appointment of Mr. Kasel annulled.

The chief ground of his complaint can be summarised as follows: the Council, contrary to Article 27 of the Staff Regulations, had reserved the post in question for a national from a particular Member State. This was arguably a misuse of discretion. He relied, in his complaint, on an agreement reached by members of the Council at the 655th meeting of the Council, to the effect that the geographical imbalance against Luxem-

---

[44] See the account of the facts, *op. cit.*, footnote 43, at 2107 *et seq.*

bourg should be redressed "in the very near future." In support of the alleged link between the Council agreement and the appointment of the Luxembourg national Kasel, Schloh pointed to a number of other factors, which for lack of space will not be listed here.

The Court called, in addition, for the documentation concerning the selection procedure, although the Council denied that there was any. To elucidate matters further, the Court called upon the Council "to state the date of the comparative examination of the candidates and any other factor which might be of use in establishing the circumstances in which the recruitment procedure was conducted."[45] This showed that on July 15, 1981 the applications which had been received in time from the 17 internal candidates (including the application from Mr. Schloh) had been examined. On July 24, the Council had examined the application received out of time from one Council official, and also the application from Mr. Kasel. The Court concluded from this[46]:

"It must be stated that the procedure as described above points to the absence of a comparative examination of the various applications validly submitted. Indeed, the Secretary-General himself states that his decision to reject the applications from within the institution was taken on the basis of 'comparative examinations' which he conducted exclusively in respect of the Council officials. In particular, of the two 'comparative examinations' mentioned in the memorandum, the first, on 15 July 1981, related to the applications submitted within the period prescribed by the vacancy notice, and the second, on 24 July 1981, related to the application of Mr. Sacchettini, also a Council official, who, however, submitted his application after the closing date. In accordance with the vacancy notice and the rules applicable to competitions, the appointing authority is required to disregard applications submitted after the expiry of the prescribed period, so that the examination of Mr. Sacchettini's application could not, as indeed was the case, have any practical effect on the examination of the applications from within the institution, validly submitted, which had already been conducted on 15 July. It follows that the sole basis on which the decision to reject the applications from within the institution was founded was the examination conducted before the expiry of the closing date for applications, namely

[45] *Op. cit.*, footnote 43, at 2128.
[46] *Op. cit.*, footnote 43, at 2130 *et seq.*, para. 35.

15 July 1981. That examination was carried out by the Secretary General in the presence of the Director General for Administration, the Director of Personnel and the Head of the Private Office. Since Mr. Kasel's application was examined separately, on 24 July 1981, it follows that there was no comparative examination of all the candidates for the post in question."

There were further disparities in the reasons given for the rejections, and these, against the background of the advertised arrangements for the selection procedure, prompted the Court to draw the conclusion that[47]:

"In view of all the circumstances and considerations set out above, it must be concluded that the treatment accorded to Mr. Kasel's application, by reason of his Luxembourg nationality, exceeds the limits within which the application of the criterion of geographical balance is justified under Article 27 of the Staff Regulations. In reality, the newly-created post was reserved for a national of a specific State in order to satisfy the requirements of the compensation which was due to be accorded to that State "in the immediate future," as envisaged by the decisions of the Council of 15 and 16 September 1981, which moreover, at the same time, emphasized the need to have regard to the necessary qualifications."

The complaint was allowed in every particular.[48]

(b) An assessment

Apart from the clear boundaries it sets on official patronage, the *Schloh* case also clarifies some major aspects of the judicial review of

---

[47] *Op. cit.*, footnote 43, p. 2131, para. 37.

[48] *Op. cit.*, footnote 43, p. 2132, para. 40; in the other case law on staff competitions, see: Case 10/82 *Mogensen* v. *Commission* [1983] E.C.R. 2397 *et seq.*; Case 9/820 *Øhrgaard and others* v. *Commission* [1983] E.C.R. 1245 *et seq.*; Case 265/81 *Giannini* v. *Commission* [1982] E.C.R. 3865 *et seq.*; Case 151/80, *De Hoe* v. *Commission* [1981] E.C.R. 3161 *et seq.*; Case 2/80 *Dautzenberg* v. *Court of Justice.* [1980] E.C.R. 3107 *et seq.*; Case 7/77 *Ritter von Wüllersdorf und Urbair* v. *Commission* [1978] E.C.R. 769 *et seq.*; Case 23/74 *Küster* v. *European Parliament* [1975] E.C.R. 353 *et seq.*; Case 188/73 *Grassi* v. *Council* [1974] E.C.R. 1099 *et seq.*; Case 21/70 *Rittweger* v. *Commission* [1971] E.C.R. 7 *et seq.*; Case 46/69 *Reinarz* v. *Commission* [1970] E.C.R. 275; Joined Cases 27 & 30/64 *Fonzi* v. *Commission of Euratom* [1965] E.C.R. 651 *et seq.*; Case 97/63 *De Pascale* v. *Commission* [1964] E.C.R. 575 *et seq.*; see also W. Schick, "Die 'Konkurrentenklage' des Europäischen Beamtenrechts—Vorbild für das deutsche Recht?" DVB1 1975, pp. 741 *et seq.*

administrative decision-making in civil service law. As far as selection procedures are concerned, what it means is that the wide discretion which the executive enjoys in the selection process cannot extend to the pursuit of unlawful ends (misuse of discretion).

The appointments policy of the Community civil service and its lawful purpose are stated in Chapter I of the Staff Regulations (Article 27): to recruit officials meeting the highest standard of ability, efficiency and integrity, on the broadest possible geographical basis.

The same governing principle appears in Article 29 which, together with Annex III of the Staff Regulations, regulates the selection process and is intended to ensure that full consideration is given to the available candidates. In Article 27, paragraphs 2 and 3, this positive statement of aims is contrasted with inadmissible motives which transgress the limits of a discretionary decision. The list of motives is not exhaustive, but some of them, in a Community of mixed ethnic and cultural composition, would be clearly inconsistent with the notion of impartial personnel management.

In addition to the grounds of discrimination in paragraph 2, there is a mention in paragraph 3 of another danger for internationally-staffed institutions: that certain posts may be treated as the special preserve of certain nationalities. In other words, paragraph 3 defines an unlawful purpose, the pursuit of which would constitute a misuse of discretion. The Court's findings in the *Schloh* judgment refer simply to a breach of Article 27(3) of the Staff Regulations; there is no explicit finding of a "misuse of discretion," and this may signify a measure of judicial reserve in a particularly delicate case. Nevertheless, the Court's inquiry was instituted by way of a plea of misuse of discretion.

As well as confirming a wrongful use of discretionary power, the judgment is interesting for its reasoning.

Summarising the procedural flaws and apparent grounds for suspicion, the Court concluded that there had been a breach of Article 27(3) of the Staff Regulations.

The legal effects of the decision would have been the same if the annulment had rested on the lack of a comparative examination of the candidates. But the Court goes much further in this case; it uses the suspicious factors to bring out the element of subjectivity in the appointment decision: the intention of the appointing authority to appoint a certain candidate, thereby misusing its discretionary power of selection.

The Court's findings make it clear that the general bar against misuse of discretion applies unreservedly to civil service law. The significance of the judgment is not confined to the case itself; rather, it lies in the explicit reminder that in civil service law there are legal limits to freedom of decision in staff appointments, a reminder which contributes to preventing official patronage in appointments in the European public service.

(ee) General principles of law as a limit on the freedom of decision

The executive's freedom of decision is also limited by general principles of law.

In the Staff Regulations, the general principle of equality is expressed in the form of a ban against discrimination, for instance in Articles 7 and 27.

The principle of proportionality also places an important restriction on the discretionary power of the executive. For instance, when imposing disciplinary measures, the appointing authority must ensure that due proportion is observed between the breach of duty and the penalty ordered.[49]

The general principle of legal certainty and of protecting legitimate expectations was central to the case of *Algera* v. *European Parliament*.[50] This principle is governed by Article 85 of the Staff Regulations, on the repayment of sums wrongly advanced.

A further group of principles emerges from the body of fundamental rights which belong to the general principles of law enshrined in the constitutions of the Member States, and which the Court has consistently upheld in its case law.[51]

There are, finally, certain specific administrative rules, such as the rule of sound administration or the use of proper administrative methods.[52]

In combination with the restraints posed by positive law, these principles set effective and appropriate limits to executive freedom of action in the civil service.[53]

---

[49] *cf.* Case 46/72 *De Greef* v. *Commission* [1973] E.C.R. 543 *et seq.*, at 555, paras. 43 to 44 and 45 to 47, which also comments on the discretionary element in disciplinary proceedings. See also Case 13/69 *Van Eick* v. *Commission* [1970] E.C.R. 3 *et seq.* (paras. 23 to 26).

[50] Joined Cases 7/56 & 3–7/57 [1957] E.C.R. 39; on the protection of legitimate expectations, see also Case 92/85 *Hamai* v. *Court* [1986] E.C.R. 3157, para. 10.

[51] See, for instance, Case 130/75 *Prais* v. *Council* [1976] E.C.R. 1589 *et seq.* (1598 *et seq.*, paras. 12 to 19).

[52] *cf.* Case 125/80 *Arning* v. *Commission* [1981] E.C.R. 2539 *et seq.*, at 2555, para. 20: "good administrative practice"; Case 105/75 *Giuffrida* v. *Council* [1976] E.C.R. 1395 *et seq.*, at 1403, paras. 15 to 17: the administration is morally bound in the interest of "proper administration."

[53] See D. Rogalla, *Dienstrecht der Europäischen Gemeinschaften*, Cologne/Berlin/Bonn/Munich 1981, pp. 49 *et seq.*

3. Conclusion

Many rules of European civil service law give the executive a measure of discretion to judge and decide matters, as this survey has shown.

Other rules, however, ensure that discretionary powers, which are often very broadly drawn, are subject to procedural and formal requirements which offer both a sounder guarantee of a correct decision and a proper balance between individual interests and the needs of the administration.

The Court treats observance of the procedural and formal requirements as an important element of any judicial review of contested personnel decisions, and this is also the main focus of its inquiries. Particularly important is the obligation to state reasons, since these will disclose the internal and subjective aspects of the administrative decision and will also play a major role in any subsequent judicial review.

In practice, however, it is difficult to prove a misuse of discretion, partly because the burden of proof is wholly on the complainant.

Nevertheless, in a few landmark cases the Court has plainly shown its determination to monitor compliance with the limits of discretionary power in civil service law and to resist the intrusion of official patronage.

The distinction ordinarily made in German administrative law between discretionary decisions and value judgments plays no part in European civil service law, where executive freedom of decision is paramount.

II. THE COMMON MARKET IN COAL AND STEEL

The European Coal and Steel Community is a classic example of a supranational administrative community.[1] The treaty on which it is based is precisely worded and implementing legislation is largely absent.[2] In their decision-making, ECSC institutions exercise broad powers.

Judicial review of such decisions is chiefly based, in practice, on Article 33 of the ECSC Treaty, and to a lesser extent on Article 36. In Article 33, the only express limit on discretion is misuse of powers. Undertakings and associations can contest general ECSC decisions only on the basis of

---

[1] E. Steindorff, *Die Nichtigkeitsklage im Recht der Europäischen Gemeinschaft für Kohle und Stahl*, Frankfurt a.M. 1952, p. 17.

[2] *Ibid.*, *op. cit.*, p. 16; it is explained that the Treaty was drafted to avoid, as far as possible, the need for special economic legislation. But see the court's decision in Case 8/55 *Fédération Charbonnière de Belgique* v. *High Authority* [1954–1956] E.C.R. 245; general decisions are "quasi-legislative measures".

this legal concept. In the survey which follows, we describe the role of discretion in executive decision-making within the Common Market in coal and steel, and the legal limits on it. The relevant material is so abundant that only a handful of key cases can be selected to illustrate the practice of the court and how the legal constraints on the ECSC executive operate.

This chapter is arranged according to the specific constraints imposed by Community law; it does not attempt to cover the whole of the subject.

The commentary which follows is therefore structured according to the causes of action in the Community legal system, which also constitute the standards of review for the conduct of ECSC institutions.

1. EXECUTIVE FREEDOM OF DECISION AND THE FRAMEWORK FOR ITS JUDICIAL REVIEW

The standards of judicial review of legal acts within the ECSC are to be found in Article 33(1) of the ECSC Treaty, expressed as causes of action.

They are modelled upon the *cas d'ouverture* of the French *contentieux administratif*, although the language used reflects the requirements of the Treaty.[3]

The court can annul decisions and recommendations of the High Authority if there is a complaint of lack of competence, infringement of essential procedural requirements, infringements of the Treaty or of a rule of law relating to its application, or misuse of powers.[4]

Under the ECSC Treaty, the review of discretionary decisions is subject to the limits already described for the judicial review of administrative decisions. The second sentence of Article 33(1) expressly states that:

> "The Court may not, however, examine the evaluation of the situation, resulting from economic facts or circumstances, in the light of which the High Authority took its decisions or made its recommendations . . ."

But the text goes on:

---

[3] F. Clever, *Ermessensmissbrauch und détournement de pouvoir nach dem Recht der Europäischen Gemeinschaften*, Berlin 1976, p. 104.
[4] The causes of action are exhaustive, and the court may not add to them; *ibid., op. cit.,* p. 105, with further references.

"... save where the High Authority is alleged to have misused its powers or to have manifestly failed to observe the provisions of this Treaty or any rule of law relating to its application."

This raises the question of the kind of "allegation" which has to be made if the court is to have wider powers of review.

The court has decided that substantiated and conclusive evidence of a misuse of discretion or of a manifest disregard will be enough.[5]

But extending its review powers does not make the court into an administrative appeal tribunal; it does not enable it, for instance, to annul a lawful decision on economic policy grounds.[6]

Even where the wider powers of review under sentence 2 of Article 33(1) of the ECSC Treaty (Part 2) are invoked, an act can be set aside only if a legal defect is established.[7]

2. THE STANDARDS OF JUDICIAL REVIEW OF DISCRETIONARY DECISIONS

(a) The aims of the Treaty as a standard of conduct for the ECSC executive

The overall goal of the ECSC is to achieve the aims set out in Articles 2 and 3 of the ECSC Treaty. Many other articles refer to them; for instance, an express reference to Article 3 appears in Article 53(1)(a) and in Article 62, and there is an implicit reference in Articles 5 and 14.

A glance at these Articles will show, however, that their requirements cannot possibly be fulfilled simultaneously or to the same degree.

The court's case law makes allowance for this, although its emphasis varies.

---

[5] cf. Case 6/54 Netherlands v. High Authority [1954–1956] E.C.R. 103, for an allegation of manifest disregard of the provisions of the Treaty; Cases 15 & 29/59 Société Métallurgique de Knutange v. High Authority [1960] E.C.R. 1, in which "serious indications" for the allegations were put forward. More recent examples include Joined Cases 154–78 & 39/79 Valsabbia v. Commission [1980] E.C.R. 907 at 992, para. 11.

[6] H.-W. Daig, Nichtigkeits- und Untätigkeitsklagen im Recht der Europäischen Gemeinschaften, Baden-Baden 1985, p. 161, no. 211.

[7] cf. Advocate-General Capotorti in Joined Cases 154, 205–206, 226–228, 263–264/78 & 31, 39, 83 & 85/79 Valsabbia v. Commission [1980] E.C.R. 907 et seq. at 1041; he stresses that the facts must be looked at in relation to the legal limits of executive action. See also Daig, op. cit., footnote 6, p. 161.

Case 8/57, *Groupement des Hauts Fourneaux et Aciéries Belges* v. *High Authority*[8] dealt with certain arrangements under the so-called scrap equalization scheme, introduced by means of a general decision based on Article 53(b) of the ECSC Treaty. Through the equalization of scrap the High Authority (now the Commission) had attempted to regulate the use of scrap in the production of crude steel and iron and to decouple the price of scrap from world market prices, in order to shield the Community from the undesired impact of fluctuating prices on the world market.[9]

Because the complaint was made according to the second sentence of Article 33(2) of the ECSC Treaty, the basis of the complaint, and the only standard of review, was a misuse of powers.

The complainants argued that the arrangements for financial equalization conflicted with, among other things, the aims laid down in Articles 2, 3, 4 and 5 of the Treaty. On the legal effects of these provisions in general, and their impact on other provisions of the Treaty, the Court commented:[10]

> "The High Authority, by using the financial arrangements provided for in Article 53, is in a position to exercise a broad influence on the market in coal and steel, while it must be borne in mind that Article 53 restricts the application of such arrangements to the procedures 'necessary for the performance of the tasks set out in Article 3 and compatible with this Treaty, and in particular with Article 65'.
>
> The express reference made to Article 3 does not release the High Authority from its duty to observe the other articles of the Treaty and in particular Articles 2, 4 and 5 which, together with Article 3, must always be observed because they establish the fundamental objectives of the Community. These provisions are binding and must be read together if they are to be properly applied. These provisions can stand by themselves and accordingly, in so far as they have not been adopted in any other provision of Treaty, they are directly applicable. If they have been adopted or are governed by other

---

[8] [1957–1958] E.C.R. 245; see the parallel proceedings in Cases 13/57, *op. cit.* 265; 9/57, *op. cit.* 319; 10/57, *op. cit.*, 339; 11/57, *op. cit.*, 357; 12/57, *op. cit.*, 375. See also B. Meister, *Ermessensmissbrauch oder détournement de pouvoir als Fehlertatbestand der Nichtigkeitsklage der Montanunion*, Bielefeld 1971, p. 105, for the "pluralité des buts" in the case law of the French Conseil d'Etat.

[9] *cf.* the description of the overall position in the Opinion of Advocate-General Lagrange in Case 50/58 *Phoenix-Rheinrohr* v. *High Authority* [1959] E.C.R. 75.

[10] [1957–1958] E.C.R. at 253; see also Case 27/58 *Compagnie des Hauts Fourneaux and others* v. *High Authority* [1960] E.C.R. 241.

provisions of the Treaty, words relating to the same provision must be considered as a whole and applied together. In practice it will always be necessary to reconcile to a certain degree the various objectives of Article 3, since it is clearly impossible to attain them all fully and simultaneously as those objectives constitute general principles which must be observed and harmonized as far as possible."

The legal requirement in Case 8/57 is apparently strict and unconditional but is mitigated by the court in certain instances, where the aims of the Treaty cannot be wholly reconciled with one another:[11]

"In pursuing the objectives laid down in Article 3 of the Treaty the High Authority must permanently reconcile any conflicts between those objectives considered individually and, when such reconciliation proves unattainable, must grant such temporary priority to one or other of them as appears necessary having regard to the economic facts or circumstances in the light of which, in carrying out the tasks entrusted to it under Article 8 of the Treaty, it adopts its decisions."

Hence in the court's view, it is permissible to give temporary preference to one aim rather than another. In Case 9/56 *Meroni* v. *High Authority*, the court explains how the choice is to be made and what aspects must be taken into consideration.[12]

"Reconciling the various objectives laid down in Article 3 implies a real discretion involving difficult choices, based on a consideration of the economic facts and circumstances in the light of which those choices are made."

In his Opinion on Case 13/57 *Eisen- und Stahlindustrie* v. *High Authority*, Advocate-General Lagrange says that with the equalization arrangements for scrap, there is a limit to this discretionary choice[13];

"That the financial arrangements made pursuant to Article 53 of the Treaty constitute indirect procedures for regularizing the markets;
 That these arrangements must correspond to one or more of the objectives listed in Article 3 of the Treaty as tasks for the Community

---

[11] *Op. cit.*, at 254.
[12] [1957–1958] E.C.R. 152.
[13] [1957–1958] E.C.R. 314.

without however sacrificing the other objectives, since it is possible that reconciliation may be required, subject to review by the Court on the conditions laid down in Article 33 . . ."

Thus the objectives which are passed over must not be completely forgotten. A further legal limit emerges from the list of prohibited measures in Article 4 of the ECSC Treaty.[14] Hence the ECSC executive is not completely free to decide its own arrangements.

(b) Misuse of powers

The judicial protection which undertakings and the associations referred to in Article 48 of the ECSC Treaty enjoy against general decisions is confined to a plea of misuse of powers.[15] Elsewhere, this is mercly one of several grounds for contesting a decision. However, this is a particularly interesting plea, because, as already explained, a substantiated allegation of misuse of powers widens the Court's authority to investigate the case. Moreover, the German translation of the standard French term *détournement de pouvoir* evokes the notion of freedom of decision under the law, an element which is not necessarily present in the other causes of action.

(aa) The concept of misuse of powers in the case law of the European Court

(1) In Case 3/64 *Chambre syndicale de la Sidérurgie française and others* v. *High Authority*,[16] Advocate-General Roemer reviewed the concept of misuse of powers in the case law of the European Court,[17] together with the procedural rules for contesting a general decision. Pointing to the abundant case-law on the question of misuse of powers, the Advocate-General explains this phenomenon as follows:

"We can speak of misuse of powers when they are used for ends other than those provided by the law; this definition has been ren-

---

[14] See W. v. Simson, *Der Gerichtshof und unbestimmte Rechtsbegriffe*, K.S.E. Vol. I, Cologne/Berlin/Bonn/Munich, 1965 pp. 396 *et seq.* (409).
[15] See the Court's judgment in Case 8/55, *Fédération Charbonnière de Belgique* v. *High Authority* [1955–1956] E.C.R. 245.
[16] [1965] E.C.R. 441.
[17] *cf.* Case 8/55 *Fédération Charbonnière de Belgique* v. *High Authority* [1955–1956] E.C.R. 245.

dered more flexible in the course of later decisions and expanded in the sense that a misuse of powers is constituted by serious lack of foresight or of care, amounting to a disregard for the purpose of the law.

The restriction 'affecting them' (*à leur egard*) provided for in the second paragraph of Article 33 must be understood in the sense of the words which express it, that is, where it concerns an undertaking which is the subject or at any rate the victim of the misuse of powers alleged by that undertaking ...

Finally, for the application to be admissible it is essential in this instance that the applicants convincingly plead a 'misuse of powers affecting them' in a sufficiently detailed form, that is to say, that they show the circumstances and reasons which give rise to a strong presumption of the existence of a misuse of powers."

(2) The "end provided by the law" may be found either in the actual source of authority, or in Articles 2 to 5 of the ECSC Treaty.

In Case 8/57 the complainants argued that the equalization arrangements for the market in scrap, introduced by the High Authority on the basis of Article 53 of the Treaty, were contrary to Articles 3 and 4 of the Treaty.[18]

One question the court had to consider was whether the equalization scheme discriminated among consumers in the Common Market, contrary to Article 3(b) of the Treaty.

It found that any infringement of the equal treatment rule in that clause might constitute a misuse of powers.[19]

However, a misuse of powers may occur not only if the general aims of the Treaty are infringed, but also if the aims pursued are not those for which authority was given.

In Case 1/54[19a] the French Government argued that a general decision by the High Authority based on Article 60 of the ECSC Treaty constituted a misuse of powers. It claimed that the purpose of the decision was to reduce the overall level of prices, rather than to prevent discriminatory practices, as Article 60 of the ECSC Treaty prescribes.

---

[18] [1957–1958] E.C.R. 245. Writers distinguish between the pursuit of "aims wholly alien to the Treaty, and the pursuit of Treaty aims by impermissible means"; *cf.* Clever, *op. cit.*, footnote 3, pp. 121 and 128.

[19] *Op. cit.*, p. 257. F. Clever disagrees: *Ermessensmissbrauch und détournement de pouvoir nach dem Recht der Europäischen Gemeinschaften*, Berlin 1967, p. 136, he argues that the discrimination must be deliberate.

[19a] *Government of the French Republic* v. *High Authority* [1954–1956] E.C.R. 1.

It argued that the proper authority for altering the general level of prices was to be found in Article 61 of the Treaty, Article 65 being the appropriate authority for combating price cartels. But the court rejected the plea of a *détournement de pouvoir*. As well as its direct obligations, under Article 60 of the Treaty, to prevent unfair competition and discriminatory practices, the High Authority was also bound to take account of the requirements of Articles 2, 3 and 4 of the Treaty. The High Authority was, therefore, also entitled to take a decision which sought to alter the general level of prices.[19b]

If one of several aims pursued simultaneously in the same decision is unlawful, this will not automatically constitute a misuse of powers. In Case 1/54, the court explains[20]:

> "Even if the grounds for the High Authority's decisions included, in addition to proper grounds, the improper one of avoiding subjecting guilty undertakings to penalties, this would not make the decisions invalid for misuse of powers, in so far as they do not detract from the main aim, which is the prohibition of unfair competitive practices and discrimination. The court considers that this is not the case."

(3) Typically, however, a misuse of powers is not an objective breach of law, but a subjective intention on the part of the executive to act unlawfully, *i.e.* contrary to the "end provided by the law."[21]

This means that a decision which is outwardly lawful may, because of the purpose for which it is taken, constitute a misuse of powers and thus be found unlawful.

The question then arises whether the executive must have deliberately pursued an aim not found in the law, or whether a mere act of negligence will suffice.

Scholars differ on this question, one which is particularly significant for the judicial review of regulatory decisions. If a misuse of powers can occur simply through negligence in pursuing the lawful end, the latter will be within reach of judicial review and will be close to a plea of *violation de la loi* (*Rechtsverletzung*). Yet there is no such plea among the standards of review in Article 33(2), second paragraph.[22]

[19b] *Op. cit.*, p. 34.
[20] [1954–1956] E.C.R. 1; see also Case 2/57 *Compagnie des Hauts Fourneaux de Chasse* v. *High Authority* [1957–1958] E.C.R. 199.
[21] See the remarks of Advocate-General Lagrange in Case 3/54 *ASSIDER* v. *High Authority* [1954–1956] E.C.R. 63 at 75, on the cardinal principle of *finalité* in administrative law.
[22] For the possibility of examining all the causes of action in paragraph 1, see above, footnote 1.

So far, apparently, the Court has made no explicit ruling on this point.

There is a clue to the subjective conditions for a misuse of powers in the definition which the court gave in Case 8/55[23], according to which a misuse of powers may also exist if, objectively speaking, the aim pursued departs from the prescribed aim, owing to a serious lack of foresight or care. As Advocate-General Roemer explains[24]:

> "The objective pursuit of another objective, expressed in another way, represents a misuse of powers where the authority responsible overlooked this consequence as a result of serious lack of foresight."

A grossly negligent disregard of the lawful objective will therefore suffice for a finding of misuse of powers.

This view has been challenged by Advocate-General Lagrange, and by writers on the subject.

Early on, in Case 8/55, Advocate-General Lagrange argued strongly that the theory of an objective misuse of powers was incomprehensible in the light of the classic definition of a *détournement de pouvoir*.[25]

Clever interprets the Court's language in Case 8/55 as meaning that the decision is incompatible with the aims of the Treaty, because it is based on manifestly serious breaches of the Treaty, and that this incompatibility may also represent a misuse of powers.[26]

In his Opinion in Cases 8–13/57, Advocate-General Lagrange also interpreted the statement as a stipulation that proof must be adduced.[27]

In the same case, however, the court employed the term in question, in its grounds of judgment, in the sense preferred by Advocate-General Roemer[28]:

---

[23] [1954–1956] E.C.R. 245.

[24] Advocate-General Roemer in Case 18/57 *Firma I. Nold KG* v. *High Authority* [1957–1958] E.C.R. 121.

[25] Advocate-General Lagrange in Case 8/55 *Fédération Charbonnière de Belgique* v. *High Authority* [1954–1956] E.C.R. 245.

[26] F. Clever, *Ermessensmissbrauch und détournement de pouvoir nach dem Recht der Europäischen Gemeinschaften*, Berlin 1967, p. 134.

[27] [1957–1958] E.C.R. 265, *Eisen- und Stahlindustrie* v. *High Authority*. Advocate-General Roemer interpretation is also challenged by B. Meister, in *Ermessensmissbrauch oder détournement de pouvoir als Fehlertatbestand der Nichtigkeitsklage des Montanvertrages*, Bielefeld 1971, pp. 147 *et seq.* This writer refers to the risk of duplicating the pleas of manifest failure to observe the Treaty, and treats the case contemplated in Article 33(2), second sentence, as an inadmissible extension of the right of petition.

[28] [1958] E.C.R. 265.

"Furthermore, although the system set up does not constitute a system of allocation, even with the view that such a system might display certain characteristics of indirect allocation it would be necessary to prove that the objective of the contested decisions was to attain this allocation by means of Article 53(b), through the expedient of a financial arrangement and, contrary to the stated objective of effecting economies in ferrous scrap and ensuring a regular supply of scrap to the market, or else, to prove that the High Authority had been motivated by a wish to evade Article 59 or that, through a serious misconception, it had failed to recognize that the contested arrangement amounted to an arrangement under Article 59. This has not been sufficiently proved in law."

Admitting a misuse of powers will be of practical importance only where an individual plea is entered against a general decision under Article 33(2), second sentence, of the ECSC Treaty. In the circumstances contemplated by Article 33(1) and (2), first alternative, it is only of academic interest.[29]

(bb) Procedural irregularity

One form in which misuse of powers occurs is the so-called *détournement de la procédure*, which is roughly translated as procedural irregularity.[30] The recognition of this type of misuse of powers dates from the Court's decision in Case 2/57.[31] There is a more recent case, however, which sheds light on the concept of procedural irregularity.

---

[29] *cf.* B. Meister, *op. cit.*, footnote 27, p. 148.

[30] *cf.* H.-W. Daig, *Nichtigkeits- und Untätigkeitsklagen im Recht der Europäischen Gemeinschaften*, Baden-Baden 1985, p. 175, no. 227; B. Meister, *op. cit.*, footnote 27, pp. 111 *et seq.*

[31] *cf.* Case 2/57 *Compagnie des Hauts Fourneaux de Chasse* v. *High Authority* [1957–1958] E.C.R. 199; Case 8/57 *Groupement des Hauts Fourneaux et Aciéries Belges* v. *High Authority* [1957–1958] E.C.R. 245. The recognition was welcomed by Advocate-General Roemer, [1965] E.C.R. 441, and by Advocate-General Reischl, [1982] E.C.R. 413 *et seq.*, the latter referring back to Roemer. Roemer, however, doubted (*op. cit.*) whether a procedural abuse under Article 33(2), second sentence, would normally meet the requirement of being committed "à leur egard." Advocate-General Reischl (*op. cit.*) expressed the same doubts in relation to Article 33(2), second sentence. Neither doubts that procedural irregularity is a distinct type of détournement de pouvoir. Advocate-General Warner at [1976] E.C.R 1412, has wrongly been thought sceptical of the plea of procedural irregularity. He does not attempt to argue against it, but simply points out that there is a connection between a procedural abuse and an allegation of abuse of powers. He rightly emphasises that it is not the failure to observe the prescribed procedure which

Joined Cases 140, 146, 221 and 226/82[32] dealt, among other things, with an application to set aside two general decisions which altered the system of steel production quotas.

These decisions did not fulfil the conditions set by the Commission in the Regulation on which they were based, nor did the procedure followed by the Commission in adopting them comply with the sole legal authority, found in Article 58 of the ECSC Treaty.[33]

The Court stated, as a general principle[34]:

"In order to resolve this issue it is useful to recall that in its judgment of 21 June 1958 in Case 8/57 (*Groupement des Hauts Fourneaux et Aciéries Belges* v. *High Authority* [1958] ECR 245) the Court held that the powers conferred on the Commission by the ECSC Treaty are limited by the specific provisions set out in Title III of the Treaty and that, in particular, such powers would be diverted from their lawful purpose if it appeared that the Commission had made use of them with the exclusive, or at any rate the main, purpose of evading a procedure specifically prescribed by the Treaty for dealing with the circumstances with which it is required to cope."

The court went on to explain how, in practice, a procedural irregularity may occur[35]:

"Since the quota system introduced by Decisions No. 2974/80, No. 1831/81 and No. 1696/82 was based on the application to all undertakings of uniform abatement rates for each category of products subject to it—unless the individual situation of the undertaking in question justified an exception—the Commission could decide upon a general increase of the quotas for a whole group of undertakings characterized by their structure only after following the procedure laid down in Article 58 of the Treaty, that is to say after consulting the Consultative Committee and obtaining the assent of the Council. Consequently, in acting pursuant to Articles 16 and 18

---

constitutes misuse of powers in a particular decision, but the purpose for which the procedure is used. See Daig, *op. cit.*, footnote 30, p. 176.

[32] Joined Cases 140, 146, 221 & 226/82 *Walzstahl-Vereinigung and Thyssen* v. *Commission* [1984] E.C.R 951 *et seq.*

[33] See the Opinion of Advocate-General Verloren van Themaat, *op. cit.*, footnote 32, pp. 887 *et seq.* (995).

[34] *Op. cit.*, footnote 32, p. 985, para. 27.

[35] *Op. cit.*, footnote 32, pp. 985–986, para. 29 and p. 986, para. 30.

of the basic decisions, the Commission also evaded the procedure specifically laid down by the Treaty for that purpose. In those circumstances the applicants' submission that Decisions No. 533/82 and No. 1698/82 were vitiated by a misuse of powers affecting them must be upheld, without its being necessary to investigate whether the considerations advanced by the Commission were capable of justifying the application of different abatement rates to the single-product undertakings and the integrated undertakings. Consequently, those two decisions must be declared void."

Here we should add that in this case, the procedural irregularity related to a misuse of powers in an area where the executive was already bound. In principle, there can be an evasion of a procedure only if the procedure is itself binding.

(cc) *The effectiveness of the plea of misuse of powers in reviewing administrative decisions*

Only a handful of legal acts have been annulled for misuse of powers. One example of a successful appeal has been mentioned in the preceding section.[36] The small number of cases is due chiefly to the difficulty of proving a case.[37] In his Opinion in Case 3/54, Advocate-General Lagrange commented on the manner in which the burden of proof is assigned[38]:

"To conclude this brief analysis of French law in the matter of misuse of powers, it must be borne in mind that case-law accepts this plea on fairly strict conditions. The concept of proof is, generally speaking, handled with considerable flexibility and, if I may say so, tact, by an administrative court, which follows the principle of judicial investigation. When, on the other hand, it is dealing with misuse of powers, it requires proof to be supplied by the plaintiff or to be clearly forthcoming from the file. The reason for this is the need for inquiry into subjective intention, which must not be the subject of *a priori*

---

[36] [1984] E.C.R. 951 *et seq.*
[37] See also H.-W. Daig, in H.v.d. Groeben, H. v. Boeckh, J. Thiesing, C.-D. Ehlermann, *Kommentar zum EWG-Vertrag* (3rd ed., Baden-Baden 1983), Article 173, p. 356 (footnote 91).
[38] *Assider* v. *High Authority* [1954–1956] E.C.R. 63.

suspicion; until the contrary is proved the Administration must be presumed to have acted in the interests of the service for which it is responsible."

Only in exceptional cases will the statement of reasons for a general decision disclose unintentionally that the authority which took it misused its powers. Hence the complainants must usually look to other evidence, which they must themselves supply.

The Court's case-law regularly presumes that the burden of proof lies on the complainant. Typically, the grounds of judgment in Joined Cases 154 etc./78 and 39 etc./79, *Valsabbia* v. *Commission* state[39]:

"Moreover, the applicants have not assembled the body of concordant evidence which might justify a finding of misuse of powers.

Therefore the applicants have not adduced proof that the Commission's powers were used for ends other than those envisaged by Article 61."

Protecting one's interests by entering a plea of misuse of powers is therefore a course beset with considerable practical difficulties, and this increases the attraction of the other pleas and standards of review.

(c) Manifest failure to observe a rule of law

The court may extend its examination to an evaluation of the situation resulting from the economic facts and circumstances if the Commission is alleged to have "manifestly failed to observe" the provisions of the Treaty or any rule of law relating to its application.[40]

For this examination to take place, it is not necessary to prove that there has been a failure to observe the applicable law. It is enough if there is circumstantial evidence indicating that the allegation is justified. But it is not enough merely to assert the existence of a "manifest failure," otherwise the submission might itself "become a mere formality."[41]

---

[39] [1980] E.C.R. 907 at 1019, para. 129; 1020, para. 130; from the earlier case law, see Case 8/55 *Fédération Charbonnière de Belgique* v. *High Authority* [1954–1956] E.C.R. 245; also Case 13/57 *Eisenund Stahlindustrie* v. *High Authority* [1957–1958] E.C.R. 265.
[40] For detailed comment, see H. W. Daig, *Nichtigkeits- und Untätigkeitsklagen*, p. 166 *ff.*
[41] An early statement by the court in Case 6/54 *Government of the Kingdom of the Netherlands* v. *High Authority of the European Coal and Steel Community* [1954–1956] E.C.R. 103 at 115.

The term "manifest" presupposes that there is a certain degree of failure to observe the Treaty provisions.[42]

As the court had already explained in Case 6/54 *Government of the Kingdom of the Netherlands* v. *High Authority*, the failure to observe the Treaty must "derive from an obvious error in the evaluation, having regard to the provisions of the Treaty . . ."[43] A manifest failure to observe a rule of law is not however a fifth plea of a different kind; it is simply a variant of an "ordinary" breach of law.

Not surprisingly, Daig asks[44] why the Court has wider powers of investigation when there is a particularly obvious breach of the Treaty. According to his interpretation, a manifest failure to observe the applicable law is really no different from "exceeding the limits of discretion."[45]

This seems a plausible argument, because if the evaluation of the overall economic situation, as a proper part of the administrative function, is beyond judicial review, any review proceedings which, exceptionally, deal with the evaluation must be a review of the use of a discretionary power.

Since, as Advocate-General Roemer points out,[46] there are always legal limits to the exercise of discretionary powers, the second alternative in the second sentence in Article 33(1) of the ECSC Treaty must refer to a manifest failure to observe the legal limits of discretion.

This does not however explain why an ordinary review of a discretionary decision, based on the plea of a breach of law, need not involve any thorough evaluation. Because the investigation is more superficial, any discretionary abuse detected in such proceedings must surely be more flagrant than a defect in the use of discretion discovered only through an evaluation of the economic facts and circumstances.

Daig attempts to dispose of this difficulty by interpreting the term "manifest" in the sense of clear or unambiguous.[47] He argues that between a lawful and an unlawful exercise of discretion there is a grey area, within which the lawfulness of any particular decision is difficult to judge; the eventual outcome will depend, to some extent, on a judicial nicety.

Hence the second sentence of Article 33(1) of the ECSC Treaty calls for a measure of judicial restraint where the decision-making activities of

---

[42] As in Case 6/54 (*cf.* footnote 41), at 115.
[43] *Op. cit.*, footnote 41, at 115.
[44] *Op. cit.*, footnote 40, p. 167.
[45] *Op. cit.*, footnote 40, p. 167.
[46] Case 34/62 *Germany* v. *Commission* [1963] E.C.R. 131 at 151; see also Advocate-General Rozès, in Case 210/81 *Demo-Studio Schmidt* v. *Commission* [1983] E.C.R. 3045 at 3070.
[47] *Op. cit.*, footnote 40, p. 168; see also Steindorff, *op. cit.*, footnote 1, p. 139.

other organs are concerned. The Court should annul a decision only if the bounds of discretion have obviously been exceeded, and this need not necessarily be proved.[48]

One may add, with Steindorff, that this sentence refers only to cases requiring an "overall evaluation" of economic facts and circumstances, cases which therefore leave considerable scope for discretion.[49]

Where other executive decisions are concerned, it acts as a reminder to the court that the discretionary considerations involved in the decision are beyond its reach unless the review cannot be carried out without going into them. There is no precedent in the case-law of a legal act being annulled for a manifest breach of law.

(d) The standards of review for the other causes of action

Misuse of powers comprises a range of defects which are difficult to demonstrate in practice. As already explained in the comparative law survey, Advocate-General Lagrange, in his Opinion in Case 3/54, pointed out that in France, the plea of *détournement de pouvoir* reached a peak between 1890 and 1930, and then lost ground to the plea of *violation de la loi* (breach of law). Breach of law is also a significant element in judicial protection against discretionary decisions by the ECSC executive, because there are always legal limits to a discretionary decision, and to exceed these constitutes a breach of law.[50] But freedom of decision is also constrained by the rules on competence, due form and due procedure, and these rules form a framework which ensures, at least, that such freedom is properly exercised. The survey below does not follow strictly the order of the causes of action. Instead, to bring out more clearly the tension which prevails between discretion and the legal limits of executive action, it describes some important aspects of the limitations on discretion, and the manner and scope of their operation.

[48] Daig, *ibid*.
[49] *Op. cit.*, footnote 1, p. 139; see also Case 154/78 *SPA Ferriera Valsabbia and others* v. *Commission* [1980] E.C.R. 907, where the Court comments on the difficulties of dealing with the complaints brought before it. These are complex cases in which the Court has broader powers of investigation and can deal with questions of legality.
[50] *cf.* Advocate-General Roemer in Case 34/62 *Germany* v. *Commission* [1963] E.C.R. 131 at 151: "So far as the exercise of discretionary powers is concerned, it obviously cannot be unlimited. Its limits fall within the scope of legal review and to exceed them can be treated as an infringement of the Treaty." See also Advocate-General Rozès, *op. cit.*, footnote 46.

(aa) The binding nature of powers conferred by the Treaty

(1) Preliminary marks

As well as being guided in its activities by the aims of the Treaty, the ECSC executive must also observe the detailed prescriptions enjoined by the Treaty functions themselves.

Here it often encounters undefined terms such as "manifest crisis" (Article 58(1), first sentence), "a system of quotas" (Article 58(2), first sentence), "a serious shortage" (Article 59(1), first sentence), "the necessary measures" (*ibid.*) etc., or again, "explicit powers of appraisal," such as in Article 58(1), paragraph 1 of the Treaty, where the High Authority has to decide if a situation of manifest crisis exists.

The following survey of case-law illustrates the Court's methods for examining the Commission's use of its undefined powers.

(2) Case law

The court's review takes place at various levels of the decision-making process.

(a) First, the institution in question must have been competent to take the decision, *i.e.* the decision must be one which lies within the competence of the Community as such, and within the specific competence of the institution itself.

A well-known case illustrating the specific competence of the High Authority and of the Community was the judgment in Case 8/55, which dealt with price-fixing by the High Authority. The complainants disputed that the High Authority was empowered to fix prices; the Court however held that it was, referring to the theory of implied powers.[51] The question of competence in this case was complex; for the details, see Chapter 6.

(b) The decision must have been taken through a proper procedure, and this involves examining the motives which prompted it.

In Case 111/63 *Lemmerz-Werke* v. *High Authority*[52] the complainant attacked a decision on interest payments which was part of an equal-

---

[51] [1954–1956] E.C.R. 245.
[52] [1965] E.C.R. 677.

isation scheme for imported scrap introduced by a general decision. It argued that this new rule was not covered by the consent earlier given by the Council under Article 53(b) of the ECSC Treaty.[53] The Court first considered whether it was necessary, under Article 53(b) of the ECSC Treaty, for such consent to be given[54]:

> "Under Article 53(b) of the Treaty the High Authority may 'with the unanimous assent of the Council, itself make any financial arrangements serving the same purposes.' As this is a provision which lays down the essential procedural requirements for the validity of certain decisions, it must be strictly construed. The effect of Article 53(b) of the Treaty is that the unanimous assent of the Council was only necessary if the introduction of a system of crediting interest affected or modified the very basis of the imported ferrous scrap equalization scheme.
>
> A system of crediting interest, established in order to compensate undertakings subject to the scheme for periods during which they had to lock up capital required to meet their obligations, appears to be necessary in order to ensure that these undertakings are not unjustifiably prejudiced by delays in payments made by other undertakings. This system, which does not modify the essential structure of the financial arrangements for equalisation, was adopted to enable it to function properly and to attain the objectives approved by the Council."

The Court goes on to explain that there is a duty to assent, derived from a secondary rule of law.

> "The second question to be answered is whether the fact that Article 13 of Decision 16/53, adopted with the unanimous assent of the Council, provided for the application of a system for the payment of interest for delay meant that the High Authority had to obtain once more the unanimous assent of the Council to any amending decision.
>
> There is no justification for the conclusion that the decisions of the High Authority taken with the unanimous assent of the Council could only be amended, even in the case of amendments not affecting the basis of such decisions, by a new decision also taken with the unanimous assent of the Council.

---

[53] *Op. cit.*, footnote 52, at 698.
[54] *Op. cit.*, footnote 52, at 699.

Therefore the complaint based on the absence of the unanimous assent of the Council is unfounded."

Departures from this rule, if the evasion is deliberate, may constitute a procedural defect. Strictly speaking, however, they will not be procedural errors, but a misuse of powers.

(c) The decisions must also be promulgated in the prescribed form. The points which are relevant here are discussed in detail in the chapter on administrative procedure.

(d) The facts underlying a decision must be complete and accurate

Since in most cases the Court is unable to make its own appraisal of the underlying facts, because this is a discretionary matter outside the scope of judicial review, (Article 33(1), second sentence, first alternative), it pays special heed to the completeness and accuracy of the facts.

This procedure is regularly adopted in French administrative cases, where an *illégalité relative aux motifs de fait*, which is a *violation de la loi*, is a ground for annulling a decision.[55] The Court follows the same procedure when it deals with questions of fact in the light of infringements of the Treaty.[56]

In Joined Cases 36/59 and others[57] the Court took a firm stance on the link between the limited review of discretionary decisions and the specific reason for reviewing the basis of the decision. These cases turned upon the authorisation of a cartel under Article 65(2) of the ECSC Treaty:

"Such authorization therefore depends on a finding which, of its very nature, comprises an assessment of the situation created by the facts or economic circumstances, and for this reason is partly immune from review by this Court. Therefore the High Authority has an absolute duty to state specific reasons for these authorizations and this rule must be strictly observed . . . so as to be in a position to examine whether the authorization was rightly granted as a matter both of fact and of law."

---

[55] See M. Fromont, *Rechtsschutz gegenüber der Verwaltung in Deutschland, Frankreich und den Europäischen Gemeinschaften*, Cologne, etc. 1967, p. 269.
[56] *cf.* Case 13/60, *Geitling, Mausegatt, President* v. *High Authority* [1962] E.C.R. 83.
[57] *Präsident, Geitling, Mausegatt, I. Nold KG* v. *High Authority* [1960] E.C.R. 423; *cf.* also Case 185/85 *USINOR S.A.* v. *Commission* [1986] E.C.R. 2079, paras. 20 *et seq.*

A distinction must be drawn between the investigation of the "facts" and the review of the evaluation of the facts.

The latter is no part of the Court's function, since, for the reasons already explained, it is not competent to examine subjective opinions and forecasts.

Facts, on the other hand, are objective data and can, in principle, be exactly demonstrated or refuted. If the Court finds flaws or omissions in the facts, however, it does not necessarily follow that the decision based on them must be annulled.

Case 13/60 was a case in point; here the Court held that[58]:

> "Such errors and omissions in the findings of fact as are referred to by the applicants do not in fact or in law affect Decision No. 16/60, and cannot therefore constitute grounds for its annulment."

If a legal act is to be annulled, therefore, it must be vitiated by factual errors or omissions.

One particular kind of factual statement is an assessment, a procedure which, by definition, dispenses with absolute and complete accuracy. The basis of calculation in the scrap equalisation scheme was an estimation of this sort.

The general decisions in question allowed for an assessment of the quantity of scrap consumed if the contributing enterprise had not submitted any consumption figures, or if the figures submitted were incomplete or were not fully documented.

Apparently, it has never been disputed that this procedure is an acceptable basis for the decision. It must be borne in mind, however, that in these cases the assessment was merely a remedy for missing or incomplete information, enabling the equalisation scheme to proceed.[59]

By way of comparison, in Case 8/65 *Acciaierie e Ferriere Pugliesi* v. *High Authority*,[60] the question in dispute was whether the preconditions existed for the High Authority to perform the assessment. The Court therefore had to consider whether there was a sufficient factual basis for the exercise of this function. It commented:

---

[58] [1962] E.C.R. 117.
[59] See Advocate-General Gand in Case 2/65 *Handelsgesellschaft Ferriera Ernesto Preo & Figli* v. *High Authority* [1966] E.C.R. 228, para. 225.
[60] [1966] E.C.R. 1.

"The defendant has not given any specific reply to the arguments thus put forward, and has limited itself to relying on the absence of complete industrial accounts for the iron foundry. It has also failed to give any precise reasons for the figures adopted. The factors put forward by the applicant have thus not been sufficiently refuted. It is thus apparent that the contested decision contains no basis for applying the rules concerning the High Authority's estimated assessments of contributions to changes under the equalization scheme."

In Case 3/67 *Fonderie Acciaierie Giovanni Mandelli* v. *Commission of the European Communities*,[61] two points were in dispute: whether the conditions for an assessment had been fulfilled, and the method and the result of the assessment actually made.

The Court, having admitted the case, took a stance on the method applied and the risks involved in communicating the facts in this way[62]:

"The method of assessment used in this case—based on an assessment of the capacity and operating times of the furnaces for the purpose of calculating the undertaking's aggregate production of steel and of thus establishing, after subtracting the consumption of the casting foundry, the production of steel for ingots—was well adapted to give a reasonable assessment of the consumption of scrap subject to contribution. Moreover, the result reached by the method used by the High Authority coincides largely with the information supplied by the applicant in the preliminary stages of the procedure. The possibility of a discrepancy between the result arrived at by such a method and the actual consumption is a risk which must be borne by the applicant, whose conduct it was that induced the High Authority to have recourse to the assessment procedure."

One point revealed by the Court's case-law is that accurate communication of the facts is the rule, and assessments merely the exception.

Hence special circumstances must exist—such as undertakings being in breach of their obligations—to justify a departure from accurate communication of the facts.

(e) As well as the investigation of questions of competence, procedure and form, and the completeness and accuracy of the facts, the question

---

[61] [1968] E.C.R. 25.
[62] *Op. cit.*, footnote 61, at 32.

arises whether there is any primary or secondary rule of law requiring the Commission to reach a particular decision, or whether its discretion is total.

The Treaty contains many undefined terms from which it is impossible to discern the force of the legal obligations which arise from them. Before turning to examples of cases, let us recall the idea from which this survey began:

The executive possesses freedom of decision wherever the lawmaker has omitted to prescribe a specific outcome and the Court cannot substitute a decision of its own.

Hence if the lawmakers (or the authors of the Treaty) use undefined terms which appear to invest the executive with decision-making powers, its actual freedom to decide will be determined by the scope of the Court's investigative powers.

The first of the decisions to which we have referred related to the quota system for regulating the steel market. When it introduced production quotas, the Commission was attempting to control a general crisis in sales by limiting the output of certain steel products.

The complainants in Joined Cases 39, etc./81[63] were a number of Greek steel enterprises, who attacked the quota allocation they had been given under a special decision. They argued that the general decision to introduce production quotas in the steel market did not apply to Greek undertakings; and secondly, that a general decision of this sort was unlawful and should therefore be annulled.[64]

The second complaint is interesting from a procedural point of view, because the general decision was attacked not because it constituted a misuse of discretion, but solely because it infringed the other grounds for action under Article 33(1) of the ECSC Treaty.

Advocate-General VerLoren van Themaat argued that this procedure was admissible.[65] The Court's case-law, he said, allowed for review of

---

[63] *Halyvourgiki* v. *Commission* [1982] E.C.R. 593.

[64] See p. 611, paras. 2 and 3.

[65] *Op. cit.*, footnote 63, p. 621; see also Advocate-General Lagrange in Case 15/57 (and also his opinion in Case 2/57, with the same plaintiff) *Compagnie des Hauts Fourneaux de Chasse* v. *High Authority* [1957–1958] E.C.R. 199 at 236, expressing a view on the review of regulatory decisions by way of general decisions, and referring to the case law of the French Conseil d'Etat:

"As far as France is concerned, I refer to two judgments of the Conseil d'Etat, among many others: *Abbé Barthélémy*, July 9, 1926. Recueil p. 713; *Marcin-Kowsky*, November 28, 1951, Recueil p. 548. These judgments are interesting because they begin by dismissing claims for the annulment of the regulation because they were submitted out of time and, immediately afterwards, give a ruling on the legality the regulation in the

procedural questions like these, although it could consider the illegality of the general decision for the purpose of annulling the special decision only in so far as the former was reflected in the latter. This meant, however, that all four causes of action were relevant in examining the legality of the general decision. In the first of their pleas, concerning the interpretation of an undefined term, the complainants argued that Greece's joining the Community meant that the Commission's finding of a "manifest crisis," within the meaning of Article 58(1), first paragraph, of the ECSC Treaty, was no longer correct.

That article stipulates that it is for the High Authority to judge whether a manifest crisis, or, in the German translation, an *offensichtliche Krise*, exists.

The Court found that the language of the article imparted a broad power of appraisal[66]:

> "The applicants' argument that the finding of a state of crisis was not representative of the situation in the Community after the accession of Greece ignores the fact that the existence of such a crisis must be ascertained in the light of the situation in the Community as a whole. Therefore the introduction of measures under Article 58 may not be ruled out even if undertakings in some Member States or some regions of the Community are less affected than others by a widespread state of crisis. In any case, it has not been proved that the effect of Greece's entry into the Community was substantially to alter the general situation of the market for steel products in the Community as a whole. The argument must therefore be rejected."

The penultimate sentence suggests, however, that if there had been a substantial change—or perhaps an obvious improvement—in the market situation, this would have reduced the scope for assessment, so that to call such a situation a "manifest crisis" would certainly have been wide of the mark. This point, of course, related to the facts covered by the rule, whereas the next question dealt with the legal consequences of a "manifest crisis" in the steel market.

context of claims brought against an individual implementing decision. However, case law accepts that the legality of the regulation can be impugned only in so far as the provisions of the regulation which formed the basis of the implementing measure are concerned. (*Dame Denayer*, February 18, 1949, Recueil p. 80 and *Sirey*, 1949, 3.40)."
He continues with a brief survey of the same point in other legal systems. However, the Court's case law shows that it has followed the French model.
[66] *Op. cit.*, footnote 63, p. 614, para. 16.

The reference in question was the reference in Article 58(1), paragraph 1, to Article 74 of the ECSC Treaty. In its grounds of judgment, the Court commented[67]:

> "Article 58(1) states that in the event of a manifest crisis if the means of action provided for in Article 57 prove to be insufficient the Commission must 'establish a system of production quotas, accompanied to the necessary extent by the measures provided for in Article 74.' In such a situation Article 74 empowers the Commission to make recommendations to the Member States with a view to introducing appropriate restrictions on imports."

The complainant enterprises argued that while the Commission, acting under Article 58(1) of the ECSC Treaty had imposed production quotas on the enterprises of the Community, it had not at the same time taken any steps under Article 74 of the Treaty to restrict imports of steel products.[68]

The legal connecting device between Article 58(1), first paragraph, and Article 74 of the ECSC Treaty is the expression "to the necessary extent" (in French: *en tant que de besoin*).

The Court interprets this, too, as authority to make an assessment, and proceeds to explain how the authority is to be exercised. The following extract from the significant passages in the judgment illustrates the Court's approach to the specific requirements of economic administrative law[69]:

> "It follows from the provisions cited that if production quotas are imposed they do not necessarily have to be accompanied by import restrictions. The introduction of such restrictions depends on the Commission's assessment of the state of the steel market and of the need to afford that market protection. That need depends in turn both on the possibility of disposing of existing production on the internal market and by external trade. But in this regard it is necessary to take into account obligations entered into by the Community towards non-member countries and the repercussions which the introduction of import restrictions might have on Community exports in general and on steel products in particular.

---

[67] *Op. cit.*, footnote 63, p. 615, para. 20.
[68] See para. 19, *op. cit.*, footnote 63, at 615.
[69] Paras. 21 and 22, *op. cit.*, footnote 63, at 616.

347

As the Court has already stressed in its judgment of 18 March 1980 in Joined Cases 154, 205, 206, 226 to 228, 263 and 264/78, 39, 31, 83 and 85/79 *SpA Ferriera Valsabbia and Others* [1980] E.C.R. 907 and Case 258/80 *Rumi* [1982] E.C.R. 487, the taking into consideration of those factors requires the assessment of a complex economic situation, which means that the link established by Article 58(1) between the introduction of production quotas and the imposition of restrictions on imports of competing products, cannot be in any way automatic. The applicants have not been able to specify circumstances which might give reason to believe that the Commission exceeded the discretion which Articles 58 and 74 of the Treaty accord to it in this matter."

There was a further problem in the interpretation of the term "appropriate levies" within the meaning of Article 58(2) of the ECSC Treaty.

The complainants took the view that the levies were not appropriate, because the Commission had based its calculations not on production capacity, but on actual production.

The Court held, however, that Article 58(2) of the Treaty places no restriction on the Commission when it has to decide the basis on which, in a given economic situation, the appropriate levies should be determined.[70] This decision is part of its rule-making function, and the Court explains[71]:

"It follows from the explanations given during these proceedings that there are no reasonable grounds for denying that the Commission's choice of the criterion based on undertakings' actual production may constitute an 'equitable basis' within the meaning of Article 58(2). Indeed that criterion, as adjusted by Article 4 of Decision No. 2974/80, constitutes, in the first place an objective basis of assessment which avoids the uncertainties inherent in determining a factor which is partly conjectural, such as production capacity; secondly, it enables total production to be reduced without altering the positions of the undertakings on the market as between each other."

The Court therefore confines itself to determining whether the criterion of "actual production" was properly applied when the levies were fixed.

---

[70] Para. 25, *op. cit.*, footnote 63, at 617.
[71] *Ibid.*

The expression "appropriate levies" in Article 58(2) of the ECSC Treaty is an example of an undefined term which must be given concrete expression in rules made by the executive before it can be applied to an individual case.[72]

In this process it must, however, be remembered that the provision is part of the legal arrangements of the ECSC for managing crisis situations. When crisis situations are to be regulated by economic legislation, the authority conferred must be of a particularly flexible kind, and the "management" which enjoys such complete authority must be capable of dealing with the particular dynamics of the situations which arise and the special interests which will become apparent.

On the other hand, however, it should not be forgotten that to fix quotas for production, for instance, is an interference with entrepreneurial freedom, and in certain cases this may ruin them, as indeed has happened.

From this point of view, the broad powers enjoyed by the Commission and the limitations on the Court's power to review the manner in which they may be used are deserving of criticism. It should be remembered, however, that Article 58 of the ECSC Treaty strikes a balance between preserving the common market and the hard cases which may result, and opts in principle for giving priority to the common market itself.

Similarly, the maintenance of the common market in coal and steel is the aim of the competition rules in Articles 65 *et seq.* of the ECSC Treaty. Even in "normal times" this market may be threatened by mergers and cartels. The decision in Case 13/60 *Geitling* v. *High Authority*[73] is an instructive example of judicial review of undefined terms in cartel law.

This case dealt with an appeal against a special decision of the High Authority refusing authorisation for the setting up of a joint selling company for the Ruhr coalmines.

Article 65(1) of the ECSC Treaty prohibits all agreements between undertakings, all decisions of associations and undertakings and all concerted practices tending to restrict competition in the common market.

Under Article 65(2), cartels may be authorised under certain conditions.

In Case 13/60, it was necessary to decide how the following terms in Article 65(2)c, paragraph 1, were to be interpreted and applied:

---

[72] For the definition of undefined terms through administrative rule-making, see W. von Simson, in: "Der Gerichtshof und unbestimmte Rechtsbegriffe," KSE, Vol. 1, p. 397.
[73] [1962] E.C.R. 83.

"The power to determine prices"

"the control of marketing"

"a substantial part of the products in question within the Common Market."[74]

The Court took each of these expressions in turn, and examined the meanings attributed to them by the High Authority.[75] It considered, for instance, whether the planned sales company would be in a position to determine prices, and drew a subtle distinction between the power to fix prices and the power to determine prices. It held that neither the Treaty itself nor the materials published on its ratification clarified the effects of the distinction for Article 65(2) of the Treaty.[76]

However, by making a comparison with Article 85(3) of the EEC Treaty and allowing for the particular regulatory function covered by Article 65 of the ECSC Treaty, the Court was able to conclude that it was the power to determine prices which was crucial.

This it defined as follows[77]:

"The power to determine prices, however, resides in a power, given to the undertaking in a position to exercise it, to establish prices at a level appreciably different from that which would be established by the effect of competition alone."

To show how this influence was exercised, the Court said:

"Thus, to show the existence of a power to determine prices, it is necessary to establish that the actual prices are, or could be, different from what they would have been in the absence of any power to fix prices."

The power to fix prices, it said, was an objective fact arising out of an easily ascertainable organisational structure. Moreover, the process itself is open to judicial review, and this is not the case with a power to determine prices[78]:

---

[74] *Op. cit.*, footnote 73, at 101.
[75] See also the analysis by G. Reinicke, "Der Gerichtshof und unbestimmte Rechts-begriffe," KSE, Vol. I, pp. 318 *et seq.* (426).
[76] Judgment, *op. cit.*, footnote 73, at 102.
[77] Judgment, *op. cit.*, footnote 73, at 102.
[78] *Ibid.*

"Such a proposition involves a subtle comparison between the actual and the potential, of a kind which must rest to a considerable extent upon informed speculation."

Despite its finding that the assessment described above was a discretionary process not open to judicial review, the Court went on, in its reasoning, to consider whether the High Authority had followed reliable indicators in reaching the conclusion that if the sales organisation was able to fix prices, it could also determine them.

After thorough investigation, it concluded that "the internal effect of the joint-selling organisation involves a certain power to determine prices. . . ."[79]

This is an example of an extensive judicial review, examining in depth the economic matters at issue.[80]

What is the influence here of German administrative law theory? These two cases show plainly that the Court does not seek to distinguish undefined terms, which may be fully tested, from areas of discretionary judgment, which may not.

Instead, its approach seems to be that a legal term should be fully tested in those respects which, objectively speaking, warrant it; other aspects which are matters for subjective judgment, or prognostic by nature, are relegated to the area of discretion and are not tested. Hence a single expression may combine a legal prescription with a discretionary power.

As for the range of judicial review, the Court is obviously not guided by the German system; instead, it investigates cases in a flexible spirit not dissimilar to the judicial practice of the French Conseil d'Etat, which draws no distinction between an undefined legal term and discretion.

This emerges with particular force from the interpretation in Case 13/60 of the expression "a substantial part of the products in question within the common market."[81]

(bb) How institutional rules constrain discretionary powers

The ECSC institutions are bound by their own rules and by the laws they have themselves enacted; this creates a certain amount of tension and makes it necessary to bring legislation up to date. The resulting

---

[79] Judgment, *op. cit.*, footnote 73, at 104.
[80] For a critical comment, see Reinicke, *op. cit.*, footnote 75, p. 428.
[81] *Ibid.*, *op. cit.*, pp. 427 *et seq.*

problems are fully examined in a separate chapter and need only be touched upon here.

It is quite a different matter, however, if discretionary authority is limited by prior statements of intent, since these have no binding force and do not feature in the Treaty as prescribed modes of action. One example is Case 2/57 *Compagnie des Hauts Fourneaux de Chasse* v. *High Authority*,[82] which dealt, once more, with the equalisation system in the scrap market. In this case, the general decision on which the system was based was alleged to constitute a misuse of discretion, since the stated aim of that decision was to ensure a regular supply of scrap to the common market, whereas the High Authority, in a previously published memorandum, had stated that the general aim of the scrap equalisation scheme was to balance the pig-iron/steel market.[83]

Because of the change of purpose, the complainant argued that there was a misuse of powers. The Court held[84]:

"This ground of complaint must be rejected because the legality of the contested decision cannot depend on its conformity or otherwise with the memoranda published by the High Authority, but only on its conformity or otherwise with the Treaty. In no sense do the memoranda contain the only possible definition of the legal objective which the High Authority is entitled to pursue. To prove an abuse of power the applicant would have had to demonstrate that the decision itself was in fact pursuing an objective other than that for the purposes of which the High Authority was entitled to act; the variation which the applicant has pointed out between the wording of the memoranda and that of the contested decision does not suffice to constitute such evidence."

A finding that the memoranda were decisive would have constrained the discretionary power of the High Authority and limited its choice of aims. This shows that freedom of decision-making can be limited only by a prior legal act of some kind.

Case 179/82 *Lucchini Siderurgica S.p.a.* v. *Commission of the EEC* involves a complex mix of discretionary constraints and exceptions to

---

[82] [1958] E.C.R. 199.
[83] Judgment, *op. cit.*, footnote 82, at 231.
[84] Judgment, *op. cit.*, at 231; in his opinion, Advocate-General Lagrange does not comment specifically on this link.

them.[85] The contested decision had imposed a fine for exceeding the quarterly steel production quota. The complainant asked for the penalty to be annulled or at least reduced.[86]

The authority to impose fines under the quota system is derived from Article 58(4) of the ECSC Treaty. The amount of the penalty is within the discretion of the High Authority.

Acting on this authority, the Commission had determined, in Article 9, paragraph 1, of Decision 2794/80 (introduction of a quota system) that for every tonne of steel products in excess of the fixed quotas, a fine of 75 ECU per tonne would be payable.

Only in exceptional cases could the fine be waived.

The complainant undertaking argued that this was an exceptional case because, during the quarter in question, it had been commissioning a reconstructed rolling-mill which, owing to the special circumstances of the start-up phase, had produced an unexpectedly large quantity of steel. This accounted for the quota being exceeded.[87]

It had, however, been suggested in writing that the temporary over-production could be compensated by reducing production to the equivalent amount in subsequent quarters, and this had in fact been done. The Commission had taken no notice of the letter. The penalty ought therefore to be revoked. But the Court did not agree with the undertaking on that point[88]:

> "It should be emphasized in this respect that the quarterly nature of the quota system established by Decision 2794/80/EEC is an essential element of the scheme. The Commission thus rightly insists on the fact that all forecasts and the fixing of quotas are based on quarterly production and that undertakings are responsible for ensuring that production does not exceed the quotas fixed for that period.
>
> That is the reason why the producer normally bears the risk of not observing the quotas. The irregular production of a rolling mill and the problems caused by relations with trade unions, on which the applicant relies, fall within a sphere of normal business risks and are not capable of exonerating the applicant from its responsibility for observing the quotas.

---

[85] [1983] E.C.R. 3089.
[86] See [1983] E.C.R. 3086 *et seq.* (3090, para. 4).
[87] *Op. cit.*, footnote 86, at 3092, para. 14.
[88] *cf. op. cit.*, footnote 86, at 3094, paras. 20 to 23.

In the same way a reduction in the production for a subsequent quarter is not capable of correcting a previous irregularity since the decisive period in applying the system is quarterly.

Thus the Commission rightly found in the contested decision that the applicant had disregarded its obligations under Community law and imposed a fine on it. Thus the application for a declaration that the contested decision imposing the fine is void must be dismissed."

Particularly interesting are the Court's comments on the ancillary plea for a reduction of the fine[89]:

"However, the applicant claims in the alternative a reduction in the fine in view of the special circumstances of the case.

As has been stated above, the fine must be fixed according to Article 9 of Decision No. 2794/80 at an amount of 75 ECU per tonne of excess production, save in exceptional cases justifying a departure from the normal rate. In this case exceptional circumstances justify such a departure.

It is not disputed that during the quarter in question the applicant encountered exceptional difficulties in observing the quota allocated and that it made a reduction in its subsequent production. Although there may be many reasons for such a reduction it must nevertheless be borne in mind in the present case that in its telex message of 7 April 1981 the applicant offered in advance to offset the excess, which indicates that it voluntarily reduced its production in order to compensate for exceeding the quota and to regularize the situation.

Since the Commission did not answer that telex message and thus regrettably neglected the rules of good administration, it left the applicant in doubt as to whether the Commission was accepting the applicant's offer. Since in those circumstances the applicant in fact reduced its production to a considerable extent to compensate for having exceeded the quota, it is necessary to recognize in its favour that there was an exceptional situation justifying the fixing of a rate lower than the normal rate."

This means, first, that the Commission ought to have exercised its discretion regarding the imposition of fines. But in the case in question, the Commission had assumed that it had no discretion but was already bound by its own decision.

---

[89] *Op. cit.*, footnote 86, at 3094, paras. 24 *et seq.*

The Court had therefore to substitute a decision of its own, acting under Article 36 of the ECSC Treaty. According to its findings the undertaking was, for technical reasons, in an exceptional position and as a result had exceeded the quotas.

It could not wholly escape being fined, and indeed this is the sort of risk an entrepreneur has to face; but because of the exceptional circumstances, an appropriate measure of discretion was called for. The Commission, however, had followed the rule blindly and had imposed the standard fine; it had thereby acted unlawfully. Since the Court, under Article 36 of the ECSC Treaty, has the power to investigate all discretionary decisions and the right to amend them, it had to look for other criteria which would justify reducing the fine.

In short, the plaintiff's case was favoured by the "honesty" of the steel enterprise and by the negligence of the Commission.

Although this made it possible to reduce the fine, the amount of the reduction had still to be determined. The Court finally decided[90]:

> "In those circumstances the fine must be reduced. In view of the amount of the reduction in production made during the second quarter of 1981 a fine of an amount equal to half that imposed, namely 205 800 ECU (LIT 272 349 546) appears appropriate."

This reasoning is disappointing. It does not show any connection between exceeding the quotas, reducing production and halving the fine. Nor does the Court itself explain this important aspect of the use of discretion. It is doubtful whether the Commission, for its part, could have satisfied the law with such a succinct statement of reasons. This case shows that the ECSC executive can voluntarily limit its exercise of discretion, but is bound by the terms governing that use in the areas which it has reserved to itself.

(cc) *How the ECSC executive is bound by general principles of law*

Despite the precision of the language in which its authority is expressed, even ECSC law cannot close all the gaps in its sources of authority without resorting to general principles of law.

---

[90] *Op. cit.*, footnote 86, at 3095, para. 28.

On a view of the case law, however, they have a less important role than in EEC affairs, for example. This may be due to the more substantial body of positive law in the ECSC, which leaves fewer gaps to be closed.

Some ECSC cases have nevertheless been decided by the Court on the basis of general principles of law, and these include cases of fundamental importance to the Community as a whole.

Among this class of cases is the judgment given by the Court in Case 4/73 *Nold* v. *Commission*,[91] which concerned the authorisation under cartel law of a new trading arrangement for the Ruhr coalmines. Under this new rule, coal was to be supplied direct only to dealers willing to conclude a two-yearly agreement to take a minimum of 6,000 tonnes a year to meet the needs of domestic and small industrial consumers.[92]

The complainant argued that because this figure was much in excess of its sales and the decision had caused it to lose its status as a wholesaler, the rule infringed both fundamental rights and the prohibition against discrimination.

The Court dealt first with the complaint of discrimination[93]:

> "Firstly, the applicant considers it to be discriminatory that, unlike other undertakings, it should lose its entitlement to direct supplies from the producer and should thereby be in a more unfavourable position than other dealers who continue to enjoy this advantage.
>
> Secondly, it invokes Article 65(2), which in a similar case to that envisaged under Article 66 authorizes joint-selling agreements only if such arrangements will make for 'a substantial improvement in the production or distribution' of the products concerned."

Article 66(1) of the ECSC Treaty defines the circumstances for which authorisation is required, and paragraph 2 states the conditions for the authorisation. Its wording suggests a tied, or non-discretionary, decision:

> "The High Authority shall grant the authorization referred to in the preceding paragraph if it finds . . ."

Here follow the special circumstances in which authorisation must be withheld. This too suggests a tied decision. The next paragraph continues, however:

---

[91] [1974] E.C.R. 491.
[92] *cf.* the summary of facts, *op. cit.*, footnote 91, at 493 *et seq.*
[93] *Op. cit.*, footnote 91, at 506, para. 8.

"In assessing whether this is so, the High Authority shall, in accordance with the principle of non-discrimination laid down in Article 4(b), take account of the size of the undertakings in the Community, to the extent it considers justified in order to avoid or correct disadvantages resulting from unequal competitive conditions."

The words "assessing whether this is so" are reminiscent of a corresponding passage in Article 33(1) of the Treaty, which refers to the freedom of the executive to judge the situation for itself.

From the German point of view, this constitutes scope for appraisal, since it is the facts underlying the authorisation which have to be assessed, the consequences remaining unaltered. The only possible modification of the legal consequences is found in the second paragraph of Article 66(2), which allows the High Authority to attach appropriate conditions to the authorisation.

In the case in question, the explicit ban against discrimination in Article 66(2) of the Treaty was not relevant, and the complainant's case turned upon the general prohibition of discrimination.

The legal question was whether the prohibition had been observed when assessing the consequences of the planned merger, and whether these consequences met the conditions for an authorisation under Article 66(2) of the ECSC Treaty.

The ban on discrimination is therefore the deciding factor in, and the boundary to, the Commission's scope for appraisal.

The Court found however that the complainant had not suffered any undue disadvantage.[94] The second complaint was that fundamental rights had been infringed[95]:

"The applicant asserts finally that certain of its fundamental rights have been violated, in that the restrictions introduced by the new trading rules authorized by the Commission have the effect, by depriving it of direct supplies, of jeopardizing both the profitability of the undertaking and the free development of its business activity, to the point of endangering its very existence.

In this way, the Decision is said to violate, in respect of the applicant, a right akin to a proprietary right, as well as its right to the free pursuit of business activity, as protected by the Grundgesetz of the Federal Republic of Germany and by the Constitutions of other

---

[94] *Op. cit.*, footnote 91, at 506 *et seq.*, para. 10; and p. 507, para. 11.
[95] *Op. cit.*, footnote 91, at 507, para. 12.

357

Member States and various international treaties, including in particular the Convention for the Protection of Human Rights and Fundamental Freedoms of 4 November 1940 and the Protocol to that Convention of 20 March 1952."

The Court, pointing out that fundamental rights were among the general principles of law which it had to uphold, went on to consider this question[96]:

"If rights of ownership are protected by the constitutional laws of all the Member States and if similar guarantees are given in respect of their right freely to choose and practise their trade or profession, the rights thereby guaranteed, far from constituting unfettered prerogatives, must be viewed in the light of the social function of the property and activities protected thereunder.

For this reason, rights of this nature are protected by law subject always to limitations laid down in accordance with the public interest.

Within the Community legal order it likewise seems legitimate that these rights should, if necessary, be subject to certain limits justified by the overall objectives pursued by the Community, on condition that the substance of these rights is left untouched.

As regards the guarantees accorded to a particular undertaking, they can in no respect be extended to protect mere commercial interests or opportunities, the uncertainties of which are part of the very essence of economic activity.

The disadvantages claimed by the applicant are in fact the result of economic change and not of the contested Decision.

It was for the applicant, confronted by the economic changes brought about by the recession in coal production, to acknowledge the situation and itself carry out the necessary adaptations."

Although the complaint of a breach of fundamental rights did not succeed in *Nold*, clearly the existence of fundamental rights requires that the High Authority (Commission), when making its economic evaluations, must take account of protected market situations and must decide whether, in the public interest, they should be restricted.

[96] *Op. cit.*, footnote 91, at 507 *et seq.*, paras. 14 and 15 at 508.

The final judgment in the 1962 case *Klöckner Werke AG, Hoesch AG* v. *High Authority* deals, once again, with the question of scrap equalisation.[97]

This decision sheds some light on the role of general principles of law in limiting the discretionary powers of Community organs. It deals with a modern variant of sovereign freedom of decision, in the form of discretionary planning decisions. The question was, how far the High Authority has discretion to decide on planning issues when it devises and introduces financial arrangements such as the scrap equalisation scheme[98]:

> "In working out the financial arrangements which it establishes for safeguarding the stability of the market, the High Authority has a duty to take account of the economic circumstances in which those arrangements have to be applied, so that the aims pursued may be attained under the most favourable conditions and with the smallest possible sacrifice by the undertakings affected. This principle of justice however must always be harmonized with the principle of legal certainty. These two principles must be so reconciled as to entail the minimum of sacrifice by persons as a whole within the Community."

This upholds, above all, the principles of proportionality and legal certainty, which may contain countervailing tendencies. It is interesting that the proportionality principle is described as a "principle of justice." Both principles are examined in a separate chapter and need not be dealt with here. The position can be summarised by saying that wherever there is room for decision-making, whether in assessing economic factors or in determining legal consequences, general principles of law play a guiding and limiting role.

3. Conclusion

This survey of the role of law in the common market for coal and steel has shown that the ECSC Treaty, despite the relative precision of its language, gives the ECSC executive considerable freedom of decision in some areas, a freedom which is also respected by the Court. Of special

---

[97] Case 17/61 [1962] E.C.R. 325.
[98] *Op. cit.*, footnote 97, at 325.

significance is the use of undefined terms, requiring complex economic judgments, to denote the discretionary powers of the executive. The Treaty's provisions on judicial protection go even further, since they exclude judicial investigation of these matters. Yet the Court is apparently prepared to review the assessment of complex economic relationships, especially in the field of cartel law. There is, however, no reliable method of ascertaining how far the review process will go. As a general guideline, it is true to say that the Court insists on judging both the facts and the observance of legal restrictions derived from the Treaty provisions, from secondary law, from administrative rules and from general principles of law.

"Misuse of powers" is significant chiefly as a basis for contesting normative decisions, rather than as an effective limit on official authority. The plea of "manifest failure to observe" a rule of law is similar, but has greater procedural significance. Where the plea of misuse of powers is substantiated, this will permit an evaluation of economic facts and circumstances, which would otherwise lie beyond the reach of judicial review.

III. THE COMPETITION LAW OF THE EEC

1. Introduction

The competition law of the European Economic Community consists chiefly of the ban on cartels, the prohibition of abuse of a dominant market position, rules on the conduct of public undertakings and monopolies, and the ban on certain state aids.

The law therefore covers threats to competition within the common market arising either from undertakings themselves or from government policies.[1] This survey focuses mainly on acts by private individuals to restrict competition and on national subsidy arrangements. It omits the considerable problems posed by public undertakings and monopolies because, apart from a legal challenge to the Commission's directive on transparency in this field, administrative cases do not often come before the Court.

---

[1] *cf.* B. Beutler, R. Bieber, J. Pipkorn, J. Streil, *Die Europäische Gemeinschaft—Rechtsordnung und Politik* (3rd ed., Baden-Baden 1987), p. 356.

It is obvious from the language of the competition rules that this is a very complex subject. The rules are full of undefined legal concepts which the Commission, as the executing agency, has to apply in each individual case. Within the compass of this study, it is hardly feasible to cover the entire range of competition law or even to review the field in any systematic fashion. For this purpose, the reader is referred to the many existing in-depth studies and commentaries and to the countless articles on the subject.[2] Here, we can deal with only a few sample terms and discretionary functions. Our chief aim is to pinpoint the essential features of the legal rules in this field.

2. The subject-matter of Articles 85 and 86 of the EEC Treaty

(a) The ban on cartels (Article 85)

Article 85(1) of the EEC Treaty forbids cartels. It prohibits agreements between undertakings, decisions by associations of undertakings and concerted practices which may affect trade between Member States and which have as their object or effect the prevention, restriction or distortion of competition within the common market. EEC cartel law, as opposed to national law, applies wherever trade between States may be affected.[3] Where there is no obstacle of this kind, the case will be confined to domestic law.[4] If the case fits both Community and national cartel law, Community law will take precedence in the event of any conflict between the two.[5]

Article 85(1), subparagraphs (a) to (e), of the EEC Treaty is an illustrative, non-exhaustive list of practices covered by the prohibition.[6] Paragraph 2 states that all the agreements and decisions prohibited in paragraph 1 are automatically void.[7] Article 85(3) of the Treaty exempts from the ban, under certain circumstances, the concerted practices and

---

[2] There is a systematic survey by H. Schröter in H. v. d. Groeben, H. v. Boeckh, J. Thiesing, C.-D. Ehlermann, *Kommentar zum EWG-Vertrag* (3rd ed., Baden-Baden 1983); see the notes on Articles 85 to 94, pp. 857 *et seq.*

[3] *cf.* H. Schröter, *op. cit.*, footnote 2, Artikel 85 Abs. 1, p. 997, no. 82.

[4] E.-J. Mestmäcker, *Europäisches Wettbewerbsrecht*, Munich 1974, p. 2.

[5] *Ibid.*

[6] *Ibid.*, *op. cit.*, footnote 4, p. 185.

[7] See H. Schröter, *op. cit.*, footnote 2, Article 85(2), p. 1002, no. 95, with citations from the case law.

decisions listed in paragraph 1.[8] Regulation 17 of February 6, 1962 contains the main governing provisions on cartels.[9] This regulation defines the powers enjoyed by the Commission under Article 87 of the Treaty when applying Articles 85 and 86. It deals with the institution of proceedings, the duty to report cartels, the Commission's right to obtain and seek information from national authorities and undertakings, and enforcement procedures where there is a breach of obligations under Regulation 17 and Articles 85 and 86 of the EEC Treaty.[10] The procedural guarantees accompanying Articles 85 and 86 of the Treaty strengthen the judicial protection afforded to the parties concerned. The procedural rights of undertakings and associations affected will be considered separately. Their significance can only be clearly understood, however, in the light of the controls derived from substantive law. We shall therefore look first at the legal powers of the Commission under Article 84 of the EEC Treaty, through one particularly illustrative case.

(aa) The subject-matter of Article 85(1) of the EEC Treaty

We have already referred to the situations covered by this Article and their legal consequences. Each of the factors involved raises difficult questions of fact and law. Hence the Commission commonly encounters problems of evidence when dealing with concerted practices and decisions by associations. Delicate inquiries may be needed to ascertain if certain undertakings are engaged in concerted practices. This particular type of prohibited market "co-operation" is especially complicated for the Commission, because of the factual problems involved. Agreements

---

[8] Article 85(3) reads as follows:
  "The provisions of paragraph 1 may, however, be declared inapplicable in the case of:
  —any agreement or category of agreements between undertakings;
  —any decision or category of decisions by associations of undertakings;
  —any concerted practice or category of concerted practices;
  which contributes to improving the production or distribution of goods or to promoting technical or economic progress, while allowing consumers a fair share of the resulting benefit, and which does not:
    (a) impose on the undertakings concerned restrictions which are not indispensable to the attainment of these objectives.
    (b) afford such undertakings the possibility of eliminating competition in respect of a substantial part of the products in question."
[9] J.O. 1962, 204 *et seq.*; O.J. Sp. Ed. 1959–1962, 60.
[10] Commission Regulation 99/63 stipulates that there is a right to be heard; *cf.* J.O. 1963, 2268; O.J. Sp. Ed. 1963–1964, 47. Schröter summarises the chief implementing regulations, *op. cit.*, footnote 2, textual commentary on Article 87, pp. 1383 *et seq.*

and decisions are legally binding,[11] whereas concerted practices form a kind of blanket term for all forms of co-operation based on agreements which are not legally binding.[12] A crucial stage in the development of this concept was reached with the so-called "dyestuffs" cases.[13]

Around the mid-1960s, some major producers of aniline dyes made a series of price increases which, in the Commission's view, represented a concerted practice incompatible with Article 85(1) of the EEC Treaty. The Commission therefore decided to impose a fine on these producers. Its decision was challenged by the dye-producers. Once of these was the British company ICI, whose case before the Court is summarised below.[14] The complainant argued that the Commission had failed to show the existence of concerted practices. The contested decision, it said, was based on market studies lacking in depth, and on a misunderstanding of the notion of "concerted practices."

The Commission, it alleged, was wrongly equating the meaning of the term with the deliberate parallel actions by members of an oligopoly, disregarding the fact that the conduct in question may be due to separate decisions by the individual companies in response to objective economic needs, especially the need to improve profitability.[15]

The Court was thus called on to elucidate the meaning of "concerted practices". The Opinion of Advocate General Mayras reflects the efforts required from both the plaintiffs and the Court simply to assemble the facts from which the question could be answered. The elaborate pleadings of the parties and the number of experts involved point to the complexity of the economic factors involved.[16] By contrast, in agricultural law cases the Court has consistently held that the institution responsible has wide scope for appraisal and broad powers to evaluate and

---

[11] cf. H. Schröter, op. cit., footnote 2, Article 85(1), p. 956, no. 12.

[12] The term itself originates in United States antitrust law. It came into the ECSC Treaty (Article 65(1)) via the French cartel law of the post-war period. The term was then incorporated in Article 85 of the EEC Treaty. See Case 14/68 Walt Wilhelm and Others v. Bundeskartellamt [1969] E.C.R. 1, with an instructive opinion by Advocate-General Roemer, pp. 17 et seq.

[13] Case 48/69 Imperial Chemical Industries Ltd. v. Commission [1972] E.C.R. 619; Case 49/69, BASF v. Commission [1972] E.C.R. 713; Case 51/69 Bayer v. Commission [1972] E.C.R. 745; Case 52/69 Geigy v. Commission [1972] E.C.R. 787; Case 53/69 Sandoz v. Commission [1972] E.C.R. 845; Case 54/69 Francolar v. Commission [1972] E.C.R. 851; Case 55/69 Cassella v. Commission [1972] E.C.R. 887; Case 56/69 Hoechst v. Commission [1972] E.C.R. 927; Case 57/69 Azienda Colori Nazionali v. Commission [1972] E.C.R. 933.

[14] Case 48/69 [1972] E.C.R. 619.

[15] Op. cit., footnote 14, p. 654, paras. 57 to 63.

[16] cf. Advocate-General Mayras, op. cit., footnote 14, p. 665.

decide matters. The difference here is that most agricultural law cases deal with Community rules, rather than individual decisions as in this instance. However, in its judgments in customs cases, to be considered later, the Court has, wherever possible, avoided using terms in a single meaning only, as if they were scientific measures.

The Court uses a different approach when resolving cartel cases. In general it examines whether the presentation of the case, which is often complex and full of economic problems, squares with the legal definition. Finally, it determines whether or not its requirements have been fulfilled. This was what it did in the case of the dye manufacturers ICI, to determine whether "concerted practices" had been followed.

The Court began with the abstract elements of the definition[17]:

> "Article 85 draws a distinction between the concept of 'concerted practices' and that of 'agreements between undertakings' or of 'decisions by associations of undertakings'; the object is to bring within the prohibition of that article a form of coordination between undertakings which, without having reached the stage where an agreement properly so-called has been concluded, knowingly substitutes practical cooperation between them for the risks of competition.
>
> By its very nature, then, a concerted practice does not have all the elements of a contract but may *inter alia* arise out of coordination which becomes apparent from the behaviour of the participants.
>
> Although parallel behaviour may not by itself be identified with a concerted practice, it may however amount to strong evidence of such a practice if it leads to conditions of competition which do not correspond to the normal conditions of the market, having regard to the nature of the products, the size and number of the undertakings, and the volume of the said market.
>
> This is especially the case if the parallel conduct is such as to enable those concerned to attempt to stabilize prices at a level different from that to which competition would have led, and to consolidate established positions to the detriment of effective freedom of movement of the products in the common market and of the freedom of consumers to choose their suppliers.
>
> Therefore the question whether there was a concerted action in this case can only be correctly determined if the evidence upon which the contested decision is based is considered, not in isolation, but as a

---

[17] *Op. cit.*, footnote 14, p. 655, paras. 64 to 67.

whole, account being taken of the specific features of the market in the products in question."

A comparison follows—too detailed to summarise here—of the facts adduced during the proceedings to furnish evidence of a concerted practice. The details are not, however, indispensable for the purpose of answering the essential query: how far is the Commission legally bound by substantive cartel law? It is the result of the judicial review which is both decisive and illuminating[18]:

"In these circumstances and taking into account the nature of the market in the products in question, the conduct of the applicant, in conjunction with other undertakings against which proceedings have been taken, was designed to replace the risks of competition and the hazards of competitors' spontaneous reactions by cooperation constituting a concerted practice prohibited by Article 85(1) of the Treaty."

It is standard practice for the Court to give a final interpretation of a term in Article 85(1) of the EEC Treaty, and this is also evident in Case 48/69, which concerned the expression "affect trade between Member States."[19] One is also struck by the Court's apodictic style when it compares the relevant market, here the market in dyestuffs, with the situation contemplated by Article 85(1). This is apparently a combination of an outside expert opinion and the Court's own views. Because of its judicial reserve towards the investigation of complex economic factors, as in the field of agriculture or customs law, the question again arises why the review should be so thorough in the particular matter of cartels. The same applies to another area already mentioned, ECSC competition law.

---

[18] *Op. cit.*, footnote 14, pp. 660–661, paras. 115 to 119.

[19] *Op. cit.*, footnote 14, p. 661, paras. 120 *et seq.* Administrative lawyers will be interested in the Commission's so-called "bagatelle" pronouncement of May 27, 1970 (O.J. 1970, C64/1 *et seq.*) which explains the notion of affecting intra-EEC trade. This statement puts flesh on the criterion of "perceptibility," which the Court had found to be an essential feature of the impairment of trade among Member States through cartel agreements; *cf.* Case 56/65 *Société Technique Minière* v. *Maschinenbau Ulm* [1966] E.C.R. 235 at 251. This is an abstract principle of interpretation which does not have binding force but is intended to reduce the need for individual decisions. Other guidelines for interpretation will be found in E. J. Mestmäcker, *Europäisches Wettbewerbsrecht*, Munich 1974, Annex VI, pp. 792 *et seq.* For the executive's (the Commission's) power to make abstract rules, see also J. Schwarze, *Die Befugnis zur Abstraktion im Europäischen Gemeinschaftsrecht*, Baden-Baden 1978, pp. 61 *et seq.*

It would be premature, however, to attempt an answer here. No survey of the legal rules applying to cartels would be complete without examining the practice of exemptions.

(bb) Exemptions under Article 85(3) of the EEC Treaty

Article 85(3) of the EEC Treaty allows exemptions, under certain conditions, from the prohibition imposed in paragraph 2. The text states that the provisions of paragraph 1 "may" be declared inapplicable.

Here a basic distinction must be made between individual and group exemptions. An individual exemption is granted through a special decision, and a group exemption by way of a regulation.[20] A group exemption simplifies administrative procedures by eliminating entire groups of decisions, agreements and concerted practices that constitute no danger to trade among the Member States.[21] Under Article 189(2) of the EEC Treaty, these exemption rules apply directly in every Member State, and no intervening administrative procedure is necessary to obtain the exemption. Undertakings may therefore carry out the exempted practices without official consent. There is, of course, the risk that they may err in their judgment that a certain practice is among those exempted, although this risk is mitigated by Regulation 17 whereby, in spite of the direct application of the group exemption, the Commission may, on request, decide by a special decision that the agreement is admissible under cartel law.[22]

Undertakings whose agreements obviously do not fall within the group exemption are expected to apply for an individual exemption. The statement in Article 85(3) of the EEC Treaty that the provisions of that paragraph "may" be declared inapplicable indicates that a discretionary decision is required from the Commission. The Court's judgment in Joined Cases 56 and 58/64 *Consten and Grundig* v. *Commission* illustrates the kind of judicial review which may take place where the Commission has decided on a special exemption.[23]

These cases concerned a contract between Grundig, the German firm of electronic equipment manufacturers, and the French firm Consten, whereby the latter was appointed sole representative for Grundig equip-

---

[20] H. Schröter, *op. cit.*, footnote 2, Article 85(3), p. 1047, no. 140.
[21] For a detailed comment, see E.J. Mestmäcker, *op. cit.*, footnote 19, pp. 308 *et seq.*
[22] *Ibid.*, *op. cit.*, footnote 19, p. 310.
[23] [1966] E.C.R. 299.

ment in France, the Saar and Corsica. Consten undertook, in addition, not to sell either on its own or another's account similar articles competing with the goods covered by the contract, and not to make deliveries, either directly or indirectly, from the contract territory to other countries. Consten was also given the right to use the Grundig name and pictorial trade marks for the sale of Grundig equipment. For its part, Grundig undertook not to supply other people in the contract territory either directly or indirectly.[24]

A number of similar agreements were also concluded with dealers in other countries. The dispute arose when these contracts were notified to the Commission under Article 4, no. 1 of Regulation 17—not itself a compulsory procedure, except where an exemption is sought under Article 85(3) of the EEC Treaty.

Initially, the Commission decided only on the Grundig/Consten contract. In Article 1 of its decision it ruled that both the contract and the supplementary agreements on trade marks were in breach of Article 85(1) of the EEC Treaty.[25] In Article 2, it refused any exemption under Article 85(3) of the Treaty. Finally, Article 3 ordered Grundig and Consten to refrain from any act which would make it impossible or difficult for other firms to procure, at will, articles covered by the contract for distribution in the territory of the contract.[26] Grundig and Consten both entered separate appeals against the decision. Because the two appeals were similar in substance, the Court decided to hear and resolve them jointly. Two questions had to be decided: whether the subject was within the ambit of Article 85(1) of the EEC Treaty, and whether the Commission had been justified in its refusal to grant an exemption.

The Court began by deciding where the burden of proof lay for establishing the facts relevant to an exemption[27]:

"The undertakings are entitled to an appropriate examination by the Commission of their requests for Article 85(3) to be applied. For this purpose the Commission may not confine itself to requiring from undertakings proof of the fulfilment of the requirements for the grant of an exemption but must, as a matter of good administration, play its part, using the means available to it, in ascertaining the relevant facts and circumstances."

[24] See the "Issues of fact and of law," *op. cit.*, footnote 23, p. 303.
[25] *Op. cit.*, footnote 23, p. 304 of the summary of facts.
[26] *cf.* the summary of facts, *op. cit.*, footnote 23, p. 304.
[27] *Op. cit.*, footnote 23, p. 347 of the judgment.

This is followed by some significant remarks on the judicial review of decisions under Article 85(3)[28]:

> "Furthermore, the exercise of the Commission's powers necessarily implies complex evaluations on economic matters. A judicial review of these evaluations must take account of their nature by confining itself to an examination of the relevance of the facts and of the legal consequences which the Commission deduces therefrom. This review must in the first place be carried out in respect of the reasons given for the decisions, which must set out the facts and considerations on which the said evaluations are based."

The restrictions on the Court's powers of review for exemption decisions are matched by a corresponding discretionary power on the part of the Commission. It is free to gather and appraise the facts for itself, but may not withhold the exemption where the legal result would be to grant one. In other words, if the factual conditions of Article 85(3) of the EEC Treaty are fulfilled, the Commission must exempt the agreement in question, and has no discretion in the matter.[29] The following extract from the Consten/Grundig decision shows that the Commission has only one option open to it[30]:

> "Since all the requirements necessary for granting the exemption provided for in Article 85(3) must be fulfilled, there is therefore no need to examine the submissions relating to the other requirements for exemption."

The Court has therefore admitted that the Commission's so-called "measure of discretion" extends only to the facts and the evaluation of them.[30a]

However, the Commission's scope for decision-making under Article 85(3) is not confined to granting or withholding an exemption. There is an intermediate state, at which it may grant the exemption subject to the undertaking fulfilling certain requirements. Here it has further scope for discretion, as the Court held in Case 17/74, *Transocean Marine Paint* v.

---

[28] *Op. cit.*, footnote 23, p. 347 of the judgment.
[29] H. Schröter, *op. cit.*, footnote 2, Article 85(3), p. 1017, no. 111, refers to "scope for discretion," which means the same thing.
[30] *Op. cit.*, footnote 23, p. 350 of the judgment.
[30a] *cf.* Case 71/74 *Trubo* v. *Commission* [1972] E.C.R. 563 at 585, para. 43; Case 45/85 *Verband der Sachversicherer e.V.* v. *Commission* [1987] E.C.R. 405, paras. 58 *et seq.*

Commission.[31] This concerned the prolonging of an exemption which had been granted by the Commission subject to certain requirements being fulfilled. As to the Commission's discretionary powers and their limits, the Court held[32]:

> "Since Article 85(3) constitutes, for the benefit of undertakings, an exception to the general prohibition contained in Article 85(1), the Commission must be in a position at any moment to check whether the conditions justifying the exemption are still present. Accordingly, in relation to the detailed rules to which it may subject the exemption, the Commission enjoys a large measure of discretion, while at the same time having to act within the limits imposed upon its competence by Article 85. On the other hand, the exercise of this discretionary power is linked to a preliminary canvassing of objections which may be raised by the undertakings."

This last sentence shows once more that discretionary authority, on the one hand, and the duty to investigate the facts fully, on the other, are closely interwoven. In the judicial review process, this is reflected in the checks made on the completeness and accuracy of the facts in the case. The entitlement to a fair hearing—which was ultimately at issue in the above decision—should help to ensure an objective presentation of the facts.[33]

In the case of the Transocean Marine Paint Association, the right to a hearing had been denied, and the Court annulled the conditions imposed and referred the matter back to the Commission. As the Court found, the decision had been imposed "in breach of procedural requirements."[34] Nevertheless, the Commission has wider discretion when making exemptions than when defining the subject of the prohibition.

(cc) Conclusion

The Court's case-law on Article 85 of the EEC Treaty shows that the

---

[31] [1974] E.C.R. 1063 *et seq.*

[32] *Op. cit.*, footnote 31, p. 1081, para. 16; on the limit to the Commission's discretion in anti-dumping matters arising from a manifest error of judgment, see Case 255/84 *Nachi Fujikoshi* v. *Commission* [1987] E.C.R. 1861, para. 26.

[33] On the right to a judicial hearing, see Advocate-General Warner *op. cit.*, footnote 31, pp. 1090 *et seq.*, also Case 234/84 *Belgium* v. *Commission* [1986] E.C.R. 2263, para. 27.

[34] *Op. cit.*, footnote 31, p. 1081, para. 20.

Commission operates under tight legal rules when applying the cartel provisions. First, it must comply strictly with the procedural and formal requirements found both in secondary legislation and in general principles of administration. Secondly, when deciding whether Commission decisions are correct according to substantive law, the Court has wide powers of review, which extend to the evaluation of complex economic factors. Decisions to grant exemptions are a different matter, because in such cases the Court gives the Commission scope to determine whether the factual conditions are present. Finally, it must be emphasised that where the ban on cartels is applied, the balance is held by the formal and substantive rules binding on the administration. It is generally true to say that the Court's case-law is equally strict towards both.

(b) Abuse of a dominant position (Article 86)

Article 86 of the EEC Treaty forbids the abuse of a dominant position, in so far as this affects trade among Member States. The expression "abuse of a dominant position" is an almost typical example of an undefined legal term. The rules found in subparagraphs (a) to (d) of this Article suggest the type of conduct which is covered by this term. The prohibition is absolute and direct in its effects; there is no possibility of exemption such as in Article 85 of the EEC Treaty.

(aa) How the term "abuse of a dominant position" is applied in individual cases

Case 27/76 *United Brands Company and others* v. *Commission*[35] concerned the legality of a Commission decision that the banana importing firm "United Brands" was guilty of abusing a dominant position and ordering it to cease the practices in question. The company was also fined 1 million units of account for similar previous acts.[36]

United Brands (UBC) appealed under the second paragraph of Article 173 of the EEC Treaty against the decision and the fine, and sought compensation for non-material damage under the second paragraph of Article 215 of the Treaty.[37]

---

[35] [1978] E.C.R. 207 *et seq.*
[36] See below.
[37] *Op. cit.*, footnote 35, p. 279, paras. 6 to 7; the compensation sought was calculated as one unit of account, as a token that non-material loss had been sustained.

The Court began its judgment by quoting the substance of the Commission's decision, in the following words[38]:

> "Article 1 of the decision declares that UBC has infringed Article 86 of the Treaty establishing the European Economic Community,
>
>   (a) by requiring its distributor/ripeners in the Belgo-Luxembourg Economic Union, Denmark, Germany, Ireland and the Netherlands to refrain from reselling its bananas while still green;
>
>   (b) by, in respect of its sales of Chiquita bananas, charging other trading parties, namely distributor/ripeners other than the Scipio Group in the Member States referred to above, dissimilar prices for equivalent transactions;
>
>   (c) by imposing unfair prices for the sale of Chiquita bananas on its customers in the Belgo-Luxembourg Economic Union, Denmark, the Netherlands and Germany (other than the Scipio Group);
>
>   (d) by refusing from 10 October 1973 to 11 February 1975 to supply Chiquita bananas to Th. Olesen A/S, Valby, Copenhagen, Denmark."

Article 2 of the decision imposes a fine of 1,000,000 units of account on UBC for the unlawful acts defined in Article 1. Under Article 3, UBC is ordered,

> "(a) to bring to an end without delay the infringements referred to in Article 1 hereof, unless it has already done so of its own accord,
>
>   (b) (i) to inform all its distributor/ripeners in the Belgo-Luxembourg Economic Union, Denmark, Germany, Ireland and the Netherlands that it has ceased to apply the prohibition on the resale of green bananas and inform the Commission that it has done so by not later than 1 February 1976;
>
>   (ii) to inform the Commission by 20 April 1976 and thereafter twice yearly not later than 20 January and 20 July for a period of two years of the prices charged during the previous six months to customers in the Belgo-Luxembourg Economic Union, Denmark, Germany, Ireland and the Netherlands."

This decision is then compared, seriatim, with the eight grounds of complaint advanced by United Brands[39]:

---

[38] *Op. cit.*, footnote 35, pp. 268 *et seq.*, paras. 3 to 5 *et seq.*
[39] *Op. cit.*, footnote 35, p. 279, paras. 6 to 7 *et seq.*

"1. It challenges the analysis made by the Commission of the relevant market, and also of the product market and the geographic market;

2. It denies that it is in a dominant position on the relevant market within the meaning of Article 86 of the Treaty;

3. It considers that the clause relating to the conditions of sale of green bananas is justified by the need to safeguard the quality of the product sold to the customer;

4. It intends to show that the refusal to continue to supply the Danish firm Th. Olesen was justified;

5. It takes the view that it has not charged discriminatory prices;

6. It takes the view that it has not charged unfair prices;

7. It complains that the administrative procedure was irregular;

8. It disputes the imposition of the fine and, in the alternative, asks the Court to reduce it."

The Court begins its examination of the specific complaints by considering whether the complainant had a dominant position on the market. It divides this examination into two parts:

first, the definition of the relevant market; second, the position of United Brands on the relevant market.[40]

The Court explains the need to define the relevant market in the following terms[41]:

"In order to determine whether UBC has a dominant position on the banana market it is necessary to define this market both from the standpoint of the product and from the geographic point of view.

The opportunities for competition under Article 86 of the Treaty must be considered having regard to the particular features of the product in question and with reference to a clearly defined geographic area in which it is marketed and where the conditions of competition are sufficiently homogeneous for the effect of the economic power of the undertaking concerned to be able to be evaluated."

[40] *Op. cit.*, footnote 35, p. 280, paras. 10 to 11.
[41] *Op. cit.*, footnote 35, p. 280, paras. 10 to 11; *cf.* also Case 226/84 *British Leyland* v. *Commission* [1986] E.C.R. 3263, paras. 3 to 10.

For the purposes of this investigation it is not necessary to go into the details of the world banana market. It suffices to say that the Court gives an accurate and conclusive definition both of the market for the product and of the territorial market, on the basis of the known facts, and that no aspects of the question are referred to the discretionary judgment of the Commission. The examination of the relevant market ends with the finding[42]:

> "It follows from all these considerations that the geographic market as determined by the Commission, which constitutes a substantial part of the common market, must be regarded as the relevant market for the purpose of determining whether the applicant may be in a dominant position."

The second step is to assess the position of United Brands on the relevant market. The Court explains how it did this[43]:

> "In order to find out whether UBC is an undertaking in a dominant position on the relevant market, it is necessary first of all to examine its structure and then the situation on the said market as far as competition is concerned.
>
> In doing so it may be advisable to take account if need be of the facts put forward as acts amounting to abuses without necessarily having to acknowledge that they are abuses."

The examination which follows is aimed at defining the economic influence of United Brands on the relevant market. This, without question, necessitates evaluating a complex economic situation, even if the issue is overshadowed by the role played by a single undertaking. Its position on the market emerges only from an analysis of the manifold inter-relationships among the undertaking concerned, its competitors and customers.

The Court made a careful examination of the known structure of United Brands and of the competition on the relevant market, and concluded that[44]:

> "The cumulative effect of all the advantages enjoyed by UBC thus ensures that it has a dominant position on the relevant market."

---

[42] *Op. cit.*, footnote 35, p. 285, para. 57.
[43] *Op. cit.*, footnote 35, p. 286, paras. 67 to 68.
[44] *Op. cit.*, footnote 35, p. 292, para. 129.

373

Here the Court makes a final determination, in an individual case, of what is meant by a "dominant position."

There is a second main group of grounds of judgment, dealing with the question whether United Brands has abused its dominant market position and thereby affected trade among Member States.[45] This question is considered in several parts. The first of these concerns the conduct of United Brands towards the ripeners (no. 1 of the Commission's decision).

The first point here is the clause forbidding the resale of green bananas. After thorough consideration, the Court concludes[46]:

> "Although it is commendable and lawful to pursue a policy of quality, especially by choosing sellers according to objective criteria relating to the qualifications of the seller, his staff and his facilities, such a practice can only be justified if it does not raise obstacles, the effect of which goes beyond the objective to be attained.
>
> In this case, although these conditions for selection have been laid down in a way which is objective and not discriminatory, the prohibition on resale imposed upon duly appointed Chiquita ripeners and the prohibition of the resale of unbranded bananas—even if the perishable nature of the banana in practice restricted the opportunity of reselling to the duration of a specific period of time—were without any doubt an abuse of the dominant position since they limit markets to the prejudice of consumers and affect trade between Member States, in particular by partitioning national markets.
>
> Thus UBC's organization of the market confined the ripeners to the role of suppliers of the local market and prevented them from developing their capacity to trade vis-à-vis UBC, which moreover tightened its economic hold on them by supplying less goods than they ordered.
>
> It follows from all these considerations that the clause at issue forbidding the sale of green bananas infringes Article 86 of the Treaty.
>
> On this point the contested decision is therefore justified."

---

[45] *Op. cit.*, footnote 35, p. 292, paras. 130 to 138 *et seq.*; for a similar approach, see Case 226/84, *op. cit.*, footnote 41, para. 11.
[46] *Op. cit.*, footnote 35, p. 295, paras. 152 to 160 and p. 296, paras. 161 to 162.

The Court also agreed with the Commission that the refusal to supply the Olesen company was an abuse of a dominant position and affected trade among Member States[47]:

> "In fact when Olesen's supplies were cut off it was unable to buy Chiquita bananas at Bremerhaven and therefore had to import into Denmark the same quantities of bananas as it did before this step was taken.
>
> It was forced to buy bananas bearing other brand names outside Denmark and to import them into Denmark.
>
> Furthermore, if the occupier of a dominant position, established in the common market, aims at eliminating a competitor who is also established in the common market, it is immaterial whether this behaviour relates to trade between Member States once it has been shown that such elimination will have repercussions on the patterns of competition in the Common Market.
>
> Consequently the refusal to supply a long-standing regular customer who buys with a view to reselling in another Member State has an influence on the normal movement of trade and an appreciable effect on trade between Member States.
>
> The finding in the decision that UBC has infringed Article 86 of the Treaty by refusing to supply Olesen is therefore justified."

The second question is the pricing policy of United Brands. The Court shared the Commission's view that UBC's practice of altering prices on a weekly basis without proper cause and charging different prices in different Member States was discriminatory and infringed Article 86[48]:

> "These discriminatory prices, which varied according to the circumstances of the Member States, were just so many obstacles to the free movement of goods and their effect was intensified by the clause forbidding the resale of bananas while still green and by reducing the deliveries of the quantities ordered.
>
> A rigid partitioning of national markets was thus created at price levels which were artificially different, placing certain distributor/ripeners at a competitive disadvantage, since compared with what it should have been competition had thereby been distorted.

[47] *cf. op. cit.*, footnote 35, pp. 289 *et seq.*, paras. 163 to 168 *et seq.*; Conclusion: paras. 198 to 203.

[48] *Op. cit.*, footnote 35, paras. 227 to 233 *et seq.*

Consequently the policy of differing prices enabling UBC to apply dissimilar conditions to equivalent transactions with other trading parties, thereby placing them at a competitive disadvantage, was an abuse of a dominant position."

Here too, the Court's final determination links the contested action with the relevant legal term. The next chapter in the Court's decision dealt with the allegation that unfair prices had been charged to certain purchasers. The Court found[49]:

"The imposition by an undertaking in a dominant position directly or indirectly of unfair purchase or selling prices is an abuse to which exception can be taken under Article 86 of the Treaty.

It is advisable therefore to ascertain whether the dominant undertaking has made use of the opportunities arising out of its dominant position in such a way as to reap trading benefits which it would not have reaped if there had been normal and sufficiently effective competition.

In this case charging a price which is excessive because it has no reasonable relation to the economic value of the product supplied would be such an abuse.

This excess could, *inter alia*, be determined objectively if it were possible for it to be calculated by making a comparison between the selling price of the product in question and its cost of production, which would disclose the amount of the profit margin; however the Commission has not done this since it has not analysed UBC's cost structure.

The Commission bases its view that prices are excessive on an analysis of the differences—in its view excessive—between the prices charged in the different Member States and on the policy of discriminatory prices which has been considered above.

The foundation of its argument has been the applicant's letter of 10 December 1974 which acknowledged that the margin allowed by the sale of bananas to Irish ripeners was much smaller than in some other Member States and it concluded from this that the amount by which the actual prices f.o.b. Bremerhaven and Rotterdam exceed the delivered Rotterdam prices for bananas to be sold to Irish

---

[49] *Op. cit.*, footnote 35, p. 305, paras. 248 to 257 and p. 306, paras. 258 to 260.

customers c.i.f. Dublin must represent a profit of the same order of magnitude.

Having found that the prices charged to ripeners of the other Member States were considerably higher, sometimes by as much as 100 per cent., than the prices charged to customers in Ireland, it concluded that UBC was making a very substantial profit."

However, this is not in itself a sufficient factual basis for the decision[50]:

"Nevertheless the Commission has not taken into account in its reasoning several of UBC's letters in which was enclosed a confidential document retracting what is said in its letter of 10 December 1974 and pointing out that the prices charged in Ireland had produced a loss.

The applicant also states that the prices charged on the relevant market did not allow it to make any profits during the last five years, excepting 1975.

These assertions by the applicant are not supported by any accounting documents which prove the consolidated accounts of the UBC group or even by the consolidated accounts for the relevant market.

However unreliable the particulars supplied by UBC may be (and in particular the document mentioned previously which works out the "losses" on the Irish market in 1974 without any supporting evidence), the fact remains that it is for the Commission to prove that the applicant charged unfair prices.

UBC's retraction, which the Commission has not effectively refuted, establishes beyond doubt that the basis for the calculation adopted by the latter to prove that UBC's prices are excessive is open to criticism and on this particular point there is doubt which must benefit the applicant, especially as for nearly 20 years banana prices, in real terms, have not risen on the relevant market."

The Court finally concludes[51]:

---

[50] Op. cit., footnote 35, p. 306, paras. 261 to 266.

[51] Op. cit., footnote 35, p. 307, paras. 261 to 266 on p. 306; for a decision which was likewise annulled for lack of sufficient factual evidence, see Case 6/72 Europemballage and Continental Can v. Commission [1973] E.C.R. 215 at 250, paras. 36 and 37. The decision against Hoffmann-La Roche for a breach of Article 86 of the EEC Treaty was also annulled partly because the evidence was insufficient; cf. Case 85/76 Hoffmann-La Roche v. Commission [1979] E.C.R. 461, at 528, para. 58.

"In these circumstances it appears that the Commission has not adduced adequate legal proof of the facts and evaluations which formed the foundation of its finding that UBC had infringed Article 86 of the Treaty by directly and indirectly imposing unfair selling prices for bananas. Article 1(c) of the decision must therefore be annulled."

(bb) Summary

The scope of judicial review of Commission decisions in such cases parallels the review process in cartel cases. When dealing with Article 86 of the EEC Treaty, the Court once again examines all the facts before deciding whether the article has been complied with or not.[52]

Expert witnesses are sometimes heard on the facts, and if elements are missing from the facts on which the decision is based, it will be annulled. Observance of the Commission's procedural requirements is also insisted upon, for the sake of protecting the impugned undertaking.

(c) Enforcement

If the conditions for an exemption are lacking and the practice is one which infringes Article 85(1) of the EEC Treaty, paragraph 2 of that article will apply, with the result that any legally binding elements in a cartel agreement are automatically void.[53] This does not apply to concerted practices, which are matters of fact and cannot be rendered ineffectual. However, the prohibition in paragraph 1 is automatic, so that the undertakings which follow such practices are also bound to desist. The same applies to undertakings which abuse their market position according to Article 86 of the EEC Treaty.

But in many instances, a prohibition or an automatic avoidance will not be enough. The Commission must enforce the line of conduct it has

---

[52] cf. Case 40/70 Sirena v. EDA [1971] E.C.R. 69, which shows that in preliminary rulings the Court prefers, for judicial reasons, simply to set guidelines for interpretation by national courts. In one such case, however, referred under Article 177 of the EEC Treaty, it made a very concrete ruling; this was Case 22/79 Greenwich Film Production v. SACEM, under Article 86 of the EEC Treaty, [1979] E.C.R. 3275 at 3289, para. 13.

[53] See H. Schröter, in H.v.d. Groeben, H. v. Boeckh, J. Thiesing, C.-D. Ehlermann, Kommentar zum EWG-Vertrag (3rd ed., Baden-Baden 1983), Artikel 85 Abs. 1, pp. 1001 et seq.; see also E.-J. Mestmäcker, Europäisches Wettbewerbsrecht, Munich, 1974, pp. 263 et seq.

prescribed, and for this purpose it may issue a restraining order and may also impose an actual or a suspended fine.[54] The fine will act as a deterrent against future infringements and help to ensure that the Commission's orders are carried out forthwith.[55]

The Commission frequently imposes a fine for past infringements (Article 15 of Regulation 17). It is free to decide the amount of the fine.[56]

Under Article 172 of the EEC Treaty and Article 17 of Regulation 17, on fines and penalty payments, the Court's jurisdiction for reviewing discretionary decisions is unlimited, and it may annul or amend a decision by the Commission to impose a fine. The rules applicable to fines differ from those applicable to penalty payments.

A penalty payment cannot be imposed once the breach for which it was ordered is at an end or the risk of a recurrence has been removed. A fine, however, may be imposed even after the act in question is over.[57] The imposition of a fine means that the conduct was wrongful, whereas a technical breach of the law will suffice for the ordering of a penalty payment. The degree of wrongfulness, however, plays a role in determining the amount of the penalty payment.[58]

Because they are different in nature, fines and penalty payments may be ordered in conjuction, without offending against the principle *ne bis in idem*.[59] A double "punishment," under both national and EEC cartel law is also admissible, although, on equitable grounds, an earlier fine will be taken into account in determining the amount of a later one.[60] According to Article 15, paragraph 2 of Regulation 17, the chief criteria to be followed by the Commission in fixing the amount of a penalty are the severity and duration of the offence.

The case-law is replete with appeals against fines and penalty payments. Case 27/76, *United Brands and others* v. *Commission*, is also an example of an appeal of this kind.[61]

As we have seen, the Commission had accused the United Brands company of abusing its dominant position on the banana market. It was

---

[54] *cf.* Article 16 of Regulation 17.
[55] *cf.* E.-J. Mestmäcker, *op. cit.*, footnote 53, p. 532.
[56] Article 15(2)(a) and Article 16(1)(a) of Regulation 17.
[57] *Ibid.*
[58] H. Schröter, *op. cit.*, footnote 2, Artikel 87, p. 1321 no. 13.
[59] *Ibid.* and E.-J. Mestmäcker, *op. cit.*, footnote 35, p. 533.
[60] In the case-law, see Case 7/72 *Boehringer* v. *Commission* [1972] E.C.R. 1281 (especially 1290, para. 3), for an example of a fine imposed in a third country. See also Case 14/68 *Walt Wilhelm and others* v. *Bundeskartellamt* [1969] E.C.R 1 at 15, para. 11.
[61] [1978] E.C.R. 207. See also above, 2(b)(aa); also Case 226/84 *British Leyland* v. *Commission* [1986] E.C.R. 3263.

ordered to pay a fine of 1 million units of account. The Commission's decision was based on four separate allegations. The Court upheld the first three of these, but found no substantial basis for the fourth, and annulled this part of the decision.[62] The Court's review was as follows[63]:

"The Commission, for the purpose of imposing a fine of one million units of account for the four infringements which it found UBC had committed, stating that the latter 'were at the very least negligent,' had regard to their gravity and duration and to the size of the undertaking."

For the gravity of the infringement, the Court simply refers to the reasons advanced by the Commission[64]:

"As far as their gravity is concerned the Commission considered them in their economic and legal setting by taking account of their combined effect and of their consequences which are manifestly inconsistent with the Treaty objectives of integrating markets and of the fact that the banana is a product which is widely consumed."

Commenting on the duration of the infringement, the Court merely repeated what the Commission had already said; but for the responsibility incurred, it looked to the arguments put by the applicant[65]:

"The applicant submits that it did not know that it was in a dominant position, still less that it had abused it, especially as, according to the case-law of the Court to date, only undertakings which were pure monopolies or controlled an overwhelming share of the market have been held to be in a dominant position.

UBC is an undertaking which, having engaged for a very long time in international and national trade, has special knowledge of anti-trust laws and has already experienced their severity.

UBC, by setting up a commercial system combining the prohibition of the sale of bananas while still green, discriminatory prices, deliveries less than the amounts ordered, all of which was to end in strict partitioning of national markets, adopted measures which it

[62] *Op. cit.*, footnote 61, p. 307, paras. 267 to 268.
[63] *Op. cit.*, footnote 61, p. 309, para. 289.
[64] *Op. cit.*, footnote 61, p. 309, para. 290.
[65] *Op. cit.*, footnote 61, p. 310, paras. 298 *et seq.*

knew or ought to have known contravened the prohibition set out in Article 86 of the Treaty.

The Commission therefore had good reason to find that UBC's infringements were at the very least negligent.

The amount of the fine imposed does not seem to be out of proportion to the gravity and duration of the infringements (and also to the size of the undertaking).

Account must however be taken of the partial annulment of the decision and the amount fixed by the Commission reduced accordingly.

A reduction of the fine to 850,000 (eight hundred and fifty thousand) units of account, to be paid in the national currency of the applicant undertaking whose registered office is situated in the Community, that is to say 3,077,000 Netherlands guilders (three million seventy seven thousand Netherlands guilders), appears to be justified."

The main yardstick in fixing the amount of the fine therefore seems to be the principle of proportionality. Here a remark by Advocate-General Mayras deserves quoting[66]:

"In this connexion the figure of one million units of account can be compared with the 'commission' paid by United Brands in 1975 to a Honduras general in an attempt to obtain a commercial advantage."

But in most cases, the principle of proportionality is applied to more "conventional" factors when fines are challenged and reviewed, as the chapter on this question will show.[67]

It will also bring out more clearly the fact that the severity of the sanction is limited chiefly by the prohibition against excess.

3. The prohibition of aid by Articles 92 et seq. of the EEC Treaty

(a) Introduction

Threats to competition in the Common Market do not stem only from

---

[66] *Op. cit.*, footnote 61, p. 350.
[67] See Chapter 5.

cartels and abuses of a dominant market position. Especially in times of economic recession, Member States step up aids to their own enterprises, or perhaps to entire sectors of their economies, and this too can distort competition. State aids have always been among the traditional instruments of economic policy, and as far as the Treaties are concerned, this remains a matter for the Member States. This is why State aids, which have to be adopted by the Member States themselves, need to be slotted into a Community framework, and this framework has been provided through the right of review conferred in Articles 92 *et seq.* of the EEC Treaty.[68]

According to Article 92(1) of the Treaty, "Save as otherwise provided in this Treaty, any aid granted by a Member State or through State resources in any form whatsoever which distorts or threatens to distort competition by favouring certain undertakings or the production of certain goods shall, in so far as it affects trade between Member States, be incompatible with the common market." This paragraph speaks cautiously of such aids being "incompatible" with the common market; it avoids using the word "prohibited," which appears in Articles 85 and 86 of the Treaty. But the meaning is the same.[69] Article 92(2) goes on to list a series of aids which are compatible with the common market. These are aids of a social character to individual consumers, aids to make good damage caused by natural disasters or exceptional occurrences, and aids to compensate for the economic disadvantages caused by the division of Germany.

Finally, paragraph 3 of Article 92 lists the aids considered to be compatible with the common market, subject to the fulfilment of certain conditions. The observance of Article 92 is monitored by the Commission according to a procedure laid down in Article 93. The Commission keeps under constant review all existing systems of state aid in the Member States (Article 93(1) of the Treaty). Under Article 93(3), Member States are bound, when planning to introduce new aids or alter existing ones, to inform the Commission in sufficient time to enable it to submit its comments.

If the Commission doubts whether existing or planned aids are compatible with Article 92(1) of the Treaty, it institutes the formal procedure in

---

[68] It is necessary to distinguish between the Community's monitoring of State aids and the grant of Community aids, which have a legal basis in the appropriate chapters of the Treaty or in Article 235. This applies particularly to the agricultural aids under Articles 38 *et seq.* of the Treaty, or regional aids through the Regional Fund.

[69] J. Thiesing, in H.v.d. Groeben, H. v. Boeckh, J. Thiesing, C.-D. Ehlermann, *Kommentar zum EWG-Vertrag* (3rd ed., Baden-Baden 1983), Artikel 93, p. 1588, no. 1.

Article 93(2). While this review is in progress, the Member States may not give legal effect to their intentions. If the Commission's doubts cannot be removed, a formal decision is issued to the Member States requiring them to alter or withdraw the aid. A decision that the aid is to be altered must be sufficiently specific to enable the Member State to model its conduct accordingly.[70] If the Member States fail to comply with the Commission's directions, the Commission can bring an action against them before the Court for infringement of the Treaty, through a procedure simplified in comparison with that under Article 169 of the Treaty.[71]

If the original doubts are not substantiated, the procedure will end without a formal decision. The Member States are simply informed of the outcome.[72] Under Article 93(2) and (3) of the Treaty the Council, acting on the application of a Member State, may, in exceptional circumstances, declare unanimously, in derogation from Article 92 of the Treaty or from the regulations provided for in Article 94, that a particular aid granted or planned by that State is compatible with the common market.[73] If the Council fails to pronounce on the matter within three months of the application, the Commission then has authority to resolve it.

Although state aids have become a key instrument of state economic policy, the number of Court decisions on the matter is surprisingly small.[73a] This may be due to the fact that the Community's monitoring of State aids has a direct influence on State planning and on State social and economic policies. It impinges not only on areas in which States have independent decision-making powers, but also on activities which, by their nature or prevalence, may be *instrumental* to the success or failure

---

[70] *cf.* Case 70/72 *Commission* v. *Germany* [1973] E.C.R. 813 *et seq.* (especially para. 23).

[71] On the relationship between this procedure and the procedure adopted for breaches of the Treaty, see D. Gilmour, "The enforcement of Community Law by the Commission in the context of State Aids," (1981) C.M.L.Rev. 63 *et seq.*

[72] In Case 120/73 *Lorenz* v. *Germany and Rheinland-Pfalz*, the Court treated it as a matter of "good administration" that Member States should be informed of the outcome of the investigation: [1973] E.C.R. 1471 at 1482, paras. 5 and 6. See also Advocate-General Reischl, *op. cit.*, p. 1493. See also Case 121/73 *Markmann* v. *Germany and Schleswig-Holstein* [1973] E.C.R. 1495; Case 122/73 *Nordsee, Deutsche Hochseefischerei* v. *Germany and Rheinland-Pfalz* [1973] E.C.R. 1511; Case 141/73 *Lohrey* v. *Germany and Hessen* [1973] E.C.R. 1527.

[73] *cf.* J. Thiesing, *op. cit.*, footnote 69, Article 93, pp. 1632 *et seq.*, nos. 30 *et seq.* p. 1633 no. 31, with references to relevant decisions.

[73a] But the number has lately been increasing. For recent developments, see M. Caspari, "The aid rules of the EEC Treaty and their application," in *Discretionary Powers of the Member States in the Field of Economic Policies and their Limits under the EEC Treaty* (ed. J. Schwarze), Baden-Baden 1988, pp. 37 *et seq.*

of governments. The monitoring of state aids therefore calls, above all, for political sensitivity on the part of those responsible, and this means that disputes are often settled out of court.[74]

We deal below with two questions of great importance to Member States. First, the exact meaning of the term "State aid" will be explored. The meaning of the term will be decisive in determining how far States are bound by Community law. Secondly, the extent of the Commission's discretionary powers when deciding on exceptions will be examined.

(b) The prohibition of State aids in Article 92(1) of the EEC Treaty

(aa) The concept of State aids

The Court's key pronouncement on the concept of a state aid is found in a decision in a Coal and Steel Community case from the year 1961, Case 30/59 *De Gezamenlijke Steenkolenmijnen in Limburg* v. *High Authority*.[75] The case turned on the interpretation of Article 4(c) of the ECSC Treaty, which states that "subsidies or aids granted by States" are incompatible with the common market in coal and steel.

The Dutch undertaking which had brought the case contested a decision by the High Authority (now the Commission) finding, in response to its application, that a German coalminers' bonus was compatible with the Treaty. The Court began its examination of the High Authority's decision by clarifying the concept of subsidies under the ECSC Treaty. The grounds of judgment are so important that they are given here in full[76]:

(a) The concept of subsidy under the ECSC Treaty

Article 4 of the Treaty reads as follows:

"The following are recognised as incompatible with the common market for coal and steel and shall accordingly be abolished and

---

[74] *cf.* M. Seidel, "Aktuelle Rechtsprobleme der Subventionsgewährung und der Beihilfe-naufsicht in der Europäischen Wirtschaftsgemeinschaft," in J. Schwarze (ed.) *Integrationsrecht*, Vol. I, Beiträge zu Recht und Politik der EG aus dem Europa-Kolleg Hamburg, Baden-Baden 1985, p. 67.

[75] [1961] E.C.R. 1.

[76] *Op. cit.*, footnote 75, p. 42 *et seq.*

> prohibited within the Community, as provided in this Treaty: ... (c) subsidies or aids granted by States, or special charges imposed by States, in any form whatsoever."

The Treaty contains no express definition of the concept of subsidy or aid referred to under Article 4(c). A subsidy is normally defined as a payment in cash or in kind made in support of an undertaking other than the payment by the purchaser or consumer for the goods or services which it produces. An aid is a very similar concept, which, however, places emphasis on its purpose and seems especially devised for a particular objective which cannot normally be achieved without outside help. The concept of aid is nevertheless wider than that of a subsidy because it embraces not only positive benefits, such as subsidies themselves, but also interventions which, in various forms, mitigate the charges which are normally included in the budget of an undertaking and which, without, therefore, being subsidies in the strict meaning of the word, are similar in character and have the same effect.

Since these definitions are not contained in the Treaty, they are acceptable only if they are substantially borne out by the provisions of the Treaty or by the objects which it pursues.

Among the declared aims of the Community, in Article 2 of the Treaty, is that it "shall progressively bring about conditions which will of themselves ensure the most rational distribution of production at the highest possible level of productivity, while safeguarding continuity of employment and taking care not to provoke fundamental and persistent disturbances in the economies of Member States."

A subsidy or aid, within the meaning of the definition given above, in itself constitutes an obstacle to the most rational distribution of production at the highest level of productivity inasmuch as, being a payment made by someone other than the purchaser or consumer, it makes it possible to fix or maintain selling prices which are not directly related to production costs and thereby to establish, maintain and develop economic activity which does not represent the most rational distribution of production at the highest possible level of productivity.

Judged on this basis, and in the sense in which they are normally defined, subsidies or aids granted by the States are incompatible with the common market because they constitute an obstacle to one of its essential aims.

In view of this, it must be recognised that subsidies and aids, in the sense in which they have traditionally been and are usually understood, are what Article 4(c) recognises as incompatible with the common market and accordingly declares abolished and prohibited.

This conclusion is confirmed by the third indent on the second paragraph of Article 5, which lays down the Community's principal task as being to "ensure the establishment, maintenance and observance of normal competitive conditions," since payment of a proportion of the costs of production by someone other than the purchaser or consumer manifestly obstructs the establishment of normal competitive conditions.

The above interpretation is confirmed by the fifth paragraph of Article 54 of the Treaty, which reads:

"If the High Authority finds that the financing of a programme or the operation of the installations therein planned would involve subsidies, aids, protection or discrimination contrary to this Treaty, the adverse opinion delivered by it on these grounds shall have the force of a decision within the meaning of Article 14 and the effect of prohibiting the undertaking concerned from drawing on resources other than its own funds to carry out the programme."

Hence in the Court's view, the concept of a subsidy is part of the wider concept of aid itself. Apparently, the Court has not defined these terms in any later decision.[77] The tendency here is the same as in the decisions of the Commission: to define the concept of aids in each particular instance. One general characteristic of the aids and subsidies covered by Article 92(1) of the EEC Treaty emerges from a comparison with the restricted concept of a subsidy in German criminal law, which also embraces Community benefits.

According to the definition in German criminal law,[78] subsidies are payments from public funds of the Federation of the Länder, or under the law of the European Communities, to firms or enterprises, granted at least to some extent

1. regardless of commercial considerations and
2. for the purpose of promoting economic development.

But within the meaning of Article 92(1) of the EEC Treaty, whether a State payment is defined as a subsidy does not depend on the form of the

---

[77] On the reasons, see above, M. Seidel (footnote 74).
[78] Paragraph 264(6) of the Penal Code.

subsidy, the recipient, the reasons for granting it or the aims pursued, but solely on its effects on trade between Member States.[79]

Recent Court judgments indicate that the Court makes no attempt to define the concept conclusively, or more precisely than in the decision quoted above. Rather, it proceeds on the basis that any state participation in an undertaking is to be regarded as an aid within the meaning of Article 92 of the EEC Treaty.[80] Nor does the Court pronounce conclusively on the binding effects of the prohibition in Article 92(1) of the Treaty. Admittedly, the lack of any abstract definition leaves the door open for future developments in State industrial policy; on the other hand, however, it reduces legal certainty, because it is impossible to predict whether a particular measure will be caught by Article 92 or not. There is a quite separate question here: whether the Commission has any discretionary powers when it classifies a particular form of State support as an aid. From the existing case-law, the obvious answer is no. The approval of aids under Article 92(3) of the Treaty is a different matter.

(bb) The approval of aids which are incompatible with Article 92(3) of the EEC Treaty

Under Article 92(3) of the EEC Treaty, certain forms of State aid are regarded as compatible with the common market: aids to promote the economic development of regions with an abnormally low standard of living or serious underemployment, and aids to promote major projects of Europe-wide significance or to remedy a serious disturbance in the economy of a Member State. This is also true of aids to promote certain economic sectors and certain areas, as long as they do not adversely affect trading conditions to an extent contrary to the Community interest. Finally, the Council may, on a proposal from the Commission and acting by a qualified majority vote, specify other categories of aid which may be regarded as compatible with the common market.

The very wording of Article 92(3) of the Treaty suggests that the Commission and the Council enjoy some freedom of decision when

---

[79] *cf.* Case 173/72 *Italy* v. *Commission* [1974] E.C.R 709 at 718, para. 18.
[80] See Case 323/82 *Intermills* [1984] E.C.R. 3809; Joined Cases 296 & 318/82 *Leuwardener Papierfabrieken* v. *Commission* [1985] E.C.R. 817 and Case 52/85 *Commission* v. *Belgium* [1986] E.C.R. 89. There is a link between Case 52/85 and Case 40/85 *Belgium* v. *Commission* [1986] E.C.R. 2321; this too deals with the question whether State participation in private enterprise is to be treated as "aid" within the meaning of Article 92 of the Treaty; para. 13 of this judgment, however, stipulates additional criteria for accepting that it is State aid.

approving aids. In Case 78/76 *Steinike & Weinlig* v. *Federal Republic of Germany*, the Court emphasised this point.[81] The question in this case was whether the German state fund to promote the marketing of agricultural, forestry and food products was a permissible form of aid. The complainant in the original proceedings, a producer and dealer in beverages, had to pay a levy to the fund for imported fruit juice concentrate.[82]

The first question put to the European Court by the German Court which handled the case was, how far may national courts rely on Article 92 of the Treaty in the context of their national legal systems, whether on the instigation of a party or of their own motion.[83]

The Court considered Articles 92 to 94 of the EEC Treaty together and concluded[84]:

> "These provisions show that the prohibition in Article 92(1) is neither absolute nor unconditional, since Article 92(3) and Article 93(2) give the Commission a wide discretion and the Council extensive power to admit aids in derogation from the general prohibition in Article 92(1)."

The Court also mentions the consequences for the parties[85]:

> "The parties concerned cannot therefore simply, on the basis of Article 92 alone, challenge the compatibility of an aid with Community law before national courts or ask them to decide as to any compatibility which may be the main issue in actions before them or may arise as a subsidiary issue. There is this right however where the provisions of Article 92 have been applied by the general provisions provided for in Article 94 or by specific decisions under Article 93(2)."

---

[81] [1979] E.C.R. 595.
[82] See the summary of the facts in the judgment, *op. cit.*, footnote 81, pp. 597 *et seq.*
[83] *Op. cit.*, footnote 81, p. 609, para. 5.
[84] *Op. cit.*, footnote 81, p. 609, para. 8. See also Case 730/79 *Philip Morris* v. *Commission* [1980] E.C.R. 2671 *et seq.*, at 2691, paras. 24 and 26. The Federal Government had asked the Court, in connection with aids to the steel industry, to annul a decision on the grant of aids in Belgium, France, Italy and Britain and to establish the principles and guidelines which are binding on the Commission when approving aids; *cf.* Case 214/83 *Germany and Wirtschaftsvereinigung Eisen- und Stahlindustrie* v. *Commission* [1985] E.C.R. 3053, para. 13.
[85] *Op. cit.*, footnote 81, p. 610, para. 10.

This does not alter the fact that the prohibition in Article 92(1) of the EEC Treaty is directly applicable to the Member States.

(c) Conclusion

It may certainly be said, in the light of the existing case law, that the prohibition on State aids is strictly binding in law. The Commission has, however, some discretionary power to make exceptions under Article 92(3) of the EEC Treaty.

IV. COMMUNITY LAW ON EXTERNAL TRADE, AND ESPECIALLY THE RULES AGAINST DUMPING

The introductory chapter surveyed briefly the various instruments comprising the Community law on external trade. The protective clauses in agricultural law will be considered in connection with the common market in agriculture. Here we are chiefly concerned with anti-dumping measures, which are specifically governed by EEC Regulation 2176/84,[1] and which the Court has considered on a number of occasions.[2]

The guiding principle here is the nature of the legal constraints on the executive, which have certain special features in the law against dumping. To prove dumping is basically extremely difficult. Both the markets in which the enterprise operates and the profits it has made must be investigated. Many companies are reluctant to reveal their own profits and

---

[1] cf. O.J. 1984, L202/1, et seq., amended by Regulation 1761/87 of June 22, 1987, O.J. 1987, L167/9 et seq. The Coal and Steel Community's anti-dumping law is stated in Decision 2177/84/EEC, O.J. 1984, L201/17 et seq. On the external trade law of the Community, see C.-D. Ehlermann, "Neuere Entwicklungen im Aussenhandelsrecht der Europäischen Gemeinschaft", in J. Schwarze (ed.), Integrationsrecht Vol. 1, Baden-Baden, 1985, 105 et seq., on anti-dumping law in particular, see p. 112; for the procedures for applying the Community's external trade rules, see p. 114 et seq.

[2] The cases so far resolved have been dominated by questions of admissibility; for instance, Case 113/77 NTN TOYO Bearing Company v. Council [1979] E.C.R. 1185 et seq. (1203 et seq., paras. 7 et seq.), in which the contested measure was annulled as a breach of the provisions of the basic regulation: p. 1209, paras. 21 to 23; see also Case 118/77 I.S.O. v. Council [1979] E.C.R. 1277 et seq., at 1291 et seq., paras. 8 et seq.; Case 119/77 Nippon Seiko v. Council and Commission [1979] E.C.R. 1303 et seq., at 1325 et seq., paras. 9 et seq.; Case 120/77 Koyo Seiko v. Council and Commission [1979] E.C.R. 1337 et seq., at 1350 et seq., paras. 7 et seq.: Case 121/77 Nachi Fujikoshi v. Council [1979] E.C.R. 1363 et seq., at 1377 et seq., paras. 4 et seq.; also Case 264/82 Timex Corporation v. Council and Commission [1985] E.C.R. 849 et seq.

losses even for the purpose of demonstrating an adverse effect, for fear
that the facts may come to the knowledge of their competitors.

But it is not merely the protection of trade secrets which makes anti-
dumping measures so difficult to enforce. Even where dumping can be
proved through third-country imports, the question remains whether it is
politically advisable to levy anti-dumping duties as a countermeasure.
Regulation 2176/84 reflects this concern in the proviso that the countermeasures must be in the Community interest. It is sometimes best to
tolerate a certain amount of dumping if countermeasures against dumped
imports would provoke a crisis in political and economic relations with
the country of origin of the cheap goods. However, private economic
interests argue for preventing dumping. Hence there are difficult
questions of fact and policy to resolve if countermeasures are adopted,
and the responsible Community institutions must have some latitude to
resolve them. It is not, however, clear how the judicial protection of the
enterprises concerned is to be secured.

Case 191/81 *FEDIOL* v. *Commission*[3] turned upon the admissibility of
a complaint by the EEC Oil Processors' Federation (FEDIOL) against an
announcement by the Commission of its intention not to institute anti-
dumping procedures in respect of the importation of soya-bean oil-cake
from Brazil.[4]

In the Commission's view, a complaint against the communication
based on Article 5(5) of EEC Council Regulation 3017/79 was not admissible, because its only effect was to give information.[5] The enterprises
concerned were certainly entitled to apply to the Court, but had no
automatic right to a hearing on the question of dumping. In this area the
Commission enjoyed a wide measure of discretion, which touched upon
the economic and political interests of the Community and of the non-
Member countries concerned.[6]

The Court confirmed that the Commission had broad discretion in
deciding whether measures should be adopted and how far they should
go[7]:

> "Whilst it is true that the Commission, when exercising the powers
> assigned to it in Regulation No. 3017/79, is under a duty to establish
> objectively the facts concerning the existence of subsidization prac-

---

[3] [1983] E.C.R. 2913 *et seq.*
[4] See the facts cited, *op. cit.*, footnote 3, p. 2929 *et seq.*
[5] *Op. cit.*, footnote 3, p. 2931, para. 11.
[6] *Op. cit.*, footnote 3, p. 2931.
[7] *Op. cit.*, footnote 3, pp. 2934 *et seq.*, para. 26.

tices and of injury caused thereby to Community undertakings, it is no less true that it has a very wide discretion to decide, in terms of the interests of the Community, any measures needed to deal with the situation which it has established."

In the Court's view, if the provisions of the Regulation are examined as a whole, they give due recognition to the justified concern of producers in the Community to have anti-dumping measures introduced, and they protect this interest by giving them a right to bring suit, together with certain procedural guarantees. The Court concludes[8]:

"It follows that complainants may not be refused the right to put before the Court any matters which would facilitate a review as to whether the Commission has observed the procedural guarantees granted to complainants by Regulation No. 3017/79 and whether or not it has committed manifest errors in its assessment of the facts, has omitted to take into consideration any essential matters of such a nature as to give rise to a belief in the existence of subsidization or has based the reasons for its decision on considerations amounting to misuse of powers. In that respect, the Court is required to exercise its normal powers of review over a discretion granted to a public authority, even though it has no jurisdiction to intervene in the exercise of the discretion reserved to the Community authorities by the aforementioned regulation."

Here we see a technique adopted by the Court in other fields as well, to secure judicial protection for individuals against an extensive discretionary authority. First, the necessary constitutional rights are upheld through the observance of procedural guarantees.[9] Secondly, the Court extends its review functions to the facts on which the discretionary decision was based. These two controlling devices have been found extremely effective in areas where the frequent complaint of misuse of powers cannot succeed for lack of evidence.[10] The same is true of the

---

[8] *Op. cit.*, footnote 3, at p. 2935, para. 30 and at p. 2936, para. 31.

[9] This is especially clear in competition law, and notably where a review is made of decisions under Articles 85 and 86 of the EEC Treaty. But strict procedural rules apply here too, and the judicial review of the substantive aspects of the decision is equally stringent; see above, Part 2, section 2 B.III.

[10] H.-W. Daig, in H.v.d. Groeben, H. v. Boeckh, J. Thiesing, C.-D. Ehlermann, *Kommentar zum EWG-Vertrag* (3rd ed., Baden-Baden 1983), Artikel 356, p. 173, footnote 92.

presence of "manifest error" and the disregard of important aspects when the appraisal is carried out. This manner of proceeding is reminiscent of the review practice of the French Conseil d'Etat, with its "contrôle minimum"; this is confined to the same elements of a discretionary decision as those singled out by the European Court. The Court's practice, however, is discernibly influenced by German administrative law which, especially in recent times, emphasises the importance of effective procedural guarantees, as we shall show in Chapter 7.

Because the Court's approach is so cautious, complaints brought by undertakings are rarely upheld. For instance, in Joined Cases 239 and 275/82 *Allied Corporation* v. *Commission*[11] the complainant did not succeed in its claim that on the basis of incomplete facts the Commission had wrongly judged the damage to European industry from dumping, according to Regulation 3017/79. The complainant was seeking annulment of a Commission Regulation which introduced a provisional anti-dumping duty on imports of certain chemical fertilisers originating in the United States, as a result of which the plaintiff's exports to the common market became more expensive.[12] The grounds of judgment show that even in anti-dumping law a "substantive" review is carried out of a discretionary decision, *i.e.* one based on the facts, not merely the procedural aspects. However, they also illustrate the caution exercised by the Court when examining economic judgments made by the Commission. This is clear from the following extract, which reproduces the Court's conclusions on the facts of the case and the Commission's assessment of them[13]:

"The arguments put forward by the applicants are not of such a nature as to constitute proof that the Commission committed a number of manifest errors in its assessment of the question whether injury was caused to the European fertilizer industry as a result of the practice of dumping, established by reference to the criteria laid down by Article 2 of Regulation No. 3017/79. Consideration of the facts put forward by the applicants therefore warrants the conclusion that the Commission could properly take the view that, after the applicants had withdrawn their undertakings, the interests of the Community called for the adoption of provisional measures forthwith, in order to prevent injury to Community producers."

[11] [1984] E.C.R. 1005 *et seq.*
[12] *Op. cit.*, footnote 11, 1026, para. 1.
[13] *Op cit.*, footnote 11, 1033 para. 24.

The criterion of "manifest error" by the authorities is a demanding one, and the result is that an anti-dumping measure will be annulled only in extreme cases. In this area, therefore, the Commission has considerable freedom of decision in matters of fact. The only strict constraints upon it which are open to judicial review are found to lie in the procedures for adopting countermeasures.

Indeed, the first time such a measure was annulled was for an infringement of the "priority of statute". Case 113/77 *Toyo Bearing Company* v. *Council*[14] dealt with an application to annul a provisional anti-dumping duty on ball bearings from Japan, under Article 15 of Regulation 459/68. The provisional duty did not in fact have to be paid; but the importer had to put up certain guarantees if it was not. Under Regulation 459/68, the Council decides whether any anti-dumping duty is definitive. Under those conditions the Regulation enables the Council to fix a definitive duty as a deterrent and to determine what guarantees are payable instead of the provisional anti-dumping duty.[15]

In the case in question the Commission, after fixing a provisional duty, had negotiated an arrangement with the Japanese firms concerned whereby they undertook to raise their prices to reflect the dumping margin. About four weeks later the Council, in Regulation 1778/77, fixed a definitive anti-dumping duty and prescribed in Article 3 that the guarantees were to be paid.[16]

The complainants argued that according to Regulation 459/68 it was not admissible that undertakings by the producers to raise prices should be accepted at the same time as a definitive anti-dumping duty was introduced. Since it was possible to collect the guarantee payments based on the provisional duty only if a definitive anti-dumping duty was introduced, there was no legal basis for Article 3.[17]

The Court defined Article 3 of Regulation 1778/77 as a collective decision, which could be individually contested under Article 173, paragraph 2 of the EEC Treaty.[18] Before examining the facts of the case, the Court cited Articles 14 and 17 of Regulation 459/68 and finally concluded[19]:

---

[14] [1979] E.C.R. 1185 *et seq.*—the so-called ball bearings cases. See also footnote 1.
[15] See the summary of the facts in the judgment, *op. cit.*, footnote 14, pp. 1190 *et seq.*
[16] *Op. cit.*, footnote 15.
[17] *Op. cit.*, footnote 14, pp. 1205 *et seq.*, para. 13.
[18] *Op. cit.*, footnote 14, p. 1205, para. 12.
[19] *Op. cit.*, footnote 14, pp. 1207 *et seq.*, paras. 17 *et seq.*

"In the light of these provisions it is unlawful for one and the same anti-dumping procedure to be terminated on the one hand by the Commission's accepting an undertaking from the exporter or exporters to revise their prices at the same time as, on the other, by the imposition on the part of the Council, at the proposal of the Commission, of a definitive anti-dumping duty.

On the contrary, under the above-mentioned Article 14, an undertaking by an exporter to revise his prices leads to termination of the proceeding so that it is impossible to apply Article 17 of Regulation 459/68. By specifying that termination of the proceeding occurs only if 'the Commission, after hearing the opinions expressed within the Committee, considers this acceptable,' Article 14 in no way implies that the Commission and, where appropriate, the Council may follow the procedure provided for until the stage reached in Article 17 and accept the undertaking only at the same time as introducing a definitive anti-dumping duty."

Two paragraphs further on is a passage which refers expressly to the priority of superior law or, in the language of a national constitution, the priority of statute[20]:

"The argument that Regulation No. 1778/77 constitutes a measure *sui generis* based directly on Articles of the Treaty and not subject to the provisions of Regulation No. 459/68 disregards the fact that the whole proceeding in question was carried out within the context of the provisions laid down by that regulation. The Council, having adopted a general regulation with a view to implementing one of the objectives laid down in Article 113 of the Treaty, cannot derogate from the rules thus laid down in applying those rules to specific cases without interfering with the legislative system of the Community and destroying the equality before the law of those to whom that law applies.

The submission is therefore well founded and it follows that the application directed against Article 3 is sound in law.

If the result of the undertakings signed by the four major Japanese producers was that, under Article 14 of the basic regulation, the proceeding should have stood terminated, it follows that there was no need to apply Article 17, which empowers the Council to order

---

[20] *Op. cit.*, footnote 14, p. 1209, paras. 21 *et seq.*

the collection of the amounts secured by way of provisional duty. The wording of Article 17 shows moreover that such a decision can be adopted only at the same time as the imposition of a definitive anti-dumping duty."

This case shows that judicial protection is guaranteed by placing a strict requirement on the executive to observe certain procedures. However, it also shows the close connection between procedural and substantive rules. These may combine in an individual case with the result that the choice of a particular procedure will exclude certain alternative solutions to the case and effectively limit the use of discretion.

V. THE COMMON AGRICULTURAL POLICY

1. Introduction

The common market for agricultural products is the most complex part of the Community legal order. Agricultural law not only embraces a multiplicity of agricultural products and operations, but itself forms an almost impenetrable maze of Community rules and national rules, adopted and applied by European institutions and by national authorities in the Member States.

At the end of the 1960s, the common agricultural policy was perceived as the ideal method for abolishing the separate agricultural markets in the Member States, by setting up a "European common market in agricultural products." Because the policy was so successful, it was seen as a prototype for the integration to be striven for in other fields.

Attitudes are much more sober nowadays. It is certainly true that the Community's agricultural policy is integrated to a degree unprecedented elsewhere, at least as far as legal integration is concerned. No other area of Community law has so many rules, and the abolition of national legal systems or quasi-systems is nowhere so far advanced as in the agricultural policy of the Community.

But this in itself is not enough to defuse the criticism engendered by the results of the common agricultural policy. In fact, the shortcomings of this policy may be largely responsible for the increasingly sceptical views now being voiced about the prospects for European unification. What concerns us here, however, is not the economic side of the Community's agricultural policy, but its complex legal regime. The brief description in the Introduction of the sources and executing organs of Community law shows that agricultural law is a particular fertile source of pronouncements about the emergence of a corpus of European administrative law. The chief legal source is Articles 38 *et seq.* of the EEC Treaty which is the basis on which the Council must formulate the Common Agricultural Policy. Now that virtually all agricultural products are handled by Community marketing organisations, this task may be considered complete, at least in a quantitative sense. Second in importance to the powers of the Council to regulate the market in agriculture are the comprehensive executive powers of the Commission, as well as of the Council, the Commission being chiefly responsible for devising appropriate rules.

Here we must look at the limits placed on the Commission when it is exercising its executive discretion, and on the Council when it acts in an executive capacity but is governed by the basic regulations.

The Member States are responsible, in practice, for applying Community agricultural law. Here it is necessary to distinguish betwecn actions by the Member States which are based directly on Community law and those based on national implementing legislation.

As for the rules enacted by the Member States, it is also necessary to distinguish between formal rules and legal instruments which set out specific requirements. The constraints on the national executing agencies will differ according to the type of regulation concerned. This applies to the chief agricultural law systems, the ones we are concerned with here. A full compendium of Community agricultural policies is hardly possible within the confines of this work; however, even a brief survey of the main problems involved in implementing this area of Community law will be of value.

2. The Council's prerogative of market regulation

The core of the Community's agricultural policy is the power to regulate the market. This prerogative embraces the wide powers conferred by Articles 38 *et seq.* of the EEC Treaty, and extends to almost all agricultural products.[1]

---

[1] *cf.* R. Boest, *Die Agrarmärkte im Recht der EWG*, Baden-Baden 1984, pp. 29 *et seq.*, especially p. 42 on the situation prevailing when the EEC was formed, with references.

(a) The task of policy-making

The origins of the Community's agricultural policy are already fully documented.[2] It was devised as a means of creating a common market in agricultural produce, by abolishing national marketing systems and setting up a Community market organisation.[3] The other aims of the CAP are set out in Article 39(1) of the EEC Treaty:

(a) to increase agricultural productivity,
(b) to ensure a fair standard of living for persons engaged in agriculture,
(c) to stabilise markets,
(d) to assure the availability of supplies,
(e) to ensure that supplies reach consumers at reasonable prices

Article 40 of the Treaty states which methods are to be used to achieve these goals. A common organisation of agricultural markets is to be established and is to take one of the three following forms, depending on the product concerned:

— common rules on competition,
— compulsory co-ordination of the various national market organisations,
— a European market organisation.

To achieve the goals stated in Article 39(1), the Council has relied mainly on Community market organisations.[4] Because of its broad but undefined powers, the Council has had to set up a political framework, which enables it to describe the resulting agricultural regulations as "European legislative acts."[5] In the sense used here, the authority concerned has therefore a "legislative discretion," and its limits will be considered below.[6] We shall also see how this differs from the legal constraints on the Community's implementing authorities—the Commission and the Member States.

---

[2] cf. H. P. Ipsen, *Europäisches Gemeinschaftsrecht*, Tübingen 1972, pp. 831 *et seq.*; R. Boest, *op. cit.*, footnote 1, pp. 42 *et seq.*, with references.
[3] On the original situation and the reasons for including the agricultural sector in the Common Market, see R. Boest, *op. cit.*, footnote 1, pp. 42 *et seq.*
[4] There is a survey, with sources, in R. Boest, *op. cit.*, footnote 1, see the Annex, pp. 329 *et seq.*
[5] See R. Boest, *op. cit.*, footnote 1, p. 116.
[6] For the concept of legislative discretion, see the introduction to Part 3 of this chapter.

(*b*) *The legal limits of constitutive authority*

Even in Community law, no discretionary power is without its legal limits.[7] What is true elsewhere is also generally true of the discretionary authority of the Council in agricultural matters, which is limited by both formal and substantive rules.[8] The formal requirements for Council decisions are that the enacting institution must possess proper authority and that both the procedure and the Council's own conduct must follow the prescribed form.

The substantive rules include restrictions as to subject-matter; these are the essence of the limits on discretion, since they directly affect the outcome of the decision.

(*aa*) *Formal constraints—proper authority and procedure*

According to Article 43(2), subparagraph 3, of the EEC Treaty, the Council is responsible for binding decisions in the agricultural sector. The Commission is empowered to act only where the Council has conferred the necessary powers on it (Article 155, fourth indent, and Article 145, second indent of the EEC Treaty). In agricultural law, as in other fields, these powers of implementation are framed in a manner which inspired legal doubt until the decision in Case 25/70.[9]

Although the power to enact implementing legislation was delegated to the Commission, this was in the form of the so-called "Management Committee" procedure.[10] This means that before a measure is adopted, the draft must be submitted to the above Committee. When it has given

---

[7] *cf.* Advocate-General Roemer in his opinion in Case 34/62 *Germany* v. *Commission* [1963] E.C.R. 131 at 149; see also Advocate-General Rozès in Case 210/81 *Demo-Studio-Schmidt* [1983] E.C.R. 3045 *et seq.* (3070).

[8] "Formal rules" means requirements as to proper authority, procedure and form. The term "substantive law" is a general term, meaning the provisions which influence the content of a legal instrument.

[9] *cf.* the statement by the respondent in the initial proceedings, in [1970] E.C.R. 1161 at 1164 on the Management Committee procedure.

[10] See H. Schmitt v. Sydow, in Groeben/Boeckh/Thiesing/Ehlermann, *Kommentar zum EWG-Vertrag* (3rd ed., Baden-Baden 1983), Article 155, p. 188, no. 149; see also *ibid. Die Verwaltungs- und Regelungsausschussverfahren der Europäischen Wirtschaftsgemeinschaft*, Heule/Brussels/Namur 1973; C. Bertram, *Das Verwaltungsausschussverfahren*, Diss. jur Bonn 1967; P. Strohmaier, *Die Befugnisse von Rat und Kommission der Europäischen Gemeinschaften zur Einsetzung von Ausschüssen*, Diss. jur Saarbrücken 1972. Other sources are quoted in H. Schmitt von Sydow, *op. cit.*, Article 162, p. 22, footnote 19.

its consent, the Commission can pass the instrument into law. If the Management Committee, consisting of Commission officials and representatives of the Member States,[11] withholds its consent, the Commission may nonetheless adopt the legal instrument, or may instead postpone doing so for one month. During that time the Council may confirm the measure or adopt a different ruling.[12]

The Court has declared this procedure lawful, although the independent right of execution which it gives the Commission is limited. In its preliminary ruling in Case 25/70 *Einfuhr- und Vorratsstelle für Getreide und Futtermittel* v. *Köster*, it decided as follows[13]:

> "Secondly, the respondent in the main action criticizes the Management Committee procedure in that it constitutes an interference in the Commission's right of decision, to such an extent as to put in issue the independence of that institution. Further, the interposition between the Council and the Commission of a body which is not provided for by the Treaty is alleged to have the effect of distorting the relationships between the institutions and the exercise of the right of decision.
>
> Article 155 provides that the Commission shall exercise the powers conferred on it by the Council for the implementation of the rules laid down by the latter. This provision, the use of which is optional, enables the Council to determine any detailed rules to which the Commission is subject in exercising the power conferred on it. The so-called Management Committee procedure forms part of the detailed rules to which the Council may legitimately subject a delegation of power to the Commission. It follows from an analysis of the machinery set up by Articles 25 and 26 of Regulation No. 19 that the task of the Management Committee is to give opinions on draft measures proposed by the Commission, which may adopt immediately applicable measures whatever the opinion of the Management Committee. Where the Committee issues a contrary opinion, the only obligation on the Commission is to communicate to the Council the measures taken. The function of the Management Committee is to ensure permanent consultation in order to guide the Commission in the exercise of the powers conferred on it by the

[11] See also H. Schmitt von Sydow, *Verwaltungs- und Regelsungsausschussverfahren*, footnote 10, p. 35.
[12] See H. Schmitt von Sydow, *ibid.*
[13] [1970] E.C.R. 1161 at 1171, paras. 8 to 10.

Council and to enable the latter to substitute its own action for that of the Commission. The Management Committee does not therefore have the power to take a decision in place of the Commission or the Council. Consequently, without distorting the Community structure and the institutional balance, the Management Committee machinery enables the Council to delegate to the Commission an implementing power of appreciable scope, subject to its power to take the decision itself if necessary.

The legality of the so-called Management Committee procedure, as established by Article 25 and 26 of Regulation No. 19, cannot therefore be disputed in the context of the institutional structure of the Community."

But it is not only the relationship between the Council and the Commission which may prove difficult; in some cases, legal conflicts also arise from the relations between both institutions and the European Parliament. Before making any important decision, the Council must consult the Assembly or Parliament. Because the obligatory process of consulting the Parliament naturally delays the decision-making process, the question arises whether a hearing can be dispensed with in some cases. This is particularly relevant with rules for the implementation of existing market regulations,[14] for example, implementing measures enacted by the Commission using its powers under Article 155, paragraph 4 of the EEC Treaty, which can be issued without consulting the Parliament.[15]

In Case 25/70 *Einfuhr- und Vorratsstelle für Getreide* v. *Köster* the Court laid down the following principles[16]:

"Both the legislative scheme of the Treaty, reflected in particular by the last indent of Article 155, and the consistent practice of the Community institutions establish a distinction, according to the legal concepts recognized in all the Member States, between the measures directly based on the Treaty itself and derived law intended to ensure

---

[14] See (2) below.

[15] This is the rule; but in some market arrangements the Council has reserved to itself the enactment of basic implementing provisions. See also (2)(a) below for an example from the common market organisation for sugar.

[16] [1970] E.C.R. 1161 at 1170, para. 6; *cf.* also Case 230/78 *Eridania* v. *Minister für Landwirtschaft und Forsten* [1979] E.C.R. 2749 *et seq.*, at 2765, paras. 7 and 8. The case concerned a provision in the sugar market organisation which enabled the Council to enact implementing measures and provisions departing from the basic regulations, without providing for a consultation of Parliament.

their implementation. It cannot therefore be a requirement that all the details of the regulations concerning the common agricultural policy be drawn up by the Council according to the procedure in Article 43. It is sufficient for the purposes of that provision that the basic elements of the matter to be dealt with have been adopted in accordance with the procedure laid down by that provision. On the other hand, the provisions implementing the basic regulations may be adopted according to a procedure different from that in Article 43, either by the Council itself or by virtue of an authorisation complying with Article 155."

Where scholars have commented on the basic regulations, they have pointed to the "resolution of a problem by regulation," in a manner not specifically prescribed by the Assembly,[17] or they look for "essential defined characteristics" of the subject, so as to distinguish the measures (basic regulations) to be adopted in a procedure according to Article 43(2), subparagraph 3.[18]

In the case already referred to, Case 25/70, the Court describes as follows the difference between a basic regulation and an implementing measure[19]:

"The measures dealt with by implementing Regulation No. 102/64 of the Commission do not go beyond the limits of the implementation of the principles of basic Regulation No. 19. The Commission was thus validly authorized by Regulation No. 19 to adopt the implementing measures in question, the validity of which cannot therefore be disputed within the context of the requirements of Article 43(2) of the Treaty."

But it is also possible to adopt through a simplified procedure rules which, like Article 24(3) of Regulation 3330/74 providing for a sugar market organisation, depart from the provisions of the basic regulation.[20] In Case 230/78 Eridania v. Minister für Landwirtschaft und Forsten, the Court confirmed that this procedure was admissible, but also made clear where its boundaries lie[21]:

---

[17] See O. Gottsman, in Groeben, Boeckh, Thiesing, Ehlermann, Kommentar zum EWG-Vertrag (3rd ed., Baden-Baden 1983), Article 43, p. 439 no. 9.
[18] R. Boest, op. cit., footnote 1, p. 224.
[19] [1970] E.C.R. 1161, at 1172, para. 7.
[20] O.J. 1974, L359/1.
[21] cf. [1979] E.C.R. 2749 et seq., at 2765, para. 8.

"Consequently it was lawful for the Council to enact an implementing regulation in accordance with the procedure referred to in Article 24(3) of Regulation No. 3330/74 which constitutes the basic regulation for the market in sugar. That outcome is not affected by the sole fact that Article 24(3) empowers the Council not only to enact implementing measures but also to determine any "derogations" from the provisions of the basic regulation, which word must be understood in this context as necessarily referring to derogations which relate to the general system for the allocation of quotas provided for by the basic regulation and which do not jeopardize the essential elements embodied in that regulation."

The Court went on to consider whether this measure by the Council went beyond the implementation of the principles of the basic regulation, and found nothing objectionable in the outcome.[22]

However, if a Parliamentary hearing is mandatory and does not take place, this will have far-reaching legal consequences. In Case 138/79 *Roquette Frères* v. *Council*, the Court regarded as a breach of essential procedural requirements the fact that the Council, when introducing a levy on isoglucose, had not obtained the views of Parliament.[23] The Council had in fact asked the Assembly for its opinion, but because the first direct elections to Parliament took place in the interim the process was, in the Council's view, unduly delayed. Because the Council regarded prompt action as necessary, it enacted the regulation without waiting for the opinion of Parliament.[24]

It is not necessary to deal here with the question, interesting though it undoubtedly is, as to how far Parliament has a duty to co-operate in the sense that it must respond with special promptness to a request from the Council to give its views on legal instruments which the Council declares to be urgent.[25] What is decisive of our purposes is that the duty to hold a hearing is among the institutional arrangements existing between the

---

[22] *Op. cit.*, footnote 21, p. 2766, para. 13.
[23] [1980] E.C.R. 3333 *et seq.* (3361, para. 37).
[24] For the factual details, see the survey of the case, *op. cit.*, footnote 23, pp. 3336 *et seq.*
[25] The Council had requested Parliament to give its opinion at a particular meeting, so that the regulation could enter into force on a date fixed by the Council. See the Council's explanations in the summary of the evidence brought by both sides, *op. cit.*, footnote 18, p. 3346C. The Court found evidence against the Council in the fact that it had omitted to call a special meeting, in spite of the alleged urgency of the matter, *cf. op. cit.*, footnote 23, p. 3361, para. 36.

Council and Parliament, *i.e.* part of the essential structure of the Community. As the Court says[26]:

> "The consultation provided for in the third subparagraph of Article 43(2), as in other similar provisions of the Treaty, is the means which allows the Parliament to play an actual part in the legislative process of the Community. Such power represents an essential factor in the institutional balance intended by the Treaty. Although limited, it reflects at Community level the fundamental democratic principle that the peoples should take part in the exercise of power through the intermediary of a representative assembly. Due consultation of the Parliament in the cases provided for by the Treaty therefore constitutes an essential formality disregard of which means that the measure concerned is void."

It is also important to note the conditions for a proper consultation[27]:

> ". . . observance of that requirement implies that the Parliament has expressed its opinion. It is impossible to take the view that the requirement is satisfied by the Council's simply asking for the opinion. The Council is therefore wrong to include in the references in the preamble to Regulation No. 1293/79 a statement to the effect that the Parliament has been consulted."

Applying these principles, the Court came to the following conclusion[28]:

> "It follows that in the absence of the opinion of the Parliament required by Article 43 of the Treaty, Regulation No. 1293/79 amending Council Regulation No. 1111/77 must be declared void without prejudice to the Council's power following the present judgment to take all appropriate measures pursuant to the first paragraph of Article 176 of the Treaty."

Because of this legal consequence of a failure to consult the Assembly, the Council must also examine carefully whether an implementing measure requires the Parliament's opinion or not. Even if these opinions have no legally binding influence on a legal instrument issued by the Council,

---

[26] [1980] E.C.R. 3333 at 3360, para. 33.
[27] *Ibid.*, para. 34.
[28] *Op. cit.*, footnote 26, p. 3361, para. 37.

they are crucial in determining whether the measure has a sound factual basis and whether the political and legal implications have been considered by the enacting institution.[29]

As we have seen, the Council enjoys a wide discretion in formulating the common agricultural policy; parliamentary control therefore plays an important part in the exercise of this discretion.

The last point to consider in connection with formal constraints is the general obligation, under Article 190 of the EEC Treaty, to give a statement of reasons; this statement should throw light on the lawmakers' intentions in enacting the rules of the market organisation. For the problems associated with this, we refer to the chapter which deals in detail with this arrangement, itself an unusual one for normative acts.[30]

(bb) The limits of the subject-matter

(1) General requirements—clarity of rules

If a common market is to be created in agricultural products by means of European market regulations, the same rules must be applied in all Member States. For this purpose it is essential to use clear terms. Otherwise there would be a risk that differences of interpretation, caused by ambiguous language, might jeopardise the uniform implementation of the rules. As the Court explained in connection with the concept of "importation"[31]:

"In fact the development of the rules in relation to agricultural policy is characterized by an effort to define and elucidate the major concepts, such as that of importation, which are intended to facilitate

---

[29] For the other ways in which Parliament can exert an influence, see E. Grabitz, T. Läufer, *Das Europäische Parlament*, Bonn, 1980, pp. 119 *et seq.* Of special interest are the agreements among institutions to consult on non-treaty questions. For the newly-introduced co-operation procedure under the Single European Act, see Article 149 of the EEC Treaty.

[30] See, for example, the Court's decision in Case 158/80 *Rewe* v. *Hauptzollamt Kiel* [1981] E.C.R. 1805 *et seq.*, in which a regulation was annulled for lack of a sufficient statement of reasons: p. 1834, para. 26.

[31] *cf.* Case 3/74 *Einfuhr- und Vorratsstelle für Getreide* v. *Pfützenreuter* [1974] E.C.R. 589 at 597, para. 10. See also Case 169/80 *Zollverwaltung* v. *Gondrans Frères* [1981] E.C.R. 1931 at 1942, para. 17.

the replacement of differing customs practices within the Member States by a uniform Community practice."

It follows that[32]:

"With this in mind, the provisions at issue must be interpreted and applied uniformly in all the Member States, so as to avoid certain patterns of trade being treated more favourably than others as a result of differing practices."

The insistence on clear rules helps to ensure that Community law rests on a constitutional basis; it also serves the purpose of integration, which calls for the use of precise terms which are capable of implementation. In individual cases, of course, it must be made clear where the implementing function lies. The powers of the Commission may be left broad and undefined, to ensure that complex matters can be flexibly but appropriately handled. At this level of market organisation, there is no risk of discrepancies in the implementation of the rules.

This is why Advocate-General Roemer was right to say, in Case 5/73 *Balkan-Import-Export GmbH* v. *Hauptzollamt Berlin-Packhof*, of the Commission's undefined authority to issue implementing rules for equalising the currencies[33]:

"Furthermore, one must not forget that the Community, particularly in the field of interest in these proceedings, has its own structure which justifies special yardsticks as regards the formulation of empowering norms."

In the initial proceedings the plaintiff, relying on Article 80(1), second sentence of the German Basic Law, with its requirement that legislative powers granted to the administration must be clearly defined, had complained against the vagueness of the Community rule which gave the Commission authority to fix the currency equalisation amounts.

When the plaintiff found that his objection was not upheld by the Court, he turned his attention to the national level, where the rules were implemented. Originally there were six, now there are 12 different national administrations, legislatures and legal systems which play a part in implementing Community law. What this means is that 12 different

---

[32] *Ibid.*
[33] [1973] E.C.R. 1091 *et seq.*, at 1130.

executives have to apply agricultural law within the framework of their constitutions, laws and administrative traditions. It also means that there are 12 constitutional systems which form the backdrop to the judicial review of administrative decisions. The different yardsticks and modes of judicial control which have emerged against this background add further disparities at the level of national implementation.

It is here, at the last stage before the legal effects reach the individual citizen of the Market, that the grave risk emerges of frustrating uniform implementation by having terminology which is too vague. The Community legislature, when framing the agricultural rules, must take account of this. Depending on the agency responsible for making the rule, the degree of precision in the terminology and the subject-matter will vary.

It is therefore possible to argue that the closer the implementing agency stands to the addressee, the more clearly the applicable rule must be formulated.

The requirement for clarity in the rules is, however, only a formal dimension of the law of market organisations. Its substantive law constraints will be considered in more detail below.

(2) The compulsory objectives of Article 39(1) of the EEC Treaty

The separate aims of the common agricultural policy have already been listed. They form a broad framework within which the Council has to legislate. As in the area of the Coal and Steel Community, it was originally uncertain what the relationship was between one aim and another. Because the goals pursued were to some extent contradictory—for example, increasing producers' earnings while ensuring reasonable prices for the consumer—it was clearly impossible to pursue all of them simultaneously.[34]

Where conflicts arose between them, there were several options for resolving them[35]: either there is a hierarchy of separate aims, from which it is possible to justify giving priority to one aim rather than another; or all the aims are equally important, with the consequence that in the event of

---

[34] cf. R. Boest, *Die Agrarmärkte im Recht der EWG*, Baden-Baden 1984, p. 107, with references, esp. to Case 5/67 *Fa. W. Beus* v. *Hauptzollamt München-Landsberger Strasse* [1968] E.C.R. 127 *et seq.* (147).
[35] See also R. Boest, *op. cit.*, footnote 34, p. 107.

a conflict, a balance must be struck between them. Finally, it is conceivable that the separate aims are equally important but that the Community legislature may, in some situations, have the power to give priority to one of them.

R. Boest correctly points out that the third solution allows a distinction to be drawn between the general direction of agricultural policy on the one hand, and specific individual measures for organising the market on the other.[36] This is significant because there is a difference here: either the entire agricultural policy favours the achievement of one individual objective and the neglect of the rest, or a part-measure for market regulation is framed in a one-sided way. Boest, in his careful examination of the case law on the common market in agriculture, has made a distinction between two different periods: first, the "older" case law which, although without expressly saying so, seems to assume an order of priority among the different aims, and secondly the "newer" case law, based on the equal importance of the aims in Article 39. Boest's theory that the Court—especially in Case 106/63 *Töpfer and others* v. *Commission of the EEC*—has accepted an order of priority among the aims, cannot, however, be verified, since the judgments are too vague on this score.[37] The "newer" case law is, however, somewhat more fruitful. In Case 5/73 *Balkan-Import-Export GmbH* v. *Hauptzollamt Berlin-Packhof*, dealing with the lawfulness of the currency equalisation system, the Court took a position expressly on the relationship of the separate aims with each other in Article 39[38]:

"Article 39 of the Treaty sets out various objectives of the common agricultural policy.

In pursuing these objectives, the Community institutions must secure the permanent harmonisation made necessary by any conflicts between these aims taken individually and, where necessary, allow any of them temporary priority in order to satisfy the demands of the economic factors or conditions in view of which their decisions are made.

---

[36] R. Boest, *op. cit.*, footnote 34, p. 108.

[37] R. Boest, *op. cit.*, footnote 34, p. 108; see the cases cited: Case 34/62 *Bundesrepublik Deutschland* v. *Commission* [1963] E.C.R. 287 at 319; Case 106/63 *Alfred Töpfer* v. *Commission* [1965] E.C.R. 405.

[38] [1973] E.C.R. 1091 *et seq.*, at 1112, para. 24; see also Case 29/77 *Roquette Frères* v. *France* [1977] E.C.R. 1835 *et seq.*, at 1843, paras. 29 to 31; Cases 279–280 & 285–286/84 *Walter Rau and others* v. *Commission* [1987] E.C.R. 1069, para. 21.

If, owing to developments in the monetary situation, preference happens to be given to the interests of the agricultural community, the Council does not by so doing contravene Article 39.

Moreover, it has not been established that the measures questioned gave rise to prices which would appear obviously unreasonable on selling to consumers."

Similarly, the Court stated in Joined Cases 63 to 69/72 *Werhahn* v. *Council*[39]:

"By temporarily giving priority to some of the objectives of Article 39, as compared with the maintenance of established positions, the institutions did not infringe paragraph 1(c) of this provision."

The institutions therefore have some discretionary scope. In the case mentioned above, Case 5/73, Advocate-General Roemer commented in his opinion[40]:

"... Since Article 39 does not refer to the lowest prices but only to *reasonable* consumer prices, *i.e.*, since it does not lay down solely the need for having regard to the interests of the consumer, therefore, having regard also to the different objectives enumerated in Article 39 of which pursuant thereto account shall be taken and which leave a wide room for discretion, one cannot really conclude that the system is invalid."

In Case 106/81 *Kind* v. *EEC*, the complaint bore on a question of public liability, the lawfulness or otherwise of the market organisation in sheep-

---

[39] [1973] E.C.R. 1229 at 1248, para. 13; see also Case 29/77 [1973] E.C.R. 1835 at 1843, paras. 29 to 31; also Advocate-General Reischl in Case 127/77 *Koningklijke Scholten-Honig* v. *Hoofdproduktschap voor Akkerbouwprodukten* [1978] E.C.R. 2033: It is in my view advisable at the beginning of the examination of this complaint to recall that the decided cases of the Court have repeatedly stressed that all the objectives of Article 39 cannot be pursued at the same time and with equal effect and it is therefore permissible to give one or other of them priority (*cf.* for example judgment of March 13, 1968 in Case 5/67 *W. Beus GmbH & Co.* v. *Hauptzollamt München* [1968] E.C.R. 83; judgment of 24 October 1973 in Case 5/73 *Balkan Import-Export GmbH* v. *Hauptzollamt Berlin Packhof* [1973] E.C.R. 1091; judgment of 2 July 1974 in Case 153/73 *Holtz & Willemsen GmbH* v. *Council and Commission of the European Communities* [1974] E.C.R. 675). The Community institutions have a wide discretion in this matter. They exercise it according to the economic circumstances. On the other hand the case-law of the Court nowhere indicates that giving preference to one objective requires evidence that in the interest of that objective it is *essential* to disregard other objectives.

[40] [1973] E.C.R. 1091 at 1127.

meat. As to whether the Council was free to set up a common market for agricultural produce—in this case for sheepmeat—the Court found that[41]:

> "In these circumstances and in view of the discretion enjoyed by the Council in implementing a common organization of the markets which is still developing and taking into account the responsibilities which are entrusted to it by Articles 39 and 40 of the Treaty in order to determine which methods appear to it most suited for the purpose of ensuring the gradual achievement of a uniform market, the fact that intervention methods vary from region to region in the Community, and the consequences of such variation do not amount to discrimination."

The case law also shows, however, that an imbalance among the different aims which is only temporary may be admitted. This is clear from the reasoning of the judgment in Case 29/77 *Roquette Frères* v. *France*, which is expressed in almost identical terms to the above case, Case 5/73 *Balkan Import-Export GmbH* v. *Hauptzollamt Berlin-Packhof*[42]:

> "As regards the validity of the basic regulation, Article 39 of the Treaty sets out various objectives of the common agricultural policy.
> In pursuing those objectives, the Community institutions must secure the permanent harmonization made necessary by any conflicts between these objectives taken individually and, where necessary, allow any one of them temporary priority in order to satisfy the demands of the economic factors or conditions in view of which their decisions are made.

---

[41] [1982] E.C.R. 2885 at 2921, para. 24. The Court's case law is consistent: Case 43/72 *Merkur-Aussenhandels-GmbH* v. *Commission* [1973] E.C.R. 1055 at 1074, para. 24 shows that the Commission has discretion when adopting implementing rules, Case 11/74 *L'Union des minotiers de la Champagne* v. *French Government* [1974] E.C.R. 877 at 885, paras. 13 to 16; Joined Cases 56–60/74 *Kampffmeyer* v. *Commission and Council* [1976] E.C.R. 711 at 744.

[42] [1977] E.C.R. 1835 at 1843, paras. 29 to 31; *cf.* also Cases 279–280 & 285 & 286/84 *Walter Rau and others* v. *Commission* [1987] E.C.R. 1069, para. 21.

If, owing to developments in the monetary situation, preference happens to be given to the requirements of stabilizing the market, Regulation No. 974/71 does not in doing so contravene Article 39."[43]

The aims are not to be understood as a random collection of projected desirable outcomes of a common agricultural policy. Rather, "it must be borne in mind in the first place ... that the several objectives of the common agricultural policy set out in Article 39 are inseparable." This was the comment of Advocate-General J. P. Warner in Case 29/77 *Roquette Frères* v. *France*, and he continues[44]:

"The compatibility with them of any particular measure adopted in pursuance of that policy cannot be judged by looking at one of them in isolation. As the Court indicated in the first *Balkan* case (in paragraph 24 of the judgment), in pursuing those objectives, the Community institutions must for ever seek to conciliate their inherent contradictions. Secondly, even if one were, impermissibly, to look at objective (b) alone, it would not be permissible to judge in isolation, by reference to that objective, a single measure adopted in implementation of the common agricultural policy, such as the fixing of m.c.a.'s. That which would fall to be judged would be the whole complex of measures adopted in implementation of that policy, including those whose effect is to bolster the incomes of farmers, not least import levies and export refunds."

Taken in their logical combination and bearing in mind the rules for achieving them, the objectives therefore provide a broad and flexible framework for the development of the common agricultural policy. The Court justifies this freedom of action through the political responsibility laid upon the Council in Articles 39 and 43 of the EEC Treaty[45]:

---

[43] *cf.* R. Boest *op. cit.*, footnote 34, p. 111.

[44] See [1977] E.C.R. 1835 at 1854.

[45] Case 138/78 *Hans-Markus Stölting* v. *Hauptzollamt Hamburg Jonas* [1979] E.C.R. 713 at 722, para. 7; see also Joined Cases 197–200/80 *Ludwigshafener Walzmühle* v. *Council and Commission* [1981] E.C.R. 3211 at 3251, paras. 37 and 39.

"It should be remembered that, in determining their policy in this area, the competent Community institutions enjoy wide discretionary powers regarding not only establishment of the factual basis of their action but also definition of the objectives to be pursued, within the framework of the provisions of the Treaty, and the choice of the appropriate means of action. This choice having been made by the Council in the

"If a measure is patently unsuited to the objective which the competent institution seeks to pursue, this may affect its legality, but on the other hand the Council must be recognized as having a discretionary power in this area which corresponds to the political responsibilities which Articles 40 and 43 impose upon it."

The development of the agricultural market through common market organisations is not, therefore, a mechanical process of implementing the law, but a process of political decision-making in a broad legal framework.

As for the requirement that the common agricultural policy must take account of the general treaty aims found in the Preamble and in Articles 2 and 3 of the EEC Treaty, Article 38(2) of the Treaty stipulates that the rules for the establishment of the common market also apply in principle to agriculture. Exceptions to these rules are possible only where the particular features of the agricultural sector call for them.[46]

A glance at Community practice shows that the aims of the agricultural policy have often been given preference over the general Treaty aims. Agriculture, in fact, is an independent sphere of integrationist policy which has often caused conflict, not least because of the principle of Community preference.[47]

However, the legal limits of Council lawmaking are not found only in the aims of Article 39(1) of the EEC Treaty and the general aims of the Treaty itself. Effective controls have been established through other guiding instruments, to be considered later. What they have in common is that they make it possible to check on the use actually made of discretionary powers by subjecting to legal scrutiny the outcome of the decision, but not the procedure involved or any other formal aspects.

(3) Review the underlying facts

It is a prior condition for every legislative decision that the object of the

---

legitimate exercise of its powers of discretion, its repercussions must be accepted by the manufacturers of secondary products, as they must by the various groups of producers concerned."

[46] See O. Gottsmann, *op. cit.*, footnote 17, Article 38, p. 358 no. 2.

[47] See R. Boest, *op. cit.*, footnote 34, p. 113; there is instructive comment on Community preference in Case 5/67 *W. Beus* v. *Hauptzollamt München-Landsberger Strasse* [1968] E.C.R. 83 at 98:

"These objectives, which are intended to safeguard the interests of both farmers and consumers, may not all be simultaneously and fully attained. In balancing these interests, the Council must take into account, where necessary, in favour of the farmers

regulation must be known. The more far-reaching the legislation, the more accurate must be the information available to the legislative body concerning the factual background of the law. The Council, before enacting, amending or supplementing a market regulation, must accordingly carefully examine the economic terrain on which it stands, and must seek to judge the consequences of its legislative intervention for the operations of the market.

In economic legislation, however, there are practical limits to the amount of factual explanation which can be provided. The complexity of the subject-matter and the impossibility of analysing the consequences except in terms of an economic forecast, mean that a complete presentation and assessment of the facts is out of the question. Moreover, subjective assessments are often called for in any statement of facts of this nature.[48]

The Court allows for this by permitting a measure of discretion with regard to the market situation and the economic data. In Case 166/78 *Italy* v. *Council*[49] a Council regulation altering the common market organisation for cereals had been challenged. The amending regulation had introduced a premium for producers of potato starch which was not granted to the competing product, maize starch. The purpose of the regulation was to create a balance between the two products.[50]

The applicant, Italy, argued that economic factors had been wrongly assessed when the disputed premium was introduced.[51] The Court dismissed this argument[52]:

> "In order to weigh the arguments put forward by the parties it should in the first instance be placed on record that it is an implication of the objective of the Community regulation at issue, which is to ensure that the organization of the market makes proper allowance for the balance between the competing products, that the Council has to assess a complex economic situation. Although some of the constituent elements of this situation may be ascertained in accordance

the principle known as 'Community preference,' which is one of the principles of the Treaty and which in agricultural matters is laid down in Article 44(2)."
[48] See Advocate-General Roemer in Case 6/54 *Kingdom of the Netherlands* v. *High Authority* [1954–1955] E.C.R. 103 at 118 *et seq.*
[49] [1979] E.C.R. 2575 *et seq.*
[50] *cf.* [1979] E.C.R. 2596, para. 4.
[51] *Op. cit.*, footnote 50, 2598, para. 11.
[52] *Op. cit.*, footnote 50, 2599, para. 14; see also Case 236/84 *Malt GmbH* v. *Hauptzollamt Düsseldorf* [1986] E.C.R. 1923, para. 15.

with objective criteria, such, for example, as the prices of raw materials which are determined by the actual organization of the market in cereals, there are others which are far more difficult to apprehend with any accuracy. This applies especially to production costs in an industry such as the one in this case, the distinguishing feature of which is the existence of a large number of undertakings of different size and economic structure and situated in different Member States. In such circumstances the discretion which the Council has when it assesses a complex economic situation is not only exercisable in relation to the nature and scope of the provisions which are to be adopted but also, to a certain extent, to the findings as to the basic facts, especially in this sense that the Council is free to base its assessment, if necessary, on findings of a general nature."

The results of this wide discretion can be seen particularly in the way in which the ban against discrimination and the principle of equal treatment are applied; both operate by bringing together at least two different situations. This problem was touched upon by the complaint lodged by Roquette Frères in Case 138/79, which we have already mentioned.[53]

The question at issue was whether the introduction of a levy on isoglucose, a sweetener substitute for sugar, discriminated against its producers as compared with sugar producers. In the preceding cases 103 and 145/77 the Court had held that it did, on the basis of Article 40(3) of the EEC Treaty, which it regarded as a special statement of the equality principle applying to the agricultural law.[54]

In applying the general principle of equality, it is necessary to begin by defining the subjects to be compared. It is the act of definition which will ultimately determine how far the principle can be used to monitor normative acts. In this process, the requirement of effective judicial protection must be reconciled with the practical possibilities for elucidating the facts and the need for flexibility in the legislation. This should be remembered when considering the Court's comments[55]:

"When the implementation by the Council of the agricultural policy of the Community involves the need to evaluate a complex economic

---

[53] [1980] E.C.R. 3333.

[54] *Koningklijke Scholten-Honig v. Hoofdproduktschap voor Akkerbouwprodukten* [1978] E.C.R. 1991 at 2003, paras. 25 to 27; Cases 279–280 & 285 & 286/84 *Walter Rau and others v. Commission* [1987] E.C.R. 1069, para. 28.

[55] *Op. cit.*, footnote 53, p. 3358, para. 25.

situation, the discretion which it has does not apply exclusively to the nature and scope of the measures to be taken but also to some extent to the finding of the basic facts inasmuch as, in particular, it is open to the Council to rely if necessary on general findings. In reviewing the exercise of such a power the Court must confine itself to examining whether it contains a manifest error or constitutes a misuse of power or whether the authority in question did not clearly exceed the bounds of its discretion."

In the outcome, the regulation on the levy withstood the subsequent review by the Court.

Another field proper to market organisation policy is the external protection of agricultural markets. The protective clauses in the agricultural market rules offer a range of measures for use, primarily, by the Commission.[56] The Council may, however, on the application of a Member State, adopt through a qualified majority a decision at odds with the Commission's. To venture a classification, protective measures fall into a grey area between (political) lawmaking and administrative action. Their proximity to legislation is seen in the discretionary powers of judgment which the Court accords where the facts are concerned. Case 112/80 *Dürbeck* v. *Hauptzollamt Frankfurt am Main-Flughafen* was based on a protective measure (a regulation) by the Commission to restrict the importation of dessert apples from Chile.[57]

This measure was, in turn, based on protective provisions under the common market organisation for fruit and vegetables. In these provisions, the Commission's discretion was limited by an entire network of data.[58] Nevertheless, the Court found that the authority was able to exercise discretion "when assessing the situation on the market in question as regards the available quantities of the products involved."[59]

The conclusion must be, in the Court's words in Joined Cases 197 and others/80 *Ludwigshafener Walzmühle* v. *Council and Commission*[60]:

"... in determining their policy in this area, the competent Community institutions enjoy wide discretionary powers regarding not only

---

[56] See C.-D. Ehlermann, *Neuere Entwicklungen im Aussenhandelsrecht der Europäischen Gemeinschaft*, Baden-Baden 1984, p. 11.
[57] [1981] E.C.R. 1095.
[58] See the summary of facts in the judgment, *op. cit.*, footnote 57, p. 1197 *et seq.*
[59] See the judgment, *op. cit.*, footnote 57, p. 1114 no. 24; see also Case 29/77 *Roquette Frères* v. *France* [1977] E.C.R. 1835 at 1842.
[60] [1981] E.C.R. 3211 at 3251, para. 37.

establishment of the factual basis of their action, but also definition of the objectives to be pursued, within the framework of the provisions of the Treaty, and the choice of the appropriate means of action."

(4) *Misuse of powers*

If an institution uses its authority for purposes other than those laid down in the Treaty, it commits a misuse of powers. There is no precedent, in the case law on market organisation, for a decision being annulled on this ground. There are, of course, cases in which a ruling has been attacked as invalid for misuse of powers.[61] The aims of the common agricultural policy are so manifold and flexible, however, that it will always be possible to assign a particular market organisation ruling to one or other of the statutory objectives.

The difficulty of proof also tends to prevent claims being successful, as also happens in Coal and Steel Community affairs. All in all, the Court seems anxious to avoid annulling decisions for misuse of powers, at least where policy measures are concerned, because to admit such a flaw would go beyond merely finding that legal boundaries had been transgressed. Because the Council is a political organ of the Communities, an annulment on this ground would be more than a mere legal setback.

(5) *How general principles of law constrain policy-making*

The various objectives found in Article 39(1) of the EEC Treaty form a broad framework, and misuse of powers is an impractical and cumbersome tool for fixing its boundaries. This, however, is not the only legal constraint on the discretionary powers of the Council. There are other controls, in the form of general principles of law, which have successfully been applied by the Court.[62]

In so doing it has relied partly on the express prohibition of discrimination found in Article 40, paragraph 2(3) of the EEC Treaty, but

---

[61] *cf.* Case 125/77 *Koningklijke Scholten-Honig N.V., De verenigde Zeetmeelbedrijven "De Bijenkorf" BV* v. *Hoofdproduktschap voor Akkerbouwprodukten* [1978] E.C.R. 1991 at 2005, paras. 42 and 43 to 45; Case 35/80 *Denkavit* v. *Produktschap voor Zuivel* [1981] E.C.R. 45 at 61 and 62, paras. 19 and 25; Case 52/81 *Faust* v. *Commission* [1982] E.C.R. 3745 at 3760, paras. 19 and 20.
[62] For a general comment, see above, Chapter 1, Introduction.

also on unwritten principles, such as proportionality and legal certainty. In addition to these, the Court has felt itself bound to uphold fundamental rights, which are general principles of law common to the Member States.

As potential causes of action, they are among the legal rules which must be observed when the Treaty is applied and implemented.[63] They will be treated separately for the purposes of this study. We shall therefore confine ourselves to the points which are relevant to this chapter, dealing with the legal constraints on the institutions, their scope for discretion and the limits of that discretion.

It is not possible to deal fully with the principles, either chronologically or by subject, nor is this attempted. Instead, we shall focus on those instances in which general principles of law have staked out the boundaries of the Council's political decision-making. We begin here with the express ban on discrimination in Article 40 of the EEC Treaty and the general principle of equality.

(a) Article 40(3), second paragraph, of the EEC Treaty, and the general principle of equality as a limit to freedom of decision

According to the provisions of Article 40 of the EEC Treaty, the market organisations to be set up by the Community institutions in pursuance of the aims of Article 39(1) of the Treaty "shall exclude any discrimination between producers or consumers within the Community." In the abstract, this means, as for instance in German constitutional law,[64] that markedly similar matters may not be treated unequally, unless there is an objective justification[65] or objective criteria for different treat-

---

[63] See H.-W. Daig, *Nichtigkeits- und Untätigkeitsklagen im Recht der Europäischen Gemeinschaften*, Baden-Baden 1985, pp. 150 *et seq.*

[64] See BVerfGE 1, p. 14 *et seq.* (52); 3, 58(135).

[65] See Case 2/77 *Hoffmann's Stärkefabriken AG* v. *Hauptzollamt Bielefeld* [1977] E.C.R. 1375 at 1396, para. 21; Joined Cases 117/76 & 16/77 *Ruckdeschel* v. *Hauptzollamt Hamburg St. Annen* [1977] E.C.R. 1753 at 1770, continuation of para. 7 on p. 1769; Case 125/77 *Koningklijke Scholten-Honig NV and others* v. *Hoofdproduktschap voot Akkerbouwprodukten* [1978] E.C.R. 1991 at 2075, continued in paras. 25 to 27 on p. 2074; Joined Cases 103 & 145/77 *Royal Scholten-Honig (Holdings) Limited* v. *Intervention Board for Agricultural Produce* [1978] E.C.R. 2037 at 2075, continued in paras. 25 to 27 at 2074; Case 54/81 *Firma Wilhelm Fromme* v. *Bundesanstalt für landwirtschaftliche Marktordnung* [1982] E.C.R. 1449 at 1464, continued in para. 7 at p. 1463 and para. 10; Case 106/81 *Julius Kind KG* v. *EEC* (claim for compensation) [1982] E.C.R. 2885 at 2921, para. 22, where reference is made both to the need for objective justification and to objective grounds for justifying unequal treatment; Case 215/85 *BALM* v. *Raiffeisen Hauptgenossenschaft* [1987] E.C.R. 1279, para. 23.

ment.[66] This also precludes similar treatment of dissimilar questions without proper cause.[67] In other words, the general principle of equality and the ban on discrimination enshrine a general prohibition against arbitrary action.

As for the matters to which these rules apply, the Court said in Case 5/73 *Balkan-Import-Export GmbH* v. *Hauptzollamt Berlin-Packhof*[68]:

> "Article 40 refers only to discrimination between producers or between consumers, while the balance to be held between the conflicting interests of these two groups is dealt with in Article 39.
>
> The Council did not, therefore, contravene Article 40 by adopting the measures in dispute."

In the ban on discrimination in agricultural law, the Court sees an expression of the general principle of equality,[69] a fundamental principle found in every constitutional system and therefore valid for every Member State.[70]

In spite of the equality principle, however, there is broad scope for legislative action.[71] As already explained, decision-making begins with the factual situation, where the Community institutions enjoy wide powers of appraisal. To some extent, they are also able to decide which sets of facts are to be compared in the event of a judicial review.[72]

This discretion includes the right to determine whether similar or dissimilar characteristics are to be given pride of place when factual circumstances are compared.[73] The institutions are also free to select the

---

[66] See Case 153/73 *Holtz & Willemsen GmbH* v. *Council and Commission of the EEC* (claim for compensation) [1974] E.C.R. 675 at 696, para. 13; Case 11/74 *Minotiers de la Champagne* v. *French Government* [1974] E.C.R. 877 at 886, paras. 22 to 23; Case 8/78 *Milac* v. *Hauptzollamt Freiburg* [1978] E.C.R. 1721 at 1732, para. 18. The Court has not, however, explained these criteria in detail: R. Boest, *Die Agrarmärkte im Recht der EWG*, Baden-Baden 1984, p. 131.

[67] See Case 13/63 *Republic of Italy* v. *Commission of the EEC* [1963] E.C.R. 357 at 384; R. Boest, *op. cit.*, footnote 66, p. 114, with references to sources.

[68] [1973] E.C.R. 1092 at 1113, para. 26.

[69] See, for instance, Joined Cases 117/76 & 16/77 *Ruckdeschel* v. *Hauptzollamt Hamburg-St. Annen* [1977] E.C.R. 1753 at 1770, continued in para. 7 at p. 1769; Cases 279–280 & 285–286/84 *Walter Rau and others* v. *Commission* [1987] E.C.R. 1069, para. 28.

[70] See the country reports in Chapter 4 below; on German constitutional law, see BVerfGE 1, 208 *et seq.*(233): "Grundbestandteil."

[71] R. Boest, *op. cit.*, footnote 67, p. 114; also see above, 1(a) (bb) (2).

[72] See also R. Boest, *op. cit.*, footnote 67, p. 149, who considers that this detracts from the meaning of the ban on discrimination.

[73] Case 106/81 *Kind* v. *EEC* [1982] E.C.R. 2885 at 2921, paras. 23 *et seq.*; there is, however, an unusual point in Case 55/75 *Balkan-Import-Export* v. *Hauptzollamt Berlin-Packhof*

criteria for unequal treatment.[74] But since these must be "objective" criteria, they are open to judicial examination.

Finally, it may be permissible in law to treat dissimilar cases similarly, or similar ones dissimilarly, in order to simplify administrative procedures and facilitate the application of a ruling.[75] This authority which the Community institutions possess to determine when flat-rate payments are appropriate and to levy them is a legal power which forms a natural corollary to its freedom of appraisal where the facts are concerned.[76]

The market developments which have to be regulated are highly complex, and there can be no question of taking account of every special feature of the market. Hence it is not necessary for the lawmaker to provide for every special case, either when investigating the facts or when determining the legal consequences, even though this may lead to some

---

[1976] E.C.R. 19 at 31, para. 14, where the Court explains: "In the Treaty there exists no general principle obliging the Community, in its external relations, to accord to third countries equal treatment in all respects and in any event traders do not have the right to rely on the existence of such a general principle." See also p. 32, para. 15.

[74] See Case 43/72 *Merkur* v. *Commission* [1973] E.C.R. 1055 at 1074, paras. 22 to 24; Case 11/74 *Minotiers de la Champagne* v. *French Government* [1974] E.C.R. 877 at 885.

[75] From the case law on the power to fix global sums, see, for
(a) skimmed-off profits:
Case 31/70 *Deutsche Getreide- und Futtermittel Handelsgesellschaft mbH* v. *Hauptzollamt Hamburg-Altona* [1970] E.C.R. 1055 at 1062, para. 6; Case 76/70 *Ludwig Wünsche & Co.* v. *Hauptzollamt Ludwigshafen/Rhein* [1971] E.C.R. 393 at 399, para. 5; Case 11/73 *Getreide-Import GmbH* v. *Einfuhr- und Vorratsstelle für Getreide und Futtermittel* [1973] E.C.R. 919 at 926, para. 6; Case 87/78 *Welding und Co.* v. *Hauptzollamt Hamburg-Waltershof* [1978] E.C.R. 2457 at 2466, para. 6.
(b) export refunds
Case 25/74 *Günter Heuck* v. *Einfuhr- und Vorratsstelle für Getreide und Futtermittel* [1974] E.C.R. 1017 at 1025 (continuation of para. 7, at p. 1024).
(c) currency equalisation amounts
Case 5/73 *Balkan-Import-Export GmbH* v. *Hauptzollamt Berlin-Packhof* [1973] E.C.R. 1091 at 1112, continuation of para. 22 at p. 1111; Case 29/77 *SA Roquette Frères* v. *French Customs Administration* [1977] E.C.R. 1835 at 1843, paras. 21 to 23, which, however, is concerned not so much with whether global amounts are permissible as with an authority to fix global amounts in a power delegated by the Council to the Commission. To justify the practice in general terms, however, the Court says that there are "compelling reasons relating to the practicability of the system"; Case 79/77 *Firma Kühlhaus Zentrum AG* v. *Hauptzollamt Hamburg-Harburg* [1978] E.C.R. 611 at 620, continuation of para. 8 at p. 619.

[76] See R. Boest, *op. cit.*, footnote 66, p. 134; for the system of currency equalisation amounts, see also P. Gilsdorf, *Der Währungsausgleich aus rechtlicher Sicht*, Cologne/Berlin/Bonn/Munich 1978, pp. 13 *et seq.* This deals with problems for trade caused by applying the currency equalisation on a flat-rate basis, but describes the scheme as inherent in the system and quite legal in itself. It also refers to equalisation methods applied in individual cases, *op. cit.*, p. 15.

loss of competitive advantage. Otherwise it would be impossible, in practical terms, to exercise administrative control over the economy. The Court has expressed this in forthright language in Case 5/73 *Balkan-Import-Export GmbH* v. *Hauptzollamt Berlin-Packhof*[77]:

> "In exercising their powers, the institutions must ensure that the amounts which commercial operators are charged are no greater than is required to achieve the aim which the authorities are to accomplish; however, it does not necessarily follow that the obligation must be measured in relation to the individual situation of any one particular group of operators.
>
> Given the multiplicity and complexity of economic circumstances, such an evaluation would not only be impossible to achieve, but would also create perpetual uncertainty on the law.
>
> An overall assessment of the advantages and disadvantages of the measures contemplated was justified, in this case, by the exceptionally pressing need for practicability in economic measures which are designed to exert an immediate corrective influence; and this need had to be taken into account in balancing the opposing interests."

It is obvious, however, that the authority to decide and set flat-rate payments will not go so far as to overburden the individual through excessive emphasis on the needs of the administration. This might happen if, for instance, the effect of the decision were to distort competition or to outweigh the costs actually incurred.[78]

All in all, these principles tend to suggest that there is only a limited measure of judicial protection against the economic "lawgiver," because the latter's freedom of appraisal begins on the factual level. The prohibition against discrimination and the general principle of equality seem rather weak restraints against discretionary power. There have nevertheless been some important cases in which the Community legislature has been baulked by these principles.

---

[77] [1973] E.C.R. 1091 at 1112, continuation of para. 22, at p. 1111.
[78] *cf.* Case 87/78 *Welding and Co.* v. *Hauptzollamt Hamburg-Waltershof* [1978] E.C.R. 2457 at 2466, para. 6:
"In fact the use of any flat-rate method presupposes by its very nature a degree of approximation.
It is sufficient that the existence of such a degree of approximation does not give rise to discrimination capable of disturbing the market of the products in question."
See also R. Boest, *op. cit.*, footnote 66, p. 135.

Case 114/76 *Bela-Mühle* v. *Grows Farm* dealt with an obligation imposed on cattle-feed producers to buy skimmed milk powder.[79]

The original case was a civil law dispute in which the plaintiff was a feed producer, "Bela-Mühle," and the defendant the owner of a business dealing in laying hens. "Bela-Mühle," in addition to the agreed purchase price, claimed a sum equivalent to the levy due according to the "compulsory purchase regulation."[80] The purpose of this regulation was to reduce excess stocks of skimmed milk powder. The regulation was attacked on the ground that it was contrary to the aims of Article 39(1) of the EEC Treaty, the prohibition against discrimination in Article 40(3), second paragraph, of the Treaty and the principle of proportionality.[81]

In the grounds of judgment, there is a curious interplay between the ban on discrimination and the proportionality principle[82]:

"Under Article 39, the objectives of the common agricultural policy are to be the rational development of agricultural production, the assurance of a fair standard of living for the whole of the agricultural community, the stabilization of markets and the availability of supplies to consumers at reasonable prices. Although Article 39 thus enables the common agricultural policy to be defined in terms of a wide choice of measures involving guidance or intervention, the fact nevertheless remains that the second paragraph of Article 40(3) provides that the common organization of the agricultural markets shall be limited to pursuit of the objectives set out in Article 39. Furthermore, the same subparagraph lays down that the common organization of the markets 'shall exclude any discrimination between producers or consumers within the Community.' Thus the statement of the objectives contained in Article 39, taken together with the rules in the second subparagraph of Article 40(3), supplies both positive and negative criteria by which the legality of the measures adopted in this matter may be appraised.

The arrangements made by Regulation (EEC) No. 563/76 constituted a temporary measure intended to counteract the consequences

---

[79] [1977] E.C.R. 1211; see also the parallel decision in Joined Cases 119 & 120/76 *Olmühle und Becker* v. *Hauptzollamt Hamburg und Hauptzollamt Bremen- Nord* [1977] E.C.R. 1269, and in Case 116/76 *Granaria BV* v. *Hoofdproduktschap voor Akkerbouwprodukten* [1977] E.C.R. 1247.

[80] See para. 1, *op. cit.*, footnote 79, p. 1219.

[81] *Op. cit.*, footnote 79, p. 1220, para. 5.

[82] *Op. cit.*, footnote 79, pp. 1220 *et seq.*, paras. 6, 7 and 8; Advocate-General Capotorti had voted to annul the regulation solely on the basis of the proportionality principle, p. 1235.

of a chronic imbalance in the common organization of the market in milk and milk products. A feature of those arrangements was the imposition not only on producers of milk and milk products but also, and more especially, on producers in other agricultural sectors of a financial burden which took the form, first, of the compulsory purchase of certain quantities of an animal feed product, and, secondly, of the fixing of a purchase price for that product at a level three times higher than that of the substances which it replaced. The obligation to purchase at such a disproportionate price constituted a discriminatory distribution of the burden of costs between the various agricultural sectors. Nor, moreover, was such an obligation necessary in order to attain the objective in view, namely, the disposal of stocks of skimmed-milk powder. It could not therefore be justified for the purposes of attaining the objectives of the common agricultural policy.

In consequence, the answer must be that Council Regulation 563/76 of March 15, 1976 is null and void."

The annulment in this case sparked off a series of compensation claims, all of which were unsuccessful.

There is a further example of the limits on the Council's discretion when formulating the common agricultural policy in Joined Cases 103 and 145/77 *Royal Scholten-Honig (Holdings) and others* v. *Intervention Board for Agricultural Produce*.[83]

The plaintiffs in the original case were producers of isoglucose, a glucose syrup which is similar in many respects to cane or beet sugar. A levy was introduced for isoglucose, explained as follows in the seventh recital of the regulation concerned (EEC No. 1111/77)[84]:

"Whereas, being a substitute product in direct competition with liquid sugar, which, like all beet or cane sugar, is subject to stringent production constraints, isoglucose therefore enjoys an economic advantage, and since the Community has a sugar surplus, it is necessary to export corresponding quantities of sugar to third countries; whereas there should, therefore, be provision for a suitable production levy on isoglucose to contribute to export costs".

[83] [1978] E.C.R. 2037.
[84] *cf.* O.J. 1977, L134/4.

Here it should be noted that the common market organisation in sugar includes a combined quota and levy system to combat excess production of sugar.[85] The A quota assigned to individual sugar producers states how much sugar is subject to unlimited intervention; the B quota prescribes the quantity of sugar on which a levy must be paid for production and storage costs. Any excess above the A and B quotas must not be brought on to the common market, but must be exported to third countries within a prescribed time period.[86] This is the background to the following comments by the Court[87]:

"Nevertheless it must be pointed out that isoglucose manufacturers and sugar manufacturers are treated differently as regards the imposition of the production levy. In fact, in contrast to the production levy provided for in Article 27 of Regulation No. 3330/74, which only affects Quota B sugar, the levy applied by Article 9 of Regulation No. 111/77 is applied to the whole of isoglucose production.

Within the limits of Quotas A and B sugar manufacturers enjoy a guarantee of marketing at the intervention price and are entitled to the benefit of the export refund system, whereas isoglucose manufacturers do not enjoy any similar advantages.

Even when account is taken of the fact that in pursuance of Article 9(2) of Regulation No. 1111/77 the amount of the production levy on isoglucose was limited to the period from 1 July 1977 to 30 June 1978 to the maximum rate of 5 units of account per 100 kg., a rate which was maintained in force for the marketing year 1978/79 by Regulation No. 1298/78, the difference in treatment still exists as the isoglucose manufacturers do not enjoy the marketing guarantees provided for manufacturers of normal sugar.

However, it is still necessary to inquire whether that difference of treatment as regards the imposition of the production levy is objectively justified."

[85] See R. Boest, *op. cit.*, footnote 66, p. 182; on the previous method of operating the sugar quota system, which still applies in this connection, see R. Börner, "Das Interventions-system der landwirtschaftlichen Marktordnungen der EWG," in *Kölner Schriften zum Europarecht*, Vol. 10, Cologne/Bonn/Munich, 1969, pp. 17 *et seq.*

[86] *cf.* Article 26, para. 1 of Council Regulation 1785/81 of June 30, 1981 on the common market organisation for sugar, O.J. 1981, L177/4 *et seq.*, which corresponds to Article 26(1) of the sugar market regulations at the time of Joined Cases 103 & 145/77; see O.J. 1974, L359/1 *et seq.*

[87] *Op. cit.*, footnote 83, p. 2080, paras. 63 to 66 and 67.

The Court goes on to examine in great detail the arguments of the Council and the Commission in justification of the amount of the levy. It is striking how closely the Court examines the Commission's economic judgment as to the proper allocation, between sugar and isoglucose producers, of the burdens caused by over-production. The Court expresses a critical view[88]:

> "By omitting to take this factor into consideration in its calculations, the Commission has considerably overestimated the charges borne by sugar manufacturers."

The Court responds to the objection raised by the Council and the Commission, that alternative methods of calculating the isoglucose levy were not practicable[89]:

> ". . . inconveniences of the type alleged cannot justify the imposition of a charge which is manifestly unequal.
> Accordingly the provisions of Regulation No. 1111/77 establishing the production levy system for isoglucose offend against the general principle of equality of which the prohibition on discrimination set out in Article 40(3) of the Treaty is a specific expression."

In this case too, the use of the equality principle has something in common with the proportionality principle, where the reference is to a "manifestly unequal charge".[90]

Both of these decisions therefore serve to illustrate the application of the latter principle. Its role in limiting discretionary power will be considered below.

(b) *How the proportionality principle limits policy-making in the law of market organisation*

Whereas the ban on discrimination and the general principle of equality apply wherever duties are imposed or benefits granted, the proportionality principle is significant for the limits it sets to intervention by the

---

[88] *Op. cit.*, footnote 83, p. 2081, paras. 78 to 80.
[89] *Op. cit.*, footnote 83, p. 2082, paras. 82 to 83.
[90] See also R. Boest, *Die Agrarmärkte im Rechte der EWG*, Baden-Baden 1984, p. 145. In his view, the principle of non-discrimination can be truly reflected only in the combination of the ban on discrimination, the proportionality principle, the essential freedom of market members and the aims of Article 39(1) of the EEC Treaty.

Community authorities.[91] The proportionality principle, also described as the prohibition of excess or the principle of minimum intervention, makes it possible to keep to a minimum the burdens imposed on individuals by the authorities. These are regarded as proportionate as long as the decisions concerned are both necessary and appropriate for their purpose, and as long as the resulting charges are reasonably proportionate to the aim in view. The principle therefore ensures that the relationship between ends and means is open to judicial examination.[92]

This has implications for the exercise of discretionary powers by legislative bodies and also, most importantly, by executive organs. The oft-quoted remark that the court will test a decision only for its legality, not for its expediency, may be qualified in the light of the proportionality principle. When this principle is applied, expediency is found in some important respects to be an essential element of legality, for instance when a legal act is tested to ascertain that it is necessary or appropriate for achieving the desired purpose. This particularly affects administrative discretion. The law's invasion of the last stronghold of independent decision-making reins in the executive still further. Whether this is a desirable development cannot be discussed here; this question will be considered in the chapter which deals in detail with the proportionality principle in the Member States and in the legal system of the European Community.

What we shall do here is to show, through examples from the case law, how the Court has used the proportionality principle to restrict the legal scope of policy-makers in market organisation. Since there are now so many cases, any review is bound to be somewhat sketchy. However, a comparison of a variety of significant cases shows up the problem areas for Community intervention. The question of the limits to discretion arises with particular urgency where the Community is intervening in the sphere of Market citizens.

It has already been shown, through the judgments in Cases 114/76 and 103 and 145/77, how the proportionality principle has been applied to the law of market organisation. These cases dealt with "crisis management" measures of agricultural policy, intended for disposing of surpluses.

But even where "ordinary" measures are concerned, Article 40(3), first paragraph, of the EEC Treaty stipulates that they must be

---

[91] See, for example, the opinion of Advocate-General Capotorti in Case 114/76 *Bela-Mühle* v. *Grows Farm* [1977] E.C.R. 1211 at 1233; A. Bleckmann, *Die Grundrechte im Europäischen Gemeinschaftsrecht*, EuGRZ 1981, pp. 257 *et seq.* (274).

[92] R. Boest, *op. cit.*, footnote 90, p. 152.

"required," and this is an important element of the proportionality principle.

This means that a measure is permissible only if there is no less stringent means of achieving the aim in view. Where intervention in the market is concerned, this means that the only permitted means of regulation are those which interfere as little as possible with the ordinary workings of the market.[93] It is clear from Article 40(2) of the EEC Treaty that even the Community agricultural policy, which at first glance is highly interventionist, relies chiefly on market forces. Common rules on competition may be the form taken by the common market organisation, but only where the product concerned does not call for stricter methods of regulation.[94]

The assumption that the market is regulated essentially by supply and demand brings with it the assumption that the participants in the market have both economic freedom and freedom to compete.[95] Any intervention in the market will therefore affect this freedom. The word "required" in Article 40(3), first paragraph, is therefore a substantive law guarantee of the freedom of each Market citizen.

The criterion of "appropriateness" refers specifically to the relationship between means and ends. The means specified in Article 40(3), first paragraph, of the Treaty may be deemed appropriate in the eyes of the Treaty's authors, since one reason why they were taken over into Community law was that they had been found useful in national farm policy.[96]

However, even this is too crude an outline. It is, in fact, the individual measures for combatting agricultural surpluses which are regularly questioned, and the Court itself has tested the appropriateness of individual aspects of market organisation, such as the licensing and deposit rules in the common market in cereals.

One example of the Court's attitude towards the question whether a measure is appropriate is Case 138/78 Stölting v. Hauptzollamt Hamburg-Jonas.[97]

This case turned on the introduction of a levy on all milk production, for the purpose of disposing of surpluses in this sector of the agricultural market.[98] The complainant in the initial proceedings argued that this was

---

[93] R. Boest, op. cit., footnote 90, p. 152.
[94] The most highly regulated market so far is the common market in sugar.
[95] cf. Case 111/76 Officier van Justitie v. van den Hazel [1977] E.C.R. 901 at 910, paras. 16 et seq.
[96] R. Boest, op. cit., footnote 90, p. 152.
[97] [1979] E.C.R. 713 et seq.
[98] The so-called responsibility levy; cf. [1979] E.C.R. 713 at 714.

not an appropriate method of reducing milk production. The Court found[99]:

> "If a measure is patently unsuited to the objective which the competent institution seeks to pursue this may affect its legality, but on the other hand the Council must be recognized as having a discretionary power in this area which corresponds to the political responsibilities which Articles 40 and 43 impose upon it."

In other words, "evidence must be brought" if a measure is to be rejected as inappropriate. This means, of course, that it is for the responsible institution to ponder in advance the suitability of the measure. As well as being necessary and appropriate, a measure must be proportionate, in the narrow sense, and this is the point we must now turn to. Weighing the usefulness of a particular measure for the public at large against the restriction placed on the protected property rights of Market citizens is a process reflected in the so-called *Hauer* decision.[100] In the earlier decisions this element was almost completely absent.[101]

The *Hauer* decision concerned a restriction of the free exercise of a professional activity and of property rights, through a prohibition against planting new vineyards for a certain period of time. The aim was to combat over-production in the Community wine market.[102] Having considered in detail why this restriction was required, the Court found[103]:

> "Therefore it is necessary to conclude that the restriction imposed upon the new planting of vines introduced for a limited period by Regulation No. 1162/76 is justified by the objectives of general interest pursued by the Community, and does not infringe the substance of the right to property in the form in which it is recognized and protected in the Community legal order."

---

[99] *Op. cit.*, footnote 97, p. 722, para. 7; *cf.* also Cases 279, 280, 285 & 286/84 *Walter Rau and others* v. *Commission* [1987] E.C.R. 1069.

[100] Case 44/79 *Lieselotte Hauer* v. *Land Rheinland-Pfalz* [1979] E.C.R. 3727.

[101] See Chapter 5 above. However, the Court's remarks in Joined Cases 99 & 100/76 *Beste Boter und Hoche* v. *Bundesanstalt für landwirtschaftliche Marktordnung* [1977] E.C.R. 861 at 873, para. 11 may also be understood in the sense of weighing up the interests involved against the interference with property rights: "It must therefore be concluded that the system of the processing deposit established by Regulation No. 1259/72 does not exceed what is appropriate and necessary to attain the objective desired."

[102] *Op. cit.*, footnote 100, p. 3741.   [103] *Op. cit.*, footnote 100, p. 3749, para. 29.

The "substance," however, is not taken into account in weighing up the property rights involved here; rather, it indicates the permissible outer limit of a restriction on property.

The principle of proportionality has proved an important and effective means of protecting the legal rights of Market citizens; let us therefore conclude with a few examples from the Court's case law in which this principle has been applied. The first of these calls for some introductory comment, which is also useful in scrutinising the executive discretion of the Commission and the Member States. It takes us into the area of trade with non-Member States.

The rules on imports and exports from and to non-Member States are a fixed and essential component of the common market in agricultural products.[104] Having created the internal market in these products, the Council also had to define the relationship between the Community and the world market in this field. The assumption was that the Community's pricing policy,[105] geared chiefly to raising producers' incomes, must be protected against imported products from the world market, which were usually cheaper, if its aim was to be achieved. The code-word "Community preference" stands for the political option for an internal market which is largely sealed off from events on the world market.

On the other hand, it was necessary to ensure that agricultural surpluses could be sold on the world market.[106] The solution chosen to meet these requirements was a system of levies and refunds on the outer boundaries of the Community, to compensate for price differences of imports and exports from world market prices.[107]

When agricultural products are imported, the difference between what is usually a lower world market price and the higher Community price is eliminated by means of a levy, and when products are exported this difference is refunded.[108] In the former case the price is brought up to the Community level, and in the latter the refund acts as an export subsidy to

---

[104] On external trade law in general, see: C.-D. Ehlermann, *Neuere Entwicklungen im Aussenhandelsrecht der Europäischen Gemeinschaft*, Baden-Baden 1984.

[105] In recent times this priority in the common agricultural policy has been questioned. Instead, more emphasis is being placed on the supply and demand aspect as a basis for pricing. See the Commission's proposals in the "Green Paper" on the reform of the common agricultural policy.

[106] See R. Boest, *op. cit.*, footnote 90, p. 185 and 218; but see also *ibid. op. cit.*, pp. 154 *et seq.*

[107] See B. Börner, *Das Interventionssystem der landwirtschaftlichen Marktordnungen der EWG*, KSE Vol. 10, Cologne/Berlin/Bonn/Munich 1969, p. 37 *et seq.*

[108] See the survey in G. Nicolaysen, *Europäisches Gemeinschaftsrecht*, Stuttgart/Berlin/Cologne/Mainz 1979, p. 127/128.

make it possible to sell the product on the world market. Because of the fluctuations in world market prices, both forms of compensation have to be fixed anew at regular intervals. This is done by the Commission, in the "Management Committee procedure" which we have already mentioned.[109]

The fixing of levies and refunds bulks large in the case law on agricultural policy.

The common market in cereals has an additional, highly controversial arrangement for external trade. With the help of so-called licences, which are not authorisations, data concerning imports and exports of these products are gathered and evaluated.[110] This makes it possible to monitor trade flows in the cereals market and to take the necessary policy decisions.[111] The licences are issued by the responsible authorities in the Member States. When they are issued, an undertaking is exacted that the goods will be imported or exported within the time-limit indicated in the licence.[112]

To ensure that this undertaking is complied with, a deposit is payable when the licence is granted, and if the goods are not exported within the set time-limit the deposit will, except in cases of force majeure, be forfeited.[113] The licensing and deposit system has proved a fertile source of disputes centred on the degree of proportion between the obligations imposed and the legal consequences.

In the proceedings for a preliminary ruling in Case 25/70 *Einfuhr- und Vorratsstelle für Getreide* v. *Köster*, the question was raised whether the export obligation and the deposit accompanying each export licence were lawful from the standpoint of proportionality. The original text states[114]:

> "It appears from the grounds of the judgment at first instance that the Verwaltungsgericht considered the undertaking attached to the issue of the import or export licences, under Article 1 of Regulation No. 102/64, and the deposit provided for by Article 7(1) of the same regulation guaranteeing the fulfilment of that obligation to be invalid, because it allegedly constitutes an *ultra vires* measure contrary

---

[109] B. Beutler, R. Bieber, J. Pipkorn, J. Streil, *Die Europäische Gemeinschaft—Rechtsordnung und Politik* (3rd ed., Baden-Baden 1987), p. 453.

[110] See G. Nicolaysen, *op. cit.*, footnote 108, 128.

[111] See Case 25/70 *Einfuhr- und Vorratsstelle für Getreide* v. *Köster* [1970] E.C.R. 1161 at 1174, para. 24.

[112] See R. Boest, *op. cit.*, footnote 90, p. 155.

[113] *Ibid.* On the proportionality question involved in the forfeiture of the deposit, see also Case 38/86 *Neumann* v. *BALM* [1987] E.C.R. 1675, para. 9.

[114] [1970] E.C.R. 1161 at 1174, para. 21.

to the principles of economic freedom and proportionality. According to the court, these principles which are intended to guarantee protection of fundamental rights form an integral part of both international law and the supranational legal order, such that a Community measure contrary to these concepts must be considered null and void."

Explanations follow of the purpose of the deposit rule and the need for the Commission to have comprehensive market information. The Court concludes[115]:

"The choice for that purpose by the Community legislature of the deposit cannot be criticized in view of the fact that that machinery is adapted to the voluntary nature of requests for licences and that it has the dual advantage over other possible systems of simplicity and efficacy.

A system of mere declaration of exports affected and of unused licences, as proposed by the respondent in the main action, would, by reason of its retrospective nature and lack of any guarantee of application, be incapable of providing the competent authorities with sure data on trends in the movement of goods. Likewise, a system of fines imposed *a posteriori* would involve considerable administrative and legal complications at the state of decision and of execution.

It therefore appears that the requirement of import and export licences involving for the licensees an undertaking to effect the proposed transactions under the guarantee of a deposit constitutes a method which is both necessary and appropriate to enable the competent authorities to determine in the most effective manner their interventions on the market in cereals.

The principle of the system of deposits cannot therefore be disputed."

But the judges went on to ask[116]:

"However, examination should be made as to whether or not certain detailed rules of the system of deposits might be contested in the light of the principles enounced by the question, especially in view of the

---

[115] *Op. cit.*, footnote 114, p. 1177, paras. 26 *et seq.*
[116] *Op. cit.*, footnote 114, p. 1177, para. 30.

allegation of the respondent in the main action that the burden of the deposit is excessive for trade, to the extent of violating fundamental rights."

The excess is judged not by the amount of the deposit, but by the costs associated with making it. However, these are not excessive, and do not point to any legal flaws in the licensing system.[117]

After dismissing two further complaints, which need not be mentioned, the Court finally concludes[118]:

"... the fact that the system of licences involves an undertaking by those who apply for them, to import or export, guaranteed by a deposit, does not violate any right of a fundamental nature. The machinery of deposits constitutes an appropriate, and in no way excessive, method for the purposes of Article 40(3) of the Treaty, for carrying out the common organization of the agricultural markets and also conforms to the requirements of Article 43."

In what follows, we focus on one particular aspect of the deposit regulation, the exception whereby the deposit is not forfeited if there is force majeure to prevent the import or export of the goods. The validity of this very narrow exception has been questioned, especially in view of the fact that the deposit is forfeited even when there is no deliberate failure to export.[119] The following extracts from the grounds of judgment in Case 25/70 show how the Court defines the concept of "force majeure," a definition in which elements of the proportionality principle are discernibly present[120]:

"The concept of force majeure adopted by the agricultural regulations takes into account the particular nature of the relationships in public law between traders and the national administration, as well as the objectives of those regulations. It follows from those objectives as well as from the positive provisions of the regulations in question that the concept of force majeure is not limited to absolute

---

[117] *Op. cit.*, footnote 114, p. 1176, para. 32.
[118] *Op. cit.*, footnote 114, p. 1176, para. 36.
[119] [1970] E.C.R. 1161 at 1176, para. 37.
[120] *Op. cit.*, footnote 119, pp. 1177 *et seq.*, para. 38 *et seq.*

impossibility but must be understood in the sense of unusual circumstances, outside the control of the importer or exporter, the consequences of which, in spite of the exercise of all due care, could not have been avoided except at the cost of excessive sacrifice. This concept implies a sufficient flexibility regarding not only the nature of the occurrence relied upon but also the care which the exporter should have exercised in order to meet it and the extent of the sacrifices which he should have accepted to that end."

After further consideration the Court finally concludes that the rule exempting the deposit only in cases of force majeure does not render the deposit system legally invalid.

It is noticeable that the Court, in paragraph 38 of its grounds of judgment, introduces the "cost of excessive sacrifice" as an element justifying force majeure. This essential process of balancing the aims of a rule against the sacrifices involved in complying with it echoes the case law on measures which have equivalent effect, such as quantitative restrictions under Article 30 of the EEC Treaty. The presence of these undefined terms does not mean that a particular solution must, or must not, be chosen; what it means is that the public authorities, in applying the law, must weigh up and evaluate the options for themselves. The Court has itself used the catchword "elasticity."[121] It would be an interesting exercise to examine how the term force majeure is interpreted in individual cases, and not merely in those where the proportionality principle is involved. We have so far dealt only with the general category of exceptions from forfeiture of deposits in cases of force majeure. Where the Member States have to apply the concept when implementing agricultural law, it will emerge whether the national authorities are free to judge when exceptions may be made. We shall look at this more closely in the context of discretionary powers in indirect, *i.e.* national, implementation.

(c) *How the demands of legal certainty limit the discretion of policy-makers*

When intervening in the market, the Community authorities have to reconcile two contradictory requirements. On the one hand, the rapidly evolving market situation calls for legislation which is as flexible as

---

[121] *Op. cit.*, footnote 119, p. 1176, end of para. 38.

possible; on the other hand, participants in the market need some consistency in the rules, so that they can base their calculations on firm foundations.[122] This simple balance becomes more complicated, however, if we add to it the manifold interests of the many undertakings which participate in the market. It will therefore come as no surprise that many cases before the European Court have turned on questions of legal certainty.

For the most part, these cases deal with situations in which transactions in progress have been affected, at various stages, by changes in the rules. Many of them have raised the problem of the retroactive effect of legal acts. In most instances this has been where changes in the law have occurred after a transaction has been concluded but before the contract has been performed, and these changes have affected the basis of the calculation.

The Court has basically forbidden retroactive decisions only where the retroactivity is genuine, that is, where the rule relates to matters already determined when the rule was enacted.[123] Exceptions may be permitted, however, if there are particularly pressing reasons.[124] In such cases the legislator has to weigh the protection of legitimate expectations against the public interest.[125]

Changes in the law relating to past events may on the other hand be admitted if the legal effects have a bearing on the future.[126] This category includes, for instance, many foreign trade transactions in which the conclusion of the contract and the date for performing it may be months apart. During this period any changes in the law, such as a reduction in

---

[122] See R. Boest, *op. cit.*, footnote 90, pp. 158 *et seq.*

[123] *cf.* Case 88/76 *Société pour l'exportation des sucres SA* v. *Commission* [1977] E.C.R. 709, paras. 16 to 19, Case 99/78 *Weingut Gustav Decker KG* v. *Hauptzollamt Landau* [1979] E.C.R. 101 at 111, para. 8; see also the opinion of Advocate-General Warner in Case 7/76 *JRCA* v. *Staatliche Finanzverwaltung* [1976] E.C.R. 1234.

[124] See Advocate-General Reischl in Case 98/78 *Racke* v. *Hauptzollamt Mainz* [1979] E.C.R. 96.

[125] Case 98/78, *Racke* v. *Hauptzollamt Mainz* [1979] E.C.R. 69 at 86, para. 20, with opinion by Advocate-General Reischl at p. 96; Case 84/81 *Staple Dairy Products Limited* v. *Intervention Board for Agricultural Produce* [1982] E.C.R. 1763 at 1777, para. 12, with references; Case 224/82 *Meiko Konservenfabrik* v. *Bundesrepublik Deutschland* [1983] E.C.R. 2539 at 2448, para. 12.

[126] See also Case 1/73 *Westzucker GmbH* v. *Einfuhr- und Vorratsstelle für Zucker* [1973] E.C.R. 723 at 729, para. 5; Case 143/73 *Sopad* v. *FORM und FIRS* [1973] E.C.R. 1433 at 1441, paras. 8 to 9; Case 2/75 *Einfuhr- und Vorratsstelle für Getreide und Futtermittel* v. *Fa. C. Mackprang* [1975] E.C.R. 607 at 617; Case 96/77 *SA Ancienne Maison Marcel Bauche and others* v. *French Customs Administration* [1978] E.C.R. 383 at 400, paras. 48 to 51; Case 125/77 *Scholten-Honig* v. *Hoofdproduktschap voor Akkerbouwprodukten* [1978] E.C.R. 1991 at 2005, paras. 37 to 41; Case 84/78, *Angelo Tomadini* v. *Amministrazione delle Finanze dello Stato* [1979] E.C.R. 1801 at 1815, para. 21.

---

refunds, may invalidate the entire calculation. Here it is necessary to distinguish whether the change in the law affects the basic structure of a market organisation or only its functioning. For example, a basic change would be the introduction of a quota system in the common market for milk and milk products, whereas the periodic adjustments of levies and refunds are everyday administrative matters which do not affect the basic structure of the market organisation.

Among the various basic methods of market regulation which interest us here, one example is the introduction of a levy on isoglucose, which we have already mentioned when discussing the anti-discrimination rule and the limits it sets on policy-making. The first attempt to introduce this levy was frustrated, as we have seen, by the anti-discrimination rule in conjunction with the proportionality principle. The second attempt was halted by the Court because the Parliament had had no opportunity to consider the matter.[127]

The following case centred on a third attempt to integrate isoglucose into the sweetener market and subject it to the same restrictions as sugar.

In Case 110/81 *Roquette Frères* v. *Council* an action was brought under Article 173(2) of the EEC Treaty against the regulation by which the Council had reintroduced the isoglucose levy, with retroactive effect.[128]

The Court made extensive comment on the particular features of this case; we shall quote here only the most significant pronouncements. At the beginning of its examination the Court restated its position on retroactivity[129]:

> "As the Court has already held, in particular in its judgments of January 25, 1979 in Case 98/78 *Racke* [1979] E.C.R. 69 and Case 99/78 *Decker* [1979] E.C.R. 101, although in general the principle of legal certainty, as the applicant states, precludes a Community measure from taking effect from a point in time before its publication, it may exceptionally be otherwise where the purpose to be achieved so demands and where the legitimate expectations of those concerned are duly respected."

The Court then goes on to consider whether a retroactive effect was necessary in the public interest. It found that this was indeed so[130]:

---

[127] See under IV.2(a)(aa) above.
[128] [1982] E.C.R. 3159; see also the parallel action against the introduction of a levy on isoglucose, Case 108/81 *Amylum* v. *Council* [1982] E.C.R. 3107.
[129] [1982] E.C.R. 3159, para. 5.
[130] *Op. cit.*, footnote 129, p. 3179, para. 8.

"In that situation the Council was lawfully entitled to consider that the objective to be achieved in the general interest, namely the stabilization of the Community market in sweeteners without arbitrary discrimination between traders, required the contested provisions to be retroactive in nature and thus the first of the conditions which the Court lays down for the applicability *ratione temporis* of a Community measure to a date prior to the date of its publication may be regarded as satisfied."

This justified interest was weighed against the possibility that the party concerned might have relied on the rule not being retroactive. The first question was whether such an expectation could in fact be justified.[131] The Court found it could not, and mentioned factors which would preclude any reliance by the undertaking concerned on the legal situation before the regulation was enacted.[132] The existing case-law on the justified expectations of the market participants can be summarised by saying that the Court poses stringent requirements on this point.[133] The market participants must not only follow closely both currency and market trends and allow for possible legislative reactions to these, but must also examine the actions of the Community institutions for portents of imminent legislation.[134]

It is not surprising, therefore, that in Case 110/81 the Court denied that any expectation worthy of protection existed. But even if the conditions were fulfilled and a justified expectation did exist, there might be compelling public interests, such as the risk of a serious perturbation of the market, which would call for the new rule to be applied immediately and without exception.[135] In the outcome, therefore, the complaint in Case 110/81 was dismissed as unfounded.

The principles defined by the Court, as explained here, form a framework within which it is possible to resolve the conflicting demands for flexible legislation and legal certainty or protection of legitimate expec-

---

[131] *Op. cit.*, footnote 129, p. 3179, para. 9.
[132] *Op. cit.*, footnote 129, p. 3180, paras. 17 *et seq.*
[133] *cf.* R. Boest *op. cit.*, footnote 90, p. 164.
[134] *cf.* Joined Cases 44–51/77, *Union Malt and others* v. *Commission* [1978] E.C.R. 57 at 81, paras. 34 to 37; Case 78/77 *Fa. Johann Lührs* v. *Hauptzollamt Hamburg-Jonas* [1978] E.C.R. 169 at 178, para. 6. Among later cases, see Case 84/81 *Staple Dairy Products Limited* v. *Intervention Board for Agricultural Produce* [1982] E.C.R. 1763 at 1777, para. 15.
[135] Case 78/77 *Fa. Johann Lührs* v. *Hauptzollamt Hamburg-Jonas* [1978] E.C.R. 169 at 177, para. 6; Case 44/79 *Lieselotte Hauer* v. *Land Rheinland-Pfalz* [1979] E.C.R. 3727 at 3742.

tations. This much wider problem is examined in depth in the chapter on "Legal certainty and protection of legitimate expectations."

(d) How fundamental rights limit policy-making in the law of market organisation

The Court includes fundamental rights among the general principles of law which it is bound to uphold.[136] Although its case law on agriculture contains few decisions in which the legality of a measure has been judged according to the benchmark of these fundamental rights, they have nonetheless played a decisive role as the protection of these rights has evolved in Community law.

One example is Case 11/70, *Internationale Handelsgesellschaft* v. *Einfuhr- und Vorratsstelle für Getreide und Futtermittel*, in which the Court was asked whether the deposit rule under the licensing system was compatible with fundamental rights guarantees.[137] On this point the Court said[138]:

> "However, an examination should be made as to whether or not any analogous guarantee inherent in Community law has been disregarded. In fact, respect for fundamental rights forms an integral part of the general principles of law protected by the Court of Justice. The protection of such rights, whilst inspired by the constitutional traditions common to the Member States, must be ensured within the framework of the structure and objectives of the Community. It must therefore be ascertained, in the light of the doubts expressed by the Verwaltungsgericht, whether the system of deposits has infringed rights of a fundamental nature, respect for which must be ensured in the Community legal system."

Another example is Case 44/79, *Hauer* v. *Land Rheinland-Pfalz*.[139] This concerned a refusal by the competent authorities in the German Land of Rheinland-Pfalz to authorise the planting of a vineyard. The application submitted by the plaintiff had been rejected on the basis that Council Regulation 1162/76 prohibited the issue of authorisations for the planting

---

[136] See Case 44/79 *Lieselotte Hauer* v. *Land Rheinland-Pfalz* [1979] E.C.R. 3727 at 3744, para. 15.
[137] [1970] E.C.R. 1125 at 1134, para. 4.
[138] *Ibid.*
[139] [1979] E.C.R. 3727.

of new vineyards for a certain period of time, even if the area was in principle suited to wine-growing.[140] The administrative court which dealt with the complaint, in Neustadt a. d. Weinstrasse, expressed a doubt whether this prohibition was compatible with two fundamental rights, the free exercise of a profession and the freedom to own property, enshrined in Articles 12 and 14 of the German Basic Law. The Court began by correcting the question as put[141]:

".... the question of a possible infringement of fundamental rights by a measure of the Community institutions can only be judged in the light of Community law itself. The introduction of special criteria for assessment stemming from the legislation or constitutional law of a particular Member State would, by damaging the substantive unity and efficacy of Community law, lead inevitably to the destruction of the unity of the Common Market and the jeopardizing of the cohesion of the Community."

In this light, the Court framed the question before it as follows[142]:

"In these circumstances the doubts evinced by the Verwaltungsgericht as to the compatibility of the provisions of Regulation No. 1162/76 with the rules concerning the protection of fundamental rights must be understood as questioning the validity of the regulation in the light of Community law. In this regard, it is necessary to distinguish between, on the one hand, a possible infringement of the right to property and, on the other hand, a possible limitation upon the freedom to pursue a trade or profession."

The Court went on to deal with the question of property rights[143]:

"The right to property is guaranteed in the Community legal order in accordance with the ideas common to the constitutions of the Member States, which are also reflected in the first Protocol to the European Convention for the Protection of Human Rights."

[140] *Op. cit.*, footnote 139, p. 3741, para. 2.
[141] *Op. cit.*, footnote 139, p. 3744, para. 14.
[142] *Op. cit.*, footnote 139, p. 3745, para. 16.
[143] *Op. cit.*, footnote 139, p. 3745, para. 17; see also Case 19/61 *Mannesmann AG* v. *High Authority* [1962] E.C.R. 357 at 374; Case 4/73 *Nold* v. *Commission* [1974] E.C.R. 491 at 507, paras. 13 *et seq.*

A reference follows to the actual text of the European Convention, evidently with a view to defining property rights within Community law in a manner likely to achieve consensus in all Member States.[144] The Court then turns to the possible restrictions involved if a right is completely withdrawn or its exercise is limited.[145]

The prohibition against planting new vineyards, in the Court's view, was no more than a restriction on use, and in the wine-growing countries of the Community this is regarded, both in the abstract and in specific instances, as compatible with the right to hold property.[146] In support of its finding that the exercise of property rights may be restricted in the public interest, the Court quotes examples of a provision of this kind in the constitutions of several Member States.[147] Its interim conclusion is as follows[148]:

"Thus it may be stated, taking into account the constitutional precepts common to the Member States and consistent legislative practices, in widely varying spheres, that the fact that Regulation No. 1162/76 imposed restrictions on the new planting of vines cannot be challenged in principle. It is a type of restriction which is known and accepted as lawful, in identical or similar forms, in the constitutional structure of all the Member States."

But, the Court continued, this finding did not deal completely with the problem raised by the administrative court[149]:

"Even if it is not possible to dispute in principle the Community's ability to restrict the exercise of the right to property in the context of the common organization of the market and for the purposes of a structural policy, it is still necessary to examine whether the restrictions introduced by the provisions in dispute in fact correspond to objectives of general interest pursued by the Community or whether, with regard to the aim pursued, they constitute a disproportionate and intolerable interference with the rights of the owner, impinging upon the very substance of the right to property.

---

[144] Similarly, B. Beutler, in EuR 1981, p. 133 ("Anmerkung zur Hauer-Entscheidung des EuGH").
[145] *Op. cit.*, footnote 139, p. 3746, para. 19.
[146] *Op. cit.*, footnote 139, p. 3747, para. 22.
[147] *Op. cit.*, footnote 139, p. 3746, para. 20.
[148] *Op. cit.*, footnote 139, p. 3747, para. 22.
[149] *Op. cit.*, footnote 139, p. 3747, para. 23.

It is therefore necessary to identify the aim pursued by the disputed regulation and to determine whether there exists a reasonable relationship between the measures provided for by the regulation and the aim pursued by the Community in this case."

This is followed by an analysis of the goals and problems of the common market organisation for wine, which concludes as follows on the initial treatment of the complaint[150]:

"Seen in this light, the measure criticized does not entail any undue limitation upon the exercise of the right to property. Indeed, the cultivation of new vineyards in a situation of continuous over-production would not have any effect, from the economic point of view, apart from increasing the volume of the surpluses; further, such an extension at that stage would entail the risk of making more difficult the implementation of a structural policy at the Community level in the event of such a policy resting on the application of criteria more stringent than the current provisions of national legislation concerning the selection of land accepted for wine-growing."

Having completed its examination, the Court stated[151]:

"Therefore it is necessary to conclude that the restriction imposed upon the use of property by the prohibition on the new planting of vines introduced for a limited period by Regulation No. 1162/76 is justified by the objectives of general interest pursued by the Community and does not infringe the substance of the right to property in the form in which it is recognized and protected in the Community legal order."

Legal literature abounds with comment on the *Hauer* decision.[152] To avoid repetition, we shall simply outline here the points relevant to the restrictions imposed on the discretionary powers of agricultural policy-making.

---

[150] *Op. cit.*, footnote 139, p. 3749, para. 29.
[151] *Op. cit.*, footnote 139, p. 3749, para. 30.
[152] *cf.* above, Beutler's remark in: EuR 1981, pp. 130 *et seq.*; J. A. Usher, *European Law Review* 1980, pp. 209 *et seq.*; L. J. Constantinesco, *Journal du droit international*, 1981, pp. 174 *et seq.*; S. Bellini, *Rivista di diritto internazionale* 1981, pp. 318 *et seq.*; M. Schweitzer, *EWR-Schriftenreihe zum europäischen Weinrecht* 1982, pp. 97 *et seq.*

Whereas the aims specified in Article 39(1) of the EEC Treaty are binding on the institutions as substantive law, guarantees of fundamental rights add a subjective dimension; individuals have a right of defence against over-zealous intervention by Community authorities. The Court's reference to the "substance" of the right to property, which is clearly borrowed from German constitutional law (Article 19(2) of the Basic Law), suggests a minimum standard which must be upheld at all costs. This, in addition to the proportionality principle, sets a further legal limit on intervention by public authorities in the protected legal sphere of the individual. Because of the particular features of this case, it is understandable that there is no pointer to the precise circumstances in which the substance of the right would have been infringed, and the legal consequences this would have. One of these legal consequences however would certainly be that the principle of compensation would come into play, a principle which is a major achievement of the liberal constitutional state.

(c) Assessment of the Council's freedom in policy-making in agricultural law

Articles 38 *et seq.* of the EEC Treaty give the Council a considerable degree of political freedom, subject to certain broad legal constraints. The creation of a market organisation may therefore be justifiably described as a legislative act in the sense originally defined. The discretionary power involved—which is a legislative power—is limited by the Treaty provisions. The most important of these are Articles 39 and 40 of the EEC Treaty, which define the aims of the common agricultural policy and provide the necessary machinery to implement it.

The prohibition of discrimination in Article 40, paragraph 3(2) also acts as a limit on discretionary power. The unwritten legal principles of equal treatment, proportionality, legal certainty and fundamental rights are further legal constraints by which the Council is bound in its decision-making. In its case law, however, the Court has always taken care to ensure that the judicial protection against market regulation measures which is available under Article 177 of the EEC Treaty does not interfere with the smooth working of the common market in agriculture. This is why the various judgments of the Court frequently refer to the latitude enjoyed by the Council to appraise and evaluate, at its own discretion, the complex economic factors involved in agricultural policy, a latitude which avoids too narrow an application of the Treaty provisions and of general principles of law. However, the Court, in stating that the Council is free in its decision-making, does not offer any firm or final definition of its own review powers. The judgments are far from uniform in this respect, because in individual cases administrative demands are weighed against the individual's need for judicial protection.

In general, it can be said that the prerogative accorded to the Community authorities in evaluating market situations, which is explained by the complexity of these situations, will in case of doubt take precedence over any considerations of judicial protection for individuals.

Procedural questions are not so important in this field, except for the obligation to furnish the grounds for a decision, this being a procedural requirement which is often allegedly infringed. Its infringement will not, however, cause the decision to be declared invalid except in rare cases.

Bearing in mind that measures of market regulation, under the Treaty, taken in furtherance of the common agricultural policy are decided on a level equivalent to a state legislature, the judicial protection offered by the Court is quite considerable, despite the recognition of wide scope for policy-making. If one considers, in particular, the limited opportunities under the laws of the Member States to scrutinise, by direct or indirect means, the legality of economic legislation, the judicial protection available at Community level may be regarded as well developed.

3. THE AUTHORITY TO IMPLEMENT BY THE COMMISSION

In the common agricultural policy, the implementing law of the Commission is the second stage of enactment, once the market regulations have been made by the Council. The Council has of course reserved to itself powers to execute its basic regulations, but most of the legislation in this area falls within the competence of the Commission.[153]

The Commission, using powers conferred on it by Article 155(4) of the EEC Treaty (now Article 145, under the Single European Act), enacts this legislation, consisting chiefly of regulations, through the Management Committee procedure and thereby adapts the agricultural law of the Community to the prevailing economic situation. The Commission has at its disposal the necessary administrative apparatus to collect and evaluate data and turn them into legal decisions. Its role is nevertheless confined to enacting supplementary legislation, referred to here as implementing

---

[153] See the general comment in B. Beutler, J. Pipkorn, J. Streil, *Die Europäische Gemeinschaft—Rechtsordnung und Politik* (3rd ed., Baden-Baden 1987), pp. 453 *et seq.*

law; it does not have to apply the law concerning market regulation.[154] It is invariably the responsibility of the national authorities to translate the rules into practice in individual cases.[155] Only in a few cases does the Commission implement Community agricultural law through individual acts.[156]

Through the implementing Regulations of the Commission it is possible to impart to an agricultural ruling by the Community the terminological exactitude it requires if it is to be simultaneously implemented in the Member States. In its legislative activity the Commission must, therefore, always ensure that the rules are suitable for practical application. Typically, in the enactment of implementing provisions there is considerable room for discretion in the process of evaluation and decision. In practical terms, the rule-making is often a routine administrative activity. We shall consider below the constraints to which the Commission is subject when it enacts implementing orders.

(a) The limitation of powers by the source of authority and by the Treaty

The implementing powers of the Commission are limited in terms of both procedural and substantive law, but are always associated with a certain freedom of decision. Two examples from the common market organisation for sugar will show how the source of authority is itself a constraining factor[157]:

Article 8 of Council Regulation 1785/81 provides for an arrangement to compensate for the costs of storing sugar products. Paragraph 2 of this

---

[154] On the terminology, see M. Zuleeg, *Das Recht der Europäischen Gemeinschaften im innerstaatlichen Bereich*, KSE Vol. 9, Cologne/Berlin/Bonn/Munich 1969, pp. 47 *et seq.*
[155] *cf.* R. Boest, *Die Agrarmärkte im Rechte der EWG*, Baden-Baden 1984, pp. 302 *et seq.*
[156] See R. Boest, *op. cit.*, footnote 155, p. 302 *et seq.* with references; see also Case 809/79R, *Fratelli Pardini S.p.A.* v. *Commission* [1980] E.C.R. 139 *et seq.*, seeking an interim order compelling the Commission to authorise the Italian Government to issue a new licence to replace a stolen one. The Court rejected this on the ground that the Commission had no power to authorise a national authority to issue an export licence on the basis of what was a Community regulation. It was for the Member States to issue these licences (148, para. 4 of the judgment).
[157] See O.J. 1981, L177/4 *et seq.*, *cf.* also Case 167/82 *Nordgetreide* v. *Hauptzollamt Hamburg-Jonas* [1983] E.C.R. 1149 *et seq.*, which concerned the fixing of an export refund for barley flakes. Although Article 6 of the basic Regulation in question defined a method of calculating the refund for processed cereal products based on five elements, derived mainly from the levies themselves, the Court found that the Commission had discretion in the matter, conferred on it by the Council in proper form (p. 1162 paras. 12 and 13).

Regulation lists the products covered by it and establishes a flat rate of reimbursement for storage costs for Member States. This is to be financed by means of a levy.

In paragraphs 4 and 5, the implementing functions are divided between the Council and the Commission; according to paragraph 4, the Council is to make the basic rules for the application of Article 8, including fixing the compensation for storage costs; according to paragraph 5, compensation rates for storage costs are to be fixed annually, through the procedure in Article 41 of Regulation 1785/81. The same applies to the other implementing provisions relating to Article 8. This is a reference to the so-called "Management Committee procedure." The vagueness of the substantive powers here conferred on the Commission is quite striking.

By contrast, the power given to the Commission in Article 16(8) of the same Regulation to fix the levies for particular sugar products is defined in fairly specific terms. Nevertheless, the wording of Article 16(7) indicates that there is some room for discretionary judgment and decision:

> "Detailed rules for the application of this Article, in particular the margin within which the variations in the factors used for calculating the levy do not require any adjustment of the levy, shall be adopted in accordance with the procedure laid down in Article 41."

Although the preceding paragraphs set the parameters for calculating the levy, Article 16, with its greater precision, gives the Commission considerable latitude to assess the complex economic factors involved.

Many examples of such wide powers could be quoted.[158] Very often, a market regulation is brought into effect only through an implementing provision by the Commission, and the legal constraints on the latter therefore warrant special attention.

It has been confirmed by the Court that such flexible powers are admissible in principle as regards Article 2 of Regulation 974/71, which governs the fixing of monetary compensation amounts by the Commis-

---

[158] cf., for instance, Case 147/81 *Merkur-Fleischimport* v. *Hauptzollamt Hamburg-Ericus* [1982] E.C.R. 1389 *et seq.*; this case turned on a broadly-worded provision in the common market organisation for beef, on the basis of which the Commission introduced a ruling that beef imported free from levies must be processed within a certain time-limit, otherwise the deposit payable would be forfeited.

The Court (*op. cit.*, p. 1396, para. 7) replied to the objection that the general power did not extent to this ruling: "The conferment of that power, expressed in general terms, implies that the Commission has the right and the duty to take all appropriate measures in order to ensure that the rules laid down by the Council are implemented in such a way as to attain fully the objectives pursued by such rules."

sion. The original complainant in Case 5/73 had argued that Article 2 of Regulation 974/71, if seen in the light of the restrictions imposed in Article 80, paragraph 1, second sentence, of the German Basic Law, was not specific enough to give the administration such legislative powers.[159]

The Court focused upon the calculation of the monetary compensation and concluded that the discretion involved was limited and the power not excessively vague.[160]

In practice, complaints are most frequently directed against the Commission for allegedly exceeding the bounds of its implementing powers, either because it has made an incomplete or inaccurate evaluation of the underlying facts or because it has adopted measures not within its authority or not in accordance with general principles of law.

Questions relating to due authority and procedure are less problematic, however. In most cases, the rulings are made through the Management Committee procedure, which the Court has declared to be admissible. Hence there are no further procedural law difficulties for the Court to deal with. The procedural requirement for the Commission to follow the Management Committee procedure is, moreover, an evident reason for the Council possessing broad implementing powers. In individual cases, the management committees enable the Member States to exercise ultimate control over the implementing decisions of the Commission.[161]

In the case law, the points referred to in this survey occur mainly in connection with the levy, refund and monetary compensation systems and also in connection with protective measures for the Community's common market in agriculture.

(aa) Establishing and weighing the facts

In the areas mentioned above, the Court allows the Commission a

---

[159] cf. Case 5/73 Balkan-Import-Export GmbH v. Hauptzollamt Berlin-Packhof [1973] E.C.R. 1091 et seq., at 1115, para. 35. The judgment of Joined Cases 133–136/85 Walter Rau and others v. Commission [1987] E.C.R. 2289, paras. 25 to 31, is also concerned with the precision of a source of authority.

[160] Op. cit., footnote 159, p. 1115, para. 35. See also the interesting opinion of Advocate-General Roemer, op. cit., pp. 1129 et seq., regarding the reflection in Community law of the German principle of explicitness, as expressed in Article 80 I 2 of the Basic Law.

[161] See O. Gottsmann, in Groeben, Boeckh, Thiesing, Ehlermann, Kommentar zum EWG-Vertrag (3rd ed., Baden-Baden 1983), Article 40, pp. 396 et seq.; J. Schwarze, Die Befugnis zur Abstraktion im Europäischen Gemeinschaftsrecht, Baden-Baden 1976, p. 52 and H.P. Ipsen, Europäisches Gemeinschaftsrecht, Tübingen 1972, pp. 442 et seq.

considerable measure of discretion in establishing and weighing the facts. This is particularly clear from the large body of case-law on the monetary compensation system.

In the early 1970s the break-up of the world monetary system, which was based on fixed parities, resulted in some marked fluctuations and jeopardised the Community's uniform farm prices. The monetary compensation system was introduced to neutralise the effects of these changing parities on the pricing structure.[162] It had emerged that the differing agricultural prices among Member States, caused by the monetary fluctuations, were leading to a reduction in trade. For instance, the 11 per cent. devaluation of the French franc in 1969 had led to an 11 per cent. increase in farm prices, expressed in units of account. To combat the inevitable rise in consumer prices, the relationship between the franc and the unit of account was frozen.

However, this created a risk of French farmers making a profit from the exchange rate when their produce crossed the border. When produce was sold to a German intervention agency, for instance, the unaltered sum paid in German marks would, because of the devaluation of the franc, yield a higher sum in francs than if the same goods were sold to a French intervention board.[163]

Through the monetary compensation system, this potential advantage is eliminated by imposing a levy, at the internal frontiers of the Community, on products and their derivatives which are subject to intervention. Conversely, a subsidy is granted if the monetary situation would result in producers incurring losses on exports to another Community country.[164]

The Council's basic Regulation, 974/71,[165] empowers the Commission to decide whether monetary compensatory amounts are payable, and on which products. According to Article 1(3) monetary compensatory amounts are levied only if monetary policies would result in disturbances to trade in the agricultural products for which intervention arrangements exist. Article 2 of Regulation 974/71 prescribes how the monetary compensatory amounts are to be calculated if there is a disturbance of this kind. According to the consistent case law of the European Court,

---

[162] See P. Gilsdorf, *Der Währungsausgleich aus rechtlicher Sicht*, Cologne/Berlin/Bonn/ Munich 1978, p. 3 *et seq.*; G. Nicolaysen, *Europäisches Gemeinschaftsrecht*, Stuttgart/ Berlin/Cologne/Mainz 1979, pp. 130 *et seq.*

[163] See the description in G. Nicolaysen, *op. cit.*, footnote 162, p. 131.

[164] On the chronology of the development of the monetary compensation system, see P. Gilsdorf, *op. cit.*, footnote 162, pp. 3 *et seq.* Nowadays, the monetary compensation system applies only in a restricted sense.

[165] See J.O. 1971, L106/1; O.J. Sp. Ed. 1971, 257.

evaluating the market surveys needed to predict the effects of monetary policies is to a considerable extent a matter of discretion[166]:

"Where a complex economic situation is to be evaluated, the administration enjoys a wide measure of discretion. In reviewing the legality of the exercise of such discretion, the Court must confine itself to examining whether it contains a manifest error or constitutes a misuse of power or whether the authority did not clearly exceed the bounds of its discretion."

The Court goes on to explain exactly what is permissible in the context of this discretionary power, which would be described from a German viewpoint as scope for appraisal[167]:

"Article 1(3) of Regulation No. 974/71 cannot be interpreted as obliging the Commission to decide case by case, or in respect of each product individually, and making distinctions according to the country of export, whether there is a risk of disturbance.

The very terms of that provision show that evaluations of a general nature may be made in this respect.

---

[166] Case 29/77 *Roquette Frères* v. *France* [1977] E.C.R. 1835 at 1842, paras. 19 to 20; see also Case 74/74 *CNTA* v. *Commission* [1975] E.C.R. 533 at 547, paras. 19 to 23; Case 4/79 *Société Coopérative, Providence agricole de la Champagne* v. *ONIC* [1980] E.C.R. 2823 at 2847, para. 27; Case 136/77 *Fa. A. Racke* v. *Hauptzollamt Mainz* [1978] E.C.R. 1245 at 1256, para. 4; Case 95/75 *Effem GmbH* v. *Hauptzollamt Lüneburg* [1976] E.C.R. 361 at 369, para. 7: invalidity of a regulation on levies on processed cereals products, containing excessive rules on pricing; Case 55/75 *Balkan Import-Export GmbH* v. *Hauptzollamt Berlin-Packhof* [1976] E.C.R. 19 at 30, para. 8; see also Advocate-General Reischl, *op. cit.*, p. 37. See also Advocate-General Capotorti in Case 131/77 *Milac and others* v. *Hauptzollamt Saarbrücken* [1978] E.C.R. 1041 at 1058, containing a thorough investigation of the Commission's use of its discretionary powers. See also Case 95/80 *Dervieu-Delahais* v. *Directeur général des douanes et droits indirects* [1981] E.C.R. 317 at 334, para. 13 on monetary compensation amounts on French exports of Roquefort cheese; Case 98/78 *Racke* v. *Hauptzollamt Mainz* [1979] E.C.R. 69 at 81, para. 5; Case 136/77 *Racke* v. *Hauptzollamt Mainz* [1978] E.C.R. 1245 at 1256, para. 4 on MCAs on table wine. *cf.* opinion of Advocate-General Warner in Case 12/78 *Republic of Italy* v. *Commission* [1979] E.C.R. 1731 at 1755, *ibid.* in Joined Cases 67–85/75 *Lesieur Cotelle and others* v. *Commission* [1976] E.C.R. 391 at 418; Case 43/72 *Merkur Aussenhandels GmbH* v. *Commission* [1973] E.C.R. 1055 at 1074, para. 23.

An example from the milk sector is Case 35/80 *Denkavit Nederland* v. *Produktschap voor Zuivel* [1981] E.C.R. 45 at 60, para. 14, and 62, para. 25; also Joined Cases 133–136/85 *Walter Rau and others* v. *BALM* [1987] E.C.R. 2289, para. 31 and Joined Cases 279–280, 285 & 286/84, para. 14. For the administration of the beef market, see Case 92/78 *Simmenthal SpA* v. *Commission* [1979] E.C.R. 777 at 810, paras. 98 to 100; *cf.* also Case 236/84 *MALT GmbH* v. *Hauptzollamt Düsseldorf*, [1986] E.C.R. 1923, para. 15.

[167] Case 29/77 *Roquette Frères* v. *France* [1977] E.C.R. 1835 at 1843, paras. 21 to 23.

In particular, compelling reasons relating to the practicability of the system of compensatory amounts enable groups of products to be taken into consideration in assessing the possibility of disturbances in trade in agricultural products."

As explained above, the authority to fix flat rates may affect the operation of the ban on discrimination as a limit to discretionary power.[168] The Commission's power of appraisal, or its discretion, as the Court calls it, rests on the factual preconditions in Article 1 of Regulation 974/71.[169] We shall deal below with its legal consequences, in terms of fixing specific compensatory amounts.

Another area in which the Commission enjoys considerable freedom of appraisal is in activating protective clauses.[170] The basic rules for these in the market systems, in their "original" state, are broadly defined. The Council, however, usually prescribes in implementing regulations the conditions under which they are to be applied and the permissible ways of doing so. The Commission then has to apply the rules to individual cases, and in the process must evaluate complex economic and political facts. Here too, the Commission possesses considerable discretionary scope.

[168] See above on the limits to freedom of policy-making in the law of market organisation. Of special note is the express denial by Advocate-General Reischl, in his opinion in Case 55/75 *Balkan-Import-Export GmbH* v. *Hauptzollamt Berlin-Packhof* [1976] E.C.R. 19 at 42, that under Regulation 974/71 the Commission also has discretion to judge economic factors in individual cases. This, he says, is exactly what it cannot do.

[169] The language used here shows that the Court is not following the German administrative law system, where the facts are referred to either by undefined legal terms, which a court may review, or by areas of discretion which are only partially open to review. There are some interesting comments on this point by the German Advocate-General, Reischl, in Case 37/70 *Rewe Zentrale* v. *Hauptzollamt Emmerich* [1971] E.C.R. 23 *et seq.* (43); he comments as follows on the interim application of Article 226 of the EEC Treaty as a basis for national monetary compensatory amounts:

"Since under Article 226 the Commission must make extremely difficult appraisals very quickly, the Court admits, as Advocate-General Gand expressed it, that although in this sphere the Commission cannot exercise a 'discretion,' it possesses a power of appraisal subject to review by the Court and I would personally add that this is a wide power of appraisal."

Here, the Advocate-General is evidently seeking to apply elements of German administrative law theory to Community law. In the French version, the term is: "*large pouvoir d'appréciation*," cf. Receuil 1977, pp. 1835 *et seq.*, 1842, paras. 19 to 20.

[170] On the application of the protective clause in general, see: C.-D. Ehlermann, *Neuere Entwicklungen im Aussenhandelsrecht der Europäischen Gemeinschaft*, Baden-Baden 1984, pp. 5 *et seq.*; Advocate-General Rozès in Case 126/81 *Wünsche* v. *Bundesrepublik Deutschland* [1982] E.C.R. 1479 at 1496, which also bears out the assertion that the Commission had exceeded its discretion in making the evaluation. See also Case 52/81 *Faust* v. *Commission* [1982] E.C.R. 3745 at 3758, para. 9, on the selective application of a protective clause and the relationship with the ban on discrimination, and on the Commission's broad discretionary powers in this area of E.C. external trade law.

Case 40/72 *Schröder* v. *Federal Republic of Germany* dealt with protective measures against imports of tomato concentrate from Greece, which at the time was an associate member of the Community, not a full member.[171] The protective clause in the common market organisation for fruit and vegetables provided for measures when the market in these products is "subject to or threatened with serious disturbances," which might jeopardise the aims enshrined in Article 39(1) of the EEC Treaty.[172] The criteria for the presence or threat of "serious disturbances" and the protective measures allowed were laid down in a Council regulation.[173] These factual elements were in a sense a supplement to the original protective clause.

While admitting that the Commission had discretion in this area, the Court examined its economic analyses and numerical data[174] and found that the Commission's evaluation must be based on the objectives set out in Article 39 of the EEC Treaty. Hence it was reasonable, in taking steps to stabilise the market, to take account of the general standard of living of the agricultural community.[175]

There follows some extremely detailed explanations of the market situation. This is not surprising, because in its implementing regulation the Council had laid down precise criteria, requiring full statistical evidence, for the existence of a market disturbance. Although some points, such as the expected quantities of imports, remained vague, there were essentially four parameters to limit discretionary judgment. In this way the Council was able to predetermine in broad outline how the Commission would act, even though the final decision was to be the Commission's own.[176]

This example shows that an essentially broad term such as "disturbance of the common market" can be further defined by secondary law rules if the authority which applies the law is told in advance which facts it is to focus on. In the final analysis, however, there is still room for independent appraisal by the Commission.[177]

The process of establishing and weighing the facts is, however, only the first step towards a protective measure. If the Commission considers that

---

[171] [1973] E.C.R. 125 *et seq.*
[172] *Op. cit.*, footnote 171, p. 139, para. 2.
[173] *cf. ibid.*
[174] *Op. cit.*, footnote 171, p. 142, para. 11 implies this.
[175] *Op. cit.*, footnote 171, p. 141, para. 9.
[176] *cf.* C.-D. Ehlermann, *op. cit.*, footnote 170, p. 11.
[177] There is instructive comment by Advocate-General Rozès in Case 345/82 *Wünsche Handelsgesellschaft* v. *Bundesrepublik Deutschland* [1984] E.C.R. 1995 at 2022, with references.

a disturbance exists or may occur in the near future, it must select the appropriate measures from the range of measures provided by the Council, mainly by means of implementing regulations. The question then arises, how far implementing powers carry legally binding effects. The legal consequences themselves depend of course on the form in which the authority has been granted in the basic regulation and how it is expressed in additional regulations by the Council. However broad or narrow the range of possible measures for the Commission to adopt, however many or few the elements in the ruling, the Commission will always be free to decide the various components of a particular measure.

What this means in practice will be explained below, with reference to the protective measures already mentioned for trade with non-Member States and the monetary compensation system.

(bb) Constraints arising from the source of authority and the Treaty

The Commission has not only to select from the catalogue of permissible protective measures; it must also determine the form each one will take, how long it will last and what it will cover. In Case 40/72, referred to above, the interesting question arose whether there was any order of priority in the measures to be adopted.[178] The Court's utterances are of course framed for a particular legal situation, and it is not possible simply to extrapolate from these; however, the example above sheds some light on how the Luxembourg judges perceive the freedom of the administration in fulfilling its tasks. This was how the Court answered the question of the order of priority among protective measures[179]:

> "Neither Article 2 of Regulation No. 1428/71 nor Article 41 of the Association Agreement on enumerating the measures provided for there, establish an order of priority between them. It is in accordance with the object aimed at by these measures that the administration can decide according to the circumstances the measures which appear to it most suitable."

The administration's freedom of appraisal emerges even more distinctly from the following considerations on the question whether a particular

[178] [1973] E.C.R. 125 at 146, paras. 30 *et seq.*
[179] *Op. cit.*, footnote 178, p. 146, para. 32.

protective measure was appropriate for preventing or removing a market disturbance[180]:

> "With regard to the possibility of there existing opportunities of circumvention, it must be observed that the legality of a Community act cannot depend on retrospective considerations of its efficacy. Since in the present case it is a question of complex economic measures, which for the purpose of their efficacy necessarily require a wide discretion and moreover as regards their effects frequently present an uncertainty factor, the observation suffices that these measures do not appear on issue as obviously inappropriate for the realization of the desired object."

The appropriateness of the measure contains an element of proportionality as well; and in this respect the executive is accorded a considerable degree of discretion, which in the text of the grounds of judgment even goes so far as to include a right to err as to the appropriateness of a particular measure.

A different kind of legal question arose in Case 345/82 *Wünsche Handelsgesellschaft* v. *Federal Republic of Germany*. The subject was a Commission regulation whereby, to afford protection against imports of tinned mushrooms from Taiwan, a licence was introduced and its issue made subject to the payment of a levy.[181]

However, in the initial implementing regulation made by the Council, the only provision expressly made was for the complete or partial introduction of a licensing system, with a schedule of minimum prices.[182] The text of the regulation gave no authority to levy an additional sum when licences were issued, nor were any restrictions placed on their issue. The complainant therefore alleged that the Commission had exceeded its authority. But the Court replied, with reference to an earlier judgment[183]:

> "It should be recalled in that regard that, as the Commission has pointed out, the Court, in its judgment of 13 May 1971 in a case concerning protective measures on the importation of dessert apples (Joined Cases 41 to 44/70 *International Fruit Company NV and others* v. *Commission* [1971] E.C.R. 411, at p. 427), held as follows:

---

[180] *Op. cit.*, footnote 178, p. 142, para. 14.
[181] [1984] E.C.R. 1995 *et seq.*
[182] *Op. cit.*, footnote 181, p. 2011, para. 22 and p. 1997 in the summary of facts.
[183] *Op. cit.*, footnote 181, 2011, para. 23.

'Since the Commission was entitled to take protective measures leading to a complete suspension of imports from third countries, it was, *a fortiori*, entitled to adopt less restrictive measures.' "

Advocate-General Rozès took a different view in these proceedings, arguing that the levy was not one of the methods expressly prescribed in the regulation. She concluded that no sufficient authority existed for the protective measure adopted by the Commission.[184]

In Case 109/79 *Maïseries de Beauce* v. *ONIC*, however, the Court found that the terms of the basic regulation had been exceeded.[185] This case brings us back to the complications of the monetary compensation system. The complainant attacked the way in which the monetary compensation amounts for certain processed maize products had been calculated. In the case in question, the total amount of compensation payable on the subsidiary products was higher than it would have been on the requisite quantity of maize.[186] A possible monetary advantage on the primary product would therefore have been over-compensated, to the detriment of trade in processed products.

The recitals to Regulation 974/71 nevertheless made it clear that the compensatory amounts must not be higher than are absolutely necessary in order to eliminate the impact of the monetary measures on the prices of the basic product.[187] From this principle that the monetary compensation is neutral, also expressed elsewhere in Regulation 974/71, the Court concludes[188]:

"Undoubtedly it is difficult in certain cases to determine the precise incidence which the monetary compensation amount fixed on the basic product has on the price of each of the derived products whose price depends on that of the basic product and in this respect, as has been stated, the Commission enjoys a wide discretion. One of the limits to that discretion however is the ceiling which prevents the sum of the monetary compensatory amounts on the products derived from a certain quantity of a basic product from exceeding the monetary compensatory amount on the quantity of the basic product from which they are obtained."

---

[184] *cf. op. cit.*, footnote 181, p. 2022 with references and pp. 2019–2020.
[185] [1980] E.C.R. 2883 at 2912, para. 41. See also Case 145/79 *Roquette Frères* v. *France (customs administration)* [1980] E.C.R. 2917 at 2937, para. 14 and 2942, para. 32.
[186] *cf. op. cit.*, footnote 185, pp. 2888 *et seq.* of the summary of facts.
[187] See *op. cit.*, footnote 185, p. 2904, para. 18.
[188] *cf. op. cit.*, footnote 185, p. 2909, para. 32.

Since this had occurred in the case at issue, the Court decided[189]:

> "The reply to the question submitted should therefore be that by adopting in various successive implementing regulations, in particular Regulation No. 938/77, a system for the calculation of the monetary compensatory amounts on products processed from maize and whose price depends on that of maize which results in establishing for the various products obtained by processing a given quantity of maize in a specific manufacturing process monetary compensatory amounts the sum of which amounts to a figure clearly in excess of that of the monetary compensatory amount fixed for that given quantity of maize, the Commission has infringed the basic regulation, Regulation No. 974/71 of the Council of 12 May 1971, and Article 43(3) of the Treaty."

The regulation issued by the Commission involved two infringements: first, of the basic regulation and secondly, of Article 43(3) of the EEC Treaty. The latter infringement, the Court explained, was a continuing and systematic over-taxation of a category of products, contrary to the rule in Article 43(3) of the Treaty, that: "such an organization (must ensure) conditions for trade within the Community similar to those existing in a national market."[190]

Here one must bear in mind that the monetary compensation amounts are levied at the internal frontiers of the Community, and such a levy must be for a purpose stated in Article 43(3b) of the EEC Treaty and must itself be financially neutral.[191] This decision by the Court also shows that in an individual case, there may be several limits to discretion in a single area.

(b) How executive discretion is constrained by general principles of law

There is one further constraint on executive freedom. Like the Council when it regulates the market, the Commission, when adopting executive measures, may not infringe general principles of law. This has already been explained in connection with the law of market organisation. The details and modifications of the principle are covered in the various

---

[189] *Op. cit.*, footnote 185, p. 2912, para. 41.
[190] *Op. cit.*, footnote 185, p. 2912, para. 40 (continued from p. 2911).
[191] The Court has commented specifically on this, *op. cit.*, footnote 185, p. 2907, para. 25.

separate chapters, and only its general application need be discussed here.

The principle of equality and the ban against discrimination frequently encounter evaluation, weighting and imposition functions which substantially reduce their effectiveness as legal protection for Market citizens. The proportionality of the measures adopted is always important where powers of intervention are created or used.[192] One query raised regarding the protective measures in the cases mentioned above was whether they were "necessary." Particular problems arise in connection with legal certainty and the protection of legitimate expectations. Because the agricultural law system has to be both reliable and flexible, there is often an area of tension which generates many legal disputes. In the past ten years monetary compensation—levied against many traders, but to the advantage of many others—has proved especially controversial. This is already clear from the decisions referred to here.

(c) Concluding comments on executive freedom in policy-making

The major burden of executive legislation lies with the Commission, which has wide scope for assessment and discretionary judgment. Although these powers are limited by the Treaty, by the particular source of authority and general principles of law, the resulting executive decisions have been found invalid in practice only in certain extreme cases. The Court exercises its review powers with varying degrees of strictness, and no generalisation can be offered on this.

A process of judicial control may be initiated by looking at certain features of the source of authority which are open to objective scrutiny. But whenever the need arises to evaluate economic facts and make predictions, the Court will go no further than deciding whether there has been any misuse of powers, any obvious transgression of the bounds of discretion or any obvious error. This will always, to some extent, involve a judgment on the performance of the administration. It must be remembered, however, that laws are being made which will necessarily include definitions of categories and financial arrangements, and these may well result, in individual cases, in a denial of justice. There are tighter constraints on discretion when the Member States have to apply this law. It

---

[192] See also the interesting comments by Advocate-General Rozès in Case 272/81 *Société RU-MI* v. *FORMA* [1982] E.C.R. 4167 at 4190, on the limits to a test of proportionality where complex economic situations have to be evaluated.

must also be remembered that the rules made by the executive merely translate into practice what the market organisations have already prescribed. The legal constraints which apply in individual cases therefore depend largely on the market organisations themselves. Where the Council opts for delegating broad powers to the Commission, it is seeking to ensure that the agricultural market will be administered efficiently and flexibly. This is quite unobjectionable from a legal point of view.

As a matter of legal policy, there cannot be any fundamental objection to the wide executive discretion which the Commission often enjoys. To argue that the authorities should be able to intervene in agricultural markets amounts to accepting that the legal fetters placed on the executing agencies will not be over-constrictive, given the complexity of the matters which they have to regulate. It is not possible to frame in advance rules to cover every conceivable situation.

Moreover, over-narrow legal constraints would reduce the flexibility of the administration, thereby reducing its effectiveness, and this would undermine the usefulness of market intervention by the public authorities. Hence it is in the interest of efficient operation of the markets, and therefore ultimately in the interest of the traders concerned, for the Commission to enjoy considerable freedom of evaluation and decision-making when implementing agricultural law. Nothing would be achieved by trying to mitigate the severities which occur under the present system through even more comprehensive and intensive legislation. Not only is the common market in agriculture already overburdened in the matter of agricultural law, but constantly changing legislation would involve a considerable loss of legal certainty for Market citizens in planning their affairs.

On the whole it is true to say that the Court focuses chiefly on the substance of the Commission's measures, and that formal and procedural complaints tend to play a subsidiary role. Complaints not infrequently centre on the obligation to furnish reasons, but even here the Court allows the Commission to confine itself to general explanations dealing only with the essential points of a decision.

4. How the Member States implement agricultural law

(a) Preliminary observation

The application of agricultural law to individual cases is a matter for the

Member States. It is they who are chiefly responsible for incorporating the marketing systems into administrative practice. We have already referred to this process of implementing agricultural law as indirect execution. "Execution" should be understood both in the sense of the "performance" of the Community's agricultural law through national legislation and in the sense of "application to individual cases."[193] This terminology, which relates to the way in which governments approach the implementation of the law, is to be distinguished from the difference between indirect and direct effect. Direct effect is the process of applying a Community rule to an individual case; indirect effect is the operation of an intervening national rule. This is a distinction drawn from the legal basis of national administrative conduct.

(b) How States exercise scope for decision-making

When considering the legal constraints under which national administrations must operate in their implementation of agricultural law, it is necessary to begin with the various ways in which the Member States may exercise their discretionary powers of judgment and decision-making. The legal conduct of States falls into two categories, rule-making and special acts. Where the Member States enact legal rules for the purpose of administering the common market in agriculture, the question arises to what extent they enjoy legislative discretion, and what legal limits there are to this discretion (see **c**). The problem of administrative discretion, however, will arise only in specific cases. The application of Community agricultural law to these cases is, essentially, what the agricultural market is all about. Because so many Community citizens are affected by it and because it covers so many subjects, it is a massive operation. On their own, the Community institutions would be unable to guarantee proper administration of the law; they must decentralise and allocate tasks to the Member States. The performance of these tasks on a decentralised basis is not, therefore, a sign that full integration is still wanting. It is, rather, a rational form of the division of labour, even in the longer term.[194]

---

[193] cf. M. Zuleeg, *Das Recht der Europäischen Gemeinschaften im innerstaatlichen Bereich*, KSE Vol. 9, Cologne/Berlin/Bonn/Munich 1969, pp. 47 *et seq.*

[194] cf. V. Götz, *Probleme des Verwaltungsrechts auf dem Gebiet des gemeinsamen Agrarmarktes*, EuR 1986, pp. 29 *et seq.* (32 *et seq.*).

However, the sheer number of agricultural regulations and the different ways in which administrations are organised and operate in the Member States lead to many conflicts in practice. The case law on administrative and executive problems applicable to individual cases in the common market in agriculture is particularly abundant.

Some selection from among these cases is therefore inevitable. A key criterion in this selection is how the cases demonstrate the kind of problems which tend to occur when seeking to achieve maximum uniformity in the implementation of Community law (see **d**).

(c) The legal constraints on rule-making in the Member States

The scope of Community farm rules may not be altered by either formal or substantive rules within the Member States,[195] This is the decisive principle where legislation by the Member States is concerned. Below we describe how it has developed and been applied in practice.

(aa) The enactment of "substantive" agricultural law by the Member States

The above principle is the outcome of a complex process of investigation[196] which impinges on significant areas of agricultural policy, marking the boundary between the legislative competence of the Community and that of Member States. For the purpose of this study, we need only describe in brief the division of powers from which result the freedom and lack of freedom, respectively, of Member States when legislating for agriculture. It is first necessary to distinguish between sectors in which there is already a common market organisation and other areas in which there is none. Where a common market organisation is in operation, the Member States are essentially deprived of all power to legislate in that

---

[195] The Court's case law is consistent on this point. See, for instance, Case 40/69 *Hauptzollamt Hamburg* v. *Bollmann* [1970] E.C.R. 69 at 79, paras. 4 and 5; Case 49/71 *Hagen* v. *Einfuhr- und Vorratsstelle für Getreide und Futtermittel* [1972] E.C.R. 23 at 34, para. 6; Case 94/77 *Fratelli Zerbone* v. *Amministrazione delle Finanze dello Stato* [1978] E.C.R. 99 at 115, paras. 22 to 27; Case 265/78 *Ferwerda BV* v. *Produktschap voor Vee en Vlees* [1980] E.C.R. 617 at 630, para. 13. See also R. Voss, *Nationale Vorschriften zur Durchführung des EWG-Rechts im Bereich des Zoll- und Agrarverwaltungsrechts*. R/W/AWD 1979, p. 659.

[196] See R. Boest, *Die Agrarmärkte im Recht der EWG*, Baden-Baden 1984, p. 261 and p. 272 "a pragmatic approach, geared to individual cases."

particular area. They may act only where expressly permitted to do so by Community law.[197]

In Case 111/76 *Officier van Justitie* v. *Van de Hazel* the Court decided, with regard to a national decision on the setting of quotas for the slaughtering of poultry[198]:

> "Once the Community has, pursuant to Article 40 of the Treaty, legislated for the establishment of the common organization of the market in a given sector, Member States are under an obligation to refrain from taking any measure which might undermine or create exceptions to it."

The Court explained this further in Case 83/78 *Pigs Marketing Board* v. *Redmond*, which dealt with a marketing system (the Pigs Marketing Scheme) which operated in Northern Ireland[199]:

> "With a view to applying that statement in the case of the Pigs Marketing Scheme it should be borne in mind that the common organization of the market in pigmeat, like the other common organizations, is based on the concept of an open market to which every producer has free access and the functioning of which is regulated solely by the instruments provided for by that organization."

Exceptionally, the Member States may make supplementary regulations, where Community law expressly authorises them to do so. However, their powers in this respect are very narrow, as far as can be seen from the case law. And even here the Court has placed the Member States under the obligation to adhere to Community regulations.[200]

Where there is no common market organisation, the Member States may of course set up market organisations of their own, but they remain bound by the general principles of the Treaty.[201] As the Court has decided in Case 68/76, the absence of a Community market organisation does not

---

[197] R. Boest comments in detail on this, *op. cit.*, footnote 196, p. 286 with additional references.

[198] [1977] E.C.R. 901 at 909, para. 13; also Case 148/85 *Direction générale des impôts* v. *Forest* [1986] E.C.R. 3449, para. 14, and Case 130/85 *Wulro B.V.* [1986] E.C.R. 2035, para. 21.

[199] [1978] E.C.R. 2347 at 2371, paras. 56 to 57.

[200] *cf.* Case 74/69 *Hauptzollamt Bremen* v. *Krohn* [1970] E.C.R. 451 *et seq.*

[201] Here reference should also be made to the careful analysis in R. Boest, *op. cit.*, footnote 196, p. 255 *et seq.*, esp. pp. 259 *et seq.* See also Case 148/85 *Direction générale des impôts* v. *Forest* [1986] E.C.R. 3449, para. 14.

amount to a legal vacuum, "since Articles 39 to 46 of the Treaty remain applicable."[202]

Having to observe the general provisions of the Treaty makes it virtually impossible for the Member States to set up national market organisations of a regulatory kind, because this would, almost inevitably, interfere with the external trade of the Community. It is forbidden, under Articles 9 and 30 of the EEC Treaty, to interfere with the trade of other Member States; and Article 113 rules that trade with non-Member countries is to be handled by the Community itself. The same principles apply to individual measures in favour of agriculture. They must also be compatible with the general provisions of the Treaty, and especially with the rules on the free circulation of goods.[203]

(bb) The enactment of "formal" implementing law

(1) Competence

"Competence" in this connection means the capacity of the national implementing agencies to formulate rules. This is a power which lies with the Member States.

We see this in Joined Cases 51–54/71 *International Fruit Company* v. *Produktschap voor Groenten en Fruit*. Here the Court also explained the starting point for Community law[204]:

> "Although under Article 5 of the Treaty the Member States are obliged to take all appropriate measures, whether general or particular, to ensure fulfilment of the obligations arising out of the Treaty, it is for them to determine which institutions within the national system shall be empowered to adopt the said measures.
> The answer to the first question must therefore be that when provisions of the Treaty or of regulations confer power or impose obligations upon the States for the purposes of the implementation of Community law the question of how the exercise of such powers and the fulfilment of such obligations may be entrusted by Member States to specific national bodies is solely a matter for the constitutional system of each State."

---

[202] Case 68/76 *Commission* v. *France* [1977] E.C.R. 515 at 531, paras. 20 to 23.
[203] See R. Boest, *op. cit.*, footnote 196, pp. 274 *et seq.*
[204] [1971] E.C.R. 1107 *et seq.*, at 1115–1116, paras. 3 and 4.

However, the Court's judgment in Case 31/78 *Bussone* v. *Italian Ministry of Agriculture* appears to suggest that the Community may, within certain limits, regulate such organisational matters itself.[205] The question at issue was whether a provision in the common market system for eggs made it compulsory for the public authorities to issue quality stamps, or whether the Member States had a free hand in the matter.[206]

It might have been expected that the Court would begin by referring to the principle in the *International Fruit* decision, omitting any detailed analysis of the provisions of the regulation, and would conclude that matters of administrative organisation are to be decided exclusively by the Member States. But the Court took a somewhat different approach[207]:

"From a comparison and joint interpretation of the first sub-paragraph of Article 17(1) and Article 26 of Regulation (EEC) No. 2772/75 and Article 5 of Regulation (EEC) No. 95/69 it is clear that those provisions do not reserve to the public authorities the exclusive right to affix the marking and to prepare and distribute labels, but that they leave the Member States entirely at liberty to entrust the organisation of and the detailed rules for supervision to the agency which they regard as being the most suitable in their internal order to carry out that task.

The discretionary power held by the Member States in this respect by virtue of the aforesaid provisions authorises them to entrust exclusively to the public authorities the preparation and distribution of bands and labels.

The first question should be answered to that effect."

This shows that certain Community arrangements for market administration are not necessarily excluded. Even the Advocate-General did not query the central issue; he spoke merely of a "relatively wide discretion" of the Member States to regulate the organisation and methods of quality control under the market organisation for eggs.[208]

In this case, however, the Court may have been relying on the actual text of the Community regulation and not seeking to pronounce on

---

[205] [1978] E.C.R. 2429 *et seq.*
[206] See the comments in the summary of facts, *op. cit.*, footnote 205, pp. 2433 *et seq.*
[207] *Op. cit.*, footnote 205, pp. 2441–2442, paras. 9 to 11.
[208] See *op. cit.*, footnote 205, p. 2451.

matters of principle. If so, its statement in the *International Fruit* case would remain valid.

Nevertheless, the discretion of Member States to set up appropriate executing agencies is limited by Article 5 of the EEC Treaty in the sense that a completely unsuitable administrative organisation would give rise to a breach of the Treaty.[209]

In practice, differences in treatment which stem from differences in procedural law from one Member State to another are much more significant and more difficult to resolve. Points of conflict between national and Community law are much more frequent in matters of procedure than in matters of organisation.[210]

(2) *The freedom of States to decide in procedural law matters*

In principle, the Member States are free to decide how their executives will act in any particular instance.

However, the Community maxim is that the scope of Community rules cannot be altered. What this means in practice will become clear from the examples which follow. They show that, unlike in the organisational field, in procedural law there are many elements of a Community system but distinct limits on its future development. Why are common principles of procedure necessary in this field?

In a material sense, Market citizens may obtain a range of benefits, such as subsidies and grants, available under the agricultural law system. On the other hand, they are also expected to contribute to it, through levies or deposits. The system can become legally effective only if there are also rules governing time limits, the impact of administrative decisions or the formal requirements to be observed.[211] Particularly important are the monitoring procedures to ensure compliance with intervention and subsidy rules. Not only do they prevent unwarranted use of Community resources; they also safeguard the principle of Community

---

[209] See Advocate-General Reischl *op. cit.*, footnote 205, p. 2452; *cf.* also Case 31/69 *Commission* v. *Italy* [1970] E.C.R. 25 on a charge that the Treaty had been infringed because the national arrangements for executing it were unsuitable. The Commission's complaint under Article 169 was dismissed as unfounded, however.

[210] See R. Boest, *op. cit.*, footnote 196, p. 288.

[211] On the "indirect conflicts" which may occur in this area, see K. E. Huthmacher, *Der Vorrang des Gemeinschaftsrechts bei indirekten Kollisionen*, Cologne/Berlin/Bonn/Munich 1985, pp. 192 *et seq.*

financing of agricultural spending, which is the cause of substantial financial transfers among the Member States. Both in practice and in policy, financial solidarity can be sustained only if all Member States strictly uphold the rules concerned.[212] The same is true when levies are raised which contribute to the Community budget.

In principle, the Member States are responsible for determining what information must be supplied to prove that the conditions for payment of a benefit are met.[213] To a large extent, however, these formalities are governed by Community law itself. The exclusion of national law is so far-reaching that a rule made by a Member State will not be admitted even if it would be more effective than the Community rule[214]:

"In these circumstances it is not necessary to consider the soundness of the German Government's argument that the supervision system set up in the Federal Republic is more effective than that provided for in Article 3 of Regulation No. 990/72. In fact, the provisions of Community regulations must be uniformly applied in all the Member States and have, so far as possible, the same effect throughout the territory of the Community. The position is no different where a regulation lays down specific measures of supervision but leaves to Member States the task of ensuring their observance by appropriate administrative measures."

When imposing Community taxes (*e.g.* levies and monetary compensatory amounts) the Member States are forbidden to make their own rules to alter the basis of calculation, the conditions under which they are payable and the sums involved.[215] The payment of benefits in an individual case must be based on a Community rule, even where the payment would appear mandatory on grounds of equity. In Case 18/72 *Granaria* v. *Hoofdproduktschap voor Veevoeder*[216] the Court laid down:

---

[212] See below in this section, on the Community sanction for misapplication of the provisions of Community law regarding liability for payments. See also O. Gottsmann, *op. cit.*, footnote 161, Article 40, pp. 410 *et seq. Ibid.*, *op. cit.*, p. 408, no. 11 on financial solidarity.

[213] *cf.* Case 6/71 *Rheinmühlen* v. *Einfuhr- und Vorratsstelle für Getreide und Futtermittel* [1971] E.C.R. 719 at 837, paras. 8 and 9; Joined Cases 205–215/82 *Deutsche Milchkontor* v. *Bundesrepublik Deutschland* [1983] E.C.R. 2633 at 2677, paras. 42 and 43.

[214] Case 819/79 *Germany* v. *Commission* [1981] E.C.R. 21 at 35, para. 10.

[215] See R. Boest, *op. cit.*, footnote 196, 293 with further references.

[216] [1972] E.C.R. 1163 at 1171, paras. 15 to 17.

> "Neither Regulation No. 120/67 nor any other provisions of Community law envisage the possibility of the national authorities of a Member State granting exemption from the obligation to pay the levy.
>
> Since, in accordance with Article 189 of the Treaty, this regulation has general application and is binding in its entirety, Member States may not, in the absence of a provision of Community law to the contrary, have recourse to national measures capable of modifying its application.
>
> Where the import of agricultural products subject to the levy system involves their being put into free circulation in the Community, exemption from the levy granted by a Member State by national measures is contrary to the distribution of powers between the Member States and the Community."

It can hardly be disputed that, on grounds of equity, it is sometimes necessary to refrain from levying dues; this has led to a whole series of Community rules under which national authorities are permitted to decide whether a particular levy will be made. This, of course, leads to problems of implementation, examples of which will be discussed below. Other problems arise where traders fail to comply with their obligations under Community law. These include the rules on the forfeiture of deposits payable under existing licensing systems and the refunding of incorrectly paid Community subsidies. As regard the deposits, it has already been explained that if the licence conditions are not observed, they are automatically forfeited. There are conclusive Community law provisions on this point.

The question of reclaiming subsidies advanced in error is a different and highly complex matter. Disputes arising in this field are governed by Article 8 of Regulation 729/70, under which Member States must claim repayment of any subsidy paid in error. There is no room for discretion in the text of Article 8. In German law, this rule conflicts with section 48(1) of the Law on Administrative Procedure, which states that public authorities have discretion to decide whether a measure is to be withdrawn. There is a reference in section 48(2) to the need to protect legitimate expectations. Apart from this, there are fixed time limits after which an administrative decision may no longer be withdrawn.

These time limits are calculated in different ways in the various Member States, so that the absence of any Community ruling in this field can lead to considerable disparities in implementation. In legal literature, such a lack of uniformity in the practice of Community law is treated as an "indirect conflict."[217] It is described as indirect because the actual subjects covered by the rules do not conflict, but rather, the arrangements in different Member States for applying them, with the result that Community law may not have the same force everywhere. The "conflict" is between looking for uniformity in Community law and finding that the administrations in the Member States are applying it differently. "Conflicts" of this kind frequently arise when subsidies incorrectly paid are reclaimed.

There is another aspect, a financial one, of reclaiming incorrectly paid subsidies, and this is referred to by the code-word "charging."[218] Articles 2 and 3 of Regulation 729/70 on the financing of the common agricultural policy stipulate that the Member States may be given refunds from the European Agricultural Guidance and Guarantee Fund only as long as their disbursements are in accordance with Community law. Unlawful payments will be charged against national budgets. Hence it is the Member States which bear the risks of making an incorrect application of Community agricultural law. The extent of the risk depends chiefly on the degree to which the decisions of Member States are governed by Community law. The less room they have for manoeuvre, the more they will naturally tend to breach the principles of legality. This problem area has generated many contentious cases before the European Court, and some of these clearly demonstrate the urgency of establishing an all-European system of administrative law.

Finally, there is the question of the refunding of duties wrongly levied.[219] Where Community levies unlawfully paid have to be refunded, the method of doing so is determined by Community law, and the Court proceeds according to the general principle of unjustified enrichment. However, national levies paid contrary to Community law must be refunded according to the rules of the Member State concerned, with the result that differing methods of refunding will inevitably lead to disparity of treatment.

(*d*) *Selected examples from the case law on problems associated with the application of agricultural law at national level*

The survey which follows attempts to illustrate the key problems

---

[217] See the study by K. E. Huthmacher (footnote 211).
[218] See Gottsmann, *op. cit.*, footnote 161.
[219] There is a detailed comment in R. Boest, *op. cit.*, footnote 196, pp. 299 *et seq.*

involved in implementation by national authorities, so that the effect of legal constraints in the final stage of operation of Community law will be easier to grasp. Reference will also be made to the possible drawbacks of uniform methods of implementation, arising from the different legal constraints under which these authorities operate.

(aa) Definition of terms

The use of undefined terms can in itself lead to unequal treatment in the implementation of the Community's agricultural law rules. For example, the undefined term "force majeure" has been pondered by the Court in a number of cases.[220] We have already referred to the meaning of "force majeure" in the context of the very strict licensing system and have also mentioned certain guidelines set by the Court for the interpretation of the term in individual cases. The following case should serve to illustrate the problem.

In Case 4/68 *Firma Schwarzwaldmilch GmbH* v. *Einfuhr- und Vorratsstelle für Fette*, a quantity of skimmed milk powder had not been delivered from France to Germany owing to machine failure.[221] We should note that this case occurred during the transitional period, when the Commission was still able to take protective measures within the Community. The licensing system served to provide the necessary data-base for the application of market-protection measures. In principle, this licensing system operated exactly like the one described above for the cereals market, *i.e.* if the obligation to import within the prescribed time limit was not complied with, the deposit paid was forfeited, unless performance had been prevented by *force majeure*. In the case in question the national authority, the German importing and storage agency for cereals, contested the existence of a circumstance of *force majeure*.

The relevant regulation stated, in Article 6 (3), that[222]:

> Cases of *force majeure* within the meaning of paragraph (2) may result from the following circumstances:

---

[220] *cf.* Case 4/68 *Firma Schwarzwaldmilch GmbH* v. *Einfuhr- und Vorratsstelle für Fette* [1968] E.C.R. 377. On the duty of Member States to inform the Commission if they are treating as cases of *force majeure* any circumstances not covered in the Community regulation, see Case 36/70 *Getreide Import GmbH* v. *Einfuhr- und Vorratsstelle für Getreide und Futtermittel* [1970] E.C.R. 1107. On the term itself, see Case 3/74 *Einfuhr- und Vorratsstelle für Getreide* v. *Pfützenreuter* [1974] E.C.R. 589 at 598, para. 8.

[221] See [1968] E.C.R. 377 at 379 in the summary of facts.

[222] See *op. cit.*, footnote 221, p. 565 in the summary of facts.

(a) war and civil disturbance
(b) a government ban on exports or imports
(c) restrictions imposed on navigation by acts of sovereignty,
(d) shipwreck
(e) mechanical failure, damage to vessel or damage to cargo
(f) strikes
(g) shipping hold-up in periods of icing-up or low water.

In paragraph 4, it was stated that Member States were bound to inform the Commission of their intention to treat circumstances other than those in paragraph 3 as circumstances of *force majeure*.[223]

In its first question, the court of first instance at Frankfurt queried whether "mechanical failure" within the meaning of subparagraph (e) included damage to dairy machines.

The Court replied that the term "mechanical failure," because it occurred in a series of other shipping problems, and because there was a similar rule in another regulation, did not refer to damage to production plant but only to means of transport. Hence damage to the machines intended for the production of the goods was not "mechanical failure" within the meaning of Article 6, paragraph 3(e) of the regulation in question.[224]

However, the list of circumstances of *force majeure* in paragraph 3 is not exhaustive. The Court, referring to the recitals of the regulation, found that this list was intended only to furnish examples of significant cases of *force majeure* and did not mean that other circumstances not mentioned in it were necessarily to be excluded.[225]

Since the situation arising for decision by the Frankfurt court did not fall under paragraph 3 of the regulation, the next question was what other circumstances might qualify as "force majeure." In the following extracts from the grounds of judgment, it must be borne in mind that the Court, in proceedings under Article 177 of the EEC Treaty, may offer only abstract guidelines for interpretation and cannot itself resolve the issue. However, the abstract framework within which the national courts must decide also limits the executive's freedom of decision. The more precisely the Court defines the terms, the more exact will be the standards of scrutiny by the

---

[223] See Case 36/70 *Getreide Import GmbH* v. *Einfuhr- und Vorratsstelle für Getreide und Futtermittel* [1970] E.C.R. 1107 at 1114, para. 5: the communication does not constitute authority, but has only declaratory force.
[224] *Op. cit.*, footnote 221, p. 385 of the judgment.
[225] *Op. cit.*, footnote 221, p. 387 of the judgment; see also opinion of Advocate-General Gand, p. 389.

courts of the Member States, and the tighter the legal constraints on national courts will eventually be.

The Court began its answer to the question about the meaning of "force majeure" by saying[226]:

> "Article 6 (2) provides that the obligation to import is cancelled where the importation cannot be effected during the term of validity of the licence owing to *force majeure*.
>
> As the concept of *force majeure* is not identical in the different branches of law and the various fields of application, the significance of this concept must be determined on the basis of the legal framework within which it is intended to take effect."

In his opinion, Advocate-General Gand had also referred to the specific legal context and rejected the idea that there could be a general standard of definition.[227]

The Court then continues[228]:

> "Thus the interpretation of the concept of *force majeure* used in the regulation in question must take into account the particular nature of the relationships in public law between the importers and the national administration, as well as the objectives of that regulation.
>
> The public interest, which requires the most accurate forecast possible of the future development of imports in each Member State and warrants the lodging of a deposit on the issue of an import licence, must be reconciled with the need, which is also a matter of public interest, for trade between States to remain unhampered by obligations which are too rigid.
>
> The threat of the loss of the deposit is intended to encourage the importers to whom a licence has been issued to fulfil the obligation to import and thus to ensure the accuracy of the forecast of the future development of imports in the general interest.
>
> It follows therefore that an importer who has shown the necessary diligence is in principle released from the obligation to import within the meaning of Article 6 of Regulation No. 136/64/EEC when circumstances outside his control make it impossible for him to effect the importation within the required period.

[226] *Op. cit.*, footnote 221, p. 395 of the judgment.
[227] *cf. op. cit.*, footnote 221, p. 392, preceded by a comparative law study.
[228] *Op. cit.*, footnote 221, p. 385 of the judgment.

Such is the case when the event which renders impossible the performance in due time of a contract which, under normal circumstances, ought to have enabled the importer to fulfil his obligation to import, is so unusual that it would have had to be considered as improbable by a prudent businessman exercising all due care.

Some of the cases enumerated in Article 6(3) appear to be based on this criterion, as they do not refer to situations corresponding to a concept of *force majeure* in the sense of absolute impossibility, but to unusual difficulties which are independent of the will of importers and which arise during the performance of the contracts.

However, recognition of a case of *force majeure* presupposes not only the occurrence of an unusual event but also that the consequences of that event could not be avoided, as for example where an importer could have obtained the goods elsewhere within the period stipulated.

In this respect, too, the importer must be expected to show all due diligence.

This being so, *force majeure* is established if the importer could only have effected the importation within the period stipulated by replacing the goods at an excessive loss taking into account, where necessary, any remedies available to him.

It must, therefore, be concluded that sufficient causal connection between the circumstances relied on as a case of *force majeure* and the failure to effect the importation must in principle be recognized when delivery in due time by the importer's supplier has become impossible within the meaning of the above definition, and when the importer can only obtain the goods elsewhere at an excessive loss.

Finally, it follows from the scheme of Article 6 of the regulation that it is for the importer to prove the existence of the circumstances necessary to constitute a case of *force majeure*"

The elements of the concept as developed by the Court—(a) an event which could not have been predicted by a prudent businessman and independent of his volition, and (b) having consequences which are avoidable only at disproportionate cost—leave room for the national authorities to make their own judgment, although the words "discretion" or "scope for appraisal" do not appear in the decision. What exactly this will mean in an individual case, and how much real scope for decision is left to the implementing authority, will be decided by the courts of the

Member States. As the Court said in reply to a question on that point in the same case[229]:

> "Within the limits of their own jurisdiction, therefore, national courts may recognize the existence of a case of *force majeure* not only when the situation relied on is included in those enumerated in Article 6(3), or when it has been recognized by the national authorities in accordance with Article 6(4), but also in other specific cases in which *force majeure* within the above mentioned exposition of the concept, justifies the application of the exemption referred to in Article 6(2).
>
> The effect of Article 6(4), which makes a general reference to the powers of the Member States, is not to limit the powers of the national courts in this respect."

The reference to the various national jurisdictions suggests, at least in theory, that the legal constraints on the administration may differ from one Member State to another, according to the prevailing review practices of the courts. In that case, uniformity of execution can be achieved only by imposing additional written formalities. This is borne out by a number of other court proceedings.[230]

This case had to do with the substantive conditions for *force majeure*; by comparison, Case 3/74 *Einfuhr- und Vorratsstelle für Getreide und Futtermittel* v. *Pfützenreuter* elucidates a procedural law aspect of the matter.[231] The court hearing the main action raised the question whether the application was time-bound, in view of circumstances of *force majeure*. The Court replied[232]:

> "Although, unlike subsequent regulations, Article 8 does not lay down a specific period within which a case of *force majeure* must be invoked, it is clear both from the wording of the Article and from the general scheme of the system initiated by the Regulation that the

---

[229] *Op. cit.*, footnote 221, p. 387 of the judgment.
[230] *cf.* Case 11/70 *Internationale Handelsgesellschaft* v. *Einfuhr- und Vorratsstelle für Getreide und Futtermittel* [1970] E.C.R. 1125, especially 1137, para. 23); Case 25/70 *Einfuhr- und Vorratsstelle für Getreide und Futtermittel* v. *Köster* [1970] E.C.R. 1161, especially 1177, para. 38; Case 158/73 *Firma E. Kampffmeyer* v. *Einfuhr- und Vorratsstelle für Getreide und Futtermittel* [1974] E.C.R. 101, especially 110, paras. 8 *et seq.*
[231] [1974] E.C.R. 589 *et seq.*
[232] *Op. cit.*, footnote 231, p. 599, paras. 10 and 11.

request must be made as soon as possible, preferably during the period of validity of the licence in question.

However, the case in point which has given rise to this reference clearly shows that it would be impossible to establish any strict and absolute rule in this matter, in view of the fact that a case of *force majeure* might possibly be invoked merely as a subsidiary point, if the party concerned considers that in the circumstances the conditions contained in the Regulation have been fulfilled.

It must be concluded that although Article 8 of Regulation 102/64 does not lay down any specified period for the introduction of a request for the consideration of circumstances of *force majeure*, it nevertheless requires the importers or exporters concerned to substantiate their claims in the fullest possible manner."

Here too, the chosen solution has a certain flexibility.

Case 49/71 *Hagen* v. *Einfuhr- und Vorratsstelle für Getreide und Futter-mittel* turned on the interpretation of the term "a valid offer" to the intervention agency.[233] In its first question, the referring court sought a decision from the European Court as to whether the terms "offer" and "offered," which are found in the relevant Community regulations, are to be interpreted in the same manner in all Member States.[234]

After some general comments on the significance of the intervention measures and the duty of intervention in some cases, the Court answered the question put to it[235]:

"As the obligation to intervene depends decisively on a prior offer, it is important that the concept of a valid offer and the conditions thereby involved shall apply throughout the Community, in order that the desired standardization of the conditions for intervention may be achieved. This requirement appears indispensable, not only because the Community authorities themselves determine those conditions, but also inasmuch as it is necessary to ensure that the additional conditions, which in certain cases the intervention agencies of each Member States are authorized to lay down, are compatible with the objectives of the intervention system. Terms used in Community law must be uniformly interpreted and implemented

[233] [1972] E.C.R. 23 *et seq.*
[234] *Op. cit.*, footnote 233, p. 34, para. 4.
[235] *Op. cit.*, footnote 233, p. 34, paras. 6 *et seq.*

throughout the Community, except when an express or implied reference is made to national law.

It follows, therefore, that although intervention agencies are empowered, under Article 5 of Regulation No. 1028/68 to adopt additional procedures and conditions for taking over, they cannot however derogate from the Community concept of an offer as contained in particular in Regulations Nos. 120/67 and 132/67.

It is appropriate therefore to reply that the terms "offer" and "offered," contained in Regulations Nos. 120/67, 132/67 and 1028/68, must be uniformly interpreted in the Member States, in accordance with the objectives of the intervention system laid down by those regulations."

The referring court put other questions relating to particulars of the original case, placing the concept of a valid offer in the context of the surrounding circumstances. But the final question was on a point of principle. The court inquired whether the Member States were permitted to enact provisions which differed from those of the Community as regards the methods of intervention and the making of offers for intervention, or to develop an administrative practice along different lines.

The Court's reply was unambiguous[236]:

"The provisions, the interpretation of which is requested, relate to essential factors in the common organization of the market in cereals. If the objectives of the common organization of the market are to be attained, the introduction of the intervention machinery must follow rules which are as uniform as possible, so as not to impede the free movement of cereals within the Community under normal market conditions.

In the absence of any clearly expressed intention on the part of the draftsmen of the Community regulations it cannot be considered permissible for Member States to derogate therefrom."

(bb) The remission of levies on grounds of equity

To achieve a balance, in the monetary compensation system, between the requirements of legal certainty and of protecting legitimate expectations, and the need for flexible and effective economic management, the

---

[236] *Op. cit.*, footnote 233, p. 38, paras. 25 *et seq.*

Commission enacted Regulation 1608/74, which enables the Member States to remit the monetary compensatory amounts in individual cases on grounds of equity. Before this, the Court had warded off attempts by the authorities in the Member States to mitigate certain hard cases by applying equity rules under domestic law. In several instances, however, the Court has also been concerned with the Community rules themselves.

From the viewpoint both of terminology and of theory, the most interesting case is Case 183/84 *Söhnlein Rheingold* v. *Hauptzollamt Wiesbanden*.[237] This is because notions of German administrative law were transposed to Community law and became the subject of discussion, having first been raised by the referring court (the Finance Court of Hesse) and the parties.

During the period November 1972 to March 1973, the plaintiff in the main action had contracted for the importation of table wine from France. In the period when the contracts were to be performed, the monetary compensatory amounts for this product were increased. This inevitably altered the basis on which the transaction had been calculated. The plaintiff accordingly requested remission of the monetary compensatory amounts equivalent to the amount of the increase, according to Articles 1 and 2 of Regulation 1608/74.

In Article 1 the Member States are authorised to remit the monetary compensation on grounds of equity, and in Article 2 the conditions are defined:

> "The authorization provided for an Article 1 may be made use of only at the request of the interested party and if such party at the time of making the request furnishes proof that:
>
> (a) in the case in question it is not necessary to levy the newly introduced or increased monetary compensation amount to compensate for the effects of the monetary measures referred to in that Article on the price of the product, and that
> (b) to levy such amount would constitute an excessive additional burden for him, which he could not avoid even taking all the necessary and normal care."

Confronted with an increase in the monetary compensatory amounts, the Government of the Federal Republic of Germany had given notice that it

---

[237] [1985] E.C.R. 3351 *et seq.*; also reproduced in DVBl. 1986, pp. 92 *et seq.*, with a note by C. H. Ule.

intended to make use of the authority conferred in Regulation 1608/74.[238] The plaintiff in the main proceedings therefore sought remission of the monetary compensation amounts, but this was refused. After an unsuccessful preliminary application the firm of Söhnlein applied to the Finance Court of Hesse, and one of the questions put by the latter court was:

> "Must Regulation (EEC) No. 1608/74 be interpreted as meaning that, where the relevant conditions are satisfied, a right to the waiver or the refund of monetary compensatory amounts exists, or do the Member States have discretion as regards not only the decision concerning the application in principle of the regulation but also the decision as to the waiver or refund in individual cases?"

The plaintiff in the main action had argued that the national authorities had no discretion in a particular case if the Member State in question had decided in principle to apply Regulation 1608/74. Rather, they were bound to implement the regulation strictly.

From the viewpoint of German law, Article 2 of the Regulation constitutes the factual element to which the principle has to be applied; the terms in it, being undefined, are in principle fully open to scrutiny by the competent courts, since the criteria for unlimited discretion, according to the theory of discretion as upheld in the Federal Republic of Germany, are not fulfilled.[239] Hence the question can also be put as follows: is the remission or refund of monetary compensatory amounts under Regulation 1608/74 binding on national authorities, or do they have discretion in the matter?

The Court replied by reiterating its previous findings on this point[240]:

> "It should be noted that Article 2 (2) leaves the competent national authorities a certain margin of discretion in determining whether the conditions required are or are not fulfilled. However, once it is accepted that the conditions are in fact fulfilled, the competent authority has no power to refuse the waiver or refund."

This means, first, that in each individual case the administration must consider whether the conditions are met ("equity, not required, excessive

---

[238] *cf.* the summary of facts in DVBl. 1986, p. 92.
[239] *cf.* Ule, *op. cit.*, footnote 237, p. 94.
[240] *Op. cit.*, footnote 237, p. 3361, para. 24.

additional burden" etc.); second, that it is free to judge whether this is the case, but if it is, it will have no further latitude in determining the legal consequences which arise.

As to whether the Court has followed the logic of the German theory of discretion, the answer must be an emphatic "no." Although the Court recognises that there is "freedom of appraisal" where the facts of the case are concerned, it uses the term in the context of the existing prerogative of appraising the facts which the executive already possesses. Nor is this based on any notion modelled on German administrative law. The plaintiff in the main action had apparently assumed this was so when arguing that the national authorities had no "discretion" to make a remission on grounds of equity, if the Member States had already decided in principle to apply Regulation 1608/74. For according to the case law of the European Court, the Member States would have only "a margin of discretion." The plaintiff considered that this margin had already been fully exploited when the decision was made in principle. Not only is this a misconception, since the matter will always be resolved by the competent authority investigating the individual case, but the theory cannot be applied as it stands to an individual case. The Court comments on this point both in this case and in the cases previously settled on the question of remission on grounds of equity.

The Commission took the view that the problem was merely one of terminology. The decisive question was whether the executive, in applying the equity clause to an individual case, had a decision-making power open only to a limited measure of scrutiny. It did have "discretion," as the Commission called it.[241] Advocate-General Mancini also thought that the national authorities had a discretion of this kind.[242]

There is no suggestion, in this case law, that the Court treats undefined terms as fully open to the scrutiny of the courts. This is already an indication that the European Court has a different approach to the review of executive decisions from that of the German administrative courts. Its approach is much more akin to the flexible review practice of the French Conseil d'Etat, to which reference has already been made in the comparative law survey.

A glance at the consequences shows the relevance of this finding to the future development of a European administrative law system.

The judgment of the European Court is an interpretation, of general validity, of Regulation 1608/74. It is for the national courts to apply it to

---

[241] cf. DVBl. 1986, p. 92 no. 22.
[242] Op. cit., footnote 237, p. 3354.

individual cases. For a German administrative court, Article 2 of Regulation 1608/74, if viewed in an exclusively "domestic" light, is full of undefined terms which a court may examine, whereas the European Court accepts that there is a measure of discretion in the matter.[243] The German approach would ensure more wide-ranging review than the Court's approach.

Since a national court, in proceedings under Article 177 of the EEC Treaty, is bound by a preliminary ruling, a German court must have regard to different, namely European, principles when applying undefined terms to an individual case, which would not be the situation in domestic law.

In German administrative law the strict division between undefined terms at the factual level and discretion where the legal consequences of a rule are concerned is set aside, at least partially, when Community law is applied to a particular case. It is replaced by the approach of the European Court, not a rigid one either in terminology or in theory, which treats scope for appraisal or discretion as being synonymous with free decision-making by the executive and subject only to the legal limits of misuse of powers, manifest error or obvious transgression of the bounds of discretion.

It is not surprising that German jurists have already raised the question whether the reduction of review powers might constitute a limitation of individual judicial protection which cannot be reconciled with Article 19, paragraph 4, of the Basic Law, and whether this might lead to the possibility of a conflict between the Federal Constitutional Court and the European Court. This question touches, broadly speaking, on the relationship between Community law and German constitutional law—a problem which we shall not examine further here.

From the viewpoint of administrative law, this case illustrates the possible objections to uniform legal constraints in the implementation of Community law and bears out the theory already advanced, that the true extent of any legal constraint becomes clear only in the course of a judicial investigation.

While the European Court, when reviewing direct administrative decisions by the Community authorities, can itself determine how far its review will go and to what extent the outcome will be affected, its views will not always be echoed when it comes to the binding effects of Community law when implemented indirectly by the Member States. Opinions will differ as to the form a judicial review of executive decisions

---

[243] See Ule, *op. cit.*, footnote 237, p. 94.

should take. And if, as in the case of the Federal Republic of Germany, ideas about judicial review are based on constitutional law principles, there is a very real risk of profound disagreement.

(cc) Reclaiming Community subsidies paid unlawfully

The decision below will show how a general principle of Community law affects the application of domestic law and how it exercises a controlling influence on administrative practice.

Joined cases 205–215/82 *Deutsche Milchkontor GmbH and others* v. *Federal Republic of Germany*[244] concerned a claim for refund of a subsidy for skimmed milk and skimmed milk powder used for animal feed, the powder being a product of Milchwerke Auetal-Beyer KG, on the basis that the recipients had not complied with the terms of the Community rules.[245]

On the applicability of Community law, the court in question, the Frankfurt administrative court, posed the question whether Article 8 of Council Regulation 729/70 of April 21, 1970 was a direct source of authority for the national agencies to seek a refund of wrongly-paid subsidies, in which case the factual conditions for making such a claim would be wholly governed by the regulation, or whether a decision at the national level was required for the claim to be effective. It was also asked whether, in the latter case, the application of domestic law would be subject to any restrictions.[246] The Court begins its reply by summarising the general principles of implementing Community law, with particular reference to agriculture. Because its statements on the question are so fundamental, they are reproduced here in full[247]:

> "According to the general principles on which the institutional system of the Community is based and which govern the relations between the Community and the Member States, it is for the Member States, by virtue of Article 5 of the Treaty, to ensure that Community regulations, particularly those concerning the common agricultural policy, are implemented within their territory. In so far as Community law, including its general principles, does not include

---

[244] [1983] E.C.R. 2633 *et seq.*
[245] See *op. cit.*, footnote 244, p. 2638 in the summary of facts.
[246] *cf. op. cit.*, footnote 244, p. 2664, para. 15.
[247] *Op. cit.*, footnote 244, p. 2665, paras. 17 *et seq.*

common rules to this effect, the national authorities when implementing Community regulations act in accordance with the procedural and substantive rules of their own national law; however, as the Court stated in its judgment of 6 June 1972 in Case 94/71 (*Schlüter & Mack* v. *Hauptzollamt Hamburg-Jonas* [1972] ECR 307), the rule must be reconciled with the need to apply Community law uniformly so as to avoid unequal treatment of producers and traders.

It is in this context, then, that Article 8(1) of Regulation 729/70 of the Council provides that 'in accordance with national provisions laid down by law, regulation or administrative action,' Member States must take the measures necessary to prevent and deal with irregularities affecting the operations of the European Agricultural Guidance and Guarantee Fund and to recover sums lost as a result of irregularities or negligence. Consequently the competent national authorities are bound to exercise all the supervision necessary to ensure that aids are granted only upon the conditions laid down by the Community regulations and that any infringement of the rules of Community law is appropriately penalized. At its present stage of development Community law does not include any specific provisions relating to the exercise of that supervision by the competent national authorities.

In accordance with those principles, the Court has repeatedly held (on 5 March 1980 in Case 265/78 *H. Ferwerda BV* v. *Produktschap voor Vee en Vlees* [1980] ECR 617, on 12 June 1980 in Joined Cases 119 and 126/79 *Lippische Hauptgenossenschaft eG and Another* v. *Bundesanstalt für landwirtschaftliche Marktordnung* [1980] ECR 1863 and on 6 May 1982 in Case 54/81 *Firma Wilhelm Froome* v. *Bundesanstalt für landwirtschaftliche Marktordnung* [1982] ECR 1449 and Joined Cases 146, 192 and 193/81 *Bay Wa AG and Others* v. *Bundesanstalt für landwirtschaftliche Marktordnung* [1982] ECR 1503) that in the absence of provisions of Community law disputes concerning the recovery of amounts unduly paid under Community law must be decided by national courts pursuant to their own national law subject to the limits imposed by Community law inasmuch as the rules and procedures laid down by national law must not have the effect of making it virtually impossible to implement Community regulations and national legislation must be applied in a manner which is not discriminatory compared to procedures for deciding similar but purely national disputes.

It follows that Article 8(1) of Regulation 729/70 does not govern the relations between the intervention agencies and the traders concerned and in particular it does not constitute a legal basis authorizing the national authorities to bring actions to recover unduly-paid aids from their recipients; such actions are governed by national law."

Having defined the field in which the law operates, the Court turned to the problem of the disparities of implementation which might arise among Member States as a result[248]:

"... the effect of such differences, which moreover in the present state of development of Community law are inevitable, is reduced by the limits to which the Court has subjected the application of national law in the decisions cited above.

In the first place the application of national law must not affect the scope and effectiveness of Community law. That would be the case in particular if the application of national law made it impossible in practice to recover sums irregularly granted. Furthermore, the exercise of any discretion to decide whether or not it would be expedient to demand repayment of Community funds unduly or irregularly granted would be inconsistent with the duty to recover such sums which Article 8(1) of Regulation No. 729/70 imposes on the national administration.

Secondly, national law must be applied in a manner which is not discriminatory compared to procedures for deciding similar but purely national disputes. This means first that in such cases the national authorities must act with the same degree of care as in comparable cases concerning solely the application of corresponding national legislation and in accordance with rules and procedures which do not make the recovery of the sums in question more difficult. Secondly, notwithstanding the principle referred to above that the exercise of any discretion to decide whether or not it is expedient to demand repayment is ruled out, the obligations imposed by national legislation on undertakings wrongly granted pecuniary advantages based on Community law must be no more stringent than those imposed on undertakings which have wrongly received similar advantages based on national law, provided that the two groups of recipients are in comparable situations and therefore different treatment is objectively unjustifiable."

---

[248] *Op. cit.*, footnote 244, pp. 2666 *et seq.*, paras. 21 *et seq.*

The only instrument which Community law has so far used for preventing wholly disparate rulings on demands for repayment of sums wrongly advanced is the principle that matters of Community interest are not to be treated differently from similar matters of domestic concern. The Court has taken a clear and unambiguous stance on this question, notwithstanding the difficulties of implementation in some cases.[249]

However, its statement that Article 8 of Regulation 729/70 precludes discretion requires closer consideration. The chief point to consider is the Court's statement that the exercise of discretion in deciding whether claiming repayment of subsidies paid without due reason is "expedient" cannot be reconciled with the obligation under Article 8 to seek repayment. Hence discretionary judgment is precluded by Article 8 only where considerations of expediency arise.

How does this impinge on section 48 of the Law on Administrative Procedure (VwVfG) of the Federal Republic of Germany? Under the terms of this statute, the revocation of unlawful administrative decisions, and the clawback of sums paid without due reason, is a discretionary matter for the authorities.[250]

There is hardly any free discretion over the clawback of payments in such cases; it is necessary to have regard to the legal protection enjoyed by the beneficiary, that is, the latter's expectation that the benefit will be secure; this expectation is expressly upheld in section 48, paragraph 2 of the VwVfG.[251] On the question how far the authorities must have regard to these and other legal considerations, the Court explained[252]:

---

[249] On this and the points which follow, see the opinion of Advocate-General Verloren van Themaat *op. cit.*, footnotes 244 *et seq.*, with references to the case-law, especially p. 2675.

[250] Section 48 VwVfG (Federal) states:

"(1) An unlawful administrative decision, even one which is unappealable, may be rescinded with future effect or retrospectively, either as a whole or in part. An administrative decision which confers or confirms a right or lawful benefit may only be rescinded subject to the reservations in paragraphs 2 to 4."

See Meyer, Borgs, *Kommentar zum Verwaltungsverfahrensgesetz* (2nd ed., Frankfurt am Main 1982), section 48, no. 2, p. 421; F. O. Kopp, *Verwaltungsverfahrensgesetz mit Erläuterungen* (4th ed., Munich 1986), section 48, pp. 794 *et seq.*

[251] section 48, para. 2, as a legal limitation on the discretionary power to reclaim or claw back benefits, is interpreted predominantly according to the principles of legal certainty and the protection of legitimate expectations. See Meyer, Borgs, *Kommentar zum Verwaltungsverfahrensgesetz*, (2nd ed., Frankfurt am Main 1982), section 48, nos. 50 and 60; F. O. Kopp, VwVfG, *op. cit.*, footnote 250, section 48, no. 51, p. 819 and no. 55. This is also explained in H. J. Knack (editor), *Verwaltungsverfahrensgesetz (VwVfG) Kommentar*, (2nd ed., Cologne/Berlin/Bonn/Munich 1982), section 48 (written by W. Klappstein) nos. 5.6.2; Stelkens, Bonk, Leonhardt, *Verwaltungsverfahrensgesetz*, Kommentar (2nd ed., Munich 1983), section 48 (written by P. Stelkens) no. 18, p. 587.

[252] *Op. cit.*, footnote 244, p. 2669 *et seq.*, paras. 30 *et seq.*

"The first point to be made in this regard is that the principles of the protection of legitimate expectation and assurance of legal certainty are part of the legal order of the Community. The fact that national legislation provides for the same principles to be observed in a matter such as the recovery of unduly-paid Community aids cannot, therefore, be considered contrary to that same legal order. Moreover, it is clear from a study of the national laws of the Member States regarding the revocation of administrative decisions and the recovery of financial benefits which have been unduly paid by public authorities that the concern to strike a balance, albeit in different ways, between the principle of legality on the one hand and the principles of legal certainty and the protection of legitimate expectation on the other is common to the laws of the Member States.

The answer to the seventh question must therefore be that Community law does not prevent national law from having regard, in excluding the recovery of unduly-paid aids, to such considerations as the protection of legitimate expectation, the loss of unjustified enrichment, the passing of a time-limit or the fact that the administration knew, or was unaware owing to gross negligence on its part, that it was wrong in granting the aids in question, provided however that the conditions laid down are the same as for the recovery of purely national financial benefits and the interests of the Community are taken fully into account."

From a German viewpoint, the question arises whether the public authority still has any "discretion" in the matter, or whether, because the whole question is narrowed down to legal considerations, the decision to recover or reclaim aids is entirely open to judicial review. This is certainly true of the review of such decisions by the West German administrative courts.[253] Discretionary decisions, once shorn of any element of expediency, if indeed such decisions still warrant the description "discretionary" in the German sense, may be fully reviewed to ascertain that the legal limits have been respected. The ultimate decision as to whether the decision was correct, for instance in weighing administrative legality against the protection of a legitimate expectation, lies with the national courts, including the German courts.

The weighing up of the considerations referred to above as "discretion"—and the case of section 48, paragraph 2 of the VwVfG there is

---

[253] See the comparative law survey above, Part 3, section 1.

in fact a duty to do this—is difficult to reconcile with what may be called discretion in the broadest sense. The elimination of the aspects of expediency produces a "discretion shell," the substance of which consists entirely of legal considerations which, according to German ideas, are subject to comprehensive judicial review.[254] As a result, the Court's ruling, seen against the background of the judicial review practice in the Federal Republic of Germany, turns a clawback decision based on discretion into a binding decision.

(e) Concluding assessment of the legal constraints in the indirect (national) implementation of the agricultural law of the European Community

The implementing organs in the Member States face an often bewildering miscellany of legal rules in the agricultural field. They have to begin with the Council's market organisations, which are supplemented and further defined in numerous executive decisions by the Commission, containing both substantive and formal requirements. The implementation of agricultural law often calls for supplementary national rules, and here a number of problems arise.

The legal starting-point is the exclusive competence of the Community to formulate substantive rules in the field of agriculture. Here the Member States have lost the right to legislate for themselves. However, they have retained the responsibility for deciding on the administration arrangements for implementing Community law. This competence to determine administrative arrangements brings with it the power to legislate on the necessary procedural and formal arrangements. At the same time, in promulgating procedural rules the Community has wider-ranging powers than in its own organisational area. Where the Community itself has laid down rules of procedure, the Court will insist that they are strictly applied.

However, serious discrepancies between national systems of procedural law can ultimately be removed only through the approximation procedure under Article 100 of the EEC Treaty, a very onerous procedure which has been only sparingly used so far. Indeed some of the existing problems of implementation which arise if the law is applied in dissimilar fashion can be attributed to disparities in the organisational

---

[254] *Ibid.*

arrangements of national administrations; some, however, are undoubtedly due to dissimilarities of procedural law between one Member State and another.

The claim of Community law to be enforced directly and uniformly throughout the Community is often frustrated by organisational and procedural differences in the Member States.

However, the Court's view is unmistakably that the substantive constraints of the agricultural law must be enforced with as few restrictions as possible, and should not be moderated by allowing scope for discretionary decisions except where unavoidable. The Court attaches the same importance to the use of clear and unambiguous terms as to a restrictive application of Community rules of equity.

Although legal constraints are relatively frequent in Community agricultural law, the danger nevertheless remains that its rules may not be uniformly implemented in the Member States, owing to different administrative arrangements, customs and practices.

VI. THE CUSTOMS UNION

The customs union is the founding core of the Community. According to Article 9(1) of the EEC Treaty, it involves all trade in goods covered by the Treaty and forbids Member States to levy customs duties on each other for imports and exports, or any charges having equivalent effect. There is also provision for a common customs tariff (CCT) in relation to third countries.

1. The significance of the customs union

With the creation of a customs union, a major step was taken towards achieving parity in conditions on the internal market. The disappearance of customs duties on trade between Member States, and the imposition of a common external tariff, were milestones of European integration. The customs union is therefore one of the most important components of the edifice.[1]

---

[1] cf. M. Beschel, in H.v.d. Groeben, H. v. Boeckh, J. Thiesing, C.-D. Ehlermann, *Kommentar zum EWG-Vertrag*, (3rd ed., Baden-Baden 1983), Article 9, p. 162 no. 7; K. Landry, "Das Zollrecht der EG," in *Das Wirtschaftsrecht des Gemeinsamen Marktes in der aktuellen Rechtsentwicklung* (edited by J. Schwarze), Baden-Baden 1983, p. 123.

Its economic significance lies in the creation of an area which transcends frontiers and a market for the economic potential of the Member States, which are better able to deal with competition on world markets by joining forces than they would be in isolation. The common external customs tariff is also an effective form of protection against the economic influence of third States.[2]

From a political standpoint, the common customs tariff enables the Community to play a role in the field of development and foreign policy.[3] A limiting factor, however, is GATT, whose preamble defines its purpose as substantially eliminating customs duties and other barriers to trade, and removing discrimination in international trade. Because the Community is bound by this international agreement, there may be restrictions on the imposition of tariffs in individual cases, especially when fixing preferential and protective duties.[4]

Customs duties are also an important source of revenue for the Community's budget, since they form part of the Community's own resources.[5] Finally, the customs union constitutes a legal regime of interlocking Community and national rules, the sheer number of which shows that customs policy, alongside agricultural law, is an area in which integration is highly advanced and which is contributing to the emergence of a European administrative law.[6]

2. Legal constraints in customs policy: the essential points

The ban on customs duties and similar levies within the Community is unconditional and immediate in its effects.[7] However, comprehensive accompanying legislation is required to bring it into practice. Of cardinal importance, and therefore a leading issue in the survey which follows, is how the authorities in the Member States apply the common customs tariff. As in agricultural law, implementation at the national level

---

[2] M. Beschel, *op. cit.*, footnote 1, p. 154 no. 1.
[3] *Ibid.*, *op. cit.*, footnote 1, p. 155 no. 2.
[4] *cf.* H. Laubereau, in R. Regul (editor), *Gemeinschaftszollrecht*, Baden-Baden 1982, pp. 365 *et seq.*
[5] See the Council Decision of April 21, 1970, O.J. 1970, L94/20, Article 2(b).
[6] On the customs union as a legal concept, see M. Beschel, *op. cit.*, footnote 1, Article 9, p. 158 no. 9.
[7] Case 26/62 *Van Gend & Loos* v. *Netherlands Customs Administration* [1963] E.C.R. 1 *et seq.*, at 25 to 26; Case 33/70 *S.A.C.E.* v. *Italian Ministry for Finance* [1970] E.C.R. 1213 *et seq.*, at 1223, paras. 14 to 16.

involves the risk that the law in force will not be interpreted and applied in the same manner at different levels.

The groundwork is the common customs tariff, which is a Council regulation and therefore applies directly in every Member State. With around 3,000 fixed tariffs, including the customs rates which are usually expressed as a percentage of the value of the goods, this is the core of external customs law.[8] In addition, there are the rules on exemptions from customs duties, which are also framed as a regulation and have the effect of amending the CCT. Taken on its own, the Community tariff does not ensure uniform treatment of individual cases. The rules establishing the conditions under which the CCT will apply must, in principle, be framed by domestic legislation.[9] In this area it was therefore necessary to devise a series of Community rules for standardizing customs law. The most important of these are Regulation 1224/80 on defining the customs value of goods,[10] and also provisions (regulations) on the origin of goods,[11] Community dispatch procedures[12] and both positive and negative trade in finished products.[13] These replace national rules.

However, there are many supplementary provisions which have not been covered by any Community rules, so that there is still a need for harmonisation. To standardise the application of the CCT throughout the Community, a number of so-called interpretative regulations have been issued since 1968, and continue to be issued, as well as many statements from the committee on the common customs tariff. This has not been enough, however, and in many instances the Court has had to interpret the CCT.

3. Applying the customs tariff nomenclature (CCT)

As already explained, the CCT contains some 3,000 tariff categories, *i.e.* descriptions of goods to which a particular customs rate is allotted.

---

[8] EEC Council Regulation 950/68 J.O. 1968, L172/1, O.J.Sp. Ed. 1968, 275.
[9] B. Beutler, R. Bieber, J. Pipkorn, J. Streil, *Die Europäische Gemeinschaft—Rechtsordnung und Politik* (3rd ed., Baden-Baden 1987), pp. 277 *et seq.*
[10] EEC Council Regulation 1224/80 O.J. 1980, L134/1, amended by EEC Council Regulation 313/80 O.J. 1980, L333/1.
[11] EEC Council Regulation 802/68 J.O. 1968, L148/1; O.J.Sp. Ed. 1968, 165, since amended several times. See the references in M. Beschel, *op. cit.*, footnote 1, Article 9, p. 159, footnote 21.
[12] EEC Council Regulation 222/77 O.J. 1977, L38/1.
[13] Council Directive 69/73, J.O. 1969, L58/1; O.J.Sp. Ed. 1969, 75, since amended several times. See M. Beschel, *op. cit.*, footnote 11, p. 160, footnote 24.

These are primarily descriptive terms, and their interpretation is essentially subjective.

However, these expressions are often supplemented by definitions such as "products of any kind for use as adhesives ..." or perhaps "scientific apparatus."

As the case law shows, this results in considerable uncertainty when the tariffs are set. Problems arise even with the interpretation of the straightforward descriptions of goods, where there are no instructions for use or supplementary definitions.

Because ambivalence in assigning an item to a particular tariff category will always jeopardise the uniform application of the CCT, the Community has rules of interpretation to ensure, as far as possible, that it is uniformly applied in the Member States. It must not be forgotten that every day, at several dozen border crossing posts, the tariffs payable on thousands of items must be ascertained. The danger of divergent decisions by the customs posts, and consequent delays in transit, will be apparent.[14] Explanations of the CCT, as guidelines for interpretation by the administration, will therefore be of special interest.

(a) *Explanations of the CCT by the Community and the Member States*

By EEC Regulation 97/69, a Committee on Common Customs Nomenclature was set up,[15] consisting of representatives of the Member States and chaired by a representative of the Commission (Article 1, paragraph 1). The Committee has the right to examine any question concerning the schedule of the CCT which may be put to it by the Chairman on his own initiative or at the request of a Member State.

Article 3, paragraph 2 of Regulation 97/69 provides that the Committee may issue an opinion, and this will be incorporated, according to paragraph 3, into corresponding Commission rules. So far, this has happened only in isolated cases. Usually, the opinion of the Committee is no more than a suggestion, which will be accepted by the Commission and issued in a collection of explanations of the European Community's

---

[14] *cf.* R. Regul, *Steuern und Zölle im Gemeinsamen Markt*, IV, Vol. 6 (1981) A/5. p. 1.
[15] J.O. 1969, L14/1; O.J.Sp. Ed. 1969, 12, amended by Council Regulation 280/77, O.J. 1977, L40/1.

customs tariff.[16] The legal standing of these has been defined as follows by the Court, in its decision in Case 74/69[17]:

> "An unofficial interpretation of a regulation by an informal document of the Commission is not enough to confer on that interpretation an authentic Community character. Such documents, which no doubt have their value for the purpose of applying certain regulations, have, however, no binding effect, and thus cannot ensure that the descriptions of the goods to which they refer have the same scope in all the Member States. The uniform application of Community law is only guaranteed if it is the subject of formal measures taken in the context of the Treaty."

But the Committee's opinions are not wholly without significance, as we see from the grounds of judgment in Case 69/76[18]:

> "The opinions of the Committee on Common Customs Nomenclature constitute an important means of ensuring the uniform application of the Common Customs Tariff by the customs authorities of the Member States, and as such they may be considered as a valid aid to the interpretation of the tariff. Nevertheless such opinions do not have legally binding force so that, where appropriate, it is necessary to consider whether their content is in accordance with the actual provisions of the Common Customs Tariff and whether they alter the meaning of such provisions."

Where the Commission, acting under Article 3 of Regulation 97/69, enacts an interpretative regulation, it has considerable freedom of decision in allocating products to the tariff categories[19]:

> "It is clear from those rules that in this field the Council has conferred on the Commission, acting in co-operation with the customs experts of the Member States, a wide discretion as to the choice between two or more tariff headings in which a given product might be classified."

---

[16] See R. Regul, *op. cit.*, footnote 14, p. 25.

[17] Case 74/69 *Hauptzollamt Bremen-Freihafen* v. *Waren-Import-Gesellschaft Krohn & Co.* [1970] E.C.R. 451 at 460, para. 9.

[18] Case 69/76 *Dittmeyer* v. *Hauptzollamt Hamburg-Waltershof* [1977] E.C.R. 231 at 238, para. 4; see also Advocate-General Warner pp. 242 *et seq.*

[19] Case 158/78 *Biegi* v. *Hauptzollamt Bochum* [1979] E.C.R. 1103 at 1117, para. 6.

The binding interpretative decisions on the CCT may not, however, introduce alterations to it.[20] The same applies to the Council's views and interpretations relating to co-operation in customs matters.[21]

If the interpretation of the tariff nomenclature is doubtful, the Member States may not make their own rules of interpretation[22]:

"The Council issued pursuant to Articles 28 and 111 of the EEC Treaty Regulation No. 950/68 concerning the Common Customs Tariff, which contains the customs tariff as an annex. The interpretation of the headings of this tariff can only be fixed if the powers vested in the Community are respected. For it follows from the very nature of the Common Customs Tariff that the individual tariff headings must have the same scope in all the Member States. This requirement would be jeopardized if, where there are difficulties in classifying a product for tariff purposes, each Member State were itself able to fix this scope by way of interpretation."

Nevertheless, the Court admits the practical necessity for Member States to make interpretative decisions in cases of doubt, although it poses considerable restrictions on the legal effects these decisions may have[23]:

"Although, where there are difficulties in classifying a product, the national administration may find it advisable to take implementing measures and to elucidate thereby the doubts raised by the description of a product, it may only do so by observing Community law, without the national authorities being able to issue rules of interpretation having binding effect."

A binding interpretation of the tariff will therefore require either formal legal interpretation by the Council or the Commission, or a decision by the Court. However, an example from the case law will show that even in the Court's pronouncements, the status of these notions of interpretation is not that of a binding legal rule.

---

[20] *Op. cit.*, footnote 19, p. 1117, para. 5.
[21] See M. Beschel, *op. cit.*, footnote 1, preliminary comments on Articles 18 to 29, p. 219 and no. 11, with references to the case law in footnote 31.
[22] Case 14/70 *Bukels* v. *Oberfinanzdirektion München* [1970] E.C.R. 1001 *et seq.*, at 1008, para. 3.
[23] *Op. cit.*, footnote 22, p. 1008, para. 4.

(b) The Court's review of the application of the CCT

In principle, it is for the customs authorities of the Member States to apply the CCT. In their activities, they are subject both to the supervision of the national courts and to the review practice of the Court of the European Communities. The Court has the last word in deciding how a term in the CCT is to be interpreted. This decision is usually made in the form of a preliminary ruling under Article 117 of the EEC Treaty. It must be borne in mind, however, that under Article 177 of the Treaty the Court may not resolve a dispute brought before a national court; it may only formulate an abstract principle of interpretation for the national court. However, the Court's technique of abstract interpretation, which is also applied to other issues within the ambit of Article 177, enables it to reach an outcome which hinges on the actual subject of the proceedings.[24]

Instances of this type of case abound, consisting mostly of a reiteration of the familiar principles as they apply to yet another tariff category. We can judge the legal force of the tariff nomenclature by looking at the principles followed in applying it.

In Case 36/71 *Henck* v. *Hauptzollamt Emden*, the question was which criteria applied to the classification of products under the CCT.[25] The Court found[26]:

> "In the interests of legal certainty and of administration the classification of goods in the Common Customs Tariff is in principle carried out on the basis of their objective characteristics."

The decision in Case 46/83 *Gerlach* v. *Inspecteur der Invoerrechten en Accijnzen*[27] shows the extent to which the Court pre-empts the decision of a national court. It also illustrates the method used to allocate a highly-specialised product to the tariff nomenclature.

The initial proceedings concerned the classification in the CCT of a fully hydrogenated animal fat from Spain, derived from fish liver.[28] Three tariff groups were available: group 15.04 A II "liver oils from fish," on which no duties are levied; group 29.01 A I "acyclic hydrocarbons," with

---

[24] The Court is confined to the factual information made available by the court dealing with the case. It may not conduct investigations of its own. See, for instance, Case 104/77 *Oehlschläger* v. *Hauptzollamt Emmerich* [1978] 791 at 797, para. 4.

[25] [1972] E.C.R. 187.

[26] *Op. cit.*, footnote 25, p. 197, para. 4.

[27] [1984] E.C.R. 841 *et seq*.

[28] *Op. cit.*, footnote 27, p. 848, paras. 1 and 2.

a customs rate of 6.7 per cent. of the value of the product; and no. 15.12, comprising "refined fats and oils from fish or ocean mammals which are hydrogenated or solidified through any other process."

The Court began its examination using the existing interpretations of the Council's nomenclature for co-operation in customs matters, which are similar in nature to the explanations of the tariff nomenclature.[29]

> "Heading 15.04 covers fats and oils, of fish and marine mammals, whether or not refined. According to the Explanatory Notes to the Customs Cooperation Council's Nomenclature, that heading covers oils and fats derived from fish and marine mammals which are extracted from the body or liver of the fish or from fish waste, and which usually have a characteristic fishy smell and a disagreeable taste. Their natural colour may vary from yellow to reddish-brown. When refined fats and oils derived from fish or marine mammals have been hydrogenated, solidified or hardened by any process, they are classified under heading 15.12. That heading covers animal or vegetable oils and fats, wholly or partly hydrogenated, or solidified or hardened by any other process, whether or not refined, but not further prepared.
>
> In its order for reference, the *Tariefcommissie* found that the product in question was transparent, colourless and odourless and that it must be regarded as completely hydrogenated. That fact is sufficient to conclude that the goods cannot be covered by heading 15.04.
>
> Neither can the goods in question be classified under heading 15.12, since they must have been prepared in order to become a colourless and odourless product and that only products which have been hydrogenated but not further prepared are covered by heading 15.12."

The Court goes on to consider whether the product in question falls under tariff heading 29.01. This time the "explanatory notes" on the customs tariff are used as an aid to interpretation[30]:

> "Heading 29.01 is formulated in the following terms:
> 'Hydrocarbons:
> A. Acyclic.'

[29] *Op. cit.*, footnote 27, p. 850, paras. 9 to 11.
[30] *Op. cit.*, footnote 27, p. 851, paras. 12 and 13.

According to Note 1(a) to Chapter 29, the headings of this chapter are to be taken as applying to 'separate chemically defined organic compounds, whether or not containing impurities.'

Furthermore, the Explanatory Notes to the Customs Tariff of the European Communities say, in relation to Chapter 29, that 'The products below are classified in this Chapter when they satisfy the following criteria as to purity:

6. Ethane and other saturated acyclic hydrocarbons (other than methane and propane), single isomers not less than 95% pure on the anhydrous product, calculated by reference to volume for gaseous products and 95% by weight for non-gaseous products.'

The reply to the first question must therefore be that a completely hydrogenated animal oil, manufactured from fish liver, which is at the same time an acyclic hydrocarbon, must be classified under subheading 29.01 A I of the Common Customs Tariff."

Within tariff classification 29.01 A a distinction is drawn between:

    I. use as fuel or heating oil and
   II. any other use.

Products classified under number 29.01 A II can be imported free of duty. Admission under this heading is, however, subject to the preconditions to be set by the responsible authorities, including, according to the relevant implementing regulations of the Commission, the production of a written authorisation for duty-free import.[31] According to the findings of the national customs service, the plaintiff in the main action had not received any such authorisation. Bearing in mind the purpose of this, the Court ruled as follows on the tariff classification in this case[32]:

"The requirement of a written authorisation issued by a competent authority is intended to make the task of the customs authorities easier and to prevent fraud. In the interests of legal certainty and the orderly working of the administration, the procedure laid down in the Community rules must be followed.

The second question must therefore be answered to the effect that a product cannot be assigned to tariff subheading 29.01 A II unless an authorisation within the meaning of Regulation No. 1775/77 is

---

[31] *Op. cit.*, footnote 27, p. 852, para. 16.
[32] *Op. cit.*, footnote 27, p. 852, paras. 17 to 19.

produced. From this it follows that the product mentioned in the second question must be assigned not to subheading 29.01 A II but to subheading 29.01 A I."

On the basis of findings of fact in the main action, the European Court will therefore proceed to make a firm and definitive classification of the product in question to the tariff nomenclature.[33] In such cases the national court has no further discretion, unless one of the parties brings forward new factual information which demands some other conclusion.

The degree to which the Court predetermines the outcome depends, however, on the particular features of the tariff categories concerned. If it is possible to classify a product solely according to properties which can be scientifically defined, the Court makes a final classification on the facts alone.[34]

If, however, the tariff category comprises a combination of features based both on the external characteristics of the product and the purpose for which it is used, or indeed its suitability for use in a particular way, the Luxembourg court is noticeably hesitant in assigning the product to a particular category.

Case 72/77 *Universiteitskliniek Utrecht* v. *Inspecteur der Invoerrechten en Accijnzen* concerned the importation, duty-free, of an ultra-violet spectral photometer.[35] From the plaintiff's point of view, the legal basis for the customs exemption was Council Regulation 1798/75 on the importation, free of the Common Customs Tariff rates, of objects of an educational, scientific or cultural character. According to Article 3 of this Regulation, equipment "imported exclusively for educational purposes or for pure scientific research . . ." is exempt from duty. The University of Utrecht, which was importing the ultra-violet spectral photometer, pointed to the "purely scientific" use to which the equipment would be put and sought customs exemption under the appropriate Regulation.

---

[33] This is not uncommon, as a glance through the relevant case law will show. See, for instance: Case 816/79 *Klaus Mecke & Co.* v. *Hauptzollamt Bremen-Ost* [1980] E.C.R. 3029 at 3041, para. 20; Case 111/77 *Bleiindustrie* v. *Hauptzollamt Hamburg-Waltershof* [1978] E.C.R. 659 at 668, para. 11 in which the classification was referred to a national court, the European Court retaining the right to consider the factual aspects. Here see above, footnote 24. See also Case 104/77 *Oehlschläger* v. *Hauptzollamt Emmerich* [1978] E.C.R. 791 at 798, para. 9; Case 62/77 *Carlsen Verlag* v. *Oberfinanzdirektion Köln* [1977] E.C.R. 2343 at 2352, para. 9, continued from p. 2351; Case 36/71 *Günter Henck* v. *Hauptzollamt Emden* [1972] E.C.R. 187 at 199, para. 12.
[34] See examples above in footnote 33.
[35] [1978] E.C.R. 189 *et seq.*

However, the application was rejected by the Netherlands financial authorities on the basis that the instrument could also be used in industry or in quality-testing laboratories. It could not therefore be regarded as scientific apparatus within the meaning of the provisions on customs exemptions.[36]

In its first question, the referring court asked whether the provisions in Regulation 1798/75 concerning the "scientific use" of equipment were based on a purely subjective criterion. If not, the court asked, does the mere fact that the equipment is used in industry or elsewhere for commercial purposes mean that no customs exemption can be granted? If this question were also answered in the negative, the court wanted to know whether there were other criteria in the relevant legal rules which must be taken into account when considering an application for a customs exemption.[37]

The Court dealt with these questions together[38]:

"The first recital in the preamble to the regulation provides that the importation into a Member State free of Common Customs Tariff duties of educational, scientific and cultural materials is to be allowed 'by all possible means.'

For the same purposes, the second recital in the preamble to the regulation at issue states that 'customs duty-free admission of educational, scientific and cultural materials must be uniform throughout the Community.' "

From the need for uniformity of implementation throughout the Community, the Court concluded[39]:

"Hence it follows that the assessment of whether or not an instrument or apparatus capable of being granted exemption from customs duties is of a 'scientific' nature within the meaning of Article 3(1) of the regulation must be based upon the objective characteristics of that instrument or apparatus.

Those characteristics must be such as to make it particularly suitable for pure scientific research.

[36] See *op. cit.*, footnote 35, p. 196, paras. 2 to 3.
[37] *Op. cit.*, footnote 35, p. 196, paras. 4 to 7.
[38] *Op. cit.*, footnote 35, p. 197, paras. 8 to 12.
[39] *Op. cit.*, footnote 35, p. 197, paras. 13 to 16.

Although the first indent of Article 3(3) defines the concept of pure scientific research as 'research carried out for non-commercial purposes,' it is none the less true that the intended use of the instrument or apparatus in question must be assessed on the basis only of its objective characteristics and not in relation to the particular end to which the institution or establishment which applied for exemption from customs duty intends to use it.

For the purposes of such assessment, the fact that the use of the instrument or apparatus requires specific scientific knowledge can be evidence of its being of a scientific nature within the meaning of the aforesaid Article 3(1)."

The national authorities are therefore accorded a power of assessment, but they must use it in the light of objective characteristics. The intention of the user, or the subjective element, is not important. In this case, the Court was careful not to curb excessively the decision-making powers of the referring court and of the national customs authorities. The reason for this is the inherent vagueness and difficulty of definition implied by "pure scientific research." Applying this term to an individual case calls for a complex process of evaluation on the part of the public authority, if it is to examine whether the item is appropriate for purely scientific research. On the other hand, reverting to the original example, hydrogenated fish liver oil can be chemically classified, without further ado, as "acyclic hydrocarbon." Both judgments clearly demonstrate how the decisions of the European Court bear on individual cases.

The judgment in Case 294/81 *Control Data* v. *Commission* shows that even where there is a direct action under Article 173, second paragraph, of the EEC Treaty, the Court does not make a complete investigation of how the term "pure scientific use" has been interpreted and applied.[40] The subject of this case was a decision by the Commission to refuse the applicant customs exemption under Regulation 1798/75 on computers of a particular type. It should be noted here that the rules for implementing the regulation provide, in some circumstances, for a decision by the Commission on exemption from customs duties.

The applicant argued that its computers were definitely to be regarded as scientific instruments or apparatus within the meaning of the Community rule. The Commission had therefore breached the Community's law in the matter of rejecting the application for customs exemption.[41]

[40] [1983] E.C.R. 911 *et seq.*
[41] *Op. cit.*, footnote 40, p. 929, para. 18.

The Court began its examination with an interesting interpretation of the applicant's argument[42]:

"It therefore asks the Court not only to declare the contested decision void but also to make a finding establishing the scientific nature of the computers in question."

Then follows a sentence which requires some explanation[43]:

"Although it is not for the Court to make such a finding within the framework of an application for a declaration that a measure is void, it must on the other hand ascertain whether the criteria applied by the Commission are in accordance with the Community rules and whether in applying those criteria the Commission took account of the objective characteristics of the computers referred to by the decision. It is therefore necessary to examine both the criteria emanating from the decision itself and those which were stated by the Commission in the course of the proceedings before the Court."

This statement has to be interpreted as meaning that the Commission has discretion in determining whether a piece of apparatus is scientific in character, and its decision may be reviewed only within narrow limits. The statement defies any other interpretation. In proceedings under Article 173 of the EEC Treaty the Court is not precluded from classifying certain matters as undefined legal concepts, as the survey on its decisions on EEC cartel law has shown.[44]

Contrary to what the reader would expect from the introduction to the case, the applicant's plea does not exceed the bounds of Article 173 of the EEC Treaty. The Court's eventual finding that the computers in question were scientific instruments is not an "added extra" to its finding that the original decision was invalid; it is the standard prerequisite for deciding that an error of definition has occurred.

The Court's reserve may be due to its respect for the decision-making powers of the Commission, since if the Court had confirmed the scientific character of the computers its only option would have been to admit the application without making any further evaluation of its own.[45] The

---

[42] *Ibid.*
[43] *Op. cit.*, footnote 40, p. 929, para. 19.
[44] See above, section III.
[45] This also explains the reserve expressed by Advocate-General Mancini in his opinion in Case 283/82 *Schoellershammer* v. *Commission* [1983] E.C.R. 4219 at 4232.

Court's attitude can be discerned from the fact that it downgrades its examination from a special exercise of definition to the level of the evaluative criteria used and their application to the product to be classified.

A different, more pragmatic approach would emphasise the difficulties which face a body of jurists in considering and appraising the technical specifications of highly complex instruments. As the judgment proceeds, it is clear that the Court is at pains to examine the Commission's evaluation as thoroughly as possible, without venturing beyond its competence by engaging in an analysis of data-processing concepts. This is apparent from the following statement[46]:

"Confronted with these conflicting points of view, the Court does not consider that it can exclude the possibility that a criterion based on the difference between the hardware and the software of a computer may be in conformity with Community rules on the duty-free importation of scientific instruments and apparatus."

The Court continued[47]:

"However, it has not been established either in the statements of the reasons on which the decision at issue is based or in the proceedings before the Court that a precise criterion of that nature was in fact applied by the Commission for the purpose of adopting the decision. Nor, furthermore, is there anything to show that if the Commission did apply such a criterion it took sufficient account of the objective characteristics of the two computers, both with regard to their hardware and to their system software."

After weighing up some further considerations advanced by the Commission, the Court finally concluded[48]:

"It must therefore be concluded that neither the statement of the reasons on which the decision at issue is based nor the Commission's arguments before the Court have made it possible for the Court to find that when the Commission adopted the decision it applied clear criteria which were in accordance with the Community regulations

[46] *Op. cit.*, footnote 40, p. 931, para. 26.
[47] *Ibid.*
[48] *Op. cit.*, footnote 40, p. 933, paras. 31 and 32.

and that in doing so it had sufficient regard for the particular objective characteristics of the two computers in question.

For that reason the decision adopted by the Commission should be declared void and the matter should be referred back to the Commission for reconsideration."

As we originally indicated, the Court confers a limited measure of discretion on the Commission.

4. Conclusion

Even the few cases summarised here are enough to show the flexibility the Court displays in examining decisions made by national and Community authorities on classification according to the CCT and its special rules. Yet it is also obvious that the Court, despite its "judicial self-restraint," is anxious to interpret the tariff terminology as clearly and precisely as it can, so as to foster uniformity of implementation.

The scope which exists for independent decision-making is confined to the factual aspects of the customs tariff. From a German point of view this is scope for appraisal, but it can be exercised only within narrow limits because it is tied to the objective characteristics of the products to be classified. The Court, when interpreting the customs law of the Community, has two main aims: to achieve legal certainty and to ensure that the administration can operate in an orderly manner. Both principles help to make the Community's customs regime more reliable and ultimately promote the justified interests of the Market's citizens, as well as the Community's aims in fiscal and trade policy.

VII. THE LEGAL CONSTRAINTS ON THE ADMINISTRATION IN THE SOCIAL SECURITY LAW OF THE EUROPEAN COMMUNITY

1. Introduction

In the area of freedom of movement, the creation of the common market requires that the mobility of workers is not hampered by the threat of losing entitlement to social benefits. The common market for workers cannot be achieved without an effective social network capable of encompassing different countries. The parallelism of economic union and the achievement of social progress through common action by the Member States was therefore strongly emphasised by the Court in Case 43/75 *Defrenne II* v. *Sabena*.[1] Nowadays, in the developed industrial nations, social policy is an indispensable element of the welfare state. Social policy can be defined as the entire range of measures to improve working and living conditions.[2] It is a broad concept, reflected in a multiplicity of different forms of State intervention. The range of measures designated as "social policy," which began with pensions and unemployment insurance, now extends to health care and the statutory control of working conditions.

Although the Community treaties set economic policy goals (to a lesser extent in the case of the Euratom treaty), there are no parallel structured rules for social policy. Articles 117 to 128 of the EEC Treaty regulate certain aspects of social policy under that heading, but the other provisions with a social dimension are scattered throughout the Treaties. This indicates that social policy in general is intended to remain the province of the Member States.[3] However, in a 1968 decision the Court pointed out that the Community may reflect social policy considerations in all its fields of activity.[4]

2.   The Community's competence in social policy, and how it is exercised

The chapter on "Social policy" (Articles 117–128 of the EEC Treaty) begins with an admission by the Member States of the need to promote improved living and working conditions for workers and to bring about the necessary improvements by means of harmonisation (Article 117). Article 118 places a duty on the Commission, in conformity with the general objectives of the Treaty, to promote close co-operation between the Member States in the social field.[5] More specifically, Article 119 lays

---

[1] [1976] E.C.R. 455 at 473, paras. 8 to 11.
[2] B. Beutler, R. Bieber, J. Pipkorn, J. Streil, *Die Europäische Gemeinschaft—Rechtsordnung und Politik* (3rd ed., Baden-Baden 1987), p. 436.
[3] *Ibid.* As a result of the Single European Act, the social policy Articles 118a and 118b have been added to the EEC Treaty.
[4] See Case 28/66 *Netherlands* v. *Commission* [1968] E.C.R. 1 *et seq.* (p. 11 of the judgment).
[5] See J. Forman, in Groeben, Boeckh, Thiesing, Ehlermann, *Kommentar zum EWG-Vertrag*, Vol. I, (3rd ed., Baden-Baden 1983), Article 118, nos. 8 *et seq.* See also a recent European Court judgment on migration policy, Joined Cases 281, 283–285 & 287/85 *Federal Republic of Germany* v. *Commission* [1987] E.C.R. 3203.

down that Member States are bound to apply the principle that men and women should receive equal pay for equal work. The European Court has attributed direct effect to this provision, and not only where the individual's relationship with his or her Member State is concerned (vertical effect) but also in relationships among individuals (horizontal effect).[6] Hence one cannot speak of administrative implementation of Article 119 of the EEC Treaty, except where it applies within a public administration. We shall therefore ignore it for present purposes, without, however, disregarding its unquestionable significance.

The Council, in implementation of its 1974 Action Programme, issued several directives on equal treatment in various fields, using its powers under Article 235 of the EEC Treaty.[7] Other legal measures in the area of social policy are the directive of February 17, 1975 on mass dismissals,[8] the directive of February 14, 1977 on the entitlement of employees in company takeovers,[9] and the directive of October 20, 1980 on the harmonisation of legal protection for employees when their employer is insolvent.[10]

Another instrument of Community social policy is the European Social Fund, which provides direct financial support for retraining and resettlement schemes in the Member States as well as assistance to be paid to workers whose employment has been curtailed or has temporarily ceased entirely as a result of a reorganisation of production.[11]

Finally, Regulation 1408/71 on social security for migrant workers is a particularly significant step towards realising the common market.[12] This regulation guarantees that an employee who has worked in another EEC Member State, either temporarily or permanently, will continue to receive social benefits such as pensions, sickness and unemployment insurance. An employee who makes use of the right to freedom of movement guaranteed in Articles 48 *et seq.* should not be exposed to any disadvantage or uncertainty with regard to his social security. This is

---

[6] See Case 43/75 *Defrenne* v. *Sabena* [1976] E.C.R. 455, paras. 21 to 24; Case 170/84 *Bilka-Kaufhaus* v. *K. Weber von Hartz* [1986] E.C.R. 1607.

[7] Council Directive 75/117 of February 10, 1975, O.J. 1975, L145/19 (directive on equal pay); Council Directive 76/207 of February 9, 1975, O.J. 1976, L39/40 (directive on equal treatment); Council Directive 79/7 of December 19, 1978, O.J. 1979, L6/24 (directive on social security).

[8] Directive 75/329, O.J. 1975, L48/29.

[9] Directive 77/187, O.J. 1977, L61/26.

[10] Directive 80/987, O.J. 1980, L283/23.

[11] On the various target groups of the fund, see W. Stabenow in Groeben, Boekh, Thiesing, Ehlermann, *op. cit.*, footnote 5, preliminary remarks to Articles 123–128, nos. 8 *et seq.*

[12] O.J. 1971, L149/2 *et seq.*

stipulated in Article 13 of Regulation 1408/71, which provides that a worker may be covered by the social security rules of only one Member State at a time. This will normally be the country in which he is employed, even if he lives in another Member State.[13] Other guaranteed arrangements cover financial payments across frontiers and the aggregation of insurance contributions according to standard principles.[14]

Regulation 1408/71 and its predecessor, Regulation 3, are concerned with an area of public administration which is very different from one Member State to another, as regards both substantive law and organisation.[15] The case law on this regulation is particularly instructive for studying the emergence of a European administrative law. The case studies which follow will therefore focus on the judgments dealing with the migrant worker regulation. However, because of the technical nature of the material and the large number of judgments, it is not possible to go into these in depth. Instead, examples will be used to show how the Court's interpretation of undefined terms in Regulation 1408/71 binds national authorities in applying the regulation and helps them to apply it uniformly.

3. Executive freedom of decision in European social law, illustrated in Regulation 1408/71 on social security for migrant workers

The area to which these provisions apply is defined in Article 4(1) of Regulation 1408/71, which states that the regulation is valid for all legal rules concerning branches of social security which affect the particular benefits listed exhaustively in this regulation. These include, for instance, sickness and maternity benefit, benefits for invalidity and occupational accident and illness, and old-age pensions. Article 4(4) contains a negative provision stipulating that the regulation does not cover social assistance or the special benefit arrangements for war victims, or special arrangements for civil servants and those on a similar footing.[16]

---

[13] There is a detailed and comprehensive survey of Regulation 1408/71 and the case law on it in K. A. Klang, *Soziale Sicherheit und Freizügigkeit im EWGV*, Baden-Baden 1986. p. 36 *et seq.* deal especially with the aims of the regulation.
[14] See K. A. Klang, *op. cit.*, footnote 13, *ibid.*
[15] The recitals to Regulation 1408/71 refer expressly to this factor.
[16] There is a detailed comment on the exact scope of Regulation 1408/71 in K. A. Klang, *op. cit.*, footnote 13, p. 41 *et seq.*

From the abundant case law on the catalogue of benefits, we shall select one case dealing with the question whether a particular benefit falls within the social security system or is a form of social assistance not covered by Regulation 1408/71.

As in Case 79/76 *Fossi* v. *Bundesknappschaft*, the European Court proceeds from the assumption that where the provision is statutory there is a legal entitlement which precludes any discretionary appraisal of individual need and individual circumstances. Where this is the case, the benefit is a social security arrangement and is covered by Article 51 of the EEC Treaty and by Regulation 3, or the more recent Regulation 1408/71, even if it would be described differently in the domestic systems of Member States.[17] This criterion does not, however, always afford a reliable definition of social assistance. Case 1/72 *Frilli* v. *Belgium* turned on the question whether a guaranteed pension income is to be defined as a social security benefit or as social assistance.[18] In the main action the plaintiff, an Italian national living in Belgium, claimed the statutory guaranteed minimum retirement income from the Ministry for Social Welfare. Her application was, however, refused, on the ground that the relevant legislation permitted payment of the guaranteed income only to foreigners whose home states had concluded a reciprocal agreement with Belgium on guaranteed minimum incomes. There was no such agreement between Belgium and Italy.[19]

The plaintiff appealed on the basis of Regulation 3 (the predecessor of Regulation 1408/71), which stipulated that a Member State's social security benefits covered by that regulation must be granted to the citizens of other Member States according to the conditions set by the host country. The point to be clarified was therefore whether the guaranteed minimum income paid under Belgian law was a social security benefit within the meaning of Regulation 3, or a form of social assistance not covered by the regulation. The European Court commented on the difficulty of its task in this case[20]:

"Under Article 1(b) of Regulation No. 3, the said regulation applies to all laws of the Member States relating to 'the social security schemes and branches of social security' set out in Article 2(1) and (2).

---

[17] [1977] E.C.R. 667 at 678, para. 6.
[18] [1972] E.C.R. 457 *et seq.*
[19] *Op. cit.*, footnote 18, p. 460 of the summary of facts.
[20] *Op. cit*, footnote 18, p. 465, paras. 11 to 13.

However, under paragraph (3) of the said article the regulation does not apply to 'social assistance and medical aid.'

Although it may seem desirable, from the point of view of applying the regulation, to establish a clear distinction between legislative schemes which come within social security and those which come within assistance, it is possible that certain laws, because of the classes of person to which they apply, their objectives and the detailed rules for their application, may simultaneously contain elements belonging to both the categories mentioned and thus defy any general classification."

The Court continued with several observations which go beyond the case in issue and indicate the ambivalent nature of minimum income arrangements[21]:

"Although, by virtue of certain of its features, national legislation on guaranteed income has certain affinities with social assistance—in particular where it prescribes need as an essential criterion for its application and does not stipulate any requirement as to periods of employment, membership or contribution—nevertheless it approximates to social security because it does not prescribe consideration of each individual case, which is a characteristic of assistance, and confers on recipients a legally defined position giving them the right to a benefit which is analogous to the old-age pensions mentioned in Article 2 of Regulation No. 3.

Taking into account the wide definition of the range of recipients, such legislation in fact fulfils a double function; it consists on the one hand in guaranteeing a subsistence level to persons wholly outside the social security system, and on the other hand in providing an income supplement for persons in receipt of inadequate social security benefits."

The Court then concludes[22]:

"Under Article 2(1)(c) of Regulation No. 3, that regulation applies to all 'old-age benefits.'

According to Article 1(s) of the same regulation the term 'benefits' is to be understood as meaning, in the widest sense, all pensions,

---

[21] *Op. cit.*, footnote 18, p. 466, paras. 14 to 15.
[22] *Op. cit.*, footnote 18, pp. 466 *et seq.*, paras. 16 to 18.

including all fractions thereof chargeable to public funds, incre-
ments, revaluation allowances or supplementary allowances.

Thus as regards a wage-earner or assimilated worker who has
completed periods of employment in a Member State, resides in that
State and is entitled to a pension there, the legislative provisions
giving all elderly residents a legally protected right to a minimum
pension are provisions which, as regards those workers, come within
the field of social security covered by Article 51 of the Treaty and
within the regulations adopted in application of that article, even
where such legislation might fall outside this classification as regards
other categories of recipients."

Accordingly, the Court concluded, the absence of a reciprocal agreement
could not be held against a worker, because "such a requirement is
incompatible with the rule of equality of treatment, which is one of the
fundamental principles of Community law and is enshrined, in this respect, in Article 8 of Regulation 3."[23]

However, the Court was also aware of the dangers of widening the field
of application of a social security system in this manner. After concluding
its investigations on the inclusion of a guaranteed minimum retirement
income within the category of social benefits for migrant workers, it took
a detailed and very general stance on the basic problem of integrating
national social security systems into the regulatory mechanism of the
European Community[24]:

"The difficulties which may occur as regards the Community rules as
the result of the application of general systems of social protection,
which have been designed for a population as a whole and are based
on requirements of nationality and residence, are inherent in the
very nature of such systems, which are intended to protect simultaneously employed persons covered as such by social security and
persons who are not thus covered.

Although these difficulties, taken as a whole, can only be resolved
within the context of a legislative action taken by the Community,
nevertheless this fact cannot adversely affect the right and duty of

[23] *Op. cit.*, footnote 18, p. 466, para. 19.
[24] *Op. cit.*, footnote 18, p. 466, paras. 20 to 22.

courts and tribunals to ensure that migrant workers receive protection wherever this proves to be possible under the principles of the social legislation of the Community, and without thereby breaking up the system set up by the national legislation in question.

Such is the case at least whenever a person having the status of an employed or assimilated worker within the meaning of Regulation No. 3 already comes, by virtue of a prior occupational activity, under the social security system of the Member State whose legislation guaranteeing a minimum income to old people is pleaded."

The national authorities are, however, bound to grant the benefit if the conditions for receiving it are met. They have no discretion to classify the social benefit concerned in a manner which departs from the definition given by the European Court. And yet Regulation 1408/71 also contains provisions which allow the authorities of the Member States a certain measure of discretion. One example worth mentioning is the judgment in Case 139/78 *Coccioli* v. *Bundesanstalt für Arbeit*, which deals with the interpretation of Article 69 of Regulation 1408/71.[25]

This article governs the payment of unemployment benefit to wholly unemployed workers who go to one or more other Member States in search of work. It provides that the worker retains his entitlement to unemployment benefit if, as well as fulfilling certain other conditions, he returns within three months to the Member State responsible for paying the benefit (Article 69(2)). If his return takes place after three months have elapsed, he loses his entitlement to benefits payable under the law of that State. However, in exceptional cases the responsible administration may extend the three-month time limit.

In the case of the plaintiff, Mr. Cioccioli, who claimed that his failure to return in time from Italy to the responsible State, the Federal Republic of Germany, was due to illness, the application was refused. The Federal Labour Office explained its refusal on the ground that it was not possible to make an exception by extending the three-month time limit under Article 69(02) of Regulation 1408/71, because it had been obvious to the applicant before the time-limit expired that there was no prospect of employment in the place where he was seeking work. Accordingly, his stay in Italy had become unnecessary some time before he fell ill. He must therefore bear the risk of being prevented by unforeseen circumstances from making a timely return to the Federal Republic.[26]

---

[25] [1979] E.C.R. 991 *et seq.*
[26] *Op. cit.*, footnote 25, p. 993 of the facts.

The Social Court in Hildesheim asked the European Court whether the German labour administration had acted within the bounds of its discretion when advancing these considerations. The Court found[27]:

> "It is for the authorities concerned to check whether the use made by the worker of the right conferred upon him by Article 69 of Regulation No. 1408/71 was in conformity with the objective for which it was instituted.
>
> Consequently it is for the competent services and institutions of the Member States to assess in each specific case the factual circumstances constituting an "exceptional case" as relied on in support of a request for extension of the period referred to in Article 69(2) of Regulation No. 1408/71.
>
> The answer to be given to the second question should therefore be that that provision does not restrict the freedom of the competent services and institutions of the Member States to take into consideration, with a view to deciding upon any extension of the period laid down by the regulation, all factors which they regard as relevant and which are inherent both in the individual situation of the worker concerned and in the exercise of effective control."

Although the competent authorities in the Member States have no discretion in determining which benefits are covered by Regulation 1408/71, they may have some discretion when granting the benefits, at least when dealing with exceptions which, in the nature of things, will hinge upon individual cases. The discretion of the national authorities is limited, however, by the general principles of Community law, as shown by Case 41/79 *Testa and others* v. *Bundesanstalt für Arbeit*.[28] While according the national labour office "wide discretion" in extending the time-limit under Article 69(2) of Regulation 1408/71, the Court found that "in exercising that discretionary power they must take account of the principle of proportionality, which is a general principle of Community law."[29]

When considering such cases the authorities must, "in order correctly to apply that principle . . . take into consideration the extent to which the period in question has been exceeded, the reason for the delay in return-

[27] *Op. cit.*, footnote 25, p. 999, paras. 8 and 9.
[28] [1980] E.C.R. 1979 *et seq.*
[29] *Op. cit.*, footnote 28, p. 1997, para. 21.

ing and the seriousness of the legal consequences arising from such delay."[30]

Hence in European social security law too, there is a prevailing tendency to avoid giving the administration unlimited discretionary powers, preferring to restrain them by general principles of its rule of law.

[30] *Ibid.*

PART 4

THE NON-CONTRACTUAL LIABILITY OF THE COMMUNITY

Unlawful conduct by the State does not merely infringe the legality principle. It can also cause damage to the parties concerned. In such cases the fact that the unlawful decision can be revoked is not a sufficient guarantee of proper judicial protection. The annulment must be accompanied by a fundamental duty to make good the damage done. We may recall that it was the notion of the constitutional State, part of the intellectual heritage of the Enlightenment, which led to the principle of compensation being accepted into the constitutional systems of the European States.[1] Although the principle appears in these systems in a variety of different forms, it is uniformly seen as a corrective for harmful conduct by the State.[2]

In the European Community, endowed as it is with sovereign powers, there is the same need for a duty of compensation. The so-called non-contractual liability of the Community is governed by Articles 34 and 40 of the ECSC Treaty, Article 215, second paragraph, of the EEC Treaty, and Article 188, second paragraph, of the Euratom Treaty. To complete our study of the legal constraints on the executive, we summarise below the main principles applying to the Community's liability for damage. Domestic rules will be mentioned only where they are relevant to Community law.

---

[1] E. W. Fuss, *Die Europäischen Gemeinschaften und der Rechtsstaatsgedanke*, 1967, p. 17.
[2] On State responsibility in general, see the international comparative survey by the International Colloquium of the Max Planck Institute for foreign public law and international law, held in Heidelberg in 1964 and published in a collection by the Max Planck Institute under the title: *Haftung des Staates für rechtswidriges Handeln seiner Organe, Länderberichte und Rechtsvergleichung*, Heidelberg, 1967.

SECTION 1

THE DEVELOPMENT OF NON-CONTRACTUAL LIABILITY IN COMMUNITY LAW

Without specifying precisely how liability arises, the EEC and Euratom Treaties[3] state that the Community, in the case of non-contractual liability, shall make good any damage caused by its institutions or by its servants in the performance of their duties in accordance with the general principles common to the laws of the Member States (Article 215, second paragraph, of the EEC Treaty, Article 188, second paragraph, of the Euratom Treaty).

This is a broadly-worded formula which, as Advocate-General Gand[4] says in one of his Opinions, ultimately means that the draftsmen of the Treaties have made the Court responsible for "settling the system of non-contractual liability." This, says the Advocate-General, is a task "of comparison and creation" which resembles the task the Court has previously had to perform in other areas. In their opinions, the Advocates-General have described on several occasions a method of legal innovation which would enable the Court to fulfil this task. This method rejects the "minimum theory," which calls for harmonisation of the legal systems of all Member States,[5] and prefers a method of "legal comparison and

---

[3] K. Roemer, *Betrachtungen zum Verhältnis Gemeinschaftsrecht—nationales Recht*, Karlsruhe 1969, p. 7, refers to the liability clause in Art. 40 of the ECSC Treaty, in which there is no mention of the "general principles of law" in the Member States, and suggests that this omission of any detailed statement of liability imposes on the Court a task of legal innovation similar to the provisions found in the EEC and Euratom Treaties.

[4] See Advocate-General Gand, Joined Cases 5, 7 & 13–24/66, *Kampffmeyer v. EEC Commission* [1967] E.C.R. 245. See also his opinion in Case 9/69 *Sayag v. Leduc* [1969] E.C.R. 337. Scholarly writings mentioning the Court's innovative mission in framing rules of official liability include, in addition to K. Roemer, *op. cit.*, footnote 141, pp. 5 and 7, H. Mosler, *Rechtsvergleichung vor völkerrechtlichen Gerichten, Internationale Festschrift für A. Verdross*, Munich/Salzburg 1971, pp. 381 *et seq.* (p. 407) and G. Zieger, "Die Rechtsprechung des Europäischen Gerichtshofes," JÖR Vol. 22 (1973), pp. 299 *et seq.* (p. 348). There is a more reserved treatment of the same point in P. Gilsdorf, *Die Haftung der Gemeinschaft aus normativem Handeln*, EuR 1975, pp. 73 *et seq.* (p. 92).

[5] A proponent of this theory is A. Heldrich, *Die allgemeinen Rechtsgrundsätze der ausservertraglichen Schadenshaftung im Bereich der Europäischen Wirtschaftsgemeinschaft*, Frankfurt am Main-Berlin 1961, pp. 18 *et seq.* See also, by the same author, "Art. 215 Abs. II des Vertrages über die Europäische Wirtschaftsgemeinschaft—ein Irrweg zu europäischer Rechtseinheit," JZ 1960, pp. 681 *et seq.* (pp. 684 *et seq.*). The theory is opposed by J. H. Kaiser, *Rechtsquellen im Recht der Europäischen Gemeinschaften*,

appraisal"[6] for the purpose of devising liability rules appropriate to the Community, its particular aims and the specific structure of its law.[7] This includes being guided by "the best elaborated national rules"[8] and choosing "from each of the Member States those solutions which . . . appear to it to be the best or . . . the most progressive."[9]

In its early judgments on the liability clauses in the EEC and Euratom Treaties the Court was somewhat reluctant to develop general principles,[10] but later made rulings containing forthright statements of the law. Subsequently, it made similar rulings applying to special questions of liability. It decided, for instance, that where rules made under domestic law are unlawful, the Community's liability for legislation expressive of economic policy decisions remains "unless a sufficiently flagrant violation

Thessaloniki 1965, p. 14. Heldrich later expressly abandoned his view. See EuR 1967, p. 349, footnote 30 (author's note).

[6] See K. Zweigert, "Der Einfluss des Europäischen Gemeinschaftsrechts auf die Rechtsordnungnen der Mitgliedstaaten," RabelsZ 28 (1964), pp. 601 *et seq.* (p. 611). See also H. P. Ipsen, *Europäisches Gemeinschaftsrecht*, section 27/3 (= p. 538) with further references.

[7] See Advocate-General Roemer's opinion in Case 5/71 *Schöppenstedt* v. *Council* [1971] E.C.R. 975 at 989: "These observations should suffice for Article 215 of the EEC Treaty, since it is widely recognised that the description of the methods of discovering the law contained in it should not be taken too literally. For Community law the criterion is not only rules which exist in *all* Member States, nor is the lowest common denominator determinative, nor does 'the rule of the lowest limit' apply. Rather what is indicated—as always when judicial decisions are arrived at by references to general principles—is a process of assessment in which above all the particular objectives of the Treaty and the peculiarities of the Community structure must be taken into account." See also his opinion in Joined Cases 63–69/72, *Wehrhahn* v. *Council* [1973] E.C.R. 1258. See also Advocate-General Gand, Joined Cases 5, 7 & 13–24/66, *Kampffmeyer* v. *Commission* [1967] E.C.R. 245 and Case 9/69 *Sayag* v. *Leduc* [1969] E.C.R. 337. See footnote 2 above.

[8] Advocate-General Roemer, *op. cit.*, footnote 7, with reference to K. Zweigert.

[9] Advocate-General Lagrange states thus in Case 14/61 *Koninklijke Nederlandse Hoogovens Staalfabrieken N.V.* v. *High Authority* [1962] E.C.R. 277. See also, with reference to Advocate-General Lagrange, J. H. Kaiser, *Rechtsquellen im Recht der Europäischen Gemeinschaften*, Thessaloniki 1965, p. 14.

[10] See the judgments in Joined Cases 5, 7 & 13–24/66 *Kampffmeyer* v. *EEC Commission* [1967] E.C.R. 330 and in Case 9/69 *Sayag* v. *Leduc* [1969] E.C.R. 329. In his opinion in the *Sayag* case Advocate-General Gand [1969] E.C.R. 337 objects to the Court's failure, in the *Kampffmeyer* case—a case on EEC law—to mention the "general principles common to the laws of the Member States" (Article 215, second paragraph, EEC Treaty), instead finding that there was a "wrongful act or omission" by the Community, in the words of Article 40 of the ECSC Treaty.

of a superior rule of law for the protection of the individual has occurred."[11]

The possibility of suing against an unlawful rule is a form of judicial protection for the individual which compensates for the lack of any direct remedy against legislative measures. Although a private individual cannot proceed directly against an unlawful decision, he may in principle seek legal redress for damage caused by it.[12] In the case-law and practice of the courts, however, the number of successful claims is very small.[13]

To conclude, Article 215, second paragraph, of the EEC Treaty, beyond its specific relevance to compensation law, has become a model rule used to fill the gaps in other areas of Community law.[14] In particular, the development of general principles of law, especially those appropriate to the Community, is justified by reference to Article 215, second paragraph, of the Treaty.[15]

---

[11] Case 5/71 *Schöppenstedt* v. *Council* [1971] E.C.R. 975 at 984. Among the case law, see also Joined Cases 9 & 11/71, *Compagnie d'approvisionnement, de transport et de crédit S.A. and Grands Moulins de Paris S.A.* v. *Commission* [1972] E.C.R. 391 and Case 59/72 *Baer-Getreide* v. *Einfuhr- und Vorratsstelle Getreide* [1973] E.C.R. 791 at 803. For a general comment see H. P. Ipsen, *Zur Haftung für normatives Unrecht nach europäischem Gemeinschaftsrecht, Festschrift für H. Jahrreiss*, Cologne/Berlin/Bonn/Munich 1974, pp. 85 *et seq.* and P. Gilsdorf, *op. cit.*, footnote 4.

[12] For further comment see J. Schwarze, "Rechtsschutz Privater gegenüber normativen Rechtsakten im Recht der EWG," in *Festschrift für Hans-Jürgen Schlochauer*, Berlin, New York 1981, pp. 927 *et seq.* (940 *et seq.*)

[13] See Case 238/78 *Ireks-Arkady GmbH* v. *Council and Commission* [1979] E.C.R. 2955 *et seq.*; Joined Cases 241 & 242 245–250/78 *DGV Deutsche Getreideverwertung and others* v. *Council and Commission* [1979] E.C.R. 3017 *et seq.*; Joined Cases 261 & 262/78 *Interquell Stärke-Chemie and others* v. *Council and Commission* [1979] E.C.R. 3045 *et seq.*; Joined Cases 64 & 113/76, 167 & 239/78, 27–28 & 45/79 *P. Dumortier and others* v. *Council* [1979] E.C.R. 3091; Case 256/81 *Pauls Agriculture* v. *Council and Commission* [1983] E.C.R. 1707 *et seq.*

[14] See Chapter 1.

[15] See above, Chapter 1.

SECTION 2

CIRCUMSTANCES GIVING RISE TO LIABILITY

A. ADMINISTRATIVE WRONGS

Administrative wrongs are specific unlawful decisions by the Community institutions which render the Community liable in consequence. The case-law shows significantly fewer compensation cases for unlawful administrative conduct, as opposed to legislative error, if complaints by Community officials are disregarded. This is due chiefly to the fact that most of the cases relate to the Community's agricultural law, which has a legal regime at Community level based mainly on written rules.

I. GENERAL PRINCIPLE

In Case 4/69 *Lütticke* v. *Commission* the Court summarised the conditions for a compensation claim against the Community[16]:

"By virtue of the second paragraph of Article 215 and the general principles to which this provision refers, the liability of the Community presupposes the existence of a set of circumstances comprising actual damage, a causal link between the damage claimed and the conduct alleged against the institution, and the illegality of such conduct."

II. PARTICULAR CONDITIONS

1. Official capacity

According to Article 215, second paragraph, of the EEC Treaty, the Community is liable for damage caused "by its institutions or by its servants," provided the damage occurs "in the performance of their

---

[16] [1971] E.C.R. 325 at 337, para. 10; on the conditions, see also Case 267/82 *Développement S.A. and others* v. *Commission*, para. 29.

508

duties." This excludes actions by the institutions which by their nature are not official duties; this might apply, for instance, to assistance with tax inquiries. What is more significant here, however, is the fact that Community servants may incur liability for acts classified as part of their duties depending on whether the individual concerned is liable in his private capacity or whether the Community itself is also liable to provide compensation.

Apparently, this question has only once featured in a case before the Court. In *Sayag* v. *Leduc*[17] the question was whether a Community official (in this case of Euratom) was acting in the performance of his duties when he caused an accident during an official journey by car. The Court considered the circumstances under which Community liability is incurred, and decided[18]:

"By referring at one and the same time to damage caused by the institutions and to that caused by the servants of the Community, Article 188 indicates that the Community is only liable for those acts of its servants which, by virtue of an internal and direct relationship, are the necessary extension of the tasks entrusted to the institutions.

In the light of the special nature of this legal system, it would not therefore be lawful to extend it to categories of acts other than those referred to above.

A servant's use of his private car for transport during the performance of his duties does not satisfy the conditions set out above.

A reference to a servant's private car in a travel order does not bring the driving of such car within the performance of his duties, but is basically intended to enable any necessary reimbursement of the travel expenses involved in the use of this means of transport to be made in accordance with the standards laid down for this purpose.

Only in the case of *force majeure* or in exceptional circumstances of such overriding importance that without the servant's using private means of transport the Community would have been unable to carry out the tasks entrusted to it, could such use be considered to form part of the servant's performance of his duties, within the meaning of the second paragraph of Article 188 of the Treaty.

It follows from the above that the driving of a private car by a servant cannot in principle constitute the performance of his duties

[17] [1969] E.C.R. 329.
[18] *Op. cit.*, footnote 17, pp. 335–336, paras. 5 to 11.

within the meaning of the second paragraph of Article 188 of the EAEC Treaty."

The actions of Community officials must therefore be directly and inherently connected with the tasks of the Community if they are to involve its liability in the sense of "duties" under the second paragraph of Article 215 of the EEC Treaty and of Article 188 of the Euratom Treaty.

2. The conduct of Community institutions or officials

The Court's "Lütticke formula" relies on the broad concept of "conduct" which gives rise to liability. This includes both acts and ommissions.[19] Conduct need not necessarily consist of enacting, or failing to enact, a legal instrument; it may also consist of an administrative measure.[20] In order to give rise to liability, however, this conduct must have specific outward effect. In Case 217/81 *Interagra* v. *Commission*, the Court therefore found that no liability was incurred by the Commission's dispatch of two telexes to the French marketing organisation FORMA, giving instructions for the interpretation of a regulation on the payment of refunds for exports of butter and butter oil to the USSR[21]:

"In its judgment of 27 March 1980 in Case 133/79 *Sucrimex* [1980] ECR 1299 the Court had the occasion to record that the application of Community provisions on export refunds is a matter for the national bodies appointed for this purpose and the Commission has no power to take decisions on their interpretation but may only express its opinion which is not binding upon the national authorities. It follows that the telex messages at issue are part of the internal co-operation between the Commission and the national bodies responsible for applying the Community rules in this field and as a

---

[19] P. Gilsdorf, in H.v.d. Groeben, H. v. Boeckh, J. Thiesing, C.-D. Ehlermann, *Kommentar zum EWG-Vertrag*, (3rd ed., Baden-Baden 1983), Artikel 215, nos. 32 *et seq.* An example of an omission found to incur liability was Case 14/78 *Denkavit* v. *Commission* [1978] E.C.R. 2497 at 2504, para. 1. Among more recent cases, see Case 244/83 *Meggle Milchindustrie* v. *Council and Commission* [1986] E.C.R. 1101.

[20] *Ibid.*

[21] [1982] E.C.R. at 2247, para. 8.

general rule that co-operation cannot make the Community liable to individuals."

Evidently, however, the Court does not exclude the possibility that in some cases internal acts of the administration may have external effects, so that damage caused by these may also incur liability.

3. The "illegality" of the conduct

The obvious requirement that the conduct which incurs liability must itself be unlawful has been further developed by the Court. It is not enough for the conduct to have violated a superior rule of law; the rule must also be one which is intended to protect the interests of the complainant.

The involvement of third parties in the infringement of the rule, included among the sources of liability, dates back to Joined Cases 9 and 12/69 *Vloeberghs* v. *High Authority*.[22] These cases turned on a refusal by the High Authority (now the Commission) to take steps requiring France to lift import restrictions on U.S. coal imported into the Community via Belgium. The Belgian coal merchants concerned were unsuccessful in their application to the High Authority for a decision under Article 88 of the ECSC Treaty, ordering France to lift the import ban. Another possible option would have been to resort to the mutual assistance measures among Member States in crisis situations provided for in Article 71 of the ECSC Treaty, under the supervision of the High Authority.[23] The Court commented as follows on the breach of this provision by the ECSC[24]:

> "Even if it is accepted that the Member States may defend themselves against such practices by the application of the mutual assistance provided for in Article 71, the duty to have recourse to the said mutual assistance is not intended to safeguard the interests of any third parties, but only the interests of the Community."

The Court also applied this finding to Article 215, second paragraph, of the EEC Treaty. It shows that the Community may be liable even in cases where the conduct incurring the liability is conduct by the Member States

---

[22] [1961] E.C.R. 197.
[23] *Op. cit.*, footnote 22, p. 208 in the summary of facts.
[24] *Op. cit.*, footnote 22, p. 217 in the judgment.

in breach of the Treaties, where the competent institutions have failed in their duty to exercise their supervisory functions with regard to the States concerned.[25]

By contrast, in the case of *Kampffmeyer and others* v. *Commission*,[26] the Court found that a rule affording protection to third parties had been infringed. This involved the approval by the Commission of a protective measure by the Federal Republic of Germany in respect of certain agricultural products. In earlier proceedings, this decision had been revoked because Article 22 of Regulation 19, on which it was based, had been wrongly applied.[27] In establishing the liability incurred by this infringement, the Court proceeded immediately from the assumption that the rule which had been violated must be one which protects third parties[28]:

"With regard to the argument that the rule of law which is infringed is not intended to protect the interests of the applicants, the said Article 22, together with the other provisions of Regulation No. 19, is directed, according to the wording of the fourth recital in the preamble to the regulation, to ensuring appropriate support for agricultural markets during the transitional period on the one hand, and to allowing the progressive establishment of a single market by making possible the development of the free movement of goods on the other. Furthermore, the interests of the producers in the Member States and of free trade between these States are expressly mentioned in the preamble to the said regulation. It appears in particular from Article 18 that the exercise of freedom of trade between States is subject only to the general requirements laid down by its own provisions and those of subsequent regulations. Article 22 constitutes an exception to these general rules and consequently an infringement of that article must be regarded as an infringement of those rules and of the interests which they are intended to protect. The fact that these interests are of a general nature does not prevent their including the interests of individual undertakings such as the applicants which as cereal importers are parties engaged in intra-Community trade. Although the application of the rules of law in question is not in general capable of being of direct and individual

---

[25] See also Advocate-General Gand, Joined Cases 5, 7 & 13–24/66, *Fa. E. Kampffmeyer and others* v. *Commission* [1967] E.C.R. 245 at 269.

[26] Joined Cases 5, 7 & 13–24/66 *Kampffmeyer* v. *Commission* [1967] E.C.R. 245 at 269.

[27] *Op. cit.*, footnote 26, p. 252 in the summary of facts.

[28] *Op. cit.*, footnote 26, pp. 262–263.

concern to the said undertakings, that does not prevent the possibility that the protection of their interests may be—as in the present case it is in fact—intended by those rules of law."

Advocate-General Gand comments on the theoretical background in his opinion[29]:

"The first condition was imposed by you in the judgment in the *Vloeberghs* case (9 and 12/60, Rec. 1961, p. 391) when you had to interpret Article 40 of the ECSC Treaty, and one may logically extend the application of it within the framework of the second paragraph of Article 215. It is based upon German law where Article 34 of the Basic Law makes a public authority liable only when the party responsible for the damage has infringed its *obligations to third parties* in the performance of a duty which has been entrusted to it; it is necessary to say, further, that if one is to believe counsel for the applicant in Case 13/66 that concept should be interpreted today in a very flexible manner. It is not without analogy with that concept of Italian law that rules which exist exclusively or principally in the public interest create, according to the circumstances, a legitimate interest allowing an action for annulment to be brought, but give no subjective right on the basis of which an action for damages may be brought. But, although it is admissible, that condition should not be followed too strictly for fear of rendering the concept of liability devoid of meaning."

The Advocate-General's concern, apparent especially in the last sentence, not to restrict the Community's liability to an excessive degree by the requirement that a rule protecting third parties has been infringed, is reflected in the case-law of the Court, as for instance in the grounds of judgment already quoted from the *Kampffmeyer* judgment.[30]

4. The "culpability" of the conduct which incurs liability

It has not yet been explained what degree of culpability must be

---

[29] *Op. cit.*, footnote 26, p. 274.
[30] See also P. Gilsdorf, in H.v.d. Groeben, H. v. Boeckh, J. Thiesing, C.-D. Ehlermann, *Kommentar zum EWG-Vertrag*, (3rd ed., Baden-Baden 1983), Artikel 215, p. 902 no. 41.

involved in the breach of a protective rule.[31] It is necessary, first, to distinguish between liability in the Coal and Steel Community under Article 40 of the ECSC Treaty, and non-contractual liability under Article 215, second paragraph, of the ECSC Treaty of Article 188, second paragraph, of the Euratom Treaty.

The Court apparently assumes, in ECSC law, that the liability involves an element of fault. In Joined Cases 19 and 21/60 and 2 and 2/61 *Société Fives Lille Cail and others* v. *High Authority*, it treated a failure by the High Authority to exercise supervision as follows[32]:

> "Whatever the reasons for this omission, it gravely neglected the duties of supervision required by a normal standard of care, and it is this shortcoming which gives rise to its liability."

Advocate-General Lagrange, in Case 33/59 *Compagnie des Hauts Fourneaux de Chasse* v. *High Authority*, states plainly[33]:

> "... the basis of liability under Article 40 of the Treaty is the 'wrongful act or omission'; this is subjective liability and the wrongful act or omission must be established."

The element of fault does not appear in the case-law on Article 215, second paragraph, of the EEC Treaty. The definition reproduced above of the conditions for liability, taken from the *Lütticke* judgment, omits any reference to the requirement that the breach of a protective rule must be culpable.

However, the following judgment in Case 5/71 *Schöppenstedt* v. *Council* contains a formulation which apparently leaves room for interpretation[34]:

> "The non-contractual liability of the Community presupposes at the very least the unlawful nature of the act alleged to be the cause of the damage."

This statement must be viewed in the context of the conditions for compensation in the event of a defective legal ruling, which were at issue

---

[31] P. Gilsdorf, *op. cit.*, footnote 30, p. 904 no. 45.
[32] [1961] E.C.R. 282 at 297 of the judgment.
[33] [1962] E.C.R. 381 at 395 of the Opinion.
[34] [1971] E.C.R. 975 at 984, para. 11.

in that case and are cited in the judgment.[35] It cannot therefore be assumed from the expression "at the very least" that the Court is reserving the right to test separately for fault before liability is established.

The remaining case-law on liability contains no further pronouncements on the condition of fault, yet it would be a mistake to assume that the Court has completely disregarded the subjective element of fault. That this is not so is clear from its findings on Article 40 of the ECSC Treaty. Unusual though it is, the requirement of a rule of third-party protection in this case shows that it has also served as a model for Article 215, second paragraph, of the EEC Treaty, although the legal sources are different. Moreover, in the Member States the requirement of fault is invariably among the conditions for State responsibility. It is therefore unlikely that the concept of Community liability can be wholly dissociated from the principle of liability based on fault. Rather, it may be assumed that the unlawfulness of the conduct is an indication of fault.[36] We shall consider below the question whether, in addition to Community liability based on fault, there is an independent duty of compensation patterned on the German concept of acts akin to expropriation.

III. DAMAGE WHICH CAN BE MADE GOOD

Article 215, second paragraph, of the EEC Treaty and Article 188, second paragraph, of the Euratom Treaty contain no definition of the nature and amount of compensation which may be made; instead, they refer to the "general principles common to the laws" of the Member States. A glance at the principles which actually apply in the Member States reveals many differences.[37] It is only in Article 40 of the ECSC Treaty that the compensation is defined exclusively in financial terms. In a somewhat sparse body of case-law on the question of damages, the Court has developed its own case-by-case approach; there are no references to comparative law.

---

[35] The passage which follows is rarely quoted. It runs:
   "Where legislative action involving measures of economic policy is concerned, the Community does not incur non-contractual liability for damage suffered by individuals as a consequence of that action, by virtue of the provisions contained in Article 215, second paragraph, of the Treaty, unless a sufficiently flagrant violation of a superior rule for the protection of the individual has occurred. For that reason the Court, in the present case, must first consider whether such a violation has occurred."

[36] See P. Gilsdorf, *op. cit.*, footnote 19, Artikel 215, p. 905, no. 46.

[37] See A. Bleckmann, in *Die Haftung des Staates* (*cf.* ref. in footnote 2), pp. 780 *et seq.*

1. The nature of the compensation

Unlike Article 40 of the ECSC Treaty, Article 215, second paragraph, of the EEC Treaty and Article 188, second paragraph, of the Euratom Treaty do not exclude restitution in kind. The general principle to which they refer is that the agent of the damage must restore the situation which would have existed if the event giving rise to liability had not occurred.[38] In the great majority of cases, however, the damage suffered would consist of financial loss, so that restitution in kind is of little practical relevance. There are also considerations of treaty law which argue against a general system of restitution in kind under Article 215, second paragraph, of the EEC Treaty and the parallel clause in the Euratom Treaty. Under Article 176 of the EEC Treaty, institutions whose acts have been declared void are required to take the necessary measures to comply with the judgment. In addition, Article 175 of the EEC Treaty offers a legal basis for claims consequent upon an annulment under Article 177 EEC, with the result that no such basis is found in Article 215, second paragraph, of the Treaty. It does, however, continue to apply where normative wrongs are concerned, since Article 173, second paragraph, and Article 175, third paragraph, pose narrower conditions for admitting claims on this basis.[39] Hence there are legal reasons why the possibility of restitution in kind on the basis of Article 215, second paragraph, is limited to a specific category of cases.

In parties' applications, however, a claim is sometimes made for compensation in the form of a restoration of the original situation.

For instance, in Case 68/77 *IFG-Interkontinentale Fleischhandelsgesellschaft* v. *Commission*,[40] which dealt with the issue of import licences in the beef market, the plaintiff had concluded a contract with the Romanian state foreign trading agency *PRODEXPORT* for deliveries of spiced cooked beef from Romania into the Community. According to Commission Regulation 1090/75, which was then in force, the issue of the import licences was dependent on the prior export of an equivalent quantity of beef, to ensure that the surplus situation on the beef market would not be worsened through the importation of meat from third countries.

However, cooked preserved beef in airtight packaging was exempt from this obligation. The transaction between IFG and the Romanian

---

[38] See A. Bleckmann, *op. cit.*, footnote 37, pp. 780 *et seq.*
[39] On this problem see P. Gilsdorf, with references, *op. cit.*, footnote 19, Artikel 215, p. 908, no. 51.
[40] [1978] E.C.R. 353 *et seq.*

agency was covered by this exception. But as a result of a flood disaster in Romania, delays occurred in deliveries of some of the meat consignments. In the meantime, a new Commission regulation came into force, which did not provide for any exceptions from the export obligation.[41] The IFG firm then applied to the Court requesting an order against the Commission to guarantee performance of the contract under the original conditions. The submissions of the complainant refer expressly to compensation in the form of "restitution in kind."[42]

The applicant in Case 90/77 *Stimming* v. *Commission* made a similar application.[43] The purpose of the application was to secure the importation free of levies of stewed pickled beef from Romania, which had become impossible because of a change in the law during the lifetime of the contract. The Court was asked to order the Commission to instruct the Federal Republic of Germany to permit the plaintiff to proceed with the imports free of levies, notwithstanding the rules in force.[44]

Both applications failed, because the conduct of the Commission had not been unlawful.[45] Otherwise, a claim for financial compensation is normally the commonest remedy sought.[46]

2. The extent of compensation

There must be a causal link between the unlawful conduct and the damage. In the past, the Court has considered the causality question in depth only where ECSC matters are concerned. The stance it has taken is similar to the German sufficiency theory, according to which the only forms of damage open to compensation are those which are not beyond the bounds of probability.[47] On this point, the Court commented in Case 36/62 *Société des Acieries du Temple* v. *High Authority*[48]:

---

[41] For the details, see the summary of facts, *op. cit.*, footnote 40, pp. 354 *et seq.*
[42] *Op. cit.*, footnote 40, p. 361.
[43] [1978] E.C.R. 995 *et seq.*
[44] *Op. cit.*, footnote 43, p. 1005, para. 2 on p. 1004.
[45] See *Stimming* v. *Commission, op. cit.*, footnote 43, p. 1009, para. 15; *IFG* v. *Commission, op. cit.*, footnote 40, p. 370, para. 11.
[46] See the Court's *Lütticke* formula, [1971] E.C.R. 325 at 337, para. 10. See also the detailed considerations of this aspect of liability in Joined Cases 197–200, 243, 245 & 247/80, *Ludwigshafener Walzmühle* v. *Council and Commission* [1981] E.C.R. 3211 at 3253, para. 46. The causal link was found to be missing in Case 169/73 *Compagnie Continentale* v. *Council* [1975] E.C.R. 177 at 135, paras. 22 to 23 *et seq.*.
[47] P. Gilsdorf, in H.v.d. Groeben, H. v. Boeckh, J. Thiesing, C.-D. Ehlermann, *Kommentar zum EWG-Vertrag* (3rd ed., Baden-Baden 1983), Article 215, no. 61.
[48] [1963] E.C.R. 289.

"The applicant submits that the wrongful act or omission which it imputes to the High Authority caused the injury of which it complains; it is, therefore, appropriate to examine this question first of all and to establish whether a causal link actually exists between the alleged wrongful act or omission and the alleged injury. For the purposes of this examination, one must not ask whether the conduct of the defendant in fact caused the error, but whether it could and should have caused such an error in the mind of a prudent person."

In the case-law on the EEC Treaty, only the Advocates-General have dealt in any detail with the causality question. An interesting comment is found in the Opinion of Advocate-General Dutheillet de Lamothe in Case 4/69 *Lütticke* v. *Commission*, referring expressly to the notion of sufficiency[49]:

"Article 215 requires in fact that there should be a causal link between the damage suffered and the fact alleged.

In the context of the ECSC Treaty the Court stated that this causal link had to be *direct*.

This is, in my opinion, also valid for the application of Article 215 of the EEC Treaty. In fact, whether in the same terms or under the slightly different description of sufficient causality (*causalité adéquate*), this requirement of a direct link between the alleged fact and the damage is found in the general principles common to the laws of all the Member States."

We need not dwell here on the problems of distinguishing direct from indirect damage, which are not touched upon in the case-law of the Court.[50] The Court has recognised loss of profit as damage entitled to compensation, provided there is sufficient evidence of the transactions on which the claim is based.[51] Where speculative transactions are concerned, it has accepted only part of the loss of profit[52]:

"The alleged injury in respect of the loss of profit is based on facts of an essentially speculative nature ... Thus the applicants may be regarded as having been aware of the abnormal speculative nature of

[49] [1971] E.C.R. 325 at 339.
[50] On this point see P. Gilsdorf, *op. cit.*, footnote 19, Artikel 215, p. 909, no. 52.
[51] See the *Kampffmeyer* decision, [1967] E.C.R. 245.
[52] *Op. cit.*, footnote 51, p. 266 of the judgment.

the transaction involved in their purchases of maize. By cancelling the transactions concerned, they avoided any commercial risk to themselves inherent in importation into the Federal Republic. Consequently it is not justifiable to acknowledge their right to recover the whole profit that they would have been able to obtain if the transaction which had been started had been performed. Taking this into account, the injury resulting from loss of profit for which the Community must be regarded as being liable cannot equitably be evaluated at a sum exceeding 10% of that which the applicants would have paid by way of levy, if they had carried out the purchases made but cancelled."

In another important case, the Court has accepted as loss of profit the damage caused to the plaintiffs through unlawfully withholding a subsidy.[53] In this case, the plaintiffs were producers of maize gritz. They claimed compensation for the damage they had suffered because the Council, contrary to the principle of equal treatment, had abolished the refunds payable on maize gritz while retaining them for maize starch.[54]

The grounds of judgment, reproduced below, illustrate how the damage is calculated and how the Court endeavours, when calculating the damage, to avoid over-compensating losses by applying the principle of mitigation of damage, which is also familiar to the law of the Member States[55]:

"This said, it is necessary to go on to examine the damage resulting from the discrimination to which the gritz producers were subjected. The origin of the damage complained of by the applicants lies in the abolition by the Council of the refunds which would have been paid to the gritz producers if equality of treatment with the producers of maize starch had been observed. Hence, the amount of those refunds must provide a yardstick for the assessment of the damage suffered.

The Council and the Commission objected to that method of calculating the damage on the ground that the gritz producers eliminated, or could have eliminated, the damage by passing on the loss

---

[53] There were several judgments; see Joined Cases 241–242 & 245–250/78, *DGV Deutsche Getreideverwertung* v. *Council and Commission* [1979] E.C.R. 3017.
[54] See the summary of facts and of the prior proceedings in the judgment, *op. cit.*, footnote 53, p. 3035, para. 1.
[55] *Op. cit.*, footnote 53, p. 3039, para. 14.

519

resulting from the abolition of the refunds in their selling prices. In principle, in the context of an action for damages, such an objection may not be dismissed as unfounded. In fact, it must be admitted that if the loss from the abolition of the refunds has actually been passed on in the prices the damage may not be measured by reference to the refunds not paid. In that case the price increase would take the place of the refunds, thus compensating the producer.

For their part, the applicants dispute that the loss was passed on in the way alleged. They state that, faced with the competition from the starch producers benefiting from refunds, they chose, as a matter of commercial policy, to sell gritz at a loss in order to retain their markets, rather than raise the prices at the risk of losing those markets. The price increases referred to by the Council and the Commission are, in the applicants' submission, due to the rise in the threshold price of maize and to the increase in production costs.

The parties have put forward statistics and other data in support of their respective submissions. Those data do not permit the conclusion advanced by the Council and the Commission to be accepted. The conclusion which emerges is rather that during the period in dispute the prices for gritz charged by the applicants and the price of starch developed along similar lines without reflecting the absence of refunds for gritz.

It follows that the loss for which the applicants must be compensated has to be calculated on the basis of its being equivalent to the refunds which would have been paid to them if during the period from 1 August 1975 to 19 October 1977 the use of maize for the manufacture of gritz used by the brewing industry had conferred a right to the same refunds as the use of maize for the manufacture of starch."

The Court takes a pragmatic attitude when it comes to ascertaining the exact amount of the loss; it refers the question to the disputants, reserving the right to resolve it if they fail to reach agreement[56]:

"The other applicants submitted a number of documents to the Court as proof of the quantities of gritz for which they may claim to be entitled to compensation and of the amounts of the refunds not paid (in) respect of those quantities. However, the Court is not in a

[56] *Op. cit.*, footnote 53, p. 3041, para. 20.

position at this stage of the procedure to give a decision on the accuracy of those data. Therefore, it is necessary to lay down by interlocutory judgment the criteria whereby the Court considers that the applicants must be compensated, leaving the amount of the compensation to be determined either by agreement between the parties or by the Court in the absence of such agreement."

Losses which the Court excludes for compensation purposes are those which are indissolubly connected with some rule or regulation, such as the deductions imposed by the ECSC scrap equalisation fund, which were the subject of Case 14/60 *Meroni and others* v. *High Authority*[57]:

"The Court cannot accept that the normal disadvantages which are bound to be inherent in the system of equalization amount to an injury giving rise to a claim for reparation and is reinforced in its view because these disadvantages affect every Community undertaking and because equalization on the other hand gives substantial advantages to all consumers of ferrous scrap, especially by maintaining the price of Community scrap at a reasonable level and by preventing much larger fluctuations of this price. In the present case it has not been shown that the disadvantage suffered by undertakings owing to the fact that they were for a time uncertain as to the final amount of their equalisation contributions is greater than the disadvantage normally inherent in the system which was chosen."

A further restriction on the duty to compensate arises if the party suffering the loss shares in the liability. This is clear from the judgment already quoted in the case of *Meroni* v. *High Authority*, where the applicants are told that they should have been prepared for the deductions imposed by the scrap equalisation scheme.[58]

An interesting contemporary example of shared liability leading to reduced compensation is the decision in Case 145/83 *Stanley George Adams* v. *Commission*.[59]

This judgment found, in brief, that the Community was in principle liable for action by the Commission which enabled the Swiss company Hoffman La Roche to identify a complainant on its staff as an informant

[57] [1961] E.C.R. 161 at 166–167 of the judgment.
[58] See also Advocate-General Roemer in Joined Cases 9 & 12/60, *Vloeberghs* v. *High Authority* [1961] E.C.R. 197 at 219 *et seq.*
[59] [1985] E.C.R. 3539.

of the Commission in a competition case.[60] The complainant, Stanley Adams, was brought before a Swiss court as a result of this identification, on a charge of disclosing industrial secrets. He also lost his pension rights from Hoffman La Roche and his newly acquired right of residence in Italy. His wife's suicide during the court proceedings in Switzerland, after she had been questioned by the Swiss police, highlights the tragic human side of this case and the consequences which may follow from administrative errors.[61]

However, the complainant himself had not acted with all due care. The Court therefore determined[62]:

> "It must therefore be concluded that the Community is bound to make good the damage resulting from the discovery of the applicant's identity by means of the documents handed over to Roche by the Commission. It must however be recognised that the extent of the Commission's liability is diminished by reason of the applicant's own negligence. The applicant failed to inform the Commission that it was possible to infer his identity as the informant from the documents themselves, although he was in the best position to appreciate and to avert that risk. Nor did he ask the Commission to keep him informed of the progress of the investigation of Roche, and in particular of any use that might be made of the documents for that purpose. Lastly, he went back to Switzerland without attempting to make any inquiries in that respect, although he must have been aware of the risks to which his conduct towards his former employer has exposed him with regard to Swiss legislation.
>
> Consequently, the applicant himself contributed significantly to the damage which he suffered. In assessing the conduct of the Commission on the one hand and that of the applicant on the other, the Court considers it equitable to apportion responsibility for that damage equally between the two parties.
>
> It follows from all the foregoing considerations that the Commission must be ordered to compensate the applicant to the extent of one half of the damage suffered by him as a result of the fact that he was identified as the source of information regarding Roche's anticompetitive practices. For the rest, however, the application must be dismissed. The amount of the damages is to be determined by

[60] *Ibid.*
[61] *Ibid.*
[62] *Ibid.*

agreement between the parties or, failing such agreement, by the Court."

In this case too, the Court therefore left it to the disputants to establish the exact amount of the damages, reserving the decision for itself in the event of their failing to agree.

Compensation may, finally, include interest and costs, such as the costs associated with concluding or terminating a contract. As for interest payments, the Court referred to the legal arrangements in the Member States when it decided, in Joined Cases 241, etc./78 *DGV Deutsche Getreideverwertung and others* v. *Council and Commission*[63]:

> "The applicants further claim that the Community should be ordered to pay interest at a rate of 6% from dates which are slightly earlier than the dates on which the actions were brought, it being alleged that the Community's liability for the unpaid refunds arose at those earlier dates.
>
> As it is a question of a claim made in relation to the non-contractual liability of the Community, pursuant to the second paragraph of Article 215, it must be considered in the light of the principles common to the legal systems of the Member States, to which that provision refers. It follows that a claim for interest is in general admissible. Taking into account the criteria for the assessment of damages laid down by the Court, the obligation to pay interest arises on the date of this judgment, in that it establishes the obligation to make good the damage. The rate of interest which it is proper to apply is 6%."

The fate of the plaintiff Stanley Adams is associated with a further type of loss for which compensation may be claimed, which can be defined as non-material or non-financial loss. The key judgment on this point was the case of *Algera and others* v. *Common Assembly*,[64] in which the transfer of certain Community officials from a contractual relationship to employee status led to a dispute. The applicants successfully appealed against the refusal to transfer them and sought compensation for both loss of income and non-material damage. The Court found that there was no financial loss, but that non-material damage had been suffered[65]:

---

[63] [1979] E.C.R. 3017 *et seq.* at 3041, paras. 21 and 22. See also Case 256/81 *Pauls Agriculture* v. *Council and Commission* [1983] E.C.R. 1707 at 1721, para. 16.
[64] [1957] E.C.R. 39.
[65] *Op. cit.*, footnote 64, pp. 66–67.

"... the wrongful behaviour of the defendant, namely the unlawful withdrawal of the application to the applicants of the Staff Regulations and the fact of having notified the orders of 12 December 1955 prematurely, which was to lead to their subsequent partial withdrawal, did cause the applicants non-material damage.

(a) Placed in a situation to which they were suited by their professional merits and which offered them every appearance of stability and permanence, the applicants found themselves without any fault on their part confronted with the prospect of a dismissal which meant the end of a career which they could legitimately rely on.

The shock caused by this action, the disturbance and uneasiness which resulted from it for those concerned, therefore caused the applicants non-material damage, for which they can claim compensation ...

(c) As to the amount which should be granted in compensation for the non-material damage, it must not be forgotten that the Common Assembly's gesture in granting them the material benefit of the orders of 12 December 1955 until the Court has given its decision was only the result of the court action and could not eliminate apprehension as to the future.

In the light of those considerations, the Court sets the damages payable to the applicants at 100 EPU units of account each."

Hence in this case, the Court fixes the amount of damages itself. So far, compensation for non-material damage has been confined to staff cases. This is doubtless due to the serious personal impact of legal relationships in this area. Nevertheless the *Stanley Adams* case shows that even in economic administrative law circumstances may arise in which legal values not reckonable in financial terms may be damaged, and in which the need for compensation for non-material damage should as a matter of principle be recognised.

B. THE PREREQUISITES OF LIABILITY FOR LEGISLATIVE WRONGS

In the *Schöppenstedt* judgment, the Court admitted that there is an inherent obligation in Community law to make restitution in the case of wrongful legislation. This remedy, which does not exist in all Member

States,[66] is however subject to special conditions which are not the same as the conditions applying to administrative error. The Court commented[67]:

> "In the present case the non-contractual liability of the Community presupposes at the very least the unlawful nature of the act alleged to be the cause of the damage. Where legislative action involving measures of economic policy is concerned, the Community does not incur non-contractual liability for damage suffered by individuals as a consequence of that action, by virtue of the provisions contained in Article 215, second paragraph, of the Treaty, unless a sufficiently flagrant violation of a superior rule of law for the protection of the individual has occurred. For that reason the Court, in the present case, must first consider whether such a violation has occurred."

Hence it is not enough that a rule of law for the protection of the individual has been breached. There must, in addition, be "a sufficiently flagrant violation of a superior rule of law." The effect will be to keep the number of those entitled to compensation as small as possible. The Court explains the reasons for this restriction in Joined Cases 83 and 94/76, 4, 15 and 40/77 *Bayerische HNL Vermehrungsbetriebe* v. *Council and Commission*[68]:

> "To determine what conditions must be present in addition to such breach for the Community to incur liability in accordance with the criteria laid down in the case-law of the Court of Justice it is necessary to take into consideration the principles in the legal systems of the Member States governing the liability of public authorities for

---

[66] See W. Morvay, "Die Haftung des Staates für rechtsetzende Akte," in *Die Haftung des Staates für rechtswidriges Verhalten seiner Organe* (*cf.* reference in footnote 2), pp. 776 *et seq.*

[67] Case 5/71 *Schöppenstedt* v. *Council* [1971] E.C.R. 975 at 984, para. 11. But see also Case 74/74 *CNTA* v. *Commission* [1975] E.C.R. 533 at 549, para. 44, concerning a Commission regulation which caused damage; here the Court found that the "violation of a superior rule of law" was sufficient. The importance of this case should not be exaggerated; it is probably a variation of language rather than of substance. On the conditions for liability for wrongful legislative measures, see Joined Cases 54–60/76 *Compagnie industrielle du Comté de Loheac* v. *Council and Commission* [1977] E.C.R. 645 at 658, paras. 8 to 9; Advocate-General Reischl in Case 49/79 *Pool* v. *Council* [1980] E.C.R. 569 at 585 and the Court's concluding remarks in Joined Cases 197–200, 243, 245 & 247/80 *Ludwigshafener Walzmühle* v. *Council and Commission* [1981] E.C.R. 3211 at 3246, paras. 17 *et seq.* with references to the earlier case-law.

[68] [1978] E.C.R. 1209 at 1224, para. 5.

damage caused to individuals by legislative measures. Although these principles vary considerably from one Member State to another, it is however possible to state that the public authorities can only exceptionally and in special circumstances incur liability for legislative measures which are the result of choices of economic policy. This restrictive view is explained by the consideration that the legislative authority, even where the validity of its measures is subject to judicial review, cannot always be hindered in making its decisions by the prospect of applications for damages whenever it has occasion to adopt legislative measures in the public interest which may adversely affect the interests of individuals."

The Court then goes on to indicate what a "sufficiently serious breach of a superior rule of law" may consist of. We recall that the case of *Bayerische HNL Vermehrungsbetriebe* dealt with the consequences of annulment of rules on the compulsory purchase of skimmed milk powder, found to be illegal owing to a breach of the ban against discrimination and of the proportionality principle. The Court did not consider this breach to be sufficiently serious. Moreover, the Court found it appropriate to require individuals to accept without compensation certain damaging effects of such a rule[69]:

"It follows from these considerations that individuals may be required, in the sectors coming within the economic policy of the Community, to accept within reasonable limits certain harmful effects on their economic interest as a result of a legislative measure without being able to obtain compensation from public funds even if that measure has been declared null and void. In a legislative field such as the one in question, in which one of the chief features is the exercise of a wide discretion essential for the implementation of the Common Agricultural Policy, the Community does not therefore incur liability unless the institution concerned has manifestly and gravely disregarded the limits on the exercise of its powers."

The considerations which follow, explaining why the Council did not manifestly and gravely disregard the limits on the exercise of its powers, do not, surprisingly, deal with the actual breach of law, but with its consequences[70]:

---

[69] *Op. cit.*, footnote 68, pp. 1224 *et seq.*, para. 6.
[70] *Op. cit.*, footnote 68, p. 1225, para. 7.

"In this connection it is necessary to observe first that this measure affected very wide categories of traders, in other words all buyers of compound feeding-stuffs containing protein, so that its effects on individual undertakings were considerably lessened. Moreover, the effects of the regulation on the price of feeding-stuffs as a factor in the production costs of those buyers were only limited since that price rose by little more than 2%. This price increase was particularly small in comparison with the price increases resulting, during the period of application of the regulation, from the variations in the world market prices of feeding-stuffs containing protein, which were three or four times higher than the increase resulting from the obligation to purchase skimmed-milk powder introduced by the regulation. The effects of the regulation on the profit-earning capacity of the undertakings did not ultimately exceed the bounds of the economic risks inherent in the activities of the agricultural sectors concerned."

In the isoglucose cases, the Court likewise found that the Community was not liable for losses occasioned by a levy on this starch product, owing to the absence of a sufficiently grave violation. The Court emphasised the condition of gravity[71]:

"Although, in its judgment of 25 October 1978, giving a preliminary ruling within the framework of a consideration of the validity of Regulation No. 1111/77, the Court found that the charges borne in pursuance of that regulation by isoglucose producers by way of production levy were manifestly unequal as compared with those imposed on sugar producers, it does not follow that, for the purposes of an assessment of the illegality of the measure in connexion with Article 215 of the Treaty, the Council has manifestly and gravely disregarded the limits on the exercise of its discretion.

In fact, even though the fixing of the isoglucose production levy at five units of account per 100 kg of dry matter was vitiated by errors, it must nevertheless be pointed out that, having regard to the fact that an appropriate levy was fully justified, these were not errors of such gravity that it may be said that the conduct of the defendant institutions in this respect was verging on the arbitrary and was thus of such a kind as to involve the Community in non-contractual liability.

[71] Joined Cases 116 & 124/77 *Amylum* v. *Council and Commission* [1979] E.C.R. 3497 at 3561 *et seq.*, paras. 18 to 21.

It must also be recalled that Regulation No. 1111/77 was adopted in particular to deal with an emergency situation characterized by growing surpluses of sugar and in circumstances which, in accordance with the principles set out in Article 39 of the Treaty permitted a certain preference in favour of sugar beet, Community production of which was in surplus, whilst Community production of maize was to a considerable extent deficient.

It follows from these considerations that the Council and the Commission did not disregard the limits which they were required to observe in the exercise of their discretion in the context of the common agricultural policy in such a serious manner as to incur the non-contractual liability of the Community."

Accordingly, not even a "manifestly unequal" measure leads to a "manifest and grave disregard" of the legal limits on the institutions, *i.e.* to a sufficiently grave violation.

In the starch and maize gritz cases the Court found that the Community was liable, having considered in conjunction the consequences and the seriousness of the violation. It will be remembered that the set of rules in question was regarded as a breach of the equality principle, because it cancelled without adequate justification the long-standing practice of treating both products equally. On the sufficiently grave violation which this involved, the Court commented[72]:

"In the circumstances of these cases, the Court is led to the conclusion that there was on the part of the Council such a grave and manifest disregard of the limits on the exercise of its discretionary powers in matters of the Common Agricultural Policy. In this regard the Court notes the following findings in particular:

In the first place it is necessary to take into consideration that the principle of equality, embodied in particular in the second subparagraph of Article 40(3) of the EEC Treaty, which prohibits any discrimination in the common organization of the agricultural markets, occupies a particularly important place among the rules of the Community law intended to protect the interests of the individual. Secondly, the disregard of that principle in this case affected a limited and clearly defined group of commercial operators. It seems, in fact, that the applicants in these cases and in the related Cases

---

[72] [1979] E.C.R. 3017 at 3038, paras. 10 *et seq.* See also the references in footnote 13.

64/76 and others, *P. Dumortier Frères S.A.* v. *Council* comprise the entire maize gritz industry of the Community. Further, the damage alleged by the applicants goes beyond the bounds of the economic risks inherent in the activities in the sector concerned. Finally, equality of treatment with the producers of maize starch, which had been observed from the beginning of the common organization of the market in cereals, was ended by the Council in 1975 without sufficient justification.

The Council's disregard of the limits imposed upon its discretionary power is rendered all the more manifest by the fact that, as the Court pointed out in its judgment of 19 October 1977, the Council has not acted upon a proposal made by the Commission in June 1975 to re-introduce the refunds for maize gritz on the ground that the absence of such refunds could foreseeably upset the balance between the breweries' raw materials costs in maize gritz and maize starch.

For those reasons the Court arrives at the conclusion that the Community incurs liability for the abolition of the refunds for maize gritz under Regulation No. 665/75 of the Council."

This indicates that the determining factors in ascertaining liability arising from a breach of law are the number of persons affected, the amount of damage they have suffered and the gravity of the breach itself. The applications so far lodged on the basis of legislative wrongs show that compensation is granted only in rare instances.[73] This has excited criticism, not only of the vagueness of the designation of a "sufficiently flagrant" breach, but also, more generally speaking, of the Court's restrictive attitude in this area.[74]

To extend the judicial protection available to individuals, it has been suggested that the concept of normative decisions should be more narrowly defined, so that only basic Council regulations would be subject to the strict liability rules described above.[75] Commission regulations would be regarded as administrative decisions and would be covered by the less restrictive conditions of liability for administrative errors. But since these

---

[73] The only successful applications in the field of economic administrative law have been the starch and maize gritz cases.

[74] For these criticisms, see B. Beutler, R. Bieber, J. Pipkorn, J. Streil, *Die Europäische Gemeinschaft—Rechtsordnung und Politik* (3rd ed., Baden-Baden 1987), pp. 263 *et seq.*; see also E. W. Fuss, *La responsabilité des Communautés Européennes pour le comportement illégal de leurs organes*, in RTDE 1981, 1 *et seq.* (7 *et seq.*, with references).

[75] *cf.* P. Gilsdorf, *op. cit.*, footnote 47; no. 68, p. 921.

regulations are undeniably normative in character and many administrative regulations contain legal formulations, an extended application of the rules for administrative error is advocated only for those regulations which are intended to adapt the basic regulation to changed conditions, through a legal reformulation of the parameters originally set out.

The case-law shows, however, that the Court has not made any such distinction. Mention may be made of the judgment in Joined Cases 194 and 206/83 *Asteris A.E. and others* v. *Commission*.[76] Here the applicants were seeking compensation for an error made in fixing the coefficient for calculating a subsidy for tomato pulp. The Court found, without comment, that the regulation in question, which consisted mainly of the results of a computation in accordance with the instructions in the basic regulation, was subject to the basic principles of liability for legislative wrongs.[77]

[76] [1985] E.C.R. 2815.
[77] *Ibid.*

SECTION 3

OTHER FORMS OF LIABILITY

A. LIABILITY FOR ILLEGAL ACTS NOT INVOLVING FAULT

In Joined Cases 63 to 69/72, *Wehrhahn* v. *Council*, the complainant had lodged a subsidiary claim for compensation for an act tantamount to expropriation[78]:

"By way of reply and as a subsidiary point the applicants cite the existence of a principle that calls for compensation by reason of an illegal intervention on the part of a public authority, comparable to an expropriation.

Without it being necessary to decide the question whether Article 215 covers such a liability, it suffices to state that since the criticised interventions involve no illegality, the submission relating thereto must be rejected."

As early as the *Kampffmeyer* decision in 1967, Advocate-General Gand[79] had mentioned this aspect, but without coming to any definite conclusion. In its judgment in the *Tezi* case the Court left the question open, finding that no illegal action was involved.[80] These examples do not however mean that compensation for acts by public authorities comparable to expropriation cannot be allowed. Nor does the fact that this form of liability is not widely recognised in the legal systems of the Member States preclude *a priori* its being adopted in Community law,[81] since the "minimal theory" in developing principles of liability was rejected early

---

[78] [1973] E.C.R. 1229 *et seq.*, at 1253, paras. 29 *et seq.* See also the opinion of Advocate General Roemer, *op. cit.*, p. 1255.

[79] In Joined Cases 5, 7 & 13–24/66 *Kampffmeyer and others* v. *Commission* [1967] E.C.R. 245.

[80] Case 59/84 *Texi Textiel B.V.* v. *Commission* [1986] E.C.R. 867, paras. 70 *et seq.*

[81] H. Steinberger, "Die fehlerhafte Amtshandlung als tatbestandliche Grundlage der Haftung des Staates im hoheitlichen Bereich," in *Haftung des Staates für rechtswidriges Verhalten seiner Organe* (ref.: footnote 2), pp. 753 *et seq.* (765).

531

on. There remain, however, genuine doubts whether it is wise to incorporate an extended form of liability of this kind in the Community's legal system.[82]

B. LIABILITY FOR LAWFUL ACTS

On a literal reading of Article 215, second paragraph, of the EEC Treaty and Article 188, second paragraph, of the Euratom Treaty, it is possible for the Community to be liable for lawful acts. However, this is a point which has not yet been finally clarified. The Court has so far dealt only once with the question of the duty to make good the consequences of lawful actions. In Joined Cases 9 and 11/71 *Compagnie d'approvisionnement and others* v. *Commission*[83] the applicants sought compensation for the losses they had suffered when an equalization subsidy for monetary measures was fixed at too low a figure. Their application, arguing that the decision in question was unlawful, was dismissed.[84] The Court commented as follows on this application for compensation for an action which was lawful but unusually damaging to the complainants[85]:

"The applicants claim that the Community incurs liability even in the absence of illegality because the applicants have suffered 'unusual and special damage' owing to the fact that they were treated less favourably than, first, importers from Member States other than France and, secondly, than German and Netherlands exporters.

Any liability for a valid legislative measure is inconceivable in a situation like that in the present case since the measures adopted by the Commission were only intended to alleviate, in the general economic interest, the consequences which resulted in particular for all French importers from the national decision to devalue the franc.

Consequently, the submission is unfounded."

---

[82] See E. W. Fuss, "Grundfragen der Gemeinschaftshaftung," EuR 1968, pp. 353 *et seq.* (362 *et seq.*).
[83] [1972] E.C.R. 245.
[84] *Op. cit.*, footnote 83, p. 391, para. 44.
[85] *Op. cit.*, footnote 83, pp. 407–408, para. 45. Likewise, in Case 267/82 *Développement S.A. and others* v. *Commission* [1986] E.C.R. 3331, para. 33, the Court rejected an argument that liability and responsibility were different notions, and justified it in this case by pointing to the damage suffered by the complainant, which was not unusually severe.

Advocate-General Trabucchi concluded from this statement that the Court had tacitly admitted the Community's liability for lawful acts, and was denying it only in the particular circumstances of this case.[86]

However, in Joined Cases 63 to 69/72 *Wehrhahn* v. *Commission*, Advocate-General Roemer rejected the notion of liability for lawful acts.[87] Legal writers are also sceptical on this point.[88] However, it is probable that the Court has not yet had the last word on the subject.

C. ABSOLUTE LIABILITY

In the legal systems of the Member States, a form of strict liability for permitting hazards is quite common.[89] Absolute liability is also significant for the Communities. It may be of practical importance where official vehicles are involved in traffic accidents or, in particular, where damage is caused by nuclear installations. However, this problem has not yet been

---

[86] See his opinion in Case 169/73 *Compagnie Continentale France* v. *Council* [1975] E.C.R. 117 at 141.

[87] [1973] E.C.R. 1229 at 1273.

[88] E. Grabitz, in Grabitz, *Kommentar zum EWG-Vertrag*, Munich, 1984, no. 44 on Article 215, with references. On a survey of national legal systems, we find liability for lawful acts (strict liability) only in France and the Federal Republic of Germany. However, the German "intervention akin to expropriation" is the result of a legal theory specially tailored to the Basic Law. Under Article 14 of the Basic Law, expropriation according to or on the basis of statute is lawful only if the statute in question provides for compensation. A ruling is seen as causing expropriation if a special sacrifice is demanded from the party concerned. However, administrative decisions may also have the effect of causing expropriation, for instance, if construction works on public highways hinder traffic and imperil business activity. The Federal Court has developed the concept of "intervention akin to expropriation" in order to provide for such unforeseen consequences of administrative conduct. It is justified by the gap in legal liability left by Article 14 of the Basic Law, in cases where the expropriation occurs not on a statutory basis but simply as a factual consequence of acts by the public authorities. See F. Ossenbühl, *Staatshaftungs-recht* (3rd ed., Munich 1983), pp. 148 *et seq.* with references. On recent instances of intervention akin to expropriation, see BGHZ 91, 20 (26 *et seq.*) and BGH, NJW 1988, pp. 478 (479 *et seq.*). In France, a similar form of liability has been developed in administrative case-law. The "théorie de la rupture de l'égalité devant les charges publiques" assumes that in normal circumstances, a citizen must accept the undesirable effects of an administrative decision. If, however, the administration imposes exceptional burdens on the individual, the State must make these good; see also the opinion of Advocate-General Capotorti in Joined Cases 83 & 94/76, 4, 15 & 40/77 *HNL Vermeh-rungsbetriebe* v. *Council and Commission* [1978] E.C.R. 1209 at 1234, with references to the French case-law, especially the decision of the Conseil d'Etat of January 14, 1938—*La Fleurette*—Receuil Lebon, p. 25.

[89] H. Steinberger, in *Haftung des Staates* (see footnote 2), p. 766.

dealt with in the case-law. Nevertheless, where atomic energy installations are concerned, it has for some time been generally agreed that liability exists under Article 188, second paragraph, of the Euratom Treaty.[90]

[90] See H. D. Mosthoff, "Die ausservertragliche Haftung der Euratom," EuR 1966, pp. 174 *et seq*.

SECTION 4

DELIMITATION OF LIABILITY SYSTEMS IN THE COMMUNITIES AND THE MEMBER STATES

In a highly complex series of cases, the Court has developed the principles whereby the respective areas in which rules of liability apply in the Communities and in the Member States can be distinguished. The governing principle is that Community liability is a subsidiary matter. This approach of the Court has sparked off criticism both of a theoretical nature and from the perspective of legal policy, to which we shall refer in one connection only.[91] Below we turn to the most important of the Court's statements on this question, in findings which must be considered, the critics notwithstanding, as precedents in this field.

The key problem arises in connection with indirect implementation. Here, the interaction between acts of Member States and Community acts can lead to situations of shared liability, which cause difficulty in selecting the appropriate remedy.

We begin with the *Kampffmeyer* decision from the year 1967.[92] In this case, the complainants applied both to a German court and to the Luxembourg court for compensation amounting to the total of levies they had paid contrary to law. In this procedural situation, the European Court decided[93]:

". . . those applicants have informed the Court that the injury alleged is the subject of two actions for damages, one against the Federal Republic of Germany before a German court and the other against the Community before the Court of Justice. It is necessary to avoid the applicants' being insufficiently or excessively compensated for the same damage by the different assessment of two different courts applying different rules of law. Before determining the damage for which the Community should be held liable, it is necessary for the national court to have the opportunity to give judgment on any

---

[91] See Advocate-General Dutheillet de Lamothe in Joined Cases 9 & 11/71, *Compagnie d'approvisionnement* v. *Commission* [1972] E.C.R. 391 at 414.

[92] Joined Cases 5, 7 & 13–24/66 *Fa. E. Kampffmeyer and others* v. *Commission* [1967] E.C.R. 245 *et seq.*

[93] *Op. cit.*, footnote 92, pp. 266–267 of the judgment.

liability on the part of the Federal Republic of Germany. This being the case, final judgment cannot be given before the applicants have produced the decision of the national court on this matter."

The Court thus circumvents the possibility of conflicting judgments by admitting that Community liability is secondary to national liability.

In Case 96/71 *Haegemann* v. *Commission* the Court continued with the same approach, although the procedural situation was different.[94] The Haegemann company was objecting to an equalization payment for wine imports from Greece, levied by the domestic authorities on the basis of a Commission regulation. In a decision addressed to the applicant, the Commission had refused to grant an exemption. The Court decided, in respect of its competence to rule on the appeal and the plea for compensation[95]:

"The countervailing charge in question is part of the own resources referred to in Article 6 of the Council Decision of 21 April 1970.

It is therefore for the competent national authorities to rule on claims for the refund of that charge.

The applicant's claim for a refund should therefore have been made to those authorities.

In these circumstances the Commission's refusal of the applicant's request is not an act capable of being the subject of an application for annulment within the meaning of Article 173 of the Treaty.

The application for annulment is therefore inadmissible.

The applicant maintains further that by reason of the defendant's behaviour it has suffered exceptional damage as a result of loss of profit, unforeseen financial outlay and losses on existing contracts.

The question of the possible liability of the Community is in the first place linked with that of the legality of the levying of the charge in question.

It has just been found that, in the context of the relationship between individuals and the taxation authority which has levied the charge in dispute, the latter question comes under the jurisdiction of the national courts.

Accordingly, at the present stage the claim for compensation for possible damage must be dismissed."

[94] [1972] E.C.R. 1015.
[95] *Op. cit.*, footnote 94, p. 1025, paras. 9 to 13.

The remainder of the case-law is lacking in consistency. In Case 43/72 *Merkur* v. *Commission*,[96] concerning compensation for damage which the complainant claimed to have suffered through the failure to fix a monetary compensatory figure for the export of barley products, the Court, with the explicit support of Advocate-General Mayras,[97] found that it was competent to decide the case[98]:

> "The Commission then maintains that the applicant should be sent back to pursue its claim before the administrative and judicial authorities in the Federal Republic of Germany, on the grounds that the event giving rise to the present dispute was the refusal by the competent customs office in that Member State to grant the applicant compensatory amounts on the exports it had made to third countries.
>
> If such a procedure were followed it would result in a reference to the Court under Article 177 of the Treaty from the German courts of the question of the validity of Regulations Nos. 1014/71 and 1687/71.
>
> But the Court already has the case before it and within its jurisdiction, and is therefore bound to see whether or not these regulations are tainted with the alleged irregularities.
>
> It would not be in keeping with the proper administration of justice and the requirements of procedural efficiency to compel the applicant to have recourse to national remedies and thus to wait for a considerable length of time before a final decision on his claim is made."

We recall that in the *Kampffmeyer* decision, the Court did not hesitate to refer the complainant to domestic remedies, which were certainly no less complex to pursue. The application by a French exporter of agricultural products was also dismissed as inadmissible. The company *Interagra* of Paris[99] applied for compensation for refunds on exports of butter and butter oil to the USSR, discontinued under a Commission regulation. The actual decision to refuse the refunds had been made by the responsible French authority (*Forma*). The Court commented as follows on the Commission's objection that the plea was inadmissible[100]:

---

[96] [1973] E.C.R. 1055 *et seq.*
[97] *Op. cit.*, footnote 96, pp. 1076 *et seq.*
[98] *Op. cit.*, footnote 96, p. 1069, paras. 5 *et seq.*
[99] Case 217/81 *Interagra* v. *Commission* [1982] E.C.R. 2233.
[100] *Op. cit.*, footnote 99, p. 2248, para. 9.

"The decision to refuse the applications for export certificates, which is said to be the cause of the damage alleged by the applicant, is therefore to be seen as having been adopted by the French intervention agency.

As the Court stated in its judgment of 12 December 1979 in Case 12/79 *Wagner* [1979] E.C.R. 3657, the purpose of the action for damages provided for in Articles 178 and 215 of the Treaty is not to enable the Court to examine the validity of decisions taken by national agencies responsible for the implementation of certain measures within the framework of the common agricultural policy or to assess the financial consequences resulting from any invalidity of such decisions."

This is followed by a pronouncement which must be regarded as typical of the contemporary case-law on the distribution of judicial competence in liability questions, wherever action has been taken or omitted by a national authority as well as a Community institution[101]:

". . .a review of the administrative acts of Member States in applying Community law is primarily a matter for national courts, without prejudice to their power to refer questions for a preliminary ruling to the Court under Article 177 of the EEC Treaty. In the circumstances the remedy to be envisaged in the present case is an action before the national courts, to which the applicant has in fact already applied."

But the case-law also shows that the remedy chosen depends, essentially, on whether acts by a Community institution or those by a national authority are the basis of liability. It is clear that in this area the legal position at present is far from satisfactory.

[101] *Op. cit.*, footnote 99, p. 2248, para. 10.

PART 5

SUMMARY AND CONCLUSION

A. THE PRESENT SITUATION

The legality of the administration is recognized, in all Member States of the European Community, as one of the pillars of the constitutional State. In every constitution, however, the executive varies in its approach, and this is especially true of the European Community itself.

On the national level, great importance is attached to the historical experience of the executive in the attribution of powers compared with other constitutional organs and individuals. In France, the weakened executive of the Fourth Republic was followed by a stronger administration in the Fifth Republic, equipped with independent legislative powers. By contrast, the dominant tendency in Germany after 1945 was to place as many legal fetters as possible on an executive which had previously been too powerful. Parliament too was to be prevented from ever again depriving itself of authority, through an express statutory reservation forbidding the delegation of legislative powers to the administration. This is clear from the wording of the key clause in the Basic Law, Article 80, paragraph 1, sentence 2. On the Community level, however, the horizontal and vertical distribution of powers reflects the functions of an inter-State institution whose powers are limited.

The position of the administration in the various constitutional systems is a consequence of its relationship to the other two powers. Its legal links with the parliament are shown by statute law to result from a binding act of will by the popular assembly. Nowadays, the law which obliges the executive to perform its administrative role is a bridge between the representatives of the sovereign authority and the actual practice of government. Administrative acts in accordance with statute have emerged, with the growth of the welfare state, as the prevalent type of administrative conduct, so that little scope for discretionary decision remains.

However, the impregnation of administrative activity by law has not produced an executive without a will of its own, a mere machine for

539

issuing legal definitions and decisions. Although, in theory, the administration's subjection to law is virtually absolute, to take this view would be to ignore the reality and the demands of State practice.

Even in its intervention role, a State legislating to protect public security and order has been unable to do without powers expressed in general terms. Moreover, rules of redress had inevitably to be stated in abstract terms when the State left behind its role as a mere protector of the existing order and began planning for the social status of many categories of citizens by means of benefits of various kinds.

The modern state apparatus would be unable to operate without relying on sufficiently abstract formulations. Legislators seek to fulfil the task of steering this ship by using undefined terms capable of comprehending many individual cases, at the same time enabling the administration to act within a broad framework through the use of enabling clauses or mandatory provisions.

This phenomenon is also to be found, at various levels, in European Community law.

In the founding treaties, and especially in the EEC Treaty, open and flexible wordings were deliberately chosen in a number of places, partly to enable the Community lawmakers to choose the right legislative formula and partly to express the lack of political unity among the contracting States, which were anxious to prevent certain future options being foreclosed and did so by framing the provisions in deliberately vague language.

Similarly, undefined legal notions abound in the normative provisions of secondary law. Here, however, it is usually the special features of the subject-matter which are responsible for the flexibility of the powers conferred. There are instructive examples of this in agricultural, foreign trade and competition law. Here, the administration at E.C. level or in the Member States has the task of applying to individual cases the broadly framed legislation adopted in these areas.

It falls to the courts to define the framework within which the administration may lay claim to independent powers of decision-making, whether in ascertaining the relevant facts or in ordering specific measures.

It is also commonly found, in domestic administrative law systems, that where the rules are vaguely formulated it is ultimately the courts which have to decide on the precise legal constraints by which the administration is bound. The German administrative courts take a comparatively strict and dogmatic view, proceeding from the assumption that the interpretation of undefined legal terms by the administration is essentially open to judicial review and that administrative discretion is confined to the freedom to select the legal consequences in specific cases on its own responsibility, the exercise of this prerogative being open to investigation only as regards observance of the legal limits of discretion.

In the other Member States, by contrast, there is no such strict division between the different levels of legal control of the executive.

Here we may mention the case law of the French administrative courts, which exercise their review powers chiefly on a case-by-case basis and tend to make room for administrative discretion and freedom of decision even where the language of the law is vague. Nor does the European Court draw any firm distinction, when determining the extent of judicial review, between "undefined legal terms" and "discretion." Instead, it uses the concept of discretion in its broadest sense, as meaning the freedom of the executive to act untrammelled either by statute or by the courts. Hence the criteria by which the Court decides on the thoroughness of its review practice are different in origin from those on which German administrative law is based. The Court sees the extent of its review as being not so much a problem of legal theory and method, but rather as a problem of judicial practice, to be resolved chiefly by apportioning the burden of decision properly as between the judiciary and the executive. Where acts of intervention are concerned, the severity of the intervention will also help to determine the extent of the judicial review.

Our survey of the case-law of the European Court in selected fields of Community law has revealed a complex picture. To avoid repetition, we shall give a summary reminder of the situation using the examples of agricultural and competition law.

In the area of agricultural law, which at Community level is dominated by normative decisions, the emphasis lies on ensuring that the common market in agriculture is capable of functioning. However, the Court frankly admits the limits on its own powers of assessment, faced with the complexity and unpredictability of market situations. The importance of the efficiency of the administration is reflected in the recognition that both Council and Commission enjoy wide discretionary powers, while the idea of an agricultural administration based on a common organization is expressed in the close ties between the national implementing agencies and Community agricultural law. The choice of language is particularly important, since it determines whether a legal principle common to the legal systems of all Member States is both sufficiently abstract and sufficiently concrete to play the guiding role proposed for it.

By comparison, the Court's extensive review powers in competition law, especially under Articles 85 and 86 of the EEC Treaty, are striking.

In this area of law, which is governed mainly by precedent, the main priority is given to judicial protection of the interests of the undertakings concerned. Even here, however, the Commission is given wide discretionary powers in individual cases.

On the whole, the Court seems surprisingly flexible in its approach to the legal constraints on other Community organs. Unlike, for instance, the case-law of the German administrative courts, there is no discernible set of principles for judicial review. Only in certain limited fields is it possible to anticipate roughly how extensive the review is likely to be, and then only where the issues involved are comparable with those in previous cases.

In a comparison with national administrative law systems, only the German system is markedly more predictable as regards the extent of judicial review.

B.   PROSPECTS FOR DEVELOPMENT

It will be clear from the foregoing that the development of legal constraints on the administration is not solely a problem of administrative law. The legality of the administration is, rather, a *matter of constitutional law* and thus a precondition for the emergence of a body of administrative law. Apart from recent trends in the reservation of statute, the basic constitutional issue of legality or adherence to statute has been widely elucidated in the Member States and in the Community. There are, however, difficulties in the area of administrative freedom of decision, especially in the German administrative law system. Areas of conflict arise mainly in the indirect implementation of Community law, and especially in agricultural law and the matter of levies. Some examples are given in Part 3, Section 2. The outward cause of potential conflict in these particular fields is the binding nature of preliminary rulings by the Court (Article 177 of the EEC Treaty) for national courts. Hence a German administrative court must in certain cases recognise a power of the German authorities to apply a rule of equity in the agricultural market as involving a discretion, although from a German point of view the conditions for such a prerogative of appraisal do not exist.

If we recall that the restrictive treatment of administrative freedom of decision in the Federal Republic of Germany is based on the constitution, the Court's greater willingness to allow such freedom may lead to constitutional conflict in certain areas.

542

Even if this does not happen, it seems rather optimistic to hope that the rigid judicial review practices of German administrative courts will be rendered more flexible through the European model.

On the other hand, conflicts of this sort are somewhat improbable in other legal systems, at least as regards the testing of discretionary decisions, since the national courts mostly adopt a flexible approach in deciding how far a review should go. Indeed it is questionable whether there is any room for European judicial practice to influence the review practices of national courts.

It is reasonable to conclude that where the legal constraints and freedoms of the administration are concerned, there will be no full-scale "dialogue between legal systems." This is because judicial controls are mostly used flexibly in the Member States; where formal tests are applied, these are defended on constitutional law grounds. Conversely, it is hardly necessary for the European Court's review practice to be supplemented by national models. The option the Court has already chosen, which is to use its review powers in an elastic way, strikes the necessary balance between enabling the administration to function properly and securing the judicial protection necessary for citizens of the Market.

CHAPTER 4

THE PRINCIPLE OF EQUALITY AND THE PROHIBITION OF DISCRIMINATION AS OBLIGATORY MAXIMS OF GOVERNMENT ACTION

A.   INTRODUCTION

I.   GENERAL PROBLEMS AND THE DEVELOPMENT OF THE PRINCIPLE; STRUCTURE AND METHOD OF THE SURVEY

The principle of equality before the law is one of the oldest and most fundamental principles of all law and is firmly rooted, as a substantive principle, in the constitutional and administrative law of every democratic constitutional system. Even though the principle may take different forms in different countries, as a legal maxim its validity is almost uniformly acknowledged in every state in the Western world.[1] What we shall be discussing in this chapter will be detailed aspects of this maxim.[2]

Far more than any other legal principle, however, the principle of equality before the law has undergone profound changes in substance and significance in the course of its development.[3]

With the Declaration of the Rights of Man and of the Citizen of August 26, 1789 the principle of equality before the law acquired political significance in western Europe for the first time.[4] In Germany the principle of equality before the law was first mentioned in the constitution of the

---

[1] cf. E. Zimmermann, *Die Preisdiskriminierung im Recht der Europäischen Gemeinschaft für Kohle und Stahl*, Frankfurt am Main 1962, pp. 30 *et seq.*, 32.
[2] See under A.V. below.
[3] See on this point K. Hesse, "Der Gleichheitssatz im Staatsrecht," AöR Vol. 77 (1951/52), pp. 67 *et seq*.
[4] See K. Hesse, *op. cit.*, footnote 3, p. 170.

Kingdom of Westphalia drawn up by Napoleon. It is also to be found in several south German constitutions, for example the Bavarian constitution of 1818 (preamble: "Equality of the Laws and before the Law") and the constitutions of Baden (§§ 7–10), Württemberg (§§ 21, 22) and Hesse (Art. 18). The Prussian constitution of 1850 proclaimed the principle of equality in its Article 4.

The imperial constitution proposed by the Frankfurt National Assembly after the revolution of 1848 contained wide-ranging provisions on equal rights, but with the failure of this attempt at German unification the proposals lapsed.

The 1867 constitution of the North German Confederation and the 1871 constitution of the German empire contained no guarantees at all on basic rights and hence no principle of equality before the law.[5]

After the 1918 revolution, Article 109 of the Weimar Constitution enshrined the principle of the equality of all Germans before the law. In its early stages of development as an element of constitutional law, the equality principle was, by its content, confined to removing differences arising from the class system.[6] Later it was seen as providing the basis for equality of rights as between men and women, until finally it came to constitute a legal foundation for demands for social and political equality.[7]

It will be clear even from this brief outline that the substance and significance of the equality principle are largely determined by the political, social and ethical ideas of the time. Thus equality emerges as an extremely dynamic principle showing no signs of regularity in its development and hence offering wide scope for divergent interpretations of its content.[8] Any attempt to determine the content of the equality principle from its present form alone therefore inevitably ends up in a more or less formal definition of only limited usefulness.[9] To comprehend the essence of the principle, its concepts, tendencies and dynamics, it is vital also to know the conditions which make its emergence possible in the first place. Only if there is a clear understanding of the preconditions necessary for

---

[5] cf. K. Hesse, ibid., pp. 170 et seq., with references to contemporary literature.
[6] cf. K. Hesse, op. cit., footnote 3, p. 171; ibid., "Der Gleichheitssatz in der neueren deutschen Verfassungsentwicklung," AöR Vol. 109 (1984), pp. 174 et seq. (175); details in, for example, R. Brunet, Le principe d'égalité en droit français, Paris 1910, pp. 54 et seq., 56 et seq.
[7] cf. K. Hesse, op. cit., footnote 3, p. 171; ibid., op. cit., footnote 6, pp. 175 et seq. Details in Brunet, ibid., pp. 71 et seq., 96 et seq., 123 et seq.
[8] Thus K. Hesse, op. cit., footnote 3, pp. 169 and 170.
[9] cf. K. Hesse, op. cit., footnote 3, p. 169.

the emergence of the equality principle, is it possible to determine its content correctly; as has been rightly said, "its practical application requires a theoretical foundation."[10]

The theoretical basis of the equality principle in law will therefore also be discussed in the following sections, which deal with the concept of equality (II), the possible orientations of the principle (III) and the concept of arbitrary action (IV). Only after that has been done will it be appropriate to examine the present form taken by the equality principle in the individual national legal orders (V) and to attempt to ascertain whether, in this or a similar form, it is also a component of Community law.

With reference to this aim of the study, it should be noted before proceeding any further that the equality principle, as a constitutional rule, requires of the legislature from the outset that in shaping its legislation it should essentially ensure that similar situations are dealt with in a similar manner and make distinctions only when these are objectively justified.[11]

For their part, too, the bodies which interpret, apply and execute the law may not draw arbitrary distinctions if there is scope for them to make an assessment or exercise their discretion; they must guarantee uniform application of the law.[12]

These basic requirements inherent in the principle are recognised in German law, for example, under Article 3 of the Basic Law.[13]

In this chapter we shall examine the extent to which the equality principle is also binding on the public authorities under Community law, both in the formulation of the relevant provisions of secondary law and in the interpretation and application of existing law.

A reading of the Treaties establishing the European Communities will show, however, that the texts do not expressly enshrine the equality principle as such, but that they do contain a number of anti-discrimination provisions, for example in Articles 4(b) and 60(1) ECSC and Articles 7, 36, 37, 40(3) subsection 2, 48(2), 49(c), 52, 60, 67, 79, 85(1)a, 86(a) and 132(5) EEC.

This raises the question not only whether the equality principle is recognised as a general legal principle of Community law but also, if it is

---

[10] Thus K. Hesse, *op. cit.*, footnote 3, p. 170.
[11] See under A.III. and A.IV. below.
[12] This is a substantive principle: it should not be confused with the requirement of formal equality of application of the law. See under A.III.1. below.
[13] See under A.V. below.

so recognised, of its relationship to the anti-discrimination provisions of the Treaties (VI).

The method used in the rest of this chapter is principally an analysis of the decisions of the Court of Justice of the European Communities. For obvious reasons it is possible here to make only a selection from the relevant cases. By giving an accurate account of the cases in question it is hoped, firstly, to illustrate the principle in concrete terms for practical purposes and, secondly, to prevent over-hasty generalisation. Since the equality principle is so widely applicable, we shall be discussing the extent of its observance not only in the administrative application of the law but also in the framing of individual legislative provisions.

II. THE CONCEPT OF EQUALITY

Lack of conceptual exactitude often leads to an incorrect interpretation of "equality" as being complete correspondence between two or more persons, objects, relationships or situations that are being compared.[14] Although this interpretation is right in stressing that the nature of the concept "equality" necessarily presupposes the existence and mutual comparison of at least two entities, it fails to recognise that the concept itself excludes any possibility of complete correspondence.[15] The objects of the comparison must differ at least in time or space if there is to be any question of their equality, since otherwise the comparison could only reveal that they were identical and hence that there was only one object.[16]

From this it follows that "equality" can never be absolutely complete, but can exist only partially—in relation to specific qualities and relationships which are examined as to the extent to which they correspond.[17]

---

[14] cf. R. Herzog, under the headword "Gleichheitssatz," in Kunst, Hermann, Grundmann, Siegfried, Schneemelcher, Wilhelm, Herzog, Roman (ed.), *Evangelisches Staatslexikon* (1st ed., Stuttgart/Berlin 1966), pp. 696 *et seq*. (696).

[15] cf. R. Herzog, *ibid.*, p. 696; K. Hesse, *op. cit.*, footnote 3, p. 172.

[16] cf. K. Hesse, *op. cit.*, footnote 3, p. 172; W. Kewenig, *Der Grundsatz der Nicht-diskriminierung im Völkerrecht der internationalen Handelsbeziehungen*, Vol. 1: *Begriff der Diskriminierung*, Frankfurt am Main 1972, p. 73; B. Börner, "Diskriminierungen und Subventionen," KSE Vol. 17, Cologne/Berlin/Bonn/Munich 1973, pp. 49 *et seq*. (51 *et seq*.) with reference to St. Thomas Aquinas's maxim: "Ibi possumus identitatem dicere, ubi differentia non invenitur."

[17] cf. R. Herzog, *op. cit.*, footnote 14, p. 697; K. Hesse, *op. cit.*, footnote 3, p. 173; W. Kewenig, *op. cit.*, footnote 16, p. 73; H. P. Ipsen, "Gleichheit," in F. L. Neumann, H. C. Nipperdey, U. Scheuner (ed.), *Die Grundrechte*, Vol. 2, Berlin 1954, pp. 111 *et seq*.

What qualities and relationships are involved in the individual case will depend on the problem at issue, that is to say on the point of view from which the comparison is actually made.[18] The validity of every judgment which confirms or denies the equality of the objects being compared can therefore be only relative. Any claim that two objects had absolute equality would lack all logical justification.[19]

Accordingly, on the basis of the concept of equality, it can immediately be said that the core problem of the equality principle is not really the determination or judgment of equality as such but the choice of the qualities and relationships whose equality or inequality is at issue in the individual case.[20] But these qualities and relationships, usually characterised as "essential," cannot be determined by objective means. Only if the reflective standpoint, the *tertium comparationis*, is adopted, can it be decided what is essential in the specific case and what can be disregarded as being inessential.[21] The selection cannot be strictly logical.[22] Thus it may happen that the same entities are equal for one person but unequal for another, because the standpoints of comparison were not the same for both persons.[23]

It will be clear from this that views as to what is equal and should be treated equally in law[24] may diverge widely and that there may well be no means of proving which view is correct.[25] This means that every judgment on equality must be confined to the individual case. No judgment can claim universal validity in this area.[26]

---

(180); also judgments in Case 1/54 *Government of the French Republic* v. *High Authority* [1954–1955] E.C.R. 1 at 21, and in Joined Cases 3–18, 25 & 26/58 *Barbara Erzbergbau AG and Others* v. *High Authority* [1960] E.C.R. 173 at 209.

[18] *cf.* K. Hesse, *op. cit.*, footnote 3, p. 174. See for example the E.C.J. decisions mentioned in footnote 17, in which the comparability of the facts is compared from the standpoint of transport (*France* v. *Commission*) and from the standpoint of the market situation (*Erzbergbau*).

[19] *cf.* K. Hesse, *op. cit.*, footnote 3, p. 173; B. Börner, *op. cit.*, footnote 16, pp. 51 *et seq.*; G. Leibholz, *Die Gleichheit vor dem Gesetz* (1st ed., Berlin 1925), pp. 51 *et seq.*

[20] *cf.* R. Herzog, *op. cit.*, footnote 14, p. 697; W. Kewenig, *op. cit.*, footnote 16, p. 73; G. Leibholz, *op. cit.*, footnote 19, p. 48.

[21] *cf.* K. Hesse, *op. cit.*, footnote 3, p. 174 on equality in general and p. 204 specifically on equality under the law; B. Börner, *op. cit.*, footnote 16, p. 52; E. Zimmermann, *op. cit.*, footnote 1, pp. 30 *et seq.* For the *tertium comparationis* in comparative law, see Introduction above.

[22] *cf.* K. Hesse, *op. cit.*, footnote 3, p. 174; B. Börner, *op. cit.*, footnote 16, p. 52 with further references.

[23] *cf.* K. Hesse, *op. cit.*, footnote 3, p. 174.

[24] See under A.III.2. below.

[25] Thus K. Hesse, *op. cit.*, footnote 3, p. 169.

[26] *cf.* E. Zimmermann, *op. cit.*, footnote 1, pp. 30 *et seq.*

III. POSSIBLE ORIENTATIONS OF THE PRINCIPLE

1. The Requirement of Formal Equality in the Application of the Law

In the nineteenth century in particular and on into the early years of the twentieth the equality principle was regarded as a purely formal legal rule with the aid of which uniform application of the law without regard to persons could be assured.[27] Interpreted in this way, the equality principle merely meant that the law had to apply to everybody, that there were therefore no persons "exempt from the law" and that legal provisions had to be put into effect "strictly," hence without regard to persons.[28] In this connection law was understood as universal law, that is to say as rules governing factual situations, rules with which everyone could comply and by the statutorily prescribed consequences of which everyone, in so complying, would be affected—whether positively or negatively.[29]

As a requirement of mere equality in the application of the law, the equality principle was thus only a confirmation of the principle of the legitimacy of the executive and the judiciary, so that alongside the latter principle it enjoyed a degree of autonomy only in the area of the exercise of official discretion.[30] It was automatically assumed that adequate regard had been had to the equality principle by the fact of the universality of the law. This was because it was assumed that the universality of the law necessarily guaranteed its material uniformity.[31]

It soon became clear, however, that this interpretation of the uniformity of the law was too narrow. It was found to be correct only when the criteria of the law did in fact apply to everyone. For it does not automatically follow from the universality of the law that the law must apply to everyone.[32] Thus the law may differentiate at will between the factual situations to be regulated without thereby surrendering any part of its

---

[27] *cf.* R. Herzog, *op. cit.*, footnote 14, p. 698. See also G. Dürig under the headword "Gleichheit," in Görres-Gesellschaft (ed.), *Staatslexikon*, Vol. 3, Freiburg 1959, pp. 985 *et seq.*; K. Hesse, *op. cit.*, footnote 6, p. 175.

[28] *cf.* R. Herzog, *op. cit.*, footnote 14, p. 698.

[29] *cf.* R. Herzog, *op. cit.*, footnote 14, p. 698. See also K. Hesse, *op. cit.*, footnote 3, p. 175.

[30] *cf.* R. Herzog, *op. cit.*, footnote 14, pp. 698 *et seq.* See also G. Leibholz, *op. cit.*, footnote 19, pp. 30 *et seq.*

[31] *cf.* R. Herzog, *op. cit.*, footnote 14, p. 699.

[32] *cf.* K. Hesse, *op. cit.*, footnote 3, p. 176.

universality. That would not occur until the law attempted to impose a numerical restriction on the parties to whom it applied.[33]

Thus material equality cannot be attained solely through the requirement of formal equality of application of the law. Interpreted as a requirement of this kind, the only function of the equality principle, ultimately, is to ensure the uniform application of the law and—connected with this—the uniformity of the legal order.

2. The Requirement of Substantive Equality Before the Law

The inadequacies of the equality principle when it is conceived of as a requirement of mere equality of application of the law, which we have just described, are avoided if the principle itself is regarded as a requirement of substantive equality before the law. In this interpretation, the equality principle springs from the original idea of justice, which means that the equal treatment which the principle demands must be just.[34] However clear and simple this interpretation of the equality principle may seem, the introduction of the concept of justice into the discussion brings in an element that eludes any possibility of formal definition.[35] The following two key maxims, which will be explained in more detail below, give at best a descriptive account of the meaning of justice: they are that each person should be granted his due (*suum cuique tribuere*) and—more specifically—that like must be treated in like manner and unlike in unlike manner.[36]

This description of justice is traditional. Originating in Aristotle's distinction between retributive and distributive justice,[37] it has lasted

---

[33] cf. K. Hesse, *op. cit.*, footnote 3, p. 176.

[34] cf. H. Henkel, *Einführung in die Rechtsphilosophie*, Munich/Berlin 1964, pp. 301 *et seq.*, particularly pp. 304 *et seq.*; R. Herzog, *op. cit.*, footnote 14, p. 698; E. Zimmermann, *Die Preisdiskriminierung im Recht der Europäischen Gemeinschaft für Kohle und Stahl*, Frankfurt am Main 1962, p. 30.

[35] cf. H. Henkel, *ibid.*, pp. 304 *et seq.*; K. Hesse, *op. cit.*, footnote 3, p. 198; G. Leibholz, *op. cit.*, footnote 19, pp. 55 *et seq.*

[36] Thus H. Henkel, *op. cit.*, footnote 34, p. 305; E. Zimmermann, *op. cit.*, footnote 34, pp. 30, 34; a different view is taken by H. Kelsen, *Reine Rechtslehre*, Vienna 1960, pp. 390 *et seq.*, who regards the principle that like must be treated in like manner and unlike in unlike manner not as an imperative of justice but as a logical requirement (especially pp. 394 *et seq.*).

[37] Aristotle, *Nicomachean Ethics*, Book 5, Chapters 5–7. *cf.* in particular H. Henkel, *op. cit.*, footnote 34, pp. 310 *et seq.*; E. Zimmermann, *op. cit.*, footnote 34, p. 30; H. Coing, *Die obersten Grundsätze des Rechts*, Heidelberg 1947, p. 31.

unchanged for two millennia as the basis of Western legal thinking.[38] In drawing this distinction, Aristotle postulated two different kinds of equality: on the one hand absolute[39] or arithmetical, on the other hand proportional or geometric equality.[40] Of these two kinds of equality the first (the absolute or arithmetical) governs retributive justice, which presupposes a relationship of mutuality and aims at securing, for instance, equality of performance and counter-performance, goods and price, or damage and compensation.[41] In this form, justice lies in a simple—arithmetical—equality. It aims to even out inequalities which have arisen and therefore systematically treats all persons in the same way.[42]

By contrast, distributive justice is based on the proportional or geometric type of equality.[43] The task of this second type of justice is to regulate the treatment of different persons when it comes to the allocation of property and obligations.[44] In particular, its aim is to ensure that every member of a community is rewarded or burdened in accordance with his merits, hence that like is treated in like manner and unlike in correspondingly unlike manner.[45]

According to the distributive philosophy, equality—and hence justice—is to be achieved by regulating each situation in due proportion.[46] Consequently, it is not a question of systematically treating everyone in the same way; rather, the crucial factor governing the distribution of property and obligations is the worth of the individual.[47]

After Aristotle's time, it was chiefly the second of the two doctrines, that of distributive justice, that was taken up and extended. Eventually it was formulated classically in the principle of *suum cuique tribuere*, enun-

---

[38] *cf.* K. Hesse, *op. cit.*, footnote 3, p. 197 with further references; H. Henkel, *op. cit.*, footnote 34, pp. 305, 310.

[39] From a purely conceptual point of view, this designation is not accurate—see under A.II. above.

[40] Schneemelcher, Wilhelm, Herzog, Roman (ed.), *Evangelisches Staatslexikon* (1st ed., Stuttgart/Berlin 1966), pp. 620 *et seq.* (621).

[41] *cf.* H.-J. Birkner, *ibid.* p. 621; H. Henkel, *op. cit.*, footnote 34, pp. 311, 315 *et seq.*

[42] *cf.* K. Hesse, *op. cit.*, footnote 3, pp. 197 *et seq.*; H. Henkel, *op. cit.*, footnote 34, p. 311.

[43] *cf.* H.-J. Birkner, *op. cit.*, footnote 40, p. 621.

[44] *cf.* H.-J. Birkner, *op. cit.*, footnote 40, p. 621; H. Henkel, *op. cit.*, footnote 34, p. 310.

[45] *cf.* H.-J. Birkner, *op. cit.*, footnote 40, p. 621; K. Hesse, *op. cit.*, footnote 4, p. 197; see also G. Leibholz, *op. cit.*, footnote 19, p. 45.

[46] Thus K. Hesse, "Der Gleichheitssatz im Staatsrecht," AöR Vol. 77 (1951/52), p. 197.

[47] *cf.* K. Hesse, *op. cit.*, footnote 46, p. 197; H. Henkel, *op. cit.*, footnote 34, pp. 310 *et seq.* On the concept of worth in this connection see H. Henkel, *ibid.*, pp. 313 *et seq.*

ciated by Cicero but usually quoted from the Roman jurist Ulpian.[48] Under this principle the requirement of substantive equality before the law is limited by the demand that each person should be granted his due and his rights, and hence that like should be treated in like manner and unlike in unlike manner.[49]

If there were such a thing as absolute equality, the last-mentioned maxim would determine the content of the equality principle once and for all. But because "equality" is relative,[50] it remains an open question, in the final analysis, how someone is to receive "his due" in the sense of *suum cuique*—through equal or unequal treatment.[51] To a certain extent this decision will always be subjective and may thus lead to considerable uncertainty about the content of the equality principle.[52] If the equality principle is regarded as a substantive legal principle derived from the concept of justice, a certain concomitant degree of legal uncertainty will generally have to be accepted.[53]

IV. THE CONCEPT OF ARBITRARY ACTION

Even if neither of the two doctrines of justice outlined above substantively lays down what legal treatment is specifically "just," they do establish negative guidelines which exclude certain solutions—those solutions, that is, which are at variance with justice.[54] All attempts to comprehend the content of the equality principle therefore concentrate

---

[48] *cf.* H.-J. Birkner, *op. cit.*, footnote 40, p. 622; K. Hesse, *op. cit.*, footnote 46, p. 197 with further references; E. Zimmermann, *op. cit.*, footnote 34, p. 30; H. Coing, *op. cit.*, footnote 37, p. 29. Ulpian, in D 1.1.10, writes: *"Justitia est constans et perpetua voluntas ius suum cuique tribuendi. Juris praecepta sunt haec: Honeste vivere, alterum non laedere, suum cuique tribuere"*—quoted in H. Coing, *ibid.*

[49] *cf.* H.-J. Birkner, *op. cit.*, footnote 40, p. 622; E. Zimmermann, *op. cit.*, footnote 1, pp. 30, 34; H. Coing, *op. cit.*, footnote 37, pp. 30 *et seq.*; R. Herzog, *op. cit.*, footnote 14, p. 698.

[50] See under A.II. above.

[51] *cf.* R. Herzog, under the headword "Gleichheitssatz," in Kunst, Hermann, Grundmann, Siegfried, Schneemelcher, Wilhelm, Herzog, Roman (ed.), *Evangelisches Staatslexikon* (1st ed., Stuttgart/Berlin 1966), p. 698; H. Henkel, *op. cit.*, footnote 34, pp. 305 *et seq.*, 308; H. Kelsen, *op. cit.*, footnote 36, p. 366. G. Jaenicke, under the headword "Diskriminierung," in K. Strupp (founder), H.-J. Schlochauer (ed.), *Wörterbuch des Völkerrechts*, Vol. 1, Berlin 1960, pp. 387 *et seq.* (390 *et seq.*), sees in the requirement that like should be treated in like manner and unlike in unlike manner only a "shifting of the problem"; similarly, B. Börner, *op. cit.*, footnote 16, p. 52, who describes this requirement as "circular reasoning."

[52] *cf.* R. Herzog, *op. cit.*, footnote 51, p. 698; K. Hesse, *op. cit.*, footnote 46, p. 198.

[53] Thus R. Herzog, *op. cit.*, footnote 51, p. 698.

[54] *cf.* H. Henkel, *op. cit.*, footnote 34, p. 309.

on the concept of arbitrary action which, as the contrary correlate of justice, means nothing less than the "radical, absolute negation" of justice[55] and consequently covers every equal and unequal treatment which is simply irreconcilable with a sense of what is right and wrong.[56]

Understood in this way, the concept of arbitrary action represents a "limiting concept," a concept from the outermost sphere of the law.[57] As such, this too is a conditioned value-concept which is just as little amenable to formal and universally valid definition as justice itself.[58] In the same way its content is also subject to constant change and is meaningful only in relation to individual cases.[59] The only general characteristics that can be derived from the concept of arbitrary action is that it is inherently in opposition to what is regarded as "reasonable" at the time and specifically to the laws and rules which should properly be complied with.[60] For "arbitrary law" is "false law," differing from it only in degree in that no reasonable grounds or no grounds which are reasonable as to their principal content can be adduced in support of the legal act in question.[61] However, even the concept of what is "reasonable" cannot be defined in objective and/or formal terms.[62]

---

[55] Thus G. Leibholz, *op. cit.*, footnote 19, p. 72; *ibid.*, "Das Verbot der Willkür und des Ermessensmissbrauchs im völkerrechtlichen Verkehr der Staaten," first published in ZaÖRV, Vol. 1, Part 1 1929, pp. 77 *et seq.*, Darmstadt reprint, p. 2. The same view was taken by Advocate-General Lagrange in his opinion in Joined Cases 8–13/57 [1958] E.C.R. 317 at 365, with reference to the anti-discrimination provisions of Articles 4(b) and 60(1) ECSC: "Ultimately it appears to me that when the rule of non-discrimination relates to a decision of the High Authority constituting intervention on the market, the scope of this rule must be appraised first and foremost in the context of this concept of arbitrariness." See also under B.II.1. below; on the relation of the anti-discrimination provisions to the equality principle, see under A.VI. below.

[56] *cf.* G. Leibholz, *op. cit.*, footnote 19, pp. 61, 73, 77; E. Zimmermann, *op. cit.*, footnote 34, pp. 36 *et seq.*; critical comments by K. Hesse, *op. cit.*, footnote 46, pp. 170 *et seq.*, 205, 206, 215, and H. P. Ipsen, *op. cit.*, footnote 17, pp. 152 *et seq.* In the context of its formal recognition in individual national legal systems (see under A.V. below), the equality principle is generally interpreted as a prohibition of arbitrary action. *cf.* for example K. Feige, *Der Gleichheitssatz im Recht der EWG*, Tübingen 1973, with reference to the individual countries; K. Hesse, *op. cit.*, footnote 6, pp. 186 *et seq.*, on cases decided by the German Federal Constitutional Court, and pp. 194 *et seq.* on supreme court decisions in some other European countries and in the United States.

[57] Thus G. Leibholz, *op. cit.*, footnote 55, p. 2.

[58] *cf.* G. Leibholz, *op. cit.*, footnote 55, p. 2.

[59] *cf.* G. Leibholz, *op. cit.*, footnote 55, p. 2; *ibid. op. cit.*, footnote 19, pp. 73, 78.

[60] Thus G. Leibholz, *op. cit.*, footnote 19, p. 72; see also H. Henkel, *op. cit.*, footnote 34, p. 309.

[61] Thus G. Leibholz, *op. cit.*, footnote 19, p. 87; see also p. 76, where this statement is related to laws.

[62] *cf.* G. Leibholz, *op. cit.*, footnote 19, p. 87. H. P. Ipsen, *op. cit.*, footnote 17, is also no doubt alluding to this when he remarks, on pp. 156 *et seq.*, that there can barely be said to

V. THE BINDING NATURE OF THE EQUALITY PRINCIPLE AS A LEGAL RULE

If equality before the law is to be a binding legal principle, it has to be recognised by the legal system in force at the time.[63]

In Western legal systems this recognition is traditionally given mainly in constitutional and administrative law,[64] which is our central concern here. A glance back in time reveals that the equality principle as a legal rule with constitutional status first appeared in the constitutions of the North American states.[65] In 1789 its validity as a principle was proclaimed by the French Revolution, to be incorporated later into various European constitutions.[66] Nowadays the idea of the equality of the citizen before the law has become so rooted in the consciousness of the peoples of the Western world that it is one of the basic principles of modern Western constitutional and administrative law.[67]

1. General Validity

Specifically, it can be said that the equality principle is enshrined as a positive precept in the national constitutions of the majority of European countries[68] and in that of the United States.[69]

In all these countries the equality principle is regarded as a substantive and comprehensively binding legal principle.[70] It is thus binding not only

be any justiciable criteria for the concept of arbitrary action; see earlier comment in footnote 56 above.

[63] Thus E. Zimmermann, *op. cit.*, footnote 34, p. 31.

[64] *cf.* E. Zimmermann, *op. cit.*, footnote 34, p. 31.

[65] *cf.* E. Zimmermann, *op. cit.*, footnote 34, pp. 31, 32; G. Leibholz, *op. cit.*, footnote 19, p. 14.

[66] *cf.* E. Zimmermann, *op. cit.*, footnote 34, pp. 31, 32; G. Leibholz, *op. cit.*, footnote 19, p. 14.

[67] *cf.* E. Zimmermann, *op. cit.*, footnote 34, p. 31. For a general discussion on this point see under A.1. above.

[68] Namely the Federal Republic of Germany, Italy, Belgium, the Netherlands, Luxembourg, Ireland, Denmark, Greece, Portugal and Spain among the Member States of the European Communities and Austria and Switzerland as Western European "third countries."

[69] Article 3(1) of the German Basic Law; Article 3(1) of the Italian constitution; Article 6(2) of the Belgian constitution; Article 11(2) of the Luxembourg constitution; Article 1(1) of the Dutch constitution; Article 40(1) of the Irish constitution; Article 4 of the Greek constitution; Article 13 of the Portuguese constitution; Article 14 of the Spanish constitution; Article 2 (*inter alia*) of the Austrian National Basic Law; Article 4 of the Swiss constitution; the 14th Amendment to the American constitution (para. 1, 2nd sentence).

[70] For an understanding of the equality principle as a substantive legal principle, see under A.III.2. and A.IV. above. For the practice followed in the individual countries, see the authors listed in footnote 56 above.

on the executive and the judiciary but also on the legislature, although this does not necessarily mean that the courts have the power to test legislative acts for their compatibility with basic rights—and hence with the equality principle.[71]

2. Special National Features

(a) French law

Among the States which maintain the equality principle as a constitutional rule, France to some extent occupies a special position. In that country the equality principle, despite being mentioned in Articles 1, 6 and 13 of the *Déclaration des droits de l'homme* of 1789, in the preamble to the 1946 constitution and in the preamble and Articles 2 and 3 of the 1958 constitution, has long been regarded only as a *principe général du droit, i.e.* as a general legal principle binding only on the authorities that interpret and apply the law.[72] This tradition was not broken until December 27, 1973, when the Conseil Constitutionnel delivered a decision to the effect that the statutory provision which was being contested in the specific case was invalid because it contravened the *principe de l'égalité*, which had been enshrined in the 1789 "Déclaration des droits de l'homme" and guaranteed anew in the preamble to the current constitution (of 1958).[73]

With this decision the Conseil Constitutionnel was continuing its "new" case law, which had started with its decision of July 16, 1971.[74]

What is fundamentally new about this line of decisions is that they also adduce the preamble to the 1958 constitution as a substantive yardstick by

---

[71] See in particular, with reference to the individual countries K. Feige, *op. cit.*, footnote 56, and R. Bernhardt, "Probleme eines Grundrechtskatalogs für die Europäischen Gemeinschaften," in Bulletin of the European Communities, supplement 5/76, pp. 19 *et seq.*

[72] *cf.* for example P. Tiffreau, "Le principe d'égalité en droit économique," in F.I.D.E., "Le principe d'égalité en droit économique," Reports, Vol. 2, The Hague 1984, Chap. 8, p. 1; F. Miclo, "Le principe d'égalité et la constitutionnalité des lois," AJ 1982, pp. 115 *et seq.* (117). See also G. Vedel, P. Delvolvé, *Droit administratif* (11th ed., Paris 1985), pp. 78 *et seq.*; A. de Laubadère, *Droit administratif*, Vol. 1, (9th ed., Paris 1984), pp. 266, 269 *et seq.*

[73] Décision No. 73–51 DC du 27 décembre 1973, Rec. p. 25. See L. Favoreu, L. Philip, *Les grandes décisions du Conseil Constitutionnel* (3rd ed., Paris 1984), pp. 274 *et seq.*; see also P. Tiffreau, *ibid.*, p. 1; F. Miclo, *ibid.*, p. 118; G. Braibant, *Le droit administratif français*, Paris 1984, pp. 222 *et seq.*; G. Vedel, P. Delvolvé, *ibid.*, pp. 398 *et seq.*

[74] See L. Favoreu, L. Philip, *ibid.*, pp. 222 *et seq.*; J.-F. Lachaume, "Les grandes décisions de la jurisprudence," *Droit administratif*, Paris 1980, pp. 22 *et seq.* See also in this

which to test proposed legislation. Since the above decision on the equality principle was pronounced, it has been beyond dispute that the 1789 "Déclaration des droits de l'homme" is also included via that preamble.[75]

Clearly the equality principle is now classified as a constitutional principle. This follows ultimately from the fact that the Conseil Constitutionnel no longer feels obliged to refer to the preamble to the 1958 constitution when citing the equality principle. It now refers only to "Article 6 of the 'Déclaration des droits de l'homme et du citoyen de 1789' "[76] or simply speaks of the "principe de l'égalité devant la loi" without quoting a specific provision.[77]

The Conseil d'Etat has long recognised the equality principle as a general legal principle. Thus it occurs as early as 1913 as the "principle of the equality of all citizens before the administrative ordinances"[78] and is formulated today— comprehensively and generally—as the "equality of the citizen before the law."[79]

In the course of its judgments the Conseil d'Etat has developed a number of groups of cases which give concrete expression to various aspects of the equality principle; examples are the equality of the sexes and equality of liability to public charges.[80]

In substance, the principle signifies, in French law also, that like must be treated in like manner and unlike in unlike manner, so that in the final analysis the equality principle requires, here too, only that arbitrary distinctions should not be made.[81]

connection G. Ress, "Der Conseil Constitutionnel und der Schutz der Grundfreiheiten in Frankreich," JöR NF Vol. 23 (1974), pp. 122 et seq.

[75] See F. Miclo, op. cit., footnote 72, pp. 115, 117 et seq.

[76] Décision No. 76–67 DC du 15 juillet 1976, Rec. p. 35. See F. Miclo, op. cit., footnote 72, p. 118.

[77] See F. Miclo, op. cit., footnote 72, p. 118; G. Braibant, op. cit., footnote 73, p. 223.

[78] C.E. 9.5.1913, Roubeau, R.D.P. 1913, p. 685, comment by Jèze. On this decision see B. Jeanneau, Les principes généraux du droit dans la jurisprudence administrative, Paris 1954, pp. 7 et seq.; K. Stahl, Die Sicherung der Grundfreiheiten im öffentlichen Recht der Fünften Französischen Republik, Hamburg 1970, p. 182; H. Krech, Die Theorie der allgemeinen Rechtsgrundsätze im französischen öffentlichen Recht, Göttingen 1973, pp. 34 et seq.

[79] Thus for example: C.E. 13.7.1956, Syndicat national des pyrotechniciens de France, Rec. p. 332; C.E. 30.4.1965, Brault, Rec. p. 255; C.E. 27.1.1967, Soc. Decker, R.D.P. 1967, p. 788. Further references in M. Waline, Droit administratif (9th ed., Paris 1963), pp. 465 et seq.; B. Jeanneau, ibid. p. 8.

[80] Detailed treatment in B. Jeanneau, op. cit., footnote 78, pp. 11 et seq.; G. Braibant, op. cit., footnote 73, p. 227. See also A. de Laubadère, op. cit., footnote 72, pp. 267 et seq.

[81] cf. F. Miclo, op. cit., footnote 72, pp. 127 et seq., especially pp. 130 et seq.; P. Braud, La notion de liberté publique en droit français, Paris 1968, pp. 216 et seq.; C.-A. Colliard,

(b) British law

The situation in the United Kingdom is characterised by the fact that the country has no written constitution. Consequently, the equality principle is not explicitly enshrined in the constitution.[82] Parliament has wide powers. An essential feature of the British constitution is that Parliament can change constitutional laws by the same majority as other laws. As a result, its legislation is not in principle bound by any higher-ranking law, and the courts have no power to declare Acts of Parliament unconstitutional.[83] Parliamentary sovereignty is, however, limited by the concept of natural justice, which is still relevant in British constitutional law. According to this concept, Parliament has been given its powers only on trust; these powers never imply complete authority to oppress or to act unjustly.[84] Thus in the United Kingdom even the legislature is bound to observe the equality principle in the form of a prohibition on arbitrarily discriminatory legislation. The executive's duty to observe the equality principle stems from the principles of the "rule of law."[85] These include statutory reservation for acts of administrative intervention, judicial review of the exercise of discretionary powers by the executive and the independence of judges. The rule of law also includes the principle of equality before the law in the sense that basically the same law applies both to individuals and to authorities.[86] The only exceptions occur in

---

Libertés publiques (6th ed., Paris 1982), p. 222; K. Feige, *op. cit.*, footnote 56, pp. 170 *et seq.*; K. Stahl, *op. cit.*, footnote 78, pp. 183 *et seq.*

[82] Instead there are a number of Acts of Parliament prohibiting individual discriminatory acts and providing remedies which enable the citizen to take action against such discriminatory acts. *cf.* for example E. C. S. Wade, A. W. Bradley, *Constitutional and Administrative Law* (10th ed., London/New York 1985), pp. 574 *et seq.*; S. A. de Smith, *Judicial Review of Administrative Action*, London 1980, pp. 44 *et seq.*; J. N. Stevens, *Constitutional and Administrative Law*, Plymouth 1984, pp. 144 *et seq.*

[83] *cf.* for example N. MacCormick, "Der Rechtsstaat und die rule of law," JZ 1984, pp. 65 *et seq.*; C. von Loeper, *Verwaltungsrechtspflege in England*, Hamburg 1983, p. 36; see also J. F. Garner, B. L. Jones, *Administrative Law* (6th ed., London 1985), p. 9.

[84] On the influence on English law of Dicey's theory, see for example P. Craig, *Administrative Law*, London 1983, pp. 27 *et seq.*

[85] A. V. Dicey, *Introduction to the study of the Law of the Constitution* (9th ed., London 1948), p. 202.

[86] A. V. Dicey, *ibid.* p. 203. For more detail see E. C. S. Wade, A. W. Bradley, *op. cit.*, footnote 82, p. 94; P. Craig, *op. cit.*, footnote 84, pp. 28 *et seq.*; O. Hood Phillips, *Constitutional and Administrative Law* (6th ed., London 1978), p. 36; H. W. R. Wade, *Administrative Law* (5th ed., Oxford 1983), pp. 23 *et seq.*, 25 *et seq.*; C. von Loeper, *op. cit.*, footnote 83, p. 38; E. Riedel, *Kontrolle der Verwaltung im englischen Rechtssystem*, Berlin 1976, pp. 231 *et seq.*, 242 *et seq.*

situations where a difference is absolutely necessary for the performance of the public task in question.[87]

On the other hand the executive is bound to observe the equality principle by the doctrine of *ultra vires*. An administrative action is *ultra vires* if the executive authority exceeds the limits of the powers conferred on it by statute in the situation in question.[88] Such an infringement of powers is said to have occurred, *inter alia*, if the action in question is "plainly/manifestly unreasonable" and therefore arbitrary.[89] In a negative sense the *ultra vires* doctrine thus also guarantees the equality principle; for, as we have demonstrated above, every arbitrary act of equal or unequal treatment must be regarded as an infringement of the requirement of substantive equality before the law.[90]

Lord Chief Justice Russell expressed this in a decision in 1898[91] when he attempted to explain the meaning of the term "unreasonable"; to quote verbatim:

> "If [by-laws] were found to be partial and unequal in their operation as between different classes; if they were manifestly injust; if they disclosed bad faith; if they involved such progressive or gratuitous interference with the rights of those subject to them as could find no justification in the minds of reasonable men, the court might well say Parliament never intended to give authority to make such rules; they are unreasonable and *ultra vires*."[92]

As far as the substance of the equality principle is concerned, an action described in the quoted decision as "unreasonable" could also be said to

---

[87] A. V. Dicey, *op. cit.*, footnote 85, p. 203. Detailed discussion with critical comments: E. C. S. Wade, A. W. Bradley, *op. cit.*, footnote 82, pp. 95 *et seq.*; P. Craig, *op. cit.*, footnote 84, pp. 28 *et seq.*; O. Hood Phillips, *ibid.* p. 36; J. F. Garner, B. L. Jones, *op. cit.*, footnote 83, pp. 10 *et seq.*; C. von Loeper, *op. cit.*, footnote 83, p. 38; E. Riedel, *ibid.* pp. 231 *et seq.*, 242 *et seq.*

[88] *cf.* S. A. de Smith, *op. cit.*, footnote 82, pp. 94 *et seq.*; C. von Loeper, *op. cit.*, footnote 83, p. 82.

[89] *cf.* de Smith, *op. cit.*, footnote 82; von Loeper, *op. cit.*, footnote 83, pp. 96 *et seq.*; on the concept of arbitrary action see A.IV. above.

[90] See under A.IV. above.

[91] *Kruse* v. *Johnson* [1898] 2 Q.B. 91. See O. Hood Phillips, *Leading Cases in Constitutional and Administrative Law*, London 1979, pp. 317 *et seq.*; S. H. Bailey, C. A. Cross, J. F. Garner, *Cases and Materials in Administrative Law*, London 1977, pp. 610 *et seq.* In detail on this decision: de Smith, *op. cit.*, footnote 82, pp. 355 *et seq.*; P. Craig, *op. cit.*, footnote 84, p. 209; H. W. R. Wade, *op. cit.*, footnote 86, pp. 752 *et seq.*; O. Hood Phillips, *op. cit.*, footnote 86, p. 602; J. F. Garner, B. L. Jones, *op. cit.*, footnote 83, pp. 72 *et seq.*

[92] *Op. cit.*, p. 99.

be "unfair," for an authority is acting "unfairly" if—*inter alia*—it discriminates on "unacceptable grounds."[93]

To sum up, it can be said that in the United Kingdom, too, the equality principle is a constitutional principle, in the form of a prohibition on discrimination, binding on the legislature and the executive.[94]

(c) Danish law

The Basic Law of the Kingdom of Denmark dating from January 15, 1953 contains no provisions guaranteeing the equality principle in general form as a principle of equality before the law.[95] Nevertheless the courts have handed down a number of judgments in which they have declared acts by the executive to be void because they were in breach of the duty to give equality of treatment.[96]

In inferring the duty to give equality of treatment, the courts have repeatedly referred to "general principles of law,"[97] "general basic principles of law"[98] or "general rules of law,"[99] thereby demonstrating, in effect, that the decisions have been based on the equality principle, which is deemed to be a general principle of law.[100]

Admission of the equality principle does not extend beyond the realm of administrative law, however.[101] As far as can be seen, the courts have not yet dealt with the question whether the equality principle has constitutional status. Legal commentators reject such status for the equality principle, because no such principle exists in Danish customary law.[102]

[93] *cf.* S. A. de Smith, *op. cit.*, footnote 82, pp. 356, 346; P. Craig, *op. cit.*, footnote 84, p. 360.

[94] *cf.* n. 84.

[95] There are merely some isolated special rules on equal treatment, such as those in Articles 70, 71 and 77 of the Danish constitution. See C. A. Nørgaard, "The principle of equality in Danish administrative law," Scandinavian Studies in law 1967, pp. 241 at 252 *et seq.*

[96] See the references in C. A. Nørgaard, *ibid.*, pp. 254 *et seq.*

[97] For example in Decisions 1958 U.f.R. 868 and 1958 U.f.R. 455 (cited by C. A. Nørgaard, *op. cit.*, footnote 95, pp. 259 *et seq.* and 262 *et seq.*).

[98] For example in Decision 1932 U.f.R. 505 (cited by C. A. Nørgaard, *op. cit.*, footnote 95, p. 258).

[99] For example in Decision 1940 U.f.R. 1030 (cited by C. A. Nørgaard, *op. cit.*, footnote 95, p. 262).

[100] *cf.* C. A. Nørgaard, *op. cit.*, footnote 95, pp. 266 *et seq.*

[101] See C. A. Nørgaard, *op. cit.*, footnote 95, p. 253.

[102] *cf.* C. A. Nørgaard, *op. cit.*, footnote 95, p. 253.

VI.   THE EQUALITY PRINCIPLE AND PROHIBITIONS OF DISCRIMINATION

The Treaties establishing the European Communities contain no provisions guaranteeing the principle of equality in a general way. Instead they contain a number of provisions forbidding discrimination and differentiation,[103] provisions which apply to specific individual areas of law[104] or cover specific individual acts of discrimination and differentiation.[105]

1.   The Concept of Discrimination and Discrimination Prohibitions in General

As a legal concept, the concept of discrimination has its origins in American commercial law. From there it gradually found its way into international contract law and the commercial law of European countries.[106]

In its original lexical meaning the term merely denotes the making of a distinction—of whatever kind.[107] As a legal concept, however, it is universally given the meaning which it has acquired in American law, that is to say a differentiation or differentiating treatment which is "unjust" or "unlawful"[108] and hence ultimately arbitrary.[109]

For discrimination to have taken place, therefore, it is necessary for there to have been an infringement of the requirement to treat like in like manner and unlike in unlike manner.[110] Conversely, however, this means

---

[103] The only specific requirement to accord equal treatment is to be found in Article 3(b) ECSC.

[104] For example Articles 4(b), 60(1) ECSC; Articles 36, 37, 40(3) subparagraph 2, 85(1a), 86(c), 95 EEC.

[105] For example Article 60(1) ECSC; Articles 7, 48(2), 49(c), 52, 60, 67, 79, 132(5) EEC.

[106] cf. E. Zimmermann, op. cit., footnote 34, pp. 14, 40 et seq.; W. Kewenig, op. cit., footnote 16, pp. 24 et seq., with further references; see also the opinions of Advocate-General Capotorti in Joined Cases 117/76 & 16/77 A. Ruckdeschel & Co. and Hansa-Lagerhaus Stroeh & Co. v. Hauptzollamt Hamburg St. Annen [1977] E.C.R. 1753 at 1777.

[107] cf. E. Zimmermann, op. cit., footnote 34, p. 29 with footnote 35; G. Jaenicke, op. cit., footnote 51, p. 387.

[108] Thus G. Jaenicke, op. cit., footnote 51, p. 388; E. Zimmermann, op. cit., footnote 34, pp. 29 et seq. Also W. Kewenig, op. cit., footnote 16, pp. 25 et seq., with further references on international and national law; J. Schwarze, "Diskriminierung bei der Vergabe öffentlicher Aufträge aus der Sicht des Gemeinschaftsrechts," in Öffentliche Aufträge und Forschungspolitik, Baden-Baden 1979, pp. 79 et seq. (83 et seq.).

[109] On the concept of arbitrary action see under I.4. above.

[110] On this requirement, which has grown out of the concept of justice, see under A.III.2. above.

that any prohibition of discrimination constitutes an application of the (substantive) equality principle.[111]

2. The Structure of Discrimination Prohibitions in Community Law

In recent times the Court of Justice has frequently made pronounce-ments on the structure of the discrimination prohibitions, doing so in the manner already described in Section 1. Thus it has repeatedly declared since 1977[112] that the prohibition of discrimination (between agricultural producers or consumers) laid down in Article 40(3) subparagraph 2 EEC is "merely a specific enunciation of the general principle of equality" and that this prohibition therefore extends beyond the actual wording of Article 40(3) subparagraph 2 EEC and also applies to relations between different commercial and industrial sectors.[113]

---

[111] cf. E. Zimmermann, op. cit., footnote 34, pp. 14, 30, 41; W. Kewenig, op. cit., footnote 16, pp. 51 et seq.; G. Jaenicke, op. cit., footnote 51, p. 390. See also Advocate-General Capotorti, op. cit., footnote 106, p. 1777; J. Schwarze, op. cit., footnote 108, pp. 83 et seq.; F. W. Jerusalem, Das Recht der Montanunion, Berlin/Frankfurt am Main 1954, p. 111, who sees the prohibition of discrimination as the modern idea of equality.

[112] Thus for example judgments in Joined Cases 117/76 & 16/77 Albert Ruckdeschel & Co. and Others v. Hauptzollamt St. Annen [1977] E.C.R. 1753; Joined Cases 124/76 & 20/77 S.A. Moulins et Huileries de Pont-à-Mousson and Others v. Office national interprofes-sionnel des céréales [1977] E.C.R. 1753 at 1812 et seq.; judgments in Case 125/77 Koninklijke Scholten-Honig NV and Others v. Hoofdproduktschap voor Akkerbouw-produkten, and in Joined Cases 103 & 145/77 Royal Scholten-Honig (Holding) Ltd. and Others v. Intervention Board for Agricultural Produce [1978] E.C.R. 1991 at 2037 et seq.; judgment in Case 245/81 Edeka-Zentrale AG v. Federal Republic of Germany [1982] E.C.R. 2745 et seq.; judgment in Case 59/83 SA Biovilac NV v. European Economic Community [1984] E.C.R. 4057; judgment in Joined Cases 201–202/85 Marthe Klensch and Others v. Staatssekretär für Landwirtschaft und Weinbau and Others [1986] E.C.R. 3477, para. 9.

[113] Thus for example ibid., [1977] E.C.R. 1753, para. 7, pp. 1812 et seq., paras. 14 to 17; [1978] E.C.R. 1991, pp. 2037 et seq., paras. 25 to 27; [1982] E.C.R. 2745, para. 11; [1984] E.C.R. 4057, para. 19. Earlier authorities taking the same view: H. von der Groeben, "Über das Problem der Grundrechte in den Europäischen Gemeinschaften," in E. von Caemmerer, H.-J. Schlochauer, E. Steindorff (ed.), Probleme des Europäischen Rechts (Festschrift for Walter Hallstein on his 65th birthday), Frankfurt am Main 1966, pp. 226 et seq. (234 et seq.); P. Pescatore, "Les droits de l'homme et l'intégration européenne," C.D.E. 1968, pp. 629 et seq. (646); L.-J. Constantinesco, "La constitution économique de la C.E.E.," R.T.D.E. 1977, pp. 244 et seq. (274); B. Börner, op. cit., footnote 16, pp. 51, 66 et seq. with reference to Arts. 4(b), 60(1) ECSC, and p. 64 with reference to the areas covered by the EEC Treaty. Advocate-General Lagrange, in his opinion in Joined Cases 8–13/57 [1958] E.C.R. 319 at 363 et seq., also assumed that the discrimination prohibitions are related to the equality principle in this way when, with regard to Article 4(b) ECSC, he described the German and French case law on the equality principle. See also Advocate-General Lagrange's opinion in Case 13/63 Italian

It can be inferred from this, for agriculture at least, that whenever an act constituting discrimination occurs there is a breach of the principle of equality, in other words that it is also—and precisely—to the concept of discrimination that we must look for information about the substance and scope of the equality principle. A more or less complete picture of the equality principle can therefore be obtained only if the self-contained case law on the concept of discrimination is also considered.

For the sake of clarity we begin the next section with a description of this case law, without however giving any answer at this stage to the question of the general recognition of the equality principle. Our investigation will go beyond the boundaries of agricultural law to cover the other discrimination prohibitions contained in the Treaties.

B. THE CONCEPT OF DISCRIMINATION

From the earliest years of its existence, when its work was still confined to the coal and steel industries, the Court of Justice frequently had cause to explain the concept of discrimination in general terms. Since then it has handed down a number of decisions in which the concept has been defined from many different standpoints.

Most of the judgments in which the Court of Justice has dealt with the concept of discrimination have revolved around the requirement that like should be treated in like manner and unlike in unlike manner[1] and around the fact that an infringement of a discrimination prohibition is ultimately deemed to occur only where there is arbitrary equal or unequal treatment.[2]

However, the Court has not always arrived at this view by the same route. Thus in some decisions the starting-point has been a purely formal consideration of the relationship between the objects being compared, in order to test, on the basis of objective criteria, whether the objects in

---

Republic v. Commission of the EEC [1963] E.C.R. 357 at 394, 408; Advocate-General Roemer's opinion in Case 5/71 Aktien-Zuckerfabrik Schöppenstedt v. Council of the European Communities [1971] E.C.R. 975 at 998, 999 et seq.; Advocate-General Mayras's opinion in Joined Cases 9 & 11/71 Compagnie d'Approvisionnement v. Commission [1972] E.C.R. 391 at 422; Advocate-General Trabucchi's opinion in Case 11/74 L'Union des Minotiers de la Champagne v. French Government [1974] E.C.R. 877 at 891.

[1] On the concept of justice and the requirement that like should be treated in like manner and unlike in unlike manner which has grown out of that concept, see under A.III.2. above.

[2] On the concept of arbitrary action see under A.IV. above.

563

question are "like" or "unlike." Other decisions, in contrast, have not initially considered the compared objects themselves at all but have immediately looked at the question whether the equal or unequal treatment complained of is "objectively justified."

Not all the Court of Justice's decisions have applied these criteria consistently and logically, however. In some instances it has declared a case of unequal treatment to be "justified," despite having stated earlier that the objects compared are "unlike"—which means that on the facts there is no discrimination.[3] It should be added, however, that it would be inappropriate to take such a pronouncement too literally. For in the final analysis its effect is simply to demonstrate clearly once again that the Court's only concern is to prevent "unjust" and hence arbitrary treatment—by whatever route it may arrive at this result in the individual case.

The other decisions deal with the forms of discrimination and a number of other characteristics which further define and delimit the concept. Since these decisions are only supplementary in their effect, we shall postpone our discussion of them (see III. below) until after we have outlined the decisions relating to the central requirement that like should be treated in like manner and unlike in unlike manner.

I. ELEMENTS OF A DISCRIMINATORY ACT

1. Unlike Treatment of Like Matters

The first attempt at a definition based on the relationship of the compared objects to each other was in 1956 in a decision given in connection with coal imports.[4] In this case the Court of Justice examined the question whether a levy imposed by a national compensation fund which represented a price rise for consumers of industrial coal, was a measure or practice constituting discrimination of the kind prohibited by Article 4(b) ECSC.

The background to the decision was that the Luxembourg Government maintained an "Office Commercial du Ravitaillement," which had a

---

[3] Thus, for example, judgments in Joined Cases 17 & 20/61 *Klöckner-Werke AG and Others* v. *High Authority* and in Case 19/61 *Mannesmann AG* v. *High Authority* [1962] E.C.R. 653 at 717 *et seq.*; judgment in Case 13/63 *Italian Republic* v. *High Authority* [1963] E.C.R. 357; judgment in Case 8/82 *Wagner* v. *Bundesanstalt für landwirtschaftliche Marktordnung* [1983] E.C.R. 371. See also under B.II.1. below.
[4] Joined Cases 7 & 9/54 *Groupement des Industries Sidérurgiques Luxembourgeoises* v. *High Authority* [1955–1956] E.C.R. 53.

monopoly in the importing of solid fuels. The monopoly was operated in conjunction with a compensation fund, which imposed a levy on industrial coal the revenue from which was used to subsidise domestic fuel. The plaintiff, which in its capacity as a steel producer was a consumer of industrial coal, took the view that the benefits to domestic fuel financed from the levy were in breach of the common market and, *inter alia*, in breach of the prohibition on discrimination contained in Article 4(b) ECSC.

The Court of Justice interpreted the term "discrimination" used in Article 4(b) ECSC systematically from the context of the Treaty,[5] referring to the characteristics of the "discriminatory practices" on pricing in which undertakings are forbidden by Article 60(1) ECSC to engage. Specifically, the Court declared:

> "The Treaty abolishes and prohibits measures or practices which discriminate between producers, between purchasers or between consumers. The concept of discrimination is specified in Article 60 of the Treaty which indicates that practices involving, within the Common Market, the application of dissimilar conditions to comparable transactions, are discriminatory."[6]

The Court did not go on to accept that the levy constituted discrimination of the kind prohibited by Article 4(b) ECSC, the reason being that the levy was a measure falling under the heading of general economic policy; under Article 26 ECSC each individual Member State is responsible for its own general economic policy.[7]

With regard to the method of systematically interpreting the term "discrimination," the Court again fell back on a decision dating from 1959.[8] The question to be decided in the case in point, among others, was whether the High Authority, by refusing to exempt primary foundries from contributions to the compensation fund in respect of imported

---

[5] On the systematics of the anti-discrimination provisions of Articles 4(b) and 60(1) ECSC, *cf.* B. Börner, "Diskriminierungen und Subventionen," in "Studien zum deutschen und europäischen Wirtschaftsrecht," KSE Vol. 17, Cologne/Berlin/Bonn/Munich 1973, pp. 49 *et seq.* (66 *et seq.*).

[6] E.C.J., *loc. cit.*, footnote 4, p. 94 of the judgment. The same point had already been made by Advocate-General Roemer in his opinion in Joined Cases 7 & 9/54 *Groupements des Industries Sidérurgiques Luxembourgeoises* v. *High Authority* [1955–1956] E.C.R. 53 at 133.

[7] E.C.J. *loc. cit.*, footnote 4, pp. 97 *et seq.* of judgment.

[8] Case 14/59 *Sociétés des Fonderies de Pont-à-Mousson* v. *High Authority* [1959] E.C.R. 215.

scrap, had committed an act of "discrimination prohibited by the Treaty."

The applicant had applied to the Court because it considered that it had been put at a disadvantage compared with competitors who were not subject to the levy, such as the secondary foundries and the integrated and independent steel foundries. Whilst the integrated steel foundries had been exempted from these contributions, the secondary foundries and the independent steel foundries were not covered by the ECSC Treaty and so were outside the Community's competence.

The applicant took the view, *inter alia*, that the High Authority had behaved in discriminatory fashion by refusing to exempt primary foundries in the same way as integrated steel foundries.

The Court stated the general principle in the following terms:

> "Discrimination consisting of the dissimilar treatment of comparable situations presupposes that there is a duty to treat all interested parties on the same footing and the possibility of so doing. In this case the High Authority could only discriminate in the manner alleged by the applicant if it was empowered and bound either to make the latter's competitors subject to equalization or to exempt the applicant therefrom."[9]

Even though in this decision the Court defines the term "discrimination" in its own words, it does not go beyond the boundaries of an individual provision—that contained in Article 3(b) ECSC—as it sees the elements of discrimination only negatively as an alleged infringement of the positive duty laid down by this provision to "ensure that all comparably placed consumers in the common market have equal access to the sources of production."[10]

---

[9] *Ibid.*, p. 494 of the judgment.

[10] The actual wording, on pp. 493 *et seq.* of the judgment, was: "The applicant claims that the defendant practised discrimination which is forbidden by the Treaty and failed to fulfil the obligation specified in Article 3(b) of the Treaty, namely to 'ensure that all comparably placed consumers in the common market have equal access to the sources of production. Both these complaints—the second of which also refers to discrimination in the broadest sense—have the same effect. In each case one applicant accuses the defendant of not having placed it in the same situation as its competitors which do not have to pay the equalization contribution and of having thus made access to scrap a greater financial burden for it than for its competitors.'" On the relationship of Article 3(b) to Article 4(b) ECSC see also Advocate-General Lagrange's opinion in Joined Cases 8–13/57 *Wirtschaftsvereinigung Eisen-und Stahlindustrie and Others* v. *High Authority* [1958] E.C.R. 317 at 361 *et seq.*; further B. Börner, *op. cit.*, footnote 5, pp. 55 *et seq.*

In the end the Court did not accept that there had been discrimination, because the applicant, *vis-à-vis* the secondary foundries, was not in a position comparable to that of the integrated steel foundries *vis-à-vis* the independent ones. The High Authority, declared the Court, had exempted the integrated steel foundries because they operated similar production installations and used the same raw materials as the independent steel foundries. The same similarity did not subsist between the applicant, which both consumed and produced pig iron, and the secondary foundries, which used pig iron but did not produce it.[11]

In the years that followed, the Court did not define the concept of discrimination except in a generalised, abstract way independently of the ECSC Treaty, This tendency had already been seen, however, in two earlier decisions in 1956.[12]

The cases with which these two decisions were concerned related to the coal production sector and specifically to the granting of compensation payments to the Belgian coal industry on account of the relatively unfavourable extraction conditions prevailing in that country. These compensation payments had at first been calculated on a uniform basis, but had later been adjusted to take account of the undertakings' individual situation.

The applicants were coal-mining undertakings whose entitlement to compensation payments had been reduced or even completely withdrawn by the change in the rules. On application from these undertakings the Court of Justice had to decide whether the conditions for a discriminatory act prohibited by Article 4(b) ECSC were fulfilled if compensation payments of the kind in question were adapted to the individual situation of parties who would otherwise be entitled to benefit. On the specific point at issue the Court stated as follows:

"That argument must be rejected. As a result of the decision contained in the letter of 28 May 1955 the disadvantages resulting from less favourable geological conditions, which are indeed one of the premises of the special provisions applying to the Belgian coal industry, no longer exist. It follows therefrom that the payment of differing rates of equalization on the basis of physical conditions of production is evidence of a desire to acknowledge differences which

[11] E.C.J. *loc. cit.*, footnote 8, pp. 494 *et seq.* of the judgment.
[12] Cases 8/55 *Fédération Charbonnière de Belgique* v. *High Authority* [1954–1956] E.C.R. 292 and 9/55 *Société des Charbonnages de Beeringen and Others* v. *High Authority* [1954–1956] E.C.R. 311.

actually exist, so as to ensure that comparable cases receive comparable benefit and, therefore, to avoid discrimination."[13]

A positive result of this judgment is that it demonstrates that discrimination is always held to exist when dissimilar advantages are granted in comparable cases. Thus the judgment goes on to state:

"On the assumption that equalization payments . . . were the same for all undertakings without regard to differences in their conditions of production, equalization would become discriminatory and its existence unjustified since, insofar as it was awarded to undertakings whose conditions of production do not suffer the disadvantages which are the very requirements of the award, it would become a subsidy. It follows that equalization must necessarily take account of the individual position of the undertakings as regards their conditions of production."[14]

The Court of Justice has given similar directions, if not in so many words, in many cases in which the meaning of discrimination had to be clarified.[15] We shall mention two of these cases here, both of them relating to agriculture, i.e. in a sector covered by the EEC Treaty.

One of the decisions, dating from 1971,[16] deals with the law on refunds. The Court had to decide, inter alia, whether the imposition of a special ceiling on refunds in intra-Community trade by Regulation 162/64[17] constituted discrimination against trade between Member States compared with trade by Member States with third countries.[18]

This question was referred to the Court of Justice by the German Federal Finance Court. It arose in the course of proceedings based on the following circumstances:

---

[13] E.C.J., ibid., pp. 321, 367 et seq. of the judgment.
[14] E.C.J., loc. cit., footnote 12, pp. 322, 369 of the judgment.
[15] See for example the judgments cited in footnotes 56, 63 and 117 below.
[16] Case 6/71 Rheinmühlen Düsseldorf v. Einfuhr- und Vorratsstelle für Getreide und Futter-mittel [1971] E.C.R. 823.
[17] Commission Regulation 162/64 of October 29, 1964 J.O. 1964, 2739.
[18] The Court of Justice examined this question without specific reference to any Treaty provisions. It is clear from the context, however, that the Court was guided by Article 40(3) subparagraph 2 EEC.

The firm of Rheinmühlen, the plaintiff, had supplied pearl barley and durum wheat to various firms in Belgium, Italy and Switzerland and on account of these exports had initially received refunds in the form of levy-free imports. The import and storage agency for cereals and fodder then reversed the decision on the refunds on the grounds that the exports—contrary to what had been stated by the plaintiff—had been to Member States, not to third countries.

The background to this decision by the import and storage agency was that Regulation 162/64 set a fixed ceiling for refunds in trade between Member States, restricting them to certain percentages of the refund rates permitted under Regulation 141/64,[19] whereas Regulation 164/64[20] set no ceiling of this or a similar kind for refunds granted in trade with third countries.

After examining whether, as a result of these arrangements, Regulation 162/64 amounted to discrimination against trade between Member States, the Court of Justice made the following general statement:

> "The non-discrimination rule would only be infringed if it were shown that the Community legislature had treated comparable situations differently."[21]

After a thorough examination of the comparability of the Community refunds on the one hand and the third-country refunds on the other,[22] the Court finally came to the conclusion that the two kinds of refund were not mutually comparable and that therefore the lowering—introduced by Regulation 162/64—of the upper limit of the intra-Community levy was not discriminatory.[23]

The second of the two decisions referred to above was delivered in 1978 and related to the law on monetary compensatory amounts.[24] In this case the Court of Justice was examining the question whether a reduction of a monetary compensatory amount which had not taken place in a specific instance owing to failure to apply a monetary coefficient was an "infringement of the principle of the prohibition on discrimination and of the

---

[19] Council Regulation 141/64 of October 21, 1964, J.O. 1964, 2666.
[20] Commission Regulation 164/64 of October 29, 1964, J.O. 1964, 2739.
[21] E.C.J., *loc. cit.*, footnote 16, para. 14.
[22] The objectives of Community agricultural law serve as *tertium comparationis* (likewise para. 14).
[23] E.C.J., *loc. cit.*, footnote 16, para. 16.
[24] Case 79/77 *Firma Kühlhaus Zentrum AG* v. *Hauptzollamt Hamburg-Harburg* [1978] E.C.R. 611.

principle of equal treatment, and in particular of the principle stated in Article 40(3) of the Treaty."[25]

This question had been referred to the Court of Justice by the Finance Court of Hamburg. The facts of the case, on which the initial proceedings had been based, were essentially as follows:

Kühlhaus Zentrum AG, the plaintiff, had withdrawn for free circulation a batch of stored frozen Argentinian beef from a public bonded warehouse which it owned. The meat had been imported under a tariff quota which the Community had opened in favour of third countries on the basis of GATT agreements. This quota permitted the levy-free import of a certain quantity of meat at a customs duty rate of 20 per cent.

The plaintiff had been charged a monetary compensatory amount of DM 1866.80 on the goods which it had withdrawn from the bonded warehouse.

It objected to this because in its opinion the levy-free importation meant that the monetary coefficient specified in Article 4(3) of Regulation 1380/75[26] should be applied to the monetary compensation. The consequence would be, the plaintiff claimed, that the monetary compensatory amount would be reduced by DM 1483.20, that is to say by the amount to be deducted from the levy if the levy were multiplied by the prescribed monetary coefficient.

On the plaintiff's claim that the failure to apply the monetary coefficient was in breach of Article 40(3) subparagraph 2 EEC the Court declared:

"... 'The exemption of the quota in question from the levy was an exceptional derogation from the Community system of determination of prices for beef and veal, so that importers who were able to benefit from that exemption were in a situation not comparable to that of other importers. Therefore, since *discrimination consists above all in treating comparable situations differently*, the facts do not

---

[25] This formulation used in para. 7 was taken by the Court from the plaintiffs' argument (p. 613 of the facts). In the text that follows we shall speak only of the "complaint of discrimination" without specifying whether all three accusations are being referred to or only the accusation of infringement of Article 40(3) EEC ("in particular"). It is, after all, irrelevant, as far as the concept of discrimination is concerned, which of the three accusations is being scrutinised. The position might be slightly different, however, with regard to the question of the possible recognition of the equality principle (see also under C below).

[26] Commission Regulation 1380 of May 29, 1975, O.J. 1975, L139/37 *et seq.*

support the complaint of discrimination as regards the application of Regulation No. 1380/75 to the goods imported as part of the quota exempted from levy."[27]

2. Like Treatment of Unlike Matters

In a number of further judgments on the concept of discrimination the Court of Justice has also made some pronouncements on the converse question, namely whether the conditions for a discriminatory act are fulfilled if dissimilar circumstances receive similar treatment.

A first, and fundamental, decision on this point was made in 1963,[28] when the court considered, among other things, whether the authorisation granted to the French Government enabling it to take protective measures under Article 226 EEC against the import of certain electrical goods from Italy was compatible with the anti-discrimination provisions of Article 7 EEC.

Specifically, the French Government had applied for authorisation to take protective measures to curb Italian imports, which had increased many times over following the general liberalisation of intra-Community trade in 1961 and 1962. The Commission had acceded to the application and had stated that the French Government was justified in imposing a special duty on imports from Italy of domestic electrical refrigerators and their accessories, where such a duty had not already been imposed beforehand at the exporting stage, i.e. in Italy.

The Italian Government took the view that the authorisation granted by the Commission was in breach of the anti-discrimination provisions of Article 7 EEC because only Italian products were subject to the duty and not products from other countries. The Commission, in the Italian Government's opinion, should have extended the special duty to imports from other Member States as well.

The Court of Justice eventually rejected the Italian Government's contention, holding that dissimilar sets of circumstances were involved.[29] On the general point the Court declared as follows:

"The different treatment of non-comparable situations does not lead automatically to the conclusion that there is discrimination. An

---

[27] E.C.J., *loc. cit.*, footnote 24, para. 8.
[28] Case 13/63 *Italian Republic* v. *Commission of the EEC* [1963] E.C.R. 165.
[29] See also under B.II.1. below.

appearance of discrimination in form may therefore correspond in fact to an absence of discrimination in substance.

Discrimination in substance would consist in treating either similar situations differently or different situations identically."[30]

The Court of Justice did not deliver any more decisions of this kind until a case in 1977 relating to social security for migrant workers.[31] The point at issue there was whether, having regard to Article 7 EEC, Article 12 of Regulation 1408/71,[32] which permits the "cumulation" of benefits (*i.e.* allows a claimant to draw more than one benefit at the same time), was also applicable (and took precedence over national anti-cumulation rules) if it had the effect of giving migrant workers benefits in excess of those available to other workers.

The question arose in the context of an action which had come before a French labour tribunal. The point at issue was the calculation of a disability pension payable to an Italian national who had worked first in France and later in Belgium. The nature and method of the calculation made by the competent Belgian administrative body was disputed.

The details of the case were as follows:

In Belgium the person concerned (the plaintiff) had fulfilled all the conditions laid down in the relevant national laws for gaining entitlement to a disability pension. In France, on the other hand, he had to rely on Article 45 of Regulation 1408/71; for calculating the benefit due to him the insurance periods actually spent in both Member States were then aggregated and the French benefit was appointed on a pro rata basis.

When the Belgian authorities learned of the payments in France, they deducted them from the disability pension under the national anti-cumulation rules. The Court of Justice, which came down in favour of the application of Article 12 of Regulation 1408/71 and hence in favour of cumulation of the benefits, ruled as follows:

"The charge that migrant workers obtain an advantage over workers who have never left their own country cannot be accepted since no

---

[30] E.C.J., *loc. cit.*, footnote 28, p. 384 of the judgment. The Court had already stated as much in auxiliary paragraphs in Joined Cases 8–9/55 and Joined Cases 32–33/58 [1955–1956] E.C.R. 322 at 369; [1958–1959] E.C.R. 320; *cf.* R. Stotz, *Die EG-Stahlkrise im Lichte der Wirtschaftsverfassung des EGKS-Vertrages*, Baden-Baden 1983, pp. 96 *et seq.*

[31] Case 22/77 *Fonds national de retraite des ouvriers mineurs* v. *Giovanni Mura* [1977] E.C.R. 1699.

[32] Council Regulation 1408/71, J.O. 1971, L149/2.

discrimination can arise in legal situations which are not comparable. Any differences which may exist to the benefit of migrant workers do not result from the interpretation of Community law but rather from the lack of any common social security system or of any harmonization of the existing national schemes, which cannot be mitigated by the mere co-ordination at present practised."[33]

Since then the Court of Justice has delivered three further decisions in which it has defined the negative side of the concept of discrimination in relation to the objects of comparison.[34] All three decisions relate to Article 40(3) subparagraph 2 EEC, which applies to agriculture. The most recent of them dates from 1982.[35] Specifically, it deals with the question whether Article 11(1) of Regulation 1998/78[36] fulfils the conditions for discrimination because it provides for compensation for the storage costs of sugar made from basic products harvested in the Community only where the sugar, "at 0.00 hours on the first day of a month," if at all, is in transit between two recognised stores within the same Member State.

This question, which was submitted to the Court of Justice by the Frankfurt Administrative Court, had arisen in the course of an action between a German agricultural products trading company (the plaintiff) and the BALM intervention agency.[37]

The background to the dispute was that the plaintiff had purchased sugar from an undertaking domiciled in France; on the last day of the month in question the sugar was in transit from a recognised store in France to a recognised store in the Federal Republic of Germany. The plaintiff had claimed compensation for the storage costs of the sugar from BALM, within whose competence the matter fell. BALM rejected the claim on the grounds that under Article 11 of Regulation 1998/78 the only goods eligible were those in transit to a recognised store within the same Member State.

---

[33] E.C.J., *loc. cit.*, footnote 31, paras. 9 to 10.
[34] Case 8/78 *Milac GmbH* v. *Hauptzollamt Freiburg* [1978] E.C.R. 1721; Case 230/78 *S.p.A. Eridania Zuccherifici Nazionali and Others* v. *Ministre de l'Agriculture et des Forêts* [1979] E.C.R. 2749; Case 8/82 *Wagner* v. *Bundesanstalt für landwirtschaftliche Marktordnung* [1983] E.C.R. 371.
[35] Case 8/82 *Wagner* v. *BALM*, *ibid.*
[36] Commission Regulation 1998/78, O.J. 1978, L231/5.
[37] Bundesanstalt für landwirtschaftliche Marktordnung (Federal Agricultural Marketing Board).

The plaintiff maintained that this rule was discriminatory. The Court of Justice pronounced as follows:

"Article 40(3) of the Treaty is concerned with the common organization of agricultural markets, including the regulation of storage, and provides in the second paragraph that the common organization must exclude any discrimination between producers or consumers within the Community. According to case-law of the court discrimination is defined as treating differently situations which are identical, or treating in the same way situations which are different."[38]

Since, in the end, the Court of Justice accepted that dissimilar circumstances were involved in this case, it found that the unequal treatment of sugar in the matter of compensation for storage costs as between transit between two Member States on the one hand and transit within the same Member State on the other did not constitute discrimination.[39]

II. DISCRIMINATION AND ARBITRARY ACTION

As already explained,[40] the concept of arbitrary action is connected with the concept of discrimination in two ways: firstly, it is used as the basis for deciding whether the objects compared are "similar" or "dissimilar" and, secondly, treatment which in itself is discriminatory is justified if it is not based on arbitrary action. Although for practical

---

[38] E.C.J., *loc. cit.*, footnotes 34, 35, para. 18. Similarly: Case 8/78 *Milac GmbH* v. *Hauptzollamt Freiburg*, *loc. cit.*, footnote 34, in which it is stated in para. 24: "The principle of non-discrimination laid down in Article 40(3) of the Treaty does not prohibit different treatment of products which are not identical, unless it results in discrimination between producers or between consumers within the Community." This statement must be seen in the light of the fact that in agriculture different products may be comparable, *i.e.* when they are substitutable and therefore in competition with each other; if the products are not substitutable they are not comparable, and so their dissimilar treatment does not amount to a prohibited discrimination under Article 40(3) subparagraph 2 EEC (see also under D. below on this point). Similarly: Case 230/78 *S.p.A. Eridania and Others*, *loc. cit.*, footnote 34, where it is stated in para. 18: "Discrimination within the meaning of Article 40 of the Treaty cannot occur if inequality in the treatment of undertakings corresponds to an inequality in the situations of such undertakings." More detail on this point under B.II.1. below.

[39] E.C.J., *loc. cit.*, footnotes 34, 35, para. 21. More detail on this point under B.II.1. below.

[40] See under B. above.

purposes it is unimportant which of these two variants is adduced in the individual case, it seems appropriate to deal with them separately here.

1. Arbitrary Action as Regards the Facts

The Court of Justice has repeatedly expressed its intention of linking the concept of discrimination factually with that of arbitrary action, starting with a line of similar decisions in 1958.[41]

In these decisions, which all relate to the system of compensatory payments for scrap metal, the Court was examining, *inter alia*, whether a supplementary rate such as that provided for in the High Authority's Decision No. 2/57 of January 26, 1957 infringed the duty of the Community institutions, laid down in Article 3(b) ECSC, to "ensure that all comparably placed consumers in the common market have equal access to the sources of production."

The decisions were based on the following circumstances:

The High Authority had adopted that particular Decision No. 2/57 as part of its reorganisation of the scrap market. In so doing it was continuing financial arrangements permitted under Article 53(a) ECSC, with the intention of, firstly, guaranteeing equality of prices as between imported and home-produced scrap and, secondly, effecting economies in scrap use.

In contrast to the existing arrangements, Decision No. 2/57 provided for a supplementary as well as a basic rate. The supplementary rate—as far as existing facilities were concerned—was levied on the consumption of additionally purchased scrap in excess of the scrap consumed during a reference period in the past. To make due allowance for the peculiarities of each individual case, the choice of this period—within certain limits— was left to the undertakings themselves.

The applicants—undertakings in the iron and steel industry and their official representatives—were of the opinion that Decision No. 2/57 was intended to make it more difficult to increase scrap use not only in percentage terms but also in absolute terms. In reality, therefore, the arrangements would not produce any savings of scrap but would tend to

---

[41] Cases 8/57 *Groupement des Hauts Fourneaux et Aciéries Belges* v. *High Authority*; and 13/57 *Wirtschaftsvereinigung Eisen- und Stahlindustrie and Others* v. *High Authority* and Cases 9/57 *Chambre Syndicale de la Sidérurgie Française* v. *High Authority*; 10/57 *Société des Anciens Etablissements Aubert et Duval* v. *High Authority*; 11/57 *Société d'Electro-Chimie and Others* v. *High Authority*; 12/57 *Syndicat de la Sidérurgie du Centre-Midi* v. *High Authority* [1957–1958] E.C.R. 245, 265, 319, 339, 357 and 375.

perpetuate the present situation to the advantage of those undertakings which had wasted scrap and to the disadvantage of those that had been economical with scrap and of new undertakings which had not been granted any reference period.

In its finding on the contention that the High Authority was in breach of Article 3(b) ECSC the Court of Justice was clearly basing its view on the comparative survey by Advocate-General Lagrange.[42] The latter, admittedly, considered that the relevant provision was not Article 3(b) ECSC but Article 4(b) of the same Treaty, because in this case—he thought—the point at issue related "merely to the rule of non-discrimination in prices."[43] But in view of the "discriminatory practices," defined in greater detail in Article 60(1) ECSC, which could be exercised in the field of undertakings' prices, the Advocate-General was compelled to define the concept of "comparability of *situations*" with regard to action by the High Authority by way of a formula.[44] To this end he looked at the national legal systems of France and the Federal Republic of Germany[45] and concluded that the equality principle was also recognised in both countries under the aspect of equality under business legislation and that there was a basic correspondence between the solutions put forward in this connection in both countries.

On the basis of this finding and of the relevant national rule in force,[46] the Advocate-General stated what was in his opinion the "best solution"[47] for Community law in these words: "Ultimately it appears to me that when the rule of non-discrimination relates to a decision of the High Authority constituting intervention on the market, the scope of this rule must be appraised first and foremost in the context of this concept of arbitrariness."[48]

The Court then stated:

> "Pursuant to a principle generally accepted in the legal systems of the Member States, equality of treatment in the matter of economic

---

[42] Advocate-General Lagrange's opinion in Joined Cases 8–13/57 [1958] E.C.R. 245 at 288.
[43] Advocate-General Lagrange, *ibid*. On the relationship between Articles 4(b) and 3(b) ECSC, see Lagrange, *ibid.*, and B. Börner, *op. cit.*, footnote 5, pp. 55 *et seq.*; see also footnote 9, above.
[44] Advocate-General Lagrange, *ibid*.
[45] Advocate-General Lagrange, *ibid*.
[46] For the general discussion of comparative law and the incorporation of national rules into Community law, see the Introduction above.
[47] On this point see the Introduction above.
[48] Advocate-General Lagrange, *loc. cit.*, footnote 42, p. 365.

rules does not prevent different prices being fixed in accordance with the particular situation of consumers or of categories of consumers provided that the differences in treatment correspond to a difference in the situations of such persons. If there is no objectively-established basis distinctions in treatment are arbitrary, discriminatory and illegal. It cannot be alleged that economic rules are unfair, on the pretext that they involve different consequences or disparate disadvantages for the persons concerned when this is clearly the result of their different operating conditions.

The supplementary rate established under Article 3(1)(b) of the contested decision applies generally and entirely to any consumption of bought scrap in excess of that relating to a reference period. The discretion conferred upon the undertakings subject to the scheme themselves to select within specially prescribed temporal limits, the period most favourable to them does not, however, mean that the criterion used for distinguishing between them thus loses its objective nature, without which it would appear arbitrary. Indeed the factual differences which this situation entails for undertakings stem from their dissimilar operating conditions and not from any legal inequality inherent in the decision."[49]

The Court of Justice had already pronounced in similar fashion but by no means so clearly in the two decisions dating from 1956 in the matter of compensation payments in the coal production sector,[50] as mentioned under 1(a) above. As already explained, the question at issue was whether the criteria for a discriminatory act as mentioned and prohibited in Article 4(b) ECSC are fulfilled if the payments are adapted to the individual situation of the beneficiary.

The Court had rejected this with the comment that a provision of this kind "is evidence of a desire to acknowledge differences which actually exist, so as to ensure that comparable cases receive comparable benefit and, therefore, to avoid discrimination."[51] The Court qualified this, however, by noting further that Article 4(b) ECSC would be infringed.

"... Only if the High Authority had not applied an objective and uniform criterion in order to check whether the individual situation

---

[49] E.C.J., *loc. cit.*, footnote 41, at 256–257.
[50] Cases 8/55 *Fédération Charbonnière de Belgique* v. *High Authority* and 9/55 *Société des Charbonnages de Beeringen and Others* v. *High Authority*, *loc. cit.*, footnote 12.
[51] E.C.J., *loc. cit.*, footnote 12, at 305. See also earlier comments under B.I.1 above.

of the undertakings satisfied the conditions fixed for the award of equalization."[52]

For its part, the Court of Justice did not see any reason to examine the matter further, since the High Authority itself had supplied a definition of the criterion used and since it was not disputed that the situation of the coal mines in question corresponded to this criterion.[53]

Another decision, which incorporates the concept of arbitrary action more or less tacitly into the criteria for discrimination via the lack of an "objectively determined reference basis," was delivered in 1962.[54] In this decision the Court made a fundamental examination of the concept of comparability contained in Article 60(1) ECSC in connection with prices.

The relevant facts underlying the dispute can be summarised as follows:

The applicant, an Italian undertaking in the steel industry, had issued to one of its customers, the firm of Orsi, a credit note for 4 258 998 lire. The High Authority considered that this credit note represented a discount off list prices, which infringed Article 60(1) ECSC. The High Authority therefore felt justified—for this and a number of other reasons—in imposing a fine of 8 000 000 lire under the provisions of Article 64 ECSC.

The applicant contested this decision, which was enforceable under Article 92 ECSC, maintaining, *inter alia*, that its relations with the firm of Orsi were not comparable with its relations with its other customers on account of personal links between the shareholders of the two companies resulting from the distribution of an estate arising from a single family undertaking.

The Court stated:

> "This contention must be rejected. The concept of comparability referred to by the Treaty is objective in nature and does not permit purely subjective factors to be taken into consideration, such as family ties which may exist between the parties. The prohibition of discrimination would otherwise lose its effect."[55]

---

[52] E.C.J., *loc. cit.*, footnote 12, at 305.

[53] E.C.J., *loc. cit.*, footnote 12, at 305; see also Advocate-General Lagrange, who names additional "purely objective criteria" in his opinion on p. 284.

[54] Case 16/61 *Acciaierie Ferriere e Fonderie di Modena* v. *High Authority* [1962] E.C.R. 289.

[55] E.C.J., *ibid.* p. 306 of the judgment. Advocate-General Roemer is less unequivocal, stating on p. 311 of his opinion: "There can be no doubt, however, that for the purposes of comparability it is also necessary to take into consideration circumstances which could be properly described as subjective factors, such as the functions exercised by the buyer

In this context two more decisions, delivered in 1962 in connection with the scrap compensation system, may be mentioned.[56] In these cases the Court of Justice was dealing with the question whether the High Authority, by including scrap obtained from within a corporate group in the additionally purchased scrap subject to the levy, was in breach of Articles 3(b) and 4(b) ECSC.

The facts on which the decisions had to be based were as follows:

To prevent scrap prices in the Community rising to the level of prices of scrap imported from third countries, the High Authority, through Decisions 22/54, 14/55, 2/57 and 16/58, had created compulsory compensation arrangements. Under these arrangements all undertakings falling within the scope of Article 80 ECSC were obliged to pay contributions, the level of which was to be calculated on the basis of the quantities of bought scrap consumed by the individual undertakings over a given period. Unlike this kind of scrap, the quantities of "own arisings" consumed were exempt from the levy (Articles 3 and 4 of Decision No. 2/57).

During the period when the compensation arrangements were in force the applicants—Klöckner-Werke AG, Hoesch AG and Mannesmann AG—were responsible, in their capacity as parent companies, for the business of several plants which had the attributes of legally independent subsidiary companies. Formerly these plants had been integrated operating departments of the applicant companies; since their

---

on the market (discounts to dealers) or the manner in which the goods bought are used (domestic fuel or for the public supply). It is certainly not easy to distinguish between relevant and irrelevant factors in this field, but unless such distinctions are made the prohibition of discrimination would be drained of all its substance because in every case there are subjective features which prevent comparison with other transactions." With regard to the discounts to dealers or functional discounts, which are connected with the attributes of a dealer and hence in Advocate-General Roemer's view with a subjective element, the Advocate-General goes on to state: "This case concerns the functions of a buyer in the market which have repercussions on the seller's markets and on his productivity and which therefore are connected objectively with the transaction concluded and with the economic activity of the supplier." Thus unlike the Court of Justice, Advocate-General Roemer regards all elements arising from the person of the party concerned or the beneficiary as "subjective features," even when it appears necessary for objective reasons that they should be taken into account. So in the final analysis the Advocate-General, too, wishes to interpret the concept of comparability in such a way that arbitrary considerations of all kinds are excluded. See on this point H.-J. Lecheler, *Die allgemeinen Rechtsgrundsätze in der Rechtsprechung des Europäischen Gerichtshofs*, Erlangen-Nürnberg 1967, p. 84.

[56] Joined Cases 17 & 20/61 *Klöckner-Werke AG und Others* v. *High Authority* and Case 19/61 *Mannesmann AG* v. *High Authority* [1962] E.C.R. 325 at 357. Reference may also be made to the prior decision in Joined Cases 32 & 33/58 *SNUPAT* v. *High Authority*; see under 3.b. below, pp. 70 *et seq.*

conversion into subsidiary companies they had been wholly-owned subsidiaries of the applicants. Later, in 1959, the subsidiaries were again
amalgamated to form single legal entities, each under the name of the
applicants.

In the applicants' view all scrap consumed by their subsidiaries
(Klöckner-Werke AG in the one case and Hoesch AG and Mannesmann
AG in the other) represented "own arisings." This was because the
applicants, as parent companies together with their subsidiaries, constituted a single economic unit within which there were no market transactions and hence no buying of scrap.

According to the High Authority, the applicants' view was incompatible with the concept of an "undertaking" on which the provisions embodying the compensation arrangements were based. It therefore
considered that it could call upon the applicants to pay the contributions.
The applicants regarded this as discrimination, since in their view they
would have been in the same position with regard to their production
conditions as those competitor undertakings which operated different
branches under a single legal personality but were not subject to the levy,
because the scrap they used was "own arisings."

In the end the Court of Justice did not accept the claim of discrimination. Specifically, it stated:

> "However, even if this assertion is factually correct and if it be
> admitted that the difference in treatment claimed brought not incon-
> siderable disadvantages to the applicants in relation to those of their
> competitors not subject to equalization charges, that of itself is not a
> sufficient ground for admitting the existence of a form of discrim-
> ination prohibited by the Treaty. For the High Authority to be
> accused of discrimination it must be shown to have treated like cases
> differently, thereby subjecting some to disadvantages as opposed to
> others, without such differentiation being justified by the existence
> of substantial objective differences. On the other hand, in this case,
> in spite of identical circumstances as regards production, the appli-
> cants by reason of their legal structure incorporating several under-
> takings were not in a similar position to that of their competitors who
> formed a single legal entity. This difference is of importance in law
> and is therefore capable of justifying different treatment."[57]

---

[57] E.C.J., *ibid.*

In the area of the EEC Treaty, too, the Court of Justice brings the arbitrary action concept into play in dealing with the question whether the objects compared are "similar" or "dissimilar."

We should first mention in this respect the decision in Case 13/63 already discussed in I.2. above.[58] As explained, the Court in that case had to decide, *inter alia*, whether an authorisation granted to the French Government enabling it to take protective measures against imports from Italy under Article 226 EEC was compatible with the discrimination prohibition contained in Article 7 EEC. The applicant, the Italian Government, claimed that this provision had been infringed because the authorisation affected only imports from Italy, whilst the other Member States remained unaffected.[59]

In stating its findings the Court of Justice first declared, generally and fundamentally, that "discrimination of substance" also exists when different situations are treated in the same way.[60] With regard to the question whether, in the specific case, "different situations" did or did not exist, the Court further commented:

"... Finally, in authorizing protective measures, the Commission is entitled to make a distinction between countries rather than between undertakings in the Common Market when there are reasonable grounds for such a distinction. This is so when it is possible to find, within a given country, a price level which is clearly different from the price level in the other countries."[61]

The outcome was that the Court considered the restriction of the protective measures to imports from Italy to be "justified" because the measures corresponded to the different relationships with Italy on the one hand and with the other Member States on the other. "Different situations" therefore call for dissimilar treatment. Only in this way can discrimination be avoided.[62]

In conclusion two more decisions, both in the agricultural sector and relating to the common organisation of the market for sugar, should be mentioned:

---

[58] Case 13/63 *Italian Republic* v. *Commission of the EEC*, *loc. cit.*, footnote 28.
[59] For details see [1963] E.C.R. 369.
[60] E.C.J., *loc. cit.*, footnote 30.
[61] E.C.J., *loc. cit.*, footnotes 28, 58, p. 178 of the judgment.
[62] E.C.J., *loc. cit.*, footnotes 28, 58, pp. 178 *et seq.* of the judgment.

The first was in 1979.[63] In this case the Court was dealing with the question, *inter alia*, whether a change in the basic quotas for sugar introduced by the Italian Government infringed the anti-discrimination provisions of the second subparagraph of Article 40(3) EEC owing to the fact that it increased the basic quotas for some sugar producers whilst at the same time reducing it for others.

This problem, which had been referred to the Court of Justice by an Italian administrative court, had arisen in the course of an action based on the following situation:

Under Article 2(2) of Regulation 3331/74[64] the Italian Republic was entitled to "alter the basic quotas of undertakings within its territory in so far as is necessary for the implementation of restructuring plans for the beet and sugar sectors."

The trend in Italian economic policy, as for as sugar is concerned, has been to shift sugar beet production from the north to the south of the country. In line with this policy, a "restructuring plan for the promotion of sugar beet growing and sugar production" put forward by S.p.A. Zuccherifici Meridionali was approved in accordance with the prevailing law.

The production quota allotted to Zuccherifici Meridionali was then increased by 6,000 tonnes by a "Decreto Interministeriale" as formally permitted under Article 2(2) of the said Regulation 3331/74. By the same "Decreto" the basic quotas of some other sugar undertakings operating in the north of the country were reduced from the crop year 1978/79 onwards.

The plaintiffs, Eridania Zuccherifici Nazionali S.p.A. and Società Italiana per l'industria degli zuccheri, were two such undertakings, whose basic quotas had been reduced by 3,104.9 and 1,855 tonnes respectively. They considered the measure to be unlawful and had instituted legal action to have the "Decreto" rescinded.

On the question of the possible infringement of the second sub-paragraph of Article 40(3) EEC the Court of Justice declared as follows:

> "Discrimination within the meaning of Article 40 of the Treaty cannot occur if inequality in the treatment of undertakings corresponds to an inequality in the situations of such undertakings. It is

---

[63] Case 230/78 *Eridania Zuccherifici Nazionali S.p.A. and Others* v. *Ministre de l'Agriculture et des Forêts* [1979] E.C.R. 2749.
[64] Council Regulation 3331/74 of December 19, 1974, O.J. 1974, L359/18.

commonly accepted that the situation in the beet and sugar sectors in Italy differs appreciably from that in the other Member States. The special situation of Italy referred to in the preambles to Regulations Nos. 3330/74 and 3331/74 has occasioned special measures intended to improve the structure of the economy in the beet and sugar sectors in Italy as a whole. In certain respects the Italian undertakings enjoy more favourable arrangements than undertakings in the other Member States. For example with regard to the system of aids; in other respects certain Italian undertakings suffer the disadvantages of the special situation of Italy. For example in the case of the reduction in their basic quotas in favour of an increase in the basic quotas of other undertakings on the basis of the restructuring plans.

Such differences in treatment are thus based on objective differences arising from the underlying economic situations; they cannot be considered discriminatory."[65]

The other ruling given on the common organisation of the market for sugar in this connection was the decision in Case 8/82,[66] outlined in I.2. above. As already explained, the point at issue in that case was whether Article 11(1) of Regulation 1998/78 fulfilled the criteria for discrimination owing to the fact that it provided for compensation for the storage costs of sugar made from basic products harvested in the Community only in cases where the sugar was in transit between two recognised stores within one Member State "at 0.00 hours on the first day of a month," if at all.[67]

The plaintiff in the main proceedings, a German agricultural products trading company, considered that this rule amounted to "discrimination between producers or consumers within the Community" as prohibited by the second subparagraph of Article 40(3) EEC.

The Court of Justice stated, first, that under its case law discrimination consisted in "treating differently situations which are identical or treating in the same way situations which are different."[68]

The Court went on to say:

"Even if it might appear to be contrary to the concept of a unified market that aid should be granted for sugar in transit between two

---

[65] E.C.J., *loc. cit.*, footnote 63, para. 18.
[66] Case 8/82 *Wagner* v. *Bundesanstalt für landwirtschaftliche Marktordnung loc. cit.*, footnotes 34, 35.
[67] See under B.I.2. above.
[68] E.C.J., *loc. cit.*, footnotes 34, 35, para. 18.

approved warehouses in a single Member State while it is refused for sugar in transit between two approved warehouses situated in different Member States, that is not in fact the case. The difference of treatment is based on requirements of supervision which may be justified objectively. Council Regulation No. 1358/77 emphasizes the need for supervision and therefore provides that the reimbursement should normally be made by the Member State in whose territory the sugar is stored."[69]

From this it follows, in the Court's opinion:

". . . the situation with regard to sugar in transit at the beginning of a month between two approved warehouses in the same Member State is not the same as that where the warehouses are situated in different Member States. In the circumstances the difference between the two situations justifies a difference in treatment which does not amount to unlawful discrimination in Community law."[70]

2. Arbitrary Action and Justification

In many decisions the Court of Justice, in deciding whether an instance of similar or dissimilar treatment amounts to discrimination, has had regard not to the relationship of the compared objects to each other but to whether or not the treatment in question is objectively justified. In so doing, the Court has taken the view that "just" treatment can ultimately be defined only negatively as "not arbitrary" and that the requirement that like should be treated in like manner and unlike—in accordance with its special features—in unlike manner does not in itself provide a solution to the problem, because it does not indicate what situations must be regarded as "like" and what as "unlike."[71]

Most of the decisions of this kind have related to the prohibition of discrimination "between producers or consumers within the Community" laid down in the second subparagraph of Article 40(3) EEC in connection with agriculture.

---

[69] E.C.J., *loc. cit.*, footnotes 34, 35, para. 19.
[70] E.C.J., *loc. cit.*, footnotes 34, 35, para. 21. See also Case 139/79 *Maizena GmbH* v. *Council of the European Communities* [1980] E.C.R. 3393, para. 28; on this decision see also under B.III.4. below.
[71] See under A.IV above.

Three of these decisions may be mentioned here to start with; in them the Court has stressed particularly clearly that the second subparagraph of Article 40(3) EEC is infringed only if the treatment in question is not based on objective considerations.

The first decision was given in 1974 on the law on intervention prices.[72] In that case the Court had to decide, *inter alia*, whether the second subparagraph of Article 40(3) EEC was infringed when the principle of regionalisation of Community prices was applied in fixing the derived intervention prices for cereals.

The question had been referred to the Court of Justice by the French Conseil d'Etat. It had arisen in the context of a lawsuit based on the following facts:

When the common organisation of the market for cereals was being set up in 1967, the Council indicated that it aimed to equalise the surpluses of the production areas and the needs of the aided areas. With this aim in mind, the intervention price system was designed in such a way that in addition to the basic intervention price there were also "derived intervention prices" which under Article 4(1) subparagraph 2 second sentence of Regulation 120/67/EEC[73] are determined in such a way "that the differences between them correspond to the price disparities in prices to be expected in a normal harvest under natural conditions of price formation on the market . . ."

Regulation 131/67/EEC[74] then introduced the principle of regionalisation of Community prices for the derived intervention prices. Under this principle five area categories were designated, and for each category criteria were set for the fixing of the derived intervention prices in order to safeguard the natural conditions of price formation.

Under these criteria special importance attaches to the costs of transport between the different areas, particularly between the surplus areas and the aided areas. But other factors as well, for example the geographical situation of the areas in question, the need of other consuming areas, imports from third countries and export possibilities, are also taken into account.

On the strength of these two regulations the Council designates the most important trading centres each year and the derived intervention

---

[72] Case 11/74 *Union des Minotiers de la Champagne* v. *French Government* [1974] E.C.R. 877.
[73] Council Regulation 120/67 of June 13, 1967, J.O. 1967, L117/2269; O.J.Sp.Ed. 1967, 33.
[74] Council Regulation 131/67 of June 13, 1967, J.O. 1967, L120/2362; O.J.Sp.Ed. 1967, 70.

prices applying to them. The rules for the crop year 1970/71 are contained in Regulation (EEC) 1210/70.[75] This regulation fixed the intervention prices for 1000 kg of common wheat at the trading centre of Compiègne (Département Marne) at 94.95 u.a. and at the trading centre of Chartres (Région Centre) at 91.77 u.a.

The millers in the Département Marne or their representative—the plaintiff—claimed that in times of surplus supply they suffered detriment on account of the price difference between the Département Marne and the Région Centre, because they were at a disadvantage when selling their products on the market of the Paris Basin. In their view the principle of regionalisation of Community prices on which the fixing of the derived intervention prices under Regulation (EEC) 1210/79 was based was therefore incompatible with the discrimination prohibition in the second subparagraph of Article 40(3) EEC.

The Court of Justice ruled on this point:

> "In an instance of unequal treatment an infringement of the discrimination prohibition can only be deemed to have occurred if it appears arbitrary. The price differences arising for cereal producers and consumers under Regulation No. 1210/70 are fixed according to objective criteria inherent in the common regulation of the market; they cannot therefore be regarded as discriminatory."[76]

The second ruling was given in 1978 and related to aids.[77] The question to be decided in this case was whether the German revaluation compensation law conflicted with the second subparagraph of Article 40(3) EEC because it differentiated between agricultural stockbreeders and stockfarmers on the one hand and industrial stockbreeders and stockfarmers on the other in the matter of an aid permissible under Community law.

This question was referred to the Court of Justice by the Finance Court of Münster. It had arisen in the course of an action, in which the following were the salient facts:

On October 24, 1969 the Government of the Federal Republic of Germany revalued the Deutsche Mark by 8.5 per cent. with effect from October 27, 1969. Since European farm prices are linked to units of account, this currency measure—assuming the value of the unit of

---

[75] Council Regulation 1210/70 of June 29, 1970, J.O. 1970, L142/20.
[76] E.C.J., *loc. cit.*, footnote 72, paras. 22 to 23.
[77] Case 139/77 *Denkavit Futtermittel GmbH* v. *Finanzamt Warendorf* [1978] E.C.R. 1317.

account remained stable—inevitably led to income losses for German farmers.

To compensate for these income losses, which the German authorities and the Commission agreed in estimating at DM 1.7 billion, the Council adopted Regulation 2464/69[78] and authorised the Federal Republic of Germany "to grant aid ... in the form of direct aid to agricultural producers" (first point in the preamble).

The procedures for administering the aids were governed by Article 1 of the regulation; paragraph 3 of that article stated: "Aid may be granted in the form of direct aids to agricultural producers in so far as they are not calculated on the basis of the price or the quantity of the product." The regulation goes on to stipulate: "Aid may be granted partly in the form of an advance to the agricultural producer when he sells his products, subject to a maximum of 3 per cent. of the selling price, to be paid either by the buyer or by an agency to be appointed by the competent national authorities."

The Council extended and modified Article 1(3) of the regulation by a decision dated January 21, 1974 in which the Federal Republic of Germany was "temporarily authorised to grant to the agricultural producers an aid in the form of compensation which the agricultural producer receives on the sale of his produce and which may not exceed 3 per cent. of the sale price." The decision permits the aid as thus modified to be paid in one of the two forms mentioned in Article 1(3) of the regulation.

On the basis of the aforesaid regulation the German Parliament adopted a "Revaluation Compensation Act" on December 23, 1969; Article 4 of the Act provides that agricultural and forestry businesses as defined in § 24(2) of the Turnover Tax Act are entitled to reduce by 3 per cent. the turnover tax (value added tax) which they are required to pay. "Agricultural and forestry businesses" in this definition are deemed to include, in particular, stockbreeding and stockfarming businesses where the animals in question are used or kept for agricultural purposes; for their part animals are deemed to be used or kept for agricultural purposes when the number of units of livestock bred and kept per hectare of land in regular agricultural use per farm year does not exceed certain limits (§ 51 of the Valuation Act, to which Article 24(2) of the Turnover Tax Act refers).

Under these provisions of German law the plaintiff was not eligible for an aid. Although the plaintiff—in addition to making animal feed—

---

[78] Council Regulation 2464/69 December 9, 1969, J.O. 1969, L312/4; O.J. Sp.Ed. 1969 (II), 527.

operated a calf fattening unit using its own home-produced milk replacement feed, it did not do so on "land in agricultural use" and was therefore regarded under German tax law as an industrial business not eligible for aid under the Revaluation Compensation Act (Article 4).

Consequently, an application for aid to an amount of 3 per cent. of the turnover achieved on the sale of its fat calves, submitted by the plaintiff with its tax return for 1974, was turned down. The plaintiff resorted to the Court of Justice to contest this decision, maintaining that the Revaluation Compensation Act was incompatible with Community law as the latter did not distinguish between agricultural and industrial stockfarming. There had therefore been *inter alia*—in the plaintiff's view—an infringement of the prohibition on discrimination in the second subparagraph of Article 40(3) EEC.

The Court of Justice rules as follows on this point:

> "In providing in paragraph 1 that the objectives of the common agricultural policy shall be *inter alia* to ensure a fair standard of living for the agricultural community, in particular by increasing the individual earnings of persons engaged in agriculture, Article 39 does not exclude the possibility of differences of treatment between the various sectors of agricultural activity, always provided that such differences of treatment are not arbitrary and are based on objective criteria. The need for different treatment of various classes of the agricultural community, in appropriate cases, is acknowledged in Article 39(2), which provides that "In working out the common agricultural policy ... account shall be taken of: (a) the particular nature of agricultural activity, which results from the social structure of agriculture and from structural and natural disparities between the various agricultural regions. Although Article 40(3) of the Treaty prohibits any discrimination between producers within the Community, and even within a single country of the Community, different treatment could be regarded as constituting prohibited discrimination only if it appears to be arbitrary."[79]

On the basis of this assessment, the Court then went on to emphasise that agricultural stockbreeders and stockfarmers, because the fodder they use is mainly produced on their own farms, are particularly subject to the hazards of land use. Industrial stockbreeders and stockfarmers are not

---

[79] E.C.J., *loc. cit.*, footnote 77, para. 15. In this connection see also Case 36/79 *Denkavit Futtermittel GmbH* v. *Finanzamt Warendorf* [1979] E.C.R. 3439, paras. 6 and 16.

exposed to the same risks, because they largely obtain their fodder requirements on the national and international market and if their national currency is revalued they are able to purchase fodder cheaply abroad.

The Court then stated:

"Accordingly, the distinction between agricultural livestock breeders and keepers and industrial livestock breeders and keepers, which German tax law makes by laying down a ratio between the head of livestock and the utilized agricultural area and which the Government of the Federal Republic of Germany adopted as an objective, albeit unmodulated, criterion as regards the granting of the aid which it is empowered to grant by the provisions of Regulation No. 2464/69, cannot be classified as discriminatory."[80]

The third decision was delivered in 1982 and related to the law on refunds.[81] In that case the Court of Justice had to decide, *inter alia*, whether a special duty levied as a so-called "claw-back" on exports of sheep meat to a Member State infringed the prohibition on discrimination in the second subparagraph of Article 40(3) EEC.

The background to the decision was as follows:

When the Council set up the common organisation of the market for sheep meat and goat meat in 1980, its objective was to equalise the markets in the various regions of the Community in order to arrive at a uniform market and a system of uniform prices.

Accordingly, Regulation (EEC) 1837/80[82] divided the Community into six regions, with separate reference prices being set for each region. The reference price is used to calculate a premium provided under Article 5 of the regulation for every ewe "to offset the loss of income which may result from the establishment of the common market organization."

In addition, the Regulation lays down a basic price for the whole Community, varying according to the season. On the basis of this price, intervention measures under Articles 6 to 9 may be taken. Here the Member States, besides aids for private storage, have a choice between the purchase of fresh sheep meat by the intervention agencies and the payment of a variable slaughtering premium.

---

[80] E.C.J., *loc. cit.*, footnote 77, para. 17.
[81] Case 106/81 *Julius Kind AG* v. *European Economic Community* [1982] E.C.R. 2885.
[82] Council Regulation 1837/80 of June 27, 1980, O.J. 1980, L183/1.

Under Article 9(1) of the Regulation, the Member State in question may, in regions where there are no purchases by intervention agencies "the Member State or Member States concerned may pay a variable slaughter premium for sheep when the prices recorded on the representative market or markets of the Member State or Member States concerned are below a 'guide level' corresponding to 85 per cent. of the basic price." Article 9(2) of the Regulation stipulates that the amount of this premium shall be equal to the difference between the guide level and the market price obtaining in the Member State in question. Finally, Article 9(3) provides that necessary measures shall be taken, so that in the event of payment of the premium under paragraph 1 an amount equal to this premium is levied if the products named in Article 1(a) leave the territory of the Member State in question. This amount, which is levied on exports and is identical to the slaughtering premium, is generally termed a "claw-back."

The plaintiff—a German undertaking importing fresh sheep meat from the United Kingdom into the Federal Republic of Germany—contested the rule in Article 9(3) of the regulation, which had the effect of increasing the price of meat exported from the United Kingdom to other Member States. The plaintiff maintained that the rule infringed the discrimination prohibition of Article 40(3) subparagraph 2 EEC, because it "created completely different conditions for the continental and British businessman on the one hand and for the German and British consumer on the other; as a result of an intervention measure the same goods were offered to the two groups at quite different prices."[83]

The Court of Justice first stated, as a general point, that the levying of an export duty under Article 9(3) of Regulation 1837/80 could not in principle be separated from the intervention arrangements which entailed the payment of a variable slaughtering premium in regions in which there were no purchases by intervention agencies. This duty was designed to compensate precisely for the effects of the slaughtering premium and thus to make it possible for products from countries or regions in which this premium was granted to be exported to other Member States without distorting their markets. For if the claw-back was not levied, produce from a country granting slaughtering premiums would arrive on other Member States' markets at considerably lower prices than the local prices and, as a result of falling price levels, would entail intervention measures the cost of which the Community would

---

[83] E.C.J., *loc. cit.*, footnote 81, p. 2897 of the statement of the facts.

then in fact have to bear a second time, albeit perhaps in a different form.[84]

The Court then declared:

> "Secondly, as regards the submission alleging discrimination it should be recalled that different treatment may not, as pointed out in the judgment of the Court of 13 June 1978 (Case 139/77 *Denkavit* [1978] E.C.R. 1317), be regarded as discrimination prohibited by Article 40(3) of the Treaty unless it appears to be arbitrary, or in other words, as stated in other judgments, devoid of adequate justification and not based on objective criteria."[85]

The Court found that the analysis of the common organisation of the market for sheep meat had shown that "objective reasons" for the intervention measures provided for in Regulation 1837/80—and thus also for the variable slaughtering premium and the claw-back—did exist and that there had therefore been no discrimination.[86]

However, the Court of Justice has not always referred to the interplay, as described above, of the concept of arbitrary action and the justification of disparity of treatment on the grounds of objective circumstances. There have been plenty of cases where it has based its rulings solely on the criterion of disparity of objective circumstances or arbitrariness of treatment. Here again we can give only a few examples from a plethora of decisions.

The first decision we would mention is a case involving competition law, where one of the points at issue was whether there had been an infringement of Article 7 EEC when a state authority had imposed sanctions owing to the existence of a cartel which was also the subject of proceedings before the Commission.[87] The specific point to be decided was whether the authority had committed "discrimination on grounds of nationality" because it had imposed the sanctions—in accordance with the powers that had been conferred on it—exclusively on its own nationals.

This question had been referred to the Court of Justice by the Restrictive Practices Chamber of the Kammergericht (Higher Regional

---

[84] E.C.J., *loc. cit.*, footnote 81, para. 21.
[85] E.C.J., *loc. cit.*, footnote 81, para. 22; in connection with the judgment in Case 139/77 referred to, see under B.II.2. above.
[86] E.C.J., *loc. cit.*, footnote 81, paras. 23 and 24.
[87] Case 14/68 *Walt Wilhelm and Others* v. *Federal Cartel Office* [1969] E.C.R. 1.

Court) of Berlin. It had arisen in the course of an action based on the following facts:

By a decision taken on November 28, 1967 the Federal Cartel Office had imposed fines under Article 38(-1) 1 in conjunction with § 1 of the Act Prohibiting Restraints on Competition on four German undertakings whose business included the manufacture of coal-tar dyes and mineral pigments. These firms were accused of having agreed among themselves, and with other—French, British and Swiss—operators in the same industry, on July 18, 1967 to raise aniline prices by 8 per cent. with effect from October 16, 1967.

The European Commission had already instituted proceedings under Articles 9(3) and 3 of Regulation 17 on an earlier occasion against the four German undertakings and a number of other, non-German, firms which also manufactured dyes and pigments. These proceedings had related to two increases in aniline prices effected in 1964 and 1965; the proceedings were then duly extended to cover the latest price increase as well, because here, too, the Commission suspected that concerted practices within the meaning of Article 85(1) EEC were involved.

The four undertakings fined by the Federal Cartel Office had instituted proceedings against the decision of November 28, 1967 in which the fine had been imposed.

On the question of alleged infringement of Article 7 EEC the Court of Justice ruled as follows:

> "Article 7 of the EEC Treaty prohibits every Member State from applying its law on cartels differently on the ground of the nationality of the parties concerned. However, Article 7 is not concerned with any disparities in treatment or the distortions which may result, for the persons and undertaking subject to the jurisdiction of the Community, from divergences existing between the laws of the various Member States, so long as the latter affect all persons subject to them, in accordance with objective criteria and without regard to their nationality."[88]

---

[88] E.C.J., *ibid.* para. 13. A similar decision relating to Article 7 EEC was the judgment in Case 118/75 *Lynne Watson and Alessandro Belmann* [1976] E.C.R. 1185. In paras. 21 to 22 of this decision the Court of Justice stated the following general opinion on the control of foreigners under the provisions of national law: "In so far as national rules concerning the control of foreign nationals do not involve restrictions on freedom of movement for persons and on the right, conferred by the Treaty on persons protected by Community law, to enter and reside in the territory of the Member States, the application of such legislation, where it is based upon objective factors, cannot constitute 'discrimination on grounds of nationality' prohibited under Article 7 of the Treaty."

Another decision which may be mentioned by way of example in this connection is a 1973 ruling on the law on monetary compensatory amounts.[89] One of the points at issue was whether the Commission had infringed the second subparagraph of Article 40(3) EEC in 1971 by failing, during the period from May 12, to August 2, to fix compensatory amounts for the export of processed barley products.

The background to the case was that on May 9, 1971 the Federal Republic of Germany and the Netherlands had widened the fluctuation bands of their currencies in relation to the official parity. This action was likely to cause difficulties for the functioning of the common organisation of the agricultural market as soon as the actual rate of exchange differed from the official parity by more than a certain margin, because it would then be possible to trade goods at a price below the intervention or purchase prices.[90]

To enable it to counter these expected difficulties, the Council decided to take "conjunctural" measures as permitted by Article 103 EEC. It accordingly adopted Regulation 974/71,[91] which introduced a system of compensatory amounts in order to compensate for the effects of currency fluctuations on the prices of basic products.

Specifically, Article 1(1) of this Regulation states that a Member State which, in connection with trading transactions, allows the existence of a rate of exchange for its currency "allows the exchange rate of its currency to fluctuate by a margin wider than the one permitted by international rules, it shall be authorised to: (a) charge on imports . . . (b) grant on exports . . . compensatory amounts . . ."

Paragraph 2 of the same article extends this right to basic products for which intervention measures are prescribed within the framework of the common organisation of the agricultural market and to processed products the price of which is geared to the price of the basic products; the last sentence of paragraph 2 stipulates that the right granted by paragraph 1 shall be exercised only if application of the currency measures referred to therein "would lead to disturbances in trade in agricultural products."

In accordance with Article 6 of Regulation 974/71, the Commission on May 17, 1971 adopted Regulation 1014/71,[92] in the annexes of which the compensatory amounts were fixed for a number of products, including,

---

[89] Case 43/72 *Merkur-Aussenhandels-GmbH* v. *Commission of the European Communities* [1973] E.C.R. 1055.
[90] See in particular Advocate-General Roemer in his opinion in Case 5/73 *Balkan-Import-Export* v. *Hauptzollamt Berlin Packhof* [1973] E.C.R. 1091 at 1118.
[91] Council Regulation 974/71 of May 12, 1971, J.O. 1971, L106/1; O.J. Sp.Ed. 1971, 257.
[92] Commission Regulation 1014/71 of May 17, 1971, J.O. 1971, L110/10.

for example, various individually specified "processed cereal products" (Annex IB).

A perusal of the list revealed, however, that processed barley products were not mentioned, which meant that compensatory amounts were neither granted on exports of barley groats and meal nor levied on imports of the same products.

In Regulation 1687/71,[93] which came into force on August 2, 1971, the Commission replaced the annexes of Regulation 1018/71 with new annexes, so that the heading "processed cereal products" now also includes "barley groats and barley meal."

The plaintiff, which had more or less specialised in the export of barley groats and meal from the Federal Republic of Germany, contended that the temporary non-inclusion of processed barley products in the compensation arrangements was incompatible with the second subparagraph of Article 40(3) EEC. It maintained that German exporters of these products were discriminated against in two respects: firstly, in comparison with exporters in other Member States in which no currency measures as defined by Article 1(1) of Regulation 974/71 had been taken and, secondly, in comparison with those German exporters exporting products which had already been included in the compensation arrangements before August 2, 1971.

On the latter part of this claim the Court of Justice made the following general point:

> "As regards the comparison made with German exporters of goods which had had the benefit of this compensatory system from the start, the different treatment of which the applicant complains would not be a violation of the principle of non-discrimination unless it appeared to be arbitrary."[94]

The Court then pointed out that the Commission, in deciding whether the application of the currency measures mentioned in Regulation 974/71 could lead to disturbances in the trade in agricultural products, enjoyed wide discretion. In conclusion the Court stated:

[93] Commission Regulation 1687/71 of August 2, 1971, J.O. 1971, L173/1.

[94] E.C.J., *loc. cit.*, footnote 89, para. 22. The Court of Justice again uses the term "arbitrary" in isolation in its judgment in Joined Cases 56–60/74 *Kurt Kampffmeyer Mühlenvereinigung KG and Others* v. *Commission and Council of the European Communities* [1976] E.C.R. 711, para. 14; in connection with this judgment, which was also delivered in relation to the second subparagraph of Article 40(3) EEC, see also under B.III.5. below.

"... Bearing in mind the exceptional nature of the compensatory amounts, the Commission does not appear to have exercised these powers in an arbitrary fashion."[95]

Another decision meriting a mention is a 1974 ruling in connection with aids,[96] in which the Court of Justice considered, *inter alia*, whether an additional aid, granted only to the oil mill operators in Italy, amounted to a breach of the anti-discrimination provisions of the second subparagraph of Article 40(3) EEC.

The facts on which this decision was based were as follows:

To set up a common organisation of the market for fats and oils, Regulation 136/66[97] was adopted in 1966; since July 1, 1967 it has been applicable to rapeseed and turnip seed. The Regulation provides for a system of basic intervention prices and derived intervention prices in order to equalise the differing costs of transporting oilseeds from the various growing areas to the oil mills.

However, after the Regulation had come into force, the Italian industry experienced difficulties because French rapeseed oil suddenly appeared on the Italian market at much lower prices than rapeseed oil produced in Italy from French seed. Since rape is not grown in Italy, the Italian oil mills are dependent on supplies of oilseed from France, the nearest area where the crop is grown.

Within the framework of Article 36 of Regulation 136/66 the Council thereupon adopted Regulation 876/67,[98] which introduced an "additional aid" for rapeseed and turnip seed produced in the Community and processed in Italy. This measure was renewed from year to year until it was finally abolished at the end of the crop year 1973–74.

During the case the Council maintained that the difficulties of the Italian industry were due mainly to the fact that the cost of transporting oilseed from France to Italy was higher than the cost of transporting the oil contained in this seed. The additional aid was thus intended only to equalise the competitive advantages arising for the Italian oil mills from the structure of the common organisation of the market.

The plaintiff, which operated an oil mill in North Rhine-Westphalia and processed—*inter alia*—rape and turnip seed, contended on the other

[95] E.C.J., *loc. cit.*, footnote 89, para. 23.
[96] Case 153/73 *Holtz & Willemsen* v. *Council and Commission of the European Communities* [1974] E.C.R. 675.
[97] Council Regulation 136/66 of September 22, 1966, J.O. 1966, 172/3025; O.J. Sp. Ed. 1965–1966, 221.
[98] Council Regulation 876/67 of November 20, 1967, J.O. 1967, L281/7.

hand that the additional aid, granted as it was only to the oil mills in Italy, infringed the EEC Treaty and in particular the prohibition of any "discrimination on grounds of nationality" contained in Article 7(1) EEC.

The Court of Justice, which held that the relevant provisions were those of the second subparagraph of Article 40(3) rather than of Article 7(1) EEC, declared on this point:

> "The objectives referred to in Article 40 of the Treaty, that is the establishment of a common agricultural policy and a common organization of agricultural markets, presupposes the adoption of common rules and criteria and the consequent exclusion of any discrimination based on the nationality or locality of the oil mills. In this light the various factors in the common organization of the markets, protective measures, aids, subsidies, etc. may be distinguished according to the areas and other conditions of production or consumption only in terms of criteria of an objective nature which ensure a proportionate distribution of advantages and disadvantages for those concerned without distinguishing between the territory of Member States. Additional subsidies limited to oil mills established in one of the Member States are therefore in general incompatible with the objectives of the common agricultural policy in so far as they are not justified by circumstances special to the whole of the national market in question."[99]

Even though the Court of Justice did not find the Council's case convincing in every respect, it nevertheless considered that the setting up of the common organisation of the market for fats and oils had created a new situation which had adverse effects on business in Italy. In view of the fact that the disputed additional aid was a temporary rather than a definitive measure,[100] the court held that the second subparagraph of Article 40(3) EEC had not been infringed.[101]

Another decision, which from the point of view of possible justification links up with the criterion of "objective circumstances," was delivered in 1977 in connection with the law on refunds.[102] One of the questions facing the Court of Justice here was whether the second subparagraph of Article

---

[99] E.C.J., *loc. cit.*, footnote 96, para. 13. Similarly: Case 8/78 *Milac GmbH* v. *Hauptzollamt Freiburg* [1978] E.C.R. 1721, para. 18; see earlier comment under footnote 38 above.

[100] On the admissibility of temporary measures during the start-up period of a common organisation of a market, see E.C.J., *loc. cit.*, footnote 96, para. 14.

[101] E.C.J., *loc. cit.*, footnote 96, paras. 15 and 17.

[102] Case 2/77 *Hoffmanns Stärkefabriken* v. *Hauptzollamt Bielefeld* [1977] E.C.R. 1375.

40(3) EEC had been infringed owing to the fact that manufacturers of maize starch were temporarily receiving a smaller refund than manufacturers of potato starch.

This question had been referred to the Court of Justice by the Finance Court of Münster. It had arisen in the course of an action based on the following facts:

In accordance with the version of Article 5 of Regulation 1125/74[103] which has been in force since August 1, 1974, Article 11 of Regulation 120/67[104] provides that a refund shall be granted: (a) for maize and common wheat used in the Community for the manufacture of starch, (b) for potato starch, (c) for groats and meal (gritz) made from maize used in the Community for the manufacture of glucose by "direct hydrolysis," and (d) for maize used by the maize industry in the Community for the production of groats and meal (gritz) used in the Community by the brewing industry in the making of beer.

In the tenth recital to Regulation 120/67 the granting of a refund on maize intended for starch manufacture is justified as follows:

"Because of the special situation on the market in starches and, in particular, the need for that industry to keep prices competitive with those for substitute products, it is necessary to ensure by means of a production refund that the basic products used by the industry are made available to it at a lower price than that which would result from applying the system of levies and common prices."

The preamble goes on to state:

"Whereas, for similar reasons and because of the interchangeability of starches with quellmehl[105] and maize groats and meal, production refunds should also be granted in respect of the latter products."

In accordance with Article 11(3) of Regulation 120/67 the Council adopted Regulation 371/67[106] in which it fixed the amounts of the refunds.

[103] Council Regulation 1125/74 of April 29, 1974, O.J. 1974, L128/12.
[104] Council Regulation 120/67 of June 13, 1967, J.O. 1967, L117/2269; O.J. Sp.Ed. 1967, 33. See footnote 73 above.
[105] Quellmehl is a product made from maize, common wheat or broken rice. See in this connection the Court of Justice's judgment in Joined Cases 117/76 & 16/77 *Albert Ruckdeschel & Co. and Others* v. *Hauptzollamt Hamburg St. Annen* [1977] E.C.R. 1753, outlined under C. below.
[106] Council Regulation 371/67 of July 25, 1967, J.O. 1967, L174/40; O.J. Sp.Ed. 1967, 219.

Article 1 of the Regulation stipulated that the amount receivable in respect of the production of maize starch was to be the difference between the threshold price of maize and a "procurement price" set at a flat rate of 68 u.a. per tonne, which was lower than the threshold price and reflected what the maize starch manufacturers considered to be a desirable and normal purchase price for maize. Article 2 of the Regulation gives the Council the power, in the event that world market prices of the basic products specified in Article 1—including maize—"show appreciable and persistent variations," to change the procurement price as well.

Regulation 371/67 was repealed and replaced by Regulation 1132/74,[107] with Article 2 being incorporated in the new Regulation as Article 7. Overall, the new rules recognised that the competitive position of the maize starch manufacturers had to be assured by making it possible for them to purchase maize at a price nearer to the world market price than the price derived from the simple application of the threshold price.

Since the crop year 1974/75 the Council, and the Commission on the Council's authority, have raised the procurement price in stages, first to 82 u.a., then to 87.45 u.a. and from April 1, 1975 to 103.10 u.a. Where the threshold price remained unchanged—as was the case with the first and last increases—this inevitably entailed a reduction in the amount of the refund.

The last increase in the procurement price was based on Regulation 3113/74.[108] Regulation 231/75[109] had the effect of removing potato starch from the scope of this measure, so that the manufacturers of maize starch temporarily received a smaller refund.

The plaintiff, a German starch manufacturing firm, claimed that this would infringe the prohibition on discrimination in the second subparagraph of Article 40(3) EEC.

The Court of Justice ruled on this point as follows:

> "In accordance with the second subparagraph of Article 40(3) of the Treaty, the common organizations of the market must exclude any discrimination between producers or consumers within the Community. Having regard to the competitive situation of maize-starch producers and potato-starch producers, Article 2 of Regulation No. 1132/74 provides that the production refund per 100 kg of potato

---

[107] Council Regulation 1132/74 of April 29, 1974, O.J. 1974, L128/24.
[108] Council Regulation 3113/74 of December 9, 1974, O.J. 1974, L332/1.
[109] Commission Regulation 231/75 of January 30, 1975, O.J. 1975, L24/2.

starch shall be equal to the average amount of the refund granted during the same marketing year per 161 kg of maize for starch manufacture. The increase in the supply price from 1 April 1975 and the subsequent reduction of the production refund in favour of maize starch producers pursuant to Article 1 of Regulation No. 3113/74 would, if the abovementioned Article 2 had been applied automatically, have been reflected in the same proportions until 31 July 1975 in the amount of the refund granted to potato-starch producers."[110]

The Court of Justice was told that under Article 3 of Regulation 1132/74 the manufacturers of potato starch were granted a refund only if they could prove that they had paid the amount of the refund to the potato producers. For this reason and because the amounts were calculated on the basis of threshold prices for maize which had been fixed in advance for the whole crop year, an immediate change in the procurement price would have meant that moneys that had been paid to the potato producers before January 31, 1975 would have had to be repaid.[111]

From this the Court of Justice concluded as follows:

"There are thus objective grounds for the difference between the treatment accorded potato-starch producers and that accorded maize-starch producers so that the transitional measure enacted in connexion with the production refund for potato starch does not constitute a discrimination against maize-starch producers."[112]

In conclusion we would mention another decision, dating from 1981 and relating to the social provisions.[113] Here the Court of Justice had to decide, *inter alia*, whether a difference in the level of remuneration for work done on a part-time basis and the same work done in the course of full-time employment represented discrimination of the kind prohibited

---

[110] E.C.J., *loc. cit.*, footnote 102, para. 19.

[111] E.C.J., *loc. cit.*, footnote 102, para. 20.

[112] E.C.J., *loc. cit.*, footnote 102, para. 21; see also Case 5/82 *Maizena GmbH* v. *Council of the European Communities* [1982] E.C.R. 4601, in which the Court of Justice—in para. 17—refers to the passage quoted. Similar ruling on the law on monetary compensatory amounts: Case 88/78 *Hauptzollamt Hamburg-Jonas* v. *Hermann Kendermann oHG* [1978] E.C.R. 2477, para. 12.

[113] Case 96/80 *J.P. Jenkins* v. *Kingsgate (Clothing Productions) Ltd.* [1981] E.C.R. 911; for later case law see Case 91/85 *Anne-Marie Clemen and Others* v. *Commission of the European Communities* [1986] E.C.R. 2853, para. 10; Joined Cases 201–202/85 *Marthe Klensch and Others* v. *Staatssekretär für Landwirtschaft und Weinbau and Others* [1986] E.C.R. 3477, para. 9.

by Article 119 EEC if the group of part-time workers consisted exclusively or predominantly of women.

This question had been referred to the Court of Justice by a British industrial tribunal. It had arisen in the course of an action between a female worker employed on a part-time basis—the plaintiff—and her employer, a manufacturer of ladies' clothing.

The background to the decision was that the employer—the defendant—had paid different wages to his male and female employees until 1975, but making no distinction—as far as hourly wages were concerned—between part-time and full-time work. Since November 1975 the pay for full-time work, *i.e.* 40 hours per week, had been the same for both male and female employees, but the hourly rate for part-time work had been 10 per cent. lower than this.

With only one exception, *all* the workers employed by the defendant on a part-time basis under these conditions were female. The exception was a male employee who had reached normal retirement age but had been allowed to continue to work for a short time after reaching that age.

The plaintiff, in her action, complained that she was being paid a lower hourly rate than one of her male colleagues who was employed full-time doing the same work. She claimed that this arrangement was in breach of Article 119 EEC.

The Court of Justice declared that the aim of Article 119 EEC was to ensure the application of the principle that men and women should receive equal pay for equal work, which that unequal treatment was forbidden under this rule only if it was based on the sex of the worker. Hence the fact that a lower hourly wage was paid for part-time than for full-time work did not constitute prohibited discrimination under Article 119 EEC if the hourly rates applied to all workers without differentiation according to sex.[114]

The Court went on to state:

> "If there is no such distinction, therefore, the fact that work paid at time rates is remunerated at an hourly rate which varies according to the number of hours worked per week does not offend against the principle of equal pay laid down in Article 119 of the Treaty in so far as the difference in pay between part-time work and full-time work is attributable to factors which are objectively justified and are in no way related to any discrimination based on sex."[115]

[114] E.C.J., *ibid.*, para. 10.
[115] E.C.J., *ibid.*, para. 11.

"Such may be the case, in particular, when by giving hourly rates of pay which are lower for part-time work than those for full-time work the employer is endeavouring, on economic grounds which may be objectively justified, to encourage full-time work irrespective of the sex of the worker."[116]

III. OTHER CHARACTERISTICS AND FORMS OF DISCRIMINATION

Going beyond the scope of the judgments we have outlined so far, which have contained basic rulings on the concept of discrimination, the Court of Justice has also on many occasions pronounced on certain further characteristics of prohibited discrimination or—negatively—has excluded certain factual elements as being incompatible with the concept of discrimination. On the basis of these judgments it is possible to arrive at a more precise definition of the concept of prohibited discrimination. Once again, however, it is possible to discuss in any detail only a few typical examples from the plethora of relevant cases.

1. Occurrence of Damage

As early as 1960—in a case involving rates and conditions for the carriage of coal and and steel—the Court of Justice examined the question whether the concept of discrimination necessarily requires that direct damage be caused.[117] Specifically, the Court had to decide whether the High Authority, by abolishing the preferential tariff rates applicable to internal carriage, had committed an act of discrimination prohibited by Articles 4(b) and 70(1) ECSC.

The facts on which this decision was based were as follows:

Right at the beginning of its activities the High Authority had drawn up a programme or work in order to fulfil its duties under the transport provisions of the ECSC Treaty and to review the preferential tariffs applicable to inland carriage.

Under this programme, surveys were carried out in the individual

---

[116] E.C.J., *ibid.*, para. 12. The same idea had already been expressed by Advocate-General Capotorti in his opinion in Case 129/79 *Macarthys Ltd.* v. *Wendy Smith* [1980] E.C.R. 1291 at 1294.

[117] Joined Cases 3–18 & 25–26/58 *Barbara Erzbergbau AG and Others* v. *High Authority* [1960] E.C.R. 373.

601

regions into the economic situation in general and the situation of the iron and steel industry in particular. On completion of these surveys the High Authority adopted the decisions complained of, which required the applicants—a number of German undertakings—to withdraw the preferential tariffs that had been granted.

The principal reason adduced by the High Authority for its decisions was that the preferential tariffs were by their nature discriminatory, because they put other undertakings, which were in a comparable position with regard to transport, at a disadvantage.

The applicants, on the other hand, maintained that the High Authority was incorrect in claiming that *every* preferential tariff was discriminatory; a preferential tariff was discriminatory only if its application had the effect of causing direct damage to a third party. The High Authority had not been able to prove that this had been the case.

The Court of Justice ruled on this point:

> "The concept of discrimination does not imply, by definition, the fact that direct damage is caused. The meaning of this concept is primarily that unequal conditions are laid down for comparable cases. The application of such unequal conditions may, it is true, bring about damage, which can then be considered as the consequence by which that discrimination may be detected. However, it would be arbitrary to reduce the concept of discrimination solely to those cases of unequal treatment in which the interested parties in fact suffer damage."[118]

The Court of Justice concluded that the question cannot turn on whether or not a preferential tariff applicable to internal transport puts other undertakings at a disadvantage, "since a perfect comparison is only possible between transport which takes place within one and the same country."[119]

2. Distortion of Competition

In 1959 the Court of Justice handed down a decision relating to the scrap compensation system, in which it pronounced in general terms on

---

[118] E.C.J., *ibid.*, p. 11 of the judgment.
[119] E.C.J., *ibid.*, p. 412 of the judgment.

the question whether measures or interventions are discriminatory when they distort competition, in particular within the meaning of Articles 2(2), 3(b), 60 and 67 ECSC.[120]

The facts behind the decision were as follows:

The applicant, Société Nouvelle des Usines de Pontlieue—Aciéries du Temple (SNUPAT), produced special steel in its plants in Saint-Michel-de-Maurienne (Savoie) using scrap of which by far the greater part came form "Régie nationale des usines Renault" in Billancourt (Seine). Régie Renault in turn was the main customer for the steel made by the applicant in its Saint-Michel plants.

The plants in Saint-Michel and Billancourt had originally—since 1921—belonged to two separate legal entities, although industrially and economically they constituted a single business. In 1946 a single legal body, Régie Renault, replaced the two former legal entities and the Saint-Michel plant was operated by Régie Renault as its own plant.

Then in 1954/55 Régie Renault decided to put the Saint-Michel plant—the present SNUPAT—on to an independent legal footing. However, it retained 99.77 per cent. of the share capital, and the links between SNUPAT and Régie Renault remained close, both in economic and financial matters and as regards executive and technical staff.

Owing to these links SNUPAT took the view that scrap obtained from the Régie Renault plants was not scrap purchased from a third party but "own arisings." It did not therefore report it to the compensation fund for imported scrap and pay a levy as required pursuant to Articles 2 and 4 of Decision No. 2/57 on scrap purchased from a third party.[121]

However, in a letter dated December 18, 1957 to the Joint Scrap Users' Bureau the High Authority maintained that scrap arising within a corporate group ("group scrap"), such as that used by SNUPAT, did not constitute levy-exempt "own arisings"; an undertaking could regard as "own arisings" only such scrap as "it generates itself in its own plants, which bear the same firm name."

The compensation fund thereupon stated that a further 23,357 tonnes of scrap obtained by the applicant were subject to the levy. The sum due was calculated to be $228,430.75 and the applicant was called upon to pay it by letter of May 12, 1958.

In the letter of December 18, 1957 referred to above the High

---

[120] Joined Cases 32–33/58 *SNUPAT* v. *High Authority* [1959] E.C.R. 127. See also the judgments in Joined Cases 17 & 20/61 *Klöckner Werke AG* v. *High Authority* and Case 19/61 *Mannesmann AG* v. *High Authority*; see under B.II.1. above.

[121] See earlier comment under B.II.1. above.

603

Authority had approved two exceptions to the rule based on its definition of "own arisings" in favour of an Italian and a Dutch undertaking; these companies had accordingly been exempted from the levy. The reason given for this decision was that the two undertakings were "spatially linked with . . . scrap-producing plants which did not belong to them" to such an extent that they formed a single industrial complex; the High Authority expressly stated that other factors, such as organisational links, were not decisive.

When SNUPAT's request that it, too, should be exempted from the levy was turned down, it appealed to the Court of Justice. The company claimed that "group scrap" should be regarded as equivalent to "own arisings." Particularly in view of the two exceptions which had been approved by the authorities, a disparity of treatment which failed to take into account such definite links as those between itself and Régie Renault was—SNUPAT maintained—"arbitrary and discriminatory," for it conferred an additional benefit on those undertakings which did not have to incur any transport costs on their scrap requirements and were thus already in an advantageous position, whereas SNUPAT's own position was made worse; instead of creating competitive equilibrium, the High Authority by its action had made an existing disequilibrium even more pronounced than before.

The Court of Justice could not accept the applicant's contention that "group scrap" should be regarded as equivalent to "own arisings." In the Court's view this result was confirmed by the concept of discrimination—"as evident, in particular, from Articles 2(2), 3(b), 60 and 67 of the Treaty."

Specifically, the Court stated:

> "On the basis of the above mentioned provisions these may be considered as discriminatory in principle and, accordingly, prohibited by the Treaty, *inter alia*, measures or interventions, even those emanating from the High Authority, which are calculated, by substantially increasing differences in production costs otherwise than through changes in productivity, to give rise to an appreciable disequilibrium in the competitive position of the undertakings concerned.
>
> In other words, any intervention attempting to distort or actually distorting competition artificially and significantly must be regarded as discriminatory and incompatible with the Treaty, whilst measures which take into account the internal organization of an undertaking

and the use by it of its own resources cannot be regarded as discriminatory."[122]

Following on from this, the Court of Justice declared that those undertakings which produced steel from scrap and used their own scrap for that purpose were recycling one of their by-products. The quantity of steel obtained from a given quantity of scrap, which had already attracted the levy, was thereby increased and this had the effect of reducing production costs and, as a result, definitely increasing productivity.[123]

From this the Court concluded that an intervention which offered an incentive to internal economies of this kind in no way distorted competition but on the contrary fostered a change in methods which would give rise to greater productivity. Such an intervention was therefore consonant with Community law, which meant that it was not discriminatory to exempt "own arisings" from the levy.[124]

By contrast, to treat "group scrap" in the same way would amount to prohibited discrimination within the meaning of Article 4(b) ECSC; for the resultant fall in production costs would be likely substantially to increase the differences in production costs in relation to those undertakings which also produced steel from scrap but were not linked to an undertaking that produced scrap.

These differences in production costs would than be the result of fortuitous geographical, administrative or financial links such as were inherent in a corporate group. They would not, however, be based on a change in productivity; for it was evident from the ECSC Treaty as a whole that the term "productivity" (rendement) referred exclusively to the result of the efforts of the individual undertaking.[125]

---

[122] E.C.J. *loc. cit.*, footnote 120, p. 143 of the judgment. The same idea was expressed again later in connection with agriculture by Advocate-General Mayras in his opinion in Case 4/79 *Société Coopérative "Providence agricole de la Champagne"* v. *Office national professionnel des céréales* [1980] E.C.R. 2823 at 2863 and by Advocate-General Capotorti in his opinion in Case 158/80 *Rewe-Handelsgesellschaft Nord mbH and Others* v. *Hauptzollamt Kiel* [1981] E.C.R. 1805 at 1852. Criticism of this reasoning in R. Stotz, *op. cit.*, footnote 30, pp. 93 *et seq.*

[123] E.C.J., *loc. cit.*, footnote 120, p. 143 of the judgment.

[124] E.C.J., *loc. cit.*, footnote 120, pp. 143 *et seq.* of the judgment.

[125] E.C.J., *loc. cit.*, footnote 120, pp. 144 *et seq.* of the judgment.

3. "Natural" Differences

In 1973 and 1980 the Court of Justice ruled in two cases that discrimination was *not* deemed to exist where the dissimilar treatment in question was caused by natural differences.

This emerges particularly clearly in a ruling given in 1980 in connection with services.[126] In that case the Court of Justice had to decide, *inter alia*, on the question whether a provision of national law prohibiting the retransmission of advertising material by cable television constituted discrimination under Articles 59 and 69 EEC, because it restricted foreign stations, owing to their geographical location, to broadcasting such advertising material exclusively within their own natural transmission areas.

The question was referred to the Court of Justice by a Belgian "Tribunal Correctionnel." It had arisen in the course of criminal proceedings brought by a number of consumer associations.

The principal defendants in the proceedings were two companies incorporated under Belgian law which operated a cable television service covering part of Belgian territory with the approval of the competent authority. The television sets of the subscribers to this service were connected to a central antenna by cable; this enabled them, for specific technical reasons, to receive Belgian and certain foreign transmissions which could not in all cases be received by private households using individual aerials.

However, the national radio and television organisations, which enjoyed a statutory broadcasting monopoly, were forbidden by Belgian law to transmit material of an advertising nature. By virtue of Article 21 of the "arrêté royal" of December 24, 1966, this prohibition applied *mutatis mutandis* to cable television.

The two companies against which criminal proceedings had been brought had not complied with Article 21 of the "arrêté" and had retransmitted foreign programmes without cutting out the integrated advertising matter. The Government had tolerated this action without imposing sanctions; one reason for this was said to be that a large proportion of the Belgian population could pick up foreign channels anyway—*i.e.* without cable. The "Tribunal Correctionnel" hearing the case stated that it could not exclude the possibility that Article 21 of the "arrêté royal" of December 24, 1966 constituted prohibited discrimination under Articles 59 and

[126] Case 52/79 *Procureur du roi* v. *Marc J.V.C. Debauve and Others* [1980] E.C.R. 833.

60 EEC, because it restricted foreign stations, on account of their geographical location, to transmitting advertising material solely within their natural transmission areas.

The Court of Justice ruled on this point as follows:

> "The national court is referring in this question to the spatial limits on the diffusion of television programmes depending, on the one hand, on the natural relief of the ground and of built-up areas and, on the other, on the technical features of the broadcasting systems used. These natural and technical factors undoubtedly lead to differences as regards reception of television signals in view of the correlation between the location of broadcasting stations and television receivers. However, such differences, which are due to natural phenomena, cannot be described as "discrimination" within the meaning of the Treaty; the latter regards only differences in the treatment arising from human activity, and especially from measures taken by public authorities, as discrimination."[127]

In a ruling given in 1973 in connection with the pricing and aid system for durum wheat, the concept of discrimination was similarly defined—albeit not too clearly and only in passing.[128] In that case the Court of Justice was considering, *inter alia*, whether discrimination prohibited by the second subparagraph of Article 40(3) EEC had been committed if the Council did not take any measures to ensure that millers in Member States where durum was *not* grown could purchase durum from third countries at a price corresponding to the price paid by millers in Member States where durum *was* grown for durum grown in those countries.

The background to the decision was that there were large surpluses in Community production of common wheat intended for bread-making, whereas there was a considerable deficit in the production of durum wheat and moreover this production was concentrated in certain areas— the Paris Basin (Beauce), southern France and southern Italy.

---

[127] E.C.J., *ibid.*, para. 21. In this connection those cases in which the differences in question were attributable to *force majeure* ought also to be mentioned. As far as we can ascertain, however, the Court of Justice has not yet examined such a case from the point of view of possible discrimination. See for example Case 31/70 *Deutsche Getreide- und Futtermittel Handelsgesellschaft mbH* v. *Hauptzollamt Hamburg-Altona* [1970] E.C.R. 1055. See also Advocate-General Capotorti's opinion in Case 68/77 *IFG-Interkontinentale Fleischhandelsgesellschaft mbH & Co. KG* v. *Commission* [1978] E.C.R. 353 at 378.

[128] Joined Cases 63–69/72 *Wilhelm Werhahn Hansamühle and Others* v. *Council of the European Communities* [1973] E.C.R. 1229.

The applicants operated mills at various places in the Federal Republic of Germany, mainly processing durum wheat to produce meal. They obtained the wheat in question principally from third countries and only to a small extent from growing areas within the Community.

Besides common wheat, durum wheat is also one of the products covered by the common organisation of the market for cereals. Under this organisation of the market a number of prices of different kinds are fixed each year for durum, including—first of all—the target price, which is assumed to set the standard for the market price. Under Article 2 of Regulation 120/67,[129] this price is "fixed for Duisburg at the wholesale stage, goods delivered to warehouse, not unloaded." In the crop year 1971/72 it was set by Regulation 1054/71[130] at 127.50 u.a.

Then there is the threshold price, which can be described as the target price projected to the frontier (i.e. Rotterdam), since it is calculated by deducting from the target price the transport costs (to Duisburg), the handling costs and the importer's margin. By means of levies, which are equal to the difference between the cif price and the threshold price, imports from third countries are raised to the level of the threshold price. Under Regulation 1120/71,[131] the threshold price for the crop year 1971/72 was 125.25 u.a.

In addition, there are the intervention prices at which the intervention agencies must buy durum. In the crop year 1971/72 there was also a basic intervention price—later abolished—which, under Article 2 of Regulation 120/67, was also fixed for Duisburg and which was set by Regulation 1054/71 at 119.85 u.a. For the other trading centres there was a uniform derived intervention price in 1971/72, fixed by Regulation 1530/71[132] at 112.44 u.a.

Finally, mention should be made of the "guaranteed minimum price," which is intended to promote the growing of durum in the Community and to this end assures the producers of a minimum income which makes it worth their while to grow this crop. This price is fixed for the trading centre in the zone with the largest surplus; in the crop year 1971/72 it was set by Regulation 1054/71 at 147.90 u.a., which meant that it was 20.40 u.a. above the target price, 28.05 u.a. above the basic intervention price and 35.46 u.a. above the derived intervention price.

---

[129] Council Regulation 120/67 of June 13, 1967, J.O. 1967, L117/2269; O.J. Sp.Ed. 1967, 3.
[130] Council Regulation 1054/71 of May 25, 1971, J.O. 1971, L115/8.
[131] Council Regulation 1120/71 of May 28, 1971, J.O. 1971, L118/3.
[132] Council Regulation 1530/71 of July 12, 1971, J.O. 1971, L162/16.

In view of the high level of this price, consumer prices for durum could have been expected to rise, with the danger that consumers would switch to cheaper common wheat; Article 10 of Regulation 120/67 therefore provided that durum production should qualify for an aid equal to the difference between the guaranteed minimum price and the intervention price for the zone with the largest surplus. Under Regulation 1530/71, the aid was 35.46 u.a. in the crop year 1971/72.

The applicants, who obtained durum—as previously mentioned—mainly from third countries and therefore at the threshold price, felt that they had been put at a disadvantage by this pricing arrangement and claimed that there had been discrimination of the kind prohibited by Article 40(3) subparagraph 2 EEC. They maintained, *inter alia*, that the French meal millers had a competitive advantage over them, in that they could obtain at the much lower intervention price French durum to which they—the applicants—had no access or the purchase of which would make little commercial sense in view of the high freight charges.

In the applicants' view, this disadvantageous situation could be avoided if the threshold price were lowered or the aid reduced, *i.e.* if the intervention price were raised.

The applicants also pointed out that the French meal millers would continue to enjoy a privileged position even if the market were opened up in the manner suggested, on account of their more favourable location in the vicinity of the producing areas.

Taking up this last point, the Court of Justice first stated:

> "This fact does not in itself constitute a prohibitive kind of discrimination but rather the consequence—that is not contrary to the rules of the Treaty—of a more advantageous location of French undertakings."[133]

The Court went on to state that the difference in prices on the German and French durum markets exceeded this advantage, which was reflected in the difference in carriage costs for meal or durum between the Paris Basin and the trading centres. Although its cause did not lie in Regulation 120/67 itself, the implementing provisions to this regulation had not taken account of the special situation on the French market and had thus contributed to maintaining the difference.

---

[133] E.C.J., *loc. cit.*, footnote 128, para. 17.

This prompted the Court of Justice to consider whether the Council should have responded to the situation and—at least temporarily—taken measures calculated to ensure similarity of competitive conditions for the meal millers of the various Member States.[134] The Court then considered in detail what latitude was available to the Council in deciding on threshold price and intervention price levels; it concluded that the levels of both prices were necessary for realising the objectives which the durum aid system was intended to achieve (expressly so in the case of the threshold price[135]) and that these objectives would be at risk if the prices were to be altered in the manner proposed by the applicants (expressly so in the case of the intervention price[136]).

On the basis of this finding, the Court of Justice concluded that although the Council had failed to compensate for the disadvantages which the German meal millers had "were indirectly subject, by reason of the fact that their French competitors enjoyed an advantage from this system" (paragraph 28, grounds of judgment), the provisions in question had not been rendered unlawful by this omission; for in adopting the provisions the Council did not have to consider at the time in question and in the light of the specific attendant circumstances whether circumstances of such a special kind conflicted with the application of provisions which would have proved successful under normal circumstances.[137]

4. "Contributory Fault"

Two Court of Justice decisions in 1980 and 1982 relating to the second subparagraph of Article 40(3) EEC demonstrated that discrimination *cannot* be deemed to exist if the similar or dissimilar treatment in question is the consequence of a free choice on the part of the affected party.

The first decision, dating from 1980, involved production quotas for isoglucose.[138] The Court of Justice had to determine, *inter alia*, whether the Council had committed a discriminatory act prohibited by the second subparagraph of Article 40(3) EEC in that, in allocating the quotas, it had not taken into account the fact that some undertakings—in the certain

---

[134] E.C.J., *loc. cit.*, footnote 128, para. 18.
[135] E.C.J., *loc. cit.*, footnote 128, paras. 19 and 20.
[136] E.C.J., *loc. cit.*, footnote 128, paras. 23 and 24.
[137] E.C.J., *loc. cit.*, footnote 128, para. 28.
[138] Case 139/79 *Maizena GmbH* v. *Council of the European Communities* [1980] E.C.R. 3393.

expectation of a change in the arrangements for isoglucose—had been sparing in their purchases during the time designated as the reference period.

The facts of the case were as follows:

In its judgment of October 25, 1978 in Joined Cases 103 and 145/77,[139] the Court of Justice had adjudged that Regulation 1111/77[140] was invalid in so far as it provided, in its Articles 8 and 9, for a production duty on isoglucose of 5 u.a. per 100 kg dry matter for the period corresponding to the sugar year 1977/78. The Court had ruled "that the system established by the above-mentioned articles offended against the general principle of equality (in those cases between sugar and isoglucose manufacturers) of which the prohibition on discrimination as set out in Article 40(3) of the Treaty was a specific expression."[141] The Court had then added, however, that this answer left the Council free to "take any necessary measures compatible with Community law for ensuring the proper functioning of the market in sweeteners."[142]

In the light of this judgment the Council had adopted Regulation 1293/79,[143] which had come into force on July 1, 1979; by virtue of this Regulation, the Council had amended Regulation 1111/77 so that it introduced a quota system for isoglucose, which was based directly on the arrangements applying to sugar. Under Article 9(1) to (3) of Regulation 1111/77—by this time in the version of Article 3 of Regulation 1293/79— the quotas had been calculated on the basis of production and capacity in the period November 1, 1978 to April 30, 1979, which had been designated as the reference period. According to Article 9(4), the basic quotas set for each undertaking in application of paragraphs 1 to 3 were set out in Annex II; the basic quota for Maizena GmbH—the applicant—was shown there as 15,887 tonnes.

Maizena GmbH was a German undertaking that processed maize into starch and starch derivatives. In its action Maizena complained, *inter alia*, that the quota arrangement as regulated by Article 9 of Regulation

---

[139] Joined Cases 103 & 145/77 *Royal Scholten-Honig (Holding) Ltd. and Others* v. *Intervention board for agricultural produce* [1978] E.C.R. 2037. See also under C. below.

[140] Council Regulation 1111/77 of May 17, 1977, O.J. 1977, L134/4.

[141] Thus E.C.J., *loc. cit.*, footnote 138, para. 6, on its judgment in Joined Cases 103 & 145/77, *loc. cit.*, footnote 139. See also under C. below.

[142] Thus E.C.J., *loc. cit.*, footnote 138, para. 6, on its judgment in Joined Cases 103 & 145/77, *loc. cit.*, footnote 139.

[143] Council Regulation 1293/79 of June 25, 1979, O.J. 1979, L162/10, corrected at O.J. 1979, L176/37.

1111/77 constituted discrimination prohibited by Article 40(3) sub-paragraph 2 EEC, because it disadvantaged those undertakings which—like itself—had been sparing in their purchases in the period designated as the reference period in view of the uncertainty about the legal framework for isoglucose.

The Court of Justice ruled on this point as follows:

> "After the judgment of 25 October 1978 the future market prospects for isoglucose were the same for all the isoglucose-manufacturing undertakings in the Community. Faced with that problem they reacted differently but the Council is not to blame for failing to take into account the commercial choices and internal policy of each particular undertaking when it adopts measures of general interest to prevent the uncontrolled isoglucose production from jeopardizing the sugar policy of the Community."[144]

The second division was delivered in 1982 and related to the law on refunds and monetary compensatory amounts in the sugar sector.[145] The Court of Justice had to decide, *inter alia*, whether the Community institutions, by reducing the representative rate of exchange of the French franc and raising the intervention price for sugar without adjusting the export refunds fixed in advance, was in breach of the anti-discrimination provisions of the second subparagraph of Article 40(3) EEC.

The matter had been referred to the Court of Justice by the Paris "Tribunal administratif." It had arisen in the following case:

Between February 7 and June 13, 1979 the French firm Jean Lion et Cie—the plaintiff in the main proceedings in Case 292/81—had been granted by the competent national agency—the Fonds d'intervention et de régularisation du marché du sucre (FIRS)—licences for the export of sugar to third countries with simultaneous prior fixing of the export refunds on the basis of a public invitation to tender and of the monetary compensatory amounts. After these licences had been granted, the Community devalued the representative rate of exchange of the French

---

[144] E.C.J., *loc. cit.*, footnote 138, para. 30.
[145] Joined Cases 292–293/81 *Société Jean Lion et Cie and Others* v. *Fonds d'intervention et de régularisation du marché du sucre F.I.R.S.* [1982] E.C.R. 3887.

franc—the so-called "green franc"—and raised the intervention price for sugar. Both measures came into force on July 1, 1979. Société Jean Lion et Cie took the view that the Community institutions, by taking these unforeseeable measures, had aggravated the financial conditions under which the exports to which the licences related were effected. It therefore requested FIRS to grant it an additional repayment for the sugar exports it had effected, to take account of the devaluation of the "green franc" and the increase in the intervention price.

When the request was not acceded to, Lion had instituted legal proceedings concerning this tacit refusal. In its defence FIRS pleaded that it had merely applied an existing set of Community rules, namely Regulation 3016/78,[146] which stipulated for the case in question that the said measures were not to be taken into account.

Lion therefore contested the validity of Regulation 3016/78, because it contained no provision concerning adaptation of the repayments for the undertakings which made use of the legally-provided possibility of prior fixing.

After the events on the currency scene which were important with regard to Case 292/81, but before September 28, 1979, the date on which the Council devalued the "green franc" again with effect from October 1, 1979, nine more French firms—the plaintiffs in the main proceedings in Case 293/81—were granted licences for the export of sugar with prior fixing of the export refunds and the monetary compensatory amounts. When FIRS again saw no reason to pay additional repayments which had been requested, the nine firms, together with Lion, instituted proceedings before the Paris "Tribunal administratif."

All 10 firms claimed, *inter alia*, that Regulation 3016/78 was incompatible with the second subparagraph of Article 40(3) EEC, because it led to unjustifiable treatment of the economic participants.

The Court of Justice ruled on this point as follows:

> "As regards the difference between the treatment of traders who have availed themselves of advance fixing and the treatment of other traders, the complaint of discrimination is once again misconceived since the purpose of advance fixing is precisely to crystallize, at the request of traders, the amount of the refund and of the monetary compensatory amounts at a date prior to the day of the exportation. The resultant difference of treatment is merely the consequence of a

---

[146] Commission Regulation 3016/78 of December 20, 1978, O.J. 1978, L359/11.

613

choice between two systems offered to traders under the regulation and they may choose one or the other freely according to their own requirements."[147]

5.   Failure to Take a Measure

The Community institutions may also be guilty of discrimination if they fail to take measures of such a nature as to compensate for a disadvantageous situation. The converse also applies, in that the Community institutions are obliged—where appropriate—to take positive action if they wish to avoid discrimination.

For logical reasons, however, such a duty exists only if the disadvantageous situation is due to human agency. For although on the one hand natural differences do not lead to discrimination,[148] it cannot be assumed—on the other hand—that failure to remove these differences also satisfies this criterion.[149]

That discrimination can be committed by omission was first[150] ruled by the Court of Justice in a decision pronounced in 1976 in connection with

---

[147] E.C.J., *loc. cit.*, footnote 145, para. 25. See also Case 22/80 *Boussac Saint-Frères SA* v. *Brigitte Gerstenmaier* [1980] E.C.R. 3427, where the question to be decided was whether the distinction drawn in § 688(1) ZPO between the domestic currency and foreign currencies in connection with debt collection in debt enforcement proceedings constituted "discrimination on grounds of nationality" as prohibited under Article 7 EEC. In para. 13 the Court of Justice stated: ". . . A distinction based on the currency in which debts are expressed, which applies only to the simplified procedure for recovery of debts, does not amount, even indirectly, to discrimination on grounds of nationality if the parties to the contract are free to select the currency in which the debt is expressed and if ordinary proceedings remain available to creditors established on the territory of the other Member States, whatever the currency in which the claim is expressed." See also footnote 164 below.

[148] See under B.III.3. above.

[149] This was expressly stated by the Court of Justice in its judgment in Case 52/79 *Procureur du roi* v. *Marc J.V.C. Debauve and Others*, *loc. cit.*, footnote 126. That judgment stated, following on from the passage in para. 21, quoted in B.III.3. above: ". . . Moreover, it should be pointed out that even if the Community has in some respects intervened to compensate for natural inequalities, it has no duty to take steps to eradicate differences in situations such as those contemplated by the national court."

[150] This emerges by inference from, for example, the judgment in Joined Cases 63–69/72 *Wilhelm Werhahn and Others* v. *Council of the European Communities*, *loc. cit.*, footnote 128, in which the Court of Justice, in the context of the second subparagraph of Article 40(3) EEC, automatically examined whether the Council ought to have taken certain measures to compensate for an existing difference, for the continuance of which it had been jointly responsible. See also under B.III.3. above.

the pricing and aid system for durum wheat.[151] The point at issue there, *inter alia*, was whether the Council was in breach of the second subparagraph of Article 40(3) EEC when it did *not* take measures to reduce the disadvantages caused to the meal millers in the Federal Republic of Germany and the Benelux countries.

The background to this decision was that Regulation 120/67[152] had provided for the fixing of a guaranteed minimum price for durum wheat in order to promote the growing of durum in the Community, as there was a substantial deficit in durum production in contrast to the situation with regard to common wheat. Article 10 of the Regulation stipulated: "Where the intervention price for durum wheat ... is lower than the guaranteed minimum price, aid shall be granted for the production of this cereal"; the amount of the aid was equal to the difference between the two prices.

In some of the regions where conditions were favourable to durum growing there was an increase in durum production as a result of the aid scheme. This was the case in particular in Beauce (France) and in southern France and southern Italy, with the result that supplies to the French and Italian mills could largely be met from domestic production. On the other hand, millers in the Federal Republic of Germany and the Benelux countries still had to obtain their supplies of durum—as before—by importing from third countries.

In the view of the Court of Justice this situation did indeed operate to the disadvantage of the German meal millers—including the applicants—in the crop years before 1974/75, because their French competitors were in a position to obtain their supplies locally at a price approaching the intervention price. The Germans, on the other hand, had to purchase the commodity at a price determined by the much higher threshold price; they could purchase supplies of durum from within the Community only in small quantities.

The applicants claimed that the Council had been aware of the fact that the provisions adopted to implement Regulation 120/67 could increase the disadvantages arising from this situation. It was the Council's duty, therefore, either to reduce the aid and thus remove the influence which the aid had on the price level of durum harvested in France or to mitigate the effect of this influence by lowering the threshold price in relation to the intervention price. In the applicants' view, the Council, by failing to

---

[151] Joined Cases 56–60/74 *Kurt Kampffmeyer Mühlenvereinigung KG and Others* v. *Commission and Council of the European Communities* [1976] E.C.R. 711.
[152] Council Regulation 120/67 of June 13, 1967, J.O. 1967, 117/2269; O.J. Sp.Ed. 1967, 33.

take these or other measures to reduce the disadvantages to the meal millers in the Federal Republic of Germany and the Benelux countries, had been in breach of the second subparagraph of Article 40(3) EEC.

Considering this case, the Court of Justice first stated that it had to be established whether the aid system—in the form created by Regulation 120/67—"wrongfully put . . . at a disadvantage"[153] the German meal millers compared with the French ones.

The Court went on to declare:

> "During the marketing years prior to 1974/75 durum wheat harvested in France has been marketed at prices consistently near the intervention price without ever approaching that of imported durum wheat. This factor justifies saying that the rules in question have profited the purchasers of durum wheat, that is to say mainly the French meal producers, rather than the growers themselves. This situation which was found and recognized by the defendant institutions during the course of the proceedings in Joined Cases 63 to 69/72 and during the present proceedings should have led them to reconsider, if not the system of aids, at least their level. The fact that the Council did not remedy this situation could have given rise to the question whether the situation was compatible with Articles 39 and 40 of the Treaty if the conditions of the market had remained unchanged."[154]

With reference to the qualification in the last sentence of this passage, the Court of Justice then stated that the market conditions for durum wheat had changed in the autumn of 1973 in such a way that maintenance of the aid scheme in the crop year 1974/75 could not be regarded as a "sufficiently qualified" infringement of—*inter alia*—the second subparagraph of Article 40(3) EEC[155] and in such a way that a lowering of the threshold price in relation to the intervention price would have jeopardized the objectives of Article 39 EEC and Community preference.[156]

6. Hidden Discrimination

The Court of Justice has ruled on many occasions and in connection

---

[153] E.C.J., *loc. cit.*, footnote 151, para. 14.
[154] E.C.J., *loc. cit.*, footnote 151, para. 15. On Joined Cases 63–69/72 referred to in this passage, see under B.III.3. above.
[155] E.C.J., *loc. cit.*, footnote 151, paras. 18 to 21.
[156] E.C.J., *loc. cit.*, footnote 151, paras. 16 and 17.

with different areas of EEC law that not only manifest but also hidden discrimination is unlawful. As will be seen from the following examples, an act of discrimination is considered to be "hidden" if it produces in fact the same result as an act of discrimination which "manifestly" involves the application of a differentiation criterion forbidden under Community law.

A first—and fundamental—ruling to this effect was delivered in 1974 in connection with freedom of movement for workers within the Community.[157] In that case one of the questions considered by the Court of Justice was whether Article 48(2) EEC as implemented by Article 7(1) and (4) of Regulation 1612/68[158] was to be interpreted as prohibiting dissimilar treatment of workers not only on grounds of nationality—as explicitly stipulated in the wording of the legislation[159]—but also on grounds of residence.

This problem was referred to the Court of Justice by the German Federal Labour Court. It had arisen in the course of a legal action instituted by an Italian national—Giovanni Maria Sotgiu—working for Deutsche Bundespost (the German Federal Post Office). The point at issue was the payment of a "separation allowance" granted to employees working away from their place of residence.

The details of the case were as follows:

Mr. Sotgiu was appointed by Deutsche Bundespost as a skilled worker under a contract of employment dated March 23, 1965. His remuneration was based on a collective agreement for employees of Deutsche Bundespost dated January 6, 1955; under Mr. Sotgiu's contract of employment all the provisions of this collective agreement applied to him directly.

Mr. Sotgiu's family had remained in Italy, so he was paid a separation allowance in the same way as the German employees who had to work

---

[157] Case 152/73 *Giovanni Maria Sotgiu* v. *Deutsche Bundespost* [1974] E.C.R. 153.
[158] Council Regulation 1612/68 of October 15, 1968, J.O. 1968, L257/2; O.J. Sp.Ed. 1968, 475.
[159] Article 7(1) of Regulation 1612/68 stipulates that "a worker who is a national of a Member State may not . . . be treated differently from national workers by reason of his nationality in respect of any conditions of employment and work . . ."; under paragraph 4 of this article "any clause of a collective or individual agreement or of any other collective regulation concerning eligibility for employment, remuneration and other conditions of work or dismissal shall be null and void in so far as it lays down or authorises discriminatory conditions in respect of workers who are nationals of the other Member States."

away from home. The amount of the allowance had initially been a uniform DM 7.50 a day for all those eligible.

At a later date, *i.e.* with effect from April 1, 1965, the separation allowance for German employees working away from home was increased to DM 10.00 a day. Employees whose homes were abroad continued to receive only DM 7.50 a day.

Mr. Sotgiu also continued to be paid the lower separation allowance, which he considered to be incompatible with the anti-discrimination provisions of Article 7(1) and (4) of Regulation 1612/68. He maintained that these provisions were to be interpreted as meaning that disparity of treatment of workers merely on grounds of residence was prohibited.

The Court of Justice ruled on this point as follows:

"The rules regarding equality of treatment, both in the Treaty and in Article 7 of Regulation No. 1612/68, forbid not only overt discrimination by reason of nationality but also all covert forms of discrimination which, by the application of other criteria of differentiation, lead in fact to the same result. This interpretation, which is necessary to ensure the effective working of one of the fundamental principles of the Community, is explicitly recognized by the fifth recital of the preamble to Regulation No. 1612/68 which requires that equality of treatment of workers shall be ensured 'in fact and in law.' It may therefore be that criteria such as place of origin or residence of a worker may, according to circumstances, be tantamount, as regards their practical effect, to discrimination on the grounds of nationality, such as is prohibited by the Treaty and the Regulation."[160]

This would not be the case, in the Court of Justice's view, if the conditions for payment of the separation allowance and the detailed rules "took

---

[160] E.C.J., *loc. cit.*, footnote 157, para. 11; the "provisions on equality of treatment . . . in the Treaty . . ." referred to here are those of Article 7 EEC as implemented in Article 48(2), 49c, 52, 60 and 67 EEC. See also judgment in Joined Cases 62–63/81 *S.A. Seco and Others* v. *Etablissement d'assurance contre la vieillesse et l'invalidité* [1982] E.C.R. 223, where it is stated with regard to Articles 59 and 60 EEC: "As the Court has repeatedly emphasised, most recently in its judgment of December 17, 1981 in Case 279/80 *Webb* [1981] E.C.R. 3305, those provisions entail the abolition of all discrimination against a person providing a service on the grounds of his nationality or the fact that he is established in a Member State other than that in which the service must be provided. Thus they prohibit not only overt discrimination based on the nationality of the person providing a service but also all forms of covert discrimination which, although based on criteria which appear to be neutral, in practice lead to the same result." (para. 8).

account of the objective differences which the situation of workers may involve according to whether their residence . . . is within the territory of the State in question or abroad." From this point of view, stated the Court, the fact that the separation allowance for workers resident in the country of employment is granted only temporarily and on condition that the worker moves house, whereas it is granted irrespective of their nationality and without limit as to time or requirement to move house to workers whose residence is abroad, could be a "valid reason" for the disparity in the levels of allowance. In any case, unequal treatment in breach of the Treaty and Regulation 1612/68 could not be said to have occurred if a comprehensive comparison of the two rules on the separation allowance showed that those workers who maintain their residence abroad are not put at an overall disadvantage compared with workers whose residence is in the country of employment.[161]

Another decision meriting consideration in this context was one in 1978 in connection with sea fisheries.[162] The specific point to be clarified was whether Ireland, by unilaterally taking certain measures to conserve fish stocks in 1977, had infringed the anti-discrimination provisions of Article 7 EEC and Article 2(1) of Regulation 101/76.[163]

The background here was that the Council, at a meeting in The Hague on October 30, 1976, has passed a resolution, formally adopted on November 3, 1976, in which it had agreed that the Member States should, by a concerted measure, extend their fishing limits off the North Sea and North Atlantic coasts to 200 miles from January 1, 1977. In the decision the Council also stressed the need to work towards joint measures to conserve Community fish stocks, whilst at the same time leaving Member States free to adopt suitable measures in cooperation with the Commission—if necessary until an arrangement came into force at Community level (Annex VI).

Immediately after the adoption of The Hague resolution the Council continued its discussions on the introduction of a joint scheme to conserve and manage fish stocks, based on a Commission proposal of

---

[161] E.C.J., *loc. cit.*, footnote 157, para. 12. See also under B.II.1 above.

[162] Case 61/77 *Commission of the European Communities* v. *Ireland* [1978] E.C.R. 417.

[163] Council Regulation 101/76 of January 19, 1976, O.J. 1976, L20/19. Article 2(1) of this Regulation stipulates: "Rules applied by each Member State in respect of fishing in the maritime waters coming under its sovereignty or within its jurisdiction shall not lead to differences in treatment of other Member States." It goes on to state: "Member States shall ensure in particular equal conditions of access to and use of the fishing grounds situated in the waters referred to in the preceding subparagraph for all fishing vessels flying the flag of a Member State and registered in Community territory."

October 8, 1976. In view of difficulties that arose, however, the Commission then put forward a fresh proposal on December 3, 1976, which was limited to the introduction of transitional measures. This proposal was subsequently amended many times to take account of differences of opinion still subsisting within the Council.

On December 13, 1976 the Irish Government, which was playing an active part in the discussions, tabled additional proposals to supplement the planned conservation measures. These proposals contained provisions such as the exclusion of factory ships, the designation of special protected areas for some fish species, the prohibition of certain fishing methods and the exclusion of fishing vessels of more than 85 feet in length or with engine capacities of more than 1000 bhp from a 20-mile band around the coasts.

During this part of the negotiations the Irish delegation constantly pointed out to the Council that conservation measures were urgently needed. The delegation indicated that Ireland would feel compelled to take action unilaterally if agreement was not soon reached. This message was repeated emphatically at a meeting of the Council on February 8 and 9, 1977, whereupon the Commission felt obliged to advise the Irish Government in writing that conservation measures could be promulgated by a Member State only if—as The Hague resolution provided—the Member State had consulted the Commission and had attempted to obtain that institution's approval.

The Irish Government nevertheless decided to wait no longer but to take unilateral measures to conserve fish stocks. Accordingly, the fisheries minister responsible first issued the "Sea Fisheries (Conservation and Rational Exploitation) Order 1977" on February 16, 1977, which made it a punishable offence for a fishing vessel to enter, remain in or fish in that part of Ireland's exclusive fishing zone which lies south of latitude 56° 30', east of longitude 12° and north of latitude 50° 30'. The "Sea Fisheries (Conservation and Rational Exploitation) (No. 2) Order 1977," issued on the same day, exempted fishing vessels of less than 33 metres registered length or less than 1100 bhp engine capacity from this ban.

After discussions with representatives of the Irish Government and of the other Member States affected, arranged at short notice, the Commission expressed serious reservations about the Irish measures in a letter of February 22, 1977 and called upon the Irish Government to refrain from implementing the measures pending the outcome of the next Council deliberations—which at that time gave grounds for expecting that agreement was near.

During the Council meeting of March 25, 1977 there did in fact prove to be a wide consensus among the Member States. However, owing to opposition from one Member State no decision could be taken, and shortly afterwards the Irish Government informed the Commission that the two orders of February 16, 1977 would enter into force on April 10, 1977. This course of action prompted the Commission to institute the procedures provided for under Article 169 EEC against Ireland and finally to bring the matter before the Court of Justice.

The Commission maintained that the Irish measures, despite the apparently neutral criteria on which they were based, were discriminatory within the meaning of Article 7 EEC and Article 2(1) of Regulation 101/76. For it had become evident that only two vessels in the Irish fishing fleet were above the limits set by the disputed orders and that of these two ships only one—definitely not the other—had fished within the exclusion zone, whereas some of the other Member States' fleets were severely affected. Moreover, the measures led to disparities of treatment as between Member States, because the Dutch fishing fleet, which consisted mainly of large ships, was almost entirely excluded from the waters in question whereas the British fleet, for example, owing to the nature of its vessels, was wholly unaffected.

The Court of Justice ruled as follows:

"As the Court has had occasion to declare in other contexts, in particular in its judgment of 12 February 1974 in Case 152/73, *Sotgiu* v. *Deutsche Bundespost* [1974] ECR 153 the rules regarding equality of treatment enshrined in Community law forbid not only overt discrimination by reason of nationality but also all covert forms of discrimination which, by the application of other criteria of differentiation, lead in fact to the same result. This certainly applies in the case of the criteria employed in the contested measures the effect of which is to keep out of Irish waters a substantial proportion of the fishing fleets of other Member States which have traditionally fished in those areas whereas under the same measures no comparable obligation is imposed on Ireland's own nationals. These measures are, accordingly, contrary both to Article 7 of the EEC Treaty, which prohibits any discrimination on grounds of nationality, and to Article 2(1) of Regulation (EEC) No. 101/76 under which rules applied by each Member State in respect of fishing in the maritime waters coming under its sovereignty or within its jurisdiction shall not lead to differences in treatment of other Member States."[164]

In its preliminary ruling in Case 96/80,[165] as outlined above, the Court of Justice applied what it had formulated in general terms concerning discrimination on grounds of nationality to cases of discrimination on the basis of a worker's sex. The question at issue in this decision, as already explained, was whether a difference in the levels of pay for work done on a part-time basis and for the same work done under full-time employment constituted discrimination as prohibited by Article 119 EEC if the group of part-time workers consisted exclusively or mainly of women. On this point the Court first stated that the fact that a lower hourly wage was paid for part-time than for full-time work did not contravene the principle of equal pay laid down in Article 119 EEC if the difference in remuneration was based on facts "which are objectively justified and have nothing to do with discrimination on grounds of sex."[166]

In the view of the Court of Justice this was "the case in particular where the employer, by paying a lower hourly wage for part-time than for full-time work, does so for objectively justified economic reasons with the aim of providing an incentive for full-time employment irrespective of the worker's sex."[167]

The Court went on to state:

"By contrast, if it is established that a considerably smaller percentage of women than of men perform the minimum number of weekly working hours required in order to be able to claim the full-time hourly rate of pay, the inequality in pay will be contrary to Article 199 of the Treaty where, regard being had to the difficulties encountered by women in arranging to work that minimum number of hours

---

[164] E.C.J., *loc. cit.*, footnote 162, paras. 78 to 80. See also the E.C.J.'s preliminary ruling of February 16, 1978—where the situation was similar—in Case 88/77 *Ministre des pêcheries* v. *C.A. Schonenberg and Others* [1978] E.C.R. 473, paras. 10 to 13. On the judgment in Case 152/73 see footnote 157 above; see also Case 22/80 *Boussac Saint-Frères SA* v. *Brigitte Gerstenmaier* [1980] E.C.R. 3427, para. 9, in which the Court of Justice repeated word-for-word the passage just quoted; on this judgment see footnote 147 above. On the nationality criterion see also Case 1/78 *Patrick Christopher Kenny* v. *Insurance Officer* [1978] E.C.R. 1489, paras. 18 to 20, and Case 237/78 *Caisse régionale d'assurance maladie* v. *Diamante Toia, épouse Lermo, Lille* [1979] E.C.R. 2645, para. 12.

[165] See under B.II.2. above.

[166] E.C.J., *loc. cit.*, footnote 115.

[167] E.C.J., *loc. cit.*, footnote 116.

per week, the pay policy of the undertaking in question cannot be explained by factors other than discrimination based on sex."[168] "Where the hourly rate of pay differs according to whether the work is part-time or full-time it is for the national courts to decide in each individual case whether, regard being had to the facts of the case, its history and the employer's intention, a pay policy such as that which is at issue in the main proceedings although represented as a difference based on weekly working hours is or is not in reality discrimination based on the sex of the worker."[169]

The Court of Justice finally answered the question brought before it by stating:

". . . that a difference in pay between full-time workers and part-time workers does not amount to discrimination prohibited by Article 119 of the Treaty unless it is in reality merely an indirect way of reducing the level of pay of part-time workers on the ground that that group of workers is composed exclusively or predominantly of women."[170]

Another area in which the Court of Justice has declared—by implication—that "hidden" discrimination is unlawful is that of the origin or destination of goods; the first decision of this kind came in 1980 and related to tax regulations.[171] In that case one of the points to be decided was whether Denmark had contravened Article 95(1) EEC by taxing spirits other than aquavit higher than aquavit itself.

The facts on which the decision was based were as follows:

Before 1980 Denmark produced in the region of 7 million litres of spirits a year, of which aquavit—at nearly 6 million litres—accounted for by far the greater part. Total spirits consumption in Denmark amounted to about 9 million litres a year; in the years 1972 to 1977 the proportion of this total accounted for by aquavit ranged between 67 and 63 per cent.

Danish spirits imports from other Member States totalled approximately 2.3 million litres in 1975 and consisted mainly of whisky, vodka, cognac, gin and rum—in that order of importance.

---

[168] E.C.J., *loc. cit.*, footnote 113, para. 13.
[169] E.C.J., *loc. cit.*, footnote 113, para. 14.
[170] E.C.J., *loc. cit.*, footnote 113, para. 15.
[171] Case 171/78 *Commission of the European Communities* v. *Kingdom of Denmark* [1980] E.C.R. 447.

Section 2 of the "Lovbekendtgørelse Nr. 151 af 4. April 1978 om afgift af spiritus m.m.," the law in force at the time of the court case and therefore the relevant one in this instance, imposed on spirits a consumption tax which bore more lightly on aquavit (at DKR 167.50 per litre of pure ethyl alcohol) than on other spirits (DKR 257.15). Under § 3 of this law the term "aquavit" was defined as covering "products containing vegetable aromatic substances" having the characteristics neither of gin, vodka, geneva, juniper gin and similar drinks nor of anisette, rum, spirits distilled from fruit, and other spirits, the typical taste of which is derived from distillation or storage.

The Commission's case was that the Danish tax regulations discriminated against spirits imported from other Member States since they prescribed a reduced rate of tax for the greater part of domestic production—i.e. aquavit—whereas imported spirits mainly attracted the higher rate of tax. Specifically, the Commission claimed that Article 95(1) EEC had been infringed.

The Danish Government, for its part, contended that the tax regulations in question did not differentiate between imported and domestic products. The spirits were taxed at the rate corresponding to the statutory tax group to which they had been allocated, irrespective of their origin; imported aquavit was taxed at the same rate as domestic aquavit, and other domestic products were taxable at the same rate as imported products.

The Court of Justice ruled as follows:

> "Viewed by itself, the tax system introduced by the Danish legislation contains incontestable discriminatory or protective characteristics. Although it does not establish any formal distinction according to the origin of the products, it has been adjusted so that the bulk of the domestic production of spirits comes within the most favourable tax category whereas almost all imported products come within the most heavily taxed category. These characteristics of the system are not obliterated by one fact that a very small fraction of imported spirits benefits from the most favourable rate of tax whereas, conversely, a certain proportion of domestic production comes within the same tax category as imported spirits. It therefore appears that the tax system is devised so that it largely benefits a typical domestic product and handicaps imported spirits to the same extent."[172]

---

[172] E.C.J., *ibid.*, para. 36. See also the E.C.J.'s preliminary ruling of February 27, 1980— where the situation was similar—in Case 68/79 *Hans Just J/S* v. *Ministry of Taxation* [1980]

IV. SUMMARY

To sum up our findings in section B of this chapter, it can be said that for discrimination of the kind prohibited under Community law to be present, "arbitrary" differentiation must have taken place.

As the Court of Justice has specifically declared, this is the case—firstly—when like has been treated in unlike manner or unlike in like manner, for which purpose the comparability of that which is being compared has to be established on the basis of objective criteria. Secondly, the action is then said to be "arbitrary" if the like or unlike treatment in question is not objectively justified.

If it is objectively justified, it cannot constitute prohibited discrimination; whether discrimination has in fact occurred is then irrelevant.

As the judgments quoted in III. show, the Court of Justice has not been content merely to explain the concept in general terms, but has in many respects further defined and delimited it.

Nevertheless, this in no way affects the central ruling, namely that public authorities commit discrimination only when they differentiate arbitrarily.

C. RECOGNITION OF THE EQUALITY PRINCIPLE AS A GENERAL LEGAL PRINCIPLE

I. AS A FUNDAMENTAL PRINCIPLE OF COMMUNITY LAW

Aside from those fundamental judgments which have held that the "fundamental rights of the person"—and hence also the principle of equality—are guaranteed under the general legal principles of Community law,[1] there have been a few decisions in which the Court of Justice has

---

E.C.R. 501, paras. 8 et seq., 12. See also Case 40/82 Commission of the European Communities v. United Kingdom of Great Britain and Northern Ireland [1982] E.C.R. 2793, where the point at issue was whether a ban on imports of poultry products into England, Wales and Scotland amounted to discrimination against goods from other Member States as prohibited under Article 30 and Article 36, second sentence EEC. Para. 40 stated: "Taken together, these facts are sufficient to establish that the 1981 measures constitute a disguised restriction on imports of poultry products from other Member States . . ."

[1] Thus for the first time in Case 29/69 Erich Stauder v. Stadt Ulm-Sozialamt [1969] E.C.R. 419, para. 7; further developed and considered in greater depth in Case 11/70 Internationale Handelsgesellschaft mbH v. Einfuhr- und Vorratsstelle für Getreide und Futtermittel [1970] E.C.R. 1125, para. 4, and Case 4/73 J. Nold, Kohlen- und Baustoffgrosshandlung v. Commission of the European Communities [1974] E.C.R. 491,

specifically ruled that the equality principle is one of the "fundamental principles" of Community law.

This was stated for the first time in two decisions on cases involving essentially the same subject matter, both handed down in 1977 in connection with the law on refunds.[2] In those cases the Court of Justice had to decide, *inter alia*, whether Article 11 of Regulation 120/67[3] led to discrimination "between producers or consumers within the Community" as prohibited under the second subparagraph of Article 40(3) EEC, owing to the fact that—in a later version—it provided for a production refund for maize when used for starch production but not when used for quellmehl production.

This matter was brought before the Court of Justice in Joined Cases 117/76 and 16/77 by the Hamburg Finance Court. It had arisen out of two lawsuits based on the following situation:

A refund had been granted on the production of quellmehl from maize in Germany since as early as 1930; this had been incorporated into the common organisation of the market for cereals—at first optionally by Article 1(1)e of Regulation 142/64[4] and later compulsorily by Article 11(1) of Regulation 120/67. This rule was identical to another rule that had been introduced, namely that a refund of corresponding amount was to be granted on maize for the manufacture of starch. The reason given for the latter refund was the need to maintain competitive prices in relation to the prices of substitute products; concerning the first-named

---

para. 13. See on this point in preference to many other works: M. Hilf, "Der Gerichtshof der Europäischen Gemeinschaften als Integrationsfaktor, dargestellt anhand der Rechtsprechung zu den Grundrechten," in: Arbeitskreis Europäische Integration (ed.), *Die Grundrechte in der Europäischen Gemeinschaft*, Baden-Baden 1978, pp. 23 *et seq.*; H. Kutscher, "Der Schutz von Grundrechten im Recht der Europäischen Gemeinschaften," in: Kutscher, Rogge, Matscher (ed.), *Der Grundrechtsschutz im Europäischen Gemeinschaftsrecht*, Heidelberg 1982, pp. 35 *et seq.*; on the latest development of the law see J. Schwarze, "Schutz der Grundrechte in der Europäischen Gemeinschaft-Grundlagen und heutiger Entwicklungsstand"—EuGRZ 1986, pp. 293 *et seq.* See also—specifically on the equality principle—Advocate-General Capotorti's opinion in Case 149/77 *Gabrielle Defrenne* v. *SABENA* [1978] E.C.R. 1365 at 1385 *et seq.*; *cf.* also Case 215/85 *Bundesanstalt für landwirtschaftliche Marktordnung* v. *Raiffeisen Hauptgenossenschaft e.G.* [1987] E.C.R. 1279.

[2] Joined Cases 117/76 & 16/77 *Albert Ruckdeschel & Co. and Others* v. *Hauptzollamt Hamburg St. Annen* and Joined Cases 124/76 & 20/77 *S.A. Moulins et Huileries de Pont-à-Mousson and Others* v. *Office national interprofessionnel des céréales* [1977] E.C.R. 1753 at 1795 *et seq.*

[3] Council Regulation 120/67 of June 13, 1967, J.O. 1967, L117/2269; O.J. Sp.Ed. 1967, 33.

[4] Council Regulation 142/64 of October 21, 1964, J.O. 1964, 2673.

refund, it was said that there was a possibility of substitution as between starch and quellmehl.

This situation lasted until August 1, 1974, when Regulation 1125/74[5] came into force and amended Article 11(1) of Regulation 120/67 to the effect that a refund was now granted only for the production of starch. Concerning the abolition of the refund for the production of quellmehl, it was said that experience had shown that the possibility of substituting starch for quellmehl for certain specific purposes in connection with human consumption was "economically slight, if not non-existent."

The plaintiffs, who manufactured quellmehl, had applied to the competent national authorities for a production refund. The application was refused with the comment that Community regulations no longer contained any provisions for the payment of a refund for the production of quellmehl.

The plaintiffs claimed, *inter alia*, that the abolition of the refund for the production of quellmehl but not for the production of starch was an infringement of the second sub paragraph of Article 40(3) EEC.[6]

On this claim the Court of Justice ruled as follows:

"The second subparagraph of Article 40(3) of the Treaty provides that the common organization of agricultural markets 'shall exclude any discrimination between producers or consumers within the Community.' Whilst this wording undoubtedly prohibits any discrimination between producers of the same product it does not refer in such clear terms to the relationship between different industrial or trade sectors in the sphere of processed agricultural products. This does not alter the fact that the prohibition of discrimination laid down in the aforesaid provision is merely a specific enunciation of the general principle of equality which is one of the fundamental principles of Community law. This principle requires that similar situations shall not be treated differently unless differentiation is objectively justified."[7]

---

[5] Council Regulation 1125/74 of April 29, 1974, O.J. 1974, L128/12.

[6] The point at issue in the parallel proceedings in Joined Cases 124/76 & 20/77 was the abolition of a refund for the production of maize groats for the brewing industry, which occurred on August 1, 1975. This refund, too, had first been granted under Article 11(1) of Regulation 120/67; and the reason given for its granting had also been the possibility of substituting starch for the product. Concerning its abolition, it was merely stated that it was "no longer required" (Council Regulation 665/75 of March 4, 1975, O.J. 1975, L72/14).

[7] E.C.J., *loc. cit.*, footnote 2, pp. 1753 *et seq.*, para. 7, and pp. 1795 *et seq.*, paras. 14 to 17.

The Court of Justice then examined whether "comparable" situations existed for quellmehl and starch and in particular whether quellmehl, in its traditional specific use, could be replaced by starch. The Court first noted in this connection that until 1974 the Community arrangements had assumed that such substitution was possible and had accordingly treated both products equally as regards refunds. In the light of this fact in particular, and because the Commission was unable to prove the contrary, the Court concluded by denying the existence of objective circumstances "which could have justified altering the previous system as was done by Regulation 1125/74, which put an end to this equality of treatment," stating that the abolition of the refund for quellmehl therefore represented "a disregard of the principle of equality."[8]

The Court of Justice gave a similar ruling one year later—in 1978—when it delivered two more decisions on the law on refunds (and levies).[9] The question involved in those cases was whether Article 2 of Regulation 1862/76[10] contravened the second subparagraph of Article 40(3) EEC in that it had reduced the refund granted in connection with the production of cereal starch on cereal starch processed into glucose with a high fructose content ("isoglucose") but had increased the refund for other forms of cereal starch.

This question was brought before the Court of Justice as Case 125/77 by a Dutch court. It had arisen during an action in which the plaintiffs contested a decision by the Dutch intervention agency requiring them, by virtue of Regulations 1862/76 and 2158/76,[11] to pay a levy on maize starch which they had processed into high-sugar glucose in the period from August 1 to October 31, 1976.

High-sugar glucose ("isoglucose") is a new natural sweetener made from cereal starch, usually maize starch. This product, which first appeared on the common market in any quantity in 1976, possesses a sweetening strength comparable to that of sugar; however, isoglucose cannot be crystallised, so it competes with sugar only in those branches of the food industry where liquid sugar is used as a raw material.

---

[8] E.C.J., *loc. cit.*, footnote 2, pp. 1753 *et seq.*, para. 10, and—correspondingly—pp. 1795 *et seq.*, paras. 22 to 23.

[9] Case 125/77 *Koninklijke Scholten-Honig NV and Others* v. *Hoofdproduktschap voor Akkerbouwprodukten*, and Joined Cases 103 & 145/77 *Royal Scholten-Honig (Holdings) Limited and Others* v. *Intervention board for agricultural produce* [1978] E.C.R. 1991 at 2037 *et seq.*

[10] Council Regulation 1862/76 of June 27, 1976, O.J. 1976, L206/3.

[11] Commission Regulation 2158/76 of August 31, 1976, O.J. 1976, L241/21.

According to the ninth recital to Regulation 2727/75,[12] "in view of the special market situation for cereal starch, potato starch and glucose produced by the 'direct hydrolysis' process it may prove necessary to provide for a production refund of such a nature that the basic products used by this industry can be made available to it at a lower price than that resulting from the application of the system of levies and common prices." It is therefore provided in Article 11(1) of this Regulation that a refund on production "may be granted (a) for maize and common wheat used in the Community for the manufacture of starch; (b) for potato starch; (c) for maize groats and meal used in the Community for the manufacture of glucose by direct hydrolysis"; Article 3 provides that the Council shall lay down the rules for the implementation of this article and the amount of the refund on production.

The Council accordingly adopted Regulation 2742/75,[13] laying down the amounts of the refund on the production of the products named. This Regulation was amended by Regulation 1862/76, which came into force on August 1, 1976. The reason given for the amendment was as follows:

"In view of the situation which will exist as from the beginning of the 1976/77 marketing year, particularly as a result of the application for that marketing year of common prices for cereals and rice, it is necessary to increase the production refunds; whereas however, given the objectives of the production refund system, such an increase should not be retained in the case of products used in the manufacture of glucose having a high fructose content; whereas the best method of implementing a measure of this type is to provide for recovery from the manufacturers concerned of the amount of the increase in production refunds according to the product used."

The refunds were then increased as provided by Article 1 of the Regulation. Article 2 inserted a new Article 5a into Regulation 2742/75, stipulating that the refund for cereal starch processed into glucose with a high fructose content should remain unchanged compared with the previous crop year; from the crop year 1977/78 onwards this refund lapsed completely. Paragraph 3 of Article 5a stipulates that Member States should recover the difference between the amounts of the refunds for cereal starch intended for the manufacture of glucose with a high fructose

[12] Council Regulation 2727/75 of October 29, 1975, O.J. 1975, L281/1.
[13] Regulation 2742/75 of October 29, 1975, O.J. 1975, L281/57.

629

content on the one hand and for cereal starch used for other purposes on the other hand.

The Commission then adopted a number of implementing provisions to Article 5a of Regulation 2742/75 in the form of Regulation 2158/76. Under the latter Regulation these provisions were to come into force on September 3, 1976; they were actually applied from August 1, 1976 onwards.

The plaintiffs were starch manufacturers who had invested fairly heavily in isoglucose manufacture. They claimed in their action, *inter alia*, that Article 2 of Regulation 1862/76 discriminated against manufacturers of starch intended for isoglucose production compared with manufacturers of starch intended for other purposes; Article 2, they submitted, therefore contravened "the principle of non-discrimination on which the Treaty is also based, ... as expressed in particular in Article 40 of the Treaty."

The Court of Justice ruled on this point as follows:

> "The second subparagraph of Article 40(3) of the Treaty provides that the common organization of agricultural markets 'shall exclude any discrimination between producers or consumers within the Community.' The prohibition of discrimination laid down in the above-mentioned provision is merely a specific enunciation of the general principle of equality which is one of the fundamental principles of Community law. This principle requires that similar situations shall not be treated differently unless the differentiation is objectively justified."[14]

The Court of Justice then considered whether "a comparable situation" applied to isoglucose and other starch industry products; in particular, the Court examined whether isoglucose in its usual specific application could be replaced by the latter products. The Court first emphasised in this connection that no competition existed either between starch and isoglucose or between isoglucose and other starch products, with the possible exception of glucose. The documentation showed, however, that the great differences in the sweetening power of isoglucose and glucose led to different applications for the two products, with the result that they, too, were not in competition with one another and therefore their situations were not comparable in this respect. Incidentally, the Court

[14] E.C.J., *loc. cit.*, footnote 9, paras. 25 to 27.

noted that isoglucose could replace sugar, at least to some extent; continuance of the refund to isoglucose manufacturers could therefore in certain circumstances eventually amount to discrimination against sugar manufacturers, who were not eligible for the same benefit. The Court of Justice concluded that Article 2 of Regulation 1862/76 did not infringe "the rule of non-discrimination between Community producers set out in the second subparagraph of Article 40(3) of the Treaty."[15]

The Court of Justice returned to the findings just quoted in a decision given in 1982.[16] The point at issue there was whether the Commission, by suspending the granting of import licences for tinned mushrooms from Taiwan and South Korea from time to time, was guilty of discrimination as prohibited by the second subparagraph of Article 40(3) EEC to the detriment of the importers concerned.

The question had been referred to the Court of Justice by a German administrative court. It had arisen in the course of an action of which the facts were as follows:

The company Edeka Zentrale AG of Hamburg was an importer of, *inter alia*, tinned mushrooms from Taiwan and South Korea. On September 25, 1978 it had applied to the Federal Office for Food and Forestry for import licences for two consignments of mushrooms from those countries. The Federal Office refused the application, giving as the reason the fact that the granting of import licences for tinned mushrooms from Taiwan and South Korea had been suspended by Regulation 1102/78.[17]

Regulation 1102/78 was adopted in conjunction with a trade agreement signed by the EEC and the People's Republic of China. Under Article 1 of the Regulation, the granting of import licences for tinned mushrooms was suspended as from May 26, 1978. However, Article 2(1) excluded from the suspension any products originating from countries "which the Commission accepts as being able to ensure that their exports to the Community do not exceed a level agreed by the Commission." Article 3 stated that Article 2 would be applied for the benefit of the People's Republic of China.

Regulation 1102/78 was based on Regulation 516/77,[18] Article 14 of which empowered the Commission to take the necessary measures if, as a result of imports or exports, the Community market for one or more of

---

[15] E.C.J., *loc. cit.*, footnote 9, paras. 28 to 32.
[16] Case 245/81 *Edeka Zentrale AG* v. *Federal Republic of Germany* [1982] E.C.R. 2745.
[17] Commission Regulation 1102/78 of May 25, 1978, O.J. 1978, L139/26.
[18] Council Regulation 516/77 of March 14, 1977, O.J. 1977, L73/1.

the products covered by the common organisation of the market for products processed from fruit and vegetables was exposed to or threatened by serious disturbances which endangered the objectives of Article 39 EEC. Article 2(2) of Regulation 521/77[19] stipulated that such measures were to be taken only in so far and for as long as they were absolutely necessary.

The Edeka company—the plaintiff—claimed, *inter alia*, that Regulation 1102/78 gave rise to discrimination of the kind prohibited by the second subparagraph of Article 40(3) EEC, because it put importers of tinned mushrooms from Taiwan and South Korea at a disadvantage compared with competitors importing the same product from the People's Republic of China.

The Court of Justice stated on this point first of all:

> "As the Court held in its judgments of 19 October 1977 in Joined Cases 117/76 and 16/77 *Ruckdeschel* v. *Hauptzollamt Hamburg-St. Annen* [1977] E.C.R. 1753 and in Joined Cases 124/76 and 20/77 *Moulins et Huileries de Pont-à-Mousson* [1977] E.C.R. 1795, the prohibition of discrimination contained in the second subparagraph of Article 40(3) of the Treaty is merely a specific enunciation of the general principle of equality which is one of the fundamental principles of Community law. That principle means that like situations should not be treated differently unless such different treatment is objectively justified."[20]

The Court of Justice further stated that the supposed difference in the treatment of the importers sprang from the distinction which Regulation 1102/78 drew between the exporting countries in question, which in turn was based on the fact that only the People's Republic of China had been willing to reduce its exports to the Community. In reality, therefore, the complaint against the disputed Regulation was a complaint against the policy pursued by the Commission when it negotiated with the People's Republic of China and with Taiwan and South Korea concerning a possible voluntary-restraint agreement.

The Court of Justice concluded from this that it was necessary to determine "whether that policy is arbitrary in nature, in particular

---

[19] Council Regulation 521/77 of March 14, 1977, O.J. 1977, L73/28.
[20] E.C.J., *loc. cit.*, footnote 16, para. 11; for the latest ruling along these lines—even if only tacit—see for example Case 59/83 *SA Biovilac NV* v. *European Economic Community* and Case 106/83 *Sermide S.p.A.* v. *Cassa Conguaglio Zucchero and Others* [1984] E.C.R. 4057, para. 19, at 4209 *et seq.*, para. 28.

whether the quantities of imports proposed by the Commission to the non-member countries concerned as the basis for an agreement of voluntary restraint were in accordance with the needs of the Community market."[21]

On this point the Court of Justice stated that, as far as 1978 was concerned, both the quantities of tinned mushroom imports offered and the quantities actually exported to the Community had been fixed on the basis of the average annual tonnages actually exported in earlier years, without any preferential treatment being granted to any of the three countries. Preferential treatment had, however, been accorded to the People's Republic of China for 1979. In this respect, however, it was clear from the information provided by the Commission that Regulation 1102/78 had remained unaltered because only the People's Republic of China had been willing from the outset to reduce its exports to the Community.

In the light of these circumstances and of the fact, on the one hand, that the Community institutions "enjoy discretion in the sphere of commercial policy" and on the other hand that "the Treaty contains no general principle which may be relied upon by traders, compelling the Community in its external relations to accord equal treatment in all respects to non-member countries,"[22] the Court of Justice concluded that the differentiation complained of was to be regarded as "objectively justified" and the claim that the second subparagraph of Article 40(3) EEC had been infringed was dismissed.[23]

When the Court of Justice describes the equality principle as a "basic principle," it is no doubt indicating that it recognises the principle as such—that the recognition is thus very wide and does not apply only to areas in respect of which a discrimination prohibition has been imposed by the Treaties.[24]

This also follows indirectly from the fact that nowadays the equality principle is sometimes declared to be applicable even when no discrimination prohibition appears to apply to the specific case—as was

---

[21] E.C.J., *loc. cit.*, footnote 16, para. 13.

[22] E.C.J., *loc. cit.*, footnote 16, para. 19. The Court of Justice is here referring to its judgment of January 22, 1976 in Case 55/75 *Balkan-Import-Export* v. *Hauptzollamt Berlin-Packhof* [1976] E.C.R. 19. See also under IV.1. below.

[23] E.C.J., *loc. cit.*, footnote 16, para. 20.

[24] For more detail see J. Schwarze, "Der Schutz des Gemeinschaftsbürgers durch allgemeine Verwaltungsrechtsgrundsätze im EG-Recht," NJW 1986, pp. 1067 *et seq.* (1069); F. Caporti, "Le principe d'égalité en droit économique: Rapport général," in Le principe d'égalité en droit économique, F.I.D.E., Rapports, Vol. 2, The Hague 1984, Chap. 3, p. 10.

accepted by the Court of Justice, for example, in 1980 in connection with the financial provisions of the EEC Treaty.

In one decision of this kind—in Case 265/78[25]—the Court of Justice was dealing with the question of the recovery of incorrectly paid export refunds by a national authority. Specifically, the point to be decided was whether Community law contained any general principle or specific provision prohibiting the application of a national legal principle—such as the principle of legal certainty in Dutch law—and the blocking of the recovery.

This question was referred to the Court of Justice by the College van Beroep voor het Bedrijfsleven, The Hague. It had arisen in the course of the following legal action:

In accordance with two export notices which it had submitted before-hand, the Rotterdam-based firm of Ferwerda had supplied two consignments of frozen beef in 1976 to Dutch ocean liners cruising in Bermudan waters. For this the firm had received the advance fixing and advance financing of the refund on exports to third countries pursuant to Regulation 1041/69.[26]

Article 6(5) of Regulation 1957/69[27] adopted for the implementation of Regulation 441/69 stated:

"The amount of the refund paid, plus any increase, shall be repaid in accordance with the provisions of this Article if the proofs referred to in paragraph 1 are not furnished within the time limit laid down. In such case, if repayment has been claimed but is not received, the deposit which was lodged shall be forfeited."

One of the items of "proofs" referred to is evidence that the goods "have reached their destination within the meaning of Article 3 of Regulation 1041/67/EEC." Under Article 3 of Regulation 192/75,[28] "supplies for victualling within the Community seagoing vessels or aircraft" is regarded as equivalent to export, as far as entitlement to payment of a refund is concerned.

This Community scheme was the subject of two circulars dated March 12 and October 15, 1976 issued in the Netherlands by the Produktschap

---

[25] Case 265/78 *H. Ferwerda BV* v. *Produktschap voor Vee en Vlees* [1980] E.C.R. 617.
[26] Council Regulation 441/69 of March 4, 1969, J.O. 1969, L59/1; O.J. Sp.Ed. 1969(I), 91.
[27] Commission Regulation 1957/69 of September 30, 1969, J.O. 1969, L250/1; O.J. Sp.Ed. 1969(II), 417.
[28] Commission Regulation 192/75 of January 17, 1975, O.J. 1975, L25/1.

voor Vee en Vlees. According to the annexes to the circulars, a trader could claim a refund in respect of the products in question for deliveries to "special destinations." One such special destination was listed in a note as "delivery for the supplying of ocean-going ships," using the wording of Article 3 of Regulation 192/75; missing, however, were the words of that article stipulating that the ships being provisioned must be "within the Community."

Under this scheme, the Ferwerda company claimed and received from the Produktschap during 1976 refunds in respect of the exporting of the meat already mentioned, concerning the destination of which, incidentally, it had given precise and correct information.

Soon afterwards the Produktschap realised its mistake and requested Ferwerda to repay the amounts of the refunds granted. It maintained that the refunds had been granted in contravention both of Article 3 of Regulation 441/69, since the Bermudas were not on the list of third countries, exports to which were eligible for refunds, and of Article 3 of Regulation 192/75, since the supply of ships was equated with exporting for the purpose of eligibility to a refund only when the supply took place within the Community.

The Ferwerda company (the plaintiff) asserted that the demand for repayment of the refunds infringed the principle of legal certainty, which was basically recognised·under Dutch law as a defence against a demand of this kind from the administration. The referring court, which supported the plaintiff on this point, wished to know whether Community law, and in particular Article 6(5) of Regulation 1957/69, forbade the application of a national legal principle such as this one.

Considering this problem, the Court of Justice first pointed out that the export refund that had been granted and paid to the Ferwerda company represented a financial benefit "financed by the Community from its own resources within the general framework of the budgetary arrangements made by Articles 199 to 209 which constitute the financial provisions of the EEC Treaty."[29]

The Court further stated:

> "The arrangements for the fixing and the conditions of collection of the financial charges which the Community is empowered to levy and which specifically constitute its own resources, such as customs duties, agricultural levies and monetary compensatory amounts, and

[29] E.C.J., *loc. cit.*, footnote 25, para. 6.

the arrangements concerning the conditions for the granting and payment of financial benefits to traders from the Community budget are laid down by the Council Decision of 21 April 1970 on the replacement of financial contributions from Member States by the Communities' own resources (Official Journal, English Special Edition 1970 (I), p. 224) and the regulations in implementation thereof, together with Regulation (EEC) No. 729/70 of the Council of 21 April 1970 on the financing of the common agricultural policy (Official Journal, English Special Edition 1970 (I) p. 218) the provisions of which were extended to monetary compensatory amounts by Article 2 of Regulation No. 2746/72 of the Council of 19 December 1972 (Official Journal, English Special Edition 1972 (28–30 December), p. 64). These provisions must be considered within the framework of the general arrangements regarding the financial provisions of the Treaty which, like the corresponding arrangements in the Member States, are governed by the general principle of equality which requires that comparable situations may not be treated differently unless difference of treatment is objectively justified."[30]

The Court of Justice concluded from this that the duties which are transferred to the Community budget and the financial benefits which are borne by this budget must be paid and levied in such a way that they uniformly bear upon or uniformly benefit all those who fulfil the conditions laid down by Community regulations for levying the charge or granting the benefit in question. This requirement implied, said the Court, that no discrimination may be made as regards the formal and material conditions under which, on the one hand, traders take action against Community charges imposed upon them and claim refunds of charges wrongly paid, or claim the financial benefits due to them under Community law, and, on the other hand, the Member States' executives, acting on behalf of the Community, levy the said charges and, where appropriate, may demand restitution of financial benefits granted unlawfully.[31]

Referring to its judgment of May 21, 1976 in Case 26/74 (*Roquette*[32]), the Court of Justice then pointed out that legal disputes on the repayment of amounts levied on behalf of the Community fell within the jurisdiction

---

[30] E.C.J., *loc. cit.*, footnote 25, para. 7.
[31] E.C.J., *loc. cit.*, footnote 25, para. 8.
[32] E.C.J., Case 26/74 *Société Roquette Frères* v. *Commission of the European Communities* [1976] E.C.R. 677.

of the national courts and had to be decided by them by applying the national law in cases where Community law did not cover the subject matter in question. In this context it was the duty of the Member States' courts, under the principle of cooperation laid down in Article 5 EEC, to provide the legal protection arising from the direct effect of the Community provisions—both when these provisions imposed obligations on individuals and when they granted them rights. It was, however, the task of each Member State's national legal system to determine which courts were competent in the matter and to regulate those procedures for the judicial assertion of claims which were intended to assure the protection of the rights arising to individuals as a result of the direct effect of Community law; these procedures were not to be less favourable than those for the assertion of similar claims arising under the country's own law and were on no account to be designed in such a way that the exercise of the rights which the national courts were required to protect was rendered impracticable.[33]

The Court of Justice further stated that the above considerations were to be found in the said Regulation 729/70, Article 8 of which obliged Member States to recover financial benefits granted as a result of irregularities, such recovery to take place "in accordance with national provisions laid down by law, regulation or administrative action." From what had been said thus far it could be seen, however, that the express reference to the individual State's laws was subject to the same limitations as the tacit condition "inasmuch as the application of national legislation must be effected in a non-discriminatory manner having regard to the procedural rules relating to disputes of the same type, but purely national, and in so far as procedural rules cannot have the result of making impossible in practice the exercise of rights conferred by Community law."[34]

The Court of Justice then referred to its judgment of June 28, 1977 in Case 118/76, *Balkan-Import-Export*,[35] in which it had applied these principles and had concluded that the application of a national hardship clause allowing the executive to absolve a creditor from charges that were due did not apply to Community-law charges "in so far as its effect would be to modify the scope of the provisions of Community law concerning the basis of assessment, the manner of imposition or the amount of a charge introduced by that law," even where all formalities connected with

[33] E.C.J., *loc. cit.*, footnote 25, para. 10.
[34] E.C.J., *loc. cit.*, footnote 25, para. 12.
[35] [1977] E.C.R. 1177.

the levying of Community charges had been transferred to the Member States' administrative authorities. Accordingly, it had to be decided whether there was a general principle or specific provision of Community law which prohibited the application of a national legal principle such as the Dutch principle of legal certainty.[36]

Since there proved to be no such rule in Community law, the Court of Justice finally came to the conclusion that it was permissible, in connection with legal disputes on the recovery of incorrectly paid export refunds by Member States' national authorities, to apply a national legal principle according to which financial benefits granted in error may not be recovered if the error is not attributable to the furnishing of incorrect information by the beneficiary or if the error, despite the furnishing of incorrect information, could easily have been avoided.[37]

In the other decision—in Joined Cases 66, 127 and 128/79[38]—the Court of Justice was faced with the question of the post-clearance recovery of Community charges. Among the points to be decided was whether a national authority has the power to institute legal proceedings for the collection of import levies which are due but have not been levied.

The matter was brought before the Court of Justice by the Corte Suprema di Cassazione, Rome. It had arisen in the course of a lawsuit between three Italian undertakings and the competent Italian administrative authority, which demanded that the undertakings should pay over import levies in respect of imports of beef made in 1968.

Detailed points to be noted are as follows:

In calculating the levies on the imports in question, the Italian authority had followed a procedure recommended by the Commission for customs duties—a procedure universally followed—whereby if customs duties were reduced in the period between the import declaration and the putting of the goods into free circulation, the most favourable duty rate was to be applied on request.

However, in a judgment of July 15, 1976 in Case 113/75 (*Frecassetti*[39]) the Court of Justice had rejected the application of this method to levies on agricultural imports from third countries, because the uniform basis

---

[36] E.C.J., *loc. cit.*, footnote 25, para. 14.
[37] E.C.J., *loc. cit.*, footnote 25, para. 21.
[38] Joined Cases 66, 127 & 128/79 *Amministrazione delle finanze* v. *Meridionale Industria Salumi and Others* [1980] E.C.R. 1237.
[39] E.C.J., [1976] E.C.R. 983.

for the calculation of levies of this kind was the rate of levy in force on the date on which the import declaration was accepted. Accordingly, the undertakings concerned should have paid higher levies than they actually had done.

Even before this judgment had been delivered, the undertakings had been called upon to pay the additional amounts, the reason being in this case that they had not satisfied a formal requirement of Italian law which determined whether the lower levy rate would be applied or not. The question then arose, however, whether and to what extent the interpretation given in the judgment quoted had any effect on legal circumstances which—like the disputed demands—had arisen before the judgment had been delivered.

The Court had regard to the fact that, first, the Italian rule had since been changed to bring it into line with the judgment in the *Frecassetti* case and, secondly, that this amendment had not started to apply until September 11, 1976, so that subsequent levies could be demanded only in respect of goods declared to customs at a later date. The September 11 date had been chosen because that was the date on which the substance of the judgment quoted had been published in the Official Journal of the European Communities (C 214).

In this situation the referring court wished to know whether the exercise of rights arising from the direct effect of a Community-law provision could be governed by an individual State's law and hence in certain circumstances also be limited by such law. The principal point to be decided in this connection was whether a national authority had the power to institute legal proceedings for the collection of Community charges which were due but had not been levied.

On this question the Court of Justice first stated:

> "The arrangements for the fixing and the conditions of collection of the financial charges which the Community is empowered to levy and which specifically constitute its own resources, such as customs duties and agricultural levies, are laid down by the Council Decision of 21 April 1970 on the replacement of financial contributions from Member States by the Community's own resources (Official Journal, English Special Edition 1970 (I), p. 224) and the regulations in implementation thereof. These provisions must be considered within the framework of the general arrangements on the financial provisions of the Treaty which, like the corresponding arrangements of the Member States, are governed by the general principle of equality which requires that comparable situations may not be

639

treated differently unless difference of treatment is objectively justified."[40]

From this the Court of Justice deduced that the system of charges which represent revenue in the Community budget must be designed in such a way that all those subject to a charge under the conditions imposed by Community arrangements are charged uniformly. This requirement entailed equality of treatment with regard to the formal and material conditions under which the undertakings take action against the Community charges imposed on them and under which they may demand a refund if they are not liable to make payment; it also entailed a corresponding harmonisation of the conditions under which the Member States' administrations, when acting on behalf of the Community, levy the charges mentioned and, if appropriate, may demand repayment of unlawfully granted financial benefits.[41]

Referring to its judgment of May 21, 1976 in Case 26/74 (*Roquette*[42]), the Court of Justice further stated that legal disputes concerning refunds of amounts levied on behalf of the Community continued to fall within the jurisdiction of the individual States' courts and that such disputes had to be decided by these latter courts according to individual States' law in cases where Community law did not cover the subject matter in question. The same comment applied—for the same reasons, specified in the judgment quoted—to proceedings and disputes relating to charges the collection of which had been transferred to the Member States' administrations to carry out on behalf of the Community.[43]

In the Court of Justice's opinion it was therefore the responsibility of the Member States' internal legal systems to lay down the procedures and conditions for the levying of Community charges in general and agricultural levies in particular and to determine which authorities should be responsible for the levying of the charges themselves and which courts should handle disputes concerning such levying. Care had to be taken in this connection to ensure that these procedures and conditions did not make the arrangements for the levying of Community charges less effective than those in existence for similar national charges.[44]

The Court further stated that this consideration had been reflected in the cited Council Decision of April 21, 1970, in which Article 6 expressly

---

[40] E.C.J., *loc. cit.*, footnote 38, para. 14.
[41] E.C.J., *loc. cit.*, footnote 38, para. 15.
[42] E.C.J., [1976] E.C.R. 677.
[43] E.C.J., *loc. cit.*, footnote 38, paras. 16 and 17.
[44] E.C.J., *loc. cit.*, footnote 38, para. 18.

provided that the Community's own resources, which included the agricultural levies, "shall be collected by the Member States in accordance with national provisions imposed by law, regulation or administrative action, which shall, where necessary, be amended for that purpose."[45]

However—the Court continued—this express reference to national laws is subject to the same limitations as the tacit reference, the necessity for which in the absence of any Community rules on the matter in question is recognised in that when national laws are applied no differentiation may be made in comparison with proceedings in which similar, but purely national, disputes are decided and in that the exercise of rights conferred by Community law is not rendered impracticable.[46]

The Court of Justice then concluded that a national arrangement for the levying of Community charges which restricted the powers granted to the administration to ensure the levying of these charges compared to its powers with regard to the levying of similar national charges was not compatible with Community law.[47]

II. AS AN ADMINISTRATIVE-LAW PRINCIPLE

But it is not only as a "basic principle" that the equality principle is—generally—emphasised. It is also viewed under the heading of "the administration's binding of itself,"[48] that is to say from the point of view that an authority may in certain circumstances be bound by its own abstract interpretative concepts[49]; from this it follows that the equality principle has also achieved importance as a specific administrative-law principle.

[45] E.C.J., *loc. cit.*, footnote 38, para. 19.
[46] E.C.J., *loc. cit.*, footnote 38, para. 20.
[47] E.C.J., *loc. cit.*, footnote 38, para. 21.
[48] This is German legal terminology; see for example I. von Münch, *Grundgesetzkommentar*, Vol. 1 (3rd ed., Munich 1985), para. 33 on Art. 3; P. Badura, *Staatsrecht*, Munich 1986, p. 99, para. 44; F. Ossenbühl, "Die Quellen des Verwaltungsrechts," in H.-U. Erichsen, W. Martens (ed.), *Allgemeines Verwaltungsrecht* (7th ed., Berlin/New York 1986), pp. 91 *et seq.*; *ibid.*, "Selbstbindungen der Verwaltung," DVBl. 1981, pp. 857 *et seq.* (860); H. P. Ipsen, "Gleichheit," in F. L. Neumann, H. C. Nipperdey, U. Scheuner (ed.), *Die Grundrechte*, Vol. 2, Berlin 1968, pp. 111 *et seq.* (147 *et seq.*).
[49] On the judgments in Case 46/71 and Case 148/73 outlined below, see also J. Schwarze, *Die Befugnis zur Abstraktion im europäischen Gemeinschaftsrecht*, Baden-Baden 1976, pp. 64 *et seq.*; see also judgment in *M. Hurnai* v. *Court of Justice of the European Communities* [1986] E.C.R. 3157, in which the principle of sound administration was regarded as not having been infringed but a contravention of the equality principle was deemed to have occurred.

An early decision which may be mentioned in this connection was given in 1972 and concerned the law relating to officials.[50] The point at issue, *inter alia*, was whether the granting of an aid is mandatory if the conditions specified in a Council Decision have been fulfilled.

The facts on which the judgment was based were as follows:

Under Article 2 of Annex VII of the Community's Staff Regulations, officials receive monthly child allowances for dependent children; by virtue of paragraph 4, "exceptionally, under special dispensation from the appointing authority accompanied by the reasons for the decision and supported by conclusive evidence, any person whom the official is legally obliged to maintain and whose maintenance involves him in considerable expense" may be treated as equivalent to a dependent child.

Relying on this provision, the plaintiff claimed an allowance for his mother who, being in need of care, lived in an old people's home at great financial cost to him.

In support of his claim he adduced, in particular, a Council Decision of April 2, 1964, which, in implementation of the article quoted, laid down objective criteria for the conditions under which a person was to be deemed equivalent to a dependent child. He contended that the allowance must be granted if the conditions specified in the Decision were fulfilled; this left no scope for the authorities to exercise discretion in the matter.

The Court of Justice rejected this interpretation. Specifically, it ruled:

"Although, in applying Article 2(4) of Annex VII to the Staff Regulations, each institution of the Community can lay down in advance and in general terms the objective criteria which it intends to observe, they cannot be regarded as other than a statement of minimum requirements, applicable in all cases, without prejudice to the exercise, in each individual case, of the discretion conferred on the administration by the Staff Regulations themselves. This discretion on the part of the administration, which is essential to enable it to take account of the manifold unforeseeable facts peculiar to each case, is not incompatible with the general principle, relied on by the applicant, of equal treatment for officials. This general principle does not mean that, in applying the provision concerned, the administration must merely carry out a mechanical application of pre-

---

[50] Case 46/71 *Georg Brandau* v. *Council of the European Communities* [1972] E.C.R. 373.

determined rules and criteria. Such an interpretation would conflict with the need for evaluation of the often complicated factual considerations peculiar to each individual case."[51]

Another decision was handed down in 1974, again in connection with the law relating to officials and again on the question of the granting of an aid.[52]

The background to the case was essentially that the applicant and her husband—both officials of the European Commission—had applied for the reimbursement of removal expenses; the nature and amount of the reimbursement claimed complied with internal guidelines.

The applicant's case was upheld, on the grounds that the administration, by issuing the guidelines, had bound itself. For, in the words of the Court of Justice:

"Although an internal directive has not the character of a rule of law which the administration is always bound to observe, it nevertheless sets forth a rule of conduct indicating the practice to be followed, from which the administration may not depart without giving the reasons which have led it to do so, since otherwise the principles of equality of treatment would be infringed."[53]

In 1983 the Court of Justice again considered the equality principle from the point of view of the administration's binding of itself, but without defining it any further, since the situations involved were dissimilar and hence the unequal treatment complained of did not from the outset contravene the principle.[54]

The subject matter of the decision was the ECSC quota system, and the background to the case was as follows:

---

[51] E.C.J., *ibid.*, paras. 11 to 14; for comparative law on this point: J. Schwarze, *op. cit.*, footnote 49, pp. 66 *et seq.* with further references; Advocate-General Warner in his opinion in Case 81/72 *Commission of the European Communities* v. *Council of the European Communities* [1973] E.C.R. 575 at 592.

[52] Case 148/73 *Raymond Louwage and Marie-Thérèse Louwage (née Moriame)* [1974] E.C.R. 81.

[53] E.C.J., *ibid.* paras. 11 to 18; a similar recent decision: Joined Cases 129 & 274/82 *Charles Lux* v. *Court of Auditors of the European Communities* [1984] E.C.R. 4127, para. 20. For comparative law on this point, see J. Schwarze, *op. cit.*, footnote 49, p. 69.

[54] Case 188/82 *Thyssen AG* v. *Commission of the European Communities* [1983] E.C.R. 3721. On the equality principle as a requirement of the *suum cuique tribuere*, see under I.3.B. above.

By a decision dated June 11, 1982 the Commission had imposed a fine of ECU 288 825 on the Thyssen company because in the first quarter of 1981 it had exceeded the production quota for a certain type of steel allocated to it pursuant to Decision No. 2794/80/ECSC.[55]

Thyssen took legal action to contest the imposition of the fine.

On the basis of Article 8(2) of the said Decision No. 2794/80, Thyssen claimed that it could carry over the quantities of steel not produced in the fourth quarter of 1980 to the first quarter of 1981. Since the Commission had developed the administrative practice of allowing undertakings which found themselves in the same situation as Thyssen to effect a carry-over in this way, the Commission could not prosecute Thyssen—so Thyssen claimed—without infringing the principle of self-binding by the administration.

On this point the Court of Justice first stated that Article 8(2) of Decision No. 2794/80/ECSC provided only for the *possibility* of carrying over the unused production quota to the next quarter.[56] The Court went on to declare:

"As regards the reference to the principle that the administration is bound by its own acts, the Commission has demonstrated that the undertakings which were allowed to carry over the unused portion of their quota had not yet, unlike Thyssen, exhausted their quota and therefore fulfilled the conditions laid down by Article 8(2) of Decision No. 2794/80 for exercising that right. Since the two situations are not comparable, no principle of Community law can be relied upon to support the claim that they should be accorded identical treatment."[57]

III. SUMMARY

As we have shown in section C, the equality principle as such is also recognised in Community law, and this recognition is comprehensive and not confined to those areas in respect of which the Treaties contain anti-discrimination provisions.

Thus it is first of all expressly and generally stated that the equality principle is a basic principle of Community law. However, the equality

---

[55] Commission Decision 2794/80/ECSC of October 31, 1980, O.J. 1980, L291/1.
[56] E.C.J., *loc. cit.*, footnote 54, para. 8.
[57] E.C.J., *loc. cit.*, footnote 54, para. 9.

principle is also mentioned, for example, in connection with the concept of "self-binding" by the executive; it follows, by inference, that it has also attained importance as a specifically administrative-law principle.

When the Court of Justice defines the content of the equality principle, it resorts to its decisions on the concept of discrimination.

It thus reduces the principle to the classic formula that "similar situations shall not be treated differently unless differentation is objectively justified."

D.   LIMITS TO THE APPLICATION OF THE EQUALITY PRINCIPLE

Even though the equality principle in itself is recognised comprehensively, that is to say beyond the ambit of the anti-discrimination provisions, there are nevertheless some subjects to which it does not apply. This should come as no surprise, for ultimately it is only a consequence of the special nature of Community law, which, although—as superior law—applying in Member States directly and with precedence over national law, is nevertheless rigorously targeted and functionally restricted to Community objectives and fields of activity.

I.   THE COMMUNITY'S EXTERNAL RELATIONS

One area to which the equality principle does not apply is that of the Community's external relations. This means that the Community is not obliged to treat all third countries—and hence also all market participants which have established trading relations with third countries—equally in every respect. This was formulated with especial clarity in a decision handed down by the Court of Justice in 1982 relating to the law on protective measures in connection with the common organisation of the market for fruit and vegetables.[1] In this case the Court had to decide, *inter alia*, whether the Commission had infringed the "discrimination prohibition"[2] by setting up a system of voluntary restraint for imports of tinned

---

[1] Case 52/81 *Offene Handelsgesellschaft in Firma Werner Faust* v. *Commission of the European Communities* [1982] E.C.R. 3745; *cf.* also Case 236/84 *MALT GmbH* v. *Hauptzollamt Düsseldorf* [1986] E.C.R. 1923, para. 21, in which the E.C.J. refers to Case 52/81.

[2] As will be clearly seen from what follows, the reference is to the discrimination prohibition contained in Article 40(3) subpara. 2 EEC; see in particular para. 25, footnote 5.

mushrooms from third countries, under which the import quota granted to each third country was to be determined without reference to the imports from that country in past years.

The facts of the case were as follows:

Protective measures against imports of tinned mushrooms into the Community from third countries were first introduced in 1974 by Regulation 2107/74,[3] in the form of a system of purchase quotas. Under this system every import required presentation of an import licence; this would be granted to the applicant for a quantity calculated on the basis of the quantity imported in an earlier period.

The Commission lifted these protective measures with effect from January 1, 1977, but on May 25, 1978—through Regulation 1102/78[4]—it adopted new protective measures which entailed the suspension of the granting of import licences for tinned mushrooms with immediate effect. Under Article 2(1) of the Regulation the import ban did not apply "for preserved mushrooms originating in third countries which the Commission accepts as being able to ensure that their experts to the Community do not exceed a level agreed by the Commission."

As there was no voluntary-restraint agreement between the Commission and Taiwan, imports of tinned mushrooms from that country were very small in relation to previous years, since the protective measures continued to be applied against third countries which were not prepared voluntarily to reduce their exports. In 1980 Taiwan declared that it was willing to limit its exports of tinned mushrooms to the Community to 1,000 tonnes, after it had ascertained that the Commission was not prepared to grant it a larger quota than this.

The Faust company, the applicant, was an undertaking domiciled in the Federal Republic of Germany, whose principal business was the import of tinned mushrooms from Taiwan on behalf of third parties. In its legal action Faust complained of Regulation 1102/78, which in its view was an infringement of the discrimination prohibition; it did not, however, complain of the system of voluntary restraint introduced by the Regulation but of the manner in which the Commission had applied the system, and in particular of the fact that the Commission's fixing of the import quotas granted to each third country within the framework of the voluntary-restraint agreement had been arbitrary, in that no account had been taken of the imports from the country in question in earlier years.

---

[3] Commission Regulation 2107/74 of August 8, 1974, O.J. 1974, L218/54.
[4] Commission Regulation 1102/78 of May 25, 1978, O.J. 1978, L139/26.

The Court of Justice ruled that this complaint was without foundation. It stated:

> "Although Taiwan certainly appears to have been treated by the Commission less favourably than certain non-member countries, it should be remembered that there exists in the Treaty no general principle obliging the Community, in its external relations, to accord to non-member countries equal treatment in all respects. It is thus not necessary to examine on what basis Faust might seek to rely upon the prohibition of discrimination between producers or consumers within the Community contained in Article 40 of the Treaty. It need merely be observed that, if different treatment of non-member countries is compatible with Community law, different treatment accorded to traders within the Community must also be regarded as compatible with Community law, where that different treatment is merely an automatic consequence of the different treatment accorded to non-member countries with which such traders have entered into commercial relations."[5]

The Court of Justice had already declared this to be fundamental law in 1976 in a decision on the law relating to monetary compensatory amounts in the market for dairy products.[6] In that case the point at issue, *inter alia*, was whether the Commission, by not exempting Bulgarian sheep's milk cheese from the payment of a compensatory amount in the same way as certain types of Italian and Swiss cheese, was in breach of the equality principle.[7]

This question had been referred to the Court of Justice by the Finance Court of Berlin. It had arisen in the course of proceedings between the firm Balkan-Import-Export, the plaintiff, and the customs authorities of the Federal Republic of Germany. Specifically, the facts were as follows:

Under Regulation 974/71[8] the Council had established a system of compensatory amounts for trade between Member States and third countries. The sixth recital to the Regulation states that these compensatory amounts may not be higher than the amounts absolutely necessary to compensate for the effects of currency measures on the prices of basic

---

[5] E.C.J., *loc. cit.*, footnote 1, para. 25.
[6] Case 55/75 *Balkan-Import-Export GmbH* v. *Hauptzollamt Berlin Packhof* [1976] E.C.R. 19.
[7] E.C.J., para. 13.
[8] Council Regulation 974/71 of May 12, 1971, J.O. 1971, L106/1; O.J. Sp.Ed. 1971(I), 257.

products for which intervention measures are prescribed; compensatory amounts should be admitted only in cases where these effects would lead to difficulties.

Accordingly, Article 1(3) of Regulation 974/71 provides that paragraph 1, which governs the granting or levying of compensatory amounts in general, "shall be exercised only where application of the monetary measures referred to in paragraph 1 would lead to disturbances in trade in agricultural products." By virtue of Article 6 it is the Commission's duty to decide, in the procedure laid down, whether there is a danger of disturbance or not.

When the Balkan-Import-Export company, on April 25, 1974, imported into Germany 14.490 kg of Bulgarian sheep's milk cheese (tariff heading 04.04 E I b 4 CCT) which it had purchased under a fairly long-term contract dated November 24, 1972 and expressed in Deutschmarks, the German customs authorities demanded that it should pay a compensatory amount of DM 9244.62, calculated on the basis of a rate of duty of DM 63.80/100 kg.

The firm in question had considered this demand incompatible with Community law and had taken the matter to the competent finance court.

The Court of Justice rules as follows:

> "Although Article 2 of Regulation No. 974/71 of the Council, by specifying the method of calculating the compensatory amounts, determines the amounts which cannot be exceeded, it does not follow that the Commission could not undertake to apply lower amounts or to grant negotiated exemptions in respect of certain third countries and for reasons relating to the exercise of other powers which it holds under the Treaty. In the Treaty there exists no general principle obliging the Community, in its external relations, to accord to third countries equal treatment in all respects and in any event traders do not have the right to rely on the existence of such a general principle."[9]

With reference in particular to the cheese from Italy, the Court then stated that the general principle of Community preference justified a divergent assessment of the danger of disturbances according to whether the products involved originated in another Member State or in a third

---

[9] E.C.J., *loc. cit.*, footnote 6, para. 14. A corresponding ruling by the Court of Justice was given in Case 245/81 *Edeka Zentrale AG* v. *Federal Republic of Germany* [1982] E.C.R. 2745, para. 19; see under C above.

country. As far as the products from Switzerland were concerned, it should be noted first of all that examination of the question whether the principle of equal treatment had been observed did not have to extend to the existence or non-existence of competition between the Swiss or Bulgarian types of cheese (as claimed), but to their comparability with regard to possible disturbances to the trade in agricultural products caused by imports. The Court of Justice went on to state that the Commission could base its assessment of the danger of disturbances on the global free-at-frontier selling prices. It was therefore irrelevant that—as the plaintiff had maintained—the actual free-at-frontier selling prices for Bulgarian sheep's milk cheese in April 1974 had been higher than the actual free-at-frontier selling prices for Swiss Emmental cheese.[10]

II. MEMBER STATES' JURISDICTION

Also outside the scope of application of the Community-law equality principle are the matters which still remain under the Member States' jurisdiction—in every case within their own territory.[11] This means that differing treatment of citizens of the Common Market cannot be remedied with the aid of the equality principle if the unequal treatment is the result of differences in national laws, regulations and administrative provisions.[12]

[10] E.C.J., *loc. cit.*, footnote 6, para. 15.
[11] Here there is a parallel with the situation in the Federal Republic of Germany, in that, for instance, the fact that a *Land* law differs from related laws in other *Länder* is not in itself regarded as a violation of the equality principle. The Federal Constitutional Court has emphasised in this regard: "In view of the federal structure of the Federal Republic of Germany, the *Land* legislature is required to observe on its territory only the general principle of equality. Where a *Land* has authority to legislate, the validity of a provision enacted by it is not dependent on whether other *Land* legislatures or the Federal Republic have adopted similar rules." (E 33, p. 224, at 231). See also, for instance, BVerfGE 42, p. 20, at 27.
[12] If differences of this kind arise, the Community can or must—depending on the situation—take action as prescribed by Article 103(2) or Articles 100 and 101 EEC. In addition, the Community will take action under Articles 30 *et seq.* EEC where the national regulations in question contravene the provisions on the free movement of goods. See, *inter alia*, Advocate-General VerLoren van Themaat's opinion in Joined Cases 197–200, 243, 245 & 247/80 *Ludwigshafener Walzmühle Erling KG and Others* v. *Council and Commission of the European Communities* [1981] E.C.R. 3211; Advocate-General Reischl's opinion in Case 31/78 *Francesco Bussone* v. *Italian Ministry of Agriculture* [1978] E.C.R. 2429; Advocate-General Capotorti's opinion in Case 233/81 *Denkavit Futtermittel GmbH* v. *Federal Republic of Germany* [1982] E.C.R. 2933.

The Court of Justice decisions to be examined here concern the various discrimination prohibitions embodied in the Treaties. The following judgments, handed down in connection with Articles 7, 40(3) sub-paragraph 2, and 119 EEC, may be mentioned by way of example.

In a ruling given in 1979 on fisheries law,[13] the Court of Justice dealt with the question, *inter alia*, whether the Dutch Government, by imposing a limit on catches of sole and plaice, had committed discrimination on grounds of nationality as prohibited by Article 7 EEC.

This question had been referred to the Court of Justice by the Economische Politierechter (judge for criminal economic matters) of the Rotterdam Arrondissementsrechtbank. It had arisen in the course of several sets of criminal proceedings instituted against fishery undertakings and deep-sea fishermen. The defendants were accused of having broken the Dutch regulations which had set quotas for catches of sole and plaice in the North Sea for 1978.[14] Before the national court the defendants maintained in their defence that the transitional period specified in Article 102 of the Act of Accession had expired on January 1, 1978 and that the imposition of measures to protect the living resources of the high seas thus fell within the Community's competence. Therefore the Dutch Government no longer had the authority to introduce the regulations on which the criminal prosecution was based. These regulations would also lead to discrimination within the meaning of Article 7 EEC against Dutch fishermen, since other Member States had applied less strict regulations to the same fishing grounds; the result was that all fishermen who were not subject to the jurisdiction of the Dutch authorities could actually fish in Dutch waters under more favourable conditions than the local Dutch fishermen.

In this case the Court of Justice ruled first of all that the Dutch Government did indeed have the authority to adopt the disputed regulations. On the matter of the discrimination complained of, the Court then went on to state:

"In this connexion it should be remembered that protective measures agreed on within the Community, in consultation with the Commission, are based on responsibility shared between the Member States, in the sense that at present each State regulates in

[13] Joined Cases 185–204/78 *Firma J. van Dam en Zonen and Others* [1979] E.C.R. 2345.
[14] These regulations were the "Regulation for the provisional arrangement of the limitation of catches for sole and plaice, 1978" and the "Regulation for the provisional arrangement of the quota system for catches of sole and plaice in the North Sea, 1978."

accordance with the provisions of its own national legislation concerning fishing quotas, the catches landed in its own ports. It cannot be held contrary to the principle of non-discrimination to apply national legislation, the compatibility of which with Community law is moreover not contested, because other Member States allegedly apply less strict rules. Inequalities of this kind, if they exist, must be eliminated by means of the consultations provided for by Annex VI to the Hague Resolution, quoted in the judgment referred to above, but they cannot be the foundation of a charge of discrimination with regard to the provisions made by a Member State which applies equally to any person under its jurisdiction, the regulations which it had adopted for fishing quotas."[15]

In short, then, national provisions such as the Netherlands fishing quota regulations cannot be regarded as discriminatory "as long as they are applied uniformly to all the fishermen under the jurisdiction of the Member State concerned."[16]

Another relevant ruling was delivered in 1978 in the field of social policy.[17] There one of the questions at issue was whether there was a general principle in Community law prohibiting discrimination between male and female workers with regard to other working conditions besides those governed by the rules on pay contained in Article 119 EEC.

This matter was brought before the Court of Justice by the Belgian Cour de Cassation. It had arisen in the course of a case brought by a former air stewardess—Gabrielle Defrenne—against the Belgian airline company Sabena. The details of the case were as follows:

Under the terms of her contract of employment with Sabena, Mrs. Defrenne was compulsorily retired on reaching the age of 40. She instituted proceedings against the airline in a Belgian labour court on the basis of Article 119 EEC, claiming that Sabena should be compelled to pay the following amounts:

---

[15] E.C.J., *loc. cit.*, footnote 13, para. 10. Basically the same: judgments in: Case 14/68 *Walt Wilhelm and Others* v. *Bundeskartellamt* [1969] E.C.R. 1, para. 13; Case 22/77 *Fonds de retraite des Ouvriers Mineurs* v. *Giovanni Mura* [1977] E.C.R. 1699, paras. 9 to 10; Case 1/78 *Patrick Christopher Kenny* v. *Insurance Officer* [1978] E.C.R. 1489, paras. 18 to 20; Case 126/82 *D.J. Smit Transport B.V.* v. *Commissie Grensoverschrijdend Beroepsgoederenvervoer* [1983] E.C.R. 73, para. 27. On the judgments in Case 14/68 and Case 22/77, see under B.I.2. and B.II.2. above.

[16] E.C.J., *loc. cit.*, footnote 13, para. 11.

[17] Case 149/77 *Gabrielle Defrenne* v. *SABENA* [1978] E.C.R. 1365.

651

1. compensation for the fact that as a female worker she had been discriminated against in the matter of pay in comparison with her male colleagues who did the same work as pursers;
2. an additional severance payment equal to the difference between the severance pay she had actually received on leaving the service and that payable to a 40-year-old purser with the same length of service who had been definitively declared unfit for work;
3. damages for the disadvantages suffered by her in relation to her pension.

Whereas the court of first instance had rejected the plaintiff's case in its entirety, the appeal court upheld this judgment only in respect of the last two claims. With regard to the first-mentioned claim for compensation, the appeal court submitted two questions to the Court of Justice for a preliminary ruling[18] and allowed the plaintiff's claim for back pay of Bfr 12,716 plus interest and costs.

Mrs. Defrenne appealed against the appeal court's judgment to the Cour de Cassation. The latter court, for its part, wanted to know if there was any general principle in Community law prohibiting discrimination between male and female workers if the discrimination in question related to matters other than pay.

On this matter, the Court of Justice ruled firstly as follows:

"The Court has repeatedly stated that respect for fundamental personal human rights is one of the general principles of Community law, the observance of which it has a duty to ensure. There can be no doubt that the elimination of discrimination based on sex forms part of those fundamental rights. Moreover, the same concepts are recognized by the European Social Charter of 18 November 1961 and by Convention No. 111 of the International Labour Organization of 25 June 1958 concerning discrimination in respect of employment and occupation. It should also be noted in this connection that the Court of Justice, in its judgments of 7 June 1972 in the *Sabbatini-Bertoni* case ([1972] E.C.R. 345) and of 20 February 1975 in the *Airola* case ([1975] E.C.R. 221), recognized the necessity that equal working conditions should be created for male and female workers employed by the Community itself under the terms of the Staff Regulations."[19]

[18] E.C.J., Case 43/75 *Gabrielle Defrenne* v. *SABENA* [1976] E.C.R. 455.
[19] E.C.J., *loc. cit.*, footnote 17, paras. 26 to 29.

The Court then stated:

"On the other hand, as regards the relationships of employer and employee which are subject to national law, the Community had not, at the time of the events now before the Belgian courts, assumed any responsibility for supervising and guaranteeing the observance of the principle of equality between men and women in working conditions other than remuneration. As has been stated above, at the period under consideration Community law contained only the provisions in the nature of a programme laid down by Articles 117 and 118 of the Treaty, which relate to the general development of social welfare, in particular as regards conditions of employment and working conditions. It follows that the situation before the Belgian courts is governed by the provisions and principles of internal and international law in force in Belgium."[20]

Specifically, the Court of Justice deduced from this:

"... that at the time of the events which form the basis of the main action there was, as regards the relationships between employer and employee under national law, no rule of Community law prohibiting discrimination between men and women in the matter of working conditions other than the requirements as to pay referred to in Article 119 of the Treaty."[21]

That leaves two decisions, both relating to the second subparagraph of Article 40(3) EEC:

One of the judgments[22] delivered in 1972, was reached against the background of the devaluation of the French franc in 1969; in this case the Court of Justice had to decide, *inter alia*, whether the Commission had committed a discriminatory act under the second subparagraph of Article 40(3) EEC by fixing the Council-approved national subsidies for imports of common wheat and meslin in such a way that the price increase suffered by the French importers and millers—which had led to the subsidies—was not offset in full.

---

[20] E.C.J., *loc. cit.*, footnote 17, paras. 30 to 32.
[21] E.C.J., *loc. cit.*, footnote 17, para. 33. See also Case 19/81 *Arthur Burton* v. *British Railways Board* [1982] E.C.R. 555, paras. 13 and 14.
[22] Joined Cases 9 & 11/71, *Compagnie d'approvisionnement de transport et de crédit SA and Others* v. *Commission of the European Communities* [1972] E.C.R. 391.

The decision was based on the following facts:

Pursuant to Article 103 EEC, the Council, on August 11, 1969, had issued Regulation 1586/69,[23] which stipulated in Article 1(1) subparagraph 1: "The intervention and purchase prices which France has to pay under the regulations on the common organisation of the agricultural market on the basis of the interventions on the internal market shall be reduced by 11.11 per cent. for the sector in question until the end of the crop year 1969/70." Article 3(1) stated: "In so far as the effects"—of, *inter alia*, the measures named in Article 1(1) subparagraph 1 and just quoted—"have to be compensated for, France shall grant subsidies on imports from Member States and third countries"; finally, Article 8 authorised the Commission to issue the necessary implementing regulations by means of which ". . . in particular the . . . subsidies on imports (shall be) fixed."

In implementation of Article 1(2) of Regulation 1586/69, the Council, on July 20, 1970, issued Regulation 1432/70,[24] of which Article 1(1) stipulates: "The following prices, which France has to pay under the regulations on the common organisation of the agricultural market on the basis of the interventions on the internal market, shall be reduced until the end of the crop year 1970/71 as follows: . . . b) the intervention price for common wheat and for durum wheat by 8.44 per cent."

Pursuant to the above-mentioned Article 8 of the Regulation 1586/69, the Commission issued Regulations 1670/69[25] and 1505/70,[26] fixing the subsidies for common wheat and meslin initially at FF 58.49 and subsequently at FF 44.43 per tonne (both in Annex, under A).

The applicants—two French undertakings specialising in grain dealing and grain processing—alleged that the Commission, by fixing the subsidies at this level, was in breach of the second subparagraph of Article 40(3) EEC. They claimed that the Commission had discriminated between the French importers and millers on the one hand and importers and millers in the other Member States on the other hand, since the latter did not suffer a price increase on imports from third countries as a result of the devaluation of the French franc.

The Court of Justice ruled as follows:

"The preamble to Regulation No. 1586/69, which was the basis for Regulation No. 1432/70, refers, in particular, to Article 103 of the

---

[23] Council Regulation 1586/69, O.J. 1969, L202/1.
[24] Council Regulation 1432/70, O.J. 1970, L159/20.
[25] Commission Regulation 1670/69, O.J. 1969, L214/7.
[26] Commission Regulation 1505/70 O.J. 1970, L166/33.

Treaty in the following terms: 'Whereas with effect from 11 August 1969, the ratio between the parity of France's currency and the value of the unit of account was altered by 11.11% (by decision of the French Republic'). Under Article 103 of the Treaty, 'Member States (shall regard) their conjunctural policies as a matter of common concern' and 'they shall consult each other and the Commission on the measures to be taken in the light of the prevailing circumstances,' while 'the Council may . . . decide upon the measures appropriate to the situation.' It is clear from Article 107 that it is for each Member State to decide upon any alteration in the rate of exchange of its currency under the conditions laid down by that provision. If such an alteration puts importers and exporters in the State concerned in a position different from that of their opposite numbers in other Member States, this disparity is the result of the actual decision of that Member State and not of Community intervention. Although the powers conferred on the Community institutions by the Treaty, in particular by Article 103(2) thereof, pursuant to which the Council adopted Regulations Nos. 1586/69 and 1432/70, include the power to alleviate, in the common interest, certain effects of a devaluation or of a revaluation, it does not follow that the Council must compensate for all these effects in so far as they are adverse to the importers or exporters of the Member State concerned. In fact, by empowering the Council to 'decide upon the measures appropriate to the situation,' without obliging it to do so, Article 103 conferred on that institution a wide power of discretion to be exercised in accordance with the 'common interest' and not with the individual interests of a specific group of traders."[27]

In conclusion the Court of Justice declared that the applicants had not even offered, let alone substantiated, any evidence that it would have been necessary in the common interest to provide full compensation for the price increase on imports from third countries which had arisen as a result of the devaluation of the French franc.

The last decision to be mentioned here was pronounced in 1982 and related to the implementation of the common organisation of the market in the Member States.[28] Specifically, the Court of Justice had to decide

---

[27] E.C.J., *loc. cit.*, footnote 22, paras. 28 to 34. Basically similar: Case 43/72 *Merkur-Aussenhandels-GmbH* v. *Commission of the European Communities* [1973] E.C.R. 1055, para. 20, and in Case 7/76 *Firma IRCA* v. *National Taxation Authority* [1976] E.C.R. 1213 para. 13.

[28] Joined Cases 141–143/81 *Gerrit Holdijk and Others* [1982] E.C.R. 1299.

whether Community law should be interpreted in such a way as to prevent the competent national agencies from retaining or adopting—for the animals' protection—unilateral rules on boxes in which fattening calves were to be reared.

This matter had been brought before the Court of Justice by a Dutch "Kantongerecht"; it had arisen in the course of several criminal cases brought against two calf fatteners and a fodder manufacturing company.

The defendants had been accused of keeping fattening calves in spaces which did not comply with the conditions laid down by Article 2b of the "Koninklijk Besluit" of September 8, 1961 concerning implementing provisions to Article 1 of the "Wet op de Dierenbescherming", as the dimensions were such that the calves could not lie on their sides without hindrance. Article 2b of the said "Besluit" stipulates: "Spaces in which fattening calves are kept must meet the following requirements . . . b) The dimensions of the spaces must be such as to permit the animals to lie without hindrance on either of their (the animals') sides and to move their heads freely when standing."

One of the defendants—the firm of Alpuro—claimed that Dutch calf fatteners were subject to stricter conditions than their competitors in other Member States and that this, in view of the fact that 90 per cent. of Dutch veal was produced for export—particularly to other Member States—was inevitably detrimental to the functioning of the common organisation of the market for beef and for milk and milk products.[29] Alpuro claimed that the rules in Article 2b of the "Koninklijk Besluit" of September 8, 1961 contravened, *inter alia*, the Community provisions on the common organisation of agricultural markets and Article 40(3) sub-paragraph 2 EEC, under which the common organisation must exclude any discrimination between producers within the Community.

In response, the Court of Justice first stated in general terms that under Community law as it then stood there were no specific provisions to protect farm animals.[30] On the two claims by the defendants the Court then ruled:

"As regards the rules on the common organization of the agricultural markets, it should in the first place be emphasized that the establishment of such an organization pursuant to Article 40 of the Treaty does not have the effect of exempting agricultural producers from

---

[29] Because skimmed milk is an essential food for fattening calves, according to Alpuro's submission.
[30] E.C.J., *loc. cit.*, footnote 28, para. 9.

any national provisions intended to attain objectives other than those covered by the common organization, even though such provisions may, by affecting the conditions of production, have an impact on the volume or the cost of national production and therefore on the operation of the Common Market in the sector concerned. The prohibition of any discrimination between producers in the Community, laid down in Article 40(3), refers to the objectives pursued by the common organization and not to the various conditions of production resulting from national rules which are general in character and pursue other objectives."[31]

The Court went on to state that in these circumstances the lack of any provisions to protect farm animals in regulations on the common organisation of agricultural markets could not be taken to imply that the national provisions had become inapplicable pending the possible subsequent enactment of Community provisions. Such an interpretation would be irreconcilable with the concern shown by the Community for the health and welfare of animals—as was clear from, *inter alia*, Article 36 EEC and a Council Resolution of June 19, 1978, (O.J. 1978, L323/12).[32]

The Court of Justice concluded that Community law as it then stood did not prevent the competent national agencies from retaining or adopting—for the animals' protection—unilateral rules on standard dimensions to be observed in the construction of calf boxes—rules which applied without differentiation both to calves intended for the internal market and to those intended for export.[33]

III. SUMMARY

The findings of our investigations in section D can be summarised by

---

[31] E.C.J., *loc. cit.*, footnote 28, para. 12. The Court of Justice ruled similarly in Case 222/78 *ICAP* v. *Walter Beneventi* [1979] E.C.R. 1163, paras. 15 and 16. Also comparable: Case 355/85 *Commissaire de police Driancourt* v. *Michel Coguet* [1986] E.C.R. 3231, paras. 8 *et seq.*; Joined Cases 80 & 159/85 *Nederlandse Bakkerij Stichting and Others* v. *EDAH B.V.* [1986] E.C.R. 3359, para. 23.

[32] E.C.J., *loc. cit.*, footnote 28, para. 13.

[33] E.C.J., *loc. cit.*, footnote 28, para. 14. See also judgments in: Case 86/78 *SA de grande Distillerie Pereux* v. *Directeur des Services fiscaux de la Haute-Saône et du Territoire de Belfort* [1979] E.C.R. 897, paras. 32 and 33 (on Article 95 EEC); Case 286/81 *Oosthoek's Uitgeversmaatschappij BV* [1982] E.C.R. 4575, para. 14 (on Articles 30 *et seq.* EEC); Joined Cases 7 & 9/54 *Groupement des Industries Sidérurgiques Luxembourgeoises* v. *High Authority* [1955–1956] E.C.R. 53 at 95, 96 (on Article 4b ECSC).

saying that, although the equality principle itself applies comprehensively, its application is restricted in two respects:

First, Community law is not contravened if traders who have entered into trading relations with third countries are treated unequally.

Secondly, disparity of treatment is automatically permitted if it arises from differences in national laws, regulations and administrative provisions.

E. THE EQUALITY OF MEMBER STATES UNDER COMMUNITY LAW

The requirement of equality of Member States under Community law is a manifestation of the equality principle in the form of a requirement of formal equality of application of the law, since it merely means that Community law must be applied *uniformly* in *all* Member States.[1] That in turn means, according to ECJ case-law, that the equality principle is also deemed to be infringed if an act of Community law is incompletely applied (I.) or if the Member States—if they are empowered to implement or execute such a legal act—unilaterally adopt supplementary or amending measures in excess of this power (II.).

I. INCOMPLETE APPLICATION OF A LEGAL ACT

1. Refusal to Implement or Execute

The application of a Community legal act is incomplete, first, if a Member State refuses to effect the necessary measures to implement or execute it. That this is an infringement of the equality principle could be deduced for the first time from a decision handed down in 1973 relating to the milk and milk products sector.[2] One of the points to be decided in that case was whether the Italian Republic, by not putting into effect the Community arrangements for the granting of non-marketing premiums

---

[1] For general comments on the requirement of formal equality of application of the law, see under A.III.1. above.
[2] Case 39/72 *Commission of the European Communities* v. *Italian Republic* [1973] E.C.R. 101.

for the products in question, was in breach of its duties under Regulations 1975/69[3] and 2195/69.[4]

The facts behind the case were as follows:

Regulation 1975/69 introduced a premium system aimed at reducing the surpluses of milk and milk products then existing in the Community by providing incentives for the slaughtering of dairy cows and the non-marketing of milk and milk products.

The necessary implementing procedures were adopted by the Commission in Regulation 2195/69; this Regulation made it incumbent on Member States to introduce, within precise time-limits, a package of implementing measures relating, for example, to the submission and checking of farmers' applications, registration of the declarations in which applicants undertook completely and finally to give up the production or sale of milk, and the payment of premiums to those eligible.

As a result of the two Regulations the competent national authorities had to accept applications for non-marketing premiums for milk and milk products from December 1, 1969 onwards, and the first premium instalments had to be paid over within three months of the lodging of the recipients' written undertakings.

Shortly after Regulations 1975/69 and 2195/69 came into force, the Italian Government brought a bill before the national Parliament containing all the provisions necessary for implementation of the system of slaughtering the non-marketing premiums; in addition, the Minister of Agriculture and Forestry instructed the provincial supervisory authorities, in anticipation of the expected law, to process the applications that had already been received.

However, in the course of the parliamentary debate doubts were expressed as to the wisdom of complying with the Community scheme of non-marketing premiums for milk and milk products; the upshot was that the provisions relating to the non-marketing premiums were cut out of the bill, with the result that these premiums were not—and never became—the subject of implementing measures in the Italian Republic.

The defendant attempted to justify its refusal to execute the provisions on non-marketing premiums by claiming that on account both of the special features of Italian agriculture and of the absence of an adequate infrastructure there would be difficulties in guaranteeing effective and

---

[3] Council Regulation 1975/69, O.J. 1969, L252/1.
[4] Commission Regulation 2195/69, O.J. 1969, L278/6.

convincing supervision and control of milk withdrawn from the market and intended for other uses. During the preparatory work on Regulation 1975/69 the Italian Government had made these difficulties known and since that time had expressed reservations about implementation of the Regulation. So, since the Regulation was adopted in the face of opposition from the Italian Republic, the defendant could not be reproached for having refused to execute the disputed provisions.

The Court of Justice stated on this point, first, that a (Council) regulation was deemed to have been validly issued in accordance with Article 43(2), third subparagraph EEC if the conditions set out in that article had been fulfilled and moreover that under Article 189 EEC a regulation was binding on the Member States "in its entirety." It was not acceptable that a Member State should apply the provisions of a Community regulation incompletely or selectively, thereby thwarting individual provisions which it opposed or which in its opinion ran counter to certain national interests.[5]

The Court of Justice further stated: particularly where implementation of an economic measure to reduce surpluses in certain products is involved, a Member State refusing to enact at the same time as the other Member States the provisions which it is required to enact jeopardises the efficacy of the jointly adopted measure and in so doing incidentally also obtains an unjustified advantage over its fellow Member States in relation to the free movement of goods.[6] If the defendant then cites in justification the preliminary work on the regulation in question, it should be noted that the general validity of a Community legal act cannot be modified by reservations or objections by Member States. Nor is it acceptable that difficulties in the performance of such a legal act should justify a Member State in unilaterally renouncing the fulfilment of its obligations; in this respect the Community's institutional system has provided the Member State concerned with the means necessary for ensuring that due account is taken of its difficulties whilst observing the principles of the common market and safeguarding the legitimate interests of the other Member States.[7]

In conclusion the Court of Justice stated:

> "In permitting Member States to profit from the advantages of the Community, the Treaty imposes on them also the obligation to

[5] E.C.J., *loc. cit.*, footnote 2, para. 20.
[6] E.C.J., *loc. cit.*, footnote 2, para. 21.
[7] E.C.J., *loc. cit.*, footnote 2, para. 22.

respect its rules. For the State unilaterally to break, according to its own conception of national interest, the equilibrium between advantages and obligations flowing from its adherence to the Community brings into question the equality of Member States before Community law and creates discriminations at the expense of their nationals, and above all of the nationals of the State itself which places itself outside the Community rules.

This failure in the duty of solidarity accepted by Member States by the fact of their adherence to the Community strikes at the fundamental basis of the Community legal order. It appears therefore that, in deliberately refusing to give effect on its territory to one of the systems provided for by Regulations Nos. 1975/69 and 2195/69, the Italian Republic has failed in a conspicuous manner to fulfil the obligations which it has assumed by virtue of its adherence to the European Economic Community."[8]

2. Delay in Implementation or Performance

Application of a Community legal act is also deemed to be incomplete if the measures necessary for its implementation or performance have not been taken within a reasonable time. That this also violates the equality principle can be deduced indirectly from a 1970 decision on the law relating to refunds.[9] In that case one of the points to be clarified was whether a Member State which fails to pay out on time the refunds provided for in a Community regulation had failed to fulfil an obligation within the meaning of Article 169 EEC.

The background to this decision was as follows:

By a number of regulations, all of which came into force on July 1, 1967, the Council had established a common organisation of the market for various agricultural products—including in particular fats, cereals, pig-

---

[8] E.C.J., *loc. cit.*, footnote 2, paras. 24 and 25. A similar ruling—referring to this passage—was given in Case 128/78 *Commission of the European Communities* v. *United Kingdom of Great Britain and Northern Ireland* [1979] E.C.R. 419, paras. 12 and 13. See also judgment in Joined Cases 52 & 55/65 *Federal Republic of Germany* v. *Commission of the EEC* [1966] E.C.R. 219 at 237.
[9] Case 31/69 *Commission of the European Communities* v. *Italian Republic* [1970] E.C.R. 25.

meat, eggs, poultry and rice—which involved, *inter alia*, the Commission's fixing uniform refunds for the whole Community for exports to third countries.

On December 21, 1967 the Commission issued Regulation 1041/67,[10] containing detailed rules for the implementation of these refunds. The Regulation obliged every Member State on whose territory the customs formalities for the exports were carried out to pay the refunds to the exporters upon application from the latter.

In a letter dated February 27, 1968 the Commission drew the Italian Government's attention to the fact that, among other things, no refunds had been paid in Italy since July 1, 1967 in respect of products of the kind specified, which in the Commission's view was a contravention of the rules on export refunds for those products.

The Italian Government replied that Decree-Law No. 59 of February 20, 1968 contained basic rules making the refunds applicable and that, moreover, this Decree-Law had made possible the release of 99 billion lire to cover the expenditure for 1968; it only remained for a few ministerial orders to come into force governing the administrative procedures necessary for putting into effect—in particular—the advance payments to exporters provided for in Article 9 of Regulation 1041/67.

In a letter dated June 20, 1968 the Commission pointed out that refunds had still not been granted in Italy in respect of any product covered by the common organisation of the market. The Commission finally brought the matter before the Court of Justice under Article 169 EEC, asking the Court to rule that the Italian Republic had infringed the above-mentioned regulations owing to its failure to make punctual payment of the refunds in respect of exports effected after July 1, 1967.

The Court of Justice first of all stated on this point as follows:

> "The entry into force on 1 July 1967 of an organization of the markets in various agricultural products with a single price and uniform levies and refunds for the entire Community involves for the exporters concerned the right to receive the said refunds and a duty on the part of the Member States to advance them, the sums advanced being reimbursed half-yearly to the States by the Commission.
>
> Although those provisions and especially Regulation No. 1041/67/EEC, allow the Member States a certain area of discretion, *inter alia*, in fixing the documents which constitute proof of the right to the

[10] Commission Regulation 1041/67, O.J. 1967, 314/9.

refund, they nevertheless involve a duty for the States to make the payment within a reasonable period in order to avoid treating exporters differently according to the frontier over which their products are exported."[11]

The Court of Justice then pointed out that the Commission was maintaining that the Italian Government had required 12 to 18 months to make the repayments, whereas the other Member States had made them within a much shorter time.[12] Nevertheless, the Court of Justice, considering the Commission's evidence not to have been sufficient to prove its case, finally ruled that there had been no infringement of the law within the meaning of Article 169 EEC and rejected the complaint.[13]

II. UNILATERAL SUPPLEMENTARY OR AMENDING MEASURES

The requirement of equality of application of the law is also deemed to be infringed if a Member State—where it is empowered to implement or execute a Community legal act—unilaterally adopts supplementary or amending measures in excess of this power; for such conduct, too, leads to the unequal application of Community law from one country to another and therefore means that Community law is not—as required—applied *uniformly* in *all* Member States.

1. Formal Measures

As far as formal supplementary or amending measures are concerned, the first Court of Justice decision to be mentioned here was delivered in 1972 on the law on refunds.[14] One of the points at issue was whether Member States may compel sugar exporters, with reference to their Community-law-based eligibility to refunds, to submit (additional) applications, which must be completed in the form prescribed by national law.

This question had arisen in the course of a preliminary hearing instituted by the Finance Court of Hamburg. The background to that hearing was as follows:

---

[11] E.C.J., *loc. cit.*, footnote 9, para. 15. See also the judgment (quoted under E.I.1.) in Case 39/72 [1973] E.C.R. 101, para. 14 (relating to slaughtering premiums).
[12] E.C.J., *loc. cit.*, footnote 9, para. 16.
[13] E.C.J., *loc. cit.*, footnote 9, paras. 17 to 23.
[14] See Case 94/71 *Schlüter & Maack* v. *Hauptzollamt Hamburg-Jonas* [1972] E.C.R. 307.

Regulation 1009/67,[15] by which the common organisation of the market for sugar was established, provided, in its Article 17, for a system of export refunds intended to compensate for the difference between sugar prices officially quoted or actually charged on the world market and Community prices. Article 17(2) stipulated that the refunds should be paid upon application by the exporters; Article 10 of Regulation 1041/67[16] required these payments to be made by the Member State on whose territory the customs formalities for the exports had been effected.

To put these provisions into effect, the Federal Republic of Germany issued an Order on EEC Export Refunds, § 6 of which stipulated among other things that the application to the competent customs authority for refunds had to be submitted in a prescribed form; incidentally, the German authorities also required that this application, like the documents mentioned in Article 10 of Regulation 1041/67, had to be submitted within the time-limit of six months laid down in the Commission Regulation.

In its submission the German Government claimed that execution of a Community regulation basically had to follow the formal and procedure requirements of national law, if—as here—it was the responsibility of the national authorities.

The Court of Justice ruled on this point as follows:

"This principle of law must be reconciled with the need to apply Community law uniformly so as to avoid unequal treatment of exporters depending on the frontier across which they export their products. Since the document referred to in Article 1 of Regulation No. 1041/67 has all the characteristics of the exporter's application under Article 17 of Regulation No. 1009/67, it is not necessary, inasmuch as the right to a refund is linked with the making of an application, to make this right conditional upon requirements other than those laid down in Article 1 of Regulation No. 1041/67. Although Member States may, therefore, for reasons of administrative organization, require exporters also to make an application in the form prescribed by national law, they may not, however, punish failure to fulfil this obligation by forfeiture of the right to a refund."[17]

---

[15] Council Regulation 1009/67, O.J. 308/1.
[16] Commission Regulation 1041/67, O.J. 314/9.
[17] E.C.J., *loc. cit.*, footnote 14, para. 11. See also Case 50/76 *Amsterdam Bulb B.V.* v. *Produktschap voor Siergewassen* [1977] E.C.R. 137, paras. 4 to 7.

Another decision which may be mentioned in this connection is the 1981 ruling on the refinancing of aids paid for the denaturing of skimmed milk powder.[18] The specific point at issue was whether the expenditure should also be borne by the EAGGF if the system of control of denaturing practised by a Member State differed from that prescribed by Community law.

The facts of the case were as follows:

Regulation 986/68[19] laid down the ground rules for the granting of aids for skimmed milk and skimmed milk powder for animal feed. Article 3(2) stipulated that the aid should not be paid until evidence of the denaturing of skimmed milk powder or processing into mixed fodder had been produced.

In implementation of this provision, Article 3 of Regulation 990/72[20] provided in respect of denatured skimmed milk powder that the denaturing should be inspected on site, that each Member State should nominate an agency responsible for carrying out this inspection and that the denaturing unit should send this agency in good time before the denaturing took place a written notification stating: its name and address, the quantity of skimmed milk powder that was to be denatured and the place and time of the denaturing; Article 10 required the Member States to take the necessary inspection measures to ensure compliance with the provisions of this regulation.

The files on the case showed that the system of denaturing inspection introduced by the German authorities at that time was based less on a direct inspection on site than on an audit of the books of the undertakings involved in the denaturing.

In view of these circumstances, the Commission refused to accept that an amount of DM 8,335,232.61 spent by the Federal Republic of Germany on aids for the denaturing of skimmed milk powder for the financial year 1973 should be charged against the EAGGF. The Commission contended that the inspection carried out by the German authorities did not oblige the denaturing units to provide the information mentioned in Article 3(2) of Regulation 990/72 on the time and place of denaturing and on the quantity of skimmed milk powder to be denatured; this informa-

---

[18] cf. Case 819/79 *Federal Republic of Germany* v. *Commission of the European Communities* [1981] E.C.R. 21.
[19] Council Regulation 986/68, O.J. 1968, L169/4.
[20] Commission Regulation 990/72, O.J. 1972, L115/1.

tion was necessary to make it possible to carry out the on-site inspection provided for in paragraph 1 of the same article.

The view was taken in the Federal Republic of Germany, however, that the disputed inspection system was more effective than that provided for by Article 3 of Regulation 990/72.

On this matter the Court of Justice first pointed out that it was a prerequisite for a Commission decision on expenditure to be borne by the EAGGF that the Commission should establish that expenditure by the national agencies had been effected in accordance with Community law. The granting of an aid did not, however, accord with Community law if it took place without the required evidential and inspection formalities having been complied with; it was therefore basically impermissible for the related expenditure to be accepted as a charge on the EAGGF.[21]

The Court of Justice further stated that Regulation 990/72 provided for inspection of denaturing on site in order to ensure an effective check on the proper performance of the denaturing and to prevent the granting of more than one aid in respect of the same batch of product. For the purpose of this inspection the undertakings were required to provide certain information to the competent national agency under Article 3(2) of the Regulation before the denaturing was carried out. When Article 10 stipulated that the Member States "shall take all measures necessary to ensure that the provisions laid down in this Regulation are complied with," this referred to all the provisions of the regulation, including Article 3.[22]

Finally the Court of Justice declared:

"In these circumstances it is not necessary to consider the soundness of the German Government's argument that the supervision system set up in the Federal Republic is more effective than that provided for in Article 3 of Regulation No. 990/72. In fact, the provisions of Community regulations must be uniformly applied in all the Member States and have, so far as possible, the same effect throughout the territory of the Community. The position is no different where a regulation lays down specific measures of supervision but leaves to Member States the task of ensuring their observance by appropriate administrative measures."[23]

---

[21] E.C.J., *loc. cit.*, footnote 18, para. 8.
[22] E.C.J., *loc. cit.*, footnote 18, para. 9.
[23] E.C.J., *loc. cit.*, footnote 18, para. 10. See also Case 12/70 *Paul Craeynest and others* v. *Belgian State* [1970] E.C.R. 905, paras. 5 to 8.

2. Substantive Measures

Member States are also deemed to have infringed the requirement of equality of application of the law if they unilaterally adopt substantive supplementary or amending measures. This was ruled by the Court of Justice in, for example, a 1979 decision on the refinancing of aids paid for the distillation of wine[24]; the specific point at issue was whether the expenditure—permissible under Community law—was also acceptable as a charge on EAGGF funds if Member States had introduced an additional aid.

The facts of the case were as follows:

In its Regulation 816/70[25] the Council had adopted additional provisions for the common organisation of the market for wine; Article 7 of the Regulation stipulated that distillation measures could be enacted if there was a danger that the granting of aids for the private storage of table wine would not by itself lead to a stabilization of prices.

In expectation that this condition would be fulfilled owing to the good harvest of 1970/71, the Council gave the go-ahead for distillation by issuing Regulation 766/72[26] and to this end introduced an aid.

The French Government, considering both the minimum price and the level of aid provided for under this arrangement to be inadequate, introduced an additional aid on a national basis.

Owing to this action, the Commission refused to accept as a charge on the EAGGF the aid paid at the rates prescribed by Regulation 766/72. It contended that the French Government, by extending the distillation arrangements to cover far larger quantities of wine than would have been put into distillation on the basis of the Community arrangements alone, had distorted the distillation arrangements as a whole.

The Court of Justice first stated on this point as follows:

"In applying Community rules the Member States cannot unilaterally adopt additional measures which are such as to compromise the equality of treatment of traders throughout the Community and thus to distort competitive conditions between the Member States."[27]

---

[24] *cf.* Joined Cases 15 & 16/76 *French Government* v. *Commission of the European Communities* [1979] E.C.R. 321.
[25] Council Regulation 816/70 of April 28, 1970, J.O. 1970, L99/1; O.J. Sp.Ed. 1970, 234.
[26] Council Regulation 766/72 of April 17, 1972, O.J. 1972, L91/1.
[27] E.C.J., footnote 24, para. 31.

The Court went on to rule that the French action was consequently incompatible with Community law. It was therefore impossible to establish what quantities of wine would have been put into distillation without this national measure and the Commission thus had absolutely no choice but to refuse to accept the expenditure as a charge on the EAGGF.[28]

A second decision important in this connection also dates from 1979.[29] Here the Court of Justice dealt with the question whether national potato-market regulations can prevent Articles 30 *et seq.* EEC from being fully effective even after the transitional period is over.

The case arose from the following facts:

The United Kingdom, before its accession to the Community, operated a national potato marketing scheme, which included controls over the import and export of main-crop potatoes. When, in 1977, the Commission pointed out to the British Government that the import restrictions would have to be lifted, the British Ministry of Agriculture nevertheless indicated that the prohibition on imports of this kind of potato would be maintained until further notice.

In the Commission's opinion, the United Kingdom, by failing to lift the import restrictions after the expiry of the transitional period on December 31, 1977, was in breach of the duties imposed on it by Article 30 EEC.

The British Government claimed that it was entitled under Article 60 in conjunction with Article 9(2) of the Act of Accession to maintain restrictions on imports until the application of a common organisation of the market; since potatoes were not yet covered by such an organisation, it did not have to terminate the national potato marketing scheme.

This interpretation the Court of Justice held, first, to be untenable, in view of the meaning and purpose of the Act of Accession and its connection with the provisions of the EEC Treaty.[30] Moreover, it would have unacceptable consequences for the equality of Member States *vis-à-vis* certain basic rules for the functioning of the common market.

Specifically, the Court stated:

"This conclusion is confirmed by a consideration of the consequences which would ensue from the alternative interpretation advocated by the United Kingdom. In a matter as essential for the

---

[28] E.C.J., *loc. cit.*, footnote 24, paras. 32 to 36.

[29] *cf.* Case 231/78 *Commission of the European Communities* v. *United Kingdom of Great Britain and Northern Ireland* [1979] E.C.R. 1447.

[30] E.C.J., *loc. cit.*, paras. 10 to 16.

proper functioning of the common market as the elimination of quantitative restrictions, the Act of Accession cannot be interpreted as having established for an indefinite period in favour of the new Member States a legal position different from that laid down by the Treaty for the original Member States. If Article 60(2) were regarded as a 'special provision' within the meaning of Article 9(2) of the Act of Accession, it would in effect establish a persisting inequality between the original Member States and the new Member States, the latter being in a position to prevent or restrict the importation of certain agricultural products coming from the Community, whereas the former would be obliged under the Treaty to refrain from any restriction on imports of the same products, even if they came from a new Member State which was making use of Article 60(2). Although it was justified for the original Member States provisionally to accept such inequalities, it would be contrary to the principle of the equality of the Member States before Community law to accept that such inequalities could continue indefinitely."[31]

III. SUMMARY

As we have shown in section E, the equality principle in the form of the requirement of formal equality of application of the law is deemed to be infringed if a Member State applies a Community legal act incompletely or if it amends or supplements it by additional measures.

The application of such a legal act is deemed to be incomplete, first, if the Member State concerned refuses to take the measures necessary for its implementation or performance.

Secondly, a Member State is deemed to apply a Community legal act incompletely if it delays implementing or performing such a legal act.

All types of amending or supplementary measures are deemed to infringe the requirement of formal equality of application of the law irrespective of their legal character; this stricture therefore covers both formal and substantive measures.

---

[31] E.C.J., *loc. cit.*, footnote 29, para. 17. See also: Case 39/70 *Norddeutsches Vieh- und Fleischkontor GmbH* v. *Hauptzollamt Hamburg St. Annen* [1971] E.C.R. 49, paras. 4 and 5; Case 93/71 *Orsolina Leonesio* v. *Italian Ministry of Agriculture* [1972] E.C.R. 287, paras. 21 to 23; Case 131/73 *Giulio and Adriano Grosoli* [1973] E.C.R. 1555, para. 8.

F.   CONCLUSION

Overall, we can conclude that nowadays the equality principle as a substantive legal tenet is not only observed in national constitutional and administrative law but is also binding on the public authorities under Community law, which takes precedence over the law of individual Member States.

Since the equality principle as such is not explicitly guaranteed under the Treaties, it was necessary to investigate whether its validity was derived from decisions of the Court of Justice.

The point of departure here was the anti-discrimination provisions enshrined in the Treaties, together with the concept of discrimination itself, on the basis of which the content of the anti-discrimination provisions can be determined in detail.

The concept of "discrimination" originated in American law; it is generally understood in the sense it acquired in that country, that is to say as differentiation or different treatment which is "unjust" or "unlawful" and therefore arbitrary.[1]

Consequently, every prohibition of discrimination can be seen as a case of application of the equality principle.

For beyond the classic requirement that like should be treated in like manner but unlike—in keeping with its characteristic features—should be treated in unlike manner,[2] the equality principle ultimately requires only that there should be no arbitrarily like or unlike treatment.[3]

In the Court of Justice's decisions the structure of the discrimination prohibitions is judged accordingly.[4] The Court has ruled, for example, that the discrimination prohibition in the sphere of agriculture as laid down in the second subparagraph of Article 40(3) EEC is "merely a specific enunciation of the general principle of equality" and that it therefore also applies—going beyond its actual wording—when relations between different branches of commerce and industry are involved.[5]

---

[1] See under A.VI.1. above.
[2] See under A.III.2. above.
[3] See under A.IV. above.
[4] See under A.VI.2. above.
[5] Thus for example Joined Cases 117/76 & 16/77 *Albert Ruckdeschel & Co. and others* v. *Hauptzollamt Hamburg St. Annen*; Joined Cases 124/76 & 20/77 *S. A. Moulins et Huileries de Pont-à-Mousson and others* v. *Office National Interprofessionnel des Céréales*; Case 4/79 *Société Coopérative Providence Agricole de la Champagne* v. *Office National Interprofessionnel des Céréales* [1977] E.C.R. 1753, paras. 7, 1812 *et seq.*, paras. 14 to 17; Case 125/77 *Koninklijke Scholten-Honig NV and others* v. *Hoofd-*

This already follows by inference from many judgments handed down by the Court of Justice on the concept of discrimination, all of which signify that even discrimination prohibited under Community law presupposes that there has been arbitrary differentiation.

Specifically, the Court has ruled that discrimination has occurred if like is treated in unlike manner or unlike in like manner, the comparability or otherwise of the objects being compared being ascertained on the basis of objective criteria.[6] Differentiation is also deemed to be arbitrary if the like or unlike treatment in question is not objectively justified.[7]

If it is so justified, it cannot be prohibited discrimination; whether or not the treatment has in fact been different then becomes irrelevant.

In the light of this case-law, the Court of Justice finally felt prompted to characterise the equality principle, in the context of its above-quoted pronouncement on the structure of the discrimination prohibitions, as a "basic principle of Community law."[8]

When the Court of Justice describes the equality principle in this way, it is doubtless indicating that it recognises the principle as such and that such recognition is consequently very wide and does not apply only to the areas of activity in respect of which discrimination prohibitions have been enacted.

This, incidentally, follows indirectly from the fact that the equality principle is nowadays also sometimes said to be applicable when no discrimination prohibition appears to apply to the specific case—as the Court has demonstrated by the example of the financial provisions of the EEC Treaty.[9]

However, the equality principle has also been mentioned, for example, in connection with "self-binding" by the executive; that means that it has achieved importance not only as a principle of Community constitutional law, but also as a specific administrative-law principle.[10]

---

produktschap voor Akkerbouwprodukten, and Joined Cases 103 & 145/77 *Royal Scholten-Honig (Holdings) Ltd. and others* v. *Intervention Board for Agricultural Produce* [1978] E.C.R. 1991, paras. 25 to 27, pp. 2037 *et seq.*, paras. 25 to 27; Case 245/81 *Edeka Zentrale AG* v. *Federal Republic of Germany* [1982] E.C.R. 2745, para. 11; Case 59/83 *SA Biovilac NV* v. *European Economic Community* [1984] E.C.R. 4057, para. 19; see also Case 215/85 *Bundesanstalt für landwirtschaftliche Marktordnung* v. *Raiffeisen Hauptgenossenschaft eG* [1987] E.C.R. 1297, para. 23.

[6] See under B.I. and B.II.1. above.

[7] See under B.II.2. above.

[8] See the judgments just quoted in footnote 5.

[9] Case 265/78 *H. Ferwerda BV* v. *Produktschap voor Vee en Vlees* [1980] E.C.R. 617 *et seq.*, para. 7; Joined Cases 66 & 127–128/79, *Amministrazione delle Finanze dello Stato* v. *Meridionale Industria Salumi Srl and others* [1980] E.C.R. 1237, para. 14.

[10] See under C.II. above.

It may further be noted here that self-binding by the executive may be accepted, even by the Court of Justice, only if the authority in question has acted lawfully.[11] Similar to, for example, German law,[12] Community law observes the principle that there can be no claim to equality of treatment in an unlawful situation.

When the Court of Justice defines the content of the equality principle, it refers to its decisions on the concept of discrimination. It thus reduces the principle to the classic formula that "similar situations shall not be treated differently unless differentiation is objectively justified."[13]

Although the validity of the equality principle itself extends very widely, there are two areas to which it does not apply.

First, in its external relations, the Community is not obliged to treat all third countries—and hence all market participants who trade with third countries—equally in every respect[14]; secondly, there can be no appeal to the equality principle in the case of unequal treatment springing from differences in national legislation—provided that the Member States are, and continue to be, competent to pass such legislation.[15] In the latter case there is a parallel with the legal situation in a country with a federal constitution. Thus with reference to the federal structure of the Federal Republic of Germany, the Federal Constitutional Court does not regard it as an infringement of the equality principle if a *Land*, within the scope of its powers, adopts regulations which do not correspond to similar regulations in other *Länder*.[16]

The equality principle is further understood as a requirement of formal equality in the application of the law, in that it implies that Community law must be applied uniformly in all Member States.

---

[11] Thus for example the E.C.J. in Case 119/81 *Klöckner-Werke AG* v. *Commission of the European Communities* [1982] E.C.R. 2627, paras. 18 and 19; in Case 14/59 *Société des Fonderies de Pont-à-Mousson* v. *High Authority* [1958–1959] E.C.R. 465 at 494; also recently in Case 188/83 *Hermann Witte* v. *European Parliament* [1984] E.C.R. 3465, para. 15; in Case 246/83 (*De Angelis*), para. 17; in Case 134/84 (*Williams*), paras. 21 *et seq*. See also for example H. Lecheler, *Die allgemeinen Rechtsgrundsätze in der Rechtsprechung des Europäischen Gerichtshofs*, Erlangen-Nürnberg 1967, p. 102.

[12] *cf*. for example I. von Münch, *Grundgesetzkommentar*, Vol. I, (3rd ed., Munich 1985), paragraph 36 on Article 3; P. Badura, *Staatsrecht*, Munich 1986, p. 99, paragraph 44; H. P. Ipsen, "Gleichheit," in F. L. Neumann, H. C. Nipperdey, U. Scheuner (ed.), *Die Grundrechte*, Vol. 2, Berlin 1968, pp. 111 *et seq*. (147 *et seq*.); see also H. Lecheler, *op. cit.*, p. 102 with references to German law.

[13] See the judgments just quoted in footnote 5.

[14] See under D.I. above.

[15] See under D.II. above.

[16] See the references in footnote 11 in section D above.

The equality principle is thus also deemed to be infringed if a Member State applies a Community legal act incompletely or if it amends or supplements it by additional measures.[17]

It can also be seen from the Court of Justice's case-law that the Court, by analogy with French law, has developed a number of groups of cases intended to provide a more concrete definition of the equality principle under various different aspects. Examples are the requirements of equality of the sexes[18] and of equality of exposure to public charges[19] and the idea of "reverse discrimination"[20]; in addition, there is the requirement addressed to Member States that when, in application of their own national law, they recover incorrectly paid Community aids or levy Community charges which have erroneously not been levied earlier, they "must be effected in a non-discriminatory manner having regard to the

---

[17] See under E above.

[18] e.g. Case 80/80 Defrenne I v. Belgian State [1971] E.C.R. 445; Case 43/75 Defrenne II v. SABENA [1976] E.C.R. 455; Case 149/77 Defrenne III v. SABENA [1978] E.C.R. 1365; Case 19/81 Burton v. British Railways Board [1982] E.C.R. 555; Case 23/83 Liefting v. Academisch Ziekenhuis bij de Universiteit van Amsterdam [1984] E.C.R. 3225; see also for example O. Quintin, L'égalité entre hommes et femmes: une réalisation spécifique de la politique sociale communautaire, RMC 1985, pp. 309 et seq. For the latest case law see also the references in M. Hilf, "Rechtsprechungsbericht," 2nd half of 1984 and 1st and 2nd quarters of 1985, EuGRZ 1985, pp. 343 et seq. (346), pp. 647 et seq. (648); 1986, pp. 456 et seq. (457); see also Case 150/85 Jacqueline Drake v. Chief Adjudication Officer [1986] E.C.R. 1995, paras. 27 et seq.; Case 237/85 Gisela Rummler v. Dato-Druck GmbH [1986] E.C.R. 2101, paras. 13 et seq.

[19] e.g. Joined Cases 14, 16–17, 20, 24, 26–27/60 & 1/61 Meroni and others v. High Authority [1961] E.C.R. 345; Case 111/63 Lemmerz-Werke GmbH v. High Authority [1965] E.C.R. 893; cf. also H. Lecheler, op. cit., footnote 11, pp. 87 et seq.; G. Zieger, "Die Recht-sprechung des Europäischen Gerichtshofs," JÖR NF Vol. 22 (1973), pp. 299 et seq. (311 et seq.). On the question of liability for infringement of this principle, cf. Advocate-General Mayras' opinion in Joined Cases 9 & 11/71 Compagnie d'Approvisionnement v. Commission of the European Communities [1972] E.C.R. 391 at 425 et seq.

[20] cf. Case 39/72 Commission v. Italy [1973] E.C.R. 101; Case 57/72 Westzucker v. Einfuhr-und Vorratsstelle für Zucker [1973] E.C.R. 321; cf. on the other hand also Case 78/76 Steinicke und Wesseling v. Federal Republic of Germany [1977] E.C.R. 595, and Case 86/78 Grandes Distilleries Peureux v. Directeur des Services Fiscaux de la Haute-Saône et du Territoire de Belfort [1979] E.C.R. 897; cf. also for example M.-A. Reitmaier, Inländerdiskriminierungen nach dem EWG-Vertrag, Kehl am Rhein/Strasbourg 1984; H. Schlachter, Discrimination à rebours. Die Inländerdiskriminierung nach der Recht-sprechung des EuGH und des französischen Conseil d'Etat, 1984; H. Weis, "Inländerdis-kriminierung zwischen Gemeinschaftsrecht und nationalem Verfassungsrecht," NJW 1983, pp. 2721 et seq.; A. Bleckmann, "Die umgekehrte Diskriminierung (discrimination à rebours) im EWG-Vertrag," RIW 1985, pp. 917 et seq.; S. D. Kon, "Aspects of Reverse Discrimination in Community Law," E.L.Rev., Vol. 6, 1981, pp. 75 et seq.; K. J. Mortelmans, "Omgekeerde discriminatie en het gemeenschapsrecht," SEW 1979, pp. 654 et seq.; see also Joined Cases 80/85 & 159/85 Nederlandse Bakkerij Stichting and Others v. EDAH B.V. [1986] E.C.R. 3358, paras. 22 et seq.

procedural rules relating to disputes of the same type, although purely national."[21]

Overall, the recognition of the equality principle in Community law is also based on comparative-law considerations: the Court of Justice sometimes refers expressly to the way the Member States regulate certain matters, as when it defines the concept of discrimination in Article 4(b) ECSC[22] and when it declares that the equality principle is applicable to the system of financial provisions contained in the EEC Treaty.[23]

It is clear from an overall assessment of the development of the relevant law that the equality principle has taken on a similar character in European Community law to that which it has acquired in German national public law.[24] As a fundamental legal principle it gives considerable protection to the citizens of the Community.

Owing to the relative flexibility with which its content may be interpreted, however, the usefulness of the equality principle as a political instrument depends in large measure on its continuing definition in specific cases. For that reason continual judicial review is clearly indispensable, as the former President of the Court of Justice, Hans Kutscher, emphasised so appositely when he responded to criticism by saying: "To leave equality under the law unprotected by judicial review would be most unwise."[25]

---

[21] Thus the E.C.J. in Case 265/78 *H. Ferwerda BV* v. *Produktschap voor Vee en Vlees*, *loc. cit.*, footnote 9, para. 10; *cf.* also Joined Cases 66, 127 & 128/79 *Amministrazione delle Finanze dello Stato* v. *Meridionale Salumi Srl and Others*, *loc. cit.*, footnote 9, para. 20. Also—with references to earlier decisions—Joined Cases 205–215/82 *Deutsche Milchkontor GmbH and others* v. *Federal Republic of Germany* [1983] E.C.R. 2633 *et seq.*, para. 19.

[22] *cf.* Cases 8/57 *Groupement des Hauts Fourneaux et Aciéries Belges* v. *High Authority* and 13/57 *Wirtschaftsvereinigung Eisen- und Stahlindustrie and others* v. *High Authority*; Cases 9/57 *Chambre Syndicale de la Sidérurgie Française* v. *High Authority*; 10/57 *Société des Anciens Etablissements Aubert et Duval* v. *High Authority*; 11/57 *Société d'Electro-Chimie and others* v. *High Authority*; 12/57 *Syndicat de la Sidérurgie du Centre-Midi* v. *High Authority* [1958] E.C.R. 231 at 257, 271 at 304 *et seq.*, 381 at 408, 421 at 445 *et seq.*, 459, at 483 *et seq.*, and 497 at 523 *et seq.* See under B.II.1. above.

[23] See the judgments quoted in footnote 9.

[24] See in particular the parallel with the interpretation of the equality principle as a prohibition of arbitrary action. See, specifically with regard to German law, K. Hesse, *Grundzüge des Verfassungsrechts der Bundesrepublik Deutschland* (15th ed., Heidelberg 1985), paragraph 438, with copious references and the author's own critical comments.

[25] See H. Kutscher, "Judicial Review of Supreme Courts and the Principle of Equality under the Law—The Role of the Bundesverfassungsgericht in Insuring Equality under the Law," Jahrbuch des Öffentlichen Rechts, N.F. Vol. 9 (1960), p. 197, 201.

PART II

CHAPTER 5

THE PRINCIPLE OF PROPORTIONALITY

A. INTRODUCTION

The proportionality principle has recently been described as "the most important general legal principle in Common Market law."[1] A mere glance at the case law of the European Court of Justice will suffice to confirm this assessment.

Whereas the proportionality principle made but an occasional and insubstantial appearance in the early decisions of the Court of Justice,[2] it has acquired an extremely important role in the judicial review of administrative decisions and rules since 1970. It should at all times be regarded as the overriding principle seeking to restrict the scope of Community rules which impose duties.[3]

Although a large number of publications have appeared on the subject of the proportionality principle, no satisfactory explanation appears to have been provided as yet for the precise scope of the Community law principle of proportionality. The Court has indeed frequently held in its decisions that measures adopted must be proportionate to the pursued

---

[1] J. Gündisch, "Allgemeine Rechtsgrundsätze in der Rechtsprechung des Europäischen Gerichtshof," in *Das Wirtschaftsrecht des Gemeinsamen Marktes in der aktuellen Rechtsentwicklung*, (1983) Baden-Baden, pp. 97 *et seq.*, 108.

[2] *cf.*, *e.g.* Case 8/55 *Fédération Charbonnière de Belgique* v. *High Authority* [1955–1956] E.C.R. 297 at 311.

[3] This is correctly pinpointed in G. Ress, "Der Grundsatz der Verhältnismässigkeit im deutschen Recht," in H. Kutscher (Joint ed.), *Der Grundsatz der Verhältnismässigkeit in europäischen Rechtsordnungen, Vorträge und Diskussionsbeiträge auf der Dt.-Franz. Juristenkonferenz am 26/27 November in Strassburg*, (1985) Heidelberg, pp. 5 *et seq.*, 38, containing further references; *cf.* also K.-V. Schiller, "Der Verhältnismässigkeitsgrundsatz im Europäischen Gemeinschaftsrecht nach der Rechtsprechung des EuGH" (1983) RIW, pp. 928 *et seq.*

677

objective, or that a certain measure was not "necessary" in order to achieve the desired effect.

However, the question as to which specific measures are regarded by the Court as being proportionate or disproportionate has not as yet been studied in any great depth. There also persists a certain degree of ambiguity on the subject of the extent to which the Community law proportionality principle is applicable in assessing the legality of national measures.

An overall review of the case law of the Court of Justice to date gives us the opportunity to improve our understanding of these issues and goes a long way towards giving satisfactory replies to those questions which remain unsolved.

Accordingly, this chapter will be concerned mainly with a study of the relevant case law. Prior to this, however, we must consider the theoretical basis of the proportionality principle, *i.e.* the concept, its role, the extent to which it has been recognised in other legal systems and its application in Community law. It is only by considering its intellectual roots that the development of this legal principle can be studied with the necessary clarity and depth.

B.   THE CONCEPT OF PROPORTIONALITY

I.   HISTORICAL ORIGINS

The notion which lies at the root of the proportionality principle can be traced back to ancient times. To engage in an extensive discourse on the many ways in which this principle has been expressed throughout the ages would, however, be to exceed by far the scope of this discussion.[1]

For the purpose of understanding the proportionality principle as it is expressed in the current case law of the European Court of Justice, it would appear sufficient to highlight two main schools of thought which have shaped the historical development of this principle from its inception.

On the one hand, there are the principles of retributive justice (*justitia*

---

[1] For an extensive treatment of this subject, *cf.* F. Wieacker, "Geschichtliche Wurzeln des Prinzips der verhältnismässigen Rechtsanwendung," in *Festschrift für Robert Fischer*, (1979) Berlin, New York, pp. 867 *et seq.*; *cf.* also L. Hirschberg, *Der Grundsatz der Verhältnismässigkeit*, (1981) Göttingen, pp. 2 *et seq.*

vindicativa) and of appropriate distributive justice (*justitia distributiva*); on the other hand, we find the notion of the liberal state, which has been making a steady advance since the end of the nineteenth century and which holds that the state should restrict itself to the achievement of objectives which are limited or capable of limitation. This source of the proportionality principle, which is no longer directly concerned with the notion of justice, is based on the premise that the law must serve a useful purpose, *i.e.* be geared to the objective it seeks to achieve, and must consequently form part of a quantifiable causal relationship between means and ends aimed at achieving a desired result.

The jurisprudential basis for this idea was developed to a considerable extent by Ihering, who, in his works entitled "Der Zweck im Recht" and "Der Kampf um's Recht" laid particular emphasis on the result element which is inherent in the law.[2] Accordingly, where intervention by the public authorities is justified by reference to social objectives, such intervention must be limited by its effectiveness and consequently also by its proportionality in relation to the interest it seeks to defend. Thus there is a causal relationship between the ends and the means as well as a normative link between the applicability of various legal rules.

II. THE ROLE OF THE PROPORTIONALITY PRINCIPLE

In the course of the last 100 years, the current protective role of the proportionality principle has developed under the influence of the natural law school.[3]

To the extent that the omnipotence of the State is made subject to certain limitations, fundamental rights and other subjective rights enjoyed by the individual are to be given their true importance.

Thus the main purpose of the proportionality principle is to give substance and meaning to the protection of fundamental freedoms. Since its effectiveness is not linked to a particular fundamental right, but covers the entire range of fundamental freedoms, it serves, in abstract terms, the purpose of achieving a proper balance and consequently also the furtherance of the principle of justice.

[2] F. Wieacker, *loc. cit.*, footnote 1, pp. 879 *et seq.*
[3] *cf.* on this subject: *Das Naturrechtsdenken heute und morgen, Gedächtnisschrift für René Marcic* (1983) Berlin.

C. THE PROPORTIONALITY PRINCIPLE IN THE LEGAL SYSTEMS OF THE MEMBER STATES AND IN INTERNATIONAL LAW

The Community law proportionality principle is often explained by reference to a principle which is common to the various national legal systems[1] and recognised in international law.[2] Accordingly, before explaining the concrete substance of the Community law proportionality principle, we must make a comparative law study of the various forms which this principle has assumed both in the national legal systems and in international law.

I. THE LEGAL SYSTEMS OF THE MEMBER STATES

1. France

The proportionality principle has never been fully recognised as a general legal principle in French legal circles.[3]

In spite of this, the idea that infringements of civil liberties must be accompanied by guarantees of proportionality is not totally absent from French law.[4] More particularly in the field of administrative law, which admits of no obligation to weigh up the interests involved,[5] the proportionality principle has been applied in certain areas.

The traditional area in which the proportionality principle is tested is, in France as elsewhere, the law of policing. In the famous *Benjamin* case,[6]

---

[1] *cf., e.g.* I. Pernice, *Grundrechtsgehalte im Europäischen Gemeinschaftsrecht*, (1979) Baden-Baden; H. Kutscher, "Zum Grundsatz der Verhältnismässigkeit im Recht der Europäischen Gemeinschaften," in: H. Kutscher (Joint ed.), *Der Grundsatz der Verhältnismässigkeit in europäischen Rechtsordnungen*, (1985) Heidelberg, pp. 89 *et seq.*, 91.

[2] *cf.* H. Kutscher, *loc. cit.*, footnote 1, p. 95.

[3] This is stated explicitly in F. Teitgen, "Le principe de proportionnalité en droit français," in: H. Kutscher (Joint ed.), *Der Grundsatz der Verhältnismässigkeit in europäischen Rechtsordnungen* (1985) Heidelberg, p. 53; *cf.* also G. Braibant, *Le droit administratif français*, (1984) Paris, p. 298.

[4] F. Teitgen, *loc. cit.*, footnote 3, p. 55.

[5] J.-M. Woehrling, "Die französische Verwaltungsgerichtsbarkeit im Vergleich mit der deutschen," (1985) NVwZ, pp. 21 *et seq.* (25).

[6] Conseil d'Etat Decision of May 19, 1933 in M. Long, P. Weil, G. Braibant, *Les grands arrêts de la jurisprudence administrative* (henceforth GAJA) (8th ed., Paris 1984), pp. 214 *et seq.*; *cf.* also on this subject G. Braibant, *loc. cit.*, footnote 3, p. 299.

the Conseil d'Etat held a decree prohibiting a meeting, issued by the Burgomaster, to be illegal on the grounds that it was disproportionate. The Court explained that the probability of a disturbance arising was not so great as to make it imperative that the gathering in question should be banned. Instead, public order could have been maintained by the adoption of less drastic policing measures.

Under French law, policing measures have the object and purpose of protecting the "ordre public." These measures often entail restrictions on the exercise of personal freedom.[7] As is the case in other systems, it is recognised in French law that there must exist a sufficiently strong relationship between such restrictions on personal freedom and the danger with which the "ordre public" is threatened as a result of exercising such freedom,[8] even if the "proportionality" concept is not often invoked for this purpose.[9]

What can be said is that a brief glance at the case law of the Conseil d'Etat reveals a certain degree of uncertainty in the manner in which the proportionality principle is applied. A good example is the case law relating to the "circonstances exceptionnelles."

Under the "circonstances exceptionnelles" doctrine, "exceptional circumstances" constitute both the precondition and the yardstick for recognising the lawfulness of decisions which normally would be illegal. Thus the Conseil d'Etat, in the *Dol et Laurent* case, held that the policing powers which may be exercised by the public authorities in the interest of maintaining law and order are subject to limitations which are different in peace-time from those which apply in times of war. The requirements of national security lend a greater degree of seriousness to the "ordre public" principle and warrant the adoption of measures which are more drastic than would otherwise be the case.[10]

Thus the court, in reviewing the police powers in question, had to exercise its discretion in the light of the necessities of war, the relevant circumstances dictated by the time and place in question, the categories of people involved and the nature of the danger. In this context, mention should also be made of the *Canal* case, in which the Conseil d'Etat held

---

[7] F. Teitgen, *loc. cit.*, footnote 3, p. 55: "La mesure de police a toujours pour but d'éviter que l'exercice des libertés individuelles occasionne un trouble à l'ordre public."

[8] F. Teitgen, *loc. cit.*, footnote 3, p. 56.

[9] Sharing this viewpoint, G. Braibant, *loc. cit.*, footnote 53, p. 299, considers that the French courts, even where they do not use the word "proportion," nevertheless have the notion of proportionality in mind.

[10] *cf.* Conseil d'Etat Decision in the *Damas, Dol and Laurent* case, February 28, 1919, in GAJA, pp. 150 *et seq.*

that whilst the circumstances which prevailed at the end of the Algerian war may have justified the establishment of a court of special jurisdiction, they nevertheless did not warrant the denial of a right of appeal against its decisions.[11]

It is apparent from an analysis of this case law that the proportionality rule is applied in principle when reviewing measures taken in the interests of the "ordre public," but in a wide variety of ways which depend on the circumstances of each individual case. The legal uncertainty which results from this state of affairs is also explained by the fact that French law does not provide any definition of the "ordre public" concept.

The extent to which the application of the proportionality principle depends on the judgment and discretion exercised by the courts[12] is revealed by the Conseil d'Etat decision in the *Action Française* case. Here, the court initially followed the Conseil's decision in the *Benjamin* case, only to consider that, in view of the importance of the freedom of the press, a total ban by the police on the sale of a certain newspaper constituted an unlawful act by the administration in spite of the prevailing extraordinary circumstances[13] (*théorie de la voie de fait*).

In the field of planning law, the proportionality principle has also found clear expression in the case law of the Conseil d'Etat.

Thus a development plan for an airfield was declared illegal on the grounds that the expense it involved would have been disproportionate to the funds available to the relevant municipality.[14]

Similarly, a plan for an arterial road was overruled as being contrary to the interests of the patients treated in a psychiatric institution close to the area concerned.[15]

Whereas the cases mentioned above constitute examples of far-reaching judicial review of administrative discretion, in which the courts assessed the relationship between restrictions on freedom of action and the public interest which forms the objective of the challenged measure, in cases of "manifest errors of discretion" lack of proportionality is accepted only where it is obvious.[16]

---

[11] Conseil d'Etat Decision in the *Canal, Robin and Godot* case, October 19, 1962, GAJA pp. 511 *et seq.*

[12] On the political influences, *cf.* F. Teitgen, *loc. cit.*, footnote 3, p. 60.

[13] *cf.* on the "voie de fait" doctrine A. de Laubadère, *Traité de droit administratif*, Vol. I, (9th ed., Paris 1984), p. 512.

[14] Conseil d'Etat Decision in the *Grassin* case, October 26, 1973, Rec. 598.

[15] Conseil d'Etat Decision in the *Société civile Sainte-Marie de l'Assomption case*, October 20, 1972, Rec. 657.

[16] *cf.* the key Conseil d'Etat Decision in the *Lagrange* case, February 15, 1961, Rec. 121; *cf.* also its decision in the *Société Librairie François Maspero* case, November 2, 1973, Rec.

Let us take as our final example the field of economic and social policy, in which the administration may actually adopt discriminatory measures where these are justified on grounds of the public interest or by reference to objectively unequal situations. In this case also, there must exist an appropriate relationship between the need for unequal treatment and the nature and scope of the measure itself.[17]

However, in a key area of economic policy, *i.e.* that of intervention in the economy, the administrative courts do not, in practice, exercise any review of proportionality.[18] Instead, the Conseil d'Etat has, in a consistent body of decisions, taken the view that the fixing of a particular price or of a parafiscal contribution amounts to a question of policy, which is not subject to the Conseil's review except in the case of legal error.

It is apparent from the above-mentioned court decisions that the principle of "proportionnalité" is applied only in certain areas and does not constitute an overriding legal principle which governs every administrative action in France. Certainly we must not lose sight of the fact that certain elements of the proportionality principle may, in however coincidental and haphazard a fashion, emerge in the form of viewpoints held in the course of debate on the general concept of justice.[19] Moreover, there are signs that the application by the administrative courts of the proportionality principle could become increasingly widespread in the future. An indication of this trend is the decision by the Conseil constitutionnel (CC) on the new French Law concerning the press of October 10–11, 1984.[20] In this case, the CC held that a restriction of freedom was legitimate only on condition that the relevant measure by the authorities was actually necessary for the realisation of the constitutional objective which is being pursued:

> "S'il est loisible au législateur, lorsqu'il organise l'exercice d'une liberté publique en usant des pouvoirs que lui confère l'article 34 de

---

611, 612; on this subject, *cf.* also F. Dreyfus, "Les limitations du pouvoir discrétionnaire par l'application du principe de proportionnalité," (1974) RDP, pp. 691 *et seq.* This review of "erreur manifeste d'appréciation" is relatively recent and has been influenced by trends in Swiss law, *cf.* U. Letourneur, *L'influence du droit comparé sur la jurisprudence du C.E. français*, (1951) Paris, p. 215.

[17] *cf.* G. Braibant, *loc. cit.*, footnote 3, p. 303.

[18] *cf.* A Mestre, *Le Conseil d'Etat protecteur des prérogatives de l'administration*, (1974) Paris, pp. 86 *et seq.*; *cf.* also M. Fromont, "Le contrôle de l'appréciation des faits économiques dans la jurisprudence administrative," (1966) AJDA, pp. 588 *et seq.*

[19] *cf.* H. D. Jarass, "Besonderheiten des französischen Verwaltungsrechts im Vergleich," (1981) DÖV, p. 813 (815, footnote 29).

[20] Nos. 84–181 DC, (1984) AJDA, p. 686; on this subject, *cf.* M. Herdegen, "Pressefreiheit und Verfassungsgerichtsbarkeit in Frankreich," (1986) ZaöRV, pp. 34 *et seq.*

la Constitution, d'adopter pour l'avenir, s'il l'estime nécessaire, des règles plus rigoureuses que celles qui étaient auparavant en vigueur, il ne peut, s'agissant de situations existantes intéressant une liberté publique, les remettre en cause que dans deux hypothèses: celle où ces situations auraient été illégalement acquises; celle où leur remise en cause serait réellement nécessaire pour assurer la réalisation de l'objectif constitutionnel poursuivi."

If measures issued by the legislator are made subject to the proportionality principle on these terms, this points to a remarkable intensification in the way in which constitutional review is applied. It is not at all inconceivable that this new development in French law finds its origin in the influence exercised by European Community law and in the case law of the Strasbourg-based organs of the European Convention on Human Rights.

The position which the proportionality principle has hitherto occupied in French administrative law is readily explained by some of its specific characteristics. In French administrative law, the "pouvoir discrétionnaire," *i.e.* the discretionary powers of the administration, plays a key role.[21] The "pouvoir discrétionnaire" itself is restricted by the prohibition of "détournement de pouvoir."[22] In this area, the degree to which the administrative courts influence and review administrative action is probably less intense than in Germany.[23] This applies especially to administrative authorities vested with discretionary powers, which, contrary to the situation under German law, tends to be the norm in France. In this respect, discretion is recognised not only in relation to the legal implications of the relevant legislative provisions, but also, in the case of undefined legal concepts, in relation to the actual contents of the rule.[24]

Especially where administrative action involves the maintenance of the "ordre public," both the "libertés publiques," which can be compared with the German "Grundrechten" (fundamental rights), and the prin-

---

[21] *cf.* A de Labaudère, *loc. cit.*, footnote 13, pp. 284 *et seq.*; G. Vedel, P. Delvolvé, *Droit administratif* (9th ed., Paris 1984), pp. 437 *et seq.*; G. Braibant, *Le droit administratif français*, (1984) Paris, pp. 239 *et seq.*; J.-M. Auby, R. Drago, *Traité de contentieux administratif*, Vol. II, (3rd ed., Paris 1984), pp. 370 *et seq.*

[22] On this subject, *cf.* C. Debbasch, *Contentieux administratif* (3rd ed., Paris 1981), pp. 798 *et seq.*; *cf.* also G. Vedel, P. Delvolvé, *loc. cit.*, footnote 21, p. 441.

[23] *cf.* H. D. Jarass, *loc. cit.*, footnote 19, p. 815; M. Fromont, "République Fédérale d'Allemagne, l'Etat de droit" (1984) RDP, pp. 1203, 1223 *et seq.*; by the same author, "Der französische Staatsrat und sein Werk" (1978) DVBl., pp. 89 *et seq.*, 93.

[24] The problems surrounding the "undefined legal concepts" in German administrative law are unknown, in this form, in French law.

ciple of "proportionnalité" provide comparatively little protection and entail but modest restrictions on the exercise of administrative discretion.[25]

As the examples drawn from the case law show, the function of the proportionality principle is to a large extent taken over by other rules in French law, in particular by judicial review based on "manifest error" (*erreur manifeste*), "infringement of the law" (*violation de la loi*) and "misuse of powers" (*détournement de pouvoir*). It is perfectly possible for these criteria for judicial review to involve certain aspects of the proportionality test.[26]

2. Federal Republic of Germany

Under German law, the proportionality principle has found its clearest expression both in the case law[27] and in the available literature.[28] Reduced to the necessity principle, which did not bear that description at that time, it appeared for the first time towards the end of the nineteenth century in the field of the law of policing.[29] The so-called *Kreuzberg* decision of the Prussian Oberverwaltungsgericht (supreme administrative court)[30] saw the adoption by the courts of the notion that the state requires special permission whenever it infringes the citizen's civil liberties. During the subsequent period, the growing incidence of judicial review of state action by the administrative courts also played an important part in shaping this area of the law. These courts were in a position to exercise this review, which was intended to keep the public authorities in check,

---

[25] *cf.* H. D. Jarass (1981) DÖV, p. 815; F. Teitgen, *loc. cit.*, footnote 3, p. 61.

[26] H. Huber, "Über den Grundsatz der Verhältnismässigkeit im Verwaltungsrecht" (1977) ZSR, pp. 1 *et seq.*, 2; G. Braibant, *loc. cit.*, footnote 3, p. 306; also, recently, J.-P. Costa, "Le principe de la proportionnalité dans la jurisprudence du Conseil d'Etat" (1988) AJDA, pp. 434 *et seq.*

[27] On the extensive case law of the Federal Constitutional Court (Bundesverfassungsgericht), *cf.* E. Grabitz, "Der Grundsatz der Verhältnismässigkeit in der Rechtsprechung des Bundesverfassungsgerichts" (1973) AöR 98, pp. 568 *et seq.*

[28] *cf.*, *e.g.* L. Hirschberg, *Der Grundsatz der Verhältnismässigkeit*, (1981) Göttingen, pp. 2 *et seq.*; M. Ch. Jakobs, *Der Grundsatz der Verhältnismässigkeit* (1985) Köln/Berlin/Bonn/München.

[29] *cf.* also on the issues stated below L. Hirschberg, *loc. cit.*, footnote 28; it is fair to state that the roots of the German proportionality principle go back considerably further. *cf.* also M. Ch. Jakobs, *loc. cit.*, footnote 28, pp. 2 *et seq.*

[30] Decision of June 14, 1882, PrOVG 9, 353, which held that the police were not permitted to take into account considerations of an esthetic nature without having been given additional authority.

independently from the administration and consequently also give administrative law a firmer outline.

In the case under review, the Prussian Oberverwaltungsgericht examined whether the measure taken by the police did not exceed in intensity that which was required by the pursued objective.[31] The court was able to rely on the general clause relating to policing in Section 10 II 17 of the ALR law in so far as the policy had been given the task of "adopting such measures as are necessary for the maintenance of public order" and consequently unnecessary measures were not covered by "police duties."[32] On the basis of these initial decisions, the necessity principle was further clarified by the courts in the course of the following decades.[33] It became generally recognised both in the available literature on administrative law[34] and in the law of policing.[35] It was only after World War Two that, in addition to the necessity principle, the proportionality principle in the more restricted sense developed into a legal principle in its own right.[36]

Similarly, there developed the notion that the legislature is also bound by the Constitution.[37]

In a number of decisions, the Federal Constitutional Court (BVerfG) introduced the so-called "prohibition of excessive measures" as well as the notion of "unreasonableness"[38]; in other decisions, the term "proportionality principle" was complemented by the addition, in brackets, of the words "prohibition of excessive measures,"[39] or the proportionality prin-

---

[31] cf. in particular PrOVG April 10, 1886; July 3, 1886, PrOVG 13, 424, 426.

[32] cf. L. Hirschberg, loc. cit., footnote 28, p. 3, containing further references.

[33] PrOVG 31, 409; 44, 342; 51, 284 (288); 313 (314 et seq.); 61, 255 (262); 78, 431; 79, 297 (306); 90, 293; Jb Sächs. OVG 7, 195 (198); 8, 131 (135 et seq.); 10, 329 (331 et seq.); 15, 42 (44).

[34] cf. O. Mayer, Deutsches Verwaltungsrecht, Volume One, (1895) Leipzig, p. 267; F. Fleiner, Institutionen des deutschen Verwaltungsrechts (2nd ed., Tübingen 1912), p. 354; W. Jellinek, Gesetz, Gesetzesanwendung und Zweckmässigkeitserwägung (1913) Tübingen, pp. 79, 289 et seq.; by the same author, Verwaltungsrecht (3rd ed., Berlin 1931), p. 439.

[35] cf. O. von Arnstedt, Das Preussische Polizeirecht, Vol. I (1905) Berlin, pp. 52 et seq.; R. Thoma, Der Polizeibefehl im Badischen Recht, (1906) Tübingen, p. 465; B. Drews, Preussisches Polizeirecht, General Part, (3rd ed., Berlin 1931), pp. 38 et seq., 62 et seq.; K. Friedrichs, Polizeiverwaltungsgesetz, (1932) Berlin, Section 14, Erl. 33.

[36] On this subject, cf. extensive treatment by L. Hirschberg, loc. cit., footnote 28, pp. 9 et seq.

[37] cf., e.g. R. von Krauss, Der Grundsatz der Verhältnismässigkeit in seiner Bedeutung für die Notwendigkeit des Mittels im Verwaltungsrecht, (1955) Hamburg; further examples in L. Hirschberg, loc. cit., footnote 28, pp. 10 et seq.

[38] BVerfGE 21, 173 (183); 48, 396 et seq.

[39] cf., e.g. BVerwGE 48, 199 (302); 49, 36 (43).

ciple was combined with the prohibition of excessive measures to form a criterion of assessment.[40] In his monograph on the subject, Hirschberg highlights in very clear terms these terminological uncertainties.[41] In the following summary, the proportionality principle, where it is not used in conjunction with the abbreviation i.s.s. (in the strict sense), will serve as a generic term for the secondary principles of suitability, necessity and proportionality in the strict sense. Accordingly, there is a unanimous opinion[42] that three factors can be distinguished which govern the applicability of the proportionality principle:

(1) First, the state measures concerned must be *suitable* for the purpose of facilitating or achieving the pursued objective.
(2) Second, the suitable measure must also be *necessary*, in the sense that the authority concerned has no other mechanism at its disposal which is less restrictive of freedom. Haverkate[43] clarifies this secondary principle further by stating that it is not the method used which has to be necessary, but "the excessive restriction of freedom involved in the choice of method."
(3) Finally, the measure concerned may not be *disproportionate* to the restrictions which it involves (proportionality i.s.s.).[44]

Similarly, the Federal Constitutional Court, ever since it pronounced the decision published in Volume 48, p. 402, has defined the proportionality principle in the following terms:

"The intervention must be suitable and necessary for the achievement of its objective. It may not impose excessive burdens on the individual concerned, and must consequently be reasonable in its effect on him."[45]

---

[40] BVerfGE 20, 351 (361); 22, 114 (123); 23, 127 (137); 28, 175 (188 *et seq.*); 36, 156 (165), 38, 348 (368).
[41] *Loc. cit.*, footnote 28, pp. 23 *et seq.*
[42] *cf.* F. E. Schnapp, "Die Verhältnismässigkeit des Grundrechtseingriffs" (1983) JuS, pp. 850 *et seq.* (852).
[43] G. Haverkate, *Rechtsfragen des Leistungsstaats*, (1983) Tübingen, p. 29.
[44] For an extensive treatment of these component principles, *cf.* M. Ch. Jakobs, *loc. cit.*, footnote 28, pp. 59 *et seq.*
[45] *cf.* also BVerfGE 63, p. 144.

Ress[46] rightly points out that the terms "excessive burden" and "reasonable" as used in this definition merely amount to paraphrases of the proportionality principle. This viewpoint was supported by the Federal Constitutional Court decision published in Volume 61, p. 126 (135 *et seq.*), where the Court, having examined the suitability and necessity of the measure, continued as follows:

> "Finally, the detention order appears to be proportionate in the strict sense in that the seriousness of the intervention and the gravity of the reasons justifying it are in adequate proportion to each other."[47]

In spite of differences in the terminology used, there is general agreement[48] that constitutional status should be conferred upon the proportionality principle, which first saw the light of day in the field of the law of policing. The Federal Constitutional Court saw itself compelled to derive the proportionality principle and the prohibition of excess measures, which "constitute general rules governing all actions by the state, from the principle that the state is ruled by law"[49]; elsewhere, the Court discerned them in the "essence of the fundamental rights themselves,"[50] which, expressing as they did the general right of freedom claimed by the citizen against the state, could be restricted by the public authorities only to the extent that this was imperative for the protection of the public interest.[51] Thus the proportionality principle plays a key role in giving substance to and realising the protection of freedom guaranteed by the Constitution.[52]

---

[46] G. Ress, "Der Grundsatz der Verhältnismässigkeit im deutschen Recht," in: H. Kutscher (Joint Editor), *Der Grundsatz der Verhältnismässigkeit in europäischen Rechtsordnungen*, (1985) Heidelberg, pp. 5 *et seq.*, 14.

[47] *cf.* also BVerfGE 14, 19 (27); 15, 226 (234); 18, 353 (362); on these decisions, E. Grabitz, *loc. cit.*, footnote 27, pp. 569 *et seq.*

[48] *cf.* K. Stern, *Das Staatsrecht der Bundesrepublik Deutschland*, Vol. I, "Grundbegriffe und Grundlagen des Staatsrechts, Strukturprinzipien der Verfassung" (1979) München, pp. 671 *et seq.*; B. Drews, G.Wacke, K. Vogel, W. Martens, *Gefahrenabwehr, Allgemeines Polizeirecht (Ordnungsrecht) des Bundes und der Länder* (9th ed., Köln/Berlin/Bonn/München 1986), p. 390.

[49] BVerfGE 19, 348; 23, 133; 43, 106; 61, 134.

[50] Consistent practice of the Federal Constitutional Court, *cf.* E 19, 242 (384 *et seq.*); 35, 401.

[51] *cf.* G. Ress, *loc. cit.*, footnote 46, p. 15; on the place occupied by the proportionality principle in the hierarchy of rules, *cf.* P. Kunig, *Das Rechtsstaatsprinzip*, (1986) Tübingen, pp. 35 *et seq.*, containing further references.

[52] *cf.* E. Grabitz, "Der Grundsatz der Verhältnismässigkeit in der Rechtsprechung des Bundesverfassungsgerichts," AöR 98 (1973), pp. 568 *et seq.*, 584; *cf.* also R. Wendt,

As has already been mentioned, the proportionality principle is generally accepted as governing both the law-making process and the application of the law.[53]

Where the legislator fails to observe the proportionality principle in enacting a statute, this should entail the illegality of such a rule, unless the statute concerned is precisely expressive of a principle which is contrary to, equally valid as or higher than the proportionality principle.[54]

As regards the application of the law which is of particular interest in the context of this study, the three elements contained in the proportionality principle also come into their own where statutes are applied by the administration in individual cases, assuming that in so doing the administration has been granted a certain amount of discretion. The latter can be so reduced in scope by the proportionality principle that only a particular decision will remain legitimate ("reduction of discretion to non existence").

Thus, for example, exceptions must be granted to a general prohibition ordered by the police force where such a prohibition, in the absence of a genuine danger, is not absolutely necessary.[55] On the other hand, the police may take drastic measures even in the case of minor offences, where such infringements have increased in frequency and cannot be prevented in any other way.[56]

Recently, an increasingly intense debate has been conducted on the question of the extent to which the proportionality principle should also be observed where no intervention has taken place. Particularly in relation to the community services administration the application of the proportionality principle has been expressly advocated.[57]

In private law, which in the Federal Republic of Germany has been influenced by the fundamental rights through the general provisions of

"Der Garantiegehalt der Grundrechte und das Übermassverbot," AöR 104, pp. 414 *et seq.* (416).

[53] On this subject, *cf.* G. Ress, *loc. cit.*, footnote 46, pp. 24 *et seq.*; M. Ch. Jakobs, *loc. cit.*, footnote 28, pp. 127 *et seq.*

[54] *cf.* M. Ch. Jakobs, *loc. cit.*, footnote 28, p. 134; *cf.* also L. Hirschberg, *loc. cit.*, footnote 28, p. 218: P. Lerche, *Übermass und Verfassungsrecht*, (1961) Köln, p. 53; M. Gentz, "Zur Verhältnismässigkeit von Grundrechtseingriffen" (1968) NJW, pp. 1600 *et seq.* (1606).

[55] *cf.* BVerfGE 34, 384 (386 *et seq.*) as regards the ban on receiving parcels for certain categories of remand prisoners.

[56] *cf.* BVerwG in (1974) NJW, p. 807; for an extensive discussion of the law of policing, *cf.* Drews, Wacke, Vogel, Martens, *loc. cit.*, footnote 48, pp. 389 *et seq.*; *cf.* also BVerwGE 45, 41 (59 *et seq.*).

[57] For examples, *cf.* M. Ch. Jakobs, *loc. cit.*, footnote 28, p. 155; *cf.* in particular G. Haverkate, *Rechtsfragen des Leistungsstaats*, (1983) Tübingen, p. 29.

the Constitution, the proportionality principle also applies in relations between private individuals. Thus the Federal Constitutional Court, in the *Lebach* decision, required that the proportionality principle be observed "in court decisions concerning conflicting provisions of private law."[58]

Among the specific areas in which the proportionality principle is applied, mention must be made of its role as a tool of interpretation,[59] which becomes relevant whenever two rights protected by the Constitution come into conflict with each other. Hesse proposes that this type of problem be solved by applying the principle of practical reconciliation,[60] under which constitutionally protected rights will be harmonised to the point where "each gains a degree of reality." Where conflicts arise, these must not be solved by giving one right precedence over the other either by means of an ill-considered "weighing up of interests" or even through an abstract "weighing up of values." Instead, the principle of the unity of the Constitution requires that an optimal solution be found: *both* rights must be restricted to certain limits in order to optimise their effectiveness. Consequently, the way in which these limits are drawn must be proportionate in each individual case; they may not be drawn any further than is necessary to reconcile both rights. In this context, the term "proportionality" means a relationship between two variable entities, *i.e.* a relationship which provides the best way of optimising both rights, rather than a relationship between a constant "objective" and one or more variable "means of achievement."

Finally, it should be mentioned that the "constitutionally faithful" interpretation applied by the Federal Constitutional Court in a consistent body of case law can be ascribed to a particular interpretation of the

---

[58] BVerfGE 35, 202 (221); *cf.* as regards company law BGHZ 4, 108 (112); *cf.* also Meyer, Hayoz, Zweifel, "Der Grundsatz der schonenden Rechtsauslegung im Gesellschafts-recht," in *Fs. H. Westermann* (1974), pp. 383 *et seq.*; on the law relating to industrial action, particular attention must also be given to the case law of the Federal Labour Court (Bundesarbeitsgericht), *cf.*, *e.g.* BAGE 23, pp. 292 *et seq.*; *cf.* also T. Mayer-Maly, "Die Grenzen des Grundsatzes der Verhältnismässigkeit für das kollektive Arbeitsrecht" (1980) ZfA, pp. 473 *et seq.*; for a critical appraisal, *cf.* E. Wolf, *Das Recht zur Aussper-rung,* (1980) pp. 288 *et seq.*, 351 *et seq.*; W. Zitscher, "Der 'Grundsatz der Verhält-nimässigkeit' im Arbeitsvertragsrecht als Blankettformel" (1983) BB, p. 1285.

[59] *cf.* on this subject G. Ress, *loc. cit.*, footnote 46, pp. 30 *et seq.*; T. Stein, "Der Grundsatz der Verhältnismässigkeit," in *Deutsche öffentlich-rechtliche Landesberichte zum X. Inter-nationalen Kongress für Rechtsvergleichung in Budapest* (K. Madlener, ed.) (1978), pp. 276 *et seq.*; K. Hesse, *Grundzüge des Verfassungsrechts der Bundesrepublik Deutsch-land* (15th ed., Heidelberg 1985), p. 27.

[60] K. Hesse, *loc. cit.*, footnote 59; *cf.* also P. Lerche, *loc. cit.*, footnote 54, pp. 125 *et seq.*

proportionality concept.[61] The Court has defined this method of interpretation in the following terms[62]:

> "Where the rule is contrary to the Constitution after having been subjected to every possible interpretation, it shall be unconstitutional as such. Where the rule admits of several interpretations, of which some comply with the constitution and others do not, the rule shall be constitutionally valid."

The rationale behind this interpretation rule is to respect the precedence of the legislature when assessing the constitutional validity of rules, since "as much of the legislator's intention must be maintained as it is possible to maintain within the terms of the Constitution."[63]

Ress[64] points to the wide-ranging and far-reaching criticisms which have been levelled at the proportionality principle. In particular, the charge is constantly made that this principle has been stretched beyond acceptable limits.[65] Thus Forsthoff[66] criticised as early as 1971 the fact that this principle had moved from the administrative law level to that of constitutional law. This, he claimed, amounted to a misjudgment of the qualititative change which such a rise in status necessarily entails, and to the unlawful subordination of legislation to certain aspects of administrative law. However, it is not possible here to probe more deeply into this criticism.[67] On the basis of the foregoing, it has been possible to outline only the main problems involved in the application of the proportionality principle. Similarly, it was impossible to examine in detail the conditions in which the proportionality principle could be applied to the services provided by the state.[68] Equally impossible was a discussion of the question whether the invocation of the proportionality principle leads to the blurring of the various demarcation lines between the fundamental

---

[61] cf. G. Ress, loc. cit., footnote 46, p. 31, containing further references.

[62] BVerfGE 19, 1(5).

[63] BVerfGE 2, 266 (282); as regards interpretation in accordance with the Constitution, cf. the examples provided in G. Ress, loc. cit., footnote 46, p. 32, footnote 112.

[64] G. Ress, loc. cit., footnote 46, p. 33.

[65] cf. E. Schmidt, "Der Strafprozess, Aktuelles und Zeitloses" (1969) NJW, pp. 1737 et seq.; E. Wolf, loc. cit., footnote 58.

[66] cf. E. Forsthoff, Der Staat der Industriegesellschaft (2nd ed., München 1971), pp. 137 et seq.; by the same author, Lehrbuch des Verwaltungsrechts, Vol. I, General Part (10th ed., München 1973), pp. 70 et seq.

[67] cf. on this subject L. Hirschberg, Der Grundsatz der Verhältnismässigkeit, (1981) Göttingen, pp. 251 et seq.; G. Ress, loc. cit., footnote 46, p. 33, in particular where the author criticises the case law of the Constitutional Court.

[68] On this subject, cf. G. Haverkate, loc. cit., footnote 57.

rights,[69] *i.e.* whether it effects a levelling out of the various fundamental freedoms.[70] Nevertheless, this section should have given a clear picture of the overriding importance attributed to the proportionality principle in German law today.

3. Italy

In Italy, the proportionality principle has come to prominence under this designation only as a result of the case law developed by the European Court of Justice.[71]

Whilst the earlier court decisions made no use of this principle where the object pursued by the rule was disproportionate to the methods used for its realisation, it has certainly been applied by the Consiglio dello Stato in its more recent decisions[72]—where, for example, it held that the remuneration of all state employees had to be commensurate with both the quality and the quality of their output.[73]

In its decision of April 24, 1974, the Consiglio even stated in express terms that the proportionality principle must be taken into account when fixing the extent of any penalty.[74]

In its decisions concerning the annulment of administrative instruments, however, the Consiglio in most cases relies on the "lack of appropriate powers" principle rather than on an infringement of the proportionality principle.[75] Even though the relationship between the method used and the object pursued is not obviously central to these decisions, they nevertheless feature concepts such as proportionality, suitability, moderation, correspondence, balance, reasonableness and justice by way of criteria for the purpose of assessing the lawfulness of both statutes and administrative instruments.[76]

---

[69] *cf.* B. Schlink, *Abwägung im Verfassungsrecht* (1976) Berlin, p. 47.

[70] *cf.* on this subject R. Wendt, *loc. cit.*, footnote 52.

[71] *cf.* G. M. Ubertazzi, "Le principe de la proportionnalité en droit italien," in H. Kutscher (Joint ed.), *Der Grundsatz der Vehältnismässigkeit in europäischen Rechtsordnungen*, (1985) Heidelberg, p. 79.

[72] *cf.* on the structure and role of the Consiglio, a recent article by F. Marriuzzo, "Struktur und Wirkungskreis der italienischen Verwaltungsgerichtsbarkeit" (1984) BayVBl., pp. 737 *et seq.*

[73] Decision of the Consiglio of October 27, 1972. This decision is based on Article 36 of the Italian Constitution, which expressly concerns the proportionality principle.

[74] The background of this case concerned the proportionality of a fine imposed as a result of an infringement of certain provisions concerning the movement of capital.

[75] G. M. Ubertazzi, *loc. cit.*, footnote 71, p. 80.

[76] G. M. Ubertazzi, *ibid.*, p. 81.

In a Consiglio decision of March 21, 1972, it was established that the proportionality principle enjoyed the same rank as the equality principle. Moreover, Ubertazzi points out that this principle is also entrenched in the European Convention on Human Rights, which has been ratified by Italy, and that consequently ordinary laws may not be applied where they infringe the proportionality principle. In every individual case, laws must be interpreted in the light of this principle.[77] Although the proportionality principle has only recently made an appearance under that name in Italian law, use has been made of other legal principles which are similar to it in content. These can be summarised as follows:

(a) the "buon andamento" principle, *i.e.* that of the proper and sound conduct of proceedings. Under this principle, legal provisions must constitute rules which are appropriate to the specific requirements of the area covered by these provisions.

This principle must be taken into consideration by all those to whom the application of the law is entrusted (especially by the courts and the administration), even where the legislator failed to take it into account.[78]

"Here, we are dealing with a rule of interpretation which is specific to each legal system, according to which any action or organisation governed by public law must be characterised by the principles of suitability, proportionality and good sense."[79]

The principle has found its main field of application through the case law of the Constitutional Court on the equality principle contained in Article 3 of the Constitution. According to this case law, it is possible to review the discretion exercised by the legislator where it infringes this principle.[80]

---

[77] *Ibid.*

[78] On this subject, *cf.* E. Capaccioli, *Manuale di diritto amministrativo*, Vol. I (1980) Padova, p. 126.

[79] *Ibid.*

[80] *cf.* Decision of the C. Cost. of May 20, 1980, No. 72, (1980) Foro it. I, 1828; Decision of April 14, 1980, No. 47, *Ibid.* (1980) I, 2673; Decisions of July 16, 1979, No. 73, *Ibid.* (1979) I, 2181; Decision of June 2, 1977, No. 100, *Ibid.* (1977) I, 1609; Decision of December 29, 1976, No. 264, *Ibid.* (1977) I, 565; Decision of May 6, 1976, No. 104, *Ibid.* (1976) I, 2563. On this subject, *cf.* also A. M. Sandulli, "Il principio di ragionevolezza nella giurisprudenza costituzionale" (1975) Dir. Soc., pp. 561 *et seq.*

In this respect, we are, according to certain authors, dealing here with a case where the legislator has exceeded his powers.[81]

(b) the "buon andamento" principle must also be observed by the administration. According to Sandulli[82] it should be applied more extensively in this case than in relation to the legislator. It is intrinsically characteristic of administrative discretion that it must be exercised in accordance with the principle of "sound administration." Administrative action must in the first place take into account the main public interest. This can often mean that considerations of secondary public interest or private interests have to be sacrificed. However, the administration must in every case, in spite of the range of options at its disposal, weigh up the main public interest against secondary interests.[83] Where the public objective can be reached through less drastic intervention, or even without having to restrict any secondary interest, the administration must endeavour to protect the main interest by less restrictive measures.[84]

(c) the "buon andamento" principle requires the administration to weigh up the various interests in appropriate fashion and to apply the rules, including the technical ones, of "proper administration."[85] In other words, the administration must act efficiently and in such a way as to produce the best possible results at the lowest cost.

(d) although administrative instruments are not normally assessed by the courts as to their effectiveness, failure to observe the "buon andamento" principle can result in a case of lack of appropriate powers.

The various elements of the *ultra vires* concept[86] have been developed by the case law of the Consiglio dello Stato. A leading work on this

---

[81] On this subject, *cf.* A. Barbera, F. Cocozza, G. Corso, "La libertà dei singoli e delle formazioni sociali. Il principio di eguaglianza," in *Manuale di diritto pubblico* (G. Amato, A. Barbera, ed.) (1984) Bologna, pp. 311 *et seq.*, containing further references.

[82] *cf.* A. M. Sandulli, *loc. cit.*, footnote 80.

[83] *cf.* A. M. Sandulli, *Manuale di diritto amministrativo*, Vol. I, (14th ed., Napoli 1984), p. 564.

[84] On this subject, *cf.* Capaccioli, *loc. cit.*, footnote 78, p. 285.

[85] *cf.* A. M. Sandulli, *loc. cit.*, footnote 83, pp. 564 *et seq.*

[86] The most common instances of *ultra vires*, as elaborated by the case law of the Consiglio, are the following:
    (1) distortion of facts
    (2) evident lack of logic

subject appeared in 1892 under the authorship of Codacci Pisanelli,[87] who himself had been considerably influenced by the French case law relating to "détournement de pouvoir."[88]

On the basis of these elements of the *ultra vires* concept, it is possible for the courts to examine more intensely whether the principle of proper administration has been observed in particular cases.

4. United Kingdom

Until recently, the search for any manifestation of the proportionality principle in English law was unproductive, since neither the case law nor the available literature mentioned this concept. This is due to the specific nature of the English legal system.[89] Thus the specific question as to the suitability of a certain measure is hardly necessary in English law, since any unsuitable measure is likely to be considered *ultra vires*.[90] Generally speaking, any authority acts *ultra vires* where it exceeds its statutory powers.[91]

The British system appears to be equally lacking in any system of review based on proportionality in the strict sense. Since Britain does not

---

(3) contradiction between administrative instruments
(4) unequal treatment
(5) evident injustice
(6) absence of conditions
(7) absence or inadequacy of instructions within the procedure
(8) errors in justification of the decision
(9) infringement or circumvention of a judicial decision.

[87] *cf.* Codacci Pisanelli, "L'eccesso di potere nel contenzioso amministrativo," in *Scritti di diritto pubblico*, (1900) Città di Castello.

[88] *cf.* on this subject Palma, "Note intorno alle nozioni di conformità alla legge ed eccesso di potere nella evoluzione della giurisprudenza" (1963) Rass. dir. pubbl.; Delfino, *L'eccesso di potere amministrativo e il giudice ordinario* (1963) Napoli.

[89] *cf.* on this subject *supra*, Chapter 2.

[90] On the *ultra vires* doctrine, *cf.* E. C. S. Wade, A. W. Bradley, *Constitutional and Administrative Law*, (10th ed., London, New York 1985), pp. 628 *et seq.*; H. W. R. Wade, *Administrative Law* (5th ed., Oxford 1983), pp. 38 *et seq.*, 348; S. A. de Smith, *Constitutional and Administrative Law* (4th ed., Suffolk 1983), pp. 558 *et seq.*; O. Hood Phillips, P. Jackson, *Constitutional and Administrative Law* (6th ed., London 1978), pp. 595 *et seq.*; J. F. Garner, B. L. Jones, *Administrative Law* (6th ed., London 1985), pp. 105, 109 *et seq.*; J. Beatson, M. H. Matthews, *Administrative Law, Cases and Materials* (1983) Oxford, p. 155.

[91] *cf.* on this subject R. Glücksmann, *Die Grenzen der Betätigung englischer Verwaltungsbehörden (The Development of the Doctrine of Ultra Vires in English Administrative Law)* (1984) Frankfurt; E. H. Riedel, *Kontrolle der Verwaltung im englischen Rechtssystem* (1976) Berlin, pp. 88 *et seq.*; C. von Loeper, *Verwaltungsrechtspflege in England*, (1983) Frankfurt, pp. 74 *et seq.*

have any constitutional provision to that effect, and above all because the powers of Parliament are in principle unlimited,[92] there is no imperative need to weigh up the restricted right against the importance of the pursued objective. Nevertheless, it would appear that, under the influence of European Community law, in particular the case law of the European Court of Justice, the proportionality principle has recently been introduced into English law. This prompted the following recent pronouncement by Advocate-General Sir Gordon Slynn[93]: "We are just about to have a case at the European Court in which an English judge wants to know what he should do with the doctrine of proportionality, which ... may be about to slip across the Channel into the United Kingdom's legal system."

Generally speaking, it is expected that through the agency of the European Court of Justice, certain principles of Continental administrative law will in future receive greater attention in Britain.[94]

The proportionality principle has definitely been used with increasing frequency by the courts in their *rationes decidendi*, particularly in cases involving Community law. Thus, for example, Lord Diplock stated in *R. v. Goldstein*: "This would indeed be using a sledge-hammer to crack a nut."[95]

In English law also, certain forms of state action have come under attack for being unreasonable or unsuitable. The case of *Kruse* v. *Johnson*[96] has become famous in this respect. This concerned the lawfulness of a bye-law, and the decision contains the following passage by Lord Chief Justice Russell:

> "If, for instance, they were found to be partial and unequal in their operation as between different classes; if they were manifestly unjust; if they disclosed bad faith; if they involved such oppressive or gratuitous interference with the rights of those subject to them as could find no justification in the minds of reasonable men, the court might well say: Parliament never intended to give authority to make such rules; they are unreasonable and ultra vires. . . . A by-law is not unreasonable merely because particular judges may think that it

---

[92] S. A. de Smith, *loc. cit.*, footnote 90, p. 73.
[93] Sir Gordon Slynn, in J. Schwarze, R. Bieber (eds.), *Eine Verfassung für Europa*, (1984) Baden-Baden, pp. 121 *et seq.*, 123.
[94] *cf.* C. v. Loeper, *loc. cit.*, footnote 91, pp. 156 *et seq.*, containing further examples of English viewpoints.
[95] [1983] 1 W.L.R. at 157.
[96] [1898] 2 Q.B. 91 at 99–100.

goes further than is prudent or necessary or convenient, or because it is not accompanied by a qualification or an exception which some judges may think ought to be there."

Akehurst invokes this decision as an example of a case where,

"when an English judge says that by-laws made by local authorities would probably be held void for unreasonableness if 'they involved such oppressive or gratuitous interference with the rights of those subject to them as could find no justification in the minds of reasonable men'..., he reaches virtually the same result as a German lawyer would reach by applying the doctrine of proportionality."[97]

If the term "proportionality" is understood as meaning "necessity," it is to a considerable extent comparable to the "duty of care" construction drawn from tort liability, which is applied in conjunction with the "reasonableness" criterion.[98]

It is, however, often unclear from the decisions of English courts why a certain measure is unjust and consequently classified as *ultra vires*.[99] Authors voicing critical opinion have observed that it is here that the absence of a developed theory of administrative action in British public law is at its most noticeable.[100]

5. Belgium

As a general legal principle, the proportionality principle has—as with French law and that of the Netherlands—for a long time been expressly applied by the Conseil d'Etat only in a small number of disciplinary cases.[101] Thus the Conseil d'Etat, in Decision No. 17,101 of June 26, 1975

---

[97] M. Akehurst, "The application of general principles of law by the Court of Justice of the European Community," in The British Yearbook of International Law (1981), pp. 29 *et seq.*, 38, footnote 4.

[98] *cf.*, *e.g.* W. V. H. Rogers, Winfield and Jolowicz, *On Tort* (12th ed., London 1984), p. 85: "The plaintiff might overcome this hurdle by showing, for example, that the policy adopted by the Home Office was so fraught with danger or so totally unrelated to the purpose of reform of offenders that no reasonable person could have adopted it," *cf.* also *Secretary of State for Education* v. *Tameside Metropolitan Borough Council* [1976] 3 All E.R. 665; *CCSU* v. *Minister for the Civil Service* [1984] 3 All E.R. 935 at 949 *et seq.*

[99] *cf.* examples provided in H. Riedel, *loc. cit.*, footnote 91, pp. 103 *et seq.*

[100] *Ibid.*, p. 105.

[101] *cf.* L. P. Suetens, "Algemene beginselen van behoorlijk bestuur in de rechtspraak van de Raad van State" (1981) Tijdschrift voor bestuurswetenschappen en publiek recht (TvB), pp. 81, 87; A. Delpérée, "Le principe de proportionnalité en droit public," in: Centre

(*Depelchin*), found that the court which is called upon to examine a case of "excès de pouvoir," must also assess whether the disciplinary penalty imposed was not disproportionate ("hors de toute proportion") to the offence committed,[102] the use of the term "toute proportion" indicating that this examination of proportionality merely involves an approximate and general assessment. All the same, the Conseil d'Etat clearly goes much further in disciplinary matters than is the case in its other decisions, in which, despite the broad terms of reference conferred on it in taking its decisions, it examines in only a very general way whether the administration, in weighing up the interests involved, was able to take its decision in all equity.[103]

An even clearer example of the Conseil d'Etat's attitude towards the proportionality principle was its Decision No. 20,116 of February 19, 1980 (*Decock*),[104] which concerned the annulment of a dismissal order. Here, the Conseil d'Etat decided that, although it was not entitled to substitute itself for the relevant authority, it nevertheless had to examine whether the infringements of which the employee concerned was accused were so serious as to merit punishment, and whether the penalty imposed was not disproportionate to the infringement. In other words, the disciplinary authorities were bound to observe the "proportionality principle," which required the penalty to be reasonably proportionate to the punishable action, to be justifiable and not to appear arbitrary.[105]

6. Denmark

In Danish administrative law, the proportionality principle is applied in a similar fashion to the way it is applied in European Community law. Thus the Danish administration must observe the proportionality prin-

---

interuniversitaire de droit comparé (ed.), *Rapports belges au Xième Congrès international de droit comparé, Budapest, 23–28 Août 1978*, (1978) Brussels, pp. 503, 510.

[102] *cf.* on this decision A. Delpérée, *loc. cit.*, footnote 101, p. 510.

[103] L. P. Suetens, *loc. cit.*, footnote 101, p. 87, with reference to the Decision of the Conseil d'Etat No. 19,244 of November 14, 1978, *Bossuyt*; Decision No. 19,271 of January 21, 1978, *Asnong*; No. 19,616 of May 14, 1979, *F. Guffens*; *cf.* also the parallels with the principle of equity (*redelijkheidsbeginsel*) contained in Article 8(1)(c) of the Netherlands AROB Law.

[104] Reproduced in (1979/80) Rechtskundig Weekblad, 2757–2762.

[105] The same reasoning was applied in Decision No. 20,347 of May 22, 1980, *Baudrin*; *cf.* on this question in its entirety L. P. Suetens, *loc. cit.*, footnote 101, pp. 87 *et seq.*

ciple in exercising its discretion for the purpose of restricting the rights of individuals.[106]

7. Greece

In the case law of the Greek Council of State it is possible to discern occasional signs that administrative discretion is beginning to be linked to the proportionality principle (*analogikótita*). To a certain extent the leading authorities have, by reference to the case law of the German Federal Constitutional Court and of the European Court of Justice, called for a more consistent recognition and application of this principle in Greek law.[107]

8. Ireland

Irish constitutional law, as shaped by the case law of the Irish Supreme Court on Article 43 in conjunction with Article 40.3.2 of the Constitution, accepts the principle that any irrational, absurd or excessive infringement by the State of individuals' property rights constitutes an "unjust attack."[108] Because its traditions are rooted in the Anglo-American legal system, Irish administrative law has hitherto had little contact with the proportionality principle.[109]

Since Ireland's accession to the European Community, however, legal principles which are alien to Anglo-American law have also been introduced into Irish administrative law.[110]

Thus the proportionality principle has been invoked by the courts in particular when endeavouring to ensure the smooth incorporation of Community law into the Irish legal system.[111]

---

[106] M. J. K. Skadhauge, "Interaction between Community Law and National Law," in: FIDE, *Rapports 12e Congrès* (1986) Paris, pp. 75 *et seq.*, 89.

[107] P. Dagtoglou, *Allgemeines Verwaltungsrecht*, Vol. a, (1st ed., Athens 1977), pp. 107 *et seq.*; by the same author, "Verfassung und Verwaltung," in K.-D. Grothmann, *Südosteuropa-Handbuch*, Vol. III, Greece (1980) Göttingen, pp. 14, 44.

[108] *cf.* on the case law of the Supreme Court J. M. Kelly, *The Irish Constitution* (2nd ed., Dublin 1984), pp. 654 *et seq.*

[109] *cf.* J. O'Reilly, "The Interaction between Community law and National Law," in FIDE, *Rapports 12e Congrès* (1986) Paris, pp. 167 *et seq.*, 176.

[110] R. M. Stout, *Administrative Law in Ireland* (1985) Dublin, p. 9; also, J. O'Reilly, *loc. cit.*, footnote 109, pp. 179 *et seq.*

[111] *cf.* the examples provided in J. O'Reilly, *loc. cit.*, footnote 109, pp. 174 *et seq.*, and in M. E. McMahon, "EEC Membership and the Irish Legal System," in: B. J. Drudy, Dermot McAleese (ed.), Irish Studies No. 3 (1984) Cambridge, pp. 57 *et seq.*, 71 *et seq.*

An example of the manner in which Irish law has derived the proportionality principle from Community law is the *Campus Oil* case.[112]

9. Luxembourg

Following the French example, the Luxembourg Conseil d'Etat examines the legality of administrative action in the light of the four grounds for bringing an "excès de pouvoir" action.[113]

This also involves assessing whether the method used is reasonably proportionate to the pursued objective.[114] Where, however, the relationship between method and objective is examined, this is not expressly described as an application of the proportionality principle.

10. The Netherlands

The administrative law of the Netherlands does not feature the proportionality principle in the sense of a uniform concept encompassing the notions of suitability, necessity and proportionality in the strict sense and having the status of a constitutional principle. Only in disciplinary law does one discern a proportionality principle described as such (*evenredigheidsbeginsel*). Article 58(2) of the Law relating to State Employees of 1929 confers jurisdiction on the State Employees Court to examine whether disciplinary measures are reasonably proportionate to the infringement committed by the employee concerned.[115] Such an examination involves the process of comprehensively weighing up the conflicting interests.[116]

If the cornerstone of the proportionality principle is taken to be the rule that the relevant rights and interests must be weighed up against each other, the earliest manifestation of this principle is that which is referred

---

[112] E.C.J. Case 72/83 *Campus Oil Ltd.* v. *Minister for Industry and Energy* [1984] E.C.R. 2727; *cf. infra* at p. 800.

[113] P. Majerus, *L'Etat Luxembourgeois*, (1983) Luxembourg, p. 202.

[114] M. G. Wivenes, "Interaction entre droit communautaire et droit national," in FIDE, *Rapports 12e Congrès*, (1986) Paris, pp. 215 *et seq.*, 227.

[115] *cf. Rapport van de commissie inzake algemene bepalingen van administratief recht (Rapport ABAR)* (5th ed., Alphen a/d Rijn 1984), p. 157; *cf.* also parallel rules in the French law relating to State employees: on this subject. *cf.* F. Teitgen, "Le principe de la proportionnalité en droit français," in: Kutscher, Ress, Teitgen, Ermacora, Ubertazzi, *Der Grundsatz der Verhältnismässigkeit in europäischen Rechtsordnungen* (1985) Heidelberg, pp. 53, 60.

[116] W. Duk, "Maatstaven voor de beoordeling van sancties" (1981) Ars Aequi, pp. 231, 234.

to by the leading authors and court decisions as the prohibition of inequitably weighing up the interests involved (*onredelijke belangenafweging*) or as the prohibition of arbitrary action (*verbod van willekeur*). This principle has its origin in the case law of the Hoge Raad[117] and was later incorporated in the text of a number of Laws.[118] Thus under Article 8(1)(c) of the AROB Law,[119] an administrative decision may be challenged if the administrative institution would not have adopted this decision had it equitably weighed up the interests involved against each other.

Whereas in the early stages the notion of arbitrary action was accepted only in cases where there was a failure to weigh up any interests at all, at present it is also acknowledged in cases where the process of weighing up the interests involved is manifestly unfair.[120] More particularly, this principle requires that the conflicting public and private interests involved should be weighed up against each other objectively and in due proportion in such a way that none of the conflicting viewpoints is misjudged as to its significance or ignored, or that, on the other hand, none of the interests has its importance exaggerated.[121] The restricted wording of the requirements that the weighing up process must be manifestly unfair entails that the degree of intensity with which the examination is carried out is relatively low. More specifically, in cases involving the judicial review of discretionary decisions, the examination involved is accordingly also described as "marginal" (*marginale toetsing*).[122] Since the weighing up of general and private interests is a task which is exclusively incumbent upon the administration, the legislator, by using these restrictive terms, wished to prevent a situation whereby the courts would substitute their judgment and decision for that of the administration.[123]

11. Portugal

In the Portuguese constitution, the proportionality principle (*princípio*

---

[117] Decision of the HR of February 25, 1949 (1949) NJ, 558; *cf.* further examples of the case law in A. M. Donner, *Nederlands Bestuursrecht, Algemeen deel* (4th ed., Alphen a/d Rijn 1974), p. 97.

[118] Article 5 ARBO Law; Article 4 BAB Law; Article 8 AROB Law.

[119] (Wet) Administratieve rechtspraak overheidsbeschikkingen (Law relating to the Judicial Review of Administrative Decisions).

[120] *Rapport ABAR, loc. cit.*, footnote 115, pp. 154 *et seq.*; A. M. Donner, *loc. cit.*, p. 98.

[121] *Rapport ABAR, loc. cit.*, footnote 115, p. 155 with examples from the case law.

[122] *Rapport ABAR, loc. cit.*, footnote 115, p. 154.

[123] A. M. Donner, *loc. cit.*, p. 98; *Rapport ABAR, loc. cit.*, footnote 115, p. 154.

da proporcionalidade) is specifically laid down in relation to the declaration of a state of siege (Article 19 VI), the maintenance of pre-trial detention (Article 28 II) and the entire field of police action (Article 272 II). The proportionality principle is basically recognised in Portuguese administrative law.[124]

12. Spain

The proportionality principle is mentioned only rarely in the decisions of the Spanish courts or the writings of the leading Spanish authors,[125] and where it is featured, it lacks any theoretical basis.[126] Nevertheless, it is taken into account by the 1978 Constitution, for example in Article 9(2), which compels the state to create all the conditions in which the freedom of the individual can be effectively exercised. The fact that, under Article 17(2), provisional detention may not last any longer than is absolutely necessary to conduct the enquiry aimed at clarifying the relevant facts, also results from the transformation of the proportionality principle into constitutional substantive law. This is also the view taken by the Spanish Constitutional Court, when it states in a certain decision that restrictions placed on the exercise of fundamental rights by persons who occupy a special position of subordination (*relación de sujeción especial*) are admissible only to the extent that they are strictly indispensable "for the carrying out of the assignment or function involved in this special relationship."[127] In its decision of October 15, 1982,[128] the Constitutional Court, referring to the case law of the European Court of Human Rights, held that it had to confine itself to examining whether the restriction was not disproportionate in relation to the fundamental right involved and to the interest in defence of which the restriction was imposed.[129]

---

[124] *cf.* M. Esteves de Oliveira, *Direito Administrativo*, Vol. 1 (2nd ed., Almedina 1984), pp. 336 *et seq.*; D. Freitas do Amaral, *Direito Administrativo*, Vol. II (1984) Lisbon, stencilled text, p. 358.

[125] *cf.* examples given in K.-P. Sommermann, *Der Schutz der Grundrechte in Spanien nach der Verfassung von 1978: Ursprünge, Dogmatik, Praxis*, (1984) Berlin, p. 245, footnote 197.

[126] K.-P. Sommermann, *loc. cit.*, footnote 125, p. 244.

[127] Decision of June 15, 1981, RA–16, 92/1980, (1981) BJC p. 259, 266 (II 15), German translation in K.-P. Sommermann, *loc. cit.*, footnote 125, p. 244.

[128] Decision 62/1982, RA–70, 185/1980 and 402/1981, pp. 919 *et seq.*

[129] *Loc. cit.*, pp. 928 *et seq.*; *cf.* also Decision 3/1983 of January 25, 1983, CI–8, 222/1982 (BJC) 1983; pp. 147, 152 *et seq.*

II. THE PROPORTIONALITY PRINCIPLE IN INTERNATIONAL LAW

1. General International Law

The proportionality principle is also an international legal principle which applies in the relations between states—more particularly in relation to reprisals, retaliatory measures and where non-execution of a treaty takes the form of non-performance.[130]

The term "reprisal" is taken as meaning a legal intervention by a state whose international law rights have been infringed against individual interests of any state which has committed an unlawful act of which the first-named state has been the victim, with a view to compelling the last-named state to redress the wrong committed.[131]

Because of the development in legal history of the law of reprisals, the retaliation principle has been replaced by the law of retorsion, which has to operate within the limits of proportionality.[132]

The proportionality principle was established in this context by the arbitration decision in the *Naulilaa* case. The relevant award states on this subject:

> "It is generally agreed that all countermeasures must, in the first instance, have some degree of equivalence with the alleged breach; this is a well-known rule."[133]

When taking defensive measures against intrusions which fall short of armed attack, such as border incidents or the penetration of aircraft into

---

[130] For an extensive treatment of the proportionality principle, *cf.* the Riphagen reports to the ILC concerning the substance, form and degrees of the responsibility in international law of states, First report, ILC Yearbook 1980 II, Part One, pp. 112 *et seq.*, 121 *et seq.*; Third Report; UN Doc. A/CN 4/354, Add. 2, of May 5, 1982, in particular the proposed Article 2 of the 5th Report, as well as Article 9(2) which replaced it, UN Doc A/CN 4/380 of April 4, 1984.

[131] This is the definition provided in A. Verdross, B. Simma, *Universelles Völkerrecht, Theorie und Praxis* (3rd ed., Berlin 1984), section 1342; *cf.* also, however, F. Berber, *Lehrbuch des Völkerrechts*, Vol. III, (2nd ed., München 1977), pp. 95 *et seq.*

[132] A. Verdross, B. Simma, *loc. cit.*, footnote 131, section 66.

[133] Thus it was stated by the Portuguese/German arbitration panel of July 31, 1928, ILR 54, p. 338; *cf.* on this subject K. J. Partsch, on the *Naulilaa* case in Wb VR II, pp. 577 *et seq.*, containing further examples; F. Berber, *loc. cit.*, footnote 131 pp. 95 *et seq.*; *cf.* also E. Thomas, on the Corfu case, in Wb VR II, pp. 311–313, which also deals with the proportionality principle; on the entire question generally, *cf.* W. G. Grewe, *Epochen der Völkerrechtsgeschichte* (1984) Baden-Baden, pp. 734 *et seq.*

703

another state's sovereign territory, military measures are also allowed solely on the basis of the proportionality principle.[134]

On the other hand, where a treaty is breached, the right of withdrawal by the other state involved is a matter which, under Article 60 of the Vienna Convention, lies entirely within its discretion. However, if a generally recognised principle that in exercising this discretion the state concerned is also bound by the proportionality principle.[135]

Also outside the international law of conflict, the proportionality principle is becoming increasingly relevant, e.g. as regards the extension of fishery zones, the lawfulness of which is certainly capable of assessment in the light of the principles of necessity and of proportionality.[136]

These few examples will suffice to show that the proportionality principle is also often applied in international law as a criterion of lawfulness.

2. The Principle of Proportionality Under the European Convention on Human Rights

The proportionality principle has assumed a particular dimension under the European Convention of Human Rights, which was concluded under the auspices of the Council of Europe. For the purpose of gauging the content of the Community law proportionality principle particular attention should be given to the case law of the Commission and the Court, being the two review bodies in relation to the Convention; however, the body of law constituted by the various national legal systems has also been a source of interpretation, e.g. as regards the case law on the term "necessary restrictions" as it occurs in Articles 8 to 11 of the Convention and in Article 2 of the Fourth Protocol.

A brief survey of the case law of the European Commission of Human Rights and that of the European Court of Human Rights reveals that the proportionality principle plays an important part in the protection of individual rights under the Convention.

---

[134] W. Kewenig, "Gewaltverbot und noch zulässige Machteinwirkung und Interventions- mittel," in: Schaumann, *Völkerrechtliches Gewaltverbot und Friedenssicherung* (1971) Baden-Baden, pp. 201 *et seq.*
[135] A. Verdross, B. Simma, *loc. cit.*, footnote 131, section 816.
[136] *Ibid.*, section 1091.

(*a*) *The case law of the European Commission of Human Rights*

In its report in the *Handyside* case,[137] the European Commission of Human Rights indicated that it was bound to observe the proportionality principle in cases involving deprivation of property.

In its decision in *X* v. *Federal Republic of Germany* of October 16, 1980,[138] the Commission held that the provisions of the German Penal Enforcement Law, under which the prison authorities retain part of the money in cash held by the prisoner by way of a bridging sum, served the public interest, and that fixing this sum at DM 1,818 was not disproportionately high.

In its decision of October 10, 1979,[139] the Commission examined, in the light of Article 11 of the Convention, whether the total ban on demonstrations during the Jura dispute complied with the proportionality requirement.

Even though in this case the Commission affirmed the proportional nature of the ban, it nevertheless expressly pointed out that the proportionality principle was one of the factors to be taken into account in assessing the "necessary nature of an intervention."

Our final example from the case law of the European Commission of Human Rights is the decision in *XYZ* v. *Italy* of December 18, 1980.[140] In this case, the Commission had to pronounce judgment on, *inter alia*, an infringement of Article 14 of the Convention. The applicants based their argument on an infringement of Article 14 inasmuch as, in the context of an action concerning the corrupt practices of the American Lockheed company, they, unlike a Minister who was also among the accused, had not obtained the right to defend their actions before Parliament.

The Commission, however, took the view that this separate treatment pursued a legitimate objective. In addition, it revealed a sensible and proportionate relationship between the pursued objective and the methods used. Accordingly, the Commission held that no infringement of Article 14 had taken place.

---

[137] Publications of the European Court of Human Rights, Series B, Vol. 22, *Handyside* case, No. 167, p. 50.
[138] *cf.* A. Bleckmann, Review of the case law, in (1982) EuGRZ, pp. 309 *et seq.* (No. 141).
[139] (1980) EuGRZ, pp. 36 *et seq.*
[140] A. Bleckmann, *loc. cit.*, footnote 138, No. 43.

(b) *The proportionality principle in the case law of the European Court of Human Rights*

The proportionality principle as applied under Article 14 of the Convention has also become a significant factor in the case law of the European Court of Human Rights.

According to the decisions made on the basis of Article 14, not every form of unequal treatment is prohibited, a degree of differentiation being permitted where it is justified on the basis of objective and appropriate criteria. This involves making an assessment of the relationship between the objective and the effect of the measure in question, in which precedence is to be given to the general principles which apply in a democratic society.[141]

Accordingly, unequal treatment is justified where the differentiation made pursues a legitimate objective and where an appropriate relationship exists between the objective pursued and the method used.[142]

In recent times, the Court has also been called upon to examine the proportionality principle in the context of Article 10 of the Convention.[143] In one particularly spectacular case it accepted that an infringement of this principle had taken place.

The applicant, a veterinary surgeon from Hamburg, had taken part in an interview with a regional newspaper in which he criticised standards of animal health care in his home town. As a result, an interim injunction had been obtained against him before the Hamburg District Court on the grounds of unfair competition. This order prohibited the applicant from publishing any further statements such as those he had made in the interview. In case of infringement of this order, he was threatened with a fine and even with a custodial sentence. This decision was justified essentially on the basis that the interview had mentioned that the applicant was the owner of an animal clinic, stating his name and address and including a photograph of him.

---

[141] *cf.* G. Ress, "Der Grundsatz der Verhältnismässigkeit im deutschen Recht," in H. Kutscher (Joint Editor), *Der Grundsatz der Verhältnismässigkeit in europäischen Rechtsordnungen* (1985) Heidelberg, p. 45.

[142] *cf.* Decision of July 23, 1968 in the Belgian Languages case, Series A, No. 6, pp. 33–34 = (1975) EuGRZ, p. 301; Decision concerning the National Trade Union of Belgian Policemen of October 27, 1975, Series A, No. 19, p. 19, No. 44 = (1975) EuGRZ, p. 565; Decision of June 13, 1979 in the *Marckx* case, in (1979) EuGRZ, p. 455, Nos. 32 *et seq.*

[143] Decision No. 10/1983/66/101 of March 25, 1985, *Dr. Sigurd Barthold* v. *Federal Republic of Germany* in (1985) EuGRZ, pp. 170 *et seq.*

The veterinary surgeon having unsuccessfully appealed against the interim injunction before all the available appellate bodies, including the Federal Constitutional Court, he demanded that an action be brought using the ordinary procedure. Although he won the action at the first instance, the relevant decision was overturned by the Hanseatische Oberlandesgericht (Court of Appeal), which reinstated in full the interim injunction. In the reasons for its decision, the Oberlandesgericht examined the proportionality of rules of professional conduct which restricted self-publicity,[144] and concluded that the relevant provision did not constitute a disproportionate infringement of the applicant's freedom of expression within the meaning of Article 5 of the Basic Law, since he had not been prevented from freely expressing his opinions, more particularly those in which he criticised situations requiring rectification, even though such statements inevitably had the effect of promoting his standing. However, there had occurred a number of actions which combined constituted an infringement of Article 7a of the rules of the relevant professional association, such as the inclusion of his full name, of his photograph and of the fact that he was the director of an animal clinic in Hamburg, as well as the comment that, during working days at least, Hamburg pet owners would have to search in vain for an available veterinary surgeon between 8 p.m. and 8 a.m.[145]

In the absence of any likelihood of success, the relevant action for failure to comply with the Basic Law was held to be inadmissible by the Federal Constitutional Court. The subsequent application before the European Commission of Human Rights was successful on the basis of an examination as to whether Article 10 of the Convention had been infringed. On this subject, the Court held that an infringement of Article 10 could be recognised as being lawful only where it was specified in a law, pursued one of the objectives set out in Article 10(2), and was "necessary in a democratic society" for the achievement of this objective.[146]

The Court, having established in this particular case that the infringement had been specified in a law and pursued a legitimate objective, concluded that, in the light of the importance attached to freedom of expression in a democratic society, the restriction in question had exceeded that which was necessary for the achievement of the legitimate objective.

---

[144] Section 7 of the Law relating to the Hamburg Chamber of Veterinary Surgeons.
[145] Which is assumed by the Court, *cf.* (1985) EuGRZ, pp. 172 *et seq.*
[146] *cf.* the Decision in the *Sunday Times* case of April 26, 1979, Series A, No. 30, p. 41, No. 65 = (1979) EuGRZ, p. 386.

D. THE PROPORTIONALITY PRINCIPLE IN COMMUNITY LAW

I. INTRODUCTION

Even now, more than 30 years after the entry into force of the first Community treaty, *i.e.* that establishing the Coal and Steel Community, the law of European integration still does not form a definitely established and complete body of law. On the contrary, Community law is a system which is constantly being developed and refined.[1]

More particularly, what European Community law still lacks is a detailed set of administrative law rules. This is why the review of administrative action is done mainly on the basis of unwritten general legal principles—hence the special importance attached to the proportionality principle in Community law.

When the development of this legal system was still in its infancy, it was French law which exercised a dominating influence,[2] as is evidenced by the fact that the concepts of the rule of law and of legal protection were realised, not primarily as a function of the protection of individual rights, but through the medium of objective administrative law principles.[3]

Thus the Court of Justice has, in the course of its creative decision-making,[4] developed an impressive array of general legal principles,[5] the most important of which will be discussed in the course of this work. As regards the proportionality principle itself, this was, by 1970 at the latest (in the ECJ decision in Case 11/70, *Internationale Handelsgesellschaft* v.

---

[1] *cf.* J. Schwarze, "Europäisches Verwaltungsrecht im Werden, Einführung und Problemaufriss," in J. Schwarze (ed.), *Europäisches Verwaltungsrecht im Werden* (1982) Baden-Baden, p. 11.

[2] On the influence of French law on the development of legal protection in the European Communities, *cf.* the eponymous work by P. Becker, (1963) Hamburg, in particular pp. 55 *et seq.*

[3] *cf.* E.-W. Fuss, *Die Europäischen Gemeinschaften und der Rechtsstaatsgedanke*, Heule (Belgium) (1967), pp. 38 *et seq.*; G. Zieger, *Das Grundrechtsproblem in den Europäischen Gemeinschaften*, (1970) Tübingen, pp. 41 *et seq.*; H. P. Ipsen, *Europäisches Gemeinschaftsrecht* (1972) Tübingen, paragraph 41/21 and 23. On the debate concerning the relative merits of subjective and objective legal protection in Germany, *cf.* H. H. Rupp, *Grundfragen der heutigen Verwaltungsrechtslehre* (1965) Tübingen, p. 8.

[4] For an extensive study on this subject, *cf.* J. Schwarze, Die *Befugnis zur Abstraktion im europäischen Gemeinschaftsrecht* (1976) Baden-Baden.

[5] On the subject of these principles, *cf.* the corresponding chapter in this work.

Einfuhr- und Vorratsstelle für Getreide und Futtermittel),[6] recognised as being the overriding principle for the purpose of setting limits to Community law measures imposing burdens.[7] Case 11/70 concerned the lodging and forfeiting of deposits for import and export licences.[8] The applicant had objected in the course of the proceedings that the forfeiture of the deposit constituted a disproportionate burden in the light of the minor delay which had occurred. For this reason, the rule in question should provide different types of measures, *e.g.* forfeiture in part or other enforcement measures.

The Court did not concur with the arguments put forward by the applicant, but held the compulsory lodging of a deposit to be lawful and, on the subject of the admissibility of its forfeiture, stated that the provision in question was the appropriate measure for the purpose of ensuring, in the general interest, the proper functioning of the organisation of the cereals market without imposing an excessive burden on importers or exporters.[9]

Subsequently, there developed an important body of case law on the subject of the proportionality principle which has, in varying degrees of intensity, affected virtually every area of administrative action governed by Community law and of Community legislation. Before analysing each field of application of this principle in the light of its own specific characteristics, we should, recalling the question raised in the introduction, first examine (a) the manner in which the Court of Justice came to "discover" the proportionality principle, and (b) the importance attached by the Court to this principle.

In other words, our starting point must be to establish the field of application and the status of this legal principle. Once we have located it properly on the Community law spectrum, this will enable us to determine the extent to which this legal principle can serve as a criterion for the review of the various forms of action by the Community institutions, and in particular the extent to which it can assist the legal protection of the Community citizen.

---

[6] *cf.* I. Pernice, *Grundrechtsgehalte im Europäischen Gemeinschaftsrecht* (1979) Baden-Baden, p. 232; *cf.* also G. Zieger, "Die Rechtsprechung des Europäischen Gerichtshofs," Jahrbuch des öffentlichen Rechts, N.F. Vol. 22 (1973), pp. 299 *et seq.*, 319.

[7] Case 11/70 [1979] E.C.R. 1125.

[8] On this problem, *cf.* R. Barents, "The System of Deposits in Community Agricultural Law, Efficiency v. Proportionality" (1985) E.L.R. 239 *et seq.*

[9] For an extensive study of this decision and the system of deposits, *cf. infra*, pp. 731 *et seq.*

II. THE SOURCES OF THE PROPORTIONALITY PRINCIPLE

1. Express Provisions in the Treaty

In his Opinion delivered in Case 11/70, *Internationale Handelsgesell-schaft* v. *Einfuhr- und Vorratsstelle*,[10] Advocate-General Dutheillet de Lamothe specifically explored the question of the legal sources from which the proportionality principle is derived and through which it entered Community law. On this subject, he stated:

> "In fact, the fundamental right invoked here—that the individual should not have his freedom of action limited beyond the degree necessary for the general interest—is already guaranteed both by the general principles of Community law, the compliance with which is ensured by the Court, and by an express provision of the Treaty.
>> — by the general principles of Community law: that has been expressly affirmed by at least two of the Court's judgments: of 29 November 1956 in *Fédération Charbonnière de Belgique* v. *High Authority* (Rec. 1955–56, p. 304) and of 13 June 1958 in *Compagnie des Hauts Fourneaux de Chasse* v. *High Authority* (Rec. 1958, p. 190).
>> — by an express provision of the Treaty: that appears in Article 40 of Title II on agriculture, from which it follows that the common organisation of the markets set up to attain the objectives set out in Article 39 may include only those measures required to attain the objectives set out in Article 39 . . .
> I shall propose the one derived from the written law, for I think that it is good judicial technique to apply unwritten law only in cases of obscurity, insufficiency or gaps in the written law and also that since Article 40 of the Treaty refers not to more or less defined aims of general interest but more precisely to the objectives listed in Article 39 it thereby ensures a more precise guarantee of the rights of individuals than the general principles of Community law."[11]

---

[10] [1970] E.C.R. 1125.
[11] [1970] E.C.R. 1147.

This approach by Advocate-General Dutheillet de Lamothe has been challenged on the grounds that the wording of Article 40 merely permits the adoption of those measures required to achieve the objectives laid down in Article 39 of the EEC Treaty and merely touches upon one aspect of the proportionality principle, *i.e.* the necessity requirement.[12]

A measure might be necessary in itself to meet legal requirements, yet entail for the person affected a disadvantage manifestly disproportionate to the desired result, namely the (re-) establishment of the legal situation. Where this is the case, the measure, although necessary in itself, cannot be imposed.[13]

In his Opinion delivered in Case 31/70, Advocate-General Roemer also appears to entertain doubts about the solution proposed by Advocate-General Dutheillet de Lamothe, where he states:

> "Although in my opinion in Case 73/69 [1970] ECR, I left open the question whether the principle of proportionality can be derived from Article 40 of the EEC Treaty or whether the words mentioned are not on the contrary intended to postulate the power of the Council to make provisions concerning the market organisations, of course there can be no doubt that the Council's wide margin of discretionary power which exists in fact under Community law on the organisation of markets is not unlimited, but is bound to the purpose inherent in the law on the organisation of markets, and that consequently it must be permissible to examine whether the use of this discretionary power is based on proper consideration."[14]

In its Decision, however, the Court adopted the solution proposed by Advocate-General Dutheillet de Lamothe,[15] although over and above the necessity principle in the strict sense, it established in the reasons for its decision that, by limiting the cancellation of the undertaking to export and the release of the deposit to cases of *force majeure*, the Community legislature

---

[12] On the subsidiary principle of necessity, *cf. infra*, pp. 859 *et seq.*

[13] *cf.* E.-W. Fuss, *Der Grundrechtsschutz in den Europäischen Gemeinschaften aus deutscher Sicht*, (1975) Heule/Brussels/Namur, p. 82.

[14] Judgment of December 15, 1970, Case 31/70 *Deutsche Getreide- und Futtermittelhandelsgesellschaft mbH* v. *Hauptzollamt Hamburg-Altona* [1970] E.C.R. 1055 *et seq.*, 1071.

[15] I. Pernice, *loc. cit.*, footnote 6, p. 47, points out that in so doing, the Court favoured a solution which in each case was based on the concrete expression of the principle in written law, even though this may be only by approximation.

"adopted a provision which, without imposing an undue burden on importers or exporters, is appropriate for ensuring the sound functioning of the organisation of the market in cereals, in the general interest as defined in Article 39 of the Treaty."[16]

Thus the Court, in addition to assessing the necessity of the measure, also effected the process of weighing up the interests involved, which is necessary for the purpose of examining the proportionality of a measure in the strict sense of the term, as a result of which the measure in question could have been held unlawful had it excessively restricted the party involved in the exercise of his rights.

2. Deriving the Proportionality Principle from that of the Rule of Law

A number of authors[17] consider the proportionality principle under Community law to be the expression of the principle of the rule of law, which is inherent in the Community law system.

The rule of law is a constitutional principle which is recognised in all Member States, even though it may assume a different appearance and substance in each individual legal system.[18]

According to German legal thinking,[19] a particular distinction should be drawn between the substantive and the formal concepts of the rule of law. In the formal sense, the rule of law requires all forms of state action to be measurable in the light of statute law. In the substantive sense, the rule of law requires the state to be a function of the notion of justice.

Article 28(1) of the Basic Law of the Federal Republic of Germany embodies the principle of the rule of law in both its formal and substantive meaning.[20]

---

[16] [1970] E.C.R. 1140, para. 25.
[17] cf. for example H. P. Ipsen, *Europäisches Gemeinschaftsrecht* (1972) Tübingen, pp. 512, 528.
[18] cf. R. v. Borries (ed.), *Europarecht von A-Z* (1982) München, p. 360.
[19] cf. K. Doehring, *Staatsrecht* (3rd ed., Frankfurt a.M. 1984), p. 234; K. Hesse, *Grundzüge des Verfassungsrechts der Bundesrepublik Deutschland* (15th ed., Heidelberg 1985), paragraph 6, footnote 2; K. Stern, *Das Staatsrecht der Bundesrepublik Deutschland*, Vol. 1, *Grundbegriffe und Grundlagen des Staatsrechts, Strukturprinzipien der Verfassung* (1979) München, paragraph 20; I. von Münch, *Grundgesetzkommentar*, Vol. I, (2nd ed., München 1981), Art. 20 Nos. 21 *et seq.*
[20] cf. the works mentioned under footnote 19.

It is legitimate, then, to ponder the question whether the notion of the rule of law can claim a similar status in Community law.

In its early stages, the Court of Justice mentioned this concept only sporadically.[21] Nevertheless, its early case law had already developed a number of general legal principles whose contents are related to the rule of law.[22] Since the Community, unlike sovereign states, requires an explicit legal basis for every binding act issued by it (*principe de compétence d'attribution*),[23] its exercise of authority is restricted "at its very source" in relation to the individual citizen.[24] The "formal" concept of the rule of law, as it is known in German law, is consequently also recognised in Community law. As a result, the Community citizen can defend himself against the Community exceeding its powers by means of act of legal protection. This state of affairs is expressed by Hans Peter Ipsen in the following terms:

> "It is consequently right to consider the principle of the limited powers of the Community organs, on which the Community treaties are based, to have the effect of a general compulsory rule based on the rule of law, the infringement of which is subject to judicial review."[25]

Ipsen regards the proportionality principle as a manifestation of the principle of the rule of law and, in particular, as an extension of the principle of competence limited by treaty.[26]

However, the Community also meets the requirements of the rule of law in its substantive sense.[27] Even though the original preoccupation of

---

[21] Thus, for example, in the judgment of February 13, 1979, Case 101/78 *Granaria* [1979] E.C.R. 623 at 637.

[22] *cf.* B. Beutler, "Grundrechtsschutz," in H. von der Groeben, H. von Boeckh, J. Thiesing, C.-D. Ehlermann, *Kommentar zum EWG Vertrag* (3rd ed., Baden-Baden 1983), p. 1483.

[23] *cf.* G. Nicolaysen, *Europäisches Gemeinschaftsrecht*, (1979) Stuttgart/Berlin/Köln/ Mainz, pp. 43 *et seq.*, 47; H. P. Ipsen, *loc. cit.*, footnotes 17, 20 to 21 *et seq.*

[24] *cf.* G. Nicolaysen, *loc. cit.*, footnote 23, p. 43.

[25] H. P. Ipsen, *loc. cit.*, footnote 17, pp. 511 *et seq.*; *cf.* also P. Pescatore, "Bestand und Bedeutung der Grundrechte in der Europäischen Gemeinschaft" (1978) EuGRZ, p. 441.

[26] H. P. Ipsen, "Die Verfassungrolle des Europäischen Gerichtshofs für die Integration," in Jürgen Schwarze (ed.), *Der Europäische Gerichtshof als Verfassungsgericht und Rechtsschutzinstanz* (1981) Baden-Baden, pp. 29 *et seq.*, 58.

[27] *cf.* M. Hilf, "Möglichkeiten und Grenzen des Rückgriffs auf nationale verwaltungsrechtliche Regeln bei der Durchführung von Gemeinschaftsrecht," in Jürgen Schwarze (ed.), *Europäisches Verwaltungsrecht im Werden, loc. cit.*, footnote 1, pp. 67 *et seq.*, 84: "It is acknowledged that the principle of the rule of law, in its individual applications, also applies in the Community legal system."

the Court of Justice was to formulate certain objective principles of administrative action complying with the rule of law,[28] these principles have a "binding effect on the Community authorities in the same way as fundamental rights in terms of the automatic protection they give to the Community citizen"[29] and subject the public authorities of the Community to the principle of justice.[30] The idea that the last-named principle applies in Community law was expressed by the Court of Justice in its decision of July 13, 1962 (*Mannesmann* v. *High Authority*), in which it described as a "principle of justice" the duty of the High Authority to achieve the pursued objectives under the best possible conditions and imposing as small a burden as possible on the enterprises involved.[31]

In its more recent case law, the Court of Justice has removed any doubts that it considers the rule of law principle to be an integral part of the Community law system. In its decision of February 13, 1979 (Case 101/78, *Granaria*) it stated for the first time that it considered "the respect for the principle of the rule of law" to be one of the basic features of the Treaty.[32]

3. The Proportionality Principle as Derived from National Rules

In Community law, the applicability of the proportionality principle is justified by reference to the national legal systems of the Member States.[33]

---

[28] E.-W. Fuss, *loc. cit.*, footnote 3, p. 38; G. Zieger, *loc. cit.*, footnote 3, p. 734.

[29] H. P. Ipsen, *loc. cit.*, footnote 17, p. 734.

[30] G. Zieger, *loc. cit.*, footnote 3, p. 40.

[31] Case 19/61 [1961] E.C.R. 717 at 749; the same view is expressed by Lord Mackenzie Stuart, *The European Community and the Rule of Law* (1977) London, p. 31: "Another rule of the same type, this time principally derived from German administrative law, but which I suggest accords with universal good sense, is that an administration should not, in the exercise of discretionary power, employ means which disturb economic interest out of all proportion to the legitimate aim sought to be achieved—what is generally known as the doctrine of proportionality, but which is more accurately to be described as the doctrine of disproportionality."

[32] [1979] E.C.R. 623 at 637; *cf.* later also, for example, Case 155/79 *AM & S Limited* v. *Commission* [1982] E.C.R. 1575 at 1610.

[33] *cf.* I. Pernice, *loc. cit.*, footnote 6, pp. 31 *et seq.*; H. Kutscher, "Zum Grundsatz der Verhältnismässigkeit im Recht der Europäischen Gemeinschaften," in H. Kutscher (Joint ed.), *Der Grundsatz der Verhältnismässigkeit in europäischen Rechtsordnungen* (1985) Heidelberg, p. 91.

The technique used to prove the existence of general legal principles is that of comparative law as a method of evaluation.[34] Where the written Community law does not contain the rules required to enable it to take a decision in a dispute, the Court has felt obliged to play a creative judicial role by elaborating such rules itself.[35]

Acting in this "quasi-rule-making capacity" in determining the precise contents of legal principles to make them relevant to Community law, the Court has drawn from the well of those values which are common to the Member States and on which their legal systems are based.[36] The proportionality principle has also been found to apply, albeit in various forms, in the legal systems of the majority of Member States.[37]

4. The Proportionality Principle as Deduced from the Treaty Provisions

Hans Kutscher, the former President of the European Court of Justice, doubts whether it is necessary to invoke the "supreme principles of the law or the legal principles which are common to the Member States as a reason for the applicability of the proportionality principle in Community law."[38] According to this author, this principle "results from, if I may be forgiven the expression, a more primitive deduction from the Treaty provisions themselves." In his opinion, the Treaties contain a large number of rules in certain areas which involve the use of measures which are "required," "justified" or "necessary," or which "cause the least disturbance" to the functioning of the Common Market.[39] Just as the Court, in the *Ruckdeschel* decision of October 1977, described the special prohibition of discrimination in Article 40(3) and (2) of the EEC Treaty as the "specific expression of the general principle of equality, which belongs to the fundamental principles of Community law," and just as it established that the provisions of a Council Regulation were to a certain extent inconsistent with the principle of equality, so by applying the same

---

[34] *cf.* on this subject *supra*, pp. 71 *et seq.*

[35] J. Schwarze, *Die Befugnis zur Abstraktion im europäischen Gemeinschaftsrecht* (1976) Baden-Baden, p. 224.

[36] J. Schwarze, *Europäisches Verwaltungsrecht im Werden* (1982) Baden-Baden, p. 13; *cf.* also G. Zieger, JöR Vol. 22 (1973), p. 349.

[37] *cf.* on this subject *supra*, Chapter 2, Section 1.

[38] H. Kutscher, *loc. cit.*, footnote 33, p. 91.

[39] *Loc. cit.*, Kutscher gives as examples Articles 36, 40(3), 48(3), 115(2) and (3) EEC.

reasoning the said Treaty provisions (and other rules) could be construed as the "specific expression" of the general principle of proportionality.[40]

5. Summary and Evaluation

The various angles from which the origin of the proportionality principle in Community law can be approached have all, regardless of the other opinions expressed, made an important contribution towards a better understanding of the basis and the present-day significance of this Community law principle. On the one hand, certain essential elements of the proportionality principle can be found in the provisions of the Treaty itself. There is certainly some scope here for finally recognising this principle as a general Community law principle through a universally applicable interpretation of the individual provisions of the Treaties.

On the other hand, there is no obvious reason why, in order to arrive at a more precise description of the proportionality principle in Community law, there should be no recourse to the technique, which has been used in other contexts, of using comparative law as a method of evaluation. Comparative analysis has certainly resulted in the proportionality principle being acknowledged as a constitutional principle in the various legal systems, whatever form it may take. It can also, as has been the case mainly in the Federal Republic of Germany, be derived from the principle of the constitutional state founded on law and justice, the applicability of which has been confirmed on several occasions recently by the European Court of Justice.

Finally, the provinces of the European Convention for the Protection of Human Rights and Fundamental Freedoms also constitute significant points of reference for the development of Community law in this respect.[41]

Accordingly, the European Court of Justice, in the *Rutili* decision, referred to the principle "enshrined in Articles 8, 9, 10 and 11 of the Convention for the Protection of Human Rights and Fundamental Freedoms, signed in Rome on November 4, 1950 and ratified by all the Member States, and in Article 2 of Protocol No. 4 to the same Conven-

---

[40] I. Pernice, *Grundrechtsgehalte im Europäischen Gemeinschaftsrecht* (1979) Baden-Baden, pp. 231 *et seq.*
[41] *cf. supra*, pp. 706 *et seq.*

tion, signed in Strasbourg on September 16, 1963, which provide, in identical terms, that no restrictions in the interests of national security or public safety shall be placed on the rights secured by the above-quoted articles other than such as are necessary for the protection of those interests in a democratic society."[42]

III. THE PROPORTIONALITY PRINCIPLE AS AN OBJECTIVE RULE

1. Its Status

The issue which gives rise to as much discussion as the question concerning the basis for the applicability of the proportionality principle is that of its status in the hierarchy of Community rules. Are we dealing with a constitutional principle, or merely with a principle of administrative law? Has it acquired a place at the level of primary Community law, which would render E.C. regulations subject to its criteria, or at an even higher level, so that it would be unlawful, for example, to remove, by means of additions or amendments to the Treaties (*e.g.* through acts of accession) certain individual areas from the ambit of this principle? Although as late as 1970 Ehlermann[43] rightly stated that the Court could apply the proportionality principle only when reviewing individual aspects of administrative action by the Community authorities and that this principle could not be recognised as constituting a criterion by which to appraise the entire field of Community action, in particular the rules adopted by the Council and the Commission, the case law of the Court on this subject has progressed considerably since then. In the meantime, the proportionality principle has developed into a general overriding principle seeking to restrict those Community legal acts—including rules—which impose burdens.[44] Therefore, the question of the status currently enjoyed by this principle should clearly be answered in the same terms as those expressed by Hans Kutscher, to wit, that the proportionality principle "is entitled to at least the same status as the rules of the

---

[42] Case 36/75 [1975] E.C.R. 1219 *et seq.* at 1232; on this subject, C. Tomuschat, "La libre circulation et le statut politique des ressortissants communautaires," in (1976) CDE pp. 58 *et seq.*, 63; A. Bleckmann on the *Rutili* case in (1976) EuGRZ, p. 265.

[43] (1970) EuR, pp. 39 *et seq.*, 47 footnote 16.

[44] *cf.* G. Ress, "Der Grundsatz der Verhältnismässigkeit im deutschen Recht," in H. Kutscher (Joint ed.), *Der Grundsatz der Verhältnismässigkeit in europäischen Rechtsordnungen* (1985) Heidelberg, p. 38.

Treaty and consequently enjoys a definitely higher status than derived Community law."[45]

Accordingly, the Court, in its decision of July 5, 1977 (*Bela-Mühle*) declared invalid Council Regulation 563/76 of March 15, 1976, relating to the compulsory purchase of skimmed-milk powder.[46]

Does it follow from the above that the proportionality principle is a constitutional, as opposed to an administrative law, principle?

In the present state of Community law, it is impossible to draw a clear distinction between constitutional principles[47] and principles of administrative law.

It is interesting to observe in this context that the majority of general legal principles have been developed, not on the basis of individual administrative acts, but through the review of the legality of regulations—both those adopted by the Council and those enacted by the Commission. In this respect, Council regulations may normally be compared with statute law, at least according to German legal thought. Commission regulations, on the other hand, could be placed on the same level as statutory orders or even mere administrative provisions.

Advocate-General Reischl defines this specific nature of Community law in the following terms: "I should almost be tempted to say that a considerable proportion of Commission action, even where we are dealing with generally applicable regulations in the shape of regulations implementing Council regulations, can be located on the borderline between proper law-making and the adoption of administrative provisions."[48]

It is not irrelevant to decide whether or not the proportionality principle also enjoys constitutional status, since Council regulations could not otherwise be assessed in the light of its requirements. Where, however,

---

[45] H. Kutscher, *Zum Grundsatz der Verhältnismässigkeit*, *loc. cit.*, (footnote 33), pp. 92 *et seq.*

[46] Case 114/76 [1976] E.C.R. 1211 at 1221; *cf.* also Case 116/76 *Granaria* [1977] E.C.R. 1222 at 1223 *et seq.*

[47] This concept is taken as meaning Community constitutional law in the substantive sense; *cf.* on this subject H. P. Ipsen, *loc. cit.*, footnote 17, 2/33 *et seq.*; by the same author, "Zur Tragfähigkeit der Verfassungsprinzipien der Europäischen Gemeinschaft," in R. Bieber (ed.), *Integrationskonzepte auf dem Prüfstand*, Vol. 19 of the series compiled by the Working Party on European Integration (Arbeitskreis Europäische Integration e.V.) (1983) Baden-Baden, pp. 9 *et seq.*

[48] G. Reischl, "Ansätze zur Herausbildung eines europäischen Verwaltungsrechts in der Rechtsprechung des EuGH. Bestandsaufnahme, Einfluss der unterschiedlichen nationalen Rechtsvorstellungen," in Jürgen Schwarze (ed.), *Europäisches Verwaltungsrecht im Werden* (1982) Baden-Baden, pp. 97 *et seq.*, 98.

we are dealing with mere administrative action, it is sufficient to review such action in the light of a corresponding administrative law principle.[49]

The fact that the proportionality principle, in the sense described above, also enjoys "constitutional status" and, being an overriding principle, constitutes a criterion of lawfulness for every Community rule, is specifically referred to by Advocate-General Capotorti in his opinion delivered in Joined Cases 83 and 94/76, 15 and 40/77.[50]

Having affirmed that every Community rule is subject to the equality principle, he notes, in relation to the proportionality principle, that "that principle too is without doubt superior to regulations and it too is aimed at the protection of individuals who derive therefrom a corresponding basic personal right."

Another factor which makes out a case for giving this principle constitutional status is the significance of the proportionality principle for the protection of the Community citizen's fundamental rights.

2. Its Function as a Substitute for Fundamental Rights

In the Court's early decisions, the proportionality principle often filled the gap left by the absence of precisely defined fundamental rights in Community law. In later decisions, this principle has, even where its effect was to place restrictions on rights similar to fundamental rights, provided a considerable degree of legal protection in Community law.[51]

This trend was already clear in the Court's decision of December 14, 1962 (*San Michele*).[52]

In this case, a number of steel manufacturers had lodged a complaint against a request made by the High Authority to transmit invoices relating to electricity consumption to the Commission for the purpose of monitoring production quotas and to provide an assurance that the invoices submitted were final.

---

[49] This is also the conclusion reached by H.-W. Rengeling, "Die Entwicklung verwaltungsrechtlicher Grundsätze durch den Gerichtshof der Europäischen Gemeinschaften" (1984) EuR, pp. 331 *et seq.*, 342 *et seq.*; *cf.* also J. Gundisch, "Allgemeine Rechtsgrundsätze in der Rechtsprechung des Europäischen Gerichtshofs," in J. Schwarze (ed.), *Das Wirtschaftsrecht des Gemeinsamen Marktes in der aktuellen Rechtsentwicklung* (1983) Baden-Baden, pp. 114 *et seq.*

[50] Judgment of May 25, 1978 *Bayerische HNL* v. *Council and Commission* [1978] E.C.R. 1209 at 1230.

[51] *cf.* H. Kutscher, "Über den Gerichtshof der Europäischen Gemeinschaften" (1981) EuR, pp. 392 *et seq.*, 404.

[52] Cases 5–11, 13–14 & 15/62 *San Michele* [1962] E.C.R. 917.

In his opinion, Advocate-General Lagrange pointed out that, according to the existing case law, the necessity to perform the examination in proportion to the objective pursued determined the limits of the powers conferred on the High Authority in applying Article 47. This did not entail, however, that the necessity principle could justify everything. The task of the administrative courts was rather, as in all other areas, to reconcile the requirements of the public interest with the observance of individual rights.[53]

The respect for individual rights was also involved in the ECJ decision of November 12, 1969 (Case 29/69, *Erich Stauder* v. *Stadt Ulm, Sozial-amt*).[54] This judgment is based on a request for a preliminary ruling made by the Stuttgart Administrative Court, in which the Verwaltungsgericht asked the ECJ whether the contents of Article 4 of Decision No. 68/71 of the Commission of February 12, 1969, which made the provision of butter at reduced prices to persons receiving social assistance conditional upon such beneficiaries revealing their name to the seller, were consistent with the general principles of existing Community law.

Without referring specifically to the object of legal protection involved, the Court made the following statement in relation to the disputed rule:

> "In a case like the present one, the most liberal interpretation must prevail, provided that it is sufficient to achieve the objective pursued by the decision in question. It cannot, moreover, be accepted that the authors of the decision intended to impose stricter obligations in some Member States than in others . . .[55]
>
> Interpreted in this way, the provision at issue contains nothing capable of prejudicing the fundamental human rights enshrined in the general principles of Community law and protected by the Court."[56]

Thus the proportionality principle is used here by the Court as an interpretation guideline,[57] more particularly in the sense of an "interpretation conforming to the Constitution or to fundamental rights" (*verfassungs- oder grundrechtskonforme Auslegung*) used in German law.[58]

---

[53] *Ibid.*, at 957.
[54] [1969] E.C.R. 419.
[55] [1969] E.C.R. 425.
[56] [1969] E.C.R. 428.
[57] G. Ress, *loc. cit.*, footnote 44, p. 40.
[58] *cf.* I. Pernice, *loc. cit.*, footnote 40, pp. 45, 230 *et seq.*

In Case 11/70, *Internationale Handelsgesellschaft* v. *Einfuhr- und Vorratsstelle für Getreide und Futtermittel,*[59] the Court, which had initially established the obligation of the Community institutions to protect fundamental rights merely by way of an obiter dictum in its *Stauder* decision, extended the scope of this obligation.

The plaintiff had claimed that the system of deposits laid down in the context of the common organisation of the cereals market infringed "the principles of freedom of action and of disposition, of economic liberty and of proportionality."[60] Having established that the

> "respect for fundamental rights forms an integral part of the general principles of law protected by the Court of Justice,"[61]

the Court merely examined the infringement of the proportionality principle in the sense of a guarantee under Community law which could possibly be violated. The Court arrived at the conclusion that by laying down the disputed system, the Community legislature, acting in the general interest as defined in Article 39 of the Treaty, had "adopted a provision which, without imposing an undue burden on importers or exporters, is appropriate for ensuring the normal functioning of the organisation of the market in cereals."[62]

This decision has been criticised[63] on the grounds that the Court examined the question whether the firm affected by the deposit system had suffered an excessive burden in a one-sided manner by approaching it from the angle of the "general interest as defined in Article 39."[64] It was further argued (a) that there is no basis in the existing legislation for evaluating the interests to be balanced against this "general interest," (b) that under the German constitutional system, fundamental rights have such a basis and thus constitute a criterion for balancing public and private interests, and (c) that, since Community law contains no fundamental rights, the examination by the Court of the question whether the burden imposed on the firm concerned was excessive had no legislative basis where it concerned itself with private interests.[65]

---

[59] [1970] E.C.R. 1125.
[60] *Loc. cit.,* p. 1134, para. 2.
[61] *Loc. cit.,* p. 1135.
[62] *Loc. cit.,* p. 1140.
[63] H. Rittstieg, "Anmerkung zu EuGH Rs 11/60" (1971) AWD, pp. 183 *et seq.*
[64] *Loc. cit.,* p. 184.
[65] *Ibid.*

Against this, Fuss[66] once again correctly holds that in the case law of the German Constitutional Court, the proportionality principle has also become a decisive criterion in relation to all rules in the field of fundamental rights. The criticism mentioned above is consequently lacking in substance.

It is interesting to note that the rights of the firm involved in the *Internationale Handelsgesellschaft* case definitely belong in the category of fundamental rights, since they concern in particular the freedom of action and of disposition and, more generally, economic liberty[67]—*i.e.* fundamental rights such as can be found in Articles 2, 9, 12 and 14 of the German Basic Law.

The Community treaties contain sufficient grounds for having these fundamental rights protected under Community law. The free movement of goods, the unrestricted provision of services, the freedom of establishment, the free movement of investment and of capital,[68] as well as the references to the rules in the Member States governing the system of property ownership,[69] all constitute objectives which testify to that fact.

In the *Nold* case,[70] the Court was once again presented with an opportunity to concern itself with the questions discussed in this chapter.

In this case, the action was brought against a Commission Decision relating to the approval of a new set of trade rules applicable to the Ruhrkohle AG Company. The plaintiff, the Nold Company, held that these rules were unlawful and considered itself to have been adversely affected by them.

Nold claimed in particular that certain fundamental rights, which were recognised by the national constitutions and which had to be considered as having been "received" into Community law, had been infringed. The company alleged in particular that the right of property ownership, as protected by Article 14 of the German Basic Law, had been infringed.

---

[66] E.-W. Fuss, *Der Grundrechtsschutz in den Europäischen Gemeinschaften aus deutscher Sicht*, Heule/Brussels/Namur, p. 85.

[67] [1970] E.C.R. 1133, para. 2. On the question of economic freedom, *cf.* Gert Nicolaysen, "Wirtschaftsfreiheit," in *Das Europa der zweiten Generation, Gedächtnisschrift für Christoph Sasse* (Bieber, Bleckmann, Capotorti *et al.*, ed.) Vol. II, (1981) Strasbourg, pp. 651 *et seq.*

[68] *cf.* Articles 12 *et seq.*, 52 *et seq.*, 106 EEC. On the question of the "freedom on the European market" conceived as a fundamental rule, *cf.* T. Oppermann, "Europäische Wirtschaftsverfassung nach der Einheitlichen Europäischen Akte," in *Staat und Wirtschaft in der EG, Kolloquium zum 65. Geburtstag von B. Börner* (1987) Baden-Baden, pp. 53, 57 *et seq.*

[69] *cf.* Article 222 EEC, 83 ECSC, and Article 36 EEC, which refers to the protection of industrial and commercial property.

[70] Case 4/73 [1974] E.C.R. 491.

On this question, the Court held:

"As the Court has already stated, fundamental rights form an integral part of the general principles of law the observance of which it ensures. In safeguarding these rights, the Court is bound to draw inspiration from constitutional traditions common to the Member States.

If rights of ownership are protected by the constitutional laws of all the Member States, and if similar guarantees are given in respect of their right freely to choose and practise their trade or profession, the rights thereby guaranteed, far from constituting unfettered prerogatives, must be viewed in the light of the social function of the property and activities protected thereunder. For this reason, rights of this nature are protected by law subject always to limitations laid down in accordance with the public interest.

Within the Community legal order it likewise seems legitimate that these rights should, if necessary, be subject to certain limits justified by the overall objectives pursued by the Community, on condition that the substance of those rights is left untouched."[71]

According to this decision, the proportionality principle therefore also embodies to a certain extent a guarantee of the substance of freedoms protected by Community law.[72]

The Court of Justice explored this aspect more thoroughly a few years later in its well-known decision in Case 44/79, *Hauer* v. *Land Rheinland-Pfalz*.[73] The background to this case was the action brought by a woman named Lieselotte Hauer against the rejection of her application for permission to plant vines on a plot of land in the Bad Dürkheim district. This request had been refused on the basis of Council Regulation 1162/76 of May 17, 1976 concerning measures designed to adjust wine-growing potential to market requirements (O.J. 1976 L135/32). Article 2 of this Regulation prohibited the granting of authorisations for the new planting of vines for a period of three years.

As regards the restrictions placed on the plaintiff's rights of ownership, the Court held:

"Taking into account the constitutional precepts common to the Member States, consistent legislative practices and Article 1 of the

---

[71] [1974] E.C.R. 507.
[72] *cf.* also G. Ress, *Der Grundsatz der Verhältnismässigkeit*, *loc. cit.*, footnote 44, p. 39.
[73] Judgment of December 13, 1979 [1979] E.C.R. 3727.

first Protocol to the European Convention for the Protection of Human Rights, the fact that an act of an institution of the Community imposes restrictions on the new planting of vines cannot be challenged in principle as being incompatible with due observance of the right to property. However, it is necessary that those restrictions should in fact correspond to objectives of general interest pursued by the Community and that, with regard to the aim pursued, they should not constitute a disproportionate and intolerable interference with the rights of the owner, such as to impinge upon the very substance of the right to property."[74]

The proportionality principle also provides a certain degree of "guarantee of substance" in relation to the protection of specific fundamental rights provided under Community law, e.g. the free movement of persons and the freedom to provide services.[75]

The right of free movement inside the Community is subject to the "ordre public" exception. The national notion of "ordre public" has also been to a large extent superseded by Community law standards.[76] For the purpose of determining the contents of the term "national interest," the effect of the proportionality principle is similar to that of a fundamental right.

In his Opinion delivered in Case 118/75, *Watson and Belmann*,[77] Advocate-General Trabucchi referred to the *Royer* decision, according to which the "deportation of an alien, which impinges on the very substance of his freedom of movement and residence," is unlawful from the point of view of the proportionality principle.[78] This circumstance was described by the Court in the following terms:

"Among the penalties attaching to the failure to comply with the prescribed declaration and registration formalities, deportation, in relation to persons protected by Community law, is certainly incompatible with the provisions of the Treaty since, as the Court has already confirmed in other cases, such a measure negates the very right conferred and guaranteed by the Treaty."[79]

---

[74] [1979] E.C.R. 3728.
[75] *cf.* on this subject *supra*, pp. 816 *et seq.*, 829 *et seq.* pp. 793 *et seq.*, 805 *et seq.*, *infra*.
[76] *cf.* I. Pernice, *Grundrechtsgehalte im Europäischen Gemeinschaftsrecht* (1979) Baden-Baden, p. 140.
[77] [1976] E.C.R. 1185, at 1201 *et seq.*
[78] *Loc. cit.*, 1209.
[79] *Loc. cit.*, 1199, para. 20.

Advocate-General Reischl also drew attention to the possible "erosion" of the freedom of movement guaranteed in the EEC Treaty, namely in his opinion in Case 8/77, *Sagulo*,[80] in which he noted that penalties resulting from the absence or invalidity of a residence permit may not be more severe than those which the relevant domestic law provides for the nationals of the Member State concerned, since any other interpretation

> "would lead to the application of penalties quite disproportionate to the criminality of disregard of the formalities with regard to control of aliens and would thus represent a direct obstacle to freedom of movement guaranteed by Community law and to that extent contrary to the EEC Treaty."[81]

In Cases 33/74, *Van Binsbergen*[82] and 39/75, *Coenen*[83] the Court was required to answer the question whether a Member State may impose a residence requirement on a provider of services in order to make him subject to domestic professional rules.[84]

From the point of view of the proportionality principle, Pernice correctly states: "In view of the unconditional guarantee of the freedom to provide services laid down in Article 59 of the EEC Treaty, it is open to question whether the Court of Justice could have ruled that the residence requirement was lawful without denying this right altogether, *i.e.* without undermining its substance."[85]

The oft-expressed viewpoint in relation to this case law that the effect of the proportionality principle in Community law is equal in significance to the fundamental rights which exist in national law has not met with universal consent.[86] It has been challenged on the grounds that, *inter alia*, the proportionality principle acquired its significance for the individual only on the basis of a legal status belonging to the latter and that it would consequently not be accurate to give the principle itself the status of a fundamental right.[87] Instead, the principle in question merely acts as a limitation on such encroachments on those rights of the citizen which do

---

[80] [1977] E.C.R. 1495, at 1508 *et seq.*
[81] *Loc. cit.*, 1512.
[82] [1974] E.C.R. 1311.
[83] [1975] E.C.R. 1547.
[84] For more details concerning the residence requirement, *cf.* below, pp. 805 *et seq.*
[85] I. Pernice, *loc. cit.*, footnote 76, p. 162.
[86] *cf.* R. Boest, *Die Agrarmärkte im Recht der EG* (1984) Baden-Baden, p. 151; A. Bleckmann (1981) EuGRZ p. 274; B. Engler, "Die Schadensersatzklage gegen die EG– geringe Erfolgschancen für den Einzelnen," in (1979) EuGRZ pp. 377 *et seq.*, 380.
[87] R. Boest, *loc. cit.*, footnote 86.

not necessarily affect fundamental rights but can be justified only in the pursuit of mainly public interests.[88]

This criticism is hardly valid in principle. At no time has it been claimed that the proportionality principle constituted a real fundamental right in itself. Thus Kutscher, in particular, has pointed out that this principle cannot be described as either a fundamental right or a subjective right.[89]

Nevertheless, as a criterion for the validity of encroachments on fundamental rights and other subjective rights, as well as on the fundamental freedoms contained in the Treaty, the proportionality principle is of considerable importance as regards the legal protection of the individual, bearing particularly in mind its role as "guarantor of substance" in relation to certain protected rights.[90] In this sense it is possible to agree with Cohen Jonathan,[91] when he describes the proportionality principle as a "principe structurel trouvant son origine dans le droit communautaire lui-même et correspondant à un droit fondamental de l'individu."

IV. THE PRACTICAL APPLICATION OF THE PROPORTIONALITY PRINCIPLE IN THE CASE LAW OF THE EUROPEAN COURT OF JUSTICE

Having explained the theoretical basis of the proportionality principle in Community law, we shall now proceed to examine its contents in detail on the basis of the case law of the European Court of Justice.

In so doing, we must differentiate among the various areas in which this principle has been applied.

The following areas of application are to be distinguished:

    (a) The organisation of agricultural markets.
    (b) The free movement of goods, in particular Article 36 of the EEC Treaty.
    (c) Trading relations with non-Member countries.
    (d) The free movement of persons.
    (e) The freedom of establishment and the freedom to provide services.

---

[88] *Loc. cit.*, p. 152 containing further examples.
[89] H. Kutscher, "Zum Grundsatz der Verhältnismässigkeit im Recht der Europäischen Gemeinschaften," in H. Kutscher (Joint ed.), *Der Grundsatz der Verhältnismässigkeit in europäischen Rechtsordnungen* (1985) Heidelberg, p. 94.
[90] On this subject, *cf.* G. Ress, *loc. cit.*, footnote 44, pp. 39 *et seq.*
[91] G. Cohen Jonathan, "La Cour des Communautés européennes et les droits de l'homme" (1978) RMC, pp. 74 *et seq.*, 86 *et seq.*

(f) Competition law.
(g) The ECSC Treaty.
(h) The internal employment law of the Community institutions.

In the course of this examination, it will inevitably be the case that certain decisions will be featured in various areas of application, in view of the many areas of overlap in this field (*e.g.* where trade with non-Member States involves agricultural produce).

1. The Organisation of Agricultural Markets

(*a*) *Introduction*

For the implementation of its agricultural policy, the Community essentially uses two administrative mechanisms: (a) the provision of incentives for the taking up or extension of certain types of economic activity, and (b) interventions, imposing burdens, in economic trends in order to prevent market irregularities. The administrative implementation of the Common Agricultural Policy is entrusted to the Member States, who in so doing apply mainly rules of domestic administrative law.[92] The ECJ is involved in disputes arising from the administration of the Common Agricultural Policy chiefly through the medium of the preliminary rulings procedure under Article 177 of the EEC Treaty, *i.e.* where the validity of national administrative measures is disputed in the light of Community law, or where the application of those measures gives rise to difficulties of interpretation.

(*b*) *Cases featuring deposits*

(*aa*) *Introduction*

Cases under the Common Agricultural Policy often concern deposits which traders must in certain cases provide by way of guarantee that they will satisfy their obligations, and which may be forfeited in case of non-performance.[93]

---

[92] *cf.* Case 39/70 *Norddeutsches Vieh- und Fleischkontor GmbH* v. *HZA Hamburg St. Annen* [1971] E.C.R. 49 at 58.
[93] For an extensive treatment of this subject, *cf.* R. Barents (1985) E.L.Rev. 239 *et seq.*

The largest category of cases involving such deposits concerns the import and export of produce coming within the scope of the common organisation of agricultural markets, which is subject to official authorisation. Imports and exports of the produce involved require the production of an import or export licence respectively. This rule is intended to provide the Community authorities with an instrument enabling them to monitor the relevant market and thus compile reliable forecasts of market trends.

The issue of the licence in question is conditional upon the lodging of a deposit intended to ensure that the movement of the goods involved is carried out within the period of validity of the licence. If the import or export of these articles does not take place, or is only partially carried out, the deposit is forfeited either wholly or in part.[94]

The second category of cases involving deposits which should be mentioned is that which relates to the provision of subsidies for private storage. The Community grants such subsidies where the applicant undertakes to store, privately and for a few months, certain goods which, by being surplus to demand, constitute a burden on the market, in order to relieve the pressure on the relevant market.

The deposit required under this heading is forfeited if the applicant fails to store the goods either correctly or by the date specified, or if he releases them before the date provided.[95] The deposit mechanism also comes into play where intervention stocks are sold at reduced prices.[96] Thus, for example, the Community releases butter from intervention stocks which may be used only for certain processing operations (*e.g.* for the production of ice-cream powder).

The price at which the butter is to be released is announced by means of an invitation to tender, in which only those who can lodge the deposit specified may participate. The deposit is forfeited if the tenderer withdraws his application before the adjudication or fails to buy the butter after the adjudication.[97] The purchase is in turn conditional upon the provision of a processing deposit, which is forfeited if the processing operation specified is not carried out, or is not carried out within the stated period.[98]

---

[94] *cf.* Article 33 of Commission Regulation 3183/80 of December 3, 1980, O.J. 1980, L338/1.
[95] *cf.* EEC Regulation 1091/80 of the Commission of May 2, 1980, O.J. 1980, L114/18; EEC Regulation 1092/80 of the Commission of May 2, 1980, O.J. 1980, L.114/22.
[96] *cf.*, *e.g.* EEC Regulation 1687/76 of the Commission of June 30, 1976, O.J. 1976, L190/1.
[97] *cf.* Article 22, EEC Regulation 262/79 of the Commission of February 12, 1979, O.J. 1979, L41/1.
[98] *cf.* Article 23, EEC Regulation 262/79, *loc. cit.*, footnote 97.

This system of deposits has recently met with considerable reservations based on the rule of law. It is alleged that the penalties which are part of the rules governing the deposits are inconsistent with general legal principles, in particular the proportionality principle. These reservations arise from the accusation that the relevant rules governing the forfeiture of deposits take but little account of the seriousness of the offence, and no account at all of the extent of the offender's guilt.[99] The question arises whether the Community system of deposits can be described as criminal law in disguise, and consequently whether the seriousness of the offence, as well as the extent of the offender's guilt, must also be taken into account in cases involving the forfeiture of deposits.

(bb) The legal nature of deposits

Tiedemann draws a distinction between two types of deposit.[100] On the one hand, there are the "repayment deposits," whose function is to secure claims for the repayment of benefits granted; on the other hand, there are the "penalising deposits," whose purpose is the carrying out of a penal sanction. The latter type especially forms the subject of Tiedemann's reservations based on the rule of law.

By contrast, Advocate-General Dutheillet de Lamothe considers that the deposits governed by Community law do not have the legal status of penalties, but serve the exclusive purpose of providing security. In his opinion in Case 11/70, he makes the following statement on this subject:

> "Up to the middle of the nineteenth century, the word 'cautionnement' had only one meaning, that given to it by Article 2011 of the French Civil Code, the old fidejussio of Roman law, that is to say, the undertaking whereby a third party intervenes in the relationship between creditor and debtor to guarantee to the creditor that he will carry out the obligations of the debtor if the debtor fails to do so.
>
> But another meaning of the word 'caution' quickly appeared, which has sometimes been called 'administrative' caution and which means the compulsory lodging of a sum of money before being able to carry out certain acts or exercise certain functions in order to guarantee any liabilities which may follow, in particular with regard

---

[99] cf. P. Tiedemann, "Das Kautionsrecht der EWG—ein verdecktes Strafrecht?" in (1983) NJW, pp. 2727 et seq., 2731.

[100] Loc. cit., footnote 99, pp. 2728 et seq.

to public authorities. The latter type of cautionnement, which from the point of view of civil law is related rather to a pledge (nantissement), is very different from the fidejussio which the cautionnement had as its first meaning.

But these two forms of cautionnement may be combined, for example, as is often the case in practice, when the caution nantissement, to coin a phrase, is itself guaranteed by a fidejussor, usually a bank.

But what really is a caution nantissement? In my opinion, it is nothing other than a form of security intended to guarantee compliance with undertakings entered into previously or at the same time.

The institution of a security is clearly only with difficulty capable of being assimilated to the institution of a penalty. A penalty is intended to punish. A security is intended to prevent and possibly to recompense.

The submission made against the disputed provisions and based on the allegation that the Community authorities are not competent to institute penalties thus in my opinion fails 'on the facts,' since those provisions did not institute a system of penalties but a system of securities."[101]

In his Opinion delivered on February 11, 1982, Advocate-General Capotorti also intimates that the forfeiture of deposits is not in the nature of being a criminal sanction in the following terms:

"It must first of all be emphasised that the forfeiture of the security provided for by Regulation 572/78 is not in the nature of a penalty but constitutes at the most a form of withdrawal of the benefit granted to importers by Regulation No. 805/68 and the implementation of the general obligation to pay the levy fixed by the Common Customs Tariff."[102]

To characterise the forfeiture of deposits as a penalty is not consistent with the specific features of the Community rules on agriculture. The object and purpose of the deposit system is to institute a type of security aimed at guaranteeing that a trader who wishes to market agricultural produce satisfies the obligations which he has voluntarily entered into as a

---

[101] [1970] E.C.R. 1144 et seq.
[102] Case 147/81 Merkur Fleischimport v. HZA Hamburg-Ericus [1982] E.C.R. 1389 at 1404.

result of the approval of his economic activity. Once he has obtained the licence, he remains free to import or export the goods involved or to meet the processing requirements. Failure to satisfy his obligations does not constitute an offence and is not as such punished with a fine or any other penalty. The trader merely forfeits his deposit, which normally deters him from failing to satisfy his obligations. The lodging of a deposit provides the administration with some guarantee that the rules relating to trade in agricultural produce will be complied with.

It is in this sense that the Court of Justice, in Case 11/70, recognised the legitimacy of the deposit system on the basis that, without the rules governing the licences or the deposits in question, both the Commission and the national authorities would lack the necessary insight into the state of the cereals market and would not be able to operate properly the various mechanisms aimed at controlling the cereals market.[103]

The Court based this appraisal on the recitals to Regulation 120/67,[104] according to which information must be supplied to the relevant authorities which will enable the latter to assess market trends on a continuous basis in order to be in a position to make proper use of the range of intervention mechanisms at their disposal. The required details are to be obtained through the process of issuing export and import licences. In order to guarantee the "correctness" of these details, it is necessary that the traders involved should actually make use of the licences awarded to them. This, in turn, is guaranteed by the lodging of deposits and by the threat of their forfeiture.

If the lawfulness of this deposit system is consequently recognised, the question which remains to be answered from the point of view of the trader is in what conditions the forfeiture of the deposit is lawful on the basis of its proportionality to the ground of non-fulfilment of obligations and to the degree of his responsibility for this. In addition, he will have an interest in establishing up to what limit the amount of the deposit required remains lawful.

These questions were the subject-matter of a series of preliminary rulings in which the Court of Justice raised the proportionality principle to the status of a decisive criterion for the validity of the deposit system and of the conditions of forfeiture of deposits.

The accusation that the deposit system is archaic by nature[105] is consequently refuted by the fact that the Court, through its use of the general

[103] [1970] E.C.R. 1135.
[104] J.O. 1967, 117/2269; O.J. Sp.Ed. 1967, 33.
[105] cf. P. Tiedemann, loc. cit., footnote 99, p. 2727.

731

legal principles—in particular here the proportionality principle—has made this area of the law an integral part of European administrative law, under which the trader's rights are protected precisely through the application of these general legal principles.[106]

(cc) The amount of the deposit

The lodging of deposits regularly burdens the trader involved with interest and other expenses.[107] The admissibility of the imposition of this burden was recognised by the Court in Case 11/70.

At the same time, however, the ECJ pointed out that the costs involved in lodging the deposit must not be disproportionate in relation to the total value of the goods and other overheads.[108] The upper limit of the charge is reached where the imposition of a deposit has the effect of a fine.[109] Bearing in mind the ultimate objective of the deposit system, i.e. to monitor the market, to make forecasts concerning future market trends and, where appropriate, to allow the adoption of planning measures, the amount of the deposit must vary according to each planning requirement.

Particularly where there is a danger of speculative transactions taking place, larger deposits are justified.[110] Deposits must be fixed in such a way that no financial benefit can accrue as a result of a failure to satisfy the obligations attached to them.[111]

(dd) Forfeiture of deposits

The relevant regulations provide that the deposit shall be forfeited if the secured obligation in question has not been fulfilled at all or within the period specified. In most cases, however, these regulations do not allow for any partial forfeiture commensurate with the seriousness of the failure

---

[106] cf. R. Barents, loc. cit., footnote 93, pp. 239, 244.

[107] The law relating to the organisation of agricultural markets provides for three types of deposit, i.e. cash deposits, bank guarantees and cheques. Normally traders use the bank guarantee, cf. P. Tiedemann, "Rechtsprobleme der Agrarmarktintervention" (1980) EuR, pp. 219 et seq., 236; for a more in-depth study of bank guarantees, cf. F. H. L. Mynssen and J. U. Boll, Die Bankgarantie (1984) Zwolle.

[108] [1970] E.C.R. 1137.

[109] This correct view is shared by R. Barents, loc. cit., footnote 93, p. 245.

[110] Case 25/70 Einfuhr- und Vorratsstelle für Getreide und Futtermittel v. Köster, Berodt and Co. [1970] E.C.R. 1161 at 1183.

[111] R. Barents, loc. cit., footnote 93.

to satisfy the relevant obligation.[112] Only in cases of *force majeure* is provision made for the relaxation of the obligation to import or export and for the release of the deposit.

The Court clarified the *force majeure* concept for the first time in a decision dating from 1968.[113] This holds that *force majeure* applies where circumstances arise which lie beyond the control of the person concerned and make it impossible for him to carry on his obligations within the period specified. The event in question must be so unusual that any person, acting with the due care which should be expected of a conscientious trader, is entitled to regard its occurrence as an improbability. Additional conditions are that the consequences of this event are not preventable, or that their prevention is possible only at disproportionate expense.[114]

In the decision it took two years later in Case 11/70, the Court amended this definition of *force majeure* in the interests of protecting the rights of the person concerned. Under this new definition, the Court does not confine the applicability of this concept to circumstances making it absolutely impossible to carry out the relevant transaction within the period of validity of the licence. Instead, it interprets this concept "in the sense of unusual circumstances outside the control of the exporter, the consequences of which, in spite of the exercise of all due care, could not have been avoided except at the cost of excessive sacrifice."[115] This broad interpretation enabled the Court to establish that

> "It therefore appears that by limiting to cases of *force majeure* the cancellation of the undertaking to export and the release of the deposit, the Community lawgiver promulgated a provision which, while not imposing an undue burden on importers or exporters, is appropriate in order to ensure the normal working of the organisation of the market in cereals, in the general interest as defined in

---

[112] *cf.* however, Article 23, EEC Regulation 262/79, O.J. 1979, L41/1.

[113] Case 4/68 *Schwarzwaldmilch GmbH* [1968] E.C.R. 562 at 575; *cf.* on this subject P. Tiedemann, (1978) RIW/AWD pp. 8 *et seq.*

[114] Case 4/68 *Schwarzwaldmilch GmbH* v. *Einfuhr- und Vorratsstelle für Fette* [1968] E.C.R. 562.

[115] [1970] E.C.R. 1139. On the need for a broad interpretation of the *force majeure* concept, *cf.* G. Reischl, "Ansätze zur Herausbildung eines europäischen Verwaltungsrechts in der Rechtsprechung des EuGH. Bestandsaufnahme, Einfluss der unterschiedlichen nationalen Rechtsvorstellungen," in J. Schwarze (ed.), *Europäisches Verwaltungsrecht im Werden* (1982) Baden-Baden, p. 108. E.-W. Fuss refers to an interpretation "contra legem," in *Der Grundrechtsschutz in den Europäischen Gemeinschaften aus deutscher Sicht* (1975) Heule/Brussels/Namur, p. 80.

733

Article 39 of the Treaty. It follows that no argument against the validity of the deposit system may be derived from the provisions limiting the release of the deposit to cases of *force majeure* only."[116]

The legal dispute on which Case 186/73 *Fleischkontor* v. *Einfuhr- und Vorratsstelle*[117] is based also involved the forfeiture of a deposit. The importer had lodged this deposit by way of security for the import of frozen beef. Before the expiry of the period of validity of the licence granted to him for this purpose, he had submitted a quantity of foreign meat to the meat inspectorate. Since the conditions concerning the veterinary inspection of meat of foreign origin stipulated by German law had not been fulfilled, the import could not take place. Thereupon the import authority declared the deposit which corresponded to the shortfall forfeited. On this point, the Court stated:

> "It is apparent from these objectives, as well as from the actual provisions of the Regulations in question, that the concept of *force majeure* is not confined to that of absolute impossibility but must be extended to include abnormal circumstances, outside the control of the importer, and which have arisen in spite of the fact that the titular holder of the licence had taken all the precautions which could reasonably be expected of a prudent and diligent trader."[118]

The Court arrived at this conclusion having made the following observation concerning the proportionality of the deposit requirement:

> "It should be borne in mind, however, that the public interest, which requires as accurate a forecast as possible of import trends in each Member State and justifies the deposit of security against the grant of authorisation to import, must be reconciled with the necessity of not hampering trade between states by too rigid obligations, a necessity which also derives from the public interest."[119]

But even where the concept of *force majeure* is given a liberal interpretation, the result is merely the fixing of an upper limit and consequently also the application of proportionality to the relationship between the duty imposed and the price demanded. This serves to mitigate the harshness of

---

[116] [1970] E.C.R 1140.
[117] [1974] E.C.R. 491 *et seq.*
[118] [1974] E.C.R. 543 *et seq.*
[119] *Ibid.*

734

the deposit system. However, what will be the situation where the obligation has been only slightly infringed but the relevant regulations nevertheless stipulate the forfeiture of the entire deposit—*i.e.* where the period specified has been only slightly exceeded, or where the infringements concerned merely involve secondary or formal obligations of a relatively minor nature?

In its decision of February 20, 1979 (Case 122/78 *Buitoni* v. *FORMA*)[120] the Court appears to have revised its opinion in this respect.

Having provided a deposit, the Buitoni Company had obtained licences for the import from non-Member States of a certain quantity of tomato purée, which it duly imported within the period of validity of the licences. Nevertheless, the French intervention board decided to refuse the release of the deposit on the grounds that the company had failed to present the supporting import documents within the period specified in Article 3 of Regulation 499/76, under which the deposit is forfeited if, except in cases of *force majeure*, the supporting documents are not submitted within a period of six months following the final day of validity of the licence. According to the third Recital of Regulation 499/76, this provision had been added for the purpose of "administrative efficiency." The Court ruled as follows:

> "That fixed penalty, which is applied to an infringement which is considerably less serious than that of failure to fulfil the obligation which the security itself is intended to guarantee, which is sanctioned by an essentially proportionate penalty, must therefore be held to be excessively severe in relation to the objectives of administrative efficiency in the context of the system of import and export licences."[121]

Consequently, the Court also allows the Commission to set a time limit, resulting in forfeiture of the deposit if exceeded, for the purpose of administrative efficiency, but with the proviso that

> "it should have sanctioned failure to comply with that period only with a penalty considerably less onerous for those concerned than that prescribing the loss of the whole of the security and more closely allied to the practical effects of such an omission."[122]

[120] [1979] E.C.R. 677.
[121] [1979] E.C.R. 685.
[122] *Ibid.*

Shortly after this case, the Court also gave a ruling along these lines on June 21, 1979 in Case 240/78,[123] in which it held that

> "the absolute nature of Article 5(2) of the above mentioned regulation is contrary to the principle of proportionality in that it does not permit the penalty for which it provides to be made commensurate with the degree of failure to implement the contractual obligations or with the seriousness of the breach of those obligations."[124]

The Court consequently interpreted the regulation involved in terms of Community law, and held the latter to be applicable in the sense that

> "the competent authority may declare the deposit forfeit in whole or in part according to the gravity of the breach of the contractual obligations."[125]

The requirement that the forfeiture of the deposit must be proportionate to the infringement in question may not, however, be interpreted as meaning that the trader has a free choice between, on the one hand, satisfying his obligations and, on the other hand, fulfilling them only in part and expecting only part of the deposit to be forfeited. Market conditions can definitely occur which require the strict fulfilment of obligations, if only in relation to the observance of time limits.

It is in this sense that the Court's decision in Case 147/81 is to be interpreted.[126] This case also concerned the forfeiture of a deposit because of a minor non-adherence to the deadline for the processing of imported beef. This deposit had been lodged by the plaintiff in order to qualify for suspension of a levy on imports of frozen beef. In the reasons for its decision, the Court pointed out in the first place that the existence and the extent of the right to suspension of the levy in this field was directly dependent on conditions and trends prevailing in the common market. Although the suspension of the levy was intended to secure adequate supplies for the processing industry in the Community, this could not, however, be at the expense of the fundamental principle of according preference to meat produced in the Community.[127]

---

[123] *Atalanta BV* v. *Produktschap voor Vee en Vlees* [1979] E.C.R. 2137.
[124] *Loc. cit.*, p. 2151.
[125] *Loc. cit.*, p. 2151; *cf.* also G. Reischl, *loc. cit.*, footnote 115, p. 108.
[126] *Merkur Fleischimport* v. *HZA Hamburg-Ericus* [1982] E.C.R. 1389.
[127] *Loc. cit.*, pp. 1396 *et seq.*

Taking into account the relatively rapid pace at which conditions were changing in this market, the Court, in relation to the accusation that the forfeiture of the deposit was disproportionate to the minor infringement of the time limit for processing, stated the following:

"Such an argument is based on a mistaken view of the objectives pursued by the arrangements in question, inasmuch as it fails to take into consideration the need to preserve the role of Community preference which could not be guaranteed, for the reasons given above, if a time-limit for processing were not prescribed for under-takings qualifying for suspension of the levy on imports. Failure to carry out the processing within the period laid down thus directly jeopardiscs the objectives pursued by the system and the penalty attached to it is by no means disproportionate."[128]

In his opinion, Advocate-General Capotorti further points out in this connection that

"the forfeiture of the security provided for by Regulation No. 572/78 is not in the nature of a penalty but constitutes at the most a form of withdrawal of the benefit granted to importers by Regulation No. 805/68 and the implementation of the general obligation to pay the levy fixed by the Common Customs Tariff."[129]

Considering the matter from this angle and taking into account the factors on which the special deposit system introduced by the relevant Reg-ulation is based, Capotorti also arrives at the conclusion that there was no justification for grading the levy according to whether there had occurred a considerable or a minor delay in the processing of the imported meat.[130] The same considerations obviously applied to the forfeiture of the deposit which related to the infringement.

Case 272/81, *Société RU-MI* v. *FORMA*[131] also concerned the forfei-ture of the entire deposit as a result of a minor infringement of the obligations involved.

[128] *Loc. cit.*, p. 1397.
[129] *Loc. cit.*, p. 1404.
[130] *Loc. cit.*, pp. 1404 *et seq.*
[131] [1982] E.C.R. 4167.

737

The plaintiff in the main action had, in the course of denaturing milk, deviated slightly from the standard laid down in the Regulation concerned.[132] As a result, the special subsidy provided for, which for this special denaturing operation (consisting in the transformation of milk powder into fodder intended for animals other than young calves) is considerably larger than that which is paid for fodder intended for calves, was not remitted and the deposit declared forfeit.

In her Opinion, Advocate-General Rozès had pointed out that it was clearly contrary to the proportionality principle

> "to impose the same sanction for the breach of two obligations laid down in the same instrument, one being a fundamental obligation and the other an obligation which is manifestly of secondary importance."[133]

However, she did not consider this issue to be conclusive in this case. Instead, the solution to this dispute depended on the question whether or not

> "the requirement (. . .) is manifestly irrelevant for the attainment of the objective of (the) Regulation."[134]

Although the Advocate-General answered this question in the affirmative and consequently concluded that the provision in question infringed the proportionality principle, the Court followed the opinion expressed by the Commission in denying that such an infringement took place. Earlier in the case, the Commission had explained what alternative monitoring systems could be devised in order to guarantee that the denatured produce could not be used for a purpose other than that which was specified, and why it had decided to proceed with the system at issue.

On this question, the Court held that

> "In view of the amount of the aid granted for the product intended for feed of animals other than young calves and in view of the risk that it might be used for other, unauthorised purposes, the Commis-

---

[132] Regulation 1844/77.
[133] [1982] E.C.R. 4187.
[134] Loc. cit., pp. 4189 et seq.

sion was entitled to stress the importance of the denaturing of skimmed-milk powder by laying down strict conditions in order to prevent any risk of unauthorised use of the product.

Although, in certain cases, the Court has declared void provisions which imposed the same penalty both for failure to fulfil an obligation which the security was intended to guarantee and for a far less serious breach such as failure to adduce proof of performance of the principal obligation within the period prescribed, the decisions concerned are not relevant in this case. The Commission was legally justified in adopting provisions which entail withholding of the aid and loss of the security for failure to fulfil the principal obligation laid down in the tendering procedure and was not obliged to vary the severity of the measure according to the gravity of the tenderer's failure to comply with that obligation. Such a measure cannot be regarded as out of proportion to the objective pursued."[135]

These decisions clearly stated the Court's position that, where an obligation intended to guarantee the achievement of the objectives specified in the relevant provision has not been fulfilled, the proportionality principle should have no mitigating effect.[136]

Exactly how fraught with difficulties this criterion of legality is in its practical application can be clearly gauged from various statements made by Advocate-General Reischl on the one hand and by the Court of Justice on the other in Case 66/82 *Fromançais S.A.* v. *FORMA*.[137]

In this case, the plaintiff in the main action had purchased butter at reduced prices for the purpose of producing bread, cakes and pastries as well as ice-cream, and had lodged a processing security. The Fromançais company having been late in its processing operations, FORMA refused to release the security.

Here, too, we must agree with Advocate-General Reischl's opinion that the seriousness of the infringement had to be judged differently according to whether the processing operations had failed to take place altogether—in which case the forfeiture of the security was perfectly justified—or whether there had been merely a delay in performing them. The Advocate-General concluded as follows:

---

[135] *Loc. cit.*, p. 4180, *cf.* Case 9/85 *Nordbutter* v. *Federal Republic of Germany*, [1986] E.C.R. 2831, paras. 12 *et seq.*
[136] *cf.* R. Barents, "The system of deposits in Community agricultural law," (1985) E.L.Rev. 247.
[137] [1983] E.C.R. 395.

> "In view of that circumstance, it is clear that there is an evident disproportion between the penalty which is imposed when the processing is not done at all and that which applies where the processing is in fact completed but the processing time limit has not been observed (. . .) Consequently there are in fact grounds on which the regulations cited in the question submitted by the national court may be held to be invalid in so far as they provide for the forfeiture of the whole processing security even where the processing is completed after the expiry of the prescribed period."[138]

The Court of Justice did not follow this opinion. Instead, it showed, in the reasons for its decision, the way to follow in assessing the compliance of a particular provision with the proportionality principle:

> "It is necessary to establish, in the first place, whether the means (that provision) employs to achieve its aim correspond to the importance of the aim and, in the second place, whether they are necessary for its achievement."[139]

The Court considered that the objective pursued by the relevant provisions, which stipulated the forfeiture of the entire security in the event of the processing deadline being exceeded, was to prevent those who benefited from the sale of butter at reduced prices from building stocks for speculative purposes[140]; without the fixing of a processing period, or if this could be extended by considerable periods, the danger would arise that the beneficiary could purchase considerable quantities of butter in order to use them for purposes other than those specified by Community law, in particular for speculative purposes.

As regards the necessity for the relevant provisions, the Court rejected the argument put forward by the plaintiff, *i.e.* that the latter had attached no importance to observing the processing deadline because the Commission had on many occasions in the past changed the relevant deadlines, in the following terms:

> "In reality, the experience gained over the years enabled the Commission in the exercise of its discretion in the economic sphere, to consider that slightly longer periods might be allowed the traders

[138] *Loc. cit.*, p. 414.
[139] *Loc. cit.*, p. 404.
[140] *Loc. cit.*, p. 404.

concerned; that must not, however, be regarded as an acknow-
ledgement that no connection exists between the processing period
and the possibility of speculation (. . .) It follows from those considerations that withholding the security in full when the periods prescribed by the Community legislator are exceeded is a step which is
proportionate to the aim pursued by Regulations Nos. 1259/72 and
232/75."[141]

The Court thus recognised the Commission's right to insist on the strict
observance of the relevant provisions, where the Commission is able to
prove that such observance is necessary in order to eliminate all risk of
speculation. The extent to which the person in question had infringed his
obligation appears to be irrelevant in this context.

Barents vividly illustrates the difficulties raised by this case law:

"Although for the administration this interpretation is favourable, as
it relates the decision to release a deposit to a simple test, if the
various conditions have been implemented or not, it may be won-
dered if the efficiency argument is not carried too far."[142]

Nevertheless, this case law can be considered established. In spite of the
doubts expressed by the Advocates-General, the Court arrived at exactly
the same conclusion in the cases cited above.

As Advocate-General Rozès rightly observed in her Opinion delivered
in Case 272/81, rules in the area of agriculture which are subject to review
in the light of the proportionality principle are most frequently adopted in
sectors

". . . in which it is necessary to assess a complex economic situation,
in the present case that of the market in milk products. Accordingly,
in that sector the Community authorities must be able to exercise a
wide discretion in the adoption of appropriate measures subject only
to the limitation that there must be no manifest infringement of a
superior rule of law."[143]

Barents points out that "this harsh regime for the trader could be mitigated, based on the obiter dictum in Case 240 from 78, that if the trader

---

[141] *Loc. cit.*, p. 406.
[142] *Loc. cit.*, footnote 136, p. 247.
[143] [1982] E.C.R. 4190.

could prove beyond doubt that he was not responsible for the (slight) deviations that the objective in question has nevertheless been fulfilled, forfeiture could be adapted to the circumstances involved."[144]

This was confirmed by the Court in a recent decision of September 24, 1985 (Case 181/84 *Fa. Man* v. *IBAP*). In this case, a dispute between E. & F. Man (Sugar) Ltd., a British trading and brokerage firm in sugar, on the one hand, and the Intervention Board for Agricultural Produce (IBAP) on the other, gave rise to the following question, addressed to the Court of Justice by the Queen's Bench Division of the High Court of Justice in accordance with Article 177 of the EEC Treaty:

> "whether Article 6(3) of Commission Regulation (EEC) No. 1880/83 is invalid for breach of principle of proportionality in that it purports to require, except in the event of force majeure, the forfeiture of the entire security in every case where, as a result of an unintentional failure on the part of the applicant, an application for an export licence is not received by the competent intervention agency within the period laid down by the legislation."[145]

The facts of the case were as follows. The Man Sugar company submitted, by a telex dated July 27, 1983, seven tenders for the export of sugar to non-member countries, having previously lodged the required deposit in the form of a bank guarantee. The following day, five of these tenders were accepted by the IBAP. Man Sugar was now obliged, in accordance with the relevant Community law provisions, to apply for export licences by August 2, 1983, at 12 noon (British time) at the latest. In fact, the relevant applications were submitted by the company to the IBAP between 3.41 and 3.57 p.m. The fact that the deadline had thus been exceeded by a few hours was because an employee, whose task it was to represent the appropriate company agent, had been slightly late in sending the relevant telex messages on account of his excessive workload.

However, the IBAP declared the deposit, which amounted to £1,670,370, forfeit, whereupon the Man Sugar company brought proceedings for the repayment of the deposit. As there was no question of *force majeure* in this case, the proportionality principle was the decisive criterion in assessing the compatibility of the disputed provision[146] with Community law.

---

[144] *Loc. cit.*, footnote 136, pp. 247 *et seq.*
[145] Para. 7, [1985] E.C.R. 2889.
[146] Article 6(3)(b) of Regulation 1880/83, O.J. 1983, L187/5.

Article 6(3)(b) of Regulation 1880/83 states:

"(3) Except in the event of force majeure, the security will be released only:
(. . .)
(b) if the recipients of the award apply for their export licence within the time-limit specified in Article 12(b) and only for the quantity for which they have fulfilled the export obligation derived from the export licence mentioned in Article 12(b). Article 33 of Regulation (EEC) No. 3183/80 remains applicable. The security is forfeited in respect of the quantity for which these conditions are not observed."[147]

After confirming the necessity of stipulating a certain deadline for submitting an application for an export licence, Advocate-General Mancini, referring to the prevailing case law, observed in relation to the disputed provision:

"The provision in question is therefore incompatible with the principle of proportionality because forfeiture is automatic, which makes it impossible to adapt the penalty in accordance with the seriousness of the delay in applying for a licence, and because the security is forfeited both for failure to comply with the time-limit and for the deliberate refusal to export."[148]

The Court followed the Advocate-General's viewpoint. In so doing, it took into account the differences in degree of the obligations in question. Referring in turn to previous decisions, which can accordingly be deemed to constitute established case law, the Court stated:

"In order to establish whether a provision of Community law is in conformity with the principle of proportionality, it is necessary to ascertain whether the means which it employs are appropriate and necessary to attain the objective sought. Where Community legislation makes a distinction between a primary obligation, compliance with which is necessary in order to attain the objective sought, and a secondary obligation, essentially of an administrative nature, it cannot, without breaching the principle of proportionality, penalize

[147] *Loc. cit.*, para. 13.
[148] Opinion of June 18, 1985, [1985] E.C.R. 2890.

743

failure to comply with the secondary obligation as severely as failure to comply with the primary obligation."[149]

Accordingly, the Court, having assessed the facts of the case in the light of the disputed provision, concluded that

"the automatic forfeiture of the entire security, in the event of an infringement significantly less serious than the failure to fulfil the primary obligation, which the security itself is intended to guarantee, must be considered too drastic a penalty in relation to the export licence's function of ensuring the sound management of the market in question."[150]

The Court certainly recognised the right of the Commission, in the interests of sound administration, "to impose a time-limit for the submission of applications for export licences."[151] However, the penalty imposed for failure to comply with this time-limit should have been fixed in such a way as to be significantly less severe for the trader concerned than forfeiture of the entire security.

In the last case to be discussed in this context,[152] the Frankfurt Administrative Court, which made a reference to the ECJ under Article 177 of the EEC Treaty, based its view that a deposit which had been declared forfeit could possibly be repaid on the general legal principle of unreasonableness, and requested that its validity in Community law be clarified.

This was one of two questions raised in the course of a lawsuit between the *Karl-Heinz Neumann* company (plaintiff) and the German *Bundesanstalt für landwirtschaftliche Marktordnung* (BALM—the Federal Board for Agricultural Market Organisation) concerning the forfeiture of a security lodged by the plaintiff on the occasion of a purchase application made in accordance with Commission Regulation 731/81 of March 19, 1981.[153]

In the context of the European Monetary System, a number of changes were made, with effect from March 23, 1981, in the major rates of

---

[149] *Loc. cit.*, para. 20; *cf.* on this subject also Case 21/85 *N.V.A. Maas & Co. S.A.* v. *BALM* [1986] E.C.R. 3537.
[150] *Loc. cit.*, para. 29; however, *cf.* also Case 137/85 *Maizena* v. *BALM* [1987] E.C.R. 4587.
[151] *Loc. cit.*, para. 30.
[152] Case 299/84 *Neumann* v. *BALM* [1985] E.C.R. 3663.
[153] On the sale of certain quantities of boned beef from stocks held by certain intervention agencies at flat-rate prices fixed in advance, O.J. 1981, L74/27.

exchange of the Community currencies. The specific exchange rates to be applied in the agricultural sector—the "green rates"—had remained unchanged on March 27, 1981, the date on which the plaintiff submitted its purchase application and lodged its security, and which, under the provisions of the relevant regulation,[154] was conclusive in determining both the sale price and the order in which the various purchase applications would be considered when allocating the available quantities of agricultural produce. The Council did not adjust the green rates to the changes in the major rates of exchange until it enacted Regulation 850/81, which was adopted on April 1, 1981, published on April 4, 1981 and entered into force in the beef sector on April 6, 1981. As a consequence, the price applicable to the meat which was the subject of the plaintiff's purchase application dropped from DM 10,112.68 to DM 9,763.01 per tonne (these being the DM equivalent of the price expressed in ECU).

On the day following the date on which the new green rates came into effect, BALM communicated to the plaintiff a "confirmation of sale" fixed at the price at which the plaintiff had submitted its application, *i.e.* DM 10,112.68 per tonne. As a result of the changes in the exchange rate, the other applicants, who had lodged their application on April 6, 1981 and thus had the benefit of the new green rate applicable to the DM, enjoyed a considerable competitive advantage. Since the plaintiff did not consider it possible to sell the meat on the German market without incurring losses, it refused to fulfil its obligation to purchase and to pay. After BALM had accordingly declared forfeit the security lodged, the plaintiff claimed restitution of the security before the administrative court.

In the reasons for its decision, the ECJ pointed out first of all that the security system, in the context of sales of beef, was intended to guarantee that the purchaser would observe the contractual obligations based on the purchase application on the one hand and the conditions of sale laid down in the relevant Regulation provisions on the other. These conditions included payment of the equivalent of the sale price, fixed in advance in ECU, in the national currency according to the green rate which applied on the date on which the application had been completed by the lodging of the security. After the leading rates of exchange of the EEC currencies had changed on March 23, 1981, it was to be expected that subsequent changes were also possible in the green currencies. From the foregoing, the Court concluded in this case that

---

[154] 2173/79 of the Commission of October 4, 1979, on implementing measures concerning the marketing of beef bought by the intervention agencies, O.J. 1979, L251/12.

"the Community regulations thus offered the prudent trader a choice. He could either lodge his purchase application and security at once, on the basis of the prevailing green rate, and run the risk that the rate would be adjusted to the advantage of competitors who submitted their application after it was adjusted, or he could himself wait for it to be adjusted and run the risk that stocks might by that time be exhausted by his competitors' applications.

If, having made this free choice, a trader refuses to accept the goods on the conditions of sale entailed thereby, the forfeiture of the security, the purpose of which is precisely to ensure that those conditions are complied with, cannot be regarded as disproportionate."[155]

On the question whether there exists in Community law a general legal principle of objective unfairness, which would enable a national authority to grant, on grounds of fairness, a remission of debt where the application of a Community rule involved a burden not envisaged by the Community legislator, the Court, referring to its earlier case law,[156] stated:

"In *Balkan Import/Export*, the Court rules that a national administration was not entitled to apply national law to an application for a remission on equitable grounds of charges due under Community law if this would alter the effect of the Community rules governing the basis and conditions of assessment or the amount of the charge in question; there was no legal basis in Community law for remitting charges on equitable grounds."[157]

This approach by the Court is based on the division of powers between the Community and the Member States, under which a national authority is not empowered not to apply a provision of Community law in a case where it considers that the application of that provision would produce a result which the Community legislator would have clearly sought to avoid, had he considered such a possibility at the time of adopting the

---

[155] Case 299/84 [1985] E.C.R. 3690; in a second decision, Case 38/86 [1987] E.C.R. 1675, para. 9, relating to the same case, the E.C.J. stated that the forfeiture of the security would not lead to any disproportionate consequences if "this purchaser, with the co-operation of the Intervention Board, received a new contract relating to the same quantities but covered by the more favourable price resulting from the alteration of the green rate."
[156] Case 118/76 *Balkan-Import-Export GmbH* v. *HZA Berlin-Packhof* [1977] E.C.R. 1177.
[157] [1985] E.C.R. 3690.

provision in question. Otherwise, the full development of the effectiveness of the provisions of Community law within the Member States could no longer be guaranteed, and the fundamental principle of the uniform application of Community law within the Community as a whole would be placed in jeopardy.[158]

(c) Skimmed-milk powder cases

The problems involved in assessing complex economic issues also form the background of the so-called skimmed-milk powder cases,[159] in which the proportionality principle, together with the objectives of the Common Agricultural Policy, constitute the decisive criterion of assessment.

These cases are based on Regulation 563/76 of the Council of March 15, 1976 relating to the obligation to purchase skimmed-milk powder held by the intervention boards and intended for use in feedstuffs.[160]

This Regulation was adopted at a time when stocks of skimmed-milk powder purchased by the intervention agencies had reached excessive proportions and all measures seeking to reduce the amount of overproduction of milk and to increase sales of skimmed-milk powder had failed. The system established by Regulation 563/76 was intended to assist in the process of reducing stocks by increasing the use of protein contained in skimmed-milk powder in animal feedstuffs. Accordingly, the granting of aids for certain vegetable protein products and for the free movement in the Community of certain imported animal feed products was made subject to the obligation to purchase certain quantities of skimmed-milk powder. The relevant implementing measures prescribed that the skimmed-milk powder be purchased at a price equivalent to approximately three times the value of the feedstuffs.

In Case 114/76, Bela-Mühle,[161] the question was raised as to whether this Regulation was valid or not. It arose in the context of civil proceedings concerning the performance of a contract for the supply of feedstuffs between a producer of concentrated feedstuffs—the plaintiff in the main

---

[158] [1985] E.C.R. 3688.

[159] cf. on this subject C. M. Schmitthoff, "The Doctrines of Proportionality and Non-Discrimination" (1977) E.L.Rev. et seq.

[160] O.J. 1976, L67/18.

[161] [1977] E.C.R. 1211; cf. the similar judgments made on the same date in Case 116/76 Granaria v. Hoofdproduktschap voor Akkerbouwprodukten [1977] E.C.R. 1247, and Joined Cases 119–120/76 Oelmühle u. Becker v. HZA Hamburg u. HZA Bremen-Nord [1977] E.C.R. 1269.

action—and the operator of a specialised battery-hen unit, being the defendant in the main action. In addition to the price agreed in the contract, the plaintiff claimed payment of an amount corresponding to the charges incurred under Regulation 563/76, the validity of which was, however, challenged by the defendant in the main action.

The Court of Justice joined together its examination of the alleged infringement of both the prohibition of discrimination and the proportionality principle. Having initially listed the objectives of the Common Agricultural Policy under Article 39, the Court made the following statement on the question of the scope of the discretion enjoyed by the appropriate authorities:

> "Although Article 39 thus enables the Common Agricultural Policy to be defined in terms of a wide choice of measures involving guidance or intervention, the fact nevertheless remains that the second subparagraph of Article 40(3) provides that the common organisation of the agricultural markets shall be limited to the pursuit of objectives set out in Article 39. Furthermore, the same subparagraph lays down that the common organisation of the markets 'shall exclude any discrimination between producers or consumers within the Community.' Thus the statement of the objectives contained in Article 39, taken together with the rules in the second subparagraph of Article 40(3), supplies both positive and negative criteria by which the legality of the measures adopted in this matter may be appraised."[162]

The Court goes on to point out that a feature of these arrangements

> "was the imposition, not only on producers of milk and milk products, but also, and especially, on producers in other agricultural sectors of a financial burden which took the form, first, of the compulsory purchase of certain quantities of an animal feed product and, secondly, of the fixing of a purchase price for that product at a level three times higher than that of the substances which it replaced. The obligation to purchase at such a disproportionate price constituted a discriminatory distribution of the burden of costs between the various agricultural sectors."[163]

---

[162] [1977] E.C.R. 1220 *et seq.*
[163] *Loc. cit.*, p. 1221.

Without pausing to weigh up the issues any further, the Court concludes as follows:

> "Nor, moreover, was such an obligation necessary in order to attain the objective in view, namely, the disposal of stocks of skimmed-milk powder. It could not therefore be justified for the purpose of attaining the objectives of the Common Agricultural Policy."[164]

An important question raised by this decision is the question of the extent to which judicial review can be brought to bear on the manner in which the Council and the Commission exercise the discretionary powers conferred on them for the purpose of implementing the Common Agricultural Policy.

This question has important implications beyond the skimmed-milk cases, as could already be concluded from the security cases. Advocate-General Capotorti makes the following pronouncement in his opinion:

> "It is beyond dispute that, although the Court is invested with the responsibility of reviewing the validity of regulations, it has no power to evaluate the wisdom of choices of economic policy made by the Council or by the Commission. It is called upon to consider whether or not there has been an infringement of the limits imposed by rules in the Treaty or general principles upon the exercise of the discretionary powers conferred on those Community institutions. It is not, therefore, for the Court to say whether in the light of the economic situation, the Council could have adopted a better provision than that the validity of which is called in question . . .
>
> This does not, however, mean that it is altogether out of the question for the Court to appraise economic considerations to the extent to which their approval is necessary in determining the legality or otherwise of the measure."[165]

More especially on the issue of examining the question whether the proportionality principle had been observed, Advocate-General Capotorti states:

> "But it is clearly no part of the Court's duties to assess the wisdom or otherwise of an aspect of economic policy adopted by the Council or

[164] *Loc. cit.*, p. 1221.
[165] *Loc. cit.*, p. 1226.

by the Commission or to go into the propriety of economic provisions on which certain decisions of those bodies were based. As to the assessment for the need for a measure or of the seriousness of the situation which led to it, there may be cases in which the Court is called upon to make it."[166]

Adopting this attitude, the Advocate-General rejects the argument put forward by the enterprises using the feedstuffs, *i.e.* that the fixing of excessive intervention prices for milk did not contribute to the stabilisation of the relevant markets but resulted in overproduction and an increase in stocks. In his view, an assessment of the wisdom of these measures would lead to an appraisal of the general economic policy adopted by the Council in the dairy sector. Instead, the Advocate-General examined the assessment made by the Council in connection with the adoption of the disputed regulation in attempting to strike a balance between the various interests involved. In this context it is particularly important to consider the question whether a regulation which, whilst furthering some of the objectives set out in Article 39 of the EEC Treaty, nevertheless runs counter to others is incompatible with this provision and consequently invalid. The Advocate-General replied to this question in the following terms:

> "Accordingly, it is not enough to establish that, in a particular intervention measure, one objective or the other is subordinated or sacrificed to the claims of another to justify the finding that the Treaty has been infringed; what must be established is that the facts do not justify the sacrifice of that objective."[167]

This viewpoint should be endorsed. In the area of economic policy decision-making it is certainly possible to envisage situations in which one particular objective which has received priority can be achieved only by measures which are incompatible with another aim stated in the same provision. National governments and parliaments are also regularly vested with this degree of discretion in elaborating their economic policy and in fixing such priorities as are necessary for this purpose.

In the case under examination, the Advocate-General considers that the decisive question is

---

[166] *Ibid.*
[167] *Loc. cit.*, p. 1228.

"whether it is permissible, in the general interest of the Community, to impose specific burdens and sacrifices upon categories outside a sector in difficulty. . . ."[168]

He examines this question in the particular context of the compatibility of the disputed measure with the proportionality principle. Having examined various other measures which could have been adopted (*e.g.* the destruction of the milk surpluses) the Advocate-General concludes by stating that "the fact that, compared with the advantage sought for the Community, that system made demands which were too heavy on certain categories of producers and consumers" leads him to conclude that the said Regulation breached the general principle of proportionality.[169]

Thus the Advocate-General does not examine the question specified above from the point of view of whether the Regulation is compatible or not with the prohibition of discrimination, since, regardless of whether a certain category could be subjected at all to burdens and duties which were totally unrelated to the sector which was the subject of the Regulation, these burdens and duties could not in any case be excessive.

In his Opinion concerning this case, the Advocate-General also examined the relationship between the prohibition of discrimination and the proportionality principle, drawing the distinction between these two concepts in the following terms:

"Non-discrimination is concerned with the relationship between various groups of persons and takes the form of equality of treatment by bodies vested with public authority, whereas the principle of proportionality means that the burdens imposed on the persons concerned must not exceed the steps required in order to meet the public interest involved. If, therefore, a measure imposes on certain categories of persons a burden in excess of what is necessary—which must be appraised in the light of the actual economic and social conditions and having regard to the means available—it violates the principle of proportionality."[170]

The sequence of decisions discussed above was continued by an important judgment of May 25, 1978 in Joined Cases 8 and 94/76, 4, 15 and

[168] *Loc. cit.*, p. 1232.
[169] *Loc. cit.*, p. 1235.
[170] *Loc. cit.*, p. 1232.

40/77,[171] which has become known as the "second skimmed-milk powder" case.

Here, several German enterprises had claimed from the Community, under Article 215(2) of the EEC Treaty, compensation for the damage which they claimed to have suffered as a result of Regulation 563/76, which had been declared invalid.

It has consistently been held in the relevant case law that the Community incurs liability in respect of its economic policy measures only where the provisions in question constitute a sufficiently serious breach of a superior rule of law protecting the individual concerned.[172]

In its *Bayerische* judgment, the Court, referring to the first skimmed-milk powder cases, identified as the infringed rule protecting the individual, only the prohibition of discrimination contained in Article 40(3)(2), and not the proportionality principle. This circumstance prompted the question whether the Court accorded higher priority to the non-discrimination principle than to that of proportionality.[173]

This question must be answered in the negative on the basis of what was stated earlier on the subject of the status of the proportionality principle. The fact that the Court, in the reasons for its *Bayerische* judgment, merely took account of the infringement of the prohibition of discrimination regulated by the Treaty, can be explained by the circumstance that, where it has been established that a rule of the Treaty has been infringed, it no longer appears necessary to have recourse to the general legal principle of proportionality. The Court acted accordingly. The fact that the infringement of the proportionality principle, established in the first skimmed-milk powder case, was not referred to does not necessarily imply an assessment of the status of this principle.

(d) Other cases concerning intervention

The enormous increase in structural surpluses, and the resulting expenditure, prompted the Community to follow a relatively cautious pricing policy and to adopt the practice of no longer guaranteeing prices or subsidies for unlimited quantities of produce. For this reason, a number of restrictive measures were adopted with a view to restoring the balance

---

[171] *Bayerische HNL Vermehrungsbetriebe GmbH and Co. KG and Others* v. *Council and Commission* [1978] E.C.R. 1209.
[172] *cf.* Case 5/71 *Schoeppenstedt* [1971] E.C.R. 975 at 984.
[173] B. Engler (1979) EuGRZ p. 377 (379).

to the markets, *e.g.* the co-responsibility levy imposed on the producer, who would share in the relevant storage or marketing costs through a levy or deduction; other methods included production quotas and guarantee thresholds which, if exceeded, envisaged a drop in the guaranteed price.

In all ECJ decisions on this subject, a major factor has been the question of the extent to which the proportionality principle is capable of placing restrictions on the discretion enjoyed by the Community institutions in taking economic policy decisions.

(*aa*) *Guarantee*

In Case 2/75, the Federal Republic of Germany was empowered to restrict intervention to certain cereals, and the question was raised whether this authorisation, provided by the Commission, also applied to cereals which, although already in transit before the decision was taken, had become the subject of an offer made to the intervention agency only after the decision. Advocate-General Warner stated the following in his opinion:

> "In my opinion, in the situation as it was, with the evident strain on the appellant's storage capacity and the threat of the breakdown of the intervention system in Germany, and having regard to the consequences that such a breakdown could have for German producers and indeed for the CAP itself, the Commission was well entitled to take the view that every ton mattered and that, as regards the traders in question, its only duty was to safeguard legal rights already acquired."[174]

(*bb*) *Co-responsibility levy*

Regarding the legality of the co-responsibility levy for milk, which was introduced by the Council in its Regulation (EEC) 1079/77 of May 17, 1977,[175] the Court's position on the issue of the proportionality of this measure, the wisdom and effectiveness of which were being challenged by the plaintiff in the main action, was as follows:

---

[174] Case 2/75 *Einfuhr- und Vorratsstelle für Getreide und Futtermittel* v. *Fa. C. Mackprang* [1975] E.C.R. 607 at 624.

[175] Regulation on a co-responsibility levy and measures seeking to extend the markets for milk and milk products, O.J. 1977, L.131/6.

"If a measure is patently unsuited to the objective which the competent institution seeks to pursue, this may affect its legality, but on the other hand the Council must be recognised as having a discretionary power in this area which corresponds to the political responsibilities which Articles 40 and 43 impose upon it. As it is directed towards restraining production in the face of surpluses observed, the co-responsibility levy contributes to the attainment of the objective of stabilizing markets. Nor does the level of the rate of levy appear to be disproportionate in relation to the facts referred to by the Council."[176]

On the subject of examining the suitability of the disputed measures, the statements made in this decision accord with the case law of the German Federal Constitutional Court (Bundesverfassungsgericht), in which even those statutes which restrict fundamental rights are not necessarily examined fully as to their suitability.[177]

Instead, the Federal Constitutional Court tends to restrict itself to examining whether the restricting legislation is "totally (*i.e.* absolutely) unsuitable."[178] In recent decisions, it has established that "a measure is suitable if the desired objective can be achieved with its assistance."[179]

Given this criterion based on the secondary principle of suitability, which constitutes a broad-meshed net indeed, we shall examine later what benefits can be derived by applying this principle in the judicial review based on the rule of law.

(cc) Fixing of threshold prices

As a flexible burden on imports, the system of levies serves the purpose of protecting Common Market price levels, which are generally speaking higher than world market prices.[180] It replaced the previous array of national measures such as customs duties, charges with equivalent effect,

---

[176] Case 138/78 *Stölting* v. *HZA Hamburg-Jonas* [1979] E.C.R. 713 at 722.

[177] *cf.* L. Hirschberg, *Der Grundsatz der Verhältnismässigkeit* (1981) Göttingen, p. 51.

[178] Thus, for example, BVerfGE 13, 97 (113); 16, 147 (181); 19, 119 (126 *et seq.*); 29, 402 (410 *et seq.*).

[179] BVerfGE 30, 292 (316); 33, 171 (187); 39, 210 (230); 40, 196 (222).

[180] *cf.* H. P. Ipsen, *Europäisches Gemeinschaftsrecht* (1972) Tübingen, p. 850; G. Nicolaysen, *Europäisches Gemeinschaftsrecht* (1979) Stuttgart/Berlin/Köln/Mainz, pp. 127 *et seq.*; B. Beutler, R. Bieber, J. Pipkorn, J. Streil, *Die Europäische Gemeinschaft—Rechtsordnung und Politik* (2nd ed., Baden-Baden 1982), p. 423.

quantitative restrictions, minimum prices, etc. The amount of the levies corresponds to the difference between the threshold price, which is fixed by the Community for one trading year, and to the best quotation on the world market, *i.e.* the so-called c.i.f. price obtained at Rotterdam, which is the largest port receiving imports of cereals. Thus the importer must pay the levy in addition to the sale price.

The fixing of the threshold price was one of the issues involved in the ECJ judgment in *Walzmühle*.[181] In this case, a number of firms sought to obtain, through the Court, compensation from the Council and the Commission for the damage which they claimed the institutions concerned had caused them by imposing an excessively high threshold price, compared with common wheat, for durum wheat imported from non-member states in 1979. The applicants considered that an infringement of the proportionality principle had been committed in that the Council, when it fixed the durum wheat prices as part of its array of mechanisms for market control, had chosen a method which had been unjustifiably prejudicial to them.

Before dealing with the concrete aspects of the proportionality issue, Advocate-General VerLoren van Themaat, in his Opinion, tackled the problem facing the Community institutions in making the appropriate choice among the options available to them. On this subject, he stated that

"even after a political decision has been taken in favour of specific priorities within the objectives of Article 39, the order of objectives chosen usually—and indeed on the market in wheat as well—still leaves considerable discretion as to the choice of the methods to be employed. By virtue of the provisions in the Treaty that discretion of the Council has to be respected by the Court. It must then be said that, according to the Court's decisions (. . .) in actions arising from non-contractual liability against the Community concerning legislative acts involving choices of economic policy that discretion may be regarded as having been exceeded only in the case of a sufficiently flagrant infringement of a 'superior' rule of law protecting the individual."[182]

---

[181] Joined Cases 197–200, 243, 245 & 247/80 *Ludwigshafener Walzmühle* v. *Council and Commission* [1981] E.C.R. 3211; *cf.* also Joined Cases 63–69/72 [1973] E.C.R. 1229 at 1259; Case 6/77 [1977] E.C.R. 1291 at 1298 (Levy).
[182] [1981] E.C.R. 3267.

However, the Advocate-General did not consider that the applicants' private interests had clearly been infringed.

The Court arrived at the same conclusion. First, it pointed out that in determining policy with respect to the fixing of agricultural prices, the relevant Community institutions enjoyed wide discretionary powers, regarding not only the establishment of the factual basis of their action but also the definition of the objectives to be pursued, within the framework of the Treaty provisions, and the choice of the appropriate means of action.[183] Next, the Court held, on the question of the proportionality of the level at which the threshold price had been fixed, that

> "in itself, recourse to differentiation of the various prices administered by the Community seems to be a method particularly well-suited to the general machinery of the market organisation and to the objective pursued in this case, namely development of durum wheat growing with a view to improving the structure of Community production as a whole."[184]

(dd) Fixing the amount of the levy

The Court has ruled in a number of cases[185] that the amount of the levy may not be fixed in such a way as to exceed that which is necessary for the achievement of the objective pursued, *i.e.* to compensate for the difference between the threshold price and the applicable world market price.

Case 95/75, *Effem GmbH* v. *Hauptzollamt Lüneburg*[186] concerned the question whether it was permissible to fix a high levy for feedstuffs without having regard to the amount of starch present.

In the reasons for its decision, the Court pointed out first of all that when fixing an export levy where a distortion of the market takes place, various economic considerations need to be taken into account. From this, the Court concluded, in relation to the case under review, as follows:

> "Consequently the fixing of a standard levy which is applicable irrespective of the quantity, whether negligible or considerable, of cereals included in the products concerned cannot comply with these

---

[183] *Loc. cit.*, p. 3251.
[184] *Loc. cit.*, p. 3253.
[185] *cf.* also R. Boest, *Die Agrarmärkte im Recht der EG* (1984) Baden-Baden, p. 155.
[186] [1976] E.C.R. 361.

provisions. An instance of this would be a levy of 26.25 u.a. per metric ton applicable to products containing only a small quantity of cereals, whilst, moreover, the standard amount of levy was several times in excess of the value of these products."[187]

In Case 73/69[188] the Court was called upon to deal with, *inter alia*, the question whether the levy which applied on the intended date of import—in this case in the field of intra-Community trade—should also be charged where the import had been delayed as a result of *force majeure* (in this case the import had been delayed because the waterways had iced over).

In his Opinion, Advocate-General Roemer initially pointed out that

> "In the present context, there is a wide area of discretion in the formation of market organisations"

and that the only issue involved here was whether the maintenance of the levy had caused the relevant traders to incur restrictions and burdens which could be regarded as discriminatory or unreasonable.[189] On the specific question raised in the case, he went on to state that

> "Finally, all this leads to the conclusion that by refraining from issuing a body of rules governing the case of *force majeure* in the intra-community cereals trade the legislature of the Community remained within the limits which its discretion must be assumed to have in the field in question. Consequently, there can be no question of a breach of the principle of proportionality."[190]

The Court followed this assessment in its decision.[191] If, however, parallels are drawn with the "security cases" discussed above, in which the Court had agreed that it was necessary to allow for *force majeure* where securities were forfeited, this decision appears to contradict this case law.

The Court did correct this decision shortly afterwards where, in a similar case, involving a delay in rail transport, it found as follows:

---

[187] [1976] E.C.R. 368; on the problem of fixing flat rates, *cf.* also Case 87/78 *Welding* v. *HZA Hamburg-Waltershof* [1978] E.C.R. 2457 at 2446.

[188] *Oehlmann* v. *HZA Münster* [1970] E.C.R. 467.

[189] [1970] E.C.R. 485.

[190] *Loc. cit.*, p. 485; on the subject of flat-rate levies in the case of loss of value of goods damaged whilst being transported, *cf.* Case 31/70 *Deutsche Getreide- und Futtermittel-handelsgesellschaft* v. *HZA Hamburg-Altona* [1970] E.C.R. 1055 at 1062.

[191] [1970] E.C.R. 476 *et seq.*

> "It follows from the sixth and seventh recitals of Regulation No. 87/62 that to make, in respect of imports of cereals from third countries, special regulations that provide for the case of force majeure, is justified by reasons of equity. It does not appear that this justification is lacking in the case of imports of cereals from Member States (. . .) While the concept of force majeure in a case such as the present implies that the failure to observe a time-limit provided for in a licence does not involve the loss of entitlement of a levy fixed in advance, this is nevertheless on condition that the delay in importation is due to exceptional circumstances and not negligence of which a prudent importer would not be guilty, either when entering into a contract to buy or to carry, or in asserting his rights against the carrier."[192]

Prior to this, Advocate-General Warner had, in his opinion, pointed to the case law of the Court which had developed between the above two cases, under which Community law could not impose on traders any burdens which were not necessary to achieve the objectives pursued by the regulation concerned.[193] A particular application of this principle, continued the Advocate-General,

> "consists in the requirement that, in appropriate cases, traders should be relieved of the consequences of events amounting to force majeure."[194]

As regards the legal consequences of infringements of the proportionality principle, he further stated:

> "It is true that the principle of proportionality has generally been thought of as one whose effect is to invalidate legislative provisions or other acts infringing it. But I do not, for my part, think that its operation should be regarded as necessarily limited in this way. We are familiar, in all our systems of law, with general principles whose effect need not be to invalidate legislative provisions but may be to supplement them."[195]

---

[192] Case 64/74 *Adolf Reich* v. *HZA Landau* [1975] E.C.R. 261 at 268.
[193] [1975] E.C.R. 274.
[194] *Loc. cit.*
[195] *Loc. cit.*

The Court accordingly considered itself to have the jurisdiction to regard the amount of the levy for imports, as fixed previously, to be applicable, even where the relevant goods were not imported within the 30-day period specified when applying for the licence, provided that the delay incurred can be attributed to circumstances which can be regarded as *force majeure*.[196]

(ee) Quota system

A further example of intervention rules in the field of agriculture which have been assessed in the light of the proportionality principle, is the quota system for the production of isoglucose.

In Case 138/79 *SA Roquette Frères* v. *Council of the European Communities*[197] the applicant applied for the invalidation of the production quota as established in Appendix 2 of Regulation 1293/79 of the Council of June 25, 1979. The applicant claimed, *inter alia*, that a quota system was the most restrictive method possible, as it both involved restrictions of competition and impinged on the right to the free pursuit of economic activity.

The Court did not concur with the applicant's arguments, ruling that

> "the laying down of quotas based on a reference period is a customary procedure in Community law and is appropriate when it is necessary to check production in a particular sector."[198]

Prior to this, Advocate-General Reischl had, in his Opinion, dealt extensively with the applicant's arguments and held, on the question of the restriction of competition, that

> "The principle of proportionality applies only to measures to which individuals are subject, and here it must be borne in mind that the principles of competition are not part of the rights to freedom and property of individuals."[199]

---

[196] *Loc. cit.*, p. 269.
[197] [1980] E.C.R. 3333; *cf.* also Case 230/78 *S.p.A. Eridemia—Zuccherifici Nazionali et al.* v. *Minister for Industry, Trade and Crafts* [1979] E.C.R. 2749 at 2786 and Case 139/80 *Maizena GmbH* v. *Council* [1980] E.C.R. 3393 at 3422.
[198] [1980] E.C.R. 3360.
[199] [1980] E.C.R. 3381.

On the argument that the quota system impinged upon the right to the free pursuit of economic activity, the Advocate-General stated:

"It is apparent from the case law that the right to free exercise of an occupation, trade or profession does not have unrestricted priority in the sense of restricting intervention by the authorities. Restrictions must be accepted in the public interest. The said right is restricted by the aims of the Community serving the general welfare. In the present case the quota arrangements do not bar access to an activity in the sense of freedom to choose a trade, an occupation or profession."[200]

There are clear parallels between these statements by the Advocate-General and the "Pharmacists" decision of the German Federal Constitutional Court (Bundesverfassungsgericht),[201] in which it was held that

"the freedom to exercise a profession (...) can be restricted by public regulation where reasonable considerations of general welfare appear to render these measures appropriate."[202]

In addition, Advocate-General Reischl, in his Opinion, stressed the similarity between the effect of the proportionality principle and that of fundamental rights.[203]

(ff) Minimum prices system

As is the case in other fields,[204] the Community, on the basis of Article 43 of the EEC Treaty and Article XIX of GATT,[205] also lays down protective measures in the field of agriculture. We are dealing here with restrictions of trade which depart from the normal rules for a limited period in order to counter an economic crisis threatened by imports. Thus Article 1 of Council Regulation 1427/71 of July 2, 1971, relating to the introduction of protective measures for products processed from fruit and

---

[200] *Loc. cit.*
[201] BVerfGE 7, p. 377.
[202] *Loc. cit.*, p. 405.
[203] *cf.* on this subject *supra*, pp. 722 *et seq.*
[204] *cf.* on the safeguard provisions in foreign trade, pp. 808 *et seq.* below.
[205] On the relationship between GATT and the European Community, *cf.* the eponymous book by M. Hilf, E.-U. Petersmann (eds.) (1986) Baden-Baden.

vegetables,[206] provided, *inter alia*, that where there existed an actual or potential disturbance of the Community market for various products which could endanger the objectives of Article 39 of the EEC Treaty, "appropriate measures may be taken in trade with non-Member States until the actual or potential disturbance has been eliminated." Council Regulation 1428/71, issued on the same day "to establish the forms of application for the protective measures applicable to processed products made from fruit and vegetables,"[207] set out, in Article 2(1), a system of minimum prices, among other things, which "if they are undercut, may make imports dependent on being effected at a higher price than the minimum price set for the product in question."

When the Commission, in July 1971, arrived at the conclusion that a serious disturbance was threatened for the Community market in tomato concentrate as a result of imports of this commodity from non-Member States, it introduced a system of minimum prices for imports of these products emanating from Greece.[208]

Case 40/72[209] concerned an application made by the Schröder company (the plaintiff in the main action) to the German Federal Office for Food and Forestry for a licence to import tins of tomato purée from Greece. This application was, however, rejected on the grounds that the company was not prepared to fulfil the conditions set out in Article 2 of Regulation 1643/71. The plaintiff lodged, without success, an objection against this rejection and finally appealed against this decision before the administrative court, which referred a number of questions to the ECJ relating to the validity of the Commission regulation concerned. In substantiation of its claim that the regulation was invalid, the Schröder company alleged that the system of minimum prices introduced by the Commission was not suitable for the achievement of the desired market stability, since the system presented considerable opportunities for evasion. On this subject, the Court held that

"With regard to the possibility of there existing possibilities of circumvention, it must be observed that the legality of a Commission act cannot depend on retrospective considerations of its efficacy. Since in the present case it is a question of complex economic measures, which for the purpose of their efficacy necessarily require

[206] O.J. 1971, L151/5.
[207] O.J. 1971, L151/6.
[208] Commission Regulation 1643/71 of July 28, 1971, O.J. 1971, L171/2.
[209] *Schröder* v. *Germany* [1973] E.C.R. 125.

a wide discretion and moreover as regards their effects frequently present an uncertainty factor, the observation suffices that these measures do not appear on issue as obviously inappropriate for the realization of the desired object."[210]

Having thus endorsed the suitability of the disputed measure, the Court, in relation to the judgment exercised by the Commission within its scope for discretion, stated that

"Having regard to the various objects of Article 39 the Commission, in weighing the disadvantages of the minimum price system for the importer against the significance of all the measures taken with regard to third countries and then deciding for the system which had been applied, has not exceeded the limits of its discretion."[211]

(gg) *Monetary compensation system*

In a series of decisions, the Court was called upon to deal with the legality of levying monetary compensatory amounts.[212]

The monetary compensation system was introduced in 1971, when, as a result of the dollar crisis, exchange rates became extremely flexible and currencies started to float. The unit of account served as the common denominator for fixing the common prices, yet the rate of the unit of account remained stable[213]; consequently, the u.a. became detached from the true value of the currencies in accordance with these exchange rate fluctuations, while prices remained the same. As a result, monetary compensation had to be introduced for intra-Community trade, the legal basis of which, Council Regulation 974/71 of May 12, 1971 "concerning certain measures of conjunctural policy to be taken in agriculture following the temporary widening of the margins of fluctuations for the currencies of certain Member States,"[214] was the subject of the decision in Case 5/73, *Balkan Import-Export* v. *Hauptzollamt Berlin-Packhof*.[215] On

---

[210] [1973] E.C.R. 142.

[211] [1973] E.C.R. 143; *cf.* also Case 59/72 *Wünsche* v. *Commission* [1973] E.C.R. 791 at 812 and Case 92/78 *Simmenthal* v. *Commission* [1979] E.C.R. 777 (Minimum price system for the sale of boned frozen beef).

[212] On this subject, *cf.* the extensive study by G. Nicolaysen, *loc. cit.*, footnote 180, pp. 130 *et seq.*

[213] To have extended the currency fluctuations to the u.a. would have led to flexible and floating agricultural prices; *cf.* G. Nicolaysen, *loc. cit.*, footnote 180 p. 131.

[214] O.J. 1971, L106/1.

[215] [1973] E.C.R. 1091.

the question of the proportionality of the monetary compensation measures, the Court stated:

> "In exercising their powers, the institutions must ensure that the amounts which commercial operators are charged are no greater than is required to achieve the aim which the authorities are to accomplish; however, it does not necessarily follow that the obligation must be measured in relation to the individual situation of any one particular group of operators. Given the multiplicity and complexity of economic circumstances, such an evaluation would not only be impossible to achieve, but would also create perpetual uncertainty in the law. An overall assessment of the advantages and disadvantages of the measures contemplated was justified, in this case, by the exceptionally pressing need for practicability in economic measures which are designated to exert an immediate corrective influence; and this need had to be taken into account in balancing the opposing interests.
>
> The Court is not satisfied, then, that in weighing up the advantages and disadvantages of the system linking compensatory amounts to the relationship with the dollar of the national currency of each Member State concerned, and in opting for the system in force, the Council imposed burdens on traders which were manifestly out of proportion to the object in view."[216]

The wide powers of discretion conferred on the Community institutions, referred to in the grounds of judgment in Case 5/73 mentioned above, were the subject of the assessment made by the Court in Case 29/77, *Roquette* v. *France*,[217] in which the legality of a change in the monetary compensatory amounts was under challenge.

Referring to the various objectives set out in Article 39 of the EEC Treaty, the Court held that

> "In pursuing those objectives, the Community institutions must secure the permanent harmonisation made necessary by any conflicts between these objectives taken individually and, where necessary, allow any one of them temporary priority in order to satisfy the demands of the economic factors or conditions in view of which their decisions were made."[218]

---

[216] [1973] E.C.R. 1112.
[217] [1977] E.C.R. 1835.
[218] [1977] E.C.R. 1843 *et seq.*

Consequently the Council may, in elaborating the monetary compensation system, make a global assessment weighing up the advantages and the defects involved in this process.

Referring to the *Roquette* decision, Advocate-General Mayras shortly afterwards pointed out, in his opinion in Case 151/77, *Peiser* v. *Hauptzollamt Hamburg-Ericus*,[219] that even the Commission must not be considered to be under an obligation to

> "decide case by case, or in respect of each product individually, and making distinctions according to the country of export, whether there is a risk of disturbance."[220]

Instead, the Advocate-General recognised that the Commission should be able to make an overall assessment in this respect, since this is the only way in which to guarantee the viability of the system.

Subsequently, the Court was called upon to tackle numerous detailed aspects of the monetary compensation system, which enabled it to assume an increasingly concrete profile. This explains why monetary compensatory amounts are necessary only where currency differences need to be compensated. Consequently, processed products are to be involved in the process of monetary compensation only in accordance with the effect of fluctuations on the basic products.[221] Monetary compensatory amounts applicable to processed products may not exceed the sum of the compensatory amounts for the basic products processed.[222] Also, the levying of the amounts may not lead to the provision of additional protection of the processing industry,[223] since according to the object pursued by the system, compensatory amounts may be levied only to the extent that compensation of the currency fluctuations and developments on the currency markets is necessary for the purpose of maintaining the system of agricultural intervention.

When short-term changes occur in the process of monetary compensation, it sometimes happens that firms which have concluded contracts subject to a monetary compensatory amount fixed at a particular level

---

[219] [1979] E.C.R. 1469.
[220] [1979] E.C.R. 1500; *cf.* also Case 11/78 *Italian Republic* v. *Commission* [1979] E.C.R. 1527; Case 95/78 *Dulciora* v. *Amministratzione delle Finanze dello Stato* [1979] E.C.R. 1549; Case 157/78 *Travigo* v. *Hauptzollamt Aachen-Nord* [1979] E.C.R. 1657.
[221] *cf.* Article 4IIb of Regulation 974/71; Case 131/77 [1978] E.C.R. 1041 at 1050; Case 12/78 [1979] E.C.R. 1731 at 1749.
[222] *cf.* Case 4/79 [1980] E.C.R. 2823 at 2848; Case 109/79 [1980] E.C.R. 2883 at 2908.
[223] Thus Advocate-General Mayras in Case 4/79 [1980] E.C.R. 2869.

experience financial losses because the monetary compensatory amount involved has changed to that firm's disadvantage before the date on which the import or export takes place.

The Commission took this possibility into account when, for example, in Article 1 of Regulation 1608/74 of June 26, 1974 "on special provisions in respect of monetary compensatory amounts,"[224] it authorised the Member States in question "to waive, on a discretionary basis (. . .) the monetary compensatory amount or so much thereof as corresponds to the increase." However, this rule, inspired by considerations of fairness, was, in accordance with Article 2(1) of this Regulation, to "apply only to imports and exports carried out pursuant to binding contracts concluded before the monetary measure referred to in that Article."

This fairness rule was the subject of the Court's judgment in Case 152/80, *Debayser* v. *FIRS*.[225] The plaintiff maintained that this system violated, *inter alia*, the proportionality principle where it resulted in commercial enterprises such as Debayser being exposed to considerable and unforeseeable fluctuations in the monetary compensatory amounts. The plaintiff had entered into the contracts in question after the monetary measures contained in Article 1 of the relevant regulation had been adopted, but before the increase in the actual monetary compensatory amounts.

In its grounds of judgment, the Court initially pointed out that

"the purpose which the provisions of that regulation were designed to fulfil was not to provide traders engaged in the performance of contracts containing pre-fixed conditions with full protection against the application of monetary compensatory amounts."[226]

As regards the alleged violation of the proportionality principle, the Court went on to state that

"Regulation No. 1608/74, being a provision providing for discretionary relief, is designed precisely to mitigate in the appropriate circumstances of fact and of law the hardship which may result for traders from the application of the monetary compensatory amounts and it also helps to prevent the introduction of the amounts from growing excessively burdensome for some of them. In these circumstances it

---

[224] O.J. 1974, L170/38.
[225] [1981] E.C.R. 1291.
[226] [1981] E.C.R. 1304.

cannot be held that such a regulation breaches the principle of proportionality by not affording traders more ample opportunity to benefit from a clause providing discretionary relief."[227]

(hh) Subsidies and denaturing premiums

The final area of the Common Agricultural Policy to be mentioned here is the category of decisions in which the Court was called upon to adjudicate in cases where subsidies or denaturing premiums were not awarded, or in cases involving claims for the refund of subsidies or denaturing premiums which had been wrongly paid.

In Case 27/72, *Aimer* v. *Einfuhr- und Vorratsstelle für Getreide*[228] the plaintiff had, during a period of two days, denatured more than 70 tonnes of common wheat—on the third day, however, this amount had dropped to 27.5 tonnes. In the relevant regulation,[229] it was provided that "the duration of the denaturing process shall not exceed one day per 40 tonnes of cereals processed." This raised the question whether this provision should be interpreted as meaning either (a) that a trader may claim the premium if he denatures a quantity of cereals amounting to less than 40 tonnes—regardless of whether he is dealing with a total or with a residual quantity—as long as the duration of the denaturing process does not exceed one day, or (b) that the author of the regulation, in addition to the duration, also intended to specify the minimum quantity which needed to be denatured per day.

In its decision, the Court pointed out that, in view of the not inconsiderable monitoring costs involved in any denaturing process, it was justifiable to make this process subject to a working rate of 40 tonnes per day in order to avoid too many checks. The case under review, however, concerned a denaturing operation which took place over a number of days. This prompted the conclusion on the part of the Court that

"if on the other hand the process of denaturing lasts several days, the objectives sought are attained if the total duration of the process does not exceed a period which is equivalent to a daily average of 40 denatured tonnes, provided that the undertaking's capacity has been

---

[227] *Loc. cit.*, p. 1307.
[228] [1972] E.C.R. 1091.
[229] Regulation 1403/69 of the Commission of July 18, 1969, J.O. 1969, L180/3, O.J. Sp. Ed. 1969 (II), 345.

used in a rational way. Consequently a balance of less than 40 tonnes denatured on any one day may be taken into consideration, if it arose as a result of a rational use of the undertaking's capacity for denaturing and provided that the maximum duration of the whole process is equivalent to an average of at least 40 denatured tonnes per day. A narrower interpretation of Article 40(3) would go beyond the objectives sought and must for this reason be rejected."[230]

Case 273/81, *Société Laitière de Gacé* v. *FORMA*[231] also concerned the non-payment of a subsidy. In this case, FORMA had refused to pay to the plaintiff in the main action a Community subsidy for caseinate produced by the plaintiff, on the basis that its water content exceeded the maximum water content fixed by the relevant regulation by 0.6 per cent.

In her Opinion,[232] the Advocate-General pointed out that the legislation at issue called for "the assessment of a complex economic situation and consequently the Community institutions are allowed a wide margin of discretion." There would consequently be a breach of the proportionality principle only "if the requirement of a maximum water content of 6 per cent. in the case of caseinate is manifestly irrelevant for the attainment of the objectives of the regulations governing the grant of an aid for the manufacture of those products."

In the course of these proceedings, the plaintiff had raised two arguments which are relevant when it comes to assessing the proportionality of the legislation in question. On the one hand, the objective which seeks to ensure the production of high quality caseinate was, in the light of the aim of promoting the processing of skimmed milk into caseinate, of secondary importance. Consequently there was a lack of proportionality if the subsidy was refused on the basis that the maximum water content had been exceeded in spite of the main objective pursued by the Community legislation having been achieved. On the other hand, it was not necessary to maintain a maximum water content in order to ensure that the product was of adequate quality, particularly as the caseinates intended for use as food were not stored for long periods.

Unlike the Advocate-General, the Court rightly rejected both arguments.[233] It noted that the objective of guaranteeing the quality of the products was an essential aspect of the Community system in question.

---

[230] [1972] E.C.R. 1097 *et seq.*
[231] [1982] E.C.R. 4193.
[232] [1982] E.C.R. 4205 at 4209.
[233] *Loc. cit.*, pp. 4202 *et seq.*

This objective, which sought to identify the products concerned on the market by virtue of their quality, was fully justified. In addition, in certain cases the possibility of a long period of storage could not be ruled out. In these circumstances, the maximum water content specified had to be strictly observed in order to eliminate the danger of reducing the flavour of the product. From the foregoing, the Court concluded that

> "the provisions of Regulation 756/70, which makes the grant of aid conditional upon strict compliance with the maximum water content, are not contrary to the principle of proportionality. The Commission was justified in taking the view that in order to sell the products in question the maintenance of high quality was necessary and that the grant of aid at a reduced rate for a product of substandard quality was not in keeping with that aim."[234]

Case 15/83, *Denkavit Nederland* v. *Hoofdproduktschap voor Akkerbouwprodukten*[235] was based on a dispute in which the plaintiff in the main action had applied for immediate payment of the subsidy for supplies of concentrated feedstuffs in loose form from the Netherlands to Belgium, after the lodging of the monthly application and the presentation of the required supporting documents giving proof of use and the relevant tables. The relevant Community regulation,[236] however, lays down a procedure which results in any delay incurred in the payment of aids in the case of exports being attributed only to the different circumstances which attend exports, *i.e.* the fact that the necessary document for intra-Community trade takes longer to reach its destination than does the national document within a Member State. Claiming a serious breach of the proportionality principle, the plaintiff in the main action argued that the disputed provisions imposed on the exporter a burden which exceeded that which was necessary for the achievement of the supervisory aim involved.

In his Opinion, Advocate-General Mancini pointed out first of all that

---

[234] *Loc. cit.*, p. 4204.
[235] [1984] E.C.R. 2171.
[236] Regulation 1725/79 of the Commission of July 26, 1979 on implementing measures for aids for milk processed into concentrated feedstuffs and for skimmed-milk powder intended for feedstuffs for calves, O.J. 1979, L199/1.

"the proportionality principle does not exclude—in fact it presupposes—consideration and co-ordination of all the requirements of the system."[237]

In the case before the Court, it was essential for the functioning of the common organisation of the market in question

"for exported feedingstuffs to be subject to stricter supervision than that required for products sold on the domestic market. The sacrifice required of traders is thus not disproportionate."[238]

The Court arrived at the same conclusion, although it held on this particular issue that

"since the purpose of those rules is to exclude the possibility of aid being paid twice, as well as that of the goods re-entering normal market channels, and thereby to prevent fraudulent practices, the formalities regarding proof must continue to be rigorously applied both to exports and to inland deliveries."[239]

In addition, the Court pointed out that disproportionate expenditure would be incurred if aid wrongly paid had to be refunded. Accordingly, it had to be stated that

"the principle of proportionality is not breached by Community rules which prescribe prior administrative supervision to ensure compliance with the conditions for the payment of aid where the sums involved are particularly large and there is a particular danger of fraud."[240]

Case 77/81, *Zuckerfabrik Franken* v. *Federal Republic of Germany*[241] concerned a refund of wrongly paid denaturing premiums for sugar. In 1972, denaturing premium allocations relating to 114,500 tonnes of sugar had been issued to this firm. After having denatured the sugar in question, it received the premiums. The company to which the plaintiff in the main action sold the denatured sugar, subject to the condition,

---

[237] [1984] E.C.R. 2188, 2193.
[238] *Loc. cit.*, p. 2193.
[239] *Loc. cit.*, p. 2186.
[240] *Loc. cit.*, p. 2187.
[241] [1982] E.C.R. 681.

stipulated in the contract, that this sugar could be used "only for the feeding of bees and that, where appropriate, evidence of its proper use shall be supplied," had sold the sugar to another firm, which failed to use it in the manner stipulated. This fact prompted BALM to claim reimbursement of the premiums from the plaintiff in the main action.

The court making the reference, which proceeded on the basis that under German law premiums wrongly paid are to be refunded, sought *inter alia* to establish, through its questions, whether the recipient of a denaturing premium allocation was answerable in the event of improper use by third parties.

The particular issue at stake here was whether the legislation in question, which in the event of improper use of the denatured sugar provided that the recipient of the denaturing premium must reimburse the latter, even where the improper use giving rise to the reimbursement was committed by a third party, exceeded that which was appropriate and necessary to achieve the desired objective.

In answering this question, the Court pointed out that the premium was paid mainly in order to permit the sugar to be marketed for use as animal feed. In the case under review involving the Federal Republic of Germany, the allocation of premiums was primarily intended to enable beekeepers to purchase sugar on cheaper terms. The Court concluded from the above that

> "where the denatured sugar had been diverted from that purpose the payment of the premium becomes pointless, and the penalty which has been laid down does not exceed what is appropriate and necessary in order to achieve the end in view."[242]

In his Opinion,[243] Advocate-General Reischl emphasised this conclusion, pointing out that "the plaintiff in the main action participated in the denaturing scheme of its own free will and with knowledge of the duty to repay which existed in certain circumstances."

This conclusion is also justified by the fact that the plaintiff in the main action was contractually able to claim damages from the third party involved.

The reimbursement of denaturing premiums wrongly paid—in this case, the denaturing of wheat—was also the subject of the ECJ decision in

---

[242] *Loc. cit.*, p. 696; *cf.* also Case 9/85 *Nordbutter* v. *Federal Republic of Germany* [1986] E.C.R. 2831, paras. 12 *et seq.*
[243] *Loc. cit.*, p. 697 at 706.

Case 54/81, *Fromme* v. *BALM*.[244] Here, BALM requested the plaintiff in the main action not only to reimburse the denaturing premium, but also to pay interest from the date of payment of the premium until the day of repayment, this interest amounting to 3 per cent. more than the discount rate applied by the Bundesbank, *i.e.* at least 6.5 per cent.

The Court making the reference sought to have the legality of this interest charge reviewed by the ECJ.

Advocate-General VerLoren van Themaat assessed this national legislation in the light of, *inter alia*, the proportionality principle. He pointed out first of all that the Court had developed this principle not only in numerous judgments concerning the Common Agricultural Policy, but also in other judgments, namely those involving safeguard clauses. In addition, it had been regularly applied by the Commission when conducting its competition policy under Article 85(3)(a) and Article 92(3) of the EEC Treaty.[245] The Advocate-General then proceeded to point out that

> "In such cases it was always a matter of applying provisions of Community law the wording of which, or the interpretation placed upon it by the Court in its decisions or by the Commission in its practice, contained the restriction that the action undertaken must be 'required' [first subparagraph of Article 40(3)], 'indispensable' [Article 85(3)] or 'justified' and 'necessary' for the objective in view (safeguard provisions of public policy). The opening words of Article 8 of Regulation (EEC) No. 729/70 of the Council, which is applicable in this case, constitutes such a clause. I accordingly consider that the principle of proportionality, as developed in many decisions of the Court, also constitutes a general principle of Community law in this case which restricts the national application of that article by Member States."[246]

In addition, Advocate-General VerLoren van Themaat held the view that

> "it follows in particular from that principle of proportionality that there must be sufficient proportionality between the interest claimed and the advantage attained through the application of a hardship provision of natural law or other means of mitigation applicable in

---

[244] [1982] E.C.R. 1449.
[245] *Loc. cit.*, p. 1476.
[246] *Loc. cit.*, p. 1477.

771

similar kinds of cases might be justified where it is made apparent that the aim of the denaturing scheme (the use of the relevant quantity of common wheat for cattle feed) has actually been attained in a specified case despite a minor infringement of the relevant Community provision."[247]

In this case, the Court arrived at the conclusion that it was compatible with Community law, in its present state, for a Member State to charge interest on Community denaturing premiums wrongly paid, but only provided that the principle of equality of treatment or the non-discrimination rule were observed.[248] The Court did not deal with the proportionality principle—which had not, in fact, been raised in the course of the proceedings.

In his Opinion in Joined Cases 146, 192 and 193/81, *Baywa* v. *BALM*,[249] Advocate-General Capotorti referred to the statements by his colleague VerLoren van Themaat in Case 54/81. *Baywa* v. *BALM* also concerned not only a claim for reimbursement of denaturing premiums wrongly paid, but also, closely related to this issue, the key question whether under Article 8(1) of Regulation 729/70 of the Council concerning the financing of the Common Agricultural Policy,[250] a Member State merely had the power to claim repayment of Community denaturing premiums irregularly allocated, or whether it was actually obliged to do so. The Court held that it was not possible to confer

"on the competent national authorities a discretion to determine, case by case, whether or not to demand repayment of premiums irregularly granted."[251]

Accordingly, the Court considered the Member States to be under an obligation to reclaim the wrongly paid premiums.[252] However, Advocate-General Capotorti, in his Opinion, held the view that the obligation for

---

[247] *Loc. cit.*
[248] [1982] E.C.R. 1465.
[249] [1982] E.C.R. 1503.
[250] J.O. 1970, L94/13; O.J. Sp.Ed. 1970 (I), 218.
[251] [1982] E.C.R. 1547.
[252] On this issue, *cf.* also O. Gottsmann in H. v.d. Groeben, H. v. Boeckh, J. Thiesing, C.-D. Ehlermann, *Kommentar zum EWG-Vertrag* (3rd ed., Baden-Baden 1983), Article 40, No. 11; H.-W. Rengeling, "Die Entwicklung verwaltungsrechtlicher Grundsätze durch den Gerichtshof der Europäischen Gemeinschaften" (1984) EuR, p. 331 (348 *et seq.*); *cf.* also Joined Cases 205–215/82 *Deutsche Milchkontor GmbH et al.* v. *Federal Republic of Germany* [1983] E.C.R. 2633.

the Member States to demand repayment in every case where premiums had been granted without any legal basis did not exclude the possibility

> "that the obligation in question, which owes its existence to a provision of Community law, may not in individual cases be qualified by certain principles recognised by the Community legal order itself, which are moreover common to all the Member States."

In his view, the proportionality principle is one such legal principle.[253]

2. The Free Movement of Goods

(a) Introduction

More than 50 per cent. of all cases brought before the Court of Justice (other than staff disputes) concern the free movement of goods. During the period which followed the famous *Cassis de Dijon* decision,[254] the proportionality principle started to play an increasingly prominent part in striking the right balance, from the point of view of the goods and interests involved, between the leading principle of the free movement of goods and the requirements of a rational system of trade. However, the proportionality principle also plays a crucial role in relation to the Member States' ability to avail themselves of the safeguard clause of Article 36 of the EEC Treaty. On this subject, the Court has repeatedly pointed out that under Article 36 only those measures can be justified which "satisfy mandatory requirements"[255] and which are "absolutely necessary"[256] for the achievements of the goal pursued.

After a prolonged and varied period of development, the Court laid the foundations for a flexible casuistic approach in relation to the free movement of goods with its key definition of measures having equivalent effect to quantitative restrictions in the *Dassonville* decision,[257] in which it held that

---

[253] [1982] E.C.R. 1547.
[254] Case 120/78 *Rewe* v. *Monopolverwaltung* [1979] E.C.R. 649.
[255] *Loc. cit.*
[256] Case 41/76 *Donckerwolcke* [1976] E.C.R. 1921.
[257] Case 8/74 [1974] E.C.R. 837.

"all trading rules enacted by Member States which are capable of hindering directly or indirectly, actually or potentially, intra-Community trade"[258]

were to be considered as measures having an effect equivalent to quantitative restrictions and thus prohibited under Article 30 of the EEC Treaty. This so-called *Dassonville* formula is exceptionally broad and, according to its wording, embraces virtually every marketing rule issued by the State which affects imports.[259] Accordingly, a more precise version of this broad definition was provided in the authoritative *Cassis de Dijon* decision.[260]

This case concerned imports of the cordial liqueur "Cassis de Dijon" from France to the Federal Republic of Germany. Under the German Branntweinmonopolgesetz (Law relating to the Monopoly in Spirits) and the regulation—adopted on the basis of this Law—concerning the minimum alcohol content of spirits intended for consumption, cordial liqueurs such as "Cassis de Dijon" require a minimum alcohol content of 25 per cent. by volume if they are to circulate freely. In France, on the other hand, an alcohol content varying between only 15 and 20 per cent. is permissible. The import licence requested by the Rewe company, the plaintiff in the main action, was refused by the German Monopoly Administration (Monopolverwaltung), on the grounds that the product could not circulate freely because its alcohol content was too low. In his Opinion, Advocate-General Capotorti, having weighed up, in broad terms, the various interests involved, observed that

"The objective of the protection of the consumer against frauds may, in fact, be attained by other means which are less harmful to trade; in relation to that objective the obstacles placed in the way of the free movement of goods are excessive and, therefore, disproportionate."[261]

In its grounds of judgment, the Court held that, in the absence of a Community system, it was for the Member States to enact all measures relating to the manufacture and sale of alcohol and alcoholic beverages applicable within its sovereign territory. Obstacles to movement within

[258] *Loc. cit.*, p. 852.
[259] *cf.* U. Everling (1982) EuR p. 303.
[260] Case 120/78 [1979] E.C.R. 649 = (1979) EuR p. 417 with annotation by E. Millarg.
[261] [1979] E.C.R. 666 at 674.

the Community resulting from disparities between the national laws relating to the marketing of the products in question had to be accepted

> "in so far as those provisions may be recognised as being necessary in order to satisfy mandatory requirements relating in particular to the effectiveness of fiscal supervision, the protection of public health, the fairness of commercial transactions and the defence of the consumer."[262]

In the event, the Court, like the Advocate-General, was of the opinion that the appropriate information—which was, in itself, necessary—could easily have been conveyed to the purchaser by requiring the origin and alcohol content to be stated on the product packaging.

Following this decision, the Court, in various decisions, has developed a number of restrictive criteria aimed at preventing the concept of measures with equivalent effect from having its scope excessively extended.[263]

In the remainder of this section, we shall endeavour first of all to present a systematic picture of the complex and sophisticated network of rules created by the case law of the ECJ on the free movement of goods. At the same time, we shall try to discover the manner in which the proportionality principle is to be pressed into service in assessing the relevant cases. As invariably happens when decisions are made on a case-by-case basis and a clear trend emerges only gradually, this can only be done retrospectively. The main focus of our interest in this context will be the "measures having equivalent effect," since it is the latter which enable the Member States to place considerable restrictions on the free movement of goods.

(b) The field of application of Article 30 EEC

Of particular importance are the so-called technical barriers to trade. These are national measures relating to the production, marketing and

---

[262] *Loc. cit.*, p. 662.
[263] For an extensive treatment of this subject, *cf.* H.-J. Rabe, "Garantien und Sicherungen des freien Warenverkehrs im Lichte der neuesten Rechtsprechung des EuGH,—Cassis de Dijon und die Folgerechtsprechung," in J. Schwarze (ed.), *Das Wirtschaftsrecht des Gemeinsamen Marktes in der aktuellen Rechtsentwicklung* (1983) Baden-Baden, pp. 41 *et seq.*; M. A. Dauses, *Rechtsprobleme eines "Systems" des freien Warenverkehrs in der Europäischen Gemeinschaft* (1984) Saarbrücken; P. Oliver, "A Review of the Case Law of the Court of Justice on Articles 30 to 36 EEC in 1984," in (1985) 22 C.M.L.Rev. 301–328.

import or export of goods, which have the effect of forming not only obstacles to the free movement of goods within the Community and to trade between the Member States, but also, in a more general sense, restrictions on free competition.[264]

(aa) Measures relating to the quality of food

In Case 15/79, *Groenveld* v. *Produktschap voor Vee en Vlees*,[265] the Court was called upon to give a ruling on the lawfulness of a Netherlands rule prohibiting the storage and processing of horsemeat in the Netherlands.

Whilst the Court saw no infringement of the provisions on the free movement of goods in this rule, on the grounds that the latter concerned "national measures which have as their specific objective the restriction of patterns of exports,"[266] the Advocate-General, in his opinion, concluded that this measure was incompatible with the proportionality principle.

The Advocate-General did not consider this rule to be necessary for the protection of fair competition and of the interests of the consumer. The appropriate method of overcoming any alleged difficulties posed by Netherlands firms was in each case a clear indication addressed to the consumer, stated on the label, concerning the nature of the product. The Advocate-General went on to state that

> "on the other hand a remedy such as that adopted in the Netherlands consisting in a complete prohibition on the production of horsemeat sausages is certainly out of proportion to that object."[267]

It is questionable whether the proportionality principle did not require a distinction to be made between a prohibition of storage and processing for the benefit of the domestic consumer and a prohibition for the purpose of exports.[268] In addition, there must be doubt as to whether the term "specified object," introduced by the Court in this decision, is

---

[264] cf. H.-J. Rabe, *loc. cit.*, footnote 263, p. 41.
[265] [1979] E.C.R. 3409.
[266] [1979] E.C.R. 3415; confirmed in Case 155/80 *Oebel* [1981] E.C.R. 1993.
[267] [1979] E.C.R. 3421.
[268] cf. M. A. Dauses, *loc. cit.*, footnote 263, p. 27.

capable of bringing out the full scope of Article 34 of the EEC Treaty. We shall not, however, probe this question any further in this chapter.[269]

The so-called "apple vinegar cases"[270] concerned Italian rules prohibiting the marketing and importation of vinegar of agricultural origin (in the case under review, apple vinegar imported from the Federal Republic of Germany) which is not derived from acetic acid obtained from wine. Accordingly to these rules, the denomination "vinegar" is restricted to wine vinegar.

In its decision of December 9, 1981, the Court arrived at the following conclusions in this case:

"Whereas it is true, as is confirmed by a consistent line of decisions of the Court, that in the absence of common rules relating to the marketing of a product it is for the Member States to regulate on their own territory all matters relating to the marketing of that product and that obstacles to movement within the Community resulting therefrom must be accepted, the fact remains that those requirements must still be acknowledged to be necessary in order to satisfy mandatory requirements such as the protection of public health, referred to in Article 36, consumer protection or fair trading, which does not appear to be the case here.

As far as fair trading and consumer protection are concerned, those needs ... may be fulfilled by means less restrictive to free movement than a prohibition of the marketing of all kinds of natural vinegars other than wine vinegar."[271]

Case 237/82, *Jongeneel Kaas* v. *Netherlands*[272] concerned a series of Netherlands provisions on the quality of cheese products. The disputed rule contained a restricted list of types of cheese which could be produced

---

[269] *cf.* on this subject R. Wägenbaur, in Groeben, Boeckh, Thiesing, Ehlermann, *Kommentar zum EWG—Vertrag* (3rd ed., Baden-Baden 1983), Article 34, Nos. 15 *et seq.*

[270] The first case (788/79 *Italian State* v. *Gill* (First Apple Vinegar case) [1980] E.C.R. 2071), concerned a reference made in the course of criminal proceedings in which an Italian importer had been charged with importing and marketing German apple vinegar; the second (Case 193/80 [1981] E.C.R. 3019—(Second Apple Vinegar case)) related to an action for infringement of the Treaty brought by the Commission against Italy concerning the repeal of the Italian measures in question.

[271] [1981] E.C.R. 3034 *et seq.*; *cf.* also the opinion of Advocate-General Sir Gordon Slynn, *loc. cit.*, pp. 3042 *et seq.*

[272] [1984] E.C.R. 483.

in the Netherlands—in essence, the traditional Dutch cheeses. Accordingly, the production of cheeses which failed to conform to these provisions was prohibited.

The main action, brought by several cheese wholesalers, was directed against this rule. The issues put to the Court included the question whether the proportionality principle took direct effect in this dispute. On this point, the Court observed, in its grounds of judgment, that

> "there is nothing to prevent a Member State from establishing an inspection agency and allowing it to exercise authority over producers, or even from requiring them to register with, or become affiliated to, that agency, provided that such measures are necessary to ensure compliance with the rules adopted in accordance with Community law.
>
> However, it is contrary to Community law for a Member State (. . .) to reserve exclusively to persons affiliated to such bodies the right to market, re-sell, import, export and offer for export domestic cheese production. It is for the national courts to ascertain whether that is the effect of the legislation submitted for its consideration, either because failure to register or to become affiliated results in prohibition of carrying on business, or because the requirement of affiliation goes beyond what is necessary to ensure compliance with the rules on quality."[273]

Earlier, Advocate-General Mancini had unambiguously replied in the affirmative to the question whether the proportionality principle took direct effect in such cases:

> "The general principle elicited by the Court from the primary and secondary provisions of Community law, and in particular from those fundamental values which are common to the legal systems of Member States, form part of the Community legal order and may therefore be relied upon by individuals before the national court which, as is well known, is also a Community court. However, that is subject to the limitation that such principles may come into operation only in cases where the application of substantive rules of Community law is involved. To be more explicit, those principles may be relied upon by individuals and will be taken into account by

[273] [1984] E.C.R. 507.

778

the courts not in any circumstances but in cases which display some connection with the legal order of the Community."[274]

(bb) *Measures concerning the marketing of products*

In their attempts to place products on the market, traders find themselves faced with many restrictions which frequently give rise to examination by the Court of Justice. These concern formalities to be completed when goods cross frontiers as well as prohibitions of, and obstacles to, their marketing.

Case 8/74 *Dassonville*, which has already been referred to,[275] involved *inter alia* the question whether Article 40 of the EEC Treaty was infringed by a national rule which prohibits the importation of products which bear a designation of origin where, in relation to such products, no official document, drawn up by the country of export, is available which certifies the right to use this designation. This question was raised in the course of criminal proceedings brought against traders with regard to a consignment of Scotch whisky which could circulate freely within France but which, although acquired legally, they had nevertheless imported in violation of Belgian law, lacking as they did a certificate of origin issued by the British customs authorities.

The Court's grounds of judgment made no specific reference to the proportionality principle. However, the underlying idea is hinted at when the Court stated

> "In the absence of a Community system guaranteeing for consumers the authenticity of a product's designation of origin, if a Member State takes measures to prevent unfair practices in this connexion, it is however subject to the condition that these measures should be reasonable and that the means of proof required should not act as a hindrance to trade between Member States and should, in consequence, be accessible to all Community nationals."[276]

Case 104/75, *de Peijper*[277] also concerned the issue, raised in the course of criminal proceedings involving the unauthorised importation of certain

---

[274] *Loc. cit.*, p. 520.
[275] [1974] E.C.R. 837.
[276] *Loc. cit.*, p. 853.
[277] [1976] E.C.R. 613.

pharmaceuticals, of the compatibility of the relevant national rules with the provisions relating to the free movement of goods.

In its grounds of judgment, the Court observed that intra-Community trade would be unduly restricted if a trader was required to supply all the details which are deemed necessary for an examination of the effectiveness and safety of certain pharmaceuticals, where the authorities of another Member State were already in possession of such details and could examine them.[278]

Earlier, Advocate-General Mayras, in his Opinion, had pointed out with reference to Cases 11/70, *Internationale Handelsgesellschaft*[279] and 8/74, *Dassonville*[280] that whilst the Member States enjoyed a large measure of freedom in regulating the market in pharmaceuticals, this freedom ended where the procedures adopted were no longer indispensable for the achievement of the goal pursued or if the same objective could be attained by means of a system which imposed fewer restrictions on free trade.[281]

As a sequel to the criminal proceedings in the *Dassonville* case, the question of the proportional nature of the national rule concerning details of the origin of certain products, which had been challenged in that case, was also raised in an action for infringement of the Treaty brought by the Commission against Belgium.[282]

The Kingdom of Belgium had subjected imports of spirits bearing a certificate of origin, which could circulate freely in other Member States as conforming to the relevant laws in the country of origin, to the fulfilment of conditions regarding the provision of evidence of the right to use this designation which were more stringent than those which applied to the same products where they were imported direct from the country of origin. The Commission saw in this system an infringement of Article 30 of the EEC Treaty.

In its decision, the Court noted in the first instance that it was not possible to say that

"to check the authenticity of a product bearing a designation of origin by the expedient of examining certificates of origin issued in the producer Member State constitutes an unreasonable measure in

---

[278] *Loc. cit.*, p. 636.
[279] [1970] E.C.R. 1125.
[280] [1974] E.C.R. 837.
[281] [1976] E.C.R. 649.
[282] Case 2/78 [1979] E.C.R. 1761.

relation to the objective of guaranteeing the authenticity of the product."[283]

Although the Court concluded from this that the action should be dismissed, on the grounds that it was unable to detect any infringement of Article 30 of the EEC Treaty, it nevertheless provided a restrictive interpretation of the disputed measure, inspired by the proportionality principle, when it held that it was necessary to emphasise

> "that the Kingdom of Belgium has a duty to ensure (...) that traders wishing to import into Belgium spirits bearing a designation of origin duly adopted by the Belgian Government and in free circulation in a regular manner in a Member State other than that of origin are able to effect such imports and are not placed at a disadvantage in relation to direct importers, save in so far as appears reasonable and strictly necessary to ensure the authenticity of those products."[284]

(cc) *Penalties*

In Case 41/76,[285] the Court was required to consider the proportionality of a penalty for a defective customs declaration, in which the origin of certain goods had not, according to the French authorities, been correctly indicated.

The Court observed in the first place that commercial policy measures taken by the Member States could also restrict trade involving goods in free circulation only if they did so in compliance with Community law. It continued, on the subject of the disputed measure, in the following terms:

> "Nevertheless the Member States may not require from the importer more in this respect than an indication of the origin of the products in so far as he knows it or may reasonably be expected to know it.
>
> In addition the fact that the importer did not comply with the obligation to declare the real origin of goods cannot give rise to the application of penalties which are disproportionate taking account of the purely administrative nature of the contravention.
>
> In this respect seizure of the goods or any pecuniary penalty fixed according to the value of the goods would certainly be incompatible

---

[283] [1979] E.C.R. 1785.
[284] *Loc. cit.*, p. 1787.
[285] [1976] E.C.R. 1921.

with the provisions of the Treaty as being equivalent to an obstacle to the free movement of goods.

In general terms, any administrative or penal measure which goes beyond what is strictly necessary for the purpose of enabling the importing Member State to obtain reasonably complete and accurate information on the movement of goods falling within specific measures of commercial policy must be regarded as a measure having an effect equivalent to a quantitative restriction prohibited by the Treaty."[286]

The question of the proportionality of a penalty was also raised in the course of criminal proceedings initiated before the Tribunal de Grande Instance of Montpellier by the *Procureur de la République* and the customs administration against the *Riviora* partners. The latter had, in December 1970 and December 1971, imported several consignments of dessert grapes of Spanish origin into France, these grapes having been despatched from Italy, where they were in free circulation. When imported into France, these consignments were accompanied by a certificate issued by the Istituto Nazionale per il Commercio Estero, which confirmed that the goods conformed to the relevant quality standards and stated Italy as being the country of origin. At the time of importation, the bilateral quota fixed by France for grapes imported from Spain had already been exhausted. As a result of an investigation conducted by the French customs authorities, the Riviora partners were charged with having imported prohibited goods by means of a false declaration of origin based on inappropriate or inaccurate documents.

The question whether Community law precluded the imposition of penal sanctions for making false declarations, where it was established that these declarations had been made in relation to imports which as such could be neither prohibited nor restricted, was answered by the Court in the following terms:

"However, as was held in the judgment of 15 December 1976 in Case 41/76—*Donckerwolcke* v. *Procureur de la République* [1976] 2 ECR 1921—such a requirement would fall under the prohibition contained in Article 30 if the importer were required to declare with regard to origin, something other than what he knows or may reason-

---

[286] [1976] E.C.R. 1937 *et seq.*; for a case which has certain similarities with this one, *cf.* Case 52/77 *Cayrol* v. *Rivoira* [1977] E.C.R. 2261, in which the question was raised of the proportionality of a penalty in the context of a civil lawsuit.

ably be expected to know, or if the omission or inaccuracy of the declaration were to attract penalties disproportionate to the nature of the contravention.

In particular, 'the criminal penalties provided for by the Code des Douanes in respect of false declarations made in order to effect prohibited imports' cannot be applied without regard being had to the fact that the present case did not concern prohibited imports.

Therefore the answer must be that, although the fact that Spanish grapes imported into France from Italy have been declared as being of Italian origin may in appropriate cases give grounds for the application of the criminal penalties provided against false declarations, it would be disproportionate to apply without distinction the criminal penalties provided in respect of false declarations made in order to effect prohibited imports."[287]

(c) Measures restricting exports (Article 34 EEC)

By way of counterpart to Article 30 EEC, Article 34 EEC prohibits quantitative restrictions and measures with equivalent effect on exports between Member States. In practice, this prohibition does not play as important a part as that contained in Article 30 EEC.

In Case 808/79, *Pardini*,[288] one of the questions raised in the course of an action brought by an Italian firm concerning the replacement of an export licence allegedly stolen from this company, related to the proportionality of the EEC Regulation on which the decision rejecting their application was based.[289]

In its grounds of judgment, the Court pointed out that, in order to establish whether the disputed measure was compatible with the proportionality principle, it was necessary to discover first of all the objectives of the rule in question. Referring to its decisions on the rules requiring deposits, it stated the objective in question as being to provide the authorities on whom the task of administering the common organisation of markets had been devolved with precise projections regarding future imports and exports. This objective required that compliance with the obligation to import or export in accordance with the licences granted

---

[287] Case 179/78 *Procureur de la République* v. *Michelangelo Riviora* [1979] E.C.R. 1147 at 1157.
[288] [1980] E.C.R. 2103.
[289] Regulation 193/75 of the Commission of January 17, 1975, O.J. 1975, L25/10.

should be guaranteed by suitable means. In the case of licences containing advance fixing certificates this requirement was all the more necessary because the double use of such licences could confer unjustified advantages on the traders and at the same time impose heavy financial burdens on the Community. Viewed in this light, the prohibition of carrying out a transaction on the basis of mere copies constituted a measure which was at the same time simple and effective, but which admittedly contained the danger that the trader might lose, without any fault on his part, the advantages attached to the original copies of the licences. The conflicting interests involved in such cases were weighed up by the Court in the following terms:

> "In the circumstances it is necessary to examine the situation of traders under the rules in force. In the first place, the risk borne by them derives from the system of advance fixing, which was created in the interests of trade and which in normal cases gives traders considerable benefits. If by requesting advance fixing traders take advantage of those benefits, it is therefore just that they should bear the disadvantages which arise from the necessity, on the part of the Community, of preventing any abuse. In particular, it is reasonable to expect the titular holders of licences or certificates to take the greatest possible care of them and to insure against the risks which cannot be eliminated to the same extent to which they insure against other commercial risks.
>
> For these reasons the risk borne by traders as a result of the provisions (...) is not disproportionate in relation to the need for control."[290]

Exports of agricultural products were also the subject-matter of Case 15/83, *Denkavit* v. *Hoofdproduktschap voor Akkerbouwprodukten.*[291] Here, the question was raised, in the context of preliminary proceedings, whether a particular system infringed, *inter alia*, the proportionality principle in addition to Article 34 of the EEC Treaty. This question arose where the subsidy specified in the provision in question, namely for milk powder which had been transformed into concentrate in one of the Member States and was supplied in tank wagons or containers, was paid one month later in the case of exports than for domestic deliveries.

---

[290] [1980] E.C.R. 2121 *et seq.*
[291] [1984] E.C.R. 2171.

In its decision, the Court explained that the objective of this system was to exclude the possibility of a subsidy being paid twice or that of the product once again entering commercial circulation—in other words, to prevent fraudulent practices. On the basis of these considerations, the Court made the following pronouncement on the preliminary question:

> "It must be stated that the principle of proportionality is not breached by Community rules which prescribe prior administrative supervision to ensure compliance with the conditions for the payment of aid where the sums involved are particularly large and there is a particular danger of fraud.
>
> Therefore even though the contested measures entail the result that aid in respect of exports is paid later than aid in respect of inland deliveries, they do not, by reason of the special conditions applicable to intra-Community transit, breach the principle of proportionality."[292]

Although arriving at the same conclusion as the Court, Advocate-General Mancini adds, for the sake of completeness,

> "I have based my arguments so far on the premise that the longer time required for the payment of aid to exporters is attributable exclusively to the supervisory measures, that is to say, it arises from the fact that they constitute a precondition for payment and require co-operation from the authorities in various countries. In the course of the oral procedure, however, it was pointed out on several occasions that the delays are also due to shortcomings on the part of the national administrative authorities. If that is the case, the problem cannot be dealt with by reference to the interpretation of Articles 6 and 7. Solving it would require a greater degree of co-operation among the States or indeed legislative action."[293]

(d) The case law relating to "mandatory requirements"

At the beginning of this section, we pointed out that in the *Cassis de Dijon* ruling, the Court had placed a considerable restriction on the interpretation of the concept of "measures having equivalent effect"

[292] [1984] E.C.R. 2187.
[293] [1984] E.C.R. 2193.

compared with the broadly-defined *Dassonville* formula. Under the latter, the Court accepted as being compatible with Article 30 of the EEC Treaty those provisions which were necessary

> "in order to satisfy mandatory requirements relating in particular to the effectiveness of fiscal supervision, the protection of public health, the fairness of commercial transactions and the defence of the consumer."[294]

The problems involved in applying these grounds of justification to domestic provisions have been correctly identified by Rabe.[295] The wording of Article 30 of the EEC Treaty does not by itself present any grounds for such a restrictive interpretation. It would have been more advisable to turn to the restriction contained in Article 30 itself, *i.e.* the "without prejudice to the following provisions" formula, and to fall back on Article 36, which under certain conditions accepts derogations from the provisions of Article 30. Rabe explicitly states that the Court did not venture down this road because it had at an early stage already decided on a strict interpretation of Article 36 and it considered that the scope of the legal concepts contained in this provision was not capable of being extended any further. As a result, the subsequently-established grounds of justification could be considered only in the context of Article 30.

In Case 113/80[296] the Court clarified the position by stating that the "mandatory requirements" criterion as a ground of justification for such measures was valid only for national provisions which applied indiscriminately to domestic and imported products. In relation to rules which related exclusively to imports and were consequently discriminatory, exceptions to Article 30 were allowed only to the extent to which they were justified under Article 36.

This case concerned an Irish rule under which certain imported souvenirs had to have either a mark of origin or the word "foreign" stamped on them. The Court stated that a national system which applied indiscriminately to domestic and to imported products could derogate from the requirements of Article 30 only if that system was justified on the grounds that it was necessary in order to comply with mandatory requirements, in particular those which concerned fairness in commercial transactions and the protection of the consumer. In this case, however,

---

[294] [1979] E.C.R. 662.
[295] *Loc. cit.*, footnote 263, p. 52.
[296] *Commission* v. *Ireland* [1981] E.C.R. 1625.

the Court concluded that the system in question did not apply indiscriminately to domestic and to imported products, but constituted a
complex set of provisions which affected exclusively imported products
and consequently was discriminatory.[297]

The four grounds of justification specified, *i.e.* the effectiveness of
fiscal supervision,[298] the protection of public health,[299] the fairness of
commercial transactions[300] and consumer protection,[301] have been
assessed by the Court in the light of the proportionality principle.
According to this assessment, the measures in question must be truly
necessary in order to satisfy a "mandatory requirement."

Thus Case 130/80, *Keldermann*[302] concerned a rule applicable in the
Netherlands, called the Broodbesluit, under which the amount of dry
matter in bread had to fall within certain limits, regardless of whether the
product in question had been produced domestically or had been
imported. A type of bun called "brioches," imported from France into
the Netherlands, did not satisfy these requirements. The Court established that this measure could present an obstacle to trade between
Member States and thereupon proceeded to examine whether it could be
justified as a "mandatory requirement."

First, the Court rejected the argument that the measure had been
adopted in order to ensure that the population should receive sufficient
nutritive matter.[303] It went on to state:

"So far as the protection of consumers is concerned, it is claimed that
the Broodbesluit introduced a clear delimitation between the

---

[297] [1981] E.C.R. 1637 *et seq.*; *cf.* also Case 249/81 *Commission* v. *Ireland* [1982] E.C.R.
4005, in which the Court held that the concept of measures having equivalent effect by no
means presupposes commercial legislation in the formal sense of the term. Instead, the
Court, in relation to a campaign aimed at encouraging the marketing and sale of Irish
products ("Buy Irish"), considered it a proven fact that the advertising in question, which
had been formally carried out by a private firm, could be attributed to the Irish Government and produced effects which were similar to those of Government action with
mandatory effect.
[298] Case 120/78 [1979] E.C.R. 649—*Cassis de Dijon.*
[299] Case 120/78 [1979] E.C.R. 649; Cases 788/79 and 193/80 [1980] E.C.R. 2071 and [1981]
E.C.R. 3019 respectively (the first and second *Apple Vinegar* Cases); Case 130/80 [1981]
E.C.R. 572—*Fabriekvoor Hoogwaardige Voedingsprodukter Kelderman BV* (*Dry Matter
in Bread*); Case 132/80 [1981] E.C.R. 995—*Fish Research.*
[300] Case 120/78 [1979] E.C.R. 649; Cases 788/79 and 193/80 [1980] E.C.R. 2071 and [1981]
E.C.R. 3019 respectively; Case 130/80 [1981] E.C.R. 572.
[301] *Ibid.*; *cf.* in addition Case 27/80 [1980] E.C.R. 3841. "Likeurbesluit."
[302] [1981] E.C.R. 527.
[303] [1981] E.C.R. 536, para. 10.

various shapes and weights of bread and thus helps to prevent consumers from being misled as to the actual quantity of bread which is being offered to them.

However, it must be observed in this connexion that the provision of suitable information for consumers may easily be ensured by appropriate means, such as requiring labelling showing, for example, the weight and specific composition of an imported product . . ."[304]

Earlier, Advocate-General Capotorti, in his opinion, had also observed that the pursued objective of protecting the consumer would be satisfied if traders were required to display details on a label indicating the essential characteristics of the product involved.[305]

Two further cases[306] concerned Belgian rules which were allegedly intended to protect the consumer.

The first concerned a Belgian provision prescribing that silver-plated articles should display hallmarks. These hallmarks had to satisfy certain requirements designed to inform the consumer about the article he had acquired. In the context of criminal proceedings brought against importers for having sold silver-plated cutlery from other Member States whose hallmarks did not comply with the relevant Belgian rules, the question was raised whether these provisions were compatible with Articles 30–36 of the EEC Treaty.

The Court held in the first instance that

> "the obligation on the part of the manufacturer or the importer to stamp silver-plated articles, which by their very nature are capable of being confused with articles made of solid silver, with special hallmarks which are indelible . . . is in principle capable of affording effective protection to consumers and of promoting fair trading."[307]

However, the Court was of the opinion that the need for (additional) protection provided by national provisions no longer arose if articles imported from another Member State had already been stamped with hallmarks in accordance with the legislation of that Member State, subject to the condition that the details supplied by this hallmark cor-

---

[304] [1981] E.C.R. 536, paras. 11 to 12.
[305] [1981] E.C.R. 592.
[306] Case 220/81 *Robertson* [1982] E.C.R. 2349 and Case 261/81 *De Smedt* [1982] E.C.R. 3961.
[307] [1982] E.C.R. 2361.

responded to the information provided by the hallmarks required by the importing Member State and were intelligible to the consumer in that country. Whether or not the relevant information for the benefit of the consumer was of equal value was to be determined by the court making the reference.

The second case concerned the shape in which margarine sold by retailers could be packaged. Belgian legislation prohibited retailers from marketing margarine and edible fat mixtures having a certain weight in any other form than that of a cube. The rationale behind this provision was, *inter alia*, to make it easier for the consumer to distinguish between butter and margarine.

The Court considered this Belgian rule on packaging to be a measure having an effect equivalent to a quantitative restriction, which could not be legally used to prevent imports of margarine in bowl-shaped tubs from Germany.

In the Court's opinion, it could not be denied that in principle legislation designed to prevent butter and margarine from being confused in the mind of the consumer was justified. However, the application by one Member State to margarine lawfully manufactured and marketed in another Member State of legislation which prescribed for that product a specific kind of packaging such as the cubic form, to the exclusion of any other form of packaging,

> "considerably exceeds the requirements of the object in view. Consumers may in fact be protected just as effectively by other measures, for example by rules on labelling, which hinder the free movement of goods less."[308]

The case law concerning problems of consumer protection is characteristic of the Court's view, as expressed in other areas, that State intervention in areas which impede harmonisation can be considered as legitimate only if in so doing the relevant authorities do not apply any measures which exceed the pursued objective.[309]

(e) Article 36 EEC

Article 36 of the EEC Treaty is invoked in cases where national

---

[308] [1982] E.C.R. 3973.
[309] See, *e.g.* Advocate-General Mancini's opinion in Case 84/82 [1983] E.C.R. 967; *cf.* also Case 193/80 [1981] E.C.R. 3019 at 3030.

provisions or measures constitute measures with equivalent effect within the meaning of Article 30 EEC, even when the restrictive *Cassis de Dijon* formula is applied, or where these provisions or measures do not apply equally to domestic and imported goods but have a discriminatory effect on imports. Such measures are, however, exempt from the prohibition contained in Article 30 EEC only if they are necessary for the protection of the interests specified in Article 36 and if they do not constitute arbitrary discrimination or a disguised restriction on trade between Member States.

The proportionality principle also has a crucial role to play in this area.[310] Under this system, it is not sufficient for a Member State to plead one of the interests specified in Article 36, since the restrictive measure in question must above all be justified. The Court will judge whether or not such measures are "justified" by examining them in the light of the proportionality principle, as can be seen from the following cases in which the latter was applied.

(aa) Protection of health

The last few years have witnessed the development of a considerable body of case law concerning measures and provisions aimed at protecting public health. In this field, the Court has allowed the Member States a wide margin of discretion and, in particular, recognised their right to determine, in the absence of any harmonising measures and subject to their observing the requirements of the free movement of goods, the extent to which they wish to ensure the protection of public health.[311]

The subject-matter of a direct action for infringement of the Treaty against *the Federal Republic of Germany*[312] was the admissibility of certain provisions of the German Meat Inspection Act, under which imports of meat products from other Member States were allowed only where the article in question had been produced in an establishment recognised by the relevant Federal Minister and, in addition, located in the country in which the animals whose meat was used in preparing the product had

---

[310] *cf.* H.-J. Rabe, "Garantien und Sicherungen des freien Warenverkehrs im Lichte der neuesten Rechtsprechung des EuGH," in J. Schwarze (ed.) *Das Wirtschaftsrecht des Gemeinsamen Marktes in der aktuellen Rechtsentwicklung* (1983) Baden-Baden pp. 41 *et seq.*

[311] M. A. Dauses, *Rechtsprobleme eines Systems des freien Warenverkehrs in der Europäischen Gemeinschaft* (1984) Saarbrücken p. 30.

[312] Case 153/78 *Commission* v. *Germany* [1979] E.C.R. 2555.

been slaughtered. The German customs authorities insisted that an official certification to this effect be produced.

In its decision, the Court concluded that the system in question was not necessary

> "either to diminish the risk of unwholesomeness of meat products imported into the Federal Republic of Germany coming from an establishment situated in another Member State, or to ensure effective health controls with regard to such products at the time of importation. Thus the requirement constitutes both an obstacle to the free movement of meat products which is superfluous and in any event disproportionate to its objective . . ."[313]

The Court saw in this system both a discrimination against those meat-producing establishments which, unlike their competitors—who obtain their supplies of fresh meat from abattoirs in their own country—import their raw materials from another Member State.[314]

In Case 272/80 ("*Pesticides*"),[315] the Court gave a similar ruling. It held that there was nothing to prevent a Member State from requiring pesticides, on public health grounds, to undergo a prior authorisation procedure, even if the product in question had already received approval in the exporting Member State and was in free circulation. However, the authorities of the Member States were required

> "to assist in bringing about a relaxation of the controls existing in intra-Community trade. It follows that they are not entitled unnecessarily to require technical or chemical analyses or laboratory tests where those analyses and tests have already been carried out in another Member State and their results are available to those authorities, or may at their request be placed at their disposal.
>
> For the same reasons, a Member State operating an approvals procedure must ensure that no unnecessary control expenses are incurred if the practical effects of the control carried out in the Member State of origin satisfy the requirements of the protection of public health in the importing Member State. On the other hand, the

---

[313] [1979] E.C.R. 2567; *cf.* on the question whether a measure is justified under Article 36 Case 251/78 [1979] E.C.R. 3369 (3391 *et seq.*, at 3405) and Case 53/80 [1981] E.C.R. 409 at 430 *et seq.*

[314] [1979] E.C.R. 2567.

[315] [1981] E.C.R. 3277; on this issue, H.-J. Rabe. *loc. cit.*, footnote 310, p. 57.

mere fact that those expenses weigh more heavily on a trader marketing small quantities of an approved product than on his competitor who markets much greater quantities, does not justify the conclusion that such expenses constitute arbitrary discrimination or a disguised restriction within the meaning of Article 36."[316]

The admissibility of charges imposed for the purpose of public health controls in the context of measures coming within the scope of Article 36 has also been raised in a number of Court decisions. Thus the Court has made it clear that it was not necessary for the purpose of protecting public health to examine all imported goods (and that the charges thereby levied were not justified); instead, it was enough to conduct spot checks.[317] In another case, the Court concluded that Article 36 could not be interpreted as allowing, in respect of inspections of imports or exports, the imposition of levies aimed at covering the cost of these checks—such charges were not essential for the purpose of carrying out the operations envisaged under Article 36 and could consequently also impair intra-Community trade.[318]

To summarise the position, charges imposed in respect of public health controls may not exceed the level necessary for the purpose of effecting these controls.[319]

In his Opinion in Case 40/82, *Commission* v. *United Kingdom*,[320] Advocate-General Capotorti stated his position on the question of what requirements must be met by the Member State when providing evidence that the measures it has adopted, and for which it invokes Article 36, are justified.[321] The State in question could not confine itself to a mere statement that the measures in question were necessary for the purpose of

---

[316] [1981] E.C.R. 3291.
[317] Case 35/76 *Simmenthal S.p.A.* v. *Italian Ministry of Finance* [1976] E.C.R. 1871 at 1887; cf. also Case 2–4/82 *Delhaize* v. *Belgium* [1983] E.C.R. 2973 at 2974, 2991 *et seq.* and Case 42/82 *Commission* v. *France* [1983] E.C.R. 1013.
[318] Case 46/76 *Bauhuis* v. *the Netherlands* [1977] E.C.R. 5 at 15, paras. 12 to 15, 19 to 20, 48 to 50.
[319] Case 30/79 *Berlin* v. *Wigei* [1980] E.C.R. 151 at 169; Case 132/80 *United Foods and van den Abeele* v. *Belgium* [1981] E.C.R. 995 at 1025.
[320] [1982] E.C.R. 2793; the subject-matter of this action for infringement of the Treaty was a system of import licences laid down by the British Government for the import of poultry products. In respect of these measures, Britain relied upon Article 36 EEC, since the measures belonged to a series of precautions taken for the protection of the health and life of poultry threatened with Newcastle disease.
[321] cf. R. Wägenbaur, in H. v.d. Groeben, H. v. Boeckh, J. Thiesing, C. D. Ehlermann, *Kommentar zum EWG—Vertrag* (3rd ed., Baden-Baden 1983), Article 36, Nos. 68 *et seq.*

protecting one of the interests specified in Article 36. Instead, the State had to demonstrate

"that these measures are necessary in order to attain the desired objective; and that it was impossible to take an alternative course of action which was equally effective and yet less liable to restrict trade. The Court, when called upon to consider whether the measures in question are lawful, must examine their merits from the point of view of their necessity and the observance of the principle of proportionality . . ."[322]

As in the case mentioned above, the British Government also invoked Article 36 in Case 124/81,[323] in particular the protection of public health and of the life of animals. In this case, the defendant Government had imposed certain restrictions both on the importation of milk and cream which had undergone UHT treatment and on the marketing of these products within its territory, for the purpose, *inter alia*, of preventing foot-and-mouth disease. The Court held on this subject that

"whilst the protection of health of animals is one of the matters justifying the application of Article 36, it must none the less be ascertained whether the machinery employed in the present case by the United Kingdom constitutes a measure which is disproportionate in relation to the objective pursued, on the ground that the same result may be achieved by means of less restrictive measures, or whether, on the other hand, regard being had to the technical constraints already mentioned, such a system is necessary and hence justified under Article 36."[324]

In the event, the Court denied the legality of the measure in question, since it would be sufficient, for the purpose of achieving the desired objective, if "the UK authorities abandoned the practice of issuing licences and confined themselves to obtaining the information which is of use to them, for example, by means of declarations signed by the importers, accompanied if necessary by the appropriate certificates."[325]

---

[322] [1982] E.C.R. 2837.
[323] *Commission* v. *United Kingdom* [1983] E.C.R. 203.
[324] [1983] E.C.R. 236.
[325] [1983] E.C.R. 236; on this topic, *cf.* P. Oliver, (1985) C.M.L.Rev. 312 *et seq.*

Case 155/82, *Commission* v. *Belgium*[326] concerned a Belgian provision in which the right to apply for approval of pesticides for non-agricultural use and phyto-pharmaceutical products was reserved to persons established in Belgium.

In this decision, the Court confirmed the right of every Member State

> "to take within its territory, in particular in a sphere in which the objective of the harmonisation of health control measures has not yet been achieved, appropriate measures in order to ensure protection of health. However, such measures are justified only if it is established that they are necessary in order to attain the objective of protection referred to in Article 36 and that such protection cannot be achieved by means which place less of a restriction on the free movement of goods within the Community."[327]

Admittedly, the requirement that a representative be established within the national territory is not seen by the Court as being capable of providing additional security from the point of view of protecting public health, which could justify an exception to the prohibition contained in Article 30.

The fact that difficulties and uncertainties in making a scientific assessment in the context of Article 36 EEC can also be taken into account is demonstrated by the decision in Case 174/82, *Sandoz*.[328] In the criminal proceedings which gave rise to this decision, the Sandoz firm had been charged with selling and supplying in the Netherlands for commercial purposes and for human consumption, without an authorisation from the responsible Minister, food and beverages to which vitamins had been added.

In this decision, the Court held that in view of the uncertainties inherent in the scientific assessment of the harmfulness of vitamins, a national system under which it was prohibited to put into circulation, without prior authorisation, food to which vitamins had been added, which had been legally placed on the market in another Member State, was essentially justified under the terms of Article 36 on grounds of protecting human health. However, the proportionality principle required

---

[326] [1983] E.C.R. 531.
[327] [1983] E.C.R. 543.
[328] [1983] E.C.R. 2445.

"that the power of the Member States to prohibit imports of the product in question from other Member States should be restricted to what is necessary to attain the legitimate aim of protecting health. Accordingly, national rules providing for such a prohibition are justified only if authorisations to market are granted when they are compatible with the need to protect health."[329]

In concrete terms, the Court considers that under the proportionality principle, the Member States must authorise marketing when the addition of vitamins to foodstuffs meets a real need, especially a technical or nutritional one.[330]

This preliminary ruling also confirmed that a preventive health policy is also covered by Article 36 of the EEC Treaty. That this gives the Member States wide scope for policy making has been confirmed in a recent series of decisions.

Case 97/83[331] concerned a Netherlands milk regulation, under which sterilised milk products could not contain any coliform bacteria and were allowed to contain only a certain maximum amount of active microorganisms. The Court was asked to rule on the compatibility of this type of system with the provisions of Articles 30 *et seq.* of the EEC Treaty. The main action involved criminal proceedings which had been brought against a Dutch importer of pasteurised milk from Germany. Although the imported milk satisfied the (less stringent) German requirements, it fell foul of the relevant rules applicable in the Netherlands.

According to the Court, this system fundamentally infringed Article 30 of the EEC Treaty. However, the Court considered it to be justified under Article 36 on grounds of public health, although it was debatable to what extent the strict Netherlands requirements were truly necessary for the purpose of protecting health. In view of the contradictory statements which had emerged during the proceedings, it concluded that this issue could not be decided with certainty in the present state of scientific research, and that in these conditions it was for the Member States to determine the level at which they wished to secure public health.[332]

What is also remarkable about this decision is that it allows the Member States to take into account particular national business customs and

---

[329] [1983] E.C.R. 2463.
[330] *Loc. cit.*, para. 19.
[331] *Criminal proceedings against CMC Melkunie BV* [1984] E.C.R. 2307.
[332] [1984] E.C.R. 2386.

that Article 36 could also justify the practice of taking account of the risk carried by a product only for certain sensitive categories of consumers.

In Case 178/84, *Commission* v. *Federal Republic of Germany* (Regulation relating to purity standards of beer) the Court confirmed its established line that barriers to trade which are based on a number of different national systems could be acceptable if they applied indiscriminately to imported and domestic products and where they were *necessary* in order to comply with mandatory requirements of consumer protection.[333] The Court went on to hold that a prohibition on the marketing of beer which did not satisfy the German beer purity regulation was not necessary, since the protection of the consumer could be guaranteed by other means—in particular by labelling rules. Accordingly, the German system offended the proportionality principle and was consequently no longer covered by Article 36 EEC.[334]

In Case 94/83, *Heijn*[335] the Court was called upon to rule on a Netherlands rule which prohibited any residue of a certain pesticide from being present in apples, whereas in respect of other types of fruit and vegetables certain tolerance levels were accepted as being inevitable. The question of the compatibility of this provision with Articles 30–36 EEC had been raised in the course of criminal proceedings in which the Heijn company had been charged with having in stock or for sale, or at any rate for supply to others, a quantity of apples intended for human consumption which constituted a potential danger to health by virtue of the presence of 1.0 milligram of the pesticide known as vinclozoline per kilogram of apples.

In its ruling, the Court confirmed that Member States enjoyed a fair amount of policy-making discretion in the context of preventive public health protection, on the understanding, however, that

"when making such regulations, Member States must take account of the fact that pesticides are substances which are both necessary to agriculture and dangerous to human and animal health. The fact that the quantities absorbed by the consumer, in particular in the form of residues of foodstuffs, can neither be predicted nor controlled justifies such measures intended to reduce the risks faced by the consumer."[336]

---

[333] [1987] E.C.R. 559, para. 28.
[334] Para. 53.
[335] [1984] E.C.R. 3263.
[336] [1984] E.C.R. 3280, para. 15.

The Court went on to state that the Member States may regulate the presence of residues of those pesticides in foodstuffs in a way which may vary from one country to another according to the climatic conditions, the normal diet of the population and their state of health.[337]

However, the Court also considered the Member States to be under an obligation to review the prescribed maximum level if it appeared to them that the reasons which led to it being fixed had changed, for example, as a result of the discovery of a new use for a particular pesticide.[338] In the event, the Court was unable to find that the system in question infringed Article 36 of the EEC Treaty.[339]

Case 247/81, *Commission* v. *Germany*[340] concerned a German provision under which medicinal products could be marketed only by pharmaceutical enterprises having their registered office in Germany. The German Government justified this measure on the basis of Article 36 EEC, claiming, *inter alia*, that the continuous supervision of the risks inherent in medicinal preparations required that the firm in question be represented by a pharmaceutical company established on German territory.

In its decision, the Court once again emphasised the right of any Member State, in the absence of appropriate harmonising measures at the level of the Community, to adopt suitable rules for the protection of public health within its territory.[341] However, in this context the Court pointed out that such measures were justified only where it was proved that they were necessary in order to achieve the objective of public health protection set by Article 36 EEC and that this goal could not be reached by methods which involved fewer restrictions on the movement of goods within the Community.[342] In the case under review, the Court concluded that the objectives of exercising supervision over medicinal products and the availability of information in case of accident

> "could be fully met by appropriate organisational measures at the stage of the examination of applications and the issue of the authorisation to place the product on the market, without there being any need for a pharmaceutical undertaking to act as an intermediary."[343]

---

[337] *Loc. cit.*, para. 16.
[338] *Loc. cit.*, para. 18.
[339] [1984] E.C.R. 3281.
[340] [1984] E.C.R. 1111.
[341] [1984] E.C.R. 1120, para. 6.
[342] *Loc. cit.*
[343] [1984] E.C.R. 1121, para. 11.

(bb) Protection of public security and public policy

In addition to the health and life of humans and animals, the protected interests referred to in Article 36 of the EEC Treaty also include public policy and public security. These are concepts for which no uniform perception exists among the Member States as to what their contents should be. To rely on the interpretation which these concepts have received in the law relating to internal security which prevails in the Member States presents the problem that Article 36 EEC, being an exception from the fundamental rule of the free movement of goods between the Member States, must be interpreted strictly.[344] Bearing this reservation in mind, the concept of "public policy and security" can be defined as meaning the entire field of fundamental rules, laid down by the sovereign authorities and incapable of being waived, which have been adopted in the interests of the political and social integrity of society.[345] Because these interests can differ appreciably from state to state, the judicial practice of the Court of Justice will have a correspondingly crucial role to play. In every individual case which comes within this particular area, the Court of Justice defines the limits imposed by Community law on the relevant measures.

In the authoritative *Campus Oil* case,[346] the Court went very far in its recognition of the national interest. The Irish High Court had referred to the Court, in accordance with Article 177 EEC, a number of questions relating to the interpretation of Articles 30, 31 and 36 EEC, in order to be in a position to assess the compatibility with the EEC Treaty of Irish rules under which importers of petroleum products are compelled to obtain a certain percentage of their requirements, at prices laid down by the relevant Minister, from a domestic firm operating a refinery on Irish territory. The background to the case is the circumstance that Ireland possesses one refinery only, whose activity can be sustained only if all importers of refined petroleum products obtain 35 per cent. of their requirements from this refinery at prices officially laid down by the state. The main proceedings were based on actions brought by six Irish petroleum firms against the legal provisions adopted in this context. The Irish Government justified the measures in question on the grounds that the refinery was of critical importance for the public security of the country.

---

[344] Case 7/68 *Commission* v. *Italy* [1968] E.C.R. 633 at 644; Case 13/68 *Salgoil* [1968] E.C.R. 679; Case 46/76 [1977] E.C.R. 5 at 15.

[345] *cf.*, *e.g.* R. Wägenbaur, *loc. cit.*, footnote 321, Article 36, No. 30.

[346] Case 72/83 *Campus Oil Ltd.* v. *Minister for Industry and Energy* [1984] E.C.R. 2727.

In its decision, the Court stated initially that

"petroleum products, because of their exceptional importance as an energy source in the modern economy, are of fundamental importance for a country's existence, since not only its economy but above all its institutions, its essential public services and even the survival of its inhabitants depend upon them. An interruption of supplies of petroleum products, with the resultant dangers for the country's existence, could therefore seriously affect the public security that Article 36 allows States to protect."[347]

Accordingly, when assessing the compatibility of these measures with Article 36 EEC, the Court concluded that

"the presence of a refinery on the national territory . . . can effectively contribute to improving the security of supply of petroleum products to a state which does not have crude oil resources of its own."[348]

Having thus endorsed the appropriateness in principle of the measures in question for the purpose of protecting public security, the Court finally examined the question of the proportionality of the disputed measures. On this issue, the Court held that

"a Member State which is totally or almost totally dependent on imports for its supplies of petroleum products may rely on grounds of public security within the meaning of Article 36 of the Treaty for the purpose of requiring importers to cover a certain proportion of their needs by purchase from a refinery situated in its territory at prices fixed by the competent minister on the basis of the costs incurred in the operation of that refinery, if the production of the refinery cannot be freely disposed of at competitive prices on the market concerned. The quantities of petroleum products covered by such a system must not exceed the minimum supply requirement without which the public security of the state concerned would be affected or the level of production necessary to keep the refinery's production capacity available in the event of a crisis and to enable it to continue

---

[347] [1984] E.C.R. 2751.
[348] [1984] E.C.R. 2753, para. 41.

to refine at all times the crude oil for the supply of which the State concerned has entered into long-term contracts."[349]

The particular question whether the system instituted by the measures concerned observed these limits had to be decided by the national court making the reference.

One of the crucial issues at stake in the *Campus Oil* case was the question whether the disputed measure, particularly where it laid down certain prices, concerned economic policy rather than public security. On this issue, the Court, in Case 7/61, *Commission* v. *Italy* took the line that "Article 36 is directed to eventualities of a non-economic kind which are not liable to prejudice the principles laid down by Articles 30 to 34, as the last sentence of this article confirms."[350] Consequently, Member States may not under any circumstances adopt on the basis of public security measures which essentially serve to protect their own economic interests. On this subject, Oliver points out that at no time before the *Campus Oil* case had the Court declared any form of price controls, which it had qualified as a purely economic measure, to be justified under Article 36.[351] This prompts him to conclude that "this judgment constitutes a highly important development of the case law, especially as regards economic considerations and Article 36."[352] However, in this context it must be borne in mind that the quantitative restrictions which, under Article 36, are exempt from the prohibition contained in Article 30 are of necessity related to the field of economics; otherwise, they would not have fallen within the scope of Article 30 EEC in the first place.[353] The reference to measures which are justified for the protection of industrial and commercial property is a clear example of this.

(cc) *Protection of industrial and commercial property*

In Case 15/74, *Centrafarm*,[354] the Court held that, on the subject of the

---

[349] [1984] E.C.R. 2755, para. 51.
[350] [1961] E.C.R. 695; confirmed in Case 95/81, *Commission* v. *Italy* [1982] E.C.R. 2187.
[351] (1985) C.M.L.Rev. 312.
[352] *Ibid.*
[353] *cf.* the appropriate view taken by Advocate-General Sir Gordon Slynn in his opinion in Case 72/83 [1984] E.C.R. 2757 at 2763.
[354] [1974] E.C.R. 1147.

protection of industrial and commercial property, a distinction had to be drawn between the existence and the exercise of these rights:

"It is clear from this same Article (Article 36), in particular its second sentence, as well as from the context, that whilst the Treaty does not affect the existence of rights recognised by the legislation of a Member State in matters of industrial and commercial property, yet the exercise of these rights may nevertheless, depending on the circumstances, be affected by the prohibitions in the Treaty. Inasmuch as it provides an exception to one of the fundamental principles of the Common Market, Article 36 in fact only admits of derogations from the free movement of goods where such derogations are justified for the purpose of safeguarding rights which constitute the specific subject-matter of this property."[355]

On the subject of trade mark law, the Court was required to deal, in a number of cases over a relatively short period, with the problem of so-called parallel imports.[356] The first of these cases[357] concerned the question whether the owner of a trade mark in Member State A could prevent a third party from importing into and marketing in Member State A a product bearing the trade mark of the owner which had been placed on the market in Member State B by the owner of the trade mark or with his permission, this third party having changed the packaging of the product and placed the owner's trade mark on the new packaging.

On the basis of the purpose of trade mark law, the Court concluded that the trade mark owner had the right to prevent the risk of confusion and to oppose any use of his trade mark which could distort the guarantee of origin. According to the Court, this guarantee must also give the consumer or final customer the assurance that a product offered to him for sale and bearing a trade mark had not, at an earlier marketing stage, been interfered with by a third party, without the trade mark owner's permission, in such a way as to affect the original condition of the product.

The Court accordingly considered the right of the trade mark owner to defend this right as inherent in trade mark law and, as a natural corollary,

---

[355] [1974] E.C.R. 1163. This has since become established case law.
[356] Case 102/77 *Hoffmann-La Roche* v. *Centrafarm* [1978] E.C.R. 1139; Case 1/81 *Pfizer* v. *Eurim-Pharm* [1981] E.C.R. 2913; Case 51/80 *Dansk Supermarked* v. *Imerco* [1981] E.C.R. 181.
[357] Case 102/77.

that a trade mark owner was in principle entitled to apply for a prohibition order against an importer of a trade marked product who, having repackaged the goods, attached the trade mark to the new packaging.[358] The Court concluded that the holder of a trade mark right which was protected in two Member States simultaneously was entitled to prevent a product to which the trade mark had been lawfully applied in one of those States from being marketed in the other Member State after it had been repacked in new packaging to which the trade mark had been affixed by a third party.[359]

Although based on the same circumstances as the previous case, *Pfizer* v. *Eurim-Pharm* differed from the one described above in that, unlike Centrafarm, Eurim-Pharm had not produced a totally new packaging featuring the protected trade mark, but had merely replaced the outer wrapping without changing the blister pack containing the medicinal product. Instead, the original trade mark affixed to the untouched blister pack was made visible through an opening in the outer packaging. In addition, Eurim-Pharm pointed out that the product had been manufactured by a subsidiary of the proprietor of the trade mark and repacked by the importer.

In its decision, the Court recalled in the first place that

"inasmuch as it creates an exception to the fundamental principle of free movement of goods in the common market, Article 30 in fact permits derogations from that principle only to the extent to which they are justified for the purpose of safeguarding the rights which constitute the specific subject matter of that property."[360]

In this concrete case, this viewpoint, based on the proportionality principle, led the Court to conclude that

"Article 36 of the Treaty must be interpreted as meaning that the proprietor of a trade mark right may not rely on that mark in order to prevent an importer from marketing a pharmaceutical product manufactured in another Member State by the subsidiary of the

---

[358] [1978] E.C.R. 1165, para. 14.
[359] *Loc. cit.*,
[360] [1981] E.C.R. 2925; *cf.* also [1981] E.C.R. 181 at 193.

proprietor and bearing the latter's trade mark with his consent, where the importer, in re-packaging the product, confines himself to replacing the external wrapping without touching the internal packaging visible through the new external wrapping, at the same time clearly indicating on the external wrapping that the product is manufactured by the subsidiary of the proprietor and re-packaged by the importer."[361]

(dd) Recent legal developments

Recently, the Court has removed national rules capable of restricting imports from the field of application of Article 30 without invoking the reasons stated in Article 36 or "mandatory requirements" within the meaning of the case law inspired by the "Cassis de Dijon" decision.

Thus in Case 155/80, *Oebel*,[362] the Court described a German rule under which the production and carriage of bakery products was restricted to certain periods (*i.e.* the so-called prohibition on night baking) as a measure of economic and social policy seeking to improve working conditions, which served the general interest and complied with the spirit of the Treaty.

The *Blesgen* case[363] involved a (Belgian) Law aimed at combating alcoholism, which prohibited the consumption and stocking of certain spirits in all places accessible to the public, in particular public houses.

The Court decided that this matter was unrelated to imports, since the disputed marketing rules made no distinction as to the origin of the beverages in question, and that their restrictive effects on trade did not exceed those which were normally associated with such provisions of trade regulation.

The explanation which has been put forward in relation to the decisions mentioned above, *i.e.* that the modest nature, or certain aspects only, of the effects of the disputed rules on the free movement of goods were in the final analysis the main reason for the Court's approach[364] has become

---

[361] [1981] E.C.R. 2927; *cf.* also [1981] E.C.R. 193, where the Court held: "The exclusive right guaranteed by the legislation on industrial and commercial property is exhausted when a product has been lawfully distributed on the market in another Member State by the actual proprietor of the right or with his consent."

[362] [1981] E.C.R. 1993.

[363] Case 75/81 [1982] E.C.R. 1211.

[364] *cf.* U. Everling, "Zur neueren EuGH—Rechtsprechung zum Wettbewerbsrecht" (1982) EuR p. 301(305).

questionable in the light of the decision in the *Duphar* case.[365,366] This concerned a Netherlands rule under which certain medicinal products were excluded from being supplied at the expense of the social security system, in order to reduce the cost of the sickness insurance scheme. Since 80 per cent. of all medicinal products consumed in the Netherlands were imported, and 70 per cent. became chargeable to the sickness insurance scheme, the exclusion of a medicinal product from the sickness insurance scheme meant, in practical terms, that it became largely excluded from the Netherlands market.

The plaintiffs in the main action raised the question whether the objective of securing the protection of human health could not have been reached in any way by applying methods which constituted a lesser threat to intra-Community trade, and whether consequently the rules in question did not run counter to the proportionality principle.

In his Opinion, Advocate-General Mancini stated on this topic that the Court could not give the final answer to this question which the plaintiffs sought, since it was appropriate to bear in mind that

"this dispute has come before the Court under Article 177 and that means that the Court may appraise the national provisions only in so far as is necessary to enable it to answer the question put by the national court. It is ultimately the responsibility of the national court to establish whether the domestic provisions are in conformity with the principle of proportionality."[367]

Advocate-General Mancini did not confine himself to this statement, but proceeded to indicate a number of guidelines which might assist the Court in solving problems such as those raised in the case under review. He pointed out that, although there were possibilities less detrimental to the free movement of goods, for example an increase in contributions, it was doubtful, "in view of the present economic situation in Europe, whether proposals of that kind would command any attention."[368]

---

[365] Case 238/82 *Duphar* v. *Netherlands* [1984] E.C.R. 523.
[366] Thus, *e.g.* H. Matthies, "Aktuelle Rechtsentwicklungen auf dem Binnenmarkt der EG," in J. Schwarze, R. Bieber (ed.)., *Das europäische Wirtschaftsrecht vor den Herausforderungen der Zukunft* (1985) Baden-Baden, pp. 25 *et seq.*, 26; on this subject *cf.* also J. Sedemund, "Europäisches Gemeinschaftsrecht" (1985) NJW p. 526 (52); P. Oliver (1985) C.M.L.Rev. 301 *et seq.*
[367] [1984] E.C.R. 552.
[368] *Ibid.*

In accordance with the questions put to it by the court making the reference, the decision does not concern itself with the proportionality principle. Instead, it acknowledges that the Member States have the power to take measures seeking to regulate the consumption of medicinal products in order to enable that the finances of their sickness insurance schemes remain in balance.

The cases mentioned above gave rise to a discussion regarding the theoretical basis of the corresponding decisions. In the course of this debate, an attempt was made to revise the interpretation given to Article 30 as a result of the key decisions in *Dassonville* and *Cassis de Dijon*, and to return to the prohibition of discrimination when considering the concept of "measures having equivalent effect to quantitative restrictions."[369] According to this way of thinking, even a system which made no distinction in its application but which compelled the importer to handle his merchandise in a certain way would have a discriminatory effect, since it would specifically affect imports. On the other hand, it would be permissible *per se* for various legislations of the Member States to produce a general effect on imports if in the process imported goods were subjected to the same conditions as domestic goods.

Matthies[370] correctly points out that these theses put forward by Marenco would result in the fundamental freedoms of the Common Market being reduced to "the same treatment as nationals." "The national markets," writes Matthies, "with their different rules relating to production and marketing remain in existence; however, all Community measures encounter within a certain Member State the same conditions as the economic agents established in that state. The creation of a single market would thus once again be made dependent to a greater extent on the process of harmonisation of laws, but at the same time the Member States' willingness to pursue this would be reduced, thus again making the realisation of the objective of the Community more remote."

This prompts Matthies to propose that account be taken of the nature of the measure. For a rule to qualify as a "measure having an effect equivalent to import restrictions" or as a "measure of trade regulation," it must have a direct effect on imports and on goods. Rules adopted in the public interest which are covered by the Treaty objectives and do not concern imports or the goods themselves, but merely their use, would fall

---

[369] *cf.* G. Marenco, "Pour une interprétation traditionelle de la mesure d'effet équivalent à une restriction quantitative" (1984) Cahiers de Droit Européen, pp. 291 *et seq.*

[370] *Loc. cit.*, footnote 366, p. 28.

outside the scope of Article 30 if the system in question necessarily and inevitably has an effect on imports.[371]

It is debatable whether a new theoretical justification for the decisions discussed under this heading is really necessary, or whether in fact it would not be preferable to assume that by adopting these decisions, the Court sought to prevent a limitless extension of the concept of "measures having equivalent effect"[372] and to add to the existing range of "mandatory requirements." One reason why the latter option is appropriate is that in the *Duphar* decision, the Court itself pointed out that Article 36 EEC was incapable of justifying this type of economic policy objective, since this provision concerned exclusively objectives of a non-economic nature.[373] In addition, Advocate-General Mancini, in his Opinion, stressed that the disputed system had to be assessed in the light of the proportionality principle. As has been demonstrated above, it is precisely this principle which, in the context of the notion of "mandatory requirements," has played an increasingly prominent part in weighing up the interests of, on the one hand, the fundamental principle of the free movement of goods and, on the other, the requirements of a reasonable system of trade. Even if the Court failed to say so expressly, it may be assumed that in the *Duphar* decision it sought to give the status of "mandatory requirement" in the context of Article 30 EEC to the objective of limiting the cost of social spending.[374]

3. The Foreign Trade Law of the Community

Trade in goods and services with non-Member States is the subject of the common commercial policy. Under Article 113 EEC, the latter includes all positive and negative official measures specifically related to international trade.[375] Once the transitional period has expired, the transfer of commercial policy-making powers to the Community excludes the possibility of the Member States conducting their own trade policy.

---

[371] *Ibid.*; *cf.* also J. Rabe, "Garantien und Sicherungen des freien Warenverkehrs im Lichte der neuesten Rechtsprechung des EuGH", in J. Schwarze (ed.), *Das Wirtschaftsrecht des Gemeinsamen Marktes in der aktuellen Rechtsentwicklung* (1983) Baden-Baden, pp. 41 *et seq.*

[372] *cf.*, *e.g.* M. A. Dauses, *Rechtsprobleme eines Systems des freien Warenverkehrs in der Europäischen Gemeinschaft* (1984) Saarbrücken p. 27.

[373] [1984] E.C.R. 542.

[374] *cf.* also J. Sedemund, *loc. cit.*, footnote 366, p. 527.

[375] *cf.* G. Nicolaysen, *Europäisches Gemeinschaftsrecht*, (1979) Stuttgart/Berlin/Köln/Mainz, p. 191.

Under Article 115 of the Treaty, however, the Commission may empower the Member States to adopt protective measures, if disparities between the trade policies of the Member States lead to deflections of trade or to economic difficulties. It has already been pointed out above that Article 115 EEC, being a rule containing an exception, must be interpreted strictly.[376]

The ECJ assesses these protective measures in the light of the proportionality principle. Thus in Case 62/70, *Bock* v. *Commission*,[377] it held that

> "the Commission, by extending the authorisation at issue to an application relating to a transaction which was insignificant in terms of the effectiveness of the measures of commercial policy proposed by the Member States concerned and which in addition had been submitted at a time when the principle of the free circulation of goods applied unrestrictedly to the goods in question, has exceeded the limits of what is "necessary" within the meaning of Article 115."

The Commission had extended the disputed authorisation to the applications for import licences which were pending before the Commission at the time when the application was made. As in previous cases, the Court to a certain extent explained the principle of non-retroactivity by reference to the proportionality principle.[378]

In his Opinion, Advocate-General Dutheillet de Lamothe had pointed out in this context that

> "the extension which (this provision) effects of rules laid down for the future to pre-existing situations was not absolutely necessary in order to attain the end pursued."[379]

The Advocate-General considered that because of the modest nature of the quantities which the plaintiffs wished to import, the risks which were inherent in the non-application of measures laid down for the future were too unimportant to justify any infringement, however small, of the principle of non-retroactivity.

The requirements which must be met by the Commission in exercising its powers under Article 115 were set out by Advocate-General Warner in

---

[376] [1976] E.C.R. 1937 *et seq.*
[377] [1971] E.C.R. 897.
[378] *cf.*, *e.g.* Advocate-General Dutheillet de Lamothe in his opinion, *loc. cit.*, p. 916.
[379] *Ibid.*

his Opinion in Case 29/75, *Kaufhof* v. *Commission*[380] in the following terms:

> "It must be satisfied that it fully understands the policy of the Member State concerned and the reasons for it, for, without that knowledge, the Commission cannot judge whether the measures proposed are 'necessary' for the protection of that policy nor whether, as required by the third paragraph of Article 115, they are those that will 'cause the least disturbance to the functioning of the common market.' "[381]

In the case under review, the Court was required to review a decision of the Commission by which the Federal Republic of Germany became empowered to take out of free circulation certain types of tinned beans emanating from the People's Republic of China. The Court established that the Commission had infringed the obligation incumbent upon it under Article 115 to verify whether the protective measures requested were necessary within the meaning of this provision. According to the Court, the Commission had neglected to examine with precision and in detail the reasons advanced by the Member State concerned in justification of the envisaged trade policy measures.

Recently, the exemption clause which is contained in legal acts laying down the common organisation of the markets for various products and whose wording has, for some time now, become standardised, has been described as the oldest extraordinary measure regulating imports from non-member States.[382] It can be found in all basic regulations in the following wording:

> "If as a result of imports or exports the Community market in the products listed in Article 1 experiences, or is threatened with, serious disturbances which may endanger the objectives set out in Article 39 of the Treaty, appropriate measures may be applied in trade with third countries until such disturbance or threat of disturbance has ceased."[383]

---

[380] [1976] E.C.R. 431.
[381] [1976] E.C.R. 452.
[382] C.-D. Ehlermann, *Neuere Entwicklungen im Aussenhandelsrecht der Europäischen Gemeinschaften* (1984) Baden-Baden p. 5.
[383] *cf.*, *e.g.* Article 29 of Regulation (EEC 1035/72—Fruit and Vegetables) J.O. 1972, L118/1; O.J. Sp.Ed. 1972 (II), 437.

These exemption clauses have been supplemented by implementing measures issued by the Council, under which the measures must, *inter alia*, be restricted to that which is strictly necessary. In its assessment of the legality of these protective measures, the Court will invoke the proportionality principle.

Case 112/80, *Dürbeck* v. *Hauptzollamt Frankfurt*[384] concerned the validity of measures issued by the Commission[385] under which eating apples emanating from Chile could be temporarily prevented from entering into free circulation. During the early part of 1979, the Commission had established that the situation in the market for eating apples within the Community was particularly critical and could have become even worse with imports of 380,000 tonnes of eating apples from non-Member States in prospect. On these grounds, the Commission considered that the conditions set out by Article 29(1)(1), first indent, of Regulation 1035/72 of the Council[386] had been fulfilled and in accordance with Article 29(2) of this Regulation[387] and Article 3 of Regulation 2707/72[388] introduced the protective measures specified in these instruments. Prior to this, the Commission had endeavoured to obtain the consent of the major exporting nations of the southern hemisphere to restrict voluntarily their exports to the Community. This attempt was successful with several countries, with the exception of Chile, which is why, following the failure of negotiations with that country, protective measures were to have been introduced.

The plaintiff in the main action, the Anton Dürbeck company, which operates a wholesale and import business in fruit and vegetables, having concluded and later cancelled a number of contracts concerning imports of eating apples from Chile, imported by air two boxes of eating apples from Chile and applied to the German customs authorities for clearance in order to place them in free circulation. This application was rejected by

---

[384] [1981] E.C.R. 1095—Apples from Chile.

[385] Regulation 687/79 of April 5, 1979, O.J. 1979, L86/18, in conjunction with Regulations 797/79 of April 23, 1979, O.J. 1979, L101/7, and 1152/79 of June 12, 1979, O.J. 1979, L144/13.

[386] Text of the provision: "Appropriate measures may be applied in trade with third countries if
—by reason of imports or exports, the Community market in one or more of the products referred to in Article 1 experiences or is threatened with serious disturbances which may endanger the objectives set out in Article 39 of the Treaty, . . ."

[387] Article 29(2) reads: "If the situation mentioned in paragraph 1 arises, the Commission shall, at the request of a Member State or on its own initiative, decide upon the necessary measures . . ."

[388] Article 3 states, *inter alia*: "Such measures may only be taken in so far, and for as long, as they are strictly necessary . . ."

the relevant customs department on the basis of the protective measures adopted by the Commission. This was the subject of the main action.

The ECJ, which had been requested to give a ruling on the question of the legality of the disputed protective measures in accordance with Article 177 EEC, observed in its decision that it was perfectly valid under Community law for the Commission to attempt to reach agreement with the exporting countries on the possibility of the latter restricting their exports to the Community before decreeing the temporary ban on imports from Chile. In this context, the Court pointed out that Article 3(2) of Regulation 2707/72 provided that

> "any protective measures decided upon by the Commission may be adopted only "in so far, and for so long, as they are strictly necessary," and implies that when the Commission believes that the conditions requisite for the application of such measures are fulfilled, it must observe the principle of proportionality underlying the Community legal order.
>
> The fact that, when adopting Regulations (. . .) the Commission took into consideration only goods which had left Chile to the exclusion of those in the course of being loaded does not amount to a failure to observe the principle of proportionality with regard to the last-mentioned products."[389]

A case which strongly resembles the one described above is Case 245/81, *EDEKA v. Federal Republic of Germany*.[390] Here, the main action had been brought against a refusal to grant import licences for two consignments of mushrooms from Taiwan and South Korea. The German Ministry for Food and Forestry had, as the representative of the Federal Republic of Germany, rejected the relevant applications made by the EDEKA company on the basis that the issue of import licences in respect of preserved mushrooms originating in Taiwan and South Korea had been suspended in pursuance of Regulation 1102/78. One of the arguments raised by the firm against this rejection was that the import restrictions imposed by the disputed regulation infringed the proportionality principle.

Since negotiations seeking to obtain voluntary restrictions on the part of the nations concerned had preceded the adoption of the protective

[389] [1981] E.C.R. 1118 *et seq.*
[390] [1982] E.C.R. 2745.

measures in this case as well, the Court took the opportunity to point out once again, by reference to the *Dürbeck* decision, that

> "the Commission's attempt, before adopting coercive measures, to obtain the agreement of supplier countries on a voluntary restriction of their exports cannot be regarded as being unacceptable from the point of view of Community law since it demonstrates the Community's effort to refrain from adopting coercive measures unless all else fails."[391]

On this issue, the plaintiff had also pointed out that Article 110 EEC precluded a total ban on imports from Taiwan and South Korea. This provision makes reference to the Member States' intention "to contribute, in the common interest, to the harmonious development of world trade, the progressive abolition of restrictions on international trade ..." Article 110 is, however, a statement of intent, which does not in principle create any legal commitments, certainly not in relation to non-Member States.[392] Accordingly, the Court rejected the plaintiff's argument in the following terms:

> "It is necessary merely to call to mind the judgment of the Court of 5 May 1981 in the previously-mentioned *Dürbeck* case, in which it was held that Article 110 of the Treaty could not be interpreted as prohibiting the Community from enacting, upon pain of committing an infringement of the Treaty, any measure liable to affect trade with non-member countries in particular where, as in the present case, the adoption of such a measure is made necessary by the risk of a serious disturbance which might endanger the objectives set out in Article 39 of the Treaty and where the measure is largely justified by provisions of Community law."[393]

In his Opinion, Advocate-General Sir Gordon Slynn examined the thesis put forward by the plaintiff, namely that instead of imposing a total ban on imports from South Korea and Taiwan and allowing only limited quantities of goods to be imported from China, the Commission should have instituted a system of reference quantities in order to give each

---

[391] [1982] E.C.R. 2757, para. 22.
[392] *cf.*, *e.g.* W. Ernst, H. F. Bescler in H.v.d. Groeben, H. v. Boeckh, J. Thiesing, C.-D. Ehlermann, *Kommentar zum EWG-Vertrag* (3rd ed., Baden-Baden 1983), Article 110, No. 4.
[393] [1982] E.C.R. 2757, para. 24.

importer a fair chance. Since, unlike Taiwan and South Korea, China was prepared to limit its exports, Advocate-General Sir Gordon Slynn considered that in view of China's willingness,

> "the imposition of protective measures is not strictly necessary in order to avoid a serious disturbance of the market. It could therefore be contrary to the principle of proportionality to adopt a reference quantity or quota system in so far as goods from that country are concerned."[394]

Case 52/81, *Faust* v. *Commission*[395] did not concern the review of the legality of a regulation laying down protective measures in the form of a preliminary ruling, but an action for damages under the second paragraph of Article 215 EEC.

In the absence of an agreement concerning voluntary restrictions between the Commission and Taiwan, imports of preserved mushrooms from that country were on the low side in 1979, since the protective measures issued by the Commission, under which only a certain amount of preserved mushrooms could be imported into the Community, continued to apply. In 1980, Taiwan declared that it was prepared to limit its imports of preserved mushrooms to the Community to 1,000 tonnes, having noted that the Commission did not intend to allow it to export more than this amount. The applicant claimed that if trade flows had continued as normal, in particular had the reference quantity system been maintained, it could have proceeded on the assumption that its market share would have reached 19.12 per cent. of imports of preserved mushrooms from Taiwan; consequently, as a result of the draconian reduction in these imports in 1979 and 1980, it had forfeited more than 100,000 US dollars in foreseeable commissions. Faust attributed these losses to the regulations by which the Commission had taken these protective measures, and considered these regulations to be incompatible with Community law. In particular, the applicant accused the Commission of having infringed the proportionality principle in that it should have pursued its objectives by proportionate methods, *e.g.* by linking the new protective measures introduced in 1978 to a system which took into account the imports which had emanated from each of the non-Member States concerned during the previous years. On this point, the Court held:

---

[394] [1982] E.C.R. 2767.
[395] [1982] E.C.R. 3745 (Mushrooms from Taiwan).

"In view of the fact that the Commission sought by means of the contested measures to achieve two equally legitimate objectives, namely stabilisation of the market and implementation of a Community policy relating to external trade, the measures adopted cannot be considered to be disproportionate to the objectives pursued. It is an unavoidable fact that changes in Community policies relating to external trade have repercussions on the prospects of traders in the sector concerned."[396]

Accordingly, the Court authorised the Commission to take account of the Community's trade policy when deciding which protective measures to adopt. On this point, Advocate-General Sir Gordon Slynn stated in his opinion that although the Community's trade policy towards non-Member States was not one of the objectives referred to in Article 39,

"there is nothing in Article 39 or 40 to suggest that account cannot be taken of the Community trade policy in selecting the means to achieve the objectives set out in Article 39."[397]

The fact that the Court had conferred on the Commission plenty of scope for evaluation with regard to the actual conditions which the relevant ground rules imposed for resorting to the exemption clause was pointed out by Advocate-General Rozès, referring to the *Faust* decision, in her Opinion in Case 345/82, *Wünsche* v. *Federal Republic of Germany.*[398]

In that case also, the Court was called upon to review the legality of protective measures relating to preserved mushrooms—this time in the context of a preliminary ruling.

The question referred was raised in the context of an action brought by the Wünsche company against the German Ministry of Food after the latter had rejected, on the basis of the protective measures adopted by the Commission, an application made by the plaintiff for the grant of an import licence "containing no reference to an additional amount of 175 ECU" for 3,500 tonnes of preserved mushrooms from the People's Republic of China.[399]

---

[396] [1982] E.C.R. 3761, para. 23.
[397] [1982] E.C.R. 3770.
[398] [1984] E.C.R. 1995 at 2014, 2022.
[399] The additional amount referred to in the request formed by the Wünsche firm was provided for in Article 1 of Regulation 3429/80, O.J. L358/66: "An additional amount of 175 ECU per 100 kg net will be charged on preserved mushrooms under tariff heading 20.02 A of the Common Customs Tariff, except for those specified in Article 4, which are

The Wünsche company had alleged, *inter alia*, that the Commission had no jurisdiction to adopt the disputed measures, since the basic Regulation of the Council comprised, on the one hand, only the procedure for awarding licences either wholly or in part or for rejecting licence applications either wholly or in part, and on the other hand a system of minimum prices, but not the measure actually adopted. On this point, the Court, referring to the decision in Joined Cases 41–44/70, *International Fruit Company et al.* v. *Commission*,[400] stated that

> "since the Commission was entitled to take protective measures leading to a complete suspension of imports from third countries, it was, *a fortiori*, entitled to adopt less restrictive measures."

In her Opinion, the Advocate-General did not confine herself to the observation that the effect of the disputed measure was less restrictive. For this measure to be lawful, she also stipulated that it must be appropriate and that the Commission had correctly assessed the conditions which prevailed in the market in question.[401]

On the question of the proportionality of the measure, which is the issue under examination here, she accordingly concluded that in this case the protective mechanism created by the Commission satisfied the proportionality requirement in that it maintained the normal trade flows and at the same time protected the Community market.[402]

4. Freedom of movement

In the recitals to Regulation 1612/68 of the Council on the implementation of Article 48 EEC, freedom of movement was identified as a fundamental right of the worker and of his family.[403] This freedom represents a significant element in the "mobility of factors of production," in that it improves the balance between supply and demand on the labour market and ensures that labour is available where the best economic

---

cleared for free trade in the Community in addition to the quantities specified in Article 2(1) and (3), during the period from 1 January 1981 to 31 March 1981."

[400] [1971] E.C.R. 426.

[401] [1984] E.C.R. 2018 *et seq.*

[402] [1984] E.C.R. 2022.

[403] Regulation (EEC) 1612/68 of the Council of October 15, 1968, on the freedom of movement of workers within the Community, J.O. 1968, L257/2; O.J. Sp.Ed. 1968(II), 475, third recital.

advantages prevail.[404] The corner stone of the freedom of movement is the free movement of persons, which in the Treaty of Rome has been regulated in express terms only in relation to workers. Under Article 48(3), workers have the right

"(a) to accept offers of employment actually made;
(b) to move freely within the territory of Member States for this purpose;
(c) to stay in a Member State for the purpose of employment in accordance with the provisions governing the employment of nationals of that State laid down by law, regulation and administrative action";
(d) to remain in the territory of a Member State after having been employed in that State, subject to conditions which shall be embodied in implementing regulations to be drawn up by the Commission."

Accordingly, under this provision freedom of movement is linked to an economic objective. In addition, it is, under Article 48(3), subject to limitations "justified on grounds of public policy, public security or public health."[405] Finally, under Article 48(4) the provisions of this Article "shall not apply to employment in the public service."

Thus in relation to the entry and residence of aliens, the Member States are entitled to apply special provisions which are justified on grounds of national "ordre public."

The resulting danger that, by abusing this reservation, the Member States could denude the guarantee of free movement of its practical

---

[404] cf. G. Nicolaysen, *Europäisches Gemeinschaftsrecht* (1979) Stuttgart/Berlin/Köln/Mainz, pp. 106 *et seq.*

[405] cf. also Article 56(1), Article 66 EEC. The rights conferred by these Articles are elaborated further in the following Community directives.

(a) Council directive 68/360 of October 15, 1968, on the abolition of restrictions on movement and residence of nationals of Member States and the members of their families within the Community (J.O. 1968, L275/13).

(b) Council Directive of May 21, 1973, on the abolition of restrictions on movement and residence within the Community of nationals of Member States with regard to establishment and the provision of services (O.J. 1973, L172/14).

(c) Council Directive of February 25, 1964, on the co-ordination of special measures concerning the movement and residence of foreign nationals which are justified on grounds of public policy, public security or public health (Directive 64/221, J.O. 1964, L56/850; O.J. Sp. Ed. 1963–1964, 117).

significance,[406] has been met by the Court with increasing strictness.[407] In this context, Pernice rightly states that where the Court, by applying the proportionality principle in guaranteeing freedom of movement, uses an instrument commonly used for the protection of fundamental rights and for the purpose of weighing up the interests involved, "it has given this guarantee the objective character of a criterion by which to assess the public interest as well as the subjective character of the Community citizen's fundamental freedoms."[408]

The other grounds on which entry can be refused or expulsion decreed have been consolidated in Directive 64/221 of February 25, 1964.[409] The latter does not contain any definition of these concepts, but—obviously in harmony which the case law of the Court—proceeds from the assumption that to determine that which is necessary to maintain "ordre public" is, for the time being, a matter for the Member States to decide.[410] Thus in the *Van Duyn* case, Advocate-General Mayras pointed out that

> "under present conditions and given the present position of the law, Member States have sole power ... to take measures for the safe-guarding of public security within their territory and to decide the circumstances under which that security may be endangered."[411]

As to the public security safeguard, he went on to state that

> "this concept remains, at least for the present, national, and this conforms with reality inasmuch as the requirements of public security vary, in time and space, from one State to another."[412]

If we examine the concept of "public policy" as it is commonly used in the internal security legislation of Germany and other countries, it is clear that its contents are determined by the social and ethical values of the

---

[406] *cf.* D. Simon, "Ordre public et libertés publiques dans les Communautés européennes. A propos de l'arrêt Rutili," in (1976) RMC p. 201(204).

[407] *cf.* I. Pernice, *Grundrechtsgehalte im Europäischen Gemeinschaftsrecht* (1979) Baden-Baden p. 129.

[408] *Loc. cit.*, pp. 140 *et seq.*

[409] *Loc. cit.*, footnote 405.

[410] *cf.* G. Druesne, "La réserve d'ordre public de l'article 48 du traité de Rome," in (1976) RTDE p. 229 (235); D. Simon, *loc. cit.*, footnote 406, pp. 206 *et seq.*; P. Selmer, "Die öffentliche Sicherheit und Ordnung als Schranke der Arbeitnehmer-Freizügigkeit gem. Article 48 Abs. 3 EWG-Vertrag," DÖV 1967, p. 323 (330 *et seq.*).

[411] Case 41/74 [1974] E.C.R. 1337 at 1357 *et seq.*

[412] *Loc cit.*, p. 1358.

day, and consequently "may vary from one country to another and from one period to another."[413]

However, in exercising their discretion with regard to the measures they adopt in relation to aliens, the Member States are bound by Community legislation and the case law of the Court of Justice. On this issue, the ECJ has increasingly applied the strict criterion of proportionality. Thus the Court clarified the objective of Directive 64/221 in the following terms in the *Bouchereau* decision[414]:

"By co-ordinating national rules on the control of aliens, to the extent to which they concern the nationals of other Member States, Directive 64/221/EEC seeks to protect such nationals from any exercise of the powers resulting from the exception relating to limitations justified on grounds of public policy, public security or public health, which might go beyond the requirements justifying an exception to the basic principles of free movement of persons."

The directive lays down that any measures concerning public policy or security (*e.g.* expulsion orders) must relate exclusively to the personal behaviour of the person affected (Article 3(1)). As a result, measures based on general considerations of prevention are inadmissible. In addition, considerations of public policy, public security and public health may not be used for economic purposes.[415] Finally, diseases and disabilities which are capable of justifying a refusal of entry into a territory or a refusal to issue first residence permit, are restricted to those listed in the appendix to the directive. If any such disease occurs after the first residence permit has been issued, it may not be taken into consideration as a factor in this context.

When the Court was requested to rule on a decision issued by the relevant French authority granting an Italian national living in France a residence permit for EEC nationals restricted by a prohibition on residence in certain French Départements, it took the opportunity to recall, by reference to the underlying principles of the European Convention on Human Rights, the particular importance of the proportionality principle. In this case, the ECJ held that

---

[413] *cf.* [1974] E.C.R. 1350; [1977] E.C.R. 1999 at 2013; *cf.* G. Nicolaysen, *loc. cit.*, footnote 404, p. 118.

[414] Case 30/77 [1977] E.C.R. 1999 at 2010, para. 15.

[415] *cf.* on the difficulties in identifying economic measures the statements cited earlier in connection with the *Campus Oil* case, pp. 777 *et seq.*

"taken as a whole, these limitations placed on the powers of Member States in respect of control of aliens are a specific manifestation of the more general principle, enshrined in Articles 8, 9, 10 and 11 of the Convention for the Protection of Human Rights and Fundamental Freedoms, signed in Rome on 4 November 1950 and ratified by all the Member States, and in Article 2 of Protocol No. 4 of the same Convention, signed in Strasbourg on 16 September 1963, which provide, in identical terms, that no restrictions in the interests of national security or public safety shall be placed on the rights secured by the above-quoted articles other than such as are necessary for the protection of those interests 'in a democratic society.' "[416]

Thus the ECJ compares the limitations to which freedom of movement is subject in the public interest under Article 48(3) with those to which the fundamental rights provided in the first paragraphs of Articles 8–11 ECHR are subject under the second paragraphs of each of these provisions.[417] In so doing, the Court emphasises once again the fundamental character of the right to freedom of movement as well as the importance of the proportionality principle in reviewing the legality of measures restricting freedom.[418]

In the *Watson and Belmann* case,[419] a British subject called Watson had for a certain period been given accommodation by Belmann, an Italian citizen. Some time later, Mrs. Watson disappeared during a journey to Venice. In the course of their search for her whereabouts, the police discovered that Belmann had failed to comply with the relevant Italian rules under which he should have notified the authorities of the presence of his guest. In the course of criminal proceedings brought against him, a number of questions concerning the compatibility of these Italian rules with Community law were raised, which were put to the European Court of Justice in accordance with Article 177 EEC.

The Court decided that in spite of the freedom of movement guaranteed by the EEC Treaty, the Member States were certainly entitled to lay

---

[416] Case 36/75 *Rutili* v. *Minister of the Interior* [1975] E.C.R. 1219 at 1232, para. 32.
[417] *cf.* A. Bleckmann, "Die Freiheiten des Gemeinsamen Marktes als Grundrechte," in Bieber, Bleckmann, Capotorti *et al.* (ed.) *Das Europa der zweiten Generation: Gedächtnisschrift für Christoph Sasse* Vol. II (1981) Strasbourg p. 665.
[418] On this subject, *cf.* I. Pernice, *loc. cit.*, footnote 407, p. 135.
[419] Case 118/75 [1976] E.C.R. 1185.

down a duty of notification on grounds of public security and public policy, provided that they did not impose an unreasonable deadline for compliance with these formalities. On the question of the penalties attaching to a failure to comply with these obligations, the ECJ stated that

"deportation, in relation to persons protected by Community law, is certainly incompatible with the provisions of the Treaty since, as the Court has already confirmed in other cases, such a measure negates the very right conferred and guaranteed by the Treaty.

As regards the other penalties, such as fines and detention, whilst the national authorities are entitled to impose penalties in respect of failure to comply with the terms of provisions requiring foreign nationals to notify their presence which are comparable to those attaching to infringements of provisions of equal importance by nationals, they are not justified in imposing a penalty so disproportionate to the gravity of the infringement that it becomes an obstacle to the free movement of persons."[420]

Penalties for infringements against legislation relating to aliens were also the subject-matter of Case 8/77, *Sagulo et al.*[421] In the context of criminal proceedings before a German court, in which two Italians and one French national were indicted for infringements of section 47 of the Law relating to Aliens, doubts had arisen as to the lawfulness of the penalties laid down for failure to possess a residence permit, even in the case of those who possessed no residence permit under the Law relating to EEC Aliens. The Italian citizens had no valid passport or identity card, whereas the French national had refused to comply with the formalities which were necessary in order to obtain a residence permit.

Although Section 15 of the Law relating to EEC Aliens made reference to the Law relating to Aliens, the German Laws incorrectly equated, even from the point of view of the terminology used, the permit issued under the Law relating to EEC Aliens ("Residence Permit for a National of a Member State of the European Communities") with the residence permit obtainable under the Law relating to Aliens. However, the ECJ had already made it clear that the permit issued under the Law relating to EEC Aliens was merely confirmatory in its effect, and consequently was not identical to the residence permit under the general Law relating to Aliens, which had a constituting effect, and that consequently the EEC

[420] [1976] E.C.R. 1199, para. 20.
[421] [1977] E.C.R. 1495.

nationals' right of residence could be said to be derived directly from the relevant Treaty provisions.[422]

In his Opinion on this decision,[423] Advocate-General Reischl pointed to the requirement of equal treatment between EEC nationals and nationals of the Member State in question, holding on the subject of the interpretation of the disputed Article 47 of the Law relating to Aliens that

> "If a national does not comply with his obligations in respect of identity cards, then under German law he is liable to a fine only for a minor offence from the point of view of its criminality. The disregard of the obligation in respect of evidence of a substantively existing right of residence by a national of another Member State of the EEC cannot be treated differently. This is in line with the previous case law of the Court. . . . An interpretation of the second subparagraph of the German Ausländergesetz to the effect that this provision is applicable also to the residence permit under Article 4 of Council Directive No. 68/360 would . . . lead to the application of penalties quite disproportionate to the criminality of disregard of the formalities with regard to control of aliens and would thus represent a direct obstacle to freedom of movement guaranteed by Community law and to that extent is contrary to the EEC Treaty."[424]

In its ruling, the Court first confirmed the viewpoint expressed in the *Watson and Belmann* decision, and held that

> "although Member States are entitled to impose reasonable penalties for infringements by persons subject to Community law of the obligation to obtain a valid identity card or passport, such penalties should by no means be so severe as to cause an obstacle to the freedom of entry and residence provided for in the Treaty."[425]

It then proceeded to point out that if a Member State had not adapted its legislation to the requirements of Community law in this sphere, it was the task of the domestic court to use its judicial discretion

---

[422] *cf.* [1976] E.C.R. 497; [1977] E.C.R. 1495; [1976] E.C.R. 1185; *cf.* also G. Nicolaysen, *loc. cit.*, footnote 404, p. 118.
[423] [1977] E.C.R. 1495 at 1509 *et seq.*
[424] *Loc. cit.*, p. 1512.
[425] [1977] E.C.R. 1506, paras. 12 to 13.

"to impose a punishment appropriate to the character and objective of the provisions of Community law the observance of which the penalty is intended to safeguard . . . but (to ensure) that the penalties imposed must not be disproportionate to the nature of the offence committed."[426]

Joined Cases 115 and 116/81[427] concerned a refusal by the Belgian authorities to allow two French nationals to reside in Belgian territory. This refusal was based on public order offences committed by the applicants. The ladies in question had allegedly operated as hostesses in a bar of questionable morality.

In his Opinion, Advocate-General Capotorti observed that the criteria of reasonableness and of proportionality were two contributory factors in restricting the Member States' powers in applying the public order safeguard clause. He went on to state:

"By those criteria, and thus having regard in each case to all the factors which characterise the personal conduct of the person concerned and also to his family situation and to any links he may have established with the country he has entered, the risk that the discretion allowed to national administration will give rise to arbitrary action is avoided."[428]

In addition to the "ordre public" safeguard, the right of freedom of movement under Article 48(4) EEC[429] is further restricted by the exercise of public authority. Whereas the public policy safeguard relates primarily to the free movement of persons, the exemption based on the exercise of public authority concerns mainly the employment opportunities available to the Community citizen within the entire territory of the Common Market. In view of the broad wording of Article 48(4) ("employment in the public service"), the exemption applies not only to officials, but also to workers and employees,[430] although it is confined to access to employment in the public service.[431] Once the employee has lawfully secured employment, he may not suffer any disadvantage in terms of conditions

---

[426] *Ibid.*
[427] *Adoui* v. *Belgium* and *Cornuaille* v. *Belgium* [1982] E.C.R. 1665.
[428] [1982] E.C.R. 1720.
[429] *cf.* also Article 55(1) EEC; this is analysed by U. H. Wittkopp, *Wirtschaftliche Freizügigkeit und Nationalvorbehalte* (1977) Baden-Baden.
[430] *cf.* G. Nicolaysen, *loc. cit.*, footnote 404, p. 107.
[431] On this subject *cf.* P. Karpenstein, *loc. cit.*, footnote 392, Article 48, No. 48.

of employment or working conditions in relation to nationals of the country concerned, as was held by the Court in Case 152/73.[432] In the main action underlying this decision, an Italian national had sued the German Postal Service, by whom he was employed, for payment of the "separation allowance" to which employees working outside the locality in which they lived were entitled under certain circumstances, but which was higher for employees residing in another locality within the Federal Republic than for employees whose residence was located abroad at the time of their appointment.

In this case also, the Court applied the proportionality principle, when it held that

> "taking account of the fundamental nature, in the scheme of the Treaty, of the principles of free movement and equality of treatment of workers within the Community, the exceptions made by Article 48(4) cannot have a scope going beyond the aim in view of which the derogation was included."[433]

However, a number of problems arise out of the question whether Article 48(4) exempts any employment in the public service or merely certain activities. In Case 149/79, *Commission* v. *Belgium*,[434] a number of Member States sought to interpret the concept of "employment in the public service," as used in Article 48(4), as referring to the interpretation of this notion under each national legal system in question.[435] In 1972, the European Parliament had also adopted this interpretation.[436]

In the above-mentioned ruling of December 17, 1980,[437] the Court reserved judgment on the action brought by the Commission against Belgium for infringement of the Treaty and established certain criteria for determining the scope of the reservations in Article 48(4) from the point of view of employment opportunities provided by the public authorities. This case concerned a number of vacancies for nurses, gardeners, joiners and railway construction workers with the Belgian state railways and the City of Brussels, for which nationals of other EC Member States

---

[432] *Sotgiu* v. *Deutsche Bundespost* [1974] E.C.R. 153.
[433] [1974] E.C.R. 162 para. 4.
[434] [1980] E.C.R. 3881.
[435] *cf.* J. Schwarze, *Die Europäische Gemeinschaft zwischen Krise und Bewahrung* (1983) Hamburg, pp. 12 *et seq.*
[436] J.O. 1972, C10 4; on this subject, U. H. Witkopp, *loc. cit.*, footnote 429, pp. 211 *et seq.*, and, on a critical note, W. Bongen, *Schranken der Freizügigkeit aus Gründen der öffentlichen Ordnung und Sicherheit im Recht der EWG* (1975) Berlin.
[437] *cf.* footnote 434.

could have applied had the Belgian authorities not refused to consider applications from aliens for these posts.

In its final judgment in this case,[438] the Court decided that henceforth the concept of public service was to be defined by reference to Community law. Any activity coming within the scope of the public authorities, which accordingly constituted an exception to the fundamental guarantee of the free movement of workers, could come within the ambit of the safeguard clause in question only where it related to posts which involved the exercise of official authority. The vacancies in question were not related to any such exemption, so that applicants from other Member States should also have access to them. This interpretation was confirmed by the Court in Case 66/85, *Lawrie Blum*,[439] in which it held that the post of trainee teacher in the education sector did not come within the scope of the Article 48(4) EEC exemption, since the duties of a trainee teacher did not involve any exercise of official authority aimed at safeguarding the general interests of the State.[440]

In recent years, the proportionality principle has also increasingly been applied by the Court in cases where the matter at issue was not the "ordre public" or "public service" exemption, but provisions of social legislation and related areas.

Thus the Reutlingen Amtsgericht (district court) referred a question to the ECJ under Article 177 EEC in order to establish whether an infringement of the free movement of workers guaranteed under Article 48 could arise from the provisions of national road traffic regulations under which any holder of a foreign driving licence who had been resident within the Federal Republic of Germany for more than one year was obliged to apply for a German driving licence.

On this issue, the referring court pointed out that the acquisition of a new driving licence could involve linguistic difficulties and give rise to disproportionate costs.[441] Even though the Court did not specifically refer to the proportionality principle, the latter did appear to have inspired it when it stated that

"it is not in principle incompatible with Community law for one Member State to require a national of another Member State who is permanently established in its territory, to obtain a domestic driving

---

[438] Judgment of May 26, 1982 [1982] E.C.R. 1845, in particular paras. 7 to 11 of the judgment.
[439] [1986] E.C.R. 2139.
[440] *Loc. cit.*, at 2147.
[441] Case 16/78 (Criminal proceedings against *Michel Choquet*) [1978] E.C.R. 2293.

823

licence for the purpose of driving motor vehicles, even if he is in possession of a driving licence issued by the authorities in his State of origin.

However, such a requirement may be regarded as indirectly prejudicing the exercise of the right of freedom of movement ... if it appears that the conditions imposed by national rules on the holder of a driving licence issued by another Member State are not in due proportion to the requirements of road safety."[442]

Case 139/78, *Coccioli* v. *Bundesanstalt für Arbeit*[443] concerned social security law. Here, the Hildesheim Social Court had referred to the Court, in accordance with Article 177 EEC, a number of questions concerning the interpretation of Article 68(2) of Regulation (EEC) 1408/71 of the Council of June 14, 1971, on the application of social security schemes to employed persons and their families moving within the Community.[444] These questions were raised in the context of a dispute in which an Italian citizen resident in the Federal Republic of Germany sought to obtain that, by way of exception, he should be granted the right to enjoy unemployment benefit by extending the three-month deadline provided in Article 69(2) of the Regulation in question. The worker concerned had, with a view to seeking employment, travelled on December 19, 1976, to Italy, where, however, according to the local employment agency, there was no prospect of obtaining employment either at that moment or for some weeks to come. Two days before the expiry of the deadline for his return, the plaintiff fell victim to pyelitis and cystitis and was unable to work until May 14, 1977. His application for unemployment benefit, made after his recovery and his consequent return to West Germany, was rejected on May 16, 1977, by the relevant authority. The latter justified its decision on the basis that, *inter alia*, the plaintiff had, contrary to the objective of Article 69, decided to continue his stay in Italy and consequently had to carry the risk of being prevented from re-entering the Federal Republic at the right time through unforeseen circumstances.

Under Article 69(1)(c) of the Regulation, any worker who is totally unemployed and fulfils the conditions for eligibility for unemployment benefit stipulated by the relevant legislation of a Member State has the right to travel to one or more other Member States in order to seek

---

[442] [1978] E.C.R. 2303, para. 9.
[443] [1979] E.C.R. 991.
[444] O.J. 1971, L149/2.

employment there. In so doing, he retains the right to payment for a maximum of three months as from the moment at which he was no longer available to the employment authorities in the Member State which he left. Under Article 69(2) of the Regulation, the relevant employment authority or the appropriate representative may extend this deadline in exceptional circumstances. On this point, Advocate-General Reischl stated in his Opinion that

> "the possibility of extending the period was provided in order to allow the competent sources in a particular case to settle such conflict situations where the normal expiry of the period and the consequent loss of entitlement to benefits would lead to disproportionate social hardship."[445]

Thereupon the Court held that

> "that provision [Article 69(2) Regulation 1408/71] does not restrict the freedom of the competent services to take into consideration, with a view to deciding upon any extension of the period laid down by the regulation, all factors which they regard as relevant and which are inherent both in the individual situation of the workers concerned and in the exercise of effective control."[446]

In Joined Cases 41, 121 and 796/79, *Testa et al.* v. *Bundesanstalt für Arbeit*[447] the questions raised also concerned the interpretation and validity of Regulation 1408/71 of the Council of June 14, 1971.[448] These questions were raised in the context of a number of legal disputes between the German Government Employment Agency (Bundesanstalt für Arbeit) and certain unemployed workers who had taken advantage of Article 69(1) of the Regulation in order to travel to Italy in search of employment but had subsequently failed to return to the Federal Republic of Germany within the three-month period specified in this provision. On these grounds, the Bundesanstalt für Arbeit had refused to pay the workers in question any further unemployment benefit on the basis of Article 69(2) of the said Regulation. This prompted the workers to bring an action before the relevant German courts, by which they sought to

---

[445] [1979] E.C.R. 1003.
[446] [1979] E.C.R. 999, para. 9.
[447] [1980] E.C.R. 1979.
[448] O.J. 1971, L149/2.

continue to receive those payments to which they would have been entitled under internal German law.[449]

In his Opinion, Advocate-General Reischl emphasised that

> "in each individual case, the competent services or institutions in the Member States must decide, when exercising their discretion as they are bound to do, whether the facts set out in an application for an extension of the period laid down in Article 69(2) of Regulation 1408/71 constitute an 'exceptional case' which justifies an exception being made to the rule. In the exercise of that discretion, which is conditioned by the meaning and purpose of the provision in question, particular consideration must be given to the length of time by which the three month period has been exceeded, the reason for the late return and also, and this seems to me to be of particular importance, the seriousness of the legal consequences in the event of a late return."[450]

Taking into account the object of the rule in question, he went on to state that

> "The loss of further entitlement is in the public interest and, as I have already argued, accords well with the principle of proportionality which must be observed. If, however, in an individual case, special circumstances prevent a return in good time and a loss of all further entitlement would, in the light of all the circumstances, be disproportionate then, as I have stated, account must be taken of the principle of proportionality by application of the hardship clause contained in the second sentence of Article 69(2)."[451]

The Court confirmed the Advocate-General in his opinion that, when taking decisions on applications for extension based on the final sentence of Article 69(2), the labour authorities concerned must take into account the proportionality principle.[452]

---

[449] *cf.* sections 106, 110(3) of the Employment Promotion Act.
[450] [1980] E.C.R. 2009.
[451] [1980] E.C.R. 2012.
[452] [1980] E.C.R. 1977, para. 21: ". . . in exercising this discretion, however, they must observe the principle of proportionality, which is a general legal principle of the Community." *cf.* also H.-W. Rengeling, "Die Entwicklung verwaltungsrechtlicher Grundsätze durch den Gerichtshof der Europäischen Gemeinschaften" (1984) EuR, p. 331 (351).

5.   Freedom to provide services and freedom of establishment

The proportionality principle has also frequently been applied in the field of the freedom to provide services and freedom of establishment, and indeed is featured in some of the leading ECJ cases in this area. In a decision which has proved a milestone in the field of freedom of establishment (*Van Binsbergen*),[453] the Court held that

"taking into account the particular nature of the services to be provided, specific requirements imposed on the person providing the service cannot be considered incompatible with the Treaty where they have as their purpose the application of professional rules justified by the general good—in particular rules relating to organisation, qualifications, professional ethics, supervision and liability—which are binding upon any person established in the State in which the service is provided . . ."[454]

This case concerned a Dutch legal adviser who was to have been barred from taking part in court proceedings on the grounds that, in the course of a lawsuit taking place in the Netherlands, he had moved his residence to Belgium. The Court considered that the requirement that a person should have a permanent place of establishment in the territory of the Member State in which the service is to be provided presented the danger that Article 59 EEC might be rendered totally ineffective, and accordingly made the legality of any restrictions in this area subject to the conditions stated above. In the event, the Court held that the exclusion from the profession concerned, based on the absence of a permanent residence, was inadmissible in relation to the person in question, since the services provided by a legal adviser in the Netherlands were subject to neither the requirement of a professional qualification nor any rules relating to the exercise of the profession.[455]

This decision was confirmed by the Court in the *Coenen* case, in which a Dutch insurance broker having his residence in Belgium objected to the fact that he had been barred from exercising his profession in the Netherlands, even though he had an office there.[456] The Court first repeated its

---

[453] Case 33/74 [1974] E.C.R. 1299.
[454] [1974] E.C.R. 1309, paras. 10 to 12.
[455] [1974] E.C.R. 1310, para. 15.
[456] Case 39/75 [1975] E.C.R. 1547.

opinion that a residence requirement applied to the provider of the service

"may, according to the circumstances, have the result of depriving Article 59 of all effectiveness, in view of the fact that the precise object of that Article is to abolish restrictions on freedom to provide services imposed on persons who do not reside in the State where the service is to be provided."[457]

The Court then proceeded to contrast the interests of the provider of the service with that of the State in preventing

"the freedom guaranteed by Article 59 being used by a person whose activities are entirely or chiefly directed towards this territory in order to avoid the professional rules which would apply to him if he resided in that State."[458]

The Court succeeded in reconciling the two conflicting interests by applying the proportionality principle and stated that the residence requirement could be allowed only as an exception

"where the Member State is unable to apply other, less restrictive measures to ensure respect for these rules."[459]

Pernice correctly points out the similarities in the reasoning process adopted by the Court in the decisions referred to above and the decisions in *Cayrol*[460] (freedom to trade) and in *Sagulo*[461] (free movement of persons) and consequently doubts where the Court could have held the residence requirement to be at all lawful without denying this right in its entirety, *i.e.* without striking at its very existence. He states: "If this were to be the case, the Community citizen would, to all practical intents and purposes, be compelled to establish himself in the foreign state, which would, in turn, prevent him from providing his services in his home country." Pernice considers this to amount to "the removal of all content from an essential individual right" and concludes that, as a result, the public interest "could not, under any circumstances, justify the perma-

---

[457] [1975] E.C.R. 1554, para. 7.
[458] [1975] E.C.R. 1555, para. 9.
[459] *Ibid.*
[460] [1977] E.C.R. 2280, para. 38.
[461] [1977] E.C.R. 1506, para. 12.

nent residence requirement, in view of the principle of the freedom to provide services."[462]

Case 279/80, Webb[463] also concerned restrictions on the freedom to provide services on grounds of public policy. Here, the Netherlands Hoge Raad sought a preliminary ruling on, *inter alia*, the question of the compatibility with Article 59 of the rule applicable in the Netherlands under which the provision of manpower to another person without authorisation by the Minister of Social Affairs was prohibited.

The Court stated first of all that the freedom to provide services

> "is one of the fundamental principles of the Treaty and may be restricted only by provisions which are justified by the general good and which are imposed on all persons or undertakings operating in the said State in so far as that interest is not safeguarded by the provisions to which the provider of the service is subject in the Member State of his establishment."[464]

The Court went on to point out that the provision of manpower constituted an extremely sensitive area from a professional and social point of view, and that consequently the Member States were free to lay down a requirement of prior authorisation for the provision of manpower in its territory, on the understanding that the authorisation in question had to be provided under the same conditions as those which applied to its own nationals.

The Court, however, also stated that

> "such a measure would be excessive in relation to the aim pursued (...) if the requirements to which the issue of a licence is subject coincided with the proofs and guarantees required in the state of establishment."[465]

For these reasons, the Court considered it to be necessary that the Member State, when processing the application for authorisation and taking the relevant decision, should take into account the documentary

---

[462] I. Pernice, *Grundrechtsgehalte im Europäischen Gemeinschaftsrecht* (1979) Baden-Baden, p. 162.
[463] [1981] E.C.R. 3305.
[464] [1981] E.C.R. 3325, para. 17.
[465] [1981] E.C.R. 3326, para. 20; *cf.* also Joined Cases 62–63/81 [1982] E.C.R. 223 on the problems raised by the social security of workers who have been temporarily employed in another Member State.

evidence and securities which the provider of the service had already presented for the purpose of exercising his activity in the Member State where he was established.

An important case for the subsequent development of Community media law[466] was the *Debauve* decision,[467] in which the proportionality principle was the subject-matter of the judicial review. Here, the Court considered the restrictions on the freedom to provide services to be permissible if they were justified on grounds of the general interest. On this subject, the Advocate-General stated that the object of these provisions clearly was not to exclude the reception of such televised items (*i.e.* advertisements) from Belgian territory altogether. All they sought to achieve in relation to each individual programme was to prevent the active propagation of such programmes beyond the circle of persons who were able to receive the programme in question directly. In his view, the circumstance that these provisions served only this limited objective did not affect their validity.[468] Applying this argument, the Court stated in its grounds of judgment:

> "Since the transmission of television signals by cable television enables them to be diffused over a wider area and improves their penetration, restrictions or prohibitions imposed on television advertising within its territory by a Member State do not lose their justification because of the fact that reception of foreign broadcasting stations is also possible throughout the national territory, or in certain areas thereof, without the intervention of any cable television system."[469]

The measure in question was thus not declared by the Court to be disproportionate. In taking this decision, the Court assumed that in the absence of harmonisation of the applicable provisions, this type of prohibition came within the power conferred on each Member State to subject television advertising in its territory to legal provisions, restrictions and even prohibitions on the grounds of public policy.[470]

---

[466] For an extensive study of this issue, *cf.* J. Schwarze (ed.), *Fernsehen ohne Grenzen* (1985) Baden-Baden. *cf.* also J. Sedemund, "Europäisches Gemeinschaftsrecht" (1986) NJW, p. 632 (633).
[467] Case 52/79 [1980] E.C.R. 833.
[468] *Loc. cit.*, p. 869.
[469] *Loc. cit.*, p. 858.
[470] *Loc. cit.*, p. 857.

Case 205/84[471] concerned restrictions on the freedom to provide services imposed for the purpose of official supervision of insurance activity. The German Law relating to Insurance Supervision (Versicherungsaufsichtsgesetz—VAG) subjects insurance companies from the Community seeking to offer their services in the Federal Republic not only to prior authorisation but also to the requirement of being established in the Federal Republic. These restrictions prompted the Commission to bring an action for infringement of the Treaty against the Federal Republic.

The Court stated that the freedom to provide services could be restricted by rules which applied equally to all persons active within the national territory and which were justified by the public interest. This was the case only where the public interest had not already been served by the rules to which the provider of services was subject in his home country. The Court acknowledged the existence of necessary considerations of public policy which justified the authorisation requirement on the grounds that it was only the requirement that all persons active in the field of insurance obtain prior authorisation which guaranteed effective supervision. The establishment requirement, on the other hand, constituted a restriction of the freedom to provide services which was infinitely more serious. Effective supervision was already made possible by the authorisation requirement. The establishment requirement was, from the point of view of treating both nationals and other Community citizens on an equal footing, justified only in relation to those insurers who had a permanent presence on the German market.[472]

In the area covered by the freedom of establishment, the Court also recently had the opportunity to concern itself with the residence requirement. In Case 182/83, *Fearon* v. *Irish Land Commission*[473] the Irish Supreme Court referred a question to the Court of Justice under Article 177 seeking an interpretation of Article 58 EEC which would enable it to assess the compatibility of Irish provisions with the EEC Treaty. This question was raised in the context of a legal dispute surrounding a decision by the Irish Land Commission to expropriate a site belonging to the plaintiff in the main action, R. Fearon and Co., Ltd., a company formed under Irish law.

The rules on expropriation contained in the disputed Land Act 1965 provided for exceptions to the expropriation of agricultural land only

---

[471] *Commission* v. *Federal Republic of Germany* [1986] E.C.R. 3755.
[472] *Loc. cit.*, pp. 225, 227, 228.
[473] [1984] E.C.R. 3677; *cf.* J. Sedemund, *loc. cit.*, footnote 466, p. 634.

where the owner—or, in the case of companies, all their shareholders—were established on the land in question or in its vicinity. The Court decided that a company formed under Irish law, whose shareholders were British nationals having already exercised their right of establishment by founding the company, enjoyed no exemption from expropriation if the British shareholders did not themselves live on the land.[474]

Accordingly, Advocate-General Darmon did not consider that the proportionality principle had been infringed here, since this principle could not be interpreted as prohibiting the national legislator from adopting rules on expropriation, such as Article 35 of the Land Act 1965, which did not discriminate on grounds of nationality.[475]

As a criterion of lawfulness, the proportionality principle plays a significant role not only in the context of the freedom of establishment, but also in relation to other measures or rules restricting professional activity.

Thus in a preliminary ruling arising from an action brought by a Netherlands national, the holder of a state diploma giving access in Belgium to the profession of lawyer, after he had been refused membership of the Bar Association in question under a Belgian regulation because of his nationality, the Court held that

> "having regard to the fundamental character of freedom of establishment and the rule on equal treatment with nationals in the system of the Treaty, the exceptions allowed by the first paragraph of Article 55 cannot be given a scope which would exceed the objective for which the exemption clause was inserted."[476]

Here, the Court resorted to the formula which it used in the *Sotgiu* case in relation to the principle of the free movement of persons,[477] and thus followed the advice given by Advocate-General Mayras, *i.e.* to apply the same reasoning process in interpreting Article 55 as that applied to Article 48(4).[478]

The decision in *Thieffry*[479] concerned the admission of a Belgian lawyer in France. Here, the plaintiff in the main action had been refused admission to the Bar with the Paris Court of Appeal, in spite of the fact that he

---

[474] [1984] E.C.R. 3686, para. 11.
[475] [1984] E.C.R. 3690.
[476] Case 2/74 *Reyners* v. *Belgium* [1974] E.C.R. 631 at 654.
[477] *cf.* footnote 432.
[478] [1974] E.C.R. 665.
[479] Case 71/76 [1977] E.C.R. 765.

held the Belgian degree of Doctor of Laws, whose equivalence had been recognised by a French university. The Court reached the conclusion that this rejection constituted a restriction which was incompatible with the freedom of establishment,[480] since in spite of the absence of the directive envisaged by Article 57 EEC, only professional regulations justified in the public interest were permissible.[481]

The proportionality principle was also featured in the final case to be considered under this heading, where the Court stated that the principle that a lawyer may have only one establishment did not mean

> "that the legislation of a Member State may require a lawyer to have only one establishment throughout the Community territory. Such a restrictive interpretation would mean that a lawyer once established in a particular Member State would be able to enjoy the freedom of the Treaty to establish himself in another Member State only at the price of abandoning the establishment he already had."[482]

6. Competition law

(a) Introduction

Among the administrative powers which the Commission exercises over the Community citizen, those which have by far the most significant impact are those which relate to competition policy.[483] The full extent of these powers of intervention becomes clear when it is considered that in the light of the increasingly extensive interpretation of Articles 85 and 86 of the EEC Treaty, the most common types of contract in the business world—*i.e.* purchase agreements, distribution agreements, licensing agreements, joint ventures, mergers or other co-operation agreements which are of considerable economic importance—increasingly depend on authorisation by the Commission.[484] Even the granting of exemptions

---

[480] *Loc. cit.*, p. 779.
[481] *Loc. cit.*, p. 777.
[482] Case 107/83 *Ordre des Avocats au Barreau de Paris* v. *Klopp* [1984] E.C.R. 2971 (2989, para. 18); on this subject, *cf.* J. Sedemund, "Europäisches Gemeinschaftsrecht" (1985) NJW, p. 526 (529).
[483] Apart from the law governing staff/management relationships. On this subject, *cf. infra*, p. 830.
[484] *cf.*, for example, J. Sedemund, "Allgemeine Prinzipien des Verwaltungsverfahrensrechts—dargestellt am Beispiel des europäischen Verwaltungsverfahrensrechts in Kar-

from the fundamental prohibition of agreements which restrict competition lies in the exclusive power of the Commission. Enterprises can be compelled by the latter to provide all the necessary information and to agree to examination of all business documents. Finally, the Commission is entitled to impose fines of up to 10 per cent. of the total turnover of a firm on grounds of infringement of Articles 85 and 86 of the Treaty. Bearing in mind these broad powers of intervention, it becomes clear that it is precisely in the field of competition "law that the proportionality principle plays an important part."[485] As Ipsen[486] has correctly stated, freedom of competition "must be understood not only as serving a business purpose, but also as an element of private law which serves to make effective fundamental constitutional principles of freedom and equality." Consequently, as the Court has since also acknowledged, it must be accorded the status of a fundamental right, and it is precisely in the field of fundamental rights that the proportionality principle plays an important role.[487]

(b) Administrative procedure in European competition law

Several aspects of the administrative procedure in European competition law,[488] which assists the process of defending competition in the Common Market against distortions as well as the penalising of infringements, are characterised by the proportionality principle. Thus Article 11 of Regulation 17 provides that the Commission, for the purpose of carrying out the tasks devolved on it by Article 89 and by rules adopted under Article 87 of the Treaty, may require of the Governments and the institutions of the Member States, as well as of undertakings and associations of undertakings, all "necessary" information. The information required by the Commission may not be disproportionate to the objective pursued by it.[489] It is generally accepted that the interest of the Commission in elucidating the facts must be weighed up against the efforts

---

tellsachen," in J. Schwarze (ed.), *Europäisches Verwaltungsrecht im Werden* (1982) Baden-Baden, p. 46.

[485] On the rights of the defence in competition law proceedings before the Commission, *cf.* A. v. *Winterfeld*, in the eponymous article in (1981) RIW, pp. 801 *et seq.*

[486] H. P. Ipsen, *Europäisches Gemeinschaftsrecht* (1972) Tübingen, p. 608. On this subject, *cf.* also T. Oppermann, "Europäische Wirtschaftsverfassung nach der Einheitlichen Europäischen Akte," *loc. cit., supra*, footnote 68, pp. 59 *et seq.*

[487] *cf. supra*, 721.

[488] *cf.* Regulation 17 of February 6, 1962, J.O. 1962, 204; O.J. Sp.Ed. 1959–1962, 87.

[489] E.C.J. [1962] E.C.R. 917 at 944.

required of the undertaking which is the subject of the investigation.[490] A crucial element in assessing whether or not the information is disproportionate to the objective pursued is the view taken by the Commission that it suffices that the information required could be important for the purpose of carrying out the procedure.[491]

Under Article 14 of Regulation 17, the Commission may, on the same grounds as those stated in Article 11 of Regulation 17, conduct all "necessary" investigations. Even these wide powers of intervention must be interpreted in the light of the proportionality requirement, since under this provision the Commission may, *inter alia*, carry out investigations on the business premises of the undertakings concerned by virtue of decisions which are immediately enforceable—which are comparable to the "searches" laid down by the German law relating to preliminary investigations—even without judicial authorisation.[492] Under German law, this gives rise to a constitutional problem in view of Article 13 of the Basic Law, since the inviolability of the citizen's residence, which is enshrined in this provision, means that searches can be carried out only on judicial instructions, and only exceptionally by the competition law bodies acting under their own authority, *i.e.* "where there is danger in delay."[493]

In Case 136/79, *National Panasonic* v. *Commission*,[494] the applicant brought an action under Article 173 EEC for the annulment of a Commission decision under which the applicant had been compelled to agree to undergo investigations pursuant to Article 14(3) of Regulation 17 of the Council. The applicant based its action on, *inter alia*, the argument that the Commission decision infringed the proportionality principle, since the case law of the Court had held that any decision to conduct investigations without a preliminary inquiry was proportionate only where the situation was particularly serious and there prevailed a situation of utmost urgency as well as the need for absolute secrecy when carrying out the investigation. The Court, however, dismissed the action, stating on the subject of proportionality that

> "The Commission's choice between an investigation by straightforward authorisation and an investigation ordered by a decision

[490] A. Gleiss-M. Hirsch, *Kommentar zum EWG-Kartellrecht* (3rd ed., Heidelberg 1978), Regulation 17 (11), No. 13.
[491] *cf.* [1960] E.C.R. 163 at 181; *cf.* also Decision 71/85/EEC, J.O. 1971, L34/13, 15.
[492] *cf.* on this subject J. Sedemund, *loc. cit.*, footnote 484, p. 60.
[493] *Ibid.*
[494] [1980] E.C.R. 2033.

does not depend on the facts relied upon by the applicant but on the need for an appropriate inquiry having regard to the special features of the case.

Considering that the contested decision aimed solely at enabling the Commission to collect the necessary information to appraise whether there was any infringement of the Treaty, it does not therefore appear that the Commission's action in this instance was disproportionate to the objective pursued and therefore violated the principle of proportionality."[495]

The reliance by the applicant on the inviolability of the residence, guaranteed by Article 8 of the ECHR, was of no avail to it either. Instead, the Court considered that the intervention which accompanied the investigation was covered by Article 8(2) of the ECHR, since it had a statutory basis in Article 14 of Regulation 17 and served the purpose of countering distortions in competition which disadvantaged the public interest.[496]

In this context, Sedemund[497] points to Article 17(2) of the Regulation relating to Crafts, under which, in Germany, the agents of the Chamber of Crafts have the power, for the purpose of supervising the activity of craft industries, to visit land and business premises belonging to the person required to supply information, and to carry out investigations and inspections on these premises. The German Federal Constitutional Court did not judge the rights of access and inspection under Article 17(2) of the Regulation relating to Crafts as constituting "searches" and, because of the narrowly defined nature of the powers involved, did not regard these powers as constituting an infringement or restriction of the inviolability of the citizen's residence.[498] However, since the powers conferred on the Commission under Article 14 of Regulation 17 are more far-reaching, it will be necessary, when weighing up the interest the Commission has in clarifying the matter under investigation and that of the undertaking involved to see its individual rights protected, to apply a strict criterion of necessity, and in any case one which is stricter than that

---

[495] [1980] E.C.R. 2060, paras. 29 to 30.
[496] *Loc. cit.*, p. 2057, paras. 19 to 20.
[497] *Loc. cit.*, footnote 484, pp. 60 *et seq.*
[498] BVerfGE 27, 1; DVBl (1971) p. 892; for a critical review of this issue, *cf.* Lepa, "Aus der Rechtsprechung des Bundesverfassungsgerichtes" (1972) JR, p. 192.

involved in, for example, the requisitioning of information under Article 11 of Regulation 17.[499]

The question could be asked at this point whether the Commission, before conducting an investigation, is compelled to clear up the matter initially by applying the less restrictive method of requesting information. The general view is that this is not the case.[500] The reason for this is that, whilst under Article 11 of Regulation 17 the Commission may demand only the information "required" by virtue of a decision to that effect, the decision to conduct an investigation, under Article 14 of Regulation 17, is not subject to the same precondition. This was confirmed by the ECJ in a corresponding case,[501] in which it decided, in relation to Article 47 of the ECSC Treaty, that the Commission could make a choice between the information procedure or the investigation procedure according to what it deemed to be the most effective. This conclusion is also justified by the fact that in certain cases, the purpose of the investigation could be achieved only by an unannounced visit.[502]

(c) Fines

A particularly far-reaching measure has generally proved to be the fines which the Commission may impose for infringements of competition law. These fines are laid down as a penalty for deliberate and negligent infringements of the prohibitions contained in Articles 85 and 86 EEC and of competition decisions issued by the Commission, and for the protection of the administrative procedure against incorrect or distorted evidence under Article 15 of Regulation 17.[503] In the context of its unrestricted right to review discretionary acts,[504] the Court assesses the seriousness of the infringement and the size of the fine in accordance with the same criteria as does the Commission. Even though in the majority of

---

[499] cf. A. Gleiss, M. Hirsch, loc. cit., footnote 490. Regulation 17, Article 14, No. 7; H. Schröter, in H.v.d. Groeben, H.v. Boeckh, J. Thiesing, C.-D. Ehlermann, Kommentar zum EWG-Vertrag (3rd ed., Baden-Baden 1983), Article 87, No. 38.

[500] cf. A. Gleiss, M. Hirsch, loc. cit., footnote 490, Regulation 17, Article 14, No. 4 et seq.

[501] E.C.J. Case 35/59 Acciaieria e tubificio di Brescia v. High Authority [1960] E.C.R. 163 at 179 et seq.

[502] H. Schröter, loc. cit., footnote 499, Article 87, No. 38, with further references in footnote 182.

[503] cf. A. Gleiss, M. Hirsch, loc. cit., footnote 490, Regulation 17, Article 15, Nos. 1 et seq.; H. Schröter, loc. cit., footnote 499, Nos. 12 et seq., 32 et seq., and N. Koch, in Eberhard Grabitz (ed.), Kommentar zum EWG-Vertrag (1986) München, under Article 87, then under Article 15 Regulation 17, Nos. 1 et seq.

[504] cf. Article 17 Regulation 17.

cases the Court confirms challenged decisions imposing fines, the Court has been known to reduce the amount of the fine and, in so doing, to make frequent use of the proportionality principle or general considerations of fairness.[505]

The upper limit for the amount of a fine, laid down in Article 15(2) of Regulation 17, is also an expression of the proportionality idea. Thus in its decision of June 7, 1983,[506] the Court held that

> "thus the only express reference to the turnover of the undertaking concerns the upper limit of a fine exceeding 1,000,000 units of account. In such a case, the limit seeks to prevent fines from being disproportionate in relation to the size of the undertaking."[507]

In the same decision, the Court also pinpointed those elements which are to be taken into account in assessing the seriousness of an infringement:

> "The nature and importance (of these factors) vary according to the type of infringement in question and the particular circumstances of the case. Those factors may, depending on the circumstances, include the volume and value of the goods in respect of which the infringement was committed and the size and economic power of the undertaking and, consequently, the influence which the undertaking was able to exert on the market."[508]

With regard to the argument raised in this case by one of the applicants, namely that the fines imposed on it had the effect of an expropriation and could possibly lead to the business in question being ruined, Advocate-General Sir Gordon Slynn stated in his Opinion that

> "the Court has shown a reluctance in the past to reduce fines on similar grounds . . . Nevertheless it is right (and consonant with the policy of Article 15(2) of Regulation No. 17) in fixing the fine to have regard to the ability of undertakings to pay them. In that connection, it seems established that the fine fixed by the Commission exceeds MDF's working capital; the accounts presented to the Court by MDF disclose a high proportion of short-term loans, and

---

[505] cf. the examples given by N. Koch, loc. cit., footnote 503, No. 79.
[506] Joined cases 100–103/80 *Musique Diffusion Française* v. *Commission* [1983] E.C.R. 1825.
[507] Loc. cit., p. 1908, para. 119.
[508] Loc. cit., p. 1909, para. 120.

unlike the other undertakings in this case, MDF remains independent. These factors in my view indicate some reduction in the fine."[509]

The Court followed the advice given by the Advocate-General and reduced the fine imposed on MDF from 800,000 ECU to 600,000 ECU. In so doing, it took account of the relatively short duration of the action constituting the infringement, of the total turnover of the company and of the other criteria relevant to the assessment of the seriousness of the infringement.[510]

In Case 107/82, *AEG* v. *Commission*,[511] Advocate-General Reischl considered a reduction in the fine imposed in this case to be appropriate on the following grounds:

"In that connection, it is material that a substantial part of the Commission's allegations cannot be upheld and that the Commission did not obtain a reliable picture of the actual effects of certain infringements on the market and consumers."[512]

The applicant had, for the purpose of marketing certain electronic entertainment products in the Common Market, registered with the Commission the "Sales agreement for Telefunken products," whose legal basis was standard contracts (E.C. obligation certificates) with qualified resale agents relating to the individual stages of trade. At the request of the Commission, the applicant had, during the subsequent period, made certain changes in these marketing conditions. Thereupon the Director-General for Competition had communicated to it in writing that he had no objections against the proposed version of the selective distribution agreements envisaged on the basis of Article 85(1) EEC. In the course of time, the Commission had, on the basis of many complaints made against the applicant by various traders, arrived at the conclusion that the actual carrying out of the selective distribution agreements by the applicant and its subsidiaries did not correspond with the standard contracts which had been registered. In the disputed decision, the Commission had established that the applicant had used its selective distribution agreements in such a way as to constitute an abuse of the law, in that the applicant had

---

[509] *Loc. cit.*, p. 1952.
[510] *Loc. cit.*, pp. 1911 *et seq.*, paras. 130 *et seq.*
[511] [1983] E.C.R. 3151.
[512] *Loc. cit.*, p. 3270.

discriminated against certain traders and directly or indirectly influenced the sales prices to be applied by the licensed traders with a view to excluding certain types of business altogether and to maintaining prices at a certain level. In addition, the Commission had imposed a fine of 1,000,000 ECU on the applicant.

The Court did not follow the proposal, put by the Advocate-General, that the fine be reduced. Instead, it held that

> "It is clear from the foregoing considerations that AEG's systematic conduct in the improper application of the selective distribution system must be regarded as having been sufficiently proved in law. The fact that the Commission has not succeeded in proving a number of individual cases does not call in question the systematic nature of AEG's improper conduct and does not affect the scope of the infringement as determined in its decision of 6 January 1982. The Court feels that it must emphasise the gravity of such an infringement, which consists in applying a selective distribution system, after the approval by the Commission, in a manner contrary to the undertaking entered into by the applicant, upon which the compatibility of the selective distribution system with Article 85 of the Treaty depended.
>
> In these circumstances, there are no grounds for fixing the fine at an amount other than that determined by the Commission."[513]

In Case 86/82, *Hasselblad* v. *Commission*,[514] the Court considered that the evidence produced by the Commission was in part inadequate and accordingly, in its decision, reduced the fines. This case concerned the accusation of concerted practices by which the applicant and six of its exclusive distribution agents had hampered, restricted or made more onerous the export of the applicant's goods within the Community. The applicant claimed that the size of the fine imposed on it was disproportionate to the infringement established and especially—given their respective turnovers—disproportionate to the fine imposed on the Victor Hasselblad company. On this point, the Court held:

> "An undertaking's turnover is only one of the factors which may be taken into account. The aim of the concerted practice established by the Commission was to prevent any imports into the United King-

---

[513] *Loc. cit.*, p. 3220, paras. 136 to 138.
[514] [1984] E.C.R. 883.

840

dom of Hasselblad cameras intended for Camera Care and as such the practice constituted a flagrant breach of the rules on competition contained in the Treaty. However, it would appear that the Commission fixed the amount of the fine on the basis of various considerations . . . which the Commission failed to prove in the proceedings before the Court. . . . A further consideration is that the applicant is not a large undertaking. In the circumstances, the Court has decided to reduce the fine from ECU 165,000 to ECU 80,000."[515]

The slender reasons given by the Court make it difficult to weigh up the interests involved and to understand clearly the reasons which were finally conclusive for the reduction of the fine or for the size of this reduction. It remains to be established to what extent the Court, in assessing the method of fixing the fine, uses precise criteria or merely applies a vague proportionality test and seeks in each individual case to arrive at a fair solution. This question cannot, however, be examined in depth under this heading.

(d) Substantive competition law

The following cases will demonstrate that the proportionality principle has played an important part not only in competition proceedings—and especially in the assessment of penalties—but also in the assessment of infringements of the substantive law of competition.

In Joined Cases 56 and 58/64, *Consten and Grundig* v. *Commission*[516] the point at issue was the circumstance that the Consten company had a right to the sole distribution in France of Grundig appliances. The distribution agreement between Consten and Grundig having been the subject of several actions based on competition law brought by Consten against other distributors of Grundig appliances, Grundig notified the exclusive distribution agreement to the Commission. The latter decided that the agreement in question constituted an infringement of Article 85 EEC, and prohibited at the same time any action which would either prevent third parties from importing into France or from exporting the products covered by the agreement as they saw fit or make such imports more difficult. The action for annulment brought by the applicants was aimed against this decision. The Federal Republic of Germany, which

[515] *Loc. cit.*, p. 911, para. 57.
[516] [1966] E.C.R. 321.

intervened in these proceedings, had invoked the proportionality principle on the basis that the Commission, by issuing its refusal, had infringed a certain exemption condition. This accusation was countered by the Commission, which stated that the proportionality principle had been developed in German administrative law in relation to the choice of means of coercion and could in no way be applied to the refusal to grant a benefit. However, the Court did not have the opportunity to adopt a position on this issue, since it was able to establish the illegal nature of the decision at an earlier stage of the proceedings.

The refusal of an exemption was, finally, the subject-matter of Case 258/78, *Nungesser* v. *Commission*.[517] Here the Court established that, under Article 85(3) of the Treaty, an exemption from the prohibition contained in Article 85(1) could be granted for those agreements between firms which contributed to the improvement of the production process or the distribution of the products or to promoting technical progress

> "and which does not impose on the undertakings concerned restrictions which are not indispensable to the attainment of those objectives."[518]

In the case under review, the applicants sought exclusive territorial protection in the Federal Republic of Germany for certain types of hybrid maize seed developed by the Institut National de la Recherche Agronomique (INRA). The Court, however, was of the opinion that as this concerned a question of seeds intended to be used for the production of maize, which is an important product for human and animal foodstuffs,

> "absolute territorial protection manifestly goes beyond what is indispensable for the improvement of production or distribution or the promotion of technical progress."[519]

7.   ECSC

(a) *Introduction*

Although the EEC law occupies a central position in the issue discussed

---

[517] [1982] E.C.R. 2015.
[518] *Loc. cit.*, p. 2073, para. 76.
[519] *Loc. cit.*, para. 77.

here, a glance at the Court's case law relating to the ECSC Treaty cannot be avoided, since this is where the relevant case law had its origins. Thus Advocate-General Dutheillet de Lamothe, in his Opinion on the famous *Internationale Handelsgesellschaft* decision, correctly invoked a Court decision of November 29, 1956,[520] when discussing the issue of the proportionality principle. In that case, the action was brought against the last of a series of decisions by which the High Authority had, in accordance with Article 26 of the Transitional Agreement, established and approved certain price lists for the sale and purchase of coal in Belgium. The subject-matter of the action was the question whether the High Authority was entitled itself to establish the price lists in question or whether its role was restricted to approving or rejecting pricing proposals made by the undertakings concerned. In the course of the oral proceedings, the applicant had pointed out that inasmuch as the undertakings could not reduce their prices to the extent laid down in the Transitional Agreement, the High Authority had at its disposal indirect methods of realising the objective set out in Article 26 (incorporation of the Belgian market into the Common Market, levelling the various price differences). One such method, for example, was to withdraw the equalisation payment from the defaulting undertakings. Since this method would have sufficed, the fixing of prices by the High Authority could not be regarded as indispensable. On this point, the Court decided[521]:

"The Court cannot accept this argument, since in accordance with a generally-accepted rule of law such an indirect reaction by the High Authority to illegal action on the part of undertakings must be in proportion to the scale of that action. For that reason, the High Authority can be empowered only to reduce equalisation payments to the extent to which the undertakings have not reduced their prices within the stated limits. In that case, undertakings always have a clear interest in risking such a reduction in equalisation and in preferring profits from prices which are too high in relative terms to higher equalisation payments corresponding to any reduction in prices which they might have made, particularly since the funds available for equalisation are on a sliding scale.

It results from the foregoing that indirect action on the part of the High Authority such as a reduction in equalisation payments is

---

[520] Case 55/56 *Fédération Charbonnière de Belgique* v. *High Authority* [1956] E.C.R. 297.
[521] *Loc. cit.*, p. 311.

insufficient to attain the objective of Article 26(2) of the Convention."

(b) Scrap metal equalisation cases

The proportionality principle also played a part in the so-called scrap metal equalisation fund of the ECSC. By introducing this fund, the Commission sought to control the use of scrap metal in the production of basic steel and iron and to remove it from world market levels, in order thus to protect the Community against the adverse effects of fluctuating world prices. In these decisions, the Court stressed the need to weigh up the interests of the public authorities against those of the private sector. Thus it held in its decision of July 12, 1958[522]:

> "Any set of economic rules necessarily has consequential effects, even on the interests of those within the jurisdiction to whom those measures are not directly addressed. A public authority has a duty to act with circumspection and to intervene only after carefully balancing the various interests concerned while so far as possible restricting the foreseeable damage to third parties."

The Court then proceeded to apply these principles by examining whether the High Authority had in that case given sufficient consideration to the interests of the basic steel producers, and replied to this question in the affirmative following a thorough exercise in weighing up the interests involved.

In a further decision on the scrap metal equalisation fund,[523] the principle of proportionality was taken into account to the extent that the Court approved the path taken by the Commission in opting for indirect methods of influencing markets, since the use of this method—in contrast with direct official intervention—guaranteed the freedom of choice of the economic agents.[524] In his Opinion on this case, the Advocate-General indicated his preference for indirect methods of influencing markets, stating that

---

[522] Case 15/57 [1958] E.C.R. 165 at 194.
[523] Case 8/57 *Groupement des Hauts Fourneaux et Aciéries Belges* v. *High Authority* [1958] E.C.R. 231.
[524] *Loc. cit.*, p. 261.

"the Treaty, if I am correct, makes provision for a graded series of steps, almost a hierarchy of means for affecting production, and recourse to direct action entirely suspending the economy of the market is only envisaged as a last resort."[525]

(c) The production quota systems

In recent times, the Court has had the opportunity, in a series of cases, to concern itself with the legality of the production quota system for steel in accordance with Article 58 of the ECSC Treaty[526] and the penalties attached to the system. These production quotas were introduced for the first time in October 1980,[527] the Commission having initially, in 1975, decided to impose on the steel-producing undertakings a duty to provide information on and to register the quantities placed on the Community market by the producers. This occurred against the background of the crisis in the steel industry in the mid-70s, which resulted from overcapacity. The limits of the discretion accorded to the Commission in elaborating this production quota system were derived from the proportionality principle as well as from the rationale of Article 58.[528]

In Case 276/80, *Padana* v. *Commission*,[529] in which the fixing of production quotas was at issue, the parties involved extensively debated the question of the extent to which the application of the proportionality principle could be the subject of judicial scrutiny. On this issue, the applicant had alleged that under this principle, intervention by the public authorities which imposed restrictions on the rights of undertakings was valid only where it was in reasonable proportion to the objective pursued. Where this could not be realised because the official intervention was unsuitable for that purpose, the measure in question would be accordingly illegal. As a result, the examination of the suitability of the legal act for the achievement of the object in view was a fundamental precondition in order to be able to answer the question whether the restriction imposed on the rights of the undertaking appeared to be suitably proportionate to

---

[525] *Loc. cit.*, p. 354; *cf.* also Joined Cases 15 & 29/59 *Société Métallurgique and others* v. *High Authority* [1960] E.C.R. 9.

[526] *cf.* on this subject F. J. Säcker-C. W. Neumann, "Rechtliche Grenzen fur die Ausgestaltung von Erzeugerquotensystemen nach Art. 58 EGKS-Vertrag" (1985) RIW, pp. 946 *et seq.*

[527] "System of Steel Producer Quotas for the Fixing of Production Quotas," General Decision of the Commission 1794/80 ECSC.

[528] F. J. Säcker-C. W. Neumann, *loc. cit.*, footnote 526, p. 947.

[529] [1982] E.C.R. 517.

the desired result. The Commission, on the other hand, adhered to the view that the application of the proportionality principle could be examined only in the context of one and the same legal act or in that of several legal acts which were dependent on each other and covered the same substantive area. Any other approach would lead to hampering those Community institutions to whom the issuing of legal acts was entrusted in the execution of their duties, since as a result the validity of any legal act could be challenged on a wide variety of grounds (external relations, state aids, social policy, economic policy, etc.) and even on the basis of facts which had occurred after the issuing of the act in question. By applying its established case law on the proportionality principle to the case under review, the Court needed only to decide whether or not the system of production quotas as such imposed excessive burdens on the undertakings which were unjustified in view of the objectives pursued.

In his Opinion, Advocate-General Reischl examined from the point of view of a possible infringement of the proportionality principle the allegation that the measures adopted were unsuitable for the achievement of the object in view, and held that[530]

"in the circumstances of a case like this an appraisal with the benefit of appraising the effectiveness of the measures adopted the decisive point is whether, at the time when they were adopted, it could be assumed that they were clearly not conducive to the aim pursued."

Recently, Advocate-General VerLoren van Themaat had occasion to state his position on the proportionality of the production quota system in his Opinion on Joined Cases 140, 146, 221 and 226/82.[531] He pointed out in the first instance that the proportionality principle also played a prominent role in other areas of the Court's case law, i.e.—as has been demonstrated earlier—in the assessment of the exceptions to the fundamental principles of a system of free trade with undistorted competition. He went on to state that

"this principle has always been taken into account in various ways in the quota systems. The first quota system consisted, of course, in the application of an abatement rate that was the same for all producers

---

[530] *Loc. cit.*, p. 551.
[531] *Walzstahl-Vereinigung und Thyssen* v. *Commission* [1984] E.C.R. 951 at 987, 994.

of specific types of steel to their best production results in a specified reference period. Various adjustments were then made to take account of restructuring investment and production cuts consistent with the interests of the Community. Save for those adjustments, it was however assumed that the relative market shares of undertakings would be frozen. It cannot be denied that the contested decisions depart from that assumption and increase the market share of the single-product undertakings at the expense of the integrated undertakings that also produce concrete reinforcing bars.

In later general decisions, the results of the market mechanism are further taken into account by taking into account not only production in the twelve best months of the basis period but also production since the introduction of the quota system.

This lessening of the quota system's rigidifying effect on the market is important in connection with the possibilities, available ever since the introduction of Article 8 of Decision No. 2794/80, of exceeding quotas to a limited extent, carrying forward a partially used quota to the next quarter and of buying, exchanging or selling quotas. It is mainly by that approach that the Commission decisions have taken into account the principle of proportionality which I deduce from Article 2 and from the Court's judgments concerning exceptions to the system of undistorted competition."[532]

Of particular import for the undertakings concerned are the penalties which the Commission imposes in the event of infringement of the production quotas. In a number of cases,[533] the undertakings in question alleged that the enforcement of the fines concerned would jeopardise the existence of the firm, since they had neither the necessary reserves nor the size required to be able to accommodate the fines imposed. In an established line of reasoning, the Court decided on this point that

"an undertaking may not rely upon the economic difficulties which it must contend with in order to exempt itself from the restrictions imposed on account of the crisis and exceed at will the production quota allocated to it. Such conduct would create increased difficulties for all the other undertakings and would eventually bring about the collapse of the entire quota system. The applicant must therefore

---

[532] *Loc. cit.*, p. 994.
[533] *cf.* for example, Case 263/82 *Klöckner* v. *Commission* [1983] E.C.R. 4143; Case 10/83, *Metalgoi* v. *Commission* [1984] E.C.R. 1271.

bear the consequences, which it was perfectly able to foresee, of its failure to submit to a discipline imposed in the general interest."[534]

In the *Queensborough* case,[535] the applicant claimed that a fine of 75 ECU per tonne of steel produced in violation of the quota system had proportionately more serious implications for a processing firm than for an integrated undertaking. The Court, on the other hand, expressed the view that this fact could not be viewed as a mitigating circumstance or be regarded as a special situation which affected only one undertaking, and that for this reason the fine could not be reduced. In the Court's opinion, the quota system would be deprived of a good deal of its effectiveness if the Commission had to take into account in each case the particular category to which the undertaking involved belonged, as well as the various differences between them.

Also in cases involving infringements of the prices and minimum prices set under Articles 60 and 61 ECSC, fines are laid down whose lawfulness has been assessed by the Court in the light of their proportionality.

In the *Valsabbia et al.* joined cases,[536] actions had been brought by a number of undertakings producing reinforcing steel for concrete against individual decisions by which the Commission had imposed fines for infringement of the system of minimum prices. The applicants claimed, *inter alia*, that complying with the system of minimum prices had imposed excessive burdens on the most productive enterprises and that the sacrifices thus demanded of them were disproportionate because of the inadequacies and omissions in Decision No. 962/77. Against this claim made by the applicants, the Commission replied that the validity of a general decision could not depend on whether other decisions, which were formally independent of it, had been adopted or not.

On this point, the Court did not consider the Commission's argument sound. Instead, it saw itself under an obligation to examine whether the omissions found in the decision had led to the imposition on the applicants of burdens which, in the light of the objectives pursued by Decision No. 962/77, had to be considered disproportionate.

The Court pointed in the first place to its judgment of October 24, 1973, in Case 5/73,[537] in which it had held that

---

[534] [1984] E.C.R. 1279 *et seq.*
[535] Case 64/84 [1985] E.C.R. 1829 *et seq.*
[536] Joined Cases 154, 205–206, 226–228, 263–264/78, 31, 39, 83 & 85/79 [1980] E.C.R. 907.
[537] [1973] E.C.R. 1091 at 1112.

"in exercising their powers, the Institutions must ensure that the amounts which commercial operators are charged are no greater than is required to achieve the aim which the authorities are to accomplish; however, it does not necessarily follow that that obligation must be measured in relation to the individual situation of any one particular group of operators."

On the basis of this scope for discretion, the Court held in the case under review that[538]

"on the whole, the system established by Decision No. 962/77 worked despite the omissions disclosed and in the end attained the objectives pursued by that decision. Although it is true that the burden of the sacrifices required of the applicants may have been aggravated by the omissions in the system, that does not alter the fact that the decisions did not constitute a disproportionate and intolerable measure with regard to the aim pursued.

In those circumstances, and taking into consideration the fact that the objective laid down by Decision No. 962/77 is in accordance with the Commission's duty to act in the common interest, and that a necessary consequence of the very nature of Article 61 of the ECSC Treaty is that certain undertakings must, by virtue of European solidarity, accept greater sacrifices than others, the Commission cannot be accused of having imposed disproportionate burdens on the applicants."

On the argument put forward by the applicants that the measures in question were inappropriate since other steps should have been taken—an argument which is constantly reiterated in a number of cases—Advocate-General Capotorti adopted the following position[539]:

"If the allegation of an infringement of the principle of proportionality is based on the inadequacy of that decision, it is not sufficient to declare that the system required to be supplemented by other measures: it would be necessary to prove that the system did not function as long as such measures were not adopted."

---

[538] [1980] E.C.R. 1017 *et seq.*, paras. 119 *et seq.*
[539] *Loc. cit.*, p. 1058.

(d) Procedural questions

Finally, let us consider two ECJ decisions which involve procedural issues and which have already been touched upon when we discussed competition law procedure.[540] These concern cases dealing with the Commission's right to demand information and to conduct investigations.

In Case 31/59, *Acciaieria* v. *High Authority*[541] the subject-matter of the action was a decision by the High Authority by which the applicant had been compelled to supply to High Authority agents and inspectors "such information as they require for the performance of their duties and to this end to provide them with all company documents and accounts, in particular invoices, documents relating to banking operations and, in particular, individual items of the profit and loss account such as, for example, the turnover account and expense account." The firm in question challenged this decision particularly with the argument that the decision went too far, since the High Authority was merely entitled to examine the profit and loss account and similar documents where these concerned the field covered by the ECSC. If, however, such information covered other areas, verification by the High Authority was inadmissible.

Advocate-General Roemer, in his Opinion, dealt extensively with the substantive conditions for and the extent of the right to information and to investigation. Under this heading, Article 47 ECSC provided the High Authority with the opportunity to make the necessary investigations and to call for the necessary information.[542] There also existed, however, a principle in Community law under which the authorities were obliged, when intervening in private life, to select the least drastic measure. This principle was expressed in Article 5 of the ECSC Treaty.[543] Referring to Article 46(1) of the German Law relating to Restrictions on Competition, he continued[544]

> "I therefore consider that as a general rule the right of the High Authority to carry out checks which represent a far-reaching intervention in the activities of an undertaking, may only be exercised where a special need for it is shown in a specific case, that is, for example, if information has been refused or if there is good reason to suspect that the information obtained is incomplete or incorrect."

[540] *cf. supra*, p. 863.
[541] [1960] E.C.R. 159.
[542] *Loc. cit.*, p. 196.
[543] *Loc. cit.*, p. 197.
[544] *Loc. cit.*, p. 199.

As regards the challenged decision, which required the presentation of all documents and accounts of the company, he stated[545]:

> "By using this extremely wide form of wording, the High Authority therefore requests documents which have already been produced and which for the purpose of Article 47 need not be produced a second time."

In addition, the Advocate-General considered that the substantive conditions for requiring information were not to be interpreted as strictly as those relating to the right to conduct investigations.

On the question whether there exists a hierarchy between the right to demand information and the right to conduct investigations, the Court stated in its decision that

> "there is nothing in the letter, spirit or aim of the first paragraph of Article 47 to prohibit information being obtained and a check being made at the same time. There has thus been no infringement of Article 47 and the applicant cannot succeed in his claim that the information must be obtained and the check made in two distinct and successive stages according to an order of priority which is not laid down in the text, provided of course that it is necessary for the checks to be made."[546]

The *San Michele* case[547] concerned a decision by the High Authority by which a number of steel producers were required, for the purpose of checking production quotas, to submit invoices concerning the consumption of electricity, as well as to give the assurance that the invoices submitted constituted a complete set.

In his Opinion, Advocate-General Lagrange pointed out that the necessity of conducting the checks constituted, proportionately to the objective pursued, the limits of the powers conferred on the High Authority in applying Article 47 and raised the question whether the objective pursued could justify every type of intervention. His reply to this question was as follows[548]:

---

[545] *Loc. cit.*, p. 205.
[546] *Loc. cit.*, p. 180.
[547] Joined Cases 5–11 & 13–15/62 [1962] E.C.R. 917.
[548] *Loc. cit.*, p. 957.

"As in everything else, it is for the administrative court to reconcile the dictates of public interest with respect for individual rights. But in this case, taking account of the circumstances, I do not think that one could see an excessive requirement in a demand for the production of invoices together with a certificate, not of their authenticity, but 'confirming that the documents supplied cover all the electrical energy consumed by the undertaking during the period' in question."

The Advocate-General also examined the question whether the financial authorities could examine the taxpayer's documents only on the latter's premises. On this point, he stated:

"It appears that the current rules in the various countries of the Community are not exactly the same in this matter. Nevertheless, it cannot be claimed that it is unknown to require the taxpayer to produce certain documents in the tax office. We have been told that in Italy revenue officials have the right to require the attendance of the taxpayer or his representative in person. In the Community, we have no rule. In my opinion it is a question of degree. The requirements of inspection must not be excessive and disproportionate to the objective sought."[549]

Accordingly, the Court examined, in its decision, the question whether the verification methods of the High Authority had exceeded what was permitted and arrived at the following conclusion[550]:

"In this case, and having regard to the circumstances, the demand for the production of the invoices at Luxembourg was not excessive and disproportionate to the aim in view. The inspections previously carried out on the spot by officials of the High Authority and of the Swiss Trust Company give reasons for seriously doubting the veracity of the declarations made by certain undertakings with regard to their consumption of scrap. Consequently, checking in detail in the offices of the High Authority constituted a more adequate method and one which moreover was less likely to disturb the functioning of the undertakings concerned than fresh inspections carried out on their premises."

[549] *Loc. cit.*, p. 958.
[550] *Loc. cit.*, p. 944.

8. Staff law cases

The proportionality principle has also been known to play a decisive role in staff disputes. Here it is sufficient to mention, for the record, the Court decision in Case 18/63, *Schmitz* v. *Commission*.[551]

The subject-matter of the action was a Commission decision not to extend the contract of employment of a first-aid attendant. This decision had been based on professional misconduct on the part of the applicant, the latter having refused to lend her assistance in an accident which had occurred in the vicinity of the building in which she was employed. Against this, the Court found that at the time, the applicant had sole charge of the first-aid department and could not leave the premises without taking steps to ensure she was replaced. The actual facts of the case had not, however, been totally clarified.

The Court arrived at the conclusion that it would be disproportionate to dismiss an employee on the basis of one particular action, regarding which it was doubtful whether it constituted a mistake. The same applied where the dismissal occurred in the form of the non-renewal of a contract which previously had been regularly renewed.[552]

V. SUMMARY

The foregoing demonstrates that the proportionality principle is applicable in virtually every area of Community law as a criterion in the assessment of the legality of actions of the Community institutions and of the national authorities, which has often had a decisive effect, in relation to both legislative and executive action. It is consequently rightly regarded as a crucial principle in limiting economic legislation and practice within the Community.[553]

However, it has also become apparent that the terminology used by the Court in relation to the proportionality principle does not present an adequate degree of clarity. In addition, it is not always clear on what basis the Court has held, in a particular decision, a certain measure to be proportionate or disproportionate. Accordingly, it would appear appropriate in the following pages to attempt to derive from the relevant case law, taken as a whole, certain indications which could give more concrete

---

[551] [1964] E.C.R. 175.
[552] *Loc. cit.*, pp. 203 *et seq.*
[553] *cf.* footnote 3.

expression to the proportionality principle and thus to give it a clearer profile in its practical application. To this end, it is necessary in the first instance to examine the extent to which certain subsidiary principles can be formulated,[554] such as, for example, the principles of suitability, necessity or proportionality in the strict sense of the term, as is the case in German law.[555] Also, it would be useful to examine the extent to which there exists a distinction between the use of the proportionality principle as a criterion for rule-making on the one hand and for administrative action on the other.[556] Accordingly, we shall examine whether different approaches are tried according to the field of administrative action in which the principle is applied.

1. Content of the proportionality principle in community law

We have pointed out on a number of occasions that the proportionality principle has been applied by the Court of Justice using a number of different wordings.[557] In so doing, the Court gives preference to expressions such as "necessary," "suitable" and "essential," and on the basis of these criteria, establishes whether a certain measure has the least restrictive effect on economic agents from the point of view of economic freedom. The question arises here whether the Court, like the German administrative courts, recognises the existence of subsidiary principles such as suitability, necessity or proportionality in the narrow sense of the term,[558] or whether, in using these concepts, all the Court does is to give concrete expression, without further differentiation, to the general principle of proportionality.[559]

---

[554] *cf.* on this subject K.-V. Schiller, (1983) RIW, p. 928; R. Boest, *loc. cit.*, footnote 245, pp. 151 *et seq.*; H.-W. Rengeling, "Der Rechtsschutz bei der Subventionierung von Konkurrenten im EWG-Recht," in D. Wilke, H. Weber (ed.), *Gedächtnisschrift für F. Klein* (1977), pp. 416 *et seq.*, 432 *et seq.*

[555] *cf. supra*, pp. 689 *et seq.*

[556] *cf.* on this subject *supra*, pp. 719 *et seq.*

[557] On this subject, H.-P. Ipsen, *Europäisches Gemeinschaftsrecht in Einzelstudien* (1984) Baden-Baden, p. 358.

[558] *cf.* K.-V. Schiller (1983) RIW, p. 929, who considers that the Community law proportionality principle corresponds substantially with its German law counterpart.

[559] *cf.* B. Beutler, in: H. v.d. Groeben, H. v. Boeckh, J. Thiesing, C.-D. Ehlermann, *Kommentar zum EWG-Vertrag* (3rd ed., Baden-Baden 1983), p. 1477; *cf.* also H.-W. Rengeling in GS-Klein, *loc. cit.*, footnote 554, pp. 432 *et seq.*

Even if it can be assumed that the proportionality principle as used in Community law had its origins in German law,[560] it would be too premature to place the Community law principle and its German counterpart on the same footing, even in its subsidiary aspects. On the one hand, account must be taken of the fact that the relevant German principle is based on a very old tradition and has, in the course of a century, experienced many concrete applications.[561] By contrast, the Community law proportionality principle has been increasingly applied in the case law of the Court of Justice only since the early seventies and is for that reason less concrete in its application than its German counterpart. On the other hand, it needs to be recalled that the Court consists of judges and Advocates-General trained in a variety of legal systems. Thus an English lawyer does not have the same experience of the proportionality principle, in its concrete expression, as his German colleague. Nevertheless, as an Advocate-General, he will certainly apply a Community law proportionality principle. Accordingly, when the Court uses expressions such as "suitability" and "necessity," as is common in German law,[562] it will normally do so only in order to give concrete expression to the general principle of proportionality, without necessarily indicating a total degree of harmony with the German terminology and theory on this subject.[563]

Although the Court's grounds of judgment in many cases make use of only one particular aspect of the proportionality principle, a total picture of the case law, especially in the opinions of the Advocates-General, reveals a clear use of certain subsidiary aspects of the proportionality test.

(a) Suitability

It is true that in a number of decisions the Court has held that a measure complied with the Community law proportionality principle only where the method used was suitable for the purpose of achieving the objective

---

[560] Lord Mackenzie Stuart, *The European Community and the Rule of Law* (1977) London, p. 31: "... derived from German administrative law ...."; one of the principal reasons for this is that it was especially the German administrative courts which referred cases to the ECJ in which disproportionality of measures had been raised.

[561] Although German law, at all levels, features a wide variety of opinions on this issue, as well as a certain lack of terminological clarity, *cf.* for an extensive study of this subject M. Ch. Jakobs, *Der Grundsatz der Verhältnismässigkeit* (1985) Köln/Berlin/Bonn/München.

[562] Here, account must also be taken of the fact that, in certain circumstances, the translators involved also influence the choice of words in the judgment.

[563] As is correctly pointed out by B. Beutler, *loc. cit.*, footnote 559, p. 1477; H.-W. Rengeling, GS-Klein, *loc. cit.*, footnote 554, pp. 432 *et seq.*

pursued.[564] However, the suitability aspect is only of secondary importance since it concerns only the relationship between the end and the means. In this connection, the leading authors have justifiably pointed out that, for example, the methods which Article 40(1) of the EEC Treaty makes available for the achievement of the objectives stated in Article 39(1) of the EEC Treaty are to be regarded as suitable and, moreover, provide the Community legislator in this respect with wide scope for prognosis and assessment.[565] In the same spirit, the Court has also held on a number of occasions that

> "it is a question of complex economic measures, which for the purposes of their efficacy necessarily require a wide discretion and moreover as regards their effects frequently present an uncertainty factor.... The observation suffices that these measures do not appear on issue as obviously inappropriate for the realisation of the desired objective."[566]

On other occasions, the Court has stated that

> "In the circumstances of a case like this with the benefit of appraising the effectiveness of the measures adopted the decisive point is whether, at the time when they were adopted, it could be assumed that they were clearly not conducive to the aim pursued."[567]

These types of wording clearly reveal a reticence on the part of the Court, in particular when it comes to assessing law-creating measures in the light of the suitability criterion. Obviously the Court is fully aware of the difficulties inherent in making an exact projection of the effectiveness of official measures. This is why the Court confines its powers of review to assessing whether, at the time when it was adopted, the measure concerned was manifestly unsuitable for the achievement of the object in view. Even if it subsequently appears that a certain measure requires additional steps if it is to achieve total effectiveness, this does not necessarily lead to the conclusion that the measure concerned is unsuitable.

---

[564] *cf.* for example Case 25/70 [1970] E.C.R. 1161 at 1177, para. 28; [1980] E.C.R. 2103 at 2120, para. 17; Joined Cases 279, 280, 285 and 286/84 (*Christmas Butter*) [1987] E.C.R. 1069, para. 34.

[565] *cf.* R. Boest, *Die Agrarmärkte im Recht der EG* (1984) Baden-Baden, p. 152.

[566] [1973] E.C.R. 142; [1979] 722; *cf.* on the scope for appraisal by the Commission also Joined Cases 133–136/85 [1987] E.C.R. 2289 (*Berlin Butter*) paras. 36 *et seq.*

[567] [1982] E.C.R. 551.

This is the position adopted by Advocate-General Capotorti in his opinion in the *Valsabbia* case[568]:

> "Therefore, I doubt whether that measure may be considered contrary to the principle of proportionality on the basis of the fact that other measures, necessary to set up an economically effective system, were not adopted. If the allegation of an infringement of the principle of proportionality is based on the inadequacy of that decision, it is not sufficient to declare that the system required to be supplemented by other measures; it would be necessary to prove that the system did not function as long as such measures were not adopted."

From the foregoing, it is clear that there will be only a small number of measures which can be said to be unsuitable. Consequently, assessing the suitability of measures can serve only to single out extreme cases of failing to meet the objective.

(b) Necessity

It is a different story with the necessity criterion, which dominates the majority of cases in which the Court has applied the proportionality principle and already featured in the early stages of the Court's case law, where the Court restricted its assessment to examining whether a measure was necessary, which was found not to be the case where it imposed an excessive burden on the person concerned.[569] In a large number of decisions, the Court has insisted that Community measures were not allowed "to exceed that which was necessary for the purpose of the verification."[570] The necessity aspect entails that a measure is permissible only if no less restrictive measure exists to achieve the objective pursued.[571] Among the various possible (and suitable) measures, only that one may be used which has the least drastic implications.[572] Thus the

---

[568] [1980] E.C.R. 1058.

[569] R. Boest, *Die Agrärmarkte im Recht der EG* (1984) Baden-Baden, p. 157.

[570] [1977] E.C.R. 801 at 873, para. 11; [1979] E.C.R. 677 at 694, 695, paras. 16, 18; [1980] E.C.R. 833 at 857 *et seq.*, paras. 18 *et seq.*; 1083 (1093, para. 6); 2103 (2112, para. 22); 2171 (2187, para. 19); [1981] E.C.R. 1291 at 1307, paras. 23 *et seq.*; [1982] E.C.R. 1389 at 1397, paras. 11 *et seq.*

[571] *cf.* R. Boest, *loc. cit.*, footnote 569, p. 152.

[572] H.-W. Rengeling, GS-Klein, *loc. cit.*, footnote 554, p. 433.

Court decided, for example, that the obligation to repay denaturing premiums in the event of the denatured sugar being used in a different manner did not exceed that which was necessary for the achievement of the objective pursued,[573] or "that under Article 36, only those measures are justified which satisfy urgent requirements" and are "absolutely necessary" for the achievement of the objective in view.[574] In another case, for example, it was held that a provision relating to packaging exceeded that which was necessary for the achievement of the objective pursued, *i.e.* consumer protection, and that the goal could have been reached just as effectively by measures which involved fewer restrictions on the free movement of goods.[575]

Assessing the necessity of a measure has the limitation that the authorities are given a great deal of scope for exercising discretion in the field of economic policy. On this point, the Court displays a great deal of reticence in exercising its powers of review. This problem is described by Advocate-General Roemer in the following terms:

"We are dealing here with a field in which the discretion of the bodies concerned is of considerable importance. In this connection, one must have due regard for the total situation within the Community, one has to weigh up—here the financial aspect again makes its appearance—whether more is to be said in favour of providing the means for storage rather than reducing stocks. Last but not least there are considerations of economic trade policy in relation to which both the world market situation and other countries' interest in the field of trade policy are of importance. All these are points of view which render it desirable to observe the greatest possible reticence from the outset and only to criticize in the event of clearly incorrect use of discretionary powers."[576]

Consequently, it is always possible that the Commission, when taking decisions relating to economic policy, holds a certain measure to be necessary on the basis of having weighed up the various interests involved, and that this measure is not the least restrictive but is the most

---

[573] [1982] E.C.R. 696.
[574] [1976] E.C.R. 1921.
[575] [1982] E.C.R. 3973.
[576] Opinion of Advocate-General Roemer in Case 72/72 [1973] E.C.R. 400.

appropriate measure for the purpose of achieving the objective pursued, *e.g.* the Common Agricultural Policy, in a particular situation.

(c) *Proportionality in the strict sense*

Finally, the Court has recently taken to using the proportionality test in the narrow sense of the term, *i.e.* that of weighing up the usefulness of the measure for the general good on the one hand against the restriction of the protected rights of the Community citizen on the other.[577]

This aspect finds clear expression for the first time in the *Hauer* decision,[578] which concerned the restriction of the free exercise of a certain profession and of property rights by a prohibition order regarding the planting of new grapevines. Having confirmed the necessity of the measure in question, the Court proceeded to require for its lawfulness that

> "the restriction is justified by the objective of general interest pursued by the Community and does not infringe the substance of the right to property in the form in which it is recognised and protected."[579]

The relationship between the means and the end must consequently be a reasonable one. Accordingly, the Court, in the so-called deposit cases, put forward the view that it would be disproportionate to allow the deposit to be forfeited without regard to the seriousness of the infringement of the duty. In this context, the ECJ refers to "a totally inappropriate relationship between the penalty applied in case of a failure to carry out the operation, and that which applies where the processing operation has actually been carried out, or where there has been a failure to observe the relevant deadline,"[580] or to the fact that a total forfeiture of the deposit would be "excessively severe in relation to the objective of simplifying administrative procedures."[581]

In the *Cassis de Dijon* case, Advocate-General Capotorti, having weighed up in a very general way the various interests involved, arrived at

---

[577] *cf.* R. Boest, *loc. cit.*, footnote 569, p. 157; *cf.* [1977] E.C.R. 873; 1221; 1264; [1979] E.C.R. 684 *et seq.*; [1981] E.C.R. 1095; [1982] E.C.R. 1397.
[578] Case 44/79 [1979] E.C.R. 3727 at 3747 *et seq.*
[579] [1979] E.C.R. 3728.
[580] [1983] E.C.R. 414.
[581] [1979] E.C.R. 685.

the conclusion that the objective of protecting the consumer against confusion could have been achieved by a measure which meant a less drastic restriction of the free movement of goods. In relation to this objective, the obstacles to free trade were excessive and consequently disproportionate to this goal.[582]

Pernice[583] considers that the way in which the Court weighs up the various interests constitutes to a certain extent an application of the principle of achieving the right balance.[584] Freedom of trade, the freedom to exercise one's profession, or freedom of competition, being Community or individual interests, have to be weighed up against public policy, safely and health, the protection of industrial and commercial property or the interest in conquering sudden economic difficulties, being "provisional" national or individual interests. The Court has made pronouncements in the same spirit, as where it stated that

> "the public interest, which requires as accurate a forecast as possible of import trends in each Member State and justifies the deposit of security against the grant of authorisation to import, must be reconciled with the necessity of not hampering trade between Member States by too rigid obligations, a necessity which only derives from the public interest."[585]

It has, however, to be pointed out that the proportionality principle cannot be equated with the principle of achieving the right balance. Instead, the proportionality principle is a negative factor in relation to this principle, which is championed by Konrad Hesse. The reason for this, as Jakobs perceptively points out, is that it is perfectly conceivable that a measure may be proportionate but greater consideration of the individual interest could nevertheless also have been achieved through a greater restriction of the public interest.[586] This consideration also applies in Community law.

---

[582] [1979] E.C.R. 666 at 674.
[583] *Grundrechtsgehalte im Europäischen Gemeinschaftsrecht* (1979) Baden-Baden, p. 232.
[584] *cf.* on this subject K. Hesse, *Grundzüge des Verfassungsrechts der Bundesrepublik Deutschland* (16th ed., 1988) Heidelberg, pp. 127 *et seq.*
[585] [1974] E.C.R. 543.
[586] *cf.* M. Ch. Jakobs, *Der Grundsatz der Verhältnismässigkeit* (1985) Köln/Berlin/Bonn/München, p. 85.

2. Differentiation according to the field of application and the form taken by the official action

The review of the case law made earlier has demonstrated that the proportionality principle is not only a criterion whereby the Court, in the context of a certain type of procedure, exercises its powers of review over law-creating measures of secondary Community legislation. Increasingly, it has also become a criterion for assessing administrative action by the Community institutions[587] and—less frequently—by the administrative authorities of the Member States, since it is the latter which are essentially involved in carrying out the Community's administrative functions.

Where the intention is to differentiate, as far as the proportionality principle is concerned, according to the type of official action involved, we are faced with the problem, detailed earlier,[588] that the majority of measures made subject to review are Commission regulations, which are difficult to classify from a legal viewpoint but which can be said to straddle the border between the creation of legal rules and the adoption of administrative measures.[589] Certainly it is possible to draw a distinction in such a way that the importance of the proportionality principle is normally greater the more scope there is for discretion, and smaller the more precise the manner in which the decision concerned has been laid down in legal provisions.[590] Thus in the deposit cases, the ECJ confines itself to indicating the upper limit, comparable to *force majeure*, which the authorities are to apply when declaring a deposit to be forfeited, whereas, when the Court is dealing with the imposition of fines under competition law, it exercises a specific verification of compliance with the proportionality principle by evaluating all the circumstances of the individual case.

If we take as our point of departure the ultimate aim of the proportionality principle, *i.e.* to protect the freedom of the individual against restrictions imposed by the public authorities, it becomes clear that it is just as necessary to assess the proportionality of the application of the law by the

---

[587] *cf.* the judgment in Case 18/63 *Schmitz* [1964] E.C.R. 175 (204).
[588] p. 720.
[589] G. Reischl, "Ansätze zur Herausbildung eines europäischen Verwaltungsrechts in der Rechtsprechung des EuGH," in J. Schwarze (ed.), *Europäisches Verwaltungsrecht im Werden* (1982) Baden-Baden, pp. 97 *et seq.*, 98.
[590] *cf.* M. Ch. Jakobs. *loc. cit.*, footnote 586, p. 138.

administration as to evaluate its law-creating function, since freedoms are capable of being restricted on both levels.[591] In addition to making a differentiation according to the level at which the action—whether law-creating or applying the law—is taken, a hierarchy needs to be established within the process of assessing proportionality according to the status of the legal interest protected, the intensity of the manner in which it is being restricted, and the weight of the public interest at stake. This is because, when examining whether a measure is compatible with the proportionality principle, the decisive factor should be in the first instance not the formal quality of the official action, but the intensity of the manner in which freedom is being restricted.

Accordingly, the ECJ, when assessing the legality of a measure in the light of the criterion of the proportionality principle, has been less inclined to make a differentiation according to the manner and the form of the action taken by the authority in question. This was clearly stated in the opinion of Advocate-General Trabucchi in Case 118/75, *Watson and Belmann*,[592] where he said

> "indeed, the principle is not confined to cases of derogation from such rights but is of general application and constitutes one of the principles which must govern action by public authorities.
>
> More generally, it must be concluded that whenever, without any possible justification based on objective requirements, the State authorities subject nationals of the other Member States to greater intrusion in their private lives and movements than that to which the nationals of that state are legally subjected, such unjustified intrusion constitutes illegal interference with the rights of the individual and one which thereby makes it more difficult to exercise them."

Having put forward a number of criteria for the legality of administrative action, regardless of the nature of the action concerned, he went on to make a differentiation according to the importance and the status of the interest protected:

> "The unlawfulness of an action is established all the more clearly where it is established that this intervention by the State infringes a fundamental right of the individual."[593]

---

[591] *cf.* G. Haverkate, *Rechtsfragen des Leistungsstaats* (1983) Tübingen, p. 15, No. 51.
[592] [1976] E.C.R. 1208.
[593] *Loc. cit.*

In his Opinion, the Advocate-General acknowledged that the requirements of present-day society and the performance by the State of its
duties demanded that certain adjustments be made to the limits of the
scope for freedom which the individual subjective right guaranteed, and
that not every restriction constituted an infringement. It must, however,
be acknowledged that an infringement took place where the individual
right concerned had been affected in its essence.[594] Thus the proportionality principle is, in this sense, credited with being a mechanism for the
protection of Community law freedoms.[595]

In Case 44/79, *Hauer* v. *Land Rheinland-Pfalz*,[596] which clearly concerned an infringement of property rights (*i.e.* a prohibition on the
planting of new vineyards), the Court examined whether the restrictions
contained in the disputed rule really served the general interest, or
whether they constituted, in view of the objective pursued, a disproportionate and unacceptable intervention in the privileges of the property
owner which affected the very essence of property rights.[597] In order to
have this established, it was necessary, according to the Court, to
examine

> "what was the objective pursued by the disputed regulation and
> whether there existed between the measures contained in the reg-
> ulation and the objective pursued by the Commission, an appro-
> priate relationship."[598]

When we are dealing with the restriction, on the basis of the general
interest, of the right of the individual to economic development guaranteed by the Community legal order, the interests of the Community
citizen are essentially to be related to the method envisaged and the
objective pursued.[599] In so doing, the interests of the general public which

---

[594] *Loc. cit.*, p. 1209.
[595] *cf.* G. Ress, "Der Grundsatz der Verhältnismässigkeit im deutschen Recht," in H.
Kutscher (Joint ed.) *Der Grundsatz der Verhältnismässigkeit in europäischen Rechtsordnungen* (1985) Heidelberg, pp. 39 *et seq.*
[596] [1979] E.C.R. 3727.
[597] *Loc. cit.*, p. 3728; *cf.* also [1974] E.C.R. 507.
[598] [1979] E.C.R. 3728.
[599] *cf.* D. Feger, *Die Grundrechte im Recht der EG—Bestand und Entwicklung*—(1984)
Bern, p. 119.

are worthy of protection have to be weighed up against the individual right affected, on the understanding that the more a regulating measure restricts the economic freedom of the individual, the more important the public protection requirement has to be.[600]

The proportionality principle occupies a similar position in Community law to that taken up by the basic rights under German law.[601] It derives its decisive importance from its position as a criterion in the process of weighing up the general interest objective pursued by the Community on the one hand, and the essential guarantee of basic rights on the other.[602] However, it is not only in the field of interventions by the Community authorities in basic rights, but also in that of intervention in the actual interests of the Community citizen and of the Member States that the proportionality principle has developed its role. Similarly, the national authorities are bound by this principle in its specific Community law dimension when they become involved with areas which "reveal a connection with Community law."[603]

E. CONCLUSION

The above survey shows that the proportionality principle constitutes an extremely variable instrument of review. Its administration is problematic since it has been applied in virtually every legal field and hardly appears to be measurable in strict terms. In addition, to extend its field of application presents the danger of giving to the courts a quasi-law making power in the field of fundamental rights.[604]

However, where, as is the case in Community law, there is no detailed and comprehensive system of administrative law, and in the absence of clearly defined rules laying down fundamental rights, making the administration subject to the law and to judicial review can take place only by

---

[600] cf. H. Claudi, *Die Bindung der EWG an Grundrechte* (1976) München, p. 420.

[601] cf. on this subject *supra*, pp. 701 *et seq.*, H. P. Ipsen, *Europäisches Gemeinschaftsrecht* (1972) Tübingen, p. 734: the principles of administrative law "guarantee that the German Community citizen enjoys protection similar to constitutional rights."

[602] B. Beutler, in H. v.d. Groeben, H. v. Boeckh, J. Thiesing, C.-D. Ehlermann, *Kommentar zum EWG-Vertrag* (3rd ed., Baden-Baden 1983), p. 1477, No. 31.

[603] cf. the opinion of Advocate-General Mancini [1984] E.C.R. 520.

[604] cf. G. Ress, *loc. cit.*, footnote 595, p. 9.

requiring a relationship to exist between the objective pursued and the methods used.[605] Consequently, the proportionality principle is correctly characterised as the "most important general legal principle in the field of Community economic law."[606]

This principle furthermore occupies a broader, special importance in the development of European administrative law. This principle is, as has been aptly suggested by the former President of the ECJ, Hans Kutscher, "a good example of the mutual process of enhancement, harmonisation and co-operation between the European legal systems in the field of constitutional law."[607] Appropriate in this context are the words of Lord Diplock, where he holds out the possibility of incorporating the proportionality principle, as inspired by some EC Member States, into English law:

> "My Lords, I see no reason why simply because a decision-making power is derived from a common law and not a statutory source it should for that reason only be immune from judicial review. Judicial review has I think developed to a stage today when, without reiterating any analysis of the steps by which the development has come about, one can conveniently classify under three heads the grounds on which administrative action is subject to control by judicial review. The first ground I would call "illegality," the second "irrationality" and the third "procedural impropriety." That is not to say that further developments on a case by case basis may not in course of time add further grounds. I have in mind particularly the possible adoption in the future of the principle of "proportionality," which is recognised in the administrative law of several fellow members of the European Economic Community; but to dispose of the instant case the three already well-established heads that I have mentioned will suffice."

[605] cf. B. Schlink, *Abwägung im Verfassungsrecht* (1976) Berlin, p. 459.
[606] J. Gündisch, "Allgemeine Rechtsgrundsätze in der Rechtsprechung des Europäischen Gerichtshofes," in J. Schwarze (ed.), *Das Wirtschaftsrecht des Gemeinsamen Marktes in der aktuellen Rechtsentwicklung* (1983) Baden-Baden, pp. 97 *et seq.*, 108.
[607] H. Kutscher, "Zum Grundsatz der Verhältnismässigkeit im Recht der Europäischen Gemeinschaften," in H. Kutscher (Joint ed.), *Der Grundsatz der Verhältnismässigkeit in europäischen Rechtsordnungen* (1985) Heidelberg, p. 95; *cf.* also J. Schwarze, "Entwicklungsstufen des Europäischen Gemeinschaftsrechts," in B. Börner, H. Jahrreiss, K. Stern (ed.), *Einigkeit und Recht und Freiheit, FS für Karl Carstens.* Vol. 1, Köln/Berlin/Bonn/München (1984), p. 259 (266).

The mutual influence between national law and Community law has, in the proportionality principle, produced an example of harmonisation or, as Kutscher[608] pertinently expresses it, "a happy development of the *ius commune europaeum* in the field of constitutional and administrative law."

---

[608] *Loc. cit.*, footnote 607, p. 95.

CHAPTER 6

LEGAL CERTAINTY AND THE PROTECTION OF LEGITIMATE EXPECTATIONS

SECTION 1

THE ORIGINS

A. INTRODUCTION

The principles of legal certainty and the protection of legitimate expectations are fundamental to Community law.[1] Yet these principles are merely general maxims derived from the notion that the Community is based on the rule of law and can be applied to individual cases only if expressed in enforceable rules. Moreover, in most instances there are other principles which run counter to legal certainty and the protection of legitimate expectations; here, the right balance will need to be struck. For instance, in the field of Community legislation the need for changes in the law can conflict with the expectation of those affected by such a change that the previous legal situation will remain in force.[2] As regards the administration of Community law, if unlawful administrative measures which create individual rights are to be revoked, the legality of the administration has to be weighed against the principles of legal certainty

---

[1] European Court of Justice, Joined cases 42 & 49/59 *SNUPAT* v. *High Authority* [1961] E.C.R. 109 at 172—Legal certainty. E.C.J., Case 112/80 *Dürbeck* v. *Hauptzollamt Frankfurt/Main-Flughafen* [1981] E.C.R. 1095 at 1120 *et seq.*—Protection of legitimate expectations.

[2] See also Chapter 3, section D.

and the protection of legitimate expectations.[3] In addition, it is possible to conceive of cases where the principle of equality may take priority over the principle of legal certainty.[4]

Whilst the principle of protecting legitimate expectations normally operates to the advantage of the Community citizen, undertaking or official in question, the principle of legal certainty may work both to their advantage—for example, to prevent the revocation of administrative measures which create rights—and to their disadvantage, by upholding the formal validity of administrative acts which impose obligations.

Accordingly, the case law of the European Court contains a wealth of different groups of cases having little more in common than their having been affected, in one form or another, by the notion of legal certainty or the protection of legitimate expectations.[5] Consequently, the problems we have to consider here are unusually complex. It seems best to begin, in this first section, by considering the significance of these two principles in the legal systems of both the Member States and the Community. In Section 2, a detailed examination of the legal systems of the Member States will give a clear picture of the extent, if any, to which legal certainty and the protection of legitimate expectations are used to test the legality of both legislative and administrative procedures. Section 3 applies the same analysis to the legal system of the European Community, and in the context the comparative survey which precedes it will be a useful aid in the academic treatment of a wide range of cases. Finally, in Section 4, the findings are reviewed in the context of an emerging corpus of European administrative law.

B.   EMERGENCE AS PRINCIPLES OF LAW

I.   RECOGNITION IN NATIONAL LAW

The principle of legal certainty is widely recognised in the Member

---

[3] This applies in particular to the question whether unlawful administrative acts may be revoked; see, for example, Joined cases 42 & 49/59, *loc. cit.*

[4] The Court found, for instance, in a claim for scrap equalisation dues outstanding owing to a failure to levy them, that in this area the principle of distributive justice took precedence over legal certainty (Case 2/70 *Riva* v. *Commission* [1971] E.C.R. 97 at 109).

[5] *cf.* also the contribution by P. Pescatore to the 12th FIDE Conference in Paris, 1986; *Les principes généraux du droit en tant que source du droit communautaire*, Rapport Communautaire, FIDE Report, pp. 17 *et seq.*; and J. Boulouis, "Quelques observations à propos de la sécurité juridique," in F. Capotorti *et al.* (eds.), *Festschrift Pierre Pescatore*, Baden-Baden 1987, pp. 53 *et seq.*

States of the Community as a general legal principle. This is true, without exception, of the six founding States. It is equally true, however, of Portugal and Spain, where the principle of legal certainty is regarded as a general rule of administrative law. In Britain and Ireland, on the other hand, there is no comparable general principle of law, but their legal systems reveal certain specific principles of administration, developed from case law, which are comparable to the rules derived from the principle of legal certainty in, for example, France or the Federal Republic of Germany. The same is true of Denmark and Greece.[6]

The principles of protecting legitimate expectations, as an independent principle of administrative and constitutional law, finds its clearest expression in the Federal Republic of Germany and in the Netherlands. Outside the EEC Member States, it has achieved a prominent position in Switzerland.[7] It was chiefly in the 1950s that the principle of protecting legitimate expectations emerged as an independent legal principle in the case law of these countries, both in administrative and in constitutional law.[8]

Among the other founder members, the principle of protecting legitimate expectation has won a certain status in Italy—inspired by German administrative law—and in Belgium, although this status is still widely challenged.[9] In France, on the other hand, the role of legitimate expectation has so far been insignificant. Because of the importance attached to the principle of legal certainty, matters which involve balancing the public interest in legal change against the individual's interest in preserving legal certainty are dealt with on the basis of objective criteria to the exclusion of subjective elements.

In the group of more recent Member States, however, it is possible to observe distinct trends towards a recognition of the principle of protecting legitimate expectations. In Britain, for example, recent judgments

---

[6] See also section 2 below.

[7] cf. the comprehensive analysis by B. Weber-Dürler, *Vertrauensschutz im öffentlichen Recht*, Basel 1983.

[8] See further under section 2; for the case law in Germany, see, *e.g.* the judgment of the Federal Administrative Court on October 28, 1959, Decisions of the Federal Administrative Court no. 9, pp. 251 *et seq.* = Neue Juristische Wochenschrift (NJW) 1960, pp. 692 *et seq.*—Revocation of illegal administrative measures creative of rights; Judgments of the Federal Constitutional Court of December 19, 1961, Decisions of the Federal Constitutional Court no. 13, p. 261; 13, p. 274 = NJW 1962, p. 291; for the Netherlands, see, *e.g.* the judgment of the CRvB of October 2, 1951, Ars Aequi II, p. 116; Judgments of October 28, 1952, December 16, 1952 and December 30, 1952, AA III, pp. 44 *et seq.*, with commentary by A. M. Donner; for Switzerland, see commentary by Weber-Dürler, *loc. cit.*, footnote 7, pp. 5 *et seq.*, 48 *et seq.*

[9] This is examined further in section 2.

refer to the importance of "legitimate expectations," and the concept is also found in the available literature,[10] which suggests that the case law of the European Court and the case law and academic writing of the Federal Republic of Germany have exercised some influence on the English legal system. In Ireland, however, no such trend is yet discernible.

In Denmark and Greece, cautious moves are also being made towards the recognition of legitimate expectations.[11] In Portugal too, the principle has been recognised in connection with the revocation of administrative measures.[12] There is no such notion in Spanish administrative law, but the related principles of good faith and the preservation of vested rights play a role here.[13]

In general, it is true to say that the principles of legal certainty and of protecting legitimate expectations, as general principles of law, have not achieved the same status in all Member States. But, as we shall show later, in many Member States specific questions of administrative law are resolved according to them, mostly in reliance on the case law, especially questions of revoking or challenging administrative measures. Naturally these decisions differ in many points of detail, but in general they observe clear time limits and weigh up the respective interests concerned, either in abstract terms or by reference to the case in point. Decisions like these are commonly seen as statements of the principle of legal certainty or, less frequently, of the principle of respecting legitimate expectations. In certain cases, however, these Member States resolve such questions without applying these general principles.

II. RECOGNITION IN COMMUNITY LAW

The principle of legal certainty was also recognised at a relatively early stage in the case law of the European Court of Justice.[14] This is in spite of

---

[10] See, for example, Lord Mackenzie Stuart, "Legitimate expectations and estoppel in Community Law and English administrative law," in: Legal Issues of European Integration, 83/1, pp. 53 *et seq.* (65 *et seq.*) with citations from the case law.

[11] For Denmark, see J. K. Skadhauge, *Danish Report on General Principles derived from the law of the Member States as Source of Community Law and National Law,* FIDE Report 1986, p. 75 (86); for Greece, see J. Iliopoulos-Strangas, *Rückwirkung und Sofortwirkung von Gesetzen—eine verfassungsrechtliche Untersuchung unter Berücksichtigung des deutschen und griechischen Steuerrechts,* Baden-Baden 1986, p. 201, with references.

[12] *cf.* D. Freitas do Amaral, *Direito administrativo,* Vol. 3, Lisbon 1985, p. 348.

[13] See Section 2 below.

[14] See, *e.g.* Joined cases 42 & 49/59, *op. cit.* footnote 1, p. 172; Joined cases 14, 16–17, 20, 24 & 26–27/60 & 1/61 *Meroni and others* v. *High Authority* [1961] E.C.R. 345 at 365 and Case

a marked absence of doctrinal reasoning processes or comparative law considerations in the text of the decisions. For example, a judgment in 1961 on the admissibility of revocation *ex tunc* of an illegal administrative measure conferring benefits states:

> "That allegation disregards the fact that the principle of respect for legal certainty, important as it may be, cannot be applied in an absolute manner, but that its application must be combined with that of the principle of legality."[15]

The principle has been described as a "rule of law of which due account must be taken in the application of the Treaty,"[16] as "the general principle of legal certainty inherent in the Community legal order,"[17] as an "essential principle,"[18] a "basic principle,"[19] or a "general principle of law."[20] The principle of legal certainty has played a role mainly in establishing whether the revocation of administrative measures conferring benefits is admissible. It is on this principle, according to the Court, that "the system of legal remedies established by the Treaty is based."[21] The Court has made use of this principle to determine the formal validity of administrative measures which impose obligations.[22] It has also been used for setting time limits in administrative proceedings.[23]

However, the principle of legal certainty also operates to restrict the "genuinely" retrospective effect of administrative rules[24] and measures.[25] More specifically, the principle is expressed in a general obligation to ensure that rules are clear and that the applicable law is foreseeable, this being a requirement addressed both to the lawmaker and to the Court itself.

13/61 *Kledingverkoopbedrijf de Geus en Uitdenbogerd* v. *Robert Bosch GmbH and others* [1962] E.C.R. 97 at 113.

[15] Joined cases 42 & 49/59, *op. cit.*, footnote 1.

[16] Case 13/61, *op. cit.*, footnote 14.

[17] Joined cases 66 & 127–128/79 *Amministrazione delle Finanze dello Stato* v. *Salumi* [1980] E.C.R. 1237 *et seq.* at 1261.

[18] Advocate-General Roemer in Case 48/72 *Brasserie de Haecht* v. *Wilkin-Janssen* [1973] E.C.R. 77 at 99.

[19] Roemer in Case 59/70 *Netherlands* v. *Commission* [1971] E.C.R. 639 at 659.

[20] Roemer, Case 48/72 *op. cit.*, footnote 18, p. 97.

[21] Case 52/83 *Commission* v. *France* [1983] E.C.R. 3707 at 3715; *cf.* also Case 59/70, *op. cit.*, footnote 19, p. 653.

[22] See below, Section 3, B. III.1.

[23] See below, Section 3, B. III.2.

[24] See further in Section 3, D.

[25] See further in Section 3, B.V.

It has taken the principle of protecting legitimate expectations longer to be given express recognition in the case law of the Court than the principle of legal certainty. However, the concept of legitimate expectations emerges at a relatively early stage as a corollary to the principle of legal certainty or the principle of the preservation of "vested rights," more particularly in the first major judgments on the admissibility of revocations of administrative measures. According to the Court's judgment in the *Algera* case, it is precisely the "confidence in the stability of the situation thus created"[26] which acts to prevent the revocation of a lawful administrative measure conferring benefits. According to the judgment in the *SNUPAT* case, what has to be taken into account when balancing the principle of legal certainty and the principle of the legality of the administration, when considering the revocation of such a measure, is the extent to which the undertakings affected by it "might arrange their affairs in reliance on the continuity of this position."[27]

From the beginning of the 1970s, the principle of protecting legitimate expectations also acquired special significance when dealing with the "false" retroactivity of regulations. From that time onwards, this principle has been expressly endorsed by the Court.[28] It is now regarded by the Court as "one of the fundamental principles of the Community,"[29] as a "constituent part of the legal order of the Community"[30] and, in the words of Advocate-General Trabucchi, "one of the superior rules of the Community legal order for the protection of individuals."[31]

According to the Court's judgment in the *CNTA* case, failure to take account of a legitimate expectation—even if the failure is attributable to the Community lawgiver—can constitute an infringement of a "superior rule of law"[32] and, under Article 215, second paragraph, of the EEC Treaty, may involve the liability of the Community.

---

[26] Joined cases 7/56 & 3–7/57 *Algera and others* v. *Common Assembly* [1957] E.C.R. 83 at 118; see below, Section 2, A.II.3(a).

[27] Joined cases 42 & 49/59 *SNUPAT* v. *High Authority* [1961] E.C.R. 109 at 173.

[28] Case 81/72 *Commission* v. *Council* [1973] E.C.R. 575 at 584; Case 1/73 *Westzucker* v. *Einfuhr- und Vorratsstelle für Zucker* [1973] E.C.R. 723 at 729 *et seq.*; Case 74/74 *CNTA* v. *Commission* [1975] E.C.R. 533 at 548 *et seq.*; on this subject, see below, Section 2, B.I.2.

[29] Case 112/80 *Dürbeck* v. *Hauptzollamt Frankfurt/Main-Flughafen* [1981] E.C.R. 1095 at 1120 *et seq.*

[30] Joined cases 205–215/82 *Deutsche Milchkontor and others* v. *Federal Republic of Germany* [1983] E.C.R. 2633 at 2669; similarly, see Case 112/77 *A. Töpfer & Co. GmbH* v. *Commission* [1978] E.C.R. 1019 at 1033.

[31] Advocate-General Trabucchi in Case 5/75 *Deuka* v. *Einfuhr- und Vorratsstelle für Getreide und Futtermittel* [1975] E.C.R. 759 at 777.

[32] Case 74/74 *op. cit.*, footnote 28, p. 549.

A systematic analysis of the various cases in which the protection of legitimate expectations has so far played a part in the case law of the Court will reveal a great variety of approaches and applications. The principle is not only binding on the administration itself, as regards the revocation of administrative measures. Because of the rules on "genuine" and "false" retroactivity, it also constrains the legislature and therefore assumes the status of a rule of constitutional law.

SECTION 2

THE PRINCIPLES OF LEGAL CERTAINTY AND THE PROTECTION OF LEGITIMATE EXPECTATIONS IN THE LAW OF THE MEMBER STATES

A. FRANCE

I. GENERAL RECOGNITION OF THE PRINCIPLES

In the hierarchy of public interests, the highest place is taken by the application of the principle of compliance with the statute law.[1] Moreover, the general interest dictates that unlawful and inexpedient situations should be eliminated.[2] This rule serves to justify the withdrawal of unlawful administrative acts.[3] The recognition of an unrestricted right to such withdrawal conflicts with the principle of legal certainty (*principe de sécurité des situations juridiques*), which is recognised as a "general principle," from which three further principles are derived: the non-retroactivity of administrative acts (*principe de non-rétroactivité des actes administratifs*), the recognition of vested rights (*respect des droits acquis*) and the inviolability of individual administrative decisions (*intangibilité des décisions individuelles*).[4] This also applies in French administrative law, especially in the revocation (*abrogation*) of unlawful administrative acts, where the two conflicting principles of legality and legal certainty have to be reconciled.[5]

According to the principle of non-retroactivity, an administrative measure (an individual measure—an "acte individuel" or regulation)

---

[1] M. Waline, "Le retrait des actes administratifs," Mélanges Mestre, Paris 1956, pp. 563, 564; J.-Y. Vincent, "Le retrait des actes adminstratifs unilatéraux," R.T.D.E., 1974, pp. 31, 32.

[2] J.-Y. Vincent, *op. cit.*, footnote 1, p. 32.

[3] J.-Y. Vincent, *op. cit.*, footnote 1, p. 32.

[4] J.-Y. Vincent, *op. cit.*, footnote 1, p. 32; G. Vedel, P. Delvolvé, *Droit administratif* (9th ed., Paris 1984), pp. 269 *et seq.*; *cf.* also A. de Laubadère, J.-C. Venezia, Y. Gaudemet, *Traité de droit administratif*, Vol. I (9th ed., Paris 1984), no. 559.

[5] P. Auvret, "La notion de droit acquis en droit administratif français," R.D.P. 1985, pp. 53, 54; M. Waline, Mélanges Mestre, *op. cit.*, footnote 1, p. 566; M. Nauwelaers, L. Fabius, "Chronique générale de jurisprudence administrative française," A.J.D.A. 1976, p. 557.

which does not have the approval of the legislature[6] cannot take legal effect before the moment when it comes into force.[7] This principle does not arise from Article 2 of the Civil Code, which concerns exclusively legislation; rather, it is one of the general principles of law, on which the case law confers the status of a legal rule.[8] It plays a decisive role in the question whether an administrative act with retroactive effect can be annulled.[9]

The recognition of vested rights also follows from the principle of legal certainty. For a "vested right" to be accepted, it is sufficient for the administrative act to create a legal situation for the person at whom it is directed, or for a third party, which individuals have an interest in maintaining.[10] Here, a distinction is drawn between those rights which have been acquired through an individual measure and those conferred on the basis of a regulation.[11] As to the former, the principle of the recognition of vested rights is the equivalent of that of the inviolable nature of the effects of an administrative act creating rights; in the latter case, the protection of vested rights is confined to the implications of a regulation which took effect in the past.[12]

II. APPLICATION TO INDIVIDUAL CASES

In French administrative law, administrative decisions can be rescinded in one of three ways: by "retrait," by "abrogation," and by "annulation." Unlike German administrative law, no distinction is drawn between lawful and unlawful decisions. Instead, the methods of rescinding them are distinguished according to their effects in time.

Thus *retrait* means revocation by the administration itself[13]; here the administrative decision is set aside from the outset (*ab initio*) and its legal

---

[6] *cf.* C.E. of February 15, 1949, *Société civile de l'école Gerson*, Rec. 98.
[7] *cf.* A. de Laubadère, J.-C. Venezia, Y. Gaudemet, *op. cit.*, footnote 4, no. 728; G. Vedel, P. Delvolvé, *op. cit.*, footnote 4, p. 269.
[8] A. de Laubadère, J.-C. Venezia, Y. Gaudemet, *op. cit.*, footnote 4, no. 728 with additional references.
[9] On the basic principle, see M. Letourneur, "Le principe de la non-rétroactivité des actes administratifs," Etudes et Documents du Conseil d'Etat, 1955, pp. 37 *et seq.*
[10] See M. Waline, *Droit administratif* (9th ed., Paris 1963), no. 949; P. Auvret, *op. cit.*, footnote 5, p. 60.
[11] P. Auvret, *op. cit.*, footnote 5, p. 67.
[12] P. Auvret, *op. cit.*, footnote 5, p. 67.
[13] See G. Braibant, *Le droit administratif français*, Paris 1984, p. 256; A. de Laubadère, J.-C. Venezia, Y. Gaudemet, *op. cit.*, footnote 4, no. 776.

effects are cancelled, both for the future and in the past.[14] *Retrait* is carried out by the administrative authority which made the decision.[15] *Abrogation*,[16] on the other hand, cancels only the future effects of the administrative decision, and does not interfere with its existing consequences.[17] Authority for an *annulation* (avoidance) lies either with a higher decision-making level, a supervisory authority[18] or, in the case of *recours pour excès de pouvoir*, with the court (*annulation contentieuse*).[19] Through an *annulation*, the past effects of the administrative decision are also cancelled,[20] the same rules applying, in principle, to *retrait*.

1. Action by the Administration

(a) Annulment of administrative decisions

In order to establish whether and to what extent an administrative decision is open to *retrait* or *abrogation*, we must known whether the decision is an individual one (*acte individuel*) or a regulation (*acte réglementaire*). A regulation is also an *acte administratif*, and as such is open to administrative or judicial review.[21] It is also important to know whether the administrative decision is lawful (*régulier*) or unlawful (*irrégulier*) and finally, whether it has conferred any rights (*créateur de droits*).[22]

An administrative decision may create legal relationships; the authorities may use it to carry out functions assigned to them by statute which create a legal relationship between the administration and the citizen.[23]

---

[14] G. Vedel, P. Delvolvé, *op. cit.*, footnote 4, p. 272.

[15] *cf.* R. Odent, *Contentieux administratif*, Paris 1970–71, p. 882; A. de Laubadère, J.-C. Venezia, Y. Gaudemet, *op. cit.*, footnote 4, no. 776.

[16] On this concept, see the detailed comment in J.-M. Auby, "L'abrogation des actes administratifs," A.J.D.A. 1967, pp. 131 *et seq.*

[17] J.-M. Auby, *op. cit.*, footnote 16, p. 131; G. Vedel, P. Delvolvé, *op. cit.*, footnote 4, p. 272; G. Braibant, *op. cit.*, footnote 13, p. 256.

[18] *cf.* R. Odent, *op. cit.*, footnote 15, p. 882; A. de Laubadère, J.-C. Venezia, Y. Gaudemet, *op. cit.*, footnote 4, no. 778, who describe this also as "retrait hiérarchique."

[19] *cf.* G. Braibant, *op. cit.*, footnote 13, p. 257.

[20] G. Braibant, *op. cit.*, footnote 13, p. 256.

[21] See G. Vedel, P. Delvolvé, *op. cit.*, footnote 4, p. 253.

[22] Unlike European Community law and German administrative law, the French terminology does not mention subjective rights, but only "droits." However, this term has essentially the same meaning as subjective rights. There is a detailed comparison of both concepts in J.-Y. Vincent, *op. cit.*, footnote 1, p. 35.

[23] E.C.J., Case 14/61 *Hoogovens* v. *High Authority* [1962] E.C.R. 511 at 565 (opinion of Advocate-General Lagrange).

This is a fairly broad category of decisions; it includes, for instance, the appointment of officials and the issuing of permits. In these cases a (subjective) right is derived from the administrative decision itself.[24]

Administrative decisions which do not confer rights are not confined to those which impose obligations; they may include decisions advantageous to the individual which are of only a declaratory nature.[25]

The case law traditionally distinguishes between attributive decisions (*décisions attributives*), *i.e.* those which have legal effects, and declaratory decisions (*decisions récognitives*).[26] In the case of declaratory administrative decisions, rights are conferred only by statute or regulation. The only function of the administrative decision is to translate them into practice, if need be through an interpretation.[27] This category includes administrative decisions which concern only payments (*décisions purement pécuniaires*)[28] and confirmatory administrative decisions.[29] Declaratory administrative decisions do not give rise to any subjective rights which can be enforced.[30] Conditional administrative decisions,[31] likewise, do not confer subjective rights on the addressee.

(aa) Retrait

(1) Individual decisions (actes individuels)

Administrative decisions which do not create rights can be withdrawn *ex tunc* and unconditionally at any time.[32] This applies equally to lawful[33]

---

[24] E.C.J. Case 14/61 *Hoogovens* v. *High Authority* [1962] E.C.R. 511 at 565 (opinion of Advocate-General Lagrange).

[25] E.C.J. Case 14/61 *Hoogovens* v. *High Authority* [1962] E.C.R. 511 at 565 (opinion of Advocate-General Lagrange); see also W. Däubler, "Der Widerruf von Verwaltungsakten im Recht der Europäischen Gemeinschaften," NJW 1965, pp. 1646, 1649.

[26] M. Nauwelaers, L. Fabius, *op. cit.*, footnote 5, p. 557 with references.

[27] E.C.J. Case 14/61 *Hoogovens* v. *High Authority* [1962] E.C.R. 511 at 565 (opinion of Advocate-General Lagrange).

[28] C.E. of October 15, 1976, *Buissière*, Rec. 419 with notes; M. Nauwelaers, L. Fabius, *op. cit.*, footnote 5, p. 557 with references to the case law.

[29] C.E. of January 15, 1943, *Thomet*, Rec. 9.

[30] M. Nauwelaers, L. Fabius, *op. cit.*, footnote 5, p. 557.

[31] C.E. of March 10, 1967, *Ministre de l'Economie et des Finances* v. *Société Saumat et Cie.*, Rec. 113.

[32] G. Vedel, P. Delvolvé, *op. cit.*, footnote 4, p. 273; J. Rivero, *Droit administratif* (11th ed., Paris 1985), no. 103.

[33] See C.E. of June 27, 1947, *Société Duchet et Cie.*, Rec. 283; C.E. of May 20, 1955, *Syndicat national autonome du cadre de l'administration générale des colonies*, Rec. 273.

and unlawful administrative decisions.[34] The distinction between administrative decisions which create rights and those which do not is sometimes illogical and contradictory and may produce inequitable results.[35] The only remedy is to pursue a claim for administrative error (*action en responsabilité pour faute d'administration*), a form of redress which is broadly defined in the case law.[36]

Administrative decisions which create rights have to be divided into lawful and unlawful decisions. *Retrait* of a lawful decision which confers rights is, in principle, impossible.[37] This rule is based on the ban on retroactivity (*principe de non-rétroactivité*).[38] Expediency considerations will not be enough to justify a *retrait*,[39] unless specifically provided by law.[40] *Retrait* will be necessary to bring into effect a court order for avoidance, and the addressee may himself apply for one.[41] In this case, the withdrawal may not cause the addressee any further disadvantage, nor may it involve any disadvantage for third parties.[42]

Two conditions, apart from the obligation to provide reasons,[43] apply to the *retrait* of administrative decisions. These conditions are stated by the Conseil d'Etat in the important precedent of the *Dame Cachet* decision of November 3, 1922.[44] First, the act may be annulled retrospectively only if the annulment is based on that unlawfulness. Second, *retrait* is permitted only within the time-limit for an appeal

---

[34] See C.E. of March 10, 1943, *Thomet,* Rec. 9; C.E. of June 17, 1955, *Silberstein*, Rec. 334; C.E. of October 15, 1976, *Buissière*, Rec. 419 with notes by M. Nauwelaers, L. Fabius, *op. cit.*, footnote 5, p. 557.

[35] See F. Batailles, "Les Beati Possidentes du droit administratif," R.D.P. 1965, p. 1072: "The situation is creative of rights if the court so finds." See also J.-Y. Vincent, *op. cit.*, footnote 1, p. 38; E.C.J., Case 14/61 *Hoogovens* v. *High Authority* [1962] E.C.R. 511 at 568 (opinion of Advocate-General Lagrange).

[36] E.C.J., Case 14/61 *Hoogovens* v. *High Authority* [1962] E.C.R. 511 at 568 (opinion of Advocate-General Lagrange).

[37] See C.E. of April 23, 1948, *Veilland*, Rec. 175; C.E. of July 23, 1976, *Sté Algéco*, A.J.D.A. 1977, p. 380 with notes by P. Thévenin.

[38] See A. de Laubadère, J.-C. Venezia, Y. Gaudemet, *op. cit.*, footnote 4, no. 778.

[39] See C.E. of March 21, 1947, *Dame Ingrand*, Rec. 430; G. Vedel, P. Delvolvé, *op. cit.*, footnote 4, p. 274.

[40] C.E. of March 29, 1968, *Manufacture française des Pneumatiques Michelin*, A.J.D.A. 1968, p. 342.

[41] M. Long, Y. Weil, G. Braibant, *Les grands arrêts de la jurisprudence administrative* (8th ed.), Paris 1984, p. 172.

[42] C.E. of July 23, 1974, *Ministre de l'Intérieur* v. *Gay*, Rec. 441.

[43] Article 1 of Law no. 79–587 of July 11, 1979, *Motivation des actes administratifs, Code administratif* (18th ed.), Paris 1985, p. 558.

[44] M. Long, Y. Weil, G. Braibant, *op. cit.*, footnote 41, p. 169; Rec. Sirey 1925, 3.9 with notes by Hauriou; R.D.P. 1922, p. 552 with an Opinion by Rivet. It has subsequently become an established precedent "which because of its enduring qualities has in fact

(*recours en annulation*), *i.e.* within two months of the publication or announcement of the decision. This time-limit may be extended if an appeal has been instituted (*recours gracieux*), if a complaint has been filed against the authority (*recours hiérarchique*)[45] or if the plea has been entered with a court lacking jurisdiction to hear it.[46] Once an appeal has been lodged, the time-limit is extended until the outcome is known.[47] After the expiry of the time-limit, the decision will be upheld, and *retrait* is no longer possible.[48]

The reason why these conditions are stipulated lies in the nature of *retrait* as a substitute for annulment by a court.[49] In the interests of legal certainty, administrative decisions which create rights must be regarded as lawful in principle. However, from the viewpoint of the administration it would appear desirable for it to be able to annul any unlawful decisions. But in so doing it must not be vested with wider powers than the courts, which are called upon in the first instance to uphold the legality principle. The unlawfulness on which the *retrait* is based must therefore be of a kind which would warrant annulment by a court. This means that the *retrait* must be based on want of jurisdiction (*incompétence*), a formal defect (*vice de forme*), an abuse of authority (*détournement de pouvoir*) or some breach of law (*violation de la loi*). In addition, it will be granted only where annulment by a court would also be a possibility;[50] if, for example, the citizen cannot be sure that the decision will be upheld, perhaps because a third party is able to appeal against it.

---

achieved the status of established law"; E.C.J., Case 14/61 *Hoogovens* v. *High Authority* [1962] E.C.R. 511 at 566 (Lagrange).
[45] C.E. of November 23, 1962, *Association des anciens élèves de l'Institut Commercial de Nancy*, A.J.D.A. 1962, p. 677; A. de Laubadère, J.-C. Venezia, Y. Gaudemet, *op. cit.*, footnote 4, no. 783.
[46] C.E. of May 25, 1928, *Reynaud*, Rec. 1928; C.E. of April 28, 1950, *Druard*, Rec. 243.
[47] See C.E. of June 12, 1936, *Kremer*, Rec. 638, with Opinion of Lagrange; C.E. of January 19, 1938, *Dlle. Achille Fould*, Rec. 55.
[48] See also C.E. of June 12, 1959, *Syndicat chrétien du ministère de l'Industrie et du Commerce*, A.J.D.A. 1960, II, p. 62 with Opinions by Mayras.
[49] A. de Laubadère, J.-C. Venezia, Y. Gaudemet, *op. cit.*, footnote 4, no. 783.
[50] The whole question is studied in detail in G. Vedel, P. Delvolvé, *op. cit.*, footnote 4, pp. 274 *et seq.*

There are three instances in which this "time-limit exemption" does not apply: administrative decisions made as a result of a deliberate deception,[51] or so gravely defective that they must be regarded as void (*inexistants*, or *nuls et non avenus*).[52] Decisions such as these may be withdrawn at any time. The time-limit will also be extended if the unlawfulness of an administrative decision results from the judicial annulment of another decision in consequence of which it was made. This is called an *acte conséquence*, and the withdrawal may take place even if the two-month time limit has already elapsed. For instance, the judicial annulment of an (unlawful) dismissal of a civil servant will justify (and even demand) the withdrawal of his successor's appointment.[53] In exceptional cases such as these, French courts may relax somewhat the rigid rules governing withdrawal.[54]

Decisions which have not yet been published or announced[55] may be withdrawn at any time.[56] Here it should also be noted that when an individual decision is announced, as far as the third party is concerned time begins to run only as from that moment. In relation to interested third parties, time begins only when they have received formal or official notification of the administrative decision.[57] Since there is no general rule that individual decisions must be published, in some cases the administration has a right to withdraw them over a period of several years, for as long as an appeal may be lodged by a third party claiming that its rights have been infringed.[58] It is also worth noting that the "interest" which is required in order for a third party to lodge a complaint is broadly interpreted in the case law. For example, as far as the law relating to subsidies is concerned, competing enterprises and business associations

---

[51] C.E. of June 17, 1955, *Silberstein*, R.P.D.A. 1955, p. 310; C.E. of March 10, 1976, *Baillet*, R.P.D. 1976, p. 1373.

[52] C.E. of July 17, 1953, *Constantin*, Rec. 381; C.E. of February 3, 1956, *De Fontbonne*, R.D.P. 1956, p. 859 with notes by M. Waline; see the detailed commentary in G. Braibant, *op. cit.*, footnote 13, pp. 260 *et seq*.

[53] C.E. of February 6, 1948, *Dlle. Mollet*; January 20, 1939, *Hollender*, Rec. 20; see also A. de Laubadère, J.-C. Venezia, Y. Gaudemet, *op. cit.*, footnote 4, no. 784.

[54] See P. Weil, "Une résurrection; la théorie de l'inexistence en droit administratif," D. 1958, Chronique, pp. 56 *et seq*.

[55] C.E. of May 6, 1966, *Ville de Bagneux*, A.J.D.A. 1966, p. 498 with notes by Puissochet, Lecat, Chronique, A.J.D.A. 1966, p. 485.

[56] See also M. Nauwelaers, L. Fabius, *op. cit.*, footnote 5, p. 557.

[57] C.E. of May 6, 1966, *Ville de Bagneux*, A.J.D.A. 1966, p. 498.

[58] C.E. of May 6, 1966, *Ville de Bagneux*, A.J.D.A. 1966, p. 498; C.E. of July 23, 1974, *Ministère de l'Aménagement du territoire, de l'Equipement, du Logement et du Tourisme* v. *Thooris*, Rec. 442; see J.-Y. Vincent, *op. cit.*, footnote 1, p. 49.

enjoy much greater freedom in France to contest the grant of subsidies than, for instance, in the Federal Republic of Germany.[59]

Treating as a whole, a comparison between the French and the Community rules for revoking decisions does not suggest that the latter offer a lesser degree of legal certainty or protection of legitimate expectations. What appears, at first sight, to be greater legal clarity in the formalistic French solution is less so on closer examination. In fact the French approach is superior only in cases where unlawful decisions creative of rights have been made public.[60] The criticism which has been expressed of the Court's "appropriate time limit"—especially the objection that it is a "sword of Damocles"[61] from the viewpoint of legal certainty—does not appear justified in view of the inherent unpredictability of the French system.

If the administrative decision is unlawful and the time limit for objecting has not expired, the administration may withdraw it, *i.e.* it has discretion to decide on a *retrait*.[62] In so doing, it must weigh the public's interest in the legality of the administration against the interest of the individual in the decision being upheld.[63] The option to withdraw becomes a duty if there is a request to this effect from the addressee or from a third party whose interests have been affected. This is clear from the nature of *retrait* as a sanction, comparable to a judicial annulment, to which the appropriate rules must apply. Hence the addressee, or a third party with standing to sue, is entitled to demand *retrait* within the time limit for an action. The refusal to grant one constitutes an *excès de pouvoir*.[64]

(2) Regulations (actes réglementaires/règlements)

It has already been pointed out that in French administrative law,

---

[59] *cf.* C.E. of November 26, 1954, *Syndicat de la raffinerie du soufre français et Société française des établissements Koch et Reis,* Rec. 620; C.E. of October 6, 1967, *Syndicat des sylviculteurs du Sud-Ouest,* Rec. 356.

[60] J.-Y. Vincent, *op. cit.*, footnote 1, p. 50.

[61] Advocate-General Lagrange's opinion in Case 14/61 *Hoogovens* v. *High Authority* [1962] E.C.R. 511 at 570.

[62] *cf.* for instance, J. Rivero, *op. cit.*, footnote 32, no. 103; A. de Laubadère, J.-C. Venezia, Y. Gaudemet, *op. cit.*, footnote 4, no. 782.

[63] M. Waline, *Mélanges Mestre, op. cit.*, footnote 1, p. 566.

[64] C.E. of February 13, 1948, *Syndicat national des statistiques,* Rec. p. 74; A. de Laubadère, J.-C. Venezia, Y. Gaudemet, *op. cit.*, footnote 4, no. 788.

regulations are subject to review by the executive or the courts.[65] They are not intended, in principle, to create rights directly for the citizen. However, this does not mean that regulations, unlike individual decisions, can never create rights.[66] What it means is that nobody has a right to insist on an *acte réglementaire* being upheld, *i.e.* to oppose its being annulled for the future. But regulations can certainly confer subjective rights which apply retrospectively. In that case, their *retrait* will be subject to the rules applying to administrative decisions creative of rights.[67] Normally, however, there must be an *acte individuel* based on the *règlement* if the legal position is to warrant protection.[68]

As regards *retrait*, the *acte réglementaire* is therefore governed by essentially the same rules as the *acte individuel*. Here too, the main question is whether it is lawful or unlawful, and whether it creates rights or not.

(bb) Abrogation

Since *abrogation* rescinds the administrative decision only *ex nunc*, and therefore has less drastic effects, the conditions to which *abrogation* is subject are not so far-reaching. However, certain requirements relating to competence and procedure and certain substantive conditions must be met. The *abrogation* must be effected by the authority which made the original decision. It must be made in the same form as the decision which is to be annulled (*règle du parallélisme des formes*).[69] Reasons must also be given for the *abrogation*.[70]

As for the substantive conditions, here too the main question is whether individual decisions or regulations are in issue, and whether or not they create rights. Unlike the rules on *retrait*, the decision does not have to be unlawful to enable *abrogation* to take place.[71]

---

[65] *cf.* above, pp. 106 *et seq.*

[66] But see, *e.g.* L. Rolland, *Précis de droit administratif* (11th ed., Paris 1957), p. 54.

[67] G. Vedel, P. Delvolvé, *op. cit.*, footnote 4, pp. 272 *et seq.*; from the same perspective, P. Le Mire, "La stabilité des situations juridiques," A.J.D.A. 1980, pp. 203–204, with references (footnote 12).

[68] *cf.* P. Le Mire, *op. cit.*, footnote 67, p. 204.

[69] *cf.* G. Vedel, P. Delvolvé, *op. cit.*, footnote 4, pp. 276 *et seq.*; J. Rivero, *op. cit.*, footnote 32, no. 103; on the principle of "parallélisme des formes" and the limits to this, see C.E. of April 10, 1959, *Fourré-Cormery*, Rec. 233 with notes by M. Waline, R.D.P. 1959, p. 1223.

[70] Article 1 of Law no. 79–587 of July 11, 1979.

[71] G. Vedel, P. Delvolvé, *op. cit.*, footnote 4, pp. 278 *et seq.*

(1) Individual decisions

Individual decisions which do not create rights or confirm the existence of rights[72] may be annulled at any time with future effect.[73]

However, if an administrative decision confirms individual rights, it may be annulled *ex nunc*, but only in the cases prescribed by law and by way of an *actus contrarius*.[74] For instance, the *abrogation* of an appointment of a civil servant may take place only by removing him from office (*révocation*) or giving him early retirement (*mise à la retraite*).[75] When the time limit for contesting the decision has elapsed, the decision cannot be revoked, since this would be an evasion of the rules on *retrait*.[76]

(2) Regulations

Règlements can be rescinded *ex nunc* or amended at any time, because even if, in some circumstances, they have created rights for the past, they can never create rights for the future.[77] Moreover, the administrative authority which has made the decision, or its hierarchical superior, is actually bound to revoke an unlawful *acte réglementaire* if requested to do so.[78] However, this obligation lasts only as long as the time limit for appeals.[79] After the time limit has expired it is still possible,[80] and may actually be compulsory,[81] not to comply with a regulation which is unlawful but has not been rescinded.

---

[72] This includes the withdrawal of permits.

[73] J. Rivero, *op. cit.*, footnote 32, no. 103; M. Long, Y. Weil, G. Braibant, *op. cit.*, footnote 41, p. 171; G. Vedel, P. Delvolvé, *op. cit.*, footnote 4, p. 279.

[74] G. Vedel, P. Delvolvé, *op. cit.*, footnote 4, p. 278; M. Long, Y. Weil, G. Braibant, *op. cit.*, footnote 41, p. 172.

[75] *Ibid.*

[76] C.E. of February 7, 1973, *Ministère de l'Education et Nguyen Van Nang,* A.J.D.A. 1975, p. 248; G. Vedel, P. Delvolvé, *op. cit.*, footnote 4, p. 279.

[77] According to the case law; *e.g.* C.E. of June 25, 1954, *Syndicat national de la meunerie à seigle,* Rec. 379; January 26, 1973, *Société Leroi et autres,* A.J.D.A. 1973, p. 252.

[78] C.E. of May 12, 1976, *Leboucher et Tarendon,* Rec. 246; with notes by Cedara, A.J.D.A. 1977, p. 261.

[79] *cf.* C.E. of January 30, 1981, *Ministère du Travail* v. *Société Afrique Europe Transaction,* Rec. 32 with an opinion by Mrs. Hagelsteen.

[80] C.E. of January 8, 1960, *Laiterie Saint-Cyprien,* Rec. 10.

[81] C.E. of November 8, 1968, *Ministère des Finances* v. *Meyer,* Rec. 557.

(b) Reclaiming benefits paid without legal justification

The question of refunding State contributions levied in error is generally dealt with in France according to Articles 1235 and 1376 of the Civil Code on unjustified enrichment.[82] There is a general time-bar after 30 years. However, special rules apply to customs duties levied without proper legal justification, and in these cases the time limit is two to three years only.[83]

Unlike in German and Dutch law, the question of refunding wrongly levied State contributions in France is not dominated by the formal correctness of the decision to levy the contributions. French administrative decisions which impose obligations cannot be challenged after the two-month time limit for appeals has elapsed. But jurisdiction to deal with claims for the repayment of State contributions and customs duties levied in error normally lies with the civil courts. These courts are not bound by the time limits for appeals in the administrative courts, so that even when a decision on a public levy has become unappealable by virtue of these time limits, a citizen may contest the decision on the ground of its unlawfulness.[84] An unlawful, but unappealable administrative decision is not a "legal basis" for a public levy, and it is therefore possible for a citizen to seek repayment.

In the opposite case too, where State benefits paid in error are being reclaimed, the principle followed is the principle of unjustified enrichment.[85] This is true especially in the area of (defective) contractual relationships between the citizen and the State.

But where a payment, such as a subsidy, has been made through or on the basis of an administrative decision creating rights, the question whether the subsidy can be reclaimed is primarily the question whether the administrative decision is itself voidable.[86] A subsidy payment made

---

[82] For a general comment, see: G. Vedel, P. Delvolvé, *Droit administratif* (9th ed.), Paris 1984, pp. 371 *et seq.*; M.-F. Furet, "L'enrichissement sans cause d'après la jurisprudence administrative," Recueil Dalloz Sirey 1967, pp. 42 *et seq.*

[83] M. Fromont, "La restitution de taxes perçues indûment par l'Etat," Länderbericht Frankreich, Geneva 1976, pp. 101 (114 *et seq.*); K. E. Huthmacher, *Der Vorrang des Gemeinschaftsrechts bei indirekten Kollisionen*, Cologne/Berlin/Bonn/Munich 1985, pp. 260 *et seq.*

[84] M. Fromont, *op. cit.*, footnote 83; K. E. Huthmacher, *op. cit.*, footnote 83.

[85] *cf.* also M.-F. Furet, *op. cit.*, footnote 82.

[86] *cf.* M. Fromont, in B. Börner, M. Bullinger, *Subventionen im Gemeinsamen Markt*, KSE Vol. 29, Cologne 1978, pp. 92 *et seq.*; H.-W. Rengeling, "Das Beihilferecht der Europäischen Gemeinschaften," in B. Börner, K. Neundörfer, *Recht und Praxis der Beihilfen im Gemeinsamen Markt*, KSE Vol. 32, Cologne 1984, p. 23 (49).

on the basis of an administrative decision creating rights may be reclaimed only within the two-month time limit for appeals following the announcement or publication of the subsidy, even if the decision is itself unlawful. However, since subsidy decisions are not usually made known to third parties, there is in practice no time limit on appeals from affected third parties or on measures by the public authorities to annul unlawful subsidy decisions.[87] Once granted, subsidies may be reclaimed without restriction except where they were approved on the basis of false information supplied by the recipient.[88]

2. Legislation—Retroactivity of Statutes and Regulations

Article 2 of the Civil Code prohibits retroactivity of statutes.[89] Since this is merely a statutory provision which may be amended at any time by the legislature, it is regarded not so much as a prohibition on the legislature to adopt statutes with retroactive effects as a rule forbidding the courts to attribute retroactive force to a statute by way of an interpretation, except where this effect is expressly stipulated by the lawmaker.[90] Regulations (*actes réglementaires, règlements*), which French administrative law regards as administrative decisions, cannot have retroactive effect unless the lawmaker has expressly stated otherwise.[91] Contrary to a view widely held in earlier literature, which looked to Article 2 of the Civil Code as the source of authority,[92] in the prevailing view this is regarded as a *principe général du droit*,[93] for which the theoretical basis is the principle of legal certainty.[94]

Here a distinction is drawn between cases of retroactivity in the narrow sense and cases in which a new measure has an impact on situations originating in the past but whose implications have not yet ceased.

---

[87] See above, footnotes 55 *et seq.*
[88] See above, footnote 51.
[89] "La loi ne dispose que pour l'avenir, elle n'a point d'effet rétroactif."
[90] M. Waline, *Droit administratif, op. cit.*, footnote 10, no. 221.
[91] See above, 1.a.
[92] M. Waline, *Droit administratif, op. cit.*, footnote 10, no. 221; see the further references in B. Jeanneau, *Les principes généraux du droit dans la jurisprudence administrative*, Paris 1954, pp. 97 *et seq.*
[93] B. Jeanneau, *op. cit.*, footnote 92, p. 98; A. de Laubadère, J.-C. Venezia, Y. Gaudemet, *op. cit.*, footnote 4, no. 728; G. Vedel, P. Delvolvé, *op. cit.*, footnote 82, p. 269, each with references to the case law.
[94] G. Braibant, *op. cit.*, footnote 13, p. 229.

Whereas retroactivity in the narrow sense is always prohibited, except in a few rare exceptions,[95] in the second category of cases it is admitted up to the point where it would encroach on vested rights (*droits acquis*).

B. GERMANY

I. GENERAL RECOGNITION OF THE PRINCIPLES

In the law of the Federal Republic of Germany, legal certainty and protection of legitimate expectations are regarded as principles of constitutional law. Many attempts have been made to trace their legal history.[1] In legal theory, both principles are usually seen as being derived from the constitutional principle enshrined in Article 20 of the Basic Law,[2] or in Articles 20 and 28 of the Basic Law.[3,4] It is argued in the first place that the principle of the rule of law makes for legal certainty.[5] This principle in turn forms the basis for the principle of the protection of legitimate expectations, which has, occasionally but also directly, been based on the principle of the rule of law.[6]

The established case law of the German Federal Constitutional Court and of the Federal Administrative Court also views the principle of legal certainty and of peace under the law, together with that of the legality of the administration, as one of the essential elements of the rule of law

---

[95] G. Vedel, P. Delvolvé, *op. cit.*, footnote 82, pp. 269 *et seq.*

[1] Among the various attempts at finding a derivation, see especially B. Weber-Dürler, *Vertrauensschutz im öffentlichen Recht*, Basle/Frankfurt am Main 1983, pp. 36 *et seq.*; G. Püttner, G. Kisker, in: VVDStRL 32 (1974), pp. 149 *et seq.* and 200 *et seq.*

[2] See, for instance, K.-A. Schachtschneider, "Das Rechtsstaatsprinzip des Grundgesetzes," JA 1978, p. 185.

[3] See D. Ehlers, "Rechtsstaatliche und prozessuale Probleme des Verwaltungsprivatrechts," DVBl. 1983, pp. 422, 425.

[4] F. E. Schnapp, in: Ingo v. Münch (ed.), *Grundgesetz-Kommentar*, Vol. 1, (3rd ed., Munich 1985), no. 21 on Article 20, with references; in addition to the writers referred to in footnotes 2 and 3, see the many references in B. Weber-Dürler, *op. cit.*, footnote 1, p. 47 (footnote 1); for a criticism of Article 20 see P. Kunig, *Das Rechtsstaatsprinzip*, Tübingen 1986, pp. 72 *et seq.*

[5] *cf.* F. O. Kopp, *Verfassungsrecht und Verwaltungsverfahrensrecht*, München 1971, p. 131; B. Weber-Dürler, *loc. cit.*, footnote 1, pp. 49 *et seq.*

[6] *cf.* Th. Maunz, "Selbstbindung der Verwaltung," DÖV 1981, pp. 497 *et seq.*; F. Ossenbühl, "Vertrauensschutz im sozialen Rechtsstaat," DÖV 1972, pp. 25, 27; V. Götz, "Bundesverfassungsgericht und Vertrauensschutz," in *Bundesverfassungsgericht und Grundgesetz, Festgabe aus Anlass des 25jährigen Bestehens des Bundesverfassungsgerichts*, 2nd Vol., Tübingen 1976, pp. 421, 423.

principle, which forms the basis of the rule of the protection of legitimate expectations.[7] Here, the Federal Constitutional Court follows a train of thought which leads successively from the rule of law principle to legal certainty, the reliability of the legal system, the ability to anticipate state intervention, the protection of legitimate expectations and the continuity of the legal system.[8]

Both the decisions of the highest courts and the majority of legal authors view the principles of legal certainty and of the protection of legitimate expectations, taken in conjunction with Article 20 of the Basic Law, as having the status of constitutional principles, equal in rank and importance to the principle of administrative compliance with the statute law.[9] The constitutional status of these principles means that they are relevant even in relation to legislative measures.[10] However, the fact that they are equal in rank to the principle of administrative compliance with the statute law means that, in cases where a conflict arises between these two notions, the interests involved will need to be weighed up against each other, taking into account the relevant circumstances of each individual case.[11]

II. APPLICATION TO INDIVIDUAL CASES

1. Action by the Administration

(a) Revocation and withdrawal of administrative decisions

In Germany, the revocation (*Widerruf*) and withdrawal (*Rücknahme*) of administrative decisions are subject to rules laid down by legislation. In addition to the many Special Rules (*Spezialnormen*)[12] laid down by

---

[7] *cf.* BVerfGE 8, 155, 172; 30, 367, 386; 30, 392, 401 *et seq.*; 45, 142, 167 *et seq.*; 59, 128, 164 *et seq.*; 60, 253, 267; BVerwGE 10, 282, 288; 11, 136, 137 *et seq.*; 56, 254, 257 and 260; 65, 174, 176; 67, 206, 209.

[8] BVerfGE 45, 142, 167 *et seq.*

[9] *cf.* H.-U. Erichsen, W. Martens, in: Erichsen, Martens (eds.), *Allgemeines Verwaltungsrecht* (7th ed., Berlin/New York 1986), pp. 247 *et seq.*

[10] F. Ossenbühl, *loc. cit.*, footnote 6, pp. 29 *et seq.*; *cf.* also BVerfGE 63, 343, 356 *et seq.*; 67, 1, 14 with further references.

[11] H.-U. Erichsen, W. Martens, *loc. cit.*, footnote 9, p. 248; *cf.* also F. Ossenbühl, *loc. cit.*, footnote 6, p. 30.

[12] *cf.* also the examples given in H.-U Erichsen, W. Martens, *loc. cit.*, footnote 9, pp. 232 and 247, and in N. Achterberg, *Allgemeines Verwaltungsrecht* (2nd ed., Heidelberg 1986), pp. 596 and 605.

Federal legislation, it is especially the Laws relating to administrative procedure (*Verwaltungsverfahrensgesetze*—VwVfG) issued both at the federal level and at that of the Länder which provide a comprehensive system of rules governing the conditions under which administrative acts may be withdrawn or repealed (Articles 48 and 49 VwVfG). Essentially, this comes down to a codification of the various criteria developed in the available literature and by the courts up to that moment.[13]

Withdrawal and revocation are two methods of repeal of administrative acts, bearing in mind that it is the last-named concept which must be regarded as the generic term.[14] The repeal of a legally valid administrative act is called revocation (*Widerruf*—Article 49 VwVfG), whereas the repeal of an unlawful administrative act is qualified as withdrawal (*Rücknahme*—Article 48 VwVfG). In assessing whether the act to be repealed is legally valid or unlawful, the factual circumstances and the legal position which applied at the moment when the act was adopted are decisive.[15] A further issue to be examined separately under each set of rules is whether the administrative act to be repealed confers benefits or imposes burdens.[16] In this context, it should be noted that administrative acts which confer benefits on their addressees may at the same time impose burdens on third parties (administrative act with third-party effect) or be such that they both confer advantages and impose burdens on the addressee (administrative act with dual effect).[17]

(aa) Revocation

(1) Revocation of administrative decisions imposing burdens

In principle, lawful administrative acts imposing burdens may be revoked, either wholly or in part, with future effect, even after they have become unchallengeable (Article 49(1) VwVfG). Revocation may, in

---

[13] *cf.* on this subject D. Göldner, "Die Rücknahme begünstigender Verwaltungsakte nach dem neuen Verwaltungsverfahrensgesetz," DÖV 1979, pp. 805, 807.

[14] *cf.* Articles 43(2), 46, 51(1) VwVfG.

[15] *cf. e.g.* U. Battis, *Allgemeines Verwaltungsrecht*, Heidelberg 1985, No. 197.

[16] Articles 48(1)(1) and (2), 49(1) and (2) VwVfG.

[17] H.-U. Erichsen, W. Martens, *loc. cit.*, footnote 9, p. 231; U. Battis, *loc. cit.*, footnote 15, No. 200.

accordance with Article 49(1) VwVfG, be prohibited only if the relevant authority is obliged to re-adopt an administrative act with the same contents, or if that authority is barred from revoking the act on other grounds, *e.g.* where it has pledged itself towards a third party not to revoke the administrative act.[18] In addition, decisions on withdrawal are a matter for the appropriate authority's discretion.

(2) Revocation of administrative decisions conferring benefits

Whereas lawfully adopted administrative decisions imposing burdens arc subject to the principle of unrestricted revocation, lawfully adopted administrative decisions conferring benefits are in principle incapable of revocation.[19] This conforms to both the principle of compliance by the administrative authorities with the statute law and the principle of the protection of legitimate expectations, both of which in this case work to the advantage of the party on whom the benefit has lawfully been conferred.[20] The legislator has solved the conflict between the interest of the addressee in maintaining the administrative act on the one hand, and that of the public interest pursued by the administrative authorities, which is that the act should be set aside, on the other hand, by making revocation subject to the fulfilment of the conditions which are set out in a restricted list contained in Article 49(2) VwVfG.[21]

Administrative measures conferring benefits may be revoked if such revocation is permitted by legal provisions (Article 49(2)(1)(1) VwVfG). Here, "legal provisions" are taken as meaning any legal rule having general effect, such as statute law, regulations and constitutions, excluding, however, administrative provisions.[22] Where the administrative act in question validly provides for the possibility of revocation, the latter is also permissible (Article 49(2)(1)(2) VwVfG). The validity of such revocation clauses is assessed in the light of Article 36 VwVfG. In such cases, the citizen will not be protected by the principle of legitimate

---

[18] H.-U. Erichsen, W. Martens, *loc. cit.*, footnote 9, p. 255; *cf.* also F. O. Kopp, *Verwaltungsverfahrensgesetz* (4th ed., München 1986), paragraph 49, No. 17 *et seq.*

[19] *cf.* H.-U. Erichsen, W. Martens, *loc. cit.*, footnote 9, p. 234.

[20] N. Achterberg, *loc. cit.*, footnote 12, p. 606; U. Battis, *loc. cit.*, footnote 15, No. 220.

[21] F. O. Kopp, *VwVfG, loc. cit.*, footnote 18, paragraph 49, No. 19 containing further references.

[22] C. H. Ule, H.-W. Laubinger, *Verwaltungsverfahrensrecht* (2nd ed., Köln/Berlin/Bonn/München 1979), paragraph 63 II 1 a; N. Achterberg, *loc. cit.*, footnote 12, p. 606; H.-U. Erichsen, W. Martens, *loc. cit.*, footnote 9, p. 235.

expectations, since he must take into account from the start the possibility of revocation in view of the express clause to that effect.

Revocation is also permissible where the administrative act in question is subject to the fulfilment of a legitimate[23] condition and the beneficiary has failed to meet it or failed to fulfil it within the period provided (Article 49(2)(2) VwVfG). The question whether the beneficiary was at fault in this non-fulfilment is irrelevant here.[24] However, the proportionality principle may in certain circumstances prevent revocation, if the condition was only a minor factor in relation to the benefit conferred.[25]

Administrative acts may also be revoked if the authorities concerned would have been entitled not to adopt them in the light of subsequent events and the public interest would be in jeopardy without their revocation (Article 49(2)(3) VwVfG). This change of circumstances may relate to considerations which are internal or external to the act.[26] The additional requirement that the public interest must be put in jeopardy means that the revocation must be necessary in order to remove or prevent a direct threat to the State, the public or important community interests.[27]

In addition, the authorities may revoke an administrative measure if they would have been entitled not to adopt it in the light of the amendment of a legal provision, on condition that (a) the beneficiary has yet to make use of the benefit conferred or has yet to receive payment on the basis of the administrative act, and (b) the public interest would be endangered without its revocation (Article 49(2)(4) VwVfG).

Finally, administrative acts may be revoked in order to prevent or remove serious infringements of the public interest (Article 49(2)(5) VwVfG). What qualifies as a serious infringement of the public interest must be determined in the light of the appropriate substantive law; in this respect, the case law relating to the concept of "major public interests" developed by the Federal Constitutional Court in cases which involved a possible restriction of the freedom to exercise one's profession (Article 12

---

[23] H.-U. Erichsen, W. Martens, *loc. cit.*, footnote 9, p. 235 containing further references.

[24] *cf.* F. O. Kopp, *VwVfG, loc. cit.*, footnote 18, paragraph 49, No. 33; W. Klappstein, in: H. J. Knack (ed.), *Verwaltungsverfahrensgesetz, Kommentar* (2nd ed., Köln/Berlin/Bonn/München 1982), paragraph 49, No. 13.

[25] W. Klappstein, in: H. J. Knack (ed.), *VwVfG, loc. cit.*, footnote 24, paragraph 49, No. 6.2; H. Meyer, in: H. Meyer, H. Borgs-Maciejewski, *Verwaltungsverfahrensgesetz* (2nd ed.), Frankfurt am Main 1982, paragraph 49, No. 25.

[26] F. O. Kopp, *VwVfG, loc. cit.*, footnote 18, paragraph 49, No. 38 with examples.

[27] BVerwG, DVBl. 1982, pp. 1004, 1005; F. O. Kopp, *VwVfG, loc. cit.*, footnote 18, paragraph 49, No. 39.

Basic Law) may serve as a guideline.[28] In view of the exceptional nature of the provision in question, the undefined concept of "serious infringement" is to be interpreted restrictively in order not to deplete the other grounds for revocation.[29]

According to Article 38(2) VwVfG, these grounds for revocation also apply to the case of promised benefits covered by Article 38(3), *i.e.* where, in the event of a change in circumstances or in the applicable law after the benefits were promised, the binding effect of the measure in question ends as from the moment when the authorities, had the subsequent changes been known to them, would not have promised these benefits or would not have been allowed to promise them on legal grounds.

Even where the circumstances provided by Article 49(2) VwVfG apply, the relevant authorities are not compelled to revoke the measure in question; here, we are dealing with a discretionary decision, as can be seen from the use of the term "may."

(bb) Withdrawal

The withdrawal of unlawful administrative acts is subject to the principle of the freedom to withdraw, *i.e.* the rule that in principle, unlawful administrative measures may at all times be set aside, wholly or in part, either retrospectively (*ex tunc*) or with effect for the future (*ex nunc*).

(1) Withdrawal of administrative decisions imposing burdens

This principle applies in full to the withdrawal of unlawful administrative decisions whose sole effect is to impose burdens.[30] More particularly, an administrative decision imposes burdens when it lays down duties, orders or prohibits certain actions, removes rights or changes them to their beneficiary's disadvantage, or when it results in other forms of legally relevant disadvantage or, conversely, in the denial of legally

---

[28] F. O. Kopp, *VwVfG, loc. cit.*, footnote 18, paragraph 49, No. 47 with further references.
[29] W. Klappstein, in: H. J. Knack (ed.), *VwVfG, loc. cit.*, footnote 24, paragraph 49, No. 6.5; N. Achterberg, *loc. cit.*, footnote 12, p. 607; H.-U. Erichsen, W. Martens, *loc. cit.*, footnote 9, p. 239.
[30] This is the prevailing view; *cf., e.g.* F. O. Kopp, *VwVfG, loc. cit.*, footnote 18, paragraph 48, No. 32.

relevant advantages.[31] Decisions on withdrawal are left to the discretion of the appropriate authority (Article 48(1)(1) VwVfG uses the word "kann" (may). However, under certain conditions the authority may be compelled to withdraw the administrative decision to the benefit of the addressee. This applies, for example, where the unlawfulness of the decision is obvious, where to maintain the original decision would be totally unacceptable, or where to rely upon the unchallengeable nature of the administrative measure would qualify as an infringement of the principle of good faith in administrative affairs.[32] As can be seen from Article 48(1)(2) VwVfG, the withdrawal of administrative decisions imposing burdens is not subject to any restrictions in time.

(2) Withdrawal of administrative decisions conferring benefits

Whereas the traditional approach by the leading authors and by the courts towards unlawful administrative decisions conferring benefits was, by reference to the principle of compliance with the statute law by the administration, based on the freedom in principle to withdraw administrative acts,[33] the idea that the expectation by the addressee, that the decisions conferring benefits will be maintained at law, should be protected has increasingly gained ground since a decision by the Berlin Administrative Court of November 14, 1956.[34] Ever since, both the leading authors and the courts have sanctioned the withdrawal of unlawful administrative decisions conferring benefits only where the public interest in the compliance by the administration with the statute law outweighs the expectation by the beneficiary that the legal situation created by the administrative decision will be maintained.[35]

At present, unlawful administrative decisions conferring benefits are governed by Article 48 VwVfG, which, in paragraphs 2 to 4, applies the principle of the freedom to withdraw, but only subject to severe restrictions. The latter result from the principles of legal certainty and of the protection of legitimate expectations, whose status in substantive law is

---

[31] F. O. Kopp, *VwVfG, loc cit.*, footnote 18, paragraph 49, No. 42.

[32] *cf.* on this subject BVerfGE 28, 122, 127; 44, 333, 336 *et seq.*; BVerfGE 27, 297, 306 *et seq.*

[33] Thus most recently E. Forsthoff, *Lehrbuch des Verwaltungsrechts*, Vol. 1, General Part, (10th ed., München 1973), p. 261.

[34] DVB1. 1957, p. 503; *cf.* also BVerwGE 9, 251 *et seq.* (confirmation of the decision of the Berlin OVG).

[35] BVerwGE 19, 188, 189 with further references; F. Ossenbühl, *loc. cit.*, footnote 6, pp. 28 *et seq.*

confirmed by this provision. Depending on the nature of the administrative measure in question, both principles are taken into account in various ways. Where the unlawful act in question confers payments in cash or in kind, the protection of legitimate expectations entails the protection of its maintenance. For other types of unlawful act conferring benefits, however, the beneficiary's legitimate expectation is protected merely by means of financial compensation.

Unlawful administrative acts which confer single or continuous payments in cash, or payments in kind which can be divided into several parts or which are the precondition for such payments, may not be withdrawn where the beneficiary had legitimately expected the decision to be maintained and this legitimate expectation is worthy of protection against withdrawal after having been weighed up against the public interest (Article 48(2)(1) VwVfG). Legitimate expectation is worthy of protection if the beneficiary has used up the benefit granted or has made arrangements in connection with it such as can no longer be rescinded or can be rescinded only at unacceptable cost (Article 48(2)(2) VwVfG). This legitimate expectation is not, however, worthy of protection where the beneficiary

(a) has obtained the administrative decision in question through deception, threats or bribery,
(b) has secured the adoption of the administrative decision on the basis of information which is substantially incorrect or incomplete, or
(c) was aware of the unlawful nature of the decision or was unaware of it as a result of his own wanton negligence (Article 48(2)(3) VwVfG).

Where the administrative decision is withdrawn, payments already made arc to be returned (Article 48(2)(5) VwVfG). Where only part of the decision is withdrawn, this rule applies only to those payments which have been conferred by the withdrawn part. In accordance with Article 48(2)(6) VwVfG, the extent to which payments are to be returned is determined by the legal provisions relating to the repayment of monies acquired unjustifiably. However, the system relating to unjustified enrichment as laid down in the German Civil Code is departed from in that anyone who, pursuant to Article 48(2)(3) VwVfG does not enjoy protection of legitimate expectation and was aware of the circumstances which resulted in the administrative decision becoming unlawful, or was unaware of them through his own wanton negligence, may not plead the loss of the monies unjustifiably acquired (Article 48(2)(7) VwVfG).

In the case of beneficiaries of administrative decisions which do not involve payments in cash or kind, Article 48(3) VwVfG confers protection of legitimate expectations not by ensuring the maintenance of the measure, but by payment of compensation for material losses incurred. The obligation to pay compensation arises only where the legitimate expectation of the party in question is worthy of protection after having been weighed up against the public interest. The question whether or not the expectation is worthy of protection is subject to the same principles as those which apply to administrative act covered by Article 48(2) VwVfG.[36] Claims for compensation are subject to application and may be instituted only within a period of one year (Article 48(3)(5) VwVfG).

Administrative decisions conferring benefits may be withdrawn only within a year from the date on which the authority in question became aware of the circumstances justifying the withdrawal. Where the beneficiary has secured the adoption of the decision through deception, threats or bribery, the authority is not bound by this deadline (Article 48(4) VwVfG).

(b) Pledges

As regards pledges, *i.e.* the undertaking by the authorities to adopt or to refrain from adopting a certain administrative act,[37] these are, in accordance with Article 38(2) VwVfG, subject to the applicable legal provisions relating to the withdrawal of unlawful administrative acts (Article 48 VwVfG) and to the revocation of lawful acts (Article 49 VwVfG). This means that pledges to adopt administrative acts conferring benefits may be either withdrawn in accordance with Article 48 paragraphs 2–4 or revoked in accordance with Article 49 paragraphs 2–5. The reservation made with reference to Article 38 paragraph 3 ("without prejudice to Paragraph 3") broadens the range of opportunities for revocation in relation to Article 49(2)(3) and (4) VwVfG. The conditions for admissibility stated in these provisions need not apply here. Under Article 38(3) VwVfG, the relevant authority already ceases to be bound by the pledge if the general circumstances and legal situation have, after the pledge was given, changed in such a way that the authority

---

[36] F. O. Kopp, *VwVfG, loc. cit.*, footnote 18, paragraph 48, No. 89 with further references.
[37] *cf.* para. 38(1) first sentence VwVfg.

in question, had it been aware of that subsequent change, would not have given that pledge or would have been unable to give it on legal grounds.[38]

(c) Recovery of payments having no legal basis

(aa) Recovery of payments made by the State

In so far as payments made by the State have been granted by means of, or on the basis of, an administrative act conferring benefits, the decisive factors in deciding whether or not they can be withdrawn, is that the enabling administrative act may be legitimately withdrawn or revoked, or that this withdrawal occurs simultaneously with the request for return. Only repeal of the enabling administrative act with effect *ex tunc* removes the legal basis for payment and can justify such a public-legal claim for compensation modelled on the (private law governing the repayment of monies acquired unjustifiably).

As has already been stated, the relevant legislation relating to administrative procedure, both at the Federal level and at that of the Länder, provides that administrative acts conferring benefits may be withdrawn with retrospective effect only if they are unlawful (Article 48(1) and (2), Article 49(2) VwVfG) and if sufficient account has been taken of the legitimate expectations of the person in question. In respect of this possibility, Article 48(2)(5) VwVfG lays down that a claim for restitution may be made, for whose detailed regulation the Law refers to the provisions of the Civil Code. If the enabling measure has not been withdrawn in this fashion, or if it is unlawful on grounds of infringing the principle of the protection of legitimate expectations, as expressed in Article 48(2) VwVfG, no subsequent recovery claim can arise.[39]

As the Federal Administrative Court has stated only recently, it is undoubtedly the case that provisions such as the German Regulation relating to Skimmed Milk Subsidies, which implements Common Agricultural Policy legislation, exclude any possibility of withdrawal at the

---

[38] For a detailed discussion, see F. O. Kopp. *VwVfG*, a.a.O. (footnote 18), Section 38, paragraphs 25 *et seq.*

[39] BVerwGE 8, 261, 264 *et seq.*; 67, 305, 312; H.-U. Erichsen, W. Martens, in: Erichsen, Martens (eds.), *Allgemeines Verwaltungsrecht* (7th ed., Berlin 1986), paragraph 18 II 3 with further references; *cf.* also on this subject J. Schwarze, *Landesbericht Deutschland*, 12th FIDE Conference, Paris 1986, Vol. II, pp. 111 *et seq.*

discretion of the administrative authorities in accordance with Article 48(1)(1) VwVfG and, in certain cases, may compel them to withdraw unlawful enabling administrative acts. However, this type of legal provision cannot exempt the administration from having due regard for the principle of legitimate expectations, whose protection is regulated by Article 48(2) VwVfG.[40]

In addition to these general rules laid down by Article 48 VwVfG, Article 44a of the Federal Budgetary Regulations (Bundeshaushaltsordnung—BHO) relating to payments (Article 23 BHO) from Federal budgetary funds extends the opportunities for recovery on the part of the Federal authorities.[41] Here also, precondition for recovery is the prior annulment of the enabling administrative decision. It is this annulment, and it only, which in turn removes the legal basis for the maintenance of the payment. For more detailed rules relating to the action for recovery, this Law—with some limitations—again refers to the provisions of the German Civil Code on the repayment of unjustifiably acquired monies.

However, this provision at the same time extends the opportunities for recovery, because under Article 44a(1) BHO even lawful decisions regarding these payments may under certain circumstances be revoked with retrospective effect, this being impossible in principle under the rules laid down by Article 49(2) VwVfG, which in this particular area does not apply.[42] It is possible to have these decisions subsequently revoked in this manner if the monies thus paid have not been used for the purpose for which they were originally granted or if the conditions attached to the payment in question have not been fulfilled or have not been complied with within the deadline imposed on the beneficiary of the payment.

Being a *lex specialis*, this provision—at least in part—takes precedence, in the area covered by it, over the rules governing claims for

---

[40] BVerwG, Decision of August 14, 1986, DVBl. 1986, p. 1205.

[41] Expenditure within the meaning of this provision refers only to those payments to which the recipient has no direct claim based on legal provisions. *cf.* on this subject P. Weides, "Widerruf und Rückforderung von Zuwendungen des Bundes und der Länder," NJW 1981, p. 841; for general comments, *cf.* also R. Grawert, "Widerruf und Erstattung im Recht der Zuwendungen—Die haushaltsrechtlichen Änderungen des Verwaltungsverfahrens," DVBl. 1981, pp. 1029 *et seq.*; R. Stober, "Zur Problematik des § 44a Abs. 1 BHO und des entsprechenden Länderrechts," DÖV 1984, pp. 265 *et seq.*

[42] This was also the reason for the inclusion of Article 44a(1) BHO; on this subject, *cf.* P. Weides, *loc. cit.*, footnote 41, pp. 843 *et seq.*

compensation (Article 48(2), (5) to (8) VwVfG) where an unlawful payment decision is withdrawn.[43]

For certain areas, German administrative law contains, in addition to the general provisions, special rules relating to recovery (which, under Article 1(1) VwVfG, take precedence over these general rules), such as, for example, Article 12 of the Federal Civil Service Remuneration Act and Article 53(2) of the Civil Service Law Framework Regulations Act as regards the recovery of payments made to state officials, and Articles 45, 47 and 50 of the Social Legislation Code for social security payments.

(bb) Recovery of duties wrongly levied by the State

Where State taxation is imposed by administrative regulation, the rule that the valid or, where appropriate, the unlawful administrative act imposing burdens forms the legal basis for the payment also applies to the claim for recovery by the citizen against the State.[44] The citizen has no opportunity to exercise the claim, governed by public law, to repayment, which is modelled on the private law action for repayment on the grounds of unjustified enrichment, as long as the administrative act imposing burdens in question retains its legal effect.[45]

Unless the administrative act concerned is null and void on grounds of exceptionally serious deficiencies under Article 44 VwVfG, the citizen involved may, even in the case of an unlawful administrative act, set aside these legal effects only by challenging this act before the administrative courts (Articles 42, 40 VwGO). The peremptory time limit applicable to this type of action amounts to only one month as from the date of publication of the administrative act or of the administrative decision rejecting the citizen's complaint (Article 74 VwGO) where the action has been preceded by a complaints procedure (Article 68 VwGO), which is also subject to time limits (Article 70 VwGO).

Once the deadline for bringing the action has expired, and after the administrative act imposing the burdens has formally taken

---

[43] cf. Article 44a(2) BHO; on this subject, cf. P. Weides, loc. cit., footnote 41, pp. 845, 847 et seq.; F. Kopp, VwVfG, loc. cit., footnote 18, paragraph 48, No. 119; R. Grawert, loc. cit., footnote 41, p. 1036.

[44] G. Langer, G. Theuerkauf, "Landesbericht Deutschland," in La restitution de taxes perçues indûment par l'Etat, Geneva 1976, p. 9(25); K. E. Huthmacher, Der Vorrang des Gemeinschaftsrechts bei indirekten Kollisionen, Köln/Berlin/Bonn/München 1985, p. 52.

[45] H.-U. Erichsen, W. Martens, loc. cit., footnote 39, paragraph 30 III.

effect, no claims for repayment may, in principle, any longer be instituted. Only in severely restricted conditions can the authority in question be compelled, even after the deadline instituting the claim has expired, to cancel an unlawful decision imposing burdens by withdrawing it.[46] Legally effective administrative acts imposing burdens are not made inapplicable or capable of being challenged even where the law on the basis of which they were adopted has been declared null and void by the Federal Constitutional Court. Under Article 79(2) of the Law relating to the Constitutional Court (BVerfGG), this type of administrative act imposing burdens remains unaffected by the invalidation of the law.[47] Only the subsequent enforcement action arising from the act in question is not permitted under this provision. Pursuant to Article 79(2)(4) VfVwG, there can be no question here of claims for repayment of taxes levied without justification, since the legally effective administrative act which imposed them, in spite of the annulment of its legal basis, remains the legal basis for the payment made.

2. Legislation—Retroactivity of Statutes and Regulations

With the exception of the explicit prohibition on retrospective legislation in criminal matters laid down in Article 103(2) of the Basic Law,[48] the admissibility of the retrospective effect of legal rules imposing burdens is assessed by the Federal Constitutional Court and the Federal Administrative Court, in their established case law, in the light of the principle of the rule of law and its corollaries, *i.e.* the principles of legal certainty and of the protection of legitimate expectations.[49] To a certain extent, the Federal Constitutional Court considers that the protection against retrospective legislation is also directly embodied in each individual and constitutionally protected right of the citizen, since in particular the right of property ownership within the meaning of Article 14 of the Basic Law[50] and the right of admission to, and the exercise of, the professions within

---

[46] H.-U. Erichsen, W. Martens, *loc. cit.*, footnote 39, paragraph 19 II; P. Badura, in Erichsen, Martens, *loc. cit.*, footnote 39, paragraph 41 V 3; K. E. Huthmacher, *loc. cit.*, footnote 44, pp. 48 *et seq.*

[47] BVerfG, Decision of October 11, 1966, BVerfGE 20, 230; G. Langer, G. Theuerkauf, *loc. cit.*, footnote 44, pp. 20 *et seq.*

[48] *cf.* on this subject P. Kunig, *loc. cit.*, footnote 4, pp. 417 *et seq.*

[49] Thus, for example, BVerfGE 13, 261, 271; 38, 139, 148 *et seq.*; 45, 142, 168 and 174; 48, 1, 25, each with further references; BVerwGE 18, 254, 261; 37, 293, 300; 67, 129, 131.

[50] *cf., e.g.* BVerfGE 45, 142, 168.

the meaning of Article 12[51] run the risk of becoming devalued or restricted by retrospective legislation.[52]

Here, the Federal Constitutional Court draws the distinction between "real" and "apparent" retrospective effect.

"Real" retrospective effect ("retroactivity") arises when a legal rule has the effect of subsequently changing actions which have been concluded and which belong to the past.[53] Rules which have this type of retroactive effect are in principle null and void, as they infringe the principle of the rule of law, and are deemed permissible only in certain exceptional circumstances.[54] Thus retrospective legislation is not subject to the protection of legitimate expectations where, *inter alia*,

  (i) the legal situation which applied at the time as from which the law provides that it shall take legal effect required the citizen to take account of the new system[55];

 (ii) the applicable law is unclear and confused[56];

(iii) the extent to which legitimate expectation has been infringed is negligible and cannot outweigh the legislator's concern to serve the public interest.[57]

"Apparent" retrospective effect, on the other hand, occurs when a legal rule, although it intervenes directly only in circumstances or legal situations which have yet to take place, nevertheless detracts from or devalues

---

[51] *cf., e.g.* BVerfGE 32, 1, 22 *et seq.*

[52] *cf.* on this subject also E.-W. Fuss, "Der Schutz des Vertrauens auf Rechtskontinuität im deutschen Verfassungsrecht und im europäischen Gemeinschaftsrecht," in *Europäische Gerichtsbarkeit und nationale Verfassungsgerichtsbarkeit, Festschrift für H. Kutscher*, Baden-Baden 1981, pp. 201, 206 *et seq.*

[53] BVerfGE 30, 367, 386; 57, 361, 391; according to one decision by the Second Chamber of the BVerfG (E63, 343, 353) a legal rule "has retrospective effect if the start of its scope in time is fixed at a moment which occurs before the date on which the rule has become legally effective"; thus also BVerfG, RIW 1986, pp. 651, 652 *et seq.*; on the changes in the approach by the BVerfG towards retroactivity, *cf.* also H. Bauer, "Neue Tendenzen in der bundesverfassungsgerichtlichen Rechtsprechung zum Rückwirkungsverbot," NVwZ 1984, p. 220; B. Pieroth, "Die neuere Rechtsprechung des Bundesverfassungsgerichts zum Grundsatz des Vertrauensschutzes," JZ 1984, pp. 971, 973; *cf.* also J. Fiedler, "Neuorientierung der Verfassungsrechtsprechung zum Rückwirkungsverbot und zum Vertrauensschutz," NJW 1988, pp. 1624 *et seq.*

[54] BVerfGE 13, 261, 270 *et seq.*; 18, 429, 439; 30, 367, 387, *et seq.*; 45, 142, 173 *et seq.*; 48, 1, 25, each with further references; on the exceptional situations, *cf.* extensive commentary in J. Iliopoulos-Strangas, *Rückwirkung und Sofortwirkung von Gesetzen*, Baden-Baden 1986, pp. 54 *et seq.*

[55] BVerfGE 13, 261, 272.

[56] BVerfGE 13, 261, 272; 30, 272, 285.

[57] BVerfGE 30, 367, 389.

legal rights which have already been secured.[58] "Apparently" retrospective legal rules in principle pass the test of the Basic Law, but may exceptionally be unconstitutional if the rule in question interferes with a legitimate expectation and the legislator's concern for the public interest does not outweigh the individual's interest in maintaining the prevailing position.[59] However, the protection of legitimate expectations has not yet reached the point where the individual concerned is safeguarded against all disappointment.[60] Certainly the public interest may require the adoption of rules which have considerable impact on situations which have their origins in the past.[61] In such cases, however, even in the case of "apparent" retrospective effect, the constitutional principle of proportionality requires the legislator to make, where appropriate, transitional arrangements.[62]

3. The Retrospective Effect of Court Decisions

In connection with changes in the case law of the highest courts which result in a deterioration of the legal position of the addressees of the rule in question, there arises, under the heading of "Limits of the retrospective effect of changes in the case law," the question whether and to what extent the principle of the protection of legitimate expectations safeguards the citizen against developments in the case law of the highest courts.[63] Certain authors are of the opinion that the citizen has a right to rely upon the continuity of this case law and that this expectation is worthy of protection. This has given rise to demands that the rule which prohibits the legislator from producing retrospective effects should extend to the case law to the extent that the latter, as a result of a temporary restriction it imposes on itself, is prevented from applying to situations having their origins in the past any change in its attitude towards the law which works to the disadvantage of the individual in question.[64]

---

[58] BVerfGE 11, 139, 146; 55, 185, 203 et seq.; 59, 128, 164 et seq.; 67, 1, 15.
[59] BVerfGE 36, 73, 82; 63, 312, 329; 67, 1, 15; cf. also BVerfGE 71, 255, 273.
[60] BVerfGE 43, 242, 286; 67, 1, 15.
[61] BVerfGE 63, 343, 357; 67, 1, 15.
[62] BVerfGE 43, 242, 288 with further references; 67, 1, 15.
[63] cf. the extensive references to the available literature in J. Burmeister, *Vertrauensschutz im Prozessrecht*, Berlin/New York 1979, p. 26, footnote 38.
[64] J. Burmeister, *loc. cit.*, footnote 63, p. 28 with further references.

The case law of the financial[65] and industrial courts[66] provides examples of this type of protection of legitimate expectation. However, the attitude of the Federal Constitutional Court and of the Federal Administrative Court towards this question tends to be dismissive, as they consider that the principles which have been developed in relation to the retrospective effect of legislation cannot be unconditionally transposed to the case law. Since a development in the case law does not result in a change in a citizen's legal position but in a correction of the interpretation of the law, the courts could not in any way be bound by certain decisions where the latter, as a result of new trends in interpretation or changed relationships, are no longer tenable.[67]

C. UNITED KINGDOM

I. GENERAL RECOGNITION OF THE PRINCIPLES

British law knows no counterpart to the notions of legal certainty or the protection of legitimate expectations, which are recognised in most states of Continental Europe as general legal principles.[1] Nevertheless, the recent case law of the highest courts, in particular the House of Lords and the Privy Council, features a number of decisions in whose *ratio decidendi* the legitimate expectations of the parties play a decisive part.[2] In addition, certain types of "estoppel" contain notions which are at least similar to these principles.[3] Also, it is possible to discern traces of the protection of legitimate expectation in the principle that decisions by the administration may not be taken unreasonably.[4] The same applies to the requirement of a fair hearing and to the rule that the negligent provision of false

---

[65] BFHE 137, 202, 205.
[66] BAG, NJW 1984, pp. 2374, 2376.
[67] *cf. e.g.* BVerfGE 18, 224, 240 *et seq.*; 38, 386, 397; 59, 128, 165; BVerfGE 28, 122, 126.
[1] L. Collins, *European Community Law in the United Kingdom* (3rd ed., London 1984), p. 210.
[2] *cf. e.g.* O'Reilly v. Mackman, [1982] All E.R. 1124; *Attorney-General of Hongkong* v. Ng Yuen Shiu, [1983] 2 W.L.R. 735; *Regina* v. Home Secretary, ex parte Khan, [1984] 1 W.L.R. 1337; *cf.* on this subject also Lord Mackenzie Stuart, "Legitimate Expectations and Estoppel in Community Law and English Administrative Law," Legal Issues of European Integration 1983/I, pp. 53, 66; P. Cane, *An Introduction to Administrative Law*, Oxford 1986, p. 112.
[3] H. W. R. Wade, *Administrative Law* (5th ed., Oxford 1982), p. 231; L. Collins, *loc. cit.*, footnote 1, p. 210; Lord Mackenzie Stuart, *loc. cit.*, footnote 2, p. 66.
[4] Lord Mackenzie Stuart, *loc. cit.*, footnote 2, p. 66.

information by the administration may give rise to an obligation to pay compensation.

1. Legitimate Expectations

The principle of legitimate expectations was featured for the first time in an English court decision on an administrative law question in connection with the guaranteed right to a lawful hearing (*audi alteram partem*), which is derived from natural justice.[5]

In *Regina* v. *Liverpool Corporation, ex parte Liverpool Taxi Fleet Operators' Association*,[6] legitimate expectations asserted themselves against a decision by a municipal authority. The latter had increased the number of taxi licences, which conflicted with a pledge given to the contrary and with the interests of the licence holders. In this case, the Court of Appeal decided that the authority in question, although free in principle to decide the policy it wished to pursue, was bound to act fairly towards all the interested parties. Accordingly, that authority could certainly have departed from its fundamental pledge, but not before having accorded the Operators' Association a lawful hearing.[7]

Recently, legitimate expectations have also been successfully invoked against the central authorities. Thus in *Council of Civil Service Unions* v. *Minister for the Civil Service*,[8] the House of Lords regarded the fact that since 1947 trade union officials had been consulted before any changes in conditions of employment were made as giving rise to a legitimate expectation of consultation.[9]

The statements by the courts in which the notion of legitimate expectations finds expression are characterised by a certain degree of ambiguity. Thus it is often unclear whether the legitimate expectation relates only to a fair hearing or extends also to obtaining the desired benefit.[10] It cannot be claimed that there has been a long-established trend in the case law on

---

[5] *Schmidt* v. *Home Secretary* [1969] 2 Ch. 149 (Lord Denning M.R.).

[6] [1972] W.L.R. 1262.

[7] *cf.* on this subject also H. W. R. Wade, *loc. cit.*, footnote 3, pp. 493 *et seq.*; J. A. Usher, *General Principles derived from the laws of the Member States as a source of Community Law—The Interaction between Community Law and National Law*, British Report for the 12th FIDE Conference, Paris 1986, pp. 303, 314 *et seq.*

[8] [1984] 3 All E.R. 935, 3 W.L.R. 1174.

[9] *cf.* on this subject also P. Cane, *loc. cit.*, footnote 2, p. 73; J. A. Usher, *loc. cit.*, footnote 7, pp. 315 *et seq.*

[10] H. W. R. Wade, *loc. cit.*, footnote 3, p. 465; *cf.* also P. Cane, *loc. cit.*, footnote 2, pp. 112 *et seq.*

this subject; what is certain, however, is that in recent times the courts have tended to favour the latter, broader viewpoint.[11] Under this new approach, the notion of legitimate expectations is applied in the field of public law in such a way that a person who seeks to obtain a benefit or a special right to which he has no legal right, *i.e.* on which he has no claim based on the common law, may definitely rely on a legitimate expectation, which is to be protected by the courts, to obtain the benefit or the special right in question.[12] The object of the exercise is not in the first instance to protect property or any other vested right, but to guarantee that the authority of the State is exercised in a fair and considerate manner.[13]

2. Estoppel

The principle of estoppel also contains elements of the protection of legitimate expectations. The underlying idea of this principle, which has its origins in private law but is also binding upon the public authorities, is to prevent any person who, by a certain representation of the facts, causes another person to act in the belief that the information thus supplied is correct, from subsequently relying on the defectiveness of this information.[14] In its most general form, the meaning of this principle is that he who enters into a legal transaction believing a certain fact to be true, is protected in his belief against the person who had supplied the relevant information.[15] In the field of public law, the estoppel principle is limited by the *ultra vires* doctrine.[16] Closely related to the notion of lawfulness, this doctrine, which is considered to constitute the fundamental principle of British administrative law, holds that an authority is acting unlawfully, *i.e. ultra vires*, if its action has no legal basis. Where an administrative authority is bound to perform certain obligations, no estoppel can either exempt it from meeting these obligations or allow it to act *ultra vires*. Neither does this principle empower an authority to transform a matter

---

[11] *cf. e.g. Schmidt* v. *Home Secretary* [1969] 2 Ch. 149; *McInnes* v. *Onslow-Fane* [1978] 1 W.L.R. 1520; *CCSU* v. *Minister for the Civil Service* [1984] 3 All E.R. 935.

[12] Lord Fraser, in *CCSU* v. *Minister for the Civil Service* [1984] 3 All E.R. 935 at 943 *et seq.*

[13] H. W. R. Wade, *loc. cit.*, footnote 3, p. 465.

[14] H. W. R. Wade, *loc. cit.*, footnote 3, p. 232; Lord Mackenzie Stuart, *loc. cit.*, footnote 2, p. 68.

[15] Thus already H. P. Ipsen, *Widerruf gültiger Verwaltungsakte*, Hamburg 1932, p. 100.

[16] H. W. R. Wade, *loc. cit.*, footnote 3, p. 233: "no estoppel can legitimate action which is ultra vires"; Lord Mackenzie Stuart, *loc. cit.*, footnote 2, p. 68; *cf.* also P. Cane, *loc. cit.*, footnote 2, pp. 228 *et seq.*

over which it has discretion into a binding commitment by giving a pledge as to its future conduct.[17]

The case law relating to estoppel contains very few examples in which the court departs from the strict *ultra vires* doctrine.[18] Most of these concern cases in which the persons in question had been disadvantaged as a result of incorrect information provided by the administration. The latter can be broken down into two categories.[19]

The first concerns the delegation of powers, which enables, for example, planning bodies to empower individual officials to take, on their own authority, certain decisions such as the granting of applications. Decisions taken by individual officials are binding upon the authorities, even in cases where a delegation of powers did not take place as such but would have been perfectly legal—in other words, where the decision came "within the ostensible authority" of the official and the addressee of the decision could not have been aware of the lack of authority.[20]

The second category concerns formal requirements. Thus a planning authority which, in processing applications, fails to apply statutorily prescribed procedures may not subsequently rely on this procedural defect.[21] Accordingly, it is possible to depart from the *ultra vires* doctrine in cases which concern merely technicalities.

II. APPLICATION TO INDIVIDUAL CASES

1. Action by the Administration

(a) Revocation of administrative decisions

In English law, there is no definitive way of establishing what are the

---

[17] Lord Mackenzie Stuart, *loc. cit.*, footnote 2, p. 68; *cf.* also Megaw L.J. in *Western Fish Products Ltd.* v. *Penwith District Council and another* [1981] 2 All E.R. 204.

[18] On the reasons for the dismissive attitude of the courts, *cf.* the extensive commentary in P. Cane, *loc. cit.*, footnote 2, pp. 229 *et seq.*

[19] On this distinction, *cf.* Megaw L.J., in *Western Fish Products Ltd.* v. *Penwith District Council and another* [1981] All E.R. 204.

[20] *Lever Finance Ltd.* v. *Westminster Corporation* [1971] 1 Q.B. 222; a similar view is expressed in *Robertson* v. *Minister of Pensions* [1949] 1 K.B. 227.

[21] *Wells* v. *Minister of Housing and Local Government* [1967] W.L.R. 1000; *cf.* also *Re L(AC) (an infant)*, [1971] 3 All E.R. 743; on these two categories and the cases included under each category, *cf.* also Lord Mackenzie Stuart, *loc. cit.*, footnote 2, pp. 68 *et seq.*; D. Foulkes, *Administrative Law* (5th ed., London 1982), pp. 184 *et seq.*; P. Cane, *loc. cit.*, footnote 2, pp. 230 *et seq.*

generally applicable rules concerning the revocation[22] of administrative decisions. This area is not subject to a general system of legislation, nor do the case law or the leading authors provide sufficient details on this question.

There is, of course, a rule which governs the interpretation of statutory powers and duties, which states that these powers and duties must, unless the relevant statute provides otherwise, be exercised "from time to time as occasion requires."[23] The rationale of this rule is to challenge the notion that a particular power is spent after having been exercised on one occasion.[24] This does not, however, apply to all powers to take decisions involving claims by the citizen. There are exceptions based on specific circumstances[25] such as, for example, the fixing of compensation or of a pension. This inability to revoke decisions in such cases is justified by reference to considerations of legal certainty and the protection of legitimate expectations.[26]

The leading decision in *Re 56, Denton Road, Twickenham* also concerned the power "to decide once and once only."[27] In this case, the War Damage Commission had provisionally declared a house owned by the plaintiff which had been destroyed during the war as a "total write-off" for the purpose of determining the amount of the compensation due. Later, this assessment was changed to "non-total write-off," which meant that the plaintiff was eligible for a higher compensatory payment, *i.e.* for rebuilding costs instead of a payment based on the property value. Six months later, the Commission once again reverted to its original assessment that the house was a "total write-off," which prompted the owner to take court action. The court held that the second assessment was to be the definitive one because

> "where Parliament confers on a body such as the War Damage
> Commission the duty of deciding or determining any question, the
> deciding or determining of which affects the rights of the subject,

---

[22] No terminological distinction is drawn between withdrawal and revocation. Both are covered by the uniform concept of "revocation."

[23] Interpretation Act 1978, s.12.

[24] *cf.* D. Foulkes, *loc. cit.*, footnote 21, p. 191.

[25] H. W. R. Wade, *loc. cit.*, footnote 3, pp. 225 *et seq.*

[26] *cf.* H. W. R. Wade, *loc. cit.*, footnote 3, p. 226: "Citizens whose legal rights are determined administratively are entitled to know where they stand."

[27] [1953] Ch. 51; [1952] 2 All E.R. 799; for a similar ruling, *cf.* also *Employment and Immigration Commission* v. *Macdonald Tobacco Inc.* (1981) 121 Daily Law Reports (3 d) 546.

such decision or determination made and communicated in terms which are not expressly preliminary or provisional is final and conclusive, and cannot, in the absence of express statutory power or the consent of the person or persons affected, be altered or withdrawn by that body."[28]

However, a practical distinction is made between revocation with effects as to the future and revocation with retroactive effect. It is also generally acknowledged among the leading writers that there is no possibility of retroactive revocation if an administrative decision is given definitive status by means of separate legislation.[29] Conversely, revocation with retrospective effect is possible if a legal rule explicitly or implicitly confers such powers.[30]

Retroactive revocation is also permissible if the addressee of an administrative decision conferring benefits has obtained this decision by fraudulently deceiving or misleading the authority in question. In such cases, the decision may at all times be revoked.[31] This exceptional rule is particularly relevant in the field of immigration law. Although a residence permit, once granted, cannot in principle be revoked, it will be declared invalid if the immigrant in question has obtained it by fraudulent deception or by withholding information which was relevant to the decision.[32]

Any authority which exercises continuing powers is not prevented from revoking a decision with effect for the future.[33] This applies in particular where the authority has taken the decision for an indefinite period or on the basis of an error.[34] This is demonstrated by the case of *Rootkin* v. *Kent County Council*,[35] in which the local education authority had indicated its readiness to bear the cost of providing a girl with transport by school bus. This decision had been taken on the assumption that the girl in question

---

[28] Vaisey, J., in *Re 56, Denton Road, Twickenham* [1952] 2 All E.R. 799 at 802.
[29] H. W. R. Wade, *loc. cit.*, footnote 3, p. 225: ". . . the decision, once validly made, is an irrevocable legal act and cannot be recalled or revised." *cf.* also Lord Mackenzie Stuart, *loc. cit.*, footnote 2, p. 71; P. Cane, *loc. cit.*, footnote 2, p. 237.
[30] Thus, *e.g.* s.36(4) of the Road Traffic Act 1960.
[31] *cf.* Lord Denning, in *Lazarus Estates Ltd.* v. *Beasley* [1956] 1 Q.B. 702 at 712: "No judgment of a court, no order of a Minister, can be allowed to stand if it has been obtained by fraud. Fraud unravels everything"; *cf.* on this subject also H. W. R. Wade, *loc. cit.*, footnote 3, p. 228.
[32] Lord Mackenzie Stuart, *loc. cit.*, footnote 2, p. 71, with reference to *R.* v. *Home Secretary, ex parte Khawaja* [1983] 2 W.L.R. 321; *cf.* also *R.* v. *Home Secretary, ex p. Zamir* [1980] A.C. 930.
[33] Lord Mackenzie Stuart, *loc. cit.*, footnote 2, p. 71.
[34] *Ibid.*; *cf.* also H. W. R. Wade, *loc. cit.*, footnote 3, p. 226.
[35] [1981] 1 W.L.R. 1186.

lived more than three miles from school and that in such circumstances there arose a statutory duty to bear the relevant costs. Having subsequently established, however, that the distance in question was less than three miles and that for this reason any decision on this issue was a matter for its discretion rather than resulting from a statutory duty, the authority revoked the decision *ex nunc*. The Court of Appeal maintained the revocation and held the principle stated in *Re 56, Denton Road* to be inapplicable where, as was the case here, the actual conditions for obtaining payment had not been met and all that had arisen was a right to request the authority to exercise its discretion. In such cases, the administrative authorities could exercise its discretion "from time to time as occasion requires," *i.e.* once the error was discovered, it could not be estopped from changing its decision.[36]

However, a revocation *ex tunc* is also permissible where the authority is under an obligation which it is bound to meet. The case of *Maritime Electric Co. Ltd.* v. *General Dairies Ltd.*[37] concerned such an obligation. Here, Maritime Electric Co., being a company established under private law but subject to public law rules, had for more than two years inadvertently undercharged the defendant for its consumption of electricity. The manner in which the charges were calculated was to be corrected in accordance with a system which prohibited the electricity company from charging higher or lower rates than those which were statutorily prescribed. The Privy Council decided that Maritime Electric was not estopped by the inadvertent undercharging from subsequently claiming the rates actually due, since neither a contract nor a mistake could render a statutory duty inoperative.

(b) Recovery of payments having no legal basis

In Britain, claims for recovery by the citizen against the State are in principle not conditional upon a challenge within a certain time limit of the administrative act levying the payment. Essentially, the English courts are not estopped by any form of "existence as a binding

---

[36] Lawton L.J., in *Rootkin* v. *Kent C.C.* [1981] 1 W.L.R. 1186 at 1195; *cf.* also *Southend-on-Sea Corporation* v. *Hodgson (Wickford) Ltd.* [1962] 1 Q.B. 416, Lord Parker C.J.: "... an estoppel cannot be raised to prevent or hinder the exercise of the discretion."
[37] [1937] 1 All E.R. 748.

force" from assessing the lawfulness of administrative acts imposing burdens.[38]

However, the opportunities for recovering monies wrongly levied are restricted, in England (and Scotland) as in other countries. Unless special provisions apply to individual cases, claims for recovery are based on the principle of the repayment of money constituting unjustified enrichment, *i.e.* the action for money paid and received.[39] Here, a distinction is made according to the reason for the incorrect levying of the charge in question.[40] It is possible to claim recovery only if the original payment was made on the basis of a "mistake of fact." If on the other hand a "mistake of law" has occurred, which also includes a mistaken interpretation of Community law,[41] it is normally impossible for the citizen to claim repayment.[42] This ground rule in turn admits of two exceptions for the benefit of the person affected: even where a "mistake of law" has occurred, the possibility of recovery is not excluded if the person having the obligation to pay had done so only under protest or if the recipient of the payment is said to be under an obligation to explain the legal position to the person making the payment.[43]

In addition, there exists in English law a time limit for the institution of claims for recovery. This takes the form of a limitation period and is normally for six years[44] (five years in Scotland).[45] This period of limitation, which in principle applies to claims arising from contract, has been extended to claims arising from the *condictio indebiti* by the case

---

[38] D. G. Valentine, "The Recovery of Dues improperly levied by a State," National Report for the United Kingdom, in *La restitution de taxes perçues indûment par l'Etat*, Geneva 1976, pp. 39 *et seq.* (41).

[39] On this subject, and on the matters discussed below, *cf.* also: A. A. Dashwood, J. W. G. Blackie, J. C. Minor, National Report for England and Scotland in J.-V. Louis (ed.), *Régime juridique des relations entre les opérateurs économiques et les organismes d'exécution du droit communautaire*, stencilled report, Brussels 1982, pp. 592 *et seq.* (619 *et seq.*).

[40] *cf.* on this subject D. G. Valentine, *loc. cit.*, footnote 38, pp. 42 *et seq.*; Decision in *Bilbie* v. *Lumley* (1802) 2 East 469; A. A. Dashwood *et al.*, *loc. cit.*, footnote 39, pp. 619 *et seq.*, 626 *et seq.*

[41] In accordance with s.3(1) of the European Communities Act 1972.

[42] *cf.* on this subject: P. Cane, *loc. cit.*, footnote 2, pp. 225 *et seq.*; P. Aubin, *Die Haftung der Europäischen Wirtschaftsgemeinschaft und ihrer Mitgliedstaaten bei gemeinschaftsrechtswidrigen nationalen Verwaltungsakten*, Baden-Baden 1982, pp. 91 *et seq.*

[43] D. G. Valentine, *loc. cit.*, footnote 38; *cf.* on this subject the decision in *Kiriri Cotton Co. Ltd.* v. *Bewani* [1960] A.C. 192.

[44] In accordance with s.9(1) of the Limitation Act 1980.

[45] In accordance with the Prescription and Limitation (Scotland) Act 1973, s.6 and Schedule I; *cf.* on this subject A. A. Dashwood *et al.*, *loc. cit.*, footnote 39, pp. 653 *et seq.*

law.[46] The time limit is extended, or begins once the mistaken nature of the payment is discovered, if and to the extent to which the legally defective nature of the payment could not have been discovered earlier even by exercising due care.[47]

As regards cases where, conversely, recovery is sought of monies paid by the State, these are, under British law, covered in the first place by a series of special provisions on the basis of which subsidies, subventions or other official payments are made. On the one hand, there are provisions such as the Industrial Development Act 1982, which empowers the grant-making authority in individual cases to insert in the letter of approval of the subsidy a provision stating that the amount in question may be recovered in certain circumstances, such as failure to satisfy the conditions stipulated.[48] On the other hand, there exist various provisions relating to agricultural subsidies which lay down more detailed rules concerning the recovery of wrongly granted subsidies. Thus, for example, the monies may be recovered (a) if conditions stipulated have not been met, (b) if the purpose for which the subsidy was made has not been, or could not be expected to be, realised or has been realised only in part or too late, (c) if the approval has been obtained on the basis of incorrect information supplied by the beneficiary and (d) if the recovery concerns agricultural subsidies paid by the Council or the Commission on the basis of Community law.[49]

Except where possible claims for the recovery of State payments wrongly made are subject to specific rules based on such legislation, the recovery procedure is modelled on the general principles of the common law, in particular those relating to "quasi-contracts."[50]

---

[46] Thus on the legal position in England: A. A. Dashwood, *loc. cit.*, footnote 39, p. 646; *Re Diplock* [1948] Ch. 465, 514.

[47] A. A. Dashwood *et al.*, *loc. cit.*, footnote 39, p. 646 (as regards England), also for Scotland *ibid.* p. 654.

[48] Industrial Development Act 1982, s.4(1); *cf.* on this subject: J. Flynn, National Report for the United Kingdom, 12th FIDE Conference Paris 1986, Vol. II, p. 355 (357 *et seq.*); T. C. Daintith, T. A. E. Sharpe, National Report for the United Kingdom, in B. Börner, M. Bullinger (eds.) *Subventionen im Gemeinsamen Markt, KSE* Vol. 29, Cologne 1978, pp. 138 *et seq.*

[49] Thus, *e.g.* Regulation 5 of the Agricultural Products Processing and Marketing Improvement Grant Regulations 1977/2112; on this subject, A. A. Dashwood *et al.*, *loc. cit.*, footnote 39, p. 607; *cf.* also Agriculture Act 1970 Part III, s.29(4) (except for alternative (d)).

[50] J. Flynn, *loc. cit.*, footnote 48; A. A. Dashwood *et al.*, *loc. cit.*, footnote 39, pp. 619 *et seq.*, 625 *et seq.*

As a result, the principles governing estoppel, the *ultra vires* doctrine, the "condictio indebiti"[51] and "legitimate expectations" also apply here. What is certain is that neither the day-to-day administrative decision-making process nor the relevant case law have so far revealed any uniform or established trends on this subject.

2. Legislation—Retroactivity of Statutes and Regulations

Laws—*i.e.* Acts—or regulations are retrospective where they remove or impinge upon vested rights acquired under the law which applied up to that moment or where they establish new obligations with effect into the past or impose new duties with similar effect.[52] However, regulations are not retrospective merely on account of relating to past events.[53]

It follows from the rule of Parliamentary sovereignty that statutes enacted by Parliament may in principle have retrospective effect.[54] The Parliamentary legislator may also empower the administration to adopt retrospective regulations.[55] Nevertheless, any retrospective legislation as such is repugnant to the concept of the rule of law.[56] Accordingly, Acts adopted by the legislator should, on grounds of protecting legitimate expectations, in principle concern only future events.[57] For this reason, retrospective legislation is rarely enacted in practice.

---

[51] A. A. Dashwood *et al.*, *loc. cit.*, footnote 39, pp. 619 *et seq.*, 625 *et seq.*, 642 *et seq.*

[52] *cf.* P. B. Maxwell, *On the Interpretation of Statutes* (11th ed.), revised by R. Wilson and B. Galpin, London 1962, p. 206; D. Foulkes, *loc. cit.*, footnote 21, p. 193.

[53] D. Foulkes, *loc. cit.*, footnote 21, p. 193; *cf.* also on this subject *Master Ladies Taylors Organisation* v. *Minister of Labour and National Service* [1950] 2 All E.R. 525.

[54] E. C. S. Wade, A. W. Bradley, *Constitutional and Administrative Law* (10th ed., London/New York 1985), pp. 614, 67 with examples (p. 67, footnote 24). The situation is different in the U.S.A., where retrospective legislation is subject to constitutional restrictions; for a comparative view, *cf.* G. Kisker, *Die Rückwirkung von Gesetzen. Eine Untersuchung zum anglo-amerikanischen und deutschen Recht*, Tübingen 1963.

[55] *cf.* D. Foulkes, *loc. cit.*, footnote 21, pp. 193 *et seq.*

[56] E. C. S. Wade, A. Bradley, *loc. cit.*, footnote 54, p. 614.

[57] E. C. S. Wade, A. W. Bradley, *loc. cit.*, footnote 54, p. 67 with reference to Willes J., in *Phillips* v. *Eyre* [1870] 6 Q.B. 1, p. 23: "Retrospective laws are, however, prima facie of questionable policy and contrary to the general principle that legislation by which the conduct of mankind is to be regulated ought . . . to deal with future acts and ought not to change the character of past transactions carried on upon the faith of the then existing law. . . . Acccordingly the court will not ascribe retrospective force to new laws affecting rights unless by express words or necessary implication it appears that such was the intention of the legislature."

D. ITALY

I. GENERAL RECOGNITION OF THE PRINCIPLES

The principles, recognised in private law, of good faith (*bona fides*) and of the protection of legitimate expectations (Articles 1153, 1175, 1337, 1414, 1433 and 1445 of the Civil Code)[1] have not hitherto found any expression in the substantive public law. There is disagreement in the literature as to whether the principle of the protection of legitimate expectations is one which applies in public law. An increasing number of authors[2] tend to follow their German counterparts in adopting the position that the principle of good faith is an unwritten constitutional rule which gives rise to the protection of the legitimate expectations of the citizen against the public authorities (both the legislature and the administration).[3] A minority remain critical of this theory,[4] holding that the hitherto established case law on the revocation of administrative acts is not so significant as to form the basis for a general principle of the protection of legitimate expectations governing the relationship between the administration and the citizen.[5]

On the other hand, the principle of the protection of legitimate expectations is generally acknowledged as being applicable when the administration concludes private law contracts. Contrary to previous assumptions,[6] both academic writers and the courts currently accept that the administrative authorities will incur pre-contractual liability if in the

---

[1] On this subject, *cf.* R. Sacco, "Affidamento," EdD, Vol. I, p. 660.

[2] *cf.* in particular F. Merusi, *L'affidamento del cittadino*, Milan 1970; by the same author, "Buona fede e tutela dell'affidamento nella programmazione economica," in *Studi sulla buona fede*, Milan 1975, pp. 731 *et seq.*

[3] *cf.* G. Guarino, "Sul regime costituzionale delle leggi di incentivazione e di indirizzo," in *Scritti di diritto pubblico dell' economia e di diritto dell'energia*, Milan 1962, p. 125; V. Bachalet, *Legge e attività amministrativa nella programmazione economica*, Milan 1975, pp. 47 *et seq.*; for a critical appraisal, *cf.* A. Barbera, *Leggi di piano e sistema delle fonti*, Milan 1968, pp. 58, 61 *et seq.*, 71, 83; L. Benadusi, "Attività di finanziamento pubblico, Aspetti costituzionali e amministrativi," Riv. trim. dir. pubbl. 1966, pp. 931 *et seq.*; C. Mortati, *Istituzioni di diritto pubblico*, Vol. I (9th ed., Padua 1975), p. 285; rejecting this view as regards legislation, *cf.* F. Capelli, Italian Report for the 12th FIDE Conference, Paris 1986, pp. 183, 208.

[4] *cf.* A. Mantero, *Le situazioni favorevoli del privato nel rapporto amministrativo*, Padua 1979.

[5] *cf.* A. Mantero, *loc. cit.*, footnote 4, p. 59.

[6] *cf. e.g.* Vela, "Riflessi giurisprudenziali in tema di responsabilità precontrattuale della pubblica amministrazione," Riv. giur. edil. 1963 I, pp. 855 *et seq.*

course of preliminary negotiations they act contrary to *bona fides* or infringe the principle of the protection of legitimate expectations.[7]

II. APPLICATION TO INDIVIDUAL CASES

1. Action by the Administration

(*a*) *Annulment of administrative decisions*

Hitherto, there have not been in Italian law any explicit legislative rules governing the avoidance of administrative decisions. However, both academic writers and the courts have in the meantime developed an authoritative system of rules on this topic. For this purpose of setting aside administrative decisions, essentially two mechanisms are available. The "annullamento" concerns the withdrawal of a mistaken and thus unlawful administrative decision, whereas the "revoca" involves the revocation of an administrative decision which, although lawful as such, is inappropriate.[8] Only a minority of authors follow German public law in drawing a distinction between administrative decisions conferring benefits and those imposing burdens.[9]

(*aa*) *Withdrawal of unlawful administrative decisions (annullamento)*

The unlawful nature (*vizi di legittimità*) of an administrative decision leads to its inapplicability (*inapplicabilità*) or makes it capable of being withdrawn (*annullabilità*).[10] The concept of inapplicability[11] is derived

---

[7] A. M. Sandulli, *Manuale di diritto amministrativo*, Vol. II (14th ed., Naples 1984), p. 1116; M. S. Giannini, "La responsabilità precontrattuale dell'amministrazione pubblica," in *Raccolta di scritti in onore di A. C. Jemolo*, Milan 1963, Vol. III, pp. 263 *et seq.*; Santucci, *Considerazioni in tema di "culpa in contrahendo" della pubblica amministrazione*, Florence 1964; established case law since decision by the Corte di Cassazione of May 8, 1963, No. 1142; *cf.* also decision of January 11, 1977, No. 93; Decision of December 1, 1978, No. 5831; F. Capelli, *loc. cit.*, footnote 3, p. 208.

[8] *cf.* M. S. Giannini, *Diritto Amministrativo*, Vol. 2, Milan 1970, p. 1083; G. Pericu, *Le sovvenzioni come strumento di azione amministrativa*, 1971, p. 304; A. M. Sandulli, *Manuale*, Vol. I, *loc. cit.*, footnote 7, pp. 694 *et seq.* G. Landi, G. Potenza, *Manuale di diritto amministrativo* (7th ed., Milan 1983).

[9] *cf. e.g.* F. Merusi, *loc. cit.*, footnote 2, pp. 80 *et seq.* and 146 *et seq.*

[10] G. Landi, G. Potenza, *loc. cit.*, footnote 8, p. 264.

[11] *cf.* on this subject E. Cannada Bartoli, *L'inapplicabilità degli atti amministrativi*, Milan 1950.

from Article 5 of Law No. 2248 of March 5, 1865, Appendix E,[12] under which the courts are to apply "both the administrative decisions and the general and local regulations to the extent that they conform to legislation." The "annullabilità," on the other hand, provides the opportunity to remove unlawful administrative acts through either an annulment act on the part of the administration or an annulment decision taken by an administrative court.[13]

Under Italian law, there are essentially three grounds on which administrative acts can be held to be illegal: lack of authority (*incompetenza*), excess of discretionary power (*eccesso di potere*) and infringement of legislation (*violazione di legge*).[14] Administrative acts which are unlawful on these grounds may be set aside either by the administrative authority which issued them (*autoannullamento*) or by a superior authority (*annullamento gerarchico*) by virtue of the administration's power of annulment by its own motion (*annullamento d'ufficio*).[15] We are dealing here with discretionary decisions.[16] Since the *annullamento d'ufficio* constitutes a means of protecting the interests of the administration, the principal criterion in such a decision will be that it is in the current public interest to have the decision withdrawn. The fact that the administrative act proves to be unlawful is not of itself sufficient to that end. The rule is rather that in individual cases the public interest in having the act withdrawn has to be weighed up against that of the citizen in maintaining the decision.[17]

For reasons of legal certainty, the withdrawal of an unlawful administrative act is no longer possible after the expiry of a certain time limit. Once this date has passed, the act is deemed to be lawful.[18]

---

[12] Legge abolitiva del contenzioso amministrativo—Law relating to the abolition of the administrative courts.

[13] G. Landi, G. Potenza, *loc. cit.*, footnote 8, p. 264.

[14] *cf.* for an extensive commentary on this subject G. Landi, G. Potenza, *loc. cit.*, footnote 8, pp. 255 *et seq.*

[15] M. S. Giannini, *loc. cit.*, footnote 8, p. 1057; G. Landi, G. Potenza, *loc. cit.*, footnote 8, p. 264; on the other forms of *annullamento, cf.* also M. S. Giannini, *loc. cit.*, footnote 8, p. 1057.

[16] This is the predominant view; *cf.*, *e.g.* G. Landi, G. Potenza, *loc. cit.*, footnote 8, p. 265; A. M. Sandulli, *Manuale*, Vol. I, *loc. cit.*, footnote 7, p. 707; M. S. Giannini, *loc. cit.*, footnote 8, p. 1059; CdS, Sez. VI, Decision of September 27, 1963, No. 475; CdS, Sez. VI, Decision of February 30, 1972, No. 279.

[17] *cf.* on this subject G. Landi, G. Potenza, *loc. cit.*, footnote 8, p. 265 with references to the case law; *cf.* also E.C.J. Case 14/61 *Hoogovens* v. *High Authority* [1962] E.C.R. 511 at 569 (opinion of Advocate-General M. Lagrange).

[18] M. Sandulli, *Manuale*, Vol. I, *loc. cit.*, footnote 7, pp. 690 and 711; *cf.* also CdS, Sez. VI, September 30, 1984, No. 654 with annotation by E. Cannada Bartoli, Foro amm. 1964, II, pp. 143 *et seq.*; CdS Sez. V, June 8, 1979, No. 296.

The fixing of this time limit in individual cases is also a matter for which the various interests involved have to be weighed up.[19]

The *annullamento* revokes the administrative act with effect from the date on which it came into force, *i.e.* its effect is *ex tunc*.[20] The revoked administrative act does not in principle give rise to any subjective rights, since it is held to be invalid from the outset.[21] Particularly as regards payments wrongly received (salaries, subsidies, etc.), limits have been set to the retrospective nature of revocation. According to the case law of the Consiglio dello Stato, such payments may be recovered only under certain conditions.[22] Where they have been received in good faith and expended for the purpose for which they were intended, they are not recoverable.[23] Under certain conditions, the implications of the revocation for the material interests of the citizen concerned are to be compensated by restitution (*restituzione*) or by payment of damages (*risarcimento*).[24]

(bb) Revocation of inappropriate administrative decisions (revoca)

Administrative decisions which present the defect of inappropriateness (*viziati nel merito*) may be set aside by revocation decreed by the administrative authority or by a judicial organ.[25] Administrative decisions are inappropriate if they are defective on grounds other than infringement of the substantive law, such as, for example, technical or economic considerations or infringement of a principle of proper administration (*regola di buona amministrazione*).[26] The withdrawal of administrative decisions in principle takes effect only *ex nunc, i.e.* the implications of the administrative decisions which have already taken place are not affected by the

---

[19] A. M. Sandulli, *Manuale*, Vol. I, *loc. cit.*, footnote 7, p. 711; *cf.* also on this subject W. Däubler, "Der Widerruf von Verwaltungsakten im Recht der Europäischen Gemeinschaften," NJW 1965, pp. 1646, 1649.

[20] A. M. Sandulli, *Manuale*, Vol. I, *loc. cit.*, footnote 7, pp. 703 *et seq.*; G. Landi, G. Potenza, *loc. cit.*, footnote 8, p. 268; R. Alessi, *La revoca degli atti amministrativi*, 1956, p. 56; M. S. Giannini, *loc. cit.*, footnote 8, p. 1062.

[21] A. M. Sandulli, *Manuale*, Vol. I, *loc. cit.*, footnote 7, p. 703; Corte di Cassazione, Decision of June 5, 1956, No. 1907; Decision of October 10, 1956, No. 3471.

[22] CdS, Sez. IV, Decision of November 23, 1971, No. 1036.

[23] CdS, Audienza Plenaria, Decision of November 28, 1970, No. 12 and of October 5, 1971, No. 7.

[24] G. Landi, G. Potenza, *loc. cit.*, footnote 8, p. 268.

[25] G. Landi, G. Potenza, *loc. cit.*, footnote 8, p. 271.

[26] *cf.* A. M. Sandulli, *Manuale*, Vol. I, *loc. cit.*, footnote 7, pp. 575 *et seq.*; G. Landi, G. Potenza, *loc. cit.*, footnote 8, p. 272.

withdrawal.[27] However, the non-retroactivity rule may be waived if withdrawal confers a benefit on the addressee and the interests of third parties are not affected.[28]

(b) Recovery of payments having no legal basis

On the question of claims for the recovery of taxes, duties and other charges wrongly levied, both the available literature and the case law consider that the rules on the unjustified acquisition of monies set out in Articles 2041 and 2042 of the Civil Code (*i.e.* the so-called *actio de in rem verso*) also apply in the field of public law.[29]

The overwhelming majority of authors and courts appear to regard the tax legislation itself as constituting the legal basis for the imposition of the tax.[30] Accordingly, the question whether the administrative act is still capable of being challenged is irrelevant in determining the enforceable nature of the citizen's claim for recovery. Although in Italy also an administrative act becomes formally effective once the time limit for challenging it has expired—this being a status which has to be accepted even by the civil courts, which in principle have jurisdiction over claims for recovery—only a few authors are willing, at least as regards the law of taxation, to conclude that the citizen is barred from enforcing a claim for recovery once the administrative act has become effective. The prevailing view is that the right to enforce recovery claims against the State is restricted in time only by the limitation period of 10 years, which applies to civil law claims in general (Article 2946 Civil Code), or, where appropriate, by such shorter periods as may be laid down by various special tax provisions.

The general 10-year limitation period has in the past repeatedly caused considerable problems to the Italian State in connection with Community

---

[27] *cf.* Corte di Cassazione, Decision of October 7, 1954, No. 3357; CdS, Sez. V, Decision of November 14, 1958, No. 857; Sez. VI, Decision of February 9, 1979, No. 72; on this subject, A. M. Sandulli, *Manuale*, Vol. I, *loc. cit.*, footnote 7, pp. 699 *et seq.*; M. S. Giannini, *loc. cit.*, footnote 8, p. 1083; R. Alessi, *loc. cit.*, footnote 20, p. 56.

[28] On this subject, *cf.* A. M. Sandulli, Vol. I, *loc. cit.*, footnote 7, p. 695.

[29] A. M. Sandulli, *Manuale*, Vol. I, *loc. cit.*, footnote 7, p. 166 with further references (footnote 115).

[30] On this subject and the matters discussed below, *cf.* F. Capelli, National Report for Italy, in *La restitution de taxes perçues indûment par l'Etat*, Geneva 1976, pp. 127 (131 *et seq.*); G. Guarino, P. de Caterini, *ibid.* pp. 135 *et seq.*; K. E. Huthmacher, *Der Vorrang des Gemeinschaftsrechts bei indirekten Kollisionen*, Köln/Berlin/Bonn/München 1985, pp. 263 *et seq.*

law, whenever an Italian charge or tax levied on intra-Community transactions has proved contrary to Community law. Thus the State saw itself
exposed to claims for recovery by the citizens affected relating back to
distant dates in the past.[31] It was apparently this consideration which
prompted the Italian legislator to incorporate into Italian law the
"transfer theory," which had been held by the ECJ, in the *Just* case,[32]
which concerned a Danish dispute, to be compatible in principle with
Community law. However, as will be explained later, the Court, in the
San Giorgio case,[33] stated that in Community law, contrary to the prevailing Italian legislation, a national legal provision may not impose on the
Community citizen the burden of proving that he has not already passed
the tax levied contrary to Community law on to his customers. Accordingly, repayment may not be denied on the basis that the person affected
has not succeeded in furnishing the required evidence.

In Italy, the admissibility of the recovery of wrongly paid State benefits
is assessed in the first place in the light of the principles governing the
revocation of administrative acts, which have already been explained
above.[34] According to the latter, the recovery of wrongly paid State
benefits is, from the point of view of the protection of legitimate expectations, admissible only on a restricted basis, particularly where the beneficiary has acquired these monies in good faith and expended them for the
purpose for which they were intended.[35]

2. Legislation—Retroactivity of Statutes

Laws enter into force on the fifteenth day following their promulgation, *i.e.* following their publication in the "Gazzetta ufficiale della
Repubblica Italiana" (Official Journal of the Italian Republic),[36] unless
the Law specifies a different date for its entry into force (Article 73 of the
Italian Constitution).[37] The same principles apply to regulations (Article
10 disp. prel. cod. civ.).

---

[31] *cf.* on such cases Section 3, A, footnotes 23a, 23b.
[32] E.C.J. Case 68/79 *Just* v. *Danish Ministry for Fiscal Affairs* [1980] E.C.R. 501.
[33] E.C.J. Case 199/82 *Amministrazione delle Finanze dello Stato* v. *San Giorgio* [1983]
E.C.R. 3595 at 3613.
[34] *cf. supra*, (a)(aa).
[35] *cf.* the decisions mentioned under footnotes 22 and 23.
[36] G. Landi, G. Potenza, *loc. cit.*, footnote 8, p. 21; G. Treves, *Principi di diritto pubblico*
(2nd ed.), Turin 1973, p. 99; *cf.* also Lupo, "La Raccolta ufficiale delle leggi e dei decreti
e la Gazzetta ufficiale della Repubblica Italiana," Riv. trim. dir. pubbl. 1981, pp. 650 *et
seq.*
[37] *cf.* on this subject G. Treves, *loc. cit.*, footnote 36, p. 99.

Article 11 disp. prel. cod. civ. contains a rule prohibiting the retroactivity of laws.[38] This rule, which has its origins in the Roman law tradition and in the principle of legal certainty, means that no law may apply to events which preceded its entry into force.[39] Since this rule is contained only in an ordinary law, it certainly applies to rules inferior to laws (regulations and other legal provisions issued by the executive), but has no binding effect on the legislature itself.[40] The latter may waive this prohibition and decree that a law should be retrospective to the extent that no constitutional obstacles prevent it from doing so.[41] The Constitution explicitly prohibits retroactivity only for criminal laws (Article 25(2)).[42] By way of analogy, this prohibition also applies to disciplinary provisions.[43] The overwhelming majority of authors[44] and administrative courts[45] adhere to the view that outside the field of criminal law, the legislature is not bound by the constitutional prohibition of retroactivity. However, laws may be defective if their retroactivity leads to the infringement of another constitutional provision.[46]

A number of theories, systematically grouped under the general heading of the protection of the *diritti quesiti* (*i.e.* vested rights), have been developed on the subject of the scope of the non-retroactivity rule. The term *diritti quesiti* is interpreted as meaning rights which have been established within the scope of a particular law on the basis of certain facts.[47] To be capable of protection, these rights must have acquired a certain degree of durability. Thus there is no *diritto quesito* where the previously applicable law had merely conferred on the beneficiary an

---

[38] The text reads as follows: "The law disposes only for the future; it shall have no retroactive effect."

[39] G. Treves, *loc. cit.*, footnote 36, p. 99.

[40] On this subject, C. Mortati, Vol. I, *loc. cit.*, footnote 3, pp. 350, 366; Vol. II (1976) p. 738; A. M. Sandulli, *Manuale*, Vol. I, *loc. cit.*, footnote 7, pp. 93 *et seq.*; G. Treves, *loc. cit.*, footnote 36, p. 99.

[41] G. Treves, *loc. cit.*, footnote 36, p. 99; G. Landi, G. Potenza, *loc. cit.*, footnote 8, p. 22; *cf.* also on this subject CdS, Sez. IV, Decision of April 30, 1955, No. 297; Cons. Stato 1955, I, p. 440; CdS, Sez. VI, Decision of July 11, 1956, No. 508, Cons. Stato 1956, I, p. 1002; G. Grottanelli de Santi, *Profili costituzionali della irretroattività delle leggi*, Milan 1970, pp. 13 *et seq.*

[42] However, the retroactivity of those rules which provide for lesser punishment is permitted; on this subject, F. Sorrentino, "Le fonti del diritto," in G. Amato, A. Barbera, *Manuale di diritto pubblico*, Bologna 1984, pp. 127 *et seq.*, 156 *et seq.*

[43] G. Landi, G. Potenza, *loc. cit.*, footnote 8, p. 22 with further references.

[44] G. Grottanelli de Santi, *loc. cit.*, footnote 41, pp. 13 *et seq.*; F. Sorrentino, *loc. cit.*, footnote 42, p. 156 with further references.

[45] C. Cost., Decision of July 8, 1957, No. 118.

[46] G. Treves, *loc. cit.*, footnote 36, p. 100.

[47] *cf.* on this subject, G. Treves, *loc. cit.*, footnote 36, p. 100.

expectation (*aspettativa*) or a legitimate interest (*interesse legittimo*).[48] If, on the other hand, the previously applicable law has conferred on the beneficiary a *diritto quesito*, the latter cannot be adversely affected by a later law.[49] The facts on which the *diritto quesito* is based cannot therefore be assessed in a different way under the new system from that which obtained under the previously applicable law.[50] Thus, for example, the appointment of an official will remain valid even if the general terms of admission to the public services have changed.[51]

E. BELGIUM

I. GENERAL RECOGNITION OF THE PRINCIPLES

The principles of legal certainty and of the protection of legitimate expectations also play a crucial role in Belgian administrative law, especially in the context of the withdrawal and revocation of administrative acts, with the principle of legal certainty taking precedence.[1]

II. APPLICATION TO INDIVIDUAL CASES

1. Annulment of Administrative Decisions

The terminology used for the avoidance of administrative decisions essentially follows the distinction between "retrait" and "abrogation" which was developed by the French writers.[2] It should be observed here that the Flemish literature does not draw this distinction but follows the Dutch leading authors in using the uniform concept of "intrekking."[3]

---

[48] G. Landi, G. Potenza, *loc. cit.*, footnote 8, p. 23.

[49] G. Landi, G. Potenza, *loc. cit.*, footnote 8, p. 23. .

[50] On the difficulties in upholding this principle, *cf.* C. Mortati, Vol. I, *loc. cit.*, footnote 3, pp. 365 *et seq.*

[51] G. Treves, *loc. cit.*, footnote 36, p. 100.

[1] L. P. Suetens, "Algemene rechtsbeginselen en algemene beginselen van behoorlijk bestuur in het Belgisch administratief recht," *Tijdschrift voor bestuurswetenschappen en publiek recht* (T.v.B.) 1970, pp. 379, 387.

[2] *cf. e.g.* J. Dembour, *Droit administratif* (3rd ed., Liège 1978), Nos. 223 *et seq.*

[3] *cf.* A. Mast, L. Dujardin, *Overzicht van het Belgisch Administratief Recht* (9th ed., Gent 1984), No. 494.

As is the case in French law, the term "retrait" means a legal action by virtue of which an administrative authority annuls *ab initio* decisions taken by it,[4] whereas "abrogation" covers the annulment *ex nunc* of an administrative instrument.[5] The system of annulment as it applies in individual cases essentially follows the theory developed by the French Conseil d'Etat.[6] Thus the following distinction is drawn in relation to the "retrait":

(1) Administrative instruments which do not confer rights on third parties may be withdrawn if the administrative authority in question is of the opinion that the general interest so requires.[7]

(2) On grounds of legal certainty, lawful administrative acts conferring rights may not be revoked,[8] unless the relevant Act expressly provides for this possibility.[9]

(3) Unlawful administrative acts conferring rights may be withdrawn under certain conditions. On this subject, the courts endeavour to reconcile the principle of legal certainty, which conflicts with the questioning of vested rights, with the principle of compliance with the statute law, *i.e.* the concern of the public authorities to remove unlawful situations:

    (a) Withdrawal may be applied at all times, regardless of any applicable statute, if the administrative act was obtained by the beneficiary through deception or if the unlawfulness is so serious that the administrative act must be deemed to be non-existent.

    (b) Withdrawal may be applied if and in so far as a statutory rule contains an express provision to that effect.[10]

    (c) In the absence of a statutory provision to that effect, withdrawal may also be applied if it is decreed within the time limit

---

[4] J. Dembour, *loc. cit.*, footnote 2, No. 224; A. Mast, J. Dujardin, *loc. cit.*, footnote 3, No. 494.

[5] J. Dembour, *loc. cit.*, footnote 2, No. 223; for an extensive study on this subject, *cf.* P. Lewalle, "L'abrogation des actes administratifs unilatéraux," in Annales de la Faculté de Droit de Liège 1970, pp. 63 *et seq.*

[6] *cf.* in particular C.E. français, November 3, 1922, *Dame Cachet*, R.D.P. 1922, p. 522.

[7] A. Mast, J. Dujardin, *loc. cit.*, footnote 3, No. 494.

[8] A. Mast, J. Dujardin, *loc. cit.*, footnote 3, No. 494, referring to the Raad van State, Decisions Nos. 1339 and 1340 of March 3, 1952, *De Troyer*; No. 6091 of February 21, 1958, *Hubert*; No. 20561 of September 17, 1980, *C.G.R. Benelux*.

[9] J. Dembour, *loc. cit.*, footnote 2, No. 224(2); an example of such a rule is Article 86 of the Law relating to Communes.

[10] Thus, for example, Article 86 of the Law relating to Communes.

for bringing an action for annulment before the Conseil d'Etat or, where such an action has already been instituted, before the verdict is pronounced.[11]

In relation to the "abrogation," the following distinction is drawn:

(1) Administrative acts which have conferred no rights[12] may be revoked at all times with effect for the future.[13]

(2) Unlawful administrative acts conferring rights, which could be annulled by the Conseil d'Etat on the grounds of their unlawful nature, may be revoked *ex nunc* within the time limit for bringing an action for annulment.

Where an action has already been instituted, the *abrogation* may also be decreed up to the date on which the verdict is pronounced.[14]

(3) The *abrogation* of a lawful administrative act conferring rights is contrary to the principle, derived from the legal certainty rule, of the inviolable nature of the effects on individuals of administrative action (*principe de l'intangibilité des effets individuels des actes administratifs*).[15]

2. Retroactivity of Administrative Decisions and Rules

In Belgian administrative law, as under the French system, the rule derived from the principle of legal certainty applies, which prohibits the retrospective effect of administrative acts—which in Belgium also include regulations (*actes réglementaires*).[16,17] This entails that, in

---

[11] A. Mast, J. Dujardin, *loc. cit.*, footnote 3, No. 494; J. Dembour, *loc. cit.*, footnote 2, No. 224(3); for established case law, *cf. e.g.* Conseil d'Etat Decision of June 6, 1969, *de Lannoy*, reproduced in R.J.D.A. 1970, p. 149.

[12] On this concept, *cf.* J. Dembour, *loc. cit.*, footnote 2, No. 210.

[13] J. Dembour, *loc. cit.*, footnote 2, No. 223(2).

[14] Conseil d'Etat, Decision of April 22, 1964, *Piron*, A.A.C.E. (Recueil des arrêts et avis du Conseil d'Etat—Section d'administration statuant au contentieux), p. 375; J. Dembour, *loc. cit.*, footnote 2, No. 223(2).

[15] J. Dembour, *loc. cit.*, footnote 2, No. 223(2), with reference to J. M. Auby, "L'abrogation des actes administratifs," A.J.D.A. 1967, pp. 131, 138.

[16] J. Dembour, *loc. cit.*, footnote 2.

[17] Established case law, *cf. e.g.* Conseil d'Etat, Decision of March 13, 1950. *Vanhaeverbeke*, R.J.D.A., p. 129; Decision of January 3, 1968, *A.S.B.L. Enseignement moyen de l'évêché de Liège*, A.A.C.E. p. 5; *cf.* also J. Dembour, *loc. cit.*, footnote 2, No. 218; for an

principle, administrative acts can produce no legal effects in relation to the period which precedes their entry into force (*i.e.* their promulgation or publication).[18] This non-retroactivity rule is not based on Article 2 of the Civil Code, since this provision applies only to the interpretation of laws.[19]

3. Recovery of Wrongly Levied Duties

Claims by the citizen against the State for the recovery of charges, taxes or customs duties wrongly levied are governed by the principles applying to the restitution of monies wrongly acquired (Articles 1235, 1376 and 1377 Civil Code) unless different rules are contained in special legislation.[20] In Belgium the latter is normally the case under tax legislation, which means that the general private law provisions apply in the first place in actions for the recovery of customs duties wrongly levied. Whilst the majority of special provisions of tax law lay down shorter limitation periods for claims for recovery, the general limitation period for bringing actions on grounds of the unjustified acquisition of monies amounts to 30 years. For this type of action jurisdiction is vested in the civil courts, which are not however bound by the expiry of the time limit for challenging administrative acts which applies to actions brought before the Conseil d'Etat. Thus here also, the enforcement of claims for recovery is not restricted in time by the date on which the tax decision becomes formally effective, but only by the expiry of the limitation period.

F. DENMARK

In Danish law, legal certainty is considered to be one of the ideas which

---

extensive study, *cf.* P. Lewalle, *Contribution à l'étude de l'application des actes adminsitratifs unilatéraux dans le temps*, Liège 1975, pp. 135 *et seq.*, 179 *et seq.*

[18] J. Dembour, *loc. cit.*, footnote 2, No. 218, which on this subject refers to the French literature and case law (also footnote 4).

[19] J. Dembour, *loc. cit.*, footnote 2, No. 218; for a different view, *cf.* M. Somerhausen, "Les principes généraux du droit administratif, in *Perspectivas del Derecho Público en la segunda mitad del siglo XX, Festschrift für Enrique Sayagues-Laso*, Vol. IV, Madrid 1969, pp. 463, 480.

[20] *cf.* on this subject and what follows, C. A. Gouthier, "Landesbericht Belgien," in *La restitution de taxes perçues indûment par l'Etat*, Geneva 1976, pp. 77 *et seq.*; K. E. Huthmacher, *Der Vorrang des Gemeinschaftsrechts bei indirekten Kollisionen*, Köln/Berlin/Bonn/München 1985, pp. 264 *et seq.*; P. Karpenstein, "Zur Wiedergutmachung

lie at the root of the democratic system. However, it is not recognised as constituting a general legal principle of such a stature as to give rise to certain requirements with which the legislature and the administration are to comply.[1] Thus the Danish constitution, the Grundlov, does not prohibit the retroactivity of legislation.[2]

Although the principles regarding the protection of vested rights and of legitimate expectations do not enjoy the status of general legal principles in this country, those involved in Danish law are well acquainted with their underlying ideas, their purpose being achieved through other rules. Thus certain rights to compensation on grounds of the loss of vested rights or actions infringing legitimate expectations may arise from Article 73 of the Constitution, which regulates the question of compensation for expropriation, or from principles of tort liability.[3]

Generally applicable time limits for challenging administrative acts do not exist in Denmark.[4] In cases of State charges wrongly paid, the person affected has a claim for compensation which is subject to a limitation period of five years.[5] The ECJ decision in *Just*[6] shows how difficult it can be actually to obtain compensation, because the Danish courts award such claims only where the person affected has not "passed on" the wrongly paid taxes to others.

Where, conversely, State benefits have been wrongly paid, it is especially the Danish provisions adopted in implementation of E.C. agricultural law which lay down special rules.[7] Unless there are separate rules governing the right to recovery, the general principles relating to the *condictio indebiti* apply. As is the case in the United Kingdom, Danish law draws a distinction between errors which concern facts and those which concern the legal implications. Here too, it may be relevant to probe the question whether the recipient may legitimately expect to

---

von Vertragsverstössen der Mitgliedstaaten gegen das Gemeinschaftsrecht," DVB1. 1977, pp. 61 *et seq.*

[1] J. K. Skadhauge, "Danish report on general principles derived from the law of Member States as source of Community law and national law," Danish Report for the 12th F.I.D.E. Conference, Paris 1986, pp. 75, 86.

[2] *Ibid.*

[3] *Ibid.*

[4] *cf.* on this subject: K. E. Huthmacher, *Der Vorrang des Gemeinschaftsrechts bei indirekten Kollisionen*, Köln/Berlin/Bonn/München 1985, p. 270.

[5] In accordance with the Danish Law No. 274 of December 22, 1908.

[6] E.C.J. Case 68/79 *Just* v. *Danish Ministry for Fiscal Affairs* [1980] E.C.R. 501; *cf.* on this subject also P. Germer, "National Report for Denmark," in J.-V. Louis, *Régime juridique des relations entre les opérations économiques et les organismes d'exécution du droit communautaire*, stencilled report, Brussels 1982, p. 244 (259).

[7] On this subject and on what follows, P. Germer, *loc. cit.*, footnote 6, pp. 254 *et seq.*

retain the benefit. The Danish courts, however, have shown a certain degree of reluctance to recognise the protection of legitimate expectations against the statute law.[8] These claims are also subject to a five-year limitation period, unless special legislation provides otherwise.

G. GREECE

The revocation of unlawful administrative measures imposing burdens,[1] in the sense of annulment *ex tunc*, is permitted at all times, and is even legally compulsory in certain cases.[2]

In relation to unlawful administrative acts conferring benefits, revocation is possible only when decreed within a "reasonable" period, unless the unlawful nature of the measure can be attributed to the intentional behaviour of the beneficiary or where the revocation is necessary in the public interest.[3]

Lawful administrative acts imposing burdens may at all times be revoked (annulment *ex nunc*), whereas lawful acts conferring benefits may be revoked with effect for the future only where the possibility of revocation is specified in the administrative act or in the law, or if it is necessary to do so in the public interest.[4]

Apart from the provisions in the Constitution prohibiting retroactivity for criminal legislation (Article 7(1)) and for tax legislation (Article 78(2)), the Greek Constitution imposes no restrictions whatsoever on the legislator in this field. Nor is it possible to derive a general rule prohibiting retroactivity from Article 77(2) of the Constitution, under which laws (with the exception of laws of interpretation) take effect only on the date of their promulgation, since this provision is addressed in the first instance to those called upon to apply the law.[5] Although Article 2 of the

---

[8] *cf.* C. Boye Jacobsen, "National Report for Denmark," 12th FIDE Conference, Paris 1986, Vol. II, p. 101 (103 *et seq.*).

[1] Following the French example, the Greek concept of administrative measures includes, in addition to individual measures, also legal rules issued by the administration. Hereafter, the notion of "administrative measure" will concern only individual measures.

[2] P. Dagtoglou, "Verfassung und Verwaltung," in K.-D. Groth (ed.), *Südosteuropa-Handbuch*, Vol. III, Greece, Göttingen 1980, pp. 13, 45.

[3] *Ibid.*

[4] *Ibid.*

[5] For an extensive study of this subject, *cf.* J. Iliopoulos-Strangas, *Rückwirkung und Sofortwirkung von Gesetzen—Eine verfassungsrechtliche Untersuchung unter Berücksichtigung des deutschen und griechischen Steuerrechts*, Baden-Baden 1986, p. 189.

Civil Code states that laws take effect for the future and have no retrospective effect, this provision, being a rule contained in an ordinary law, is not binding upon the legislature but merely on the courts and the executive.[6] Recently, the Greek Council of State, for the purpose of assessing retrospective legislation, has applied, in addition to the constitutional principles, the rule relating to the protection of legitimate expectations. Thus any infringement of the principle of the protection of legitimate expectations is held to be legitimate only on grounds of public interest.[7]

The repayment of duties wrongly levied is governed by the principles which apply to the repayment of monies wrongly acquired, unless special legislative provisions provide otherwise.[8] Claims of this nature are to be instituted before the civil courts and are subject to a 20-year limitation period. Although Greece has its separate system of administrative courts, before which the time limit for challenging administrative acts is 60 days, this deadline does not affect the enforcement of claims on grounds of monies wrongly acquired.

H. IRELAND

As is the case in British law, neither legal certainty nor the protection of legitimate expectations are recognised as constituting general legal principles. As in the United Kingdom, account is certainly taken of the protection of legitimate expectations in the context of the requirement that court proceedings be lawfully conducted, in particular the guarantee of a fair hearing.[1] This applies, for example, in cases of the revocation of permits. However, the principle is not explicitly recognised as such.

Article 15(5) of the Irish Constitution prohibits the retroactivity of criminal legislation.[2] Although this provision is expressly restricted to the criminal law, the Irish courts tend to oppose the "injurious retrospection" of statutes.[3] However, this does not amount to a general rule prohibiting the retroactivity of statutes imposing burdens. Instead, retroactivity is

---

[6] J. Iliopoulos-Strangas, *loc. cit.*, footnote 5, pp. 191 *et seq.*

[7] J. Iliopoulos-Strangas, *loc. cit.*, footnote 5, p. 201, containing further references.

[8] *cf.* on this subject, K. E. Huthmacher, *Der Vorrang des Gemeinschaftsrechts bei indirekten Kollisionen*, Köln/Berlin/Bonn/München, p. 267.

[1] *cf.* R. M. Stout, *Administrative Law in Ireland*, Dublin 1985, pp. 363 *et seq.*

[2] Article 15(5) of the Irish Constitution: "The Oireachtas shall not declare acts to be infringements of the law which were not so at the date of their commission."

[3] *cf.* on this subject, J. M. Kelly, *The Irish Constitution* (2nd ed., Dublin 1984), pp. 87 *et seq.*, containing further references to the case law.

considered permissible where it is explicitly provided or clearly intended by the legislature.[4] The retroactivity of statutory instruments is permissible whenever a parent statute expressly confers this power.[5]

In a case decided by the Supreme Court,[6] in which certain provisions of the 1967 income tax legislation were held to be unconstitutional and which concerned the scope in time of the decision as well as the financial implications of any claims for compensation which could arise, the highest Irish court relied in full on the reasoning of the ECJ in the second *Defrenne* case,[7] in particular Grounds of Judgment 71–75. In Ground 74, the Court had held that

> "as the general level at which pay would have been fixed cannot be known, important considerations of legal certainty affecting all the interests involved, both public and private, make it impossible to reopen the question as regards the past."

I. LUXEMBOURG

In the Luxembourg legal system, the principle of legal certainty is applied in the same manner as in French and Belgian administrative law. Here too, this rule plays a crucial part in the context of the retrospective revocation of administrative decisions (*retrait*) and of the retroactivity of laws.[1]

Under the established case law of the Luxembourg Conseil d'Etat, the retrospective revocation of defective or unlawful administrative acts conferring rights is permissible within the time limit provided for challenging the instrument in question before the administrative courts.[2]

---

[4] Thus, *e.g.* O'Byrne, J., in *Irish Land Commission* v. *Dolan*, [1930] I.R. 235; *cf.* also s.21(1)(c) of the Interpretation Act 1937.

[5] *cf.* 1(3) Seanad Resolution of 1978 on a Select Committee on Statutory Instruments, reproduced in R. M. Stout, *loc. cit.*, footnote 1, p. 51.

[6] *Murphy* v. *Attorney-General* [1982] I.R. 241.

[7] Judgment of April 8, 1976, Case 43/75 [1976] E.C.R. 455 at 480; *cf.* also on the *Murphy* case J. O'Reilly, "The Interaction between Community Law and National Law," Irish Report for the 12th FIDE Conference, Paris 1986, pp. 167, 177 *et seq.*

[1] *cf.* G. Wivenes, "Les principes généraux communs aux droits des Etats membres en tant que source du droit communautaire. Interaction entre droit communautaire et droit national," Luxembourg report for the 12th FIDE Conference, Paris 1986, pp. 215, 222.

[2] *cf. e.g.* C.E. lux., Decision of August 6, 1956, Bull. de doc. communale, No. 4, p. 26, Rec. C.E. 1956; Decision of December 17, 1975, Bull. de doc. communale, No. 16, p. 163, Rec. C.E. 1975; G. Wivenes, *loc. cit.*, footnote 1, p. 222.

The adoption of laws is subject to a rule prohibiting retroactivity (*principe de non-rétroactivité*) which is also derived from the principle of legal certainty. Here too, the courts have consistently held that, in the field of administrative law, neither laws nor the regulations adopted for their implementation may apply to the past, unless the legislature has expressly provided an exception to that effect.[3]

J. THE NETHERLANDS

I. GENERAL RECOGNITION OF THE PRINCIPLES

In the legal system of the Netherlands, the general principles of proper administration include the rule that the public authorities may not disappoint expectations raised by their actions.[1] This principle applies not only to all types of administrative action,[2] but also to the legislature.[3] In theoretical terms, this principle, which for some time now has been recognised by the courts,[4] in particular by the Centrale Raad van Beroep (CRvB), is derived from the notion of the rule of law.[5] However, opinions are divided on the question whether, and to what extent, a distinction must be drawn between the principle of legal certainty and that of the protection of legitimate expectations.[6] In the older case law, cases where

---

[3] *cf.* C.E. lux, Decision of June 13, 1978, Rec. C.E. 1978; G. Wivenes, *loc. cit.*, footnote 1, pp. 222 *et seq.*, containing further references.

[1] *Rapport van de Commissie inzake algemene bepalingen van administratief recht (Rapport ABAR)* (5th ed., Alphen a/d Rijn 1984), p. 187; A. M. Donner, *Nederlands Bestuursrecht, Algemeen Deel* (4th ed., Alphen a/d Rijn 1974), p. 104; M. Scheltema, "Enkele gedachten over het vertrouwensbeginsel in het publiek recht," RMT (Rechtsgeleerd Magazijn Themis) (1984), p. 538; S. Prechal, T. Heukels, "Algemene beginselen in het Nederlandse recht en het Europese recht: rechtsvergelijking en interactie," SEW 1986, pp. 287, 293; J. Mertens de Wilmars, "De Europese Gemeenschappen en het Administratief Recht," SEW 1962, pp. 660, 677; an extensive survey of the relevant literature and case law can be found in the Opinion of Advocate-General M. R. Mok of the Hoge Raad (HR), Decision of June 23, 1982, AB (Administratiefrechterlijke Beslissingen) 1982, p. 121.

[2] *cf.* M. R. Mok, *loc. cit.*, footnote 1, p. 121.

[3] M. Scheltema, *loc. cit.*, footnote 1, p. 543.

[4] *cf., e.g.* CRvB (Centrale Raad van Beroep), decision of October 2, 1951, AA (Ars Aequi) II, p. 116; Decisions of October 28, 1952, December 16, 1952, and December 30, 1952, AA III, pp. 44 *et seq.*, with annotation by A. M. Donner.

[5] M. Scheltema, *loc. cit.*, footnote 1, pp. 545 *et seq.*

[6] *cf.* on this subject, *ABAR Report*, *loc. cit.*, footnote 1, pp. 188 *et seq.*

rights were changed to their beneficiaries' disadvantage (*e.g.* reductions in public service pay) were invariably assigned to the principle of legal certainty.[7] By certain authors the rule of the protection of legitimate expectations is considered to derive from the legal certainty principle. Others advocate drawing a distinction between the two, on the basis that both principles have different objectives. Others still are of the opinion that the principle of the protection of legitimate expectations leaves no room for a separate principle of legal certainty.[8] In the most recent decisions of the judicial section of the Raad van State, both principles are used virtually interchangeably.[9] This has reduced the relevance of the theoretical debate on the desirability of a distinction.

The question of when a legitimate expectation has been raised and in what circumstances it is capable of protection cannot be answered in general terms. The case law has developed a number of criteria which may assist in finding an answer[10]:

(a) the expectation must have been raised by an action on the part of the authority within whose power the matter in question falls. An exception to this rule arises where the person affected could reasonably be expected to rely upon the appearance that the authority had this power.

(b) the following are regarded as the recognised sources of legitimate expectation: administrative dispositions, contracts, commitments, information and administrative regulations (*pseudo-wetgeving*) governed by public law.[11]

(c) the degree of care displayed by the person affected in establishing the basis for the expectation is subject to average requirements, taking into account different levels of ability.

(d) a further consideration is the extent to which the expectations raised by the authority prompted the action by the person affected. This has to be taken into account where the person in

---

[7] *cf.* the references to the case law in the *ABAR Report, loc. cit.*, footnote 1, p. 189 footnote 167 *et seq.*, and in A. M. Donner, *loc. cit.*, footnote 1, p. 103 footnote 1.

[8] On the state of affairs in this debate, *cf. ABAR Report, loc. cit.*, footnote 1, with numerous references.

[9] *cf.* AR (Afdeling Rechtspraak van de Raad van State), Decisions of May 17, 1982, May 13, 1985 and May 24, 1982, De Gemeentestem 6729.

[10] *ABAR Report, loc. cit.*, footnote 1, p. 190.

[11] *cf.* also M. Scheltema, *loc. cit.*, footnote 1, p. 539; S. Prechal, T. Heukels, *loc. cit.*, footnote 1, p. 294.

question made certain arrangements in the light of these expectations. This so-called "arrangements factor" is a necessary condition if the object of the exercise is to succeed in protecting the legitimate expectation *contra legem*.

(e) in individual cases, vital public interests may lead to a denial of the individual's otherwise legitimate expectations.[12]

II. APPLICATION TO INDIVIDUAL CASES

1. Action by the Administration

(a) Annulment of administrative decisions

No terminological distinction is drawn between revocation and withdrawal. Both are covered by the term "intrekking." Where the public authority takes administrative decisions, the rights which are thereby conferred on the addressee are in principle inviolable.[13] Under certain conditions, however, it is possible to revoke them or to change them subsequently. Here too, this involves striking the right balance between the conflicting principles of lawfulness and legal certainty, *i.e.* deciding which of these two principles may claim priority in individual cases.[14]

(aa) Annulment of lawful administrative decisions conferring benefits

In principle, the "intrekking" *ex tunc* of lawful administrative decisions conferring benefits on the basis of a subsequent change in administrative practice or in the underlying situation is impossible on grounds of legal certainty.[15] Even annulment *ex nunc* is possible only by way of exception. Such an exception may apply if, at the time of revocation—*i.e.* after the underlying situation had changed[16]—the administrative decision in

---

[12] *cf.* on this point also *ABAR Report*, *loc. cit.*, footnote 1, pp. 196 *et seq.*
[13] *ABAR Report*, *loc. cit.*, footnote 1, p. 191; A. M. Donner, *loc. cit.*, footnote 1, p. 266.
[14] *cf.* P. de Haan, Th. G. Drupsteen, R. Fernhout, *Bestuursrecht in de sociale Rechtsstaat* (2nd ed., Deventer 1978), p. 283; A. M. Donner, *loc. cit.*, footnote 1, p. 266.
[15] *cf.* P. de Haan, Th. G. Drupsteen, R. Fernhout, *loc. cit.*, footnote 14, p. 284, with reference to M. Scheltema, "Gebondenheid van overheid en burgers aan eigen voorafgaand handelen," VAR (Vereniging voor Administratief Recht)—Geschrift LXXIV (1975), p. 20; S. Prechal, T. Heukels, *loc. cit.*, footnote 1, p. 295.
[16] S. Prechal, T. Heukels, *loc. cit.*, footnote 1, p. 295 (footnote 72).

question could have been refused and the public interest takes precedence over the interests of the individual affected.[17] In addition, compensation may, where appropriate, be payable.

(bb) Annulment of unlawful administrative decisions conferring benefits

In principle, unlawful conduct on the part of the addressee warrants the annulment of an administrative act conferring benefits, even retrospectively.[18]

Various special laws confer explicit powers of corrective annulment.[19] Under these provisions, the conditions for annulment are met if the information supplied by the beneficiary is so incorrect or incomplete that his application would have resulted in a different decision had the true and complete information been available at the time of considering this application.[20] In the case of administrative decisions with long-term effects, the beneficiary may under certain conditions be under an obligation to inform the authorities of a change of circumstances. Failure to fulfil this obligation may result in annulment with retrospective effect going back to the time at which the change occurred.[21]

The power to annul need not, however, be expressly stated in a statute.[22] Even in the absence thereof, the revocation of an unlawful administrative decision *ex tunc* is permissible if its unlawful nature is attributable to culpable behaviour on the part of the beneficiary and the decision would not have been taken had the true relevant facts been available.[23] An exception is made in cases where the beneficiary cannot be accused of culpable behaviour and the annulment of the decision would cause him disproportionate damage.[24] In such cases it is also possible to maintain the administrative decision with effect for the future.[25]

---

[17] P. de Haan, Th. G. Drupsteen, R. Fernhout, *loc. cit.*, footnote 14, p. 285; M. Scheltema, "Gebondenheid," *loc. cit.*, footnote 15, p. 25.

[18] *ABAR Report, loc. cit.*, footnote 1, p. 220.

[19] *e.g.* Article 9 of the Law relating to Imports/Exports; Article 98 of the General Regulations relating to State Officials, Article 12(a) of the Law relating to Aliens.

[20] *cf. ABAR Report, loc. cit.*, footnote 1, p. 221.

[21] CRvB, Decision of December 19, 1977, Dutch Official Journal 1978, p. 285; KB (Koninklijk Besluit) of June 23, 1978, Dutch Official Journal 1979, p. 9.

[22] CBB (College van Beroep voor net Bedrijfsleven), Decision of December 27, 1977, Dutch Official Journal 1978, p. 334.

[23] *cf. ABAR Report, loc. cit.*, footnote 1, pp. 220 *et seq.*

[24] *ABAR Report, loc. cit.*, footnote 1, p. 221; CRvB, Decision of February 18, 1975, Dutch Official Journal 1976, p. 68.

[25] *Ibid.*

The opportunities for annulment are considerably restricted where the responsibility for the unlawful nature of the decision lies with the administrative authority. In such cases, the applicable rule is that the decision may not be revoked retrospectively if the beneficiary was entitled to rely upon the lawful nature of the decision.[26] On the other hand, annulment *ex nunc* is in principle possible.[27] This rule, however, also admits of exceptions where the beneficiary would suffer disproportionate damage as a result of such an annulment.[28]

(b) Recovery of State benefits wrongly paid

The recovery of benefits wrongly paid is subject to the same ground rules as those which apply to the annulment of administrative decisions conferring benefits.[29] Thus, for example, under the legal system which applies to State officials, the right of the administration to recover an excess amount paid in salaries is not recognised by the courts on grounds of legal certainty.[30] In the law relating to pensions (Article 132 Pensions Act), the recovery of excess amounts paid is possible in cases where the recipient had intentionally caused the overpayment by supplying incorrect information. The same approach is observed in the field of social security.[31]

(c) Recovery of wrongly levied duties

As is the case in Germany, the recovery of duties wrongly levied by the State, such as taxes and customs duties, is impossible once the time limit for bringing a challenge, which in most cases is 30 days, has expired. The

---

[26] cf. *ABAR Report, loc. cit.*, footnote 1, p. 223; A. M. Donner, *loc. cit.*, footnote 1, p. 226; P. de Haan, Th. G. Drupsteen, R. Fernhout, *loc. cit.*, footnote 14, p. 283; also the case law, *cf., e.g.* KB of June 4, 1976, Dutch Official Journal 1976, p. 182; KB of November 29, 1979, Dutch Official Journal 1980, p. 177.

[27] *ABAR Report, loc. cit.*, footnote 1, p. 224.

[28] *ABAR Report, loc. cit.*, footnote 1, p. 225, with reference to CRvB, Decision of November 24, 1971, Dutch Official Journal 1972, p. 269.

[29] cf. A. M. Donner, *loc. cit.*, footnote 1, p. 265.

[30] A. M. Donner, *loc. cit.*, footnote 1, pp. 265 *et seq.*, with reference to CRvB, Decision of March 23, 1937, Dutch Official Journal 1937, p. 497.

[31] A. M. Donner, *loc. cit.*, footnote 1, p. 266.

legal effectiveness of the decision imposing burdens is unaffected by the general action for recovery.[32]

2. Legislation—Retroactivity of Statutes and Regulations

Article 16 of the Netherlands Constitution contains a rule explicitly prohibiting the retroactivity of criminal legislation. Apart from this, there is no general bar on retroactivity. Even the rule contained in Article 88 of the Constitution, under which laws enter into effect only after their promulgation, docs not prevent the legislature from giving retrospective effect to a legislative provision.[33]

The Centrale Raad van Beroep (CRvB) initially derived a general rule prohibiting the retroactivity of regulations from Article 4 of the Law[34] containing the general principles applicable to the legislation of the Kingdom.[35] Although the wording of this provision appears to be clear, it cannot give rise to a general rule prohibiting retroactivity[36] since, according to the CRvB's interpretation, this prohibition would also have to have been applied to those regulations which retrospectively confer benefits on the citizen.[37] More recently, however, the CRvB, like the other courts,[38] has adopted the practice of assessing regulations directly in the light of the principle of legal certainty.[39] Thus a provision imposing a reduction in pensions was held to be invalid only to the extent to which it worked retrospectively and consequently infringed legal certainty.

The applicability of the principles of the protection of legitimate expectations and of legal certainty does not give rise in this context to a

---

[32] J. S. Buiting, "National Report Netherlands," in *La restitution de taxes perçues indûment par l'Etat*, Geneva 1976, pp. 159 *et seq.*; K. E. Huthmacher, *Der Vorrang des Gemeinschaftsrechts bei indirekten Kollisionen*, Köln/Berlin/Bonn/München 1985, pp. 259 *et seq.*

[33] *cf.* C. A. J. M. Kortmann, *De Grondwetsherziening*, Deventer 1983, p. 248; M. Scheltema, *loc. cit.*, footnote 1, p. 541.

[34] *Wet houdende algemene bepalingen der wetgeving in het Koninkrijk* of April 24, 1852, Article 4: "The law is binding only for the future and has no retroactive effect."

[35] CRvB, Decision of October 31, 1935, Dutch Official Journal 1936, p. 168; Decision of April 3, 1963, Dutch Official Journal 1964, p. 75.

[36] C. W. van der Pot, *Handboek van het Nederlands Staatsrecht*, revised by A. M. Donner (11th ed.), Zwolle 1983, p. 445, containing further references.

[37] M. Scheltema, *loc. cit.*, footnote 1, p. 541.

[38] *cf. e.g.* HR (Hoge Raad) Decision of March 7, 1979, NJ (Nederlandse Jurisprudentie) 1979, p. 319.

[39] *cf.* CRvB Decision of October 20, 1983, Dutch Official Journal 1984, p. 100 with annotation by v. Eijck; *cf.* however also the case law of the Judicial Section of the Raad van State, *cf.* on this subject M. Scheltema, *loc. cit.*, footnote 1, p. 543.

comprehensive ban on retroactivity. Thus the CRvB also holds retrospective provisions to be permissible where the formal legislator explicitly so provides.[40] Nor does the principle of the protection of legitimate expectations preclude legislative amendments with effect for the future.[41]

K. PORTUGAL

The principle of legal certainty (*princípio da segurança*, or *certeza nas relações jurídicas*) is recognised in Portuguese law.[1]

In relation to the revocation of administrative acts, the term *revogação* is used. Revocation is defined as the subsequent removal (*extinção*), either wholly or in part, of the effects caused by an unlawful or inappropriate administrative act.[2]

With respect to revocation, a distinction is made according to whether

(a) it is made by the authorities on their own initiative (*revogação oficiosa*) or as a result of an application to that effect,

(b) it is pronounced by the authority which issued the administrative act, or by some other authority,

(c) it is based on the unlawfulness or only on the inappropriate nature of the measure, and

(d) it takes effect for the future (*revogação abrogatória*) or for the past (*revogação anulatória*).[3]

Administrative acts which are lawful but inappropriate may be revoked only *ex nunc*, whereas unlawful acts may also be revoked *ex tunc*.[4] Administrative acts which establish rights may not, in principle, be revoked, for reasons of the protection of legitimate expectations (*principio geral da protecção da confiança*) or of the recognition of vested rights (*respeito pelos direitos adquiridos*), unless they are unlaw-

---

[40] M. Scheltema, *loc. cit.*, footnote 1, p. 541, with reference to CRvB, Decision of December 11, 1980, Dutch Official Journal 1981, p. 200, with annotation by van der Net.

[41] M. Scheltema, *loc. cit.*, footnote 1, p. 544.

[1] *cf.* D. Freitas do Amaral, *Direito Administrativo*, Vol. III, Lisbon 1985, p. 346, 353.

[2] M. Esteves de Oliveira, *Direito Administrativo*, Vol. I Coimbra 1984, pp. 603 *et seq.*; additional definitions, mostly on similar lines, in M. Caetano, *Direito Administrativo*, Vol. I, (10th ed., Coimbra 1984), pp. 531 *et seq.*; D. Freitas do Amaral, *loc. cit.*, footnote 1, p. 327.

[3] D. Freitas do Amaral, *loc. cit.*, footnote 1, pp. 334 *et seq.*

[4] D. Freitas do Amaral, *loc. cit.*, footnote 1, p. 339.

ful.[5] On the other hand, administrative acts which do not establish any rights may be revoked at any time.[6] Administrative acts are said to establish rights if they confer new subjective rights on another person, extend existing subjective rights or remove restrictions on the exercise of existing rights.[7]

Unlawful administrative acts which establish rights may be revoked by the authority which made the measure or by a superior organ either within the time limit laid down by the relevant legislation for making the challenge, or until such time as the challenge is made.[8] Depending on whether the administrative act has been issued by a local authority or by the central administration, the statutory time limit is between three and twelve months.[9]

It is a general principle both of public and of private law that laws may not apply retrospectively, unless they constitute rules of interpretation.[10] In addition to a specific prohibition of retroactivity in respect of criminal legislation (Article 29), the 1976 Constitution[11] also features a non-retroactivity rule for laws imposing burdens. Thus Article 18(3) of the Constitution stipulates that "Laws which restrict rights, freedoms and guarantees must be of a general and abstract character, and may neither apply retrospectively nor restrict the extent or the scope of the essential contents of the provisions of the constitution."

L. SPAIN

I. GENERAL RECOGNITION OF THE PRINCIPLES

In principle, the legal certainty rule (*seguridad jurídica*),[1] the principle

---

[5] D. Freitas do Amaral, *loc. cit.*, footnote 1, p. 348.
[6] Article 18, No. 1, Law relating to the Supreme Administrative Court (*Lei Orgânica do Supremo Tribunal Administrativo—LOSTA*): D. Freitas do Amaral, *loc. cit.*, footnote 1, p. 348.
[7] D. Freitas do Amaral, *loc. cit.*, footnote 1, p. 349.
[8] Article 83 No. 2, 357 and 411 Administrative Code (*Código Administrativo*); Article 18 No. 2 LOSTA (*cf.* footnote 6), *cf.* on this subject M. Caetano, *loc. cit.*, footnote 2; M. Esteves de Oliveira, *loc. cit.*, footnote 2, p. 608; D. Freitas do Amaral, *loc. cit.*, footnote 1, pp. 358 *et seq.*
[9] D. Freitas do Amaral, *loc. cit.*, footnote 1, pp. 361 *et seq.*
[10] M. Caetano, *loc. cit.*, footnote 2, p. 139.
[11] In the revised version of 1982.
[1] *cf.* F. Garrido Falla, *Tratado de Derecho Administrativo*, Vol. I (General Section) (9th ed., Madrid 1985), p. 407; E. García de Enterría, T. R. Fernández, *Curso de Derecho Administrativo I* (4th ed., Madrid 1984), p. 603.

of good faith (*buena fe*)[2] and the observance of vested rights (*derechos adquiridos*)[3] are all recognised in Spanish administrative law. Indeed, the legal certainty rule has, since 1978, enjoyed constitutional status. In addition to other fundamental principles relating to the rule of law, Article 9(3) of the 1978 Constitution expressly guarantees legal certainty.

II. APPLICATION TO INDIVIDUAL CASES

1. Action by the Administration—Annulation of Administrative
    Decisions

As regards the avoidance of administrative decisions, Spanish law draws a distinction between "anulación" and "revocación." The exact meaning of these concepts is subject to a variety of opinions. Some authors use the term *anulación* where the administrative act has been revoked by the same authority which had issued it, and apply the term *revocación* to cases where the avoidance is pronounced by a superior authority.[4] Others are of the opinion that, regardless of the authority which decrees it, "anulación" relates to the avoidance of those measures which were already defective at the time when they were issued, whereas the term "revocación" applies to those administrative acts which have become unlawful or inappropriate as a result of subsequent circumstances.[5] The prevailing view, supported by the decided cases, makes a distinction according to whether the avoidance was pronounced on the basis of the unlawfulness of the administrative acts—in which case the term "anulación" is used—or whether it was decreed on grounds of inappropriateness—in which case the term "revocación" applies.[6] It is this distinction which will be observed here.

---

[2] Tribunal Supremo, Decision of March 31, 1975; *cf.* also R. Entrena Cuesta, *Curso de Derecho Administrativo*, Vol. I (8th ed., Madrid 1983), p. 156.
[3] E. Garcïa de Enterrïa, T. R. Fernándes, *loc. cit.*, footnote 1, p. 602.
[4] *cf.* R. Entrena Cuesta, *loc. cit.*, footnote 2, p. 254.
[5] *Ibid.*
[6] R. Entrena Cuesta, *loc. cit.*, footnote 2, p. 255; F. Garrido Falla, *loc. cit.*, footnote 1, pp. 719 *et seq.*; Tribunal Supremo, Decision of April 21, 1961.

(a) Revocación

In seeking to ascertain whether the administration may on its own initiative revoke lawful administrative acts whose effects conflict with the public interest, it must be established first of all whether the act in question confers rights on the addressee or on third parties, or whether it has formed the basis for a judicial decision. Where neither circumstance applies, there is nothing to prevent the "revocación" from being decreed.[7] If, however, one of these conditions is fulfilled, the principle of irrevocability applies.[8]

Article 16 of the *Reglamento de Servicios de las Corporaciones locales* forms an exception to this principle. This provision confers on the authority in question the opportunity to decree the "revocación" of an authorisation if it establishes new criteria which determine what constitutes the public interest. If the authority uses this power, it is obliged to pay compensation to the recipient of the authorisation.

(b) Anulación

As in the case of "revocación," a distinction is also made here between administrative acts establishing rights and those which do not do so. If the administrative act confers no rights on the addressee, there is nothing to prevent the avoidance from being decreed on legal grounds, regardless of whether the administrative authority was acting on its own initiative or as a result of an administrative complaint (*recurso*).[9]

In relation to administrative acts establishing rights, however, it is necessary to establish whether the "anulación" was pronounced by the relevant authority on its own initiative or in response to an administrative complaint. If a complaint has been lodged, the authority in question may in principle revoke the unlawful administrative measure. However, in the case of "anulación de oficio," the rights conferred by the administrative

---

[7] *cf.* Article 369, *Ley de Régimen Jurídico de la Administración del Estado* (L.R.J.); Article 27, 1 L.R.J.; Articles 109 and 110 *Ley de Procedimiento Administrativo*; *cf.* also F. Garrido Falla, *loc. cit.*, footnote 1, pp. 723 *et seq.*; R. Entrena Cuesta, *loc. cit.*, footnote 2, p. 255; J. González Pérez, "La revocación de los actos administrativos en la jurisprudencia española," Revista de Administración Pública, 1950, pp. 149, 361.

[8] F. Garrido Falla, *loc. cit.*, footnote 1, p. 724; *cf.* also R. Entrena Cuesta. *loc. cit.*, footnote 2, p. 255.

[9] R. Entrena Cuesta, *loc. cit.*, footnote 2, p. 256.

act on the addressee must be taken into consideration for reasons of legal certainty.[10]

The essential rules which apply in the case of "anulación de oficio" are contained in Articles 109 *et seq.* of the Law relating to Administrative procedure (*Ley de Procedimiento Administrativo (L.P.A.)*).

Under this system, the administration may at all times rectify errors of fact and of calculation (Article 111).[11]

The administration may also, subject to a prior opinion by the Consejo de Estado in which it indicates its consent, declare an administrative act void (*acto nulo de pleno derecho*) (Article 109 L.P.A.). Unlawful administrative acts which are not null and void are merely voidable. In their case, it must be established whether the unlawfulness is obvious (*manifiesto*) or not. If the latter is the case, the "ilegalidad ordinaria" will apply. Where on the other hand the unlawfulness is obvious, in the sense that it does not have to be concluded by interpretation beforehand but is clearly and indisputably[12] apparent merely by comparing the administrative act with the legislative provision,[13] the administrative authority may decree the "anulación" after a consenting prior opinion by the Consejo de Estado and subject to a time limit of four years (Article 110(2) L.P.A.).[14]

If the unlawfulness is not obvious, the administrative act may not be revoked by the relevant authority on its own initiative, even where the Consejo de Estado has established its unlawful nature. Under current legislation, revocation requires both a statement that the administrative act is prejudicial to the public interest, and a challenge brought before the administrative courts (Article 110(1) L.P.A.). This procedure is conducted over two stages. In the first, the administrative authority declares that the administrative act endangers the public interest, Here, too, the applicable time limit is four years. During the second stage, a challenge must be brought before the relevant administrative court within a period of two months of the said declaration.[15] It is the latter court which will then decide whether or not the "anulación" of the challenged decision should be pronounced.

---

[10] *Ibid.*; *cf.* also E. Garcïa de Enterrïa, T. R. Fernández, *loc. cit.*, footnote 1, pp. 602 *et seq.*
[11] *cf.* also Tribunal Supremo, Decision of March 15, 1971.
[12] Tribunal Supremo, Decision of April 6, 1963.
[13] Tribunal Supremo, Decision of January 26, 1961.
[14] *cf.* on this subject F. Garrido Falla, *loc. cit.*, footnote 1, p. 731; Garcïa de Enterrïa, T. R. Fernández, *loc. cit.*, footnote 1, p. 607; R. Entrena Cuesta, *loc. cit.*, footnote 2, p. 259.
[15] *cf.* on this subject F. Garrido Falla, *loc. cit.*, footnote 1, pp. 731 *et seq.*; E. Garcïa de Enterrïa, T.-R. Fernández, *loc. cit.*, footnote 1, pp. 606 *et seq.*; R. Entrena Cuesta, *loc. cit.*, footnote 2, p. 259.

2. Legislation—Retroactivity of Statutes and Regulations

Article 2(3) of the *Código civil* states: "Laws shall have no retroactive effect unless they state otherwise." As is the case under French law,[16] this provision constitutes a rule of interpretation: if a law contains no express instruction, it must be accepted that it can have no retrospective effect whatsoever. Laws may confer retroactivity upon themselves without being subject to any restriction.[17] However, the present Constitution, which took effect in 1978, has made this extremely wide-ranging rule of interpretation subject to certain limitations. Thus Article 9(3) of the Constitution contains the principle of "the non-retroactivity (*irretroactividad*) of rules which have an unfavourable or restrictive effect on the rights of individuals."[18] The term "rules" is taken as meaning legal rules of any type.

---

[16] *cf.* Article 2 *Code Civil*, also on this subject, M. Waline, *Droit Administratif* (9th ed., Paris 1963), No. 221.

[17] F. Garrido Falla, *loc. cit.*, footnote 1, p. 336.

[18] For an extensive analysis of this issue, *cf.* F. Garrido Falla, *loc. cit.*, footnote 1, pp. 337 *et seq.*

SECTION 3

THE PRINCIPLES OF LEGAL CERTAINTY AND OF THE PROTECTION OF LEGITIMATE EXPECTATIONS IN COMMUNITY LAW

A.   INTRODUCTION

I.   THE DEVELOPMENT OF THESE PRINCIPLES IN THE CASE LAW OF THE COURT OF JUSTICE

The principles of legal certainty and of the protection of legitimate expectations have become accepted as general legal principles in the case law of the Court of Justice, without causing either its judges or its Advocates-General to feel compelled, in their decisions or opinions respectively, to find an explicit basis for these principles in either legal theory or in comparative law. However, the same cannot be said for the development of concrete principles of constitutional and administrative law which have become applicable as rules derived from the general legal principles, such as the rules regarding the admissibility of the revocation of administrative instruments conferring benefits,[1] the rules which decide when revocation should be applied *ex nunc* or *ex tunc*,[2] the time limit within which the right to revoke instruments may be exercised[3] and the consequences of administrative measures which are unlawful merely in part.[4] These too have a more extensive basis in comparative law, as is the case in relation to the scope, both in time and in substance, of rule

---

[1] Joined Cases 7/56 & 3–7/57 *Algera et al.* v. *Common Assembly* [1957–1958] E.C.R. 39; also Advocate-General Lagrange, *ibid.* pp. 69 *et seq.*

[2] Advocate-General Lagrange in Case 14/61 *Hoogovens* v. *High Authority* [1982] E.C.R. 253.

[3] Advocate-General Roemer in Case 111/63 *Lemmerz-Werke* v. *High Authority* [1965] E.C.R. 893 at 938.

[4] Joined Cases 7/56 & 3–7/57, *loc. cit.*, footnote 1.

changes, more particularly the retroactivity of rules,[5] the extent to which the legislature may bind itself[6] and the "vested rights" of officials.[7]

The development of the principles of legal certainty and the protection of legitimate expectations has been considerably influenced by the following decisive factors: on the one hand, the recognition of these legal principles, or of the administrative principles to be derived from them, by the Court of Justice often constitutes a response to statements to that effect made by the parties involved in the case and to questions posed by the courts making the reference in the context of Article 177 EEC. Where the adoption of a particular administrative instrument or regulation, or some other type of action by the Community organs, is assessed in the light of the principles of legal certainty or of the protection of legitimate expectations, this will in most cases be the result of an action brought before, or a question referred to, the Court of Justice. Since the mid-1970s, it is especially the principle of the protection of legitimate expectations which has been invoked with particular frequency.[8] The large number of decisions in which this concept is mentioned should not blind us to the fact that the Court has seldom seen in the outcome a reason for accepting that a particular legitimate expectation was worthy of protection.

On the other hand, it should be noted that at times the Opinions of the Advocates-General are particularly marked by those legal systems with which they are personally familiar. This applies, for example, to the influence exerted by French administrative law on the Opinions of Advocate-General Lagrange in the early cases concerning the revocation of administrative instruments,[9] and to the extent to which, on the subject of the retroactivity of regulations, the Opinions of Advocates-General

---

[5] Advocate-General Warner in Case 7/76 *IRCA* v. *Amministrazione delle Finanze delle Stato* [1976] E.C.R. 1213 at 1235 *et seq.*; Advocate-General Roemer in Case 1/73 *Westzucker* v. *Einfuhr- und Vorratsstelle für Zucker* [1973] E.C.R. 723 at 736 *et seq.*; the same in Case 17/67 *Neumann* v. *Hauptzollamt Hof/Saale* [1967] E.C.R. 591 at 628.

[6] Advocate-General Warner in Case 81/72 *Commission* v. *Council* (Officials' Salaries) [1973] E.C.R. 575 at 592 *et seq.*

[7] Advocate-General Capotorti in Case 127/80 *Grogan* v. *Commission* [1980] E.C.R. 869 at 900.

[8] *cf.* on this subject also P. Pescatore, *Les principes généraux du droit en tant que source du droit communautaire, Rapport Communautaire*, FIDE Report 1986, pp. 17 *et seq.* (35 *et seq.*).

[9] In particular Joined Cases 7/56 & 3–7/57, *Algera et al.* v. *Common Assembly* [1957–58] E.C.R. 39 at 69 *et seq.*; Joined Cases 42 & 49/59 *SNUPAT* v. *High Authority* [1961] E.C.R. 53 at 90 *et seq.*; Case 14/61 *Hoogovens* v. *High Authority* [1962] E.C.R. 511 at 277 *et seq.*

Roemer and Reischl in the *Westzucker*[10] and *Isoglucose*[11] cases are modelled on the German case law regarding the protection of legitimate expectations. Similarly, the influence of English legal thinking in the Opinions of Advocate-General Warner in the 1973 *Commission* v. *Council (Officials' Salaries)* case is unmistakable.[12]

However, the early case law on the question of the admissibility of the revocation of unlawful administrative instruments is also a good example of a compromise, which takes the form of "comparative law taken as a tool of evaluation," between various attempts at finding solutions based on the administrative law systems of the Member States. Whilst the case law on the revocation of administrative instruments establishing rights has tended to follow the patterns set by French administrative law,[13] the Court, in the *SNUPAT* case, clearly applied concepts of German administrative law in the case of so-called declaratory administrative instruments by weighing up the need to protect legitimate expectations against the *ex tunc* revocation of an administrative instrument conferring benefits.[14] Advocate-General Lagrange hailed this differentiated approach in the following terms:

> "In this way the case law of the Court, in so far as it invokes national laws (as it does to a large extent) to define the rules of law relating to the application of the Treaty, is not content to draw on more or less arithmetical 'common denominators' between the different national solutions, but chooses from each of the Member States those solutions which, having regard to the object of the Treaty, appear to it to be the best or, if one may use the expression, the most progressive. That is the spirit, moreover, which has guided the Court hitherto."[15]

II. LEGAL CERTAINTY AND THE PROTECTION OF LEGITIMATE EXPECTATIONS AS PRINCIPLES OF CONSTITUTIONAL AND ADMINISTRATIVE LAW

As the Court of Justice stated in the *CNTA* case mentioned above, the principles of legal certainty and of the protection of legitimate expecta-

---

[10] Advocate-General Roemer in Case 1/73, *loc. cit.*, footnote 5, pp. 738 *et seq.*

[11] Advocate-General Reischl in Case 108/81 *Amylum* v. *Council* [1982] E.C.R. 3107 at 3144.

[12] Advocate-General Warner in Case 81/72, *loc. cit.*, footnote 6, pp. 592 *et seq.*; in this case, however, the Court did not follow the proposed solution put forward by its Advocate-General.

[13] Joined Cases 7/56 & 3–7/57, *loc. cit.*, footnote 1.

[14] Joined Cases 42 & 49/59, *loc. cit.*, footnote 9.

[15] Advocate-General Lagrange in Case 14/61, *loc. cit.*, footnote 9. pp. 570 *et seq.*

tions constitute "superior rules of law,"[16] which could also form the basis for Community liability for injustice caused by its legislation. "The submission that there has been a breach of this principle is admissible in the context of proceedings instituted under Article 173, since the principle in question forms part of the Community legal order."[17] As general principles of Community constitutional and administrative law, these principles are generally accorded priority status over other E.C. instruments, regardless of whether the latter are rules of Community law or administrative decisions. In fact, in this respect no distinction in principle is made between various types of regulation—*i.e.* Council regulations, independent Commission regulations or derived Commission regulations.[18] According to the case law of the ECJ, these legal instruments of the Community organs are all subject to review as to their lawfulness in the light of the principles of legal certainty and the protection of legitimate expectations. However, distinctions are drawn along these lines as regards the effect of these principles on individual instruments—*i.e.* Community administrative instruments—on the one hand, and on rules of Community law on the other.

The principles of administrative law have turned out to be those rules which the Court of Justice drew from the principles of legal certainty and the protection of legitimate expectations and applied to the field of executive action by the administration. In the famous *Algera* case, the ECJ was faced with the problem that written Community law provided no body of rules on the issue of the revocation of administrative instruments. The method it adopted in order to fill the existing legislative gap was formulated by the Court in the following terms[19]:

> "Unless the Court is to deny justice, it is therefore obliged to solve the problem by reference to the rules acknowledged by the legislation, the learned writing and the case law of the member countries."

However, the principles of administrative law thus developed cannot be accorded equal status with the general principles of legal certainty and the

---

[16] Case 74/74 *CNTA* v. *Commission* [1975] E.C.R. 533 at 548 *et seq.*

[17] Case 112/77 *A. Töpfer* v. *Commission* [1978] E.C.R. 1019 at 1033. In Case 170/86 *Deetzen* v. *HZA Hamburg/Jonas* [1988] E.C.R. 2535, the Court held partly invalid a Council regulation, as completed by the Commission, on the grounds of infringement of the principle of the protection of legitimate expectation.

[18] M. Akehurst, "The Application of General Principles of Law by the Court of Justice of the European Community," in *The British Yearbook of International Law 1981* (1982), p. 29 (45 *et seq.*).

[19] Joined Cases 7/56 & 3–7/57, *loc. cit.*, footnote 1, p. 118.

protection of legitimate expectations. A gap in the body of rules which has been filled by the Court by the concrete application of general legal principles can also be filled in a different manner by the Community legislator as soon as the latter decides to intervene in the area in question. The formula adopted by the Court—*e.g.* on the subject of the revocation of unlawful administrative instruments conferring benefits—amounts to no more than a proposal. Where the legislature declines to intervene, this proposal may certainly acquire a permanent status.[20] However, although the concrete principles of administrative law, developed by the Court of Justice by applying the principles of legal certainty and of the protection of legitimate expectations, may as such be binding on the administration when enforcing Community law in the individual area in question, they cannot bind the Community legislature. Nevertheless, the latter is compelled to take into account the general principles of legal certainty and the protection of legitimate expectations, in their capacity of overriding constitutional principles, when enacting written legal rules.

III. THE AREAS IN WHICH THESE PRINCIPLES APPLY

In relation to the principles of legal certainty and of the protection of legitimate expectations, three different areas of application must be distinguished, which at the same time form the boundaries of the following analysis.

1. Legal Certainty and the Protection of Legitimate Expectations as Applied to Direct Executive Action by the Administration

The field of direct administration, *i.e.* executive action by the Community authorities, forms the centre of gravity of our analysis. Here, it is possible to discern a number of administrative principles which are related to the principles of legal certainty and the protection of legitimate expectations. More specifically, these are the rules governing the revocation or the withdrawal of administrative instruments,[21] drawing the par-

---

[20] J. Schwarze, *Die Befugnis zur Abstraktion im europäischen Gemeinschaftsrecht*, Baden-Baden 1976, p. 120.
[21] In most cases, the decisions of the Court of Justice reveal no clear distinction between these two concepts, which are drawn from German law. In the context of this approach, it is accordingly only the notion of revocation which normally applies.

ticular distinction between the revocation of lawful and unlawful decisions, the revocation of administrative instruments conferring benefits and those imposing restrictions, and the revocation of administrative instruments establishing rights and those which are purely declaratory. To this must be added a large number of rules relating to special grounds for revocation.

This category also includes the principles relating to the formal applicability of administrative instruments imposing restrictions as well as a number of rules governing time limits to be observed in certain types of administrative procedure. Disputes involving the recovery of payments wrongly made or of duties which were incorrectly not levied have also been settled by the Court in the context of direct executive action by the administration.[22]

Finally, this category also comprises a number of principles which come under the heading of the cases in which the administration binds itself, featuring especially the rule under which the administration is bound by the pledges it has given. The general question of the retroactivity of administrative instruments has also been handled by the Court in this context.

In view of the small number of areas in which the Community authorities are themselves responsible for executive action, the scope for the Court to develop principles of administrative law in the field of direct executive action has so far been fairly restricted. This can be seen from the fact that direct executive action covers certain areas of ECSC law, especially the so-called scrap metal equalisation fund, which existed in the early stages of ECSC law but has in the meantime been abolished, but recently also the quota systems applying to steel products on the one hand and EEC competition law on the other. Relevant cases arising out of disputes involving Community officials also account for a considerable proportion of such decisions. In spite of the variegated nature of these individual areas, the case law of the Court reveals, in a number of individual cases in which the principles of legal certainty and the protection of legitimate expectations have been applied, a considerable degree of consistency in the approach adopted, which can reasonably claim to be generally binding. Thus the principles developed by the ECJ on the subject of the revocation of administrative instruments constitute general administrative principles in the sense that they are not confined to a specific area of Community administrative law. The precedents relating to the revocation of administrative instruments in the field covered by the

---

[22] For further analysis, *cf.* section 3, B.IV below.

ECSC on the one hand and those resulting from the staff cases on the other have exercised a mutual influence and reinforced each other. Only the concept of "vested rights" appears to have acquired a special area of application in civil service law.[23] The principles developed by the Court in the field of direct executive action can accordingly be considered to form a kind of basis for the general field of administrative law.

2. Legal Certainty and the Protection of Legitimate Expectations in the Field of Indirect Executive Action by the Administration

Since there are considerable areas of Community law, in particular the law of agriculture, which are implemented and enforced not by the Community institutions but by the authorities of the Member States (*i.e.* the so-called indirect administration), the question can be raised here as to which general principles of Community administrative law, if any, are to be applied in addition to the domestic rules of enforcement and implementation. From the point of view of legal certainty and the protection of legitimate expectations, the impact of Community law on, for example, the principles governing the recovery of Community moneys wrongly paid comes to mind. Similar considerations apply to the collection of Community duties which were incorrectly not levied or, conversely, to the repayment of Community duties levied contrary to Community law.

A solution based on Community law in this field could be allied to, for example, the principles developed by the Court in the field of direct executive action by the administration on the subject of the revocation of administrative instruments conferring benefits or of the compliance with formal requirements of administrative instruments imposing restrictions. This would undoubtedly require a uniform application of substantive Community law in all Member States. However, the significance attached by the case law of the Court of Justice to the Community law principles of legal certainty and the protection of legitimate expectations has so far been relatively low.

On the other hand, those categories of cases in which national authorities levy, in accordance with their domestic legal system, duties and taxes contrary to directly effective Community law do not fall within the scope

---

[23] However, these principles are also relevant in connection with the retroactivity of agricultural regulations.

of the Community law principles of legal certainty and the protection of legitimate expectations.[23a]

The question whether, and the extent to which, the citizen may claim repayment of moneys paid contrary to Community law will be decided in accordance with national rules relating to reimbursement. Where these rules restrict the opportunities for reimbursement from the point of view of legal certainty, this will be based not on the Community law principle of legal certainty but on domestic considerations in this area.[23b]

3. Legal Certainty and the Protection of Legitimate Expectations as Applied to Community Legislative Action

The principles of legal certainty and of the protection of legitimate expectations have played an important part in the judicial review of legislation. Prominent among the issues raised in this regard has been the question whether and to what extent the adoption of retrospective rules is permissible. In so doing, it has been necessary to reconcile the interest which the party in question has in stable legal relations with the requirements of a flexible system of legislation adjusted in the light of changes in circumstances. On the basis of the rulings pronounced by the Court on this subject, the principles of legal certainty and of the protection of legitimate expectations have emerged as principles of (Community) constitutional law. There is a clear distinction to be made between these principles and the rules which apply to executive action, particularly from the point of view of the extent to which they have applied in concrete

---

[23a] By way of illustration, *cf.* Case 61/79 *Amministrazione delle Finanze dello Stato* v. *Denkavit Italiana* [1980] E.C.R 1205, in which the Italian authorities had levied phytosanitary charges on imports of milk and dairy products, contrary to Article 13(2) EEC.

[23b] *cf., e.g.* Case 199/82, *Amministrazione delle Finanze dello Stato* v. *San Giorgio* [1983] E.C.R. 3595 (rules relating to the burden of proof). A distinction needs to be drawn between this question and that which seeks to establish whether directly effective Community law takes precedence over these national considerations of legal certainty; *cf.* on this subject Case 45/76 *Comet* v. *Produktschap voor Siergewassen* [1976] E.C.R. 2043; Case 68/79 *Just* v. *Danish Ministry for Fiscal Affairs* [1980] E.C.R. 501 *et seq.*; Case 811/79 *Amministrazione delle Finanze dello Stato* v. *Ariete* [1980] E.C.R. 2545 *et seq.*; Case 61/79, *loc. cit.*, footnote 23a; Case 199/82, *loc. cit.*, footnote 23b; Case 309/85 *Barra* v. *Belgian State; City of Liège* [1988] E.C.R. 355, paras. 16 *et seq.* The fact that Community law does not absolutely exclude the possibility of taking account of considerations of national legal certainty is shown by the decision in Case 33/76 *Rewe* v. *Landwirtschafts-kammer Saarland* [1976] E.C.R. 1989 at 1998.

cases. However, the case law of the Court on the retroactivity of regulations also reveals a number of general rules aimed at establishing whether or not there is a legitimate expectation in a particular case, which may be applied in the field of direct executive action by the administration.

IV. THE PRINCIPLES OF LEGAL CERTAINTY AND THE PROTECTION OF LEGITIMATE EXPECTATIONS AS CONCEPTS

Since the range of the effects of the principles of legal certainty and of the protection of legitimate expectations in Community law is very broad, it is possible, in the context of this survey, to mention only a few general areas in which they have been applied and certain general features of such application, which will be subjected to further analysis in the more specific sections which follow.

1. The Principle of Legal Certainty

In German constitutional and administrative legal doctrine, which together with that of the Netherlands has developed probably the most extensive theoretical analysis of this topic, the principle of legal certainty, as a structural principle based on objective criteria, has been derived mainly from the rule of law concept.[24] The principle of the protection of legitimate expectations, on the other hand, appears to be an expression, taking the form of a subjective right, of legal certainty, which is equal in rank in the hierarchy of rules. As far as can be ascertained, the Court has failed to adopt a decisive position on the fundamental theoretical question whether there is a link—in the sense of one being derived from the other—between legal certainty and the protection of legitimate expectations. There exists, however, a series of decisions in which it is clearly assumed that there is a correlation between these two legal princi-

---

[24] On the legal position in Germany, *cf.* F. Ossenbühl, "Die Bindung der Verwaltung an die höchstrichterliche Rechtsprechung," AöR 92 (1967), p. 478 (484); P. Kunig, *Das Rechtsstaatsprinzip*, Tübingen 1986, p. 195 with further references; E. W. Fuss, "Der Schutz des Vertrauens auf Rechtskontinuität im deutschen Verfassungsrecht und europäischen Gemeinschaftsrecht," in *Festschrift für Hans Kutscher*, p. 201 (203); BVerfGE 13, p. 261 (271); BVerwG, NJW 1961, p. 1130 (1131); for a critical approach, *cf.* G. Püttner, "Vertrauensschutz im Verwaltungsrecht," VVDStRL 32 (1974), p. 200 (203). On this subject, and on the legal position in Switzerland, *cf.* B. Weber-Dürler, *Vertrauensschutz im öffentlichen Recht*, Basel and Frankfurt 1983, pp. 47 *et seq.*, 51 *et seq.*

ples. Thus, for example, in the *Westzucker* case, it is stated, in connection with the review of the admissibility of the false retroactivity of a regulation, that it must be established whether the regulation "thus interpreted infringes a principle of legal certainty by which the confidence of persons concerned deserves to be protected (Vertrauensschutz)."[25] In cases featuring the true retroactivity of regulations, the formula normally used is worded as follows:

> "Although in general, the principle of legal certainty precludes a Community measure from taking effect from a point in time before its publication, it may exceptionally be otherwise where the purpose to be achieved so demands and where the legitimate expectations of those concerned are duly respected."[26]

Similarly, according to the case law of the ECJ, it is necessary, in connection with the *ex tunc* revocation of unlawful administrative instruments conferring benefits, to weigh up the principle of the conformity of administrative action with the relevant statute against the principle of legal certainty, and in so doing to take into account the citizen's legitimate expectations.[27] In other cases, however, the principle of the protection of legitimate expectations is applied without any reference to the possibility of a correlation with the principle of legal certainty. This is especially, and frequently, the case with the judicial review of the false retroactivity of regulations and with the appraisal of the binding effect of information and commitments. In some cases, the principle of legal certainty is associated with the protection of vested rights, on the understanding, however, that there is a clear distinction between legal certainty and the effects of the principle of the protection of legitimate expectations.[28] The overall impression is that although the ECJ in certain individual cases applies the principles of legal certainty and of the protection of legitimate expectations separately from each other, it nevertheless assumes that, in theoretical terms, there is a close correlation between these two principles in the sense of one being derived from the other. Here, legal certainty in many cases is used as a legal principle based on objective criteria, whilst the recognition of legitimate expectations serves to protect subjective rights.

---

[25] Case 1/73 *Westzucker* v. *Einfuhr- und Vorratsstelle für Zucker* [1973] E.C.R. 723 at 729.

[26] Case 98/78 *Firma A. Racke* v. *Hauptzollamt Mainz* [1979] E.C.R. 69 at 86.

[27] *e.g.* Joined Cases 42 & 49/59 *SNUPAT* v. *High Authority* [1961] E.C.R. 53.

[28] *cf., e.g.* Advocate-General Mayras in Case 35/78 *N.G.J. Schouten BV* v. *Hoofdproduktschap voor Akkerbouwprodukten* [1978] E.C.R. 2543 at 2563; by the same, opinion in Case 90/77 *Firma H. Stimmig KG* v. *Commission* [1978] E.C.R. 997 at 1013.

However, the principle of legal certainty can also have the effect of protecting individuals in specific cases.

In this context, it is appropriate to recall the formula used by the German Federal Constitutional Court, which holds that for the citizen, legal certainty means above all the protection of legitimate expectations.[29] In practice, the principle of legal certainty also frequently has this beneficial effect for citizens under Community law also.

As an objective principle, legal certainty requires the maintenance of a legal situation and consequently also its stability and "inalienable nature."[30] In addition, it follows from this principle that the Community legislature has the duty to formulate the rules adopted by it in clear and precise terms.

However, the compliance of Community constitutional enactments with the rule of law requires more than the guarantee of legal continuity. Where administrative action infringes the applicable law, the principle of compliance with the statute law by the administration also demands that the unlawful circumstances in question be eliminated. However, the compliance of administrative action with statute law can in certain cases come up against the principle of legal certainty, such as, for example, when an unlawful administrative instrument conferring benefits is to be revoked with retroactive effect. In such circumstances, the administration is obliged to weigh up both principles against each other and to decide in each individual case which principle should enjoy priority.[31]

The principle of legal certainty is also to be observed in cases where certain legal relations are changed for the future. According to the case law of the Court of Justice, this applies especially in the case of the revocation *ex nunc* of unlawful administrative instruments conferring benefits, where it assumes that even this type of revocation is permissible only within a "reasonable period." However, this question has not been conclusively settled under Community law. Where in this type of case observance of legal certainty works to the advantage of addressees of the administrative instrument conferring benefits, the guarantee of stable legal relations may in other cases work to the disadvantage of the indivi-

---

[29] BVerfGE 13, p. 261 (271)—on this subject also B. Weber-Dürler, *loc. cit.*, footnote 24, p. 48.

[30] *cf.* P. Badura, "Die Rechtsprechung des Bundesverfassungsgerichts zu den verfassungs-rechtlichen Grenzen wirtschaftlicher Gesetzgebung im sozialen Rechtsstaat," AöR 92 (1967), pp. 382 *et seq.* (393).

[31] This has been regularly upheld by the Court *cf., e.g.* Joined Cases 42 & 49/59 *SNUPAT* v. *High Authority* [1961] E.C.R. 53 at 87. Advocate-General Lagrange in Case 14/61 *Hoogovens* v. *High Authority* [1962] E.C.R. 253 at 286.

dual citizen. There are ample examples of this in the case law of the Court of Justice. Mention should be made in this connection of the acceptance by the Court, on grounds of legal certainty, of the legal validity of administrative instruments after the expiry of certain time limits,[32] and of the possibility of excluding the retroactivity of decisions pronouncing the avoidance or the invalidity of Community instruments under Article 174(2) of the EEC Treaty, as a result of which the citizen is denied claims for the repayment of duties paid, which were levied on the basis of the rule which has now been held invalid.[33]

2. The Principle of the Protection of Legitimate Expectations

In the context of a staff dispute involving the question of the protection of legitimate expectations, the Court established that "this right extends to any individual who is in a situation in which it appears that the administration's conduct has led him to entertain reasonable expectations."[34] In practice, there has developed a widely ramified case law in which it is hard to discern a consistent pattern. Consequently, it is necessary on this subject to refer to the following account of individual administrative principles which have evolved on the basis of the fundamental concept of the protection of legitimate expectations, *i.e.* the statements made by the Court on the subject of the revocation of administrative instruments, on the circumstances in which the administration binds itself and on the true or false retroactivity of rules.

Whereas in certain Member States the principle of the protection of legitimate expectations has either established itself with great difficulty or has failed to do so altogether, it has been accepted as constituting a principle of Community law by the Court of Justice, without the need for any detailed reasons for such acceptance.

The protection of legitimate expectations is a principle which is closely related to that of legal certainty, which is binding not only on administrative action but also on the Community legislature. Especially the scope in time of rules is conditioned to a considerable extent by the principle of the protection of legitimate expectations.

---

[32] For further details, *cf.* section 3, B. III.1 below.
[33] For further details, *cf.* section 3, C.4 below.
[34] Case 289/81 *Mavrides* v. *European Parliament* [1983] E.C.R. 1731 at 1744.

The familiar problem, under national constitutional law, of the admissibility of the retroactivity of instruments laying down rules defines this difficult problem area, whose co-ordinates are formed by the requirement of legislative flexibility on the one hand, and the expectation of the person to whom the rule is addressed that the previous legal situation will continue to apply on the other.

In the field of Community administrative action, the notion of the protection of legitimate expectations becomes particularly important where the issue involved is whether an unlawful administrative instrument conferring benefits should be revoked *ex nunc* or *ex tunc*. Here, the cancellation of the unlawful decision is permissible only if the person to whom the rule is addressed did not have an expectation, which was worthy of protection, that the legal situation in question would be maintained.[35]

As regards the conditions in which the protection of legitimate expectations can be guaranteed, it is hardly possible—at least not on the basis of the case law of the Court of Justice in its present state of development—to compile a universally binding and definitive list of relevant circumstances. On the one hand, the individual cases in which this principle is applied cover a wide range of issues and require a different examination depending on their specific circumstances. On the other hand, the following account of the case law developed by the Court will demonstrate that it is only very seldom that the principle of the protection of legitimate expectations has ultimately benefited the individual citizen. In the majority of its decisions, the Court has contented itself with the observation that the case in question did not present the conditions necessary for protecting a legitimate expectation. This allowed the question to remain open as to what additional conditions should have been met in the case in question. However, it is possible to discern in the relevant decisions certain circumstances which must be present, either individually or cumulatively, in order to justify the protection of a legitimate expectation.

From an objective viewpoint it is, according to those decisions, an action on the part of the Community institutions justifying legitimate expectations which is necessary for there to be a guarantee of protection of legitimate expectations. This action may take the form of the adoption of a lawful or unlawful administrative instrument conferring benefits. However, justified expectations which are worthy of protection under certain conditions may also be created by consistent administrative prac-

---

[35] For further details, *cf.* section 3, B.II.3.b below.

tice, by information supplied or statements made or by pledges, and may ensure that the administration is bound by its own actions.[36]

The expectation of a person may also concern the continuation of a legal position. This can be disrupted by the legislature, for example by the adoption of retroactive rules. However, if we are dealing here with a so-called "false retroactivity," *i.e.* a change in the relevant legal position which relates to events which arose in the past but which have yet to be fully completed, the guarantee of the protection of legitimate expectations presupposes an additional practical expression of the general legal relationships which are based on the legal position which applied up to the moment in question. Such a practical expression may occur through an administrative instrument conferring benefits which was adopted before the change in the legal position occurred. In the case law of the Court of Justice on this subject, however, it is especially pledges made by the Community institutions and the adoption of certain provisions, to wit, the undertaking by individuals of concrete commitments towards the administration, which have played a decisive part in this area.

Where one of the objective criteria for entertaining a legitimate expectation is actually present, the principle of the protection of legitimate expectations can protect individual rights or specific interests of the person affected against any infringements in the past or in the future, as long as certain additional subjective conditions are met—in Community law also, it is only a concrete expectation which is protected. Apart from this type of concrete expectation, the Court seems at most prepared to recognise a purely objective element of expectation in relation to a revocation *ex tunc* of lawful administrative instruments establishing rights or conferring benefits.[37]

The expectation of the person in question, which must have a subjective basis, must also be recognisable to an outsider and therefore be capable of acquiring an objective dimension. This entails in the first place that the affected party must not have acted in such a way as to preclude his reliance on the expectation.[38] In addition, the subsequent frustration of the alleged legitimate expectation by the infringement of the acquired legal position or of the individual interest must not have been foreseeable by the person affected.[39]

---

[36] For further details, *cf.* section 3, B.VI below.
[37] This can certainly be inferred from the decision in Joined Cases 7/56 & 3–7/57 *D. Algera et al.* v. *Common Assembly* [1957–1958] E.C.R. 39 at 63.
[38] *cf., e.g.* the judgment in Case 14/81 *Alpha Steel* v. *Commission* [1982] E.C.R. 749 at 764 *et seq.*
[39] Advocate-General Mayras in Joined Cases 44–51/77 *Union Malt* v. *Commission* [1978] E.C.R. 57 at 90.

Knowledge of the unlawful nature of an administrative instrument,[40] the fact that the conditions for the promised adoption of an administrative instrument are not fulfilled,[41] as well as the foreseeable nature of a change in the legal position by a retroactive regulation, all exclude the possibility of guaranteeing the protection of legitimate expectations. Here, the criteria for the relevance of the subjective element of expectation are different according to whether we are dealing with the expectation that an individual instrument will be maintained, or with the expectation that a legal situation created by a rule-making instrument will continue to apply. In the former case, what is required is a concrete and individual expectation, whereas in the second case, the ECJ applies the criterion of the "knowledge of a reasonable trader." Only if the persons in question, on the basis of "all the essential factors known at the time,"[42] were entitled to assume that the rights or interests acquired by them would remain guaranteed, could there be said to be a "legitimate expectation worthy of protection."[43]

Moreover, the Court—admittedly not in all cases—requires a certain degree of active participation in the raising of the expectation. At the domestic law level too, controversy also surrounds the question whether the granting of protection to legitimate expectations requires any type of active participation in creating the expectation; however, this question cannot be assessed in a uniform manner in relation to all possible cases in which the notion of the protection of legitimate expectations could be applied.[44] It has already been pointed out that the adoption of certain provisions may give rise to the protection of legitimate expectations, especially where false retroactivity has occurred. This applies, for example, to cases where certain commitments are entered into towards the official authorities. According to the case law of the Court of Justice, protection of legitimate expectations can be given in such cases, even if no administrative instrument has been adopted or no explicit undertaking has been given by the administration to the person in question. Other specific cases will be dealt with in the section in which the relevant case law is analysed.

Finally, whenever an expectation which is intrinsically legitimate enters into the judge's calculations, this normally presupposes a process

---

[40] *cf.*, *e.g.* Case 14/61 *Hoogovens* v. *High Authority* [1962] E.C.R. 253 at 273 *et seq.*

[41] *cf.*, *e.g.* Case 228/84 *Pauvert* v. *Court of Auditors* [1985] E.C.R. 1973.

[42] Advocate-General Reischl in Case 108/81 *Amylum* v. *Council* [1982] E.C.R. 3107 at 3148.

[43] Advocate-General Reischl in Case 108/81, *loc. cit.*, footnote 42.

[44] On this subject, in general terms, *cf.* B. Weber-Dürler, *Vertrauensschutz im öffentlichen Recht*, Basel and Frankfurt 1983, pp. 96 *et seq.*

of weighing up the interests of the person affected in having his legitimate expectation protected against the public interest. Here too the case law of the Court of Justice reveals certain similarities with the legal position in a number of Member States.[45] This type of specific balancing of interests is encountered in all court decisions involving Community law in which the notion of the protection of legitimate expectations is applied, with the exception of cases which concern the revocation *ex tunc* of lawful administrative instruments conferring benefits. Here, the expectation of the individual that the administrative instrument will be maintained normally prevails over the public interest in having the instrument revoked, without requiring any special examination of the relative importance of the two interests.

Where the citizen in question has a justified interest in the protection of his legitimate expectation which in a particular case could expect to take precedence over the public interest in a different outcome, this may, as is the case in the national legal systems,[46] essentially have two different types of legal implication, *i.e.* either the guaranteed protection of the maintenance of the instrument or payment of compensation. According to the case law of the Court of Justice, any infringement of the requirement that legitimate expectations must be protected "does not automatically mean that the disputed measure is void but may in certain circumstances justify the award of damages if the person concerned has suffered injury as a result."[47] Which legal remedy is to apply will depend on the circumstances of each individual case.

3. Vested Rights

On the issue of legal certainty and the protection of legitimate expectations, the question whether or not there are "vested rights" is often raised not only in the case law of the Court of Justice but also, and especially, in the Opinions of the Advocates-General. Particularly in the staff cases and on questions of agriculture the parties often invoke such rights in order to obtain a declaration that the revocation of an administrative instrument conferring benefits is inadmissible, or in order to secure the inapplicability of a legislative amendment in their particular case, or the avoidance of the amending regulation.

---

[45] On this subject, *cf., e.g.* B. Weber-Dürler, *loc. cit.*, footnote 44, pp. 112 *et seq.*
[46] *cf.* on this subject B. Weber-Dürler, *loc. cit.*, footnote 44, pp. 128 *et seq.*; G. Püttner, "Vertrauensschutz im Verwaltungsrecht," VVDStRL 32 (1974), p. 200 (217).
[47] Case 289/81 *Mavrides* v. *European Parliament* [1983] E.C.R. 1731.

Among the legal systems of the Member States, the doctrine of the protection of vested rights is to be found especially in France (*droits acquis*) and in Italy (*diritti quesiti*).[48] In Switzerland also this principle has played, and continues to play, an important part in constitutional and administrative law.[49] Here, vested rights demand a certain degree of consistency on the part of the legislature in the face of changes in the legal position.[50] However, they also provide an argument in favour of the irrevocability of administrative instruments conferring benefits,[51] the obligation to protect vested rights having been derived from the principle of legal certainty. Expressed in this form, the protection of vested rights has also become part of Community law, although it must be stated that it is hard to draw a clear distinction between this concept and the (general) notion of the protection of legitimate expectations. The fact that both these principles have been recognised on an equal basis in the Court's case law reflects the desire to accommodate the various approaches and traditions enshrined in the legal systems of the Member States rather than a concern to recognise the protection of two separate rights or objectives.

Accordingly, in the detailed analysis which follows, the case law on the subject of vested rights has been examined together with that which relates to the protection of legitimate expectations and analysed in an integrated way according to certain categories of cases or in relation to specific administrative law principles. In particular the protection of vested rights prompts two questions: (a) what are the effects of the recognition of vested rights in cases of the revocation of administrative instruments conferring benefits, and (b) what is their influence if the legal position is changed by the legislature? In particular it needs to be established whether vested rights are capable of excluding the possibility of revoking administrative instruments or of preventing new regulations becoming generally applicable to the holders of such rights. In both cases, we must examine what special characteristics a right must possess if citizens are to be entitled to invoke it as a vested right.

Here it is not possible to discern finally, on the basis of the case law of the Court of Justice, whether the concept of vested rights concerns only

---

[48] *cf.* on this subject *supra*, section 2 A. and D.
[49] *cf.* on this subject K. Klett, *Verfassungsrechtlicher Schutz "wohlerworbener Rechte" bei Rechtsänderungen, anhand der bundesgerichtlichen Rechtsprechung*, Bern 1984, and B. Weber-Dürler, *loc. cit.*, footnote 44, pp. 63 *et seq.*
[50] K. Klett, *loc. cit.*, footnote 49, pp. 115 *et seq.*, 202 *et seq.*
[51] B. Weber-Dürler, *loc. cit.*, footnote 44, pp. 64 *et seq.*

some very special categories of rights[52] or whether it includes all subjective rights where the latter have been created as a result of an individual instrument conferring benefits. More especially, the opinions of the Advocates-General on the retroactivity of agricultural regulations point in the latter direction.[53]

Moreover, vested rights, as concepts, are characterised especially by their inherent inability to be revoked. Thus in the *Algera* case, the Court of Justice had already emphasised the following points when highlighting the characteristics of vested rights:

> "First of all, an error of reasoning which is liable to lead in this connexion to a vicious circle must be eliminated: it consists in asserting the existence of a vested right, and then inferring therefrom that that right cannot be revoked. In fact, if the right conferred by an administrative measure can be unilaterally revoked by the administration, then the simple fact is that it does not constitute a vested right."[54]

Thus it is possible for vested rights to arise especially from lawful administrative instruments establishing rights. Here, their vested nature results from the inadmissibility of revocation *ex tunc* and, normally, of revocation *ex nunc*.[55] This applies in the first instance to cases in which the legal position has not changed. As regards the question of the significance of vested rights when the legal position changes as a result of new legal provisions, the resistance of vested rights to legislation is regularly acknowledged as one of their characteristics in national law.[56] This characteristic is also attributed to vested rights by the case law of the Court of Justice, where the latter states that although regulations take immediate effect as from the date of their adoption or of their entry into force, they may not, in case of doubt, infringe vested rights. Accordingly, the notion

---

[52] *cf.* on the history of vested rights, B. Weber-Dürler, *loc. cit.*, footnote 44, pp. 63 *et seq.*; K. Klett, *loc. cit.*, footnote 49, pp. 9 *et seq.*, 91 *et seq.* and 118 *et seq.*

[53] *cf., e.g.* Advocate-General Reischl in Case 64/80 *Giuffrida and Campogrande* v. *Council* [1981] E.C.R. 693 (712); Advocate-General Trabucchi, Case 5/75 *Deuka* v. *Einfuhr- und Vorratsstelle für Getreide und Futtermittel* [1975] E.C.R. 759 at 777; by the same, opinion in Case 74/74 *CNTA* v. *Commission* [1975] E.C.R. 533 at 555 *et seq.*; Advocate-General Mayras in Case 112/77 *Töpfer & Co. GmbH* v. *Commission* [1978] E.C.R. 1019 at 1037; by the same, opinion in Case 90/77 *Firma H. Stimmig KG* v. *Commission* [1978] E.C.R. 997 at 1013.

[54] Joined Cases 7/56 & 3–7/57 *Algera* v. *Common Assembly* [1957] E.C.R. 39.

[55] *cf.* in detail on this subject *supra* in the national section dealing with France, Section 2, A.II.1.

[56] *cf. supra* examples under Footnotes 48–50.

of vested rights also assists the Court in the interpretation of regulations which change an existing legal situation.

B. DIRECT EXECUTIVE ACTION

The following analysis of Community law is based on the duality presented by the various forms of action, which also dominates national law. In both legal systems, a distinction is drawn between abstract and general rule-making on the one hand, and concrete and individual administrative action on the other.[1]

The Treaties apply this distinction not only where they outline the available forms of administrative action (Article 189 EEC; Article 161 EAEC; Article 14 ECSC), but also in relation to legal protection against Community action.

Thus under the EEC and EAEC systems, private parties may in principle institute proceedings only against decisions addressed to them, but not against regulations (Article 173, second paragraph, EEC, Article 146, second paragraph, EAEC).[2]

Under the ECSC Treaty, the legal protection afforded to undertakings against rule-making instruments—which exists in addition to the opportunities with which they are also presented under this Treaty to bring actions against individual decisions—is restricted in that the only ground on which they may challenge general decisions is that of misuse of powers (Article 33, second paragraph, ECSC).

It is on this fundamental distinction between legal rules and individual instruments in Community law, having regard to the differences in the principles which govern their structure and the forms in which they

---

[1] E.-W. Fuss, "Rechtssatz und Einzelakt im europäischen Gemeinschaftsrecht," NJW 1964, pp. 327 et seq., 945 et seq. (946 et seq.); H.-W. Daig, in H. v. d. Groeben, H. v. Boeckh, J. Thiesing, C.-D. Ehlermann, Kommentar zum EWG-Vertrag (3rd ed., Baden-Baden 1983), Article 189, No. 58; H. P. Ipsen, Europäisches Gemeinschaftsrecht, Tübingen 1972, 21/14; Case 18/57 Nold v. High Authority [1958–1959] E.C.R. 89 at 112; Advocate-General Lagrange in Case 30/59 De Gezamenlijke Steenkolenmijnen in Limburg v. High Authority [1961] E.C.R. 1 at 73.

[2] cf. on this subject J. Schwarze, "Rechtsschutz Privater gegenüber normativen Rechtsakten im Recht der EWG," in I. v. Münch (ed.), Festschrift für Schlochauer, Berlin 1981, pp. 927 et seq.

appear, that our analysis of the field of application of the principles of legal certainty and of the protection of legitimate expectations is based.

In the first place, we shall examine administrative action in the form of individual instruments.

For the purpose of this analysis, we shall substitute the term "administrative act" for the terms "individual decision" as used in the ECSC Treaty, "decision" as used in the EEC and EAEC Treaties and "decision" or "act" as used in the Staff Regulations, this being the terminology which is occasionally encountered in the judgments of the Court of Justice[3] and in the Opinions of the Advocates-General.[4]

Our analysis opens with a survey of the substantive conditions which must be met if an instrument is to qualify as an administrative act in European Community law [see 1]. We then proceed to draw the line of distinction between administrative acts and regulations, especially in the light of the problems caused by the intermediate forms between rule-making instruments and individual acts [see 2]. Finally, we shall examine the extent to which the classification of administrative acts normally applied in national law is also used in Community law, and proceed to define certain individual key concepts from the doctrine of administrative acts for use in the detailed analysis which follows [see 3].

I. ADMINISTRATIVE ACTS

1.   Conditions which must be met by Community Administrative Acts

The formal conditions, in particular the questions of jurisdiction, the applicable procedure, the granting of judicial hearings and the duty to give reasons, will not be dealt with here.[5] From the substantive viewpoint,

---

[3] Joined Cases 7/56 & 3–7/57 *Algera et al.* v. *Common Assembly* [1957] E.C.R. 39; Joined Cases 42 & 49/59 *SNUPAT* v. *High Authority* [1961] E.C.R. 53; Case 14/61 *Hoogovens* v. *High Authority* [1962] E.C.R. 253; Joined Cases 4–13/59 *Mannesmann et al.* v. *High Authority* [1960] E.C.R. 249 at 290: "administrative measure establishing individual public rights."

[4] Advocate-General Roemer in Joined Cases 4–13/59 *Mannesmann et al.* v. *High Authority* [1960] E.C.R. 249 at 336 *et seq.*; opinion by the same Advocate-General in Case 15/60 *Simon* v. *Court of Justice* [1961] E.C.R. 239 at 273; Advocate-General Lagrange in Case 14/61 *Hoogovens* v. *High Authority* [1962] E.C.R. 253; Advocate-General Reischl in Case 14/81 *Alpha-Steel* v. *Commission* [1982] E.C.R. 749 at 782.

[5] *cf.* on this subject *infra*, Chap. 7.

the decisive criterion for what constitutes an administrative act is that it should be obviously intended to confer rights or impose duties,[6] or to "have legal effects,"[7] on those to whom the act is addressed. Consequently, whilst not every action of the Community authorities in individual cases is an administrative act, merely because it is apt to produce legal effects, but may also constitute a non-binding recommendation, an opinion or even merely an item of information or clarification, on the other hand it cannot meet the conditions for qualifying as an administrative act if it is not intended to produce legal effects.[8]

Viewed in this light, the criterion that administrative acts must be designed to produce legal effects occupies—as Advocate-General Roemer points out in the "Cement" case—a prominent position.[9] In this case, the applicant had challenged an item of information given by the Commission under Article 15(6) of Regulation 17. This provision states that the Commission may inform the undertakings concerned that, on the basis of a preliminary examination, it is of the opinion that a certain action or agreement between undertakings infringes the prohibition of cartels laid down in Article 85(1) EEC, and that an exemption under Article 85(3) would probably not be granted. Under Article 15(6) of Regulation 17, such a communication entails the consequence that the provision of Article 15(5) of this Regulation, that properly notified practices and agreements undertaken during the period between the notification and the Commission decision under Article 85(3) of the EEC Treaty, (which is often made much later), are not subject to the threat of fines. Although this type of communication by the Commission is referred to in Article 15(6) only as an item of information, the Court, agreeing with the Advocate-General, considered that it qualified as a "decision" within the meaning of Articles 173/189 EEC.

---

[6] Joined Cases 23–24 & 52/63 *Usines Emile Henricot* v. *High Authority* [1963] E.C.R. 467 at 484; also, similar judgments in Case 28/63 *Hoogovens* v. *High Authority* [1963] E.C.R. 253 and Joined Cases 53–54/63 *Lemmerz-Werke et al.* v. *High Authority* [1963] E.C.R. 517 at 538. In this case, subordinate organs had, without a formal decision to that effect by the High Authority itself, submitted certain statements and communicated to the undertakings in question requests for payment and statements of account.

[7] Case 54/65 *Compagnie des Forges de Châtillon* v. *High Authority* [1966] E.C.R. 529 at 544; *cf.* also Case 22/70 *Commission* v. *Council* [1971] E.C.R. 263 at 277, and Case 182/80 *Gauff* v. *Commission* [1982] E.C.R. 799 at 817.

[8] H.-W. Daig, in H. v. d. Groeben, H. v. Boeckh, J. Thiesing, C.-D. Ehlermann, *Kommentar zum EWG-Vertrag* (3rd ed.), Baden-Baden 1983, Article 189, No. 82; Advocate-General Roemer in Joined Cases 8–11/66 *Cimenteries C.B.R. Cementbedrijven N.V. et al.* v. *Commission* [1967] E.C.R. 75 at 102.

[9] Advocate-General Roemer, *ibid.*; H. G. Schermers, *Judicial Protection in the European Communities* (3rd ed., Deventer 1983), paragraph 245.

Although the Court had held, in the *Henricot et al.* case,[10] that any administrative act had to meet the condition that it conferred rights or imposed duties on those to whom it was addressed, it abandoned this formula in a subsequent decision,[11] in which the facts of the case were the same, and did likewise in the "Cement" case.[12] It would appear that the Court was justified in doing this, since in a large number of cases the Court had also acknowledged as "administrative acts" communications by the Commission which did not even establish a right but had merely, in an individual case, confirmed the existence of a right granted by a regulation and to this end interpreted, where necessary, the underlying rule[13]; in other words, it had, by way of a declaratory decision, given a binding confirmation of a legal relationship.[14] Here, the instruments in question could be either acts which worked to the citizen's advantage or measures which imposed burdens on him.[15]

In reply to an objection raised by the Commission in the "Cement" case that an agreement which infringed Article 85(1) EEC was prohibited even if no prior decision had been taken,[16] the Court pointed out that information given in accordance with Article 15(6) of the Competition Law Regulation, in relation both to the question whether there had been an infringement of Article 85(1) EEC and to the question whether Article 85(3) EEC was applicable, presupposes "an evaluation of elements of fact and of law," in which the Commission has "some discretion" when judging whether the conditions of paragraph 3 have been met. This reinforces the Commission's obligation to take a decision declaring that all the conditions of Article 85(1) are satisfied and that application of Article 85(3) is not justified.[17] Here, it appears that in Community law

---

[10] *cf.* the decisions mentioned *supra* (footnote 6).

[11] Case 54/65, *loc. cit.*, footnote 7—in this case, the applicants had appealed against a subsequent and this time formal decision of the High Authority, by which they claimed that legally effective "pledges" by the High Authority had been wrongly revoked *ex tunc.*

[12] Joined Cases 8–11/66, *loc. cit.*, footnote 8, p. 122.

[13] Thus Advocate-General Lagrange in Case 14/61 *Hoogovens* v. *High Authority* [1962] E.C.R. 253 at 277 *et seq.*

[14] M. Wegmann, *Die Nichtigkeitsklage Privater gegen Normativakte der Europäischen Gemeinschaften*, Berlin 1976, p. 28.

[15] *cf.* on this subject the cases involving exemptions from the scrap equalisation fund (*e.g.* Joined Cases 42 & 49/59 *SNUPAT* v. *High Authority* [1961] E.C.R. 53) on the one hand, and the cases in which contributions to the scrap equalisation fund which had not been levied were subsequently demanded (*cf.*, *e.g.* Case 2/70 *Riva* v. *Commission* [1971] E.C.R. 97) on the other.

[16] E.C.J. in Joined Cases 8–11/66, *loc. cit.*, footnote 8, pp. 116, 123.

[17] E.C.J., *ibid.* p. 123; *cf.* also Joined Cases 42 & 49/59 *SNUPAT* v. *High Authority* [1961] E.C.R. 53. In reply to the objection raised by the intervening party that the decision in

also the application of the law to individual cases does not constitute a mechanical process in which the relevant authority is "en quelque façon nulle."[18] Although it is true that the prohibition of Article 85(1) EEC produces effects without requiring any "prior decision to that effect" (Article 1, Regulation 17), Article 15(5) of that Regulation states that such fines shall be imposed in respect of acts taking place between the notification and the final decision by the Commission only where the Commission has, in the course of a preliminary examination conducted in accordance with Article 15(6) of the Regulation, confirmed that the conditions for the applicability of Article 85(1) EEC Treaty have been met. This involves intervening in the legal interests of undertakings. Although the item of information does not directly establish any rights or duties, it is designed to produce legal effects and consequently constitutes an administrative act.

From this decision it can also be seen, as the Court has stated on a number of occasions,[19] that the legal nature of a communication by a Community organ can be established on the basis of objective factors and does not depend on the denomination attributed to it by its author, even if, as was the case in this decision, that denomination is based on a rule of derived Community law.[20]

Generally speaking, it is possible to discern a tendency on the part of the ECJ, when faced with the task of drawing the difficult line between the non-binding instrument which is not an act and the administrative act which is open to challenge, to give priority to the interest of the citizen in having his rights protected in cases admitting of any doubt. As the Court held on the subject of the absence of a clear legal definition of the term "informed" under Article 15(6) of Regulation 17, "the silence of the text in a matter which affects the protection of the rights of individuals cannot be construed in the manner most unfavourable to them."[21]

---

question was not an individual one but merely a general decision, the Court stated that "the application of General Decision No. 2/57 to a concrete case constitutes a decision."

[18] H.-U. Erichsen, W. Martens, in H.-U. Erichsen, W. Martens, *Allgemeines Verwaltungs-recht* (7th ed., Berlin 1986), Paragraph 11 II 4, on the characteristics of "rules" in the case of the so-called confirmatory administrative measure in German administrative law.

[19] Thus, *e.g.* in Joined Cases 19–22/62 *Fédération Nationale de la Boucherie* v. *Commission* [1962] E.C.R. 1003 (1020).

[20] H.-W. Daig, in H. v. d. Groeben, H. v. Boeckh, J. Thiesing, C.-D. Ehlermann, *Kommentar zum EWG-Vertrag* (3rd ed., Baden-Baden 1983), Article 189, Nos. 54, 83 with further references.

[21] Joined Cases 8–11/66, *loc. cit.*, footnote 8; *cf.* in the same sense H.-W. Daig, *loc. cit.*, footnote 20, Article 189, No. 81.

On the other hand, communications, statements and items of information without legal effect, such as a statement that "the matters raised are being investigated," do not qualify as administrative acts. The Court held that this type of communication made by the High Authority did not constitute a decision which rendered an action for refusal to act inadmissible.[22] Nor did the mere announcement of a later decision, accompanied by a request to "be so good as to wait a little longer," constitute an administrative act.[23]

In many cases, the final decision which is formally notified to the citizen is preceded by preparatory measures taken with varying degrees of formality. On this issue, the Court of Justice was faced with the question whether these measures were open to challenge on an individual basis. In the *Henricot* case,[24] which has already been referred to, the Court expressed the view that it followed "from the natural meaning of the word that a decision marks the culmination of a procedure within the High Authority and is thus the definitive expression of its intentions."[25] In other cases, on the other hand, it has been held that individual procedural steps, or even mere provisional decisions, could constitute administrative acts which were open to challenge.[26]

However, an essential element which must be present in any Community law administrative act is a certain degree of external effect.[27] Where the Court has denied individual acts issued by the Community authorities the status of a "decision" on the grounds that they were not designed to produce legal effects, the yardstick by which this refusal was made was in each case the absence of any external legal effect. The required legal relations may, in the particular case, come into being between the Community and the Community citizen, between the Community and a Member State, or between a Community authority as employer and its officials. Purely internal communications, on the other hand, although capable of imposing direct obligations on the recipient thereof, cannot

---

[22] Joined Cases 42 & 49/59 *SNUPAT* v. *High Authority* [1961] E.C.R. 53 at 74. This case concerned an action by the applicant seeking to revoke a decision granting an exemption from the scrap equalisation payment to another firm.

[23] Case 79/70 *H. Müllers* v. *Economic and Social Committee* [1971] E.C.R. 689 at 697.

[24] *cf.* the decisions mentioned *supra* under footnote 6.

[25] Joined Cases 23, 25 & 52/63, *loc. cit.*, footnote 6, p. 484; *cf.* similarly Case 182/80 *H.P. Gauff* v. *Commission* [1982] E.C.R. 799 at 817: "...by which a procedure laid down by law is concluded...."

[26] *cf.* on this subject in particular the E.C.J. judgment in Case 60/81 *IBM* v. *Commission* [1981] E.C.R. 2639 at 2652 *et seq.*, and F. H. Wenig, in E. Grabitz, *Kommentar zum EWG-Vertrag*, Article 173, No. 13.

[27] For general comments on this, *cf.* H. P. Ipsen, *loc. cit.*, footnote 1, 22/17–20.

961

normally do so in relation to third parties.[28] Accordingly, such communications are not open to challenge by the latter. However, we have already pointed out[29] that such decisions which intrinsically are purely internal to the administrative department in question may in certain individual cases also produce legal effects in relation to third parties.[30] However, in the absence of any intention to that effect, these instruments cannot constitute administrative acts under Community law.[31]

Where the Court, in connection with the examination of the admissibility of an action for annulment of a legal act, has established that there can be a decision within the meaning of the second paragraph of Article 173 EEC only if the legal effects which it is intended to produce are capable of "affecting the interests of the applicant by bringing about a distinct change in his legal position,"[32] we are dealing, not with yet another obligatory characteristic of administrative acts under Community law, but with a procedural requirement for bringing the action under the second paragraph of Article 173 EEC. Not every administrative act under Community law constitutes a decision open to challenge by the appropriate complainant within the meaning of the second paragraph of, respectively, Article 173 EEC, Article 146 EAEC or Article 33 ECSC.[33] Although the conditions for the admissibility of actions for annulment under the ECSC Treaty are different from those required by the EEC and EAEC Treaties, in each case the ability to bring the action is subject to the condition that the complainant can show that his interests have been adversely affected.[34] Whereas under the EEC Treaty an action for annulment under the second paragraph of Article 173 is admissible only if it is brought against an individual decision addressed to the complainant or against a decision issued in the form of a ruling or addressed to a third party which is of "direct and individual concern" to the complainant, it is also the case in this context that a condition for the admissibility of the

---

[28] *cf., e.g.* Case 20/58 *Phönix-Rheinrohr AG* v. *High Authority* [1958–1959] E.C.R. 165 (183); H. G. Schermers, *loc. cit.*, footnote 9, paragraph 232.

[29] For a case in which the administration is bound by its own internal directives, *cf.* Case 148/73 *Louwage* v. *Commission* [1974] E.C.R. 81.

[30] *cf.* only H.-W. Daig, *loc. cit.*, footnote 20, Article 189, No. 49.

[31] However, the position is different where we are dealing with individual decisions based on the Staff Regulations, which then become, in relation to the officials, administrative measures within the meaning of the definition given here.

[32] Case 60/81 *IBM* v. *Commission* [1981] E.C.R. 2639 at 2651; *cf.* also Joined Cases 8–11/66 *Cimenteries C.B.R. Cementbedrijven N.V. et al.* v. *Commission* [1967] E.C.R. 99 at 122; Case 182/80, *loc. cit.*, footnote 25, p. 817.

[33] The Commission in Joined Cases 8–11/66, *loc. cit.*, footnote 32, p. 115.

[34] H.-W. Daig, *loc. cit.*, footnote 20, Article 173, Nos. 27, 43; M. Wegmann, *loc. cit.*, footnote 14.

action for annulment is an infringement of the legal interests of the complainant.[35] In relation to an action for annulment under the second paragraph of Article 33 ECSC, on the other hand, as is the case under French law,[36] it is not necessary for there to have been individual concern; however, the applicant must be able to claim "that the decision concerns it" and to support its claim "by an appropriate statement explaining the interest which it has in having the decision declared void."[37]

There is no infringement of the applicant's interests, and therefore no administrative act open to challenge, if, for example, the act in question is merely an administrative act establishing rights and conferring benefits.[38] Although it constitutes an administrative act, this type of measure is no more open to challenge than if it were an administrative act addressed to a third party[39] but which does not infringe his interests by intervening in his legal position. It is precisely such an infringement of interests which is a precondition which has to be met if the applicant is to be deemed to have been concerned within the meaning of the second paragraph of Article 33 ECSC, or directly and individually concerned as required by the second paragraph of Article 173 EEC or Article 146 EAEC.[40]

The criterion of the infringement of interests has also been of assistance to the Court when faced with actions brought for annulment even against those acts which, although they do not constitute a formal decision within the meaning of the fourth paragraph of Article 189 EEC, are nevertheless capable of infringing the legal position of the applicant. This is the case, for example, with the term "informed" used in Article 15(6) of Regulation 17.[41] However, by applying this criterion, the Court, in the *IBM* case, also denied title to sue where the case concerned merely the

[35] H.-W. Daig, *loc. cit.*, footnote 34; Case 60/81, *loc. cit.*, footnote 32.
[36] M. Fromont, *Rechtsschutz gegenüber der Verwaltung in Deutschland, Frankreich und den Europäischen Gemeinschaften*, Köln/Berlin/Bonn/München 1967, pp. 215 *et seq.*; M. Wegmann, *loc. cit.*, footnote 14, p. 21.
[37] Case 30/59 *De Gezamenlijke Steenkolenmijnen in Limburg* v. *Commission* [1961] E.C.R. 1 at 39.
[38] On this concept, *cf.* Advocate-General Lagrange in Case 14/61 *Hoogovens* v. *High Authority* [1962] E.C.R. 253—the position could be different if the administrative measure at the same time rejects any more far-reaching application by the person affected and consequently imposes a burden on the latter.
[39] For a case in which the E.C.J. acknowledged the fact that a firm had been directly and individually concerned by an administrative measure addressed to a Member State, *cf.* Joined Cases 41–44/70 *International Fruit Company* v. *Commission* [1971] E.C.R. 411 at 421 *et seq.*
[40] H.-W. Daig, *loc. cit.*, footnote 20, Article 173, No. 43.
[41] Joined Cases 8–11/66 *loc. cit.*, footnote 32.

initiation of restrictive agreement proceedings and the communication of information within the meaning of Article 2 of Regulation 99/63.[42] Here, the ECJ arrived at the conclusion that the procedural steps undertaken by the Commission had produced no effects on the legal position of the parties in question and had not led to any infringement of their interests.[43]

However, the Court did not concur with the opinion of Advocate-General Slynn, who agreed with that of Advocate-General Roemer in the aforementioned "Cement" case,[44] requiring the infringement of "considerable interests."[45]

2. Differentiating Administrative Acts from Regulations

The text of the fourth paragraph of Article 189 EEC (Article 161 EAEC) states that:
"A decision shall be binding in its entirety upon those to whom it is addressed." Regulations, on the other hand, have "general application" (Second paragraph of Article 189 EEC and Article 161 EAEC). Although this distinction between "decisions" and "regulations" appears at first sight to be clear-cut, in practice it has given rise to a large number of demarcation problems. In the area covered by the ECSC Treaty, the distinguishing criteria between individual decisions on the one hand and general decisions on the other were developed only by the relevant case law.[46]

Difficulties can arise particularly in cases where only a limited number of undertakings or private persons are actually affected by a Community instrument. The Court has on numerous occasions been required to decide whether this type of instrument was a "collective decision"[47] open

---

[42] Case 60/81 *IBM* v. *Commission* [1981] E.C.R. 2639 at 2651 *et seq.*
[43] Case 60/81, *loc. cit.*, footnote 42, p. 2653.
[44] Roemer in Joined Cases 8–11/66, *loc. cit.*, footnote 32, p. 138.
[45] Slynn in Case 60/81, *loc. cit.*, footnote 42, p. 2662.
[46] *cf.*, *e.g.* Roemer in Joined Cases 7 & 9/54 *Groupement des Industries Sidérurgiques Luxembourgeoises* v. *High Authority* [1955–1956] E.C.R. 53 at 118 *et seq.* Lagrange in Case 8/55 *Fédération Charbonnière de Belgique* v. *High Authority* [1955–1956] E.C.R. 197 at 247 *et seq.*
[47] Case 113/77 *NTN Toyo Bearing* v. *Commission* [1979] E.C.R. 1191 at 1205.

to challenge under Article 173 EEC, *i.e.* a bundle of individual decisions open to challenge,[48] or a regulation which was not open to challenge by the Community citizen or by undertakings. Particularly relevant in this context is the provision laid down in the second paragraph of Article 173, second alternative, EEC, under which natural and legal persons may also challenge those decisions "which, although in the form of a regulation . . . is of direct and individual concern to the former." However, the type of decision thus defined is not identical to that of Community collective decisions. On the one hand, even a "decision" which is expressly described as such may be addressed not only to one individual or enterprise but also to several undertakings or private persons. In such cases, we are merely dealing with "individual acts joined together," to which, in his Opinion in the *Fédération Charbonnière de Belgique* case, Advocate-General Lagrange, with reference to the national legal systems of the Member States, applied the term "décisions collectives."[49] On the other hand, it is also possible, in principle, for a decision issued as a regulation to concern only one undertaking directly and individually, so that it may be open to challenge under the second paragraph of Article 173, second alternative, EEC, without fulfilling the conditions required for collective decisions.

Under the case law of the Court of Justice, a collective decision is open to challenge in the same way as an ordinary decision if the act in question, in spite of having been issued as, or forming part of, a regulation, concerns only a limited number of undertakings, *i.e.* those mentioned in the regulation. By way of example we refer to the Japanese ball bearings cases.[50] Here, the ECJ decided that the action brought by the undertaking concerned against Regulation 1778/77[51] was admissible. The challenged

---

[48] Joined Cases 41–44/70 *International Fruit Company* v. *Commission* [1971] E.C.R. 411 at 422; Advocate-General Lenz in Case 232/81 *Agricola Commerciale Olio S.r.l. et al.* v. *Commission* [1984] E.C.R. 3881 at 3910: "A bundle of individual measures conferring individual rights and similar benefits."

[49] Advocate-General Lagrange in Case 8/55, *loc. cit.*, footnote 46, p. 249; Advocate-General Lenz in Case 232/81, *loc. cit.*, footnote 48; "General Decision conferring benefits."

[50] Case 113/77 *NTN Toyo Bearing* v. *Commission* [1979] E.C.R. 1191 at 1205; the same formula is used in Case 118/77 *I.S.O.* v. *Commission* [1979] E.C.R. 1277 at 1294; Case 119/77 *Nippon Seiko* v. *Commission* [1979] E.C.R. 1303 at 1327; Case 120/77 *Koyo Seiko* v. *Commission* [1979] E.C.R. 1337 at 1353; Case 121/77 *Nachi Fujikoshi* v. *Commission* [1979] E.C.R. 1363 at 1379; *cf.* on this subject W. v. Simson, 'Anforderungen an die Rechtmässigkeit des Verwaltungshandelns der EG-Behörden—Erfahrungen aus Prozessen vor dem EuGH," in J. Schwarze (ed.), *Europäisches Verwaltungsrecht im Werden*, Baden-Baden 1982, p. 23 (37 *et seq.*).

[51] Regulation 1778/77 of the Council of July 26, 1977, O.J. 1977, L196/1.

provision had ordered the definitive collection of an anti-dumping duty, which had been imposed upon the undertakings specified in the regulation.

These principles were confirmed by the Court in its decision in the *Allied Corporation* case of 1984, which had substantially the same background.[52] Article 13(2) of the Anti-dumping Regulation[53] provides that "anti-dumping or countervailing duties, whether provisional or definitive, shall be imposed by regulation." The Court held that "measures imposing anti-dumping duties are liable to be of direct and individual concern to those producers and exporters who are able to establish that they were identified in the measures adopted by the Commission or the Council. . . ."[54] This was the case in relation to three United States exporters of chemical fertilizers.[55] The action for annulment brought by them was accordingly held admissible. Although the Court in this decision expressly refers to the Japanese ball-bearings cases, it did not describe the act in question as a "collective decision," perhaps because its ambiguity became fully apparent in this case.[56] In addition to being a decision in relation to the producers and exporters mentioned by name, the challenged measure at the same time constituted a genuine regulation, *i.e.* in relation to all independent importers of the fertilisers in question who were not mentioned by name, such as for example another applicant in this case, whose action was accordingly rejected as being inadmissible.[57]

However, those legal acts which do not mention the parties affected by it by name but define them on the basis of abstract criteria can also constitute collective administrative acts under Community law, with the result that they are open to challenge under the second paragraph of Article 173 EEC. The object and purpose of this provision is precisely to avoid a situation whereby the Community organs would have the power to deprive the parties actually affected by a legal act of the

---

[52] Joined Cases 239 & 275/82 *Allied Corporation* v. *Commission* [1984] E.C.R. 1005 at 1030.
[53] Regulation 3017/79, O.J. 1978, L339/1.
[54] Joined Cases 239 & 275/82, *loc. cit.*, footnote 52.
[55] *cf.*, Regulations 1967/82, O.J. 1982, L214/7 (Article 1 amended by Regulation 2302/82, O.J. 1982, L246/5), and 349/81, O.J. 1981, L39/4 (Article 2).
[56] Advocate-General VerLoren van Themaat in Joined Cases 239 & 275/82, *loc. cit.*, footnote 52, p. 1041.
[57] E.C.J., *ibid.*, p. 1031; *cf.* also Case 307/81 *Alusuisse* v. *Commission* [1982] E.C.R. 3463 at 3472.

opportunity to challenge it merely by virtue of the form they chose to give to that measure or by an abstract definition of the parties affected.[58]

Particularly relevant in this context is the decision in the *International Fruit Company* case. Article 1 of the measure in question, *i.e.* Regulation 983/70,[59] provided that a system of import licences for dessert apples, which had been introduced by Regulation 459/70,[60] was to apply to all applications made within a certain period prior to the adoption of Regulation 983/70.

In this case, the Court arrived at the conclusion that this Article was "not a provision of general application within the meaning of the second paragraph of Article 189 of the Treaty, but must be regarded as a conglomeration of individual decisions taken by the Commission under the guise of a regulation ... each of which decisions affects the legal position of each author of an application for a licence. Thus the decisions are of individual concern to the applicants."[61] Although the applicants had not been mentioned by name in the challenged Regulation 983/70, they had nevertheless been singled out on the basis of an abstract criterion, *i.e.* a certain period within which their applications for import licences had been filed. However, the issue which decided the matter as far as the Court of Justice was concerned was that in so doing, the Regulation had made reference to a completed event in the past. "It follows that when the said regulation was adopted, the number of applications which could be affected by it was fixed. No new application could be added."[62]

In other cases also,[63] the Court considered that a decisive factor in separating collective administrative acts open to challenge (without necessarily using this or a similar term on every occasion) from regulations not open to challenge was the question whether the circle of addressees of the measure, if defined on the basis of abstract criteria, was based exclusively on a past event. This was the situation, for example, in

---

[58] Case 101/76 *Koninklijke Scholten Honig N.V.* v. *Council and Commission* [1977] E.C.R. 797 at 806; *cf.* also Advocate-General Lenz in Case 232/81 *loc. cit.*, footnote 48, p. 3903, containing further references.

[59] J.O. 1970, L116/35.

[60] J.O. 1970, L57/19; O.J. Sp.Ed. 1970, L57/145.

[61] Joined Cases 41–44/70 *International Fruit Company* v. *Commission* [1971] E.C.R. 411 at 422.

[62] Joined Cases 41–44/70, *loc. cit.*, footnote 61.

[63] *cf.* on this subject Case 232/81 *Agricola Commerciale Olio* v. *Commission* [1984] E.C.R. 3881 at 3895 *et seq.*; Case 307/81 *Alusuisse Italia SpA* v. *Council and Commission* [1982] E.C.R. 3463 at 3470; Case 222/83 *Municipality of Differdange et al.* v. *Commission* [1984] E.C.R. 2889.

the decision of Case 100/74, *CAM* v. *Commission*.[64] In this case, the applicant had challenged a Commission regulation of October 4, 1974, which affected only those exporters of cereals for whom permission to export had been fixed in advance before July 26, 1974 and who on October 7, 1974 were still in possession of valid export licences. In this case, the Court concluded that the challenged "regulation," by adopting these distinguishing criteria, "affects a fixed number of traders identified by reason of the individual course of action which they pursued or are regarded as having pursued during a particular period."

> "Such a measure, even if it is one of a number of provisions having a legislative function, individually concerns the person to whom it applies in that it affects their legal position because of a factual situation which differentiates them from all other persons and distinguishes them individually just as in the case of the person addressed."[65]

According to this case law of the Court, the important issue to establish is whether, once the legal act has been adopted, other persons could become affected by it or new circumstances could come into being to which the measure could be applied.[66] Where this possibility is excluded, we are faced with a "bundle of individual decisions," *i.e.* a "collective administrative act"; if it is not, we are dealing with a regulation. It is irrelevant in this connection whether the regulation actually concerned only one trader or a certain number of traders which was known at the time of adopting the regulation. For a measure to qualify as a regulation, it is sufficient that, at least in theory, other persons could become affected by the act.

In establishing this distinction, a factor which counts just as little as the question whether the circle of persons affected at the time of adopting the regulation was determined or capable of being determined, is the number of traders affected.[67] As the Court made clear in the *Scholten Honig* case, "the nature of a measure as a regulation is not called into question by the possibility of determining more or less precisely the number or even the identity of the persons to whom it applies at a given moment as long as it is

---

[64] Case 100/74 *CAM* v. *Commission* [1975] E.C.R. 1393.
[65] E.C.J. *ibid.*, p. 1403; also in a similar case: Case 88/76 *Exportation des Sucres* v. *Commission* [1977] E.C.R. 709 at 726 and Advocate-General Reischl, *ibid.*, p. 731.
[66] H.-W. Daig, in H. v. d. Groeben, H. v. Boeckh, J. Thiesing, C.-D. Ehlermann, Article 189, No. 62.
[67] Advocate-General Reischl in Case 101/76, *loc. cit.*, footnote 58, p. 811.

established that it is applied by virtue of an objective legal or factual situation defined by the measure in relation to the objective of the latter."[68] Here, the Council had increased the refunds on the manufacture of products based on wheat starch, but had at the same time decided that in future the manufacture of certain products, *i.e.* glucose having a high content of fructose, would be excluded from this increase. As the Court observed, this regulation affected the applicant only "by virtue of its capacity of a producer of glucose."[69] It was irrelevant in this context that only a limited number of undertakings, in this case four, had in fact been affected by this provision and the number of undertakings could not be increased in the short term because of the required investment and expertise.[70] Here, the legally relevant criterion for determining the circle of parties concerned was the future production of glucose and not, as had been the case in relation to the export refunds fixed in advance mentioned in the cases referred to earlier, a past event—in this case, the circumstance that the applicant had already produced glucose up to that point.

Although in all these cases the demarcation between "collective decisions" on the one hand, and "real" regulations on the other was relevant to the Court of Justice in the first place from the point of view of the admissibility of an action, this distinction could also become increasingly important for the substantive appraisal of the facts of a case.

Thus Advocate-General Lenz, in his Opinion in the "Olive Oil" case in 1984,[71] concluded from the fact that the measure in question was not a "real" regulation but a "general measure in favour of those persons, that is, a group of individual acts which confers favourable individual rights upon them,"[72] that on the question of the admissibility of a later revocation of this general measure, the "general principles of law concerning revocation of administrative acts"[73] had to be applied, instead of the principles relating to the retroactivity of regulations.[74]

---

[68] Case 101/76, *loc. cit.*, footnote 58, p. 808; *cf.* also, for a similar ruling, Case 64/80 *F. Giuffrida and G. Campogrande* v. *Council* [1981] E.C.R. 693 at 703.

[69] Case 101/76, *loc. cit.*, footnote 58, p. 807.

[70] This is according to the statements made by the applicant, cited at p. 804.

[71] Lenz in Case 232/81 *Agricola Commerciale Olio* v. *Commission* [1984] E.C.R. 3881 at 3900 *et seq.*

[72] Lenz, *ibid.*, p. 3910; here, Lenz is referring to Regulation 71/81; whilst the challenged regulation 2238/81 concerns the applicant directly and individually (as is confirmed by the E.C.J. at p. 3896) and is to be regarded as a general decision, this is a doubtful proposition in relation to Regulation 71/81 in the light of the criteria set out above.

[73] Advocate-General Lenz, *ibid.*

[74] In this case, the E.C.J. concluded that the "sole ground advanced by the Commission in order to justify the revocation of the Regulation in question cannot be upheld in the light

3. Classification of Administrative Acts

(a) Declaratory administrative acts and acts establishing rights

The distinction between administrative acts establishing rights and declaratory (or confirmatory) administrative acts forms the basis for the case law of the Court of Justice, at least in the initial major ECSC decisions on the question of the revocation of administrative acts. Composed to this issue, the distinction between administrative acts conferring benefits and acts imposing burdens, which is derived from German law, is of lesser significance. In so doing, the Court clearly intended to be guided by French administrative law, to which Advocate-General Lagrange expressly refers in his Opinion in the *Hoogovens* case:

> "A measure which creates rights is a measure by which a public authority exercises a power conferred on it by law or by regulation, in the fulfilment of its public service, and which creates legal relations between the administration and those subject to it, such as the appointment of an official or the grant of an authorisation; there the right derives from the measure. In the second category are, for example, the financial relations, debts and credits of the State or of public organisations, contested revenue claims, and so forth; in these cases, the right derives solely from the law or regulation, and the measure does no more than apply the law or regulation, interpreting it if need be.
>
> This does not, of course, mean that measures creating rights can never be found in the second category. But they can exist only where a special competence is conferred on the administration, permitting it, in the exercise of limited discretionary powers, to create a new legal situation, as, for example, by granting benefits under certain conditions."[75]

Here, the distinction drawn by the Court between both types of administrative acts differs from that made in French administrative law between "actes créateurs de droit" and "actes récognitifs" in that the ECJ includes among the administrative acts establishing rights only those acts which

---

of the relevant circumstances," so that "there is no need to examine whether the Commission could have revoked the regulation if circumstances were different..." (p. 3898).

[75] Advocate-General Lagrange in Case 14/61 *Hoogovens* v. *High Authority* [1962] E.C.R. 253.

confer subjective rights on the parties affected,[76] whereas in France this type of additional condition is not stipulated.[77] The Court has, for example, described as an administrative act establishing rights the appointment of officials and their assignment to a particular salary bracket,[78] and direct or indirect subsidies for the price of scrap metal were also identified by the Court as "administrative measures producing subjective rights."[79]

In the case of an order for the payment of contributions towards the scrap equalisation fund, on the other hand, we are in its opinion dealing with a purely declaratory administrative act.[80] The measure allocating an expatriation allowance on the basis of Article 47(3) of the Staff Regulations was also deemed to be a confirmatory administrative act.[81]

Finally, in another case, the Court denied the status of an administrative act establishing rights to a decision of the High Authority, by which the latter had exempted certain undertakings from payment of contributions, pointing out that "the High Authority has no power to grant derogations or exemptions from the payment of equalisation contributions, but power only to declare that the obligation to pay the levy does not arise from the basic Decisions."[82,83] Accordingly, the measure in question was an unlawful confirmatory administrative act conferring benefits.[84]

The distinction between administrative acts establishing rights and declaratory acts has played an important part, especially on the question

---

[76] Thus stated expressly by the E.C.J. in this case (footnote 75), p. 549; *cf., e.g.* also Case 159/82 *Verli-Wallace* v. *Commission* [1983] E.C.R. 2711 at 2719 and Advocate-General Lagrange in Joined Cases 7/56 & 3–7/57 *Algera et al.* v. *Common Assembly* [1957] E.C.R. 39; also the opinion by the same Advocate-General in Joined Cases 42 & 49/59 *SNUPAT* v. *High Authority* [1961] E.C.R. 53.

[77] H. Lecheler, *Der Europäische Gerichtshof und die allgemeinen Rechtsgrundsätze*, Berlin 1971, p. 78.

[78] Joined Cases 7/56 & 3–7/57, *loc. cit.*, footnote 76, p. 117.

[79] Joined Cases 4–13/59 *Mannesmann AG et al.* v. *High Authority* [1960] E.C.R. 249 at 290.

[80] *cf., e.g.* Case 108/63 *Merlini* v. *High Authority* [1965] E.C.R. 1; Case 2/65 *Handelsgesellschaft Preo and Figli* v. *High Authority* [1966] E.C.R. 559; Case 67/69 *Simet* v. *Commission* [1971] E.C.R. 197; Case 2/70 *Riva* v. *Commission* [1971] E.C.R. 97; *cf.* in addition Case 14/61 *Hoogovens* v. *High Authority* [1962] E.C.R. 253 and Case 111/63 *Lemmerz-Werke* v. *High Authority* [1965] E.C.R. 893 at 911.

[81] Advocate-General Roemer in Case 15/60 *Gabriel Simon* v. *Court of Justice* [1961] E.C.R. 239 at 272.

[82] In this case the general decision on the establishment of the scrap equalisation fund system.

[83] Case 14/61 *Hoogovens* v. *High Authority* [1962] E.C.R. 253—*cf.* also Case 111/63 *Lemmerz-Werke* v. *High Authority* [1965] E.C.R. 893 at 911 and Advocate-General Lagrange in Case 14/61, *loc. cit.*, pp. 90 *et seq.*

[84] Advocate-General Roemer in Case 111/63, *loc. cit.*, footnote 83, pp. 934 and 937.

of the admissibility of the revocation of administrative acts. As will be explained later in detail, the Court considered that, in the case of administrative acts establishing rights, the decisive criterion was in the first place that the revocation should be pronounced "within a reasonable period"[85]—thus following, cautiously but unmistakably, the case law developed by the French administrative courts.[86] On the other hand, the ECJ has tended to apply German legal thinking where it states that, in its opinion, the criterion for assessing the lawfulness of the revocation *ex tunc* of declaratory administrative acts should be the weighing up of the conflicting public and private interests.[87]

However, the Court has not invariably drawn a strict distinction between these two categories of administrative act.[88] More particularly, there is a lack of recent judgments in which this distinction is explicitly referred to. In more recent times, the ECJ tends to use general notions such as the "retroactive withdrawal of a legal measure which has conferred individual rights or similar benefits,"[89] or of the "withdrawal of an unlawful measure."[90] Accordingly, it is extremely doubtful whether the distinction originally drawn by the Court continues to have the same relevance.

(b) Administrative acts conferring benefits and imposing burdens

The distinction between administrative acts conferring benefits and those which impose burdens is also used in Community law. Although the concept of "legal measures conferring individual rights or similar benefits" is occasionally featured in the case law of the Court of Justice, the latter would appear often to make this distinction without applying it

---

[85] Thus, *e.g.* in Joined Cases 7/56 & 3–7/57, *loc. cit.*, footnote 76, p. 119; *cf.* also on this distinction Case 14/61, *loc. cit.*, footnote 83, p. 272.

[86] Advocate-General Lagrange in Joined Cases 7/56 & 3–7/57, *loc. cit.*, footnote 76, pp. 162 *et seq.*; opinion by the same Advocate-General in case 14/61, *loc. cit.*, footnote 83, pp. 277 *et seq.*

[87] *cf. e.g.* Case 14/61, *loc. cit.*, footnote 83, p. 272.

[88] Case 56/75 *Raymond Elz* v. *Commission* [1976] E.C.R. 1097 at 1109; Case 54/77 *Anton Herpels* v. *Commission* [1978] E.C.R. 585 at 598; note in particular the attitude of the parties to this question in the *Herpels* case; here, the Commission advocated drawing a distinction between administrative measures creating rights and confirmatory measures; it took the view that here, as in the *Elz* case, they were dealing with confirmatory administrative measures.

[89] Case 159/82 *Verli-Wallace* v. *Commission* [1983] E.C.R. p. 2711 at 2718 *et seq.*; however, the Court also pointed out that the administrative measure which was subsequently revoked had "granted [the applicant] the individual right to take part in the tests of this competition" (p. 2719).

[90] Case 14/81 *Alpha Steel* v. *Commission* [1982] E.C.R. 749 at 764.

explicitly. Administrative acts conferring benefits were involved, for example, in the question of the permissibility of the revocation and withdrawal of administrative acts issued under Community law.

Thus the Court observed in the *SNUPAT* case that "the retroactive withdrawal of a legal measure which has conferred individual rights or similar benefits is contrary to the general principles of law."[91] The concept of "legal measures conferring individual rights or similar benefits" is also used in the *Verli-Wallace* case—in which reference is made to the *SNUPAT* case.[92] In this case, a Commission official brought an action against the decision by which her admission to a competitive examination was revoked by her administrative department. In the opinion of the Court, the decision in question related to a legal measure which conferred individual rights or similar benefits, since "the original admission of the applicant to the competition at issue gave her a personal right to take part in the tests for the competition."[93]

However, declaratory administrative acts may also confer benefits.[94] This is demonstrated by, for example, the manner in which the aforementioned *SNUPAT* case was decided.[95] Although the exemption in question constituted an administrative act which conferred benefits on the intervening parties in this case, the Hoogovens and Breda companies, it was, in the Court's opinion, merely declaratory in character, since the High Authority had no authority to grant exemptions but was merely empowered to establish whether or not there existed a duty to make the equalisation payments or not.[96] The *Simon* case[97] also concerned a declaratory administrative act conferring benefits; Advocate-General Roemer makes express reference here to a measure conferring individual rights or similar benefits,[98] whilst the Court uses the term "privilege."[99] Although the Court does not explicitly state that the act in question is a declaratory administrative act, it may be assumed, on the basis of the criteria applied in other cases,[100] that this is in fact what it is. The term "legal measure

---

[91] Joined Cases 42 & 49/59 *SNUPAT* v. *High Authority* [1961] E.C.R. 53.

[92] Case 159/82, *loc. cit.*, footnote 89, pp. 2718 *et seq.*

[93] Case 159/82, *loc. cit.*, footnote 89, p. 2719.

[94] Advocate-General Roemer in Case 111/63 *Lemmerz-Werke* v. *High Authority* [1965] E.C.R. 893 at 934, 937.

[95] Joined Cases 42 & 49/59, *loc. cit.*, footnote 91.

[96] This was the view of the Court in the following decision: Case 14/61 *Hoogovens* v. *High Authority* [1962] E.C.R. 253.

[97] Case 15/60 *Gabriel Simon* v. *Court of Justice* [1961] E.C.R. 239.

[98] Advocate-General Roemer, *ibid.*, p. 273.

[99] E.C.J., *ibid.*, p. 259.

[100] Advocate-General Lagrange in Case 14/61 *Hoogovens* v. *High Authority* [1962] E.C.R. 253.

imposing burdens," on the other hand, which was intended as a counter-part of the concept of "measures conferring individual rights and similar benefits," is not explicitly used by the Court. However, legal measures imposing burdens frequently occur in this context, namely in the many decisions by the Court on the question of the subsequent assessment applied under the scrap equalisation fund system of the ECSC Treaty. In these cases, the regular cause of the action was a decision by the High Authority by which the latter withdrew from the firms in question an earlier administrative act imposing a burden, in which a certain amount had been fixed by way of contribution towards the scrap equalisation fund, and at the same time claimed a new and higher amount.[101] The fact that the original measure thus acquires a kind of dual effect was not acknowledged by the Court in these cases—after all, it was theoretically possible to attribute to these administrative acts, in addition to the clearly imposed burden, a beneficial effect in the sense that they fixed the mandatory contributions once and for all.[102] However, the Court specifically rejected this view and held a subsequent increased assessment to be permissible.[103]

Finally, there also exist in Community law administrative acts which acquire a dual effect in the sense that the decision imposes a burden on one Community citizen and benefits another at the same time. Examples of this possible outcome are the *SNUPAT* and *Hoogovens* cases, which have already been mentioned.[104] Both actions arose from an exemption decision in the context of the scrap equalisation fund. On the one hand, this decision benefited the Breda and Hoogovens firms, as it exempted from the obligatory contributions certain types of bought scrap acquired by these firms as being their own arisings, whereas on the other hand it imposed a burden on all other firms, including the applicant in the *SNUPAT* case, since on account of this exemption they had to pay a proportionately higher amount to the scrap equalisation fund. Strictly speaking, however, the *SNUPAT* action was not brought against this administrative act but against the tacit decision by the High Authority, which imposed burdens on *SNUPAT*, not to revoke the exemption decision taken in 1956/57, although the Court had already, in another

---

[101] *cf.*, *e.g.* Case 2/70 *Riva* v. *Commission* [1971] E.C.R. 97; Case 108/63 *Merlini* v. *Commission* [1965] E.C.R. 1.

[102] This had also been pointed out by the applicant in Case 2/70, *loc. cit.*, footnote 101 (pp. 101, 115).

[103] Case 2/70, *loc. cit.*, footnote 101, p. 108; Advocate-General Roemer, *ibid.*, p. 115.

[104] Joined Cases 42 & 49/59, *SNUPAT* v. *High Authority* [1961] E.C.R. 53; Case 14/61 *Hoogovens* v. *High Authority* [1962] E.C.R. 253.

case,[105] established the unlawful nature of the decision to exempt "own scrap."[106]

(c) Unlawful administrative acts which are completely null and void

Community law also applies the rule that "the adoption of an administrative measure creates a presumption as to its validity."[107]

As the Court stated in the *Algera* case, which has already been mentioned, "the unlawful nature of an individual administrative measure entails its complete nullity[108] only in certain circumstances which do not occur in the present action."[109] The same considerations apply in the case of administrative measures imposing burdens.[110] Accordingly, where an administrative measure is not null and void by way of exception, the legally effective character even of an unlawful administrative measure may be set aside only by an annulment pronounced by the Court (a declaration that it is void by virtue of Articles 173 EEC, Article 146 EAEC and 33 ECSC) or through revocation by the authority which issued the administrative measure in question.[111] As is the case in national law, Community law imposes, in the interests of legal certainty, certain restrictions both on the extent to which unlawful administrative measures

---

[105] Joined Cases 32–33/58 *SNUPAT* v. *High Authority* [1959] E.C.R. 53.

[106] Joined Cases 42 & 49/59, *loc. cit.*, footnote 104.

[107] Joined Cases 7/56 & 3–7/57 *Algera et al.* v. *Common Assembly* [1957–1958] E.C.R. 39; on this topic and on the issues dealt with subsequently, *cf.* H. P. Ipsen, *Europ. Gemeinschaftsrecht*, Tübingen 1972, 24/8; H.-W. Daig, in H. v. d. Groeben, H. v. Boeckh, J. Thiesing, C.-D. Ehlermann, *Kommentar zum EWG-Vertrag* (3rd ed., Baden-Baden 1983), Article 174, No. 7; H. G. Schermers, *Judicial Protection in the European Communities* (3rd ed., Deventer 1983), paragraphs 213 *et seq.*; W. Däubler, "Der Widerruf von Verwaltungsakten im Recht der Europäischen Gemeinschaften," NJW 1965, p. 1646 (1647); *cf.* also Case 3/59 *Federal Republic of Germany* v. *Commission* [1960] E.C.R. 53, Case 11/81 *Dürbeck* v. *Commission* [1982] E.C.R. 1251 (1266).

[108] Both the Court and the Advocates-General at times also use the terminology drawn from French law and describe the administrative measure which is absolutely void as a "non-existent measure."

[109] Joined Cases 7/56 & 3–7/57, *loc. cit.*, footnote 107.

[110] *cf.* for example Joined Cases 15–33, 52–53, 57–109, 116–117, 123, 132 & 135–137/73 *Kortner-Schots et al.* v. *Commission* [1974] E.C.R. 177 at 190 *et seq.* on the question of the formal legality of administrative measures; also *cf.* Case 36/64 *SOREMA* v. *High Authority* [1965] E.C.R. 447 at 459 and Advocate-General Roemer, *ibid.*, p. 467.

[111] Joined Cases 7/56 & 3–7/57, *loc. cit.*, footnote 107; H. P. Ipsen, *loc. cit.*, footnote 107; H. G. Schermers, *loc. cit.*, footnote 107; M. van Empel, "L'acte public inexistant et le droit communautaire," CDE 1971, p. 251.

imposing burdens are open to challenge and on the revocation of measures conferring benefits. If, on the other hand, the administrative measure is null and void, an application made against it is, according to the Court's decision in the *Tubes de la Sarre* case, "inadmissible for want of subject matter since the act which impugns it is, in law, non-existent."[112]

Apart from those cases in which the Court has denied an act issued by the Commission the status of a "decision" in the absence of an intention to create direct legal effects,[113] this is, as far as can be ascertained, the only case hitherto in which the ECJ has pronounced the nullity of an administrative act issued by the High Authority.[114] Here, the Court concluded that the contentious "reasoned opinion" made by the High Authority in accordance with the fourth paragraph of Article 54 ECSC—which was not, however, open to challenge—should be held to be non-existent since it lacked the reasoning, which was not only "prescribed by Articles 5, 15 and 54 para. 4 of the Treaty," but also "constitutes an essential, even a constitutive, element of such an act."[115] Even though the statements by the Court are based on the details of an action against reasoned opinions made in accordance with the fourth paragraph of Article 54 ECSC, it is not possible to conclude from them a general legal principle under which an administrative measure which lacks proper reasons is not only unlawful and consequently challengeable, but also null and void *per se*.[116] In any case, the Court, in other cases concerning infringements of the duty to give reasons, has not treated the legal measure in question as null and void but has merely set it aside as the occasion demanded.[117]

In other decisions also, the Court has restricted itself merely to considering the possibility of the absolute nullity of an administrative act, without applying it in practice.

The 1969 *Commission* v. *France* case is an example of this. Here, the ECJ appears to examine the question of the nullity of a Commission decision: "If this allegation were valid, the aforementioned decision

---

[112] Joined Cases 1 & 14/57, *Tubes de la Sarre* v. *High Authority* [1957–1958] E.C.R. 105 at 113.

[113] *cf.* on this subject the examples given in footnote 9.

[114] H. G. Schermers, *Judicial Protection in the European Communities* (3rd ed., Deventer 1983), paragraph 217.

[115] Joined Cases 1 & 14/57, *loc. cit.*, footnote 112.

[116] H. G. Schermers, *loc. cit.*, footnote 114; A. M. van Empel, *loc. cit.*, footnote 111, p. 273.

[117] *cf.*, *e.g.* Case 18/57 *Firma Nold KG* v. *High Authority* [1959] E.C.R. 89 at 114 *et seq.*, as well as Joined Cases 8–11/66 *Cimenteries C.B.R. Cementbedrijven N.V. et al.* v. *Commission* [1967] E.C.R. 75 at 94.

would lack all legal basis in the Community legal system."[118] In this case, the Government of the French Republic had, in the context of an action for breach of the Treaty brought by the Commission for failure to observe a decision concerning the illicit nature of certain protective measures, claimed that the Community lacked jurisdiction in this matter. However, France had neglected to challenge the original decision within the time limit set by the third paragraph of Article 173 of the EEC Treaty. Although the decision thus became incapable of being challenged *per se*, and no plea of illegality is provided for against administrative measures,[119] both the Advocate General[120] and the Court,[121] following his example, saw fit to examine whether the decision made by the Commission should be held to be completely null and void on grounds of, *inter alia*, lack of authority on the part of the Commission. In this case, however, the ECJ concluded that the Community, and the Commission acting on its behalf, had the necessary authority.

According to the case law of the Court, it is thus possible, at least in theory, for an administrative act to be declared null and void on grounds of lack of authority, even after the time limit for challenging the measure has expired. However, the *Commission* v. *France* case mentioned above has two special features. On the one hand, it was not the special powers of a Community institution within the Community system which were under scrutiny but, more generally, the demarcation of the jurisdiction of the Community in relation to that of the Member States which was called into question. On the other hand, the case in question concerned an action for breach of the Treaty. The Court also emphasised this point with regard to the necessity of examining the possibility of pronouncing the absolute nullity of the act,[122] so that it is doubtful whether this case law expresses a general principle which could also be relied upon by an individual citizen in a legal dispute with the Community.[123]

Another case of absolute nullity on grounds of "apparent infringement of rules of jurisdiction" was, in the opinion of Advocate-General

---

[118] Joined Cases 6 & 11/69, *Commission* v. *French Republic* [1969] E.C.R. 523 at 540.

[119] Advocate-General Roemer, *ibid.* pp. 550 *et seq.*; Case 3/59 *Federal Republic of Germany* v. *High Authority* [1960] E.C.R. 121 at 139; Case 36/64 *SOREMA* v. *High Authority* [1965] E.C.R. 447 at 459.

[120] Advocate-General Roemer, Joined Cases 6 & 11/69, *loc. cit.*, footnote 118, pp. 551 *et seq.*

[121] E.C.J., *ibid.*, pp. 540 *et seq.*

[122] E.C.J., *loc. cit.*, footnote 121.

[123] L. J. Brinkhorst, I. M. Verougstraete, "Annotation to Joined Cases 6 & 11/69," [1970] C.M.L.Rev. 479 (485); H. G. Schermers, *loc. cit.*, footnote 114, para. 216.

Roemer, that of *Société Fives Lille et al.*[124] The Advocate-General pointed out that the legal systems of France, the Netherlands and Germany also drew the distinction between mere unlawfulness and *absolute nullity*.[125] However, the Court failed to follow the Opinion of its Advocate-General on this point.

Finally, the Court itself held, in the famous *Kortner-Schots* case, that the measure in question—in this case a legal rule[126]—could not "be termed 'non-existent,' originating as it does with the competent authority and taken with due regard for the procedural and formal conditions laid down by the Treaties."[127]

To sum up, then, it can be stated that the absolute nullity of an administrative act is not totally unknown in Community law, but that such cases are extremely rare and that consequently an administrative measure, if found to be unlawful, will in most cases merely be set aside through a judicial decision pronouncing its annulment or by an *actus contrarius* on the part of the issuing authority. The complete avoidance of administrative measures, which is at the same time expressive of the principle of compliance with the relevant legislation and an infringement of the principle of legal certainty, has not as yet been fully recognised in Community law.[128]

From a procedural viewpoint, it must be observed that the actions which can be brought under the Community treaties do not give the Community citizen the opportunity to bring a declaratory action, as is, for example, possible in German law for the purpose of establishing the nullity of an administrative measure (*cf., e.g.* Article 43 VwGO). The action for avoidance under Article 173 EEC (Article 146 EAEC, Article 33 ECSC) has the object of setting aside the administrative measure in question and does not restrict itself to establishing its nullity. As a result, actions against absolutely null and void administrative acts are not permissible in the absence of subject-matter for that action.[129] Where in such cases the Court fails to use the possibility of ordering, by way of exception, the winning party to pay costs in accordance with Article 69(3) of the

---

[124] Advocate-General Roemer in Joined Cases 19 & 21/60; 2–3/61 *Société Fives Lille* v. *High Authority* [1961] E.C.R. 611 at 669.

[125] Advocate-General Roemer, *ibid.*; on the Netherlands law, *cf.* the same Advocate-General in his opinion in Joined Cases 4–13/59 *Mannesmann et al.* v. *High Authority* [1960] E.C.R. 249 at 327 *et seq.*

[126] Article 4(3) Annex VII to the Staff Regulations.

[127] Joined cases 15–33, 52, 53, 57–109, 116–117, 123, 132 & 135–137/73 *Kortner-Schots et al.* v. *Council, Commission and Parliament* [1974] E.C.R. 190 at 197.

[128] *cf.* on this subject H. G. Schermers, *loc. cit.*, footnote 114, paragraph 213.

[129] *cf.* on this subject also H. G. Schermers, *loc. cit.*, footnote 114, paragraph 219.

Rules of Procedure, or at least of setting the relevant costs off against each other,[130] these must be borne by the applicant.[131] It is especially for this reason that Advocate-General Lagrange, in another case which concerned the question whether a "decision" of the High Authority, for want of proper authority on the part of the official who had issued it, was merely unlawful or actually null and void, advocated that the solution which would pronounce the measure unlawful be adopted, particularly as he considered this to be "more correct from a legal viewpoint."[132]

II. REVOCATION OF ADMINISTRATIVE ACTS

1. Introduction

The doctrine of the revocation and withdrawal of administrative acts, which forms a key element of general administrative law, has, as is the case in the national legal systems, been developed in Community law on the basis of the legal principles of legal certainty and of the protection of legitimate expectations.

Particularly on this issue the Court has displayed its explicit concern that the rules of European administrative law should be elaborated on the basis of a comparative assessment of the legal systems of the Community Member States.

In the absence of any reference to this question in the Treaties, and since derived Community law contains only a few detailed rules on this subject, the unwritten general legal principles as developed by the case law of the Court of Justice will occupy a particularly important place.

The logical point of departure for the principles which have thus been developed on the revocation of administrative measures is, as far as the

---

[130] As occurred in Case 28/63 *Hoogovens* v. *High Authority* [1963] E.C.R. 231 at 236. In this decision, which has a slightly different background, the Court concluded that the instruments in question were not "decisions" but non-binding written communications by the Commission.

[131] Thus, *e.g.* in Joined Cases 1 & 14/57, *loc. cit.*, footnote 112, pp. 233, 237.

[132] Advocate-General Lagrange in Joined Cases 15 & 29/59 *Société Métallurgique de Knutange* v. *High Authority* [1960] E.C.R. 9 at 34; when the Advocate-General states that the decision is "void," this reflects French terminology, which uses the term "nullité" even in relation to what would normally be described as "Anfechtbarkeit" (contestability) within the meaning of German administrative law; an administrative measure which is absolutely void is characterised as an "acte inexistant" or as an "acte quasi inexistant"; it is this meaning which is intended where Advocate-General Lagrange states that "although there is a decision . . .": on this subject, *cf.* W. Däubler, "Der Widerruf von Verwaltungsakten im Recht der Europäischen Gemeinschaften," NJW 1965, p. 1646 (1647).

ECJ is concerned, the rule prohibiting the courts from denying justice. In an early decision, *i.e.* the *Algera* case, to which we have already referred several times, the Court emphasised that "unless the Court is to deny justice" it was obliged to "solve the problem by reference to the rules acknowledged by the legislation, the learned writing and the case law of the member countries."[1]

As regards the terminology used in the analysis which follows, we shall apply exclusively to the subsequent rescission of administrative measures the term "revocation," which concept will be explained in greater detail as and when it arises; we shall not use the term "withdrawal," even though both terms ("Widerruf" and "Rücknahme") occur in the German texts of the Court's decisions.

Accordingly, any similarity with German administrative law is excluded from the outset, since the language used in the Court's decisions, in which German is often merely a language into which the text has been translated, does not admit of the distinction,[2] made in German administrative legislation, between the withdrawal of unlawful administrative measures (Article 48 BVwVfG) and the revocation of lawful administrative measures (Article 49 BVwVfG).

Here too, the account which follows must be restricted to the bare outlines and cannot give an opinion on each individual decision taken from an extensive and variegated case law.

2. The Revocation of Administrative Acts in Written Law

Written rules concerning the revocation of Community administrative acts can be found in the competition law of the ECSC and of the EEC, as well as in the Staff Regulations.[3]

---

[1] Joined cases 7/56 & 3–7/57 *Algera et al.* v. *Common Assembly* [1957–1958] E.C.R. 39.

[2] A different situation applies in Regulation 3318/85 of the Commission of November 27, 1985 on the annulment or revocation of authorisations for processing under customs control (O.J. 1985, L 317/13); here, a distinction is made between annulment, which takes effect "from the date of issue of the authorisation" and revocation, which normally becomes effective from the date of its notification (Article 3(1)); similar considerations apply to Regulation 3787/86 of December 11, 1986.

[3] *cf.* in addition the rules mentioned *supra* (footnote 2).

(a) Revocation under Article 65(2), fourth paragraph, ECSC

Under Article 65(2), first paragraph, of the ECSC Treaty, the High Authority—now the Commission—may, under certain circumstances, authorise certain specialisation or joint-buying or joint-selling agreements, even if they restrict competition. Such authorisations are administrative measures conferring benefits. Under the third paragraph of this provision, such authorisations may be granted under certain conditions and for a limited period. Under the fourth paragraph, the High Authority may revoke or amend such an authorisation "if it finds that as a result of a change in circumstances the agreement no longer meets these requirements (*i.e.* those stated in the first paragraph of Article 65(2))[4] or that the actual results of the agreement or of the application thereof are contrary to the requirements (*i.e.* those stated in the third paragraph)[5] for its authorisation."

By way of derogation from the general principle of the irrevocability of administrative measures conferring benefits, this provision empowers the High Authority to revoke these administrative measures, at least for the future,[6] if a change of circumstances occurs or if the conditions attached to the original authorising decision are infringed.

In both *SOREMA* cases, which date from the 1964–65 period,[7] the ECJ had the opportunity to adopt a certain position on these provisions. In this case, the High Authority had initially granted an authorisation for the joint buying of fuel by OKU, an undertaking established by a group of mining companies. This authorisation was extended for the last time by Decision 3/62 of March 28, 1962 until December 31, 1967, subject to the condition that the participation of SOREMA, one of the OKU partner

---

[4] Case 67/63 *SOREMA* v. *High Authority* [1964] E.C.R. 321 at 352.

[5] Advocate-General Lagrange in Joined Cases 36–38 & 40/59 *Präsident Ruhrkohlenverkaufsgesellschaft mbH et al.* v. *High Authority* [1960] E.C.R. 885 at 981; *cf.* also R. Krawielicki, *Das Monopolverbot im Schumanplan* (1952) Tübingen, p. 29. The Court also appears to adhere to the view that these requirements are those of the third paragraph and not the "conditions" of the first paragraph, as can be seen from its judgment in Case 67/63, *loc. cit.*, footnote 4, and in particular from the following decision in Case 36/64 *SOREMA* v. *High Authority* [1965] E.C.R. 447 at 462; for a different viewpoint, *cf.* W. Wiesner, *Der Widerruf individueller Entscheidungen der Hohen Behörde der EGKS*, Hamburg 1966, p. 39.

[6] The Court has not yet had the opportunity to decide whether *ex tunc* revocation would also be possible (as is expressly provided for in the corresponding rules laid down in Article 8(3) of Regulation 17 in respect of some of the areas covered by this provision).

[7] Case 67/63 *SOREMA* v. *High Authority* [1964] E.C.R. 321, and Case 36/64 *SOREMA* v. *High Authority* [1965] E.C.R. 447.

companies, in this concern should be ratified only in respect of a transitional period which was to be fixed by a later decision. By a Decision of April 30, 1963, the High Authority ruled that this transitional period should end on June 30, 1963. By its judgment in the first *SOREMA* case, the Court had set aside this decision on the grounds of infringement of the duty to give reasons.[8] Thereupon the High Authority issued a new decision of July 15, 1964, which this time provided reasons and by which it revoked the original decision, which had authorised the participation of SOREMA, as from September 30, 1964. This decision formed the subject-matter of the second *SOREMA* case.[9] In the opinion of the ECJ, it remained an open question in this case whether the High Authority's decision which was being challenged amounted "either to a decision under the third subparagraph of Article 65(2) to refuse to renew the authorisation previously granted or to a decision under the fourth subparagraph to revoke it."[10] The objection raised by the applicant that, by stipulating the condition that the expiry of the transitional period would be fixed at a later date, the High Authority had arrogated to itself a right to which it was not entitled under the Treaty, was rejected by the Court as being unfounded, as was the plea that this renewed decision lacked proper reasons. Instead, the decision had, according to the Court, been sufficiently reasoned, both in relation to the rejection of a renewed authorisation and as regards the revocation of the original authorisation.[11] The action brought by SOREMA was accordingly dismissed.

Unlike Advocate-General Roemer, who, referring to the case law of the Court on the revocation of administrative measures conferring benefits, considered that an assessment of the relative merits of all the interests involved was necessary in order to reply to the question whether the original decision was capable of being revoked,[12] the Court did not see fit to take into account any consideration relating to the protection of legitimate expectations—in any case, no such consideration had been advanced by the applicant. Moreover, this case concerned only an *ex nunc* revocation.

---

[8] Case 67/63, *loc. cit.*, footnote 7, pp. 352 *et seq.*
[9] Case 36/64, *loc. cit.*, footnote 7.
[10] E.C.J., *ibid.*, p. 459; also in Case 67/63, *loc. cit.*, footnote 7, p. 352.
[11] Case 36/64, *loc. cit.*, footnote 7, p. 462.
[12] Roemer, *ibid.*, p. 472. The Advocate-General, however, assumed that the measure in question was not, in fact, a revocation within the meaning of Article 65(2), fourth paragraph, ECSC, since according to the submissions of the High Authority the conditions for obtaining permission had not existed from the beginning and the administrative measure was consequently unlawful from the beginning (pp. 468, 472).

In addition, the ECJ observed that the High Authority did not have any discretion on the question whether or not to take a revocation decision:

"The High Authority must revoke the authorisation in particular if it finds that the actual results of the agreement or of its application are contrary to the requirements for its authorisation."[13]

What this special case, which concerns the ECSC competition law, shows is that even a lawful administrative measure may be revoked, at any rate *ex nunc*, if circumstances have changed or if the conditions which were attached to the original administrative measure no longer apply.

(b) Revocation under Article 8(3) of Regulation 17 (EEC)

Article 8(3) of Regulation 17 (EEC) applies a similar system to EEC competition law.[14] Under Article 85(3) of the EEC Treaty, the Commission may exempt from the prohibition of cartels contained in paragraph 1 certain agreements between undertakings, decisions by associations of undertakings or concerted practices. Such exemption decisions are administrative measures conferring rights[15] and similar benefits, which may, however, receive retroactive effect under Article 6(1) of Regulation 17. Article 8(3) of this Regulation provides that such an exemption measure may be revoked under certain conditions.[16]

Under Article 8(3)(a), this revocation may be pronounced *ex nunc*, if there has been a change in any of the facts which were basic to the decision. Where the parties commit a breach of any obligation attached to the exemption (b), where the decision is based on incorrect information or was induced by deceit (c), or where the parties abuse the exemption (d), the decision may be revoked with retroactive effect.[17] Because the set

---

[13] E.C.J. *ibid.*, p. 462.

[14] Regulation 17 of the Council of February 6, 1962, J.O. 1962, 204; O.J. Sp.Ed. 1959–1962, 87, pp. 204 *et seq.*

[15] Unlike the negative test under Article 2 of Regulation 17, which is not a constitutive but a confirmatory administrative measure: H. Schroter, in Groeben, Boeckh, Thiesing, Ehlermann, *Kommentar zum EWG-Vertrag* (3rd ed., Baden-Baden 1983), Article 87, Nos. 35, 36; Gleiss, Hirsch, *Kommentar zum EWG-Kartellrecht* (3rd ed., Heidelberg 1978), on Regulation 17, Article 2, No. 13; Case 31/80 *NV L'Oréal and SA L'Oréal* v. *PVBA "De Nieuwe AMCK"* [1980] E.C.R. 3775 at 3793; Advocate-General Reischl, *ibid.*, p. 3803.

[16] For a detailed study of these conditions under Article 8(3) of Regulation 17 *cf.* Gleiss, Hirsch, *loc. cit.*, footnote 15, Article 8, Nos. 6 *et seq.*

[17] Article 8(3) Regulation 17.

of circumstances mentioned under (b), (c) or (d) above cannot give rise to any legitimate expectation on the part of the beneficiaries that the exemption, once granted, will continue to apply, those beneficiaries must take into account the possibility of a retroactive revocation. It will be understood, however, that any revocation pronounced will take retroactive effect only from the moment when one of the circumstances stated in subparagraphs (b) to (d) of this provision, such as an infringement of an obligation (subparagraph b), became realised.[18] Any retroactivity which took effect from an earlier date would be incompatible with the principle of the protection of legitimate expectations. In the case of revocation on grounds of incorrect information innocently supplied, any retroactive revocation would give rise to problems in view of the principle of the protection of legitimate expectations. If, on the other hand, we are dealing merely with a change in circumstances, any benefits granted should be maintained at least for the past. The provisions of Article 8(3)(a) satisfy the principles of legal certainty and of the protection of legitimate expectations on this point. Where an exemption decision is revoked, this completely eliminates its effectiveness. In the case of *ex tunc* revocation also (Article 8(3)(b) to (d)), the effectiveness of the exemption is in principle completely removed. However, such cases raise the question whether the revocation is also capable of retroactively eliminating effectiveness under private law of the underlying agreement.

As is the case with the area covered by Article 65(2) ECSC, a distinction must be drawn here also between the revocation of administrative measures which are still effective and the rejection of an application for renewal of an exemption granted for a limited period. Article 8(2) of Regulation 17 makes provision for the latter contingency and states that the exemption may be renewed if the conditions set by Article 85(3) EEC continue to be met.

(c) *Revocation in the Staff Regulations*

The Community Staff Regulations also contain a number of special provisions relating to revocation. Community officials are appointed by

---

[18] Gleiss, Hirsch, *loc. cit.*, footnote 15, Article 8, No. 19.

administrative measures ("decisions" within the meaning of Article 25 Staff Regulations). The appointment decisions constitute "individual administrative measures giving rise to an individual right"[19] if they are legally valid and effective.

The dismissal of an official is also decided by an administrative measure ("decision" within the meaning of Article 25 Staff Regulations). It takes the form of a revocation of the measure conferring benefits which is constituted by the appointment or the promotion in question. Mention should be made of the following possibilities: dismissal for departmental reasons (Article 50 Staff Regulations, for political appointees), automatic dismissal, which is pronounced if, for example, an official loses the nationality of one of the Member States (Article 49, in conjunction with Articles 28(a), 13, 39, 40, 41(4) and (5) Staff Regulations), dismissal for unsatisfactory performance of duties (Article 51 Staff Regulations), and, finally, removal from office as the ultimate disciplinary punishment (Article 86(2)(f) Staff Regulations). According to the circumstances in question, some of these provisions state that the official may continue to receive his regular earnings for a certain period or that a pension may be payable; on the other hand, the official in question may also be deprived of any pension payments acquired.

In making these decisions, the appointing boards enjoy a certain degree of discretion. Nevertheless, their decisions are open to review by the Court of Justice. Unlike the rule stated in Article 85 of the Staff Regulations, which concerns the recovery of emoluments wrongly paid, the relevant provisions do not expressly require that, during the weighing-up process which must be a feature of every individual case, legitimate expectations which are worthy of protection or vested rights must be taken into account.

Constituting as they do a special set of rules applicable to the conditions of employment of E.C. officials, these Regulations hardly appear to be capable of acquiring a more general significance which could extend to other areas of Community law.[20] As is the case with the competition law provisions which have been mentioned above, these rules relating to revocation also constitute legislative exceptions to the general principle of the irrevocability of lawful administrative measures conferring benefits.[21]

---

[19] Joined Cases 7/56 & 3–7/57 *Algera et al.* v. *Common Assembly* [1957–1958] E.C.R. 39.
[20] W. Wiesner, *Der Widerruf individueller Entscheidungen der Hohen Behörde der EGKS*, Hamburg 1966, p. 78.
[21] W. Wiesner, *loc. cit.*, footnote 20, pp. 52 *et seq.*

3.   General Legal Principles Regarding the Revocation of
     Administrative Acts

Apart from these special rules, it was left to the Court to develop
certain principles regarding the admissibility of the revocation of administrative acts by way of unwritten principles of Community law.

In the Algera case, which dates from 1957, Advocate-General
Lagrange suggested to the Court that Community law should also draw

"the traditional distinction between adopted decisions and illegal
decisions."[22]

The Court followed this proposal. When assessing the admissibility of the
revocation of lawful or unlawful administrative measures, the ECJ
applied two opposite principles which have, on the basis of the established case law developed on the subject, become general principles of
Community law, but have yet to be elaborated in greater detail, namely
the irrevocability of lawful administrative measures conferring benefits
on the one hand and the revocability of unlawful administrative measures
on the other.

(a) The revocation of lawful administrative acts

The background to the Algera case was as follows. The applicants,
being employees of the Common Assembly of the ECSC, had all been
brought within the ambit of the Community Staff Regulations by an
administrative act dated December 12, 1955 and assigned to certain
salary brackets. After they had failed to agree to a new set of conditions
governing their salary bracket, the decisions which brought them within
the scope of the Community Staff Regulations, as well as those which
specified the salary brackets which had originally been agreed, were
revoked by a decision of July 12, 1956, and the contracts of employment
which had applied until December 12, 1955, were "reinstated." The
actions in this case were brought against this revocation decision. The

---

[22] Lagrange in Joined Cases 7/56 & 3–7/57 Algera et al. v. Common Assembly [1957–1958]
E.C.R. 39.

Court took advantage of this case to deal extensively for the first time with the question of the revocation of administrative measures conferring benefits. Then as now, the Treaties provided no rules concerning the revocation of administrative measures. Nevertheless, the Court recognised that here they were dealing with

> "a problem of administrative law which is familiar in the case law and learned writing of all the countries of the Community."[23]

Having made a comparative study of this issue, the Court acknowledged that in all six Member States (as they were then)

> "an administrative measure conferring individual rights on the person concerned cannot in principle be withdrawn, if it is a lawful measure; in that case, since the individual right is vested, the need to safeguard confidence in the stability of the situation thus created prevails over the interests of an administration desirous of reversing its decision."[24]

Here, the Court adopted a position different from that which it entertained in relation to unlawful administrative measures, and decided that there was no case for applying the spirit of the protection of legitimate expectations by weighing up the interests involved in this particular case. Unless one of the exceptional circumstances set out below applied,[25] the protection of legitimate expectations took precedence here in principle over the possibly competing interest of the authority in question to correct its original decision. In the *Algera* case, the ECJ concluded that

> "the Assembly was competent as regards the application of staff regulations, so that that application is valid and irrevocable."[26]

On the other hand, the ECJ considered that the assignment of departmental rank and the placing of the officials in question in certain salary brackets was unlawful and was capable of being revoked.[27]

In addition to this decision in the *Algera* case, the Court, in two other staff cases, set aside a decision by which a lawful administrative measure

---

[23] Cases 7/56 & 3–7/57, *loc. cit.*, footnote 22.
[24] Joined Cases 7/56 & 3–7/57, *loc. cit.*, footnote 22; Advocate-General Lagrange, *ibid.*
[25] On this subject, *cf. infra* 3(d).
[26] Joined cases 7/56 & 3–7/57, *loc. cit.*, footnote 22.
[27] E.C.J., *ibid.*

conferring benefits had been revoked on the grounds that this revocation had been inadmissible.[28]

In a decision made some time before the *Algera* judgment, *i.e.* in the *Kergall* case, the Court was called upon to rule on the admissibility of a decision of the President of the Common Assembly by which the latter had revoked part of the compensation allocated to the applicant because his contract of employment had not been extended. In support of his decision, the President had claimed that the applicant had not accepted this benefit and intended to bring the matter before the Court of Justice. Without referring to principles of Community law or national law, the Court concluded that the fact of bringing an action could not justify changing the decision to the applicant's disadvantage.[29]

In a more recent decision, made in the *Verli-Wallace* case, the ECJ set aside a Commission decision on the grounds that "the retroactive withdrawal of a legal measure" which had conferred individual rights or similar benefits was "contrary to the general principles of law."[30] In this case, the Commission had revoked its original decision admitting the applicant to a competitive examination. The Court, however, held that the original decision admitting the applicant to the examination was lawful. Since that decision had conferred on the applicant a "personal right," it could not be subsequently revoked.[31]

The rule prohibiting the revocation of lawful administrative measures conferring benefits applies in principle to retroactive revocation. On the other hand, the case law of the Court gives no clear indication on what is the position in relaxation to *ex nunc* revocation. Although in the *Algera* case, the ECJ held the *ex nunc* revocation of a lawful administrative measure conferring benefits to be illegal,[32] it is doubtful whether this rule could be extended to the revocation of administrative measures which are

---

[28] The Court has also elevated to the status of a principle of Community law the prohibition of the retroactive revocation of lawful administrative measures in Joined Cases 42 & 49/59 *SNUPAT* v. *High Authority* [1961] E.C.R. 53; however, the Court concluded by describing the instrument in question as an unlawful administrative measure.

[29] Case 1/55 *Kergall* v. *Common Assembly* [1955–1956] E.C.R. 1 at 28.

[30] Case 159/82 *Verli-Wallace* v. *Commission* [1983] E.C.R. 2711 at 2718 *et seq.*; also in this sense, the decision in Joined Cases 42 & 49/59, *loc. cit.*, footnote 28, to which the Court refers here; *cf.* also Advocate-General Lenz in Case 232/81 *Agricola Commerciale Olio S.r.l. et al.* v. *Commission* [1984] E.C.R. 3881 at 3910.

[31] Case 159/82, *loc. cit.*, footnote 30, p. 2719.

[32] The statement by the Court that the admission to the Staff Regulations was lawful and could therefore not be revoked applies here even to a mere *ex nunc* revocation. The E.C.J. did not exclude the possibility of revoking admission to the Staff Regulations with effect for the future, but only prohibited it for the past.

purely declaratory.[33] More particularly, the Court's decision in the *Simon* case[34] would appear to stand in the way of such a generalised application. In this case, the applicant, being an employee of the Court of Justice, had, by a decision by the President of the Court of March 15, 1958, obtained a separation allowance as provided in Article 47(3) of the Staff Regulations. Article 47 conferred such a separation allowance on employees residing at a distance exceeding 25 kilometres from the offices of the institution. In the course of an examination carried out by the auditor, it was later established that the Court had based its decision granting the separation allowance on the distance over the ground, whereas the High Authority had in similar cases applied the distance as the crow flies. Accordingly, the President's Committee decided, on May 9, 1960, that although the applicant, who was not entitled to a separation allowance if the latter was based on the distance as the crow flies, could retain the amounts he had thus received in the past, this payment would be discontinued in line with an interpretation of the Staff Regulations which was adjusted to the practice adopted by the High Authority, and that these payments would be "absorbed" by an "advance in grade and step."[35]

The applicant, invoking the decision in the *Algera* case, considered this to be an infringement of vested rights and consequently an inadmissible revocation of a lawful administrative measure conferring benefits.

Advocate-General Roemer agreed with the applicant on this point and observed that a correct interpretation of the Regulations implied that the distance over the ground was as valid a criterion as the distance as the crow flies. Since the revoked administrative measure (of March 15, 1958) was lawful, there was no possibility of revoking it as long as the text of the regulations remained unamended.[36]

Although the Court also concluded that the revocation of the original administrative measure was inadmissible, its reasons for doing so were different. The Court held in the first place that no vested rights had been infringed by the revocation:

> "The decision granting the separation allowance to the applicant has not been revoked retroactively but only amended in respect of the future. Further, the allowance has been maintained ad personam

---

[33] This is clearly also the assumption made by H.-J. Rüber, *Der Gerichtshof der Europäischen Gemeinschaften und die Konkretisierung allgemeiner Rechtsgrundsätze*, Diss. Köln 1970, p. 180.

[34] Case 15/60 *Simon* v. *Court of Justice* [1961] E.C.R. 239.

[35] Case 15/60, *loc. cit.*, footnote 34, p. 248.

[36] Advocate-General Roemer in Case 15/60, *loc. cit.*, footnote 34, p. 276.

until the amount of the allowance is absorbed by subsequent advancements.

If the administrative authority becomes aware that a certain allowance has been granted as a result of a wrong interpretation of a legal provision, it has the power to amend the previous decision.

Even if in certain cases in view of vested rights withdrawal on grounds of unlawfulness does not have a retroactive effect, it always takes effect from the present."[37]

The Court then proceeded to examine whether the new administrative measure of May 9, 1960, by which the original administrative measure had been revoked, was itself lawful in substantive terms and whether the interpretation of Article 47(3) of the Staff Regulations which had been applied was free from legal defects. This was not, in the Court's opinion, the case: the provision in question had to be interpreted in the same way as it had been at the time of issuing the original administrative measure (of March 15, 1958). Since the administrative measure which effected the revocation in turn lacked any basis in substantive law, it was, in the Court's opinion, unlawful and should therefore be set aside.[38]

Clearly the Court considered the decision of March 15, 1958 to be a declaratory administrative measure.[39] It is a special characteristic of declaratory measures that the authority in question has no discretion in issuing them, which is not the position in relation to administrative measures establishing rights.[40] Where the measure is lawful—as is the case here[41]—there is no possibility of revoking it, at any rate if the circumstances of the case and the legal situation[42] remain the same, since the authority in question is not free to issue a decision which differs from the original administrative measure made for an indefinite period. Thus the revocation already failed the test of the compliance of administrative action with the relevant legislation. There could be no question here of any legitimate expectation worthy of protection. Accordingly, the Court clearly saw no reason to examine whether the applicant had relied upon the maintenance of the benefit conferred.

---

[37] Case 15/60, *loc. cit.*, footnote 34, pp. 259 *et seq.*
[38] E.C.J. *ibid.*, *p. 263.*
[39] Thus also H.-J. Rüber, *loc. cit.*, footnote 33, p. 180, and W. Wiesner, *loc. cit.*, footnote 20, pp. 61 *et seq.*
[40] Advocate-General Lagrange in Case 14/61 *Hoogovens* v. *High Authority* [1962] E.C.R. 253 at 277.
[41] This has also recently been the assumption made by the E.C.J., without stating so expressly.
[42] *cf.* on this subject *infra*, III (d), (dd), (ee).

The above formula used by the Court in rejecting the plea of infringe-ment of vested rights also indicates that the ECJ would in principle allow without reservation the revocation of a lawful declaratory administrative measure conferring benefits with effect for the future if, unlike the situation which applied in the *Simon* case, a different decision needed to be taken on the grounds of a change in the relevant circumstances or legal situation. This view may have been inspired by French administrative law, under which the revocation of lawful declaratory administrative measures, even when they confer benefits, is in principle admissible.[43]

(b) *The revocation of unlawful administrative acts*

Accordingly, whilst lawful administrative measures may not, at least in principle, be revoked retroactively, the revocation of unlawful admin-istrative measures is perfectly admissible, subject, however, to the revok-ing authority fulfilling certain conditions. In particular, the Court draws a distinction between the revocation of unlawful administrative measures creating rights and unlawful declaratory measures. Whereas unlawful administrative measures creating rights may be revoked only within a reasonable period, as is the case in French law,[44] every individual case of revocation of unlawful declaratory administrative measures must involve a weighing up of the interests in question, as required under the German and Netherlands legal systems.[45] This distinction was put to the Court by Advocate-General Lagrange in the following context:

"In this way the case law of the Court, in so far as it invokes national laws (as it does to a large extent) to define the rules of law relating to the application of the Treaty, is not content to draw on more or less arithmetical 'common denominators' between the different national solutions but will select from the various legal systems those solu-tions which, having regard to the objects of the Treaty, appear to it to

[43] W. Wiesner, *loc. cit.*, footnote 20, p. 47; W. Däubler, "Der Widerruf von Verwaltungs-akten im Recht der Europäischen Gemeinschaften," NJW 1965, p. 1646 (1650). However, the *ex tunc* revocation of such an administrative measure would, if it were not inadmissible, have to be judged in the light of the protection of legitimate expectations in Community law, contrary to what would be the case under French law.
[44] For more details, *cf. supra* Section 2 A.
[45] For more details, *cf. supra* Section 2, B and J.

be the best or, if one may use the expression, the most progressive. This is the spirit, moreover, which has guided the Court hitherto."[46]

In the *Algera* case,[47] which has already been referred to in connection with the revocation of lawful administrative measures, the Court had also to rule on the question of the revocability of unlawful administrative measures creating rights, *i.e.* those which conferred rank of service and those which assigned the employees concerned to certain salary brackets. Here too, in the absence of any rules in the Treaties or in derived Community law, the Court referred to the legal systems of the Member States in this context:

> "If on the other hand the administrative measure is illegal, revocation is possible under the law of the Member States. The absence of an objective legal basis for the measures affects the individual right of the person concerned and justifies the revocation of the said measures. It should be stressed that whereas this principle is generally acknowledged, only the conditions for its application vary."[48]

The resulting comparative analysis of the legal systems of the then six Member States led to the following decisive conclusion:

> "In agreement with the Advocate-General's opinion, the Court accepts the principle of the revocability of illegal measures at least within a reasonable period of time, such as that within which the decisions in question in the present dispute occurred."[49]

As regards the assignment of officials to certain salary brackets or the conferment of rank of service, the original administrative measures could consequently be revoked. Accordingly, the action was dismissed on this point as being unfounded.[50] The condition that the measure should be revoked within a "reasonable period of time" had been proposed to the Court by Advocate-General Lagrange with reference to the law which applied in France:

---

[46] Advocate-General Lagrange in Case 14/61 *Hoogovens* v. *High Authority* [1962] E.C.R. 253 at 277 *et seq.*
[47] Joined Cases 7/56 & 3–7/57 *Algera et al.* v. *Common Assembly* [1957–1958] E.C.R. 39.
[48] Joined Cases 7/56 & 3–7/57, *loc. cit.*, footnote 47, p. 55.
[49] E.C.J. *loc. cit.*, footnote 47, p. 56.
[50] E.C.J. *loc. cit.*, footnote 47, p. 64.

"In France, according to the thoroughly consistent—one might almost say classical—case law of the Conseil d'Etat, the withdrawal of individual decisions which have created rights is possible when they are illegal, but only within the time limit laid down for the commencement of legal proceedings or, if proceedings have been commenced, up to the time when judgment is delivered."[51]

In the *Hoogovens* case, Advocate-General Lagrange advocated, for the purpose of clarifying the concept of "reasonable period of time," the application of French law, which

"lays down the same limitation period for the revocation of an illegal measure creating rights as for legal proceedings—a principle which the Algera judgment does not preclude. That is the only real means of ensuring legal certainty. In that way the definitive nature of the measure results from an objective and easily established criterion, namely the expiration of the period of limitation for proceedings, whereas an appeal to the concept of "a reasonable period of time" leaves an uncertainty, like a sword of Damocles, hanging over the head of the person concerned—uncertainty both as to the possibility of an ultimate dispute and as to the appraisal which the Court might make, in the event of such dispute, regarding the meaning of a reasonable period of time."[52]

The Court did not follow this proposal. It did not explicitly use the relevant time limits for bringing a challenge applicable in Community law as a criterion, or in any other way provide a binding interpretation of the term "reasonable period." In the facts underlying the *Algera* case,[53] the administrative measures in question had been revoked within a period of seven months following their adoption, this being a period which, according to the Court's decision, was reasonable, at least in this case.

In the *Alpha Steel* case,[54] dating from 1982, the Commission had revoked an administrative measure of December 19, 1980 on February 24, 1981. The Court considered this time limit to be reasonable, taking into account the fact that the Commission had been called upon to

---

[51] Advocate-General Lagrange in Joined Cases 7/56 & 3–7/57, *loc. cit.*, footnote 47, p. 80.
[52] Advocate-General Lagrange in Case 14/61 *Hoogovens* v. *High Authority* [1962] E.C.R. 253 at 277.
[53] Joined Cases 7/56 & 3–7/57 *Algera et al.* v. *Common Assembly* [1957–1958] E.C.R. 39.
[54] Case 14/81 *Alpha Steel* v. *Commission* [1982] E.C.R. 749 at 764—moreover, this case did not concern the revocation of administrative measures creating rights but confirmatory administrative measures; however, the E.C.J. did not adopt a position on this matter.

process a large amount of information concerning the various undertakings and the applicant had failed to show that delaying of the decision until February 24, 1981 had been to its disadvantage.

In a decision dating from 1987, the Court decided, at least in relation to the case before it, that the revocation by the Commission of a subsidy decision in the context of the EAGGF two years after the latter had been made had not occurred within a reasonable period of time. Here, the decisive factor for the Court was clearly the fact that the Commission could have made it clear, immediately after the adoption of the original administrative measure, that the conditions for the granting of the funds did not apply.[55]

Nevertheless there exists as yet no generally applicable clarification of the concept of a "reasonable period of time." This would appear to be necessary if Community law is to provide a greater degree of legal certainty on the question of the revocation of administrative measures creating rights.

The revocation of unlawful declaratory administrative measures, unlike that of administrative measures creating rights, presupposes, according to the case law of the Court, a process of weighing up the interests involved in each individual case, following the principle of the protection of legitimate expectations. Here, the ECJ follows the example set by the legal systems of Germany and the Netherlands.[56] According to French law on the other hand, declaratory administrative measures may be revoked—even retroactively—without requiring this process of weighing up the interests involved.[57]

On the question of the revocability of unlawful declaratory administrative measures, the starting point for the Court is its decision in the *SNUPAT* case.[58] The background to this case is as follows:

In accordance with the provisions adopted by the High Authority regarding the scrap equalisation fund, contributions were payable in respect of so-called bought scrap, whereas the relevant companies' "own arisings" were exempted from this obligatory contribution. A contentious issue in this regard was the question whether the so-called "group scrap," *i.e.* the scrap supplied by companies belonging to the same group,

---

[55] Case 15/85 *Consorzio Cooperative d'Abruzzo* v. *Commission* [1987] E.C.R. 1005.
[56] Advocate-General Lagrange in Case 14/61 *Hoogovens* v. *High Authority* [1962] E.C.R. 253 at 277.
[57] On the legal position in France, *cf.* under Section 2 A below, and Advocate-General Lagrange in Case 14/61, *loc. cit.*, footnote 56, pp. 277 *et seq.*
[58] Joined Cases 42 & 49/59 *SNUPAT* v. *High Authority* [1961] E.C.R. 53 (second *SNUPAT* judgment).

was to be regarded as "own arisings" or as "bought scrap." By a decision of July 17, 1959 in Joined Cases 32 and 33/58, *i.e.* the First *SNUPAT* Decision,[59] the Court ruled that group scrap had to be regarded as bought scrap.

For its part, the Joint Agency of Scrap Users (GBSV), whose task it was to settle this matter, had, in the case of the Breda and Hoogovens companies, the intervening parties in the second *SNUPAT* case, decided in 1956 to exempt from the scrap equalisation fund, as constituting own arisings, scrap which was supplied to these companies by other firms with whom they had formed a local association. Initial reservations expressed by the High Authority representative with the GBSV in relation to this arrangement were abandoned by the High Authority by a letter dated December 18, 1957, which was published in the Official Journal of February 1, 1958. The applicant (SNUPAT) requested the High Authority, following the decision made on July 17, 1959, to revoke these exemptions granted to the Hoogovens and Breda companies as well and to reassess accordingly the contributions claimed from all other scrap users. The applicant brought this tacit rejection before the Court by means of an action for refusal to act.

The ECJ in the first place confirmed its decision in the *Algera* case:

> "The legality of the refusal to withdraw the disputed exemptions with retroactive effect depends in the first place on the legality of the exemptions themselves. In fact, if these are legal, it follows that the High Authority was justified in refusing to withdraw them since the retroactive withdrawal of a legal measure which has conferred individual rights or similar benefits is contrary to general principles of law."[60]

However, the Court concluded by establishing that the exemptions granted to the Breda and Hoogovens companies were unlawful[61]; consequently, it remained to be decided whether they were capable of being revoked or whether the High Authority had rightly rejected revocation. The intervening parties were of the opinion that a retroactive withdrawal infringed the principle that "once they have been granted, benefits cannot be withdrawn."[62]

---

[59] Joined Cases 32–33/58 *SNUPAT* v. *High Authority* [1959] E.C.R. 127.
[60] E.C.J., *loc. cit.*, footnote 58.
[61] E.C.J., *loc. cit.*, footnote 58.
[62] Cited in E.C.J., *ibid.*

The ECJ countered this statement in the following terms:

"That allegation disregards the fact that the principle of respect for legal certainty, important as it may be, cannot be applied in an absolute manner, but that its application must be combined with that of the principle of legality; the question which of these principles would prevail in each particular case depends upon a comparison of the public interest with the private interests in question, that is to say:

on the one hand the interest of the beneficiaries and especially the fact that they might assume in good faith that they did not have to pay contributions on the ferrous scrap in question, and might arrange their affairs in reliance on the continuance of this position.

on the other hand, the interest of the Community in ensuring the proper working of the equalisation scheme, which depends on the joint liability of all undertakings consuming ferrous scrap; this interest makes it necessary to ensure that other contributors do not permanently suffer the financial consequences of an exemption illegally granted to their competitors."[63]

Since the amounts at which the contributions had been fixed were purely "provisional in character,"[64] and since it had also to be established whether it was appropriate to apply the principle under which retroactive withdrawal was generally possible "in cases in which the administrative measure in question has been adopted on the basis of false or incomplete information provided by those concerned,"[65] the Court ruled that the contested decision was unlawful "because it is based on the notion, which is incorrect in law, that the disputed exemptions were legal and that the High Authority had no power to withdraw them."[66]

Since "the appraisal of this fact and of the respective importance of the interests in question and consequently the decision whether or not to withdraw the irregular exemption with retroactive effect"[67] devolved in the first place on the High Authority, the Court referred the decision

---

[63] E.C.J., *ibid.*
[64] E.C.J., *loc. cit.*, footnote 58.
[65] On the subject of revocation on grounds of false or incomplete information by the persons involved, *cf.* under 3(d)(cc) below.
[66] E.C.J., *loc. cit.*, footnote 58.
[67] E.C.J., *ibid.*

back to the High Authority. In the Court's view, the latter enjoyed a measure of discretion on this issue. However, as the ECJ was to state later in the *Hoogovens* decision, this recognition did not amount to denying "the jurisdiction of the Court to see whether the decision of the High Authority rests on a correct application of the Treaty, of the basic Decisions and of the rules recognised by the *SNUPAT* judgment, and whether it is accordingly justified in law."[68]

Following the administrative measure issued on June 14, 1961, by which the High Authority revoked retroactively, with reference to the (second) *SNUPAT* decision, the exemptions granted to the Hoogovens firm, the undertaking concerned challenged this measure on the basis that, *inter alia*, "a retroactive withdrawal would not be permissible in this case because the reasonable period of time within which such a withdrawal would be possible had long since expired."[69]

In his Opinion, Advocate-General Lagrange stated that the exemptions had not been revoked within a "reasonable period" in the sense attributed to this term by the *Algera* judgment, since between the measure granting the exemption of December 18, 1957 and the decision to revoke it of July 14, 1961, a period of nearly three-and-a-half years had elapsed. Nevertheless, he considered the revocation of the exemptions to be permissible in principle because the latter constituted merely declaratory administrative measures to which the rule that revocation was permissible only within a reasonable period did not apply.[70]

The Court followed the Advocate-General in drawing the distinction between declaratory administrative measures and measures creating rights in the following terms:

> "Moreover, there is a distinction to be drawn, because the rule which requires that withdrawal must take place within a reasonable period of time varies in substance and extent according to the circumstances.
>
> In fact, this rule, which may be of considerable importance where it is a question of decisions creating individual rights, is of less significance where it is a question of purely declaratory decisions.
>
> There can be no doubt that the exemption granted to the applicant could not constitute a measure creating rights, as the High Authority

---

[68] Case 14/61 *Hoogovens* v. *High Authority* [1962] E.C.R. 253; *cf.* also on this subject Advocate-General Lagrange, *ibid.*, p. 279.
[69] Cited in E.C.J., *loc. cit.*, footnote 68, p. 272.
[70] Lagrange, *loc. cit.*, footnote 68, pp. 280 *et seq.*

has no power to grant derogations or exemptions from the payment of equalisation contributions, but power only to declare that the obligation to pay the levy does not arise from the basic decisions. Its decision to regard group ferrous scrap recovered by an undertaking which is locally integrated with the consumer undertaking as own arisings was therefore only a declaratory measure."[71]

From the foregoing, it followed that

"the test of 'the reasonable period of time' is only one of the factors to be taken into consideration in weighing up the various interests and that in this case it is of relatively little weight."[72]

In this decision, the ECJ confirmed its practice, initiated in the *SNUPAT* case earlier, of making a distinction in principle in the manner in which it treated the revocation of administrative measures creating rights (as was the case in the *Algera* decision) on the one hand, and declaratory measures (such as that which formed the subject-matter of the *SNUPAT* and *Hoogovens* cases) on the other. Whereas unlawful administrative measures creating rights could in principle be revoked retroactively only within a "reasonable period," this criterion constitutes, in relation to declaratory measures, "only one of the factors to be taken into consideration in weighing up the various interests."[73]

In the case, however, the Court was unable to confirm the existence, in practice, of a legitimate expectation which was capable of protection:

"As to the period after this date, the applicant knew that the undertakings subject to the financial arrangement were showing a clear inclination to bring before the Court the question whether the Decisions relating to the institution and application of the equalisation system were justified and, in particular, to make an issue of situations in which there was, or appeared to be, an element of discrimination. In these circumstances, the applicant could not—strictly speaking—feel certain at any time that the distinction made between ferrous scrap circulating within the Hoogovens-Breedband group and ferrous scrap circulating within other industrial groups would be upheld by the Court."[74]

---

[71] E.C.J., *loc. cit.*, footnote 68.
[72] E.C.J., *loc. cit.*, footnote 68.
[73] E.C.J., *loc. cit.*, footnote 68.
[74] E.C.J., *loc. cit.*, footnote 68.

On the question of weighing up the interests of the parties involved, the ECJ decided that in this case the public interest took precedence over the private interest and that consequently the revocation had been correctly decreed.[75] In his Opinion, Advocate-General Lagrange gave a more extensive set of reasons for this approach:

"In general, it is the public interest, represented here by respect for legality, which should prevail. The only exception is where that respect may demand such a sacrifice on the part of the private interests that the public interest involved cannot justify it."[76]

The question whether it was possible for the revocation to take effect retroactively or whether it could apply only *ex nunc* was answered by Advocate-General Lagrange by reference to the case law of the German Federal Administrative Court (Bundesverwaltungsgericht). The latter had, in a case dating from 1957, ruled that

"Any intelligent appraisal should be based exclusively on the particular background of the case, taking reasonable account of the interests of the parties involved, in particular the legal nature of the contents of the defective administrative measure, the grounds for its revocability, and the objective pursued by the intended revocation. If the object of the revocation can be realised only by giving it retroactive effect, the authority in question must also be in a position to set aside the unlawful administrative measure retrospectively. . ."[77]

The Court concluded by following the Advocate-General's opinion and rejected the applicant's action as being unfounded.

The background to the *Lemmerz-Werke* case[78] was very similar to the facts underlying the *SNUPAT/Hoogovens* series. In April 1956, the Lemmerz-Werke firm started its bought scrap processing operations. On May 20, 1957, the German Scrap Consumers Association (Deutsche Schrottverbrauchergemeinschaft—DSVG) addressed a letter to the applicant informing it of a decision of the Scrap Equalisation Fund Committee by which certain undertakings, including the applicant, had

---

[75] E.C.J., *loc. cit.*, footnote 68.
[76] Advocate-General Lagrange, *ibid.*
[77] BVerwG, NJW 1958, pp. 154 *et seq*.
[78] Case 111/63 *Lemmerz-Werke* v. *High Authority* [1965] E.C.R. 893.

the mandatory contributions for bought scrap imposed on them with effect from February 1, 1957 only. By letter dated July 19, 1961, the High Authority informed the applicant that an error had been committed in making the applicant subject to this system of mandatory contributions. By a decision of November 6, 1963, the High Authority claimed from the applicant payment of those contributions which had not been levied for the period between April 1956 and January 1957. This decision was based in the first instance on the consideration that the applicant had not been validly exempted from the relevant contributions for the period preceding February 1, 1957; accordingly, any such exemption was revoked retroactively. The applicant appealed to the Court against this decision. The latter left open the question whether the communication issued by the DSVG of May 20, 1957 could, in fact, be regarded as an exemption. Since the institutions attached to the Scrap Equalisation Fund were not in any case empowered to grant exemptions, any such exemption was to be regarded as an unlawful (confirmatory) administrative measure,[79] whose revocation was, in the circumstances of this case, permissible:

> "The High Authority can revoke illegal decisions, even retroactively, provided that in certain exceptional circumstances proper consideration is given to the principle of legal certainty. Although such consideration is in the first instance a matter for the High Authority, it is, however, subject to review by the Court."[80]

For the ECJ, the main question to be considered here was whether

> "the defendant paid sufficient regard to the extent to which the applicant was able to rely on the legality and the continuance of the exemption in question."[81]

However, the Court did not consider that any infringement of the principle of the protection of legitimate expectations had occurred in this case, because

---

[79] Contrary to the view taken by Advocate-General Roemer, Case 111/63 *Lemmerz-Werke* v. *High Authority* [1965] E.C.R. 893 at 934, the Court does not describe the exemption decision expressly as a confirmatory administrative measure, but leaves the question open.

[80] Case 111/63, *loc. cit.*, footnote 79, p. 911.

[81] E.C.J., *ibid.*

> "it could not have escaped the applicant's notice that the basic decisions which set up the equalisation scheme did not provide for exemptions and that in the matter of public contributions such exemptions cannot be presumed."[82]

Moreover, the applicant could rely upon the continuation of the exemptions only for a brief period. In any case, as from mid-1958, a number of circumstances had arisen which gave the applicant no reason to assume that any such exemption would be maintained, such as the publication of General Decision No. 13/58 of July 30, 1958, giving the High Authority the right where necessary to set aside decisions of the Equalisation Fund and of the Joint Office and to adopt such measures as were necessary as a result of any such annulment. Although six years had elapsed between the exemption decision (1957) and its revocation (1963), the Court concluded that a retroactive revocation was permissible in this case. The plea raised by the applicant that the right of revocation had lapsed[83] was also held to be unfounded by the Court.[84] The action was therefore dismissed.

Finally, the *Châtillon* case[85] also had a background similar to those described above. This dispute also involved the assessment of a contribution to the Scrap Equalisation Fund. The applicant had considered as "scrap," within the meaning of the general provisions mentioned above, certain quantities of ARMCO-iron waste which it had sold, and had consequently deducted these amounts from the contribution assessment. By letters dated June 12, 1958 and August 12, 1958, the Equalisation Fund stated its agreement with this manner of calculation. Following the transfer of powers from the Scrap Equalisation Fund to the High Authority, the latter notified the applicant on August 17, 1961 that its method of assessment would be subjected to an audit. On June 8, 1963, the applicant received a statement in which, contrary to the practice followed hitherto, the ARMCO waste was to be included retrospectively in the assessment. On August 21, 1965, the High Authority issued a formal decision to that effect. The applicant brought an action against this decision.

Referring once again to the form of words used in the *Lemmerz-Werke* case, the Court held that

---

[82] E.C.J., *ibid.*
[83] Case 111/63 *Lemmerz-Werke* v. *High Authority* [1965] E.C.R. 893 at 905.
[84] E.C.J., *loc. cit.*, footnote 83; *cf.* also Advocate-General Roemer, *ibid.*, p. 938, for a contrary view.
[85] Case 54/65 *Châtillon* v. *High Authority* [1966] E.C.R. 529.

1001

> "the High Authority has the power to revoke decisions and may even do so retroactively, subject in exceptional cases to considerations of legal certainty."[86]

This principle was applied by the ECJ, even though the contested decision of August 21, 1965 did not concern a "typical case" of revocation of an administrative measure. Contrary to the Advocate-General's statements on this issue,[87] the Court did not consider the revoked communications made by the Equalisation Fund of June 12, 1958 and August 12, 1958 as a decision in the formal sense, but merely as an unlawful "statement." However, in the Court's opinion, the permissible nature of retroactive revocation extended even further in the case of measures which were mere statements rather than formal decisions.[88]

However, the Court deemed it appropriate to consider the extent to which it was reasonable for the applicant to rely upon the original statement. In its decision, the ECJ considered the revocation to be permissible, since the applicant could reasonably expect to rely upon the effectiveness of the position adopted by the Fund only for a relatively short time. In substantiation of its decision, the Court also referred in this case to the above-mentioned General Decision No. 13/58 of July 30, 1958, by which the High Authority had given itself the right to revoke the measure in question.[89] It was not possible for the applicant to rely upon the decision on the ultimate fate of the statement being taken within a short period. In addition, the High Authority had already notified the applicant as early as August 1961 that the inclusion of the ARMCO production waste in the assessment would be the subject of a new audit.[90]

The long-established principles concerning the revocation of unlawful administrative measures also apply to the question of retroactive revocation. Here, the Court endeavours to guarantee a degree of legal certainty by making the revocation subject to the observance of a reasonable period or by obliging the administrative authority in question to take into account the legitimate expectations of the citizen and to weigh up the conflicting interests involved.

The Court has also, however, been called upon to consider the question whether the revocation of an unlawful administrative measure, even if in certain cases it could not operate retroactively, was at least

---

[86] Case 54/65, *loc. cit.*, footnote 85, p. 545.
[87] Advocate-General Gand, *ibid.*, pp. 555 *et seq.*
[88] E.C.J., *loc. cit.*, footnote 85, p. 545.
[89] *cf. supra* on Case 111/63 *Lemmerz-Werke* v. *High Authority* [1965] E.C.R. 893.
[90] Case 54/65, *loc. cit.*, footnote 85, p. 545.

permissible *ex nunc*. In respect of administrative measures which did not create any rights, namely declaratory measures, the Court's reply was as straightforward as it was clear:

> "If the administrative authority becomes aware that a certain allowance has been granted as a result of a wrong interpretation of a legal provision, it has the power to amend the previous decision. Even if in certain cases in view of vested rights withdrawal on grounds of unlawfulness does not have a retroactive effect, it always takes effect from the present."[91]

The above-mentioned *Simon* case illustrates this. In this case, the applicant suffered the withdrawal of a separation allowance which had been paid for some considerable time. In the *Hoogovens* case[92] the Court went somewhat further, holding that, faced with the unlawfulness of an administrative measure, the High Authority had not only the right to revoke that instrument *ex nunc*; where failure to revoke infringed the interests of a third party, this right would become a duty:

> "The Court, in the *SNUPAT* judgment, found that such exemptions were illegal. This finding obliged the High Authority to take steps to withdraw the exemptions.
>
> The question, however, whether the withdrawal should be made retroactive or should take effect only *ex nunc* was not decided by the Court."[93]

Whilst the High Authority also enjoys a certain degree of discretion in assessing the question whether it should revoke retroactively an unlawful administrative measure, this body is accordingly compelled to rule the measure in question invalid *ex nunc*.

Both these judgments concerned declaratory administrative measures. Here, the Court does not give any guarantee that legitimate expectations will be protected against *ex nunc* revocation if the measure turns out to be unlawful. On this point, the position is the same as in French law, where the revocation, at least as from the present, of unlawful measures which are merely declaratory is permitted without reservation.[94] At the same

---

[91] Case 15/60 *Simon* v. *Court of Justice* [1961] E.C.R. 239 at 259 *et seq.*
[92] Case 14/61 *Hoogovens* v. *High Authority* [1962] E.C.R. 253.
[93] E.C.J., *loc. cit.*, footnote 92.
[94] *cf.* under Section 2 A below; H. Lecheler, *Der Europäische Gerichtshof und die allgemeinen Rechtsgrundsätze*, Berlin 1971, p. 78.

time the legal protection of the Community citizen has not progressed as far as the German legal system, where Article 48 of both the Law relating to administration at the federal level and those which regulate Länder administration contain a binding provision compelling the administration to observe any legitimate expectation, even in the case of *ex nunc* revocation.

However, it has yet to be conclusively stated whether the principle of the freedom to revoke administrative measures *ex nunc* in Community law applies only to declaratory measures or also to those which create rights.

As is revealed by the *Algera* decision,[95] the restrictions in time which apply to the revocation of unlawful administrative measures creating rights do not appear to be confined to the question of retroactivity. Instead, the Court has made the permissible nature of the *ex nunc* revocation[96] also conditional in principle upon the observance of a "reasonable period of time." The statement by the ECJ that revocation is permissible "at least within a reasonable period of time"[97] is not restricted to the retrospective effects of revocation, although by using the words "at least" the Court has left itself the opportunity to allow *ex nunc* revocation even where a reasonable period has not been observed. It has also been proposed to the Court[98] that, when reviewing the admissibility of the revocation of administrative measures, it should completely abandon the distinction between administrative measures creating rights and declaratory measures on which the French case law on this subject is based.

However, it appears from the Court's decision in the *Elz* case,[99] which dates from 1976, that the ECJ, as is the case in France,[100] still assumes that

---

[95] Joined Cases 7/56 & 3–7/57 *Algera et al.* v. *Common Assembly* [1957–1958] E.C.R. 39.

[96] The revocation of a classification in a certain salary bracket which has been found to be unlawful should in any case take effect only *ex nunc*; *cf.* also on this subject M. Schlockermann, *Rechtssicherheit als Vertrauensschutz in der Rechtsprechung des EuGH*, Diss. München 1984, pp. 36 *et seq.*

[97] Joined Cases 7/56 & 3–7/57 *Algera* v. *Common Assembly* [1957–1958] E.C.R. 39.

[98] Thus, for example, by the applicant in Case 54/77 *A. Herpels* v. *Commission* [1978] E.C.R. 585 (593); this consideration also forms the basis for the opinion of Advocate-General Mayras in this case (pp. 605 *et seq.*); similarly also Advocate-General Reischl in Case 56/75 *Elz* v. *Commission* [1976] E.C.R. 1097 at 1115 *et seq.*

[99] Case 56/75 *Elz* v. *Commission* [1976] E.C.R. 1097.

[100] In France also the principle applies whereby the freedom to revoke unlawful administrative measures applies only to measures which are not creative of rights, *i.e.* to declaratory administrative measures and the "revocable decisions" which are assimilated to these. On the other hand, administrative measures creating rights and which are not merely "revocable" are revocable, even *ex nunc*, only within the time limit for bringing the challenge—*cf.* under Section 2 A below.

an unlawful administrative measure creating rights cannot be freely revoked, even *ex nunc*, and that the admissibility of its revocation is subject to special conditions.

The facts of the *Elz* case were as follows:

Although Article 17(2) of Annex VII to the Staff Regulations merely allows the Commission, by way of derogation from paragraph 1 of this provision, and if requested to do so, to pay part of an official's salary at his place of residence, instead of at his place of work and in the currency of the country where his place of work is situated, the applicant had for a number of years received, at his request, his entire salary at his place of residence. The action brought by the applicant was against the decision by the Commission no longer to grant him this "benefit" in the future, but instead to pay his salary in principle at his place of work, in accordance with Article 17(1).

Unlike Advocate-General Reischl, the Court did not expressly describe as an "administrative measure conferring benefits" the practice of paying the salary at the employee's residence, although the ECJ held the latter to infringe the relevant Staff Regulations. However, the Court did follow the Advocate-General's conclusion and confirmed the permissible nature of the "revocation":

> "The immediate withdrawal of such a benefit based on a situation which is not in conformity with the Staff Regulations cannot infringe the principle that vested rights must be respected."[101]

As Advocate-General Reischl also explains,[102] this statement in the first place confirms the principle, developed by the Court in the *Hoogovens* and *Simon* cases, of the freedom to revoke *ex nunc* unlawful declaratory administrative measures. Unlike Advocate-General Reischl,[103] however, the Court clearly assumed that *ex nunc* revocation of unlawful administrative measures is not always unconditionally permissible. Although the applicant had relied upon the protection of vested rights,[104] which was the objective of the "reasonable period" requirement, the Court considered the permissible nature of the revocation to be justified by the consideration that

---

[101] Case 56/75, *loc. cit.*, footnote 99, p. 1109.
[102] Advocate-General Reischl, *loc. cit.*, footnote 99, pp. 1115 *et seq.*
[103] Advocate-General Reischl, *loc. cit.*, footnote 99, pp. 1115 *et seq.*
[104] Cited in E.C.J., *loc. cit.*, footnote 99, p. 1102.

> "the continuation of the benefit during the period in question appears to be a measure of a precarious nature which entails no implied decision on the part of the institution which might create rights in favour of the person concerned."[105]

Conversely, therefore—and this is where the Court confirms its ruling in the *Algera* case—the principle of the unconditional freedom to revoke *ex nunc* does not apply in the case of administrative measures creating rights.[106]

Although this conclusion appears to have the desirable effect, there are some doubts whether the unconditional *ex nunc* revocation of declaratory administrative measures is compatible with the principle of the protection of legitimate expectations.[107] So far, the Court has failed to adopt a clear position on this issue.

The decision in the *Herpels* case,[108] which arose some years later, merely confirmed the principles which had already been formulated and provided no clarification of the question whether the *ex nunc* revocation of an unlawful administrative measure was universally permissible.

The applicant entered the employment of the High Authority of the ECSC in Luxembourg on September 18, 1961; as from that date, he was in receipt of a separation allowance, which was described as an expatriation allowance in the uniform Staff Regulations. Having been transferred from Luxembourg to Brussels in June 1968, he continued to receive the expatriation allowance. On the occasion of a general audit, the Directorate-General in charge of this operation concluded that this allowance had become unjustified as from the time when the applicant was transferred to Brussels. Accordingly, the High Authority refused to make any more payments after January 1, 1976. The action was brought against this decision, the applicant pleading, *inter alia*, an infringement of vested rights as well as the protection of legitimate expectations.

As had been the case in the *Simon* and *Elz* decisions, this dispute also involved the revocability of a declaratory administrative measure.[109] The Court restated the established principles in the following terms:

---

[105] E.C.J., *loc. cit.*, footnote 99, p. 1109.
[106] *cf.* in this sense also the Commission in Case 54/77 *Herpels* v. *Commission* [1978] E.C.R. 585 (592).
[107] H. Lecheler, *Der EuGH und die allgemeinen Rechtsgrundsätze*, Berlin 1971, p. 81.
[108] Case 54/77 *Herpels* v. *Commission* [1978] E.C.R. 585.
[109] Thus also the Commission, *ibid.*, p. 592; neither Advocate-General Mayras nor the Court adopt a position on this issue.

"Although the retroactive withdrawal of a wrongful or erroneous decision is generally subject to very strict conditions, on the other hand the revocation of such a decision as regards the future is always possible."[110]

The Court justified this view by reference to the special nature of the Staff Regulations:

"In any event, under the law relating to the public service the irregular grant or continued payment of elements of remuneration cannot create vested rights such as to prevent revocation. Article 85 of the Staff Regulations on the recovery of undue payment confirms this distinction by making recovery subject to well-defined conditions while recognising by implication that undue payments may be stopped.
Officials, who are deemed to have knowledge of that provision, cannot rely on legitimate expectation in this respect."[111]

Thus the fact that there is no need for the protection of any legitimate expectation follows from a presumption of knowledge of a provision which—prudently, from the Court's point of view—precisely does not regulate the circumstances of the case.[112] It is accepted that what we are dealing with here is merely one of the grounds on which the reasoning behind the decision is based, and not a new principle. In any case, it should not be concluded conversely from this statement that an unlawful administrative measure cannot in principle be revoked, even for the future, if the person in question had, or could have had, no knowledge of the relevant revocation provision.

An additional special feature of this case was that the provision of Article 9(b) of the ECSC Staff Rules of 1956,[113] which in the Court's view applied in this case, explicitly provided for the possibility of revoking *ex nunc* the allowance paid up to the date in question where, as was the case here as a result of the employee's transfer to Brussels, the conditions for

---

[110] E.C.J., *loc. cit.*, footnote 108, p. 598.
[111] E.C.J., *loc. cit.*, footnote 108, p. 598.
[112] Article 85 Staff Regulations.
[113] This provision reads: "Employees who, as a result of being transferred to another department, are obliged to change their residence to a place situated at less than 25 km from the place in which they were established prior to their transfer, shall forfeit the right to such payments" (cited in Case 54/77, *loc. cit.*, footnote 108, pp. 597 *et seq.*).

the allocation of an allowance are cancelled for the future,[114] so that the applicant was unable to base his alleged legitimate expectation on the original payments, which had been correctly made before his transfer to Brussels.

Finally, a kind of summing up is provided by the decision in the *Alpha Steel* case dating from 1982.[115]

On January 29, 1981, the Alpha Steel company brought an action under the second paragraph of Article 33 ECSC for the annulment of an administrative measure issued by the Commission on December 19, 1980, by which the latter had, in accordance with General Decision No. 2794/80 ECSC, fixed the applicant's steel production quotas for the first quarter of 1981. By a further individual decision of February 24, 1981—*i.e.* after the action had been brought—the Commission set aside the contested administrative measure and reduced the production quota granted even further, on the grounds that, when taking the decision of December 19, 1980, it had by mistake applied the provision contained in Article 4(3) of General Decision No. 2794/80 wrongly to the applicant's advantage.

In the course of the oral proceedings, the applicant claimed in relation to this new administrative measure of February 24, 1981 that the Commission could not withdraw a decision which formed the subject-matter of an action, or at least that it could not replace that decision by another one which was even more disadvantageous to the applicant.

Referring to its earlier case law, the ECJ stated that

> "the withdrawal of an unlawful measure is permissible, provided that the withdrawal occurs within a reasonable time and provided that the Commission has had sufficient regard to how far the applicant might have been led to rely on the lawfulness of the measure."[116]

On the question whether there existed a legitimate expectation worthy of protection, the Court took the view that the applicant lacked any expectation.[117] Although the applicant had brought the action in order to increase the quota, by bringing the action the applicant had—still according to the Court—deprived itself of any expectation, or at least any expectation of

---

[114] For general observations on revocation on the grounds of changed circumstances, *cf.* under 3(d) (ee) below.

[115] Case 14/81 *Alpha Steel* v. *Commission* [1982] E.C.R. 749.

[116] E.C.J., *ibid.*, p. 764.

[117] E.C.J., *loc. cit.*, footnote 115, p. 764.

maintaining the original quota. In addition, the applicant also knew, according to the findings of the Court, that the Commission had made an error in applying Article 4(3) of General Decision No. 2794/80. Finally, the Court maintained, a reasonable period had also been observed between the issuing of the first administrative measure (December 19, 1980) and its revocation (February 24, 1981):

> "The delay on the part of the Commission in rectifying the mistake may be attributed, at least in part, to the fact that it had to process information concerning a large number of undertakings. The applicant has not shown in what manner it was adversely affected by the time which was allowed to elapse before February 24, 1981."[118]

In its statement of reasons, the Court not only referred to decisions on both measures creating rights (*Algera*[119]) and declaratory measures (*Hoogovens*[120] and *Lemmerz-Werke*[121]). The ECJ also integrated the conditions for admissibility developed in relation to the two categories, *i.e.* the "reasonable period" requirement on the one hand and the protection of legitimate expectations on the other. This would appear to indicate a tendency towards disregarding the distinction between administrative measures creating rights and declaratory measures in the future. However, such an interpretation is not binding. Since the ECJ in this case concluded that the revocation was possible on the grounds that both these conditions had been fulfilled, it was not necessary for it to decide which of these criteria had been decisive.

The fact that the revocation of the administrative measure which had been originally contested had been decided only after the action had been brought was considered by the Court to be permissible. On this issue also, Advocate-General Reischl made reference to the statements made in the *Algera* decision on the legal position in France, under which revocation after the bringing of the action challenging the decision was permissible where it was decided before the judgment was given.[122] According to the Court, this manner of proceeding had, in spite of its permissible nature, a bearing on the allocation of costs. It appeared equitable to the ECJ "for the Commission to pay that part of the applicant's costs which might have

---

[118] E.C.J., *loc. cit.*, footnote 115, p. 764.
[119] Joined Cases 7/56 & 3–7/57 *Algera et al.* v. *Common Assembly* [1957] E.C.R. 83.
[120] Case 14/61 *Hoogovens* v. *High Authority* [1962] E.C.R. 253.
[121] Case 111/63 *Lemmerz-Werke* v. *High Authority* [1965] E.C.R. 893.
[122] Advocate-General Reischl, in Case 14/81, *loc. cit.*, footnote 122, p. 749 (783), with reference to Joined Cases 7/56 & 3–7/57.

been avoided if the Commission had given a proper statement of the reasons on which its first decision was based."[123]

(c) Special characteristics of the revocation of measures imposing burdens

The case law examined so far applies in the first place to administrative measures conferring benefits. On the subject of measures imposing burdens, the case law of the ECJ contains only a few decisions on the problems surrounding their revocation. This comes as no surprise in view of the different level at which the conflicting interests are situated.[124]

The situation is somewhat different only in relation to measures having a dual character. Thus, for example, the "exemption decision" which formed the subject-matter of the *SNUPAT*[125] and *Hoogovens*[126] cases constituted an unlawful administrative decision which on the one hand conferred benefits on Hoogovens, whilst on the other imposing burdens on SNUPAT. As can be seen from the *Hoogovens* judgment, the High Authority was justified in revoking that measure *ex tunc* and indeed compelled to revoke it *ex nunc*.[127] In spite of its dual effect, it is clear that the ECJ attached greater importance to the weighing up of interests from the point of view of the permissible nature of the revocation of a measure conferring benefits.[128] In any case, the Court upheld the application made by SNUPAT on the grounds that the contested tacit decision of the High Authority by which it had refused to revoke the administrative measure in question was unlawful, because it was based on the mistaken assumption that the contested exemptions were lawful and that the High Authority had no power to revoke them.[129]

The special category of cases concerning the subsequent levying of scrap equalisation fund contributions, revoking in the process an earlier administrative measure imposing fewer burdens, will be discussed elsewhere.[130] Thus in the *Riva* case, the Court rejected the argument of

---

[123] Case 14/81, *loc. cit.*, footnote 122, p. 771; the applicant had initially pleaded that the decision which was challenged and later revoked was not properly reasoned.

[124] *cf.* on this subject H. Lecheler, *Der Europäische Gerichtshof und die allgemeinen Rechtsgrundsätze*, Berlin 1971, p. 75.

[125] Joined Cases 42 & 49/59 *SNUPAT* v. *High Authority* [1962] E.C.R. 53.

[126] Case 14/61 *Hoogovens* v. *High Authority* [1962] E.C.R. 253.

[127] E.C.J., *loc. cit.*, footnote 126.

[128] Joined Cases 42 & 49/59, *loc. cit.*, footnote 125. Case 14/61, *loc. cit.*, footnote 126.

[129] Joined Cases 42 & 49/59, *loc. cit.*, footnote 125, p. 174.

[130] See IV. 2 below.

the applicant that the High Authority could not, after a period of several years, revoke and replace by a measure imposing greater burdens an administrative measure which fixed the mandatory contribution by the applicant to the scrap equalisation fund and which had not been contested by the applicant itself. Instead, the High Authority had the "duty to rectify all legal or factual errors and all assessments which experience showed to be inaccurate or incomplete."[131]

Moreover, mainly from the viewpoint of their formal legal effect, *i.e.* the question whether administrative measures are open to challenge after the expiry of the time limit for bringing the challenge, administrative measures imposing burdens have been the subject-matter of the relevant case law of the ECJ concerning the principle of legal certainty.[132]

(d) Special grounds for revocation

(aa) Revocation as laid down by statute

In Community law also, the principle applies that revocation is at all times possible where and to the extent that the legal rule on which the measure is based explicitly provides for the possibility of revocation. In such cases, the issuing of the administrative measure does not create an unconditional and vested right; nor does it give rise to any legitimate expectation that it will be maintained, so that the revocation of lawful administrative measures—in certain cases even retroactively—is permissible under the conditions specified in the relevant statute. By way of example we would refer to the special provisions of ECSC and EEC competition law which have already been examined elsewhere (Article 65(2), fourth paragraph, ECSC; Article 8(3) of Regulation 17 EEC).[133]

The unwritten general principles of administrative law concerning the revocation of administrative measures have been overtaken or even displaced by sets of written rules. What is certain is that the right of the administrative authorities to revoke measures is likely to be extended by such explicit provisions. In individual cases, doubts can arise whether, given the availability of special provisions in writing, it is permissible also to apply general principles relating to revocation or whether the rules

---

[131] Case 2/70 *Riva* v. *Commission* [1971] E.C.R. 97 at 108.
[132] For further details, *cf.* III, 1 below.
[133] *Supra*, II, 2.

stated in Treaty law or in derived legislation are decisive to the extent of excluding the possibility of revocation based on the general principles. This question exercised Advocate-General Roemer in the second *SOREMA* case.[134] He considered that the authorisation granted by the High Authority was an administrative measure which was unlawful from the very beginning, since the conditions which had to be fulfilled for the granting of the authorisation had not been met from the outset. Accordingly, he took the view that, although there was no reason to revoke the measure under the special provisions of Article 65(2), fourth paragraph, of the ECSC Treaty, the relevant general principles did apply. A different interpretation "would be defensible only if the Treaty set out unequivocally the exclusive character of the conditions which could justify revocation." It was the very strictness of the rules governing competition which suggested "that respect for the principle of competition must be ensured by all means available, and thus, inter alia, by applying general principles of law to the revocation of defective administrative measures."[135]

The Court did not consider these issues, however, since it held that the administrative authority had fulfilled the conditions for revoking the measure under Article 65(2)(4) on the grounds that the conditions stipulated for the granting of the authorisation had not been met.[136] Apart from this judgment, the case law of the ECJ has so far revealed no decisions in which the Court was called upon to give a ruling on a conflict between the written and the unwritten rules on the revocation of administrative measures.

(bb) Measures explicitly subject to revocation

The revocation even of lawful administrative measures conferring benefits should also be uncontroversial if the measure, when taken, was lawfully declared subject to revocation. Such an express statement restricts the possibility of the emergence of any vested right or legitimate expectation in the maintenance of the legal situation created by the measure in question. Thus Advocate-General Lagrange, in his opinion in the *Algera* case, when faced with the question whether bringing an employee within the ambit of the Staff Regulations had created vested rights, stated that the decision contained no reservations or other provi-

---

[134] Advocate-General Roemer in Case 36/64 *SOREMA* v. *High Authority* [1965] E.C.R. 447.
[135] Advocate-General Roemer, *loc. cit.*, footnote 134, p. 469.
[136] E.C.J., *loc. cit.*, footnote 134, p. 463.

sions which allowed the conclusion that the decision in question was of a temporary nature.[137]

As far as can be ascertained, there are no Community court decisions which specifically seek to establish in what circumstances the administrative authority may legitimately make an administrative measure subject to revocation.[138] Where the person in question has a right to the adoption of an administrative measure, such a reservation should be inadmissible, as long as it is not specifically provided for by legislation. Where, on the other hand, the authority in question has a discretion in adopting an administrative measure conferring benefits, this could be a ground for holding a provision making the measure in question subject to revocation to be lawful.

An example of a certain type of reservation can be found in the previously mentioned *SOREMA* case.[139] Under Article 2(2) of Decision No. 3/62, the High Authority had reserved the right to revoke the decision authorising SOREMA (*i.e.* 15 wholesalers established in France who had formed an association) to link up with OKU (a joint marketing organisation of West German mining companies). According to the applicant in Case 36/64 (second *SOREMA* case), the High Authority had, by stipulating this reservation, arrogated to itself a right to which it was not entitled. Accordingly, the revocation which was being challenged in this case was unlawful. The Court noted that the applicant had itself neglected to challenge Decision No. 3/62, which contained the reservation, within the time limit for bringing the action. Moreover, by issuing the original decision and revoking it, the High Authority had remained within the terms of Article 65(2) of the ECSC Treaty.[140]

Since this provision explicitly confers on the High Authority a right of revocation, the reservation expressed in the original decision merely amounts to a declaratory reservation. This type of reservation should give rise to relatively few problems.[141]

(cc) Revocation on the grounds of false or incomplete information

There is a further ground for revocation where "the administrative

---

[137] Advocate-General Lagrange in Joined Cases 7/56 & 3–7/57 *Algera et al.* v. *Common Assembly* [1957–1958] E.C.R. 39.
[138] *cf.* on this subject W. Wiesner, *Der Widerruf individueller Entscheidungen der Hohen Behörde der EGKS*, Hamburg 1966, pp. 83 *et seq.*
[139] Case 36/64 *SOREMA* v. *High Authority* [1965] E.C.R. 447.
[140] Case 36/64, *loc. cit.*, footnote 139, p. 459 (461).
[141] *cf.* W. Wiesner, *loc. cit.*, footnote 138, pp. 83 *et seq.*

measure in question has been adopted on the basis of false or incomplete information provided by those concerned."[142] This was the ruling of the Court in the *SNUPAT* case, making reference to the legal systems of the Member States. Accordingly, even those administrative measures which are lawful, either *per se* or otherwise, may be revoked if they have been made on the basis of false or incomplete information supplied by the parties in question. In addition, following the *SNUPAT* decision any such revocation may also at all times be retroactive.[143]

This ground for revocation is not only acknowledged as constituting an unwritten principle. It is also featured in the written Community law, such as, for example, in the provisions of Article 8(3) of Regulation 17 (EEC) in relation to the revocation of a decision allowing a cartel. In addition to the fraudulent acquisition of the exemption, the innocent and unconscious[144] provision of incorrect information is also mentioned as a ground for revocation by this Article. Under paragraph 3(2) of this provision, the Commission is also empowered in such cases to revoke the measure retroactively, on the understanding, however, that in the context of its discretionary decision-making power it is also bound by the proportionality principle.[145] More particularly in the case of incorrect information innocently supplied, the Commission will need to take into account the legitimate expectation acquired by the person concerned in the exemption when considering the possibility of revoking the measure retroactively.[146] Similar restrictions in relation to the freedom to revoke on the basis of false or incomplete information, decreed by the Court, would appear to apply to the corresponding unwritten general principles of administrative law.[147]

---

[142] Joined Cases 42 & 49/59 *SNUPAT* v. *High Authority* [1961] E.C.R. 53.

[143] In the case on which this decision was based, the Court finally arrived at the conclusion, in the following decision, that Hoogovens could not be accused of having supplied incorrect or incomplete information (Case 14/61 *Hoogovens* v. *High Authority* [1962] E.C.R. 253.) This issue was also discussed by Advocate-General Roemer in Case 111/63 *Lemmerz-Werke* v. *High Authority* [1965] E.C.R. 911 at 936. However, here too he arrived at the conclusion that incorrect or incomplete information had not been supplied by the undertaking.

[144] This is the general view: Gleiss, Hirsch, *Kommentar zum EWG-Kartellrecht* (3rd ed., Heidelberg 1978), Regulation 17, Article 8 No. 12.

[145] Gleiss, Hirsch, *loc. cit.*, footnote 144, Nos. 3, 19.

[146] On this subject, *cf.* II.2(b) above.

[147] W. Wiesner, *loc. cit.*, footnote 138, pp. 63 *et seq.*, goes even further where he suggests that the E.C.J. decision in the *SNUPAT* case must be interpreted restrictively as meaning that the Court held that there was a special ground of revocation only in the case of deception, and not in the case of incorrect information innocently supplied.

(dd) Changes in the legal situation

The question whether the revocation of an administrative measure is permissible can also arise when, in relation to the rule on which the administrative measure is based, a change occurs in the legal situation. A distinction must be made here between a change made by the legislature on the one hand and the repeal of a rule or a statement by the ECJ on the non-applicability of the rule on the other.

In the first instance, the legal rule in question may be amended, repealed or replaced with another rule by the Council or by the Commission. To revoke retroactively any administrative measure which, at least originally, was lawful and based on a legal provision which previously was applicable will in such cases be permissible if the new regulation itself has had "genuine" retroactivity[148] attributed to it and the latter is, by way of exception, lawful. Normally, however, the retrospective revocation, based on a retroactive regulation, of an administrative measure conferring rights will infringe vested rights and accordingly be unlawful. This would, for example, be the case in relation to the recovery of benefits paid on the basis of a new retroactive regulation.[149] The protection of legitimate expectations and vested rights is the problem which will need to be considered as a matter of priority when examining the question of the permissible nature of the retroactivity of the regulation.[150]

A case which will be more difficult to assess is that of the withdrawal of a benefit granted for the future on the basis of the rule which applied up to a certain date. It is a precondition for the protection of vested rights here that

> "the facts creating the rights occurred under a provision existing before the amendments subsequently introduced by the Community authority."[151]

In other words, it is necessary for a right to have been created—such as a measure fixing in a binding way the amount of a claim or the nature and

---

[148] On the distinction between genuine and unreal retroactivity, *cf. infra*, under D.II.1.

[149] On the prohibition of retroactive changes in the Staff Regulations which work to the officials' disadvantage, *cf.* Advocate-General Capotorti in Case 127/80 *Grogan* v. *Commission* [1982] E.C.R. 869 (898); opinion by the same Advocate-General in Case 167/80 *Curtis* v. *European Parliament* [1981] E.C.R. 1499 at 1552 *et seq.*; Advocate-General Mayras, in Case 28/74 *Gillet* v. *Commission* [1975] E.C.R. 463 at 478.

[150] On this subject, *cf.* Section 3, D below.

[151] Advocate-General Capotorti in Case 167/80, *loc. cit.*, footnote 149, referring to the decision by the E.C.J. in Case 28/74, *loc. cit.*, footnote 149, p. 473.

size of some other benefit—which is to exist indefinitely in the future and independently of any subsequent amendment in the legal situation, this right having been created by an administrative measure made by virtue of the old legal system. Only then would the withdrawal of this benefit for the future constitute a revocation of an administrative measure which originally was lawful and created rights.[152]

The Court was faced with such a situation—at least according to the applicant—in the *Grogan* case.[153] The applicant objected to a decision by the Commission of October 23, 1979 by which it informed him that on the basis of Regulations 3085/78 and 3086/78 (EEC/ECSC/EURATOM) on the adjustment of the correcting coefficients as applied to the salaries and pension payments of officials and other employees of the E.C., the relevant pension payments were to be gradually reduced from Bfrs. 30,145 to Bfrs. 13,080. The applicant was of the opinion that the decision of March 25, 1975, by which he had been retired from his post in the interests of the service, had already definitively created for his benefit a right to a pension based on rates of exchange current at that time. If this was indeed the case, the amending Regulations 3085/78 and 3086/78 would definitely have been given retroactive effect. The revocation based on such a regulation, even if the former allowed him to retain the payments already received in the past and merely reduced future benefits—would, in his opinion, infringe the vested rights of the applicant[154] and therefore in normal circumstances be inadmissible.

Advocate-General Capotorti denied that such vested rights had been created on the basis of the earlier version of the legal rule in question. Instead, the situation was that

---

[152] According to Gleiss, Hirsch, *loc. cit.*, footnote 144, revocation on grounds of a changed legal situation, *e.g.* in cases of exemptions granted under Article 85(3) EEC, is not permissible, since the provisions of Article 8(3)(a) of Regulation 17 apply only to a change in the material circumstances and not to a change in the legal situation (Annotation to Article 8 Regulation 17, No. 6).

[153] Case 127/80 *Grogan* v. *Commission* [1982] E.C.R. 869. *cf.* also the parallel cases of *Curtis* v. *European Parliament*, Case 167/80 [1981] E.C.R. 1499 and [1982] E.C.R. 931; Case 164/80 *Pasquale* v. *Commission* [1982] E.C.R. 909; also, in a similar group of cases, Case 817/79 *Buyl* v. *Commission* [1982] E.C.R. 245; Case 543/79 *Birke* v. *Commission* [1982] E.C.R. 4425; Joined Cases 532–534, 567, 600, 618 & 660/79 *Amesz et al.* v. *Commission* [1982] E.C.R. 4465 and Case 779/79 *Bruckner* v. *Commission* [1982] E.C.R. 4525.

[154] On the notion of vested rights, *cf.* Advocate-General Capotorti in Case 127/80, *loc. cit.*, footnote 153, p. 898; also opinion by the same Advocate-General in Case 167/80, *loc. cit.*, footnote 153, p. 1553.

"the circumstances giving rise to a former official's right to be paid a specific amount each month, by way of pension, arise when each monthly payment falls due."[155]

The Court also held that the plea of infringement of vested rights was unfounded.[156]

Neither the Advocate-General nor the Court applied the principles relating to the revocation of administrative measures in this case. The new decision of October 23, 1979, which was made on the basis of a change in the legal situation, cannot be regarded as an administrative measure revoking the original administrative decision. Both the decision of March 25, 1975 and that of October 23, 1979 were merely declaratory measures by which the right of the applicant was established on the basis of the applicable rules. The original administrative measure does not entitle its author to create a right which is immune to changes in the legal situation. The new administrative measure, which takes away for the future the benefit granted in the past, is merely a (new) rule[157] based on a changed legal situation and not a revocation of a lawful administrative measure creating rights and conferring benefits. The fact that the ECJ is nevertheless prepared to guarantee the protection of legitimate expectations, namely when corresponding assurances have been given by the Community organs or where insufficient attention has been paid to the need for transitional arrangements,[158] is closely related to the question whether the "unreal" retroactivity of the underlying regulation is permissible. This issue will be examined later.[159]

The issue of the permissible nature of revocation, or the question whether there is a duty to revoke even administrative measures which were originally lawful or legally valid, also arises in the context of proceedings in disputes before the Court between the Community and a third

---

[155] Advocate-General Capotorti in Case 127/80, *loc. cit.*, footnote 153; opinion by the same Advocate-General in Case 167/80, *loc. cit.*, footnote 153, on the justification of this type of vested rights by the earlier legal provision: "there is nothing in the text of this provision to justify such an interpretation; moreover, a provision of this type would be both absurd and nonsensical" (p. 1553).

[156] Case 127/80, *loc. cit.*, footnote 153, pp. 880 *et seq.*

[157] On the legal situation in Germany, *cf.* F. O. Kopp, *Verwaltungsverfahrensgesetz* (4th ed., München 1986), Article 49, Nos. 41, 35 and Article 48, Nos. 20 *et seq.*

[158] For example, Case 127/80, *loc. cit.*, footnote 153, pp. 884 *et seq.*—here, the Court arrived at the conclusion that the envisaged transitional system should have been twice as long, in order not to infringe the legitimate expectations of the person receiving the pension. The decision based on the amending regulation was accordingly set aside.

[159] *cf.* Section 3, D.II.3 below.

party seeking to establish whether a rule on which the administrative measure is based is void (Articles 173 and 174 EEC) or inapplicable (Article 184 EEC). From the point of view of legitimate expectations and legal certainty, it is also conceivable that on the basis of an appropriate Court decision the relevant authorities were entitled to revoke administrative measures conferring benefits which had been adopted in relation to third parties, whilst being at the same time compelled, where appropriate, to revoke an administrative measure imposing burdens adopted on the basis of the regulation which had been declared null and void.

Decisions by which the Court declares a contested instrument null and void in accordance with Article 174 EEC (147 EAEC, 33 ECSC) in principle take effect *ex tunc* and *erga omnes*. Where the Court holds a regulation to be null and void, the legal instrument which up to that time was regarded as valid is henceforth deprived retrospectively of its validity; it is to be regarded as "non-existent."[160] The Court, however, can, under the second paragraph of Article 174 EEC, "if it considers it necessary, state which of the effects of the regulation which it has declared void shall be considered as definitive." More particularly, this gives the Court the opportunity to deny or reduce the retroactivity of the avoidance by reference to the principle of legal certainty or to certain vested rights.[161] If the Court, by virtue of this provision, denies the retroactivity of the avoidance of a regulation, it will be necessary to assess the permissible nature of the revocation of an administrative measure which has been adopted on the basis of the regulation prior to it being declared void, in the light of the above-mentioned principles relating to the revocation of lawful administrative measures. In other words, whereas administrative measures creating rights and effective for the future should not be revoked *ex nunc*, declaratory measures may be thus revoked.

If on the other hand the Court has failed to take the opportunity to restrict the retroactivity of the avoidance, it is possible in principle to revoke, even retroactively, all administrative measures made on the basis of the regulation in question. Where we are dealing with administrative measures imposing burdens, there already arises a duty to revoke from the provisions of Article 176 EEC, under which the Community institution in question "shall be required to take the necessary measures to

---

[160] Case 22/70 *Commission* v. *Council, ("AETR")* [1971] E.C.R. 263 (279).
[161] Advocate-General Trabucchi in Case 91/75 *HZA Göttingen* v. *Miritz* [1976] E.C.R. 217 (238); H. W. Daig, in Groeben, Boeckh, Thiesing, Ehlermann, *Kommentar zum EWG-Vertrag* (3rd ed., Baden-Baden 1983), Article 174, Nos. 3 *et seq.*

comply with the judgment of the Court of Justice."[162] The same considerations apply if the administrative measure imposing burdens has already
become unchallengeable by the third party concerned because of the
expiry of the time limit.[163] If on the other hand we are faced with the
revocation of an administrative measure conferring benefits, the
authority, in spite of the retroactive nature of the avoidance of the
regulation, will need to observe the principle of the protection of legitimate expectations when reviewing the revocation of the administrative
measures adopted on the basis of that regulation.[164] Here, taking account
of legitimate expectations in individual cases can lead to the inadmissibility of revocation *ex tunc*. So far, there is no case law on this subject.
However, there are certain parallels with the *SNUPAT* case, which has
been examined in detail earlier.

Once the ECJ had, in the first *SNUPAT* case,[165] made a binding
interpretation of General Decision 2/57, the High Authority, as the Court
stated in the second *SNUPAT* judgment,[166] should, because of the resulting unlawfulness of the exemptions granted to the Hoogovens and Breda
firms, have considered the question whether these exemptions were open
to revocation. Consequently, a compulsory examination resulted from a
binding interpretation, made by the Court in another case, of the rule on
which the administrative measures granting the exemptions were based;
from this examination, it appeared that the administrative measures

---

[162] In relation to the avoidance of tacit decisions by the Commission, the Court, with
reference to the provision of Article 176 EEC, has expressly held that the Commission
must "withdraw or at least render inapplicable" any later decision merely confirming this
tacit decision: Joined Cases 45 & 49/70 *Bode* v. *Commission* [1971] E.C.R. 465 at 476.

[163] Opinion of Advocate-General Trabucchi in Joined Cases 15–33, 52–53, 57–109, 116–117,
123, 132 & 135–137/73 *Kortner-Schots et al.* v. *Council, Commission and Parliament*
[1974] E.C.R. 177 at 195: "It is, however, legitimate to raise the question of retroactivity
also in relation to third parties." The Court, however, has, in a decision concerning
indirect administrative action, ruled that the measures to be adopted by the relevant
authorities on the basis of the decision by the E.C.J. (Article 176 EEC) could also take the
form of the adoption of a new regulation having retroactive effect, which could accordingly at a later stage form a valid legal basis (Case 110/81 *SA Roquette Frères* v. *Council*
[1982] E.C.R. 3159 at 3181; Advocate-General Reischl, in his opinion in Joined Cases
108, 110 & 114/81 [1982] E.C.R. 3139 at 3145 *et seq*. This may, however, be called into
question if the annulled rule was unlawful only because of procedural defects (T. C.
Hartley, *The Foundations of European Community Law*, Oxford 1981, p. 461).

[164] G. Bebr, *Judicial Control of the European Communities*, London 1962, p. 131; H. W.
Daig, in Groeben, Boeckh, Thiesing, Ehlermann, *Kommentar zum EWG-Vertrag* (3rd
ed., Baden-Baden 1983), Article 174, No. 6, Article 176, Nos. 9 *et seq.*; W. Däubler,
"Der Widerruf von Verwaltungsakten im Recht der Europäischen Gemeinschaften,"
NJW 1965, p. 1648 (with further references).

[165] Joined Cases 32–33/58 *SNUPAT* v. *High Authority* [1959] E.C.R. 127.

[166] Joined Cases 42 & 49/59 *SNUPAT* v. *High Authority* [1961] E.C.R. 53.

which up to that time had constituted valid measures were unlawful in the absence of any legal basis. As has been explained elsewhere, these circumstances led the Court, in the subsequent *Hoogovens* case, to conclude that, in view of the unlawfulness of the purely declaratory administrative measures conferring benefits, the High Authority was obliged to issue an *ex nunc* revocation and, in addition, had to examine whether it was appropriate also to revoke the measure retroactively, bearing in mind any legitimate expectation which was worthy of protection and weighing up the conflicting interests involved.[167] Even in the case of the retroactive annulment of a legal provision on which the administrative measure conferring benefits was based, these principles were applicable.

Particularly in relation to administrative measures imposing burdens, however, there is another combination of circumstances which is of importance in practice. In view of the greatly reduced right of the Community citizen to bring a direct action against general decisions (Article 33 ECSC) and against regulations (Article 173 EEC, Article 146 EAEC), a particularly important role is played by the incidental plea of non-applicability of the underlying rule under Article 184 EEC (156 EAEC) from the point of view of the legal protection of individuals against the effects of unlawful regulations. According to the established case law of the Court, since this provision expresses a general principle, it can also be applied in the area covered by the ECSC Treaty[168] and in the law governing E.C. staff.

Where the Court has established that a particular rule is unlawful in an action brought under the second paragraph of Article 173 EEC in which the applicant pleads the unlawfulness of the rule on which the measure imposing burdens is based, the first consequence of such an outcome is its inapplicability under Article 184 EEC. It will also result in the unlawfulness of the administrative measures which are based on this rule and are being challenged by the action; these measures will consequently need to be set aside by the ECJ.[169]

However, it may be that the rule which has now been incidentally held unlawful has been applied in a large number of cases for many years, without the administrative measures adopted on the basis of this reg-

---

[167] Case 14/61 *Hoogovens* v. *High Authority* [1962] E.C.R. 253.
[168] Joined Cases 32–33/58, *loc. cit.*, footnote 165.
[169] J. Schwarze, "Rechtsschutz Privater gegenüber normativen Rechtsakten im Recht der EWG," in *Festschrift für H.-J. Schlochauer*, Berlin 1981, p. 927 (938); H. W. Daig, in Groeben, Boeckh, Thiesing, Ehlermann, *Kommentar zum EWG-Vertrag* (3rd ed., Baden-Baden 1983), Article 184, No. 11.

ulation being challenged by the parties affected by them. Here, the question arises whether the administrative authority in question is in such cases also compelled to revoke automatically those administrative measures imposing burdens which were adopted on the basis of the regulation which is now held to be unlawful and which were no longer open to challenge, as would be regarded as acceptable in the case of an annulment.[170] On this question, the same principles apply which the ECJ elaborated on the subject of the formal validity of the relevant administrative measures in the *Kortner-Schots* case, *i.e.* that decisions in which the unlawfulness of a regulation has been established merely by way of incidental plea

> "have the authority of *res judicata* only in relation to the parties involved at that time. It is right moreover to point out that they could not have pronounced the annulment of the regulatory provision involved, within the meaning of Article 174 first paragraph, but that they simply placed on record the inapplicability of this provision and consequent upon this pronounced the annulment of the individual decisions taken on that basis."[171]

The view that such incidental decisions have only a limited effect is generally accepted today.[172] The provision of Article 184 merely seeks to protect the parties involved in a particular case against the application of unlawful regulations, without calling into question the continued existence of the regulation itself.[173]

In the same way that the Court, in the *Kortner-Schots* case, concluded from this fact that the applicants could no longer rely on the unlawfulness, established incidentally in another case, of the rule underlying these administrative measures once the time limit for bringing the action had elapsed,[174] it may be concluded here that, contrary to what is entailed by the avoidance of a rule under Articles 173 and 174 EEC, the administrative authority in question has no duty to revoke such measures.

---

[170] *cf. supra* under footnote 163; Advocate-General Trabucchi in Joined Cases 15–33 *et al./73, loc. cit.*, footnote 163, p. 195.

[171] Joined Cases 15–33 *et al./73, loc. cit.*, footnote 163, p. 191.

[172] J. Schwarze, *loc. cit.*, footnote 169, p. 938 with further references; H. W. Daig, in Groeben, Boeckh, Thiesing, Ehlermann, *Kommentar zum EWG-Vertrag* (3rd ed., Baden-Baden 1983), Article 184, Nos. 14 *et seq.*

[173] Thus the E.C.J. in Joined Cases 31 & 33/62 *Wöhrmann and Lütticke* v. *Commission* [1962] E.C.R. 1027 at 1942.

[174] Joined Cases 15–33 *et al.*, 73, *loc. cit.*, footnote 163, p. 191.

On the other hand, it should be accepted in principle that in such cases a right to revoke these measures does exist. Where, however, administrative measures conferring benefits on third parties have been adopted on the basis of regulations which have been held to be unlawful in incidental proceedings under Article 184 EEC, their revocability must be assessed in the light of the relevant general principles. In particular, legitimate expectations, if worthy of protection, and vested rights will, where appropriate, need to be respected.[175]

(ee) Changes of circumstances

As can be seen from the rules of written Community law described above, the possibility of revoking a measure which, at least initially,[176] was lawful again cannot in principle be excluded if the relevant circumstances have changed on an issue which is crucial to the adoption of the administrative measure in question. Thus, for example, Article 8(4)(c) of Competition Regulation 127 (EEC) permits in such cases the revocation *ex nunc* of an exemption decision. A similar rule is found in Article 65(2), fourth paragraph, ECSC. The Staff Regulations also provide, under certain conditions, for the possibility of revocation on grounds of changed circumstances. A typical example is automatic dismissal (Article 49 of the Staff Regulations), which may be based on the loss of citizenship of one of the Member States of the Community or the deprivation of civic rights (Article 28a of the Staff Regulations).

The provision in Article 9(b) of the ECSC Staff Rules, which played an important part in the *Herpels* case, also anticipated the possibility of revocation *ex nunc* due to changed circumstances.[177] When the ECJ established that the applicant, contrary to his statements, was not based in a place which was situated more than 25 kilometres from his new

---

[175] This can be concluded from the grounds of judgment of the E.C.J. in Case 92/78 *Simmenthal* v. *Commission* [1979] E.C.R. 777.

[176] It cannot be concluded from the present case law of the E.C.J. whether or not changed circumstances can render unlawful a measure which was originally lawful. In Case 232/81 *Agricola Commerciale Olio et al.* v. *Commission* [1984] E.C.R. 3881, Advocate-General Lenz contradicted the viewpoint that a measure had become "gradually unlawful" because of changed circumstances by referring to the "general consideration that an originally lawful measure, as long as it exists, is deemed to continue to be lawful" (p. 3911). The Court has failed to take up this argument.

[177] This provision read as follows: "Officials who, as a result of a new posting, take up residence less than 25 kilometres from the place where they resided before their entry into the service lose the right to the allowance . . ." (ECSC Staff Regulations of 1956, cited in Case 54/77 *Herpels* v. *Commission* [1978] E.C.R. 585 at 590 *et seq.*).

domicile and that consequently the provisions of Article 9(b) of the Staff Rules applied to him, it became perfectly clear that the payment of the expatriation allowance should have been revoked *ex nunc* immediately after his transfer to Brussels.[178] The change in circumstances was enough to justify *ex nunc* revocation. There could be no question here of any legitimate expectation or vested rights.[179]

However, all this relates to special rules. It therefore does not necessarily follow that in Community law generally the revocation of an administrative measure which, at least initially, was lawful is permissible on the grounds of a change in circumstances.[180] As has already been stated, however, the grounds of judgment in the *Simon* case[181] prompt the conclusion that the Court, at least in the case of administrative measures conferring benefits which are merely declaratory, assumes that such instruments may be freely revoked *ex nunc* if a change in circumstances arises.

In such cases, the principle which states that administrative action must comply with the relevant statute also favours revocation since, as a result of the change in circumstances, the administrative measure has come into conflict with the applicable legal rules. The principle of the freedom to revoke *ex nunc* can, however, be inequitable if allowance has to be made for the fact that the person affected had a legitimate expectation in the maintenance of the benefit, since it is not always the person affected who must bear the responsibility for the change in circumstances.

However, a particular distinction must also be made here between actual changes in circumstances and a changed perception of unchanged circumstances by the relevant authorities. Where there has been merely a change in perception by the authorities, this can justify revocation only if any legitimate expectation the person affected may have has been adequately protected.[182]

The revocation of administrative measures creating rights must, unless it is expressly permitted, be only a restricted possibility even when a

---

[178] E.C.J., *loc. cit.*, footnote 177, p. 598, Advocate-General Mayras, *ibid.*, p. 604.

[179] This question was relevant for the E.C.J. in that the Commission had, over a period of seven-and-a-half years, failed to revoke the original administrative measure (allocation of an expatriation allowance) on the basis of changed circumstances; E.C.J., *loc. cit.*, footnote 177, p. 598; also Advocate-General Mayras, *ibid.*, pp. 605 *et seq.*

[180] *cf.* W. Wiesner, *Der Widerruf individueller Entscheidungen der Hohen Behörde der EGKS*, Hamburg 1966, p. 68.

[181] Case 15/60 *Simon* v. *Court of Justice* [1961] E.C.R. 239.

[182] *cf.* on the legal situation in cases covered by Article 8(3)(a) of Regulation 17: Gleiss, Hirsch, *Kommentar zum EWG-Kartellrecht* (3rd ed., Heidelberg 1978), Article 8 of Regulation 17, No. 8.

change in circumstances has occurred. Where in such cases, as a result of the new circumstances, the conditions for the adoption or the maintenance of the measure no longer apply, there is a stronger case for permitting *ex nunc* revocation than where the new circumstances merely constitute factors which influence the discretion exercised by the authority in question. In the latter situation, *ex nunc* revocation should normally not be permissible either.

(e) Summary

This section can be summed up as follows:

Lawful administrative measures creating rights may not be revoked in principle—*i.e.* where no special grounds for revocation apply. In such cases the legitimate expectation on the part of the person concerned that the situation created by the administrative measure will be maintained will take precedence over the interests of the administration in changing the legal situation. According to the Court's decision in the *Algera* case,[183] *ex nunc* revocation is also normally inadmissible in the case of lawful administrative measures creating rights. Whether this applies unreservedly to lawful declaratory administrative measures as well cannot be clearly established from the present state of the case law.

Unlawful administrative measures, on the other hand, can be revoked in principle. "The absence of an objective legal basis for the measure affects the individual right of the person concerned."[184] As the Court has ruled, initially in relation to the revocation of a measure creating rights, such a revocation is permissible "at least within a reasonable period of time."[185] As regards the revocation of declaratory administrative measures, the administrative authority in question has to take into consideration the extent to which the person affected had a legitimate expectation that the measure concerned was lawful.[186] In the *Alpha Steel* case, which dates from 1982, the Court did not—at least in express terms—restrict to the revocation of declaratory measures the obligation on the part of the administration to guarantee the protection of legitimate expectations.[187]

---

[183] Joined Cases 7/56 & 3–7/57 *Algera et al.* v. *Common Assembly* [1957–1958] E.C.R. 39.
[184] Joined Cases 7/56 & 3–7/57, *loc. cit.*, footnote 183.
[185] E.C.J., *ibid.*
[186] Joined Cases 42 & 49/59 *SNUPAT* v. *High Authority* [1961] E.C.R. 53 (172), Case 14/61 *Hoogovens* v. *High Authority* [1962] E.C.R. 253.
[187] Case 14/81 *Alpha Steel* v. *Commission* [1982] E.C.R. 749 at 764; however, this case also concerned the revocation of a merely declaratory administrative measure.

In particular, a distinction must be drawn between the retroactive and the *ex nunc* revocation of unlawful administrative measures. In the case of the former, the administration has to take into account any legitimate expectation in the lawful nature of the administrative measure[188] or else decree the revocation only within a reasonable period.[189] Where a conflict arises with the principle of legal certainty, particular importance is given to the principle under which the administration must comply with the relevant legislation when, as was for example the case with the exemptions from the scrap equalisation fund (which only took effect in the past anyway), the mere act of revoking the measure *ex nunc* no longer has any effect.[190] *Ex nunc* revocation is, at least with regard to declaratory administrative measures, normally permissible without reservation,[191] and under certain conditions is even compulsory.[192] Here, the question of legitimate expectation is irrelevant. However, there has been no clear position on the part of the case law on the question whether this unconditional revocation of unlawful beneficial administrative measures also applies in the case of measures creating rights. According to the *Algera* decision, the rule restricting the permissible nature of revocation to a "reasonable period" in such cases also applies to *ex nunc* revocation. The more recent decisions continue to prompt the conclusion that the Court gives greater protection to the maintenance of an unlawful administrative measure creating rights than to a merely declaratory administrative measure.[193]

4. General conditions for the lawful nature of revocation decisions

(a) *Where no forfeiture has occurred*

The general conditions for the lawfulness of a revocation decision

---

[188] Joined Cases 42 & 49/59 *SNUPAT* v. *High Authority* [1961] E.C.R. 53; Case 14/61, *loc. cit.*, footnote 186; Case 14/81, *loc. cit.*, footnote 187, p. 764.

[189] Joined Cases 7/56 & 3–7/57, *loc. cit.*, footnote 183.

[190] Advocate-General Lagrange in Case 14/61, *loc. cit.*, footnote 186.

[191] Case 15/60 *Simon* v. *Court of Justice* [1961] E.C.R. 239 at 259 *et seq.*

[192] Thus, at any rate, Case 14/61 *Hoogovens* v. *High Authority* [1962] E.C.R. 253; the administrative measure which benefited the applicant and was later revoked was at the same time a measure imposing burdens in relation to other scrap metal users.

[193] *cf.* Commission in Case 54/77 *Herpels* v. *Commission* [1978] E.C.R. 585 at 592.

include the requirement that the administrative authority in question has not forfeited its right to revoke.

The question of the forfeiture of the right to revoke played a particularly important role in the *Lemmerz-Werke* case.[194] Although the High Authority had already had knowledge of the unlawfulness of the applicant's exemption from certain payments in November 1958 and the German Regional Office had, unsuccessfully, demanded that the mistake in question be rectified in relation to the applicant, the exemption was formally revoked only in 1963. The applicant brought an action against this administrative measure and raised, *inter alia*, a plea of forfeiture. The Court examined this question, although it had already rejected the claim that the applicant had a legitimate expectation in the continued existence of the exemption,[195] and concluded that the High Authority had not forfeited the right to which it was entitled.[196] The reason for this was, according to the ECJ, that although the approach adopted by the German Regional Office had given rise to criticism, it nevertheless appeared understandable that the authority in question had the expectation that its instructions would be transmitted properly and promptly.[197] Advocate-General Roemer, on the other hand, came to the conclusion that the defendant had forfeited its right of revocation because of its negligent administration.[198] In support of this view, he referred *inter alia* to the Law relating to Administrative Procedure (*Verwaltungsverfahrensgesetz*)— then in draft form—which fixed the time limit for setting aside an administrative measure at a period of one year as from the time when the facts which justified the revocation became known.[199]

A failure to remain within the time limit which leads to a forfeiture of the authority's right to revoke is not necessarily the same as exceeding the "reasonable period" within which the authority, according to the *Algera* decision, must in principle revoke an unlawful administrative measure

---

[194] Case 111/63 *Lemmerz-Werke* v. *High Authority* [1965] E.C.R. 911.

[195] For a critical note on this issue, *cf.* H. Lecheler, *Der Europäische Gerichtshof und die allgemeinen Rechtsgrundsätze*, Berlin 1971, p. 102, who rightly points out that there is no question of forfeiture, as a corollary of the good faith principle, where the person concerned himself lacks good faith; *cf.* also H.-J. Rüber, *Der Gerichtshof der Europäischen Gemeinschaften und die Konkretisierung allgemeiner Rechtsgrundsätze*, Diss. Köln 1970, p. 291.

[196] Case 111/63, *loc. cit.*, footnote 194, p. 913.

[197] E.C.J., *loc. cit.*, footnote 194, p. 913.

[198] Advocate-General Roemer, *loc. cit.*, footnote 194, p. 938.

[199] Advocate-General Roemer, *ibid.*; *cf.* on the recent state of affairs on this subject Article 48(4) of the German Laws relating to Federal and Land Administrative Procedure.

creating rights.[200] On the one hand, the reasonable period within the meaning of the *Algera* decision commences, as is the case in France, with the adoption of the administrative measure creating rights[201] and not with the time when the administrative authority had knowledge of the circumstances which gave rise to the unlawfulness and therefore also to the revocability of the measure in question. On the other hand, the period elapsing between the time when the revocable nature of the measure became known and the revocation itself can also be important if the measure in question is merely declaratory, although according to the case law of the ECJ in the *Hoogovens* decision the reasonable period within the meaning of the *Algera* decision forms only one of the factors to be taken into account when weighing up the interests involved.[202]

(b) Principles governing form and procedure

The revocation of an administrative measure is a decision within the meaning of the second paragraph of Article 173 EEC (Article 146 EAEC) or an individual decision within the meaning of the second paragraph of Article 33 ECSC. Accordingly, the general principles governing form and procedure must be respected in this context as well. Revocation in particular must be reasoned. As the Court stated in the *Hoogovens* case, the statement of reasons will be considered adequate "when it enables both the parties concerned and the Court to discover the essential elements of the High Authority's reasoning."[203] This applies particularly in relation to the process of weighing up the interests involved from the viewpoint of the protection of legitimate expectations. The ECJ stated that in this connection,

"the contested Decision makes clear the reasons which led the defendant to give preference in this case to the principle of legality.

---

[200] Joined Cases 7/56 & 3–7/57, *Algera et al.* v. *Common Assembly* [1957–1958] E.C.R. 39.
[201] Advocate-General Lagrange in Case 14/61 *Hoogovens* v. *High Authority* [1962] E.C.R. 253. In relation to the starting point of this period, the decision in Case 15/85 *Consorzio Cooperative d'Abruzzo* v. *Commission* [1987] E.C.R. 1005, clearly also starts from this assumption. At the same time, the Court, in establishing that a reasonable period had not been observed, pointed to the fact that the Commission, immediately after the adoption of the administrative measure revoked by the challenged decision, had the opportunity to become acquainted with the facts which justified the revocation, and that a revocation which was made only two years afterwards would consequently be inadmissible as infringing the principles of legal certainty and of the protection of legitimate expectation.
[202] Case 14/61, *loc. cit.*, footnote 201.
[203] Case 14/61, *loc. cit.*, footnote 201.

Moreover, if the defendant did not think it necessary to take note of the effects—effects of some consequence no doubt—which a withdrawal *ex tunc* would, on a concrete appraisal of the interests involved, entail for the applicant, that is easily explained by the fact that, in the opinion of the High Authority, the well-known prosperity of the applicant company reduced the relative importance of those effects in the context of the balance of interests.

This reasoning emerges clearly from the scheme of the contested decision, both for the party to whom it was addressed and for the Court, so that the statement of reasons cannot be said to be substantially inadequate in this regard."[204]

As the Court ruled in the *Kortner-Schots* case,[205] however, even a revocation of an administrative measure which has not been adequately reasoned can become formally valid and consequently not open to challenge if the action has not been brought within the time limit.

Finally, from a substantive point of view, account must be taken of the fact that, according to the case law of the Court, the revocation on grounds of unlawfulness of an administrative measure conferring benefits is in principle permissible only to the extent that the measure in question actually turns out to be unlawful. If the measure is unlawful only in part but valid in every other respect, revocation is normally inadmissible. In the *Algera* case, the Court was called upon to deal with this particular question, since in the opinion of the ECJ the appointment itself had been lawful and only the attribution of a certain rank of service and the classification of the employee concerned in a particular salary bracket were unlawful. Although Advocate-General Lagrange concluded that both parts of the original administrative measure were unlawful,[206] the Court arrived at a different conclusion:

"Adopting the interpretation followed in most modern legislative systems, according to which partial unlawfulness does not entail the revocability of the measure in its entirety, unless that measure is deprived of its raison d'être if the unlawful part is removed, the

---

[204] E.C.J., *ibid.*, p. 553.
[205] Joined Cases 15–33, 52–53, 57–109, 116–117, 123, 132 & 135–137/73 *Kortner-Schots* v. *Council, Commission and Parliament* [1974] E.C.R. 177.
[206] Advocate-General Lagrange in Joined Cases 7/56 & 3–7/57 *Algera et al.* v. *Common Assembly* [1957–58] E.C.R. 39.

Court rejects the argument that the various elements of the orders are indissociable."[207]

(c) *The exercise of discretion and the duty to observe the law*

The decisive statements by the ECJ on the issue of discretion or the duty to observe the law on the part of the authorities in taking decisions on the revocation of administrative measures can be summarised as follows:

With regard to unlawful measures conferring benefits—at least those which are confirmatory in character—a distinction must be drawn between *ex tunc* revocation and mere revocation for the future. Whilst the authority in question is compelled to revoke an unlawful declaratory administrative measure *ex nunc*,[208] it may exercise its discretion in relation to retroactive revocation.[209] This exercise of discretion involves in the first instance a process of weighing up the two conflicting interests,[210] *i.e.* the public interest, which is dominated by the principle of compliance with the relevant statute, and the individual interest of the person in question, which seeks to ensure that the confidence placed by that person in the maintenance of the administrative measure is protected. However, the Court at all times reserves the right in such cases to examine whether the revocation decision made by the High Authority "disclosed a substantial error of judgment in considering any position acquired by the applicant for which it could claim protection,"[211] or whether, as stated in the *Alpha Steel* case, "the Commission has had sufficient regard to how

---

[207] E.C.J., *ibid.* pp. 126 *et seq.*
[208] Case 14/61 *Hoogovens* v. *High Authority* [1962] E.C.R. 253.
[209] Joined Cases 42 & 49/59 *SNUPAT* v. *High Authority* [1961] E.C.R. 53.
[210] Joined Cases 42 & 49/59, *loc. cit.*, footnote 209. For the sake of completeness, it should be pointed out that when taking a decision on the revocation of an administrative measure conferring benefits, the authority in question is bound to observe not only the principle of the protection of legitimate expectation but also the principles of equality and of proportionality; W. Wiesner, *Der Widerruf individueller Entscheidungen der Hohen Behörde der EGKS*, Hamburg 1966, p. 107, takes as an example the prohibition of arbitrary action—which is, however, of limited authority (Case 25/60 *de Bruyn* v. *European Parliament* [1962] E.C.R. 43 at 63—dismissal of an official of the European Parliament); on the principle of proportionality, mention must be made here of Case 14/61 *Hoogovens* v. *High Authority* [1962] E.C.R. 253—revocation decision: "no stricter than is necessary in the circumstances . . ."
[211] Case 111/63 *Lemmerz-Werke* v. *High Authority* [1965] E.C.R. 893 at 911.

far the applicant might have been led to rely on the lawfulness of the measure."[212]

In relation to administrative measures creating rights, the Court did not, in the *Algera* case,[213] stipulate in express terms a legal duty to revoke unlawful administrative measures—not even in relation to revocation for the future only—but merely stated that revocation within a certain time limit was permissible.

However, the relevant authority definitely has a duty to revoke administrative measures creating rights where this is expressly stipulated, as is the case, for example, with the provisions of Article 65(2), fourth paragraph, ECSC. Under this rule, the High Authority must "revoke an authorisation if it finds that as a result of a change in circumstances the agreement no longer meets these requirements."[214]

As regards unlawful administrative measures imposing burdens, the question whether there exists a duty to revoke arises in particular after the expiry of the time limits for challenging the administrative measure which has been adopted and which is subsequently, in the course of a different procedure, found to be an unlawful administrative measure. As has already been stated elsewhere,[215] it must be assumed that, where the rule on which the administrative measure is based is declared void under Article 173 or 174 EEC (Articles 146, 147 EAEC, Article 33 ECSC), the authority in question is in principle obliged to revoke all administrative measures adopted on the basis of that rule—at least for the future—whilst it is under no such obligation in the event of a mere declaration of inapplicability under Article 184 EEC (156 EAEC—similar considerations also apply to the ECSC Treaty and the Staff Regulations). In such cases, revocation is a matter for the discretion of the authority concerned. Here the persons affected have no right to revocation.

According to the ECJ decision in the *Bode* case, "where the Court annuls the decision, the author of that decision is under an obligation [under Article 176 EEC] to revoke or at least not to apply a subsequent decision which merely confirms that first one."[216]

---

[212] Case 14/81 *Alpha Steel* v. *Commission* [1982] E.C.R. 749 at 764.
[213] Joined Cases 7/56 & 3–7/57 *Algera et al.* v. *Common Assembly* [1957–1958] E.C.R. 39.
[214] Case 36/64 *SOREMA* v. *High Authority* [1965] E.C.R. 447 at 462. The corresponding provision in EEC competition law (Article 8 Regulation 17), on the other hand, makes the decision subject to the Commission's discretion.
[215] *Supra*, B.II.3.(d)(dd).
[216] Joined Cases 45 & 49/70 *Bode* v. *Commission* [1971] E.C.R. 465 at 476.

5. Legal implications of an infringement of legitimate expectations in the event of revocation of administrative measures

In Community law, account is taken of the principle of the protection of legitimate expectations when considering the question of the revocable nature of administrative measures conferring benefits—where appropriate, by protecting the latter's maintenance. As has already been explained in detail, the case law of the ECJ holds that normally, a lawful administrative measure cannot, whereas an unlawful measure in principle can, be revoked where this is necessary following the weighing-up of the interests involved, and in particular where a reasonable time limit is allowed and any legitimate expectation worthy of protection has been taken into account.

On the other hand, the Court does not yet appear to have considered the possibility of ruling that the revocation of an unlawful administrative measure conferring benefits is admissible whilst at the same time granting compensation to the person affected in respect of the infringement of his legitimate expectation,[217] as is, for example, provided under Article 48(3) of the German Laws relating to Administrative Procedure in the event of revocation of unlawful administrative measures which do not confer any financial payments or severable benefits in kind.

In the *Algera* case,[218] the question of compensation for breach of official duty caused by the revocation of an administrative measure was discussed. On this issue, the Court considered that a distinction had to be drawn in the following terms. Although the revocation of the decision allowing the persons in question to come within the ambit of the Staff Regulations was unlawful and therefore constituted an official error, it did not cause the applicants to suffer any material disadvantage once the ECJ had set aside the administrative measures which imposed the revocation. On the other hand, the applicants did suffer material loss in the future as a result of the lawful revocation of the decision which graded them in certain salary brackets. "However," stated the Court, "that fact is not the consequence of wrongful acts or omissions, since the revocation of the classification is lawful; consequently the said deprivation does not

---

[217] The position is different, however, in the event of infringement of the principle of the protection of legitimate expectations by failure to satisfy pledges given originally; *cf.* on this subject under IV.
[218] Joined Cases 7/56 & 3–7/57 *Algera et al.* v. *Common Assembly* [1957] E.C.R. 39.

confer any entitlement to compensation."[219] Only the non-material damage, *i.e.* the "shock caused by this action, the disturbance and uneasiness which resulted from it for those concerned" were, in the Court's view, deserving of compensation.[220] In the event of the permissible revocation of an unlawful administrative measure by which a financial payment or an exemption from an obligatory payment has been granted, the recognition of a right to damages should normally, in economic terms, be equivalent to the waiver of the revocation.[221] Where, on the other hand, the revocation of an administrative measure is unlawful according to the case law of the ECJ, either because the original administrative measure was lawful or, in the case of unlawful administrative measures, because the protection of legitimate expectations excludes the possibility at least of retroactive revocation, the ECJ will declare the challenged revocation decision void. This avoidance is in principle retroactive and compels the administrative authorities to proceed to a "restitutio in integrum" and, where appropriate, to the repayment of amounts wrongly collected or to the subsequent collection of amounts wrongly deducted.[222]

III. TIME LIMITS FOR REMEDIES AND ADMINISTRATIVE PROCEDURES

1. Time limits for remedies and the formal validity of measures

"The periods within which applications must be lodged are intended to safeguard legal certainty."[1] This general principle has also been confirmed by the ECJ in respect of Community law. The limit limits "were laid down with a view to ensuring clarity and legal certainty"[2] and accord-

---

[219] E.C.J., *ibid.*

[220] E.C.J., *loc. cit.*, footnote 218.

[221] *cf.* Advocate-General Lagrange, *loc. cit.*, footnote 218, p. 92; E.C.J., *ibid.*, p. 67.

[222] Advocate-General Lagrange, *loc. cit.*, footnote 218, p. 90; for the area covered by the ECSC, this is contained in Article 34, first paragraph, second sentence, ECSC, and for that of the EEC in Article 176 EEC.

[1] Case 156/77 *Commission* v. *Belgium* [1978] E.C.R. 1881 at 1896; also: "the principle of legal certainty which governs the system of actions" (E.C.J., *ibid.*, p. 1897) and Case 52/83 *Commission* v. *France* [1983] E.C.R. 3707 at 3715 *et seq.*; *cf.* Case 59/70 *Netherlands* v. *Commission* [1971] E.C.R. 639 at 653; Joined Cases 122–123/79 *Schiavo* v. *Council* [1981] E.C.R. 473 (491); this case concerns the time limits for bringing complaints under Article 90 of the Staff Regulations.

[2] Case 227/83 *Sophie Moussis* v. *Commission* [1984] E.C.R. 3133 at 3146; established case law, *cf.* also: Case 79/70 *H. Müllers* v. *Economic and Social Committee* [1971] E.C.R. 689 at 697.

ingly constitute "public policy."[3] They are designed to prevent "Community measures which involve legal effects from being called into question indefinitely."[4] Accordingly, they satisfy the "need for legal certainty, indispensable to the proper functioning of the Community institutions."[5] This achieves the objective that "on the expiry of certain time limits, the administration may know clearly what matters may be included as incontestable in the provisions which it makes."[6]

Although the Court has constantly reiterated these general positions, the principle of legal certainty will not play a direct role in the assessment of the admissibility of appeals against Community administrative measures; instead, it will have only an indirect bearing on this issue by its expression through concrete legal rules, such as precisely the time limits for bringing appeals, and by its role as a complementary rule of interpretation. Unlike the part played by the principle of the protection of legitimate expectations in relation to the revocation of administrative measures conferring benefits, the principle of legal certainty is not normally used as a direct criterion in assessing the admissibility of an application in individual cases.

Whereas, in the relevant case law of the Court of Justice on administrative measures conferring benefits, priority is usually given to the question whether, or under what conditions, the authority is entitled at a later stage to revoke an administrative measure which it has issued—in other words, the substantive validity of the measure is affected[7]—with regard to administrative measures imposing burdens the primary problem that arises is whether a measure of this kind can still be contested by the person affected after a certain period has elapsed or whether the application is inadmissible due to the formal validity[8] of the measure imposing burdens. A kind of intermediate position is occupied by the administrative measures which have a dual effect, in particular measures conferring

[3] Case 79/70, *loc. cit.*, footnote 2; Case 4/67 *Müller* v. *Commission* [1967] E.C.R. 468 at 497 and Case 24/69 *T. Nebe* v. *Commission* [1970] E.C.R. 145 at 152.
[4] Case 156/77, *loc. cit.*, footnote 1; Case 76/83 *Usines Gustave Boël and Fabrique de fer de Maubeuge* v. *Commission* [1984] E.C.R. 859 at 874.
[5] Joined cases 15–33, 52–53, 57–109, 116–117, 132 & 133–137/73 *Kortner-Schots* v. *Council, Commission and Parliament* [1974] E.C.R. 177 at 190, or Case 24/69, *loc. cit.*, footnote 3.
[6] Advocate-General Roemer in Case 20/65 *Collotti* v. *Court of Justice* [1965] E.C.R. 847 at 854.
[7] H. P. Ipsen, *Europäisches Gemeinschaftsrecht* (1972) Tübingen, No. 25/1–2.
[8] In relation to formal validity, the E.C.J. normally refers to "legality," as it does in Case 265/82 *Usinor* v. *Commission* [1983] E.C.R. 3105 at 3114 and in Case 81/83 *Acciaierie e Ferrierie Busseni SpA* v. *Commission* [1984] E.C.R. 2951 at 2961; Case 76/83, *loc. cit.*, footnote 4; *cf.* on the other hand Advocate-General Mancini in Case 52/83 *Commission* v. *France* [1983] E.C.R. 3707 at 3718: "final."

benefits on the addressee but imposing burdens on third parties. For these measures both revocability and contestability may be doubtful.

Thus as a result of the distinction between formal and substantive validity, formal validity normally becomes a relevant factor in assessing the admissibility of an application against an administrative measure imposing burdens.[9] Substantive validity, on the other hand, is in most cases an important factor in assessing whether or not an appeal against the revocation of an administrative measure conferring benefits is well-founded.[10] For the purpose of establishing whether a measure imposing burdens is contestable or not, it is immaterial whether the administrative measure in question is lawful or unlawful. Formal validity is precisely, in the words of the Court of Justice, the concrete expression of the need to prevent "Community measures which involve legal effects from being called into question indefinitely."[11] On the other hand, a decisive factor in assessing whether or not an administrative measure conferring benefits is revocable is the question whether the measure concerned was lawful or unlawful. However, where the Court, when considering the revocation of unlawful administrative measures establishing rights, emphasises the criterion of a reasonable time limit, this amounts to waiving a clear distinction between formal validity on the one hand and substantive validity on the other—as indeed occurs in French administrative case law.[12] Although in other areas of Community law where the question of the revocable nature of administrative measures conferring benefits arises, considerable importance is attached to protection of the legitimate expectation of the person affected by the revocation, this criterion plays no part when the admissibility of appeals against administrative measures imposing burdens is being examined. In such cases, the principle of legal certainty as expressed in the time limits for applying legal remedies is normally[13] used against the citizen.

[9] Or an administrative measure conferring benefits but imposing burdens on third parties, as in Joined Cases 42 & 49/59 *SNUPAT* v. *High Authority* [1961] E.C.R. 53.

[10] Or against the application by a third person adversely affected by a measure for revocation of the latter, rejected by the authority, as in Joined Cases 42 & 49/59, *loc. cit.*, footnote 9.

[11] Case 76/83, *loc. cit.*, footnote 4, pp. 874 *et seq.*; *cf.* also Case 34/65 *Mosthaf* v. *Commission* [1966] E.C.R. 781 (797), Case 156/77 *Commission* v. *Belgium* [1978] E.C.R. 1881 at 1896.

[12] According to French case law, an administrative measure conferring benefits and creating rights which is not revoked by the authority or challenged by a third party within the time limits prescribed is a lawful measure; *cf.* Advocate-General Lagrange in Case 14/61 *Hoogovens* v. *High Authority* [1962] E.C.R. 253 at 277 *et seq.*

[13] An exception to this rule is once again the person who benefits from an administrative measure with effects for third parties, who can also derive benefits from the validity of the measure in question—*cf. e.g.* Case 4/67 *Müller* v. *Commission* [1967] E.C.R. 488 at 497 *et seq.*, Case 24/69 *T. Nebe* v. *Commission* [1970] E.C.R. 145 at 152.

(a) Conditions for and consequences of the existence of formal validity

The precondition for the existence of the formal validity of a measure is the expiry of the time limit for using the remedy.

Time limits for using remedies are contained both in Community primary law and in the rules of derived legislation. Thus, for example, the actions for annulment under Article 173 EEC must "be instituted within two months of the publication of the measure, or of its notification to the plaintiff, or, in the absence thereof, of the day on which it came to the knowledge of the latter, as the case may be" (Article 173, third paragraph). Actions for annulment under Article 33 ECSC "must be instituted within one month of the notification or publication, as the case may be, of the decision or recommendation" (Article 33, third paragraph, ECSC). The days on which the time limits for using these remedies begin to run are determined individually by applying the provisions of Article 80(1) and (2) of the Rules of Procedure.

Only measures against which remedies may be used are capable of acquiring "validity." Accordingly, those measures which do not produce any direct external legal affects and are consequently not contestable—e.g. the adoption of provisional positions[14]—cannot acquire "validity."[14]

The existence of formal validity is not dependent on the administrative measure in question being properly reasoned. This at any rate was the view taken by the ECJ, which in so doing followed the opinion of Advocate-General Trabucchi, in the *Kortner-Schots et al.* case.[15] The background to this case was as follows. The applicants, being officials of E.C. institutions, had, as a result of their marriage, their expatriation allowance either withdrawn or refused under Article 4(3) of Annex VII of the Staff Regulations. It was only after the Court, in the *Sabbatini-Bertoni*[16] and *Chollet-Bauduin*[17] cases, had decided that this provision of the Staff Regulations constituted arbitrary discrimination between male and female officials and was consequently inapplicable, that the respondent Community institutions granted the expatriation allowances with

---

[14] Case 2/71 *Federal Republic of Germany* v. *Commission* [1971] E.C.R. 669 at 676.
[15] Joined Cases 15–33/73 *Kortner-Schots, loc. cit.*, footnote 5.
[16] Case 20/71 *Sabbatini-Bertoni* v. *European Parliament* [1972] E.C.R. 345.
[17] Case 32/71 *Chollet-Bauduin* v. *Commission* [1972] E.C.R. 363.

effect from January 1, 1972. However, they refused to pay subsequently any allowances for earlier periods. The action brought by the applicants sought to obtain retroactive payment of allowances as from the moment at which these had been withdrawn or refused. However, since the decisions in question had all been taken a considerable time before these proceedings—longer ago than the three months (Article 90 Staff Regulations) specified as a time limit for bringing complaints under Article 91 of the Staff Regulations, the Court, in examining the admissibility of the actions, had to deal with the issue of the (formal) validity of the decisions in question.

To the objection raised by the applicants that the time limit for bringing the complaint had not begun to run against them, since the contentious decisions by which the expatriation allowances had been withdrawn had not been properly notified to them in accordance with Article 25 Staff Regulations, and more particularly since these decisions had not been properly reasoned, the Court held that

> "the applicants had knowledge of the decisions resulting in the withdrawal or refusal to them of the expatriation allowance more than three month before the making of the administrative complaint. The sending of the monthly salary statement has the effect of starting the time for appeal running where it clearly shows the decision taken."[18]

Advocate-General Trabucchi stated in even clearer terms that

> "Where a sufficiently clear and exact rule of the Regulations is currently being applied, explicit and detailed reasoning need not be held indispensable. In any case, within such a framework, once an actual decision is known, the question of the reasons on which it is based could be raised at once and lack of reasons may prove a sufficient defect to secure annulment of the decision, provided action is taken within the time limits set; but such a defect is of course quite unable to prevent time from running."[19]

[18] Case 15–33/73, *loc. cit.*, footnote 5, p. 189.
[19] Advocate-General Trabucchi, *ibid.*, p. 194.

With the expiry of time limits for bringing complaints, the administrative measure becomes (formally) "legal,"[20] "definitive,"[21] and consequently "final,"[22] and an action brought against it becomes inadmissible:

> "Failure to observe a time-limit entails the loss of the actual right to bring an action, that is to say, of the opportunity to bring the facts forming the subject of the action before the Court for examination of the substance of the case."[23]

On the other hand, the expiry of the time limit for bringing an action does not by itself lead to a measure acquiring substantive validity. Unless the person in question has himself challenged an administrative measure imposing burdens within the relevant time limits, this circumstance does not prevent the authority from revoking the administrative measure, only to replace it by a measure imposing even greater burdens—on the assumption that the other requirements for doing so have been met. This question has played a relevant part in Community law in relation to the levying of outstanding contributions to the scrap equalisation fund.

In the *Riva* case,[24] for example, the High Authority had, by an administrative measure of December 4, 1969, revoked its original decision of December 18, 1963, and fixed, for the period between March 10, 1957, and November 30, 1958, new (and higher) contributions towards the scrap equalisation fund, after an audit had established that the decision of December 18, 1963, was based on incorrect calculations. Since the applicant had lodged no appeal against the decision of December 18, 1963, the Commission considered, on the basis of what it termed the "principle of *res judicata*," that the decision in question had become "final, not only in relation to the undertaking concerned, but also in relation to the Community authorities."[25]

The ECJ, however, rejected this viewpoint and held that instead, the Commission was compelled

---

[20] Case 265/82 *Usinor* v. *Commission* [1983] E.C.R. 3105, and the other judgments mentioned in footnote 8; also Advocate-General Roemer in Case 36/64 *SOREMA* v. *High Authority* [1965] E.C.R. 447 at 467: "validity."

[21] Advocate-General Mancini in Case 52/83 *Commission* v. *France* [1983] E.C.R. 3707 at 3718.

[22] Case 15–33/73 *Kortner-Schots, loc. cit.*, footnote 5, p. 191.

[23] Case 20/65 *Collotti* v. *Court of Justice* [1965] E.C.R. 1111 at 1117.

[24] Case 2/70 *Riva* v. *Commission* [1971] E.C.R. 97.

[25] Cited by the E.C.J., *ibid.*, p. 108.

"to rectify all legal or factual errors and all assessments which experience showed to be inaccurate or incomplete."[26]

The Advocate-General justified this viewpoint in the following terms:

"In fact, the principle of *res judicata* in relation to administrative decisions which can be raised against the administrative authorities which make those decisions does not exist in the manner which the applicant claims. What is more, it is generally recognised that despite the expiry of the period for lodging an appeal, the administrative authorities can in any case re-examine and, if necessary, revoke their decisions, for example where public policy requires it."[27]

Accordingly, administrative instruments which have become formally valid, may at all times be set aside by the relevant authority in accordance with the principles relating to the revocation of administrative instruments.

Formally valid administrative measures may not, however, be challenged by an action brought by the person affected, even if the authority in question agrees or co-operates with such an action. Since the time limits for lodging appeals are part of "public policy,"[28] they are not "subject to the discretion of the parties."[29]

The observance of the deadlines for lodging appeals, which is mandatory and automatic,[30] takes into account

"*inter alia* the fact that in an administration decisions relating to the situation of a particular member of staff may frequently affect the position of other officials."[31]

---

[26] E.C.J., *ibid.*; a similar position is adopted in the decisions in Case 2/65 *Prio and Figli* v. *High Authority* [1966] E.C.R. 559—here Advocate-General Gand, p. 578, and Case 108/63 *Merlini* v. *High Authority* [1965] E.C.R. 1 at 16.

[27] Advocate-General Roemer, *loc. cit.*, footnote 24, p. 115.

[28] Case 79/70 *H. Müllers* v. *Economic and Social Committee* [1971] E.C.R. 689 at 697; Case 4/67 *Müller* v. *Commission* [1967] E.C.R. 488 at 497; Case 24/69 *T. Nebe* v. *Commission* [1970] E.C.R. 145 at 152.

[29] Case 227/83 *S. Moussis* v. *Commission* [1984] E.C.R. 3133 (3146), with further references.

[30] Advocate-General Roemer in Case 24/69, *loc. cit.*, footnote 28, p. 155; in this sense also E.C.J. in Case 4/67, *loc. cit.*, footnote 28, p. 497.

[31] Case 24/69, *loc. cit.*, footnote 28, p. 152; also Case 4/67, *loc. cit.*, footnote 28, p. 497, and Joined Cases 122–123/79 *Schiavo* v. *Council* [1981] E.C.R. 473 at 491—on the time limit for bringing complaints under Article 90 of the Staff Regulations.

This type of situation is not uncommon in the system of staff regulation within the Community institutions. Appointment and promotion decisions are constantly being challenged by those undergoing open competitions or by those who are otherwise affected by them.[32] Here, the principle of legal certainty expresses itself for the benefit of a third party—*i.e.* the person deriving benefits from the administrative measure which is subject to a challenge brought after the official time-limit—in the principle of formal validity.

Under Article 91(2) of the Staff Regulations, an appeal is admissible only if a complaint brought under Article 90(2) of the Regulations has previously been lodged with the appropriate authority against the administrative measure imposing the burden in question within a period of three months and this complaint has been rejected either expressly or implicitly[33]—*i.e.* where an internal preliminary procedure has taken place. Under Article 91(3) of the Staff Regulations, any appeal against this decision rejecting the complaint must be brought within a further period of three months.

These rules prompt the question of the implications for an appeal if the authority in question takes a decision rejecting an application by the applicant in spite of the time limits which apply to the complaints procedure having expired. This situation formed the background to the *Moussis* decision,[34] dating from 1984. The applicant, a Commission official, had lodged a complaint against a Commission decision of June 8, 1982, but failed to do so within the official three-month time limit as laid down in Article 90(2) of the Staff Regulations. Instead, she had waited until January 11, 1983, to lodge an application under Article 90(1) seeking to review the relevant decision. The decision dated January 20, 1983, which explicitly rejected this application, was challenged by the applicant after the administrative complaint lodged within the time limit against the decision referred to in the previous sentence was rejected on July 14, 1983. The Court concluded that the original administrative decision of June 8, 1982, was valid on the basis that the time limit for bringing the

[32] *cf. e.g.* the facts of Case 4/67, *loc. cit.*, footnote 28.
[33] Staff Regulations as amended by Regulation 1473/72 of June 30, 1972, J.O. 1972, L160/1; on the subject of the observance of the principle of legal certainty, the case law of the E.C.J. on the time limits for bringing actions also applies "for the time limits for lodging complaints which, from a procedural point of view, precede the time limits for bringing actions and have the same legal character, since they contribute towards the rules relating to the equal opportunities for legal protection aimed at securing legal certainty"—thus the E.C.J. in Joined Cases 122–123/79, *loc. cit.*, footnote 31.
[34] Case 227/83 *Moussis* v. *Commission* [1984] E.C.R. 3133.

application had not been observed and that consequently the application of January 11, 1983, made by the applicant was inadmissible:

> "These time limits are a matter of public policy and are not subject to the discretion of the parties or the Court, since they were laid down with a view to ensuring clarity and legal certainty. . . .
>
> The fact that the Commission, for reasons related to its staff policy, deals with the substance of a request, even though it is inadmissible, cannot have the effect of derogating from the system of mandatory time limits laid down in Articles 90 and 91 of the Staff Regulations and re-establishing a right of action which is definitively time-barred."[35]

Thus the fact that, although the relevant period had expired, a decision had been taken in the administrative complaints procedure which preceded the appeal, did not, on grounds of legal certainty, lead to the applicant being reinstated in her former rights, the exercise of which was subject to time limits. She was not permitted to re-enact the appeal procedure, and the validity of the decision, once it entered into effect, was not interrupted.[35a]

Applicants in such appeals could also face problems arising from the provision contained in Article 91(2)(2) of the Staff Regulations,[36] under which a complaint which has been lodged within the time limits provided but has not yet received an express ruling is deemed to have been tacitly rejected on expiry of the time limit. Such a tacit decision is also open to challenge. Here too, the non-observance of the time limit for bringing the appeal leads to the formal validity of the decision rejecting the application.

In the case of *Müllers* v. *Economic and Social Committee*,[37] the Court held inadmissible an appeal brought by the applicant against a decision of

---

[35] Case 227/83, *ibid.*, p. 3146.

[35a] Under the German system it is normally possible, in cases where the authority in question fails to reject an objection which has been lodged too late as being inadmissible and gives a ruling on that objection, to appeal against this decision; BVerwGE 57, p. 342 (344); BVerwG, NVwZ 1983, p. 608; established case law. This does not apply, however, where the rights of third parties could be infringed by the decision, in particular in the case of administrative measures with third party effect; BVerwG, DÖV 1969, p. 142; DÖV 1982, p. 940. This case law of the BVerwG is the subject of controversy; *cf.* F. O. Kopp, *VwGO* (7th ed., München 1986), Article 70 No. 9 (with further references).

[36] Article 91(2)(2) in conjunction with Article 90(2)(5) of the Staff Regulations as amended by Regulation No. 1473/72, *loc. cit.*, footnote 33.

[37] Case 79/70 *Müllers* v. *Economic and Social Committee* [1971] E.C.R. 689 at 697.

the Economic and Social Committee which merely confirmed a tacit decision of this body against which an appeal had been lodged outside the permitted time limits. The applicant had, within the prescribed time limits, lodged a complaint against a decision, whereupon the authority in question informed him that before any ruling was made on this application, it wished to obtain the opinion of the administrative heads of the Community institutions. In addition, he was requested to "be so good as to wait a little longer for the final solution of the matter." Because this communication did not constitute a decision but announced that such a decision would be forthcoming at some later date, the Court considered that, since the time limit of two months laid down in Article 91(2) of the Staff Regulations had expired, it had to be assumed that the defendant had tacitly rejected the complaint as being unfounded:

> "Although it is correct that at that time the defendant still hoped to be able to give a favourable reply to the complaint, this does not alter the fact that it is not for the parties who are directly concerned to extend at their own convenience the periods laid down in Article 91 of the Staff Regulations since these are matters of public policy and rigorous compliance with them is calculated to ensure the clarity and certainty of legal solutions."[38]

The Court gave a similar ruling in the case of *T. Nebe* v. *Commission.* Here, the Commission, replying to a complaint lodged by the applicant on August 3, 1966, informed the latter on August 24, 1966, that "the case was being thoroughly examined" and that the applicant would receive a decision as soon as this examination "was brought to a definite conclusion." It was only after a reminder dated October 2, 1968, that the Commission rejected the complaint on March 14, 1969—*i.e.* more than three years later. Here too, the Court held the appeal which followed to be inadmissible on grounds of it having been brought outside the prescribed time limit.[39]

A later, explicit ruling which merely confirms the tacit decision is not capable of removing the formal validity, once it has come into effect, of the tacit administrative measure which has not been challenged within the relevant time limits. More particularly, the Court held in the *Müllers*[40]

---

[38] E.C.J., *loc. cit.*; *cf.* on this subject also Advocate-General Dutheillet de Lamothe, who on this issue, rejecting to the claim made by the applicant, refers to the corresponding case law of the French Conseil d'Etat (p. 701).

[39] Case 24/69, *loc. cit.*, footnote 28, p. 151.

[40] Case 79/70, *loc. cit.*, footnote 37, p. 698.

and *Nebe*[41] cases that since this express decision had imposed no burdens, this did not lead to a re-opening of the opportunity to bring an appeal. Thus the appeals in question, even where they were aimed at the express decision which had been made outside the prescribed time limit, were inadmissible.

Although these cases presented the peculiarity that the applicants might have had the opportunity initially to contest the Commission's interim decisions on a provisional basis, it was established case law that

> "an express decision which simply confirms an implied decision does not have the effect of starting the period for lodging an appeal to the Court against the implied decision running afresh and in addition that an applicant has no interest in contesting the express decision which simply confirms the implied decision."[42]

The Court took a similar decision in the *W. Vinck* v. *Commission* case,[43] which was also a staff case. In general terms, the ECJ had already established in the *SNUPAT* case that

> "a measure which merely confirms a previous measure cannot afford those concerned the opportunity of reopening the question of the legality of the measure which is confirmed."[44]

The same considerations apply in cases where the authorities refuse to revoke legally valid administrative measures imposing burdens. Unless special requirements are stipulated,[45] the person who fails to challenge an administrative measure imposing burdens on him within the prescribed time limits has no right to bring an action for the revocation of the administrative measure. The decision which rejects such revocation is merely an administrative measure which confirms the original decision and is not capable of undermining the formal validity of the original administrative measure once it has taken effect.[46]

---

[41] Case 24/69, *loc. cit.*, footnote 28, p. 152.
[42] Advocate-General Dutheillet de Lamothe in Case 79/70, *loc. cit.*, footnote 37, p. 700.
[43] Case 52/70 *W. Vinck* v. *Commission* [1971] E.C.R. 601 at 609.
[44] Joined Cases 42 & 49/59 *SNUPAT* v. *High Authority* [1961] E.C.R. 53.
[45] Thus, for example, where "new circumstances" arise—*cf.* under (d) (ee).
[46] In this sense also, the judgment in Joined Cases 15–33, 52, 53, 57–109, 116, 117, 123 & 135–137/73 *Kortner-Schots et al.* v. *Council, Commission and Parliament* [1974] E.C.R. 177 at 191.

By way of example we refer to the decision in the *Gunnella* case.[47] The salary of the applicant, an official of the Commission, had been changed by a decision of October 5, 1965. No expatriation allowance had been granted. On August 30, 1971, she applied for an expatriation allowance. This application was rejected by a decision of March 9, 1972. The action brought against this decision was held inadmissible by the Court, on the grounds that the applicant should have brought the action against the 1965 decision. The communication of March 9, 1972 "only confirmed the previous decision whereby the Commission refused to grant the applicant the expatriation allowance." Accordingly, "such a communication could not have the effect of setting a fresh time limit in the applicant's favour."[48]

Thus the applicant was prevented from obtaining even for the future payment of the expatriation allowance to which she considered herself entitled.[49]

In this way, the administrative measure, whether lawful or unlawful, acquires, in the interests of legal certainty, absolute protection of validity even in relation to its effects for the future only.

As the ruling in the case of *Federal Republic of Germany* v. *Commission*[50] shows, the principle of the non-contestability of a merely confirmatory decision also applies in the case of an administrative measure addressed to the Member States.

The Commission had, in a communication of March 2, 1970, informed the Government of the Federal Republic of Germany of the balance of the European Social Fund accounts for the financial year 1969, and, by a letter of March 6, 1970, communicated to it the amount to be allocated to the Federal Republic of Germany. The Federal Minister for Financial Affairs, who considered this amount to be too small, objected to this communication by letter of March 25, 1970. The Commission rejected this objection by letter of November 6, 1970. The ECJ decided that the communication of the balance of accounts had to be considered as a final and therefore contestable decision, against which, however, the applicant had failed to bring an action within the two-month period prescribed by the third paragraph of Article 173 EEC. Moreover it could not

> "repair that omission by instituting proceedings against a subsequent letter refusing to reconsider the measures in question."[51]

---

[47] Case 33/72 *Gunnella* v. *Commission* [1973] E.C.R. 475.
[48] *Ibid.* p. 481.
[49] On this subject the applicant, *ibid.*, p. 478.
[50] Case 2/71 *Federal Republic of Germany* v. *Commission* [1971] E.C.R. 669.
[51] E.C.J., *loc. cit.*, p. 677.

Accordingly, the action was dismissed as inadmissible.

Even an administrative measure which was based on an earlier decision which had already become unchallengeable but whose substance exceeded the latter could, as a mere confirmatory administrative measure, be covered by the formal validity of the original measure. This is confirmed by, for example, the judgment in the *Collotti* case.[52] On the basis of the ECJ decision of July 7, 1964,[53] the appointing authority had, by a decision of July 21, 1964, classified the applicant in a new salary bracket with retroactive effect from January 1, 1962, and paid him outstanding amounts due by way of salary. The applicant, who did not agree with this new classification and considered that the authority in question had failed to take the reasoning behind the judgment to its logical conclusion, brought a new action, not against the decision of July 21, 1964, but against the decision relating to future pension payments made on February 18, 1965, and based on the changed classification. The Court concluded that this new decision merely confirmed that of July 21, 1964. Accordingly, it was not "capable of reviving the right to bring an action which was already forfeited."[54]

(b) Exceptions to the principle of formal validity

The principle of the formal validity of measures following the expiry of the time limits for bringing an action is not totally unrestricted. Exceptions to this principle can arise particularly in connection with the absolute nullity of administrative measures, with the occurrence of new circumstances and with the plea of illegality.

(aa) The absolute nullity of administrative measures

The absolute nullity (as opposed to the mere challengeability) of administrative measures, which is only beginning to find cautious acceptance in Community law, constitutes one of the exceptions to the formal validity of administrative measures. As has already been explained elsewhere,[55] the case law of the ECJ does not in principle rule out the

---

[52] Case 20/65 *U. Collotti* v. *Court of Justice* [1965] E.C.R. 1111.

[53] In Case 70/63 *U. Collotti* v. *Court of Justice* [1964] E.C.R. 937.

[54] E.C.J., *loc. cit.*, footnote 52, p. 1117; also Advocate-General Roemer, *ibid.*, pp. 1122 *et seq.*

[55] *Supra*, I.3.(c).

possibility that an administrative measure could be regarded as absolutely void on grounds of, for example, a flagrant infringement of the conditions under which the authority in question exercises its powers.[56] If necessary, an applicant may also invoke the absolute nullity of an administrative measure where the time limits for bringing an action against the measure in question have expired.[57] The absolute nullity of the administrative measure thus prevents it from becoming formally valid. In such cases the principle of the compliance by the administration with the relevant statute takes precedence over that of legal certainty.

(bb) New circumstances

Restrictions placed on the validity of measures by the occurrence of new circumstances are closely linked to the case law of the Court of Justice on confirmatory administrative measures.[57a]

Although the occurrence of new circumstances does not normally result in a formally valid measure becoming challengeable once again, they can nevertheless remove the effect of the validity, namely in relation to the challengeability of a decision confirming the substance of the original administrative measure. Thus in the *SNUPAT* case,[58] the ECJ decided that although a purely confirmatory measure could not in principle give the persons involved the opportunity to call into question once again the lawfulness of the confirmatory measure, this principle did not apply

> "if there is a new fact of such a character as to alter the essential circumstances and conditions which governed the adoption of the first measure."[59]

---

[56] *cf. e.g.* Joined Cases 6 & 11/69 *Commission* v. *France* [1969] E.C.R. 523 at 540, and Advocate-General Roemer, *ibid.* pp. 551 *et seq.*; also opinion by the same Advocate-General in Joined Cases 19, 21/60 & 2–3/61 *Société Fives Lille* v. *High Authority* [1961] E.C.R. 611 at 669 and E.C.J. in Joined Cases 15–33 *et al.*/73 *Kortner-Schots, loc. cit.*, footnote 46, p. 197; this concerned the absolute nullity of a legal rule.

[57] As in Joined Cases 6 & 11/69, *loc. cit.*, footnote 56.

[57a] *cf. supra* under footnote 40 *et seq.*

[58] Joined Cases 42 & 44/59 *SNUPAT* v. *High Authority* [1961] E.C.R. 109.

[59] *Ibid.*, p. 158; *cf.* also Joined Cases 109/63 & 13/64 *C. Muller* v. *Commission* [1964] E.C.R. 1411 at 1436 *et seq.*; Case 326/82 *H. Aschermann et al.* v. *Commission* [1984] E.C.R. 2253 at 2263 with further references; Case 46/64 *Schoffer* v. *Commission* [1965] E.C.R. 1063 at 1071; also Case 127/84 *Esly* v. *Commission* [1985] E.C.R. 1437 at 1446.

In other cases, the ECJ has restricted the conditions which have to be satisfied in this area by making the partial derogation from the formal validity of a measure dependent on the occurrence of "important" new circumstances.[60] In the case of *C. Muller* v. *Commission*,[61] the applicant had, on August 28, 1963, lodged an administrative complaint against the decision made in December 1962 which classified him in a certain salary bracket, which he considered to be too low. At the same time, he had applied for inclusion in a higher bracket. In the absence of any reply from the Commission, the applicant brought an action on December 23, 1963. The ECJ held the action to be inadmissible on grounds of expiry of the time limit for bringing the challenge, inasmuch as it was aimed against the classification decision of December 1962. The action brought against the tacit rejection of the application of August 28, 1963, on the other hand, was admissible. Whilst the Court held on the one hand that

> "the Commission was not required, unless important new facts arose, to reconsider a decision which could no longer be contested,"[62]

it nevertheless considered that an important new fact had arisen, as the Commission had, on July 29, 1963, taken a decision by which it had communicated a new table concerning the activities and range of duties connected with individual administrative posts; according to the applicant, this new table justified his being graded in a higher salary bracket. The Court arrived at the conclusion that

> "the publication of this table could in fact be regarded as a sufficiently important new fact to enable the applicant to request the Commission to grade him in accordance with the new provisions."[63]

Therefore, although the action against a valid original administrative measure is inadmissible, it may be admissible in the event of new circumstances arising where the action in question is aimed at the rejection of an application to amend the original administrative measure imposing burdens.

---

[60] Thus in Joined Cases 109/63 & 13/64, *loc. cit.*, footnote 59; Case 326/82, *loc. cit.*, footnote 59.
[61] Joined Cases 109/63 & 13/64, *loc. cit.*, footnote 59.
[62] *Ibid.*, p. 1436.
[63] *Ibid.*, p. 1436.

The Court gave a similar ruling in the case of *Tontodonati* v. *Commission*.[64] Here, the Court acknowledged as a new fact the reorganisation of an administrative department which had led to the applicant's range of duties being extended. In spite of the fact that the original classification decision was unchallengeable, it was in order for the applicant to call on the Commission

> "to review his position in the administration in view of the changes which had taken place in the structure of the department to which he belonged."[65]

Where such new circumstances arise, a decision of the authority in question rejecting an application to change the original administrative measure is not merely a confirmatory administrative measure which is covered by the formal validity of the original administrative measure. Unlike a merely confirmatory administrative measure, such a "second decision" (*Zweitbescheid*)[66] is a "measure imposing burdens" (*beschwerende Massnahme*), and any action brought against it is therefore admissible.[67]

A further example of an important new fact within the meaning of this case law could also be the annulment, under Article 173 EEC (Article 146 EAEC and Article 33 ECSC) of a rule on which an administrative measure is based in the context of proceedings brought by a third party. If in the course of such proceedings the Court declares a regulation null and void, this annulment takes effect in principle *erga omnes* and, unless the Court has availed itself of the opportunity available to it under the second paragraph of Article 174 EEC (second paragraph of Article 147 EAEC) to restrict the retroactivity of the judgment, it also has retroactive effect. Thus the regulation may, where appropriate, be retroactively deprived of its validity, *i.e.* it must be "deemed non-existent."[68] Quite apart from the question whether or to what extent the relevant authority is obliged, in view of the provisions of the first paragraph of Article 176 EEC (Article 149 EAEC, Article 34 ECSC), to revoke an administrative measure

[64] Case 28/72 *Tontodonati* v. *Commission* [1973] E.C.R. 779.
[65] *Ibid.* p. 784.
[66] On this notion in German administrative law, *cf.* F. O. Kopp, *Verwaltungsverfahrensgesetz* (4th ed., 1986), Article 35, No. 38.
[67] Case 28/72, *loc. cit.*, footnote 64, p. 784; *cf.* also Advocate-General Reischl in Case 173/80 *Blasig* v. *Commission* [1981] E.C.R. 1649 at 1664.
[68] Case 22/70 *Commission* v. *Council*, *"AETR"* [1971] E.C.R. 263 at 279; *cf.* H. W. Daig, in: Groeben, Boeckh, Thiesing, Ehlermann on Article 175, No. 7.

imposing burdens on a third party based on a rule which has been declared null and void for the future, the question also arises here whether the formal validity of such an administrative measure has been undermined. Advocate-General Trabucchi dealt with this issue in the *Kortner-Schots* case.[69] However, in this case, the regulation on which the contentious administrative measure was based had not been declared void, but had merely been declared unlawful by way of incidental plea under Article 184 EEC. Therefore, there could be no question of a derogation from the formal validity of the measure in this concrete case. However, Advocate-General Trabucchi observed in his Opinion that

> "if the judgments cited had annulled the rule in the Regulation that was recognised as unlawful, there might have been some question of retrospective effect in relation to third parties."[70]

The grounds of judgment in this case also reveal[71] that the Court would consider the annulment of a Regulation as being an important new fact, which could also be invoked by third parties against the plea of formal validity raised in respect of administrative measures imposing burdens on them. In particular the rejection of an application made in such cases by the person in question to change, at least with effect for the future, the administrative measure based on the rule which is henceforth regarded as void should not be regarded as merely an unchallengeable administrative measure which merely confirms the original measure.

On the other hand, judgments which merely establish by way of incidental plea brought under Article 184 EEC the unlawful nature of the rule on which the administrative measure challenged by a third party is based,

> "have the authority of *res judicata* only in relation to the parties involved at that time. It is right to point out moreover that they could not have pronounced the annulment of the regulatory provision involved, within the meaning of Article 174, first paragraph, but that they simply placed on record the inapplicability of this provision and consequent upon this pronounced the annulment of the individual decisions taken on that basis. In these circumstances, the judgments

---

[69] Advocate-General Trabucchi in Joined Cases 15–33, 52–53, 57–109, 116–117, 123, 132 & 135–137/73 *Kortner-Schots et al.* v. *Council, Commission and Parliament* [1974] E.C.R. 177—*cf.* on the background to this case *supra*, footnote 15.

[70] Advocate-General Trabucchi, *ibid.*, p. 195.

[71] E.C.J. *ibid.* pp. 190 *et seq.* (paras. 35 to 38).

cannot be relied upon by parties who at the appropriate time omitted to make use of the possibilities of appeal offered to them by the Treaty."[72]

This was the reply given by the ECJ to the objection raised by the applicants that their actions were admissible, in spite of the expiry of the time limits for bringing the action, because of the occurrence of new facts, namely the judgments in the *Sabbatini* and *Bauduin* cases.

"Any other view," states Advocate-General Trabucchi, "would jeopardise the rule of public policy implicit in the general adoption of fixed procedural time limits, applied in our case by Article 91 of the Staff Regulations, and the principle of legal certainty would thereby be impaired."[73]

In the judgment in the *Kortner-Schots* case, the question was also considered whether any "change in administrative practice" constituted a new fact which was capable of undermining the formal validity of an administrative measure. The applicants considered that such a change in administrative practice had occurred when the Community institutions had, on the basis of the judgments of June 7, 1972,[74] paid the expatriation allowances which had previously been withheld with effect from July 1, 1972, even though the change in the relevant legal position was brought about only by the Council Regulation of February 26, 1973. However, the ECJ rejected this view in the following terms:

"The general change in direction of administrative practice following upon those judgments must in the present circumstances be considered as the anticipated application of a formal amendment in the Staff Regulations but must not be understood as permitting the retrospective re-opening of a situation resulting from decisions taken in relation to the applicants, which at the expiry of the time limits for appeals had become final."[75]

---

[72] *Ibid.*, p. 191.
[73] Advocate-General Trabucchi, *ibid.*, p. 195.
[74] In Case 20/71 *Sabbatini* v. *European Parliament* [1972] E.C.R. 345, or Case 32/71 *Bauduin* v. *Commission* [1972] E.C.R. 363.
[75] Cases 15/33 *et al./73, loc. cit.*, footnote 69, p. 191.

On this question, Advocate-General Trabucchi drew a distinction between the *ex nunc* effect of a change in administrative practice and the *ex tunc* effect sought by the applicants:

> "A new fact consisting of a change in administrative practice following a changed interpretation of certain rules in the regulations on the part of the Administration, could in the case of officials be relevant for the purpose of allowing an action which would otherwise be barred to them as a result of the running of time. But such an action would be conceivable only insofar as it was aimed at obtaining a change in their situation for the future, and not at calling in question once again the way in which that situation had been regulated prior to the change in administrative practice constituting the new fact. This new fact, then, does not have the effect of reopening the time limits within which a decision must be challenged, but, because of the change introduced at the time it occurs, it provides the basis for the official to make a fresh request aimed at changing the current situation, even if this situation results from a decision of long standing which can no longer be challenged. It is in a situation exactly like the present one that the party concerned would have been within his rights in claiming that the Administration should adopt in his case a position in conformity with the new practice followed. But, in this respect, the applicants have already received full satisfaction before lodging the present appeals."[76]

Finally, a judgment obtained by a third party in which an administrative measure adopted in relation to the latter is revoked on grounds of unlawfulness does not constitute a new fact which could serve to justify the review of an administrative measure which has become valid. The fact that in the course of that procedure the Court establishes that an administrative measure is unlawful does not in any way change the formal validity of an administrative measure adopted in relation to a third party which is possibly "just as unlawful."

In the judgment in the case of *Schoffer* v. *Commission*, in which the applicant invoked the occurrence of such an allegedly new fact, the Court held that

> "apart from the actual parties in proceedings before the Court, the only persons concerned by the legal effects of a judgment of the

---

[76] Advocate-General Trabucchi, *ibid.*, p. 196.

Court annulling a measure are the persons directly affected by the measure which is annulled. Such a judgment can only constitute a new fact as regards those persons."[77]

(cc) The plea of illegality

Under Article 184 EEC (Article 156 EAEC, Article 36, third paragraph, ECSC)[78] the parties to a legal dispute may, by way of incidental plea, raise the inapplicability of a regulation (or of a general decision within the meaning of the ECSC Treaty), even if the time limits for using the direct action remedy against the contentious decision have themselves already expired. Individual decisions, on the other hand, cannot normally be the subject-matter of incidental pleas. The unlawfulness of a formally valid administrative measure can in principle no longer be relied upon by means of a plea of illegality in the context of another administrative measure based on the legally valid administrative measure.

> "The limitation period for bringing an action fulfils a generally recognised need, namely the need to prevent the legality of administrative decisions from being called into question indefinitely, and this means that there is a prohibition on reopening a question after the limitation period has expired."[79]

Consequently, it is established ECJ case law that

> "an applicant cannot, in an application for a declaration that an individual decision is void, raise an objection of illegality relating to another individual decision addressed to him which has become final."[80]

---

[77] Case 46/64 *Schoffer* v. *Commission* [1965] E.C.R. 1063 at 1071; also Advocate-General Gand, *ibid.*, pp. 1075 *et seq.*; also Joined Cases 50–51, 53–54 & 57/64 *Loebisch* v. *Councils of EEC/Euratom/ECSC* [1965] E.C.R. 1080 at 1090.

[78] According to the case law of the E.C.J., this provision expresses a general principle which is applied beyond the special field of application of Article 36 ECSC; Case 9/56 *Meroni* v. *High Authority* [1958] E.C.R. 9 at 26.

[79] Case 3/59 *Federal Republic of Germany* v. *High Authority* [1960] E.C.R. 125 at 139.

[80] Case 265/82 *Usinor* v. *Commission* [1983] E.C.R. 3105 at 3114; *cf.* also Case 270/82 *Estel NV* v. *Commission* [1984] E.C.R. 1195 at 1214; Case 348/82 *IRO* v. *Commission* [1984] E.C.R. 1409 at 1415 and Case 64/84 *Queenborough Rolling Mill Comp.* v. *Commission* [1985] E.C.R. 1829 at 1853.

This legal principle serves the "interests of legal peace and legal certainty."[81] To deviate from it would

> "be impossible to reconcile with the principles governing the legal remedies established by the Treaty and would jeopardise the stability of that system and the principle of legal certainty on which it is based."[82]

This applies, for example, in cases where the administration has, in an individual decision which in the meantime has become valid, reserved the right to revoke that decision at some later date. In those circumstances the undertaking affected may no longer, in the context of an action brought against the later revocation decision, claim that the authority had reserved this right to revoke in an unlawful manner.[83]

Moreover, an undertaking which has been fined by the Commission for infringement of the fixed steel production quotas may not, in the context of an appeal against the fine (Article 36, second paragraph, ECSC) raise the plea that the quota system, which in the meantime has become legally valid, is unlawful.[84]

The same considerations apply to an action brought by a Member State against a decision taken in accordance with the first paragraph of Article 88 ECSC, in which the High Authority has decided that the Member State in question has infringed one of its obligations under the Treaty. Here too, the Member State is in principle prevented from claiming, in the course of an action brought against the decision establishing the breach of the Treaty, that an individual decision of the administrative authority which it has infringed but not challenged within the prescribed deadlines is unlawful.[85]

This also applies to the procedure brought in accordance with the second subparagraph of Article 93(2) EEC for infringement by a Member State of a decision made under the first subparagraph of Article 93(2), by

---

[81] Advocate-General Roemer in Joined Cases 6 & 11/69 *Commission* v. *France* [1969] E.C.R. 523 at 551.

[82] Case 52/83 *Commission* v. *France* [1983] E.C.R. 3707 at 3715.

[83] Case 36/64 *SOREMA* v. *High Authority* [1965] E.C.R. 447 at 459; Advocate-General Roemer, *ibid.*, p. 467.

[84] Case 265/82, *loc. cit.*, footnote 80, p. 3114; also Case 81/83 *Acciaierie e Ferriere Busseni SpA* v. *Commission* [1984] E.C.R. 2951 at 2961, and Case 21/64 *Machiorlati Dalmas* v. *High Authority* [1965] E.C.R. 241 at 259.

[85] *cf., e.g.* Joined Cases 6 & 11/69, *Commission* v. *France* [1969] E.C.R. 523 at 543 *et seq.*; on this subject also, Advocate-General Roemer, *ibid.*, p. 552; also Case 3/59 *Federal Republic of Germany* v. *Commission* [1960] E.C.R. 116 at 139.

which the Commission decides that State aids are incompatible with Community law. It would be contrary to the principle of legal certainty

> "to allow a Member State to which a decision adopted under the first subparagraph of Article 93(2) has been addressed a further opportunity to call into question the validity of that decision on the occasion of an application referred to in the second subparagraph of that Article, in spite of the expiry of the period laid down in the third paragraph of Article 173 of the Treaty."[86]

On the other hand, according to the case law of the ECJ, it is possible to call into question the validity of a Community measure, in spite of the expiry of the time limits laid down in the third paragraph of Article 173, by means of the preliminary rulings procedure under Article 177 of the EEC Treaty.[87] This applies, for example, in cases where the undertaking affected pleads, before a national court in the course of an action brought against a national administrative measure, the unlawfulness of a decision, made by the Commission in relation to a Member State, which forms the basis for the national administrative measure:

> "It would be taking the need for legal certainty a long way to preclude quite generally a challenge in the national courts to the validity of such acts on the basis that the Community measure was itself invalid and thereby also to preclude a reference under Article 177 once the time limit for seeking annulment had gone."[88]

This issue presents no problems where the undertaking in question is not directly and individually affected by the decision addressed to the Member State, since in such cases the undertaking has no right of action on its own against the Commission measure. Consequently, the administrative measure in question cannot acquire formal validity against that undertaking. According to Advocate-General Slynn, the plea of illegality is possible even if the undertaking in question could have brought an action against the Commission decision itself, being directly and individually concerned by the latter:

---

[86] Case 52/83, *loc. cit.*, footnote 82, p. 3715; also Case 156/77 *Commission* v. *Belgium* [1978] E.C.R. 1851 at 1896.

[87] Case 156/77, *loc. cit.*, footnote 86, p. 1897; in this sense also Case 216/82 *University of Hamburg* v. *HZA Hamburg-Kehrwieder* [1983] E.C.R. 2771 at 2778 and Advocate-General Slynn, *ibid.*, pp. 2795 *et seq.*

[88] Advocate-General Slynn, Case 216/82, *loc. cit.*, footnote 87, p. 2796.

"A party who could have applied under Article 173 for annulment and did not do so, is not barred from challenging the validity of an act because the time for seeking annulment has gone."[89]

On this question, the Court held:

"According to the general principle of law which finds its expression in Article 184 of the EEC Treaty, in proceedings brought under national law against the rejection of his application, the applicant must be able to plead the illegality of the Commission's decision on which the national decision adopted in his regard is based."[90]

The question whether this also applies if the person affected could have brought an action against the Commission directly himself is not answered by this decision. The Court clearly assumed that in the case before it it was not absolutely certain that such a right of action existed.[91]

2. Time Limits in Administrative Proceedings

The ECJ has emphasised the need for strict observance of existing time limits as a requirement imposed by the need for legal certainty, not only in relation to the use of legal remedies. The legal certainty principle also has an important part to play when it comes to assessing whether or not certain measures were adopted within the prescribed time limits in the course of administrative proceedings, in particular where no express time limits were laid down for these measures in the written Community law.

This applies, for example, in relation to the duty to "raise the matter "with the Commission, laid down in the first paragraph of Article 35 ECSC (second paragraph of Article 175 EEC and of Article 148 EAEC), which must necessarily precede any action for failure to act.[92] Although these provisions lay down in each case certain time limits for bringing the

---

[89] Advocate-General Slynn, *loc. cit.*, footnote 87, p. 2797; the Commission also adopted this position: *cf.* pp. 2782 *et seq.*; this view was, however, rejected by Advocate-General Mayras in Case 59/77 *de Bloos* v. *Bouyer* [1977] E.C.R. 2359 at 2381; *cf.* also H. W. Daig, in Groeben, Boeckh, Thiesing, Ehlermann on Article 177, No. 28.

[90] Case 216/82, *loc. cit.*, footnote 87, p. 2788.

[91] E.C.J., *ibid.* pp. 2787 *et seq.*

[92] *cf.* on this subject also Case 17/57 *de Gezamenlijke Steenkolenmijnen in Limburg* v. *High Authority* [1959] E.C.R. 1 at 8 and Advocate-General Lagrange, *ibid.*, pp. 14 *et seq.*—on Article 35 ECSC; the second paragraph of Article 175 EEC and of Article 148 Euratom expressly provide for this condition for the admissibility of proceedings for failure to act.

action in the event of a tacit rejection of the objection raised (Article 35 ECSC) or in that of the continued failure to act by the authority in spite of having been called upon to act (Article 175 EEC, Article 148 EAEC), they lay down no time limit within which the person affected may "raise the matter" with the authority which has failed to act.

In the case of *Netherlands* v. *Commission*,[93] the Court was called upon to decide whether the possibility of addressing this type of application to the authority in question was subject to any time limits. By a letter dated December 4, 1968, the High Authority had informed the French Government that, in its view, certain measures of financial assistance to the French steel industry did not infringe any Treaty provisions. This letter was brought to the attention of the applicant, the Government of the Netherlands, on December 9, 1968. It was not until June 24, 1970 that the latter addressed to the Commission an application in accordance with the first paragraph of Article 35 ECSC in order to prompt the Commission to act against the measures taken by the French Government. The Court was faced with the question whether it was still possible at this stage to raise the matter with the Commission. The Court stated that it followed

> "from the common purpose of Articles 33 and 35 that the requirements of legal certainty and of the continuity of Community action underlying the time-limits laid down for bringing proceedings under Article 33 must also be taken into account—having regard to the special difficulties which the silence of the competent authorities may involve for the interested parties—in the exercise of the rights conferred by Article 35. Thus it is implicit in the system of Articles 33 and 35 that the exercise of the right to raise the matter with the Commission may not be delayed indefinitely."[94]

Although in such cases it is impossible to apply the notion of formal validity—in the absence of a Commission decision capable of acquiring legal validity[95]—the Court uses similar arguments to those it applied to highlight the need to observe the deadlines for bringing the relevant

---

[93] Case 59/70 *Netherlands* v. *Commission* [1971] E.C.R. 639; *cf.* on this subject also H. G. Schermers, *Judicial Protection in the European Communities* (3rd ed., Deventer 1983), paragraphs 71, 336.

[94] E.C.J., *ibid.* p. 653.

[95] Neither letter from the High Authority, *i.e.* those of December 4, 1968 and of December 9, 1968, constituted decisions which were challengeable, and therefore capable of becoming legally valid, in relation to the applicant; *cf.* also Advocate-General Roemer, *loc. cit.*, footnote 93, p. 658.

1055

action in order to satisfy the requirement of legal certainty. Here too, the principle of legal certainty works to the disadvantage of the applicant in question. On the other hand, the principle of legal certainty benefits those parties—in this case, the French Government and the recipient of the French measures of financial assistance—against whom the applicant may no longer bring administrative proceedings because of the expiry of the relevant time limit. It is precisely the latter consideration which played an important part in the Court's decision in this particular case.[96]

This case law applies in principle also where it is permissible for private parties to bring actions for failure to act, and it can be extended to the corresponding provisions of the EEC Treaty[97] and the Euratom Treaty.

However, the application by the Court of this type of "administrative time limit"—which is moreover not established with precision—is not totally devoid of problems. The fact that it is possible to raise the principle of legal certainty precisely against the application of deadlines which are not laid down by legislation is shown by the opinion of the Advocate-General in this particular case:

> "The idea of establishing by means of case law (as the Treaty is silent on this point)—a limitation period for raising matters with the administration above all conflicts with the basic principle of legal certainty, particularly as neither by means of analogy nor on the basis of comparative law is it possible to ascertain what period may be regarded as reasonable."[98]

Since the measures adopted by the French Government, which the applicant considered to be contrary to Community law, had already been taken before the Commission stated its position in December 1968, Advocate-General Roemer did not consider that the admissibility of the action presented any problems as regards the protection of the legitimate expectation of the persons affected by the French measures. Nor was there any question here of the right to bring the action being forfeited, so that according to the viewpoint expressed by the Advocate-General, the action against the tacit rejection of the application made under the first paragraph of Article 35 ECSC was admissible in spite of the delay in "raising the matter" with the Commission.

---

[96] E.C.J., *loc. cit.*, footnote 93, p. 654; *contra, cf.* Advocate-General Roemer, *ibid.*, p. 659.
[97] H. W. Daig, in Groeben, Boeckh, Thiesing, Ehlermann, on Article 175, No. 19, which refers to "forfeiture" in this respect.
[98] Advocate-General Roemer, *loc. cit.*, footnote 93, p. 659.

A similar set of circumstances, in which the principle of legal certainty militates against the introduction by the Court of procedural time limits, is at the basis of the case law of the Court on time limits for bringing proceedings against infringements of EEC competition law.

In 1970, in the case of *ACF Chemiefarma* v. *Commission* and in a series of similar cases,[99] the Court was called upon to decide whether, in the absence of appropriate legislation,[100] it was acceptable to impose a time bar on infringements of competition law on the basis of general legal principles. The applicant relied upon the fact that the alleged infringements were time-barred, the Commission having taken action against them only after a number of years had passed. The ECJ rejected this plea in the following terms:

> "In order to fulfil their function of ensuring legal certainty limitation periods must be fixed in advance. The fixing of their duration and the detailed rules for their applications come within the powers of the Community legislature."[101]

The Court therefore adopted a different line from that which it took in the case mentioned earlier,[102] which concerned the raising with the Commission of certain matters under Article 35 ECSC prior to commencing an action for failure to act, and rejected, with reference to the principle of legal certainty, the judicial imposition of time limits for the bringing of administrative proceedings.

Advocate-General Gand, on the other hand, had advised the Court to confirm the existence of a time limit. He too started from the assumption that limitation periods should in principle be determined in a general way and beforehand and that the obligation to observe merely a "reasonable period" was not sufficient:

> "Although legal certainty is not a factor justifying the existence of limitation periods it is nevertheless inseparable from it. Short of depriving legal certainty of a major part of its force, limitation

---

[99] Case 41/69 *ACF Chemiefarma* v. *Commission* [1970] E.C.R. 661; *cf.* on this subject also Case 44/69 *Buchler* v. *Commission* [1970] E.C.R. 733 at 752 *et seq.* and Case 45/69 *Boehringer* v. *Commission* [1970] E.C.R. 769 at 798 *et seq.*; on this subject and on what follows, *cf.* also H. G. Schermers, *loc. cit.*, footnote 93, paragraph 73.

[100] Regulation 2988/74 was not adopted until later; *cf. infra* at footnote 107.

[101] Case 41/69, *loc. cit.*, footnote 99, p. 687.

[102] Case 59/70 *Netherlands* v. *Commission* [1971] E.C.R. 639; Advocate-General Roemer specifically invoked the judgment in Case 41/69.

periods could not be fixed case by case in terms of the particular nature of the proceedings."[103]

Nevertheless a cursory glance at the legal systems of the Member States prompted the Advocate-General to advise the Court to recognise the existence of a limitation period:

"I am able to find first of all that as a general rule the various legal systems, and not only those of the Member States, accord a place to periods of limitations. This procedure expresses a common truth in legal terms, that is, that time is the great healer, that after a more or less extensive period there always comes a point when, in the relationships of society, the past can no longer be called in question and even if it was wrongful it is better to wipe the slate clean. Nevertheless it is always the legislature which at the same time as it establishes the limitation period lays down the details for its application in terms of moral and legal concepts as the tactical and pragmatic requirements of the society in which it is to be applied.

The reasons at the basis of this process are also valid for the system of European law which is developing and no consideration peculiar to this system requires that this process be excluded. Since the absence of any provision by the Community legislature may not be interpreted as an intention to dispense with a principle so widely recognised, the Court can only recognise its existence."[104]

The Advocate-General concluded by proposing a limitation period of five years.

Two years later, the ECJ moderated its stance on the judicial imposition of limitation periods.

In a series of fundamentally similar cases, the applicants relied upon a time bar when the Commission, in 1967, brought proceedings against them in respect of infringements of competition law committed in 1964.[105] Here too, the Court pointed out that in order to fulfil its function, a

---

[103] Advocate-General Gand in Case 41/69, *loc. cit.*, footnote 99, p. 728.

[104] Advocate-General Gand, Case 41/69, *loc. cit.*, footnote 99, pp. 727 *et seq.*

[105] Case 48/69 *ICI* v. *Commission* [1972] E.C.R. 619: Case 49/69 *BASF* v. *Commission* [1972] E.C.R. 713; Case 51/69 *Bayer* v. *Commission* [1972] E.C.R. 745; Case 52/69 *Geigy* v. *Commission* [1972] E.C.R. 787; Case 53/69 *Sandoz* v. *Commission* [1972] E.C.R. 825; Case 54/69 *Francolor* v. *Commission* [1972] E.C.R. 851; Case 55/69 *Cassella* v. *Commission* [1972] E.C.R. 887; Case 56/69 *Hoechst* v. *Commission* [1972] E.C.R. 927 and Case 57/69 *ACNA* v. *Commission* [1972] E.C.R. 933.

limitation period had to be set in advance by the Community legislature. However, it added the following qualification:

"Although in the absence of any provisions on this matter, the fundamental requirement of legal certainty has the effect of preventing the Commission from indefinitely delaying the exercise of its power to impose fines, its conduct in this case cannot be regarded as constituting a bar to the exercise of that power as regards participation in the concerted practices of 1964 and 1965."[106]

Thus the Court applied in these cases the principle of legal certainty to the benefit of the undertakings in question—even though it failed to swing the outcome of the case in their favour.

It was not until well over two years after these judgments that the Council, on November 26, 1974, adopted a regulation on limitation periods applicable to the bringing of actions and enforcement proceedings in the law relating to the free movement of goods and to competition.[107] Article 1 of this Regulation fixes limitation periods of three to five years.

The Court was faced with a similar problem in the context of the law of the EEC relating to the monitoring of State aids.[108] Under Article 93(3) EEC, Member States must notify the Commission of any planned introduction of or changes in their system of State aids in sufficient time to enable the Commission to state its position on these. Where appropriate, the Commission can then bring an action against a Member State under Article 93(2) EEC. Until this preliminary examination by the Commission is completed, the Member State in question may not, under the third paragraph of Article 93(3) EEC, implement the planned measures ("suspensive effect").

In the preliminary proceedings in *Lorenz* v. *Federal Republic of Germany*,[109] the Court was called upon to decide whether the period available to the Commission to conduct this examination is subject to limitation. Neither Article 93 EEC nor the regulation implementing its provisions lays down a specific period to that effect. The Court held on this issue that

---

[106] Case 48/69, *loc. cit.*, footnote 105, p. 653; on this subject it uses the same text in the other judgments cited in footnote 105.

[107] O.J. 1974, L319/1.

[108] *cf.* on this subject also M. Seidel, "Das Verfahren in Beihilfesachen," EuR 1985, p. 22 (37 *et seq.*).

[109] Case 120/73 *Lorenz* v. *Federal Republic of Germany and Rheinland-Pfalz* [1973] E.C.R. 1471; *cf.* on this judgment also the annotation by H. P. Ipsen, 1974, p. 153.

"in the absence of any regulation specifying this period, the Member States cannot unilaterally terminate this preliminary period which is necessary for the Commission to fulfil its role. The latter, however, could not be regarded as acting with proper diligence if it omitted to define its attitude within a reasonable period. It is appropriate in this regard to be guided by Articles 173 and 175 of the Treaty which, in dealing with comparable situations, provide for a period of two months. When this period has expired, the Member State concerned may implement the plan, but the requirements of legal certainty involve that prior notice should be given to the Commission."[110]

The Court thus took a different attitude to that which it adopted in the case of limitation periods for actions for infringements of competition law by creating itself a legal rule which fixed a clear limitation period.[111]

Also when it comes to interpreting the limitation periods laid down by the Commission, the principle of legal certainty can play an important part, since this principle, as the Court stated in the case of *Federal Republic of Germany and Bundesanstalt für Arbeit* v. *Commission*, requires

"that a provision laying down a preclusive period, particularly one which may have the effect of depriving a Member State of the payment of financial aid its application for which has been approved and on the basis of which it already incurred considerable expenditure, should be clearly and precisely drafted so that the Member States may be made fully aware of the importance of their complying with the time-limit."[112]

In this case, the Commission had, by a decision of December 23, 1977, given approval to a number of grants by the Social Fund in respect of certain measures of the German Federal Labour Agency. After the relevant payments for these measures had been made from the Social Fund, the Commission rejected applications for payment of the remain-

---

[110] Case 120/73, *loc. cit.*, p. 1482; also, using the same text, Case 121/73 *Markmann* v. *Federal Republic of Germany and Land Schleswig-Holstein* [1973] E.C.R. 1495 at 1506; Case 122/73 *Nordsee, Deutsche Hochseefischerei GmbH* v. *Federal Republic of Germany and Land Rheinland-Pfalz* [1973] E.C.R. 1511 at 1522 and Case 141/73 *Lohrey* v. *Federal Republic of Germany and Land Hessen* [1973] E.C.R. 1527 at 1538 *et seq.*

[111] J. Thiesing, in Groeben, Boeckh, Thiesing, Ehlermann on Article 93, No. 44.

[112] Case 44/81 *Federal Republic of Germany and Bundesanstalt für Arbeit* v. *Commission* [1982] E.C.R. 1855 at 1877.

ing amounts, on the basis that these applications had not been submitted within the period laid down by Article 4(1) of the Commission Decision of July 27, 1978 on the administration of the European Social Fund. Since the Court, by reference to the principle of legal certainty, interpreted the rules laying down this time limit in such a way that they failed to lay down a recognisable limitation period, it set aside the decision challenged by the applicant.

IV. RECOVERY AND SUBSEQUENT ASSESSMENT

In Community law, the rules relating to the recovery of payments wrongly made from Community funds on the one hand and the subsequent collection of Community duties which have incorrectly not yet been levied on the other play a special role.[1]

For the purpose of assessing both the recovery and the subsequent collection decisions of the Community institutions, the Court has not referred to the rules concerning the revocation of administrative measures and has made only limited use of the general principles of the protection of legitimate expectation and of legal certainty, although these had been proposed to the Court on various occasions by the parties or by the Advocate-General.[2]

1. Recovery of Payments Wrongly Made

The recovery of payments wrongly made is regulated only in a number of special cases in Community law.[3] Particularly important in this regard is Article 85 of the Staff Regulations.[4]

---

[1] It is not possible to discuss under this heading the sizeable case law of the E.C.J., especially that which has been developed recently, on the question of the recovery or the obligation to repay in the case of Community administrative action undertaken through the authorities of the Member States. This will be dealt with later—as will the Regulations which have resulted therefrom, i.e. Nos. 1430/79 and 1697/79.

[2] cf., e.g. Case 106/76 F. Gelders—Deboeck v. Commission [1977] E.C.R. 1623 at 1628 et seq. on the subject of recovery; W. Wiesner, Der Widerruf individueller Entscheidungen der Hohen Behörde der EGKS, Hamburg 1966, pp. 54 et seq.; Case 2/70 Riva v. Commission [1971] E.C.R. 97 at 101 on the subject of subsequent levies; cf. also Advocate-General Lagrange in Case 20/58 Phönix—Rheinrohr v. High Authority [1958–1959] E.C.R. 165, on the subject of subsequent levies; Advocate-General Roemer in Cases 4–13/59 Mannesmann et al. v. High Authority [1960] E.C.R. 249 at 336 et seq. on the subject of recovery.

[3] cf., e.g. Article 8(2) of Regulation 23/58 of October 30, 1958, J.O. 1958, L481.

[4] Article 85 Staff Regulations as amended by Council Regulation 1473/72 Euratom/ECSC/EEC of June 30, 1972, J.O. 1972, L160/1; O.J.Sp.Ed. 1972, 703.

In the absence of a statutory basis for the right of recovery, the Court applied in these cases the principles governing unjustified enrichment.[5]

(a) Article 85 of the Staff Regulations

The most important specific legislative provision governing the right of recovery is contained in Article 85 of the Staff Regulations:

> "Any sum overpaid shall be recovered if the recipient was aware that there was no due reason for the payment or if the fact of the overpayment was patently such that he could not have been unaware of it."[6]

(aa) Absence of legal basis

Under this provision, the first condition for the recovery of the sum is that the payment was made "without due reason." In the case of *Kuhl* v. *Council*,[7] Advocate-General Mayras considered that this criterion was satisfied where

> "his (*i.e.* the official's) total remuneration is higher than would result from a lawful application of the terms of the Regulations and the provisions for putting them into effect."[8]

Normally, the legal basis for a payment to an official is a regulation or a provision in the Staff Regulations, but not an administrative measure creating rights. Accordingly, the payment itself can be classified only as a fact or as a confirmatory administrative measure. There already exists an absence of "due reason" within the meaning of Article 85 of the Staff Regulations by virtue of the fact that the material conditions stipulated in the regulation or in the provision of the Staff Regulations have not been or are no longer being fulfilled. The case of *Kuhl* v. *Council* concerned the continued payment of an education allowance, the conditions for which were no longer met after the children of the applicant moved their

---

[5] On this subject, *cf.* under (b) below at p. 1068.
[6] *cf.* footnote 4.
[7] Case 71/72 *Kuhl* v. *Council* [1973] E.C.R. 705.
[8] Advocate-General Mayras in Case 71/72, *loc. cit.*, footnote 7, p. 714 (719 *et seq.*).

residence. The applicant had notified the appointing authority of this fact only at a much later stage. The action was aimed at the consequent recovery of the allowance wrongly paid. The mere fact that the payment had been made contrary to the applicable law meant that it lacked any legal basis.[9] The action was dismissed.

The background to the case of *Meganck* v. *Commission* was very similar.[10] Here, the Commission claimed repayment of an allowance paid to the applicant and of a certain amount paid by way of daily allowance. The applicant had notified the Commission—albeit somewhat late—of a change in his domestic circumstances. The Commission had nevertheless in error continued to pay part of the allowance to the applicant. The payments wrongly made were subsequently reclaimed by means of the challenged decision. Here too, the absence of legal basis resulted from the mere fact that the conditions for payment laid down in the regulation were no longer met.

In the case of *Gutmann* v. *Commission*,[11] the absence of legal basis for the payment resulted merely from the fact that, contrary to what was claimed by the applicant, the conditions for the payment of a reinstallation allowance were not met.

Conversely, however, it is not invariably the case that the fact that the conditions for the payment of an allowance are met means that the payment has a legal basis.

This emerges very clearly from the Court's judgment in the case of *Mulligan* v. *Commission*.[12]

In the course of his employment with the Press and Information Office of the delegation of the Commission in Washington D.C., the applicant had obtained an accommodation allowance. The legal basis for this payment was Article 14(1) of Annex VII to the Staff Regulations, under which the appointing authority may, in certain special cases, undertake to pay part of the official's accommodation expenses. It was the Commission's practice to pay only a rent allowance, and not a mortgage subsidy for an apartment or house which the official acquired as his own property. Thereupon the applicant set up a company which bought a house and rented it to him. He then applied for and obtained a rent allowance for this house on the basis of Article 14(1) of Annex VII to the Staff Regulations. When the Commission learned that the applicant was himself

---

[9] Case 71/72, *loc. cit.*, footnote 7, p. 705 (712).
[10] Case 36/72 *F. Meganck* v. *Commission* [1973] E.C.R. 527.
[11] Case 92/82 *M. Gutmann* v. *Commission* [1983] E.C.R. 3127.
[12] Case 235/83 *A. A. Mulligan* v. *Commission* [1984] E.C.R. 3379.

the owner of the house in which he resided through the company which he had set up, it reclaimed the allowance which in its view had been wrongly paid.

The ECJ rejected the action brought against this decision. Advocate-General Slynn stated his conviction that Article 14(1) of Annex VII to the Staff Regulations would also allow payment of an allowance in respect of ownership and that consequently, although the Commission had

> "misinterpreted the width of Article 14, the Director-General of Personnel was entitled, under the discretion given by that Article, to authorise allowances only in respect of rent."[13]

Although in the opinion of the Advocate-General the payment was consistent with the relevant rule, he denied that there was a legal basis in respect of it.

The Court explicitly left open the question whether Article 14 had been wrongly applied. However, it held that there was no legal basis on the grounds that the payment of the accommodation allowance required an express authorisation and such an authorisation had not been given to the applicant. Instead, the authorisation granted to the applicant related only to a rented house. The Court went on to state that the applicant had, moreover, been aware of this.[14]

This decision of the Court is of particular interest from the point of view of the theory surrounding administrative measures creating rights.

The payment of the accommodation allowance did not have its legal basis—or at least its sole basis—in a legal rule (Article 14(1) of the Annex to the Staff Regulations) but in the authorisation decision as an administrative measure creating rights.

Consequently, in terms of German administrative law, the payment of the accommodation allowance would have lacked a legal basis only if the authorisation measure had been eliminated beforehand by revocation.[15] When the admissibility of the revocation was being assessed, it should have been examined whether the legitimate expectation by the applicant that the administrative measure would be maintained was worthy of protection.

---

[13] Advocate-General Slynn in Case 235/83, *loc. cit.*, footnote 12, p. 3389 (3392).
[14] Case 235/83, *loc. cit.*, footnote 12, p. 3379 (3387).
[15] This was also the view taken by Advocate-General Roemer in Joined Cases 4–13/59, *Mannesmann et al.* v. *High Authority* [1960] E.C.R. 296 at 336 *et seq.*

In this case, an argument against the protection of the applicant's legitimate expectation was the fact that the decision authorising the allowance had been based on incorrect information supplied by the applicant.

However, it is not possible to conclude from the current case law of the ECJ whether under Community law it is necessary to examine whether these conditions for revocation have been fulfilled. Under the legal systems of the other Member States, the lawfulness of a recovery decision rarely depends on the admissibility of the (prior) revocation of the authorising administrative measure.

The Court is more inclined to base the protection of the legitimate expectations of the person affected on the criterion of the "actual awareness of the irregularity" as stated in Article 85 of the Staff Regulations.[16]

The question of the revocation of an authorising administrative decision was also raised by the parties involved in the case of *Deboeck* v. *Commission*.[17]

Here, the applicant objected to the reclaiming of a family allowance which had been granted to her and which, according to the Commission, had to be repaid under Article 67(2) of the Staff Regulations because the applicant's husband had obtained a Belgian family allowance having the same value.

While the Commission claimed that the right of recovery could be concluded from this provision alone, the applicant alleged that the Commission could base the claim for recovery only on Article 85 of the Staff Regulations. However, this provision did not apply if the relevant conditions were met, since the Commission had a legal basis for granting the family allowance. As the manner in which other officials in similar circumstances had been treated showed, the Commission had tacitly decided, on the basis of an opinion of the Legal Service, that a deduction under Article 67(2) of the Staff Regulations could not be made on the basis of the Belgian family allowance paid in this case. There was no possibility of revoking this decision.

On this issue, the applicant relied upon the Court judgment in the case of *Elz* v. *Commission*.[18] Here, the ECJ had rejected the possibility of taking account of vested rights on the basis that the conduct of the

---

[16] *e.g.*: Case 36/72 *F. Meganck* v. *Commission* [1973] E.C.R. 527 at 534.
[17] Case 106/76 *F. Gelders—Deboeck* v. *Commission* [1977] E.C.R. 1623 at 1628 *et seq.*
[18] Case 56/75 *R. Elz* v. *Commission* [1976] E.C.R. 1097.

Commission entailed "no implied decision on the part of the institution which might create rights in favour of the person concerned."[19]

According to the applicant, however, the measure in question constituted just such a Commission decision.

Neither the Court nor the Advocate-General were required to adopt a position on this issue. They concluded that the case should be decided in favour of the applicant because, contrary to the Commission's view, the Belgian family allowance could not be taken into account for the purposes of Article 67(2) of the Staff Regulations.

(bb) Other conditions for the recovery of payments

Even payments made without a legal basis can, under Article 85 of the Staff Regulations, be reclaimed only if the recipient knew, or must have known, that they had no legal basis.

According to the Court, knowledge of the absence of a legal basis requires evidence of the actual knowledge of the recipient.[20]

If there is no evidence that the recipient was actually aware of this, the next question to be answered is whether the absence of any legal basis was so obvious that the recipient should have noticed it.

This obvious absence was held by the Court to exist in the case of *Kuhl* v. *Council*,[21] since it should have been clear to the applicant that the payments had been wrongly made.

In the case of *Meganck* v. *Commission*,[22] the Court, in examining whether there was "actual knowledge," tried to establish to what extent the recipient was himself responsible for the unlawful nature of the payments made to him.

To the extent that the applicant had failed to communicate the change in his domestic circumstances, the Court stated that the applicant had

> "placed himself in an irregular situation by his own conduct"; therefore he could not "rely on his good faith to be released from the obligation to return the sums overpaid during this period."[23]

However, in relation to the allowance which had continued to be paid in part to the applicant in spite of his having communicated the relevant

---

[19] Case 56/75 *loc. cit.*, footnote 18, p. 1097 (1109).
[20] Case 71/72 *A. Kuhl* v. *Council* [1973] E.C.R. 705 at 712.
[21] Case 71/72, *loc. cit.*, footnote 20.
[22] Case 36/72 *F. Meganck* v. *Commission* [1973] E.C.R. 527 at 534.
[23] Case 36/72, *loc. cit.*, footnote 22.

changes, the Court held that here there was no obvious absence of lawfulness, since the applicant could not have concluded the absence of a legal basis from his salary statements.[24]

(cc) The procedural context of the right of recovery

Where a right of recovery is justified according to the Court's findings, the latter will dismiss the action. If this is not the case, the recovery decision is set aside.

However, the Court does not consider it necessary

"to order the Commission to pay the applicant the sums claimed, since the annulment of the contested decision will in itself cause the Commission to take a new decision in accordance with the judgment given."[25]

Such an obligation arises for the Community institutions from the provisions of Articles 176 EEC, 149 EAEC and 34 ECSC.

On the other hand, the annulment of the recovery decision does not normally give rise to the obligation to pay interest on arrears:

"It is usual for such errors, the commission of which either benefits or prejudices the official concerned, to be rectified as soon as they are discovered without the matter of claiming interest on account of delay being raised by either party."[26]

The situation may be different in the event of "serious" errors which "go beyond the framework of errors and rectifications which frequently occur in calculating monthly salaries."[27]

---

[24] Case 36/72, loc. cit., footnote 22.
[25] Case 106/76 F. Gelders—Deboeck v. Commission [1977] E.C.R. 1623 at 1635. cf. on this subject the German case law, which, in addition to a general action regarding payment, also provides for the possibility of a declaratory action against the State, because it can be assumed that the State may also be subject to declaratory judgments in view of the binding force of legislation; BGHZ 28, p. 126 at para. 256 ZPO; cf. also BVerwGE 36, p. 179 (181); for more detailed study, cf. F. O. Kopp, Verwaltungsgerichtsordnung— Kommentar (7th ed., München 1986), para. 43, No. 28; Redeker, v. Oertzen, Verwaltungsgerichtsordnung—Kommentar (8th ed., Berlin/Köln/Mainz 1985), para. 43, Annotation 26.
[26] Case 106/76, loc. cit., footnote 25, p. 1623 (1635).
[27] Case 106/76, loc. cit., footnote 25.

(b) *The principle of unjustified enrichment*

In the *Mannesmann* decision,[28] the Court was presented for the first time with the opportunity to tackle the issue of recovery of moneys without a legislative basis. In this case, the applicants had brought actions against individual decisions of the High Authority by which the latter had reclaimed equalisation contributions paid from the scrap equalisation fund. According to the High Authority, the preconditions for these payments had not been met. There was no body of written rules available laying down a duty to repay payments wrongly made from the scrap equalisation fund.

In examining the admissibility of the right of recovery, the Court focused on the question whether undertakings affected had acquired financial benefits without good reason by receiving these payments.

According to the viewpoint expressed by the Court and by the Advocate-General, this was not so in this particular case.

Whereas the Court concentrated its attention on the absence of enrichment, Advocate-General Roemer stated his view at length on the legal basis for the payment, holding that this basis resided in a non-revocable authorising measure by the administration:

> "In trying to situate in the well-known categories of national administrative law the legal actions which have taken place within the framework of the equalisation scheme, one is led to the observation that every payment of equalisation supplements, which constitute public law subsidies, implies an administrative measure in which the existence of a right to equalisation is established after an examination of the conditions for its existence."[29]

According to the Advocate-General, such an authorising administrative measure had been tacitly enacted and formed the legal basis for the equalisation payment in this particular case.

This legal basis would have been absent only if the authorisation measure had been lawfully revoked. However, such a revocation would have been unlawful from the point of view of the protection of legitimate expectations—here the Advocate-General adopted a comparative approach by referring to the national legal systems, namely those of the Netherlands and of the Federal Republic of Germany.

---

[28] Joined Cases 4–13/59 *Mannesmann et al.* v. *High Authority* [1960] E.C.R. 249.
[29] Advocate-General Roemer in Joined Cases 4–13/59, *loc. cit.*, footnote 28, p. 296 (336).

The statements made by the Advocate-General on the connection between the rules on revocation and the repayment of moneys wrongly paid failed to be reflected in the Court's judgment or in its subsequent case law.

The reason for this may be that this connection is unknown in the majority of legal systems of the Member States.[30]

2. Subsequent Collection of duties which were incorrectly not Levied

Like the recovery of payments wrongly made, the subsequent collection of duties which were incorrectly not levied is situated in an area of conflict between the principle of compliance by the administration with the relevant legislation and the principle of legal certainty.

The principle of the compliance by the administration with the relevant legislation requires, as does the principle of equality as regards public burdens,[31] that public taxes be correctly levied. The principle of legal certainty, on the other hand, gives rise to the need to take into account the interests of the person affected, the latter having a legitimate expectation that he will no longer be subject to any claims which relate to past events.

A balance is struck between these conflicting principles, as they affect certain aspects of indirect administration, by Regulation 1697/79.[32]

As regards direct administration, the Court has stated its position in a number of judgments which relate to disputes concerning the scrap equalisation fund.

Although this equalisation system for scrap consumers existed for only a relatively short period, from April 1, 1954 to November 30, 1958, it took several more years before it was finally wound up. The nature of the equalisation system led to a close interrelation between the statements of account communicated to the individual undertakings in question, which were subject to frequent corrections. These in turn gave rise to the subsequent levying of amounts which in some cases were quite considerable. As a result, the undertakings affected called upon the Court of Justice to rule that the decisions imposing these subsequent levies were

---

[30] cf. on this subject Section 2.
[31] Joined Cases 14, 16–17, 20, 24, 26–27/60 & 1/61 *Meroni et al.* v. *High Authority* [1961] E.C.R. 345 at 365.
[32] O.J. 1979, L197/1. For more details, cf. C.II.3 below.

null and void. In the course of these proceedings, the question was raised whether on the one hand the High Authority could revoke the initial contribution decision and on the other, whether the revoked initial decision could be replaced by a second decision imposing even greater burdens.

On the subject of the revocation of earlier contribution decisions, the Court drew a distinction between them according to their nature. Certain undertakings had been exempted, by means of decisions of the High Authority which subsequently turned out to be unlawful,[33] from the duty to contribute towards the scrap equalisation fund.

These exemptions were described by the Court as benefits granted[34] which were, however, merely declaratory and did not create any rights.[35] The Court took the view that any question of revoking these exemption decisions required the weighing up of the public interest in levying the contributions in a correct manner and of the legitimate expectation by the individual that a legal situation, once established, would continue to apply.[36]

In each of the cases in question the Court ruled that the public interest in levying the contributions in a correct manner took precedence over other considerations.[37]

In the case of *Riva* v. *Commission*,[38] on the other hand, the initial decision had already imposed a certain contribution to the equalisation fund, which was increased by the later decision.

The Court took a different line from that taken in the exemption cases, holding that there was no scope here for weighing up the interests involved but ruling instead that

"The Commission therefore had the right and the duty in the very interest of the contributors to the equalisation scheme, to see that the latter always operated on just principles, which were both legally and factually sound. In consequence, it was its duty to rectify all legal

---

[33] Joined Cases 42 & 49/59 *SNUPAT* v. *High Authority* [1961] E.C.R. 53 and Case 14/61 *Hoogovens* v. *High Authority* [1962] E.C.R. 253.
[34] Joined Cases 42 & 49/59, *loc. cit.*, footnote 33, p. 109 (172 *et seq.*); Case 111/63 *Lemmerz-Werke* v. *High Authority* [1965] E.C.R. 893 at 911.
[35] Case 14/61 *Hoogovens* v. *High Authority* [1962] E.C.R. 253.
[36] Case 14/61, *loc. cit.*, footnote 35, p. 511 (548); Case 111/63, *loc. cit.*, footnote 34, p. 893 (911).
[37] Case 14/61, *loc. cit.*, footnote 35, p. 511 (552); Case 111/63, *loc. cit.*, footnote 34, p. 893 (911 *et seq.*).
[38] Case 2/70 *Riva* v. *Commission* [1971] E.C.R. 97.

or factual errors and all assessments which experience showed to be inaccurate or incomplete."[39]

Obviously, the Court did not in this case take into account the fact that the first contribution conferred benefits as well as imposing burdens, in that it laid down a certain contribution which was actually smaller.

In addition to the question of the admissibility of the revocation, this case raised the issue of the time limits within which it was permissible for the authorities to correct the first decision by means of a measure fixing a new amount.

On this question, the Court held—once again in the *Riva* case, in which the amount in question was fixed after a period of eight years—that

> "the absence of provisions relating to the barring by time of the powers of organisations competent to draw up estimates on their own authority of the quantities and periods for which undertakings are subject to the duty to contribute to the equalisation scheme is explained by the desire of the legislature that in this respect the principle of distributive justice should prevail over that of legal certainty."[40]

However, Advocate-General Roemer held the view that

> "the complete exclusion of the period of limitation for the equalisation of scrap could in fact disregard entirely the principle of legal certainty."[41]

Accordingly, the Advocate-General favoured the solution of applying by way of analogy General Decision 5/65[42] concerning the limitation period for the allocation of costs laid down in Articles 49 and 50 ECSC. This decision provides for a limitation period of three or six years.

---

[39] Case 2/70, *loc. cit.*, footnote 38, p. 97 (108).
[40] Case 2/70, *loc. cit.*, footnote 38, p. 97 (109).
[41] Advocate-General Roemer in Case 2/70, *loc. cit.*, footnote 38, p. 112 (116).
[42] J.O. 1965, p. 695; O.J.Sp.Ed. 1965–1966, 38.

1071

V. *RETROACTIVITY OF ADMINISTRATIVE MEASURES*

1. General Observations

The problem of the retroactivity of an administrative measure arises whenever a measure takes effect for the past and thus certain events acquire a new legal dimension.

The recovery of a payment made in the past or the *ex tunc* revocation of an administrative measure both constitute examples of the retroactive effect of administrative measures. Thus where, for example, an authorisation is retroactively revoked, that which was originally authorised, and therefore lawful, is subsequently regarded as unlawful.

The question of the extent to which the principles of legal certainty and of the protection of legitimate expectations militate against the retrospective revocation of administrative measures has already been discussed.[1] In the following sections, we shall provide examples of some more categories of cases in which the retroactivity of administrative measures on the one hand and the protection of the individual's legitimate expectation on the other play a special part.

2. Examples of the Retroactivity of Administrative Measures

(a) *The law on the supervision of subsidies*

In the law relating to the supervision of subsidies, the problem of retroactivity arises when the Commission, by a decision made under Article 93(2) EEC,[2] establishes that a State subsidy is contrary to Community law and orders the Member State in question to recover the unlawful subsidy granted.

---

[1] *cf.* Section 3, B. II above.
[2] "If, after giving notice to the parties concerned to submit their comments, the Commission finds that aid granted by a State or through State resources is not compatible with the Common Market having regard to Article 92, or that such aid is being misused, it shall decide that the State concerned shall abolish or alter such aid within a period of time to be determined by the Commission."

Although as an administrative measure such a decision is addressed to the Member State in question, it naturally impinges on the legal situation of the recipient of the State subsidy.[3]

In *Commission* v. *Federal Republic of Germany*,[4] a case which concerned the coal mining industry, the Court established in principle that the Commission, in the context of a decision under Article 93(2) EEC, can also order the Member State in question to recover the aids already granted contrary to the Treaty.[5]

In this case, the Commission had brought an action against the Federal Republic of Germany on the grounds that the Federal Republic had failed to comply with a decision under Article 93(2) EEC in that, *inter alia*, it had omitted to recover aids already paid from the recipients.

According to the Court, however, it could not clearly be concluded from the Commission decision that the Federal Republic of Germany had been called upon to recover the amounts paid by way of State aids.

Accordingly, the Court did not need to consider the issue of protecting the legitimate expectations of the recipient undertaking.

Advocate-General Mayras, on the other hand, had, in his opinion, proposed to the Court that a distinction be drawn between existing and new subsidies:

"It follows therefore from the system created by Article 93(2) concerning existing aid that, if the Commission has the power to decide whether certain aid is incompatible with the Common Market, its decision only takes effect in the future. Moreover, in accordance with a general principle of law commonly recognised by Member States and this Court, it cannot have retroactive effect. Such a decision creates rights and is not declaratory. It is from this decision and from this alone, that the prohibition of aid or the obligation to alter it is derived.

To interpret Article 93 in any other way would mean ignoring the rights acquired by third parties, would destroy all legal certainty and would lead in the end to insuperable difficulties in the application of the Article.

The position is quite different if the Commission is considering a scheme for new aid or for the alteration of existing aid. In fact, a

---

[3] Case 169/84 *Compagnie Française de l'Azote (COFAZ)* v. *Commission* [1986] E.C.R. 408 *et seq.*
[4] Case 70/72 *Commission* v. *Federal Republic of Germany* [1973] E.C.R. 813.
[5] Case 70/72, *loc. cit.*, footnote 4, p. 813 (829).

scheme cannot give rise to any subjective right. It has therefore been thought to be possible, in such a case, to confer on the Commission the exceptionally wide power to oppose the implementation of projected measures if it considers that they are incompatible with the Common Market within the meaning of Article 92."[6]

It is only recently, in the case of *DEUFIL* v. *Commission*,[7] that the Court has considered the issue of the protection of legitimate expectations in relation to new State aids.

Here, the applicant had obtained a subsidy for the conversion of a factory. The subsidy was to serve the purpose of replacing polyamide yarns by polypropylene yarns. This subsidy had not been notified.

The Commission had established that the subsidy was incompatible with the Common Market and had instructed the Federal Republic of Germany to recover the payments made.

The applicant claimed that the repayment instruction infringed the principle of the protection of legitimate expectation. It had received the payments on the basis of legally valid decisions and correct information.

The Court rejected this argument in the following terms:

"Since the contested amount undoubtedly constitutes aid within the meaning of Article 92(1), the Commission should have been informed of the intention to grant it in accordance with Article 93(3) and the aid should not have been granted before the end of the procedure initiated by the Commission. According to Article 93(2), the Commission is to decide that the State concerned is to abolish or alter the aid if it finds that it is not compatible with the common market. Where, contrary to the provisions of Article 93(3), the proposed aid has already been granted, that decision may take the form of an order to the national authorities to recover the aid.

It follows that the failure to include polypropylene yarns in the aid code cannot justify a legitimate expectation on the part of the applicant of such a nature as to prevent the Commission, in the decision in which it finds that the aid is incompatible with the common market, from ordering the German authorities to recover that aid."[8]

---

[6] Advocate-General Mayras in Case 70/72, *loc. cit.*, footnote 4, p. 833 (835).
[7] Case 310/85 *DEUFIL GmbH & Co. KG* v. *Commission* [1987] E.C.R. 901.
[8] Case 310/85, *loc. cit.*, footnote 7, paras. 24 to 25.

This prompts the conclusion that a subsidy granted without the required notification cannot form a valid basis for a legitimate expectation on the part of the recipient of the aid which is capable of protection.[9] However, in relation to existing subsidies[10] there are fundamental considerations relating to the protection of legitimate expectations and legal certainty which militate against giving retroactive effect to a later prohibition decision on the part of the Commission.[11]

(b) Authorisations for protective measures

In this context, it is especially the additional authorisations addressed to the Member States to adopt protective measures (Article 115 EEC, Article 226 EEC and on the basis of special agricultural regulations) that are of interest.[12]

The measures in question are generally acknowledged to be decisions within the meaning of the fourth paragraph of Article 189 EEC, which are to be regarded as administrative measures within the meaning of the terminology used in this context and can be challenged by those individually concerned under the terms of the second paragraph of Article 173 EEC.[13]

By issuing a decision, the Commission gives a Member State the opportunity to adopt protective measures in the shape of laws and regulations as they apply under the national legal system. The authorisation to adopt protective measures is granted partly with retroactive effect in order to authorise the Member State itself to adopt retroactive measures and even to approve retroactively a national measure which has already been adopted. This is normally achieved by fixing the date on which the authorisation takes effect at a moment which precedes the publication or even the adoption of the measure itself. Thus this type of decision

---

[9] J. Thiesing, in Groeben, Boeckh, Thiesing, Ehlermann, *Kommentar zum EWG-Vertrag* (3rd ed., Baden-Baden 1985), on Article 93 No. 19; G. von Wallenberg, in E. Grabitz, *Kommentar zum EWG-Vertrag*, München 1983, on Article 93, No. 22, 64 *et seq.*

[10] On the concept of existing aids: *cf.* Case 120/73 *Lorenz* v. *Federal Republic of Germany and Land Rheinland-Pfalz* [1973] E.C.R. 1471 at 1482.

[11] J. Thiesing, *loc. cit.*, footnote 9; G. von Wallenberg, *loc. cit.*, footnote 9, No. 64.

[12] *cf.*, *e.g.* Joined Cases 106–107/63 *A. Töpfer et al.* v. *Commission* [1965] E.C.R. 547 at 556—this case concerned an authorisation to take protective measures under Article 22 of Regulation 19/62, on the basis of which the issuing of import licences can be postponed under certain conditions.

[13] C. Vedder, in E. Grabitz, *Kommentar zum EWG-Vertrag*, München 1986, under Article 115, No. 30.

authorising protective measures acquires a certain degree of real retroactivity which the ECJ basically considers to be unlawful if applied to regulations.[14]

The authorisation to adopt protective measures can, however, also be given only unreal retroactivity. In that case, the authorisation is valid for measures in relation to import applications which were applied for before the granting of the authorisation but not yet allowed[15] or for consignments for which an import application has not yet been made but which are already in the process of being transported to the country of importation.[16] Having regard to the fact that these authorisations for protective measures serve as a basis for national legal provisions, some authors are of the opinion that the question whether retroactivity is permissible should be answered in the same way as that which seeks to establish whether regulations may have retroactive effect.[17]

This viewpoint has not, however, been adopted by the case law up to the present.[18] Instead, the Court has been concerned to find a reasonable solution for each individual case, and in so doing has tended to concentrate not so much on the principle of the protection of legitimate expectations but rather, with varying degrees of clarity, on the principle of proportionality.

In the case of *Rewe* v. *Hauptzollamt Emmerich*,[19] the Commission had, on the basis of the substantial revaluation of the Deutschmark on October 27, 1969, authorised the Federal Republic of Germany, by a decision of October 30, 1969, to adopt a number of protective measures with effect from October 27, 1969.

On this issue, the Court held:

> "The transitional protective measures (...) could not have been capable of attaining their objective fully if they had not been applicable from the entry into force of the new parity of the German mark.

---

[14] *cf.* Section 3 D.

[15] Case 62/70 *Bock* v. *Commission* [1971] E.C.R. 897; Case 29/75 *Kaufhof AG* v. *Commission* [1976] E.C.R. 431; Case 1/84 *Ilford* v. *Commission* [1984] E.C.R. 423.

[16] Case 2/75 *Einfuhr- und Vorratsstelle für Getreide* v. *Mackprang* [1975] E.C.R. 607.

[17] Thus expressly in M. Schlockermann, *Rechtssicherheit und Vertrauensschutz in der Rechtsprechung des EuGH*, Diss. München 1984, pp. 66 and 114; also Advocate-General Dutheillet de Lamothe in Case 37/70 *REWE—Zentrale* v. *Hauptzollamt Emmerich* [1971] E.C.R. 39 at 46.

[18] Doubts concerning the similarity of the facts are also expressed by Advocate-General Warner in Case 7/76 *IRCA* v. *Amministrazione delle Finanze dello Stato* [1976] E.C.R. 1229 at 1235.

[19] Case 37/70 *REWE—Zentrale* v. *Hauptzollamt Emmerich* [1973] E.C.R. 23.

It was thus proper to fix at this same date the point when the protective measures authorised could take effect."[20]

In the case of *Einfuhr- und Vorratsstelle für Getreide- und Futtermittel* v. *Mackprang*,[21] the Commission had, with a view to avoiding distortions, authorised the Federal Republic of Germany, with effect from May 8, 1969, to confine its intervention obligations to cereals harvested internally. The Court established that the protective measure also applied to those goods which, at the time of its adoption, were already in the process of being transported to the Federal Republic of Germany.

> "Accordingly, the application ... is in accordance with the purpose of the intervention system and does not, as was argued by the respondent in the national proceedings, constitute an infringement of the principle of protection of legitimate expectation of the individual, but a justified precaution against purely speculative activities."[22]

In the cases of *Bock* v. *Commission*[23] and *Kaufhof AG* v. *Commission*,[24] the Court expressly examined in the light of the proportionality principle the extension of a protective measure to import applications which had already been made but on which a decision had not yet been taken. This principle has found expression in the provisions of the first paragraph of Article 115 EEC in that the Commission is authorised to adopt only the "necessary protective measures."

In both cases, the Court considered that the "necessity" of the adopted measures was not apparent, as a result of which the decisions authorising the protective measures were set aside.

Similarly, the Court held in the *Ilford* v. *Commission* judgment[25] that the necessity of a retroactive authorisation of protective measures had to be justified by the authorising decision itself.

---

[20] Case 37/70, *loc. cit.*, footnote 19, p. 23 (37).
[21] Case 2/75 *Einfuhr- und Vorratsstelle für Getreide* v. *Mackprang* [1975] E.C.R. 607 at 617.
[22] Case 2/75, *loc. cit.*, footnote 21, p. 607 (617).
[23] Case 62/70 *Bock* v. *Commission* [1971] E.C.R. 897.
[24] Case 29/75 *Kaufhof AG* v. *Commission* [1976] E.C.R. 431.
[25] Case 1/84 *Ilford* v. *Commission* [1984] E.C.R. 423.

(c) Regulations challengeable under the second paragraph of Article 173 EEC as being decisions

Decisions authorising protective measures form merely a subgroup of regulations which are open to challenge as being decisions.

By way of introduction, it has been shown that this type of regulation constitutes, in relation to the undertakings which are directly and individually affected, a kind of collective administrative measure.[26]

In the case of *Roquette Frères* v. *Council*,[27] the Court tackled the question of the admissibility of such regulations taking retroactive effect.

The applicant had brought an action against the retroactive reintroduction of a production and sales quota for isoglucose, after a previous regulation with similar contents had been annulled by the Court on procedural grounds. Since the regulation affected the applicant directly and individually, the latter was able to bring an action under the second paragraph of Article 173 EEC.

The applicant claimed that such an unreal regulation could not acquire any retroactivity, any more than "real decisions" under Article 191 EEC could. Under the latter provision, decisions take effect on being notified. The ECJ did not uphold this argument, stating that

"As regards the possibility of retroactively adopting a measure, following a declaration of nullity by the Court, no distinction may, in the case of measures adopted in the present case, be drawn between a regulation and an individual decision. In fact, whether Regulations Nos. 1293/79 and 1592/80 were followed by individual implementing measures, as was usually the case in fixing the levy due from each producer undertaking, or whether they fixed directly and individually the undertakings' quotas, in either case, it must be decided whether the principle of legal certainty protecting those concerned precluded the provisions of those regulations from being retroactively reinstated and under what conditions such retroactivity might be held to be proper."[28]

---

[26] *cf.* Section 3, B.I.2 above.

[27] Case 110/81 *Roquette Frères* v. *Council* [1982] E.C.R. 3159: on this subject, Advocate-General Reischl in Case 108/81 *Amylum* v. *Council* [1982] E.C.R. 3139 at 3144 *et seq.*

[28] Case 110/81, *loc. cit.*, footnote 27, p. 3159 (3182).

Consequently, we are dealing here with a case in which the retroactivity of a collective administrative measure is to be judged in the light of the general principles on the retroactivity of legal rules.[29]

VI. SELF-BINDING ACTION BY THE AUTHORITIES AND THE PROTECTION OF LEGITIMATE EXPECTATIONS

1. Principles

The question whether the administration may bind itself towards the citizen by means of acts other than formal administrative measures also arises under Community law.

The notion of the authorities binding themselves on the basis of consistent administrative practice is a familiar one in German law. Where the administration has followed a certain practice in a continuous way, this confers on the citizen a right to expect a consistent use of discretionary powers by the administration in question.[1] Thus the authority concerned may not depart from its administrative practice in an arbitrary manner in individual cases, *i.e.* by infringing the principle of equality.

This notion that the administration may bind itself by following a consistent administrative practice has also been applied to Community law by the Court of Justice.

Thus in the staff case of *Louwage* v. *Commission*,[2] the ECJ stated, in relation to an internal directive, that

> "although an internal directive has not the character of a rule of law which the administration is always bound to observe, it nevertheless sets forth a rule of conduct indicating the practice to be followed, from which the administration may not depart without giving the reasons which have led it to do so, since otherwise the principle of equality of treatment would be infringed."

---

[29] *cf.* also, however, Advocate-General Lenz in Case 232/81, *Agricola Commerciale Olio* v. *Commission* [1984] E.C.R. 3881 at 3910.

[1] F. Ossenbühl, in H.-U. Erichsen, W. Martens (eds.), *Allgemeines Verwaltungsrecht* (7th ed., Berlin/New York 1986), pp. 91 *et seq.*

[2] Case 148/73 *Louwage* v. *Commission* [1974] E.C.R. 81 at 89; *cf.* also J. Schwarze, *Die Befugnis zur Abstraktion im europäischen Gemeinschaftsrecht*, Baden-Baden 1976, pp. 69 *et seq.*; Case 188/82 *Thyssen* v. *Commission* [1983] E.C.R. 3721 at 3734.

The principle of equality of treatment can thus compel the authority not to depart arbitrarily from an administrative practice which has been applied to a third party. However, the principle of the protection of legitimate expectations may also result in the authority in question being bound by the administrative practice it has previously followed in relation to a person similarly affected.

In the case of *Commission* v. *Council*,[3] the Court applied this rule to legislative action in the following terms:

> "It appears, therefore, that by its Decision ... the Council ... assumed obligations which it has bound itself to observe for the period it has defined. This followed from the rule of protection of the confidence that the staff could have that the authorities would respect undertakings of this nature. Whilst this rule is primarily applicable to individual decisions, the possibility cannot by any means be excluded that it should relate, where appropriate, to the exercise of more general powers."

In the remainder of this section, the concept of "self-binding administrative action" will cover all those circumstances in which the authority in question is bound by its earlier administrative practice, without it being necessary that the binding nature should result from an administrative measure adopted in relation to the addressee.

The main points of reference to emerge from the case law as it stands at present are: (a) consistent administrative practice, (b) the provision of information or of statements of the authority's position, and (c) the giving of explicit undertakings or pledges.[4] According to the extent to which the authorities in question are bound by such action, a distinction can be drawn as set out below.

2. Administrative Practice and Linked Administrative Measures

In a number of ECJ cases, the parties have claimed that the authority in

---

[3] Case 81/72 *Commission* v. *Council, Staff Remuneration* [1973] E.C.R. 575 at 584.
[4] The terminological differentiation customary in German administrative law between an "undertaking" (*Zusage*) and a "pledge" (*Zusicherung*) is not normally followed in European law. The two terms are used interchangeably.

question was bound by previous administrative practice.[5] However, the Court has in most cases failed to uphold this claim.

In the case of *Société Fives Lille et al.* v. *High Authority*,[6] the applicants invoked, in support of their claim for equalising transport charges, the practice followed up to that time by the regional office of the Scrap Equalisation Department of the High Authority. After two of the applicants had failed to obtain an answer from the High Authority in respect of their applications, they brought an action for failure to act. The Court declared this action to be inadmissible, since the Authority was not compelled to take action, because

> "neither any provision of the Treaty nor any decision of general or individual application which would constitute a rule laid down for the implementation thereof provided for or governed any allowance whatever as transport parity. Without its being necessary to examine whether these decisions formally preclude the practice regularly followed in respect of and to the advantage of the applicants, they could not in any case, in the absence of a general foundation in law, constitute rules laid down for the implementation of the Treaty which could create for the High Authority a duty to act in a particular manner."[7]

In the *Klöckner* v. *High Authority*[8] and *Mannesmann* v. *High Authority*[9] cases, the applicants claimed that the High Authority had improperly acted contrary to its earlier practice. On this issue, the ECJ held that

> "moreover, the administrative authority is not always bound by its previous actions in its public activities by virtue of a rule which, in relations between the same parties, forbids them to *venire contra factum proprium*."[10]

---

[5] Joined Cases 19 & 21/60 & 2–3/61 *Société Fives Lille et al.* v. *High Authority* [1961] E.C.R. 611 at 629; Joined Cases 17 & 20/61 *Klöckner et al.* v. *High Authority* [1962] E.C.R. 659 at 666; Case 47/75 *Federal Republic of Germany* v. *Commission* [1976] E.C.R. 569 at 576, 584; Case 188/82 *Thyssen* v. *Commission* [1983] E.C.R. 3721 at 3726; Case 1252/79 *Lucchini* v. *Commission* [1980] E.C.R. 3753 at 3757.

[6] Joined Cases 19 & 21/60 & 2–3/61, *loc. cit.*, footnote 5, p. 611.

[7] Joined Cases 19 & 21/60 & 2–3/61, *loc. cit.*, footnote 5, p. 611 (642).

[8] Joined Cases 17 & 20/61, *loc. cit.*, footnote 5, p. 659.

[9] Case 19/61 *Mannesmann et al.* v. *High Authority* [1962] E.C.R. 717.

[10] Joined Cases 17 & 20/61, *loc. cit.*, footnote 8, p. 659 (689); Case 19/61, *loc. cit.*, footnote 9, p. 717 (752); *cf.* on this subject H. Lecheler, who agrees with this statement in *Der EuGH und die allgemeinen Rechtsgrundsätze*, Berlin 1971, p. 100.

In the case of *Federal Republic of Germany* v. *Commission*,[11] which concerned the granting of payments from the EAGGF, the Federal Republic had argued that, in an earlier case, the Commission had acknowledged a certain claim for payment and that, by now rejecting the relevant application, it was therefore infringing the principle of the protection of legitimate expectations. The Court found for the applicant without needing to consider this argument.

Advocate-General Trabucchi, on the other hand, took the opportunity to adopt a position in extensive terms on the question of the relationship between self-binding administrative action and the protection of legitimate expectations.

According to the Advocate-General,

> "when exercising a discretion, an administrative authority is always at liberty to adopt a different view from those previously taken on particular issues. The adoption at a particular time of one of the possible alternatives does not deprive the authority of the power to take a different view in future."[12]

Consequently, in relation to changes in the administrative practice itself the administration should not feel itself bound in any way.

The Advocate-General considered that the principle of the protection of legitimate expectations was relevant only in relation to the side effects of the change in administrative practice, *i.e.* as regards the question whether the citizen affected was entitled to any compensation arising from the infringement of his legitimate expectation:

> "In saying this, I am not trying to deny the importance of respect for the principle of legitimate expectation, the legal effect of which in the Community legal order the Court has had occasion to recognise in its previous decisions. What must be borne in mind here is that the principle assumes its essential importance in determining the existence, if any, of the blame which is the foundation of the liability of public authorities for compensation for damage suffered by an interested party because of the unforeseeable shift of attitude by the administration concerning the settlement of a given problem."[13]

---

[11] Case 47/75 *Federal Republic* v. *Commission* [1976] E.C.R. 569.
[12] Advocate-General Trabucchi, in Case 47/75, *loc. cit.*, footnote 11, p. 582 (589).
[13] Advocate-General Trabucchi in Case 47/75, *loc. cit.*, footnote 12, p. 582 (589).

Since then, however, the Court, in the case of *Rijn-Schelde-Verolme* v. *Commission*,[13a] has recognised the possibility of taking account of the principle of legitimate expectations even in relation to previous administrative action. By a decision of December 19, 1984, the Commission had declared incompatible with the Common Market a subsidy given by the Netherlands Government to the applicant in 1982 for the purpose of restructuring the shipbuilding industry.

The aid in question, which had been notified, was intended to supplement, on grounds of disproportionate increases in costs, a programme of aids to the shipbuilding industry which the Commission had approved in 1981.

The Court set aside the Commission's decision on the grounds that, *inter alia*, the decision had had insufficient regard for the applicant's legitimate expectation:

> "It is further apparent from the documents before the Court that the aid in question concerned a sector which since 1977 had been in receipt of aid granted by the Netherlands Government and that that aid was intended to meet additional costs of an operation which had also been in receipt of an authorised aid. The applicant had therefore reasonable grounds for believing that the Commission's doubts no longer existed and that the aid would encounter no objection."[13b]

However, there can be no question whatsoever of legitimate expectation capable of protection and of binding the administration if the earlier administrative practice in question was unlawful. The case of *Lucchini* v. *Commission*[14] can be cited by way of example. In this case, a fine had been imposed on the applicant on grounds of infringement of a system of minimum prices. In the course of its action against the decision imposing the fine, the applicant unsuccessfully invoked the protection of legitimate expectation, in the sense that in the past, the Commission had, in similar cases, not insisted on the strict observance of the minimum price system. On this issue, the Court stated that

> "It is necessary to observe first of all that a concession on the part of the authorities cannot make an infringement legitimate, still less justify making that infringement more serious. The fact that the

---

[13a] Case 223/85 *Rijn-Schelde-Verolme* v. *Commission* [1987] E.C.R. 4617.
[13b] Case 223/85, *loc. cit.*, footnote 13a, para. 16.
[14] Case 1252/79 *Lucchini* v. *Commission* [1980] E.C.R 3753.

Commission may have shown some laxity as regards alignment not on specific price lists but on a basic price formed by the minimum price in no way justifies selling at prices lower than the minimum prices or the failure to take into consideration extras for quality or quantity. Moreover, it has not been shown that producers in other Member States benefited from a concession enabling them not to charge the extras for quality or quantity."[15]

More particularly on the subject of the principle of the protection of legitimate expectations, Advocate-General Capotorti stated that

"conduct of the authorities which is outside the normal application of the law to which it is itself subject cannot . . . give rise to a legitimate expectation on the part of a person subject to those authorities."[16]

A special category of consistent administrative practice is the administrative measure as part of a linked series. This category is characterised by the fact that an administrative measure conferring benefits and limited in time is adopted on a regular basis in relation to the same person. Here, the consistent administrative practice takes the form of a series of administrative measures; however, each individual measure is limited in time and does not bind the administration beyond the time limit in question. This gives rise to the question whether the citizen in question has a legitimate expectation that the administrative measure conferring benefits will be regularly repeated, *i.e.* whether the series of measures will continue.

The notion of the linked series of administrative measures has yet to be applied as such in the case law of the Court.

However, the ECJ did, in the case of *SOREMA* v. *High Authority*,[17] concern itself with the rejection of an application for the renewal of an authorisation under the third paragraph of Article 65(2) ECSC.[18]

---

[15] Case 1252/79, *loc. cit.*, footnote 14, p. 3753 (3783): Case 2/82 *HZA Krefeld* v. *Maizena* [1982] E.C.R. 4601 (4615) on practices by the Member States which have been approved by the Commission contrary to Community law; Case 316/86 *HZA Jonas* v. *Krücken* [1988] E.C.R. 2213.

[16] Advocate-General Capotorti in Case 1252/79, *loc. cit.*, footnote 14, p. 3766 (3771).

[17] Case 67/63 *SOREMA* v. *High Authority* [1964] E.C.R. 321 (352); Case 36/64 *SOREMA* v. *High Authority* [1965] E.C.R. 447 at 459, 461 *et seq.*

[18] "Authorisations may be granted subject to specified conditions and for limited periods. In such cases the High Authority shall renew an authorisation once or several times if it finds that the requirements of subparagraphs (a) to (c) are still met at the time of renewal."

The Court did not adopt a definitive position on the question whether the decision in question was a rejection of an application for renewal or the revocation of a long-term authorisation. According to its findings, either interpretation would have been permissible. More particularly, the ECJ did not examine the question whether this was a rejection of the renewal of an authorisation in the light of the principle of the protection of legitimate expectations. Instead, under the judgment in question it appears to be sufficient that the Commission decided that the conditions for renewing the authorisation had not been fulfilled.

3. Information and Explanation

Mere items of information and of explanation issued by the administration are in principle insufficient to bind the authorities as to their future action, *i.e.* as to their decision whether they should adopt or not adopt a certain administrative measure.

This does not apply, however, if the information or explanations are to be considered in good faith as legally binding statements and consequently acquire the regulatory force of administrative measures.

In the case of *Richez-Parise* v. *Commission*,[19] the applicants had voluntarily resigned from their posts with the Communities. The pension rights granted to them by a decision were however lower than they had been led to expect from the relevant information provided by the Commission before the applicants' resignations.

The applicants alleged in the first place that the information supplied had given them a legitimate expectation. This expectation was worthy of protection even if the information in question did not have the status of an administrative measure. The information had been supplied by one of the appropriate Commission departments. In such cases any subsequent departure from this information infringed vested rights. The Court, however, did not uphold these arguments:

> "These statements were supplied solely by way of information and were not capable of determining rights which the applicants were to derive from a given legal situation. It is not therefore possible to concede that the statements have the character of measures creating rights for the addressees. The appointing authorities, being obliged

---

[19] Joined Cases 19–20, 25 & 30/69 *D. Richez–Parise et al.* v. *Commission* [1970] E.C.R. 325.

to apply Regulation No. 259/68 in defining the applicants' pecuniary rights, could not apply the incorrect interpretation adopted in those statements once they had become aware of the more accurate interpretation. The argument based on a supposed violation of vested rights is therefore unfounded."[20]

By way of incidental plea, the applicants had requested the Court to order the Commission to pay damages, since they had applied for retirement from their post as a result of the error conveyed by the information in question.

On this question, the Court stated that

"Apart from the exceptional instance, the adoption of an incorrect interpretation does not constitute in itself a wrongful act. Even the fact that the authorities request those concerned to obtain information from the competent departments does not necessarily involve those authorities in an obligation to guarantee the correctness of information supplied and does not therefore make them liable for any injury which may be occasioned by incorrect information. Although such rectification was possible as early as April 1968 it was deferred without any justification until the end of 1968. The failure to make such a correction is, on the other hand, a matter of such a nature as to render the Communities liable."[21]

Nevertheless, in this particular case the ECJ did not admit the claim for compensation, because the applicants had failed to establish adequately any causal link between the error induced by the information and their decision to resign voluntarily from their posts with the Communities.

However, in the case of *Fiehn* v. *Commission*,[22] which was based on similar facts, the Court was of the opinion that a different interpretation needed to be placed on the causal link in question. Here, the ECJ arrived at the conclusion that it was actually the incorrect information supplied which had caused the applicant to apply for retirement from her post.

Other points of clarification addressed to the public in general or to individuals which lack the status of administrative measures cannot in principle cause the administration to be bound as to its subsequent decisions in certain areas.

[20] Joined Cases 19–20, 25 & 30/69, *loc. cit.*, footnote 19, p. 325 (337).
[21] Joined Cases 19–20, 25 & 30/69, *loc. cit.*, footnote 19, p. 325 (339).
[22] Case 23/69 *A. Fiehn* v. *Commission* [1970] E.C.R. 547.

In the case of *Geitling et al.* v. *High Authority*,[23] the Court of Justice consequently dismissed as inadmissible an action brought by a group of undertakings and challenging a written communication by the High Authority. In this document, the High Authority had informed the addressees that it intended in future to grant no more authorisations under Article 65(2) ECSC. The Court judged this communication to be

"simply a notice which does not bind the High Authority for the future ... Moreover, neither these grounds themselves nor the contested parts of the letter of notification of February 21, 1959 are such as to affect the applicants adversely because they are not binding on the addressees of the decision and on the other hand they do not bind the High Authority on exercising in the future its power of authorisation."[24]

The Court applied a similarly strict interpretation in the case of *Salerno et al.* v. *Commission*.[25] In these cases, the applicants, employees of the European Association for Co-operation (EAC), relied upon a decision by the European Parliament and on certain explanations concerning the budget in support of their claim to be brought retrospectively under the terms of employment of the Community. On this issue, the Court's position was as follows:

"Contrary to the applicants' claim, a resolution of the Parliament is not binding and cannot give rise to the legitimate expectation that the institutions will comply with it. With regard to the remark in the budget for the 1982 financial year, it can neither confer individual rights on the applicants nor give rise to any legitimate expectation."[26]

By way of exception, however, the legitimate expectation of the citizen induced by mere explanations by the administration may also be worthy of protection.

In the case of *Châtillon* v. *High Authority*,[27] the High Authority had assured the applicant that it would not take into account certain sales of

---

[23] Joined Cases 16–19/59 *Geitling et al.* v. *High Authority* [1960] E.C.R. 45.
[24] Joined Cases 16–19/59, *loc. cit.*, footnote 23, p. 45 (64).
[25] Joined Cases 87 & 130/77, 22/83 & 9–10/84 *V. Salerno et al.* v. *Commission* [1985] E.C.R. 2525.
[26] Joined Cases 87 & 130/77, 22/83 & 9–10/84, *loc. cit.*, footnote 25, p. 2525 (2542).
[27] Case 54/65 *Châtillon* v. *High Authority* [1966] E.C.R. 529.

scrap metal when fixing the latter's contribution towards the scrap equalisation fund.

The Court considered this statement to be not a formal decision but a mere statement, since the obligatory formal and procedural requirements needed for the adoption of an administrative measure had not been met. In spite of this, however, the Court examined in the light of the various principles governing the revocation of administrative measures conferring rights whether the High Authority could repudiate the original statement by means of formal decisions.[28] The ECJ, however, concluded by rejecting the notion that the applicant had an overriding legitimate expectation capable of protection.

In the case of *Mavrides* v. *European Parliament*[29] also, the Court confirmed that in principle, mere explanations were capable of giving rise to the protection of legitimate expectation.

Here, the applicant challenged the rejection of his application which he had submitted in response to an advertisement of a vacancy published in the Official Journal. In the applicant's opinion, the appointing authority had applied the special recruitment procedure as laid down in Article 29(2) of the Staff Regulations without any prior notification and had, in the process, imposed an additional condition for admission in the form of an age limit. According to the applicant, this manner of proceeding had infringed the principle of legitimate expectations, since the advertisement in question had implied an undertaking that the conditions for admission as stated were restrictively listed.

Although the Court did not tackle the question of the undertaking, it ruled that

> "if the appointing authority decides to fill a post under Article 29(2) of the Staff Regulations and if, for that reason, it does not clearly state all the conditions required of the candidates, it must nevertheless indicate in an appropriate manner that the procedure in question constitutes a derogation from the normal provisions relating to recruitment. In any event, an infringement of that requirement does not automatically mean that the disputed measure is void but may in certain circumstances justify the award of damages, if the person concerned has suffered injury as a result."[30]

---

[28] Case 54/65, *loc. cit.*, footnote 27, p. 529 (545).
[29] Case 289/81 *Mavrides* v. *European Parliament* [1983] E.C.R. 1731.
[30] Case 289/81, *loc. cit.*, footnote 29, p. 1731 (1745).

Since the applicant had not submitted a claim to that effect, the Court was not required to give a ruling on that point.

That an infringement of the principle of legitimate expectations does not automatically need to be rectified by the annulment of the administrative measure in question is all the more obvious in cases where the rights of third parties could thus be violated. This would be the case where another applicant had been recruited during the intervening period. On the other hand, it would be possible in such cases to bring an action for damages without prejudice to the rights of third parties.

4. Undertakings and Pledges[31]

Recently, the ECJ has concerned itself with a particular category of administrative statement, namely pledges and undertakings. Officials and firms alike regularly invoke alleged undertakings or pledges given by a Community institution in support of their claim that the institution in question has thereby bound itself. In this manner, the Community authorities would be compelled to adopt an administrative measure conferring benefits on the person affected or to refrain from adopting or carrying out a measure imposing burdens.[32]

As far as can be ascertained, the Court has yet to uphold the objection that by giving an undertaking in the course of exercising their discretion the relevant authorities have effectively bound themselves.

This may be one of the reasons why the case law has so far failed to set out definitive criteria which have to be met by a measure if it is to qualify as a binding undertaking. However, it is possible to discern in the case law as it stands certain essential characteristics which an effective undertaking must possess. Thus it is required in the first place that the measure in question should definitely constitute an undertaking. It is necessary that the authority should have committed itself to a certain formal manner of proceeding.

---

[31] cf. footnote 4.

[32] This principle was also invoked by the applicants in the following cases (in addition to those already mentioned): Case 2/80 Dautzenberg v. Court of Justice [1980] E.C.R. 3107—assurance of promotion; Case 78/83 Usinor v. Commission [1984] E.C.R. 4177—fine imposed for exceeding steel quotas; Cases 303 & 312/81 Klöckner v. Commission [1983] E.C.R. 1507—fine imposed for exceeding steel quota; Case 228/84 Pauvert v. Court of Auditors [1985] E.C.R. 1973; Case 188/82 Thyssen v. Commission [1983] E.C.R. 3721 at 3734.

In the case of *Klöckner-Werke* v. *Commission*,[33] the Court doubted whether the authority in question had thus bound itself. Here, the applicant challenged the imposition of a fine for having exceeded its steel quotas. In support of its claim, the applicant invoked a telephone conversation, in the course of which the Head of Cabinet of the Vice-President of the Commission had, in the context of his efforts to conclude a "Eurofer II" agreement, promised to the Chairman of the applicant's Board of Directors that the Commission would "solve the problem" if the applicant undertook to take part in the relevant negotiations. The problem in question concerned the fact that the applicant wished to produce more in the course of the first quarter of 1981 than was possible under the quotas which had been previously communicated to it but which were merely provisional. The applicant was of the opinion that this undertaking bound the Commission in its decision on the imposition of the fine. On this issue, the Court held that

> "Klöckner's argument must be disallowed first on account of the general nature of the utterances ascribed to Mr. Defraigne. The use of the expression "solve the problem," even if examined in the context as expounded by the applicant, cannot be regarded as a commitment to engage in a specific course of action."[34]

Moreover, to be effective an undertaking has to be given by the appropriate authority. That much was expressed in the case of *Frubo* v. *Commission*,[35] which concerned competition law, in the following terms:

> "In the letter, the Director-General of Competition, taking note of a specific amendment to the agreement which the applicants were prepared to accept, states that, in his view, the agreement as thus amended can, notwithstanding the remaining restriction on competition, qualify for exemption under Article 85(3). Expressed in these terms, the opinion given could not convey any impression that it committed the Commission, nor moreover is the signatory authorised to enter into such a commitment."[36]

Where oral assurances have been given by individual officials, then, to be effective,

---

[33] Joined Cases 303 & 312/81, *loc. cit.*, footnote 32, p. 1507.
[34] Joined Cases 303 & 312/81, *loc. cit.*, footnote 32, p. 1507 (1529).
[35] Case 71/74 *Frubo* v. *Commission* [1975] E.C.R. 563.
[36] Case 71/74, *loc. cit.*, footnote 35, p. 563 (582).

"the general rules of law governing the exercise of administrative authority and the validity or efficacy of compromises would have required that this assurance be expressly approved by the responsible officers of the High Authority."

This was the ruling given by the Court in another case, in response to a claim made by the applicant that High Authority officials had given her an assurance that under certain conditions it would not impose any surcharges for the delayed payment of certain joint contributions due.[37]

In relation to the formal requirements which an assurance had to meet if it was to be regarded as effective, Advocate-General Reischl observed in the above-mentioned *Klöckner* case, invoking "national law," that

"if it is necessary for the administrative measure whose adoption was envisaged by the assurance to be stated in writing, "then a promise having the same effect may be regarded as effective only if it is made in writing."[38]

However, in certain individual cases it is possible that to rely upon the lack of jurisdiction of the authority which gave the assurance could mean infringing the principle of good faith.[39]

Also it is necessary, from a substantive point of view, for the assurance to be lawful if it is to be regarded as binding the authority which gave it.

This was made clear by the Court in the previously quoted case of *Klöckner* v. *Commission*:

"Even if it were hypothetically possible to accept that the utterances attributed to Mr. Defraigne concerned the non-enforcement of the fine, such a declaration would be devoid of legal force, for if the "promise" related to a waiver of the legal consequences of overproduction officially determined, it would be illegal inasmuch as Article 9 of Decision 2794/80 requires the Commission to impose the fine whenever production in excess of the quotas is determined."[40]

---

[37] Case 21/64 *Macciorlati Dalmas & Figli* v. *High Authority* [1965] E.C.R. 241 at 258—follow-up decision to the judgment in Case 1/63 *Macciorlati Dalmas & Figli* v. *High Authority* [1963] E.C.R. 653, in which the E.C.J. set aside the challenged decision on the grounds of inadequate reasoning.

[38] Advocate-General Reischl in Joined Cases 303 & 312/81 *Klöckner* v. *Commission* [1983] E.C.R. 1507 at 1547.

[39] Advocate-General Warner in Case 2/80 *Dautzenberg* v. *Court of Justice* [1980] E.C.R. 3119 at 3121.

[40] Joined Cases 303 & 312/81 *Klöckner* v. *Commission* [1983] E.C.R. 1507 at 1530; *cf.* also opinion by Advocate-General Reischl, p. 1534 (1545).

A corresponding ruling was given by the Court in the case of *Thyssen* v. *Commission*:

"The argument concerning the promise allegedly made by certain Commission officials must also be rejected, since no official can give a valid undertaking not to apply Community law. No legitimate expectation can therefore have been aroused by such a promise, even if one was made."[41]

Finally, there can also be no question of an assurance being effectively binding on the authority which gave it if the authority in question, in giving the assurance, made a mistake concerning the actual conditions which applied and the person affected knew, or should have known, this.

In the case of *Pauvert* v. *Court of Auditors of the EC*,[42] the applicant invoked an assurance given to him that he would be promoted, which by itself did not confer the promotion but merely put it in prospect. The authority in question had made an error in assuming that the conditions for obtaining the promotion in question had been fulfilled.

The Court assessed the facts as follows:

"Once it had discovered its error, it was impossible for it to promote him to the post since this would have been contrary to the conditions set out in the vacancy notice. The appointing authority therefore had no other choice than to recommence the procedure, which necessarily meant revoking the undertaking given to the applicant. It follows that the applicant may not base his claims on the validity of that undertaking.

Since the applicant was in the best position to know that he did not fulfil the conditions laid down in the vacancy notice, he is also debarred from founding his action on a breach of the principle of the protection of legitimate expectation because such expectation on his part may not be created by an undertaking vitiated by the mistake of fact described above."[43]

---

[41] Case 188/82 *Thyssen* v. *Commission* [1983] E.C.R. 3721 at 3734 *cf.* also Advocate-General Slynn in Case 78/83 *Usinor* v. *Commission* [1984] E.C.R. 4201 at 4204.
[42] Case 228/84 *Pauvert* v. *Court of Auditors* [1985] E.C.R. 1973.
[43] Case 228/84, footnote 42, p. 1973, para. 14.

The position on the conditions under which an assurance may constitute a self-binding measure by the administration, and the implications thereof, can accordingly be summarised as follows:

Any assurance which is formally or substantively unlawful is inappropriate as a basis for any legitimate expectation on the part of the person affected. It does not constitute self-binding action on the part of the administration. The position is different, however, if for the administration to rely upon the unlawfulness of the assurance would be incompatible with the principle of good faith. However, where the person affected has based a legitimate expectation on the effectiveness of an unlawful assurance whose illegal nature was not apparent to him, the question can also be raised, in a Community law context, whether the authority in question, even if it is not obliged by the assurance in view of its unlawfulness, is nevertheless obliged to pay compensation in respect of the infringement of the citizen's legitimate expectation. As far as can be ascertained, the ECJ has not yet had occasion to give a ruling on this issue.

Yet if the assurance is legally effective, any legitimate expectation on the part of the person affected as to the fulfilment of the assurance is in principle worthy of protection. The administration is bound by its assurance when a decision is taken at a later stage. However, in such cases also, and particularly where third-party rights are involved which run counter to such an outcome, the general statement made by the Court in the case of *Mavrides* v. *European Parliament* applies, *i.e.* that any infringement of the principle of the protection of legitimate expectation

> "does not automatically mean that the disputed measure is void," but may in certain circumstances "justify the award of damages."[44]

C. INDIRECT EXECUTIVE ACTION

I. PRINCIPLES

1. Introduction

Indirect executive action is characterised by the fact that substantive

---

[44] Case 289/81 *Mavrides* v. *European Parliament* [1983] E.C.R. 1731 at 1744.

Community law is enforced by the authorities of the Member States. In this context, reference is made to the "servicing function" of national law.[1] This "servicing function" finds its concrete expression in the fact that the provisions of the Member States' law of administrative procedure are also geared to the implementation of Community law.

However, given the extent to which the substantive provisions of Community law refer to the administrative law of procedure of the Member States, there exists a danger of divergence in the manner in which the Member States implement Community administrative law. These potential divergences represent an area of tension with the principle of the *uniform* application of Community law in all Member States.

This tension is relieved in part by the fact that at the level of Community law uniform procedural rules have been created, which complement the substantive Community law and thus render superfluous the involvement of the administrative law of the Member States.

In this context, mention should be made of the Council Regulations of July 2, 1979 on the repayment or remission of import or export duties,[2] as well as the Regulation of July 24, 1979 concerning the post-clearance recovery of import duties or export duties.[3] These Regulations, however, cover only specific areas of customs and agricultural law.[4]

The other areas of Community law, however, remain subject to implementation by the Member States in accordance with the provisions which apply nationally.

It is in order to reduce the inherent risk of divergent executive action that in recent years a number of attempts have been made in the literature to find a solution to this problem.[5] In particular, the proposals advanced seek to ensure that the general principles of Community law will also find expression in indirect executive action.[6]

---

[1] V. Götz, "Probleme des Verwaltungsrechts auf dem Gebiet des gemeinsamen Agrarmarktes" (1986) EuR p. 29.

[2] Regulation 1430/79, O.J. 1979, L175/1.

[3] Regulation 1697/79 O.J. 1979, L197/1.

[4] V. Götz, "Probleme des Verwaltungsrechts auf dem Gebiet des gemeinsamen Agrarmarktes" (1986) EuR p. 29 (36).

[5] K. E. Huthmacher, *Der Vorrang des Gemeinschaftsrechts bei indirekten Kollisionen*, Köln/Berlin/Bonn/München 1985, pp. 134 *et seq.*; A. Weber, "Verwaltungs-Kollisionsrecht der Europäischen Gemeinschaften im Lichte neuerer Rechtsentwicklungen," EuR 1986 p. 1(3).

[6] Bleckmann, *Europarecht*, (4th ed., Köln/Berlin/Bonn/München 1985), pp. 85 *et seq.*; by the same author, "Artikel 5 EWG-Vertrag und die Gemeinschaftstreue," DVBl. 1976, p. 483 (486); H.-W. Rengeling, "Rechtsgrundsätze beim Verwaltungsvollzug des Europäischen Gemeinschaftsrechts," KSE Vol. 27, Köln/Bonn/Berlin/München 1977, p. 239;

2. Case Law of the Court of Justice

However, the Court has, through a case law which must now be regarded as established, declined to "lay down general substantive and procedural rules, which can be promulgated only by the competent authorities" as regards the implementation of Community law through the national authorities.[7]

Instead, the ECJ has consciously avoided filling apparent gaps in Community law, but has regularly held that, in the present state of development of Community law, that law must be formally implemented by the Member States' authorities by applying national rules of administrative law "in so far as Community law, including its general principles, does not include common rules to this effect."[8]

The Court has also, however, expressly stated that the national procedural law must, when Community law is being implemented, also observe certain minimum standards. These minimum standards can best be summed up by the formulae "prohibition of discrimination between Community law and national law findings of fact" and "prohibition of the inability to enforce Community law in practice."

By way of example, we reproduce below the statements made by the Court in the case of *Deutsche Milchkontor* v. *Federal Republic of Germany*[9]:

> "In the absence of provisions of Community law, disputes concerning the recovery of amounts unduly paid under Community law must be decided by national courts pursuant to their own national law subject to the limits imposed by Community law, inasmuch as the rules and procedures laid down by national law must not have the effect of making it virtually impossible to implement Community regulations and national legislation must be applied in a manner which is not discriminatory compared to procedures for deciding similar but purely national disputes. . . .
>
> In the first place, the application of national law must not affect the scope and effectiveness of Community law. That would be the

---

K. E. Huthmacher, *Der Vorrang des Gemeinschaftsrechts bei indirekten Kollisionen*, Köln/Berlin/Bonn/München 1985, pp. 134 *et seq.*

[7] In particular Case 130/79 *Express Dairy Foods* v. *Intervention Board for Agricultural Produce* [1980] E.C.R. 1887 (1900); *cf.* also U. Everling, "Elemente eines europäischen Verwaltungsrechts," DVBl. 1983, pp. 649 (653 *et seq.*).

[8] Joined Cases 205–215/82 *Deutsche Milchkontor et al.* v. *Federal Republic of Germany* [1983] E.C.R. 2633 at 2665.

[9] Joined Cases 205–215/82, *loc. cit.*, footnote 8, p. 2633 (2665, 2666).

case in particular if the application of national law made it impossible in practice to recover sums irregularly granted. ...

Second, national law must be applied in a manner which is not discriminatory compared to procedures for deciding similar but purely national disputes. This means first that in such cases the national authorities must act with the same degree of care as in comparable cases concerning solely the application of corresponding national legislation and in accordance with rules and procedures which do not make the recovery of the sums in question more difficult.

Secondly ... the obligations imposed on undertakings wrongly granted pecuniary advantages based on Community law must be no more stringent than those imposed on undertakings which have wrongly received similar advantages based on national law, provided that the two groups of recipients are in comparable situations and therefore different treatment is objectively unjustifiable."

II. RELEVANCE OF THE PRINCIPLES OF THE PROTECTION OF LEGITIMATE EXPECTATIONS AND OF LEGAL CERTAINTY IN INDIRECT EXECUTIVE ACTION

1. Introduction

Against the background of the case law stated above, we must now examine in detail what part the principles of the protection of legitimate expectation and of legal certainty play in the implementation of Community law by the national authorities.

This question has hitherto been debated in particular under the following three headings[10]:

---

[10] On the debate on this subject in the available German literature, *cf.* P. Aubin, *Die Haftung der Europäischen Wirtschaftsgemeinschaft und ihrer Mitgliedstaaten bei gemeinschaftsrechtswidrigen nationalen Verwaltungsakten*, Baden-Baden 1982; M. Hilf, "Möglichkeiten und Grenzen des Rückgriffs auf nationalen verwaltungsrechtliche Regeln bei der Durchführung von Gemeinschaftsrecht," in J. Schwarze, ed., *Europäisches Verwaltungsrecht im Werden*, Baden-Baden 1982, pp. 67 *et seq.*; H.-W. Rengeling, "Die Entwicklung verwaltungsrechtlicher Grundsätze durch den Gerichtshof der Europäischen Gemeinschaften," EuR 1984, p. 331; by the same author, "Rechtsgrundsätze beim Verwaltungsvollzug des Europäischen Gemeinschaftsrechts," KSE Vol. 27, Köln/Bonn/Berlin/München 1977, p. 239; A Weber, "Verwaltungskollisionsrecht der Europäischen Gemeinschaften im Lichte neuerer Rechtsentwicklungen," EuR 1986 p. 1; by the same author, "Anfechtbarkeit und Aufhebbarkeit gemeinschaftsrechtswidriger nationaler Verwaltungsakte," BayVbl 1984, p. 321; B. Winkler, "Die Durchsetzung der Pflicht zur Rückforderung einer gemeinschaftsrechtswidrigen Beihilfe nach deutschem

(a) the recovery of amounts paid contrary to Community law (2.)
(b) the subsequent levying of amounts not collected contrary to Community law (3.)
(c) the repayment of amounts levied contrary to Community law (4.)

2. Recovery of Amounts paid Contrary to Community Law

Unlike the repayment or the waiver of import and export duties or their subsequent collection, the recovery of aids, export refunds or denaturing premiums under the Common Agricultural Policy is not governed by any general provisions in Community law. Under the general principles relating to the implementation of Community law described above, recovery proceedings will consequently be conducted basically in accordance with national law.

However, Article 8 of Regulation 729/70[11] states:

> "The Member States in accordance with national provisions laid down by law, regulation or administrative action shall take the measures necessary to ... recover sums lost as a result of irregularities or negligence."

In a series of requests for preliminary rulings, the Court was faced with the question which sought to establish how far the duties incumbent upon the national administration extend and, in particular, whether the undertakings concerned may invoke the principles of legal certainty and of the protection of legitimate expectations against the recovery proceedings in question.

A leading decision in relation to this question is that in the *Ferwerda* case of 1980.[12] Here, the undertaking in question had, in the underlying dispute, invoked the principle of legal certainty against an action brought

---

und europäischem Recht," DVBl. 1979, p. 263; Bastein, "Zur Bestandskraft rechtswidriger Ausfuhrerstattungsbescheide," ZfZ 1974 p. 198; V. Götz, "Probleme des Verwaltungsrechts auf dem Gebiet des gemeinsamen Agrarmarktes," EuR 1986, p. 29.

[11] Regulation 729/70 of April 21, 1970, J.O. 1970, L94/13; O.J.Sp.Ed. 1970, 218.

[12] Case 265/78 *Ferwerda* v. *Produktschap voor Vee en Vlees* [1980] E.C.R. 617 at 627—the question posed by the referring court in this case concerned the compatibility with Article 6(5) of Regulation 1957/69—the Advocate-General, however, did not consider that this provision was applicable in this case (p. 638). The Court left this question open but did not consider that this provision contained any Community rules for the recovery of export subsidies wrongly granted (p. 632).

by the national administrative authority for the recovery of export refunds wrongly paid.

The ECJ stated first of all that the question of the recovery of amounts incorrectly paid had to be decided by the national authorities, applying national law, subject to their observing the "prohibition of discrimination." On this subject, the Member States were obliged to apply, in accordance with Article 5 EEC,

> "the legal protection made available as a result of the direct effect of the Community provisions."[13]

However, in so doing the rules applied by the Member States

> "may in no case be laid down in such a way as to render impossible the exercise of the rights which the courts must protect."[14]

Here, account needs to be taken of the fact that the principle of legal certainty, as expressed in national law, may not

> "in all cases constitute a defence against a claim for the recovery of Community financial benefits wrongly granted. It must in each case be considered whether such application does not jeopardise the very basis of the rule providing for such recovery and whether it does not result in practice in frustrating such recovery."[15]

In relation to the compatibility with the Treaty of the national legal provisions in question, the Court held that

> "an application of a principle of legal certainty based on national law whereby financial benefits wrongly conferred on a trader may not be recovered if the error committed was not due to incorrect information supplied by the recipient or if, despite the fact that the information was incorrect though supplied in good faith, the error could

---

[13] Case 265/78, *loc. cit.*, footnote 12, p. 617 (629).
[14] Case 265/78, *loc. cit.*, footnote 12, p. 617 (629).
[15] Case 265/78, *loc. cit.*, footnote 12, p. 617 (630).

easily have been avoided, does not in the present state of Community law conflict with the general principle thereof."[16]

This ruling was subsequently largely confirmed in a series of decisions.[17]

In the *BayWa* case,[18] the Court clearly stated that the national authorities could not exercise any discretion in relation to the recovery of Community funds wrongly paid in view of the clear duty of recovery imposed on those authorities by Article 8 of Regulation 729/70.

The Court made a similar ruling in the *Deutsche Milchkontor* case,[19] but in so doing also stated that considerations based purely on expediency should be totally alien to such decisions.

On the other hand, Community law does not prevent national provisions from

"having regard, in excluding the recovery of unduly-paid debts, to such considerations as the protection of legitimate expectation, the loss of unjustified enrichment, the passing of a time limit or the fact that the administration knew, or was unaware owing to gross negligence on its part, that it was wrong in granting the aids in question, provided however that the conditions laid down are the same as for the recovery of purely national financial benefits and the interests of the Community are taken fully into account."[20]

Such considerations of legitimate expectation and of legal certainty also form part of Community law.

---

[16] Case 265/78, *loc. cit.*, footnote 12, p. 617 (631).

[17] Cases 119 & 126/79 *Lippische Hauptgenossenschaft* v. *BALM* [1980] E.C.R. 1863; Case 54/81 *Firma W. Fromme* v. *BALM* [1982] E.C.R. 1469; Joined Cases 146 & 192–193/81 *BayWa AG* v. *BALM* [1982] E.C.R. 1503; Joined Cases 205–215/82 *Deutsche Milchkontor et al.* v. *Federal Republic of Germany* [1983] E.C.R. 2633; Case 130/79 *Express Dairy Foods* v. *Intervention Board for Agricultural Produce* [1980] E.C.R. 1887 at 1900.

[18] Joined Cases 146 & 192–193/81, *loc. cit.*, footnote 17, p. 1535; *cf.* also opinion of Advocate-General Capotorti p. 1537 at 1546 *et seq.*

[19] Joined Cases 205–215/82, *loc. cit.*, footnote 17, p. 2633 (2666); *cf.* also opinion of Advocate-General VerLoren van Themaat, p. 2674 (2676); A. Weber, "Verwaltungskollisionsrecht der Europäischen Gemeinschaften im Lichte neuerer Rechtsentwicklungen" (1986) EuR p. 1 (18 *et seq.*); *cf.* also A. Mattfeld, "Annotation to Decision in Joined Cases 205–215/82" (1984) EuR p. 174 (177 *et seq.*); H.-W. Rengeling, "Die Entwicklung verwaltungsrechtlicher Grundsätze durch den Gerichtshof der Europäischen Gemeinschaften," (1984) EuR p. 331 (353 *et seq.*); D. Schrimpf, *Die ergänzende Anwendung des nationalen Rechts bei der Effektuierung des Gemeinschaftsrechts durch die Mitgliedstaaten, dargestellt am Beispiel der Nacherhebung von gemeinschaftsrechtswidrig gewährter Geldzahlungen*, Diss. Würzburg 1983, p. 139.

[20] Joined Cases 205 & 215/82 *Deutsche Milchkontor et al.* v. *Federal Republic of Germany* [1983] E.C.R. 2633 at 2669 *et seq.*

"The fact that national legislation provides for the same principles to be observed in a matter such as the recovery of unduly-paid Community aids cannot, therefore, be considered contrary to that same legal order."[21]

Consequently the fact that these principles are also recognised in Community law justifies their being taken into consideration by the Member States in implementing Community law.[22] In so doing, it is left to the national authorities and courts to strike the right balance between the principle of the legality of the administration on the one hand and that of legal certainty and the protection of legitimate expectation on the other.[23]

Whereas the cases mentioned above seek to establish to what extent the *national* principles of legal certainty and of the protection of legitimate expectation are compatible with Community law, the case of *Zuckerfabrik Franken* v. *Federal Republic of Germany*[24] in a certain sense reverses the question.

This case concerned the recovery of a denaturing premium which the plaintiff had obtained for denaturing sugar as animal feed. The sugar in question had subsequently been used, contrary to the agreement, not as animal feed but as a core binder.

The plaintiff challenged the recovery decision by advancing, *inter alia*, the argument that the German provisions which also provided for the

---

[21] *cf.* footnote 20.

[22] *cf.* on this subject Advocate-General Capotorti in Joined Cases 146 & 192–193/81 *BayWa AG* v. *BALM* [1982] E.C.R. 1537 at 1547; A. Mattfeld, "Annotation to Joined Cases 205–215/82," EuR 1984, p. 174 (177).

[23] This case law of the Court of Justice, with its clear distinction between the essential duty to recover on the one hand—excluding considerations of discretion—and the admissibility of the observance of the general principle of the protection of legitimate expectation on the other, which is also recognised in Community law, has recently been confirmed in relation to the German law on implementing Community law by the Federal Administrative Court—BVerwG, Decision of August 14, 1986, DVBl. 1986, p. 1205. With reference to the case law of the E.C.J. in the *Milchkontor* decision, the Federal Administrative Court observes that in the provisions of Article 9(2)(1) of the German Regulations on State Aids (Skimmed Milk), which provides that aids wrongly received must be repaid, in relation to the revocation of authorising decisions and the recovery of aids considerations of discretion are excluded (Article 48(1)(1) VwVfG) but not considerations based on the protection of legitimate expectation (article 48(2) VwVfG). The Federal Administrative Court bases this viewpoint mainly on the consideration that "the possibility in principle of invoking a right to the protection of legitimate expectation against the revocation of administrative measures conferring benefits is part of the constitutional obligations embodied in the principle of the rule of law."

[24] Case 77/81 *Zuckerfabrik Franken* v. *Federal Republic of Germany* [1982] E.C.R. 681.

possibility of recovery in the case of the improper use of sugar by third parties, infringed the *Community law* principle of legal certainty.

The Court rejected this argument in the following terms:

"As regards the principle of legal certainty it is quite plain from all the considerations set out above that traders to whom the provisions in question apply were fully aware of the requirement that the denatured sugar must be used exclusively for animal feed. They ought therefore reasonably to have expected that penalties would be provided for failure to observe that requirement and that such penalties would be incurred by the only person who was in a legal relationship with the competent authorities of the Member States. In those circumstances national rules providing for the refund of premiums unduly paid, even when third parties were responsible for the use contrary to the intended purpose, do not amount to a breach of the principle of legal certainty."[25]

This observation is interesting inasmuch as the Court appears to state that in doubtful cases, the principle of legal certainty should also be observed by the national authorities of the Member States as a (third) element among the "minimum standards" applicable under national law when implementing Community law.

3. Subsequent Recovery of Amounts not Levied Contrary to Community Law

In the course of these proceedings, the national authorities, at a date later than that on which collection should have taken place, claim duties due under Community law which have not so far been collected, or at least not collected for their full amount.[26]

The legal basis for subsequent recovery is to be found in Community law,[27] whilst the conditions of enforceability of such claims for recovery—until such time as there is a Community law system—are assessed under national law.

---

[25] Case 77/81, *loc. cit.*, footnote 24, p. 681 (695).
[26] *cf.* Case 216/78 *Beljatzky* v. *HZA Aachen-Süd* [1979] E.C.R. 2273; Case 217/78 *S.A.N. Corman and Fils* v. *HZA Aachen-Süd* [1979] E.C.R. 2287; Case 827/79 *Amministrazione delle Finanze* v. *Acampora* [1980] E.C.R. 3731.
[27] *cf.* footnote 26.

(a) Regulation 1697/79

In respect of certain aspects of subsequent recovery, Community rules have displaced national law, namely Regulation 1697/79,[28] which came into effect on July 1, 1980.

This Regulation is concerned with import and export duties relating to goods which have been submitted for customs procedures which involve an obligatory payment of such duties.

This Regulation will not be discussed in detail here[29] except to draw attention to the second recital, viewed in the light of the Community law principle of the protection of legitimate expectations:

> "Whereas the post-clearance recovery of import duties or export duties involves some degree of prejudice to the certainty which persons liable for payment have the right to expect from official acts having financial consequences; whereas it is therefore appropriate to limit the possible scope of action of the competent authorities in this field by fixing a time-limit after which the original determination of the import duties or export duties must be considered as definitive."

(b) The application of national law as a complementary tool

Unless appropriate rules have been enacted at the Community law level, subsequent recovery remains subject to national rules for the purposes of enforcement.

This is clearly shown by, for example, the judgment in the *Salumi* case.[30] This case concerned the subsequent recovery of import levies for beef imports. In calculating the levy, the Italian customs authority had applied a procedure advocated by the Commission, which the ECJ had

---

[28] O.J. 1979, L197/1.

[29] *cf.* on this subject, *e.g.* M. Müller, in R. Regul (ed.), *Gemeinschaftszollrecht*, Baden-Baden 1981, pp. 1353 *et seq.*; R. Christiansen, "Erlass, Erstattung und Nacherhebung von Eingangs- und Ausfuhrabgaben," ZfZ 1980, p. 354; K. Friedrich, "Die EWG-Verordungen über Nacherhebung und Erlass bzw. Erstattung von Eingangs- und Ausfuhrausgaben," RIW/AWD 1982, p. 35; D. Schrimpf, *Die ergänzende Anwendung des nationalen Rechts bei der Effektuierung des Gemeinschaftsrechts durch die Mitgliedstaaten, dargestellt am Beispiel der Nacherhebung von gemeinschaftsrechtswidrig nicht erhobenen Geldleistungen und der Rückforderung gemeinschaftsrechtswidrig gewährter Geldzahlungen*, Diss. Würzburg, 1983 pp. 168 *et seq.*

[30] Joined Cases 66 & 127–128/79 *Amministrazione delle Finanze dello Stato* v. *Salumi et al.* [1980] E.C.R. 1237.

later, in a preliminary ruling, ruled contrary to Community law. As a result, the undertakings concerned had paid levies at too low a rate.

In its decision, however, the ECJ gave a ruling only on the (preliminary) question whether the interpretation applied in the context of an earlier preliminary procedure should also be applied in the relationship between the Italian authorities and all other undertakings. Accordingly, this raised the question whether the interpretation by the Court of Justice had given rise to a duty on the part of the national authorities to claim payments from *all* undertakings which found themselves in the same situation. The Court replied in the affirmative as follows:

> "The interpretation which, in the exercise of the jurisdiction conferred on it by Article 177 of the EEC Treaty, the Court of Justice gives to a rule of Community law clarifies and defines where necessary the meaning and scope of that rule as it must be or ought to have been understood and applied from the time of its coming into force. It follows that the rule as thus interpreted may, and must, be applied by the courts even to legal relationships arising and established before the judgment ruling on the request for interpretation, provided that in other respects the conditions enabling an action relating to the application of that rule to be brought before the courts having jurisdiction are satisfied."[31]

Only exceptionally as in the *Defrenne* case,[32] may the Court,

> "in application of the general principle of legal certainty inherent in the Community legal order and in taking account of the serious effects which its judgment might have, as regards the past, on legal relationships established in good faith, be moved to restrict for any person concerned the opportunity of relying upon the provision as thus interpreted with a view to calling in question those legal relationships."[33]

However, where no such restriction as to the retroactivity of the judgment is laid down in the judgment itself, the effect of the retrospective application of the interpretation decision means, according to Advocate-General Reischl, that

---

[31] Joined Cases 66 & 127–128/79, *loc. cit.*, footnote 30, p. 1237 (1260); *cf.* also the opinion of Advocate-General Reischl in this case, p. 1264 (1269).
[32] Case 43/75 *Defrenne* v. *Sabena* [1976] E.C.R. 455.
[33] Joined Cases 66 & 127–128/79, *loc. cit.*, footnote 30, p. 1237 (1261).

"a supplementary charge may be made as respects levies which were undercharged owing to an erroneous application of the agricultural market regulations and the enforcement of such rights must, in principle, be protected by the national courts."[34]

However, the Court failed to tackle the issue of the extent to which the principles of the protection of legitimate expectation are relevant to the enforcement of subsequent recoveries. Advocate-General Reischl, however, states on this issue that

"consequently if the supplementary charge for the difference is now claimed before the national courts, those courts too will have to consider whether the levy made by the appropriate authority was incorrect and whether that error might not have been detected by the party liable to pay the levy, in other words, whether the subsequent charge, in the individual case, may not be barred by the principle of the protection of legitimate expectation, which is known to the legal systems of all the member states."[35]

4.   Repayment of Amounts Levied Contrary to Community Law

In respect of claims made by the citizen for the repayment of amounts charged contrary to Community law, the basic rule also applies that issues which arise from such repayment are governed by national law where no Community system applies.

(a) Regulation 1430/79[36]

As from July 1, 1980, repayments of or reductions in import and export duties are subject, in all the Member States, to the binding rules contained in Regulation 1430/79. The Regulation includes a series of substantive and procedural rules which, as to their scope,[37] displace the

---

[34] Opinion of Advocate-General Reischl in Joined Cases 66 & 127–128/79, loc. cit., footnote 30, p. 1265 (1271).

[35] Advocate-General Reischl in Joined Cases 66 & 127–128/79, loc. cit., footnote 30, p. 1265 (1272).

[36] O.J. 1979, L175/1.

[37] cf. for more details M. Müller, "Erstattung und Erlass von Eingangs- und Ausfuhrabgaben," in R. Regul (ed.), Gemeinschaftszollrecht, Baden-Baden 1981, p. 1315; R. Christiansen, "Erlass, Erstattung und Nacherhebung von Eingangs- und Ausfuhrabgaben," ZfZ 1980, p. 354; K. Friedrich, "Die EWG-Verordnungen über Nacherhebung

relevant national rules which have hitherto applied. In particular, this rule applies to the national provisions regarding the legal validity of decisions on duties or limitation periods. On this subject, Article 2(2) of the Regulation in most cases lays down a period, to be applied in a uniform way throughout the Community, of three years. Within this period, the persons affected must submit applications for repayment to the appropriate national authorities. Where the authorities have, within this period, themselves established that there is an entitlement to repayment, this must take place automatically. Thus the undertakings concerned are on the one hand accorded a right to repayment recognised under Community law, yet on the other hand are subject to a time limit for the purpose of enforcing the claim in the interests of legal certainty.

Particular mention must also be made here of Article 13, under which "in special circumstances duties may be repaid if the party concerned has not acted with any fraudulent intent." This clause, qualified by the Court as a

"general provision on equitable grounds,"[38]

has subsequently been amended by Regulation 1672/82.[39]

As with subsequent recoveries, a committee procedure has also been provided for the observance of the repayment regulation.[40] Although under this procedure the Member States may themselves decide to reject an application for repayment, they are not alone in having the power to decide on such applications. This can occur only on the basis of a decision issued by the Commission after consultation with the appropriate committee and addressed to the particular Member State. The Commission decision in question can be challenged by the affected party under the second paragraph of Article 173 of the EEC Treaty.[41]

Exactly which situations come within the scope of Regulation 1430/79 is a question which has yet to be finally clarified.[42]

---

und Erlass bzw. Erstattung von Eingangs- und Ausfuhrausgaben," RIW/AWD 1982, p. 35.

[38] Case 283/82 *Papierfabrik Schoellershammer* v. *Commission* [1983] E.C.R. 4219 at 4225.

[39] Regulation 1672/82 of June 24, 1982, O.J. 1982, L186/1.

[40] By Regulation 1575/80 of June 20, 1980, O.J. 1980, L161/13 which was adopted on the basis of Article 13(2) of this Regulation.

[41] Case 283/82 *Papierfabrik Schoellershammer* v. *Commission* [1983] E.C.R. 4219.

[42] *cf.* A. Weber, "Verwaltungskollisionsrecht der Europäischen Gemeinschaften im Lichte neuerer Rechtsentwicklungen," EuR 1986, p. 1 (8 with further references); P. Aubin, *Die Haftung der Europäischen Wirtschaftsgemeinschaft und ihrer Mitgliedstaaten bei gemeinschaftsrechtswidrigen nationalen Verwaltungsakten*, Baden-Baden 1982, pp. 160 *et seq.*; K. E. Huthmacher, *Der Vorrang des Gemeinschaftsrechts bei Kollisionen*, Köln/

The only matter to be governed directly by the Regulation is the reimbursement of payments where the applicable Community law has been incorrectly enforced beforehand by the national authorities.

However, it is doubtful whether the Regulation also applies in relation to the retrospective effects of regulations which have subsequently been declared unlawful by the Court of Justice. The text of Article 2(1) of Regulation 1430/79[43] appears to be worded in sufficiently broad terms to admit this. The application of this Regulation in cases in which "incorrect" Community law has been implemented would undoubtedly contribute towards the goal of equality of treatment of all traders in the Member States, which is frequently urged by the Court of Justice. Hitherto it has been possible for the Court to leave open the question of the extent of the field of application of Regulation 1430/79.[44]

However, in judgments which concerned the legal position prior to the entry into effect of this Regulation,[45] the Court has on several occasions dealt with claims for repayment made by citizens subsequent to the relevant Community Regulation being declared invalid.

In such cases, the Court has itself imposed time limits on the effect of the unlawfulness of the Regulation in question, as a result of which there was no longer any scope for claims by the citizen for repayment when this claim was instituted in accordance with Community law.

Berlin/Bonn/München 1985, pp. 23 *et seq.*; on the other hand, M. Müller, in R. Regul (ed.), *Gemeinschaftszollrecht*, Baden-Baden 1982, p. 1327, who on this subject refers to a unanimous decision by the Committee for Customs Exemption (Member States and Commission) of June 30, 1980; *cf.* on this subject also D. Schrimpf, *Die ergänzende Anwendung des nationalen Rechts bei der Effektuierung des Gemeinschaftsrechts durch die Mitgliedstaaten*, Diss. Würzburg 1983, pp. 36 *et seq.*; Advocate-General Lenz in his opinion on Case 33/84 *SpA Fragd* v. *Amministrazione delle Finanze dello Stato* [1985] E.C.R. 1606 at 1609 *et seq.*

[43] "Import duties may be refunded or waived where it can be demonstrated to the competent authorities that the amount recorded in the accounts
—relates to goods for which no customs liability has arisen or for which the customs liability has been extinguished for a reason other than payment of the corresponding amount or limitation;
—exceeds for whatever reason the amount that can legally be levied."

[44] Case 130/79, *Express Dairy Foods* v. *Intervention Board for Agricultural Produce* [1980] E.C.R. 1887.

[45] Regulation 1439/79 does not have retroactivity—Case 113/81, *Reichelt* v. *Hauptzollamt Berlin-Süd* [1982] E.C.R. 1957 at 1965.

In the cases of *Providence Agricole* v. *ONIC*[46] and *Roquette Frères* v. *French Customs Administration*,[47] the Court declared null and void a regulation on the basis of which monetary compensatory amounts had been levied by the national authorities. The possibility of the annulment having effect for the period before the making of the judgment was excluded by the ECJ on the following grounds:

"In this case it is necessary to apply by analogy the second paragraph of Article 174 of the Treaty, whereby the Court of Justice may state which of the effects of the regulation which it has declared void shall be considered as definitive, for the same reasons of legal certainty as those which form the basis of that provision. On the one hand the invalidity of the regulation in this case might give rise to the recovery of sums paid but not owed by the undertakings concerned in countries with depreciated currencies and by the national authorities in question in countries with hard currencies which, in view of the lack of uniformity of the relevant national legislation, would be capable of causing considerable differences in treatment, thereby causing further distortion in competition."[48]

This decision by the ECJ has been subject to frequent criticism.[49] Thus the Lille Tribunal d'Instance made the observation that

"after it had interpreted Community law for the purpose of replying to the questions referred to it for a preliminary ruling and had exhausted its powers, the Court took the step, for which there was no basis in law, of adding to the opinion it had thereby given a comment based on a provision which was not applicable to the situation under consideration. Far from amounting to a complementary statement which assisted it in its task of interpretation, the step taken by the

---

[46] Case 4/79, *Société Coopérative Providence Agricole de la Campagne* v. *ONIC* [1980] E.C.R. 2823.
[47] Case 145/79, *Roquette Frères* v. *French Customs Administration* [1980] E.C.R. 2917; *cf.* also Case 109/79, *Maiseries de Beauce* v. *ONIC* [1980] E.C.R. 2883.
[48] Case 4/79, *loc. cit.*, footnote 46, p. 2823 (2853).
[49] *cf.* P. Aubin, *Die Haftung der Europäischen Wirtschaftsgemeinschaft und ihrer Mitgliedstaaten bei gemeinschaftsrechtswidrigen nationalen Verwaltungsakten*, Baden-Baden 1982, pp. 161 *et seq.*; K. E. Huthmacher, *Der Vorrang des Gemeinschaftsrechts bei indirekten Kollisionen*, Köln/Berlin/Bonn/München 1985, pp. 23 *et seq.*; *cf.* also the references to the available French literature in the arguments of the parties in Case 112/83, *Société des produits de maïs SA* v. *Administration des douanes et droits indirects* [1985] E.C.R. 732 (739), and in G. Isaac, "La modulation par la Cour de Justice des CEE des effets dans le temps de ses arrêts d'invalidité," CDE 1987, pp. 444 *et seq.*

Court constitutes the deliberate expression of a choice whereby preference is given to the principle of legal certainty over that of legality and to the authority of the Community legal order over the national legal order."[50]

On this issue, the Court stated first of all that

"the Court's power to impose temporal limits on the effects of a declaration that a legislative act is invalid, in the context of preliminary rulings under indent (b) of the first paragraph of Article 177, is justified by the interpretation of Article 174 of the Treaty having regard to the necessary consistency between the preliminary ruling procedure and the action for annulment provided for in Articles 173, 174 and 176 of the Treaty, which are two mechanisms provided by the Treaty for reviewing the legality of acts of the Community institutions. The possibility of imposing temporal limits on the effects of the invalidity of a Community regulation, whether under Article 173 or Article 177, is a power conferred on the Court by the Treaty in the interests of the uniform application of Community law throughout the Community."[51]

However, the ECJ proceeded to narrow down the terms of this statement by adding:

"It must be pointed out that where it is justified by overriding considerations, the second paragraph of Article 174 gives the Court discretion to decide, in each particular case, which specific effects of a regulation which has been declared void must be maintained. It is therefore for the Court, where it makes use of the possibility of limiting the effect on past events of a declaration in proceedings under Article 177 that a measure is void, to decide whether an exception to that temporal limitation of the effects of its judgment may be made in favour of the party which brought the action before the national court or of any other trader which took similar steps before the declaration of invalidity or whether, conversely, a declaration of invalidity applicable only to the future constitutes an adeq-

---

[50] Cited by the Commission in Case 112/83, *loc. cit.*, footnote 49, p. 732 (736).
[51] Case 112/83, *loc. cit.*, footnote 49, p. 732 (747); *cf.* also Case 33/84, *Fragd* v. *Amministrazione delle Finanze dello Stato* [1985] E.C.R. 1613 at 1618.

uate remedy even for traders who took action at the appropriate time with a view to protecting their rights."[52]

Accordingly, the ECJ decided that the effect of a judgment—including that which declares a measure to be void—can be restricted on grounds of legal certainty even in the context of an examination of the validity of a measure under Article 177 EEC. Consequently, the problem posed by the uniform settlement of claims for repayment does not even arise in such cases.

However, it would then no longer be necessary for reasons of legal certainty to restrict the effect of a judgment establishing the invalidity of a certain measure if the implementation of claims for repayment was regulated in a uniform manner and on a Community-wide basis. This objective could be achieved if Regulation 1430/79 was to be applied and interpreted in the extensive sense described above.[53]

(b) The application of national law as a complementary tool

Where a claim for repayment has been lodged and no Community rule can be applied, the claim in question will be settled in accordance with national law.

Thus in the case of *Roquette Frères* v. *Commission*, the ECJ held that

> "it is clear from the provisions on the Community's own resources ... that the national authority must ensure on behalf of the Community and in accordance with provisions of Community law that Regulation No. 2/71, these collections shall be made by Member States in accordance with national provisions laid down by law, regulation or administrative action. Disputes in connexion with the reimbursement of amounts collected for the Community are thus a matter for the national courts and must be settled by them under national law in so far as no provisions of Community law are relevant."[54]

As the Court stated shortly after this judgment in the *Express Dairy Foods* case, this applies to both the formal and the substantive law:

---

[52] Case 112/83, *loc. cit.* footnote 49, p. 732 (747); Case 33/84, *loc. cit.*, footnotes 51, p. 1613 1628 .

[53] P. Aubin, *Die Haftung der Europäischen Wirtschaftsgemeinschaft und ihrer Mitgliedstaaten bei gemeinschaftsrechtswidrigen nationalen Verwaltungsakten*, Baden-Baden 1982, p. 161.

[54] Case 26/74, *Société Roquette Frères* v. *Commission* [1976] E.C.R. 667 at 686.

> "In the regrettable absence of Community provisions harmonising procedure and time limits, the Court finds that this situation entails differences in treatment on a Community scale. It is not for the Court to issue general rules of substance or procedural provisions, which only the competent institutions may adopt."[55]

The two limits mentioned earlier also apply in the case of repayment of duties levied contrary to Community law, as can be seen from the following passage:

> "In the absence of Community rules however, the necessary reference to national law is nevertheless subject to limits, the need for which has been acknowledged inasmuch as the application of national legislation must be effected in a non-discriminatory manner having regard to the procedural rules relating to disputes of the same type, but purely national, and in so far as procedural rules cannot have the result of making impossible in practice the exercise of rights conferred by Community law."[56]

The Court further held that

> "it is for the national authorities to decide as to the recovery of sums unduly charged on the basis of Community regulations which have been declared invalid."[57]

However, in view of the reference to the provisions of national law in this area, it will in principle also be the national rules on the validity of administrative measures and on limitation periods, which are different in every Member State,[58] which will apply. The manner in which the conflict between the principle of legal certainty and that of the compliance of the administration with the relevant legislation is settled in individual cases in this field will consequently also be determined in accordance with the

---

[55] Case 130/79, *Express Dairy Foods* v. *Intervention Board for Agricultural Produce* [1980] E.C.R. 1887 at 1900.
[56] *cf.* footnote 55.
[57] *cf.* footnote 55.
[58] *cf.* on this subject a comparative study by K. E. Huthmacher, *Der Vorrang des Gemeinschaftsrechts bei indirekten Kollisionen*, Köln/Berlin/Bonn/München 1985, pp. 259 *et seq.*

national provisions applicable in the Member States and with their interpretation by the domestic courts.

On this issue, the Court has found that

> "the protection of rights guaranteed in the matter by the Community legal order does not require the grant of an order for the recovery of charges improperly levied in conditions such as would involve an unjustified enrichment of assigns and that from the point of view of Community law there is therefore nothing to prevent national courts from taking account in accordance with their national law of the fact that it has been possible for charges unduly levied to be incorporated in the prices of the undertaking liable for the charge and to be passed on to the purchasers of the product in question."[59]

The only exception to this rule arises where the substantive law itself excludes the possibility of repayment. This was accepted by the Court in the *International Chemical Corporation* case.[60]

In this case, the plaintiff had obtained aids for the purchase of skimmed-milk powder and was obliged to lodge a deposit in respect thereof. Since the applicant had failed to fulfil its obligation to purchase, the Italian financial authorities had declared the deposit forfeited.

The Regulation in question had been declared null and void by the ECJ in the context of a different preliminary ruling.

However, the ECJ concluded from the (void) Regulation that the parties affected would pass the deposits on to other undertakings. Accordingly,

> "the existence during the entire period in which (the Regulation) applied of a scheme especially designed with a view to spreading the effects of a measure of economic policy destroys the basis of an action for the recovery of securities which have been provided and declared forfeit even if a similar action could be successfully brought under national law alone. In this regard, it does not matter whether the operator has actually passed on the charge or whether he has decided not to do so for reasons connected with the financial policy of his undertakings."[61]

---

[59] Case 130/79, *Express Dairy Foods* v. *Intervention Board for Agricultural Produce* [1980] E.C.R. 1887 at 1900.

[60] Case 66/80, *International Chemical Corporation* v. *Amministrazione delle Finanze dello Stato* [1981] E.C.R. 1191.

[61] Case 66/80, *loc. cit.*, footnote 60, p. 1191 (1218).

It is possible that the Court saw fit to take the far from uncontroversial decision[62] to exclude unconditionally any possibility of repayment because the alternative of restricting the retroactivity of the judgment decreeing the invalidity, used in other cases, was not—or was no longer—available in this particular instance.

According to Advocate-General Reischl,[63] such a restriction on retroactivity, arrived at by extrapolating the second paragraph of Article 174 EEC, must, for reasons of legal certainty, also be expressed in the judgment establishing invalidity—as is the case with interpretation decisions. However, the Court did not avail itself of this opportunity in its judgment.

III. SUMMARY

In conclusion, it can be stated that the Community law principles of legal certainty and of the protection of legitimate expectations have hitherto been of very limited relevance to the case law of the ECJ on indirect executive action.

More particularly, these principles have not been used by the Court in order to bring about uniformity in the field of executive action by the administration in the Member States. Instead, it is essentially the relevant national rules which apply when it comes to carrying out Community law in this context.

At best, the Court has given to the principles of legal certainty and of the protection of legitimate expectations the status of minimum standards to be observed in the implementation of Community law by the national authorities. Here too, however, their scope remains restricted to an obligation imposed on the Member States to observe certain limits to their freedom of action, whilst the actual process of weighing up the interests of legal certainty and of the protection of legitimate expectations on the one hand, and the obligation on the part of the administration to

---

[62] For a critical study, cf. P. Aubin, *Die Haftung der Europäischen Wirtschaftsgemeinschaft und ihrer Mitgliedstaaten bei gemeinschaftsrechtswidrigen nationalen Verwaltungsakten*, Baden-Baden 1982, p. 168; cf. also the debate on the paper by Advocate-General Reischl, "Ansätze zur Herausbildung eines europäischen Verwaltungsrecht in der Rechtsprechung des EuGH—Bestandsaufnahme der unterschiedlichen nationalen Rechtsvorstellungen," in J. Schwarze (ed.), *Europäisches Verwaltungsrecht im Werden*, Baden-Baden 1982, p. 112 (114); K. E. Huthmacher, *Der Vorrang des Gemeinschaftsrechts bei indirekten Kollisionen*, Köln/Berlin/Bonn/München 1985, p. 23.
[63] Advocate-General Reischl, in Case 66/80, footnote 60, p. 1224 (1236).

comply with the relevant legislation on the other remains the prerogative of the national legal systems.

The main area in which the principle has been applied and which holds out the prospect of further developments in the ECJ case law in this area is probably that of the recovery of Community funds wrongly paid. Although in the meantime an established case law has developed in this field, the question whether the procedures followed by Member States in recovering—or failing to recover—such sums are compatible with Community law will continue to be raised in individual cases.

However, there are certain essential legal areas in which the application of national principles of administrative law is currently excluded by virtue of either Regulation 1430/79 on the recovery or the waiver of Community duties or Regulation 1697/79 on the subsequent recovery of Community duties. Here, there are a number of provisions relating to limitation periods which are currently governed by uniform Community standards and which take account of the principle of legal certainty.

On the other hand, the question whether these regulations also apply if a provision of substantive Community law has been declared invalid in the context of a preliminary ruling remains unanswered. On this issue, the Court has hitherto attempted to take into account both the need to apply Community law in a uniform way and considerations of legal certainty by excluding the possibility that the effects of the judgment in question could extend to events of the past.

D. NORMATIVE INSTRUMENTS

The case law of the Court on the principles of legal certainty and of the protection of legitimate expectations shows that these principles have become particularly relevant in the context of the review of legislative instruments of the Community. At present, nearly 100 decisions have been made concerning the question of the retroactivity of Community normative instruments. It is possible to discern an increasing trend on the part of the undertakings affected to invoke an infringement of the principle of the protection of legitimate expectations in the course of their defence. However, as far as can be ascertained, there are only a few instances in which the undertakings in question have invoked this principle successfully against the actual or apparent retroactivity of a rule.[1]

---

[1] Case 74/74 *CNTA* v. *Commission* [1975] E.C.R. 533; Case 78/74 *DEUKA* v. *Einfuhr- und Vorratsstelle für Getreide und Futtermittel* [1975] E.C.R. 421, and Case 5/75 *ibid.* [1975]

Apart from those which relate to the enforcement of economic law, there are a number of decisions in staff cases in which the principle of the protection of legitimate expectations has also been successfully pleaded against unexpected changes in the applicable law. However, the decisive factor here was not so much the notion that the retroactivity of the amending provision was inadmissible as the idea that the legislator had to a certain extent bound himself.[2]

Altogether, the questions arising from the retroactivity of legal rules in Community law deserve a good deal of attention if only because there are considerable areas in which the Community institutions only enact legislation whilst leaving any executive action relating thereto to the national authorities. In addition, the decisions in which the Court has given concrete expression to the principle of the protection of legitimate expectations—albeit subject to certain restrictions—in the light of the so-called "apparent" retroactivity of legal rules are relevant to the entire field covered by the administrative law of the Community.

I. THE DUTY OF THE LEGISLATOR TO OBSERVE, IN PRINCIPLE, THE RULES OF LEGAL CERTAINTY AND THE PROTECTION OF LEGITIMATE EXPECTATIONS

There can no longer be any doubt that in Community law the legislator is also, in the execution of his task, bound by the overriding principles of legal certainty and of the protection of legitimate expectations. Thus, for example, in the context of the question whether it was possible to raise the infringement of the principle of the protection of legitimate expectations in the course of an action for annulment against a Commission regulation, the Court ruled that the principle of the protection of legitimate expectations

> "forms part of the Community legal order with the result that any failure to comply with it is an 'infringement of the Treaty or of any rule of law relating to its application.' "[3]

E.C.R. 759; Case 224/82 *Meiko-Konservenfabrik* v. *Bundesrepublik Deutschland* [1983] E.C.R. 2539; Case 170/86 v. *Deetzen* v. *HZA Hamburg-Jonas* [1988] E.C.R. 2355. *cf.* on these decisions also K.-D. Borchardt, "Vertrauensschutz im Europäischen Gemeinschaftsrecht," EuGRZ, p. 309.

[2] Case 81/72 *Commission* v. *Council* [1973] E.C.R. 575—*cf.* on this subject H. P. Ipsen, Annotation in EuR 1973, p. 333; Case 127/80 *Grogan* v. *Commission* [1982] E.C.R. 869, and other parallel decisions.

[3] Case 112/77 *A. Töpfer* v. *Commission* [1978] E.C.R. 1019 at 1032—here, however, the action for annulment by private parties under the second paragraph of Article 173 EEC is

Nevertheless, from a very early stage onwards the Court claimed for itself jurisdiction to assess the admissibility of the retroactivity of legislative instruments, without however providing any concrete details on the conditions which had to be fulfilled for this admissibility.

Thus in the case of *Neumann* v. *Hauptzollamt Hof/Saale*, decided in June 1967, the Court stated, on the question of the authority of the legislator to determine himself, in accordance with Article 191 EEC, the moment at which regulations take effect that[4]

> "the wide liberty granted to the authors of a regulation cannot, however, be considered as excluding all review by the Court, particularly with regard to any retroactive effect. An institution cannot, without having an adverse effect on a legitimate regard for legal certainty, resort without reason to the procedure of an immediate entry into force."

Thus it became an established rule that the legislature was also bound by the principles of legal certainty and of the protection of legitimate expectations. At present, the Court confines itself to the terse statement that the fact that the legislature is thus bound belongs to the "fundamental principles of the Community."[5]

The first decision in which the Court effectively applied the principle of the protection of legitimate expectations—admittedly with the assistance of other considerations—against a rule-making instrument was the well-known ruling on staff remuneration in 1973.[6]

On March 21, 1972, the Council had, in accordance with Article 65 of the Staff Regulations, taken a decision on the procedures it intended to follow in the future when fixing the new salary levels of Community officials, subject to the express proviso that this would not give rise to "vested rights" on the part of the officials. However, by a Regulation of December 12, 1972 "on the harmonisation of officials' salaries and benefits," the Council took advantage of the first opportunity which arose to depart from its earlier decision in a way which disadvantaged the officials. Although in the course of the judicial proceedings brought as a result of this regulation, Advocate-General Warner, in an exhaustive comparative

admissible only under conditions which, as in this case, are capable of depriving the legal instrument of its character as a genuine regulation.
[4] Case 17/67 *Neumann* v. *Hauptzollamt Hof/Saale* [1967] E.C.R. 591 at 611.
[5] Case 112/80 *Dürbeck* v. *Hauptzollamt Frankfurt/Main—Flughafen* [1981] E.C.R. 1095 at 1120.
[6] Case 81/72 *Commission* v. *Council* [1973] E.C.R. 575 *et seq.*

analysis, rejected the notion that the legislature could effectively bind itself and consequently proposed that the action for annulment brought by the Commission against the Council regulation be dismissed,[7] the Court found for the applicant on the following grounds[8]:

> "Taking account of the particular staff/employer relationship which forms the background to the implementation of Article 65 of the Staff Regulations, and the aspects of consultation which its application involved, the rule of protection of the confidence that the staff could have that the authorities would respect undertakings of this nature implies that the Decision of 21 March 1972 binds the Council in its future action. Whilst this rule is primarily applicable to individual decisions, the possibility cannot by any means be excluded that it should relate, when appropriate, to the exercise of more general powers."

In this decision, it is interesting to note that the Court used the infringement of the principle of the protection of legitimate expectation not only to award a claim for damages, but also to accept that the legislature had bound itself, with the result that the latter was prevented from amending the relevant legal position once again in the short term.

Admittedly the Court qualified its principled position by adding the following consideration:

> "Furthermore, the adjustment each year of remunerations provided for in Article 65 only constitutes an implementing measure of an administrative rather than a legislative nature, and is within the framework of the Council's application of that provision."[9]

In its decision in the *Westzucker* case,[10] which followed shortly afterwards, the Court was called upon to review, in the context of a preliminary ruling, the compatibility of an agricultural regulation by the Council with the principle of the protection of legitimate expectations. Here, the Court unreservedly acknowledged that the principle of the protection of

---

[7] [1973] E.C.R. 592 *et seq.*
[8] [1973] E.C.R. 584.
[9] *Ibid.*
[10] Case 1/73 *Westzucker GmbH* v. *Einfuhr- und Vorratsstelle für Zucker* [1973] E.C.R. 723 *et seq.*

legitimate expectations was a rule which the Community legislature was also bound to observe.[11]

In this case, it was beyond dispute that the regulation in question, which amended a provision contained in an earlier regulation, could have no "actual" retroactivity.

In his opinion, Advocate-General Roemer made particular reference to the case law of the German Federal Constitutional Court relating to the problem of retroactivity. He arrived at the conclusion that the new regulation did not impinge upon legal positions which were already acquired ("vested rights"). At the same time, he examined the question whether the principle of the protection of legitimate expectations had not been infringed in this particular case.[12]

The Court did not follow the Advocate-General, stating first of all that

"according to a generally accepted principle . . . the laws amending a legislative provision apply, unless otherwise provided, to the future consequences of situations which arose under the former law."[13]

The ECJ went on to examine whether the legitimate expectation of the person affected, which was worthy of protection, had not been infringed by the adoption of the new regulation. Although the Court replied in the negative to this question, it was to arrive at a different conclusion shortly afterwards in Case 74/74.[14]

Thus the foundations for the subsequent case law had been laid. In addition, it became clear, as early as in the *Westzucker* case, that the concept of the protection of legitimate expectation exceeds the scope of the protection of the maintenance of the legal positions of individuals or that of "vested rights"—which were not relevant in this case.[15] This principle also extends to "mere" legitimate expectations.

In relation to rule-making acts, the principles of the protection of legitimate expectations and of legal certainty have played their part in the context of both claims for compensation under Article 215 EEC and preliminary rulings under Article 177 EEC. Although on several occasions the Advocates-General have proposed that the principle of the

---

[11] P. Gilsdorf, "Vertrauensschutz, Bestandsschutz und Rückwirkungsbegrenzung im Gemeinschaftsrecht," RIW 1983, pp. 22, 23.
[12] *cf.* Advocate-General Roemer in Case 1/73 *Westzucker GmbH* v. *Einfuhr- und Vorratsstelle für Zucker* [1973] E.C.R. 738 at 740.
[13] [1973] E.C.R. 729.
[14] Case 74/74 *CNTA* v. *Commission* [1975] E.C.R. 523 *et seq.*
[15] The same applies to Case 81/72 mentioned above, *Commission* v. *Council* [1973] E.C.R. 575 at 584.

protection of legitimate expectations should be relevant only in the context of claims for damages,[16] the Court has refused to entertain such a restrictive interpretation. As the Court noted in Case 112/77, which has already been mentioned, the principle of the protection of legitimate expectations must also, where appropriate, be observed in the context of an action for annulment under the second paragraph of Article 173 EEC.[17] In addition, the principle of the protection of legitimate expectations can also be relevant when used in support of a plea of illegality raised against the underlying regulation in the course of an action against an administrative measure. ECJ decisions to that effect exist both in the context of the ECSC[18] and in that of the staff cases.[19]

Finally, the Court has disregarded opinions to the contrary expressed in certain quarters[20] where, in considering the question whether or not the legislature was bound by the principles of legal certainty and of the protection of legitimate expectations, it has made no distinction in principle between Council regulations on the one hand and Commission regulations—in particular those which are derived from Council regulations—on the other.[21] The Council is bound just as strongly to observe these principles as the Commission. Conversely, the prohibition of retroactivity applies with equal force to derived Commission regulations as it does to key regulations made by the Council.

---

[16] *cf., e.g.* the opinion of Advocate-General Mayras in Case 151/77 *Kaiser KG* v. *Hauptzollamt Hamburg-Ericus* [1979] E.C.R. 1469 at 1502; Advocate-General Reischl in Case 88/76 *Exportation des sucres* v. *Commission* [1977] E.C.R. 709 at 727 and Advocate-General Trabucchi in Case 47/75 *Germany* v. *Commission* [1976] E.C.R. 569 at 589 *et seq.*

[17] Case 112/77 *A. Töpfer* v. *Commission* [1978] E.C.R. 1019 at 1032; *cf.* on this issue also Advocate-General Reischl in Case 88/76 *Exportations des sucres* v. *Commission*, who doubted whether the principle of the protection of legitimate expectations "was at all appropriate" in the context of an action for annulment.

[18] Case 258/80 *Romi* v. *Commission* [1982] E.C.R. 487 and Case 276/80 *Padano* v. *Commission* [1982] E.C.R. 517—actions under Article 33 (2) ECSC—and Case 235/82 *Ferriere San Carlo SpA* v. *Commission* [1983] E.C.R. 3949 at 3965—action under the second paragraph of Article 36 ECSC.

[19] Case 127/80 *V. Grogan* v. *Commission* [1980] E.C.R. 869.

[20] *cf., e.g.* the comparative analysis made by Advocate-General Warner in Case 7/76 *IRCA* v. *Amministrazione delle Finanze dello Stato* [1976] E.C.R. 1213 at 1236 *et seq.*, also, M. Akehurst, "The Application of General Principles of Law by the Court of Justice of the European Community," in *British Yearbook of International Law 1981*, p. 29.

[21] P. Gilsdorf, "Vertrauensschutz, Bestandsschutz und Rückwirkungsbegrenzung im Gemeinschaftsrecht," RIW 1983, p. 22 at 28 *et seq.*

II. THE PROTECTION OF LEGITIMATE EXPECTATIONS IN RELATION TO CHANGES IN LEGAL POSITIONS—THE RETROACTIVITY OF RULES

The main field of application of the principles of legal certainty and of the protection of legitimate expectations is the review of rule-making acts from the point of view of retroactivity. After the Court had, in the cases cited above ("Remuneration of Officials" and "Westzucker"),[22] made it known that it was in principle also prepared to assess Community legislative acts in the light of these principles, the question whether the retroactivity of rules was admissible has played an important part in the case law of the ECJ. The central question, according to the Court, was whether regulations could be given "retroactive effect in the proper sense of the expression."[23] Although the Court had already at an early stage made it clear that the "actual" retroactivity of legal acts would be fraught with problems, it has on successive occasions succeeded in evading the question of setting out in detail the conditions for the admissibility of such retroactivity. In most cases, it took the view that such "actual" retroactivity did not apply in the particular case before it. Accordingly, a more decisive criterion in this respect will be constituted by the principles which the Court has developed for the purpose of distinguishing between the various categories of cases, and in particular on the subject of "actual" retroactivity.

1. Principles Relating to the Validity of Legal Rules in Time and in Substance

Under Article 191 EEC, regulations enter into force on the date specified in them or, in the absence of such specification, on the twentieth day following their publication. The date of publication is deemed to be the day on which the Official Journal containing the text of the regulation actually becomes available. The Court has stated on this subject that

"a fundamental principle in the Community legal order requires that a measure adopted by the public authorities shall not be applicable to

---

[22] Case 81/72 *Commission* v. *Council* [1973] E.C.R. 575 *et seq.*; Case 1/73 *Westzucker GmbH* v. *Einfuhr- und Vorratsstelle für Zucker* [1973] E.C.R. 723 *et seq.*

[23] Case 74/74 *CNTA* v. *Commission* [1975] E.C.R. 523 *et seq.*

those concerned before they have the opportunity to make themselves acquainted with it."[24]

In principle, the Community institutions are free to determine the time at which a legal act enters into effect.[25] In so doing, they are bound to observe the principles of legal certainty, of the protection of legitimate expectations and of proportionality. Thus in Case 17/67,[26] the ECJ was called upon to rule whether it was possible for a Regulation to determine that it would enter into effect on the date of its publication. Although the Court made its ruling on the basis that the immediate entry into effect could not have been laid down without good reason, it arrived at the conclusion that in this case it had been necessary to decree that the measure in question should take immediate effect in order to prevent commercial agreements seeking to circumvent the disputed regulation from being concluded between the time of publication and the moment of entry into force.

By virtue of its entry into force, the regulation in question becomes, in principle, applicable to every situation which comes within its scope. This will not give rise to any problems in relation to events which occur after the entry into force of the regulation. It is, however, more difficult to establish under what conditions it is permissible to subject to the authority of a regulation events which have occurred before its publication.

(a) Actual retroactivity

There is "actual" retroactivity where a rule is to be introduced by the legislature in respect of events which have already been concluded.[27] This "actual" retroactivity may result either from the fact that the entry into effect of a regulation is fixed for a date which occurs before the date of its publication or from the circumstance that the regulation applies to situations which have not only come into existence but have also actually been concluded before its entry into effect. Here, the terminology used is

---

[24] Thus the E.C.J. declared in Case 98/78 *Racke* v. *Hauptzollamt Mainz* [1979] E.C.R. 69 at 84.

[25] Case 57/72 *Westzucker GmbH* v. *Einfuhr- und Vorratsstelle für Zucker* [1973] E.C.R. 321 at 341.

[26] Case 17/67 *Neumann* v. *Hauptzollamt Hof/Saale* [1967] E.C.R. 591 *et seq.* at 611.

[27] Advocate-General Roemer in Case 1/73 *Westzucker GmbH* v. *Einfuhr- und Vorratsstelle für Zucker* [1973] E.C.R. 733 *et seq.* at 738; P. Gilsdorf, *loc. cit.*, footnote 21, p. 27.

drawn especially from the case law of the German Federal Constitutional Court, which makes a distinction between "actual" and "apparent" retroactivity—a concept which has, however, in recent times become subject to numerous qualifications.[28]

On the subject of "actual" retroactivity, the established case law of the Court is that

> "in general, the principle of legal certainty precludes a Community measure from taking effect from a point in time before its publication."[29]

However, exceptions to this rule are in theory permissible where

> "the purpose to be achieved so demands, and where the legitimate expectations of those concerned are duly respected."[30]

This exception has assumed relevance only for the fixing in the short term, and subject to corrections, of the monetary compensatory amounts in the context of the Common Agricultural Policy.

(b) Apparent retroactivity

"Apparent retroactivity" is deemed to be the applicability of legislative acts to events which originated in the past but which have yet to be definitively concluded.

The problems surrounding this issue have become particularly acute in cases in which the conditions of repayment are changed after the issuing of export licences but before the export of agricultural products. Here, the question arises whether export refunds are governed by the old legal

---

[28] *cf.* only the decision of the BVerfG of May 14, 1986, RIW 1986 pp. 651 *et seq.* (657), in which it was claimed that the category of cases concerning actual retroactivity, as with that concerning apparent retroactivity, is an expression of the fundamental notion that only overriding public interests or a legitimate expectation on the part of the individual which is worthy of protection but no longer available can justify or even require a derogation, for the benefit of the freedom of action on the part of the legislator, from the prohibition of retroactivity which is inherent in the rule of law. *cf.* also J. Fiedler, "Neuorientierung der Verfassungsrechtsprechung zum Rückwirkungsverbot und zum Vertrauensschutz," NJW 1988, pp. 1624 *et seq.*

[29] Case 98/78 *Racke* v. *Hauptzollamt Mainz* [1979] E.C.R. 69 at 86: Case 99/78 *Decker* v. *Hauptzollamt Landau* [1979] E.C.R. 101 *et seq.* at 111; Case 224/82, *Meiko-Konservenfabrik* v. *Federal Republic of Germany* [1983] E.C.R. 2539 *et seq.* at 2548.

[30] *Ibid.*

rules applicable at the time when the licences were issued, or whether the law which applies at the time at which the export actually takes place is the valid one.

On this issue the Court, in accordance with its established case law, states that

> "according to a generally accepted principle, the laws amending a legislative provision apply, unless otherwise provided, to the future consequences of situations which arose under the former law."[31]

The Court has, ever since its decision in the 1973 *Westzucker* case mentioned above, also applied this principle to the disadvantage of the persons in question, *i.e.* where the change in legal position adversely affects their interests. As will be discussed in greater detail later, the Court is thus faced with the question of the safeguarding of vested rights and of the protection of legitimate expectations.

The Court has not as yet used the term "apparent retroactivity." Only in the *CNTA* case has it referred to a regulation having no "retroactive effect in the proper sense of the expression."[32]

2. The Conditions for the Admissibility of Actual Retroactivity—a Detailed Survey

Both the Court and the Advocates-General have, in a series of decisions, held the unrestricted retroactivity of rules to be inadmissible. Thus the Advocates-General have pointed out in, *inter alia*, various staff cases that the provisions of the Staff Regulations could at all times be amended, but only if the amending provisions had "no retroactive effect to the detriment of the employees"[33]—so as not to impair vested rights.

---

[31] Case 1/73, *loc. cit.*, footnote 22, p. 729; Case 143/73 *Société des produits alimentaires et diététiques (Sopad) SA* v. *Fonds d'orientation et de régularisation des marchés agricoles (Forma) et Fonds d'intervention et de régularisation du marché du sucre (Firs)* [1973] E.C.R. 1433 at 1441; Case 96/77 *S.A. Ancienne Maison Marcel Bauche and S.a.r.l. François Dequiquis* v. *French Customs Authority* [1978] E.C.R. 383 at 400; Advocate-General Capotorti, *ibid.* p. 411; Case 125/77 *Scholten Honig* v. *Hoofdproduktschap voor Akkerbouwprodukten* [1978] E.C.R. 1991 at 2005; Case 40/79 *Mrs. P.* v. *Commission* [1981] E.C.R. 361 *et seq.* at 373.

[32] Case 74/74 *CNTA* v. *Commission* [1975] E.C.R. 533 at 548.

[33] Advocate-General Mayras in Case 28/74 *Gillet* v. *Commission* [1975] E.C.R. 463 at 478; Advocate-General Capotorti in Case 167/80 *Curtis* v. *Commission and European Parliament* [1981] E.C.R. 1499 at 1551, and the same Advocate-General in Case 127/80 *Grogan* v. *Commission* [1982] E.C.R. 869 at 898.

In a judgment relating to social security law, the Court held that a certain Regulation provision had entered into effect retroactively, but that

> "nevertheless this retroactive effect cannot prejudice in any way the persons whose entitlement to benefit was acquired before the publication of Regulation No. 130."[34]

In addition, the Court has consistently rejected the retroactivity of Regulation provisions which define more closely the tariff positions of the Common Customs Tariff.

Since such regulations were "of a legislative nature," they could not "have any retroactive effect." Accordingly, they could not "be applied for the purpose of determining the classification of products imported before its entry into force."[35]

In the case of *Regina* v. *Kent Kirk*, the Court ultimately resorted expressly to the legal systems of the Member States and to the provisions of the European Convention on Human Rights on the question of the retroactivity of penal provisions. In the course of criminal proceedings based on an infringement of the fisheries legislation of a Member State, the ECJ was called upon to give a preliminary ruling on the question whether a Council Regulation of January 25, 1983, by which, with retroactive effect from January 1, 1983, certain national protective measures, which were intrinsically contrary to Community law as contravening the prohibition of discrimination, were approved by way of a transitional arrangement, could acquire retroactive effect also in relation to national (penal) provisions. On this issue, the Court held that[36]

> "the principle that penal provisions may not have retroactive effect is one which is common to all the legal orders of the Member States and is enshrined in Article 7 of the European Convention of Human Rights and Fundamental Freedoms as a fundamental right; it takes its place among the general principles of law whose observance is ensured by the Court of Justice.

[34] Case 100/63 *Kalsbeek-van de Veen* v. *Sociale Verzekeringsbank* [1964] E.C.R. 1214 at 1234.

[35] Case 77/71 *Gervais-Danone* v. *Hauptzollamt München* [1971] E.C.R. 1127 at 1137; also, *e.g.* Case 158/78 *P. Biegi* v. *Hauptzollamt Bochum* [1979] E.C.R. 1103 at 1119, and Case 196/80 *Anglo-Irish Beef Company* v. *Minister for Agriculture* [1981] E.C.R. 2263 at 2282.

[36] Case 63/83 *Regina* v. *Kent Kirk* [1984] E.C.R. 2689 at 2718; *cf.* also on a similar case, Case 82/71 *Italian Public Ministry* v. *SAIL* [1972] E.C.R. 119; Advocate-General Roemer *ibid.* p. 152.

> Consequently the retroactivity provided for in Article 6(1) of
> Regulation No. 170/83 cannot be regarded as validating *ex post facto*
> national measures which imposed criminal penalties, at the time of
> the conduct at issue, if those measures were not valid."

In this decision, the Court specifically gave to the prohibition of the
retroactivity of penal provisions the status of an autonomous principle of
Community law.

However, when it came to formulating general principles for dealing
with the actual retroactivity of rules—apart from the proviso of judicial
review already mentioned and the statements made by the Court in
relation to certain particular categories of circumstances—the Court for a
long period adopted a rather reticent stance. At regular intervals, the
ECJ was able to meet the plea of inadmissible retroactivity with the
observation that the rule in question was not subject to any actual
retroactivity. Thus, until recently there has been no adequate answer to
the question whether, and in what conditions, the Court would hold the
actual retroactivity of a rule to be permissible.

The first extensive comparative analysis of the relevant principles in
the legal systems of the Member States and in the ECHR can be found in
the opinion of Advocate-General Warner in the 1976 case of *IRCA* v.
Amministrazione delle Finanze dello Stato.[37] Here, the Commission had,
by a regulation of March 23, 1973, adjusted the monetary compensatory
amounts for certain products. The regulation in question provided that it
would enter into force on the day of its publication (April 7, 1973) but
would already apply to import transactions concluded on or after
February 26 or March 5, 1973. The imports which formed the basis of the
main action before the Italian court had taken place on March 22, 1973,
i.e. on the day before the adoption of the Regulation in question.

Advocate-General Warner considered this to be a case of actual
retroactivity. On the basis of an exhaustive comparative survey, he
proposed that the Court should rule as follows[38]:

> "Where a provision of the Treaty directly authorises the Council or
> the Commission to legislate, the analogy is with a national Parlia-
> ment empowered to enact statutes. Subject to the limitation that
> legitimate expectations may not be defeated, the Institution con-
> cerned is free to legislate retroactively, but it will be presumed not to

---

[37] Advocate-General Warner in Case 7/76, [1976] E.C.R. 1213 at 1234 *et seq.*
[38] Advocate-General Warner, *ibid.* pp. 1238 *et seq.*

do so. Its acts will be held to have retroactive effect only if and in so far as their terms evince, either expressly or by necessary implication, a clear intention that they should have that effect. Where however the Commission needs the authority of the Council to legislate, it can only do so within the bounds of the authority expressly or by necessary implication conferred upon it by the Council. It cannot therefore legislate retroactively unless thereunto so authorised by the Council."

According to Advocate-General Warner, the regulation in question was a derived regulation, on the understanding that the Commission had not obtained authorisation to enact retroactive measures. As a result, he considered the Regulation to be invalid.

The Court did not follow the opinion of its Advocate-General in this matter. It did not consider the Regulation to be one with retroactive effect, since it was intended only to adjust the monetary compensatory amounts in the short term, and such changes were already "inherent in the system."[39]

The principles governing the issue of "actual" retroactivity, which were later to be confirmed in a series of judgments, were formulated for the first time in the cases of *Racke* v. *Hauptzollamt Mainz*[40] and *Decker* v. *Hauptzollamt Landau*,[41] which were decided on the same day.

Here, the Commission had, in close succession, initially introduced monetary compensatory amounts for a certain product and subsequently, in two further Regulations, changed the applicable amounts. Each of these three Regulations specified that the date on which it would start to apply was one which preceded by fourteen days its publication (or entry into force).[42] On this question, the ECJ initially stated the following principle[43]:

"Although in general the principle of legal certainty precludes a Community measure from taking effect from a point in time before its publication, it may exceptionally be otherwise where the purpose

---

[39] E.C.R. *ibid.* p. 1228.
[40] Case 98/78 *Racke* v. *Hauptzollamt Mainz* [1979] E.C.R. 69.
[41] Case 99/78 *Decker* v. *Hauptzollamt Landau* [1979] E.C.R. 101.
[42] These regulations were to enter into force on the date on which they were published, but at the same time fixed a certain date as being the time on which they were to become applicable. The publication was however delayed.
[43] Case 98/78, *loc. cit.*, footnote 40, p. 86; also Case 99/78, *loc. cit.*, footnote 41, p. 111.

to be achieved so demands and where the legitimate expectations of those concerned are duly respected."

The need for the retroactive effect of the regulation in question was justified by the ECJ by reference to the special conditions to which monetary compensatory amounts are subject. In addition, the retroactivity in question was only a short-term one. As was the case in the *IRCA* judgment, the ECJ emphasised that the very nature of the system required an immediate adjustment to changes in exchange rates; the Court also recognised in this instance the need for retroactivity in relation to the possible inclusion of new categories of products in the system of monetary compensatory amounts.

On the subject of the observance of the principle of the protection of legitimate expectations, the Court held that

"traders must expect any appreciable change in the monetary situation possibly to entail the extension of the system to new categories of goods and the fixing of new amounts. In this case, on the date laid down for the applicability of the new amounts, the Commission adopted special measures for them to be brought to the attention of the various sectors of industry concerned."[44]

In conclusion, the ECJ saw no reason to declare the regulation in question invalid.

The Court was faced with a similar situation in the *Staple Dairy Products* case.[45] Here too, the case concerned monetary compensatory amounts. On April 23, 1980, the Commission had adopted a regulation which was published on April 26, 1980 and by which the period of validity of another regulation, which was originally due to expire on March 31, 1980, was extended with effect from April 1, 1980 on the understanding, however, that the "individual rights of the persons affected" would not be infringed.

The Court decided that this reservation had to be interpreted as meaning that it would apply only in cases in which definitive administrative measures had already been adopted by the appropriate authorities for the

---

[44] E.C.J. *ibid.*
[45] Case 84/81, *Staple Dairy Products* v. *Intervention Board for Agricultural Produce* [1982] E.C.R. 1763 *et seq.*

benefit of the persons affected between April 1 and 25, 1980. For the rest, however, the Regulation was applicable to those transactions which had been concluded between April 1 and 25. Referring to the above-mentioned formula applied in the *Racke* and *Decker* cases, the Court did not see fit in this case to call into doubt the lawfulness of the retroactivity in question. Retroactivity was necessary in order to avoid any distortions arising from the gap in time. No legitimate expectation could be protected here, on the grounds that

> "the history of the rules in question, as well as their scope and purpose, were such as to lead traders to conclude" that the rules which applied until 31.3.1980 "would be maintained for some time."[46]

Of particular interest, even though once again the persons affected failed to benefit from them, are the decisions of the Court, made in 1982,[47] on the question of the introduction of a system of production quotas for isoglucose. One of the relevant Council regulations having been declared void on grounds of an infringement of essential procedural requirements—namely the failure to consult Parliament—by a decision of October 29, 1980 in the *Roquette Frères*[48] case, the Council once again enacted the provisions of the annulled Regulation, having this time observed the necessary formalities, by a Regulation of February 10, 1981, which applied retroactively to the period between July 1, 1979 and June 30, 1980. On the question of the validity of the Regulation, the ECJ initially referred once again to the formula used in the *Racke* decisions. It then proceeded to justify the need for the retroactive reintroduction of the rules set aside by the Court's earlier decision in the following terms:

> "Thus the Council was lawfully entitled to consider that the objective to be achieved in the general interest, namely the stabilisation of the Community market in sweeteners without arbitrary discrimination between traders, required the contested provisions to be retroactive in nature, and thus the first of the conditions which the Court lays down for the applicability *ratione temporis* of a Community measure

---

[46] E.C.J. *loc. cit.*, footnote 45, p. 1778.
[47] Case 108/81 *Amylum* v. *Council* [1982] E.C.R. 3107; Case 110/81 *Roquette Frères* v. *Council* [1982] E.C.R. 3159 and Case 114/81 *Tunnel Refineries* v. *Council* [1982] E.C.R. 3189.
[48] Case 138/79 *SA Roquette Frères* v. *Council* [1980] E.C.R. 3333; also Case 139/79 *Maizena GmbH* v. *Council* [1980] E.C.R. 3393.

to a date prior to the date of its publication may be regarded as satisfied."[49]

The Court also did not consider that a legitimate expectation had been infringed here, and it proceeded to explain why there was no justified expectation, even in the objective sense, in this case.[50] According to the Court, the reason for this was particularly that the undertakings in question had been informed in such a way as to enable them to assess the situation correctly, and especially that it could not have escaped the applicants' attention that the decisions of October 29, 1980 had expressly endorsed the substantive lawfulness of the regulation which it had set aside; also, there could be no doubt that the Council had the definite intention of imposing a quota system on the production of isoglucose.[51]

The Court did not share the reservation expressed by the applicants that the principles which had been developed in relation to retroactivity in the short term in the field of monetary compensatory amounts were not capable of being extended to the case of a far-reaching change in the legal position, as was the case here.

The Court thus answered in the affirmative a question which was the subject of dispute between the parties, i.e. whether it was permissible for the legislature to replace, with retroactive effect, a rule annulled by the Court by a new rule whose substance was the same as the previous one, pointing out that the substantive validity of the regulation in question had been confirmed by the earlier judgment.[52]

In the cases which concerned the "retroactive" introduction of steel production quotas,[53] the ECJ, even though the general decision in question did not in its view possess "actual" retroactivity, also arrived at the conclusion that the criteria developed in the *Racke* decision for the admissibility of "actual" retroactivity had definitely been fulfilled in this case.[54]

---

[49] Case 108/81 *loc. cit.*, footnote 47, pp. 3131 *et seq.*; *cf.* on this subject extensively Advocate-General Reischl, pp. 3146 *et seq.*

[50] *cf.* also Advocate-General Reischl, p. 3148.

[51] E.C.J., *loc. cit.*, pp. 3132 *et seq.*

[52] Case 108/81 *loc. cit.*, footnote 47, pp. 3133 *et seq.*; Case 110/81, *loc. cit.*, footnote 47, pp. 3181 *et seq.*; Case 114/81, *loc. cit.*, footnote 47, p. 3209.

[53] Case 258/80 *Rumi* v. *Commission* [1982] E.C.R. 487; confirmed in Case 276/80 *Padana* v. *Commission* [1982] E.C.R. 517 at 541 and Case 235/82 *Ferriere San Carlo SpA* v. *Commission* [1983] E.C.R. 3449 at 3965; *cf.* on this subject also M. Schlockermann, *Rechtssicherheit als Vertrauensschutz in der Rechtsprechung des EuGH*, Diss. München, p 1984, p. 64.

[54] Case 258/80, *loc. cit.*, footnote 53, p. 503.

In a further decision, however, the Court declared invalid a provision contained in a Commission regulation on the grounds that it infringed the principle of the protection of legitimate expectations. In the course of the preliminary ruling procedure in the case of *Meiko-Konservenfabrik* v. *Federal Republic of Germany*,[55] the ECJ was called upon to rule on the validity of Regulation 2946/80 of October 2, 1980, published in the Official Journal of October 3, 1980, by which July 31, 1980 had been retroactively fixed as a deadline by which certain contracts had to be submitted to the relevant authorities for the purpose of obtaining financial assistance.

Here too, the Court first referred to the generally accepted principles governing retroactivity, and then stated that

> "by retroactively subjecting the payment of aid to the forwarding of the contracts by 31 July 1980 the Commission acted in breach of the legitimate expectation of the persons concerned, who, having regard to the provisions in force at the time the contracts were concluded, could not reasonably have anticipated the retroactive imposition of a time-limit for forwarding the contracts which coincided with the time-limit for their conclusion."[56]

The Court saw no reason to proceed to a special examination of the question whether, and if so, to what extent, this retroactivity was necessary given the objective pursued. The ECJ concluded by declaring the regulation invalid to the extent that it fixed July 31, 1980 as the relevant deadline.

The position can be summarised by saying that the Court has not excluded the possibility of permitting the actual retroactivity of regulations. In so doing, it applies equal standards to Council regulations and to those issued by the Commission; also, the ECJ draws no distinction between the power to issue primary legislation and the authority to enact secondary legislation. Although "real" retroactivity is in principle not permissible, this rule admits of certain exceptions. The main criterion to be applied in this regard will be whether "the purpose to be achieved demands" that the rule in question be given retroactive effect. It is clear from the relevant case law that not every consideration based on the object to be achieved will be acceptable.

---

[55] Case 224/82 *Meiko-Konservenfabrik* v. *Federal Republic of Germany* [1983] E.C.R. 2539.
[56] E.C.J. *ibid.* p. 2549.

Instead, the retroactivity in question must be necessary for the achievement of the objective, which itself must serve the public interest.[57]

The case law of the Court gives no support to the view that, if a "compelling interest" is involved, the existence of any legitimate expectation is irrelevant.[58] The decision in the *Meiko* case would appear to refute this view, since here the regulation in question was declared invalid solely on the basis of an infringement of the principle of the protection of legitimate expectations, without considering the issue of the interest pursued by the retroactivity of the regulation.

Accordingly, it must be assumed that account must be taken at all times of the legitimate expectation of the person in question. However, the case law as it stands at present indicates that the requirements which must be met for such legitimate expectation to be acknowledged are relatively high. Even a justified legitimate expectation would not serve to exclude retroactivity altogether, since according to the words used by the ECJ, it is sufficient for this legitimate expectation to have been "duly respected."[59] In the final analysis, it will be necessary to weigh up the conflicting interests, in the course of which a decisive factor will be the principle of proportionality, which is also recognised in Community law.[60]

3. The Conditions for the Operation of Apparent Retroactivity of Normative Acts

(a) *The protection of legitimate expectations as a restriction on the legislator's freedom to legislate*

It is the established case law of the Court of Justice that normally, in relation to changes in the legal position, traders

"are unable to invoke a vested right in order to maintain a certain benefit,"[61] that "Community institutions enjoy a margin of discre-

---

[57] *cf.* Advocate-General Slynn in Case 84/81, *loc. cit.*, footnote 45, p. 1783.
[58] This question is raised by F. Lamoureux, "The Retroactivity of Community Acts in the Case Law of the Court of Justice," C.M.L.Rev. 1983, p. 269 (292); *cf.* on this subject also M. Schlockermann, *loc. cit.*, footnote 53, p. 78.
[59] Case 98/78, *loc. cit.*, footnote 40, p. 86, established case law.
[60] On this principle, *cf.* Chapter V.
[61] *e.g.* Case 230/80 *SpA Eridania* v. *Minister für Landwirtschaft und Forsten* [1979] E.C.R. 2749 at 2768; Case 59/83 *SA Biovilac* v. *EEC* [1984] E.C.R. 4057 at 4080; for a similar ruling, *cf.* Joined Cases 197–200, 243 248 & 247/80, *Ludwigshafener Walzmühle et al.* v. *Council and Commission* [1981] E.C.R. 3211 at 3251; Case 26/77 *Balkan Import-Export GmbH* v. *Hauptzollamt Berlin-Packhof* [1977] E.C.R. 2031 at 2045.

tion in the choice of the means needed to achieve their policies" and that "traders are unable to claim that they have a legitimate expectation that an existing situation which is capable of being altered by decisions taken by those institutions within the limits of their discretionary powers will be maintained."[62]

In these judgments, the Court has emphasised the essential freedom enjoyed by the legislature to alter for the future the fundamental legal conditions in which traders operate, even if the changes made work to the disadvantage of certain firms, or in some cases to the disadvantage of all firms in a certain industrial sector. In particular, the plea of infringement of fundamental rights or of the principle of the protection of legitimate expectations has been rejected where the actions in question are based only on the circumstance that the trading position of the firms in question has deteriorated as a result of changes in the legal position.

Similar considerations apply in the field of staff disputes. Here too, the Community legislature may in principle change the provisions of the Staff Regulations at any time, with effect for the future, even if such changes work to the disadvantage of the officials. Normally, the latter will not be able to rely, in relation to such changes, upon vested rights which guarantee the maintenance of a certain legal position.[63]

This general and broad freedom of action enjoyed by the legislature admits of exceptions in the current state of the ECJ case law only where the general legal relationship to which a large number of traders[64] are subject has found a certain degree of concrete expression. For this to be the case, it is not even necessary that the interests in question should be individual legal positions acquired on the basis of an earlier administrative measure. It is, however, necessary that concrete obligations should have been imposed or provisions enacted, or that certain assurances should have been given by the relevant authorities.

---

[62] Case 52/81 *W. Faust* v. *Commission* [1982] E.C.R. 3745 at 3762; similarly, Case 245/81 *Edeka* v. *Federal Republic of Germany* [1982] E.C.R. 2745 at 2758 and Case 14/81 *Alpha Steel* v. *Commission* [1982] E.C.R. 749 at 769.

[63] *cf.* on this subject, *e.g.* Case 28/74 *Gillet* v. *Commission* [1975] E.C.R. 463; Advocate-General Capotorti in Case 817/79 *Buyl* v. *Commission* [1982] E.C.R. 245, opinion in [1981] E.C.R. 1512 at 1553; opinion by the same Advocate-General in Case 127/80 *V. Grogan* v. *Commission* [1982] E.C.R. 869 at 898; *cf.* also Advocate-General Lagrange already in Joined Cases 7/56 & 3–7/57 *Algera et al.* v. *Common Assembly* [1957] E.C.R. 39.

[64] The same applies to the law relating to staff disputes—*cf.* in particular on this subject Case 81/72 *Commission* v. *Council* [1973] E.C.R. 575 *et seq.*

Thus the principle of the protection of legitimate expectations ultimately occupies an important position in relation to changes in the legal position which take effect for the future, especially as regards contracts which are already in the course of completion at the time of publication, or other events which have started to take effect at this time.

Here, it is in principle the formula regarding the "apparent" retroactivity which has been regularly used by the Court since the *Westzucker* decision which applies[65]:

> "According to a generally accepted principle, the laws amending legislative provisions apply, unless otherwise provided, to the future consequences of situations which arose under former laws."

Where in such cases—as in certain subsequent decisions—the reservation is expressed that the immediate applicability applies "inasmuch as the intended exportation had not yet taken place and an adjustment of the intervention price had not been made,"[66] this formula reveals essentially a mere rule of interpretation. This is not tantamount to stating that there are vested rights here which in principle exclude the possibility that a regulation could apply to events which have already been concluded to the detriment of the person in question. The legislature would not be prevented in principle from withdrawing individual legal positions once again by means of an administrative measure.[67] Instead, the withdrawal of such individual rights should be assessed against the principle of the protection of legitimate expectations. Then the question becomes one of legislative formulation or of the scope of the quite far-reaching definition of "actual retroactivity," namely whether the enactment of rules is also a question of "actual" or "apparent" retroactivity in relation to events which have already been completed.

In the case law as it stands at present, the principle of the protection of legitimate expectation has played a part especially where the concrete expression of the legal relationship had not reached the level of a justification of individualised, definitive legal interests or of "vested rights." Significant in this regard is, for example, the *CNTA* decision,[68] a decision

---

[65] Case 1/73 *Westzucker* v. *Einfuhr- und Vorratsstelle* [1973] E.C.R. 723 at 729; *cf.* also on this subject Case 68/69 *Bundesknappschaft* v. *Brock* [1970] E.C.R. 171 at 178.

[66] Case 1/73, *loc. cit.*, footnote 65; in this sense also Advocate-General Roemer, *ibid.*, pp. 738 *et seq.*; Advocate-General Trabucchi in Case 74/74 *NTA* v. *Commission* [1975] E.C.R. 533 at 555.

[67] *cf.* on this subject also Case 74/74, *loc. cit.*, footnote 66, as well as Case 37/73 *Filli Variola SpA* v. *Amministrazione italiana delle Finanze* [1973] E.C.R. 981 *et seq.*

[68] Case 74/74 *CNTA* v. *Commission* [1975] E.C.R. 533 *et seq.*

relating to monetary compensatory amounts in the field of agricultural policy, the frequent short-term changes to which have often presented the Court with issues relating to the protection of legitimate expectation as regards contracts which were already in the course of completion but not yet fully completed at the time of publication of the amending regulation. The CNTA company had obtained an export licence for a certain product, arranged for the export refunds to be fixed in advance and lodged the required deposit.

Shortly before these proceedings, monetary compensatory amounts had been introduced for the product in question. These amounts, which could not be fixed in advance, were revoked again by the Commission at short notice, before the export envisaged by CNTA could be effected. Thereupon the applicant brought an action for damages. In principle, the applicant succeeded in its action.[69] In support of its application, the applicant claimed that "the withdrawal of the compensatory amounts with immediate effect destroyed the expectation which he had of their maintenance when he sought the advance fixing of aid and refunds on exports, thus definitively undertaking with the competent authorities to carry out commercial transactions from which he could not withdraw save under pain of forfeiting the deposit lodged."[70]

On this question, the Court initially held that

> "the system of compensatory amounts cannot be considered tanta-mount to a guarantee for traders against the risks of alteration of exchange rates.
>
> The ECJ conceded, however, that "the application of the compensatory amounts in practice avoids the exchange risk, so that a trader, even a prudent one, might be induced to omit to cover himself against such risk. In those circumstances, a trader may legitimately expect that for transactions irrevocably undertaken by him because he has obtained, subject to a deposit, export licences fixing the amount of the refund in advance, no unforeseeable alteration will occur which could have the effect of causing him inevitable loss, by re-exposing him to the exchange risk."

The Court then arrived at the conclusion that the Commission had

---

[69] This action succeeded only in principle, because the applicant ultimately failed to prove that damage had occurred; on this subject cf. [1976] E.C.R. 797 et seq.
[70] Case 74/74, loc. cit., footnote 68, p. 548.

"violated a superior rule of law, thus rendering the Community
liable by failing to include in Regulation 189/72 transitional measures
for the protection of the confidence which a trader might legitimately
have had in the Community rules."[71]

Here, the principle of the protection of legitimate expectations was
applied, although at the time at which the change in the law occurred the
granting of monetary compensatory amounts had not yet assumed the
concrete form of individualised legal interests.[72] At that moment, the
applicant had not yet acquired a valid right to the performance of a
certain obligation.[73] Instead, the Court considered that all that was
involved here was legitimate expectations. However, this was a case in
which a general legal relationship had found concrete expression in that
transactions were affected which had already been concluded and in
respect of which the applicant had entered into obligations towards, *inter
alia*, the relevant authorities. The applicant could no longer resile from
these obligations without forfeiting the deposit lodged. At the same time,
the Commission had, through its actions, caused the applicant to refrain
from safeguarding itself against any exchange rate risk. According to the
Court, the Commission should have taken this circumstance into account
by making transitional arrangements in respect of contracts which were
already in the course of completion.

Since this decision, this case law has been confirmed in principle in a
number of instances, but generally without benefiting the persons
affected. This case law can be summarised in the following terms[74]:

For the principle of the protection of legitimate expectations to be applicable, an objective basis must exist for this principle in the shape of an
expectation which is worthy of protection. Because of the broad freedom
of action enjoyed by the legislature, the mere existence of a legal rule is
not normally a suitable basis for a legitimate expectation which must be

---

[71] *Ibid.* p. 549.

[72] To apply this principle only *because* there were no vested rights involved, as the Advocates-General sometimes appear to be suggesting, (*cf.* Advocate-General Trabucchi,
p. 553; also Advocate-General Mayras, in Case 35/78 *Scholten* v. *Hoofdproduktschap
voor Akkerbouwprodukten* [1978] E.C.R. 2543 at 2563), is to restrict the concept of the
protection of legitimate expectations too narrowly to a protection of "justified
expectations."

[73] *cf.* Advocate-General Trabucchi in Case 74/74, *loc. cit.*, footnote 68, pp. 555 *et seq.*

[74] *cf.* on this subject also P. Gilsdorf, "Vertrauensschutz, Bestandsschutz und Rückwirkungsbegrenzung im Gemeinschaftsrecht," RIW 1983, p. 22 at 25 *et seq.* and M. Schlockermann, *loc. cit.*, footnote 53, pp. 81 *et seq.*

taken into account. Adequate grounds for a solid expectation can be provided on the one hand by the fact of having entered into certain obligations towards the authorities, or on the other hand by a course of conduct on the part of the authorities giving rise to specific expectations—which in certain circumstances may arise out of a commitment entered into by the authorities.

By reference to the decision in the *CNTA* case, the Court stated in the *Tomadini* case, for example, which also concerned monetary compensatory amounts, that[75]

> "in the context of economic rules such as those governing the common organisation of agricultural markets, if in order to deal with individual situations the Community institutions have laid down specific rules enabling traders in return for entering into certain obligations with the public authorities to protect themselves—as regards transactions definitively undertaken—from the effects of the necessarily frequent variations in the detailed rules for the application of the common organisation, the principle of respect for legitimate expectations prohibits these institutions from amending those rules without laying down transitional measures, unless the adoption of such a measure is contrary to an overriding public interest. On the other hand, the field of application of this principle cannot be extended to the point of generally preventing new rules from applying to the future effects of situations which arose under the earlier rules in the absence of obligations entered into with the public authorities. This is particularly true in a field such as the common organisation of markets, the purpose of which necessarily involves constant adjustment to the variations of the economic situation in the various agricultural sectors."

The plea of infringement of the principle of the protection of legitimate expectations was rejected by the Court, since this case concerned intra-Community trade, "in respect of which there is no refund or levy and consequently no advance fixing."[76]

On the same grounds, the Court also rejected the arguments invoking the principle of the protection of legitimate expectations in the *Dürbeck*

---

[75] Case 84/78 *A. Tomadini S.n.c.* v. *Amministrazione delle Finanze dello Stato* [1979] E.C.R. 1801 at 1814 *et seq.*

[76] E.C.J. *ibid.* p. 1815; on the other hand, those cases in which a licence had been granted for trade with non-member states were expressly exempted.

case.[77] This case did not concern monetary compensatory amounts; instead, the Commission had included in a measure of agricultural protection (an import ban) contracts which had been concluded before the adoption of the regulation but which had not yet been completed.

The protection of legitimate expectations is not restricted to the maintenance of the legal framework for the completion of transactions which have given rise to concrete obligations from which the persons in question cannot free themselves, at any rate without accepting certain disadvantages.

The protection of legitimate expectation can also be relevant where the Community legislature changes with a certain period of notice—for example by observing a reasonable transitional period—the legal position in relation to circumstances about which the legislature, by its actions, had aroused concrete expectations of stability in the person affected.

This was expressly highlighted by the Court in a recent case which concerned the co-responsibility levy for milk.[77a] The relevant legal dispute concerned the question whether a farmer could be excluded from the allocation of a milk production quota for which no co-responsibility levy had been charged on the grounds that he had produced no milk during the period which was used for the calculation of the size of the quota, although this interruption in his production activity was caused by the fact that he had obtained a premium for not selling any milk, the right to which is dependent on his refraining from producing milk during a certain period. The plaintiff considered that his legitimate expectation had been infringed particularly because the milk quota system was introduced after he had decided to apply for the premium for not selling milk and to interrupt his production of milk.

> "It must be conceded . . . that a producer who has voluntarily ceased production for a certain period cannot legitimately expect to be able to resume production under the same conditions as those which

[77] Case 112/80 *Dürbeck* v. *Hauptzollamt Frankfurt/Main-Flughafen* [1981] E.C.R. 1095 at 1120; for a similar situation, *cf.* also Case 68/77 *IFG-Interkontinentale Fleischhandelsgesellschaft* v. *Commission* [1978] E.C.R. 353 at 369 and Case 90/77 *Firma H. Stimmig KG* v. *Commission* [1978] E.C.R. 995 at 1005 *et seq.*

[77a] Case 170/86 *Georg von Deetzen* v. *Hauptzollamt Hamburg-Jonas* [1988] E.C.R. 2355. For more details of this decision and on the development of the relevant case law, *cf.* K.-D. Borchardt, "Vertrauensschutz im Europäischen Gemeinschaftsrecht," EuGRZ 1988, p. 309.

previously applied and not to be subject to any rules of market or structural policy adopted in the meantime.

The fact remains that such a producer, as in the present case, has been encouraged by a Community measure to suspend marketing for a limited period in the general interest and against payment of a premium; he may legitimately expect not to be subject, upon the expiry of his undertaking, to restrictions which specifically affect him precisely because he availed himself of the possibilities offered by the Community provisions."[77b]

Consequently the regulation was declared invalid to the extent that it provided for no allocation of a reference quantity to producers who, by fulfilling the obligations on production attached to the granting of the premium for not selling milk, failed to produce any milk in the course of the relevant reference period.

In the field of agricultural policy, mention should also be made of the two *DEUKA* cases,[78] which also belong to the small number of decisions which have had a successful outcome for the person affected and in which the principles of legal certainty and of the protection of legitimate expectations have been effectively applied against rule-making measures.

In this case, the ECJ was called upon to decide whether two regulations, under which denaturing premiums for soft wheat had been reduced in the course of a certain financial year, were also applicable from the moment of their entry into force to the consignments purchased before this date in respect of which the denaturing process had not yet been completed. The basis for the legitimate expectation was not formed by concrete obligations, but merely by certain expectations of stability as well as decisions related to those expectations, which had been based on the practice hitherto applied, whereby premium adjustments were effected only at the end of the financial year[79]:

"Article 4 of Regulation No. 172/67, in its original version, suggests that it is normal for denaturing operations to be determined in the context of the cereal marketing year.... It cannot therefore be considered abnormal for a denaturing undertaking to arrange its projects in the light of the entire crop year.

[77b] Paras. 12 *et seq.* of the judgment.

[78] Case 78/74 and Case 5/75 *DEUKA* v. *Einfuhr- und Vorratsstelle für Getreide und Futtermittel* [1975] E.C.R. 421 at 759.

[79] Case 78/74, *loc. cit.*, footnote 78, p. 433; also case 5/75, *loc. cit.*, footnote 78, p. 771.

> Accordingly, for the sake of legal certainty, Regulation No. 849/70 had to be applied in such a way that there might still benefit from the system under Article 4(2) of Regulation No. 1403/69 those quantities of goods in respect of which it was established that they were purchased before the coming into force of Regulation No. 849/70, provided the request under Article 4(2) of Regulation No. 172/67 was made ... before 1 June 1970."

Staff disputes have also produced decisions in which legitimate expectation was based on expectations raised by the legislator himself. This applies on the one hand to the above-mentioned decision in the "Officials' Remuneration" case.[80] Because the Council had in this case taken a specific decision regarding its future procedures when adjusting salary levels, it had bound itself in such a way as to justify the protection of a legitimate expectation:

> "The rule of protection of the confidence that the staff could have that the authorities would respect undertakings of this nature, implies that the Decision ... binds the Council in its future action."[81]

The Council could not, "to escape this obligation, plead this discretion, the exercise of which it has itself determined."[82]

There exists another series of judgments, which have already been mentioned in connexion with the admissibility of the revocation of administrative measures where the legal position has changed, in which the applicants have in some instances successfully invoked the principle of the protection of legitimate expectations. In the *Grogan* case,[83] although the Court made it clear that the persons affected could not invoke the principle of the protection of legitimate expectations in support of an appeal against a change in the legal situation which, with effect for the future, worked to their disadvantage,[84] the officials involved could

---

[80] Case 81/72 *Commission* v *Council* [1973] E.C.R. 575; *cf.* also the other decision in Case 70/74 [1975] E.C.R. 795; in this case, as in other similar cases noted below, the protection of legitimate expectation was not discussed from the viewpoint of an alleged retroactivity; these cases, however, concerned the application of a rule to existing transactions (contractual relations).

[81] Case 81/72, *loc. cit.*, footnote 80, p. 584.

[82] Case 70/74, *loc. cit.*, footnote 80, p. 827.

[83] Case 127/80 *V. Grogan* v. *Commission* [1982] E.C.R. 869; also Case 164/80 *Luigi de Pasquale* v. *Commission* [1982] E.C.R. 909, and Case 167/80 *D. Curtis* v. *European Parliament* [1982] E.C.R. 931.

[84] Case 127/80, *loc. cit.*, footnote 83, p. 884.

nevertheless justifiably plead the protection of legitimate expectations on the grounds that the Council had, for a long period, neglected to make the necessary adjustment in the relevant exchange rates[85]:

> "Whilst there may be some explanation for the Council's inaction it must none the less not be overlooked that pensioners benefiting from that inaction were entitled to expect the Council to take account of the situation in which they had been placed by the prolonged application of the system temporarily used. That is particularly true in the case of pensions, since they are intended to ensure that officers who have left the service of the Communities enjoy an adequate standard of living. It follows that after failing to act for a period extending over a number of years, the Council could not, without failing to protect pensioners' legitimate expectations, lay down a transitional period for the progressive reduction of the amounts paid which lasted only ten months. A period of at least twice that length should have been envisaged for that process."

Advocate-General Capotorti, on the other hand, was of the opinion that

> "the expectation is relevant only if it is based on assurances given by the other party."

In his view, no such assurances had been forthcoming in this case.[86]

On a number of occasions, the Court has made it clear that the making of concrete arrangements is a necessary[87] but not a sufficient condition[88]

---

[85] E.C.J., *ibid.* p. 885.

[86] Advocate-General Capotorti, *ibid.* p. 901; by the same Advocate-General also in Case 167/80, *loc. cit.*, footnote 83 in [1981] E.C.R. 1551; in this sense also the Court in Case 817/79 *Buyl* v. *Commission* [1982] E.C.R. 245 at 266.

[87] *cf., e.g.* Joined Cases 95–98/74, 15 & 100/75, *Coopératives Agricoles de Céréales* v. *Commission and Council* [1975] E.C.R. 1615 at 1639; in the staff cases mentioned earlier, however, this is expressed only to a limited extent.

[88] *cf.* Case 84/78 which has already been mentioned, *loc. cit.*, footnote 75, and Case 52/81 *W. Faust* v. *Commission* [1982] E.C.R. 3745 at 3762; similarly Case 245/81 *Edeka* v. *Federal Republic of Germany* [1982] E.C.R. 2745 at 2758, and Case 14/81 *Alpha Steel* v. *Commission* [1982] E.C.R. 749 at 769; also, the decision in Case 125/77 *Scholten Honig* v. *Hoofdproduktschap voor Akkerbouwprodukten* [1978] E.C.R. 1191 at 2005 prompts the same conclusion; whether or not the Court also considers this case to be one of "apparent retroactivity" is not the main point (M. Schlockermann, *Rechtssicherheit als Vertrauensschutz in der Rechtsprechung des EuGH*, Diss. München 1984, p. 88), since the "apparent" retroactivity is just as permissible according to the case law of the E.C.J.; however, the Court failed to find in favour of a legitimate expectation in this case also, *inter alia* because of the "dispositive nature" of the original rule—this is also the conclusion reached by M. Schlockermann, *loc. cit.*, p. 130.

for allowing the protection of legitimate expectation. Thus, according to the relevant case law, there is no reason to protect any legitimate expectation if the Commission

> "conveyed nothing to importers which could have justified the expectation that, regardless of the development of conditions on the market, the previous rules would be maintained without alteration during the time when prior contracts were to be performed."[89]

In the *Scholten-Honig* case, Advocate-General Reischl observed that

> "there can only be said to be a breach of the principle of the legitimate expectation that a given legal position would continue if, having regard to all the relevant circumstances and especially to the conduct of the Community institutions, there were grounds for being absolutely certain that a specific legal situation would not be altered."[90]

Moreover, the advantage which was subsequently forfeited, or the legal consequences which were beneficial to the person in question in the application of the then prevailing law, must have been a matter of concrete expectation. This was not the case in, for example, the *Westzucker* decision,[91] to which reference has already been made.

In addition, the arrangements made, in respect of which the protection of legitimate expectation is desired, must have resulted precisely from the Community measure which gave rise to the legitimate expectation. Accordingly, a causal link is needed between the arrangement made by the Community citizen and the action undertaken by the Community institutions.[92]

From a subjective viewpoint, it is a precondition for the recognition of a legitimate expectation worthy of protection that the infringement of the trader's rights or interests must have been "unforeseeable."

> "The interference with that right or with those interests must have been unforeseeable, it must have occurred without warning and with

---

[89] Case 68/77 *IFG-Interkontinentale Fleischhandelsgesellschaft mbH & Co. KG* v. *Commission* [1978] E.C.R. 353 at 369.

[90] Advocate-General Reischl, in Case 125/77, *loc. cit.*, footnote 88, p. 2032.

[91] Case 1/73 *Westzucker GmbH* v. *Einfuhr- und Vorratsstelle für Zucker* [1973] E.C.R. 723 at 729.

[92] *cf.* on this subject Joined Cases 95–98/74, 15 & 100/75, *Union Nationale des Coopératives Agricoles de Céréales et al.* v. *Commission and Council* [1975] E.C.R. 1615 at 1638 *et seq.*

immediate effect and without any transitional measures of such a nature as to enable a prudent trader to avoid losses or to be compensated for them."[93]

In negative terms, this means that no legitimate expectation can be protected if it was "foreseeable" that a change in the legal situation would occur on the basis of the actions of the authorities or of the contents of the existing rules.[94]

This last-named principle has been expressly applied by the Court in a number of cases.[95] Although the notion of "unforeseeability" involves a subjective criterion, the latter nevertheless becomes objectively quantifiable by virtue of the fact that the Court normally does not consider the matter from the individual viewpoint of the undertaking concerned, but uses the criterion of the ability of a "prudent trader"[96] to foresee these circumstances. Thus for example in the *CNTA* case, the ECJ conceded that the consequences in question could not have been foreseen by a "prudent trader."[97] Similar considerations applied in the *DEUKA* cases, where the ECJ pointed out that it could not "be considered abnormal" for the undertakings in question to make certain arrangements.[98]

In most instances, however, the ECJ has confirmed that the change in the relevant rules was foreseeable and has consequently denied the existence of a legitimate expectation worthy of protection on the part of

---

[93] Advocate-General Mayras in Joined Cases 44–51/77 *Groupement d'Intérêt économique "Union Malt" et al.* v. *Commission* [1978] E.C.R. 57 at 90.

[94] *cf., e.g.* Case 146/77 *British Beef Company Ltd.* v. *Intervention Board for Agricultural Produce* [1978] E.C.R. 1347 at 1355.

[95] Joined Cases 95–98/74, 15 & 100/75, *loc. cit.*, footnote 92, p. 1639; Joined Cases 44–51/77, *loc. cit.*, footnote 93, pp. 81 *et seq.*; Case 97/76 *Merkur* v. *Commission* [1977] E.C.R. 1063 at 1076 *et seq.*; Case 78/77 *J. Lührs* v. *Hauptzollamt Hamburg-Jonas* [1978] E.C.R. 169 at 178: Case 96/77 *SA Ancienne Maison Marcel Bauche et al.* v. *French Customs Administration* [1978] E.C.R. 383 at 400; Case 245/81 *Edeka-Zentrale AG* v. *Federal Republic of Germany* [1982] E.C.R. 2745 at 2758; Case 74/74 *CNTA* v. *Commission* [1975] E.C.R. 533 at 549 and Case 276/82 *B.V. Roomboterfabriek "De beste boter"* v. *Produktschap voor Zuivel* [1983] E.C.R. 3331, para. 21.

[96] Joined Cases 95–98/74, 15 & 100/75, *loc. cit.*, footnote 92; Case 97/76, *loc. cit.*, footnote 95; Case 78/77, *loc. cit.*, footnote 95; Case 74/74, *loc. cit.*, footnote 95; Case 95/78 *Dulciora SpA* v. *Amministrazione delle Finanze dello Stato* [1979] E.C.R. 1549 at 1570; Case 152/80 *Debayser* v. *Firs* [1981] E.C.R. 1291 at 1306 *et seq.*

[97] Case 74/74, *loc. cit.*, footnote 95, p. 549.

[98] Case 78/74 and Case 5/75 *DEUKA* v. *Einfuhr- und Vorratsstelle für Getreide und Futtermittel* [1975] E.C.R. 412 at 433 and [1975] E.C.R. 759 at 771.

the person affected.[99] In so doing, the Court normally sets the ability to foresee events at a very high level.

The relevant circumstances are deemed to be "foreseeable" not only when proposals relating to changes in the legal situation are made by the Commission to the Council and are published, or at least become known to the traders in question,[100] but also when the existing rules[101] or developments in the relevant market which were known to the traders involved[102]—or even trends in exchange rates[103]—make a reaction on the part of the Community authorities likely.

Closely linked to the above-mentioned question of the unforeseeable nature of the change made in the legal situation is the question whether in addition the justified nature of the legitimate expectation claimed needs to be tested.[104] The ECJ tackled this issue in, for example, the *Mackprang* case, which concerned the admissibility of the retroactivity of an administrative measure conferring the authority to adopt protective measures. Here, the Court concluded that there could be no protection of legitimate expectation, since the measure in question constituted a "justified precaution against purely speculative activities."[105]

The lack of sufficient grounds for the protection of legitimate expectation also played a part in the *Grogan* case. Advocate-General Capotorti observed that[106]:

---

[99] *cf.* on this subject extensively M. Schlockermann, *Rechtssicherheit als Vertrauensschutz in der Rechtsprechung des EuGH*, Diss. München 1984, pp. 93 *et seq.*

[100] *cf.* on this subject Case 97/76, *loc. cit.*, footnote 95, p. 1077 and Joined Cases 95–98/74, 15 & 100/75, *loc. cit.*, footnote 92, p. 1638.

[101] Case 146/77, *loc. cit.*, footnote 94.

[102] Joined Cases 44–51/77, *loc. cit.*, footnote 93, pp. 81 *et seq.*; Case 78/77, *loc. cit.*, footnote 95, pp. 177 *et seq.*; Case 96/77, *loc. cit.*, footnote 95, p. 400: Case 245/81, *loc. cit.*, footnote 95, p. 2758—a published trade agreement was a suitable medium for announcing a new starting point in the Community's commercial policy; Case 276/82, *loc. cit.*, footnote 95, para. 21.

[103] Joined Cases 95–98/74, 15 & 100/75, *loc. cit.*, footnote 92, p. 1639; Case 146/77, *loc. cit.*, footnote 94, pp. 1355 *et seq.*; Case 152/80, *loc. cit.*, footnote 96, p. 1306; Case 97/76, *loc. cit.*, footnote 95, p. 1078.

[104] *cf.* on this subject T.C. Hartley, *Foundations of European Community Law*, Oxford 1981, p. 134; generally also P. Pescatore, in *Die allgemeinen Rechtsgrundsätze, die den Rechtsordnungen der Mitgliedstaaten gemeinsam sind, als Quelle des Europarechts. Gegenseitige Einwirkung des Europarechts und des nationalen Rechts*, FIDE Report 1986, p. 40.

[105] Case 2/75 *Einfuhr- und Vorratsstelle* v. *Mackprang* [1975] E.C.R. 607 at 617; *cf.* on this subject also M. Schlockermann, *loc. cit.*, footnote 99, p. 113; T. C. Hartley, *loc. cit.*, footnote 104, p. 113.

[106] Case 127/80 *Grogan* v. *Commission* [1982] E.C.R. 869 at 902; *cf.* on this subject also P. Pescatore, *loc. cit.*, footnote 104.

"the Community administration preferred, it would appear, to allow a situation the absurdity of which was evident to persist. . . . But it is precisely for that reason that the situation could not give rise to any legitimate expectation on the part of those benefiting from it. The procedure which was being followed was manifestly contrary to the principle of equal treatment."

For this reason also, the applicant officials could not in principle appeal against a change in the legal situation effective for the future by relying on the principle of the protection of legitimate expectations.

The same considerations applied in the *Töpfer* case. Here too, the plea that a legitimate expectation had been infringed failed on the grounds that, *inter alia*, the applicant had no

"right to the continuance of these incorrect calculations."[107]

The last-named cases are closely linked to the question whether the legal change in question was foreseeable or not, which is a decisive factor in the recognition of legitimate expectation which is worthy of protection, in that the legitimate expectation was not deemed to be worthy of protection because, and insofar as,[108] the basis for the absence of any entitlement to the maintenance of certain advantages was obvious to the persons affected.

However, even where the legitimate expectation is justified, the persons affected have not invariably succeeded in their action. As the Court stated in the *Tomadini* case, which has already been mentioned, although the Community legislator is in such cases obliged in principle to make transitional arrangements for transactions which have not yet been completed, this rule does not apply where "the adoption of such (transitional) measures is contrary to an overriding public interest."[109] In such cases, it is permissible to refrain from adopting transitional measures, in spite of the existence of a legitimate expectation.

This process of striking a balance between the interest of the protection of legitimate expectation on the one hand and the public interest on the other already played a decisive part in the *CNTA* case. Here, the ECJ

---

[107] Case 112/77 *Töpfer* v. *Commission* [1978] E.C.R. 1019 at 1032.

[108] As cogently indicated by M. Schlockermann, *loc. cit.*, footnote 99, p. 138.

[109] Case 84/78 *A. Tomadini S.n.c.* v. *Amministrazione delle Finanze dello Stato* [1979] E.C.R. 1801 at 1815; also in Case 97/76, *loc. cit.*, footnote 95, p. 1077, where the claim of legitimate expectation was, however, rejected on other grounds; *cf.* on this subject also Advocate-General Mayras in Joined Cases 44–51/77, *loc. cit.*, footnote 93, p. 90.

held, on the subject of the Community's tort liability, that the latter is incurred where

> "in the absence of an overriding matter of public interest," the Commission fails to make provision for transitional arrangements.[110]

In this particular case, however, the Court did not consider that there existed such an "overriding matter of public interest." The position was different, however, in the *Dürbeck* case,[111] where the ECJ decided, on the question whether the scope of certain protective measures (*i.e.* an import ban) extended to contracts already concluded, that

> "in view of the needs which the temporary suspension of imports met, transitional measures which exempted contracts already entered into from the suspension of imports would have robbed the protective measures of all practical effect by opening the Community market in dessert apples to a volume of imports likely to jeopardise that market."[112]

In the *Lührs* case, the Court also held that the failure to adopt transitional measures was justified on the basis of an overriding public interest. This interest was perceived as the need for the unhampered functioning of the Common Market.[113] However, in this particular case no legitimate expectation worthy of consideration was found, so that it was not necessary to weigh up the various interests involved.

Finally, it will be necessary here, as it is in the case of actual retroactivity or possibly in that of the revocation of administrative measures, to strike a balance between the various conflicting interests which are worthy of protection. Hitherto, however, the Court has been reluctant to do so, because it has already on numerous occasions made the existence of legitimate expectation subject to very high requirements. Here too, special attention should be paid to the principle of proportionality.[114]

---

[110] Case 74/74 *CNTA* v. *Commission* [1975] E.C.R. 533 at 549.
[111] Case 112/80 *Dürbeck* v. *Hauptzollamt Frankfurt/Main-Flughafen* [1981] E.C.R. 1095 at 1121.
[112] E.C.J. *ibid.* p. 1121; this concerned the validity of a regulation enacting protective measures.
[113] Case 78/77, *loc. cit.*, footnote 95, p. 177.
[114] *cf.* Case 74/74, *loc. cit.*, footnote 110; the same applies, under different circumstances, to the decision in Case 78/77, *loc. cit.*, footnote 95, p. 178; *cf.* in this sense also Advocate-General Dutheillet de Lamothe in Case 62/70 *Firma Bock* v. *Commission* [1971] E.C.R. 897 at 916.

In cases of apparent retroactivity, however, the basis on which the various interests will, where appropriate, need to be weighed will be the exact opposite to that which will be used in the case of "actual" retroactivity. Whereas an overriding public interest is necessary if "actual" retroactivity is to be considered admissible at all, it is necessary in the case of apparent retroactivity for there to exist an overriding legitimate expectation if the immediate applicability of the measure in question to events of the past is to be excluded.[115]

(b) Legal consequences

Where the Court establishes that the principle of the protection of legitimate expectations has been infringed by the process of apparent retroactivity, the legal consequences will relate in the first place to the applicable procedure. As was mentioned at the beginning of this study, the Court has concerned itself with practically the entire gamut of the possible legal implications of this question.

The ruling in the *CNTA* case awarded damages to the applicant, on the substance of the case, on the grounds that the principle of the protection of legitimate expectations had been infringed. The Commission had "violated a superior rule of law, thus rendering the Community liable."

With regard to the assessment of the amount of compensation, the Court went on to state that

> "the maintenance of the compensatory amounts was in no way guaranteed to the applicant and that it would not therefore legitimately expect under all circumstances to make the profits which would have accrued to it from the contract under the system of compensatory amounts. The protection which it may claim by reason of its legitimate expectation is merely that of not suffering loss by reason of the withdrawal of those amounts."[116]

Similar sentiments were expressed by Advocate-General Mayras in the *Töpfer* case:

---

[115] *cf.* also M. Schlockermann, *loc. cit.*, footnote 99, pp. 142 *et seq.*

[116] Case 74/74 *CNTA* v. *Commission* [1975] E.C.R. 533 at 549 *et seq.—cf.* on this subject also the final decision in this case; [1976] E.C.R. 795; in particular Advocate-General Trabucchi, pp. 807 *et seq.*

"Since this submission is in the highest degree subjective, it is necessary to ascertain first of all the nature of the damage alleged. In fact the protection of the legitimate expectation of traders in the continuance of a given legal situation can only have the purpose of sheltering them from any positive damage which they have suffered precisely as a result of that expectation, but not of indemnifying them against loss of profits."[117]

Contrary to the viewpoints expressed by certain Advocates-General, however, in the case of apparent retroactivity also, the relevance of the principle of the protection of legitimate expectations is not confined to the award of damages, since it can also prompt the inapplicability of the provisions in question in individual cases when these provisions are being interpreted. Examples of this possibility, taken from the law relating to the common agricultural policy, are the two *DEUKA* decisions, in which the ECJ ruled that the new rules did not yet apply to certain transactions made in the past.[118] The first case concerned the validity of a rule raised during a preliminary ruling procedure. The Court arrived at the conclusion that "interpreted in this way, Regulation 849/70 contains no provision the validity of which could be doubted."[119]

The Court also held a regulation to be inapplicable on the grounds of an infringement of the principle of the protection of legitimate expectations in the previously mentioned staff dispute underlying the *Grogan* case. In the course of an action against an administrative measure adopted on the basis of the regulation in question, the ECJ held that

"in the absence of transitional arrangements which were lawful, the Commission was not entitled to apply Regulations Nos. 3085/78 and 3086/78 to the applicant and that consequently the contested decision must be annulled."[120]

In other cases concerning the common agricultural policy, the Court has, hitherto without success for those affected, discussed the infringement of the principle of the protection of legitimate expectations by a case of apparent retroactivity when assessing the validity of legal rules in the

---

[117] Case 112/77 *A. Töpfer & Co. GmbH* v. *Commission* [1978] E.C.R. 1019 at 1037.
[118] Case 78/74 and Case 5/75 *DEUKA* v. *Einfuhr- und Vorratsstelle für Getreide und Futtermittel* [1975] E.C.R. 471 at 433 and 759 at 771.
[119] Case 78/74, *loc. cit.*, footnote 118, p. 433; in Case 5/75, a request for an interpretation had been made under Article 177 EEC.
[120] Case 127/80, *loc. cit.*, footnote 106, p. 885.

context of a preliminary ruling procedure.[121] Following the decision in the *Töpfer* case, the principle of the protection of legitimate expectations can also be relevant in the context of an action for annulment brought under the second paragraph of Article 173 EEC.[122] Some Advocates-General, however, have expressed the view that

"a breach of legitimate expectation docs not lead to the review of the legality or the assessment of the validity of a regulation."[123]

In relation to an action for annulment, Advocate-General Reischl stated his opinion that

"the revocation of a sovereign act with effect *erga omnes* . . . might thus affect the interests of third parties and so raises questions of legal certainty."

Therefore such revocation should, in his view, take place only if it can be proved that

"the expectation of the economic sector concerned in general has been disregarded," and not only that of the applicant.[124]

The Court has yet to give a ruling which adopts this stance. However, if the conditions stated by Advocate-General Reischl are to be applied, it should be possible to establish the invalidity or the nullity of a regulation on the grounds that the principle of the protection of legitimate expectations has been infringed[125] where, as the Court accepted in relation to the actual retroactivity of regulations in the *Meiko* case, the ECJ has declared the subsequent fixing of a time limit to be invalid.[126]

---

[121] Case 78/77 *J. Lührs* v. *Hauptzollamt Hamburg-Jonas* [1978] E.C.R. 169 *et seq.*; Case 146/77 *British Beef* v. *Intervention Board* [1978] E.C.R. 1347; Case 125/77 *Scholten Honig* v. *Hoofdproduktschap voor Akkerbouwprodukten* [1978] E.C.R. 1991 *et seq.*

[122] Case 112/77, *loc. cit.*, footnote 117, p. 1032.

[123] Advocate-General Mayras in Case 151/77 *Kaiser & Co. KG* v. *Hauptzollamt Hamburg-Ericus* [1979] E.C.R. 1469 at 1502—assessment of validity under Article 177 EEC.

[124] Advocate-General Reischl in Case 88/76 *Exportation des sucres* v. *Commission* [1977] E.C.R. 709 at 736.

[125] For a more restrictive interpretation, *cf.* also P. Gilsdorf, "Vertrauensschutz, Bestandsschutz und Rückwirkungsbegrenzung im Gemeinschaftsrecht," RIW 1983, p. 27.

[126] *cf. supra* under footnote 55; this decision was at the same time based on an infringement of the principle of equal treatment; *cf.* also the decision in Case 70/83 *Kloppenburg* v. *Finanzamt Leer* [1984] E.C.R. 1075 on the question of the validity of directives in the case of statutorily imposed retroactivity; *cf.* on this subject also the judgment of the BVerfG of April 8, 1987, BVerfGE 75, pp. 223 *et seq.*

(c) *The special case of the retroactivity of directives*

In principle, it is possible for analogous questions relating to the permissible nature of retroactivity to arise in connection with directives in the same way as they occur in relation to regulations. This follows from the fact that the ECJ has been known to confer, under certain circumstances, direct effect, in relation to the Community citizen, on directives addressed to Member States when these legal acts have not been incorporated into the relevant national law within the time-limit provided.[127]

Under the second paragraph of Article 191 of the EEC Treaty, directives take effect upon their notification to those to whom they are addressed (*i.e.* all or some of the Member States). In many cases, the directive imposes on the Member States a date by which it has to be incorporated into national law. This issue has so far given rise to two interesting questions which the Court has been obliged to consider.

In the first instance, in the *Ratti* case,[128] the Court was called upon to decide whether a directive could also acquire direct effect for the benefit of a private person as from the date on which it was published and before the time limit for incorporating the directive into national law had expired. In the course of criminal proceedings brought before an Italian court, the accused Ratti had invoked the principle of the protection of legitimate expectations on the basis that he had complied with the provisions stated in the relevant directive before the expiry of the period stipulated for its incorporation. Accordingly, the direct effect of the directive in question should be recognised in advance in his case, as a result of which the inadmissibility of the criminal proceedings which arose from the directive should be taken into consideration for his benefit.

However, the Court came to the conclusion that

> "since a directive by its nature imposes obligations only on Member States, it is not possible for an individual to plead the principle of "legitimate expectation" before the expiry of the period prescribed for its implementation."[129]

---

[127] Case 148/78 *Ratti* [1979] E.C.R. 1629 at 1642, 1645; Case 47/74 *Van Duyn* v. *Home Office* [1974] E.C.R. 1337, and Case 9/70 *Grad* v. *Finanzamt Traunstein* [1970] E.C.R. 825 at 838.

[128] Case 148/78, *loc. cit.*, footnote 127.

[129] Case 148/78, *loc. cit.*, footnote 127, p. 1645.

Accordingly, although the directive becomes effective in relation to the Member States on the date of its notification, it acquires the force of law in relation to the citizen at the earliest with the expiry of the period provided in the directive for its incorporation into national law. It is therefore not possible for it to apply retrospectively to events which occurred before this date.

In a further decision,[130] the Court was called upon to decide whether a directive could apply retroactively as from a date prior to its notification to the disadvantage of the undertakings affected. The background to this case was as follows: the Sixth VAT Directive should have been incorporated by the Member States by January 1, 1978 at the latest. On June 26, 1978 the Council adopted the Ninth Directive in this area, which was notified to the Member States on June 30, 1978 and by which they were now empowered, by way of derogation from the corresponding provision in the Sixth Directive, to implement the latter directive by January 1, 1979 at the latest. The Federal Republic of Germany, however, fulfilled this obligation only by a Law of November 26, 1979, with effect from January 1, 1980.

Initially, the Court had, in the 1982 *Becker*[131] and *Grendel*[132] cases, decided that, under certain conditions, the provisions of the Sixth Directive had direct effect for the benefit of the persons in question as from January 1, 1979, if the Member States concerned had failed to incorporate the directive into national law within the required time. In the *Kloppenburg* case, the ECJ had to rule whether this direct effect of the Sixth Directive also applied to the period between January 1, 1978—*i.e.* the expiry date of the original time limit—and June 30, 1978, the date on which the extension of the relevant deadline by the Ninth Directive was published, or whether the Ninth Directive could retroactively cancel out a direct effect which had already come into force. On this subject, the ECJ held that[133]:

> "In that regard it is necessary to emphasise, as the Court has already done on several occasions, that Community legislation must be unequivocal and its application must be predictable for those who are subject to it. Postponement of the date of entry into force of a measure of general application, although the date initially specified

---

[130] Case 70/83, *loc. cit.*, footnote 126.
[131] Case 8/81 *Becker* v. *Finanzamt Münster-Innenstadt* [1982] E.C.R. 53.
[132] Case 255/81 *Grendel* v. *Finanzamt für Körperschaften* [1982] E.C.R. 2301.
[133] Case 70/83, *loc. cit.*, footnote 126, p. 1086.

has already passed, is in itself liable to undermine that principle. If the purpose of an extension is to deprive individuals of the legal remedies which the first measure has already conferred upon them, such an effect in practice raises the question of the validity of the amending measure.

However, such a question of validity could arise only if the intention to produce the above-mentioned effect were expressly stated in the amending measure. That is not so in the case of the Ninth Directive. The text of that directive merely extends the period of transposing the Sixth Directive into national law in favour of those Member States which were unable to complete, within the period initially prescribed, the legislative procedure required for amending their legislation on value-added tax. It contains nothing to indicate that the extension alters the position of economic operators in relation to transactions carried out by them prior to the entry into force of the measure altering the period allowed for implementation.

It follows that the Ninth Directive must be interpreted as not having retroactive effect in that regard."

According to Advocate-General VerLoren van Themaat, the legal position acquired by the private parties involved on the basis of the original date for incorporation

"unquestionably falls within the scope of the principle of legitimate expectation which is recognised by the Court and of which proper account must be taken if a provision is to be accorded retroactive effect."[134]

With this judgment, the Court made it clear that in case of doubt, directives too could not acquire actual retroactivity.[135] Moreover, in the Court's opinion, retroactive directives would give rise to as many problems from the point of view of the protection of legitimate expectation as corresponding regulations. Because of the wording of the referral, the ECJ was not required to give a ruling on a further problem which the Advocate-General raised in the course of his opinion. This concerned the question whether, from the point of view of retroactivity, the decisive date was that on which the directive which changed the legal position was

---

[134] Advocate-General, *ibid.* pp. 1091 *et seq.*
[135] Here, the Advocate-General refers to the decision in Case 212–217/80 *Amministrazione delle Finanze dello Stato* v. *Salumi* [1981] E.C.R. 2735 at 2751.

notified to the Member States or, in the interests of the Community citizen, that on which the directive in question was published in the Official Journal, *i.e.* the date on which the citizen was in a position to know about this change in the law. Referring to a passage from the *Racke* case,[136] which has already been cited above, the Advocate-General opted for the latter date.[137]

III. OTHER MEANS BY WHICH THE LEGISLATURE CAN BE BOUND BY THE PRINCIPLES OF LEGAL CERTAINTY AND THE PROTECTION OF LEGITIMATE EXPECTATIONS

Finally, there are certain other ways in which the legislature can be bound by the principles of the protection of legitimate expectations and of legal certainty, which will be mentioned here in brief.

1. Expectation of Changes in the Legal Position

On the one hand, considerations of legitimate expectation may also be relevant when undertakings have made certain arrangements in the expectation that the existing legal situation would be changed in a certain way.

Thus, for example, in the context of an action for damages, the applicant had invoked the "legitimate confidence of the citizen in the correct application of the Treaty" and had consequently also relied on the expectation that the amendment of a certain provision, which was actually effected subsequently, would be applicable to earlier events. On this question, the Court held:

> "Nor has it been proven, moreover, that the legitimate expectations of those concerned were disappointed, since no Community measure forecast the introduction of arrangements other than those fixed in 1967. Consequently the applicants' claim for the retroactive application of a new system to transactions freely concluded under old rules, which moreover protected them from the risks of the world market, cannot be taken into consideration."[138]

---

[136] Case 98/78 *Racke* v. *Hauptzollamt Mainz* [1979] E.C.R. 69.
[137] Advocate-General VerLoren van Themaat in Case 70/83, *loc. cit.*, footnote 126, p. 1093.
[138] Case 54/76 *Compagnie Industrielle du Compte de Loheac* v. *Council and Commission* [1977] E.C.R. 645 at 659 *et seq.*

In the *Unifrex* case (1984), the ECJ was called upon to give a ruling on the question whether the principle of legal certainty could be infringed if the Community legislator had failed to change certain monetary compensatory amounts, even though this had been standard practice whenever changes occurred in the currency rates of exchange. In this case also, the Court, like the Advocate-General, rejected the notion that any expectation to that effect constituted a legitimate expectation.[139]

The same consideration applied to the decision in the *Eximo* case,[140] which dates from the same year. Here, the applicant had allegedly relied upon the Commission to provide, in the event of a change in the intervention price, certain adjusting amounts in respect of export subsidies which were fixed in advance. The Court held that[141]

> "if, as is alleged, its sole price was fixed not on the basis of that amount but in the expectation of an adjustment of which neither the amount nor the time at which it would fall due could be ascertained at the time in question, the applicant voluntarily assumed a risk whose consequences cannot be attributed to the Community."

Although up to this point pleas of the infringement of the principle of the protection of legitimate expectations by the failure to change the legal situation, or to change it in time, this case law does not automatically exclude the possibility that legitimate expectations in this area may need to be protected. This would be the case, for example, if assurances to that effect had been obtained.

2. The Clear and Predictable Nature of the Legal Position

In this context, certain judgments have already been discussed earlier in which the Court, in the course of interpreting a legislative rule, raised certain issues. In the *Salumi* case,[142] it was held, in connexion with the formula which holds that in case of doubt, rules shall acquire no retroactive effect:

---

[139] Case 281/82 *S.a.r.l. Unifrex* v. *Commission and Council* [1984] E.C.R. 1969 at 1985 and 1993; on a similar case *cf.* also Advocate-General Mayras in Joined Cases 12, 18 & 21/77 *Debayser* v. *Commission* [1978] E.C.R. 553 at 580.

[140] Case 62/83 *Eximo* v. *Commission* [1984] E.C.R. 2295.

[141] E.C.J., *ibid.* p. 2312; *cf.* also Advocate-General Lenz, *ibid.* at p. 2321.

[142] Joined Cases 212–217/80 *Amministrazione delle Finanze dello Stato* v. *Salumi* [1981] E.C.R. 2735.

"This interpretation ensures respect for the principles of legal certainty and the protection of legitimate expectation, by virtue of which the effect of Community legislation must be clear and predictable for those who are subject to it."[143]

The Court took a similar decision in the *Kloppenburg* case.[144]

In the course of a preliminary ruling procedure which concerned the proper tariff applicable to a particular type of cheese, and in which both the national customs authorities and the Commission had relied upon a possible interpretation of the relevant provision which was more unfavourable to the undertaking in question, the ECJ held[145]:

"Even assuming that the interpretation advocated by the Commission is in accord with the logic of the system of monetary compensatory amounts, nevertheless it is for the Community legislature to adopt the appropriate provisions. The principle of legal certainty requires that rules imposing charges on the taxpayer must be clear and precise so that he may know without ambiguity what are his rights and obligations and may take steps accordingly."

Although the rules referred to are initially those which result from the interpretation of the written law, they also impose corresponding obligations on the Community legislator.

---

[143] E.C.J., *ibid.* p. 2751.
[144] Case 70/83, *loc. cit.*, footnote 126, p. 1088.
[145] Case 169/80 *Zollverwaltung* v. *Gondrand Frères* [1981] E.C.R. 1931 at 1942.

SECTION 4

SUMMARY

A. LEGAL CERTAINTY AND THE PROTECTION OF
   LEGITIMATE EXPECTATIONS AS GENERAL LEGAL
   PRINCIPLES

At the beginning of this survey[1] we drew attention to a number of
essential conceptual distinctions in the administrative law of the Member
States, which can be discerned in particular from an examination as to
whether the administrative law system in question applies a special principle of the protection of legitimate expectations in addition to the principle
of legal certainty, or whether, as is more traditional, it makes no such
express distinction. Both principles have in common that they determine,
inter alia,[2] the legal effects, the validity or the applicability of legal
measures taken by the administration or by the legislator. Above all, both
principles may conflict with the principle under which the administration
has to comply with the relevant legislation.

These conceptual distinctions become particularly apparent when the
"legal certainty solution," applied especially in France, is based in the
first place on objective factors such as the expiry of certain time limits, the
existence of vested rights or the retroactivity of legal acts. By contrast, the
recognition of the principle of the protection of legitimate expectations,
which finds its clearest expression in the legal systems of Germany and
the Netherlands, involves taking into consideration the subjective legal
interests of the citizen in question. The conflict between opposing public
and private interests is resolved not only in the light of objective legal
criteria and through the general process of weighing up the interests
involved, but also by taking into account the citizen's legitimate expectation (a subjective element). In this system, the principle of legal

---

[1] For more details on the subject discussed here, *cf. supra* Section 3, A.IV.
[2] In addition, the principle of legal certainty plays, in Community law and in the national
legal systems, the important role of ensuring that the legal situation is clear and predictable for all interested parties (*cf.* on Community law, *e.g.* Section 3, D.III.2); on the
situation in the Netherlands, *cf.* S. Prechel, T. Henkels, Netherlands Report for the 12th
FIDE Congress in Paris in 1986, Vol. 1, p. 239 (246).

certainty is applied mainly to the disadvantage of the citizen,[3] or as a neutral principle.[4]

Community law has been influenced by these two concepts, which are familiar to the legal orders of the Member States. Although the principle of the protection of legitimate expectations is clearly and widely recognised, there are a large number of Court judgments which, even where they constitute positive decisions for the benefit of the citizen concerned, at times tend to recall the "legal certainty solution" described above, in particular where, in cases which involve the revocation of administrative measures conferring benefits or the retroactivity of regulations, the existence of vested rights, or their absence, is established in individual cases.

In addition—and this applies to Community law also—the general legal principles of legal certainty and of the protection of legitimate expectations must be defined in more concrete terms if they are to serve as practicable tools.

On this issue, a comparative analysis of the concrete rules of constitutional and administrative law of the Member States and the Community which have been derived from these two principles reveals only a modest amount of common ground. On the one hand, certain rules are known only to a small number of legal systems, and their concrete expression reveals at least a considerable degree of disparity. On the other hand, there are a number of principles in the various legal systems which reveal broad similarities and even a considerable degree of parallel thinking. This is shown conclusively by an examination of some of the distinct categories of cases which are familiar both in Community law and basically in the legal systems of most Member States. On this subject, it should be observed once again that the essential differences between the majority of Continental systems of administrative law on the one hand and the Anglo-Saxon systems on the other are also discernible in respect of the two principles of legal certainty and of the protection of legitimate expectations. Thus it is possible to observe notable differences in the English and Irish systems. However, Danish law also reveals considerable differences from the corresponding rules which are applicable in the other European systems of administrative law.

---

[3] Thus for example when an action against a measure which has become valid is dismissed as being inadmissible; cf. in Community law *supra*, Section 3, B.III.1.

[4] *cf. supra*, footnote 2.

B. REVOCATION OF ADMINISTRATIVE MEASURES

As can be seen from an analysis of the principles which govern the revocation of administrative measures which confer benefits in the legal systems of the Member States and in Community law,[5] it is possible to discern—initially in relation to the factual background to the decisions in question—far-reaching parallels in relation to the decisive criteria for drawing the distinction between the various categories of underlying facts.

Thus a distinction is generally drawn between the revocation of lawful and of unlawful administrative measures,[6] and between the admissibility of revocation *ex tunc* and *ex nunc*.[7] Considerable differences are also noticeable in the rules governing the revocation of administrative measures creating rights and those which are merely declaratory.[8] In certain legal systems, on the other hand, a distinction is drawn between the revocation of administrative measures conferring benefits and those imposing burdens.[9]

Also on the subject of the legal consequences involved, there are certain essential similarities between the legal systems of the Member States and the Community legal order.

Thus the general rule is that the revocation of unlawful administrative measures is in principle permissible where it is not expressly obligatory. This certainly applies to revocation *ex nunc*, but in many cases also to *ex tunc* revocation. On the other hand, the revocation of lawful administrative measures is in principle inadmissible; this certainly applies to *ex tunc* revocation, and often also to revocation for the future.

More particularly, the following distinction can be made:

The retroactive revocation of unlawful measures is generally subject to the fulfilment of certain conditions. In some Member States, this applies

---

[5] *cf.* on this subject in detail *supra*, Section 3, B.II for Community law and Section 2 for the individual national legal systems.

[6] In Community law and in France, Italy, Luxembourg, the Netherlands, Belgium, Greece, Germany, Spain and Portugal.

[7] In Community law and in France, Italy, Luxembourg, the Netherlands, Belgium, Greece, Portugal, Germany and the United Kingdom.

[8] In France, Luxembourg, Belgium, Spain and Portugal; this is also gradually being introduced into Community law.

[9] In Germany, the Netherlands and Greece; gradually being introduced in Italy and in Community law.

in principle to all administrative measures conferring benefits,[10] whereas in other States this is so only in relation to the revocation of administrative measures creating rights, while in these countries the revocation of merely declaratory administrative measures is at all times held to be permissible.[11]

Where in such cases the *ex tunc* revocation of unlawful administrative measures is dependent on certain conditions being met, the observance of time limits, which are subject to wide variations in the Member States, is often considered to be necessary.[12] In many instances a process of weighing up the public and private interests involved is also required.[13] In relation to the latter category of interests, it is the legitimate expectation worthy of protection of the citizen in question which will be the decisive criterion—this is particularly the case in the administrative law systems of Germany and the Netherlands, but also in that of Community law, especially in relation to the revocation of merely declaratory administrative measures.

Up to a certain point, the *ex nunc* revocation of unlawful administrative measures is at all times held to be permissible in the Community Member States. However, this applies only to the revocation of merely declaratory measures. The revocation of administrative measures creating rights, on the other hand, is subject to the observance of certain time limits.[14]

In the administrative law systems of Germany and the Netherlands, on the other hand, it is considered necessary to strike a balance between the interests involved, or to take into account any legitimate expectation worthy of protection, even in the case of the *ex nunc* revocation of unlawful administrative measures. The legal position in Community law on this point has not yet been determined in a conclusive manner. Although it is clear that the revocation of merely declaratory measures is permissible without the observance of special conditions, this is probably not so in relation to the revocation of administrative measures creating rights.[15]

Finally, even the *ex tunc* revocation of administrative measures creating rights is also generally permissible, particularly where the measure in

[10] In Germany, Italy, the Netherlands and in Community law.
[11] In France, Belgium, Portugal and Spain.
[12] In France, Italy, Luxembourg, Belgium, Greece, Portugal, Spain and in Community law (in the latter case at least in relation to administrative measures creating rights).
[13] In France, Italy, Belgium, Greece, the Netherlands, Germany and in Community law (in the latter case at least in relation to declaratory measures).
[14] Thus in France and Belgium.
[15] On this issue, *cf.* for more details Section 3, B.II.3.b above.

question has been adopted on the basis of incorrect information or through deception on the part of the person affected.[16]

The revocation of lawful administrative measures, on the other hand, is usually permissible in the majority of Member States only if certain conditions have been met, and even where this is the case, revocation will be permitted only *ex nunc*.[17] This is certainly so for measures creating rights[18]: here, *ex tunc* revocation is basically not allowed. This also appears to be the situation in Community law. The administrative law of the Member States and the Community lays down a wide variety of detailed conditions to be observed for the *ex nunc* revocation of lawful administrative measures conferring benefits. Such revocation is permissible, *inter alia*, where the possibility of revocation is laid down by statute,[19] where either the factual situation[20] or the legal position[21] has changed, in the event of overriding public interests[22] or within certain time limits.[23] Although the solutions proposed in the individual legal systems as regards a reasonable balance of interests in the event of the revocation of administrative measures conferring benefits accordingly reveal a large number of similarities, there nevertheless exist certain notable differences. This applies on the one hand in relation to the time limits for revocation, which in the individual legal systems are subject to a wide variety of durations—assuming that a time limit has been specified at all. In Community law, the ECJ, with its as yet unspecified "reasonable period" formula,[24] has shown itself to be extremely flexible. This applies

---

[16] This applies for example in France, Belgium, the Netherlands, Germany and the United Kingdom, and also in Community law.

[17] In France, Italy, Belgium, Portugal, Germany, the Netherlands and in Community law.

[18] Declaratory administrative measures can normally be revoked without difficulty in, for example, France. The same applies in relation to the *ex nunc* revocation of lawful administrative measures.

[19] France, Belgium and Germany.

[20] Germany and the Netherlands; in Community law, this certainly applies in relation to declaratory administrative measures, and in France certainly in so far as there are no vested rights which would receive protection even in the case of a change in the legal position.

[21] In Germany; in Community law, certainly insofar as the original administrative measure did not create vested rights capable of protection. (The same applies in Italy).

[22] Germany, the Netherlands and Spain.

[23] France (time limit for challenging administrative measures) and Germany (time limit which starts from the moment at which the grounds for revocation become known under Article 48(4) and Article 49(2) VwVfG).

[24] *cf.* on this subject the decision in Case 15/85 *Consorzio Cooperative d'Abruzzo* v. *Commission* [1987] E.C.R. 1005; here, the E.C.J. held that a revocation decreed by the Commission after the expiry of a period of two years, in spite of having knowledge of the grounds for revocation, had not been made within a "reasonable period," so that the

also to the distinction made in particular in the administrative systems of France, Belgium, Luxembourg, Spain and Portugal—which in some cases has considerable repercussions—between the revocation of administrative measures creating rights and those which are merely declaratory. In response to pressure exerted in this direction by Advocate-General Lagrange, the Court has, at least in the early stages of its case law, resorted to this distinction. However, this resulted to a certain extent in a legal position which was more favourable towards the person concerned by taking account of his legitimate expectation that the measure will be maintained, especially in the case of the *ex tunc* revocation of unlawful administrative measures which are declaratory.

A further essential difference in the legal systems of the Member States concerns the protection of legitimate expectations *contra legem*. On this point, the Court applies the principles recognised in the administrative law of Germany and the Netherlands.

Although in this way Community law, by taking into account the legitimate expectation of individual citizens which is worthy of protection, provides a more solid type of protection than is available under the traditional system of French administrative law,[25] particularly in relation to the *ex tunc* revocation of unlawful administrative measures which are declaratory,[26] the person concerned enjoys greater protection under Community law in relation to the *ex tunc* revocation of unlawful measures creating rights than he would in Germany or the Netherlands. The reason for this is that provided the Court continues to consider that in relation to the latter category the expiry of a reasonable period is in certain conditions sufficient to exclude the possibility of revocation, the protection afforded will not depend on the provision of evidence of a concrete legitimate expectation on the part of the person concerned which is worthy of protection.

revoking measure had to be set aside as infringing the principles of legal certainty and of the protection of legitimate expectations.

[25] The same applies to Belgium, Portugal and Spain as well.

[26] The position of the Court of Justice in the case of the *ex nunc* revocation of unlawful administrative measures creating rights is not as yet very clear. With regard to the *ex nunc* revocation of unlawful declaratory measures, the legal position tends to follow the systems of France, Belgium, Portugal and Spain.

C. RECOVERY OF PAYMENTS MADE WITHOUT A LEGAL BASIS

Although this survey is devoted mainly to the development of general legal principles in Community administrative law, it is not possible to neglect under this heading the various national principles of administrative law. These will be particularly relevant in connection with the recovery under Community law also of payments made without legal justification. As has already been extensively explained,[27] in relation to indirect executive action, *i.e.* the implementation of Community law by the national authorities, and in relation to the subsequent settlement of duties levied or State aids given contrary to Community law but on the basis of national legal provisions, the Court refers in each case to the applicable national principles governing executive action by the administration. However, the Court has hitherto been extremely reluctant to assess the compatibility of these national administrative principles with the substantive Community law, and has done so only by applying the criterion formed by certain limits to the freedom of action enjoyed by the Member States.

The relevant national principles of administrative law reveal considerable mutual differences. Even within the legal orders of the individual Member States there exist in certain areas of law rules which are extremely disparate.

Whether in Community law or in the law of the Member States, these principles do not, in most instances, have their origins in either the principle of legal certainty or in that of the protection of legitimate expectation. They are shaped mainly by the principle of the compliance by the authorities with the relevant statute. The latter principle can be used in support of both claims for repayment made by the citizen against the State, in the case of duties wrongly paid, and, conversely, claims by the State against the citizen for the recovery of State payments wrongly made or made without a legal basis in some other way. In particular, the right of recovery by the State can also give rise to problems concerning the observance of the equality principle[28] or of the proportionality principle.[29]

---

[27] *Supra*, Section 3, C.II.2.
[28] *cf.* Section 3, C.II.2.
[29] *cf.* for Community law, *e.g.* Case 288/85 *Hauptzollamt Hamburg-Jonas* v. *Plange Kraftfutter GmbH & Co.* [1987] E.C.R. 611.

In this context, the principle of legal certainty can be relevant in relation to duties wrongly levied, particularly where it takes the form of time limits for the enforceability of recovery claims by the citizen. This principle can also play an important part in the converse case of the recovery by the State of payments wrongly made or made without a legal basis in some other manner. In certain Member States, the principle of the protection of legitimate expectations is also relevant in this context.

More particularly, a comparative examination of the Community law principles applicable to direct executive action by the administration on the one hand and the principles of administrative law applicable in the Member States on the other presents the following picture:

I. THE OBLIGATION TO REPAY IN THE CASE OF UNLAWFULLY PAID PUBLIC LEVIES

As is the case in Community law,[30] the legal systems of the majority of Member States apply principles relating to the formal and substantive validity of administrative measures. Although in many Member States these principles also apply basically to the contestability of those administrative measures which have imposed a tax or any other type of State duty on the person in question, it is only in Germany and the Netherlands[31] that they are relevant in relation to the further question whether and, where appropriate, within what time limits an unlawful duty may be recovered from the State by the citizen. Only in these Member States does the expiry of the time limit for challenging the administrative measure imposing the duty also exclude the possibility of recovering a duty levied contrary to the relevant substantive law. Even unlawful, but unchallenged, administrative measures retain their legal validity on the expiry of the time limit, with the result that there can be no public law or civil law claims based on unjustified enrichment against the State. The measure, which is legally valid even if it is unlawful, constitutes the "legal basis" for the levy and excludes the possibility of recovery proceedings against the State.

On the other hand, in all other Member States[32]—particularly in view of the jurisdiction conferred on the civil courts in relation to actions for recovery—it is possible for the person concerned to claim the recovery of duties unlawfully levied, even after the expiry of any time limit to be

---

[30] On this subject, *cf.* extensively *supra*, Section 3, B.III.1.
[31] *cf.* in detail on this subject Section 2 *supra*.
[32] *cf.* in detail on this subject Section 2 *supra*.

observed for the purpose of challenging the underlying administrative measure. The unlawfulness of the payment is based solely on the unlawfulness of the imposition of the duty. It is also possible to enforce the recovery of payments made without legal justification even after the expiry of the time limits for challenging the underlying measure fixing the duty in question.

This rule applies unreservedly to the legal systems of Belgium, Luxembourg and Greece. In Italy[33] and France[34] it is certainly frequently proposed that a similar system to that which applies in Germany and the Netherlands be introduced, *i.e.* that the validity of the administrative measure should be taken into consideration and that the latter should, even where it is unlawful, be regarded as the basis for the relevant payment. However, so long as, in these countries, claims of unjustified enrichment, even in the field of tax law, remain within the jurisdiction of the civil courts, such proposals will have little relevance in practice, since the civil courts are not bound to observe the time limits for challenging measures that apply before the administrative courts. Accordingly, here too the duty to repay is based solely on the unlawfulness of the imposition of the levy. The only restriction to apply to this duty is formed by the limitation periods, which are much longer than the period of one month for challenging administrative measures which applies in Germany and the Netherlands; depending on the Member State concerned—and also depending on the area of jurisdiction within certain Member States—these can reach a maximum of 20 years.[35]

Mainly because of the different form assumed by legal protection against the State in the United Kingdom, Ireland and also in Denmark, the fact that the acquisition of legal validity by the underlying administrative measure can constitute an obstacle to claims for recovery on the part of the citizen is a notion which is unknown in these countries. Here too, however, claims for recovery are subject to the restriction of limitation periods, *e.g.* six years in the United Kingdom.[36] The same applies in Denmark, where the duty to repay subsists only for a period of five years, and then only where damage has been caused, so that there is no duty of

---

[33] *cf.* Section 2 *supra* and G. Guarino, P. de Caterini, Italian National Report in Hirsch, Junod, Macheret, *La restitution des taxes perçues indûment par l'Etat*, Geneva 1976, pp. 135 *et seq.*

[34] *cf.* on this subject Section 2 *supra* and M. Fromont, French National Report, *loc. cit.*, footnote 33, pp. 101 *et seq.*

[35] Thus in Greece, *cf.* on this subject K. E. Huthmacher, *Der Vorrang des Gemeinschaftsrechts bei indirekten Kollisionen*, Köln/Berlin/Bonn/München 1985, p. 267.

[36] *cf.* on this subject Section 2 *supra* and K. E. Huthmacher, *loc. cit.*, footnote 35, p. 268.

repayment in the particular case where the person in question has passed on the unlawful tax to third parties.[37]

Clearly inspired by the fact that in the *Just* case[38] this Danish rule was held by the ECJ to comply with Community law, Italy introduced a similar system; however, it did so in such a way that, in a later case, the Court declared it unlawful from the point of view of the indirect implementation of Community law, in that the person concerned was at all times compelled to furnish evidence that the damage had not been passed on.[39] The introduction of the notion of "passing on" into Italian law accordingly constitutes a striking example of the influence exerted by the various European legal systems on each other through the agency of the ECJ—even if, in this case, the influence was not a particularly positive one.

The foregoing applies to the legal position in the Member States. As regards the legal position at the level of the Community, a distinction needs to be drawn between direct executive action, *i.e.* the implementation of Community law by the Community institutions themselves, and indirect executive action, *i.e.* the implementation of that law by the authorities of the Member States.

In relation to direct executive action, although the ECJ, as has been extensively explained elsewhere,[40] has developed a series of rules governing the formal validity of administrative measures imposing burdens, no decision made on this subject has, as far as can be ascertained, related to any action for recovery connected with the challenge of an administrative measure imposing burdens in the form of duties or fines wrongly levied. Accordingly, it is as yet impossible to tell whether, in such cases also, the Court would invariably regard the expiry of the time limits for bringing the relevant challenge as the decisive criterion. It is certainly appropriate to make this assumption, since the ECJ would hardly be inclined to admit claims for repayment through a generous interpretation of, for example, the second paragraph of Article 215 of the EEC Treaty and by applying the general limitation periods, even though the applicant had neglected

---

[37] *cf. supra*, Section 2, as well as K. E. Huthmacher, *loc. cit.*, footnote 35, p. 270; *cf.* on this subject, and in particular on the question of passing on damages to third parties as it applies in Denmark, Case 68/79 *Just* v. *Danish Ministry of Fiscal Affairs* [1980] E.C.R. 501; for a critical view, *cf.* also P. Aubin, *Die Haftung der Europäischen Wirtschaftsgemeinschaft und ihrer Mitgliedstaaten bei gemeinschaftsrechtswidrigen nationalen Verwaltungsakten*, Baden-Baden 1982, p. 89.

[38] Case 68/79, *loc. cit.*, footnote 37.

[39] Case 199/82 *Amministrazione delle Finanze dello Stato* v. *San Giorgio* [1983] E.C.R. 3595 at 3613.

[40] *Supra*, Section 3, B.III.1.

to bring an action, within the time limits prescribed for such challenges by the second paragraph of Article 173 EEC,[41] against the measure itself which imposed the burden.

On the subject of claims for repayment in the context of indirect administrative action, the Court refers to the national principles of administrative law and to the procedural law of the Member States, unless the matter in hand is subject to express provisions of Community law.[42] Although the national principles, through the imposition of time limits for bringing challenges or of limitation periods in relation to recovery claims for duties levied wrongly or for too high an amount, can thus make a contribution towards legal certainty—admittedly only at their own level—the wide disparities mentioned above in the length of these periods in the various Member States, in spite of being driven by similar motives, in practice endanger the uniform application of Community law. This is why the Court is constantly being expected to contribute, through its case law, towards the harmonisation of recovery formalities. However, the Court has not seen fit to do so. In the face of these wide disparities among the national legal systems, it would scarcely be feasible to formulate, on a comparative basis, adequate principles of Community law which would be "common to the laws of the Member States."[43] Accordingly, the ECJ is right to confine itself to subjecting the Member States to certain external limits in their freedom of action, such as the limitations imposed by the "impossibility in practice" or the "prohibition of discrimination," and for the rest to refer to the possibility of harmonisation by the Community legislator.[44]

In certain areas of indirect executive action, the Community legislator has risen to this challenge by adopting Regulation 1430/79 on the reimbursement of, or exemption from, import or export duties.[45]

As regards the specific question raised by claims for recovery in the event of the legal rule on which the administrative measure imposing burdens is based being set aside by the competent court, it is possible to observe some interesting trends in the case law on this subject.

---

[41] This was rejected by the ECJ specifically in relation to the general action for damages: Case 59/65 *Schreckenberg* v. *Commission* [1966] E.C.R. 815 at 827; confirmed in Case 543/79 *A. Birkel* v. *Commission and Council*, part judgment of November 12, 1981 [1981] E.C.R. 2669 at 2695; *cf.* on this subject P. Gilsdorf, in Groeben, Boeckh, Thiesing, Ehlermann, *Kommentar zum EWG-Vertrag*, Article 215, No. 59.

[42] For more details on this subject, *cf.* Section 3, C.II.4.

[43] *cf.* the wording of the second paragraph of Article 215 EEC.

[44] On this subject, *cf.* in detail *supra*, Section 3, C.I.2.

[45] Council Regulation 1430/79 of July 2, 1979, O.J. 1979, L175/1.

Article 79(2) of the German BVerfGG provides that administrative measures which are no longer open to challenge and are based on a rule which has been declared void, are not affected by that annulment. Payments previously made on the basis of this administrative measure imposing burdens can no longer be reclaimed.

By applying the second paragraph of Article 174 EEC by analogy to the preliminary ruling procedure, the ECJ has, in a series of cases, imposed a similar restriction on judgments declaring the invalidity of measures. As a result, the persons affected could not institute any claims relating to duties wrongly paid. Whilst the Court was guided mainly by considerations of legal certainty in this context, more recent decisions reveal that such a denial of recovery proceedings could be reasonable only in certain circumstances such as those which apply in Germany, *i.e.* only in cases where the action for repayment had not been brought within the stipulated time limit.[46]

Whilst such a restriction of the retroactive effect of the annulment of regulations in Community law could also, on grounds of legal certainty, be appropriate in relation to direct executive action, it is particularly relevant in relation to the implementation of Community law by the authorities of the Member States. In this area, and particularly in cases where the relevant Community regulation has been annulled or declared invalid, this restriction could, in view of the disparities which exist among the limitation periods which apply in the Member States, and subject to any relevant provision in Regulation 1430/79,[47] make a contribution towards the uniform enforcement of claims for recovery.

Finally, this case law constitutes a further example of the mutual influence between the legal systems of the individual Member States on the one hand and Community law on the other.[48] Thus, for example, the Irish Supreme Court in 1982,[49] dealing with the question of the effect in time of a decision concerning the compatibility of an Irish tax law with the Constitution, referred to the judgment by the ECJ in the *Defrenne* case,[50] in which the second paragraph of Article 174 EEC was applied in this manner for the first time.

---

[46] For more details on this subject, *cf.* Section 3, C.II.4a, under footnote 52.

[47] On this subject, *cf.* Section 3, C.II.4a, above.

[48] On the influence exerted by the case law of the BVerfG: *cf.* U. Everling, *Das Vorabentscheidungsverfahren vor dem Gerichtshof der Europäischen Gemeinschaften*, Baden-Baden 1986, pp. 67 *et seq.*; by the same author, "Auf dem Wege zu einem europäischen Verwaltungsrecht," NVwZ, p. 1(9).

[49] *Murphy* v. *Attorney-General* [1982] I.R. 241.

[50] Case 43/75 *Defrenne* v. *Sabena* [1976] E.C.R. 455 at 480.

II. THE RECOVERY OF PAYMENTS WRONGLY MADE BY THE STATE

The recovery of payments wrongly made by the State is subject to such a wide variety of rules within the individual Member States that it seems hardly possible to make a general comparative assessment on this issue. Being subject to variations according to the area in question, the relevant issues relating to recovery are usually closely linked to the legal basis of each payment in question.

In many instances there exist special legislative provisions on this matter in the Member States which not only lay down the conditions under which payments can or must be made, but also state the circumstances in which the recovery of payments made can be held to be permissible or even necessary.

It is also common to encounter within the legal systems of the Member States provisions of a purely contractual nature between the party making the payment and its beneficiary, as is the case, for example, in relation not only to the legal system governing the public services but also to the granting of financial subsidies.[51] Unless in such cases the conditions of recovery are also the subject of contractual provisions, they are governed by the civil law principles relating to the restitution of monies which constitute unjustified enrichment or by public law provisions especially enacted for this purpose.[52]

If the granting of subsidies is laid down in an administrative measure, the possibility of recovering them is normally governed by the principles regarding the revocation of administrative measures conferring benefits,[53] which have already been discussed elsewhere.[54]

Although the area of recovery is subject to a wide variety of individual rules—e.g. in relation to the applicable time limits—these nevertheless reveal a certain general trend in the sense that, on the one hand, recovery is widely regarded as permissible if the payment in question is based on incorrect information supplied by the recipient.[55] The same rule certainly applies in the case of incorrect information deliberately supplied. On the other hand, in most cases the converse rule applies whereby the possibility of recovering even sums which have been unlawfully paid is normally

[51] cf. on this subject the national reports submitted to the 12th FIDE Congress in Paris 1986, Vol. 2.
[52] Thus for example in the Netherlands, Germany, and probably also in France, the United Kingdom and Denmark.
[53] Thus for example in the Netherlands, Germany, Italy and France.
[54] cf. summary in this section, supra, under B.
[55] Thus for example in Germany, the Netherlands, the United Kingdom and France.

excluded, and the person concerned is therefore protected, where the payment received has already been expended and the recipient could legitimately assume that he would remain in possession of the sums paid because he could regard the amount in question as having been lawfully paid.[56]

The Court of Justice has hitherto had little opportunity to develop, for the benefit of Community law, general principles relating to the recovery of payments wrongly made.

In the field of direct executive action by the administration, there exist—specifically in the law relating to staff disputes—special provisions concerning the recovery of payments lacking a legal basis. However, the Court has already applied general principles derived from the legal systems of the Member States in relation to the restitution of monies constituting unjustified enrichment.[57]

Whilst the Court, in applying the provisions relating to recovery contained in Article 85 of the Staff Regulations, has established no link with the principles it has developed on the revocation of administrative measures conferring benefits, this rule nevertheless reveals a striking resemblance to the national rules of the Member States regarding the recovery of payments lacking legal justification; here too, the knowledge, or at least the possible knowledge, of the lack of legal justification on the part of the recipient constitutes an essential criterion for the admissibility of any such recovery.[58]

Similar rules to those which govern claims instituted by citizens against the State apply in the field of indirect executive action by the administration. According to the case law of the Court, the recovery of payments wrongly made in this area is governed by the principles which apply in the Member State in question, unless Community law itself has regulated the issue and on condition that certain limits imposed by Community law on the freedom of action enjoyed by Member States are not exceeded.[59]

Accordingly, the national principles and provisions of the Member States, which have already been mentioned and which are subject to wide variations, also apply in this context, on the understanding that, from a

---

[56] Germany, the Netherlands and Italy; this is not, however, generally recognised in the United Kingdom, Ireland or Denmark.
[57] cf. on this subject *supra*, Section 3, B.IV.1.
[58] For more details cf. *supra*, Section 3, B.IV.1.
[59] cf. on this subject *supra*, Section 3, B.II.2.

Community law point of view, it is not prohibited, and in certain circumstances is indeed necessary, to take into account considerations of legal certainty and of legitimate expectation.[60]

D. THE RETROACTIVITY OF RULES

In the majority of Member States of the Community the principles which govern the retroactivity of legal rules are less sharply defined and sophisticated than those which relate to the revocation of (individual) administrative measures.[61]

However, in this context it must be observed first of all that, at least in France and in Belgium, the retroactivity of regulations, "actes réglementaires," is in principle subject to largely similar rules to those which apply to the retroactivity of administrative measures. Moreover, in this respect a distinction is often drawn between the principles governing the retroactivity of ordinary Laws on the one hand and those which apply to regulations and other forms of secondary legislation on the other.[62] As has already been explained earlier,[63] however, the ECJ has not applied this distinction to Community law; rather, the retroactivity of derived Commission regulations is not subject to any rules which are essentially different from those which apply to Council regulations or directives.

It must also be observed that, both in a number of Member States and in Community law, the actual retroactivity of a rule is distinguished from the mere applicability of the rule to past events or its applicability (*ex nunc*) to transactions which have been initiated but not yet completed.[64]

Serious doubts are often expressed on the subject of the (actual) retroactivity of legal rules.[65] However, it is only in certain Member States that this retroactivity is prohibited in principle by the Constitution, and even where this is the case,[66] the prohibition applies only to penal laws.[67] Moreover, in certain instances the rule that, in case of doubt, laws and other rules shall have no (actual) retroactive effect is itself contained in

---

[60] *cf.* on this subject *supra*, Section 3, C.II.2.
[61] *cf.* on this subject *supra*, Section 2.
[62] France, Luxembourg, Belgium, the Netherlands and the United Kingdom.
[63] Section 3, D.
[64] Thus in France, the United Kingdom, the Netherlands and Germany and in Community law.
[65] France, Belgium, the Netherlands, Luxembourg, Germany and in Community law.
[66] The position is different in Portugal.
[67] This is the position in Italy, the Netherlands, Greece, Spain, Germany and Ireland.

ordinary laws.[68] However, ordinary laws cannot bind the legislator himself, and he may depart from them when adopting new laws in the formal sense. Nevertheless, in many cases the legislator is certainly bound if he may confer retroactive effect on a legal rule only where the appropriate Parliamentary law so provides.[69]

As regards the application of the law, all that can be concluded from the foregoing is that "in case of doubt" legal rules cannot acquire "actual" retroactivity,[70] which is a rule of interpretation which the Court has also extended to Community law.[71]

Although the prohibition, "in case of doubt," of the retroactivity of secondary legislation is often justified by reference to considerations of legal certainty[72] or of legitimate expectation,[73] these principles cannot in most instances bind the legislator himself.[74]

Where the ECJ,[75] taking into consideration the principle of legal certainty as well as the legitimate expectation which in individual cases is worthy of protection, holds the "actual" retroactivity of rules of Community law to be inadmissible and on that basis has declared invalid the relevant provisions of Community law, it thus clearly exceeds the level of protection generally acknowledged by the legal systems of the Member States. Both in this context and, in particular, where in principle a legitimate expectation is recognised in relation to the apparent retroactivity of Community law rules, the Court has clearly been guided mainly by the case of the German Constitutional Court.[76] It is precisely the notion of the protection of legitimate expectation, even in relation to the apparent retroactivity of laws, that is a legal concept which has hitherto been largely alien to the other Member States. The Court may also have been guided by the consideration that when it is assessing the validity of rules of

---

[68] France and Italy.

[69] This is the position in France, Luxembourg, the Netherlands, Greece, Ireland and Germany; cf. on this subject also Advocate-General Warner in Case 7/76 IRCA v. Amministrazione delle Finanze dello Stato [1976] E.C.R. 1213 at 1236 et seq.

[70] This is the position in France, Belgium, the United Kingdom, Ireland and Spain.

[71] Joined Cases 212–217/80 Amministrazione delle Finanze dello Stato v. Salumi [1982] E.C.R. 2735 at 2751.

[72] This is the case in France, Belgium, the Netherlands and Luxembourg.

[73] This is the case in the Netherlands, Greece and the United Kingdom.

[74] The position is different in Portugal.

[75] Section 3, D.I.2.

[76] M. Akehurst, "The application of General Principles of law by the Court of Justice of the European Community," BYIL, 1981 (82), p. 29 (38); for a clear opinion on this subject, cf. opinions by Advocate-General Warner in Case 7/76, loc. cit., footnote 69, and Advocate-General Roemer in Case 1/73 Westzucker v. Einfuhr- und Vorratsstelle für Zucker [1973] E.C.R. 723 at 738 et seq.

Community law, it is, in the final analysis, dealing with legal measures issued by institutions which have less direct democratic legitimacy than the Parliaments of the Member States.

E.   CONCLUDING OBSERVATIONS

This survey can accordingly be concluded by stating that, on the one hand, the principles of legal certainty and of the protection of legitimate expectations do not have equal importance in the legal systems of the individual Member States. Whilst the legal certainty principle is widely recognised, the notion of protecting legitimate expectation, in contrast, tends to be alien to them.

On the other hand, it can be observed that, mainly because of the similarity in the types of problem faced by administrative law in the Member States, a number of principles and rules have been developed through a number of individual cases which reveal certain definite parallels. Whilst in this way the Member States have at their disposal a wide range of rules concerning the revocation of administrative measures, the validity or legal force of administrative acts, the recovery of payments wrongly made and the retroactivity of administrative measures and rules, these rules are not invariably regarded as an expression of the principle of legal certainty. However, this general legal principle plays a decisive role in many Member States precisely in this context, whilst the principle of the protection of legitimate expectations in most cases plays only a modest part, if it is recognised at all. In Community law, it may be observed that the ECJ has developed a considerable number of concrete legal principles in relation to direct executive action by the Community or to the rule-making powers of the Community legislator. In so doing, the Court has often been guided by the legal systems of the Member States and the rules which apply there. The various concepts used in the individual Member States have exercised considerable influence, varying according to the Member State in question, in this field. Although initially it was French administrative law which had a particularly strong impact on the development of Community law, the decisive influence exerted by German constitutional and administrative law should not be disregarded either, this being particularly noticeable in the recognition of the principle of the protection of legitimate expectations in Community law.

By its constant willingness to take account of considerations of legitimate expectation in its decisions or to compel the Community institutions to observe this principle, the Court has taken an important step in the direction of protecting the legitimate interests of the individual—even, where necessary, *contra legem.*

Whilst the principle of the protection of legitimate expectations has assumed the form of a lifeline at various levels of the legal process for many people concerned—as witness the sizeable increase during the last ten years in the number of cases in which one of the parties has relied upon this principle—it is as well to guard against an excessive degree of euphoria in this regard. In reality, considerations of legitimate expectation have hitherto assisted the parties in only a very small number of instances. Although the Court never ceases to emphasise the need to protect the legitimate expectations of the person concerned, it has frequently concluded the case in question by ruling that it did not feature any legitimate expectation or that the expectation was unworthy of protection.

The principle of legal certainty, on the other hand, has been successfully invoked in a much larger number of cases, quite frequently—particularly in decisions on the formal validity or effectiveness of administrative measures—against the applicant concerned.

Whilst the development of individual legal principles in the field of direct administrative action, or in that of the rule-making powers of the Community legislator, has certainly not yet reached its final chapter, this survey has nevertheless served to demonstrate that the case law of the Court already reveals at this stage a number of clearly defined rules for various types of circumstances and problems.

On the other hand, the Court has been far less eager to develop Community law principles in relation to indirect executive action in the implementation of Community law.

It is quite understandable that on this issue, the Court is prepared—even if its endeavours in this regard have sometimes produced unfortunate results—to accept the absence of uniformity in the various principles applied by the Member States, without attempting to secure further legal uniformity through its case law.

In this area there is clearly an urgent need, in the interests of the uniform application of Community law, to achieve a degree of harmonisation in the relevant substantive and procedural provisions applying in the Member States which will go beyond the positive efforts undertaken in this regard by Regulations 1430/79 and 1697/79. However, in view of the many considerable divergences among the national legal systems which prevail to this day, it would be overtaxing the Court to expect it to shoulder the entire burden in this field[77] or even to develop the common rules which are currently lacking.

The existing Treaties have left the Member States free to determine their own rules on indirect executive action in the absence of Community regulations on the subject. Accordingly, it is the Community legislator who has the prime responsibility for securing further harmonisation in the relevant law on the basis of Articles 100, 100a or 235 of the EEC Treaty.

---

[77] G. Reischl, "Ansätze zur Herausbildung eines europäischen Verwaltungsrechts in der Rechtsprechung des EuGH—Bestandsaufnahme, Einfluss der unterschiedlichen nationalen Regelungen" in J. Schwarze (ed.), *Europäisches Verwaltungsrecht im Werden* (1982) Hamburg, p. 97 (113); sympathy for this view is also expressed by M. Hilf, "Möglichkeiten und Grenzen des Rückgriffs auf nationale verwaltungsrechtliche Regeln bei der Durchführung von Gemeinschaftsrecht," in J. Schwarze (ed.), *loc. cit.*, p. 67 (83).

CHAPTER 7

PRINCIPLES OF ADMINISTRATIVE PROCEDURE UNDER THE RULE OF LAW

A. INTRODUCTION

I. THE SUBJECT-MATTER OF THE INVESTIGATION

The investigation which is to be undertaken in this chapter is concerned with administrative procedure. The reply to the question as to what constitutes the subject-matter of the law governing administrative procedure would appear at first sight to create no problems given the apparently analogous separation of substantive and procedural law in judicial proceedings.[1]

However, differences already emerge from the fact that in judicial proceedings substantive law offers the court an evaluatory standard against which to analyse and weigh up the conduct of third parties, whereas procedural law is itself a norm of conduct for the Court.[2] On the other hand, for the administration, both procedural law and substantive law represent binding norms of conduct.[3] The administration is moreover

---

[1] The fact that this similarity is only superficial is widely recognised; *cf.* P. Badura, "Das Verwaltungsverfahren," in: Erichsen & Martens (eds.), *Allgemeines Verwaltungsrecht* (7th ed., 1986 Berlin/New York), p. 343; also K. A. Bettermann, "Das Verwaltungsverfahren," VVDStRL 17 (1958), p. 118 at 120.

[2] See on this Bettermann, *op. cit.*, footnote 1, p. 120 with a reference to J. Goldschmidt, *Der Prozess als Rechtslage*, 1925, pp. 227 *et seq.*, as well as K. A. Bettermann, "Verwaltungsakt und Richterspruch," in: *Gedächtnisschrift für Walter Jellinek*, (1955), p. 361 at 362 to 369; Badura, footnote 1, also makes a similar point, pp. 343 *et seq.*; W. Henckel, *Prozessrecht und materielles Recht*, Göttingen 1970, p. 121.

[3] Bettermann, *op. cit.*, footnote 1, p. 121.

both a decision-making body and a "party,"[4] a conflict of interest which could not arise in judicial proceedings.

This situation leads to a considerably more highly developed interdependence of procedural law and substantive law in the administrative decision-making process.[5] It leads above all to the situation in which many substantive rulings contain procedural rules, and on the other hand, substantive rulings are occasionally to be found in procedural law.[6]

In view of the difficulties of achieving a precise demarcation, a descriptive subdivision of and distinction between substantive and procedural administrative law would thus appear appropriate.[7] The starting point of such a description may best be the notion of means and ends, originating in Austria,[8] whereby the law of administrative procedure is seen as the means of administrative action, and alternatively substantive administrative law determines the content, subject-matter and purpose of an action by reference to the desired outcome. Rules of administrative procedure thus determine how the decision-making process develops, and in that context, bearing in mind the introductory remarks about the notion of administration, it is the sovereign (*i.e.* public-law) relationship between the administration and the citizen which will be the central object of the investigation.[9]

The need for a "proper" decision-making process as being of fundamental importance for an administration inspired by the rule of law has since come to be fully recognised outside the borders of Germany itself.[10]

The stage of development reached in this area will first be examined in a European comparison. Thereafter the detailed form and content of administrative procedural rules will be carefully examined.

---

[4] Badura, *op. cit.*, footnote 1, p. 344.
[5] Badura, *ibid.*
[6] Badura, *ibid.*
[7] *cf.* however the legalistic definition in the *Bundes-verwaltungsverfahrensgesetz* of May 25, 1976, BGB1. I 1976, p. 1253 at §9:
"Administrative procedure in the sense of this law is the externally effective activity of authorities which is aimed at the examination of necessary preconditions, the preparation and adoption of administrative acts or the conclusion of a contract governed by public law; it includes the adoption of an administrative act or the conclusion of a contract under public law."
[8] The Austrian origin of this "means-end" or "production-product" definition is mentioned by Bettermann, *op. cit.*, footnote 1, p. 121, footnotes 11 to 12.
[9] See on this above Chapter 1; given this approach, references to procedural rules in the context of fiscal activities of the administration will be confined to individual cases.
[10] *cf.* on this below A.II.1.

II. THE CHANGING MEANING OF THE LAW OF ADMINISTRATIVE PROCEDURE

1. The Notion of Procedure in the Member States

Ever since the founding of the European Community, the significance accorded to the law of administrative procedure in the literature, the case law and not least the legislative process has increased considerably. Something which used to seem relevant as, at best, a postscript to the regulation of substantive questions, has now acquired its own autonomous field of application.

This development, which will be articulated in detail below with reference to Community law, has not occurred in isolation from the laws of the Member States, but rather reflects an already existing trend in those laws.

Thus in Germany discussions concerning administrative procedure have been going on for many years. However, since 1976 and the adoption of the *Verwaltungsverfahrensgesetze* (laws on administrative procedure) there has naturally been a considerable shift in emphasis. It has long been debated in Germany whether a codification of the law of administrative procedure would be sensible and if so whether it would be possible to formulate it satisfactorily.[11] Between the first discussions of the Conference of Ministers of the Interior in 1957 and the adoption of the *Bundesverwaltungsverfahrensgesetz* in 1976, almost two decades elapsed, and in this time numerous commissions and scientific committees grappled with the topic and elaborated various proposals and model

---

[11] *cf.* the references to the various stages of elaboration of the *Verwaltungsverfahrensgesetz*: see in particular P. Badura in: Erichsen & Martens, *Allgemeines Verwaltungsrecht* (7th ed., 1986 Berlin/New York), pp. 336 *et seq.* See also on this F. O. Kopp, *Verwaltungsverfahrensgesetz* (4th ed., Munich 1986), prefacing note to §1 para. 2; Ule, Laubinger, *Verwaltungsverfahrensrecht* (3rd ed., 1986), p. 25 as well as the official statement of reasons for the draft text of the law, BT-Drucksache 7/910 in I. Allgemeiner Teil; Musterentwurf eines Verwaltungsverfahrensgesetzes 1963, Cologne/Berlin, 1964, p. 57; Leonhardt, in P. Stelkens, H. J. Bonk, K. Leonhardt, *Verwaltungsverfahrensgesetz*, Kommentar, (2nd ed., 1983), (cited as StBL), Introduction, paras. 27 *et seq.*, also with further references to the pre-war developments, *op. cit.*, footnotes 3 *et seq.*

solutions.[12] Even after the adoption of the *Bundesverwaltungsverfahrens-gesetz*[13] and the laws linked to it including the Abgabenordnung of 1977 (Tax Regulation) (1977),[14] Parts I and X of the *Sozialgesetzbuch* (Social Code)[15] and the *Verwaltungsverfahrensgesetze* of the *Länder*,[16] the question of the purpose and significance of regulating administrative procedure was still being debated.

Most recently, the decision of the Federal Constitutional Court of December 20, 1979 (the *Mülheim-Kärlich* decision, so called after the location of a proposed nuclear power station) gave it a new dimension. In that case the Federal Constitutional Court made the following statement on the *constitutional law* requirements for a proper administrative procedure:[17]

---

[12] *cf.* in particular on this the Federal Minister of the Interior (ed.), *Bericht der Sachverständigenkommission für die Vereinfachung der Verwaltung*, Bonn 1960; *Verhandlungen des 43. Deutschen Juristentages*, Vol. I, Part 2 A (Report by Spanner), Vol. II, Part D, 2nd section (Reports by K. v. d. Groeben *et al*); K. A. Bettermann and E. Melichar, "Das Verwaltungsverfahren," VVDStRL 17 (1959), p. 118–182 and pp. 183 *et seq.*; *cf.* the "Musterentwurf," *op. cit.*, footnote 11, pp. 54 *et seq.*; only Schleswig-Holstein amongst the *Länder* had already adopted a Landesverwaltungsgesetz in 1967. See *Allgemeines Landesverwaltungsgesetz des Landes Schleswig-Holstein* of April 18, 1967, GVB1. 1967, p. 131; *cf.* also the Landtagsdrucksache 5/871 on the draft law, and K. v. d. Groeben, "Über die Notwendigkeit eines allgemeinen Verwaltungsgesetzes," DVBl. 1966, pp. 289 *et seq.*

[13] *(Bundes-)Verwaltungsverfahrensgesetz* (VwVfG) of May 25, 1976, BGB1. I 1976, p. 1253.

[14] *Abgabenordnung* (1977), of March 16, 1976, BGBl. I 1976, p. 613.

[15] *Sozialgesetzbuch* Part I of December 11, 1975, BGBl. I 1975, p. 3015; Part X of August 18, 1980, BGBl. I 1980, p. 2218.

[16] The laws on administrative procedure of the *Länder*, in alphabetical order: *Baden-Württemberg*: Verwaltungsverfahrensgesetz für Baden-Württemberg (LVwVfG) of June 21, 1977 (GBl. p. 227); *Bavaria*: Bayerisches Verwaltungsverfahrensgesetz (BayVwVfG) of December 23, 1976 (GVBl. p. 544); *Berlin*: Gesetz über das Verfahren der Berliner Verwaltung of December 8, 1976 (GVBl. p. 2735); *Bremen*, Bremisches Verwaltungsverfahrensgesetz (BremVwVfG) of November 15, 1976 (GBl. p. 243); *Hamburg*: Hamburgisches Verwaltungsverfahrensgesetz (HmbVwVfG) of November 9, 1977 (GVBl. p. 333); *Hessen*: Hessisches Verwaltungsverfahrensgesetz (HVwVfG) of December 1, 1976 (GVBl. p. 454); *Lower Saxony*: Vorläufiges Verwaltungsverfahrensgesetz für das Land Niedersachsen (Nds. VwVfG) of December 3, 1976 (GVBl. p. 311); *North Rhine-Westphalia*: Verwaltungsverfahrensgesetz für das Land Nordrhein-Westfalen (VwVfG.NW) of December 21, 1976 (GV. NW. p. 438); *Rhineland-Palatinate*: Landesgesetz über das Verwaltungsverfahren in Rheinland-Pfalz (Landesverwaltungsverfahrensgesetz—LVwVfG) of December 23, 1976 (GVBl. p. 308); *Saarland*: Saarländisches Verwaltungsverfahrensgesetz (SVwVfG) of December 15, 1976 (ABl. p. 1151); *Schleswig-Holstein*: Allgemeines Verwaltungsgesetz für das Land Schleswig-Holstein (Landesverwaltungsgesetz—LVwG—) in the version of March 19, 1976 (GVBl. p. 181).

[17] Federal Constitutional Court, judgment of December 20, 1979, 1 BvR 385/77—BVerfG E 53, 30 at 65 *et seq.*

"As regards the constitutional law evaluation (. . .) it can be deduced from the settled case law of the Federal Constitutional Court that basic rights must be protected by procedure and that basic rights should accordingly influence not only the whole substantive law, but also procedural law, in so far as this is of significance for ensuring the effective protection of basic rights. This case law has been developed as regards the protection of basic rights from Article 14(1) of the Basic Law (. . .) and Article 12(1) of the Basic Law (. . .). Furthermore, both Senates of the Federal Constitutional Court have already explicitly decided that Article 2(2) of the Basic Law also requires a procedural framework which observes this basic right."

Thereafter, it has not been merely the question of the significance of administrative procedure for the effective protection of basic rights which has been in the foreground of discussions of legal policy and doctrine.[18] In addition, the Association of German Teachers of Public Law at its 1982 conference, under the banner of "Administrative procedure in administrative efficiency and legal protection,"[19] reverted to the fundamental question of how administrative performance and the protection of the rights of the individual can be properly balanced in the articulation of an administrative procedure.

On the one hand, it had become apparent in legal practice and in debates around legal policy that normative guarantees of procedural safeguards and of individual rights of participation which are too extensive must necessarily lead to a deterioration in the level of administrative efficiency. However, it was not just the "political costs of the state under the rule of law"[20] which came under scrutiny. Another aspect not to be

---

[18] *cf.* from the comprehensive literature: J. Held, *Der Grundrechtsbezug des Verwaltungsverfahrens*, Berlin 1984, in particular pp. 95 *et seq.*; H. J., Konrad (ed.), *Grundrechtsschutz und Verwaltungsverfahren*, Berlin 1985; H. Goerlich, *Grundrechte als Verfahrensgarantien*, Baden-Baden 1981; F. Ossenbühl, "Grundrechtsschutz im und durch Verfahrensrecht," in *Festschrift für Kurt Eichenberger*, Basel/Frankfurt 1982, pp. 183 *et seq.*; H. W. Laubinger, "Grundrechtsschutz durch Gestaltung des Verwaltungsverfahrens," VerwArch 73 (1982), pp. 60 *et seq.*; J. Feuchthofen, "Der Verfassungsgrundsatz des rechtlichen Gehörs und seine Ausgestaltung im Verwaltungsverfahren," DVBl. 1984, pp. 170 *et seq.*, with further references.

[19] *cf.* R. Wahl & J. Pietzcker, "Verwaltungsverfahren zwischen Verwaltungseffizienz und Rechsschutzauftrag," VVDStRL 41 (1983), pp. 151 *et seq.* and pp. 193 *et seq.* See further F. Ossenbühl, "Verwaltungsverfahren zwischen Verwaltungseffizienz und Rechtsschutzverfahren," NVwZ 1982, p. 465.

[20] This was the accurate characterisation given by F. Scharpf, *Die politischen Kosten des Rechtsstaats*, Tübingen 1971; *cf.* also F. Hufen, *Fehler im Verwaltungsverfahren*, Baden-Baden 1986, p. 25; R. Wahl, "Die bürokratischen Kosten des Rechtsstaates," Die

ignored was that administrative procedures subject to formal requirements with guaranteed participation rights for those affected could assist
in creating more informed attitudes and thus lead to a better decision.[21] It
is also clear that the citizens affected are more likely to accept the
subsequent administrative decision if they have had an opportunity from
an early stage to participate in the relevant procedures, and perhaps to
influence them through their involvement.[22] Finally, a formal administrative procedure guarantees for the citizen the transparency and openness
of the bureaucratic decision-making process. It can thus make a decisive
contribution to the protection of the rights to freedom and equality of the
individual.

To that extent it is possible to say that von Jhering's famous saying that
"formality (is) the sworn enemy of the arbitrary, and the twin sister of
freedom"[23] today remains equally valid.

In conclusion, one can say that improvements in administrative procedure serve the aim of improving legal protection generally.[24] Conventional judicial legal protection which operates through *ex post facto*
control has, by comparison, distinct disadvantages and problems: the
possibility of lengthy proceedings, the danger of creating *faits accomplis*
and the frequently difficult process of reconstructing highly complex
factual relationships.[25] If the interests of those involved are already
protected through an appropriate administrative procedure, the need for

Verwaltung 1980, pp. 273 *et seq.* and J. Schwarze, "Administrative Leistungsfähigkeit als
verwaltungsrechtliches Problem," DÖV 1980, p. 581 at 588.

[21] See, in particular, R. Steinberg, "Komplexe Verwaltungsverfahren zwischen *Verfahrens-
effizienz* und Rechtsschutzauftrag," DÖV 1982, p. 619 at 620 with reference to the case
law of the Federal Constitutional Court (*inter alia* BVerfG E 42, 64 at 73; 53, 30 at 76).

[22] *cf.* R. Steinberg, *op. cit.*, footnote 21, p. 619 at 622 (with further references); similarly,
E. Schmidt-Assmann, "Verwaltungsverantwortung und Verwaltungsgerichtsbarkeit,"
VVDStRL 34 (1976), p. 221 at 229 and W. Schmidt, "Die Verwaltungsgerichtsbarkeit an
den Grenzen des Verwaltungsrechtsschutzes," NJW 1978, p. 1769 at 1776.

[23] R. v. Jhering, *Vom Geist des römischen Rechts*, Part 2, (4th ed., 1883 reprinted 8th ed.,
Basel), p. 471.

[24] F. O. Kopp, *op. cit.*, footnote 11, preliminary note to § 1 para. 32; J. Schwarze, *Der
funktionale Zusammenhang von Verwaltungsverfahrensrecht und verwaltungsgerichtlichem Rechtsschutz*, Berlin 1974, p. 48; R. Wahl, *op. cit.*, footnote 19, p. 151 at 161; P.
Häberle, "Grundrechte im Leistungsstaat," VVDStRL 30 (1972), p. 43 at 86, 90 & 125 *et
seq.*; R. Steinberg, *op. cit.*, footnote 21, p. 619 at 622.

[25] J. Pietzcker, *op. cit.*, footnote 19, p. 193 at 202 with further references, footnote 23; K.
Hesse, "Bestand und Bedeutung der Grundrechte in der Bundesrepublik Deutschland,"
EuGRZ 1978, p. 427 at 434 *et seq.*

subsequent judicial protection may be less urgent,[26] that is, the protection may not need to be so stringent, even though legal protection through an administrative procedure cannot entirely replace legal protection through the courts.[27] In this way administrative procedure in Germany[28] has become a core attribute of an administration aiming to ensure respect for the rule of law.

In English law too, recent years have seen tendencies towards a strengthening of the procedural rights of persons affected by administrative decisions.

That said, historically English law, including administrative law, has been more strongly inclined towards procedure than continental legal orders. Back in 1723, the Court of King's Bench[29] quashed a decision of the University of Cambridge depriving Dr. Bentley of his academic degrees on the mere ground that he had accused the Vice-Chancellor of the University of "foolish behaviour" (*stulte egit*). The Court decided against the University because it had failed to give the party concerned the opportunity to be heard. Thus certain unfavourable administrative decisions may not be adopted without following the principles of "natural justice." These principles, which were intended originally to secure the fairness of court procedure, were extended in part to administrative procedures. Thus, one may not be the judge in one's own case,[30] and

---

[26] This was the justification provided in the *Musterentwurf*, *op. cit.*, footnote 11, pp. 56, 62, 65; J. Schwarze, *op. cit.*, footnote 24 at pp. 17, 35, 44 *et seq.*; F. O. Kopp, *op. cit.*, footnote 11, preliminary note to §1, para. 33 with further references; R. Steinberg, *op cit.*, footnote 21, p. 619 at 620.

[27] F. O. Kopp, *op. cit.*, footnote 11, preliminary note to §1, para. 33; E. Schmidt-Assmann, *op. cit.*, footnote 22, VVDStRL 34 (1976), p. 221 at 266; Finkelnburg & Lässig, *Kommentar zum Verwaltungsverfahrensgesetz*, Düsseldorf 1979, preliminary note to §9, para. 30; *cf.* also H. Bickel & K. F. Meyer, "Begleitende Verwaltungskontrolle—Eine Alternative zum nachträglichen Verwaltungsrechtsschutz?", in B. Rüthers & K. Stern (eds.), *Freiheit und Verantwortung im Verfassungsstaat*, Munich 1984, pp. 67 *et seq.*

[28] In the German-speaking legal sphere procedural notions first became established in Austria. The Austrian law on administrative procedure dates from 1925. *cf.* on the notion of procedure in Austria in particular W. Antoniolli & F. Koja, *Allgemeines Verwaltungsrecht*, Vienna 1986, pp. 554 *et seq.*

[29] *R. v. Chancellor of Cambridge University* [1723] 1 Stra. 557, cited in O. Hood Phillips, *Constitutional and Administrative Law* (7th ed., 1987), p. 672; *cf.* also J. Garner & B. L. Jones, *Administrative Law* (6th ed., 1985), p. 143, footnote 15.

[30] *cf.* for instance J. Garner & B. L. Jones, *Administrative Law* (6th ed., 1985), London, pp. 137 *et seq.*; D. Foulkes, *Administrative Law* (5th ed., London 1982), pp. 247 *et seq.*; E. C. S. Wade & A. W. Bradley, *Constitutional and Administrative Law*, (10th ed., London/New York 1985), p. 642.

most importantly, a person affected by an administrative decision has a right of appeal[31] before it is adopted.[32]

At times, the strict control of administrative procedures by reference to such procedural requirements has been exercised only very sparingly.[33] Only since the decision of the House of Lords in 1964 in *Ridge* v. *Baldwin*,[34] characterised by some as a "landmark decision," has the "duty to act fairly" been fully enforced.[35]

The Parliamentary Reports "On Ministers' Powers"[36] and "On Administrative Tribunals and Enquiries"[37] are of central significance for the development of administrative law in England, in particular the principles of administrative procedure. Both reports emphasise particularly strongly the importance of the principle of natural justice and thus of a fair administrative procedure. In England legal protection against administrative decisions often takes the form of an appeal to a tribunal (itself part of the administration, although frequently independent) or of a formal inquiry. Both procedures are considerably more formalised than the classic continental European administrative procedure.[38] A number of general principles which govern the constitution of such tribunals or inquiries as well as the establishment of a supervisory organ (Council) are contained in the so-called Tribunals and Inquiries Acts of 1958 and 1971.[39]

---

[31] *cf.* also H. W. R. Wade, *Administrative Law*, Oxford 1982, pp. 441 *et seq.*, who covers the problems of a "fair hearing" in particular detail in a separate chapter; *cf.* furthermore De Smith & Evans, *Judicial Review of Administrative Action*, London 1980, pp. 156 *et seq.*; D. Foulkes, *Administrative Law* (5th ed., London 1982), pp. 221 *et seq.*; J. Garner & B. L. Jones, *Administrative Law* (6th ed., 1985), pp. 136 *et seq.*, pp. 142 *et seq.*

[32] In the literature it comes out clearly that the guarantee of natural justice has become one of the central questions of judicial control of administrative action, of equal importance with the concept of *ultra vires*, *cf.* E. C. S. Wade & A. W. Bradley, *Constitutional and Administrative Law*, (10th ed., London/New York 1985), p. 642.

[33] See in particular S. A. de Smith, "The Right to a Hearing in English Administrative Law," Harv. L. Rev. 68 (1955), pp. 569 *et seq.*

[34] *Ridge* v. *Baldwin* [1964] A.C. 40 (House of Lords, *per* Lord Reid).

[35] *cf.* also H. W. R. Wade, *op. cit.*, footnote 31, p. 461; E. C. S. Wade & A. W. Bradley, *Constitutional and Administrative Law*, *op. cit.*, footnote 30, pp. 647–651.

[36] *Committee on Ministers' Powers*, Report, London 1932 (1963), Cmnd. 4060.

[37] *Committee on Administrative Tribunals and Enquiries*, London, 1957 (1962), Cmnd. 218.

[38] On the procedures *cf.* H. W. R. Wade, *op. cit.*, footnote 31, pp. 776 *et seq.*; E. C. S. Wade & A. W. Bradley, *op. cit.*, footnote 30, pp. 703 *et seq.* (Tribunals), p. 713 (Inquiries); J. Garner & B. L. Jones, *op. cit.*, footnote 29, pp. 229 *et seq.* (Tribunals), pp. 273 *et seq.* (Inquiries).

[39] On the Tribunals and Inquiries Act 1971, *cf.* J. Garner & B. L. Jones, *op. cit.*, footnote 29, pp. 244 *et seq.*; H. W. R. Wade, *op. cit.*, footnote 31, pp. 796 *et seq.*

Legal protection through appeals to ordinary courts is possible in particular where errors of law are alleged. These include procedural defects.[40]

This trend[41] towards stricter guarantees of procedural rights has also become apparent in other common-law legal systems.

Thus, in Ireland, it is important to mention that the administration is bound to observe so-called "constitutional justice,"[42] which in the opinion of Irish authors places even more wide-ranging obligations on the administration than in English law.[43]

With regard to the USA it is sufficient at this point to refer to the "Due Process Clause" contained in the 5th and 14th Amendments to the United States Constitution,[44] which gave a great impetus to procedural law thinking in that country.[45] It is no coincidence that the Administrative Procedure Act[46] is a sophisticated tool for the control of the administration by law.

In the French legal order a variety of tendencies is to be discerned in recent times, and this places a greater weight on administrative procedure than in the past. This is notable in particular because the French legal

---

[40] On the possibilities for court review of tribunal decisions, *cf.* H. W. R. Wade, *op. cit.*, footnote 31, pp. 787 *et seq.*, as well as pp. 814 *et seq.*; S. A. de Smith, *op. cit.*, footnote 33, pp. 126 *et seq.*

[41] E. C. S. Wade & A. W. Bradley, *op. cit.*, footnote 30, p. 701 also take a similar approach: "However (. . .) there is a strong tendency in public law in Britain for principles derived from the work of the courts, such as the doctrine of natural justice, to be applied to administrative decisions. The same tendency applies to the development of institutions within government."

[42] On "Constitutional Justice" in Ireland, which is deduced from Article 40.3.1 of the Constitution, *cf.* D. G. Morgan, *Constitutional Law of Ireland*, 1985, p. 213.

[43] On this *cf.* D. G. Morgan, *op. cit.*, footnote 42, p. 213; R. M. Stout, *Administrative Law in Ireland*, Dublin 1985, pp. 133 *et seq.* with reference to Henchy J., *The State (Gleeson)* v. *Minister for Defence and the Attorney-General* [1976] I.R. 280 at 294.

[44] 5th Amendment to Federal acts; 14th Amendment to State acts; on procedural due process, *cf.* from the case-law of the U.S. Supreme Court, for example, *Board of Regents of State Colleges* v. *Roth*, 408 U.S. 564 (with further references) (1972); *Goldberg* v. *Kelly*, 397 U.S. 254 (1970); as well as E. Gellhorn & B. Boyer, *Administrative Law and Process*, St. Paul, Minn. 1981, pp. 139 *et seq.*

[45] On the procedural problems cited here, *cf. inter alia* W. Gellhorn, C. Byse & P. Strauss, *Administrative Law*, Mineola, New York, p. 23; *cf.* also E. Gellhorn & B. Boyer, *op. cit.*, footnote 44, pp. 139 *et seq.*; H. D. Jarass, "Besonderheiten des amerikanischen Verwaltungsrechts im Vergleich—zugleich ein Beitrag zum Stellenwert des Verwaltungsverfahrens," DÖV 1985, pp. 377 *et seq.*

[46] Administrative Procedure Act 1946, as amended, Public Law 404–79th Congress, approved June 11, 1946, 60 Stat. 237–244; the text is reprinted in W. Gellhorn *et al.*, *Administrative Law, op. cit.*, footnote 44, pp. 1115 *et seq.* On the emergence and significance of the Act *cf.* also J. S. Williams, "Fifty Years of the Law of the Federal Administrative Agencies—and beyond," (1970) 29 Federal Bar Journal 1.

tradition is governed by the notion that the most important reason for providing legal protection against the administration is not the protection of the rights of the individual, but rather to ensure that the administration adheres to law and statute (*principé de légalité*).

In the context of the control of the administration greater weight was traditionally placed on the substantive result rather than on adherence to a particular means for adopting the decision.[47]

However, in recent years in France, several laws have been adopted which improve the procedural rights of parties concerned. Thus the law "relative au contrôle de la concentration économique et à la répression des ententes illicites et des abus de positions dominantes,"[48] of July 19, 1977 contains significant guarantees of the rights of the defence in anti-trust proceedings.[49]

Even clearer as examples are the changes wrought through the law of July 17, 1978 on the right of access to files[50] and through the law of July 11, 1979 on the duty to give reasons for administrative acts,[51] and finally, through the decree of November 28, 1983 "concernant les relations entre l'administration et les usagers."[52] Also worthy of mention is the French data protection legislation, which contains regulations on access to information held by the administration.[53]

---

[47] *cf.* on this M. Rott, *Das verwaltungsrechtliche subjektive Recht im Spiegel seiner Entwicklung im deutschen liberalen Rechtsstaat und in der französischen "théorie des droits subjectifs des administrés,"* Dissertation, Giessen, 1976; M. Fromont, *Rechtsschutz gegenüber der Verwaltung in Deutschland, Frankreich und den Europäischen Gemeinschaften,* Cologne 1967, p. 2014; J.-M. Woehrling, "Die französische Verwaltungsgerichtsbarkeit im Vergleich mit der deutschen," NVwZ 1985, p. 21 at 23; *cf.* however the criticism of the overemphasis on the difference in G. Vedel & P. Delvolvé, *Droit administratif* (9th ed., Paris 1984), p. 744.

[48] Law no. 77–806 of July 19, 1977, (French) J.O. of July 20, 1977, p. 3833.

[49] *cf.* for instance the judgment of the Conseil d'Etat of March 13, 1981, *S.A.R. Armand Pellerin et Cie et Fédération nationale du négoce du tissu*, RDP 1981, p. 1436, as well as the case note by Y. Gaudemet, RDP 1981, p. 1428; *cf.* also D. Linotte, "Chronique générale des réformes administratives françaises," RDP 1978, p. 215 at pp. 225 *et seq.*, with respect to the anti-trust Law no. 77–1189: "Contrôle de la concentration économique et répression des ententes illicites et des abus de positions dominantes," (French) J.O. of October 26, 1977, p. 5223.

[50] Law no. 78–753 of July 17, 1978, (French) J.O. of July 18, 1978, p. 2851. On the most recent case law see the references in Le Conseil d'Etat, *Etudes et documents*, no. 38 (1987), pp. 102 *et seq.*

[51] Law no. 79–587 of July 11, 1979, (French) J.O. of July 12, 1979, p. 1711, including the explanations in the Prime Minister's Circular of August 31, 1979, (French) J.O. of September 4, 1979, p. 2146.

[52] Decree no. 83–1025 of November 28, 1983, (French) J.O. of December 3, 1983, p. 3492.

[53] Law no. 78–17 of January 6, 1978, (French) J.O. of January 7, 1978, p. 227.

The provisions noted above indicate a changed understanding of the role of the citizen in the administrative process. Citizens have been given extensive rights and opportunities for influencing the decision-making process. It is also notable that special complaints commissions have been created which act, not merely on the application of a citizen, to ensure that these new rights are safeguarded, and possess the authority to intervene directly with the administration in order to ensure that the rights are implemented.[54] Seen from this angle, there is more than simply a difference in terminology in the change from the language of the "administré" to that of the "usager" (de l'administration).[55]

In Italy, which does not yet have a law on administrative procedure, it is also possible to discern an increased interest in the problems of administrative procedure. A codification is planned. A commission of experts set up by the Government in 1984 has already devised a draft law on the subject.[56] Proposals on this matter have been made before,[57] so that even in Italy it is possible to see the evolution of the debate, although concrete measures on the part of the legislature have so far been lacking.[58]

Denmark, too, as the "representative" of the Scandinavian legal tradition, has taken a major step very recently towards securing procedural rights. Through Law no. 571 of December 19, 1985 ("Forvaltningslov") and Law no. 572 of the same date ("Om offentlighed i forvaltningen") the rights of those affected and of the public in general *vis-à-vis* the

---

[54] Judgment of the Conseil d'Etat of May 19, 1983, no. 40–680—*Bertin*, Rec. 1983, p. 207; (=AJDA 1983, p. 434, no. 71); *cf.* also the decisions printed at AJDA 1983, pp. 341 *et seq.*, no. 62–70; on this see also C. B. Lasserre & J. M. Delarue, "Accès du public aux documents administratifs," AJDA 1983, p. 402.

[55] This is the title of the decree of November 28, 1983, *op. cit.*, footnote 52.

[56] On September 7, 1984 (*cf.* Atti parlam. Camera dei deputati, leg. IX) two Commissions of Experts were set up under the Prime Minister for institutional problems. The Commission chaired by Prof. Massimo Severo Giannini (which has three sub-commissions) has been concerned *inter alia* with the question of administrative procedure.

[57] *cf.* on this G. Cataldi, *Il procedimento amministrativo nei suoi attuali orientamenti giuridici e non giuridici*, Milan 1967; ISAP, *La procedura amministrativa*, Vicenza 1964. *cf.* also F. Benvenuti, in C. H. Ule (ed.), *Verwaltungsverfahrensgesetze des Auslands*, Berlin 1967, p. 157, with comprehensive references.

[58] On the most important studies on administrative procedure *cf.* A. M. Sandulli, *Il procedimento amministrativo*, Milan 1940, (new edition 1959); F. Benvenuti, "Funzione amministrativa, procedimento, processo," Riv. trim. dir. pubbl. 1952, pp. 118 *et seq.*; G. Berti, *La pubblica amministrazione come organizzazione*, Padua 1968, p. 220; M. Nigro, "Procedimento amministrativo e tutela giurisdizionale contro la pubblica amministrazione," in AA.VV. L'azione amministrativa fra garanzia ed efficienza, "Problemi di amministrazione pubblica" (comment), footnote 1, 1981, pp. 21 *et seq.*

administration have been comprehensively codified and strengthened,[59] although even before the passing of these laws there existed a well-developed tendency to ensure the control of the administration through the provision of (administrative) procedural rights.

The growing significance of thinking around the question of procedure is expressed in one final point. In the more recent constitutions, in particular of the new Member States, a number of express guarantees of rights in administrative procedure are anchored as basic rights, or at the very least, there is a duty to introduce them which is imposed by way of an instruction to the legislature. Thus the Portuguese Constitution runs as follows[60]:

Article 267, paragraph 4:

> "The exercise of administrative activities will be the subject of a special law which will secure the rationalisation of the instruments available to administrative authorities and the participation of citizens in decision-making processes and determinations by which they are affected."

and Article 268, paragraphs 1, 2:

> "1. Citizens have the right, upon request, to be informed by the administration about the progress of any procedures in which they have a direct interest as well as to be informed of those definitive decisions which affect them.
> 2. Administrative acts with external effects must be notified to those persons who have an interest in them in so far as they are not already officially published and they must contain an express legal basis if they affect the rights or legally protected interests of citizens."

---

[59] Law no. 571 of December 19, 1985, "Forvaltningslov"; Law no. 572 of December 19, 1985, "Lov om offentlighed i forvaltningen." Except as regards local administration, the laws came into force on January 1, 1987. cf. K. Borgsmidt, "Ein Verfahrensgesetz und Neugestaltungen im dänischen Verwaltungsrecht," DÖV 1988, p. 70.
[60] German translation in A. Thomashausen, "Die revidierte Verfassung der Republik Portugal von 1976," JöR 32 (1983), p. 443 at 495.

Similar guarantees are to be found in the Spanish Constitution of 1978[61] and in the Greek Constitution of 1975.[62] The significance of administrative procedure in these legal systems can already be seen in the type and legal quality of the safeguards for procedural rights of citizens *vis-à-vis* the administration.

Legal developments within the framework of the Council of Europe also confirm the tendency towards increased protection of the citizen under administrative procedures in Europe.

The Committee of Ministers of the Council of Europe, by Resolution no. 31 of 1977, laid down certain essential principles, and thus also the general standard which has since been achieved, described in the Preamble in the following terms[63]:

> "Considering that, in spite of the differences between the administrative and legal systems of the member states, there is a broad consensus concerning the fundamental principles which should guide the administrative procedures and particularly the necessity to ensure fairness in the relations between the individual and administrative authorities."

In the annex to the Resolution five rights and duties are enumerated, which the law on administrative procedure of each of the Member States of the Council of Europe is required to guarantee:

---

[61] *cf.* Article 105 of the Spanish Constitution:
"La ley regulará:
(a) La audiencia de los ciudadanos, directamente o a través de las organizaciones y asociaciones reconocidas por la ley, en el procedimiento de elaboración de las disposiciones administrativas que les afecten.
(b) El acceso de los ciudadanos a los archivos y registros administrativos, salvo en lo que afecte a la seguridad y defensa del Estado, la averiguación de los delitos y la intimidad de las personas.
(c) El procedimiento a través del cual deben producirse los actos administrativos, garantizando, cuando proceda, la audiencia del interesado."
There is in any case a comparatively long tradition of procedural administrative law in Spain. *cf.* above, Chap. 2, Spain.

[62] Article 20, para. 2 of the Greek Constitution of 1975, *cf.* P. Pavlopoulos *et al.*, "Procédure administrative non contentieuse et problèmes juridiques en Grèce: La garantie constitutionelle du principe 'audi alteram partem,' " Annuaire européen d'administration publique, 1978 I (1979), pp. 427 *et seq.*

[63] Resolution no. 31 of 1977 of the Committee of Ministers of the Council of Europe "On the protection of the individual in relation to the acts of administrative authorities" adopted by the Committee of Ministers on September 28, 1977, Council of Europe, Information Bulletin on legal activities, June 1978, p. 45.

— the right to a hearing before the administration;
— the right of access to essential facts;
— the right to legal advice;
— the duty of the administration to give reasons for its decisions;
— the duty of the administration to indicate the possibilities for legal challenge to its decision.

These principles are repeated and in part extended in Recommendation no. 2 of 1980 as regards the exercise of discretionary powers by an authority.[64]

2. The Significance of the Notion of Procedure Within the Community

Having regard to the method of formulating law in the form of the general principles of administrative law discussed in detail above,[65] it was obvious that the "broad consensus" with regard to the introduction of effective procedural guarantees in the Member States, which was mentioned in the Council of Europe resolution,[66] must also influence European Community law in this field.

The founding Treaties have little to say on matters of administrative procedure.

Probably the best known of these rules is the provision in Article 190 of the EEC Treaty,[67] which even now still extends beyond the comparable protection in the Member States in so far as it contains a duty to give reasons in respect of normative acts.[68]

The duty to give reasons is however "considerably relaxed"[69] in the case law, in so far as it applies to normative acts, but it has retained its function of a guarantee in respect of administrative procedure.[70]

---

[64] Recommendation no. 2 of 1980 of the Committee of Ministers concerning the exercise of discretionary powers by administrative authorities, adopted by the Committee of Ministers on March 11, 1980, Council of Europe, Information Bulletin on legal activities, June 1980, p. 50.

[65] cf. above, Chapter 1.

[66] cf. the Preamble of Resolution 31 of 1977 of the Council of Europe, *supra*, footnote 63.

[67] Of importance is for instance also Article 191 EEC on the notification and publication of legal acts; cf. also Article 15 ECSC.

[68] See on this in more detail below, F.II.2 (comparative survey of the duty to give reasons).

[69] Advocate-General Reischl, Cases 275/80 & 24/81 *Krupp* v. *Commission* [1981] E.C.R. 2489 at 2526.

[70] cf. *inter alia* J. Sedemund, "Allgemeine Prinzipien des Verwaltungsverfahrensrechts, dargestellt am Beispiel des Verwaltungsverfahrens der EG in Kartellsachen," in J. Schwarze (ed.), *Europäisches Verwaltungsrecht im Werden*, Baden-Baden 1982, p. 45 at 56; H. H. Scheffler, *Die Pflicht zur Begründung von Massnahmen nach den europäischen*

Rights of defence for persons affected are also provided for in part in the Treaties.[71] With regard to the language of the procedure and questions of competence, there exist in the Treaties either the power to adopt the relevant regulations[72] or general principles.[73]

Moreover, the Community legislature has been active in instituting improvements to the *status quo*. In accordance with the task laid down in Article 217 EEC, a regulation on the language question was adopted.[74] Furthermore, in 1961 the Staff Regulations came into force, and these give individual rights to Community officials.[75]

Right back in 1962/63 competition Regulations 17/62[76] and 99/63[77] were adopted, and these give certain procedural rights to the undertakings concerned. The fact that only a certain minimum standard was codified is understandable given the time of adoption. Nonetheless, looking at these provisions from the standpoint of the time, they do provide an above average level of protection.

The increased level of interest in the law of administrative procedure on the part of the Community legislature can be best discerned from the recently adopted provisions in the field of anti-dumping law, which are detailed in Regulation 2176/84[78] and Decision 2177/84/ECSC.[79]

These provisions are of note not simply on account of the detailed regulation of the rights of the defence which they offer. They are formulated so that both the undertaking suffering from the dumping and the

Gemeinschaftsverträgen, Berlin, 1974, p. 214; H.-W. Daig, in H. v.d. Groeben *et al.*, *Kommentar zum EWG-Vertrag* (3rd ed., Baden-Baden 1983), Article 190, para. 6 (para. 7 at the end), is rather doubtful on this point.

[71] *cf.* Articles 36(1), 46(2), 54(4), 66 § 5(2), 88(1), ECSC; Article 5(2) 2nd sentence, 46(2), 1st sentence, 141 Euratom; there are no equivalent rules for private parties in the EEC Treaty; Article 169 EEC contains a comparable provision only for the Member States; on the rights to participation and a hearing on the part of Member States see the E.C.J. judgment in Case 290/83 *Commission* v. *France* [1985] E.C.R. 440.

[72] *cf.* for example Article 217 EEC, and see on this below at C.

[73] *cf.* on this below at B on competence (*compétence d'attribution*).

[74] Regulation 1 on the language question, J.O. 1958, 385/17; O.J. Sp. Ed. 1952–1958, 59.

[75] Staff Regulations of December 18, 1961 in *Handbuch des Europäischen Rechts*, no. 1A 67/11, p. 57 in the version then in force (without annexes); *cf.* in the original Regulation 31/62 of December 18, 1962; J.O. 1962, 45/1385; O.J. Sp. Ed. 1959–1962, 135; modified by Regulation 259/68/EEC/Euratom/ECSC of February 29, 1968, J.O. 1968, L56/1; O.J. Sp. Ed. 1968, 30, as well as further amendments.

[76] Regulation 17 of February 6, 1962, J.O. 1962, 204; O.J. Sp. Ed. 1959–1962, 87, with later amendments.

[77] Regulation 99/63 of July 25, 1963, J.O. 1963, 2268; O.J. Sp. Ed. 1963–1964, 47 with later amendments.

[78] Regulation 2176/84 of July 23, 1984, O.J. 1984, L201/1, as amended by Council Regulation 1761/87 of June 22, 1987, O.J. 1987, L167/9.

[79] Decision 2177/84/ECSC of July 27, 1984, O.J. 1984, L201/17.

undertakings accused of it have roles to play as parties to the proceedings, and the Commission adopts a kind of arbitral function within a form of adversarial proceedings. Equally important, however, is the adoption of identically worded rules for the EEC[80] and ECSC[81] fields, since this represents a step towards an internal Community harmonisation of procedural law.

Even so, the Community has not gone beyond laying down normative rules for individual fields of law.

Here too, given the absence of written law, the task has fallen on the European Court of making a decisive contribution towards the development of an administrative law based on the rule of law.

It should be noted that the case law of the Court is characterised by a tendency to give an extensive interpretation of provisions on legal protection within its own court procedure as well as to develop general procedural guarantees for the parties concerned in administrative procedure, more especially the latter in recent times.

The selection of examples from the case law which follow may make a contribution towards a closer characterisation of the central principles underpinning the legal developments in question, thus facilitating a deeper understanding of the subsequent detailed analyses.

In the first case discussed here, Case 6/60, *Humblet*,[82] which dates from the early years of the Court's jurisprudence, the European Court was required to decide whether an official of the Coal and Steel Community, who considered that his rights had been infringed by a failure to observe the Protocol on Privileges and Immunities of the Community on the part of a Member State (his State of origin), could bring an action before the Court on that ground.

The ECSC Treaty contains no provision which would allow a private party to appeal direct to the Court on account of an infringement of the Treaty by a Member State.[83] Despite this, the Court of Justice found that the official did have a claim in respect of breach of the Protocol, based on Article 16, which provides that "any dispute concerning the interpreta-

---

[80] Regulation 2176/84.
[81] Decision 2177/84/ECSC.
[82] See Case 6/60 *J. Humblet* v. *Belgium* [1960] E.C.R. 559; *cf.* on this W. v. Simson, "Der Gerichtshof und unbestimmte Rechtsbegriffe," KSE 1, pp. 396 *et seq.* at p. 404; O. Riese, "Über den Rechtsschutz innerhalb der Europäischen Gemeinschaften," EuR 1966, pp. 24 *et seq.* at p. 30, who is in agreement; and P. Pescatore, KSE 1, pp. 547 *et seq.*, who is particularly critical.
[83] See on this expressly [1960] E.C.R. 559 at 571.

tion or application of the present Protocol shall be submitted to the Court."

Since the protocol grants the claimant an individual right, he must also have the correlative procedural right to seek a remedy if that substantive right is interfered with.[84]

The Court of Justice justified this finding with the concluding remark that:

> "In these circumstances it is proper to apply the principle whereby, in case of doubt, a provision establishing guarantees for the protection of rights cannot be interpreted in a restrictive manner to the detriment of the individual concerned."[85]

The second example to be mentioned here, the judgment of the Court of Justice in Joined Cases 8–11/66[86] concerns a dispute in the field of competition law.

A substantial number of Belgian, Dutch and German undertakings in the cement industry, the future applicants, had concluded a contract known as the "Noordwijks Cement Accoord," which had the object of perpetuating and reorganising a division of the Dutch cement market which had been in existence for decades.[87] This agreement had been properly notified to the Commission, thereby acquiring provisional protection against a fine in respect of the agreement in question under

---

[84] On this conclusion on the existence of a correlative procedural right matching a substantive right, see also from the case law of the Court of Justice its decisions in Case 175/73 *Syndicat Général du Personnel des organismes européens* v. *Council* [1974] E.C.R. 917 at 925 and Case 18/74 *Syndicat Général du Personnel des organismes européens* v. *Commission* [1974] E.C.R. 933 at 944. In that case the Court of Justice deduced from the freedom of association guaranteed in Article 24a of the Staff Regulations a *locus standi* under the second paragraph of Article 173 EEC. However, it rejected a claim based on Article 91 of the Staff Regulations. This provision was intended only for individual disputes.

[85] [1960] E.C.R. 559 at 572. The Court of Justice had already made use of this principle in the earlier Joined Cases 7 & 9/54 *Groupement des Industries Sidérurgiques Luxembourgeoises* v. *High Authority* [1956] E.C.R. 175 at 191 in order to justify recognising the right of action of an association of undertakings: "... In the opinion of the Advocate General, there is no provision of the Treaty which requires that the speciality of the producers must be linked to the special field of the dispute. The silence of the Treaty on this point cannot be interpreted to the disadvantage of the undertakings and associations. For this reason the applicant's right (in accordance with the provisions of Articles 33 and 35(3) ECSC) to institute proceedings before the Court cannot in this instance be contested."

[86] Joined Cases 8–11/66 *S.A. Cimenteries C.B.R. Cementbedrijven et al.* v. *Commission* [1967] E.C.R. 75.

[87] The facts are set out in detail in the "facts" part of the judgment ([1967] E.C.R. 79) and in the opinion of Advocate-General Roemer ([1967] E.C.R. 96).

1189

Article 15(5) of Regulation 17.[88] The Commission took a provisional negative position on the agreement and subsequently informed the undertakings involved in accordance with Article 15(6) of Regulation 17 that on the basis of a preliminary examination it was of the opinion that the conditions relating to the application of Article 85(1) EEC were present and that the application of Article 85(3) EEC would not be justified. In accordance with Article 15(6) of Regulation 17 as cited by the Commission, the undertakings lost by virtue of this communication the provisional protection against fines acquired through notification.

The undertakings concerned sought the annulment of the communication. The Commission considered the claim to be inadmissible. It argued that it had issued only a notice, not a decision within the meaning of Article 189 EEC. Furthermore Article 15(6) of Regulation 17 did not provide for the adoption of measures with the character of a decision. The Court of Justice rejected both of the Commission's defences.

In the opinion of the Court, the Commission's communication did amount to a decision which could be challenged in the Court, because it affected the favourable legal position under Article 15(5) of Regulation 17 which the applicants had acquired by virtue of notification of the agreement and burdened them with a considerable financial risk.

Furthermore it could not be deduced from the absence of the word "decision" in Article 15(6) or from the provisional nature of the procedure provided for in this provision that the Commission could content itself with the issue of a mere notice, since, in particular, the expression "notice" was not used in this provision either. In confirming its view of the law, the Court concluded by noting that:

> "The silence of the text in a matter which affects the protection of the rights of individuals cannot be construed in the manner most unfavourable to them."[89]

Where there are existing gaps in the regulatory structure, where the Treaties and secondary Community law are silent, the Court of Justice

---

[88] Article 15(5) of Regulation 17 provides that a fine cannot be imposed in respect of a prohibited cartel agreement for activities which take place "after notification to the Commission and before its decision in application of Article 85(3) of the Treaty, provided they fall within the limits of the activity described in the notification."

[89] [1967] E.C.R. 92. Advocate-General Roemer made a similar comment in his opinion, making an explicit reference to the judgment of the Court in *Humblet* (*supra*, footnote 82) ([1967] E.C.R. 105).

will thus guarantee the necessary legal protection through its own extensive interpretation or through a decision which makes law.[90]

The Court of Justice has pursued this conception of an extensive interpretation of the provisions on legal protection in the Treaties right up to the present day.[91] In the field of economic law this is particularly visible in the area of anti-dumping law, where the Court of Justice has guaranteed legal protection for the manufacturers and exporters concerned even as regards anti-dumping measures adopted in the form of a regulation,[92] although the EEC Treaty has in principle excluded the standing of individuals to challenge regulations on the basis of the second paragraph of Article 173 EEC.[93] Beyond this, the most recent questions of principle settled in this field by the Court of Justice concern the institutional framework of the Community. In Case 294/83,[94] in which the French political grouping *Les Verts* brought an action against the European Parliament seeking a fair distribution of money to fund an information campaign leading up to the direct elections to the Parliament, the Court was once more faced with the problem of ensuring a system of comprehensive judicial protection with a view to guaranteeing the operation of the Community on the basis of the rule of law. In that particular case it concluded in favour of making Parliament a defendant, a position not explicitly laid down in the Treaty, with the justification that

---

[90] See also, in addition to the examples cited here, above all the judgment of the Court in Case 25/62 *Plaumann* v. *Commission* [1963] E.C.R. 95. In that case the Court of Justice held that a decision of the Commission addressed to a Member State could in principle be challenged by a private individual as a decision within the meaning of the second paragraph of Article 173 EEC, (a decision addressed to another person) and, to justify this finding, based itself on the following extensive interpretation of the Treaty ([1963] E.C.R. 107): "Moreover provisions of the Treaty regarding the right of interested parties to bring an action must not be interpreted restrictively. Therefore the Treaty being silent on the point, a limitation in this respect may not be presumed."

[91] See in more detail J. Schwarze, "Stellung und Funktionen des Europäischen Gerichtshofes im Verfassungssystem der EG," in *Fortentwicklung des Rechtsschutzes in der Europäischen Gemeinschaft*, (J. Schwarze (ed.)), Baden-Baden 1987, p. 13 at 21.

[92] Case 113/77 *NTN Toyo Bearing* v. *Council* [1979] E.C.R. 1185, at 1205, para. 11; identical formulations can be found in the other "ball-bearing" cases; Case 307/81 *Alusuisse* v. *Council and Commission* [1982] E.C.R. 3463, para. 9; Cases 239 and 275/82, *Allied Corporation* v. *Commission* [1984] E.C.R. 1005 at 1030, paras. 12 & 14; Case 53/83 *Allied Corporation* v. *Council* [1985] E.C.R. 1621.

[93] For a more detailed doctrinal evaluation of the case law of the European Court see J. Schwarze, "Rechtsschutz gegen Anti-Dumpingmassnahmen der EG—Zu Verfahren und richterlicher Kontrolle auf dem Gebiet der Aussenwirtschaftsverwaltung der Gemeinschaft," EuR 1986, p. 217.

[94] Case 294/83 *Parti écologiste "Les Verts"* v. *Parliament* [1986] E.C.R. 1339. *cf.* in this context also the decision in the budgetary dispute of July 3, 1986 Case 34/86 *Council* v. *Parliament* [1986] E.C.R. 2155.

"an interpretation of Article 173 of the Treaty which would exclude measures adopted by the European Parliament from those which could be attacked would lead to a result which is contrary both to the spirit of the Treaty as expressed in Article 164 thereof and to its overall structure."[95]

In so far as the principle of the most comprehensive judicial protection possible is secured and recognised in Community law, it is also possible to discern clearly the corresponding tendencies towards the protection of the rule of law in the development of procedural rights in administrative procedure. Advocate-General Trabucchi stressed in a 1973 case before the Court the significance of the judicial control of procedural rights of the individual in the following terms:

"(...) an examination, in which the function of the Court will become all the more apparent as it involves itself in an affair completely impregnated with illegal activity, to see whether the rights of the defence of the applicant have been infringed in any respect and to ensure that procedure, the "shield of justice," has indeed been observed in its essential requirements."

Amongst the various rights intended for the protection of citizens, the principle of the right to a hearing before the administration is of particular significance.[96] On this point, in the competition case *Transocean Marine Paint Association*, the Court of Justice held that in addition to the specific guarantees to a hearing, it should be recognised as a general principle of Community law that "a person whose interests are perceptibly affected by a decision taken by a public authority must be given the opportunity to make his point of view known."[97] In his Opinion in this same case, Advocate-General Warner reached the conclusion that there should be general recognition of the principle of *audi alteram partem* as against the administration, following a careful comparative analysis of the administrative laws of the Member States.[98]

---

[95] Judgment of April 23, 1986, *supra*, footnote 94, at p. 1364, para. 25.

[96] Advocate-General Trabucchi in Case 46/72 *De Greef* v. *Commission* [1973] E.C.R. 543 at 558.

[97] Case 17/74 *Transocean Marine Paint Association* v. *Commission* [1974] E.C.R. 1063 at 1081; *cf.* also Case 85/76 *Hoffmann-LaRoche* v. *Commission* [1979] E.C.R. 461 at 511.

[98] Advocate-General Warner in *Transocean Marine Paint, op. cit.*, footnote 97, [1974] E.C.R. 1063 at 1090–1092. In the literature see M. Waline, in *Le Conseil d'Etat du Grand-Duché de Luxembourg, Livre Jubilaire*, 1957, pp. 495 *et seq.* On the meaning of this principle in Community law see in particular Lord Mackenzie Stuart, *The European Communities and the Rule of Law*, 1977, p. 32 and C.-D. Ehlermann, D. Oldekop, "Due Process," in FIDE *Rapports du 8ème Congrès*, June 22–24, 1978, pp. 11.1–11.20, *cf.* also

The method for developing the procedural rights of the individual as against the administration emerges clearly from the recently decided staff case of *De Compte*.[99] In a case based on unusual circumstances, the Court of Justice annulled a disciplinary measure taken against a financial official of the European Parliament on account of certain missing sums of money on the following grounds[100]:

> "It follows from a rule common to most of the legal systems of the Member States that the principle of *audi alteram partem* in an inquiry (...) requires that the official charged or his representative should be given an opportunity to be present (before the Disciplinary Board of the administration) when witnesses are heard and to put to them any questions which the official considers useful for his defence."

Naturally it is not only the Continental legal concepts which now play a role in the development of procedural rights of the defence in Community law. The decision in the case of *A. M. & S.*,[101] in which the Court of Justice recognised the concept of the confidentiality of correspondence with a lawyer (legal privilege), which is particularly well-developed in English law, shows clearly how the influence of the common law is growing in the development of general principles of Community law.[102]

The recently decided case of *Stanley Adams* shows how effectively general principles of administrative law can contribute to the protection

---

Advocate-General Warner, "Due Process," FIDE, *op. cit.*, pp. 1.1 *et seq.*; L. Goffin, "La jurisprudence de la Cour de Justice sur les Droits de la Défense," CDE 1980, pp. 127 *et seq.*; F. C. Jeantet, "La défense dans les procédures répressives en droit de la concurrence," RTDE 22 (1986), p. 53.

[99] Case 141/84 *De Compte* v. *European Parliament* [1985] E.C.R. 1951 *et seq.*; *cf.* also the Order of the President of July 3, 1984, Case 141/84R [1984] E.C.R. 2575.

[100] *De Compte*, *supra*, footnote 99, at p. 1966, para. 17.

[101] Case 155/79 *A.M. & S. Europe Ltd.* v. *Commission* [1982] E.C.R. 1575; see in more detail on this J. Schwarze, "Das Verhältnis von deutschem Verfassungsrecht und europäischem Gemeinschaftsrecht auf dem Gebiet des Grundrechtsschutzes im Spiegel der jüngsten Rechtsprechung," EuGRZ 1983, p. 117 at 120. On "legal privilege" see also *idem*, "Grenzen für die Ermittlungstätigkeit der Kommission als Wettbewerbsbehörde der EG—Zum Auskunftsverweigerungsrecht, Legal Professional Privilege und Schutz der Geschäftsgeheimnisse im Europäischen Kartellrecht," in J. Schwarze (ed.), *Der Gemeinsame Markt. Bestand und Zukunft in wirtschaftsrechtlicher Perspektive*, Baden-Baden 1987, p. 159 at 168.

[102] On the need for a balance between Continental legal conceptions and principles of the common law *cf.* for instance P. Pescatore, "Abschied vom Gerichtshof der Europäischen Gemeinschaften," EuR 1985, p. 341 at 343; W. v. Simson, "Das Common Law als Verfassungsrecht," Der Staat 16 (1977), pp. 75 *et seq.*

of the privacy rights and fundamental rights of the Community citizen.[103] Here the Court of Justice ordered compensation to be paid to a person who had given information to the Commission indicating a breach of the competition rules by his own former employer, the firm of Hoffmann-La Roche, where the Commission had not completely safeguarded his anonymity.

Furthermore, in addition to the development of unwritten general principles, the Court of Justice has also been eager to ensure that procedural rights included in normative acts are fully respected. Thus with respect to the duty to give reasons, it reached the following conclusion[104]:

> "Thus it is not sufficient that the Member States as addressees of the decision, are aware of the reasons as a result of their participation in the preliminary procedure and that the applicant as the person directly and individually concerned, is able to deduce these reasons by comparing the decision in question with similar earlier decisions. It is further necessary that the applicant should be enabled in practice to defend its rights and the Court should be able effectively to exercise its power of review on the basis of the statement of reasons."

Finally, the most recent case law expresses in an instructive form the connection between the guarantee of procedural rights in administrative procedure and legal protection in the context of judicial proceedings. Thus the Court has decided on numerous occasions that "where a regulation accords applicant undertakings procedural guarantees entitling them to request the Commission to find an infringement of Community rules, those undertakings should be able to institute proceedings to protect their legitimate interests."[105] The right of petition accorded by administrative procedure can be pursued as such through judicial pro-

---

[103] Case 145/83 *Stanley Adams* v. *Commission* [1985] E.C.R. 3539; the information which Mr. Adams gave later led to the competition proceedings in Case 85/76 *Hoffmann-La Roche* v. *Commission* [1979] E.C.R. 461. On administrative confidentiality, see also Advocate-General Lenz, opinion of January 22, 1986, Case 53/85 *AKZO Chemie* v. *Commission* [1987] E.C.R. 1965.

[104] *cf.* from the more recent case law Case 294/81 *Control Data Belgium* v. *Commission* [1983] E.C.R. 911 at 928, para. 14; Case 185/83 *Rijksuniversiteit Groningen* v. *Inspecteur der Invoerrechten* [1984] E.C.R. 3623 at 3641; also Case 69/83 *Luxembourg* v. *Court of Auditors* [1984] E.C.R. 2447 at 2466; Case 41/83 *Italy* v. *Commission* [1985] E.C.R. 873; *cf.* on the analysis of the case law and literature below, F.II.3 (duty to give reasons).

[105] Case 169/84 *COFAZ* v. *Commission* [1986] E.C.R. 391 at 414; in the field of anti-dumping law *cf.* Case 191/82, *FEDIOL* v. *Commission* [1983] E.C.R. 2913, at 2935, para. 28, and in competition law Case 26/76 *Metro* v. *Commission* [1977] E.C.R. 1875 at 1902, para. 13, also Case 210/81 *Demo-Studio Schmidt* v. *Commission* [1983] E.C.R. 3045 at

ceedings, without the complainant needing to prove that he or she is directly and materially concerned by the decision.

Naturally in Community law too, the procedural rights of those affected by administrative decisions will come up against limits, especially where the unconditional guarantee of such rights would make it impossible to achieve an administrative goal laid down by law. Thus in the case of *National Panasonic* the Court of Justice held that it is quite permissible for the Commission, as the responsible competition authority with the task of seeking out breaches of the competition rules, to conduct investigations of undertakings suspected of violations without giving prior notice.[106]

In the *IBM* case, which also originated in competition law, the Court of Justice was called upon to define the distinction between the executive powers of the Commission and the procedural rights of the parties concerned. In this case the Court held that the undertaking was not justified in appealing against the initiation of proceedings under competition law and the communication of a statement of objections with the following argument: a claim, at such an early stage of proceedings, would be incompatible "with the system of the division of powers between the Commission and the Court and of the remedies laid down by the Treaty, as well as the requirement of the sound administration of justice and the proper course of the administrative procedure to be followed in the Commission."[107]

The requirement to have regard to the functional capacity of the administration is not simply restricted to the right to a hearing. Thus, for example, Advocate-General Roemer considered that in the context of the duty to give reasons laid down in Community law, a brief statement of reasons would be sufficient where this appeared unavoidable on grounds of administrative efficiency[108]:

3063, para. 14. In its most recent case law on subsidy law the Court put other undertakings on the same footing as the complainant because of "the fact that the undertaking was at the origin of the complaint which led to the opening of the investigation procedure, the fact that its views were heard during that procedure and the fact that the conduct of the procedure was largely determined by its observations": Case 169/84, *supra*, para. 24. *cf.* on this in particular also Case 264/82 *Timex* v. *Council and Commission* [1985] E.C.R. 849 at 865, para. 13. But the Court of Justice has also indicated that not every aspect of a case, and certainly not obligations which fall exclusively on Member States, will give rise to a right of complaint for the individual. Case 174/84 *Bulk Oil* v. *Sun International* [1986] E.C.R. 559, para. 61.

[106] Case 136/79 *National Panasonic* v. *Commission* [1980] E.C.R. 2033 at 2053.
[107] Case 60/81 *IBM* v. *Commission* [1981] E.C.R. 2639 at 2654.
[108] Advocate-General Roemer in Case 41/70 *International Fruit Co. et al.* v. *Commission* [1971] E.C.R. 411 at 441 with reference to Case 16/65 *Schwarze* v. *Einfuhr- und*

"In addition, from the decided cases, the fact that the Commission only had 24 hours to prepare and issue the protective measure at issue must also be taken into consideration. This factor naturally requires a different standard for the statement of reasons than may be expected for measures which are drafted in normal circumstances."

Yet quite independently of the individual requirements for administrative conduct, the Court of Justice has always stressed the general significance of a properly ordered procedure.[109] A good example of this would be the steel market. Within the framework of the organisation of the market (a system of production quotas) the Commission argued that it must alter the production quotas for structural steel, because as a result of the recession in the building trade demand was falling sharply, a drop in prices was threatening and certain undertakings (so-called single-product undertakings) particularly affected were facing exceptional difficulties.[110]

The Commission could have granted these undertakings special production quotas, following a special examination of their case. It could also have taken measures under Article 58 ECSC to provide general assistance for the group of undertakings affected. This, however, would have required a complex consultation and examination process.

Instead of this the Commission decided on a general alteration of the quota regulation so that the affected groups in exceptional difficulties were allowed additional production quotas.

The Court annulled this decision on the following ground[111]:

"In order to resolve this issue it is useful to recall that in its judgment of 21 June 1958[112] the Court held that the powers conferred on the Commission by the ECSC Treaty are limited by the specific provisions set out in Title II of the Treaty and that, in particular, such powers would be diverted from their lawful purpose if it appeared that the Commission had made use of them with the exclusive, or at

---

Vorratsstelle für Getreide [1965] E.C.R. 877; *cf.* also Case 31/59 *Acciaieria e Tubificio di Brescia* v. *High Authority* [1960] E.C.R. 71 at 97; *cf.* also Case 69/83 *Luxembourg* v. *Court of Auditors* [1984] E.C.R. 2447 at 2466.

[109] Cases 140, 146, 221 & 226/82 *Walzstahl-Vereinigung und Thyssen* v. *Commission* [1984] E.C.R. 951 at 984 *et seq.*

[110] For the facts *cf.* paras. 9 *et seq.*, *supra*, footnote 109, pp. 978 *et seq.*

[111] E.C.J. *op. cit.*, footnote 109, [1984] E.C.R. 951 at 985, paras. 27 to 30.

[112] With reference to Case 8/57 *Groupements des Hauts-Fourneaux et Aciéries belges* v. *High Authority* [1958] E.C.R. 98.

any rate the main, purpose of evading a procedure specifically prescribed by the Treaty for dealing with the circumstances with which it
is required to cope.

In this regard it is clear from the preambles to the contested
decisions and from the explanations of the Commission summarised
above that the Commission was in fact pursuing the aims of Article
14 of the basic decisions and that in founding its action on Articles 16
and 18 of those decisions it not only avoided the restrictions laid
down in Article 14 but also sought to avoid the examination of each
individual case prescribed by that Article.

(. . .) (Furthermore) the Commission could decide upon a general
increase of the quotas for a whole group of undertakings characterised by their structure only after following the procedure laid down
in Article 58 of the Treaty, that is to say after consulting the Consultative Committee and obtaining the assent of the Council. Consequently, in acting pursuant to Articles 16 and 18 of the basic
decisions, the Commission also evaded the procedure specifically
laid down by the Treaty for that purpose."

In summary, this review provides the picture of developments in the
Community which is to be expected, given developments in the Member
States: the establishment of an administrative procedure in Community
law is regarded as essential having regard to the general principles of the
rule of law and in particular of legal protection. For this reason the law on
administrative procedure is becoming increasingly important in investigations of general administrative law principles in European law.

III. SUMMARY

Following this examination of the importance in principle of the law of
administrative procedure, the legal standards and principles of procedure
will now be examined in detail. In this context the development of the
decision-making process will be set out. Thus questions of competence
and procedural language must first be dealt with. Only then can legal
approaches to the gathering of information by authorities be examined in
more detail.

Thereafter the "rights of the defence" of both those directly affected
and of third parties will be addressed. This term, akin to the French
concept of "droits de la défense" includes the right of the person affected
to participation and information during the administrative procedure.

1197

Finally the rules on the formulation of the decision will be examined, that is on the authority's wording of the decision, the statement of reasons and the communication of the decision. In conclusion we shall consider which procedural defects would make the result of the procedure unlawful, thus enabling the Court to annul the decision. The investigation will include, where appropriate, comparative perspectives.

B. COMPETENCE

The question of the jurisdiction of the European Community can be posed at three levels. First, the Community must be competent as an organisation. Secondly, the competent institution must have acted. Thirdly, the process whereby the institution reached its decision must accord with its own internal rules of procedure.

I. COMMUNITY COMPETENCE

Where Community competence is at issue, it is necessary to establish in what areas and with what legal instruments the Community has the power to act.[1] The decisive factor is the particular substantive issue and how in

---

[1] *cf.* on Community competence in general A. Bleckmann, *Europarecht* (4th ed., Cologne 1984), etc., p. 58; H. P. Ipsen, *Europäisches Gemeinschaftsrecht*, Tübingen 1972, pp. 20/21 *et seq.*; G. Nicolaysen, *Europäisches Gemeinschaftsrecht*, Stuttgart, etc., 1979, p. 43; L.-J. Constantinesco, *Das Recht der Europäischen Gemeinschaften I*, Baden-Baden 1977, p. 264; *cf.* also R. Priebe, *Entscheidungsbefugnisse vertragsfremder Einrichtungen im Europäischen Gemeinschaftsrecht*, p. 75 with comprehensive further references in footnote 18. Of course, there are limited possibilities for altering the Community's framework of competence through Article 235 EEC (see G. Nicolaysen, *op. cit.* p. 45) and the so-called "minor revision" process under the ECSC Treaty (see L.-J. Constantinesco, *op. cit.* p. 265), but it is not possible thereby to create a new Community; *cf.* G. Nicolaysen, *op. cit.* p. 47; similarly A. Bleckmann, *op. cit.* p. 145; *cf.* in this context also R. Priebe, *op. cit.* who sees Article 235 as sufficient within limits as a legal basis for altering the Community's framework of competence. On the question of how far the express integration of new areas of policy, such as for example protection of the environment, into Community competence through the Single European Act will in future exclude, or at least hinder, recourse to Article 235 EEC, see in particular the contributions of F. G. Jacobs, G. Nicolaysen and J. A. Usher in the volume *Structure and dimensions of European Community policy* (eds. J. Schwarze & H. G. Schermers), Baden-Baden 1988. On the significance of the principle of the limited individual delegation for the organisational authority of the Community, *cf.* M. Hilf, *Die Organisationsstruktur der Europäischen Gemeinschaften*, Berlin, etc., 1982, pp. 310 *et seq.* See also J. A. Usher, "The Scope of Community Competence—Its Recognition and Enforcement," JCMSt 24 (1985/86), pp. 121 *et seq.*; R. Böhm, *Kompetenzauslegung und Kompetenzlücken im Gemeinschaftsrecht*, Frankfurt 1985.

practice it is regulated under the Treaties.[1a] To that extent we are dealing with a question which is in principle one of Community constitutional law, and which cannot be considered in depth because it transcends the boundaries of this investigation, limited to the specific problems of administrative law.

For such matters, reference should be made to the existing comprehensive works on the Community legal order. This work sketches only a few cases in which the administrative-law features of Community competence are visible.

As regards the areas in which the Community institutions themselves directly implement Community law, it will suffice to refer to competence in the areas of competition law, anti-dumping law, the regulation of the market in the field of the ECSC and the new Community trade policy instrument.[2]

In very recent times the question has re-emerged in the field of competition law whether the Community can validly address legally enforceable decisions to undertakings and persons which have their registered office permanent domicile outside the sovereign territory of the Member States.[3]

[1a] *cf.* from the recent case law of the Court, its judgment of July 9, 1987 in Joined Cases 281, 283–285 & 287/85, *Germany, etc.* v. *Commission*: migration policy, competence of the Community [1987] E.C.R. 3203. In that case, at para. 28, the Court had the following statement to make on the competence of the E.C. Commission in the area of migration policy:

"(w)here an article of the EEC Treaty—in this case Article 118—confers a specific task on the Commission it must be accepted, if that provision is not to be rendered wholly ineffective, that it confers on the Commission necessarily and per se the powers which are indispensable in order to carry out the task."

[2] *cf.* on this U. Everling, "Elemente eines europäischen Verwaltungsrechts," DVBl 1983, pp. 649 *et seq.* at p. 650; on the new trade policy instrument see C.-D. Ehlermann, "Neuere Entwicklungen im Außenhandelsrecht" in J. Schwarze (ed.), *Integrationsrecht*, Baden-Baden 1985, pp. 105 *et seq.* at pp. 113, 115 (*passim*); in contrast the technical implementation of export licences etc. falls within the sole jurisdiction of the Member States, Case 217/81 *Interagra* v. *Commission* [1982] E.C.R. 2233 at 2257.

[3] This question is particularly evident in the field of competition law; anti-dumping law and market regulation in the ECSC field, which also have international relevance, have only an "internal" effect, because the actual fixing of tariff duties or limitation of production through quotas can occur only "internally," so that problems of jurisdiction cannot occur. *cf.* on this problem A. Deringer, "The Common Market Competition Rules, with particular reference to non-member countries" 12 (1963) I.C.L.Q. 582 (*passim*); M. Kalmansohn, "Application of EEC Art. 85 and 86 to foreign multinationals," LIEI 1984/2, pp. 1 *et seq.*; P. Kunig, "Völkerrecht und Fusionskontrolle," WuW 1984/9, pp. 700 *et seq.*; K. M. Meessen, "Der räumliche Anwendungsbereich des EWG-Kartellrechts," EuR 1973, pp. 18 *et seq.*; R. Kovar, "Droit communautaire de la concurrence et droit international," CDE 1986, pp. 127 *et seq.*; P. M. Schmitt, "EG-Kartellrecht, Praxis und Verordnungen," in *Schwerpunkte des Kartellrechts* 1983/84, FIW-Schriftenreihe

In the so-called "Wood Pulp decision,"[4] the Commission based its claim to have the jurisdiction to issue a prohibition pursuant to Article 85(1) EEC against undertakings situated outside the Community on the fact that the trading activities of these undertakings have an effect within the common market.[5]

In a second decision worthy of mention,[6] the Commission forbade a cartel in the aluminium market. Amongst the members of this cartel were the external trade organisations of several Eastern Bloc States.

On its jurisdiction to issue "cease and desist" orders in such circumstances the Commission had the following to say[7]:

> "It follows that the applicability of Article 85, since it relates to trading activities, is not defeated by claims of sovereign immunity. Such claims are properly confined to acts which are those of government and not of trade. Even if the foreign trade organisations were indistinguishable under Socialist law from the State, no sovereign immunity would attach to their participation in the Brandeis agreements, since this was an exclusively commercial activity."

The argument that the existence of effects within the Common Market is sufficient to give the Community jurisdiction, was set out in more detail as follows by the Community with reference to the case law of the Court[8]:

> "Others of the participants were outside the common market but traded into the territory. In its Judgment of 25 November 1971, the Court of Justice held 'the fact that one of the undertakings which are parties to the agreement is situated in a third country does not

---

[4] (Vol. 112), Cologne, etc., 1985, p. 121 at 134 *et seq.*; E. Nerep, *Extraterritorial Control of Competition under International Law*, Vols. 1 and 2 *passim*, Stockholm 1983; M. Haymann, *Extraterritoriale Wirkungen des EWG-Wettbewerbsrechts*, Zürich 1974, *passim*.

[4] Commission Decision of December 19, 1984 (85/202/EEC) regarding a procedure under Article 85 EEC (IV/29.725-Woodpulp), O.J. 1985, L85/1. See the opinion of Advocate-General Darmon in Joined Cases 89, 104, 114, 116–117 & 125–129/85 *A. Ahlström oy* v. *Commission* [1988] E.C.R. 5193.

[5] *Ibid.*, para. 79.(p. 14f.).

[6] Decision of the Commission of December 19, 1984 (85/206/EEC) regarding a procedure under Article 85 EEC (IV/26.870—Aluminium imports from Eastern Europe) O.J. 1985, L92/1.

[7] *Ibid.*, O.J. 1985, L92/37, para. 9.2. It is noteworthy that these arguments were rather more hypothetical in character, since the Commission had made it clear in setting out the facts that these were legally independent external trade organisations (*cf.* O.J. 1985, L92/2, para. 1.2.3); *cf.* on this problem in detail, R. Kovar, "Droit communautaire de la concurrence et droit international," CDE 1986, pp. 127 *et seq.* at p. 130.

[8] *Ibid.*, O.J. 1985, L92/48 at para. 14.6.

prevent application of Article 85 since the agreement is operative on the territory of the common market' (Case 22/71 'Béguelin' [1971], paragraph 11, page 949). The Béguelin case concerned a vertical exclusive distribution agreement between a non-Community manufacturer and a Community distributor. The reasoning must be equally applicable to horizontal agreements between competitors where some are in the Community and some outside. Moreover there is no reason to distinguish in such horizontal agreements between those restrictions accepted towards each other by those within the common market and those outside, and those restrictions accepted towards each other by those wholly outside, subject always to the overall requirement that there be a substantial effect on trade between Member States."

Both the case law and legal writers bear this out,[9] in so far as the infringing activities have an effect within the territory of the Community[10] or in so far as the infringing activities can be directly attributed to the non-Community person or undertaking because it has acted through a dependent subsidiary based in the Community.[11]

By way of example it is possible to cite a decision of the Court of Justice, an Article 86 competition law case in which two undertakings, one with its registered office in the Community (Europemballage) and the other based outside the territory of the Community (Continental

[9] cf. for example H.-W. Daig, *Nichtigkeits- und Untätigkeitsklagen im Recht der Europäischen Gemeinschaften*, Baden-Baden 1985, p. 121 para. 155, footnote 425.

[10] The "Effects doctrine"; cf. the detailed comparative conclusions of Advocate-General Mayras in the *ICI* case, Case 48/69 *ICI* v. *Commission* [1972] E.C.R. 619 at 692–697; also on the special problems in the ECSC context. cf. also the decisions of the Court in Case 22/71 *Béguelin* v. *G.L. Import Export* [1971] E.C.R. 949 at 959, paras. 12 *et seq.*; Case 48/69, *ICI* v. *Commission* [1972] E.C.R. 619 at 661, paras. 126 *et seq.*; similarly in the parallel proceedings Case 52/69 *Geigy* v. *Commission* [1972] E.C.R. 787 at 835, para. 42 and Case 53/69 *Sandoz* v. *Commission* [1972] E.C.R. 845 at 849; IBM later once more vigorously contested the jurisdiction of the Community, in particular of the Commission, cf. Case 60/81 *IBM* v. *Commission* [1981] E.C.R. 2639; since the claim was inadmissible, the Court did not decide this question.

[11] To this extent too, the comparative law investigations of Advocate-General Mayras, who looked at U.S. and international law, are fundamental: Case 48/69 *ICI* v. *Commission* [1972] E.C.R. 619 at 690 *et seq.*; see also p. 662, para. 131; Case 52/69 *Geigy* v. *Commission* [1972] E.C.R. 787 at 835, paras. 43 *et seq.*; Case 6/72 *Europemballage and Continental Can* v. *Commission* [1973] E.C.R. 215 at 241, paras. 14 *et seq.* In more recent cases the jurisdiction of the Community and the Commission in this respect has not been contested: cf. Case 27/76 *United Brands* v. *Commission* [1978] E.C.R. 297; Case 22/78 *Hugin* v. *Commission* [1979] E.C.R. 1869; Case 85/76 *Hoffmann-La Roche* v. *Commission* [1979] E.C.R. 461.

Can) were accused of the abuse of a dominant position. Faced with the argument that the Community had no jurisdiction with regard to Continental Can, the Court held[12]:

> "It is certain that Continental caused Europemballage to make a take-over bid to the shareholders of TDV in the Netherlands and made the necessary means available for this. On 8 April 1970 Europemballage took up the shares and debentures in TDV offered up to that point. Thus this transaction, on the basis of which the Commission made the contested decision, is to be attributed not only to Europemballage, but also first and foremost to Continental. [Community law] is applicable to such an acquisition, which influences market conditions within the Community. The circumstance that Continental does not have its registered office within the territory of one of the Member States is not sufficient to exclude it from the application of Community law."

Thus both administrative practice and case law are striving to cover every possible factual situation which may lead to a disturbance of or interference with the Common Market.[13] This principle was developed in the context of competition law, but is not limited in its application to this field.

II. INSTITUTIONAL COMPETENCE

The distribution of competence among the institutions of the Community is laid down in the Treaties. Thus the Commission essentially holds the competence to ensure executive implementation. The competence to adopt normative legal acts lies primarily with the Council in the EEC and Euratom areas, although the Commission does possess a number of its own law-making powers. For the most part the Commission's legislative activity, aside from its basic right to propose legislation to the Council, consists of the adoption of implementing measures on the basis of a delegated law-making power under Article 155(4) EEC.[14] In the ECSC field, in contrast, the Commission has the major role as the

---

[12] Case 6/72 *Europemballage and Continental Can* v. *Commission* [1973] E.C.R. 215 at 242, para. 16; similar points are made in Case 48/69 *ICI* v. *Commission* [1972] E.C.R. 619 at 661, paras. 125 to 141.

[13] J. Sedemund, "Europäisches Gemeinschaftsrecht," NJW 1986, 632 at 637 has a similar view.

[14] See now Article 145 (3) EEC, which was added by Article 10 of the Single European Act.

legislator, although in a number of cases it requires the prior assent of the Council.

The fact that Community competence is shared by various institutions not only guarantees an appropriate accomplishment of the tasks of the Community, but also serves the purpose of controlling the exercise of sovereign power within the Community. Of course the Community-law principle of the separation of functions does not provide a *status quo* immutable in every respect. However, whenever an attempt is made to depart from the structure of competences laid down in the Treaties, the question is posed in principle whether the proposed alteration infringes the institutional framework of the E.C. and is therefore unlawful. The question at issue here is whether it is possible to transfer competence from one institution to another, and whether it is permissible to create new authorities and to give them competence. Both questions were overwhelmingly answered in the negative in earlier years.[15] However, the intervening years have seen a certain change in attitude.[16]

The transfer of competence from the Council to the Commission is expressly provided for in Article 155(4) EEC as well as in Article 145(3), which was added subsequently.[17] The Court has affirmed in this context that it is permissible to create so-called management committees and regulatory committees. These management committees are made up of representatives of the Member States. They give an opinion on regulations which the Commission wishes to adopt on the basis of the legislative power delegated to it within the framework of Article 155(4) EEC. If the Committee does not agree with the proposal of the Commission, then the Council itself must decide.

---

[15] *cf.* K. Holderbaum, "Chancen für eine europäische Kartellbehörde," EuR 1967, p. 116 at 125, 128; U. Everling, "Zur Errichtung nachgeordneter Behörden," *Festschrift für C. F. Ophüls*, Karlsruhe 1965, p. 33 at 42 (the creation of such authorities is desirable, but not attainable without an alteration of the Treaty); H. P. Ipsen, *Europäisches Gemeinschafts-recht*, Tübingen 1972, 20/48, p. 439, with further references, who differentiates even further between the various possibilities for delegation.

[16] M. Hilf, "Die abhängige juristische Person," ZaÖRV 1976, p. 551 (2.1, 557 *et seq.*, 2.3, 564 *et seq.*), who considers it permissible to transfer powers to bodies not provided for in the Treaty in so far as no sovereign executive powers are delegated; *cf.* also R. Priebe, *Entscheidungsbefugnisse vertragsfremder Einrichtungen*, Baden-Baden 1979, p. 90 at 104, 123, 157, who bases his views on Article 235 EEC as an authorising provision; *cf.* finally H. Schmitt v. Sydow, in H. v.d. Groeben *et al.*, *Kommentar zum EWG-Vertrag* (3rd ed., 1983), Baden-Baden, Article 162 (Articles 15, 16 Merger Treaty), para. 25; also J.-V. Louis, "Le Fonds européen de coopération monétaire," CDE 9 (1973) pp. 255 *et seq.*; M. Hilf *Die Organisationsstruktur der Europäischen Gemeinschaften*, Berlin, etc., 1982, pp. 316 *et seq.* (with further references).

[17] Article 124(4) Euratom; *cf.* H. P. Ipsen, *op. cit.*, footnote 15, 20/50, p. 440.

Since the failure to agree has no external legal effects but simply resurrects the Council's competence, the Court held that the introduction of this procedure was permissible. Justifying it in the face of various arguments, it held as follows[18]:

"Article 155 provides that the Commission shall exercise the powers conferred on it by the Council for the implementation of the rules laid down by the latter. This provision, the use of which is optional, enables the Council to determine any detailed rules to which the Commission is subject in exercising the power conferred on it. The so-called Management Committee procedure forms part of the detailed rules to which the Council may legitimately subject a delegation of power to the Commission. It follows from an analysis of the machinery set up by Articles 25 and 26 of Regulation 19 that the task of the Management Committee is to give opinions on draft measures proposed by the Commission, which may adopt immediately applicable measures whatever the opinion of the Management Committee. Where the Committee issues a contrary opinion, the only obligation on the Commission is to communicate to the Council the measures taken. The function of the Management Committee is to ensure permanent consultation in order to guide the Commission in the exercise of the powers conferred on it by the Council and to enable the latter to substitute its own action for that of the Commission. The Management Committee does not therefore have the power to take a decision in the place of the Commission or the Council.

Consequently, without distorting the Community structure and the institutional balance, the Management Committee machinery enables the Council to delegate to the Commission an implementing power of appreciable scope, subject to its power to take the decision itself if necessary.

The legality of the so-called Management Committee procedure, as established by Articles 25 and 26 of Regulation No. 19, cannot therefore be disputed in the context of the institutional structure of the Community. The respondent in the main action has also criticised the Management Committee procedure inasmuch as that machinery has deprived the Court of Justice of certain of its functions by instituting a right of annulment reserved to the Council for measures taken by the Commission.

---

[18] Case 25/70 *Einfuhr- und Vorratsstelle für Getreide* v. *Köster* [1970] E.C.R. 1161 at 1171, paras. 9 *et seq.*

1204

That objection is based on a false analysis of the Council's right to take over the decisions. The procedure laid down by Article 25 of Regulation No 19 has the effect of enabling the Council to substitute its own action for that of the Commission where the Management Committee gives a negative opinion. The system is therefore arranged in such a way that the implementing decisions adopted by virtue of the basic regulation are in all cases taken either by the Commission or, exceptionally, by the Council. These measures, whatever their author, are capable of giving rise in identical circumstances either to an application for annulment under Article 173 or to a reference for a preliminary ruling under Article 177 of the Treaty. It therefore appears that the exercise by the Council of its right to take over the decision in no way limits the jurisdiction of the Court of Justice."

This argument, which bases the lawfulness of the Management Committee procedure on the discretion of the Council to pass implementing measures, will have to be reconsidered in the light of the changes in the provisions of the Treaty introduced by the Single European Act. In accordance with Article 145(3) EEC the Council of Ministers is now under the obligation to delegate to the Commission the necessary powers to ensure the implementation of the legal acts which it passes. The delegation is to be made in accordance with the principles and rules which the Council laid down in its decision of July 13, 1987.[18a] This provides for four procedures.

Whereas in Procedure I the Commission is not bound by a contrary opinion on the part of the Management Committee, under Procedures II and III, as under the previous management and regulatory committee systems, the Council has the task of adopting the implementing measures on which the Committee has given a negative opinion. The exercise of the Commission's power to adopt protective measures is subject to a special committee procedure which, as in Procedure III, provides for a controlling jurisdiction on the part of the Council.

Furthermore, with its reference in Case 25/70 to the "institutional structure," the Court is referring back directly to its earlier decision in *Meroni*, in which it rejected a delegation of powers to an organ not

---

[18a] Council Decision 87/373/EEC, O.J. 1987, L197/33; *cf.* on this C.-D. Ehlermann, "Compétences d'exécution conférées à la Commission—la nouvelle décision-cadre du Conseil," RevMC 1988, 232. The European Parliament challenged this decision on October 5, 1987, *cf.* O.J. 1987, C321/4; the action was dismissed as inadmissible. See Case 302/87 *European Parliament* v. *Council* [1988] E.C.R. 561.

provided for in the Treaties on the grounds of the particular content of that delegation, but did not exclude the possibility in principle of such a delegation[19]:

> "However, the possibility of entrusting to bodies established under private law, having a distinct legal personality, and possessing powers of their own, the task of putting into effect certain 'financial arrangements common to several undertakings' as mentioned in subparagraph (a) of Article 53 (ECSC) cannot be excluded. (. . .) Hence the power of the High Authority to authorise or itself to make the financial arrangements mentioned in Article 53 of the Treaty gives it the right to entrust certain powers to such bodies subject to conditions to be determined by it and subject to its supervision."

However, the Court attaches a number of pre-conditions to the possibility of delegating powers, thus ensuring a very limited scope for such delegations[20]:

— The delegation must be express.[21]
— The Commission as the delegating authority can delegate only powers which it actually has.[22]

---

[19] Case 9/56 *Meroni & Co.* v. *High Authority* [1957–1958] E.C.R. 133 at 151; however, the ECSC Treaty provides specifically in Article 53 for the creation of such institutions; *cf.* also the opinion in Case 1/76 *Laying-up Fund for Inland Waterway Vessels* [1977] E.C.R. 741 at 760.

[20] See on this H. Schmitt v. Sydow, in H. v.d. Groeben *et al.*, *op. cit.*, footnote 16, Art. 162 (=15, 16 Merger Treaty) para. 25; *cf.* also H. P. Ipsen, *op. cit.*, footnote 15, 20/62 p. 444; M. Hilf in *Die Organisationsstruktur der Europäischen Gemeinschaften*, Berlin, etc., 1982, pp. 314 *et seq.* tends to go further.

[21] Case 9–10/56 *Meroni & Co.* v. *High Authority* [1957–1958] E.C.R. 133 at 151:
"A delegation of powers cannot be presumed, and even when empowered to delegate its powers the delegating authority must take an express decision transferring them."

[22] *Ibid.*, at p. 149:
"Decision No. 14/55 did not make the exercise of the powers which it conferred upon the Brussels agencies subject to any of the conditions to which it would have been subject if the High Authority had exercised them directly.
Even if the delegation resulting from Decision No. 14/55 appeared as legal from the point of view of the Treaty, it could not confer upon the authority receiving the delegation powers different from those which the delegating authority itself received under the Treaty.
The fact that it is possible for the Brussels agencies to take decisions which are exempt from the conditions to which they would have been subject if they had been adopted directly by the High Authority in reality gives the Brussels agencies more extensive powers than those which the High Authority holds from the Treaty."

— Only powers of execution or implementation may be delegated.[23]
— Discretionary powers in particular may not be transferred; the attribution of such powers to particular institutions is an essential aspect of the overall organisational framework of the Community.[24]
— The institutional balance may not be disturbed, and in particular the possibilities existing for the legal protection of individuals may not be damaged.[25]

The limitation on the authority to transfer its powers to other bodies applies not just to the Commission, but also in a similar way to the Council. Thus the Court has decided that the Council is not permitted to empower administrative commissions to adopt legal acts with normative effects.[26]

The limits thus established apply both to the transfer of powers to new bodies and to transfers to bodies which already exist.[27] In this way, the

---

[23] *Ibid.*, at p. 152:
"In any event, under Article 53 as regards the execution of the financial arrangements mentioned therein, it is only the delegation of those powers 'necessary for the performance of the tasks set out in Article 3' which may be authorised.
Such delegations of powers, however, can only relate to clearly defined executive powers, the use of which must be entirely subject to the supervision of the High Authority."

[24] *Ibid.*, at p. 152:
"The objectives set out in Article 3 are binding not only on the High Authority, but on the 'institutions of the Community . . . within the limits of their respective powers, in the common interest.'
From that provision there can be seen in the balance of powers which is characteristic of the institutional structure of the Community a fundamental guarantee granted by the Treaty in particular to the undertakings and associations of undertakings to which it applies.
To delegate a discretionary power, by entrusting it to bodies other than those which the Treaty has established to effect and supervise the exercise of such power, each within the limits of its own authority, would render that guarantee ineffective."
For an alternative view, see M. Hilf, *op. cit.*, footnote 20, p. 319, with further references, who argues that in so far as the delegating institution has sufficient powers of control, a transfer of discretionary powers should not be unlawful. Hilf refers only to the transfer of administrative discretion (non-political discretion), *cf.* p. 317, with a reference to R. Priebe, *Entscheidungsbefugnisse vertragsfremder Einrichtungen im Europäischen Gemeinschaftsrecht*, Baden-Baden 1979, pp. 110 *et seq.*

[25] *cf. ibid.*, quotation in footnote 24; similarly Case 25/70 *Einfuhr- und Vorratsstelle für Getreide* v. *Köster* [1970] E.C.R. 1161 at 1171–2, paras. 9 and 12.

[26] Case 98/80 *Romano* v. *INAMI* [1981] E.C.R. 1241 at 1256, para. 20.

[27] H. P. Ipsen, *op. cit.*, footnote 15, 20/62, p. 444: "generally applicable in Community law"—with reference to Advocate-General Roemer in Cases 9–10/56 *Meroni* v. *High Authority* [1957–1958] E.C.R. 133 at 177; *cf.* also R. Priebe, *op. cit.*, footnote 24, p. 172 (fundamental agreement with the *Meroni* case law, a proposal of legal policy to extend it,

institutional balance, the protection of which is of particular significance in this context,[28] can be secured in a variety of ways. It is for instance conceivable that it may be secured through rights of supervision and control, through the possibility of a complaint to the "genuinely" competent institution, and through securing of legal protection in such a way that equally effective legal protection is assured despite the delegation.[29]

In practice the Commission has made use of the possibility of creating new bodies with autonomous legal personality.[30] In so doing, however, it has transferred no executive powers. For the most part such bodies, in so far as they may exercise Community powers, may act only to confer benefits (through financial measures) in the fields of research and co-operation, or technical assistance for associated countries.

Judicial protection is guaranteed here; non-contractual liability claims may largely be brought directly before the European Court.[31] The Commission has instituted a possibility of seeking annulment, in so far as it

---

p. 173); H. Schmitt v. Sydow, in H. v.d. Groeben *et al.*, *op. cit.*, footnote 16, Article 162, para. 25.

[28] M. Hilf, *op. cit.*, footnote 20, p. 315.

[29] M. Hilf, *op. cit.*, footnote 20, p. 319 at 321.

[30] On the bodies with legal capacity *cf.* in particular M. Hilf, *op. cit.*, footnote 20, pp. 131 *et seq.*; in this context reference should be made to:
—The European Fund for Monetary Cooperation, founded by Regulation 907/73 of April 3, 1973, O.J. 1973, L89/2;
Executive powers: none;
Other powers: open market policy on currencies; gives assistance on the technical settlement of balances; it is essentially an instrument of co-operation between the central banks of the Member States.
—The European Centre for the Development of Vocational Training, founded by Regulation 337/75 of February 10, 1975, O.J. 1975, L39/1;
Executive powers: none;
Other powers: only coordination and research tasks.
—The European Foundation for the Improvement of Living and Working Conditions, founded by Regulation 1365/75/EEC of May 26, 1975, O.J. 1975, L139/1;
Executive powers: none;
Other powers: only research and coordination tasks, the organisation of conferences, etc., the conclusion of study contracts.
—The European Agency for Cooperation, founded by Regulation 3245/81 of October 26, 1981 O.J. 1981, L328/1;
Executive powers: none;
Other powers: the right to appoint staff and put them at the disposal of the ACP states, coordination and advisory tasks.
On the other existing special bodies and units *cf.* M. Hilf, *op. cit.*, footnote 20, pp. 24, 31, 48, 71 *et seq.*, 166 *et seq.*

[31] Regulation 907/73, footnote 30, Statute 9; Regulation 337/75, footnote 30, Article 17(2); Regulation 1365/75, footnote 30, Article 21(2); Regulation 3245/81, footnote 30, Article 18(2).

provides for a right of referral or complaint to itself.[32] The right of referral is effectively secured. If the Commission does not act within a certain time limit (two months), the referral is deemed to be tacitly dismissed by the Commission,[33] so that the complainant may take action directly against this decision under Article 173 of the Treaty.

The independent agencies have not so far, however, had a significant role to play in the case law.[34]

III. THE COMPETENCE OF THE DECISION-MAKING INSTITUTION

The most important body concerned with the direct implementation of Community law is, except in the field of staff matters,[35] the Commission. The Commission is a collegiate body, which takes its decisions as a body with collective responsibility, if necessary by vote.[36]

There are, however, a number of departures from this basic principle which are necessary to prevent the Commissioners becoming overburdened, and in order to accelerate procedure.[37] On the one hand the Commission has introduced a written procedure, which means that instead of requiring a collegial sitting, a submission can be made by one of the members of the Commission and distributed to the others. If none of

---

[32] Regulation 337/75, footnote 30, Article 18; Regulation 1365/75, footnote 30, Article 22; Regulation 3245/81, footnote 30, Article 19(1).

[33] Regulation 337/75, footnote 30, Article 18(2) and (3); Regulation 1365/75, footnote 30, Article 22(2) and (3); Regulation 3245/81, footnote 30, Article 19(2)–(5).

[34] cf. however Case 126/83 STS Consorzio v. Commission [1984] E.C.R. 2769 at 2777, paras. 10 et seq.

[35] In staff law each institution determines who within it shall exercise the tasks of the appointing authority: Article 2 of the Staff Regulations. This special feature can be justified on the grounds of the autonomy of each institution to organise itself internally.

[36] Article 17 of the Merger Treaty; cf. H. Smit, P. Herzog, The Law of the European Community—A Commentary on the EEC Treaty, New York, 1984, updated, Article 163.04, p. 5–248, Article 163.07, p. 5–251; H. Schmitt v. Sydow, in H. v.d. Groeben et al., op. cit., footnote 16, Article 163, para. 4; J. Amphoux in J. Mégret et al. (eds.), Le droit de la CEE, Brussels, 1979, Vol. 9, Article 163, note 3, p. 258; cf. also H. P. Ipsen, Europäisches Gemeinschaftsrecht, Tübingen, 1972, 20/48, p. 439. In practice, however, most decisions are taken unanimously, so that all are capable of supporting the decision vis-à-vis the outside world (a purely pragmatic approach, without any normative basis).

[37] cf. J. Amphoux, in J. Mégret et al. (eds.), op. cit., footnote 36, Article 163, note 14, p. 266, which refers to the fact that without some opportunity of relieving its burden the Commission would find itself "devant le choix entre l'hypocrisie et la paralysie"; M. Hilf, op. cit., footnote 20, p. 313 makes a similar point.

them objects within a specified time period (generally five days), the suggestion is deemed to be adopted.[38]

This procedure raises no doubts of a legal nature, since it preserves the basic responsibility of all the Commissioners and merely alters the voting procedure in a way that is not crucial.[39]

Furthermore, the Commission may vest decision-making authority for particular fields in individual Commissioners, allowing the adoption of decisions, for example, in the areas of competition law, anti-dumping law and the Common Agricultural Policy. Greatest use of this possibility is made in the agricultural field, which is characterised by a plethora of technical regulatory needs. The legal basis for this is Article 27 of the provisional rules of procedure of the Commission[40]:

> "Subject to the principle of collegiate responsibility being respected in full the Commission may empower its members to take, in its name and subject to its control, clearly defined measures of management or administration.
>
> Officials may also be empowered to take such measures if this is indispensable for the Commission properly to be able to fulfil its tasks.
>
> Unless they have been delegated to him personally powers vested in an official shall be valid for his deputy.
>
> Powers conferred in this way may not be sub-delegated except to the extent expressly laid down in the enabling decision. The provisions of this article shall not affect the rules concerning delegation in respect of financial matters and staff administration."

The legitimacy of this transfer is problematic, since it diminishes the responsibility of the collegiate body as a whole.[41] However, the pressure

---

[38] H. Schmitt v. Sydow, in H. v.d. Groeben *et al.*, Article 163, no. 9; J. Amphoux, in J. Mégret *et al.* (eds.) *op. cit.*, footnote 36, Article 163, note 9.

[39] J. Amphoux, in J. Mégret *et al.* (eds.), *op. cit.*, footnote 36, Article 163, note 9; H. Smit, P. Herzog, *op. cit.*, footnote 36, Article 163.04; H. Schmitt v. Sydow, in H. v.d. Groeben *et al.*, *op. cit.*, footnote 16, Article 163, no. 9 also agrees with the conclusion; also on further simplifications of procedure, such as for example the preparation of the proposals by the chefs de cabinet, in connection with the tacit adoption procedure.

[40] Communication 67/426/EEC of July 6, 1967, J.O. 1967, 147/1 read together with the rules of procedure of the Commission, O.J. 1963 p. 181, in the version of the Decision 75/461/Euratom/ECSC/EEC of July 23, 1975, O.J. 1975, L199/43.

[41] *cf.* on this also J. Amphoux, in J. Mégret *et al.* (eds.), *op. cit.*, footnote 36, Vol. 5, Article 163, notes 10 *et seq.*, pp. 262 *et seq.*; H. Smit, P. Herzog, *op. cit.*, footnote 36, Article 163.08; H. Schmitt v. Sydow, in H. v.d. Groeben *et al.*, *op. cit.*, footnote 16, Article 163, nos. 12 *et seq.*, assumes, incorrectly, that where decisions are taken, there is nothing

of work and the technical nature of many such decisions make a delegation of this type necessary, especially since it does not give the Commissioner concerned a blank cheque but limits the decision-making authority
to measures of a management and administrative nature. Advocate-
General Reischl justified this transfer in the following terms[42]:

> "In truth, according to the Commission there was a perfectly proper
> decision of the Commission which was in accordance with Article
> 27(1) of the Rules of Procedure in force for the time being, that is to
> say, a decision *authorising* one of its members to take measures
> relating to the business of the Commission and of its administration.
> In point of fact this assurance, which is not denied, should be
> sufficient, just as there can be no doubt that the authority delegated
> to the Commissioner is covered by Article 27 of the present Rules of
> Procedure, since fixing the production quotas is a purely arithmetical
> application of the Decision No. 2794/80/ECSC which contains all the
> necessary criteria for the purpose and does not leave any scope for
> discretion."

The ECJ too has affirmed the validity of the transfer of the so-called
authority to sign[43]:

> "The applicant asserts that the notice of objections, for which Article
> 2 of Regulation No. 99/63 of the Commission makes provision, is
> irregular because it is signed by the Director-General for Competi-
> tion *per procurationem* although, according to the applicant, no such
> delegation of powers on the part of the Commission is permitted.
>
> It is established that the Director-General for Competition did no
> more than sign the notice of objections which the Member of the
> Commission responsible for problems of competition had previously
> approved in the exercise of the powers which the Commission had
> delegated to him. Therefore that official did not act pursuant to a

---

against assignment of authority; *cf.* also P. Schindler, "Zur Problematik der Ermächtigung einzelner Mitglieder und Beamter der Kommission der Europäischen Wirtschaftsgemeinschaft (EWG) bzw. der Europäischen Gemeinschaften (EG) zum Erlaß von
Verordnungen auf agrarrechtlichem Gebiet," DVBl. 1970, pp. 605 *et seq.* (*passim*).

[42] Advocate-General Reischl, Case 275/80, etc. *Krupp* v. *Commission* [1981] E.C.R. 2489
at 2524; the Court in Case 48/69 *ICI* v. *Commission* [1972] E.C.R. 619 at 649, para. 12,
took a similar position, holding that it was permissible for the statement of objections to
be checked by the Commissioner on the basis of the delegation of powers by the whole
Commission.

[43] Case 48/69 *ICI* v. *Commission* [1972] E.C.R. 619 at 649, paras. 11 *et seq.*

delegation of powers but simply signed as a proxy on authority received from the Commissioner responsible.

The delegation of such authority constitutes a measure relating to the internal organisation of the departments of the Commission, in accordance with Article 27 of the provisional Rules of procedure adopted under Article 16 of the Treaty of 8 April 1965 establishing a single Council and a single Commission."

In addition to the delegation of actual decision-making powers, there are also delegations of powers of investigation to officials. This is permissible, otherwise it would be impossible to conceive of investigations of undertakings in accordance with Article 14 of Regulation 17/62 (Competition Regulation).[44]

Finally, it would be appropriate to mention one or two particular features of the law relating to staff. The Staff Regulations provide that each institution must establish who holds the powers of the "appointing authority."[45] To that extent, individual powers are delegated to high-ranking officials. This practice was condoned by the Court when it characterised this transfer of powers as a management measure, with respect to which further delegation would also be permissible.[46] In this respect, the Court has also stated that defects in jurisdiction will not be investigated by the Court of its own motion,[47] but an express finding to that effect will always lead to annulment.[48]

C. THE LANGUAGE QUESTION

In a Community, consisting of twelve Member States, with not inconsiderable executive powers, there is a need for special precautions to be taken to ensure that all citizens can communicate with the Community administration and that conversely its communications are notified to those affected in a form which is comprehensible to them.[1] Thus the

---

[44] Regulation 17/62 of February 6, 1962, O.J. 1962, 204; O.J. Sp.Ed. 1959–1962, 87.
[45] Article 2(1) of the Staff Regulations; cf. also Case 101/79 Vecchioli v. Commission [1980] E.C.R. 3069 at 3086.
[46] Case 46/72 De Greef v. Commission [1973] E.C.R. 543 at 552, paras. 14 et seq.; Case 25/68 Schertzer v. Parliament [1977] E.C.R. 1729 at 1741.
[47] Case 101/79 Vecchioli v. Commission [1980] E.C.R. 3069 at 3088, para. 19.
[48] Case 48/70 Bernardi v. European Parliament [1971] E.C.R. 175 at 185, paras. 30 et seq.
[1] On the significance of this cf. J. Thiesing, in H. v.d. Groeben et al., Kommentar zum EWG-Vertrag, (3rd ed., Baden-Baden 1983), Article 217 no. 12; cf. also Report of the European Parliament by Nyborg, EP-Doc 1–306/82.

regulation of the language question is provided for in the Treaties (Article 217 EEC[2]). This task was fulfilled by Regulation 1/58.[3] The essential provisions of this regulation are in brief as follows:

Article 1:
The official languages and the working languages of the institutions of the Community shall be Danish, Dutch, English, French, German, Greek, Italian, Portuguese and Spanish.

Article 2:
Documents which a Member State, or a person subject to the jurisdiction of a Member State sends to institutions of the Community may be drafted in any one of the official languages selected by the sender. The reply shall be drafted in the same language.

Article 3:
Documents which an institution of the Community sends to a Member State or a person subject to the jurisdiction of a Member State shall be drafted in the language of that State.

Article 4:
Regulations and other documents of general application shall be drafted in the nine official languages.

Article 5:
The Official Journal of the Communities shall be published in the nine official languages.

It is noteworthy here that Gaelic, the original and official language of Ireland, is not included, presumably because English is generally spoken and used in Ireland.[4] The costs occasioned by these language rules are

---

[2] Article 190 Euratom is identical. The ECSC Treaty contains no comparable provision: a decision of the Foreign Ministers is the basis for the language regulation, *cf.* H. Smit, P. Herzog, *The Law of the European Community—A Commentary on the EEC Treaty*, New York, as at 1984, Article 217.03 (p. 6–114).

[3] Regulation 1 determining the language to be used by the EEC, J.O. 1958, 17/385; O.J. Sp.Ed. 1952–1958, 59 as amended by the 1972 Act of Accession and the 1979 Act of Accession.

[4] See also H. Smit, P. Herzog, *op. cit.*, footnote 2, Article 217.03, p. 6–115; *cf.* also J. Thiesing, in H. v.d. Groeben *et al.*, *op. cit.*, footnote 1, Article 217, no. 2; the position is different as regards procedure before the European Court, *cf.* Article 29 of the Statute of the Court, although the judgments are not published in Gaelic (Irish) (Article 30(2) of the Statute of the Court).

considerable. The accession of Spain and Portugal increased the number of possible language combinations from 42 to 72 (an increase of 72.5 per cent.).[5]

However, as regards dealings with citizens, no alterations to the language rule have been discussed, for it is scarcely imaginable that persons affected by Community law should be expected to express themselves in a foreign language about matters crucial to their interests.[6] Moreover, the language regulation facilitates the achievement of effective judicial protection, as this necessarily presupposes that those participating can understand the language of the procedure. However, in the case of one or two legal acts, there have been departures from the requirement of "all languages" (cf. for example the decision on a uniform passport).[7]

The Court of Justice has only seldom been required to deal with the language question. However, it has held that the communication of a decision in a further (foreign) language in addition to the actual language of the proceedings is not unlawful.[8] The Court of Justice has also dealt with the language question as regards international trade (with non-E.C. undertakings)[9]:

> "According to Article 3 of the above mentioned Regulation, written documents which any organ of the Community sends to a person subject to the jurisdiction of a Member State, are to be drawn up in the language of that State. As the applicants have their registered office in a third State, the choice in the present case of the official language of the decision had to be based on what relations existed within the Common Market between the applicants and one State or another of the Community. Europemballage had opened an office in Brussels and set out its written observations in the administrative

---

[5] cf. J. Thiesing, op. cit., footnote 1, Article 217, no. 11; H. Kusterer, "Das Sprachenproblem in der Europäischen Gemeinschaft," EuArch 1980, p. 693 at p. 696; the report of the Budgetary Committee of the Parliament (Dankert) EP-Doc 1– 42/79, Annex, p. 21, and the Nyborg report on multilingualism, EP-Doc 1–306/82 take the same view; cf. also the E.C. Commission: *The transitional period and the institutional implications of enlargement*, Bull. Supp. 2/78, p. 9.

[6] For the internal workings of the institutions, the Budgetary Committee of the European Parliament has demanded changes with the goal of reducing costs, cf. Dankert Report, footnote 5, p. 21. The Commission, however, has been noticeably reluctant to bring forward a proposal: Bull. Supp. 2/78, p. 9.

[7] O.J. 1981, C241/1; cf. also J. Thiesing, op. cit., footnote 1, Article 217, no. 14, with further references in footnote 36.

[8] Case 40/73, etc. *Suiker Unie* v. *Commission* [1975] E.C.R. 1663 at 1930, para. 113.

[9] Case 6/72 *Europemballage and Continental Can* v. *Commission* [1973] E.C.R. 215 at 241, para. 12.

process in French. The facts of the case being as indicated, it is not evident that the choice of the French language as the official language of the decision offended against Article 3 of Regulation 1/58 of the Council."

A breach of the language regulation is invariably an infringement of an essential procedural requirement.[10] An infringement however will not necessarily lead to annulment if the content has been correctly understood by the addressee.[11]

"The failure to communicate a Dutch version of the draft minutes thus constitutes an irregularity in drawing up that document which is capable of affecting its validity. It is clear, however, from the arguments put forward by the applicant that it was able in due time to acquaint itself with the contents of the minutes. The applicant has not alleged that this resulted in the minutes' containing substantial inaccuracies or omissions with regard to it. It must therefore be concluded that the irregularity which has been found did not in this case have harmful consequences capable of vitiating the administrative procedure."

D. ADMINISTRATIVE POWERS TO COLLECT INFORMATION, AND THE LEGAL LIMITS GOVERNING THEM

To facilitate the performance of the tasks entrusted to it under the E.C. Treaties, the Commission has been given administrative powers to collect information. The following section examines the competence which the Commission possesses in this field, the form which information-collecting procedures take, and the legal limits to which it is subject when seeking evidence.

---

[10] H. W. Daig, *Nichtigkeits- und Untätigkeitsklagen im Recht der Europäischen Gemeinschaften*, Baden-Baden 1985, p. 129, no. 166, footnote 453.
[11] Case 41/69 *ACF Chemiefarma* v. *Commission* [1970] E.C.R. 661 at 686, paras. 29 *et seq.*; H. Smit, P. Herzog, *op. cit.*, footnote 2, Article 217.04, p. 6–119, with further references, are in agreement.

I. THE COMMISSION'S POWERS TO COLLECT INFORMATION

1. Powers to collect information provided for in the Treaties

Under Article 213 EEC and Article 187 Euratom, the Commission has the power, for the performance of the tasks entrusted to it, to collect the necessary information from Member States and individuals and to carry out checks. The Council, according to the Treaty provisions, lays down the limits and conditions which will apply.[1]

The powers possessed by the Commission within the framework of Article 47 ECSC are more wide-ranging.[2] That provision directly gives the power to the High Authority to collect the "information it requires" and to make "necessary checks." Furthermore, this provision is directly applicable and requires no implementing measures on the part of the Council.[3]

These Treaty provisions are not, however, the only ones which give the Commission the discretion ("may") to avail itself of powers to collect information. One should mention here at least the following provisions: Articles 43, 75, 79, 87, 103 and 235 EEC. Article 213 EEC represents, however, the main provision,[4] the limits of which may not be exceeded.[5]

Early on, the Court of Justice decided that the rights of the Commission to collect information and conduct investigations are independent of each other, and that a right to carry out an investigation without a prior request for information may be admitted.[6]

So far the Council has not given the Commission a general power to require information, but in Regulations and Directives it has laid down in more detail the powers established in the Articles cited above.[7]

---

[1] *cf.* the complete list of the Regulations and Directives which have so far been adopted in H. v.d. Groeben *et al.*, *Kommentar zum EWG-Vertrag*, Baden-Baden (3rd ed.), Article 213, no. 24.

[2] Specific rights of information are contained also in Articles 65 and 66 ECSC.

[3] F. Gillmeister, *Ermittlungsrechte im deutschen und europäischen Kartellordnungswidrigkeitenverfahren*, Baden-Baden 1985, p. 126.

[4] W. Hummer, in E. Grabitz, *Kommentar zum EWG-Vertrag*, updated to May 1986, Article 213 no. 5.

[5] H. Smit, P. Herzog, *The Law of the European Economic Community*, New York, 1976, 213.04.

[6] Case 31/59 *Acciaieria e Tubifino di Brescia* v. *High Authority* [1960] E.C.R. 71, at 80.

[7] *e.g.*, Article 11 of Regulation 17, J.O. 1962, 204; O.J. Sp.Ed. 1959–1962, 87.

The provisions of the EEC Treaty essentially provide for three types of rights to collect information and conduct investigations[8]:

(a) statistical: the collection of data to draw up statistics, balance sheets and surveys.[9]
(b) inquisitorial: the examination and bringing under official control of legally relevant factual situations. The request for information takes place in two stages and is aimed primarily at individuals; a duty on Member States to provide information is laid down in specific Treaty provisions: *e.g.* Articles 14(6), 15(1) and 31(2) EEC.[10] Furthermore, it is possible to deduce a general duty to do so from Article 5 EEC. Every Member State also has a general right to refuse to reveal information under Article 223 EEC with regard to matters which are necessary to ensure the protection of its essential security interests.

Inquisitorial rights, which may also be enforced against the will of the party affected, are granted to the executive on the basis of a Regulation or Directive of the Council. In individual cases, they are implemented in the form of a decision of the Commission.[11]

The most important inquisitorial rights exist in the field of competition law,[12] trade law and the common agricultural policy.

(c) miscellaneous: the Commission in principle has discretion with regard to its intervention. If it does intervene, the following legal limitations apply to the exercise of its powers to collect information.
— The information must be used by the Commission in order to fulfil the tasks with which it is entrusted.
— It must be necessary to this end for the Commission to seek information. Information can be sought only if it is actually necessary; mere convenience is not sufficient.[13] The "necessity" is also

---

[8] So far, it is only in the inquisitorial field that the Council has given the Commission the power to conduct investigations; *cf.* H. v.d. Groeben, *et al.*, *op. cit.*, footnote 1, Article 213, no. 33.

[9] Comprehensive references can be found in H. v.d. Groeben, *op. cit.*, footnote 1, Article 213 no. 24, note 34.

[10] *cf.* H. v.d. Groeben *et al.*, *op. cit.*, footnote 1, Article 213 no. 18.

[11] W. Hummer, in E. Grabitz, *op. cit.*, footnote 4, Article 213 nos. 2, 21.

[12] See on this in more detail Council Regulation 17, footnote 7.

[13] W. Hummer, in E. Grabitz, *op. cit.*, footnote 4, Article 213, no. 10.

further limited by the principle of proportionality.[14] The "necessity" of a measure can be reviewed by the Court of Justice.[15]

— At least where the EEC and Euratom Treaties are concerned, the Council must have defined the Commission's right to collect information in accordance with the provisions of the Treaty.

2. Powers to collect information provided for in secondary legislation

Of great practical significance in the field of E.C. competition law is Regulation 17/62,[16] adopted by the Council as the first measure implementing Articles 85 and 86 EEC, and in the field of anti-dumping law Regulation 2176/84.[17]

Using both these Regulations it is proposed to demonstrate that the Commission's powers to collect information may take a great variety of forms.

(a) Regulation 17/62

Under Article 3 of Regulation 17, the Commission acts either upon the application of a Member State or of a natural or legal person claiming a legitimate interest, or on its own initiative.

In order to clarify a doubtful factual situation, the Commission may direct requests for information or decisions requiring information to the undertakings concerned,[18] or it may carry out investigations even on the spot.[19]

---

[14] Case 136/79 *National Panasonic* v. *Commission* [1980] E.C.R. 2033 at 2059; Case 155/79 *A.M. & S.* v. *Commission* [1982] E.C.R. 1575 at 1609 *et seq.*
[15] F. Gillmeister, *op. cit.*, footnote 3, p. 126 with further references.
[16] Commission Decision No. 2177/84/ECSC of July 27, 1984 is largely identical to Council Regulation 2176/84.
[17] O.J. 1984, L201/1; as amended by Council Regulation 1761/87 of June 22, 1987, O.J. 1987, L167/9.
[18] *cf.* Article 11 of Regulation 17.
[19] *cf.* Article 14 of Regulation 17.

(aa) The request for information under Article 11 of Regulation 17

In order to perform the duties entrusted to it under Articles 87 and 89 EEC, the Commission may collect all the information it requires from the Governments and responsible authorities of the Member States, as well as from undertakings and associations of undertakings.

In the two-stage procedure for collecting information, the first stage consists of a formal request for information, to which the addressee need not necessarily accede.[20] Only a formal decision to seek information, a decision open to challenge before the Court of Justice, imposes a duty on the addressee to give information,[21] and such a decision may be enforced.[22,23]

If one looks at the actual practice of the Commission, it would be better to talk of a three-stage procedure, since the Commission often precedes the formal request for information with an informal request to supply information.[24]

The wide-ranging right to information laid down in Article 11 of Regulation 17 extends to indirect questions of law, knowledge of which is essential for the implementation of the competition rules.[25]

The Commission may, as mentioned above, demand only such information as is necessary for the fulfilment of the tasks entrusted to it.[26] Thus the concept of necessity represents the limit upon the right to information.[27] It is a precondition of the undefined legal concept of "necessity," which is subject to full review by the Court, that the information requested is appropriate for the achievement of the stated aim and represents the least restrictive means of achieving it.[28]

---

[20] A. Gleiss, M. Hirsch, *Kommentar zum EWG-Kartellrecht*, (3rd ed., Heidelberg 1978), Article 11 of Regulation 17, no. 2.

[21] C. Canenbley, *Verfahrensregeln der Kommission der Europäischen Gemeinschaften*, in XI. Internationales EG-Kartellrechts-Forum, Munich 1986, p. 74 at 75.

[22] The Commission's right to information from the Member States cannot be enforced; the Commission must pursue an enforcement action under Article 169 EEC; *cf.* A. Gleiss, M. Hirsch, *op. cit.*, footnote 20, Article 11 of Regulation 17, no. 4.

[23] A. Gleiss, M. Hirsch, *op. cit.*, footnote 20, Article 11 of Regulation 17, no. 2.

[24] If this request is not fulfilled, the Commission often bypasses the formal request for information, which will in any case usually be in vain, and immediately addresses a formal decision to the undertaking; *cf.* on this A. Gleiss, M. Hirsch, *op. cit.*, footnote 20, Article 11 of Regulation 17, no. 2.

[25] F. Gillmeister, *op. cit.*, footnote 3, p. 130.

[26] A. Gleiss, M. Hirsch, *op. cit.*, footnote 20, Article 11 of Regulation 17, no. 12.

[27] F. Gillmeister, *op. cit.*, footnote 3, p. 131.

[28] On the details see Chap. 5 on the principle of proportionality.

Those to whom such a decision is addressed must respond to the demand for information if it is necessary and is thus under a duty to provide information unless they have a right to refuse information,[29] which may exist on one of the following grounds[30]:

— the right to refuse information on grounds of the protection of national security[31]; this ground is largely governed by Article 223 EEC;
— the right to refuse information on grounds of the protection of professional secrets[32];
— the right to refuse information on grounds of protection against self-incrimination, at least where the Commission requires the information exclusively for the purpose of establishing facts justifying the imposition of a fine.[33] There is, however, no basic right to refuse information on grounds of the protection of business secrets. However, the Commission may not give such information to third parties without authorisation.[34]

(bb) The authority to conduct investigations under Article 14 of Regulation 17

In order to fulfil its tasks under E.C. competition law, the Commission may further conduct all necessary investigations of undertakings and associations of undertakings. It has extensive powers to assist it (the Commission) in investigating such undertakings.

Here too the Commission may use a two-stage procedure: on the one hand, a non-binding request to carry out an investigation (Article 14(2)) and on the other, the order to submit to an investigation (Article 14(3)). The two forms of request to conduct an investigation need not follow one

---

[29] *cf.* on this C. Canenbley, *op. cit.*, footnote 21, p. 74 at 83, who demonstrates the multiplicity of the problems here.
[30] *cf.* on this W. Hummer, in E. Grabitz, *op. cit.*, footnote 4, Article 213 nos. 15 *et seq.*
[31] *cf.* on this in detail F. Gillmeister, *op. cit.*, footnote 3, pp. 138 *et seq.*
[32] *cf.* on this in detail F. Gillmeister, *op. cit.*, footnote 3, pp. 141 *et seq.*
[33] F. Gillmeister, *op. cit.*, footnote 3, pp. 149 *et seq.* C. S. Kerse, *EEC Antitrust Procedure*, (2nd ed., London 1988), p. 112 has doubts about this.
[34] F. Gillmeister, *op. cit.*, footnote 3, pp. 149 *et seq.* C. S. Kerse, *op. cit.*, footnote 33, p. 86 with further references.

after the other, but it is a matter for the Commission's discretion which procedure it makes use of.[35]

The Commission is also under no obligation to request information before it carries out an investigation. According to the case law of the Court it is free to choose whichever procedure it wishes, provided it acts in accordance with the requirements of expediency.[36]

Article 14 provides the Commission with very extensive powers to collect information, and this has provoked a number of proposals for improvements, in particular from the United Kingdom.[37]

Under Article 14 of Regulation 17 the Commission can make an independent decision as to whether it is convinced by the correctness and completeness of the information provided to it, and it may also ascertain further facts which have not yet been required via a request for information.[38] The Commission's investigation procedures are likewise subject to the requirement of necessity[39]; thus just as in the case of a request for information, there must be a balance in the investigation procedure between the interests of the Commission in establishing the facts and the interests of the undertaking concerned in protecting its own affairs.[40] However, it is natural that in the investigation procedure, which interferes more radically with the interests of the parties affected, a different standard should apply from that applicable to information procedures.[41]

The right to conduct investigations is limited by reference to:

— the risk of self-incrimination[42];
— the protection of legal professional privilege.[43]

---

[35] C. Canenbley, op. cit., footnote 21, p. 74 at 75; A. Gleiss, M. Hirsch, op. cit., footnote 20, Article 14 of Regulation 17, no. 4.

[36] Case 31/59 Acciaieria e Tubifino di Brescia v. High Authority [1960] E.C.R. 71 at 79.

[37] House of Lords Select Committee on the European Communities, Competition Practice, Session 1981–82, 8th Report, Page xii, paras. 24, 25; H. W. Kreis, "Commission procedures in competition proceedings—recent reforms in practice and law," in B. E. Hawk, Antitrust and trade policies of the European Economic Community, New York 1983, p. 145 at 150, footnote 19 with further references.

[38] In this context the author of the Regulation works primarily from the assumption of investigations by authorities of the Member States (Article 13 of Regulation 17) and only subsidiarily of investigations by the Commission (Article 14 of Regulation 17).

[39] cf. the relevant details in Chapter 5 on the principle of proportionality.

[40] A. Gleiss, M. Hirsch, op. cit., footnote 20, Article 14 of Regulation 17, no. 7.

[41] See, among others, A. Gleiss, M. Hirsch, op. cit., footnote 20, Article 14 of Regulation 17, no. 7.

[42] F. Gillmeister, Ermittlungsrechte im deutschen und europäischen Kartellordnungswidrigkeitenverfahren, Baden-Baden 1985, pp. 203 et seq. Doubts on the recognition of such a right are expressed by C. S. Kerse, op. cit., footnote 33, p. 112.

[43] cf. Case 155/79 A.M. & S. v. Commission [1982] E.C.R. 1575.

(b) Powers to collect information under anti-dumping law

In contrast, the powers of the Commission to collect information under anti-dumping law are extremely limited.

In order to protect against damaging imports from abroad, the Council has adopted a basic Regulation[44] on protection against dumped or subsidised imports from non-EEC countries; this is the basis for the adoption of anti-dumping regulations applying to particular goods.[45]

In Article 7 of the Regulation the introduction and conduct of the anti-dumping procedure is laid down. The Commission has at its side an Advisory Committee made up of representatives of the Member States.[46] The Commission conducts the investigation at the level of the Community[47] and collects all necessary and relevant information for that purpose.[48]

However, the Commission has no means at its disposal for enforcing the handing over of or examination of documents.[49] It may of course request the Member States to pass information to it, to undertake all necessary investigations and checks and to carry out investigations in third states,[50] that is, to undertake investigations in its stead.[51] However, in practice very little use is made of this possibility.[52] In that context the Member States themselves have no more extensive powers to collect information than the Commission itself possesses.[53]

The only enforceable measure which the Commission may take under the anti-dumping Regulation is the authority under Article 7(7)b of the Regulation[54] to adopt a provisional or final decision on the basis of the available information if the party affected delays or refuses to give

---

[44] Regulation 2176/84, O.J. 1984 L210/1 as amended by Council Regulation 1761/87/EEC, O.J. 1987 L167/9; the corresponding decision in the ECSC field is No. 2177/84, O.J. 1984 L201/7.

[45] See on this in more detail, J. Schwarze, "Rechtsschutz gegen Anti-Dumpingmassnahmen der EG—Zu Verfahren und richterlicher Kontrolle auf dem Gebiet der Aussenwirtschaftsverwaltung der EG," EuR 1986, p. 217 at 219.

[46] J. Schwarze, op. cit., footnote 45, p. 221.

[47] Regulation No. 2176/84, Article 7(1)c, O.J. 1984 L201/1.

[48] Regulation No. 2176/84, Article 7(2)a, op. cit., footnote 47.

[49] J.-F. Beseler, Die Abwehr von Dumping und Subventionen durch die Europäischen Gemeinschaften, Baden-Baden 1980, footnote 15, p. 126.

[50] Regulation No. 2176/84, Article 7(3)a, op. cit., footnote 48.

[51] J. Schwarze, op. cit., footnote 45, p. 224.

[52] J.-F. Beseler, op. cit., footnote 49, footnote 15, p. 127.

[53] J. Schwarze, op. cit., footnote 45.

[54] cf. the identical wording in Article 6 of the New Trade Policy Instrument, O.J. 1984 L252/1.

information. Such a decision may not be challenged on the grounds that it is based on inadequate information, due to a lack of cooperation.[55]

In conclusion it can be stated that there are under the ECSC Treaty and the EEC Treaty a multiplicity of Regulations and Directives (of which those in the fields of competition law and anti-dumping law are only two examples) which give the Commission the authority to collect information under a variety of conditions.

No duty to proceed to a complete investigation can be derived from the express wording of the provisions discussed here.[56]

The Court of Justice has laid down in its case law the duty to bring comprehensive proof and thus to provide the best possible justice in each individual case. One reason for the adoption of a duty to proceed to a complete investigation lies in the fact that the interpretation of the Court of Justice based on the investigation carried out by the Commission may be of wide-ranging significance. The decision will often act as a precedent for further cases.[57]

II. THE DUTY TO MAKE A COMPLETE INVESTIGATION—AS ELABORATED BY THE COURT OF JUSTICE

In principle, the Court of Justice works from the assumption that the Commission is under an obligation to discover the actual circumstances of each individual case in as much detail as possible and to evaluate them on that basis.

1. The earlier case law

(a) Individual examples from a variety of fields of law

The Court of Justice has always emphasised in its case law the principle of the duty to make an investigation which is as comprehensive as possible.

---

[55] Case 53/83 *Allied Corporation* v. *Council* [1985] E.C.R. 1621 at 1658, para. 13.
[56] *cf.* on this in German law §§24, 26 VwVfG.
[57] U. Everling, "Der Beitrag des Europäischen Gerichtshofes zur Entwicklung der Gemeinschaft," in S. Magiera (ed.), *Entwicklungsperspektiven der Europäischen Gemeinschaft*, Berlin 1985, p. 195 at 202.

It is already discernible in a decision on the prolongation of the authorisation for the Ruhr coal-selling agencies of February 12, 1960[58] in which the Court of Justice confirmed that the High Authority was under an obligation to examine carefully, at the appropriate time, subsequent applications for authorisation which might come in the future from the agencies involved.[59]

In a decision of May 10, 1960,[60] delivered shortly thereafter, on whether it was permissible for the Deutsche Bundesbahn to give special rates for the transport of mineral fuels for the iron and steel industry and for the transport of iron ores, the principle that the administration is under an obligation, in applying the law, to have regard to the concrete facts of an individual case was reaffirmed, although it was stated on this occasion in a negative form.

The applicants (who were the German undertakings affected by the abolition of the special favourable rates) alleged that the High Authority was under an obligation to set out all the grounds on which it might have justified the maintenance of the special rates under Article 70(4) ECSC,[61] but the Court of Justice stated expressly "that the High Authority could confine itself to assessing the concrete cases which were submitted to it." It then went on to hold that "it should also be noted that the High Authority was scarcely justified in undertaking the development of a general theory on the subject matter of the fourth paragraph of Article 70."[62]

In the *Hoogovens* case,[63] the Court of Justice expressly affirmed the obligation of the administration, in particular in the case of discretionary decisions, to establish the special circumstances of the individual case and to have regard to them. In this case the Authority was expressly enjoined

---

[58] Joined Cases 16–18/59 *Geitling, Mausegatt and Präsident* v. *High Authority* [1960] E.C.R. 17.

[59] *Ibid.*, at p. 25: "... and in no way rules out its amending its viewpoint set out above after thorough examination of subsequent applications by the parties; moveover in such an event it would be under an obligation to make such an examination."

[60] Joined Cases 3–18, 25, 26/58, *Barbara Erzbergbau AG and others* v. *High Authority* [1960] E.C.R. 173.

[61]. Article 70(4) ECSC provides as follows: "The application of special internal rates and conditions in the interest of one or more coal- or steel-producing undertakings shall require the prior agreement of the High Authority, which shall verify that they are in accordance with the principles of this Treaty; it may make its agreement temporary or conditional."

[62] *Barbara Erzbergbau, supra*, footnote 60, at p. 197.

[63] Case 14/61 *Koninklijke Nederlandsche Hoogovens en Staalfabrieken N.V.* v. *High Authority* [1962] E.C.R. 253.

not to disregard the concrete situation of the party affected. These proceedings were preceded by the well-known *SNUPAT* cases.[64]

The question which was left open in the *SNUPAT* judgment was whether the withdrawal of the exemption, which it was established in that case had been unlawfully granted, could have retrospective effect, or simply effect for the future; this question was central to the decision in *Hoogovens*.[65]

The central argument of the applicant, and in this it was followed by the Court of Justice, was that in balancing the interests involved in choosing between retrospective and future withdrawal of an unlawful exemption, the concrete situation of the parties should be borne in mind.[66]

The Court of Justice accepted the applicant's contentions, at least in principle. An administrative decision, such as that taken by the High Authority, may not simply be based on "general and abstract considerations" without "referring expressly or by implication to (the party's) actual position in particular."[67] In this way, it limited the application of official discretionary decisions to the concrete circumstances of the individual case.

The case of *Ferriera Ernesto Preo & Figli* is also worthy of note. The Italian company Ferriera Ernesto Preo & Figli commenced steel production on October 1, 1956 using an electric furnace with a capacity of 6–8 metric tons.[68] In order to ascertain the amounts of ferrous scrap liable to equalisation, the Société Anonyme Fiduciaire Suisse carried out two investigations at the company's premises. The first inspection, the results of which were communicated to the company by a letter from the Director of the "Market" Division, and to which it confirmed its express agreement in reply to the High Authority, took place in September 1958 and covered the period from October 1, 1956 to December 31, 1957. The second inspection, the results of which were considerably less favourable to the company and eventually formed the basis of the equalisation contribution later claimed by the High Authority, was carried out in

[64] Joined Cases 32, 33/58 *Société Nouvelle des Usines de Pontlieue Aciéries du Temple (SNUPAT)* v. *High Authority* [1959] E.C.R. 32, as well as Joined Cases 42, 49/59 *Société Nouvelle des Usines de Pontlieue Aciéres du Temple (SNUPAT)* v. *High Authority* [1961] E.C.R. 53.

[65] *Hoogovens, supra*, footnote 63, at p. 253.

[66] *Ibid.*, at 269–270.

[67] See the arguments of the applicant. See on this *Hoogovens, supra*, footnote 63, at p. 259.

[68] Case 2/65 *Handelsgesellschaft Ferriera Ernesto Preo & Figli* v. *High Authority* [1966] E.C.R. 219; for the facts see the "Facts" section of the judgment, at pp. 220–221 and the details given in Advocate-General Gand's Opinion, pp. 228–229.

February 1961 and covered the entire period from the commencement of furnace operations to the termination of the equalisation scheme on November 30, 1958.

The company sought the annulment by the Court of Justice of the fixing of the amount of the assessable ferrous scrap and the fixing of the equalisation contribution by the High Authority on the basis of this amount.

The applicant[69] contested in its claim neither the structure and functioning of the equalisation scheme nor the High Authority's right to make an estimated assessment of the contributions if sufficient documents were not furnished by the undertaking concerned.

It was, however, of the opinion that the High Authority had wrongly failed to take into account the special circumstances of its case, and had based itself when fixing the contribution solely on a theoretical criterion which did not take into consideration the actual circumstances of its case.[70]

Finally, it alleged that the statement of reasons in the decision which was challenged contained no reference to the extent to which the High Authority had taken into account in its calculations the re-use of scrap arisings.

The Court of Justice ultimately annulled the High Authority's decision on the grounds that it was in breach of essential procedural requirements[71]:

> "Since arisings often represent a considerable percentage of the ferrous scrap with which the furnace is charged, it is not sufficient to show that account has been taken of them. It is essential to indicate, and indeed to give a statement of reasons for, the average percentage adopted in the case in question for the purpose of calculating their significance. The lack of this information (which moreover appears easy to supply) constitutes a serious hindrance of an adequate defence of the undertakings concerned and the necessary review by the Court."

It is clear from this decision that the Court of Justice regards the obligation of the administration to ascertain and take account of special circum-

---

[69] See on the arguments of the applicant, the details in the "Facts" section of the judgment, [1966] E.C.R. 221–224.

[70] This is the actual argument of the applicant. See the details in the "Facts" part of the judgment, [1966] E.C.R. 222.

[71] *Ibid.*, at 226.

stances when dealing with individual cases, as something more than a requirement of substantive law which must be observed exclusively for its own sake and which is limited to the field of administrative discretion.

Rather, it regards this obligation as a necessary element of every application of the law by the administration to an individual case, which must be observed also on account of its procedural relevance to the protection of the legitimate defence of the party affected. However, the principle that appropriate regard should be had to the needs of the administration also co-exists side-by-side with this principle in the case law of the Court of Justice.

It is thus easier for the Court of Justice to require the strict implementation of the duty to give reasons, in so far as its fulfilment does not make the activities of the administration either unnecessarily more difficult or impossible.

Finally, the principle of the obligation on the administration to ascertain and take into account all special circumstances in individual cases fulfils a function for the work of the Court of Justice itself. So long as the Court of Justice continues to insist on its generally negative attitude to the taking of additional evidence in proceedings,[72] it must place that much greater weight upon the fullest possible taking and evaluation of evidence by the administration if the necessary judicial reviewability of the administrative decisions which have been challenged is not to be hindered.

The case law of the Court of Justice offers numerous further examples of this viewpoint, with the Court of Justice indicating that the administration should in principle always undertake a comprehensive examination of the individual cases when applying the law to that case. It wishes if possible to see all factual questions decided at the level of the administration.

Examples of this can be found in almost all areas of the law in which legal disputes may come before the Court of Justice.

Thus in interpreting Article 85(1) EEC, the Court of Justice opposed attempts by the Commission, in the early days of the development of

---

[72] See on this in particular K. Zweigert, "Empfiehlt es sich, Bestimmungen über den Rechtsschutz zu ändern?" in *Zehn Jahre Rechtsprechung des Gerichtshofs der Europäischen Gemeinschaften*, KSE 1, Cologne, etc., 1963, p. 580 at 589. See from the more recent case law, however, Case 145/83, *Stanley Adams* v. *Commission* [1985] E.C.R. 3539, where the Court of Justice undertook a thorough hearing of the evidence. On the possibilities of a more detailed judicial scrutiny of the facts in consequence of the creation of a Court of First Instance attached to the Court of Justice, see U. Everling, "Die Errichtung eines Gerichts erster Instanz der Europäischen Gemeinschaften," in J. Schwarze (ed.), *Fortentwicklung des Rechtsschutzes in der Europäischen Gemeinschaft*, Baden-Baden 1987, p. 39.

European competition law, to argue that certain factual situations, defined using an abstract standard which it had itself developed, automatically fell within the prohibition in that article.

In its judgment in Case 56/65 of June 30, 1966,[73] the Court rejected the view put forward by the Commission[74] that certain types of agreement which are restrictive of competition (in that case exclusive dealing agreements) fell—at least given the further condition that they had a perceptible anti-competitive effect on trade between Member States[75]—*per se* within the prohibition of Article 85(1) EEC.

The Court of Justice referred expressly to this in its judgment[76]:

> "In order to be prohibited as being incompatible with the Common Market under Article 85(1) of the Treaty, an agreement between undertakings must fulfil certain conditions depending less on the legal nature of the agreement than on its effects on 'trade between Member States' and its effects on 'competition.'
>
> Thus as Article 85(1) is based on an assessment of the effects of an agreement from two angles of economic evaluation, it cannot be interpreted as introducing any kind of advance judgment with regard to a category of agreements determined by their legal nature. Therefore an agreement whereby a producer entrusts the sale of his products in a given area to a sole distributor cannot automatically fall under the prohibition in Article 85(1). But such an agreement may contain the elements set out in that provision, by reason of a particular factual situation or of the severity of the clauses protecting the exclusive dealership.
>
> (. . .)
>
> The prohibition of such an agreement depends on one question alone, namely whether, taking into account the circumstances of the case, the agreement, objectively considered, contains the elements constituting the said prohibition as set out in Article 85(1)."

Time and again, in the field of E.C. competition law, the Court of Justice has demanded the investigation and subsequent consideration of each individual case where the law is to be applied by the administration. And

---

[73] Case 56/65 *Société Technique Minière (LTM)* v. *Maschinenbau Ulm GmbH (MBU)* [1966] E.C.R. 235.
[74] For the view of the Commission see the details in the "Facts" part of the judgment, at pp. 239–240.
[75] See on this [1966] E.C.R. 240.
[76] *Ibid.*, at p. 248.

this in spite of the clear administrative and practical difficulties thereby caused, which can be seen in the large number of cases to be decided and in the economic complexity of those cases, which will be the result of requiring the taking and evaluating of evidence. The examples of the fact that the Court of Justice has accepted a comprehensive duty to investigate where the competition authority is dealing with individual cases extend from a decision handed down shortly after the judgment in Case 56/65, *STM* v. *Maschinenbau Ulm*,[77] in the case of *Grundig and Consten* of July 13, 1966,[78] the first case in which a decision of the Commission applying EEC competition law to an individual case was challenged before the Court of Justice,[79] to the well known case of *National Panasonic*.[80]

As is well known, *Grundig and Consten*[81] concerned a decision of the Commission to refuse an exemption from the prohibition under Article 85 EEC[82] for an exclusive agreement between the German manufacturer Grundig and the French trader Consten governing exclusive dealing arrangements for radios and televisions in France, the Saarland and Corsica.[83] The Court of Justice denied the Commission the benefit of a presumption, in so far as it held that the Commission could not neglect the concrete circumstances of the individual case when taking evidence; the Commission had argued that it was not the task of the competition authority, but solely a matter for the undertaking affected, to prove the existence of the conditions for the granting of an exemption under Article 85(3) EEC.

According to the view of the Court of Justice, any undertaking may require the Commission to investigate in its context an application for an exemption under Article 85(3) EEC. "As a matter of good administration," the Commission may not confine itself to requiring from the undertaking proof of the fulfilment of the requirements for the grant of an exemption but must play its part, using the means available to it, in ascertaining the relevant facts and circumstances.[84]

In the case of *Portelange* v. *Smith Corona Marchant International*, concerning the provisional validity of duly notified agreements, the Court

---

[77] See above, footnote 73.
[78] Joined Cases 56 & 68/64 *Consten GmbH and Grundig-Verkaufs-GmbH* v. *Commission* [1966] E.C.R. 299.
[79] *cf.* Advocate-General Roemer in his opinion, [1966] E.C.R. 352.
[80] See Case 17/74 *Transocean Marine Paint Association* v. *Commission* [1974] E.C.R. 1063.
[81] See above, footnote 78.
[82] Under para. 3 of this provision.
[83] See the facts of the case as set out in the "Facts" section of the judgment, [1966] E.C.R. 303–4.
[84] [1966] E.C.R. 347.

of Justice once more expressed the opinion that the Commission must examine the concrete circumstances of each individual case when applying European competition law. It went on to hold[85] that:

> "the question whether such an agreement is in fact prohibited depends on the appraisal of economic and legal factors which cannot be assumed to be present in the absence of an explicit finding that the individual agreement in question not only contains all the factors mentioned in Article 85(1), but does not qualify for the exemption provided by Article 85(3).
>
> So long as such a finding has not been made, every agreement duly notified must be considered valid."

Finally, in the field of competition law, the Court of Justice held, in the *Transocean Marine Paint Association* case, which concerned the lawfulness of placing conditions on the grant of an extension of an exemption under Article 85(3) EEC without giving the undertakings concerned the opportunity to be heard, that:

> "... accordingly, in relation to the detailed rules to which it may subject the exemption, the Commission enjoys a large measure of discretion, while at the same time having to act within the limits imposed upon its competence by Article 85. On the other hand, the exercise of this discretionary power is linked to a preliminary canvassing of objections which may be raised by the undertakings."[86]

Outside competition law the Court of Justice has held that the obligation on European institutions to have regard to the special circumstances of an individual case when applying the rules of the Treaty to it extends also to the field of transport policy.[87]

In the field of law governing the employment of Community officials, the view of the Court of Justice requiring the institutions, when applying the law to individual cases, to examine the individual circumstances of

---

[85] Case 10/69 *SA Portelange* v. *SA Smith Corona Marchant International, etc.* [1969] E.C.R. 309 at 316.

[86] [1974] E.C.R. 1080. In the event, the Court of Justice annulled the Commission's decision on the grounds that the undertakings concerned had been given insufficient opportunities to be heard.

[87] Case 28/66, *Netherlands* v. *Commission* [1968] E.C.R. 1; see on this also Joined Cases 3–18, 25 & 26/58, *Barbara Erzbergbau* v. *High Authority* [1960] E.C.R. 373.

each case, when taking and evaluating evidence, comes out particularly clearly.

In its decision of March 19, 1964 concerning the selection process for the post of Director of Internal Affairs in the Directorate-General for Administration, the Court of Justice expressly held, when considering a claim by a disappointed applicant for the post, that the appointing authority had "wide discretionary powers" in appointing officials under Article 45 of the Staff Regulations. Such powers implied, according to the Court, "great freedom (. . .) in making the decision, (but) there must at the same time be a scrupulous consideration of personal files each containing comparable information. This second factor provides the necessary guarantee that powers will be exercised in full knowledge of the facts."[88]

The obligation to examine the concrete circumstances of the individual case appears here almost to be a necessary balance to the wide discretionary powers given to the administration, as a corrective which, from the point of view of the protection of fundamental principles of the rule of law in administrative action, makes the granting of a discretionary power to the executive tolerable in the first place.

(b) The special problems arising in the law of customs duties and levies

A number of special factors apply in the context of the Common Customs Tariff and the law on levies, since on the one hand in these fields, the necessity for administration on a large scale was quite clear, whereas on the other hand the undertakings required to pay the duties demanded the most exact consideration possible of the individual characteristics of the goods concerned.[89]

Of the numerous cases which have come before the Court of Justice, only a small number can be highlighted in this section; these illustrate particularly clearly the legal problem and the way in which it is dealt with by the Court of Justice, including certain modifications of the point of view taken by the case law.

---

[88] Case 27/63 *Gottfredo Raponi* v. *Commission* [1964] E.C.R. 129 at 137; in the event the Court of Justice annulled the decision on the grounds of an insufficient examination of the applicant's individual case (infringement of Article 45(1), first paragraph, of the Staff Regulations). See [1964] E.C.R. 138. A similar case is Case 188/73 *Grassi* v. *Council* [1974] E.C.R. 1099 at 1109.

[89] *cf.* on this in detail J. Schwarze, *Die Befugnis zur Abstraktion im europäischen Gemeinschaftsrecht*, Baden-Baden 1976, pp. 89 *et seq.*

One decision of the Court deserves particular consideration.[90] It had to decide whether a regulation which provided for the imposition of a levy on the import of products processed from fruit and vegetables in addition to a customs duty which was charged on "the various added sugars contained in the products,"[91] was to be interpreted as meaning that an imported good was automatically subject to the levy if the amount of sugar measured by refractometry exceeded a certain level, or whether it was to be treated as subject to a levy as a good with "added sugar" only if sugar had in fact been added to it.

At the root of the request for a preliminary ruling referred by the Berlin Finanzgericht was the import of "morello cherries in spirit," which a German company was importing in large quantities in barrels from Yugoslavia.

The German customs authorities initially took the view that the import of these cherries, although subject to duty and in some respects to taxes, was not subject to a levy. However, after an analysis carried out by the *Zolltechnische Prüfungs- und Lehranstalt* had revealed that the sugar content of these products exceeded the level of 9 per cent. fixed in the Additional Note No. 2 to Chapter 20 of the Common Customs Tariff, which was included as an annex to Council Regulation 950/68 of June 28, 1968, the customs authorities changed their opinion and required a levy to be paid on the imported cherries.

The importers affected by this argued against the imposition of the import levy. They maintained that there had been no sugar added to the cherries. They offered evidence to support this assertion.

The customs authorities, however, refused to change their mind and relied upon a presumption in the evidentiary process: where the sugar content exceeded 9 per cent., goods were subject to a levy even if no sugar had in fact been added. It was therefore for legal reasons unnecessary to take the importers' evidence.

In order to make it easier to understand the case, the following section will sketch out the essential legal aspects.[92] As has already been mentioned, a levy can be imposed under Article 2(1) of Regulation 865/68 under certain conditions where products processed from fruit are

---

[90] Case 3/71, *Gebrüder Bagusat* v. *HZA Berlin-Packhof* [1971] E.C.R. 577.

[91] See Article 2 of Regulation 865/68 of the Council of June 28, 1968 on "the common organisation of the market in products processed from fruit and vegetables" (O.J. Sp.Ed. 1967–8 p. 225) read in conjunction with Article 9 of this Regulation and the provisions under the Common Customs Tariff (Additional Note No. 2 to Chapter 20, Tariff Position 20.06-B-I-e).

[92] They are all reproduced in the judgment, footnote 90, p. 587.

imported containing added sugars of various types. The levy is determined according to paragraphs 2–6 of that Article in conjunction with Annexes I to III, which provide both for fixed sugar contents and for a method of investigation, according to which under certain conditions there can be a departure from the assumed values and the real sugar content can be established. Furthermore, Article 9(2) of this Regulation provides that "the general rules for the interpretation of the Common Customs Tariff and the special rules for its application shall apply to the tariff classification of the products covered by this regulation." According to Additional Note No. 2, which is attached to Chapter 20 of the Common Customs Tariff annexed to Regulation 950/68 of June 28, 1968, "the products classified under heading No. 20.06 shall be considered as "containing added sugar" when the "sugar content" thereof exceeds by weight the percentages given hereunder, according to the kind of fruit concerned: pineapples, grapes (. . .) per cent., other fruits (. . .) 9 per cent."

Whereas the plaintiff in the national action continued to argue before the Court of Justice that the levy provided for in Article 2(1) of Regulation 865/68 could be imposed only where sugar had actually been added to the product in question,[93] the Commission supported instead the view of the German customs authorities which it had represented before the Finanzgericht. Thus it argued that the methods of approximation provided for in Regulation 865/68, together with the Additional Note to the Common Customs Tariff, created a legal fiction according to which even products containing only natural sugar were considered as "containing added sugar" if the sugar content actually exceeded the percentage given.[94] As the basis for its view the Commission relied on the fact that the entire system set up by the Additional Note No. 2 would collapse if it were assumed that Regulation 865/68 does not form the basis for a legal fiction, for in that case the customs authorities would have to ascertain for each individual good whether it contained added sugar or not, which for practical and scientific reasons it would be incapable of doing.[95]

---

[93] See on this the details in the judgment at [1971] E.C.R. 587.

[94] The view of the Commission is recited in the judgment at p. 587. There is a difference between the arguments of the German customs administration (the defendant in the national action) and the Commission, in so far as the latter reached the conclusion that there was a legal fiction through interpretation of Regulation 865/68 in conjunction with the Additional Note No. 2 to Chapter 20 of the Common Customs Tariff, whereas the former based its conclusion directly on the Additional Note No. 2. (See on this difference the statement of the Commission in the proceedings before the Court of Justice at p. 582 and the details in Advocate-General de Lamothe's Opinion, p. 596.

[95] See the details in the Advocate-General's Opinion, p. 597.

The Court did not follow the Commission.[96] Even the administrative difficulties, which in other circumstances would be almost insuperable, did not in its view allow a departure from the declared goal of the regulation which is, in accordance with the structure of the organisation of the market in sugar, solely to place a levy on sugar used in the processing of fruit, not on the natural sugar to be found in the fruits themselves. Nor did it allow the customs authorities to apply a generalisation as regards the taking and evaluating of evidence in the strictest sense, which would permit them to assume in every case that they may, without allowing contradictory evidence, impose a levy on the imported product wherever the threshold value of 9 per cent. sugar content was exceeded.

In view of the clear wording of Article 2(1) of Regulation 865/68 ("import levy on the various added sugars contained in the products") paragraphs 2 *et seq.* of the same article could only be applicable to the cases in which sugar had actually been added in so far as they determined the "details of the application of the levy and its amount," but they could not form the basis, even read in conjunction with the other provisions mentioned here, of an irrebuttable presumption that a levy be imposed. Even the Additional Note No. 2 of Chapter 20 of the Common Customs Tariff could not alter the basis of charge for an agricultural levy, and Article 9(2) of Regulation 865/68 referred to it only for the purposes of the "tariff classification" of the goods coming under that Regulation.

The Court of Justice then added:

> "Accordingly, this additional note can have no other purpose except to give guidance, on the basis of the total sugar content, to facilitate the tariff classification of products within the category of fruit subject either to a customs duty and a levy, or to a customs duty alone. In view of the provisions of Regulation 865/68 the effect of that note is to establish that products with a sugar content of less than 9 per cent. are exempt from the levy, whilst creating, in the case of products with a higher sugar content, a presumption with regard to classification against which evidence in rebuttal may be brought. When such a product has a sugar content exceeding 9 per cent., it is therefore open to the importer to prove, where appropriate, that it contains only natural sugar."[97]

---

[96] See the Court at [1971] E.C.R. 587.
[97] [1971] E.C.R. 588.

The reasoning of the Court's decision is very illuminating.

Where the Court of Justice on the one hand proceeds from the assumption that Article 2 of Regulation 865/68 allows the imposition of a levy only where the imported product actually contains added sugar, then it is in fact protecting a basic principle flowing from the concept of hierarchy of norms, that is, that where taxes are levied the detailed rules concerning the basis of assessment cannot change the basis of charge[98] (in the case of the raising of taxes, the chargeable event). This is an argument which Advocate-General de Lamothe stated expressly in his Opinion when examining the relationship between Article 2(1) of Regulation 865/68 (the basis of charge or chargeable event)[99] and paragraphs 3 and 4 of this article (the basis of assessment)[100,101] and it must apply also where the detailed rules concerning the basis of assessment which are referred to do not belong directly to the same category of legal provisions as the basis of charge.[102]

On the other hand, in so far as it required the importer to carry the burden of proving that a product prima facie falling within tariff 20.06-B-I-e as containing more than 9 per cent. sugar content does not in fact contain added sugar, the Court of Justice does give sufficient weight to the corresponding requirements of administrative practice.

It thus allowed the administration to assimilate other cases to an existing case as regards the taking and evaluation of evidence—not in an absolute sense, however (which would mean that wherever there was an abstract measure of more than 9 per cent. sugar content, a levy would be imposed), but in the limited sense that starting from a basis of 9 per cent. sugar content the imposition of a levy could be assumed and it was for the importer to prove that no sugar had in fact been added.

Since the Court of Justice in its interpretation of the relevant legal provisions correctly fixed upon Article 2(1) of Regulation 865/68 as the starting point for its analysis, it expressly left open the further question addressed by Advocate-General de Lamothe as to whether the Additional Note No. 2 to chapter 20 of the Common Customs Tariff itself raised an irrebuttable or, as the Advocate-General would have it, only a rebuttable presumption in the proceedings.[103]

---

[98] The Court uses this expression in its judgment, at p. 588.
[99] The corresponding French expression is "fait générateur."
[100] In French: "modalités de l'assiette."
[101] See on this Advocate-General de Lamothe, [1971] E.C.R. 595, who uses the two French expressions given above.
[102] The Court also expressly emphasised this contrast: [1971] E.C.R. 588.
[103] See Advocate-General de Lamothe, [1971] E.C.R. 596.

Whereas in the field of constitutional law the Court of Justice has seen fit, in the interests of developing integration, to depart occasionally from the express wording of the Treaties when considering fundamental questions concerning the construction and evolution of the Community,[104] when acting as an administrative court in the evaluation of the legality of actual administrative actions in individual cases it has generally adhered expressly to the text of provisions of Community law.

The so-called *Caribou* case[105] offers the most instructive example of this: a German importer had imported frozen caribou meat from Greenland into the Community in 1970. Whereas the Greenland authorities had declared when asked that caribous lived in the wild and were captured by hunting, the German customs office concerned had instead classified the imported goods not as "game" under tariff 02.04-B of the Common Customs Tariff but, following a statement of the Commission according to which "reindeer are held to be domestic animals," as falling under tariff 02.04-C-III ("other meat and edible meat offals").

The difference in view was not without significance, for the Common Customs Tariff places no duty on game imported from third countries but does so on meat from domestic animals which is imported into the Common Market.

On a request for a preliminary ruling from the Finanzgericht of Hamburg the Court of Justice held that "the Explanatory Notes to the Common Customs Tariff, although an important factor as regards interpretation, (. . .) cannot, in contradiction to the text of the Common Customs Tariff, eliminate all differences of classification as [sic] between the meat of wild and domestic animals of the same species."[106]

2. The more recent case law

These principles have been further developed and articulated in the more recent case law. In his opinion in Case 19/77, *Miller Internationale Schallplatten GmbH*, an appeal against a fine imposed by the Commis-

---

[104] See on this for instance the decisions in Case 26/62, *Van Gend en Loos* v. *Netherlands Administration of Finance* [1963] E.C.R. 1 on the "direct" effect of Article 12 EEC, and Case 22/70, *Commission* v. *Council (ERTA)* [1971] E.C.R. 263 on the competence of the Community in external affairs. In both cases the Advocates-General (*cf.* Advocate-General Roemer [1963] E.C.R. 22 in Case 26/62 and Advocate-General Dutheillet de Lamothe [1971] E.C.R. 289 in Case 22/70) each referred to the contradictory wording of the Treaties.

[105] Case 149/73 *Witt* v. *HZA Hamburg-Ericus* [1973] E.C.R. 1587.

[106] [1973] E.C.R. 1593.

sion for an infringement of the competition rules, Advocate-General Warner proposed "(the remission of) the case to the Commission to reconsider the amount of the fine in the light of the evidence now proffered by Miller . . . ; (this) would be the correct course, because its adoption would respect the principle that the ascertainment of the facts (. . .) is in the first instance, a matter for the Commission."[107]

A similar line is followed in the decision in *SA Musique Diffusion Française etc.* v. *Commission*, which also concerned an action for annulment (Article 173 EEC) against a competition decision of the Commission. The four applicants belonged to the European distribution network for hi-fi equipment manufactured by Pioneer Electronic in Tokyo. The major part of the Pioneer products sold in Europe were imported by a subsidiary, Pioneer Electronic (Europe) based in Antwerp. At the time of the contested decision, three independent trading companies were entrusted with exclusive dealerships in France, the Federal Republic of Germany and the United Kingdom. In the contested decision, the Commission had established that the four applicants had participated in a concerted practice which infringed Article 85(1) EEC. It imposed fines upon them.

The Court of Justice once more highlighted the comprehensive duty of the Commission to obtain full information when it stated that:

> "The procedural safeguards contained in Article 19(1) of Regulation No. 17 and in Regulation No. 19/63 are an application of the fundamental principle of Community law which requires the right to a fair hearing to be observed in all proceedings, even those of an administrative nature."[108]

From this principle flows the most comprehensive duty possible on the Commission to investigate the case and evaluate the evidence.

In Case 9/83, *Eisen und Metall AG* brought an action for a declaration before the Court of Justice in which it claimed that a decision imposing a fine under Decision No. 1836/81/ECSC was void. The applicant had been required by the Commissioner to pay this fine because it had not fulfilled the obligations imposed upon it under Decision No. 1836/81/ECSC to

---

[107] Case 19/77, *Miller Internationale Schallplatten GmbH* v. *Commission* [1978] E.C.R. 131 at 163.
[108] Cases 100–103/80, *Musique Diffusion Française* v. *Commission* [1983] E.C.R. 1825 at 1827.

publicise price lists, conditions of sale and practices forbidden in the steel trade.

The Court of Justice emphasised in its decision that Articles 36 and 47 ECSC and Articles 11 and 14 of Decision No. 1836/81 had delegated to the Commission the power to carry out investigations and to conduct checks, which it may invoke if it wishes to establish the existence of unlawful practices:

> "It is required to carry out further enquiries or to request additional information only if it considers that the information already at its disposal is not sufficient for its purpose."[109]

It appears clear from this decision that where the facts are unclear or information is insufficient, there is a comprehensive obligation to investigate imposed on the Commission. Furthermore, it is the Commission which must assess whether there are still gaps which must be clarified in any particular case. That body is however subject to subsequent control on the part of the Court of Justice.[110]

3. Conclusion

An overview of the numerous relevant decisions shows that the Court of Justice works from a basic assumption that the competent authority is subject to an obligation to clarify the concrete circumstances of each individual case as comprehensively as possible and to evaluate them as such.

The Court of Justice sees this obligation as a requirement to be observed in principle wherever the law is to be applied by the administration, which must be followed also on the grounds of its procedural impact on the protection of the legitimate rights of defence of the person affected.

The obligation on the administration to clarify the special circumstances governing the application of the law in an individual case and to take these into consideration also fulfils an important function for the Court's own proceedings. It makes it possible for the Court to adhere to its generally negative attitude towards the consideration of additional evidence in proceedings before it.

---

[109] Case 9/83, *Eisen und Metall AG* v. *Commission* [1984] E.C.R. 2071 at 2087.
[110] B. Börner, *Studien zum deutschen und europäischen Wirtschaftsrecht*, Vol. III, KSE 30, Cologne, etc., 1980, p. 171 at 176/177.

In the field of law governing Community officials, the Court's principle that the authority is obliged to examine the concrete circumstances of the individual case emerges particularly clearly. In customs and excise law, however, the Court of Justice has not closed its eyes to the necessities of modern large-scale administration. Thus in that field it has allowed the customs authorities the benefit of a standardised approach to the evaluation of individual cases, although only within the framework of the relevant statutory provisions.

III. LIMITS PLACED UPON INVESTIGATORY POWERS

1. The principle of proportionality and "legal privilege"

Legal limitations upon the investigatory powers of the Commission are derived not only from the Treaties themselves and from relevant secondary sources of law, but also in particular from general principles of law which the Court of Justice has developed. The judgment in the case of *National Panasonic* is illustrative of the Court's approach in this field[111]:

The applicant, an English company, was unexpectedly visited by two officials of the Commission authorised to examine all the company papers on the business premises, on the grounds that there was a suspicion of an infringement of Articles 85 and 86 EEC.

The Commission officials began their investigation of the company papers without waiting for the anticipated arrival of the company's legal adviser, and left seven hours later taking with them a number of photocopies of business documents and notes from the applicant's papers.

National Panasonic brought an action seeking the annulment of the Commission's decision to investigate, the destruction of the papers so far collected, and the discontinuing of further investigative activities. The applicant claimed in particular that the Commission's measures were in breach of the principle of proportionality.

---

[111] Case 136/79, *National Panasonic* v. *Commission* [1980] E.C.R. 2033.

The Court of Justice expressly recognised in this case that the principle of proportionality placed legal limitations on the Commission's investigative activities. Administrative measures aimed at the collection of evidence must not be out of proportion to the goal sought to be achieved through the measure.

In the case in question, however, the Court of Justice rejected the contention that there had been an infringement of this principle.[112]

Not long afterwards, the *A.M. & S.* case was decided.[113] The judgment contains statements on the legal limits on the investigative activities of the Commission in the field of E.C. competition law. A.M. & S. Europe Ltd. (A.M. & S.), a company under English law, refused to produce certain papers during an investigation under Article 14 of Regulation 17. It relied upon the principle of "legal privilege", which according to the rules of the common law guarantees the confidentiality of written communications between lawyer and client. The protection under the common law extends to both independent and employed lawyers. The Commission did not accept the company's refusal, but ordered it to submit to a further investigation and to facilitate access to certain business documents. A.M. & S. appealed against this decision to the Court.

The following three questions emerged during the proceedings as being crucial[114]:

— Is there a principle in Community law providing for the confidentiality of written communications between lawyer and client, and if so, what is the scope of the protection?
— Does such a principle limit the Commission's rights to carry out investigations under Article 14 of Regulation 17?
— Who decides whether any particular document is protected against access by the administrative authority?

In its judgment, the Court of Justice decided that the confidentiality of written communications between lawyer and client is in principle guaranteed under Community law.[115] It thus agreed with Advocate-General Sir Gordon Slynn, who after a comprehensive comparative analysis of the existence and scope of the protection of confidentiality in the individual

---

[112] [1980] E.C.R. 2060, para. 30.
[113] Case 155/79 *A.M. & S.* v. *Commission* [1982] E.C.R. 1575.
[114] See in more detail J. Schwarze, "Das Verhältnis von deutschem Verfassungsrecht und europäischem Gemeinschaftsrecht auf dem Gebiet des Grundrechtsschutzes im Spiegel der jüngsten Rechtsprechung," EuGRZ 1983, p. 117 at 120.
[115] [1982] E.C.R. 1610.

Member States had come to the conclusion that such protection should be recognised in Community law.[116]

As regards the scope of the protection of confidentiality between lawyer and client, the Court held that it applied only to correspondence between an undertaking and an independent lawyer established in a Member State, and not to that with a lawyer employed within the company. Thus the case law of the Court of Justice remains some way behind the protection provided in the United Kingdom, but equally extends some way beyond the standard in the legal systems of continental Europe.[117]

The decision whether a document falls under the protection of confidentiality cannot, according to the Court of Justice, be decided by a national court or by an arbitral tribunal, but must be decided at Community level.[118]

The Commission, however, does not possess a definitive power of decision but only a power of investigation by virtue of Regulation 17.[119] This power of investigation is limited by the protection of the confidentiality of correspondence with a lawyer. The Court of Justice based its opinion on the fact that in the interpretation of Regulation 17, elements common to the legal orders of the Member States must also be taken into account.[120]

Thus in this judgment the Court of Justice made two major findings: first, it recognised the principle of the confidentiality of written communications between an independent lawyer and client as a fundamental right or a right akin to a fundamental right within the Community legal order,[121] and second, it established that this principle sets defined limits to the Commission's power of investigation.

2. Prohibitions on the use of evidence

As a consequence of an infringement of written Community law or of general principles of law in the course of collecting evidence, there may be a prohibition on the use of that evidence.[122]

[116] Conclusions of Advocate-General Slynn, at pp. 1651 *et seq.*, especially p. 1654.
[117] J. Schwarze, *op. cit.*, footnote 114, p. 122; [1982] E.C.R. 1611, para. 21.
[118] Para. 30.
[119] J. Schwarze, *op. cit.*, footnote 114, at p. 122.
[120] *Ibid.*, p. 121.
[121] *Ibid.*, p. 122.
[122] See on this with detailed examples B. Börner, *op. cit.*, footnote 110, p. 172.

The Treaties do not provide for an express prohibition on the use of evidence.

However, the case law of the Court has recognised that in principle such prohibitions may apply under Community law. A good example is Case 197/80.[123]

In this case *Ludwigshafener Walzmühle* brought an action against the Council and Commission under Article 178 and the second paragraph of Article 215 EEC for compensation for loss which it claimed to have suffered as a consequence of the fixing of a comparatively high threshold price.

In the area which concerns us, the Court was required to decide whether to allow the submission of a particular document; it held

> "that there exists thus a doubt both as to the actual nature of the contested document and as to whether the interveners obtained it by proper means. In the circumstances, the document must be removed from the file, together with quotations from it included in the inter-vening parties' statement."[124]

Furthermore the Court emphasised in the *Musique Diffusion* case discussed above[125] that in its own decision it may not make use of those documents which the Commission itself had wrongly used in reaching its decision, without giving the undertaking the right to be heard.

3. Various limitations on the powers of investigation in the context of competition proceedings and anti-dumping proceedings

The Commission's powers of investigation take a variety of forms. Competition and anti-dumping proceedings provide significant examples of this.

The structure of the basic competition Regulation 17 is in two parts. In

---

[123] Joined Cases 197–200, 243, 245 & 247/80 *Ludwigshafener Walzmühle, etc.* v. *Council and Commission* [1981] E.C.R. 3211.
[124] [1981] E.C.R. 3245, para. 16.
[125] Joined Cases 100–103/80 *Musique Diffusion Française* v. *Commission* [1983] E.C.R. 1825.

the cases in which an undertaking[126] does not voluntarily submit to the Commission's request for information or to carry out an investigation, the Commission may force it to submit by threatening to impose a periodic penalty.[127]

In contrast, none of these sanctions are provided for in the anti-dumping regulation. There, checks and investigations are possible only where there is the willing cooperation of the undertakings concerned. Correspondingly, the level of judicial protection available in competition proceedings is not necessary since the information is provided on a voluntary basis.[128]

Illustrative of the differences between the competition and anti-dumping procedures is Case 53/85, *AKZO Chemie* v. *Commission*, decided recently by the Court of Justice.[129]

In his Opinion in this case the Advocate-General emphasised in particular the difference between the competition and anti-dumping procedures and the limitations on the powers of investigation in each.

Thus Advocate-General Lenz stated that "competition proceedings before the Commission are not to be understood as adversary proceedings between the complainant and the undertaking concerned"[130] and that they are therefore quite different from anti-dumping proceedings where the complainant and the undertaking concerned stand in an adversary relationship to each other, so that the complainant has more comprehensive procedural rights.

E.   RIGHTS OF DEFENCE

I.   SURVEY

The concept of rights of defence, which is discussed in this section, is a translation of the French concept of "droits de la défense." In French law, this heading includes those rights which are given to parties affected by

---

[126] *cf.* Article 11 of Regulation 17/62: the competent authorities of the Member States and undertakings and associations of undertakings; Article 14 of Regulation 17: undertakings and associations of undertakings.

[127] Article 11(5) of Regulation 17; Article 14(3) of Regulation 17.

[128] *cf.* opinion of Advocate-General Lenz of January 22, 1986 in Case 53/85 *AKZO Chemie* v. *Commission* [1986] E.C.R. 1965 at 1980.

[129] *Ibid.*

[130] Advocate-General Lenz at [1986] E.C.R. 1979.

administrative proceedings, in order that they may protect their rights and interests *vis-à-vis* the administration. It epitomises the principle that there needs to be a counterbalance to the sovereign powers of the administration, giving the party concerned the possibility of ensuring that the advantage held by the administration in terms of knowledge and experience is to some extent neutralised. Rights of defence exist in all the legal systems of the Member States. However, they take a great variety of forms.

The following remarks are intended to identify the subject-matter of this chapter and to serve as an introduction to the individual expositions.

A party affected cannot defend himself so long as he is unaware of the fact that administrative proceedings affecting him have been started. On the other hand, the authority has an interest in ensuring that it can undertake its investigations, at least in the initial phase, with a minimum of disturbance. As soon as the authority reaches a provisional conclusion in its investigation of the facts, the other party must know what allegations are made against him as well as the factual basis for the decision, so that he himself may state his views.

The principle that no one may be condemned before he has been given the opportunity of defending himself rests on very ancient traditions, common across Europe. It is, literally, as old as the Bible, as the following quotation from the well-known English case of *Dr. Bentley* shows very clearly[1]:

"Even God himself did not pass sentence upon Adam before he was called upon to make his defence."

The provision of a right to a hearing concludes the investigatory procedure on the part of the authority, which forms the basis for the actual decision of the administration.

Below, the rights of the defence,[2] and in particular the rules governing the right to a hearing in so far as they are recognised in the Member States, will be examined, before the relevant legal situation in the Community is described and analysed in more detail.

---

[1] *Dr. Bentley's Case* (1723) *R. v. Chancellor of Cambridge University* (1723) 1 Star. 557 cited in O. Hood Phillips, *Constitutional and Administrative Law* (7th ed., 1987), p. 672; *cf.* also J. F. Garner, B. L. Jones, *Administrative Law*, (6th ed., London 1985), p. 143, note 14.

[2] On the content of the "droits de la défense" see the comparative-law section below, as well as, in particular, C.-D. Ehlermann, D. Oldekop, "Due Process," FIDE 1978, p. 11.3.

II. A COMPARISON OF MEMBER STATES' LAWS

1. The "droits de la défense" in France

French administrative law is characterised by the fact that it places a greater emphasis on the public interest in ensuring the "légalité" of administrative actions, rather than on the protection of the subjective rights of the individual.[1] This basic conception is reflected in greater detail in the rules governing the provision of legal protection against sovereign acts of the administration.[2]

Even so, French administrative law has not been blind to the fact that the citizen must be put in a position where he can defend himself against the administration. Indeed, although the right of the administration to take a prior decision ("décision préalable") remains uncontested,[3] the rights of defence of the individual ("droits de la défense") have been increasingly recognised even in France.

(a) The development of a general legal principle

The starting point for the development of a relevant general principle of law is the law governing disciplinary proceedings against public officials. Their rights of defence were first expressly guaranteed in Article 65 of the law of April 22, 1905[4]:

---

[1] cf. on this M. Rott, *Das verwaltungsrechtliche subjektive Recht im Spiegel seiner Entwicklung im deutschen liberalen Rechtsstaat und in der französischen "théorie des droits subjectifs des administrés,"* Diss. Giessen 1976, *passim*; M. Fromont, *Rechtsschutz gegenüber der Verwaltung in Deutschland, Frankreich und den Europäischen Gemeinschaften*, Cologne 1967, p. 204; J. Woehrling, "Die französische Verwaltungsgerichtsbarkeit im Vergleich mit der deutschen," NVwZ 1985, p. 21 at 23; *cf.* however the criticism of the overemphasis on this distinction in G. Vedel, P. Delvolvé, *Droit administratif*, (9th ed., Paris 1984), p. 744.

[2] M. Fromont, *op. cit.*, footnote 1, p. 204; *cf.* also above, Introduction, A.II.1.

[3] The "privilège du préalable" results from the fact that the administration may adopt enforceable measures ("décisions exécutoires"). If the citizen contests the legality of the administrative decision, he must bring a claim; the administration forces the citizen to adopt the unfavourable role of the plaintiff. A claim against administrative acts has no suspensory effect, and, in contrast at least to German law, interim protection of the individual under the law is not well developed. *cf.* J. Schwarze, "Der vorläufige Rechtsschutz ("sursis à exécution") im französischen Verwaltungsrecht," DVBl. 1987, p. 1037.

[4] Law of April 22, 1905; *cf.* on this J.-M. Auby, R. Drago, *Traité de contentieux administratif*, (3rd ed., Paris 1984), Vol. 2, No. 1211.

"Tous les fonctionnaires civils et militaires, tous les employés et ouvriers de toutes administrations publiques ont droit à la communication personnelle et confidentielle de toutes les notes, feuilles signalétiques et tous autres documents composant leur dossier, soit avant d'être l'objet d'une mesure disciplinaire ou d'un déplacement d'office, soit avant d'être retardés dans leur avancement à l'ancienneté."

This duty on the administration to communicate to the official confidentially and personally all his personnel files,[5] which must in all essential respects be complete,[6] recurs in similar vein in other provisions governing the employment of officials, such as Article 67 of the Law of October 19, 1946,[7] in Article 3 of the *Ordonnance* of February 4, 1959,[8] as well as in Article 40 of the Law of April 28, 1952.[9]

From the first, these provisions were interpreted extensively.[10] Thus officials whose appointment was ineffective[11] and public employees who had come into an employment relationship on the basis of a contract of employment based on custom[12] were held to enjoy the benefit of these rules. Even disguised disciplinary measures[13] may be imposed only if the party concerned has first been given access to files and the opportunity to

[5] J. Puisoye, "La jurisprudence sur le respect des droits de la défense devant l'administration," A.J.D.A. 1962, pp. 79 *et seq.* at p. 85.
[6] A. de Laubadère *et al.*, *Traité de droit administratif*, (8th ed., Paris 1986), Vol. 2, p. 111, paras. 208–210.
[7] "Loi relative au statut général des fonctionnaires," Law of October 19, 1946.
[8] Order No. 59244 of February 4, 1959, "relative au statut général des fonctionnaires," (French) J.O. Feb. 1959, pp. 1947 *et seq.* at p. 2146.
[9] Law no. 52432 of April 28, 1952, "Loi portant statut général du personnel des communes et établissements publics communaux," (French) J.O. April 1952, p. 4349.
[10] J.-M. Auby, R. Drago, *op. cit.*, footnote 4, no. 1211. Examples include:
—the revocation of "privileges," C.E. judgment of June 17, 1936, *Gauthier*, Recueil Lebon, p. 659.
—procedures in "purges" of the administration, C.E. judgment of October 26, 1945, *Aramu*, Recueil Lebon, p. 213.
—application to representatives of the state in private organisations, C.E. judgment of July 9, 1937, *Fuster*, Recueil Lebon, p. 690; C.E. judgment of November 4, 1946, *Clary*, Recueil Lebon, p. 252.
[11] J. Puisoye, "La jurisprudence sur le respect des droits de la défense devant l'administration," A.J.D.A. 1962, p. 80; C.E. judgment of July 15, 1936, *Brion*, Recueil Lebon, p. 777.
[12] J. Puisoye, *op. cit.*, footnote 11, p. 80; C.E. judgment of May 14, 1947, *Vogler*, Recueil Lebon, p. 499; similarly C.E. judgment of May 18, 1939, *Du Chalard*, concerning employees with fixed-term contracts.
[13] C.E. judgment of June 26, 1957, *Katz*, *cf.* Long, Weil, Braibant, *Les grands arrêts de la jurisprudence administrative*, (8th ed., Paris 1984), p. 283.

1246

be heard. The Conseil d'Etat has even accepted that the President of the Republic, where he acts using special powers under Article 16 of the French Constitution,[14] may dismiss officials only in so far as he observes these formalities.[15]

These principles were later transferred to other fields of administrative activity.[16] Thus an "adversarial" procedure must be used where the administration wishes to exercise criminal justice powers.[17] If a legal person has been involved, however, this applies only where its "vital interests" have been interfered with.[18]

The case law also extended the field of the application of the rights of defence still further.[19]

A general principle of law was thus formulated in such a way that all measures "of a certain gravity" must be adopted using an adversarial procedure, that is using a procedure in which the party concerned is informed of the existence of the procedure and the essential allegations,

---

[14] Article 16 de la Constitution française du 4 octobre 1958: "Lorsque les institutions de la République, l'indépendance de la Nation, l'intégrité de son territoire ou l'exécution de ses engagements internationaux sont menacées d'une manière grave et immédiate et que le fonctionnement régulier des pouvoirs publics constitutionnels est interrompu, le Président de la République prend les mesures exigées par ces circonstances, après consultation officielle du Premier ministre, des présidents des Assemblées ainsi que du Conseil constitutionnel.
Il en informe la Nation par un message.
Ces mesures doivent être inspirées par la volonté d'assurer aux pouvoirs publics constitutionnels, dans les moindres délais, les moyens d'accomplir leur mission.
Le Conseil constitutionnel est consulté à leur sujet.
Le Parlement se réunit de plein droit.
L'Assemblée Nationale ne peut être dissoute pendant l'exercice des pouvoirs exceptionnels."
[15] C.E. judgment of October 23, 1964, d'Oriano, Recueil Lebon, p. 486, in Long et al., op. cit., footnote 13, p. 284; also the enforced early retirement of officials requires a hearing, cf. M. Waline, RDP 1956, pp. 330 et seq. at 332.
[16] B. Genevois, "Conclusions sous l'arrêt du Conseil d'Etat du mai 9, 1980, Sté Etablissements Cruse," A.J.D.A. 1980, p. 483.
[17] M. Waline, "Le principe audi alteram partem," Livre jubilaire du Conseil d'Etat luxembourgeois, 1957, p. 498.
[18] M. Waline, op. cit., footnote 17, p. 499.
[19] B. Genevois, op. cit., footnote 16, p. 484; M. Waline, op. cit., footnote 17, p. 502; J. Puisoye, op. cit., footnote 11, pp. 79 et seq.; from the case law cf. the leading case of the Conseil d'Etat of May 5, 1944, Dame Trompier Gravier, cited in B. Genevois, A.J.D.A. 1980, p. 482; cf. also prior to that the judgment of the Conseil d'Etat of October 28, 1938, Coache, and June 17, 1930, Ribeyrolles, referred to by M. Waline, op. cit., footnote 17 at p. 498, as well as the judgment of the Conseil d'Etat of May 9, 1980, Sté Etablissement Cruse, A.J.D.A. 1980, p. 483.

in order to give him or her the opportunity of examining the files and adopting a position on them.[19a]

It is clear that the question of the gravity of a measure is of particular importance, since it determines the need to introduce an adversarial procedure.[20] The point at which a "certain gravity" is reached cannot be definitively stated. The tendency of the case law is to assume that this condition is satisfied where, and to the extent that, existing rights are interfered with. Thus, for example, prohibitions on the exercise of a trade and the withdrawal of permits are regarded as measures which cannot be adopted without an adversarial procedure.[21] On the other hand, the mere rejection of a request, that is the refusal to grant new rights, is not seen as "grave" in this sense.[22]

In the case law this distinction is articulated through the concepts of "mesure de retrait" (adversarial procedure necessary) and "mesure de refus" (permissible without adversarial procedure).[23] The French literature offers a variety of definitions for this distinction; the essential and common element of these is the question of the existence of a right which has been interfered with.[24] Whether in a particular case the interference with the right has grave consequences for the party concerned is, however, less significant; if there is an interference with existing rights, then the rights of defence must normally be observed.[25]

The overwhelming majority opinion is that a further criterion for the necessity of a "procédure contradictoire" is whether or not it is alleged that the party concerned is in some way personally at fault,[26] or whether purely objective conditions require an act on the part of the authority.

[19a] See on this below in more detail.

[20] M. Waline, *op. cit.*, footnote 17, p. 501; J. Puisoye, *op. cit.*, footnote 11, p. 80; J.-M. Auby, R. Drago, *op. cit.*, footnote 4, no. 1211.

[21] B. Genevois, *op. cit.*, footnote 16, p. 483; M. Waline, *op. cit.*, footnote 17, p. 502 with further references; J.-M. Auby, R. Drago, *op. cit.*, footnote 4, no. 1211; *cf.* from the case law the judgments of the Conseil d'Etat of October 15, 1954, *Bontemps*, Recueil Lebon, p. 438 and of May 9, 1980, *Sté Etablissement Cruse*, Recueil Lebon, p. 217 as well as the judgment of February 6, 1981, *Sté Varoise de transport*, Recueil Lebon, p. 52.

[22] *cf.* the authors cited in footnote 21 as well as the judgment of the Conseil d'Etat of May 4, 1962, *Dame Ruard*, Recueil Lebon, p. 296.

[23] *cf.* B. Genevois, *op. cit.*, footnote 16, p. 483 as well as the judgment of the Conseil d'Etat cited in footnote 22.

[24] M. Waline, *op. cit.*, footnote 17, pp. 502 *et seq.*; J.-M. Auby, R. Drago, *op. cit.*, footnote 4, no. 1211 with further references.

[25] *cf.* B. Genevois, *op. cit.*, footnote 16, p. 438; *cf.* also the judgments of the Conseil d'Etat of March 7, 1958, *Epoux Speter*, Recueil Lebon, p. 152 and of December 9, 1974, *Matherey*, Recueil Lebon, p. 830.

[26] Conclusions du Commissaire du Gouvernement M. Gentot sur CE November 27, 1970: *Agence Maritime-Fret, Compagnie Générale Transatlantique et autres*, RDP 1971, 1004;

The recognition of rights of defence of this nature as general principles of law is today of greatest significance wherever equivalent statutory protection has not yet been instituted.

This was expressly confirmed by Commissaire du Gouvernement Genevois in his observations on a judgment of the Conseil d'Etat in which Letourneur's definition was used to adapt the scope of the general principle to new conditions.[27]

This definition reveals one limitation upon the "droits de la défense." So-called "mesures de police," the adoption and implementation of which by the administration is possible without the need to observe further formalities,[28] can occur in the absence of an adversarial procedure.

In so far as such an adversarial procedure is necessary, however, it has the following advantages for the party concerned.[29]

The administration must inform him of the existence of the procedure and of its intention to apply penalties, unless such notification is impossible. In the notification it must give, it is not bound by any formality; the nature of the investigation is irrelevant to the effectiveness of the measure.[30]

The object of the procedure must be made clear to the party concerned, and the allegations made against him must be communicated in full. If one allegation is missing, then (at least in staff cases) the decision

---

cf. also M. Waline, "Obligation de communiquer le dossier avant toute mesure d'éviction prise en considération de la personne de l'agent," Conseil d'Etat of December 9, 1955, *Garysas*, RDP 1956, p. 333; *cf.* also the judgment of the Conseil d'Etat of June 24, 1949, *Nègre*, Recueil Lebon, p. 304.

[27] B. Genevois, *op. cit.*, footnote 16, p. 483 with reference to the classic definition of Letourneur; *cf.* also M. Waline, note on the judgment of the Conseil d'Etat of December 9, 1955, *Garysas*, RDP 1956, p. 334.

[28] *cf.* on the definition and the state of views on this question M. Waline, note on the judgment of the Conseil d'Etat of March 6, 1970, *Ministre de l'Interieur* v. *Sideyn et Desonneville*, RDP 1970, pp. 1042 *et seq.*; B. Genevois, *op. cit.*, footnote 16, p. 483; A. de Laubadère *et al.*, *Traité de droit administratif*, Paris 1984, Vol. 1, p. 345, para. 717; see on this also the judgments of the Conseil d'Etat of February 2, 1977, *Demoiselles Picon*, and June 24, 1949, *Nègre*, Recueil Lebon, pp. 56 and 304.

[29] *cf.* also J.-M. Auby, R. Drago, *op. cit.*, footnote 4, Vol. 2, no. 1216.

[30] Judgments of the Conseil d'Etat of February 14, 1951. *Geoffroy* and *Dame Hélaine*, Recueil Lebon, p. 91.

subsequently adopted will be unlawful,[31] unless the allegation was of a totally subordinate nature.[32] If the party concerned knows the allegations or must necessarily be aware of them from the circumstances, then the failure to communicate them will exceptionally not lead to the annulment of the subsequent decision.[33]

After the communication of the objections, the party concerned must have the opportunity of defending himself effectively. That means first and foremost that he must be given "sufficient time" to prepare his defence and to give his views. The time given, which must be "reasonable,"[34] is in practice rather short, and the case law has generally regarded around nine days as sufficient.[35] On the other hand three days is generally too short.[36] It depends on the circumstances and the complexity of the individual case.

The authority is under the obligation actually to have regard to the opinion. The party concerned must be able effectively to influence the decision through his statement. That means that the measure may not in fact have been adopted before the opinion is received.

It is worthwhile mentioning the long-standing controversy in the literature as to whether, and to what extent, the protection given by the "droits de la défense" through a "procédure contradictoire" is of a different nature from that given by the right which is described by the phrase "audi alteram partem," but this is of minimal practical significance in this context.

Whereas some authors argue that this (foreign) rule is essentially identical in the results it gives to the French case law,[37] others regard the principle of "audi alteram partem" as an objective guarantee, whereas

---

[31] Judgment of the Conseil d'Etat of March 28, 1958, *Ministre de l'Education Nationale* v. *Dufresne*, Recueil Lebon, p. 204; *cf.* also J.-M. Auby, R. Drago, *Traité de contentieux administratif* (3rd ed., 1984), Vol. 2, no. 1172.

[32] Judgment of the Conseil d'Etat of February 20, 1953, *Foerst*, Recueil Lebon, p. 83.

[33] Judgment of the Conseil d'Etat of June 30, 1950, *Constantin*, Recueil Lebon, p. 840; *cf.* on this J. Puisoye, A.J.D.A. 1962, p. 79.

[34] *cf.* Long *et al.*, *Les grands arrêts de la jurisprudence administrative* (8th ed., Paris 1984), p. 283 with further references, as well as M. Waline, *op. cit.*, footnote 17, p. 505; *cf.* from the case law of the Conseil d'Etat, the judgments of August 11, 1968, *Coopération d'Insémination artificielle de la Vienne*, cited in J.-M. Auby, R. Drago, *op. cit.*, footnote 31, no. 1216, as well as of January 20, 1956, *Nègre*, Recueil Lebon, p. 24.

[35] Judgment of the Conseil d'Etat of January 26, 1912, *Lalanne*.

[36] Judgment of the Conseil d'Etat of June 22, 1938, *Albonico*.

[37] J. Lemazurier, "Vers une démocratie administrative: du refus d'informer au droit d'être informé," RDP 1980, p. 1239; M. Waline, "Obligation de communiquer le dossier," RDP 1956, p. 330; M. Waline, note on the judgment of the Conseil d'Etat of January 20, 1956, *Palm*, RDP 1956, p. 569.

the French rules are limited to the cases in which the party concerned is alleged to have been subjectively at fault.[38]

Regardless of its outcome, this discussion shows that the French legal system too is open to trends and concepts found in foreign legal systems[39] and will compare them with its own legal concepts. It is possible that this has also contributed to the fact that procedural rights are now protected largely through statutes.

(b) The formulation of statutory protective rights

The significance of the rights of defence for a proper administrative procedure has now to a large extent been recognised by the legislature as well. The task which has long been accomplished as regards public officials has now been carried over into the general administration.

A first step in this direction was taken by the adoption of the competition Law of July 7, 1977.[40] The concern of those affected that the very wide-ranging powers given to the Commission de la Concurrence could lead to excessive power in the hands of the administration, without effective counterbalance, was allayed by the guarantee given to procedural rights.

With the *Ordonnance* of December 1, 1986, French competition law was re-enacted.[41] Article 18 of the *Ordonnance* prescribes an adversarial procedure for investigations by the Conseil de la Concurrence intended to establish anti-competitive practices.[42]

---

[38] G. Vedel, P. Delvolvé, *Droit administratif*, (9th ed., Paris 1984), p. 392.

[39] M. Waline, *op. cit.*, footnote 37, RDP 1956, p. 330 at 334: "Au nombre de ces principes généraux du droit figure, d'après la jurisprudence du Conseil d'Etat, celui qui est souvent exprimé, spécialement sous la plume des juristes étrangers, par la bréve formule latine audi alteram partem et que l'on peut définir avec M. le Conseiller d'Etat Letourneur (Etudes et documents, fasc. 5, 1951, p. 25) par les termes suivants: 'le principe d'après lequel un acte individuel grave ne peut être pris par l'administration sans entendre, au préalable, la personne que cet acte est susceptible de léser dans ses intérêts moraux et matériels.' "

[40] Law no. 77–806 of July 19, 1977 concerning the control of concentrations of economic power and the regulation of unlawful agreements and the misuse of a dominant position on the market, (French) J.O. 1977, pp. 3833 *et seq.* The law extended above all the *Ordonnance* no. 45–1483 of June 30, 1945, (French) J.O. 1945, pp. 4150 *et seq.*, which was the earlier basis for French competition law.

[41] *Ordonnance* no. 86–1243 of December 1, 1986 on the removal of price controls and on freedom of competition, (French) J.O. 1986, pp. 14773 *et seq.*

[42] *cf.* in particular on the question whether Article 44 of the *Ordonnance* is still covered by Article 16 of Law no. 77–806 (see footnote 40): Y. Gaudemet, note on the judgment of the Conseil d'Etat of May 22, 1985, *Cabot*, RDP 1987, p. 233.

1251

This implies in particular that the allegations must be communicated to the party alleged to be responsible for the breach of the competition rules (Article 21(1)). Then he will be given during the course of the procedure a report on the procedure and on the opinions of the parties involved as well as the documents which form the basis of the report. The parties may then adopt a position on the report within two months (Article 21(2) and (3)).

The dangers that confidential information may be passed on or disseminated during the procedure before the Conseil de la Concurrence should be reduced by Articles 23 and 24:

Article 23:

"Le président du Conseil de la concurrence peut refuser la communication de pièces mettant en jeu le secret des affaires, sauf dans le cas où la communication ou la consultation de ces documents est nécessaire à la procédure ou à l'exercice des droits des parties. Les pièces considérées sont retirées du dossier."

Article 24:

"Sera punie des peines prévues à l'article 378 du code pénal la divulgation par l'une des parties des informations concernant une autre partie ou un tiers et dont elle n'aura pu avoir connaissance qu'à la suite des communications ou consultations auxquelles il aura été procédé."

Article 44 of the *Ordonnance* refers as regards the control of mergers only to Articles 21(2) and 23–25.

In sum, these provisions are intended to ensure that the procedural rights of the parties concerned are protected in competition proceedings.[43]

Of considerably greater general application are the guarantees of procedural rights introduced by the Law of July 17, 1978,[44] which address

---

[43] *cf.* in general on the new French competition Law H. Lob, "Das neue französische Recht der Wettbewerbsbeschränkungen," RIW 1988, p. 92.

[44] Law no. 78–753 of July 17, 1978 concerning various measures for improving relations between the administration and the citizen and various measures of an administrative law, social law and revenue law nature (French) J.O. 1978, pp. 2851 *et seq.*, as extended by Law no. 79–587 of July 11, 1979, (French) J.O. 1979, p. 1711.

the right of access to files. It guarantees on the one hand the principle that a petitioner has the right to know of the documents which refer to him or her by name.[45] On the other hand, documents which do not recognisably refer to any particular person may be seen by anyone (Article 1(1)). The proof of a special legal interest is not necessary.[46] The claim is directed towards the authorities and organisations named in Article 2 of the Law, that is almost the entire national and local state administration, including associated bodies.

In Article 6 of the Law the exceptions are dealt with. Some of these exceptions (concerning for example secrets of the government's deliberations, state secrets, investigation files in current customs and tax proceedings) play a general exclusionary function. In the face of these, private interests cannot be relied upon as against those interests intended to be protected by the introduction of the limitation. A person cannot however be denied access to the files which concern him on the grounds that they contain information about his private life, his trade and business secrets and his state of health.

The concept of "documents" is defined broadly in Article 1(2) of the Law. On the other hand, it excludes in particular the "avis" of the Conseil d'Etat and of the administrative courts. The same also applies to data held on computer which do not refer to a person.[47]

If the authority refuses to produce the documents—production includes in principle making available a copy at the expense of the person requesting it (Article 4b)—then the person concerned can and must[48] apply to the "Commission d'accès aux documents administratifs," which will issue a definitive administrative decision within precisely defined time limits.

The significance of the right of access to documents is indirectly strengthened by a decree of November 28, 1983.[49] The decree has the effect of reconciling these rules with those of the "procédure contradictoire." Article 8 of the decree provides:

---

[45] On the question of who is affected by files which recognisably refer to particular persons, cf. D. Linotte, "La motivation obligatoire de certaines décisions administratives françaises," RDP 1980, p. 1699; B. Lasserre, J.-M. Delarue, "Accès du public aux documents administratifs," A.J.D.A. 1983, p. 402.

[46] The limitation on the right of access is constituted by the concept of abuse of rights, cf. B. Lasserre, J.-M. Delarue, op. cit., footnote 45, p. 402.

[47] cf. Law no. 78–17 of January 6, 1978, (French) J.O. 1978, pp. 227 et seq.

[48] Judgment of the Conseil d'Etat of March 19, 1983, Bertin, Recueil Lebon, p. 745; B. Lasserre, J.-M. Delarue, op. cit., footnote 45, p. 408.

[49] Ordonnance no. 83–1025 of November 28, 1983 concerning relations between the administration and the citizen, (French) J.O. 1983, pp. 3492 et seq.

"Sauf urgence ou circonstances exceptionelles, sous réserve des nécessités de l'ordre public et de la conduite des relations internationales, et exception faite du cas où il est statué sur une demande présentée par l'intéressé lui-même, les décisions qui doivent être motivées en vertu de la loi du 11 juillet 1979[50] susvisée ne peuvent légalement intervenir qu'après que l'intéressé ait été mis à même de présenter des observations écrites.

Toute personne qui est concernée par une décision mentionnée au premier alinéa du présent article doit être entendue, si elle en fait la demande, par l'agent chargé du dossier ou, à défaut, par une personne habilitée à recueillir ses observations orales. Elle peut se faire assister ou représenter par un mandataire de son choix.

L'administration n'est toutefois pas tenue de faire droit aux demandes d'audition répétitives ou manifestement abusives par leur nombre et leur caractère systématique."

As regards a considerable number of unfavourable administrative decisions,[51] the person affected is given a prior right to be heard, and this prohibition on reaching a decision without giving the person concerned the opportunity to be heard is indirectly buttressed by a duty on the authority to provide information with respect to the existence of the procedure and the possibility of taking a position. Only when taken in conjunction with the right of access to files is the right to defend oneself in knowledge of all allegations and circumstances effectively guaranteed.

Otherwise, this decree introduces a number of "technical" improvements. Thus the authorities are obliged to give information about the distribution of competences, not only between the various bodies involved but also by indicating the competent party dealing with the substance of the issue within each body. If authorities receive letters, files or petitions in respect of matters for which they are not competent, then they must of their own accord forward these to the correct body (Article 7, 5, first subparagraph, first sentence, of the decree). The decree also contains improvements in the legal position of the individual, for instance with regard to the suspension of time limits where petitions have been misdirected, the need to confirm receipt by the authority or the duty to refer to documents which are missing (Article 5). It is interesting in this

---

[50] Law no. 79–587 of July 11, 1979 concerning the duty to give reasons for administrative acts, (French) J.O. 1979, p. 1711 (amended on p. 1822).
[51] Article 1 of the Law of July 11, 1979, provides:
  "Les personnes physiques ou morales ont le droit d'être informées sans délai des décisions administratives individuelles défavorables qui les concernent."

context that a confirmation of receipt must contain information about relevant legal remedies which refers to the fact that a petition is regarded as rejected at the end of a specified period of time and that this implicit rejection may be challenged in court (Article 5, first subparagraph, third sentence).

Finally, the Law of January 6, 1978 is worthy of mention, even though it is not always of importance in the context of administrative decisions.[52] It regulates in particular the right of the citizen to have access to information which is stored about him in computer files. The Law is concerned primarily with so-called "informations nominatives" that is, under Article 4, those matters which permit direct or indirect reference to the identity of a particular person.

The person concerned has in this respect not only a right to information (Articles 34, 35) and, in so far as false or outdated information is stored, to rectification (Article 36). The authorities must furthermore rectify information on their own initiative, and must communicate such a rectification to any person who has received information from the computer file which has been rectified (Article 38). Special rules apply to computer files which are covered by the protection of secrecy (Article 39) and those containing medical data (Article 40).

The enforcement of the law is supervised by a "Commission nationale de l'Informatique et des Libertés."[53]

Together with the law governing the duty to give reasons, which is considered below,[54] it can be concluded that a picture emerges in French law of a well-developed level of legislative protection for the rights of defence of citizens.

2. The right to a hearing in German administrative procedure[1]

(a) General observations

The right to a hearing also forms part of the classic rules of the general

---

[52] Law no. 78–17 of January 6, 1978, French J.O. 1978, pp. 277 *et seq.*

[53] Judgment of the Conseil d'Etat of May 19, 1953, *Bertin*, Recueil Lebon, p. 208; *cf.* also B. Lasserre, J. Delarue, *op. cit.*, footnote 45, p. 402, who also take a position on the distinction between the tasks of this body and the competence of the "Commission d'accès aux documents administratifs."

[54] See the law cited in footnote 50.

[1] A review in the English language on this subject is to be found in G. Ress, *Due Process in the administrative procedure*, FIDE 1978, pp. 4.1 *et seq.*

law of procedure in the Federal Republic of Germany. Since its conception, it has primarily been implemented in the field of judicial procedure.[2] After the end of the Second World War and the experiences of the Third Reich[3] the right to a hearing in accordance with the law was inserted in the Constitution as a basic right. Article 103(3) of the Basic Law provides that:

> "In the courts everyone shall be entitled to a hearing in accordance with the law."

This basic right is not directly transferable to the law of administrative procedure.[4]

In the field of administrative procedure, there were at first only rules on the right to be heard in various individual laws.[5] On the basis of the principle of the rule of law and other general constitutional principles, however, the administrative courts increasingly moved towards the position of recognising the right to a hearing even where it was not actually specifically enshrined in law.[6]

Since the middle of the seventies, moves towards codification have led to the comprehensive recognition of this right in the general part of administrative law. Thus the principle was laid down in the following terms in §28 of the *Verwaltungsverfahrensgesetz* (Law on administrative procedure: VwVfG)[7]:

> "§28 The hearing of parties

[2] K. Leonhardt, in P. Stelkens, H. J. Bonk, K. Leonhardt, *Verwaltungsverfahrensgesetz— Kommentar*, (2nd ed., Munich 1982), §28, para. 5.

[3] On the historical development, *cf.* P. Badura, in: H.-U. Erichsen, W. Martens (eds.), *Allgemeines Verwaltungsrecht*, (7th ed., Berlin/New York 1986), §36 II (pp. 336 *et seq.*).

[4] W. Clausen, in H. J. Knack, *Verwaltungsverfahrensgesetz, Kommentar*, Cologne etc. (2nd ed., 1982), §28, note 2.1.

[5] K. Leonhardt, *op. cit.*, footnote 2, §28, para. 5, (with reference to §90 BBG & §23 WPflG); H. Meyer, H. Borgs-Maciejewski, *Verwaltungsverfahrensgesetz*, (2nd ed., Frankfurt 1982), §28, para. 1 with further references.

[6] H. Meyer, H. Borgs-Maciejewski, *op. cit.*, footnote 5, §28, para. 1; K. Leonhardt, *op. cit.*, footnote 2, §28, para. 5; F. O. Kopp, *Verwaltungsverfahrensgesetz mit Erläuterungen*, (4th ed., Munich 1986), §28, para. 1 also with further references.

[7] VwVfG of May 25, 1976, BGBl. I 1976, p. 1253; this Federal law does not apply to the administrative activities of the federal states. They have, however, adopted laws which are materially identical. *cf.* on this the national report on the Federal Republic of Germany above in Chapter 2.

(1) Before an administrative act may be adopted which interferes with the rights of a party involved, that person must be given the opportunity of expressing his opinion on the facts relevant to the decision.

(2) A hearing need not be given where it is not required by the circumstances of the individual case, in particular where:
1. an immediate decision appears necessary on the grounds of danger if there is a delay or danger to the public interest;
2. a hearing would endanger the observance of a time limit crucial to the decision;
3. it is not intended to depart in any manner which would be detrimental to a party from the factual statements which he has made in a petition or a declaration;
4. the authority wishes to adopt a general disposition, large numbers of similar administrative acts, or administrative acts using automatic equipment;
5. measures are to be taken by way of administrative enforcement.

(3) A hearing shall not take place where it would conflict with a compelling public interest.

As regards the field of finance and tax law, which has traditionally been subject to special rules, §91 of the *Abgabenordnung* (taxation regulations: AO) offers an almost identical provision.[8]

---

[8] *Abgabenordnung* (Taxation Regulation) of March 3, 1976 (AO 1977), BGBl. I 1976, p. 613.

§91 Hearing of parties:

(1) Before an administrative act may be adopted which interferes with the rights of a party involved, that person must be given the opportunity of expressing his opinion on the facts relevant to the decision. This applies in particular where it is intended to depart in a way which operates to the disadvantage of the person subject to taxation from the facts as declared in the tax declaration.

(2) A hearing need not be given where it is not required by the circumstances of the individual case, in particular where
1. an immediate decision appears necessary on the grounds of danger if there is a delay or danger to the public interest;
2. a hearing would endanger the observance of a time limit crucial to the decision;
3. it is not intended to depart in any manner which would be detrimental to a party from the factual statements which he has made in a petition or a declaration;
4. the financial authority wishes to adopt a general disposition, large numbers of similar administrative acts or administrative acts using automatic equipment;
5. measures are to be taken by way of enforcement.

(3) A hearing shall not take place where it would conflict with a compelling public interest.

1257

In the field of social law too a specific provision on hearings for parties has been created in §24 of the *Sozialgesetzbuch* (Social Code: SGB).[9]

In so far as individual areas of administration are not covered by these fundamental provisions,[10] it can be assumed that the provision in §28 VwVfG counts at least as the expression of a general legal concept.[11] Support for this argument can be drawn from the fact that the codification has in many respects followed the guiding principles which were already previously recognised by the case law.[12]

(b) Those entitled to be heard

A party is entitled to be heard if an administrative act interferes with his rights. The concept of a party is defined more precisely in §13 VwVfG.[13] It includes those making and opposing petitions, as well as those to whom the authority wishes to address the administrative act. Furthermore, the administration must hear those persons who have a legal interest in the outcome of the procedure in accordance with §13(2) VwVfG, which means that their rights or legally protected interests[14] must be capable of being affected by the result of the procedure.[15] In addition, the administrative act must interfere with the rights of the party. There is no consensus on the interpretation of this formulation. According to one view in the literature the duty to accord a hearing is triggered only in the

---

[9] *Sozialgesetzbuch*, Tenth Book, Administrative Procedure, of August 8, 1980, BGBl. I 1980, p. 1461 (SGB (X)).

[10] On further special provisions laid down in specific laws *cf.* W. Clausen, *op. cit.*, footnote 4, §28, note 7.

[11] F. O. Kopp. *op. cit.*, footnote 6, §28, para. 64; *cf.* also R. Wimmer, "Die Wahrung des Grundsatzes des rechtlichen Gehörs," DVBl. 1985, p. 773 at 775; W. Clausen, *op. cit.*, footnote 4, §28, note 2.1 (with further references); H. Rüping, "Verfassungs- und Verfahrensrecht im Grundsatz des rechtlichen Gehörs," NVwZ 1985, p. 304 at 308.

[12] F. O. Kopp, *op. cit.*, footnote 6, §28, para. 1 (with further references); K. Leonhardt, *op. cit.*, footnote 2, §28, para. 5.

[13] *cf.* the corresponding parallel provisions in other laws, for example, §12 SGB(X), §78 AO.

[14] F. O. Kopp, *op. cit.*, footnote 6, §13, para. 17, §28, paras. 9, 12; H. Meyer, H. Borgs-Maciejewski, *op. cit.*, footnote 5, §28, para. 7 in conjunction with §13, para. 9; a critical view on the legally protected interests is provided by W. Clausen, *op. cit.*, footnote 4, §28, note 3.2.

[15] The possibility suffices; K. Leonhardt, *op. cit.*, footnote 2, §28, para. 9; F. O. Kopp, *op. cit.*, footnote 6, §28, paras. 11, 17; H. Meyer, H. Borgs-Maciejewski, *op. cit.*, footnote 5, §28, para. 10.

case of genuinely unfavourable administrative decisions, which as a rule do not include the refusal to grant a benefit.[16]

On the other hand, others argue from the essence and purpose of the provision, which is intended to protect citizens from unexpected burdens. Thus in the case of the refusal of a petition aimed at securing a favourable administrative decision as well, a hearing is required.[17]

(c) Exceptions to the duty to grant a hearing

The duty to hear the parties involved is not guaranteed without exception. Both §28(2) and (4) VwVfG and also the (identical) §91 AO and §24 SGB (X) contain a variety of exceptions. These differ from one another only in so far as §24 SGB (X) contains a (narrower) exclusive list of exceptions, whereas the other provisions are drafted in the form of a general clause ("in particular").[18]

The first group of exceptions concerns the cases where there is urgency. They are characterised by the fact that either because of external circumstances (danger resulting from delay—§28(2) No. 1 VwVfG) or because of the threat of a time period expiring (§28(2) No. 2 VwVfG) the authority must act particularly quickly in order to be able effectively to fulfil its tasks.[19] In these cases the authority has a discretion not to grant a

---

[16] N. Achterberg, *Allgemeines Verwaltungsrecht*, (2nd ed., Heidelberg 1986), p. 160; W. Clausen, *op. cit.*, footnote 4, §28, note 3 (with further references); K. Leonhardt, *op. cit.*, footnote 2, §28, para. 10; BVerwGE 66, 184 at 186 (with further references); BVerwG (of April 30, 1981, 3 C 135.77) Buchholz 451.74, §8 KHG Nr. 3; *cf.* on the whole question also H.-W. Laubinger, "Erforderlichkeit der Anhörung," VerwArch 1984, p. 55 at 56 *et seq.*; official statement of reasons for the VwVfG, §24 I, Bundestagsdrucksache 7/910, p. 51; Bundessozialgericht, judgment of March 1, 1979 (AZ: 6 RKa 17/77), SozR 1200 §34 SGB I No. 8.

[17] F. O. Kopp, *op. cit.*, footnote 6, §28, para. 10; R. Wimmer, *op. cit.*, footnote 11, p. 776 with further references; P. Badura, *op. cit.*, footnote 3, §40 III 2, p. 259; H. Meyer, H. Borgs-Maciejewski, *op. cit.*, footnote 5, §28, para. 9 (with further references); C. H. Ule, H.-W. Laubinger, *Verwaltungsverjahrensrecht*, (2nd ed., Cologne etc. 1978), p. 122; H. Maurer, *Allgemeines Verwaltungsrecht*, (5th ed., Munich 1986) Chaps. 19/20, p. 382; OVG Münster, NVwZ 1983. p. 746 (=DÖV 1983, p. 986); F. Mayer, F. O. Kopp, *Allgemeines Verwaltungsrecht*, (5th ed., Stuttgart etc. 1985), section 43 3 e (p. 368) (with further references); H. J. Wolff, O. Bachof, *Verwaltungsrecht III*, (4th ed., Munich 1978), §156 IV d 2.

[18] W. Clausen, *op. cit.*, footnote 4, §28, note 4; H. Meyer, H. Borgs-Maciejewski, *op. cit.*, footnote 5, §28, para. 20.

[19] See on this K. Leonhardt, *op. cit.*, footnote 2, §28 para. 23; W. Clausen, *op. cit.*, footnote 4, §28 note 4.1. with examples and further references; H. Meyer, H. Borgs-Maciejewski, *op. cit.*, footnote 5, §28 para. 21 (with further references).

hearing before adopting the decision.[20] To that extent the hearing must in any case take place as soon as possible.[21]

A second type of exception concerns primarily the public interest. That includes on the one hand cases in which enforcement measures are to be taken against the party concerned. If these measures were made known to the party beforehand, then the danger of the enforcement being frustrated would be too great, and in any case, material questions will have generally been discussed when the enforcement claim was granted.[22] Here too the authority has a discretion as to whether to grant a hearing.

On the other hand, the hearing may be omitted where the authority wishes to take a general disposition[23] or to adopt either large numbers of similar administrative acts or administrative acts using automatic equipment (*e.g.* traffic lights). The large numbers of persons who would have to be heard and the lack of an individual differentiation among them in most cases would here lead to a burden which would exceed the capacities of the authority.[24]

In contrast a hearing is not permissible (§28(3) VwVfG) where it conflicts with a "compelling public interest."[25] Such compelling public interests must be particularly important and must clearly outweigh the not inconsiderable significance of the right to a hearing.[26] The hearing may also be denied only in so far as there exists a public interest. The exclusion of the hearing may therefore possibly apply only to particular questions.[27]

The third large category of exceptions which should be mentioned contains the cases in which a hearing need not be held within the meaning

---

[20] W. Clausen, *op. cit.*, footnote 4, §28 note 4; H. Meyer, H. Borgs-Maciejewski, *op. cit.*, footnote 5, §28 para. 20.

[21] K. Leonhardt, *op. cit.*, footnote 2, §28 para. 22.

[22] K. Leonhardt, *op. cit.*, footnote 2, §28 para. 32; W. Clausen, *op. cit.*, footnote 4, §28 note 4.5; H. Meyer, H. Borgs-Maciejewski, *op. cit.*, footnote 5, §28 para. 27 (with further references).

[23] General dispositions are administrative acts with a concrete ruling which are addressed to numerous persons (*e.g.* a traffic sign); *cf.* §35(1) VwVfG; see on this also P. Stelkens, *op. cit.*, footnote 2, §35 paras. 129 *et seq.*

[24] H. Meyer, H. Borgs-Maciejewski, *op. cit.*, footnote 5, §28 para. 24; K. Leonhardt, *op. cit.*, footnote 2, §28 para. 27.

[25] *cf.* on this F. O. Kopp, *op. cit.*, footnote 6, §28 para. 56 (with further references); on the question when the need to preserve confidentiality, and thus the duty to refuse access to files, follows from the "nature of the case," *cf.* VGH Munich, DÖV 1978, p. 336.

[26] K. Leonhardt, *op. cit.*, footnote 2, §28 para. 33; H. Meyer, H. Borgs-Maciejewski, *op. cit.*, footnote 5, §28 para. 28 (with further references); W. Clausen, *op. cit.*, footnote 4, §28 note 5.

[27] F. O. Kopp, *op. cit.*, footnote 6, §28 para. 58.

and purpose of the provisions.[28] One statutorily regulated example is where the authority wishes to take a decision only on the basis of the matters of fact put forward by the petitioner. To hear the petitioner in such circumstances would, other than in exceptional cases, be a pure formality[29] and would furthermore be procedurally uneconomic.[30]

(d) The type and scope of the hearing

According to the wording of the law, the hearing takes place "on the facts relevant to the decision."

From this formula has arisen the argument as to whether the hearing is limited to establishing the factual circumstances relevant to the decision[31] or whether it may also cover questions of law.[32]

It is argued by some[33] that the rules of law which determine the relevance of the facts may be the subject of the hearing, even though the party has no right to conduct a detailed legal discussion.[34] It is said that this extensive construction presents no real obstacle to the "disciplined" conduct of the procedure, that is to leaving irrelevant and on occasions also querulous arguments on questions of law and fact unheeded.[35]

---

[28] H. Meyer, H. Borgs-Maciejewski, *op. cit.*, footnote 5, §28 para. 23.

[29] K. Leonhardt, *op. cit.*, footnote 2, §28 para. 25.

[30] W. Clausen, *op. cit.*, footnote 4, §28 note 4.3.

[31] G. Ress, *op. cit.*, footnote 1, p. 4.11; C. H. Ule, H.-W. Laubinger, *op. cit.*, footnote 17, p. 123; W. Clausen, *op. cit.*, footnote 4, §28 note 3.3; K. Leonhardt, *op. cit.*, footnote 2, §28 para. 12; H. Meyer, H. Borgs-Maciejewski, *op. cit.*, footnote 5, §28 para. 16.

[32] So states F. O. Kopp, *op. cit.*, footnote 6, §28 para. 15; M. Wallerath, *Allgemeines Verwaltungsrecht*, (3rd ed., 1985), §9 I 3 e, p. 260; H. Maurer, *op. cit.*, footnote 17, Ch. 19/20 p. 382; H.-W. Laubinger, *op. cit.*, footnote 16, pp. 70 *et seq.* (with comprehensive further references), who correctly distinguishes between the right of the party concerned to put forward his view of the law (which he (Laubinger) considers to be covered) and the duty of the authority to communicate its view of the law before the conclusion of the administrative procedure.

[33] F. O. Kopp, *op. cit.*, footnote 6, §28 para. 15; H. Maurer, *op. cit.*, footnote 17, ch. 19/20 p. 383.

[34] H. Meyer, H. Borgs-Maciejewski, *op. cit.*, footnote 5, §28 para. 16; F. O. Kopp, *op. cit.*, footnote 6, §28 para. 20; K. Leonhardt, *op. cit.*, footnote 2, §28 para. 13 (with further references); for a different view, *cf.* R. Wimmer, *op. cit.*, footnote 11, p. 777.

[35] F. O. Kopp, *op. cit.*, footnote 6, §28 para. 19 (with further references); H. Rüping, *op. cit.*, footnote 11, p. 307; K. Leonhardt, *op. cit.*, footnote 2, §28 para. 14; W. Clausen, *op. cit.*, footnote 4, §28 note 3.3.

In normal circumstances, the authority need give the party only one opportunity before the adoption of the administrative decision[36] to make his views known. It fulfils this duty if it informs him of the initiation of the procedure,[37] irrespective of whether the person concerned makes use of the opportunity to be heard.[38] Only if in the course of the procedure, after the hearing has taken place, new questions arise on which the person affected has not been able to express a view, is a further hearing required.[39] The person affected must be given sufficient time to prepare his opinion.[40]

It is for the authority to choose whether the hearing takes a written or oral form.[41]

The authority is prohibited from basing its decision on any information on which the other party has not been able to make observations.

(e) Rights of objection

In specific areas, in particular the law governing environmental pollution and nuclear power,[42] third parties who are affected not only have a right to be heard, but also in addition a right to formulate "objections,"

---

[36] K. Leonhardt, in P. Stelkens, H. J. Bonk, K. Leonhardt, *Verwaltungsverfahrensgesetz-Kommentar*, (2nd ed., Munich 1982), §28 para. 16; on whether it is permissible subsequently to make good the omission of a hearing *cf*. BVerwGE 66, p. 184 at 187 *et seq.*

[37] F. O. Kopp, *op. cit.*, footnote 6, §28 paras. 5, 22, 25; H. Meyer, H. Borgs-Maciejewski, *op. cit.*, footnote 5, §28 para. 17.

[38] F. O. Kopp, *Verwaltungsverfahrensgesetz mit Erläuterungen*, (4th ed., Munich 1986), §28 para. 5; W. Clausen, *op. cit.*, footnote 4, §28 note 3.4.

[39] F. O. Kopp, *op. cit.*, footnote 38, §28 para. 22 (with further references); K. Leonhardt, *op. cit.*, footnote 36, §28 para. 13; H. Meyer, H. Borgs-Maciejewski, *op. cit.*, footnote 5, §28 para. 17; OVG Lüneburg, MDR 1975, p. 786 at 788; OVG Münster, NJW 1978, p. 1764 at 1765.

[40] Bundesverfassungsgericht (BVerfG) E 49, 212 at 216; BVerwG, NJW 1976, 588; OVG Lüneburg, DVB1. 1973, p. 505 at 506; OVG Münster, NJW 1978, p. 1764 at 1765; M. Wallerath, *op. cit.*, footnote 32, §9 I 3 e) p. 259; W. Clausen, *op. cit.*, footnote 4, §28 notes 3.4, 3.6; K. Leonhardt, *op. cit.*, footnote 36, §28 para. 17; H. Meyer, H. Borgs-Maciejewski, *Verwaltungsverfahrensgesetz*, (2nd ed., 1982), §28 para. 14.

[41] F. O. Kopp, *op. cit.*, footnote 38, §28 para. 28; W. Clausen, *op. cit.*, footnote 4, §28 note 3.7 (with further references); C. H. Ule, H.-W. Laubinger, *op. cit.*, footnote 17, p. 124; H. Meyer, H. Borgs-Maciejewski, *op. cit.*, footnote 40, §28 para. 15; P. Badura, *op. cit.*, footnote 3, §40 II 3 (p. 359); BVerwGE 20, p. 160 at 166; VGH Munich, BayVwBl 1964, p. 24.

[42] §7 of the Regulation on procedures for the authorisation of installations under §7 of the *Atomgesetz* (AtVfV) of February 18, 1977, BGBl. I 1977, p. 280; §10(3) of the *Gesetz zum Schutz vor schädlichen Umwelteinflüssen* (Law on protection against damaging environmental pollution) (BImSchG) of March 14, 1974 as amended by the Law of October 4, 1985, BGBl. I 1985, p. 1950.

that is to express their doubts about a proposal in a formalised procedure.[43] The authority must take into account the objections, which within a certain period may be the subject of adversarial discussion. Such rights are provided for in the course of the planning and authorisation of certain types of "intrusive installations" which are made public by announcement.[44]

Such rights frequently also give rise to the "objector's burden." A person who raises no objections, in spite of his rights, cannot after the expiry of the time limit for objection raise a claim regarding interferences which he could have objected to during the course of the authorisation procedures (preclusion).[45]

(f) Complementary rights

The picture of the right to a hearing given here would be incomplete if one were not to refer at this stage to the complementary rights which give full efficacy to the right to a hearing. The most important point in this context is that the authority must provide the person affected with advice and information. §25 VwVfG[46] provides as follows:

> "The authority should encourage the deposition of declarations, the forwarding of petitions or the rectification of declarations or petitions, where these have clearly not come forward inadvertently or because of lack of knowledge, or where they have been incorrectly deposed or forwarded. It shall provide, in so far as is necessary, information about the rights of the persons concerned in the administrative procedure, and about the duties placed upon them."

---

[43] On the concept of the objection *cf.* C. H. Ule, H.-W. Laubinger, *Bundesimmissionsschutzgesetz, Kommentar*, Darmstadt 1978, §10 para. 8 (with further references); G. Feldhaus, W. Vallendar, *Bundesimmissionsschutzrecht*, Vol. I A, Wiesbaden 1985/86, §10 note 14; H. Schmatz, M. Nöthlichs, *Immissionsschutz–Kommentar zum Bundesimmissionsschutzgesetz*, Berlin 1979, §10 notes 8.1, 8.4; VGH Baden-Württemberg, DVBl. 1977, pp. 345 *et seq.*; VG Freiburg, DVBl. 1976, p. 807 at 809.

[44] This is the case in authorisation procedures under nuclear energy law and environmental protection law, *cf.* above, footnote 42.

[45] *cf.* §10(3) 3 BImSchG; §7(1) 2 AtVfV (above, footnote 42); see on this G. Feldhaus, W. Vallendar, *op. cit.*, footnote 43, §10 note 15; C. H. Ule, H.-W. Laubinger, *op. cit.*, footnote 43, §10 para. 9 (with further references); H. Schmatz, M. Nöthlichs, *op. cit.*, footnote 43, §10 notes 8.5, 8.6; C. H. Ule, "Zur rechtlichen Bedeutung von Ausschlussfristen im Verwaltungsverfahren und im Verwaltungsprozess," BB 1979, p. 1009.

[46] §89 AO; similar are §14–16 SGB (I) Social Code, General Part, of December 11, 1975, BGBl. I 1975, p. 3015; on the further rules to be found in specific laws see M. Wallerath, *op. cit.*, footnote 32, p. 256, footnote 36.

1263

This approach, which originates in the field of social law, was already recognised in principle even before the codification of administrative procedure,[47] but does not lead to a completely limitless claim for assistance *vis-à-vis* the authority, which would render superfluous the task of those whose job it is to give legal advice[48]; it only serves to counterbalance the most salient differences in state of knowledge among the various people affected[49] and is therefore to be understood as an expression of the principle of the welfare state.

So long as the persons affected are making obvious, that is recognisable, errors the authority should move of its own accord towards rectification.[50] In that context, what is obvious is interpreted broadly, even though the authority is not under an obligation to establish the errors in the conduct of the person affected by undertaking an extensive legal analysis.[51] The errors must be apparent to the authority. §25 VwVfG also covers information on the precise nature of a petition, which means that the authority owes a duty to a party who makes a claim to advise him with respect to the legal provision on which the petition can be based.[52]

Beyond that, it is generally only in response to a petition by a party[53] that the authority is under an obligation to provide information on rights and duties in administrative procedure. The duty to give information exists only to the extent that the party is innocently in ignorance of these rights[54] and needs the information in order effectively to protect his

---

[47] *cf.* H. Meyer, H. Borgs-Maciejewski, *op. cit.*, footnote 40, §25 para. 2; K. Leonhardt, *op. cit.*, footnote 36, §25 para.4; F. O. Kopp, *op. cit.*, footnote 38, §25 para. 1; BVerwGE 16, p. 156 at 159; 52, p. 70 at 79; BGHZ 15, p. 305 at 312.

[48] The giving of legal advice would be unlawful: F. O. Kopp, *op. cit.*, footnote 38, §25 para. 6.

[49] K. Leonhardt, *op. cit.*, footnote 36, §25 para. 3; K. Koch (ed.) *Abgabenordnung 1977*, (2nd ed., Cologne etc. 1979), §89 para. 7; H. Meyer, H. Borgs-Maciejewski, *op. cit.*, footnote 40, §25, para. 4 (with further references).

[50] K. Leonhardt, *op. cit.*, footnote 36, §25 para. 7; M. Wallerath, *op. cit.*, footnote 32, p. 256; J. Pipkorn, "Auskunftsansprüche gegenüber Verwaltungsbehörden," DÖV 1970, p. 171 at 172.

[51] K. Leonhardt, *op. cit.*, footnote 36, §25 para. 9; K. Koch, *op. cit.*, footnote 49, §89 para. 7.

[52] K. Leonhardt, *op. cit.*, footnote 36, §25 para. 11; BVerwGE 17, p. 178 at 179.

[53] H. Meyer, H. Borgs-Maciejewski, *op. cit.*, footnote 42, §25 para. 14; K. Leonhardt, *op. cit.*, footnote 36, §25 para. 14 (with further references); F. O. Kopp, *op. cit.*, footnote 38, §25 para. 9.

[54] K. Leonhardt, *op. cit.*, footnote 36, §25 para. 15; F. O. Kopp, *op. cit.*, footnote 38, §25 para. 10.

rights,[55] and in that context it is normally only a party involved in the procedure who can request the information.[56]

The duty to give information is limited to the relations arising in an actual current procedure,[57] as the authority should not be overburdened by these demands.

On the other hand, §25 VwVfG does not exclude the possibility that the authority may in an individual case, on the grounds of general legal principles, be under a duty to give more extensive advice.[58] In particular, the authority which has to take a discretionary decision must give the person affected information about the existence and content of general administration instructions which determine more precisely the nature of the exercise of discretion. The BVerwG has held with regard to this[59]:

> "According to a general principle of law which is not affected by the narrower formulation of §25 of the Law on administrative procedure of May 25, 1976 (BGB1. I p. 1253) adopted by Land Berlin— VwVfG—any person who is uncertain about the existence and extent of a right which is accorded to him and to that extent is reliant upon information imparted to him, may request the necessary information from the administration. Thus when requested in an individual case the authority must in principle provide information on the relevant directives on the exercise of discretion, as knowledge of these will be necessary for an effective pursuit of legal remedies in so far as they demonstrate how, as a rule, discretion will be exercised. This, in turn, provides a right to equal treatment."

It is also important that the authority itself must clarify the facts on its own initiative.[60] In order to give a view on the outcome of the investigations, the person affected must know these facts.[61] He has the opportunity to achieve this by inspecting the files on the case, and this possibility exists in addition to and independently of the existing duty on the authority to

---

[55] F. O. Kopp, *op. cit.*, footnote 38, §25 para. 10.
[56] K. Leonhardt, *op. cit.*, footnote 36, §25 para. 16.
[57] W. Clausen, in H. J. Knack, *Verwaltungsverfahrensgesetz, Kommentar*, (2nd ed., Cologne etc. 1982), §25 note 4.2; F. O. Kopp, *op. cit.*, footnote 38, §25 para. 2.
[58] F. O. Kopp, *op. cit.*, footnote 38, §25 para. 11 (with further references); see on this H. Meyer, H. Borgs-Maciejewski, *op. cit.*, footnote 40, §25 para. 15.
[59] BVerwG, judgment of September 16, 1980, E 61, p. 15, at 20; in agreement is F. O. Kopp, *op. cit.*, footnote 38, §25, para. 11.
[60] *cf.* §24 VwVfG, §20 SGB (X), §88 AO.
[61] K. Leonhardt, *op. cit.*, footnote 36, §29 para. 8; F. O. Kopp, *op. cit.*, footnote 38, §29 para. 2.

provide information.[62] A corresponding right is documented in §29 VwVfG[63]:

§29 Access to files by parties

(1) The authority must allow the other parties access to the files concerning the procedure to the extent that knowledge is necessary for the exercise or protection of their legal interests. Until the administrative procedure has been concluded, this provision does not apply to drafts of decisions or work leading directly to the preparation of such documents.

(2) The authority is not obliged to grant access to files in so far as this would damage the proper performance of the tasks of the authority, or knowledge of the contents of the files would harm the welfare of the *Bund* or of a *Land* or to the extent that proceedings must remain confidential by law or by their nature, in particular because of the legitimate interests of those involved or third parties.

(3) Access to files is granted in the premises of the authority which has charge of them.

(...)

§29 lays down the principle of limited public access to files.[64] This means that the authority must give the person affected access to files if knowledge about the files is necessary for the assertion or defence of rights,[65] in so far as there are no grounds for refusal.[66]

In principle, only a person who is formally involved in the procedure and whose *legal* interests require access is entitled to inspect the files (§13 VwVfG).[67]

---

[62] On this see §25 VwVfG.

[63] §25 SGB (X) is similar; the taxation regulation contains no general right of access to files, cf. F. Klein, G. Orlopp, *Abgabenordnung*, (2nd ed., Munich 1979), §90 note 4; K. Koch, *op. cit.*, footnote 49, §91 para. 5.

[64] K. Leonhardt, *op. cit.*, footnote 36, §29 para. 6; similarly F. O. Kopp, *op. cit.*, footnote 38, §29 para. 2.

[65] F. O. Kopp, *op. cit.*, footnote 38, §29 paras. 7 *et seq.*; K. Leonhardt, *op. cit.*, footnote 36, §29 paras. 6, 7.

[66] F. O. Kopp, *op. cit.*, footnote 38, §29 paras. 13 *et seq.*; K. Leonhardt, *op. cit.*, footnote 36, §29 para. 7; *cf.* on the individual exempting provisions immediately below.

[67] K. Leonhardt, *op. cit.*, footnote 36, §29 para. 12; similarly F. O. Kopp, *op. cit.*, footnote 38, §29 para. 7.

§29(2) VwVfG deals with the exceptions to the right of access to files. On the one hand, the authority is not obliged to provide access to files if and in so far as the functional capacity of the authority would be handicapped.[68] That means, for instance, that the period of time available for perusal may be limited because the authority cannot supervise the party concerned for many hours when he or she is inspecting the files.[69] The authority may also hand the files over to the other party for perusal. Lawyers in particular are often sent files for examination in their offices. Drafts of a decision do not need to be disclosed.[70]

Access can on the other hand be refused where the welfare of the *Bund* or of a *Land* may thereby suffer harm.[71] In practice, an important limitation is that access may be refused to the extent that the proceedings are to remain confidential by law or by their nature. Into the latter category falls, in addition to the confidentiality of personnel and examination files,[72] the protection of the legitimate privacy of interested third parties. In particular, the State cannot interfere with their private sphere by making information known to third parties.

Following the judgment of the Federal Constitutional Court in the population census case,[73] in which for the first time the right of the citizen to the protection of his "own" personal data was considered and protected under the constitution as a basic right,[74] this exception will carry a considerable weight.

The data protected under this principle concern not just the actual personal part of the private sphere; on the contrary business secrets and production information of legal persons are included under this concept.[75] In principle a right of refusal will also exist in respect of such

---

[68] F. O. Kopp, *op. cit.*, footnote 38, §29 para. 19; K. Leonhardt, *op. cit.*, footnote 36, §29 para. 19; W. Clausen, *op. cit.*, footnote 57, §29 note 5.1 (with further references).
[69] F. O. Kopp, *op. cit.*, footnote 38, §29 para. 20.
[70] See §29(1) second sentence VwVfG.
[71] K. Leonhardt, *op. cit.*, footnote 36, §29 para. 20; similarly F. O. Kopp, *op. cit.*, footnote 38, §29 para. 23.
[72] C. H. Ule, H.-W. Laubinger, *op. cit.*, footnote 17, p. 128; see on this also H. Meyer, H. Borgs-Maciejewski, *op. cit.*, footnote 40, §29 para. 23.
[73] BVerfGE 65, p. 1 (judgment of December 15, 1983, 1 BvR 209/83 etc.) = EuGRZ 1983, p. 577.
[74] BVerfGE 65, 1 at 42 *et seq.*
[75] F. O. Kopp, *op. cit.*, footnote 38, §29 para. 27; K. Leonhardt, *op. cit.*, footnote 36, §29 para. 21; H. Meyer, H. Borgs-Maciejewski, *op. cit.*, footnote 40, §29 para. 21.

documents as have been passed to the authority by third parties with a guarantee of confidentiality.[76]

Whether the refusal of access to files may serve to protect the person affected against himself is doubtful (*e.g.* in the case of a negative medical report).[77] It is possible that a rule may come into play here which is expressly provided for in the field of social law, namely that access to files in such cases is mediated via a doctor in the confidence of the party concerned.[78]

The right of access to files does not include a right to demand extracts or copies, although the authority is under an obligation to exercise its discretion in accordance with its obligations when considering such a request.[79]

(g) The consequences of non-observance or inadequate observance of the procedural rights

The consequences of a failure to give an adequate hearing or a failure to observe the complementary rights are not dealt with in quite the same way. In particular, in the fields where the right to a hearing is dealt with by specific legislative provision there are departures from the general rule.[80] That rule is that the implementation of the hearing cannot be made the subject of a specific process before the courts, but comes under judicial

---

[76] H. Meyer, H. Borgs-Maciejewski, *op. cit.*, footnote 40, §29 para. 22; M. Wallerath, *op. cit.*, footnote 32, §9 I 3, p. 258; OVG Koblenz, DVBl. 1977, p. 425 at 426; OVG Münster, DÖV 1980, p. 222 at 222.

[77] In favour: F. O. Kopp, *op. cit.*, footnote 38, §29 paras. 27, 29; W. Clausen, *op. cit.*, footnote 57, §29 note 5.3; OVG Münster, DVBl. 1974, p. 382 No. 149 (= RIA 1974, p. 34) (still before the adoption of the law); against: H. Meyer, H. Borgs-Maciejewski, *op. cit.*, footnote 40, §29 para. 21; K. Leonhardt, *op. cit.*, footnote 36, §29 para. 21.

[78] §25(2) SGB (X) provides as follows:
(2) In so far as the files contain details about the state of health of a party involved, the authority may instead have the files transmitted to the party through a doctor. It must transmit the files through a doctor in so far as there is a danger that access to the files would cause disproportionate harm to the party, in particular to his health. In so far as the files contain details which might harm the evolution and development of the personality of the party, the first and second sentences of this provision shall apply correspondingly subject to the condition that the content of the files may also be transmitted through a servant of the authority who is capable and qualified to undertake this task through his training as well as his personal and professional experience. The right under para. 1 is not limited.

[79] K. Leonhardt, *op. cit.*, footnote 36, §29 para. 27; it is different in the field of social law; §25(5) SGB (X) expressly accords a right to the taking of copies.

[80] *cf.* for example BVerwG, DVBl. 1986, p. 153 at 154 on the principles of the right to a hearing in proceedings under §§91 *et seq.* BDO.

1268

control only when taken together with the act which is "affected" by it[81] (§44a VwVfGO).

Furthermore, if the hearing was omitted it can normally be held at a later stage, or defects may be corrected in retrospect if the person affected is given a renewed opportunity to be heard before the end of the preliminary procedure[82] (§45(1) No. 3 read in conjunction with (2) of the VwVfG[83]; cf. also §126 AO).

In the face of the strict wording of §45 VwVfG, the Federal Administrative Court has allowed the correction of defects as regards the hearing even during the judicial process.[84] This decision has however been criticised in the literature and in lower courts.[85]

Finally, under §46 VwVfG (§127 AO) the decision may be annulled only if a different decision might possibly have been taken if a hearing had occurred.[86] This final limitation does not apply in social law affairs under §42 2nd sentence SGB (X).

In this context it should be noted that these legislative decisions are regarded by some academic commentators[87] as incorrect as a matter of legal policy and doubtful under the rule of law, in particular since they frequently deprive of sanction an infringement of material procedural law.

3. The rights of the defence in Italy

Administrative procedure is not regulated in one single law in Italy. Rather there exist in many individual laws provisions for specific fields of

---

[81] F. O. Kopp, *op. cit.*, footnote 38, §28 para. 59; K. Leonhardt, *op. cit.*, footnote 36, §28 para. 34; W. Clausen, *op. cit.*, footnote 57, §28 note 6; for a different view, *cf.* H. Meyer, H. Borgs-Maciejewski, *op. cit.*, footnote 40, §28 para. 29.

[82] BVerwGE 61, p. 45 at 50.

[83] On the conditions governing correction *cf.* W. Clausen, *op. cit.*, footnote 57, §28 note 6; U. Battis, *Allgemeines Verwaltungsrecht*, Heidelberg, 1985, para. 185; OVG Münster, DVBl. 1981, p. 689 at 690; VG Berlin, DVBl. p. 196 at 197; *cf.* also BVerwG, DVBl. 1986, p. 153 at 154.

[84] BVerwGE 61, p. 45 at 50.

[85] F. O. Kopp, *op. cit.*, footnote 38, §45 paras. 19 *et seq.*, 24 *et seq.*; F. O. Kopp, *Verwaltungsgerichtsordnung*, (7th ed., Munich 1986), §113 paras. 31 *et seq.*; H. Mandelartz, "Anhörung, Absehen von Anhörung, Nachholen der unterbliebenen Anhörung—Zur Relativierung des Verfahrensrechts," DVBl. 1983, p. 112 at 115.

[86] W. Clausen, *op. cit.*, footnote 57, §28 note 6.

[87] *cf.* the references in P. Stelkens, in Stelkens, Bonk & Leonhardt, *VwVfG*, (2nd ed., Munich 1983), §46, para. 2.

law, such that it must be said that there is a certain splintering of the relevant law.[1]

Here we shall in general emphasise only the most important features of the administrative process, as they have been developed in particular in academic writings.[2]

Reference should first be made, as a general constitutional requirement, to the principle of "buon andamento" (proper procedure) of the administration. Article 97(1) of the Constitution provides for the application of this principle in the organisation of offices and authorities. According to the majority view, it follows from this principle that the administration must act according to criteria of efficacy. Academic literature regards a proper administrative procedure as one of the most important means of ensuring effective administrative action.[3] However, the difficulty of defining the criteria according to which the performance capacity of the administration is to be measured is emphasised. The principle of "buon andamento" as such has not received any more precise formulation in the case law. Academic literature, however, has sought to define this principle.

Some authors argue that these are not legal rules of conduct but issues such as, for example, the efficiency and speed of administrative action, the better weighing up of interests and the avoidance of harm to those concerned.[4]

---

[1] *cf.* F. Favara, I. M. Braguglia, "Les garanties légales dans la procédure administrative," FIDE 1978, p. 7.3; R. Grawert, "Grenzen und Alternativen des gerichtlichen Rechtsschutzes in Verwaltungsstreitsachen, Rechtsvergleichender Bericht: Deutschland—Italien," DVBl. 1983, p. 973 at 980.

[2] Amongst the most important studies of administrative procedure *cf.* A. M. Sandulli, *Il procedimento amministrativo*, Milan, 1940 (new edition 1959); F. Benvenuti, "Funzione amministrativa, procedimento, processo," Riv. trim. dir. pubbl. 1952, pp. 118 *et seq.*; G. Berti, *La pubblica amministrazione come organizzazione*, Padua, 1968, p. 330; M. Nigro, "Procedimento amministrativo e tutela giurisdizionale contro la pubblica amministrazione" in AA.VV. *L'azione amministrativa fra garanzia ed efficienza*, "Problemi di amministrazione pubblica" (commenti) No. 1, 1981, pp. 21 *et seq.*; G. Pastori, *La procedura amministrativa*, Milan, 1964; U. Allegretti, *L'imparzialità amministrativa*, Padua, 1965, pp. 224 *et seq.*; G. Berti, "La struttura procedimentale della pubblica amministrazione," Dir. e soc. 1980; M. S. Giannini, *Istituzioni di diritto amministrativo*, Milan, 1981, Vol. II, pp. 813 *et seq.*; G. Cataldi, *Il procedimento amministrativo nei suoi attuali orientamenti giuridici e non giuridici*, Milan, 1967; S. Cassese, "Il privato e il procedimento amministrativo," Arch. giur. 1970, pp. 25 *et seq.*

[3] *cf.* M. S. Giannini, *op. cit.*, footnote 2, Vol. I, p. 263; A. M. Sandulli, *Manuale di diritto amministrativo*, (14th ed., Naples 1984), Vol. I, p. 516; A. Andreani, *Il principio costituzionale di buon andamento della pubblica amministrazione*, Padua, 1979; *cf.* also F. Favara, I. M. Braguglia, *op. cit.*, footnote 1, p. 7.1.

[4] *cf.* A. M. Sandulli, *op. cit.*, footnote 3, p. 517; R. Resta, "L'onere di buona amministrazione," in *Scritti giuridici in onore di S. Romano*, Padua, 1940, Vol. II, pp. 103 *et seq.*

According to Marzuoli,[5] the principle of "buon andamento" falls within the field of rules governing administration under the law. The "good conduct of administration" is not to be understood as a guarantee in an individual case, but as a projection with regard to the "success" of administrative action actually undertaken.[6]

An expression of this principle to be found in the substantive law is contained, for example, in the Law of July 11, 1980, No. 312, one of the most important more recent laws on the organisation of the work of the administration. According to Article 21, the organisation of the work of public officials (and employees) should follow the principles of responsibility and participation, in order to secure democracy, "buon andamento" and impartiality (para. 1). Furthermore, the organisation of the administration should seek to achieve the goals of efficiency, economy and profit maximisation. Article 22 provides for the adoption of rules governing the organisation of work which are aimed at the recovery of productivity and the improvement of the performance of the administration.

According to the principle of administration under the law, every administrative measure must be adopted on the basis of a procedure determined by law. In spite of the multiplicity and variety of the individual administrative procedures,[7] academic writings have elaborated a general procedural typology which consists of two (or sometimes three) phases.[8]

(1) The preparatory phase

The first phase covers the collection of all the statements and information necessary for a decision. It is in turn divided into three further steps:

— **the step of initiation:** the procedure is opened by a so-called act of initiation. This act can be triggered by the authorities responsible for the decision, by other authorities, or on the initiative of private individuals.[9]

---

[5] *cf.* on administration under the law Fois, *Legalità (principio di)*, EdB, Vol. XXIII, 1973, pp. 659 *et seq.*

[6] On the concept of legality as the "proper application of the law" see F. Satta, *Principio di legalità e pubblica amministrazione nello Stato democratico*, Padua, 1969, p. 95.

[7] On the typology of individual administrative procedures *cf.* A. M. Sandulli, *op. cit.*, footnote 3, pp. 571 *et seq.*

[8] *cf.* A. M. Sandulli, *op. cit.*, footnote 3, p. 575.

[9] On this see Meloncelli, *L'iniziativa amministrativa*, Milan, 1976.

— **the step of investigation:** after the step of initiating the procedure there follows an investigatory stage in which as a rule the factual and legal bases for the decision are collected by the authority responsible for the decision. The authority has a broad discretion at its disposal with regard to undertaking and if necessary repeating or widening the investigation. The case law therefore works from the assumption that the investigation can at any time be reopened.[10]

— **the hearing of parties involved and other administrative bodies:** the Italian legal order does not recognise a general principle according to which the parties affected must necessarily be heard in the course of the administrative procedure. A hearing may be provided for by law, or may be arranged by the administration itself.[11]

It is provided in individual laws that the authority which decides must (or may) take into account reports from other administrative organs or authorities.[12]

In the 1963 draft of a law on administrative procedure mentioned already above,[13] in accordance with its basic philosophy, the rights of the defence are included only in a very rudimentary form.[14] The draft provides for participation in technical inquiries (Article 28) and provides that after the adoption of the administrative act, reports and results of inquiries must also be made available to the persons affected (Article 36). It is also provided in Article 26 that the person affected must be informed about the initiation of the procedure. Finally, Article 41(4) of the draft states that every administrative act which was adopted without following the procedure set out would be unlawful and could be annulled.[15]

---

[10] *cf.* CdS, Sez. II, judgment of January 20, 1976, N.2023, in G.C.d.S. 1979, Vol. I, p. 75. On the investigatory stage *cf.* R. Perez, "L'acquisizione di notizie da parte della pubblica amministrazione," Riv. trim. dir. pubbl. 1968, p. 1371; F. Levi, *Inchiesta amministrativa, Novissimo dig.*, Vol. VIII, pp. 509 *et seq.*

[11] See on this G. Berti, "Procedimento, procedura, partecipazione," in *Studi in memoria di Guicciardi*, Padua, 1975, pp. 779 *et seq.*

[12] See on this F. Franchini, *Il parere nel diritto amministrativo*, Milan, 1944–45; A. Amorth, *La funzione consultiva e i suoi organi*, AC 1961; F. Trimarchi, *Funzione consultiva e amministrazione democratica*, Milan, 1974; G. Correale, *Parere (diritto amministrativo)*, EdD, Vol. XXXI, pp. 676 *et seq.*

[13] *cf.* above, Introduction under footnote 56.

[14] *cf.* F. Benvenuti, "Einführung (Italien)," in C. H. Ule, *Verwaltungsverfahrensgesetze des Auslandes*, Berlin 1967, p. 157 at 168.

[15] The text of the draft is reprinted as a bill dated May 31, 1963 (Lucifredi), Documenti, Camera dei Deputati, IV Legislatura, N. 81; German translation in C. H. Ule, *op. cit.*, footnote 14, pp. 176 *et seq.*

What is not provided for, however, is the right of the person affected to have access to the files even during the procedure. There is also no obligation on the authority to grant a hearing to the person affected outside technical inquiries concerning the result of the inquiries and on the proposed measures.[16]

(2) The constitutive phase

During this second phase the administrative measure is determined and adopted. Thus it is sometimes also called the phase of "conclusion."

In so far as the authority consists of an individual (*e.g.* the Minister) there are no special rules of decision. This is different where the authority is a collegiate body or the law provides for the participation of several bodies. In this case the term "complex act" is used, since the conclusion of the measure is subject to the voluntary decision of several bodies.[17]

The provisions on the notification of an administrative act are based on those of the rules of civil procedure. A duty to give a statement of reasons exists only with limitations.[18]

(3) The phase in which the act becomes fully effective

This phase is of significance only where the law exceptionally makes the effectiveness of a measure subject to the control of special institutions, *e.g.* a court of auditors. This means that a measure which has already been formally adopted can become effective only if either no control must be undertaken in the individual case, or where the consent of the controlling body has already been granted.

4. The rules of natural justice in the United Kingdom

When analysing the law in the United Kingdom, it should be borne in mind that there are different legal orders, namely England and Wales with its "true" common law system on the one hand and Scotland with its

---

[16] Critical remarks in F. Benvenuti, *op. cit.*, footnote 14 at p. 168.
[17] *cf.* A. M. Sandulli, *op. cit.*, footnote 3, p. 580.
[18] See on this below (duty to give reasons).

special rules on the other.[1] This separation of legal orders continues to exist on the basis of the "Act of Union."[2] The differences with regard to the principle to be discussed here are limited, but it does seem necessary to refer to the distinction nonetheless.

The principle of "audi alteram partem" rests on notions long recognised in the English legal tradition.[3]

Already in *Dr. Bentley's case* in 1723[4] which we discussed above, the courts recognised the necessity of according the person affected a minimum level of rights even in administrative proceedings. The University could not therefore deprive the plaintiff of all academic degrees without first giving him the right to be heard.

The foundations of this decision were the principles of "natural justice," which essentially mean[5] that no-one may be the judge in his own cause and each party must be given the opportunity of putting forward his views. Despite these early precedents, however, the review of administrative decisions in this connection remained restricted. It is important to note that the right to a hearing is limited to decisions in individual cases. Measures of the legislature require no hearing[6]—this follows from the principle of Parliamentary sovereignty.[7] Nor is a prior hearing neces-

---

[1] *cf.* on this J. D. B. Mitchell, "Due Process," FIDE 1978, p. 10.

[2] See on this S. A. de Smith, "Right to a Hearing," Vol. 68 Harv. L. Rev. (1955), 569 at 596 (with further references).

[3] The oldest reported case of 1615 (*Bagg's Case*) concerns the removal from office of an official, *cf.* 77 Eng. Rep. 1271 (K.B. 1615). It represents the leading case on the *remedy of mandamus* in such cases; *cf.* S. A. de Smith, *op. cit.*, footnote 2, p. 572.

[4] *R. v. Chancellor of the University of Cambridge* I Str. 557, 93 Eng. Rep. 698 (K.B. 1723) cited in S.A. de Smith, *op. cit.*, footnote 2, p. 572; *cf.* also J. F. Garner, B. L. Jones, *Administrative Law*, (6th ed., London 1985), p. 143; with regard to rule of *nemo judex* in *causa sua* which also falls within the rules of natural justice, Stevens refers to the case of *Dr. Bonham* in 1610, I. N. Stevens, *Constitutional and Administrative Law*, Plymouth, 1982, p. 225.

[5] *cf.* on this J. F. Garner, B. L. Jones, *op. cit.*, footnote 4, p. 136; I. N. Stevens, *op. cit.*, footnote 4, p. 224.

[6] D. Foulkes, *Administrative Law*, (5th ed., London 1982), pp. 237 *et seq.*; see also H. W. R. Wade, *Administrative Law*, (5th ed., London 1982), pp. 506 *et seq.*

[7] *cf.* on this in general A. V. Dicey, *Introduction to the study of the Law of the Constitution*, (10th ed., London 1960), p. 39; O. Hood Phillips, P. Jackson, *Constitutional and Administrative Law*, (7th ed., London 1987), p. 59 (with further references); *cf.* J. Harvey, L. Bather, *The British Constitution and Politics*, (5th ed., London 1982), p. 9, as well as the House of Lords in *Edinburgh and Dalkeith Railway Co.* v. *Wauchope* [1842] 8 Cl. & F. 710; 1 Bell. 252, at 278–279, *per* Lord Campbell:

"All that a Court of Justice can do is to look to the Parliament roll: if from that it should appear that a Bill has passed both Houses and received the Royal Assent, no Court of Justice can enquire into the mode in which it was introduced into Parliament, nor into what was done previous to its introduction, or what passed in Parliament during its progress in its various stages through both Houses," confirmed in the decision of the

sary before the adoption of regulations (delegated legislation) by the executive.[8]

The courts began[9] by dividing measures of the executive into two groups: those "of administrative (or executive) function" and those "of judicial (or quasi-judicial) character."

In the case of measures in the first group, there should be no right to a hearing. Only when the authority is simultaneously adopting a judicial decision are the principles of "natural justice" to be observed.[10]

The distinction between "judicial" and "administrative"[11] procedure is based on two criteria. On the one hand there is the question[12] whether an adversarial procedure is to be adopted. In that context it is normally assumed that a subordinate administrative authority can be the "opponent" of the citizen concerned where a decision is taken by the competent Minister. An administrative hierarchy which regards local and state administration as a single unit is thus not recognised.

The second important criterion[13] is the question whether an issue is to be dealt with simply on the basis of questions of fact and law (that applies to judicial procedure) or whether a policy decision[14] is necessary (that applies to administrative procedure).

It is essential for the understanding of the development of the law that Parliament has since the middle of the nineteenth century been ever more aware of the need to adopt statutory rules to govern the actions of the administration. Since the courts must have regard to the sovereignty of

House of Lords by Lord Reid, *Pickin* v. *British Railways Board* [1974] A.C. 765, quoted in O. Hood Phillips, P. Jackson, *op. cit.*, footnote 52.

[8] *cf.* H. W. R. Wade, *op. cit.*, footnote 6 at p. 506; J. F. Garner, B. L. Jones, *op. cit.*, footnote 4, p. 147; *Bates* v. *Lord Hailsham* [1972] 3 All E.R. 1019.

[9] D. Foulkes, *op. cit.*, footnote 6, pp. 233 *et seq.*; J. F. Garner, B. L. Jones, *op. cit.*, footnote 4, p. 144; S. A. de Smith, *op. cit.*, footnote 2, p. 596; I. N. Stevens, *op. cit.*, footnote 4, pp. 228 *et seq.*; H. W. R. Wade, *op. cit.*, footnote 6, pp. 458 *et seq.*; with general reference to the decision of the Privy Council in *Nakkuda Ali* v. *Jayaratne* [1951] A.C. 66 as well as *R.* v. *Metropolitan Police Commissioner, ex p. Parker* [1953] 2 All E.R. 1717.

[10] See in *Nakkuda Ali* v. *Jayaratne* [1951] A.C. 66, Privy Council *per* Lord Radcliffe.

[11] On the origin and basis for the distinction *cf.* H. W. R. Wade, *op. cit.*, footnote 6, p. 449 (with further references).

[12] S. A. de Smith, *op. cit.*, footnote 2, at pp. 592, 596.

[13] This was the classic position and definition adopted by the Committee on Ministers' Powers, Cmnd. 4060 (1932/1964), p. 73; J. F. Garner, B. L. Jones, *op. cit.*, footnote 4, p. 145; *cf.* also S. A. de Smith, *op. cit.*, footnote 2, p. 596.

[14] On the concept of "policy" in English law *cf.* M. Bernhardt, *Die rechtliche Bedeutung der Erklärung einer "policy" in der englischen Verwaltungspraxis. Dargestellt am Beispiel der Rückübereignung enteigneter Grundstücke*, Diss. Freiburg i. Br. 1975, *passim.*

Parliament and the "rule of law,"[15] the common law principles could be observed only where it could be assumed that the legislature desired them in fact to be applied. Up to the 1950s, there were ever fewer occasions when this assumption was made.[16]

In particular, if the statute contained procedural rules, as was increasingly the case, the applicability of the principles of natural justice, where it was not expressly provided for, was hardly ever accepted by the courts.[17]

Finally, the variety of different forms of statutorily determined administrative interventions had become so great with various Committees, Tribunals and Inquiries, that the relevant administrative procedures were investigated by two Parliamentary committees and proposals brought forward to standardise them.[18]

In so far as these are of interest here, it should be noted that this involved[19] the standardization of procedures governing Inquiries and Tribunals[20] as well as the recognition of the notion that there will be fairness and good relations between administration and citizen where[21]

— the party affected is informed of the procedure;

[15] "Supremecy of Parliament," cf. on this A. V. Dicey, op. cit., footnote 7, p. 39; O. Hood Phillips, P. Jackson op. cit., footnote 7, pp. 59 et seq., each with further references; cf. above also Chap. 2, the national report on the United Kingdom.

[16] cf. similarly J. F. Garner, B. L. Jones, op. cit., footnote 4, p. 144; S. A. de Smith, op. cit., footnote 2, p. 596 (with further references); this view departs from the dicta in Cooper v. Wandsworth Board of Works [1863] 14 C.B. (N.S.) 180; per Byles J:

"It seems to me that the board are wrong whether they acted judicially or ministerially. I conceive they acted judicially, because they had to determine the offence, and they had to apportion the punishment as well as the remedy. That being so, a long course of decisions beginning with Dr. Bentley's case, and ending with some very recent cases, establish that, although there are no positive words in a statute requiring that the party shall be heard, yet the justice of the common law will supply the omission of the legislature."

It was only in the decision in Ridge v. Baldwin [1964] A.C. 40 that the judges finally returned to these words, see immediately below.

[17] S. A. de Smith, op. cit., footnote 2, p. 593 (with further references, in particular in notes 152 and 153, with many cases as examples).

[18] Committee on Ministers' Powers, Report April 1932, Command Papers (Cmnd.) 4060 (Reprint 1963); Committee on Administrative Tribunals and Enquiries, July 1957, Command Papers (Cmnd.) 218 (Reprint 1962), the so-called "Franks Report."

[19] cf. J. D. B. Mitchell, op. cit., footnote 1, p. 10.3.

[20] By the Tribunals and Inquiries Act 1971, 41 Statutes 248.

[21] cf. Committee on Ministers' Powers, Report, Cmnd. 4060 (1932/63) p. 116 (IV,V,VI); Committee on Administrative Tribunals and Enquiries, Report, Cmnd. 218, 1957/1962, pp. 91 et seq. (9, 10, 12, 15, 19, 22, 23); on this see also J. D. B. Mitchell, op. cit., footnote 1, p. 10.5.

— he is given the opportunity of putting his views;
— the person charged with making the decision is impartial;
— reasons are given for the decision;
— the decision contains information about the possibility of legal challenge.[22]

Because of the variety of the subject-matter and the traditional distinction between the local and national administration no general codification of these rules resulted from the review. However, the aim was rather that of a certain standardisation of individual laws, in so far as the Tribunals and Inquiries Act 1971[23] put forward certain general recommendations.

The principles set out may also have influenced the House of Lords, which in the case of *Ridge* v. *Baldwin*,[24] to be discussed below, restored the rules of natural justice to their central position within administrative law, by returning to the notions which formed the original basis of the case law.[25]

The analysis here will cover two fields of law:

— *audi alteram partem* as a general principle of law (natural justice, duty to act fairly);
— *audi alteram partem* as provided for in specific statutes.

As regards the relationship between the two fields the following remarks should be made: according to the general notion of the rules of law and the supremacy of Parliament, statutes prevail over the general common

---

[22] Committee on Administrative Tribunals and Enquiries, *op. cit.*, footnote 21, p. 92 (23).
[23] 41 Statutes 248.
[24] [1964] A.C. 40 (H.L.).
[25] *cf. Board of Education* v. *Rice* [1911] A.C. 179 at 182, *per* Lord Loreburn, L.C.

"Comparatively recent statutes have extended, if they have not originated, the practice of imposing upon departments or officers of State the duty of deciding or determining questions of various kinds. In the present instance, as in many others, what comes for determination is a matter to be settled by discretion, involving no law. It will, I suppose, usually be of an administrative kind; but sometimes it will involve matter of law as well as matter of fact, or even depend upon matter of law alone. In such cases the Board of Education will have to ascertain the law and also to ascertain the facts. I need not add that in doing either they must act in good faith and listen fairly to both sides, for that is a duty lying upon everyone who decides anything. But I do not think they are bound to treat such a question as though it were a trial. They have no power to administer an oath, and need not examine witnesses. They can obtain information in any way they think best, always giving a fair opportunity to those who are parties in the controversy for correcting or contradicting any relevant statement prejudicial to their view."

cf. also S. A. de Smith, *op. cit.*, footnote 2, p. 577, with further references in note 58.

law. However, today (in contrast to a period during the 1950s) a statute will be interpreted so as not to conflict with the rules of natural justice, in so far as it does not expressly provide otherwise. This rule of construction assists the implementation of general principles of law where the legislature has adopted incomplete provisions.[26]

(a) The current significance of the general principle of law

The current role of the principles of natural justice has altered in certain essential respects by virtue of a number of more recent cases.

The starting point for the more recent development was the case of *Ridge* v. *Baldwin*.[27] A high-ranking police officer was tried for "conspiracy." He was acquitted, but was forced during the course of the trial to admit to having behaved wrongfully. His employer, the local watch committee, dismissed the plaintiff without more ado on the basis of certain official statutory powers. The House of Lords held that this measure was unlawful as the party was not given the opportunity to be heard.

The House of Lords[28] established that the principle of *audi alteram partem* is also applicable in situations where rights accorded to authorities by statute are concerned, which are not in their nature "quasi-judicial."

In subsequent cases, however, it became clear that the distinction between "judicial" and "administrative" decisions had not become totally obsolete.[29]

The first type of decision (judicial decision) is more closely tied to the principles of natural justice which govern judicial procedure, whereas the only condition placed upon "administrative decisions" is that the administration acts "fairly"[30]:

---

[26] On this phenomenon *cf.* above Chapter 2, the National Report on the United Kingdom.
[27] [1964] A.C. 40; [1963] 2 All E.R. 66 (H.L.); this decision is described by J. F. Garner, B. L. Jones, *op. cit.*, footnote 4, p. 144 as a "landmark decision"; also by H. W. R. Wade, *op. cit.*, footnote 6, p. 461; similarly I. N. Stevens, *op. cit.*, footnote 4, p. 230; J. D. B. Mitchell, *op. cit.*, footnote 1 at p. 109 is less convinced.
[28] By a majority of four to one (Lord Evershed dissenting); *cf.* also H. W. R. Wade, *op. cit.*, footnote 6, pp. 462 *et seq.*; J. F. Garner, B. L. Jones, *op. cit.*, footnote 4, p. 144.
[29] J. F. Garner, B. L. Jones, *op. cit.*, footnote 4, p. 145.
[30] J. F. Garner, B. L. Jones, *op. cit.*, footnote 4, p. 145 (with further references); see also H. W. R. Wade, *op. cit.*, footnote 6, p. 467, who sees the separation of the concepts as unnecessary, although he refers clearly to the flexibility of the system thereby achieved.

"I myself think that even if an immigration officer is not acting in a judicial or quasi-judicial capacity, he must at any rate give the immigrant an opportunity of satisfying him of the matters in the subsection, and for that purpose let the immigrant know what his immediate impression is so that the immigrant can disabuse him. That is not, as I see it, a question of acting or being required to act judicially, but of being required to act fairly. Good administration and an honest or bona fide decision must, as it seems to me, require not merely impartiality, not merely bringing one's mind to bear on the problem, but of acting fairly, and to the limited extent that the circumstances of any particular case allow, and within the legislative framework under which the administrator is working, only to that limited extent do the so-called rules of natural justice apply, which in a case such as this is merely a duty to act fairly."[31]

On the basis of this decision the courts have moved towards posing the question whether the procedural rights accorded in each case were sufficient.[32] In this context, an essential determining factor for the level of the duty to grant a hearing becomes clear: a judicial decision demands a more comprehensive hearing than an administrative one.

The case law has, however, in the meantime recognised a whole variety of further determining factors which define more precisely the "whether" and the scope of the right to be heard.[33]

· Particularly significant in this context is the question of the gravity of the interference or—to put it another way—the issue of how much reliance the party concerned may have placed on the continuation or creation of a particular state of affairs.[34]

---

[31] *Re K(H) (an infant)* [1967] 1 All E.R. 226 at 231 *per* Parker C.J. (QBD); *cf.* J. F. Garner, B. L. Jones, *Administrative Law*, (6th ed., London 1985), p. 147.

[32] J. F. Garner, B. L. Jones, *op. cit.*, footnote 31, p. 146; H. W. R. Wade, *Administrative Law*, (5th ed., Oxford 1982), p.467; I. N. Stevens, *op. cit.*, footnote 4, p. 231; *cf.* also the statement of Lord Denning M.R. that: "The rules of natural justice—or of fairness—are not cut and dried. They vary infinitely" in *R. v. Home Secretary, ex p. Santillo* [1981] Q.B. 778 (C.A.).

[33] See on this S. A. de Smith, "Right to a Hearing" (1955) Vol. 68 Harv. L. Rev. 569 at 581 *et seq.*; H. W. R. Wade, *op. cit.*, footnote 32, at pp. 491 *et seq.*; J. F. Garner, B. L. Jones, *op. cit.*, footnote 31, pp. 142 *et seq.*

[34] *cf.* O. Hood Phillips, P. Jackson, *Constitutional and Administrative Law*, (7th ed., London 1987), p. 673 with a reference to Lord Denning.

Duties to accord a hearing exist in particular in the cases in which there is an interference with existing rights.[35] Even the withdrawal of authorisations (licences) normally requires a hearing.[36] On the other hand, the decision regarding the extension of a licence or its initial award is subject to strict procedural guarantees only where the party concerned has a "legitimate expectation" in that respect.[37]

Thus a foreigner whose residence permit had expired could be refused its renewal without a hearing, although a decision to shorten its duration would require a hearing.[38]

It is also of significance how substantial was the interference, as insignificant interferences do not necessarily require a prior hearing.[39]

A further determining factor for the type and scope of procedural guarantees is the level of discretion involved.[40] In contrast to most continental European countries,[41] in the United Kingdom a prior hearing is not always necessary where a broad discretion is being exercised. In particular the dismissal of public officials normally requires no hearing,[42] unless one is provided for by statute.

An important factor for determining the scope of the right to be heard is, ultimately, whether the decision is final.[43]

---

[35] I. N. Stevens, *Constitutional and Administrative Law*, Plymouth, 1982, p. 234; H. W. R. Wade, *op. cit.*, footnote 32, pp. 496 *et seq.*; see also on this D. Foulkes, *Administrative Law*, (5th ed., 1982), p. 239.

[36] J. F. Garner, B. L. Jones, *op. cit.*, footnote 31, p. 149 (with further references).

[37] J. F. Garner, B. L. Jones, *op. cit.*, footnote 31, p. 149; *Schmidt* v. *Secretary of State for Home Affairs* [1969] 1 All E.R. 904 (C.A.); *Cinnamond* v. *British Airports Authority* [1980] 2 All E.R. 368; see also H. W. R. Wade, *op. cit.*, footnote 32, p. 496: "No distinction is drawn," *cf.* however the statement which directly follows this on the various degrees of hearings. Also *ibid.*, p. 465 as well as the references on p. 496, footnote 14.

[38] *Schmidt* v. *Secretary of State for Home Affairs* [1969] 1 All E.R. 904, *per* Lord Denning; *cf.* also *R.* v. *Secretary of State for the Home Department, ex p. Hosenball* [1977] 3 All E.R. 452: limitation on the right to a hearing on official secrets grounds.

[39] S. A. de Smith, *op. cit.*, footnote 33, p. 587 with further references, especially in footnote 120.

[40] *cf.* J. F. Garner, B. L. Jones, *op. cit.*, footnote 31, pp. 153 *et seq.*; S. A. de Smith, J. M. Evans, *Judicial Review of Administrative Action*, (4th ed., London 1980), p. 186; similarly also Lord Reid in *Ridge* v. *Baldwin* [1963] 2 All E.R. 66; *cf.* also *Russell* v. *Duke of Norfolk* [1949] 1 All E.R. 109; a different view is taken by H. W. R. Wade, *op. cit.*, footnote 32, pp. 491 *et seq.*

[41] *cf.*, *e.g.* the reports on France, Belgium, Spain and Germany, *passim*.

[42] H. W. R. Wade is to that extent in agreement, *op. cit.*, footnote 32, p. 491, footnote 86 (with further references); *R.* v. *Darlington School Governors* (1844) 6 Q.B. 682; *Ridge* v. *Baldwin* [1964] A.C. 40 at 66, *per* Lord Reid.

[43] See on this D. Foulkes, *op. cit.*, footnote 35, p. 238 (with further references to the case law); H. W. R. Wade, *op. cit.*, footnote 32, pp. 504 *et seq.*; J. F. Garner, B. L. Jones, *op. cit.*, footnote 31, p. 155.

A provisional rule or the undertaking of certain investigatory actions cannot so easily be described as unfair where they occur without notification to the party concerned as a final decision which definitively determines the rights of the party.[44] The fairness of the individual steps must be examined in the light of the procedure as a whole.[45]

Lord Pearson held in this context that[46]:

"Fairness does not necessarily require a plurality of hearings or representations and counter-representations. If there were too much elaboration of procedural safeguards, nothing could be done simply and quickly and cheaply. Administrative or executive efficiency and economy should not be too readily sacrificed."

It thus becomes immediately clear that the functional capacity of the administration is an issue which is to be taken into account when deciding whether a particular way of acting is unfair, and thus whether there is need for more consideration to be given to the interests of the party concerned. The significance of this factor is also clear in another context, where national security is involved.[47]

Lord Denning M.R. said on this point[48]:

"But this is no ordinary case. It is a case in which national security is involved, and our history shows that, when the State itself is endangered, our cherished freedoms may have to take second place. Even natural justice itself may suffer a set-back. Time after time Parliament has so enacted and the courts have loyally followed."

In so far as national security is involved, or where confidentiality must be preserved *vis-à-vis* third parties, it is possible to have limitations upon the "duty to act fairly," but at the very least the allegation should normally be

---

[44] J. F. Garner, B. L. Jones, *op. cit.*, footnote 31, p. 155; *Wiseman* v. *Borneman* [1971] A.C. 297 (H.L.); *Pearlberg* v. *Varty* [1972] 2 All E.R. 6; *Balen* v. *Inland Revenue Commissioners* [1978] 2 All E.R. 1033.

[45] H. W. R. Wade, *op. cit.*, footnote 32, p. 504.

[46] *Pearlberg* v. *Varty* [1972] 2 All E.R. 6; on this see J. F. Garner, B. L. Jones, *op. cit.*, footnote 31, p. 155.

[47] *R.* v. *Secretary of State for the Home Department, ex p. Hosenball* [1977] 3 All E.R. 452 (C.A.).

[48] [1977] 3 All E.R. 452 at 457.

made known to the party concerned, which is generally possible without endangering the interests to be protected.[49]

Lord Denning M.R. stated on this[50]:

> "But, without disclosing every detail, I should have thought that the Board ought in every case to be able to give the applicant sufficient indication of the objections raised against him such as to enable him to answer them. That is only fair. And the Board at all costs must be fair. (. . .)"

If the matters are so secret that they cannot even be communicated in generalised form, then the authority should not use this information.[51]

In conjunction with the protection of primary "public interests" one should also mention the cases in which a right to a hearing is not accorded because the decision must be taken in an emergency[52] or where a prior hearing would defeat the purpose of the procedure.[53]

Finally, the question whether the person concerned has himself in some way made it more difficult to obtain a hearing may affect the decision whether or to what extent a hearing is to be granted. The authority needs only to offer the opportunity of a hearing. If the person concerned frustrates the receipt of this offer, then he cannot later complain that he has not been able to state his views.[54]

The spectrum of rights which can be mediated through the principle of *audi alteram partem* is very wide. It includes at one extreme almost all guarantees of a judicial process such as[55]:

---

[49] H. W. R. Wade, *op. cit.*, footnote 32, p. 482; J. F. Garner, B. L. Jones, *op. cit.*, footnote 31, p. 156; S. A. de Smith, *op. cit.*, footnote 33, p. 585.

[50] *R.* v. *Gaming Board for Great Britain, ex p. Benaim and Khaida* [1970] Q.B. 417, [1970] 2 All E.R. 528 at 534 (C.A.).

[51] H. W. R. Wade, *op. cit.*, footnote 32 at p. 482 (exceptions in cases of national security); *Canterbury Building Society* v. *Baker* [1979] 2 N.S.W.L.R. 265 quoted in H. W. R. Wade, *op. cit.*, footnote 32 at p. 482.

[52] S. A. de Smith, *op. cit.*, footnote 33, p. 586, with further references; H. W. R. Wade, *op. cit.*, footnote 32, p. 472.

[53] H. W. R. Wade, *op. cit.*, footnote 32, p. 473 with reference to *Norwest Holst Ltd.* v. *Secretary of State for Trade* [1978] Ch. 201.

[54] S. A. de Smith, *op. cit.*, footnote 33, p. 587, with further references; I. N. Stevens, *op. cit.*, footnote 35, p. 235.

[55] O. Hood Phillips, P. Jackson, *op. cit.*, footnote 34, p. 606; J. F. Garner, B. L. Jones, *op. cit.*, footnote 31, p. 145; *cf.* I. N. Stevens, *op. cit.*, footnote 35, p. 233.

(a) oral negotiations,[56] including the right actually to participate in negotiations taking place, or to request their adjournment[57];

(b) the clear notification of all allegations[58];

(c) all evidence should be made available to all those involved;

(d) they should have the opportunity to call witnesses, and to cross-examine those called by the other side;

(e) the obligation to hear each side only in the presence of the other;

(f) the right to legal representation[59];

(g) the opportunity of expressing a view on all questions of fact and law.

On the other hand in certain circumstances it may be sufficient to provide only a minimum standard of fairness, and in that context points (b), (c) and (g) in any case belong to the absolute minimum of rights which must be guaranteed.[60]

Thus it appears clear that the principle of *audi alteram partem* covers a wider range of rules than does for example the principle of the guarantee of a hearing in accordance with the law in German law.

It guarantees both access to files (in English practice, in fact, rather the right to be informed of the content, or in certain circumstances to receive certain documents) and also the actual substantive procedural rights, namely to be informed of the procedure and to be able to express an opinion.[61]

The exact scope of the procedural guarantees cannot, according to what has been said, be defined in the abstract in isolation from specific

---

[56] H. W. R. Wade, *op. cit.*, footnote 32, p. 482 (on the need for these and on exceptions to the rule; with further references); O. Hood Phillips, P. Jackson, *op. cit.*, footnote 34, p. 673 (generally not required); D. Foulkes, *op. cit.*, footnote 35, p. 228 (may be required in the case of particularly grave interferences).

[57] D. Foulkes, *op. cit.*, footnote 35, p. 229, with further references from the case law.

[58] D. Foulkes, *op. cit.*, footnote 35, p. 228 (with further references), p. 229 (with further references).

[59] D. Foulkes, *op. cit.*, footnote 35, pp. 235 *et seq.*

[60] *cf.* D. Foulkes, *op. cit.*, footnote 35, pp. 228 *et seq.*

[61] H. W. R. Wade, *op. cit.*, footnote 32, p. 479; I. N. Stevens, *op. cit.*, footnote 35, p. 233; Lord Denning M.R. in *Kanda* v. *Government of Malaya* [1962] A.C. 322:

"If the right to be heard is to be a real right which is worth anything, it must carry with it a right for the accused man to know the case which is made against him. He must know what evidence has been given and what statements have been made affecting him: and then he must be given a fair opportunity to correct or contradict them."

cf. also *Attorney-General* v. *Ryan* [1980] A.C. 718; *cf.* on the other hand *Local Government Board* v. *Arlidge* [1915] A.C. 120; *William Denby & Sons Ltd.* v. *Minister of Health* [1936] 1 K.B. 337; S. A. de Smith is doubtful on this point, *op. cit.*, footnote 33, p. 590; J. D. B. Mitchell, "Due Process," FIDE 1978, p. 10.10.

legislative rules, but can be stated only in the context of individual cases using the criteria cited here.

These have been stated clearly by the courts[62] and by the standard authors[63]:

> "The requirements of natural justice must depend on the circumstances of the case, the nature of the inquiry, the rules under which the tribunal is acting, the subject-matter to be dealt with, and so forth."[64]

This approach, which focuses on individual cases, does not always make the problem any less for authorities and the parties concerned. The ability to foresee any particular decision is thereby considerably restricted. Thus the procedural rights laid down in individual statutes in practice play a major role.

However, the principle of *audi alteram partem* has not so far lost its fundamental importance. See on this Lord Reid in the "landmark decision" of *Ridge* v. *Baldwin*[65]:

> "The principle of audi alteram partem goes back many centuries in our law and appears in a multitude of judgments of judges of the highest authority. In modern times opinions have sometimes been expressed that natural justice is so vague as to be practically meaningless. But I would regard these as tainted by the perennial fallacy that because something cannot be cut and dried or nicely weighed or measured therefore it does not exist."

(b) Statutory rules

In many cases and in many areas, there are statutory rules which make it possible for the party concerned to raise opposition to administrative measures which have been adopted or are planned.[66]

---

[62] *cf.* also Lord Lane C.J. in *R.* v. *Commission for Racial Equality, ex p. Cottrell and Rothon* [1980] 3 All E.R. 265 at 271; *cf.* also Lord Denning M.R. in *R.* v. *Gaming Board for Great Britain, ex p. Benaim and Khaida* [1970] 2 All E.R. 528 at 533 (C.A.).

[63] D. Foulkes, *op. cit.*, footnote 35, p. 223 (with further references); H. W. R. Wade, *op. cit.*, footnote 32, p. 474; J. F. Garner, B. L. Jones, *op. cit.*, footnote 31, p. 146.

[64] *Russell* v. *Duke of Norfolk* [1949] 1 All E.R. 109 at 118 (C.A.), *per* Tucker L.J.; *cf.* also Lord Upjohn in *Durajappah* v. *Fernando* [1967] 2 A.C. 337 at 349 (P.C.).

[65] [1964] A.C. 40 at 66, *per* Lord Reid.

[66] J. D. B. Mitchell, *op. cit.*, footnote 61, p. 10.10.

The two essential types of procedure are so-called "tribunal" decisions and so-called "inquiries."[67] The former are generally used where only questions of fact and law are at issue, whereas the latter are used where the matter is one of the "policy" to be pursued by the administration and as a rule the Minister is entitled to take the final decision.[68]

For both procedures, what is important is a general connection to the original administrative procedure. The fact that a party may receive a "fair hearing" in a later phase generally leads to the outcome that he need not be given this right in the initial phase.[69] Thus in the cases in which a party may request a hearing before a tribunal, or request that an inquiry should take place, it is frequently the case that the rules set out above apply only in a very limited form in the initial proceedings.

In this context it is important to note a duty on the administration to inform the party of the possibility of such an "adversarial" procedure. If it omits to refer to this, then the decision may be declared void on this ground.[70]

The basis for both tribunals and inquiries is the Tribunals and Inquiries Act 1971,[71] which deals with the subject only in a partial manner, since many individual statutes contain the actual implementing rules.[72]

(aa) *Tribunals*

Tribunals have been set up in a great variety of areas. They exist, for instance, in the field of agricultural law, data protection law, education

---

[67] J. D. B. Mitchell, *op. cit.*, footnote 61, pp. 10.10 *et seq.*; J. F. Garner, B. L. Jones, *op. cit.*, footnote 31, p. 229.

[68] J. F. Garner, B. L. Jones, *op. cit.*, footnote 31, p. 273; H. W. R. Wade, *op. cit.*, footnote 30, p. 783.

[69] *cf.* only H. W. R. Wade, *Administrative Law*, (5th ed., 1982), p. 473 at 489; *Pearlberg* v. *Varty* [1972] 2 All E.R. 6 (H.L.); *Wiseman* v. *Borneman* [1971] A.C. 297 (H.L.); *cf.* also Parker J. in *Hanily* v. *Minister of Local Government and Planning* [1952] 2 Q.B. 444 at 452.

[70] "Mandatory procedural requirement"; *cf.* on this J. F. Garner, B. L. Jones, *op. cit.*, footnote 31, p. 237 (footnote 15 in conjunction with p. 136); *R.* v. *Lambeth London BC, ex p. Sharp, The Times*, December 28, 1984, quoted in J. F. Garner, B. L. Jones, *op. cit.*, footnote 31, p. 136, footnote 19; *Lee* v. *Dept. of Education and Science* [1967] 66 L.G.R. 195 (Donaldson J.) quoted in S. H. Bailey, D. J. Harris, B. L. Jones, *Civil Liberties, Cases and Materials*, London 1980, p. 336.

[71] 41 Statutes 248.

[72] *cf.* on the regulatory content also J. D. B. Mitchell, *op. cit.*, footnote 61, p. 10.11.

law, immigration law, national health service law, social security law, revenue law, etc.[73]

Tribunal proceedings are initiated by an appeal. A party will have the right to appeal and this will be provided for in the statute regulating that particular area.[74] The Tribunals and Inquiries Act 1971[75] contains only general basic rules. The admissibility of the appeal, the organisation of the tribunal and the essential procedural principles will be contained in the individual statutes governing each substantive area.[76]

In spite of the differences in individual cases, it is possible to describe a typical procedure,[77] which, in the words of the Parliamentary Committee, is intended to serve the following principles:

> "Tribunals are not ordinary courts, but neither are they appendages of Government Departments. Much of the official evidence (...) appeared to reflect the view that tribunals should properly be regarded as part of the machinery of administration, for which the Government must retain a close and continuing responsibility. (...) We do not accept this view. We consider that tribunals should properly be regarded as machinery provided by Parliament for adjudication rather than as part of the machinery of administration. The essential point is that in all these cases Parliament has deliberately provided for a decision outside and independent of the Department concerned, either at first instance (...) or on appeal from a decision of a Minister or of an official in a special statutory position (...). Although the relevant statutes do not in all cases expressly enact that tribunals are to consist entirely of persons outside the Government service, the use of the term 'tribunal' in legislation undoubtedly bears this connotation, and the intention of Parliament to provide for the independence of tribunals is clear and unmistakable."[78]

---

[73] *cf.* the list in J. F. Garner, B. L. Jones, *Administrative Law*, (6th ed., London 1985), pp. 269–272, or in H. W. R. Wade, *op. cit.*, footnote 69, pp. 824–828; *cf.* also I. N. Stevens, *Constitutional and Administrative Law*, Plymouth, 1982, p. 280; these lists are in any case incomplete: there are about 2,000 various tribunals; *cf.* O. Hood Phillips, P. Jackson, *Constitutional and Administrative Law*, (7th ed., London 1987), p. 637.

[74] H. W. R. Wade, *op. cit.*, footnote 69, p. 787.

[75] 41 Statutes 248.

[76] J. D. B. Mitchell, *op. cit.*, footnote 61, p. 10.12.

[77] J. F. Garner, B. L. Jones, *op. cit.*, footnote 73, p. 230.

[78] Committee on Administrative Tribunals and Enquiries (Franks Committee) Report, Cmnd. 218 (1957/62) para. 40.

The proceedings normally take place before three "judges," who are independent.[79] The Chair is a lawyer and sometimes—except in Scotland—an official of the competent Ministry,[80] and the two assessors ("wing-men") are frequently appointed from amongst the interest groups representing the parties in dispute.[81]

Before the proceedings begin, the parties are informed of the allegations which they must defend themselves against and of the facts as stated by the administration in its decision.[82] This occurs if possible in the form of a coherent document, in which the essential questions of fact and law are dealt with.[83]

The tribunal then conducts a public, and in practice mainly oral,[84] hearing on the questions of fact and law.[85] The public may[86] be excluded on grounds of national security or on grounds of some confidential interest of one of the parties.[87]

It is intended that the proceedings should take place in an informal atmosphere, and in some exceptional cases, therefore, legal representation is not permitted.[88] Evidentiary rules are based on those in the courts,

[79] H. W. R. Wade, *op. cit.*, footnote 69, p. 784; J. F. Garner, B. L. Jones, *op. cit.*, footnote 73, p. 235.

[80] To that extent the statement of the Franks Committee may possibly have been too precipitate; *cf.* J. F. Garner, B. L. Jones, *op. cit.*, footnote 73, p. 235; H. W. R. Wade, *op. cit.*, footnote 69, p. 785; on the situation in Scotland, *cf.* J. D. B. Mitchell, *op. cit.*, footnote 61, p. 10.4.

[81] J. F. Garner, B. L. Jones, *op. cit.*, footnote 73, p. 235; H. W. R. Wade, *op. cit.*, footnote 69, p. 285.

[82] J. D. B. Mitchell, *op. cit.*, footnote 61, p. 10.12; J. F. Garner, B. L. Jones, *op. cit.*, footnote 73, p. 237.

[83] Committee on Administrative Tribunals and Enquiries (Franks Committee), *op. cit.*, footnote 78, para. 72; in agreement are J. F. Garner, B. L. Jones, *op. cit.*, footnote 73, p. 237.

[84] I. N. Stevens, *op. cit.*, footnote 73, p. 282; on the exceptions with only a written procedure, *cf.* H. W. R. Wade, *op. cit.*, footnote 69, p. 805.

[85] J. F. Garner, B. L. Jones, *op. cit.*, footnote 73, p. 238; J. D. B. Mitchell, *op. cit.*, footnote 61, p. 10.12; H. W. R. Wade, *op. cit.*, footnote 69, p. 803; I. N. Stevens, *op. cit.*, footnote 73, p. 282.

[86] A few tribunals always meet in private, such as the Mental Health Review Tribunal or various tax tribunals; *cf.* J. F. Garner, B. L. Jones, *op. cit.*, footnote 73, p. 238; H. W. R. Wade, *op. cit.*, footnote 69, p. 807 with further references.

[87] *cf.* J. F. Garner, B. L. Jones, *op. cit.*, footnote 73, p. 673; H. W. R. Wade, *op. cit.*, footnote 69, p. 807, 810.

[88] O. Hood Phillips, P. Jackson, *op. cit.*, footnote 73, p. 673 (with further references); in detail H. W. R. Wade, *op. cit.*, footnote 69, p. 805; J. F. Garner, B. L. Jones, *op. cit.*, footnote 73, p. 239.

but are handled with more flexibility.[89] The individual has access to all evidence which the "opposition" (the administration) has introduced into the procedure. He has the right to express his opinion in the proceedings on all questions of fact and law.[90]

The tribunals decide the dispute and are frequently obliged to give reasons for their decision, and in any case must do so if requested by the party affected.[91]

(bb) Inquiries

"Inquiries" represent a further type of administrative procedure, which takes the form of a formal procedure.[92] In contrast to tribunals, an inquiry does not normally reach a binding decision, but prepares a recommendation for the Minister to decide.[93] The apparent difference in that regard is minimal in practice, since the Minister generally adheres to the proposals of the inquiry; there exist, however, clear differences with regard to the legal classification and evaluation of these two types of body.

With regard to procedure, which must be conducted in a manner which is fair and impartial and in which the general principles of natural justice discussed above must be observed,[94] the following concerns of the Franks Committee have been largely put into effect.[95]

The inquiry is generally chaired by an official from the authority with power of decision.[96] Only in Scotland are independent persons,[97] fre-

---

[89] H. W. R. Wade, *op. cit.*, footnote 69, p. 805; J. F. Garner, B. L. Jones, *op. cit.*, footnote 73, p. 241. The following are permitted: hearsay evidence; expert knowledge on the part of the judges; no strict application of the "best evidence" rule in proof of documents.

[90] H. W. R. Wade, *op. cit.*, footnote 69, p. 805. The rules of natural justice must be strictly observed in the proceedings (*cf.* s.12 of the Tribunals and Inquiries Act 1971).

[91] In detail H. W. R. Wade, *op. cit.*, footnote 69, p. 812; I. N. Stevens, *op. cit.*, footnote 73, p. 282; O. Hood Phillips, P. Jackson, *op. cit.*, footnote 73, p. 646; J. F. Garner, B. L. Jones, *op. cit.*, footnote 73, p. 243.

[92] See on this J. D. B. Mitchell, *op. cit.*, footnote 61, p. 10.13; J. F. Garner, B. L. Jones, *op. cit.*, footnote 73, pp. 273 *et seq.*

[93] J. F. Garner, B. L. Jones, *op. cit.*, footnote 73, p. 273, (with further references); H. W. R. Wade, *op. cit.*, footnote 69, p. 831.

[94] H. W. R. Wade, *op. cit.*, footnote 69, p. 837 with further references, footnotes 35–41; *cf.* also Lord Diplock in *Bushell* v. *Secretary of State for the Environment* [1981] A.C. 75 at 95.

[95] J. F. Garner, B. L. Jones, *op. cit.*, footnote 73, p. 278.

[96] J. F. Garner, B. L. Jones, *op. cit.*, footnote 73, p. 278; J. D. B. Mitchell, *op. cit.*, footnote 61, pp. 10.4, 10.13; *cf.* also the Franks Committee, *op. cit.*, footnote 78, paras. 293–304.

[97] *Ibid.*

quently lawyers, entrusted with this task. The Chair alone is responsible for the conduct of the proceedings, even when he has assistants at his disposal, which will occur only in major cases.

As regards the procedure itself, it should be noted that the party affected must be informed in good time before the inquiry begins of all the details of his case.[98] The communication should contain information on the "policy" of the Ministry (not only the local body), so that the parties can put forward the relevant issues.[99]

The object of the procedure should be the decision which is challenged, even if the analysis extends beyond what the individual has argued.[100] In principle, a fair if simple and inexpensive procedure should be conducted. The provisions necessary to achieve this are contained in the statutes dealing with each individual subject.[101]

The rights of third parties (in particular of neighbours) are taken into account only in special cases. They are not in general formally involved in the inquiry, and must accept that a part of the inquiry procedure is not public.[102]

The report of the inspector is directed to the Minister, and in spite of a contrary recommendation of the Franks Committee,[103] it is not always made available to the parties; even after the decision of the Minister, publication, which generally does occur, does not always rest upon a legal duty,[104] but on an administrative practice. These details are, however, controversial, for the principle of ministerial responsibility to Parliament gives the inspector's report political weight as well. If the Minister should not follow his proposal, he makes himself vulnerable to attacks from his political opponents.[105]

---

[98] Committee on Administrative Tribunals and Inquiries (Franks Committee), *op. cit.*, footnote 78, paras. 280 *et seq.*; J. F. Garner, B. L. Jones, *op. cit.*, footnote 73, p. 278.

[99] Franks Committee, *op. cit.*, footnote 78, paras. 286 *et seq.*; J. F. Garner, B. L. Jones, *op. cit.*, footnote 73, p. 278; in practice only policy statements of local authorities are published, *cf.* H. W. R. Wade, *op. cit.*, footnote 69, p. 845.

[100] Franks Committee, *op. cit.*, footnote 78, paras. 306 *et seq.*; J. F. Garner, B. L. Jones, *op. cit.*, footnote 73, p. 279; see also the detailed comment in H. W. R. Wade, *op. cit.*, footnote 69, pp. 849–853.

[101] Franks Committee, *op. cit.*, footnote 78, para. 310; J. F. Garner, B. L. Jones, *op. cit.*, footnote 73, p. 279.

[102] J. F. Garner, B. L. Jones, *op. cit.*, footnote 73, p. 283 (with further references).

[103] Franks Committee, *op. cit.*, footnote 78, paras. 343–346.

[104] J. F. Garner, B. L. Jones, *op. cit.*, footnote 73, p. 280, who indicate that there is now a statutory duty to publish in many areas.

[105] H. W. R. Wade, *op. cit.*, footnote 69, p. 845 (with further references); J. D. B. Mitchell, *op. cit.*, footnote 61, p. 10.14; J. F. Garner, B. L. Jones, *op. cit.*, footnote 73, pp. 279–280.

In one or two major cases the attempt has been made to limit the subject-matter of the procedure in order to preserve the capacity of the competent inspector to act.[106]

(c) Legal consequences

In the case law and the literature there is some uncertainty about the consequences of a breach of the principles of natural justice and the duty to act fairly.[107] It is controversial whether decisions which are made incorporating an infringement of these rules are void, that is void *ab initio*, or only voidable.[108]

It is a basic rule of English administrative law that *ultra vires* decisions are void, and many breaches of the rules of natural justice are treated as conduct which is *ultra vires*.[109] However, it follows on practical and in particular procedural grounds that even legal acts which come into being subject to an infringement of procedural rules may be operative, in particular when time limits for bringing challenges have expired[110] or there are in a particular case no grounds of claim.[111]

---

[106] J. F. Garner, B. L. Jones, *op. cit.*, footnote 73, p. 277.

[107] See on this J. F. Garner, B. L. Jones, *op. cit.*, footnote 73, pp. 158 *et seq.*; I. N. Stevens, *op. cit.*, footnote 73, p. 238.

[108] In favour of voidness:

J. F. Garner, B. L. Jones, *op. cit.*, footnote 73, p. 158 (with further references); H. W. R. Wade, *op. cit.*, footnote 69, pp. 468 *et seq.* at 470 (with further references); I. N. Stevens, *op. cit.*, footnote 73, p. 238; *Anisminic Ltd.* v. *Foreign Compensation Commission* [1969] 1 All E.R. 208 (H.L.); *cf.* also excerpts in S. H. Bailey, D. J. Harris and B. L. Jones, *op. cit.*, footnote 70, p. 199; see also *Ridge* v. *Baldwin* [1963] 2 All E.R. 66 at 81, *per* Lord Reid:

"A decision given without regard to the principles of natural justice is void."

cf. also the Privy Council in *Calvin* v. *Carr* [1979] 2 All E.R. 440; statements which hold such decisions to be (only) voidable: Lords Evershed and Devlin in *Ridge* v. *Baldwin* [1964] A.C. 40, [1963] 2 All E.R. 66 (H.L.); *F. Hoffmann-La Roche & Co. AG* v. *Secretary of State for Trade and Industry* [1975] A.C. 295; [1974] 2 All E.R. 1128 (H.L.); Lord Denning M.R. in *R.* v. *Secretary of State for the Environment, ex p. Ostler* [1977] 3 All E.R. 90 (C.A.); it is interesting finally to note the remark of Lord Denning M.R. that decisions are void according to the rules of legal theory, but in practice only voidable, *Lovelock* v. *Minister of Transport* (1980) 40 P. & C.R. 366, quoted in D. Foulkes, *op. cit.*, footnote 35, p. 253.

[109] J. F. Garner, B. L. Jones, *op. cit.*, footnote 73, pp. 158 *et seq.*; H. W. R. Wade, *op. cit.*, footnote 69, pp. 486 *et seq.*; at 470 and 310.

[110] J. F. Garner, B. L. Jones, *op. cit.*, footnote 73, p. 159; H. W. R. Wade, *op. cit.*, footnote 69, pp. 471, 314; *cf.* also Lord Diplock in *Hoffmann-La Roche* v. *Secretary of State for Trade and Industry* [1975] A.C. 295.

[111] H. W. R. Wade, *op. cit.*, footnote 69, p. 314; J. F. Garner, B. L. Jones, *op. cit.*, footnote 73, p. 159; *Hounslow London Borough Council* v. *Twickenham Garden Developments Ltd.* [1971] Ch. 233 at 259, *per* Megarry J.:

The dispute concerning the type of nullity can remain undecided here. What is important, however, is to establish that infringements against the principles of natural justice often have the consequence of leading to the annulment of the decision concerned, if an admissible claim is brought. There are limits in so far as the only plaintiff who can establish the unlawfulness of the act is one who should have been protected by the principle of natural justice.[112]

Where there has been an infringement of the principle of natural justice but in the court's opinion where the measure adopted is appropriate, the latter may, if it involved the exercise of discretion, be upheld and the infringement treated as merely giving rise to liability.[113] However, such cases are rare and recognised only within narrow limits (*e.g.* abuse of rights by the plaintiff).[114]

Finally, there are decisions which appear to indicate that an infringement of the procedural principles of natural justice can be taken into account only in proceedings which seek directly to challenge the act, whereas in proceedings in which the validity of the act is only a preliminary question or is otherwise only of indirect relevance,[115] an infringement produces no effects.[116]

"A decision reached by a tribunal wholly outside its jurisdiction and in complete defiance of natural justice is about as void as anything can be; but if nobody who is entitled to challenge or question it chooses to do so, it remains in being. Yet to describe such a decision as being "voidable" is to use that word in a sense that is not only very special but liable to mislead."

[112] J. F. Garner, B. L. Jones, *op. cit.*, footnote 73, p. 160 (with further references) (footnotes 1–3) with reference to the decision of the Privy Council: *Durayappah* v. *Fernando* [1967] 2 All E.R. 152; H. W. R. Wade, *op. cit.*, footnote 69, p. 314 (with further references).

[113] *Glynn* v. *Keele University* [1971] 2 All E.R. 89; *cf.* also *Malloch* v. *Aberdeen Corp* [1971] 1 W.L.R. 1578 at 1595 and 1600; *Cinnamond* v. *British Airports Authority* [1980] 1 W.L.R. 582; [1980] 2 All E.R. 368; on the exercise of "discretion" by courts in these cases *cf.* also H. W. R. Wade, "Nudism and Natural Justice" (1971) 87 L.Q.R. 320; as well as *Ward* v. *Bradford Corp* [1972] 70 L.G.R. 27, quoted in D. Foulkes, *op. cit.*, footnote 35, p. 242; *cf., ibid.*, footnote 13. Lord Denning as the presiding judge later had doubts on the correctness of his own judgment (interview in *The Guardian* of December 20, 1978) quoted in D. Foulkes, *op. cit.*

[114] H. W. R. Wade, *op. cit.*, footnote 69, p. 476 with further references; J. F. Garner, B. L. Jones, *op. cit.*, footnote 73, p. 159; critical on the acceptance of this argument, D. Foulkes, *op. cit.*, footnote 35, at p. 241.

[115] So-called collateral challenges or proceedings; on the admissibility of this argument *cf.* H. W. R. Wade, *op. cit.*, footnote 69, pp. 296 *et seq.*

[116] J. F. Garner, B. L. Jones, *op. cit.*, footnote 73, p. 160.

5. The rights of defence in Belgium

Belgian law originally recognised the principle of the guarantee of a hearing only in the field of procedural law in civil and criminal cases, and then as an expression of the safeguarding of the "droits de la défense."[1] Its recognition in administrative law, in particular for procedures involving "administration active" occurred in the context of a rather long process of development in which the courts, in particular the Conseil d'Etat,[2] and the legislature only gradually accepted the principle. However, in individual fields there are examples which demonstrate that the legislature did recognise at an early stage the principle of the right to a hearing before the administration.[3]

It is undoubtedly the case that the legislature has played a decisive role in this context, in that it has constantly extended the right to a hearing to new fields,[4] and thus has given the judges the opportunity of making their own contribution to a wide dissemination of the principle. In Belgian economic law such an extension has proved to be especially relevant. The starting point for the principle of the right to a hearing before the administration was the law governing the discipline of public officials. On the grounds of the similarity of such matters to criminal proceedings, the person threatened with a disciplinary measure was given the right to a prior hearing.[5] The case law has then extended this requirement of a hearing. On the one hand, public servants now have the right to be heard in the context of non-disciplinary measures, where their interests are affected,[6] unless the measures were enacted exclusively in the interests of the service.

---

[1] W. J. Ganshof van der Meersch, "Le droit de la défense," *Mélanges en l'honneur de J. Dabin*, Brussels 1963, Part II, p. 569 at pp. 597 and 598.
[2] See on this J. Sarot, W. Deroover, "Le droit de la défense," *Administration publique* 1984, p. 193 at 195 *et seq.*
[3] Article 2(2) of the Décret sur la presse of July 20, 1831 provided that:
"Quiconque aura méchamment et publiquement attaqué la force obligatoire des lois ou provoqué directement à y désobéir, sera puni ...
Cette disposition ne préjudiciera pas à la liberté de la demande ou la défense devant les tribunaux ou toutes autres autorités constituées."
cf. M. Hayoit de Termicourt, *Répertoire pratique du droit belge*, Part IV, Droit de la défense, para. 12, p. 280; *cf.* also J. Sarot, W. Deroover, *op. cit.*, footnote 2, p. 193; Ch. Huberlant, "Le droit de la défense," FIDE 1978, p. 2.4.
[4] Ch. Huberlant, *op. cit.*, footnote 3, pp. 2.6, 2.10, *passim*; J. Sarot, W. Deroover, *op. cit.*, footnote 2, pp. 198 *et seq.*
[5] Ch. Huberlant, *op. cit.*, footnote 3, pp. 2.5 *et seq.*
[6] Ch. Huberlant, *op. cit.*, footnote 3, p. 2.10.

On the other hand, disciplinary measures even against those who are not public servants may not be taken without a hearing.[7] Thus, for example, a school student may not be expelled from a school without being given the opportunity to state his or her position.[8] The right to a hearing is now recognised as a general principle of law, although not without limits and exceptions.

The recognition is based on three considerations[9]:

On the one hand, the right to a hearing is contained as a core element in numerous individual laws. On the other hand, it is a right which corresponds to the principles of the "bonne administration" and a "procédure équitable."[10] Finally, such a right flows from the duty on the administration adequately to prepare its decisions.[11]

In individual cases the long-existing practice of the authority to hear the parties affected has become the basis for the recognition of a legally binding rule.[12] A hearing must be granted, for example, where an administrative act is revoked, in particular on the revocation of a licence or permit. If personal misconduct plays a role, the duty to give a hearing is frequently based on the notion that this is in fact a quasi-disciplinary measure which requires a prior hearing.[13]

However, even decisions which are adopted in the public interest may require a hearing, on account of the grave consequences for the party affected. The substantive material on this subject is not, however, copious.[14] However, the principle of the right to a hearing is less well recognised and developed in the field of "mesures de police" than it is today in the field of disciplinary measures. In sum, the principle of the right to a hearing is recognised by the case law as significant in the following areas outside public service law[15]:

---

[7] J. Sarot, W. Deroover, *op. cit.*, footnote 2, p. 193; Ch. Huberlant, *op. cit.*, footnote 3, p. 2.14.

[8] C.E. belge, Judgment no. 14.865 of July 5, 1971 (*Willockx*); Judgment no. 15.038 of December 2, 1971 (*De Laet*); Judgment no. 18.207 of April 1, 1977 (*Rochet*).

[9] J. Sarot, W. Deroover, *op. cit.*, footnote 2, p. 197; *cf.* also Ch. Huberlant, *op. cit.*, footnote 3, p. 2.30.

[10] See on this also C.E. belge, Judgment no. 21.595 of November 25, 1981 (*Allard*).

[11] J. Sarot, W. Deroover, *op. cit.*, footnote 2, pp. 193 & 198; C.E. belge, Judgment no. 16.217 of January 30, 1974 (*Lobijn*); Judgment no. 19.281 of December 5, 1978 (*Van Bergen*); Judgment no. 21.037 of March 17, 1981 (*Speleers*).

[12] Ch. Huberlant, *op. cit.*, footnote 3, p. 2.17; C.E. belge, Judgment no. 3405 of May 20, 1954; Judgment no. 2558 of June 11, 1953 (*Creteur*).

[13] Ch. Huberlant, *op. cit.*, footnote 3, p. 2.16.

[14] Ch. Huberlant, *op. cit.*, footnote 3, pp. 2.16, 2.30.

[15] J. Sarot, W. Deroover, *op. cit.*, footnote 2, p. 197 with further references.

— in the case of quasi-disciplinary measures;
— in the case of declarations that a building is unfit for human habitation and on the closure of buildings and businesses;
— in the case of declarations of buildings as historic monuments;
— in the field of the law of the economy.[16]

In the following fields the legislature has recognised a right to a hearing:

— in local and regional planning law, in particular in the "aménagement du territoire" and under the building regulations[17];
— in revenue proceedings concerning the raising of direct taxation[18];
— in immigration law.[19]

With regard to the exercise of the right it is recognised that there are limitations and exceptions. Thus emergency measures may in principle be adopted without the person affected being heard.[20] Also the hearing must not in the concrete case lead to excessive pressure on the authority, that is it must have regard to the "nécessités du service."[21]

Exceptions to the right to a hearing exist in certain cases of restricted decisions.[22] Thus the removal from office of an official who has been deprived of his civil rights by court decision may occur without a hearing.[23] Also the dismissal of military chaplains on the grounds of a decision of church authorities does not require a prior hearing.[24] Overall, the authority is obliged to grant a more detailed hearing where it has a wider

---

[16] Ch. Huberlant, *op. cit.*, footnote 3, pp. 2.15 *et seq.*, with the limitation that the "case material" is still sparse.

[17] J. Sarot, W. Deroover, *op. cit.*, footnote 2, p. 198; even a public hearing is provided for: Law of March 29, 1962, Articles 9, 13 & 21; *cf.* C.E. belge, Judgment no. 21.236 (and others) of June 11, 1981 (*Van den Bulcke*).

[18] J. Sarot, W. Deroover, *op. cit.*, footnote 2, p. 199; Ch. Huberlant, *op. cit.*, footnote 3, p. 2.21.

[19] Ch. Huberlant, *op. cit.*, footnote 3, pp. 2.19 *et seq.*; J. Sarot, W. Deroover, *op. cit.*, footnote 2, p. 199.

[20] J. Sarot, W. Deroover, *op. cit.*, footnote 2, p. 200; Ch. Huberlant, *op. cit.*, footnote 3, p. 2.18; C.E. belge, Judgment no. 15.581 of November 27, 1972 (*Huybrechts*); Judgment no. 16.217 of January 30, 1974 (*Lobyn*); Judgment no. 19.281 of November 22, 1978 (*Van Bergen*).

[21] J. Sarot, W. Deroover, *op. cit.*, footnote 2, p. 200; *cf.* also C.E. belge, Judgment no. 22.527 of October 12, 1982 (*Roulen*).

[22] J. Sarot, W. Deroover, *op. cit.*, footnote 2, p. 200 at 203.

[23] C.E. belge, Judgment no. 18.398 of July 18, 1977 (*Van Daele*); *cf.* also Judgment no. 16.328 of March 26, 1974 (*Detournay*).

[24] C.E. belge, Judgment no. 16.993 of April 22, 1975 (*Van Grembergen*); Judgment no. 12.086 of December 2, 1966 (*Gielen*).

discretionary power than it does in the case of restricted administrative decisions.[25]

The case law considers the exact observance of the provisions on the right to a hearing to be less important where the measures adopted by the authority are only of a provisional nature.[26]

In principle, the guarantee of the right to a hearing in administrative proceedings requires that the person concerned is informed of all allegations against him and the object of the procedure.[27] The communication must normally take place on the initiative of the authority, and it is only exceptionally the case that the person affected must himself request the communication of the "griefs" (objections). The authority must normally inform the person concerned of the opportunity of stating his views.[28]

The person entitled to be heard must then be given the time to prepare his or her defence.[29] In particular, he must be given the opportunity of entrusting a lawyer with the representation of his interests.[30] In certain

---

[25] J. Sarot, W. Deroover, *op. cit.*, footnote 2, pp. 197, 203 with a reference to C.E. belge, Judgment no. 13.939 of February 5, 1970 (*Lamalle*); Judgment no. 18.208 of April 1, 1977 (*Grynpas*); Judgment no. 22.149 of March 26, 1982 (*Boschloos*).

[26] J. Sarot, W. Deroover, *op. cit.*, footnote 2, p. 200; C.E. belge, Judgment no. 20.710 of November 14, 1980 (*Van den Eynde*).

[27] Ch. Huberlant, *op. cit.*, footnote 3, p. 2.32 (with further references); J. Sarot, W. Deroover, *op. cit.*, footnote 2, p. 201, *cf.* also the decisions cited there: Judgment no. 7.212 of September 15, 1959 (*Mahy*); Judgment no. 4.168 of March 22, 1955 (*De Meyer*); Judgment no. 4.510 of July 14, 1955 (*Vandenbussche*); Judgment no. 4.539 of July 29, 1955 (*Freney*); Judgment no. 5.480 of February 1, 1957 (*Michel*); Judgment no. 5.580 of March 28, 1957 (*Van Loo*); Judgment no. 11.288 of June 3, 1965 (*Sovet*); Judgment no. 11.430 of October 6, 1965 (*De Kerpel*); Judgment no. 15.467 of July 26, 1972 (*Doyen*); Judgment no. 16.022 of September 26, 1973 (*Schollaert*); Judgment no. 21.595 of November 25, 1981 (*Allard*).

[28] C.E. belge, Judgment no. 4.163 of March 18, 1955 (*Mombach*); Judgment no. 13.363 of January 9, 1969 (*Magery*); Ch. Humberlant, *op. cit.*, footnote 3, p. 2.32 (with further references).

[29] Ch. Huberlant, *op. cit.*, footnote 3, p. 2.32 (with further references); J. Sarot, W. Deroover, *op. cit.*, footnote 2, p. 201.

[30] Ch. Huberlant, *op. cit.*, footnote 3, p. 2.32 (with further references); J. Sarot, W. Deroover, *op. cit.*, footnote 2, p. 201, with the following references from the case law: Judgment no. 2.937 of November 20, 1953 (*Bury*); Judgment no. 13.783 of November 12, 1969 (*Demarest*); Judgment no. 14.067 of April 21, 1970 (*Meulepas*); Judgment no. 14.864 of July 5, 1971 (*Willockx*); Judgment no. 15.150 of February 9, 1972 (*Jongbloet et C.A.P. Ostende*); Judgment no. 15.419 of July 4, 1972 (*Rummens*); Judgment no. 16.686 of October 22, 1974 (*Buyle*); Judgment no. 16.284 of March 6, 1974 (*Goethals*); Judgment no. 17.022 of May 20, 1975 (*De Nul*); Judgment no. 16.938 of March 19, 1975 (*De Graeve*); Judgment no. 18.207 of April 1, 1977 (*Rochet*); Judgment no. 19.452 of February 16, 1979 (*Gijsel*); Judgment no. 21.437 of October 6, 1981 (*Van Brussel*); Judgment no. 23.626 of October 26, 1983 (*Decafmeyer*).

cases, above all in the field of disciplinary measures, the person concerned must be allowed access to the files,[31] although only where he requests this.[32] The hearing does not necessarily take the form of an oral hearing. In principle the authority decides the form which the hearing will take, unless a specific form is provided for by statute.[33]

As regards the relationship between statutory rules and the general principles of law, it is the case that the former will prevail where the statutory rules contain specific provisions on the type and the form of the protection.[34] It is presumed that a statutory rule is conclusive, so that if in an individual case a (partial) rule of general administrative law would be more favourable to the person affected in a case covered by specific legal rules, he or she cannot benefit from this.[35]

In conclusion it remains to be said that according to the Belgian view, in particular that of the case law, the "droits de la défense" in their essence protect first and foremost the interests of those affected by administrative decisions. However, this principle is simultaneously intended to further the goals of the administration. Thus the authority may, by granting a hearing, improve the basis of its own decision and thereby the decision itself. It is recognised as a limitation upon the right to a hearing that the administration may not be unduly burdened by this duty.[36]

6. The right to a hearing in Denmark

In Denmark too the right to a hearing is recognised. The person affected must be notified of the commencement of the proceedings,[1] and he must have the opportunity of familiarising himself with the factual

---

[31] J. Sarot, W. Deroover, *op. cit.*, footnote 2, p. 201; C.E. belge, Judgment no. 905 of June 4, 1951 (*Paternotte*); Judgment no. 906 of June 4, 1951 (*Demolin*); Judgment no. 9.086 of December 22, 1961 (*Vandermotten*); Judgment no. 12.878 of March 19, 1968 (*De Roo*).

[32] Ch. Huberlant, *op. cit.*, footnote 3, p. 2.32 (with further references).

[33] J. Sarot, W. Deroover, *op. cit.*, footnote 2, p. 201 with the following references from the case law of the C.E. belge: Judgment no. 3.956 of December 24, 1954 (*Blondiau*); Judgment no. 9.206 of February 27, 1962 (*Dekeyser*); Judgment no. 13.407 of February 14, 1969 (*Piette*); Judgment no. 20.097 of February 5, 1980 (*Vercauteren*); Judgment no. 20.347 of May 22, 1980 (*Baudrin*); Judgment no. 22.149 of March 26, 1982 (*Boschloos*).

[34] J. Sarot, W. Deroover, *op. cit.*, footnote 2, p. 201.

[35] C.E. belge, Judgment no. 22.672 of November 19, 1982 (*Marceli*); *cf.* also J. Sarot, W. Deroover, *op. cit.*, footnote 2, p. 201.

[36] J. Sarot, W. Deroover, *op. cit.*, footnote 2, p. 204.

[1] N. E. Holm, "Due process in Danish administrative procedure," FIDE 1978, pp. 3.12 *et seq.*

material held by the authority,[2] and he must be able to state his views to the administration on this material.[3] The basis for the recognition was previously the explicit regulation of these various partial principles in many individual laws. Particularly important in this context was the "Law on access by the public to documents in official files,"[4] of 1970.

On the basis of experiences gained with this law, and of proposals by the Parliamentary Ombudsman, which had in part already been taken up in administrative practice,[5] two new laws were passed at the end of 1985 which provide a comprehensive codification of the procedural aspects of the relationship between the public, the parties and the administration. In Law no. 571 of December 19, 1985, "Forvaltningslov," which is the actual law on administrative procedure, the procedural guarantees for the parties are laid down.[6] Law no. 572 "Om offentlighed i forvalt-ningen," as the title says, deals with the relationship between the public and the administration.[7] This law thus derives from the tradition begun by the laws on "open files," which has developed in the Scandinavian countries.[8]

The "Forvaltningslov" concerns the relationship between the party concerned and the administration. The question of who is a party is not dealt with in the law. §9 talks only of "der er part i en sag." In accordance with prior understanding, it can be assumed that the question of the "characteristic of involvement" is closely linked to the problem of having a sufficient legal interest in the outcome of the procedure. The decisive question is thus whether and if so, to what extent, a legal or natural person has an interest in the case and how closely this interest is linked to the outcome of the decision.[9]

According to §1 the law is in practice applicable to the entire field of official administration, in particular in the context of proceedings before

---

[2] N. E. Holm, *op. cit.*, footnote 1, pp. 3.6 *et seq.*

[3] N. E. Holm, *op. cit.*, footnote 1, pp. 3.4 *et seq.*

[4] Law no. 280 of June 10, 1970, (1975) 19 *Scandinavian Studies in Law*, pp. 173 *et seq.*; also (1973) 21 *American Journal of Comparative Law* 470.

[5] N. E. Holm, *op. cit.*, footnote 1, pp. 3.13 *et seq.*

[6] Law no. 571 of December 19, 1985, "Forvaltningslov," Karnov 1985, pp. 6279 *et seq.* See on this in detail, K. Borgsmidt, "Ein Verfahrensgesetz und Neugestaltungen im däni-schen Verwaltungsrecht," DÖV 1988, p. 70.

[7] Law no. 572 of December 19, 1985 "om offentlighed i forvaltningen," Karnov 1985, pp. 6282 *et seq.* In more detail, see K. Borgsmidt, *op. cit.*, footnote 6.

[8] N. E. Holm, "The Danish system of open files in public administration," (1975) 19 *Scandinavian Studies in Law* 153; K. A. Frøbert, "Stärkung der staatsbürgerlichen Rechte," *Dänische Rundschau* 1971, p. 34; S. V. Anderson, "Open records laws in Scandinavia," *Statsvetenskaplig Tidskrift* (77) 1974, p. 37.

[9] N. E. Holm, *op. cit.*, footnote 1, p. 3.11.

administrative authorities (§2).[10] In addition to rules on the impartiality of those responsible for the decision and fundamental principles on the representation of the parties by representatives and lawyers (§§3–8) the most important rights of the defence are codified in this law.

§9 lays down the duty on the authority to ensure that the party has access to the files if he so requests.[11] Normally the files to which access is requested should be described precisely. The right extends to all files in the administrative procedure, including records to which reference is made in the files. According to §11 I the authority may not take the decision until the party has had the opportunity of inspecting the files.[12] Only where an immediate decision is required by the public or private interests provided for in paragraph 2 can there be a departure from this rule.

In §§12–15 the exceptions are defined in more detail. Access to internal working papers is excluded. §12 defines as internal documents those drafts which are put together for the purposes of preparation and management of the facts by the authority.[13] In §14 certain other documents are in principle excluded from the right of access. Documents of the Council of State, documents which are prepared by an authority for another administrative body, as well as those documents which form part of the preparation and negotiation of proposals and measures in the E.C. field are not accessible to the party.

§15 further provides that access to files may be refused in a particular case in order to protect prevailing public or private interests (of third parties). Thus production of files may be refused in particular on grounds of national security or on other grounds of foreign policy or external economic policy. According to §15 one interest worthy of protection is the safeguarding of the efficiency and economy of the administration. In principle the authority takes the decision on the provision of access to files (§16 I). It has a period of 10 days in which to answer the person concerned, and if it needs more time it must communicate the special reasons for this within the time limit. The right of access to files includes the right to prepare at one's own expense copies or extracts from the documents made available (§16 III). If the access to files is not provided,

---

[10] cf. the similar (but narrower) practice hitherto, N. E. Holm, op. cit., footnote 1, p. 3.7.
[11] Similar up to now has been Article 10 of the 1970 Law, cf. N. E. Holm, op. cit., footnote 1, p. 3.6.
[12] As before, the authority may set a time limit for the other party to make a statement, cf. N. E. Holm, op. cit., footnote 1, p. 3.6.
[13] This is similar to the earlier legal situation (Article 5 of the 1970 Law), cf. N. E. Holm, op. cit., footnote 1, p. 3.8.

then §17 provides for certain time limits, in particular limitation periods for claims. The law also provides in §§19–21 for the hearing of the parties. §19 lays down that the authority must refer the party to any information which operates to his disadvantage where this is of significance to the proceedings. This provision is new,[14] but it used already to be the case that the authority had to inform the party about the procedure where:

— the authority itself has obtained information which is not irrelevant to the outcome of the procedure;
— the party does not know the information;
— it is possible that the party may doubt the correctness or completeness of the information;
— this is not information to which access by the other party is prohibited.[15]

The new Law derives from these principles. §19 contains also the exceptions to the right to a hearing, which are similar to those for access to files. In §20 a hearing is provided for in conjunction with the modification of existing decisions. In §21 it is provided that a party may request the suspension of the decision until he has had the opportunity to express a view.[16] This right can be set aside where prevailing public or private interests require this, in order to make it possible to adhere to a statutory time limit, and in order to have regard to contrary rules in other laws. The Law also provides that unfavourable administrative decisions must be reasoned (§§22–24). Finally, administrative acts must include information about remedies against them including details about the competent court and the time limit for bringing a claim (§§25, 26).

The second Law mentioned here, no. 572, deals with the rights of the public vis-à-vis the administration.[17] In order to exercise these rights it is not necessary for a person to have a particular link with, or closeness to, a particular procedure. This is the essential difference from Law no. 571.

The Law applies to all records of the national and local administration as well as to those of a few various public bodies of various types (§1). Everyone has the right to inspect the records of the authority unless the

---

[14] N. E. Holm, op. cit., footnote 1, p. 3.12.
[15] N. E. Holm, op. cit., footnote 1, p. 3.13; on the legal situation even before the seventies cf. also N. Michelsen, Das rechtliche Gehör im Verwaltungsverfahren der Europäischen Gemeinschaften, Diss. Hamburg 1975, p. 162 (with further references).
[16] N. E. Holm, op. cit., footnote 1, pp. 3.4 et seq.; N. Michelsen, op. cit., footnote 15, pp. 161 et seq.
[17] On the Danish (and Scandinavian) tradition of "open files" cf. supra, footnote 8.

wide exceptions which are provided for in §§7–14 do not exclude access. Excluded first and foremost are those documents for which limitations on the right of access to files for parties to administrative proceedings will apply (internal working documents, State Council documents, files on legislative proceedings and documents regarding E.C. proposals, etc.). In addition §§12 and 14 provide particular protection for those interested parties whose private affairs and business secrets may be affected by the right of access to files. Both laws came into effect on January 1, 1987, although with regard to local authorities the "Forvaltningslov" partly came into force only on January 1, 1989 (§33 Law no. 571, §17 Law no. 572).

7. The rights of defence in Greece

In spite of some efforts to achieve codification,[1] administrative procedure in Greece is not regulated in detail by statute. Apart from the right to a hearing which will be discussed below,[2] the Constitution contains hardly any rules which govern administrative procedure.[3] However, following initially the French model,[4] the case law has developed a number of minimum requirements for the procedural framework.[5] Thus the administration is bound also within the context of procedural law to respect the fundamental principle of respect for human dignity, the principle of democracy and the principle of administration under the law.[6] It is the administration's task to establish the facts on its own initiative. It can take into account suggestions put forward by the parties.

---

[1] *cf.* the draft of the Commission on the reorganisation of the public service, submitted in accordance with the decision of the Prime Minister of February 1, 1958, as set out in A. Tsoutsos, *Das Recht auf Gehör*, Athens, 1966, pp. 356 *et seq.*; M. Stassinopoulos, *Le droit de la défense devant les autorités administratives*, Paris, 1976, p. 74, who refers to his own draft, as does T. J. Panagopoulos, "Das Verwaltungsverfahrensrecht in Griechenland," DVBl. 1977, p. 145 at 155.

[2] *cf.* above, Introduction A.II.1.

[3] T. J. Panagopoulos, *op. cit.*, footnote 1, p. 155 (with further references); P. Pavlopoulos, A. Calageropoulos & S. Lytras, "Procédure administrative non contentieuse et problèmes juridiques en Grèce: La garantie constitutionnelle du principe *audi alteram partem*," *Annuaire Européen d'Administration publique* 1978 I (1979), p. 427.

[4] M. Stassinopoulos, *op. cit.*, footnote 1, *passim*; T. J. Panagopoulos, *op. cit.*, footnote 1, p. 154.

[5] This development had begun even before the new Constitution came into force, *cf.* M. Stassinopoulos, *op. cit.*, footnote 1, as well as T. J. Panagopoulos, *op. cit.*, footnote 1, p. 156.

[6] T. J. Panagopoulos, *op. cit.*, footnote 1, p. 156.

It must investigate the facts as fully as possible.[7] In so doing it may make use of various forms of evidence, and in certain circumstances, may hear witnesses. The parties must contribute to the clarification of the facts by putting what they know at the disposal of the authority.[8] The principle of *audi alteram partem* is of particular significance.

The guarantee of the right to a hearing is a guarantee with a tradition in Greece. M. Stassinopoulos, the former President of the Greek Council of State, emphasised its significance in a monograph which first appeared in 1974. In that work it is assumed that the principle of *audi alteram partem* is one of great antiquity,[9] which while it originally determined only the nature of judicial proceedings, later came to play an important role in proceedings before the administration as an expression of the principle of the rule of law.[10]

The legal basis for the recognition of the rights of the defence (*droits de la défense*), of which the right to a hearing forms a central pillar, is in the first instance the Greek Constitution itself[11]:

Article 20 (right to a hearing)

"(1) ...
(2) The right of an interested party to a prior hearing also applies to all activities of or measures taken by the administration which operate to the detriment of his rights or interests."

The Greek Council of State has held that the "droit de la défense"

"n'est pas une simple formalité, mais le droit élémentaire de la personne poursuivie d'être entendue et d'exposer ses explications."[12]

---

[7] M. Stassinopoulos, *op. cit.*, footnote 1, pp. 135 *et seq.*, with a reference to the Judgment 512/1968 of the Greek Council of State; *cf.* also T. J. Panagopoulos, *op. cit.*, footnote 1, p. 157.

[8] T. J. Panagopoulos, *op. cit.*, footnote 1, p. 157.

[9] M. Stassinopoulos, *op. cit.*, footnote 1, p. 49.

[10] P. Pavlopoulos *et al.*, *op. cit.*, footnote 3, p. 428; M. Stassinopoulos, *op. cit.*, footnote 1, pp. 54 *et seq.*; T. J. Panagopoulos, *op. cit.*, footnote 1, p. 157.

[11] Quoted in P. Dagtoglou, "Die Beteiligung von Personen, die von grenzüberschreitenden Umweltverschmutzungen betroffen sein können, am griechischen Verwaltungsverfahren," in *Grenzüberschreitende Verfahrensbeteiligung im Umweltrecht der Mitgliedstaaten der Europäischen Gemeinschaften*, Annales Universitatis Saraviensis, Cologne, etc., 1985, p. 359 at 360; P. Pavlopoulos *et al.*, *op. cit.*, footnote 3, pp. 428–431; M. Stassinopoulos, *op. cit.*, footnote 1, pp. 80 *et seq.* (on the previous constitution).

[12] Judgment quoted by M. Stassinopoulos, *op. cit.*, footnote 1, p. 82.

The legislature is bound by this principle as it is by any other constitutional provision.[13] That is, not only in areas in which a right to a hearing is explicitly provided by law, but also where there are no special rules, the right is recognised even if not without limits.[14] The question then arises of what is meant by "droit de la défense" or "droit d'une audition." Stassinopoulos includes three essential elements in the "droits de la défense"[15]:

— the right of concerned parties to be informed of the proceedings and of the files;
— the right to be able to put forward their point of view on the proceedings;
— the duty on the administration to take account of these views.

A concerned party is the future addressee of the administrative act[16]; third parties (*e.g.* neighbours) may have a right to be heard, but must claim it in writing.[17] Excluded in principle from the provisions of Article 20(2) of the Greek Constitution are general dispositions and other acts which do not relate to particular persons.[18] In the course of the administrative procedure, the duty in Greece to provide the concerned parties with the opportunity to be heard operates in the following manner: the party must in principle be informed, on the initiative of the administration, of the existing procedure, only thus can he make effective use of the rights which are guaranteed to him.[19]

With regard to the right of access to files, the Greek Council of State has decided that[20]:

"Les autorités publiques ainsi que les personnes morales de droit public doivent, sur demande des administrés, leur communiquer les éléments concernant leur personne qui résultent de leurs archives

---

[13] M. Stassinopoulos, *op. cit.*, footnote 1, p. 84.
[14] P. Pavlopoulos *et al.*, *op. cit.*, footnote 3, p. 429.
[15] M. Stassinopoulos, *op. cit.*, footnote 1, p. 49; similar is P. Pavlopoulos *et al.*, *op. cit.*, footnote 3, pp. 434 *et seq*.
[16] M. Stassinopoulos, *op. cit.*, footnote 1, p. 163; P. Pavlopoulos *et al.*, *op. cit.*, footnote 3, p. 343 (legal persons may also be "concerned persons").
[17] M. Stassinopoulos, *op. cit.*, footnote 1, p. 159.
[18] P. Pavlopoulos *et al.*, *op. cit.*, footnote 3, p. 432.
[19] P. Pavlopoulos *et al.*, *op. cit.*, footnote 3, p. 435.
[20] Greek Council of State Judgment no. 2196/1969 quoted in P. Pavlopoulos *et al.*, *op. cit.*, footnote 3, p. 434; on access to files see also T. J. Panagopoulos, *op. cit.*, footnote 1, p. 157.

ainsi que d'autres documents, sauf si cette communication est exclue expressément par un texte ou si elle est en mesure de nuire à l'intérêt public."

This basic right of access to files is limited in practice to access to individual parts of files. In order to gain access to files at all, the party concerned must make a request in which the reasons for the necessity of access to files are set out individually.[21] The limitations on access to files result in particular from the rules on official secrets. Above all internal documents (such as advisory minutes of collegiate bodies) must not be made public.[22]

The unjustified refusal of access to files cannot be challenged in isolation, but can be brought forward as a ground for nullity in the context of judicial review of the (main) administrative decision.[23]

The notification about the proceedings, which must be given in writing,[24] and is also a requirement to the other party to state his views, must be sufficiently comprehensive to enable him to discern the nature and content of the measure with which he is threatened in order that he may have an adequate basis for his defence.[25] The time limit within which the other party must state his views must also correspond to this principle. It must be appropriate given the gravity of the affair and the severity of the possible interference.[26]

The authorities are also obliged, within certain limits, to give the other party advice and information. This applies in particular where a party is making requests which the authority knows will operate to his disadvantage.[27]

The hearing normally takes place within the written procedure. On the request of the other party the authority may allow an oral hearing,[28] unless otherwise provided for in a specific statute. Where new facts subsequently emerge, there must be a rehearing and renotification[29]; in

---

[21] P. Pavlopoulos *et al.*, *op. cit.*, footnote 3, p. 435.

[22] P. Pavlopoulos *et al.*, *op. cit.*, footnote 3, p. 435.

[23] P. Pavlopoulos *et al.*, *op. cit.*, footnote 3, p. 435.

[24] M. Stassinopoulos, *op. cit.*, footnote 1, p. 169; P. Pavlopoulos *et al.*, *op. cit.*, footnote 3, p. 435 (service is also necessary).

[25] M. Stassinopoulos, *op. cit.*, footnote 1, p. 169; P. Pavlopoulos *et al.*, *op. cit.*, footnote 3, p. 435.

[26] M. Stassinopoulos, *op. cit.*, footnote 1, pp. 173 *et seq.* with further examples from French case law.

[27] T. J. Panagopoulos, *op. cit.*, footnote 1, p. 157.

[28] M. Stassinopoulos, *op. cit.*, footnote 1, pp. 180 *et seq.*

[29] P. Pavlopoulos *et al.*, *op. cit.*, footnote 3, p. 436.

this context it is crucial that the authority is subject to a duty to ensure the full investigation of the facts.[30]

The duty to grant a hearing would be meaningless if it were not linked with the obligation to take into account the party's statement and to have regard to the arguments and facts as they have been put forward.[31] Only thus can the goal of the hearing be achieved, namely that the administration is put in the position where it can make its decision on the basis of a comprehensive factual picture.[32]

In the case law it is recognised that the administrative decision will be annulled where the hearing has been denied without good cause.[33] Thus the withdrawal of a driving licence must be preceded by a hearing on the grounds of its punitive character.[34] Even the setting of a fine on the grounds that a condition in a licensing decision for an industrial undertaking was not observed may not be undertaken without a prior hearing.[35] In that context the need for a hearing as the expression of the "principes généraux du droit" was emphasised.

On the other hand, there is no need for a hearing before urgent "mesures de police" are taken[36] if the urgency of the measure is demonstrable.[37] A hearing used to be unnecessary where the authority had rejected a request by the person concerned. The Greek Council of State put this in the following terms:

> "Considérant qu'une audition préalable n'est imposée à l'Administration pour refuser des permis ou des autorisations de toute sorte, réclamées par les administrés, sauf les cas où cette formalité est prescrite expressément par la loi, ou résulte de l'ensemble de ses dispositions."[38]

---

[30] M. Stassinopoulos, *op. cit.*, footnote 1, pp. 135 *et seq.*, with reference to Decision no. 512/1968 of the Greek Council of State.

[31] P. Pavlopoulos *et al.*, *op. cit.*, footnote 3, p. 436.

[32] P. Pavlopoulos *et al.*, *op. cit.*, footnote 3, p. 436.

[33] P. Pavlopoulos *et al.*, *op. cit.*, footnote 3, p. 431; Greek Council of State Judgment no. 2383/1976; *cf.* also the judgments 657/1976, 2078/1976, 3291/1976, 539/1977, 1003/1977, 1652/1977, 1900/1977, 1965/1977, 1134/1978.

[34] Greek Council of State, Judgment no. 2309/1964, quoted in M. Stassinopoulos, *op. cit.*, footnote 1, p. 134.

[35] Greek Council of State, Judgment no. 3485/1971, quoted in M. Stassinopoulos, *op. cit.*, footnote 1, p. 134.

[36] M. Stassinopoulos, *op. cit.*, footnote 1, p. 138.

[37] M. Stassinopoulos indicates here a contrast with French law and bases his opinion on arguments derived from German law (*op. cit.*, footnote 1, pp. 137 *et seq.*).

[38] Greek Council of State, Judgment no. 2281/1968, quoted in M. Stassinopoulos, *op. cit.*, footnote 1, p. 139.

This case was decided before the adoption of the 1975 Constitution, so that it appears doubtful whether such a limitation upon the right to a hearing would today be supportable.[39] No statement capable of generalisation to the effect that the party concerned has a general right to participate in the procedure follows from the constitutional guarantee of the right to a hearing. The case law has limited the right to a hearing to future addressees, even where other third parties affected may be able to challenge the subsequent administrative act.[40]

8. The right to a hearing in Ireland

The period 1921/22 saw the establishment of the Irish Free State. Up to this point the legal system followed the English model.[1] It is therefore not surprising that in Ireland too the principles of "natural justice," under the particular influence of the 1937 constitution also described as "constitutional justice," have played a decisive role in shaping the law in this field.[2]

As a result of its recognition as "superior" law (constitutional law) by the courts,[3] and the ascription of the principles of "natural justice" to the field of constitutional law, the development of the principle of the right to a hearing has subsequently followed a rather different path to that in England.[4]

---

[39] However, the case law has remained restrictive under the new Constitution, *cf.* P. Dagtoglou, *op. cit.*, footnote 11, p. 360.

[40] *cf.* P. Dagtoglou, *op. cit.*, footnote 11, p. 360.

[1] *cf.* the national report on Ireland; *cf.* also A. K. Asmal, "Administrative Law in Ireland," Rev. Int. d. S. Adm. 34 (1968), pp. 109 *et seq*.

[2] The rule is deduced indirectly from the Constitution (Article 34(1)), *cf.* J. M. Kelly, *The Irish Constitution*, Dublin, (2nd ed., 1984), p. 229; also D. G. Morgan, *Constitutional Law of Ireland*, Dublin, 1985, p. 213 (Article 40(3)(1)); however, the concept of constitutional justice goes further, *cf.* for instance R. M. Stout, *Administrative Law in Ireland*, Dublin, 1985, p. 133; *cf.* also the Supreme Court in *McDonald* v. *Bord na gCon* [1965] I.R. 217, quoted in part in R. M. Stout, *op. cit.*; on the evolution *cf.* also A. K. Asmal, *op. cit.*, footnote 1, pp. 109 *et seq*.

[3] *cf.* J. P. Casey, "Ireland" in E. V. Heyn, *Geschichte der Verwaltungsrechtswissenschaft in Europa*, Frankfurt 1982, p. 94.

[4] *cf.* A. K. Asmal, *op. cit.*, footnote 1, p. 110.

In Ireland laws are to be interpreted "in conformity with the Constitution"[5] so that they do not infringe the principles of "constitutional justice."[6] Amongst the recognised principles of constitutional justice belongs, as in England, the principle of *audi alteram partem*.[7] However, as it did in England, this principle originally applied only to judicial proceedings.

Thus in Ireland too the distinction is recognised between those administrative actions which impose on the administration a duty to act judicially, and those administrative measures which are of a purely administrative nature and which do not form the basis for a claim to "constitutional justice."[8]

The criteria for drawing this distinction between the two types of administrative measures are broadly speaking the following[9]:

If an administrative procedure is intended to have external effects, and thus lead to a decision which determines the rights and duties of the parties, then there will be a duty to act judicially, that is the principles of *audi alteram partem* will apply.

The position is different in the case of a purely internal procedure in which no external decision is to be made. The distinction is, however, difficult to draw in practice.

A typical division occurs in the context of the investigation of the facts. So long as the authority is only considering opening an administrative

---

[5] The "presumption of constitutionality" also means that the court must choose the interpretation which corresponds to the constitution, *cf.* P. Coffey, "Constitutional Law—Procedural Curbs on Powers of Compulsory Acquisition" (1984) Vol. 6 D.U.L.J. p. 152 at 153 (with further references); J. P. Casey, *op. cit.*, footnote 3, p. 101; Supreme Court in *East Donegal Co-op. Ltd.* v. *Attorney General* [1970] I.R. 317; *Loftus* v. *Attorney General* [1979] I.R. 221; *Irish Family Planning Association* v. *Ryan* [1979] I.R. 295 at 313 (Supreme Court), *per* O'Higgins J.

[6] F. Murphy, "Report on due process in administrative procedures in Ireland," FIDE 1978, p. 6.5; *East Donegal Co-op. Ltd.* v. *Attorney General* [1970] I.R. 317 (Supreme Court, *per* Walsh J.):
"(. . .) proceedings, procedures, discretions and adjudications which are permitted, provided for or prescribed by an Act of the Oireachtas are to be conducted in accordance with the principles of constitutional justice. In such case any departures from these principles would be restrained and corrected by the courts."

[7] D. G. Morgan, *op. cit.*, footnote 2, p. 212.

[8] F. Murphy, *op. cit.*, footnote 6, p. 6.6.

[9] *cf.* in particular P. Coffey, *op. cit.*, footnote 5, p. 154 (with further references); J. M. Kelly, *op. cit.*, footnote 2, p. 223; F. Murphy, *op. cit.*, footnote 6, pp. 6.3, 6.6 (with further references); from a somewhat different starting point *cf.* on the question of when a right to a hearing exists: R. M. Stout, *op. cit.*, footnote 2, pp. 136 *et seq.*, in particular on this p. 140 (with further references); *cf.* also A. K. Asmal, *op. cit.*, footnote 1, p. 114.

procedure and is merely collecting factual material to this end, then this is an internal procedure. Only where the authority has decided to commence the proceedings and a formal "inquiry" takes place must the party affected be heard.[10] However, this distinction operates independently of the question whether this procedure amounts to an interference with existing rights or merely affects privileges or expectations.[11]

In this context it is worth mentioning a problem of administrative process. Not all administrative acts may be challenged before the courts.[12] To that extent it is also impossible to argue an infringement of the principles of natural justice. Where the administration is obliged to respect the principles of natural justice, it must above all give the other party, that is the petitioner or a future addressee of an administrative act, the opportunity to be heard or to be involved in the procedure. Other interested parties also have a right to be heard.[13]

On the other hand, where a duty exists to make a public announcement and to take into account the view of persons who are more or less unconcerned by a measure it is the exception.[14] Such exceptions exist in the field of planning law and for the issuing of betting licences. In terms of its content, the duty to act judicially and to satisfy the principles of natural justice can be divided into a number of sub-principles.

In the first place there is the obligation to inform the party concerned of the existence of the procedure.[15] He is thus given the opportunity of establishing the object of the procedure. He must be notified in good time.[16] He must be informed which facts the authority wishes to take into

[10] J. P. Casey, *op. cit.*, footnote 3, p. 102 (with further references); similarly R. M. Stout, *op. cit.*, footnote 2, p. 140.

[11] This is different from the position in England, *cf.* J. P. Casey, *op. cit.*, footnote 3, p. 102; *Ingle* v. *O'Brien* [1975] 109 *Irish Law Times Reports* 7 (High Court); *Moran* v. *Attorney General* [1976] I.R. 400.

[12] The authorisation of the Attorney General which used to be necessary before claims could be brought against the State has now been dispensed with, *cf.* J. P. Casey, *op. cit.*, footnote 3, p. 101; *cf.* also *Macauley* v. *Minister for Posts and Telegraphs* [1966] I.R. 345 (High Court); on the earlier situation and in general *cf.* A. K. Asmal, *op. cit.*, footnote 1, p. 114.

[13] F. Murphy, *op. cit.*, footnote 6, p. 6.8; similarly D. G. Morgan, *op. cit.*, footnote 2, p. 212.

[14] F. Murphy, *op. cit.*, footnote 6, p. 6.8.

[15] D. G. Morgan, *op. cit.*, footnote 2, p. 212; F. Murphy, *op. cit.*, footnote 6, p. 6.8; R. M. Stout, *op. cit.*, footnote 2, p. 147; *Irish Family Planning Association* v. *Ryan* [1979] I.R. 295 (Supreme Court).

[16] F. Murphy, *op. cit.*, footnote 6, p. 6.8 (with further references); R. M. Stout, *op. cit.*, footnote 2, p. 150 (with further references).

consideration and to make the basis of its decision.[17] The party has in principle the right to see all documents. If the administration refuses access to files with regard to certain confidential documents, then it is a matter for a court to decide even before the conclusion of the administrative procedure on a petition by the party whether the administration is correct to withhold the documents.[18]

Only when the party has information on the state of knowledge of the authority is it possible for him, in the next phase, to put forward his viewpoint,[19] offer further information or evidence,[20] and to express an opinion on the legal position. The authority may not subsequently unilaterally obtain new material without informing the other party thereof.[21]

It is of great practical significance that the evidence may be challenged by the other side.[22] However, the authority is not obliged to reveal its position on the law to the other party. It is sufficient if it articulates the factual circumstances in the manner in which it has so far established them.[23] Moreover, natural justice is not guaranteed limitlessly[24].

> "The time was short and decision was urgent. There was no opportunity for debate or parley. Indeed, in the circumstances to permit or seek such opportunity 'of a hearing' might have defeated the very object and purpose of the section. There may be many cases in which justice requires that those to be affected by action of this kind should receive notice and be heard. I am quite satisfied that this was not one of such cases."

If the other party makes use of the opportunity to state his view in a hearing, then the authority is obliged to take account of this opinion and

---

[17] R. M. Stout, *op. cit.*, footnote 2, pp. 148 *et seq.*, pp. 184 *et seq.*; F. Murphy, *op. cit.*, footnote 6, p. 6.8; *Kiely* v. *Minister for Social Welfare* [1977] I.R. 267 at 280 *et seq.* (Supreme Court).

[18] F. Murphy, *op. cit.*, footnote 6, p. 6.9; R. M. Stout, *op. cit.*, footnote 2, pp. 176 *et seq.* (with further references); *Murphy* v. *Lord Mayor of Dublin* [1972] I.R. 215 (also sometimes cited as *Murphy* v. *Corporation of Dublin*) (Supreme Court); *Geraghty* v. *Minister for Local Government* [1976] I.R. 153.

[19] R. M. Stout, *op. cit.*, footnote 2, pp. 154 *et seq.*

[20] *Kiely* v. *Minister for Social Welfare* [1977] I.R. 267 at 281.

[21] J. P. Casey, *op. cit.*, footnote 3, p. 102; *Killiney and Ballybrack Development Association* v. *Minister for Local Government* [1978] *Irish Law Times Report* 295 (High Court) quoted in J. P. Casey, *op. cit.*, footnote 3, p. 102.

[22] *Kiely* v. *Minister for Social Welfare* [1977] I.R. 267 at 280 (Supreme Court); F. Murphy, *op. cit.*, footnote 6, p. 6.8; R. M. Stout, *op. cit.*, footnote 2, p. 185.

[23] F. Murphy, *op. cit.*, footnote 6, p. 6.9.

[24] *The State (Lynch)* v. *Cooney* [1982] I.R. 337 (Supreme Court, *per* O'Higgins C.J.); *cf.* also J. M. Kelly, *op. cit.*, footnote 2, p. 224.

to assimilate it into its work.[25] However, the authority is not under a general duty to document what form this consideration has taken in the reasons which it gives for its decision, if such are necessary.

Such duties also exist in the procedures of various tribunals and in the case of inquiries, which in Ireland as in the United Kingdom are rather extensive.[26]

If the authority has infringed the duty to grant the right to a hearing, then the decision will be annulled.[27] This remedy does not in principle depend on proving that a different substantive decision would have been possible if a hearing had been granted.[28] The strictness of this remedy is justified on the grounds that the infringement of constitutional principles is particularly serious.[29]

9. The "droits de la défense" in Luxembourg

In Luxembourg the rights of defence are codified with general application in the Law of December 1, 1978 and in a supplementary *Règlement* of June 8, 1979. The statutory rules essentially build on the principles developed in the case law. Alongside these are specific provisions in individual statutes which require the other party to be heard and to be given information. Thus the revocation of a driving licence[1] requires the prior hearing of the party affected, as does a deportation order or the revocation of an immigrant's residence permit.[2] Still more comprehensive are the procedural rights and right to a hearing which exist in the field

---

[25] *Irish Family Planning Association* v. *Ryan* [1979] I.R. 295 (Supreme Court); J. P. Casey, *op. cit.*, footnote 3, p. 102.

[26] *cf.* J. P. Casey, *op. cit.*, footnote 3, p. 99; on this see also A. K. Asmal, *op. cit.*, footnote 1, p. 109, *passim*.

[27] *cf.* P. Coffey, *op. cit.*, footnote 5, p. 156.

[28] *Ibid.*, *cf.* Supreme Court, *per* Finlay P., in *O'Brien* v. *Bord na Móna* [1983] I.L.R.M. 314 at 322, quoted by P. Coffey, *op. cit.*, footnote 5, p. 156:
"It is not part of the function of this court (. . .) to decide on the wisdom of such a policy. It is equally clear (. . .), where (. . .) there is a failure by the deciding authority properly to hear the objections and representations of the owner of the land before deciding to acquire it, that that deficiency cannot be supplied by subsequent proof that even if such objections and representations had been heard and considered it is improbable that a different decision would have been reached."

[29] *cf.* *Re Haughey* [1971] I.R. 217 (Supreme Court).

[1] F. Schockweiler, "Due Process," FIDE 1978, p. 8.2, with regard to Article 90 of the Luxembourg Road Traffic Law and the "Lorse" judgment of the Conseil d'Etat (Lux).

[2] F. Schockweiler, *op. cit.*, footnote 1, p. 8.2.

of law governing "noisome or dangerous businesses" (pollution law)[3] and in town and country planning.[4]

The case law has further developed the rule that the administration must adopt an adversarial procedure in areas in which the party concerned is particularly gravely affected, and that the party should have the opportunity of stating his views in this context.[5] This applies, as is typical of developments in other Member States too, in the first instance to disciplinary proceedings. Here the party concerned must be given the opportunity to defend himself, which includes the right of access to the files on the procedure.[6] The position is similar as regards measures which interfere with the other party's property rights or where fines or penalties are to be imposed in economic law.[7] The *Règlement* of June 8, 1979 applies this rule in Article 9 to all administrative activities in general.

The other party has the right to legal advice, even where he is required to be present in a meeting.[8] He also has the right of access to files, and, at his own expense, can request copies of documents.[9] The administration must explain to the other party the implications of the proposed decision.[10] Thereafter the party generally has the possibility of submitting a written opinion, but only exceptionally is an oral hearing necessary on the basis of a specific statutory rule.[11] Generally it is only the actual addressee who must be heard[12], the only exceptions to this are provided for in specific laws, for instance in pollution law[13] and building regulations, including environmental planning.[14]

The Law of December 1, 1978 as well as the supplementary *Règlement* of June 8, 1979 have in general extended procedural rights, building on the principles developed by the case law. Worthy of note are:

---

[3] F. Schockweiler, *op. cit.*, footnote 1, p. 8.4.
[4] F. Schockweiler, *op. cit.*, footnote 1, p. 8.5, with reference to the Law of March 20, 1974.
[5] F. Schockweiler, *op. cit.*, footnote 1, p. 8.2.
[6] F. Welter *et al.*, "Rapport présenté aux Colloques entre les C.E. Belge, Néerlandais, Français, Italien, Luxembourgeois et le Bundesverwaltungsgericht," Colloque de Rome March 4, 5 and 6, 1968, p. 165 at 170 and 177; F. Schockweiler, *op. cit.*, footnote 1, p. 8.3.
[7] F. Schockweiler, *op. cit.*, footnote 1, p. 8.3; Welter *et al.*, *op. cit.*, footnote 6, p. 177.
[8] F. Schockweiler, *op. cit.*, footnote 1, p. 8.3.
[9] F. Schockweiler, *op. cit.*, footnote 1, p. 8.3.
[10] F. Schockweiler, *op. cit.*, footnote 1, p. 8.3.
[11] F. Schockweiler, *op. cit.*, footnote 1, p. 8.3.
[12] F. Schockweiler, *op. cit.*, footnote 1, p. 8.3.
[13] F. Schockweiler, *op. cit.*, footnote 1, p. 8.5.
[14] F. Schockweiler, *op. cit.*, footnote 1, p. 8.5.

— a right on the part of the person concerned to be informed of procedures which he has not requested[15];
— a right to be informed about the factual material and the legal position, including the right of access to files;
— the right of access to files for third parties who can show a legitimate interest.[16]

If the authority withholds individual parts or documents from the files on the grounds of overriding public or private interests (of third parties), then the information contained therein may not be used for the decision.[17]

10. The right to a hearing in the Netherlands

In the Netherlands, too, there must frequently be a hearing before administrative acts can be adopted.[1] Thus numerous individual laws provide for a corresponding duty on the party of the administration. This is generally a duty to grant a hearing before the adoption of intrusive acts.[2] A hearing is also required where it is proposed to withdraw a benefit (*e.g.* a permit or licence).[3]

Apart from these specific rules Dutch administrative law also recognises a general principle to the effect that the administration must hear the other party under certain conditions which are defined more closely. This principle is derived from two considerations:

[15] F. Schockweiler, *Le contentieux administratif et la Procédure administrative non contentieuse en droit luxembourgeois*, p. 87, in particular footnote 362.
[16] F. Schockweiler, *op. cit.*, footnote 15, p. 94.
[17] F. Schockweiler, *op. cit.*, footnote 1, p. 8.4.
[1] See the *Rapport van de commissie inzake algemene bepalingen van administratief recht* (cited as the Rapport ABAR), (5th ed., Alphen a/d Rijn 1984), p. 128; D. H. Kok, FIDE 1978, "Due Process," pp. 9.4 *et seq.*; it is however not permissible to deduce from the absence of a comprehensive codification of procedural administrative law that there is no right to a hearing, see N. Michelsen, *Das rechtliche Gehör im Verwaltungsverfahren der Europäischen Gemeinschaften*, Diss. Hamburg 1975, p. 164.
[2] *cf. Rapport ABAR, op. cit.*, footnote 1, p. 128, with a reference to Articles 34 and 38 of the Law governing the Council of State, Article 14 AROB-law; Article 109 of the Law governing the provinces, Articles 21 and 22 of the Law governing environmental protection, Article 31(2) of the Law on immigration, Article 82 of the general public service regulations; *cf.* also D. H. Kok, *op. cit.*, footnote 1, pp. 9.4 *et seq.*, with comprehensive further references.
[3] D. H. Kok, *op. cit.*, footnote 1, p. 9.4 (figure 2.4).

On the one hand the administration is subject to a special duty of care (*zorgvuldigheidsbeginsel*), which is intended to ensure that the administration takes account of the interests of the citizens, if it adopts administrative acts. A duty may flow from this in individual cases to require the party concerned to make known his views before the adoption of the measure.[4]

On the other hand, the principles of official may form the basis for a duty to grant a hearing. There may be non-contractual liability in particular where an authority has acted without giving any prior warning, thus completely surprising the party affected.[5] In order to avoid such liability, prior information and a hearing of the citizen are required.

According to the so-called ABAR Report, which contains a proposal for the codification of administrative procedure, under Article 6 the authority should, in cases in which this can reasonably occur, offer to interested parties the opportunity of asserting their interests either in writing or orally.[6] The limits of the duty to grant a hearing lie in the word "reasonably," as well as in Article 7 of the draft, which provides for the following exceptions from the basic requirement of a hearing:

— the parties have no reservations about the decision;
— the administration has no discretion;
— the parties have already been heard in some other way;
— the decision would thereby be greatly delayed.

In the first place the persons concerned, that is to say those citizens who are addressed by the administrative act, have the right to a hearing[7] insofar as they are not specifically mentioned in the law.[8] In some areas, in particular in the field of town and country planning, even the general public, *i.e.* all citizens, have the right to give an opinion, even if the administration is not obliged to invite everyone personally to express his view.[9] The right to be heard for public interest groups has in the meantime (since 1975) been provided for by law. Under certain conditions they can defend the interests of their members.[10]

If the authority acts on its own initiative, the hearing will generally occur only after the authority has almost completed the internal processes of making up its mind.[11] If, however, a third party must be heard on a

---

[4] *Rapport ABAR, op. cit.*, footnote 1, p. 129 with reference to the AR of December 12, 1979, AB 1981, 7 and CRvB of October 11, 1977, AB 1979, 45; D. H. Kok, *op. cit.*, footnote 1, p. 9.6 (item 2.9 with further references); in the literature this general principle of law is in part also based on the notion that the administration must treat the other party fairly; *cf. Rapport ABAR, op. cit.*, footnote 1, p. 133; Nicolai, "Algemene beginselen van behoorlijk bestuur," in Duk, Loeb & Nicolai, *Bestuursrecht*, Amsterdam 1981, p. 62; W. Dok, "De zachte kern van het bestuursrecht," RMT 1978, pp. 564 *et seq*.
[5] D. H. Kòk, *op. cit.*, footnote 1, p. 9.7 (item 2.10).
[6] On this see D. H. Kok, *op. cit.*, footnote 1, p. 9.7 (item 2.11).
[7] D. H. Kok, *op. cit.*, footnote 1, p. 9.7.   [8] D. H. Kok, *op. cit.*, footnote 1, p. 9.8.
[9] D. H. Kok, *op. cit.*, footnote 1, p. 9.8.   [10] D. H. Kok, *op. cit.*, footnote 1, p. 9.9.
[11] D. H. Kok, *op. cit.*, footnote 1, p. 9.10 (item 2.21).

petition of the party concerned, then the hearing will mostly take place quite soon after the commencement of the proceedings.[12]

In many cases it is sufficient for the purposes of informing the other party if, for example, plans are made public, and permission to inspect documents is granted.[13] However, where a special private interest is affected, the procedure must be notified to the other party personally.[14] An infringement of the right to a hearing leads to the annulment of the decision only where the other party's legal defence has been seriously damaged.[15] According to the type of procedure, oral and written hearings are possible, but generally the authorities also allow the oral elaboration of written views.[16]

The authority need not state or specifically elaborate upon the legal position on which it wishes to base the planned decision, although this is generally clear from the context and the materials which have been made known.[17]

The question whether and in what conditions, as well as to what extent, the other party must be given access to files in an administrative procedure has since 1978 been regulated in the Law on openness of the administration.[18] According to Article 1(1) and (2) of this Law a petition which is directed at an organ of the public service for the provision of information which is contained in files for internal use must in principle be accepted. The administrative organ concerned provides the information by allowing access by the petitioner to the files which contain the desired details through the provision of copies.[19] The petitioner need not establish a specific legal interest. The provision of information is excluded where it would endanger national security or where specific interests of the State prevail over the interest in the provision of information. State interests worthy of protection include, for instance, the concern for foreign policy interests, economic matters and the requirements

---

[12] *Ibid.*

[13] D. H. Kok, *op. cit.*, footnote 1, (item 2.22; *cf.* also p. 9.11, item 2.23).

[14] D. H. Kok, *op. cit.*, footnote 1, p. 9.11 (item 2.22).

[15] *Rapport ABAR, op. cit.*, footnote 1, p. 128; D. H. Kok, *op. cit.*, footnote 1, p. 9.11 (item 2.24); AR of June 5, 1980, AB 1981, p. 125.

[16] D. H. Kok, *op. cit.*, footnote 1, p. 9.12 (items 2.25, 2.26).

[17] D. H. Kok, *op. cit.*, footnote 1, p. 9.13 (item 2.28).

[18] "Wet openbaarheid van bestuur," of November 9, 1978, which entered into force on May 1, 1980, Staatsblad 1978, No. 581.

[19] Article 5 of the decision concerning the openness of the administration of October 12, 1979, Staatsblad 1979, No. 590.

of criminal justice. Information need not be provided where the rights of third parties prevail over the interest in the provision of information.[20]

11. The rights of defence in Portugal

As already mentioned,[1] the Portuguese Constitution contains essential guarantees of the procedural rights of interested parties. The principles of adminstrative law (legality, impartiality etc.) are set out in Article 266. Article 267 lays down the general rules which determine the direction of the proper performance of administrative tasks[2]:

Article 267 (the structure of the administration)

1. Public administration shall be organised in such a way as to avoid bureaucratisation, to bring its organs closer to the people and to guarantee the participation of those affected in administrative activities, in particular through the agency of public associations, popular mass organisations or other forms of democratic representation.
2. (...)
3. (...)
4. The exercise of administrative activities shall form the subject of a specific law which will ensure the rationalisation of the measures at the disposal of administrative bodies and the participation of citizens in the formulation of decisions and resolutions concerning them.

The law on administrative procedure provided for in para. 4 has not yet been adopted.[3] However, there is now a draft law.[4] The provision in Article 267 is to be understood by the legislature as a programmatic statement which itself is not yet directly applicable. This means that in proceedings before the administrative courts an individual cannot rely

---

[20] *cf.* on the whole issue Article 4 of the "Wet openbaarheid van bestuur."

[1] *cf.* the national report on Portugal, above, Chapter 2, (Section 10).

[2] Previously Article 268 IV; *cf.* on the text then in force A. Thomashausen, "Die revidierte Verfassung der Republik Portugal von 1976," JöR 32 (1983) p. 443 at 495.

[3] *cf.* D. Freitas do Amaral, *Direito Administrativo*, Vol. I, Lisbon 1986, p. 132; Vol. III, Lisbon 1985, p. 242.

[4] *Projecto de Código de Processo Administrativo Gracioso*, Ed. da Presidência do Conselho, 1980; on the codification attempts in general *cf.* also D. Freitas do Amaral, Vol. I, *op. cit.*, footnote 3, pp. 114 *et seq.*

upon the fact that the administrative procedure has not respected the principles laid down in Article 267.[5]

Other provisions in the Constitution are, however, of immediate and direct application. The assumption is made that the rules on procedure which are laid down in the Constitution or in laws generally represent essential requirements of form. If there is an infringement of these, the measure adopted as a consequence must be annulled.[6]

A few such essential individual guarantees are contained in Article 268 of the Constitution.[7] This provision lays down:

Article 268

1. Citizens have the right, on application, to be informed by the administration about the progress of all procedures in which they have a direct interest as well as to be informed of those definitive decisions which concern them.
2. (...)
3. Interested parties are provided with a remedy to be exercised in the courts against any definitive and enforceable administrative acts, regardless of the form or type, in order to establish the unlawfulness of such act or in order to facilitate the assertion of a right or a legally protected interest.

With regard to data stored on computer, all citizens have a right to information (Article 35 I of the Portuguese Constitution). Also worthy of mention is the right of the party concerned to be heard, which is laid down at least in the case of disciplinary proceedings in Article 269 III of the Portuguese Constitution.[8]

12. The right to a hearing in Spain

In Spain the guarantee of a hearing has long belonged to the essential

---

[5] D. Freitas do Amaral, Vol. III, *op. cit.*, footnote 3, p. 242.

[6] M. Esteves de Oliveira, *Direito Administrativo*, Coimbra 1984, Vol. I, p. 460 (with further references); M. Caetano, *Manual de Direito Administrativo*, (10th ed., Coimbra 1984) Vol. I, p. 471; D. Freitas do Amaral, Vol. I, *op. cit.*, footnote 3, p. 243.

[7] On Article 268(2) of the Portuguese Constitution *cf.* below, the section on the duty to give reasons.

[8] Article 269(3) provides: "in disciplinary proceedings the accused has the right to be heard and to defend himself."

According to D. Freitas do Amaral, Vol. III, *op. cit.*, footnote 3, p. 278, this is an essential procedural requirement.

guarantees of the protection of the individual even as regards administrative procedure. In contrast to countries falling within the French legal tradition, the recognition of this right is not a recent occurrence, but dates from before the time of Franco.[1]

Thus Article 91 LPA provides[2]:

Audiencia del interesado

1. Instruidos los expedientes, e inmediamente antes de redactar la propuesta de resolución, estos se pondràn de manifiesto a los interesados para que, en un plazo no inferior a diez días ni superior a quince, aleguen y presenten los documentos y justificaciones que estimen pertinentes.
2. La audiencia será anterior al informe de la Asesoría Jurídica o al dictamen del Consejo de Estado.
3. Se podrá prescindir del trámite de audiencia cuando no figuren en el expediente ni sean tenidos en cuenta en la resolución otros hechos ni otras alegaciones y pruebas que las aducidas por el interesado.

The current status of the principle of *audi alteram partem* becomes immediately apparent when one realises that it is specifically recognised and guaranteed in the Constitution of 1978.[3]

---

[1] Even before the Law of 1958 which today regulates administrative procedure, there was a codification of rules of procedural administrative law, *cf.* under V of the statement of reasons for the Law (Civitas, *Legislación de la justicia administrativa*, (7th ed., Madrid 1985), p. 113) and the "Ley de Bases de Procedimiento Administrativo" of October 19, 1889, (*cf.* here Article 2 No. 10); *cf.* on this also E. Serrano Guirado, "El trámite de audiencia en el procedimiento administrativo," Revista de Administración Pública, No. 4/1951, p. 129 at 137 (with further references).

[2] *Ley de Procedimiento Administrativo*, Law of July 17, 1958, in the version of Law 164/1963 of December 2, 1963; *cf.* C. H. Ule, *Verwaltungsverfahrensgesetze des Auslands*, Berlin 1967, Vol. II, p. 788. Article 91 provides in translation:

(1) When the investigation has been completed,* and directly before the adoption of the proposal for a decision, the files are to be published to the parties concerned. The parties may, within a time limit of not less than 10 or more than 15 days, present the documents and justifications which appear to them to be essential.

(2) The hearing shall occur before the legal office (Asesoria juridico) presents its opinion or the Council of State delivers its judgment.

(3) The hearing is not necessary where no facts or evidentiary material is addressed or considered in the decision apart from those which the party concerned has himself presented.

*"instruidos los expedientes": *instrucción* is the entire process of establishing the basis for the decisions, *cf.* the title of Chapter III LPA (before Article 81).

[3] Boletin Oficial del Estado (BOE) of December 29, 1978, p. 1.

Article 105(c) of the Constitution provides:

La ley regulará: (. . .)

    (c) El procedimiento a través del cual deben producirse los actos administrativos, garantizando, cuando proceda, la audienci del interesado.[3a]

This heightened protection for the principle of a hearing in administrative procedure also accords with ideas which have been represented with great regularity in the case law of the highest court for many years. Thus at various times the Supreme Court has held that the right to a hearing must be recognised in all laws on judicial procedure.[4] This is a principle of legal ethics,[5] an axiom which affects all spheres of civil, criminal and administrative law.[6] Furthermore, it has spoken of this principle as being a norm of the natural law of the administration[7] and a "principio general de derecho."[8] The literature too describes this principle as a codified general principle of law of the highest status.[9]

The right to a hearing is open to every "interesado" (interested party). Article 23 LPA defines who is an "interesado"[10]:

Se consideran interesados en el procedimiento administrativo:

[3a] Translation: The law shall regulate:
    (c) the procedure by which administrative acts are to be adopted, guaranteeing, where necessary, the hearing of the party concerned.

[4] cf. R. Entrena Cuesta, *Curso de Derecho Administrativo*, Vol. I/1, (8th ed. Madrid 1983), p. 288; E. Serrano Guirado, *op. cit.*, footnote 1, p. 137 (with further references); judgment of the Supreme Court of March 10, 1956.

[5] Judgment of July 9, 1943; cf. also E. Serrano Guirado, *op. cit.*, footnote 1, p. 138.

[6] Judgments of April 30, 1928 and December 31, 1928.

[7] Judgment of the Supreme Court of February 19, 1963.

[8] Cited in F. Garrido Falla, *Tratado de Derecho Administrativo*, Vol. I, (9th ed., Madrid 1985), p. 680.

[9] R. Entreno Cuesta, *op. cit.*, footnote 4, p. 288 with reference to the quotation cited from the English case of Dr. Bentley (1723) *R. v. Chancellor of the University of Cambridge* 1 Str. 557; 93 Eng. Rep. 698 (K.B. 1723); F. Garrido Falla, *op. cit.*, footnote 8, p. 680 (with further references).

[10] cf. C. H. Ule, *op. cit.*, footnote 2, p. 769; in translation this Article states:
    The following are defined as "interested parties" for the purposes of administrative procedure:
    (a) those persons who wish to exercise rights or legitimate interests;
    (b) those persons who, although they have not initiated the proceedings, nonetheless claim rights which may be directly affected by the decision;
    (c) those persons whose personal and directly legitimate interests may be affected by the decision and who take part in the procedure before the adoption of a definitive decision.

(a) Queines lo promuevan como titulares de derechos o intereses legítimos.
(b) Los que sin haber iniciado el procedimiento ostenten derechos que puedan resultar directamente afectados por la decisión que en el mismo se adopte.
(c) Aquellos cuyos intereses legítimos, personales y directos puedan resultar afectados por la resolución y se presenten en el procedimiento en tanto no haya recaído resolución definitiva.

The right to a hearing can be broken down into a number of parts. First the authority must inform the interested parties of the procedure and the results of the investigations (the content of the files). This duty is expressed in the wording of the Law itself. Article 91(1) LPA requires notification also to be made to those interested parties who have not actually themselves initiated the procedure. (That includes in particular those persons cited in Article 23 (b)).[11] The authority must therefore in certain circumstances undertake investigations to ascertain whose legal interests may be directly affected by an administrative act.

Exceptionally, a hearing may be denied under Article 91(3) LPA if the authority is to base its decision entirely on matters which the interested parties themselves have brought forward.[12] In special cases a public hearing is also possible, and in that instance the documents must be made available for public inspection for at least 20 days in the premises of the authority, following an announcement in the Official Gazette.[13]

The notification of the procedure is normally linked to an offer of access to the files. This follows from the text of Article 91(1) LPA, which provides for the publication of the files.

According to the text of the Law, this publication should be unrestricted. However, a ministerial circular of October 22, 1958 provides for limitations, although the validity of this circular is in doubt since an inferior ministerial statement cannot limit rights guaranteed by law. The contents of the circular provide that parts of the files may be withheld from the parties in so far as publication could harm the public (protection of state secrets) or individual third parties.

The right to a hearing and the corresponding duties of the administration are not dependent on whether or not the interested party wishes to

---

[11] F. Garrido Falla, *op. cit.*, footnote 8, p. 680 (note 94); R. Entrena Cuesta, *op. cit.*, footnote 4, p. 288; Supreme Court judgment of June 17, 1942; judgment of June 21, 1955.
[12] R. Entrena Cuesta, *op. cit.*, footnote 4, p. 288; Supreme Court, judgment of February 16, 1965.
[13] R. Entrena Cuesta, *op. cit.*, footnote 4, p. 284.

make use of his right to a hearing. The *audiencia* must also be offered where the other party does not intend to make a statement.[14]

The interested parties have the right to bring forward all defences and evidence which appear appropriate to them, that is they may express an opinion on all questions of fact and law, and the authority is obliged to take cognizance of these statements.

The Law contains no references to exceptions in cases of urgency or where there is a risk that enforcement may be frustrated by the party who wishes to be heard. In the recitals accompanying the Law,[15] it is clearly the intention that through very short time limits the procedure should be managed in an efficient and effective manner. Those entitled to be heard have only 10 to 15 days at their disposal in which to exercise their right. Whether such a time limit suffices in complicated administrative procedures must be in doubt. It is however well known that the administration does in practice sometimes depart from this statutory time limit.

An infringement of the right to a hearing will make the decision voidable if the interested party was in some way handicapped in his defence (*indefensión*) (Article 48(2) LPA).[16] The principles of economy of process require that the decision should not be annulled where the interested party has ultimately been able to put forward his arguments.[17] In view of the existence of an adversarial procedure, the grant of a hearing at a later stage of the procedure will suffice.[18]

On the other hand, those defects of procedure which have deprived the interested party of his rights or have handicapped him in his defence are considered to be so essential that they must be observed on the initiative of the administration itself.[19] Even claims which in themselves are inadmissible oblige the court to examine whether the act corresponds to the correct procedure and can in exceptional cases lead to the annulment of

[14] R. Entrena Cuesta, *op. cit.*, footnote 4, p. 289.

[15] Civitas, *op. cit.*, footnote 1, §5, pp. 107 *et seq.*, 112 *et seq.*

[16] E. García de Enterría, T.-R. Fernández, *Curso de Derecho Administrativo*, Vol. I, (4th ed., Madrid 1984), p. 595; R. Entrena Cuesta, *op. cit.*, footnote 4, p. 290; F. Garrido Falla, *op. cit.*, footnote 8, p. 682; Supreme Court, judgments of May 17, 1972 and September 23, 1974; *cf.* also the judgment of January 22, 1982.

[17] E. García de Enterría, T.-R. Fernández, *op. cit.*, footnote 16, p. 595; Supreme Court, judgment of February 8, 1982.

[18] E. García de Enterría, T.-R. Fernández, *op. cit.*, footnote 16, p. 595.

[19] R. Entrena Cuesta, *op. cit.*, footnote 4, p. 264; Supreme Court, judgments of February 28, 1962, January 8, 1963 and January 25, 1966.

the decision even though the claim would, if it had been a defect of substantive law, have been dismissed on grounds of inadmissibility.[20]

III. RIGHTS OF DEFENCE IN COMMUNITY LAW

1. Normative rules

In the ECSC Treaty there are provisions in a number of articles which prescribe the hearing of the parties affected by a proposed measure, or of the interest groupings which represent them. Such provisions are contained, for example, in Articles 36(1) (for all procedures involving financial penalties), 46(2), 54(5), 66(5), second paragraph and 88(1) ECSC. Thus Article 66(5), second paragraph provides, for example:

> ". . . the High Authority, (. . .) after giving the parties concerned the opportunity to submit their comments, shall order (any necessary measures)."

Article 58(2), first paragraph, ECSC provides in similar vein:

> "The High Authority shall, on the basis of studies made jointly with undertakings and associations of undertakings, determine the quotas on an equitable basis."

Some of the ECSC provisions included in the Treaties themselves do not extend as far as the guarantees contained in secondary EEC law, which will be examined below. However, the Commission in principle grants the parties concerned the same rights as those applicable in EEC law.[1] The slightly newer EEC and Euratom Treaties also contain analogous provisions. Thus the Euratom Treaty provides for relevant rules in Articles 5(2), second sentence, 46(2), first sentence and 141. The provisions in the EEC Treaty (Articles 93(2), first sub-paragraph; 169, first para-

---

[20] R. Entrena Cuesta, *op. cit.*, footnote 4, p. 264; Supreme Court, judgments of October 5, 1961, May 24, 1968 (with further references) and July 1, 1975; the latter judgment differentiates with respect to the grounds which would cause the claim to be inadmissible.

[1] C.-D. Ehlermann, D. Oldekop. "Due Process in administrative procedure," FIDE 1978, p. 11.6; in the field of anti-dumping law the position in EEC and ECSC law has been harmonised by the adoption of identically worded measures: Regulation 2176/84 of July 23, 1984, O.J. 1984, L201/1 and Decision 2177/84/ECSC, O.J. 1984, L201/17).

graph concern only the position of Member States without actually directly providing at least for the right of private parties affected by a decision to be heard, as in the other Treaties. This is not surprising, however, when one remembers that the EEC Treaty as a *traité-cadre* includes more by way of tasks for the legislature than does, for example, the ECSC Treaty, which has been described as a *traité-loi* and which itself contains numerous concrete administrative powers.[2]

Nonetheless, even in the field of EEC law, the secondary law offers grounds for arguing that there are actually numerous guarantees of procedural rights. This is the case, above all, in the law concerning Community officials, for their disciplinary rules in particular, which, as the comparative survey has shown, have also traditionally fulfilled a function in the Member States as a "trendsetter," wherever the question of implementing guarantees of legal protection for parties in administrative proceedings has been at issue. Thus Article 87 of the Staff Regulations provides[3]:

> "The appointing authority shall have the right to issue a written warning or a reprimand without consulting the Disciplinary Board, on a proposal from the official's immediate superior or on its own initiative. The official concerned shall be heard before such action is taken. Other measures shall be ordered by the appointing authority after the disciplinary procedure provided in Annex IX has been completed. This procedure shall be initiated by the appointing authority after hearing the official concerned."

Annex IX also guarantees the official's right to a hearing. Officials have the right, at all times and without restriction to inspect their personal files, in particular in the context of disciplinary proceedings.[4]

For competition proceedings Article 19 of Regulation 17 (competition regulation)[5] is relevant:

---

[2] On this categorisation *cf.* above, Introduction; *cf.* also C.-D. Ehlermann, D. Oldekop. *op. cit.*, footnote 1, p. 11.2.

[3] Staff Regulations of December 18, 1961, in: *Handbuch des Europäischen Rechts*, No. I A67/3, p. 59 in the version then in force; *cf.* in the original Regulations 31/61 and 11/61 of December 18, 1961, J.O. 1962, 45/1385; O.J. Sp.Ed. 1959–1962, 135; modified by Regulation 259/68 of February 29, 1968, J.O. 1968, L56/1; O.J. Sp.Ed. 1968, 30 and further amendments.

[4] Article 26 of the Staff Regulations (footnote 3); Article 2 of Annex IX of the Staff Regulations; *cf.* on this C.-D. Ehlermann, D. Oldekop, *op. cit.*, footnote 1, p. 11.10.

[5] J.O. 1962, 204, O.J. Sp.Ed. 1959–1962, 87.

"Article 19. Hearing of the parties and of third persons.

(1) Before taking decisions as provided for in Articles 2, 3, 6, 7, 8, 15 and 16, the Commission shall give the undertakings of associations of undertakings concerned the opportunity of being heard on the matters to which the Commission has taken objection.

(2) If the Commission or the competent authorities of the Member States consider it necessary, they may also hear other natural or legal persons. Applications to be heard on the part of such persons shall, where they show a sufficient interest, be granted.

(3) Where the Commission intends to give negative clearance pursuant to Article 2 or take a decision in application of Article 85(3) of the Treaty, it shall publish a summary of the relevant application or notification and invite all interested third parties to submit their observations within a time limit which it shall fix being not less than one month. Publication shall have regard to the legitimate interest of undertakings in the protection of their business secrets."

This Regulation provides expressly for the hearing of parties concerned with regard to the "matters to which the Commission has taken objection." The communication required by the Commission in accordance with this provision is determined in greater detail in Article 2 of Regulation 99/63,[6] an implementing Regulation which was adopted on the basis of Article 24 of Regulation 17:

"(1) The Commission shall inform undertakings and associations of undertakings in writing of the objections raised against them. The communication shall be addressed to each of them or to a joint agent appointed by them.

(2) The Commission may inform the parties by giving notice in the *Official Journal of the European Communities*, if, from the circumstances of the case, this appears appropriate, in particular where notice is to be given to a number of undertakings but no joint agent has been appointed. The notice shall have regard to the

---

[6] J.O. 1963, 2268; O.J. Sp.Ed. 1963–1964, 47.

legitimate interest of the undertakings in the protection of their business secrets.

(3) A fine or periodic penalty payment may be imposed on an undertaking or association of undertakings only if the objections were notified in the manner provided for in paragraph 1.

(4) The Commission shall when giving notice of objections fix a time limit up to which the undertakings and associations of undertakings may inform the Commission of their views."

The consequences of a failure to communicate in particular cases are expressed very clearly here. Paragraph 3 provides expressly that the particularly grave financial penalties which the Commission may impose cannot be imposed without a comprehensive communication of the objections.

In anti-dumping proceedings also, the commencement of the proceedings must be notified to the party concerned. Since in such proceedings all the parties concerned are not necessarily known to the Commission, the Community legislature has brought in a double procedure in order to inform the parties of the introduction of the proceedings. Article 7 of Regulation 2176/84 provides[7]:

"Initiation and subsequent investigation

(1) Where, after consultation it is apparent that there is sufficient evidence to justify initiating a proceeding the Commission shall immediately:

(a) announce the initiation of a proceeding in the *Official Journal of the European Communities*; such announcements shall indicate the product and countries concerned, give a summary of the information received, and provide that all relevant information is to be communicated to the Commission; it shall state the period within which interested parties may make known their views in writing and may apply to be heard orally by the Commission in accordance with paragraph 5.

(b) so advise the exporters and importers known to the Commission to be concerned as well as representatives of the exporting country and the complainants."

---

[7] Regulation 2176/84 and Decision 2177/84/ECSC, *supra*, footnote 1.

The double protection for the parties concerned through direct contact and simultaneous publication in the Official Journal is a clear sign of the high status which is accorded to the communication of the commencement of the proceedings.[8]

The individual elements of the right to a hearing are further protected in Article 7(4)–(7) of Regulation 2176/84.

2. The existence of a general principle of law

The principle that the rights of the defence of the parties concerned, in particular the right to a hearing, are to be protected has a decisive significance even above and beyond the field of written law. The Court of Justice[9] has, with the support of the literature,[10] recognised the principle of *audi alteram partem* in general as an essential procedural rule for administrative proceedings.

More than ten years after Advocate-General Warner[11] in the *Transocean Marine Paint* case recommended the recognition of such a general principle of law, having regard to the legal systems of the Member States, the tendency continues for the significance of this principle to increase. This can be seen also from a resolution of the Council of Europe since adopted which approves this principle. Thus Resolution (77)31 "on the protection of the individual in relation to the acts of Administrative Authorities" provides.[12]

---

[8] *cf.* also A. Weber, "Das Verwaltungsverfahren im Antidumpingrecht der EG," EuR 1985, p. 1 at 15.

[9] Case 17/74 *Transocean Marine Paint* v. *Commission* [1974] ECR 1063 at 1080; Case 85/76 *Hoffmann-La Roche* v. *Commission* [1979] E.C.R. 461 at 511; Case 136/79 *National Panasonic* v. *Commission* [1980] E.C.R. 2033 at 2058 (para. 21).

[10] I. Pernice, *Grundrechtsgehalte im Europäischen Gemeinschaftsrecht*, Baden-Baden 1979, p. 41; J.-P. Warner, "Due process in administrative procedure," FIDE 1978, p. 1.6; J. Sedemund, "Allgemeine Prinzipien des Verwaltungsverfahrensrechts," in J. Schwarze (ed.), *Europäisches Verwaltungsrecht im Werden*, Baden-Baden 1982, p. 45 at 47 *et seq.*; C.-D. Ehlermann, D. Oldekop, *op. cit.*, footnote 1, p. 11.2 and *passim*; A. Weber, *op. cit.*, footnote 8, p. 15; L. Goffin, "La jurisprudence de la Cour de Justice sur les droits de la défense," CDE 1980, p. 127; O. Due, "Le respect des droits de la défense dans le droit administratif communautaire," CDE 1987, p. 383.

[11] Advocate-General Warner in Case 17/74 *Transocean Marine Paint* v. *Commission* [1974] E.C.R. 1063 at 1088; similarly also in Case 113/77 *NTN Toyo Bearing Co.* v. *Council* [1979] E.C.R. 1185 at 1261 *et seq.*

[12] Resolution of September 28, 1977, Council of Europe, Information bulletin on legal activities, June 1978, p. 45; Advocate-General Warner refers expressly to this in the Japanese Ball Bearing case (*NTN Toyo Bearing*), [1979] E.C.R. 1185 at 1262; *cf.* also *ibid., op. cit.*, footnote 10, p. 1.7.

"Right to be heard

1. In respect of any administrative act of such nature as is likely to affect adversely his rights, liberties or interests, the person concerned may put forward facts and arguments and, in appropriate cases, call evidence which will be taken into account by the administrative authority.
2. In appropriate cases the person concerned is informed, in due time and in a manner appropriate to the case, of the right stated in the preceding paragraph."

The Court of Justice has also repeatedly strengthened the application of the right to a hearing in administrative procedure under Community law.[13]

In the following sections we shall therefore examine the detailed conditions as well as the nature and scope of the right to a hearing. First we shall look at the duty of the authority to inform the person concerned of the initiation of a procedure.

Then we shall examine when and to what extent the authority must inform the person concerned of the complaints made and of the factual material in support of them. Finally the nature and scope of the possibility of submitting observations will be analysed.

3. Rights of defence for third parties

The rights of defence are intended primarily to protect the interests of those parties who will be adversely affected by a proposed measure. It is not always easy to ascertain who is adversely affected apart from those who are the direct addressees of the decision.

National law itself recognises the possible effects on third parties of administrative decisions. That is the idea that an administrative decision

---

[13] The principle was first recognised in the law governing the disciplining of officials, *cf.* Case 32/62 *Alvis* v. *Council* [1963] E.C.R. 49, 55, *cf.* also Advocate-General Lagrange, [1963] E.C.R. 60, which refers also to the legal systems of the Member States and to the principle of "bonne administration"; *cf.* also Case 80/63 *Degreef* v. *Commission* [1964] E.C.R. 391 at 406; as regards the law of procedure (European Court procedure), the principle was recognised in the *SNUPAT* cases (Cases 42 and 49/59 *SNUPAT* v. *High Authority* [1961] E.C.R. 53; more recent cases, other than those already cited, include Cases 100–103/80, *Musique Diffusion Française* v. *Commission* [1983] E.C.R. 1825 at 1880, para. 10; Case 85/76 *Hoffmann-La Roche* v. *Commission* [1979] E.C.R. 461 at 512, para. 11; Case 121/76 *Moli* v. *Commission* [1977] E.C.R. 1971 at 1979, paras. 19 *et seq.*; *cf.* also Advocate-General Mayras, [1977] E.C.R. at 1982.

may affect persons other than the immediate addressees. Frequently a favourable decision directed at the addressee will adversely affect a competitor, so that the latter will need adequate protection under the law to defend his interests. This fact is recognised in Community law. Examples of this in written law are to be found in anti-dumping and competition law.

Article 19(2) of Regulation 17[14] allows the possibility of hearing third parties, which in the view of the Commission also includes disadvantaged competitors where they have initiated the proceedings through a complaint. In the view of Advocate-General Lenz,[15] such complainants generally have a sufficient interest as required by Article 19(2), which automatically restricts the discretion of the Commission under Articles 5 and 7 of Regulation 99/63[16] with regard to their participation in the proceedings. In the field of anti-dumping law (in both the ECSC and EEC contexts) the participation of the complainant is expressly provided for. Article 7(1)(a) of Regulation 2176/84 and Decision No. 2177/84[17] oblige the Commission to grant a hearing where one is requested; as a whole, the anti-dumping proceedings are of an adversarial nature, which means that the complainant and the accused party deal with each in an adversarial relationship before the Commission, which adopts simultaneously the role of an arbitrator.

In contrast to the (future) addressee of an administrative decision, the hearing of third parties is not required in competition law to be initiated by the authority itself, but is required only if the party so requests. This was recognised back in 1966 by the Court of Justice,[18] in part even before the coming into force of the express provisions of Community law:

---

[14] See above, footnote 5.
[15] Advocate-General Lenz, Opinion of January 22, 1986, Case 53/83 *AKZO Chemie* v. *Commission* [1986] E.C.R. 1965 at 1966 *et seq.*
[16] J.O. 1963, 2268; O.J. Sp.Ed. 1963–1964, 47.

Article 5: "If natural or legal persons showing a sufficient interest apply to be heard pursuant to Article 19(2) of Regulation 17, the Commission shall afford them the opportunity of making known their views in writing within such time limit as it shall fix."

Article 7: "(1) The Commission shall afford to persons who have so requested in their written comments the opportunity to put forward their arguments orally, if those persons show a sufficient interest or if the Commission proposes to impose on them a fine or periodic penalty payment.

(2) The Commission may likewise afford to any other person the opportunity of orally expressing his views."

[17] *cf.* above, footnote 1.
[18] Cases 56 and 58/64 *Consten and Grundig* v. *Commission* [1966] E.C.R. 399 at 346.

"Although it is desirable that the Commission should extend its inquiries as far as possible to those who might be affected by its decisions, the mere interest in preventing an agreement to which they are not parties from being declared illegal so that they may retain the benefits which they derive *de facto* from the situation which results from that agreement cannot constitute a sufficient basis for establishing a right for the other concessionaires of Grundig to be called automatically by the Commission to take part in the proceedings concerning the relationship between Consten and Grundig."

In that context, it must also be borne in mind that it is precisely when several parties are involved in the procedure that certain documents are to be regarded as confidential and must not be open to inspection.

In its most recent case law the Court of Justice has furthermore decided in principle that for competition law the rights under administrative procedure of a person who makes a complaint about an infringement of the competition rules under Article 4(2) of Regulation 17 do not extend as far as the right of the defence (*droits de la défense*) of those undertakings who are actually the subjects of the Commission's administrative procedure, and are limited in any case where they threaten to interfere with the rights of the latter category of undertakings:

"The cases relied on by the applicants concern the right to a fair hearing of companies in respect of which the Commission carries out an investigation. Such an investigation, however, does not constitute adversary proceedings between the companies concerned; it is a procedure commenced by the Commission, upon its own initiative or upon application, in fulfilment of its duty to ensure that the rules on competition are observed. It follows that the companies which are the object of the investigation and the companies which have submitted an application under Article 3 of Regulation No. 17/62, having shown that they have a legitimate interest in seeking an end to the alleged infringement, are not in the same procedural situation and the latter cannot invoke the right to a fair hearing as defined in the cases relied on.

As is clear in particular from the judgment of 28 March 1985 in Case 298/83, *CICCE* v. *Commission* [1985] ECR 1105, the complainants must, on the other hand, be given the opportunity to defend their legitimate interests in the course of the administrative proceedings, and the Commission must consider all the matters of fact and of law which they bring to its attention. However, the procedural rights of the complainants are not as far-reaching as the right to a fair hearing of the companies which are the object of the Commission's investigation. In any event, the limits of such rights are reached where they begin to interfere with those companies' rights to a fair hearing.

In its judgment of 24 June 1986 in Case 53/85, *AKZO Chemie BV and AKZO Chemie UK Ltd.* v. *Commission* [1986] ECR 1965, the Court held that the obligation of professional secrecy laid down in Article 214 of the Treaty and Article 20(2) of Regulation No. 17 is mitigated in regard to complainants, and that the Commission may communicate to them certain information covered by the obligation of professional secrecy in so far as it is necessary to do so for the proper conduct of the investigation. The Court emphasized in that judgment, however, that a complainant may not in any circumstances be provided with documents containing business secrets, and set out the manner in which the company under investigation may act to prevent such disclosure."[19]

4. General limitations upon the rights of defence

The rights of defence, including the right to a hearing, are guaranteed only within certain limits. There are a number of general matters which allow the administration to depart, at least temporarily, from the requirement to grant a hearing. These exceptional circumstances are however difficult to categorise,[20] so that the groups of cases gathered together here are not definitive but represent only typical examples.

(a) The risk that the purpose of the decision may be defeated

A departure from the right to a hearing is allowed in a case where prior knowledge on the part of the party concerned would defeat the purpose of the decision. This exception follows the law in the Member States.[21]

In the case law this limitation upon the right to a hearing has been articulated in conjunction with the powers of investigation of the Com-

---

[19] See Joined Cases 142 and 156/84 *BAT and Reynolds* v. *Commission* [1987] E.C.R. 4487 at 4572, paras. 19 to 21.

[20] As expressly stated by Advocate-General Warner, Case 136/79 *National Panasonic* v. *Commission* [1980] E.C.R. 2033 at 2068; *cf.* also *ibid.*, *op. cit.*, footnote 10, p. 1.6.

[21] J.-P. Warner, *op. cit.*, footnote 10, p. 1.7.

mission in competition proceedings. Under Article 14 of Regulation 17[22] the Commission can, by decision, undertake certain checks in the business premises of undertakings. For this purpose, the officials of the Commission charged with carrying out the investigation have the following powers:

— to examine the books and other business records;
— to take copies of or extracts from the books and business records;
— to ask for oral explanations on the spot;
— to enter any premises, land and means of transport of undertakings.

The firm National Panasonic Deutshland had applied to the Commission for negative clearance or an exemption under Article 85(3) EEC. The Commission undertook an investigation in the premises of the English sister company without having previously informed the company of its intention. The relevant formal decision was transmitted to the manager on the morning of the undertaking at the premises of the company. The Advocate-General justified this procedure as follows[23]:

"A right to be heard may however exist although no legislation expressly confers it. (. . .) Nevertheless, the rule that a person whose rights are liable to be affected by an administrative decision is entitled to be heard by the authorities concerned is only a general rule. It is subject to exceptions.

(. . .)

One of the exceptions must be, in my opinion, where the purpose of the decision would or might be defeated if the right were accorded. One comes back here, of course, to the Commission's point that the purpose of carrying out an investigation without warning is to forestall the possible destruction or concealment of relevant documents. Nor is it as if an undertaking affected by such an investigation were left without a remedy. Its right to have the decision of the Commission reviewed by the Court is expressly preserved by Article 14. True, that remedy can only be invoked, if the Commission is

---

[22] cf. above, footnote 5.
[23] Advocate-General Warner in *National Panasonic*, *supra*, footnote 20, [1980] E.C.R. 2068; with reference to the *Transocean Marine Paint* decision, *supra*, footnote 11; see also J.-P. Warner, *op. cit.*, footnote 10, p. 1.7.

right, after the investigation has taken place, but that does not make it an ineffective remedy.

The Court may, as the Commission concedes, if it holds the decision to have been unlawful, order the Commission to return to the undertaking any copies of documents obtained as a result of the investigation and to refrain from using any information so obtained."

(b) The gathering of evidence

The Court of Justice too thought that what the Commission had done in this case was ultimately lawful, but it took a rather different approach to the law. The Court held that the investigation decision constituted a subordinate interim procedure which merely served the purpose of securing sufficient evidence, the use of which would later be determined by decision.[24]

In so holding, the Court of Justice may have been thinking of a statement by Advocate-General Roemer,[25] who argued in an earlier decision on related questions:

"The applicant was informed, at least briefly, by a letter from the High Authority of July 9, 1964, that the results of the inspection carried out by Fidital were unsatisfactory (which then prompted the commissioning of an expert to ascertain the extent of the applicant's production). Not only that, but there is no *duty* on the part of the High Authority in any kind of administrative proceedings to hear the observations of the parties concerned on preparatory measures prior

---

[24] Case 136/79 *National Panasonic* v. *Commission* [1980] E.C.R. 2033 at 2058, para. 21; the possibility of subsequent annulment is also raised by Advocate-General Warner, [1980] E.C.R. 2069 as well as by C.-D. Ehlermann, D. Oldekop, *op. cit.*, footnote 1, p. 11.4; *cf.* on this question also A. Gleiss, M. Hirsch, *Kommentar zum EWG-Kartellrecht*, (3rd ed., Heidelberg 1978), Regulation 17, Article 14, para. 4, as well as P. J. Kuyper, T.P.J.M. van Rijn, "Procedural guarantees and investigatory methods in European Law, with special reference to competition," (1983) 2 Yearbook of European Law, p. 1 at 12, and J. M. Joshua, "Proof in contested EEC Competition cases—A comparison with the Rules of Evidence in Common Law," (1987) E.L.Rev. 315.

[25] Case 3/67 *Mandelli* v. *Commission* [1968] E.C.R. 25 at 41 *per* Advocate-General Roemer.

to the issue of a final decision (although such consultation may of course be useful)."

Thus, it is to be taken into consideration that a temporary burden which does not represent an irreparable imposition as a result of a procedure for collecting evidence will have less grave effects than a definitive infringement decision.

The Court of Justice is very reluctant to grant interim legal protection. In principle, the party must wait for the main decision itself before bringing a challenge.[26]

In that case, however, this principle could be applied only to a limited extent, since the main proceedings were directed primarily at National Panasonic Deutschland, and not against the English sister company. The latter was burdened therefore only by the enforcement measure itself.

In this context the Court of Justice has made clear in its most recent case law that the possibility of challenging the final decision renders any challenge to individual procedural measures inadmissible only where, in the later procedure concerning the substance of the matter, all effects of the administrative measure which was to be challenged can be removed. Hence the granting of access to files containing confidential documents is capable of specific challenge. Before the adoption of such a decision, the person who may be adversely affected by such access must be given the opportunity to be heard and he must be given the chance of actually making a challenge.[27]

Since in the *National Panasonic* case the investigation decision represented a separate burden which could not necessarily be removed by a challenge in the main proceedings the provision of legal protection, quite apart from the arguments of the Advocate-General, was justified from this point of view.[28]

In so far as no rights of third parties are affected or the decision imposes no irreversible burdens which could not be removed through a challenge

---

[26] Case 60/81 *IBM* v. *Commission* [1981] E.C.R. 2639, reiterated once more recently by the Court of Justice in Case 53/85 *AKZO Chemie* v. *Commission* [1986] E.C.R. 1965 at 1989 para. 16.

[27] [1986] E.C.R. 1965 at 1989, paras. 16 *et seq*.

[28] Advocate-General Warner in *National Panasonic*, [1980] E.C.R. 2069; however, it should be noted that the need to adopt a formal decision (which is not necessarily an obvious precondition) represents to a certain degree also a guarantee of the rule of law and the (*ex post facto*) protection of the law. The question whether a formal decision is necessary for forcible implementation was previously controversial under the ECSC Treaty, *cf. National Panasonic* [1980] E.C.R. 2055, para. 11 at the end; *cf.* Case 31/59 *Acciaieria di Brescia* v. *High Authority* [1960] E.C.R. 71 at 82 as well as Advocate-General Roemer at 95 *et seq*.

in the main proceedings, the exclusion of certain measures for the collection of evidence from the requirement of a prior hearing of the party concerned is totally justified. As shown above, the legal orders of the Member States also recognise exceptions from the rights of the defence for investigatory measures.[29]

In this context it would be appropriate to add the following rider. In principle an authority has the right to initiate preliminary inquiries. This should be separated from the question whether such measures interfere with the rights of individuals. If there is such an interference, the relevant procedural principles must be observed, although these do not apply to the gathering of information in general.[30]

The issue whether a surprise action really increased the rewards to be gained in the gathering of evidence depends on the individual case and should be seen as a separate exceptional circumstance, just as Advocate-General *Warner* suggested.[31]

(c) Insignificant interferences

In an isolated case which has not so far apparently been repeated, the Court of Justice held that a measure which interferes only to an insignificant extent with the rights of the individual may be adopted without a hearing. In the case in question the issue concerned the consequences of the reorganisation of an office within the Commission. The Court of Justice was of the opinion that although the applicant was in some way adversely affected, there was no need for a hearing, in particular because he had the opportunity of bringing a complaint under the Staff Regulations.[32]

(d) Danger in delay

Under the legal orders of the Member States the right to a hearing is

---

[29] *cf.* the comparative section above, as well as P. J. Kuyper, T.P.J.M. van Rijn, *op. cit.*, footnote 24.

[30] *cf.* on this Cases 60 and 190/81R *IBM* v. *Commission* [1981] E.C.R. 1857 at 1863, para. 10.

[31] In Case 136/79 *National Panasonic* v. *Commission* [1980] E.C.R. 2033 at 2069.

[32] Joined Cases 33 and 75/79 *Kuhner* v. *Commission* [1980] E.C.R. 1677 at 1698, para. 25, *cf.* also the headnote no. 7, p. 1679; Advocate-General Mayras was not of the opinion that the interference was so insignificant and he recommended the annulment of the decision (*cf.* p. 1720 with a detailed comparative analysis of the position in the Member States).

frequently excluded in a case where measures are to be adopted immediately in order to remove some actual danger.[33] This point is also justified in principle under Community law, but must remain limited to extreme circumstances.

Thus, for example, it is possible for a Community official to be immediately suspended on suspicion of embezzlement,[34] or for interim measures to be adopted in the field of anti-dumping where the threatened damage is great, in both cases even before the person concerned is informed. However it is specifically provided in Article 7(7)(a) of Regulation 2176/84 (anti-dumping regulation) and in Decision No. 2177/84,[35] that the procedural guarantees may not in principle be limited by the possibility of adopting interim measures.[36]

As far as is known, the Court has had no opportunity of discussing his point.

(e) The impossibility of granting protection

For the rest, situations are conceivable in which the communication of the

---

[33] This had already been established by J.-P. Warner in his General Report for FIDE, cf. op. cit., footnote 10, p. 1.7; cf. also the comparative details in particular on France; in the case of measures in the interests of public safety or public health the authority may proceed without hearing or informing the party concerned: C.E. of February 20, 1953, Dame Cozic-Savoure, Recueil Lebon, p. 86; C.E. of April 25, 1958, Société Laboratoires Geigy, Recueil Lebon, p. 236; for the Federal Republic of Germany a reference to §28(2) no. 1 VwVfG will suffice.

[34] This possibility results in the case of staff disciplinary measures from Article 88 of the Staff Regulations (see above, footnote 3) according to which interim measures may be adopted "forthwith." It is apparent from a comparison with Article 87, in which in contrast to Article 88 the right to a hearing is specifically mentioned, that such interim measures may be adopted without a hearing. The most recent case (De Compte) was clearly considerably less grave, although the official who was under suspicion was in the meantime moved to a different position; before the final measures could be adopted, however, he had to be given a hearing, cf. Case 141/84 H. de Compte v. Parliament [1985] E.C.R. 1951 at 1966, paras. 16 et seq.

[35] See above footnote 1.

[36] cf. on the importance of maintaining a Community which is capable of functioning, a notion which may lend itself in individual cases to a limitation of rights of the defence: H. P. Ipsen, "Das Verhältnis des Rechts der Europäischen Gemeinschaft zum nationalen Recht (Bensheim-Referat)," in Aktuelle Fragen des europäischen Gemeinschaftsrechts, Stuttgart 1965, p. 1 at 17 et seq.; H. P. Ipsen, Europäisches Gemeinschaftsrecht, Tübingen 1972, Ch. 10/40 et seq.; G. Nicolaysen, Europäisches Gemeinschaftsrecht, Stuttgart etc. 1979, p. 12, p. 64; A. Bredimas, Methods of interpretation and Community law, Amsterdam etc. 1978, pp. 70 et seq.; H. Kutscher, "Methods of Interpretation as seen by a judge at the Court of Justice," in Court of Justice of the European Communities (ed.), Judicial and Academic Conference, Luxembourg 1976, I, pp. 44 et seq.; P. Pescatore, "Les objectifs de la Communauté Européenne comme principes d'interprétation dans la

commencement of proceedings and the granting of a hearing are objectively impossible,[37] such as, for example, where the person concerned cannot be reached or where he or she knowingly frustrates attempted communications from the Commission.

In the field of economic law, there is a possibility of the procedure being initiated by an announcement in the Official Journal, C Series, thus achieving the effect of notifying this to persons whose residence is unknown.[38] The latter possibility is also offered in cases in which it is uncertain or unknown whether there are further persons concerned by the proceedings who should be informed of them. Since such cases are quite possible in the field of anti-dumping law, an announcement of the commencement of the proceedings in the Official Journal is expressly provided for.[39]

In summary, therefore, this group of cases, on which there have not so far been any decisions, is only of minor importance. However, they should be recognised. The justification for such an exception flows directly from the Roman law principle: "Impossibilium nulla obligatio est."[40]

(f) The petition of the person concerned

One further exception applies where the administrative procedure rests upon a petition by the party concerned.[41] Since he knows of the procedure, it would be pure formalism to inform him of it. However, this applies only in so far as the Commission wishes to decide on the basis of

---

jurisprudence de la Court de Justice," in *Miscellanea Ganshof van der Meersch* 1974, Vol. II, pp. 325 *et seq.*; R. Ormand, "L'utilisation particulière de la méthode d'interprétation des traités selon leur 'effet utile' par la Cour de Justice des Communautés Européennes," RtDE 1976, p. 624 at pp. 626, 628, *passim*; C. Hamson, "Methods of Interpretation: A critical assessment of the results," in *Judicial and Academic Conference, op. cit.*, Luxembourg 1976, II pp. 1 *et seq.* is more doubtful.

[37] *cf.* for instance Advocate-General Warner's reference to the "Commentaries" to the Resolution No. (77)31 of the Council of Europe, referred to earlier where, at point 18, sentence 3, the impossibility of a hearing is expressly cited as an exception; Advocate-General Warner, Case 113/77 *NTN Toyo Bearing* v. *Council* [1979] E.C.R. 1185 at 1262; *cf.* also the reprint in Warner, *op. cit.*, footnote 10, p. 1.17.

[38] *cf.* Article 2(2) of Regulation 99/63 of July 25, 1963, O.J. Sp.Ed. 1963–64, 47, *cf.* above, footnote 6.

[39] Article 7(1) letter (a) of Regulation 2176/84 and Decision No. 2177/84/ECSC; *cf.* above, footnote 1.

[40] Celsus, D.50.17.185.

[41] See thus J.-P. Warner, "Due process in administrative procedure," FIDE 1978, p. 1.7.

facts which the person concerned himself has brought forward. If it departs from these and comes to a conclusion which is unfavourable to the petitioner, then the duty to hear the person with regard to this change will revive.

5. The Content of the Rights of the Defence at the Different Phases of the Procedure

(a) *The opening of the procedure*

The principle of the guarantee of a hearing requires in principle that the person concerned should be informed of the commencement of the proceedings, since without such information he or she cannot submit observations on the objections. This principal is as uncontroversial in European law[42] as in the national legal orders.[43]

Problems occur with regard to the question of when this communication must be made. Some authors suggest that the person concerned is to be informed at as early a stage as possible on the commencement of the proceedings, in order that he may be integrated as effectively as possible into the work of investigating the case.[44] On the other hand, others emphasise that the Commission must first become clear about its own aims and the basis for its actions and this clarity is to be acquired only through the most undisturbed preliminary inquiry which can be achieved.[45]

In the practice of economic law, the formal initiation of the procedure generally occurs only through a communication to the person concerned on the conclusion of comprehensive preliminary investigations.[46] In competition law this notification often coincides with the communication of

---

[42] C.-D. Ehlermann, D. Oldekop, "Due process in administrative procedure," FIDE 1978, p. 11.6; J. Sedemund, "Due process in administrative procedure," Reprint, p. 9.11; L. Goffin, "La jurisprudence de la Cour de justice sur les droits de la défense," CDE 1980, p. 127 at 128; P. J. Kuyper, T.P.J.N. van Rijn, *op. cit.*, footnote 24, p. 12.

[43] *cf.* General Report by J.-P. Warner, *op. cit.*, footnote 41, p. 1.7, as well as E.II (comparative section).

[44] J. Sedemund, *op. cit.*, footnote 42, p. 11.

[45] Similarly C.-D. Ehlermann, D. Oldekop, *op. cit.*, footnote 42, p. 11.3, who however consider exceptions to be conceivable, *cf.* also F. Graupner, "Commission decision-making on competition questions," (1973) 10 C.M.L.Rev. 291 and 298; J. Sedemund, *op. cit.*, footnote 42, p. 10, takes a different view.

[46] L. Goffin, *op. cit.*, footnote 42, p. 128; J. Sedemund, *op. cit.*, footnote 42, p. 9.

the statement of objections.[47] The Court of Justice,[48] following its Advocate-General[49] has held that this procedure is lawful:

"Neither the provisions in force nor the general principles of law require notice of the decision to initiate the procedure to establish an infringement to be given prior to notification of the objections adopted against the interested parties in the context of such proceedings.

It is the notice of objections alone and not the decision to commence proceedings which is the measure stating the final attitude of the Commission concerning undertakings against which proceedings for infringement of the rules on competition have been commenced.

Accordingly, the fact that the Commission did not separate, chronologically and physically, notification of the above decision from the notice of objections cannot affect the rights of defence."[50]

A procedural separation between the two acts on the part of the administration may be desirable from the point of view of the person concerned and could also offer an advantage for the Commission in so far as it might have at its disposal a more complete factual picture if the person concerned were possibly heard at an earlier stage.[51]

However, there seem to be no doubts of a legal nature in principle in acknowledging that the Commission has the right to decide on the formal commencement of proceedings only once the preliminary investigations are complete. In anti-dumping law this procedure is in fact expressly provided for even though here even the preliminary investigations are determined by the law. In competition law, the fact that it is possible to determine in a particularly comprehensive manner what the object of the administrative procedure will be speaks in favour of a combination of the

---

[47] L. Goffin, *op. cit.*, footnote 42; P. J. Kuyper, T.P.J.N. van Rijn, *op. cit.*, footnote 24, p. 12.
[48] Case 57/69 *ACNA SpA* v. *Commission* [1972] E.C.R. 933 at 947, paras. 10 to 13.
[49] *Ibid.*, at 697.
[50] In the French version of the judgment the phrase used is "droits de la défense" (*op. cit.*, para. 12); the apparent restriction in the German version to the right to a hearing in the narrower sense rests only upon the translation.
[51] J. Sedemund, *op. cit.*, footnote 42, p. 4. On the importance of a comprehensive fact-finding process see also J. Davidow, "EEC fact-finding procedures in competition cases," (1977) 14 C.M.L.Rev. 175 *et seq.*

commencement of proceedings and the communication of the statement of objections.[52]

This point is justified not only in competition proceedings, but also in anti-dumping law, since here the complexity of the proceedings is so great that it is only after undisturbed preliminary work that the main proceedings can be implemented in a structured manner. In this field even preliminary investigations are expressly provided for.[53] Worthy of special mention in this context are administrative acts which are aimed at the collection of evidence and fact-finding. The problems which these raise have already been considered above.

The best known examples are investigation decisions under Article 14(3) and (4) of Regulation 17 and the decision requiring information under Article 11(5) of Regulation 17.

These measures do indeed represent an interference in the rights of the person concerned, but these administrative acts give rise to rights on the part of persons concerned to a hearing only within the limit[54] highlighted above.[55]

It is only where such procedural measures are intended to bring about definitive states of affairs (e.g. the communication of confidential information to third parties) that the Commission is obliged at this stage of the procedure to hear the party concerned.[56] Quite rightly, reference is made to the comparable situation in many Member States.[57]

The formal commencement of an administrative procedure has as its most important legal consequence the fact that the parties, or other persons concerned, must be heard.[58] In an individual case the formal commencement of proceedings also has further legal effects. For

---

[52] The importance of this information for the effective exercise of the right to a hearing cannot be underlined too heavily. *cf.* C.-D. Ehlermann, D. Oldekop, *op. cit.*, footnote 42, p. 11.6.

[53] *cf.* A. Weber, "Das Verwaltungsverfahren im Antidumpingrecht der EG," EuR 1985, p. 1 at 12.

[54] The leading case is Case 136/79 *National Panasonic* v. *Commission* [1980] E.C.R. 2033 at 2055; see also A. Gleiss, M. Hirsch, *op. cit.*, footnote 24, Regulation 17, Article 14, note 4 (there described as being the general view).

[55] Since a request for information by decision under Article 11(5) of Regulation 17 necessarily must be preceded by an informal request for information, the possibility of being heard is thus indirectly provided: *cf.* A. Gleiss, M. Hirsch, *op. cit.*, footnote 24, Regulation 17, Article 11, note 24.

[56] Case 53/85 *AKZO Chemie* v. *Commission* [1986] E.C.R. 1965 at 1992, para. 29.

[57] *cf.* the comparative law section above; also P. J. Kuyper, T.P.J.N. van Rijn, "Procedural guarantees and investigatory methods in European Law, with special reference to competition," (1983) 2 YEL 1 at 12.

[58] C.-D. Ehlermann, D. Oldekop, *op. cit.*, footnote 42 at p. 11.6.

example, one should refer to Article 9(3) of Regulation 17, according to which the commencement of competition proceedings under Community law excludes the competence of the national authorities.[59]

(b) *Explanation about the content of the objections (communication of the statement of objections)*

Rights of the defence and the right to be heard can properly be protected only where the person concerned has sufficient information about the objections made against him, or, to put it more generally, when he is sufficiently informed about the material object of the procedure.[60]

Advocate-General Warner[61] has expressed the necessary link between sufficient information and adequate legal defence in the following terms:

> "I do not think that the applicant in the present case was given such an opportunity (to defend his interests), because he was never told the real reason why it was proposed that he should retire.
>
> In the oft-quoted words of Lord Morris of Borth-y-Gest (Current Legal Problems 1973, p.11) 'If someone has a right to be heard, he must be entitled to know what he needs to be heard about'."

On the other hand, the attempts of the Court of Justice not to overstretch the duties to provide information by placing too great a burden upon them are clearly apparent. Thus the Court has held[62] that in competition law a succinct statement of the essential objections will suffice:

> "Article 19(1) of Regulation 17 obliges the Commission, before taking a decision in connection with fines, to give the persons concerned the opportunity of putting forward their point of view with

---

[59] *cf.* on this J. Temple Lang, "The procedure of the Commission in competition cases," (1977) 14 C.M.L.Rev. 155 at 156 (with further references).

[60] J. Sedemund, *op. cit.*, footnote 42, p. 9–11; L. Goffin, *op. cit.*, footnote 42, p. 128; P. J. Kuyper, T.P.J.N. van Rijn, *op. cit.*, footnote 57, p. 12; C.-D. Ehlermann, D. Oldekop, *op. cit.*, footnote 42, p. 11.6.

[61] Advocate-General Warner in Case 34/77 *Oslizlok* v. *Commission* [1978] E.C.R. 1099 at 1124; with reference to Case 19/70 *Almini* v. *Commission* [1971] E.C.R. 623 at 630; in the first-mentioned case the Court of Justice did not, as proposed by the Advocate-General, annul the decision on account of such a defect, because in its view the notification was in fact sufficient, [1978] E.C.R. 1114, para. 25.

[62] Case 45/69 *Boehringer* v. *Commission* [1970] E.C.R. 769 at 799, para. 9; also Case 85/76 *Hoffmann-La Roche* v. *Commission* [1979] E.C.R. 461 at 512, para. 10.

regard to the complaints made against them. (. . .) The notice of complaints fulfils this requirement since it sets forth clearly, albeit succinctly, the essential facts on which the Commission relies. The requirement imposed on the Commission by Article 19 is met when in the course of the administrative procedure it supplies the details necessary to the defence."

In that context it is not necessary for the person concerned to be taken through every detail of the consequences of his actions. In particular the size of the fine which may be imposed need not be indicated in advance in the case of a competition infringement[63]:

"In this regard it need only be recalled, that to give indications as regards the level of fines envisaged, before the undertaking has been invited to submit its observations on the allegations against it, would be to anticipate the Commission's decision and would thus be inappropriate.

In the statement of its objections of 5 March 1980 the Commission expressly indicated that it intended to fine Michelin NV an amount to be fixed by taking into account the duration and gravity of the infringement which it regarded as serious. In doing so the Commission gave Michelin NV the opportunity to defend itself not only against the finding of an infringement but also against the imposition of a fine."

On the other hand, the boundaries beyond which conciseness in the communication of objections may not go are already set out more precisely in Article 4 of Regulation 99/63, as well as in the case law where this provision does not apply. Matters which are not contained in the statement of the objections may not be dealt with by the Commission in its final decision.[64] Furthermore, the person concerned may even assume that documents which are known to the Commission but are not cited in the statement of objections are without relevance for the procedure[65]:

"As regards the documents mentioned only in the decision (letter of 29 June 1976 from TFR's Münster sales office; ATF memorandum of

---

[63] Case 322/81 *Michelin* v. *Commission* [1983] E.C.R. 3461 at 3500, para. 19; with reference to Cases 100–103/80 *Musique Diffusion Française etc.* v. *Commission* [1983] E.C.R. 1825.
[64] Case 45/69 *Boehringer* v. *Commission* [1970] E.C.R. 769 at 799, para. 9; Case 107/82 *AEG* v. *Commission* [1983] E.C.R. 3151 at 3192.
[65] Case 107/82 *AEG* v. *Commission* [1983] E.C.R. 3151 at 3193, para. 26.

7 July 1977; ATF memorandum of 20 October 1978), the Commission contends that these were documents with which the applicant was already familiar as they came from its own offices and that they were used only to confirm objections already raised.

In this connection, it must be observed that the important point is not the documents as such but the conclusions which the Commission has drawn from them. Since these documents were not mentioned in the statement of objects, AEG was entitled to take the view that they were of no importance for the purposes of the case. By not informing the applicant that these documents would be used in the decision, the Commission prevented AEG from putting forward at the appropriate time its view of the probative value of such documents. It follows that these documents cannot be regarded as admissible evidence for the purposes of this case."

A precondition for a sufficient communication on the part of the authority is that the meaning and context of the allegations is made clear to the persons concerned. It does not suffice if he can only guess the intention of the Commission. Advocate-General Warner has illustrated this as follows in an anti-dumping case[66]:

"But it renders idle, if I may say so, such comments on the part of the Commission as that those who were concerned on behalf of the Big Four, and of their subsidiaries and associates, must have been able to infer, from the Commission's enquiries as to their prices, as to their costs, as to their profits and losses, and so forth, what it was that the Commission regarded as relevant. There again, if I am right about the law, it was not enough for the Commission to put those persons in a position to indulge in conjecture. The Commission's duty was to tell them, as clearly and as fully as the circumstances permitted, what its case against them was.

That being so I need not take up much time in discussing the various examples that were given to us on behalf of the Applicants of matters that were relied upon by the Commission in reaching its findings but on which they were afforded no opportunity of making observations to the Commission."

---

[66] Advocate-General Warner, in Case 113/77 *NTN Toyo Bearing Co.* v. *Council* [1979] E.C.R. 1185 at 1264; these arguments apply to the legal situation before the coming into force of Regulation 3017/79 and Regulation 2176/84.

It is important, however, that the Commission is basically in the position to be able to articulate further or make more precise the statement of objections during the course of the procedure. Advocate-General Reischl has summarised the case law of the Court on this point as follows[67].

> "In that connection the applicant has primarily objected that the *Mammoth* case was not contained in the statement of objections but was mentioned for the first time in the contested decision, which presumably must be construed as meaning that that case must be left out of account owing to the infringement of the right to be heard in the administrative procedure. ... As far as the first part of those arguments is concerned it must be admitted that in a decision under Article 85 only the infringements mentioned in a statement of objections may be set out and that if new facts are being alleged against an undertaking the statement of objections must be supplemented so that the undertaking concerned has the opportunity of making its views known (judgments in Cases 41/69 and 51/69). It is however also the case that a decision may set out further evidence in support of facts already alleged (judgment of Case 54/69) and that a supplementary statement of objections is called for, *inter alia*, only if the proof of disputed infringements is to be based on considerably altered facts (judgment in Case 51/69)."

In that case[68] the Court of Justice was of the view that this case law was satisfied only where the person concerned was made aware that a particular document was to be used against him, thus imposing even stricter requirements than did the Advocate-General.[69]

(c) *Access to files*

(aa) *The duty to communicate individual documents*

The Court of Justice has extended the relatively loose requirements as

---

[67] Case 107/82 *AEG* v. *Commission* [1983] E.C.R. 3226 at 3237 with further references.
[68] Case 107/82 *AEG* v. *Commission* [1983] E.C.R. 3151 at 3193; *cf.* the quotation above at footnote 65.
[69] Advocate-General Reischl in *AEG* [1983] E.C.R. 3238: "Furthermore it should not be overlooked that the Commission is relying on a document which was copied at ATF's premises with the latter's knowledge; for the applicant it is therefore not an unknown

regards the communication of the statement of objections (*i.e.* the object of the procedure) by imposing an obligation on the administration, if it is so requested, to make available to the person concerned further details, in particular the text of certain documents,[70] especially when the Commission intends to refer to these:

> "The applicant complains that during the administrative procedure the defendant did not inform it of all the elements of fact relied on in support of the conclusions contained in the notice of objections. It is argued that this failure to provide information, despite the repeated requests of the applicant, prevented it from defending itself during the course of the administrative procedure.
>
> During that procedure, the undertakings concerned must be informed of the essential elements of fact on which the Commission bases its objections against them.
>
> However, it is not necessary for the contents of the file to be made available in their entirety. The Commission's notice of objections, sent to the applicant by letter of 11 December 1967, sets out all the facts necessary for determining the objections taken into consideration."

A general right to inspect files exists only in specific areas of administrative law. Community officials have the express right to inspect their own personal files. Article 26(6) of the Staff Regulations[71] provides:

> "An official shall have the right, even after leaving the service, to acquaint himself with all the documents in his file."

This right extends not only to the official but also to the person whom he chooses to assist him in his defence; the Court[72] has held that this is an essential rule of a proper procedure:

---

document but a document which it ought to have expected might be used. There has therefore been no infringement of the applicant's right to be heard in spite of the absence of any specific notification concerning the *Mammouth* case. . ."

[70] Case 51/69 *Bayer* v. *Commission* [1972] E.C.R. 745 at 771, para. 7; *cf.* also Cases 100–103/80 *Musique Diffusion Française etc.* v. *Commission* [1983] E.C.R. 1825 at 1881, para. 14: "provided that, in the course of the administrative procedure, it has made available to the undertakings all the information necessary for their defence."

[71] Staff Regulation (Regulations 31/61 and 11/61, J.O. 1962, 45/1385; O.J. Sp.Ed. 1958–1962, 135; *Handbuch des Europäischen Rechts* I A 67/3, *cf.* footnote 3.

[72] Case 115/80 *Demont* v. *Commission* [1981] E.C.R. 3147 at 3157, paras. 10 *et seq.*; *cf.* also Case 206/81 *Alvarez* v. *European Parliament* [1982] E.C.R. 3369 at 3374; less clear is Case

"The second paragraph of Article 4 of Annex IX to the Staff Regulations, which provides that 'when the official appears before the Disciplinary Board he shall have the right to submit observations in writing or orally, to call witnesses and to be assisted in his defence by a person of his own choice', appearing in the specific context of Annex IX to the Staff Regulations, that provision merely concerns the matters governed by that annex and is based on the fundamental requirement that respect for the rights of the defence, including the right of the official concerned to be assisted by counsel, is all the more important when the disciplinary proceedings to which he is subject are likely to result in the imposition of particularly severe disciplinary measures.

For those reasons it must be stated that the refusal of the Commission to allow the applicant's counsel access to the disciplinary file in the course of the proceedings which resulted in the contested disciplinary measure is without any legal foundation either in the letter or in the spirit of the provisions of the Staff Regulations relating to disciplinary matters, but rather constitutes a breach of a fundamental legal principle which the Court is bound to uphold within the Community legal order."

As regards an expulsion order against an EEC national by the authorities of a Member State, Article 9 of Directive 64/221[73] provides for the protection of the rights of the defence, which Advocate-General Warner[74] understood as meaning that the person concerned must be allowed to inspect administrative documents:

"I respectfully agree with the view expressed by Mr. Advocate-General Capotorti in the opinion that he delivered recently in Case 98/79[75] that, in a case where Article 9 applies, (...) the person concerned must be supplied with all the material on which the administrative authority may found its decision, so that he may at least make representations thereon to the independent body. The reference in Article 9(1) to 'rights of the defence' clearly imports that

---

26/63 *Pistoj* v. *Commission* [1964] E.C.R. 341 at 354; *cf.* also J.-P. Warner, "Due Process in administrative procedure," FIDE 1978, p. 1.8.

[73] Directive 64/221 of February 25, 1964, J.O. 1964, 850; O.J. Sp.Ed. 1963–1964, 117.

[74] Advocate-General Warner, in Case 131/79 *R.* v. *Secretary of State for Home Affairs, ex p. Santillo* [1980] E.C.R. 1585 at 1612.

[75] Author's note: Advocate-General Capotorti, in Case 98/79 *Pecastaing* v. *Belgium* [1980] E.C.R. 691 at 718 *et seq.*

the person concerned should have the protection of what English-speaking lawyers generally call 'the rules of natural justice' and French-speaking lawyers call 'les droits de la défense'. It is contrary to those rules to withhold from a person, so that he cannot comment on it, material that is to be taken into account in reaching a decision affecting him."

Although there is no general right of access to files in Community law, in practice the Commission facilitates the inspection of all documents which the person concerned actually indicates, in so far as these are not internal or confidential documents.[76]

In so doing it is acting in accordance with a legal duty. The Commission must present the actual documents which originate from outside the authority and which it wishes to rely upon at the request of the person concerned, so that the latter may make his views known[77]:

> "In this regard it should be recalled that the necessity to have regard to the rights of the defence is a fundamental principle of Community law which the Commission must observe in administrative procedures which may lead to the imposition of penalties under the rules of competition laid down in the Treaty. Its observance requires *inter alia* that the undertaking concerned must have been enabled to express its views effectively on the documents used by the Commission to support its allegation of an infringement."

It accords with the general approach of the Court of Justice not to make this consideration the basis of a right of access to files in the sense of a right to the production of the entire bundle.[78]

In the case of disciplinary proceedings, the Advocates-General have tended to suggest an extension of this right so that certain adverse

[76] J.-P. Warner, "Due process in administrative procedure," FIDE 1978, p. 1.8; C.-D. Ehlermann, D. Oldekop, "Due process in administrative procedure," FIDE 1978, p. 11.10; P. J. Kuyper, T.P.J.N. van Rijn, *op. cit.*, footnote 57, p. 19 with further references; *cf.* also I. v. Bael, "Ten years of EEC anti-dumping enforcement," (1979) 13 Journal of World Trade Law, 395 at 400; in so far as ECSC (competition and market regulation) law contains fewer wide-ranging rights for parties, the Commission actually grants the same rights as in the EEC field, *cf.* C.-D. Ehlermann, D. Oldekop, *op. cit.*, p. 11.3.

[77] Case 322/81 *Michelin* v. *Commission* [1983] E.C.R. 3461 at 3498, para. 7; *cf.* also C. Canenbley, "Verfahrensregeln der Kommission der EG," in *Studienvereinigung Kartellrecht e.V.* XI Internationales EG-Kartellrechtsforum, Munich 1986, p. 74 at 88.

[78] Cases 43 and 63/82 *VBVB and VBBB* v. *Commission* [1984] E.C.R. 19 at 59, paras. 23 *et seq.*; so also Case 51/69 *Bayer* v. *Commission* [1972] E.C.R. 745 at 769, para. 7; similarly Advocate-General VerLoren van Themaat, in *VBVB and VBBB* [1984] E.C.R. 99; *cf.* also Cases 56 and 58/64 *Consten and Grundig* v. *Commission* [1966] E.C.R. 299 at 338; also of interest are Joined Cases 100–103/80 *Musique Diffusion Française* v. *Commission* [1983] E.C.R. 1825 at 1881, para. 14; also Case 209/78 etc., *Van Landewyck et al.* v.

documents should in any case be produced by the authority on its own initiative[79]:

"On the other hand it is certainly possible to infer, from certain judgments of the Court, that the contents of a document need only be communicated if the document is of such a nature as to have a decisive influence on the final decision (judgment of 3 February 1971, *Rittweger* v. *Commission*[1971] ECR 7). I do not think it is possible to extend that principle to apply to disciplinary matters and the failure to bring the statements, especially seeing that they were unfavourable, to the knowledge of the applicant constitutes an infringement of an essential procedural requirement."

The Commission need not accede to a request by the person concerned to inspect the whole bundle of files so long as it does not interfere with the rights of the defence with regard to individual documents.[80]

Although the right to a hearing, and where appropriate access to files, is accorded in the first instance to the person concerned, the competitor, in particular where he has initiated the proceedings, may also have a legitimate interest in following up the treatment of his complaint, including within limits a right to challenge the unjustified abandonment of the proceedings.[81]

Commission [1980] E.C.R. 3125 at 3237, para. 39; *cf.* also Advocate-General Gand in Case 41/69 *ACF Chemiefarma* v. *Commission* [1970] E.C.R. 661 at 770; "The Court has already had to apply Article 19 of Regulation 17 in the *Grundig* case and you ruled that the proceedings before the Commission are *administrative* proceedings, which implies that the undertakings concerned must be enabled to submit their observations on the complaints which the Commission considers that it must make with regard to them, that to this end they must be informed of the facts upon which the complaints of the Commission are based, although it is not necessary that the entire contents of the file should be communicated to them." The right of access to the whole bundle of files is however demanded by the literature: *cf.* L. Goffin, "La jurisprudence de la Cour de justice sur les droits de la défense," CDE 1980, p. 127 at 132 (with further references); J. Sedemund, "Allgemeine Prinzipien des Verwaltungsverfahrensrechts," in J. Schwarze (ed.), *Europäisches Verwaltungsrecht im Werden*, Baden-Baden 1982, p. 45 at 48 *et seq.* (with further references); *ibid.*, "Due process," *op. cit.*, footnote 42, pp. 15 *et seq.* I. van Bael recognises in particular the limitations placed by the confidentiality of documents originating from third parties, *op. cit.*, footnote 76, p. 400.

[79] Advocate-General Rozès in Case 791/79 *Demont* v. *Commission* [1981] E.C.R. 3105 at 3128.

[80] Case 209/78 etc., *Van Landewyck et al.* v. *Commission* [1980] E.C.R. 3125 at 3237, paras. 37 *et seq.*; *cf.* also Advocate-General Gand, in Case 41/69 *ACF Chemiefarma* v. *Commission* [1970] E.C.R. 661 at 770; *cf.* footnote 78.

[81] *cf.* Case 264/82 *Timex* v. *Council and Commission* [1985] E.C.R. 849; Case 191/82 *Fediol* v. *Commission* [1983] E.C.R. 2913 at 2932–36; on the position of the petitioner *cf.* also

In the field of anti-dumping law this is expressly provided for in Article 7(4) of Regulation 2176/84. Here the administrative procedure is organised in the form of contentious proceedings, that is the "complainant" and "party accused" play a role which is at least similar to that of the parties in court proceedings.[82]

Competition proceedings are otherwise organised. Advocate-General Lenz expressed this as follows[83]:

> "There is no basis whatever in Regulation No.17 for a comparable right of access to documents. A complainant under Article 3(2)(b) of Regulation No.17 is not legally entitled to be heard under Article 19 of that regulation. Like other third parties, he must, according to Article 19(2), be able to show a sufficient interest in order to be heard. He will generally be able to do so if he has been affected by the conduct of the undertaking against which competition proceedings have been initiated. Under Regulation No.17, however, he is not automatically entitled to take part in the proceedings but must make an application to do so."

Any right of an individual to receive or inspect a document can be exercised on his behalf by a lawyer.[84]

Clearly building on the specific privileges of lawyers under Anglo-American law, the Commission has even made information available to lawyers which it would not have been able to communicate to the person concerned (business secrets of third parties), with the condition, of course, that it must not be forwarded to the client.

Advocate-General Lenz did not state in his Opinion in the *AKZO-Chemie* case whether he believed such a procedure, which the Commission used in that case, to be lawful.[85]

---

the Order of January 17, 1980 in Case 792/79R *Camera Care* v. *Commission* [1980] E.C.R. 119 at 127 *et seq.*; the statement of the Commission in its Thirteenth Report on Competition Policy, note 74b, at 63 is doubtful in so far as it intends to limit the right of access to files of undertakings which it alleges to have committed an infringement of Articles 85 and 86 EEC.

[82] Advocate-General Lenz, in Case 53/85 *AKZO Chemie* v. *Commission* [1986] E.C.R. 1965 at 1979.

[83] *Ibid.*

[84] Case 115/80 *Demont* v. *Commission* [1981] E.C.R. 3147 at 3157, paras. 10 *et seq.*; *cf.* also J.-P. Warner, *op. cit.*, footnote 76, p. 1.8.

[85] Advocate-General Lenz in *AKZO*; the fact that such privileges are at any rate conceivable is shown by Case 155/79 *A.M. & S. Europe* v. *Commission* [1982] E.C.R. 1575 at 1610 *et seq.*, paras. 18–27, which removed correspondence with lawyers from the investigatory powers of the Commission (legal privilege).

1346

(bb) Limits and exceptions

(1) General limits

The right to inspect certain files is not guaranteed without limits. Reference should be made not just to confidential documents, which will be discussed below, but also to internal memoranda or drafts of decisions of the administration,[86] which under national law are often excluded from the right of access of private individuals. In addition, military and other State secrets must not be revealed through this procedure.[87]

With the exception of disciplinary matters, where the principle of unlimited access to disciplinary and personal files is secured and where the law requires such files always to be kept complete, the exclusion of internal documents and drafts of decisions from inspection is permissible.[88]

In the field of anti-dumping law internal documents (including those of the Member States) are expressly exempted from inspection under Article 7(4)(a) of Regulation 2176/84.[89] Although in competition law there is no parallel rule, here also the practice of the Commission[90] of excluding internal documents from inspection is justified by reference to similar approaches in the Member States.[91] In particular, the Commission considers the reports of the Inspectors on the results of investigations of undertakings to be in part confidential.[92]

There is a controversy with regard to documents of the so-called Advisory Committee on Restrictive Practices,[93] composed of representatives of the Member States, which must give an opinion on certain decisions of the Commission, although such opinions do not in any way

---

[86] cf. J.-P. Warner, op. cit., footnote 76, p. 1.8; P. J. Kuyper, T.P.J.N. van Rijn, "Procedural guarantees and investigatory methods in European Law, with special reference to competition," (1983) 2 YEL 1 at 19.

[87] cf. J.-P. Warner, op. cit., footnote 76, p. 1.8.

[88] J.-P. Warner, op. cit., footnote 76, p. 1.8; P. J. Kuyper, T.P.J.N. van Rijn, op. cit., footnote 86, p. 19.

[89] Regulation 2176/84 of July 23, 1984, O.J. 1984, L201/1; Decision 2177/84/ECSC of July 27, 1984, O.J. 1984 L201/17.

[90] cf. the Twelfth Report on Competition Policy (1982), para. 35, p. 40; Thirteenth Report on Competition Policy (1983) para. 74b, p. 65; Fourteenth Report on Competition Policy (1984), para. 46, p. 54.

[91] cf. on this also J.-P. Warner, op. cit., footnote 76, p. 1.8.

[92] cf. on this the Thirteenth Report, op. cit., footnote 90, note 74b, at 63.

[93] cf. Article 10 of Regulation 17; also on the importance of this provision see the Thirteenth Report on Competition Policy (1983), note 79.

bind the latter. This opinion is regarded by the Commission as an internal matter, so that the person concerned cannot insist on knowing its content, although in practice it is of considerable importance for the later decision of the Commission. The withholding of these documents by the Commission has therefore been heavily criticised from a number of quarters.[94]

Finally, the Court of Justice has also recognised in staff cases that documents containing information which may harm the person concerned (*e.g.* negative medical reports) need not be communicated, or need be made available only once certain precautions have been taken.[95]

(2) Confidential documents

The most important limitation placed upon the Commission when it is communicating the object of the proceedings are the business secrets of third parties, in particular of those who have given information to the Commission.

The Court of Justice and the Advocates-General have made various references to this matter. Thus Advocate-General Warner has stated[96].

> "I have no doubt, and DCL does not dispute, that the Commission has power, indeed is under a duty, to excise from such a complaint passages revealing the complainant's business secrets. There are, in my opinion, probably also cases where the Commission must avoid disclosing the complainant's identity—which may even necessitate suppressing the complaint altogether—in order to safeguard the complainant from possible reprisals."

---

[94] See on this J. Mégret *et al.*, *Le droit de la CEE*, Vol. 4, Brussels 1972, Article 85–90, note 68, p. 147; J. Sedemund, *op. cit.*, footnote 78, p. 54; J. Mertens de Wilmars, in *Europees Kartelrecht* Post doctorale Leergang 1967/68 (unpublished), Antwerp etc. 1969, p. 251 (with further references).

[95] Case 75/77 *Mollet* v. *Commission* [1978] E.C.R. 897 at 907, paras. 15 *et seq.*, Advocate-General Mayras, [1978] E.C.R. 913; Case 121/76 *Moli* v. *Commission* [1977] E.C.R. 1971 at 1978, paras. 14 *et seq.*; Advocate-General Mayras at p. 1982; *cf.* also J.-P. Warner, *op. cit.*, footnote 72, p. 1.8.

[96] Advocate-General Warner, in Case 30/78 *Distillers Co.* v. *Commission* [1980] E.C.R. 2229 at 2295; similarly Advocate-General Mayras, in Case 40/73 *Suiker Unie etc.* v. *Commission (Sugar Cartel)* [1975] E.C.R. 1663 at 2084.

The Court of Justice too has clearly highlighted the duty which exists in certain circumstances to maintain secrecy and the consequences which result from this[97]:

> "Once the Commission had decided that the information obtained during the investigation was covered by the principle of the non-disclosure of business secrets, it was under the duty, by virtue of Article 20 of Regulation No. 17, not to disclose it to Michelin NV. Consequently it could not use that information to support its decision in this case if the refusal to disclose it reduced Michelin NV's opportunity to express its views on the accuracy or scope of, the information or on the conclusions drawn from it by the Commission."

Normative rules are the basis for this limitation. The most important of these is contained in Article 214 EEC[98] which provides as follows:

> "The members of the institutions of the Community, the members of committees, and the officials and other servants of the Community shall be required, even after their duties have ceased, not to disclose information of the kind covered by the obligation of professional secrecy, in particular information about undertakings, their business relations or their cost components."

However, beyond the scope of this general rule there exist a number of provisions which govern the Community's obligation of secrecy in the context of the direct administration of the law.[99]

---

[97] Case 322/81 *Michelin* v. *Commission* [1983] E.C.R. 3461 at 3499, para. 8; *cf.* also Case 107/82 *AEG* v. *Commission* [1983] E.C.R. 3151 at 3192, para. 24; Case 234/84 *Belgium* v. *Commission* [1986] E.C.R. 2263, para. 29.

[98] Similar, and in part more wide-ranging, are Articles 24–27, and 194 Euratom; also Article 47(2) ECSC.

[99] Further provisions are to be found in a variety of legal measures on the exchange and communication of information. *cf.* on this the references which go beyond the examples below, which are limited only to administrative law, in J. Amphoux, in H. Smit, P. Herzog, *The Law of the European Economic Community*, New York, 1976, Article 214.02, p. 6–66; also as regards the relations of the Member States *inter se*, Directive 77/780 of December 12, 1977, O.J. 1977, L322/30, on the coordination of laws, regulations and administrative provisions relating to the taking up and pursuit of the business of credit institutions provides for the protection of professional and official secrets. The Court has already had occasion to consider this provision: *cf.* Case 110/84 *Gemeinde Hillegom* v. *Hillenius* [1985] E.C.R. 3947.

Thus Article 20 of Regulation 17 provides[100]:

"(1) Information acquired as a result of the application of Arts. 11, 12, 13 and 14 shall be used only for the purpose of the relevant request or investigation.

(2) Without prejudice to the provisions of Arts. 19 and 21, the Commission and the competent authorities of the Member States, their officials and other servants shall not disclose information acquired by them as a result of the application of this Regulation and of the kind covered by the obligation of professional secrecy.

(3) The provisions of paragraphs 1 and 2 shall not prevent publication of general information or surveys which do not contain information relating to particular undertakings or associations of undertakings."

The reference contained in Article 20(2) to the right to a hearing provided for in Article 19 appears at first sight to be hardly meaningful and useful. The Court of Justice[101] has considered in more detail the relationship of these two provisions in a case in which the Commission had refused to disclose certain information on grounds of professional secrecy:

"This rule (Article 20(2)) must, as the express reference to Article 19 confirms, be reconciled with the right to be heard.

The said Article 20 by providing undertakings from whom information has been obtained with a guarantee that their interests, which are closely connected with observance of professional secrecy, are not jeopardized, enables the Commission to collect on the widest possible scale the requisite data for the fulfilment of the task conferred upon it by Articles 85 and 86 of the Treaty without the undertakings being able to prevent it from doing so, but it does not nevertheless allow it to use, to the detriment of the undertakings involved in a proceeding referred to in Regulation No. 17, facts, circumstances or documents which it cannot in its view disclose if such a refusal or disclosure adversely affects that undertaking's opportunity to make known effectively its views on the truth or

---

[100] O.J. Sp.Ed. 1959–62, p. 87; also Article 19(3) and Article 21(2) of Regulation 17, cf. also Article 2(2) second sentence of Regulation 99/63, J.O. 1963, 2268, O.J. Sp.Ed. 1963–1964, 47.
[101] Case 85/76 Hoffmann-La Roche v. Commission [1979] E.C.R. 471 at 512, para. 13, cf. also Case 53/85 AKZO v. Commission [1986] E.C.R. 1965 at 1991, paras. 26 et seq.

implications of those circumstances, on those documents or again on the conclusions drawn by the Commission from them."

The equivalent provision in anti-dumping law provides considerably more detail; Article 8 of Regulation 2176/84 states[102]:

"Confidentiality
(1) Information received in pursuance of this Regulation shall be used only for the purpose for which it was requested.
(2) (a) Neither the Council, nor the Commission, nor Member States, nor officials of any of these, shall reveal any information received in pursuance of this Regulation for which confidential treatment has been requested by its supplier, without specific permission from the supplier.
   (b) Each request for confidential information shall indicate why the information is confidential and shall be accompanied by a non-confidential summary of the information, or a statement of the reasons why the information is not susceptible of such summary.
(3) Information will ordinarily be considered to be confidential if its disclosure is likely to have a significantly adverse effect on the supplier or the source of such information.
(4) However, if it appears that a request for confidentiality is not warranted and if the supplier is either unwilling to make the information public or to authorise its disclosure in generalised or summary form, the information in question may be disregarded. The information may also be disregarded where such request is warranted and where the supplier is unwilling to submit a non-confidential summary, provided that the information is susceptible of such summary.
(5) This Article shall not preclude the disclosure of general information by the Community authorities and in particular the reasons on which decisions taken in pursuance of this Regulation are based, or disclosure of the evidence relied on by the Community authorities in so far as necessary to explain those reasons in court proceedings. Such disclosure must take into account the legitimate interest

[102] Article 8 of Decision No. 2177/84/ECSC is identical and both provisions build on Regulation 3017/79 of December 20, 1979, O.J. 1979, L339/1, which also contains a very similar provision in Article 8.

of the parties concerned that their business secrets shall not be divulged."

This provision becomes more understandable when one considers the position and interests of the participants: the Commission's informants generally have an interest in the "condemnation" of the persons concerned because they are generally in competition with them. If they consider their information so confidential that they do not wish their competitors to have access to it, then this information will be disregarded and the competitor will be able to continue with what may be dumping. The informant is in a conflict in this situation. In these circumstances one must accept that he will behave in a way which accords with his interests, and his decision must be regarded as binding.[103]

Under Article 214 EEC, not only the officials, but also the institutions themselves are under an obligation of secrecy.[104] Otherwise the obligation would provide no effective protection for the informants concerned. Furthermore, the confidential character must also be maintained where the information which the authority has obtained no longer falls within the jurisdiction of the Community.[105]

The Court of Justice has emphasised the significance of the obligation of secrecy in a recent case.[106] In the celebrated case of the former employee of Hoffmann-La Roche, Stanley Adams,[107] who gave important evidence to the Commission about anti-competitive conduct on the part of the Swiss undertaking with the request that it should be handled in confidence, this obligation of secrecy plays a decisive role. The Commission later confirmed to Hoffmann-La Roche the existence of certain papers, from which the latter could deduce the identity of the informant. Once this was uncovered, criminal proceedings were subsequently taken in Switzerland against Adams, who was sentenced to a year in prison.

---

[103] On the treatment of confidential information in anti-dumping law cf. also S. Riesenfeld, "The treatment of confidential information in anti-dumping cases," (1984) 21 C.M.L.Rev. 553 with comparative references to U.S. procedural law. On confidentiality in court proceedings cf. Case 236/81 Celanese Chemical & Co. v. Commission [1982] E.C.R. 1183 at 1186; as well as Case 155/79 A.M. & S. Europe v. Commission [1982] E.C.R. 1575 at 1613.
[104] cf. J. Amphoux, in H. Smit, P. Herzog, op. cit., footnote 99, Article 214.04, p. 6–67.
[105] cf. Case 31/59 Acciaieria di Brescia v. High Authority [1960] E.C.R. 71; cf. also J. Amphoux, op. cit., footnote 99, Article 214.05, p. 6–69.
[106] The question of when the requirement of secrecy of an undertaking is so great that the Commission may not by enforcement measures require the relevant documents is to be viewed separately from this problem. On the latter cf. above (fact-finding); also Case 155/79 A.M. & S. Europe v. Commission [1982] E.C.R. 1575 at 1612, para. 27.
[107] Case 145/83 Adams v. Commission [1985] E.C.R. 3539.

In this case the Court of Justice held as regards the general significance of the obligation of secrecy[108]:

"As regards the existence of a duty of confidentiality it must be pointed out that Article 214 of the EEC Treaty lays down an obligation, in particular for the members and servants of the institutions of the Community 'not to disclose information of the kind covered by the obligation of professional secrecy, in particular information about undertakings, their business relations or their cost components.' Although that provision primarily refers to information gathered from undertakings, the expression 'in particular' shows that the principle in question is a general one which applies also to information supplied by natural persons, if that information is 'of the kind' that is confidential. That is particularly so in the case of information supplied on a purely voluntary basis but accompanied by a request for confidentiality in order to protect the informant's anonymity. An institution which accepts such information is bound to comply with such a condition."

It can be seen that the obligation of secrecy extends well beyond pure business information. The Court of Justice based this conclusion on the text of Article 214 EEC ("in particular").

It is in principle irrelevant as regards the question of confidentiality how the information has reached the Commission, that is whether it was given voluntarily or on the basis of some legal duty, and whether it came directly from the "object of protection" or via third parties[109]; all that emerges from the *Stanley Adams* case on such matters is the fact that it was clear why in that case there was no doubt about the confidential nature of the information.

---

[108] Case 145/83 [1985] E.C.R. 3587, para. 34.
[109] A. Gleiss, M. Hirsch, *Kommentar zum EWG-Kartellrecht*, (3rd ed., Heidelberg 1978), Regulation 17, Article 20, para. 11; J. Amphoux, *op. cit.*, footnote 99, Article 214.05, p. 6–68.

Also confidential are those documents the publication of which could adversely affect the persons concerned,[110] although this need not necessarily mean financial disadvantage.[111] An important indicator that information is confidential is its express designation as confidential by the person from whom it originates.[112] However, the Commission has a right to check this. It must make a decision about the nature of the documents in question, where appropriate after hearing those who are relying upon the confidentiality, and in some circumstances even by means of a formal decision, that is, one which is reasoned within the meaning of Article 189(4) EEC.[113]

However, in the context of competition law, where it has a right to order a compulsory investigation, the Commission is obliged to examine particularly closely on its own initiative certain interests in secrecy. In contrast, in the field of anti-dumping law, in which the information is generally communicated voluntarily, it can orient itself instead according to the attitude of the informant.[114]

Not everything which the supplier so argues is in fact really confidential.[115] That applies in particular where the Commission has obtained the information through the exercise of its powers to carry out checks and inspections. On the other hand, information which the supplier does not actually so describe, may in fact be confidential, because, for instance, the need to preserve secrecy results from the nature of the case[116]:

"The Community institutions are bound by Article 214 of the EEC Treaty to respect the principle of confidential treatment of informa-

---

[110] As the legal definition in Article 8(3) of Regulation 2176/84, footnote 89, provides; *cf.* otherwise J. Amphoux, *op. cit.*, footnote 99, Article 214.05, p. 6–68 (with further references); F. Luchaire, "Le devoir d'information et ses limites," in Centro italiano di Studi giuridici (ed.), *Actes officiels du Congrès international d'Etudes sur la C.E.C.A.*, Milan (1957) 1958, Vol. IV, p. 195 at 203; J. Grunwald, in H. v.d. Groeben *et al.*, *Kommentar zum EWG-Vertrag*, (3rd ed., Baden-Baden 1983), Article 214, para. 16.

[111] J. Grunwald, *op. cit.*, footnote 110, Article 214, para. 16.

[112] Advocate-General Lenz, in Case 53/85 *AKZO Chemie* v. *Commission* [1986] E.C.R. 1965 at 1977 (with further references); A. Gleiss, M. Hirsch, *op. cit.*, footnote 109, Regulation 17, Article 20, para. 12.

[113] Case 53/85 *AKZO Chemie* v. *Commission* [1986] E.C.R. 1965 at 1992, para. 29. The most recent case law builds on this decision: Joined Cases 142 & 156/84 *BAT and Reynolds* v. *Commission* [1987] E.C.R. 4487, para. 21. See on this in more detail above III, 3: rights of the defence of third parties.

[114] See on this in detail Advocate-General Lenz in [1986] E.C.R. 1965.

[115] See on this A. Gleiss, M. Hirsch, *op. cit.*, footnote 109, Regulation 17, Article 20, para. 13; J. Grunwald, *op. cit.*, footnote 110, Article 214, paras. 16, 17.

[116] Case 268/84 *Timex* v. *Council and Commission* [1985] E.C.R. 849 at 870, para. 29.

tion about undertakings, particularly about undertakings in non-member countries which have expressed their readiness to co-operate with the Commission, even if no express request for such treatment is received under Article 8 of Regulation 3017/79 (to that extent identical to Regulation 2176/84)."

If, however, the supplier of the information has given it freely, then a "secret" in the true sense of the word does not (any longer) exist.[117] The same applies where the information is already available to the public in general,[118] for which purposes availability to specialists in the field will suffice.[119] Even so communication to the "public" is required, that is publication of the knowledge regardless of membership of certain organisations or associations. The Court of Justice has stated in this regard that[120]:

"Information in the nature of a trade secret given to a trade or professional association by its members and thus having lost its confidential nature *vis-à-vis* them does not lose it with regard to third parties. Where such an association forwards such information to the Commission in proceedings commenced under Regulation No. 17, the Commission cannot rely on the provisions of Articles 19 and 20 of that regulation to justify passing on the information to third parties who are making complaints. Article 19(2) gives the latter a right to be heard and not a right to receive confidential information."

In this context the question how far an undertaking can rely upon the secrecy of the information is important. In general this is not the case where the secret is "unlawful," in so far and to the extent that this is provable. Advocate-General Lenz has given detailed consideration to this matter[121]:

"It is true that in academic legal writing it is accepted that infringements of Articles 85 and 86 of the EEC Treaty of the kind which must

---

[117] J. Amphoux, *op. cit.*, footnote 99, Article 214.05, p. 6–69.
[118] *cf.* Advocate-General Lenz, in Case 53/85 *AKZO Chemie* v. *Commission* [1986] E.C.R. 1976 (*cf.* also para. 12 of the opinion).
[119] F. Luchaire, *op. cit.*, footnote 110, p. 203; similar is J. Amphoux, *op. cit.*, footnote 99, Article 214.05, p. 6–69.
[120] Case 209/78 *Van Landewyck* v. *Commission* [1980] E.C.R. 3125 at 3239, para. 46.
[121] Advocate-General Lenz in Case 53/85 *AKZO Chemie* v. *Commission* [1986] E.C.R. 1981, with reference to A. Gleiss, M. Hirsch, *op. cit.*, footnote 109, Regulation 17, Article 21, para. 6.

be the subject of decisions whose publication is required by Article 21 may also be covered by business secrecy; in such a case there is no legitimate interest in non-disclosure and thus it does not constitute an obstacle to publication.

That view appears to be correct with regard to publication of the Commission's *final* decision. However, according to Article 21(2), even that decision must be published in a way which has regard to the legitimate interest of undertakings in the protection of their business secrets. It may be argued that the interest in the protection of business secrets can no longer be regarded as legitimate once there has been a finding in the administrative procedure that the competitive rules of the Treaty have been infringed.

In this case, access to the applicants' documents has already been granted before the official hearing of the undertakings concerned under Article 19(1) of Regulation No. 17. It is quite possible that at such a hearing and in the subsequent consultation of the Advisory Committee on Restrictive Practices and Monopolies required by Article 10(3) of Regulation No. 17, factors may emerge which show the conduct of the undertakings concerned in a different light. It is only when those two further stages of the procedure have been completed and if the Commission has found that the competition rules of the Treaty have been infringed that it would seem proper to override the interest of the undertakings concerned in the protection of their business secrets. However, until the completion of those two stages, which provide a certain degree of protection also for the undertakings concerned, the Commission may not as a rule reveal the business secrets of those undertakings."

Where the existence of a secret is demonstrated, the Commission is prevented from publishing the information on grounds of the protection of confidentiality. If it wishes to take a decision which adversely affects a third party it must give him the opportunity of submitting his observations on the document if it wishes to base its decision on this information.[122] In so far as the information is covered in other places, it can keep the confidential document to itself.[123] The Court of Justice has held that the Commission is in certain circumstances even obliged to request the

---

[122] Case 322/81 *Michelin* v. *Commission* [1983] E.C.R. 3461 at 3499, para. 8; see further above, footnote 97; *cf.* also Case 107/82 *AEG* v. *Commission* [1983] E.C.R. 3151 at 3192, paras. 22 *et seq.*; Case 85/76 *Hoffmann-La Roche* v. *Commission* [1979] E.C.R. 471 at 512, para. 14.

[123] *cf.* Case 107/82 *AEG* v. *Commission* [1983] E.C.R. 3151 at 3193, end of para. 30.

supplier of information to allow its release,[124] but it must in any case give him an opportunity to be heard before the decision.[125]

The general principle applies that the Commission must of its own accord seek to give the person concerned the most comprehensive information possible about the allegations against him[126]:

> "It follows that in the present case the Commission ought to have made every effort, as far as was compatible with the obligation not to disclose business secrets, to provide the applicant with information relevant to the defence of its interests, choosing, if necessary on its own initiative, the appropriate means of providing such information. Mere disclosure of the items referred to in the calculation of the normal value without any figures does not satisfy those imperative requirements. That conclusion is all the more warranted in view of the fact that Timex was entirely dependent for the defence of its interests on the factors on which the Commission based its calculation."

It may suffice in an individual case, at least in the field of anti-dumping law, to transmit to the person concerned a non-confidential summary of the confidential document.[127]

With regard to the consequences of an infringement of the obligation to respect secrecy, the decision may be annulled on account of the defective fact-finding, if the "betrayal" of the secret could have affected the content of the decision subsequently adopted.[128] In so far as the communication of the secrets represents a separate decision, this may be annulled on grounds of infringement of the requirement of confidentiality.[129] Furthermore, it is possible to bring a non-contractual liability claim if the publication has led to further loss.[130]

---

[124] Case 45/69 *Boehringer* v. *Commission* [1970] E.C.R. 769 at 796, para. 14, *cf.* also p. 807, para. 59; as well as the parallel proceedings in Case 44/69 *Buchler* [1970] E.C.R. 753, para. 14; *cf.* also C.-D. Ehlermann, D. Oldekop, "Due process in administrative procedure," FIDE 1978, p. 11.10.

[125] For the contrary case see Case 53/85 *AKZO Chemie* v. *Commission*, *supra*, footnote 113, with further references.

[126] Case 264/82 *Timex* v. *Council and Commission* [1985] E.C.R. 849 *et seq.* at 870, para. 30.

[127] *cf. Timex*, footnote 126, with reference to Article 8, in particular Article 8(2)(b), (3), (4) II of Regulation 2176/84, see above, footnote 89.

[128] Case 209/78 *Van Landewyck* v. *Commission* [1980] E.C.R. 3125 at 3239, para. 47.

[129] Advocate-General Lenz, in Case 53/85 *AKZO Chemie* v. *Commission* [1986] E.C.R. 1972.

[130] Case 145/83 *Adams* v. *Commission* [1985] E.C.R. 3539 at 3590, para. 44; *cf.* Advocate-General Reischl, Case 209/78 *Van Landewyck* v. *Commission* [1980] E.C.R. 3125 at 3300.

(d) The nature and extent of the provision of a hearing

(aa) The object and degree of the hearing

For the purposes of the right to a hearing and the actual implementation of this right the principle applies that the Commission must give the persons concerned the opportunity of submitting observations on the matters of fact which it intends to make the basis for its decision. This has been confirmed by the Court[131]:

> "By virtue of Article 102(1) of the Staff Regulations an unfavourable opinion by the Establishment Board binds the appointing authority. Before issuing such an opinion this Board must however afford the person concerned an opportunity to submit his comments on the factors capable of influencing his integration. The requirement is satisfied when the person concerned has been heard by the said Board in connexion with the factors in the report which formed the basis for its decision and from which it drew its conclusions.
>
> A different situation would obtain if the conclusions of the report had been amended after hearing new witnesses without the issue of any invitation to the servant concerned to submit fresh comments thereon. This did not happen in the present case. The applicant was aware of the report on him drawn up by his superiors. It is not disputed that he submitted his comments on this report, that he lodged written statements and that he was heard by the Establishment Board.
>
> The fact that the minutes of the hearings of the persons who appeared before the said Board were not communicated to the applicant and that he himself was not the last to be heard is not such as to affect the regularity of the procedure followed, since these hearings in no way altered the conclusions in his superiors' reports, which the Establishment Board adopted."

---

[131] Case 26/63 *Pistoj* v. *Commission* [1964] E.C.R. 341 at 354; a similar judgment is Case 40/85 *Belgium* v. *Commission* [1986] E.C.R. 2321, paras. 25 *et seq.*, para. 31; *cf.* also Case 9/83 *Eisen- und Metall AG* v. *Commission* [1984] E.C.R. 2071 at 2085 *et seq.*, where reference is made, in the context of the Commission's duties in relation to fact-finding, to the fact that the framework which it sets for these determines the scope of the rights of the defence.

As mentioned above,[132] both the persons concerned, that is the later addressees of the administrative decision, and interested third parties, in particular competitors, will be heard; the latter must apply to be heard.[133] The hearing extends to questions of fact and law. The earlier view of the Commission, whereby it saw itself as obliged in anti-dumping proceedings to communicate only the factual basis of the decision, not the calculations (based on legal considerations), was rejected by Advocate-General Warner in the first case which concerned a procedure of this type[134]:

"Their submission (that of the Council and Commission) was that it was a principle of very limited application in an anti-dumping investigation, and that for (the following) reasons:

The provisions of Article 6 of the Anti-Dumping Code and the corresponding provisions of Regulation No. 459/68 refer only to the presentation and disclosure of 'information,' a word apt to describe factual material gathered by or supplied to the investigating authority, but not the way in which that material is used (in calculations or otherwise) by the investigating authority. (...)

As to the fourth point, it seems to me that the Commission's interpretation of the word 'information' as used in Article 6 of the Anti-Dumping Code (and in Article 10(4) of Regulation No. 459/68) is too narrow. In the first place that word must be interpreted in the light of the purpose mentioned in the preamble to the Agreement laying down the Anti-Dumping Code 'to provide for equitable and open procedures as to the basis for a full examination of dumping cases.' (...)

Lastly, the Commission's interpretation seems to me inconsistent with the opening sentence of paragraph 9 of Article 6 which provides that 'Throughout the anti-dumping investigation all parties shall have a full opportunity for the defence of their interests.' It was suggested on behalf of the Commission that that sentence was only an introduction to the next sentence, providing for meetings between 'parties ...' I see no reason, however, for thus limiting its scope."

[132] See above, E.III.2 and 3.
[133] Joined Cases 56 & 58/64 *Consten and Grundig* v. *Commission* [1966] E.C.R. 299 at 346.
[134] Advocate-General Warner, in Case 113/77 *NTN Toyo Bearing* v. *Council* [1979] E.C.R. 1185 at 1261 *et seq.*

The degree and scope of the obligation to grant a hearing are not always identical, but rather a variety of factors are to be taken into account which determine more precisely their range. This applies in the first instance to the legal nature of the measures. A hearing on a legislative provision is only exceptionally required,[135] that is where the individual can challenge the measure in court, or to put it another way, the conditions in the second paragraph of Article 173 EEC are satisfied[136]:

> "I agree of course that, in general, no one has a right to be heard during the process of preparation of legislation such as he has in the process of preparation of an administrative decision affecting him individually and directly. But, just as it seems to me that an instrument such as Regulation 1778/77 is to some extent a hybrid, so also it seems to me that an anti-dumping investigation may also be, for present purposes, a hybrid. In so far as it may lead to a finding that a particular exporter has been guilty of dumping and, on the basis of that finding, result in the imposition of an anti-dumping duty on his products *nominatim*, it has enough of the characteristics of a procedure preparatory to a decision of individual and direct concern to him."

The Court of Justice has taken a distinctly more restrictive view with regard to the hearing of officials before measures for the reorganisation of an authority are adopted, but has recognised a certain minimum standard of procedural rights[137]:

> "The applicant considers that in view of the important consequences which the abolition of his former branch and his transfer to other duties entailed for him that measure ought to have been preceded by thorough consultation to enable him to express his opinion on the question whether the measure planned was in the interests of the service. As to that complaint it need only be remarked that, although the Staff Regulations contain precise guarantees of officials' rights under them, the Community administration is not under any duty to seek the individual views of officials on measures of reorganization which may affect their individual position. The only guarantee

---

[135] On the normal case: Advocate-General Reischl, in Case 125/77 *Scholten-Honig NV* v. *Hoofdproduktschap* [1978] E.C.R. 1991 at 2014.

[136] Advocate-General Warner, in Case 113/77 *NTN Toyo Bearing* v. *Commission* [1979] E.C.R. 1185 at 1262.

[137] Case 37/81 *Seton* v. *Commission* [1983] E.C.R. 1789 at 1811.

afforded to officials by the Staff Regulations in this regard is the duty laid down in Article 25 of the Staff Regulations to state the grounds on which individual decisions which may adversely affect their position under the Staff Regulations are based."

Finally, a similar situation applies in the field of public procurement, where the interested undertakings are guaranteed at least a minimum standard of procedural guarantees, but not, however, a comprehensive right to a hearing.[138] Modifications with regard to the type and scope of the hearing are also necessary where the proper functioning of the administrative authority would be seriously hindered by a prior hearing. Advocate-General Warner has discussed this in detail[139]:

"As to the second point, there is no doubt that the right to be heard is subject to the general proviso that it must be compatible with the requirements of efficient administration—see, for instance, paragraph 18 of the Explanatory Memorandum appended to the Resolution on the Protection of the Individual in relation to the Acts of Administrative Authorities adopted by the Committee of Ministers of the Council of Europe on 28 September 1977 (No. 77(31)), which goes on to say: 'If, for instance, the taking of the administrative act cannot be delayed, the person concerned need not be heard. The same applies whenever it is for other pertinent reasons impossible or impracticable to hear him.' The application of that exception must however, in my opinion, be kept within proper bounds. If, here, the Commission's case had been that it had done all that was reasonably possible in the time available, and having regard to the complexities of the investigation, to apprise each of the Japanese exporters of its tentative conclusions on the question of dumping by that exporter,

[138] Case 182/80 *Gauff* v. *Commission* [1982] E.C.R. 799 at 814 and 823; the alleged infringement of the right to a hearing (*cf.* p. 814, para. 7) was not discussed by the Court of Justice, because it did not consider that there was an annullable act. Advocate-General Rozès stated that the undertaking had had the opportunity to make its views known.
[139] Advocate-General Warner, in Case 113/77 *NTN Toyo Bearing* v. *Commission* [1979] E.C.R. 1185 at 1262; *cf.* the Court itself, Case 37/81, etc., *Seton* v. *Commission* [1983] E.C.R. 1789 at 1806, para. 17, with regard to the consultation of an administrative Committee, *cf.* also Advocate-General Roemer, in Case 20/59 *Italy* v. *High Authority* [1960] E.C.R. 325 at 349, who considered that a further hearing, should the authority change its mind on the law, amounted in that case to superfluous formalism, whereas the Court in its judgment in Case 31/69 *Commission* v. *Italy* [1970] E.C.R. 25 at 33 held that a hearing (that is the provision of the opportunity for one) was required even where it was clear that the person concerned would make no use of it.

and of the way in which it had reached those conclusions, and to give to each of those exporters an opportunity to make representations thereon, and if the facts as placed before this Court had been consistent with that case, I would have held that the Commission was entitled to succeed on the present issue."

Furthermore, the severity of the interference is of significance as regards the hearing which must be granted. The Court of Justice has emphasised this point in staff cases in conjunction with disciplinary proceedings[140]:

"Appearing in the specific context of Annex IX to the Staff Regulations, that provision merely concerns the matters governed by that annex and is based on the fundamental requirement that respect for the rights of the defence, including the right of the official concerned to be assisted by counsel, is all the more important when the disciplinary proceedings to which he is subject are likely to result in the imposition of particularly severe disciplinary measures."

It is worthy of note also that the Court of Justice has held that a particularly wide discretionary power requires corresponding procedural guarantees, in particular an adequate hearing[141]:

"Under the provisions of Article 50 of the Staff Regulations of Officials 'an official holding a post in Grades A1 or A2 may be retired in the interests of the service by decision of the appointing authority.' As a corollary to the discretion conferred on the institutions by Article 29(2) as regards appointments at this level, the appointing authority enjoys wide discretionary powers in so far as retirement from the service and dismissal of officials belonging to these grades are concerned. The Staff Regulations do not limit the reasons which may justify a retirement under Article 50, since these could lie in the objective requirements of the service as well as in the assessment of the officials' specific qualities in relation to such requirements. The exercise of discretionary powers which are so widely defined nevertheless requires that the official concerning

---

[140] Case 115/80 *Demont* v. *Commission* [1981] E.C.R. 3147, at 3158, para. 11; Joined Cases 33 & 75/79 *Kuhner* v. *Commission* [1980] E.C.R. 1677 at 1698, para. 25; Case 125/80 *Arning* v. *Commission* [1981] E.C.R. 2539 at 2554, *cf.* Advocate-General Rozès, at p. 2564.
[141] Case 19/70 *Almini* v. *Commission* [1971] E.C.R. 623 at 630, paras. 8 *et seq.*

whom such a measure is contemplated should first have an opportunity of effectively defending his interests."

(bb) Procedure for the hearing

The German concept of "hearing" ("Anhörung") could lead to the
assumption that an oral "hearing" ("Anhören") on the arguments is
necessary. The Court of Justice,[142] however, maintains that it is generally
a matter for the Commission to decide whether to offer the person
concerned the opportunity of making written observations or to offer an
oral hearing, in so far as the question is not governed by specific
provisions.

Such specific rules are to be found in Article 7(1) read in conjunction
with Article 9 of Regulation 99/63[143] as well as Article 7(5) and (6) of
Regulation 2176/84[144] (equivalent to Decision No. 2177/84/ECSC), in
which a contentious procedure is provided for.

Advocate-General Reischl has summarised the crucial principles
applying here as follows[145]:

> "It follows from these provisions that the Commission has a dis-
> cretion with regard to the hearing. There is a right to a hearing only if
> sufficient interest is shown and even then it is basically only a written
> procedure. Oral hearings are to be arranged only where sufficient
> interest is shown or where the Commission proposes to impose a fine
> or periodic penalty payment on those concerned. It is moreover
> clear, and Article 9 of Regulation No. 99/63 must be so understood,
> that contentious proceedings are not the rule."

The right to a hearing does not mean that the hearing must actually take
place. Rather it suffices if the Commission provides the opportunity for
the person concerned to state his views. If the person concerned does not
make use of this opportunity, then the administrative procedure will

---

[142] Case 209/78 *Van Landewyck* v. *Commission* [1980] E.C.R. 3125 at 3232; *cf.* Advocate-
General VerLoren van Themaat, in Case 9/83 *Eisen- und Metall AG* v. *Commission*
[1984] E.C.R. 2071 at 2093; in agreement (and with references to the legal orders of the
Member States) is J.-P. Warner, "Due process in administrative procedure," FIDE 1978,
p. 1.8.

[143] See above, footnote 100.

[144] See above, footnote 89.

[145] Advocate-General Reischl, in Case 209/78 *Van Landewyck* v. *Commission* [1980]
E.C.R. 3125 at 3293.

continue without him being heard. The Court of Justice has held in this regard[146]:

> "After trying several times to secure the appearance of the applicant, the Audit Board was entitled to continue even in his absence. (. . .) In those circumstances the Audit Board was entitled to adopt the disciplinary measure in the absence of the applicant. That method of proceeding is all the more justified because the Audit Board, by the successive adjournments to which it had consented, had amply taken account of the state of health of the applicant and of his wish to be assisted by counsel. It appears from the whole of the foregoing that the disciplinary authority both during the preliminary stages of the proceedings and by its conduct at the time of the meeting of 26 March 1968, respected the rights of the defence, the failure to hear the applicant being attributable exclusively to the behaviour of the latter."

In that context there exists in any case a duty on the Commission to offer a hearing, which means that even where it is clear that the person entitled to be heard intends not to make use of this right the offer must be made.[147]

Furthermore a further hearing must be offered if the authority takes a new view on the underlying factual situation, such as, for instance, broadening the allegations against an undertaking on the grounds of further factual information, even if not every alteration of the view of the administration requires a repetition of the hearing[148]:

> "The Commission has the right and where appropriate the duty to institute fresh inquiries during the administrative procedure if it appears from the course of that procedure that additional investigations are necessary. Such inquiries would render it necessary to send an additional statement of objections to the undertakings concerned

---

[146] Case 12/68 *X* v. *Audit Board* [1969] E.C.R. 109 at 115, paras. 13 *et seq.*; *cf.* also Case 43/74 *Guillot* v. *Commission* [1977] E.C.R. 1309 at 1331, paras. 60 *et seq.*; also Case 3/66 *Alfieri* v. *Parliament* [1966] E.C.R. 437 at 451; a similar case is Case 13/63 *Italy* v. *Commission* [1963] E.C.R. 165 at 174; this concerned the right of a Member State to be heard.

[147] The Court of Justice has stated this explicitly with regard to the hearing which must be given to a Member State in the context of Article 169 EEC enforcement proceedings, *cf.* Case 31/69 *Commission* v. *Italy* [1970] E.C.R. 25 at 33, para. 13; to that extent in the Court's view the functional capacity of the administration is not affected.

[148] Case 51/69 *Bayer* v. *Commission* [1972] E.C.R. 745 at 770, para. 11; a similar case is Joined Cases 40/73, etc., *Suiker Unie* v. *Commission* [1975] E.C.R. 1663 at 1990, paras. 434 *et seq.*

only if the result of the investigations led the Commission to take new facts into account against the undertakings or to alter materially the evidence for the contested infringements. The rights of the defence of the undertakings are not infringed by such inquiries if the decision terminating the administrative procedure does not hold against the undertakings concerned any facts other than those set out in the notice of objections. Additional evidence for the facts taken into consideration and amendments concerning the precise course of the facts included in the contested decision in the light of information furnished by the undertakings concerned to the Commission during the course of the administrative procedure does not in any way constitute an infringement of the rights of the defence."

There is agreement that the authority must give the person concerned sufficient time to prepare his defence.[149] The Court of Justice has had no occasion, so far, to annul a decision on grounds of the infringement of this principle. It has, however, often examined the length of time available between the communication of the statement of objections or the invitation to be heard and the hearing itself, but so far it has always concluded that this period has in each case been sufficient.[150]

In so doing the Court of Justice and the Advocates-General have taken into account that a procedure must be pursued expeditiously.[151] The length of the fact-finding procedure does not offer a necessary justification for a comparably long time limit for the hearing,[152] since the Commission must first establish the facts, whereas the undertaking could ascertain the object of the proceedings even before the communication of the individual objections on the basis of the nature of the investigation pursued by the Commission.[153] The Court has also taken into consideration the possibility of further written observations being submitted even after the (oral) hearing.[154]

---

[149] Advocate-General Mayras expressly so argued in Case 48/69 *ICI* v. *Commission* [1972] E.C.R. 619 at 707:
"Finally, upon receipt of the notice of objections, the applicants should have been given a reasonable time for presenting their written observations."
[150] Joined Cases 40/73 etc. *Suiker Unie* v. *Commission* [1975] E.C.R. 1663 at 1952, paras. 94 to 98, *cf.* Advocate-General Mayras, at p. 2084; Case 27/76 *United Brands* v. *Commission* [1978] E.C.R. 207 at 307, para. 270.
[151] In the *Suiker Unie* Cases, [1975] E.C.R. 1663 at 1952, para. 96.
[152] *Ibid.*, para. 98; *cf.* also Advocate-General Mayras at p. 2084.
[153] Advocate-General Mayras in *Suiker Unie* [1975] E.C.R. 1663 at 2084.
[154] Case 51/69 *Bayer* v. *Commission* [1972] E.C.R. 745 at 770, para. 14; Advocate-General Mayras, in parallel case of *ICI*, [1972] E.C.R. 619 at 700.

Where a time limit of only three days was fixed in certain disciplinary proceedings, the Commission was saved only by the fact that further hearings took place later[155]:

"It is in fact common ground that the hearing on 28 September 1978 was followed by two further hearings on 19 January and 13 April 1979, at which the applicant was not only heard again but was also able to submit in evidence explanatory statements and to have witnesses examined whom he had himself called. Despite the shortness of the period which was allowed him before his first hearing, the applicant was therefore put in a position, before the contested decision to reprimand him was adopted, to prepare his defence under conditions which were in conformity with the requirements of the aforementioned principle."

For the case in which an oral hearing does occur, the case law has laid down certain general guidelines. These include that the authority which conducts the hearing is not obliged to send to it the official(s) empowered to take the decision.[156] The hearing will suffice if it is held before a sufficiently qualified official who is specifically entrusted with this task,[157] and who compiles a report on the course of the hearing. If a number of officials are involved, not all of them need participate in every section of the hearing. The presence of one representative will suffice.[158]

The permissibility of holding a hearing before a representative is based, after some initial hesitation on the part of the Court[159] in the context of disciplinary law, on the fact that the hearing does not represent

---

[155] Case 115/80 *Demont* v. *Commission* [1981] E.C.R. 3147 at 3156, para. 5.

[156] The hearing before the representative is expressly provided for in Article 9(1) of Regulation 99/63 (footnote 100); *cf.* also the Twelfth Report on Competition Policy (1982), para. 36, p. 41; Thirteenth Report (1983), para. 75, p. 66; Fourteenth Report (1984), para. 46, p. 54.

[157] Case 46/72 *De Greef* v. *Commission* [1973] E.C.R. 543 at 553, paras. 20 and 24; *cf.* in detail Advocate-General Trabucchi, at 554 *et seq.*, *cf.* also Advocate-General Reischl, in Case 209/78, etc., *Van Landewyck* v. *Commission* [1980] E.C.R. 3125 at 3300.

[158] Case 209/78 etc. *Van Landewyck* v. *Commission* [1980] E.C.R. 3125 at 3234, para. 27; *cf.* also Advocate-General Reischl at p. 3300; Advocate-General VerLoren van Themaat, in Case 43/82, etc., *VBVB, etc.* v. *Commission* [1984] E.C.R. 19 at 103, and similarly the Court in this case at p. 57, para. 16.

[159] Case 35/67 *Van Eick* v. *Commission* [1968] E.C.R. 329 at 343; a narrow view is to be found in the conclusions of Advocate-General Gand, in Case 12/68 *X* v. *Audit Board* [1969] E.C.R. 109 at 120.

an exercise of sovereign powers but is rather a technical measure similar to other aspects of the fact-finding process.[160]

Meanwhile, in the field of competition law, the Commission has begun to entrust hearings to a special official (hearing officer), so that the latter can conduct a neutral hearing which is separate from and unburdened by previous investigations.[161] His tasks are laid down in the so-called terms of reference.[162] A certain independence and detachment from the usual hierarchy of the authority is secured by the fact that the hearing officer has direct access to the responsible member of the Commission (Article 6 of the terms of reference). The independence is limited, since the fact that the official remains bound by instructions is not thereby removed.

The Commission itself has summarised the expectations and hopes which it has attached to this new procedure as follows[163]:

"The Hearing Officer's task is to ensure that the hearing is properly conducted and thus to contribute to the objectiveness of the hearing itself and of any subsequent decision. In performing his duties he ensures that the rights of the defence are respected, while taking account of the need for effective application of the competition rules in accordance with the regulations in force and the principles laid down by the Court of Justice. He also ensures that in the preparation of draft Commission decisions in competition cases due account is taken of all the relevant facts, whether favourable or unfavourable to the parties concerned. (. . .)

The Hearing Officer organizes preparations for the hearing, fixing the date, duration and place; he may also let the undertakings concerned know in advance the matters on which he would particularly like them to set forth their points of view. To this end he may organize a meeting with the parties concerned and, if necessary, with the relevant Commission departments to prepare for the hearing. He may also ask for prior submission in writing of the main content of

---

[160] cf. in detail Advocate-General Trabucchi, in Case 46/72 De Greef v. Commission [1973] E.C.R. 543 at 553.

[161] Twelfth Report on Competition Policy (1982), para. 36, p. 41; Thirteenth Report on Competition Policy (1983) para. 75, p. 66; on this see C. Canenbley, op. cit., footnote 77, p. 91 also with regard to possible further developments.

[162] The terms of reference are reprinted as an annex to the Thirteenth Report on Competition Policy (1983), p. 273.

[163] Twelfth Report on Competition Policy (1982), para. 36, p. 41; cf. also the Thirteenth Report on Competition Policy (1983), para. 75, p. 64; Fourteenth Report (1984), para. 46, p. 49.

statements by persons who are to speak on behalf of the undertakings concerned."

This procedure could operate as a model for other areas of the law, but it should first be secured in legislation through a binding legal act.

The minutes of the hearing which the official in question will compile must correctly reflect the content of the discussion so that complete and correct bases for advice and decision exist for the body which is to make the decision (generally the Commission). Omissions or mistakes can affect the effectiveness and lawfulness only if the decision might possibly have been different if the minutes had been correct.[164] The recording on tape of what is said to make it easier to compile the minutes does not infringe the rights of the parties.[165]

Records are not always made. It is reported that in the field of antidumping law[166] records of hearings have deliberately not been made in order not to hinder open discussion. This is doubtful on the twin grounds that a procedure with such wide-ranging consequences should be pursued with a certain level of formality, and that as a result of a lack of evidence about the statements made, neither the Commission nor the other parties will have the opportunity of basing their arguments on the information so obtained.[167]

With regard to the oral hearing, it is permissible to oblige the representatives of the undertaking themselves to appear. Of course, they can always be accompanied and advised by their lawyers, but not necessarily represented by them[168]:

"Article 9(2) of Regulation 99/63, which provides that undertakings may be represented only by a duly authorized agent appointed from among their permanent staff or by legal representatives or represen-

---

[164] cf. altogether on this Case 44/69 Buchler v. Commission [1970] E.C.R. 733, para. 17; also the parallel case of Boehringer decided at the same time, Case 45/69 [1970] E.C.R. 769 at 796, para. 17, cf. also Advocate-General Gand, [1970] E.C.R. at 709; also finally Case 51/69 Bayer v. Commission [1972] E.C.R. 745 at 771, para. 17.

[165] This applies even where an undertaking knows nothing of the recording, cf. Case 188/82 Thyssen v. Commission [1983] E.C.R. 3721 at 3722, paras. 5 and 12.

[166] I. van Bael, "Ten Years on EEC anti-dumping enforcement," (1979) 13 Journal of World Trade Law, 395 at 401.

[167] I. van Bael, op. cit., footnote 166, is also critical.

[168] Case 49/69 BASF v. Commission [1972] E.C.R. 713 at 730, para. 11; also Advocate-General Mayras, [1972] E.C.R. 700; for other statements on legal representation, cf. Case 115/80 Demont v. Commission [1981] E.C.R. 3147 at 3157; a narrower version is Case 124/75 Perinciolo v. Council [1976] E.C.R. 1953 at 1965, cf. Advocate-General Reischl, at p. 1973; the remarks of J.-P. Warner, op. cit., footnote 142, p. 1.8 should finally be noted.

tatives authorized by their constitution, is justified by the fact that as a general rule those persons are the best informed as to the facts and technical or economic aspects of their undertakings' actions which may be of decisive importance in applying the rules on competition. The hearing of the parties concerned cannot serve any useful purpose if those persons do not take part. (...)."

Whether this argument, which derives from EEC competition law, can be extended to anti-dumping law is doubtful, as the production of evidence is essentially a voluntary matter in the latter type of proceedings.[169]

At the hearing, the person entitled to be heard can support his arguments with motions to hear evidence and can bring evidence generally.[170] The authority is, however, not obliged to follow up every motion if it considers the facts to be adequately clarified.[171] The party being heard also has no right to the last say,[172] so long as he has been able to state his views on all arguments and evidence. And even this rule has been restricted in its application by the Court in cases in which the Commission has based itself in part on further supplementary arguments, provided always that the person concerned has had at least an indirect opportunity to make observations.[173] On the other hand, the hearing of evidence and hearings which are of importance for the procedure should not occur if the addressee of the future administrative act has been excluded. At least where there is a contentious proceeding the person concerned must have the opportunity of participating in the taking of evidence.[174] The authority is obliged to acknowledge the observations of the person concerned and to take them into account.[175] However, in spite of a number of

---

[169] On this question see Advocate-General Lenz, in Case 53/85 *AKZO Chemie* v. *Commission* [1986] E.C.R. 1965 at 1978.

[170] Advocate-General Roemer, in Case 35/67 *Van Eick* v. *Commission* [1968] E.C.R. 320 at 352 *et seq.*; *cf.* for anti-dumping proceedings Article 5(2) and Article 7(1)(a) of Regulation 2176/84 (= Decision 2177/84/ECSC) (*cf.* above, footnote 89); *cf.* EEC competition proceedings, see Article 3(3) of Regulation 99/63 (*cf.* above, footnote 100).

[171] Advocate-General Roemer, in Case 26/63 *Pistoj* v. *Commission* [1964] E.C.R. 341 at 362; also *ibid.* in Case 35/67 *Van Eick* v. *Commission* [1968] E.C.R. 329 at 352 *et seq.*, with comparative references. If the authority has inadequate counter-evidence, then there may be an evidentiary defect which leads to the annulment in whole or in part of the decision, *cf.* Case 27/76 *United Brands* v. *Commission* [1978] E.C.R. 207 at 306, paras. 261 *et seq.*

[172] Case 26/63 *Pistoj* v. *Commission* [1964] E.C.R. 341 at 354, and Advocate-General Roemer at 361.

[173] Case 209/78 *Van Landewyck* v. *Commission* [1980] E.C.R. 3125 at 3246, para. 73.

[174] Case 141/84 *De Compte* v. *European Parliament* [1985] E.C.R. 1951 at 1966, paras. 16 *et seq.*

[175] N. Michelsen, *Das rechtliche Gehör im Verwaltungsverfahren der Europäischen Gemeinschaften*, Diss. Hamburg 1975, p. 200; *cf.* also Case 40/73, etc., *Suiker Unie et al.* v. *Commission* [1975] E.C.R. 1663 at 1953, paras. 100 *et seq.*; in another context a similar

warnings by the Advocates-General,[176] the administrative body does not need to deal with the arguments of the other party in its statement of reasons for the decision.[177] The duty to take account of the observations is limited to the internal process whereby the authority makes up its mind.

The Court of Justice put this recently as follows[178]:

"It is clear from the provisions of Article 36 that the abovementioned obligation cannot be understood as requiring the Commission to put forward its counter-arguments in relation to the arguments put forward in its defence by the party concerned. The rights of the defence are guaranteed by that article since it provides the party concerned with an opportunity to put forward its arguments. The Commission cannot be required to reply to those arguments, to carry out further inquiries or to hear witnesses for the party concerned, where it considers that the preliminary investigation of the case has been sufficient, for that would be likely to render the procedure for establishing an infringement too cumbersome and extend its duration unnecessarily. That submission must therefore be rejected."

It is thus extremely difficult to prove that the authority has not taken into account the evidence put forward by the parties.[179]

IV. SUMMARY

Taken as a whole, the investigation has shown that the Community law practice in principle enables a person who is directly or indirectly affected by an administrative procedure to defend his rights and interests. The person concerned must be notified of the commencement of the proceedings and must be clearly informed of the subject-matter of the procedure. In order better to determine the nature of the allegations he can have

case is Case 27/76 *United Brands* v. *Commission* [1978] E.C.R. 207 at 306, paras. 261 *et seq.*
[176] Advocate-General Roemer, in Case 29/67 *De Wendel* v. *Commission* [1968] E.C.R. 263; also critical is N. Michelsen, *op. cit.*, footnote 175, p. 200.
[177] See on this also Case 209/78 etc. *Van Landewyck* v. *Commission* [1980] E.C.R. 3125 at 3244, paras. 64 *et seq.*; Case 7/82 *Gesellschaft zur Verwertung von Leistungsschutzrechten* v. *Commission* [1983] E.C.R. 483 at 500, para. 12; *cf.* also Case 5/83 *Barbara Erzbergbau AG* v. *High Authority* [1960] E.C.R. 173 at 196.
[178] Case 9/83 *Eisen- und Metall AG* v. *Commission* [1984] E.C.R. 2071 at 2086, para. 32.
[179] *cf.*, for example, Case 40/73, etc., *Suiker Unie et al.* v. *Commission* [1975] E.C.R. 1663 at 1928, paras. 100 *et seq.*

access to the documents used by the Commission, in so far as these are not on some particular ground confidential. He also has the possibility of putting forward in full his view of the factual situation and the legal position. If one compares the position in the Community with that in the Member States, it becomes apparent that the protection under Community law departs as regards certain points of detail from that guaranteed in the Member States, but not as regards the principles on which it is based. Community law does not lead to a maximisation of legal protection in the sense that it supplements the various possibilities of protection under the national legal orders. Rather it is a question of balancing the needs of a functionally efficient administration against achieving the optimum of procedural guarantees for the individual.

It can be seen that in Community law today it is in principle an appropriate balance between the requirements of the effective protection of rights of the defence for the individual and the safeguarding of administrative efficiency which is sought. Moreover, in particular as regards the regulation of the modern economy, including the competition and external trade law of the Community, it will in the future remain a primary task first and foremost of the Court of Justice continually to develop the procedural protection of those persons affected by such regulation, but without thereby endangering the functional capacity of the Community institutions.

F.   THE DECISION-MAKING PROCESS

I.   THE FORMULATION OF THE DECISION

1.   General Comments

Once the Commission has found the facts and the parties have been able to avail themselves of their procedural rights, the Commission (or other competent body) must decide how it wishes to proceed. There are in principle three routes which can be taken:

1. The authority adopts the measure which had been requested, or which it had in mind.
2. The authority takes the formal decision to discontinue proceedings or to reject the petition.

1371

3. The authority makes no formal decision, the proceedings remain pending, or are ended by the conclusion of a settlement.

The first two types of decision are often taken where the facts have been investigated and satisfactorily established, so that the authority may take a definitive decision.

In the administrative practice of the Community, however, the third variation is a not infrequent means of ending the procedure without the Commission having to adopt a definitive decision.[1] The crucial reasons for this will be discussed below.

In some areas, there are also time limits placed on administrative decisions to be taken by the Commission. If it fails to take a decision within a certain period, then it is assumed to have taken a negative decision.[2] This rule, which is based on the French model, is intended to ensure that the authority cannot undermine the legal protection of the citizen through its indecision or delaying tactics. The time limit cannot be extended, according to the case law, so that even where the Commission promises further investigations, a definitive decision must be assumed which cannot be annulled after the expiry of the relevant limitation period.

This was made very clear by the Court of Justice in the case of *Richez-Parise*[3]:

"Under Article 91 of the Staff Regulations, where the competent authority takes no decision in respect of a request or a complaint within two months from the date on which it was lodged, this shall be deemed to constitute an implied decision rejecting it against which an appeal may be lodged within two months.

The two periods set out in Article 91 are together intended to ensure, within the Community institutions, the legal certainty which

---

[1] In this context the possibility that there may be no majority for either the rejection or the adoption of a legal act has no role to play in practice, even if this is possible under the Community legal order; *cf.* J. Amphoux, in J. Mégret *et al.*, *Le droit de la CEE*, Vol. 9, Brussels 1979, Article 163, note 2 (p. 258).

[2] In particular in staff cases: *cf.* Article 90(2)(3) of the Staff Regulations, as well as with regard to complaints about the activities of new bodies created by the Community; see also Article 35(3) ECSC; *cf.* above, the section on competence.

[3] Case 40/71 *Richez-Parise* v. *Commission* [1972] E.C.R. 73 at 79, paras. 5 *et seq.* The same considerations applied when the Court held in Case 13/83 *Parliament* v. *Council* (transport policy) [1985] E.C.R. 1513 at 1590, that the enumeration of measures which have already been adopted is not to be regarded as a (definitive) opinion, and thus does not exclude an action for failure to act under Article 175 EEC.

is indispensable to their proper functioning. The parties may not, therefore, extend them at will.

The letter of 15 December 1970 whereby the Director of Personnel informed the applicant that the question raised by her was under consideration by the departments of the Commission but that they had not yet reached a final conclusion did not constitute a decision in response to the request. It could not, on the other hand, by itself have any other legal effect, in particular that of extending the periods prescribed by Article 91 of the Staff Regulations. Since the departments of the Commission had not taken any decision within two months in reply to the request of 10 September 1970, the letter of 15 December could not have interrupted the period of two months available to the applicant for bringing before the Court the implied rejection resulting from this silence."

2. The Possibilities of Informal Settlement

In the field of economic law, and above all in the enforcement of competition and anti-dumping law, the Commission is burdened by a large case load. The number of cases which have to be dealt with on the one hand and the complexity of the administrative procedure on the other together mean that in competition law, for instance, the Commission adopts many fewer decisions granting exemptions and negative clearances than it receives notifications.[4] With the consent if not the active encouragement of those sectors of the economy concerned,[5] the Commission has sought to find means of overcoming this flood of proceedings. It has developed a variety of methods for concluding proceedings without adopting formal decisions whilst still ensuring that the undertakings concerned benefit from a certain level of legal certainty.

---

[4] cf. Commission, *Tenth Report on Competition Policy* (1980), Brussels 1981, para. 104; *Twelfth Report on Competition Policy* (1982) 1983, para. 62; *Sixteenth Report on Competition Policy*, (1986) 1987, para. 44; cf. H. Schröter, "Schwerpunkte der Verwaltungspraxis und der Rechtsprechung zum EG-Kartellrecht," in *Schwerpunkte des Kartellrechts*, Issue 100, Cologne, etc., 1982, pp. 67 *et seq.*; J. Lindemann, "Das Kartellrecht der EWG und seine Anwendungspraxis—ein Wettbewerbsnachteil für die europäische Industrie?" in J. Schwarze, R. Bieber (eds.), *Das europäische Wirtschaftsrecht vor den Herausforderungen der Zukunft*, Baden-Baden 1985, p. 203 at 207, 209; on the problem of numbers see M. Caspari, "Wettbewerbspolitik im Bereich der Vertriebsvereinbarungen," in Studienvereinigung Kartellrecht, XI. Internationales EG-Kartellrechtsforum, Munich, 1986, p. 27 at 29 *et seq.*

[5] cf. J. Lindemann, *op. cit.*, footnote 4, p. 209.

Thus in the field of competition law, for example, the Commission has made use of so-called comfort letters (administrative letters), in order to communicate to an undertaking (in particular one seeking a negative clearance or an exemption) that it does not believe, on the basis of the facts available, that there has been a breach of the competition rules.[6] The importance of comfort letters has, however, decreased since the Court of Justice attributed only very limited legal effects to them, in particular on the grounds of the almost total exclusion of publicity, and above all the exclusion of competitors from the proceedings.[7]

The Commission, however, has continued its practice of sending out comfort letters. It has at least introduced a higher level of formality into its procedure in the last few years. Thus the announcements are published, in order to give interested third parties the opportunity of making observations.[8]

In spite of the limited legal effects of such administrative statements, described above,[9] the undertakings concerned have indicated to the Commission their interest in a rapid statement, since they will thereby gain at least a certain security with regard to the attitude of the Commission. They can also use the comfort letters as persuasive evidence in proceedings before national courts.[10]

In addition, in order to relieve itself of further administrative burdens in the field of block exemptions under Article 85(3) EEC,[11] the Commis-

---

[6] *cf.* above, the section on competence, as well as V. Korah, "Comfort Letters—Reflections on the Perfume Cases," (1981) 6 E.L.Rev. 14; A. v. Winterfeld, "Neuere Entwicklungen bei der Vereinfachung und Beschleunigung von Kartellverwaltungsverfahren," RIW 1984, pp. 929 *et seq.*; C. Canenbley, "Verfahrensregeln der Kommission der Europäischen Gemeinschaften," in Studienvereinigung Kartellrecht, XI. Internationales EG-Kartellrechtsforum, Munich, 1986, p. 74 at 89; D. Waelbroeck, "New forms of settlement of antitrust cases and procedural safeguards: is regulation 17 falling into abeyance?" in (1986) 11 E.L.Rev. 268; as well as the judgments of the Court in Case 253/78, etc., *Procureur de la République et al.* v. *Giry, Guerlain et al.* [1980] E.C.R. 2327; Case 37/79 *Marty* v. *Lauder* [1980] E.C.R. 2481; Case 99/79 *Lancôme* v. *Etos* [1980] E.C.R. 2511; Case 31/80 *L'Oréal* v. *De Nieuwe Amck* [1980] E.C.R. 3775.

[7] See the cases cited above, footnote 6, as well as C. Canenbley, *op. cit.*, footnote 6, p. 90.

[8] *cf.* Commission, *Twelfth Report on Competition Policy* (1982), p. 38, para. 30; 1983 (13), p. 61, para. 72; also C. Canenbley, *op. cit.*, footnote 6, p. 74 at 90; D. Waelbroeck, *op. cit.*, footnote 6, p. 271. On comfort letters see also C. S. Kerse, *EEC Antitrust Procedure*, London, 1988, p. 193.

[9] See above, the section on competence.

[10] J. Lindemann, *op. cit.*, footnote 4, p. 210; in agreement is D. Waelbroeck, *op. cit.*, footnote 6, p. 280; C. Canenbley, *op. cit.*, footnote 6, p. 74 at 90; *cf.* also Case 253/78, etc., *Procureur de la République et al.* v. *Giry et al.* [1980] E.C.R. 2327 at 2374, para. 13.

[11] *cf.* Regulation 2349/84, O.J. 1984, L219/15; Regulation 417/85, O.J. 1985, L53/1; Regulation 418/85, O.J. 1985, L53/5. This solution is already to be found in Council Regulation 1017/68 on the application of the competition rules in the field of transport, J.O.

sion has introduced a new procedure, the so-called opposition procedure,[12] which is intended to introduce greater legal certainty. In principle,
a block exemption is intended to bring about a lightening of the administrative load. The specific aim is to make it unnecessary to have an
administrative procedure with regard to a specific agreement, which is, as
a matter of law, exempted from the prohibition in Article 85(1) by virtue
of the group exemption.

Previously, if agreements extended beyond the boundaries of the
group exemption, they were prohibited and where appropriate required
individual exemption. This is the novelty of the so-called opposition
procedure. Where an agreement does not entirely accord with the individual provisions of the group exemption regulation, then the undertakings
party to it may notify the agreement, in so far as it does not contain certain
special clauses which are always prohibited (so-called black list).[13] If the
Commission has not opposed the agreement within six months of the
notification, it will be regarded as approved. In order to satisfy the
objections raised by the Court of Justice to comfort letters, some even
more extensive duties with regard to publication and participation are
provided for. It is nonetheless doubtful whether the Commission has
thereby achieved its goal of strengthening legal certainty.[14] Attaching an
implicit rejection to the expiry of a particular time limit is in no way

---

1968, L175/1; O.J. Sp.Ed. 1968, 302, Article 12; *cf.* Commission, *Thirteenth Report on Competition Policy* (1983), p. 64, para. 73, on the differences: J. S. Venit, "The Commission's opposition procedure—between the Scylla of ultra vires and the Charybdis of Perfume," (1985) 22 C.M.L.Rev. 167 (note 2 at the end). Similar solutions were put forward before the adoption of Regulation 17 (in the Deringer Report, EP-Doc 57/61, pp. 23, 39, 52); they are still called for today by lawyers; *cf.* J. Sedemund, "Due Process," Offprint, p. 25, with further references also on the point that the legal certainty offered by the result of such an "opposition procedure" must be increased.

[12] *cf. Thirteenth Report on Competition Policy* (1983), p. 62, para. 73; (14) (1984), p. 55, para. 47; (15) (1985), p. 54, para. 47 as well as (16) (1986), p. 40, para. 29; *cf.* also on this J. S. Venit, *op. cit.*, footnote 11, pp. 167 *et seq.*; J. R. Beversluis, "De Oppositieproce-dure in Commissie Verordening 2349/84," SEW 1986, pp. 229 *et seq.*; D. Waelbroeck, *op. cit.*, footnote 6, pp. 272 *et seq.*; *cf.* also J. Lindemann, "Kartellrecht der EWG," *op. cit.*, footnote 4, p. 209; C. Canenbley, *op. cit.*, footnote 6, pp. 78 *et seq.* The description "Widerspruchsverfahren" (opposition procedure) in German is unfortunate because (given the identical formulation in §§68 *et seq.* VwGO) it can create the impression that it is an appeal procedure.

[13] On the course of the procedure: *Thirteenth Report on Competition Policy* (1983), simi-larly in the Fourteenth Report; J. S. Venit, *op. cit.*, footnote 11, pp. 171 *et seq.* On the Form A/B which is to be used *cf.* Regulation 2526/85, O.J. 1985, L240.

[14] So also J. S. Venit, *op. cit.*, footnote 11, pp. 173, 181, 182, 201; more optimistic (although without reference to the actual rules) is J. Sedemund, *op. cit.*, footnote 11, p. 25; D. Waelbroeck, *op. cit.*, footnote 6, pp. 273 *et seq.*, who considers both the effects of "non-opposition" (pp. 273 *et seq.*) and those of "opposition" (p. 279).

unusual, but is based on models to be found in the Member States (France). It is also sensible since it assists the party concerned in achieving a satisfactory level of legal protection.

However, if one establishes a fiction as here of a positive decision of an authority, then a legal situation is created which the Commission itself could only have contrived by exercising its discretion, and which gives rise to legal advantages for the party who benefits from the decision without the appropriate discussions having taken place before the decision-making body.[15]

Such a procedure would be doubtful even if the Commission, as is not inconceivable, formally reached the decision routinely not to oppose agreements (in a group decision), because it would then be exercising its discretion in ignorance of the individual facts. It is also questionable whether a Group Exemption Regulation can introduce a procedure which departs so radically from the principles laid down in Regulations 17 and 99/63.[16] Finally doubts exist with regard to the question whether the opposition procedure is actually covered by the Regulation which provides for the adoption of block exemption regulations (Regulation 19/65[17]) because it deviates from the anticipated outcome of a block exemption which is to provide for an automatic exemption.[18] It remains to be seen what position the Court of Justice and, where appropriate, the courts and competent authorities of the Member States will actually take on the details of the legal effects of the new procedure.

In this context further considerable doubts are raised once again by the question whether an interested party can oblige the Commission to adopt an individual decision. This may be of interest to concerned parties, because an individual decision has more comprehensive legal effects, in particular in so far as it limits the competence of national authorities and courts, than a comfort letter or "non-opposition."[19]

A further way of ending the proceedings without the adoption of a formal decision is the conclusion of a settlement on the subject-matter of the procedure.

---

[15] See above, the section on competence as well as Case 9/56 *Meroni* v. *High Authority* [1957–1958] E.C.R. 133; *cf.* Case 25/70 *Einfuhr- und Vorratsstelle Getreide* v. *Köster* [1970] E.C.R. 1161 at 1171–1172, paras. 9 and 12.
[16] See on this also J. S. Venit, *op. cit.*, footnote 11, pp. 177–182.
[17] Regulation 19/65 of March 2, 1965, J.O. 1965, 533; O.J. Sp.Ed. 1965–1966, 35.
[18] J. S. Venit, *op. cit.*, footnote 11, pp. 177 *et seq.*
[19] On this question see also J. S. Venit, *op. cit.*, footnote 11, p. 194; on the law hitherto *cf.* A. v. Winterfeld, *op. cit.*, footnote 6, RIW 1984, p. 930. The Commission has stated with regard to exemption decisions under Article 85(1) EEC that it will send a comfort letter

In anti-dumping law Article 10 of Regulation 2176/84[20] provides explicitly for the conclusion of such an agreement (or undertaking, as it is called in that context):

"(1) Where during the course of an investigation, undertakings are offered which the Commission, after consultation, considers acceptable, the investigation may be terminated with the imposition of provisional or definitive duties. (...)

(2) The undertakings referred to under paragraph 1 are those under which:

(a) the subsidy is eliminated or limited, or other measures concerning its injurious effects taken, by the government of the country of origin or export; or

(b) prices are revised or exports cease to the extent that the Commission is satisfied that either the dumping margin or the amount of the subsidy, or the injurious effects thereof, are eliminated. In case of subsidization the consent of the country of origin or export shall be obtained. (...)

(5) The Commission may require any party from whom an undertaking has been accepted to provide periodically information relevant to the fulfilment of such undertakings, and to permit verification of pertinent data. Non-compliance with such requirements shall be construed as a violation of the undertaking."

The Commission has also made use of settlements in the field of competition law. Particularly well-known is the settlement agreed with IBM on certain of its marketing practices. By this means, a particularly extensive and also politically sensitive administrative procedure was brought to an end.[21] It is, however, worthy of note that IBM has retained for itself the right to withdraw from the settlement, while the Commission would be able to continue with the (old) proceedings, or bring new ones, if it were to discover that the settlement was not adequate or was being infringed.[22]

---

only if the undertaking is in agreement, cf. Thirteenth Report on Competition Policy (1983), p. 62.

[20] Regulation 2176/84, O.J. 1984, L201/1; (Decision No. 2176/84/ECSC, O.J. 1984, L201/17 is identical).

[21] cf. J. P. Raines, "Common Market Competition Policy: The EC-IBM Settlement," JCMSt (XXIV) 1985/86, p. 137; V. Korah, EEC Competition Law and Practice, Oxford, 1986, p. 57; C. S. Kerse, EEC Antitrust Procedure, London, 1988, p. 197; D. Waelbroeck, op. cit., footnote 6, p. 269, also on the relative frequency of such procedures.

[22] J. P. Raines, op. cit., footnote 21, p. 144.

In particular in the case of complex proceedings with many individual points of fact and a legal position presenting special difficulties, such a solution has attractions for both sides. Of course, it must not be permitted to undermine the fundamental point that the administration remains bound by the law. It must further be ensured that the possible claims of competitors which exist where formal decisions are adopted are not excluded by the fact that a settlement has rendered a formal decision unnecessary.

At least in those fields in which the Commission has no special powers to conclude such settlements, this way of ending the proceedings must remain the exception.[23]

3. The Possibilities of Adopting Interim Measures

In the field of anti-dumping law provisional measures which operate up to the conclusion of the administrative procedure are expressly provided for in Regulation 2176/84 in the form of provisional duties.[24] Article 11 provides:

> "(1) Where preliminary examination shows that dumping or a subsidy exists and there is sufficient evidence of injury caused thereby and the interests of the Community call for intervention to prevent injury being caused during the proceeding, the Commission, acting at the request of a Member State or on its own initiative, shall impose a provisional anti-dumping or countervailing duty. In such cases, release of the products concerned for free circulation in the Community shall be conditional upon the provision of security for the amount of the provisional duty, definitive collection of which shall be determined by the subsequent decision of the Council under Article 12(2)."

Such measures with limited temporal effect (Article 11(5) of Regulation 2176/84) are intended to avoid the possible irreparable damage which might occur during the course of the proceedings and secure the claim for the duty, since the definitive collection of the duty will only later be determined. Provisional protective measures are available in staff cases,

---

[23] D. Waelbroeck, *op. cit.*, footnote 6, p. 270 refers to the problems for third parties and the rights of the Member States.
[24] *cf.* above, footnote 20.

where Article 88 I of the Staff Regulations provides for suspension "forthwith."[25]

The Court of Justice has held in the well-known decision of *Camera Care* that the Commission may, in the case of a clear infringement of the competition rules which might lead to irreparable harm to a third party, prohibit the conduct of the undertaking which is seen as anti-competitive up to the conclusion of the competition proceedings.[26] Such interim measures on the part of the Commission are permissible. The conditions under which an interim order may be made have yet to be determined conclusively, as so far there has been little practical experience with this new instrument.[27] The following criteria are essential for determining whether the adoption of interim measures in the field of competition law is permissible and, where appropriate, necessary[28]:

— a prima facie infringement of the competition rules of the Treaty;
— a consequent threat to the vital interests of the party affected by the infringement;
— the interests of the party causing the damage and those of the person suffering it must be evaluated in relation to each other.

If these conditions are fulfilled the Commission may adopt interim measures. These should not deprive the main proceedings of their object, and the Commission may adopt only such measures as it would be empowered to adopt in the final decision.

---

[25] Staff Regulations of December 18, 1961, Regulation 31/61, O.J. Sp.Ed. 1959–1962, 135, in the version of Regulation 259/68/EEC/Euratom/ECSC, O.J. Sp.Ed. 1968, 26; *cf. Handbuch des Europäischen Rechts*, item I A67/11.

[26] Case 792/79 *Camera Care* v. *Commission* [1980] E.C.R. 119; Case 228/82, etc., *Ford* v. *Commission* [1984] E.C.R. 1129 at 1161 *et seq.*, paras. 17 *et seq.*; *cf.* on this and on the question of interim measures in competition law generally, J. Temple Lang, "The powers of the Commission to order interim measures in competition cases," (1981) 18 C.M.L.Rev. 49; C. S. Kerse, *EEC Antitrust Procedure*, London, 1988, pp. 158 *et seq.*; Burnside, "Enforcement of EEC Competition Law by interim measures," (1985) 19 *Journal of World Trade Law* 34; J. Temple Lang, "Procedure in Community competition cases—some recent developments," in Studienvereinigung Kartellrecht, XI. Internationales Kartellrechtsforum, Munich 1986, p. 94.

[27] *cf.* on the practical significance of this J. Temple Lang, "Procedure in Community competition cases," *op. cit.*, footnote 26, p. 95 with reference to the *Ford* decision (O.J. 1982, L256/20) and the *ECS/AKZO* decision (O.J. 1983, L252/13).

[28] *cf.* Case 792/79 *Camera Care* v. *Commission* [1980] E.C.R. 119 at 129 *et seq.*, paras. 17 *et seq.*; Case 228/82, etc., *Ford* v. *Commission* [1984] E.C.R. 1129 at 1161 *et seq.*, paras. 17 *et seq.*; J. Temple Lang, "Procedure in Community competition cases," *op. cit.*, footnote 26, pp. 97–102.

4.   The Process for Adopting the Decision

The body empowered to adopt the measure does not always act completely autonomously in reaching its decision; sometimes other bodies must be involved. In particular, where legislative measures are to be adopted, the consultation of the Economic and Social Committee and the Parliament may be required. In the ECSC field, the Council may sometimes be required to give its consent to measures which the Commission (High Authority) then adopts.[29]

The position is similar as regards the adoption of implementing measures under Article 155(4) EEC, where the delegation of powers takes the form of a committee procedure.[30] Finally in competition law the Advisory Committee must be heard before formal decisions are adopted,[31] and in anti-dumping law the Member States are to be consulted.

As a rule the participation takes the form of a hearing, which means that the body in question must be given the opportunity of adopting an opinion,[32] although the competent authority is not obliged to adhere to this recommendation or to deal with its contents.[33] The fact that the consultation has taken place need only be mentioned (Article 190 EEC).

Only in circumstances where exceptionally the competent authority requires the consent of the body consulted are there any further requirements. The Commission adopts its decisions by reaching a conclusion as a

---

[29] *cf.* for instance Article 198 EEC, Article 137 EEC, for example, in conjunction with Article 235 EEC, Article 100(2), Article 87(1), Article 63, Article 57, Article 49 EEC; the position is similar for the other Treaties, *cf.* in particular Article 14 ECSC in conjunction with Article 19(1) (Advisory Committee), Article 20, Article 26 in conjunction with Article 58, §1(1) (*consent* of the Council, *consultation* of the Advisory Committee) ECSC.

[30] On the Committee procedure see above, the section on competence.

[31] "Advisory Committee on Restrictive Practices," governed by Article 10 of Regulation 17 on the unlawfulness of keeping the content of the statements of the Committee entirely secret, *cf.* J. Sedemund, "Allgemeine Prinzipien des Verwaltungsverfahrensrechts, dargestellt am Beispiel des Verwaltungsverfahrens der EG in Kartellsachen," in J. Schwarze (ed.), *Europäisches Verwaltungsrecht im Werden*, Baden-Baden 1982, p. 45 at 54.

[32] Case 138/79 *Roquette Frères* v. *Council* [1980] E.C.R. 3333 at 3360, para. 33, also on the limits of delaying tactics by the body to be consulted; see on this H.-W. Daig, in H. v.d. Groeben *et al.*, *Kommentar zum EWG-Vertrag*, (3rd ed., Baden-Baden 1983), Article 190, para. 18.

[33] Case 4/54 *Industrie Siderurgiche Associate* v. *High Authority* [1954–1955] E.C.R. 91 at 100; Case 6/54 *Netherlands* v. *High Authority* [1954–1955] E.C.R. 103 at 111; Advocate-General Roemer, in Case 3/67 *Mandelli* v. *Commission* [1968] E.C.R. 25 at 41; H.-W. Daig, *op. cit.*, footnote 32, Article 190, para. 19.

college upon them,[34] as it is required to do by the Treaty.[35] This requires
the consent of the majority of the members of the Commission.[36] Important questions are generally decided upon after discussion, generally by
consensus.[37]

To relieve the burden upon the Commissioners, however, two further
procedures have become common. Like the Council voting procedure,
the Commission agenda has so-called A-points, which are questions on
which agreement has previously been reached in a discussion between the
Chefs de Cabinet. Such proposals are frequently adopted en bloc,
generally without specific discussion.[38]

Further assistance is provided by the written procedure; thus a proposal for a decision from one of the Commissioners is sent to all the
members of the Commission. If none object within a certain time limit
(generally five days), the proposal is adopted by default.[39]

Both procedures have proved themselves invaluable given the weight
of tasks falling upon the Commission. As mentioned above, there have
also, within limits, been extensive delegations of powers to the individual
members of the Commission.[40]

5. The Presentation of the Decision

The presentation of the decision itself follows certain standardised
rules.[41] Both normative acts and individual decisions must contain the

---

[34] See above, the section on competence.
[35] On the decision-making process cf. H. P. Ipsen, *Europäisches Gemeinschaftsrecht*,
Tübingen 1972, 14/25 (p. 363); H. Schmitt v. Sydow, in H. v.d. Groeben *et al.*, *op. cit.*,
footnote 32, Article 163, paras. 1 *et seq.*; H. Smit, P. Herzog (eds.), *The Law of the
European Economic Community—A Commentary on the EEC Treaty*, New York, etc.,
1976, *et seq.*, Article 163.04, p. 5–247; J. Amphoux, in J. Mégret *et al.* (eds.), *Le droit de
la CEE*, Vol. 9, Brussels 1979, Article 163, pp. 258 *et seq.*
[36] H. Smit, P. Herzog, *op. cit.*, footnote 35, Article 163.03, p. 5–246.6.
[37] H. Smit, P. Herzog, *op. cit.*, footnote 35, p. 5–249; H. Schmitt v. Sydow, *op. cit.*,
footnote 35, Article 163, para. 8.
[38] H. Smit, P. Herzog, *op. cit.*, footnote 35, Article 163.03, p. 5–248; H. Schmitt v. Sydow,
op. cit., footnote 35, Article 163, para. 4.
[39] cf. J. Amphoux, in J. Mégret *et al.* (eds.), *op. cit.*, footnote 35, pp. 260 *et seq.* (also with
statistical references, p. 261, note 8); H. Schmitt v. Sydow, *op. cit.*, footnote 32, Article
163, paras. 9 *et seq.*
[40] See above, the section on competence as well as H. Schmitt v. Sydow, *op. cit.*, footnote
32, paras. 12 *et seq.*; J. Amphoux, *op. cit.*, footnote 35, pp. 262 *et seq.* (with further
references).
[41] cf. L.-J. Constantinesco, *Das Recht der Europäischen Gemeinschaften I*, Baden-Baden
1977 p. 588, paras. 521 *et seq.*; cf. on this also Article 11–15 of the Rules of Procedure of
the Council of July 24, 1979, O.J. 1979, L268/1, in which these rules are laid down; the

description of the type of legal act, the name of the body adopting it, the number of the measure and the date.

Then follow the reasons for the decision, which are required under Article 190 EEC, which include first a reference to the legal basis and to any necessary consultations of other bodies, and then the actual statements containing the reasons.

Finally comes the body of the decision (which is enforceable if this is a financial measure), that is the regulations, rules and declarations which make up the content of the measure. Only these are binding, even if they are to be interpreted in the light of the reasons. At the end it is usual to find the addressee of the measure, or a statement that the measure is of general application.

An infringement of these rules does not necessarily, in the view of the Court of Justice,[42] automatically lead to the nullity of the measure:

"Decision 22/60 prescribes in such a detailed manner the formal presentation of measures of the High Authority in order clearly to distinguish the nature of measures by using standard forms. Failure to comply with that requirement nevertheless does not entail the nullity of measures when they are unquestionably individual decisions taken on the implementation of a scheme previously established by means of a general decision adopted in accordance with the formal requirements prescribed by Decision 22/60. That is precisely the case with the contested notifications which constitute no more than the application of Article 3 of Decision 2794/80 under which the Commission fixes quarterly production quotas for each undertaking and notifies them of it. The submission that the contested notifications did not comply with the formal requirements laid down by Decision 22/60 must therefore be rejected."

6.   Information about Remedies

The Court of Justice has never required the persons concerned by a decision to be made aware of their right to make an appeal.[43] This point of

---

Commission proceeds in a similar manner; see for the ECSC Decision No. 22/60 of September 7, 1960, J.O. 1960, p. 1248.
[42] Case 275/80 etc. *Krupp* v. *Commission* [1981] E.C.R. 2489 at 2511, para. 9; the arguments of the applicant (p. 2494) and the conclusions of Advocate-General Reischl (p. 2523) are also interesting.
[43] Advocate-General Gand, in Case 41/69 *ACF Chemiefarma* v. *Commission* [1970] E.C.R. 661 at 713; see also H. P. Ipsen, *op. cit.*, footnote 35, Ch. 24/24, p. 517.

view has been the object of some critical comment in the literature,[44] in particular because the limitation period of two months for bringing claims under Article 173(2) EEC is considered to be very short.[45] This criticism appears at root to be not unjustified.

Even the Resolution of the Council of Europe, "On the protection of the individual in relation to the acts of administrative authorities," which has been referred to by Advocate-General Warner,[46] for example, on a number of occasions requires such information to be given.[47]

Exceptionally, Articles 11(5) and 4(2) of Regulation 17 require an indication that the decisions taken under those provisions (formal request for information; decision ordering an undertaking to submit to an investigation) can be reviewed by the Court of Justice.[48] For the rest, the necessity for an indication of remedies available has since come to be recognised at least in part in the legal orders of a number of Member States.[49] This changed overall situation[50] leads to the conclusion that the conditions for the recognition of a corresponding general principle are now present.

---

[44] H. P. Ipsen, *op. cit.*, footnote 35, Ch. 24/24, p. 517; C. H. Ule, "Diskussionsbeitrag," in *Zehn Jahre Rechtsprechung des Gerichtshofes der Europäischen Gemeinschaften*, KSE 1, Cologne 1965, p. 508; similarly Constantinesco L.J., *op. cit.*, footnote 41, p. 631, para. 565.

[45] Article 173(3) EEC, *cf.* also Article 80(2) of the Rules of Procedure of the Court in conjunction with Article 1 of Annex II, with regard to the extension through so-called distance periods, according to the place of residence of the applicant. Article 33 ECSC even provides for a limitation period of only one month, *cf.* on the criticism: H.-W. Daig, *Nichtigkeits- und Untätigkeitsklagen im Recht der Europäischen Gemeinschaften*, Baden-Baden 1985, p. 297 (para. 413 with further references).

[46] *cf.* for example Advocate-General Warner, in Case 113/77 *NTN Toyo Bearing* v. *Council* [1979] E.C.R. 1185 at 1262.

[47] Resolution (77) 31 of the Council of Europe (Adopted by the Committee of Ministers of the 275th meeting of the Ministers' Deputies) Council of Europe, Information Bulletin on legal activities, June 1978, p. 45:
   V. Indication of remedies
   "Where an administrative act which is given in written form adversely affects the rights, liberties or interests of the person concerned, it indicates the normal remedies against it, as well as the time-limits for their utilisation."

[48] Regulation 17 of February 6, 1962, J.O. 1962, 204; O.J. Sp.Ed. 1959–1962, 87; *cf.* on this Case 136/79 *National Panasonic* v. *Commission* [1980] E.C.R. 2033 at 2056, para. 25; in the context of these decisions, the Commission makes available to undertakings an Explanatory Note containing their essential procedural rights, *cf. Thirteenth Report on Competition Policy* (1983), p. 63, para. 74a; the text is reprinted at pp. 270 *et seq.*

[49] *cf.* above, the sections on France, Spain, Germany and Denmark.

[50] Advocate-General Gand based his conclusions, which rejected such a requirement, on the view that it was only in Germany that the need for an indication of remedies was recognised, *cf.* Case 41/69 *ACF Chemiefarma* v. *Commission* [1970] E.C.R. 661 at 713.

If such a general principle of law were recognised, then an infringement of it would normally lead, as it does in the legal orders of the Member States, to an interruption of the limitation period. Given the generally negative attitude of the Court of Justice towards the extension of limitation periods, even in cases in which the administration unfairly relies upon the expiry of the time limit,[51] it remains to be seen how the Court of Justice would react to a claim brought out of time in such circumstances. It seems rather improbable that the Court would annul an entire decision simply because it lacks an indication of remedies, given the viewpoint which it adopted in the *ACF Chemiefarma* case. In that case,[52] the Court dismissed a submission concerning the absence of an indication of remedies as lacking in foundation, since the claim was brought within time.

II. THE DUTY TO GIVE REASONS

1. Introduction

In the Community as in the Member States, it is one of the pillars of the rule of law that the administration is bound by the law.[1]

One element of the safeguarding of administrative enforcement under the law in the Community[2] is the duty to give reasons laid down in Article 190 EEC and the corresponding provisions in the other Treaties. It extends beyond the administrative sphere of application to the Community legislature, which is obliged to give reasons for regulations, directives, and general decisions, just as the administration is required to provide reasons for its individual acts. The duty to give reasons requires the responsible body to be clear as to the reasons for a measure which it intends to adopt, and thus promotes self-regulation.[3]

---

[51] *cf.* Case 209/83 *Valsabbia* v. *Commission* [1984] E.C.R. 3089 at 3097; Case 79/70 *Müllers* v. *Economic and Social Committee* [1971] E.C.R. 689 at 697; the latter case reiterates the long-standing view that the indication that the situation of an official is to be further examined does not interrupt a limitation period which is running in respect of an (implied) negative decision; *cf.* also H.-W. Daig, *op. cit.*, footnote 45, p. 51, para. 52.

[52] Case 41/69 *ACF Chemiefarma* v. *Commission* [1970] E.C.R. 661 at 692, para. 97.

[1] On the principle of the rule of law, *cf.* in particular Chapter 3.

[2] Advocate-General Reischl, in Case 89/79 *F. Bonu* v. *Council* [1980] E.C.R. 553 at 566; Advocate-General Mayras, in Case 33/79 *Kuhner* v. *Commission* [1980] E.C.R. 1677.

[3] The Court of Justice and the Advocates-General have not apparently so far discussed this point, *cf.* however from the literature H.-W. Daig, in H. v.d. Groeben *et al.*, *Kommentar zum EWG-Vertrag*, (3rd ed., Baden-Baden 1983), Article 190 para. 5; H. P. Ipsen, *Europäisches Gemeinschaftsrecht*, Tübingen 1972, Ch. 24/25; J.-V. Louis, in J. Mégret *et al.*, *Le Droit de la Communauté économique européenne*, Vol. 10.1, Brussels, 1983,

Further, in particular in the case of administrative acts, it also has an important function as an indication of unlawful, inappropriate[4] or even abusive considerations which may have entered the decision-making process of the adopting authority and thus serves the purpose of providing protection against arbitrary conduct.[5] In the following section, the sphere of application and the scope of the duty to give reasons in European Community law will be set out, in order to demonstrate clearly the importance of this principle for the legal protection of the individual.[6]

2. The Duty to give Reasons in the Legal Orders of the Member States

In order better to appreciate the meaning and extent of, as well as the limitations upon, the duty to give reasons in Community law (Article 190 EEC), the first part of this discussion will be devoted to a comparative survey of the legal position in the Member States.[7]

(a) The duty to give reasons in France

The duty to give reasons for administrative acts is regulated by the Law of July 11, 1979.[8] The statutory duty to give reasons applies to all unfavourable administrative decisions. The reasons must be in writing and

---

Article 190, note 2 (p. 502); L.-J. Constantinesco, *Das Recht der Europäischen Gemeinschaften I*, Baden-Baden 1977, para. 522, p. 590.

[4] *cf.* for instance Case 24/62 *Germany* v. *Commission* [1963] E.C.R. 63 at 69; Case 292/81 *Lion et Cie* v. *Loriet S.A.* [1982] E.C.R. 3887, at 3909, para. 18; Case 155/80 *Rewe* v. *HZA Kiel* [1981] E.C.R. 1805 at 1833; *cf.* also Advocate-General Lagrange, in Case 36/59 *Präsident et al.* v. *High Authority* [1960] E.C.R. 423 at 439; also H. P. Ipsen, *op. cit.*, footnote 3, Ch. 24/25; L. J. Constantinesco, *op. cit.*, footnote 3, para. 522, p. 590; J. V. Louis, *op. cit.*, footnote 3, Article 190, para. 2.

[5] Advocate-General Roemer, in Case 16/61 *Acciaierie Ferriere e Fonderie di Modena* v. *High Authority* [1960] E.C.R. 423 at 451; Advocate-General Lagrange, Case 36/59 *Präsident et al.* v. *High Authority* [1960] E.C.R. 423 at 439.

[6] *cf.* on the protective function of the duty to give reasons *vis-à-vis* the public and Parliament also Advocate-General Lagrange, in Case 36/59, etc., *Präsident et al.* v. *High Authority* [1960] E.C.R. 423 at 451; with regard to the addressees see Advocate-General Roemer, in Case 2/56 *Geitling* v. *High Authority* [1957–1958] E.C.R. 3 at 25.

[7] *cf.* on the development of the law in the Member States H.-H. Scheffler, *Die Pflicht zur Begründung von Massnahmen nach den europäischen Gemeinschaftsverträgen*, Berlin, 1974, pp. 41 *et seq.*

[8] Loi No. 79–587, (French) J.O. of July 12, 1979, p. 1711; Recueil Dalloz Sirey, p. 261 (with further references to the Travaux préparatoires). *cf.* on this A. de Laubadère, *Traité administratif*, (9th ed., Paris 1984), Vol. I, p. 340, para. 709; Linotte, "La motiva-

must contain the essential matters concerning the factual and legal situation (Article 3). An exception to the duty to give reasons exists in cases of special urgency; on the application of the person concerned, however, the authority must communicate the reasons for the adoption of the administrative act retrospectively (Article 4). The type and scope of the reasons are described in more detail in the Prime Minister's "circulaire du 31 août 1979."[9] This provides that the duty to give reasons extends not only to administrative decisions of the actual State administration, but also to decisions of local authorities, public bodies or authorised private persons (Section III of the Circular). The reasons must be clear and precise, and the essential grounds for the adoption of the actual decision must be articulated (Section IV).

An incomplete or absent statement of reasons for an administrative act can be rectified retrospectively. If this does not occur, the administrative act is unlawful for breach of the duty to give reasons and can be annulled by the administrative courts.[10]

The reasoning of laws, regulations and general dispositions is not dealt with in the Law of July 11, 1979. Thus the position is as it was also for administrative acts before the adoption of the Law of July 7, 1979: there is a duty to give reasons only where this is expressly provided for,[11] or where the reasons are necessary in order to ensure effective judicial control of the administration.[12] An infringement of the duty to give reasons also leads in this context to the unlawfulness of the act adopted.[13]

(b) The duty to give reasons in the Federal Republic of Germany

In the Federal Republic of Germany early recognition was given to the significance of the duty to give reasons for an administrative procedure

---

tion obligatore de certaines décisions administratives," RDP 1980, p. 1699; *cf.* also the Law of July 17, 1978.

[9] *cf.* Rec. Dalloz-Sirey, Paris, 1979, pp. 308 *et seq.*

[10] A. de Laubadère, *op. cit.*, footnote 8, p. 341.

[11] *cf.* for instance the duty to give a "motivation" for the refusal of authorization of divisions in the Law of January 15, 1943, on this A. de Laubadère, *op. cit.*, footnote 8, p. 340, para. 708; H.-H. Scheffler, *op. cit.*, footnote 7, p. 33; E. Schott, *Der Begründungszwang für Akte der Exekutiven der Europäischen Gemeinschaften*, Diss. Saarland 1971, p. 32.

[12] A. de Laubadère, *op. cit.*, footnote 8, p. 340, para. 708; M. Fromont, "Der Rechtsschutz gegen Massnahmen der Verwaltung im Europa der Sechs," EuR 1969, p. 202 at 210; J.-M. Auby, R. Drago, *Traité de Contentieux Administratif II*, (3rd ed., Paris 1984), para. 1171, p. 305.

[13] J.-M. Auby, R. Drago, *op. cit.*, footnote 12, para. 1172, pp. 306 *et seq.*

which is subject to the rule of law and for the protection of the interests of the individual. From this the courts, and later academic writers, concluded that in certain circumstances there was a duty to give reasons even though statutory provisions were not at first in place for all fields of administration.[14]

Meanwhile, the duty to give reasons for administrative acts has been enshrined in statute in the Law on administrative procedure (VwVfG).[15] Legislation, that is the adoption of laws, regulations and general rules, does not fall under the Law on administrative procedure, and such measures therefore in principle require no statement of reasons. Nonetheless, under Article 80(1) third sentence of the Basic Law, delegated regulations must state their legal basis, and thus always contain at least a "fragment of a statement of reasons."[16]

Under §39(1) second sentence of the Law on administrative procedure, the statement of reasons must contain the essential grounds of fact and law which have induced the administration to adopt the decision. In the case of discretionary decisions the underlying viewpoint on which the administration based its decision must also be stated. A standard-form statement of reasons which fits every case is not sufficient.[17] However, it is permissible for the reasons to refer to sources of information to which the person concerned has access. In particular, reference may be validly

[14] cf. Zschacke, "Die Begründung der Verwaltungsakte und ihre Bedeutung im Verwaltungsstreitverfahren," NJW 1954, p. 413 with further references to the then existing laws; M. Voucko, Die Pflicht zur Begründung von Verwaltungsakten, Frankfurt, 1967, passim; F. O. Kopp, Verwaltungsverfahrensgesetz mit Erläuterungen (VwVfG), (4th ed., Munich 1986), §38, para. 2; cf. also R. Kolzer, "Zum Begründungsgebot im geltenden Verwaltungsrecht," DÖV 1985, p. 9; W. Schick, "Notwendigkeit und Funktion der Begründung von Verwaltungsakten," JuS 1971, p. 1 with further references; J. Lücke, Begründungszwang und Verfassung, Tübingen 1987, pp. 28 et seq.; BVerfGE 6, p. 32 at 44; BVerfGE 40, p. 276 at 286; BVerwGE 5, p. 95 at 98, with further references to the earlier case law.

[15] Article 15 VwVfG (Verwaltungsverfahrensgesetz of May 25, 1976, BGBl. I 1976, p. 1253); similar or identical are the laws on administrative procedure adopted by the Länder, cf. for example the Hamburgische Verwaltungsverfahrensgesetz of November 9, 1977, GVBl. 1977, p. 333, and the Verwaltungsverfahrensgesetz Nordrhein-Westfalen of December 21, 1976, GVBl. 1976, p. 438; in the field of taxes and levies cf. §121 AO (Abgabenordnung of March 16, 1976), BGBl. I 1976, p. 613; in the field of social law see §35 SGB X (Sozialgesetzbuch—Zehntes Buch, administrative procedure of August 18, 1980, BGBl. I 1980, p. 1469; J. Lücke, op. cit., footnote 14, p. 28.

[16] cf. Article 80(1) 3rd sentence of the Basic Law; on this see J. Lücke, op. cit., footnote 14, p. 33 on the duty to give reasons for parliamentary decisions.

[17] cf. OVG Münster, NVwZ 1982, p. 326; VGH München, NJW 1981, p. 1001; F. O. Kopp, Verwaltungsverfahrensgesetz, (4th ed., Munich 1986), §39, para. 6; H. Meyer, in H. Meyer, H. Borgs-Maciejewski, Verwaltungsverfahrensgesetz, (2nd ed., Frankfurt 1982), §39, para. 25; K. R. Schwarze, in H. J. Knack, Verwaltungsverfahrensgesetz—Kommentar, (2nd ed., Cologne etc. 1982), §39 note 6.1.

made to correspondence and to the oral hearings which preceded the decision.[18]

In any case §44a of the *Verwaltungsgerichtsordnung* (VwGO: Code of Administrative Court Procedure) provides that infringements of the duty to give reasons may not be made the object of a separate claim, that is the fulfilment of this duty cannot be enforced through a special claim, but any defects may be taken into consideration only within the context of the (main) proceedings against the administrative act for which reasons should be given.[19]

Under §46 VwVfG the annulment of an administrative act for infringement of the requirements of form and procedure, which include the duty to give reasons, can be demanded only in circumstances where a different decision would in fact have been adopted. The basis for this rule is a concern about economy of process.[20]

Therefore the absence of a statement of reasons affects the legality of an administrative act only where either it is a discretionary act or the defect in reasoning also has material consequences, for instance because certain factual circumstances were not taken into consideration.[21]

(c) The duty to give reasons in Italy

Italian administrative law does not recognise a general duty to give reasons.[22] In addition to the cases in which the duty to give reasons is expressly laid down by statute, the courts have developed in a vast line of

---

[18] BVerwGE 38, 191 at 194; F. O. Kopp, *op. cit.*, footnote 17, §39, paras. 7, 8; K. R. Schwarze, *op. cit.*, footnote 17, §39, note 6.1.

[19] *cf.* on this F. O. Kopp, *Verwaltungsgerichtsordnung*, (7th ed., Munich 1986), §44a paras. 1, 2 with blunt criticism of this provision.

[20] F. Ossenbühl, "Zur Bedeutung von Verfahrensmängeln im Atomrecht," NJW 1981, p. 375 at 376; F. O. Kopp, *Verwaltungsverfahrensgesetz*, *op. cit.*, footnote 17, §46 para. 3 is critical of the result; *cf.* also BVerwG, judgment of October 7, 1980, E 61, p. 45 at 49 (NJW 1981, p. 1682).

[21] OVG Münster, NJW 1981, p. 936 (with further references); H. Meyer, *op. cit.*, footnote 17, §46 paras. 1, 19 *et seq.*; P. Stelkens, in P. Stelkens *et al.*, *Verwaltungsverfahrensgesetz*, *Kommentar*, (2nd ed., Munich 1983), §46 para. 7 with further references.

[22] *cf.* on the duty to give reasons in Italian law, C. Mortati, *Istituzioni di Diritto Pubblico*, (9th ed., Padua 1975), Vol. I, p. 251; C. Mortati, "Necessità di motivazione e sufficienza della motivazione," Giur. it. 1943 III, p. 1; A. M. Sandulli, *Manuale di Diritto Amministrativo*, (14th ed., Naples 1984), Vol. I, pp. 673 *et seq.*; G. Landi, G. Potenza, *Manuale di Diritto Amministrativo*, (7th ed., Milan 1983), p. 237; R. Iannotta, "La motivazione come modo di attuazione del principio di imparzialità amministrativa," Foro amm. 1975 II, pp. 525 *et seq.*; M. S. Giannini, *Diritto amministrativo*, Milan, 1970, Vol. 1, pp. 569 *et seq.*

cases groups of decisions in which the duty of the administration to give reasons for its decisions results "from the nature of the matter."[23] This applies in particular to negative or unfavourable administrative decisions, as well as to discretionary decisions. In so far as there exists a duty to give reasons, the authority must set out in writing the considerations which led it to the adoption of the administrative act. It will suffice, however, if the grounds of the decision are available simply in the documents which accompany the decision.[24] Exceptionally a tacit statement of reasons is also permissible.[25] The statement of reasons sets out the circumstances of fact and law which were decisive for the formation of the decision by the authority.[26] The infringement of the duty to give reasons does not necessarily lead to the annulment of the decision by the administrative courts, but rather only where a different decision would have been taken on the facts. The position is different for discretionary decisions: here insufficient reasons will generally lead to the annulment of the administrative act, because the judge may not put his discretion in the place of the discretion of the authority.[27]

(d) The duty to give reasons in the United Kingdom

English law does not recognise a general duty to give reasons. As regards the legislative context, this follows from the fundamental concept of the "supremacy of Parliament," that is the notion that the actions of Parliament neither require a justification nor are subject in any way to the control of the courts.[28]

---

[23] On the development of the case law, cf. in particular M. S. Giannini, Diritto amministra-tivo, Vol. I, pp. 569 et seq. with further references, p. 573.

[24] On reasoning "per relationem," cf. C. Mortati, op. cit., footnote 22, p. 250; G. Landi, G. Potenza, op. cit., footnote 22, p. 237.

[25] E. Schott, op. cit., footnote 11, p. 44.

[26] C. Mortati, op. cit., footnote 22, p. 250; the fact that a process of weighing up interests has occurred need only be mentioned by the authority, cf. E. Schott, op. cit., footnote 11, p. 45.

[27] cf. A. Sandulli, op. cit., footnote 22, p. 675, with reference to two contradictory decisions of the Council of State (CdS, Sez. II of March 16, 1976, No. 375/75 and CdS, Sez. VI of October 18, 1977, No. 798/77).

[28] On the supremacy of Parliament, cf. O. Hood Phillips Constitutional and Administrative Law, (6th ed., London 1978), pp. 45 et seq.; I. N. Stevens Constitutional and Administrative Law, Plymouth 1984, pp. 31 et seq.; H. W. R. Wade Administrative Law, (5th ed., Oxford 1982), pp. 26 et seq.

However, it is recognised that the reasoning of administrative decisions is an important element of administrative justice.[29] The judicial starting point is the general principle of *audi alteram partem*, which belongs to the rules of "natural justice" and requires that the person concerned is informed of the object of the procedure.[30] In order to exercise his rights to a hearing and to defend himself properly, it is necessary, in the eyes of English law, for the person concerned to know of matters which the authority has taken into consideration.[31] The duty to give reasons for administrative acts may further be laid down in a specific statute. That is for example the case for "tribunal" decisions in section 12(1) of the Tribunals and Inquiries Act 1971.[32] Furthermore the Housing (Homeless Persons) Act s.8(4), and the Housing Act 1980, s.5, contain specific duties to give reasons.[33] The infringement of one of the duties to give reasons laid down in statute or based on general principles of law has in a number of cases led to the quashing of decisions by the courts.[34] Nonetheless it would be incorrect to deduce from this a general rule that the infringement of the duty to give reasons is always sanctioned by the quashing of the decision. It is rather the case that in judicial proceedings the reasons may be stated retrospectively. Only where this does not occur and the decision appears on these grounds to be arbitrary and without foundation will it be quashed by the courts.

(e) The duty to give reasons in Belgium

Since Belgian administrative law has been considerably influenced by the French model, it is hardly surprising that the duty to give reasons in

---

[29] H. W. R. Wade, *op. cit.*, footnote 28, p. 486; D. Foulkes *Administrative Law*, (5th ed., London 1982), p. 254; P. P. Craig *Administrative Law*, London, 1983, p. 277.

[30] *cf.* on this above, E.II.4.

[31] I. N. Stevens, *op. cit.*, footnote 28, p. 233; P. P. Craig, *op. cit.*, footnote 29, p. 278; *cf.* however, the comment of Lord Denning M.R. in *Selvarajan* v. *Race Relations Board* (1976) "suffice it that the broad grounds are given (. . .)"; J. F. Garner *Administrative Law*, (5th ed., London 1979), p. 133; *McInnes* v. *Onslow-Fane* [1978] 3 All E.R. 211.

[32] *cf.* the compilation in J. F. Garner, *op. cit.*, footnote 31, p. 171 with further references to s.12 of the same Act; further D. Foulkes, *op. cit.*, footnote 29, p. 255 with further references to the case law.

[33] D. Foulkes, *op. cit.*, footnote 29, pp. 256 *et seq.* with further references; *cf.* also P. P. Craig, *op. cit.*, footnote 29, p. 278 with further references.

[34] *Giraudan & Co.* v. *Minister of Housing* [1966] 3 All E.R. 696; *Padfield* v. *Minister of Agriculture* [1968] 1 All E.R. 694 (H.L.); the latter decision was described by Lord Denning M.R. in *Breen* v. *Amalgamated Engineering Union* [1971] 2 Q.B. 175 at 190 as a "landmark in modern administrative law"; *Minister of National Revenue* v. *Wrights Canadian Ropes Ltd.* [1947] A.C. 109 at 123.

Belgium is not of general application since, as previously in France, there is no general statutory provision for such a duty.[35] In contrast to Article 97 of the Belgian Constitution, which lays down a duty on courts to give reasons for their decisions, such an obligation applies to the administration only where it is expressly provided for by statute.[36] However, every act of the administration of a legal nature must be based on statutory grounds. In order to facilitate the review of a decision the administration may be obliged in certain circumstances to make its reasons clear even where a corresponding obligation is not provided for by law.[37]

If a statement of reasons is required, it is subject to strict conditions. The statement of reasons must set out the manner in which the various conditions to which the application of the relevant legal power is subject are satisfied in each individual case. The mere repetition of the text of the law or general arguments will not be considered adequate. The considerations and legal approach of the administration must be reflected in the statement of reasons. If the statement of reasons is absent or incomplete, the administrative act will be unlawful, regardless of whether the considerations not expressed in the statement of reasons were actually applied or not.[38]

(f) The duty to give reasons in Denmark

In Danish law there are a number of specific statutory rules which impose on the relevant authority the duty to give reasons for a decision owed to the person concerned.[39] Apart from these special cases, there

---

[35] J. Dembour *Droit administratif*, p. 285, note 1. Thus the administrative act must rest on grounds (*motifs*); it is only their actual statement by the authority (*motivation*) which is not always compulsory.

[36] *e.g.* Article 87 of the Law on local authorities; *cf.* also A. Mast, J. Dujardin *Overzicht van het Belgisch Administratief Recht*, Ghent, 1984, para. 565, pp. 545 *et seq.*; A. Mast, "La motivation comme instrument du contrôle par le Conseil d'Etat de l'exercice du pouvoir discrétionnaire de l'administration," Travaux du Centre National de Recherches de Logique, Brussels, Bruylant 1978, pp. 367 *et seq.*; F. M. Remion, "La motivation des actes administratifs en droit belge," *Rapport belge au VIIIe Congrès de Droit Comparé*, Brussels, C.I.D.C. 1970, pp. 668 *et seq.*

[37] A. Mast, J. Dujardin, *op. cit.*, footnote 36, para. 565; Conseil d'Etat judgment No. 8477 of March 7, 1961, *Gemeinde Schoten*; No. 16.358 of April 9, 1974, *Schiepers and de Plecker*; No. 19.177 of October 10, 1978, *Wastiels*.

[38] H.-H. Scheffler *Die Pflicht zur Begründung von Massnahmen nach den europäischen Gemeinschaftsverträgen*, Berlin, 1974, p. 33; Wigny *Droit administratif—principes généraux*, (4th ed., Brussels 1962), p. 151 with examples from the case law.

[39] N. E. Holm, "Due process in Danish administrative procedure," FIDE 1978, p. 3.15.

was previously no general legal duty on the authorities to give a statement of reasons. However, the administrative practice tends to involve the communication of a statement of reasons if one is requested, so long as the petitioner was adversely affected by the decision.[40] Since the adoption of the *Forvaltningslov* of December 19, 1985[41] the relationship between the administration and persons concerned by administrative acts is now governed by statute.[42] The sixth Chapter of this code contains detailed rules on the duty to give reasons. Section 22 provides that a written administrative act must normally include a written statement of reasons. Under §23 the addressees of an oral administrative act have the right to demand a written statement of reasons if their petition has not been accepted in full.

Section 24 lays down the scope of the duty to give reasons. In principle, the statement of reasons must set out both the factual and the legal position. The scope and type of the statement to be provided are dependent on the significance of the matter for the person concerned. If the authority has exercised a discretion, it is particularly important that the considerations underlying the discretion should be set out.[43]

The Law also lays down the limits to and exceptions from the duty to give reasons. Under §24(3) read in conjunction with §15 the scope of the duty to give reasons will be limited in so far as it is necessary to ensure the protection of certain public and private interests (*e.g.* public security).[44]

An administrative act which infringes the duty to give reasons is unlawful and can be annulled by the courts.

(g) *The duty to give reasons in Greece*

In Greece the duty to give reasons is in principle recognised as a *principe général du droit*, specifically as a supplementary right to the right to a hearing.[45] Here there is a duty to give reasons for administrative acts,

---

[40] N. E. Holm, *op. cit.*, footnote 39, p. 3.16.
[41] Law No. 571 of December 19, 1985, "Forvaltningslov."
[42] On the distinction between this Law and the provisions of Law No. 572 of December 19, 1985 "om offentlighed i forvaltningen," *cf.* above, V.2 on the rights of the defence in Denmark.
[43] This was earlier administrative practice, *cf.* N. E. Holm, *op. cit.*, footnote 39, p. 3.16.
[44] The limitations on the duty to give reasons cited here correspond to those contained in the 1972 draft law, *cf.* N. E. Holm, *op. cit.*, footnote 39, p. 3.16.
[45] Th. I. Panagopoulos, "Das Verwaltungsverfahren in Griechenland," DVBl. 1977, pp. 154 *et seq.*; M. Stassinopoulos *Le droit de la défense devant les autorités administratives*, Paris, 1976, p. 190.

which is derived from the principles of the rule of law and of administration under the law, where a statement of reasons is provided for by law or where one is necessary from the nature of the act.[46] The latter category of acts which require a statement of reasons includes, for example, unfavourable administrative decisions. Furthermore the Greek administrative courts appear to be tending to include an increasingly wide range of administrative acts within the scope of the duty to give reasons. The important aspect of this development is that according to a decision of the Greek Council of State the authority is obliged to deal in the statement of reasons with the contentions of the other party.[47] On the other hand, the urgency of a measure or other reasons of administrative efficiency may limit or exclude the duty to give reasons.[48] An administrative act which breaches the duty to give reasons is unlawful and may be annulled.

(h) The duty to give reasons in Ireland

The rules on the duty to give reasons in Ireland, like the rest of administrative law in this country, are similar to those governing English law.[49] Although in Ireland the control of legislation by the courts is possible and the notion of the supremacy of Parliament is becoming less and less significant,[50] the introduction of a duty to give reasons for legislative acts has hardly been discussed.

However, as regards the reasoning of administrative acts, a distinctive Irish tradition has grown up since independence and under the application of the 1937 Constitution.[51] On the basis of Article 40(3) of the Constitution the principle of natural (or constitutional) justice[52] is emphasised as aiming to ensure, as in England, a fair procedure for the person concerned.[53] However, there is in Ireland a certain scepticism

---

[46] Th. Panagopoulos, op. cit., footnote 45, p. 156.
[47] Greek Council of State, Judgment no. 2184/1973.
[48] Th. Panagopoulos, op. cit., footnote 45, p. 158.
[49] B. Chubb The Government and Politics of Ireland, London, etc., 1974, p. 296; A. K. Asmal, "Administrative Law in Ireland," Revue Internationale des Sciences Administratives (1968), 34, p. 109.
[50] B. Chubb The Constitution and Constitutional Change in Ireland, Dublin, 1979, pp. 72 et seq.
[51] Article 34.4.3 of the Constitution; J. M. Kelly The Irish Constitution, Article 34.3.2, p. 270 as well as the National Report for Ireland, above.
[52] J. M. Kelly, op. cit., footnote 51, p. 229 with further references.
[53] R. Grimes, P. Horgan Law in the Republic of Ireland, Portmarnock/Dublin, 1981, p. 102; B. Chubb Constitutional Change, p. 78 with reference to Macavley v. The Minister for

towards "administrative law" of the French variety, in particular because under the Irish conception the control of the administration is an aspect of political control by Parliament.[54] Thus a duty to give reasons can be derived only with limitations from the principle of natural justice[55]; a duty to give reasons for official decisions is thus recognised only where it is specifically provided for by statute or regulation. The courts however have increasingly moved towards asking authorities for documentation on the factual and legal position.[56] In a number of cases which relate both to formal inquiries and to simple administrative decisions, the authorities have been obliged in the first instance to provide records of the evidence put forward and the factual knowledge which they have acquired in the course of investigations. This should be compiled with the actual decision. The compilation should also be made available to the person concerned. In so far as a "policy" is of significance for the decision, the principles which it incorporates should be made clear so that the person concerned can understand the background to the decision.[57] The legal basis which can lead to the quashing of a decision if there has been an infringement of these rules was summarised by Kingsmill-Moore J. delivering a judgment of the Supreme Court. In a case involving a house owner, who was refused without reasons the necessary consent of the local authority to sell her house, he held as follows[58]:

> "If so, he has refused to divulge the policy or principle which he has in mind to the applicant, and so has deprived her of the opportunity to which I think she is entitled, of conforming with or contesting such a principle or policy. Nor has he thought it right to enlighten the Court except in so far as he admitted under cross-examination that he personally did not favour sales ... and that over a period of some six years he had never consented to a sale ... in the absence of any

Posts and Telegraphs [1965] I.R. 70; *Byrne* v. *Ireland and the Attorney General* [1966] I.R. 345 (cited in B. Chubb).

[54] B. Chubb, *op. cit.*, footnote 49, p. 297 (with further references) with reference to *Local Government Board* v. *Arlidge* [1915] A.C. 120 at 136, *per* Lord Shaw.

[55] *cf.* on English law above; A. K. Asmal, *op. cit.*, footnote 49, p. 109 at 113.

[56] In *Re Dunleary's Estate* [1952] I.R. 86 at 90; *The State (McGeough)* v. *Louth County Council*, I.L.T.R. 107, 13 at 25; *Murphy* v. *Dublin Corporation and Minister for Local Government* [1972] I.R. 215; *Geraghty* v. *Dublin Corporation* [1976] I.R. 153; *Russel* v. *Minister for Local Government* [1976] I.R. 195.

[57] R. M. Stout *Administrative Law in Ireland*, Dublin, 1985, pp. 195 *et seq.* (with further references).

[58] Kingsmill-Moore J., in *The State (McGeough)* v. *Louth County Council*, I.L.T.R. 107, p. 13 at 25, cited in Stout, *op. cit.*, footnote 57, p. 200.

further elucidation or explanation on his part, he has unfortunately left himself open to the suggestion that his attitude towards applications for consent to sell has been arbitrary, capricious and obstructive. Such a suggestion may be unfair and entirely erroneous. The Manager may have acted on grounds ... which may have been reasonable ... It is ... regrettable that he has made no effort to meet this suggestion. He could clearly have done so by stating his reasons for the information of the Court, which could then have given him guidance as to their legality. Instead ... he contends that the Act gives to him the unfettered right to refuse or give consent ... according to his personal views which are to remain unexplained and unrevealed."

The rejection was quashed as arbitrary and groundless.

(i) The duty to give reasons in Luxembourg

Administrative law in Luxembourg does not recognise a general principle requiring the administration to put down the reasons for its actions in a formal statement.[59] On the other hand, it is the rule in Luxembourg that administrative actions must always be based on substantive considerations.[60] Furthermore the *Règlement* of June 8, 1979 has laid down a duty to give reasons for the main sectors of administrative activity. This requires the following acts to be reasoned: the rejection of a petition; the revocation or retrospective amendment of an existing administrative act; decisions on a complaint against the administration; administrative acts which have involved the participation of a further body which has given a recommendation which has not been followed. A statement of reasons is also required in the latter category of cases where the authority follows the recommendation but intends to take a decision which departs from existing practice.[61] The lack of a statement of reasons can be subsequently

---

[59] F. Welter *et al.*, "Rapport présenté aux Colloques entre les C. E. Belge, Néerlandais, Français, Italien, Luxembourgeois et le Bundesverwaltungsgericht," Colloque de Rome, March 4, 5, 6, 1968, p. 171, 14.

[60] F. Schockweiler, "Due process in administrative procedure," FIDE 1978, p. 8.2; F. Welter, *op. cit.*, footnote 59, p. 175, 22.

[61] F. Schockweiler *Le Contentieux administratif et la Procédure administrative non contentieuse en droit luxembourgeois*, pp. 96 *et seq.*

rectified in proceedings before the administrative courts. The infringement of the duty to give reasons will lead to the annulment of the administrative act only if a different decision would have been taken in that matter had the requirement to give reasons been duly followed,[62] that is where the inadequate statement of reasons demonstrates that the authority has in fact made an incorrect decision in that case. Thus the Conseil d'Etat annulled the revocation of an authorisation under economic law, because a justification for the act could not be discerned from either the measure itself or the files. The object of the decision was primarily the question of the material justification, that is the legal basis for the measure.[63]

(j) *The duty to give reasons in the Netherlands*

The duty to give reasons operates as a general principle in the Netherlands which applies only to individual acts of the administration, not to normative measures.[64] In addition there are individual laws in which the duty to give reasons is specifically regulated.[65] The so-called principle of reasoning (*motiveringsbeginsel*) is recognised in both the courts and the literature as a fundamental principle of proper administration. This principle is applied in two contexts: in the procedural sense, as a duty to give reasons (*motiveringsplicht*), and in the substantive sense as the principle of adequate grounds (*beginsel van draagkrachtige motivering*).[66] In the procedural sense unfavourable administrative dispositions require a statement of reasons which reveals the motives for the actions of the administration.[67]

---

[62] *Ibid.*

[63] C.E. of May 13, 1953, *Mey*, cited in F. Welter, *op. cit.*, footnote 59, p. 176.

[64] P. de Haan *et al.*, *Bestuursrecht in de sociale Rechtsstaat*, Deventer 1978, p. 40 "motiveringsbeginsel"; in part with a different view see M. Fromont, "Der Rechtsschutz gegen Massnahmen der Verwaltung im Europa der Sechs," Europarecht 1969, p. 210, who also claims to see many exceptions in Dutch law and in particular considers the judge to be justified in examining the grounds on which the decision is based; *cf.* also the report of the Dutch Association of Administrative Law on general provisions of administrative law, translated by C. H. Ule, *Verwaltungsverfahrensgesetze des Auslandes*, Berlin, 1967, Vol. I, pp. 364 *et seq.* ("Rapport ABAR").

[65] P. de Haan *et al.*, *op. cit.*, footnote 64, p. 40 (implicit); H.-H. Scheffler *Die Pflicht zur Begründung von Massnahmen nach den europäischen Gemeinschaftsverträgen*, Berlin, 1974, p. 28.

[66] G. A. van Poelje, A. M. Donner *Nederlands Bestuursrecht*, Vol. I, Alphen, 1974, p. 278; P. de Haan *et al.*, *op. cit.*, footnote 64, p. 38; Rapport ABAR, pp. 138, 166.

[67] P. de Haan *et al.*, *op. cit.*, footnote 64, p. 40.

The extent to which the statement of reasons must clarify the motives behind the decision depends on the circumstances of the individual case. In general it will suffice if the following are apparent from the statement of reasons: the factual conditions of the decision, the statutory provisions on which it is based and, in the case of discretionary decisions, the evaluatory standard which was used or the criteria which were seen as decisive. In the case of favourable administrative dispositions there may be no need to provide a statement of reasons, providing that there is no duty to give reasons laid down in law and the interests of third parties are not adversely affected.[68]

The principle of reasoning in substantive law, that is the requirement that the statement of reasons must be sufficient to sustain unfavourable decisions on the part of the administration originates in the case law of the chamber deciding economic disputes and is used particularly frequently by the judicial section of the Council of State as a sort of standard of control.[69] It requires, on the one hand, that the decision and its statement of reasons are based on the correct factual basis. On the other hand, it requires that the decision is correctly derived, both factually and legally, from the statement of reasons.[70]

The significance of the principle of reasoning in the case law of the judicial section can be discerned from the fact that a great variety of defects of form and content are often apparent in a weak statement of reasons. Thus in a series of cases in which this principle was applied, the administrative disposition in question could also have been annulled on other grounds, e.g. for infringement of the law, of the principle of the protection of legitimate expectations, or of the principle of equality.[71]

An administrative measure with an insufficient statement of reasons will normally be annulled, since only then will the administration observe the duty in the future.[72]

[68] Rapport ABAR, p. 141.
[69] A. M. Donner, "Misbruik van beginselen," RMT 1978, p. 377 at 378; Rapport ABAR, p. 166.
[70] Rapport ABAR, pp. 166 et seq.; P. de Haan et al., op. cit., footnote 64, p. 40; cf. also CBB November 6, 1959, SEW 1960, p. 37; CBB February 11, 1972, AB 1972, p. 100.
[71] Rapport ABAR, pp. 172 et seq.; cf. A. M. Donner, op. cit., footnote 69, p. 378.
[72] G. A. Poelje, A. M. Donner, op. cit., footnote 66, p. 269.

(k) The duty to give reasons in Portugal

The need to give reasons for administrative decisions is laid down in the Portuguese Constitution itself. Article 268(2) provides[73]:

> "2. Administrative acts with external effects must be notified to those who have an interest in them in so far as they are not required to be published officially; they require an express statement of reasons wherever they affect the rights or legally protected interests of citizens."

This provision was given concrete force through the statutory decree No. 256-a/77 of June 17, 1977.[74] Article 1 deals in detail with the question of which acts require a statement of reasons. Any duties to give reasons which are laid down in specific laws remain unaffected by the decree. The administrative acts which are subject to the duty to give reasons under Article 1 of the decree include, in particular, the following:

— those which wholly or in part refuse, allow to lapse, limit or otherwise adversely affect rights or entitlements, or which impose burdens or sanctions;
— those which affect legally protected interests through the exercise of discretion;
— those which decide disputes or appeals;
— those which were adopted in opposition to a petition or in the face of opposition from the person affected, or opposition from other official bodies;
— those which depart from practice in comparable cases;
— those which have the effect of revoking, amending or suspending any of the above acts.

This means that almost all unfavourable administrative acts are subject to the duty to give reasons. Under Articles 2 and 3 of the decree, the statement of reasons must satisfy three requirements:

— it must be express;

---

[73] German text in A. Thomashausen, "Die revidierte Verfassung der Republik Portugal von 1976," JöR 32 (1983), p. 443 at 496.
[74] cf. ·D. Freitas do Amaral *Direito Administrativo*, Vol. III, Lisbon, 1985, pp. 244 *et seq.*; M. Caetano *Manuel de Direito Administrativo*, (10th ed., Coimbra 1984), Vol. I, pp. 477 *et seq.*; M. Esteves de Oliveira *Direito Administrativo*, Coimbra, 1984, Vol. I, pp. 467 *et seq.*

— it must state the factual and legal position on the basis of which the decision was adopted;
— it must be clear, coherent and comprehensive.

Articles 4 and 5 contain special rules for oral administrative acts[75]; special rules also apply to administrative acts which are implicitly adopted if the authority fails to act (acto tácito).[76]

Where the statement of reasons for an administrative act does not correspond to the requirements of the Constitution or the Statutory Decree described above, then the infringement of these procedural requirements, which are seen as essential, will be sufficient for the administrative act to be vulnerable to challenge.

(*l*) *The duty to give reasons in Spain*

In Spanish law too, the duty to give reasons is relevant only to administrative decisions. Laws and other normative acts need not be reasoned.

Article 43 of the Law on administrative procedure (LPA)[77] expressly provides for a duty to give reasons in the administrative field. According to Article 43(1) of the LPA all unfavourable administrative decisions must be reasoned.[78] In the process of reasoning their decision, Spanish authorities must state the factual circumstances on which they based themselves. They must also indicate how these facts fulfil the conditions for the application of a legal norm, which contains the regulation necessary for adopting the administrative measure.[79]

---

[75] D. Freitas do Amaral, *op. cit.*, footnote 74, Vol. III, p. 247.

[76] M. Caetano, *op. cit.*, footnote 74, Vol. I, pp. 474 *et seq.*; M. Esteves de Oliveira, *op. cit.*, footnote 74, Vol. I, pp. 477 *et seq.*

[77] Ley de Procedimiento administrativo of July 17, 1958, in the version of December 2, 1963 and further amendments, cited in E. García de Enterría, T.-R. Fernández *Curso de Derecho Administrativo*, (4th ed., Madrid 1984), Vol. 1, pp. 523 *et seq.*; also *Legislación de la Justicia Administrativa*, Ed. Civitas, (7th ed., Madrid 1985).

[78] F. Garrido Falla *Tratado de Derecho Administrativo*, (9th ed., Madrid 1985), Vol. I (Parte General), p. 688 states that this is a codified general principle of law.
  Article 43(1) LPA provides:
  1. Serán motivados, con sucinta referencia de hechos, y fundamentos de Derechos:
    (a) Los actos que limiten derechos subjectivos.
    (b) Los que resuelvan recursos.
    (c) Los que se separan del criterio seguido en actuaciones precedentes o del dictamen de organos consultivos.
    (d) Aquellos que deban serlo en virtud se disposiciones legales.
    (e) Los acuerdos de suspensión de actos que hayan sido objeto de recurso.

[79] E. García de Enterría, *op. cit.*, footnote 77, p. 523.

The Spanish Constitutional Court has held that the duty to give reasons is an imperative precondition for the person concerned to be able to defend himself before the law.[80] An infringement of the wide-ranging duty to give reasons does not, however, always lead to the nullity or voidability of the administrative act. According to Article 48(2) LPA a defect of form will give rise to voidability only where the defect in the reasons indicates the presence of a substantive defect, in particular that improper considerations may have been taken into account in the exercise of a discretion.[81] The highest Court has held in this regard that an "elementary principle of the economy of process forbids the annulment of decisions and actions of the administration (. . .) where in spite of the continuing existence of the defect with all its consequences one can logically see that an administrative act will be adopted which will be identical to the one which it is argued should be annulled."[82]

3. The Duty to give Reasons in European Community Law

(a) *The significance of the duty to give reasons*

In contrast to most other principles of the law of procedure, the duty to give reasons is actually laid down in the Treaty itself. Under Article 190 EEC, regulations, directives and decisions must state the reasons on which they are based. This provides Community law with a duty to give reasons encompassing both normative and administrative acts derived directly from its constitution.[83]

The statement of reasons for a sovereign measure is primarily intended to assist the addressees, they will discover from the reasons what motives have induced the authority to adopt the measure, thus enabling them

---

[80] Tribunal Constitucional, Decision of July 17, 1981; cited in E. Garcia de Enterrïa, *op. cit.*, footnote 77, p. 524; Tribunal Constitucional, Decision of June 16, 1982; cited in E. Garcïa de Enterrïa, *op. cit.*, footnote 77, p. 524.

[81] *cf.* on this however F. Garrido Falla, *op. cit.*, footnote 78, p. 689, who considers the significance of the duty to give reasons to be very small in the case of restricted decisions, but argues that the sanction should always be the voidability of the decision.

[82] Judgment of November 6, 1963, Administrative law section; cited by E. Garcïa de Enterrïa, *op. cit.*, footnote 77, p. 597.

[83] On the notion of the EEC Treaty as the Constitution of the EEC *cf.* J. Schwarze, R. Bieber *Verfassungsentwicklung in der Europäischen Gemeinschaft*, Baden-Baden 1984, pp. 3 *et seq.*

more easily to judge the chances of success of any challenge to the act.[83a] Furthermore, the duty to give an objectively conclusive statement of reasons forces the competent authority to consider keenly the issues and thus promotes administrative self-regulation.[84] A detailed statement of reasons also gives the Member States and institutions with *locus standi* under the first paragraph of Article 173 EEC,[85] and those persons with *locus standi* under the second paragraph of that Article,[86] the opportunity, given a more detailed knowledge of the factual and legal position, to estimate their own possibilities of securing legal redress. This effect of protecting third parties has only a limited influence upon the scope of the duty to give reasons; it is the reflection, not the actual goal, of the duty to give reasons. In the foreground there is always the relationship between the authority and the addressee of sovereign measures. The duty to give reasons is one of the essential procedural requirements within the meaning of the first paragraph of Article 173 EEC, breach of which gives rise to a claim.

[83a] See, on the link between the duty to give reasons and effective legal protection, most recently the particularly instructive judgment of the Court of Justice of October 15, 1987 in Case 222/86 *Heylens* [1987] E.C.R. 4097 at 4117, para. 15:
  "Effective judicial review, which must be able to cover the legality of the reasons for the contested decision, presupposes in general that the court to which the matter is referred may require the competent authority to notify its reasons. But where, as in this case, it is more particularly a question of securing the effective protection of a fundamental right conferred by the Treaty on Community workers, the latter must be able to defend that right under the best possible conditions and have the possibility of deciding, with a full knowledge of the relevant facts, whether there is any point in their applying to the courts. Consequently, in such circumstances the competent national authority is under a duty to inform them of the reasons on which its refusal is based, either in the decision itself or in a subsequent communication made at their request."
[84] J. V. Louis, in J. Mégret *et al. Le droit de la Communauté économique européenne*, Brussels, 1983, Vol. 10, Article 190, note 2 (p. 502); H. P. Ipsen *Europäisches Gemeinschaftsrecht*, Tübingen, 1972, Ch. 24/25 (p. 517); Constantinesco L.J. *Das Recht der Europäischen Gemeinschaften I*, Baden-Baden, 1977, para. 522, p. 590; H.-H. Scheffler *Die Pflicht zur Begründung von Massnahmen nach den europäischen Gemeinschaftsverträgen*, Berlin, 1974, pp. 48 *et seq.*; E.-W. Fuss *Die Europäische Gemeinschaft und der Rechtsstaatsgedanke*, Heule, 1967, p. 73.
[85] J. V. Louis, *op. cit.*, footnote 84, Article 173 note 27; H. Smit in H. Smit, P. Herzog (eds.), *The Law of the European Economic Community, A Commentary on the EEC Treaty*, New York, etc., 1976, Article 190, p. 5–632; H.-H. Scheffler, *op. cit.*, footnote 84, p. 66; J. Streil, in B. Beutler *et al. Die Europäische Gemeinschaft—Rechtsordnung und Politik* (3rd ed., Baden-Baden 1987), p. 251; also the Court of Justice has emphasised the role of the Member States, *cf.* for example Case 294/81 *Control Data Belgium NV SA* v. *Commission* [1983] E.C.R. 911 at 928, para. 14.
[86] *cf.* Article 173(2) EEC, 146(2) Euratom, Article 33(2) ECSC; *cf.* on this also J. Streil, *op. cit.*, footnote 85, p. 253, as well as J. V. Louis, *op. cit.*, footnote 84, Article 173 note 27/29.

The infringement of the duty to give reasons may lie in a total absence of a statement of reasons[87]; it is also conceivable that the statement of reasons may be marred by internal inconsistencies and thus fail to constitute an effective statement.[88] It is questionable whether an incomplete statement of reasons actually constitutes an infringement of the duty to state reasons. Since, according to a consistent line of case law, the authority is obliged to state only the essential criteria for the decision, the legal basis and the factual conditions,[89] the statement of reasons will be incomplete only where the authority has failed to communicate one of the decisive reasons for the decision. The Court of Justice has been hesitant when considering this point[90]:

> "With regard more particularly to decisions imposing a fine, the statement of reasons is to be considered sufficient if it indicates clearly and coherently the considerations of fact and of law on the basis of which the fine has been imposed on the parties concerned, in such a way as to acquaint both the latter and the Court with the essential factors of the Commission's reasoning."

If these conditions are fulfilled, then the authority has satisfied its duty to state reasons. To be distinguished from this are submissions concerning defects of substance which, as breaches of the Treaty within the meaning of Article 173(1) EEC, give rise to a claim. Indications of a defect of substance can be revealed in the statement of reasons. To that extent, the

---

[87] H.-W. Daig, in H. v.d. Groeben *et al. Kommentar zum EWG-Vertrag*, Baden-Baden (3rd ed., 1983), Article 190, note 3. As regards the control of State aids decisions of the Commission the Court of Justice has recently decided that there will be an infringement of the duty to state reasons under Article 190 EEC where the authority confines itself to "quoting the words of Article 92(1) of the Treaty without discussing the characteristics of North Rhine-Westphalia's aid programme in order to show that it was incompatible with the common market within the meaning of Article 92(1) of the Treaty": see Case 248/84 *Federal Republic of Germany* v. *Commission* [1987] E.C.R. 4013 at 4142, para. 21.

[88] *e.g.* Case 158/80 *REWE* v. *HZA Kiel* [1981] E.C.R. 1805 at 1834, para. 26.

[89] *e.g.* Case 7/77 *Wüllerstorff* v. *Commission* [1978] E.C.R. 769 at 781; *cf.* also Advocate-General Lagrange in Case 2/54 *Italy* v. *High Authority* [1954–1955] E.C.R. 37 at 60: "In other words, the High Authority must state the reasons for its own decision as it stands and is in no way bound to *refute* contrary or different opinions," as well as Advocate-General Roemer, in Case 41/70, etc., *International Fruit Co.* v. *Commission* [1971] E.C.R. 411 at 441: "the obligation to state reasons (properly understood) only requires the giving of technical and legal considerations upon which, in the opinion of the issuing authority, the measure is based."

[90] Case 41/69 *Chemiefarma* v. *Commission* [1970] E.C.R. 661 at 690, para. 78; similar are Case 292/81 *Lion et Cie.* v. *Soc. Lorriet* [1982] E.C.R. 3887 at 3909, para. 18; Case 176/82 *Nebe* v. *Commission* [1983] E.C.R. 2475 at 2487, para. 21; Case 325/82 *Commission* v. *Germany* [1984] E.C.R. 777 at 793, para. 8.

statement of reasons is an authoritative source of information.[91] That applies in particular to the control of discretion where the Court of Justice must almost exclusively base the judicial review on the considerations which the Commission has put in the statement of reasons[92]:

> "As for the 'infringement of an essential procedural requirement,' which in this case is the absence or insufficiency of grounds for the Decision, in such matters this is always partly linked to the substance, that is, to the legality, since, as you have several times had occasion to recall, the requirements of the reasons for the decision vary according to the more or less discretionary nature of the power exercised and must enable the Court to exercise its power to review the legality of the actions of the High Authority while observing the limits of the discretionary power which result as much from the nature of the applications for annulment as from the restrictions of Article 33."

Nonetheless, it is important to adhere to the principle of the distinction between the infringement of the duty to state reasons, as an essential procedural requirement, on the one hand, and its function as an indicator of substantive defects in the decision to be examined, on the other hand. It is consistent with this distinction for the decision-making body to be able to satisfy the duty to give reasons where it puts forward the conceptions on which the decision is based, without regard to the substantive correctness of the reasons given.

(b) Measures which are subject to the duty to give reasons

In the fields of EEC and Euratom law, Articles 190 EEC and 162 Euratom require all legal acts, with the exception of opinions of the Council of Ministers, which are not legally binding, to state the reasons on which they are based. As regards opinions of the Commission in the

---

[91] H.-W. Daig, *op. cit.*, footnote 87, Article 190, para. 3 at the end; J. V. Louis, *op. cit.*, footnote 84, Article 190, para. 3 with further references; H.-H. Scheffler, *op. cit.*, footnote 84, p. 71; Advocate-General Lagrange, in Case 34/62 *Germany* v. *Commission* [1963] E.C.R. 131 at 142 and also previously Case 2/56 *Geitling* v. *High Authority* [1957–1958] E.C.R. 3 at 15.

[92] Case 66/63 *Netherlands* v. *Commission* [1964] E.C.R. 533 at 553.

context of infringement proceedings, Article 169 EEC provides for a specific duty to give reasons.[93]

In the ECSC field, Article 15 ECSC requires decisions, recommendations and opinions of the High Authority to be reasoned, which includes under "decisions" both general decisions (which correspond to EEC Regulations) and individual measures (which correspond to EEC Decisions). The (binding) recommendation cited in Article 15 ECSC corresponds to the EEC Directive within the meaning of Article 189 EEC.

Whereas under ECSC law only measures of the High Authority (Commission) need be reasoned, under EEC/Euratom law Council acts, too, are subject to the duty to give reasons. This difference can be explained by the fact that under the ECSC the High Authority carries the main decision-making burden, whereas under the EEC the Council of Ministers has this role. The duties to give reasons set out for the EEC/Euratom field on the one hand, and the ECSC on the other, are therefore, taking into consideration the differences which are specific to each Treaty, equivalent. It is therefore correct that the Court of Justice (implicitly)[94] and Advocate-General Roemer (explicitly)[95] should assume that there are no differences between the duty to give reasons under the ECSC Treaty and under the EEC and Euratom Treaties.[96]

With regard to secondary sources of law, it is apparent that duties to give reasons are provided for only in so far as a duty to give reasons already exists under the Treaty.[97] In staff cases, it is the rule that all institutions must state reasons for unfavourable decisions addressed to officials.[98]

It is questionable whether, in addition to the requirement to give reasons for sovereign acts, there is also a need to give reasons for legal

---

[93] *cf.* for example, Case 325/82 *Commission* v. *Germany* (butter cruises) [1984] E.C.R. 777 at 793, para. 8; Case 301/81 *Commission* v. *Belgium* [1983] E.C.R. 467 at 477, para. 8.
[94] Case 24/62 *Germany* v. *Commission* [1963] E.C.R. 63 at 69.
[95] Advocate-General Roemer, in Case 24/62 *Germany* v. *Commission* [1963] 63 at 73 and 79; Case 34/62 *Germany* v. *Commission* [1963] E.C.R. 131 at 152; Case 108/63 *Merlini* v. *High Authority* [1965] E.C.R. 1 at 18.
[96] This is also stated by H. P. Ipsen, *Europäisches Gemeinschaftsrecht*, Tübingen 1972, Ch. 24/25; R. H. Lauwaars, in H. Smit, P. Herzog, *op. cit.*, footnote 85, Article 190.03 (with further references), p. 5–626; G. le Tallec, C.-D. Ehlermann, "Die Begründungspflicht für Rechtsakte der Europäischen Gemeinschaften," AWD/RIW 1966, 149 at 153; H.-H. Scheffler, *op. cit.*, footnote 84, p. 19.
[97] *cf.* for example Article 25(2) of the Staff Regulations of December 18, 1961, in *Handbuch des Europäischen Rechts* I A 67/11 (=Regulation 31/61 of December 18, 1961, O.J. Sp.Ed. 1959–1962, 135, with various amendments). Article 11(5) of Regulation 17, J.O. 1962, 204; O.J. Sp.Ed. 1959–62, 87; Article 14(3) of Regulation 17.
[98] *cf.* the Staff Regulations, in particular Article 25.

acts which fall under private law. This question has become controversial in the context of the termination of civil law contracts of service.[99] In such contracts it is usual to incorporate expressly the provisions of the Staff Regulations which are intended to apply also, where appropriate, to other employers. In so far as reference is made to Article 25 of the Staff Regulations, there will be a duty to state reasons when such contracts are terminated. The exercise by the Community of its rights to create or alter relationships in the context of other private law contracts is not however, according to the Court of Justice, subject to a duty to give reasons. It has reached this conclusion on the grounds that negative effects on third parties in connection with the conclusion of a civil law contract occur only indirectly; thus a decision to conclude, for example, a contract' for services does not require a statement of reasons either *vis-à-vis* the successful tenderer, because he or she is not thereby burdened, or *vis-à-vis* the unsuccessful applicant, because he or she is not the addressee of the decision.[100]

(c) The form of the statement of reasons

Once it is established that a particular measure of a Community institution must be reasoned, the issue arises of the form in which this is to occur. One question is whether the statement of reasons must take the same form as the legal act itself.

The starting point for this discussion can be derived from the text of the relevant provisions. In so far as Articles 15 ECSC, 190 EEC and 162 Euratom provide that legal acts "shall state the reasons" on which they are based,[101] this indicates that in general the statement of reasons will share the same form as the legal act to which it refers, because both are intimately linked together.[102]

---

[99] Case 43/59 etc. *Lachmüller* v. *Commission* [1960] E.C.R. 463; Case 44/59 *Fiddelaar* v. *Commission* [1960] E.C.R. 535; Case 25/60 *De Bruyn* v. *Parliament* [1962] E.C.R. 43; Case 110/75 *Mills* v. *European Investment Bank* [1976] E.C.R. 1613; Case 25/68 *Schertzer* v. *Parliament* [1977] E.C.R. 1729; Case 25/80 *De Briey* v. *Commission* [1981] E.C.R. 637.

[100] Case 56/77 *Agence européenne d'Interims* v. *Commission* [1978] E.C.R. 2215 at 2234; Advocate-General Reischl, at p. 2244, *cf.* also 2242; from a different viewpoint see Advocate-General Mayras, in Case 23/76 *Luigi Pellegrini & C.S.a.s.* v. *Commission* [1976] E.C.R. 1807 at 1827.

[101] French text: "sont motivés,"
German text: "sind mit Gründen versehen,"
Italian text: "sono motivati,"
Dutch text: "met redenen omkleed."

[102] E. Schott *Der Begründungszwang für Akte der Exekutiven der Europäischen Gemeinschaften*, Saarbrücken, 1973, p. 97; J. V. Louis, in J. Mégret, etc., *Le droit de la*

In its case law on staff affairs, the Court of Justice has excluded the possibility of an oral statement of reasons, on the grounds that a statement of reasons in that form would make it impossible for the judge to review the reasons which determined the administration's action.[103] Although the law governing Community officials is a special case, both of the arguments in favour of the requirement of a written statement of reasons—clarity concerning the relevant reasons for the decisions, and evidentiary certainty—apply outside that field. The further argument that third parties may have a legally protected interest in the matter also speaks in favour of a written articulation of the reasons. Only thus can the possibility be excluded that the authority may seek at a later stage to justify its action with reasons which did not even exist at the time when the act was adopted.[104] Thus the statement of reasons must be issued at the same time as the decision.[105]

In principle it is the case that the statement of reasons, which must be in the form laid down for the legal act, must contain the considerations of fact and law which determined the decision. The Court of Justice has, however, articulated a series of points which in individual cases will determine the scope of the necessary statement of reasons.

(d) The scope of the duty to give reasons

With regard to the scope of the duty to give reasons, the Court of Justice distinguishes according to the type of measure in question. In Case 18/62 the Court of Justice made clear that the duty to give reasons will vary in its scope according to whether the act in question is a general decision with the character of a Regulation, or an individual act.[106] In the

---

Communauté économique européenne, Brussels 1983, Vol. 10, Article 190, note 12 at the end.

[103] Case 18/65 etc. *Gutmann* v. *Commission* [1966] E.C.R. 103 at 116; similar is Case 791/79 *Demont* v. *Commission* [1981] E.C.R. 3105 at 3116, para. 12.

[104] *cf.* J. V. Louis, *op. cit.*, footnote 102, Article 190 note 11; H.-H. Scheffler *Die Pflicht zur Begründung von Massnahmen nach den europäischen Gemeinschaftsverträgen*, Berlin, 1974, p. 192; R. H. Lauwaars, in H. Smith, P. Herzog (eds.), *The law of the European Economic Community, A commentary on the EEC Treaty*, New York, etc., 1976, Article 190.06, p. 5–631; *cf.* also Case 1/55 *Kergall* v. *European Parliament* [1954–1956] E.C.R. 151 at 157.

[105] *cf.* H. P. Ipsen *Europäisches Gemeinschaftsrecht*, Tübingen, 1972, Ch. 24/25 (p. 519); similar is E. Schott, *op. cit.*, footnote 102, p. 98.

[106] Case 18/62 *Emilia Barge* v. *High Authority* [1963] E.C.R. 259 at 281; Case 5/67 *W. Beus GmbH & Co.* v. *HZA München-Landsberger Strasse* [1968] E.C.R. 83 at 95; Case 87/78 *Welding and Co.* v. *HZA Hamburg-Waltershof* [1978] E.C.R. 2457 at 2467, para. 10; see

following section, we shall therefore discuss in more detail the question how the duty to give reasons for individual acts has taken shape in the case law. We shall then look at the requirements attached to the duty to give reasons in the case of normative acts.

(aa) *Individual acts*

The most comprehensive case law on the reasoning of individual acts is to be found in staff cases. According to Article 25(1) second sentence of the Staff Regulations, "any decision embodying a complaint against an official shall state the reasons on which it is based." These include all measures of the appointing authority which affect the official's employment relationship. Measures internal to the service are excluded in principle from the duty to state reasons, unless they represent dispositions having an adverse effect on the addressee.[107] The Court of Justice emphasised in *Kley* that such an adverse effect need not necessarily consist of an interference with material interests[108]:

> "Even though a transfer decision may not affect the material interests or rank of an official it may, having regard to the duty in question, and to the circumstances, adversely affect the morale and the future prospects of the employee concerned. In these circumstances, it cannot be considered *a priori* that such a decision is not capable of adversely affecting the person concerned.
> The objection must therefore be rejected."

Thus there is a wide-ranging duty to give reasons for all acts which affect the status of an official, so long as the interference brought about by the legal act attains a certain degree.[109] The duty to give reasons ceases to apply only where the addressee of the measure is not adversely affected, for example through promotion.[110] On the other hand, the decision

---

also Advocate-General Trabucchi, in Case 78/74, *DEUKA* v. *Einfuhr- und Vorratsstelle für Getreide* [1975] E.C.R. 421 at 438; *cf.* also the judgment of the Court at p. 431, para. 6.

[107] Case 18/65 etc. *Gutmann* v. *Commission* [1966] E.C.R. 103 at 116.

[108] Case 35/72 *Kley* v. *Commission* [1973] E.C.R. 679 at 688, paras. 4 to 6.

[109] Case 75/79, etc., *Kuhner* v. *Commission* [1980] E.C.R. 1677 at 1695, para. 14.

[110] Case 188/73 *D. Grassi* v. *Parliament* [1974] E.C.R. 1099 at 1108, paras. 11 to 12.

concerning the complaint of the rejected competitor adversely affects that person and must therefore be reasoned.[111]

Starting from the principle that the addressee of a legal act is to be put in a position by the statement of reasons such that he will be able to discern substantive defects and to estimate the possibilities of securing legal redress, the Court of Justice has evolved the necessary scope of the statement of reasons from the concrete circumstances of each case.[112] That makes it more difficult to make abstract statements about the scope of the duty to give reasons in staff cases. On the other hand, it is apparent from the case law in staff cases that certain circumstances are given particular weight. That applies, for example, to the participation of the official concerned in the decision-making process. In Case 25/80 the Court of Justice articulated this as follows[113]:

> "Moreover, it is clear from the documents before the Court that the applicant had every opportunity during the personal conversations and numerous exchanges of memoranda to put forward his defence. For the same reason the applicant cannot complain that the decision itself failed to set out the reasons on which it was based; such a failure was in any case justified by virtue of the discretion which Article 47(2) confers on the competent authority."

At the core of this decision lies the notion that participation in the procedure, like the duty to give reasons, serves to enable the party concerned to protect his interests and that consequently there will be only a limited need for a statement of reasons for the legal act if the person concerned has been able to ensure that his interests are recognised through participation in the procedure.

A further characteristic of the case law on staff matters is the circumstance that a decision on a staff question is generally preceded by a lengthy process during which the decision is formulated, for instance, within the Personnel Office. In its decision the authority may refer back

---

[111] Case 27/63 *Paponi* v. *Commission* [1964] E.C.R. 129; Case 94/63, etc., *Bernusset* v. *Commission* [1964] E.C.R. 297; Case 151/80 *De Hoe* v. *Commission* [1981] E.C.R. 3161 at 3174, para. 13.

[112] *e.g.* Case 176/82 *Nebe* v. *Commission* [1983] E.C.R 2475 at 2478, para. 11, as well as Case 75/85 *Valerio Raganelli* v. *Commission* [1986] E.C.R. 2775 at 2795, para. 12.

[113] Case 25/80 *Alain de Briey* v. *Commission* [1981] E.C.R. 637 at 646, para. 9.

to this process and need not articulate in more detail circumstances which are already known to the person concerned.[114]

As regards examinations, it is recognised that the statement of reasons for a decision on an examination is limited by the requirements of confidentiality.[115] However, the Court of Justice requires a statement of reasons to be given which enables the person concerned in each case to protect his or her interests.

The fact that the requirements governing the statement of reasons must relate to the actual possibilities available to the authority was demonstrated starkly by the Court of Justice in an agriculture case[116]:

> "The degree of precision of the statement of reasons for such a decision must be weighed against practical realities and the time and technical facilities available for making such a decision. A specific statement of reasons for each individual decision fixing a free-at-frontier price as envisaged by the Finanzgericht would mean the publication and technical evaluation of all the facts submitted by the exporting Member State or gathered by the Commission's staff for several hundreds of prices requiring to be fixed. In view, first, of the time available for the issue of the decisions and, secondly, of the number of prices to be fixed, the requirement of such a specific statement of reasons would be incompatible with the proper functioning of the machinery provided for in Regulation No. 19 of the Council and Regulation No. 89 of the Commission. The preparation and drafting of this kind of statement of reasons would take up so much time that the determination of prices would run the risk of being, to some extent, out of date by the time it was issued."

In competition law it has been recognised since the *IBM* case that it is only the legal acts which conclude the competition proceedings which must be reasoned, and not the preparatory measures.[117] Final decisions must, however, be the more thoroughly reasoned the greater the discretionary

[114] Case 791/79 *Demont* v. *Commission* [1981] E.C.R. 3105 at 3116, para. 12; Case 37/81 *Seton* v. *Commission* [1983] E.C.R. 1789 at 1813, para. 47; Case 8/83 *Bertoli* v. *Commission* [1984] E.C.R. 1649 at 1660, para. 11.
[115] Case 89/79 *Bonu* v. *Council* [1980] E.C.R. 553 at 562, para. 5.
[116] Case 16/65 *Firma C. Schwarze* v. *Einfuhr- und Vorratsstelle für Getreide und Futtermittel* [1965] E.C.R 877 at 888.
[117] Case 60/81 *IBM* v. *Commission* [1981] E.C.R. 2639 at 2653 *et seq.*, in particular also the detailed comparative analysis of Advocate-General Slynn, pp. 2659 *et seq.*

power of the Commission.[118] The connection between the scope of the duty to give reasons and the breadth of an administrative discretion has been stressed in the literature.[119] Some have attempted[120] to make use in Community law of the distinction which is still used in Germany between discretion (*Ermessen*) (on the legal side) and scope for assessment (*Beurteilungsspielraum*) (on the factual side); as we showed above,[121] no such distinction has so far been drawn in Community law.

The Court of Justice has already emphasised, in the case of *Präsident etc.* v. *High Authority*, the link between the range of the available discretion and the scope of the duty to give reasons[122]:

> "After prohibiting (Article 65(1)) cartels in a general way, the Treaty confers upon the High Authority (Article 65(2)) the power to authorize specialization agreements or joint-buying or joint-selling agreements, but subjects the exercise of that power to a finding by the High Authority that the conditions set out in subparagraphs (a), (b) and (c) of paragraph (2) are met. That finding, by its very nature, comprises an assessment of the situation created by the economic facts or circumstances and, accordingly, is partially outside the jurisdiction of the Court.
>
> The obligation to state specific reasons for decisions granting authorizations is rendered necessary and must be strictly observed by the reason of the fact that review by the Court is limited and that the authorization requested is subject to the finding by the High Authority that the conditions set out in Article 65(2) exist and are met.
>
> Those reasons must enable the interested parties and, in the event of legal proceedings, the court, to verify the factors by virtue of

---

[118] Case 56/64 *Grundig and Consten* v. *Commission* [1966] E.C.R. 299 at 338 and 385 and the opinion of Advocate-General Roemer, at 352.

[119] H.-W. Daig *Nichtigkeitsklagen und Untätigkeitsklagen im Recht der Europäischen Gemeinschaften*, Baden-Baden 1985, p. 142, para. 182 with further references; R. H. Lauwaars, in H. Smit, P. E. Herzog (eds.), *The law of the European Economic Community—A Commentary on the EEC Treaty*, New York, etc., 1976, Article 190.05, p. 5–629; J. V. Louis, in J. Mégret *et al.*, *Le Droit de la Communauté économique européenne*, Vol. 10, Brussels 1983, Article 190, note 5, p. 504, with further references to those opposed to such a distinction.

[120] E. Schott *Der Begründungszwang für Akte der Exekutiven der Europäischen Gemeinschaften*, University of Saarland 1971, pp. 108 *et seq.*

[121] Vol. 1, pp. 280 *et seq.*

[122] Case 36/59 etc. *Präsident Ruhrkohlen-Verkaufsgesellschaft et al.* v. *High Authority* [1960] E.C.R. 423 at 439.

which the High Authority concluded that the conditions required for obtaining its authorization were met so as to be able to examine whether that conclusion was right both in fact and in law."

This decision was later confirmed in its result.[123] A particular role has been played in recent years in the ECSC field by the decisions which have imposed fines on undertakings which have exceeded their production quotas. In this context, the statement of reasons is intended to contribute to the avoidance of the impression that the fine is arbitrary.[124]

It is generally the case that the standard by which the statement of reasons will be judged is that of a "person who is concerned by and competent in the matter."[125] When determining the extent of the reasons, whatever knowledge the person concerned actually has is to be taken into account.[126] In one case the Court of Justice even put forward the view that a (partially) incorrect statement of reasons was compensated for by the prior knowledge of the person affected[127]:

"Although the High Authority may have been too positive in the fourth recital to its decision, when it stated that the accounts of an undertaking are indivisible, this cannot invalidate the decision adopted in this instance which, as is shown by the earlier correspondence between the parties, seeks to check whether factors concerning the production of iron and steel are not to be found in the part of the accounts which deals with the undertaking's engineering production."

The case law on the reasoning of individual acts is in all fields of law purposive in nature. It is intended in all circumstances to enable the person concerned to protect his rights, but also simultaneously not to interfere with the functional capacity of the administration by imposing excessive requirements upon it with regard to the statement of reasons. The statement of reasons is a source of information regarding substantive

---

[123] e.g. Case 56/64 etc. *Grundig and Consten* v. *Commission* [1966] E.C.R. 229 at 338 and Case 185/85 *Union Sidérurgique du Nord et de l'Est de la France USINOR S.A.* v. *Commission* [1986] E.C.R. 2079, paras. 20 *et seq.*

[124] Advocate-General Roemer, Case 16/61 *Acciaierie Ferriere e Fonderie di Modena* v. *High Authority* [1962] E.C.R. 289 at 322; as well as Case 29/67 *Société de Wendel & Cie SA* v. *Commission* [1968] E.C.R. 263 at 289.

[125] Opinion of Advocate-General Reischl in Case 275/80 *Krupp* v. *Commission* [1981] E.C.R. 2526.

[126] Case 275/80 *Krupp* v. *Commission* [1981] E.C.R. 2512, para. 13.

[127] Case 31/59 *Acciaieria e Tubificio di Brescia* v. *High Authority* [1960] E.C.R. 71 at 81.

defects. The duty to state reasons thus makes a significant contribution to the judicial control of the legality of administrative action.

(bb) Normative acts

Regulations and general decisions, given their nature as general and abstract norms, do not require reasoning to the same extent as individual measures:

> "(The statement of reasons for such a measure) may be confined to indicating the general situation which led to its adoption, on the one hand, and the general objectives which it is intended to achieve on the other.
>
> Consequently, it is not possible to require that it should set out the various facts, which are often very numerous and complex, on the basis of which the regulation was adopted, or *a fortiori* that it should provide a more or less complete evaluation of those facts."[128]

The actual scope of the duty to give reasons can once more be described only by reference to individual cases.

In the field of agriculture it is apparent that measures of an essentially technical nature require only a limited statement of reasons. The reasons need not cover all details which are to be dealt with in an implementing measure.[129] If a Regulation is adopted within the framework of a general regulatory system, then for the purposes of the evaluation of the statement of reasons the focus should be on all the Regulations with their statements of reasons.[130] In spite of the generally slight requirements placed on the reasons to be given for a Regulation, the Court of Justice did annul a Regulation for breach of the requirement to give reasons in Case 158/80. This concerned Regulation 3023/77, which authorized the Member States to exempt certain imports of goods from agricultural levies, which would otherwise have been due under Regulation 1544/69. The Court of Justice held[131]:

---

[128] Case 5/67 *Firma W. Beus GmbH & Co.* v. *HZA München-Landsberger Strasse* [1968] E.C.R. 83 at 95.
[129] Case 87/78 *Welding & Co.* v. *HZA Hamburg-Waltershof* [1978] E.C.R. 2457 at 2468.
[130] Case 41/70 etc. *International Fruit Company* v. *Commission* [1971] E.C.R. 411 at 423; Case 292/81 etc. *Lion et al.* v. *F.I.R.S.* [1982] E.C.R. 3887 at 3924.
[131] Case 158/80 *REWE-Handelsgesellschaft Nord MbH and REWE-Markt Steffen* v. *HZA Kiel* [1981] E.C.R. 1805 at 1834.

"The statement of reasons on which Regulation No. 3023/77 was based does not fulfil that requirement. It does not in fact provide any explanation of the reason for which the Council, on finding that Regulation No. 1544/69, contrary to a practice which had developed, should not be applied in the circumstances set out above, considered it necessary to establish a special system of exemptions applicable to that type of situation. Such a contradiction in the statement of reasons is all the more serious inasmuch as it concerns a provision empowering the Member States to grant exemptions, albeit on a small scale, from import duties, which constitute an essential part of the common agricultural policy. In those circumstances the statement of reasons does not provide any legal justification for the contested provisions of the regulation and accordingly it does not appear necessary to consider their basis in order to establish whether they are compatible with the rules of the common market."

On these grounds the Regulation was annulled.

In the field of anti-dumping law, a special feature could result from the fact that the anti-dumping duties are laid down by Regulation, although they amount not to general abstract rules, but individual and specific ones. The Court of Justice has held that direct claims against anti-dumping duties under Article 173(2) EEC by directly and individually concerned foreign exporters are admissible.[132] The question then arises whether the fact that the foreign exporters are directly and individually concerned has an effect on the necessary scope of the statement of reasons. One argument in favour of taking into account the interests of the foreign exporters in the reasoning of an anti-dumping regulation is that the person affected by the anti-dumping regulation can effectively challenge the regulation under the second paragraph of Article 173 only if he can prove that the necessary conditions to prove the existence of dumping, assumed by the Council to be present, are not satisfied. This in turn presupposes that the Regulation is adequately reasoned. A further consideration is the fact that the Commission would not in practice find it difficult to set out in detail the relevant considerations with regard to the

---

[132] The leading cases are the ball-bearing cases: Case 113/77 *NTN Toyo Bearing Co.* v. *Council* [1979] E.C.R. 1185 at 1205; Case 118/77 *Import Standard Office* v. *Council* [1979] E.C.R. 1277 at 1293; Case 119/77 *Nippon Seiko K.K. et al.* v. *Council* [1979] E.C.R. 1303 at 1326; Case 120/77 *Koyo Seiko Co. Ltd. et al.* v. *Council and Commission* [1979] E.C.R. 1337 at 1352; Case 121/77 *Nachi Fujikoshi Corporation et al.* v. *Council* [1979] E.C.R. 1363 at 1378, as well as more recently Case 255/84 *Nachi Fujikoshi Corporation et al.* v. *Council* [1987] E.C.R. 1861.

1413

detailed material which it must in any case work through in order to establish the existence and margin of the dumping. Thus regulations imposing anti-dumping duties have come to occupy an intermediate position in the typology of legal acts between general/abstract and individual/concrete measures. The consequences of this for the scope of the duty to give reasons became clear in Case 53/83, *Allied Corporation* v. *Council*[133]:

> "According to Article 13(3) of Regulation No. 3017/79, the amount of anti-dumping duties may not exceed the dumping margin and should be less if such lesser duty would be adequate to remove the injury.
>
> It follows that when the Council adopts an anti-dumping regulation it is required to ascertain whether the amount of the duties is necessary in order to remove the injury. In this case, however, there is nothing in the documents before the Court to suggest that the Council took into consideration that aspect of the matter.
>
> In the preamble to Regulation No. 101/83, the Council deals in detail with the question whether the injury was caused by imports from the United States or by sales on the French market by producers established in other Member States. It does not however discuss the question of the amount of duties necessary in order to remove the injury; its only reference in that connection is the Commission's view that 'lower levels would constitute a bonus for Allied Corporation's withdrawal from its undertaking and subsequent non-cooperation and the withdrawal from their undertakings by Kaiser and Transcontinental.' That consideration is not relevant to the application of Article 13(3) of the Regulation. Examination of the case has not disclosed any other factors indicating that the Council took into account that article in fixing the amount of the anti-dumping duties. It must therefore be concluded that the regulation was adopted in disregard of Article 13 and that it must therefore be declared void."

The statement of reasons which must accompany an anti-dumping regulation has thus been assimilated more to the statement of reasons for an individual act, since it must include more than just a general statement about the overall situation. This case law has demonstrated that the Court of Justice proceeds, even when considering the concrete terms of the

[133] Case 53/83 *Allied Corporation* v. *Council* [1985] E.C.R. 1621 at 1659.

statement of reasons for a normative legal act, not in a schematic, but rather in a pragmatic and purposive manner.

In the field of the ECSC Treaty, the statement of reasons for general decisions likewise need not be so detailed as that required for an individual measure.[134]

> "According to the case law of the Court (...) the statement of reasons on which Community measures are based must be appropriate to the nature of the measure in question: it must show clearly and unequivocally the reasoning of the Community authority which issued the measure, so as to allow those concerned to take cognizance of the justification for the measure adopted and to enable the Court to exercise its powers of review. In the case of a measure in the nature of a regulation, such as the general decision in dispute, the statement of reasons cannot be required to specify the often very numerous and complex matters of law or of fact constituting the subject-matter of such instruments, as long as those matters fall within the framework of the whole of which they form part."[135]

It is thus permissible, in the context of a regulatory framework which is composed of a number of general decisions, to focus upon the various statements of reasons as a whole.

Above all it must be concluded that the statement of reasons required for normative acts is not as important as that required for individual acts. The duty to give reasons does, however, ensure that a certain level of publicity is given to the motives of the legislature.

The gradations in the scope of the duty to give reasons between normative acts and individual measures are overwhelmingly approved of in the literature.[136] Thus reference is made to the fact that legislative

---

[134] Case 18/62 *Emilia Barge* v. *High Authority* [1963] E.C.R. 259 at 280.
[135] Case 311/81 etc. *Klöckner Werke AG* v. *Commission* [1983] E.C.R. 1549 at 1571, para. 32.
[136] H.-H. Scheffler, *Die Pflicht zur Begründung von Massnahmen nach den europäischen Gemeinschaftsverträgen*, Berlin, 1974, p. 183; R. H. Lauwaars, in H. Smit, P. E. Herzog (eds.), *The Law of the European Economic Community—A Commentary on the EEC Treaty*, New York, etc., Article 190.05, p. 5–628; H.-W. Daig, in H. v.d. Groeben *et al.*, *Kommentar zum EWG-Vertrag*, (3rd ed., Baden-Baden 1983), Article 190, para. 10; J. V. Louis, in J. Mégret *et al.*, *Le droit de la Communauté économique européenne*, (Brussels, 1983), Vol. 10, Article 190, note 6; G. Le Tallec, C.-D. Ehlermann, "Die Begründungspflicht für Rechtsakte der Europäischen Gemeinschaften," RIW 1966, p. 149; E. Schott, *Der Begründungszwang für Akte der Exekutiven der Europäischen Gemeinschaften*, University of the Saarland 1971, p. 146.

measures are mostly subject to no duty to give reasons in national law, and that legislative acts by their very nature cannot be reasoned in such detail. Even so, the reasoning of normative acts in Community law must not be reduced to a formality, since, given the secrecy of the deliberations of the Council and Commission, the institutions which are called upon to apply the law rely very heavily upon detailed information about the meaning and purpose of a regulation in order to effect an appropriate interpretation of its provisions.

III. NOTIFICATION

A decision must be notified before it can have any effect *vis-à-vis* the person concerned.[1] The notification must be to the addressee; notification is not required to those who are indirectly affected,[2] even where they have *locus standi* to bring an action for annulment under the second paragraph of Article 173 EEC.

Although this is expressly required only in staff cases, and in some aspects of competition proceedings,[3] a decision must be in writing. This results not only from the duty to give reasons (Article 190 EEC) and the duty to append a copy of the act under challenge to any action for annulment, but also from the very nature of the problem.[4] However, the Court of Justice[5] has held that it is sufficient that an undertaking should be informed only of the essential contents of a decision in a letter from the Director-General. Both the Advocate-General[6] and the Court of Justice[7] have held that this form of notification will suffice.

Thus no "notification" (*Zustellung*) in the German sense of the word, meaning a formal handing over of the document, is necessary. Rather it

---

[1] Article 191, second paragraph, EEC = 163, second paragraph, Euratom, similarly Article 15, second paragraph, ECSC in conjunction with Decision No. 22/60/ECSC of September 7, 1960, J.O. 1960, 1248.

[2] H.-W. Daig, in H. v.d. Groeben *et al., Kommentar zum EWG-Vertrag*, (3rd ed., Baden-Baden 1983), Article 191, note 17.

[3] *cf.* Article 25(1) 1st sentence of the Staff Regulations (*Handbuch des Europäischen Rechts* I A 67/11 p. 16), as well as Article 2(1) of Regulation 99/63 (communication of the statement of objections).

[4] H.-W. Daig, *op. cit.*, footnote 2, para. 18; M. Waelbroeck, in J. Mégret *et al.* (eds.), *Le droit de la Communauté économique européenne*, Vol. 10, parts 1 and 2, Brussels 1983, Article 191, note 10.

[5] Case 14/63 *Forges de Clabecq* v. *High Authority* [1963] E.C.R. 357 at 375.

[6] Advocate-General Lagrange, in Case 14/63 *supra*, footnote 5.

[7] *cf.* on this R. H. Lauwaars, in H. Smith, P. Herzog (eds.), *The Law of the European Economic Community—A Commentary on the EEC Treaty*, New York, 1976.

will suffice if the decision has reached the sphere of control of the recipient and he could have knowledge of it.[8] In principle the document can be sent by ordinary post,[9] although in some fields notification through recorded delivery or registered post is provided for,[10] a rule which, for reasons of the security of evidence, should also apply where there is no express requirement.[11] Once the decision has been thus notified, it comes into force, which means that the limitation period begins to run[12] (Article 173, third paragraph, read in conjunction with Article 81(1) Rules of Procedure).

The form of notification just described does not apply when the authority adopts measures in the form of regulations, for example, in the anti-dumping field. In that case official publication in the Official Journal is provided for in Article 191(1) EEC[13] and this will suffice.

Furthermore, it is laid down in some instances that certain communications must be directed to the persons concerned, so that, in particular, they may protect their procedural rights. The same conditions apply in principle to such communications as do also to the notification of decisions.[14] In some cases publication in the Official Journal is also necessary,[15] that is official publication in addition to communication. This applies above all where it is uncertain who might possibly have a legally protected interest in participating in the proceedings. This becomes especially clear in the context of anti-dumping proceedings, where the

---

[8] Case 8/56 *ALMA* v. *High Authority* [1957–1958] E.C.R. 95 at 98; Case 42/85 *Cockerill-Sambre* v. *Commission* [1985] E.C.R. 3753 at 3756; H.-W. Daig, in H. v.d. Groeben *et al., op. cit.*, footnote 2, Article 191, para. 18; in agreement is R. H. Lauwaars, *op. cit.*, footnote 7, Article 191.05, p. 5–640.

[9] H.-W. Daig, in H. v.d. Groeben *et al., op. cit.*, footnote 2; Article 191, para. 18 at the end.

[10] *cf.*, *e.g.* for procedural communications in competition law Article 10 of Regulation 99/63 (no decisions); Article 26(3) of the Staff Regulations, *cf.* also Article 4 of Decision 22/60/ECSC, J.O. 1960, p. 1248.

[11] *cf.* H.-W. Daig, in H. v.d. Groeben *et al.*, *op. cit.*, footnote 2, Article 191, para. 18 at the end.

[12] H.-W. Daig, in H. v.d. Groeben *et al.*, *op. cit.*, footnote 2, Article 191, para. 19; *cf.* also M. Waelbroeck, in J. Mégret, *op. cit.*, footnote 4, Article 191, notes 9, 12; *cf.* Case 42/85 *Cockerill-Sambre* v. *Commission*, *supra*, footnote 8, p. 3756.

[13] Article 163, first paragraph, Euratom, similarly Article 15, third paragraph, ECSC, on these also H.-W. Daig, in H. v.d. Groeben *et al.*, *op. cit.*, footnote 2, Article 191, para. 1.

[14] *cf.* Article 7(1)(b) of Regulation 2176/84 of July 23, 1984, O.J. 1984, L201/1, as well as measures within the framework of Regulation 99/63, in particular communication of the statement of objections, informal request for information, request to submit to an investigation.

[15] Such obligatory rules on publication are to be found *inter alia* in Article 21 of Regulation 17, Article 7 of Regulation 2176/84 (Decision No. 2177/84/ECSC O.J. 1984, L201/17).

communication of the commencement of proceedings to known interested parties as well as publication in the Official Journal is provided for.[16] Publication in the Official Journal in addition to notification to the addressees is, of course, always permissible,[17] insofar as the interests of the parties in maintaining confidentiality are not adversely affected.

The notification must be in the "correct" language, that is the language of the addressee[18]; where a document is published in the Official Journal, of course, versions in all the Community languages will in any case have to be prepared. Particular problems are presented by notification outside the territory of the Member States, since the exercise of sovereign powers extraterritorially is controversial under international law.[19] The Court of Justice has solved these problems pragmatically insofar as it has held that notification by post to undertakings outside the EEC, or to dependent undertakings actually "inside,"[20] is sufficient, in circumstances where the undertakings brought a claim before the Court,[21] since it thereby became clear that they did know of the content of the decision.

[16] cf. Article 7 of Regulation 2176/84, equivalent to Decision No. 2177/84/ECSC.

[17] H.-W. Daig, in H. v.d. Groeben et al., op. cit., footnote 2, Article 191, para. 23 (with further references) with reference to Decision No. 22/60/ECSC, Article 4(2), Article 89(2) second sentence EEC; cf. also M. Waelbroeck, in J. Mégret et al. (eds.), op. cit., footnote 4, Article 191, note 11.

[18] cf. Article 3 of Regulation No. 1 on the language question, O.J. Sp.Ed. 1952–58, p. 59, as amended by the Acts of Accession of 1972, 1979, 1985; H.-W. Daig, Nichtigkeits- und Untätigkeitsklagen im Recht der Europäischen Gemeinschaften, Baden-Baden 1985, para. 166, p. 129; M. Waelbroeck, in J. Mégret et al. (eds.), op. cit., footnote 4, Article 191, note 10.

[19] Advocate-General Mayras in Case 48/69 ICI v. Commission [1972] E.C.R. 619 at 198, 701.

[20] cf. on the questions of competence in relation to such undertakings the section on competence above.

[21] Case 52/69 Geigy v. Commission [1972] E.C.R. 787 at 823, para. 11; Case 48/69 ICI v. Commission [1972] E.C.R. 619 at 651, paras. 34 et seq.; Case 6/72 Europemballage and Continental Can v. Commission [1973] E.C.R. 215 at 241, paras. 7 et seq.; B. Barack, The application of the competition rules (antitrust law) of the European Economic Community to enterprises and arrangements external to the common market, Deventer, 1981, pp. 221 et seq.; C. S. Kerse, EEC Antitrust Procedure, London, 1981, p. 150, item 6.44; R. Kovar, "Droit communautaire de la concurrence et droit international," CDE 1986, pp. 127 et seq.; A. Deringer, "The Common Market competition rules, with particular reference to non-member countries," (1963) 12 ICLQ 582; P. M. Schmitt, "EG-Kartellrecht, Praxis und Verordnungen," in Schwerpunkte des Kartellrechts 1983/84, FIW Schriftenreihe, Issue 112, Cologne etc., 1985, p. 121 at 134 et seq.; Advocate-General Mayras, in Case 48/69 ICI v. Commission [1972] E.C.R. 619 at 701.

If administrative measures are adopted by regulation, then publication in the Official Journal will be necessary if the regulation is to be validly adopted.[22]

In the case of decisions, proper notification is likewise a fundamental prerequisite of validity.

Notification is not, however, a prerequisite for adoption. A decision comes into being through the resolution adopting it. If, prior to notification, the competence to adopt the act is removed, the decision will nonetheless be valid and lawful.[23] The Court of Justice has also held that a decision which is directed to a number of persons and is not properly notified to one of those persons will operate *vis-à-vis* that person if he, for example through a subsidiary company, has learnt of the existence of the decision and is challenging it.[24] The Court of Justice based its argument *inter alia* on Article 173(3) EEC[25]:

> "The last paragraph of Article 173 of the Treaty provides that the period for instituting proceedings for the annulment of individual measures of the Commission starts to run from the date of notification of the decision to the applicant or, in the absence thereof, from the day on which it comes to the knowledge of the latter.
> In the present case it is established that the applicant has had full knowledge of the text of the decision and that it has exercised its right to institute proceedings within the prescribed period."

Defects in the notification of a decision do not make it unlawful, but only restrict its effect,[26] so that they cannot in principle lead to annulment.[27]

---

[22] H.-W. Daig, in H. v.d. Groeben *et al., op. cit.*, footnote 2, Article 191, para. 14; H. P. Ipsen, *Europäisches Gemeinschaftsrecht*, 21/43, p. 464; H.-J. Rabe, *Die Befugnis des Rates und der Kommission der Europäischen Wirtschaftsgemeinschaft zum Erlass von Verordnungen*, Hamburg 1962, p. 28.

[23] Case 3/58, etc. *Barbara Erzbergbau AG* v. *High Authority* [1960] E.C.R. 173 at 188.

[24] Similarly R. H. Lauwaars, in H. Smit, P. Herzog, *op. cit.*, footnote 7, Article 190.05, p. 5–641; also H.-W. Daig, in H. v.d. Groeben *et al., op. cit.*, footnote 2, Article 191, para. 20.

[25] Case 48/69 *ICI* v. *Commission* [1972] E.C.R. 619 at 652; *cf.* also the parallel proceedings in Case 52/69 *Geigy* v. *Commission* [1972] E.C.R. 787.

[26] Case 48/69 *ICI* v. *Commission* [1972] E.C.R. 619 at 652, also Case 52/69 *Geigy* v. *Commission* [1972] E.C.R. 787; *cf.* also M. Waelbroeck, in J. Mégret *et al., op. cit.*, footnote 4, Article 191, note 10.

[27] In that context it is however possible that an act will be annulled because a preparatory measure (for instance the statement of objections in competition law) was not notified.

Where there are differences between the version notified to the addressee and the version published in the Official Journal, the notified version will prevail.[28]

G. LEGAL CONSEQUENCES OF PROCEDURAL DEFECTS

From the grounds for review set out in Article 173 EEC[1] it becomes immediately clear that the infringement of an essential procedural requirement will lead to the annulment of the act in question.

The Court of Justice and the Advocates-General have confirmed this point on numerous occasions and have held that the "vices de forme" will make the act voidable[2] and that the Court of Justice must have regard to such defects where appropriate on its own initiative, that is not necessarily because the parties themselves have raised them.[3] However, the actual annulment of measures which are adopted in the course of an administrative procedure is limited in principle to the act which formally concludes the procedure.[4] Only where separate legal effects result from specific measures adopted during the course of the procedure which go

---

[28] Cases 56 and 58/64 *Consten and Grundig* v. *Commission* [1966] E.C.R. 299 at 337; H.-W. Daig, in H. v.d. Groeben *et al.*, *op. cit.*, footnote 2, Article 191, para. 23; M. Waelbroeck, in J. Mégret *et al.*, *op. cit.*, footnote 4, Article 191, note 11.

[1] See also Article 146 Euratom; Article 33 ECSC is similar.

[2] Case 18/57 *Nold* v. *Commission* [1959] E.C.R. 41, 51–53; Case 8/66, etc., *Cimenteries et al.* v. *Commission* [1967] E.C.R. 75 at 93; Case 80/63 *De Greef* v. *Commission* [1964] E.C.R. 391 at 406; Case 21/70 *Rittweger* v. *Commission* [1971] E.C.R. 7 at 18, paras. 36–41; *cf.* also Case 1/57, etc., *Société des usines à tubes* v. *High Authority* [1957] E.C.R. 105 at 112, with regard to the statement of reasons for an opinion, the absence of which led the Court of Justice to describe the act as "non-existent"; this statement has not been repeated. *cf.* on this H. P. Ipsen, *Europäisches Gemeinschaftsrecht*, Tübingen 1972, §24/20–25; G. Le Tallec, C.-D. Ehlermann, "Die Begründungspflicht für Rechtsakte der Europäischen Gemeinschaften," RIW/AWD 1966, p. 149 at 153; L. Goffin, "La jurisprudence de la Cour de justice sur les droits de la défense," CDE 1980, p. 127 at 141 *et seq.*; H.-W. Daig, *Nichtigkeits- und Untätigkeitsklagen im Recht der Europäischen Gemeinschaften*, Baden-Baden 1985, p. 129, para. 167; R. H. Lauwaars, in H. Smit, P. Herzog (eds.), *The Law of the European Economic Community—A Commentary on the EEC Treaty*, New York, 1976, Article 190.07, p. 5–632, and Supplement.

[3] Case 18/57 *Nold* v. *Commission* [1959] E.C.R. 41 at 51; in agreement: R. H. Lauwaars, in H. Smit, P. Herzog *op. cit.*, footnote 2, Article 190.07, p. 5–632; a different position is to be found in Case 2/54 *Italy* v. *High Authority* [1954–56] E.C.R. 37 at 52.

[4] See on this Case 60/81 *IBM* v. *Commission* [1981] E.C.R. 2639 at 2652, para. 10.

beyond the conduct of the procedure itself can these be challenged separately.[5]

In that context what matters is not so much the description of the act as its content[6]:

"In order to ascertain whether the measures in question are acts within the meaning of Article 173 it is necessary, therefore, to look to their substance. According to the consistent case law of the Court any measure the legal effects of which are binding on, and capable of affecting the interests of, the applicant by bringing about a distinct change in his legal position is an act or decision which may be the subject of an action under Article 173 for a declaration that it is void. However, the form in which such acts or decisions are cast is, in principle, immaterial as regards the question whether they are open to challenge under that article. In the case of acts or decisions adopted by a procedure involving several stages, in particular where they are the culmination of an internal procedure, it is clear from the case law that in principle an act is open to review only if it is a measure definitively laying down the position of the Commission or the Council on the conclusion of that procedure, and not a provisional measure intended to pave the way for the final decision."

Insofar as the possibility of challenge is open, the ground for review is limited to infringements of *essential* procedural requirements, and thus it should not be a source of surprise that a number of limitations have been developed in the case law, which correspond to the requirements of the economy of process in proceedings before the Court of Justice and to the needs of the functional capacity of the administration.[7]

---

[5] See the Court of Justice in the *IBM* case, Case 60/81, *supra*, footnote 4, p. 2652, para. 11; *cf.* also Case 8–11/66 *Cimenteries et al.* v. *Commission* [1967] E.C.R. 75 at 91–93; *cf.* on this J. Schwarze, *Die Befugnis zur Abstraktion im Europäischen Gemeinschaftsrecht*, Baden-Baden 1976, p. 218; W. v. Simson, "Anforderungen an die Rechtmässigkeit des Verwaltungshandelns der EG-Behörden," in J. Schwarze (ed.), *Europäisches Verwaltungsrecht im Werden*, Baden-Baden 1982, pp. 23 *et seq.*, at p. 35; *cf.* also Case 136/79 *National Panasonic* v. *Commission* [1980] E.C.R. 2033, in which it was assumed that the claim was admissible.

[6] Case 60/81 *IBM* v. *Commission* [1981] E.C.R. 2639 at 2651, para. 9; similar is Case 113/77 *NTN Toyo Bearing Co.* v. *Commission* [1979] E.C.R. 1185 at 1203, and in particular 1205, para. 11; see on this W. v. Simson, *op. cit.*, footnote 5, p. 37.

[7] On the workload of the Court of Justice *cf.* Commission, *Twentieth General Report on the Activities of the European Communities*, 1986 (1987), pp. 414 *et seq.* On the possibility that this load may be lightened through the setting up of the court of first instance see U.

Advocate-General Reischl has expressly emphasised this aspect[8]:

"I have a mind to accept that the duty to give a statement of reasons was, in the circumstances, fulfilled in that way. However, I consider that the fact that the contents of the above-mentioned memoranda were not repeated in the transfer decision does not itself justify speaking of an infringement of *essential* procedural requirements. Consequently, it is impossible to justify annulment of the transfer decision by reference to the second paragraph of Article 25 of the Staff Regulations of Officials."

In accordance with the goal of securing comprehensive legal protection for the individual through the form of the procedure, the decisive question for the Court of Justice is whether the applicant's rights of the defence or possibilities for legal redress are adversely affected by the procedural defect.[9] Advocate-General VerLoren van Themaat has argued in this regard:

"Nevertheless the infringements established are in my view set out in the decision with sufficient clarity to enable the applicant to defend itself in the proceedings before the Court against the infringements with which it is charged. (...) Moreover, the fact that the arguments put forward by the applicant before the Court were in substance already set out in its reply to the Commission of 20 September 1982 (see Annex 2 to the Commission's defence) confirms that the decision did not in that respect infringe the right of the defence as regards the applicant."

Everling, "Die Errichtung eines Gerichts erster Instanz der Europäischen Gemeinschaften," in J. Schwarze (ed.), *Fortentwicklung des Rechtsschutzes in der Europäischen Gemeinschaft*, Baden-Baden 1987, pp. 39 *et seq.*
[8] Advocate-General Reischl, in Case 61/76 *Geist* v. *Commission* [1977] E.C.R. 1419 at 1441; similarly Advocate-General Reischl, in Case 181/78 etc., *Van Paassen* v. *Staatssecretaris* [1979] E.C.R. 2063 at 2090; see also Advocate-General Lagrange in Case 20/58 *Phoenix AG* v. *High Authority* [1959] E.C.R. 75 at 96; apparently the Court of Justice considers defects with regard to the consultation of institutions as always essential: Case 6/54 *Netherlands* v. *High Authority* [1954–56] 103 at 112; *cf.* also Case 138/79, *Roquette Frères* v. *Council* (Isoglucose case) [1980] E.C.R. 3333 at 3360, paras. 32–37).
[9] Advocate-General VerLoren van Themaat, in Case 9/83 *Eisen- und Metall AG* v. *Commission* [1984] E.C.R. 2071 at 2092; also Advocate-General Reischl, in Case 25/80, *De Briey* v. *Commission* [1981] E.C.R. 637 at 657; Advocate-General Roemer, in Case 29/67, *De Wendel* v. *Commission* [1968] E.C.R. 263 at 290.

In this context one should also look at statements on the possible rectification of procedural defects. It is not in dispute that rectification is possible up to the conclusion of the administrative procedure, because the procedure represents a single unit, the legality of which is to be judged as a whole[10]:

> "It is in fact common ground that the hearing on 28 September 1978 was followed by two further hearings on 19 January and 13 April 1979, at which the applicant was not only heard again but was also able to submit in evidence explanatory statements and to have witnesses examined whom he had himself called. Despite the shortness of the period which was allowed to him before his first hearing, the applicant was therefore put in a position, before the contested decision to reprimand him was adopted, to prepare his defence under conditions which were in conformity with the requirements of the aforementioned principle."

Considerably more problematic, and also the subject of criticism in the literature,[11] is the view put forward in the case law that defects in procedure may still be rectified during the course of the procedure before the Court of Justice[12]:

[10] Case 115/80, *Demont* v. *Commission* [1981] E.C.R. 1347 at 3156, para. 5; Case 107/82, *AEG* v. *Commission* [1983] E.C.R. 3151 at 3193, para. 29; this also emerges indirectly in the decisions of July 7, 1981 (Cases 60 & 190/81RE) and of November 11, 1981 (Case 60/81), *IBM* v. *Commission* [1981] E.C.R. 1857 and 2639, where the administrative procedure is understood as a unit, the conclusion of which cannot be anticipated by the Court.

[11] *cf.*, *e.g.* L. Goffin, "La jurisprudence de la Cour de justice sur les droits de la défense," CDE 1980, p. 127 at 142; J. Sedemund, "Allgemeine Prinzipien des Verwaltungsverfahrensrechts—dargestellt am Beispiel des Europäischen Verwaltungsverfahrens in Kartellsachen," in J. Schwarze (ed.), *Europäisches Verwaltungsrecht im Werden*, Baden-Baden 1982, p. 45 at 53; H. H. Scheffler, *Die Pflicht zur Begründung von Massnahmen nach den europäischen Gemeinschaftsverträgen*, Berlin 1974, pp. 201 *et seq.*; H. P. Ipsen, *Europäisches Gemeinschaftsrecht*, Tübingen 1972, 24/25, p. 519 (rectification only for the purposes of correcting editorial oversights); R. H. Lauwaars, in H. Smit, P. Herzog, *op. cit.*, footnote 2, Article 190.06, p. 5–631 (with further references); somewhat more restrained is M. Waelbroeck, in J. Mégret *et al.* (eds.), *Le droit de la CEE*, Brussels 1983, Vol. 10, Article 190, para. 11.

[12] Case 85/76 *Hoffmann-La Roche* v. *Commission* [1979] E.C.R. 461 at 512, para. 14; similar also is Advocate-General Mayras, in Case 27/76, *United Brands* v. *Commission* [1978] E.C.R. 207 at 347 with reference to the *ICI* decision, which in fact makes no reference to rectification in the course of the proceedings before the Court, *cf.* Case 48/69 *ICI* v. *Commission* [1972] E.C.R. 619 at 651; in similar vein is the Court already in Case 16/65 *Schwarze* v. *Einfuhr- und Vorratsstelle für Getreide* [1965] E.C.R. 877 at 888, where the particular problems of the statement of reasons of a regulation in fact played a role.

"It (Article 20 of Regulation No. 17) does not nevertheless allow it (the Commission) to use, to the detriment of the undertakings involved in a proceeding referred to in Regulation No. 17, facts, circumstances or documents which it cannot in its view disclose if such a refusal or disclosure adversely affects that undertaking's opportunity to make known effectively its views on the truth or implications of those circumstances, on those documents or again on the conclusions drawn by the Commission from them.

However if such irregularities have in fact been put right during the proceedings before the Court they do not necessarily lead to the annulment of the contested decision insofar as remedying them at a later stage has not affected the right to be heard."

There is no reliable basis for this view to be found in the legal orders of the Member States. Thus, for instance, French case law requires a clear break to be interpolated after the conclusion of the administrative procedure. In Germany literature and case law are still in dispute on the admissibility of the so-called deferred statement of reasons.[13]

Even the Court of Justice had the following to say in a decision (*France v. Commission*) handed down just one week before the *Hoffmann-La Roche* judgment quoted above[14]:

"The applicant Government challenges the legality of the Commission's refusal to accept financial responsibility for those amounts, arguing that the anomalies found to exist contravene only subsidiary formal requirements and that they were, moreover, rectified subsequently. As regards the relevance of subsequent rectification it should be observed that in the context of an application for annulment under Article 173 of the Treaty the legality of the contested

---

[13] *cf.* section V.2, and L. Goffin, *op. cit.*, footnote 11, p. 127 at 143, with further references; in part with a different view with regard to the earlier French position H. H. Scheffler, *op. cit.*, footnote 11, pp. 189 *et seq.*, although limited to the question of the deferred statement of reasons. On German law, *cf.* §45 VwVfG, which according to its wording allows for rectification only up to the conclusion of the preliminary proceedings, *cf.* on this F. O. Kopp, *Verwaltungsverfahrensgesetz*, (4th ed., Munich 1986), §45, paras. 19, 21, 24, 25; F. O. Kopp, *Verwaltungsgerichtsordnung*, (7th ed., Munich 1986), §113, paras. 33 *et seq.*; *cf.* BVerwG of October 7, 1980, BVerwGE 61, 45 at 50, which recognises rectification even in the course of judicial proceedings; this decision has, however, been expressly rejected by H. Mandelartz, "Anhörung, Absehen von Anhörung, Nachholung der unterbliebenen Anhörung—Zur Relativierung eines Verfahrensrechts," DVBl. 1983, p. 112 at 115 with comprehensive further references.

[14] Case 15/76, etc., *France* v. *Commission* [1979] E.C.R. 321 at 336, paras. 6 *et seq.*; *cf.* also Case 1/55 *Kergall* v. *Assembly* [1954–56] E.C.R. 151 at 157.

measure must be assessed on the basis of the elements of fact and of law existing at the time when the measure was adopted.

Rectification subsequent to that date cannot therefore be taken into account for the purposes of such an assessment."

It is true that in that case the issue was the rectification of procedural defects for which the authorities of the Member States were responsible, but the result could be carried over to the administrative procedure of the Commission, in particular since the Court of Justice based itself in the decision on a general conception of Article 173 EEC.[14a]

Advocate-General Warner[15] has subsequently reconsidered this question in depth, and has rejected the result reached in the *Hoffman-La Roche* decision:

"(The view of the Court of Justice in *France* v. *Commission*) must in my opinion be right, if only because the Court's jurisdiction under Article 173 is to 'review the legality of acts of the Council and the Commission,' which must mean their legality at the time they were adopted. The ruling in the *Hoffman-La Roche* case has been criticized by learned writers, and I think with good reason. To hold that, in a case like the present, the Commission's infringement of an undertaking's right to be heard does not vitiate the Commission's decision if that undertaking is subsequently given a fair hearing in this Court, would, it seems to me, amount to saying that the Commission may neglect essential procedural requirements with impunity because either the undertaking concerned will not appeal to this Court or, if it does, the irregularity can be put right in the course of the appeal."

[14a] *cf.* on this Case 195/80, *Michel* v. *Parliament* [1981] E.C.R. 1861 at 1876, para. 22, in which the Court of Justice did not allow the retrospective insertion of a statement of reasons.

[15] Advocate-General Warner, in Case 30/78, *Distillers Co.* v. *Commission* [1980] E.C.R. 2229 at 2297; also other Advocates-General have expressed negative views on the deferment of reasons; *cf.* Advocate-General Roemer, in Case 1/55, *Kergall* v. *Assembly* [1954–56] E.C.R. 151 at 171; Advocate-General Roemer, in Cases 18 and 35/65, *Gutmann* v. *Commission* [1966] E.C.R. 103 at 128; similarly with regard to the conduct of national authorities before the Court of Justice Advocate-General Roemer, in Case 2/68, *Ufficio Imposte* v. *Commission* [1968] E.C.R. 435 at 448; also Advocate-General Lagrange, in Case 20/58, *Phoenix-Rheinrohr AG* v. *High Authority* [1959] E.C.R. 75 at 97 with regard to a statement of reasons offered not during the judicial proceedings, but after the conclusion of the actual administrative procedure. The literature cited above in footnote 11 is also in opposition to the view of the Court of Justice in Case 85/76, *Hoffmann-La Roche* v. *Commission* [1979] E.C.R. 461.

Such cases are to be distinguished from those in which, for example, the particular urgency of the procedure may justify the omission of the hearing and the complaint arising from this omission can be tolerated because the applicant will be given during the course of the proceedings before the Court the possibility of legal redress and of putting forward his own viewpoint.[16]

The most important limitation on annulment is represented by reasons of economy of process. The administration should not be forced to reconvene a procedure where it is clear that the result in a lawful procedure will be identical to that reached in the previous defective one. The Court of Justice has held on many occasions that defects in the statement of reasons or in communications during the course of the proceedings will lead to annulment only where it is possible that they have had an influence on the content of the decision[17]:

> "The Court finds that even assuming that the contested decision is vitiated by the two breaches of procedural requirements alleged, an applicant has no legitimate interest in securing the annulment of a decision for a formal defect where the administration has no discretion and is bound to act as it did. In such a case the annulment of the contested decision could only give rise to another decision substantially identical to the decision annulled."

Even as regards hearings, the Court has held that there will be no annulment of the decision if the omission of the hearing has not had the effect of limiting the applicant's possibilities for redress. Such was the case in particular where, for instance, the communication of the statement of objections contained an incomplete or ambiguous formula, or the decision was drafted in the wrong language. If the person concerned

---

[16] *cf.* for instance Advocate-General Capotorti, in Case 13/82, etc., *Arantzamendi-Osa* v. *Staatsanwalt* [1982] E.C.R. 3927 at 3944.

[17] Case 117/81 *Geist* v. *Commission* [1983] E.C.R. 2191 at 2207, para. 7; also Case 9/76, *Morello* v. *Commission* [1976] E.C.R. 1415 at 1422; Case 30/78, *Distillers Co.* v. *Commission* [1980] E.C.R. 2229 at 2264, para. 26, also Advocate-General Warner with further references, p. 2290; Case 41/69 *ACF Chemiefarma* v. *Commission* [1970] E.C.R. 661 at 686, paras. 47–53.

To some extent of a different view are the Advocates-General, *cf.* Advocate-General Mayras, in Joined Cases 33 and 75/79, *Kuhner* v. *Commission* [1980] E.C.R. 1677 at 1703: the E.C.J. held that the statement of reasons was adequate; Advocate-General Reischl, in Case 89/79, *Bonu* v. *Council* [1980] E.C.R. 553 at 567: here the Court reached a similar conclusion, at p. 563, para. 7.

1426

correctly understood the document, then the procedural defect would have no effect on the outcome of the procedure[18]:

> "Under the terms of Article 3 of Regulation No. 1 of the Council, documents which an institution of the Community sends to a person subject to the jurisdiction of a Member State shall be drafted in the language of such State.
>
> The failure to communicate a Dutch version of the draft minutes thus constitutes an irregularity in drawing up that document which is capable of affecting its validity.
>
> It is clear, however, from the arguments put forward by the applicant that it was able in due time to acquaint itself with the contents of the minutes.
>
> The applicant has not alleged that this resulted in the minutes' containing substantial inaccuracies or omissions with regard to it.
>
> It must therefore be concluded that the irregularity which has been found did not in this case have harmful consequences capable of vitiating the administrative procedure."

This is also the argument underlying a decision of the Court of Justice to refuse annulment of a decision, on the grounds that the statement of reasons, which contained internal contradictions, was "not decisive."[19]

Occasionally the Court or the Advocates-General have come down in favour of annulment without analysing the relevance of the procedural defect in the text of the judgment or in their opinions, respectively.[20] In these cases, perhaps the Court of Justice chose not to bring the substantive questions into the foreground on the grounds that there were no unambiguous answers to them.

The link to the possible influence on the result of the procedure corresponds to the position under national law,[21] where annulment of an administrative act is similarly out of the question where an identical one

---

[18] Case 41/69 *ACF Chemiefarma* v. *Commission* [1970] E.C.R. 661 at 686, paras. 48/52, *cf.* Advocate-General Gand, at p. 707.

[19] Case 123/75, *Küster* v. *Parliament* [1976] E.C.R. 1701 at 1712, paras. 30 *et seq.*; *cf.* also Advocate-General Reischl, at p. 1717.

[20] Case 89/79, *Bonu* v. *Council* [1980] E.C.R. 533 at 563, para. 7, similarly Advocate-General Reischl at p. 567 (no reasons had been given); also Advocate-General Mayras, in Cases 33 and 75/79, *Kuhner* v. *Commission* [1980] E.C.R. 1677 at 1703, also for the case of a defective statement of reasons. The Advocate-General referred to the general applicability of the decision in the case of *Bonu* even outside the field of staffing.

[21] See above, the Reports on Spain, France, England and Germany.

would simply be readopted. For these purposes considerations of securing the efficiency of the administration are decisive. The administration should not be burdened with having to reopen a procedure which ultimately would not lead to a different decision.

In this context, reference should also be made to the fact that in cases where the procedural defects have affected only one part of the measure, the Court of Justice has annulled it only to the extent of the defect and, correspondingly, has then proceeded, for instance, to reduce the level of the fine imposed[22]:

> "Although, as a result of their diligence, the applicants thus gained knowledge of the whole of the statement made by Mr. Mason just before the hearing, it is not disputed that they were not acquainted or were only partially acquainted with the other documents mentioned above before the Commission adopted its decision. Therefore they did not have the opportunity, in due time, of making known their views on the contents and the scope of those documents or of obtaining and putting forward, where appropriate, evidence to the contrary. It follows that the Commission was wrong to have based its decision on the contents of those documents.
>
> Since the findings which the Commission based on those documents, which did not come to the applicants' notice, relate to matters which are of purely secondary importance in relation to the infringements found to have been committed in Articles 1 and 2 of the decision, that breach of the right to a fair hearing cannot affect the validity of the whole of the decision. Instead, it is appropriate for the Court to disregard the contents of those documents when considering the substantive validity of the decision."

Insofar as the Court of Justice can exceptionally substitute its own discretion for that of the Commission (review "de pleine juridiction"—in particular as regards the amount of a fine in competition law), the Court of Justice is able, in the case of procedural defects, instead of annulling the decision, to substitute it with another according to its own views.

---

[22] Case 100/80, etc., *Musique Diffusion Française* v. *Commission* [1983] E.C.R. 1825 at 1885, para. 29; *cf.* also para. 134; similarly Case 107/82 *AEG* v. *Commission* [1983] E.C.R. 3151 at 3193, para. 30; *cf.* on contradictory but non-essential parts of a statement of reasons, which do not lead to nullity: Case 41/69 *ACF Chemiefarma* v. *Commission* [1970] E.C.R. 661 at 690, para. 86, also Advocate-General Gand, at 724; also Case 123/75 *Küster* v. *Parliament* [1976] E.C.R. 1701 at 1712, para. 32.

Advocate-General Roemer has summarised this as follows[23]:

> "This defect does not, admittedly, mean that the Decision must be annulled and referred back to the High Authority. The Court of Justice itself can amend the penalty and fix a different amount under Article 36 of the Treaty on the basis of the picture which has emerged in the course of the proceedings, because in these circumstances the Court is adjudicating with unlimited jurisdiction ("pleine juridiction"). The lack of statement of reasons may however have an effect upon the decision as to costs because it was, in part at least, the cause of the appeal."

A special case should finally be mentioned. In spite of an infringement of essential procedural requirements, the Court has maintained in force a measure in the context of anti-dumping law where the applicant bringing a claim as a competitor wished to see the imposition of a higher anti-dumping duty and thus a greater burden upon the undertaking thereby affected. The result chosen by the Court of Justice here follows from the adherence to the goal of protecting the interests of the applicant as the non-addressee of the administrative decision[24]:

> "Since the anti-dumping duty was therefore imposed in breach of the essential procedural requirements laid down in Article 7(4)a of Regulation No. 3017/79, Article 1 of Regulation No. 1882/82 must be declared void, and it is unnecessary to consider the other submissions advanced by the applicant in support of the same claim.
>
> However, the aim of the action is not to have the provision in question declared void but to have it replaced by a more stringent measure fixing a higher anti-dumping duty on mechanical watches and imposing such a duty on mechanical watch movements. The anti-dumping duty imposed by the provision declared void should therefore be maintained, in accordance with the second paragraph of Article 174 of the EEC Treaty, until the competent institutions adopt the measures needed to comply with this judgment."

---

[23] Advocate-General Roemer, in Case 16/61 *Acciaierie Ferriere e Fonderie di Modena* v. *High Authority* [1962] E.C.R. 289 at 322; similarly Advocate-General Lagrange in Case 25/60 *Leda de Bruyn* v. *Parliament* [1962] E.C.R. 21 at 39; in agreement are G. Le Tallec, C.-D. Ehlermann, *op. cit.*, footnote 2, p. 149 at 153, with further references.

[24] Case 264/82 *Timex* v. *Council and Commission* [1985] E.C.R. 849 at 870.

Summing up, it can be seen that the Court of Justice, which focuses on achieving justice in individual cases, always protects the procedural rights of the persons concerned where the infringement has had an effect upon those rights such that it would only have been possible to reach a more favourable outcome. If, however, the substantive legal position is clear and the persons concerned could not have altered any aspect of it, then the Court will generally hold that the measure should remain in force in order to protect the functional capacity of the administration and the effective safeguarding of Community law.[25]

H. SUMMARY

As the above analysis has shown, the legal protection of the Community citizen is realised to a growing extent through the application of general principles of law in the field of the law governing administrative procedure. Apart from the rules contained as a starting point in the Treaties and in secondary sources of Community law, the Court of Justice has been developing right up to the present the essential principles of an administrative procedure subject to the rule of law.

The rights of the defence of the individual, which are differentiated one from another in numerous ways, have a central place in the (overall) system of legal protection under the Treaties.[1]

If, at the outset of the Community, the development of European administrative law could be identified as falling within French conceptions of legal protection against the administration (*cf.* Article 33 ECSC, Article 173 EEC), today it is the influence of English law as regards the safeguarding of a fair administrative procedure, and above all the influence of German administrative law, which are most visible. At least, it is the latter legal system[2] which adheres to similar solutions in core areas to those which are being articulated in the European context as a common standard.

---

[25] Thus also H.-W. Daig, *Nichtigkeits- und Untätigkeitsklagen im Recht der Europäischen Gemeinschaften*, Baden-Baden 1985, p. 130, para. 167.

[1] See above, section E.

[2] On the procedural thinking in German administrative law see in particular E. Schmidt-Assmann *Das allgemeine Verwaltungsrecht als Ordnungsidee und System*, Heidelberg 1982, pp. 35 *et seq.*

Fritz Werner's apt description of current German administrative law as amounting to a "konkretisiertes Verfassungsrecht,"[3] applies in a modified form also to the European Community.

It is notable how the evolving European administrative law has adopted, in addition to actual administrative principles, a remarkable number of constitutional conceptions from the Member States and has integrated these into a synthesis appropriate to the needs of the Community.

The recently decided case of *Heylens*[4] provides graphic and impressive evidence of this approach. In that case the Court of Justice had to decide whether it was compatible with the principle of free movement of workers (Article 48 EEC) for a national provision on access to a profession (in that case that of football trainer) to require a national diploma or the corresponding equivalent certificate from another Member State, but not to provide in a case of rejection by the administration (non-recognition of the foreign diploma as equivalent) that reasons must be given for the refusal and to provide no remedy of a judicial nature against that refusal. The Court of Justice answered this question in the negative and referred to the fact that the free movement of workers (Article 48 EEC) is a fundamental right of Community law, for the safeguarding of which adequate legal protection must be ensured.

The principle of effective legal protection is described by the Court as a "general principle of Community law which underlies the constitutional traditions common to the Member States and has been enshrined in Articles 6 and 13 of the European Convention for the Protection of Human Rights and Fundamental Freedoms."[5]

The evolution of the law in the field of administrative law, and in that context in particular in the fields of administrative procedure and legal process,[6] is thus in the European context decisively influenced by constitutional law.

---

[3] F. Werner, DVBl. 1959, p. 527.
[4] Case 222/86 [1987] E.C.R. 4097.
[5] [1987] E.C.R. 4117, para. 14.
[6] In *Heylens*, *supra*, footnote 4, the Court had the following to say about effective legal control of the administration and on the administration's duty to give reasons, at [1987] E.C.R. 4117:
"Effective judicial review, which must be able to cover the legality of the reasons for the contested decision, presupposes in general that the court to which the matter is referred may require the competent authority to notify its reasons. But where, as in this case, it is more particularly a question of securing the effective protection of a fundamental right conferred by the Treaty on Community workers, the latter must also be able to defend the right under the best possible conditions and have the possibility of deciding, with a full

1431

On the other hand, it remains the case that the safeguarding of an administrative procedure subject to the rule of law and of effective legal protection should not be regarded as an end in itself, but that the goal should always be that of providing the optimum, not maximum procedural protection, in contrast to and in counterbalance against the conditions which determine the functioning and performance of the administration.

knowledge of the relevant facts, whether there is any point in their applying to the courts. Consequently, in such circumstances the competent national authority is under a duty to inform them of the reasons on which its refusal is based, either in the decision itself or in a subsequent communication at their request."

CHAPTER 8

CONCLUSION

I. THE EVOLUTION OF EUROPEAN ADMINISTRATIVE LAW

The administrative law of the European Community has now grown into a comprehensive structure of legal norms. An overview of the legal principles of administration according to the law, equality of treatment, proportionality, legal certainty and the protection of legitimate expectations as well as the guarantee of fair and due process, analysed in previous chapters, demonstrates that the Community now has access to a structure of rules of administrative law which is entirely comparable with those of the Member States. However, the analysis of the legal principles which have largely evolved out of the jurisprudence of the European Court of Justice has revealed considerable variance and gaps in the existing system. The process of building up and evolving a system of administrative law is not yet completed. A European administrative law in the sense of a complete and doctrinally mature system[1] is still only in the process of evolution.[2]

If the above investigation has succeeded in making it easier to find one's way through this process of legal development, in promoting the transparency, comparability and efficacy of European administration and thus in alleviating the everyday work of the European institutions

---

[1] On the development of systematic structures in administrative law *cf.* in particular E. Schmidt-Assmann *Das allgemeine Verwaltungsrecht als Ordnungsidee und System*, Heidelberg 1982, see also J. Schwarze, "Zum Nutzen einer Systembildung für die Kontrolle der Staatsgewalt," DVBl. 1974, pp. 893 *et seq.*

[2] *cf.* for an introduction and outline of the problem J. Schwarze (ed.), *Europäisches Verwaltungsrecht im Werden*, Baden-Baden 1982, p. 11.

and the national administrations, as well as promoting the legal protection of the Community citizen, then it will have achieved its essential goal.

II. THE INTERDEPENDENCE OF NATIONAL (EUROPEAN) ADMINISTRATIVE LEGAL ORDERS AND THE DEVELOPMENT OF A COMMON EUROPEAN LAW

The investigation has brought to light the multiple forms taken by the interconnections between the administrative law of the European Community and the administrative laws of the Member States, as well as occasionally the other States belonging to the Council of Europe. A number of particularly significant examples should be recalled once more here.

(1) Already in the Introduction we have discussed how national conceptions had influenced administrative law in the Community. French administrative law exercised a decisive influence on the formulation of central concepts and in particular on the system of legal protection in the Treaties (Articles 33 ECSC, 173 EEC).[3] Subsequently German administrative law also exercised a significant influence on Community law principles; one example of this would be the great importance acquired by the principle of proportionality, adopted from German law.[4] Following the accession of the United Kingdom, English law, in particular as regards the development of procedural guarantees for individuals, has also had an impact on legal developments in the Community.[5] However,

---

[3] On the influence of French law cf. H.-W. Daig Nichtigkeits- und Untätigkeitsklagen im Recht der Europäischen Gemeinschaften, Baden-Baden 1985, pp. 21 et seq.; P. Becker Der Einfluss des französischen Verwaltungsrechts auf den Rechtsschutz in den Europäischen Gemeinschaften, Hamburg 1963, pp. 55 et seq.

[4] See above, p. 856. On the influence of German law cf. also above, p. 672 (principle of equality); Chapter 6 Conclusion (protection of legitimate expectation contra legem and protection of legitimate expectation in the case of false retroactivity).

[5] cf. in particular Case 155/79 A.M. & S. v. Commission [1982] E.C.R. 1575, where the European Court recognised the principle which is particularly well developed in English law of the confidentiality of correspondence with lawyers (legal privilege). See especially the opinions of the British Advocates-General Warner and Slynn, op. cit. pp. 1612 et seq. at p. 1633; pp. 1642 et seq. at pp. 1651–1653. See in more detail on the A.M. & S. decision J. Schwarze, "Grenzen für die Ermittlungstätigkeit der Kommission als Wettbewerbsbehörde der EG," in J. Schwarze (ed.), Der Gemeinsame Markt. Bestand und Zukunft in Wirtschaftsrechtlicher Perspektive, Baden-Baden 1987, p. 159 at pp. 168–173. cf. on the influence of British procedural principles also the discussions of Advocate-General Warner on the right to a hearing in Case 17/74 Transocean Marine Paint v. Commission [1974] E.C.R. 1063 at 1088, as well as the right of access to files in Case 131/79 R. v. Secretary of State for Home Affairs [1980] E.C.R. 1612. From the literature see in

1434

even the administrative law conceptions and principles of other Member States have played a significant role in the construction of the general principles of Community law. The fact that the Court of Justice was developing the administrative law of the Community, taking into account the rules recognised in legislation, learned writing and case law of the Member States[6] and using the method of evaluatory comparative law, was recognised and described at an early stage of its evolution.[7]

(2) There is less awareness, on the other hand, of the influence of European Community law in the other direction on the general administrative law of the Member States.

(a) An example of such an effect can be found in the case of the indirect implementation of Community law, that is in the areas in which the administrations of the Member States must implement Community law. There is a consistent line of case law from the Court, in which it works from the assumption that the national authorities will in principle use the administrative law principles of their national legal systems when implementing Community law. However, the procedures of national administrative law must not make the achievement of the purpose of the Community rule impossible or lead to a discriminatory application.[8] In individual cases this can lead to conflicts between Community law, which takes priority in its application, and the national law concerned. Thus, although §48(1) of the German Law on Administrative Procedure (VwVfG) provides that the revocation of an administrative act lies basically within the discretion of the authority, German administrative authorities may not, within the field of application of Regulation 729/70,

---

particular D. Lasok, J. W. Bridge *Law and Institutions of the European Communities*, (4th ed., London 1987), p. 155.
[6] This is the formulation used by the European Court in the ground-breaking decision in Joined Cases 7/56 & 3–7/57 *Algera* v. *Common Assembly* [1957–1958] E.C.R. 39 at 55.
[7] See for instance already K. Zweigert, "Der Einfluss des Europäischen Gemeinschaftsrechts auf die Rechtsordnungen der Mitgliedstaaten," RabelsZ 26 (1964), pp. 601 *et seq.* From the more recent literature see in particular H.-W. Daig, "Zur Rechtsvergleichung und Methodenlehre im Europäischen Gemeinschaftsrecht," in H. Bernstein *et al.* (eds.), *Festschrift für K. Zweigert*, Tübingen 1981, pp. 395 *et seq.*; P. Pescatore *Le recours, dans la jurisprudence de la Cour de justice des Communautés européennes, à des normes déduites de la comparaison des droits des Etats membres*, R.I.D.C. 1980, pp. 337 *et seq.*, as well as E. García de Enterría, in *Tratado De Derecho Comunitario Europeo* (eds. E. García de Enterría, J. D. Gonzáles Campos and S. Muñoz Machado), Madrid 1986, Vol. 1, p. 658.
[8] Case 205–215/81 *Deutsche Milchkontor GmbH* v. *BRD* [1983] E.C.R. 2633 at 2665–6 and the decisions cited there. See in more detail above Vol. 1, pp. 459 *et seq.*

exercise any discretion in the revocation of wrongly paid subsidies.[9] Article 8 of Regulation 729/70 in fact obliges the Member States to require the repayment of wrongly paid premiums. A contrary interpretation of the provision would damage the uniform application of Community law in the various Member States.[10] A further example is offered by the *Söhnlein Rheingold* decision, where the Court of Justice came to the conclusion that a German administrative court, when considering a case in which a discretionary rule is to be applied by German authorities in the context of the common agricultural policy, must recognise a degree of discretion, although from the national point of view the relevant conditions for the existence of discretion on the part of the administration are not present.[11] In such cases involving indirect conflicts[12] the decisions of the Court of Justice, mostly occurring in the context of the preliminary ruling procedure under Article 177 EEC, have led to a partial sectoral modification of national administrative law and law of administrative procedure.[13]

(b) It is more difficult to prove that the administrative law of the European Community has also influenced the administrative laws of the Member States in areas of exclusively national competence, that is, apart from the implementation of Community law. In this context, what is at issue is not an effect which is based on the supremacy of Community law or which is enforced by court decision. On the contrary, we are dealing here with the gradual growth of influence through persuasion and the voluntary recognition of a number of aspects of European law by national law.

At the 1986 FIDE Congress in Paris, which dealt *inter alia* with the question of the interaction between the general principles of Community law and those of national law, C. Mégret summed up the position as

---

[9] Joined Cases 146, 192–193/81 *BayWa* v. *BALM* [1982] E.C.R. 1503 at 1535. The law on the implementation of the common organisation of the market as amended to October 27, 1986 (BGBl. I 1986, p. 1397) provides in §10(I) that decisions which wrongfully confer a benefit must be revoked, within the scope of the application of the law (without exercise of discretion), and for the rest the law refers to §48(2–4) VwVfG.

[10] Joined Cases 146 & 192–193/81, *supra*, footnote 9.

[11] Case 183/84 [1985] E.C.R. 3351; DVBl. 1986, p. 92 with a note by C. H. Ule. For more details see Vol. 1, pp. 454 *et seq.*

[12] *cf.* K. E. Huthmacher *Der Vorrang des Gemeinschaftsrechts bei indirekten Kollisionen*, Cologne/Berlin/Bonn/Munich 1985.

[13] See more detail in G. Ress, "Wichtige Vorlagen deutscher Verwaltungsgerichte an den Gerichtshof der Europäischen Gemeinschaften," in: *Die Verwaltung* 1987, p. 177 at pp. 200 *et seq.*

follows in her General Report: "que les principes généraux communautaires n'ont que peu d'incidence sur le contenu des principes nationaux:
cela peut se comprendre dans la mesure où il s'agit, par hypothèse, d'un
domaine qui demeure de la compétence exclusive des Etats Membres."[14]
Indeed, it is only occasionally possible to prove a direct impact of Community law on national administrative laws.[15] However, a certain level of
influence can be assumed when national courts apply legal principles
which are recognised in Community law but have not yet been recognised, or at least not yet in this form, in national law.

The President of the Court of Justice of the European Communities,
Lord Mackenzie Stuart,[16] Advocate-General Sir Gordon Slynn[16a] and
J. A. Usher[17] have all recently referred to the fact that parallels with
Community legal principles have become visible in English admin-
istrative law.[18]

The most important case to mention in this context is *Council of Civil
Service Unions* v. *Minister for the Civil Service*[19] where the House of Lords
recognised the principle of the protection of legitimate expectation in
public law and for the first time applied it to a central authority. Lord
Mackenzie Stuart has said of this decision:

[14] C. Mégret, Rapport général, FIDE Rapports 12e Congrès I, Paris 1986, p. 1 at 13.
[15] Such proof is possible in particular where the national legislature or courts expressly refer
to principles of Community law. Thus the Irish Supreme Court, when deciding the
question of the temporal effects of a decision on the constitutionality of an Irish tax law,
referred to the *Defrenne II* judgment of the European Court (*Murphy* v. *Attorney
General* [1982] I.R. 241); see for more details above Chapter 6 (comparative survey of
Ireland). *cf.* also J. O'Reilly *The Interaction between Community Law and National Law:
Irish Report*, FIDE Rapports, 12e Congrès I, Paris 1986, p. 167 at pp. 177–179.
[16] A. J. Mackenzie Stuart, "Recent Developments in English Administrative Law—the
Impact of Europe?", in F. Capotorti *et al.* (eds.), *Du droit international au droit de
l'intégration. Liber Amicorum P. Pescatore*, Baden-Baden 1987, p. 411.
[16a] Gordon Slynn, "But in England there is no ..." in: *Festschrift für Wolfgang Zeidler*,
Berlin/New York 1987, Vol. 1, p. 397.
[17] J. A. Usher *General Principles Derived from the Law of the Member States as a Source of
Community Law—The Interaction between Community Law and National Law*, FIDE
Rapports 12e Congrès I, Paris 1986, p. 303 at 312 *et seq.*
[18] *cf.* also P. Pescatore, EuR 1985, p. 341 at 343, who in his Farewell Address to the
European Court of Justice stressed the interpenetration of "civil law" and "common law"
as a consequence of the accession of the United Kingdom to the European Community as
a particularly significant development. On the changes in English law wrought by accession to the European Community see Lord Scarman in his Hamlyn Lectures *English
Law—the New Dimension*, London 1974. See on this the discussion by W. v. Simson,
"Das Common Law als Verfassungsrecht," Der Staat, Vol. 16 (1977), p. 75. See most
recently with a comprehensive review J. W. Bridge, "Abstract Law and Political Reality
in the Post-European-Accession British Constitution," in Denning Law Journal (1987),
p. 23.
[19] [1984] 3 All E.R. 935.

"Can one here detect the influence of Community law or at least that of some of the Member States? It is at least possible to suggest the answer is yes. The concept of recognising that a failure to respect legitimate expectations may give rise, in public law, to a remedy is a novelty in English law and lacks discernible English parentage. To find the true ancestry one does not have to look far across the Channel."[20]

In this decision, Lord Diplock analysed the various grounds for the nullity of acts done in exercise of a prerogative power—illegality, irrationality and procedural impropriety—and added that he considered the adoption in the future of the principle of proportionality, recognised in the administrative laws of several Member States of the European Community, to be conceivable.[21]

In contrast to the traditional independence of the common law from continental legal developments, therefore, English administrative law is proving to be quite receptive to European law influences. That may be linked to the fact that an autonomous administrative law, separate from private law, was late in developing in England, is doctrinally not yet so mature and solidified and in consequence appears to be more open to stimuli from other legal orders.

The situation is different in France. The former Judge at the European Court of Justice and Honorary Advocate-General at the Cour de Cassation A. Touffait emphasised some time ago that in France, in contrast to other Member States, there is little interest in Community law.[22] It is hard to see any impact on the part of European law on French administrative law, at least outside the areas involving the indirect implementation of Community law by French authorities. The minute influence of the general principles of administrative law recognised by the European Court of Justice on French law may be traced back to the customary French conception of the supremacy of national law.[23] As has been mentioned, it is also the case that in its origins Community law emerged in

---

[20] A. J. Mackenzie Stuart, *op. cit.*, footnote 16, p. 417.

[21] [1984] 3 All E.R. 950. See on this also Sir Gordon Slynn in his Statement in the volume *Eine Verfassung für Europa* (eds. J. Schwarze, R. Bieber), Baden-Baden 1984, p. 123.

[22] A. Touffait, "Réflexions d'un magistrat français sur son expérience de juge à la Cour de justice des Communautés européennes," R.I.D.C. 1983, p. 283 at 284.

[23] *Ibid.* p. 288: "Cette idée de la suprématie de la loi nationale qui ne saurait être mise en accusation devant quelque autorité que ce soit est toujours ancrée dans l'esprit de nombreux juristes français qui axent toutes leurs réflexions juridiques sur cette notion fondamentale et ils ne conçoivent pas que les conséquences tirées de la loi puissent être mises en échec par un principe supérieur."

close concordance with French legal conceptions, so that there was in any case little room for the Community to exercise an influence in return on French administrative law. Nevertheless, the most recent efforts of the Conseil constitutionnel to subject legislative acts to intensified review using the criterion of proportionality do demonstrate that French public law and in particular constitutional case law is not entirely closed to European influences.[24]

(3) It is possible to discern, not just in France but also in other Member States of the Community, the pattern whereby principles from national administrative laws are used in the construction of principles of Community law on the one hand, while these same principles in turn have an impact on national administrative laws, mediated through the case law of the Court of Justice. This pattern is particularly evident from the example of the adoption of the principle of proportionality, derived from German law.[25] A further example is the manner, described above,[26] in which the Italian legislature has emulated the Danish rule on refunds of payments, which has been recognised by the European Court of Justice.

Furthermore, quite independently of Community law, national administrative laws have borrowed from other more developed legal systems. The most important example is the traditional extension of French administrative law into that of other European and non-European countries.[27] As regards the control of the administration, the extensive use of

---

[24] See the decision of the Conseil constitutionnel of October 10/11, 1984 on the new French media law. See on this in detail *supra*, Vol. 2, p. 667. The Conseil d'Etat seems, in contrast, to be less open to influences from Europe. Of the recent case law of the C.E. the decision of December 8, 1978 (*G.I.S.T.I.*), Rec. 493 is particularly worthy of note. It involves the right to lead a normal family life, which is extended in France also to resident aliens. By creating this "home-made" legal principle the C.E. avoided having to apply the ECHR. See also J.-F. Flauss, "Le juge administratif français et la Convention européenne des droits de l'homme", AJDA 1983, p. 387.

[25] *cf.* the comparative survey above Vol. 2, pp. 663 *et seq. cf.* on Italian law recently also F. Capelli, "I principi generali come fonte di diritto," Dir.com.scambi.int. 1986, p. 541 at 551 or alternatively the French version *ibid.*, *Les principes généraux en tant que source du droit*, FIDE Rapports 12e Congrès I, Paris 1986, p. 183 at 206. On this also P. Mengozzi, in *Trattato di diritto privato*, Vol. 1, (ed. Pietro Rescigno), Turin 1987, p. 185 at 223. Further in general on the interaction between national judges and the Court of Justice with primarily Italian examples P. Mengozzi, "Il guidice nazionale di fronte al diritto comunitario," Estratto da *Contratto e Impresa*, Vol. II (1986), N3, p. 792.

[26] Chapter 6, Conclusions.

[27] *cf.* Le Conseil d'Etat, *Livre jubilaire*, Paris 1952, p. 481 ("Le rayonnement du Conseil d'Etat et le droit administratif à l'étranger"). On the relations between the Conseil d'Etat and other countries *cf.* most recently also the reports of the Anglo-French Conference on protection under administrative law in Conseil d'Etat 1987, *Etudes et documents* No. 38, p. 215.

1439

the institution of the Ombudsman, which originated in the Scandinavian law systems, is impressive proof of how an idea recognised as successful will be taken up by other States and introduced, sometimes in altered form, into their own systems of administrative control.[28]

(4) Finally, the activities of the Council of Europe have not been without impact on the administrative laws of the signatory states and of the European Community.

Thus in his Opinion in the first ball-bearing case[29] Advocate-General Warner referred to a Resolution of the Committee of Ministers of the Council of Europe[30] in order to argue that the right to a hearing in administrative proceedings should be made compatible with the requirements of an efficient administration.

The European Convention on Human Rights has, of course, made the foremost contribution to the creation of a common European standard of human rights.[31] The practice of the organs set up by the Convention in, for instance, the field of legal procedural guarantees or in giving effect to the principle of proportionality[32] has, however, in so far as it affects the acts of the executive, in a wider sense also created an area of common European administrative law.

(5) If one takes into consideration all the instances of interaction between national and European principles, then the thesis which we formulated in the introduction of the basic possibility of the development of a European *ius commune* in the field of administrative law would seem to be fully confirmed. A particular contribution to the harmonisation and unification of systems of administrative law can be made by the fact that the economic, scientific and technical questions which the administrations must all address in, for instance, the field of environmental law, know no national boundaries. J. Rivero referred to this fact in his work on

---

[28] *cf.* the proof of this in the national reports, *supra* Vol. 1, pp. 95 *et seq.*
[29] Case 113/77 *NTN Toyo Bearing Co.* v. *Council* [1979] E.C.R. 1185 at 1262.
[30] The Committee of Ministers of the Council of Europe of September 28, 1977, Resolution No. 77(31) on the Protection of the Individual in Relation to the Acts of Administrative Authorities. On this matter see most recently also the Recommendation of the Committee of Ministers No. R(87) 16 of September 17, 1987, reprinted in Neue Verwaltungsrechtliche Zeitschrift, 1988, p. 708.
[31] *cf.* J. A. Frowein, "Der europäische Menschenrechtsschutz als Beginn einer europäischen Verfassungsrechtsprechung," JuS 1986, p. 845 at 850.
[32] *cf.* J. A. Frowein, W. Peukert *Europäische Menschenrechtskonvention, EMRK-Kommentar*, Kehl/Strasbourg/Arlington 1985, Introductory Note Article 8–11, para. 15. See for more details *supra*, pp. 705 *et seq.*

the perspectives for the development of a common European administrative law, which has laid the foundations for further work.[33]

Against this background, the international administrative law principle of territoriality, which prescribes that the provisions of national public law will have no effects outside the relevant State boundaries, loses part of the justification for its existence.

The German Federal Administrative Court was recently required to decide a claim brought by a Dutch citizen who had complained about the partial authorisation given under nuclear energy law for the building of a nuclear power station in the border area.[34] In the authorisation proceedings conducted by the administration the objections of the plaintiff, who lived in a Dutch border town only 25 km from the proposed site of the power station, were declared inadmissible. The Administrative Court rejected the Dutchman's challenge against this finding. Since national law cannot lay claim to validity outside national boundaries, the partial authorisation is valid in principle only inside the Federal Republic of Germany. The plaintiff could not therefore claim that his rights had been interfered with. Thus he could not bring a claim. The Federal Administrative Court quashed the decision of the Administrative Court and referred the case back. Referring to the novel dangers of nuclear power, which do not stop at State borders, the Federal Administrative Court decided that the relevant provision of the German law on atomic energy accorded third party protection not only to persons living inside the country, but also at the very least to citizens of the Member States of the European Atomic Energy Community. In the authorisation proceedings conducted under administrative law the protection of third parties from other States must be considered.

Since the plaintiff's legal position as regards his procedural rights had been interfered with by the proceedings of the authorisation authority and since this procedural defect could have consequences as regards his legal position under substantive law, the BVerwG accepted the Dutch

---

[33] J. Rivero, "Vers un droit commun européen: nouvelles perspectives en droit administratif," in M. Cappelletti (ed.), *New Perspectives for a Common Law of Europe*, Leyden/London/Boston 1978, p. 389 at 403.

[34] BVerwG, judgment of December 17, 1986, DVBl. 1987, p. 375 with a note by A. Weber, also reported in EuGRZ 1987, p. 116 with a note by Beyerlin. *cf.* also A. Weitbrecht, "Zur Rechtsstellung ausländischer Grenznachbarn im deutschen Umweltrecht," NJW 1987, 2132. On the principle of territoriality and its limits in administrative law literature, see the fundamental work of K. Vogel *Der räumliche Anwendungsbereich der Verwaltungsrechtsnorm*, Frankfurt a.M./Berlin 1965.

person's right to claim and referred the matter back to the Administrative Court.

In other Member States cross-boundary participation in proceedings regarding environmental law has been practised for rather longer.[35] Just one example of this would be the proceedings conducted before the Tribunal Administratif de Strasbourg against the French nuclear power station at Cattenom, in which the plaintiffs included the Saarland and numerous local authorities from the Saarland and Rhineland-Palatinate as well as German citizens.[36]

Thus in environmental law in particular, especially where authorisation for large projects is involved, there will today be a legal relationship between the citizens of one State and the administration of another. This development is unlikely not to have an impact on the development of European administrative law. The European Community has adopted a Directive on the environmental impact of projects, which provides in particular for the unification of investigatory procedures.[37]

Judicial review of the discretion exercised by the administration when it authorises a large project also offers an example of a possible trend towards approximation between French and German administrative law. In France, where a much greater weight is placed on securing the efficacy of administrative action and the Conseil d'Etat has traditionally been reticent in exercising its right of verification in terms of groups of cases, a recent tendency to extend judicial control can be discerned.[38] The Federal Republic of Germany, on the other hand, has tended to see the

---

[35] cf. for details the contributions in G. Ress (ed.), *Grenzüberschreitende Verfahrensbeteiligung im Umweltrecht der Mitgliedstaaten der Europäischen Gemeinschaften*, Cologne/Berlin/Bonn/Munich 1985.

[36] Tribunal Administratif de Strasbourg, decision of September 8, 1986, EuGRZ 1986, p. 575 and judgment of June 16, 1987. See also the reference procedure under Article 150 Euratom—Case 187/87 with opinion of Advocate-General Slynn of June 8, 1988, [1988] E.C.R. 5013. Further references in K. Lenaerts, "Nuclear Border Installations: A Case Study" (1988) E.L.Rev. 159, as well as B. Bender, R. Sparwasser *Umweltrecht*, Heidelberg, 1988, p. 9.

[37] Council Directive 85/337 of June 27, 1985 on the assessment of the effect of certain public and private projects on the environment, O.J. 1985, L175/40. With regard to the legal situation then prevailing in certain European countries, T. Bunge (DVBl. 1987, p. 819 at 825) refers to a "European version" of environmental impact evaluation, which can be contrasted with the American version by virtue of its comparatively detailed legal provisions. On the problems of implementing the E.C. Directive in German law see R. Wahl, "Thesen zur Umsetzung der Umweltverträglichkeitsprüfung in das deutsche öffentliche Recht," DVBl. 1988, p. 86.

[38] On this development and the contrary tendency in Germany cf. chiefly M. Bullinger, "Unbestimmte Gesetzesbegriffe in der neueren deutschen und französischen Verwaltungsrechtsprechung," in *Festschrift für H. Jahrreiss*, Cologne/Berlin/Bonn/Munich 1974, p. 19 at 31; for a comparative treatment of administrative discretion more recently

---

opposite trend. In the beginning judicial protection against administrative decisions involving authorisations for large projects extended very widely. Thus the extensive elucidation of the available technical details by the Freiburg Administrative Court in the proceedings concerning the Wyhl nuclear power station led M. Fromont to remark that "le juriste français est frappé de stupeur devant une telle hardiesse."[39] Since then, it has become increasingly clear in Germany that there are political costs to the rule of law.[40] Extensive legal protection, in practice frequently in the form of prior legal protection against large projects,[41] has raised the question whether too low a status has not in the interim come to be attached to the authority to act and to the responsibility of the executive.[42] More recent decisions of the Federal Administrative Court have rather tended to move towards limiting judicial control of the substance of large projects[43] and, in compensation, placing strict requirements on the fairness of the authorisation proceedings.[44] The European Court has also gone down this road by reducing judicial control in the context of complex administrative decisions (*e.g.* as regards the common commercial policy) to strict observance of procedure and the prevention of any abuse of discretion and has left the evaluation of the substance largely to the administration, which has greater specialist expertise in such matters.[45]

(6) The examples given here of the interactions between the different administrative legal orders cannot, however, hide the fact that in many

---

see the contributions in M. Bullinger (ed.), *Verwaltungsermessen im modernen Staat*, Baden-Baden 1986.

[39] M. Fromont, "République Fédérale d'Allemagne. Les événements législatifs et jurisprudentiels survenus en 1976," RDP 1978, p. 395 at 439.

[40] *cf.* F. Scharpf. *Die politischen Kosten des Rechtsstaats*, Tübingen, 1970.

[41] See for a comparative discussion of this J. Schwarze, "Der vorläufige Rechtsschutz (sursis à exécution) im französischen Verwaltungsrecht—Rechtsgrundlagen und Rechtsprechungspraxis im Vergleich zum deutschen Verwaltungsrecht—," DVBl. 1987, p. 1037.

[42] See on this the supple formulation adopted by F. Ossenbühl, DVBl. 1978, p. 1: "The authorisation of nuclear power stations requires judicial confirmation."

[43] *cf.* in particular BVerwG, judgment of July 12, 1985, DÖV 1986, 74 (*Main-Danube Canal*) on what traditionally characterises French law, that is the greater attention paid to the interests of the administration and the grounds of public welfare; BVerwG, judgment of December 19, 1985, NVwZ 1986, p. 208 on the power of the executive to establish and evaluate the risk factors in atomic law.

[44] A particularly clear example is BVerwG, judgment of December 5, 1986, NVwZ 1987, p. 578 (*Second Munich Airport*).

[45] See from the case law most recently the judgment of July 14, 1988, in Case 188/85 *Fediol* v. *Commission* [1988] E.C.R. 4193. For more details see J. Schwarze, "Rechtsschutz gegen Antidumpingmassnahmen der EG—Zu Verfahren und richterlicher Kontrolle auf dem Gebiet der Aussenwirtschaftsverwaltung der Gemeinschaft," EuR 1986, p. 217 at 239. In

---

areas the resistance of national administrative laws to external influences is as great as ever.[46] In particular in those areas where national constitutional conceptions act to shape administrative law, the possibilities of evolving common European standards are limited. Thus the analysis of the principles of administration according to law and the freedom of the administration to take decisions has led to the result that in this area so far it can hardly be said that there has been a marked dialogue between the different legal systems. Furthermore, the differences in political and administrative culture between the civil law and common law systems, in spite of all tendencies towards rapprochement, cannot be ironed out in the short term.[47]

(7) Summing up, it can be stated today that against the background of frequently similar requirements and problems for public administration in the modern Western European industrial countries similar or at least comparable legal principles have been formulated in large part to govern administrative action.

In contrast to the scepticism sometimes uttered with regard to the comparability of different administrative law systems,[48] European administrative law offers instead a fertile field for applying the methods of comparative law. That this is not a new insight can be seen from the arguments put forward back in 1870 by Lorenz von Stein in his *Handbuch der Verwaltungslehre und des Verwaltungsrechts mit Vergleichung der Literatur und Gesetzgebung von Frankreich, England und Deutschland* as regards "the national form of internal administrative law and comparative legal science"[49]:

---

detail most recently on the discretion of the Council and Commission J. L. Dewost and I. van Bael in their contributions to the volume *Discretionary Powers of the Member States in the Field of Economic Policies and their Limits under the EEC Treaty* (ed. J. Schwarze), Baden-Baden 1988, p. 165 and p. 173.

[46] *cf.* for example the discussion of the different forms taken in the Member States by the principles of legality, the separation of powers, judicial control of administrative action, the protection of fundamental rights and the general conception of the State in U. Everling, "Auf dem Wege zu einem europäischen Verwaltungsrecht," NVwZ 1987, p. 1 at 2–4.

[47] *cf.* in general on this also O. Kahn-Freund, "Common Law and Civil Law—Imaginary and Real Obstacles to Assimilation," in M. Cappelletti (ed.), *New Perspectives for a Common Law of Europe*, Leyden/London/Boston 1978, p. 137.

[48] *cf.* for instance U. Scheuner, "Der Einfluss des französischen Verwaltungsrechts auf die deutsche Rechtsentwicklung," DÖV 1963, p. 714 on the particular national features of administrative law.

[49] L. v. Stein, *Handbuch der Verwaltungslehre und des Verwaltungsrechts mit Vergleichung der Literatur und Gesetzgebung von Frankreich, England und Deutschland*, Stuttgart, 1870, p. 51.

"Without doubt in each State this internal administration, alongside its general European development, as we have characterised it, has also an individual form, in which it differs in many respects from all others and thus must first and foremost be looked at as an autonomous whole.

On the other hand, the major fundamentals of life are identical in all States and are equally shaped by the mutuality of civilised behaviour, science and experience. On closer inspection it is unquestionably the case that in the field of internal administration the differences between laws as regards this development is much less significant than it may appear at first sight."

In comparative administrative law it can also be seen that functionally similar legal principles may sometimes be quite differently categorised and defined in doctrinal terms in the various legal systems. The functional method[50] must therefore be the cardinal principle when applying comparative law in the field of administrative law. Thus, the principle of proportionality recognised in German law, which requires State interference with the freedom of citizens to be suitable and necessary and not disproportionate to the aim sought to be achieved, has, in many Member States, at least until recently, no conceptual but rather a functional equivalent. The Italian Council of State, when considering whether official powers have been exceeded or whether the principle of the "buon andamento" of the administration has been breached, will occasionally have regard to the relationship between the means of the interference and the purpose of the measure[51]; in English administrative law, when the "reasonableness" of a measure is considered, this includes also the necessity of the administrative action in question.[52] The same legal principle can therefore take quite different forms from a doctrinal and conceptual point of view. In contrast, it may also be the case that the same concepts have different meanings in the various legal systems. Thus the European Court sometimes uses the concept of "discretionary powers," which

[50] On functionalism as the methodological basis of comparative law, *cf.* in particular K. Zweigert, H. Kötz *Einführung in die Rechtsvergleichung auf dem Gebiete des Privatrechts*, Vol. 1, (2nd ed., Grundlagen, Tübingen 1984), pp. 34 *et seq.*

[51] *cf.* G. M. Ubertazzi, "Le principe de proportionnalité en Droit Italien," in *Der Grundsatz der Verhältnismässigkeit in europäischen Rechtsordnungen* (ed. German Section of the International Commission of Jurists), Heidelberg 1985, p. 79. See for more details *supra*, Vol. 2, p. 676.

[52] See for more details *supra*, p. 697.

originates in German terminology, without, however, adopting the distinction lying at the heart of the dominant German doctrine between discretionary powers as regards the facts of the case and discretion as regards legal consequences.[53]

In conclusion, it can be stated that the administrative law systems of the European Community, its Member States and the Member States of the Council of Europe offer, because of their concordance in matters of principle and despite all national particularities, a worthwhile and so far wrongly neglected field of research into comparative law.[54]

III. EUROPEAN ADMINISTRATIVE LAW BETWEEN CASE LAW AND STATUTE

(1) European administrative law has, like the administrative laws of the Member States, very largely evolved out of case law. What the French Conseil d'Etat did for French administrative law through its creative law-making,[55] the European Court of Justice has initiated in similar manner for the evolving edifice of European administrative law.

Where written Community law does not contain the rules necessary for the resolution of a legal dispute, the Court of Justice has felt itself called upon to construct these using creative judicial law-making. Ever since the *Algera* decision,[56] when the Court of Justice, under pressure from the principle that the judge never refuses to give judgment, itself developed rules governing the revocation of beneficial administrative acts, the Court has come a long way down the road of constructing unwritten general principles of Community law. This road, at least in the early years of case law, has not always been entirely straight. Thus shortly after

---

[53] See for more details *supra*, p. 280.

[54] Furthermore, it may naturally make sense to include the administrative laws of non-European countries in the comparison, and in particular to refer to the experiences of U.S. administrative law, *cf.* for example B. Schwartz, H. W. R. Wade *Legal Control of Government, Administrative Law in Britain and the United States*, Oxford 1972.

[55] On the formative power of the Conseil d'Etat in the development of French administrative law see M. Fromont, "Le système français de protection juridictionnelle du citoyen contre l'administration" in *Festschrift für C.-F. Menger*, Cologne/Berlin/Bonn/ Munich 1985, p. 886 and J.-M. Woehrling, "Die französische Verwaltungsgerichtsbarkeit im Vergleich mit der deutschen," NVwZ 1985, pp. 21 *et seq.*, who in any case would like to see the intervention of the legislature at least in the field of administrative procedure, *op. cit.*, p. 26. For a critical reflection on the decline in the current importance of the Conseil d'Etat in the development of general administrative law principles in France, see J. Robert, "Conseil d'Etat und Conseil constitutionnel," RDP, p. 1151 at 1152. See for more details *supra*, pp. 100 *et seq.*

[56] Joined Cases 7/56 & 3/57 *Algera* v. *Assembly* [1957–1958] E.C.R. 39.

the judgment in *Algera*, where the Court derived from the silence of the Treaty a duty upon it to develop the law, in the *Campolongo* decision[57] the Court refused to award interest on the grounds of delay, because Community law did not contain the necessary legal rule. Although, as P. Mathijsen has said,[58] the obligation on the debtor to pay interest if he is in arrears is almost an elementary principle, the Court of Justice refused in this instance to extend written Community law by resorting to an unwritten general principle.

The Court took a different approach a short time later in its judgment in the *San Michele* case,[59] concerning the permissibility of measures of investigation taken by the High Authority:

> "As there is no express rule on this matter in Community law it is for the Court to determine whether the measures of investigation taken by the High Authority were excessive. In this case, and having regard to the circumstances, the demand for the production of the invoices at Luxembourg was not excessive and disproportionate to the aim in view."[60]

(a) The authority of the Court of Justice in principle to undertake creative law-making is today hardly in dispute. The reasons why, from the point of view of national constitutional law, there is in principle no objection to cautious legal development by the Court of Justice were stated most recently by the German Federal Constitutional Court in its *Kloppenburg* decision.[61]

The constitutional complainant Gerda Kloppenburg claimed exemptions from VAT arising out of credit transactions in her VAT declaration, relying on the sixth EEC VAT directive. The tax office rejected the exemption. Mrs. Kloppenburg challenged this decision before the Finance Court of Lower Saxony. On a reference for a preliminary ruling from the Finance Court, the Court of Justice held that a person who arranges credit transactions may rely directly upon the corresponding provision in the directive during the period after the expiry of the time limit when the provision had not yet been implemented in national law.[62]

---

[57] Joined Cases 27 & 39/59 *Campolongo* v. *High Authority* [1960] E.C.R. 391.
[58] See P. Mathijsen, "La Cour de Justice et les notions juridiques non précisées," KSE 1, p. 430 at 433.
[59] Joined Cases 5–11 and 13–125/62 *San Michele* v. *High Authority* [1962] E.C.R. 449.
[60] [1962] E.C.R. 462.
[61] BVerfFG—2 BvR 687/85 of April 8, 1987, BVerfGE 75, 223 ([1988] 3 C.M.L.R. 1).
[62] Case 70/83 *Kloppenburg* v. *Finanzamt Leer* [1984] E.C.R. 1075.

The Finance Court accordingly exempted the transactions from VAT. On appeal, the Federal Finance Court quashed the decision of the Finance Court for breach of Articles 20 III and 24 I of the Basic Law and rejected the claim.[63] *Inter alia* it held that powers had not been transferred to the European Economic Community to give similar effects to Directives as those attributed to Regulations, not even through the development of the law. The preliminary ruling of the European Court left untouched the competence of the referring court to decide what law to apply. Since in this case it was German law and not European Community law which was at issue, there was no need for a further reference to the Court. The plaintiff then brought constitutional proceedings against this decision, which was quashed by the Federal Constitutional Court, which referred the matter back.[64] The Federal Constitutional Court held that the Federal Finance Court had arbitrarily denied its obligation to refer the question once more to the European Court. In so doing it had breached Article 101 I second sentence of the Basic Law, which guarantees that no one shall be deprived of his or her lawful judge. On the question concerning us here regarding the authority of the Court of Justice to develop the law, the Federal Constitutional Court had the following to say[65]:

> "There can be no objection from the viewpoint of the Act ratifying the EEC Treaty of Article 24(1) of the Basic Law to the method of judicial development of the law used by the Court of Justice. It is true that the Court has not been given authority to extend at will the jurisdiction of the Community in this way, but neither can there be any doubt that it was the intention of the Member States to provide the Community with a court which would ascertain and apply the law by methods developed over centuries of common European legal tradition and refinement of law. In Europe the judge was never merely 'la bouche qui prononce les paroles de la loi.' Roman law, the English common law and the German Gemeines Recht were to a large extent the creation of the judges in the same way as in more

---

[63] Bundesfinanzhof of April 25, 1985, EuR 1985, p. 191 ([1989] 1 C.M.L.R. 873). See on this the critical note by C. Tomuschat, "Nein und abermals Nein! Zum Urteil des BFH vom 25.4.1985 (V R 123/84)," EuR 1985, p. 346.

[64] BVerfG *op. cit.*, footnote 61; [1988] 3 C.M.L.R. 19.

[65] *Op. cit.*, p. 243. On case law from the German point of view see most recently the President of the Federal Administrative Court H. Sendler, "Richterrecht—rechtstheoretisch und rechtspraktisch," NJW 1987, p. 3240, as well as F. Ossenbühl *Richterrecht im demokratischen Rechtsstaat*, Bonn 1988.

recent times in France, for instance, the development of general legal principles of administrative law by the Conseil d'Etat or, in Germany, general administrative law, large parts of the law of employment or security rights on private law business transactions. The Community Treaties must also be construed in the light of common European legal tradition and refinement of the law. In view of this it is mistaken to think that the Court of Justice of the Communities is prohibited from using the method of developing the law. The Federal Constitutional Court has already on occasion assumed, without causing a furore, that the Court of Justice may develop subjective rights of private individuals from general legal principles (BVerfGE 37, 271; BVerfGE 73, 339) (See [1974] 2 C.M.L.R. 540 and [1987] 3 C.M.L.R. 225).

(b) The European Court of Justice has commented upon the relationship between legislation and case law[66] in the creation of administrative law principles in particular in the context of the problem of judicial recognition of time limits not provided for in written law. In a number of cases where such limits upon the exercise of particular rights were not provided for in either the Treaties or secondary legislation, it has filled the existing gaps by establishing a number of abstract determinations, but mostly without setting up any rigid rules. Thus by reference to the system established in Articles 33 and 35 ECSC, it made the exercise of the rights provided for in Article 35 ECSC dependent upon observing a "reasonable time limit," although the Treaty contains no express rule.[67]

Advocate-General Roemer, on the other hand, considered it wrong for an exclusionary time limit to be introduced by case law.[68] In another place, the Court appealed to the responsibility of the Community legislature for the construction of legislative provisions and thereby called upon it to act. Thus in its decision in *Express Dairy Foods*, the Court held that: "In the regrettable absence of Community provisions harmonising procedure and time limits (on the reimbursement of sums wrongly paid) the Court finds that this situation entails differences in treatment on a Community scale."[69] In his Opinion in this case Advocate-General Capotorti

---

[66] See in general on the relationship between legislation and case law in the Community J. Schwarze, "Funktionen des Rechts in der Europäischen Gemeinschaft," in *ibid.* (ed.), *Gesetzgebung in der Europäischen Gemeinschaft*, Baden-Baden 1985, pp. 9 *et seq.*
[67] Case 59/70 *Netherlands* v. *Commission* [1971] E.C.R. 639 at 653.
[68] [1971] E.C.R. 659.
[69] Case 130/79 *Express Dairy Foods* v. *IBAP* [1980] E.C.R. 1887 at 1900.

referred even more clearly to the fact that "the Council is exercising its power to regulate matters with lamentable slowness."[70] Further examples have been analysed in the section above concerned with the principle of legal certainty.[71]

In particular the decisions concerned with the prescription of breaches of the competition rules for lapse of time show that the Court of Justice will not simply put itself in the place of the legislature where written rules are lacking. In the proceedings concerned the so-called quinine cartel,[72] when the applicants, undertakings in the pharmaceutical industry which had been fined by the Commission for operating a prohibited cartel agreement, argued *inter alia* that the alleged contravention had lapsed through passage of time, the Court of Justice rejected this defence on the grounds that the relevant competition provisions did not provide for a limitation period and it was therefore not a matter for the Court of Justice to establish this:

> "In order to fulfil their function of ensuring legal certainty, limitation periods must be fixed in advance. The fixing of their duration and the detailed rules for their application must come within the powers of the Community legislature."[73]

In the proceedings which occurred two years later against the dyestuffs manufacturers,[74] the Court again rejected the applicants' claim of lapse of time, although on this occasion together with a warning note to the Community legislature indicating that it could itself determine the limitation of actions in cases where the Commission had delayed excessively, by reference to the general principle of legal certainty. In another case, concerning the rules governing equalisation contributions for scrap metal in the coal and steel sector the Court once more refused to set its own abstract limitation period on the grounds that this would contradict the intentions of the legislature.[75] These examples show that the Court is fully aware of the primary competence of the legislature in the law-making

---

[70] [1980] E.C.R. 1910.
[71] *Supra*, Chapter 6.
[72] Case 41/69 *ACF Chemiefarma*, Case 44/69 *Buchler* and Case 45/69 *Boehringer* [1970] E.C.R. 661, 733 and 769.
[73] [1970] E.C.R. at 683, 750–1 and 795.
[74] See above all the judgment of the Court of Justice in Case 48/69 *ICI* v. *Commission* [1972] E.C.R. 619 at 653.
[75] Case 2/70 *Riva* v. *Commission* [1971] E.C.R. 97 at 109.

process and does not arrogate to itself an unlimited authority to set abstract rules in the sense of an attribution of competence.[76]

In consequence of the reticence of the Court of Justice as regards the issue of the judicial introduction of limitation periods in competition law, the Community legislature was eventually constrained to act. Two years after the dyestuffs cases the Council adopted a Regulation concerning limitation periods in proceedings and the enforcement of sanctions under the rules of the European Economic Community relating to transport and competition.[77]

(2) In addition, there are a number of rules of secondary law which, while they do not have general application to the implementation of administrative law but are valid for only one or more substantive fields, do correspond in terms of their content to the rules of the general part of an administrative law.[78]

(a) An example of partial consolidation in recent times is Commission Regulation 2220/85 of July 22, 1985 introducing common implementing provisions regulating securities for agricultural products.[79] Before the adoption of this Regulation the numerous provisions in the individual agricultural market regulations which required the provision of a security, with a guarantee to pay a particular sum of money if a given obligation was not fulfilled, were interpreted in a variety of ways. By regulating more closely the form of the security to be given the new Regulation is intended to contribute to increased uniformity and thus to prevent unequal conditions of competition.[80] Further examples of this are furnished by Council Regulations 1676/85[81] and 1677/85[82] of June 11, 1985 on the value of the unit of account and the conversion rates to be used within the framework of the common agricultural policy, and on monetary compensatory amounts in the agricultural sector. After various regulations had introduced the ECU as the unit of account for the common agricultural policy, the existing rules no longer corresponded to reality or to practical exigencies. The new regulation concerning the value of the unit of account and the conversion rates is intended to

---

[76] See for more details J. Schwarze *Die Befugnis zur Abstraktion im europäischen Gemein-schaftsrecht*, Baden-Baden 1976, pp. 204 *et seq.*
[77] Council Regulation 2988/74, O.J. 1974, L319/1.
[78] *cf.* the examples mentioned *supra*, pp. 42 *et seq.*
[79] O.J. 1985, L205/5, as amended by O.J. 1987, L113/31.
[80] *cf.* the preamble, O.J. 1985, L205/5.
[81] O.J. 1985, L164/1 as amended by O.J. 1987, L88/42.
[82] O.J. 1985, L164/6.

provide a coherent set of rules.[83] Moreover, the new regulation on monetary compensatory amounts is intended to improve access to the much amended provisions in this field. For reasons of clarity and efficacy it was therefore advisable, as is stated in the preamble,[84] to effect a consolidation and republication of the amended version.

In other contexts, it would appear that awareness is gradually growing within the institutions of the Community that at least a partial consolidation would remove uncertainties in many fields and would facilitate the application of the law.

The Council requested the Commission in a Resolution adopted back in November 1974 to prepare proposals for the consolidation of regulations or directives which have been frequently amended, since it is desirable, for reasons of legal clarity and to facilitate the dealings of those involved with such legal acts, to bring together frequently amended legal acts of the Council into a single text.[85] In its final report to the European Council in Milan (June 28–29, 1985) the Ad hoc Committee for a People's Europe recommended *inter alia* that "steps be taken to accelerate the systematic consolidation and simplification of Community law."[86] The European Council gave its support to the proposals of the Committee.[87] The Commission too has also concerned itself on a number of occasions with the question of the consolidation of Community law. According to an internal document of the Commission, legal acts which have been amended more than 10 times should be replaced and consolidated.[88] This is not a matter of introducing substantively new law, but of bringing together existing rules and setting them out in a coherent fashion in order to bring about greater transparency. Moreover, in most cases what is

---

[83] *cf.* the preamble *supra*, footnote 81, p. 1.

[84] *Op. cit., supra*, footnote 82, p. 6.

[85] Council Resolution of November 26, 1974 concerning consolidation of its Acts, O.J. 1975, C20/1. In this field some progress has since been achieved. *cf.* for instance most recently the consolidations in the wine sector by Council Regulations 822/87 and 823/87 of March 16, 1987 on the common organisation of the market in wine, and on laying down special provisions relating to quality wines produced in specified regions (O.J. 1987, L84/1 and 59) where in the preamble the consolidation is expressly based on the fact that the numerous provisions in this field were to be found in various issues of the Official Journal and were hard to use, so that there was a consequent lack of clarity. An excellent factual analysis of Community legislation and its lack of legal guarantees is provided by C. Tomuschat, "Normenpublizität und Normenklarheit in der Europäischen Gemeinschaft," in *Festschrift für H. Kutscher*, Baden-Baden 1981, pp. 461 *et seq.*

[86] E.C. Bull. Supp. 7/85, p. 20.

[87] E.C. Bull. Supp. 7/85, p. 31.

[88] "Codification du droit communautaire" of March 25, 1987, SEC (87)509 (internal document).

involved is a "vertical" consolidation, that is the addition of subsequent amendments to the original legal act. It is rarer for consolidation to involve the "horizontal" bringing together of several different legal acts in one text.[89] As regards content, most of the consolidations of that type have taken place in the agricultural sector.[90]

(b) Apart from this, no intention to undertake a larger consolidation in administrative law can currently be discerned. It is not only the legal competence to undertake an overall consolidation of the general part of European Community administrative law which is lacking, but also the political will to make the necessary extension of competence possible within a reasonable time. The limitations which the structure of powers under the Treaties places upon a comprehensive consolidation of administrative law, in particular in the field of indirect administrative implementation by the Member States, were set out earlier in the Introduction.[91] It would appear very doubtful whether a general consolidation of administrative law could be achieved. Thus at the Hamburg conference on "The development of European administrative law," H. P. Ipsen remarked that he regarded such a project as even bolder than the draft of a Community constitution.[92]

Indeed, the time may not yet be ripe for a comprehensive consolidation of European administrative law.[93] The inertia of an administrative law set

[89] On the concepts of horizontal and vertical consolidation cf. G. Isaac, "La codification du droit communautaire," Rev. Europ. 1977, p. 90.

[90] cf. Codification des règlements agricoles communautaires (Rapport d'information diffusé à la Commission, à la demande de M. Dalsager) of November 5, 1981, SEC (81) 1725 (internal document). See previously also the Commission Memorandum to the Council of November 5, 1973, Improvement of the Common Agricultural Policy, E.C. Bull. Supp. 17/73, point 28.

[91] pp. 45 et seq.

[92] In K. Iliopoulos, "Bericht über die Podiumsdiskussion," in J. Schwarze (ed.), Europäisches Verwaltungsrecht im Werden, Baden-Baden 1982, p. 123.

[93] On almost every occasion when a legal or constitutional consolidation has been planned, there has been a fundamental debate whether such a move, as a major leap forward, should be preferred to a step-by-step gradual development of the existing law and whether in particular the time is ripe to accomplish such a change. The "classical" discussion in this context is the dispute between Thibaut (Über die Notwendigkeit eines allgemeinen bürgerlichen Rechts für Deutschland, 1814) and Savigny (Vom Beruf unserer Zeit für Gesetzgebung und Rechtswissenschaft, also 1814) concerning the introduction of a general civil law in Germany. cf. volume by J. Stern containing the two contributions to the debate with an introduction and commentary, Thibaut und Savigny, 1914, reprinted by the Wissenschaftliche Buchgesellschaft, Darmstadt, 1959. See also St. Gagner, Studien zur Ideengeschichte der Gesetzgebung, Stockholm/Uppsala/Gothenburg 1960, pp. 15 et seq. On the style and signification of consolidation in general see H. Schneider, Gesetzgebung, Heidelberg 1982, para. 426. On the perspectives today for a Community

up by case law can be seen from the striking example of the efforts to achieve a consolidation of German law of administrative procedure.[94] In this case a long period of time was needed in order to overcome opposition to achieving a statutory regulation of administrative procedure, which was largely based on the point of view that such a change would be an unnecessary and even damaging obstacle to administrative efficiency.

The remaining differences between the various administrative laws of the Member States which continue to exist despite the tendency towards convergence described here may create additional difficulties with regard to agreement on a statutorily grounded European administrative law. Moreover, the case law material and the investigations done into this material in academic literature to which a statutory regulation would attach itself cannot yet be regarded as sufficient for such an undertaking.

A premature consolidation of administrative law, if it is not in the end to involve anything more than the adoption of general clauses which are capable of and require further construction, would run the risk of setting up a rigid and inflexible system of rules of law which in any case would have to be modified by numerous exceptions tailored to individual cases.[95] Putting such an untimely end to a continuing process of legal development would in any case specifically conflict with the evolutionary nature of Community law.[96] Experience further teaches that far-reaching attempts to effect judicial consolidations at least should not be undertaken too early but only in the light of rather longer lines of case law and a sufficient volume of cases and academic commentary.[97]

---

system of private law see P.-Chr. Müller- Graff, "Privatrecht und europäisches Gemeinschaftsrecht," in *Staat und Wirtschaft in der EG, Kolloqium zum 65. Geburtstag von Bodo Börner*, (eds. P.-Chr. Müller-Graff, M. Zuleeg) Baden-Baden 1987, pp. 17 *et seq.*

[94] *cf.* with references to the individual stages of development P. Badura, in H.-U. Erichsen, W. Martens *Allgemeines Verwaltungsrecht* (7th ed., Berlin/New York 1986), pp. 339 *et seq.* with references; R. Mussgnug, "Das allgemeine Verwaltungsrecht zwischen Richterrecht und Gesetzesrecht," in *Richterliche Rechtsfortbildung: Festschrift der Jur. Fak. zur 600-Jahr-Feier d. Ruprecht-Karls-Universität Heidelberg* 1986, pp. 203 *et seq.* as well as most recently G. Chr. von Unruh, "Kodifiziertes Verwaltungsrecht," NVwZ 1988, p. 690. On the question whether the Law on administrative procedure has proved itself in practice see H. Hill *Zehn Jahre Verwaltungsverfahrensgesetz*, Speyrer Arbeitshefte 78, 1987, with copious references.

[95] *cf.* also R. Mussgnug, *op. cit., supra*, footnote 94, p. 227 on the general limits to the consolidation of the general part of administrative law.

[96] See in general on the evolutionary nature of European Community law W. v. Simson, " 'Das Recht' in den Europäischen Gemeinschaften," in *Festschrift für Hans von der Groeben zum 80. Geburtstag*, Baden-Baden 1987, p. 391, as well as R. Bieber, G. Ress (eds.), *Die Dynamik des Europäischen Gemeinschaftsrechts*, Baden-Baden 1987.

[97] An example of a failed judicial consolidation is offered by the early case law of the German Bundesgerichtshof on interferences analogous to expropriation. The system

(3) In conclusion, therefore, it is to be welcomed if the Court of Justice continues to develop in a cautious and pragmatic way its case law on the principles of general administrative law. Simultaneously, within the framework of Community powers, partial statutory consolidations should be attempted[97a] where specific substantive problems require it. This would be the case in particular where overwhelming arguments relating to legal certainty made statutory regulation necessary (for instance to set time limits) or where the inactivity of the legislature would have the consequence of a lack of uniformity and a discriminatory application of Community law in the Member States, which could not effectively be prevented by case law alone. This would be the case, for instance, by reason of the very technical nature of the detailed rules required.

IV. THE INTEGRATION FUNCTION OF EUROPEAN CONSTITUTIONAL AND ADMINISTRATIVE LAW

(1) If in conclusion one were to evaluate once more the contribution of European administrative law, in the form which it has adopted as a result of the case law of the European Court, to European integration, then one would have to begin by emphasising the great importance of the general administrative law principles in the practice of the Court itself. The vast majority of actions, challenging the legality of Community legal acts at least raise the question whether the unwritten general principles of law have been breached. Even in competition law, where the focus of the investigation is primarily on the interpretation and application of Articles 85 and 86 EEC and the relevant regulations, it is also customarily argued that general procedural principles have not been observed. Occasionally the decisions of the Court and the Opinion of the Advocates-General would appear to be models of the tests to be undertaken using general principles of law. An example of this is provided by the Opinions of

---

established in BGHZ 6, 270 governing interferences analogous to expropriation proved to be too rigid and inflexible and had therefore to be subsequently replaced or modified in respect of certain essential points. On the subsequent alterations of the system see for instance F. Ossenbühl, *Staatshaftungsrecht*, (3rd ed., Munich 1983), p. 146.

[97a] Thus Ole Due, judge at the European Court of Justice, asked the question whether for the field of law governing administrative procedure the time had not come, by reason of the essentially compatible legal development of national administrative laws and the case law of the European Court, for attempts to be made to achieve a corresponding (partial) consolidation at Community level ("Le respect des droits de la défense dans le droit administratif communautaire," CDE 1987, p. 383 at 396).

Advocate-General J. Mischo in the reference for a preliminary ruling in *Maizena* v. *BALM*[98] where he considered whether a particular agricultural regulation providing for a security was compatible with the principles of legality, *ne bis in idem, in dubio pro reo* and *nulla poena sine culpa,* as well as the principle of proportionality.

This case also shows that there is no closed class of general principles of law, such as those principles analysed in the preceding chapters. Thus the principles of *nulla poena sine lege, ne bis in idem, in dubio pro reo* and *nulla poena sine culpa* originally developed under criminal law can also be applied within administrative law, in particular where the issue, as in the case of the loss of a deposit in agricultural law or the imposition of fines in competition law, concerns not exactly criminal penalties but at least burdensome administrative measures. Advocate-General Mischo stressed the predominating fundamental rights elements of these principles as follows: "Great rigour must be observed in regard to fundamental rights, and what some people regard as principles of criminal law, others might regard as fundamental rights or as principles of administrative law designed to provide traders with adequate legal protection."[99]

Similarly, what were originally principles of civil law can acquire an administrative law dimension. Thus the Court has had occasion to consider, for example, the principles of the charging of compound interest[100] and the coming into effect of a declaration of intent by delivery to the recipient,[101] which are not laid down in written Community law.

(2) The general principles of law initially became significant in administrative law as a means of filling gaps. This technical function appears right back in the *Algera* judgment concerning the revocability of administrative acts, which we have discussed on a number of occasions. Since Community law contained no relevant provisions, the Court, in order to avoid the accusation that it was denying justice, was required to have recourse to unwritten principles of law.[102]

The problem of the incompleteness of written law is known in all legal systems. The desire for perfection, raised by the Prussian *Allgemeines Landrecht* and the other great codifications of the eighteenth and early

---

[98] Case 137/85 *Maizena* v. *BALM* [1987] E.C.R. 4587 at 4594.
[99] *Op. cit.* at p. 4598.
[100] Case 67/69 *Simet* v. *Commission* [1971] E.C.R. 197 at 208.
[101] Case 8/56 *ALMA* v. *High Authority* [1957–1958] E.C.R. 95 at 99.
[102] Joined Cases 7/56 & 3–7/57 *Algera* v. *Assembly* [1957–1958] E.C.R. 39 at 61.

nineteenth centuries, proved very early to be unrealisable.[103] The problem of filling gaps is a particularly urgent one in Community law. This is primarily because of the fragmentary nature of this legal system. The founding Treaties obviously could not clarify every question which might at some time prove relevant in the course of later developments. In controversial fields the contracting parties went further with compromise formulas intentionally left vague. Community law could also not, as a newly formed legal order, rely upon its own legal tradition. From the outset, the EEC Treaty was intended as a "law-making treaty" to require normative activity by the political organs, the Council and the Commission, in order to create a legal substratum to the "traité cadre." This task was not always so simply realisable, because the necessary political consensus required within the Council was difficult to achieve. After 1966, when the so-called Luxembourg Accords in practice virtually introduced unanimity for important Council decisions, it became even more difficult for the Council to carry out the legislative tasks set before it. On the other hand, the Community developed early into an autonomous legal order separate from those of the Member States. The Court of Justice set down the decisive markers with the well-known cases of *Van Gend en Loos*[104] and *Costa* v. *ENEL*.[105] Out of the tension between the fundamental claim to autonomy by Community law, which excludes direct recourse to other legal systems, and the incompleteness of the written law, it becomes clear how important are the general principles of law here as an instrument for filling gaps.

(3) The validity and importance of the general principles of law have been extended and strengthened on several levels in the case law of the Court.

(a) At the outset the Court primarily used the general principles of law simply to fill the gaps which arose in relation to the need to render justice.[106] The *Algera* decision[107] is the paradigm of this. Increasingly, however, the general principles were applied in order to fill gaps in the

---

[103] See for more details, M. Kriele *Theorie der Rechtsgewinnung, entwickelt am Beispiel der Verfassungsinterpretation*, (2nd ed., Berlin 1976), pp. 60 *et seq.* On the various forms taken by general principles of law in particular in the case law of international courts see in particular G. Bosco *Lezioni di diritto internazionale*, Milan 1987, p. 57 with further references.

[104] Case 26/62 *Van Gend en Loos* v. *Nederlandse Administratie der Belastingen* [1963] E.C.R. 1 at 12.

[105] Case 6/64 *Costa* v. *ENEL* [1964] E.C.R. 585 at 593.

[106] *cf.* C.-W. Canaris *Die Feststellung von Lücken im Gesetz*, Berlin 1964, p. 141.

[107] *Op. cit.*, footnote 102.

law which appeared out of the unscheduled incompleteness of the Treaties only when one applied an evaluatory approach and which were not necessarily evident from the outset.[108] In this way, the Court established the application first of the principles of legality common to the Member States and then of fundamental rights.

(b) In the early years the Court tended primarily to measure the executive acts of the Commission against the general principles of administrative law. At issue in particular were individual decisions in the coal and steel field and decisions relating to officials. Later the Court started to scrutinise increasingly the normative acts of the Council and Commission to ensure their compatibility with superior unwritten law. In this context, *inter alia*, numerous regulations and implementing regulations in customs and agricultural law became subject to judicial review.

Although the general principles of law served in the first instance to bind the administration to the law, it is the case that the acts of the Community legislature are now also measured against these standards. To that extent they have, at least in part, taken on the form of constitutional principles.[109]

(c) Parallel to this development can be found a further change in the understanding of the general principles of law. Whereas originally they were understood primarily as an objective standard against which to judge the legality of actions of the Community institutions, they are now

---

[108] In this context the Court of Justice has a certain discretionary scope within which to "find" gaps in the law, in order then to fill them using a general principle of law, *cf.* H. G. Schermers, "Algemene rechtsbeginselen als bron van gemeenschapsrecht," SEW 1983, p. 514 at 526.

[109] The distinction between constitutional and administrative law principles is used here in a formal sense, namely whether the principle also binds the legislature or is restricted in its application only to the conduct of the administration. Thus, as in national law, it is not excluded, as for instance, in the case of the principle of proportionality, which in German law was first treated as a principle of executive law and only later as a constitutional principle (on this see for instance K. Hesse *Grundzüge des Verfassungsrechts der Bundesrepublik Deutschland*, (15th ed., Heidelberg 1985), p. 73 as well as Drews, Wacke, Vogel & Martens *Gefahrenabwehr*, Cologne/Berlin/Bonn/Munich (9th ed. edited by K. Vogel and W. Martens p. 390), that one and the same principle, with perhaps a variance in significance and with different scope, may be of both constitutional and administrative law nature. On the intensive discussion on the significance and constitutional position of "principes généraux du droit" in French law see, among many other writers, G. Braibant, *Le droit administratif français*, Paris 1984, pp. 220 *et seq.* See also on the dual function of the general principles of law in binding both actual Community legislation and also the conduct of the Member States F. Capotorti, "Il diritto comunitario non scritto," Diritto com. scambi intern. 1983, p. 410.

regarded increasingly from the point of view of the protection of the individual.

A clear expression of this development is the case law of the Court of Justice on fundamental rights, the doctrinal basis of which is to be found in the general principles of law within the Community legal system. This development has been documented and commented upon by many writers[110] and need not be dealt with here in detail.

The famous *Stauder* case (1969) marks the first decision in which the Court expressly recognised that the general principles of Community law which must be observed also include fundamental rights attaching to the individual.[111] Shortly thereafter, in the *Internationale Handelsgesellschaft* case (1970), the Court formulated the principles of adequate protection for fundamental rights in the Community in such a way that the fundamental rights to be respected at Community level were those integrated into the structure and objectives of the Community.[112] As the *Nold* decision of 1974 subsequently showed, the basis for the development of Community law fundamental rights includes not only the common constitutional traditions of the Member States, but also the international Treaties governing the protection of human rights, which the Member States had participated in or to which they had acceded, in particular the European Convention on Human Rights and Fundamental Freedoms.[113] Thereafter, the Court of Justice reiterated its principles on the protection of fundamental rights in the *Hauer*[114] case in 1979 and went a step further

---

[110] *cf.* in place of many B. Beutler, Annex C "Grundrechtsschutz" in Groeben *et al.*, *Kommentar zum EWG-Vertrag*, (3rd ed., Baden-Baden 1983); *Law of the European Communities* (ed. D. Vaughan), Vol. 1, London 1986, pp. 361 *et seq.*; J. Boulouis *Droit institutionnel des Communautés européennes*, Paris 1984, p. 156 as well as J. Schwarze, "Schutz der Grundrechte in der Europäischen Gemeinschaft—Grundlagen und heutiger Entwicklungsstand," EuGRZ 1986, p. 293, all with further references.

[111] Case 29/69 *Stauder* v. *Stadt Ulm* [1969] E.C.R. 419 at 425.

[112] Case 11/70 *Internationale Handelsgesellschaft* [1970] E.C.R. 1125 at 1134.

[113] Case 4/73 *Nold* v. *Commission* [1974] E.C.R. 491 at 507. On the significance of the ECHR for the protection of fundamental rights in the Community see most recently R. Bernhardt, "Neue Entwicklungstendenzen in der Rechtsprechung des Europäischen Gerichtshofes für Menschenrechte," *Vorträge aus dem Europa-Institut der Universität des Saarlandes*, 1987, p. 13.

[114] Case 44/79 *Hauer* v. *Rheinland-Pfalz* [1979] E.C.R. 3727.

by expressly referring to the Joint Declaration by the European Parliament, the Council and the Commission of April 5, 1977 on the application of and respect for fundamental rights in the Community.[115,116]

(4) With the benefit of hindsight it can be seen that the interplay between national courts, in particular the Federal Constitutional Court, and the European Court of Justice has proved itself useful in the concretisation of the rule of law in the Community. The European Court has reacted with great sensitivity to the essentially justified demands from national courts[117] that the deficiency in Community law as regards the protection of fundamental rights should be overcome. The recognition of the achievements of the Court of Justice can hardly be put better than it was most recently by the Federal Constitutional Court in a remarkably pro-integrationist decision. In that case the Federal Constitutional Court held that its doubts as regards fundamental rights had essentially been overcome, and correspondingly it found that[118]:

> "So long as the European Communities, and in particular the case law of the European Court, generally ensure an effective protection

---

[115] O.J. 1977, C103/1. On the legal status of this Declaration see M. Hilf, "Die gemeinsame Grundrechtserklärung des Europäischen Parlaments, des Rates und der Kommission vom 5. April 1977," EuGRZ 1977, p. 158.

[116] Case 44/79 *supra*, footnote 114, at p. 3747. See also the Preamble to the Single European Act, in which the Member States determined "to work together to promote democracy on the basis of the fundamental rights recognised in the constitutions and laws of the Member States, in the Convention for the Protection of Human Rights and Fundamental Freedoms and the European Social Charter, notably freedom, equality and social justice."

[117] *cf.* the judgment of the Italian Corte Costitutionale No. 183 of 1973, of December 27, 1973 [1974] 2 C.M.L.R. 372 and the "Solange" decision of the Federal Constitutional Court BVerfGE 37, 271 ([1974] 2 C.M.L.R. 549) which was in any case modified by BVerfGE 52, 187 ([1980] 2 C.M.L.R. 531 at 537) (the "Vielleicht" decision), as well as the (not directly concerned with the European Community) Eurocontrol decisions BVerfGE 58, 1; 59, 63. See for more detail J. Schwarze, "Das Verhältnis von deutschem Verfassungsrecht und europäischem Gemeinschaftsrecht auf dem Gebiet des Grundrechtsschutzes im Spiegel der jüngsten Rechtsprechung," EuGRZ 1983, p. 117. In general on constitutional reticence on the part of the courts of the Member States see most recently G. Olmi, "Les hautes juridictions nationales, juges du droit communautaire," in *Liber Amicorum P. Pescatore, op. cit.* footnote 16, p. 499.

[118] BVerfGE 73, 339 at 387 ([1987] 3 C.M.L.R. 225 at 265). On this see H. P. Ipsen, "Das Bundesverfassungsgericht löst die Grundrechts-Problematik. Zum "Mittlerweile" Beschluss des 2. Senats vom 22. Oktober 1986," EuR 1987, p. 1; M. Hilf, "Solange II: Wielange noch Solange?" EuGRZ 1987, p. 1 as well as G. C. Rodriguez Iglesias & U. Wölker, "Derecho Comunitario, Derechos Fundamentales y Control de Constitucionalidad," Revista de Instituciones Europeas 1987, p. 667. The doubts with regard to the adequacy of European fundamental rights standards do not, however, appear to have been removed in all Member States; *cf.* on the situation in Denmark, for example, R.

of fundamental rights as against the sovereign powers of the Communities which is to be regarded as substantially similar to the protection of fundamental rights required unconditionally in the Basic Law, and in so far as they generally safeguard the essential content of fundamental rights, the Federal Constitutional Court will no longer exercise its jurisdiction to decide on the applicability of secondary Community legislation cited as the legal basis for any acts of German courts or authorities within the sovereign jurisdiction of the Federal Republic of Germany, and it will no longer review such legislation by the standard of the fundamental rights contained in the Constitution."

Also informative is the list compiled by the Federal Constitutional Court in this decision of the legal principles which the European Court has recognised as fundamental rights and as binding standards against which the sovereign acts of the Community institutions are to be judged[119]:

"Side by side with the express guarantee of liberties contained in the Community Treaties themselves the foreground was occupied naturally by the fundamental rights and freedoms relating to economic activities, such as the right to property and freedom to pursue economic activities. In addition to that it cited other basic rights, such as freedom of association, the general principle of equal treatment and the prohibition on arbitrary acts, religious freedom or the protection of the family, as standards for assessment. The European Court has generally recognised and consistently applies in its decisions the principles, which follow from the rule of law, of the prohibition of excessive action and of proportionality as general legal principles in reaching a balance between the common interest objective of the Community legal system and the safeguarding of the essential content of fundamental rights. It has recognised the prohibition of retrospection as an emanation of the basic principle of legal certainty and has recognised the rule against double penalties and likewise the obligation under the rule of law to state reasons for individual decisions. ... (The Court), having recourse to the constitutional traditions common to all Member States and to Article 13 of

Gralla, *Der Grundrechtsschutz in Dänemark*, Frankfurt/M-Bern/New York 1987, pp. 449 *et seq.*
[119] BVerfGE, *op. cit.*, pp. 380/381 ([1987] 3 C.M.L.R. 225 at 260–1). The comprehensive references to the decisions of the European Court cited by the Federal Constitutional Court are omitted here.

the European Convention on Human Rights, categorised the claim to effective judicial protection for the safeguarding of personal rights as a constituent part of the guarantees for fundamental rights under Community law. It regarded the duty to grant a legal hearing as an essential requirement of a fair procedural system."

These constitutional principles of Community law also put in place, from the perspective of the administration and the citizen who faces it, the essential coordinates of European administrative law. Remarkably, the Federal Constitutional Court cites in the context of fundamental rights *inter alia* legal certainty, the duty to state reasons and the right to a hearing. It thus recognises that the European protection for fundamental rights which was established by case law takes the form not only of notional categories of fundamental rights, but also of objective general principles of law which from a functional perspective, and from the point of view of the objective to be achieved, are frequently of equal status.[120]

What Fritz Werner correctly said of German administrative law, namely that it amounted to "concretised constitutional law,"[121] can also be said in the European Community, albeit in a different form. The administrative law emerging in this context derives to a notable extent from the constitutional conceptions of the Member States and integrates these into a synthesis specific to the needs of the Community. The recently decided case of *Heylens*[122] is a particularly notable example of the close relationship between Community constitutional and administrative law. When the Court of Justice in that case describes the free movement or workers (Article 48 EEC) as a Community fundamental right, which must be guaranteed by effective judicial remedies and when it derives from this the concrete finding that if a (negative) decision[123] has been

---

[120] *cf.* also Beutler, Bieber, Pipkorn & Streil *Die Europäische Gemeinschaft—Rechtsordnung und Politik*, (3rd ed., Baden-Baden 1987), p. 221. On the lines of connection between administrative law principles and fundamental rights *cf.* J. Schwarze, "The Administrative Law of the Community and the Protection of Human Rights" (1986) C.M.L.Rev. 401.

[121] F. Werner, "Verwaltungsrecht als konkretisiertes Verfassungsrecht," DVBl. 1959, p. 527.

[122] Case 222/86 [1987] E.C.R. 4097. See *supra*, Chapter 7 conclusions.

[123] In this case the non-recognition of a foreign licence to practise as a football trainer as an equivalent diploma. The relevant passage of the judgment runs as follows ([1987] E.C.R. 4117): "Effective judicial review, which must be able to cover the legality of the reasons for the contested decision, presupposes in general that the court to which the matter is referred may require the competent authority to notify its reasons. But where, as in this case, it is more particularly a question of securing the effective protection of a fundamental right conferred by the Treaty on Community workers, the latter must also be able

taken, the competent authorities must communicate the reasons for their decision to the person concerned to enable him to judge the possible success or failure of any judicial review of the decision, then one sees the fluid cross-over, or at least the structural interaction, between constitutional and administrative protection at Community level.

(5) General principles of administrative law under the rule of law and fundamental rights thus complement each other in a positive manner and have proved, as a whole, to be an effective instrument for setting legal limits on the exercise of Community power.

These rights are not, however, unlimited. On the contrary, they must be balanced against the public interest. In particular the interest of the Community in having an efficient and effective administration must be taken into account.[124] Thus Advocate-General Warner, referring back to a Resolution of the Council of Europe, argued that the right to a hearing is undoubtedly "subject to the general proviso that it must be compatible with the requirements of efficient administration."[125] Furthermore, the Court itself has for example decided that the duty on the Commission laid down in Article 36 ECSC to give the person concerned the opportunity to make representations before the imposition of a financial sanction or of a penalty payment does not include the duty to put forward its counter-arguments in relation to the arguments in its defence put forward by the party concerned. Otherwise, continued the Court, "that would be likely to render the procedure for establishing an infringement too cumbersome and extend its duration unnecessarily."[126]

The fundamental rights recognised and given concrete form by the Court of Justice are subject to similar general reservations in the interests of the Community.[127] It appears legitimate to the Court "that these rights should, if necessary, be subject to certain limits justified by the overall

---

to defend that right under the best possible conditions and have the possibility of deciding, with a full knowledge of the relevant facts, whether there is any point in their applying to the courts. Consequently, in such circumstances the competent national authority is under a duty to inform them of the reasons on which its refusal is based, either in the decision itself or in a subsequent communication made at their request." See for more details *supra*, the conclusions to Chapter 7.

[124] *cf.* in this context J. Schwarze, "Administrative Leistungsfähigkeit als verwaltungsrechtliches Problem," DÖV 1980, p. 581.

[125] Case 113/77 *NTN Toyo* v. *Council* [1979] E.C.R. 1185 at 1262.

[126] Case 9/83 *Eisen und Metall AG* v. *Commission* [1984] E.C.R. 2071 at 2086.

[127] *cf.* B. Beutler, Annex C "Grundrechtsschutz," in Groeben *et al.*, *Kommentar zum EWG-Vertrag*, (3rd ed., Baden-Baden 1983), paras. 30 *et seq.*

objectives pursued by the Community, on condition that the substance of these rights is left untouched."[128]

Such a balancing between the rights of the party involved in the administrative procedure and the interests of the administration in a swift and efficient conclusion of the proceedings or between the fundamental rights of the Community citizen and the goals of the Community cannot be undertaken in general or abstract terms. On the contrary the Court must in each case weigh up and balance out the competing interests having regard to the actual facts of the situation. In individual cases one might take issue with the results of such an evaluation by the Court of Justice. Overall, however, in the vast majority of cases the Court has succeeded in remarkable fashion in achieving a fair balance between the individual's interest in the protection of the law and the interests of the Community.

(6) If one takes actual protection of fundamental rights and guarantees in the form of general principles of administrative law together, then it can be seen that Community law today offers a high standard of legal protection for the Community citizen against the exercise of Community power.[129] In recognising and implementing the principles of legality and the Community's own fundamental rights the European Court has achieved a remarkable feat of development. The rule of law, in particular in the form of general administrative law principles, and the protection of fundamental rights are today not only recognised in principle as points of reference within the Community constitutional system, but in many types of cases actually concretely enforceable. They thus not only represent objective basic principles for European integration. They further provide enforceable rights for the citizen in the Community.

In this way the Court has also contributed to the realisation of substantive justice, which, as Everling has correctly argued, "dignifies and legitimates an effective human unit, which the Community now represents above and beyond being a mere collection of states."[130] The Court of Justice has concentrated on transferring to the Community level the principles of the rule of law and of the liberty of citizens which lend

---

[128] Case 4/73 *Nold* v. *Commission* [1974] E.C.R. 508.

[129] On the legal position of the individual in the European Community *cf.* also F. G. Jacobs (ed.), *European Law and the Individual*, Amsterdam/New York/Oxford 1976.

[130] U. Everling, "Der Gerichtshof als Entscheidungsinstanz," in J. Schwarze (ed.), *Der Europäische Gerichtshof als Verfassungsgericht und Rechtsschutzinstanz*, Baden-Baden 1983, p. 137. On the particular significance of "personal rights" for Community citizens in this context see the memorable statement by David Edward, "Community Law. Integration and diversity," *Journal of the Law Society of Scotland*, February 1986, p. 51 at 57.

legitimacy to state power at a national level, and has thereby strengthened the supranational authority of the Community legal order. From this point of view, the case law of the Court can also contribute to improving the legitimacy of the Community in the eyes of citizens and thus politically to promoting integration to a significant extent. The pro-integrationist function of European constitutional and administrative law is today of particular significance in the face of public criticism in particular of the administration of the common agricultural policy as well as the continuing divergent national interests in Europe.

V. FINAL REMARKS

If we attempt to draw out a summary which is easy to recall and as short as possible from the entire investigation, we shall end up with the following formulation:

The European Community can today justifiably claim for itself the honour (also) of being an administrative law Community. On the basis of comparative law, an interaction has developed within the framework of the European Community which does not merely use national administrative law principles as sources of law for the newly evolving European administrative law. On the contrary, Community law has now started to exercise an influence upon national legal systems and, as a medium and catalyst, it is beginning to contribute to a convergence and approximation of administrative laws in Europe.

As regards the future perspectives for the completion of E.C. administrative law, at present and for the foreseeable future, all hopes, with the exception of partial and sectoral legislative codifications, rest upon a gradual, cautious and pragmatic further development of case law in the Community.

BIBLIOGRAPHY

Achour, Y.B., Cassese, S.   *Aspekte der internationalen Verwaltung*, Baden-Baden, 1985.

Achterberg, N.   *Allgemeines Verwaltungsrecht* (2nd ed., Heidelberg 1986).

Adamovich, L.K., Funk, B.-C.   *Algemeines Verwaltungsrecht* (2nd ed., Vienna 1984).

Akehurst, M.   "Equity and General Principles of Law", International and Comparative Law Quarterly 1976, p. 801.
"The application of general principles of law by the Court of Justice of the European Communities", BYIL 1981 (1982), p. 29.

Amato, G., Barbera, A.   *Manuale di diritto pubblico*, Bologna, 1984.

Amerasinghe, C.F.   "Détournement de pouvoir in International Administrative Law", ZaöRV 44 (1984), p. 439.

American Society of International Law   *The Emerging European Constitution*. Proceedings of the 72nd annual meeting, Washington D.C., August 27–29, 1978.

Andersen, P.   *Ungültige Verwaltungsakte (mit besonderer Berücksichtigung der Ungültigkeitsgründe)*, Mannheim/Berlin/Leipzig, 1927.

Andersen, P., Christensen, B.   "Le Conseil d'Etat et le droit administratif danois", in: *Le Conseil d'Etat, Livre jubilaire*, Paris, 1952, p. 585.

Anderson, Stanley V.   "Open records laws in Scandinavia", Statsvetenskaplig Tidskrift (77) 1974, p. 37.

André, A.   *Beweisführung und Beweislast im Verfahren vor dem Europäischen Gerichtshof*, KSE Vol. 6, 1966.
"Konkurrierende Ersatzansprüche vor deutschen Gerichten und dem EuGH", NJW 1968, p. 331.

Anschütz, G.   "Allgemeine Begriffe und Lehren des Verwaltungsrechts nach der Rechtsprechung des OVG (Preuss.)", reprinted in: DVBl. 1985, p. 156.

Antoniolli W., Koja F.   *Allgemeines Verwaltungsrecht* (2nd ed., Vienna 1986).

Antoniou, T.   *Europäische Integration und griechische Verfassung*, Frankfurt a.M./Berne/New York, 1985.

Apollis, G.   "Le principe d'égalité de traitement en droit économique communautaire", RMC 1980, p. 72.

Arendt, E.   "Le silence de l'administration en droit luxembourgeois", in: *Le Conseil d'Etat, Livre Jubilaire*, Luxembourg, 1957, p. 555.

von Arnim, H.H.   "Der strenge und der formale Gleichheitssatz", DÖV 1984, p. 85.

Arrighi de Casanova, J.   "A quoi sert le contentieux administratif des licenciements économiques?", AJDA 1985, p. 579.

Aschenbrenner, G.   "After Kupferberg—the Direct Effect of the provisions of the Free Trade Agreement between the EFTA Countries and the EEC", in: *Revue suisse de droit international de la concurrence 20* (1984), p. 23.

Asmal, A.K.   "Administrative Law in Ireland", Revue internationale des sciences administratives, 34 (1968), p. 109.

1467

Aubin, P.   *Die Haftung der Europäischen Wirtschaftsgemeinschaft und ihrer Mitgliedstaaten bei gemeinschaftsrechtswidrigen nationalen Verwaltungsakten*, Baden-Baden, 1982.

Auby, J.-M.   "L'abrogation des actes administratifs", AJDA 1967, p. 131.

Auby, J.-M., Drago, R.   *Traité de contentieux administratif* (3rd ed., Paris 1984).

Auby, J.-M., Ducos-Ader, R.   *Droit public* (8th ed., Paris 1981).
Institutions administratives (4th ed., Paris 1978).

Auby, J.-M., Fromont, M.   *Les recours contre les actes administratifs dans les pays de la Communauté économique européenne*, Paris, 1971.
Untersuchung über den Rechtsschutz gegen Wirtschaftsverwaltungsakte im Recht der Mitgliedstaaten der Europäischen Wirtschaftsgemeinschaft, Studien der Kommission—Schlussbericht, Reihe Wettbewerb—Rechtsvergleichung No. 12, 1971.

Auvret, P.   "La notion de droit acquis en droit administratif français", RDP 1985, p. 53.

Bachof, O.   "Die Dogmatik des Verwaltungsrechts vor den Gegenwartsaufgaben der Verwaltung", VVDStRL 30 (1972), p. 193.

Badura, P.   *Das Verwaltungsrecht im liberalen Rechtsstaat*, Göttingen, 1967.
Staatsrecht, Munich, 1986.

van Bael, I.   "Discretionary powers of the Commission and their legal control in trade and antitrust matters", in: *Discretionary Powers of the Member States in the Field of Economic Policies and their Limits under the EEC Treaty* (ed. J. Schwarze), Baden-Baden, 1988, p. 173.

Bähr, O.   *Der Rechtsstaat* (2nd ed., Darmstadt 1963), (unamended reprint of 1st ed., Kassel-Göttingen 1864).

Bailey, S.H., Cross, C.A., Garner, J.F.   *Cases and Materials in Administrative Law*, London, 1977.

du Ban, B.   "Les principes généraux communs et la responsabilité non contractuelle de la Communauté", CDE 1977, p. 397.

Barav, A.   "La répétition de l'indu dans la jurisprudence de la Cour de justice des Communautés européennes", CDE 1981, p. 507.
"L'incidence du droit communautaire sur le pouvoir répressif national", *Gedächtnisschrift für L.-J. Constantinesco*, Cologne/Berlin/Bonn/Munich 1983, p. 9.

Battis, U.   *Allgemeines Verwaltungsrecht*, Heidelberg, 1985.

Bauer, H.   "Neue Tendenzen in der bundesverfassungsgerichtlichen Rechtsprechung zum Rückwirkungsverbot", NVwZ 1984, p. 220.

Bazex, M.   "La réforme de la concurrence", AJDA 1985, p. 593.

Beatson, J.   " 'Public' and 'Private' in English Administrative Law", (1987) L.Q.R. 34.

Beatson, J., Matthews, M.H.   *Administrative Law—Cases and Materials*, Oxford, 1983.

Bebr, G.   "Agreements concluded by the Community and their possible Direct Effect: From International Fruit Company to Kupferberg", (1983) 20 C.M.L.Rev. 35.
Development of judicial control of the European Communities, The Hague/Boston/London, 1981.

1468

Judicial Control of the European Communities, London, 1962.

"Preliminary Rulings to the Court of Justice: Their Authority and Temporal Effect", (1981) 18 C.M.L.Rev. 475.

Remedies for breach of Community law, London, 1980.

Becker, Joachim   *Die Anwendbarkeit der Theorie von den implied powers im Recht der Europäischen Gemeinschaften*, Diss. Münster, 1976.

Becker, Jürgen   "Informales Verwaltungshandeln zur Steuerung wirtschaftlicher Prozesse im Zeichen der Deregulierung", DÖV 1985, p. 1003.

Becker, P.   *Der Einfluss des französischen Verwaltungsrechts auf den Rechtsschutz in den Europäischen Gemeinschaften*, Hamburg, 1963.

Behrens, P.   "Voraussetzungen und Grenzen der Rechtsfortbildung durch Rechtsvereinheitlichung", RabelsZ 1986, p. 19.

Bellini, S.   Rivista di diritto internazionale 1981, p. 318.

Bellis, J.-F.   *L'application du droit national dans la mise en oeuvre de la politique agricole commune*, 1981.

Bender, B., Sparwasser, R.   *Umweltrecht*, Heidelberg, 1988.

Bénoit, F.-P.   "Les fondements de la justice administrative", in: Mélanges M. Waline, Vol. II, Paris, 1974, p. 283.

Berger, M.   "Die Gleichheit von Frau und Mann in Österreich", EuGRZ 1983, p. 614.

Bernhard, A.   "Aperçu sur l'oeuvre juridictionnelle des Commissaires du Gouvernement durant la seconde moitié du XIXe siècle", in: *Le Conseil d'Etat. Livre Jubilaire*, Paris, 1952, p. 299.

Bernhardt, M.   *Zur rechtlichen Bedeutung der Erklärung einer "policy" in der englischen Verwaltungspraxis. Dargestellt am Beispiel der Rückübereignung enteigneter Grundstücke*, Freiburg.

Bernhardt, R.   "Eigenheiten und Ziele der Rechtsvergleichung im öffentlichen Recht", ZaöRV 24 (1964), p. 431.

"Probleme eines Grundrechtskatalogs für die Europäischen Gemeinschaften", Bulletin der Europäischen Gemeinschaften, Supplement 5/76, p. 19.

"Quellen des Gemeinschaftsrechts: Die 'Verfassung' der Gemeinschaft", in: Kommission der EG (ed.), *Dreissig Jahre Gemeinschaftsrecht*, Luxemburg, 1983, p. 77.

"Zur Auslegung des europäischen Gemeinschaftsrechts", in: *Festschrift für H. Kutscher*, Baden-Baden, 1981, p. 17.

Bertossa, F.   *Der Beurteilungsspielraum*, Reihe: Abhandlungen zum Schweizer Recht N.F. 489, Berne, 1984.

Beseler, J.-F.   *Die Abwehr von Dumping und Subventionen durch die Europäischen Gemeinschaften*, Baden-Baden, 1980.

Bettermann, K.-A   "Das Verwaltungsverfahren", VVDStRL 17 (1959), p. 118 "Zur Verfassungsbeschwerde gegen Gesetze und zum Rechtsschutz des Bürgers gegen Rechtssetzungsakte der öffentlichen Gewalt", AöR 86 (1961), p. 130.

Beutler, B., Bieber, R., Pipkorn, J., Streil, J.   *Die Europäische Gemeinschaft, Rechtsordnung und Politik* (3rd ed., Baden-Baden, 1987).

Beversluis, J.R.   "De Oppositieprocedure in Commissie Verordening 2349/84", SEW 1986, p. 229.

Beyerlin, U.   "Umgekehrte Rassendiskriminierung und Gleichbehandlungsgebot in der amerikanischen Verfassungsrechtsprechung", ZaöRV 39 (1979), p. 496.

Bickel, H., Meyer, K.F.   "Begleitende Verwaltungskontrolle—Eine Alternative zum nachträglichen Verwaltungsrechtsschutz?", in: Bernd Rüthers, Klaus Stern (eds.), *Freiheit und Verantwortung im Verfassungsstaat, Festgabe zum 10jährigen Jubiläum der Gesellschaft für Rechtspolitik*, Munich, 1984, p. 67.

Bieber, R.   "Verfahrensregeln—Skizze einer verborgenen Quelle des Gemeinschaftsrechts", in: F. Capotorti et al. (eds.), *Festschrift für P. Pescatore*, Baden-Baden, 1987, p. 25.

Bieber, R., Ress, G.   *Die Dynamik des Europäischen Gemeinschaftsrechts*, Baden-Baden, 1987.

Biever, T.   "De l'irresponsabilité de l'Etat législateur. Esquisse de droit luxembourgeois", in: *Le Conseil d'Etat, Livre Jubilaire*, Luxembourg, 1957, p. 457.

Birk, R.   "Auswirkungen der Rechtsprechung des EuGH zur Gleichbehandlung von Frauen und Männern beim Berufszugang", Neue Zs f. Arbeits- u. Sozialrecht 1984, p. 145.

Birkner, H.-J.   "Stichwort 'Gerechtigkeit', " in: Hermann Kunst and Siegfried Grundmann together with Wilhelm Schneemelcher and Roman Herzog (eds.), *Evangelisches Staatslexikon*, Stuttgart/Berlin, 1966, p. 620.

Bleckmann, A.   "Art. 5 EWGV und die Gemeinschaftstreue", DVBl. 1976, p. 483.

"Das Ziel des gerichtlichen Rechtsschutzes: Schutz des Einzelnen oder objektive Kontrolle der vollziehenden Gewalt? Die Rolle der Klagebefugnis", in: H. Mosler (ed.), *Gerichtsschutz gegen die Exekutive*, Vol. 3, Cologne/Berlin/Bonn/Munich, 1971, p. 21.

"Der allgemeine Gleichheitssatz beim Zusammenwirken des Europäischen Gemeinschaftsrechts mit dem nationalen Recht", NJW 1985, p. 2856.

"Der Rechtsstaat in vergleichender Sicht. Zugleich ein Beitrag zur Rechtsquellenlehre des Europäischen Gemeinschaftsrechts", GYIL 20 (1977), p. 406.

"Die Beihilfenkompetenz der Europäischen Gemeinschaft—Ein Beitrag zum Prinzip der begrenzten Ermächtigung", DÖV 1977, p. 615.

"Die Personenverkehrsfreiheit im Recht der EG", DVBl. 1986, p. 69.

"Die Rechtsprechung des Europäischen Gerichtshofs zur Gemeinschaftstreue", RIW/AWD 1981, p. 653.

"Die Rolle der richterlichen Rechtsschöpfung im Europäischen Gemeinschaftsrecht", in: *Gedächtnisschrift für L.-J. Constantinesco*, Cologne/Berlin/Bonn/Munich, 1983, p.61.

"Die umgekehrte Diskriminierung (discrimination à rebours) im EWG-Vertrag", RIW 1985, p. 917.

"Eine allgemeine Theorie des Verwaltungsrechts, zu einem neuen französischen Versuch", Die Verwaltung 1978, p. 489.

1470

Europarecht (4th ed., Cologne/Berlin/Bonn/Munich 1985).

"Gedanken zur Repressalie, ein Versuch der Anwendung der Interessenjurisprudenz auf das Völkergewohnheitsrecht", in: *Festschrift für H.-J. Schlochauer*, Berin, etc., 1981, p. 193.

"Zum Ermessensmissbrauch im europäischen Gemeinschaftsrecht", in: *Festschrift für H. Kutscher*, Baden-Baden, 1981, p. 25.

"Zur Entwicklung europäischer Grundrechte", DVBl. 1978, p. 457.

"Zur Funktion des Gewohnheitsrechts im Europäischen Gemeinschaftsrecht", EuR 1981, p. 101.

Bode, I.   *Die Diskriminierungsverbote im EWG-Vertrag*, Göttingen, 1968.

Böhm, R.   *Kompetenzauslegung und Kompetenzlücken im Gemeinschaftsrecht*, Frankfurt, 1985.

Börner, B.   "Das Beweisverwertungsverbot im Gemeinschaftsrecht. Zur Methode der Gewinnung ungeschriebener Rechtsgrundsätze des Gemeinschaftsrechts", in: *Festschrift für H. P. Ipsen*, Tübingen, 1977, p. 557.

Die Entscheidungen der Hohen Behörde, Tübingen, 1965.

"Diskriminierungen und Subventionen", in: *Studien zum deutschen und europäischen Wirtschaftsrecht*, KSE Vol. 26, 1973, p. 49.

"Subventionen—Unrichtiges Europarecht?", in: *Festschrift für K. Carstens*, Vol. 1., Cologne/Berlin/Bonn/Munich, 1984, p. 63.

Börner, B., Bullinger, M. (eds.)   *Subventionen im Gemeinsamen Markt*, KSE Vol. 29, 1978.

Böner, B., Neundörfer, K. (eds.)   *Recht und Praxis der Beihilfen im Gemeinsamen Markt*, KSE Vol. 32, 1984.

Boest, R.   *Die Agrarmärkte im Recht der EWG*, Baden-Baden, 1984.

Bonn, A.   *Der Staatsrat des Grossherzogtums Luxemburg*, Luxembourg, 1984.

Le contentieux administratif en droit luxembourgeois, Luxembourg, 1966.

"L'examen du fait par le Conseil d'Etat. Etude de jurisprudence luxembourgeoise", in: *Le Conseil d'Etat, Livre Jubilaire*, Luxembourg, 1957, p. 529.

Borchardt, K.-D.   "Vertrauensschutz im Europäischen Gemeinschaftsrecht. Die Rechtsprechung des EuGH von Algera über CNTA bis Mulder und von Deetzen", EuGRZ 1988, p. 309.

Borgsmidt, K.   "Ein Verfahrensgesetz und Neugestaltungen im dänischen Verwaltungsrecht", DÖV 1988, p. 70.

Bosco, G.   *Lezioni di diritto internazionale*, Milanø, 1987.

Bothe, M.   "Die Bedeutung der Rechtsvergleichung in der Praxis internationaler Gerichte", ZaöRV 36 (1976), p. 280.

Die Kompetenzstruktur des modernen Bundesstaates in rechtsvergleichender Sicht, Beiträge sum ausländischen öffentlichen Recht und Völkerrecht, Vol. 69, Berlin/Heidelberg/New York, 1977.

Boulouis, J.	*Droit institutionnel des Communautés européennes*, Paris, 1984.
Braga, S.	"Zur Methode der rechtsvergleichenden Arbeit", in: *Gedächtnisschrift für L.-J. Constantinesco*, Cologne/Berlin/Bonn/Munich, 1983, p. 99.
Braibant, G.	*Le droit administratif français*, Paris, 1984.
Braibant, G., Questiaux, N., Wiener, C.	*Le contrôle de l'administration et la protection des citoyens*, Paris, 1973.
Braud, P.	*La notion de liberté publique en droit français*, Paris, 1968.
Braun, W.	"Offene Kompetenznormen—ein geeignetes und zulässiges Regulativ im Wirtschaftsverwaltungsrecht?", VerwArchiv 76 (1985), p. 158.
Brauneder, W.	"Formen und Tragweite des deutschen Einflusses auf die österreichische Verwaltungswissenschaft 1850–1914", in: Erk Volkmar Heyen (ed.), *Wissenschaft und Recht der Verwaltung seit dem Ancien Régime*, Frankfurt a.M. 1984, p. 249.
Brealy, M.	"The Burden of Proof before the European Court", (1985) E.L.Rev. 250.
Bridge, J.	"National Legal Tradition and Community Law: Legislative Drafting and Judicial Interpretation in England and the European Community", in: Journal of Common Market Studies, Vol. XIX (1980/81), p. 351.
	"Procedural Aspects of the Enforcement of European Community Law through the Legal Systems of the Member States", (1984) E.L.Rev. 28.
Bridge, J.W.	"Abstract Law and Political Reality in the Post-European-Accession British Constitution", in: Denning Law Journal 1987, p. 23.
van den Brink, H.	"Niederlande", in: E. V. Heyen (ed.), *Geschichte der Verwaltungsrechtswissenschaft in Europa*, Frankfurt a.M. 1982, p. 117.
Brohm, W.	"Die Dogmatik des Verwaltungsrechts vor den Gegenwartsaufgaben der Verwaltung", VVDStRL 30 (1972), p. 245.
	"Die staatliche Verwaltung als eigenständige Gewalt und die Grenzen der Verwaltungsgerichtsbarkeit", DVBl. 1986, p. 321.
	"Verwaltung und Verwaltungsgerichtsbarkeit als Steuerungsmechanismen in einem polyzentrischen System der Rechtserzeugung", DÖV 1987, pp. 265, *et seq.*.
	"Zum Funktionswandel der Verwaltungsgerichtsbarkeit", NJW 1984, p. 8.
Brownlie, I.	*Principles of Public International Law* (3rd ed., Oxford 1979).
Brunet, R.	*Le principe de l'égalité en droit français*, Paris, 1910.
Buch, H., Dumont, M.	"La procédure d'élaboration des actes des autorités administratives", in: *Rapports présentés aux colloques entre les Conseils d'Etat Belge, Néerlandais*, Français, Italien, Luxembourgeois et le Bundesverwaltungsgericht, Rome, 1968, p. 19.
Bülck, H.	"Zur Dogmengeschichte des europäischen Verwaltungsrechts", in: *Festschrift für H. Kraus*, Würzburg 1964, p. 29.

Bünten, W.   *Staatsgewalt und Gemeinschaftshoheit bei der innerstaat-lichen Durchführung des Rechts der Europäischen Gemeinschaften durch die Mitgliedstaaten*, Berlin, 1977.

Bullinger, M.   "Das Ermessen der öffentlichen Verwaltung", JZ 1984, p. 1001.
Das Verwaltungsrecht in der DDR", Freiburger Rechts- und Staatsw. Abh. Vol. 23, 1966.
"Umbildung des Verwaltungsrechts durch Planung in der DDR", in: J. H. Kaiser (ed.), *Planung I*, Baden-Baden, 1965, p. 189.
"Unbestimmte Rechtsbegriffe in der neueren deutschen und französischen Verwaltungsrechtsprechung", in: *Festschrift für H. Jahrreiss*, Cologne/Berlin/Bonn/Munich, 1974, p. 19.
Vertrag und Verwaltungsakt, Stuttgart, 1962.
Verwaltungsermessen im modernen Staat, Baden-Baden, 1986.

Burdeau, G.   *Droit constitutionnel et institutions politiques* (20th ed., Paris 1984).
Manuel de droit constitutionnel et institutions politiques (20th ed., Paris 1984).

Burmeister, J.   "Selbstbindung der Verwaltung—Zur Wirkkraft des rechtsstaatlichen Übermassverbots, des Gleichheits-satzes und des Vertrauensschutzprinzips", DÖV 1981, p. 503.
Vertrauensschutz im Prozessrecht, Berlin/New York, 1979.

Butler, W.   *International Law in Comparative Perspective*, Alphen aan den Rijn, 1980.

Buttgenbach, A.   *Manuel de droit administratif*, Brussels, 1959.

Caeiros, A.   "L'effet direct des accords internationaux conclus par la CEE", RMC 1984, p. 526.

Caetano, M.   "La protection juridictionnelle du particulier contre le pouvoir exécutif au Portugal", in: H. Mosler (ed.), *Gerichtsschutz gegen die Exekutive*, Vol. 1, Cologne/Berlin/Bonn/Munich, 1970, p. 887.
"L'influence française sur l'évolution du droit ad-ministratif portugais", in: *Le Conseil d'Etat, Livre jubilaire*, Paris, 1952, p. 535.
Manual de Direito Administrativo, Vol. 1, 10th ed., 3rd reprint, Coimbra, 1984; Vol. 2, 9th ed., Coimbra, 1983.

Calogeropoulos, A.   "L'administration chargée des relations avec les Com-munautés européennes", in: Annuaire européen d'ad-ministration publique, II, 1979, p. 564.

Cambier, C.   *Droit administratif*, Brussels, 1968.

Canaris, C.-W.   *Die Feststellung von Lücken im Gesetz* (2nd ed., Berlin 1983).

Cane, P.   *An Introduction to Administrative Law*, Oxford, 1986.

Canenbley, C.   "Verfahrensregeln der Kommission der Europäischen Gemeinschaften", in: *Studienvereinigung Kartellrecht, XI. Internationales EG-Kartellrechtsforum*, Munich, 1986, p. 74.

Capelli, F.   "Der Anspruch auf Rückerstattung der an den italie-nischen Staat gezahlten Statistik- und Verwaltungsge-bühren", RIW/AWD 1970, p. 545.

	"I principi generali come fonte di diritto", Dir. comun. scambi int. 1986, p. 541; French version, "Les principes généraux en tant que source du droit", FIDE Rapports 12e Congrès I, Paris, 1986, p. 183.
Capotorti, F.	"Il diritto comunitario non scritto", Dir. comun. scambi int. 1983, p. 409.
	"Le principe d'égalité en droit économique: Rapport général", in: *Le principe d'égalité en droit économique*, F.I.D.E., Rapports Volume 2, The Hague, 1984, Chap. 3.
Cappelletti, M. (ed.)	*New Perspectives for a Common Law of Europe*, Florence, 1978.
Cappelletti, M., Cohen, W.	*Comparative Constitutional Law*, Indianapolis/New York/Charlottesville (Virginia), 1979.
Cappelletti, M., Seccombe, M., Weiler, J.H.H.	"Integration Through Law: Europe and the American Federal Experience. A General Introduction", in: *Integration Through Law*, Vol. 1, Book 1, Berlin/ New York, 1986.
Carré de Malberg, R.	*Contribution à la Théorie générale de l'Etat*, Vol. 1, Paris, 1920.
Casey, J.P.	"Ireland", in: E. V. Heyen (ed.), *Geschichte der Verwaltungsrechtswissenschaft in Europa*, Frankfurt a.M., 1982, p. 89.
Caspar, B.	*Die einheitliche Anwendung des Gemeinschaftsrechts und sein Vorrang vor nationalem Recht*, Göttingen, 1978.
Caspari, M.	"The aid rules of the EEC Treaty and their application", in: *Discretionary Powers of the Member States in the Field of Economic Policies and their Limits under the EEC Treaty* (ed. J. Schwarze), Baden-Baden, 1988, p. 37.
	"Wettbewerbspolitik im Bereich der Vertriebsvereinbarungen", in: *Studienvereinigung Kartellrecht, XI. Internationales EG-Kartellrechtsforum*, Munich, 1986, p. 27.
Cassan, H.	"Le principe de non-discrimination dans le domaine social à travers la jurisprudence récente de la Cour de Justice des Communautés européennes", RTDE, Vol. 12 (1976), p. 259.
Catsiapis, J.	"Les dix ans de la Constitution grecque du 9 juin 1975", RDP 1987, p. 399.
Centre National de la Recherche Scientifique	*Le Conseil d'Etat, 1799–1974*, Paris, 1974.
Cerexhe, E.	"L'égalité de traitement dans l'ordre juridique communautaire", in: *Mélanges offerts à Pierre-Henri Teitgen*, Paris, 1984, p. 33.
Cerutti, G.	"Potestà discrezionali della commissione e provvedimenti cautelari d'urgenza in tema di diritto comunitario della concorrenza", Riv. dir. europeo 1985, p. 159.
Chabanol, D.	"Contrôle de légalité et liberté de l'administration", AJDA 1984, p. 14.
Chapel, Y. (ed.)	*Formation et perfectionnement des fonctionnaires internationaux et européens, Education and in-service training of international and European civil servants*, Bruges, 1976.
Christensen, B.	"Der gerichtliche Rechtsschutz des Einzelnen gegenüber der vollziehenden Gewalt in Dänemark", in: H.

	Mosler (ed.), *Gerichtsschutz gegen die Exekutive*, Cologne/Berlin/Bonn/Munich, 1969, p. 113.
Christiansen, R.	"Erlass, Erstattung und Nacherhebung von Eingangs- und Ausfuhrabgaben", Zeitschrift für Zölle und Verbrauchssteuern 1980, p. 354.
Chubb, B. (ed.)	*A Source Book of Irish Government*, Dublin, 1964.
	The Constitution and Constitutional Change in Ireland, Dublin, 1978, reprinted 1982.
	The Government and Politics of Ireland, London/ Oxford/New York, 1974.
Clark, D.N., Sufrin, B.E.	"Constitutional Conundrums. The Impact of the United Kingdom's Membership of the Communities on Constitutional Theory", in: M. P. Furmeston, R. Kerridge, B. E. Sufrin (eds.), *The Effect on English Domestic Law of Membership of the European Communities and of Ratification of the European Convention on Human Rights*, The Hague, 1983, p. 32.
Claudi, H.	*Die Bindung der EWG an Grundrechte*, Munich, 1976.
Clever, F.	*Ermessensmissbrauch und détournement de pouvoir nach dem Recht der Europäischen Gemeinschaften*, Berlin, 1967.
Coffey, P.	"Constitutional Law—Procedural Curbs on Powers of Compulsory Acquisition", 6 (1984) Dublin University Law Journal, p. 152.
Cohen-Jonathan, G.	"La Cour des Communautés et les droits de l'Homme", RMC 1978, p. 74.
Coing, H.	*Die obersten Grundsätze des Rechts*, Heidelberg, 1947.
Colin, J.-P.	*Le Gouvernement des Jugés dans les Communautés Européennes*, Paris, 1966.
Colliard, C.-A.	*Libertés publiques* (6th ed., Paris 1982).
Collins, L.	*European Community Law in the United Kingdom* (3rd ed., London 1984).
Commissie van Maarseveen	*Rapport ABAR (Algemene bepalingen administratief recht)*, V.A.R.-geschrift LXXII, Groningen, 1974.
Committee on Administrative Tribunals and Enquiries	London, 1957 (Command Papers), Cmnd. 218 (Reprinted 1962).
Committee on Ministers' Powers Report	London, 1932 (Command Papers), Cmd. 4060. (Reprinted 1963).
Le Conseil d'Etat	*Son histoire à travers les documents d'époque, 1799–1974*, Paris, 1974.
Le Conseil d'Etat du Grand-Duché de Luxembourg	*Livre jubilaire 1856–1956*, Luxembourg, 1957.
Constantinesco, L.-J.	*Das Recht der Europäischen Gemeinschaften*, Vol. 1, *Das institutionelle Recht*, Baden-Baden, 1977.
	"La constitution économique de la C.E.E.", RTDE 1977, p. 244.
	Rechtsvergleichung, Vol. I: *Einführung in die Rechtsvergleichung*, Cologne/Berlin/Bonn/Munich, 1971.
	Rechtsvergleichung, Vol. II: *Die rechtsvergleichende Methode*, Cologne/Berlin/Bonn/Munich, 1983.
	Rechtsvergleichung, Vol. III: *Die rechtsvergleichende Wissenschaft*, Cologne/Berlin/Bonn/Munich, 1983.
Constantinesco, V., Hübner, U.	*Einführung in das französische Recht*, Munich, 1974.
Corsos, D.	"Die Organisation der Verwaltung und die Rechtsstellung der Beamten nach der griechischen Verfassung von

	1975", in: *Festschrift für C. H. Ule*, Cologne/Berlin/Bonn/Munich, 1977, p. 529.
Council of Europe	*Forms of public participation in the preparation of legislative and administrative acts*, Strasbourg, 1978.
Craig, P.P.	*Administrative Law*, London, 1983.
de Crayencour, J.-P.	*Die Europäische Gemeinschaft und die Freizügigkeit der freien Berufe. Gegenseitige Anerkennung der Diplome*, Sammlung Europ. Perspektiven, Brussels, 1983.
Crijns, F.C.L.M.	*Het Europese perspectief van het Nederlandse staatsrecht*, Zwolle, 1984.
Cruz-Villalón, P.	"Zwei Jahre Verfassungsrechtsprechung in Spanien", ZaöRV 43 (1983), p. 70.
Däubler, W.	"Der Widerruf von Verwaltungsakten im Recht der Europäischen Gemeinschaften", NJW 1965, p. 1646.
Dagory, J.	"L'interprétation du droit et le rôle du juge dans les organisations internationales", in: Brown C. Melville: *The Court of Justice of the European Community*, 1983.
Dagtoglou, P.	"Die Beteiligung von Personen, die von grenzüberschreitenden Umweltverschmutzungen betroffen sein können, am griechischen Verwaltungsverfahren", in: G. Ress (ed.), *Grenzüberschreitende Verfahrensbeteiligung im Umweltrecht der Mitgliedstaaten der Europäischen Gemeinschaften*, Cologne/Berlin/Bonn/Munich, 1985.
	"Die griechische Verfassung von 1975, Eine Einführung", JöR N.F. 32 (1983), p. 355.
	"Verfassung und Verwaltung", in: Klaus-Detlev Grothusen (ed.), *Südosteuropa-Handbuch*, Vol. III, Göttingen, 1980.
Daig, H.-W.	*Nichtigkeits- und Untätigkeitsklagen im Recht der Europäischen Gemeinschaften*, Baden-Baden, 1985.
	"Zur Rechtsvergleichung und Methodenlehre im Europäischen Gemeinschaftsrecht", in: *Festschrift für K. Zweigert*, Tübingen, 1981, p. 395.
Damkowski, W.	*Die Entstehung des Verwaltungsbegriffs*, Cologne/Berlin/Bonn/Munich, 1969.
Dauses, M.A.	"La protection des droits fondamentaux dans l'ordre juridique communautaire", Rev. europ. 1984, p. 16.
David, R.	*Les grands systèmes de droit contemporains* (8th ed., Paris 1982).
Davis, K.C.	*Administrative Law* (6th ed., St. Paul Minn. 1978).
Debbasch, C.	*Contentieux administratif* (3rd ed., Paris 1981).
	Institutions et droit administratifs, 2—L'action et le contrôle de l'administration (2nd ed., Paris 1986).
Degen, M.	"Klageverfahren und Klagegründe im französischen Verwaltungsprozess", Die Verwaltung 1981, p. 157.
Delcamp, A.	"La région, nouvelle collectivité territoriale", AJDA 1986, p. 195.
Delvaux, B.	"Rapport sur l'égalité des Luxembourgeois devant le service public", in: Travaux de l'Association Henri Capitant des amis de la culture juridique française, Paris, 1965, p. 23.
Delvolvé, P.	"L'exécution des décisions de justice contre l'administration", in: Etudes et documents du Conseil d'Etat 1983–1984, No. 35, p. 105.

Dembour, J.   *Droit administratif* (3rd ed., Liège 1978).

Demeter, W.   *Die Begründungspflicht für Verwaltungsentscheidungen im deutschen, französischen und europäischen Recht*, Munich, 1974.

Dennewitz, B.   *Die Systeme des Verwaltungsrechts*, Hamburg, 1948.

Deringer, A.   "The common market competition rules, with particular reference to Non-Member Countries", 12 (1963) ICLQ p. 582.

Dewost, J.-L.   "Les pouvoirs discrétionnaires du Conseil des ministres", in: *Discretionary Powers of the Member States in the Field of Economic Policies and their Limits under the EEC Treaty* (ed. J. Schwarze), Baden-Baden, 1988, p. 165.

Dicey, A.V.   *Introduction to the study of the Law of the Constitution* (9th ed., London 1948).

Dicke, D.   "Der Irrtum bei der Verwaltungsmassnahme", in: Zs. f. Schweizer Recht 1984, p. 525.

Dörr, D.   "Die Verjährung vermögensrechtlicher Ansprüche im öffentlichen Recht", DÖV 1984, p. 12.

Dolzer, R.   "Zum Begründungsgebot im geltenden Verwaltungsrecht", DÖV 1985, p. 9.

Donner, A.M.   "Misbruik van beginselen", Rechtsgeleerd Magazijn Themis 1978, p. 377.

Donner, A.M. *et al.* (eds.)   *Nederlands Bestuursrecht, Algemeen Deel*, Vol. I (4th ed., Alphen aan den Rijn 1974).

Drews, B., Wacke, G., Vogel, K., Martens, W.   *Gefahrenabwehr—Allgemeines Polizeirecht (Ordnungsrecht) des Bundes und der Länder*, Cologne/Berlin/Bonn/Munich (9th ed. revised by K. Vogel and W. Martens, 1986).

Druesne, G.   "La jurisprudence de la Cour de justice des Communautés européennes en matière agricole (1958–1977). Troisième thème: Principe d'égalité de traitement", RMC 1978, p. 568. "Sixième thème: Principe de sécurité juridique", RMC 1979, p. 136.

Due, O.   "Le respect des droits de la défense dans le droit administratif communautaire", CDE 1987, p. 383.

Due, O., Gulmann, C.   "Constitutional implications of the Danish accession to the European Communities", (1972) C.M.L.Rev. 256.

Dürig, G.   "Stichwort 'Gleichheit' in: Görres-Gesellschaft (ed.), *Staatslexikon*, Vol. 3 (6th ed., Freiburg 1959), p. 983.

Duk, W.   "Maatstaven voor de beoordeling van sancties", Ars Aequi 1981, p. 231.
"De zachte Kern van het bestuursrecht", Rechtsgeleerd Magazijn, Themis, 1978, p. 564.

Duk, W., Leob, Nicolai   *Bestuursrecht*, Amsterdam, 1981.

Duverger, M.   *Eléments de droit public* (9th ed., Paris 1981).

Eberle, C.-E.   "Gesetzesvorbehalt und Parlamentsvorbehalt", DÖV 1984, p. 485.

Edward, D.   "Community Law, Integration and Diversity", Journal of the Law Society of Scotland 1986, p. 51.

Ehlermann, C.-D.   *Der Rechnungshof der Europäischen Gemeinschaften*, Baden-Baden, 1976.
"Die Errichtung des europäischen Fonds für währungspolitische Zusammenarbeit", EuR 1973, p. 193.

	"Die Europäische Gemeinschaft und das Recht", in: *Festschrift für K. Carstens*, Vol. I, Cologne/Berlin/ Bonn/Munich, 1984, p. 81.
	"Neuere Entwicklungen im Aussenhandelsrecht der Europäischen Gemeinschaften", in: J. Schwarze (ed.), *Integrationsrecht*, Baden-Baden, 1985, p. 108.
Ehlers, D.	"Rechtsstaatliche und prozessuale Probleme des Verwaltungsprivatrechts", DVBl. 1983, p. 422.
Eilschou Holm, N.	"Danish Report on Due Process in Administrative Procedures", in: FIDE, *Due process in the administrative procedure, Rapports du 8ème congrès, 22–24 Juni 1978*, Vol. 3, Copenhagen, 1978, p. 3.1.
	"The Danish system of open files in public administration", Scandinav. Studies in Law 1975, p. 153.
Eisenmann, C.	*Cours de droit administratif*, Paris, 1982.
Emery, C.T., Smythe, B.	"Error of law in administrative law", in: (1984) L.Q.R. 612.
van Empel, M.	"L'acte public inexistant et le droit communautaire", CDB 1971, p. 251.
Engelhardt, H.	"Die neueste Entwicklung der Rechtsprechung zum Staatshaftungsrecht", in: NVwZ 1985, p. 621.
Engler, B.	"Die Schadensersatzklage gegen die EG—Geringe Erfolgschancen für den Einzelnen", EuGRZ 1979, p. 377.
Entrena Cuesta, R.	*Curso de derecho administrativo I* (*Concepto, fuentes, relacion juridico-administrativa y justicia administrativa*) and *II* (*Organización administrativa*) (8th ed., Madrid 1983).
Erichsen, H.-U.	"Die sog. unbestimmten Rechtsbegriffe als Steuerungs- und Kontrollmassnahmen im Verhältnis von Gesetzgebung, Verwaltung und Rechtsprechung", DVBl. 1985, p. 22.
	"Freiheit—Gleichheit—Teilhabe. Prolegomena zu einem Verwaltungsrecht des Leistungsstaates", DVBl. 1983, p. 289.
	Verfassungs- und verwaltungsrechtsgeschichtliche Grundlagen der Lehre vom fehlerhaften belastenden Verwaltungsakt und seiner Aufhebung im Prozess, Frankfurt a.M., 1971.
Erichsen, H.-U., Martens, W. (eds.)	*Allgemeines Verwaltungsrecht* (8th ed., Berlin/New York 1988).
Ermacora, F.	"Das Verhältnismässigkeitsprinzip im österreichischen Recht sowie aus der Sicht der Europäischen Menschenrechtskonvention", in: Hans Kutscher *et al.* (eds.), *Der Grundsatz der Verhältnismässigkeit in europäischen Rechtsordnungen*, Heidelberg, 1985, p. 67.
Esser, J.	*Grundsatz und Norm in der richterlichen Fortbildung des Privatrechts* (2nd ed., Tübingen 1984).
Esteves de Oliveira, M.	*Direito Administrativo*, Vol. I (2nd ed., Coimbra 1984).
Evans, J.M., de Smith, S.A.	*Judicial Review of Administrative Action* (4th ed., London 1980).
Everling, U.	"Auf dem Wege zu einem europäischen Verwaltungsrecht", NVwZ 1987, p. 1.
	Das Vorabentscheidungsverfahren vor dem Gerichtshof der EG, Baden-Baden, 1986.

"Der Beitrag des Europäischen Gerichtshofes zur Entwicklung der Gemeinschaft", in: S. Magiera (ed.), *Entwicklungsperspektiven der Europäischen Gemeinschaft*, Berlin, 1985, p. 195.
"Der Gerichtshof als Entscheidungsinstanz", in: J. Schwarze (ed.), *Der Europäische Gerichtshof als Verfassungsgericht und Rechtsschutzinstanz*, Baden-Baden, 1983, p. 137.
"Die Mitgliedstaaten der EG vor ihrem Gerichtshof", EuR 1983, p. 101.
"Elemente eines europäischen Verwaltungsrechts", DVBl. 1983, p. 649.
"Vom Zweckverband zur Europäischen Union—Überlegungen zur Struktur der Europäischen Gemeinschaften", in: *Festschrift für H. P. Ipsen*, Tübingen, 1977, p. 595.
"Zur Rechtsstruktur einer Europäischen Verfassung", Integration 1984, p. 1214.

Faber, H.	*Verwaltungsrecht*, Tübingen, 1987.
Faller, H.-J.	"Zur Entwicklung der nationalen Verfassungsgerichte in Europa", EuGRZ 1986, p. 42.
Favoreu, L.	"Actualité et légitimité du contrôle juridictionnel des lois en Europe occidentale", RDP 1984, p. 1147.
Favoreu, L. (ed.)	*Cours Constitutionnelles Européennes et droits fondamentaux*, Paris, 1982.
Favoreu, L., Philip, L.	*Les grandes décisions du Conseil Constitutionnel* (3rd ed., Paris 1984).
Feger, D.	*Die Grundrechte im Recht der EG, Bestand und Entwicklung*, Frankfurt a.M./Berne/New York/Nancy, 1984.
Feige, K.	*Der Gleichheitssatz im Recht der EWG*, Tübingen, 1973.
Feuchthofen, J.	"Der Verfassungsgrundsatz des rechtlichen Gehörs und seine Ausgestaltung im Verwaltungsverfahren", DVBl. 1984, p. 170.
F.I.D.E.	*Le principe d'égalité en droit économique, Rapports* Vol. 2, Den Haag, 1984.
Fiedler, J.	"Neuorientierung der Verfassungsrechtsprechung zum Rückwirkungsverbot und zum Vertrauensschutz", NJW 1988, p. 1624.
Fikentscher, W.	*Methoden des Rechts in vergleichender Darstellung*, Vols. I–III, Tübingen, 1975.
Finbarr, M.	"Report on due process in administrative proceedings in Ireland", in: FIDE, *Due process in the administrative procedure*, Vol. 3, Copenhagen, 1978.
Finkelnburg, K., Jank, K.P.	*Vorläufiger Rechtsschutz im Verwaltungsstreitverfahren* (3rd ed., Munich 1986).
Flauss, J.-F.	"Le juge administratif français et la Convention européenne des Droits de l'homme", AJDA 1983, p. 387.
Fleiner, F.	*Institutionen des Deutschen Verwaltungsrechts*, Tübingen, 1928 (reprinted 1960).
Fleiner, F., Gerster, T.	*Grundzüge des allgemeinen und schweizerischen Verwaltungsrechts* (2nd ed., Zürich 1980).
Fleming, J.O.	*The Law of Torts* (6th ed., Sydney 1983).
Flume, W.	*Steuerwesen und Rechtsordnung*, Göttingen, 1952.

Forrester, I.S.	"Legal Professional Privilege: Limitations on the Commission's Powers of Inspection—Following the AM & S Judgment", (1983) C.M.L.Rev. 75.
Forsthoff, E.	*Die Verwaltung als Leistungsträger*, Stuttgart-Berlin, 1938.
	Lehrbuch des Verwaltungsrechts (10th ed., Munich/Berlin 1973).
Foulkes, D.	*Administrative Law* (5th ed., London 1982).
Frank von Fürstenwerth, J.	*Ermessensentscheidungen im Aussenwirtschaftsrecht*, Cologne/Berlin/Bonn/Munich, 1985.
Freitas do Amaral, D.	*Direito Administrativo*, Vol. I–IV, Lisbon, 1984–1986.
Freudenschuss, H.	"Die Diskriminierungsverbote der Europäischen Menschenrechtskonvention und der Rassendiskriminierungskonvention im österreichischen Recht", EuGRZ 1983, p. 623.
Friedrich, K.	"Die EWG-Verordnungen über Nacherhebung und Erlass bzw. Erstattung von Eingangs- und Ausfuhrabgaben", RIW/AWD 1982, p. 35.
Frøbert, K.A.	"Stärkung der staatsbürgerlichen Rechte", Dänische Rundschau 1971, p. 34.
Fromont, M.	"Der französische Staatsrat und sein Werk", DVBl. 1978, p. 89.
	"Der Rechtsschutz des Einzelnen im niederländischen Verwaltungsrecht. Vergleich mit dem deutschen und französischen Recht", DÖV 1972, p. 405.
	"Die französische Kommunalverfassung", DVBl. 1985, p. 421.
	"La protection provisoire des particuliers contre les décisions administratives dans les Etats Membres des Communautés européennes", RISA (Revue internationale des sciences administratives), Vol. 50 (1984), p. 309.
	"La restitution de taxes perçues indûment par l'Etat en droit français", in: *La restitution de taxes perçues indûment par l'Etat*, Geneva, 1976.
	"Le pouvoir discrétionnaire et le juge administratif français", in: *Festschrift für H. Jahrreiss*, Cologne/Berlin/Bonn/Munich, 1974, p. 67.
	"Le système français de protection juridictionnelle du citoyen contre l'administration", in: *Festschrift für C.-F. Menger*, Cologne/Berlin/Bonn/Munich, 1985, p. 309.
	Rechtsschutz gegenüber der Verwaltung in Deutschland, Frankreich und den Europäischen Gemeinschaften, Cologne/Berlin/Bonn/Munich, 1967.
	"République Fédérale d'Allemagne—l'Etat de droit", RDP 1984, p. 1203.
	"République Fédérale d'Allemagne—Les événements législatifs et jurisprudentiels survenus en 1976", RDP 1978, p. 395.
	"Staatshaftungsrecht in Frankreich", DÖV 1982, p. 925.
	"Verwaltungsgerichtsbarkeit in Frankreich und Italian", in: *Die Entwicklung der österreichischen Verwaltungsgerichtsbarkeit, Festschrift österreichisches Verwaltungsgericht*, Vienna, 1970, p. 127.

1480

Fromont, M., Reig, A. (eds.)   *Introduction au droit allemand, Tome II: Droit public—Droit pénal*, Paris, 1984.

Frowein, J. Abr.   "Der europäische Menschenrechtsschutz als Beginn einer europäischen Verfassungsrechtsprechung", JuS 1986, p. 845.

"Die rechtliche Bedeutung des Verfassungsprinzips der parlamentarischen Demokratie für den europäischen Integrationsprozess", EuR 1983, p. 301.

"Eigentumsschutz im Europarecht", in: *Festschrift für H. Kutscher*, Baden-Baden, 1981, p. 189.

"Randbemerkungen zu den Grenzen des Richterrechts in rechtsvergleichender Betrachtung", in: *Richterliche Rechtsfortbildung, Erscheinungsformen, Auftrag und Grenzen. Festschrift der juristischen Fakultät zur 600-Jahr-Feier der Ruprecht-Karls-Universität Heidelberg, Heidelberg*, 1986, p. 555.

Frowein, J. Abr.   *Europäische Menschenrechtskonvention, EMRK-Kommentar*, Kehl/Strasbourg/Arlington, 1985.

Fuss, E.-W. (ed.)   *Der Beitrag des Gerichtshofes der Europäischen Gemeinschaften zur Verwirklichung des Gemeinsamen Marktes*, Baden-Baden, 1981.

Der Grundrechtsschutz in den Europäischen Gemeinschaften aus deutscher Sicht, Heule/Brussels/Namur, 1975.

"Der Schutz des Vertrauens auf Rechtskontinuität im deutschen Verfassungsrecht und europäischen Gemeinschaftsrecht", in: *Festschrift für H. Kutscher*, Baden-Baden, 1981, p. 201.

"Die allgemeinen Rechtsgrundsätze über die ausservertragliche Haftung der Europäischen Gemeinschaften", in: *Festschrift für H. Raschhofer*, Kallmünz 1977, p. 43.

Die Europäischen Gemeinschaften und der Rechtsstaatsgedanke, Heule (Belgium), 1967.

Die rechtsstaatlichen Grundlagen der Europäischen Gemeinschaften, Hamburg, 1960, (typewritten version of dissertation).

"Die Verantwortung der nationalen Gerichte für die Wahrung des europäischen Gemeinschaftsrechts", in: *Gedächtnisschrift für Chr. Sasse*, Vol. 1, Baden-Baden, 1981, p. 171.

"Rechtssatz und Einzelakt im Europäischen Gemeinschaftsrecht", NJW 1964, pp. 327, 945 and 1600.

"Rechtsstaatliche Bilanz der Europäischen Gemeinschaften", in: *Festschrift für G. Küchenhoff*, Berlin, 1972, p. 781.

"Zur Zulässigkeit der Schadensersatzklage wegen Gemeinschaftshaftung für rechtswidrige Verordnungen", in: *Festschrift für H. P. Ipsen*, Tübingen, 1977, p. 617.

Gagner, St.   *Studien zur Ideengeschichte der Gesetzgebung*, Stockholm/Uppsala/Gothenburg, 1960.

Gammeltoft-Hansen, H., Gomard, B., Philip, A. (eds.)   *Danish Law—A General Survey*, Copenhagen, 1982.

1481

Ganshof van der Meersch, W. J. — "Aspects de la mise en oeuvre d'une sauvegarde collective des droits de l'homme en droit international—La Convention Européenne", in: *Mélanges Fernand Dehousse*, Paris/Brussels 1979, Vol. 1, p. 193.
"Le droit de la défense", in: *Mélanges en l'honneur de J. Dabin*, Brussels, 1963, Part 2, p. 569.
Pouvoir de fait et règle de droit dans le fonctionnement des institutions politiques, Brussels, 1957.

Garcïa de Enterrïa, E., Fernandez, T.-R. — *Curso de derecho administrativo*, Vol. 1, 4th ed., Vol. 2, 2nd ed., Madrid, 1984.

Garcïa de Enterrïa, E., González Campos, Julio D., Muñoz Machado, S. (eds.) — *Tratado de derecho Comunitario Europeo*, 3 volumes, Madrid, 1986.

Garner, J.F. — "England", in: E. V. Heyen (ed.), *Geschichte der Verwaltungsrechtswissenschaft in Europa*, Frankfurt, 1982, p. 51.

Garner, J.F., Jones, B.L. — *Administrative Law* (6th ed., London 1985).

Garner, J.W. — *French administrative law*, New Haven, 1924.

Garrido Falla, F. — "Der gerichtliche Rechtsschutz des Einzelnen gegenüber der vollziehenden Gewalt in Spanien", in: H. Mosler (ed.), *Gerichtsschutz gegen die Exekutive*, Vol. 2, Cologne/Berlin/Bonn/Munich, 1970, p. 989.
"Spanien-Einführung", in: C. H. Ule (ed.), *Verwaltungsverfahrensgesetze des Auslandes*, Vol. II, Berlin, 1967, p. 743.
Tratado de derecho administrativo, Vol. I (*Parte general*) (9th ed., Madrid 1985); Vol. II (*Parte general: conclusión*) (7th ed., Madrid 1985).

Gazier, F. — "Aperçu sur l'oeuvre juridictionnelle des Commissaires du Gouvernement depuis 1900", in: *Le Conseil d'Etat, Livre Jubilaire*, Paris, 1952, p. 303.
"Etude sur les établissements publics", E.D.C.E. No. 36 (1984–1985), p. 13.

Geffroy, J.-B. — "Service public et prérogatives de puissance publique, Réflexions sur les déboires d'un couple célèbre", RDP 1987, p. 49.

Geidel, R.-P. — "Der sozial-ökonomische Rat der Niederlande", JöR N.F. 32 (1983), p. 219.

Geisseler, A. — *Reformbestrebungen im englischen Verfassungsrecht*, Frankfurt/Berne/New York, 1985.

Gellhorn, E., Boyer, B. — *Administrative Law and Process* (2nd ed., St. Paul Minn. 1982).

Gellhorn, W., Byse, C., Strauss, P.L. — *Administrative Law* (7th ed., Mineola/New York (USA) 1979).

Genevois, B. — "Der Conseil d'Etat und das Gemeinschaftsrecht: Antagonismus oder Komplementarität?", EuR 1985, p. 355.

Gern, A. — "Analogie im Verwaltungsrecht", DÖV 1985, p. 558.

Gicquel S., Hauriou, A. — *Droit constitutionnel et institutions politiques* (8th ed., Paris 1985).

Gillmeister, F. — *Ermittlungsrechte im deutschen und europäischen Kartellordnungswidrigkeitenverfahren*, Baden-Baden, 1985.

Gilsdorf, P. — "Die Haftung der Gemeinschaft aus normativem Handeln auf dem Hintergrund der Rechtsprechung des Europäischen Gerichtshofs", EuR 1975, p. 73.
"Vertrauensschutz, Bestandskraft und Rückwirkung im Gemeinschaftsrecht", RIW/AWD 1983, p. 22.

1482

Gitter, W.	*Sozialrecht* (2nd ed., Munich 1980).
Glaesner, H.-J.	"Die Einheitliche Europäische Akte", EuR 1986, p. 119.
Gleiss, Hirsch	*Kommentar zum EWG-Kartellrecht* (3rd ed., Heidelberg 1978).
Glücksmann, R.	*Die Grenzen der Betätigung englischer Verwaltungsbehörden*, Frankfurt/Main, 1984.
Gneist, R.	*Der Rechtsstaat und die Verwaltungsgerichte in Deutschland*, 3rd ed.; Darmstadt, 1966 (reprint of the 2nd ed., of 1879).
Göldner, D.	"Die Rücknahme begünstigender Verwaltungsakte nach dem neuen Verwaltungsverfahrensgesetz", DÖV 1979, p. 805.
Goerlich, H.	*Grundrechte als Verfahrensgarantien*, Baden-Baden, 1981.
Götz, V.	"Der allgemeine Gleichheitssatz und die Rechtsanwendung im Verwaltungsrecht", NJW 1979, p. 1478.
	"Probleme des Verwaltungsrechts auf dem Gebiete des gemeinsamen Agrarmarkts", EuR 1986, p. 29.
Götz, V., Klein, H.H., Starck, C. (eds.)	*Die öffentliche Verwaltung zwischen Gesetzgebung und richterlicher Kontrolle*, Munich, 1985.
Goffin, L.	"La jurisprudence de la Cour de justice sur le droit de la défense", CDE 1980, p. 127.
Gomes Canotilho, Vital Moreira	*Constituição da Republica Portuguesa*, Coimbra, 1980.
Gomes Canotilho, José Joaquim	*Direito Constitucional* (2nd ed., Coimbra 1980).
Goose, P.-E.	*Die Normenkontrolle durch den französischen Conseil Constitutionnel*, Berlin, 1973.
Grabitz, E.	"Der Grundsatz der Verhältnismässigkeit in der Rechtsprechung des Bundesverfassungsgerichts", AöR 98 (1973), p. 36.
	Gemeinschaftsrecht bricht nationales Recht, Hamburg, 1966.
Grabitz, E., Läufer, T.	*Das Europäische Parlament*, Bonn, 1980.
Gralla, R.	*Der Grundrechtsschutz in Dänemark*, Frankfurt/M.-Berne/Bonn/New York, 1987, p. 449.
Grassl, M.	"Vertrauensschutz bei der Aufhebung rechtswidriger begünstigender Verwaltungsakte", Die Sozialgerichtsbarkeit 1985, p. 145.
Graulich, P., Guilitte P., van Loon, J.F., Glastra, van Holk, L.E.	*Guide to foreign legal materials*, New York, 1968.
Grawert, R.	"Grenzen und Alternativen des gerichtlichen Rechtsschutzes in Verwaltungsstreitsachen", DVBl. 1983, p. 973.
	"Widerruf und Erstattung im Recht der Zuwendungen—Die haushaltsrechtlichen Änderungen des Verwaltungsverfahrens", DVBl. 1981, p. 1029.
Gregory, R., Hutchesson, P.	*The Parliamentary Ombudsman*, London, 1975.
	The Parliamentary Ombudsman, A Study in the Control of Administrative Action, London, 1975.
Greig, D.W.	*International Law* (2nd ed., London 1976).
Grimes, R.H., Horgan, P.T.	*Introduction to Law in the Republic of Ireland*, Dublin, 1981.

von der Groeben, H.	"Über das Problem der Grundrechte in der Europäischen Gemeinschaft", in: *Festschrift für W. Hallstein*, Frankfurt am Main 1966, p. 226.
von der Groeben, H., von Boeckh, H., Thiesing, J., Ehlermann, C.-D.	*Kommentar zum EWG-Vertrag* (3rd ed., Baden-Baden 1983).
von der Groeben, H., Thiesing, J., Ehlermann, C.-D.	*Handbuch des Europäischen Rechts*, loose leaf publication, Baden-Baden, 1988.
Grossmann, U.	*Der Widerruf begünstigender Verwaltungsakte im Recht der EG*, Cologne, 1964.
Grote, R.	"Ermessenslehre und Ermessenspraxis in Frankreich", NVwZ 1986, p. 269.
Grunwald, J.	"Die Entwicklung des Gemeinschaftsrechts", EuR 1983, p. 344.
Gündisch, J.	"Allgemeine Rechtsgrundsätze in der Rechtsprechung des Europäischen Gerichtshofs", in: Schwarze J. (ed.), *Das Wirtschaftsrecht des Gemeinsamen Marktes in der aktuellen Rechtsentwicklung,*, Baden-Baden, 1983, p. 97.
Guillaume, G.	"La France devant la Cour de justice des Communautés européennes", Bulletin des Juristes Européens 1985, p. 37.
Gundersen, F.	"Das Diskriminierungsverbot im EWG-Vertrag", NJW 1975, p. 472.
Gusy, C.	"Administrativer Vollzugsauftrag und justizielle Kontrolldichte im Recht der Technik", DVBl. 1987, p. 497.
de Haan, P., Drupsteen, Th.G., Fernhout, R.	*Bestuursrecht in de Sociale Rechtsstaat* (2nd ed., Deventer 1978).
Häberle, P.	"Grundrechte im Leistungsstaat", VVDStRL 30 (1972), p. 43.
Haefliger, A.	"Der Gleichheitssatz im Verhältnis zu anderen verfassungsmässigen Rechten und zur Europäischen Menschenrechtskonvention", in: *Mélanges André Grisel*, Neuchâtel, 1983, p. 79.
Händel, H.	*Grossbritannien*, Vol. I, *Staat und Verwaltung*, Munich, 1979.
Hagel-Sørensen, K., Rasmussen, H.	"The Danish Administration and its Interaction with the Community Administration", (1985) C.M.L.Rev. 273.
Hahn, H.J.	*Funktionenteilung im Verfassungsrecht europäischer Organisationen*, Baden-Baden, 1977. "Zur Drittwirkung von EG-Richtlinien", RIW/AWD 1982, p. 503.
Hailbronner, K.	"Ziele und Methoden völkerrechtlich relevanter Rechtsvergleichung", ZaöRV 36 (1976), p. 190.
Hallstein, W.	*Die Europäische Gemeinschaft* (5th ed., Düsseldorf/Vienna 1979).
Hardt, H.-J.D.	"Die allgemeinen Verwaltungsgrundsätze", DÖV 1971, p. 685. "Die Revisibilität der algemeinen Verwaltungsrechtsgrundsätze", DVBl. 1973, p. 235.
Harlow, C., Rawlings, R.	*Law and Administration*, London, 1984.
Hartley, T.C.	"Concurrent Liability in EEC Law: A Critical Review of the Cases", (1977) E.L.Rev. 249. *The Foundations of European Community Law*, Oxford, 1981.

Harvey, J., Bather, L.   *The British Constitution and Politics* (5th ed., London 1982).

Hatje, A.   *Der Rechtsschutz der Stellenbewerber im Europäischen Beamtenrecht*, Baden-Baden, 1988.

Hauriou, A., Gicquel, J., Gelard, P.   *Droit constitutionnel et institutions politiques* (7th ed., Paris 1980).

Hauriou, M.   *Précis de droit administratif et de droit public* (12th ed., 1933).

Haverkate, G.   *Rechtsfragen des Leistungsstaats—Verhältnismässigkeitsgebot und Freiheitsschutz im leistenden Staatshandeln*, Tübingen, 1983.

Heberlein, I.   "Auswirkungen der Verwaltungsverfahrensgesetze auf die Dogmatik des Verwaltungsrechts", Speyerer Forschungsberichte 24, Speyer 1981, p. 357.

Heiermeier, B.   *Rechts- und Sprachfiguren des Verwaltungshandelns. Eine übersetzungswissenschaftliche Untersuchung im Sprachenpaar Französisch-Deutsch*, Heidelberg, 1983.

Held, J.   *Der Grundrechtsbezug des Verwaltungsverfahrens*, Berlin, 1984.

Heldrich, A.   "Art. 215 Abs. 2 des Vertrages über die Europäische Wirtschaftsgemeinschaft—Ein Irrweg zu europäischer Rechtseinheit", JZ 1960, p. 681.

Hempfer, W.   *Die nationalsozialistische Staatsauffassung in der Rechtsprechung des Preussischen Oberverwaltungsgerichts*, Berlin, 1974.

Henke, W.   'Juristische Systematik der Grundrechte", DÖV 1984, p. 1.

Henkel, H.   *Einführung in die Rechtsphilosophie*, Munich/Berlin, 1964.

Henrichs, H.   "Die Rechtsprechung des Europäischen Gerichtshofs in Personalsachen", EuR 1980, p. 134.

"Die Rechtsprechung des Europäischen Gerichtshofs in Personalsachen", EuR 1985, p. 171.

Herdegen, M.   *Die Haftung der EWG für fehlerhafte Rechtsetzungsakte*, Berlin, 1983.

"Pressefreiheit und Verfassungsgerichtsbarkeit in Frankreich. Die Entscheidung des Conseil Constitutionnel zum neuen französischen Pressegesetz vom 10./11. Oktober 1984", ZaöRV 46 (1986), p. 34.

"The relation between the principles of equality and proportionality", (1985) C.M.L.Rev. 683.

"Zur Haftung für fehlerhafte Verordnungen im Recht der EWG", NVwZ 1984, p. 344.

Herlitz, N.   "Legal Remedies in Nordic Administrative Law", AJCL 1966/67, p. 687.

Hermann, H.-J.   "Die Entwicklung des Rechtsschutzes in der Europäischen Gerichtsbarkeit", RabelsZ. 1981, p. 413.

Herzog, R.   "Die Verfassung der Bundesrepublik Deutschland", in: J. H. Kaiser (ed.), *Verwaltung und Verwaltungswissenschaften in der Bundesrepublik Deutschland*, Baden-Baden, 1983, p. 12.

"Stichwort 'Gleichheitssatz', " in: *Evangelisches Staatslexikon* (edited by Hermann Kunst and Siegfried Grundmann together with Wilhelm Schneemelcher and Roman Herzog) (1st ed., Stuttgart/Berlin 1966), p. 696.

1485

Hesse, K.   "Der Gleichheitsgrundsatz im Staatsrecht", AöR 77 (1951/52), p. 167.
"Der Gleichheitssatz in der neueren deutschen Verfassungsentwicklung", AöR 109 (1984), p. 174.
Grundzüge des Verfassungsrechts der Bundesrepublik Deutschland (16th ed., Heidelberg/Karlsruhe 1988).

Heyen, Erk. V. (ed.)   *Geschichte der Verwaltungsrechtswissenschaft in Europa*, Frankfurt a.M., 1982.
Otto Mayer—Studien zu den geistigen Grundlagen seiner Verwaltungsrechtswissenschaft, Berlin, 1981.
Wissenschaft und Recht der Verwaltung seit dem Ancien Regime, Europäische Ansichten, Frankfurt a.M., 1984.

Hilf, M.   "Der Gerichtshof der Europäischen Gemeinschaften als Integrationsfaktor—dargestellt anhand der Rechtsprechung zu den Grundrechten", in: Jochen Abr. Frowein *et al.* (eds.), *Die Grundrechte in der Europäischen Gemeinschaft*, Baden-Baden, 1978, p. 23.
"Die gemeinsame Grundrechtserklärung des Europäischen Parlaments, des Rates und der Kommission vom 5. April 1977", EuGRZ 1977, p. 158.
Die Organisationsstruktur der Europäischen Gemeinschaften, Berlin/Heidelberg/New York, 1982.
"Möglichkeiten und Grenzen des Rückgriffs auf nationale verwaltungsrechtliche Regeln bei der Durchführung von Gemeinschaftsrecht", in: J. Schwarze (ed.), *Europäisches Verwaltungsrecht im Werden*, Baden-Baden, 1982, p. 67.
"Solange II: Wielange noch Solange?", EuGRZ 1987, p. 1.
"The Role of Comparative Law in the Jurisprudence of the Court of Justice of the European Community", in: *The Limitation of Human Rights in Comparative Constitutional Law/La Limitation des Droits de l'homme en Droit Constitutionnel Comparé*, Cowansville, 1986, p. 549.

Hilf, M., Petersmann, E.-U. (eds.)   *GATT und Europäische Gemeinschaft*, Baden-Baden, 1986.

Hill, H.   *Zehn Jahre Verwaltungsverfahrensgesetz*, Speyerer Arbeitshefte 78, 1987.
"Die öffentliche Verwaltung zwischen Gesetzgebung und richterlicher Kontrolle", DVBl. 1985, p. 998.
"Rechtsbehelfe gegen behördliche Verfahrenshandlungen (§ 44a VwGO)", Jura 1985, p. 61.
"Verfahrensermessen der Verwaltung", NVwZ 1985, p. 449.

Hirsch, A. *et al.* (eds.)   *La restitution de taxes perçues indûment par l'Etat*, Schweizerische Beiträge zum Europarecht Vol. 18, Geneva, 1976.

Hirschberg, L.   *Der Grundsatz der Verhältnismässigkeit*, Göttingen, 1981.

Hochbaum, M.   *Das Diskriminierungsverbot in EGKS und EWG*, Baden-Baden/Bonn, 1962.

Höhn, E.   *Gewohnheitsrecht im Verwaltungsrecht*, Abh. z. schweiz. Recht n.F. No. 340, Berne, 1960.

Höhn, R.   *Das ausländische Verwaltungsrecht der Gegenwart*, Berlin, 1949.

Hoffmann-Becking, G.

Normaufbau und Methode—Eine Untersuchung zur Rechtsprechung des Gerichtshofs der Europäischen Gemeinschaften, Tübingen, 1973.

Holleaux, A.

"Les nouvelles lois françaises sur l'information du public", RISA 1981, p. 191.

Hood Phillips, O.

Leading Cases in Constitutional and Administrative Law (3rd ed., London 1979).

Hood Phillips, O., Jackson, P.

Constitutional and Administrative Law, London.

Hrbek, R.

"Relations of Community Bureaucracy with the Social-Political Environment", in: J. Jamar, W. Wessels (eds.), *Community Bureaucracy at the Crossroads*, Brussels, 1985, p. 105.

Hubeau, F.

"La répétition de l'indu en droit communautaire", RTDE 1981, p. 442.
Le principe de la protection de la confiance légitime dans la jurisprudence de la Cour de justice des Communautés européennes", CDE 1983, p. 143.

Huber, H.

"Der Sinnzusammenhang des Willkürverbots mit der Rechtsgleichheit", in: *Mélanges André Grisel*, Neuchâtel 1983, p. 127.

Hufen, F.

Fehler im Verwaltungsverfahren, Baden-Baden, 1986.

Huthmacher, K.E.

Der Vorrang des Gemeinschaftsrechts bei indirekten Kollisionen. Eine Studie zum Verhältnis von EG-Recht zum nationelen Vollzugsrecht, dargestellt am Beispiel des Konflikts zwischen materiellem EG-Recht und nationalen Rechtsmittelfristen, Cologne/Berlin/Bonn/Munich, 1985.

v. Ihering, R.

Geist des römischen Rechts, Part 2, 4th ed., 1883 (reprinted as 8th ed., Basle).

Iliopoulos-Strangas, J.

"Grundrechtsschutz in Griechenland", JöR NF 32 (1983). p. 395.
Rückwirkung und Sofortwirkung von Gesetzen—eine verfassungsrechtliche Untersuchung unter Berücksichtigung des deutschen und griechischen Steuerrechts, Baden-Baden, 1986.

Imboden, M.

Staat und Recht, Basle/Stuttgart, 1971.

Institut Français des Sciences Administratives

Le contrôle de l'administration par elle-même, Editions du Centre National de la Recherche Scientifique, Paris, 1983.

Inst. de Recherches Juridiques Strasbourg

Les Communautés européennes et le droit administratif français, Travaux des journées d'études, Paris, 1972.

Ipsen, H.P.

"Das Bundesverfassungsgericht löst die Grundrechts-Problematik. Zum 'Mittlerweile'—Beschluss des 2. Senats vom 22. Oktober 1986", EuR 1987, p. 1.
Europäisches Gemeinschaftsrecht, Tübingen, 1972.
Fusionsverfassung Europäische Gemeinschaften, Bad Homburg/Berlin/Zürich, 1969.
"Gleichheit", in: Neumann, F.L., Nipperdey, H.C., Scheuner, U. (eds), *Die Grundrechte*, Berlin, 1954, Vol. 2, p. 111.
"Zur Tragfähigkeit der Verfassungsprinzipien der Europäischen Integration", in: *Integrationskonzepte auf dem Prüfstand*, Vol. 19 of Schriftenreihe des Arbeitskreises Europäische Integration, Baden-Baden, 1983, p. 9.
"Uber Supranationalität", in: *Festschrift für U. Scheuner*, Berlin, 1973, p. 211.

1487

Ipsen J.   "Verbindlichkeit, Bestandskraft und Bindungswirkung
                                 von Verwaltungsakten—Versuch einer begrifflichen
                                 Klärung", Die Verwaltung, 1984, p. 169.
                                 "Verfassungsrechtliche Schranken des Richterrechts",
                                 DVBl. 1984, p. 1102.
Isaac, G.   "La codification du droit communautaire", Rev.
                                 Europ. 1977, p. 90.
Jacobs, F.G. (ed.)   European Law and the Individual, Amsterdam/New
                                 York/Oxford, 1976.
Jaconelli, J.   "Constitutional Review and Section 2 (4) of the
                                 European Community Act 1972", Int. and Comp. Law
                                 Quart. 1979, p. 65.
Jacot-Guillarmod, O.   Droit communautaire et droit international public.
                                 Etudes des sources internationales de l'ordre juridique
                                 des Communautés européennes, Geneva, 1979.
Jacqué, J.-P.   "The principle of equality in economic law", (1985)
                                 C.M.L.Rev. 135.
Jacqué, J.-P., Bieber R.,   Le Parlement européen, Paris, 1984.
  Constantinesco, V.,
  Nickel, D.
Jaenicke, G.   "Stichwort 'Diskriminierung', " in: Wörterbuch des Völ-
                                 kerrechts (founded by Karl Strupp/ed. Hans-Jürgen
                                 Schlochauer), Vol. 1, Berlin, 1960, p. 387.
Jakobs, M.Ch.   "Bericht über die Arbeitssitzung der Wissenschaftlichen
                                 Gesellschaft für Europarecht am 22.09.1983 in Bonn",
                                 DVBl. 1983, p. 1182.
                                 "Der Grundsatz der Verhältnismässigkeit", DVBl.
                                 1985, p. 97.
James, P.S.   Introduction to English Law (11th ed., 1985).
Jarass, H.D.   "Besonderheiten des amerikanischen Verwaltungs-
                                 rechts im Vergleich", DÖV 1985, p. 377.
                                 "Besonderheiten des französischen Verwaltungsrechts
                                 im Vergleich", DÖV 1981, p. 813.
Jeanneau, B.   Les principes généraux du droit dans la jurisprudence
                                 administrative, Paris, 1954.
Jeantet, F.-C.   "La défense dans les procédures répressives en droit de
                                 la concurrence", RTDE 22 (1986), p. 53.
Jellinek, H.   "Ermessensausübung durch Verwaltungsbehörden",
                                 ZRP 1981, p. 68.
Jellinek, W.   Verwaltungsrecht (3rd ed., Offenburg 1931), (reprinted
                                 1948).
Jennings, I.W., Ritter, G.A.   Das britische Regierungssystem, Cologne/Opladen,
                                 1958.
Jerusalem, F.   Das Recht der Montan-Union, Berlin/Frankfurt a.M.,
                                 1954.
Jesch, D.   Gesetz und Verwaltung (2nd ed., Tübingen 1968).
Jèze, G.   Les principes généraux du droit administratif, 3 vols.,
                                 Paris, 1934–1936.
Joliet, R.   Le droit institutionnel des Communautés européennes,
                                 Liège, 1981.
Jordana, L.   "Le Conseil d'Etat espagnol et les influences françaises
                                 au cours de son évolution", in: Le Conseil d'Etat, Livre
                                 jubilaire, Paris, 1952, p. 521.
Joshua, J.M.   "Proof in Contested EEC Competition Cases. A Com-
                                 parison with the Rules of Evidence in Common Law",
                                 (1987) E.L.Rev. 315.

Jung, H.

Kahn-Freund, O.

Kaiser, J.H.

(ed.)

Kalbe, P.

Karpenstein, P.

Karwiese, D.

Kasten, H.-H.

Kegel, G.

Kelly, J.M.

Kelsen, H.
Kerse, C.S.
Kewenig, W.

Kirchhof, F.

Kirchhof, P.

Kirchner, E., Williams, K.

Kisker, G.

Klaiber, K.-P.

"Ein erstinstanzliches Gericht für die Europäischen Gemeinschaften", EuGRZ 1986, p. 229.
"Common Law and Civil Law—Imaginary and Real Obstacles to Assimilation", in: M. Cappelletti (ed.), *New Perspectives for a Common Law of Europe*, Leyden/London/Boston, 1978, p. 137.
"Vergleichung im öffentlichen Recht", ZaöRV 24 (1964), p. 391.
Verwaltung und Verwaltungswissenschaft in der Bundesrepublik Deutschland, Baden–Baden, 1983.
"Europäisches Agrarrecht—Internationales Verwaltungsrecht im Werden", DVBl. 1975, p. 753.
"Gemeinschaftsrecht und nationale Rechtsbehelfsfristen—Anmerkung zu den Rs 33/76 und 45/76", Zeitschrift für Zölle und Verbrauchssteuern 1977, p. 360.
"Die Entwicklung des Gemeinschaftsrechts", EuR 1980, p. 264.
"Zur Tragweite des Art. 48 Abs. 4 EWG-Vertrag", in: *Gedächtnisschrift für L.-J. Constantinesco*, Cologne/Berlin/Bonn/Munich, 1983, p. 377.
"Zur Wiedergutmachung von Vertragsverstössen der Mitgliedstaaten gegen das Gemeinschaftsrecht", DVBl. 1977, p. 61.
Kontrolle der Verwaltung durch ordentliche Gerichte und allgemeine Verwaltungsgerichte nach italienischem Recht, Frankfurt a.M., 1986.
"Entwicklung eines Europäischen Allgemeinen Verwaltungsrechts", DÖV 1985, p. 570.
"Sinn und Grenzen der Rechtsangleichung", in: *Angleichung des Rechts der Wirtschaft in Europa*, KSE Vol. 11 (1971), p. 9.
"Equality before the law in Three European Jurisdictions", The Irish Jurist 1983, p. 259.
"Judicial Protection of the Individual against the Executive in the Republic of Ireland", in: H. Mosler (ed.), *Gerichtsschutz gegen die Exekutive*, Vol. 1, Cologne/Berlin/Bonn/Munich, 1969, p. 425.
The Irish Constitution (2nd ed., Dublin 1984).
Reine Rechtslehre (2nd ed., Vienna 1960).
EEC Antitrust Procedure (2nd ed., London 1988).
Der Grundsatz der Nichtdiskriminierung im Völkerrecht der internationalen Handelsbeziehungen, Vol. 1: *Begriff der Diskriminierung*, Frankfurt a.M., 1972.
"Der Verwaltungsakt auf Zustimmung", DVBl. 1985, p. 651.
"Revisibles Verwaltungsrecht", in: *Festschrift f. Chr.-F. Menger*, Cologne/Berlin/Bonn/Munich, 1985, p. 813.
"The Legal, Political and Institutional Implications of the Isoglucose Judgements 1980", Journal of Com. Market Stud. 22 (1983/84), p. 173.
Die Rückwirkung von Gesetzen. Eine Untersuchung zum anglo-amerikanischen und deutschen Recht, Tübingen, 1963.
Die Aufhebung von Verwaltungsakten im französischen Recht, Mainz, 1967.

Klang, K.A. — *Soziale Sicherheit und Freizügigkeit im EWGV*, Baden-Baden, 1986.

Klein, F. (ed.) — *Lehrbuch des öffentlichen Finanzrechts*, Darmstadt/Neuwied, 1987.

Klett, K. — *Verfassungsrechtlicher Schutz "wohlerworbener Rechte" bei Rechtsänderungen, anhand der bundesgerichtlichen Rechtsprechung*, Berne, 1984.

Klisch, R. — *Gesetz und Verordnung in der Verfassung der 5. französischen Republik vom 4. Oktober 1958*, Berlin, 1971.

Kloepfer, M. — "Der Vorbehalt des Gesetzes im Wandel", JZ 1984, p. 685.

Knack, H.J. (ed.) — *Verwaltungsverfahrensgesetz, Kommentar* (2nd ed., Cologne/Berlin/Bonn/Munich 1982).

Knapp, B. — *Grundlagen des Verwaltungsrechts* (2nd ed., Basle/Frankfurt a.M. 1983).

Knapp, W. — "Der Oberste Gerichtshof der Vereinigten Staaten und die Auslegung des Gleichheitssatzes", JöR N.F. 23 (1974), p. 421.

Koch, P. — *Die Klagebefugnis Privater gegenüber Europäischen Entscheidungen gemäss Art. 173 Abs. 2 EWGV*, Frankfurt, 1981.

König J. — *Die Tatsachenermittlung im Verfahren vor dem Gerichtshof der Europäischen Gemeinschaften*, Münster, 1972.

König, K., von Oertzen, H.J., Wagener, F. (eds.) — *Öffentliche Verwaltung in der Bundesrepublik Deutschland*, Baden-Baden, 1981.

Koenig, P. — *Die Kontrolle der Verfassungsmässigkeit in Frankreich und in der BRD*, Cologne/Berlin/Bonn/Munich, 1985.

Kötz, H. — "Gemeineuropäisches Zivilrecht", in: *Festschrift für K. Zweigert*, Tübingen, 1981, p. 481.

Koja, F. — *Allgemeines Verwaltungsrecht. Lehr- und Handbuch für Studium und Praxis* (2nd ed., Vienna 1986).

Komendera, W. — *Normenkonflikte zwischen EWG- und BRD-Recht—insbesondere Kollisionen*, Heidelberg, 1974.

Kommers, D.P. — "Der Gleichheitssatz: Neuere Entwicklungen im Verfassungsrecht der USA und der Bundesrepublik Deutschland", in: Christoph Link (ed.), *Der Gleichheitssatz im modernen Verfassungsstaat*, Baden-Baden, 1982, p. 31.

Kon, S.D. — "Aspects of Reverse Discrimination in Community Law", (1981) E.L.Rev. 75.

Konrad, H.J. (ed.) — *Grundrechtsschutz und Verwaltungsverfahren*, Berlin, 1985.

Kontogeorga-Theocharopoulou, D. — "Les bases constitutionnelles de l'organisation administrative de l'Etat en Grèce (L'influence de la Constitution hellénique de 1975 sur l'organisation administrative de l'Etat)", in: Journées de la Société de Législation Comparée 1981, p. 525.

Koopmans, T. — "Europe and its Lawyers in 1984", (1985) C.M.L. Rev. 9.
"Stare decisis in European Law", in: O'Keefe D., Schermers, H. (eds.), *Essays in European Law and Integration*, Deventer, 1982, p. 11.
Vergelijkend publiekrecht, Deventer, 1978.

Kopp, F.O. — "Die Bestandskraft von Verwaltungsakten", DVBl. 1983, p. 393.

1490

	Die Vertretung des öffentlichen Interesses in der Verwaltungsgerichtsbarkeit, Passau, 1982.
(ed.)	*Entwicklungen im Staatschaftungsrecht*, Passau, 1982.
	Verwaltungsgerichtsordnung (Kommentar) (7th ed., Munich 1986).
	Verwaltungsverfahrensgesetz (Kommentar) (4th ed., Munich 1986).
Korah, V.	"Comfort Letters—Reflections on the Perfume Cases", (1981) E.L.Rev. 14.
Korber, H.	"Der Aufbau des Verwaltungsverfahrens zur Aufhebung belastender Verwaltungsakte", DÖV 1985, p. 309.
Korinek, K.	*Beiträge zum Wirtschaftsrecht, Festschrift für K. Wenger*, Vienna, 1983.
(ed.)	"Gedanken zur Bindung des Gesetzgebers an den Gleichheitsgrundsatz nach der Judikatur des Verfassungsgerichtshofes", in: *Festschrift für E. Melichar*, Vienna, 1983, p. 39.
Kortmann, C.A.J.M.	"Das niederländische Grundgesetz vom 17. Februar 1983", JöR N.F. 33 (1984), p. 175.
Kovar, R.	"Das Verhältnis von Gemeinschaftsrecht und nationalem Recht", in: *Dreissig Jahre Gemeinschaftsrecht*, Brussels/Luxembourg, 1981, p. 119.
	"Droit communautaire de la concurrence et droit international", CDE 1986, p. 127.
	"Droit communautaire et droit procédural national", CDE 1977, p. 236.
Krarup, O.	"Judicial control of administrative powers", Scandinavian Studies in Law 1971, p. 143.
Krasney, O.E.	"Zur Anhörungspflicht im Verwaltungsverfahren", NVwZ 1986, p. 337.
Krawielicki, R.	*Das Monopolverbot im Schumanplan*, Tübingen, 1952.
Krech, H.	*Die Theorie der allgemeinen Rechtsgrundsätze im französischen öffentlichen Recht*, Göttingen, 1973.
Kriele, M.	*Theorie der Rechtsgewinnung—entwickelt am Problem der Verfassungsinterpretation*, Schriften zum Öffentlichen Recht, Vol. 41 (2nd ed., Berlin 1976).
Krüger, H.	"Die Funktion der Verwaltungs- und Verfassungsgerichtsbarkeit in einigen Staaten Osteuropas", DÖV 1986, p. 45.
Kunig, P.	*Das Rechtsstaatsprinzip. Überlegungen zu seiner Bedeutung für das Verfassungsrecht der Bundesrepublik Deutschland*, Tübingen, 1986.
Kuss, K.-J.	"Die sowjetische Diskussion um den gerichtlichen Verwaltungsrechtsschutz", VerwArchiv 77 (1986), p. 145.
Kutscher, H.	"Community law and the National Judge", (1973) 89 L.Q.R. 487.
	"Der Gerichtshof der Europäischen Gemeinschaften 1952–1982, Rückblick—Ausblick", Integration 4/83, p. 149.
	"Der Gerichtshof der Europäischen Gemeinschaften", EuGRZ 1978, p. 503.
	"Der Schutz von Grundrechten im Recht der Europäischen Gemeinschaften", in: Deutsche Sektion der Int. Juristenkommission (ed.), *Der Grundrechtsschutz*

	im Europäischen Gemeinschaftsrecht, Heidelberg, 1982, p. 35.
	"Thesen zu den Methoden der Auslegung des Gemeinschaftsrechts aus der Sicht eines Richters", in: *Begegnungen von Justiz und Hochschule* I—1, Luxembourg, 1976.
	"Über den Gerichtshof der Europäischen Gemeinschaften", EuR 1981, p. 392.
	"Zum Grundsatz der Verhältnismässigkeit im Recht der Europäischen Gemeinschaften", in: Deutsche Sektion der Int. Juristenkommission (ed.), *Der Grundsatz der Verhältnismässigkeit in europäischen Rechtsordnungen*, Heidelberg, 1985, p. 89.
Kutscher, R.	*Das französische Konfliktsgericht (Tribunal des Conflits—Sein Beitrag zur Kompetenzverteilung zwischen ordentlichen Gerichten und Verwaltungsgerichten in Frankreich*, Mainz, 1983.
Lachaume, J.-F.	*Droit administratif*, Paris, 1980.
Ladeur, K.-H.	"Die rechtliche Kontrolle planerischer Prognosen", Natur und Recht 1985, p. 81.
Lafferière, E.	*Traité de la juridiction administrative et des recours contentieux*, 2 Vols. (2nd ed., Paris/Nancy 1986).
Lamoureux, F.	"The Retroactivity of Community Acts in the Case Law of the Court of Justice", (1983) C.M.L.Rev. 269.
Landi, G., Potenza, G.	*Manuale di Diritto Amministrativo* (7th ed., Milan 1983).
Landon, P.	*Histoire abrégée du recours pour excès de pouvoir des origines à 1954*, Paris, 1962.
Landry, K.	"Das Zollrecht der EG", in: J. Schwarze (ed.), *Das Wirtschaftsrecht des Gemeinsamen Marktes in der aktuellen Rechtsentwicklung*, Baden-Baden, 1983, p. 123.
Lange, K.	"Probleme des Vertrauensschutzes im Verwaltungsrecht, Wirtschaft und Verwaltung 1979, p. 15.
Langheit, T.	*Souveränität und Verfassungsstaat*, Cologne, 1984.
Langrod, G.	"France", in: E.V. Heyen (ed.), *Geschichte der Verwaltungsrechtswissenschaft in Europa*, Frankfurt a.M., 1982, p. 67.
Larenz, K.	*Methodenlehre der Rechtswissenschaft* (5th ed., Berlin/Heidelberg/New York/Tokyo 1983).
Lasok, D., Bridge, J.W.	*An introduction to the Law and Institutions of the European Communities*, London, 1973.
	Law and Institutions of the European Communities (4th ed., London 1987).
Lasok, P.	*Unwritten Principles of Community Law*, Vortäge, Reden und Berichte aus dem Europa-Institut/No. 8, Saarbrücken, 1982.
Latournerie, R.	"Essai sur les méthodes juridictionnelles du Conseil d'Etat", in: *Le Conseil d'Etat, Livre Jubilaire*, Paris, 1952.
de Laubadère, A., Venezia, J.-C., Gaudemet, Y.	*Traité de droit administratif*, Vol. 1 (9th ed., Paris 1984), Vol. 2 (8th ed., Paris 1986).
Laubinger, H.-W.	"Grundrechtsschutz durch Gestaltung des Verwaltungsverfahrens", VerwArchiv 1982, p. 60.

"Zur Erforderlichkeit der Anhörung des Antragstellers vor Ablehnung seines Antrages durch die Verwaltungsbehörde", VerwArchiv 1984, p. 55.

The Law Reform Commission   *Working Paper No. 8, Judicial Review of Administative Action, The Problem of Remedies*, Dublin, 1979.

Lecheler, H.   *Der Europäische Gerichtshof und die allgemeinen Rechtsgrundsätze*, Berlin, 1971.
Die allgemeinen Rechtsgrundsätze in der Rechtsprechung des Europäischen Gerichtshofs, Erlangen/Nuremberg, 1967.

Le Conseil d'Etat   *Livre jubilaire*, Paris, 1952.

Léger, J.   "Le bilan: la décennie 1974–1985, le constat: une crise salutaire", Etudes et documents du Conseil d'Etat 1983–1984 (No. 35), p. 328.

Leibholz, G.   *Die Gleichheit vor dem Gesetz* (2nd ed., Berlin 1959).
"Stichwort 'Gleichheit der Staaten,' " in: Karl Strupp (founder) und Hans-Jürgen Schlochauer (ed.), *Wörterbuch des Völkerrechts*, Vol. 1, Berlin, 1960, p. 694.
"Das Verbot der Willkür und des Ermessensmissbrauchs im völkerrechtlichen Verkehr der Staaten", ZaöRV I, Part 1, 1929, p. 77, reprinted Darmstadt.

Lepace, F.,   "La participation du Conseil d'Etat à l'élaboration des
Vander Stichle, A.   lois et des arrêts", in: *Rapports présentés aux colloques entre les Conseils d'Etat Belge, Néerlandais, Français, Italien, Luxembourgeois et le Bundesverwaltungsgericht*, Rome, 1968, p. 7.

Lerche, P., *et al.* (eds.)   *Verfahren als staats- und verwaltungsrechtliche Kategorie*, Heidelberger Forum Vol. 21, Heidelberg, 1984.

Letemendia, M.   "La rétroactivité en droit communautaire", CDE 1977, p. 518.

Letourneur, M.   "Le principe de la non-rétroactivité des actes administratifs", E.D.C.E. 1955, p. 37.
"Les 'principes généraux du droit' dans la jurisprudence du Conseil d'Etat", E.D.C.E. 1951, p. 19.

Lévy, M.   "De quelques limites d'un 'taylorisme contentieux', " AJDA 1985, p. 602.

Liesch, L.   "Bestand und Bedeutung der Grundrechte in Luxemburg", EuGRZ 1981, p. 84.

Link, C.   *Der Gleichheitssatz im modernen Verfassungsstaat*, Baden-Baden, 1982.

Lipphardt, H.-R.   "Grundrechte und Rechtsstaat", EuGRZ 1986, p. 149.

Lob, H.   "Das neue französische Recht der Wettbewerbsbeschränkungen", RIW 1988, p. 92.

Löden, D.   "Zur Klagebefugnis von Natur- und Umweltschutzverbänden nach französischem Recht", DVBl. 1978, p. 676.

von Loeper, C.   *Verwaltungsrechtspflege in England*, Frankfurt, 1983.

Loesch, A.   "Le Conseil d'Etat, Comité du Contentieux", in: *Le Conseil d'Etat, Livre Jubilaire*, Luxembourg, 1957, p. 507.

Loewenstein, K.   *Staatsrecht und Staatspraxis von Grossbritannien*, Vols. 1 and 2. Berlin/Heidelberg/New York, 1967.

Long, M., Weil, P.,   *Les grands arrêts de la jurisprudence administrative* (8th
Braibant, G.   ed., Paris 1984).

Louis, J.-V.   *Die Rechtsordnung der Europäischen Gemeinschaften*, Brussels, 1980.

(ed.) *Régime juridique des relations entre les opérateurs écono-miques et les organismes d'exécution du droit commu-nautaire*, duplicated report, Brussels, 1982.

Maass, R. "Beamtenrechtliche Konkurrentenklage in Form der vorbeugenden Feststellungsklage", NJW 1985, p. 303.

MacCormick, D.N. "Der Rechtsstaat und die rule of law", JZ 1984, p. 65.

Mackenzie Stuart, Lord A.J. "Legitimate Expectations and Estoppel in Community Law and English Administrative Law", L.I.E.I. 1983/1, p. 53.

"Recent Developments in English Administrative Law—the Impact of Europe?" in: F. Capotorti *et al.* (eds.), *Du Droit international au droit de l'intégration. Liber Amicorum P. Pescatore*, Baden-Baden, 1987, p. 411.

The European Communities and the Rule of Law, London, 1977.

Mackenzie Stuart, Lord A.J., "Judicial Decision as a source of Community law", in:
Warner, J.P. *Festschrift für H. Kutscher*, Baden-Baden, 1981, p. 273.

Maiwald, B. "Rückwirkung im Europäischen Gemeinschaftsrecht", NJW 1983, p. 1951.

Majerus, P. *L'Etat Luxembourgeois*, Luxembourg, 1983.

Manitakis, A. "L'illicéité comme élément de la responsabilité de l'Etat en droit hellénique", in: Journées de la Société de Légis-lation Comparée 1984, p. 17.

Marcoux, L. "Le concept de droits fondamentaux dans le droit de la Communauté économique européenne", RIDC 1983, p. 691.

Marenco, G. "Pour une interprétation traditionnelle de la mesure d'effet équivalent à une restriction quantitative", CDE 1984, p. 291.

Mariuzzo, F. "Struktur und Wirkungskreis der italienischen Verwal-tungsgerichtsbarkeit", BayVBl 1984, p. 737.

Martens, J. "Die Rechtsprechung zum Verwaltungsverfahrens-recht", NVwZ 1985, p. 158.

Martens, W. "Tendenzen der Rechtsprechung zum Sofortvollzug der Zulassung von grosstechnischen Anlagen", DVBl. 1985, p. 541.

Mast, A., Dujardin, J. *Overzicht van het Belgisch Administratief Recht* (9th ed., Geneva 1984).

Mathijsen, P. "La Cour de Justice et les notions juridiques non préci-sées", KSE 1 (1965), p. 430.

Mathijsen, P.S.R.F. A guide to European Community Law (4th ed., London 1985).

Matthies, H. "Die Verfassung des Gemeinsamen Marktes", in: *Gedächtnisschrift für C. Sasse*, Vol. 1, Baden-Baden, 1981, p. 115.

Maunz, Th. "Selbstbindung der Verwaltung", DÖV 1981, p. 497.

Maurer, H. *Allgemeines Verwaltungsrecht* (5th ed., Munich 1986).

Max Planck Inst. f. ausländ. *Gerichtsschutz gegen die Exekutive*, 3 part-volumes,
öffentl. Recht u. Cologne/Berlin/New York, 1969.
Völkerrecht (ed.)

Haftung des Staates für rechtswidriges Verhalten seiner Organe, Länderberichte und Rechtsvergleichung, Cologne/Berlin, 1967.

Verfassungsgerichtsbarkeit in der Gegenwart, Länder-berichte und Rechtsvergleichung, Cologne/Berlin, 1962.

Mayer, F., Kopp, F.	*Allgemeines Verwaltungsrecht* (5th ed., Stuttgart/Munich 1985).
Mayer, O.	*Deutsches Verwaltungsrecht*, Vol. 1, Vol. 2 (3rd ed., Munich/Leipzig 1924).
	Theorie des französischen Verwaltungsrechts, Strasbourg, 1886.
Mayer-Tasch, P.-C., Contiades, I.	*Die Verfassungen der nicht-kommunistischen Staaten Europas* (2nd ed., Munich 1975).
Mayntz, R.	*Soziologie der öffentlichen Verwaltung*, Heidelberg/Karlsruhe, 1978.
Meessen, K.M.	"Zur Theorie allgemeiner Rechtsgrundsätze des internationalen Rechts: Der Nachweis allgemeiner Rechtsgrundsätze des Europäischen Gemeinschaftsrechts", JIR Vol. 17 (1974), p. 289.
Mégret, C.	"La politique agricole commune et le principe de non-discrimination dans la jurispurdence de la Cour de justice des Communautés européennes", RTDE 1979, p. 480.
	"Rapport général", FIDE *Rapports 12e Congrès*, I, Paris, 1986, p. 1.
von Meibom, H.	"Lückenfüllung bei den Europäischen Gemeinschaftsverträgen", NJW 1968, p. 2165.
Meier, G.	"Gemeinschaftsrecht und mitgliedstaatliches Gemeinrecht", EuR 1970, p. 324.
	"Rechtsschutzmöglichkeiten bei gemeinschaftsrechtswidrigen deutschen Rechtsnormen", RIW/AWD 1980, p. 850.
Meister, B.W.	*Ermessensmissbrauch oder détournement de pouvoir als Fehlertatbestand der Nichtigkeitsklage des Montanvertrages*, Bielefeld, 1971.
Melichar, E.	"Das Verwaltungsverfahren", VVDStRL 17 (1959), p. 183.
Menger, C.-F.	"Die allgemeinen Grundsätze des Verwaltungsrechts als Rechtsquellen", in: *Festschrift für W. Bogs*, Wiesbaden 1967, p. 89.
Mengozzi, P.	"Il giudice nazionale di fronte al diritto comunitario", Contratto e Impresa 1986, p. 792.
Menzel, E., Ipsen K.	*Völkerrecht* (2nd ed., Munich 1979).
Merk, W.	*Deutsches Verwaltungsrecht*, Vol. 1, Berlin, 1962.
Mertens de Wilmars, J.	"De Europese Gemeenschappen en het administratief recht", SEW 1962, p. 660.
	"Remedies for breach of Community Law", CDE 1981, p. 379.
Mestre, J.-L.	"Les fondements historiques du droit administratif français", in: Etudes et documents du Conseil d'Etat 1982–1983 (No. 34), p. 63.
Meyer, H., Borgs-Maciejewski, H.	*Verwaltungsverfahrensgesetz* (2nd ed., Frankfurt am Main 1982).
Meyer, K.F.	"Begleitende Verwaltungskontrolle—Eine Alternative zum nachträglichen Verwaltungsrechtsschutz?" in: B. Rüthers/K. Stern (eds.), *Freiheit und Verantwortung im Verfassungsstaat*, Munich, 1984, p. 67.
Meyer, P.	"Dänemark", in: E.V. Heyen (ed.), *Geschichte der Verwaltungsrechtswissenschaft in Europa*, Frankfurt, 1982, p. 19.

Meyn, K.-U.	*Die Verfassungskonventionalregeln in Verfassungssystem Grossbritanniens*, Göttingen, 1975.
Michelsen, N.	*Das rechtliche Gehör im Verwaltungsverfahren der Europäischen Gemeinschaften*, Diss. Hamburg, 1974.
Miclo, F.	"Le principe d'égalité et la constitutionnalité des lois", AJDA 1982, pp. 115 and 243.
Mitchell, J.D.B.	"Verwaltungskontrolle in Grossbritannien", Verw-Archiv 1973, p. 163.
Mössner, J.M.	"Rechtsvergleichung und Verfassungsrechtsprechung", AöR 99 (1974), p. 192.
Monaco, R.	*Lineamenti di diritto pubblico europeo* (2nd ed., Milan 1975).
Morgan, D.G.	*Constitutional Law of Ireland*, Dublin, 1985.
Mortelmans, K.J.	"Omgekeerde discriminatie en het gemeenschapsrecht", SEW 1979, p. 654.
Mosler, H., Bernhardt, R. (eds.)	*Grundrechtsschutz in Europa—Europäische Menschenrechts-Konvention und Europäische Gemeinschaften*, Berlin/Heidelberg/New York, 1977.
Müller, M.	"Erstattung und Erlass von Eingangs- und Ausfuhrabgaben nach neuem Gemeinschaftsrecht", Zeitschrift für Zölle und Verbrauchssteuern 1979, p. 290. "Nacherhebung von Eingangs- und Ausfuhrabgaben", in: Rudolf Regul (ed.), *Gemeinschaftszollrecht*, Baden-Baden, 1982, p. 1351. "Nacherhebung von Eingangs- und Ausfuhrabgaben nach neuem Gemeinschaftsrecht", Zeitschrift für Zölle und Verbrauchssteuern 1980, p. 98.
Müller-Graff, P.-Chr.	"Privatrecht und europäisches Gemeinschaftsrecht", in: P.-Chr. Müller-Graff/M. Zuleeg (eds.), *Staat und Wirtschaft in der EG, Kolloquium zum 65. Geburtstag von Bodo Börner*, Baden-Baden, 1987, p. 17.
Münch, F.	"Einführung in die Verfassungsvergleichung", ZaöRV 33 (1973), p. 126.
v. Münch, I. (ed.)	*Grundgesetz-Kommentar*, Vol. 1 (3rd ed., Munich 1985).
Mussgnug, R.	"Das allgemeine Verwaltungsrecht zwischen Richterrecht und Gesetzesrecht", in: *Festschrift der Juristischen Fakultät zur 600-Jahr-Feier der Ruprecht-Karls-Universität Heidelberg*, Heidelberg, 1986, p. 203.
Nauwelaers, M., Fabius, L.	"Chronique générale de jurisprudence administrative française", AJDA 1976, p. 557.
Nerep, E.	*Extraterritorial Control of Competition under International Law*, Stockholm, 1983, Vols. 1 and 2.
Neville Brown, L., Jacobs, F.G.	*The Court of Justice of the European Communities*, London, 1977.
Nicolaysen, G.	*Europäisches Gemeinschaftsrecht*, Stuttgart/Berlin/Cologne/Mainz, 1979. "Wirtschaftsfreiheit", in: *Das Europa der zweiten Generation, Gedächtnisschrift für C. Sasse*, Strasbourg, 1981, p. 651. "Zur Theorie von den Implied Powers in den Europäischen Gemeinschaften", EuR 1966, p. 129.
Nicholaysen, G., Rabe, H.-J. (eds.)	*Europäische Gemeinschaft. Verfassung nach drei Jahrzehnten*, Baden-Baden, 1982.
Nielsen, G.T.	"Constitutional and Administrative Law", in: Hans Gammeltoft-Hansen, Bernhard Gomard, Alan Philip

	(eds.), *Danish Law—A general survey*, Copenhagen, 1982.
Nørgaard, C.A.	"The principle of equality in Danish administrative law", Scandinavian studies in law 1967, p. 241.
Odent, R.	*Contentieux administratif*, Paris, 1970–1971.
von Oertzen, H.-J.	"Zur erstinstanzlichen Zuständigkeit des OVG nach dem Beschleunigungsgesetz", DÖV 1985, p. 749.
Oliver, P.	"A review of the case law of the Court of Justice on Art. 30 to 36 EEC in 1984", (1985) C.M.L.Rev. 301.
Olmi, G.	"Les hautes juridictions nationales, juges du droit communautaire", in: *Liber amicorum P. Pescatore*, Baden-Baden, 1987, p. 499.
Ophüls, C.-F.	"Die Geltungsnormen des Europäischen Gemeinschaftsrechts", in: *Festschrift für O. Riese*, Karlsruhe, 1964, p. 1.
	"Quellen und Aufbau des Europäischen Gemeinschaftsrechts", NJW 1963, p. 1697.
Oppermann, T.	"Europäische Wirtschaftsverfassung nach der Einheitlichen Europäischen Akte", in: *Staat und Wirtschaft in der EG, Kolloquium zum 65. Geburtstag von B. Börner*, Baden-Baden, 1987, p. 53.
O'Reilly, J.	"The Interaction between Community Law and National Law: Irish Report", FIDE *Rapports 12e Congrès* I, Paris, 1986, p. 167.
Ortlepp, B. Chr.	*Das Vertragsverletzungsverfahren als Instrument zur Sicherung der Legalität im Europäischen Gemeinschaftsrecht*, Baden-Baden, 1987.
Ossenbühl, F.	"Die gerichtliche Überprüfung der Beurteilung technischer und wirtschaftlicher Fragen in Genehmigungen des Baus von Kraftwerken", DVBl. 1978, p. 1.
	"Die Quellen des Verwaltungsrechts", in: Erichsen, H.-U., Martens, W. (eds.), *Allgemeines Verwaltungsrecht* (8th ed., Berlin/New York 1988), p. 63.
	"Grundrechtsschutz im und durch Verfahrensrecht", in: *Festschrift für Kurt Eichenberger*, Basle/Frankfurt a.M., 1982, p. 183.
	Richterrecht im demokratischen Rechtsstaat, Bonn, 1988.
	"Verwaltungsverfahren zwischen Verwaltungseffizienz und Rechtsschutzauftrag", NVwZ 1982, p. 465.
	"Zum Problem der Rücknahme fehlerhafter begünstigender Verwaltungsakte", DÖV 1964, p. 511.
	"Zumutbarkeit als Verfassungsmassstab", in: *Festgabe zum 10. Jubiläum der Gesellschaft für Rechtspolitik*, Munich, 1984, p. 315.
Pactet, P.	*Institutions politiques—Droit constitutionnel* (7th ed., Paris 1985).
Palauro, R.	*Haftungsrelevante Probleme der allgemeinen verwaltungsrechtlichen Zusage*, Konstanz, 1983.
Panagopoulos, T.I.	"Das Verwaltungsverfahrensrecht in Griechenland", DVBl. 1977, p. 154.
	"Griechenland", in: E.V. Heyen (ed.), *Geschichte der Verwaltungsrechtswissenschaft in Europa*, Frankfurt, 1982, p. 81.
Papier, H.-J.	"Zur verwaltungsgerichtlichen Kontrolldichte", DÖV 1986, p. 621.

Pavlopoulos, P., Calogeropoulos, A., Lytras, S.	"Les recours administratifs et le recours pour excès de pouvoir en droit grec", in: *Annuaire européen d'administration publique* I, 1978, p. 437. "Les structures de l'administration centrale grecque", in: *Annuaire européen d'administration publique* I, 1978, p. 446. "Procédure administrative non contentieuse et problèmes juridiques en Grèce", *Annuaire européen d'administration publique* I, 1978, p. 427.
Peiser, G.	*Droit administratif* (10th ed., Paris 1981).
La Pergola, A., Del Duca, P.	"Community Law, International Law and the Italian Constitution", AJIL 79 (1985), p. 598.
Pernice, I.	*Grundrechtsgehalte im Europäischen Gemeinschaftsrecht*, Baden-Baden, 1979. "Verfassungsentwurf für eine Europäische Union", EuR 1984, p. 126.
Pescatore, P.	"Abschied vom Gerichtshof der Europäischen Gemeinschaften", EuR 1985, p. 401. "Bestand und Bedeutung der Grundrechte in den Europäischen Gemeinschaften", EuGRZ 1978, p. 441. "Das Zusammenwirken der Gemeinschaftsrechtsordnung und der nationalen Rechtsordnungen", EuR 1970, p. 307. "Die 'Einheitliche Europäische Akte'—Eine ernste Gefahr für den Gemeinsamen Markt", EuR 1986, p. 153. "Die Menschenrechte und die europäische Integration", Integration 2/69, p. 103. *Introduction à la science du droit*, Luxembourg, 1960. "La carence du législateur et le devoir du juge", in: *Gedächtnisschrift für L.-J. Constantinesco*, Cologne/Berlin/Bonn/Munich, 1983, p. 559. "L'application judiciaire des traités internationaux dans la Communauté européenne et dans ses Etats membres", in: *Mélanges offerts à Pierre-Henri Teitgen*, Paris, 1984, p. 355. "Le recours dans la jurisprudence de la Cour de justice des Communautés européennes, à des normes déduites de la comparaison des droits des Etats membres", RIDC 1980, p. 337. "Les droits de l'homme et l'intégration européenne", CDE 1968, p. 629. "L'exécutif communautaire: justification du quadripartisme institué par les traités de Paris et de Rome", CDE 1978, p. 387. *L'ordre juridique des Communautés européennes—Etudes des sources du droit communautaire*, Liège, 1975.
Peters, H.	*Lehrbuch der Verwaltung*, Berlin/Göttingen/Heidelberg, 1949.
Petzold, H.	*Die Gewaltenteilung in den Europäischen Gemeinschaften*, Göttingen, 1966.
Philip, J.	"EEC Competition Law and Privilege against self-incrimination in English Law", L.I.E.I. 1981, p. 49.
Pieroth, B.	"Die neuere Rechtsprechung des BVerfG zum Grundsatz des Vertrauensschutzes, JZ 1984, pp. 568 and 971.

1498

	"Interpretationsproblem § 48 IV VwVfG", NVwZ 1984, p. 681.
Pietzcker, J.	"Das Verwaltungsverfahren zwischen Verwaltungseffizienz und Rechtsschutzauftrag", VVDStRL 41 (1983) p. 193.
van der Pot, C.W.	*Handboek van het Nederlandse Staatsrecht*, revised by A.M. Donner (11th ed., Zwolle 1983).
Poulitsas, M.	"L'influence de l'institution du Conseil d'Etat français sur le Conseil d'Etat hellénique", in: *Le Conseil d'Etat, Livre jubilaire*, Paris, 1952, p. 539.
Prechal, S., Heukels, T.	"Algemene beginselen in het Nederlandse recht en het Europese recht: rechtsvergelijking en interactie", SEW 1986, p. 287.
Priebe, R.	*Entscheidungsbefugnisse vertragsfremder Einrichtungen im Europäischen Gemeinschaftsrecht*, Baden-Baden, 1979.
Püttner, G.	"Der Schutz wohlerworbener Rechte im Gemeinschaftsrecht", EuR 1975, p. 218.
Quadri, R., Monaco, R., Trabucchi, A.	*Trattato istitutivo della comunità europea del carbone e dell'acciaio (Commentario)*, Milan, 1970.
de Quadros, F.	"Portugal", in: E.V. Heyen (ed.), *Geschichte der Verwaltungsrechtswissenschaft in Europa*, Frankfurt/Main, 1982, p. 161.
Quintin, O.	"L'égalité entre hommes et femmes: une réalisation spécifique de la politique sociale communautaire", RMC 1985, p. 309.
Rabe, H.-J.	*Die Befugnis des Rates und der Kommission der Europäischen Wirtschaftsgemeinschaft zum Erlass von Verordnungen*, Hamburg, 1962.
	"Garantien und Sicherungen des freien Warenverkehrs im Lichte der neuesten Rechtsprechung des EuGH", in: J. Schwarze (ed.), *Das Wirtschaftsrecht des Gemeinsamen Marktes in der aktuellen Rechtsentwicklung*, Baden-Baden, 1983, p. 41.
Rack, B., Wimmer, N.	"Das Gleichheitsrecht in Österreich", EuGRZ 1983, p. 597.
Radbruch, G.	*Rechtsphilosophie* (5th ed., Stuttgart 1956).
Rahn, H.-G.	"Zum Recht der Ausfuhrerstattungen", RIW/AWD 1980, p. 563.
Rasmussen, H.	*On law and policy in the European Court of Justice*, Dordrecht, 1986.
	"Über die Durchsetzung des Gemeinschaftsrechts in Dänemark", EuR 1985, p. 66.
Reckhorn-Hengemühle, M.	*Der spanische "recurso de amparo" und die deutsche Verfassungsbeschwerde*, Diss. jur. Osnabrück, 1987.
Redeker, K., v. Oertzen, H.-J.	*Verwaltungsgerichtsordnung—Kommentar* (8th ed., Berlin/Cologne/Mainz 1985).
Regul, R.	*Gemeinschaftszollrecht*, Baden-Baden, 1982.
Reiners, E.	"Die Normenhierarchie in den Gründerstaaten der Europäischen Gemeinmschaften", JöR 23 (1974), p. 1. *Die Normenhierarchie in den Mitgliedstaaten der Europäischen Gemeinschaften* (2 vols.), Hamburg, 1971.
Reinicke, G.	"Der Gerichtshof und unbestimmte Rechtsbegriffe", in: *Zehn Jahre Rechtsprechung des Gerichtshofs der Europäischen Gemeinschaften*, KSE Vol. 1, 1965, p. 418.

Reischl, G.

"Die Funktion der Generalanwälte in der Europäischen Rechtsprechung", in: J. Schwarze (ed.), *Der Europäische Gerichtshof als Verfassungsgericht und Rechtsschutzinstanz*, Baden-Baden, 1983, p. 121.
"Ansätze zur Herausbildung eines europäischen Verwaltungsrechts in der Rechtsprechung des EuGH—Bestandsaufnahme, Einfluss der unterschiedlichen nationalen Rechtsvorstellungen", in: J. Schwarze (ed.), *Europäisches Verwaltungsrecht im Werden*, Baden-Baden, 1982, p. 97.

Reitmaier, M.A.

Inländerdiskriminierung nach dem EWG-Vertrag, Kehl a. Rh./Strasbourg, 1984.

Rengeling, H.-W.

"Das Zusammenwirken von Europäischem Gemeinschaftsrecht und nationalem, insbesondere deutschem Recht—zu verwaltungsrechtlichen und prozessrechtlichen Fragen—", DVBl. 1986, p. 306.
"Die Entwicklung verwaltungsrechtlicher Grundsätze durch den Gerichtshof der Europäischen Gemeinschaften", EuR 1984, p. 331.
"Fragen zum allgemeinen Verwaltungsrecht in der Europäischen Gemeinschaft", in: *Festschrift fur H.U. Scupin*, Berlin, 1983, p. 475.
"Verwaltungsverfahrens- und Verwaltungsprozessrecht im Verhältnis zum Europäischen Gemeinschaftsrecht", DÖV 1981, p. 366.
Gemeinschaftsrecht und nationaler Rechtsschutz, *Gedächtnisschrift für Chr. Sasse*, Vol. 1, Baden-Baden, 1981, p. 197.
Rechtsgrundsätze beim Verwaltungsvollzug des Europäischen Gemeinschaftsrechts, KSE Vol. 27, Cologne/ Berlin/Bonn/Munich, 1977.
"Nationaler Verwaltungsvollzug von Gemeinschaftsrecht: Die Gemeinschaftskompetenzen", EuR 1974, p. 216.

Rescigno, P. (ed.)

Trattato di diritto privato, Vol. 1, Turin, 1987.

Ress, G.

"Der Grundsatz der Verhältnismässigkeit im deutschen Recht", in: Kutscher, Hans *et al.* (eds.), *Der Grundsatz der Verhältnismässigkeit in europäischen Rechtsordnungen*, Heidelberg, 1985, p. 5.
"Die Bedeutung der Rechtsvergleichung für das Recht internationaler Organisationen", ZaöRV 36 (1976), p. 227.
"Der Conseil Constitutionnel und der Schutz der Grundfreiheiten in Frankreich", JÖR NF Vol. 23 (1974), p. 122.
Grenzüberschreitende Verfahrensbeteiligung im Umweltrecht der Mitgliedstaaten der Europäischen Gemeinschaften, Cologne/Berlin/Bonn/Munich, 1985.
"Wichtige Vorlagen deutscher Verwaltungsgerichte an den Gerichtshof der Europäischen Gemeinschaften", Die Verwaltung 1987, p. 177.

Rheinstein, M.

Einführung in die Rechtsvergleichung (2nd ed., Munich 1987).

Richer, L.

"Des droits du juge à ceux du justiciable", AJDA 1986, p. 278.

Rideau, J.

"Le rôle des Etats membres dans l'application du droit communautaire", in: Annuaire français de droit international XVIII (1972), p. 864.

Riedel, E.H.

Kontrolle der Verwaltung im englischen Rechtssystem, Berlin, 1976.

Riegel, R.

"Aktuelle Fragen des gemeinschaftsrechtlichen Verfahrens- und Haftungsrechts unter besonderer Berücksichtigung der neueren Rechtsprechung des EuGH", DVBl. 1978, p. 469.
"Zum Problem der allgemeinen Rechtsgrundsätze und Grundrechte im Gemeinschaftsrecht", NJW 1974, p. 1585.

Rinck, H.-J.

"Tendenzen in der Rechtsprechung europäischer Verfassungsgerichte zum Gleichheitssatz", DVBl. 1961, p. 1.

Ritterspach, T.

"Probleme der italienischen Verfassungsgerichtsbarkeit; 20 Jahre Corte Costituzionale", AöR 104 (1979), p. 137.

Rittner, F.

Wirtschaftsrecht (2nd ed., Heidelberg 1987).

Rivero, J.

Droit administratif (11th ed., Paris 1985).
"Vers un droit commun européen: nouvelles perspectives en droit administratif", in: M. Cappelletti (ed.), *New Perspectives for a common law of Europe*, Florence, 1978, p. 398.

Rix-Mackenthun, Ch.

Die Funktion des britischen Parlaments und die Mitgliedschaft in den Europäischen Gemeinschaften. Zur Bedeutung der Parlamentssouveränität für die britische Verfassungsordnung und der Vorrang des EG-Rechts, Frankfurt, 1984.

Robert, J.

"Conseil d'Etat und Conseil constitutionnel", RDP 1987, p. 1151.

Robinson, G.O., Gellhorn, E., Bruff, H.H.

The administrative process (2nd ed., St. Paul Minn. 1980).

Rodriguez Iglesias, G.C., Wölker, U.

"Derecho Comunitario, Derechos Fundamentales Y Control De Constitucionalidad", Revista de Instituciones Europeas 1987, p. 667.

Rogalla, D.

Dienstrecht der Europäischen Gemeinschaften, Cologne/Berlin/Bonn/Munich, 1981.

Rogers, W.V.H.

Tort (12th ed., London 1984).

Rolland, L.

Précis de droit administratif (11th ed., Paris 1957).

Ross, A.

Theorie der Rechtsquellen, Ein Beitrag zur Theorie des positiven Rechts auf der Grundlage dogmenhistorischer Untersuchungen, Leipzig/Vienna, 1929.

Rothenbücher, N.

Verwaltungsrechtsschutz in den Niederlanden. Zur Entstehung einer allgemeinen Verwaltungsgerichtsbarkeit mit vergleichenden Anmerkungen zum deutschen Recht, Heidelberg, 1978.

Rott, M.

Das verwaltungsrechtliche subjektive öffentliche Recht im Spiegel seiner Entwicklung im deutschen liberalen Rechtsstaat in der französischen "théorie des droits subjectifs des administrés", Diss. Giessen, 1976.

Rouquette, R.

"Chronique de l'actualité du droit public économique: la maîtrise d'ouvrage publique", AJDA 1985, p. 596.

Rousseau, Ch.

Droit international public, Vol. IV—*Les relations internationales*, Paris, 1980.

1501

Rüber, H.-J.   *Der Gerichtshof der Europäischen Gemeinschaften und die Konkretisierung allgemeiner Rechtsgrundsätze*, Cologne, 1970.

Rüping, H.   "Verfassungs- und Verfahrensrecht im Grundsatz des rechtlichen Gehörs", NVwZ 1985, p. 304.

Ruiter, D.W.P.   "Die niederländische Kommunalverfassung", DVBl. 1983, p. 658.

Rupp, H.H.   "Art. 3 GG als Massstab verfassungsgerichtlicher Gesetzeskontrolle", in: Christian Starck (ed.), *Bundesverfassungsgericht und Grundgesetz—Festgabe aus Anlass des 25jährigen Bestehens des Bundesverfassungsgerichts*, Vol. II, Tübingen, 1976. p. 364.
Grundfragen der heutigen Verwaltungsrechtslehre, Tübingen, 1965.

Rupprecht, W.   *Die Nachprüfungsbefugnis des Europäischen Gerichtshofes gegenüber Ermessensentscheidungen der Exekutive in der Montanunion und in der Europäischen Wirtschaftsgemeinschaft*, Kiel, 1962.

Sachs, M.   "Zur dogmatischen Struktur der Gleichheitsrechte als Abwehrrechte", DÖV 1984, p. 411.

Sandulli, A.M.   *Manuale di Diritto Amministrativo*, Vols. 1 and 2 (14th ed., Naples 1984).

Santamaria Pastor, J.A.   *Sobre la génesis del Derecho Administrativo español en el siglo XIX (1812–1845)*, 1973.

Saripoulos, N.N.   *Das Staatsrecht des Königreichs Griechenland*, Tübingen, 1909.

Scarman, Lord L.   "The shifting state: public administration in a time of change", Public administration 63 (1985), p. 1.
English Law—The New Dimension, London, 1974.

Schachtschneider, K.-A.   "Das Rechtsstaatsprinzip des Grundgesetzes", JA (ÖR) 1978, p. 185.

Schack, F.   "Analogie und Verwendung allgemeiner Rechtsgrundsätze bei der Ausfüllung von Lücken in den Normen des Verwaltungsrechts", in: *Festschrift fur R. Laun*, Hamburg, 1948, p. 275.

Scharpf, F.   *Die politischen Kosten des Rechtsstaats*, Tübingen, 1970.

Schechter, M.C.   "The rule of reason in European Competition Law", L.I.E.I. 1982, p. 1.

Scheffler, H.-H.   *Die Pflicht zur Begründung von Massnahmen nach den Europäischen Gemeinschaftsverträgen*, Berlin, 1974.

Scheltema, M.   "Enkele gedachten over het vertrouwensbeginsel in het publiekrecht", RMT (Rechtgeleerd Magazijn Themis) 1984, p. 538.

Scherer, J.   "Das Rechnungsabschlussverfahren—Ein Instrument zur Durchsetzung europäischen Verwaltungsrechts?", EuR 1986, p. 52.

Schermers, H.G.   "Algemene rechtsbeginselen als bron van gemeenschapsrecht", SEW 1983, p. 514.
Judicial Protection in the European Communities (3rd ed., Deventer 1983).

Scheuing, D.H.   "Rechtsprobleme bei der Durchsetzung des Gemeinschaftsrechts in der Bundesrepublik Deutschland", EuR 1985, p. 229.

Scheuner, U.   "Der Einfluss des französischen Verwaltungsrechts auf die deutsche Rechtsentwicklung", DÖV 1963, p. 714.

	"Die Einwirkung der verfassungsrechtlichen Feststellung der Nichtigkeit von Rechtsnormen auf vorgängige Hoheitsakte", BB 1960, p. 1253.
Schiller, K.-V.	"Weisungsrecht der EG nach dem EWG-Vertrag bei nationalem Verwaltungsvollzug von EG-Recht", RIW/AWD 1985, p. 36.
	"Der Verhältnismässigkeitsgrundsatz im Europäischen Gemeinschaftsrecht nach der Rechtsprechung des EuGH", RIW/AWD 1985, p. 928.
Schilling, T.	"Die Anhörungsregelung des Verwaltungsverfahrensgesetzes im Lichte des Grundgesetzes", VerwArchiv 1987, p. 45.
Schindler, P.	"Zur Problematik der Ermächtigung einzelner Mitglieder und Beamter der Kommission der Europäischen Wirtschaftsgemeinschaft (EWG) bzw. der Europäischen Gemeinschaften (EG) zum Erlass von Verordnungen auf agrarrechtlichem Gebiet", DVBl. 1970, p. 605.
Schlachter, H.	*Discrimination à rebours. Die Inländerdiskriminierung nach der Rechtsprechung des EuGH und des französischen Conseil d'Etat*, 1984.
Schlockermann, M.	*Rechtssicherheit als Vertrauensschutz in der Rechtsprechung des EuGH*, Munich, 1984.
Schmidt, W.	"Die Verwaltungsgerichtsbarkeit an den Grenzen des Verwaltungsrechtsschutzes", NJW 1978, p. 1769.
Schmidt-Assmann, E.	"Funktionen der Verwaltungsgerichtsbarkeit", in: *Festschrift für C.-F. Menger*, Cologne/Berlin/Bonn/Munich, 1985, p. 107.
	Das allgemeine Verwaltungsrecht als Ordnungsidee und System, Heidelberg, 1982.
	"Verwaltungsverantwortung und Verwaltungsgerichtsbarkeit", VVDStRL 34 (1976), p. 221.
Schmidt-Eichstaedt, G.	"Der Konkretisierungsauftrag der Verwaltung beim Vollzug öffentlich-rechtlicher Normen", DVBl. 1985, p. 645.
Schmidt-Salzer, J.	*Der Beurteilungsspielraum der Verwaltungsbehörden*, Berlin, 1968.
Schmitthoff, C.M.	"The Doctrines of Proportionality and Non-Discrimination", (1977) E.L.Rev. 329.
Schnapp, F.E.	"Die Verhältnismässigkeit des Grundrechtseingriffs", JuS 1983, p. 850.
Schneider, H.	*Gesetzgebung*, Heidelberg, 1982.
Schnitzler, A.F.	*Vergleichende Rechtslehre* (2nd ed., Basle 1961).
Schoch, C.	*Methode und Kriterien der Konkretisierung offener Normen durch die Verwaltung. Eine Untersuchung von Theorie und Praxis*, Zürich, 1984.
Schoch, F.K.	"Nachholen der Begründung und Nachschieben von Gründen", DÖV 1984, p. 401.
Schott, E.	*Der Begründungszwang für Akte der Exekutiven der Europäischen Gemeinschaften*, Saarbrücken, 1971.
Schrimpf, D.	*Die ergänzende Anwendung des nationalen Rechts bei der Effektuierung des Gemeinschaftsrechts durch die Mitgliedstaaten, dargestellt am Beispiel der Nacherhebung von gemeinschaftsrechtswidrig nicht erhobenen*

	Geldleistungen und der Rückforderung gemeinschafts-rechtswidrig gewährter Geldzahlungen, Würzburg, 1983.
Schröder, M.	"Zwischenbilanz zum Streikrecht der Europäischen Beamten—zugleich ein Beitrag zu den Rechtsquellen des Europäischen Gemeinschaftsrechts", ZBR 1984, p. 1.
	"Plangewährleistung im europäischen Gemeinschafts-recht", NJW 1979, p. 1729.
Schulte, B.	"Auf dem Weg zu einem Europäischen Sozialrecht? Der Beitrag des EuGH zur Entwicklung des Sozialrechts in der Gemeinschaft", EuR 1982, p. 357.
Schunck, E., De Clerck, H.	*Allgemeines Staatsrecht und Staatsrecht des Bundes und der Länder* (12th ed., Siegburg 1986).
Schwabe, J.	"Das Wiederaufgreifen unanfechtbarer Verwaltung-sakte", JZ 1985, p. 545.
Schwaiger, H.	"Mitgliedstaatliche Verfassungsmässigkeit und sekun-däres Gemeinschaftsrecht", AWD/RIW 1972, p. 265.
Schwartz, B.	*Administrative Law* (2nd ed., Boston/Toronto 1984).
Schwartz, B., Wade, H.W.R.	*Legal Control of Government—Administrative Law in Britain and the United States*, Oxford, 1972.
Schwartz, I.E.	"EG-Rechtsetzungsbefugnisse, insbesondere nach Arti-kel 235—ausschliesslich oder konkurrierend?", EuR 1976, special issue, p. 27.
Schwarz, O.	"Ungeregelte Fragen der unmittelbaren Anwendung der am 1.7.1980 in Kraft getretenen EWG VO Nr. 1697/79", RIW/AWD 1980, p. 481.
Schwarze, J.	"Administrative Leistungsfähigkeit als verwaltungs-rechtliches Problem", DÖV 1980, p. 581.
	"Das allgemeine Völkerrecht in den innergemeinschaft-lichen Rechtsbeziehungen", EuR 1983, p. 1.
	"Das Verhältnis von deutschem Verfassungsrecht und europäischem Gemeinschaftsrecht auf dem Gebiet des Grundrechtsschutzes im Spiegel der jüngsten Recht-sprechung", in: *Festschrift für Werner von Simson*, Baden-Baden, 1983, p. 343.
(ed.)	*Das Wirtschaftsrecht des Gemeinsamen Marktes in der aktuellen Rechtsentwicklung*, Baden-Baden, 1983.
(ed.)	*Der Europäische Gerichtshof als Verfassungsgericht und Rechtsschutzinstanz*, Baden-Baden, 1983.
	Der funktionale Zusammenhang von Verwaltungsver-fahrensrecht und verwaltungsgerichtlichem Rechts-schutz, Berlin, 1974.
	"Der Schutz des Gemeinschaftsbürgers durch allge-meine Verwaltungsrechtsgrundsätze im EG-Recht", NJW 1986, p. 1067.
	"Der vorläufige Rechtsschutz (sursis à exécution) im französischen Verwaltungsrecht—Rechtsgrundlagen und Rechtsprechungspraxis im Vergleich zum deut-schen Verwaltungsrecht—", DVBl. 1987, p. 1037.
	Die Befugnis zur Abstraktion im europäischen Gemein-schaftsrecht—Eine Untersuchung zur Rechtsprechung des EuGH, Baden-Baden, 1976.
	"Diskriminierung bei der Vergabe öffentlicher Aufträge aus der Sicht des Gemeinschaftsrechts", in: *Öffentliche*

	Aufträge und Forschungspolitik, Baden-Baden, 1986, p. 79.
	"Entwicklungsstufen des Europäischen Gemeinschaftsrechts", in: *Festschrift für Karl Carstens*, Cologne/Berlin/Bonn/Munich, 1984, p. 259.
(ed.)	*Europäisches Verwaltungsrecht im Werden*, Baden-Baden, 1982.
	"Funktionen des Rechts in der Europäischen Gemeinschaft", in: J. Schwarze (ed.), *Gesetzgebung in der Europäischen Gemeinschaft*, Baden-Baden, 1985, p. 9.
	"Grenzen für die Ermittlungstätigkeit der Kommission als Wettbewerbsbehörde der EG, in: J. Schwarze (ed.), *Der Gemeinsame Markt—Bestand und Zukunft in wirtschaftsrechtlicher Perspektive*, Baden-Baden, 1987, p. 159.
	"Rechtsschutz gegen Anti-Dumpingmassnahmen der EG", Europarecht 1986, p. 217.
	"Rechtsschutz Privater gegenüber normativen Rechtsakten im Recht der EWG", in: *Festschrift für H.-J. Schlochauer*, Berlin/New York, 1981, p. 927.
	"Schutz der Grundrechte in der Europäischen Gemeinschaft—Grundlagen und heutiger Entwicklungsstand", EuGRZ 1986, p. 293.
	"The Administrative Law of the Community and the Protection of Human Rights", (1986) C.M.L.Rev. 401.
	"Zum Nutzen einer Systembildung für die Kontrolle der Staatsgewalt", DVBl. 1974, p. 893.
Schweitzer, M.	"Die Verwaltung der Europäischen Gemeinschaften", Die Verwaltung 1984, p. 137.
Sedemund, J.	"Allgemeine Prinzipien des Verwaltungsverfahrensrechts—dargestellt am Beispiel des europäischen Verwaltungsverfahrensrechts in Kartellsachen", in: J. Schwarze (ed.), *Europäisches Verwaltungsrecht im Werden*, Baden-Baden, 1982, p. 45.
	"Europäisches Gemeinschaftsrecht", NJW 1984, p. 1268.
	"Europäisches Gemeinschaftsrecht", NJW 1986, p. 632.
Seidel, M.	"Das Verwaltungsverfahren in Beihilfesachen", EuR 1985, p. 21.
Seidler, H.-H.	*Rechtsschutz bei staatlicher Wirtschaftsplanung*, Berlin, 1973.
Sendler, H.	"Die Entwicklung des Verwaltungsrechts in der Bundesrepublik Deutschland", in: J.H. Kaiser (ed.), *Verwaltung und Verwaltungswissenschaften in der Bundesrepublik Deutschland*, Baden-Baden, 1983, p. 27.
	"Die öffentliche Verwaltung zwischen Scylla und Charybdis", NJW 1986, p. 1084.
	"Richterrecht—rechtstheoretisch und rechtspraktisch", NJW 1987, p. 3240.
Serrano Guirado, E.	"El trámite de audiencia en el procedimiento administrativo", Revista de Administración Pública, No. 4/1951, p. 129.
Shapiro, M.	"Administrative Discretion", The Yale Law Journal 1983, p. 1487.

Siedentopf, H.

"Vergleichende Anmerkungen zur Ausbildung des Füh-rungsnachwuchses der Verwaltung", DÖV 1984, p. 529.

von Simson, W.

"Anforderungen an die Rechtmässigkeit des Verwal-tungshandelns der EG-Behörden—Erfahrungen aus Prozessen vor dem EuGH", in: J. Schwarze (ed.), *Europäisches Verwaltungsrecht im Werden*, Baden-Baden, 1982, p. 23.

"Das Common Law als Verfassungsrecht", Der Staat 16 (1977), p. 75.

" 'Das Recht' in den Europäischen Gemeinschaften", in: *Festschrift für Hans von der Groeben*, Baden-Baden, 1987, p. 391.

Skadhauge, J.K.

Danish report on general principles derived from the law of member states as source of Community law and national law, FIDE 1986.

Skouris, W.

"Französisches Verwaltungsprozessrecht", DVBl. 1978, p. 945.

"Les incidences de la constitution hellénique de 1975 sur le droit administratif", RDP 1982, p. 113.

"L'illégalité de l'action administrative comme fonde-ment de la responsabilité de la puissance publique en Grèce", in: Journées de la Société de Législation Com-parée 1984, p. 51.

Verletztenklagen und Interessentenklagen im Verwal-tungsprozess, Cologne/Berlin/Bonn/Munich, 1979.

Slynn, Sir G.

" 'But in England there is no ...' " in: *Festschrift für Wolfgang Zeidler*, Berlin/New York, 1987, Vol. 1, p. 397.

"Statement", in: J. Schwarze/R. Bieber (eds.), *Eine Verfassung für Europa*, Baden-Baden, 1984, p. 121.

Smith, L.J.

"A European Concept of Condictio Indebiti?" (1982) C.M.L.Rev. 269.

de Smith, S.A.

"The Right to a Hearing in English Administrative Law", Harvard Law Review 68 (1955), p. 569.

de Smith, S.A., Evans, J.M.

Judicial Review of Administrative Action (4th ed., London 1980).

de Smith, S.A., Street, H., Brazier, R.

Constitutional and Administrative Law (4th ed., Har-mondsworth (Middlesex) 1981), (reprinted 1983).

Soell, H.

Das Ermessen der Eingriffsverwaltung, Heidelberg, 1973.

Söllner, R.

Art. 5 EWGV in der Rechtsprechung des Europäischen Gerichtshofes, Munich, 1985.

Sørensen, M.

"Autonomous legal orders: Some considerations relat-ing to a system's analysis of international organisations in the world legal order", I.C.L.Q. 32 (1983), p. 559.

Somerhausen, M.

"Les principes généraux du droit administratif", in: *Per-spectivas del Derecho Público en la segunda mitad del siglo XX, Homenaje a E. Sayagues-Laso*, Vol. 4, Madrid, 1969, p. 464.

Sommermann, K.-P.

"Der Defensor del Pueblo: ein spanischer Ombuds-man", AöR 1985, p. 267.

Der Schutz der Grundrechte in Spanien nach der Verfas-sung von 1978. Ursprünge, Dogmatik, Praxis, Berlin, 1984.

Spiliotopoulos, E. "Les compétences du pouvoir local en Grèce", in: Annuaire européen d'administration publique III (1980), p. 267.

Sprung, R., König, B. (eds.) *Entscheidungsbegründung*, Vienna/New York, 1974.

Stadler, R. *Die Berufsfreiheit in der EWG*, Munich, 1980.

Stahl, K. *Die Sicherung der Grundfreiheiten im öffentlichen Recht der Fünften Französischen Republik*, Hamburg, 1970.

Starck, C. "Die Anwendung des Gleichheitssatzes", in: Christoph Link (ed.), *Der Gleichheitssatz im modernen Verfassungsstaat*, Baden-Baden, 1982, p. 51.

Stassinopoulos, M. *Le droit de la défense devant les autorités administratives*, Paris, 1976.
Traité des actes administratifs, Paris, 1954.
"Long, M., Weil, P., Braibant, G.—*Les grands arrêts de la jurisprudence administrative*", RDP 1970, p. 820.

Steenblock, W. "Anmerkungen zum Urteil des BayVGH v. 20.5.1983, Rücknahme eines rechtswidrigen begünstigenden Verwaltungsaktes", DÖV 1984, p. 216.

Stein, Ekkehart *Staatsrecht* (10th ed., Tubingen 1986).

Stein, Eric "Lawyers, Judges and the Making of a Transnational Constitution", AJIL 75 (1981), p. 1.

von Stein, L. *Die Verwaltungslehre*, 8 parts in 10 volumes (1st–2nd eds., Stuttgart 1866–1884), reprinted: Aalen, 1962.

Steinberg, R. "Komplexe Verwaltungsverfahren zwischen Verwaltungseffizienz und Rechtsschutzauftrag", DÖV 1982, p. 619.

Steindorff, E. *Der Gleichheitssatz im Wirtschaftsrecht des Gemeinsamen Marktes*, Berlin, 1965.
"Die Nichtigkeitsklage im Recht der EGKS", Frankfurt/M., 1952.

Steiner, J. "Equality and Equity under Community Law", (1985) E.L.Rev. 21.

Steiniger, W. *Einführung in das dänische Rechtssystem (Arbeitspapier Nr. 3 des Lorenz-Von-Stein-Instituts für Verwaltungswissenschaften)*, Kiel, 1982.

Stern, K. *Das Staatsrecht der Bundesrepublik Deutschland*, Vol. 1 (2nd ed., Munich 1984).
Ermessen und unzulässige Ermessensausübung, Berlin, 1964.

Stevens, J.N. *Constitutional and Administrative Law*, Plymouth, 1984.

Stober, R. "Zur Problematik des § 44 a Abs. 1 BHO und des entsprechenden Länderrechts", DÖV 1984, p. 265.

Stolleis, M. "Die Verwaltungsgerichtsbarkeit im Nationalsozialismus", in: *Festschrift für C.-F. Menger*, Cologne/Berlin/Bonn/Munich, 1985, p. 57.

Storost, U. "Die Verwaltungsrechtslehre E. Forsthoffs als Ausdruck eines politischen Verfassungsmodells", in: E.V. Heyen (ed.), *Wissenschaft und Recht der Verwaltung seit dem Ancien Régime*, Frankfurt, 1984, p. 163.

Stotz, R. *Die EG-Stahlkrise im Lichte der EG-Wirtschaftsverfassung des EGKS-Vertrages*, Baden-Baden, 1983.

Stout, R.M. *Administrative Law in Ireland*, Dublin, 1985.

Strasser, D. *Die Finanzen Europas* (2nd ed., Brussels/Luxembourg 1982).

Streil, J.
"Europäisches Verwaltungsrecht im Werden, Fachtagung des Arbeitskreises Europäische Integration e.V. Hamburg (18.–20). Juni 1981)", EuR 1981, p. 269.

Le Tallec, G., Ehlermann, C.-D.
"Die Begründungspflicht für Rechtsakte der Europäischen Gemeinschaften", AWD/RIW 12 (1966), p. 149; RMC 1966, p. 179 (in French).

Teitgen, F.
"Le principe de proportionnalité en Droit Français", in: Deutsche Sektion der Intern. Juristenkommission (ed.), *Der Grundsatz der Verhältnismässigkeit in europäischen Rechtsordnungen*, Heidelberg, 1985, p. 53.

Temple Lang, J.
"Procedure in Community competition cases—some recent developments", in: *Studienvereinigung Kartellrecht, XI. Internationales Kartellrechtsforum*, Munich, 1986, p. 94.

Tettinger, P.J.
Besonderes Verwaltungsrecht—Kommunalrecht, Polizei- und Ordnungsrecht, Heidelberg, 1986.

Tetzel, C.
"Anwendbares Verwaltungsverfahrensrecht beim Vollzug von europäischem Gemeinschaftsrecht", RIW/ AWD 1982, p. 336.

Thieme, W.
Verwaltungslehre (4th ed., Cologne/Berlin/Bonn/Munich 1984).

Thomashausen, A.
"Der Freiheitsbegriff, die Grundrechte und der Grundrechtsschutz in der neuen Portugiesischen Verfassung vom 2. April 1976", EuGRZ 1981, p. 1.
"Die revidierte Verfassung der Republik Portugal von 1976—Eine Einführung", JöR N.F. 32 (1983), p. 443.
Verfassung und Verfassungswirklichkeit im neuen Portugal, Berlin, 1981.

Tiedemann, P.
"Das Kautionsrecht der EWG—ein verdecktes Strafrecht?" NJW 1983, p. 2727.

Tiffreau, P.
"Le principe d'égalité en droit économique", in: F.I.D.E., *Le principe d'égalité en droit économique, Rapports volume 2*, The Hague, 1984, Chapter 8.

Timmermans, C.W.A.
"Verboden discriminatie of (geboden) differentiatie", SEW 1982, p. 426.

Toftegaard, N.G.
"Constitutional and Administrative Law", in: Hans Gammeltoft-Hansen, Bernhard Gomard, Allgen Philips (eds.), *Danish Law*, Copenhagen, 1982.

Tomuschat, C.
"Die Rechtsetzungsbefugnis der EWG in Generalermächtigungen—insbesondere in Art. 235 EWGV", EuR 1976, special issue, p. 45.
"Nein und abermals Nein! Zum Urteil des BFH vom 25.4.1985", EuR 1985, p. 346.
"Normenpublizität und Normenklarheit in der Europäischen Gemeinschaft", in: *Festschrift für H. Kutscher*, Baden-Baden, 1981, p. 461.
Verfassungsgewohnheitsrecht?—Eine Untersuchung zum Staatsrecht der Bundesrepublik Deutschland, Heidelberg, 1972.

Toth, A.G.
Legal Protection of Individuals in the European Communities, Vol. I, *The Individual and Community Law*, Vol. II, *Remedies and Procedures*, Amsterdam/New York/Oxford, 1978.

Touffait, A.
"La jurisprudence de la Cour de justice des Communautés européennes en matière de sécurité sociale

	des travailleurs européens qui se déplacent", in: *Mélanges offerts à Pierre-Henry Teitgen*, Paris, 1984, p. 511.
	"Réflexions d'un magistrat français sur son expérience de juge à la Cour de justice des Communautés européennes", RIDC 35 (1983), p. 283.
Tourdias, M.	"La loi du 6 janvier 1986", AJDA 1986, p. 275.
Tsatsos, T.	"Der gerichtliche Rechtsschutz des Einzelnen gegenüber der vollziehenden Gewalt in Griechenland", in: H. Mosler (ed.), *Gerichtsschutz gegen die Exekutive*, Vol. 1, Cologne/Berlin/Bonn/Munich, 1969, p. 277.
Tschira, O., Schmitt Glaeser, W.	*Verwaltungsprozessrecht* (9th ed., Stuttgart/Munich/ Hanover 1988).
Ubertazzi, G.M.	"Le principe de proportionnalité en Droit Italien", in: Deutsche Sektion der Intern. Juristenkommission (ed.), *Der Grundsatz der Verhältnismässigkeit in europäischen Rechtsordnungen*, Heidelberg, 1985, p. 79.
Ule, C.H.	"Ein neuer Anlauf?" DVBl. 1985, p. 939.
	"Gesetzlichkeit in der Verwaltung durch Verwaltungs- verfahren und gerichtliche Kontrolle in der DDR", DVBl. 1985, p. 1029.
	"Rechtsstaat und Verwaltung", VerwArchiv 1985, p. 129.
	Verwaltungsprozessrecht (9th ed., 1987).
	Verwaltungsverfahrensgesetze des Auslandes, Berlin, 1967.
Ule, C.H., Laubinger, H.W.	*Verwaltungsverfahrensrecht* (3rd ed., Cologne/Berlin/ Bonn/Munich 1986).
Ureges, J.A.Jr. (ed.)	*Public administration, History and Theory in Contem- porary Perspective*, New York/Basle, 1982.
Usher, J.A.	"Exercise by the European Court of its Jurisdiction to Annual Competition Decisions", (1980) E.L.Rev. 287.
	"General Principles Derived from the Law of the Mem- ber States as a Source of Community Law—The Interac- tion between Community Law and National Law", FIDE *Rapports 12e Congrès* I, Paris, 1986, p. 303.
	"The 'Good Administration' of European Community Law", in: Current Legal Problems 1985, Vol. 38, p. 269.
	"The gradual widening of EC policy, in particular on the basis of articles 100 and 235 EEC Treaty", in: *Structure and Dimensions of European Community Policy* (ed. J. Schwarze, H. G. Schermers), Baden-Baden, 1988, p. 25.
Vandersanden, G., Barav, A.	*Contentieux communautaire*, Brussels, 1977.
Vaughan, D. (ed.)	*Law of the European Communities*, Vol. 1, London, 1986.
Vedel, G.	"Discontinuité du Droit constitutionnel et continuité du Droit administratif: le rôle du juge", in: *Mélanges M. Waline*, Paris, 1974, Vol 2, p. 777.
	"Le précédent judiciaire en droit public", in: U. Blau- rock (ed.), *Die Bedeutung von Präjudizien im deutschen und französischen Recht*, Frankfurt, 1985, p. 75.
Vedel, G., Delvolvé, P.	*Droit administratif* (9th ed., Paris 1984).
Verdross, A., Simma, B.	*Universelles Völkerrecht—Theorie und Praxis* (3rd ed., Berlin 1984).

VerLoren van Themaat, P.   "Quelques réflexions sur les méthodes d'intégration en europe occidentale et en europe orientale", in: *Mélanges Fernand Dehousse* Vol. 2, Paris, 1979, p. 95.

Vincent, J.-Y.   "Le retrait des actes administratifs unilatéraux", RTDE 1974, p. 31.

Vogel, K.   *Der räumliche Anwendungsbereich der Verwaltungs-rechtsnorm*, Frankfurt a.M./Berlin, 1965.

Völker, E.L.M.   "The direct effect of international agreements in the Community's legal order", in: LIEI 1983, p. 131.

Voss, R.   "Nationale Vorschriften zur Durchführung des EWG-Rechts im Bereich des Zoll- und Agrarverwaltungs-rechts", RIW/AWD 1979, p. 657.

"Das Verhältnis von europäischer Gerichtsbarkeit und nationalen Gerichten im Lichte der jüngsten Recht-sprechung", in: J. Schwarze (ed.), *Das Wirtschaftsrecht des Gemeinsamen Marktes in der aktuellen Rechtsent-wikklung*, Baden-Baden, 1983, p. 11.

Wade, E.C.S., Phillips, G.G., Bradley, A.W.   *Constitutional and Administrative Law* (9th ed., Bungay (Suffolk) 1979).

Wade, E.C.S., Bradley, A.W.   *Constitutional and Administrative Law* (10th ed., London/New York 1985).

Wade, H.W.R.   *Administrative Law* (10th ed., Oxford 1982).

Wägenbaur, R.   "Das Verbot steuerlicher Diskriminierung nach dem EWG-Vertrag im Lichte der Rechtsprechung des Gerichtshofs", EuR 1969, p. 20.

Waelbroeck, D.   "New Forms of Settlement of Antitrust Cases and Pro-cedural Safeguards: Is Regulation 17 falling into abeyance?" (1986) 11 E.R.L.Rev. 268.

Waelbroeck, M.   "La nature du droit au remboursement de montants payés contrairement au droit communautaire", in: *Liber Amicorum J. Mertens de Wilmars*, Antwerp, 1982, p. 429.

Wagner, F. Sosa   "Die spanische Gemeindeverwaltung", DVBl. 1986, p. 930.

Wahl, R.   "Die bürokratischen Kosten des Rechts- und Sozial-staates", Die Verwaltung 1980, p. 273.

"Thesen zur Umsetzung der Umweltverträglichkeit-sprüfung in das deutsche öffentliche Recht", DVBl. 1988, p. 86.

"Verwaltungsverfahren zwischen Verwaltungseffizienz und Rechtsschutzauftrag", VVDStRL 41 (1983) p. 151.

Waline, M.   *Droit administratif* (9th ed., Paris 1963).

"Le retrait des actes administratifs", in: *Mélanges Mestre*, Paris, 1956, p. 563.

Wallerath, M.   *Allgemeines Verwaltungsrecht* (3rd ed., Siegburg 1985).

Warner, J.-P.   "The relationship between European Community Law and the national laws of Member States", (1977) 93 L.Q.R. 349.

Wassermann, R.   "Zur Bedeutung, zum Inhalt und zum Umfang des Rechts auf Gehör", Deutsche Richterzeitung 1984, p. 425.

Weber, A.   "Anfechtbarkeit und Aufhebbarkeit gemeinschafts-rechtswidriger nationaler Verwaltungsakte", BayVBl 1984, p. 321.

"Das Verwaltungsverfahren im Antidumpingrecht der EG", EuR 1985, p. 1.

	"Die Spanische Verfassung von 1978", JöR N.F. 29 (1980), p. 210.
	"Verwaltungskollisionsrecht der Europäischen Gemeinschaften im Lichte neuerer Rechtsentwicklungen", EuR 1986, p. 1.
Weber-Dürler, B.	*Vertrauensschutz im öffentlichen Recht*, Basle, 1983.
Wegmann, M.	*Die Nichtigkeitsklage Privater gegen Normativakte der Europäischen Gemeinschaften*, Berlin, 1976.
Weides, P.	"Die Jahresfrist für Rücknahme und Widerruf von begünstigenden Verwaltungsakten", DÖV 1985, p. 431.
	"Widerruf und Rückforderung von Zuwendungen des Bundes und der Länder", NJW 1981, p. 841.
	"Zur Anwendbarkeit der Rücknahmefrist des § 48 IV 1 VwVfG bei Rechtsanwendungsfehlern der Behörde", DÖV 1985, p. 91.
Weis, H.	"Inländerdiskriminierung zwischen Gemeinschaftsrecht und nationalem Verfassungsrecht", NJW 1983, p. 2721.
Weitbrecht, A.	"Zur Rechtsstellung ausländischer Grenznachbarn im deutschen Umweltrecht", NJW 1987, p. 2132.
Welter, F.	"Discours", in: *Le Conseil d'Etat, Livre Jubilaire*, Luxembourg, 1957, p. 33.
Welter, F., Goldmann, A., Maul, R., Baden, F.	"La procédure d'élaboration des actes administratifs en droit luxembourgeois", in: *Rapports présentés aux colloques entre les Conseils d'Etat Belge, Néerlandais, Français, Italien, Luxembourgeois et le Bundesverwaltungsgericht, Colloque de Rome*, 1968, p. 165.
Werner, F.	" 'Verwaltungsrecht als konkretisiertes Verfassungsrecht,' " DVBl. 1959, p. 527.
Werner, W.	"Zulässigkeit verwaltungsrechtlicher Arrangements im Aussenhandel", RIW/AWD 1984, p. 369.
Wessels, W.	"Transnationale Verwaltungsverflechtung als Herausforderung für die Beamtenforbildung", Verwaltung und Fortbildung, 1984, p. 58.
Weyreuther, F.	"Zur richterlichen Umdeutung von Verwaltungsakten", DÖV 1985, p. 126.
Wiarda, G.J.	*Algemene beginselen van behoorlijk bestuur*, V.A.R.-geschrift XXIV, Haarlem, 1952.
Wieland, J.	"Die Entwicklung der Wirtschaftsregulierung in den Vereinigten Staaten von Amerika", Die Verwaltung 1985, p. 84.
Wielinger, G., Gruber, G.	*Einführung in das österreichische Verwaltungsverfahrensrecht*, Graz, 1984.
Wiener, C.	*Vers une codification de la procédure administrative*, Paris, 1975.
Wiesner, W.	*Der Widerruf individueller Entscheidungen der Hohen Behörde der EGKS*, Hamburg, 1966.
van Wijk, H.D., Konijnenbelt, W.	*Hoofdstukken van administratief recht*, 's-Gravenhage, (4th ed., 1979).
Wimmer, N.	"Grundtypen der Verwaltung im internationalen Vergleich", Die Verwaltung 1983, p. 417.
Wimmer, R.	"Die Wahrung des Grundsatzes des rechtlichen Gehörs—Dauerauftrag für das Bundesverfassungsgericht", DVBl. 1985, p. 773.

Winkler, B. "Die Durchsetzung der Pflicht zur Rückforderung einer gemeinschaftsrechtswidrigen Beihilfe nach deutschem und europäischem Recht", DVBl. 1979, p. 263.

Winkler, R. "Anrechnung amerikanischer Kartellstrafen auf EWG-Kartellbussen?" AWD/BB 1972, p. 565.

Winterfeld, A. von "Neuere Entwicklungen bei der Vereinfachung und Beschleunigung von Kartellverwaltungsverfahren vor der EG-Kommission", RIW/AWD 1984, p. 928.

Wittkopp, U.H. *Wirtschaftliche Freizügigkeit und Nationalstaatsvorbehalte*, Baden-Baden, 1977.

Wivenes, M.G. "Interaction entre droit communautaire et droit national", in: FIDE, *Rapports 12e Congrès*, Paris, 1986, p. 215.

Woehrling, J.-M. "Die französische Verwaltungsgerichtsbarkeit im Vergleich mit der deutschen", NVwZ 1985, p. 21.
"Die gerichtliche Kontrolle der Verwaltung im französischen Recht", Verwaltungswissenschaftliche Informationen 1985, p. 36.

Wohlfarth, J. "Die Freiheit des Personenverkehrs und der Vorbehalt der öffentlichen Ordnung", in: E.-W. Fuss (ed.), *Der Beitrag des Gerichtshofes der Europäischen Gemeinschaften zur Verwirklichung des Gemeinsamen Marktes*, Baden-Baden, 1981, p. 85.

Wolf, M. *Gerichtsverfassungsrecht aller Verfahrenszweige* (6th ed., Munich 1987).

Wolff, H.J. "Rechtsgrundsätze und verfassungsgestaltende Grundentscheidungen als Rechtsquellen", in: *Gedächtnisschrift für W. Jellinek*, Munich, 1955, p. 33.

Wolff, H.J., Bachof, O., Stober, R. *Verwaltungsrecht*, Vol. I (9th ed., Munich 1974), Vol. II (5th ed., Munich 1987), Vol. III (4th ed., Munich 1978).

Yardley, D.C.M. *Principles of Administrative Law*, London, 1981.

Zacher, H.F. "Elemente der Rechtsstaatlichkeit", in: Stimmen der Zeit, Vol. 203—No. 6 (June 1985), p. 413.

Zehetner, F. "Verzugszinsen im Preisrecht der Europäischen Gemeinschaft für Kohle und Stahl", RIW/AWD 1979, p. 311.

Zeidler, W. "Gedanken zum Verhältnis von Rechtswissenschaft und Rechtsprechung", BayVBl 1985, p. 491.

Zemanek, K. "Was kann die Vergleichung staatlichen öffentlichen Rechts für das Recht der internationalen Organisationen leisten?" ZaöRV 24 (1964) p. 453.

Zieger, G. *Das Grundrechtsproblem in den Europäischen Gemeinschaften*, Tübingen, 1970.
"Die Rechtsprechung des Europäischen Gerichtshofs, eine Untersuchung der Allgemeinen Rechtsgrundsätze", JöR N.F. 22 (1973), p. 299.

Zimmerli, U. "Der Grundsatz der Verhältnismässigkeit im öffentlichen Recht", ZSR 1978 (97), p. 9.

Zimmermann, E. *Die Preisdiskriminierung im Recht der Europäischen Gemeinschaft für Kohle und Stahl*, Frankfurt am Main, 1962.

Zuleeg, M. *Das Recht der Europäischen Gemeinschaft im innerstaatlichen Bereich*, Cologne, 1969.

	"Demokratie und Wirtschaftsverfassung in der Rechtsprechung des Europäischen Gerichtshofes", EuR 1982, p. 21.
Zweigert, K.	"Das grosse Werk Ipsens über Europäisches Gemeinschaftsrecht", EuR 1972, p. 308.
	"Der Einfluss des Europäischen Gemeinschaftsrechts auf die Rechtsordnungen der Mitgliedstaaten", RabelsZ (1964), p. 601.
	"Stichwort 'Rechtsvergleichung', " in: Strupp, Schlochauer, *Wörterbuch des Völkerrechts*, Vol. 3, Berlin, 1962.
Zweigert, K., Kötz, H.	*Einführung in die Rechtsvergleichung*, Vol. 1: *Grundlagen* (2nd ed., Tübingen 1984).
Zweigert, K., Puttfarken, H.-J.	*Rechtsvergleichung*, Darmstadt, 1978.

INDEX

Access to files
individual documents, duty to
  communicate, 1341–1346
limits and exceptions,
  confidential documents, 1348–1357
  general limits, 1347–1348
Administration
direct executive action by. *See* **Executive
  action**
European Community, concept in, 20–24
executive power, as component of, 11
France, 12–14
Germany, 15–16
indirect executive action by. *See*
  Executive action
material concept of, 12
meaning, 15
Member States, concept in, 11–20
organisational concept of, 12
state activities as whole termed as, 11
Administrative act
benefits, conferring, 972–975
burdens, imposition of, 972–975,
  1010–1011
classification of,
  benefits, acts conferring, 972–975
  burdens, acts imposing, 972–975
  declaratory administrative acts,
    970–972
  rights, acts establishing, 970–972
  unlawful administrative acts
    completely null and void, 975–979
conditions which must be met by,
  957–964
declaratory, 970–972
lawful, revocation of, 986–991
regulations, demarcating from, 964–969
revocation of,
  general legal principles regarding,
    burdens, measures imposing,
      1010–1011
    generally, 986
    lawful administrative act, 986–991
    special grounds for revocation,
      changes of circumstances,
        1022–1024

Administrative act—*cont.*
revocation of—*cont.*
  general legal principles regarding—
    cont.
    special grounds for revocation—
      cont.
      false or incomplete information,
        revocation on grounds of,
        1013–1014
      legal situation, changes in,
        1015–1022
      measures explicitly subject to
        revocation, 1012–1013
      statute, revocation laid down by,
        1011–1012
      summary, 1024–1025
    unlawful administrative act,
      991–1010
  generally, 979–980
  lawful nature of decisions, general
    conditions for,
    discretion, exercise of, 1029–1030
    form, principles governing,
      1027–1029
    law, duty to observe, 1029–1030
    no forfeiture has occurred,
      1025–1027
    procedure, principles governing,
      1027–1029
  legitimate expectation, legal
    implications of infringement of,
    1031–1032
  Staff Regulations, 984–985
  written law, in,
    Article 65(2), fourth paragraph,
      ECSC, under, 981–983
    Article 8(3) of Regulation 17 (EEC),
      under, 983–984
    generally, 980
    Staff Regulations, 984–985
rights, establishment of, 970–972
unlawful, revocation of, 991–1010
Administrative law
basic contention, 3
constitutional law, integration function
  of, 1455–1465

Administrative law—*cont.*
  evolution of, 1433–1434
Administrative law protection. *See*
  Protection
Administrative law systems
  Member States, of, 97–99
Administrative measures
  retroactivity of. *See* **Retroactivity**
  revocation of, 1156–1159
Administrative procedure
  changing meaning of law of,
    Community, significance of notion of
      procedure within, 1186–1197
    Member States, notion of procedure
      in, 1175–1186
  competence,
    Community, 1198–1202
    decision-making institution, of,
      1209–1212
    generally, 1198
    institutional, 1202–1209
  decision-making process. *See* **Decision-making**
  defence, rights of. *See* **Defence, rights of**
  European competition law, in, 834–837
  generally, 1430–1432
  information, administrative powers to
    collect. *See* **Information**
  language question, 1212–1215
  procedural defects, legal consequences
    of, 1420–1430
  rule of law, under,
    changing meaning of law,
      Community, significance of notion
        of procedure within, 1186–1197
      Member States, notion of procedure
        in, 1175–1186
    competence. *See* competence *above*
    decision-making process. *See*
      Decision-making
    defence, rights of. *See* **Defence, rights of**
    generally, 1430–1432
    information, administrative powers to
      collect. *See* **Information**
    language question, 1212–1215
    procedural defects, legal consequences
      of, 1420–1430
    subject-matter of investigation,
      1173–1174
    summary, 1197–1198
Administrative structure. *See* **Structure of administration**
Administrative tribunal
  quasi-judicial activity, 20

Administrative wrongs
  general principle, 508
  nature of, 508
  particular conditions,
    culpability of conduct, 513–514
    illegality of conduct, 511–513
    institutions, conduct of, 510–511
    official capacity, 508–510
    officials, conduct of, 510–511
Agricultural levies
  external protection of common market
    includes, 30
Agricultural markets
  organisation of,
    deposits,
      amount of, 732
      cases featuring, 727–747
      forfeiture of, 732–747
      legal nature of, 729–732
    generally, 727
    intervention, other cases concerning,
      co-responsibility levy, 753–754
      denaturing premiums, 766–773
      generally, 752–753
      guarantee, 753
      levy,
        co-responsibility, 753–754
        fixing amount of, 756–759
      minimum prices system, 760–762
      monetary compensation system,
        762–766
      quota system, 759–760
      subsidies, 766–773
      threshold prices, fixing of, 754–756
      skimmed-milk powder cases,
        747–752
  See also **Common agricultural policy**
Aid
  Articles 92 *et seq.*, prohibition by,
    381–389
  granting of, 387–389
  state aids,
    concept of, 384
    prohibition of, 384–389
    subsidy under ECSC Treaty, concept
      of, 384–387
Analogy
  admissibility of reasoning by, 54–55
Anglo-Saxon law
  customary law, role of, 56
Anti-dumping. *See* **Dumping**
Appeals
  review distinguished from, 177
Arbitrary action
  concept of, 553–554

Arbitrary action—*cont.*
  discrimination and,
    facts, arbitrary action as regards,
      575–584
    generally, 574–575
    justification, arbitrary action and,
      584–601
  facts, as regards, 575–584
  justification, and, 584–601
Aristotle
  sovereign activity, forms of expression of,
    11
Audit procedure
  communications, practice of issuing, 24n
  information notes, practice of issuing,
    24n
Authenticity
  general principles of law, of, 66–68

Bachof, Otto
  comparative law, on, 93
Belgium
  administrative law protection, 157–159
  administrative structure, 159–160
  Conseil d'Etat, 155, 156–157
  constitutional basis of administrative law,
    156–157
  decision-making process, 1390–1391
  defence, rights of, 1292–1296
  discretion, doctrine of, 287–289
  essential characteristics of system,
    154–160
  French influence on, 154
  legal certainty, principle of,
    administrative decisions,
      avoidance of, 918–920
      retroactivity of, 920–921
    general recognition of, 918
    individual cases, application to,
      918–921
    rules, retroactivity of, 920–921
    wrongly levied duties, recovery of, 921
  legality principle,
    comparative law review, 222–223
    statutory constraints and discretion,
      287–289
  legitimate expectation, principle of,
    administrative decisions,
      avoidance of, 918–920
      retroactivity of, 920–921
    general recognition of, 918
    individual cases, application to,
      918–921
    rules, retroactivity of, 920–921
    wrongly levied duties, recovery of, 921

Belgium—*cont.*
  Luxembourg, history of, 181
  origin and development, 154–156
  proportionality, principle of, 697–698
  public service, concept of, 18n
  reasons, duty to give, 1390–1391
  sources of law, 156–157
  statutory constraints and discretion,
    287–289
Benefits
  administrative acts conferring, 972–975
Binding instrument
  non-binding statement distinguished
    from,
    European Court, distinguishing
      criteria used by, 236–239
    positive law distinctions, 235–236
Bradley, A.W.
  administrative law, description of, 17
Britain. *See* **United Kingdom**
Budget
  allocation of resources, 27
  expenditure, implementation of, 26–27
  income, implementation of, 26
  internal Community administration,
    26–27
  ultimate executive responsibility for
    indirect implementation of, 27
Building law
  comparative law, 94
Burdens
  administrative act imposing, 972–975,
    1010–1011

CCT. *See* **Common customs tariff**
Caetano, M.
  Portugese administrative law,
    significance of work for development
    of, 193
Cartels
  ban on,
    exemptions under Article 85(3),
      366–369
    generally, 28, 361–362, 369–370
    subject-matter of Article 85(1),
      362–366
  regulation of, 28
  See also **Competition law**
Case law
  Common Market in coal and steel. *See*
    European Coal and Steel
    Community
  common agricultural policy. *See*
    Common agricultural policy

Case Law—*cont.*
  community civil service, law of. *See* **Civil service**
  competition law. *See* **Competition law**
  customs union. *See* **Customs union**
  dumping, rules against, 389–395
  European Court of Justice. *See* **European Court of Justice**
  external trade, 389–395
  mandatory requirements, relating to, 785–789
  proportionality, principle of. *See* **Proportionality, principle of**
  social security law, legal constraints on administration in. *See* **Social security**
  statute and, European administrative law between, 1446–1455
Central government
  Ireland, 179
  United Kingdom, 151
Certainty. *See* **Legal certainty**
Certiorari
  scope of application of claim of, 18
Civil law
  comparative law, one-sided orientation of, 76
Civil service
  law in general, 302–303, 325
  legal constraints, operation of,
    formal conditions of decision, review of,
    formal rules, 306
    functional authority and procedure, 304–305
    subject-matter of decisions, review of,
      accuracy of underlying facts, 307–308
      completeness of underlying facts, 307–308
      freedom of decision,
        general principles of law as limit to, 324
        misuse of discretion as limit to, 319–324
      self-regulation by administration,
        recruitment, discretion in appointments constrained by conditions of, 313–315
        remuneration, force of discretionary guidelines on, 316–319

Civil service—*cont.*
  legal constraints, operation of—*cont.*
    subject-matter of decisions, review of—*cont.*
      source of authority, limits to discretionary power in,
        Case 59/81, *Commission* v. *Council of European Communities*, 308–313
        evaluation process, 311–312
        generally, 308
        grounds of decision, 308–311
        salary weightings, adjustment of, 312–313
Classification of administrative acts. *See* **Administrative act**
Coal. *See* **European Coal and Steel Community**
Commercial practices
  illicit, measures against, 29–30
Commercial property
  protection of, 800–803
Common European law
  development of, interdependence of national administrative legal orders and, 1434–1446
Common agricultural policy
  case law,
    generally, 395–396
    implementing law of Commission, 440–453
    market regulation, Council's prerogative of, 396–440
    Member States, implementation of agricultural law by, 453–480
  implementing law of Commission,
    general principles of law, executive discretion constrained by, 451–452
    generally, 440–441
    policy-making, executive freedom in, 452–453
    source of authority, limitation of powers by,
      constraints arising from source of authority, 448–451
      establishing and weighing facts, 443–448
      generally, 441–443
    Treaty, limitation of powers by,
      constraints arising from Treaty, 448–451
      establishing and weighing facts, 443–448
      generally, 441–443
  indirect implementation, 34–36, 46

Common agricultural policy—*cont.*
market regulation,
Council's prerogative of,
constitutive authority, legal limits of,
formal constraints, 398–404
generally, 398
policy-making, Council's freedom
in, 439–440
proper authority and procedure,
398–404
subject-matter, limits of, 404–439
generally, 396
policy-making, task of, 397
subject-matter, limits of,
Article 39(1), compulsory
objectives of, 406–411
clear rules, 404–406
discretion of policy-makers, effect
of legal certainty on, 431–435
equality as limit to freedom of
decision, 416–423
examining underlying facts,
411–415
general principles of law, policy-
making constrained by,
415–440
general requirements, 404–406
market organisation, policy-
making in law of, 423–431,
435–439
misuse of powers, 415
proportionality principle, effect
of, 423–431
effect of, 35
Member States, implementation of
agricultural law by,
concluding assessment of legal
constraints, 479–480
decision-making, how States exercise
scope for, 454
national level, at,
definition of terms, 463–469
equity, remission of levies on
grounds of, 469–474
generally, 462–463
reclaiming Community subsidies
paid unlawfully, 474–479
preliminary observation, 453–454
rule-making, legal constraints on,
formal implementing law,
enactment of,
competence, 457–459
procedural law matters, freedom
of States to decide in, 459–462
generally, 455

Common agricultural policy—*cont.*
Member States, implementation of
agricultural law by—*cont.*
rule-making, legal constraints on—
cont.
substantive agricultural law,
enactment of, 455–457
objectives, 34
Common customs tariff
application of,
Community, explanations by, 483–485
court's review of, 486–494
generally, 482–483
Member States, explanation by,
483–485
external protection of common market
through, 36–37
GATT, effect of, 481
See also **Customs union**
Communications
audit procedure, issued in course of, 24n
Comparative law
administrative law in particular, 89–92
Belgium. *See* Belgium
civil law, one-sided orientation towards,
76
Denmark. *See* **Denmark**
European and national law, mutual
influences of, 93–95
France. *See* **France**
fundamentals of,
aims and functions,
generally, 78
judicial law making, 81–82
legislature, creation of new law by,
78–79
statutes, interpretation of, 81–82
supply of solutions, enrichment and
extension of, 78
unification of law, 79–81
concept, 77–78
functions. *See* aims and functions
above
generally, 76–77
method, 82–85
Germany. *See* **Germany**
Greece. *See* **Greece**
Ireland. *See* **Ireland**
Italy. *See* **Italy**
legality principle. *See* **Legality principle**
Luxembourg. *See* **Luxembourg**
national law, assistance in interpretation
of, 82n
Netherlands. *See* **Netherlands**
Portugal. *See* **Portugal**

Comparative law—*cont.*
public law,
characteristics, 85–87
methodology, 87–88
unification of laws, chances of, 88–89
Spain. *See* **Spain**
United Kingdom. *See* **United Kingdom**
Compensation
administrative wrong, for,
extent of compensation, 517–524
generally, 515
nature of compensation, 516–517
agricultural markets, organisation of,
762–766
Competence
Community, 1198–1202
decision-making institution, of,
1209–1212
generally, 1198
institutional, 1202–1209
Competence d'attribution
principle of, 40, 50
Competition law
abuses, regulation of, 28
administration external to Community,
27–28
aid, prohibition by Articles 92 *et seq.*,
generally, 381–384, 389
state aids,
concept of, 384
granting of, 387–389
prohibition of, 384–389
Articles 85 and 86, subject-matter of,
cartels, ban on,
exemptions under Article 85(3),
366–369
generally, 361–362, 369–370
subject-matter of Article 85(1),
362–366
dominant position, ban on,
generally, 370, 378
individual cases, application in,
370–378
enforcement, 378–381
cartels. *See* **Cartels**
concerted practices, meaning, 363–365
distortion of competition, concept of
discrimination and, 602–605
dominant position. *See* **Dominant
position**
enforcement of sanctions, 43–44
fines,
imposition of, 28
proportionality, principle of, 837–841
generally, 360–361

Competition law—*cont.*
limitation periods in proceedings, 43–44
mergers, regulation of, 28
proceedings,
investigation, limitation on powers of,
1242–1243
limitation periods in, 43–44
proportionality, principle of,
administrative procedure, 834–837
fines, 837–841
generally, 833–834
substantive competition law, 841–842
subsidies, regulation of, 28
substantive, 841–842
Concerted practices
meaning, 363–365
Concrete situation
idea of, 21
Conduct
administrative wrongs, liability for. *See*
Administrative wrongs
unlawful administrative. *See* **Legality
principle**
Confidential documents
defence, rights of, 1348–1357
Conseil d'Etat
Belgium, 155, 156–157
comparative administrative law, 91
crucial role of, 3
European Court of Justice, parallels
with, 9
France. *See* **France**
Constitution
basis of administrative law, 98
Belgium, 156–157
Denmark, 162–163
France, 103–104
Germany, 116–117
Greece, 167–168
Ireland, 174–175
Luxembourg, 182
Portugal, 194–196
United Kingdom, of, unwritten and
flexible nature of, 98, 143
Constitutional law
administrative law, integration function
of, 1455–1465
legal certainty, principle of, 940–942
legitimate expectation, protection of,
940–942
status, 70
See also **Constitution**
Court of Justice. *See* **European Court of
Justice**

Culpability
conduct which incurs liability, of,
513–515
Currency
debt collection, in connection with, 614n
Customary law
ancient customs, 56
Anglo-Saxon legal sphere, role in, 56
constitutional conventions, 56
English legal system, in, 57
formation of, 57–58
France, 56
Germany, 56
instant, 58
legal rules having character of, existence
of, 58–59
preconditions for recognition, 56–57
source of law, as, 55–59
United Kingdom, 57, 143–144
Customs duties
external protection of common market
includes, 30
information, administrative powers to
collect, 1231–1236
subsequent collection of duties
incorrectly not levied, 1069–1071
wrongly levied, recovery of,
Belgium, 921
Germany, 897–898
Netherlands, 930
Customs tariff. *See* **Common customs tariff**
Customs union
generally, 480, 494
legal concept, as, 481
legal constraints in policy, essential
points of, 481–482
significance of, 480–481
See also **Common customs tariff**

Damage
administrative wrong, liability for. *See*
Administrative wrongs
occurrence of, concept of discrimination
and, 601–602
Debt collection
currency of, 614n
Decision-making process
administrative act. *See* **Administrative**
act
formulation of decision,
general comments, 1371–1373
informal settlement, possibilities of,
1373–1378
interim measures, possibilities of
adopting, 1378–1379

Decision-making process—*cont.*
formulation of decision—*cont.*
presentation of decision, 1381–1382
process for adopting decision,
1380–1381
remedies, information about,
1382–1384
freedom of decision. *See* **Legality**
principle
informal settlement, possibilities of,
1373–1378
information about remedies, 1382–1384
interim measures, possibilities of
adopting, 1378–1379
notification, 1416–1420
presentation of decision, 1381–1382
process for adopting decision, 1380–1381
reasons, duty to give,
Belgium, 1390–1391
Denmark, 1391–1392
France, 1385–1386
generally, 1384–1385
Germany, 1386–1388
Greece, 1392–1393
Ireland, 1393–1395
Italy, 1388–1389
Luxembourg, 1395–1396
measures subject to, 1403–1405
Netherlands, 1396–1397
Portugal, 1398–1399
scope of duty,
generally, 1406–1407
individual acts, 1407–1412
normative acts, 1412–1416
significance of, 1400–1403
Spain, 1399–1400
statement of reasons, form of,
1405–1406
United Kingdom, 1389–1390
remedies, information about, 1382–1384
Defects
procedural, legal consequences of,
1420–1430
Defence, rights of
content of,
files, access to,
individual documents, duty to
communicate, 1341–1346
limits and exceptions,
confidential documents,
1348–1357
general, 1347–1348
hearing,
degree of, 1358–1363
extent of, 1358–1370
nature of, 1358–1370

Defence, rights of—*cont.*
  content of—*cont.*
    hearing—*cont.*
      object of, 1358–1363
      procedure for, 1363–1370
      objections, explanation about content
        of, 1338–1341
      opening of procedure, 1335–1338
  general limitations upon,
    delay, danger in, 1332–1333
    evidence, gathering of, 1330–1332
    generally, 1328
    insignificant interferences, 1332
    petition of person concerned,
      1334–1335
    protection, impossibility of granting,
      1333–1334
    risk that purpose of decision may be
      defeated, 1328–1330
  general principle of law, existence of,
    1324–1325
  generally, 1370–1371
  hearing. *See* content of *above*
  Member States' laws, comparison of,
    Belgium, 1292–1296
    Denmark, 1296–1300
    France, 1245–1255
    Germany, 1255–1269
    Greece, 1300–1305
    Ireland, 1305–1309
    Italy, 1269–1273
    Luxembourg, 1309–1311
    Netherlands, 1311–1314
    Portugal, 1314–1315
    Spain, 1315–1320
    United Kingdom, 1273–1291
  normative rules, 1320–1324
  overview, 1243–1244
  third parties, for, 1325–1328
Delay
  defence, rights of, general limitations
    upon, 1332–1333
  legal act, implementation or performance
    of, 661–663
Delegated legislation
  Italy, 131
  quasi-legislative function, 20
  United Kingdom, 144
  unlawfulness in, 219
Denmark
  administrative doctrine, 18n
  administrative law protection, 164–166
  administrative structure, 166
  comparative administrative law, 91
  complaints procedures, 165

Denmark—*cont.*
  constitutional basis of administrative law,
    162–163
  decision-making process, 1391–1392
  discretion, doctrine of, 289
  equality principle, binding nature of, 560
  essential characteristics of system,
    161–166
  hearing, right to, 1296–1300
  legal certainty, principle of, 921–923
  legality principle,
    content of, 223–225
    form of principle, 223–225
    statutory constraints and discretion,
      289
    unlawful administrative conduct, 225
  legitimate expectation, principle of,
    921–923
  local government, 166
  ombudsman, institution of, 165–166
  origin and development of administrative
    law, 161–162
  proportionality, principle of, 698–699
  reasons, duty to give, 1391–1392
  sources of law, 163–164
  statutory constraints and discretion, 289
Deposits
  agricultural markets, organisation of. *See*
    Agricultural markets
Development. *See* **Origin and development**
Development control
  comparative law, 94
Dicey, A.V.
  administrative law, denial of existence of,
    16
  rule of law doctrine, on, 140–141
Direct executive action. *See* **Executive
  action**
Direct implementation
  example of, 23–24
  external administration,
    agricultural levies, 30
    agricultural products, market in, 30
    competition law, 27–28
    customs duties, 30
    European Atomic Energy
      Community, 31–32
    European Coal and Steel Community,
      31
    European Investment Bank, 32, 33
    illicit commercial practices, measures
      against, 29–30
    individual treaty obligations,
      suspension of, 33–34
    national subsidies, granting of, 28–29

Direct implementation—*cont.*
  external administration—*cont.*
    quantitative restrictions, 30
    regional policy, absence of, 30–31
    social policies, 30
    third countries, dumped or subsidised
      imports from, 29
  generally, 25
  implied powers, doctrine of, 48
  internal Community administration,
    budget, implementation of, 26–27
    material resources, management of, 25
    personnel management, 25
    service agencies, management of, 25
    treaty provisions, 26
  secondary law,
    legal basis of Act, 48–50
    present position, 43–45
  sources of law, 43–45, 48–50
Discretion
  administrative, 298
  decisions, judicial review of,
    executive freedom of decision, 299–300
    France, 263–269
    Germany, 277–279
  doctrine of,
    Belgium, 287–289
    Denmark, 289
    France, 261–263
    Germany, 270–277
    Greece, 290
    Ireland, 290–291
    Italy, 279–281
    Luxembourg, 291
    Netherlands, 291–293
    Portugal, 293–294
    Spain, 294
    technical discretion distinguished from
      free discretion, 280n
    United Kingdom, 281–282
  free, technical discretion distinguished
    from, 280n
  legislative, 298
  reasons, obligation to state, link with, 301
  technical, distinguished from free
    discretion, 280n
Discrimination
  arbitrary action, and,
    facts, as regards, 575–584
    generally, 574–575
    justification, and, 584–601
  characteristics and forms of,
    competition, distortion of, 602–605
    generally, 601
    hidden discrimination, 616–624

Discrimination—*cont.*
  characteristics and forms of—*cont.*
    measure, failure to take, 614–616
    natural differences, 606–610
    occurrence of damage, 601–602
    own contributory fault, 610–614
  competition, distortion of, 602–605
  concept of,
    discriminatory act, elements of,
      like treatment of unlike matters,
        571–574
      unlike treatment of like matters,
        564–571
    generally, 563–564, 625
    prohibition of discrimination and,
      561–562
  damage, occurrence of, 601–602
  discriminatory act, elements of,
    like treatment of unlike matters,
      571–574
    unlike treatment of like matters,
      564–571
  hidden, 616–624
  measure, failure to take, 614–616
  natural differences, 606–610
  own contributory fault, 610–614
  prohibition of,
    concept of discrimination and, 561–562
    equality principle and, 561–563
    structure of, 562–563
  See also **Equality, principle of**
Documents
  confidential, rights of defence, 1348–1357
Dominant position
  abuse of,
    generally, 370, 378
    individual cases, application in,
      370–378
  prohibition of abuse of, 28
  See also **Competition law**
Dumping
  anti-dumping,
    duty, introduction of, 29
    information, administrative powers to
      collect, 1222–1223, 1242–1243
  third countries, imports from, protective
    mechanism against, 29, 44
Duties. *See* **Customs duties**

EAEC. *See* **European Atomic Energy
  Community**
ECSC. *See* **European Coal and Steel
  Community**
EEC Treaty
  Articles 85 and 86. *See* **Competition law**

EEC Treaty—*cont.*
  invalidity, declaration of, effects of,
    243–248
  legal act, avoidance of, 242
  legal instrument, nullity of, 239–240
EIB. *See* **European Investment Bank**
Employment
  internal Community administration, 25
  public service, in, free movement of
    workers not applied to, 20
Enforcement action
  European Court, before, 27n, 33
England and Wales
  separate legal system, existence of, 140n
  See also **United Kingdom**
Environmental protection
  comparative law, 94
Equality, principle of
  administrative-law principle, 641–644
  arbitrary action,
    concept of, 553–554
    discrimination and,
      facts, arbitration action as regards,
        575–584
      generally, 574–575
      justification, arbitrary action and,
        584–601
  concept of equality, 548–549
  conclusions on, 670–674
  development of, 545–548
  discrimination. *See* **Discrimination**
  external relations of Community, effect
    of, 645–649
  formal equality, requirement of, 550–551
  freedom of decision, as limit to, 416–423
  fundamental principle of Community
    law, as, 625–641
  general legal principle, recognition as,
    administrative-law principle, 641–644
    fundamental principle of Community
      law, 625–641
    generally, 644–645
  general problems, 545–548
  jurisdiction of Member States, effect of,
    649–657
  legal act, incomplete application of,
    delay in implementation or
      performance, 661–663
    performance, delay in, 661–663
    refusal to implement or execute,
      658–661
  legal rule, binding nature as,
    British law, 558–560
    Danish law, 560
    French law, 556–557

Equality—*cont.*
  legal rule, binding nature as—*cont.*
    general validity, 555–556
    generally, 555
    special national features,
      British law, 558–560
      Danish law, 560
      French law, 556–557
  limits to application of,
    external relations of Community,
      645–649
    generally, 645, 657–658
    jurisdiction of Member States, 649–657
  Member States,
    Community law, equality under,
      generally, 658, 669
    legal act, incomplete application of,
      delay in implementation or
        performance, 661–663
      performance, delay in, 661–663
      refusal to implement or execute,
        658–661
    unilateral supplementary or
      amending measures,
      formal measures, 663–666
      generally, 663
      substantive measures, 667–669
    jurisdiction of, effect of, 649–657
  method of survey, 545–548
  possible orientations of,
    formal equality, requirement of,
      550–551
    substantive equality, requirement of,
      551–553
  structure of survey, 545–548
  substantive equality, requirement of,
    551–553
  unilateral supplementary or amending
    measures,
    formal measures, 663–666
    generally, 663
    substantive measures, 667–669
  See also **Discrimination**
Equity
  remission of levies on grounds of,
    469–474
Error
  unlawful administrative conduct,
    258–259
Establishment
  freedom of, proportionality principle
    and, 827–833
Estoppel, principle of
  United Kingdom, 903–904

Euratom
administrative tasks undertaken by,
32–33
European Investment Bank compared
with, 33
functional decentralisation, example of,
23
investment programmes, promotion of,
32
primary law, 39–42
Treaty, effectiveness of legal instrument,
239–240
European Atomic Energy Community
supply Agency of. *See* **Euratom**
tasks of, 31–32
European Coal and Steel Community
case law,
executive freedom of decision,
326–327
generally, 325–326, 359–360
judicial review,
executive of ECSC, aims of Treaty as
standard of conduct for,
327–330
framework for, 326–327
misuse of powers,
concept of, 330–334
generally, 330
plea of, effectiveness of, 336–337
procedural irregularity, 334–336
other causes of action, standards of
review for,
binding nature of powers,
340–351
general principles of law, how
ECSC executive is bound by,
355–359
institutional rules, constraint of
discretionary powers by,
351–355
rule of law, manifest failure to
observe, 337–339
standards of, 327–359
fines, right to impose, 31
loans, right to take out and offer, 31
prices, right to fix, 31
primary law, 39–42
production quota systems, 845–849
proportionality, principle of,
generally, 842–844
procedural questions, 850–852
production quota systems, 845–849
scrap metal equalisation cases, 844–845
rates, right to increase, 31
scrap metal equalisation cases, 844–845

European Coal and Steel Community
—cont.
Treaty,
legal instrument, nullity of, 240
subsidy under, concept of, 384–387
undertakings, binding production quotas
for, right to fix, 31
European Commission
administrative jurisdiction, 26
budget, implementation of, 26–27
Human Rights, of, case law of, 705
European Community
administration, concept of, 20–24
administrative law Community, as, 3–10
appropriate supplementation and
growth, law dependent on, 4
civil service. *See* **Civil service**
implementation mechanisms, access to, 8
Member States. *See* **Member States**
non-contractual liability. *See* **Non-contractual liability**
secondary sources of law, rules of
administrative law written into, 4
Treaty. *See* **EEC Treaty**
European Convention on Human Rights
proportionality principle under,
704–707
European Court of Human Rights
comparative administrative law, 91–92
proportionality principle in case law of,
706–707
European Court of Justice
binding instruments, non-binding
statements distinguished from,
236–239
case law,
Common Market in coal and steel. *See*
**European Coal and Steel
Community**
common agricultural policy. *See*
Common agricultural policy
Community civil service, law of. *See*
Civil service
competition law. *See* **Competition law**
complete investigation, duty to make,
1223–1239
customs union. *See* **Customs union**
dumping, rules against, 389–395
external trade, 389–395
indirect executive action, principles of,
1095–1096
legal certainty, principle of,
development of, 938–940
legitimate expectation, protection of,
development of principle of,
938–940

European Court of Justice—*cont.*
case law—*cont.*
    proportionality principle in. *See*
      proportionality principle *below*
    social security law, legal constraints on
      administration in. *See* **Social**
      security
Conseil d'Etat, parallels with, 9
enforcement action before, 27n, 33
European Community based on law,
    description of, 4
functional comparative law, 83–84
general principles of law. *See* **General**
    principles of law
indirect executive action, principles of,
    1095–1096
judge-made law, 59–64
judicial decisions, expansion of
    administrative law through, 5
legal certainty, principle of, development
    of, 6, 938–940
legitimate expectations, protection of,
    development of, 6, 938–940
non-binding statements, binding
    instruments distinguished from,
    236–239
non-discrimination, principle of,
    recognition of, 6
political repercussions of judgments of, 9
proportionality principle,
    case law, practical application in,
      agricultural markets, organisation
        of. *See* **Agricultural markets**
      competition law. *See* **Competition**
      law
      ECSC. *See* **European Coal and Steel**
      Community
      foreign trade law, 806–814
      free movement of goods. *See* **Free**
        movement of goods
      freedom of establishment, 827–833
      freedom of movement, 814–826
      generally, 726–727
      services, freedom to provide,
        827–833
      staff law cases, 853
    recognition of, 6
public authority, right to hearing before
    adverse decision taken by, 6
public postal services, interpretation of
    concept of, 21n
public service, development of concept
    of, 20–21
European Investment Bank
administrative tasks undertaken by, 32

European Investment Bank—*cont.*
Euratom compared with, 33
financial economy of Community,
    significance for, 32
European Social Fund
administration of, 21
deconcentrated administration, example
    of, 23
Evidence
defence, rights of, general limitations
    upon, 1330–1332
investigatory powers, limits placed upon,
    1241–1242
Executive action
direct,
    administrative acts,
      classification of,
        benefits, acts conferring, 972–975
        burdens, acts imposing, 972–975
        declaratory administrative acts,
          970–972
        rights, acts establishing, 970–972
        unlawful administrative acts,
          975–979
      conditions which must be met by,
        957–964
      regulations, demarcating from,
        964–969
      revocation of,
        general legal principles regarding,
          986–1025
        generally, 979–980
        lawful nature of decisions, general
          conditions for, 1025–1030
        legitimate expectation,
          infringement of, legal
          implications of, 1031–1032
        written law, in, 980–985
    administrative proceedings, time limits
      in, 1054–1061
    duties incorrectly not levied,
      subsequent collection of,
      1069–1071
    formal validity of measures. *See* time
      limits *below*
    generally, 956–957
    legal certainty, application of, 942–944
    legitimate expectation, protection of,
      application of, 942–944
    recovery of payments wrongly made,
      generally, 1061–1062, 1160–1161
    Staff Regulations, Article 85 of,
      generally, 1062
      legal basis, absence of, 1062–1066

Executive action—*cont.*
direct—*cont.*
recovery of payments, wrongly made—
cont.
Staff Regulations, Article 85 of—
cont.
other conditions for recovery,
1066–1067
procedural context of right of
recovery, 1067
state, by, 1166–1168
unjustified enrichment, principle of,
1068–1069
unlawful public levies, obligation to
repay in case of, 1161–1165
retroactivity of administrative
measures,
decisions, regulations challengeable
as being, 1078–1079
generally, 1072
protective measures, authorisations
for, 1075–1077
subsidies, supervision of, law on,
1072–1075
self-binding action by authorities,
explanation, 1085–1089
information, 1085–1089
linked administrative measures,
administrative practice and,
1080–1085
pledges, 1089–1093
principles, 1079–1080
undertakings, 1089–1093
time limits,
administrative proceedings, in,
1054–1061
formal validity of measures,
absolute nullity of administrative
measures, 1044–1045
exceptions to principle of,
1044–1054
existence of, conditions for and
consequences of, 1035–1044
illegality, plea of, 1051–1054
new circumstances, 1045–1051
remedies, for,
exceptions to principle of formal
validity, 1044–1054
existence of formal validity,
1035–1044
generally, 1032–1034
indirect,
generally, 1112–1113
legal certainty, application of,
944–945, 1096–1113

Executive action—*cont.*
indirect—*cont.*
legitimate expectation, protection of,
application of, 944–945,
1096–1113
principles,
Court of Justice, case
law of, 1095–1096
generally, 1093–1094
recovery of amounts paid, 1097–1101
repayment of amounts levied,
generally, 1104
national law, application as
complementary tool, 1109–1112
Regulation 1430/79, 1104–1109
subsequent recovery of amounts not
levied,
generally, 1101
national law, application as
complementary tool, 1102–1104
Regulation 1697/79, 1102
Executive freedom of decision
administrative discretion, 298
case law,
Common Market in Coal and Steel. *See*
**European Coal and Steel
Community**
common agricultural policy. *See*
Common agricultural policy
Community civil service. *See* **Civil
service**
competition law. *See* **Competition law**
customs union. *See* **Customs union**
social security law, legal constraints on
administration in. *See* **Social
security**
discretionary decisions, judicial
protection in, 299–300
dumping, rules against, 389–395
external trade, 389–395
legislative discretion, 298
migrant workers, social security for,
497–503
mode of procedure, explanation of, 301
reasons, obligation to state, link between
discretion and, 301
terminology of EC law, 296–298
Executive power
administration as component of, 11
functions of government, division of, 17
legislative power, distinguished from, 17
Parliament-created statutes, limitation
through, 208
sovereign activity, form of expression of,
11

Expectation. *See* **Legitimate expectation, protection of**
Expenditure
budget, implementation of, 26
Exports
measures restricting, proportionality principle and, 783–785
External relations of Community
equality principle, limits to application of, 645–649

Facts
arbitrary action as regards, 575–584
Fault
illegal act not involving, liability for, 531–532
own contributory fault, concept of discrimination and, 610–614
Federal Republic of Germany. *See* **Germany**
Files
access to. *See* **Access to files**
Fines
competition law, infringement of, 28, 837–841
European Coal and Steel Community, imposed by, 31
undertakings acting in breach of Treaty, imposition relating to, 28
Food
quality of, measures relating to, 776–779
Force majeure
circumstances of, 463–464
meaning, 463–468
Foreign trade law
proportionality, principle of, 806–814
Foundation treaty
formulation of, 79
France
acte de gouvernement, theory of, 263
actes administratifs, actes de gouvernement distinguished from, 263n
administrative law protection, 108–111
administrative structures, 111–112
Belgian administrative law, influence on, 154
comparative administrative law, 89–91
Conseil d'Etat,
case law, influence of, 91
crucial role of, 3
European Court of Justice, parallels with, 9
judicial review of discretionary decisions, extent of, 263–269

France—*cont.*
constitution, 103–104
customary law, recognition of, 56
decision-making process, 1385–1386
discretion,
doctrine of, fundamentals of, 261–263
judicial review of decisions, 263–269
droits de la défense in,
general legal principle, development of, 1245–1251
generally, 1245
statutory protective rights, formulation of, 1251–1255
EC law as source of law, 105
equality principle, binding nature of, 556–557
essential characteristics of system, 100–113
judicial review of discretionary decisions, extent of, 263–269
legal certainty, principle of,
action by administration,
administrative decisions, avoidance of,
abrogation, 882–883
generally, 876–877
retrait, 877–882
reclaiming benefits paid without legal justification, 884–885
general recognition of, 874–875
individual cases, application to, 875–886
regulations, retroactivity of, 885–886
statutes, retroactivity of, 885–886
legality principle,
comparative law review, 212–214
statutory constraints and discretion,
doctrine of discretion, fundamentals of, 261–263
judicial review of discretionary decisions, extent of, 263–269
legitimate expectation, principle of,
action by administration,
administrative decisions, avoidance of,
abrogation, 882–883
generally, 876–877
retrait, 877–882
reclaiming benefits paid without legal justification, 884–885
general recognition of, 874–875
individual cases, application to, 875–886
regulations, retroactivity of, 885–886
statutes, retroactivity of, 885–886

France—*cont.*
  Luxembourg, history of, 181
  material concept of administration, 12–14
  origin and development of administrative
    law, 100–102
  Parliament, law-making powers of, 104
  police, functions of, 266
  predominant role of, 261
  private law and administrative law,
    demarcation between, 105
  proportionality, principle of, 680–685
  reasons, duty to give, 1385–1386
  rule-making powers of government, 103
  sources of law, 104–108
  statutory constraints and discretion in,
    discretion, doctrine of, fundamentals
      of, 261–263
    judicial review, extent of, 263–269
Franks Committee
  Report on Administrative Tribunals and
    Enquiries, 91
Free movement of goods
  Article 30 EEC, field of application of,
    food, quality of, measures relating to,
      776–779
    generally, 775–776
    penalties, 781–783
    products, marketing of, measures
      concerning, 779–781
  Article 36 EEC,
    commercial property, protection of,
      800–803
    generally, 789–790
    health, protection of, 790–797
    industrial property, protection of,
      800–803
    public policy, protection of, 798–800
    public security, protection of, 798–800
    recent legal developments, 803–806
  exports, measures restricting, 783–785
  mandatory requirements, case law
    relating to, 785–789
  proportionality principle, application of,
    773–806
Free movement of workers
  public service, not applied to
    employment in, 20
Freedom of decision. *See* Legality principle
Freedom of individual
  absolute all-powerful State, guaranteed
    against, 11
Freedom of movement
  proportionality, principle of, 814–826
  social security law. *See* Social security

Functionality
  comparative law, application of principle
    to, 82–85
  negative side of principle, 82
Fundamental rights
  proportionality principle as substitute
    for, 719–726
Future
  administration as active arrangement
    aimed at, 16

General Agreement on Tariffs and Trade
  (GATT)
  common customs tariff, effect on, 481
General principles of law
  administrative act, revocation of,
    burdens, measures imposing,
      1010–1011
    circumstances, changes in, 1022–1024
    false information, revocation on
      grounds of, 1013–1014
    generally, 986
    incomplete information, revocation on
      grounds of, 1013–1014
    lawful administrative act, 986–991
    legal situation, changes in, 1015–1022
    measures explicitly subject to
      revocation, 1012–1013
    special grounds for revocation,
      1011–1024
    statute, revocation laid down by,
      1011–1012
    summary, 1024–1025
    unlawful administrative act, 991–1010
  authenticity, 66–68
  content of, methods for determining,
    71–75
  defence, rights of, 1324–1325
  equality principle, recognition of,
    administrative-law principle, as,
      641–644
    fundamental principle of Community
      law, as, 625–641
    generally, 644–645
  generally, 64–66
  Germany, 218
  legal certainty, principle of, 1154–1155
  legitimate expectation, protection of,
    1154–1155
  status, 68–71
Germany
  administration, concept of, 15–16
  administrative courts, introduction of,
    115
  administrative law protection, 122–126

Germany—*cont.*
administrative structure, 126–127
comparative administrative law, 89–91
constitutional basis of administrative law,
116–117
customary law, recognition of, 56
decision-making process, 1386–1388
delegated rule-making, unlawfulness in,
219
development of administrative law
doctrine, 3
discretion,
decisions, how courts test, 277–279
doctrine of, basic features of, 270–277
essential characteristics of system,
114–127
general principles of law, 218
hearing, right to,
complementary rights, 1263–1268
exceptions to duty to grant hearing,
1259–1261
general comments, 1255–1258
objection, rights of, 1262–1263
procedural rights, non-observance or
inadequate observance of,
consequences of, 1268–1269
scope of hearing, 1261–1262
those entitled to be heard, 1258–1259
type of hearing, 1261–1262
legal certainty, principle of,
action by administration,
payments having no legal basis,
recovery of,
duties wrongly levied by State,
897–898
payments made by State, 895–897
pledges, 894–895
revocation,
benefits, administrative decision
conferring, 889–891
burdens, administrative decision
imposing, 888–889
generally, 887–888
withdrawal,
benefits, administrative decision
conferring, 892–894
burdens, administrative decision
imposing, 891–892
generally, 887–888, 891
court decisions, retroactive effect of,
900–901
general recognition of, 886–887
individual cases, application to,
887–901
regulations, retroactivity of, 898–900

Germany—*cont.*
legal certainty, principle of—*cont.*
statutes, retroactivity of, 898–900
legality principle,
comparative law review, 214–219
fundamental rights, constraints placed
by, 218
general principles of law, constraints
placed by, 218
primacy of statute, 214
requirement of statute,
field of application, 215–217
reserved area, content of statutes in,
217
statutory constraints and discretion,
courts test of decisions, 277–279
doctrine of discretion, basic features
of, 270–277
unlawful administrative conduct,
delegated rule-making,
unlawfulness in, 219
generally, 218
unlawful administrative act, 218–219
legitimate expectation, principle of,
action by administration,
payments having no legal basis,
recovery of,
duties wrongly levied by State,
897–898
payments made by State, 895–897
pledges, 894–895
revocation,
benefits, administrative decision
conferring, 889–891
burdens, administrative decision
imposing, 888–889
generally, 887–888
withdrawal,
benefits, administrative decision
conferring, 892–894
burdens, administrative decision
imposing, 891–892
generally, 887–888, 891
court decisions, retroactive effect of,
900–901
general recognition of, 886–887
individual cases, application to,
887–901
regulations, retroactivity of, 898–900
statutes, retroactivity of, 898–900
origin and development of administrative
law, 114–116
Plenary Chambers, jurisdiction of, 119
proportionality, principle of, 685–692
public law dispute, concept of, 122

Germany—*cont.*
  reasons, duty to give, 1386–1388
  sources of law, 117–122
  statutory constraints and discretion in,
    courts test of discretionary decisions,
      277–279
    discretion, doctrine of, basic features
      of, 270–277
Goods
  free movement of. *See* **Free movement of**
    goods
Government
  functions, division of, 17
  independent source of power, no place
    as, 12
  state activities as whole termed as, 11
Greece
  administration, concept of, 18n
  administrative instruments, theory of,
    168
  administrative law protection, 170–171
  administrative structure, 171–172
  constitutional basis of administrative law,
    167–168
  decision-making process, 1392–1393
  defence, rights of, 1300–1305
  discretion, doctrine of, 290
  essential characteristics of administrative
    law, 167–172
  legal certainty, principle of, 923–924
  legality principle,
    applicability of, 225–226
    statutory constraints and discretion,
      290
    unlawful administrative conduct, 226
  legitimate expectation, principle of,
    923–924
  local government, 171–172
  origin and development of administrative
    law, 167
  proportionality, principle of, 699
  reasons, duty to give, 1392–1393
  rule-making powers of administration,
    168
  sources of law, 168–170
  statutory constraints and discretion, 290
Guarantee
  agricultural markets, organisation of, 753

Health, protection of
  proportionality, principle of, 790–798
  standards laid down by EAEC, 31–32
Hearing. *See* **Defence**, rights of
Hierarchy of rules
  Member States, relationship between
    Community and, 252–253

Hierarchy of rules—*cont.*
  within Community law, 248–252
High Authority
  ECSC Treaty use of concept of, 21
History
  proportionality, concept of, 678–679
  See also **Origin and development**
Hood Phillips, O.
  executive and legislative functions,
    distinction between, 17
Human rights. *See* **European Court of**
  Human Rights

Illegal act
  fault, not involving, liability for, 531–532
Illegality
  conduct, of, 511–513
  plea of, time limits for remedies,
    1051–1054
Implementation mechanisms
  access to, 8
Implementation of law
  direct. *See* **Direct implementation**
  indirect. *See* **Indirect implementation**
Implied powers
  doctrine of, 48
Imports
  third countries, from, protective
    mechanisms against, 29, 44
Income
  budget, implementation of, 26
Indirect executive action. *See* **Executive**
  action
Indirect implementation
  common agricultural policy, 34–36,
    46
  common customs tariff, external
    protection through, 36–37
  example of, 23–24
  generally, 34
  main areas of, 34
  secondary law,
    legal basis of Act, 50–53
    present position, 45–47
  sources of law, 45–47, 50–53
Individual case
  idea of, 21
Individual decision. *See* **Administrative act**
Industrial property
  protection of, 800–803
Information
  administrative powers to collect,
    anti-dumping law, powers under,
      1222–1223, 1242–1243

Information—*cont.*
  administrative powers to collect—*cont.*
    Commission, powers of,
      secondary legislation, information
        provided for in,
          anti-dumping law, powers under,
            1222–1223, 1242–1243
          generally, 1218
          Regulation 17/62, 1218–1221
      treaties, information provided for in,
        1216–1218
    competition proceedings, 1242–1243
    Court of Justice, complete
      investigation as elaborated by,
      case law,
        earlier, 1223–1236
        more recent, 1236–1238
        customs duties, special problems
          arising in law of, 1231–1236
        generally, 1238–1239
        levies, special problems arising in
          law of, 1231–1236
        variety of fields of law, examples
          from, 1223–1231
    generally, 1215
    investigatory powers, limits placed
      upon,
      evidence, prohibition on use of,
        1241–1242
      legal privilege, 1239–1241
      proportionality, principle of,
        1239–1241
  decision-making process, remedies
    relating to, 1382–1384
  false, revocation of administrative act on
    grounds of, 1013–1014
  incomplete, revocation of administrative
    act on grounds of, 1013–1014
  self-binding action by authorities,
    1085–1089
Information notes
  audit procedure, issued in course of, 24n
Inquiries
  natural justice, rules of, 1288–1290
Institutions
  administrative wrong, liability for,
    510–511
  competence, 1202–1209
  decision-making, competence of,
    1209–1212
  direct administrative implementation of
    law, 23–24
  indirect implementation of law, 23–24
  measures, requirement to pass special
    committee before passing, 41

Instruments
  normative. *See* **Normative instruments**
Interest groups
  consultation of, 41n
International law
  general, 703–704
  proportionality principle in,
    European Commission of Human
      Rights, case law of, 705
    European Convention on Human
      Rights, under,
    case law,
      European Commission of Human
        Rights, of, 705
      European Court of Human
        Rights, of, 706–707
    generally, 704
    European Court of Human Rights,
      case law of, 706–707
    general international law, 703–704
Interpretation
  principles of, 257–258
Ireland
  administration, concept of, 18
  administrative law protection, 177–179
  administrative structure, 179–180
  British system compared with, 173–174
  central administration, 179
  constitutional basis of administrative law,
    174–175
  decision-making process, 1393–1395
  discretion, doctrine of, 290–291
  Emergency Powers Acts, 175
  essential characteristics of system,
    173–180
  hearing, right to, 1305–1309
  judicial review, 177–178
  legal certainty, principle of, 924–925
  legality principle,
    comparative law review, 226–227
    statutory constraints and discretion,
      290–291
  legitimate expectation, principle of,
    924–925
  local government, 179
  natural justice principle, interpretation
    of, 177
  origin and development of administrative
    law, 173–174
  proportionality, principle of, 699–700
  reasons, duty to give, 1393–1395
  sources of law, 175–177
  state liability, extension of, 174n
  state prerogatives, reduction of, 174n
  statutory constraints and discretion,
    290–291

Italy
administration, concept of, 19n
administrative law protection, 134–137
administrative structures, 137–139
decision-making process, 1388–1389
defence, rights of,
    constitutive phase, 1273
    generally, 1269–1271
    preparatory phase, 1271–1272
    so-called phase in which act becomes
      fully effective, 1273
delegated legislation, 131
discretion, doctrine of, 279–281
essential characteristics of systems,
    128–139
legal certainty, principle of,
    action by administration,
      administrative decisions, avoidance
        of,
        generally, 912
        inappropriate administrative
          decisions, revocation of,
          914–915
        unlawful administrative decisions,
          withdrawal of, 912–914
        payments having no legal basis,
          recovery of, 915–916
      general recognition of, 911–912
      individual cases, application to,
        912–918
      statutes, retroactivity of, 916–918
legality principle,
    comparative law review, 220
    statutory constraints and discretion,
      279–281
legitimate expectation, principle of,
    action by administration,
      administrative decisions, avoidance
        of,
        generally, 912
        inappropriate administrative
          decisions, revocation of,
          914–915
        unlawful administrative decisions,
          withdrawal of, 912–914
        payments having no legal basis,
          recovery of, 915–916
      general recognition of, 911–912
      individual cases, application to,
        912–918
      statutes, retroactivity of, 916–918
origin and development of administrative
    law, 128–132
proportionality, principle of, 692–695
provisional legislative instruments, 131

Italy—*cont.*
reasons, duty to give, 1388–1389
sources of law, 132–134
statutory constraints and discretion in,
    279–281

Judge-made law
comparative law, fundamentals of, 81–82
convergence of both systems of, 98
function and significance of, 5n
source of law, as, 59–64
Judicial law making. *See* **Judge-made law**
Judicial power
France, 13
functions of government, division of, 17
natural justice, procedural guarantees of,
    effect of, 18
sovereign activity, form of expression of,
    11
Judicial review
appeal distinguished from, 177
discretionary decisions, in. *See*
    Discretion
ECSC, case law of. *See* **European Coal
    and Steel Community**
France, 263–269
grounds for, 40
Ireland, 177–178
Netherlands, 189–190
See also **Protection**
Jurisdiction
Member States, of, equality principle
    and, 649–657
Justification
arbitrary action and, 584–601

Kaiser, Joseph H.
comparative law, on, 77

Lafferrière, Edouard
Language question
administrative procedure, principles of,
    1212–1215
Lawful act
liability for, 532–533
French administrative law, development
    of, 102
Legal act
authority to act, 247–248
avoidance of,
    EEC Treaty, effects of avoidance
      under, 242
    legal consequences of, 240–243
    validity pending avoidance, 241–242

Legal act—*cont.*
  avoidance of—*cont.*
    void regulation, continuing
      applicability of, 242–243
  incomplete application of,
    delay in implementation or
      performance, 661–663
    performance, delay in, 661–663
    refusal to implement or execute,
      658–661
Legal certainty, principle of
  administrative law, as principle of,
    940–942
  administrative measures, revocation of,
    1156–1159
  areas in which applicable,
    community legislative action, 945–946
    direct executive action. *See* **Executive**
      action
    indirect executive action. *See*
      Executive action
  Belgium. *See* **Belgium**
  Community law, recognition in, 870–873
  Community legislative action,
    application to, 945–946
  concept, as, 946–949
  constitutional law, as principle of,
    940–942
  Court of Justice, development in case law
    of, 938–940
  Denmark, 921–923
  direct executive action. *See* **Executive**
    action
  European Court of Justice recognition of,
    6
  France. *See* **France**
  general legal principle, as, 1154–1155
  generally, 946–949, 1170–1172
  Germany. *See* **Germany**
  Greece, 923–924
  indirect executive action. *See* **Executive**
    action
  Ireland, 924–925
  Italy. *See* **Italy**
  Luxembourg, 925–926
  national law, recognition in, 868–870
  Netherlands. *See* **Netherlands**
  normative instruments. *See* **Normative**
    instruments
  origins,
    generally, 867–868
    principle of law, emergence as,
      Community law, recognition in,
        870–873
      national law, recognition in, 868–870

Legal certainty, principle of—*cont.*
  Portugal, 932–933
  principle of law, emergence as,
    Community law, recognition in,
      870–873
    national law, recognition in, 868–870
  recovery of payments wrongly made. *See*
    Executive action
  retroactivity. *See* **Retroactivity**
  Spain. *See* **Spain**
  United Kingdom. *See* **United Kingdom**
  vested rights, 953–956
Legal instrument
  effectiveness of, 239
  invalidity of, 243–248
  nullity of,
    avoidance of legal act, legal
      consequences of,
      effects of avoidance, 242
      general, 240–241
      validity pending avoidance, 241–242
      void regulation, continuing
        applicability of, 242–243
    grounds of claim,
      ECSC Treaty, 240
      EEC Treaty, 239–240
      Euratom Treaty, 239–240
    invalidity, declaration of, effects of,
      243–248
Legal privilege
  investigatory powers, limits placed on,
    1239–1241
Legal protection. *See* **Protection**
Legal remedies. *See* **Remedies**
Legal rule
  binding nature of equality principle as.
    See **Equality, principle of**
Legality principle
  administrative freedom of decision. *See*
    freedom of decision *below*
  Belgium. *See* **Belgium**
  Denmark. *See* **Denmark**
  development, prospects for, 542–543
  executive freedom of decision. *See*
    freedom of decision *below*
  foundation of, 230–231
  France. *See* **France**
  freedom of decision,
    administrative,
      Belgium, 287–289
      Denmark, 289
      France, 261–269
      generally, 294–295
      Germany, 270–279
      Greece, 290

Legality principle—*cont.*
  freedom of decision—*cont.*
    administrative—*cont.*
      Ireland, 290–291
      Italy, 279–281
      Luxembourg, 291
      Netherlands, 291–293
      Portugal, 293–294
      Spain, 294
      United Kingdom, 281–287
  executive,
    administrative discretion, 298
    civil service law,
      generally, 302–303, 325
      legal constraints, operation of,
        304–324
    common agricultural policy,
      Commission, implementing law
        of, 440–453
      generally, 395–396
      market regulation, Council's
        prerogative of, 396–440
      Member States, implementation
        of law by, 453–480
    competition law,
      aid, prohibition of, 381–389
      generally, 360–361
      subject-matter of Articles 85 and
        86, 361–381
    customs union,
      Customs Tariff Nomenclature,
        application of, 482–494
      generally, 480, 494
      legal constraints in policy, 481–482
      significance of, 480–481
    dumping, rules against, 389–395
    European Coal and Steel
      Community,
      generally, 325–326, 359–360
      judicial review, 326–359
    external trade, 389–395
    judicial protection in discretionary
      decisions, 299–300
    legislative discretion, 298
    mode of procedure, explanation of,
      301–302
    reasons, obligation to state, link
      between discretion and, 301
    social security law,
      legal constraints on administration
        in, 494–503
      migrant workers, 497–503
      social policy, Community's
        competence in, 495–497
    terminology, 296–298

Legality principle—*cont.*
  generally, 212
  Germany. *See* **Germany**
  Greece. *See* **Greece**
  Ireland. *See* **Ireland**
  Italy. *See* **Italy**
  legality of administration, concept of, 209
  liability. *See* **Non-contractual liability**
  Luxembourg. *See* **Luxembourg**
  Netherlands. *See* **Netherlands**
  non-contractual liability. *See* **Non-
    contractual liability**
  Portugal. *See* **Portugal**
  present situation, 539–542
  prospects for development, 542–543
  sources of legality, 247–248
  sovereign power, legal delimitation of,
    208–211
  Spain. *See* **Spain**
  state governed by law, state as, 207–211
  statute,
    primacy of,
      Germany, 214
      Netherlands, 227–228
    requirement of,
      Germany, 215–217
      Netherlands, 228–229
    principle,
      reserved treaty powers, 253–256
      secondary legislation, treaty
        reservation in, 256–257
    terminology, 253
  superior law, priority accorded to,
    hierarchy of rules,
      EC and Member States, relationship
        between, 252–253
      within Community law, 248–252
    principle, 234
  survey of EC law,
    authority to act, 247–248
    binding instrument distinguished
      from non-binding statement,
      European Court, distinguishing
        criteria used by, 236–239
    positive law distinction, 235–236
    generally, 235
    legal acts, 247–248
    legal instruments,
      effectiveness of, 239
      invalidity of, 243–247
      nullity of, 239–247
    sources of legality, 247–248
  terminology,
    generally, 233
    statute, requirement of, 253

Legality principle—*cont.*
underlying structures,
generally, 233–234
interpretation, principles of, 257–258
requirement of statute,
principle,
reserved treaty powers, 253–256
secondary legislation, treaty
reservation in, 256–257
terminology, 253
superior law, priority accorded to,
hierarchy of rules,
EC and Member States, in
relationship between,
252–253
within EC law, 248–252
principle, 234
survey of EC law,
binding instrument distinguished
from non-binding statement,
235–239
effectiveness of legal instruments,
239
generally, 235
non-binding statement,
distinction between binding
instrument and, 235–239
nullity of legal instruments,
239–248
United Kingdom. *See* **United Kingdom**
unlawful administrative conduct,
conclusions on survey, 232
Denmark, 225
error, sources of, 258–259
Germany,
delegated rule-making,
unlawfulness in, 219
generally, 218
unlawful administrative act, 218–219
Greece, 226
revocability, principle of, 259
variations in expression of, 231–232
Legislation. *See* **Statutes**
Legislative action
legal certainty, application of, 945–946
legitimate expectation, protection of,
application of, 945–946
Legislative power
executive power, distinguished from, 17
France, 12–13
functions of government, division of, 17
sovereign activity, form of expression of,
11
Legislature
creation of new law by, 78–79

Legitimate expectation, protection of
administrative law, as principle of,
940–942
administrative measures, revocation of,
1156–1159
areas in which applicable,
community legislative action, 945–946
direct executive action. *See* **Executive
action**
indirect executive action. *See*
Executive action
Belgium. *See* **Belgium**
Community law, recognition in, 870–873
Community legislative action,
application to, 945–946
concept, as, 946, 949–953
constitutional law, as principle of,
940–942
Court of Justice, development in case law
of, 938–940
Denmark, 921–923
France. *See* **France**
general legal principle, as, 1154–1155
generally, 949–953, 1170–1172
Germany. *See* **Germany**
Greece, 923–924
Ireland, 924–925
Italy. *See* **Italy**
Luxembourg, 925–926
national law, recognition in, 868–870
Netherlands. *See* **Netherlands**
normative instruments. *See* **Normative
instruments**
origins,
generally, 867–868
principle of law, emergence as,
Community law, recognition in,
870–873
national law, recognition in, 868–870
Portugal, 932–933
principle of law, emergence as,
Community law, recognition in,
870–873
national law, recognition in, 868–870
protection of, European Court of Justice
recognition of, 6
recovery of payments wrongly made. *See*
Executive action
retroactivity. *See* **Retroactivity**
Spain. *See* **Spain**
United Kingdom. *See* **United Kingdom**
vested rights, 953–956
Levies
agricultural, external protection of
common market includes, 30

Levies—*cont.*
agricultural markets, organisation of. *See*
Agricultural markets
co-responsibility, 753–754
equity, remission on grounds of, 469–474
fixing amount of, 756–759
information, administrative powers to
collect, 1231–1236
subsequent collection of duties
incorrectly not levied, 1069–1071
unlawful public, obligation to repay in
case of, 1161–1165
Liability. *See* **Non-contractual liability**
Local government
Denmark, 166
Greece, 171–172
Ireland, 179
United Kingdom, 151–152
Luxembourg
administrative law protection, 184–186
administrative structure, 186
constitutional basis of administrative law,
182
decision-making process, 1395–1396
discretion, doctrine of, 291
droits de la défense in, 1309–1311
essential characteristics of system,
181–186
legal certainty, principle of, 925–926
legality principle,
comparative law review, 227
statutory constraints and discretion,
291
legitimate expectation, principle of,
925–926
origin and development of administrative
law, 181–182
proportionality, principle of, 700
public service, concept of, 19n
reasons, duty to give, 1395–1396
sources of law, 182–184
statutory constraints and discretion, 291

Mandatory requirements
case law relating to, proportionality
principle and, 785–789
Marketing
products, of, measures concerning,
779–781
Material resources
internal Community administration, 25
Maximalist theory
general principles of law, content of,
71–72

Mayer, Otto
French administrative law, book on, 3
Measures
failure to take, concept of discrimination
and, 614–616
formal, 663–666
substantive, 667–669
unilateral supplementary or amending,
formal measures, 663–666
generally, 663, 669
substantive measures, 667–669
Mechanical failure
meaning, 464
Member States
administration, concept of, 11–20
administrative law systems, essential
characteristics of, 97–99
agricultural law, implementation of. *See*
Common agricultural policy
Belgium. *See* **Belgium**
Denmark. *See* **Denmark**
equality of,
generally, 658
incomplete application of legal act,
delay in implementation or
performance, 661–663
performance, delay in, 661–663
refusal to implement or execute,
658–661
unilateral supplementary or amending
measures,
formal measures, 663–666
generally, 663, 669
substantive measures, 667–669
France. *See* **France**
Germany. *See* **Germany**
Greece. *See* **Greece**
hierarchy of rules in relationship between
Community and, 252–253
Ireland. *See* **Ireland**
Italy. *See* **Italy**
jurisdiction of, equality principle and,
649–657
liability systems in, delimitation of,
535–538
Luxembourg. *See* **Luxembourg**
Netherlands. *See* **Netherlands**
Portugal. *See* **Portugal**
Spain. *See* **Spain**
United Kingdom. *See* **United Kingdom**
Migrant worker
social security rules, application of, 47,
54, 497–503
Minimalist solution
general principles of law, concept of, 71

Misuse of powers
common agricultural policy, relating to,
415
ECSC, case law relating to. *See* **European
Coal and Steel Community**
Movement, freedom of. *See* **Freedom of
movement**

National administrative law
basic contention, 3
common European law, development of,
interdependence with, 1434–1446
executive action. *See* **Executive action**
See also **Public law**
National authorities
budget, implementation of, 26
indirect implementation. *See* **Indirect
implementation**
National rules
proportionality principle derived from,
714–715
Natural differences
discrimination, concept of, 606–610
Natural justice
Ireland, 177
judicial function, procedural guarantees
binding organs exercising, 18
United Kingdom. *See* **United Kingdom**
Necessity
proportionality principle, content of,
857–859
Netherlands
administrative law protection, 191–192
administrative structure, 192
constitutional basis of administrative law,
188–189
decentralised unitary state, principle of,
192
decision-making process, 1396–1397
discretion, doctrine of, 291–293
essential characteristics of system,
187–192
hearing, right to, 1311–1314
judicial review, grounds for, 189–190
legal certainty, principle of,
action by administration,
administrative decisions, avoidance
of,
benefits, lawful decision
conferring, 928–929
generally, 928
unlawful decision conferring
benefits, 929–930
state benefits wrongly paid, recovery
of, 930

Netherlands—*cont.*
legal certainty, principle of—*cont.*
action by administration—*cont.*
wrongly levied duties, recovery of,
930–931
general recognition of, 926–928
individual cases, application to,
928–932
regulations, retroactivity of, 931–932
statutes, retroactivity of, 931–932
legality principle,
comparative law review, 227–229
primacy of statute, 227–228
requirement of statute, 228–229
statutory constraints and discretion,
291–293
legitimate expectation, principle of,
action by administration,
administrative decisions, avoidance
of,
benefits, lawful decision
conferring, 928–929
generally, 928
unlawful decision conferring
benefits, 929–930
state benefits wrongly paid, recovery
of, 930
wrongly levied duties, recovery of,
930–931
general recognition of, 926–928
individual cases, application to,
928–932
regulations, retroactivity of, 931–932
statutes, retroactivity of, 931–932
Luxembourg, history of, 181
origin and development of administrative
law, 187–188
proportionality, principle of, 700–701
public administration, concept of, 19n
reasons, duty to give, 1396–1397
Royal Commissioner, functions of,
192
sources of law, 189–191
statutory constraints and discretion in,
291–293
New law
legislature, creation by, 78–79
Non-binding instrument
binding force, acquisition of, 58n
Non-binding statement
binding instrument distinguished from,
European Court, distinguishing
criteria used by, 236–239
positive law distinctions, 235–236

Non-contractual liability
absolute liability, 533–534
administrative wrongs,
  compensation,
    extent of, 517–524
    nature of, 516–517
  culpability of conduct, 513–515
  damage which can be made good,
    compensation,
      extent of, 517–524
      nature of, 516–517
    generally, 515
  general principle, 508
  illegality of conduct, 511–513
  institutions, conduct of, 510–511
  nature of, 508
  official capacity, 508–510
  officials, conduct of, 510–511
  particular conditions,
    culpability of conduct, 513–515
    illegality of conduct, 511–513
    institutions, conduct of, 510–511
    official capacity, 508–510
    officials, conduct of, 510–511
circumstances giving rise to,
  administrative wrongs. *See*
    administrative wrongs *above*
  legislative wrongs, 524–530
delimitation of liability systems, 535–538
development of, 505–507
generally, 504
illegal act not involving fault, liability for,
  531–532
lawful act, liability for, 532–533
legislative wrongs, prerequisites of
  liability for, 524–530
Non-discrimination
European Court of Justice, principle
  recognised by, 6
Normative instruments
defence, rights of, 1320–1324
generally, 1113–1114
legal certainty, principle of,
  legal position,
    clear and predictable nature of,
      1152–1153
    expectation of changes in,
      1151–1152
  legislator's duty to observe, 1114–1118
legitimate expectation, protection of,
  legal position,
    clear and predictable nature of,
      1152–1153
    expectation of changes in, 1151–1152
  legislator's duty to observe, 1114–1118

Normative instruments—*cont.*
legitimate expectation, protection of—
  cont.
  retroactivity of rules,
    actual retroactivity,
      admissibility of, conditions for,
        1122–1130
      detailed survey, 1122–1130
      principles relating to, 1120–1121.,
    apparent retroactivity,
      admissibility of, conditions for,
        1130–1151
      directives, special case of,
        1148–1151
      legal consequences, 1145–1147
      legislator's freedom to legislate,
        restriction of, 1130–1145
      principles relating to, 1121–1122
    generally, 1119
    validity of legal rules, principles
      relating to, 1119–1122
  retroactivity. *See* legitimate expectation,
    protection of *above*
Northern Ireland
separate legal system, existence of, 140n
See also **United Kingdom**
Notification
decision-making process, 1416–1420
Nuclear field
investment programmes, promotion by
  Euratom of, 32

Offer
meaning, 468–469
valid offer, meaning, 468
Official capacity
administrative wrong, conditions of,
  508–510
Officials
administrative wrongs, liability for,
  510–511
staff regulations, 25
Ombudsman
Denmark, 165–166
Origin and development
Belgium, 154–156
Denmark, 161–162
France, 100–102
generally, 98
Germany, 114–116
Greece, 167
Ireland, 173–174
Italy, 128–132
legal certainty, principle of, 867–873

Origin and development—*cont.*
  legitimate expectation, principle of,
    867–873
  Luxembourg, 181–182
  Portugal, 193–194
  United Kingdom, 140–143
Orlando, V.E.
  new Italian school of public law, founder
    of, 130n

Parliament
  executive power, control of, 208
  legislative role principally located in, 17
  sovereignty of, 145
  supremacy of, 17
Payments wrongly made, recovery of. *See*
  Executive action
Penalties
  free movement of goods, proportionality
    principle and, 781–783
Personnel management
  internal Community administration, 25
Petition
  defence, rights of, general limitations
    upon, 1334–1335
Planning control
  comparative law, 94
Plea
  illegality, of, time limits for remedies,
    1051–1054
Pledges
  Germany, 894–895
  self-binding action by authorities,
    1089–1093
Police
  France, functions in, 266
Portugal
  administrative law protection, 197–198
  administrative structure, 198
  constitutional basis of administrative law,
    194–196
  decision-making process, 1398–1399
  defence, rights of, 1314–1315
  discretion, doctrine of, 293–294
  essential characteristics of system,
    193–198
  legal certainty, principle of, 932–933
  legality principle,
    comparative law review, 229–230
    statutory constraints and discretion,
      293–294
  legitimate expectation, principle of,
    932–933
  origin and development of administrative
    law, 193–194

Portugal—*cont.*
  proportionality, principle of, 701–702
  public administration, concept of, 19
  reasons, duty to give, 1398–1399
  rule of law, democratic state based on,
    concept of, 195
  sources of law, 196
  statutory constraints and discretion,
    293–294
Postal services
  public, interpretation by European Court
    of concept of, 21n
Powers
  organisational separation of, 11
Premiums
  agricultural markets, organisation of,
    766–773
Prerogative writ
  scope of application of, 18
Prices
  agricultural markets, organisation of,
    754–756, 760–762
Primary law
  written, 39–42
Principles of law. *See* **General principles of**
  law
Private law
  public law, absence of distinction
    between, 84
Privilege. *See* **Legal privilege**
Procedural defects
  legal consequences of, 1420–1430
Procedure. *See* **Administrative procedure**
Proceedings
  time limits in, 1054–1061
Production quota system
  proportionality, principle of, 845–849
Products
  marketing of, measures concerning,
    779–781
Prohibition
  scope of application of claim of, 18
Property
  commercial, protection of, 800–803
  industrial, protection of, 800–803
Proportionality, principle of
  agricultural markets, organisation of,
    deposits,
      amount of, 732
      cases featuring, 727–747
      forfeiture of, 732–747
      legal nature of, 729–732
    generally, 727
    intervention, other cases concerning,
      co-responsibility levy, 753–754

Proportionality, principle of—*cont.*
agricultural markets, organisation
of—*cont.*
intervention, other cases
concerning—*cont.*
denaturing premiums, 766–773
generally, 752–753
guarantee, 753
levy,
co-responsibility, 753–754
fixing amount of, 756–759
minimum prices system, 760–762
monetary compensation system,
762–766
quota system, 759–760
subsidies, 766–773
threshold prices, fixing of, 754–756
skimmed-milk powder cases, 747–752
Belgium, 697–698
case law,
European Convention on Human
Rights. *See* European Convention
on Human Rights *below*
European Court of Justice. *See*
European Court of Justice *below*
Community law, in, generally, 708–709
competition law,
administrative procedure, 834–837
fines, 837–841
generally, 833–834
substantive, 841–842
concept of proportionality,
historical origins, 678–679
role of principle, 679
content of,
generally, 854–855
necessity, 857–859
strict sense, proportionality in,
859–860
suitability, 855–857
Denmark, 698–699
differentiation according to field of
application, 861–864
European Coal and Steel Community,
generally, 842–844
procedural questions, 850–852
production quota systems, 845–849
scrap metal equalisation cases,
844–845
European Commission of Human
Rights, case law of, 705
European Convention on Human
Rights,

Proportionality, principle of—*cont.*
European Convention on Human
Rights—*cont.*
case law,
European Commission of Human
Rights, of, 705
European Court of Human Rights,
of, 706–707
generally, 704
European Court of Human Rights,
case law of, 706–707
European Court of Justice,
case law, practical application in,
agricultural markets, organisation
of. *See* agricultural markets,
organisation of *above*
competition law. *See* competition
law *above*
ECSC. *See* European Coal and Steel
Community *above*
foreign trade law, 806–814
free movement of goods. *See* free
movement of goods *below*
freedom of establishment, 827–833
freedom of movement, 814–826
generally, 726–727
services, freedom to provide,
827–833
staff law cases, 853
recognition by, 6
express provisions in Treaty, 710–712
foreign trade law, 806–814
France, 680–685
free movement of goods,
Article 30 EEC, field of application of,
food, quality of, measures relating
to, 776–779
generally, 775–776
marketing of products, measures
concerning, 779–781
penalties, 781–783
Article 36 EEC,
commercial property, protection of,
800–803
generally, 789–790
health, protection of, 790–797
industrial property, protection of,
800–803
public policy, protection of, 798–800
public security, protection of,
798–800
recent legal developments, 803–806
exports, measures restricting, 783–785
generally, 773–775
mandatory requirements, case law
relating to, 785–789

Proportionality, principle of—*cont.*
  freedom of establishment, 827–833
  freedom of movement, 814–826
  generally, 677–678, 853–854, 864–866
  Germany, 685–692
  goods, free movement of. *See* free
    movement of goods *above*
  Greece, 699
  international law, in,
    European Convention on Human
      Rights, under,
      case law,
        European Commission of Human
          Rights, of, 705
        European Court of Human
          Rights, of, 706
        generally, 704
      general international law, 703–704
      generally, 680
  investigatory powers, limits placed upon,
    1239–1241
  Ireland, 699–700
  Italy, 692–695
  Luxembourg, 700
  Member States, legal systems of, in,
    Belgium, 697–698
    Denmark, 698–699
    France, 680–685
    generally, 680
    Germany, 685–692
    Greece, 699
    Ireland, 699–700
    Italy, 692–695
    Luxembourg, 700
    Netherlands, 700–701
    Portugal, 701–702
    Spain, 702
    United Kingdom, 695–697
  movement, freedom of, 814–826
  national rules, derived from, 714–715
  Netherlands, 700–701
  objective rule, as,
    fundamental rights, substitute for,
      719–726
    status, 717–719
  official action, form taken by, 861–864
  Portugal, 701–702
  role of, 679
  rule of law, derived from, 712–714
  services, freedom to provide, 827–833
  sources of,
    evaluation, 716–717
    express provisions in Treaty, 710–712
    national rules, derived from, 714–715

Proportionality, principle of—*cont.*
  sources of—*cont.*
    rule of law, deriving principle from,
      712–714
    treaty provisions, deduced from,
      715–716
  Spain, 702
  staff law cases, 853
  strict sense, in, 859–860
  Treaty provisions, deduced from,
    715–716
  United Kingdom, 695–697
Protection
  Belgium, 157–159
  Denmark, 164–166
  France, 108–111
  generally, 98
  Germany, 122–126
  Greece, 170–171
  Ireland, 177–179
  Italy, 134–137
  judicial. *See* **Judicial review**
  Luxembourg, 184–186
  Portugal, 197–198
  United Kingdom, 147–151
Public administration. *See* **Administration**
Public authority
  hearing before adverse decision taken by,
    right to, 6
Public corporation
  United Kingdom, 152
Public health
  comparative law, 94
Public interest
  administration concerned with, 16
Public law
  characteristics of, 85–87
  comparative law used to assist
    interpretation of, 82n
  European law and, mutual influences of,
    93–95
  methodology of comparative law, 87–88
  political power, pressure through
    exercise of, 87
  private law, absence of distinction
    between, 84
  regulatory scope of, 85–86
  unification of law, chances of, 88–89
  written and unwritten law, mixture of
    layers of, 86
Public policy
  protection of, proportionality principle
    and, 798–800
Public security
  protection of, proportionality principle
    and, 798–800

Public service
criterion of, 14
European Court of Justice, development
of concept by, 20–21
free movement of workers not applied to
employment in, 20

Quantitative restrictions
external protection of common market
includes, 30
Quasi-judicial
actions of administrative authorities
described as, 18
Quota system
agricultural markets, organisation of,
759–760
production, proportionality principle
and, 845–849

Reasons. *See* **Decision–making process**
Recovery of payments wrongly made. *See*
Executive action
Regional policy
comprehensive, absence of, 30–31
Regulations
demarcating administrative acts from,
964–969
retroactivity of,
France, 885–886
Germany, 898–900
Netherlands, 931–932
Spain, 937
United Kingdom, 910
void, continuing applicability of, 242–243
Remedies
decision-making process, relating to,
information about, 1382–1384
natural justice, rules of, 1290–1291
time limits for. *See* **Time limits**
Research
European Atomic Energy Community,
promotion by, 31
Retroactivity
actual, 1120–1121, 1122–1130
administrative measures, of,
decisions, regulations challengeable as
being, 1078
examples, 1072–1079
generally, 1072
protective measures, authorisations
for, 1075–1077
subsidies, supervision of, law on,
1072–1075
apparent, 1121–1122, 1130–1151

Retroactivity—*cont.*
normative instruments, relating to. *See*
Normative instruments
regulations, of. *See* **Regulations**
rules, of, 1168–1170
statutes, of. *See* **Statutes**
Review. *See* **Judicial review**
Revocability
unlawful administrative act, of, 259–260
Revocation
administrative act, of. *See* **Administrative
act**
administrative measures, of, 1156–1159
Rivero, Jean
comparative law, on, 93–94
Romagnosi, G.D.
Italian legal theory dominated by, 128
Rule of law
administrative procedure under. *See*
Administrative procedure
Portugal as democratic state based on,
195
proportionality principle derived from,
712–714
Rule-making
delegated. *See* **Delegated legislation**
Rules
retroactivity of, 1168–1170

Safety
protection of, standards laid down by
EAEC, 31–32
Scotland
separate legal system, existence of, 140n
See also **United Kingdom**
Scrap metal equalisation cases
proportionality, principle of, 844–845
Secondary law
generally, 42
legal basis of Act,
direct implementation, 48–50
generally, 47–48
indirect implementation, 50–53
legislature, creation of new law by, 79
present position,
direct implementation, 43–45
generally, 42–43
indirect implementation, 45–47
Treaty reservation in, 256–257
Secondary legislation
information, administrative powers to
collect, 1218–1223
Self-binding action by authorities. *See*
Executive action

Service agencies
internal Community administration, 25
Services
freedom to provide, proportionality
principle and, 827–833
Skimmed-milk powder
agricultural markets, organisation of,
747–752
Social arrangement
administration as, 16
Social law
comparative law, 94
Social policy
administration external to Community,
30
Community's competence in, 495–497
Social security
indirect implementation, 46–47
legal constraints on administration in,
executive freedom of decision,
497–503
generally, 494–495
social policy, Community's
competence in, 495–497
migrant workers, application of rules to,
47, 54, 497–503
Sources of law
Belgium, 156–157
concept of, 38
customary law, 55–59
Denmark, 163–164
France, 104–108
general principles of law,
authenticity, 66–68
generally, 64–66, 75
methods for determining content of,
71–75
status, 68–71
generally, 38, 98
Germany, 117–122
Greece, 168–170
Ireland, 175–177
Italy, 132–134
judge-made law, 59–64
Luxembourg, 182–184
Portugal, 196
United Kingdom, 143–147
written law,
analogy, admissibility of reasoning by,
54–55
generally, 38–39, 55
inadequacy of, 53–54
primary law, 39–42
secondary law,
generally, 42

Sources of law—*cont.*
written law—*cont.*
secondary law—*cont.*
legal basis of Act,
direct implementation, 48–50
generally, 47–48
indirect implementation, 50–53
present position,
direct implementation, 43–45
generally, 42–43
indirect implementation, 45–47
Sovereign activity
Aristotle, forms of expression
distinguished by, 11
Sovereign power
legal delimitation of, 208–211
Spain
administrative law protection, 203–204
administrative structure, 204–205
codification of administrative law, 98
constitutional basis of administrative law,
200–201
decision-making process, 1399–1400
discretion, doctrine of, 294
essential characteristics of system,
199–205
hearing, right to, 1315–1320
legal certainty, principle of,
action by administration, 934–936
administrative decisions, avoidance of,
934–936
general recognition of, 933–934
individual cases, application to,
934–937
regulations, retroactivity of, 937
statutes, retroactivity of, 937
legality principle,
comparative law review, 230
statutory constraints and discretion,
294
legitimate expectation, principle of,
action by administration, 934–936
administrative decisions, avoidance of,
934–936
general recognition of, 933–934
individual cases, application to,
934–937
regulations, retroactivity of, 937
statutes, retroactivity of, 937
Ordinary Laws, 201n
Organic Laws, 201n
origin and development of administrative
law, 199–200
Outline Laws, 201
proportionality, principle of, 702
public administration, concept of, 19n

Spain—*cont.*
  reasons, duty to give, 1399–1400
  sources of law, 201–202
  statutory constraints and discretion in,
    294
Staff law cases
  proportionality, principle of, 853
  Staff Regulations,
    recovery of payments wrongly made,
      1062–1067
    revocation of, 984–985
Stahl, Julius
  state governed by law, idea of, 207
Stare decisis doctrine
  United Kingdom, 144–145
State
  recovery of payments wrongly made by,
    1166–1168
  state governed by law, as, 207–211
State activity
  Aristotelian differentiation of forms of,
    11
Status
  general principles of law, of, 68–71
  proportionality principle as objective
    rule, 717–719
Statutes
  administrative act, revocation of,
    1011–1012
  case law and, European administrative
    law between, 1446–1455
  interpretation of, 81–82
  primacy of,
    Germany, 214
    Netherlands, 227–228
  requirement of,
    Germany, 215–217
    Netherlands, 228–229
    principle,
      reserved treaty powers, 253–256
      secondary legislation, treaty
        reservation in, 256
      terminology, 253
  retroactivity of,
    France, 885–886
    Germany, 898–900
    Italy, 916–918
    Netherlands, 931–932
    Spain, 937
    United Kingdom, 910
  See also **Judge-made law**
Steel. *See* **European Coal and Steel
  Community**
Structure of administration
  Belgium, 159–160

Structure administration—*cont.*
  Denmark, 166
  France, 111–112
  generally, 99
  Germany, 126–127
  Greece, 171–172
  Ireland, 179–180
  Italy, 137–139
  Luxembourg, 186
  Portugal, 198
  United Kingdom, 151–152
Subsidies
  agricultural markets, organisation of,
    766–773
  anti-subsidy duty, introduction of, 29
  competition procedures, 28
  national, granting of, 28
  reclaiming when unlawfully paid,
    474–479
  review of, practical effectiveness of,
    28–29
  supervision of, 1072–1075
Suitability
  proportionality principle, content of,
    855–857
Supervision
  subsidies, of, 1072–1075
Supply Agency of EAEC. *See* **Euratom**

Terminology
  executive freedom of decision, 296–298
  legality principle, 233
  statute, requirement of, 253
Third countries
  dumped or subsidised imports from,
    protective mechanisms against, 29,
    44
Third party
  defence, rights of, 1325–1328
Time limits
  administrative proceedings, in,
    1054–1061
  remedies, for,
    formal validity of measures,
      exceptions to principle of,
        absolute nullity of administrative
          measures, 1044–1045
        generally, 1044
        illegality, plea of, 1051–1054
        new circumstances, 1045–1051
    existence of,
      conditions for, 1035–1044
      consequences of, 1035–1044
    generally, 1032–1034

Trade
external, Community law on, 389–395
foreign trade law, proportionality
principle and, 806–814
New Trade Policy Instrument,
introduction of, 29
Transport
enforcement of sanctions, 43–44
limitation periods in proceedings, 43–44
Treaties
competence d'attribution principle
governing, 40
ECSC. *See* **European Coal and Steel
Community**
EEC. *See* **EEC Treaty**
information, administrative powers to
collect, 1216–1218
internal Community administration,
legal bases of, 25–26
primary law, as, 39–42
reserved treaty powers, 253–256
secondary legislation, treaty reservation
in, 256–257
Tribunal
natural justice, rules of, 1285–1288
quasi-judicial activity, 20

Ultra vires doctrine
elements of, 694–695
United Kingdom, 145–147, 282–286
Undertakings
self-binding action by authorities,
1089–1093
Unification of law
chances of, 88–89
comparative law, fundamentals of, 79–81
transnational, 79–81
United Kingdom
administrative law protection, 147–151
administrative structure, 151–152
central government, 151
comparative administrative law, 91
constitution, unwritten and flexible
nature of, 98, 143
Crichel Down case, misuse of
administrative power in, 150
customary law, role of, 57, 143–144
decision-making process, 1389–1390
delegated legislation, 144
discretion, doctrine of, 281–282
England and Wales, existence of separate
legal system in, 140n
equality principle, binding nature of,
558–560

United Kingdom—*cont.*
essential characteristics of system,
140–153
Irish and British systems compared,
173–174
legal certainty, principle of,
action by administration,
administrative decisions, revocation
of, 904–907
payments having no legal basis,
recovery of, 907–910
general recognition of,
estoppel, 903–904
generally, 901–902
individual cases, application to,
904–910
regulations, retroactivity of, 910
statutes, retroactivity of, 910
legality principle,
comparative law review, 220–222
statutory constraints and decision,
generally, 281–282
natural justice, principle of, 286–287
ultra vires doctrine, 282–286
legitimate expectation, principle of,
action by administration,
administrative decisions, revocation
of, 904–907
payments having no legal basis,
recovery of, 907–910
estoppel, principle of, 903–904
general recognition of, 901–904
individual cases, application to,
904–910
regulations, retroactivity of, 910
statutes, retroactivity of, 910
local government, 151–152
natural justice, principle of,
current significance of general
principle of law, 1278–1284
essential characteristics of
administrative law, 146–147
generally, 286–287, 1273–1278
legal remedies, 1290–1291
statutory rules,
generally, 1284–1285
inquiries, 1288–1290
tribunals, 1285–1288
Northern Ireland, existence of separate
legal system in, 140n
origin and development of administrative
law, 140–143
proportionality, principle of, 695–697
public administration, concept of, 16–18
public corporations, 152

United Kingdom—*cont.*
public law and private law, absence of
distinction between, 84
reasons, duty to give, 1389–1390
Scotland, existence of separate legal
system in, 140n
sources of law, 143–147
stare decisis doctrine, 144
statutory constraints and discretion in,
generally, 281–282
natural justice, principle of, 286–287
ultra vires doctrine, 282–286
ultra vires doctrine, 145–147, 282–286
United States of America
public administration in, 20n
Unjustified enrichment
recovery of payments wrongly made,
1068–1069
Unlawful administrative conduct. *See*
Legality principle

Vested rights
legal certainty, principle of, 953–956
legitimate expectation, protection of,
953–956

Wade, E.C.S.
administrative law, description of, 17
Wales. *See* **England and Wales**
Words and phrases
administration, 15
parliamentary supremacy, 17n
Workers
free movement of, not applied to
employment in public service, 20

Workers—*cont.*
migrant, application of social security
rules to, 47, 54, 497–503
See also **Freedom of movement**
Written law
administrative act, revocation of,
Article 65(2), fourth paragraph,
ECSC, under, 981–983
Article 8(3) of Regulation 17 (EEC),
under, 983–984
generally, 980
Staff Regulations, 984–985
analogy, admissibility of reasoning by,
54–55
generally, 38–39, 55
inadequacy of, 53–54
primary law, 39–42
secondary law,
generally, 42
legal basis of Act,
direct implementation, 48–50
generally, 47–48
indirect implementation,
50–53
present position,
direct implementation, 43–45
generally, 42–43
indirect implementation,
45–47
Wrongs
administrative. *See* **Administrative
wrongs**
legislative, prerequisites of liability for,
524–530